W9-CCW-353

HANDBOOK OF RESEARCH ON CURRICULUM

HANDBOOK OF RESEARCH ON CURRICULUM

A Project of the American Educational Research Association

Philip W. Jackson
EDITOR

MACMILLAN PUBLISHING COMPANY
New York

Maxwell Macmillan Canada
Toronto

Maxwell Macmillan International
New York Oxford Singapore Sydney

Macmillan Publishing Company
A Division of Macmillan, Inc.
866 Third Avenue, New York, N.Y. 10022

Macmillan, Inc., is part of
the Maxwell Communication
Group of Companies

Maxwell Macmillan Canada, Inc.
1200 Eglinton Avenue East, Suite 200
Don Mills, Ontario M3C 3N1

Library of Congress Catalog Card Number: 91-12373

Printed in the United States of America

printing number
1 2 3 4 5 6 7 8 9 10

Library of Congress Cataloging-in-Publication Data

Handbook of research on curriculum : a project of the American Educational Research Association / edited by Philip W. Jackson.
p. cm.
Includes index.
ISBN 0-02-900385-7
1. Education—United States—Curricula. I. Jackson, Philip W. (Philip Wesley). II. American Educational Research Association.
LB1570.H264 1992
375'.00973—dc20 91-12373
CIP

CONTENTS

Preface ix
Contributors xiii

Part 1
CONCEPTUAL AND METHODOLOGICAL PERSPECTIVES 1

1 Conceptions of Curriculum and Curriculum Specialists 3
Philip W. Jackson

2 Curriculum Studies and the Traditions of Inquiry: The Scientific Tradition 41
Linda Darling-Hammond and Jon Snyder

3 Curriculum Studies and the Traditions of Inquiry: The Humanistic Tradition 79
Yvonna S. Lincoln

4 Methodological Issues in Curriculum Research 98
Decker F. Walker

5 Curriculum Evaluation and Assessment 119
George F. Madaus and Thomas Kellaghan

Part 2
HOW THE CURRICULUM IS SHAPED 155

6 Constructing a History of the American Curriculum 157
Herbert M. Kliebard

7 Curriculum Policy 185
Richard Elmore and Gary Sykes

8 Curriculum Stability and Change 216
Larry Cuban

9 The Relationship Between Culture and Curriculum: A Many Fitting Thing 248
Alan Peshkin

10 Conceptions of Knowledge 268
Francis Schrag

11 Curriculum Ideologies 302
Elliot W. Eisner

12 Organization of the Curriculum 327
John I. Goodlad and Zhixin Su

13 School Organization and Curriculum 345
Charles E. Bidwell and Robert Dreeben

14 Teacher as Curriculum Maker 363
D. Jean Clandinin and F. Michael Connelly

15 Curriculum Implementation 402
Jon Snyder, Frances Bolin, and Karen Zumwalt

16 Textbooks in School and Society 436
Richard L. Venezky

Part 3

THE CURRICULUM AS A SHAPING FORCE 463

17 Students' Experience of the Curriculum 465
Frederick Erickson and Jeffrey Shultz

18 Curriculum and Pedagogy 486
Walter Doyle

19 Cognition and Curriculum 517
Carl Bereiter and Marlene Scardamalia

20 The Moral Aspects of the Curriculum 543
Hugh Sockett

21 Curriculum Differentiation: Opportunities, Outcomes, and Meanings 570
Jeannie Oakes, Adam Gamoran, and Reba N. Page

22 Low Income African-American Children and Public Schooling 609
Dorothy S. Strickland and Carol Ascher

23 The Curriculum and Linguistic Minorities 626
Lily Wong Fillmore and Lois M. Meyer

24 Gender and the Curriculum 659
Nel Noddings

Part 4
TOPICS AND ISSUES WITHIN CURRICULAR CATEGORIES 685

25 Curriculum Research in Writing and Reading 687
Judith A. Langer and Richard L. Allington

26 Literature and the English Language Arts 726
Arthur N. Applebee and Alan C. Purves

27 Problematic Features of the School Mathematics Curriculum 749
Thomas A. Romberg

28 Science and Technology 789
Peter J. Fensham

29 Social Studies 830
Gerald Marker and Howard Mehlinger

30 Research in Foreign Language Curriculum 852
Myriam Met and Vicki Galloway

31 Vocational Education 891
George H. Copa and Caryl B. Bentley

32 Becoming Knowledge: The Evolution of Art Education Curriculum 945
Dennie Palmer Wolf

33 Physical Education 964
Mary A. Steinhardt

34 The Extracurriculum 1002
Laura E. Berk

Name Index 1045
Subject Index 1069

PREFACE

For readers interested in how this publication came into being, the essential facts are these: The initial idea for the *Handbook* came from Lloyd Chilton, then education editor for Macmillan, who suggested it to William Russell, Executive Secretary of the American Educational Research Association. Russell passed the idea along to Ian Westbury, then current Vice President of Division B (Curriculum Studies) of the Association. It was Westbury who shepherded the proposal through its review by the Publications Committee and the Council of the Association, whose members approved the project early in 1989. A short time later Richard Shavelson, then current President of AERA, invited me to become its editor, an invitation that I readily accepted.

My first move as editor was to appoint an Editorial Advisory Board, whose job it would be to aid in planning the *Handbook* and in nominating authors for its various chapters. The members of that Board are listed in the front of this book. Between the time the Board was appointed and its first meeting in the spring of 1989 I co-taught (with William Pattison) a graduate seminar at the University of Chicago that focused on the dual question of how to organize such a handbook and what its contents might look like. The suggestions and recommendations that grew out of that seminar were reported to the Advisory Board at its first meeting. When the Board and I met in the spring of that year what we found especially attractive about the prospect of producing such a handbook, and what surely must have partially accounted for the AERA Council's enthusiastic endorsement of the project, was the possibility of creating a volume that would do for the field of the curriculum what the first of the three *Handbooks of Research on Teaching* had done for that area of educational research and scholarship and what both of the subsequent volumes in that series had ably advanced. What those three volumes had done, according to our assessment, was to give conceptual and methodological definition to an area of inquiry while at the same time reviewing past achievements in a way that increased the field's attractiveness to a new generation of scholars and researchers. We aspired to similar goals for the proposed *Handbook of Research on Curriculum*. At the same time, given the close relationship between teaching and curricular issues, we were also aware of the inevitability of there being considerable overlap in the contents of the volume we were planning and the three earlier *Handbooks*. Thus, from the start those three volumes served as models whose achievements we aspired to but whose specific contents we wished to avoid duplicating more than was necessary.

During the Board's two-day deliberations it established a number of guidelines that helped to shape the overall structure of the *Handbook*, the selection of its authors, and the specific advice and recommendations given them. The Board first decided that the primary focus of the *Handbook* would be on research and scholarship having to do with the curriculum of elementary and secondary schools. Its members further decided that the *Handbook* would be divided into four parts. Part 1 was to deal principally with methodological and conceptual issues, with how curricular matters are thought about and studied. Part 2 was to treat the many forces that shape the curriculum, from the most global—such as social, political, and economic forces—to the most microscopic—such as the efforts of individual classroom teachers to invent curricular materials or to modify those that are commercially available. Part 3 was to look at the curriculum as a shaping force. It would examine the impact of the curriculum on special groups of students, such as minorities, as well as its influence in general. Part 4 was to examine curricular issues having to do with the conventional subject matter areas of math, science, social studies, foreign languages, and so forth. One chapter was to move beyond those conventional categories to consider the educative significance of extracurricular activities.

During its meeting the Board also laid out what it hoped would become four common features of the volume's individual chapters. These were subsequently communicated to all of the *Handbook*'s authors. The desired commonalities were the following:

1. Each chapter was to offer as much of a historical perspective on its topic as was reasonably attainable, given the constraints of space and time, plus the availability of appropriate material. In making this recommendation the Board realized that few if any of the *Handbook*'s authors would be professionally trained historians, but it wished nonetheless to encourage a retrospective orientation throughout, with each chapter offering a perspective that was as historical in substance as its author or authors

could manage within the constraints that have been mentioned.

2. Each chapter was to present the best scholarly and empirical knowledge available on its topic, though none was required to review all of the studies that might be included under its rubric. Authors were encouraged to make judgments concerning the scholarly importance of the material being reviewed, though they were also advised to offer a comprehensive review that would at least touch upon those writings that comprise the forefront of current knowledge and thought in their respective areas of expertise.
3. Each chapter was to offer its readers a reasonably up-to-date bibliography, one that would be of particular use to those who might wish to continue their exploration of a topic.
4. Each chapter was to include, where it seemed appropriate, comments and suggestions that would point to needed research and promising avenues of investigation. The needs and interests of graduate students in education were to be considered uppermost in the fulfillment of this recommendation.

Beyond these four hoped-for commonalities, the Board also recommended to authors that they do their best to report upon international studies that bore upon their assigned topic. The Board recognized that access to foreign publications, in addition to language barriers, would prevent many authors from moving very far in this direction. Nonetheless, they wished to promulgate, where possible, an increased awareness of the international character of educational research and scholarship.

With respect to the selection of authors, the Board decided to begin by inviting the best-qualified persons they could think of to write each of the chapters, even if it seemed unlikely that the person nominated would accept the invitation. As might be expected, this policy resulted in almost all of the nominees being salient figures within their respective areas of specialization. Invited authors were to be told that they could choose to work with one or more coauthors if they so wished but that the editor would communicate directly with the invitees only and would hold each of them responsible for the completion of his or her assignment. No member of the Board nominated himself or herself as an author, but it did turn out that almost all of them were nominated as a first choice by one or more of their fellow Board members. One sign of the widely perceived importance of the project is revealed by the fact that all but two or three of the initial roster of thirty-odd invitees accepted the invitation.

Because almost all of the authors are well-known researchers and scholars who have published a great deal in their respective fields, I was free to be very light-handed as an editor. All manuscripts were read by two readers, one an outside expert who was asked to comment on the chapter's substantive adequacy and the other an editorial assistant who worked out of my office and who principally checked manuscripts for stylistic consistencies, completeness of references, and other problems of formatting. As chief editor I reviewed every chapter, though I seldom called for major changes beyond those recommended by the two readers.

So much for how the *Handbook* came into being and for a description of the policies that guided its overall design. What of the final product? Will it realize its planners' hopes? That question must obviously be answered by the *Handbook*'s readers. I can say without fear of contradiction that a lot of people worked very hard to bring the book into being (see the Acknowledgments). Thus, if hard work alone could determine the outcome of such an enterprise, which of course it cannot do, its success would be assured. Lacking that assurance and lacking now as well the opportunity to change anything, all of us who have had a hand in its making can only hope for the best. We trust that future editions will rectify whatever shortcomings this volume may be found to have.

ACKNOWLEDGMENTS

Readers may not be aware that none of the *Handbook*'s authors received any payment for writing their chapters. The editor, the members of the Advisory Board, and all of the outside readers also served without compensation. Thus, the first and largest debt of gratitude rightfully belongs to that total collection of people who gave freely and generously of their time and energy to make the *Handbook* possible. Thanks are also due the many understanding administrators—deans and department heads, principally—who sanctioned the involvement of their faculty in the project and provided various forms of institutional support. They shall remain unnamed for fear of failing to mention them all, but their contributions are no less appreciated because of their anonymity.

Those who served as outside readers comprise a clearly identifiable group whose members included Richard Beach, F. Michael Connelly, Catherine Cornbleth, Michael Day, Robert Dreeben, Edgar Epps, Jay Featherstone, John I. Goodlad, Patricia Graham, Paul Gump, Jerome Hausman, George Hillocks, Herbert Kliebard, Hope Jensen Leichter, Milbrey McLaughlin, John Meyer, Fred Newmann, Jeannie Oakes, June Phillips, Lauren Resnick, Emily Robertson, Flora Rodriguez-Brown, James F. Sallis, William Schubert, Richard Shavelson, Decker Walker, Ian Westbury, Arthur Wirth, and Karen K. Zumwalt. Through their characteristically prompt and thorough reading of drafts of all of the chapters, these men and women greatly strengthened the overall quality of the *Handbook*.

I am grateful to Lloyd Chilton of Macmillan, not only for suggesting the *Handbook* in the first place but also for serving as such a genial adviser and guide during its production. I am also grateful to the Council of AERA and to Richard Shavelson, now a past President of the Association, for inviting me to be the *Handbook*'s editor. Michael Sander of Macmillan ably saw the volume through the final stages of its production.

The University of Chicago graduate students who were enrolled in the seminar that generated suggestions for the Advisory Board included Dora Aksoy, Ellen Anderson, Robert Boostrom, Yu Cheng, Ina Ruth Eavenson, Carl Heine, Barry Kissane, Mmantsetsa Marope, Nancy Miller, Scott Salk, George Snyder, Mary Sukola, Denisse Thompson, Steven Vryhof, and John Whitehurst. William Pattison, with whom I co-taught that seminar, was among its most enthusiastic participants and provided several helpful suggestions of his own. I feel fortunate to have had him as a teaching partner.

Three editorial assistants served the *Handbook* project at different times. Craig Cunningham, who was the first of them, reviewed each chapter as it arrived and offered a detailed critique of its contents, which was usually transmitted directly to the author after I had reviewed it. His was a massive undertaking, performed with consummate skill and sensitivity. Gerald Pillsbury and Robert Boostrom helped to achieve consistency in final drafts of chapters and to work with edited copy from the publisher. Each did an outstanding job, for which I remain grateful. John Yukawa helped to organize and photocopy the chapters at each stage of the editing process, thus greatly easing the job of the editorial assistants.

I am immensely indebted to the Board of the Benton Center for Curriculum and Instruction at the University of Chicago for providing a portion of the project's cost. The Center's support of the enterprise was both direct and indirect. In addition to financial aid, it provided a congenial environment in which to carry out my editorial duties. Finally, I must thank Diane Bowers, the Center's Administrative Assistant, for her outstanding managerial skill and her unflagging commitment to the success of the project, both of which were invaluable in bringing it to fruition.

Philip W. Jackson
University of Chicago
September 1991

CONTRIBUTORS

Philip W. Jackson, Editor

Richard L. Allington
Professor of Education
Department of Reading
University at Albany
State University of New York
Albany, New York

Arthur N. Applebee
Director
National Research Center on Literature Teaching and Learning
University at Albany
State University of New York
Albany, New York

Carol Ascher
ERIC Clearinghouse on Urban Education
Teachers College
Columbia University
New York, New York

Caryl B. Bentley
Graduate Research Assistant
Department of Vocational and Technical Education
College of Education
University of Minnesota, Twin Cities Campus
St. Paul, Minnesota

Carl Bereiter
Professor
Centre for Applied Cognitive Science
Ontario Institute for the Study of Education
Faculty of Education
University of Toronto
Toronto, Canada

Laura E. Berk
Professor
Department of Psychology
Illinois State University
Normal, Illinois

Charles E. Bidwell
William Claude Reavis Professor of Sociology, Education and Public Policy Studies
University of Chicago
Chicago, Illinois

Frances Bolin
Associate Professor
Teachers College
Columbia University
New York, New York

D. Jean Clandinin
Associate Professor
Department of Elementary Education
Faculty of Education
University of Alberta
Edmonton, Canada

F. Michael Connelly
Director
Joint Centre for Teacher Development
Ontario Institute for the Study of Education
Faculty of Education
University of Toronto
Toronto, Canada

George H. Copa
Professor and Chairperson
Department of Vocational and Technical Education
College of Education
University of Minnesota, Twin Cities Campus
St. Paul, Minnesota

Larry Cuban
Professor of Education
School of Education
Stanford University
Stanford, California

Linda Darling-Hammond
Professor
Co-Director of the National Center for Restructuring Education, Schools, and Teaching (NCREST)
Teachers College
Columbia University
New York, New York

Walter Doyle
Professor of Education
Division of Teaching and Teacher Education
College of Education
The University of Arizona
Tucson, Arizona

Robert Dreeben
Professor
Department of Education and the College
University of Chicago
Chicago, Illinois

Elliot W. Eisner
Professor of Education and Art
Stanford University
Stanford, California

Richard Elmore
Professor
Graduate School of Education
Harvard University
Cambridge, Massachusetts

Frederick Erickson
Professor of Education
Graduate School of Education
University of Pennsylvania
Philadelphia, Pennsylvania

Peter J. Fensham
Professor of Science Education
Faculty of Education
Monash University
Clayton, Victoria, Australia

Lily Wong Fillmore
Professor
School of Education
Division of Language and Literacy
University of California at Berkeley
Berkeley, California

Vicki Galloway
Associate Professor
Department of Modern Languages
Georgia Institute of Technology
Atlanta, Georgia

Adam Gamoran
Associate Professor of Sociology and Educational Policy Studies
University of Wisconsin at Madison
Madison, Wisconsin

John I. Goodlad
Professor and Director
Center for Educational Renewal
College of Education
University of Washington
Seattle, Washington

Philip W. Jackson
David Lee Shillinglaw Distinguished Service Professor of Education and Psychology
University of Chicago
Chicago, Illinois

Thomas Kellaghan
Director
Educational Research Centre
St. Patrick's College
Dublin, Ireland

Herbert M. Kliebard
Professor of Curriculum and Instruction and Educational Policy Studies
University of Wisconsin at Madison
Madison, Wisconsin

Judith A. Langer
Professor of Education
School of Education
University at Albany
State University of New York
Albany, New York

Yvonna S. Lincoln
Professor of Higher Education
Department of Educational Administration
Texas A & M University
College Station, Texas

George F. Madaus
Boisi Professor of Education and Public Policy
Director, The Center for the Study of Testing, Evaluation, and Educational Policy
Boston College
Chestnut Hill, Massachusetts

Gerald W. Marker
Professor of Education
Indiana University
Bloomington, Indiana

Howard D. Mehlinger
Professor of Education and History
Director of the Center for Excellence in Education
Indiana University
Bloomington, Indiana

Myriam Met
Coordinator of Foreign Languages
Montgomery County Public Schools
Rockville, Maryland

Lois M. Meyer
Assistant Professor
School of Education
Department of Elementary Education
San Francisco State University
San Francisco, California

Nel Noddings
Professor and Associate Dean
School of Education
Stanford University
Stanford, California

Jeannie Oakes
Professor and Vice Chair
Graduate School of Education
University of California at Los Angeles
Los Angeles, California

Reba N. Page
Assistant Professor of Education
University of California at Riverside
Riverside, California

Alan Peshkin
Professor of Education
University of Illinois at Urbana-Champaign
Urbana, Illinois

Alan C. Purves
Professor of English and the Humanities
Director, Center for Writing and Literacy
University at Albany
State University of New York
Albany, New York

Thomas A. Romberg
Sears Foundation-Bascom Professor of Education
University of Wisconsin at Madison
Madison, Wisconsin

Marlene Scardamalia
Professor
Centre for Applied Cognitive Science
Ontario Institute for the Study of Education
Faculty of Education
University of Toronto
Toronto, Canada

Francis Schrag
Professor of Educational Policy Studies and Philosophy
University of Wisconsin at Madison
Madison, Wisconsin

Jeffrey Schultz
Professor of Education
Chairman, Education Department
Beaver College
Glenside, Pennsylvania

Jon Snyder
Research Associate
Teachers College
Columbia University
New York, New York

Hugh Sockett
Research Professor and Director of the Center for Applied Research and Development in Education
George Mason University
Fairfax, Virginia

Mary A. Steinhardt
Assistant Professor
Department of Kinesiology and Health Education
University of Texas at Austin
Austin, Texas

Dorothy S. Strickland
State of New Jersey Professor of Reading
Graduate School of Education
Rutgers University
New Brunswick, New Jersey

Zhixin Su
Assistant Professor
Department of Social and Philosophical Foundations
California State University
Northridge, California

Gary Sykes
Associate Professor
Departments of Educational Administration and Teacher Education
Michigan State University
East Lansing, Michigan

Richard L. Venezky
Unidel Professor of Educational Studies
University of Delaware
Newark, Delaware

Decker F. Walker
Professor of Education
Stanford University
Stanford, California

Dennis Palmer Wolf
Senior Research Associate
Graduate School of Education
Harvard University
Cambridge, Massachusetts

Karen Zumwalt
Associate Professor
Teachers College
Columbia University
New York, New York

Part

∽ 1 ∽

CONCEPTUAL AND METHODOLOGICAL PERSPECTIVES

1

CONCEPTIONS OF CURRICULUM AND CURRICULUM SPECIALISTS

Philip W. Jackson
UNIVERSITY OF CHICAGO

A look at the entries under the heading "curriculum" in any of the annual volumes of *Education Index* reveals two major kinds of writing on the subject, one rather narrowly focused, the other quite broad. The more narrowly focused kind, which makes up the bulk of the entries, is mostly about the installation or evaluation of specific subjects or topics within the curriculum of a particular school or set of schools. It deals with matters as disparate as the introduction of sex education in junior high schools, for example, to an evaluation of the new math in three counties of Tennessee, for another. Much of it is detailed and technical.

The more broadly focused kind of writing deals with topics like the construction of general theories and principles of curriculum development or broad perspectives on the curriculum as a whole or on the status of curriculum as a field of study. A lot of it appears in textbooks designed for courses on the curriculum, though a fair amount is published as articles in professional journals. The perspective from which many of these more general articles and books are written is that of an observer looking down or out on a vast field of human endeavor. The view is from a distance, its scope broad and all-encompassing. The questions that serve to guide such a view focus on the curriculum as a topic of concern in its own right and as a field of professional endeavor. This chapter treats such questions. It examines the answers given them over the past several decades, particularly since the emergence of curriculum as a special field of study in colleges and university departments of education.

How do curriculum matters look from such a distance? The answer, in a nutshell, is not very well, at least not as well as a tally of the entries under "curriculum" in *Education Index* would lead one to expect. The amount written about topics like the pros and cons of sex education or the benefits of this or that curricular innovation leads one to expect an enthusiastic and optimistic report from those who comment on the state of the field in general. Enthusiasm and optimism, however, are far from what one finds. Indeed, were one to choose a single word to capture both the state of affairs reported on as well as the recurrent mood of those doing the reporting, it would have to be the adjective "confused."

"Confusion" is the dominant condition remarked on by observer after observer (e.g., Barrow 1976; Harap 1937; Joyce 1971; Macdonald 1975; Taba 1962; Walker 1980). Its companion is "conflict" (e.g., Egan 1978; Eisner and Vallance 1974; Harap 1937). Others speak of a field that is "amorphous" and "elusive" (Goodlad 1985), "in disrepair" (Joyce 1971), "moribund" (Heubner 1976; Schwab 1969), "driven into disarray" (Foshay 1975), and suffering from "severe disorientation" (Egan 1978). One commentator complains about the "chaotic state of curriculum terminology" (Kliebard 1975); another about its "ill-defined epistemology" (Goodlad 1985), made evident by the fact that its subject matter varies markedly from one textbook to the next; yet a third talks of there being "great disenchantment" concerning the hope of amassing empirical generalizations that will turn into general laws and later coherent theory

The general textbooks examined in the preparation of this chapter include Beane, Toepfer, and Alessi (1986); Caswell and Campbell (1935); Doll (1964); Firth and Kimpston (1973); Gress and Purpel (1978); Hass, Bondi, and Wiles (1974); Inlow (1973); Jenkins and Shipman (1976); McNeil (1977); Oliver (1965); Orlosky and Smith (1978); Saylor and Alexander (1974); Schubert (1986); Smith, Stanley and Shores (1957); Stratemeyer et al. (1957); Taba (1962); Tanner and Tanner (1980); Taylor and Richards (1979); and Zais (1976).

(McNeil 1977). I myself have wondered (only half in jest) whether there is such a thing as a "field" of curricular studies after all (Jackson 1980). Others have recommended that its practitioners abandon most of their current practices (Schwab 1970). In short, if we rely solely on reports such as these, most of them from "insiders," that is, people who are themselves curriculum specialists, the picture of what is happening at the level of theory building and of making pronouncements about the curriculum in general looks gloomy indeed.

Why might that be so? What are the sources of the confusion and conflict that so many observers have remarked on? Is this a temporary state of affairs, a phase that has to be outgrown perhaps, or is it permanent, a reflection of the way discussions of curriculum always have been and must forever remain? And, whether temporary or permanent, is such a condition necessarily undesirable, no matter how discomforting and disheartening it may strike some observers? Might it be that some of the conflict, such as that generated by competing views of what our schools are for, for example, constitutes a healthy tension that needs to be preserved and managed rather than eliminated or resolved?

Such are some of the questions I shall explore in this chapter. The chapter contains three parts, each of which concentrates on a set of issues that has been around for quite some time and that presently continues to generate its share of the confusion and conflict that various observers have noted. The first part deals with issues that I shall call "definitional," the second with ones called "perspectival," and the third with ones called "professional." Because the meanings of these three terms are not self-evident, a word of explanation is in order before moving on to a more detailed treatment of each one.

Definitional issues chiefly concern what the word "curriculum" might be taken to mean. They deal with its range of applicability as a term. *Perspectival* issues are those that treat the dominant curricular outlooks, that is, the different ways we might look on the overall content of the curriculum. *Professional* issues deal with curriculum as a field of specialized endeavor. They ask what it means to be a curriculum specialist. They also probe the relationships between such specialists and other groups, particularly teachers and school administrators.

To preview what lies ahead let me say at the start that most of the sources of confusion we will be examining have to do with controversy over choices that individuals seemingly face in each of the three domains I have mentioned: choices over what the word "curriculum" should refer to; over what perspective to take on the curriculum as a whole; and over how curriculum specialists, particularly those who work in colleges and universities, should make use of their time and energy. Some of these choices, I conclude, are false ones in that they need not be made, at least not as they are usually presented. Others, it seems, are unavoidable and perhaps even desirable. What makes some of them even more confusing than they would normally be is the added assumption, sometimes explicitly stated but more often merely implied, that the choice is between a definition, a point of view, or a way of working that is true *sub specie aeternitatis*, and one that is not. That assumption, I shall claim, is always unnecessary and is usually pernicious in its effect.

PART I. DEFINITIONAL ISSUES

Harold Rugg (1936), who was among the founding fathers of what is today called the field of curriculum, once called curriculum "an ugly, awkward, academic word" (18). His reasons for calling it ugly and awkward are easy enough to understand. It is certainly not a pretty word and not the easiest to use either. The question of whether to anglicize its plural, for example—should it be curricula or curriculums?—may give the fastidious writer or speaker momentary pause. But what of "academic"? Why did he call it that? Was it because the word tends to be used mostly by academics? Or was he trying to say something more evaluative than descriptive? We might easily imagine that the adjective "academic" was a derogatory term to Rugg as it was to many other curriculum reformers of the day.

Whatever might have been Rugg's objection to the word "curriculum," it is evident that educators at all levels of schooling use it a lot these days, thus making it less academic, at least in the sense of its being more commonplace than it once was. However, a special subgroup of academics, particularly those whose writings we will be looking at in this chapter, engage in lengthy discussions about what the word "curriculum" *means*—how it should be defined—an activity that others who are not so engaged sometimes describe as academic in a pejorative sense, meaning that it has little or no connection with events in the workaday world of educational practice. This multiplicity of meanings causes one pair of textbook authors to observe, "It is a truism, perhaps, to say that one can find at least as many definitions of curriculum as one can find curriculum textbooks" (Gress and Purpel 1978, 1). They are not alone. Others have said much the same thing. But consider the claim: As many definitions as there are textbooks? Why should that be? Why do so many textbook authors in particular feel called on to offer their own definition? Are they just splitting hairs, as critics have charged them with doing, or is there more to it than that?

We first might observe that many of the definitions one finds in textbooks resemble one another very closely, which would suggest that the differences among them are not of great moment and thus needlessly contribute to a sense of conflict and confusion since the authors basically agree with one another. Consider, for instance, the following trio of definitional statements taken from texts whose publication dates span almost a half century:

> Curriculum is all of the experiences children have under the guidance of teachers. (Caswell and Campbell 1935)
>
> Curriculum encompasses all learning opportunities provided by the school. (Saylor and Alexander 1974)

Curriculum [is] a plan or program for all experiences which the learner encounters under the direction of the school. (Oliva 1982)

The definitions implied or explicitly stated in those three sentences are obviously not identical. One talks about "learning opportunities," the other two about "experience." One calls curriculum a plan or program; the other two do not. But neither are they worlds apart. All three limit the term "curriculum" to what goes on in school or under the guidance of teachers. They all insist that the term should cover *all* of the "experiences" or "learning opportunities" that the school offers, and not just those associated with the teaching of certain subjects or the use of special teaching methods such as lecturing or recitation. In short, the similarities among the three are fully as striking as are the differences, if not more so. Other definitions that would easily meld with the ones given could readily be found.

What this tells us is that even though there may be as many definitions as there are curriculum textbooks, we need not concern ourselves with anything like all of them if we wish to understand the confusion over definitions that so many observers complain about. What we must concentrate on instead are those differences that yield quite different ways of acting on or thinking about the curriculum. When we do so, what we discover are not the limitless options that critics complain about but, instead, a relatively small number of truly dissimiliar definitions of curriculum, each of which leads to a distinguishably different set of practices.

We should also note at the start that almost all of the definitions we run across in textbooks are actually *re*definitions. They are proposals to *replace* the *standard* meaning of curriculum with one that is presumed to be superior in some way. Thus, everyone who sets out to establish a *new* definition, even if it is only one that is to have jurisdiction within the space of a single article or is being recommended for use by professional educators only, is implicitly criticizing the *old* definition, the one already in force in common speech. (They may be criticizing other *re*definitions as well, but that need not concern us at this point.) It further means that those who offer a new definition are seldom if ever solely concerned with how a word is used. Instead, they are putting forward an argument of some kind in which their preferred definition plays a part. They are trying to persuade as much as describe or define. Moreover, we may not be able to tell from the definition alone what is being argued and why. The contentious nature of this process is a topic to which we shall return.

Let us begin, then, with the definition that serves as a point of departure for all the others: the standard, dictionary definition of curriculum. What is it? And what, in broadest terms, is said to be wrong with it?

The Traditional Definition

The *Oxford English Dictionary* (*OED*) defines curriculum as "A course; *spec.* a regular course of study or training, as at a school or university (The recognized term in the Scottish Universities)." The earliest citation of usage, following that definition, is to a record, in Latin, from the University of Glasgow in 1633. The first English usage cited is from an 1824 report on German universities by J. Russell, who wrote, "When the German student has finished his curriculum. . . ."

Webster's New International Dictionary, Second Edition, offers a definition that closely resembles the one in the *OED*. The definition it gives for curriculum is "*a* A course, esp., a specified fixed course of study, as in a school or college, as one leading to a degree. *b* The whole body of courses offered in an educational institution, or by a department thereof;—the usual sense." Both dictionaries note the etymology of the word from the Latin "curriculum," which, according to *Cassell's Latin-English Dictionary*, refers variously to running, a race course, and a chariot.

How did a word that originally referred to athletic events come to be used in an educational context? David Hamilton (1989) has recently sought to answer that question or at least to speculate on what the proper answer might be. The story he tells of the word's origin is interesting in what it reveals about the ideological and social movements from which the educational term "curriculum" arose. (In the process of his investigation, Hamilton ran across a use of the word some 50 years earlier than the first one cited in the *OED*. He reports its appearance in the 1582 records of the University of Leiden.) In essence, Hamilton contends that the standardization of university studies in European centers of learning during the second half of the 16th century reflected the need for greater administrative control brought on by the state control of the universities and also by the Protestant reform movement. As he points out, the organizational arrangement to which the word "curriculum" was applied, i.e., educational programs that lasted for several years and were structured internally, brought "both structural wholeness and sequential completeness" to the course of study (45). Hamilton's main point, which he spells out in some detail, is that the curriculum, as a form of organization, was essentially an instrument of social efficiency that was motivated both "externally" and "internally," by a combination of administrative and pedagogical authorities. At the heart of the word's educational usage, therefore, lies the idea of an organizational structure imposed by authorities for the purpose of bringing order to the conduct of schooling.

In sum, the dictionary definition makes clear that by the middle of the 19th century the common use of the word as meaning simply a course of study was more or less established and was routinely applied not just to the subjects studied in colleges and universities but to precollegiate levels of schooling as well. The question we now must ask is, what is wrong with that way of defining the word "curriculum"? Why have modern educators sought to change it?

What Is Wrong with the Conventional Definition?

The most common complaint against the conventional definition of curriculum is that it is too narrow, that its coverage is not broad enough. This complaint is not to be confused, however, with a similar one about the curriculum itself, though the word and its referent are so closely related that it is easy to see how such confusion could occur. Moreover, some who want the term itself to have broader coverage may also want the curriculum under its old definition to be expanded as well, though the two goals do not always go together, as we shall see. All this means is that there is a difference between wanting to see *new courses added to the curriculum* and wanting to see *the term applied to something other than courses of study*. In this section of the chapter I shall only be concerned with the latter state of affairs.

What does it mean to call the *definition* of curriculum too narrow? What makes it so? How might it be broadened? What else might the word refer to beyond a course of study? Why might someone recommend such a change?

Answers to that set of questions are not easy to find because they are not the kinds of questions that those who propose new definitions typically address directly, even though one might expect them to. Thus, there are few if any prepared answers to draw on. Moreover, the history of those changes in definition that have won at least some support does not unfold neatly and sequentially, thus providing a chronological structure that we might readily use as a narrative framework. Some definitions, such as those suggested by Franklin Bobbitt, for example, introduce several changes of meaning all at once, without bothering to highlight the significance of each one by separating it from the others. Others use the word in a new way without ever bothering to say so.

To cope with these difficulties I shall discuss four or five proposed changes of definition, not in the exact order in which they occurred, but as they might have emerged if the process had proceeded one step at a time and more or less progressively. I shall begin with Dewey, whose early educational writings establish the need for an expanded definition, and then move to Bobbitt, whose definition encapsulated a whole series of changes but did so without bothering to separate them, as has already been said.

Dewey and Bobbitt were seminal figures in the story of how our notions of the curriculum came to expand, but neither was solely responsible for the widespread acceptance of the ideas he propounded. Though an immensely influential spokesperson for his own point of view, neither was a voice in the wilderness. Many other educators of the day were saying much the same thing. I have chosen these two men as starting points chiefly because each was so well known in his day and each pointed the way toward a broadly expanded definition of curriculum.

Following a brief discussion of Dewey's and Bobbitt's ideas I shall examine two additional efforts to extend the definitional jurisdiction of the word "curriculum." One seeks to expand the term to cover what are purported to be the *negative* outcomes of schooling. The other differentiates among several *different* curricula within every single school, assigning to each a definition of its own. Both of these more recent shifts in the definition of the curriculum (postprogressive, one might call them) explicitly address the possibility, if not the inevitability, of there being shortcomings in the operation of our schools. These too, it is argued, deserve to be acknowledged by finding a place for them within the general rubric of curriculum. The perspective that includes these negative outcomes is naturally more pessimistic than any that have preceded it and is often tinged with cynicism as well.

Dewey's Curricular Misgivings

In *The Child and the Curriculum* (1902), which was not the first publication in English with "curriculum" in the title but was certainly among the first (Schubert [1984] lists two others, C. A. Bowsher's *The Absolute Curriculum* [1900] and H. S. Weet's *The Curriculum in Elementary Education* [1901]), Dewey appears to have no quarrel with the standard definition of the curriculum as "the course of study met in school [that] presents material stretching back indefinitely in time and extending outward indefinitely in space" (5). He also accepts the basic assumption behind that definition, which is that knowledge organized along subject matter lines is what must ultimately be mastered by students. What, then, is the problem? "It is," says Dewey, "just to get rid of the prejudicial notion that there is some gap in kind (as distinct from degree) between the child's experience and the various forms of subject-matter that make up the course of study" (11). If we could only get rid of the notion of "subject-matter" as being something that is "fixed and ready-made in itself" and the allied notion of the child's experience being "hard and fast," we would realize, Dewey argued, "that the child and the curriculum are simply two limits which define a single process" (11). The job of the teacher is essentially to bridge that gap. How might that be accomplished? By a process of what Dewey called "continuous reconstruction, moving from the child's present experience out into that represented by the organized bodies of truth that we call studies" (11).

One way in which Dewey seeks to get rid of both the "hard and fast" category of the child's experience and the "fixed and ready-made" character of the school subjects, thus revealing them to be the "two limits" of a "single process," is by showing how the child's ordinary interests and activities already point in the direction of those ossified remnants of experience known as the subjects of study. Thus, when the young child is playfully exploring the idea of distance, let us say, by trying to see how far an object can be thrown, he or she is already on a path of inquiry leading to those forms of organized knowledge known as geometry and physics. These rudimentary exploratory activities might be called precurricular in the conventional sense since they do not entail the paraphernalia of formal instruction. Yet the good teacher, according to Dewey, would not only sense their curricular significance and seize on them for educational purposes when he or she witnessed them but also arrange for such experiences to take place rather than waiting for them to happen spontaneously. In this view the teacher becomes a planner and manager of educational experiences.

It is significant that Dewey's influential pamphlet was called *The Child and the Curriculum* rather than *The Student and the Curriculum* and that it focused almost exclusively on the lower levels of schooling. For it is precisely the difference between *the young child's* interests and insights, on the one hand, and those embedded in the formal course of study, on the other, that provides such a striking contrast and highlights the need for some kind of transitional activities to bridge the gap. Had Dewey focused initially on college students, for example, or even on high schoolers, the gap between natural interest and organized subject matter might not have seemed as great and the need for a shift of emphasis from subject matter content to the learner's experiences might have seemed less imperative.

Even though Dewey did not himself seek to redefine the curriculum in a formal sense, which is to say he did not directly assert, "Here is what the word 'curriculum' should mean," it is clear that his views and others like them challenged the conventional definition. They did so via a line of reasoning encapsulated in the following set of questions: If teachers were to ready their students for formal studies by arranging experiences that took advantage of the students' natural interests and inclinations, should not such experiences be considered a *part* of their formal studies, even if only a preparatory part? Moreover, when older students had outgrown the need for such activities and were prepared to undertake formal studies of history, let us say, or mathematics, would not the teacher *still* be obliged to arrange and organize experiences that made such study possible? And would not *those* experiences, even if they involved nothing more than reading textbooks or memorizing historical dates, be an integral part of those studies and thus a part of the curriculum? In short, are not *planned experiences* of one kind or another all the teacher has to work with, no matter how old his or her students and no matter what subject is being taught? If we accept this argument, why not think of the curriculum as consisting of *different sets of experiences*, some dealing with mathematics, others with history, still others with geography, and so forth? Finally, if we conceive the curriculum as *consisting* of those experiences, we are only a step away from treating those experiences as though they *were* the curriculum. Note Kliebard's (1975, 44) claim that the idea of experience is too vague and subjective.

This line of reasoning or something close to it seems to have taken hold among vast numbers of educators, especially among those who became the vanguard of the progressive movement around the turn of the century and in the years preceding World War I. By the time of J. Franklin Bobbitt's ground-breaking text on the subject, the definition of the curriculum as educative experience was almost commonplace. Bobbitt's book not only helped to confirm what many others were coming to see but also stretched the boundaries of the "new" definition in two important ways.

Curriculum as Educative Experience

Fewer than 16 years after Dewey's *The Child and the Curriculum*, Franklin Bobbitt's *The Curriculum* (1972 [1918]) appeared. It is today widely acknowledged to have been the first text in what was soon to become a burgeoning field of professional activity (Caswell 1966). I shall return to some of the central ideas of Bobbitt's text in the next section of this chapter. For now, however, my concern is with the way he defined his key term.

"As applied to education," Bobbitt (1972) writes, the curriculum "is that *series of things which children and youth must do and experience* by way of developing abilities to do the things well that make up the affairs of adult life; and to be in all respects what adults should be" (42; emphasis in original). A few paragraphs further on he introduces a pair of formal definitions:

> The curriculum may, therefore, be defined in two ways: (1) it is the entire range of experiences, both undirected and directed, concerned in unfolding the abilities of the individual; or (2) it is the series of consciously directed training experiences that the schools use for completing and perfecting the unfoldment. Our profession [by which he presumably meant educators at large] uses the term usually in the latter sense. (43)

Bobbitt's pair of definitions clearly acknowledge the centrality of the concept of experience that we have already noted. However, they extend the boundaries of the curriculum as experience in two important ways. They do so first by making room within the definition for out-of school experiences. This meaning is implied in the initial statement quoted above and made clear in the first of the paired definitions. It is *the entire range* of experience, Bobbitt tells us, that constitutes the curriculum in its broadest sense. It is everything that children and youths must do to become the kinds of adults they "should be." The second radical shift in Bobbitt's definition rests on his distinction between *directed* and *undirected* experience, which he uses to characterize the curriculum that operates outside of school. The distinction is understandable enough when we think about the sources of our common knowledge. People clearly do pick up a lot of valuable information and skill in the course of everyday life, some of which is consciously delivered by parents, among others, and some not. Fair enough, one might say, but does not the same thing happen in school? Why does Bobbitt restrict his second definition, the one that he says educators use, to directed experiences alone? Why not make the two definitions exactly parallel?

Bobbitt's failure to acknowledge the likelihood of undirected educative experiences operating within the confines of schools might have been nothing more than an oversight on his part. Nonetheless, the omission is consonant with a view of schools that sees them as places in which everything that goes on is, or should be, purposeful and planned. To allow the school to operate through experiences that are unplanned, i.e., undirected, might be seen as tantamount to having it accomplish a portion of its work by chance. Given Bobbitt's insistence on the importance of careful planning, it is easy to see why he might have balked at the thought of condoning such practices. In any event, it remained for others who followed to round out the four-fold set of possibilities—in school/out of school, directed/undirected—implicit in the distinctions Bobbitt's definitions contain.

Before we leave Bobbitt's notion of an out-of-school curriculum—a curriculum of life, one might say—it is worth noting that the idea, at least as a figure of speech, is still in use. Cremin (1976), for example, speaking of the educative function of the home and of other institutions outside the school, declares that

> Every family has a curriculum, which it teaches quite deliberately and systematically over time. Every church and synagogue has a curriculum. . . . And every employer has a curriculum. . . . One can go on to point out that libraries have curricula, museums have curricula, Boy Scout troops have curricula, and day-care centers have curricula, and most important, perhaps, radio and television stations have curricula—and by these curricula I refer not only to programs labeled educational but also to news broadcasts and documentaries (which presumably inform), to commercials (which teach people to want), and to soap operas (which reinforce common myths and values). (22)

An author of a recent textbook (Schubert 1986) advises his readers to "Live as if your life were a curriculum for others, and balance that principle by realizing that every life you meet could be a curriculum for you if you perceive with sufficient perspective" (423).

At the same time it is fair to say that usage as broad as that recommended by Cremin and Schubert is rare. Few people these days, whether professional educators or members of the public at large, speak of the curriculum in such sweeping terms. Indeed, it is doubtful that many did in Bobbitt's day either. A curriculum that has nothing to do with schools and schooling was and remains more a metaphor than a term to be taken literally.

Expanding the Idea of the School Curriculum to Include the Unplanned Components of Experience

Although Bobbitt himself did not include undirected experiences in his definition of the school's curriculum, it would be a mistake to think that the idea of doing so waited for those who came after him. Dewey, for one, well before Bobbitt's book on the curriculum, clearly recognized the importance within schools of what he called "incidental learning," by which he meant not just haphazard scraps of knowledge or skill picked up while learning something else but, rather, those enduring changes of great importance, such as "a delight in thinking for the sake of thinking" (Dewey 1960 [1933], 226). Other educators of Dewey's day and possibly earlier doubtless recognized the same thing. It is clear, however, that within 10 or 20 years *after* Bobbitt's book definitions of the curriculum routinely included *all* of the experiences, planned and unplanned, that occur under the auspices of the school. The definition by Caswell and Campbell, given previously, is typical.

The move to include everything that goes on in school under the rubric of curriculum entails risks that seem not to have been foreseen by those who first endorsed the idea. An all-enveloping notion of what the curriculum includes sounds fine as long as it operates within a perspective that focuses exclusively on the desirable outcomes of schooling. It makes sense, perhaps, to look on all incidental learning of a positive nature as being a part of the school's overall mission and, therefore, as belonging to its curriculum.

But what if the outcomes of schooling are not all positive? What if some students develop attitudes and even gain knowledge in school that is in some sense harmful or undesirable? Is the definition of curriculum that includes all of the experiences that take place in school broad enough to take in those unwanted experiences as well? Can a curriculum, in short, have a dark side?

Unwanted Outcomes of Schooling Perceived as Curricular

We all know that going to school makes some students unhappy. Moreover, it has done so for centuries. Shakespeare's "whining schoolboy . . . creeping like snail/ Unwillingly to school" serves as a classic instance of our widespread recognition of that ancient truth. We also recognize and have done so for quite a time that some of the negative attitudes generated in school—a dislike of mathematics, for example—can stay with a person for years. Until quite recently, however, most people looked on such unwanted outcomes of schooling as the product of unfortunate events—the result of having a particularly inept teacher, for example—events for which no one could hold the system as a whole responsible.

In recent years, however, there has been a growing suspicion that the untoward outcomes of schooling may occur more frequently and more systematically and may be more pervasive in their overall effects than anyone had previously imagined. Moreover, at least some of these negative outcomes are now believed to be the product not of inept teachers but of institutional qualities over which teachers may have little control. Instead of focusing on the positive incidental learnings that Dewey spoke of—the good that schools do—interest began to shift sometime in the 1960s to the possibility that schools do harm and do it systematically to many, if not all, students.

Because the two sets of outcomes—the positive and the negative—are so markedly different, there has grown a tendency to speak of there being two separate curricula in every school: one explicitly endorsed, the other not. The latter has been referred to as the unintended; the unwritten (Dreeben 1976); the unstudied (Overly 1970); and possibly most popular of all, the hidden curriculum (Jackson 1968).

The suggestion that there might be something called a hidden or unintended or unwritten or unofficial curriculum has occasioned a lot of discussion and debate over the past two decades (Dreeben 1976; Giroux and Purpel 1983; Gordon 1981, 1982, 1983, 1984, 1988a, 1988b; Lakomski 1988; Martin 1976; Snyder 1970; Vallance 1973, 1982). Much of the controversy turns on the question of whether there really is such a thing and, if so, what if anything should be done about it. One student of the topic poses the problem and its solution in this way: "If the unwritten curriculum is really unwritten, hidden, tacit, or latent, how do we know it is there and has an impact that we should pay attention to? Actually, we do not know in any hard, empirical sense; the evidence for its existence and effects is rather thin, and for all we know it may go the way of phlogiston" (Dreeben 1976, 114). However, Dreeben backs away quickly from such a skeptical conclusion. "There is a case to be made, however," he reports, "largely on grounds of plausibility and to a lesser extent of suggestive empirical evidence" (114). To date at least, Dreeben's cautious conclusion appears to prevail, though not uncontested.

What is chiefly of interest within the context of this chapter is less the argument over whether there truly *is* a hidden or latent or tacit curriculum than the willingness of large numbers of educators to suspect that there might be. The suspicion that the schools might be *systematically* affecting students in ways that are both unattended and undesirable is a notion that Bobbitt and his contemporaries could hardly have been expected to have entertained. Such a view would not have been congenial with the spirit of their times. That it *is* congenial with the intellectual climate of today tells us as much about the times, perhaps, as it does about the schools. We shall return to this observation at the end of this section.

The Curriculum Defined Temporally

There is yet another way of talking about multiple curricula within schools beyond the now common distinction between the official or intended curriculum, on the one hand, and the hidden or unintended curriculum, on the other. This additional way of slicing the curriculum pie focuses on the difference between what the school plans to accomplish and what it succeeds in doing. The central distinction on which such a perspective rests resembles the one between the intentional and the unintentional in that it too calls our attention to aspects of schooling that heretofore may have been overlooked or even concealed in some way. But the emphasis in this case is on the *unaccomplished* or, more positively, the *partially accomplished* rather than on the *unintended*. The impetus to make such a distinction comes from the common observation that schools do not always deliver everything they promise. Since the promise comes before the delivery, this perspective has a temporal dimension that most other outlooks lack.

The gap between curricular plans and their fulfillment can take a number of forms. We can easily envision the major ones by thinking of some of the curricular arrangements we might find in a high school or college where there are many course offerings and lots of students. There is first the possibility of a discrepancy between the course announcements in the school catalog or course bulletin and the courses that are actually taught. Latin, for example, may be "on the books" without there being any such classes for students to attend. The set of announcements is sometimes referred to as the "official" curriculum, whereas the actual offerings have been called the "enacted" curriculum (Zumwalt 1988). At a more refined level, there are differences, perhaps inevitably, between what appears in the teacher's guide or textbook, the latter being a part of what I have just called the "enacted" curriculum, and what is actually taught in class, which might go by some other name, such as the "delivered" curriculum. There is further the distinction between what is taught ("delivered") and what the students grasp or understand. The latter some have wanted to call the "experienced" or "received" curriculum. At each stage of this extended process the curriculum seems to shrink, like a piece of melting ice, until all that is left of it are its enduring effects in the form of the knowledge and skills that students retain. But even these fade and atrophy through disuse, as we all know, making the residue of our school experience a continually diminishing one.

Perhaps the ultimate in this tendency to name a variety of different curricula, each of which depends on the central notion of there being an officially sanctioned curriculum and others that relate to it in various ways, is the proposal for something called "the null curricula." This refers to those course offerings or experiences that were *not* offered, making it, in effect, the curriculum that might have been (Eisner 1979; Flinders, Noddings, and Thornton 1986).

Making Sense of the Definitional Shifts

What shall we make of all these efforts to redefine the word "curriculum"? How shall we judge their significance? One possibility is to ask whether they add up to what one pair of textbook writers refers to as "conceptual progress" (Tanner and Tanner 1980). Another is to determine whether they mirror a "more sophisticated" view of the curriculum than the one contained in the the standard dictionary definition, as at least one writer claims they do (Zumwalt 1988). Can either be so? Can any or all of the redefinitions be looked on as improvements over the dictionary definition? Do they bring us any closer to something that might be called a *true* definition of curriculum? Do they reflect an increased awareness of curricular matters over the old way of looking at things?

Before addressing those last two possibilities directly (only to reject them both), we might pause to note that none of the redefinitions has clearly won the day in the sense of having replaced the old definition. Moreover, the replacement has occurred neither in common speech nor in the shoptalk of educators. Today, as in the past, when someone uses the word "curriculum," chances are that he or she is referring to nothing more nor less than the course of study of a school or university, i.e., the standard dictionary definition, and not to the educative experiences that take place outside of school nor even those occuring in school, for that matter. The persistence of the standard definition does not by itself mean that all of the attempts at redefinition are of little or no value. But it does indicate that none of those efforts has succeeded in supplanting the old.

I turn now to the question of whether any or all of the redefinitions bring us closer to the truth. Though some people who offer new definitions may perceive themselves as seeking a *true* definition of curriculum and perhaps as having found one, the number who do so appears to be small and diminishing. (A variant of the practice of making up a new definition of curriculum is to examine common usage and from that seek to identify what the term, as commonly used, logically entails; see, e.g., Winchester [1977].) Moreover, the view that there exists an eternal and unchanging reality outside of experience to which all definitions seek to conform (a view usually ascribed to Plato) no longer has the hold it once did within the intellectual community at large. In its place we find increasing adherence to a conception of human experience whose variants go by a variety of names, which include pragmatics, antiessentialism, hermeneutics, interpretive social science, deconstruction, and critical theory. That shift, whose beginnings can be traced at least back to the writings of Dewey, is now noticeable among today's educational writers.

This is hardly the place to explicate that emerging view (see, for example, the recent writings of Cavell [1988], Fish [1989], Geertz [1983, 1988], Rorty [1989], Smith [1988], and others), but a few of its features must be noted if we are to understand its implications for the topic at hand. Among them is the realization that all experience is necessarily situational and contextualized, that there is no privileged position outside of experience from which to achieve a free and independent (i.e., noncontextualized) perspective, and that the power of rhetoric is crucial in determining the superiority of one view over another. What those features mean within the present context is that there is no definition of curriculum that will endure for all time and that it is foolish to search for one, that every definition serves the interest of the person or group putting it forward, and that it is always appropriate to ask what the local consequences of adopting this or that definition might be.

But even if we give up the notion of there being something like a universal, nonchanging definition of curriculum, what about the possibility of an increased awareness of all that curriculum entails? If we can get no closer to eternal truth than the concept of opinion allows, can we nonetheless become more "sophisticated" in our view? Can we expand our awareness of what the idea of curriculum includes, and indeed, do we not do exactly that when, for example, we become newly conscious of the possible ill effects of the traditional curriculum and invent a term like "the hidden curriculum" to help us keep that possibility firmly in mind? It is certainly the case that when we first come upon what we perceive to be a new insight such as the one just mentioned we *feel* as though our perceptual world has suddenly expanded and we typically wonder how we ever could have been so naive as to have overlooked what we now see as being virtually self-evident. But this experience of having moved to a more sophisticated view is a very common occurrence and in itself cannot be taken as evidence of progress no matter how powerful the accompanying feeling might be. Every generation, as we know, believes itself to be more sophisticated than the preceding one. But that does not make it so. What is called for in addition is an argument that will make the case for progress convincing.

What does all this say about efforts to redefine the word "curriculum"? If these efforts can never achieve truth and if the criterion of sophistication rests only on belief and argument, should the project be abandoned? There are some who think it should. Zais (1976, 93), for example, calls the activity "not a very productive enterprise." Portelli (1987) calls the hope for help from redefinitions "a myth." Goodlad (1979), speaking of the range and variability of the content of graduate education courses that bear the label "curriculum," expresses his impatience with the process of generating new definitions in this way:

> Who is to say that one of these courses deserves the word "curriculum" attached to it and the others do not? that one is right and the others are wrong? Yet this is the box we get ourselves into in attempting some single, proper definition of curriculum, a questionable activity in which curriculum specialists have far too long engaged. We need definitions, of course, to carry on productive discourse, but attempts to arrive at a single one have inhibited discourse. If someone wishes to define "curriculum" as a course of studies, this is legitimate—and certainly not bizarre. Let us begin there and see where it takes us. If someone wishes to begin with curriculum as "the experiences of students," let us see where this carries us. But let us not begin by throwing out each definition and seeking only to substitute another that merely reflects a different perspective. We can readily see what a short distance this has taken us. (44–45)

Goodlad's advice is clear enough. He does not insist that we give up trying to redefine the word "curriculum." He does question, however, whether "some single, proper definition of curriculum" will ever be found and he comes close to advocating that we abandon *that* goal. But he then goes on to acknowledge that definitions are important, that they are helpful in carrying on discourse. His only concern, therefore, is that we take seriously whatever definition we might adopt, that we "begin there and see where it takes us" before abandoning it in favor of another one "that merely reflects a different perspective."

The latter suggestion will doubtless strike many as wise counsel, yet it contains two elements that should give pause to anyone inclined toward the kind of interpretivist position adopted in this chapter. First is the assumption that one *begins* with a definition of whatever kind and moves on from there. A rival position from an interpretivist perspective would call attention to the fact that every definition, particularly every self-consciously constructed one, is the product of someone's reasoning. It stands at the end point of a supporting argument. In short, it has a history. Hypothetically, one may *start* with that definition as a given and simply move on from there, as Goodlad recommends, but that is not what usually happens. Typically we choose to adopt a definition, in part at least, because of the reasoning that lies behind it. We do not just say, here is someone's definition of the curriculum; let us follow it and see where it takes us. Rather, we ask not only where it *goes* but also where it *comes from* and *why*.

The second point of contention that would probably be raised by an interpretivist would focus on the word "merely" in Goodlad's admonition. He warns against dropping one definition in favor of another that, as he puts it, "*merely* reflects a different perspective." The question is whether any definition, new or old, can do more than that. The difference between any pair of definitions, the interpretivist wants to insist, is always one of perspective. Why, then, the "merely"? What else might we expect our definitions to do? In fairness to Goodlad, perhaps he was only warning against the folly of seeking change for change's sake and was not suggesting that something other than a perspective, something like a "real" or "true" definition, might one day be attained, but the way his warning is worded leaves the door open to that possibility, which the interpretivist, and apparently Goodlad himself, seeks to deny.

Getting Rid of Definitional Confusion

I began by looking on the bewildering array of definitions of curriculum as one source of the confusion commentators complain about when they try to describe the state of the field. Having surveyed the major shifts of definition that have been proposed over the past several decades, we are now in a position to reassess that complaint. The basic question we must ask is whether the reported confusion is a reasonable and understandable response to the state of affairs as I have described them.

It is so if we start with the assumption that every word ought to have a single, correct meaning. Then the fact that almost every textbook on curriculum offers its own definition of its key term could reasonably be a source of confusion, for it would mean that they all could not possibly be right; yet it might be hard to tell which of them, if any, was correct. Not only do some observers appear to hold such a belief as an operating assumption, but so too do some of the definers. The latter will feel no confusion, of course, for they obviously believe their own definition to be the correct one. The former, however, have a perfect right to feel confused as long as they cling to the assumption of there being a single, correct definition of the term.

Even after we abandon that assumption, however, as more and more educational observers and commentators seem to be doing of late, we still may be left feeling puzzled by the proliferation of available meanings, but we would be so for quite different reasons than before. The key question now becomes not which one is right but, rather, what purpose does each definition serve? Why is it being put forward and who stands to gain what by adopting it? What would be the consequences of doing so?

To give such questions substance, let us return briefly to the idea of there being one or many out-of-school curricula. Why would anyone urge us to believe that to be so? Whose interests would be served by such a move? What difference would the idea make in our own thinking? What courses of action might flow from it? Such would be a few of the questions we might want answered.

Consider the answers a close look at Bobbitt's (1972 [1918]) curricular writings might give. The ultimate source of the school's curriculum for Bobbitt turns out to have been the society at large. He believed the school's job was to rectify the deficiencies of knowledge and skill that result from society's oversight or malfunctioning. The school, in other words, was to take over those educational tasks that other institutions, like the family, the church, and the workplace, were not fulfilling adequately. Bobbitt's task for the curriculum maker (whom he also called the curriculum discoverer) was to explore the workaday world, looking for signs of human weakness and deficiency that schooling might repair. These were to become the school's objectives.

Given the complementary relationship Bobbitt envisioned between the school and society (very different from Dewey's, incidentally) his readiness to posit an out-of-school curriculum whose deficiencies were to be repaired by the school becomes quite understandable. By stretching the idea of curriculum to encompass much that goes on within the society at large, Bobbitt in effect transforms that society into a kind of superschool whose educational function stands in need of supplementation.

What does such a view accomplish? It clearly gave Bobbitt and his fellow curriculum workers a job to do, and an important one to boot. What could be more pressing than to determine what the schools should be teaching by finding out what the society at large was failing to teach? The parallels between school and society, as Bobbitt viewed them, are important in another way. Curriculum workers obviously work on curriculum. If society at large has a curriculum in need of repair or supplementation, who would be better able to work on such a task than students of curriculum? Further implications and consequences of Bobbitt's notions are left for readers to work out on their own.

Consider, in contrast, Cremin's (1976) talk about museums, day-care centers, and radio and television programs having curricula. He too wanted to extend the idea of curriculum to out-of-school institutions but with a very different goal in mind than the one that occupied Bobbitt's thoughts. Cremin's purpose was not to suggest that the school take over where the society fails, at least not necessarily. Rather it was to call attention to "the multiplicity of institutions that educate" and by so doing to put the schools in their place, so to speak, to see them as but one of many educative agencies that relate to one another in complicated ways. Cremin called these networks of educative institutions "configurations" (30). His goal, in other words, was to highlight the limitations of public schooling as a kind of antidote to an exaggerated view of the schools' importance. He labeled his outlook "an ecological approach to education," one "that views educational institutions and configurations in relation to one another and to the larger society that sustains them and is in turn affected by them" (36). What are the consequences of such a view? Some are obvious; others less so. Cremin pointed out some of each kind. With respect to institutional goals, for example, it means that the modern school of education "must become directly concerned with all the roles, occupations, and professions that are involved with education. It must professionalize or further professionalize some of these—day-care workers, for example—and it must certainly illuminate all of them" (83). Or, with respect to curriculum,

> it means that courses of study should draw their problems, their data, and their examples from a variety of educational situations, and that practice teaching and field instruction should be undertaken in a broad range of educational institutions. Moreover . . . it also means that persons preparing to teach should be afforded experience with more than one type of educational institution, with more than one kind of clientele, and with more than one particular age group. . . ." (84)

I leave the further consequences of Cremin's view for readers to work out on their own, as I did with those of Bobbitt. The point of offering the two examples is simply to show that the idea of there being an out-of-school curriculum can be put forward for a variety of different reasons. These examples remind us that definitions are pieces of arguments. Whatever definition of the curriculum we come up with, it functions within a larger set of beliefs about what the schools should be doing, how we should look at them, and so forth. We may, as Goodlad suggests, choose to start with such a definition and see where it takes us. But we would also do well to consider why we have made such a choice in the first place.

Are Redefinitions Necessary?

Finally we need to ask whether any of the redefinitions we have considered are necessary *as definitions*. Could their authors have done without them and still have gotten by? Can we in turn do the same? What is to stop us, for example, from talking about the possibility of our schools contributing to the development of harmful attitudes and habits without introducing the notion of a hidden curriculum? Or to take another example, can we not acknowledge that the curriculum is rarely delivered as planned without speaking of there being two separate curricula, one planned and the other enacted? What would be lost, in short, if we restricted the use of the word to its dictionary definition?

An answer to that last question calls on the notion of rhetoric. Whatever else we might wish to say about the usefulness and necessity of terms like "the hidden curriculum" or "the enacted [as opposed to the official] curriculum" we can surely testify to their power as figures of speech. For better or for worse, people remember such phrases and put them to use. That alone speaks to one aspect of their usefulness and necessity. A function they clearly serve is to provide a language for helping us to think and talk about a variety of curricular issues that might otherwise be overlooked.

But that rhetorical function can also be turned into an argument for getting rid of such language. Some would insist that terms like "the hidden curriculum" are "merely" rhetorical. Worse, they serve to generate belief in something that may not exist at all. However, those who would dismiss the "merely rhetorical" would do well to note that a similar criticism can be leveled at the conventional definition of curriculum, the one that appears in dictionaries. After all, *that* term once referred to a race course. Its first application to education was surely a metaphorical and, hence, a rhetorical one. We no longer see it as such, of course, but that is only because we have become so accustomed to its use in the dictionary sense that we no longer respond to it as the figure of speech it once was.

I said at the start of this section that all definitions are parts of arguments. The rhetorical structures in which definitions are lodged and play an important part are attempts to persuade us of the value of looking at something in a particular way and of later using a word or phrase to stand for that perception. We may disagree with that way of looking, but we nonetheless cannot avoid making use of the definition even while expressing our disagreement. Is it valuable, for instance, to think of there being something called a hidden curriculum? It may or may not turn out to be so, but even those who oppose the use of the term and who argue against it are momentarily caught in its ideational grasp. And so it is with all of the other ways of defining the word "curriculum." All we can do in the final analysis is to proffer reasoned arguments in support of one definition over the other.

PART II. PERSPECTIVAL ISSUES

This section deals chiefly with different ways of looking at curriculum content. It treats those outlooks on curriculum matters that one commonly finds discussed in curriculum textbooks. Underlying the descriptions to follow is the question of how they relate to the sense of confusion mentioned at the beginning of the chapter.

Multiple Perspectives on Curriculum Content

How many ways are there of thinking about what the schools are for and what their curricular content should be? Are there as many perspectives on curriculum content as there are definitions of curriculum? In a trivial sense, possibly so. If we took every noteworthy statement that has ever been offered about what our schools should be doing and compared it in detail with every other one, we would probably discover that each has unique curricular consequences of one kind or another. However, we would doubtless find great similarities as well, which would allow us to group the different outlooks in various ways. How many such groupings might we readily identify?

If we allow those who have written most broadly about curricular matters to do the grouping for us, the number of global perspectives turns out to be somewhere between two and six. Both Dewey and Bobbitt, for example, only speak of two. Today's writers of curriculum textbooks typically mention three or more. Schubert (1986), for example, employs three categories. Tanner and Tanner (1980) make use of four, as does McNeil (1977). Kliebard (1987), who offers an historical overview of the subject, also has a grouping of four curricular outlooks. In Eisner and Vallance's (1974) presentation of representative essays from competing points of view, the number moves up to five.

Not only is the total number of perspectives typically fewer than six but also there is considerable agreement among today's writers about the substantive thrust of most of the outlooks and even about what to call them. Further, the shift from Dewey's and Bobbitt's pair of categories to today's three or more reflects the emergence of points of view that were not as fully articulated when Dewey and Bobbitt wrote as they have since become. To reveal this agreement and to make clear some of the changes that have led to an increased number of perspectives, I shall examine a representive sampling from the above list of writings, beginning with Dewey's and Bobbitt's views, which, though dichotomous, turn out to be so in a rather complicated way.

Bipolarity in Curricular Thought

The most fundamental split of allegiance among people who think about education, whether laypersons or professionals, has to be between those who want change of one kind or another (proponents of reform) and those who prefer to keep things pretty much as they are (the defenders of the status quo). This division is inherently unstable, of course, at least hypothetically, for if those who wanted the schools changed were suddenly successful in their efforts we might expect them to reverse their positions, at least with respect to the desirability of change. The reformers presumably would then become defenders of the status quo and vice versa. In reality, however, the changes that do occur are seldom conclusive. As a result, the educational reformers (who in this century were for years referred to as progressives) retain their original agenda even when gains (in their terms) have been made and the defenders of the status quo (commonly called traditionalists or conservatives) continue to battle to keep things as they are or, if necessary, return them to the way they once were.

In the writings of both Dewey (1899, 1902) and Bobbitt (1972 [1918], 1924) the line between these two positions is sharply drawn. On the one side stand the conservative forces, prepared to defend the status quo. The curriculum they want to keep in place contains the standard school subjects, rigorously and uniformly taught. On the other side are aligned the forces of change, eager to see the schools become "modernized." The curriculum they favor is one that is sensitive to both the nature of the child and the social needs of the day. In gross outline, this is the picture that both Dewey and Bobbitt portray. Dewey labels the two positions "the old education" and "the new education." Bobbitt calls the two adversaries "the advocates of culture" and "the utilitarians."

What is especially interesting about these portrayals is that neither Dewey nor Bobbitt himself takes sides on the issue, or at least they try to avoid doing so. Indeed, the point of both their arguments is not only that one need not choose between these two alternatives but also that it would be folly to do so. Dewey says that "common sense recoils" at the thought of carrying either point of view to its "logical conclusion" (1902, 10). He speaks of "the radical fallacy" inherent in the "pleadings" of each position. Bobbitt employs a different strategy in his argument but comes to a similar conclusion. He claims that both sides are right. To choose one over the other, he says, "is like asking the question, 'Which shall the tree produce, the flower or the fruit?' " (6). The problem, as he sees it, is how to retain both outlooks by putting each in its proper place.

Thus, though both Dewey and Bobbitt present their readers with a dichotomous view of curricular affairs, the two positions they describe constitute the horns of a dilemma. Either both choices lead to undesirable consequences (Dewey) or they both are so attractive that one cannot choose between them (Bobbitt). Consequently, each author offers a third position of his own, one that promises a way out of the dilemma, either by preserving the best of both options, as Bobbitt seeks to do, or by avoiding the excesses of both, as Dewey hopes to accomplish. In short, what first looks like an either-or situation turns out not to be so after all.

The strategy both Dewey and Bobbitt employ is as old as rhetoric itself. First one presents an apparent choice that turns out not to be genuine because it entails too many undesirables. Then one offers a resolution that looks as though it combines the best or avoids the worst of both options. Not only is such a resolution attractive but also the person making it appears to be a model of fairness and moderation, speaking with the voice of reason. It is also noteworthy that the original positions, which are almost immediately rejected, are presented without occupants. That is, no one is named as a spokesperson for either position. No quotations are offered. No references are cited. What is provided are sketches, one might even say caricatures, rather than fully developed and sympathetically presented alternatives. The argument, in short, uses straw men as props.

This may sound like a criticism of Dewey and Bobbitt as expositors but it is not intended to be. And if it were it would be quite off the mark because neither man was *trying* to be a fair-minded and neutral observer of the educational scene who just happened to have a contrary opinion of his own. Both were themselves deeply committed advocates of well-formulated positions that each had by then worked out in some detail. Neither sought to leave his readers wondering what to believe or on which side to cast their votes. The writings of both Dewey and Bobbitt were designed to dispel confusion, not to breed it.

As a matter of fact, it is not quite accurate to say that Dewey and Bobbitt presented dichotomies that they then rejected in favor of their own views. For it turns out that the position each man finally takes is closer to one side of the dichotomy than the other. After warning of its excesses,

Dewey ultimately sides with the new education over the old, which is doubtless why even today he is usually classified as an educational progressive, though he was harshly critical of many practices associated with the progressive movement from the start. Though Bobbitt finds room for both the culture-minded and the utilitarian points of view, he winds up being much more sympathetic with the latter than with the former. His utilitarian bias is clearly evident in the emphasis he gives to the knowledge found to be useful in the workaday world. In short, both men wind up on the side of reform even though each rejects a stereotypic image of the cause he ultimately espouses.

This discussion brings up yet another aspect of the reform and conservative split, which is that both sides have linkages to more encompassing worldviews. There are, as we all know, conservative and reform positions on any number of issues, from politics to religion, from tastes in art to social customs. Moreover, most such differences have a long history. It is as if the world has always been divided into these two warring camps, which may be why Dewey and Bobbitt cannot help but side more with one than the other. Perhaps as a result of disposition or upbringing or both everyone leans more toward one side of this ancient dichotomy than toward the other.

These reflections on the rhetorical force of both Bobbitt's and Dewey's writings and on the bias each man ultimately reveals toward one or another of the dichotomous views he presents are not only not intended to be critical, as has already been said, but also are intended to suggest that similiar questions might profitably be raised about every presentation of a curricular position, no matter who presents it. What makes such questions relevant is that all writing is rhetorical in the sense of seeking to persuade someone of something. Confusion arises when we fail to acknowledge its rhetorical status or when its authors seek to disguise that fact from us or when someone tries to persuade us to take actions that are unnecessary or impossible. All of these possibilities are real ones when it comes to the modern presentation of curricular positions, as we shall presently see.

Beyond the Old-New Dichotomy: The Splintering of the Reform Agenda

Imagine two people who want to see the schools change and another two who want to see them remain the same. Now ask which pair is more likely to be at odds over the substance and details of what they want to have happen. The answer should be obvious. The pair bent on reform is more likely to disagree with each other than is the pair that wants the schools to stay as they are. The wish to change remains directionless until someone specifies what form the change is to take, whereas the wish to have things stay the same calls for no further elaboration. Anyone who prefers stability to change is, by definition, already committed to the current state of affairs.

Thus, it should come as no surprise to find that school reformers as a group do not share a unified vision of the direction in which the schools should move. They all may be committed to the idea of change, but they have very different notions about the direction that change should take. The differences between Dewey and Bobbitt are instructive in this regard. Both men were advocates of reform, but when it came to specifying the changes that should be made, they diverged markedly. Dewey focused principally on the psychological nature of the learner. He believed that teachers should begin their curriculum planning with those psychological considerations in mind. Bobbitt was more concerned with social conditions outside the school. He called for detailed studies of those conditions to identify what needed to be taught.

Disagreements between those who lean toward the psychological as the starting place for their ideas and those who are more socially oriented recur often in the history of educational thought. They gain expression in a variety of ways. Sometimes, as with the above depiction of Dewey and Bobbitt, what is at issue looks quite specific and even open to compromise. In Dewey's and Bobbitt's case a focal issue seems to be where to locate the source of one's educational objectives. At other times, however, the differences have deeper roots, which reach down to fundamental questions about what the schools are for, that is, what their ultimate mission should be. In fact, Dewey and Bobbitt were worlds apart on some of these fundamental questions as well.

On one side of this recurring split within reform groups as a whole is the view of the school as serving the individual, contributing to personal development, a means of freeing his or her potential. On the other side is the view of the school as an instrument of social reform on a grand scale, a means for helping to bring a new society into being. The phrases "individual development" and "social reform" epitomize what each side of this division stands for.

The group of educational reformers that banded together under the banner of progressivism during the first half of this century provides a fascinating case study of how this divided allegiance toward the primacy of the individual, on the one hand, and the primacy of the social, on the other, worked itself out organizationally, leading ultimately to a fundamental split within the progressive movement (Cremin 1961). In the next section of this chapter, when we turn to how some of today's curriculum specialists see their mission, we will encounter a renewed working out of that same division. For the time being we need only note the potential for such a split to occur, giving rise to *three* positions—two reform-oriented and one conservative—in place of the earlier two.

Beyond the Fundamental Trichotomy

Virtually all of the mappings of curricular thought that one finds in textbooks and also in more specialized accounts limn the contours of the three positions we have just outlined. The names applied to them are not always the same, but the three forms remain easily recognizable. What gets added beyond those three is largely a matter of choice, though not entirely. There is widespread acknowledgment of a fourth position occupied by individuals of a technological or hyperrational bent who seem less interested in where the schools are going or should go than in how effectively and efficiently they are getting there. Beyond that fourth alternative further additions truly are idiosyncratic.

To illustrate how these basic orientations are portrayed in textbooks and elsewhere I turn now to three presentations of them, the first by a textbook writer (McNeil 1977), the second by the editors of a collection of essays (Eisner and Vallance 1974), and the third by a historian of curricular thought (Kliebard 1987). Each contains a fairly typical set of categories. I start with the textbook.

McNeil (1977) begins with the following assertion: "There are four prevailing conceptions of the curriculum: humanistic, social reconstructionist, technological, and academic. Holders of these viewpoints have different ideas about what should be taught, to whom, when, and how." He continues,

> Those with a humanistic orientation hold that the curriculum should provide personally satisfying experiences for each individual. The new humanists are self-actualizers, who see curriculum as a liberating process that can meet the need for growth and personal integrity. They should not be confused with those persons in a liberal arts tradition who regard the "humanities" as separate disciplines, such as art, music, or literature, and who attempt to deal with the human being through cultural creations.
>
> Social reconstructionists stress societal needs over individual needs. They place primary responsibility on the curriculum to effect social reform and to derive a better future for society.
>
> The technologists view curriculum-making as a technological process for producing whatever ends policymakers demand. This is not a neutral orientation, because holders have a commitment to method that in turn has consequences for curriculum goals and content.
>
> Persons with an academic orientation see curriculum as the vehicle by which learners are introduced to subject matter disciplines and organized fields of study. (1)

McNeil concludes his summary with the claim, "Readers who understand these four positions will be better able to formulate their own ideas regarding purpose, content, method, organization, and evaluation of curriculum" (1). He then proceeds to elaborate on each orientation in four brief chapters of 10 or 15 pages each. His four "conceptions of curriculum" closely parallel the four categories that have already been discussed. Instead of pausing here to discuss them in more detail, however, let us move on to the next formulation.

Eisner and Vallance (1974) describe "five orientations" in their overview of contemporary curricular thought: "the cognitive processes approach, curriculum as technology, curriculum for self-actualization and consummatory experiences, curriculum for social reconstruction, and academic rationalism" (3). They are quick to point out, however, that the five categories they use are "somewhat arbitrary" and "do not necessarily exhaust the ways in which positions can be characterized or identified" (2). To show that this is so they proceed to name a few of the categories they considered incorporating into their own outline but ultimately rejected for one reason or another. Among the rejects were "child-centered versus society-centered," "values education versus skills training" and "moral education as opposed to the three R's." The five orientations they settled on refer to "a range of distinct conceptual biases that emerged repeatedly in a rather comprehensive survey of current literature in and related to the field" (2). Here is how they describe each of them.

> The cognitive process orientation to curriculum seeks to develop a repertoire of cognitive skills that are applicable to a wide range of intellectual problems. In this view subject matter, as typically defined, is considered instrumental to the development of intellectual abilities that can be used in areas other than those in which the processes were originally refined. . . . These abilities, it is argued, will endure long after the particular content or knowledge is forgotten or rendered obsolete by new knowledge. (19)
>
> The technological orientation to curriculum is one that is preoccupied with the development of means to achieve prespecified ends. Those working from this orientation tend to view schooling as a complex system that can be analyzed into its constituent components. The problem for the educator or educational technologist is to bring the system under control so that the goals it seeks to attain can be achieved. (49)
>
> In the [self-actualization, or curriculum as consummatory experience] orientation to curricular thought . . . [s]chooling is to become a means of personal fulfillment, to provide a context in which individuals discover and develop their unique identities. Curriculum, in this view is a pervasive and enriching experience with implications for many dimensions of personal development. (105)
>
> Social reconstructionists see schooling as an agency of social change, and they demand that education be relevant both to the student's interests and to society's needs. Curriculum is conceived to be an active force having direct impact on the whole fabric of its human and social context. (135)
>
> The major goal of academic rationalists as far as curriculum is concerned is to enable students to use and appreciate the ideas and works that constitute the various intellectual and artistic disciplines. Academic rationalists argue that ideas within the various disciplines have a distinctive structure and a distinctive set of contributions to make to the education of man. Indeed, acquisition of these structures is largely what education is about. (161)

Once again, there is a clear similarity between four of the five categories Eisner and Vallance use and those we have already discussed. The groupings they refer to as academic rationalism, curriculum for self-actualization, curriculum for social reconstruction, and curriculum as technology bear a striking resemblance to McNeil's four categories as well as to the four outlined earlier in this section.

It is informative to compare these two formulations with a more historically oriented perspective, such as the one presented by Kliebard (1987), which looks at the emergence of four "interest groups" during the early part of the 20th century, "each with a distinct agenda for action" and each of which was partially to determine the course of the modern American curriculum" (xi). These were "the humanists," whom Kliebard describes as "the guardians of an ancient tradition tied to the power of reason and the finest elements of the Western cultural heritage" (27); "the developmentalists," described as those who believed "the curriculum riddle could be solved with ever more accurate scientific data, not only with respect to the different stages of child and adolescent development, but on the nature of learning" (28); "the social efficiency educators," who sought to apply "the standardized techniques of industry to the business of schooling" (28); and "the social meliorists," who "saw the schools as a major, perhaps the principal, force for social change and social justice" (29). As Kliebard tells the story, "The twentieth century became the arena where these four versions of what knowledge is of most worth and of the central functions of schooling were presented and argued." He concludes that in "the end, what became the American curriculum was not the result of any decisive victory by any of the contending parties, but a loose, largely unarticulated, and not very tidy compromise" (29).

New Wine in Old Bottles?

When placed alongside Kliebard's historical account, McNeil's four categories, together with those of Eisner and Valance, make it look as though all of the old curriculum debates are still very much alive. Is that really so, or does their memory just linger on? The answer turns out to be a bit of both.

The language in which some of these curricular positions were previously framed has changed considerably. Old slogans have disappeared; so too have some of their organizational embodiments. The Progressive Education Association, for example, which for so long championed what was once called child-centered education, no longer exists. (For a history of its demise, see Cremin 1961.) The phrase "social reconstruction" lacks the currency today that it enjoyed in the 1930s; so does the phrase "social efficiency." There is also less talk these days about social engineering than when Bobbitt wrote. Even today's conservatives, who by definition are opposed to change, have been transformed by their critics into today's *neo*conservatives.

All such changes aside, the similarities between the new and the old positions, at least as described in textbooks and elsewhere, are sufficient to create the impression of there being a reasonable amount of continuity between then and now, even when the points of comparision are decades apart. What we have today is new wine in old bottles, or so it would appear.

Let us go over the four recurring categories once again, seeking to incorporate some of the differences in emphasis that have emerged from the preceding discussion. There is first the conservative or reactionary position, whose advocates either want no change or else wish to restore the subjects and methods that have made up the curriculum and instructional procedures of the past. Next come two reform positions. The advocates of one are part of a long tradition of educational criticism that goes back to Rousseau and beyond. They propose having the nature of the individual learner be the central consideration in shaping both curriculum and instruction. Advocates of the other reform position are also part of a tradition of criticism, though one that is not quite as venerable as the first and also rather more social than educational in its focus. They wish to use the curriculum of the school as an instrument of social change. Finally, there is a position that has less to do with change or no change in the curriculum than with monitoring, regularizing, and evaluating the curriculum-instructional nexus. The advocates of this position are chiefly concerned with the effective management of the entire educational process.

This grouping of four leaves out the category that Eisner and Vallence referred to as the "cognitive process orientation." The argument for including it is that it too has its counterpart in the past as well as the present. Though the term "cognitive process" is decidedly modern, the argument that says that the chief function of the school should be mental training of one kind or another has been around for some time. What Eiser and Vallance call "cognitive process orientation" is only the modern version of that argument. Its principal advocates are psychologists of one kind or another (i.e., educational; developmental; child; or most recently, cognitive psychologists), though many practicing educators also find the position attractive (see, e.g., Resnick and Klopfer 1989).

Viewers, Viewpoints, and the Viewed

What is the connection among these four (or five) categories and the sense of confusion that we spoke of at the start of the chapter? One possibility is that some of the confusion arises over the difficulty of making a choice. The exposition of these four viewpoints in many textbooks creates the impression that everyone has or should have a position on such matters. Either we should adopt one of the positions that have been outlined or invent one of our own. We have already noted advice to that effect in McNeil's (1977) text. McNeil, we will recall, accompanied his presentation of the four positions with the suggestion that his readers "formulate their own ideas regarding the purpose, content, method, organization, and evaluation of curriculum." The language in which these ideas are presented—the use of words like "orientation," "outlook," and "perspective"—serves to reinforce the notion that everyone should have a position of his or her own on such matters. Indeed, the root metaphor contained in the expression "points of view" suggests that one has no choice but to view whatever it is from one angle or another.

The importance of making up one's mind about which perspective to take is heightened by the fact that the four orientations are usually depicted as competing with one another for our allegiance. Not only must the viewer look, in other words, but the choice of any one perspective rules out the others, partly because the different orientations are commonly presented as answers to a single question, such as what should our schools be for? Or what should their curriculum be? As the title of Eisner and Vallance's (1974) collection of essays emphasizes, these are *conflicting* conceptions of curriculum.

Nor is this sense of being confronted with choices that are mutually exclusive just a matter of language. There are logical incompatibilities between and among certain of the positions as well. It is impossible, for example, to be content with the curriculum as it stands (i.e., be a conservative) and also want to see it change (i.e., be a reformer of either of the two types). The two positions are mutually exclusive. Similarly, there is no way that one may be chiefly concerned with adjusting the curriculum to the needs of the individual learner and at the same time be chiefly concerned with using the schools to effect major social changes. One simply cannot be *chiefly* interested in two things at once.

Add to these logical impossibilities the fact that different interests, apart from those entailed in the choices themselves, propel us in different directions and it becomes evident that there are *psychological* as well as *logical* barriers to adopting certain combinations of the four positions. To take only one example, although there seems to be no *necessary* conflict between a concern for efficiency and effectiveness, on the one hand, and any of the remaining three positions, on the other, some of the combinations seem rather unlikely. For example, someone who assigned prime importance to matters of efficiency would not be expected to be keenly concerned with fitting the curriculum to the needs of individual students. Such a combination is possible, of course, but not very likely. Other mismatches of this kind can easily be imagined.

What all of this comes to can be summed up in the form of a syllogism: (1) An important decision about where one stands with respect to the curriculum has to be made by everyone; (2) most other people have already made up their minds about such matters; (3) to be like most people one had better hurry up and join one or another of these communities of belief or else forge one's own convictions from a combination of those available.

That such a line of reasoning might well lead to confusion is readily understandable. After all, it is often difficult to make up one's mind about important matters under the best of conditions, doubly so when the choice is between such far-reaching and global perspectives. In this instance, however, the confusion is unnecessary because the choice, at least as usually presented, does not have to be made. The logic of the argument I have just outlined is fundamentally flawed.

To see its flaws we first must acknowledge that any perspective on competing schools of curriculum thought must be sufficiently removed from its objects of observation to have them stand out as discrete entities. To be a perspective on perspectives it must, in short, take a bird's-eye view. The person who adopts such a view, if he or she is trying to be fair, as is usually the case, must at least give the appearance of objectivity, of being a dispassionate if not disinterested observer of the scene. Not all curriculum textbooks seek to do this; Tanner and Tanner (1980), for example, comes down strongly on the side of a particular point of view, as does Stratemeyer et al. (1957).

But an apparent attitude of objectivity coupled with the overt or covert suggestion that the reader make a choice about such matters, which is the way these orientations usually appear in curriculum textbooks, only heightens the confusion created by the choice alone. If the person who lays out the choices does not declare where he or she stands on such matters, the reader is left to guess why. Is it because that person has not yet *taken* a position, in which case the reader might well wonder why he or she is being encouraged to do so. One possibility is that the author simply declines to reveal his or her position, which makes one wonder how objective the presentation has been after all. Either way, a puzzling situation becomes more puzzling.

Another clue that the choice as presented is not a real one is revealed by the terms used to describe the persons who are said to hold the various positions. Who calls oneself a new humanist or a self-actualizer or a social reconstructionist or an academic rationalist? The answer is, no one does. These are not terms that people apply to themselves. Nor are they terms that are inscribed on banners or used as club names or the names of professional organizations. Rather, they are names that if used at all outside of textbooks, are applied to people by others. Even then, it is hard to imagine someone saying, "I know Sue, she's a self-actualizer" or "Poor old Harry, the last of the academic rationalists." And if they are *not* in use as labels of self-identification or as the names of organizations, one wonders why not. Is it because people have thought of using them but have chosen not to because they did not like them? Or might it be that people ordinarily do not think in such terms at all? The latter is the more likely possibility.

Moreover, it is not just that the language is wrong, that few if any educators declare themselves to be self-actualizers or academic rationalists or whatever. What is also wrong or at least misleading is the suggestion that most people wind up adopting one or another of these general views on the curriculum, no matter what they are called. Some people might do so, of course. But does everyone? *Need* everyone? The first of those questions is empirical and properly calls for a survey of some kind to determine how many practicing educators have even thought about the curriculum in such global terms, much less worked out a clear and consistent position of the kind we have been discussing. But we need not wait for such a study to predict with confidence at least one of its outcomes, which is that the results will be mixed. Some people will have given thought to such matters, but by no means everyone. Moreover, it is a fair bet that the number who have *not* done so will be far from trifling.

But what of the normative question? Even if it turns out that few people have given thought to such matters, is it desirable that more of them, or perhaps all of them, do so? A piece of the argument that says that they should depends on one's answer to the question of how broad curricular decisions get made and who should have a voice in making them. If teachers and building-level administrators are to be among the decision makers, so the argument goes, they surely must cultivate as broad a perspective as possible. Counterbalancing this argument is the view that most teachers and administrators *inherit* a curriculum when they accept their jobs and there is relatively little they can do to modify or change it globally. From this point of view there is little need for them to concern themselves with broad curricular issues. Needless to say, the view that says they should adopt a global perspective and the one that says they should not are truly in conflict.

The Issue Restated

Let me be clear about what is *not* being claimed in my criticism of the customary practice of facing teachers or teachers-to-be with a set of alternative positions on curricular matters and then encouraging them to make a choice. I am not denying that many educators, perhaps even most, would feel a strong proclivity, a flow of sympathy perhaps, toward one or another of the positions we have outlined. Here is where words like "orientation" come in handy. Once the four positions have been described to them, most people probably do feel drawn more toward one or more of them than the others: preoriented, let us say, already turned in that direction themselves. They may at the same time feel a corresponding antipathy toward one or more of the other positions. Those eventualities are not in dispute.

I am also not denying that the four positions, as they appear in many textbooks and elsewhere, have the ring of authenticity, as stereotypes commonly do. Even when the positions are sketchily presented (which turns out to be the only way they *can* be portrayed), one can almost visualize the person who would feel most at home within each position. One might even feel as though one had encountered such persons before and perhaps could name one or two of them if asked. As caricatures they are dead ringers for the stereotypes most of us already possess. That much I also grant.

What I do insist, however, is that the four (or five) perspectives do not hold up as being genuinely inhabitable—all natural proclivities and stereotypes notwithstanding. Few, if any people, living or dead, turn out to be occupants of these abstract positions, and for good reason, which is that the positions as usually presented are insufficiently contextualized and situated. In a word, they are too academic.

The common textbook advice that calls on beginning teachers to choose one of these points of view as their very own (or "construct" their own position) is at the very least psychologically naive because whatever choices there are about such matters have probably already been made long before the descriptions were encountered. Such choices are built into what was described as a natural proclivity toward one or another of the positions. Moreover, if a *change* of position is wanted or is thought desirable by someone other than the neophyte, chances are that the would-be convert would be more readily persuaded by a person speaking from *inside* one or another of the perspectives rather than by someone offering a bird's-eye view of all the options. This statement is true not only because the view would be presented in greater detail but also because it would be presented less dispassionately, with greater involvement, and more persuasively.

Talk of persuasive arguments on behalf of any of these positions may appear to contradict what was just said about there being few if any occupants of these academic positions. The apparent contradiction, however, turns out to be false. For when we turn to actual cases we find people who at first glance fit each stereotype all right, but the view each offers is highly idiosyncratic and when seen from the inside does not speak for the position as a whole.

Consider what might happen if we sought advocates of each position. We would certainly have no difficulty finding representative texts. The names of prominent authors, both past and present, come readily to mind. Robert Hutchins or Mortimer Adler could speak for the academic conservative, Carl Rogers or Maxine Greene for the self-actualizer, George Counts or Michael Apple for the social reconstructionist, Edward Thorndike or Robert Glaser for the technologist, and so on. In short order, in other words, we could assemble spokespersons for the different points of view. If we then proceeded to read a representative text by any of them, however, what we would discover is a perspective that is at once more detailed, more passionately argued, and more limited in the scope of its applicability than any synoptic overview portrays them as being, whether the latter is found in a textbook or elsewhere.

It is easy enough to understand what it means to call the positions contained in such representative texts more detailed and more passionately argued (at least in the sense of being more one-sided). What it means to describe them as being more limited in the scope of their applicability, however, may not be so clear. What this refers to is the fact that each text has a lot to say about some issues but little or nothing about others. Mortimer Adler, for example, tends to disregard the earliest years of schooling, Carl Rogers is silent on the possibility of social reform, George Counts never addresses the place of educational measurement, Edward L. Thorndike virtually overlooks the implications of a psychodynamic perspective on human nature, and so on.

I draw from this discussion two important lessons. One is that even our exemplars of "pure types" turn out to be impure when we examine them closely. The other is that what may seem at first to be conflicting views do not conflict on all fronts. Indeed, on several fronts some positions have nothing to say at all.

Kliebard's (1987) historical account reveals the same thing, only in an slightly different way. He clearly intimates that the four interest groups whose trajectories he traced were not always battling one another, at least not on all fronts. As he points out, "so many things were happening at once" that he chose to abandon "a strict chronological rendering of the story" (xiii). Instead, he relates one part of it to something like its natural conclusion, then circles back to pick up another thread. To reiterate, this means that positions that look as though they are polar opposites (e.g., the conservative and either of the reform positions) turn out not to be in conflict at all on a number of educational issues. What this result means for the neophyte is that he or she would probably be better off worrying about the pros and cons of particular issues of special interest or ones that touch on actual working conditions than trying to decide which of the four or five basic perspectives he or she should adopt.

What about the possibility of a composite view, made up of a little of this and a little of that? The problem with that option becomes one of deciding what the criteria are by which the parts are to be chosen. Next comes the question of how they should be assembled, i.e., how the parts relate to one another. Moreover, when we look at how almost any of our representative spokespersons came to the views they hold, what we find is that neither method—i.e., choosing a "standard model" or constructing a "custom-made" point of view—is the way overarching perspectives usually become developed. This result should not surprise us. Hardly anyone sits down and says, "I think I need an overall point of view with respect to the curriculum. Let's see, shall I adopt one that is already made or should I make up my own?" What is more likely to happen is for a person to become excited or puzzled or annoyed about an educational issue of some magnitude and in the process of trying to articulate his or her views on *that* issue, a process that may take a long time and may endure a number of setbacks and even reversals of opinion, something like an enduring perspective on a variety of issues begins to emerge. One thinks here of how Dewey's disappointment with the education being provided for his own children colored his thoughts about what a school might seek to do and of how Bobbitt's (1972 [1918]) chagrin over his failure to impose an American-style curriculum on schools in the Philippines led to his far-reaching formulation of a more "scientific" way of proceeding.

Career Choice as a Mode of Expressing One's Curricular Bias

Having already introduced the possibility that most people are naturally inclined toward one or another of the modal curricular perspectives, I move now to two additional observations. The first is that one's proclivity toward any such perspective, toward an academically conservative position, for example, or toward a point of view that looks with favor on the promise of educational measurement, is in all likelihood not an isolated bias toward a set of educational undertakings. Rather, it reflects a more enveloping motivational structure whose objects of preference and desire cover a wide range of human affairs. Second, I observe that an obvious way of giving expression to one's "natural" inclinations, whether they be educationally focused or more broadly diffused, is through one's choice of career.

The person who likes numbers and is interested in scientific matters would in all probability be more naturally drawn toward a career as an educational tester or an evaluation expert than toward one as a kindergarten teacher or a teacher of dance. Someone who is strongly attracted to literature and to cultural affairs in general is more likely to choose high school or college teaching, with its strong academic emphasis, than to become a specialist in educational tests and measurement. It is surely no accident, incidentally, that the modern Great Books movement was spurred by collaboration between a lawyer (Robert Maynard Hutchins) and a philosopher (Mortimer Adler) working within the framework of a private university that already had a reputation for academic rigor. It is also no accident that those who call on the schools to become instruments of social reform are less likely to be classroom teachers and school-building administrators than college and university professors and other social commentators.

This is not to say that everyone is lucky enough to wind up in a career that gives full and satisfying expression to his or her natural inclinations. Many people make ill-considered and regrettable choices, we know; countless others, unfortunately, have little or no choice to make. Nonetheless the pull toward one line of work rather than another is likely felt to some degree by us all, whether we are free to act on it or not. What this means within the domain of curricular affairs is simply that the forces that incline teachers or school administrators or university professors toward one conception of curriculum or another are probably of a piece with those that pull them toward this or that educational specialty. The choice, in brief, is far from academic. Seldom is it the clear-cut, rational process that textbook writers and others so often make it out to be.

A final point about the forces that initially incline us and ultimately guide us toward one curricular position or another: Those forces include social influences of many different kinds. As we move in one direction or another we become enmeshed in a host of social networks whose members support and encourage us along the way. There are courses to take, books and magazines to read, meetings to attend, friendships to cultivate, and organizations to join. All of these connections, when successful, serve to affirm and deepen our emerging sense of commitment and identification with this or that outlook on educational affairs. The availability and variety of these forms of social support attest to both the complexity and the duration of the process of developing an enduring affiliation with a particular point of view. They also reveal the parochial quality of all such affiliations.

The Interpretive Nature of the Different Perspectives

When one thinks of all the organizations one might join and of the many journals and books one might read if one became interested in the promise of educational measurement, say, or the preservation of our cultural heritage through education, it becomes easy to see that each of the perspectives we have been discussing is inadequately described as a fixed position from which to gaze on curricular affairs. Rather, we might more accurately think of each of our four or five orientations as something like a way of life, shared by a company of believers who form a loosely knit social network of the kind that the literary critic Stanley Fish (1980, 1989) speaks of as "an interpretive community."

It is also easy to see that each such community has, as it were, its "party line," which includes a broadly sanctioned set of beliefs; a body of writings, some of which may attain near-canonical status; and a cluster of well-known personages, some of whom may be highly revered and looked on as spokespersons for the group as a whole whereas others are spoken of as "the enemy." These communities almost always have a special vocabulary, if not a full-fledged language, complete with buzzwords that have a special meaning and significance within the community that they do not have outside of it. All of these features of interpretive communities help us to understand why they are called interpretive.

What is not so easy to see is that the overviews we have been discussing—the bird's-eye perspectives—are also interpretations, fully as much as are the views they report on. What makes this fact difficult to perceive is that the overviews are usually presented as being factual or close to it. They are reports *on* points of view rather than points of view themselves, or so it seems. They give the appearance, in other words, of standing above rhetoric and above interpretation. What is becoming increasingly evident, however, to a growing number of today's social scientists and literary critics is that there can be no position *outside* interpretation; there is no noninterpretive stance. There are only *ways of looking*, a category that includes *ways of looking at ways of looking*, which of course embraces the point of view being taken here.

I have already partially acknowledged the interpretive nature of the overviews by noting that the terms used to label the various perspectives are typically not the ones used by the people who subscribe to the outlook in question. Few people, I pointed out, call themselves self-actualizers or academic-rationalists, for example. That in itself should be enough to show readers the interpretive nature of the descriptions.

At the same time, in fairness to the three overviews used as examples, I must also point out that in each case the author or authors seemed aware of the tentativeness of the categories being used. Eisner and Vallence (1974) openly acknowledge the "somewhat arbitrary" character of their taxonomy. They admit that theirs is "not necessarily" the only way of organizing such an overview. Thus, they leave the door open to other frameworks. But at the same time their "not necessarily" implies that theirs may indeed turn out to be the only way of looking at things after all. To be more in line with the emerging interpretivist perspective, however, they should have reversed their words. They might better have insisted that theirs is *necessarily not* the only way of slicing the pie. By virtue of its being *their* way, there have to be others. The same holds of course for the other two overviews that have been discussed.

But what of the fact that there is such similarity among the three sets of categories? Isn't that evidence *against* an interpretivist reading of each one? Doesn't it imply that there is an objective reality being reported on after all? Not at all. It only implies that that particular framework for ordering the phenomena is presently dominant and, on the basis of three examples, seems to be widely shared.

Let us suppose that we do accept, at least for the time being, the interpretive nature not only of the three overviews we have been discussing but also of all overviews, no matter who puts them forward or how insistent their claim to objectivity. What would be the consequences of doing so? Does it discredit them as outlooks? Would such an acceptance force us to *dis*believe any of them? Again, the thoroughgoing interpretivist would say, "Not at all." Knowing them to be interpretations does not affect our willingness to believe or disbelieve them. We may still find them convincing or not and for basically the same reasons we might have given before adopting an interpretivist stance, though the interpretivist would rule out one very crucial justification for taking any position whatsoever, which is the claim that the point of view in question represents the truth, plain and simple.

What, then, is the advantage (or disadvantage) of seeing them as interpretations? Only this: Once seen as interpretations their persuasive character comes to the fore. We become aware that they are part of someone's effort to persuade us of something and that awareness triggers a number of questions that we might not otherwise be inclined to ask, such as these: Whose interests are being served by this effort to persuade? Are they interests I share or wish to share? What does the argument ask me to do? How might it affect the distribution of power? Do I wish to be a party to that arrangement?

Many persons would be quick to call such questions political, and so they seem to me as well. But calling them that need have no effect whatsoever on where we side once we have answered them. We remain as free as ever to join forces with any person or group we wish—though not really free, as we have seen, for we begin our search for answers already faced in one direction or another, our proclivities preestablished, our inclinations making us lean this way or that. Our direction can always be changed, of course, but that takes some doing.

The process of persuasion, with its juggling of interests and power, is starkly clear in the dichotomies that Dewey and Bobbitt presented. Dewey (1902), we will recall, spoke of the new education and the old education. Bobbitt (1972 [1918]) told of there being "culture people" and utilitarians. Yet if we look carefully at what is said about either dichotomy, we see that neither is presented in much detail. Both are stereotypes. Dewey mentions no one who speaks for the old education or the new. Bobbitt gives no examples of either "culture people" or utilitarians. In short, in his presentation of "the way things are" neither Dewey nor Bobbitt even pretends to offer his readers a serious choice. The way each talks about both alternatives makes clear that he wants *both* sides of the dichotomy to be rejected in favor of his own view, which he then proceeds to explicate in great detail. Should we criticize either Dewey or Bobbitt for presenting such a "one-sided" view? Certainly not. Seeing them to be one-sided, however, which is the same as seeing them as presenting interpretations rather than objective descriptions of the way things are, enables us to weigh their arguments in ways we might not be inclined to do as long as we believe from the start that either or both men are simply speaking the truth. Is this kind of skepticism a good thing? From a certain perspective, yes.

The point about interpretation and its political nature has no more special significance within a curricular context than it does elsewhere. All views of the curriculum are clearly interpretive and they are certainly political in the sense of being put forward with persuasive force and of having consequences that will serve the interests of some but not all. This factor does not make them in any way unique, however, for the same could be said about all attempts to persuade us to believe or do anything.

PART III. PROFESSIONAL ISSUES

Most accounts of curriculum as a field of professional endeavor (e.g., Caswell 1966; Seguel 1966) place its founding shortly after World War I and its heyday somewhere in the mid- to late 1930s. Bobbitt's book, *The Curriculum*, which appeared in 1918, is usually cited as the field's first professional text. By the beginning of World War II there were curriculum specialists of one kind or another in most school systems. At about that time departments of curriculum were also becoming commonplace in colleges and schools of education, the first one having been founded at Teachers College, Columbia University, in 1937. The fact that the subject could be studied in colleges and universities obviously gave credibility to its status as a field of professional endeavor, for as Goodlad (1985) once remarked, speaking as though to a doubting Thomas, "If there wasn't a field of the curriculum, why would there be departments of curriculum?" (142).

Divisions of Labor Within the Field of Curriculum

Part of the answer to what departments of curriculum train their graduates to do is revealed in the titles of curriculum specialists, who are also referred to generically as curriculum workers; curricularists; and most generic of all, perhaps, curriculum persons, the last a term used by Heubner (Pinar 1975, 215). Those who work directly on projects to modify a particular curriculum or piece of one go by a number of different names: curriculum makers; curriculum developers; curriculum designers; curriculum evaluators; curriculum directors; curriculum coordinators; and curriculum advisors, a term used to refer to specialists in one or more subject matter areas, such as mathematics or social studies. Directors, coordinators, and advisors are titles usually reserved for curriculum specialists working in school systems. Developers, designers, and evaluators may be found either in schools or in universities or colleges. Additionally, there are two terms reserved exclusively for university-based specialists: professors of curriculum and curriculum theorists.

What do all these people do and how does their activity relate to the sense of confusion that supposedly plagues the field of curriculum? In short, what is problematic or confusing about the work of curriculum specialists? The answer to that broad question centers, I believe, on the narrower one of what the university-based specialists do—that is, the professors of curriculum and the curriculum theorists—and, more particularly, on what people think they *should* be doing. There appear to be two answers to the narrower question, one long-standing and still dominant, the other more recent and yet to be fully articulated.

The long-standing answer says that university-based specialists should be of direct, practical help to classroom teachers and school administrators as the latter go about the day-to-day business of trying to improve the curriculum of their schools. This is not to say that the specialists must actually *work* in schools. It is only to insist that what they teach and write should have clear relevance to the curriculum-improvement efforts of practitioners.

The more recent answer, the one that remains to be fully articulated, calls for the university-based specialist to be doing something different, something other than serving the practitioner's need for technical help in the arduous business of curriculum improvement and reform, though exactly what they should be doing instead is not entirely clear. One possibility is for them to begin working even more closely with practitioners than they have in the past. Another possibility is for them to bring to bear on educational matters in general the outlooks of scholarly disciplines and political perspectives that heretofore have been overlooked or largely ignored.

The central issue, then, is whether the dominant perspective on the work of the university-based curriculum specialist has finally run its course and now needs to be replaced by something different or whether there is still vitality in what has become the traditional mission of such specialists. To see how this issue unfolds historically, we shall examine three versions of the dominant perspective at different stages of its development. The three we shall concentrate on, with only passing reference to others, are those of Franklin Bobbitt, Ralph Tyler, and Joseph Schwab. Following a look at the advice these three men gave to practitioners and by indirection to their university-based colleagues, we shall turn to the writings of those who seek to replace the dominant perspective with something different. Before treating either set of ideas about what university-based curriculum specialists should be doing it is helpful to consider briefly what the situation was like before curriculum specialists of any kind arrived on the scene. The purpose in doing so is to identify some of the sources of influence on curricular matters with which specialists would later have to deal.

How Curricula Came into Being Before There Were Curriculum Specialists

I have already pointed out that there were no curriculum specialists, as such, until around the time of World War I. But obviously there were curricula before then. How did they come into being before there were experts to help form them? An adequate answer to that question would require a detailed historical account, which I cannot begin to undertake here. (For an important part of the answer see Kliebard 1987.) I can, however, name some of the obvious forces and influences that helped to shape the curriculum before there were curriculum specialists (forces that continue to shape it today, I might add).

To begin, there are the precedents of custom and tradition. One reason why certain subjects remain in the curriculum is simply that they have been there for such a long time. Indeed, some portions of the curriculum have been in place for so long that the question of how they got there or who decided to put them there in the first place has no answer, or at least not one that anyone except a historian would be able to give. As far as most people are concerned, they have just "always" been there, or so it seems. (For an interesting lampoon of how custom can rigidify the curriculum, see Benjamin 1939.)

Another reason for certain subjects being there is that they are so obviously useful that they need no further justification. The three R's would be a case in point. It seems so obvious to just about everyone that we all need to know how to read, write, and figure that no further argument has to be mustered to retain such studies as a mandatory part of the school curriculum.

A third reason for the curriculum having the shape it has is that some group of acknowledged authorities (though not curriculum specialists per se) initially determined that such and such should be part of the curriculum, and so it stays. These authorities may have been school officials, such as superintendents or members of state boards, but they also may have been outsiders, such as a national commission whose advice some other body of authorities has chosen to accept.

Yet another powerful source of influence resides in the textbooks and other instructional material used in class. Elementary reading texts, such as McGuffy's Readers or the more modern Dick-and-Jane series, are widely acknowleged as having shaped both the method and the content of instruction in the early grades for decades. The shaping force of commercially prepared instructional materials in the upper grades and beyond is hardly less powerful. Years before Bobbitt's time the textbook writers of the day were curriculum specialists without title.

These sources of influence on the curriculum are so obvious and so familiar that little more need be said about them at this point. Even this rudimentary a sketch should suffice to remind us, however, of two fundamental points. The first is that educators seemed to get along quite well without curriculum specialists until recently, if by getting along well we simply mean that they did not have to bother trying to construct curricula on their own. The second point, which is really an elaboration of the first, is that before there were curriculum specialists, teachers and administrators seldom had to decide themselves what subjects to teach or in what order or in what detail to teach them. Those decisions were already made for them, in large measure, by forces over which they had little or no control. Moreover, the same remains true today. As happened before curriculum specialists ever appeared on the scene, today's teachers, for the most part, continue to inherit more than they invent. The curriculum that provides the framework of their daily activity is largely a kind of "given" that was firmly in place long before they got there.

It is when the practitioners' curricular inheritance is radically challenged in some way and when the task of replacing it with something else cannot be accomplished by the forces that usually do that job that the services of a curriculum specialist, a curriculum *maker* as Bobbitt was to call him or her, become attractive, if not a downright necessity. But even then the call for such services need not emerge at once.

Dewey, for example, did not call on curriculum specialists for help, even though he proceeded to found a school whose curriculum was to make a radical break with the past. He had no choice, of course, because there were no specialists to call on. The curriculum developers in Dewey's school were the teachers themselves. Reports of how the staff worked together to produce a curriculum (Dewey 1899) make clear the magnitude of the task. In Dewey's school the standard curriculum of the usual school subjects was not so much abandoned as it was looked on as a far-off goal from the perspective of the early grades, something to be attained at the end of the road perhaps but certainly not at the beginning. Teachers were to decide how to bridge the gap between the child and the curriculum by considering what children were like as psychological beings and by keeping in mind where the process was headed (i.e., toward those bodies of knowledge that are encapsulated under the traditional headings of science, math, and so forth). They were then to devise projects and activities that were designed to make use of the child's current interests while leading in incremental steps toward the mastery of traditional subjects. That was a tall order and there is some question as to whether Dewey and his teachers actually carried it off (Schwab 1978). Dewey's account of the process well dramatizes the magnitude of what it means for a group of practitioners to undertake a radical revision of the curriculum. Had Dewey and his staff been able to wait a couple of decades for Franklin Bobbitt to arrive on the scene, they might have welcomed his help.

Bobbitt's Program of Curriculum Improvement

Bobbitt's (1972 [1918]) arrival as an advice giver to practicing educators came with the publication of his book, *The Curriculum*. The Western world was just beginning to recover from the ravages of World War I. The social and economic disruptions of that event were to have profound implications for education. In Bobbitt's view, "The present social *debacle* demonstrates the inadequacy of types of education upon which we have relied in the past" (284). What was wrong, as he saw it, was that a "program never designed for the present day has been inherited." He continued, "Any inherited system, good for its time, when held to after its day, hampers social progress. It is not enough that the system, fundamentally unchanged in plan and purpose, be improved in details. . . . New duties lie before us. And these require new methods, new materials, new vision" (iii–iv). In the following remarks Bobbitt sums up his book's purpose and proceeds to comment on the magnitude of the job ahead:

> We here try to develop a point of view that seems to be needed by practical school men and women as they make the educational adjustments now demanded by social conditions; and needed also by scientific workers who are seeking to define with accuracy the objectives of education. It is the feeling of the writer that in the social reconstructions of the post-war years that lie just ahead of us, education is to be called upon to bear a hitherto undreamed-of burden of responsibility and to undertake unaccustomed labors. (v)

The two important points for us to note about Bobbitt's position are, first, the enormity of the task facing educators and, second, Bobbitt's identification of the two groups who are to do most of the work: "practical school men and women" and "scientific workers." We also might note what the respective task of each group is to be. The school people are to "make the educational adjustments" demanded by the changed social conditions; the scientific workers are to "define with accuracy the objectives of education." Who are these scientific workers, whom Bobbitt also calls "curriculum discoverers"? They are, for the most part, Bobbitt's own graduate students, working toward advanced degrees in education. Where does Bobbitt position himself with respect to this division of labor? He is in a supraordinate position. His task, presumably, is to "develop a point of view" that will serve the needs of both groups: practitioners and curriculum workers.

Bobbitt does not say where his scientific workers stand, hierarchically, with respect to the practitioners, but the implication that they occupy a position above them yet somewhat lower than Bobbitt himself seems inescapable. It is they who are to "particularize" what Bobbitt calls "the controlling purposes of education." "The scientific task preceding all others," he remarks, "is the determination of the curriculum" (41–42). It seems, then, that from Bobbitt's point of view the university-based curriculum specialist has a dual allegiance: to serve the needs of school practitioners, on the one hand, and those of graduate students, on the other. These specialists seek to fulfill their obligations to these groups in a variety of ways. They teach courses and write books and articles for both of them. They also may guide the "scientific studies" of their graduate students and perhaps even engage in such studies on their own. They also may have direct contacts with groups of practitioners by serving as curriculum consultants to schools and school districts.

I have already pointed out that Bobbitt sees the task of revitalizing the curriculum as being huge. He speaks of "a slow-moving program covering a long series of years" (1972 [1918], 285). Elsewhere he talks of the process continuing "indefinitely" (287) and predicts "a generation-long program of curriculum improvement" (1924, 6). Why must the process take so long? For two reasons, presumably. One is that it simply takes a long time to conduct the studies in which curriculum objectives are "discovered" and then to identify the pupil experiences through which those objectives are to be attained. Bobbitt speaks of there being "innumerable" specific objectives and "countless" pupil experiences. The second reason is political. Change must be introduced slowly to be acceptable. Bobbitt warns school superintendents against trying "to advance more rapidly than teachers, school board, and community are prepared for" (1972 [1918], 288). "The school superintendent will remember," he says, "that inertia is as much a factor in the general human economy as dynamic forces; that the conservation of gains is as important as making further gains" (287).

Bobbitt summarizes the key ideas of his point of view as follows:

> The central theory is simple. Human life, however varied, consists in the performance of specific activities. Education that prepares for life is one that prepares definitely and adequately for these specific activities. However numerous and diverse they may be for any social class, they can be discovered. This requires only that one go out into the world of affairs and discover the particulars of which these affairs consist. These will show the abilities, attitudes, habits, appreciations, and forms of knowledge that men need. These will be the objectives of the curriculum. They will be numerous, definite, and particularized. The curriculum will then be that series of experiences which children and youth must have by way of attaining those objectives. (42)

Bobbitt's plan was simple from one point of view but complicated from another. The description of the process as consisting of two phases, one in which curriculum objectives are "discovered" and the other in which experiences are devised by which those objectives can be obtained, sounds simple enough. But neither of those two phases is uncomplicated. The discovery process promises to take a long time, years or even a whole generation, and the number of community and school people who are to have a say in the process makes it clear that that phase involves a lot of political maneuvering and negotiating as well. Bobbitt's advice on how to deal with disagreements within and between the different "levels" of participants in the process preserves in each instance the traditional line of authority. Thus, if there is disagreement between the board and the superintendent, the board will decide; if between the superintendent and the principal, the superintendent will decide; if between the principal and the teachers, the principal will decide; and so forth. He envisioned no particular difficulty with this procedure, however, because he believed that in the final analysis, "As the vision of the different levels is thus passed on to each other, each can make the corrective which is necessary because of his special position within the field. The vision, judgment, understanding, and decision of each level can thus gradually become the vision, judgment, and decision of all the levels" (1924, 286).

What Bobbitt offered, in the final analysis, was a curious blend of empirical facts, vision, sage advice, and common sense. He tacitly recognized that the process of deciding what the schools should teach was a complicated political decision in which many different parties were to have their say. He also recognized that the decision was fundamentally a local affair, that the curriculum was to suit a particular constituency, which included not only a certain group of students but also a group of adults who had their own ideas about what those students should know. At the same time he was committed to the idea that the objectives of education were ultimately discoverable through empirical investigations.

Bobbitt's (1924) confidence in the possibility of "scientific" investigations, which were to result in the "discovery" of curriculum objectives, existed side by side with his commitment to localism. The juxtaposition of those two points of view yielded curious results at times, as in the following statement:

> Every school system should formulate its own objectives. It is probable that before long we shall have a generally acceptable professional statement of specific educational objectives. When that time comes, the local labors can be greatly lightened. To date, however, no city has gone far enough to provide a sufficient model for any other. (40)

What does that funny combination of present and future amount to? When the time comes that "a generally acceptable professional statement of specific educational objectives" is in hand, what labor will be left for the locals to perform? Bobbitt does not directly answer that question, but what he appears to mean is that the finished statement of specific objectives will be used as a kind of catalog from which local curriculum makers might choose those objectives best suited to their own needs.

The total process, as Bobbitt (1924) envisions it, unfolds in a stepwise fashion:

1. "The first step is to analyze the broad range of human experience into major fields," such as health activities, citizenship activities, spare-time activities, and so forth. As Bobbitt points out, "The lines can be drawn in any number of ways. Each curriculum-making group will make the divisions that seem best to it for its purposes" (8).
2. "The second step is to take [the major fields of human action], one after the other, and analyze them into their more specific activities." One starts with "rather large" units and "break[s] them up into smaller ones." This process is to continue until the curriculum makers have found "the quite specific activities that are to be performed" (9).
3. "The activities once discovered, one can then see the objectives of education. These latter are the *abilities* to perform in proper ways the activities. The two are cognate, but not identical" (10).

It is at level 3, presumably, that the "scientifically derived" objectives will be of benefit to the local group, for as Bobbitt points out, "As they approach the units that are minute, numerous and interrelated with each other, and especially when accuracy demands quantitative definition, careful scientific assembling of the facts becomes necessary" (10). Above that level, "simple observation" is all that is needed, at least "so long as there is virtual unanimity on the part of all objective-minded analysts of the situation" (9).

In the final analysis, what does Bobbitt's advice to the local curriculum makers amount to? It recommends a general plan of attack, which says, start with a very broad, all-enveloping conception of the activities in which humans engage and move to progressively narrower and more concrete specifications of what humans need to know in order to do those things. It recommends that the process be led by educators but that it enlist the help and support of many groups within the community, including "salesmen," "physicians and nurses," "civic and social workers," "religious workers," and others. It argues for the use of whatever "scientific" studies of human activities are available. It acknowledges the magnitude of the total process and urges that the pace of progress not be allowed to outstrip the readiness of the local community, including its teachers and school administrators, to accept change. All of this advice is couched within a larger framework of criticism of the status quo, which sets the stage for the steps to be taken.

Tyler's Rationale: The Curriculum Specialist as Rational Guide

If any single volume deserves to be called the Bible of curriculum making it is certainly Ralph Tyler's *Basic Principles of Curriculum and Instruction*, which began as a syllabus for a course Tyler taught at the University of Chicago during the 1930s and 1940s and was subsequently published by the university's press in 1949. It has gone through dozens of printings and several translations since then and is still widely sold. A more influential text within the field of curriculum would be hard to name.

Basic Principles (1949) is a curious book in a number of ways. For one thing it is small for a book of such huge reputation and such an imposing title. It contains only 128 pages. Tyler himself refers to it as "this small book" in his introduction. For another thing it is not immediately evident what kind of a book it is. Tyler makes clear at the start what it is *not*. He says it is not a textbook because "it does not provide comprehensive guidance and readings for a course" (1). He also might have added that unlike most textbooks, *Basic Principles* does not contain a single footnote or reference. It also has no index. Nor is it "a manual for curriculum construction," Tyler says, because "it does not describe and outline in detail the steps to be taken by a given school or college that seeks to build a curriculum" (1). The two crucial words in that explanation appear to be "detail" and "given." The book certainly does describe and outline steps that schools and colleges *in general* might take to build a curriculum, though it does not do so for any *given* school and arguably does not do so in sufficient detail to be called a manual.

What kind of book, then, is it? Tyler does not say. Instead, he talks about what the book does or tries to do. He says it "attempts to explain a rationale for viewing, analyzing and interpreting the curriculum and instructional program of an educational institution" (1). A few sentences further on he says the book "outlines one way of viewing an instructional program as a functioning instrument of education." He repeats the word "rationale" three more times in his brief introduction, which ends by calling the book "a rationale by which to examine problems of curriculum and instruction." Indeed, the book itself ends by reminding its readers that "the purpose of the rationale is to give a view of the elements that are involved in a program of instruction and their necessary interrelations" (128). The emphasis Tyler places on this term explains why the contents of the book are commonly referred to as "Tyler's rationale" or even "the Tyler rationale."

But the use of the word "rationale" is another of the book's oddities, for it is not common to so describe "a way of viewing." The modern definition of the word, according to Webster, describes a rationale as being "the underlying reason, rational foundation, ground" for something, and that is how the word is commonly used today. But the dictionary also lists another usage, now rare, which is "an explanation or exposition of the principles of some opinion, action, hypothesis, phenomenon, or the like." It is *that* sense that fits Tyler's use of the word, for he does indeed offer an exposition of at least some of the principles that constitute his own opinion about how to look comprehensively at matters of curriculum and instruction. To call that a rationale is not only fitting but economical.

The key to Tyler's rationale consists of four broad questions, queries that a goodly number of today's curriculum specialists, thanks to Tyler, probably know by heart.

1. What educational purposes should the school seek to attain?
2. What educational experiences can be provided that are likely to attain these purposes?
3. How can these educational experiences be effectively organized?
4. How can we determine whether these purposes are being attained?

Tyler devotes a separate chapter of his book to each of these questions. For each one he explicates what the question seeks to discover and proceeds to offer suggestions about how it might be answered. He warns from the start that his book does not contain answers to his four questions since "the answers will vary to some extent from one level of education to another and from one school to another" (1–2). All the book offers, then, is "an explanation of the procedures" (2) by which the questions might be answered.

Even though *Basic Principles* is a thin volume, the contents of each of its chapters cannot be summarized here, not even in outline form. The first one, entitled "What Educational Purposes Should the School Seek to Attain?" is worth commenting on briefly, however, to link its contents to what has already been said about Bobbitt's point of view. Also, it is by far the largest chapter in the book, taking up 60 of the book's 128 pages. Commenting on the chapter's length, Tyler says, "We are devoting much time to the setting up and formulation of objectives because they are the most critical criteria for guiding all the other activities of the curriculum-maker" (62).

In that critical first chapter Tyler begins by identifying three sources of educational objectives, each of which "has certain values to commend it" and "should be given some consideration in planning any comprehensive curriculum program" (5): (1) studies of the learners themselves, (2) studies of contemporary life outside of school, and (3) suggestions from subject matter specialists. There is a twofold problem in consulting these sources, however: Too many objectives will be generated, and some will be inconsistent with others.

To remedy this situation Tyler recommends using two "screens" that are supposed to filter out unwanted—i.e., unimportant and inconsistent—objectives. The first of these is the "educational and social philosophy" to which the school is committed. The second is "what is known about the psychology of learning." He calls for each local school to state its philosophy in sufficient detail to allow curriculum makers to check every proposed objective against it, noting whether the objective was in harmony, in opposition, or unrelated to the philosophy's main points. Those that were in harmony would be deemed most important. His suggestions about how to use what is known about the psychology of learning as a screen are rather more ambiguous. After giving some examples to show how specific psychological findings might be in keeping with some educational objectives but not with others, he concludes, "It is helpful to write down the important elements of a defensible psychology of learning, and then to indicate in connection with each main point what possible implications it might have for educational objectives" (43).

Tyler concludes his first chapter with a lengthy discussion of the form objectives should take. He warns against vagueness and recommends that each objective indicate the kind of behavior to be developed in the student and the area or content of life to which the behavior is to be applied. This degree of precision is necessary, he argues, not only so that teachers know how to proceed in planning learning experiences designed to reach the objectives but also so that the success of their efforts can later be evaluated. The discussion contains numerous examples of good and poor objectives.

Does Tyler Improve on Bobbitt?

In their conceptions of what a university-based curriculum specialist ought to be doing, Bobbitt and Tyler see eye to eye. They both agree that at least one job of such a specialist is to give advice to practitioners on how to revise the curriculum of their schools. A second task, which both theorists endorse but in different ways, is to conduct studies that shed light on what should be taught or on how various curricula could be evaluated. A third task is to train a cadre of specialists who will move to other university posts, where they will become professors in their own right and behave as their mentors have done before them.

In addition to agreeing on these points, Bobbitt and Tyler also share a broad understanding of the process by which curricula are and should be formed. This understanding contains several points that require elaboration. They both appreciate the complexity of putting a curriculum together. They conceive of the process as taking a long time (perhaps as never ending) and as involving the cooperation of many different people inside and outside of the school and at all levels of the school hierarchy. They realize that the process entails potential disagreement and conflict (though neither dwells on those eventualities) whose resolution calls for the art of compromise. In this sense, then, they both acknowledge the political nature of the task. They are both sensitive to the particularized quality of curricular plans. They see that every curriculum must fit a particular setting, a school or school district, and that to do so it must be responsive to local conditions. This requirement means tailoring both the objectives and the learning experiences not only to the students being served but also to the demands and expectations of the larger community.

The goal of both men is to bring some order and regularity to this complex process, thereby making the task more manageable. They seek to do so by providing a conceptual framework whose structure consists of steps to be taken or jobs to be done. For both of them the central job for those doing the actual planning is to decide what goals or objectives the school should seek to attain. That task accomplished, the next step, in the views of both men, is to devise learning experiences that promise to achieve those goals and objectives.

Both men are optimistic about the curricular benefits of empirical investigations of various kinds. For Bobbitt the chief form of those investigations should be studies of activities carried on within the society at large. Tyler calls for such investigations as well but also looks toward psychological studies of learning as a source of help. Both hope that such investigations will ultimately put the process of curriculum development on a firmer scientific footing than before, will lighten the burden of decisions that local practitioners must make, and will help to eliminate unimportant and unrealizable objectives. At the same time, both men are cautious in their predictions about how soon such aid will be on hand.

Finally, both men share a spirit of practicality and optimism that infuses almost every page of their writings. Both have a liberal's faith in the contribution of rationality to the continued improvement of social and educational affairs. Here is the way Bobbitt (1924) puts it: "In fields of uncertainty, for guidance, the best thought is always safer than no thought; and definite formulations better than vague unformulated attitudes and opinions" (107). Had he been asked to comment on that opinion, Tyler would doubtless have agreed.

How, then, was Tyler different than Bobbitt? Though he was clearly working within the same tradition as Bobbitt and, therefore, shared many of the same assumptions, values, and goals, Tyler both extended and refined Bobbitt's view. He extended it by going beyond Bobbitt's two-step model of (1) defining educational objectives and (2) devising learning experiences. Tyler added two additional steps to that process, one having to do with organizing learning experiences and the other with evaluating them. He further refined the first step of defining objectives by calling for the development of a school philosophy and for the perusal of psychological studies, both of which were to be used as "screens" for weeding out unwanted objectives and for reducing their overall number.

Tyler also placed a different emphasis on some components of the process than did Bobbitt. Though both included the idea of activity analysis, for example, Tyler gave it far less emphasis than did Bobbitt. Though both acknowledged that curriculum improvement can proceed piecemeal as well as across the board, Tyler was more willing than Bobbitt to accept the fact that most improvements were likely to occur on a small scale.

> Although a school-wide attack is preferable in getting a rational revision of the curriculum, improvements can be made if only a part of the instructional program can be dealt with. Thus, curriculum building can be undertaken for a single subject like mathematics, or a single grade, like the ninth, or even for the courses offered by an individual teacher. Within the limits in which the curriculum is to be rebuilt, the same general rationale can be used. (Tyler 1949, 127–128)

Though both offer numerous examples of the process in action, Bobbitt's are more likely to be specific objectives drawn chiefly from his work with the Los Angeles school system, whereas Tyler cites illustrations of how parts of the process were carried on by curriculum groups working in several different locations.

Finally, throughout *Basic Principles* Tyler is more tentative and modest in his approach than is Bobbitt in either of his two books on the subject. Tyler points out at the start that his is only *one* rationale, and he encourages his readers to examine others. He emphasizes that the sequence of steps he recommends are not ones that everyone should follow. Though he remains committed to the belief that all four of his basic questions must be addressed sooner or later, he emphatically rejects a lockstep approach to answering them. The difference is a relative one, however, for Bobbitt (1924) too offers his share of cautions and qualifications, which soften what might otherwise be characterized as a dogmatic tone. Here he is, for example, on the wisdom of not waiting until scientific activity analyses have given us "the finalities": "There is no promise of such a thing in our generation. And what is more, the practical world is not operated by the method of postponement of its labors until science is complete. It uses what is available until there is something better" (100–101). Each man, we must remember, insists that his is only one point of view among many.

Given that what both Bobbitt and Tyler offer are only "points of view," is one any better than the other? It is difficult not to see Tyler's as being the more "advanced" of the two, if only because, as has been said, it seeks to be more comprehensive, by virtue of the coverage it gives to later stages of the curriculum-development process, and more refined, by virtue of its taking more things into account when it treats the processes of defining objectives and devising educational experiences. At the same time it is important to note that both men adhere to the same conception of the role of the university-based curriculum specialist, which is one of being an advice giver to groups of practitioners who want to improve the curriculum of their schools. In that respect, at least, the two points of view are on a par with each other. They both lie within the single tradition of curriculum specialist as advice giver to practitioners.

The Curriculum Specialist as Advice Giver to Practitioners: Why Listen?

Before moving on to yet a third point of view, that of Joseph Schwab, who also conceives of his role as one of helping practitioners engage in the process of curriculum development, I wish to pause briefly to consider the status of Bobbitt's and Tyler's authority as advice givers. I do so not only to set the stage for Schwab, whose contribution to the advice-giving tradition is unlike that of his predecessors in several important respects, but also to prepare the way for the tacit rejection of that tradition by a noticeable number of today's university-based curriculum specialists.

The questions to be addressed take the form of a spate of challenges that one might imagine coming from a doubting Thomas, who aggressively asks, "Why should anyone bother to read or listen to what Bobbitt or Tyler has to say, much less try to follow their advice? What are the sources of their authority? If all they offer are points of view, as they themselves openly concede they are doing, why should anyone take them seriously? What makes them convincing?" Under normal conditions the person confronted by such a brazen questioner might reasonably respond, "Go read their work for yourself and find out!" But here I would like to do the questioners' reading for them, or at least a portion of it. Why indeed have Bobbit's and Tyler's books been so widely read over the years? *That* is the question.

A small piece of the answer surely has to do with the authority of the printed word and with the fact that both men wrote and spoke as university professors. Those facts alone would suffice to win them an initial hearing, in all probability, but possibly not much more than that. To move beyond such superficial appeals we must turn to the texts themselves. Here we find a complicated set of rhetorical devices and other methods of persuasion, many of which we have already mentioned. Most notable among these qualities in the strong appeal to common sense. When Bobbitt tells his readers that they must determine what their educational goals are before they devise ways of achieving them, who among them would bother to question such advice? It seems to be the natural thing to do. The same is true about Tyler's four questions. What comes after we select our goals and devise ways of achieving them? Well, naturally, we have to organize those ways and, after we have tried them out, determine whether or not we have been successful. What could be more obvious?

This is not to say that such prescriptions are invulnerable to challenge. Indeed, none of them is closed to attack. But all such challenges, at least at the start, are burdened by the disadvantage of seeming to oppose common sense. In any case, both Bobbitt and Tyler have already anticipated their appearance without their content. Each leaves plenty of room for other ways of doing things, including even reversing such "natural" processes as the ones just named.

Beyond the commonsense qualities of both Bobbitt's and Tyler's advice there lies an acknowledgement of the reader's (i.e., the practitioner's) plight, a recognition of how complex schools are and a fundamental respect for the enterprise in which school people are engaged. Moreover, this attitude of respect and appreciation is for the most part tacit rather than explicit, which means it never comes across sounding like flattery and false praise. The presence of examples and illustrations extend the reader's sense of the authors being at home among school people. These devices help to make points clear, as they are designed to do, but they also communicate important information about the authors' experience. They inform readers that the authors have been around, that they know what they are talking about. They also reveal that other schools and school districts have already undertaken what the authors are recommending.

The reasoning processes revealed in these texts are peculiar in their effectiveness. On the one hand, the quality of the arguments from section to section often leaves much to be desired. Few of them unfold logically, in a step-by-step manner. They skip around. They contain lapses, contradictions, redundancies, and inconsistencies. Key words shift their meanings. On the other hand, the very lack of logical coherence and consistency is somehow compelling. Precisely *because* the reasoning lacks logical precision and tightness it feels comfortable and easy to follow. The starts and stops give an almost conversational tone to the texts. Close readers might become puzzled from time to time, but they never doubt the authors' sincerity and forthrightness. Though the authors are both professors, they speak in plain language, without pretension.

The lack of pretension goes beyond the texts' workaday prose and down-to-earth reasoning. The volumes are epistemologically unpretentious as well. They offer opinions and points of view rather than facts and knowledge. Tyler's rationale is indeed a rationale in the dictionary sense of the word, as we have seen, even though we had to revert to a now rare use of the term to find its meaning. It is, quite simply, an exposition of opinion. It is not a theory, a model, a system, a taxonomy, an algorithm, a recipe, or a formula. It lacks the epistemological pretentions of all of those terms. Bobbitt too, though he goes on at somewhat greater length than Tyler about the potential benefits to curriculum makers of "scientific investigations," ends his *How to Make a Curriculum* (1924) with an admission that effectively deflates whatever high hopes his earlier talk of a science of curriculum might have aroused. "It must be admitted," he says on the very last page of his text, "that these principles are as yet pretty uncertain . . ." (286). Pretty uncertain they were, yet powerfully influential in their day. And all the more so, we might guess, because of the way Bobbitt presented them. (This assessment of both Bobbitt and Tyler is far more charitable than that of many other critics. For a far less charitable view, see Heubner [1966] and Kliebard [1970]).

Returning now to the questions with which this subsection began, we are ready to sum up our reply to the doubting Thomas. Our answer is that these texts were very persuasive in their day (and Tyler's *Basic Principles* remains so to the present) not solely because of what they said, the ideas and opinions they contained, but also because of how they said it. They were and are rhetorically effective for the reasons given, for their commonsense, reasonable, frank, unpretentious, and readily understandable approach to the almost universal problem of "how to make a curriculum," as Bobbitt puts it, or closer to actuality, how to make an existing curriculum better than it already is.

The enthusiastic reception of first Bobbitt's and later Tyler's point of view also creates a genuine problem for all the curriculum specialists who followed in their footsteps. The problem, of course, has been where to go from there, how to improve on Tyler's rationale. This may seem paradoxical, for both Bobbitt and Tyler, as we have repeatedly pointed out, insisted that theirs were only points of view. Supposedly, therefore, they left plenty of room for others to offer views of their own. But where are they? Why has Tyler's perspective, which effectively eclipsed that of Bobbitt, dominated the scene for a such a long time?

Part of the answer has already been given. It is that Tyler's point of view, and Bobbitt's before him, took quick possession of what might be called the commonsense solution to the problem of curriculum improvement, leaving little room to maneuver without rejecting the problem itself, which common sense also forbade. That is, once we have accepted the notion that the curriculum specialist should try to help practitioners make better curricula, the suggestion that we begin by trying to figure out what we want the school to accomplish sounds like the most reasonable thing in the world to do. So does the next step of deciding what it is we want the students to *do* to reach those goals; and the step after that, of trying to organize learning activities; and so forth. In other words, *from a commonsense point of view*, what questions would we substitute for the four Tyler recommends? If we can think of none, the only choice remaining is to work within the framework Tyler provides, to refine and elaborate the master's suggestions. This is not unimportant work, of course, and there is enough of it to keep legions of workers busy for years, but it is definitely derivative.

Having said all this, we must quickly acknowledge that common sense can be wrong. It is not always the sure guide to action that tradition makes it out to be. And this statement applies not only to the solutions to problems but also to the problems themselves, for they too are as likely to be the products of common sense as are their remedies. But if to move beyond Tyler is to move beyond common sense, how is it to be accomplished? How are curriculum specialists to enter a post-Tylerian world? And fully as important for their long-term success, how are they to bring others along with them, particularly if they cannot appeal to common sense?

Before turning to the work of a number of university-based curriculum specialists who have recently tried to answer these questions, let us consider the latest, if not the last, prominent figure to contribute significantly to what I shall from now on refer to as the Tylerian tradition. Schwab's writings on the subject are of interest as much for how they deviate from Tyler as for what they owe to him.

Schwab's Practical: The University-Based Curriculum Specialist as Educator of School-Based Curriculum Specialists

If Tyler's book is curious as a genre, being neither a textbook nor a curriculum manual nor almost anything else we might care to name, Schwab's (1969, 1970, 1973, 1983) four papers on curriculum building are equally so, though not because they defy categorization. It is easy enough to say what they are in a superficial sense, which is a set of scholarly essays on curriculum matters whose combined length comes to about the same number of pages as Tyler's *Basic Principles*. To describe their contents, however, is quite another matter. The titles of the essays do not help greatly: (1) "The Practical: A Language for Curriculum," (2) "The Practical: Arts of Eclectic," (3) "The Practical 3: Translation into Curriculum," and (4) "The Practical 4: Something for Curriculum Professors To Do."

Schwab (1978) himself offers a suggestion about why his essays might be difficult to describe: because "the educationist community has no common apparatus for recognizing such papers" (320). What kind of papers are they that share this fate? They are ones, Schwab tells us, "which propose alternatives to present or envisaged practices, discriminate possible consequences (good or bad) of alternatives, trace these consequences to their further probable effects, and in other ways contribute to the responsible deliberation necessary for defensible choices of new or altered practices" (320) Do Schwab's four essays accomplish all those things? It would be a generous critic who said they did but a blind one who concluded they did not try.

In essence, what Schwab does in his essays is to offer a stinging critique of the field of curriculum and then proceed to recommend how its deficiencies might be corrected. His opening salvo leaves no mistake of its intention to wound. "The field of curriculum is moribund," Schwab announces at the start. It is so, we are told, because of an "inveterate, unexamined, and mistaken reliance on *theory*" (287). The remedy, he concludes, is to transfer "curriculum energies" from the "theoretic" to "three other modes of operation," which he calls "the practical," "the quasi-practical," and "the eclectic." What Schwab means by those terms and how and why he proposes to effect the transference from one to the others make up the heart of his four essays.

Schwab spends a lot of time in his essays discussing theory and practice in general, for it turns out that the problem he identifies within the field of the curriculum, its "frustrated state" as he calls it, is not peculiar to that line of endeavor. It happens everywhere. "All fields of systematic intellectual activity are marked by rhythms which involve such crises," he says (299). To economize, I will skip over those portions of his argument that seek to explain the problem in its most general terms so that I may concentrate instead on how Schwab sees it as affecting curriculum specialists. Further, I shall forego reiterating Schwab's detailed listing of the "signs of exhaustions and failures" that culminate "in a large increase in the frequency of published papers and colloquiums marked by *a flight from the subject of the field*" (301). It is enough to say that such signs of flight (he lists six of them) are in Schwab's view endemic within the field of curriculum.

The key questions whose answers I shall seek to summarize in Schwab's terms are the following:

1. What is "the art of the practical" and how does it relate to the curriculum?
2. What is the role of the school-based curriculum specialist who seeks to practice that art?
3. What is the role of the university-based specialist, the professor of curriculum?

The art of the practical according to Schwab is in essence the art of deliberation, at least that is its method. Its outcome is a decision of some kind, its subject matter is a concrete and specific set of circumstances, and its problems are "constituted of conditions which we *wish* were otherwise and we think they *can be made* to be otherwise" (289). As applied to curricular matters this means that improvement will almost always be piecemeal rather than across the board and that changes "must be so planned and so articulated with what remains unchanged that the functioning of the whole remains coherent and unimpaired" (312). It means a focus on "the diagnosis of the ills of the curriculum," on "the frictions and failures of the curricular machine," rather than on change instigated by the latest theory-inspired fad. It also means generating "the greatest possible number and fresh diversity of alternative solutions to problems," which are needed for a variety of reasons, not the least being that freshly perceived problems, which deliberation seeks to anticipate, require fresh solutions (315–316).

Schwab recommends that a team be organized within each school to undertake the tasks of curriculum revision. Each team would comprise eight or ten regular members: four to six teachers, the principal, a school board member, and one or two student representatives. In addition, the group would call on outside consultants from time to time who would principally be drawn from two categories: "professorial academics," to serve as subject matter specialists, and social scientists, such as sociologists and psychologists, who would offer advice on "nonintellective" matters. The group would be led by a curriculum chairperson, who would be specially trained for the job and would occupy a new position within the school's organizational structure.

The curriculum chairperson, as Schwab describes the role, has three principal functions. The first is to monitor the proceedings of the curriculum-making group, "pointing out to the group what has happened in the course of their deliberations, what is currently taking place, what has not yet been considered, what subordinations and superordinations may have occurred which affect the process in which all are engaged" (368). The last of these monitoring duties is made necessary, according to Schwab, because it is easy (and apparently common) for one member of the group — the scholar-specialist, for example—to "overawe" or "overwhelm" the others, creating an imbalance of authority and influence. The chairperson "is to function as a countervailing force of these common tendencies" (368).

The chairperson's second function is to oversee the "embodiment" of the curriculum in concrete, material objects. This task means taking the curriculum purposes and the reasons for them as formulated by the planning group and seeing that those formulations are "realized," a process that entails "constructing materials for students, guides for teachers, and patterns of teaching and learning which are appropriate." Schwab believes that this work can rarely be done by the planning group itself. It requires the collaboration of others, and it is the job of the curriculum specialist "to instigate, administer, and chair this process" (369).

The third function of the chairperson is to help in identifying and communicating the planning group's underlying values, which in turn give rise to the group's stated intentions. Schwab derives the need for such help from his belief that the values of the planning group can only rarely be identified by "merely rational" means, that is, just by reading or listening to the stated intentions. On the strength of that belief he proceeds to explain what else is needed: "Only if there is added to rational scrutiny of a proposed segment of the curriculum the felt experience of it, an undergoing of it in imagination and empathy, only then can it be identified with some confidence as probably appropriate" (370). Schwab has little more to say about this process of discerning the "deep intentions" of the planning group beyond insisting that the curriculum specialist "instigate, encourage, and monitor" it.

Schwab (1983) spells out the role of the professor of curriculum in his fourth and final essay, which carries the subtitle "Something for Curriculum Professors to Do." The none-too-subtle jibe embedded in that title is a topic to which I shall return. For now I need only note its clear insinuation, repeated elsewhere in the essay, which is either that professors of curriculum have nothing to do or, if we tie together the messages in Schwab's opening and closing essays, that they typically spend their time doing the wrong sort of thing, theorizing rather than becoming involved in the practical.

In a nutshell, the job of the professor of curriculum, in

Schwab's view, is to educate the curriculum specialists whose functions we have just described. What those specialists need to know and be able to do, according to Schwab, includes the following:

- Skillful use of the rhetorics of persuasion (which includes knowing how to elicit participation in small-group settings and person-to-person encounters)
- Experience in deliberation
- Ability to read "learned" journals and the habit of doing so
- Ability to guide teacher-colleagues to the use of journals
- Knowledge of curricular practices throughout the country
- Knowledge of the behavioral sciences that contribute to the guidance of educational practice
- "Nodding" acquaintance with some of the academic fields from which school curricula are drawn

The way the would-be curriculum chairperson is to obtain the requisite skills and knowledge is through a series of seminars and internship experiences that would culminate in the preparation of a doctoral dissertation, which would consist of "a report, analysis, and assessment" of an internship in the office of a curriculum chairperson within an actual school. The task of the professor of curriculum would be to cochair the training seminars with professors from other parts of the university and to oversee the internship experiences of the candidate. He or she would also be expected to engage in scholarship that "would inform, advise and refresh their former students working in the schools." In doing so they "would attend to what they perceive as evils and vicissitudes of our government and society" and "would perform a similar task with respect to the tastes, mores, and attitudes of our fellow citizens in their daily lives" (1983, 263).

Does Schwab Improve on Tyler?

To place Schwab within the same tradition as Bobbitt and Tyler may seem an odd thing to do, given some of the obvious differences between him and them. But he himself confirms the justification of that placement. "It will be clear from these remarks that the conception of curricular method proposed here is immanent in the Tyler rationale," Schwab (1978) declares near the end of his first essay (320). And it *is* clear in certain respects, though unclear in others, as we shall see.

Schwab remarks on two major differences between his views and those of Tyler; these also turn out to be weaknesses of the Tyler rationale as he (Schwab) sees them. The first is Tyler's heavy emphasis on the process of defining educational objectives. The trouble with that emphasis, according to Schwab, is that the objectives are usually too ambiguous and equivocal. They do not provide enough "concrete matter" to fuel the process of deliberation. Furthermore, the failure to deliberate leads to what Schwab calls "delusive consensus," a form of false agreement.

The second weakness that Schwab notes is that those who use the Tyler rationale are not trained for the deliberative procedures it requires. This is not a direct criticism of Tyler's views, but it implies that Tyler did not fully appreciate the complexity and difficulty of what he was calling on school people to do. Schwab's own depiction of some of the misunderstandings and misperceptions to be handled by the curriculum chairperson serves to highlight those difficulties.

These being the chief differences, how, then, do Schwab's views *resemble* those of Tyler? If we turn again to Schwab's (1978) own assessment for an answer, the similarities are twofold. Tyler, like Schwab, "calls for a diversity of talent" (320). Both he and Tyler also, again in Schwab's words, "insist on the practical and eclectic treatment of a variety of factors" (320). What that means, presumably, is that both men realized that the process of curriculum development is complicated from beginning to end. This may sound as though it contradicts what has just been said about Schwab's hint that Tyler may not have fully appreciated all that the process of deliberation entails, but that particular shortcoming (if it was one) would not have prevented Tyler from sharing other aspects of Schwab's own appreciation of the complexity of the *overall* process.

In addition to those similarities and differences that Schwab himself names there are several others worthy of mention. Chief among the similarities is the fact that Schwab and Tyler share a common understanding of what they are about, one that Bobbitt shared as well. *All three seek to be of help to practitioners who want to improve the curriculum of the schools in which they work.* That is their chief goal. They have different ideas about how to get there, true enough, but there is no wavering in their pursuit of that overall mission.

Yet having said that Schwab joins with Tyler and Bobbitt in seeking to help practitioners build better curricula, one must also acknowledge that he seems further removed somehow from the day-to-day business of school affairs than do either of his predecessors. He also differs from them in ways that go beyond those he himself mentions. The question is how to interpret these differences. Do they represent what might be thought of as "natural extensions" of the Tylerian tradition or do they portend a radical break with that tradition? In other words, was Schwab simply marching along the same road that Bobbitt and Tyler had traveled before him, or was he, while holding aloft the same banner, beginning to veer off in a different direction entirely?

There is something to be said on both sides of that question. Consider, for instance, Schwab's focus on the piecemeal nature of curriculum development, his insistance that improvement be focused on local problems. At first glance, it may look as though he was merely facing up to conditions that both Bobbitt and Tyler tacitly acknowledged. Bobbitt clearly understood that the pace of curriculum change would have to be adjusted to local circumstances. He saw that it would be folly to move too fast. Tyler too recognized that in some schools the unit of change might be only a single course or the program within one grade level only. So from one point of view Schwab seems only to be articulating an insight that was already immanent in the two earlier views.

What one must notice, however, is that Schwab's piecemeal approach does not begin with an animating vision of some kind, as is characteristic of both Bobbitt and Tyler. Thus, at least on this point, what looks to be similiar between his view and theirs is really quite different. Bobbitt, we will recall, began with the conviction that something was drastically wrong with the schools of our nation. They were unresponsive to surrounding social conditions. He was further convinced that the remedy for that condition lay in a generation-long effort of curriculum revision. Though he does not voice as grandiose a vision as does Bobbitt, Tyler does remark on the importance of an overarching perspective. He recommends that every school develop its own set of convictions about what it is trying to do. (He called it "a philosophy," as most educators do.) He also differs from Dewey in this respect, a point made by one of his critics (Kliebard 1970). Faced with the task of choosing from among an overwhelming number of objectives, curriculum planning groups are to use their self-generated "philosophy" as a kind of filter to separate the gold from the dross.

Schwab does not talk about how the schools might address social change on a grand scale. Nor does he recommend that practicing educators concern themselves with such broad issues. On the contrary, he expresses misgivings about having curriculum planning groups spend time on statements of objectives. Agreeing on ideals is too easy, Schwab (1978) says. What is needed instead is to concentrate on oiling the squeaky wheel, on coping with the "frictions and failures of the curricular machine" (315).

This focus on the concrete and the immediate makes Schwab's curriculum planning groups sound as though they would function more like troubleshooters than like educational idealists who were propelled by a vision of what the schools might become. Yet that depiction of what Schwab calls for is not entirely fair, for he does go on to point out that the group would be charged with problem *finding* as much as with problem *solving*. So it is not that they would simply respond to problems that everyone already sees. Problem finding entails identifying difficulties that are not yet perceived as such, which could mean introducing a new conception of what is educationally desirable. Schwab also points out that planning groups will inevitably seek to enact a set of values that will not be self-evident in the group's stated intentions. (One job of the curriculum chairperson, as we have seen, is to communicate these values to those responsible for putting the group's intentions to work.) In this way as well, Schwab tacitly acknowledges the operation of higher purposes in the shaping of the curriculum.

At the same time it remains true that Schwab is far less of an idealist than was Bobbitt and is much less tolerant of idealistic thinking on the part of practitioners than Tyler seems to have been. This is not intended as a criticism. It is only to point out that in this respect at least Schwab seems to have drifted away from Bobbitt and Tyler rather than to have moved one step further in the same direction. It is possible, of course, to see Schwab's drift from idealism as being immanent in Tyler's move to group-generated "philosophies," but Schwab's explicit rejection of Tyler's emphasis on objectives makes the difference between the two of them seem qualitative rather than one of degree.

One noteworthy feature of a problem-centered, as opposed to a vision-centered, conception of curriculum improvement is that the former has nothing to set it in motion beyond the recognition of an immediate difficulty or the expectation that such difficulties are bound to occur. It also has nothing to establish its long-term future beyond the tacit understanding that problems, like wonders, never cease or, to adopt Schwab's own metaphor, that the curricular machinery will always be breaking down and thus be in constant need of repair. In short, in a problem-centered approach there is no source of external guidance beyond what Schwab calls the "values" of individual group members, which may or may not become fully "realized."

The most striking difference between Schwab's four essays and the writings of Bobbitt and Tyler lies in their rhetoric. As instruments of persuasion the two sets of documents are worlds apart. They address different audiences. They employ different arguments. They use different vocabularies. They draw on different backgrounds of experience and understanding. And most important of all, they exhibit vastly different attitudes toward the field of curriculum and toward its university-based specialists.

Schwab's (1978) orientation toward his subject is fundamentally critical. He begins by declaring the field of curriculum moribund and he continues to lambast his principal audience (professors of curriculum) throughout his essays. He accuses them of "fleeing the field" in a variety of different ways (301–302). He depicts them as desperately pursuing academic respectability (243). He describes them as "sadly wanting" in "active intellectualism" (263). His worst slam of all perhaps comes in his insinuation that they basically have nothing to do (see above). Schwab escapes his own criticism by never identifying himself as a professor of curriculum. When spoken of as a group, the latter are always referred to as "they" rather than "we." Schwab was himself a professor of education at the University of Chicago when he began his series of essays. Moreover, he was a member of the special field of Curriculum and Instruction within the Department of Education at the university.

Schwab's own "intellectualism" is abundantly evident in his writing. He presents his position systematically, almost schematically at times, with multiple reasons for almost every move, each of which he goes on to explain in some detail. He interjects arcane words and expressions (e.g., "polyfocal conspectus" and "entitative theory"). He refers a lot to Freud and reveals a broad acquaintance with various psychological theories. He speaks of science with obvious familiarity. He mentions Aristotle and Sartre. The overall rhetorical stance is one of an academic of more than moderate intellectuality addressing an audience of fellow academics, many of whom he does not think too highly of.

When Schwab speaks concretely about curricular affairs he typically draws his examples from colleges and universities. In this way too he distances himself from the day-to-day affairs of schooling far more than did either Bobbit or Tyler.

There is, then, a fundamental tension, almost a contradiction, in Schwab's position, one that bears directly on the question of what university-based curriculum specialists ought to be doing. On the one hand, Schwab urges those members of his audience who have not already done so to give up their pursuit of theory and to become more school-oriented and practical in their concerns. On the other hand, he also invites them to become more intellectual, like himself perhaps, to read broadly, to steep themselves in the social sciences, and to become critical essayists who comment insightfully on the social injustices and hypocrisies of the day as they bear on educational affairs. What Schwab is conjuring, it would seem, is an image of the university-based curriculum specialist as a Renaissance man or woman, a person capable of bridging the age-old gap between theory and practice.

What about Schwab himself? Does he model the role he describes? Well, yes and no. His performance as an essayist reveals some disturbing contradictions. He argues persuasively against various ways of "fleeing the field," one of which takes the form of "discourse about the discourse of the field." But his essays are full of such talk. He seeks to be down-to-earth and practical in his recommendations, to the point of making firm suggestions about each school's curriculum planning committee. But he pays no attention to the key question of whether most schools can afford to hire a curriculum chairperson, who holds a doctorate, and if not—since it seems obvious that most elementary schools, for example, will not be able to employ such a person on a full-time basis—how these specialists might be shared among several schools without making a mockery of Schwab's talk about how essential it is for them to perform a variety of important tasks, many of which seem extremely time-consuming.

The question is, Can Schwab's ideal be realized by a significant number of curriculum specialists? This question asks not whether it is *possible* for individuals to budget their time and energy so that they maintain the recommended balance between school-oriented and more academically oriented pursuits but whether such a balance is *likely* for most or even many individuals, given considerations of time and energy and also given what we know about human predilections for one kind of activity and way of life over another. The possibility of a perfect balance remains; but the likelihood, judging from what we already know about the directions people have taken, is that the choice facing most of today's curriculum specialists lies between moving toward a closer involvement with school affairs and with the mechanics of curriculum change, on the one hand—closer perhaps than Bobbitt or Tyler or Schwab ever managed to attain or even to picture—*or* on the other hand, moving toward a deeper immersion in academic scholarship and writing, activities whose relationship to the usual question of how to improve the existing curriculum may be indirect or tangential at best.

I shall close this overview with a quick look down both of these paths, which diverge like a parting of the ways from the unstable combination of the theoretical and the practical outlined in Schwab's closing essay. To call the division "a parting of the ways" is doubly significant, for not only are the activities and the writings I am about to consider associated with the work of curriculum specialists who have traveled different career paths but also they tend to originate in different geographical locations. One comes chiefly from Great Britain and Canada, the other from the United States, though the exceptions to that generalization are many.

Moving Toward Practice: The Curriculum Specialist as Consultant

As we have already seen, the principal way in which Schwab keeps the Bobbitt-Tyler tradition alive is by adhering to the goal of trying to help groups of practitioners who want to improve the curriculum of their schools. If Schwab may be said to have gone further in that direction than did either of his predecessors, it is through his focus on the interpersonal complexities of curriculum decision making. Schwab seems to be more aware than were either Bobbitt or Tyler of the difficulties that face a group of individuals who represent quite different interests and who must come together on a recommended course of action. To cope with those demands, according to Schwab, the school-based curriculum specialist must be well schooled in the arts of deliberation and group management. The job of the university-based specialist, in this view, is essentially to provide training experiences for those team leaders.

A different model of involvement with practice is evident in the curriculum development projects that sprang up in Britain during the mid- to late 1960s (MacDonald and Walker 1976; Reid 1979b). Some aspects of that difference reflect broad cultural dissimilarities; others are confined to educational practice. Among the latter, for example, is the tradition of teacher autonomy in Great Britain, which translates into a long-standing belief in the teacher as curriculum maker, a belief so long-standing, in fact, that one observer, Stuart McClure, refers to it as "an English myth." He goes on to explain, "To refer to this as a myth is not to denigrate it. It is a crucial element in the English educational idea. It is the key to the combination of pedagogic, political, and administrative initiatives which provide the drive for curriculum reform in England and Wales . . ." (as quoted in MacDonald and Walker 1976, 32). Partially as a result of this belief, teachers and teacher associations have played a much more central role in curriculum change in England and Wales than they have in the United States. During the period of curriculum reform that got underway in Britain during the 1960s, for example, it was groups of teachers and teacher associations that initiated many of those efforts (e.g., Stenhouse 1980).

Within this model the role of the university-based specialist is rather like that of Schwab's curriculum team leader. He or she works directly with a team of teachers, usually from several schools, on a specific project, such as the design of a curriculum for primary school French or high school mathematics. Each project usually lasts two or three years, after which the team disbands. What they produce in addition to a teachers' handbook and actual instructional materials is usually a report on the project itself in the form of a case history. For detailed reports on the workings of such teams, see Stenhouse (1980b), as well as Reid and Walker (1975). A related genre includes historical case histories of how particular parts of the curriculum came into being; see, for example, Goodson (1983).

A rather different form of involvement with practitioners, one that blurs the traditional distinction between curriculum development and in-service training, focuses on individual teachers, rather than teams, with the university-based specialist serving as a kind of confidant who helps the teacher reflect on his or her teaching practices in a way that leads to changes of different kinds, including curricular ones. One variant of this way of working is called action research (Jenkins and Shipman 1976). The written documents that come out of such cooperative interchanges include teachers' journals, diaries, autobiographies, life histories, and what one pair of curriculum specialists refer to as "narratives of experience" (Connelly and Clandinin 1988; see also Clandinin 1986; Elbaz 1983; Oberg 1987).

These two strategies for moving closer to practice entail marked changes in the traditional relationship between the university-based specialist and the practitioner—so marked, in fact, that Connelly and Clandinin (1988) speak of there being two separate traditions of school reform, one of which seeks to control teachers and the curriculum, the other of which "stresses the legitimacy of each teacher's personal knowledge of classrooms" (xv). Without taking sides on that question at this point, one can readily acknowledge that the kinds of involvement I have just described call for a more collegial relationship between the specialist and the practitioner than the one that usually prevails. Instead of playing the role of the outside expert who tells others how to make a curriculum or what principles to follow or how to deliberate, the specialist becomes more of a participant in the process, a coworker perhaps, someone who gets his or her hands dirty like everyone else. One question that quickly emerges under these changed conditions has to do with the expertise of the specialists. If they are no longer in the business of delivering advice on how to make a curriculum, in what sense may we still call them specialists? Wherein lies their expertise?

A sampling of books and articles written by adherents of a more practitioner-oriented point of view reveals plenty to write about after the goal of discovering general principles of curriculum has been abandoned (see, e.g., Stenhouse 1980b; Barrow 1984; Connelly and Clandinin 1988.) To begin with, there remains the task of trying to convince others (both practitioners and specialists) that this is the way to move. This step calls for criticism of the status quo and of the recent past as well as positive statements about where to go next. The mixture of criticism and advice in Schwab's four essays is paradigmatic of this kind of writing.

There also remain questions of technique and procedure, even when the overall advice calls for total immersion in the particularities of a localized curriculum project or in the reflections and daily activities of one teacher. Here, too, one might draw on Schwab's essays for examples, his detailed recommendations on how to form a curriculum planning group as an instance, though others are equally plentiful. If the goal is to encourage teachers to keep journals or to write about their professional development, two activities that have grown in popularity of late, one still might wish to offer suggestions about how to proceed. In short, the search for rules, suggestions, and other forms of casual advice does not end with the abandonment of the grand scheme that was supposed to fit all situations.

As part of the search for enduring outcomes from such activities there are reports to be written not only for the benefit of the participants in the projects and for individual teachers but also for others who might draw lessons of various kinds from what happened. These take the form of case studies, life histories, anecdotal accounts, and so forth. What readers are supposed to gain from such reports is not always clear. Sometimes the goal is to convey specific advice, as in the report of a flawed curriculum project such as *Man: A Course of Study*, for example, where the principal message seems to be "If you are going to try something like this, don't do it this way" (Jenkins in Stenhouse 1980b). At other times the report seems to be chiefly an instrument for encouraging others to try the same thing (Clandinin 1986).

But having acknowledged that a lot remains to be said and done after the decision to move closer to practice has been made, there are still the questions of whether and how all this activity fits together to make up a field of endeavor called curriculum or curriculum studies. An even more basic question concerns the centrality of the process of curriculum improvement within that field. How widespread and enduring is that process and how pervasive need it be to justify the existence of a nationwide cadre of specialists to deal with it?

We have already seen how Bobbitt, Tyler, and Schwab have dealt with that question, each in his own way. Bobbitt saw the need for curriculum change as massive. It was made necessary by vast social changes to which the schools must adjust, and it promised to be a task that would take years, possibly generations, to complete, even with the help of a veritable army of specialists. Tyler was somewhat less grandiose in his vision of the future of curriculum reform, but he too clearly saw the task to be a huge one, fueled by constant changes in society and by the steady growth of knowledge. Schwab's conception of the need for change is more modest than either of his predecessors. He does talk about drawing on the knowledge of specialists, both within subject matter domains and within the social sciences in general, but what drives the need for change in his view are more internal matters rather than outside forces, "frictions and fractures" of "the curricular machinery." He implies that such breakdowns occur constantly, requiring the services of a full-time, resident specialist. But he does not go on to say why that is so, except to imply that curricular imperfections are always present if one looks closely enough.

The difference between Bobbitt's call for a nationwide program of curriculum change and Schwab's talk about the constant need to fix broken curricular machinery reflects a marked diminution in the scope of the curriculum specialist's mission that appears to have taken place during the intervening 50 years. The question we now must ask is whether even Schwab's vision might be too ambitious, both insofar as its conception of the need for change is concerned as well as whether each school should have an in-house specialist to help address it. We are led to this question by the examples already given of close involvement of university-based specialists with teams of practitioners and with individual teachers. The sporadic and ad hoc nature of these arrangements challenges the assumption that the need for change is constant and pervasive. Also, if the agenda for change is established by practitioners rather than by an outside expert, who is to say that it must always be curricular? Perhaps what needs changing in a particular school or classroom are institutional arrangements, instructional methods, grouping procedures, and so on. Indeed, in some environments perhaps nothing needs changing at all, at least for the time being. What happens then to the in-residence curriculum specialist? Should he or she be fired?

One way around such projected difficulties is to reject them as possibilities, to insist that there will *always* be curricular deficiencies that need addressing, even though they may not be recognized as such by many or even most insiders. This is the position Schwab takes. He implies that if a planning team within a school looks at its curriculum long enough, problems are bound to appear. He is probably right, if for no other reason than that such a close look would probably locate "problems" almost anywhere, especially if that is what one was looking *for*. But what kind of problems are they that can be discerned only by close and penetrating examination? Are they ones that a planning committee or an individual teacher ought to be working on? The way we answer this question determines in large measure the future of curriculum as a field of endeavor *whose central professional task is that of giving advice to practitioners as they try to improve the curriculum*.

If the specialist brings no special knowledge or vision to the task of *establishing the need for change*, if he or she turns out to be only a facilitator of the change process *without substantive involvement in the question of what needs changing and why*, one then begins to wonder in what sense the label *curriculum* specialist is appropriate. Perhaps something like discussion leader or Schwab's term, "deliberator," would be more suitable. This does not mean that to deserve this title the curriculum specialist must be the sole definer of the need for change, but it does mean having a view of such matters and a voice in their determination. To give that up would indeed be to flee the field, though not quite in the way Schwab suggested. He saw the line of flight leading chiefly in the opposite direction, away from practice rather than toward it. The possibility of fleeing the field through a greater involvement in practice was not something he contemplated. Will it become real for a significant number of today's university-based curriculum specialists? That remains to be seen.

Moving Toward the Academy: The Curriculum Specialist as Generalist

The other path leading away from Schwab's idealized conception of the curriculum specialist points toward the world of the academy. The role it invites the latter to adopt is that of a critic of educational affairs in general. Schwab's (1983) description of what this might entail reveals it to be an ambitious intellectual undertaking. These individuals, he tells us,

> would attend to what they perceive as evils and vicissitudes of our government and society. They would try to convince readers that these troubles exist, show the threats they pose, and suggest ways in which alteration of school practice might help ameliorate the conditions discussed. . . . Some curricularists would perform a similar task with respect to the tastes, mores, and attitudes of our fellow citizens in their daily lives. . . . They might question the ubiquity and intensity of competition in our way of life and ask how the schools might contribute to the lessening of it, or concern themselves with the inanities of television entertainment, or face the question of means by which schools could go beyond mere propinquity in lessening the xenophopias and racisms which afflict us. [They would report] on changes in knowledge and attitude which might be important in consideration of curriculum changes . . . [and on] advances in knowledge of learning processes and modes of teaching, as they might modulate efforts to improve school curricula. (263–264)

Who would be the audience of these essays and reports? The curriculum professors' colleagues, former students, and the public at large, Schwab tells us. He does not mention classroom teachers or administrators as being among their readers, an omission that may have been deliberate or accidental but one that bears comment all the same as it foreshadows a difficulty soon to be discussed.

In the late 1960s and early 1970s there emerged a group of curriculum professors whose writings sounded as though they had taken Schwab's advice to heart, even though his fourth essay (from which the preceding quotation was taken) was not to appear for at least a decade and Schwab himself was to be among those with whom the group as a whole was said to differ. Some members of this group spoke of what they were doing as *reconceptualizing* the task of the curriculum specialist, particularly with respect to the role of theory in curricular affairs. The term stuck, and before long the group itself became known as *the reconceptualists* (MacDonald 1975).

From the start the group had no formal program or statement of purpose. As one of the more prominent of their members has remarked recently, "There is no Reconceptualist point of view, or even points of view" (Pinar 1988). What bound the group together ideationally was a broadly shared outlook that had three salient features. The first of these was a dissatisfaction with the Tylerian perspective, which had been a dominant force in the curriculum field for such a long time. The second was an eclectic intellectualism, intent on exploring bodies of knowledge and intellectual traditions that educators heretofore had not drawn on heavily. These freshly explored (by educators) intellectual terrains included psychoanalytic theory, phenomenology, existentialism, hermeneutics, and literary criticism. The third salient feature, though not shared by all, was a left-wing political bias that drew on Marxist and neo-Marxist thought and concerned itself with issues of racial and ethnic inequalities, feminism, the peace movement, and so forth.

Because the subject matter of the reconceptualists' writings is so varied, it is not possible to summarize their output or to say very much about their accomplishments to date in substantive terms. It is clear, however, that as a group their writings have become salient through the publication of edited volumes (Apple and Weis 1983; Giroux, Penna, and Pinar 1981; Barton and Lawn 1981; Molnar and Zahorik 1977; Pinar 1974, 1975, 1988a); through the founding of a journal, *The Journal of Curriculum Theorizing*, devoted almost exclusively to reconceptualist writings; and through independent publications of individual members of the group, some of whom have become prominent in their own right (see, e.g., the works of Apple 1979, 1982; Giroux 1981; and Pinar 1988). The group has also sponsored several annual conferences that have featured papers by its members. For a brief history of the group's early years, see Pinar (1988).

What all this writing adds up to in the way of influence within the field of curriculum is not entirely clear, however. William Pinar, one of the chief organizers and editors of the conferences and publications of the group and a frequent contributor to those publications, believes that its influence has been great, so great in fact that "the Tylerian dominance has passed" (1988a, 8). Pinar continues, "Like a disappearing star in another galaxy, however, it takes some time for everyone, depending upon his or her location, to see this. The fact is that to a remarkable extent reconceptualization has occurred" (8).

But has "the Tylerian dominance" become the "disappearing star" that Pinar makes it out to be? It depends, as he points out, on where one stands. From the standpoint of many educational practitioners the light may not yet have gone out entirely or even have been dimmed, for that matter. Pinar acknowledges that this is so in a footnote to the preceding quotation in which he says, "While the academic field of curriculum studies has been reconceived, the major ideas which constitute the contemporary field of study have yet to make their way to colleagues in elementary and secondary schools. If there is a 'second wave,' such schools will be its site" (13). This casual remark about the major ideas of the reconceptualists not yet having made their way to classroom teachers and school administrators is crucial if we are to understand the long-term significance of the move toward the academy on the part of university-based curriculum specialists. The obvious question to which it gives rise is, Why has this not yet happened? Is it simply a matter of time before it will? Pinar talks of a "second wave," a metaphor that carries the connotation of inevitability. But he also qualifies that expectation with an "if," which suggests that he himself has doubts about it happening. Why so? Is it that he suspects his "colleagues in elementary and secondary schools" may not read very much and therefore might be slow to get the news? Or might the source of the difficulty lie deeper?

To pursue this line of questioning, let us return to that portion of Schwab's (1983) advice to professors of curriculum in which he talked about their obligations to become educational critics in the broadest sense. Recall that the audience for that criticism, according to Schwab, was to include the professor's academic colleagues, former students, and the public at large. With the exception of the second category, which was made up of the school-based curriculum team leaders, no mention was made of practitioners at all. Was this an oversight on Schwab's part? Did he just forget to mention classroom teachers and school administrators? Or might he have had a reason for not doing so? We will never know for sure, of course, but it seems likely that their exclusion was not an oversight.

Schwab advised his readers, who were already members of the academy, even though marginally so, to write about the kinds of issues that would chiefly be of interest to other academy members. True, he wanted them to write for a wider audience as well, an audience that surely would have included practitioners. Speaking of "the evils and viscissitudes" of our government and society, Schwab (1983) urged professors of curriculum to "try to convince readers that these troubles exist, show the threats they pose, and suggest ways in which alteration of school practice might help ameliorate the conditions discussed" (263). This kind of writing, he hoped, "would thus inject into the lives of educators an element of active intellectualism which is sadly wanting" (263). But the important point is that it would specifically *not* address the day-to-day problems of how to put a curriculum together or even the techniques of how to deliberate. It would not be practical at all, at least not in a narrow, technical sense.

What would be its purpose? It would be to "inform, advise, and refresh"; to "rouse thought and debate"; to "inject into the lives of educators an element of active intellectualism." One cannot be certain that Schwab chose each of those words with care but even if he did not they nonetheless direct our attention to forms of intellectual sustenance that have little or nothing to do with the conventional task of helping a group of practitioners build a better curriculum.

The emergence of the reconceptualists, not to mention the warm reception Schwab's own writings have enjoyed among university-based specialists, shows that there is indeed an audience for that kind of sustenance. Will it ever include large numbers of practitioners? Pinar's observation about the major ideas of the reconceptualists not yet making their way to colleagues in elementary and secondary schools suggests that the latter remain relatively uninterested in what the former are doing and that the long-term prospect of a vast readership among practitioners for the kind of writing he and his colleagues have been producing is not very good.

What would it mean if that were so? What if some professors of curriculum gave up trying to help practitioners cope with the techniques involved in curriculum improvement? Would they still be deserving of their title or would they have to call themselves something else—professors of education, perhaps? (Something like this possibility has already been suggested; see, e.g., Barrow [1976, 1984]; Egan [1988]). That may be the answer. Let those who wish to make a career of addressing broad educational questions abandon the pretense of being curriculum specialists and simply think of themselves as generalists. The question of what title to use seems trivial compared to whether useful services are being performed. And what more useful service could there be than the one Schwab speaks of as informing, advising, and refreshing one's colleagues; one's former students; and with luck, the public at large?

There remains, however, the nagging worry triggered by Pinar's (1988a) observation about practitioners failing to read what he and his colleagues have written, or at least failing to do so in great numbers. Most authors would naturally like to have their work reach as large an audience as possible. But all such considerations aside, what should the specialist-turned-generalist make of a readership that largely excludes classroom teachers and school administrators? *Should* that be a source of concern?

The answer to that question depends on one's conception of educational change, which for analytic purposes can be subdivided into three components: (1) an idea of what changes are most needed, (2) an understanding of how they might come about, and (3) a set of beliefs about the role one might play in that process. If, on the one hand, one believes that vast changes are called for, that the actions of practitioners are instrumental in bringing them about, and that there are specific steps that one believes ought to be taken (all of which Bobbitt believed, for example), clearly it matters a lot whether practitioners listen to what one says. If, on the other hand, one thinks that the schools are functioning rather well as they are or that the principal agents of change are policymakers rather than practitioners, if one's critique of the status quo stops short of recommending steps to be taken, or finally if one holds to any combination of those three fundamental positions, it matters much less that relatively few practitioners are listening.

There is no question of where Bobbitt stood with respect to all three of these attitudes toward change. He was convinced that massive curricular changes were needed, that they had to be undertaken by practitioners (with outside help, of course), and that he himself knew the main steps that had to be taken. Tyler is much less clear on the scope of the undertaking, but he, like Bobbitt, sees the task as one for practitioners to initiate and shoulder. He also has a lot of concrete suggestions about how to proceed. Schwab is close to silent on the question of need (except for acknowledging that there probably will always be one); he believes, with Bobbitt and Tyler, that the practitioners' role is crucial, and he has several specific suggestions about how the planning groups should be formed and how their leaders should function, but not much beyond that.

Within the last set of possibilities, the one having to do with steps to be taken turns out to be decisive in separating those specialists who move toward practice from those who move toward the academy. It is clear that both groups are convinced of a need for change. Both also see the practitioner as central in effecting that change. What the academy-oriented specialists appear to lack, however, are concrete suggestions about how to proceed. Moreover, they are far less inclined than are their practice-oriented colleagues to become personally involved in the day-to-day affairs of schooling. Schwab might have described them as "fleeing the field," as becoming overly involved in theory to the neglect of practice.

These are certainly familiar complaints, which are often leveled at academics in general—not without justification from time to time, we must add. But we must also defend, as would Schwab himself, the legitimacy of backing off from practical affairs at least far enough to gain perspective on the whole and also of seeking to effect change through altering the way people look at the world and think about it, rather than through telling them what to do. That defense applies to education as to all other fields of human endeavor. The argument that says that practicing educators, working in an applied field, need only concern themselves with steps to be taken is plainly shortsighted. The way practitioners see their world and think about it surely has as much of a shaping effect on what they do as do any number of explicit rules or principles they may be trying to follow.

What, then, does this discussion say about the missing audience of practitioners for those educational writings that contain few if any suggestions about what to do next? It seems to say that their absence is a problem that needs to be addressed, though not necessarily and certainly not exclusively by those who are doing the writing. It is easy and all too common to castigate the authors for not being sufficiently down-to-earth and the would-be audience for not being sufficiently bookish or for lacking intellectual curiosity. It is also comforting to believe that if the writing is powerful and insightful enough the right audience will one day chance upon it. But the blame pointed in both directions may be unfair, and the hope of the problem belatedly rectifying itself may be false. Perhaps what is needed are new means for bringing the best of such writings to the attention of practitioners. These would include new kinds of publications, new forms of advertising, new educational efforts by teachers' unions and professional organizations, and more. Perhaps there are lessons to be learned in this regard by studying the myriad ways in which works of art and literature are brought to the attention of the public at large.

Textbook writers might object that they have been trying to do this for some time, of course, and so they have. Pinar (1988a), for example, notes with obvious approval the inclusion of reconceptualist work in Schubert's textbook and predicts its wide use by "responsible scholars" (7). Schwab (1978), for one, was well aware of the need for such efforts. He called for the establishment of new journals and for various other forums "connecting the series from teacher, supervisor, and school administrator at one end to research specialists at the other" (319). Without denigrating the impact of such efforts, it is clear that they are not all that is needed.

There is an additional consideration that can only be touched on in closing. It is related to the question of what practitioners are willing to read but bears even more directly on the future of curriculum as a field of study. It begins by asking whether curriculum change on a massive scale (Bobbitt) or even on the more modest scale of continuous tinkering (Tyler and Schwab) remains the issue it once was. There are signs that it is not. Certainly the days of nationwide curriculum reform that swept the country in the 1960s are long past. Similiar movements in other nations seem to have ceased as well.

There continues to be a lot of curricular activity—witness the huge amount of writing on specific topics that was mentioned at the start of this chapter. But discussion of these topics and the activity of curriculum development in these specialized areas tend to be dominated by specialists in particular subject matter fields rather than by specialists whose domain of expertise is the curriculum in general or curriculum improvement across the board. Also, today's emphasis on special populations of students, such as those described as being "at risk," and the focus on teaching basic skills may make the most pressing educational problems of the day seem more instructional than curricular. Perhaps, in short, there is no longer the need for the services of curriculum specialists that there once was. If this were so (and the supposition that it might be calls for empirical verification) it might mean that today's specialists and those still in training have little choice but to "flee the field," as Schwab might put it, because the field itself no longer contains the opportunities for service that were once there.

There is another possibility, of course, at least hypothetically, and that is to respond to current conditions by seeking to rejuvenate the field from within, which is what the reconceptualists have obviously sought to do and may be what those who are moving closer to practitioners are seeking to do as well. Can that be accomplished? Will either group succeed in recapturing the spirit of optimism and the sense of mission that clearly marked the first two or three decades of the emergence of curriculum as a field of study? Is it even desirable that such an attempt be made? These are questions to be addressed by tomorrow's educational leaders, who may or may not wish to think of themselves as curriculum specialists.

I return, finally, to the sense of confusion spoken of at the start of this chapter. Having completed my examination of that form of the confusion that centers on the question of what curriculum specialists are supposed to know and do, I must now ask whether the condition that so many have remarked on and complained about is remediable. The answer, I fear, is no. The variety of intellectual pursuits available to those who wish to contribute to an understanding of educational matters in general or curricular matters in particular is truly vast in number and therefore a bit daunting, if not downright unsettling, in its multiplicity. The boundaries of the field are diffuse, so much so that one may wonder sometimes whether it has any boundaries at all. To some, that condition is troublesome; to others, it is exhilarating; to all, it can become confusing at times.

References

Apple, Michael W. 1975. "Commonsense Categories and Curriculum Thought." In *Schools in Search of Meaning*, edited by James B. MacDonald and Esther Zaret, 116–148. Washington, DC: Association for Supervision and Curriculum Development.

Apple, Michael W. 1979. *Ideology and Curriculum*. London, Boston: Routledge & Kegan Paul.

Apple, Michael W. 1982. *Education and Power*. London, Boston: Routledge & Kegan Paul.

Apple, Michael W., and Lois Weis, eds. 1983. *Ideology and School Practices*. Philadelphia, PA: Temple University Press.

Association for Supervision and Curriculum Development. 1976. *Milwaukee Curriculum Theory Conference, University of Wisconsin–Milwaukee*. Washington, DC: ASCD.

Bantock, G. H. 1980. *Dilemmas of the Curriculum*. New York: Wiley.

Barrow, Robin. 1976. *Common Sense and the Curriculum*. London: George Allen & Unwin.

Barrow, Robin. 1984. *Giving Teaching Back to Teachers: A Critical Introduction to Curriculum Theory*. London, Ont.: Althouse Press.

Barton, Len, and Martin Lawn, 1981. *Rethinking Curriculum Studies*. New York: Halsted Press.

Beane, James A., Conrad F. Toepfer, Jr., and Samuel J. Alessi, Jr. 1986. *Curriculum Planning and Development*. Boston: Allyn & Bacon.

Beauchamp, George A. 1968. *Curriculum Theory*. Wilmette, IL: Kagg Press.

Beauchamp, George A. 1972. Basic components of a curriculum theory. *Curriculum Theory Network* 10: 16–22.

Bellack, Arno A. 1969. History of curriculum thought and practices. *Review of Educational Research* 39(3): 283–292.

Benjamin, Harold. 1939. *The Saber-Tooth Curriculum*. New York: McGraw-Hill.

Bloom, Benjamin S., ed. 1956. *Taxonomy of Educational Objectives; The Classification of Educational Goals. Handbook I: Cognitive Domain*. New York: McKay.

Bobbitt, J. Franklin. 1924. *How to Make a Curriculum*. Boston: Houghton Mifflin.

Bobbitt, J. Franklin. 1972 [1918]. *The Curriculum*. New York: Arno Press.

Bowsher, Columbus A. 1900. *The Absolute Curriculum*. Champaign, IL: Bowsher.

Broudy, Harry S. 1976. Review of curriculum theorizing: The reconceptualists. *Teachers College Record* 77(4): 639–641.

Caswell, Hollis L. 1966. "Emergence of the Curriculum as a Field of Professional Work and Study." In *Precedents and Promise in the Curriculum Field*, edited by Helen F. Robison, 1–11. New York: Teachers College Press.

Caswell, Hollis L., and Doak S. Campbell. 1935. *Curriculum Development*. New York: American Book Co.

Cavell, Stanley. 1988. *In Quest of the Ordinary*. Chicago: University of Chicago Press.

Clandinin, D. Jean. 1986. *Classroom Practice: Teacher Images in Action*. London: Falmer.

Connelly, F. Michael. 1985. "Definitions of Curriculum." In *International Encyclopedia of Education: Research and Studies*, vol. 2, edited by Torsten Husén and T. Neville Postlethwaite, 1160–1163. Oxford: Pergamon.

Connelly, F. Michael, and D. Jean Clandinin. 1988. *Teachers as Curriculum Planners*. New York: Teachers College Press.

Connelly, F. Michael, and Freema Elbaz. 1980. "Conceptual Bases for Curricular Thought: A Teacher's Perspective." In *1980 Yearbook: Considered Action for Curriculum Improvement*, edited by Arthur W. Foshay, 95–119. Washington, DC: Association for Supervision and Curriculum Development.

Cremin, Lawrence A. 1956. "The Problem of Curriculum Making: A Historical Perspective." In *1956 Yearbook: What Shall the High Schools Teach?* 6–26. Washington, DC: Association for Supervision and Curriculum Development.

Cremin, Lawrence A. 1961. *The Transformation of the School: Progressivism in American Education*. New York: Knopf.

Cremin, Lawrence A. 1976. *Public Education*. New York: Basic Books.

Dewey, John. 1899. *The School and Society*. Chicago: University of Chicago Press.

Dewey, John. 1902. *The Child and the Curriculum*. Chicago: University of Chicago Press.

Dewey, John. 1956. *The Child and the Curriculum; The School and Society*. Chicago: University of Chicago Press.

Dewey, John. 1960 [1933]. *How We Think*. Lexington, MA: Heath.

Doll, Ronald C. 1964. *Curriculum Improvement: Decision-making and Process*. Boston: Allyn & Bacon.

Dreeben, Robert. 1976. The unwritten curriculum and its relation to values. *Journal of Curriculum Studies* 8(2): 111–124.

Egan, Kieran. 1978. What is curriculum? *Curriculum Inquiry* 8(1): 65–72.

Egan, Kieran. 1982. On the possibility of theories of educational practice. *Journal of Educational Studies* 14(2): 153–165.

Eggleston, J. 1977. *The Sociology of School Curriculum*. London: Routledge & Kegan Paul.

Eisner, Elliot W. 1978. Humanistic trends and the curriculum field. *Journal of Curriculum Studies* 10(2): 197–204.

Eisner, Elliot W. 1979. *The Educational Imagination*. New York: Macmillan.

Eisner, Elliot W., and E. Vallance, eds. 1974. *Conflicting Conceptions of the Curriculum*. National Society for the Study of Education Series on Contemporary Educational Issues. Berkeley, CA: McCutchan.

Elbaz, Freema. 1983. *Teacher Thinking: A Study of Practical Knowledge*. London: Croom Helm.

Elbaz, Freema, and R. Elbaz. 1981. Literature and curriculum: Toward a view of curriculum as discoursive practice. *Curriculum Inquiry* 11(2): 105–122.

Flinders, D. J., N. Noddings, and S. J. Thornton. 1986. The null curriculum: Its theoretical basis and practical implications. *Curriculum Inquiry* 16(1): 33–42.

Firth, Gerald R., and Richard D. Kimpston. 1973. *The Curricular Continuum in Perspective*. Itasca, IL: Peacock.

Fish, Stanley. 1980. *Is There a Text in This Class?* Cambridge, MA: Harvard University Press.

Fish, Stanley. 1989. *Doing What Comes Naturally*. Durham, NC: Duke University Press.

Foshay, Arthur W. 1975. "Forward." In *Curriculum Development: Theory Into Practice*, Daniel Tanner and Laurel N. Tanner. New York: Macmillan.

Fox, Seymour. 1985. The vitality of theory in Schwab's conception of the practical. *Curriculum Inquiry* 15(1): 63–89.

Geertz, Clifford. 1983. *Local Knowledge*. New York: Basic Books.

Geertz, Clifford. 1988. *Works and Lines*. Palo Alto, CA: Stanford University Press.

Giroux, Henry. 1981. *Ideology, Culture, and the Process of Schooling*. Philadelphia, PA: Temple University Press.

Giroux, Henry A., Anthony N. Penna, and William F. Pinar, eds. 1981. *Curriculum and Instruction: Alternatives in Education*. Berkeley, CA: McCutchan.

Giroux, Henry, and David Purpel. 1983. *The Hidden Curriculum and Moral Education: Deception of Discovery?* Berkeley, CA: McCutchan.

Goodlad, John I. 1985. "Curriculum as a Field of Study." In *International Encyclopedia of Education*, vol. 2, edited by Torsten Husen and T. Neville Postlethwaite, 1141–1143. Oxford: Pergamon.

Goodlad, John I., and associates. 1979. *Curriculum Inquiry: The Study of Curriculum Practice*. New York: McGraw-Hill.

Goodlad, John I., Renata von Stoephasius, and N. Frances Klein. 1966. *The Changing School Curriculum*. New York: Fund for the Advancement of Education.

Goodson, Ivor. 1983. *School Subjects and Curriculum Change*. London: Falmer.

Gordon, David. 1981. The immorality of the hidden curriculum. *Journal of Moral Education* 10(1): 3–8.

Gordon, David. 1982. The concept of the hidden curriculum. *Journal of the Philosophy of Education* 16(2): 187–198.

Gordon, David. 1983. Rules and the effectiveness of the hidden curriculum. *Journal of the Philosophy of Education* 17(2): 207–218.

Gordon, David. 1984. The magic of science, technological consciousness and the hidden curriculum. *Curriculum Inquiry* 14 (4): 367–399.

Gordon, David. 1988a. Education as text: The varieties of education hiddenness. *Curriculum Inquiry* 18(4): 426–449.

Gordon, David. 1988b. The rebirth of the hidden curriculum: Phlogiston as Priestley might explain it to Lavoisire. *Curriculum Inquiry* 18(4): 465–70.

Gordon, Peter, and Denis Lawton. 1978. *Curriculum Change in the Nineteenth and Twentieth Centuries*. London: Hodder and Stoughton.

Gress, James R., and David E. Purpel, eds. 1978. *Curriculum: An Introduction to the Field*. Berkeley, CA: McCutchan.

Hameyer, Uwe, and others. 1986. *Curriculum Research in Europe*. Published under the auspices of the Secretary General of the Council of Europe. Lisse, Switzerland: Swets and Zeitlinger B.V.

Hameyer, Uwe, Karl Frey, and Henning Haft, eds. 1983. *Handbuch der Curriculumforschung*. Weinheim und Basel: Beltz.

Hamilton, David. 1989. *Toward a Theory of Schooling*. London: Falmer.

Harap, Henry, ed. 1937. *The Changing Curriculum*. New York: D. Appleton-Century.

Hass, Glenn, Joseph Bondi, and Jon Wiles. 1974. *Curriculum Planning: A New Approach*. Boston: Allyn & Bacon.

Hirst, Paul H. 1974. *Knowledge and the Curriculum*. London: Routledge & Kegan Paul.

Huebner, Dwayne. 1966. "Curricular Language and Classroom Meanings." In *Language and Meaning*, edited by James B. Macdonald and Robert R. Leepers, 8–26. Washington, DC: Association for Supervision and Curriculum Development.

Huebner, Dwayne. 1976. The moribund curriculum field: Its wake and our work. *Curriculum Inquiry* 6(2): 153–167.

Hutchins, Robert M. 1953. *The Conflict in Education*. New York: Harper & Brothers.

Inlow, Gail M. 1973. *The Emergents in Curriculum*, 2nd ed. New York: Wiley.

Jackson, Philip W. 1968. *Life in Classrooms*. New York: Holt, Rinehart and Winston.

Jackson, Philip W. 1980. Curriculum and its discontents. *Curriculum Inquiry* 10(2): 159–172.

Jenkins, David, and Marten D. Shipman. 1976. *Curriculum: An Introduction*. London: Open Books.

Joyce, Bruce R. 1971. "The Curriculum Worker of the Future." In *The Curriculum: Retrospect and Prospect*, edited by Robert M. McClure, 307–355. Chicago: University of Chicago Press.

Kelly, A. 1982. *The Curriculum: Theory and Practice*, 2nd ed. London: Harper & Row.

Kliebard, Herbert M. 1970. Reappraisal: The Tyler rationale. *School Review* 78(2): 259–272.

Kliebard, Herbert M. 1975. "Persistent Curriculum Issues in Historical Perspective." In *Curriculum Theorizing*, edited by William Pinar, 39–50. Berkeley, CA: McCutchan.

Kliebard, Herbert. 1977. Curriculum theory: Give me a "for instance." *Curriculum Inquiry* 6(4): 257–269.

Kliebard, Herbert M. 1987. *The Struggle for the American Curriculum 1893–1958*. New York: Routledge & Kegan Paul.

Lakomski, Gabriele. 1988. Witches, weather gods, and phlogiston: The demise of the hidden curriculum. *Curriculum Inquiry* 18(4): 451–463.

McClure, Robert M. 1971. *The Curriculum: Retrospect and Prospect*. Seventieth Yearbook of the National Society for the Study of Education, Part I. Chicago: University of Chicago Press.

MacDonald, Barry, and Rob Walker. 1976. *Changing the Curriculum*. London: Open Books.

Macdonald, James B. 1975. "Curriculum Theory." In *Curriculum Theorizing*, edited by William Pinar, 5–16. Berkeley, CA: McCutchan.

McNeil, John D. 1977. *Curriculum: A Comprehensive Introduction*. Boston: Little, Brown.

Martin, Jane Roland. 1976. What should we do with the hidden curriculum when we find one? *Curriculum Inquiry* 6(2): 135–152.

Molnar, Alex, and John A. Zahorik, eds. 1977. *Curriculum Theory*. Washington, DC: Association for Supervision and Curriculum Development.

Musgrave, Peter William. 1978. *The Moral Curriculum: A Sociological Analysis*. London: Methuen.

Oberg, Antoinette. 1987. Using construct theory as a basis for research into teacher professional development. *Journal of Curriculum Studies* 19(1): 55–65.

Oliva, Peter F. 1982. *Developing the Curriculum*. Boston: Little, Brown.

Oliver, Albert J. 1965. *Curriculum Improvement: A Guide to Problems, Principles, and Procedures*. New York: Dodd, Mead.

Orlosky, Donald E., and B. Othanel Smith. 1978. *Curriculum Development: Issues and Insights*. Chicago: Rand McNally.

Overly, Norman V. 1970. *The Unstudied Curriculum: Its Impact on Children*. Washington, DC: Association For Supervision and Curriculum Development Elementary Education Council.

Pinar, William. 1974. *Heightened Consciousness, Cultural Revolution, and Curriculum Theory*. Berkeley, CA: McCutchan.

Pinar, William, ed. 1975. *Curriculum Theorizing: The Reconceptualists*. Berkeley, CA: McCutchan.

Pinar, William. 1978. Notes on the curriculum field. Address at the 1978 American Educational Research Association. *Educational Researcher* 7(8): 5–12.

Pinar, William F. 1988a. *Contemporary Curriculum Discourses*. Scottsdale, AZ: Gorsuch Scarisbrick.

Pinar, William F. 1988b. The Reconceptualization of curriculum studies, 1987: A personal retrospective. *Journal of Curriculum and Supervision* 3(2): 157–167.

Portelli, John P. 1987. On defining curriculum. *Journal of Curriculum and Supervision* 2(4): 354–367.

Pring, Richard. 1976. *Knowledge and Schooling*. London: Open Books.

Purpel, David E. 1988. *The Moral and Spritual Crisis in Education: A Curriculum for Justice and Compassion in Education*. Granby, MA: Bergin and Garvey.

Purpel, David E., and Maurice Belanges. 1972. *Curriculum and the Cultural Revolution*. Berkeley, CA: McCutchan.

Reid, William A. 1979a. Schools, teachers, and curriculum change: The moral dimension of theory-building. *Educational Theory* 29(4): 325–336.

Reid, William A. 1979b. *Thinking About the Curriculum: The Nature and Treatment of Curriculum Problems*. Boston: Routledge & Kegan Paul.

Reid, William A., and Decker F. Walker. 1975. *Case Studies in Curriculum Change*. London: Routledge & Kegan Paul.

Resnick, Lauren B., and Leopold E. Klopfer, eds. 1989. Yearbook: *Toward the Thinking Curriculum: Current Cognitive Research*. Washington, DC: Association for Supervision and Curriculum Development.

Reynolds, William M. 1989. *Reading Curriculum Theory: The Development of a New Hermeneutic*. New York: P. Lang.

Richmond, Kenneth W. 1979. *The School Curriculum*. London: Methuen.

Robison, Helen F., ed. 1966. *Precedents and Promise in the Curriculum Field*. New York: Teachers College Press.

Rorty, Richard. 1989. *Contingency, Irony, and Solidarity*. New York: Cambridge University Press.

Rugg, Harold. 1926a. *Curriculum Making: Past and Present*. Twenty-sixth Yearbook of the National Society for the Study of Education, Part I. Bloomington, IL: Public School Publishing.

Rugg, Harold. 1926b. *The Foundations of Curriculum-Making*. Twenty-sixth Yearbook of the National Society for the Study of Education, Part II. Bloomington, IL: Public School Publishing.

Rugg, Harold. 1936. *American Life and the School Curriculum*. Boston: Ginn.

Saylor, J. Galen, and William M. Alexander. 1974. *Planning Curriculum for Schools*. New York: Holt, Rinehart and Winston.

Schubert, William H. 1982. Return of curriculum inquiry from schooling to education. *Curriculum Inquiry* 12(2): 221–232.

Schubert, William H. 1984. *Curriculum Books: The First Eighty Years*. Lanham, MD: University Press of America.

Schubert, William H. 1986. *Curriculum: Perspective, Paradigm, and Possibility*. New York: Macmillan.

Schwab, Joseph J. 1969. The practical: Arts of eclectic. *School Review* 79(4): 493–542.

Schwab, Joseph J. 1970. *The Practical: A Language for Curriculum*. Washington, DC: National Education Association.

Schwab, Joseph J. 1973. The practical 3: Translation into curriculum. *School Review* 81(4): 501–522.

Schwab, Joseph J. 1978. *Science, Curriculum and Liberal Education: Selected Essays, Joseph J. Schwab*, edited by Ian Westbury and N. J. Wilkof. Chicago: University of Chicago Press.

Schwab, Joseph J. 1983. The practical 4: Something for curriculum professors to do. *Curriculum Inquiry* 13(3): 239–265.

Seguel, Mary Louise. 1966. *The Curriculum Field: Its Formative Years*. New York: Teachers College Press.

Selden, Steven. 1977. Conservative ideology and curriculum. *Educational Theory* 27(3): 205–222.

Smith, Barbara Herrnstein. 1988. *Contingencies of Value*. Cambridge, MA: Harvard University Press.

Smith, B. Othanel, William O. Stanley, and J. Harlan Shores. 1957. *Fundamentals of Curriculum Development*. Yonkers-on-Hudson, NY: World Book Company.

Snyder, B. R. 1970. *The Hidden Curriculum*. New York: Knopf.

Sockett, Hugh. 1976. *Designing the Curriculum*. London: Open Books.

Stenhouse, Lawrence A. 1980a. Curriculum research and the art of the teacher. *Curriculum* 1(1): 40–44.

Stenhouse, Lawrence A. 1980b. *Curriculum Research and Development in Action*. London: Heinemann Educational Books.

Stenhouse, Lawrence A. 1985. "Curriculum Research, Artistry and Teaching." In *Research as a Basis for Teaching: Readings from the Work of Lawrence Stenhouse*, edited by Jean Rudduck and David Hopkins. London: Heinemann Educational Books.

Stenhouse, Lawrence A. 1988. Artistry and teaching: The teacher as focus of research and development. *Journal of Curriculum and Supervision* 4(1): 43–51.

Stratemeyer, Florence B., and others. 1957. *Developing a Curriculum for Modern Living*. New York: Teachers College Press.

Taba, Hilda. 1962. *Curriculum Development: Theory and Practice*. New York: Harcourt, Brace & World.

Tanner, Daniel, and Laurel N. Tanner. 1980. *Curriculum Development*. New York: Macmillan.

Tanner, Laurel N. 1988. *Critical Issues in Curriculum*, Eighty-seventh Yearbook of the National Society for the Study of Education, Part I. Chicago: University of Chicago Press.

Taylor, Philip H. 1979. *New Directions in Curriculum Studies*. Lowes, England: Falmer Press.

Taylor, Philip H., ed. 1986. *Recent Developments in Curriculum Studies*. Windsor, England: NFER-Nelson.

Taylor, Philip H., and Colin M. Richards. 1979. *An Introduction to Curriculum Studies*. Windsor, England: NFER Publishing Company.

Taylor, Philip H., and J. Walton, eds. 1973. *The Curriculum: Research, Innovation and Change*. London: Ward Lock.

Tyler, Ralph W. 1949. *Basic Principles of Curriculum and Instruction*. Chicago: University of Chicago Press.

Unruh, Glenys G., and Adolph Unruh. 1984. *Curriculum Development: Problems, Processes, and Progress*. Berkeley, CA: McCutchan.

Vallance, Elizabeth. 1973. Hiding the hidden curriculum: An interpretation of the language of justification in nineteenth century educational reform. *Curriculum Theory Network* 4(1): 5–21.

Vallance, Elizabeth. 1982. The hidden curriculum and qualitative inquiry as states of mind. *Journal of Education* 162(1): 138–151.

Walker, Decker F. 1980. "A Barnstorming Tour of Writing on Curriculum." In *1980 Yearbook: Considered Action for Curriculum Improvement*, edited by Arthur W. Foshay, 71–81. Washington, DC: Association for Supervision and Curriculum Development.

Walker, Decker, and Jonas Soltis. 1986. *Curriculum and Aims*. New York: Teachers College Press.

Weet, H. S. 1901. *The Curriculum in Elementary Education*. Rochester, NY: University of Rochester Press.

Westbury, Ian, and William Steiner. 1971. Curriculum: A discipline in search of its problems. *School Review* 79(2): 243–267.

Winchester, Ian. 1977. Concept elucidation and educational issues. *Curriculum Inquiry* 7(4): 331–342.

Zais, Robert S. 1976. *Curriculum: Principles and Foundations*. New York: Harper & Row.

Zumwalt, Karen. 1988. "Beginning Professional Teachers: The Need for a Curricular Vision of Teaching." In *Knowledge Base for the Beginning Teacher*, edited by Maynard C. Reynolds, 173–184. Oxford: Pergamon.

2

CURRICULUM STUDIES AND THE TRADITIONS OF INQUIRY: THE SCIENTIFIC TRADITION

Linda Darling-Hammond and Jon Snyder
TEACHERS COLLEGE, COLUMBIA UNIVERSITY

This chapter treats the history of scientific approaches to curriculum studies from two vantage points, one conceptual and the other methodological. From a conceptual perspective, the scientific tradition offers curriculum workers a framework for thinking about—and making judgments about—curriculum. A scientific approach seeks to justify curricular decisions by reference to a growing base of knowledge about the nature of learning and the effects of teaching choices on various learning outcomes. This approach might be viewed as standing in contrast to, or complementary with, approaches that seek to justify curricular decisions on more purely philosophical or humanistic grounds, referencing values and beliefs as the cornerstones of evaluative judgments and actions (see the chapter by Lincoln in this *Handbook*).

From a methodological perspective, the scientific tradition offers a range of procedures for attempts to understand and advance curricular theory and practice by grounding them empirically in systematic studies of student learning and classroom undertakings. Although the results of these studies may be represented in quantitative form (we will devote special attention in this chapter to statistical representations of curriculum investigations), a wide range of observational and descriptive strategies have been used in building a knowledge base for curriculum decision making. The domain of such investigations includes most centrally the four curriculum "commonplaces" described by Schwab (1966). Thus it includes the empirical study, based in part on psychological and other theories (e.g., social, political, and economic) of students and their learning, teachers and their teaching, subject matter and its structure, and the contexts for curriculum enactment.

By our definition, then, the scientific tradition of curricular inquiry asks the question "How can curriculum decisions be informed by what we know or can discover about how and what children learn in relation to how and what they are taught?" A secondary question, which undergirds many statistical analyses and comparative studies based on survey research, is "How can we describe and compare students' curriculum encounters and their influences on learning?" The scientific tradition's methods for answering these questions involve systematic observation and data analysis.

The philosophic tradition asks fundamental questions about whether children *should* be taught certain things or in certain ways, based on what we believe are just and appropriate educational goals and means. Its methods—many of them treated in this *Handbook's* chapter on the humanistic tradition of curriculum inquiry—involve interpretive analysis, critical theory, hermeneutics, and other means for illuminating the ideas and values underlying curricular pursuits. This distinction does not place the two traditions of inquiry in opposition to each other, as each must dip from the other's stream, but it points to their differing emphases; concerns; and to some extent, standards of proof.

Any attempt to create a divide between the two breaks down, of course, as values about education and judgments about goals implicitly and explicitly influence decisions about what shall be scientifically studied and how curriculum "outcomes" shall be measured. And observations about the world and relationships within it, derived from systematic investigation as well as personal observation, influence philosophers' ideas about goals, norms, and values.

These kinds of distinctions, although they serve to give us an initial boundary for our work, have proven especially problematic in recent years, giving rise to "paradigm wars" that have seemed to place in opposition the "objectivist-quantitative-positivist-scientific" research tradition and the "interpretive-qualitative-hermeneutic-humanistic" tradition (Gage 1989). These common clumpings of descriptors would seem to exclude from the range of scientific endeavors those that use qualitative methods of conducting and reporting research or those that seek to take subjects' intentions or interpretations of events into account. They would meanwhile seem to deny qualitative researchers and assorted humanists any claims to organized, dispassionate (or at least open-minded) inquiry.

These clusterings of adjectives are symptomatic of how particular methods have, in the view of some, become bound up with theories and ideologies, and all of them confused with particularistic perceptions of what it means to be "scientific" in one's investigations. There are many reasons why these associations in goals, means, and method have been configured in this way and placed in ostensible conflict. These are part of our story and we shall return to them in greater depth. For now, we note that our construction of the scientific tradition of curriculum inquiry does not bundle goals, methods, and attributions in the manner sketched above. Following in the footsteps of those who launched the tradition—John Dewey, Jean Piaget, and others—we define scientific approaches as encompassing all empirical research methods that systematically examine curriculum, teaching, learning, and their interrelationships.

One of the major sources of conflict in the history of scientific curriculum inquiry involves sharp differences in views about the uses to which resulting knowledge should be put: for control of the curriculum and of teachers and learners or for their own use in enriching their teaching and learning efforts. These differences in aims, we believe, have contributed to the paradigm wars, which raise to the fore questions of the intentions and uses of research as well as its presumptions and methods.

John Dewey's quest for the sources of a "science of education" was aimed at the enrichment of the teacher's capacity for heightened understanding and intelligent decision making rather than the control of his or her behavior. Noting that those who see "uniformity of procedure" as the end result of science have got it backward, Dewey (1929) contended,

> Command of scientific methods and systematized subject matter liberates individuals; it enables them to see new problems, devise new procedures, and, in general, makes for diversification rather than for set uniformity. . . . (12)
>
> This knowledge and understanding render [the teacher's] practice more intelligent, more flexible and better adapted to deal effectively with concrete phenomena of practice . . . . Seeing more relations he sees more possibilities, more opportunities. His ability to judge being enriched, he has a wider range of alternatives to select from in dealing with individual situations. (20–21)

As the range of administrative and policy uses to which curriculum studies and data are put is continually expanding, these observations are particularly prescient. Currently, many would use studies of curriculum effects to limit teachers' judgments and constrain classroom practice to set routines. Meanwhile, some policies advocate managing schools with reference to statistical indicators alone, rather than more messy encounters with the real students, teachers, content, and contexts that make up the educational process (Darling-Hammond and Wise 1985; Wise 1979). There are continuing questions concerning whether curriculum research will be used by educators to deepen their judgments with greater understanding of how diverse children learn in a wide range of cognitive and subject matter domains, or whether the search for uniform procedures and outcomes will turn curriculum research into control mechanisms aimed at narrow measures of learning and schooling. Following what must necessarily be a too-sketchy outline of the major lines of research that have formed the scientific tradition of curriculum inquiry in this century, we will turn our attention at the close of the chapter to some of the recent uses to which these inquiries have been put and their implications for teaching and learning.

The questions we explore in this chapter are, with some narrowing of scope, a partial retrospective on those that Dewey (1929) raised:

> What are the ways by means of which the function of education in all its branches and phases—selection of material for the curriculum, methods of instruction and discipline, organization and administration of schools—can be conducted with systematic increase of intelligent control and understanding? What are the materials upon which we may—and should—draw in order that educational activities may become in a less degree products of routine, tradition, accident and transitory accidental influences? From what sources shall we draw so that there shall be steady and cumulative growth of intelligent, communicable insight and power of direction? (9–10)

We discuss the routes that have been taken to pursue a "science for curriculum," if you will, by describing the ways in which researchers have sought to (1) investigate student learning in order to derive a more scientific basis for curriculum design and (2) examine, describe, and compare curricular activities and their variously defined effects.

Distinctions often made between curriculum and instruction will become very blurry in this chapter, as research on both curriculum and teaching have increasingly made them. The "curriculum," as it is received by students, cannot in their view be divorced from the way in which it is conveyed to them. Neither, we believe, can it be evaluated without attention to how it is transmitted. Teaching methods, in turn, are clearly influenced by the nature of both curriculum content and its assessment, another fine line that is increasingly difficult to maintain in the real world of schools.

As we will describe, the scientific tradition in curriculum studies has by the nature of its goals had to treat matters of curriculum, teaching, and testing or evaluation simultaneously. In fact, its findings are contingent on how these closely related activities are defined and addressed. To eliminate instructional methods and assessment from our consideration, then, would obscure a substantial part of the story and eradicate most of its meaning. Although we do not take the extreme view that "curriculum is the study of any and all educational phenomena" (Egan 1978), we do see the instructional interactions of teachers and learners as part of the intended and unintended school curriculum. In this sense, our view of the curriculum domain is similar to Bruner's (1966):

> A curriculum reflects not only the nature of knowledge itself but also the nature of the knower and the knowledge-getting process. It is an enterprise par excellence where the line between subject matter and methods grows necessarily indistinct. . . . Knowledge is a process, not a product. (72)

As we trace inquiries into the nature of learning and the nature and effects of curriculum, we devote a substantial section to various efforts to "quantify" the curriculum, that is, to describe various aspects of curriculum content and its enactment in numerical or statistical terms, for purposes of evaluation, comparison, or monitoring.

Currently, a greatly renewed level of activity in the development of educational indicators, including curriculum indicators, is occurring at the national and state levels as well as cross-nationally. These efforts involve the collection of data, usually by survey methods, and their aggregation for statistical analysis and representation to depict comparisons among groups or trends over time. These apparently simple, statistical representations of educational conditions and events have enormous appeal and are persuasive in motivating political action of various kinds, ranging from general support of education to specific curricular mandates intended to rectify perceived problems suggested by the indicators. We describe this "movement" as it has evolved and discuss the kinds of curriculum study these data collections have engendered and are likely to encourage and support in the future.

Efforts at curriculum quantification (and the quantification of curriculum "results") come about for both scientific and policy reasons. Attempts to study phenomena for the purpose of comparison require the development of standard metrics, whether they are used to determine relative effectiveness in the cause of scientific advancement or to promote more equitable allocation of opportunities in the cause of just policy making. Of course, in either case, uses of such metrics other than promoting equity or effectiveness are also possible, including the tracking of students in ways that deny access to curricular opportunities (see the chapter by Oakes, Gamoran, and Page in this *Handbook*) and the narrowing of curriculum goals to only those that can be easily measured in standardized form. The promise and pitfalls of attempts to measure curriculum and its outcomes are also treated in this chapter.

Obviously, this is a tall order. We cannot do full justice to this complex terrain, but we will attempt to provide the reader with a map and a compass for negotiating its topography and shifting borders. As a first step on this journey, we begin with a discussion of the possibilities and limits of scientific study as a means for understanding curriculum, and we treat first the confusion of scientism for science, which so often obscures our path.

The Possibilities and Limits of Scientific Inquiry

Earlier we sought to delimit this chapter's subject by distinguishing scientific, empirical approaches from "humanistic" or philosophic orientations. The former, we acknowledged, tend to be viewed as an objective enterprise, asking what are the measured effects of various amounts and kinds of curricular experiences. The latter are often viewed as more subjective, asking what are the benefits, using normative referents, of a certain quality or nature of curricular experience. Immediately, though, we began to hedge on the usefulness of this dichotomy since the attempt to bring meaning to events must always, if it is to be successful, eventually both confront their qualitative nature and interpret them in terms of some norms, values, or goals.

Thus, "scientific" study, as it is sometimes narrowly construed, is useful but not sufficient for developing a full understanding of curriculum. Its virtues are that it allows a systematic view of events and provides a set of potentially powerful methods for uncovering relationships between these events and their consequences. Its counting and categorizing capabilities provide a means for monitoring, comparing, and evaluating educational offerings and results over time, between jurisdictions, and among groups of students. These can be used to indicate where there may be shortcomings in the system or inequities in opportunities provided to children, thus stimulating changes in policy or practice.

But matters of philosophy and values cannot be ignored if scientific inquiries are to be intellectually honest, theoretically sound, and practically useful. Those who would like to engage in science may err in their interpretations of findings if they believe that biases or normative points of view do not exist merely because they have not been made explicit. Furthermore, their findings may be irrelevant or meaningless if they have not given careful thought and consideration to the *nature* and *quality* of what they are observing, measuring, or evaluating. And finally, reductions of experience to that which can be quantified always risk ignoring important factors that are not easily measured in favor of those that are, no matter how trivial they may be.

As Dewey recognized long ago, neither empiricism nor measurement in and of itself produces science. We must bring meaning to these activities via theory and thought, which first produce ideas about the principles that may govern relationships among events and then immediately question and test their generalizability. This step must be taken with constant reference to the still thornier questions of goals. Toward what ends is this inquiry directed and its findings applicable? In what sense are these the ends we claim to be seeking? "A hard and fast distinction between [psychological methods and social and philosophical questions]," Dewey (1929) claimed, "is fraught with danger" (61).

Throughout this chapter, we will examine three sets of recurrent issues that have been raised by efforts to develop and study curriculum scientifically. *Normative issues*, whether implicit or explicit, underlie research decisions about what is worth studying and what factors or consequences are worth taking into account. *Theoretical issues* crop up as explanations are sought for the phenomena observed. To understand the place and meaning of an inquiry in the greater scheme of things we must examine the theory or model relied on (again, this may be implicit or explict) and the assumptions about education, teaching, and learning that guide the search for cause and effect. *Measurement issues* arise as decisions are made about what to measure and how to measure it. Once again, layers of values, goals, and assumptions must be excavated along with technical matters to make sense of the metrics and evaluate their validity for particular uses.

Science and Scientism in the Study of Curriculum

Although these issues have not always been ignored in the ongoing pursuit of a science of education, they have sometimes been unacknowledged and neglected. Claims of "objectivity" have sometimes been made for any tool or finding that can be reduced to numerical terms or presented in a standardized fashion, without regard to the manner in which it was concocted or the perspective that initially made it seem worth concocting. And as we shall see in the course of this discussion, some of the underlying, unexamined assumptions about the nature of human learning and behavior that have driven efforts to manage schools and children "scientifically" and "objectively" have been proven untenable by genuine scientific study, using the methods and thought processes of science rather than merely its cloak.

Lack of deeper reflection about the alternate meanings of results, inadequate testing of discrete findings, and leaps of inference about their applicability to diverse situations have frequently led to what we call "scientism" in education. This is the adoption or prescription, under the mantle of scientific applications, of specific educational procedures to be unvaryingly used to produce specific results. When these attempts to establish rational, objective procedures for assuming control of uncertain situations are based on misinterpretations of the relationship between means and ends, students and teachers may suffer the dysfunctional consequences of what Wise (1979) terms "hyperrationalization." Hyperrational curriculum policies are those that carefully prescribe "inputs" or "processes" to attain specific "outputs" even when cause-effect relationships are unknown or indeterminate.

Such initiatives, especially when they are ostensibly "research-based" are among the reasons for the paradigm wars mentioned earlier. A rush to generalization and application of correlational findings; tendencies to oversimplify the nature of learning, the goals of curriculum, and the acts of teaching; and attempts to use scientific findings to control rather than inform teaching are among the side effects of early enthusiasms for "curriculum science" that have engendered serious backlash.

Perhaps because of the zeal with which "scientific" (too often merely technocratic) solutions to difficult and complex problems have been adopted, reactions against the research touted in their support have also been severe. Attempts to correct shortcomings in one or another approach have led to the rejection of whole conceptions rather than correctives, augmentations, or peaceful coexistence. Gage (1989) characterizes objections to "scientific" research on teaching as stemming from three major perspectives —the antinaturalist, interpretivist, and critical theorist critiques.

The first critique is that the scientific tradition's attempts at prediction and control have extended beyond what is possible and desirable in explaining or shaping such human, and thus variable, affairs as teaching and learning. Second, the focus on observable behaviors of the tradition's "quantitative, objectivity-seeking researchers" (Gage 1989, 137) ignores the meaning perspectives of teachers and students and imposes assumptions of uniformity where they are not warranted. Third, the findings of a positivistic "technical orientation aimed at efficiency, rationality, and objectivity" (138) are applicable only if existing schooling and teaching structures are accepted as a given. They do not reach beyond the status quo to issues of how schools might produce qualitatively different and more socially just outcomes.

These factors may have contributed to the more fundamental problem. Many of those who claimed the mantle of science, in the early days of this century and since, asserted objectivity by virtue of measurement and experimentation, abdicating responsibility for the perspectives and sensibilities that informed their choices of what should be studied and how as well as what explanations and uses for results would be sought.

The role of self-consciousness in inquiry—acknowledgment of one's own frame of reference, theoretical base, goals, and bases for judgment—has often been recognized, if not always fully enacted, by those who may be classified as philosophic, humanistic, or qualitative investigators. Part of their critique is that many who voice a preference for "hard" science have seemed less prone to self-reflection or reflection about the meaning of the measures they develop and report. Satisfied that what is empirical and classifiable must also thus be true and useful, they have sometimes substituted the taxonomies and trappings of science for the substance of scientific theory building and the rigors of testing alternative explanations. In contrast, truthful empiricists strive to verify their ideas by observation, seeking methods that—although always only approximations—can counteract individual predilections as the sole basis for conclusions and actions.

In his effort to reconcile the two camps, Gage (1989) suggests that the objectivist-scientific and interpretive-humanistic paradigms may contribute to each other, producing more fruitful insights by sharing methods, revising assumptions, illuminating intentions, and revamping measurements better to reflect a range of authentic and important actions and outcomes on the part of students and teachers (143–144). Acknowledging that the "scientific" tradition has much to gain by paying greater attention to a range of methods and meanings, Gage seeks recognition as well that the scientific method, more thoughtfully applied, can still be of positive benefit to the attainment of moral goals as well as the technical improvement of education.

A key issue in the paradigm wars is the conceptions of teaching and curriculum that underlie both research specifications and researchers' intentions for the uses to which research results will be put.

Conceptions of Teaching in Curriculum Research

Different conceptions of teaching and curriculum are embodied in research that seeks uniformly applicable rules for practice as opposed to understandings of context-dependent interactions and outcomes. In the first case, teaching is the work of a laborer, an assembly-line worker, applying a well-defined curriculum according to standard operating procedures. In the second, teaching is viewed more as a profession or an art, requiring wide-ranging knowledge and well-developed judgment in evaluating how to approach a curriculum that itself is context-responsive (Darling-Hammond, Wise, and Pease 1983).

The lines of research we discuss in this chapter have differed in the degree to which uniformity, predictability, and environmental controls are assumed or even considered in the design and goals of curriculum studies. These traits of the teaching environment vary, in turn, depending on the assumptions that are made about learners and learning. The more variable learners and learning contexts or modes are thought to be, the more likely researchers are to seek to understand the subjective realities of those engaged in either teaching and learning and the less likely to try to specify one best method for accomplishing their tasks.

In cautioning against giving way to pressures "to convert the results of statistical inquiries and laboratory experiments into directions and rules for the conduct of school administration and instruction," Dewey (1929, 18) explained the problem as well as it has been before or since:

> No conclusion of scientific research can be converted into an immediate rule of educational art. For there is no educational practice whatever which is not highly complex; that is to say, which does not contain many other conditions and factors than are included in the scientific finding. . . . The significance of one factor for educational practice can be determined only as it is balanced with many other factors. (19)

This is essentially the same conclusion Cronbach (1975) reached after some years of trying to uncover rules for educational practice that might be revealed by taking into account the interactions between student aptitudes and the nature of specific treatments. Having earlier understood the limits of proceeding on the basis of small, bivariate correlations between teaching practices and outcomes, he had sought a more complex but still predictable set of answers. He discovered that interaction effects that may be identified from teaching research are not confined to easily translatable two- or even three-way interactions, thus limiting the prospects of achieving generalizable rules for practice:

> An ATI [aptitude-treatment interaction] result can be taken as a general conclusion only if it is not in turn moderated by further variables. . . . Once we attend to interactions, we enter a hall of mirrors that extends to infinity. However far we carry our analysis—to third order or fifth order or any other—untested interactions of a still higher order can be envisioned. (119)

Cronbach (1975) concluded that the search for empirical generalizations "in a world in which most effects are interactive" should give way to "response sensitive" research, which takes exceptions seriously and makes continual adjustments on the basis of individual, context-specific responses (121–122).

Interestingly, two men who spent their careers seeking to establish a framework for a scientific basis for curriculum and teaching decisions never doubted that teaching is itself not a science but an art *informed by* science. Gage (1978) explained that a science of teaching is not an appropriate goal because it "implies that good teaching will some day be attainable by closely following rigorous laws that yield high predictability and control" (17). Using science to achieve practical ends, he argues, requires artistry—the use of judgment, intuition, and insight in handling the unpredicted; knowledge of when to apply which laws and generalizations and when not to; the ability to make clinical assessments of how multiple variables affect the solution to a problem. His words harken back to Dewey (1929), who wrote,

> When, in education, the psychologist or observer and experimentalist in any field reduces his findings to a rule which is to be uniformly adopted, then, only, is there a result which is objectionable and destructive of the free play of education as an art . . . . But this happens not because of scientific method but because of departure from it. (13–14)

Use of scientific inquiry has established the complexity of teaching occasioned by the multidimensional nature of learning, not to mention the even more complicated nature of life in classrooms (Jackson 1968). The question of whether teaching is conceived of as an art versus a science is not arcane; it drives research and policy today.

In the final analysis, the struggles to harness science in the service of education have been less over research methods or even findings than over their uses. If science seeks to increase our capacity to understand and control our affairs, the fundamental questions concern who will control science—and what uses will be made of its fruits. Who will seek to exert control and over what or whom? These questions have been central in the unfolding history of curriculum inquiry and action.

We examine how scientific inquiry—and the debate(s) over its goals and uses—have shaped curriculum studies by examining the nature of learning, in the first instance, and the nature of curriculum and its outcomes, in the second.

SCIENTIFIC STUDY OF LEARNING AS A BASIS FOR CURRICULUM

A major part of the scientific tradition in curriculum inquiry has been based on the efforts of researchers—particularly psychologists—to understand learning so as to better inform curriculum development and teaching. Several areas of psychological research have helped to shape curricular ideas and studies. They include those branches of psychological inquiry we categorize in our discussion below as behaviorist, developmentalist, cognitive structuralist, and cognitive scientist. We include in this section the work of cognitive psychologists and others who work on questions of cognition and information processing. This section describes how psychological theory and research in these areas have interacted with curricular theory, research, and practice, directly and indirectly shaping the kinds of research questions asked, studies undertaken, and answers found.

To a notable extent, these distinctions among lines of scientific inquiry have paralleled distinctive schools of thought in curriculum work, as suggested by the use of analogous categories in Eisner and Vallance's (1974) discussion of competing conceptions of curriculum and Kliebard's (1982) historical treatment of curriculum development.

Though relationships have been forged between studies of learning and curriculum research, the nature of the psychology-curriculum connection is complicated and problematic. In 1892, William James warned teachers to be cautious in looking for direct, immediate applications:

> I say moreover that you make a great, a very great mistake, if you think that psychology, being a science of the mind's laws, is something from which you can deduce definite programmes and schemes and methods of instruction for immediate schoolroom use. Psychology is a science, and teaching is an art; and sciences never generate arts directly out of themselves. An intermediary inventive mind must make the application, by using its originality. . . . The teaching must *agree* with psychology, but must not necessarily be the only kind of teaching that would agree; for many diverse methods of teaching may equally well agree with psychological laws. (Quoted in Wolfson 1985, 54)

In addition to the practical problems of deriving applications in a setting more variable and complex than the laboratory are the questions of what types of knowledge are desired and what kinds of learning are to be sought. As we discuss below, different psychological perspectives have differing epistemological underpinnings. Each perspective's conception of knowledge influences research decisions about the kinds of learning to be examined and the ways in which learning is assessed, thus determining the nature and findings of the research. These conceptions, then, should also be considered in judgments about whether and how the findings of research might be used in curriculum decision making.

Few of the significant protagonists of any of the four areas of research discussion in this section would suggest that the area of learning they study is the entirety of the human learning experience. And the categories are permeable: Many studies could be placed under more than one rubric. Whether or not these categories most aptly describe the distinctions among areas, it is certainly true that in combination these lines of inquiry offer insights about a wide range of learning experiences of concern to curriculum theorists and practitioners.

The Behaviorist Perspective

It might be said that Locke (1947 [1690]) provided much of the epistemological underpinnings for the behaviorist perspective:

> Let us suppose the mind to be, as we say, white paper void of all characters, without any ideas. How comes it to be furnished? Whence comes it by that vast store which the busy and boundless forms of man has painted on it with an almost endless variety? Where has it all the materials of reason and knowledge? To this I answer, in one word, from EXPERIENCE. In that all our knowledge is founded; and from that it ultimately derives itself. (65)

This view attributes knowledge and its acquisition to external rather than internal sources. The mind is a "tabula rasa": an empty slate to be filled by force of experience or, in the words of later behaviorists, by reinforcements of presenting stimuli. In this sense, the acquisition of knowledge is largely a receptive activity since it is the actions of external events on the organism that provide the stimulus reinforcements that lead to new behaviors or learning. Human variability, to the extent that it exists, is caused by the fact that different people have experienced different reinforcements.

As B. F. Skinner (1961) put it many years later,

> Inner entities or events do not "cause" behavior, nor does behavior "express" them. . . . In an acceptable explanatory scheme the ultimate causes of behavior must be found *outside* the organism. . . . We can predict and control behavior, we can modify it, we can construct it according to specifications—and all without answering the explanatory questions which have driven investigators into the study of the inner man." (253–254; emphasis in original)

The key research question for behaviorists concerns what external events (stimuli and reinforcers) can produce the desired behavioral responses (learning). "A student is 'taught' in the sense that he is induced to engage in new forms of behavior and in specific forms upon specific occasions'' (Skinner 1961, 161). Pavlov's classical conditioning; Watson's (1930) stimulus substitution; and Thorndike's (1913) work on learning curves, mental nerve pathways, and the laws of exercise and effect are early behaviorist answers to this basic research question.

Of equal importance to the answers advanced were the methodological criteria for testing them. Watson (1913) argued that since it is impossible to validate the introspective reports of the learner, the psychological scientist should rely on external behavior. Skinner (1961) took up the claim, calling ''mentalist'' theories ''purely inferential'' in nature and essentially nonverifiable. And because he found their explanations unnecessary to effectuate the goals of prediction and control, he and his followers also deemed them largely unnecessary as avenues of study.

Attention to observable behavior was accompanied by the development of methods that relied heavily on quantifiable aspects of behavior. As Verhave (1959) points out, Skinner's discovery of the ''frequency of responding'' as a dependent variable in the investigation of factors controlling voluntary behavior was a major contribution to experimental methods of observation. In the decades that followed, results of research were reported in terms of ratios and intervals and frequencies and curves, using running-time meters, impulse counters, and cumulative recorders of various kinds.

Foreshadowing later educational studies guided by observed frequencies of student and teacher behaviors and aimed at such dependent variables as time on task and proportion of behavioral objectives achieved, these early studies had a significant influence on what became viewed as the predominant paradigm for scientific method:

> The consequences of Skinner's initial modest and seemingly trivial experiment have been staggering. Ever since 1930, and at a positively accelerated rate the end of which is not yet in sight, hundreds of rats and pigeons, as well as mice, turtles, chimpanzees, fish, cats, dogs, college students, mentally defective persons, psychotic patients and naval trainees, have been pushing doors, pressing levers, nosing plastic disks, and pulling all sorts of switches, unwittingly producing cumulative records. (Verhave 1959; reprinted in Ulrich, Stachnik, and Mabry 1966, 33)

Attention to the presence or absence of behaviors in various amounts over particular periods of time provided a standard metric for observing, presenting, and comparing results of experiments. This development gave a great push to the systematic study of interventions and outcomes. By and large, however, this set of methods did not attend to the meaning of behaviors or the meanings and future utility of learning acquired and manifested in these ways. Skinner (1961), in fact, explicitly rejected this kind of inquiry, defining the production of right answers or correct responses—rather than such vague constructs as understanding or the development of analytic ability—as the goal of education:

> It is true that the techniques which are emerging from the experimental study of learning are not designed to ''develop the mind'' or to further some vague ''understanding'' of mathematical relationships. They are designed, on the contrary, to establish the very behaviors which are taken to be evidences of such mental states or processes. . . . The behavior in terms of which human thinking must eventually be defined is worth treating in its own right as the substantial goal of education. (156)

Skinner advanced experimental studies of behavior as a methodology, and conditioning as a construct, to their logical conclusions. Starting from the presumption that behavior that is rewarded will be repeated (i.e., learned), behaviorists argued that complex forms of behavior can be shaped by rewarding each step in the right direction, using the principles of operant conditioning, contingent reinforcement, and behavioral chaining. Early in his career, Skinner demonstrated that a pigeon could be ''taught'' to steer a guided missile (Phillips and Soltis 1985). He also found the behaviorist paradigm adequate for analyzing the reinforcements that produce scientists' decisions to engage in certain lines of inquiry (''The Flight from the Laboratory,'' 1958) as well as the literary behaviors of poets (''The Alliteration in Shakespeare's Sonnets: A Study in Literary Behavior,'' 1939, both in Skinner 1961).

Skinner's great faith that complex learning could be easily produced by presenting discriminative stimuli or cues and immediately reinforcing correct responses led him to resurrect the idea of a teaching machine (Skinner 1954, 1958), introduced earlier without great success by Pressey (1926, 1932). The early machines were simple devices that presented factual information in small dollops, posed questions or simple tasks (often fill-in-the-blank statements) for students to respond to, and gave immediate feedback about the correctness of the responses when the machine operator turned a knob or opened a slot.

It was not long before it became clear that the simple gadgetry of these teaching machines was not the main point, however. As Holland (1960) noted, it was a ''new technology'' of education, a ''behavioral engineering of teaching procedures'' that was the distinguishing characteristic of the new approach to instruction, whether mechanized or not. His summary of the principles underlying this technology characterizes the considerations that predominate in the behaviorist influence on curriculum work: immediate reinforcement for correct answers; many opportunities for correct performance; gradual progression of individual, discrete skills to establish complex repertoires; and use of reinforcement strategies for maintaining student attention and participation.

As this list suggests, much of the influence of behavioral research on curriculum studies has been to direct attention to the manner of presentation of material rather than to the nature of the material itself. Perhaps because of the behavioral emphasis on inducing specific behaviors in the form of right answers and confidence that these can be produced in any area, behaviorists have tended to ignore questions about what kinds of curriculum content are worthy of study (and what kinds of right answers are worthy of production), focusing more on how any content should be presented for most efficient mastery. In fact,

Thorndike (1924) attacked the classical notion of discipline-based curriculum by showing that the classical disciplines are no more effective for "training the mind" than are more practical subjects. His attacks helped to hasten the decline of the mental discipline approach to curriculum development and to legitimize the inclusion of vocational and other practical subjects in the curriculum.

Implications of Behavioral Research for Curriculum. Among the contributions to curriculum theory and development of this work and its later refinements are a number of ideas that have contributed to the organization of lessons and texts: the use of reinforcements and frequent feedback to students during the course of instruction (e.g., written or verbal checks on understanding and frequent tests and quizzes), the provision of opportunities for guided practice (intensive practice for simple skills that are easily overlearned and intermittant practice for more complex skills), and the use of classical conditioning cues to engender automatic responses (e.g., the repetitious use of flash cards in teaching vocabulary or computation). Current cognitive theory builds on some of these ideas, for example, practice in basic skills until they become automatic, which is thought to free mental energies for more complex operations.

These precepts have also been the basis for a variety of programmed instruction and individualized instruction initiatives that allow students to move at their own pace through a set of prepackaged curriculum materials (some recently computerized in computer-aided instructional programs). Though some researchers once held high hopes for the effectiveness of such technologies, many of the assumptions underlying these strategies—such as those concerning the importance of careful sequencing of material, control of student responses, and repetition to achieve mastery—have been called into question by studies that have found that they frequently do not produce the anticipated learning gains (Good and Brophy 1986; Horak 1981; Martin and Pavan 1976).

One of the limitations of behaviorally oriented approaches to curriculum building is that the research base cannot account for the complexities of classroom life. The notion of stimulus control attainable in a Skinner box is not applicable to the multidimensional interactions typical of learning in large group settings, where it is frequently difficult to know what behavior is being reinforced at any time or which of many dozens of concurrent stimuli may be serving as a reinforcement.

Another shortcoming has been the assumption that the production of specific behaviors in certain circumstances signifies desired learning. Erlwanger (1975) found that students who consistently scored well on the criterion-referenced tests associated with an individualized programmed instruction package nonetheless misunderstood the underlying mathematical concepts and could not apply them to new types of problems. His findings are similar to those of others (see, e.g., Peterson 1979; Schoenfeld 1987; and Talmage and Rasher 1980) whose work indicates that highly structured curricular approaches aimed at the sequential teaching of discrete subskills may produce "successful" student performance on tests of those subskills without producing sufficient mastery of the overarching concepts to allow generalization to other applications or problem-solving exercises.

Ultimately, the quest to define effectiveness must always confront questions of what kinds of learning are to be sought and toward what ends. That these questions have long bedeviled behavioral attempts to establish principles for the efficient production of learning is suggested by Dewey's (1929) assessment of the contributions and shortcomings of stimulus-response research, rejoined in the historic debate between B. F. Skinner and Carl Rogers before the American Psychological Association in 1956 (Ulrich, Stachnik, and Mabry 1966). Although acknowledging the usefulness of psychological advances in explaining influences on behavior, Dewey complained that, too often, narrow behavioral measures of skills attainment (chosen for ease of specific, short-term measurement) failed to take into account the other abilities, preferences, and disabilities that are also influenced (or neglected) by the stimulus or treatment selected for its efficiency on only one narrow criterion. By avoiding questions of educational goals and values, limited findings could presume to encompass everything worth knowing.

In the same vein, agreeing that the advances of behavioral science were important and impressive, Rogers posed in 1956 a central criticism taken up again more recently by participants in the "paradigm wars": "The major flaw I see in [Skinner's] review of what is involved in the scientific control of human behavior is the denial, misunderstanding, or gross underestimation of the place of ends, goals or values in their relationship to science" (quoted in Ulrich, Stachnik, and Mabry 1966, 309).

Interestingly, Rogers chose very nearly the same example of the problem as Dewey (1929) had chosen nearly 30 years earlier:

> If I value knowledge of the "three R's" as a goal of education, the methods of science can give me increasingly accurate information on how this goal may be achieved. If I value problem-solving ability as a goal of education, the scientific method can give me the same kind of help. Now, if I wish to determine whether problem-solving ability is "better" than knowledge of the three R's, then scientific method can also study those two values but *only* in terms of some other value which I have subjectively chosen. . . . It is important that this choice be made explicit, since the particular value which is being sought can never be tested or evaluated, confirmed or denied, by the scientific endeavor to which it gives birth. (310)

That the same issues are still being raised 30 years later may have been predicted by Skinner's (1961) response: "I cannot quite agree that the practice of science requires a prior decision about goals or a prior choice of values. . . . Any list of values is a list of reinforcers—conditioned or otherwise" (33).

Untroubled by the possibility of different points of view on the question of goal choices, Skinner (1961) traced his hopes for a science of behavior to the 18th-century doctrines of human perfectibility: "As more and more causal relations are demonstrated, a practical corollary becomes difficult to resist: it should be possible to *produce* behavior according to plan simply by arranging the proper conditions" (3). That this behavior should, by virtue of its planned production, be desirable is not subject to doubt:

> In a modern school, there is usually a syllabus which specifies what every student is to learn by the end of the year. . . . But some will be poor in particular subjects, others will not study, others will not remember what they have been taught, and diversity is assured. Suppose, however, that we someday possess such effective educational techniques that every student will in fact be put in possession of all the behavior specified in a syllabus. . . . Should we reject such a system on the grounds that in making all students excellent it has made them all alike? (13)

It is possible that it is this underlying philosophy, which happily resolves the problems of ends by equating excellence with those behaviors that can be controlled and produced, is one source of current criticism that the pursuit of "positivistic social science" produces answers that "can only be implemented in an authoritarian, manipulative, bureaucratic system" (Cazden, quoted in Gage 1989, 136).

Behavioral research has evolved substantially since those days when euphoria about achieving human perfectability seemed to obscure questions of what short- and long-term ends were being sought. It has also incorporated perspectives that allow for investigation into the "inner workings" of the mind and psyche. Social learning theorists, for example, consider cognitive, behavioral, and environmental factors as they examine how the learner mediates stimulus input (see, e.g., Bandura 1977).

This work has led to an understanding of how it is that different people will respond distinctively to the same stimulus, depending on the meaning that a common stimulus takes on for the individual, depending in turn on his or her prior learning and experience. These understandings have been operationalized in a variety of ways in curriculum work, ranging from the development of "cues" incorporated in curriculum materials, to help learners attend in similar ways to the relevant aspects of a task, to the development of cognitive behavior-modification techniques, which help learners examine and model particular thinking strategies (Meichenbaum 1977; Meichenbaum and Goodman 1971).

The contributions of the behaviorist perspective include its insights regarding the effects on students' behaviors of a wide variety of reinforcements, which occur intentionally and unintentionally in classrooms, and its efforts to understand how these reinforcements may be used more systematically to produce desired learning. We have devoted substantial space to this line of work because the power of its paradigm and methods in this century has been so great that they have influenced other traditions by providing the standards either for emulation or for counterreaction. At times, this perspective and the experimental research methods undergirding its earliest advances have appropriated the term "scientific" as their own, seeming to exclude other ways of observing and explaining from the realm of scientific endeavor. Although such extreme claims are rarely made today, the rifts in view are still evident in both basic research and curricular interpretations of its meaning.

For its many contributions, by and large, we must look outside of the behaviorist orientation for explanations of how certain interventions produce their effects, why they seem to be more effective in some circumstances than in others, and whether the effects produced support or detract from other desirable goals. We turn to some of these questions as we examine other perspectives.

The Developmental Perspective

Whereas the behaviorist sees childhood as a blank slate, ready to be written on by experience, the developmentalist sees it as a "biologically useful phase whose significance is that of progressive adaptation to a physical and social environment" (Piaget 1970, 153). The developmentalist looks primarily within the organism for an explanation of how and why it learns, rather than without. And the developmentalist attends to progressive changes or stages in perception and cognition as signposts for those explanations of learning.

Elements of the developmental perspective can be found in the works of, among others, Rousseau, Pestalozzi, Froebel, and Montessori (see Rusk 1969, for a concise summary). However, these classic educational theorists operated on intuitive knowledge and practical observations of child development, rather than on systematic empirical study. Though Piaget would be the first to acknowledge the role of colleagues in the establishment of a scientific basis for the developmentalist perspective (those he often mentioned include Baldwin 1975; Claparede 1975; Groos 1976; Isaacs 1930; Stern 1930), it is not without reason that he is considered the father of this perspective. Consequently, his work is the focal point for the following discussion.

Educated originally in biology and, later, philosophy and logic, Piaget was seeking a genetic epistemology. Starting with the view that intelligence is an adaptive feature of the human organism, he sought to understand how progressively more powerful mental structures are developed over the course of childhood. His work suggested to him that like the tadpole, who breathes through different organs than the adult frog, the child grows through a series of qualitatively distinct mental stages, each of which represents not just more knowledge but also a different kind of knowledge, born of a new cognitive structure for organizing and using what has been learned (Piaget 1970).

The essential research questions guiding the developmental perspective involve how cognitive (and related physical and psychological) functions develop, how these functions influence learning, and how this learning in turn allows humans to develop more fully their creative and adaptative abilities. The concomitant curricular questions ask how the kinds of learning associated with these developmental stages can be supported through curricular strategies. Piaget, however, concerned himself largely with the epistemological questions, believing that the implications of his work for educational theory and practice ought to be explicated by those more directly involved in these fields.

His research methods, essentially clinical in nature, were aimed at understanding how knowledge is acquired. Rather than seeking to quantify behavioral responses, he sought to describe the quality of children's thinking. He examined children's thought processes by, for example, presenting them with ingeniously designed tasks involving the manipulation of concrete materials. Correct or incorrect completion of the task was less important than the children's explanation of their reasoning, which was elicited through informally structured interview techniques. Protocols were developed for everything from manipulation of the materials to verbalizations and expressions (surprise, excitement, mimicry, etc.). Extensive qualitative analysis of these data produced categories used to describe and analyze the various stages of cognitive development (Fischer 1964).

Piaget saw children as internally motivated, exploratory beings, always engaged in information processing and constantly searching for relevant stimuli to inform them about the effects of their actions:

> Actually, in order to know objects, the subject must act upon them, and therefore transform them; he must displace, correct, combine, take apart, and reassemble them. From the most elementary sensorimotor actions (such as pushing and pulling) to the most sophisticated intellectual operations, which are interiorized actions, carried out mentally (e.g., joining together, putting in order, putting into one-to-one correspondence), knowledge is constantly linked with actions or operations, that is, with transformations. (Quoted in Mussen 1970, 704)

Borrowing from the biological notions of assimilation, accommodation, and equilibration, Piaget explained the process of learning as a continual matching of one's mental constructs with one's experiences in the environment. Step by step, by amassing and organizing schema, operations, and structures and by assimilating and accommodating toward equilibrium, the child develops intelligence in discrete, sequential stages. Though Piaget's work as popularized has been viewed as nearly synonymous with this stage theory of development, stage theory is neither his construct alone, nor is it, arguably, his major contribution to our understanding of learning. However, both because this concept has been so important to some areas of curriculum theory and development and because it has been subject to frequent debate, we explore it more extensively below.

Developmental Stages and Debates. Stage concepts of development exist in a variety of areas regarding different types of learning: physical, cognitive, psychological, and moral (e.g., Erickson, 1963; Gesell, 1940; and Kohlberg, 1981). These developmental theories include notions of staged progress based on maturation and readiness as well as prior learning. They suggest that one level cannot be reached before certain prior levels of maturation and development have been achieved and that seeking certain types of learning or behavior change before a level of readiness has been attained is not productive. In terms of curriculum development, these theories have been used to guide judgments of when children are deemed likely to learn particular kinds of concepts in particular ways (thus when they should be presented in the curriculum) and to alert teachers to look for signs of student readiness when making pedagogical decisions in their work. The ideas have had their greatest impact on early childhood programs, justifying the traditional kindergarten and a general emphasis on hands-on learning opportunities for young children.

Many studies across differing areas seem to support stage concepts of development. For example, Gesell and his colleagues studied the development of physical abilities and other skills closely associated with school tasks, such as fine motor skills, visual skills, and other perceptual abilities, finding support for the notion that performances taught before readiness levels have been reached are attained inefficiently, sometimes only superficially (without transferability), and often at cost to other developing abilities (Gesell 1940; Gesell and Thompson 1929).

However, many learning theorists of the behavioral tradition reject the notion of qualitative stages in intellectual development, believing that with proper conditioning and sequencing of instruction, learning can be induced at any time by moving learners through successive approximations of the desired behaviors. Others accept the general ideas of staged development but insist that instruction can stimulate new operational understandings if it is presented in a form and a level appropriate to the child's stage of development (e.g., Bruner 1966).

Much of the debate has centered around whether development can be "induced" (see, e.g., Kuhn 1974) or readiness taught (a peculiarly American preoccupation). In some experiments, critics have sought to train children in a short period of time to master concepts, such as conservation, that Piaget argued would require years of broad-based natural experience as a foundation. Though the children could give correct answers to specified questions, Piaget and his colleagues argued that they did not have a full operational understanding of the concept as demonstrated in further studies, in which the children were required not only to produce correct verbal responses but also to apply their knowledge and defend it in the face of counterarguments. (Inhelder, Sinclair, and Bovet 1974; Piaget 1970).

A much larger-scale test of these developmental propositions took place during the 1970s in the province of North Rhein-Westphalia in Germany. There, the rush to induce readiness and to speed learning led to a desire by legislators to replace traditional play kindergartens (based substantially on developmental principles regarding active and concrete, rather than symbolic, learning for young children) with early-learning experiences that would hasten the acquisition of academic skills. The new policy was tested by creating a large number of these academic kindergartens and comparing their effects over a five-year period against those of play kindergartens.

Teams of researchers from two different universities

using different methods found that at the age of 10, children from 50 play kindergarten programs compared to those from 50 early-learning programs did differ significantly, but not in the direction expected. Children who had attended play kindergartens were not only better adjusted socially and emotionally in school but also more cognitively advanced in reading, mathematics, and other subjects tested, as well as excelling in creativity and intelligence, "industry," and "oral expression." The researchers concluded that the effort to override developmental considerations had not succeeded, and the academic kindergartens were discontinued (Ewert and Braun 1978; Tietze 1987; Winkelmann, Hollaender, Schmerkotte, and Schmalohr 1979).

In their review of the debates regarding readiness, Good and Brophy (1986) note that research on attempts similar to the "conservation teaching" efforts, in this case to teach preadolescents to use formal operations, also produced mixed findings.

> Taken together, the Swiss and American work suggests that cognitive development is more open to meaningful stimulation through instruction than Piaget thought, but that Piaget was correct in stating that there are limits on what can be accomplished with a given child, and on whether it will be worth the effort involved. In any case, this controversy involved differences not only in beliefs about what is possible, *but also in beliefs about what a particular cognitive achievement means.* (71; emphasis added)

Once again, we find that different explanations of how learning occurs rest ultimately on different views of what valuable learning consists of and how it is demonstrated. These differences in views are also reflected in the design of curriculum materials and methods of curriculum evaluation.

Piaget (1970) was much troubled by what he felt were superficial definitions and measurements of learning, which in turn drove short-sighted curriculum decisions that turn schooling into "the pursuit of ephemeral and largely artificial results" rather than "the formation of the intelligence and good working methods" (108). "Psychology," he claimed, "has too often chased the shadow instead of the fox, by searching for applications, and more particularly for measurements, before understanding the formative mechanisms and the significance of the factors measured" (109).

Implications of Developmental Theory for Curriculum. The ideas of staged development and readiness have been widely used in curriculum decisions concerning when certain kinds of material may be most effectively presented, offering a rationale for sequencing based on learner characteristics as well as on the organization of subject matter. Much of the developmentalist influence on curriculum has also centered on the concepts of learning through active and self-regulated interaction with the environment. If knowledge is constructed by the individual learner operating on the environment, the curriculum must provide students with surroundings and materials that are worth exploring and with opportunities for active engagement. The notion that curriculum construction includes the creation of a "learning environment"—an arrangement of materials to be examined and manipulated in the classroom—derives from this view.

Equally important to a developmental outlook on curriculum is the centrality of students' interest as both an indicator of readiness and an engine for propelling exploration and learning. Engendering interest is not to be confused with letting children do whatever they want; it "requires above all that [children] should will what they do; that they should act, not that they should be acted upon" (Claparede, quoted in Piaget 1970, 152).

"Experiential learning," "discovery learning," and the use of "developmentally appropriate" methods and environments that seek to provide children with opportunities to act on materials suited to their stages and modes of learning are among the curricular commitments that emanate from a developmentalist perspective. These have been widely adopted in early-childhood programs. Such curricular initiatives as Open Education, the School Curriculum Improvement Study (SCIS Science), the School Mathematics Study Group (SMSG Math), the use of Cuisenaire rods in mathematics instruction, and a variety of hands-on science programs, are a few of the more widely known innovations that have emerged from a developmental orientation (for reviews, see Deans 1963; Frost and Rowland 1969).

In addition to raising different curricular concerns, active education also involves a different role and training for the teacher since the aim is to respond to individual students' initiatives and evidence of readiness rather than instructing them in a more routine and didactic manner. The teacher's attention is focused more on the processes of students' thinking and their understanding of concepts than the production of right answers. His or her activity is aimed at encouraging exploration, discovery, and valuable social interaction—including discussion and testing of ideas among students—rather than imparting information (Ginsburg and Opper 1979; Hooper and DeFrain 1980). These activities require the teacher to have knowledge of cognitive, physical, social, and psychological development, as well as subject matter. Without such knowledge, "the teacher cannot properly understand the students' spontaneous procedures, and therefore fails to take advantage of reactions that appear to him quite insignificant and a mere waste of time" (Piaget 1970, 69).

These ideas about teaching and learning have led to the construction of a "mediating variable" paradigm for understanding how students learn (e.g., Doyle 1978; Lowyck 1986; McDonald 1988; Peterson 1988; Webb 1980). This approach stresses the role of the learner in "determining *what* is processed, *how* it is processed, and therefore *what* is learned" (Doyle 1978, 171). It undergirds a concept of reciprocal teaching, which demands continual adjustment by the teacher to the student's changing needs, interests, and understandings, accompanied by a necessarily pliable concept of curriculum. These ideas and recent cognitive research combine to forge a more highly developed constructivist view of knowledge, consistent with Piaget's theories but not so dependent on orthodox views of stage determinism (Resnick 1989). Other work built on a developmentalist foundation is incorporated in current theories of cognition and perception (e.g., Resnick 1989; Peterson and Swing 1982; Vygotsky 1962) and is discussed in subsequent sections.

Piaget's work has been constructively criticized in recent years on methodological grounds, including, for example, tests of whether his inferences about children's abilities would be sustained if they were presented with differently chosen cognitive tasks. Criticisms have also been raised about limitations of his work stemming from its emphasis on the development of logical thinking about physical and spatial relationships rather than the development of social and cultural knowledge (e.g., Donaldson 1978; Ives 1980; Lee 1989).

Nevertheless, the essence of the developmentalist orientation—and the epistemological message of most import to curriculum—remains a strong foundation of evolving learning theories. That children are actively engaged in constructing knowledge and mediating their own learning, that their accommodative and assimilative efforts evolve through stages exhibiting qualitatively different modes of processing and organizing information, and that these processes are aimed at adapting to and mastering the environment are cornerstones of much research and theory building today.

The Cognitive Structuralist Perspective

The cognitive structuralist perspective on learning draws together threads of both the behaviorist and developmentalist traditions. Research in this tradition recognizes the role of associations, repetition, and reinforcement in learning, while also recognizing that learning involves active and systematic mental processes that construct cognitive maps to guide understanding.

Drawing on the ideas of Gestalt psychology, cognitive structuralists view knowledge acquisition as the building of patterns or configurations designed to make sense out of experience. These, in turn, rely on the sense made of prior experience, as well as on the structure of the presenting situation. During the learning process, the learners extract and categorize similarities between what they already understand and what they are now encountering (Lennenberg 1967). The means by which sense data are processed is an important area of study, as are the roles of selective perception and prior experience in learning (Eccles 1964; Galambos 1961; Hebb 1949; Lashley 1950).

Gestalt psychologist Max Wertheimer (1959) observed that just as various artistic techniques such as highlighting, framing, and contrasting affect how viewers perceive visual objects, so techniques for presenting information affect how it will be perceived by learners. He emphasized that learning could be more effective if learners were explicitly taught the structure of the content to be learned and the relationships among components.

These ideas provided the basis for work by Ausubel (1963) and others (e.g., R. E. Mayer 1984) on presentational techniques for encouraging "meaningful reception learning," as well as for work by Bruner (1963, 1966) and others (e.g., Shulman and Keislar 1966) on structuring discovery learning situations. Although the learner is a receptor in the first instance and an actor in the second, these works share the view that learners are guided in the sense-making process by the knowledge structures they encounter in the environment, including the constructions of knowledge represented in language and in subject matter disciplines. The central research question of this perspective asks how learning is influenced by the structures used to organize both prior learning and current teaching.

This construction of the learning puzzle was framed by earlier basic research that focused on the role of insight in problem solving. Typical were experiments with chimpanzees in which simple problem-solving attempts were varied by the arrangement of needed tools in the environment (Kohler 1959). The structuring of the discovery learning situation proved to have great influence on successful problem solving and the ability to apply this learning in analogous situations.

Jerome Bruner is best known for his application of these ideas to the school curriculum. He extended the developmental concepts of Piaget, tying different modes of knowledge representation associated with cognitive development to different teaching strategies. He devoted much of his attention to methods of discovery learning that would produce insights leading to concept acquisition and transfer.

Undergirding these methods was a commitment to use language and disciplinary structure in the cause of successful discovery. "Grasping the structure of a subject is understanding it in a way that permits many other things to be related to it meaningfully. To learn structure, in short, is to learn how things are related" (Bruner 1963, 7; see also Hirst 1974; Phillips and Soltis 1985; Schwab 1965). Thus, paying explicit attention to the structure of a discipline in framing learning situations can enhance the acquisition of concepts. This view therefore argues for disciplinary expertise as a critical component in developing curricular methods that will help learners translate their experience into more powerful systems of notation, ordering, and thought (Bruner 1966).

Structuralists also look to the relationships between language and thought for clues about learning. Vygotsky (1962) examined the ways in which children use language to verbalize their internal thinking processes and to move from pseudoconcepts to actual concept formation. Not only does the use of language help children to express their independently arising thoughts, but also the expression of thoughts in language aids in the further development of thinking and conceptual organization. In other words, verbalization is a functional instrument for learning.

In addition, the availability of rich language experiences in the environment allows learners to gain access to the preexisting knowledge structures embedded in language, so that they will have ready-made concepts or cognitive structures at their disposal when they are ready to understand and use them (e.g., Corbett 1971). Having heard it, a child may use the term "half hour" as a pseudoconcept to denote an indefinite block of time, but when he or she is capable of understanding that this term represents one half of an hour, the availability of this language facilitates the acquisition of the abstract concept, thus enhancing further development and learning.

This tradition's attention to the role of perception in information reception and learning has also led to research on how different modes of perception are related to differing cognitive styles (e.g., Kagan and Kogan 1970; Sigel and Coop 1974). Attention to these differences in information-processing approaches have supported more recent work on different dimensions of ability and intelligence that are demonstrated in distinct types and modes of performance (see, e.g., Gardner 1983; Gardner and Hatch 1989; Sternberg 1985). In sum, the structuralist perspective looks both within and without the learner for an understanding of how information is perceived, processed, and later used as a foundation for additional insight and knowledge structuring.

Implications of Structuralist Theory for Curriculum. The curricular implications of structuralist research are many and wide-ranging. Because much of the research has focused on learning for problem solving and transfer rather than for recognition or recall, the curriculum and teaching strategies examined—and the criteria for their evaluation—have often differed substantially from those studied by behavioral researchers. However, concern for the effects of environmental cues and conditions is present in both traditions. At the same time, structuralists attend to the nature of the learner and his or her mental processes as well as the learner's need to operate on the environment in order to learn from it. Many of the curricular orientations of a structuralist perspective share deep roots with "developmental" initiatives.

One large group of initiatives clusters under the general rubric of discovery learning. These are attempts to construct learning situations to exploit students' curiosity and natural motivation so that they will discover principles and concepts for themselves in a manner that will allow them to apply similar insights in new situations. The curriculum challenge is to find ways to structure the learning situation to allow students to draw productively on their prior learning experiences—linking the familiar to the unfamiliar—in encountering novel tasks.

Seen in the British "infant" (i.e., primary) schools and many Montessori schools, some manifestations of discovery learning call for the flexible use of space to create learning centers or areas for individual and small-group exploration activities, designed to provide hands-on opportunities for investigation that capitalize on students' readiness and interests.

Bruner sought to use these ideas in the development of an elementary social studies curriculum, Man: A Course of Study (MACOS), as did Schwab in his Biological Science Curriculum Study (BSCS). Similar principles have been used in developing discovery approaches to early mathematics learning, many of which draw from Gestalt psychology an emphasis on the interconnectedness of concepts rather than on the sequential presentation of discrete subskills (e.g., Frost and Rowland 1969; Kamii and DeClark 1985). Similar emphases are present in "whole language" approaches to reading and writing, as we describe in more detail below. These ideas have also been used in the development of techniques that may be applied across curricular areas, such as inquiry training (Joyce and Weil 1980; Suchman 1962) and the use of simulation activities, allowing students to tackle problems through systematic experimentation and inquiry. These methods seem especially to aid concept acquisition, application, and retention (Case 1975; Cohen 1969; Cohen and Bradley 1978; Coleman, Livingston, Fennessey, Edwards, and Kidder 1973; Singer 1977).

In addition, although researchers have often found little difference between discovery learning strategies and traditional methods on conventional achievement measures, a number of studies have concluded that inquiry-oriented education produces more positive outcomes on affective measures such as students' attitudes, self-concepts, and curiosity (Gage 1985; Horwitz 1979; Peterson 1979; Walberg, Schiller, and Haertel 1979).

Other applications of structuralist research have emphasized the structuring of content so that it can be more easily received by students. Ausubel's (1968) work on advance organizers focused on how the learner's selective perception could be targeted on the relevant aspects of content to be learned and how the content could be framed in terms already familiar to the learner. This work was based on the precept that ". . . the most important factor influencing the meaningful learning of any new idea is the state of the individual's existing cognitive structure at the time of learning" (Ausubel and Robinson 1969, 143).

Related work has included organizers that structure lessons around key principles, which help learners prepare a mental map for receiving and organizing the information (R. E. Mayer 1984; Stone 1982), or models, analogies, and metaphors, which help learners link new concepts to familiar ones (R. E. Mayer 1984). These strategies seem to promote the retention and transfer of concepts and the ability to use them in later problem solving (Bromage and Mayer 1981; R. E. Mayer 1979).

The structuralists' concern for building on the learner's prior knowledge and experiences as the basis for incorporating new concepts representing still more powerful knowledge constructions is a major foundation of the whole language approach to literacy (see, e.g., Moffett and Wagner 1976). To the structuralist, language is not only the medium of exchange but also the tool with which the learner orders reality. Thus, the acquisition of written and oral language skills must be embedded in the experience of the learner rather than viewed as a hierarchical series of subskills leading only to mastery of the techniques of reading or writing. These ideas shape research on whole language curricular strategies (Goodman n.d.; Goodman, Haussler, and Strickland 1982; Halliday 1975; Huff and Kline 1987; Well 1981) and their evaluation (e.g., Cooper and Odell 1977; Genishi and Dyson 1984). Acknowledgment of the ways in which culture shapes knowledge and perception is also a basis for concerns about multicultural curriculum. If the prior experiences of learners shape the ways in which they perceive and organize their subsequent experiences, and if both of these are culturally influenced (from the vantage points of different cultures in the case of many students and the school experience), efforts to establish links between the familiar and the novel must be based on an understanding of these cultural influences on the structure of knowledge (see, e.g., Banks and Banks 1989).

Research emerging from the structuralist orientation has brought a number of important curriculum issues to the surface:

- How can the learner's internally developed and the school or curriculum developer's externally applied cognitive structures be identified? How does one determine what structure(s) should inform instruction?
- If the mere recognition or recall of information can signify a pseudoconcept rather than a true conceptual understanding of the underlying structure of a domain of knowledge, can traditional achievement measures be used to understand student outcomes? If not, what means can be used to measure the effectiveness of such curricula?
- If external structures of knowledge are significant educative forces, how shall we decide what external structures to apply in curriculum development? How shall we understand those that already exist—in the dominant culture and in other cultures as well?

Serious political, sociological, and ethical questions were raised as structuralist-inspired curricula were designed for use in public schools. Bruner's MACOS, in particular, was a lightening rod of public conflict, in part because its cultural relativism was troubling to some groups unaccustomed to thinking in those terms. The importance of understanding culturally based knowledge structures and their influences on perception and learning are also brought to the fore as issues of multicultural curriculum content and culture-fair testing are considered.

More than any of the other research traditions thus far discussed, the structuralist perspective places the subjective values that are embedded in curricular goals and intentions in the foreground of the picture, where the learner's constructions of reality and the curriculum worker's implicit view of valued learning intersect.

The Cognitive Science Perspective

Whereas many cognitive structuralists emphasize the structure of the content to be learned, cognitive psychologists and cognitive scientists who follow an information-processing paradigm for examining learning tend to focus more on the cognitive structures built up by the learners themselves. The perspectives are complementary rather than competing. To a large extent, they share a common research foundation, which rests on the concept of innate sense making:

> This seeing of like and unlike, of putting together and classifying apart . . . is the mechanism through which reality is organized. . . . The world is a vast elaborated *metaphor*. . . . Nature does not come to the child in ordered fashion, but the child is equipped to perceive parts of it, and is born with one intellectual capacity that surpasses all others: the ability to see resemblances. (Bolinger 1980, 191)

Like developmentalists, cognitive psychologists assume that humans develop increasingly powerful cognitive structures for organizing and applying their knowledge. They posit that the mind selects data from current sensory stimulus and integrates it "with knowledge of previous experiences to yield a perception, an understanding, an expectation, a plan of action, or some combination of these reactions" (Calfee 1981, 25).

This information-processing model, also the basis for structuralist work (see, e.g., Shavelson 1974), assumes that the human mind uses "frameworks" to organize information into memory. These frameworks, what the structuralists might call maps, are variously described as schema (J. R. Anderson 1976), frames (Goldstein and Papert 1977), prototypes (Posner 1969), and networks (Anderson and Bower 1973). Regardless of the label, the framework "is a formalized metaphor, a mental tool for tackling new problems and filling the gaps in everyday experience in an intelligent manner so that life becomes understandable and events are under our control" (Calfee 1981, 29).

Support for this orientation derives from early research on memory emanating from a constructivist approach, which contrasts sharply with the associationist approach undergirding behavioral learning theories. In contrast with Ebbinghaus's (1964 [1885]) efforts to study "pure" memory by looking for clues to the recall of nonsense syllables or unconnected words, Bartlett (1932) studied memory as it occurs in real-life circumstances, where contexts for learning, including prior experience, are always present. In his studies of short-term and long-term recall of stories, Bartlett found that subjects remembered far more than the associationist theories derived from rote learning of unconnected words would have suggested. He also found that whereas subjects remembered well those aspects of stories related to the main idea, they often misremembered or distorted some aspects of the stories. Often, the distortions substituted ideas or activities more familiar to the subjects' own experience or culture for those less familiar—and consequently, less easily interpreted.

On the basis of his work, Bartlett suggested that people were involved in a process of exerting "effort after meaning" when they encountered new information, seeking to understand the new and unfamiliar by connecting it to existing cognitive structures or schemas. They would actively construct meanings for the stories rather than trying to interpret merely the words, and they would reconstruct the stories from memory, refiltering them through additional schema, at the time of recall. Later research has supported and refined many of Bartlett's ideas (see, e.g., Spiro 1977; for a review, see Good and Brophy 1986), yielding insights on not only memory and recall but also the interpretation and application of information.

The unique contribution of the cognitive science perspective is its sharpened focus on the process of thinking and the relationship between mental processes and performances. Whereas a behavioral psychologist might examine the number of correct responses following a particular teaching stimulus, the cognitive psychologist "would attempt to answer the questions: What is going on in the student's head during the instructional process? . . . What cognitive processes does a learner engage in while completing intellectual tasks?" (Peterson and Swing 1982, 482).

The key research question is not "How do people learn or develop?" or "What conditions produce particular behaviors?" but "What do people do when they think?" What is the "*process* or operation, by which a given organism achieves an intellectual response?" (McNemar 1964, 881). This question is seen as a necessary foundation for the kinds of theories generated by the other three orientations. Glaser (1988, 35) is quite optimistic in this regard: "We are entering a time when the discovered properties of competence should inform investigations and theories of learning and instruction."

As suggested by Glaser's reference to competence, research within the cognitive science orientation makes a conscious decision to study performance—and to study it within a framework that acknowledges the roles of development, cognitive structure, and behavioral change as an indicator of learning:

> Turning to the performance-learning-development dimension, our emphasis on performance again represents a scientific bet. We recognize that what sort of information processing system a human becomes depends intimately on the way he develops. . . . Yet acknowledging this, it still seems to us that we have too imperfect a view of the system's final nature to be able to make predictions from the development process to the characteristics of the structures it produces. . . . The study of learning, if carried out with theoretical precision, must start with a model of a performing organism, so that one can represent, as learning, the changes in the model. . . . The study of learning takes its cue, then, from the nature of the performance system. If performance is not well understood, it is somewhat premature to study learning. (Newell and Simon, quoted in Glaser and Bassok 1988, 3)

Performance of mental tasks, however, is not defined in purely behavioral terms. "Behavior is observed to draw inferences about mental processes, but, in a dramatic departure from behaviorism, the mind, not behavior is of central interest" (Floden 1981, 79). Like early behaviorists, though, many cognitive scientists strive to find ways to represent and test their theories with high levels of formal precision. "Our explanations are operational and do not depend on vague, mentalistic concepts" (Larkin, McDermott, Simon, and Simon 1980, 1336).

The explanations of mental performance developed from cognitive science research have become highly expanded. This research demonstrates how learning is influenced not only by how information is presented but also by the learner's understanding of the learning goals, by the schemas or framework used to interpret and process information, by prior knowledge (including conceptions and misconceptions) and the manner in which it is addressed in a new context, and by his or her own learning strategies (Good and Brophy 1986; R. Mayer 1982).

Much of this research has been conducted by observing how learners' performances on certain types of tasks are influenced by different modes of information presentation. Other studies have started with subjects who perform with varying degrees of proficiency and have sought to understand how their information-processing strategies differ. This latter approach has recently produced a great deal of work comparing the mental processes of experts with those of novices in various fields of endeavor.

The expert-novice comparisons reveal that the experts' abilities to process and organize large amounts of information effectively are related to the means by which they use "chunking" strategies for processing and have complex, highly developed conceptual schema for organizing and interpreting information by using generalized principles but drawing on a substantial amount of domain-specific knowledge (Chi, Feltovich, and Glaser 1981; Chi, Glaser, and Farr 1988; Chi, Glaser, and Rees 1982; Ericsson and Staszewski 1988; Simon 1979). By contrast, novices will focus on specific aspects of problems and try to encode or solve them, without reference to a "big picture" that allows for explanation and broader interpretation (Newell and Simon 1972; Shulman and Elstein 1975).

Implications of Cognitive Theory for Curriculum. Much of this work comes together in certain areas of research pointed more or less directly at curriculum issues. For example, expert-novice studies conducted with children on specific performance tasks in reading and mathematics demonstrate the mental processes used by more and less proficient performers (who are often at developmentally different stages as well). Just as "more capable" readers perform many subcomponents of reading with a degree of automaticity (e.g., decoding and interpreting word meanings), so children who are more proficient at arithmetic have encoded certain kinds of quantitative knowledge in their memories so that they can perform more complex problems without resorting to individual counts for each operation (Fuson 1982).

One implication drawn from this work is that lower-level component skills need to be reinforced until they become automatic so that more of the child's working memory can be relieved for comprehension (Glaser 1988). This requirement might suggest substantial drill and practice on "basic" or rote skills even if comprehension and problem solving are sought.

However, additional research suggests that readers and problem solvers use both "bottom-up" and "top-down" strategies in their effort to construct meaning; that is, they understand what they are doing not only by processing discrete subparts of the problem but also by activating useful schemas for interpreting the task and relating it to their experience and existing ways of knowing (R. Anderson 1984; Davis 1984). The development of useful schemas, a higher-order cognitive task, is itself an aid to comprehension and more proficient performance. Part of this process of schema development and activation involves providing sufficient domain-specific knowledge and experience so that learners have some cognitive structures on which to hang new information. The other aspect of the task is finding ways to link this new information to prior knowledge and experience. These notions support the concepts of cognitive structuralists regarding such strategies as whole language instruction, which seeks to use the learner's own experience in conjunction with a language-rich environment to develop and activate cognitive structures that support the learning of reading and writing. They also suggest that since thinking and problem-solving processes rely heavily on domain-specific knowledge, the teaching of thinking and problem solving ought to occur in a specific subject matter context rather than as generalized heuristics and ought to allow opportunities for knowledge synthesis and application rather than passive acquisition of disconnected bodies of information (Brown 1985; Ennis 1989; Perkins and Salomon 1989; Shulman and Elstein 1975).

These ideas give shape to a number of principles for curriculum development regarding the structuring of learning opportunities. Research on the development of expertise in teachers also provides insights into the kinds of knowledge teachers must acquire to construct and manage the learning process (Leinhardt and Greeno 1985; Leinhardt, Weidman, and Hammond, 1984; Shavelson and Stern 1981; for reviews, see Ben-Peretz, Bromme, and Halkes 1986; Berliner 1987; Clark and Peterson 1986; Clark and Yinger 1977).

For the cognitive scientist, a curriculum should provide students with "frameworks for arranging knowledge in organizational networks that differ substantially from the results of natural experience" (Calfee 1981, 19). The instructional challenge is that preexisting knowledge structures must be assessed and transferred to the formal abstractions of school learning (Curtis and Glaser 1981). Based on this conception, the teacher's task is to "assist students to identify and use a large repertoire of learning methods" (McKeachie, quoted in Phillips and Soltis 1985). Recent research on metacognition (e.g., Brown 1980; Haller, Child, and Walberg 1988; Peterson 1988) and error analysis (e.g., Clancey 1987) is part of a growing body of work that promises to inform us about how students can systematically develop more effective information-processing strategies that with the guidance of skilled teachers can help them "learn how to learn."

Efforts to understand cognitive functioning better have also led to new understandings of intelligence, with profound implications for the curriculum and its assessment. Based on his studies of cognitive capacity and symbol use, Gardner (1983) became persuaded that different psychological processes are involved in handling linguistic, mathematical, pictorial, gestural, interpersonal, and other kinds of symbol systems, and these are associated with multiple intelligences. Cross-cultural studies of cognition (Brown, Collins, and Duguid 1989; Lave 1988) suggest that these intelligences are culturally grounded and susceptible to nurture and development, as their demonstration is dependent on prior experiences and familiarity with task demands. Not only does this work press self-consciously for a broadened school curriculum, one more inclusive of activities and performances beyond those requiring linguistic and logical-mathematical symbol use (such as the arts and kinesthetic activities), but it also redefines the role and nature of testing in education and the goals of schooling itself: Together these demands for assessments that are intelligence-fair, are based on culturally valued activities, and take place within a familiar context naturally lead to an approach that blurs the distinctions between curriculum and assessment. Drawing information from the regular curriculum ensures that the activities are familiar; introducing activities in a wide range of areas makes it possible to challenge and examine each intelligence in an appropriate manner. Tying the activities to inviting pursuits enables students to discover and develop abilities, which in turn increase their chances of experiencing a sense of engagement and of achieving some success in their society (Gardner and Hatch 1989, 6–7).

The Contributions of Scientific Inquiry to Curriculum Work

As the preceding sections have indicated, several lines of empirical inquiry into the nature of learning have had important implications for curriculum thinking and development. Behavioral research has drawn our attention to the importance of environmental conditions and cues in the shaping of learning. Developmental research has described how cognitive strategies evolve through maturation and how this development can be supported through opportunities for active engagement with the environment. Research focusing on cognitive structures has illustrated how perception and presentation influence information processing and interpretation. Cognitive scientists have extended this work to demonstrate how schema development and activation, along with conscious changes in information-processing strategies, can enhance learning.

Over time, the distinctions among various research perspectives have become increasingly blurred. Behaviorally inspired learning psychologists concerned with manipulating the environment have begun to attend to learners' active internal mental processes (e.g., Corno and Rohrkemper 1985; Weinstein and Mayer 1985), and developmental psychologists have begun to attend to environmentally induced changes in performance (e.g., Palincsar and Brown 1984). Current cognitive research tends to examine the interactions between learners' constructions of reality and external stimuli that may pose new information suggesting structural changes. They seek ways to accommodate or address learners' developmental or cognitive differences while structuring the environment (i.e., the curriculum and its presentation) for heightened success.

Similarly, disputes among perspectives rooted in different definitions and operationalizations of "learning" have begun to reconcile as scientists have broadened the range of types of learning they investigate and have more sharply defined their constructs. Earlier efforts to define different kinds of learning (see, e.g., Bloom, Englehart, Furst, Hill, and Krathwol 1956; Gagné 1977; Gagné and Briggs 1979) have been extended and refined, allowing researchers to investigate more carefully the types of curriculum and instruction appropriate to various learning goals. Current work often distinguishes between types of knowledge and learning (e.g., figurative versus operational knowledge and rote versus meaningful learning) and within these distinctions to specific types of tasks and performances. These advances ought to allow for more sophisticated and less dogmatic applications of learning theory in research on curriculum and teaching.

Curriculum workers have drawn on these areas of research as they have sought to develop curricula that incorporate organizational principles and methods thought to encourage learning. We have discussed how the differences in the types of learning examined and explanatory factors investigated by various lines of research have often given rise to very different inferences—sometimes competing and sometimes complementary—concerning curriculum implications. These varying inferences about what scientific studies of learning "tell" the curriculum designer are also apparent in the design of research concerning the curriculum itself. As we describe in the next section, empirical studies of curriculum and its effects are themselves based on ideas about what types of learning are sought and which explanatory factors are important to examine.

EMPIRICAL INVESTIGATIONS OF CURRICULUM

In this section, we trace the ways in which the curriculum itself has been studied and how, in some instances, inquiries into student learning have shaped research about the curriculum and its effects. In the United States, empirical inquiry into curriculum has its roots as far back as the early 19th century. Because so many research efforts have been associated with the struggle to establish a common system of public schools, to evaluate its curriculum, and to define its future course, a major thrust of investigations has been to describe the curriculum and its effects in terms useful to policymakers responsible for controlling the schools.

This link to policy has led to an emphasis among many empirical studies on describing what students study and what they know in pragmatic and quantifiable terms. The quest for useful statistical indicators of educational offerings and outcomes derives from this source. The policy link has also strengthened the reflections of each historical era's predominant political and social ideologies in the design and intentions of research of the times. As we describe below, curriculum studies adopt outcome measures in response to (or occasionally in reaction against) prevailing political, social, and economic goals for schooling.

At the same time, schools often adopt curriculum innovations in response to what they believe scientific studies have found. Likewise, desired changes are frequently defended on scientific grounds, whether or not the claims are justified. Thus, our examination of the scientific tradition traces the uses made of science for curriculum decision making as well as the uses made of scientific methods for curriculum study. To set a context for this exploration, we first discuss the social and educational goals of curriculum investigations and the attendant rationales for various efforts to introduce statistical studies of curriculum.

Goals of Curriculum Inquiries

Empirical investigations of curriculum have aimed to reveal what it is that students are being taught and what it is that they are learning. These sound like purely descriptive activities, prone to easy objectification; however, since studies must aim at specific areas with a manageable number of objectives and variables, they must necessarily decide to examine those specific elements of curriculum, teaching, and learning that are thought to be in some sense important and worthy of study.

The goals of curriculum inquiries, then, become quickly bound up with goals of the curriculum itself, and these in turn with the goals of various actors within society for the education of young people. Competing conceptions of curriculum goals dictate different topics for and, often, approaches to research about curriculum (Eisner and Vallance 1974). Though policymakers, parents, teachers, administrators, and students all have ideas about what education is for—and hence what the curriculum ought to consist of and what studies ought to look for—these ideas are rarely explicit. Researchers, too, often fail to describe how their views of education's purpose and goals influence the studies they choose to conduct and the measures they use to designate success or failure of a curriculum effort.

Of particular importance for the course of curriculum investigations in U.S. public education is the fact that the common school was created primarily to meet the state's need for an educated citizenry in a country aiming at democracy and made up of immigrants. Those on all sides of pedagogical and political divides agree that "the reason that so much of our social resources are devoted to education is that the reproduction of our social, economic, and political system depends heavily on preparing the young to understand and participate in that system" (Levin 1979, 15).

State goals include socialization to a common culture (education to meet social needs), inculcation of basic democratic values and preparation for citizenship (education to meet political needs), and preparation for occupational life (education to meet economic needs). Because the public school is embedded in an egalitarian legal system, equality of educational opportunity is an additional important value that has become both a goal of education and a measure of its processes (Wise and Darling-Hammond 1984, 1–2).

It is important to recognize that the state's interest is not the same as parents' interests or individual students' interests or even those of particular groups of parents and students. Individuals have different social, economic, and political goals and very often disagree on how to pursue even the commonly held goals. The tension between state goals and individual goals is addressed, if not resolved, by allowing some diversity in public schools and escape hatches to private schools. Especially during times of social ferment, allowances for alternative curricula and "individual differences" are made. However, concerns about efficiency in the cause of the public purse and uniformity in the cause of administrative ease and the appearance of equality have militated against too much diversity.

Given the state's interest in public education, its interest in curriculum investigations has been primarily to provide information useful for monitoring the schools' attention to its goals and developing policies that will better control those specific school outcomes related to perceived social, political, and economic needs. Another rationale for curriculum studies—to inform better the decisions and actions of school practitioners about the varied consequences of their work with students—has also been present but often to a lesser degree.

The pursuit of societal goals necessarily requires some reduction in curriculum goals. To evaluate the acquisition of that "certain amount of positive knowledge" described by a 19th-century school superintendent as essential (Tyack 1974, 49), someone must define precisely what it is, and thus what it is not, as well.

These definitions, responding to government needs to prove the worth of public education, have often tended to be narrowly utilitarian (Cremin 1965), focusing on discrete pieces of knowledge or types of behavior and skills thought to be directly related to the social welfare. Sometimes, they explicitly exclude other kinds of knowledge or action beneficial to the individual but not obviously and directly useful to the greater society. As one educator said in 1909,

> Ordinarily a love of learning is praiseworthy, but when this delight in the pleasures of learning becomes so intense and so absorbing that it diminishes the desire and the power of earning, it is positively harmful. Education that does not promote the desire and power to do useful things—that's earning—is not worth the getting. (Quoted in Callahan 1962, 10)

Dewey (1929) offered an example of this conflict between social goals for the curriculum and personal goals, which shaped curriculum studies then and still does today:

> Social needs and conditions are said to dictate, for example, the necessity of instruction in reading, writing, and number at a fairly early age. It is also recognized that these are useful factors in later personal growth, being the means of opening up learning in a variety of subjects. So far the two aspects seem to be in harmony. But suppose the question of how children learn most effectively to master these skills then be taken up in isolation, and methods are devised to promote the ready acquisition of the skills in question. . . . The larger question is what other habits, including tastes and desires, are being collaterally formed. . . . Unfortunately, experience shows that the methods which most readily and efficiently bring about skill to read (or write, or figure) in its narrower sense of the ability to recognize, pronounce and put together words, do not at the same time take care of the formation of attitudes that decide the uses to which the ability is to be put. This is the more important issue. (62–63)

Dewey then criticized his psychologist colleagues in much the same manner as the "alternative paradigm" proponents have done in recent years.

> It will not do for the psychologist to content himself with saying in effect: "These other things are none of my business; I have shown how the child may most readily and efficiently form the skill. The rest is up to somebody else." It will not because as one skill is acquired, other abilities, preferences and disabilities are also learned, and these fall within the province of the psychological inquirer. The social question is intertwined with the psychological. (63–64)

The thorny issue of curriculum goals has arisen throughout the last century or more, in which curriculum has been observed and shaped by scientific inquiry. This issue has proved especially important when investigations and reports turn quantitative in orientation.

"Quantifying" the Curriculum

In much the same way that the state's role in education, and its obligation to provide education accountably, points at certain kinds of curriculum goals, so, too, it encourages quantification of many aspects of curriculum. Policymakers try to "count" curriculum so that they can assess what is occurring in classrooms too numerous to be visited and so that they can evaluate the extent to which goals for the educational system are being met. Ways of measuring curriculum are also useful for controlling it. Precision appears to be enhanced when we can report—or legislate—that students receive X hours of this, or Y courses in that. Metrics must be devised to meet these needs since a constant way of counting is necessary when comparisons are to be made or when standardization is sought.

For reasons also related to the need for comparison and standardization, scientists, too, require measurement. Their measures are intended to serve different ends—aiding description, aggregation of data, replication of studies, and further hypothesis testing—and may be based on more detailed observations or sophisticated conceptions of ends and means and the relationship between the two. However arrived at and initially used, though, scientists' measurements may be seized on by others to serve different ends. Their context and meaning may be meanwhile forgotten, if ever known, by the users. Or regrettably, their meaning and appropriate inference may never have been given much attention by their creators to begin with.

Decisions about what curricular content, processes, and outcomes should be measured can have far-reaching implications for what is taught and learned in schools as well as what is studied and transmitted in research communities. The influence of scientifically derived and used measures is felt as they accumulate to form a body of findings that can be said to constitute well-tested knowledge in an area. Most researchers will continue to work around those areas already viewed as well defined rather than create new definitions or constructions.

The import of politically derived and used measures, such as today's educational indicators and their earlier predecessors, is felt as they direct the attention of school people and the public to the specific concerns suggested by published data (e.g., low test scores) and to particular interpretations of those data suggested by the ways in which they are presented (e.g., differential average performance between different schools). These presentations will tend to suggest a certain definition of the problem and its first-order solutions.

The indicators themselves may be used as arbiters of incentive systems, as is the case, for example, with current policy uses of test scores for allocating rewards to schools and teachers and conferring or denying educational opportunities to students. This practice forces actions that are intended to influence the measurements, redirecting curriculum goals and/or reshaping other educational processes in schools. Below we discuss efforts to measure curriculum both to evaluate and to standardize practice.

Early Curriculum Indicators: The Search for One Best System

During the 19th century, American educators began to search for a way to standardize education across the nation. Convinced that "one best system" (Tyack 1974) could be found, well-intentioned reformers advocated abandoning the traditional model of local control for a centralized educational structure based on principles of scientific management. Though the "scientific movement," as it has come to be called, was not based on studies of children, learning, or schooling, its use of the term "science" legitimized both the changes it sought and the curriculum studies it spawned.

The origins of this movement were manifold. American schools in the 18th and early 19th centuries were often haphazardly run and staffed by unqualified teachers. At the same time, German and Prussian schools offered a centralized and rigorously structured alternative model. The industrial revolution had given America its own paradigm for industrial efficiency. And American educational reformers, zealous to turn the nation's schools into modern, uniform institutions, established themselves in positions of authority in states, cities, and universities throughout the nation.

Following the introduction of graded texts with *McGuffey's Eclectic Readers* in 1836, the reformers borrowed the Prussian system of age-grading and began to establish standards and uniform examinations by which the grades would be defined. As early as 1844, Samuel Gridley Howe devised a set of uniform written tests to be administered in lieu of less easily quantified oral examinations to the top class at each of Boston's grammar schools. He hoped these tests would provide "positive information, in black and white" (in Tyack 1974, 35) about the degree to which the city's students had mastered the material in their textbooks. The focus on short-answer, factual recall in these examinations—and the emphasis on finding a means for "counting" curriculum acquisition—is suggested by the fact that the tests were reported to embody 57,873 possible right answers (out of which, on the average, students answered only 17,216 correctly).

Tyack (1974, 36) notes that Howe's "empirical muckraking" was a tool for effectuating much larger political ends. Howe used what he could claim as scientific test results to charge that the Boston schools required a total organizational overhaul, along with a full-time professional superintendent. As the practice caught on, uniform tests were sometimes used throughout a state, and scores were used to compare schools and teachers.

These changes represented a shift not just in practice but also in concept. The idea that schools could be run along the model of factories had been nascent in the American psyche since the industrial revolution; as the 19th century progressed, the metaphor took strong hold of the nation's spirit. Schools were no longer to be informal institutions in which a community acquainted its youngest members with the written word and the fundamentals of arithmetic; rather, they represented the most efficient means to produce a product, whose uniformity and quality could be carefully monitored by a series of appropriate tests.

Efforts to quantify the curriculum got a great boost from the convergence of a heightened state role in education in the latter half of the 19th century with the enthusiastic application of "scientific management" techniques to education. These efforts sought detailed specification of curriculum goals, objectives, content, and processes to guide the work of the teacher. They also outlined an input-process-product model for curriculum studies that guided the work of researchers for many decades. This model can be characterized by Bobbitt's (1913) seven principles for defining the educational process:

(I) Definite qualitative and quantitative standards must be determined for the product [read: "student"].

(II) Where the material that is acted upon by the labor processes passes through a number of progressive stages on its way from the raw material to the ultimate product, definite qualitative and quantitative standards must be determined for the product at each of these stages [read: "grade levels"].

(III) Scientific Management finds the methods of procedure [read: "curriculum and teaching methods"] which are most efficient for actual service under actual conditions, and secures their use on the part of the workers [read: "teachers"].

(IV) Standard qualifications [read: "teacher characteristics and behaviors"] must be determined for the workers.

(V) The management must train its workers previous to service in the measure demanded by its standard qualifications. . . .

(VI) The worker must be kept up to standard qualifications for his kind of work for his entire service.

(VII) The worker must be kept supplied with detailed instructions as to the work to be done, the standards to be reached, the methods to be employed and the appliances to be used [read: "curriculum content, goals, processes, and tools"]. (Quoted in Callahan 1962, 81–90)

As noted earlier, the search for control through application of scientific management principles could not be justified on the grounds that this form of management was based on systematic, empirical studies of education. In that sense, the term "scientific" was misleading, though politically persuasive. Instead it was drawn from an engineering approach to the organization of factory work. Indeed education's debt to industry for this approach was repaid by its drawing the standards for students—and the dependent variables for many studies—from the requirements of industrial occupations. As in industry, investigations of the work focused on the measurement of time spent and economies achieved.

Curriculum Counting. Obviously, the quest for a scientifically managed educational system required the development of many kinds of measures: To use the factory metaphor so explicitly adopted, measures of inputs, measures of processes, and measures of outputs were required to design and manage the enterprise.

During the 19th century, inputs were measured in terms of time and texts, processes by teaching methods, and outputs by students' test scores (though we will see that tested "intelligence" was later defined as an input to the schooling process). Alongside the attempts to develop a perfectly defined and sequenced set of curriculum texts, a great deal of attention was devoted to the measurement of time spent on the learning of various subjects. In 1890, 82 large cities engaged in a study that reported the amount of time devoted to different curricular subjects during the 8 years of elementary school. Of 7,000 total hours, the study found, for example, that spelling consumed 516 and arithmetic 1,190 (Tyack 1974, 46–47).

Typical of the efforts of scientific managers was Newton, Massachusetts, Superintendent Frank Spaulding's calculation of the costs of pupil recitations in each subject: When he found that "5.9 pupil recitations in Greek are of the same value as 23.8 pupil recitations in French," he declared that "when the obligations of the present year expire, we ought to purchase no more Greek instruction at the rate of 5.9 recitations per dollar. The price must go down, or we shall invest in something else" (quoted in Callahan 1962, 73). Thus, time and money spent became the grist of both curriculum studies and curriculum itself.

Similarly, the 1893 Committee of Ten, headed by Harvard University President Charles Eliot, issued its recommendations for the secondary school curriculum in terms of the numbers of years that should be devoted to each of nine subjects deemed essential for "life preparation." By 1909, a majority of high schools across the country claimed to have implemented the recommendations; however, there was no standard definition of a "year." Was a year the amount of time a rural child spends in the classroom between performing necessary farm and life-related chores? Or was it the amount of time the son of a scion of society gives to studying Greek with a private tutor?

A team of researchers funded by the Carnegie Foundation observed and interviewed school people around the country to answer this question (Tompkins and Gaumnitz 1954). The product of this empirical work was the Carnegie unit—an attempt to regularize and quantify high school credits in terms of time. The Carnegie unit, which defined 1 year of study as 120 sixty-minute sessions, has remained the standardized definition of a year for a half century.

Output studies consisted largely of the compilation of test results in which the tests were derived directly from the texts prescribed. Even after many decades of efforts to refine the "one best system," the results of these studies indicated that the system was not working for everyone. One response to this problem was to study the "process" as well as the inputs to education. Like early behaviorists, researchers sought to identify stimuli and reinforcements in the classroom environment that could account for differences in learning. The goal was to find out what the schools were doing wrong as a means for revising the system so that it would work as planned.

One of the more influential process studies was undertaken by Joseph Mayer Rice (1913). Originally a journalist, Rice concluded after a 36-city tour of schools that American education was in a catastrophic state. In 1895, Rice began research into the teaching of spelling to explain why some students succeeded where others failed. With a sample of 16,000 students, he set out to discover superior techniques of teaching spelling. His behaviorally inspired underlying assumptions—that more drill would improve performance—were not borne out by his results, and he blamed teachers for giving away answers through their careful enunciation of words while administering tests. Though he could not identify the one best way to teach spelling, Rice's disgust with what he found in schools eventually persuaded him that the standardization of schooling was the only way to force administrators and teachers to do the "right" thing. His position, like that of many others, "evolved from outraged humanitarian to a zealot for the elimination of waste in the curriculum through the application of the kind of scientific management that was so successful in industry" (Kliebard 1982, 21).

Eliminating curriculum waste meant a tighter focus on objectives and outcomes and a clear focus on measures of inputs, costs, and outputs. It also came to mean allocating curriculum opportunities "efficiently" so that energy was not wasted on those who, it was perceived, would not profit from the expense.

Differentiating Curriculum. A second response to the problem of poor system outputs was to blame individual students by documenting their lack of capacity. The creation and widespread promulgation of IQ tests at the turn of the century provided a tool for this strategy. Though Alfred Binet protested as a "brutal pessimism" the idea that "the intelligence of an individual is a fixed quantity" (quoted in Kamin 1974, 5), many scientific psychologists were persuaded otherwise. In 1912, for example, Henry Goddard's testing experiments at Ellis Island established to his own satisfaction (and, sadly, to that of many others) that 83 percent of Jews, 80 percent of Hungarians, 79 percent of Italians, and 87 percent of Russians were feebleminded (Kamin 1974).

Well-known and respected scientists such as Lewis Terman, Henry Goddard, Robert Yerkes, Edward Thorndike, and Carl Brigham all vouched for the scientific validity of intelligence testing. Meeting under the auspices of the Eugenics Research Association (ERA) and the National Research Council (the political arm of the ERA), these men were also among the leadership of the American Psychological Association. Consequently, their ideas gained great currency in the scientific and research communities, encouraging substantial work on the development of more scientifically constructed measures (at least in terms of their statistical properties) and more widely used tests.

Researchers used the tests as measures of educational input, in which intelligence was viewed as "raw material" for schooling, or as measures of outputs, in which intelligence was viewed as its "product." School people used them to differentiate the curriculum students would receive. And as schools were pressed by business groups and civic leaders to be more efficient and businesslike, educational reformers seeking to extend the reach of the common school urged them to sort their pupils and educate them according to their future roles in society (Cremin 1961; Cubberly 1947 [1919]).

Institutions such as the Carnegie Foundation supported the use of IQ tests to maintain quality control. Though many proponents felt that using such instruments to track students more efficiently would enhance social justice, the rationales for tracking were often frankly racially motivated.

> Children of this group [Indians, Mexicans, and blacks] should be segregated in special classes. . . . They cannot master abstractions, but they can often be made efficient workers. There is no possibility at present of convincing society that they should not be allowed to reproduce, although from a eugenic point of view they constitute a grave problem because of their unusually prolific breeding. (Terman, quoted in Oakes 1985, 36)

The advent of IQ testing provided the scientific justification for tracking, along with the tools to implement it with efficiency and precision. Tracking, along with age-grading, offered the promise of more efficient standardization of curriculum within groups, on the assumption that the key variables predicting educational performance could be predetermined and used as the basis for grouping decisions. The search for such predictors has continued, drawing heavily on techniques developed in the behaviorist tradition and producing a line of studies seeking a means for identifying which curriculum "treatments" are likely to be most effective with different types of students (see, e.g., Cronbach 1975; Cronbach and Snow 1977; also Good and Power 1976).

An Alternative Research Tradition: The Quest for Responsive Curriculum

Another research tradition arose from a set of commitments very different from those driving the scientific management movement. When the National Education Association (NEA) and the U.S. Department of Education issued a set of Cardinal Principles for Secondary Education in 1918, the students attending secondary schools had become much more diverse than they were when the Committee of Ten had met 25 years earlier, and educational theory had begun to attend to issues of pedagogy and learning as factors important to educational outcomes. In contrast to the narrow concerns for measurable outputs intended to produce efficient workers, the Cardinal Principles aimed to produce in students "the knowledge, interests, ideals, habits, and powers to shape the self and society to noble ends" (NEA 1918).

Perhaps the leading spokesperson for this vision of education was John Dewey. For Dewey, any curriculum was an act of creation, an experiment to lead to a better social system, not an end in and of itself (Dewey 1929). His goal was an improved social order based on an education grounded in the needs of children and a science of how they best learn. For him, empirical research was a means for inquiring into the nature of learning, of teaching, and of schools, not for measuring the number of right answers on a test or developing more efficient methods of standardization and control.

Dewey's plea for educational research to create a science of education based on an empirical understanding of the strivings of students, teachers, and schools did not result in an immediate outpouring of work. But by 1932, with the country in the midst of the Great Depression, scientific management deemed a failure, and no level of sufficiency in Greek or Latin capable of guaranteeing individual advancement or societal well-being, a remarkable research project was undertaken by the Progressive Education Association (PEA).

Led by many of the most prominent curriculum theorists of the time, the PEA steadfastly refused to outline a single philosophy statement, but it did "endorse by common consent, the obvious hypothesis that the child rather than what he studies should be the centre of all educational effort and that a scientific attitude toward new educational ideas is the best guarantee of progress" (Burton Frank, president of the PEA, quoted in Cremin 1961, 258).

Frankly developmentalist in their orientation, the progressives saw the efforts of prior reformers to standardize curriculum and create quantifiable indicators for measuring it as one impediment to the objective understanding of educational results:

> It is an amazing fact that our schools . . . know little of the results of their work. It is even more amazing that they seldom attempt

> seriously to find out what changes schooling brings about in students. . . . How can this lack of knowledge . . . be explained? There are doubtless many causes but one of the most obvious is the universal emphasis upon the accumulation of credits for promotion, graduation, and admission to college. (Smith and Tyler 1942, xvii)

In the rush to quantify schooling, the measures themselves became more important than the underlying goals:

> What goes on the school record becomes the real objective of the student, no matter what the school *says* its purposes are. . . . One of the major reasons for the over-emphasis upon these limited objectives is that results in these fields are more easily measured than in other less tangible areas. . . . Because instruments of appraisal in other areas have not been available, the teacher tends to neglect other objectives and to strive only for results that can be ascertained with relative ease and objectivity. (Smith and Tyler 1942, xvii-xviii)

The PEA heard teachers complain that the problem with education was an overemphasis on externally prescribed inputs in the form of standardized and regulated courses of study. Colleges demanded specific courses and tests for admission, and school districts managed schooling by reference to Carnegie units, prescribed texts, and other tests. Based on this analysis, the PEA designed the Eight Year Study, an experimental study in which 30 secondary schools were invited to offer to their students whatever the local school people, students, and community felt would be best for them. Meanwhile, over 300 colleges agreed to accept students from these experimental schools based on recommendations from school staffs without requiring specific credits or test results.

The Eight Year Study followed the 2,108 graduates from these schools throughout their high school and college careers. Of these graduates, 1,475 were paired student for student with graduates of conventional schools, matched as closely as possible with respect to sex, age, race, scholastic aptitude scores, home and community background, and vocational and avocational interests. The classes entering college in 1936, 1937, 1938, and 1939 were included in the study, which sought to evaluate such attributes as cultural and social development, practical competence and physical fitness, emotional balance and character, and intellectual achievements.

New evaluation tools had to be created for the studies because existing instruments did not measure many of the constructs of concern and existing achievement tests tended to measure factual recall of information rather than broader curriculum concepts and analytic abilities. New instruments were needed for measuring not only student growth but also teacher growth and changes in curricular inputs and processes. Each element was observed and assessed over the course of the study.

School people themselves were also engaged in evaluating their progress and its outcomes since part of the "treatment" was to develop a system in which teachers, students, parents, and administrators would be directly engaged in defining and designing a student-centered curriculum. The curriculum was defined as being constructed in its enactment, not predesigned for faithful implementation. In fact, the researchers observed that schools that tried to replicate a precreated path made "a serious mistake and the results were unsatisfactory. Genuine reconstruction does not come that way. All teachers, all faculties must go through the hard experience of thinking their own problems through" (Aikin 1942, 131–132).

Using this wide array of criteria and measures, the study reported that graduates of the experimental schools equaled or exceeded their counterparts from nonexperimental schools in every assessment area, "whether success is judged by college standards, by the students' contemporaries, or by the individual students" (Chamberlin, Chamberlin, Drought, and Scott 1942, 208). Whether the measure was grade point average or resourcefulness in new situations, receipt of academic honors or intellectual drive, precision in thinking or extracurricular participation, the experimental school graduates outscored their counterparts (Smith and Tyler 1942).

Two other analyses pointed more directly at curricular effects. The graduates of the six schools whose programs differed most sharply from the conventional schools and those of the six whose programs differed least were compared with their respective control groups. The graduates of the most experimental schools were "strikingly more successful than their matchees. Differences in their favor were much greater than the differences between the total Thirty Schools and their comparison group" (Chamberlin, Chamberlin, Drought, and Scott 1942, 209).

The researchers then examined two of the most successful schools, deliberately chosen to be quite different in size, setting, students' socioeconomic characteristics, and nature of the program offered. This investigation led to the conclusion that "the important characteristics of both schools were their willingness to undertake a search for valid objectives; organizing curricula and techniques and setting them in motion in order to attain the objectives; and finally, measuring the effectiveness of curricula and techniques by appropriate evaluation devices" (Chamberlin, Chamberlin, Drought, and Scott 1942, 182). In other words, it was the *process* rather than the *content* of the developed curriculum that seemed to make the most difference for success. Teachers and administrators reported that it was the collective thinking stimulated by this process that engendered the vitality, willingness to change, and conviction to continue that changed the life of the school (Aikin 1942).

Given the magnitude of this research and the decisiveness of the findings, it seems odd that the Eight Year Study seems to have had so little influence on the course of curriculum development or, for that matter, curriculum studies in the subsequent half century. No other experimental research on this scale involving longitudinal data collection of this nature has been conducted since. Perhaps the intervention of a world war dimmed attention and enthusiasm. Perhaps, once these discoveries were made, their import for public policy affecting the mass of schools was too complicated to contemplate. Perhaps, as Lawrence Cremin (1965) put it, "Progressive education, after all, demanded infinitely skilled teachers, and it failed because such teachers could not be recruited in sufficient numbers'' (56). Whatever the reason, the next major cycle of empirical studies suggested that although the experiment died, its research methods lived on, exerting at least some influence on how curriculum and teaching would be investigated thereafter.

Research on Teaching: The Curriculum Enacted

The period after World War II, especially the post-Sputnik years, was characterized by a great deal of curriculum development activity, most of it stimulated by large congressional funding allocations to improve education in the cause of ''national defense'' (i.e., to catch up to the Russians in science and technology). The largest projects were in mathematics and science, followed by foreign language initiatives, with the humanities and social studies an afterthought. The first major grant was given in 1956 to the PSSC (Physical Sciences Study Committee), followed shortly by the SMSG (School Mathematics Study Group), BSCS (Biological Science Curriculum Study), CHEM Study (Chemical Education Materials Study), and many others. By 1967 there were more than 70 such projects in science alone (Grobman 1968).

Some of these projects drew explicitly on several areas of learning research. For example, the SMSG and a number of other elementary mathematics curriculum initiatives drew heavily from Piaget's research on child development and from the structuralist ideas of Gestalt psychology in stressing discovery and insight methods for concept acquisition (Frost and Rowland 1969). An emphasis on disciplinary structure was prominent in many of the secondary curriculum projects, especially PSSC physics. Bruner's BSCS curriculum was more eclectic, though also heavily influenced by structuralist theory. Initially the project developed three course versions of high school biology; ultimately, it developed others based intentionally on alternative premises about the implications of research for curriculum design and goals (Tanner and Tanner 1980).

Though some of these large-scale projects had built-in methods for experimentation, feedback, and revision, very few included systematic independent evaluations before, during, or after their implementation (Ford Foundation, 1972; Frost and Rowland 1969; Tanner and Tanner 1980). Typically, the projects' funders—The National Science Foundation, the U.S. Office of Education, or major foundations—asked the curriculum developers to evaluate their own projects rather than sponsoring independent assessments of their use and outcomes. This lack of independence and the tendency of sponsors and developers to want their research to endorse their innovations, led to more than a few efforts to make the data ''come out'' in support of the curriculum projects' effectiveness (Grobman 1968; Tanner and Tanner 1980).

Nonetheless, the projects broke important ground for curriculum research. In addition to a raft of input-output studies seeking to establish the effects of the curriculum changes on test scores (e.g., Braden 1967; Finlay 1962; Livermore and Ferris 1962; W. V. Mayer 1971), there were investigations of project implementation that ultimately broadened researchers' conceptions of curriculum and expanded the horizons of curriculum inquiry. The nearly exclusive emphasis on curriculum content that had characterized the projects at their start necessarily grew to include concerns for curriculum enactment, as it became clear that the dissemination of new materials was insufficient to produce the desired changes.

First came the discovery that teachers' curriculum translations were so varied as to negate the concept of a common curriculum. For example, a BSCS study revealed that teachers teaching the same lessons from the same course versions to classes of similar ability levels taught so differently that ''there really is no such thing a BSCS curriculum presentation in the schools'' (Gallagher 1967, 17).

Then came the finding from Harvard's Project Physics course and other studies that teachers' values, classroom behaviors, and the resulting social learning climate in classrooms were strongly related to students' achievement and attitudes (Rothman, Welch, and Walberg 1969; Walberg and Rothman 1969). Finally, researchers discovered that the process of curriculum implementation and school change was itself a set of complex variables strongly influencing outcomes (Carlson 1965). In combination, these studies moved the field toward a much more holistic and integrated view of curriculum and instruction:

> From an initial concern with questions of whether the materials were intellectually sound and could be learned by students, many project evaluations have come to include questions about optimal sequencing, grade level placement, teaching styles, learning styles, and the change process. . . . This broader view is not a matter of empire building; rather it reflects an increased understanding of the complexity of the educative process. . . . (Grobman 1968, 5–6)

Subsequent research followed up on these issues, though not always in a fully integrated fashion. During the 1960s and 1970s, ongoing social concerns for school outcomes spurred, on the one hand, the development of large-scale national data bases on schooling (discussed in the next section) and, on the other, studies of classroom life.

These studies have taken on several forms. One line of work, commonly called ''process-product'' research, has sought to discern generalizable strategies for effective curriculum implementation by correlating specific teacher behaviors with student outcomes (Dunkin and Biddle 1974; Medley 1977). Another, which might be termed ecological, contextual, or intentionalist research, has sought to understand the context for curriculum use by observing and describing classroom life and teachers' instructional decision making (Clark and Peterson 1986; Doyle 1978; Jackson 1968). Over time, these lines of work have evolved into distinctive paradigms, which are said to be among those at war (Gage 1989; Gage and Needels 1989), as the two areas of work have sought, by and large, to understand teaching from different vantage points and to influence it—and the development of curriculum ideas—in different ways.

Early on, the divide was not pronounced. Studies of classroom life looking for distinctions among more and less effective teaching strategies often investigated teaching content, processes, contexts, intentions, and outcomes holistically. For example, Tikunoff, Berliner, and Rist (1975) used ethnographic observation techniques to collect detailed information about the classroom climates and teaching patterns in classrooms where student achievement varied greatly. Their findings were derived from qualitative analysis of the transcribed field notes, which were later organized into 61 dimensions of classroom life, 21 of which showed significant differences between more and less successful classrooms.

The kinds of variables they identified as important—for example, classroom conviviality and engagement, promotion of cooperation and student self-sufficiency, teacher structuring of material, spontaneity, and pacing to students' needs—are high-inference variables representing broad constructs rather than specific, discrete actions of teachers. Similarly, a review of early research in this vein by Rosenshine and Furst (1971) cited high-inference variables suggesting context-dependent patterns of teaching aimed at responsiveness to students' interests and needs as key to teacher effectiveness. Many of these variables also represent important features of curriculum enactment supported by research on learning as well. The list includes such instructional elements as clarity, variability, enthusiasm, use of student ideas and general indirectness, use of structuring comments, use of various types of questioning and probing, task-oriented behaviors, student opportunity to learn criterion material, and adjusting instructional levels to the appropriate level of difficulty for students.

Later studies aiming to test and verify these claims began to use highly structured observation systems, many of them low-inference instruments designed to tally the presence and frequency of specific teacher behaviors. Experiments designed to test the effects of these classroom variables developed highly specified behavioral guidelines for training teachers whose classrooms would constitute the experimental group for comparisons (Anderson, Evertson, and Brophy 1979; Good and Grouws, 1979).

Eventually the importance of curriculum content and context disappeared from view. "If teachers vary in effectiveness, then it must be because they vary in the behaviors they exhibit in the classroom" (Dunkin and Biddle 1974, 13). In addition, the behaviorist orientation exerted criteria for both the process of teaching and its products that pressed for not only observable but also quantifiable student and teacher behaviors (e.g., time on task and achievement test scores).

Although this work pointed to some key constructs for guiding teaching, such as time and opportunity to learn the desired content and "active teaching" behaviors that structure and monitor students' learning (Brophy and Evertson 1976; Good and Brophy 1986), the quest for specific lists of teaching behaviors that would consistently lead to increased student achievement has been a troubled one. Apparently inconsistent and contradictory findings about what behaviors belong on the list (Doyle 1978; Dunkin and Biddle 1974; Shavelson and Dempsey-Atwood 1976) have plagued research developers and users.

The most extensive process-product study of teacher effectiveness, the Beginning Teacher Evaluation Study, conducted for California's Commission for Teacher Preparation and Licensing, contributed to the discomforts associated with this quest. After that monumental effort, "The researchers . . . concluded that linking precise and specific teacher behavior to precise and specific learning of pupils (the original goal of the inquiry) is not possible at this time" (Bush 1979, 15; see also McDonald and Elias 1976).

Some researchers have addressed the problem of inconsistent research findings by reference to interaction effects and attention to other situation-specific variables. This line of research has found that effective teaching behaviors and instructional strategies seem to vary for students of different socioeconomic, mental, and psychological characteristics (e.g., Brophy and Evertson 1974, 1977; Cronbach and Snow 1977; Peterson 1976), and for different grade levels and subject areas (Gage 1978; McDonald and Elias 1976). Some have hoped that this research would yield clear guidelines for practice, given the specifications of a particular teaching context (Medley 1977).

But the world has proved still more complicated, as Cronbach (1975) pointed out when he raised cautions about the limits of the line of aptitude-treatment interaction research he had helped to launch 20 years earlier. Not only are the important contextual variables too numerous to accommodate in two- or three-way interactional analyses (Anderson 1982; Centra and Potter 1980; McKenna 1981), but also the effectiveness of various teaching behaviors depends both on the goals of instruction and on the responses of students.

Furthermore, some of the claims for differentiating teaching behaviors by student type have relied heavily on prototypes that would deliver a substantially different, more controlling, and intellectually less challenging curriculum to lower-socioeconomic-status children than to middle-class children (Medley 1977, 113–130). These claims are made by assuming causation in correlational findings about existing differential teacher behaviors in diverse settings, thus reifying the status quo rather than questioning the appropriateness of existing differentiations of educational offerings (see Oakes, this volume).

The broader goals problem is visible when lists of teaching behaviors and their associations with "product" variables are arrayed with respect to distinctly different, though equally desirable, outcomes. For example, Medley's (1977) lists of teacher behaviors and their associations with student achievement and student self-concept includes several that are positively related with one but negatively related with the other. Other research also suggests that desirable affective outcomes of education—independence; curiosity; and positive attitudes toward school, teacher, and self—seem to result from teaching behaviors that are different from those prescribed for increasing student achievement on standardized tests of basic skills (Horwitz 1979; McKeachie and Kulik 1975; Peterson 1979; Traub, Weiss, and Fisher 1973).

Similarly, in reviewing the competing claims of research

in the 1960s and 1970s concerning the effectiveness of "direct instruction" versus "indirect instruction," Darling-Hammond, Wise, and Pease (1983) concluded that they are aimed at entirely different curriculum goals. These two instructional approaches, which have had distinct and substantial influences on curriculum ideas, typify the debates about learning theory and assessment that have occurred over the past century.

Direct instruction, which includes a variety of teaching acts defined in later process-product studies as effective teaching behaviors, is defined by Rosenshine (1979) as occurring in

> academically focused, teacher-directed classrooms using sequenced and structured materials. It refers to teaching activities where goals are clear to students, time allocated for instruction is sufficient and continuous, coverage of content is extensive, the performance of students is monitored, questions are at a low cognitive level . . . and feedback to students is immediate and academically oriented. In direct instruction, the teacher controls instructional goals, chooses materials appropriate for the student's ability, and paces the instructional episode. The goal is to move the students through a sequenced set of materials or tasks. Such materials are common across classrooms and have a relatively strong congruence with the tasks on achievement tests. (38)

Direct instruction is characterized by frequency of single-answer questions and drill, large-group instruction, and opportunities for "controlled practice." These strategies are built into prepackaged curriculum materials that adopt this view. Teaching behaviors that are discouraged include the use of higher-order, divergent, or open-ended questions; exploration of students' ideas; student-initiated discourse or choice of activities; and conversation about personal experience or about subject matter tangential to the immediate objectives of the lesson at hand. In this sense, direct instruction contrasts with "teacher indirectness" (Flanders 1965) and with approaches generally ascribed to "open" rather than "traditional" instruction (Horwitz 1979; Peterson 1979). Many of the instructional ideas associated with indirect instruction—use of discovery methods and inquiry-oriented materials—were built into the curriculum reform initiatives of the 1960s.

Various studies (Berliner 1979; Evertson and Brophy 1973; Soar 1972) have found support for direct instruction in terms of its effects on student achievement, primarily on basic skills achievement tests. In contrast, teacher *indirectness* has been found to have positive effects on student achievement, variously measured through standardized tests and a range of other evaluations (for reviews, see Dunkin and Biddle 1974; Glass et al. 1977; Horwitz 1979). Patterns of teaching behaviors associated with teacher indirectness are also identified more frequently in studies investigating strategies for increasing complex cognitive learning, problem-solving ability, and creativity (McKeachie and Kulik 1975; Peterson 1979; Soar 1977; Soar and Soar 1976). Darling-Hammond et al. (1983) conclude that research conclusions depend on the nature of curriculum goals:

> If markedly different teaching behaviors lead to divergent results that can be deemed equally desirable, there is no way to identify a single construct called effective teaching, much less delimit its component parts. One can, at best, pursue alternative models of effective teaching, making explicit the goals underlying each. This has yet to become part of the empirical research base on teaching effects, although educational philosophers and organizational theorists have treated the issues of goal specification in more explicit terms. (296–297)

Another set of problems with the quest for effective teaching behaviors has been the difficulty of generalizing from one context to the next. For example, teaching behaviors that have sometimes been found to be effective often bear a distinctly curvilinear relation to achievement. That is, a behavior that is effective when used in moderation can produce significant and negative results when used too much (Peterson and Kauchak 1982; Soar 1972) or when applied in the wrong circumstances (Coker, Medley, and Soar 1980; McDonald and Elias 1976).

Research on the stability and generalizability of measures of teaching behaviors lends support to a context-specific view of teaching. In general, specific, discrete measures of teacher behaviors—especially those derived from low-inference ratings of behavior—are neither stable over time nor generalizable across different teaching situations (e.g., subjects, grade levels, and student characteristics) (Shavelson and Dempsey-Atwood 1976; Stodolsky 1984). In other words, teachers adjust their behaviors to the changing demands of the teaching context. These kinds of findings undermine the continuing quest for a general use, teacher-proof curriculum or a highly specific recipe for implementation accompanying curriculum materials.

Researchers who adopt an ecological perspective for investigating teaching point out that reciprocal causality limits the applicability of behavioristically specified process-product research findings (Doyle 1979). Research grounded in this perspective finds that what students do affects teachers' behaviors and that the complexity of classroom life calls for teaching strategies responsive to environmental demands. As Doyle notes,

> Traditionally, research on teaching has been viewed as a process of isolating a set of effective teaching practices to be used by individual teachers to improve student learning or by policymakers to design teacher education and teacher evaluation programs. The emphasis in this tradition has been on predicting which methods or teacher behaviors have the highest general success rate, and much of the controversy over the productivity of research on teaching has centered on the legitimacy of propositions derived from available studies. . . . [The ecological approach] would seem to call into question the very possibility of achieving a substantial number of highly generalizable statements about teaching effectiveness. (203–204)

Doyle (1978, 169) contends that the process-product paradigm for research leads us to focus on behaviors that promise to be "context-proof, teacher-proof, and even student-proof" even though they may not be the most important behaviors in bringing about learning. He proposes instead the use of a "mediating process" paradigm that takes into account the students' responses and the psychological processes that govern learning. Ecological analysis of teaching, as Doyle describes it, encompasses three basic features that are consonant with the research strategy advocated by Cronbach (1975): (1) a vigorously naturalistic approach, (2) a direct focus on environment-behavior relationships, and (3) a concern for the adaptive significance of behaviors in an environment (Doyle 1979, 188–189).

This approach is consonant with an intentionalist thesis for studying teaching that examines teachers' *reasons* for adopting particular behaviors in different classroom situations rather than simply examining behaviors (Fenstermacher 1978; Shavelson and Stern 1981). Studies of teachers' thought processes (Clark and Peterson 1986) have also been joined by research on students' mediating thought processes (Wittrock 1986). These approaches to studying curriculum enactments suggest different variables for study as well as different methods.

For example, those who argue that "the quality and appropriateness of students' thinking produces differences in students' academic achievement" (Peterson and Swing 1982, 230) need to find curriculum methods that allow students to reveal their thinking, not just their overt behaviors. In line with the findings of cognitive psychologists, researchers engaged in studying classroom work from a mediating process paradigm find that students' abilities to diagnose their own learning problems (and teachers' abilities to help them do so) are key determinants of performance. Furthermore, of methodological interest, some research has found that "observers' judgments of off-task behavior were found to be unrelated to students' reports of attending as measured by the interview" (Peterson and Swing 1982, 232). Their results suggest that "students' reported thought processes may be better predictors of student achievement than observations of student behavior" (236).

In responding to criticisms of process-product research, Gage and Needels (1989) suggest accommodations between the behaviorist and ecological-intentionalist paradigms:

> Future research should aim at developing theory based on cognitive information-processing conceptions of learning. Such theory would begin to explain why teacher discourse of different kinds results in differences in student knowledge and comprehension. Future research should also rest on more complete conceptualizations. Thus new formulations should include (a) the student cognitive processes mediating between process and product variables and (b) the teachers' thought processes associated with process variables. The study of teaching processes should be conducted with a variety of methods, including ethnographic methods. Product variables should be measured with criterion-referenced achievement tests and unobtrusive measures. Relationships between process and product variables should be studied with the whole variety of methods mentioned above. (294)

Although these adaptations of the process-product approach may allow the thoughts of students and teachers to creep into the mix, they will probably not provide the teaching recipes or teacher-proof curricula that many policymakers have sought. Nor will they settle the questions of educational and curricular goals that have defined much of the battleground. These same questions characterize current debates about how to measure and represent schools' curriculum offerings and outcomes, bringing us full circle to contemporary educational indicators and their efforts to evaluate and stimulate curriculum change.

Statistical Research on Schooling: The Quest for More Meaningful Curriculum Indicators

Alongside studies of curriculum enactment in classrooms have been continuing efforts to collect large-scale survey data about schooling for gauging the conditions of education and their effects. These data and their analysis are often closely linked to government monitoring functions and policy agendas, thus enhancing their political as well as scientific interest.

Earlier we noted that the collection of statistical information about American schools was an important stimulus for reform during the common school movement in the mid-19th century. Spurred by desires to pressure local communities to improve schools and to equalize educational opportunities after the Civil War, the U.S. Department of Education (later changed to the U.S. Office of Education) was founded in 1867 with the major purpose of collecting such information (Travers 1983; Warren 1974). Its most publicized data were enrollment statistics, but as concerns about efficiency emerged, information was also collected about graduation rates and costs (Callahan 1962). Whereas states and localities developed and published information about curriculum "inputs" and "outcomes," no federal government initiatives to investigate what students learned in school emerged until the 1960s (Murnane 1987).

A series of educational "indicator" movements have waxed and waned over more than a century alongside political concerns over education. Indicators can be simply defined as individual or composite statistics that reflect important features of a system, such as education, health, or the economy (Shavelson, McDonnell, and Oakes 1989), though more complex definitions are available (see, e.g., Jaeger 1978, 285–287). Their "overriding purpose . . . is to characterize the nature of a system through its components, their interrelations, and their changes over time. This information can then be used to judge progress—toward some goal or standard, against some past benchmark, or by comparison with data from some other institution or country" (Shavelson, McDonnell, and Oakes 1989, 4). Thus, indicators are intended to be evaluative in nature, not merely informative. "Statistics qualify as indicators only if they serve as yardsticks" (5).

Though social indicators aim to monitor the health or status of an enterprise with a major goal of informing policy, their history indicates that promises of policy applications are often overblown. They cannot provide the kind of specifically designed and detailed information necessary for answering fundamental research questions or evaluating specific programs or policies. Neither can they define what is good education or desirable legislation (De Neufville 1975; Shavelson, McDonnell, and Oakes 1989; Sheldon and Parke 1975).

> What social indicators may do reasonably well is to describe the state of the society and its dynamics and thus improve immensely our ability *to state problems in a productive fashion, obtain clues as to promising lines of endeavor, and ask good questions* [emphasis added]. . . . The fruits of these efforts will be more directly a contribution to the policy-maker's cognition than to his decisions. Decision emerges from a mosaic of inputs, including valuational and political, as well as technical components. (Sheldon and Parke 1975, 698)

Though indicators do not provide policy answers, they do provide policy fodder and are powerful political tools. Because national indicators are derived from large-scale survey data bases made up of information collected from very large numbers of school districts, schools, and classrooms, they are political because of their costs as well as their policy functions. At the same time, the governance structure of American education places states and their concerns between the data collectors and their data sources (Murnane 1987), adding to both the costs and the range of political concerns.

Consequently, the development of educational indicators has had a checkered history, with complaints about quality and concerns about political implications colliding with erratic congressional impulses to spend money for educational data collection. Nonetheless, since the launching of Sputnik and the civil rights movement propelled federal concerns about education in the 1950s and 1960s, large-scale federal education data-collection efforts have become institutionalized, even if their funding has grown only in fits and starts.

Currently collected educational data are the grist for indicators, but no full-blown system of educational indicators has yet been created. The U.S. Department of Education regularly publishes statistical information in its *Digest of Education Statistics* and *The Condition of Education* series, using data from large-scale survey efforts. In recent years, the latter series has attempted to perform a more comparative, evaluative function and has assumed the title *Educational Indicators*, but it yet lacks a systematic framework for suggesting how components of the system are linked to one another. Increasingly, though, educational data are being put to use as policy signals, and attention is turning to the development of curriculum indicators.

Two major federal initiatives in the 1960s were the precursors to much curriculum indicators work today. The Equality of Educational Opportunity Survey (EEOS) provided achievement test score information on 645,000 children in public schools along with rudimentary information about school-level resources. The first major analysis of these data, reported in what came to be known as the Coleman Report (Coleman and Campbell 1966), documented large inequalities in achievement between minority-group children and white children and between children from different socioeconomic groups and from different regions of the country. Though the analysis did not study detailed curriculum variables, it found a positive relationship between student achievement and "a curriculum that offers greater challenges, more laboratories, and more (cocurricular) activities." However, the report's finding that the strong relationships between students' background characteristics and achievement outcomes overwhelmed the schooling measures it did investigate produced the popularized version of its conclusions, that "schools don't make a difference."

Criticized on methodological and interpretive grounds, the Coleman report only stimulated more research on school factors that *do* make a difference. A classic "input-output" study reminiscent of those conducted during the scientific management era (though infinitely more elaborate), the Coleman Report fueled efforts to investigate school processes along with inputs in order to explain outcomes. As we discuss below, contemporary research using more sophisticated methods and richer school- and classroom-level data has opened up the "black box" of schooling to identify the different curricular experiences that seem to produce, or at least contribute to, disparities in achievement.

The second major initiative in the 1960s was the creation of the National Assessment of Educational Progress (NAEP), under the intellectual leadership of Ralph Tyler (who had earlier played a leading role in the evaluation of the Eight Year Study and a great many other seminal curricular development and measurement initiatives). Since 1969, the NAEP has provided periodic assessment of student performance in reading, mathematics, and science—and occasionally in writing, history, and other areas as well. As Murnane (1987) notes, the NAEP achievement trend data raised questions that the study was not designed to answer: Why, for example, did the achievement of black 9-year old students climb steadily and more quickly than that of white students throughout the 1970s? And why has 17-year-olds' performance seemed to decline for more than a decade in most subject areas, especially on tasks requiring critical thinking and problem-solving skills?

Though the data set could not support analyses of many curriculum questions of interest, that did not stop educators and policymakers from making curriculum-related claims to explain the findings and from acting on them (Tanner and Tanner 1980, 732–733). Over time, the samples of students' achievement test performance have been supplemented by more descriptive information about school organizational variables, staffing patterns and characteristics, and teachers' classroom practices.

The same kind of data base elaboration has occurred with the federal longitudinal surveys launched to examine the school and out-of-school experiences and outcomes for cohorts of students over time: the national longitudinal studies of the high school classes of 1972, 1980, and 1982 (these last two dubbed the High School and Beyond [HSB] studies). A new cohort of 8th and 11th graders to be followed for a number of years was launched in 1988 as part of the NELS (National Education Longitudinal Studies) project.

In addition to these federal data bases, several international assessments of student achievement have been conducted under the auspices of the International Association for the Evaluation of Educational Achievement (IEA). Assessments of mathematics achievement (McKnight et al. 1987) and science achievement (Raizen and Jones 1985) found curricular effects nearly equal to the influence of students' background characteristics (Wolf 1977). Earlier assessments of reading and literature achievement discovered more pronounced influences of home background, as might be expected in these subjects, but also a strong effect of schooling on students' cognitive styles as demonstrated in the study of literature (Purves 1975). The low ranking of the United States on the recent IEA assessments was one stimulus for a wide range of educational reform proposals (National Science Board 1983). It was also a stimulus for the creation of more indicators.

Partly in response to the concern that the IEA tests might have low curricular validity for U.S. schools (and hence suggest lower achievement for U.S. students than they should), the U.S. government persuaded a group of countries to take part in an international assessment of mathematics and science achievement using items from its own NAEP tests. The International Assessments of Educational Progress (IAEP), however, produced the same results, with U.S. students scoring very near the bottom on most measures (Educational Testing Service 1989). The release of these cross-national statistics has been an important motivator for the decade of school reform throughout the 1980s and for a resurgence of funding for mathematics and science education, including a new wave of curriculum development initiatives.

More important than the data on achievement outcomes are the strides made in these studies toward an understanding of curriculum "inputs" and "processes." The Second International Mathematics Study, for example, examined the type of mathematics taught in the 20 countries involved, in terms of both curricular content and methods. It found few relationships between achievement outcomes and such gross measures of curriculum access as time allocated to mathematics or class size but considerable links between outcomes and measures of curriculum *goals* (what students are expected to learn at different grade levels), curriculum *intensity* (the extent to which certain areas of study are emphasized), curricular *organization* (the ways in which topics and skills are structured and sequenced), and curriculum *differentiation* (the extent to which different expectations are applied to different groups of classes and students) (McKnight et al. 1987). The IAEP study confirmed cross-national differences in the extent to which students are exposed to different types of curricular content in science and mathematics (Educational Testing Service 1989).

Ongoing concerns over the status of mathematics and science instruction, triggered by these indicators and fueled by the more wide-ranging educational reform movement of the 1980s, have produced even greater efforts to construct systems of indicators that can be used to monitor inputs, processes, and outcomes at the state, national, and cross-national levels. The National Academy of Sciences convened a panel to explore what indicators of mathematics and science education should be used (Murnane and Raizen 1988). Meanwhile, the National Science Foundation has sponsored research to design a national monitoring system (Shavelson, McDonnell, and Oakes 1989; Shavelson, McDonnell, Oakes, and Carey 1987) and state-level systems (Council for Chief State School Officers 1989). Other initiatives are arising independently. For example, the international Organization for Economic Cooperation and Development (1987) has begun an effort to define indicators that can be used cross-nationally.

These efforts have begun to produce some consensus about the components of an indicator system. Relying still on industrial terminology, the reports construct models of inputs (e.g., fiscal and material resources, teacher quality, and student background) and relate them to processes (e.g., school factors, curriculum variables, and teaching variables) and outputs (e.g., achievement, participation, attitudes, and aspirations), with increasing concern for school and community contexts.

The objectives of these efforts are to construct data systems that will be used on a regular basis to assess educational conditions, monitor progress toward social goals (e.g., equity or greater participation in certain types of activities or courses), and provide aids to policy analysis and planning. At the same time, researchers look to these data bases as a means for exploring relationships among educational variables that may explain, or at least hint at, aspects of schooling, curriculum, and teaching that influence student learning.

Looking for School Effects. The advent of these rich data sets—in some cases replete with longitudinal information about students' tested achievement, high school course taking, school environments, family circumstances, vocational paths, and post-high school educational experiences—has provided opportunities to look more closely for "school effects" on students' accomplishments. In the national longitudinal studies, the schooling data include fairly gross measures of curriculum experiences, such as track placements, course titles, and students' perceptions of the kinds of schoolwork they've been asked to do. The NAEP and the IEA studies have sometimes included much more detailed accounts by teachers of the content and teaching methods they use in particular subjects.

The availability of these kinds of data have permitted broad-scale analyses of what kinds of students are afforded what types of curricular experiences, as well as analyses of whether curricular offerings and teaching strategies vary among schools of different types, across sectors (or even nations), and over time.

For example, assessment data from many sources show disparities between non-Asian minority students and white and Asian students in overall mathematics achievement. At the same time, analyses of data from the HSB surveys demonstrate dramatic differences among students of various racial and ethnic groups in mathematics course taking. These data also demonstrate that for students of all racial and ethnic groups, mathematics course taking is strongly related to achievement, so that for students with similar course-taking records, achievement test score differences by race or ethnicity virtually disappear. More recent research demonstrates that the availability of these key courses varies substantially among schools serving different racial and socioeconomic populations of students (Oakes in press). Thus, the "black box" that was the missing stuff of schooling in early input-output studies is opened.

Similarly, analyses of cross-national data show marked differences in course content and student course-taking patterns across countries, with U.S. students' low levels of achievement in mathematics, especially at the 12th-grade level, potentially explained by the fact that much smaller proportions of U.S. students tend to encounter certain kinds of content or take advanced-level courses (McKnight 1987). Researchers conducting these studies have coined the phrase "opportunity-to-learn" as a construct for investigating curricular access as suggested by the content to which students are exposed. This exposure may differ by virtue of school policies, controlling access to courses, or by teacher decisions, controlling access to certain kinds of knowledge or learning tasks.

These studies have also begun to investigate the ways in which curriculum content is conveyed. The IEA mathematics study obtained detailed information from teachers about their teaching strategies and activities, finding instruction dominated by textbooks with little use of other resources (such as computers, calculators, and manipulatives) and heavy use of "tell and show" approaches for U.S. teachers. The researchers concluded,

> This use of abstract representations and of strategies geared to rote learning, along with class time devoted to listening to teacher explanations followed by individual seatwork and routine exercises, strongly suggests a view that learning for most students should be passive—teachers transmit knowledge to students who receive it and remember it mostly in the form in which it was transmitted. . . . In the light of this, it is hardly surprising that the achievement test items on which U.S. students most often showed relatively greater growth were those most suited to performance of rote procedures. (McKnight et al. 1987, 81)

In the IAEP study, students were surveyed about their classroom activities, reporting the extent to which they spent time listening to the teacher lecture, doing independent seatwork, reading the text, performing or watching experiments, working in small groups, or working with another classmate (Educational Testing Service 1989). These indicators showed informative differences. In contrast to their peers in other countries, for example, U.S. students reported low levels of involvement in science experimentation and relatively little cooperative group work in mathematics.

Similar data collected in the U.S. longitudinal studies of the high school classes of 1972 and 1980 depict differences in teaching strategies across school sectors (public, parochial, and private independent schools) and over time. Such comparisons indicate substantial differences between private and public schools in the frequency with which high school students report being asked to engage in such activities as writing tasks and student-centered discussions (much more of both in private schools) and using teaching machines or computers (more in public schools). The data also show a decline in the use of certain teaching strategies between 1972 and 1980, depicting possible changes in instructional philosophies over time.

The large-scale survey data bases providing such tantalizing clues to school-related differences in student performance are beginning to yield to more powerful statistical methods that can examine the effects of classroom-level differences in instruction as well as school- or district-level differences in educational resources and policies. These include the use of such tools as hierarchical linear modeling (Raudenbush 1988; Raudenbush and Bryk 1986), which allows simultaneous explanation of within- and between-school variations in schooling conditions and outcomes.

Attempts to find school effects on achievement have frequently been frustrated by the difficulties associated with using single-level methods for analyzing multilevel data (Burstein and Miller 1981; Cronbach 1976). These include limitations due to aggregating individual and classroom-level data to the school level at which variation is obscured (or conversely, ignoring school-level effects of such variables as group socioeconomic status when individual measures are used), failure to take account of the interdependence of variables occurring at different levels, and inability of single-level methods to examine how school factors may operate differently across schools in producing student outcomes (Lee and Bryk 1988).

One strategy for finding school effects was developed by "effective schools" researchers, who started by identifying unusually effective schools, i.e., those that produced student outcomes substantially better than would be predicted on the basis of student background characteristics, and then examining their characteristics. Starting with statistical identification of outliers (Klitgaard and Hall 1973), effective schools research went on to study and categorize the observable characteristics of these schools, identifying such school organizational variables as academic press and the monitoring of student progress as key to heightened student outcomes (Brookover, Beady, Flood, Schweitzer, and Wisenbaker 1977; Edmonds 1979). Though most such studies have paid little attention to more specific curricular variables, continued work in this vein could do so.

A second, related strategy has been to pursue multilevel statistical analysis of survey data alongside case study analysis of school types that seem to produce different outcomes for low-income and minority students. Statistical studies that suggest a weaker relationship between student background and outcomes in Catholic than in public schools (Coleman, Hoffer, and Kilgore 1982; Hoffer, Greeley, and Coleman, 1985) have been supplemented by field research suggesting school organizational variables similar to those described in the "effective schools" literature that may produce this result (Bryk, Holland, Lee, and Carriedo 1984; Hill, Foster, and Gendler 1990). Further probing of the HSB data with hierarchical methods indicates that certain types of school conditions and practices, which are more prevalent in Catholic than public schools, are associated with higher and more equitably distributed achievement among students. These include higher levels of academic course taking among all students and fewer differences among their programs of study (Lee and Bryk 1988).

From a variety of angles, then, investigations of these large-scale data bases have begun to illuminate the nature and distribution of curricular opportunities available to students and to suggest how these may be associated with what students learn. At the same time, recent forays into the data have raised discontent with their ability to answer certain kinds of research and policy questions (Murnane 1987) and with the measures of curriculum and learning themselves.

Looking for Policy Answers. As this discussion intimates, the quest to understand how schools affect student learning is also a quest to figure out how to change schools so that they perform more effectively and more equitably. As data become available that hint at educational problems, the desire to make the data useful for solving those problems grows stronger. Where clear answers are not possible, both the studies and their data sources may be criticized.

> Improved indicators lead to new analyses that raise new questions and call into question the usefulness of the new indicators. But the new questions would not have been identified without the improved indicators. . . . What has happened . . . is that users of indicators have come to appreciate the importance of things not captured by existing indicators. In other words, sophistication leads to dissatisfaction, which leads to redefined goals. These evolving definitions of goals have created new demands for indicators. (Murnane 1987, 102)

Among the new demands for educational indicators is the desire for more detailed and fine-grained information about the nature of students' educational and out-of-school experiences to support research about "what matters" in the production of educational outcomes. Another desire is for survey collections to include the kind of information about school experiences that might support evaluations of specific programs or policies. Still another is for more intense sampling of students, classrooms, schools, and districts to support finer-grained comparisons among educational jurisdictions. All of these issues have been raised in recent public discussions about the future of the major National Center for Education Statistics data bases: NAEP, NELS, and the newly created SASS (Schools and Staffing Surveys) (Center for Education Statistics 1986; National Center for Education Statistics 1985).

All of these demands pose issues of costs and burdens on respondents' time and school resources. They raise many knotty questions: For example, at what point does information greed produce lower-quality data because demands on schools are overwhelming or because it provokes outright refusals on the part of schools and teachers to participate in data collections? But the demands pose more weighty scientific issues as well. As large-scale survey collections are pressed into greater duties, will the answers sought and inferences made exceed the capacity of the data to be honestly illuminating?

There are at least three sets of dangers. First, overzealous efforts to push data beyond their proper limits may yield wrong answers. For example, attempts to answer difficult questions about causal relationships (e.g., program effects) by using statistical methods to partial out information from large, cross-sectional data sets—a request often made by policymakers of the NAEP data—are inappropriate and likely to produce spurious findings (National Center for Education Statistics 1985). The attempt to draw inferences where none are truly supportable can have real-world effects beyond the besmirching of scientific canons. Programs, along with hypotheses, may rise or fall in the process.

Second, the mere publication of indicator data can change behavior in ways that invalidate the indicator. When such data are used in incentive systems, so that decisions and rewards or sanctions are based on the data, these effects are exacerbated. Haney and Madaus (1986) have documented the effects on curriculum and teaching of "high stakes" testing programs—those that base decisions about students or school programs on test results—in several countries. The tendency to "teach to the test" under such circumstances can invalidate the inferences that are made about test score meanings because the assumption that student performance on the items sampled on the test fairly represents the broader domain of curriculum goals has been violated.

The furor created by the Cannell report in 1987—which reported the statistically impossible finding that virtually all states claim average student achievement test scores above the national norm—caused a hard look at how indicators used as performance measures change behavior in ways that inflate scores on those measures (Koretz 1988). In addition to teaching to the test, these include encouraging poor students to be absent on test days, "helping" students take the test, and outright cheating.

The fact that policymakers intend to look at indicator data as a basis for making changes in policy occasions other kinds of behavioral responses. Oakes (1986) reports that state-level indicator systems have produced a variety of pressures for misreporting:

> In some states currently collecting indicator data about school processes, school administrators have been reported to encourage students to "exaggerate" their responses to particular questions about school experiences. In other areas, informal teacher-networks have spread the word among their colleagues to deflate their salary figures and inflate their teaching-load numbers on state data-collection instruments, reasoning that the resulting data might bring about more favorable policies in both areas. These pressures are likely to be proportionate to what can be lost or gained by indicators. (30)

These examples suggest responses that make it difficult for indicator interpreters to know what their statistics represent. A third danger is that the use of indicators may actually create perverse incentives, pushing school policies and practices in directions positively antithetical to those that many policymakers and educators might desire.

Some dysfunctional consequences have already been reported from efforts to use test scores for making decisions about student placements, teacher bonuses and careers, and even school funding. These include placing large numbers of low-scoring students in special education placements so that their scores won't "count" in school reports, excluding low-scoring students from admission to schools where transfers are requested and encouraging such students to drop out when they are old enough (or to stay away in the meanwhile), and reducing what is taught to both the content and the format of the test itself (Darling-Hammond and Wise 1985; Koretz 1988; Talmage and Rasher 1980).

Concerns about comparisons among schools, districts, or states are born of worries that inaccurate or unfair inferences will be made about the causes or meanings of differences in practices or outcomes and that these inferences will be used to support decisions that could be harmful to some students or schools. Such concerns prevented the use of NAEP scores to support comparisons among states when the assessment was first created, but with current enthusiasms for indicators running high, an experiment with state-level comparisons has recently been launched. Though endorsing the comparisons, the Council of Chief State School Officers (1988) has also given voice to its members' concerns:

> Some are worried that Federal, state, and local policymakers may misuse the data, making inappropriate inferences and drawing unwarranted cause and effect conclusions. Fears are expressed that the test will be very influential, and with that influence, foster a national curriculum. Still others fear that the compromises that might be made on objectives will result in an assessment that measures the least common denominator and discourages badly needed curriculum reform. (1)

Murnane (1987) speculates that behavioral responses to the new state-by-state NAEP comparisons may include efforts to exclude low-scoring children from the tested sample, focus instruction on the skills to be tested, and teach test-taking skills. He notes that the extent to which "teaching to the test" is problematic depends largely on judgments about the quality of the tests and what they measure.

The possibility that instruction will be driven by performance measures is one that has engendered increased concern in recent years, as knowledge about human learning and performance has suggested that currently used norm-referenced multiple-choice tests fail to measure higher-order cognitive skills and abilities well (Reznick 1987; Sternberg 1985). If such tests drive instruction, many fear that these kinds of skills and abilities are likely to be neglected (Haney and Madaus 1986; National Academy of Education 1987).

In fact, steady declines and low absolute levels in students' higher-order thinking and problem-solving abilities as measured by the NAEP tests in reading, writing, mathematics, and science have been attributed by NAEP officials and representatives of the National Councils of Teachers of English and Mathematics, among others, to the emphasis on basic skills testing and associated "fill-in-the-blanks teaching" in U.S. schools throughout the 1970s and 1980s (National Academy of Education 1979; National Research Council 1979; Office of Productivity, Technology and Innovation 1980). Their criticism, we note, is made possible by the availability of one set of indicators depicting trends that raise hypotheses about the uses and effects of another. Thus we see that as indicators become more widely used, their uses produce pressures to improve the quality of information they provide.

Looking for Better Measures. As survey research and test score data return to center stage as tools for both researchers and policymakers, concerns are being raised about the validity and utility of the measures used to produce indicators and about the uses to which the indicators are put. These concerns are closely related. It may always be true that in some sense statistics can "lie," but no one much cares if they are not being used in ways that affect people's lives. As educational indicators are used for a wider variety of purposes—e.g., decisions about student placement, promotion, and graduation; arbiters of teacher retention and, in some places, wages; triggers for district or state intervention in school affairs—issues of measurement come to the fore.

In arguing for new indicators of reading education, John Guthrie (1987) aptly described the political rationale for improved measurement:

> Reading assessments are being deployed by administrators to shape the curriculum. . . . Tests can be used to set standards and goals, which will influence the content of curricula. Because indicators are not merely passive statistics but are proactive agents of change, they must be selected carefully. . . . (1)

> Even though the search for reading indicators takes place in a policy context which requires measures that are manageable, it is critical to avoid radical oversimplification. The hazard of being simplistic is that Johnny's reading will be misunderstood, teachers will be mislead, parents will be outraged, and policymakers will be frustrated in their attempts to improve reading achievement. (5)

Guthrie argues for measures of reading achievement that "are grounded in research on metacognition and information processing" (21) and that extend beyond current measures of decoding and literal comprehension to include analytic, inferential, and research skills, along with indicators of active reading use. In addition, he argues for indicators of instructional processes that stress not only the quantity of instruction students receive but also the "quality," i.e., "research-based features of exemplary teaching programs" (18). These include attention to the teaching of cognitive processes, instructional strategies for reflective reading, inferencing, use of students' background knowledge, and so on.

Researchers in other fields make similar urgings for substantial changes in assessment goals and methods. In evaluating the achievement data needed to construct an indicator system for mathematics and science education, Shavelson, McDonnell, and Oakes (1989) claim that NAEP

> shares certain weaknesses with other tests. . . . The tests generally fail to meet the criteria of cognitive fidelity [ability to assess stu-

dents' knowledge and conceptual understanding], process relevance [ability to assess students' application of concepts and skills], and curricular relevance [ability to measure the content students have been taught]. (157)

Shavelson, McDonnell, and Oakes argue for tasks that demand more realistic problem-solving skills, using assessment techniques such as clinical interviews (Piaget and Inhelder 1964) and stimulated recall (Shulman and Elstein 1975) as well as demonstrations of abilities to construct experiments and find solutions. Similarly, Romberg (1987) argues for new indicators of mathematics achievement that rely on contemporary understanding of cognition and that bring "school mathematics" more in line with the field of mathematics as a discipline.

A wide variety of other measurement issues concern the validity of inferences that will be drawn from measures ranging from coursework counts to curriculum coverage measures. These include construct validation concerns, data quality, aggregation questions, and a host of other features of data collection and statistical manipulation (Guiton and Burstein 1987; Shavelson, McDonnell, and Oakes 1989).

Interrelationships among variables in an indicator system affect the inferences drawn from changes in the measures used to approximate a construct; so do context changes, which affect the meanings of measures. Guiton and Burstein (1987) provide a useful example of how reforms aimed at increased course requirements for graduation may actually result in watered-down course content or an increase in the dropout rate, thus making indicators difficult to interpret:

In the first instance, the indicator (number of academic courses) would suggest positive effects due to reform efforts, but achievement scores would not improve (leaving us to question the relationship between coverage and achievement). In the second instance . . . improved achievement scores would support the perceived relation between coverage and achievement, but the concomitant reduced student participation would lead to ambiguous interpretations of the indicator (i.e. Is an increase in the number of courses taken good or bad?). (13)

Finally, the measurement questions come down to educational goals and social values. What is it that we want to encourage? And how can our systems of observation and enumeration help us to steer a course toward those ends?

Conclusions

The scientific tradition of inquiry has, over more than a century, given us the capacity to understand learning in more sophisticated and powerful ways and the ability to study curriculum and teaching with greater scope as well as insight. The fruits of this research have shown a potential for informing policy as well as practice. It is this potential that has stirred the debates over method and meaning that have grown more heated in the last decade. These debates symbolize the greater social issues raised by science and power: Who defines what knowledge is worth having? And how will the knowledge be used?

As the sources of a science of education (Dewey 1929) have been uncovered and explored, it has become increasingly clear that their effective use as guides for curriculum and teaching relies on their ability to inform the complex decisions of school practitioners rather than to prescribe from the perch of laboratory or statehouse what those decisions should be. As Bertrand Russell (1958) suggested, it is in pursuit of scientific "temper" (a concern for the process of inquiry and knowledge gathering) rather than technique (the production of unvarying "truths") that a scientific basis for the art of teaching (Gage 1978) and for the development of curriculum is likely to be found.

References

Aikin, Wilford. 1942. *Adventure in American Education. Vol 1: Story of the Eight Year Study*. New York: Harper & Brothers.

Anderson, Carolyn S. 1982. The search for school climate: A review of the research. *Review of Educational Research* 52(3): 368–420.

Anderson, John R. 1976. *Language, Memory and Thought*. Hillsdale, NJ: Erlbaum.

Anderson, John R., and Gordon H. Bower. 1973. *Human Associative Memory*. New York: Wiley.

Anderson, Linda, Carolyn Evertson, and Jere E. Brophy. 1979. An experimental study of effective teaching in first-grade reading groups. *Elementary School Journal* 79(4): 193–223.

Anderson, Richard. 1984. "Role of the Reader's Schema in Comprehension, Learning, and Memory." In *Learning to Read in American Schools: Basal Readers and Content Texts*, edited by Richard Anderson, J. Osborn, and R. Tierney, 243–257. Hillsdale, NJ: Erlbaum.

Ausubel, David P. 1963. *The Psychology of Meaningful Verbal Learning: An Introduction to School Learning*. New York: Grune & Stratton.

Ausubel, David P. 1968. *Educational Psychology: A Cognitive View*. New York: Holt, Rinehart and Winston.

Ausubel, David P., and Floyd G. Robinson. 1969. *School Learning: An Introduction to Educational Psychology*. New York: Holt, Rinehart and Winston.

Baldwin, James M. 1975. *Thought and Things: A Study of the Development and Meaning of Thought on Genetic Logic*. New York: Arno Press.

Bandura, Alfred. 1977. *Social Learning Theory*. Englewood Cliffs, NJ: Prentice Hall.

Banks, James A., and Cherry A. McGee Banks. 1989. *Multicultural Education: Issues and Perspectives*. Boston: Allyn & Bacon.

Bartlett, Sir Frederic C. 1932. *Remembering*. Cambridge: Cambridge University Press.

Ben-Peretz, Miriam R., R. Bromme, and R. Halkes, eds. 1986. *Advances of Research on Teacher Thinking*. Lisse: Swets and Zeitlinger.

Berliner, David C. 1979. "Tempus Educare." In *Research on Teaching: Concepts, Findings, & Implications*, edited by Penelope Peterson and Herbert Walberg, 120–135. Berkeley, CA: McCutchan.

Berliner, David C. 1987. In pursuit of the expert pedagogue. *Educational Researchers* 15(7): 5–13.

Bloom, Benjamin S., Max Englehart, Edward Furst, Walker Hill, and David Krathwol. 1956. *Taxonomy of Educational Objectives: The Classification of Educational Goals. Handbook I: Cognitive Domain*. New York: Longmans Green.

Bobbitt, Franklin. 1913. "The Supervision of City Schools: Some General Principles of Management Applied to the Problem of City-School Systems." In *The Twelfth Yearbook of the National Society of the Study of Education*, Part I, edited by Franklin Bobbitt, J. W. Hall, and J. D. Wolcott. Bloomington, IN: NSSE.

Bolinger, Dwight L. M. 1980. *Language—The Loaded Weapon*. White Plains, NY: Longman.

Braden, Albert C. 1967. Study of success in college physics. *Science Education* 51: 461–463.

Bromage, Bruce, and Richard Mayer. 1981. Relationship between what is remembered and creative problem-solving performance in science learning. *Journal of Educational Psychology* 73(4): 451–461.

Brookover, Wilbur B., Charles Beady, Patricia Flood, John Schweitzer, and Joe Wisenbaker. 1977. *Schools Can Make a Difference*. East Lansing: Michigan State University, Center for Urban Affairs.

Brophy, Jere E., and Carolyn Evertson. 1974. *Process-Product Correlations in the Texas Teacher Effectiveness Study: Final Report*. Austin, TX: Research and Development Center for Teacher Education.

Brophy, Jere E., and Carolyn Evertson. 1976. *Learning From Teaching: A Developmental Perspective*. Boston: Allyn & Bacon.

Brophy, Jere E., and Carolyn M. Evertson. 1977. "Teacher Behavior and Student Learning in Second and Third Grades." In *The Appraisal of Teaching: Concepts and Process*, edited by G. D. Borich, 79–95. Reading, MA: Addison-Wesley.

Brown, A. 1980. "Metacognitive Development and Reading." In *Theoretical Issues in Reading Comprehension*, edited by Rand Spiro, Bertram Bruce, and William F. Brewer. Hillsdale, NJ: Erlbaum.

Brown, Ann. 1985. "The Importance of Diagnosis in Cognitive Skill Instruction." In *Thinking and Learning Skills: Research and Open Questions*, vol. 2, edited by Susan Chipman, Judith Segal, and Robert Glaser. Hillsdale, NJ: Erlbaum.

Brown, John S., A. Collins, and P. Duguid. 1989. Situated cognition and the culture of learning. *Educational Researcher* 18(1): 32–42.

Bruner, Jerome. 1963. *The Process of Education*. New York: Vintage Books.

Bruner, Jerome. 1966. *Toward a Theory of Instruction*. New York: Norton.

Bryk, Anthony S., P. B. Holland, V. E. Lee, and R. A. Carriedo. 1984. *Effective Catholic Schools: An Exploration*. Washington, DC: National Catholic Education Association.

Burstein, Lee, and M. David Miller. 1981. "Regression-Based Analyses of Multilevel Educational Data." In *Reanalyzing Program Evaluations*, edited by Robert F. Boruch, P. M. Wortman, and D. S. Cordray. San Francisco, CA: Jossey-Bass.

Bush, Robert N. 1979. Implications of the BTES. *The Generator* 9(1): 13–15.

Calfee, Robert. 1981. "Cognitive Psychology and Educational Practice." In *Review of Research in Education*, vol. 9, edited by David C. Berliner, 3–74. Washington, DC: American Educational Research Association.

Callahan, Raymond E. 1962. *Education and the Cult of Efficiency*. Chicago: University of Chicago Press.

Carlson, Richard O. 1965. *Adoption of Educational Innovations*. Eugene: Center for Advanced Study of Educational Administration, University of Oregon.

Case, Robbie. 1975. Gearing the demands of instruction to the developmental capacities of the learner. *Review of Educational Research* 45(1): 59–87.

Center for Education Statistics. 1986. *The National Assessment of Educational Progress and the Longitudinal Studies Program: Together or Apart? Report of a Planning Conference, December 11, 1986*. Washington, DC: Office of Educational Research and Improvement, U.S. Department of Education.

Centra, John A., and David A. Potter. 1980. School and teacher effects: An interrelational model. *Review of Educational Research* 50(2): 273–291.

Chamberlin, Dean, Enid Chamberlin, Ned Drought, and William Scott. 1942. *Adventure in American Education, Vol. 4: Did They Succeed in College?* New York: Harper & Brothers.

Chi, Michelene, Paul J. Feltovich, and Robert Glaser. 1981. Categorization and representation of physics problems by experts and novices. *Cognitive Science* 5:121–152.

Chi, Michelene, Robert Glaser, and M. Farr, eds. 1988. *The Nature of Expertise*. Hillsdale, NJ: Erlbaum.

Chi, Michelene, Robert Glaser, and E. Rees. 1982. "Expertise in Problem Solving." In *Advances in the Psychology of Human Intelligence*, vol. 1, edited by Robert J. Sternberg, 7–75. Hillsdale, NJ: Erlbaum.

Clancey, William J. 1987. *The Knowledge Engineer as Student. Word Bases for Asking Good Questions*. Technical Report STAN-CS-87-1183. Palo Alto, CA: Department of Computer Science, Stanford University.

Claparede, Edouard. 1975. *Experimental Pedagogy and the Psychology of the Child*, translated by M. Louch and H. Holman. New York: Arno Press.

Clark, Christopher, and Penelope Peterson. 1986. "Teachers' Thought Processes." In *Handbook of Research on Teaching*, 3rd ed., edited by Merlin C. Wittrock, 255–296. New York: Macmillan.

Clark, Christopher, and R. Yinger. 1977. Research on teacher thinking. *Curriculum Inquiry* 7(4): 279–394.

Cohen, K. 1969. "The Effects of Two Simulation Games on the Opinions and Attitudes of Selected Sixth, Seventh, and Eighth Grade Students." Document ED 031 766. Washington, DC: Educational Resources Information Center.

Cohen, Robert B., and Robert H. Bradley. 1978. Simulation games, learning, and retention. *Elementary School Journal* 78(4): 247–253.

Coker, Homer, Donald M. Medley, and Robert Soar. 1980. How valid are expert opinions about effective teaching? *Phi Delta Kappan* 62(2): 131–134, 149.

Coleman, James S., and Ernest Campbell. 1966. *Equality of Educational Opportunity*. Washington, DC: U.S. Government Printing Office.

Coleman, James S., Thomas Hoffer, and Sally Kilgore. 1982. *High School Achievement: Public, Catholic and Private Schools Compared*. New York: Basic Books.

Coleman, James S., Samuel Livingston, Gail Fennessey, Keith Edwards, and Steven Kidder. 1973. The Hopkins games program: Conclusions from seven years of research. *Educational Researcher* 2(8): 3–7.

Cooper, Charles, and Lee Odell. 1977. *Evaluating Writing: Describing, Measuring, Judging*. Buffalo: State University of New York.

Corbett, Edward. 1971. *Classical Rhetoric for the Modern Student*. New York: Oxford University Press.

Corno, Lyn, and M. Rohrkemper. 1985. "Self-regulated Learning." In *Research on Motivation in Education*, vol. 2, edited by Russel Ames and Carole Ames. Orlando, FL: Academic Press.

Council of Chief State School Officers. 1988, March. *On Reporting Student Achievement at the State Level by the National Assessment of Educational Progress*. Washington, DC: CCSSO.

Council of Chief State School Officers. 1989. *State-by-State Indicators of Science and Mathematics Education: Preliminary Report*. Washington, DC: CCSSO State Education Assessment Center.

Cremin, Lawrence A. 1961. *The Transformation of the School: Progressivism in American Education, 1876–1957*. New York: Vintage Books.

Cremin, Lawrence A. 1965. *The Genius of American Education*. New York: Vintage Books.

Cronbach, Lee J. 1975. Beyond the two disciplines of scientific psychology. *American Psychologist* 30(2): 116–127.

Cronbach, Lee J. 1976. *Research on Classrooms and Schools: Formulations of Questions, Design, and Anaylsis*. Palo Alto, CA: Stanford Evaluation Consortium.

Cronbach, Lee J., and Richard E. Snow. 1977. *Aptitudes and Instructional Methods: A Handbook for Research on Interactions*. New York: Irvington.

Cubberly, Ellwood P. 1947 [1919]. *Public Education in the United States: A Study and Interpretation of American Educational History*. Boston: Houghton Mifflin.

Curtis, Mary E., and Robert Glaser. 1981. "Changing Conceptions of Intelligence." In *Review of Research in Education*, vol. 9, edited by David C. Berliner, 111–150. Washington, DC: American Educational Research Association.

Darling-Hammond, Linda, and Arthur E. Wise. 1985. Beyond standardization: State standards and school improvement. *The Elementary School Journal* 85(3): 315–336.

Darling-Hammond, Linda, and Arthur E. Wise. 1985. Beyond standardization: State standards and school improvement. *The Elementary School Journal* 85(3): 315–336.

Darling-Hammond, Linda, Arthur E. Wise, and Sara R. Pease. 1983. Teacher evaluation in the organizational context: A review of the literature. *Review of Educational Research* 53(3): 285–328.

Davis, Robert. 1984. *Learning Mathematics: A Cognitive Science Approach to Mathematics Education*. London: Croom Helm.

Deans, Edwina. 1963. *Elementary School Mathematics: New Directions*. Washington, DC: U.S. Department of Health, Education, and Welfare.

De Neufville, J. I. 1975. *Social Indicators and Public Policy: Interactive Processess of Design and Application*. New York: Elsevier.

Dewey, John. 1900. *The School and Society*. Chicago: University of Chicago Press.

Dewey, John. 1929. *The Sources of a Science of Education*. New York: Horace Liveright.

Donaldson, Margaret. 1978. *Children's Minds*. New York: Norton.

Doyle, Walter. 1978. "Paradigms for Research on Teacher Effectiveness." In *Review of Research in Education*, vol. 5, edited by Lee S. Shulman, 163–198. Itasca, IL: Peacock.

Doyle, Walter. 1979. "Classroom Tasks and Students' Abilities." In *Research on Teaching*, edited by Penelope L. Peterson and Herbert J. Walberg, 183–205. Berkeley, CA: McCutchan.

Dunkin, Michael J., and Bruce Biddle. 1974. *The Study of Teaching*. New York: Holt, Rinehart and Winston.

Ebbinghaus, Herman. 1964 [1885]. *Memory*, translated by H. Ruger and C. Bussenius. New York: Dover.

Eccles, John. 1964. *The Physiology of Synapses*. New York: Academic Press.

Edmonds, Ronald. 1979. Effective schools for the urban poor. *Educational Leadership* 37(1): 15–24.

Educational Testing Service. 1989. *A World of Differences: An International Assessment of Mathematics and Science*. Princeton, NJ: ETS.

Egan, Kieran. 1978. What is curriculum? *Curriculum Inquiry* 8(1): 71.

Eisner, Elliot W., and Elizabeth Vallance, eds. 1974. *Conflicting Conceptions of Curriculum*. Berkeley, CA: McCutchan.

Ennis, Robert. 1989. Critical thinking and subject specificity: Clarification and needed research. *Educational Researcher* 18(3): 4–10.

Erickson, Eric. 1963. *Childhood and Society*, rev. ed. New York: Norton.

Ericsson, K. Anders, and J. Staszewski. 1988. "Skilled Memory and Expertise: Mechanisms of Exceptional Performance." In *Complex Information Processing: The Impact of Herbert A. Simon*, edited by David Klahr and K. Kotovsky. Hillsdale, NJ: Erlbaum.

Erlwanger, Stanley. 1975. Case studies of children's conceptions of mathematics, part I. *Journal of Children's Mathematical Behavior* 1(2): 157–283.

Evertson, Carolyn M., and Jere E. Brophy. 1973. *High-Inference Behavioral Ratings as Correlates of Teaching Effectiveness*. Austin: Research and Development Center for Teacher Education, University of Texas.

Ewert, O. M., and Braun, M. 1978. Ergebnnisse und Probleme vorschulischer Foerderung. In *Struktu foerderung im Bildungswesen des Landes Nordrhein-Westfalen. Eine Schriften-reihe des Kultusministers, vol. 34: Modellversuch Vorklasse in NW-Abschlussbericht*. Koeln: Greven.

Fenstermacher, Gary D. 1978. "A Philosophical Consideration of Recent Research on Teacher Effectiveness." In *Review of Research in Education*, vol. 6, edited by Lee S. Shulman. Itasca, IL: Peacock.

Finlay, Gilbert C. 1962, spring. The Physical Science Study Committee, *School Review* 70.

Fischer, Hardi. 1964, June. The psychology of Piaget and its educational implications. *International Review of Education*: 431.

Flanders, Ned. 1965. *Interaction Analysis in the Classroom: A Manual for Observers*. Ann Arbor: University of Michigan Press.

Floden, Robert. 1981. "The Logic of Information-processing Psychology in Education." In *Review of Research in Education*, vol. 9, edited by David Berliner, 75–110. Washington, DC: American Educational Research Association.

Ford Foundation. 1972. *A Foundation Goes to School*. New York: Ford Foundation.

Frost, Joel, and Thomas G. Rowland. 1969. *Curricula for the Seventies: Early Childhood through Early Adolescence*. Boston: Houghton Mifflin.

Fuson, Karen. 1982. "An Analysis of the Counting-on Solution Procedure in Addition." In *Addition and Subtraction: A Cognitive Perspective*, edited by Thomas P. Carpenter, James Moser, and Thomas A. Romberg, 67–83. Hillsdale, NJ: Erlbaum.

Gage, Nathaniel L. 1978. *The Scientific Basis of the Art of Teaching*. New York: Teachers College Press.

Gage, Nathaniel L. 1985. *Hard Gains in the Soft Sciences: The Case of Pedagogy*. Bloomington, IN: Phi Delta Kappa.

Gage, Nathaniel L. 1989. The paradigm wars and their aftermath: A historical sketch on research on teaching since 1989. *Teachers College Record* 91(2): 135–150.

Gage, Nathaniel L., and Margaret C. Needels. 1989. Process-product research on teaching: A review of criticisms. *The Elementary School Journal* 89(3): 253–300.

Gagné, Robert. 1977. *The Conditions of Learning*, 3rd ed. New York: Holt, Rinehart and Winston.

Gagné, Robert, and L. Briggs. 1979. *Principles of Instructional Design*, 2nd ed. New York: Holt, Rinehart and Winston.

Galambos, R. 1961. A Glia-neural theory of brain function. *Proceedings of the National Academy of Sciences* 47: 129–136.

Gallagher, James J. 1967, January. Teacher variation in concept presentation. *BSCS Newsletter* (30).

Gardner, Howard. 1983. *Frames of Mind: The Theory of Multiple Intelligences*. New York: Basic Books.

Gardner, Howard, and Thomas Hatch. 1989. Multiple intelligences go to school: Educational implications of the theory of multiple intelligences. *Educational Researcher* 18(8): 4–10.

Genishi, Celia, and A. Dyson. 1984. *Language Assessment in the Early Years*. Norwood, NJ: Ablex.

Gesell, Arnold, and H. Thompson. 1929. Learning and growth in identical infant twins. *Genetic Psychology Monographs* 6: 1–24

Gessell, Arnold Lucius. 1940. *The First Five Years of Life: A Guide to the Study of the Preschool Child from the Yale Clinic of Child Development*. New York: Harper & Brothers.

Giles, H., S. McCutchen, and A. Zechiel. 1942. *Adventure in American Education, Vol. 2: Exploring the Curriculum*. New York: Harper & Brothers.

Ginsburg, Herbert, and Sylvia Opper. 1979. *Piaget's Theory of Intellectual Development*, 2nd ed. Englewood Cliffs, NJ: Prentice Hall.

Glaser, Robert. 1988. Cognitive science and education. *International Social Science Journal* 40(1): 21–44.

Glaser, Robert, and M. Bassok. 1988. *Learning Theory and the Study of Instruction*. Pittsburgh: Learning Research and Development Center.

Glass, Gene V., D. Coulter, S. Hartley, S. Hearold, S. Kahl, J. Kalk, L. Sherretz. 1977. *Teacher "Indirectness" and Pupil Achievement: An Integration of Findings*. Boulder: Laboratory of Educational Research, University of Colorado.

Goldstein, Ira, and S. Papert. 1977. Artificial intelligence, language, and the study of knowledge. *Cognitive Science* 1: 84–123.

Good, Thomas S., and Jere E. Brophy. 1986. *Educational Psychology*, 3rd ed. White Plains, NY: Longman.

Good, Thomas S., and Douglas A. Grouws. 1979. The Missouri mathematics effectiveness project: An experimental study in fourth-grade classrooms. *Journal of Educational Psychology* 71 (3): 355–362.

Good, Thomas S., and Colin N. Power. 1976. Designing successful classroom environment for different types of students. *Journal of Curriculum Studies* 8(1): 1–6

Goodman, Kenneth. n.d. *Language and Literacy: The Selected Writings of Kenneth S. Goodman*, vols. 1 and 2, edited by Frederick Gollasch. London: Routledge & Kegan Paul.

Goodman, Yetta, Myna Haussler, and Dorothy Strickland, eds. 1982. *Oral and Written Language Development Research: Impact on the Schools*. Urbana, IL: National Council of Teachers of English.

Grobman, Hilda. 1968. *Evaluation Activities of Curriculum Projects*. Chicago: Rand McNally.

Groos, Karl. 1976. *The Play of Man*. New York: Arno Press.

Guiton, Gretchen, and Leigh Burstein. 1987. "Steps in Construct Validation Within a Conceptual Framework for the Educational System." Los Angeles: Center for Research Evaluation, Standards and Student Testing, University of California at Los Angeles.

Guthrie, John T. 1987. *Indicators of Reading Education*. New Brunswick, NJ: Center for Policy and Research in Education, Eagleton Institute of Politics, Rutgers University.

Haller, Eileen, David A. Child, and Herbert J. Walberg. 1988. Can comprehension be taught? A quantitative synthesis of word studies. *Educational Researcher* 17(9): 5–8.

Halliday, Michael A. K. 1975. *Learning How to Mean*. New York: Elsevier.

Haney, Walt, and George Madaus. 1986. "Effects of Standardized Testing and the Future of the National Assessment of Educational Progress." Working paper for the NAEP study group. Chestnut Hill, MA: Center for the Study of Testing, Evaluation and Educational Policy.

Hebb, Donald O. 1949. *Organization of Behavior*. New York: Wiley.

Hill, Paul T., Gail E. Foster, and Tamar Gendler. 1990. *High Schools with Character: Alternatives to Bureaucracy*. Santa Monica, CA: Rand.

Hirst, Paul H. 1974. "Liberal Education and the Nature of Knowledge." In *Knowledge and the Curriculum. A Collection of Philosophical Papers*, edited by Paul H. Hirst. London: Routledge & Kegan Paul.

Hoffer, Thomas, Andrew M. Greeley, and James S. Coleman. 1985. Achievement growth in public and Catholic schools. *Sociology of Education* 58(2). 74–97.

Holland, James G. 1960. Teaching machines: An application of principles from the laboratory. *Journal of the Experimental Analysis of Behavior* 3: 275–287.

Hooper, Frank H., and John DeFrain. 1980. On delineating distinctly Piagetian contributions to education. *Genetic Psychology Monographs* 101:151–181.

Horak, Virginia M. 1981. A meta-analysis of research findings on individualized instruction in mathematics. *Journal of Educational Research* 74(4): 249–253.

Horwitz, Robert. A. 1979. "Effects of the 'Open Classroom.'" In *Educational Environments and Effects: Evaluation, Policy and Productivity*, edited by Herbert J. Walberg. Berkeley, CA: McCutchan.

Huff, Roland, and C. Kline. 1987. *The Contemporary Writing Curriculum: Rehearsing, Composing, and Valuing*. New York: Teachers College Press.

Inhelder, Bärbel, Hermine Sinclair, and Magili Bovet. 1974. *Learning and the Development of Cognition*. Cambridge, MA: Harvard University Press.

Isaacs, Susan. 1930. *Intellectual Growth in Young Children*. London: Routledge & Sons.

Ives, William. 1980. Preschool children's ability to coordinate spatial perspectives through language and pictures. *Child Development* 51(4): 1303–1306.

Jackson, Philip. 1968. *Life in Classrooms*. New York: Holt, Rinehart and Winston.

Jaeger, Richard M. 1978. "About Educational Indicators: Statistics on the Conditions and Trends in Education." In *Review of Research in Education*, vol. 6, edited by Lee S. Shulman, 276–315. Washington, DC: American Educational Research Association.

Joyce, Bruce, and Marsha Weil. 1980. *Models of Teaching*, 2nd ed. Englewood Cliffs, NJ: Prentice Hall.

Kagan, Jerome, and Nathan Kogan. 1970. "Individual Variation in

Cognitive Processes." In *Carmichael's Manual of Child Psychology*, vol. 1, 3rd ed., edited by Paul H. Mussen. New York: Wiley.

Kamii, Constance, and Georgia DeClark. 1985. *Young Children Reinvent Arithmetic*. New York: Teachers College Press.

Kamin, Leon J. 1974. *The Science and Politics of IQ*. New York: Wiley.

Kliebard, Herbert. 1982. Education at the turn of the century: A crucible for curriculum change. *Educational Researcher* 11(1): 16–24.

Klitgaard, Robert E., and George R. Hall. 1973. *A Statistical Search for Unusually Effective Schools: Prepared for the Carnegie Corporation of New York*. Santa Monica, CA.: Rand.

Kohlberg, Lawrence. 1981. *The Philosophy of Moral Development*. San Francisco: Harper & Row.

Kohler, Wolfgang. 1959. *The Mentality of Apes*. New York: Vintage Books.

Koretz, Daniel. 1988. Arriving in Lake Wobegon: Are standardized tests exaggerating achievement and distorting instruction? *American Educator* 12(2): 8–15, 46–52.

Kuhn, Deanna. 1974. Inducing development experimentally: Comments on a research paradigm. *Developmental Psychology* 10: 590–600.

Larkin, Jill, J. McDermott, D. Simon, and H. Simon. 1980. Expert and novice performance in solving physics problems. *Science* 208: 1335–1342.

Lashly, Karl S. 1950. In search of the engram. *Symposia of the Society for Experimental Biology* 4: 454–482.

Lave, Jean. 1988. *Cognition in Practice*. Cambridge: Cambridge University Press.

Lee, Patrick. 1989. Is the young child egocentric or sociocentric? *Teachers College Record* 90(3): 375–391.

Lee, Valerie E., and Anthony S. Bryk. 1988. Curriculum tracking as mediating the social distribution of high school achievement. *Sociology of Education* 61(2): 78–94.

Leinhardt, Gaea, and James Greeno. 1985. *The Cognitive Skill of Teaching*. Pittsburgh: University of Pittsburgh.

Leinhardt, Gaea, C. Weidman, and K. Hammond. 1984. "Introduction and Integration of Classroom Routines by Expert Teachers." Paper presented at the annual meeting, American Educational Research Association, New Orleans.

Lennenberg, Eric H. 1967. *Biological Foundations of Languages*. New York: Wiley.

Levin, Henry M. 1979. *Educational Vouchers and Social Policy*. Palo Alto, CA: Institute for Research on Educational Finance and Governance.

Livermore, Arthur H., and Frederick L. Ferris, Jr. 1962, December 7. The chemical bond approach course in the classroom. *Science*: 318.

Locke, John. 1947 [1690]. *An Essay Concerning Human Understanding*. London: Dent.

Lowyck, Joost. 1986. "Post-Interactive Reflections of Teachers: A Critical Appraisal." In *Advances of Research on Teacher Thinking*, edited by Miriam Ben-Peretz, Rainer Bromme, and R. Halkes, 172–185. Lisse, Switzerland: Swets and Zeitlinger.

McDonald, F. J., and P. Elias. 1976. *Executive Summary Report: Beginning Teacher Evaluation Study, Phase II*. Princeton, NJ: Educational Testing Service.

McDonald, Joseph P. 1988. The emergence of the teacher's voice: Implications for the new reform. *Teachers College Record* 89(4): 471–486.

McKeachie, William J., and J. A. Kulik. 1975. "Effective College Teaching." In *Review of Research in Education*, vol. 3, edited by F. N. Kerlinger, 165–209. Itasca, IL: Peacock.

McKenna, Bernard H. 1981. "Context/Environment Effects in Teacher Evaluation." In *Handbook on Teacher Evaluation*, edited by Jason Millman. Beverley Hills, CA: Sage.

McKnight, Curtis C., F. J. Crosswhite, J. A. Dossey, E. Kifer, S. O. Swafford, K. J. Travers, and T. J. Cooney. 1987. *The Underachieving Curriculum: Assessing U.S. School Mathematics from an International Perspective*. Champaign, IL: Stipes Publishing.

McNemar, Quinn. 1964. Lost: Our intelligence? Why? *American Psychologist* 19: 871–882.

Martin, Lyn S., and Barbara N. Pavan. 1976. Current research on open-space, non-grading, vertical grouping, and team teaching. *Phi Delta Kappan* 57(5): 310–315.

Mayer, Richard. 1982. "Learning." In *Encyclopedia of Educational Research*, vol. II, 5th ed., edited by Harold E. Mitzel. New York: Free Press.

Mayer, Richard E. 1979. Can advance organizers influence meaningful learning? *Review of Educational Research* 49(2): 371–383.

Mayer, Richard E. 1984. Aids to text comprehension. *Educational Psychologist* 19: 30–42.

Mayer, William V. 1971, February. The impact of BSCS Biology on college curricula. *BSCS Newsletter* 42.

Medley, Donald M. 1977. *Teacher Competence and Teacher Effectiveness*. Washington, DC: American Assocation of Colleges for Teacher Education.

Meichenbaum, Donald H. 1977. *Cognitive-Behavior Modification*. New York: Plenum.

Meichenbaum, Donald H., and J. Goodman. 1971. Training impulsive children to talk to themselves: A means of developing self-control. *Journal of Abnormal Psychology* 77: 115–126.

Moffett, James, and Betty J. Wagner. 1976. *Student Centered Language Arts and Reading K–13*. Boston: Houghton Mifflin.

Murnane, Richard. 1987. Improving education indicators and economic indicators: The same problems? *Educational Evaluation and Policy Analysis* 9(2): 101–116.

Murnane, Richard, and Senta Raizen. 1988. *Improving Indicators of the Quality of Science and Mathematics: Grades K–12*. Washington, DC: Conference Board on the Mathematical Sciences.

Mussen, Paul H., ed. 1970. *Carmichael's Manual of Child Psychology*. New York: Wiley.

National Academy of Education. 1987. *The Nation's Report Card*. Cambridge, MA: NAE.

National Assessment of Educational Progress. 1979. *Changes in Mathematical Achievement, 1973–78*. Denver: NAEP.

National Center for Education Statistics. 1985. *Synthesis of Invited Papers: Elementary/Secondary Education Data Redesign Project*. A public discussion draft edited by Leslie J. Silverman and Richard C. Taeuber. Washington, DC: NCES.

National Education Association. 1918. *Report of the Commission on the Reorganization of Secondary Education*. Washington, DC: U.S. Government Printing Office.

National Research Council. 1979. *The State of School Science*. Washington, DC: Commission on Human Resources.

National Science Board Commission on Precollege Education in Mathematics, Science and Technology. 1983. *Educating Americans for the 21st Century: Source Materials*. Washington, DC: National Science Foundation.

Newell, Allen, and Herbert A. Simon. 1972. *Human Problem Solving*. Englewood Cliffs, NJ: Prentice Hall.

Oakes, Jeannie. 1985. *Keeping Track: How Schools Structure Inequality*. New Haven, CT: Yale University Press.

Oakes, Jeannie. 1986. *Educational Indicators: A Guide for Policymakers*. Santa Monica, CA: Rand.

Oakes, Jeannie. In press. *Multiplying Inequalities*. Santa Monica, CA: Rand.

Office of Productivity, Technology, and Innovation. 1980. *Learning*

Environments for Innovation. Washington, DC: Department of Commerce.

Organization for Economic Cooperation and Development. 1987. *International Conference on Educational Indicators: Conclusions and Follow-up*. Paris: OECD Education Committee.

Palincsar, Annemarie, and Ann Brown. 1984. Reciprocal teaching of comprehension-fostering and comprehension-monitoring activities. *Cognition and Instruction* 1(2): 117–175.

Perkins, David, and Gavriel Salomon. 1989. Are cognitive skills context bound? *Educational Researcher* 18(1): 16–25.

Peterson, K., and D. Kauchak. 1982. *Teacher Evaluation: Perspectives, Practices and Promises*. Salt Lake City: Center for Educational Practice, University of Utah.

Peterson, Penelope. 1979. "Direct Instruction Reconsidered." In *Research on Teaching: Concepts, Findings and Implications*, edited by Penelope Peterson and Herbert Walberg. Berkeley, CA: McCutchan.

Peterson, Penelope. 1988. Teachers' and students' cognitional knowledge for classroom teaching and learning. *Educational Research* 17(5): 3–14.

Peterson, Penelope L. 1976. "Interactive Effects of Student Anxiety, Achievement Orientation, and Teacher Behavior on Student Achievement and Attitude." Doctoral dissertation, Stanford University, Palo Alto, CA.

Peterson, Penelope, and Susan R. Swing. 1982. Beyond time on task: Students' reports of their thought processes during classroom instruction. *Elementary School Journal* 82(5): 481–491.

Phillips, Denis C., and Jonas Soltis. 1985. *Perspectives on Learning*. New York: Teachers College Press.

Piaget, Jean. 1969. *The Psychology of Intelligence*. Totowa, NJ: Littlefield, Adams & Co.

Piaget, Jean. 1970. *Science of Education and the Psychology of the Child*. New York: Penguin Books.

Piaget, Jean, and Bärbel Inhelder. 1964. *The Early Growth of Logic in the Child*, translated by L. Lunzer and D. Papert. London: Routledge & Kegan Paul.

Posner, Michael I. 1969. "Abstraction and the Process of Recognition." In *The Psychology of Learning and Motivation*, edited by Gordon H. Bower and J. T. Spencer. New York: Academic Press.

Pressey, Sidney L. 1926. Simple apparatus which gives tests and scores and teaches. *School and Society* 23(586): 373–376.

Pressey, Sidney L. 1932. A third and fourth contribution toward the coming "industrial revolution" in education. *School and Society* 36(934): 668–672.

Purves, Alan C. 1975. Culture and the deep structure of the literature curriculum. *Curriculum Inquiry* 5(2): 145–149.

Raizen, Senta A., and Lyle V. Jones, eds. 1985. *Indicators of Precollege Education in Science and Mathematics: A Preliminary Review*. Washington, DC: National Academy Press.

Raudenbush, Stephen W. 1988. Applications of hierarchical linear models in educational research: A review. *Journal of Educational Statistics* 13(2): 85–116.

Raudenbush, Stephen W., and Anthony S. Bryk. 1986. A hierarchical model for studying school effects. *Sociology of Education* 59: 1–17.

Resnick, Lauren B. 1987. *Education and Learning to Think*. Washington, DC: National Academy Press.

Resnick, Lauren B. 1989. Developing mathematical knowledge. *American Psychologist* 44(2): 162–169.

Rice, Joseph M. 1913. *Scientific Management in Education*. New York: Hinds, Nobel, and Eldridge.

Romberg, Thomas A. 1987, April. "School Mathematics Indicators." Paper prepared for the annual meeting, American Educational Research Association, Washington, DC.

Rosenshine, Barak. 1979. "Content, Time and Direction Instruction." In *Research on Teaching: Concepts, Findings and Implications*, edited by P. Peterson and H. Walberg, 28–56. Berkeley, CA: McCutchan.

Rosenshine, Barak, and N. Furst. 1971. "Research on Teacher Performance Criteria." In *Research in Teacher Education: A Symposium*, edited by B. Otthanel Smith, 37–72. Englewood Cliffs, NJ: Prentice Hall.

Rothman, Arthur I., Wayne Welch, and Herbert J. Walberg. 1969. Physics teacher characteristics and student learning. *Journal of Research in Science Teaching* 6(1): 63.

Rusk, Robert R. 1969. *The Doctrines of the Great Educators*, 4th ed. New York: St. Martin's Press.

Russell, Bertrand. 1958. *Religion and Science*. Oxford: Oxford University Press.

Rutter, M., 1979. *Fifteen Thousand Hours: Secondary Schools and Their Effects on Children*. Cambridge, MA: Harvard University Press.

Schoenfeld, Alan H. 1987. "What's All the Fuss About Meta Cognition?" In *Cognitive Science and Mathematics Education*, edited by Alan H. Schoenfeld, 189–215. Hillsdale, NJ: Erlbaum.

Schwab, Joseph J. 1965. "Structure of the Disciplines: Meanings and Significances." In *The Structure of Knowledge and the Curriculum*, edited by G. Ford and L. Pugno. Chicago: Rand McNally.

Schwab, Joseph J. 1966. *The Teaching of Science as Inquiry*. Cambridge, MA: Harvard University Press.

Shavelson, Richard J. 1974. Methods for examining representations of a subject-structure in a student's memory. *Journal of Research in Science Teaching* 11(3): 231–249.

Shavelson, Richard J., and Nancy Dempsey-Atwood. 1976. Generalizability of measures of teacher behavior. *Review of Educational Research* 46(4): 553–612.

Shavelson, Richard J., Lorraine M. McDonnell, and Jeannie Oakes, eds. 1989. *Indicators for Monitoring Mathematics and Science Education: A Sourcebook*. Santa Monica, CA: Rand.

Shavelson, Richard J., Lorraine McDonnell, Jeannie Oakes, and Neil Carey. 1987. *Indicator Systems for Monitoring Mathematics and Science Education*. Santa Monica, CA: Rand.

Shavelson, Richard J., and Paula Stern. 1981. Research on teachers' pedagogical thoughts, judgements, decisions and behavior. *Review of Educational Research* 51(4): 455–498

Sheldon, Eleanor B., and Robert Parke. 1975. Social indicators. *Science* 188(4189): 693–699.

Shulman, Lee, and A. Elstein. 1975. "Studies of Problem Solving, Judgement, and Decision Making: Implications for Educational Research." In *Review of Research in Education*, vol. 3, edited by F. Kerlinger. Itasca, IL: Peacock.

Shulman, Lee, and E. Keislar, eds. 1966. *Learning by Discovery*. Chicago: Rand McNally.

Sigel, Irving E., and Richard H. Coop. 1974. "Cognitive Style and Classroom Practice." In *Psychological Concepts in the Classroom*, edited by Richard Coop and Kinnard White, 250–275. New York: Harper & Row.

Simon, Herbert A. 1979. "Information Processing Models of Cognition." In *Annual Review of Psychology*, edited by M. Rosenzweig and L. Porter, 363–396. Palo Alto, CA: Annual Reviews.

Singer, R. 1977. To err or not to err: A question for the instruction of psychomotor skills. *Review of Educational Research* 47: 479–498.

Skinner, B. F. 1954. The science of learning and the art of teaching. *Harvard Educational Review* 24: 86–97.

Skinner, B. F. 1958. Teaching Machines. *Science* 128: 969–977.

Skinner, B. F. 1961. *Cumulative Record*. New York: Appleton-Century-Crofts.

Smith, Eugene, and Ralph W. Tyler. 1942. *Adventure in American Education, vol. 3: Appraising and Recording Student Progress.* New York: Harper & Brothers.

Soar, Robert S. 1972. *Follow Through Classroom Process Measurement and Pupil Growth.* Gainesville: Institute for Development of Human Resources, University of Florida.

Soar, Robert S. 1977. "An Integration of Findings from Four Studies of Teacher Effectiveness." In *The Appraisal of Teaching: Concepts and Process,* edited by G. D. Borich, 96–103. Reading, MA: Addison-Wesley.

Soar, Robert S., and Ruth M. Soar. 1976. An attempt to identify measures of teacher effectiveness from four studies. *Journal of Teacher Education* 27: 261–267.

Spearman, Charles E. 1927. *The Abilities of Man.* New York: Macmillan.

Spiro, Rand J. 1977. "Remembering Information from Text: Theoretical and Empirical Issues concerning the 'State of Schema' Reconstruction Hypothesis." In *Schooling and the Acquisition of Knowledge,* edited by Richard Anderson, Rand J. Spiro, and William E. Montague. Hillsdale, NJ: Erlbaum.

Stern, William. 1930. *Psychology of Early Childhood Up to the Sixth Year of Age,* translated by Anna Barnwell. London: Allen.

Sternberg, Robert J. 1985. *Beyond IQ.* New York: Cambridge University Press.

Stodolsky, Susan. 1984. Teacher evaluation: The limits of looking. *Educational Researcher* 13(9): 11–22.

Stone, C. 1982. "A Meta-Analysis of Advance Organizer Studies." Paper presented at the annual meeting, American Educational Research Association, New York.

Suchman, J. Richard. 1962. *The Elementary School Training Program in Scientific Inquiry.* Report to the U.S. Office of Education, Project Title VIII, Project 216. Urbana: University of Illinois.

Talmage, Harriet, and Sue Pinzur Rasher. 1980, November. Unanticipated outcomes: The perils to curriculum goals. *Phi Delta Kappan* 62: 194–198.

Tanner, Daniel, and Laurel Tanner. 1980. *Curriculum Development: Theory Into Practice.* New York: Macmillan.

Thorndike, Edward L. 1913. *Educational Psychology: The Psychology of Learning.* New York: Teachers College Press.

Thorndike, Edward L. 1924. Mental discipline in high school studies. *Journal of Educational Psychology* 15: 1–22, 83–98.

Tietze, Wolfgang. 1987. A structural model for the evaluation of preschool effects. *Early Childhood Research Quarterly* 2(2): 133–159.

Tikunoff, William J., David C. Berliner, and Ray C. Rist. 1975. *An Ethnographic Study of the Forty Classrooms of the Beginning Teacher Evaluation Study Known Sample.* Technical Report No. 75-10-5. San Francisco, CA: Far West Laboratory.

Tompkins, Ellsworth, and Walter H. Gaumnitz. 1954. *The Carnegie Unit: Its Origin, Status, and Trends.* Bulletin No. 7: 4–19. Washington, DC: U.S. Department of Health, Education, and Welfare.

Traub, Ross, Joel Weiss, and Charles Fisher. 1973. *Openness in Schools: An Evaluation of the Wentworth County Roman Catholic School Board Schools.* Toronto: Educational Evaluation Center, Ontario Institute for Studies in Education.

Travers, Robert M. W. 1983. *How Research Has Changed American Schools: A History From 1840 to the Present.* Kalamazoo, MI: Mythos Press.

Tyack, David. 1974. *The One Best System.* Cambridge, MA: Harvard University Press.

Ulrich, Roger, Thomas Stachnik, and John Mabry, eds. 1966. *Control of Human Behavior.* Glenview, IL: Scott, Foresman.

Verhave, Thom. 1959, March 26–27. "Recent Developments in the Experimental Analysis of Behavior." In *Proceedings of the Eleventh Research Conference.* Chicago: University of Chicago.

Vygotsky, Lev S. 1962. *Thought and Language,* translated by Eugenia Hanfmann and Gertrude Vaker. Cambridge, MA: MIT Press.

Walberg, Herbert J., and Arthur I. Rothman. 1969. Teacher achievement and student learning. *Science Education* 53: 256–257.

Walberg, Herbert J., Diane Schiller, and Geneva D. Haertel. 1979. The quiet revolution in educational research. *Phi Delta Kappan* 61(3): 179–183.

Warren, Donald R. 1974. *To Enforce Education: A History of the Founding Years of the United States Office of Education.* Detroit: Wayne State University Press.

Watson, John B. 1913. Psychology as the behaviorist views it. *Psychological Review* 20: 158–177.

Watson, John B. 1930. *Behaviorism.* New York: Norton.

Webb, Noreen W. 1980. A process-outcome analysis of learning in group and individual settings. *Educational Psychologist* 15(2): 69–83.

Weinstein, Claire E., and Richard Mayer. 1985. "The Teaching of Learning Strategies." In *Handbook of Research On Teaching,* 3rd ed., edited by Merlin C. Wittrock, 315-327. New York: Macmillan.

Well, C. Gordon. 1981. *Learning Through Interaction: The Study of Language Development.* New York: Cambridge University Press.

Wertheimer, Max. 1959. *Productive Thinking,* rev. ed. New York: Harper.

Winkelmann, W., A. Hollaender, H. Schmerkotte, and E. Schmalohr. 1979. Kognitive Entwicklung und Foerderung von Kindergarten und Vorklassenkindern. *Bericht uber eine laengsschnittliche Vergleischsuntersuchung zum Modellversuch des Landes Nordrhein-Westfalen,* vol. 2. Kronberg, Ger.: Scriptor.

Wise, Arthur E. 1979. *Legislated Learning: The Bureaucratization of the American Classroom.* Berkeley: University of California Press.

Wise, Arthur E., and Linda Darling-Hammond. 1984. Education by voucher: Private choice and the public interest. *Educational Theory* 34(1): 29–47.

Wittrock, Merle C. 1986. "Students' Thought Processes." In *Handbook of Research on Teaching,* 3rd ed., edited by Merlin C. Whittrock, 297–314. New York: Macmillan.

Wolf, Richard M. 1977. *Achievement in America.* New York: Teachers College.

Wolfson, Bernice. 1985. "Psychological Theory and Curricular Thinking." In *Current Thought on Curriculum: 1985 ASCD Yearbook,* edited by Alex Molnar, 53–72. Alexandria, VA: Association for Supervision and Curriculum Development.

3

CURRICULUM STUDIES AND THE TRADITIONS OF INQUIRY: THE HUMANISTIC TRADITION

Yvonna S. Lincoln
TEXAS A&M

The title of this chapter is slightly misleading, in that it leads readers to believe that the humanistic tradition is a singular phenomenon, a unitary tradition. In fact, what is typically grouped under the humanist tradition is an aggregation of perspectives on curricular matters, some of which bear as little resemblance to one another as they bear to the scientific or rationalistic tradition. Included among those perspectives are historical studies; critical theories; literary analyses; philosophical examinations; and hermeneutic, narrative, autobiographical, political, economic, artistic, and interpretive investigations of curriculum and its meaning.

The rise of curriculum studies is argued to be a phenomenon of this century (Pinar and Grumet 1988), although curricular studies in the United States date back over 100 years. After the turn of the century, curriculum was sometimes treated as an extension of administrative responsibility, with managerial rather than philosophical overtones. Widespread investigations into curriculum philosophy are a peculiarly late-20th-century phenomenon, and histories of this development—a large part of what this chapter is about—are often histories of the still living.

It is always risky to try to capture a field in foment, and especially so when many bellwether spokespersons are alive and furiously at work. The "organization" that one imposes on such a history bears a heavy burden: It can be dismissed as inaccurate, attacked as incomplete, or disparaged as an effort to see order where there is none or to create order where others prefer the autonomy of ambiguity. Such organization rarely enjoys the approbation of those engaged on the front lines of the debates, and as a result, this chapter will simply attempt to provide the reader with an introduction and a framework, the purpose of which is what Karl Weick (1985, 127) calls "a little cognitive economy, and some peace of mind." Since any historical examination, whether of contemporary or past history, is a *reconstruction*—an attempt to achieve understanding and/or impose meaning—many such histories of any given event (or set of events) can potentially be useful, depending on the purposes to which they are put. In effect, reconstructions serve as *rival hypotheses*, illuminating aspects of a phenomenon or event to which persons might wish to attend. Almost always, reconstructions are revisions, and thus they become revisionist history. The purpose of this history, therefore, is merely to set a stage for the discussion of newer and emergent traditions.

Let me say at the outset that I am not a curriculum theorist. My early training was in history, and I am a humanist by tradition—a perspective that I bring to educationist work—and a researcher in the history of academic work and thought. My own interests have been in the effects of the scientific paradigm on education (and the social sciences more broadly) and in the framing of an alternative paradigm as a guide to future inquiries. Thus, I bring a view that is both inside the arguments surrounding the shift from a solely scientific mode of curriculum development and outside the field of curriculum theory per se. This is not an altogether unuseful position, as those who know Theodore Brown's (1988) work on Kuhn and its relation to curriculum theory will attest.

The humanist *traditions* go by many names, generally indicating their analogic or metaphoric disciplinary or methodological roots. Thus, there are political themes, for instance, the work of Michael Apple (1975; 1979) or Henry Giroux (1981); feminist work (Leslie Roman's 1989 feminist materialist ethnographies, e.g.); poststructuralist themes, as for instance in Cherryholmes (1988); phenomenological and autobiographical perspectives, for instance the work of Grumet (1983) or Pinar (1988a); Marxists and neo-Marxists; historical work, such as that of Barry Franklin (1988a, 1988b) or Tanner and Tanner (1990); economic critiques; the aesthetic criticism of both Aoki (1988) and Eisner (1979) fit well here, as does the commentary of those who utilize literary theory as a mode of curriculum discourse analysis.

Where did the foment have its beginning? What has been instrumental in prodding a whole generation of curriculum theorists to criticize the work of some of their early predecessors and attempt to expand the perspectives brought to curriculum work? What were the issues to which they responded so forcefully? And where do the humanists appear to be heading at this moment? These are legitimate questions that might be proposed or to which speculation might be addressed, and the remainder of this chapter will deal with some of these issues in one way or another.

A HISTORY OF QUIET REVOLUTION

Where did the humanistic traditions come from? And why did such traditions arise at all? Pinar's (1975, 1988a, 1988b), Schubert's (1986), and Tanner and Tanner's (1990) accounts and histories of the early curriculum developers and the debates regarding their work are useful and insightful commentaries and historical accounts. Some of the reconstruction here will rely on their analyses.

What Is a "Humanistic" Tradition?

Humanism has several different definitions, depending on a given writer's purpose. Reese (1980), in the *Dictionary of Philosophy and Religion*, defines humanism in two ways important to this chapter: "In the Renaissance . . . the term [humanism] signified a return to the Greek sources and individual criticism and interpretation in contrast to the tradition of . . . religious authority. [But] in more recent centuries the term has been often used in contrast to theism, locating in man the source of goodness and creativity" (235). But Reese refers also to the work of William James, among others, where ". . . humanism is taken as the view which stands in contrast to philosophical absolutism. . . . [And] the stress is, hence, upon an open universe, pluralism, and human freedom" (235).

The centrality of humankind, as both the source and the measure of human achievement, is the core of humanism. During the Renaissance, the idea of humanism challenged theism, particularly as theism dictated—by analogy if no longer by theology—the design and structure of civil governments and political and social systems.

The humanism of the 19th and 20th centuries, often labeled "secular humanism" to denote "an approach to life divorced from the influence of religion" (Reese 1980, 519), reflected an increasing commitment to the concepts of openness, plurality, social justice achieved by cooperation among persons, conditionality, ethical decisions situated in contexts, and temporal and secular concerns. Thus humanism as a philosophical concept can be thought of as an evolving tradition, increasingly challenging to absolutist philosophies on metaphysical, epistemological, and political grounds.

In the academic disciplines, humanism has maintained a strong presence. But the press to abandon humanistic traditions and move to "scientific," and largely quantitative, investigations has created the situation in which, even in history, it is not unknown to hear a call for a return to the strong value bases of the discipline and therefore to the human judgment some feel is being lost in historiography (Lincoln 1989).

In the arts and humanities, the resurgence of interest in humanism has come about partly in response to a perceived absolutist tendency in science, particularly scientific method. The hypothetico-deductive, verificationist emphasis of much of the hard sciences has led to a reexamination of interpretivist methodologies; interest in hermeneutics; phenomenological philosophies; reconsideration of the problematic and conditional nature of knowledge (Hesse 1980); and serious exploration of how knowledge is produced, by whom, and for what purposes (Bleier 1986; Langland and Gove 1981).

Clearly, a return to humanism as a philosophical stance has implications that are not only metaphysical but also epistemological and methodological. Conducting curriculum inquiry from a humanistic perspective, rather than from that of a scientific method, necessitates that knowledge become situated, probably historically and socially located, and problematic, conditional, and nonabsolutist. Such a shift away from science and toward the humanities means that a wide variety of methodological modes and analytic tools can be utilized, including historical and economic analyses; cultural interpretation; artistic connoisseurship and criticism; literary analysis; and feminist, Marxist, and critical methods, among others.

Thus, the stance of humanism not only challenges absolutist philosophical underpinnings. It also opens curriculum study to questions about the nature of knowledge itself; suggests that knowledge may come in many types or forms; and holds that there are multiple, nonpositivist ways to gather and interpret such knowledge.

Education as a discipline has been no more immune to the scientific explosion than any other facet of human life. The wonders of technology suggested that John Stuart Mills's prediction that we could engineer utopia as we had engineered the industrial revolution seemed entirely possible. Much of the current press for humanistic and interpretive approaches to curriculum theory has arisen in response to a perceived overly scientific, overly technological approach to schooling, which arose in the early part of this century. How did scientific advances shape curriculum development?

In the early part of the 20th century, curriculum developers, like most thoughtful people, were impressed with the success of the industrial revolution in the West and enchanted with its achievements in the world of science, technology, and the mechanization of heavy piecework into assembly-line production, a system that made mass production of consumer goods possible, desirable, and profitable. The metaphor of the giant clockwork, the universe as a machine, had been realized in capitalist economies, and the same metaphor was being translated into the schooling arena (Guba and Lincoln 1981). This "translation" was not an ahistorical or epiphenomenal event. The work of Max Weber on bureaucracies as models of organizational efficiency, the studies of Frederick Taylor on time and motion in production activities (Morgan 1986), and the development of the Alpha tests to sort and screen large numbers of Army recruits for the World War I effort (Guba and Lincoln 1981) bespoke an interest in "engineering" human efficiency, production, and motion, which could then be harnessed to the needs, demands, and interests of a capitalist economy. It is not surprising that "engineering" the public schools, especially given their rapid influx of immigrant children from the 1880s onward into the 20th century, for whom inculcation of capitalist, nonagrarian values was critical to supply the primary and secondary labor markets of capitalism, appeared to be a forward-thinking and "scientific" goal (Morgan 1983). The adoption of a hierarchical, bureaucratic model for public schooling, with its metaphoric base in the machine, all its parts working in harmony to produce goods, and its physical situation in the factory, with raw goods as inputs and products as outputs, drew spokespersons who were eloquently clear regarding the role of the schools. So, for instance, Ellwood Cubberley (1916) could argue that schools were manufacturing units and, to do their jobs, must model themselves on the factory:

> Every manufacturing establishment that turns out a standard product or a series of products of any kind maintains a force of efficiency experts to study methods or procedures and to measure and test the outputs of its works. Such men ultimately bring the manufacturing establishment large returns, by introducing improvements in processes and procedure, and in training the workmen to produce larger and better output. Our schools are, in a sense, factories in which the raw products (children) are to be shaped and fashioned into products to meet the various demands of life. The specifications for manufacturing come from the demands of twentieth-century civilization, and it is the business of the school to build its pupils according to the specifications laid down. This demands good tools, specialized machinery, continuous measurement of production to see if it is according to specifications, the elimination of waste in manufacture, and a large variety in the output. (1916, 338)

Pupils as products of a routinized process dominated the thinking of many, although not all, curricular specialists for decades to come. The production metaphor was singularly amenable to the influence of Frederick Taylor's scientific management movement, transferred from industry to schooling; to the rising cult of efficiency (Callahan 1962); and to the adoption of vocabulary from both industry (e.g., school plant, superintendent, outputs, cost-per-pupil ratios, and the like) and the military (e.g., chain of command, line and staff, and lines of communication; see David L. Clark [1985] for a larger discussion of the adoption of Weberian, military terminology to the work of the schools, particularly to its administration).

The early work of Franklin Bobbitt (1912) continued this tradition. Describing himself as an "educational engineer," he set about to "eliminate waste" in education, primarily by investigating how physical plants might be more effectively utilized to turn out educated products. Bobbitt's translation of worker and school plant efficiency into a theory of schooling ultimately had the effect of ". . . ma[king] the child the object on which the bureaucratic machinery of the school operate[d]" (Kliebard 1975, 36).

The strong resurgence of the humanist tradition is, in part, a reaction to the perceived objectification of children, which inheres in the scientific movement in schooling. Indeed, a strong and growing literature has arisen criticizing the concept of objectivity in scientific (positivistic) inquiry (Hesse 1980) and on the effects of objectification on human subjects in general (Bleier 1984; Keller 1985; Langland and Gove 1981; Lincoln and Guba 1985).

But a "standardization" of product was not the only goal of the schooling experience, some have argued. A hidden curriculum was masked by the siren song of educating children at the most efficient cost for a new industrial world. This was the political goal—the social agenda—of "social control" (Franklin 1988b). At the same time that the Western world was industrializing, creating a powerful physical and capital plant for consumer and durable goods, the social, psychological, and political terrain was also being remapped. The work of Freud was receiving widespread attention in the United States after 1920, studies of eugenics and biological determinism were widely discussed (Selden 1988), and the idea of social control as a function of the schools achieved its ascendency (Franklin 1988a, 1988b).

Both social control and the eugenics movement found comfortable niches in the bureaucratized, production-oriented environment of the schools of the first half of the century and in the social reaction to waves of immigrants. To some extent, the racism inherent in the eugenics movement and the social control reflective of a desire to fuel the means of production continue to persist today, stimulating ongoing criticism by the humanist theorists. Of the two, social control has probably had the most profoundly disturbing effect, and it has drawn the sternest criticism from one group of the new generation of curriculum theorists (Franklin 1988a, 1988b).

The production model of curriculum, with its emphasis on "social efficiency" (Kliebard 1971) and its accompanying agenda of social control (Franklin 1988b), is argued to have waned during the period of the Great Depression. It was to reappear, "muted," some years later, during the course of what Kliebard (1971, 89) terms the electronic or technological revolution. The coercive authority of social control (Franklin 1988a) was replaced by a call for specification of educational outcomes that if achieved would produce the desired "educational products." Social control as a movement appeared to be replaced by the psychological behaviorists, for whom objectives replaced physical punishments in attaining desired "educational products" (Franklin 1988a). The price of adopting an efficiency model for an intellective and expressive process has been high, argue some:

> The bureaucratic model, along with its behavioristic and technological refinements, threatens to destroy, in the name of efficiency, the satisfaction that one may find in intellectual activity. . . .
>
> The tragic paradox of the production metaphor applied to curriculum is that the dehumanization of education, the alienation of means from ends, the stifling of intellectual curiosity carry with them very few compensations. . . . The particularization of the educational product, it turns out, is tantamount to its trivialization. (Kliebard 1971, 91)

One productive way to interpret the criticisms of Franklin and Kliebard is to note the concern of society as a whole with the "cult of efficiency" (Callahan 1962)—a concern that expresses itself today in a widespread worry over whether the United States is losing its technological edge to other industrialized countries. The production metaphor of schooling, like other metaphors in use then or today, was rooted in modernism, progressivism, and a plethora of contemporary social understandings, some widely shared, with varying degrees of sophistication. At some distance, understandings must necessarily be conditional and revisionist. Nevertheless, social control and efficiency appear to be hallmarks of early 20th-century theorists; whether or not those goals were translated into classroom practice, and therefore, the shaping of students, is in fact unknown and probably unknowable.

The mechanistic, industrial model for schooling promulgated by efficiency experts does not represent the whole, nor is the foregoing intended to buttress the argument implicitly made by some (Pinar 1988a) that mechanism was the sole influence on schooling. To so argue is to ignore a long tradition of classroom observation studies and the work of Dewey and others, whose curricular theorizing should be placed solidly in the humanistic tradition. But the relative emphasis on production rather than humanism is not to be missed, especially between 1920 and 1970.

The production metaphor of schooling spawned a generation of curriculum theorists, later dubbed the conceptual empiricists (Pinar 1988a) because of their focus on scientific management, efficiency, reduction of waste in the schooling process, production of a carefully engineered educational "product" that would fit into an appropriate slot in industrial society, and a focus on the school as the location for these factorylike activities. The generation that followed the conceptual empiricists—with their emphasis on observable and measurable behavior—took as their focus the tasks a curriculum developer or practitioners needed to consider. This group of curriculum theorists came to be labeled the Tylerian "traditionalists."

The Tylerian Traditionalists

Ralph W. Tyler's "model" for curriculum development was first published as the syllabus for Education 360 at the University of Chicago (where Tyler taught for nearly a quarter of a century) in 1949. A year later, the university press prepared *Basic Principles of Curriculum and Instruction* (1950) as a professional publication, and it has remained in print continuously since then. (Strangely enough, the book is considered among curriculum theorists to be one of the most influential ever written on the curriculum and instruction, but it enjoys a second reputation also, that of being a classic and one of the most influential and seminal works in the field of program evaluation. Tyler's thinking on both curricular and evaluation matters have shaped generations of thinkers to this day.)

Unlike earlier theorists, Tyler was little interested in mechanistic and production models of schooling per se; his experience with the Eight Year Study (Smith and Tyler 1942) was essentially a democratic, rather than authoritarian, exercise in creating and reorganizing curricula. Instead, Tyler (1950) was interested in helping his students think about the "parameters" of study of the curriculum; to this end, he organized his syllabus around four major questions:

1. What educational purposes should the school seek to attain?
2. How can learning experiences be selected which are likely to be useful in attaining these objectives?
3. How can learning experiences be organized for effective instruction? and
4. How can the effectiveness of learning experiences be evaluated?

The emphasis for Tyler was not on what should be taught (a matter to be determined by the students whom one is teaching, not by enduring absolutist principles, as Tyler was to make clear in the Eight Year Study) but rather on what should be considered when either analyzing or developing curriculum (Schubert 1986, 170) or when selecting instructional strategies. The focus for Tyler is of critical importance. Tyler was writing largely for individuals: either classroom teachers who were developing curricula or administrators who might be providing supervision to such persons. The larger social context in which schooling was occurring—political, social, and economic—did not inform *Basic Principles*, a fact for which Tyler was to be criticized in later years.

What Tyler did not provide, however, was less important at the time than what he did provide: a clear, simple, direct, and highly useful statement of principles to guide curriculum development and evaluation. This statement—especially the four categories—was sufficiently compelling that successive generations of curriculum theorists have turned to it as a way of organizing their own thinking.

Tyler and others who worked either within his general framework or within his tradition (such as Taba, Smith, Stanley and Shores, and Saylor and Alexander, among others) are termed variously the "theoretics" (Schwab 1970), the later "conceptual empiricists" (Pinar 1975), or the "social behaviorists" (Schubert 1986). Probably most accurately, they are social behaviorists, since much of this work focuses on behaviors that can be elicited or derived from curricular interventions, although it is inaccurate to attribute to Tyler and his colleagues the same behavioral agendas that may be ascribed to curriculum theorists such as Cubberley. Tyler was interested not in behaviors consonant with production needs but in those behaviors that would indicate retention and mastery of the concepts, ideas, and skills chosen by teachers as the appropriate objectives for a given lesson.

Criticism of the Tyler work and its followers has come in two forms: criticism of the lack of attention to political aspects of the curriculum and criticism of the lack of attention to how practical dilemmas encountered in specific milieus dictate how research on curriculum should proceed (Schwab 1970). For purposes of this chapter in tracing the reemergence of the humanistic traditions, the first criticism of Tyler's work is probably the most significant. The work is labeled "traditionalist" largely because of its emphasis on curricular objectives (what should the curriculum attempt to do?), student behaviors (what should students know and/or be able to do?), and teacher activities (what should a teacher do in delivering the curriculum?). But Tyler's work, as powerful as it has been to shape generations of theorists, left open and unaddressed questions regarding pluralism and politics inhering in the curriculum, the economics of curricular decisions, and potentially contested social and cultural dimensions of the curriculum.

Tyler's emphasis on behavioral objectives should not obscure his basically egalitarian approach to curricular theorizing. The central point to the Eight Year Study (Smith and Tyler 1942) was the assessment and evaluation of a nontraditional curriculum designed for a nontraditional student population. But subsequent critics of Tyler's work have pointed out that there were gaps in his work, and it was to those gaps that some—though not all—of Tyler's critics addressed themselves.

The Reconceptualists: Criticism and Dissent

The criticism of Tyler's work and the work of the other behaviorists, or "traditionalists," marked the beginning of a long period of criticism of the curriculum and curriculum studies from many quarters. Some of this criticism came not from other "traditional" theorists (Schwab 1970) but from curricular theorists whose roots were in political analysis, from historians, and from those whose work represented nonmainstream theorists who found a forum for their criticisms.

Huebner (1974), Pinar (1975), Jackson (1980), and Tanner and Tanner (1979), among others, were to become instrumental as lightning rods in drawing attention to a fugitive and scattered, but growing, body of literature that criticized the Tyler traditionalists and the behaviorists and social control curricularists before them. The American Educational Research Association Division B addresses of Huebner and Pinar in the mid-1970s, coupled with the publication of Pinar's *Curriculum Theorizing: The Reconceptualists* (1975), drew attention to serious criticisms from scholars "discontented" with the traditionalists and traditional curriculum theory. The discontents who produced those criticisms are characterized by Pinar (1975) as "reconceptualists." Because Pinar has been instrumental in focusing criticism of earlier curriculum theorists, and because he has collected some of the pivotal work in two collections (1975, 1988a, 1988b), his work has been used to structure a portion of this chapter. That is an arbitrary decision, adopted principally because Pinar utilizes categories that are recognized in other disciplines and, indeed, in other subdisciplines of education research. There are other approaches to organizing the material, but the strength of choosing Pinar's classification schema is twofold: One, it resembles, in tracing the various humanistic traditions, other disciplinary currents (e.g., in sociology); and two, it represents this author's own explorations of emergent paradigm inquiry. Much of the terminology—for instance, labeling Tyler a "traditionalist"—descends from Pinar's popularization of the term. And Pinar's term for the students he trained and colleagues working in the same field, the "reconceptualists," is not perhaps a label which other curricular theorists, whether working in the tradition or not, would approve. But I believe that Pinar's appropriation of this label for himself and others is indicative of his intent to draw attention to both the idea and the possibility of *reconceiving* the curriculum in terms that are both broader and at the same time more humanistic than he believed curriculum theorizing to have been in the earlier part of the 20th century. His most compelling and persuasive characteristics, for my purposes and in light of my own values as a scholar, are his sense of contestation surrounding curriculum studies—a contestation that is likely to grow more fierce rather than less in the coming decades—and the openly ideological stance that he takes on inquiry. The commitment to discourse that makes explicit its value premises represents a major break with traditional science and a political commitment that is highly resonant with all forms of new paradigm inquiry.

The key problem with adopting the set of terms, labels, and arguments Pinar proposes is that it necessarily limits discussion of other possibilities for tracing the humanistic tradition. As noted, the reconceptualists did not invent humanism, and in fact, represent the vocal reemergence of a long line of inquiry and theoretical work. But their discontent and dissent touched a nerve in the curriculum world, largely because curriculum studies seemed to that group to be dormant and lacking in serious internal criticism. It is also problematic that Pinar's (1975) earlier work draws the boundaries for much of the contemporary discussion of curriculum. However, that is as much a linguistic problem as it is a problem with curriculum theory. Those who give "names" or labels to phenomena tend to have both their labels and their names remembered until new labels can be defined and defended. The very function of a label, stereotype, metaphor, or simile is to cut short long discussions by drawing on associational characteristics and linking ground and referent into some common understanding. In short, because Pinar labels, he maintains some control over the debate. The justice of this may be debated (and has been, vigorously), but the reality of it cannot be.

The philosophical and practical consequences of taking the reconceptualists seriously are severalfold. First, one has to examine whether or not their "cut" at the field of curriculum withstands outside analysis, and it is probably the case that it both does and does not. It does not because it misses much of the work of Dewey and others in his tradition; but it probably does withstand analysis on the major premise, which many earlier curriculum theorists missed, ignored, or were not interested in—the interaction between curricula and political, social, economic, cultural, and artistic forces, which exerted powerful influences over the design and shape of what is taught in the American schools. Practically speaking, the reconceptualists appeared not to be coupled tightly to British theorists who mounted the same criticisms a generation earlier, although many of the contemporary reconceptualists have drawn heavily on the work of Ricouer, Foucault, and other French social theorists in illuminating their own work. In focusing early on the problems of the American curriculum, the link with traditions other than the peculiarly American experience were glossed over or ignored.

But another and more serious practical consequence of taking their work seriously is that their assumptional base must be debated. That set of assumptions contrives to set curriculum and curriculum theory in a larger social, historical, economic, and cultural theater: a theater where some children are privileged and others are not, where learning is divorced from its intellectual energy and excitement (Kliebard 1971), and where schooling produces "products" to be consumed for industrial and technological purposes rather than active citizens. The result of their criticisms has been largely what was intended. The field of curriculum, curriculum theory, and curriculum inquiry is characterized by vigorous debate, energy, and a plethora of compelling arguments. Among the debates are what curriculum is, how one should inquire into curricular matters (Short 1984), what influences social and historical forces have exerted and continue to exert on the curriculum (Apple 1979; Giroux 1981), and who should determine the curriculum (Giroux n.d.a, n.d.b). Thus, Pinar's (1975) metaphoric throwing down of the gauntlet has created a climate that did not entirely exist before. Conceptions of curriculum have expanded and the debates have been enlarged to include voices not heard before. Terms and terminology—a "dictionary for languages not spoken" (Lincoln 1985)—have been created, and they have enriched the debate over the aims and purposes of the American curriculum. Their criticisms may not be complete or even accurate. But they have been effective in opening a whole field of inquiry to revolutionary ideas.

The field of curriculum responded to the criticisms of Pinar, Huebner, and others. Jackson (1980) characterized those criticisms as a "litany," not without its conceptual merits, to which many in the field might subscribe. As a result, the field's "probable agreement with some of the items on the list also means that the total set of complaints cannot be discarded as crank letters" (167). Those complaints included

- The Tyler rationale is out-of-date, and we have little or nothing to replace it with.
- Our present ways of thinking and talking about schools and schooling do not do justice to the complexity and dignity of the human condition.
- The control of the curriculum is in the hands of technologists, test makers, textbook publishers, and school administrators.
- Our schools are losing sight of humanistic values and goals.
- Curriculum workers have little to offer teachers that is of direct help to them.
- The aesthetic, ethical, and spiritual dimensions of the educational experience are being ignored.
- Our schools are damaging to many students, particularly to children of the poor and oppressed minorities. (167)

Although the Jackson litany of complaints was accurate, it was only one perspective (albeit a significant one) on what was wrong with the field of curriculum studies. Others were also mounting criticisms.

Kliebard (1975), a historian of education, viewed the Tyler rationale as limited also, mainly because it failed to take into account a sufficient historical perspective in order to grapple with persistent issues that had descended virtually untouched from the previous century. Kliebard (1975, 39) suggested that "involvement with the past . . . [is useful] as a kind of dialogue across generations" and noted that the "a-historicity" of previous formulations of curriculum theory had led to those perennial issues remaining unaddressed. In addition to the ahistorical posture of contemporary curriculum theory, Kliebard observed that two other problems plagued then current theory: an ameliorative orientation and a lack of definition of the field. With respect to the ameliorative orientation of curriculum studies, Kliebard noted that the undergirding interest of most curriculum theorists appeared to be in doing immediate good (or solving immediate problems), rather than engaging in long-range research with few, if any, immediate payoffs (40–41). The latter problem—the lack of definition—he noted revolved about the "paucity of ordered conceptions of what the curriculum field is, and [what] its relationship [is or ought to be] to cognate fields" (43–44). These three problems seemed to Kliebard to be paramount, but two others, one that questioned the role of curricular objectives and one that questioned the propriety and utility of curriculum differentiation for different identifiable groups in school populations, were also deemed persistent and particularly irksome (47–48).

Pinar (1975) calculated that among the dissenters there were, in reality, two kinds of reconceptualists: those who, like Kliebard and his colleagues, mounted criticisms of what was and who were dissatisfied with current curricular discourse, and those whom he termed "postcritical" (a term he now regrets)—scholars who were critical of prevailing traditionalist curriculum theory but who were also concerned with the "creation of the new," the generation of new forms of curricular discourse. The latter group's challenge might be considered "a marriage of two cultures: the scientific . . . [with] the artistic and the humanistic" (xi–xii). With respect to the former, significant criticism of what had been was mounted, with powerful commentary, by Mann (1975), Molnar and Zahorik (1977), Mooney (1975), and others. But the second variety of reconceptualists—those originally deemed "postcritical"—had additional concerns besides critical commentary on the present state of the art.

These latter reconceptualists are actually a diverse group and cannot be characterized readily or simply by a single definition; they "represent schools of thought, or discourses, within curriculum studies" (Pinar 1988a, vi). Pinar notes that they have taken as their concerns "the political dimensions of curriculum"; the "internal and existential experience of the public world"; "matters of temporality, transcendence, consciousness and politics"; the "nature of the educational experience"; and the disciplined understanding of the educational experience, particularly in its "political, cultural, gender and historical dimensions" (vi–xi and 2). The situation now is rather more complicated than it first appeared: Reaction to what was considered mainstream has no more unity than the original mainstream, which had been opposed. The forms of criticism originally mounted have formed "traditions" with adherents of their own (Short 1987).

At least some part of the reconceptualists' work can be traced to a reaction against the extreme *rationality* inherent in the scientific management movement's influence on curriculum studies. Macdonald (1988b) has explained the use of rationality as a form of fear, anxiety, or tension regarding the unknown.

> Rationality . . . is painting by the numbers. No matter how much information rationalists accumulate, or how many concepts they identify, they won't learn about those aspects of reality that frightened them into being cautious in the first place. . . . The point here is to emphasize that almost all of our curriculum theory efforts are attempts to explain (flatten out), which are usually intended to lead to prediction and control. (103)

The political, emotive, expressive, artistic, or humanistic, being basically unpredictable, uncontrolled, and uncontrollable, were elements missing from curriculum theory and, therefore, underattended as aspects of curriculum theorizing. Reconceptualism's intent was to redress this imbalance, although such a concern might not have been expressed in quite that way originally.

The work of the reconceptualists has not been without its critics. Tanner and Tanner (1979) in particular have mounted a scathing attack on the early Pinar work, most especially his attempts to characterize the reconceptualists as "heirs" to the curriculum field, for what they believed to be his "criticism promulgated as theory" (9); the "absence of an identifiable reconceptualist theory" (9); the adoption by Pinar of Habermas's category system without understanding the basis of the original classification schema; Pinar's classification of the work of Tyler, Taba, and others of that generation as "traditionalist" (11); and his (and others') attempts "to substitute a radical critique of society for a curriculum theory" (11). In retrospect, some of these criticisms are well taken. It is not particularly the case that Pinar or his colleagues are "heirs" to the field any more than others. And it was the case that reconceptualists had no identifiable, recognizable theoretical base as such. Criticism of mainstream theoretical approaches substituted for integrated theory, which could be identified as "reconceptualist." And Tanner and Tanner were probably correct in their assessment of Pinar's purposes as largely political, but this partly misses the point that some newer theoretical formulations, for instance, critical theory, do have embedded in them radical critiques of society (Fay 1987).

However, Pinar and other reconceptualists, even those who disagree strongly with theorists who consider themselves reconceptualists, understood all too well that schools were run by society. Their interest was precisely in schools as social institutions and in curricula as the instruments of a particular form of social legitimation and organization. As such, schools could be criticized simultaneously with criticizing the larger social structure committed to preserving and maintaining schools as they have existed historically, a point to which later neo-Marxists and critical theorists would return often. The reflection of society's goals in schooling processes left both schools and society in criticism's way.

Pinar's account of the curriculum field is regarded as "revisionist history" by some (Connelly 1990), "organized according to the notion of reconceptualism." But historic revisionism itself has a long history and is often undertaken precisely to accomplish what the antirevisionists resist: the interpretation of historic currents and events in fresh or startling ways in light of new evidence or insights. This is not to argue that all historical revisionism is sound or salutary; it is not. But it is to comment that some revisionism is healthy and that revisionism itself can, or should, be accepted as neutral until its premises are inspected. The premises of the curricular reconceivers have attained a legitimacy that suggests they ought at least to be conditionally accepted.

As to the most compelling of the criticisms—that the educational reformers (reconceptualists) offered no integrated theory of curriculum of their own ("nothing is more striking than the absence of an identifiable reconceptualist theory" [Tanner and Tanner 1979, 9])—it is also well taken. There is still no coherent "program," no curriculum in place, no practical application of a critical pedagogy (Simon 1988), nor is there likely to be one within the very near future. Just as humanistic theories are not fully explicated or integrated—and may well not be integratable—critical pedagogical practices are also not fully explicated. What we have are several bodies of curriculum thought, each of which represents a specific set of criticisms or a mode of addressing concerns with traditional curricula. Rather than thinking of any or all of them as "theories," which suggests a certain coherence and integration, it probably would be more productive to think of them as points of reference on a curricular compass, as strands to an epic story, or as doors by which one might enter the curriculum arena, depending on what one's research or practice needs might be.

Among the strands, foci, or points of view that are readily recognizable could be included the categories that Pinar

(1988a) has utilized: those of political analysis, particularly those that focus on social consciousness and cultural politics; aesthetic criticism; phenomenological studies, including the work on autobiography as a form of critical pedagogy; historical studies, including much of what would have earlier been termed "critical studies" (rather than postcritical studies); and feminist studies, with their emphasis on gender-related aspects of the educational experience (Pinar 1988a, 1988b). Others that he does not mention might include the poststructuralist inquiries of Cherryholmes (1988); the work on deconstructionism of Lather (1989); or in his later work, arguments directed at the education community more broadly for expanding inquiry in phenomenological directions (Lincoln 1985; Lincoln and Guba 1985). But his categories will serve as the organizers for the subsequent discussion, in part because the categories have meaning both within and outside of curriculum theorizing; i.e., they have heuristic value in, for instance, educational research, educational philosophy, school administration inquiries, and higher education as a field of study. For another reason, any category system is a human construction; one function of categories is to impose a common level of discourse between and among communicants. Since these categories are widely understood, they are consequently shared and therefore convenient.

RECONCEPTUALISTS, HUMANISTS, AND OTHER CRITICS

As curricular theorists, political analysts, aesthetic critics, phenomenologists, historians, and feminist scholars all share a common belief: that most curricular theory up to and including the traditionalists is too narrow and that it fails to grasp adequately aspects of the curricular process that have profound meaning for educational outcomes and for individuals—teachers and students—who experience the processes. The extent to which these humanistic traditions overlap depends to a large extent on what their early work and intellectual training consisted of and to what traditions they now feel they owe their scholarly allegiance. In some instances, their root connections are visible; in others, they are not.

Short (1984, 1986, 1987) commented that the field of curriculum theorizing has undergone major shifts from the early 1970s to the mid- to late 1980s partly because of the rise of nonpositivistic methods and traditions of scholarship and inquiry. The reconceptualists represent just such a shift, although Short's analysis of it is far less positive, sanguine, or exuberant than Pinar's (1975, 1988a). Short (1987) noticed that the shift involved

> the tendency for curriculum scholarship to coalesce around each new method that has gained legitimacy, sometimes around particular interpretations of method. The shift from positivistic to a whole range of newer . . . forms of inquiry has occurred in a climate of uncertainty and defensiveness where acceptance has often been problematic. . . . But the net result of this situation in many cases has been to work, publish, and discuss curriculum research in isolated enclaves somewhat protected from the interaction of tough critics of an approach or of its use in a particular study. While this isolationist tendency has gradually softened as time has passed (interactions and mutual criticism is, admittedly, more frequent now than they were in the mid-1970s), there still remains what might be called a kind of irrational allegiance on the part of some persons to a particular method or a particular interpretation of a method long after a need to sharpen or modify or to abandon a method has become clear to others. (7)

Those outside the newer traditions, including but not limited to positivists, may feel that it is time for more interaction and criticism, whereas those inside the newer traditions may still feel the need to defend their positions. Both sides probably have valid points to make, although the new levels of interactions noted by Short will undoubtedly bring about the dialogue and criticism needed by all curriculum theorists with and among one another. For the moment, it is the case that work in newer traditions has been salutary in helping the field of curriculum rethink itself. Whether various traditions and interpretations become accepted models and methods for curriculum inquiry over time or not, those traditions will nevertheless have created a *climate* in which ardent criticism, dialogue, and reshaping of a field can take and has taken place.

The relationship between traditions, when they exist, are not always easy to locate, perhaps in part because of the "isolationist" tendencies noted by Short. But where it is possible to see links and connections, this chapter will attempt to provide them. Nevertheless, the reader is free to draw his or her own connections or to comprehend the traditions as separate and particular interpretations or methods. Both are possible and, occasionally, even desirable.

The Curricular Historians' Views

Historians of curriculum, those who have studied the effects of various social movements on curriculum and those who have commented on theoretical and conceptual gaps in curriculum theory, form a diverse group. Their numbers and diversity prevent a full discussion of their contributions to historical analyses of curricular issues, but review of the more salient arguments will give the reader some sense of their legacy and the legitimacy of their criticisms.

Two concerns emerge as central. First and foremost has been the absence of a coherent, communicable, and integrated theory of curriculum, even though scholars and administrative theorists had provided practical and technical advice to those whose role it was to supervise the development and delivery of curriculum. The second concern of historians and some reconceptualists has been the inattention of earlier curricular theorists to the interaction of *context*—cultural, gender-related, social, and historical—with the process of curriculum development.

Tyler's *Basic Principles of Curriculum and Instruction* (1950) had provided the first clear guide to the questions that must direct, manage, and control any curriculum development project, even though attention had been paid to curriculum as a field of specialization before the turn of the century. Nevertheless, curriculum specialists working in the years immediately after World War II believed that however complete the Tyler rationale might be relative to earlier curriculum theory, it still failed to take into account aspects of curriculum building that were of some significance socially and, therefore, that the rationale provided a less than complete theoretical base for curriculum development. The criticism leveled at Tyler and his followers was less that the rationale provided was inadequate or incomplete but rather that it was directed largely to classroom teachers and to instructional supervisors and failed in the larger social arena to take account of political and cultural factors impinging on the curriculum development process (Kliebard 1975, 44). Kliebard and others have criticized the Tyler rationale because it appears to represent the "embodiment of a production model of how the process of teaching and learning proceeds" (45). The production model was one focus of criticism of pre-World War II models for curriculum development. Criticism of that "embodiment" has continued to this day.

But curriculum theory in general—beyond the Tylerian rationalists—was problematic. According to Kliebard (1975), curricular reform and reformists faced several difficulties. Among those were the problem referred to earlier in this chapter: a generally ahistorical posture, which has eventuated in a "lack of knowledge" regarding even "the basic facts in recent curriculum history" (40). One consequence of this ahistoricity has been "an uncritical propensity for novelty and change rather than funded knowledge or a dialogue across generations" (41). (In fact, if one wished to mount a criticism of the reconceptualists apart from theory, it might be that they generally chose to forgo creating a "dialogue across generations," as Kliebard had hoped. Instead, opting for a kind of broad critique, they often found themselves on the defense against the very traditions they hoped to persuade. The relative emphasis on criticism versus dialogue brought about some rancorous exchanges in the field in the early years of the debates.)

Another problem reformists faced was a distinctly "ameliorative orientation," the focus of which has been too heavily weighted in favor of "doing good" over conducting long-range research projects, the value of which may not be immediate (1975, 41). Finally, there has been the "lack of definition" in the field itself. With respect to the latter, Kliebard noted that the "paucity of ordered conceptions of what the curriculum field is" (43) contributes to a lack of agreement regarding terminology in the field. This state has resulted in ongoing problems among theorists about what ordinary and much-used terms mean, a condition that persists to this day. Consistent reading of the core journals in curriculum inevitably leads to the question, What does this label or term mean in *this* particular article since it clearly does not mean what it meant in the last one about the same topic?

Curricular theorists interested in looking at curriculum in some historic way have focused their attention on the place of curriculum in a larger social context, particularly on social control (Anyon 1988; Franklin 1988a), on self-control as the appropriate ideology of schooling (Franklin 1988b), and on radical criticism of the role of the public schools in fostering the production goals of the capitalist economy over the goal of producing critical and liberated individuals (Apple 1975, 1979, 1984, 1986; Apple and Weiss 1983; Giroux n.d. b; Giroux 1981; Giroux and Simon 1984; Gitlin 1983).

The work of Michael Apple deserves special credit for its criticism of the production emphasis in American schooling. Although it is generally fair to note that later curriculum theorists were less consciously concerned with the creation of educational *products* than were earlier curricular theorists such as Cubberley, Seeley, Finney, and Bobbitt, nevertheless, the heritage of those early curricular theorists can still be felt today. The criticisms of Apple and his students, Giroux, and others, however, reflect the observation that the "commitment to using the curriculum to achieve cultural uniformity is as much a part of the contemporary curriculum as it was a part of the field during the formative days" (Franklin 1988b, 81).

In that spirit, critics of the production model have introduced into curriculum theory and curricular discourse terms that were not part of the field's vocabulary until recently: "cultural hegemony," "social reproduction," "resistance," "hidden curriculum," and "marginalization" (Apple 1975; Giroux 1983b). Their criticisms have taken aim at the assumption that the processes of schooling can and should legitimately function to create "cultural homogeneity." This homogeneity in turn would act to preserve and maintain, through the process of schooling, existing social, cultural, political, economic, and structural arrangements within society.

Franklin (1988b) points out, as does Apple (1975, 1979, 1984, 1986, 1988) in a set of lengthier arguments, that "just as a reliance on the principles of scientific management and on behaviorism allowed early curriculum theorists to use the curriculum as an instrument of social control, behaviorism allows them to use the curriculum to the same end" (Franklin 1988b, 82). Although Franklin noted that the terms of the discourse were altered shortly before World War II, the effect—of attempting to use the curriculum as a device for ensuring social control—was precisely the same. Changing terminology did not alter the fundamental aims of the behaviorists; it merely "mask[ed] what is essentially a coercive process dedicated to cultural uniformity behind the language of democracy" (82). The pervasiveness of the scientific-technical model, especially in its systems-model incarnation, has failed to give way, even in the face of pointed identification and scathing criticism.

But social control, self-control, and the scientific production model as social movements were not the only "scientific" claims that gained a foothold in American education. Two others, biological determinism and the eugenics movement, interacted powerfully to institutionalize sexism and racism in the curriculum (Apple 1975; Selden 1988).

Selden's (1988) analysis, particularly, points out how historical notions of the characteristics of the races reinforced cultural, social, and economic as well as educative stereotypes, leading to "a picture of a racially and economically stratified society run in harmony with the laws of nature" (54). The messages of racial purity, a master race, and selective eugenics and even genocide (see, e.g., Grant 1921, *The Passing of the Great Race*) to create a biologically superior race were far more widespread than is generally realized. Lest the reader believe that these ideas represent the far fringe of Western civilization, biological determinism and eugenics were characteristic, as Selden (1988) argues, of more progressive arguments for school curricula and a schooling agenda. Arguments essentially proposed that only by moving toward more racial purity, and away from less suitable matches between races, could a better world be socially and racially engineered (56–62; see also Helen C. Putnam 1919, whom Selden cites).

The historians' work has been directed chiefly to understanding how and under what conditions curriculum came to be developed and what the implications were and are of the social trends that fed into curricular projects. Their curriculum criticism, whether from the right or left or a centrist ideological position (and many historians would probably count themselves as centrists), has attempted to demonstrate that curriculum development efforts, especially during the early 20th century, consciously and with painful accuracy reflected the orientation of the larger public, especially with respect to a rising tide of immigrants and great concern about maintaining "racial purity."

The Political Analysts

Perhaps no one's work is more well known in the realm of political and economic analysis than Michael Apple's (1975, 1979, 1984, 1986, 1988a, 1988b). To him the field owes such terms as "hegemony," "reproduction or correspondence theory," and "resistance theory." Additionally he has mentored a new generation of curricular theorists and scholars, whose work has had a profound impact on curriculum discussion. Together, they have done much to shape some of the debates around a Marxist, critical theorist, political, or economic focus. Included in this group of political analysts are Henry Giroux (1981, 1983a, 1983b), who has focused primarily on constructions of culture, ideology, critical theory, resistance, and marginality and, more recently, on school reform efforts; Jean Anyon (1988); and others. James Macdonald (1975, 1988a, 1988b) also joins this group of social psychologists, sociologists, economists, and political analysts in some of his later work.

What do the political analysts have to say? This is an extremely complex question, and indeed, there are persons who spend the bulk of their professional reading time attempting to keep up with the work of Apple, Giroux, and others in this vein. The group also includes Foucault in France and numbers of the British theorists and researchers whose work complements and enlarges what is being done on this side of the Atlantic.

Also among these theorists are Paulo Friere, who produced the seminal *Pedagogy of the Oppressed* (1970), Hans-Georg Gadamer (1976), Jürgen Habermas (see, e.g., *Knowledge and Human Interest*, 1971), and Paul Ricouer (1978). The influences of such persons on political analysis (even though, for instance, Gadamer would have to be considered a hermeneuticist) has been to make clear that "Critical theory recognizes the role of human interest in knowledge formation and creation . . . [and while] science, critical theory claims, has an interest in control . . . critical theory has an interest in emancipation" (Macdonald 1988a, 107).

The political analysts' most important contribution to curricular theory has been to demonstrate, in such a way that no curriculum research can ever again ignore it, that curriculum, like inquiry more broadly (Lincoln and Guba 1985), is not a neutral or value-free entity, that curricula are not produced in a vacuum absent from political or social ideology. Although the idea that it might be sounds naive today, one legacy of a positivist social science was the assertion and assumption that scientific "findings" could be objective, without taint of human bias (providing, of course, that studies were carried out without contaminating influences in methodologically correct, "pure" ways) and free of political ideology. Nowhere was this any more true than in the field of curriculum development, where it was felt that if scholars could uncover basic knowledge types that students needed to master, curriculum could be "engineered" to produce students who mastered the social, civic, personal, and intellective knowledge they needed to be model citizens, parents, and workers. The work of Apple and others undertaking political, economic, and cultural analyses of schooling has provided ample demonstration that ideology and ideological concerns permeate curriculum efforts more profoundly than we might have suspected (see, e.g., King 1986).

Macdonald (1988a) makes clear that the goals of schooling have been in conflict for centuries (a contest between idealism and realism, he notes). The major break with the history of curriculum in this century is represented by "enter[ing] into the work of curriculum for the sake of human liberation, rather than shaping and controlling behavior, or understanding, per se, as end points" (158), a position that one might argue would represent the aims of many political analysts, whatever their other ideological agendas.

A central theoretical concern of these analysts (and no effort is made here to separate the political analysts from the cultural or economic analysts who have worked on curriculum) is that "knowledge cannot be separated from human interest" (Macdonald 1975, 286). That is, there is no knowledge outside the social and cultural forms and norms that contribute to its creation. This assertion stands in stark contrast to conventional scientific philosophy, which postulates that knowledge stands apart from, and exists outside of, those who "discover" it; objectivism "deludes the knower by projecting an image of a self-subsistent world of facts structured in a lawlike manner; and thus conceals the *a priori* constitutions of these facts" (287). A guiding premise, then, of the work of these analysts has been connecting the content, form, and purpose of the curriculum to larger social structures, which create the conditions of empowerment for some (Anyon 1988) and marginalization, disempowerment, and impoverishment for others (Bromley 1989).

The efforts to uncover the "hidden curriculum," to trace the ways by which knowledge is socially constructed, to find ways in which to give voice to the marginalized, and to expose the bias and power relations located in curriculum and in broader conceptions of schooling have been the focus of this body of work. The creation of forms of schooling that create dialogic movement toward human liberation has been in the forefront of critical efforts. As Macdonald (1988a) expressed this aim,

> There is little reason that I can see to propose to the young that the freeing of the human spirit, mind and body from arbitrary social and psychological constraints—that is, the liberation of human potential in a framework of democratic rights, responsibilities and practices—leading toward better realization of justice, equality, liberty, and fraternity—should not be reflected in our own work with schools. Thus, I think we should work toward change in the direction of human liberation. (158)

Central to this work of human liberation are the concepts of ideology and ideological struggle, with ideology representing the entire system of cultural values, norms, beliefs, attitudes, ethical systems, modes of justice, and institutional and social artifacts. Ideological struggle, for the political analyst, is located in the work of both schools as institutions and individuals, whose primary change process is coming to terms with ideologies that are limiting, defeating, marginalizing or that reify dominant and, by definition, oppressive ideologies. This realization is the core of the educational process, revolving around recognizing and shedding divided or false consciousness and internalizing a new consciousness. The new consciousness should, the critical theorists argue (Fay 1987), provide the "ideological moment" for an individual to act, to create change in her or his circumstances, and to institute greater justice for others who are also marginalized, without "voice," or oppressed.

Toward that end, the political analyst provides two sets of learning tools: research on the curricular, cultural, or economic structures that oppress or marginalize and a pedagogy, commonly grounded in community work (such as that espoused by Friere 1970), designed to provide confrontational and dialectic interaction, which forces those marginalized to understand and locate the sources of their marginalization. The interaction further encourages them to seek means and modes of movement toward liberation or emancipation. The agenda, as Macdonald (1988a) sees it, involves "asking persons to transcend the limitation and restrictions of their social conditioning and common sense and to venture beyond by seeing and choosing new possibilities. . . . it is rather a process of helping others see possibilities and helping them free themselves." (163).

The conviction that social and structural arrangements are embedded in the curriculum and schooling is a powerful one. Political analysts argue, not without strong evidence, that "unequal distributions of power and authority, undemocratic and unpalatable work arrangements, economic, and other stratifications and unequal opportunity, and one's future social class position" (Anyon 1988, 184) reside in those hidden or largely unexamined processes. The so-called "hidden curriculum" (Jackson 1968), by which attitudes, values, beliefs, and norms are communicated in schools, without discussion (implicitly) but powerfully and effectively, function to shape behavior, to control, and ultimately to teach children that one set of activities is to be rewarded and one is not. Conflict, in particular, argues Apple (1975), is a social activity around which carefully structured boundaries and parameters are set, the ultimate function of which is to socialize children politically to the extent that their own internal conflicts will not be open to discussion, debate, or dialogic expression.

A dominant theme of the political analysts is criticism of the "dominant normative structure of the larger society," using the vehicle of criticism of the educational enterprise (Apple 1975, 90). This criticism is accomplished through modes of analysis and inquiry that demonstrate to educators, researchers, teachers, and citizens that there are "concrete linkages between personal, social and economic injustice and education's models of inquiry" (90). Whether the topic is the curriculum (Giroux 1983b), school administration and bureaucratic modes of management, models for inquiry commonly used in educational research (Lather 1986a, 1986b,1987), or teacher labor markets (Apple 1984), the themes bear resemblance across researchers and theoreticians: Schooling and the curriculum as it operates in the schooling process perpetuate forms of oppression, injustice, and social class structures, which in turn act to limit democracy and emancipation. Thus, exposure of the ways in which curriculum operates to achieve these unjust social ends is the first step in restoring schools to their appropriate place in fostering empowerment, transcendence, and liberation. This is a political as well as an inquiry goal for this group of curricularists.

The modes of inquiry associated with such analysis are primarily, though not solely, Marxist, materialist, or critical theorist. Although each of these three generally holds to a realist ontology, they all do constitute a major break with conventional science in that their preferred epistemologies are monistic rather than dualistic, and their methodologies are interactive rather than interventionist, as is classical science. Thus, political analysts have more in common with hermeneuticists and phenomenologists than they do with logical positivists. Their typical inquiry stance is dialectic in nature, focusing on the conflict that inheres in pluralistic social structures.

The pedagogy that proceeds from these analyses, although incomplete in either practice or theory (Simon 1988, 1–2), is dialogic in form and emancipatory in intent. The focus of such inquiry—and its accompanying pedagogy—is often structural; that is, the central concern is frequently with organizational structures and the structure of social arrangements, particularly those that maintain power relationships; distribute wealth or education inequitably; or render marginal a class, or classes, of persons.

Their criticisms, although sometimes arcanely argued, have provided a turning point in curriculum research. It is difficult to ignore the careful, systematic inquiry of the political analysts in curriculum research. Their efforts to characterize curriculum as part of a series of oppressive social structures and their success in provoking debate regarding the larger ends of curriculum (Berman 1984; Short 1987) have proven persuasive even to those who do not consider themselves political analysts per se.

The Aesthetic Critics

But other scholars have also figured strongly in the great curriculum debates of the past 15 years. Among the other voices heard, those of the aesthetic critics and art educators have also proven compelling. Critics of schooling who attack educational processes on aesthetic grounds do so primarily because "the intimate connection between imagination and the intellectual has been forgotten, overlooked, and neglected—especially in our schools" (Broudy 1988, 334). A central thesis of these critics is that art and aesthetics education has been sold as an *instrumental*, rather than as an *expressive*, form of curriculum and that as such it has lost considerable ground in contemporary debates about returning schools to the "basics." When classed as an instrumental end, rather than as an expressive means, aesthetics and art curricula are viewed as "frills," to be abandoned or offered in truncated ways, not central to the core to which schools are to be dedicated.

The aesthetic critics make several powerful arguments for returning aesthetic education to the central core of school curricula. Their arguments stem in part from critical theory and in part from 20th-century art itself, and the approach is almost purely phenomenological. Padgham (1988, 360) notes that the "views of this group differ from the more traditional curriculum theorists in that the emphasis is placed on the nature of the relationship between the teacher and the learner." Whereas in traditional curriculum theory, the relationship between the two is between the expert and the seeker, in more contemporary, and certainly in reconceptualist, criticism, the relationship between teacher and taught is dialogic, emphasizing not meaning that is "inherited" from previous learners but rather meaning that is derived from the experience of the learner and that the learner constructs (Greene 1974). The final source of knowledge, according to Padgham (1988), is "within the individual . . . [where] through a dialogical encounter . . . the individual begins to discover that he creates meaning . . . and the major emphasis then is not placed on the known [facts to be digested], but rather on the unknown, and it is through contact with the unknown that the individual comes to know himself" (374). The centrality of the self in the knowing and coming-to-know process is one of the humanistic precepts shared by the feminist critics, the phenomenologists, and the critical theorists and political analysts. It is a very *postmodern* concept.

Beyer (1988) argues that several presuppositions more or less sequentially affect aesthetic education in the United States. First, the supposition abroad is that the arts are for those who have the leisure, wealth, and taste to partake of them, and indeed the structure of artistic endeavor in the Western world has largely created a patronage system for art consumption buttressed by wealth, power, and prestige. Second, to appreciate art and aesthetic modes, one must also be trained in the creation of such products. And finally it is presumed that children of the working classes have neither the need nor the desire for artistic or aesthetic experiences.

The aesthetic critics refute these stereotypic assumptions and argue otherwise. Broudy (1983, 1988) makes the case compellingly that to understand a world fraught with images and image making, we must have aesthetic education to help children connect images to the words they read. Without the images to create meaning in the words, children will not read, he argues, and thus there is a functional—in addition to an aesthetic—linkage to literacy.

Beyond that, however, the creative moment in individuals is believed to be intimately connected to self-knowledge, both to dialogical processes within the individual and between the individual and others in his or her world. Aesthetic education functions to release and liberate expressive and imaginative potential in the self, and thus has empowering aspects that are overlooked in the treatment of art as an instrumental mode of curriculum. The power of imaging and imagination are blocked when artistic and expressive forms of teaching and learning are removed from the curriculum. The result, Broudy and others argue, is an impoverishment of the power of the individual to engage in certain kinds of dialogic interactions.

> Contemporary curriculum theory . . . places the emphasis on the finding. . . . In the traditional approach to curriculum the emphasis is placed on the seeking. The student is led to believe that there is something out there which he is to find. . . . In the new curriculum theory the emphasis is placed on what to do with what one finds; it attempts to use the known to assist the individual in finding his way, of knowing that he might generate new knowledge for himself. (Padgham 1988, 376)

Dialogic aspects of curriculum are central to the argument for aesthetic critics. Interactions between form and content—long believed to be separate entities by the more traditional curriculum theorists (Broudy 1988; Padgham 1988)—have become crucial; in some sense, the medium is the message. Form becomes an aspect of content, and content cannot exist without form; some congruence between the two is realized to be both appropriate and necessary (Buescher 1986; Eisner 1979).

In this framework of contemporary assumptions regarding aesthetic criticism and curriculum, other aspects of schooling come under scrutiny, as one might well suppose. Critical theorists and neo-Marxists point out that artistic creations have immediate bearing on the representations of social life with which individuals are confronted, and Beyer (1988, 390) argues that both Marx and Engels "repeatedly point to the necessity of creating works which typify the development of social and historical forces." Those forces that have shaped a culture and that would serve to illuminate the condition of the working classes particularly ought to be a subject of artistic interest, albeit without sacrificing "artistic integrity or aesthetic excellence" (390).

In addition to social and expressive life, Beyer argues that ethical considerations should also be a part of an aesthetics curriculum. One possibility for such a curriculum would be a demonstration of the relationships between and among images of an aesthetic nature, the individual's and larger society's consciousness, and ethical standards for conduct (393–396). The idea of linking aesthetic images to ethical systems is hardly a new one. Much of medieval, and particularly religious, forms such as painting, stained glass, altar pieces, and even architecture communicated theological lessons about good, evil, right, wrong, and the moral narratives of the Judeo-Christian tradition. But the solid and unmoving nature of most of those forms, contrasted with the highly mobile, kinesthetic quality of film-as-art, television, public concerts, museums (a "modern" invention), art galleries, and other aesthetic exhibitions, demands a reexamination of public images alongside public and private moral and ethical standards. As expressions of social consciousness, artistic and aesthetic creations, like the curriculum, reflect social arrangements and structures whose unconscious purposes may be oppression rather than the freeing of the human spirit or the elevation of humankind to new levels of consciousness.

To summarize, the aesthetic critics have argued that aesthetic education, and indeed aesthetic curricula in general, have been marginalized; abstracted from the flow of daily life; divorced from common, public, and community concerns. In addition, aesthetic appreciation has increasingly accrued as a social given to powerful and privileged classes and, in the educational reform currents of "back to the basics," has been treated as a commodity to be purchased by those educationally and economically privileged enough to afford its consumption. Finally, this treatment has led to the impoverishment in the emotional, feeling, expressive, and appreciative education of those who could most use such a connection between the intellectual and the imaginative.

Proposals to reconnect the imaginative and expressive to the intellective are varied, but they most often assert the primacy of the individual's ascription of meaning to his or her experience, a kind of critical subjectivity (Gauthier 1982), and the interactive and dialectical-dialogical nature of the teacher-learner relationship. In both respects, the aesthetic critics share assumptions to which the phenomenologists and postmodernists would likely assent.

The Phenomenologists

There is no "economical" or single definition of phenomenology. Credit for the original work in phenomenology is ordinarily given to Husserl, and the short answer to "What is it?" is often that it is a scientific discipline of description of how the world is experienced by persons (Reese 1980). Elaborations of the original formulations of Husserl have been presented by Heidegger, Husserl's student, and Hans-George Gadamer, Heidegger's student. Each of these philosophers has worked to eliminate some of the problems with the original formulations, and phenomenology enjoys a status today as a soundly conceived philosophical school, the bent of which is to return experience to the lived rather than the instrumental or conceptual world and to view the conceptual world as one given meaning and mediated by the lived, present being and temporal experience (Beyer 1986b; Cherryholmes 1988, 1989; Gauthier 1982; Grumet 1983; Huebner 1974).

What individual researchers and theoreticians in curriculum studies do with phenomenology, how they handle it, and to which aspects they pay particular attention determine the particular focus of any given piece of research. There is simply no single, unilateral expression of phenomenology and its meaning for curriculum studies or pedagogy. This lack of a sharp, hard, univocal focus creates difficulties in characterizing or summarizing the work of phenomenologists, but it also creates compensations in the form of richness, depth, and multiple approaches to the use of phenomenology in curricular studies.

If summary were possible, it would be necessary to note that the phenomenologists themselves are increasingly concerned with the abstractions represented by the scientific, technological, and instrumentalist approaches to curriculum that prevailed during the first half of this century. The notion of a curriculum as a set of concepts, ideas, and facts to be mastered; students as empty vessels waiting to be filled with those concepts; and pedagogy as a set of techniques to be acquired by teachers is often rejected by contemporary curricularists. This rejection is buttressed by both a body of evidence and a set of moral suasions that children are themselves capable of rich inner lives, that their experience is worth eliciting and building on, and that pedagogy is a form of interactive relationship rather than a bag of tricks to be assembled in the teaching process (van Manen 1988).

Like that of the aesthetic critics and the feminist critics to some extent, the emphasis of the phenomenologists has consistently resided in the meanings attached to the lived experience of the world and in the dialectical relationship between that lived experience and the social and structural experience given as scientific and technical concepts (the "received view" of society). Thus, phenomenology has demanded of its theoreticians, practitioners, and ethnographers that they search for and uncover deeper social structures and the larger connections between inner life and the outer world.

The mere description of schooling and learning experiences is not enough and has been criticized as essentially sterile (Smith 1988). The provision of description without unpacking its social meaning and context may be compared by analogy to qualitative research done in a positivist tradition: The forms are there, but little research context has changed if the paradigm has not shifted (Lincoln and Guba 1985). Locating the research in its social milieu and using it dialogically are what provide power to newer forms of phenomenological curriculum research. Without context and without dialogic interaction, phenomenology is absent.

The language phenomenologists use, the terms they choose to represent thought, derive from a deliberate attempt to break with the instrumentalist-technocratic-systems orientation of the rationalists. Determined attempts to break the bonds of formal scientific, and conventional, discourse is one way of forcing the reader, analyst, researcher, teacher, or dialogic "other" to confront a worldview that is unfamiliar; that is brought away from second-order concepts and back to "being"; and that captures, at least in part, the emotional, psychological, social, kinesthetic, and moral experiences of another. Aoki (1988, 406) observed that the phenomenologists have "interests in reconceptualizing the curriculum, in understanding alternative paradigms or ideologies within which curriculum thought is embedded, in transcending instrumentalism in curriculum thought to embrace beingness and critical consciousness, and in viewing schools engaged in a search for situational meaning."

The phenomenologists' central objection is to a curriculum model, or set of models, more accurately, that creates a "conceptual theoretical world . . . devoid of the sense of historicity . . . [the end point of which] is an objectified world within which even people are transformed into objects, their subjectivities reduced out" (Aoki 1988, 410). The criticism, which is equally powerfully advanced as a criticism of positivism in general and as a paradigm for human sciences (Lincoln and Guba 1985), is that "Obscured or missing is the first order [phenomenological] meaning structure underlying the second order structure of facts, generalizations, laws and theories" (Aoki 1988, 410). Phenomenologists abjure the implicit assumption of conventional science that the "facts" are all that there is to a matter. Like constructivist psychologists or Gestalt therapists, phenomenologists act from two premises: that knowledge is a human construction and that social life is an enacted, meaning-embedded experience, inseparable from human beliefs and values.

So the phenomenologists, although not rejecting the second-order world—the world of concepts, facts, theories, and laws—nevertheless believe the ends-means instrumentalism of this technological, rationalistic worldview is a profoundly mistaken, or at least seriously limited, orientation for curriculum building and for curriculum research and scholarship. They argue, some more strongly than others, that the second-order focus is an emotionally and psychologically empty and artistically, aesthetically, and socially debilitating form of curriculum, which not only serves to denigrate the inner lives of its "consumers" (and possibly producers and transmitters) but also alienates students from their basis of meaning and context. Primacy in curricular matters ought, these researchers argue, to emphasize "the quality of life experiences within a lived situation . . . [as] what matters" (Aoki 1988, 412). It is not that second-order concepts and the world of conventional science is not important; it surely is. But phenomenologists would have pedagogy reflect a dialogic relationship between first-order (inner) and second-order (outer, nomological) worlds rather than an instrumental focus. The emphasis on dialogic, dialectical relationships—whether between first- and second-order worlds or between teacher and taught, or between the lived experience and the "received" experience, as in the case of feminist theorists—is what marks the phenomenologist.

The relative emphasis on meaning, context, and the lived experience of schooling should not obscure the fact that phenomenologists are also interested in reason, logic, and instrumentality. They surely are. But their central concern has been to balance the perceived overemphasis of the latter with consideration of the expressive power of the former (Eisner 1982). The relatively scant attention paid to the former ends in schooling during the first half of this century are of enormous concern to those trained in, or later persuaded by, phenomenology.

The Feminist Theorists

Of all the humanistic traditions, perhaps none has been so profoundly critical and potentially radical to curriculum studies—and indeed, to all the academic disciplines—as feminist theory. Feminist theorists have cut across disciplinary lines, examining the roles of women in history, sociology, family life, economic structures, education and pedagogy, the arts, and the sciences. Feminists, female scientists, and feminist theorists have sought in the past two decades to delineate the dominance of a patriarchal system and its debilitating effects on women and men alike. As Tuana (1989, vii) notes, feminist scientists "have uncovered the complex interconnections of sexist, racist, and classist biases grounding theories of human nature, and in doing so have seen the ways in which such biases permeate the entire structure of science. Feminist critiques of science have thus begun to focus on the ideologies, politics, epistemologies, economies, and metaphysics of traditional science." In the process, these scholars have attacked the conventional paradigm for inquiry—the scientific method—as an institutionalized form of objectifying the world, which removes persons from their center of being by dehumanizing them as research "objects" (Bleier 1984, 1986; Keller 1985). Of the humanistic traditions, none has more potentially radical and radicalizing consequences than the study of the social structures that oppress and negate and relegate to second-class status half the world's population.

One of the many sources of power in feminist theory has been its intuitive, psychological, and scientific links to other significant social changes (Harding 1986): a new ecological awareness, rooted in concerns for human habitats and the environment; peace movements; the rise of civil rights demands; studies of parenting, loving, nurturing, and caring, which point to the impoverishment of men as well as women when men are removed from such concerns; and studies of how ethical systems are generated between and among the sexes (Grumet 1983, 1988a, 1988b; Lather 1987). All of these influences can be seen in various forms in curriculum studies, particularly as they reflect critical theory, aesthetic criticism, and phenomenology. But no group has grounded its potent criticisms of the instrumental curriculum more squarely in sexism than the feminist theorists.

About what are the feminist theorists concerned? In his introduction to the work of some feminist theorists, Pinar (1988a) describes an avenue some feminist theorists and researchers have taken, although it clearly does not represent all feminist theorists:

> No serious curriculum scholar ignores developments in . . . [the] . . . area . . . of the relations among gender, values, and curriculum. [Here, we can see] the scale of the problem of sexism, linking it to the world's armament and environmental crises. [Macdonald and Macdonald (1988, 477–487)] rightly link politics, economics, and culture with the production of gendered personalities in family and school. . . . Sexism permeates all aspects of the school, including its organization, status hierarchy, and curriculum. . . . The so-called hidden curriculum of the school reiterates familiar sex-role stereotyping. No aspect of school life seems to escape these influences. (476–477)

That no aspect of school life seems to escape these influences has not been lost on the feminist theorists, who have undertaken to explore the ways in which sexism operates to reify existing social arrangements from the larger culture to schools; to examine the patriarchal patterns that predominate in school hierarchies; to observe the ways in which sex segregation takes place in school activities; to criticize curricular materials themselves for evidence of sex-role stereotyping; or to connect the world of teacher training and the university to the subjugation of women and the creation and amplification of tension and hostility, particularly among women who might otherwise support and nurture one another (Apple 1984; Miller 1986; Pinar and Miller 1982).

A pivotal concept to feminist studies is the concept of hegemony, crudely defined in *Webster's New Collegiate Dictionary* (seventh edition) as "preponderant influence or authority." But the concept is much more extensively elaborated as "the permeation throughout civil society . . . including a whole range of structures and activities, beliefs, morality, etc., that is in one or another way supportive of the established order and the class interests that dominate it" (Boggs 1976, cited in Macdonald and Macdonald 1988, 477).

Hegemony works in two ways: by providing a sense of what is orderly and "right" for the society as a whole and by operating as an enculturation and acculturation system for the young, particularly in schools, as part of the formal curriculum. Feminist theorists have undertaken the task of uncovering and delineating the forms and structures that operate in hegemonic fashion, creating roles for both men and women that desiccate and truncate their emotional and social lives.

The focus, then, has been threefold for the feminist theorists. First, some theorists have been intent on structural analyses of curricula, pedagogies, and practices that support sexism and undermine women as human beings and place them in restrictive roles. In this effort, such theorists have tried to provide evidence of sexism, sexist practices, and their debilitating effects on girls and boys and men and women (Grumet 1983).

Second, the feminist theorists have been attempting to create a theory or theories that would guide curriculum, pedagogical training, and dialogic relationships, in the hope that such theories, grounded in the phenomenologically lived experiences of women, could lead to a more general understanding of how we might train women and men to be first and most simply human beings. Above all, the feminist theorists have concerned themselves with ways of thinking about curriculum that might allow both genders to move toward caring, nurturing, responsible, knowing, meaningful humanity (Lauritzen 1989). Such theories are not likely to be complete for some time, but drawing on preliminary work on ethical systems (Gilligan 1982) and women's ways of knowing (Belenky, Glinchy, Goldberger, and Tarule 1986), the feminist curricular theorists are creating new theories of how women experience the world and their relationships differently from the way men experience them. That is a beginning for those who would like to see new, fresh, noninstrumental, phenomenologically oriented theories replace those of the conventional, objectivist, patriarchal scientist.

Third, the feminists have tried, with some measure of success, to suggest ways in which the relationships within schools, between school and family, between teacher and student (Kenway and Modra 1989), and between teachers and administrators might be incrementally altered to bring about a rethinking of the ethos and ethic of schooling (Macdonald and Macdonald 1988). A fundamental concept in such a program to feminist theorists is the idea of resistance, or the rejection of socially ascribed roles, behaviors, feelings, and experiences that are often laid on women. Resistance is a form of consciousness-raising within individuals, a defiance of stereotyping, a stubborn refusal to accept social definitions of one's meanings and experiences when social definitions do not match one's own subjective inner experiences. Resistance implies the struggle for a definition of the self that is rooted in the unique subjectivity of individuals, without regard to gender.

Neither the influence nor the potential of the feminist theorists for reconceptualizing the curriculum should be underestimated. Like the critical theorists, with whom they often make common cause, "critical" has two meanings for feminists. The first relates to the discovery of the structures that repress and stultify inner worlds and outer social life, or the raising of "critical consciousness." The second "critical" relates to their position on contemporary social class and caste arrangements: unrelenting analysis and censure of the prevailing and predominant patriarchal system. This reproof, in the form of careful, painstaking "heartwork," extends from analyses of who does the bulk of the housework and child care in the nuclear family to how economic labor markets function to depress the wages for "women's work." Both microanalyses and macroanalyses (Apple 1984, 1986) are viewed as appropriate and meaningful in the effort to uncover and put on trial the systematic denigration of one class of individuals for the benefit of another.

The links between research on women and feminist issues and phenomenology deserve to be stressed again. Renewed interest in how women experience the world differently from men has led to natural alliances between phenomenologists, who stress the primacy of lived meanings of persons over second-order theories of the world, and feminists. There is in many respects a natural collegiality between the philosophical underpinnings of phenomenology and the findings of feminist theorists, particularly those whose focus has been on meaning or on curriculum, more broadly. Although not all feminist theorists would assert an allegiance to phenomenology, and not all phenomenologists would feel comfortable with feminist theorists, nevertheless there is a mutuality of worldview that strengthens both. Thus, it is not unusual to hear feminist theorists talking in terms and languages that are resonant with those of phenomenologists. The bond is probably a profound humanism and the concern for human liberation and realization of potential. Feminist theorists would focus first on the liberation of women from oppression but also on the possibility of the liberation of all human beings from oppressive structures.

CONCLUSION

There is no single "humanistic" tradition. There are several, each with its own particular focus and its unique wedge into curricular and pedagogical matters. In spite of this multiple focus, the humanistic traditions share important assumptions among themselves.

The first such shared assumption is that historical perspectives can and should be periodically reexamined, principally to see what might have been overlooked or to provide a fresh account of what we thought we meant. Historians, critical theorists, feminists, and others in this tradition have emerged mindful of the premise that we have histories and that those histories, social and individual, will determine what we will be tomorrow, unless we make decisions regarding how things will be different. The image of history and historicity, and the persuasion that history is not a scientific (i.e., instrumental) enterprise, has reemerged as a guiding precept to the new curriculum theorists.

A second theme to emerge among the new humanists is the realization that knowledge is a socially constructed entity, emerging from a socially designated "priesthood" of science, and therefore is suspect with regard to its social and class preoccupations (Bleier 1984, 1986). Knowledge does not exist "out there" waiting for humans to wrench it from the unwilling arms of a greedy Nature (and the reader should note the sexist and force-filled images of this description of how knowledge is accrued since such images have been prevalent for several centuries in the Western world). Rather, it is created from the meaning made by individuals and groups, and as such is subject to renegotiation and revision as social restructuring demands it. Understanding the socially constructed nature of knowledge both undermines the priesthood of science and at the same time makes more precarious, tentative, uncertain, underdetermined, conditional, and exploratory our own sense of knowledge of the world. It makes both mandatory and urgent more intensive study of meaning-making activities, both social and individual.

A third theme to emerge, and one that has yet to be understood or comprehended in its entirety, is the interrelatedness of our social and pedagogical, and therefore curricular, theories with our larger theological, moral-ethical, environmental, and psychological needs. Although some are working at the borders of such work (Sissela Bok, Hans Kung, Jean Houston, among others), we may be simply seeing the beginning of a global paradigm shift, a change in the social, scientific, and moral consciousness of civilization. That argument has been advanced and continues to be advanced (e.g., arguments being advanced in disciplines outside education, in Lincoln 1989; Lincoln and Guba 1985) by serious scholars in a variety of disciplines.

Whatever position one wishes to take on the possibility of a paradigm shift, nevertheless, a fourth characteristic theme emerges from the new humanists: a stunning rejection of what science and conventional mind-body dualism philosophies have done to individuals, and to societies, and a scathing criticism of the underpinnings of science and objectivism. The new curricular humanists point to the damage wreaked on children and to the fatal flaws of schools in failing to teach children what they need to understand to enable humanity to survive. And despite the understanding that science has provided untold miracles, the new humanists cast a cold eye on what the rationalists and the empirical-analytic school have done to create starved and alienated personalities.

What began as a radical but small group of critics of contemporary curriculum theory has now become a groundswell. Scholars writing about curricular matters today cannot avoid taking into account one or many of the critical schools of curriculum discourse. As a result, the reconceivers of curriculum studies are not just postulating that a new world could exist but also creating it—voice by voice, criticism by criticism, scholar by scholar.

References

Anyon, Jean. 1988. "Schools as Agencies of Social Legitimation." In *Contemporary Curriculum Discourses*, edited by William F. Pinar, 175–200. Scottsdale, AZ: Gorsuch Scarisbrick.

Aoki, Ted Tetsuo. 1988. "Toward a Dialectic Between the Conceptual World and the Lived World: Transcending Instrumentalism in Curriculum Orientation." In *Contemporary Curriculum Discourses*, edited by William F. Pinar, 402–416. Scottsdale, AZ: Gorsuch Scarisbrick.

Apple, Michael W. 1975. "The Hidden Curriculum and the Nature of Conflict." In *Curriculum Theorizing: The Reconceptualists*, edited by William Pinar. Berkeley, CA: McCutchan.

Apple, Michael W. 1979. *Ideology and Curriculum*. London: Routledge & Kegan Paul.

Apple, Michael W. 1984. Teaching and "women's work": A comparative historical and ideological analysis. *Journal of Education* 166(3): 455–473.

Apple, Michael W. 1986. *Teachers and Texts*. London: Routledge & Kegan Paul.

Apple, Michael W. 1988a. Curricula and teaching: Are they headed toward excellence? *NASSP Bulletin* 32:14–25.

Apple, Michael W. 1988b. Curriculum in the year 2000: Tensions and possibilities. *Phi Delta Kappan* 64 (5): 321–326.

Apple, Michael W., and L. Weiss, eds. 1983. *Ideology and Practicing Education*. Philadelphia, PA: Temple University Press.

Bateson, Gregory. 1972. *Steps to an Ecology of Mind*. New York: Ballantine Books.

Belenky, Mary Field, Blyth M. Glinchy, Nancy R. Goldberger, and Jill M. Tarule. 1986. *Women's Ways of Knowing*. New York: Basic Books.

Berlak, Ann. 1989. "Angles of Vision on Emancipatory Pedagogy: Some "Takes" on the First Five Weeks." Paper presented at the annual meeting, American Educational Research Association, San Francisco, CA.

Berman, Edward H. 1984. State hegemony and the schooling process. *Journal of Education* 166(3): 239–253.

Beyer, Landon E. 1984. Field experience, ideology, and the development of critical reflexivity. *Journal of Teacher Education* 35(3): 36–41.

Beyer, Landon E. 1986a. Critical theory and the art of teaching. *Journal of Curriculum and Supervision* 1(3): 221–232.

Beyer, Landon E. 1986b. The reconstruction of knowledge and educational studies. *Journal of Education* 168(2): 113–135.

Beyer, Landon E. 1988. "Art and Society: Toward New Directions in Aesthetic Education." In *Contemporary Curriculum Discourses*, edited by William F. Pinar, 380–399. Scottsdale, AZ: Gorsuch Scarisbrick.

Beyer, Landon E. 1989. The social and educational conditions for democracy. *Journal of Curriculum and Supervision* 4:178–186.

Bleier, Ruth. 1984. *Science and Gender: A Critique of Biology and Its Theories on Women*. Oxford: Pergamon.

Bleier, Ruth, ed. 1986. *Feminist Approaches to Science*. New York: Pergamon.

Bobbitt, John Franklin. 1912. The elimination of waste in education. *Elementary School Teacher* 12: 258–265.

Boggs, Carl. 1976. *Gramsci's Marxism*. South Hampton, England: Camelot Press.

Bromley, Hank. 1989. Identity politics and critical pedagogy. *Educational Theory* 39: 207–223.

Broudy, Harry S. 1983. The humanities and their uses: Proper claims and expectations. *Journal of Aesthetic Education* 17(4): 125–138.

Broudy, Harry S. 1988. "Aesthetics and the Curriculum." In *Contemporary Curriculum Discourses*, edited by William F. Pinar, 332–342. Scottsdale, AZ: Gorsuch Scarisbrick.

Brown, Theodore M. 1988. "How Fields Change: A Critique of the 'Kuhnian' View." In *Contemporary Curriculum Discourses*, edited by William F. Pinar, 16–30. Scottsdale, AZ: Gorsuch Scarisbrick.

Brubaker, Dale L., and Gayle Brookbank. 1986. James B. Macdonald: A bibliography. *Journal of Curriculum and Supervision* 1(3): 215–221.

Buescher, Thomas M. 1986. Appreciating children's aesthetic ways of knowing: An interview with Elliot Eisner. *Journal for the Education of the Gifted* 10(1): 7–15.

Cain, Bonnie C. n.d. "Participatory Research: Research with Historic Consciousness." Working Paper no. 3, Participatory Research Project, Toronto, Ontario.

Callahan, Raymond E. 1962. *Education and the Cult of Efficiency: A Study of the Social Forces That Have Shaped the Administration of the Public Schools*. Chicago: University of Chicago Press.

Cherryholmes, Cleo H. 1988. *Power and Criticism: Poststructural Investigations in Education*. New York: Teachers College Press.

Cherryholmes, Cleo H. 1989. "Agency, Structure, and Rational Choice in Educational Attainment: Poststructural Considerations." Paper presented at the annual meeting, American Educational Research Association, San Francisco.

Clark, David L. 1985. Emerging Paradigms in Organizational Theory and Research." In *Organizational Theory and Inquiry: The Paradigm Revolution*, edited by Yvonna S. Lincoln, 43–78. Newbury Park, CA: Sage.

Connelly, Michael. 1990. Personal communication.

Cubberley, Ellwood P. 1916. *Report of the Survey of the Public System of Salt Lake City, Utah: Salt Lake Survey Committee*. Salt Lake City: Salt Lake City Grocer Printing Company.

Dallmayr, Fred R. 1985. Pragmatism and hermeneutics. *The Review of Politics* 47: 411–430.

Davis, O. L., Jr. 1983. Liberating learning. *Educational Leadership* 23: 58–60.

Eisner, Elliot W. 1979. *The Educational Imagination*. New York: Macmillan.

Eisner, Elliot W. 1982. *Cognition and Curriculum*. New York: Longman.

Fay, Brian. 1987. *Critical Social Science*. Ithaca, NY: Cornell University Press.

Franklin, Barry M. 1988a. "Self Control and the Psychology of School Discipline." In *Contemporary Curriculum Discourses*, edited by William F. Pinar, 31–49. Scottsdale, AZ: Gorsuch Scarisbrick.

Franklin, Barry M. 1988b. "Whatever Happened to Social Control? The Muting of Coercive Authority in Curriculum Discourse." In *Contemporary Curriculum Discourses*, edited by William F. Pinar, 80–90. Scottsdale, AZ: Gorsuch Scarisbrick.

Freire, Paolo. 1970. *Pedagogy of the Oppressed*. New York: Continuum.

Gadamer, Hans-Georg. 1976. *Philosophical Hermeneutics*. Berkeley: University of California Press.

Gauthier, Michael G. 1982. Narcissus in the classroom: The pedagogical implications of subjective criticism. *Journal of Education* 164(3): 238–255.

Gilligan, Carol. 1982. *In a Different Voice*. Cambridge, MA: Harvard University Press.

Giroux, Henry A. n.d.a. "Border Pedagogy in the Age of Postmodernism." Mimeograph.

Giroux, Henry A. n.d.b. "Postmodernism and the Discourse of Educational Criticism." Mimeograph.

Giroux, Henry A. 1981. *Ideology, Culture and the Process of Schooling*. Philadelphia, PA: Temple University Press.

Giroux, Henry A. 1983a. Ideology and agency in the process of schooling. *Journal of Education* 165(1): 12–33.

Giroux, Henry A. 1983b. *Theory and Resistance in Education*. South Hadley, MA: Bergin and Garvey.

Giroux, Henry A., and Roger Simon. 1984. Curriculum study and cultural politics. *Journal of Education* 166(3): 226–238.

Gitlin, Andrew. 1984. "School Structure and Teacher's Work." In

Ideology and Practicing Education, edited by Michael Apple and L. Weiss, 193–212. Philadelphia, PA: Temple University Press.

Goodson, Ivor F. 1988. *The Making of Curriculum: Collected Essays*. Philadelphia, PA: Falmer.

Grant, Madison. 1921. *The Passing of the Great Race, or the Racial Basis of European History*. New York: Scribners.

Greene, Maxine. 1974. "Cognition, Consciousness and Curriculum." In *Heightened Consciousness: Cultural Revolution and Curriculum Theory*, edited by William F. Pinar, 69–87. Berkeley, CA: McCutchan.

Greene, Maxine. 1985. Consciousness and the public space: Discovering a pedagogy. *Phenomenology + Pedagogy* 3: 69–83.

Grumet, Madeleine R. 1983. The line is drawn. *Educational Leadership* 40: 28–38.

Grumet, Madeleine R. 1988a. *Bitter Milk: Women and Teaching*. Amherst: University of Massachusetts Press.

Grumet, Madeleine R. 1988b. "Bodyreading." In *Contemporary Curriculum Discourses*, edited by William F. Pinar, 453–474. Scottsdale, AZ: Gorsuch Scarisbrick.

Guba, Egon G., and Yvonna S. Lincoln. 1981. *Effective Evaluation*. San Francisco, CA: Jossey-Bass.

Habermas, Jürgen. 1971. *Knowledge and Human Interest*. Boston: Beacon Press.

Habermas, Jürgen. 1973. *Legitimation Crisis*. Boston: Beacon Press.

Haggerson, Nelson L. 1985. Curriculum as figurative language: Exalting teaching and learning through poetry. *Illinois School Research and Development* 22: 10–17.

Harding, Jan, ed. 1986. *Perspectives on Gender and Science*. London: Falmer.

Hesse, Mary. 1980. *Revolutions and Reconstructions in the Philosophy of Science*. Bloomington: Indiana University Press.

Heubner, Dwayne. 1974. "Curriculum as Concern for Man's Temporality." In *Heightened Consciousness: Cultural Revolution and Curriculum Theory*, edited by William F. Pinar. Berkeley, CA: McCutchan.

Jackson, Philip W. 1968. *Life in Classrooms*. New York: Holt, Rinehart and Winston.

Jackson, Philip W. 1980. Curriculum and its discontents. *Curriculum Inquiry* 10: 159–172.

Johnson, Harold T. 1968. *Foundations of Curriculum*. Columbus, OH: Charles E. Merrill.

Keller, Evelyn Fox. 1985. *Reflections on Gender and Science*. New Haven, CT: Yale University Press.

Kenway, Jane, and Helen Modra. 1989. Feminist pedagogy and emancipatory possibilities. *Critical Pedagogy Networker* 2(2 and 3): 1–17.

King, Nancy R. 1986. Recontextualizing the curriculum. *Theory into Practice*, 25: 36–40.

Kliebard, Herbert M. 1971. "Bureaucracy and Curriculum Theory." In *Freedom, Bureaucracy, and Schooling*, 1971 Yearbook, edited by Vernon Haubrich, 74–92. Washington, DC: Association for Supervision and Curriculum Development.

Kliebard, Herbert M. 1975. "Persistent Curriculum Issues in Historical Perspective." In *Curriculum Theorizing: The Reconceptualists*, edited by W. F. Pinar, 39–50. Berkeley, CA: McCutchan

Langland, Elizabeth, and Walter Gove, eds. 1981. *A Feminist Perspective in the Academy*. Chicago: University of Chicago Press.

Lather, Patti. 1986a. "Issues of Data Trustworthiness in Openly Ideological Research." Paper presented at the annual meeting, American Educational Research Association, San Francisco, CA.

Lather, Patti. 1986b. Issues of validity in openly ideological research: Between a rock and a soft place. *Interchange* 17: 63–84.

Lather, Patti. 1987. "Feminist Perspectives on Empowering Research Methodologies." Paper delivered at the annual meeting, American Educational Research Association, Washington, DC.

Lather, Patti. 1989. "Deconstructing/Deconstructive Inquiry: The Politics of Knowing and Being Known." Paper delivered at the annual meeting, American Educational Research Association, San Francisco, CA.

Lauritzen, Paul. 1989. "Seeing and Caring: Reflections on the Education of the Emotions." Paper presented at the annual meeting, American Educational Research Association, San Francisco, CA.

Lawn, Martin, and Len Barton, eds. 1981. *Rethinking Curriculum Studies: A Radical Approach*. London: Croom Helm.

Lemish, Peter. 1989. "Cultural Conflict and the Curriculum." Paper presented at the annual meeting, American Educational Research Association, San Francisco, CA.

Lincoln, Yvonna S., ed. 1985. *Organizational Theory and Inquiry*. Newbury Park, CA: Sage.

Lincoln, Yvonna S. 1989. "Trouble in the Land: The Paradigm Revolution in the Academic Disciplines." In *Higher Education: Handbook of Theory and Research*, edited by John S. Smart, 57–133. New York: Agathon Press.

Lincoln, Yvonna S., and Egon G. Guba. 1985. *Naturalistic Inquiry*. Newbury Park, CA: Sage.

Macdonald, James B. 1975. "Curriculum and Human Interests." In *Curriculum Theorizing: The Reconceptualists*, edited by William Pinar, 283–298. Berkeley, CA: McCutchan.

Macdonald, James B. 1986. The domain of curriculum. *Journal of Curriculum and Supervision* 1: 205–214.

Macdonald, James B. 1988a. "Curriculum, consciousness, and social change." In *Contemporary Curriculum Discourses*, edited by W. F. Pinar, 156–174. Scottsdale, AZ: Gorsuch Scarisbrick.

Macdonald, James B. 1988b. "Theory-Practice and the Hermeneutic Circle." In *Contemporary Curriculum Discourses*, edited by W. F. Pinar, 101–113. Scottsdale, AZ: Gorsuch Scarisbrick.

Macdonald, James, and Susan Colberg Macdonald. 1988. "Gender, Values, and Curriculum." In *Contemporary Curriculum Discourses*, edited by W. F. Pinar, 476–485. Scottsdale, AZ: Gorsuch Scarisbrick.

Mann, John Steven. 1975. "Curriculum criticism." In *Curriculum Theorizing: The Reconceptualists*, edited by W. F. Pinar, 133–148. Berkeley, CA: McCutchan.

Miller, Janet L. 1986. Women as teachers: Enlarging conversations on issues of gender and self-concept. *Journal of Curriculum and Supervision* 1(2): 111–121.

Molnar, Alex, and John A. Zahorick, eds. 1977. *Curriculum Theory*. Washington, DC: Association for the Study of Supervision and Curriculum Development.

Mooney, Ross L. 1975. "The Researcher Himself." In *Curriculum Theorizing: The Reconceptualists*, edited by W. F. Pinar, 175–208. Berkeley, CA: McCutchan.

Morgan, Gareth. 1986. *Images of Organization*. Newbury Park, CA: Sage.

Padgham, Ronald E. 1988. "Correspondences: Contemporary Curriculum Theory and Twentieth Century Art." In *Contemporary Curriculum Discourses*, edited by William F. Pinar, 359–379. Scottsdale, AZ: Gorsuch Scarisbrick.

Pinar, William F., ed. 1975. *Curriculum Theorizing: The Reconceptualists*. Berkeley, CA: McCutchan.

Pinar, William F., ed. 1988a. *Contemporary Curriculum Discourses*. Scottsdale, AZ: Gorsuch Scarisbrick.

Pinar, William F. 1988b. The reconceptualization of curriculum studies, 1987: A personal retrospective. *Journal of Curriculum and Supervision* 3: 157–188.

Pinar, William F., and Madeleine R. Grumet. 1988. "Socratic

Caesura and the Theory-Practice Relationship." In *Contemporary Curriculum Discourses*, edited by W. F. Pinar, 92–100. Scottsdale, AZ: Gorsuch Scarisbrick.

Pinar, William F., and J. L. Miller. 1982. Feminist curriculum theory: Notes on the American field, 1982. *Journal of Educational Thought* 16: 217–224.

Putnam, Helen C. 1919. Practical aspects of niological science in school administration: The problem of janitor services. *Journal of Proceedings and Addresses of the Forty-eighth Annual Meeting of the National Educational Association*, 964. Winona, MN: NEA.

Ramsey, Peter D. K. 1983. Fresh perspectives on the school transformation-reproduction debate: A response to Anyon from the Antipodes. *Curriculum Inquiry* 13: 295–319.

Reese, W. L. 1980. *Dictionary of Philosophy and Religion: Eastern and Western Thought*. Atlantic Highlands, NJ: Humanities Press.

Ricouer, Paul. 1978. In *The Philosophy of Paul Ricouer*, edited by Charles Reagon and David Stewart. Boston: Beacon Press.

Roman, Leslie G. 1989. "Double Exposure: The Politics of Feminist Materialist Ethnography." Paper presented at the annual meeting, American Educational Research Association. San Francisco, CA.

Rosario, Jose R. 1986. Excellence, school culture, and lessons in futility: Another case against simplistic views of educational change. *Journal of Curriculum Studies* 18: 31–43.

Rosario, Jose. 1988. "Harold Rugg on how we came to know: A view of his aesthetics." In *Contemporary Curriculum Discourses*, edited by William F. Pinar, 343–358. Scottsdale, AZ: Gorsuch Scarisbrick.

Schubert, William H. 1986. *Curriculum: Perspective, Paradigm, and Possibility*. New York: Macmillan.

Schwab, Joseph J. 1970. *The Practical: A Language for Curriculum*. Washington, DC: National Educational Association.

Selden, Steven. 1984. Objectivity and ideology in educational research. *Phi Delta Kappan* 67: 281–283.

Selden, Steven. 1987. Professionalization and the null curriculum: The case of the popular eugenics movement and American educational studies. *Educational Studies* 18: 221–38.

Selden, Steven. 1988. "Biological Determinism and the Normal School Curriculum: Helen Putnam and the NEA Committee on Racial Well-being, 1910–1922." In *Contemporary Curriculum Discourses*, edited by William F. Pinar, 50–64. Scottsdale, AZ: Gorsuch Scarisbrick.

Short, Edmund C. 1984. "Another Look at Curriculum Knowledge.'" Unpublished paper.

Short, Edmund C. 1986. A historical look at curriculum design. *Theory Into Practice* 25: 3–9.

Short, Edmund C. 1987. "Curriculum Research in Retrospect." Paper delivered at the Society for the Study of Curriculum History, Washington, DC.

Simon, Roger I. 1988. For a pedagogy of possibility. *Critical Pedagogy Networker* 1: 1–4.

Slater, Phillip. 1977. *The Wayward Gate*. New York: Beacon Press.

Smith, David G. 1988. "Experimental Eidetics as a Way of Entering Curriculum Language from the Ground Up." In *Contemporary Curriculum Discourses*, edited by William F. Pinar, 417–436. Scottsdale, AZ: Gorsuch Scarisbrick.

Smith, E. and Ralph W. Tyler. 1942. *Appraising and Recording Student Progress*. New York: Harper & Row.

Strayer, George D. 1920. *Some Problems in City School Administration*. Yonkers-on-Hudson, NY: World Book Company.

Tanner, Daniel, and Laurel N. Tanner. 1979. Emancipation from research: The reconceptualist prescription. *Educational Researcher* 8: 8–12.

Tanner, Daniel, and Laurel Tanner. 1990. *History of the School Curriculum*. New York: Macmillan.

Tuana, Nancy, ed. 1989. *Feminism and Science*. Bloomington: Indiana University Press.

Tyler, Ralph W. 1950. *Basic Principles of Curriculum and Instruction: Syllabus for Education 360*. Chicago: University of Chicago Press.

van Manen, Max. 1985. Hope means commitment. *The History and Social Science Teacher* 20: 42–44.

van Manen, Max. 1988. "The Relation Between Research and Pedagogy." In *Contemporary Curriculum Discourses*, edited by William F. Pinar, 437–452. Scottsdale, AZ: Gorsuch Scarisbrick.

Weick, Karl E. 1985. "Sources of Order in Underorganized Systems: Themes in Recent Organizational Theory." In *Organizational Theory and Inquiry: The Paradigm Revolution*, edited by Yvonna S. Lincoln, 106–136. Newbury Park, CA: Sage.

Willower, Donald J. 1985. "Marxian Critical Theory and Educational Administration: A Criticism." Paper presented at the annual meeting, American Educational Research Association, Chicago.

§ 4 §

METHODOLOGICAL ISSUES IN CURRICULUM RESEARCH

Decker F. Walker

STANFORD UNIVERSITY

These are interesting times for anyone concerned with the methodology of research in education. The old order, based on an empirical-scientific-positivist doctrine, has lost its grip on the field, and no new doctrine has yet achieved dominance, so the educational researcher planning a study today faces an open field bright with possibilities. Curriculum researchers stand to benefit enormously from this new freedom. We can now study what we have always talked about and believed to be important—aims, purposes, plans, interests, beliefs, values, thoughts, feelings, attention, experience, intuition, involvement, content, subjects, activities . . . everything. We will not be told any more that such things are mentalistic, cannot be operationally defined, or are unmeasurable, and if we are, we can reply with ideas taken from any of dozens of cogent critiques of positivistic behavioral science published in the most prestigious journals of the field. The kinds of studies curriculum researchers have always judged to be most informative—case studies, direct observation, expert judgments, etc.—are now acceptable in refereed journals. The climate has never been better for acceptance of new methods.

Along with this new freedom, however, comes the responsibility to choose. So many options can lead to confusion and indecision in the most experienced researcher. Designing a study that the entire research community will applaud is harder now that so many competing standards are being applied. Furthermore, the freedom is not guaranteed to continue. A new orthodoxy could be taking shape even now as the flood of new publications on research methodology emerges from the presses each month and settles on the landscape. When a new prevailing view coalesces out of this flood, the new doctrine could impose new limits that would be equally unwelcome.

The only way curriculum researchers can defend against the closing in of unwelcome new methodological limits is to develop countervailing methodological ideas. This task entails more than writing about the metaphysics of inquiry. It means translating philosophical doctrine into concrete methods of inquiry and guidelines for when and how to employ them in our research. Even further, it means demonstrating the value of our methods by using them in studies that we and others find informative and persuasive.

Advocates of methodological diversity in educational research have, for a time at least, achieved their purpose. This chapter urges curriculum researchers to turn their attention to building a body of methods and methodological doctrine well suited to curriculum research, a mission I believe to be essential for defending the gains achieved.

The chapter consists of two main parts. The first part offers a roughly chronological account of methodological writing about curriculum research. This account necessarily follows the broad outlines of the larger body of writing on the more general topic of the methodology of educational research. Readers already familiar with the early history of educational research may want to skip to the section on the recent controversy over qualitative and quantitative methods. The second part of the chapter explores the possibility of developing a stance on methodology that is more directly related to curriculum research as we know it. Starting from assumptions about the practical character of work in curriculum, some conceptual foundations are proposed for a practice-centered research methodology. The methods used in one type of curriculum research—formative research—are briefly reviewed for the purpose of identifying the important methodological issues raised. The chapter closes with some reflections on the important but limited part I think methodology should play in the improvement of curriculum research in the years ahead.

METHODOLOGICAL WRITING ABOUT CURRICULUM RESEARCH

Some fields of study are virtually defined by their methods. What would remain of psychology if all traces of the psychological experiment were magically wiped out, of cognitive science without think-aloud interviews, of sociology without the survey, or of anthropology without ethnography? It is commonly believed that reliance on systematic methods is the most important difference between knowledge gained through research and mere speculation or opinion. In the contemporary behavioral and social sciences methodology plays a central role. Its rules and principles govern judgments about the quality of work in the field. Methodological norms serve as criteria for judging research reports, and they also play a major role in the peer evaluations of researchers for appointments and promotions and in the awarding of status and honors.

Emergence of a Concern for Method in the Study of Human Affairs

Such a central role for methods is a relatively recent development in the centuries-long history of scholarship. As Levine (1986) writes,

> The quest to identify a kind of knowledge that enjoys a privileged status over commonsense perceptions and understandings of the world has been pursued since the very beginnings of reflections about how we know. The record of responses to that quest provides a capsule summary of the major moments in the history of human speculation. The idea of the Good, the authority of Revelation, the clear and distinct truths of geometry, the controlled outcomes of investigation, the self-understanding by humans of human projects, the demystified grasp of real historic forces, the quantification of metric operations, the analysis of unconscious expressions, the enlightenment that follows disciplined meditation—these are some of the well-known historical candidates for that privileged position. (271)

Levine goes on to note, "In the past two centuries in the West, and increasingly throughout the world the single most popular candidate [for the status of privileged knowledge] has been known generically as 'science'" (271).

The elements of the contemporary scientific stance on method were well known in the scientific community by the end of the 17th century. Conventionally the story begins with Francis Bacon's empiricism and its revolutionary insistence that all knowledge must be based on observation, not authority. Descartes's (1980 [1637]) methodical rationalism is the next major step:

> The first rule was to accept as true nothing that I did not know to be self evidently so; that is to say, to avoid carefully precipitancy and prejudice, and to apply my judgement to nothing but that which showed itself so clearly and distinctly to my mind that I should never have occasion to doubt it. The second was to divide each difficulty I should examine into as many parts as possible, and as would be required the better to solve it. The third was to conduct my thoughts in an orderly fashion, starting with what was simplest and easiest to know, and rising little by little to the knowledge of the most complex, even supposing an order where there is no natural precedence among the objects of knowledge. The last rule was to make so complete an enumeration of the links in an argument, and to pass them all so carefully under view, that I could be sure I had missed nothing.

Finally came the capstone of the edifice, the experiment, generally credited to Galileo. The methodologies of all the modern sciences at least until the current generation of Feyerabend (1983), Kuhn (1962), Lakatos (1978), and Popper (1965) are elaborations on these basic elements.

Traditional humanistic fields of study, like philosophy and history, have their methods, of course, but methods do not play the same central role in the humanities. Methods are not the fundamental basis on which humanists rest the authority of their knowledge claims but rather are tactical devices that provide good materials to be worked on by the scholar's learning, experience, talent, and character. It is recognition in texts of these human qualities, not the details of the scholar's methods, that compels the humanist's assent. Methods books in the humanities offer general advice, and the reader must make extremely complex judgments when applying the advice to particular cases, in sharp contrast to the scientific community's specific rules and principles, whose application requires merely technical skill. Questions of technique in the humanities mainly concern narrowly procedural matters such as how to authenticate documents or how to manage notes (Barzun 1977). Except for these scholarly minutiae, adherence to methodological norms has seldom been a major consideration in the humanities, where faith in the reason, judgment, and creative power of educated individuals has always been fundamental. Emphasis on method in research is an innovation of those academic upstarts, the scientists.

In recent decades, though, the humanities have taken on many of the trappings of scientific disciplines: research journals, where once scholarly books and reflective essays were the stock in trade; government-sponsored and foundation-supported research; and in some cases a collection of distinctive research methods. Where once there was simply the interpretation of texts, there is now a bewildering variety of distinctly formal methods of interpreting texts—the new criticism, psychoanalytic criticism, Marxist criticism, hermeneutics, semiotics, and so on. Within both the humanities and the behavioral and social sciences, methodological affiliations play a central role in defining a scholar's reference group and sometimes also friends and enemies. Within the larger academic community, the relative standing of different disciplines is strongly influenced by the general perception of the objectivity, power, and rigor of each discipline's methods, with fields using "hard" methods receiving more prestige than those using "soft" ones.

Emergence of a Concern for Methods in Educational Research

Until the turn of this century, education as a field of study could be described as following the model of the humanities. Those seeking graduate degrees in education studied the history of education, philosophy of education, educational theory, and educational psychology (then more speculative than scientific), along with their practical studies. Scholarly writing in education was devoid of technicalities and, except for gratuitous jargon, could generally be understood by any educated person. Some schools or departments of education kept a small fund to defray some of the expenses of faculty research, but there were few external sources of funding for research. There were few discussions of research methods in professional writing and few, if any, books on research methodology in education. Method played a minor role in educational research, as it did in the humanities generally (Cronbach and Suppes 1969).

By the 1890s, under the influence of German precedents, a significant, organized body of American scholars working in education began to advocate the establishment of a science of education (Cremin 1963; Cronbach and Suppes 1969; De Landsheere 1988). William James's *Principles of Psychology* (1890) and *Talks to Teachers on Psychology* (1899) and E. L. Thorndike's *Animal Intelligence* (1911) were early landmarks in this development. The National Society for the Scientific Study of Education, founded in 1901 as a successor to the National Herbart Society, served as a focus for many of these efforts. "Scientific" was dropped from the title in 1910, but the movement for a science of education continued to gain strength in academic circles and was especially influential in the years from 1910 to 1930 (De Landsheere 1988). In his memoir, *That Men May Understand*, Harold Rugg (1941) sketches educational research in 1918 in this way:

> The new "child accounting" was being born: Thorndike had just published his original studies of the school population. Strayer, Elliott, and Cubberley had question-blanked school finance in cities and states. Courtis was making his original series of arithmetic tests. The new science of educational psychology was emerging from the pioneer laboratory studies in learning; experimental methods of laboratory psychology were being taken over into education. (181)

The first great success of the movement for a science of education was the discrediting of the classics around the turn of this century. Defenders of the classics rested their case on the claim that studying Latin and Greek literature disciplined all the faculties of the mind. When careful studies by Thorndike, Judd, and other psychologists and educational researchers failed to detect the claimed effects, this rationale was no longer convincing to the uncommitted, and partly as a result, the classics lost their central place in the secondary school curriculum (Cremin 1963; Cronbach and Suppes 1969; Krug 1964).

Leaders of the education profession were striving to raise the status of the field from that of a trade taught to high school graduates in normal schools to that of a full-fledged academic field of study in colleges and universities (Cronbach and Suppes 1969). They faced strong opposition from faculty members in the traditional fields. Rugg (1941) writes of the science of education as being born "in spite of the jeers of the established academicians—the physical and natural scientists and the classicists" (181). Even those educators who set no great store by the vision of education as a science applauded the movement's role in legitimizing education as a field of study.

Tensions between scientific and humanistic traditions were present from the beginnings of educational research. Although education as a field of study within universities was born under the banner of science, the faculties of the newly formed departments, colleges, and schools of education included both scientists, trained mostly in psychology, sociology, and statistics, and humanists, who had studied philosophy, history, or education. John Dewey's pragmatic philosophy, committed to a broad conception of democracy and featuring the notion of experience as the fundamental human reality, was held in high regard, and his essentially humanistic methods of work were widely imitated. Although Dewey was a staunch supporter of science and of the movement for a science of education during this period, his own researches in education were either too practical (as in his work with the Laboratory School and his book *Schools of Tomorrow* [1915], written with his daughter, Evelyn) or too theoretical (i.e., philosophical) to meet the methodological canons of educational science, as it later came to be understood. After the 1920s most doctoral candidates in education at major universities were at least exposed to the methods of quantitative, experimental science through graduate courses in research methods.

The Rise of a Scientific Methodological Tradition in Educational Research

The Great Depression and World War II diverted attention from academic matters, but the influence of the vision of a science of education grew steadily within schools and departments of education. When things settled down after the war, psychologists were in control of methodological standards for research in education, and the prevailing view on educational research was behaviorist and positivist (Bloom 1968; Cronbach and Suppes 1969; De Landsheere 1988). Prevailing behaviorist psychological doctrine declared the proper study of humankind to be the body's observable motions and physical changes. All else was inference and, as such, open to question. In particular, talk about ideas, thoughts, feelings, concepts, and other "mentalistic" entities was discouraged. The doctrine of positivism asserted that all knowledge must be capable of being reduced to direct observations that could be verified by any competent observer. Thus, both the educator's and the researcher's judgments were ruled out of order, and most traditional notions people held about themselves and their actions—ideas such as honor, good, evil, wit, grace, beauty, and pleasure—could only be admitted to the realm of positive knowledge if they were recast in terms of things that could be directly observed. To the most rigorous methodologists of the time the only way to be certain that something was scientifically observable was to create a test or other measuring instrument that could be shown to be reliable and valid according to the elaborate rules of educational and psychological measurement.

According to the doctrine prevailing in this period, among the studies that led to positive knowledge, the experiment was king. The experiment was, in the words of an influential methodological treatise of the 1960s, "the only means for settling disputes regarding educational practice . . . the only way of verifying educational improvements, and . . . the only way of establishing a cumulative tradition in which improvements can be introduced without the danger of a faddish discard of old wisdom in favor of inferior novelties" (Campbell and Stanley 1963, 172). Thus, beginning in the postwar years and continuing into the 1970s, educational research, to meet the highest methodological standards, had to be cast in terms of an experiment in which observable variables were measured with instruments that conformed to elaborate technical standards. For nearly three decades, from the 1940s to the 1970s, neither complaints from researchers holding other views nor criticisms from practicing educators nor devastating philosophical critiques of positivism and behaviorism sufficed to free educational research from the hegemony of this prevailing "scientific" methodology.

Then, in less than a decade, support for the once-dominant view collapsed. Future historians will need to sort out the reasons as well as anyone can, but some are plain enough. As more scholars from other social science disciplines began to do work in education, they brought with them other, more varied, less doctrinaire ideas about method. New developments in the history and philosophy of science provided new reconstructions of the logic of science to replace the discredited positivism, and many respected educational researchers embraced these new notions of what it meant to be scientific. Many, citing historian of science Thomas Kuhn as the authority, began to refer to the behaviorist-positivist-psychological doctrine on methodology as simply one paradigm, one way of being scientific. In psychology itself, the stronghold of positivistic scientific ideals, cognitive science was successfully challenging the behaviorist hegemony.

However complex the underlying reasons for it, the public manifestation of the fall from dominance of the positivist-scientific methodology was a series of debates conducted at conferences and published in research journals during the 1980s on the issue of qualitative methodology. Before moving ahead with this story, we need to backtrack briefly to review the development of methodological thought about curriculum research.

Methodological Traditions in Curriculum Research

Methodology in curriculum research developed as an integral part of this larger history. Prior to the emergence of the movement for a science of education, scholarly work on curriculum was largely historical or philosophical, leavened with more or less attention to practical matters. The most esteemed works on curriculum were philosophical and did not differentiate curricular concerns from other aspects of education. Herbart's (1895 [1838]) *The Science of Education*, Locke's (1892 [1690]) *Some Thoughts Concerning Education*, and Rousseau's (1899 [1762]) *Émile* were classics of the type. Standing in only slight contrast were Froebel's (1891 [1826]) *The Education of Man*, and Pestalozzi's (1987 [1781]) *Leonard and Gertrude*, works based on the authors' experience in developing innovative schools. Even the latter works, however, presented systematic theories of education along with practical suggestions. In the United States, the works of the most influential educational leaders, such as William T. Harris, the idealist, Hegelian philosopher who became superintendent of schools in St. Louis and later the national commissioner of education, followed the European style and what might be termed applied humanistic models. Pre-20th-century curriculum work was rightly seen as an integral part of pedagogical theory. The only method in evidence was logical deduction of curricular proposals from theoretical assertions about education and related matters.

Beginning as early as the 1890s in the United States, many of those who would later become prominent figures in curriculum research joined the movement to create a science of education. Prominent early curriculum researchers who enlisted in the crusade included Franklin W. Bobbitt and William W. Charters (scientific curriculum making and educational efficiency), Guy T. Buswell (arithmetic), S. A. Courtis (spelling), Ernest Horn (spelling), Harold Rugg (statistics and later social studies), and Guy M. Whipple (arithmetic). Much of the curriculum innovation during this period was initiated by specialists in the various subjects of the curriculum, and most of these specialists adopted a scientific viewpoint. The psychology of school subjects flourished after 1910, and specialists in the teaching of various school subjects constituted the bulk of many faculties of education by the 1930s. School surveyists collected data about the curriculum actually offered in schools and school systems and prescribed curriculum reforms.

Some of these early studies remain interesting models for research on curriculum. Some, such as Thorndike and Lorge's (1938) studies of the frequency of words in everyday published material, were purely descriptive but yielded interesting and useful facts nonetheless. Others, such as Joseph Mayer Rice's (1897) studies of the relation of time spent on spelling to spelling test performance, were far ahead of their day in methodological sophistication. By the 1930s, though, the most influential curriculum researchers were more concerned about reforming the curriculum and responding to the social problems of the Great Depression than about doing more sophisticated studies of the existing curriculum.

The progressive transformation absorbed the energies of most curriculum scholars during the Great Depression, and quantitative work declined in influence. As an amusing illustration of many progressives' disdain for scientific rigor in educational research, in 1933 the *Journal of Higher Education*, with a largely progressive editorial board, published a study on "Permanence of Learning" by Ralph W. Tyler of the Bureau of Educational Research at Ohio State University, a study whose methods would be almost qualitative by today's standards. Yet it appeared in a section of the journal called "With the Technicians."

Most writing on curriculum issues during the progressive era was either philosophical in form, reflecting in part the influence of John Dewey, or practical in the tradition of Pestalozzi and Froebel, trying out new practices in schools and writing about what happened. George S. Counts's (1932) *Dare the School Build a New Social Order*, William Heard Kilpatrick's (1926) *Foundations of Method*, and Harold Rugg and Ann Shumacher's (1928) *The Child-Centered School* are prominent works on curriculum typical of the period. They are strongly committed to a progressive vision, written for teachers as well as professional and lay leaders, and they rarely cite evidence from research to support their claims. Methodologically, curriculum research during the progressive era reverted to earlier scholarly patterns, only this time the writing was more frankly partisan and ideological.

But at the same time other researchers, less noted but possibly as influential in schools, continued to develop a scientific approach to curriculum. Carleton Washburne, for example, superintendent of schools in Winnetka, Illinois, worked with his faculty to develop extensive graded, self-instructional materials to support individualized learning in basic subjects. Field experiments were carried out in schools and classrooms during the progressive era that would still be considered good examples of curriculum research. Some of them combined methods that today would be called qualitative with quantitative measurement. Ellsworth Collings (1923), for instance, carried out a year-long experiment with a project curriculum. Harold Fawcett (1938) in *The Nature of Proof* reported an experiment in teaching high school geometry by a kind of guided classroom discovery in which students first examined the rules of effective reasoning they used in familiar situations and then applied them to geometry. Fawcett used a second geometry class as a control for the experimental class and employed a variety of outcome indicators. The Eight Year Study (Smith and Tyler 1942) remains one of the most extensive field experiments ever done in education. Schools that experimentally changed their programs to approximate more closely their educational ideals were compared with similar schools that continued their conventional programs. A wide spectrum of effects on students were monitored with techniques that today would be considered both qualitative and quantitative, and the study continued searching for effects until students finished college.

The reign of behaviorism in psychology and education in American universities during and after World War II split the curriculum research community. Advocates of behavioral objectives, including Benjamin Bloom (1968), James Popham (1969), and many others, sought to express all educational goals in the form of statements about the behavior expected of students—a direct application of the behaviorist and positivist programmes. Many curriculum researchers and educational practitioners followed their lead. Accountability movements found the behavioral objectives doctrine to be a convenient vehicle for bringing centralized educational reforms into schools and classrooms. At one point the legislature in California enacted a law requiring all teachers to state their goals in measurable terms so that tests could be constructed to assess whether their students had met their goals. Bloom (1968) and Tyler (1949) urged a broader, less strictly behavioral conception of objectives but still insisted that they should be measurable. A vigorous methodological debate sprang up about the value of behavioral objectives (Eisner 1969; Popham 1969). The opposition was broadly humanistic; among the chief opponents were Elliot Eisner (1969), trained in art and aesthetics, and Herbert M. Kliebard (1970), trained in history. The extreme reductionism of the behaviorist position—every purpose of education was to be stated in the form "The student should be able to . . ." followed by an observation statement describing the student's manifest behavior—was a difficult position to defend both practically and philosophically, and many prominent educational scientists disassociated themselves from the behaviorist position (Cronbach 1971; Glass 1972).

By the late 1960s curriculum theorizing became the humanistically oriented scholarly alternative to research in the behaviorist tradition. The establishment of the *Curriculum Theory Network* in 1968 and the *Journal of Curriculum Theorizing* in 1979 helped to give this activity legitimacy and identity. Writers such as Michael Apple (1979), Madeleine Grumet (Pinar and Grumet 1976), and William Pinar (1980) published essays that combined social and literary criticism with elements of philosophy into a fresh blend of broadly humanistic scholarship that defied scientific norms of objectivity.

Meanwhile, beginning in the 1960s, curriculum researchers found their leadership over the school curriculum under challenge. Scientists from universities were put in charge of projects to develop curriculum materials in science, and mathematicians, language researchers, and professors of history and English worked on new curriculum materials for their subjects (Ford and Pugno 1964). Later in that decade, reformers like Paul Goodman (1964) and John Holt (1966) inspired a reform movement called Open Education, explicitly modeled on British infant schools. Later still, politicians allied with behavioral and social scientists to legislate new educational programs for the early education of disadvantaged children (Wirt and Kirst 1982). A few curriculum researchers participated in these reform movements (Bloom 1971; Eisner 1971; Stenhouse 1975), but others found themselves on the sidelines of their own professional specialty.

Many curriculum researchers found themselves reacting to others' curriculum initiatives, which necessitated shifts in their research styles. A genre of curriculum criticism arose in the 1960s, similar to much earlier progressive criticism of the traditional curriculum but also reflecting the rhetoric of contemporary lay critics (Eisner 1976; Kliebard 1970; Young 1971). Criticism offered a way for curriculum scholars to comment on the curriculum work others were doing. Curriculum evaluation blossomed once more as curriculum researchers struggled to assess the merits of the many new reform projects being urged on the schools in response to one crisis after another (Eisner 1969; Parlett and Hamilton 1976; Stake 1978; Welch 1979). Some curriculum researchers, detached from struggles to reform the curriculum, began to study the realities of curriculum work in classrooms, schools, and other settings with an inquiring rather than a reforming purpose (Doyle 1977; D. Walker 1971; Westbury and Bellack 1971).

Older traditions of curriculum research continued to be vital. Some humanistically inclined scholars continued to write theory as scholars in the universities for practitioners in the schools, just as Dewey, Counts, Kilpatrick, and Rugg had done (Bantock 1968; Broudy 1974; Foshay 1970; Hirst 1974; Schwab 1970). John Goodlad and associates (Goodlad and Klein 1970) continued to travel around the country reporting on conditions in schools, much as Horace Mann had done more than a century earlier. Historical studies were pursued with renewed vigor by some curriculum researchers (Kliebard 1977; Schubert 1980; Tanner and Tanner 1975). This brings us to the 1970s, where we can pick up the story of the debate over qualitative methods in education. It is worth noting before we leave the more specialized topic of methodology in curriculum research that the writings on curriculum in the decades before 1970 were almost entirely devoid of writing about research methods.

The Debate Over Qualitative Methodologies in Education

The emergence of this issue to prominence in the educational research community is reflected in a striking way in the methodology chapters of the successive editions of the *Handbook of Research on Teaching*. The first handbook (Gage 1963) contained no hint of the issue. Its chapter on research methodology, "Experimental and Quasi-Experimental Designs for Research on Teaching" by Donald Campbell and Julian Stanley, was a partisan manifesto for the currently dominant scientific, methodological doctrine. The point of view they articulated so forcefully in their chapter expressed that doctrine more clearly and succinctly than it had ever been expressed before—a scientific ideal, with a realist, positivist epistemology and a commitment to controlled experiments as the most valid way of confirming knowledge claims. They relegated all study designs except experiments to the lowest category of rigor, case studies, which they judged to have "such a total absence of control as to be of almost no scientific value" (176). They went further, labeling all experiments in which subjects were not randomly assigned to treatments "quasi-experiments" to emphasize their shortcomings in comparison to "true" experiments.

Challenges to this scientific methodological doctrine were clearly in evidence in the *Second Handbook of Research on Teaching* (Travers 1973). Among its 13 chapters on methods, most reflected the dominant scientific paradigm, but some challenged it. Among the challengers were three chapters on the sociology and social psychology of teaching, in which the authors argued for broadening standards of accepted methods in scientific research, and two chapters on traditional curriculum concerns, which asserted the need for additional methods beyond those of science: MacDonald and Clark's chapter on "Critical Value Questions and the Analysis of Objectives and Curricula" and Price's chapter, "Of the Impact of Theory of Knowledge on Thought about Education." Qualitative methods, as such, were not treated explicitly in the second handbook.

The third edition of the handbook (Wittrock 1986) included a full chapter on qualitative methods. Even the chapter on *quantitative* methods by Linn included an approving discussion of qualitative methods as particularly appropriate for the goal of discovering knowledge. And another chapter, "Theory, Methods, Knowledge, and Research on Teaching" by Biddle and Anderson, developed this position at greater length. A slightly later international handbook on educational research (Keeves 1988) also devoted almost a quarter of its nearly 150 chapters to nonquantitative topics. In less than two decades the research methods that eventually came to be labeled qualitative had gone from the status of pariah to full acceptance by the educational research community.

The debates surrounding the relatively rapid acceptance of qualitative methods were spectacular public displays. The issue appeared with great frequency on the programs of annual meetings of the American Educational Research Association (AERA) throughout the 1980s, and most issues of that organization's house organ, *Educational Researcher*, still contain an article or letter on this controversy. It has dominated methodological discussions in the educational research community for nearly two decades. And no wonder. Not only the future direction of research in the field but also researchers' reputations, their influence within the research community, and the likelihood of their research proposals being accepted and their research reports published all depended on the outcome.

Although qualitative methods appear to be widely accepted today, the substantive intellectual issues that divide advocates of quantitative and qualitative methodologies have not been resolved. The debate has subsided more because the two sides have already said what they have to say than because anything has been settled. But at least some movement can now be discerned in a sprawling, confusing set of issues and arguments. The earliest major debate was over the positivist-experimental-scientific methodology expressed so clearly in Campbell and Stanley's (1963) chapter in the first handbook. This doctrine had long been the subject of criticism by humanists and others outside the psychological and educational research mainstream, but within a few years of its publication attacks on this doctrine came from within the scientific establishment as well. Bracht and Glass (1968) argued that Campbell and Stanley's methodology guarded only against threats to the *internal* validity of studies, i.e., the validity of conclusions about the study itself, and it neglected other equally serious threats to *external* validity, i.e., to the generalizability of the study's findings to situations other than those studied. Bracht and Glass maintained that when both internal and external validity are considered, the certainty gained from an experiment is not in principle greater than from other research designs.

Later, Cronbach (1975) delivered an address to the American Psychological Association, on the occasion of receiving a Distinguished Scientific Contribution Award, in which he questioned "too narrow an identification with science" and argued that instead of amassing experimentally tested scientific generalizations, "the special task of the social scientist in each generation is to pin down the contemporary facts. Beyond that, he shares with the humanistic scholar and the artist in the effort to gain insight into contemporary relationships, and to realign the culture's view of man with present realities" (126). Cronbach's rejection of the Campbell and Stanley doctrine was perhaps extreme among the community of scientific methodologists. He eventually concluded, "All social scientists are engaged in case studies" (Cronbach 1982, 75) and pronounced the Campbell and Stanley vision of a science of education to be infantile:

> Fortunately, today's profession is coming to see the rationalist, scientistic ideal as no more than an infantile dream of omnipotence. The present mood, one hopes, bespeaks an institution on the brink of adulthood . . . aware that waiting for its Newton is as pointless as waiting for Godot. (61)

Many other prominent figures closely identified with scientific research traditions urged a broadening of prevailing standards for research methods, including Robert Ebel (1967), Philip Jackson (1968), and Lee Shulman (1970). Even Donald Campbell himself abandoned his earlier position and extolled the benefits of quasi-experimental designs and case studies as well as action research and qualitative knowing (Campbell 1975, 1978; Cook and Campbell 1979).

Among those outside the methodological mainstream, the ethnographic methods of the anthropologists were probably the most alien to the prevailing doctrine. Ethnography soon gained attention as an alternative to experimental methods in educational research (Lutz and Ramsey 1974; Rist 1977; Smith and Geoffrey 1968; Wolcott 1973). Even more important, from a methodological standpoint, the way anthropologists justified their methods made a stark contrast with the concepts employed in mainstream scientific doctrine. Instead of ruling out alternative interpretations by controlling against threats to validity, anthropologists sought to discover a group's shared categories of meaning and perception by close observation and questioning of informants while guarding against ethnocentrism by a rigorous personal discipline. Soon educational researchers were citing ethnographic methods approvingly and using similar language to justify ethnographic studies of schools and classrooms (Shulman 1978). Similar use was made of certain styles of work in sociology (Denzin 1970; Goffman 1974).

Among professional educators one of the most outspoken opponents of the prevailing scientific doctrine was Eisner (1976). He criticized the limits that prevailing scientific methodological standards imposed on educational research and argued that the scientific search for general laws obscured the uniqueness of the particular. He maintained that scientific approaches tended to objectify knowledge and thus drained feeling out of experience: "To know what people feel, to know what behavior *means*, we must go beyond behavior" (138). He contrasted artistic and scientific approaches to qualitative research, claiming that scientific methods used literal but not figurative language; sought validity in contrast to illumination; focused on manifest behavior, not experience and meaning; sought generalizations but not heightened awareness of the particular; employed standardized forms of language rather than expressive forms; constrained inventiveness and personal interpretation; emphasized impersonal methods over the experience and judgment of the investigator; excluded emotions and sensory experience from knowing; and sought a singular, monopolistic truth rather than appreciation of diverse and relative meanings (Eisner 1981).

Philosopher Denis Phillips was one of the few who staunchly defended scientific methodological standards in his writing. He maintained steadfastly that natural science was still an appropriate model for research in education (Phillips 1983, 1986, 1987). He countered arguments to the contrary by pointing out instances in which various branches of natural science had successfully coped with problems similar to those faced by educational research. For instance, Cronbach (1975) had argued that educational phenomena were simply too complex, with too many interacting variables. It would be totally impractical, so Cronbach argued, to study these complex situations by conducting experiments and controlling for all the variables and their interactions. Phillips countered this point by citing successes of scientists in studies of meteorology, the behavior of fluids, and evolutionary biology, all complex, highly interacting systems. Other supposed limitations of scientific methods Phillips (1986) classified as pragmatic and argued that such pragmatic difficulties were "no bar in principle to the social sciences and educational research being naturalistic endeavors" (i.e., using the methods of the natural sciences) (65). The problem with Phillips's response is that no one, certainly not Cronbach, was asserting a problem of principle. Rather, Cronbach's (1975) argument was that the track record of experimenters who had actually tried to cope with the complexity through factorial designs was poor and that *as a strictly empirical finding*, no firm, substantial generalizations had emerged after more than half a century of effort by the world's best scientific students of human behavior.

Phillips (1981) also defended the scientist's traditional standard of objective truth against the weaker standards proposed by some advocates of qualitative methodology, such as giving a coherent and credible account, a position stated most explicitly by Dippo (1988). Phillips argued against relativism and holism and in favor of Karl Popper's (1965) view that although it was impossible to prove that a proposition was true, it was at least possible to say that it has survived our best efforts to prove it false. Phillips defended the experiment as a logically superior research design, endeavoring to win back some territory once claimed by Campbell and Stanley. Phillips (1983) even defended some aspects of positivism that he believed were unjustly attacked, but his was a lonely voice and even he did not try to defend the sweeping claims for experimental science made earlier by Campbell and Stanley (1963).

A detailed consideration of even the main arguments on both sides of this issue is far beyond the scope of this chapter. The most that can be done here is to summarize the territory gained, lost, and still contested by the parties. My reading of the results to date, and the issue is still joined, is that the Campbell and Stanley brand of narrow scientism is dead, abandoned by the leading figures on the scientific side. Advocates for building a science of education can still be found, but its image is quite different from the behaviorist, positivist image of a few decades ago. The image of science embraced by today's leading figures acknowledges that science works within assumptions that cannot themselves be tested and that the transition from one paradigm to another is a social and political process even more than a logical one. It recognizes that all observations are theory laden and therefore that observations cannot by themselves disprove theories. It follows Popper (1965) in demanding that theories be subjected to the most rigorous possible tests in an effort to falsify them, with those that best survive being regarded as the provisional truth, subject to falsification at any time. This conception of science has room within it for a wide range of methods, and what sort of methodological standards for educational research may eventually be promulgated in its name is not yet clear.

Against this revamped science of education is pitted a mixed band of researchers marching from all directions under many banners such as qualitative, interpretive, ethnographic, clinical, action, holistic, and naturalistic, armed with the most diverse views imaginable and united only in the common opposition to a narrowly scientific methodology. At the rate books on qualitative methodology are appearing I calculate that there will be a distinct published position on qualitative methodology for each qualitative researcher in the United States by the year 2000 (my favorite few: Argyris, Putnam, and Smith 1985; Becker 1986; Bogdan and Biklen 1982; Burgess 1985; Carr 1989; Cohen and Manion 1980; Ericksson and Simon 1984; Fetterman 1988; Hopkins 1985; Hustler, Cassidy, and Cuff 1986; McKernan 1988; Oja and Smulyan 1989; Spindler 1982; van Manen 1990; R. Walker, 1985; Woods 1986; Yin 1984). Qualitative methods, even though no one is quite sure what they are, have won a place for themselves in the methodological mainstream. Advocates and practitioners of qualitative research methods have been elected to high office in the AERA and appointed to the prestigious National Academy of Education. Even in educational psychology, qualitative methods for studying cognition have been accepted. Mentalistic terms and qualitative interpretations of verbal protocols are now found in nearly every journal of educational psychology.

Qualitative methods have been accepted into the methodological mainstream, but my informal network indicates that suspicion of them remains widespread among scientifically trained researchers. Many doubtlessly endorse Phillips's (1987) demand that qualitative researchers be pressed to answer the fundamental question, Why should this account be believed? Indeed, many qualitative researchers are eager to establish standards for qualitative methods. For instance, Spindler (1982, 6–7) offers these standards for ethnographies:

- Observations are contextualized.
- Questions for study emerge as the study proceeds.
- Observation is prolonged and repetitive.
- The native's view of reality is brought out.
- Effort is made to understand the participants' sociocultural knowledge.
- Instruments are generated in the field.
- A transcultural perspective is present.
- Tacit knowledge is brought to light.
- Inquiry disturbs the setting as little as possible.
- The ethnographer must elicit informants' knowledge in a natural form.

Smith and Glass (1987, 278) list eight issues to be raised about the quality of what they call naturalistic studies.

1. Time spent collecting data
2. Access to data
3. "Naturalness" of the data
4. Researcher self-criticism
5. Logical validity
6. Confirmation
7. Descriptive adequacy
8. Significance

Qualitative researchers face a delicate situation in considering how to respond to pressure to establish standards of quality for qualitative methods. If they respond with standards that are too limiting or too draconian, they could surrender the very qualities that make qualitative methods a genuine alternative to scientific methods, such qualities as openness to surprising events and encouragement to speculate and to rely on one's intuitions. Some qualitative methods books already look as intimidatingly technical as quantitative ones. Miles and Huberman (1984), for instance, list dozens of methods for merely recording data: coding, event listing, site analysis form, memoing, effects matrix, contact summary form, time-ordered matrix, and so on.

Qualitative researchers may be better off enduring their critics' charges of methodological softness than sacrificing their methodology's distinctive strengths. An obsession with avoiding error can interfere with many humanly important experiences such as spontaneity, caring, joy, love, and adventure, as well as with the willing suspension of disbelief presupposed in literary and artistic experience. What if an obsessive search for objective truth should turn out to be inhumane, as Roszak (1970) conjectures?

> The sciences, in their relentless pursuit of objectivity, raise alienation to its apotheosis as our only means of achieving a valid relationship to reality. Objective consciousness is alienated life promoted to its most honorific status as the scientific method. Under its auspices we subordinate nature to our command only by estranging ourselves from more and more of what we experience, until the reality about which objectivity tells us so much finally becomes a universe of congealed alienation. (72)

None of the intellectual issues that divide these two camps has yet been resolved, and I doubt if they will ever be. For one thing, the discourse has persistently levitated to the stratosphere of abstraction. A debate that begins with the question, What methods should we use to study education? is hardly underway before the debaters are discussing such questions as, Is objectivity possible? Should we aspire to truth or merely to a credible and coherent account? Granted, these are philosophically important questions, but somehow the prime methodological issue—What kinds of methods should educational researchers use?—gets lost in the discussion. If these abstract philosophical issues must be resolved before we can move ahead on the methodological question, the whole history of philosophy suggests that we may be in for a long wait.

But the connection between these abstract philosophical issues and the methodological questions may not be as tight as it seems. On those occasions when the debate does get down to the question of what methods are most valuable for studying certain educational phenomena and problems, the two camps tend to fall apart. Researchers and research methodologists with unimpeachable scientific credentials—Donald Campbell, Thomas Cook, Lee Cronbach, and Gene Glass, for example—turn out to support case studies and other qualitative methods, and anthropologists committed to qualitative methods who have long been critical of a restrictive scientific methodology—Ray Rist, George Spindler, and David Fetterman, for example—turn out to be critical of many methods called qualitative and to favor methodological standards for qualitative research as strict in their own way as those of Campbell and Stanley. Thus, failure to resolve fundamental epistemological and metaphysical issues may not portend a total stalemate on methodological issues.

Another reason why the debate is unlikely to proceed to a prompt resolution is that the two sides have seldom engaged in a real dialogue. Rather, they have flung well-worn charges at one another's weak spots. Advocates of qualitative methods attack behaviorist and positivist doctrines. Defenders of a science of education do not defend these doctrines but rather defend more contemporary scientific doctrines. Advocates of scientific methodology attack qualitative methods as soft and charge that they provide no good reason for a prudent person to believe their conclusions. Qualitative advocates do not say why their methods should be believed but instead point to the ways in which they include more of human experience than the methods considered legitimate in scientific methodology.

Apparently, the two groups have different concerns. The major concern of advocates of a science of education is verification of knowledge claims, how to find truth in a world filled with error, fraud, and deception. Therefore, they talk about truth, warrant, and error, and they insist on imposing rules and standards on investigations to guard against potential errors. The major concern of advocates of qualitative methodology, in contrast, is the adequacy of research data and findings to the richness, complexity, and subtlety of educational phenomena as people experience them. Therefore, they bridle at what they see as rigid, narrow limitations imposed by the rules of scientific procedure. And neither side really responds to the other's concerns.

The issue in this debate is not well posed, either. Neither side possesses a clearly stated methodological doctrine. Positivism is a (reasonably) clear position on methodological issues, and its merits can be and have been productively debated. But most members of the quantitative camp are not positivists except in the vague sense of "tends to be sympathetic to many positivist positions." Many researchers and methodologists use numbers, graphs, tables, and other quantitative techniques without subscribing to positivism. Many advocate experiments as powerful methods for gaining knowledge but do not endorse the use of standardized tests and other quantitative techniques of educational measurement. What unites each camp is not belief in a common doctrine but rather the kind of attitudinal orientation that unites people on the left or right of the political spectrum. It takes great faith in the powers of reason to suppose that such differences can be resolved through abstract argument alone.

It is unlikely that the issues dividing these camps will ever be resolved, any more than will the tensions between what William James called the tough-minded and the tender-minded. They represent contrasting but equally defensible attitudes. Quantitative types are more skeptical and also more cautious. They want higher standards of confirmation and more protection against errors. The qualitative types are bolder and more accepting of the possibility of error, but they want more assurances that methodological standards will not rule important realms of human experience out of bounds. Surely these are both desirable. How could one be given priority over the other as a matter of principle in all cases? Ours is a pragmatic civilization, and the obvious pragmatic response to this tension would be to let researchers exercise their individual judgment about particular studies and see when each gives the most satisfactory results. This is probably what will happen but it will take many years.

The Qualitative Debate in Curriculum

Curriculum researchers helped to initiate the debate over qualitative methods and played an active role in advocating qualitative methods from the start. Philip Jackson's *Life in Classrooms*, published in 1968, although clearly a rigorous, disciplined work, pointedly did not conform to Campbell and Stanley's (1963) standards. Jackson's own description in the preface reveals that he is clearly aware of this and is intentionally applying quite different standards to his own work.

> Stylistically, the book is a melange. Descriptions of empirical studies are interlaced with speculative asides, tabular materials sometimes share the page with the most unquantifiable assertions. . . . But the mixture is not without purpose. Classroom life, in my judgment, is too complex an affair to be viewed or talked about from one single perspective. . . . We must not hesitate to use all the means of knowing at our disposal. (vii)

Jackson argued that the tactics of the learning theorist and the human engineer were not likely to advance education as far or as fast as was generally supposed, and he suggested instead that researchers adopt the goal of "discovering what really goes on in classrooms" through observational studies (175). There, in the heyday of narrowly scientific methodological standards, was a defiantly qualitative study, and furthermore the author advocated more of the case studies Campbell and Stanley had declared to be of almost no scientific value. As it happened, the direction of educational research in the following two decades conformed much more closely to Jackson's than to Campbell and Stanley's visions.

Except for a thoughtful essay, "Is There a Best Way of Teaching Harold Bateman?" in which he explored the difficulties of using scientific principles in dealing with particular cases, Jackson (1970) did not lend his pen to polemics on behalf of qualitative research methods. Elliot Eisner emerged as the chief spokesperson for qualitative methods among curriculum researchers. Almost half of his book *The Educational Imagination* (1979) was devoted to methodological issues. He opened the pivotal chapter on connoisseurship and criticism with a quotation from Thomas Kuhn (1962) to the effect that a paradigm shift requires a complete reconstruction of the foundations of a field, and he set about to offer such a reconstruction of the foundations of research methodology in curriculum. Eisner criticized scientific approaches to the study of education on a variety of grounds. He lamented that "rationality has been conceived of as scientific in nature, and cognition has been reduced to knowing in words" (357). He rejected the model of the natural sciences as "probably inappropriate for most of the problems and aims of teaching, learning, and curriculum development" (358). He charged that "the canons of behavioral science have too often determined what shall be studied and what shall be regarded as important in education" (359) and that "Operationalism and Measurement" (sic) have focused so heavily on behavior that the quality of the student's experience has been generally ignored or seriously neglected (361). He rejected the scientist's criterion of truth in favor of utility: "What we can productively ask of a set of ideas is not whether it is *really* true but whether it is useful" (241). For scientific validity he proposed to substitute the standard of a coherent account that is "referentially adequate" (244), this adequacy to be judged qualitatively and subjectively. Eisner issued such a direct challenge to several of the core values and beliefs of educational science that it was no coincidence when Phillips (1983, 1986, 1987) singled out Eisner's views for special criticism in his rejoinders to critics of scientific research methodology.

As a complement to scientific methods, Eisner (1979) proposed two alternative forms of inquiry derived from the arts—educational connoisseurship and educational criticism. Connoisseurship and criticism call on the researcher's extensive first-hand experience with the objects of expertise. They require an ability to perceive subtle particulars and to infer the rules that govern people's patterned conduct. Criticism, Eisner maintained, is "the art of disclosing the qualities of events or objects that connoisseurship perceives" (223). Critics create a rendering of a situation, providing pointers to what is significant about it. Eisner argued that critics should use metaphor and other figurative forms of language to supplement and enrich what they could communicate discursively. In contrasting connoisseurship and criticism to quantitative methods of inquiry, Eisner emphasized the differences in the language used and the tendency of quantitative methods to rely on procedures and to define in advance what was to be looked for. (Eisner's ideas about criticism and related ideas are described at greater length in Ross 1988.)

We can glimpse something of the radical challenge Eisner's methods pose to scientific methodological doctrines in an exchange between a practitioner of educational criticism and a traditional anthropologist and ethnographer. Barone (1987a) published the paper "On Equality, Visibility, and the Fine Arts Program in a Black Elementary School: An Example of Educational Criticism." Rist (1987) responded, and Barone (1987b) published a rejoinder in the same issue of *Curriculum Inquiry*. Barone had observed art classes in a largely black elementary school in much the way a movie critic would attend a screening of a film. Based on what he saw, Barone (1987a) reported finding many serious problems in the classroom, problems so serious as to indicate that students not only were being poorly educated and miseducated but also were being not so subtly demeaned by the teacher. Barone's language was vivid and he did not hold back his personal impressions and interpretations. Rist's (1987) response to Barone's paper, entitled "Research in the Shadows," was extremely critical. He found Barone's methods to be inadequately controlled and unsystematic. Rist demanded methods of inquiry and reporting that were clear and complete enough to make the grounds of the critic's claims explicit. He described Barone's account of the classroom as consisting of "entertaining accounts of surface behaviors" (448) and "adjective-laden descriptions" (450), and he suggested that Barone's paper was an effort "to garb personal ideological views in the respectable cloak of academic research" (447). In his rejoinder Barone (1987b) insisted that his educational criticism was "a highly disciplined reflection upon and recasting of the content of the researcher's experiences into a narrative form with a potential for reeducating the perceptions of its readers" (460).

If two qualitative researchers can differ so completely on the merits of the methods used in a single study, imagine how the scientific community must feel about the lack of methodological standards for qualitative methods. Such differences increase the pressure on qualitative researchers to establish minimal methodological standards for qualitative research, and they increase the risk of rejection by the mainstream research community of research that uses qualitative methods. Perhaps accepted methodological standards, even if they are confining, are not so bad as methodological controversy.

Meanwhile, other curriculum researchers who had long been doing research in a manner quite different from the Campbell and Stanley (1963) ideal discovered that they had been using qualitative methods all along. Maxine Greene's (1967, 1978) writings on education in the mode of literary criticism were easily recognized as kindred forms by advocates of qualitative research. The curriculum theorizing of Michael Apple (1979), William Pinar and Madeleine Grumet (1976), and others certainly did not fit a scientific model and so came also to be identified as qualitative. Curriculum evaluators such as David Hamilton (1976) and Robert Stake (1978), who advocated interpretive case studies and dissented from the prevailing scientific orientation, clearly deserved to be classified as qualitative researchers. It turned out that many, perhaps most, well-known curriculum researchers were already using qualitative methods. The eventual widespread acceptance of qualitative methods by the mainstream of the methodological community in education brought curriculum work closer to the mainstream and doubtlessly gave it greater salience in the broader educational research community.

New studies using nonstandard methods once scorned by the arbiters of methodological merit soon began to appear. For instance, dozens of researchers began to study teachers' curriculum work. Clandinin (1985), Connelley (1972), and Elbaz (1983) studied teachers' practical knowledge by using a variety of methods, including interviews and diaries. Doyle (1977) made careful observations of classrooms much in the manner Jackson (1968) had earlier proposed, gleaning powerful insights into the social and ecological patterns at work there. Berk (1980) and Pinar (1980, 1981) explored the possibilities of life histories as a way to gain insight into a person's educational experiences. Almost as though they had been waiting to be freed from the bonds of a narrow scientism, a new generation of curriculum researchers put to use a profusion of innovative methods, a profusion that continues to the present day.

Implications of the Qualitative Debate for Curriculum Research

Most curriculum researchers are delighted with the greater freedom they now have to use a variety of methods. Any method imaginable is publishable today, and very likely some curriculum researcher is using it already. One may still be asked to explain it and justify it. One may even have to respond publicly to critics as Barone did. But researchers are no longer restricted by blanket proscriptions against case studies, participant observations, self-report data, or any other particular method. Methods that were nearly always rejected by journals and blacklisted by methodological authorities only a decade ago are now fully accepted. Curriculum researchers have reason to celebrate. We now have plenty of methods in great diversity, and we can choose freely among them according to our judgment of which are best suited to our problems.

On the other hand, the Barone and Rist exchange shows that there are still unwritten, generally accepted standards and that the methodological innovator runs some risk in flouting them. Qualitative methodologists are under pressure to provide warrants stronger than the researcher's testimony and the simple plausibility of the report. Eisner and others (Donmoyer 1989; Jacob 1988; Peshkin 1982; von Manen 1990) have begun the important work of formulating philosophically well-grounded frameworks for justifying qualitative methods. Their hope is that as qualitative methodology matures, curriculum researchers will be able to use ideas from these emerging frameworks to develop specific rationales for their choice of particular methods for particular studies. Perhaps, but how long will researchers have to wait until alternative philosophical frameworks appear in print, are discussed, and gain acceptance? We have already had nearly two decades of controversy, and as indicated earlier in this chapter, none of the philosophical issues have been resolved; there is good reason to suspect that many of them may never be resolved.

In the second part of this chapter, I propose to explore the possibility of developing a methodology especially suited to curriculum research. Suppose we set out to build a methodology by studying the research we actually do and find most useful. We examine the methods used in the most successful instances of curriculum research and see if we can explain why they worked particularly well. From such investigations we should be able to generate some more general principles that could become the foundation of a methodology particularly suited to curriculum research. With luck, the findings of these methodological investigations will complement the results of more abstract philosophical speculations and speed the day when curriculum researchers will have a criticized body of methodological principles for choosing among the many methods now available.

TOWARD A METHODOLOGY FOR CURRICULUM RESEARCH

The purpose in this section is to examine the character of curriculum research and to ask what sort of methodology might be appropriate for it. Since curriculum research is essentially any research that illuminates a curriculum problem or advances our ability to deal with it, its examination must begin with some conception of the character of curriculum problems. This is not the place to discuss various conceptions of curriculum, but to proceed with this discussion some position on the subject must be sketched in.

The Character of Curriculum Work

I take curriculum to be a field of practice, primarily. Fundamentally, curriculum work consists of the delivery of certain services and the resolution of certain kinds of problems that arise in schools and the agencies associated with schools. Specifically, curriculum work is concerned with services and problems related to the purposes and content of the educational program of the school and how these are organized in time, in relation to one another, and in relation to the people involved and to the physical and social milieu. The primary problems of the curriculum, then, are practical in the root sense of being capable of being resolved only through taking action in the situation (Schwab 1970).

Thought can be brought to bear on curriculum work by considering, through deliberation, what should be done in particular situations. Research assists deliberation by discovering and validating knowledge that decision makers can then use to identify and pose problems, discover and generate alternative possible courses of action, assess the strengths and limitations of each possible course of action, and weigh all the considerations to decide what to do. Research contributes by informing the decisions faced in practice, informing them not only with specific facts but also with ways of perceiving curricular situations, thinking about them, and acting in them.

This conception of curriculum work defines the environment in which curriculum research must function. This environment is, first, the world of schools. Hence, it is an active more than a contemplative environment, one in which people have jobs to do and deadlines to meet. There is little time for decision making. It is a lean environment, one in which the claims on resources far exceed the supply, so that the resources available for making considered decisions are meager. It is an environment full of routines and traditional patterns of conduct deeply ingrained in teachers and students and comfortably familiar to parents and the public. When decisions are made to change the curriculum, these routines and traditions must be altered. The decisions that shape a school's curriculum are widely distributed over time and space and necessarily involve accommodations among many individuals and agencies whose exact configuration changes all the time. Thus curriculum researchers must look broadly at all aspects of the environment and cannot focus exclusively on any particular part of the educative process, such as the development of curriculum plans and materials, teacher planning, teaching, school administration, or educational policymaking.

The conditions of curriculum work are also suffused with moral considerations, for practical problems are inescapably moral. To act in a situation (or to recommend an action to another or not to act when action is possible) is to incur a moral responsibility for the reasonably foreseeable consequences of the action on those affected by it. Since a practical problem, by definition, can be resolved only through action, all practical problems are inescapably moral. Whether the researcher who supplies knowledge that informs the deliberation that leads to an action shares a moral responsibility for the consequences of that action is a difficult moral question. It depends on how great a role the knowledge played in the decision, on the extent to which the researcher could reasonably have foreseen what the consequences of using the knowledge would be, and on the balance between good and bad uses to which the knowledge could be put. But anyone who sets out to do curriculum research intends to supply knowledge for use in deliberation (in contrast to the image, at least, of the pure researcher who gives no thought to possible uses), and therefore curriculum research is destined from the start for use in a morally charged environment. Curriculum research must come equipped with ways to incorporate moral concerns into the research plans, operations, and findings.

It is also a political environment. Since the school is a public institution, an integral part of the polity, deciding what to do about curriculum problems in schools is also inherently a political act. In an open society, certainly, and perhaps in any society, any activity that is inherently moral and political is likely to be contested and, from time to time, embroiled in controversy. This certainly has been true of curriculum work. Curriculum research, therefore, must be capable of making constructive contributions in controversial situations.

The Nature of Curriculum Research

What kinds of research could do the best job of informing deliberations in such an environment? Resource constraints favor studies that yield particularly useful findings quickly and at low cost. Reviews of research relevant to decisions would certainly fit this description. When the decision would benefit from new data about many individuals, collecting facts from surveys and existing records would be particularly appropriate. Simple, unstructured interviews and observations would often be useful. Case studies of situations such as the one under discussion could be very helpful, indeed. Historical studies of similar situations could provide a useful perspective. Philosophical studies could suggest ways of thinking about certain situations or reveal hidden flaws in the ideas being used. If some scholar published a theoretical analysis of the whole problem, suggesting its dimensions, causes, and cures, that would surely be useful.

Time-consuming, expensive, or difficult methods would have to yield a great deal more useful information than these simple methods to justify their greater expense, and even then they would not be useful when, as often happens, the decision could not wait for a study to be completed. Curriculum work is not, in general, a favorable environment for controlled laboratory experimentation, though quick field experiments whose treatments could be incorporated seamlessly into the ongoing work of the school could be useful.

The point is obvious. Curriculum research is shaped by the environment in which it must function. Curriculum researchers have not been particularly concerned to develop sophisticated research methods that guard against the many threats to the validity of these simple methods because the simple, ordinary methods perform well under the real conditions of curriculum work, better than more sophisticated methods. When we shift the context of the research to an academic environment in which researchers are vying with one another to falsify theories, these simple methods become almost useless because any competent researcher could easily cast doubt on a conclusion supported only by evidence obtained from such crude, uncontrolled methods. But when the goal is to inform decisions in a timely manner, decisions that will otherwise be made with little or no factual basis, these simple, straightforward methods outshine more elaborate, sophisticated, and specialized ones.

This line of thought suggests that curriculum researchers should be wary of methodological standards and doctrines borrowed from academic disciplines, both humanities and sciences. When examples of good research are needed, curriculum researchers should look first to other practical fields, such as social work, business, law, journalism, architecture, and other practical and professional fields concerned with people and their institutions, and only then, and warily, look to academic disciplines. When we borrow methods and techniques from other fields, we should be sure they will be useful in a curricular environment.

Before we go searching for models from other fields, though, let us look at the best research now being done on curriculum. We may find that the methods we use are more defensible than we think.

An Example: Methodology of Formative Curriculum Research

I will examine briefly the methods actually used in one small corner of curriculum research and identify the methodological issues that arise in connection with their use. As readers of this *Handbook* will certainly realize, curriculum research covers a large and varied body of work. In the short space remaining in this chapter, all that can be done is to review some small corner of the field. I have chosen a corner familiar to me: research intended to inform the development of curriculum materials. The analysis could equally well be carried out with research intended to inform teachers' classroom curriculum work or curriculum evaluation or any other phase or facet of curriculum work. The present limited and cursory analysis of one small body of work is only a beginning, intended merely to suggest what a more complete analysis would show.

A broad overview of research related to curriculum development would go something like the following. Two broad types of methods for curriculum development are widely practiced: systematic methods based on ends-means reasoning and naturalistic methods based on deliberation (D. Walker 1990, 468–499). Developers, theorists, and researchers have proposed a variety of types of extensions and elaborations to both types of methods. For instance, curriculum evaluators have long maintained that developers need more factual information on crucial issues than they typically have. Tyler (1949) emphasized this point and suggested that developers carry out studies of students and communities as a basis for curriculum development. Some have urged developers to pay special attention to the naive conceptions students bring to any new subject (Case 1978; Posner, Strike, Hewson, and Gertzog 1982). Advocates of systematic methods based on objectives have long maintained that developers should be more systematic about stating their purposes and ensuring that activities lead to their achievement (Bloom 1968; Bobbitt 1924; Gagné and Briggs 1979; Popham 1969).

A number of studies of curriculum development have been conducted, mostly descriptive, including Riley (1984a, 1984b, 1984c) and D. Walker (1971). Frey, Frei, and Langeheine (1989) studied the impact of using different models of curriculum development in a series of curriculum conferences on the process of development and the resulting product. Recently Tamir (1988) conducted a remarkable experiment in which several curriculum development teams worked in parallel. Some of them were given additional information about the students for which the curriculum was designed. The plans produced by the two sets of teams were measurably different in ways that could plausibly be traced to the greater information given to some of the teams. Furthermore, after all teams were shown the additional information, those who had completed their work without it became dissatisfied and insisted on redoing it.

Edward L. Palmer's (1974) evaluations of the children's television program "Sesame Street" set new standards of specificity and intensity in formative evaluation. He focused on measuring children's attention to television programming by providing attractive distractions such as might be found in children's homes and measuring the fraction of time they watched the television programming. Since then, there have been numerous notable achievements in the formative evaluation of materials for educational technology. Many of these are reviewed in Flagg (1990). For instance, White (1984) carried out an extensive series of clinical studies of individual students, probing their understanding of Newton's laws of motion, and then designed and formatively evaluated several versions of interactive computer programs, documenting as she did so the impact of successive versions on children's performance and understanding.

Over the past two decades extensions of and elaborations on the informal, commonsense studies often associated with the development of educational materials have proliferated to such an extent that some now speak of a new branch of research, formative research, which may be defined as research carried out "to inform the decision-making process during the design, production, and implementation . . . of an educational program with the purpose of improving the program" (Flagg 1990, 23). Formative researchers use such methods as reviewing research, consulting experts, constructing conceptual models, measuring characteristics of the intended audience for the educational program, and trying out prototypes in laboratories and in realistic field settings. They seek to learn about such matters as the readiness and needs of the audience, the value of the content to society and to the audience, the appeal of the planned program to the audience, the receptivity of teachers to it, and its utility and appeal for both students and teachers. Formative research is usually eclectic in its choice of techniques for eliciting data, including self-reports (in the form of diaries, interviews, or questionnaires), observations, tests, and records. Because most formative research takes place under severe limitations of time and resources, simple, direct methods predominate, including case studies, open-ended observations, quick and informal analyses of existing data and available products, and relatively uncontrolled experiments in both field and laboratory. Formative researchers frequently employ a strategy called triangulation, which uses a variety of simple methods to compensate for their separate weaknesses instead of using one method that is more controlled and sophisticated but requires more time and resources.

A number of specific methods seem to be especially useful in formative research, including

- Shadowing: Students are followed through their daily routines in an effort to discover conditions in their lives and aspects of their conduct that should be taken into account in designing an educational program.
- Think-aloud technique: Students are asked to think aloud as they engage in some portion of an educational program in an effort to find out about their subjective mental and emotional states.
- Stimulated recall: Students are given a recording or account of an educational activity they have recently experienced and asked to recall what they were thinking at each of several points.
- Distraction technique: Students are exposed simultaneously to two or more competing stimuli, one of which is the portion of an educational program being tested, so that their relative attention to the educational program can be measured.
- Confederates: Students are asked to tell another student about something that was presented to them earlier, so that their understanding of it can be made explicit in a natural way.
- The Oz paradigm: Researchers act as resources for students, answering questions, giving advice, and facilitating their learning in an effort to discover what sorts of supports to build into a product under development (named for the tactic of simulating a machine employed by the Wizard of Oz).
- Staggered case studies: To investigate an ongoing or long-term program, researchers can start two classrooms using the same program, one begun several weeks after the other; thus problems discovered in the first class can be corrected for the second and the corrections can be tested.

Many of these techniques as well as others especially useful in formative studies are described in Flagg (1990).

Why should we believe the findings of formative studies that use methods such as these? The answer will of course depend, just as it does for standard experimental research, on how skillfully the researcher has deployed these methods. And standard scientific criteria such as replicability still apply. But formative research draws its greatest credibility from (1) the close similarity between the situation in which data are collected and the situation of ultimate interest (trying out prototype materials in a classroom can be very close to using final versions in typical classrooms) and (2) the compelling face validity of the data collected (observations of classroom interaction, test scores, and so on).

However, methods of formative research, like all other methods, have their limitations, and hence the need for methodology. One reason to doubt many formative studies is that formative researchers usually accept the developers' basic beliefs and values. On the one hand, if they did not, the developers could easily reject the findings of the formative research on the grounds that they spring from an alien conceptual framework that the team and its sponsors had already examined and rejected. On the other hand, if the formative researcher accepts the developer's beliefs and values uncritically, the research loses its power to identify faulty assumptions the developers may be making.

Also, formative research that embraces the perspective of the developers unfairly neglects the perspectives of other interested parties, such as other educators who may not accept the developers' conceptual framework. This is a particular example of a general methodological problem in studies of curriculum practice: how to accommodate the diversity of values, perceptions, and interests of those who are legitimately involved in the practice, typically including students, teachers, parents, and school officials, as well as researchers in all their diversity. Should researchers be encouraged to strive for impartiality or rather to embrace freely and frankly one of the contending views? Or is another stance better?

A second methodological concern that arises with special force in formative research is the generalizability problem: how to justify applying the findings from one situation being studied to many others not being studied (Cronbach 1982a). Formative studies are often designed around a particular set of activities, plans, or materials and involve detailed observations of students' and teachers' use of these materials. To which potential users do the findings of such studies apply? To which implementations of the program being studied do the findings apply? To what other programs might the findings apply? We are constantly guessing.

To carry out the many studies that would be needed to yield valid statistical estimates of the generality of the findings would take more money than the development effort, and by the time they were completed the issues driving the development would probably have changed.

Furthermore, it is difficult to see how product-oriented formative research could contribute to the development of a research community. The benefits of such research could usually be expected to contribute directly to the improved quality of the product and also perhaps to the enlightenment of the developers, and maybe even to the enlightenment of developers of similar products. But in many cases what is learned will not be of sufficient generality to justify publication of a book or journal article. If the benefits such research brings to practice are important enough for us to encourage people to do this kind of research, how can we reward excellence and locate incompetence? Since the audience for reports of such research would be so small, normal reliance on the vigilance of the community of researchers seems impractical. Is such research, then, compatible with the traditions and structures of academia—journals, professional associations, and publish or perish? Should these traditions and structures be changed to acknowledge the importance of this kind of research?

A third methodological issue confronting formative researchers is the question of the relation of the program under study to the contexts in which it will be used. All too often formative research reflects the easy assumption that results obtained in field tests are due to characteristics of the program. But the available evidence (e.g., House, Glass, McLean, and Walker 1978) strongly suggests that programs succeed or fail in various settings depending on the timing of the effort in relation to other events at the site, on the personalities and attitudes of those involved at the site, on the history of the organization and its characteristics, on community attitudes, and on a host of other factors in the local context. The national curriculums developed in science and mathematics in the post-Sputnik period worked well when field-tested in favored suburban schools convenient to the colleges where they were developed. They did not always work so well in inner-city schools or poor rural schools (Welch 1979). An alternative methodological assumption more consistent with recent experience is that programs should be expected to assume different forms in different contexts and that any study of a program is really a study of the program-in-context (Cronbach 1982a). This alternative assumption requires the use of methods that are in some way sensitive to the interactions and interdependencies of program and context, possibly multiple, parallel case studies or an intensive ethnographic approach in a few contrasting contexts.

Observational studies of curriculums in use in classrooms raise the now familiar methodological questions about how to determine the validity of the interpretations observers make of what they see. Should observers be expected to compare rival interpretations of their observations in an effort to determine which interpretations best explain their observations? Or is it sufficient, as some advocates of qualitative research methods argue, to offer a plausible interpretation that is consistent with the observations?

But observational studies of curriculum also raise another equally fundamental but less discussed methodological difficulty: how to identify the purposes of the actors observed. It is much more difficult to determine why a teacher or student did something than it is to determine that they did it, and yet information about purpose is usually crucial in understanding curriculum practice. So-called objective indicators, such as time spent in various kinds of activities, allocation of resources, and the distribution of verbal markers of importance in the flow of information are certainly useful, but they are, at best, indirect and fallible indicators of purpose. Interviews and other forms of self-report data can be informative, but as we all know, people are not always or necessarily aware of their purposes or always willing to tell a researcher the whole truth and nothing but the truth. It is by no means clear that these easily measurable indicators are invariably superior to the empathic understanding and intuition of a talented, knowledgeable, and sensitive observer and interpreter. Other methods might be adapted for illuminating purposes. For instance, economists study people's priorities by looking at how they trade off one good against another when offered an exchange. It might be possible to study students' or teachers' classroom purposes in a similar way. In any event, finding methods to reveal the purposes of teachers and students and to validate claims researchers make about their purposes remains a continuing methodological challenge for curriculum researchers.

Even this cursory examination of some methods actually employed in one body of curriculum research has uncovered several methodological issues that have received relatively little attention in recent years from those who write about such issues in curriculum research:

- How do we study curriculum practices in relation to their contexts rather than as isolated, independent factors?
- How do we do justice in research to the differing values, interests, and perspectives of all those involved in curriculum practice?
- How do we reconcile research that meets the practical need for detailed studies of specific curriculum practices with traditional methodological standards and the institutional structures and procedures of the research community?
- How do we identify purposes when studying curriculum practice?

It seems likely that paying close attention to the actual methods we use in curriculum research could reveal many fresh methodological issues. If curriculum researchers were to carry out careful analyses along these lines for the most important curriculum problems addressed, analyze the methods used in specific studies in detail, and clearly formulate each issue by using examples, I believe we would have a much clearer grasp of our own priorities as a field and could then develop methodological principles well suited to our own problems. A comparison of the results of such an analysis with the traditional canons of scientific research and humanistic scholarship and with emerging qualitative methodological frameworks could lead to a fruitful dialogue.

On the Role of Methodology in Improving Curriculum Research

Curriculum researchers would surely do more to improve curriculum practice by handling important methodological issues better. Scientific experiments would surely yield better information about the cause-effect relations between the curriculum program and the outcome if they were designed to include data on how the program interacts with the classroom and school contexts. This aspect could be achieved by controlling for contextual factors; by measuring them; or by making them the focus of parallel, independent investigation. Curriculum criticism, curriculum theorizing, and other forms of humanistically oriented research would surely make a greater contribution to curriculum improvement if the writing reported more specifics and explored more thoroughly and critically various ways in which these might be interpreted. Developing alternative methodologies for qualitative research would surely expand the researcher's repertoire of methods and might enable research to embrace a wider range of human experience. The development of a distinctive methodology for research in curriculum along the lines suggested previously would help curriculum researchers to design studies better suited to the realities of curriculum work.

But there are not that many curriculum researchers and there are many urgent curriculum problems. Is the development of better research methods and methodologies the best use of their time and talents? Should curriculum researchers be urged to turn away from their current preoccupations and pay greater attention to their methods? Should those preparing for or just beginning careers as curriculum researchers be encouraged to invest more time and effort in developing their methodological skill and expertise? All the attention being given to methodological issues in conferences and journals and the flood of recent publications on research methods would suggest so. The potential contributions of new methods from cognitive science and anthropology, to name only two prominent sources, seem great. More sophisticated and powerful methods would certainly help curriculum researchers compete for funds and prestige with researchers from other disciplines.

For all these reasons and more, my judgment is that we should pay more attention to methods and methodology than we have, but not a great deal more, and that we should focus our efforts carefully. Above all, we must not be seduced by the overemphasis on methodology so prevalent in the academic disciplines. We must not expect salvation from new methods or new ways of thinking about methodology.

In a paper entitled "The Art of Social Science," sociologist Robert Redfield (1948) addressed a puzzlement in the social sciences that bears a close resemblance to the situation today in curriculum research. He noted that some of the greatest works of social science, such as Sumner's (1906) *Folkways*, de Tocqueville's (1898) *Democracy in America*, and Veblen's (1934) *The Theory of the Leisure Class*, used research methods of low scholarly repute among social scientists, and furthermore, these giants of the field virtually ignored methodological rules in writing their great works. "There is nowhere in them any procedure, any kind of operation upon facts to reach conclusions which might not occur to any intelligent and generally educated person" (Redfield 1948, 182). How, then, to account for the greatness of their contribution to our understanding of humankind in society? Redfield's meditations on this puzzle led him to suggest three additional qualities, independent of methodological rigor, that contribute to excellence in social science research: sympathetic understanding of people; the ability to see the general in the particular; and freshness and independence of viewpoint, "a clear-headed willfulness to take another look" (186). He concluded that if "programs for making social scientists . . . [are] made up [only] of training in techniques and the opportunity to take part in some kind of research in which the procedures are already determined and the problems set by some established master [then] . . . we are not likely to have great social scientists or to have many books written that are as illuminating and as influential as those by Sumner, Veblen, and De Tocqueville" (189).

Behavioral and social scientists are notorious for a tendency to worship method. Many of them believe that sophisticated methods are what mainly distinguish their findings from common sense, speculation, and received wisdom. An overreliance on method, however, has characterized many behavioral and social science disciplines during much of their history. The Campbell and Stanley (1963) doctrine is an outgrowth of such an excess in experimental psychology and psychological measurement, and the history of the various behavioral and social science disciplines is replete with other examples. The notion that "the most serious difficulties which confront behavioral science are 'methodological,' and that if only we hit on the right methodology, progress will be rapid and sure," which the distinguished philosopher of social science Abraham Kaplan (1964) calls the myth of methodology, is also a danger facing advocates of qualitative methodology today. Kaplan makes a compelling case that "methodology is far from being a sufficient condition for scientific achievement. Methodological programmes enforce a conformity on researchers that may inhibit bold, adventurous moves and prevent researchers from exploring productive lines of thought and inquiry" (24).

A greater danger than inhibition in education's present state of methodological anarchy is distraction and dissipation. Curriculum researchers, caught up in the excitement of trying new methods, may waste time polishing their new toys and fail to make headway against any important problem. If this were to happen, curriculum research could go the way of educational measurement, a field that lavishes energy on perfecting sophisticated techniques for constructing standardized tests and analyzing numerical data, while it virtually ignores the more important problem of how to help teachers get better information about what their students know. It would be a dubious achievement if curriculum researchers developed sophisticated techniques for, say, connoisseurship and criticism or critical ethnography or quantitative studies of course taking, at a similar cost.

In addition to the danger of going overboard in our concern for methodology, we face the danger of steering by the wrong star. It is tempting to compete with the academic disciplines on their terms, searching for methods as rigorous as the psychologists' or as subtle as the literary critics', even though we know that their methods serve a different function in a different context. It is easy to mistake sophistication for quality. Methods do not have to be fancy, complicated, new, or mysterious to be good. A recent example of research in mathematics education illustrates this point dramatically.

Uri Treisman (Henkin and Treisman 1984; Treisman 1983), while a graduate student working with Professor Leon Henkin at the University of California at Berkeley, carried out a chain of studies that were by traditional standards methodologically primitive but nevertheless exceptionally productive. Treisman was assigned to teach a section of a large introductory college mathematics course. This was an honors class, but even so, the students from disadvantaged minority groups—African-American and Hispanic students—received lower grades than other students in the class. Treisman could have attributed this result to genetics or early deprivation and let the matter rest, but he did not. He continued asking questions. He noticed that another minority group, Asian-American students, did better than the class as a whole, a result that also reflected national trends. Believing that these students were all of high academic ability since they all met the entry requirements for an honors course, Treisman decided to see if he could observe any differences in how the two contrasting groups of students prepared for the class.

He arranged to shadow individual students, noting when, where, how, and how long they studied for the mathematics class. He found to his surprise that the disadvantaged minority students actually spent more hours studying than the Asian-Americans, but they typically studied alone, and when they studied, they spent more time reading the assigned textbook pages and studying their class notes and relatively less time attempting the homework problems. When they got stuck on a homework problem, virtually their only strategy was to try one method of solution over and over again. By contrast, the Asian-American students spent only a small proportion of their time reading. They met regularly as a group to review the homework problems, and they spent most of their time in these groups discussing the most difficult problems. If someone in the group could solve a problem, that person explained it to the ones who could not. If no one in the group could solve a problem, they discussed it and tried to work it out together. If this failed, someone would consult the instructor about the problem.

At this point Treisman could have written a paper announcing his intriguing finding and reporting his experience with a little-known qualitative research method. But he and his colleagues pressed on. Suspecting that these group problem-solving sessions could account for some of the difference between the performance of the two groups of students, he initiated an honors workshop for minority students enrolled in the course. In this honors workshop he coached the students to follow the same group problem-solving process he had observed among the Asian-American students. Sure enough, the minority students in the honors workshop performed as well as the rest of the class.

By any reasonable standards for curriculum research, this is an outstanding study. The researcher focused his attention on the crucial practical problem, observed practices closely, kept himself open to a wide variety of evidence at every stage of the inquiry, compared circumstances in which a practice seemed to succeed with circumstances in which it failed, searched for factors in the situation that could be changed, redesigned practices to reflect what he thought he had learned from his observations, and tested the new practices by using the standards of achievement actually employed in the real course. His results have been widely reported and have already begun to influence research and practice in mathematics education (Gillman 1990). And all this work was accomplished in three years on a modest budget.

By the prevailing methodological standards of the behavioral and social sciences, in contrast, these studies are merely intriguing observations that prove nothing. Their methods were primitive and completely lacking in controls. The samples were small and not randomly selected. The classroom experiment was intriguing, but the treatment was not theoretically well specified and was administered to only one small group. Since the researchers were the instructors, their influence is a plausible alternative explanation for the students' gains. The studies were not grounded in an explicit theoretical framework; the researchers cannot even provide a convincing theoretical interpretation of the causes of the improvement they observed among the minority students. A hard-nosed methodologist of the Campbell and Stanley (1963) variety would pronounce on this work the same judgment they pronounced on case studies: "Such a total absence of control as to be of almost no scientific value" (176).

I can almost hear the voice of a methodologist I know. He is saying, "These people may have stumbled onto something. We had better put someone with real methodological training onto this problem and see if there is anything to it." That is a reasonable attitude for someone seeking to build a science of education, but is it a reasonable attitude for someone seeking to improve professional practice? Should curriculum researchers follow the academic's lead and discount the achievement of the Berkeley researchers while showering the "good methodologist" with academic honors, or should we rather honor the Berkeley researchers as exemplary practice-centered methodologists? I think the latter is the wiser choice for curriculum researchers.

Neither lack of methods nor of ideas about methods is the crucial factor limiting the contribution of curriculum research to curriculum improvement. Never before have so many researchers had so many methods to choose from, so many different ideas about which methods work best and why, and so much freedom to choose. We could exhaust ourselves in an orgy of methodological promiscuousness and still not try half the methods and ideas available. And that is another danger we face.

In my opinion the most serious obstacles to better research in curriculum today are problems of commitment and organization. We need curriculum researchers who are wedded to the goal of bringing about improvements in important curriculum problem areas—researchers who will persist doggedly, pursue the problem wherever it leads, try new methods when they seem useful, and design chains of studies that inform one another and that deepen and progress over decades. We need curriculum researchers whose loyalty to their problem and to the research enterprise is so strong that they would be willing to put their deepest beliefs to the test of practice rather than judging practice by the standard of their beliefs. We need curriculum researchers for whom learning how to build a better curriculum seems more important than building a science of education or even, dare one think it, a brave new world. Curriculum researchers with such an inquiring attitude and unshakable commitment would be able to find or invent the methods they need.

To recruit and sustain such dedicated curriculum researchers, we will need to develop an institutional infrastructure to support their work. I am not at all certain about what kinds of support are needed. The following suggestions are mere gestures toward the kinds of actions members of the curriculum research community will need to consider. Graduate training for research is crucial, but it is not clear what kind of preparation will encourage the kind of researchers we need. Methodological eclecticism makes enormous demands on our ability to learn new methods as we need them. Certainly one course in quantitative methods and one in qualitative, which seems to be the emerging pattern, will be inadequate. My own inclination would be toward extended participation in research from the first year of graduate study, along the lines suggested by Gray and Meighan (1980). But we need to discuss many proposals and experiment with several of the most promising. How do you teach someone to make adroit use of a variety of simple methods in the dogged pursuit of knowledge about a problem?

Curriculum researchers may need established forums in which to discuss curriculum problems with reflective practitioners who are also concerned about finding better solutions, as well as more forums for discussion among ourselves, especially dialogue with those whose problem seems most unlike ours: The researcher doing microscopic studies of children working with textbooks would benefit from working with the student of curriculum policy studying textbook selection. We need support for the kinds of collaborative studies that would be most helpful in addressing those problems—case studies, observational studies, fact collecting, intensive clinical interactions with students and teachers, and simple field trials of promising programs. We need publication outlets for such studies. The several fine journals on general curriculum research now published in English together with the subject matter journals and journals specializing in the different ages and grades of schooling still do not provide enough pages for reporting this work. It will be detailed and probably of interest mainly to a small audience. We should investigate the possibilities of electronic publishing with referees who appropriately apply practice-centered standards.

Most of us should probably write less, study more, and circulate our papers and discuss them in the spirit of making our work more defensible and more widely useful. Suydam (1985) set a useful precedent. She edited abstracts and critiques of 11 varied practice-centered studies in mathematics education, called *Investigations in Mathematics Education*.

Whatever directions the development of research methodology in curriculum may take, researchers would do well to reflect deeply on both the promise and the limitations of methodological reform as a strategy for improving research and to adopt research support policies that treat methodological rigor and sophistication as only one component of excellence in research.

References

Apple, Michael. 1979. *Ideology and Curriculum*. London: Routledge & Kegan Paul.

Argyris, Chris, Robert Putnam, and Diana McLain Smith. 1985. *Action Science*. San Francisco: Jossey-Bass.

Bantock, G. H. 1968. *Culture, Industrialisation, and Education*. London: Routledge & Kegan Paul.

Barone, Thomas E. 1987a. On equality, visibility, and the fine arts program in a black elementary school: An example of educational criticism. *Curriculum Inquiry* 17(4): 431–433.

Barone, Thomas E. 1987b. Research out of the shadows. *Curriculum Inquiry* 17(4): 453–459.

Barzun, Jacques. 1977. *The Modern Researcher*. New York: Harcourt Brace.

Becker, Howard S. 1986. *Doing Things Together*. Evanston, IL: Northwestern University Press.

Berk, Len. 1980. Education in lives: Biographic narrative in the study of educational outcomes. *Journal of Curriculum Theorizing* 2(2):188–155.

Bloom, Benjamin. 1968. "Some Theoretical Issues Relating to Educational Evaluation." In *Educational Evaluation: New Means, New Roles*, Sixty-sixth Yearbook, Part II, edited by Ralph W. Tyler, 26–50. Chicago: National Society for the Study of Education.

Bloom, Benjamin. 1971. "Mastery Learning and Its Implications for Curriculum Development." In *Confronting Curriculum Reform*, edited by Elliot Eisner. Boston: Little, Brown.

Bobbitt, Franklin W. 1924. *How to Make a Curriculum*. Boston: Houghton Mifflin.

Bogdan, R. C., and S. K. Biklen. 1982. *Qualitative Research in Education*. Boston: Allyn & Bacon.

Bracht, Glenn H., and Gene V. Glass. 1968. External validity of experiments. *American Educational Research Journal* 20(4): 437–474.

Broudy, Harry. 1974. *General Education: The Search for a Rationale*. Bloomington, IN: Phi Delta Kappa Educational Foundation.

Burgess, Robert G. 1985. *Field Methods in the Study of Education*. London: Falmer.

Campbell, Donald T. 1975. Degress of freedom and the case study. *Comparative Political Studies* 8(2): 178–193.

Campbell, Donald T. 1978. "Qualitative Knowing and Action Research." In *The Social Context of Method*, edited by M. Brenner, P. Marsh, and M. Brenner. New York: St. Martin's Press.

Campbell, Donald T., and Julian Stanley. 1963. "Experimental and Quasi-Experimental Designs for Research on Teaching." In *Handbook of Research on Teaching*, edited by N. L. Gage. Chicago: Rand McNally.

Carr, Wilfred. 1989. Action research ten years on. *Journal of Curriculum Studies* 21(1): 85–90.

Case, Robbie. 1978. A developmentally based theory and technology of instruction. *Review of Educational Research* 48: 339–363.

Clandinin, Jean. 1985. Personal practical knowledge: A study of teachers' classroom images. *Curriculum Inquiry* 15(4): 361–383.

Cohen, Louis, and Lawrence Manion. 1980. *Research Methods in Education*, 2nd ed. Dover, NH: Croom Helm.

Collings, Ellsworth. 1923. *An Experiment with a Project Curriculum*. New York: Macmillan.

Connelley, F. Michael. 1972. The functions of curriculum development. *Interchange* 3:161–171.

Cook, Thomas D., and Donald T. Campbell. 1979. *Quasi-Experimentation: Design and Analysis Issues for Field Settings*. Chicago: Rand McNally.

Cooley, William, and William Bickel. 1986. *Decision-Oriented Educational Research*. Boston: Kluwer-Nijhof.

Counts, George S. 1932. *Dare the School Build a New Social Order?* New York: John Day.

Cremin, Lawrence. 1963. *The Transformation of the School*. New York: Vintage Books.

Cronbach, Lee J. 1971. "Mastery Learning and Its Implications for Curriculum Development." In *Confronting Curriculum Reform*, edited by Elliot Eisner. Boston: Little, Brown.

Cronbach, Lee J. 1975. Beyond the two disciplines of scientific psychology. *The American Psychologist* 30(2): 116–126.

Cronbach, Lee J. 1982a. *Designing Evaluations of Educational and Social Programs*. San Francisco: Jossey-Bass.

Cronbach, Lee J. 1982b. "Prudent Aspirations for Social Inquiry." In *The Social Sciences: Their Nature and Uses*, edited by William Kruskal. Chicago: University of Chicago Press.

Cronbach, Lee J., and Patrick Suppes, eds. 1969. *Research for Tomorrow's Schools*. London: Macmillan.

Cronbach, Lee J. 1982. *Designing Evaluations of Educational and Social Programs*. San Francisco: Jossey-Bass.

De Landsheere, G. 1988. "History of Educational Research." In *Educational Research, Methodology, and Measurement: An International Handbook*, edited by John P. Keeves. Oxford: Pergamon.

Denzin, Norman. 1970. *The Research Act: Introduction to Sociological Methods*. Chicago: Aldine.

Descartes, René. 1980 [1637]. *Discourse on Method*, translated by Donald A. Cress. Indianapolis: Hackett.

Dewey, John, and Evelyn Dewey. 1915. *Schools of Tomorrow*. New York: Dutton.

Dippo, Don. 1988. Making ethnographic research count. *Curriculum Inquiry* 18(4): 481–488.

Donmoyer, Robert. 1987. Beyond Thordike/Beyond Melodrama. *Curriculum Inquiry* 17(4): 353–363.

Donmoyer, Robert. 1989. Theory, practice, and the double-edged problem of idiosyncracy. *Journal of Curriculum and Supervision* 4(3): 257–270.

Doyle, Walter. 1977. Learning the classroom environment: An ecological analysis. *Journal of Teacher Education* 28: 22–34.

Ebel, Robert. 1967. Some limitations of basic research in education. *Phi Delta Kappan* 49(2): 81–84.

Eisner, Elliot. 1969. "Instructional and Expressive Educational Objectives: Their Formulation and Use in Curriculum." In *Instructional Objectives*. AERA Monograph Series on Curriculum Evaluation. Washington, DC: American Educational Research Association.

Eisner, Elliot, ed. 1971. *Confronting Curriculum Reform*. Boston: Little, Brown.

Eisner, Elliot. 1976. Educational connoisseurship and criticism: Their form and function in educational evaluation. *The Journal of Aesthetic Education* 10(3–4): 135–150.

Eisner, Elliot. 1979. *The Educational Imagination*. New York: Macmillan.

Eisner, Elliot. 1981. On the differences between scientific and artistic approaches to qualitative research. *Educational Researcher* 10(4): 5–9.

Elbaz, Freema. 1983. *Teacher Thinking: A Study of Practical Knowledge*. London: Croom Helm.

Ericksson, K. Anders, and Herbert A. Simon. 1984. *Protocol Analysis: Verbal Reports as Data*. Cambridge, MA: MIT Press.

Fawcett, Harold, ed. 1938. *The Nature of Proof*, Thirteenth Yearbook. Washington, DC: National Council of Teachers of Mathematics.

Fetterman, David M., ed. 1988. *Qualitative Approaches to Evaluation in Education: The Silent Scientific Revolution*. New York: Praeger.

Feyerabend, Paul K. 1983. *Against Method*. London: Verso.

Flagg, Barbara. 1990. *Formative Evaluation for Educational Technologies*. Hillsdale, NJ: Erlbaum.

Ford, G. W., and Lawrence Pugno. 1964. *The Structure of Knowledge and the Curriculum*. Chicago: Rand McNally.

Foshay, Arthur. 1970. *Curriculum for the Seventies: An Agenda for Invention*. Washington, DC: Association for Supervision and Curriculum Development.

Frey, Karl, Alphons Frei, and Rolf Langeheine. 1989. Can curriculum development models really influence the curriculum? *Journal of Curriculum Studies* 21(16): 553–559.

Froebel, Friedrich. 1891 [1826]. *The Education of Man*, translated by W. N. Hailmann. New York: Appleton.

Gage, Nathaniel L., ed. *Handbook of Research on Teaching*. Chicago: Rand McNally.

Gagné, Robert, and Leslie Briggs. 1979. *Principles of Instructional Design*. New York: Holt, Rinehart and Winston.

Geertz, Clifford, ed. 1973. *The Interpretation of Cultures*. New York: Basic Books.

Gillman, Leonard. 1990. *Focus* 10(1): 7–10.

Glass, Gene V. 1972. The wisdom of scientific inquiry on education. *Journal of Research in Science Teaching* 9(1): 3–18.

Goffman, Irving. 1974. *Frame Analysis*. New York: Harper Colophon Books.

Goodlad, John, and Frances Klein. 1970. *Behind the Classroom Door*. Worthington, OH: Jones.

Goodman, Paul. 1964. *Compulsory Mis-Education*. New York: Horizon Press.

Gray, Paul S., and Phyllis Meighan. 1980. Learning research methods by doing research. *Improving College and University Teaching* 28: 160–165.

Greene, Maxine 1967. *Existential Encounters for Teachers*. New York: Random House.

Greene, Maxine. 1978. *Landscapes of Learning*. New York: Teachers College Press.

Hamilton, David, ed. 1976. *Beyond the Numbers Game*. London: Macmillan.

Henkin, Leon, and Uri Treisman. 1984. Final Report: University of California Professional Development Program, ERIC ED 2669932.

Herbart, Johann Friedrich. 1895 [1838]. *The Science of Education*, translated by Henry M. Felkin and Emmie Felkin. Boston: Heath.

Hirst, P. H. 1974. *Knowledge and the Curriculum*. London: Routledge & Kegan Paul.

Holt, John. 1966. *How Children Fail*. London: Pitman.

Hopkins, D. 1985. *A Teacher's Guide to Classroom Research*. Milton Keynes, England: Open University Press.

House, Ernest R., Gene V. Glass, Leslie D. McLean, and Decker F. Walker. 1978. No simple answer: Critique of the follow through evaluation. *Harvard Educational Review* 48(2): 128–160.

Hustler, D., T. Cassidy, and T. Cuff, eds. 1986. *Action Research in Classrooms and Schools*. London: Allen & Unwin.

Jackson, Philip. 1968. *Life in Classrooms*. New York: Holt, Rinehart and Winston.

Jackson, Philip. 1970, spring. Is there a best way of teaching Harold Bateman? *Midway*: 15–28.

Jacob, Evelyn. 1988. Clarifying qualitative research: A focus on traditions. *Educational Researcher* 17(1): 16–24.

James, William. 1890. *The Principles of Psychology*. New York: Henry Holt.

James, William. 1899. *Talks to Teachers on Psychology: And to Students on Some of Life's Ideals*. New York: Henry Holt.

Kaplan, Abraham. 1964. *The Conduct of Inquiry*. San Francisco: Chandler.

Keeves, John P., ed. 1988. *Educational Research, Methodology, and Measurement: An International Handbook*. Oxford: Pergamon.

Kilpatrick, William H. 1926. *Foundations of Method*. New York: Macmillan.

Kliebard, Herbert. 1970. The Tyler rationale. *School Review* 78: 259–272.

Kliebard, Herbert. 1977. "Bureaucracy and Curriculum Theory." In *Curriculum and Evaluation*, edited by Arno Bellack and Herbert Kliebard. Berkeley, CA: McCutchan.

Krug, Edward. 1964. *The Shaping of the American High School*. Madison: University of Wisconsin Press.

Kuhn, Thomas. 1962. *The Structure of Scientific Revolutions*. Chicago: University of Chicago Press.

Lakatos, Imre. 1978. *The Methodology of Scientific Research Programmes*. Cambridge, England: Cambridge University Press.

Levine, David O. 1986. *The American College and the Culture of Aspiration*. Ithaca, NY: Cornell University Press.

Locke, John. 1892 [1690]. *Some Thoughts Concerning Education*. Cambridge, England: Cambridge University Press.

Lutz, F. W., and M. A. Ramsey. 1974. The use of anthropological field methods in education. *Educational Researcher* 3(10): 5–9.

McKernan, Jim. 1988. The countenance of curriculum action research: Traditional, collaborative, and emancipatory-critical conceptions. *Journal of Curriculum and Supervision* 3(3): 173–200.

Miles, Matthew, and Michael Huberman. 1984. *Qualitative Data Analysis: A Sourcebook of New Methods*. Beverly Hills, CA: Sage.

Oja, Sharon N., and Lisa Smulyan. 1989. *Collaborative Action Research: A Developmental Approach*. London: Falmer.

Palmer, Edward L. 1974. "Formative Research in the Production of Television for Children." In *Media and Symbols: The Forms of Expression*, edited by David Olson, 303–329. Chicago: University of Chicago Press.

Parlett, M., and Hamilton, D. 1976. "Evaluation as Illumination: A New Approach to the Study of Innovatory Programmes." In *Beyond the Numbers Game*, edited by D. Hamilton. London: Macmillan.

Peshkin, Alan. 1982. "The Researcher and Subjectivity: Reflections on an Ethnography of School and Community." In *Doing the Ethnography of Schooling*, edited by George Spindler. New York: Holt, Rinehart and Winston.

Pestalozzi, Johann Heinrich. 1987 [1781]. *Leonard and Gertrude*, translated by Eva Channing. Boston: Heath.

Phillips, Denis C. 1976. *Holistic Thought in Social Science*. Palo Alto, CA: Stanford University Press.

Phillips, Denis C. 1983. After the wake: Postpositivist educational thought. *Educational Researcher* 12(5): 4–5.

Phillips, Denis C. 1986. *Philosophical Issues in Educational Research*. Bentley: Western Australian Institute of Technology.

Phillips, Denis C. 1987. *Philosophy, Science, and Social Inquiry*. New York: Pergamon.

Pinar, William. 1980. Life history and educational experience, Part I. *Journal of Curriculum Theorizing* 2(2): 59–212.

Pinar, William. 1981. Life history and educational experience, Part II. *Journal of Curriculum Theorizing* 3(1): 259–286.

Pinar, William F., and Madeleine Grumet. 1976. *Toward a Poor Curriculum*. Dubuque, IA: Kendall/Hunt.

Popham, W. James. 1969. *Objectives and Instruction in Instructional Objectives*. AERA Monograph Series on Curriculum Evaluation. Washington, DC: American Educational Research Association.

Popper, Karl. 1965. *Conjectures and Refutations*. New York: Harper.

Posner, George, Kenneth A. Strike, Peter W. Hewson, and William A. Gertzog. 1982. Accommodation of a scientific conception: Toward a theory of conceptual change. *Science Education* 662: 211–227.

Redfield, Robert. 1948. The art of social science. *The American Journal of Sociology* 54: 181–190.

Rice, Joseph Mayer. 1897. The futility of the spelling grind. *The Forum* 23: 162–173.

Riley, Judith. 1984a. An explanation of drafting behaviors in the production of distance education materials. *British Journal of Educational Technology* 15: 226–238

Riley, Judith. 1984b. The problems of drafting distance education materials. *British Journal of Educational Technology* 15: 192–204.

Riley, Judith. 1984c. The problems of revising drafts of distance education materials. *British Journal of Educational Technology* 15: 205–226.

Rist, Ray C. 1977. On the relations among educational research paradigms: From disdain to detente. *Anthropology and Education* 8: 177–194.

Rist, Ray C. 1987. Research in the shadows. *Curriculum Inquiry* 17(4): 447–452.

Ross, Dorene D. 1988. "An Introduction to Curriculum Criticism." In *Qualitative Research in Education: Focus and Methods*, edited by Robert R. Shermine and Rodman B. Webb, 162–174. London: Falmer.

Roszak, Theodore. 1970. *The Making of a Counter Culture*. London: Faber & Faber.

Rousseau, Jean Jacques. 1899 [1762]. *Émile*, translated by Eleanor Worthington. Boston: Heath.

Rugg, Harold O. 1941. *That Men May Understand*. New York: Doubleday, Doran and Company.

Rugg, Harold O., and Ann Shumaker. 1928. *The Child-Centered School*. New York: World Book Company.

Schubert, William. 1980. *Curriculum Books: The First Eighty Years*. Washington, DC: University Press of America.

Schwab, Joseph. 1970. *The Practical: A Language for Curriculum*. Washington, DC: National Education Association.

Shulman, Lee S. 1970. Reconstruction of Educational Research. *Review of Educational Research* 40(3): 371–396.

Shulman, Lee S. 1978. *Relating Theory to Practice in Educational Research*. East Lansing, MI: Institute for Research on Teaching.

Smith, Eugene R., Ralph W. Tyler, and the evaluation staff. 1942. *Appraising and Recording Student Progress*. New York: Harper & Brothers.

Smith, Louis M., and William Geoffrey. 1968. *The Complexities of an Urban Classroom: An Analysis Toward a General Theory of Teaching*. New York: Holt, Rinehart and Winston.

Smith, Mary Lee, and Gene V. Glass. 1987. *Research and Evaluation in Education and the Social Sciences*. Englewood Cliffs, NJ: Prentice Hall.

Spindler, George. 1982. *Doing the Ethnography of Schooling*. New York: Holt, Rinehart and Winston

Stake, Robert. 1978. The case study method in social inquiry. *Educational Researcher* 7(2): 5–8.

Stenhouse, Lawrence. 1975. *An Introduction to Curriculum Research and Development*. London: Heinemann.

Sumner, William Graham. 1906. *Folkways*. Boston: Ginn.

Suydam, Marilyn, ed. 1985. *Investigations in Mathematics Education* 18(4): 1–73.

Tamir, Pinchas. 1988. The role of pre-planning curriculum evaluation in science education. *Journal of Curriculum Studies* 20(3): 257–262.

Tanner, Daniel, and Laurel Tanner. 1975. *Curriculum Development: Theory Into Practice*. New York: Macmillan.

Thorndike, Edward L. 1911. *Animal Intelligence*. New York: Macmillan.

Thorndike, Edward L., and Irving Lorge. 1938. *A Semantic Count of English Words*. New York: Institute of Educational Research, Teachers College, Columbia University.

Tocqueville, Alexis de. 1898. *Democracy in America*. New York: Century.

Travers, Robert M. W., ed. 1973. *Second Handbook of Research on Teaching*. Chicago: Rand McNally.

Treisman, P. Uri. 1983. Improving the performance of minority students in college-level mathematics. *Innovation Abstracts* 5(17): 1–5.

Tyler, Ralph. 1949. *Basic Principles of Curriculum and Instruction*. Chicago: University of Chicago Press.

van Manen, Max. 1990. *Researching Lived Experience*. Albany: State University of New York Press.

Veblen, Thorstein. 1934. *The Theory of the Leisure Class*. New York: Modern Library

Walker, Decker. 1971. The process of curriculum development: A naturalistic model. *School Review* 80: 51–65.

Walker, Decker. 1990. *Fundamentals of Curriculum*. San Diego, CA: Harcourt Brace Jovanovich.

Walker, Rob. 1985. *Doing Research: A Handbook for Teachers*. London: Methuen.

Welch, Wayne. 1979. "Twenty Years of Science Curriculum Development: A Look Back." In *Review of Research in Education*, vol. 7, edited by David C. Berliner. Washington, DC: American Educational Research Association.

Westbury, Ian, and Arno Bellack. 1971. *Research Into Classroom Processes*. New York: Teachers College Press.

White, Barbara. 1984. Designing computer games to help physics students understand Newton's Laws of Motion. *Cognition and Instruction* 1: 69–108.

Wirt, Frederick, and Michael W. Kirst. 1982. *Schools in Conflict*. Berkeley, CA: McCutchan.

Wittrock, Merlin C., ed. 1986. *Handbook of Research on Teaching*, 3rd ed. New York: Macmillan.

Wolcott, Harry F. 1973. *The Man in the Principal's Office*. New York: Holt, Rinehart and Winston.

Woods, Peter. 1986. *Inside Schools: Ethnography in Educational Research*. London: Routledge & Kegan Paul.

Yin, R. K. 1984. *Case Study Research: Design and Methods*. Beverly Hills, CA: Sage.

Young, Michael F. D. 1971. *Knowledge and Control*. London: Collier-Macmillan.

5

CURRICULUM EVALUATION AND ASSESSMENT

George F. Madaus
BOSTON COLLEGE

Thomas Kellaghan
EDUCATIONAL RESEARCH CENTRE
ST PATRICK'S COLLEGE, DUBLIN

The terms "curriculum," "evaluation," and "assessment" do not have generally agreed-upon meanings. "Curriculum" is used in a variety of senses—from describing a specific course or program, which may be implemented in one class or across the nation, to referring to all of a student's experiences in school. There are difficulties also with the terms "evaluation" and "assessment," which are sometimes used as synonyms, both in everyday language and in the professional literature, and sometimes to denote quite different things. Just as these terms themselves must be considered problematic, so too are the relationships among them. For example, for some commentators, the curriculum should be defined in terms of its aims and objectives and is entirely antecedent to assessment and evaluation. For others, assessment and evaluation procedures may be used to determine the curriculum. Further, many concepts frequently used in the context of curriculum, assessment, and evaluation, such as aims, objectives, processes, standards, accountability, and teacher appraisal, are also problematic and assume different roles and levels of importance in differing models.

Lack of clarity in the meanings of assessment and evaluation is due in part to the fact that since the 1960s, there has been a growth in emphasis on testing in American education and a broadening of the functions for which tests are used. Partly as a reaction against this development, the term "assessment" has become more popular and is being used to denote a broader range of information and techniques than those associated with the standardized multiple-choice test.

Lack of clarity can also be attributed to the enormous growth, also since the 1960s, in the use of program evaluation in general and of curriculum evaluation in particular. In this situation, old procedures have sometimes been used for purposes for which they were not originally intended, while new procedures are also being developed to meet new needs. Conceptual clarification has often lagged behind the application of procedures, with the result that the implications of particular procedures are not always fully appreciated. This fact would seem to be particularly true in the case of standardized tests of achievement, which occupy a major position in both assessment and evaluation efforts.

We begin the chapter with a consideration of terminology, followed by a brief description of major historical developments in the evaluation component of the curriculum. Then we describe classroom assessment practice, which of course is directed primarily toward student appraisal, though it may also be used for curriculum evaluation. The components of the curriculum that might be considered in a formal evaluation are then outlined, followed by a description of major approaches in the methodology of evaluation. We then consider the appropriateness of a commonly used procedure, multiple-choice tests, for curriculum evaluation. Next we consider how evaluation can serve policy and in particular how evaluation is used as a mechanism of power. Finally, we consider relationships among assessment, evaluation, and curriculum and how assessment and evaluation can affect curricular practice.

TERMINOLOGY

We shall not attempt to define "curriculum" in this chapter because the question of definition is dealt with elsewhere in this *Handbook*. Rather, we will consider the curriculum in operational terms as consisting of six major components, described below, any of which could attract the attention of an evaluator. Describing the curriculum in terms of these components allows for a variety of emphases in defining a curriculum since the components cover content, process, and product, as well as the context in which the curriculum is implemented. Further, it allows us to consider interactions between different aspects of the curriculum; for example, the relationship between a planned curriculum and how it is actually implemented in schools or the relationship between the context of curriculum implementation, including student characteristics, and student outcomes.

Our concern in this chapter is with assessment and evaluation. "Assessment" may be defined as an activity designed to show what a person knows or can do. Thus, it is concerned with the appraisal of individuals. As we shall see, assessment in the classroom is based largely on a teacher's observations of students as they go about their normal learning activities. Often a teacher will use information derived from the assessment of students to make important curriculum decisions, such as modifying teaching methods, reorganizing the class, emphasizing or re-presenting topics, or changing the pace of instruction.

Many definitions of and approaches to "evaluation" are to be found in the literature (see Madaus, Scriven, and Stufflebeam 1983; Murphy and Torrance 1987; Stufflebeam and Shinkfield 1985; Worthen and Sanders 1987). One that has exerted considerable influence was that proposed by Tyler (1949): "The process of evaluation is essentially the process of determining to what extent the educational objectives are actually being realized by the program of curriculum and instruction" (105–106). Here the emphasis is on the appraisal of a program or project rather than of an individual. There is also an emphasis on outcomes, though this is not an essential aspect of program evaluation. Indeed an overemphasis on outcomes is unsatisfactory since information about outcomes does not necessarily tell us anything about other important aspects of a curriculum, such as the quality of its objectives or the way in which it has been taught. As Scriven (1967) has pointed out, a history curriculum that consisted only of the memorization of names and dates could not be regarded as "good," no matter how well students had memorized the specified information. When new curricula in mathematics, science, and foreign languages as well as projects to promote equality of opportunity, such as Head Start, were introduced in the 1960s, a variety of questions were raised. Did the new programs identify students who had previously been neglected? Did the programs respond to the valid needs of the students? Were the programs based on sound theoretical and practical principles? Were the programs being operated competently and efficiently? (Joint Committee on Standards for Educational Evaluation 1981). These questions could not be answered by evaluations that focused exclusively on the achievement of educational objectives.

Dissatisfaction with the limitations of the Tylerian, or "objectives," approach, along with increased political and financial support for evaluation, led to the development during the 1970s of a host of different approaches to the assessment of the value and effectiveness of various educational activities. In response to this development and in recognition of a need to monitor and strengthen evaluation practices, the Joint Committee on Standards for Educational Evaluation (1981) developed a set of evaluation standards and provided a broad definition of evaluation as "the systematic investigation of the worth or merit of some object" (program, project, or materials) (12). The definition allows for a variety of ways of evaluating programs other than by determining if program objectives are being realized.

Much evaluation activity relates to specific programs in schools. However, curricula may also be evaluated at the national level, usually by using tests or exercises, sometimes specially devised, which are either controlled or underwritten by government authorities. In England, national surveys of reading achievement go back to 1948. More recently, the Assessment of Performance Unit of the Department of Education and Science has been monitoring standards of achievement in a broader range of subjects (see Gipps and Goldstein 1983). In the United States, the National Assessment of Educational Progress (NAEP) program has been monitoring standards since 1969. These approaches are designed to assess the effects of curricula in schools throughout the nation; to identify weaknesses and strengths in student achievement; and presumably, on the basis of this information, to improve the achievement levels of students. They will assume increasing importance in the coming decade as NAEP is used to make comparisons between states and as the monitoring of progress toward the realization of President Bush's and the governors' national educational goals commences.

At the national level, the term "educational indicator" (which was developed from the terms "economic indicators" and "social indicators") has been used in the description of key aspects of the condition of an educational system, or of significant parts of it, which might be useful to policymakers (see Johnstone 1981; Oakes 1986). Examples of the use of indicators are to be found in the United States (National Center for Education Statistics 1985) as well as in an international context (Bottani 1990; Nuttall 1990a). Indicators may refer to inputs into the educational system (e.g., pupil-teacher ratio and opportunity to learn) or to outputs (e.g., student achievement). They may be used to monitor an educational system over time, to evaluate its performance (e.g., the extent to which it provides equality of opportunity for girls), or to make international comparisons. The term "indicator" may also be used to describe aspects of individual curricula (Oakes and Carey 1989).

As well as evaluation at the national level, external testing has been mandated in the United States by state boards or legislatures as part of their efforts at educational reform. At last count, some 48 states required some sort of elementary and secondary school testing (Pipho and Hadley 1984). Almost every large education reform report has called for more centralized testing (Madaus 1988), and recently almost all efforts at the state level to mandate educational reform have recommended the inclusion or expansion of the use of tests (Pipho 1985).

In keeping with our definitions, in this chapter we generally use the term "assessment" to refer to the appraisal of individuals and the term "evaluation" to refer to the appraisal of programs, curricula, or institutions (see McCormick and James 1983). However, it would be very difficult and artificial to adhere to this distinction all the time, partly because of the way the terms are used in everyday language: "Evaluation" is frequently used in the context of student appraisal, and one also hears of "assessing" program effects. Further, there are conditions in which the distinction blurs, for example, when data on individuals (assessment) may be aggregated for use in the appraisal of a program (evaluation). Finally, although assessment may be regarded as the evaluative component of the curriculum delivery system, like other aspects of the curriculum, it too may be the subject of evaluation. Thus, for example, we may inquire into the appropriateness of a particular form of assessment (e.g., the use of standardized tests) or into how a form of assessment affects other aspects of the curriculum.

MAJOR HISTORICAL DEVELOPMENTS IN THE EVALUATION COMPONENT OF THE CURRICULUM

The history of curriculum evaluation and assessment is closely intertwined with the histories of testing, educational research, and program evaluation. The emphasis that evaluation and assessment have received and the form they have taken at different points in history reflect differences in the importance accorded to such diverse factors as beliefs about the nature of education and the determinants of school achievement, the importance of accountability, and the purpose of evaluation. In this section, we will first describe general trends in curriculum evaluation history, followed by a description of changes that have occurred in techniques of assessment and evaluation and then by a consideration of the important role played by standardized testing today.

Historical Trends in Curriculum Evaluation

In an 1918 history, Leonard Ayres claimed that "measurements in education are fifty years old if we count from the oldest beginnings of which we have records" (9). However, tests and examinations had been used as devices for stimulating efforts to learn and for administrative and accountability purposes in education for a considerably longer time. Certainly, the 16th century had many examination enthusiasts. For example, Philip Melancthon, the great Protestant German teacher, is quoted as saying in his *De Studiis Adolescentum* that "no academical exercise can be more useful than that of examination. It whets the desire for learning, it enhances the solicitude of study while it animates the attention to whatever is taught" (quoted in Hamilton 1853, 769). The 16th century also saw the Jesuits develop and introduce a system of emulative examinations in their schools and colleges across Europe. The Jesuits can probably take credit for the widespread acceptance of examinations as a means of raising educational standards in European universities.

For what is perhaps the earliest record linking assessment directly to a specific curriculum, we can go back even further. In a 1444 contract between the town fathers of Treviso and its schoolmaster, the schoolmaster's salary varied according to the level of attainment of pupils—measured by a viva voce examination—on the *Donat* or on Alexandre de Villedieu's *Doctrinal*, which together formed the grammar curriculum of the time. Based on student performance, the schoolmaster received four levels of reward, ranging from a half ducat for proficiency in the alphabet and the beginning of the *Donat* to two ducats for success in stylistic exercises or rhetoric (Aries 1962).

The Treviso contract is important for several reasons. First, Philippe Aries (1962) argues that the evaluative reward categories associated with the curriculum are the beginning of the separation of schools into grades or classes based in part on the curriculum covered and, although Aries does not say it, in part by passing examinations for promotion. Second, it is the earliest reference to the use of examinations for teacher accountability. Third, it is one of the earliest references—predated perhaps only by the Chinese mandarin civil service examinations—to the use of the technology of testing in the interest of centralized, hierarchical, managerial control. Testing in Treviso was accorded bureaucratic sponsorship as an administrative device to ensure that certain educational outcomes were obtained. Much of the testing that goes on today (particularly mandated, high-stakes testing), its sponsorship, financial base, character, and use, is also essentially bureaucratic and only secondarily educational, or if it is educational, it is educational as conceived by policymakers.

The concept of holding teachers accountable for student mastery of a basic skills curriculum through the device of coupling their pupils' examination results with monetary rewards turned out to be an enduring one. It reappeared in 18th-century Ireland (Burton 1979) and again in 19th-century Great Britain (Bowler 1983; Montgomery 1967; Sutherland 1973) Ireland (Coolahan 1975; Madaus 1979), Australia (Hearn 1872), and Jamaica (Gordon 1968) in a scheme known as Payment by Results. Recent variations of the concept include the performance-contracting movement of the 1960s (Levine 1971), present attempts to link merit pay or vouchers to pupil test performance (Lerner 1981; Shanker 1986), and proposals to pay students for good test performance (Hughes 1979; Laffer 1982). In all of these schemes, tests are an important defining component of the curriculum.

There were many contemporary critics of the Payment by Results scheme. Matthew Arnold, a school inspector in England at the time, rendered a classic indictment of the scheme when he described it as: "a game of mechanical contrivance in which teachers will and must learn how to beat us. It is found possible by ingenious preparation to get children through the . . . examination in reading, writing and ciphering, without their really knowing how to read, write and cipher" (quoted in Sutherland 1973, 52). Arnold's observations illustrate how high-stakes tests are believed to influence both teacher and pupil behavior. Examinations, through the associated rewards or sanctions, are perceived to exercise prescriptive authority on the curriculum and teaching, delimiting and eventually defining what and how things are taught and learned. We will return to this concept later.

Payment by Results was not the only system of evaluation used in the 19th century. Most evaluations of social agencies and their functions during this period of great reform were more informal and impressionistic in nature, often taking the form of government-appointed commissions (royal commissions in the United Kingdom and presidential commissions in the United States). In the United Kingdom, the school inspectorate played a major role through their contributions to annual reports on the conditions of schools and on pupil achievement. Inspectors' reports contained a mine of information about school districts, school buildings, managers, teachers, monitors, discipline, quality of instruction, and student achievements in a variety of curricular areas. It is of interest also that at this time inspectors were not unaware of the problems of evaluating schools, in particular, problems of subjectivity and unreliability (Commissioners of National Education in Ireland 1889, 138).

The assumption in Payment by Results schemes that all students would learn if taught properly was common at least through the first half of the 19th century, when schools dealt with small numbers of pupils. For example, Matthew Arnold, commenting on education in Germany, observed that "the assigned work of the year (the curriculum) is well within a child's power . . . and if children are not fit [to be promoted], unless there is some special reason, the teaching has not been right" (Royal Commission on Education 1886, 211). The idea that children, if taught properly, would not fail to learn was not limited to Europe. When written examinations were introduced to the Boston public schools in 1845, correspondence between Samuel Gridley Howe and Horace Mann relating to how to use the results clearly show that this concept was recognized (Mann 1845).

Belief in the ability of all students to learn if properly taught began to be eroded when compulsory attendance and the abolition of child labor forced educators in the latter part of the 19th century to deal for the first time with diverse populations never before of concern. Two developments in testing provided the basis and rationalization for the change of heart about the relationship among the curriculum, teaching, and learning early in this century. First, there had been up to this time at least an implicit assumption of an absolute standard of proficiency—students should be able to master all the content of a test or examination. Thorndike (1918) reports on a scale book developed in 1864 by George Fisher, which assigned numbers to degrees of proficiency in various subjects (Ayres 1918). Thorndike also proposed two types of educational measurement: one asking how well a pupil performs a certain uniform task, the second asking how hard a task a student could perform. Both involve absolute rather than relative interpretations of student performance. Thorndike opined that measurements by relative position—the order-of-merit method—although useful, should soon give way to an absolute rating, however rough.

Thorndike's hope soon vanished. The idea of interpreting test scores in terms of absolute proficiency or achievement began to be replaced by relative or normative standards of achievement. That is, the median score of students across a district became the standard of acceptable achievement in terms of the curriculum. Ballou (1916) describes how this system worked in the Boston public schools in the first decade of the century: "A further result [of testing] is to furnish each teacher with a standard [district level median performance] by which she may judge whether her class is above or below the general standard for the city" (63). Here is a hint of the advent of nationally normed tests, which appeared soon after World War I. The proliferation of school surveys between 1910 and 1920 also reinforced the idea of national standards or norms of performance, based on the average test performance of students in a grade (Madaus and Stufflebeam 1984, Travers 1983). Standardized tests developed by Courtis, Ayres, and Thorndike were popular in part because they had rudimentary normative data (Tyack and Hansot 1982). Test interpretation, rather than being anchored in curriculum material, became a function of the performance of the examinee relative to some normative group. Relative population performance rather than the mastery of curriculum content or skills became the valuing criterion.

Faced with large numbers of diverse students being forced to attend school and with large numbers not doing well and being retained in grade (Ayres 1909), acceptable achievement levels on tests were relativized. However, one could still argue that if teachers taught properly this move toward norm-referenced interpretation of achievement would not have been really necessary. One solution to poor performance advocated at the time was better grouping practices (Resnick 1981). The advent of IQ tests in the early part of this century provided an explanation for poor pupil performance as well as a method for forming homogeneous groups for instruction.

Educational theorists such as Pestalozzi, Herbart, Froebel, Emerson, Parker, and Dewey believed that intelligence, although absolute, was educable (Snow and Yalow 1982). However, toward the end of the first decade of the century, the ability level of students began to be used to "explain" why many students could not be expected to do well. Educators could now shift the explanation for poor achievement away from teaching and onto a lack of "ability." For example, in 1918, Charles Judd, then director of the School of Education at the University of Chicago, argued that the problem of "unsatisfactory school results is to be traced to the native limitations in the ability of [the] child or to the home atmosphere in which the child grows up" (152). Judd goes on to extoll the virtues of "scientific" measurement:

> We all understand now, in definite scientific terms that children are different from one another, and that the best we can hope for is improvement—not absolute achievement of ideals.
>
> With the theoretical ideal of perfection overthrown, there is now an opportunity to set up rational demands. We can venture to tell parents with assurance that their children in the fifth grade are as good as the average if they misspell fifty percent of a certain list of words. We know this just as well as we know that a certain automobile engine cannot draw a ton of weight up a certain hill. No one has a right to make unscientific demands of the automobile or of the school. (153)

Likewise, Terman (1919) argued that "teachers must learn to use tests [or] the universal grading of children according to mental ability must remain a utopian dream" (291). Terman got his wish. "The testing technology became accepted, and an increasingly influential feature of American life" (Cronbach 1975, 1). The idea that all students could learn if properly taught did not reemerge until the 1960s (Bloom 1968, Bruner 1966, Edmonds 1980).

The credo of the "scientific" nature of tests was captured by Thorndike's (1918) dictum, "whatever exists at all exists in some amount" (16). Thorndike saw that education's concern was with changes in human beings, and he believed that these changes could be known only through the products produced by them—"things made, words spoken, acts performed, and the like" (16). Measurement's job was to define the amount of the product so "that competent persons will know how large it is, with some precision, and that this knowledge may be conveniently recorded and used" (16). Thorndike argued that this creed was held by physicists, chemists, and physiologists and that "in general, the nature of educational measurements is the same as that of all scientific measurements" (16–17).

Dedication to this credo became for many an unswerving secular faith rivaling any religion. The symbolism of "scientific" or "objective" accuracy ascribed to testing has always been extremely important when tests are used for bureaucratic or administrative purposes. This potent symbolism can give test scores almost magical qualities, particularly in the minds of laypersons (Bell and Grant 1974). Unfortunately, it also has the effect of shifting the focus of much of the discussion about what is wrong with schools, or why certain groups perform poorly on tests, away from critiques of the curriculum, the delivery of instruction, and other systemic problems of the schools (National Commission on Testing and Public Policy 1990).

"Scientific" tests of both achievement and "intelligence" quickly began to serve as selection devices to identify talent and to place students in the "proper" curriculum for their ability level. For example, a survey of 200 school superintendents by Haggerty (1918) revealed that tests were being used for six general purposes, all of which had implications for curriculum: changes in classification of pupils, in school organization, in courses of study, in time devoted to subject, in methods of instruction, and in methods of supervision.

Behaviorism, operationalism, and testing all became essential ingredients of the curriculum during the scientific movement in education around the turn of the century. Not surprisingly, under the influence of the scientific movement, evaluation of the curriculum also increased during that period. Many school systems carried out comprehensive surveys, which included analyses of expenditure, dropout rates, and promotion rates, as well as the new objective tests of achievement in arithmetic, spelling, handwriting, and English composition (Madaus and Stufflebeam 1984). Tests were also used for curriculum evaluation. Rice's (1897) classic studies used tests of spelling to pinpoint weaknesses in the curriculum and to provoke curriculum revision (Cronbach 1983).

However, as the testing movement developed in the 1920s, there was a shift from the use of tests to assess curricula to their use to assess the efficiency of teachers and school systems in delivering the curriculum. This use declined in the 1930s, when tests were used almost exclusively to make judgments about individual students—to assign grades, to diagnose learning difficulties, and to place students in instructional groups (Cronbach 1983).

The years immediately following World War II were marked by considerable expansion in educational facilities and programs but relatively little formal evaluation effort. However, some important developments relating to how evaluations of the curriculum were conceptualized and operationalized did take place. These included a growth in the availability and use of standardized tests, the emergence of operational or behavioral objectives made popular by Ralph Tyler (see Madaus and Stufflebeam 1989; Smith and Tyler 1942; Tyler 1934, 1949; Tyler and Waples 1930), and the development of taxonomies designed to help educators articulate objectives (Bloom 1956; Krathwohl, Bloom, and Masia 1964).

The idea that educational outcomes needed to be defined in terms of identifiable behavior and in operational terms was the keystone of Tyler's Eight Year Study. Tyler's rationale is depicted by a triangle, at the apex of which are the objectives that lead to the development of learning experiences, which in turn lead to evaluation of the extent to which objectives were realized. As Travers (1983) notes, "the simplicity of the formula, and its appearances of logicality, gave it instant appeal across the country" (152). Ostensively a way of developing curriculum, Tyler's rationale became a blueprint for test development, with a corresponding neglect on the learning-experiences leg of the triangle (see, e.g., Bloom 1950, 1966, 1969; Bloom, Hastings, and Madaus 1971). Although Tyler saw evaluation as deriving from the objectives of the curriculum, in time it was the tests themselves that came to define and make explicit, and in some cases even create, the curriculum and objectives (Travers 1983).

In the late 1950s and early 1960s, the call for the evaluation of large-scale curriculum development projects, supported by federal funds, led to a period of revitalization and reorientation in evaluation activity (Stufflebeam and Webster 1983; Worthen and Sanders 1987). A variety of approaches are represented in the evaluation activity of the time: definition of objectives for curricula in the Tylerian tradition, development of new nationally standardized tests to reflect the objectives and content of new curricula, use of field experiments to evaluate curricula, and use of professional judgment to rate proposals and to check on the efforts of contractors (Madaus and Stufflebeam 1984).

Dissatisfaction with the relevance and utility of these approaches soon grew, however. It was felt, for example, that they did not provide adequate information on the implementation of curricula and that they often used measures of outcome that were insensitive to program goals. In reaction to this situation many new conceptualizations of evaluation began to emerge in the 1960s and 1970s. These new ideas recognized the need to evaluate goals, assess inputs, examine the implementation and delivery of services, measure intended and unintended program outcomes, and make judgments about the merit or worth of the object being evaluated.

It is only in the last 15 years or so that evaluation has developed as a field distinct from, though related to, the older disciplines of research and testing. Universities now offer courses in evaluation, in-service courses are also available, professional journals exist, and a set of standards for program evaluation has been developed. Further, a wide variety of approaches to evaluation has been advanced (e.g., goal-free, naturalistic, transactional, responsive, adversarial, and judicial). We shall return to some of these new developments when we consider methods of evaluation.

Changes in Assessment Techniques

We will now outline briefly developments in assessment techniques as an integral part of the curriculum, ranging from oral and product evaluation to written, and ultimately, standardized test procedures.

Evaluating Products. Initially, the medieval guilds required an apprentice to supply a product as a final proof of competence. The product was evaluated according to well-defined criteria by the master craftspersons (Hoskins 1968). The crystal maker's "apprentice bowl" is a modern example of apprentice certification.

Oral Examinations. Aristotle offered rules for examination in the *Topics*, offering suggestions to both the questioner and answerer in the didactic exchange (Perreiah 1984). In the medieval universities, the apprentice scholar, once a year, demonstrated mastery of the subject before the masters by responding orally to a set of previously known questions. The results of this disputation were *qualitatively* evaluated by the masters according to the examinee's ability to demonstrate a traditionally approved form of rhetoric. (See Perreiah 1984 for a detailed treatment of the oral disputation.) The viva voce examination was designed to reveal the student's "ability to remember relevant and acceptable knowledge, the ability to present it in eloquent form, and a tacit conformity to orthodoxy, educational and social" (Hoskins 1968, 138). Instruction and learning were geared to helping students attain these three curriculum goals.

At a more popular level, Martin Luther, though not the inventor of the catechism, developed and enhanced it as an educational medium. The catechetical approach is of particular interest in the context of testing as an aspect of the curriculum since it has a set content and is also a form of instruction that is entirely based on oral questioning and answering. The approach, which was adopted by the counter-Reformers (particularly Canisius and Bellarmine) as well as by the Reformers, enjoyed considerable popularity for four centuries, creating during that time a new popular, religious, vernacular literature (Tynan 1985).

The Written Examination. The first major change in the technology of evaluation in the West was the introduction of written examinations. (China, of course, which had long had the advantage of paper, included written sections in mandarin civil service examinations.) Written examinations were found in 14th-century Europe. Baccalarii at the University of Paris exchanged their views in writing, before the oral disputation and the oral exchanges themselves were recorded (Perreiah 1984). Farrell (1938) provides accounts of examination compositions in Jesuit schools in the 16th century. However, it was not until the 18th century, as paper became more readily available, that the written examination was introduced systematically into European schools. When mathematics was introduced as part of the curriculum, first at Cambridge and later at Oxford, it became apparent that the oral disputation was not suitable (Wiseman 1961).

Qualitative Ranking. When written questions were known in advance and the oral mode was used in examining much of the curriculum, both the oral and written products of several days had to be *qualitatively* assessed according to traditionally acceptable answers. Around 1750, people were ranked within class. At the heart of the ranking system was the presumption that examiners singly and in concert could rank a person's total performance (Hoskins 1968). Rothblatt (1982) notes that at Oxford and Cambridge in the early 19th century, character was more important than proficiency and "harmonious integration of mind and body preferable to expert accomplishment" (5).

Quantitative Marks. Inevitably, partiality crept into qualitative evaluations, and in 1792 William Farish introduced the next momentous technical innovation in evaluation: assigning *quantitative* marks to individual questions. "Quality" could not be mathematized; individual marks, however, could be summed and an individual's performance and consequent overall ranking compared to others. Former qualitative categories of student performance "yielded to the precision tool of the mark" (Hoskins 1968, 144). The introduction of a quantitative score might well be considered the first step in the development of the field of psychometrics, which is so dependent on a total test score. At any rate, the combination of students responding in writing to a set of standardized questions, together with the ability to rank performance based on quantitative marks, led to a common set of questions defining a common curriculum. As Hoskins observed, the quantitative symbol of the mark had assumed supreme significance, and a generation later the questions posed had a factual "right" answer rather than being judged qualitatively: "Narrow specialization and examination based on the principle of testable knowledge became the new parameters of undergraduate education . . . and with it a new intellectualist ideal, what we now call proficiency or the acquisition of skills" (145). Thus, factual knowledge and technical competence in specific subjects, rather than rhetorical style across the entire curriculum, assumed prominence in evaluation and in schools.

The emphasis on factual knowledge and technical competence led to examining and licensing entrants to certain professions. For example, in 1815, the Society of Apothecaries was granted the right to examine "since it was not a profession 'fit for gentlemen,' social accomplishments played no part, and technical competence was demanded" (Carr-Saunders and Wilson 1933).

Essay Examinations. For the remainder of the 19th century, the examination was basically what we would call today the essay examination. Students had to write extended answers to set questions, and the answers were scored by subject matter specialists by assigning points. The essay examination had been introduced into the Boston public schools by Horace Mann in 1845. The questions were printed and distributed to students throughout the entire city so that all students sat for the examination at the same time. Mann, as superintendent of instruction for the Commonwealth, used these test results for bureaucratic, accountability, and political purposes (see Travers 1983 for a detailed treatment of written examinations in Boston). The practice quickly spread throughout the country and, in addition to being used to judge the effectiveness of teachers and schools, began to be used for decisions about the grade-to-grade promotion of students. By 1888, the superintendent in Cincinnati complained that when these essay tests were used to determine the promotion and classification of children they perverted

> the best efforts of teachers, and narrowed and grooved their instruction; they have occasioned and made well-nigh imperative the use of mechanical and rote methods of teaching; they have occasioned cramming and the most vicious habits of study; they have caused much of the overpressure charged upon schools, some of which is real, they have tempted both teachers and pupils to dishonesty; and last but not least, they have permitted a mechanical method of schools supervision. (White 1888, 518)

The essay examination eventually came under criticism in two historic studies by Starch and Elliot (1912, 1913), who showed that a student's grade on an essay test varied substantially according to who read the examination. One marker might be more lenient or severe than another. Further, marks varied even when read by the same person on different occasions. These findings have been replicated (e.g., Hartog and Rhodes 1935; Madaus and Macnamara 1970). Present methods of reading essay examinations can help reduce the difficulties of marking essays.

Short-Answer Examinations. About the same time as essay tests were under criticism, a host of standardized tests using the short-answer format began to appear. By 1918, 109 such tests were available (Monroe 1918). In these tests, students could respond to a question by producing a word, number, or short phrase. This format lent itself to easier scoring, increasingly by clerks, as in the case of the Army Alpha Test, the first group-administered intelligence test. During the first decade of this century, when the efficiency movement was in full flower (see Callahan 1962), short-answer tests were increasingly used by school districts (Travers 1983). As the factory metaphor seized education, the new technology of the short-answer format facilitated the use of testing by administrators in the interest of efficiency, supervision, and bureaucratic control.

Multiple-Choice Questions. Shortly after World War I another major innovation in the technology of testing was introduced in the schools—the selection mode of responding. Students no longer had to produce a product—even a short answer—but instead had to select the right answer from among competing alternatives. The technology of the multiple-choice item changed very little over the following 50 years (Buros 1977).

Like its short-answer counterpart, the multiple-choice technology lends itself to bureaucratic, centralized evaluation in which efficiency and cost effectiveness are highly valued. From the 1920s, multiple-choice standardized tests began to be used on a wide scale by administrators. Writing in the 1927 National Society for the Study of Education Yearbook, *The Foundations of Curriculum Making*, a committee of outstanding educators, including Bagley, Bobbitt, Charters, Counts, Judd, Kelly, Kilpatrick, and Rugg, pointed out the dangers involved, noting that "one of the most potent forms of curriculum-control is the measurement of uniform examinations and standardized tests" (Rugg 1927, 25). The committee argued that "to serve a useful purpose, tests must be fitted to the requirements of the curriculum and to the requirements of method" (25). The committee went on to condemn the use of standardized tests by administrators to evaluate the product of education: "We have reference specifically to the rigid control over the school curriculum exercised by those administrative examinations which over-emphasize the memory of facts and principles and tend to neglect the more dynamic outcomes of instruction" (25).

Standardized Testing Today

Today, standardized testing is endemic in elementary and secondary education in the United States. Depending on the assumptions made, between 33 million and 71 million individual tests are administered under state mandate, between 69 million and 218 million as part of traditional school district testing programs, between 12 million and 31 million to special populations, for a total of between 114 million and 320 million tests per year (Haney, Madaus, and Lyons in press).

An admittedly rough but interesting index of the increased attention to testing was developed by Haney (1981), who measured the number of column inches in the *Education Index* between 1930 and 1987 devoted to "tests and scales" and, for comparative purposes, to "curriculum." He found that the average number of column inches devoted to "curriculum" increased only modestly in the last 57 years. It rose from 50 to 100 inches in the 1930s and 1940s and to only 100 to 150 in recent years. In sharp contrast is the dramatic increase in the space devoted to "testing"—from only 10 to 30 inches in the 1930s and 1940s to well over 300 in the 1980s. The correlation between average column inches devoted to testing and year is a whopping 0.91 (Haney, Madaus, and Lyons in press). This is strong evidence that testing has become more important than other curriculum issues.

Another interesting indirect indicator of the growing popularity of standardized testing in the elementary and high school (ELHI) market can be found in an examination of brokerage house evaluations of companies offering stock. Two companies doing test-related business in the ELHI market, National Computer Systems (NCS) and Scan-Tron Corporation (SCNN), are the subjects of such evaluations. Both sell optical-mark reading (OMR) equipment and expendable answer sheets; NCS also carries out test development under contract. Perusal of these evaluations shows that the stock market is certainly aware of the profit potential associated with an increased demand for testing in general and for accountability, state-mandated testing programs in particular (Cicchetti 1987). Taken together, these indicators demonstrate the growth in importance of ELHI testing in this country as well as its preeminence and predominance over the curriculum.

ASSESSMENT BY TEACHERS

Assessment is an integral part of curriculum and is acknowledged to be one of the teacher's most complex and important tasks (Linn 1990; Stiggins, Conklin, and Bridgeford 1986). Jackson (1968) has noted that tests are as indigenous in teaching and learning as are textbooks or pieces of chalk. Since the teacher is in daily contact with students and since the nature of teaching necessitates continuous assessment of the extent to which students carry out tasks or acquire knowledge and skills, the teacher's role must be regarded as central in the evaluation activities of the school.

It would seem obvious that in planning and carrying out instruction, teachers attend to, and take into account, a variety of kinds of information about students. Among these factors are students' general ability and/or achievement, gender, participation in class, self-concept, social competence, independence, classroom behavior, and work habits. Of these, achievement seems to be the most important; there is evidence that teachers' judgments about ability and student motivation and effort rely heavily on judgments about achievement, though account may also be taken of students' problematic behavior and work habits (Shavelson and Stern 1981).

Despite the centrality of assessment in teaching, we know relatively little about the actual practices of teachers in schools (Stiggins, Conklin, and Bridgeford 1986). This lack is perhaps not surprising given the fact that whereas assessment may logically be distinguished from other aspects of school activity, in practice the distinction may not be very clear. Although a formal test or examination is clearly designed to appraise students' performance, assessment is not confined to such activity. When a teacher asks a student a question or even looks over the student's shoulder at what he or she is writing, the teacher may well be making judgments about the student's progress as well as attempting to advance or improve the student's knowledge and skills. On the basis of such judgments, the teacher is likely to come to some kind of more general judgment about a student's progress, set objectives for the future, and reach decisions about the learning experiences that are most likely to help a student reach the objectives that are set. Obviously, this is a very complex procedure. For the most part, it is subjective, informal, immediate, and ongoing, involving a continuous monitoring of student behavior, scholastic performance, and responsiveness to instruction. Little of it ever comes to the surface in the form of numerical data (Morrison 1970).

It is in the grading of students that the assessment activity of teachers becomes most overt in the American school system. Grades represent, first, a communication link among students, their parents, and school decision makers and, second, an attempt to motivate students to learn—two purposes that may be at odds with each other (Stiggins, Frisbie, and Griswold 1989). However, research on the underlying methods of grading—what factors teachers take into account and how they weigh and interpret these factors—is extremely limited. On the basis of an in-depth analysis of the grading practices of a small number of volunteer teachers, Stiggins, Frisbie, and Griswold conclude that there is much ambiguity in what teachers do.

Students, for their part, perceive performance on teacher-made, objective tests as the principal source of information for grading, more important than performance on projects, homework, class discussion, or other academic products and performances. This is perhaps not surprising given the amount of testing students undergo; a study in three California high schools found that the median numbers of quizzes and course exams per semester were 9 in English, 22 in mathematics, 6 in social studies, and 7 in science (Haertel, Ferrara, Korpi, and Prescott 1984).

In comparison with other areas of assessment, assessing cognitive ability and scholastic performance has received the most attention in the literature. Furthermore, most research has been concerned with the development of standardized objective methods to assess performance. A preoccupation with the technical refinement of such methods has meant that other major issues in assessment have received relatively little attention—issues such as the role of assessment in the work of the school; the effects of using standardized tests; an examination of teachers' informal methods of assessment; and the assessment of equally important, if more elusive, noncognitive variables.

A variety of informal and formal methods is available to teachers for assessment. Among the informal methods are observing students in class, asking questions, giving quizzes, monitoring learning activities, examining homework, and talking to other teachers and parents. More formal procedures include teacher-made tests, which are often objective; tests provided as part of textbook series; and standardized tests (see Crooks 1988).

In one study of classroom evaluation, a sample of principals and teachers in 91 school districts throughout the United States were asked about their testing practices and test use patterns. Principals reported about the use of test results for school-level decisions and communication, and teachers reported on classroom uses (Herman and Dorr-Bremme 1983). In the case of principals, at both primary and secondary levels, teacher opinions and recommendations carried more weight than tests (teacher-made, standardized, norm-referenced test batteries or minimum-competency tests) for a variety of functions—curriculum evaluation; student class assignment; teacher evaluation; and reporting to parents, the district, or the public. When tests were used, most attention was paid to required tests (standardized, minimum-competency, and referenced to district curriculum objectives), and they were used mainly for curriculum evaluation decisions and for communications with parents and school district personnel. Required tests, particularly minimum-competency tests, played a more important role in decisions about the assignment of students to classes at secondary than at primary level. Further, among required tests, minimum-competency test results were more influential at the secondary level, whereas standardized, norm-referenced tests were more influential at the primary level.

At the classroom level, teachers also reported that the results of required tests were not as influential as their own observations, students' classwork, and the results of tests they had developed themselves in making decisions about student placement in a curriculum, grouping, or assigning grades. The results of required tests, although not as important as other sources of evidence, were regarded as somewhat useful in planning instruction and in assigning or reassigning students to groups.

A number of tentative conclusions can be drawn from research about classroom assessment practices in the United States. First, a substantial amount of student time is involved in activities that are formally assessed: Estimates, which do not include informal evaluation activities, of from 2 to 15 percent have been reported (Crooks 1988; Goodlad 1984). Second, teachers, both elementary and secondary, use a variety of sources of information, the most important being their own observations of students' work, to make a variety of decisions about curricula and students (Dorr-Bremme and Herman 1986; Herman and Dorr-Bremme 1983; Salmon-Cox 1982). Third, teachers' key assessment tool is "performance assessment," that is, the observation and rating of student behavior and products in contexts in which students actually demonstrate proficiency (Stiggins and Bridgeford 1985). Fourth, many teachers also make use of paper-and-pencil tests that they construct themselves. The great preponderance of questions on such tests, for a variety of reasons (ease of construction, ease in marking, and high reliability), tend to emphasize factual knowledge of terms and rules rather than more complex thinking skills (Crooks 1988; Fleming and Chambers 1983). Fifth, the amount of time devoted to formal assessment increases as students move through the grades. The lower figure (2 percent) cited is more typical in elementary school classes; the higher figure (15 percent), in high school classes (Crooks 1988; Goodlad 1984). Sixth, the nature of classroom assessment varies at different grade levels. In the higher grades, teachers are more likely to use their own assessments and teacher-made objective tests than published tests (Dorr-Bremme, Herman, and Doherty 1983; Stiggins and Bridgeford 1985). Seventh, the nature of assessment also varies by curriculum area. In assessing performance in mathematics and science, teachers tend to rely on objective-type tests. Performance assessment is more common in the language arts (e.g., writing), in science (e.g., lab work), and in social science discussion (e.g., group participation) (Stiggins and Bridgeford 1985). Finally, teachers tend to store and retrieve information on student performance in their heads rather than on paper (Stiggins and Bridgeford 1985).

FORMAL EVALUATION OF THE CURRICULUM

It seems reasonable to assume that most curriculum evaluation by teachers is informal and secondary to their concern with assessing the extent to which they have been successful in raising the level of achievement of individual students. However, a teacher may adopt more formal procedures to evaluate the curriculum he or she teaches. Indeed, the Tyler model was designed mainly as a training device to help teachers prepare valid classroom tests and as an evaluation tool in a situation in which the statement of objectives and the appraisal of educational outcomes are considered to be an integral aspect of curriculum building efforts (Cronbach 1983). Although this evaluation approach originally focused on the local school or school district, developments in evaluation over the past two decades have had a broader focus and were organized from outside schools rather than from within them. Much of the literature on evaluation centers on this broader focus when making suggestions about the scope, objectives, and techniques of evaluation. Most of what we will consider in this section relates to formal evaluation activities, usually carried out by bodies external to the school. In its formality, it contrasts sharply with the type of informal evaluation carried out by teachers that we considered in the last section.

Formal evaluation activity can focus on a variety of aspects or domains of curricula (see Goodlad, Klein, and Tye 1979; Oakes and Carey 1989). Some evaluation models explicitly cover a range of components. For example, Stufflebeam's (1983) CIPP model involves four aspects: context evaluation (involving needs assessment), input evaluation (to identify and assess competing strategies), process evaluation, and product evaluation. Similarly, Stake (1967) distinguishes three elements in the educational process as the focus of evaluation: antecedents (conditions existing prior to teaching and learning), transactions (e.g., pupil-teacher interactions), and outcomes (interpreted in a broad sense to include immediate and long-range, cognitive and conative, and personality and community-wide outcomes). (For taxonomies of major evaluation models, see House 1983 and Stufflebeam and Webster 1983.)

Formal evaluation activity can also make use of a variety of methods, which we will consider in greater detail below. In practice, however, an evaluator has to select particular domains and particular methods. Even in an elaborate evaluation, compromises will be required about the aspects that can be included (Oakes and Carey 1989). The evaluator should be aware that choices regarding domains and methods will reflect a particular model of education (e.g., whether education is conceptualized in the terms of industry or of human development) and may have ethical and political implications since the findings may play a role in decision making about changes in the educational system (Coomer 1986).

We shall consider the curriculum as being made up of six major components: (1) context; (2) general aims of the total school curriculum; (3) objectives of specific curricula or learning units; (4) curriculum materials, in which content, subject matter, and skills have been selected and placed in a particular sequence and may take various forms of documentation, including syllabi, teachers' guides, textbooks, workbooks, software, and other material; (5) transactions, usually in a classroom, in which teachers deliver or teach various aspects of the content, subject matter, skills, and values that students are expected to experience, acquire, or learn, as well as other subject matter, skills, and values that may not be intended in the curriculum but to which students are exposed in a variety of activities in the classroom and outside it; (6) outcomes of the transactions among curricular materials, teachers, and students, which may be intended or unintended.

Context

Any curriculum will take into account, implicitly or explicitly, the planned and intended context of implementation. Of major importance in considering context are the characteristics of the participating students—their current level of knowledge and skills (e.g., in reading, mathematics, or physics) and their needs and interests. Tyler (1949) stressed the importance of students' needs as a source for formulating educational objectives. Apart from a consideration of objectives, however, information on context is necessary to evaluate the appropriateness of recommended or utilized curricular materials and procedures as well as the extent to which student outcomes can be judged as satisfactory.

The selection of objectives and educational experiences, the relative emphasis given to different areas in the curriculum, and the placement and sequencing of material may also be evaluated as appropriate or inappropriate in the light of other contextual factors: the philosophy of education of the school, conditions and problems of contemporary life (especially the demands that will be made on students in their everyday life), the nature of subject matter, and the psychology of learning (see Tyler 1949).

Broad Educational Aims

The evaluation of broad educational aims is difficult since people differ in what they perceive the overall aim and purpose of education to be. Indeed, the view that aims can be specified for education at all is based on an assumption, which has been questioned, that the means and ends of education can be separated. For Dewey (1939), the distinction was problematic since "Every condition that has to be brought into existence in order to serve as means is, *in that connection*, an object of desire and an end-in-view, while the end actually reached is a means to future ends as well as a part of valuations previously made" (43).

Although the distinction between ends and means may be merely temporal and relational, it does appear to have had considerable intuitive appeal in the study of curricula and of education. However, although there might be considerable agreement that education has the general aim of producing desired changes in individuals (Marler 1975), there is no agreement on which characteristics should be changed or how they should be changed. To accept that education is directed toward such objectives as self-realization or happiness or, as Schwab (1989) has put it, "has something to do with a good and happy life for the men and women our students will become" (4) helps us only a little. For evaluation purposes, at least, it is still necessary to define what we mean by "a good and happy life" or whatever term we select, to justify its selection, and to specify how education might contribute to its realization. Very often, however, the inability to operationalize or to measure goals efficiently means that they get lip-service only.

Educators have long debated what the aims of general education should be. Such a debate is likely to continue as long as people differ in their political, economic, and moral perspectives, which color people's values. For example, even if everyone were to agree that "good citizenship" was an acceptable goal of education, differences would continue to exist in defining good citizenship, depending on whether an individual's political views espoused monarchism, communism, or one of a variety of kinds of democracy (laissez-faire individualism or pragmatic liberalism) (see Brubacher 1955). Definitions of the aims of education or of the attributes of an educated person ultimately must have recourse to value positions, that is, beliefs that some things are better than others and hence desirable. Many people make judgments about the aims and purposes of education on the basis of such value positions. At a professional level, philosophers use analytic procedures that attempt to make the values underlying people's positions explicit and examine how the values are justified by those who hold them.

It may be that some aims of education (particularly those involving ideas of vocational preparation) could be defined operationally for evaluation purposes. In practice, however, most aims for general education are probably better considered as "ideals," which do not actually exist and toward which schools are expected to direct their activities without ever actually achieving them.

Objectives of Specific Curricula or Learning Units

It is precisely because a statement of the general aims of education may lack the specificity needed to provide a basis for designing classroom instructional activities that some theorists recommend that the general aims should be "translated" into more specific objectives that are adjusted to the content of courses and the particular needs of groups of students (see Taba 1962). These more specific objectives may themselves vary in their level of specificity (Wheeler 1967). They may relate to a total course (e.g., seventh-grade mathematics) or to shorter learning units, such as a chapter in a textbook or a topic in a course, or even to an individual class period. (See Bloom, Madaus, and Hastings 1981 for a discussion of the problem of specificity in defining objectives.)

The view that objectives should be stated clearly in terms of behavior in the field of education was a reflection of the practice in industry in the early part of this century. By the time Tyler (1949) published his important work, *Basic Principles of Curriculum and Instruction*, the objectives approach had been firmly established. For example, Bobbitt (1918) had recommended that teachers should write their objectives clearly, and he set an example by listing several hundred himself. Around the same time, Charters's (1924) "job analysis" of teaching reinforced the industrial analogue (see also Ayres 1918; Ballou 1916; Thorndike 1918).

The resilience and general acceptability of the objectives approach can be seen in the work of a committee that recently reported in Great Britain on criteria for national tests at ages 7, 11, 14, and 16 in conjunction with the introduction of a national curriculum. The committee started from the assumption that a school can function effectively only if it has adopted clear aims and objectives and ways of gauging whether or not they have been achieved (Department of Education and Science 1987).

Tyler had contributed to the development of the objectives approach, when between 1934 and 1942, as director of evaluation of the famous Eight Year Study, he saw his job as facilitating staffs in the 30 participating schools in formulating educational objectives and then in developing assessment techniques to measure them. Stripped to the bare bones, Tyler's approach involved seven steps: formulating objectives, classifying the objectives, refining and defining the objectives, identifying situations for assessing the objectives, selecting and trying out promising ways to assess the objectives, improving appraisal methods, and interpreting results. The approach had two foci, behavioral objectives and assessment. The development of the learning experiences, a component found in the Tyler rationale, flows theoretically from the behavioral objectives. However, when the model has been used for evaluation, this aspect very often gets very little attention.

The objectives approach received a considerable boost with the publication of taxonomies of educational objectives (Bloom 1956; Krathwohl, Bloom, and Masia 1964). Objectives were divided into three major categories (cognitive, affective, and psychomotor) and were hierarchical in nature. The cognitive taxonomy became a short-hand device for defining objectives, describing cognitive functions, and analyzing test items during the post-Sputnik development era of the 1960s. It was assumed, since every effort was made to avoid value judgments about objectives and behavior in constructing the taxonomies, that they could be used in a system expressing any philosophy of education (Bloom 1956).

The taxonomies were closely tied to the ideas of testing and evaluation. Krathwohl, Bloom, and Masia (1964) say that they provide "a convenient system for describing and ordering test items, examination techniques, and evaluation instruments" and that they are also useful in "comparing and studying educational programs" (5).

A number of other taxonomies of objectives related to educational achievement have been produced, including Gagné's (1977) categorization of learning tasks in terms of the conditions under which they are learned. More recently, attention in the field of cognitive psychology is being given to the conceptualization of the cognitive functioning that underlies the educational goals of taxonomies. Attention is also being paid to ways of formulating the content specialist's educational goals, so that account is taken of how students organize and use information (Greeno 1989; Haertel and Calfee 1983; Snow and Lohman 1989).

Another close relative of the Tyler model was the behavioral- or instructional-objectives movement prominent in the 1960s. The specificity of the definition and the level of detail, however, went well beyond Tyler's original concept (see Popham 1969). The behavioral-objectives movement was swept in by several related factors including management-based objectives, task analysis deriving from applications of industrial psychology to military training (MacDonald-Ross 1973), and programmed instruction (Gagné 1965; Glaser and Reynolds 1964; Mager 1962). (For criticism of the behavioral-objectives approach see Case 1975; Duchastel and Merrill 1977; Eisner 1969; Gardner 1977; Jackson 1968; MacDonald and Clark 1973.)

Although the objectives in the Tylerian model were subject to evaluation themselves in terms of their appropriateness for students, many commentators on the taxonomies have pointed to a need for a more wide-ranging and rigorous evaluation of objectives. The importance of considering what is included and emphasized in curricula is obvious when one considers the not unexpected finding of studies that different curricular content and emphasis produce correspondingly different patterns of achievement (Walker and Schaffarzick 1974). If the precise objectives and corresponding content specified for particular courses influence substantially what students learn, it would seem important to determine whether the objectives and content are in the first place worthwhile and defensible.

A major problem in requiring objectives to be clearly stated is that it can lead to a distortion of the curriculum since some objectives lend themselves more readily to this procedure than do others. For example, cognitive competencies and knowledge (particularly literacy and numeracy skills) are more easily specified than are aspects of personality, character, or social development (e.g., the development of "good" work habits, respect for law and order, and the development of standards for what is "right" and "wrong"), even though the latter may be regarded as important educational goals by teachers and the general public (see Gallup 1985; Gallup and Clarke 1987). Further, the more specific the statement of objectives, in general, the easier it is to measure whether or not they have been achieved. Thus, cognitive objectives are more likely to be tested than noncognitive ones, and within the cognitive arena, objectives that measure specific lower-order competencies (e.g., involving the recognition or recall of factual information) are more likely to be tested than higher-order ones (e.g., thinking creatively or analytically).

Not all approaches to evaluation require a statement of objectives. Scriven (1973) has proposed "goal-free evaluation," in which the evaluator is not told the purpose of a program; rather, the evaluation involves finding out what the program is actually doing, without knowing what it is trying to do. Presumably, if a program is successful in achieving its stated goals and objectives, this will become obvious to the evaluator during the course of evaluation.

As an addition to "instructional" objectives, Eisner (1969) has suggested the use of "expressive" objectives, which do not specify outcomes of instruction in the same way. Rather they are used to describe "an educational encounter"—that is, a problem or task to be tackled—not what students are expected to learn as a result of the encounter. Specific examples of expressive objectives are "to interpret the meaning of *Paradise Lost*" or "to visit the zoo and discuss what was of interest there." Objectives viewed in this way would appear to relate more to transactions and process (considered below) than to the traditional Tylerian view of objectives.

Curricular Materials

Curricular materials may take various forms: a formal description of a syllabus, a curriculum guide, lesson plans, textbooks, supplementary reading materials, workbooks, laboratory equipment, and audiovisual aids. Not all curricula make use of all these materials.

In some educational systems, the formal description of curriculum as set out in a syllabus is an important curriculum document. The description is usually presented in terms of the subjects to be studied and the aspects of the subjects that should be studied. For example, the recently promulgated National Curriculum in Britain is of this type (Department of Education and Science 1987).

A number of questions can be asked about such syllabus documents in the context of evaluation. First, do they provide a rationale for the inclusion of the knowledge, content, skills, and processes specified? In practice, such a rationale is rarely presented since the choice of material for a syllabus is not usually regarded as problematic, despite the fact that material choice at any particular level and the criteria for the inclusion or exclusion of material inevitably reflect certain values. Thus, it is reasonable to expect that an attempt be made, either in presenting the curriculum or in its evaluation, to make explicit the value framework on which the curriculum is based.

Second, and at a more concrete level, we can ask if syllabus materials are stated in sufficient detail to provide an adequate guide for implementation. Many syllabi state only the content to be covered; they do not describe the precise skills the student should acquire or the level at which the content should be covered. This situation obviously could lead to considerable variation in the way in which curricula are implemented. In practice, teachers often rely on other guides to implementation: textbooks, the tradition of the school, and the tradition of examinations.

These other influences on curriculum practice may also be evaluated. The evaluation of curriculum materials assumes a particular importance when objectives are not explicitly stated, in which case it is necessary to examine the materials to determine the objectives they imply. Like a toaster or car, a textbook can also be evaluated according to preset criteria: readability, coverage of material, sexism, even durability of binding. Characteristics of the students for whom the curriculum is intended (e.g., grade level and level of achievement) are also relevant in the evaluation of materials.

Transactions and Process

In some educational philosophies, the process of education, particularly what happens in the classroom, is regarded not only as being more important than the outcomes but also as being the only thing that matters (see Kelly 1989). Even if one does not espouse this position, the fact remains that statements about skills and content, which may be translated into short-term objectives, have to be translated into procedures designed to achieve the objectives. One of the major criticisms of evaluations that focus only on output is that the antecedents of achievement are hidden in the so-called "black box," with the result that we do not even know if there has been adequate implementation of the planned curriculum; much less do we know what factors in its delivery might have contributed to or hindered the achievement of the proposed objectives (see Cronbach 1983).

The need for curriculum indicators to provide information on what students had the opportunity to learn has been stressed by Oakes and Carey (1989). In addition to examining curricular goals, textbooks, and materials, they suggest that other curricular domains that warrant attention are the breadth of content coverage, the depth of coverage, and the mode and sequence of content presentation.

Evaluation of processes, including classroom interactions, may be combined with evaluation of other aspects of curricula. Thus, studies of program implementation may be combined with a study of program objectives or outputs (see Fullan and Pomfret 1977). Some evaluation approaches, however, pay little attention to outcomes expressed as end-of-program objectives and instead set out only to provide descriptions of program activities. These approaches do not just reflect a shift in emphasis from one part of the curriculum to another. They often imply a discontentment with the ability of quantitative empirical approaches in evaluation (as exemplified in attempts to ascertain whether or not the goals of a curriculum have been achieved) to take into account many important aims of education or to describe the educational process in a meaningful way. In their attempts to find meaning, evaluators may adopt a phenomenological rather than an empirical approach. The approach that one takes will be of more than academic interest if, as it has been argued, the forms of evaluation widely employed can have a profound influence on the character of teaching, the content of curricula, and the kinds of goals that schools seek to attain (Eisner 1983).

Alternatives to traditional empirical methods attend to the settings in which learning occurs and to teaching transactions. They focus more on program activities than on program intents, they attempt to respond to audience requirements for information, and they take into account the different values of the people involved in a program (Guba 1978; Parlett and Hamilton 1972; Stake 1983). We shall describe these in greater detail below.

Outcomes

Those who stress the importance of outcomes in education claim that it is reasonable to ask in the context of evaluation, What happens to students? What do they learn? As a result of being exposed to a curriculum, do they develop cognitively, emotionally, morally, and physically?

There are many reasons why such questions have been asked in the past. First, policymakers or administrators have felt the need to monitor or supervise district or building-level personnel (Resnick 1981). Second, there has been recurring dissatisfaction with educational achievement or standards and with schools' success in promoting equality of opportunity. Third, there has been a general bureaucratic drive—in education and elsewhere—toward efficiency and productivity (Hall 1977; McNeil 1988; Winner 1986). The tendency to make educational procedures more rational led eventually to what Wise (1979) has called "hyperrationalization." Fourth, the fact that schools have had to deal with increasing numbers of diverse students created a need to explain differences in performance and to classify and group students for more efficient instruction. Fifth, the findings of the Coleman et al. (1966) report, in which variance in school input measures seemed to contribute little to school achievement, helped produce a shift in education, from a concentration on inputs to one on outputs. Acceptance of a metaphor of schools as factories or pipelines served to reinforce this shift (McNeil 1988; Madaus 1985; Wise 1979).

For a variety of reasons, standardized testing became the preferred means of measuring outcomes. Testing was perceived to be an efficient, inexpensive, administratively convenient, quantifiable, and objective way of serving the needs of accountability. Again, whereas many problems of low achievement were perceived to be rooted in the instructional delivery system, these did not lend themselves to mandates or legislative solutions, but testing did. Further, testing permitted policymakers to appear to be addressing such problems (Cuban 1986; Madaus 1985, 1986; Wise 1979). Finally, those inclined to bureaucratic solutions to education problems also had the clout to ensure that testing was adopted (Cuban 1986; Resnick 1981): Witness federal legislation that included standardized testing provisions, e.g., the National Defense Education Act of 1958, the Elementary and Secondary Education Act of 1965, and the Education for All Handicapped Children Act of 1975 (P.L. 94–142). Likewise, state-level policymakers first turned to test results for information about schools and populations of at-risk students but soon realized that test results could also be used as an administrative mechanism to drive or implement policy. As a result, state-mandated assessment programs rose from 1 in 1960 to 32 in 1985, and state-level basic skills and minimum-competency programs went from 1 in 1972 to 34 in 1985 (Office of Technology Assessment 1987).

The Tyler rationale demands that the tests used to evaluate curricula should be based on an explicit curriculum domain as set out in the stated goals, objectives, and syllabi of the curriculum. However, tests could be based, and in practice often are, on two other domains (Nitko 1989; Schmidt, Porter, Schwille, Floden, and Freeman 1983). The first is an a priori domain based on social criteria of what is regarded as important for all students to learn. Such a domain may be established by a variety of agents who are not directly associated with particular schools or programs (e.g., state commissions and test publishers). Examples of tests based on an a priori domain are those used in various state-assessment programs, the tests used in the National Assessment of Educational Progress, and commercial standardized tests.

The second domain that can be used as a source of test content and emphasis is the instructional delivery domain—what is actually taught in the classroom. Although a curriculum may be prescribed for schools, teachers may vary considerably, even within the same school, in the topics they ignore and cover and the relative emphasis they give to different areas of the curriculum. Therefore, the curriculum as delivered by teachers or received by students can be quite different from the curriculum as stated. This domain is rarely recorded in written form. One would expect teacher-made tests to reflect the instructional delivery domain rather than a domain based on the stated curriculum or an a priori domain.

Tests based on an a priori domain are likely to be less sensitive to school curricula than tests based on the curriculum or instructional domains (Leinhardt and Seewald 1981; Madaus 1979). This view was apparently accepted by the Florida Fifth Circuit Court in *Debra P.* v. *Turlington* (see Madaus 1983). However, it can be argued that different courses may and even should promote the same general understandings and that an a priori test could be designed to assess them. If a student's general educational growth is more important than mastery of specific lesson material, a test that measures general and particularly higher-order educational knowledge and skills, and assesses a student's ability to apply knowledge acquired in school, might be more valuable than one closely geared to instructional experiences. It can also be argued that whereas a test based on curriculum objectives may tell you how well the curriculum is achieving its objectives, if you want to know how well the curriculum is serving the national interest, you have to measure all the outcomes that might be worth striving for (Cronbach 1983). This argument really brings us back to the point at which we started our consideration of the formal evaluation of the curriculum—the evaluation of aims and objectives.

METHODS OF EVALUATION

From our description of the components of a curriculum that might be evaluated, it follows that a wide range of methods would be required for a comprehensive evaluation. Most people would probably agree that different components require different methods. For example, the evaluation of the aims or objectives of a curriculum might require philosophical analysis, whereas the evaluation of outputs might require the administration of tests to students. Most people, however, would probably not agree on which component of a curriculum should receive the most attention in evaluation. Often, only one or two aspects are chosen, and for logistic and financial reasons, that might be all that is feasible (Oakes and Carey 1989). Although to some extent the components or domains of the curriculum that are chosen for evaluation will determine the method, this is not entirely the case. For any particular component, one can find disagreement among evaluators regarding the most appropriate approach. The disagreement relates particularly to a number of interrelated factors: the formality or informality of the approach, reliance on objective or subjective measures, and the extent to which empirical quantitative procedures or more qualitative ones are used.

As we have seen, the assessment methods of teachers in the classroom are for the most part informal and are based primarily on subjective observations of students' scholastic behavior, which may be supplemented by more objective methods of assessment. Although most teacher evaluation probably has as its prime purpose the evaluation of student progress, it seems reasonable to assume that teachers also use the information they derive from student assessment to make inferences about their own effectiveness as well as about the appropriateness of various aspects of the curriculum (e.g., the level of difficulty of concepts and skills, the way in which these are sequenced, and the need for giving more time and emphasis to certain areas). Some commentators have argued that such self- and curriculum evaluation should play a larger role in the work of teachers. If it is true that there are severe problems in implementing accountability procedures that are located outside the school and that much research conducted outside the field of practice has had little impact on teaching, it might seem that the only forms of evaluation and curriculum development likely to prove satisfactory are those that are at least school-based and most probably teacher-based (see Kelly 1989; Nuttall 1981; Skilbeck 1976; Stenhouse 1975). Although self-evaluation of work is no doubt a characteristic of "good" if not of all teachers, it has to be recognized that such evaluation is difficult. Further, many teachers would probably need considerable assistance in developing the skills and techniques needed for proper and effective evaluation of themselves and of the curricula they implement.

Evaluations of curricula that are not carried out by teachers may also use a variety of procedures. The procedures may not even be based on observations of the work of the school. For example, one of the most public and influential evaluations of the American school system was based on activities in space that had been initiated by a foreign country. When it was learned that the Soviet Union had launched Sputnik in 1957, judgments were formed about the inadequacy of science programs in American schools, and what were perhaps the most extensive efforts ever to reform school curricula followed. At a less dramatic level, parents and employers may make inferences about the adequacy of schools in general or of particular schools without having made any direct contact with the schools. Such evaluations are likely to be based on observers' experiences with individual products of the school or on comments that they read in the press or hear.

More formal evaluations are also carried out on various aspects of school curricula. The traditional procedures used in these evaluations, and which were common in the 1960s, were based largely on methods that had proved useful in advancing knowledge in the physical sciences. Thus they included "objective" forms of measurement and experimental or quasi-experimental designs, using as far as was feasible randomization of subjects and control of treatments. In Stake's (1983) words, traditional empirical methods were "preordinate, emphasizing statement of goals, use of objective tests, standards held by program personnel, and research-type reports" (292).

Although such methods are still in use, particularly "objective" forms of measurement, there has been increasing interest since the 1960s in the exploration of alternatives to traditional research procedures, not just in evaluation but more generally in educational research. Many commentators felt that traditional approaches were not providing the kind of information that policymakers or teachers needed to make decisions about school curricula and other programs, not least because the designs in use were too narrow to identify and examine the full range of impacts of complex educational activities (Guba 1969; Stufflebeam 1983). To provide this information, Guba (1978) advocated a methodology that he regarded as uniquely suited to evaluation's needs, which were not to establish universal laws but to make possible judgments about some phenomenon.

Increased interest in methods other than those of traditional educational research also occurred, partly as a response to the social and political climate of the 1960s and 1970s. To reflect the increasing democratic impetus of the times, it was felt that the opinions and perspectives of all participants, and not simply those in power, should be solicited; further, those opinions and perspectives should be valued equally and an attempt should be made to understand them. This step involved challenging the idea that members of powerful groups have the right to define the way things "really are" and that, in general, their perspectives and opinions are more valuable than those of the less powerful (Becker 1970).

The term "qualitative" is often used to describe the alternatives to traditional approaches that have arisen in recent years. The term is not easily defined, partly because it is derived from several research traditions and partly because of the use of a variety of terms that, if not quite identical in meaning, are closely related. The main traditions from which qualitative research comes are ethnographic work (carried out largely in cross-cultural contexts) and case studies (used in cross-cultural studies but also found in medical and psychiatric work, particularly psychoanalysis).

Five major approaches to qualitative research and evaluation can be identified: interpretive, artistic, systematic, theory-driven, and critical/emancipatory (see M. L. Smith 1987 for a description of the first four). Many of the alternatives to quantitative evaluation have characteristics that fit into more than one of these approaches.

In interpretive approaches, the investigator studies the acts, meanings, and significance ascribed to events by actors in a particular social context (e.g., teachers and students) (Eisner 1983). It is crucial in understanding this approach to appreciate its assumption that acts imply purposeful constructions on the part of an actor that can be understood only from the actor's point of view (to be distinguished from observable behavior). A philosophical assumption underlying the approach is that although meanings of things are formed through social interaction, an individual's use of meaning is not an automatic application of these socially derived meanings; rather, meanings are modified through interpretive processes recurring within the individual (Jacob 1987). Thus, mind creates reality, and an objective world separate from the perceptions of the person cannot be known. Social knowledge is gained by *Verstehen* (subjective, participative understanding) and cannot be verified by appeal to external criteria.

The artistic approach involves the presentation of a narrative account of what the investigator has discovered. Again, *Verstehen* is an important aspect of this approach. Essentially, it is rooted in intuition and is based on experience and observation (Eisner 1981). In Eisner's (1983) words, the evaluator is considered to be a connoisseur, focusing on "the qualities of the relationship that exists between teacher and student and the kinds of devices that the teacher employs to stimulate interest, to reward, to explain, and to manage" (344).

Systematic approaches seem very similar to traditional approaches in a number of respects. They are based on a realist epistemology insofar as investigation is directed at "a real world" outside of individuals. However, proponents of systematic approaches deny the position often ascribed to positivism, that the external world determines absolutely the one and only correct view that can be taken of it, independently of the process or circumstances of viewing it. Although attempts may be made to show that a study provides "objective," valid, reliable evidence (through triangulation or replication), this is likely to be done by descriptions and logical analyses rather than by statistical techniques, as in the traditional positivist approach.

Theory-driven approaches strive to understand the meanings of people (as do the interpretivists) but go beyond these to explain meanings and acts in a deterministic framework of social structures and forces (e.g., Willis 1977). Hence, unlike the interpretivists but like the traditional positivists, they are interested in issues such as validity and reliability.

Finally, critical/emancipatory approaches probably constitute the most radical departures from tradition (see Coomer 1986). In these approaches, discourse toward a critical social science is primarily concerned with ways of generating knowledge that turn critical thought into what Habermas (1974) has called "emancipatory action." The ultimate goal is a critical social science that alleviates oppression by supporting "the emergence of people who know who they are and are conscious of themselves as active and deciding beings, who bear responsibility for their choices and who are able to explain them in terms of their own freely adopted purposes and ideals" (Fay 1987, 74).

This conception of social science is so far removed from traditional views that it is not included in recent descriptions of qualitative research provided by M. L. Smith (1987) and Jacob (1987). However, some of the ideas advocated in the critical/emancipatory approach, particularly the "construction of meaning" through negotiation with participants, are already in evidence in evaluation practice as well as in some recommendations for teaching.

It should not be concluded from our attention to qualitative methods that they now dominate the evaluation scene. Such is far from being the case. There is still a strong view that methods derived from the physical sciences and used widely in educational research provide the strongest basis for drawing inferences about cause-effect relationships. In this view, if the findings of studies in the past have been less than adequate in meeting the needs of policymakers, the solution may not be to discontinue more traditional approaches but to produce better designs and to supplement studies with information obtained by other means so as to produce information that is more relevant to policy decisions (see Greenberg and Robins 1978).

Perhaps the strongest evidence of the continuing influence of traditional methods in the field of evaluation is to be found in the heavy reliance on standardized tests in the evaluation of curricula and students. Because of the continuing importance of tests in evaluation, we will describe three of their very basic concepts.

First, a test is meant to represent a particular *domain* of knowledge, skills, or abilities. A domain is a body of knowledge, skills, or abilities, which is defined so that you can decide whether a particular piece of knowledge or a particular skill or task is part of the domain. In the context of curriculum, a content domain is of course a familiar concept to teachers. Test domains, however, are not limited to academic achievement or curricular areas. A test domain might focus on one of a wide range of more abstract traits such as intelligence, functional literacy, mathematics problem-solving ability, or reading-comprehension ability. Many tests used in education and other fields purport to measure such abstract domains, technically called constructs, which have been defined as theoretical ideas "developed to explain and to organize some aspects of existing knowledge" (American Educational Research Association 1985, 29).

It is always important to question critically the appropriateness of a particular domain for a particular use. The question "Is this the correct domain?" is central to proper test use. It is easy to use an inappropriate domain in making decisions about people or institutions. For example, in a legal challenge to Florida's use of a minimum-competency test for graduation, the judge ruled that there was insufficient proof that the test measured things taught in school (see Madaus 1983). Again, some employers use a standard school-related or academic basic skills reading test to screen job applicants on the assumption that "basic reading skills" are essentially the same in school and on the job. However, the ability of school-based tests of basic reading to predict job performance varies enormously from job to job; many workers are able to perform jobs competently even when the reading material is well above their tested reading levels on scholastic tests (Datta 1982; Stedman and Kaestle 1987).

Second, there are a very large number of questions that one could theoretically ask a student about most domains. One way to reduce this large number of potential questions is to define the domain more precisely, though not all domains can be readily divided into subdomains. For example, the domain of fourth-grade arithmetic might be divided into four sections, or facets. We might limit the addition facet of the domain to tasks involving three or fewer digits, with no carrying. However, even with a limited content domain, there are still an enormous number of questions one could conceivably ask students to answer. The way around the problem is to draw a *sample* of questions from the domain that represents its important parts. It is this sample that constitutes a test.

Third, what we are really interested in is a student's performance in the domain rather than his or her performance on the particular sample of questions that make up the test. Thus, test performance, a sample of behavior from the domain, is used to make a broader, more general *inference* about a student's performance relative to the entire domain of interest. Based on the inference made, the test user describes and/or makes a decision about a test taker or group of test takers. The appropriateness or correctness of an inference and resulting descriptions or decisions about a person's performance relative to a domain, made on the basis of test performance, is called "test validity" and is the central and most important concept in testing (American Educational Research Association 1985; for a more detailed discussion of validity see Messick 1989).

THE USE OF STANDARDIZED MULTIPLE-CHOICE TESTS IN CURRICULUM EVALUATION

In this section, we will consider some aspects of multiple-choice tests that can affect their appropriateness as instruments in curriculum evaluation. Problems can arise whether the tests are teacher-made for classroom use or are of the standardized commercial variety. However, the latter have characteristics (e.g., the use of item selection techniques and norm referencing) that do not apply to the former and that affect their suitability for curriculum evaluation. The latter also are more likely to be used in a high-stakes context and so are more likely to have a greater impact on teaching and learning. We shall see that developments in testing technology (e.g., electronic scoring and computerized testing) are likely to create additional problems in the use of multiple-choice tests for curriculum evaluation. For a detailed treatment of all standardized tests, see Linn (1989).

Concern with the use of multiple-choice tests reflects a more basic concern in the field of measurement: that the method used—whether it involves supply- or selection-type items, students' oral competence, written competence, performance competence, or the evaluation of a product—can have important consequences. Historically, the consequences that have been regarded as most important and have been alluded to most frequently are that the method of measurement influences teaching and how and what pupils study and that areas that are not tested will get less attention from both teachers and students. (For a discussion of the influence of testing on instruction see Crooks 1988; Frederiksen 1984; Madaus 1988; Popham 1983; Popham, Cruse, Rankin, Sandifer, and Williams 1985; Stodolsky 1988). Less frequently recognized is the possibility that a measurement method may have a differential impact on the observed performance of males and females (see Bolger and Kellaghan 1990).

It is interesting to see what skills get the attention of policymakers and test makers at the elementary and secondary level—what test publishers call the ELHI market. Adam Smith (1846) and John Stuart Mill (1874) had advocated that every citizen should be able to read and write. During the Payment by Results era, emphasis was clearly on the three R's. For example, Hearn (1872) argued that because the examinations concentrated on reading, writing, and arithmetic instruction, "higher branches of instruction" (11) were neglected. Buros (1977) noted a shift in the 1940s from subject-centered to more general tests of reading and computation. The back-to-basics movement and the minimum-competency testing movement of the 1970s zeroed in on basic skills (Popham 1981). For example, Stodolosky (1988) notes that most accountability systems use standardized tests in what people regard as the "essential" or "basic" subjects of reading and mathematics but not in what are seen to be the "enrichment" fields such as social studies and science. The distinction between "skills" and "frills" in testing for administrative accountability also reinforces this bias. She concludes that "a very significant effect of testing programs is a narrowing of educational objectives to conform to those in the test" (4).

Although one can build multiple-choice items measuring higher-order cognitive skills, items measuring recall tend to predominate on many professionally constructed tests (see, e.g., Little 1982). Even professional item writers are biased toward items measuring recall of information, even after explicit instruction on writing higher-order items (Frederiksen 1984).

American children do well on lower-order NAEP exercises but poorly on tests of higher-order skills. This situation may be due in part to the fact that much of the testing they encounter in school, in both standardized and teacher-made tests, measures lower-order skills. This is a hypothesis in need of investigation. Obviously, it does little good to have a curriculum designed to develop higher-order thinking skills if teaching and learning are directed at getting students over the hurdle of a test measuring factual knowledge of lower-order skills.

There are two other issues related to item format that have implications for the curriculum and that need considerably more attention than they have received. First, one needs to remember that in constructing a test each multiple-choice item is a building block in the total structure. Generally, each item contributes one point to a person's total raw (untransformed) score. However, we know very little about why students answer multiple-choice questions in the way they do. We need to know considerably more about what items written by adults from certain middle-class backgrounds mean to students of different ages, genders, cultural backgrounds, and languages. Elementary children can answer standard test questions incorrectly for very good reasons, and conversely they can get them right for incorrect or trivial reasons. Children's answers can be based on experiences, associations, and observations that do not readily occur to adult item writers (Haney and Scott 1987; Meier 1973, 1981). Thus, it is important to realize that the inferences we make about student knowledge, or the possession of a skill or construct, depend on an accumulation of inferences at the item level. If students are getting items wrong for reasons that have nothing to do with performance, decisions or assumptions based on such experiences are compromised.

Second, and related to the emphasis in multiple choice tests on factual knowledge, is the preoccupation built into achievement tests on getting the right answer and getting it quickly. How or why a student arrives at an answer is neglected. Duckworth (1987) notes that "it is the quick right answer that is appreciated. Knowledge of the answer ahead of time is, on the whole, more valued than ways of figuring it out" (64). And this tendency is often built into the way in which the curriculum is delivered.

Another important issue in considering the use of multiple-choice tests is the practice of norm referencing. When a person's score on a standardized test is interpreted in terms of his or her performance relative to a norm group, the relative position of the person's score in the distribution determines in some sense whether the score is good or bad. The normative approach, which is based on maximizing differences between test takers and reflects an individual-differences model, tells us nothing directly about what a student has actually learned in terms of the content or skills encompassed in the curriculum. For curriculum evaluation, however, more absolute interpretations may be required. Although knowledge of a person's relative standing can be useful, an inability to make absolute interpretations detracts from a test's usefulness in guiding individual students or in making inferences about curricular, program, or school effectiveness (Cronbach 1969; Madaus, Airasian, and Kellaghan 1980).

Norm-referenced testing was not seriously challenged until Glaser's (1963) seminal article called for absolute rather than relative score interpretation. Glaser's call for criterion-referenced measurement was taken up by test developers. However, the "criterion-referenced," "objective-referenced," or "curriculum-referenced" tests marketed did not refer performance to an underlying scale that described what students at different points could most likely do or not do. Instead, the scores told test users whether students mastered certain objectives on the basis of whether they answered correctly a fixed number of questions (generally three or four out of five) related to the particular objective. Further, most of the commercially available "criterion-referenced," "objective-referenced," or "curriculum-referenced" tests eventually reported normative data about performance. (For a review of the technology of criterion-referenced testing see Berk 1986.)

The developers of *The Degrees of Reading Power Test* (Koslin, Zeno, and Koslin 1987) took Glaser's advice and reported student performance in terms of the type of material that can actually be read. Beaton (1988) has used advanced statistical scaling techniques, coupled with the considered judgment of subject matter specialists, to provide scores on the NAEP exercises in reading and mathematics. These scores are meant to communicate to educational policymakers what students falling at different points on the scale know and can do. Further research along the lines of Beaton's work, together with cooperation between psychometricans and subject matter specialists, is needed to determine whether it is possible to describe particular curriculum areas or major aspects of a particular curriculum in terms of underlying performance or of a content-related scale.

The multiple-choice format led in 1927 to a recommendation by Ruch and Stoddard that the total score on the tests be used as the criterion to compute item discrimination indexes (Buros 1977). The item discrimination index and the related index of item difficulty (i.e., the percentage of examinees answering the item correctly) became the principal criteria for selecting items for inclusion on standardized achievement tests. Another criterion for item selection was showing a grade-to-grade increase in performance, a practice criticized by Buros (1977) since it can lead to the exclusion of items that are an important part of the curriculum at particular grade levels.

The process of selecting test questions, based on their ability to differentiate between grades and between high scores and low scores on the total test, shifted emphasis from measuring the mastery of knowledge and skills included in the curriculum to a differentiation between individuals and grades (Buros 1977). The process also led to the elimination of questions that subject matter specialists thought were good and the inclusion of ones thought to be poor. As early as 1936, Hawkes, Lindquist, and Mann pointed out that one consequence of discarding easy items is that if instruction has been good, very important and fundamental items, answered correctly by most students, are eliminated (see also Cronbach 1971).

When used to build tests applicable across a wide range of curricula, item selection techniques tend to eliminate specific-knowledge items in favor of those measuring a more general underlying trait. When this happens, the tests become more general in the content and skills they measure and, consequently, more highly related to general ability and home background than to school-specific achievement (Anderson 1972; Madaus, Airasian, and Kellaghan 1980). More recently, Carroll (1987) pointed out that many of the more difficult tasks used in the NAEP reading assessment—those measuring so-called higher-order thinking—resemble tasks found on tests of verbal and scholastic aptitude. Although he recognizes that it may be unpopular, he wonders if these exercises may be a measure of the verbal ability of the nation's youths, and if this is so, he points out that the research literature does not hold out much hope of improvement, given what we know about teaching a curriculum geared to higher-order skills.

The twin needs of developing representative national norms and national commercial feasibility dictated another important development in the technology of test development. Content for most standardized achievement tests is selected from content and skills common across 10 or 12 of the most widely used textbooks or curriculum guides in a particular subject at a particular grade. Because tests include only common curricular content and objectives, they often inadequately reflect the specific content and objectives of particular schools. In fact, techniques of selecting common objectives work best at the elementary level. Consequently, at the secondary school level, standardized achievement tests tend to be more difficult versions of elementary tests, and few commercially viable subject-specific achievement tests are available.

In 1925, subject matter tests were developed for a Pennsylvania survey, which had as its purpose a determination of the relationship between the secondary school curriculum and the college curriculum. During the 1930s, subject-specific tests were developed by the Cooperative Test Service and the Iowa Every-Pupil Testing Program. However, in the 1940s, these tests disappeared in favor of tests of the abilities needed to continue one's education. The emphasis switched from determining what was learned at earlier levels to predicting success at higher levels. These tests took the form of more general reading and aptitude tests (Buros 1977).

The multiple-choice format was rendered even more efficient and cost-effective by the addition to the testing technology of the electronic scoring machine developed in the 1950s by E. F. Lindquist (1954). The technology of optical scanning has made large-scale testing programs for college admission, statewide assessment, and minimum-competency testing administratively convenient and cost-effective. Further, with the exception of short writing samples, optical-scanning technology has "for all practical purposes, driven out other types of examinations, at least for large-scale testing programs" (Frederiksen 1984, 194). Once again, the advent of a new technology in testing proved to be more useful in the service of bureaucracy and centralized control than in the service of curriculum evaluation.

Low-cost optical scanners are now being marketed for classroom use. Schools are provided with these machines if they agree to purchase a fixed number of consumable scanning forms, which can be used with teacher-made tests or for various administrative uses. One company has an agreement with textbook publishers to provide answer sheets for their accompanying tests. The scanner scores the answer sheets to give teachers immediate feedback on student performance on end-of-unit or chapter tests (Haney, Madaus, and Lyons in press).

So far, optical scanning machines work only with selection-type items. Testing specialists and curriculum and subject matter specialists need to focus much more on the quality and impact of text-embedded tests on teaching and learning. Further, care should be exercised so that electronic technology, in the name of speed or efficiency, is not allowed to dictate how aspects of the curriculum are measured, as defined by state departments of education or by the ubiquitous textbook.

There is a final development that we believe will have serious consequences for the curriculum—computerized testing. The advent of relatively low-cost computers may make it possible to design new modes of testing, in which students supply their answers rather than just select a correct alternative. To date, however, most uses of computerized testing have been to make the multiple-choice format more efficient. For example, computer-adaptive testing combines the computer's computational power with item response theory to permit an examinee to take a shorter version of a multiple-choice test (Madaus 1986).

THE EVOLUTION OF EVALUATION AS A MECHANISM OF POWER

Evaluation can service policy in two ways. First, information can inform policymakers about the state of education or about the performance or achievements of certain groups of children. For example, in the 1960s, discrepancies between the average test scores of majority and minority students were used to lobby for new compensatory programs such as Head Start and Title I. More recently, declining test score data were used politically and simplistically by the National Commission on Excellence in Education to support a picture of a "rising tide of mediocrity" in American education and to argue for the need for reform recommendations (Stedman and Kaestle 1985; Stedman and Smith 1983). Again, a recent study of the Chicago public schools used dropout statistics and test information to describe the effectiveness of the city's secondary schools. It was found that of the 25,500 who entered the system, only 14,000 graduated. Among graduates, 36 percent (20 percent of the original class) read above the national average, 36 percent read above the ninth-grade level but below the national level, and 28 percent read below the ninth-grade level (Moore and Davenport 1989). The effects on education, curriculum, teaching, and learning of using evaluation information of this kind may be indirect, but not any less powerful for being so. Effects flow eventually from legislation or from changes that are the result of lobbying or of advocacy. The use of tests to lobby for educational changes may eventually result in using those same test scores as "output" measures to evaluate the subsequent success of the mandated programs.

Second, evaluation information serves policy when it is used as an administrative device to implement policy. Policymakers realize that they cannot mandate what goes on in the classroom. However, they believe that if they use test results as an accountability device, coupling test performance with important rewards or sanctions, teachers, building-level administrators, superintendents, curricula, and instructional delivery systems will eventually conform to the test (Haertel 1989; Madaus 1985).

There are many examples in history in which evaluation has been used in the exercise of power by policymakers or administrators in the service of accountability, centralization, or control. There are many reasons why evaluation procedures have been employed for such bureaucratic ends. Historically, policymakers have used the power, which they perceived to be inherent in a high-stakes external examination, to correct defects or abuses or to reform the educational system. Over the past 200 years, external examinations have been mandated to help eliminate patronage; to open access to groups hitherto excluded; to ensure that all students will acquire basic literacy and numeracy skills; to establish and maintain standards of excellence; to hold teachers, students, or schools accountable for learning; and to allocate scarce resources to the most able or deserving. Policymakers' intent in mandating external examinations has been corrective rather than malevolent or punitive. Examinations, when coupled with rewards or sanctions, have been perceived as a practical, efficient, and cheap means of correcting what are considered to be defects in the educational system. When examinations and other forms of tests are used to address practical problems, abstract principles about test validity and unintended negative consequences seem remote.

The late French philosopher-historian Michel Foucault (1977) elaborated on the connection between evaluation and the exercise of control and power in educational matters. For him, the exercise of power was not "simply a relationship between partners, individual or collective; [but it was] a way in which certain actions modify others" (189). In an apt, but unintended, description of what a high-stakes test can do, Foucault (1982) saw power as a "total structure of actions brought to bear upon possible actions; it incites, it induces, it seduces, it makes easier or more difficult, in the extreme it constrains or forbids absolutely, it is nevertheless always a way of acting upon an acting subject or acting subjects by virtue of their acting being capable of action" (189). A set of actions on other actions confers power because those who control it can use the results to control the actions of the examinees, as well as school personnel.

Although Foucault is essentially correct, it is likely that the power to control the actions of teachers, students, and administrators lies less in evaluation per se than in the ability of those in control of a testing program to affix important rewards or sanctions to test results. That is, although intractable properties of the testing technology, such as administrative convenience, quantifiability, efficiency, and low cost, are unavoidably linked to particular institutionalized patterns of power and authority, it is ultimately the specific features of how a test is used and what follows from the use that confer the power and authority. (See Winner 1986 for a discussion of how many technologies are highly compatible with centralized, hierarchical, managerial control.) For example, Travers (1983) notes that in the period 1920 to 1940, teachers and children did not seem to be bothered by standardized tests:

They knew virtually nothing was ever done with the results. When the teacher spent the morning giving a test, it was an easy morning for him or her, and a not unpleasant one for most of the pupils. Such tests were much less threatening to the children than a test prepared by the teacher on which a grade might depend. (145)

This atmosphere began to change in the late 1960s, when tests began to be "employed to make keep-or-kill decisions about educational programs. Big dollars . . . were riding on the results of achievement tests . . . the days of penny-ante assessment were over" (Popham 1983, 23). In the 1970s, with the advent of minimum-competency testing linked to student graduation or placement, and later the use of standardized tests to evaluate teachers or fix merit pay, the ante was raised further (Haertel 1989; Madaus 1985; Madaus and McDonagh 1979).

Foucault (1977) points out that the older guild examinations simply validated or certified an apprentice's acquired aptitude. However, the written test, with standardized questions, which all examinees had to answer, went beyond the certification function and became a mechanism to exchange knowledge. The introduction of the written examination was, for Foucault, "the beginnings of a pedagogy that functions as a science" (187). The teacher and later the policymaker, through the test, defined what was expected, and the test in turn forced students to reveal periodically how their learning was progressing. Thus, the written examination "guaranteed the movement of knowledge from the teacher to the pupil, but it extracted from the pupil a knowledge destined and reserved for the teacher" (187). The examination became a mechanism "that linked to a certain type of the formation of knowledge a certain form of the exercise of power" (187).

Foucault (1977) also saw that the written examination could be used as a disciplinary tool. The examinee was perceived as an object and, in turn, was objectified by the examination results. The examination not only places examinees in a "field of surveillance" but also "situates them in a network of writing . . . in a whole mass of documents that captures and fixes them" (189). The examinee becomes a "describable, analyzable object" and the examination the "ceremony of this objectification" (190). The examination is a ritualized and "scientific" method of fixing individual differences, by the "pinning down of each individual in his own particularity" (187). Thus, the written examination is for Foucault a "new modality of power in which each individual [described by Foucault as "calculable man"] receives as his status his own individuality, and in which he is linked by his status to the features, the measurements, the gaps, the 'marks' that characterize him and make him a case" (192).

It was when the examination in England became a device to induce students to work hard that students perceived it as a disciplinary tool. Rothblatt (1982) reports that a world of student slang based on negative examination experiences sprang up. Many words for failing, cheating, and survival strategies came into the vernacular.

The new written examination also took on bureaucratic features. It became possible for the first time to accumulate and aggregate student marks, organize them, rank them, classify them, form categories, determine averages, fix norms, describe groups, compare results across units of aggregation, and fix individuals and groups in a population distribution. Thus, the documentation provided by the written examination, and later by the quantifiable mark, gave those in charge of it the ability not only to objectify individuals but also to form, describe, and objectify groups. This ability, in turn, eventually opened up a whole new mechanism for program and school-level accountability.

Foucault's description of the examination as a mechanism of power was based on his experience with the free-response format examination widely used in Europe. He makes no mention of the additional power of objectification associated with the development of the selection or objective-type item. The objective, multiple-choice, true-false item format could be corrected by a clerk, without the need to make qualitative judgments about answers. With the development of the selection mode came the recognition and exploitation of its efficiency and commercial possibilities through the introduction of national norms, separate answer sheets, and eventually high-speed electronic scoring. All these features made the processing of large numbers of test responses both efficient and cost-effective and, as such, bureaucratically attractive.

The new twin technologies of the selection mode and electronic scoring made it possible to keep the entire student population of a school district or a state under surveillance and normalizing judgment. They facilitated the easier documentation of the individual through his or her quantitative test scores. The classification and aggregation of individual results made the formation and comparison of groups easier than in the past. Accountability became cheaper and administratively more convenient. The end result is that the multiple-choice test, with cut scores that are linked to rewards or sanctions, is now a major administrative device in the hands of district and state-level policymakers, designed to control the actions of students, teachers, and administrators.

Foucault (1977) described the function of all discipline as "essentially *corrective*" (179, emphasis in original). As an example of the corrective potential of examinations, he offers the following from Jean-Baptiste de la Salle, the founder of the teaching order of Christian Brothers:

Of all penances, impositions are the most honest for a teacher, the most advantageous for the parents; they make possible to "derive, from the very offences of the children, means of advancing their progress by correcting their defects"; to those, for example, "who have not written all that they were supposed to write or who have not applied themselves to doing it well, one can give some impositions to write out or learn by heart." (190)

Jeremy Bentham (1960 [1816]), like de la Salle, recognized the corrective information teachers could receive from testing and its potential to guide further instruction; he insisted on "constantly testing the pupil's knowledge, in such a way as to ensure that concepts have been fully grasped and understood, and not merely memorized" (81).

When an examination is school-based and in the hands of the teachers—as is the case in the de la Salle and Bentham examples—Foucault is essentially correct. Information derived from quizzes, tests, recitations, and homework can guide teachers' actions and those of their students toward correcting poor performance and improving learning. Scriven (1967) has labeled this type of evaluation "formative"; it is directed primarily at the improvement of learning while instruction is ongoing, rather than at grading, marking, or ranking, forms of evaluation that are characterized as "summative." If testing is strictly summative in nature, coming as it does at the end of a fixed instructional period (a term, semester, or year), it is generally too late for the teacher to do much in the way of corrective action, at least for that class. Nonetheless, the summative, grading function associated with internal tests is a powerful mechanism of discipline and control in the hands of the teacher, particularly for those students who value school achievement and high grades.

An examination becomes a mechanism of bureaucratic power in the hands of the district or state when the test results are linked directly to rewards or sanctions perceived to be important. Since the 18th century, political theorists and policymakers have recognized that tests perceived to have high stakes can be used to modify the behavior of administrators, teachers, and students (see Mill 1859; A. Smith 1846).

Policymakers over the years have believed that they could force instruction into line by mandating a high-stakes test. By attaching rewards or sanctions to a test, they believed that instruction would eventually adjust to preparing students for the examination, which came to define the curriculum. A classic illustration of these beliefs is contained in the Irish Intermediate Education Act of 1878, which set up a seven-member board with the duty "to promote intermediate secular education in Ireland in the manner provided by this act; that is to say 1) By instituting and carrying on a system of public examinations of students" (Intermediate Education Act 1878, Clause 5). Here is a clear example that those 19th-century policymakers realized that a system of public examinations was a mechanism for defining education and the curriculum. The system of examinations would determine the curriculum; teaching methods; and the criteria of success for students, teachers, and parents (Madaus 1985).

Another example, this time from the present century, graphically illustrates how policymakers viewed the power of an important external examination to bring about changes, without directly dealing with either curriculum or the instructional delivery system (Madaus and Greaney 1985). Prime Minister of Ireland Eamon DeValera, arguing in parliament for a system of certification examinations at the end of primary school, said in 1941,

> But if we want to see that a certain standard is reached and we are paying the money, we have the right to see that something is secured for that money. The ordinary way to test it and try to help the whole educational system is by arranging our tests in such a way that they will work in a direction we want. (Dail Eireann 1941, col. 119)

These examples are not peculiar to their time or place. The sentiments they reflect can also be found in contemporary America. For example, when Senator Bill Bradley of New Jersey drafted a new bill, modeled on Chapter 1 of the Elementary and Secondary Education Act but targeted exclusively on disadvantaged students in secondary school, he linked continued funding to a school's improvement in the pass rate on a state-approved basic skills test and/or a decrease in the school's dropout rate (Haney, Madaus, and Lyons in press). The recent wave of reform reports also contains proposals dealing with testing that embrace a strong bureaucratic belief in the power of external tests to direct the efforts of those in education (Madaus 1985).

Foucault's characterization of the examination as a mechanism of disciplinary power, and his further characterization of a system of discipline as being essentially corrective, generates a paradox. Although an examination used as a mechanism of power can be corrective in the short term, in the longer term the bureaucratic imperative associated with it may corrupt the system it was designed to correct or improve. If, as Foucault theorized, the power of tests affects the actions of those involved, and if the rewards or sanctions associated with a test coerce teachers, students, and administrators to prepare for it, this very coerciveness may eventually become corrosive, leading to cramming, coaching, and narrowing of the curriculum.

If the results of a test are perceived by students, teachers, administrators, parents, or the general public to be linked to important decisions, they may be regarded as being of the high-stakes variety. Such tests are directly linked to such important decisions as graduation, promotion or placement of students, evaluation or rewarding of teachers or administrators, allocation of resources to schools or school districts, and school or school-system certification. In all of these examples, policymakers have mandated that the results of an appraisal are to be used automatically to make decisions (Madaus 1988). In contrast to a high-stakes evaluation, a *low-stakes* one is perceived as having no direct ties to important rewards or sanctions.

High-stakes tests generally are administered at critical junctures in the educational process, where the policymaker can exert the most leverage on the actions of students, teachers, or administrators. Thus, they are always summative in nature, which limits their scope for corrective action. It is obviously too late to affect the decision made on the basis of one's test performance *after* the fact. Thus, it is clear to all players that any correction has to come *before* the examination is given if the student is to avoid sanctions, such as denial of certification or of admission to the next level of education, or if teachers' salaries or conditions of employment are not to be adversely affected. This realization inevitably leads to coaching in the tradition of the test, which in turn can corrupt the test's validity.

The initial strategy of power—the high-stakes test—eventually gives rise to legitimate counterarguments. Eventually, the coercive power exerted by the test may be perceived by those adversely affected as punitive, not corrective, in nature. This perception explains a great deal of the criticism directed at such test use over the years. More important, it gives rise to reform movements and eventually to the adoption of a counterstrategy to combat the perceived abuses.

Today, throughout the world, counterstrategies are being put forward to overcome perceived corrupting influences associated with established testing programs. What is interesting is that, on the one hand, in Europe, Africa, and Australia, proposals are being made to reform the narrowing, elitist, university-dominated aspects of their external examination systems by including internally controlled, school-based, teacher assessments of student performance, in some ways similar to practices in American education. American policymakers, on the other hand, have come to distrust teachers' assessments of students and administrators' assessments of teachers. They feel that the primarily internal system of low-stakes testing in operation in schools has been corrupted by social promotion and a lowering of standards. One strategy being proposed to reform these defects is to adopt the older European system of external, high-stakes examinations.

THE RELATIONSHIP BETWEEN EVALUATION AND THE CURRICULUM

Although assessment and evaluation have always been seen as integral parts of the curriculum, there are two basically different views on the nature of this relationship. In the first, assessment and evaluation are seen as being defined by the curriculum, flowing from its goals, and reflecting instruction that has taken place (Tyler 1949). The alternative view of the relationship is best captured by variations on the current metaphor of measurement-driven instruction (MDI) (Popham 1983, 1987a, 1987b, Popham, Cruse, Rankin, Sandifer, and Williams 1985): Assessment and evaluation, when defined independently of the curriculum, have the potential to exercise immense impact on it.

Instruction-Driven Measurement

A recent important court decision has affirmed the need to look beyond explicit curriculum domains (of the Tyler type) and a priori ones (of the Popham type) and to link directly assessment and evaluation, particularly testing, to the instructional delivery system. In a case challenging Florida's use of a minimum-competency test as a high school graduation requirement, the Fifth Circuit ruled that a test used for such purposes must have instructional validity. (For a complete discussion of the minimum-competency testing movement see Jaeger 1989.) The jurists concluded, "We believe that the state administered a test that was, at least on record before us, fundamentally unfair in that it may have covered matters not taught in the schools of the state." (*Debra P.* v. *Turlington*, 644 F.2d 397 and 404, 5th Cir. 1981). The decision implicitly incorporated McClung's (1979) description of instructional validity: "Even if the curricular objectives of the school correspond with the competency test objectives, there must be some measure of whether the school district's stated objectives were translated into topics actually taught in the district's classrooms" (682). The court ruled that Florida should not use the test "to deprive its high school seniors of the economic and educational benefits of a high school diploma until it has demonstrated that the [test] is a fair test of that which is taught in its classrooms" (644 F.2d at 408).

"Instructional validity" is not a term recognized in the joint AERA, American Psychological Association, and National Council on Measurement in Education (1985) standards. It falls most comfortably under the rubric of content-related evidence, which has always been the most important facet of validity for achievement tests. Five reasons may be offered for the rather singular devotion to content validation. First, the use of the adjective "content" to modify the noun "validity" conjures up, in the mind of educators, the image of subject matter coverage rather than of hypothetical constructs. Second, publishers of standardized achievement tests emphasize content validity in their manuals when they describe how they survey the most widely used textbooks and curriculum guides, review syllabi of large districts, and consult with subject matter specialists. Third, although skills have always been emphasized in achievement tests, they are not generally thought by educators to be constructs. For many, it is perfectly clear from the public performance of the task whether or not one has the skill in question. Fourth, if the test is content-valid—that is, it truly represents a content domain—it is considered valid for all kinds of people. Fifth, content validation involves consensual judgment about the relationship of the test items to the test domain, and as such is cheap, feasible, and relatively simple to carry out (Madaus 1983).

The idea of curricular and instructional validity, that is, relating test items to the objectives of the curriculum and then relating the test to instruction, has been around at least since the 1920s (see Cureton 1951; Ebel 1956; Furst 1958; Greene, Jorgensen, and Gerbrich 1943; Lee 1936; Noll 1957; Ross and Stanley 1954; Ruch 1929; Stanley and Hopkins 1972; Woody and Sangren 1933; Wrightstone, Justman, and Robbins 1956). Many commentators took for granted that the domain of interest in educational achievement testing was the curricular and instructional emphasis of the school. For example, in 1929, Ruch wrote that "validity is in general the degree to which a test parallels the curriculum and good teaching practices'' (28).

Haney (1983) presents an interesting analysis of the relationships among high-stakes tests, the curriculum, and material actually taught. He also shows the scope of the discussion of content validity by both the state's and plaintiff's witnesses in the *Debra P.* trial. The defendant's witnesses focused on test items, test specifications, and skill objectives, whereas the plaintiffs used a broader conceptual net to include the components of instruction, curriculum materials, and curriculum programs.

Interestingly, the relationships among test results, learning, and degree of instructional effectiveness fall outside the parameters of discussion of either party. However, at least two very important questions arise when we consider these relationships. First, does the provision of instruction in itself provide adequate opportunity to learn, or does the instruction have to be "effective"? What of the student who fails the tests because instruction has been poor? This situation, after all, provides one ostensible reason for accountability programs that tie teacher evaluations or salaries to student test performance—which brings us back to the argument articulated by Mann (1845), that students will not fail to learn, as indicated by the test, if taught properly.

A second question relates to the very complex validity issue of whether or not the test is an adequate measure of what students actually have learned and can do. On the basis of poor test performance, one should never infer the absence of an ability; the best one can say is that for whatever reason, the student did not display the ability. Many educators have been struck by the incongruity between inferences about poor "abilities" (e.g., reading and numeracy) based on test performance and the apparently similar skills being displayed in everyday contexts (reading the sports page and making complicated calculations in shops) (see Walkerdine 1988). Part of the reason for failing to display what one can do or has learned has to do with the way a person encounters a test item, perhaps the way in which it is worded. Students can also simply refuse to perform on a test.

The relationships among instruction, test items, skills and knowledge tested, and textbooks have been the subject of considerable analysis (Airasian and Madaus 1983). For example, Nitko (1989) presents a detailed discussion of how to design tests that are integrated with instruction, and Leinhardt (1983) conceptualizes the overlap among tests, texts, and instruction by a Venn diagram and suggests techniques to estimate it. Another approach has involved investigations of the overlap in the coverage of commercial standardized tests and topics covered in different textbooks. For example, researchers at the Institute for Research on Teaching found that the proportion of topics presented in five major norm-referenced, standardized achievement tests that received more than cursory treatment in three widely used mathematics textbooks was never higher than 50 percent (Schmidt, Porter, Schwille, Floden, and Freeman 1983). As Walter Heaney pointed out, the school systems' practice of choosing the norm-referenced test that most closely represents their curriculum (often their adopted textbook) or of aligning their curriculum to the test vitiates comparisons based on test norms since the norms were developed by using many districts without such alignment.

The Tyler model was used mainly as a training device to help teachers prepare valid classroom tests and as an evaluation tool, in which stating and appraising educational objectives are an integral aspect of curriculum building efforts (Cronbach 1983). The definitive history of the impact of the "evaluation school"—its related "technical" and technological outcome-oriented philosophy, its apparent rationality and emphasis on predefined objectives, and its test-builder friendliness on American education in general and on the field of curriculum in particular—has yet to be written. However, it is certainly safe to say that it was a boon to testing.

Tyler's "evaluation school" originally involved the local school or district since the objectives would, according to his thinking, necessarily differ from school to school and district to district. As a consequence, the model was never a very practical one for building commercial norm-referenced tests since a common core of behavioral objectives was not as easy to identify as were common content or topics found in textbooks or curriculum guides. One of the reasons for the instrument development effort of the Eight Year Study was the inappropriateness of commercial standardized achievement tests to the goals of the progressive schools (Smith and Tyler 1942).

Further, for Tyler the first criterion of adequate achievement test construction was the faithful representation of the objectives of instruction. Psychometric concerns, relating to reliability and the use of item selection techniques to maximize differences, did not figure prominently in Tyler's design of achievement tests. Neither did he emphasize administrative convenience, machine scorability, or efficiency, factors all now associated with the selection mode of response. Tyler's evaluation model, with its emphasis on matching test items to the objectives of instruction, has coexisted since the 1930s with the standardized testing model, emphasizing common content, individual differences, and psychometric item selection procedures. However, adaptation of Tyler's objective-based approach in the service of accountability led to a virtual abandonment of his emphasis on building instruments that most directly permitted students to demonstrate their achievements as defined by the curriculum.

Measurement-Driven Instruction (MDI)

The idea of measurement-driven instruction (MDI) in recent years grew out of a disillusionment with the behavioral-objectives approach, which had failed to yield the instructional improvements hoped for by its proponents. Popham (1983) feels that the failure of the approach was due to the fact that educators were "overwhelmed by interminable lists of miniscule behavioral objectives. Too many targets turned out to be no targets at all" (27). Thus,

Popham argues that "we should make certain that the achievement tests we now hope will serve as instructional targets contain a reasonable number of assessment foci, so teachers can organize their instructional efforts around a reasonable number of instructional foci" (25)—a de facto curriculum. Also, MDI has roots in the direct-instruction model, the goal of which is to "move students through a sequenced set of materials or tasks. Such materials are common across classrooms and have a strong congruence with the tasks on achievement tests" (Rosenshine 1976, 38).

At first blush there would appear to be two essential ingredients in MDI. First, there must be a clear concept of desired goals, and second, the test must well and truly measure them. But there is a third element that the driver of the MDI vehicle needs to fuel the engine—high stakes associated with the results (Airasian 1987; Madaus 1985).

Recent evidence shows that the public, teachers, and students look favorably on the use of MDI as part of the reform effort. A 1987 Gallup poll asked about measures that would "help a lot" to improve education in the basics. Requiring students to pass standardized tests in basic skills to earn a high school diploma was looked on with favor by 81 percent of the general public and ranked second in the list of ten options; 62 percent of teachers approved, giving the option a rank of six. Requiring remedial courses for students who fail to pass standardized tests was endorsed by 73 percent of the public (rank of six) and by 63 percent of teachers (rank of five). Finally, 68 percent of the public (rank of seven) and 45 percent of teachers (rank of eight) endorsed the option of "requiring that students pass standardized tests to go from junior to high school" (National Education Association 1988).

In another study of an opportunity sample of 285 teachers from low-stakes testing states, most teachers reported that current testing oriented teachers and students to stated goals and increased emphasis on basic skills. They also reported that testing made them work harder and improved some factors. The test helped teachers to focus on a common curriculum as expressed by state objectives and measured by state tests, with particular emphasis on basic skills (Stake and Theobald 1988; see also the National Center of Effective Secondary Schools 1987). Haertel, Ferrara, Korpi, and Prescott (1984) interviewed 1,200 students in five San Francisco schools and found that two thirds of them felt that minimum-competency testing was a good idea; only 1 in 10 disagreed. Students saw the tests as ensuring the quality of a high school diploma, measuring necessary basic skills, providing feedback about their performance in school, and calling the teacher's attention to learning problems. Thus, it seems that if a plebiscite were held, MDI would win in a landslide.

Measurement-driven instruction can have both positive and negative effects in the hands of policymakers. On the positive side is the fact that historically, when reformers met resistance in making curricular changes, they were able to overcome it by instituting changes in external, high-stakes examinations. Soon thereafter, the curricular reforms became the focus of instruction and learning. This result occurred in chemistry in Australia (G. C. Morris 1969); in physics, mathematics, and chemistry in Ireland (Madaus and Macnamara 1970); in the primary school curriculum in Belgium (Hotyat 1958); in modern language in the New York Regents examination (Tyler 1963); and in modern math on the College Entrance Examination Board (CEEB) mathematics achievement tests (Commission on Mathematics 1959). Bowler (1983) cites studies supporting the belief that when Payment by Results controlled the curriculum in the British Isles, literacy increased markedly.

On the negative side, the drivers who steer the MDI vehicle are either the policymakers or the test constructors, not teachers or curriculum specialists. It is the policymakers who mandate the broad objectives on which the tests will focus. In the United States, the emphasis of MDI is on the easily measurable three R's (Cuban 1986; Stodolsky 1988).

It is assumed in MDI that the test is a good measure of the objectives. However, the bureaucratic need to test all students in the state at certain grades ensures that for reading and mathematics, at least, the multiple-choice format will be employed. It is almost axiomatic that less efficient tests are driven out by more efficient ones (Frederiksen 1984). This result, in turn, puts further emphasis on lower-order thinking skills at the expense of higher-order skills, which do not lend themselves so readily to the selection mode of response.

Several commentators have noted that as a result of MDI, minima tend to become maxima (Bowler 1983; National Commission on Excellence in Education 1983; Stodolsky 1988). Further, educational outcomes tend to become valued as a function of their measurability (Holmes 1911). This point can be illustrated in the Connecticut Department of Education's definition of an effective school as one "that brings children from low-income families to the minimum basic skills mastery level which now describes the minimally successful performance for middle-income children" (Gauthier 1983, 2).

EVIDENCE RELATING TO THE EFFECTS OF ASSESSMENT AND EVALUATION ON CURRICULA

We have seen that much educational reform has been based on the assumption that assessment and evaluation procedures can be used to shape curricula. Tyler's proposals for evaluation were directed toward improving educational outputs. Similarly, proposals regarding the use of public examinations assumed that the examinations would redirect the activities of schools, teachers, and students. More recently, minimum-competency testing and other forms of examinations are being proposed as mechanisms to improve educational standards in this country, while in Africa, the reform of public examinations is perceived as a way of improving the quality of education and of making it more relevant to the needs of students (Eisemon, Patel, and Abagi, 1987; Heyneman 1987; Kellaghan and Greaney 1991). Evidence on the precise effects of assessment and evaluation on school curricula and practice, however, is hard to come by. Much of it is impressionistic in nature, though often based, it must be accepted, on the observations of people in close contact with schools.

In this section, we shall review this topic, considering evidence that is impressionistic as well as evidence that is more firmly grounded in the empirical tradition. We shall distinguish between low-stakes (usually school-controlled) assessment or evaluation and high-stakes (usually externally controlled) assessment or evaluation since this distinction seems important when one is considering the degree of impact that assessment or evaluation is likely to have on curricula and school practice.

Some of the findings of research would seem to relate to assessment or evaluation in both high- and low-stakes situations. For example, it would seem that whether assessment is high-stakes or low-stakes, the use of higher-order questions, rather than questions that require verbatim recall, tends to enhance retention, transfer of learning, interest, and development of learning skills. A further general finding of reviews on the topic indicates that the influence of assessment tends to be specific to the content of the test used; that is, where there is an effect, it relates mainly to the kind of topics and skills that are contained in a test (Crooks 1988; Felker and Dapra 1975; Frederiksen 1984; LeMahieu 1984).

Perhaps the most striking evidence on the relationship between assessment and curriculum practice is to be found in an anecdote of a researcher on the selection and training of U.S. naval personnel during World War II (Fredericksen 1984). It was found that the best tests for predicting grades given by instructors were written verbal and reading-comprehension tests. This did not seem to make much sense, given that the tasks of gunners were maintaining, adjusting, and repairing guns. The researcher found that training classes consisted of lectures and demonstrations of how to use the equipment, rather than having students actually use it. The researcher then designed performance tests in which students were required to demonstrate competence by, for example, removing and replacing the extractor plunger on an antiaircraft gun. Few of the students could perform the tasks. However, new students soon found out what the new tests were like and began practicing the assembly and disassembly of guns. The instructors also turned from lecturing to more practical work with guns and gun mounts. At the end of the course, students did much better on the performance tests on which students following the older instructional method had fared so badly. Further, the predictive validity of the verbal and reading tests dropped, and the validity of the mechanical aptitude and mechanical knowledge tests improved. The interesting point of this anecdote is that no attempt was made to change the curriculum or teacher behavior. The dramatic changes in curriculum and achievement came about solely through a change in testing.

Low-Stakes Testing

In addition to these findings, research reviews, relating to in-school low-stakes assessment, indicate that the use of assessment, which most often takes the form of teacher questioning, is positively related to student achievement. Certainly, students who are not assessed at all are at a disadvantage. For greatest effect, questions should be directed to as many students as possible and the difficulty level of the questions should be appropriate to the students' level of skill and knowledge—that is, not too easy or not too difficult for the majority of students. Assessment soon after studying a topic tends to enhance long-term retention. Furthermore, assessment that is moderately frequent results in gains in student performance (LeMahieu 1984). To be effective, feedback should be provided to students on their performance, and it should be immediate rather than delayed. Again, feedback is enhanced if errors of knowledge and understanding are identified (Crooks 1988; Frederiksen 1984).

A number of possible mechanisms can be suggested to explain how assessment might help to promote student learning. First, assessment directs teachers' and students' attention to particular topics and skills. Second, responding to questions or testing requires active participation on the part of students, to process the material being assessed. Third, assessment provides practice for students on material, which helps to consolidate learning. And finally, assessment can provide feedback that clarifies understanding and corrects misconceptions (see Crooks 1988).

Research findings on the effects of commercial, standardized measures of achievement on school practice tend to be less positive than findings on the effects of assessment by teachers. We have already noted Travers' (1983) observation that standardized tests, when used in American schools in the 1930s and 1940s, had little impact. This conclusion was largely substantiated in an experimental study of testing in Irish schools in the 1970s (Kellaghan, Madaus, and Airasian 1982). Although the reactions of both teachers and students to the testing program were very positive, the program produced few effects on school practice and organization, teachers, parents, or students. Aspects of these findings are corroborated in studies carried out in the United States (Boyd, McKenna, Stake, and Yachinsky 1975; Salmon-Cox 1981, 1982; Stetz and Beck 1978) and in Britain (Gipps 1984).

The lack of strong effects in the Irish study may be attributed to the fact that the testing program did not involve high stakes, such as graduation or promotion decisions, teacher evaluations, or award of funds (Madaus 1989). However, it is possible that other factors also contributed to the findings. For example, since the agency that sponsored the testing was a research organization, it did not have the authority to impose pressure on parents or teachers. The failure to find more positive results might also have been due to the fact that tests were not seen by teachers as being integrated with instructional materials and procedures. This is not an unlikely hypothesis, given that the Irish educational system had very little experience of standardized tests at the time.

High-Stakes Testing

Many if not most accountability testing programs have mandated sanctions or rewards directly and overtly linked to test performance. Other programs, without explicit high-stakes mandates, can take on the characteristics of high-stakes tests when people perceive that important sanctions or rewards are associated with performance. For example, when test results are used by newspapers to rank districts across a state or schools across a district, the results are perceived as an important indicator of what is to be valued in education (Center for the Study of Testing, Evaluation, and Educational Policy 1986). In this case, the test results have important, though perhaps unintended, consequences.

Although high-stakes testing programs are often initiated with the intention of improving educational quality and standards, an historical review of the effects of such programs over many years in several countries indicates that they are perceived to have a variety of negative effects on school curricula, teaching, and learning. A neglected, rich source of evidence on this topic is the observations of writers, found in poetry, short stories, novels, plays, and biographies (Rafferty 1985). On a more empirical note, Bowler (1983), in her history of Payment by Results (PBR) in England, examined the annual reports of the Department of Education, statistical data, school log books, and the testimony of numerous commentators; she concluded that PBR "had a reactionary and deleterious effect upon the educational system and upon teachers and students engaged in the life of the school" (162). The Cross Commission, which was set up to look into the PBR scheme, sent detailed questionnaires to teachers, school inspectors, and other interested parties and, although it did not call for the abolition of PBR, it found the system was carried too far, was too rigidly applied, and needed to be modified in the interests of teachers, of students, and of education itself (Bowler 1983).

Perhaps the most obvious effect of high-stakes examinations is the alignment that takes place between curricula and the examinations' objectives. Evidence is to be found in a study of the Regents' examination in New York State, in which as one would expect, it was found that most teachers were aware of the objectives being tested. Further, the achievements of students in 61 school districts were closer to the examination objectives than to the objectives specified in local curricula (Spaulding 1938). Tyler (1963) also reported that in his Eight Year Study, new curriculum proposals were poorly received by teachers if their objectives differed from those on which college-entrance tests were based. Other studies have noted a tendency on the part of teachers to direct their attention toward areas they know will be covered by standardized tests in district or city testing programs (Stodolsky 1988). Faced with a choice between objectives that are explicit in a syllabus and ones that are implicit in examinations, students and teachers generally choose the latter.

In England, the evidence on the impact of high-stakes examinations on the curriculum—given to the Taunton Commission as far back as 1868 and for the Beloe Report in 1960—was similar, leading to the conclusion that "the examination dictates the curriculum and cannot do otherwise; it confines experimentation, limits free choice of subject, hampers treatment of subjects, encourages wrong values in the classroom" (quoted in Kelly 1989, 152). Other commentators have noted similar effects in England (see Bell and Grant 1974; Broadfoot 1984; Gordon and Lawton 1978; Holmes 1911; Koerner 1968; N. Morris 1961), in Africa (Eisemon, Patel, and Abagi 1987; Little 1982), in India (Gayen, Nanda, Duari, Dubey, Bhattacharyya 1961; Mukerji 1966; Srinivasan 1971), in Ireland (Madaus and Macnamara 1970), and in Japan (Cummings 1980). In the United States, White (1888), commenting on the effect on teacher practices of high-stakes tests used for grade-to-grade promotion in Cincinnati, observed that few teachers could resist the influence of the test "and teach according to their better judgment. They shut their eyes to the needs of the pupil and put their strength into what will 'count' in the examination" (518).

Recently, directors of state-level testing programs, when asked if as a result of testing teachers spent more time teaching to the objectives of tests, almost unanimously said yes. Those who looked positively on the test effects felt that tests focused instruction on important objectives, whereas those who saw the effects in a negative light worried about areas that were deemphasized or not taught at all (Shepard 1989a). Whether the effect is considered to be positive or negative, one thing that is clear is that the curriculum tends to become narrowed and to focus on the academic. Areas measured by the test will receive time; areas not measured will not (National Commission on Testing and Public Policy 1990; Stake, McTaggart, and Munski 1985; Stodolsky 1988; Turner 1984). Given this situation, it is not surprising that recent shifts have been detected in early childhood curricula away from social, emotional, and physical goals for children toward academic ones (see Cunningham 1989; Kamii in press; Meisels 1989; National Commission on Testing and Public Policy 1990; Shepard 1989b; Shepard and Smith 1986, 1989; Smith and Shepard 1987, 1988). Further, the shift is not only toward the academic area but also toward basic skills, if that is what the test measures.

High-stakes testing has been reported to affect teaching as well as curricula. Bowler (1983) reports that the Payment by Results system in Britain strengthened preexisting instructional methods such as drill, rote teaching, and emphasis on mechanical learning, delaying the emergence of child-centered teaching and learning for decades. In this country, Cuban (1986), like Bowler, feels that contemporary high-stakes testing has intensified already existing teacher-centered, direct instruction. He describes what happens to the teacher's instructional practices, particularly in low-income, high-minority districts in the following formula:

Competency-based curricula + direct instruction + standardized tests = measurement-driven teaching and higher test scores. He argues that in this situation, the emphasis in the national and state reform reports calling for graduates with flexible thinking skills and a strong desire for learning is frustrated: "The harnessing of teacher-centered instruction to recent state mandates that detail curricular content, specify fact-filled textbooks, and evaluate student performance by means of multiple-choice test items pours concrete over an already durable pedagogy" (10). In a similar vein, Stodolsky (1988) contends that accountability pressure for student attainment in mathematics may be one reason why teachers are slow to change their teaching methods or to use efforts appropriate for serious learning. More damaging still is her observation that "The dislocation to students and teachers caused by preparation for external exams is often severe, and instructional momentum is sometimes lost for the rest of the school year" (108).

Teaching to the high-stakes test can be a comfortable form of pedagogy. It also becomes a defensive act because it satisfies, "superficially at least, the observable demands of teaching" and helps the teacher to maintain authority and efficiency (McNeil 1988, 434).

Apart from effects on the scope and emphasis of the curriculum and on teaching methodology, high-stakes testing is likely to cause considerable effort to be put into test preparation. For example, Shepard (1989a) found a wide range of test preparation practices in use, from fostering testwiseness to teaching the test. She also found that some states provide material for test preparation.

A further observation relating to test preparation is that reading instruction can center on having students read short passages and answer multiple-choice questions. A recent study in the Boston public schools found that much of the curriculum in "reading" might not fit many definitions of that activity. Worksheets, vocabulary drills, and multiple-choice questions about short passages often were the main focus of attention. The stories that students read were very short, often easy, and boring; rarely were students given entire books to read. Further, just as classroom reading instruction had come to imitate the important reading tests, remediation programs involved simple test preparation (Wheelock and Dorman 1989). Given this situation, it is not surprising that Wodtke, Harper, Schommer, and Brunelli (1985), in their study of ten kindergartens that used standardized reading tests, found that pressure to increase test scores produced "tester effects," leading to large variations in testing conditions.

In the light of such findings, a longtime advocate of standardized tests, Albert Shanker (1988), president of the American Federation of Teachers (AFT), recently reassessed his support:

> Since the reputation of a school, its principal, its teachers and the school board and superintendent depends largely on test scores, schools are devoting less time to reading real books, writing essays, and discussing current events and more and more time teaching kids strategies for filling in blanks and choosing the answers to multiple-choice questions. This destroys much of the value of these tests, which only tell you something if they are an independent measure of what the student knows. (7)

In a study for the Arizona State Department of Education, nine "test preparation activities" were identified and classified according to their degree of ethicalness: training in testwiseness (ethical); checking answer sheets to make sure that each has been properly completed (ethical); increasing student motivation to perform on the test through appeals to parents, students, and teachers (ethical); developing a curriculum based on the content of the test (unethical); preparing objectives based on items on the test and teaching accordingly (unethical); presenting items similar to those on the test (unethical); using *Scoring High* or other test preparation activities (unethical); dismissing low-achieving students on testing day to boost artificially group test scores (unethical); presenting items verbatim from the test to be given (unethical). Nearly 60 percent of the teachers and administrators reported practicing with sample questions in the weeks before the test, and 41 percent reported regularly using some sort of commercial test preparation material. Variation was found in the way exclusionary policies were implemented, but 10 percent of the teachers admitted to using current test items as practice for the test (Haladyna, Nolen, and Hass 1989; see also Cannell 1989 and National Association of Test Directors 1986 for examples of teachers "cheating" to help students on tests).

A major problem underlying the use of high-stakes tests, arising in particular from test preparation procedures, is that the inferences that can be made from actual test performance may be distorted. Any measurement of the status of an educational institution, no matter how well designed and well intentioned, inevitably changes its status (Campbell 1975). When a high-stakes test is mandated, it will influence, in intended and unintended ways, the curriculum, teaching, and learning. These changes in the instructional delivery system in turn can render obsolete the validity of the inferences, descriptions, and decisions made on the basis of best performance.

Test preparation activities are likely to be based on teachers' inferences about the kind of intellectual activity required by questions on previous tests. Students will then be prepared to meet the questions' demands. Thus, it may not be the curriculum objectives that become the focus or target of instruction but the selection-type questions that are used to operationalize them (Haetel 1989). If this is the case, teachers will corrupt the curricular skills of interest and reduce them to the level of strategies in which the examinee is drilled. Thus, practices initiated in response to the testing mandate will corrupt the test's ability to serve as a valid indicator of student achievement.

The essay component of the Irish Primary Certificate (IPC) examination illustrates the cycle of how the test first distorts teaching and the teaching subsequently distorts inferences that can be made from the test (Madaus and Greaney 1985). Students sitting for the IPC had to write a short essay on a topic that changed each year (e.g., a bicycle ride, 1946; a day in the bog, 1947; a bus tour, 1948). Because of the IPC's perceived importance, at least some teachers taught generations of Irish children to memorize a series of stock sentences that could be used with any prompt (e.g., "I awakened early, jumped out of bed and had a quick breakfast. My friend was coming to our house at nine o'clock as we were going for a ______ fill in the prompt ______"). As a result of this type of teaching to the test, a high score on the subsequent writing examination was no longer a valid indicator of well-developed writing skills. Rather, the test results became a measure of students' ability to memorize, recall, and use the stock responses with that year's prompt.

A recent report by John Jacob Cannell (1987), a West Virginia physician, which may prove to be a watershed study, provides a case study of how the use of an indicator for decision making can distort the social processes it is intended to monitor. Cannell discovered that "no state is below average at the elementary level on any of the six major nationally normed, commercially available tests" (1). This finding is popularly portrayed as the "Lake Wobegon effect," after that mythical town where all students are above average. Given the fact that state- and national-level reformers based their arguments for change and for using tests for accountability on low test scores, the "Lake Wobegon effect" should have been a cause for celebration. The reforms, it might be argued, had led to the desired effect—improved test performance. However, this news became the cause of serious concern rather than national elation. Cannell initially blamed the startling results on corrupt norms and "dumbing down" the content of the test. However, another possible hypothesis is that the mandated test had become so important that teachers adjusted their teaching to the test, producing the subsequent rises, but without a concomitant improvement in the skills that the tests were originally designed to measure. (For further details of Cannell's study, see *Educational Measurement Issues and Practices* 1988, 7[2].)

People simply did not believe Cannell's results or his explanations. Policymakers and test publishers argued that his data and statistics were wrong or that his negative explanations were wrong and that the high achievement reflected real improvement, or if he was right, the results were inflated because of outdated norms and increased familiarity with the tests (Shepard 1989a). Reanalysis, however, confirmed Cannell's results; the "Lake Wobegon effect" is real. Further, data from NAEP contradict the argument that all of the gains reflect improved skills levels (Linn, Graue, and Sanders 1989; see also Koretz 1988).

The effects of high-stakes testing are not limited to the educational experiences of students at the grade at which the tests are administered. For example, it has been observed that the impact of high-stakes reading tests in grades 3 and 4 has "trickled down" to the lower primary grades. Pressure to improve reading scores in upper primary grades has led to pressure on teachers in the lower grades to begin to place more emphasis on reading skills. Such an emphasis may come at the expense of other, more traditional goals (Cunningham 1989). The trickle-down phenomenon is not limited to the United States. It has also been observed in Africa, where teachers use the multiple-choice format of national examinations not only in their classroom tests but also in their teaching methodology in the early grades of primary school (Kellaghan and Greaney 1991).

A number of other strategies and tactics that are designed to lead to improved test scores are being used in schools. One administrative gambit is to exclude children who are potential low scorers (students in special education or students for whom English is a second language) from the tested population (Murnane 1987). A related tactic is that of "red shirting" kindergarten students—a term borrowed from collegiate football, whereby freshmen or injured players are kept on the team without playing but without losing a year's eligibility. Retaining students in kindergarten or not letting them enter in the first place because they do not have the necessary "readiness" should, in the long run, contribute to higher test scores, if for no other reason than that the children are a year older when they take the tests (see Smith and Shepard 1988 for a discussion of validity issues surrounding the use of "readiness" tests for entrance or retention).

A further consequence of high-stakes testing is the grade retention of students. For example, in time-series analyses of promotion rates in Irish schools, it was found that when the primary certificate examination was made compulsory, there was an overall decrease in promotion rates (Madaus and Greaney 1985). It would appear that pupils who were not likely to pass the examination were prevented from failing it by not being allowed to sit for it. Thus, schools achieved relatively high pass rates for the pupils who actually took the examination. Retention based on a high-stakes test, either in the early childhood years or in the upper grades, assumes that students will benefit from the treatment they receive in the repeated year. In other words, the assumption is made that the high-stakes achievement tests used for promotion decisions —often called "gates tests"— are valid. That is, they aid in the selection of students who will benefit from the treatment they receive during the additional year. However, there is no supporting evidence to suggest that this is the case. On the contrary, a growing body of research indicates that retention does not result in clear-cut benefits (Shepard and Smith 1986).

There are also indications that failing a high-stakes test may increase the likelihood of early dropout (Kreitzer, Haney, and Madaus 1989). This subject needs much more systematic research. The National Commission on Testing and Public Policy (1990) points out that concentrating on testing for selection or retention avoids consideration of the harder issue of specifying appropriate goals and of the instructional and systemic problems that impede their realization.

If tests and testing are important, ancillary commercial activities are likely to develop around them. In Japan, for example, it is common for Japanese parents to enroll their children in special extra-study schools known as *juku* (Fallows 1987). The use of private tutors for coaching pupils after school is also a feature of the Kenyan system (Eisemon,

Patel, and Abagi 1987). There is little doubt that the public perceives such services as helpful and is willing to pay for them.

Companies have long recognized the financial potential of developing materials that teachers can use to help them prepare their students for high-stakes tests (Bowler 1983). The rise of state-mandated minimum-competency or high-stakes basic skills tests in the United States has led publishers to design materials to train pupils to take them. As a result, there has been a large growth of test-coaching companies, particularly since the 1980s (Haney, Madaus, and Lyons in press). These companies are offering practice tests that closely resemble commercially available, standardized achievement batteries employed in many high-stakes state-level programs. Included in this hidden dimension of test preparation materials are end-of-chapter tests, which textbook publishers provide to schools when a text is adopted.

Some of the commercially prepared material is designed to familiarize students with the test format, scoring rules, guessing strategies, and test-anxiety reduction techniques. Such material is certainly appropriate and is not destructive of either instruction or test validity (Haladyna, Nolen, and Hass 1989; Mehrens and Kaminski 1988; Shepard and Kreitzer 1987). However, as the commercial material begins to resemble more closely the high-stakes tests, its use by teachers to prepare students will serve to undermine the validity of the inferences one might make from the test to a larger domain of interest.

There is much we do not know about the use of test preparation materials, whether commercial or prepared by school districts. For example, we do not know how extensive the practice of test preparation is; how much of it is inappropriate; what the associated dollar, instructional, and teacher costs are; what types of districts and teachers are most apt to use test preparation material; and what types of students receive this type of preparation. A recent attempt to estimate the costs associated with test preparation found that the figure would be $387 million a year on the conservative assumption that 20 percent of the teachers in the country spent five days a year in test preparation (National Commission on Testing and Public Policy 1990).

CONCLUSION

This survey of the field of curriculum evaluation and assessment indicates that it is a complex area of study, with close relationships to program evaluation, testing, and educational research. It is also complex in its area of application since curriculum evaluation can raise issues relating to bureaucratic control and accountability, as well as to the more traditional concepts of curriculum adequacy and effectiveness.

A summary position of the state of curriculum evaluation is difficult to present since the field has been in a state of flux for the past two decades under the constant and increasing pressure to provide evaluation information as a basis for a range of decisions. In attempts to provide "relevant" information, a variety of approaches other than empirical ones associated with traditional educational research are being explored. Although these developments are generally enriching the field of evaluation study, they also carry with them the seeds of divisiveness and polarization in the field.

The common practice of relying on outcome measures (most usually standardized test scores) as a primary indicator of the success of a program or curriculum, though still common, raises a number of issues. First, the concentration on output measures ignores other aspects of programs (e.g., characteristics of students and curriculum implementation). Second, the perceived effect of a program may be a function of the type and content of the test measure that is used, and thus provide an incorrect evaluation of the effectiveness of a curriculum. Third, when test data are used to make critical decisions about curricula, schools, or teachers, they can have important, if unintended, negative consequences on what goes on in schools (Frechtling 1989).

In this review, considerable attention has been given to the issue of testing. This emphasis reflects the position that despite recent advances in the field of evaluation, testing (particularly multiple-choice testing) continues to occupy a central role in evaluation activities. There are many situations, however, in which the use of multiple-choice tests is inappropriate; there are other cases in which their use would appear to have undesirable effects on curricula and school practice to the point that their use is counterproductive.

It is in response to this situation that there have recently been proposals, both in this country and in Great Britain, to place less emphasis on multiple-choice tests in favor of what has come to be called "alternative" or "authentic" assessment (Haney and Madaus 1989; National Commission on Testing and Public Policy 1990; Raizen and Kaser 1989; Resnick and Resnick in press; Wiggins 1989). The growing assessment movement employs exercises that ask students, often in tasks that are longer and more complex than those involved in traditional tests, to supply answers, produce products, and perform experiments. The assessments may be based on observations of students while they are engaged in the normal learning activities of their programs of study (Department of Education and Science 1988). Much research is going to be required to develop the new procedures into workable assessment systems (Nuttall 1990b), particularly if those systems are to meet adequately the variety of objectives that are being posited for them: reflecting the learning outcomes they purport to measure and allowing users to arrive at clear decisions about students' achievements (Black, Hall, Martin, and Yates 1989).

More than new forms of assessment and evaluation, however, will be needed to escape the bureaucratic power of testing. If the new forms are used for the same purposes as the systems they are designed to replace, and without attention to underlying systemic reasons for such problems as poor student achievement, it would appear that the new modes will eventually be open to corruption in the way the older ones were. Foucault would understand these developments on both sides of the Atlantic and would probably be amused. In both Britain and the United States, testing is being perceived as a solution to a policy problem without necessarily seeing that over time the solution can have inherent and corrupting effects on teaching and learning and eventually on the tests themselves.

References

Airasian, Peter W. 1987. State mandated testing and educational reform: Context and consequences. *American Journal of Education* 95(3): 393–412.

Airasian, Peter W., and George F. Madaus. 1983. Linking testing and instruction: Policy issues. *Journal of Educational Measurement* 20(2): 103–118.

American Educational Research Association, American Psychological Association, and National Council on Measurement in Education. 1985. *Standards for Educational and Psychological Testing*. Washington DC: American Psychological Association.

Anderson, Richard C. 1972. How to construct achievement tests to assess comprehension. *Review of Educational Research* 42(2): 145–170.

Aries, Phillipe. 1962. *Centuries of Childhood: A Social History of Family Life*, translated by R. Boldick. New York: Vintage Books.

Ayres, Leonard P. 1909. *Laggards in the Schools*. New York: Russell Sage Foundation.

Ayres, Leonard P. 1918. "History and Present Status of Educational Measurements." In *The Measurement of Educational Products*. Seventeenth Yearbook of the National Society for the Study of Education, Part II, edited by Guy M. Whipple, 9–15. Bloomington, IL: Public School Co.

Ballou, Frank. 1916. "Work of the Department of Educational Investigation and Measurements, Boston, Massachusetts." In *Standards and Testing for the Measurement of the Efficiency of Schools and School Systems*. Fifteenth Yearbook of the National Society for the Study of Education, Part I, edited by Guy M. Whipple, 61–68. Bloomington IL: Public School Co.

Beaton, Albert. 1988. *Expanding the New Design: The NAEP 1985–86 Technical Report*. Princeton, NJ: Educational Testing Service.

Becker, Howard S. 1970. *Sociological Work. Method and Substance*. Chicago: Aldine.

Bell, Robert, and Nigel Grant. 1974. *A Mythology of British Education*. London: Panther.

Bentham, Jeremy. 1960 [1816]. "Chrestomathic." In *Studies in the History of Education, 1780–1820*, edited by Brian Simon. London: Lawrence & Wishart.

Berk, Ronald A., ed. 1986. *A Guide to Criterion-Referenced Construction*. Baltimore, MD: Johns Hopkins University Press.

Black, Harry, John Hall, Sue Martin, and John Yates. 1989. *The Quality of Assessments*. Edinburgh: Scottish Council for Research in Education.

Bloom, Benjamin S. 1950. *The Idea and Practice of General Education*. Chicago: University of Chicago Press.

Bloom, Benjamin S., ed. 1956. *Taxonomy of Educational Objectives: The Classification of Educational Goals, Handbook 1, Cognitive Domain*. New York: McKay.

Bloom, Benjamin S. 1966. The role of the educational sciences in curriculum development. *International Journal of Educational Sciences* 1(1): 5–16.

Bloom, Benjamin S. 1968. Learning for mastery. *University of California Comment* 1(2): 1–12.

Bloom, Benjamin S. 1969. "Some Theoretical Issues Relating to Educational Evaluation." In *Educational Evaluation*. Sixty-eighth Yearbook of the National Society for the Study of Education, Part II, edited by Ralph W. Tyler, 26–50. Chicago: University of Chicago Press.

Bloom, Benjamin S., Thomas Hastings, and George F. Madaus. 1971. *Handbook of Formative and Summative Evaluation of Student Learning*. New York: McGraw-Hill.

Bloom, Benjamin S., George F. Madaus, and Thomas Hastings. 1981. *Evaluation to Improve Student Learning*. New York: McGraw-Hill.

Bobbitt, J. Franklin. 1918. *The Curriculum*. Boston: Houghton Mifflin.

Bolger, Niall, and Thomas Kellaghan. 1990. Method of measurement and gender differences in scholastic achievement. *Journal of Educational Measurement* 27(2): 165–174.

Bottani, Norberto. 1990. The background of the CERI/OECD project on international educational indicators. *International Journal of Educational Research* 14(4): 335–342.

Bowler, Rosemary. 1983. "Payment by Results: A Study in Achievement Accountability." Doctoral dissertation, Boston College.

Boyd, John, Bernard H. McKenna, Robert E. Stake, and J. Yachinsky. 1975. *A Study of Testing Practices in the Royal Oak (Michigan) Public Schools*. Royal Oak, MI: Royal Oak City School District.

Broadfoot, Patricia, ed. 1984. *Selection, Certification and Control: Social Issues in Educational Assessment*. New York: Falmer.

Brubacher, John S. 1955. "The Challenge to Philosophize About Education." In *Modern Philosophies and Education*. Fifty-fourth Yearbook of the National Society for the Study of Education, Part 1, edited by Nelson H. Henry, 4–16. Chicago: National Society for the Study of Education.

Bruner, Jerome. 1966. *Toward a Theory of Instruction*. Cambridge, MA: Belknap Press of Harvard University Press.

Buros, Oscar K. 1977. Fifty years in testing: Some reminiscences, criticisms, and suggestions. *Educational Researcher* 6(7): 9–15.

Burton, Edward. 1979. Richard Lowell Edgeworth's Education Bill of 1979: A missing chapter in the history of Irish education. *Irish Journal of Education* 13(1): 24–33.

Callahan, Raymond E. 1962. *Education and the Cult of Efficiency*. Chicago: University of Chicago Press.

Campbell, Donald T. 1975. "Assessing the Impact of Planned Social Change." In *Social and Public Policies: The Dartmouth/OECD Conference*, edited by Gene M. Lyons. Hanover, NH: Public Affairs Center, Dartmouth College.

Cannell, John J. 1987. *Naturally Normed Elementary Achievement Testing in America's Public Schools: How All Fifty States Are Above the National Average*. Daniels, WV: Friends for Education.

Cannell, John J. 1989. *The "Lake Wobegon" Report: How Public Educators Cheat on Standardized Achievement Tests*. Albuquerque NM: Friends for Education.

Carroll, John B. 1987. The National Assessments in Reading: Are we misreading the findings? *Phi Delta Kappan* 68(6): 424–430.

Carr-Saunders, Alexander M., and P. A. Wilson. 1933. *The Professions*. Oxford: Clarendon Press.

Case, Robbie. 1975. Gearing the demands of instruction to the developmental capacities of the learner. *Review of Educational Research* 45(1): 59–87.

Center for the Study of Testing, Evaluation, and Educational Policy. 1986. *An Evaluation of the Kentucky Essential Skills Tests in Mathematics and Reading. Report submitted to the Kentucky Department of Education*. Chestnut Hill, MA: Boston College.

Charters, W. W. 1924. *Curriculum Construction*. New York: Macmillan.

Cicchetti, P., ed. 1987. "Corporate and Industry Research Reports." (microfiche). Eastchester, NY: JA Micropublishing.

Coleman, James S., Ernest Q. Cambell, Carol J. Hobson, James McPartland, Alexander M. Mood, Frederick D. Weinfeld, and Robert L. York. 1966. *Equality of Educational Opportunity*. Washington DC: Office of Education, U.S. Department of Health Education and Welfare.

Commissioners of National Education in Ireland. 1889. *The Fifty-fifth Report (for the Year 1888)*. Dublin: Her Majesty's Stationery Office.

Commission on Mathematics. 1959. *Program for College Preparatory Mathematics, USA*. New York: College Entrance Examination Board.

Coolahan, John M. 1975. "The Origins of the Payment by Results Policy in Education and the Experience of it in the National and Intermediate Schools of Ireland." Master's thesis, Trinity College, Dublin.

Coomer, Donna L. 1986. "Reformulating the Evaluation Process." In *Critical Perspectives on the Organization and Improvement of Schooling*, edited by Kenneth A. Sirotnik and Jeannie Oakes, 163–204. Boston: Kluwer-Nijhoff.

Cronbach, Lee J. 1969. "Validation of Educational Measures." In *Proceedings of the 1969 Invitational Conference on Testing Problems. Toward a Theory of Achievement Measurement*, chaired by Philip H. Dubois, 35–52. Princeton, NJ: Educational Testing Service.

Cronbach, Lee J. 1971. "Test Validation." In *Educational Measurement*, 2nd ed., edited by Robert L. Thorndike, 443–507. Washington, DC: American Council on Education.

Cronbach, Lee J. 1975. Five decades of public controversy over mental testing. *American Psychologist* 30(1): 1–14.

Cronbach, Lee J. 1983. "Course Improvement Through Evaluation." In *Evaluation Models. Viewpoints on Educational and Human Services Evaluation*, edited by George F. Madaus, Michael S. Scriven, and Daniel L. Stufflebeam, 101–115. Boston: Kluwer-Nijhoff.

Crooks, Terence J. 1988. The impact of classroom evaluation practices on students. *Review of Educational Research* 58(4): 438–481.

Cuban, Laurence. 1986. Persistent instruction: Another look at constancy in the classroom. *Phi Delta Kappan* 68(1): 7–11.

Cummings, William K. 1980. *Education and Equality in Japan*. Princeton, NJ: Princeton University Press.

Cunningham, Anne E. 1989. "Eeny, Meeny, Miney, Moe: Testing Policy and Priorities in Early Childhood Education." Paper commissioned by the National Commission on Testing and Public Policy. Chestnut Hill, MA: NCTPP, Boston College.

Cureton, Edward E. 1951. "Validity." In *Educational Measurement*, edited by E. F. Lindquist, 621–694. Washington DC: American Council in Education.

Dail Eireann (Parliament of Ireland). 1941, May 28. Dail Debates.

Datta, Lois-ellin. 1982. "Employment-Related Basic Skills." In *Education and Work*. Eighty-first Yearbook of the National Society for the Study of Education, Part II, edited by Harry F. Sieberman, 140–168. Chicago: University of Chicago Press.

Department of Education and Science and Welsh Office (Great Britain). 1987. *The National Curriculum 5–16. A Consultation Document*. London: Her Majesty's Stationery Office.

Department of Education and Science and Welsh Office (Great Britain). 1988. *National Curriculum Science for Ages 5 to 16*. London: Her Majesty's Stationery Office.

Dewey, John. 1939. *Theory of Valuation*. Chicago: University of Chicago Press.

Dorr-Bremme, Donald W., and Joan L. Herman. 1986. *Assessing Student Achievement: A Profile of Classroom Practices*. CSE Monograph No. 11. Los Angeles: Center for the Study of Evaluation, University of California.

Dorr-Bremme, Donald W., Joan L. Herman, and Victor W. Doherty. 1983. *Achievement Testing in American Public Schools. A National Perspective*. Los Angeles: Center for the Study of Evaluation, University of California.

Duchastel, Philippe C., and Paul F. Merrill. 1977. The effects of behavioral objectives on learning: A review of empirical studies. *Review of Educational Research* 43(1): 53–69.

Duckworth, Eleanor. 1987. *"The Having of Wonderful Ideas" and Other Essays on Teaching and Learning*. New York: Teachers College Press.

Ebel, Robert L. 1956. Obtaining and reporting evidence on content validity. *Educational and Psychological Measurement* 16(3): 294–304.

Edmonds, Ronald R. 1980, fall. Schools count: New York City's school improvement project. *Harvard Graduate School of Education Association Bulletin* 25: 33–35.

Eisemon, Thomas O., Vilma L. Patel, and Jared Abagi. 1987. Read these instructions carefully. Examination reform and improving health education in Kenya. *International Journal of Educational Development* 7(1): 1–12.

Eisner, Elliot W. 1969. "Instructional and Expressive Educational Objectives: Their Formulation and Use in Curriculum." In *Instructional Objectives*. AERA Monograph Series on Curriculum Evaluation 3, edited by W. James Popham, Elliot W. Eisner, H. J. Sullivan, and Louise L. Tyler. Chicago: Rand McNally.

Eisner, Elliot. 1981. On the difference between scientific and artistic approaches to qualitative research. *Educational Researcher* 10(4): 5–9.

Eisner, Elliot. 1983. "Educational Connoisseurship and Criticism: Their Form and Functions in Educational Evaluation." In *Evaluation Models: Viewpoints on Educational and Human Services Evaluation*, edited by George F. Madaus, Michael S. Scriven, and Daniel L. Stufflebeam, 335–347. Boston: Kluwer-Nijhoff.

Fallows, James. 1987, March. Gradgrind's heirs. *Atlantic*: 16–24.

Farrell, Allan P. 1938. *The Jesuit Code of Liberal Education. Development and Scope of the Ratio Studiorum*. Milwaukee, WI: Bruce Publishing Company.

Fay, Brian. 1987. *Critical Social Science: Liberation and Its Limits*. Ithaca, NY: Cornell University Press.

Felker, Daniel B., and Richard A. Dapra. 1975. Effects of question type and question placement on problem solving ability from prose material. *Journal of Educational Psychology* 67(3): 380–384.

Fleming, Margaret, and Barbara Chambers. 1983. Teacher-made tests: Windows on the classroom. *New Directions for Testing and Measurement* (19): 29–38.

Foucault, Michel. 1977. *Discipline and Punish, The Birth of the Prison*, translated by A. Sheridan. New York: Viking.

Foucault, Michel. 1982. "The Subject and Power of Critical Inquiry." In *Afterword to Beyond Structuralism and Hermeneutics*, edited by Hubert I. Dreyfus and Paul Robinow. Chicago: University of Chicago Press.

Frechtling, Joy A. 1989. "Administrative Uses of School Testing

Programs." In *Educational Measurement*, 3rd ed., edited by Robert L. Linn, 475–483. New York: Macmillan.

Frederiksen, Norman. 1984. The real test bias: Influence of testing on teaching and learning. *American Psychologist* 39(3): 193–202.

Fullan, Michael, and Alan Pomfret. 1977. Research on curriculum and instruction implementation. *Review of Educational Research* 47(2): 335–397.

Furst, Edward J. 1958. *Constructing Evaluation Instruments*. New York: McKay.

Gagné, Robert M. 1965. "The analysis of Instructional Objectives in the Design of Instruction." In *Teaching Machines and Programmed Learning, Vol. 2. Data and Directions*, edited by Robert Glaser. Washington, DC: National Education Association.

Gagné, Robert M. 1977. *The Conditions of Learning*, 3rd ed. New York: Holt, Rinehart and Winston.

Gallup, Alec M. 1985. The Gallup poll of teachers' attitudes toward the public schools. Part 2. *Phi Delta Kappan* 66 (5): 323–330.

Gallup, Alec M., and David L. Clark. 1987. The 19th annual Gallup poll of the public's attitudes towards the public schools. *Phi Delta Kappan* 69(1): 17–30.

Gardner, Leonard. 1977. Humanistic education and behavioral objectives: Opposing theories of educational science. *School Review* 85(3): 376–394.

Gauthier, William J. 1983. *Instructionally Effective Schools: A Model and a Process*, Monograph No. 1. Hartford: State of Connecticut, Department of Education.

Gayen, A. K., P. D. Nanda, P. Duari, S. D. Dubey, and N. Bhattacharyya. 1961. *Measurement of Achievement in Mathematics: A Statistical Study of Effectiveness of Board and University Examinations in India, Report 1*. New Delhi: Ministry of Education.

Gipps, Caroline. 1984. Issues in the use of standardized tests by teachers. *Bulletin of the British Psychological Society* 37: 153–156.

Gipps, Caroline, and Harvey Goldstein. 1983. *Monitoring Children: An Evaluation of the Assessment of Performance Unit*. London: Heinemann.

Glaser, Robert. 1963. Instructional technology and the measurement of learning outcomes: Some questions. *American Psychologist* 18: 519–521.

Glaser, Robert, and J. Reynolds. 1964. "Instructional Objectives Programmed Instructions: A Case Study." In *Defining and Educational Objectives*, edited by C. Mauritz Lindvall. Pittsburgh: University of Pittsburgh Press.

Goodlad, John I. 1984. *A Place Called School*. New York: McGraw-Hill.

Goodlad, John I., M. Frances Klein, and Kenneth A. Tye. 1979. "The Domains of Curriculum and Their Study." In *Curriculum Inquiry. The Study of Curriculum Practice*, edited by John I. Goodlad, 43–76. New York: McGraw-Hill.

Gordon, Peter, and Denis Lawton. 1978. *Curriculum Change in the 19th and 20th Centuries*. New York: Holmes and Meier.

Gordon, Shirley C. 1968. *Reports and Repercussions in West Indian Education, 1835–1933*. London: Ginn.

Greenberg, David H., and Philip Robins. 1978. The changing role of social experiments in policy analysis. *Journal of Policy Analysis and Management* 5(2): 340–362.

Greene, Harry, Albert Jorgensen, and J. Raymond Gerbrich. 1943. *Measurement and Evaluation in the Secondary School*. New York: Longmans Green.

Greeno, James G. 1989. A perspective on thinking. *American Psychologist* 44(2): 134–141.

Guba, Egon G. 1969. The failure of educational evaluation. *Educational Technology* 9(4): 29–38.

Guba, Egon G. 1978. *Toward a Methodology of Naturalistic Inquiry in Educational Evaluation*. Los Angeles: Center for the Study of Evaluation, University of California.

Habermas, Jurgen. 1974. *Theory and Practice*. London: Heinemann.

Haertel, Edward. 1989. "Student Achievement Tests as Tools of Educational Policy: Practices and Consequences." In *Test Policy and Test Performance: Education, Language and Culture*, edited by B. Gifford, 25–50. Boston: Kluwer Academic Publishers.

Haertel, Edward, and Robert Calfee. 1983. School achievement: Thinking about what to test. *Journal of Educational Measurement* 20(2): 119–132.

Haertel, Edward, Steven Ferrara, Meg Korpi, and Barbara Prescott. 1984. Testing in Secondary Schools: Student Perspectives." Paper presented at the annual meeting, American Educational Research Association, April 23–27, New Orleans.

Haggerty, M. E. 1918. "Specific Uses of Measurement in the Solution of School Problems." In *The Measurement of Educational Products*. Seventeenth Yearbook of the National Society for the Study of Education, edited by Guy M. Whipple, 25–40. Bloomington, IN: Public School Co.

Haladyna, Thomas M., Susan B. Nolen, and N. S. Hass. 1989. *Report to the Arizona Legislature: Test Score Pollution*. Phoenix: Arizona State University West Campus.

Hall, Edward T. 1977. *Beyond Culture*. Garden City, NY: Doubleday.

Hamilton, W. 1853. *Discussions in Philosophy and Literature, Education and University Reform*, 2nd ed. London: Longman.

Haney, Walt, 1981. Validity, vaudeville, and values: A short history of social concerns over standardized testing. *American Psychologist* 36(10): 1021–1034.

Haney, Walt, 1983. "Validity and Competency Tests." In *The Courts, Validity and Minimum Competency Testing*, edited by George F. Madaus, 63–93. Boston: Kluwer-Nijhoff.

Haney, Walt, and George F. Madaus. 1989. Searching for alternatives to standardized tests: Whys, whats, and whethers. *Phi Delta Kappan* 70(9): 683–687.

Haney Walt, George F. Madaus, and Robert Lyons. In press. *The Fractured Market Place for Standardized Testing*. Boston: Kluwer Academic Publishers.

Haney, Walt, and Laurie Scott. 1987. "Talking with Children About Tests: An Exploratory Study of Test Item Ambiguity." In *Cognitive and Linguistic Analysis of Test Performance*, edited by Roy O. Freedle and Richard Duran, 298–368. Norwood, NJ: Ablex.

Hartog, Philip, and Edmund C. Rhodes. 1935. *An Examination of Examinations*. London: Macmillan.

Hawkes, Herbert E., E. F. Lindquist, and C. R. Mann. 1936. *The Construction and Use of Achievement Examinations*. Boston: Houghton Mifflin.

Hearn, W. E. 1872. *Payment by Results in Primary Education*. Melbourne: Stellwell and Knight.

Herman, Joan L., and Donald W. Dorr-Bremme. 1983. Uses of testing in the schools: A national profile. *New Directions for Testing and Measurement* (19): 7–17.

Heyneman, Stephen P. 1987. Uses of examinations in developing countries: Selection, research, and education sector management. *International Journal of Educational Development* 7(4): 251–263.

Holmes, Edmund G. A. 1911. *What Is and What Might Be: A Study of Education in General and Elementary in Particular*. London: Constable.

Hoskins, Keith. 1968. The examination, disciplinary power and rational schooling. *History of Education* 8: 135–146.

Hotyat, Fernand. 1958. "Evaluations in Education." In *Reports on an International Meeting of Experts held at the UNESCO Institute for Education*, edited by UNESCO. Hamburg: UNESCO.

House, Ernest R. 1983. "Assumptions Underlying Evaluation Models." In *Evaluation Models*, edited by George F. Madaus, Michael S. Scriven, and Daniel L. Stufflebeam. Boston: Kluwer-Nijhoff.

Hughes, R. N. 1979, March 15. Education could pay. *New York Times*.

Intermediate Education Act (Ireland). 1878. 41, 42, Vict. C.66

Jackson, P. W. 1968. *Life in Classrooms*. New York: Holt, Rinehart and Winston.

Jacob, Evelyn. 1987. Qualitative research traditions: A review. *Review of Educational Research* 57(1): 1–50.

Jaeger, Richard. 1989. "Certification of Student Competence." In *Educational Measurement*, 3rd ed., edited by Robert Linn, 485–514. New York: Macmillan.

Johnstone, James N. 1981. *Indicators of Education Systems*. Paris: UNESCO.

Joint Committee on Standards for Educational Evaluation. 1981. *Standards for Evaluation of Educational Programs, Projects and Materials*. New York: McGraw-Hill.

Judd, Charles H. 1918. "A Look Forward." In *The Measurement of Educational Products*. Seventeenth Yearbook of the National Society for the Study of Education, Part II, edited by Guy M. Whipple. Bloomington, IN: Public School Co.

Kamii, Constance, ed. In press. *Achievement Testing in Early Childhood Education. The Games Grown-Ups Play*. Washington, DC: National Association for the Education of Young Children.

Kellaghan, Thomas, and Vincent Greaney. 1991. *Using Examinations to Improve Education: A Study in Fourteen African Countries*. Washington, DC: World Bank.

Kellaghan, Thomas, George F. Madaus, and Peter W. Airasian. 1982. *The Effects of Standardized Testing*. Boston: Kluwer-Nijhoff.

Kelly, Albert V. 1989. *The Curriculum. Theory and Practice*, 3rd ed. London: Chapman.

Koerner, James D. 1968. *Reform in Education: England and the United States*. New York: Delacorte Press.

Koretz, Daniel. 1988. Arriving in Lake Wobegon. Are standardized tests exaggerating achievement and distorting instruction? *American Educator* 12(2): 8–15, 46–52.

Koslin, Bertram L., Susan Zeno, and Sandra Koslin. 1987. *The DRP: An Effectiveness Measure in Reading*. New York: College Board.

Krawthwohl, David R., Benjamin S. Bloom, and Bertram B. Masia. 1964. *Taxonomy of Educational Objectives: The Classification of Educational Goals. Handbook II: Affective Domain*. New York: McKay.

Kreitzer, Amelia E., Walt Haney, and George F. Madaus. 1989. "Competency Testing and Dropouts." In *Dropouts from School: Issues, Dilemmas, and Solutions*, Part II, edited by Lois Weis, Eleanor Farr, and Hugh G. Petrie, 129–152. New York: State University of New York.

Laffer, A. B. 1982, June 9. For better schools, pay achievers. *Education Week*: 24.

Lee, J. M. 1936. *A Guide to Measurement in Secondary Schools*. New York: Appleton Century.

Leinhardt, Gaea. 1983. Overlap: Testing whether it is taught. In *The Courts, Validity and Minimum Competency Testing*, edited by George F. Madaus. Boston: Kluwer-Nijhoff.

Leinhardt, Gaea, and Andrea M. Seewald. 1981. Overlap: What's tested, what's taught? *Journal of Educational Measurement* 18(2): 85–96.

LeMahieu, Paul G. 1984. The effects on achievement and instructional content of a program of student monitoring through frequent testing. *Educational Evaluation and Policy Analysis* 6(2): 175–187.

Lerner, Barbara. 1981. The minimum competency testing movement: Social, scientific, and legal implications. *American Psychologist* 36(10): 1057–1066.

Levine, Donald M., ed. 1971. *Performance Contracting in Education. An Appraisal: Toward a Balanced Perspective*. Englewood Cliffs, NJ: Educational Technology Publications.

Lindquist, Everet F. 1954. "The Iowa Electronic Test Processing Equipment." In *1953 Invitational Conference on Testing Problems*, corporate ed., 160–168. Princeton, NJ: Educational Testing Service.

Linn, Robert L., ed. 1989. *Educational Measurement*, 3rd ed. New York: Macmillan.

Linn, Robert L. 1990. Essentials of student assessment: From accountability to instructional aid. *Teachers College Record* 91(3): 422–436.

Linn, Robert L., M. Elizabeth Graue, and Norris M. Sanders. 1989. "Comparing State and District Test Results to National Norms: Interpretations of Scoring 'Above the National Average.'" Paper presented at the annual meeting, American Educational Research Association, San Francisco.

Little, Angela. 1982. "The Role of Examinations in the Promotion of 'The Paper Qualification Syndrome.'" In *Paper Qualification Syndrome (PQS) and Unemployment of School Leavers. A Comparative Sub-Regional Study*. Addis Ababa: International Labour Office.

McClung, M. S. 1979. Competency testing programs: Legal and educational issues. *Fordham Law Review* 47: 652–712.

McCormick, Robert, and Mary James. 1983. *Curriculum Evaluation in Schools*, 2nd ed. London: Routledge & Kegan Paul.

Macdonald, James B., and Dwight Clark. 1973. "Critical Value Questions and the Analyses of Objectives and Curriculum." In *Second Handbook of Research on Teaching*, edited by Robert M. W. Travers, 405–412. Chicago: Rand McNally.

MacDonald-Ross, Michael. 1973. Behavioral objectives: A critical review. *Instructional Science* 2(1): 1–52.

McNeil, Linda M. 1988. Contradictions of control, Part 2. Teachers, students and curriculums. *Phi Delta Kappan* 70(6): 432–438.

Madaus, George F. 1979. Testing and funding: Measurement and policy issues. *New Directions for Testing and Measurement* (1): 53–62.

Madaus, George F. ed. 1983. *The Courts, Validity and Minimum Competency Testing*. Boston: Kluwer-Nijhoff.

Madaus, George F. 1985. Public policy and the testing profession—You've never had it so good? *Educational Measurement: Issues and Practices* 4(4): 5–11.

Madaus, George F. 1986. "The Perils and Promises of New Tests and New Technologies: Dick and Jane and the Great Analytical Engine?" In *Proceedings of the 1985 ETS Invitational Conference*, corporate ed., edited by Eileen E. Freeman, 87–101. Princeton NJ: Educational Testing Service.

Madaus, George F. 1988. "The Influence of Testing on the Curriculum." In *Critical Issues in Curriculum*. Eighty-seventh Yearbook of the National Society for the Study of Education, Part 1, edited by Laurel N. Tanner, 83–121. Chicago: University of Chicago Press.

Madaus, George F. 1989. "The Irish Study Revisited." In *Test Policy and Test Performance: Education, Language, and Culture*, edited by Bernard R. Gifford, 63–89. Boston: Kluwer-Nijhoff.

Madaus, George F., Peter W. Airasian, and Thomas Kellaghan. 1980. *School Effectiveness: A Reassessment of the Evidence*. New York: McGraw-Hill.

Madaus, George F., and Vincent Greaney. 1985. The Irish experience in competency testing: Implications for American education. *American Journal of Education* 93(2): 268–294.

Madaus, George F., Thomas Kellaghan, Ernest A. Rakow, and Denis

King. 1979. The sensitivity of measures of school effectiveness. *Harvard Educational Review* 49(2): 207–230.

Madaus, George F., and John T. McDonagh. 1979. Minimum competency testing: Unexamined assumptions and unexplored negative outcomes. *New Directions for Testing and Measurement* (3): 1–15.

Madaus, George F., and John Macnamara. 1970. *Public Examinations: A Study of the Irish Leaving Certificate.* Dublin: Educational Research Centre, St. Patrick's College.

Madaus, George F., Michael Scriven, and Daniel L. Stufflebeam. 1983. *Evaluation Models. Viewpoints on Educational and Human Service Evaluation.* Boston: Kluwer-Nijhoff.

Madaus, George F., and Daniel L. Stufflebeam. 1984. Educational evaluation and accountability: A review of quality assurance. *American Behavioral Scientist* 27(5): 649–672.

Madaus, George F., and Daniel L. Stufflebeam, eds. 1989. *Educational Evaluation: The Classic Works of Ralph W. Tyler.* Boston: Kluwer-Nijhoff.

Mager, Robert F. 1962. *Preparing Objectives for Programmed Instruction.* San Francisco: Fearon Publishers.

Mann, Horace. 1845. *Mann Papers.* Boston: Massachusetts Historical Society.

Marler, Charles D. 1975. *Philosophy and Schooling.* Boston: Allyn & Bacon.

Mehrens, William A., and John Kaminski. 1988. "Using Commercial Test Preparation Materials: Fruitful, Fruitless or Fraudulent?" Paper presented at the annual meeting, National Council on Measurement in Education, New Orleans.

Meier, Deborah. 1973. *Reading Failure and Tests,* Occasional Paper. New York: City College of New York.

Meier, Deborah. 1981. Why reading tests don't test reading. *Dissent* 28(3): 457–766.

Meisels, Samuel J. 1989. High-stakes testing in kindergarten. *Educational Leadership* 46(7): 16–22.

Messick, Samuel. 1989. "Validity." In *Educational Measurement,* 3rd ed., edited by Robert L. Linn, 13–103. New York: Macmillan.

Mill, John Stuart. 1859. *On Liberty.* In *Essential Works of John Mill,* 1961, edited by Max Lerner. New York: Bantam Books.

Monroe, Walter S. 1918. "Existing Tests and Standards." In *Measurement of Educational Products,* Seventeenth Yearbook of the National Society for the Study of Education, Part II, edited by Guy M. Whipple, 71–104. Bloomington, IN: Public School Co.

Montgomery, Robert J. 1967. *Examinations: An Account of Their Evolution as Administrative Devices in England.* Pittsburgh: University of Pittsburgh Press.

Moore, Donald R., and Suzanne Davenport. 1989. *The New Improved Sorting Machine.* Chicago: Design for Change.

Morris, G. C. 1969. "Educational Objectives of Higher Secondary School Science." Doctoral dissertation, University of Sydney, Australia.

Morris, Norman. 1961. "An Historian's View of Examinations." In *Examination and English Education,* edited by S. Wiseman, 1–43. Manchester, England: Manchester University Press.

Morrison, A. 1970. Some aspects of assessment in the classroom. *Scottish Educational Studies* 2(1): 95–101.

Mukerji, Shridhar N. 1966. *History of Education in India: Modern period.* Baroda, India: Acharya Book Depot.

Murnane, Richard J. 1987. Improving education indicators and economic indicators: The same problems? *Educational Evaluation and Policy Analysis* 9(2): 101–116.

Murphy, Roger, and Harry Torrance, eds. 1987. *Evaluating Education: Issues and Methods.* London: Harper & Row.

National Association of Test Directors. 1986. *Cheating on Standardized Tests.* Portland, OR: Multnomah ESD.

National Center for Education Statistics. 1985. *Indicators of Education, Status and Trends.* Washington, DC: U.S. Department of Education.

National Center of Effective Secondary Schools. 1987. Standardized testing: Problem or solution? *Newsletter* 2(2). Madison: School of Education, University of Wisconsin.

National Commission on Excellence in Education. 1983. *A Nation at Risk: The Imperative for Educational Reform.* Washington, DC: U.S. Government Printing Office.

National Commission on Testing and Public Policy. 1990. *From Gatekeeper to Gateway; Transforming Testing in America.* Chestnut Hill, MA: NCTPP, Boston College.

National Education Association. 1988. *NEA Research/Gallup Opinion Polls: Public and K–12 Teacher Members. Spring 1987 Annual Public Polls. Response.* Washington, DC: NEA.

Nitko, Anthony. 1989. "Designing Tests That Are Integrated with Instruction." In *Educational Measurement,* 3rd ed., edited by Robert L. Linn, 447–474. New York: Macmillan.

Noll, Victor H. 1957. *Introduction to Educational Measurement.* Boston: Houghton Mifflin.

Nuttall, Desmond L. 1981. *School Self-Evaluation: Accountability with a Human Face?* London: Schools Council.

Nuttall, Desmond L. 1990a. The functions and limitations of international educational indicators. *International Journal of Educational Research* 14(4): 327–333.

Nuttall, Desmond L. 1990b. Proposals for a national system of assessment in England and Wales. *International Journal of Educational Research* 14(4): 373–381.

Oakes, Jeannie. 1986. *Educational Indicators: A Guide for Policymakers.* Santa Monica, CA: Rand.

Oakes, Jeannie, and Neil Carey. 1989. "Curriculum." In *Indicators for Monitoring Mathematics and Science Education; A Sourcebook,* edited by Richard J. Shavelson, Lorraine M. McDonnell, and Jeannie Oakes, 96–122. Santa Monica, CA: Rand.

Office of Technology Assessment. 1987. *State Educational Testing Practices: Background Paper.* Washington, DC: Office of Technology Assessment, U.S. Congress.

Parlett, Malcolm, and David Hamilton. 1972. *Evaluation as Illumination: A New Approach to the Study of Innovatory Programs,* Occasional Paper No. 9. Edinburgh: Centre for Research in the Educational Sciences, University of Edinburgh.

Perreiah, Alan R. 1984. Logic examinations in Padua circa 1400. *History of Education* 13(2): 85–103.

Pipho, Chris. 1985. Tracking the reforms, Part 5: Testing. Can it measure success of the reform movement?. *Education Week*: 19.

Pipho, Chris, and Conn Hadley. 1984. *State Activity—Minimum Competency Testing,* Clearinghouse Notes. Denver: Education Commission of the States.

Popham, W. James. 1969. "Objectives and instruction." In *Instructional Objectives.* American Educational Research Association Monograph Series on Curriculum Evaluation, No. 3, edited by W. James Popham, Elliot Eisner, H. J. Sullivan, and Louise L. Tyler. Chicago: Rand McNally.

Popham, W. James. 1981. The case for minimum competency testing. *Phi Delta Kappan* 63(2): 89–92.

Popham, W. James. 1983. Measurements as an instructional catalyst. *New Directions for Testing and Measurement* (17): 19–30.

Popham, W. James. 1987a. The merits of measurement-driven instruction. *Phi Delta Kappan* 68(9): 679–682.

Popham, W. James. 1987b. Middle-minded emotionalism. *Phi Delta Kappan* 68(9): 687–689.

Popham, W. James, Keith L. Cruse, Stuart C. Rankin, Paul D. Sandifer, and Paul L. Williams. 1985. Measurement-driven instruction: It's on the road. *Phi Delta Kappan* 66(9): 628–635.

Rafferty, Martin. 1985. "Examinations in Literature: Perceptions from Nontechnical Writers of England and Ireland from 1850 to 1984." Doctoral dissertation, Boston College.

Raizen, Sentra A., and Joyce S. Kaser. 1989. Assessing science learning in elementary school: Why, what and how? *Phi Delta Kappan* 70(9): 718–722.

Resnick, Daniel P. 1981. Educational policy and the applied historian: Testing, competency and standards. *Educational Policy* 14: 539–559.

Resnick, Lauren B., and Daniel P. Resnick. In press. "Assessing the Thinking Curriculum: New Tools for Educational Reform." In *Cognitive Approaches to Assessment*, edited by Bernard Gifford and Michael C. O'Connor. Boston: Kluwer Academic Publishers.

Rice, Joseph M. 1897. The futility of the spelling grind. *Forum* 23: 163–172

Rosenshine, Barak V. 1976. "Classroom Instruction." In *Psychology of Teaching Methods*. Seventy-fifth Yearbook of the National Society for the Study of Education, Part II, edited by N. L. Gage, 335–371. Chicago: University of Chicago Press.

Ross, Clay C., and Julian C. Stanley. 1954. *Measurement in Today's Schools*, 3rd ed. Englewood Cliffs, NJ: Prentice Hall.

Rothblatt, Sheldon. 1982. Failure in early nineteenth century Oxford and Cambridge. *History of Education* 11(1): 1–21.

Royal Commission on Education, Great Britain. 1886. *Minutes of Evidence, Wednesday, 7 April. Mathew Arnold, Esq. Further Examined*. London: Her Majesty's Stationery Office.

Ruch, Giles M. 1929. *The Objective of New Types of Examination: An Introduction to Educational Measurement*. New York: Scott, Foresman.

Rugg, Harold O., ed. 1927. *The Foundations of Curriculum Making*. Twenty-sixth Yearbook of the National Society for the Study of Education. Chicago: National Society for the Study of Education.

Salmon-Cox, Leslie. 1981. Teachers and standardized achievement tests: What's really happening? *Phi Delta Kappan* 62: 631–634.

Salmon-Cox, Leslie. 1982. *Social Functions of Testing*, Technical Report. Pittsburgh: Learning Research and Development Center, University of Pittsburgh.

Schmidt, William H., Andrew C. Porter, John R. Schwille, Robert E. Floden, and Donald J. Freeman. 1983. "Validity as a Variable: Can the Same Certification Test Be Valid for All Students?" In *The Courts, Validity and Minimum Competency Testing*, edited by George F. Madaus, 133–151. Boston: Kluwer-Nijhoff.

Schwab, Joseph J. 1989. Testing and the curriculum. *Journal of Curriculum Studies* 21(1): 1–10.

Scriven, Michael S. 1967. "The Methodology of Evaluation." In *Perspectives of Curriculum Evaluation*, edited by Ralph Tyler, Robert Gagné, and Michael S. Scriven, 39–83. Chicago: Rand McNally.

Scriven, Michael S. 1973. "Goal-Free Evaluation." In *School Evaluation: The Politics and Process*, edited by Ernest House. Berkeley, CA: McCutchan.

Shanker, Albert. 1986, October 26. Power v knowledge in St. Louis: Professional under fire. *New York Times*.

Shanker, Albert. 1988, April 24. Exams fail the test. *New York Times*.

Shavelson, Richard J., and Paula Stern. 1981. Research on teachers' pedagogical thoughts, judgments, decisions, and behavior. *Review of Educational Research* 51(4): 455–498.

Shepard, Lorrie A. 1989a. "Inflated Test Score Gains: Is It Old Norms or Teaching to the Test?" Paper presented at symposium on "Cannell Revisited: Accountability, Test Score Gains, Normative Comparisons and Achievement" at the annual meeting, American Educational Research Association, San Francisco.

Shepard, Lorrie A. 1989b. Why we need better assessments. *Educational Leadership* 46(7): 4–9.

Shepard, Lorrie A. and A. Kreitzer. 1987. "The Texas Teacher Test." Paper presented at the annual meeting, American Educational Research Association, Washington, DC.

Shepard, Lorrie A., and Mary L. Smith. 1986. Synthesis of research on school readiness and kindergarten retention. *Educational Leadership* 44(3): 78–86.

Shepard, Lorrie A., and Mary L. Smith. 1989. Escalating academic demand in kindergarten: Counterproductive policies. *Elementary School Journal* 89(2): 135–146.

Skilbeck, Malcolm. 1976. "Openness and Structure in the Curriculum." In *Open University Course Unit 26*. Milton Keynes, England: Open University Press.

Smith, Adam. 1846. *An Inquiry into the Nature and Causes of the Wealth of Nations*. Edinburgh: Adam & Charles Black, and William Tait.

Smith, Eugene R., and Ralph W. Tyler. 1942. *Appraising and Recording Student Progress*. New York: Harper & Row.

Smith, Mary L. 1987. Publishing qualitative research. *American Educational Research Journal* 24(2): 173–183.

Smith, Mary L., and Lorrie A. Shepard. 1987. What doesn't work: Explaining policies of retention in the early grades. *Phi Delta Kappan* 69(2): 129–134.

Smith, Mary L., and Lorrie A. Shepard. 1988. Kindergarten readiness and retention: A qualitative study of teachers' beliefs and practices. *American Educational Research Journal* 25(3): 307–333.

Snow, Richard E., and David F. Lohman. 1989. "Implications of Cognitive Psychology for Educational Measurement." In *Educational Measurement*, 3rd ed., edited by Robert L. Linn, 263–331. New York: Macmillan.

Snow, Richard E., and Elanna Yalow. 1982. "Education and Intelligence." In *Handbook of Human Intelligence*, edited by Robert J. Sternberg, 493–585. Cambridge, England: Cambridge University Press.

Spaulding, F. T. 1938. *High School and Life: The Regent's Inquiry into the Character and Cost of Public Education in New York*. New York: McGraw-Hill.

Srinivasan, Joseph T. 1971. "Annual Terminal Examinations in the Jesuit High Schools of Madras, India." Doctoral dissertation, Boston College.

Stake, Robert E. 1967. The countenance of educational evaluation. *Teachers College Record* 68: 523–540.

Stake, Robert E. 1983. "Program Evaluation, Particularly Responsive Evaluation." In *Evaluation Models. Viewpoints on Educational and Human Services Evaluation*, edited by George F. Madaus, Michael S. Scriven, and Daniel L. Stufflebeam, 287–310. Boston: Kluwer-Nijhoff.

Stake, Robert E., Robin McTaggart, and Marilyn Munski. 1985. *An Illinois Pair: A Case Study of School Art in Champaign and Decatur*. Urbana: CIRCE, University of Illinois.

Stake, Robert E., and Paul Theobeld. 1988. Teachers in seven states: Testing as helping schools. Educational assessment and policy use. *Newsletter of ECAP Researchers* (5).

Stanley, Julian C., and Kenneth D. Hopkins. 1972. *Educational and Psychological Measurement and Evaluation*. Englewood Cliffs, NJ: Prentice Hall.

Starch, D., and E. C. Elliot. 1912. Reliability of grading high school work in English. *School Review* 21: 442–457.

Starch, D., and E. C. Elliot. 1913. Reliability of grading work in mathematics. *School Review* 21: 254–259.

Stedman, Lawrence C., and Carl F. Kaestle. 1985. The test score decline is over: Now what? *Phi Delta Kappan* 67(3): 204–210.

Stedman, Lawrence C., and Carl F. Kaestle. 1987. Literacy and reading performance in the United States, from 1880 to the present. *Reading Research Quarterly* 22(1): 8–43.

Stedman, Lawrence C., and Marshall S. Smith. 1983. Recent reform proposals for American education. *Contemporary Education Review* 2(2): 85–104.

Stenhouse, Lawrence. 1975. *An Introduction to Curriculum Research and Development*. London: Heinemann.

Stetz, F. P., and Michael D. Beck. 1978. "A Survey of Opinions Concerning Uses of Standardized Tests." Paper presented at the annual meeting, National Council on Measurement in Education, Toronto.

Stiggins, Richard J., and Nancy J. Bridgeford. 1985. The ecology of classroom assessment. *Journal of Educational Measurement* 22(4): 271–286.

Stiggins, Richard J., Nancy F. Conklin, and Nancy J. Bridgeford 1986. Classroom assessment: A key to effective education. *Educational Measurement: Issues and Practice* 5(2): 5–17.

Stiggins, Richard J., David A. Frisbie, and Philip A. Griswold. 1989. Inside high school grading practices: Building a research agenda. *Educational Measurement: Issues and Practice* 8(2): 5–14.

Stodolsky, Susan S. 1988. *The Subject Matters: Classroom Activity in Math and Social Studies*. Chicago: University of Chicago Press.

Stufflebeam, Daniel L. 1983. "The CIPP Model for Program Evaluation." In *Evaluation Models. Viewpoints on Educational and Human Services Evaluation*, edited by George F. Madaus, Michael S. Scriven, and Daniel L. Stufflebeam, 117–141. Boston: Kluwer-Nijhoff.

Stufflebeam, Daniel L., and Anthony J. Shinkfield. 1985. *Systematic Evaluation*. Boston: Kluwer-Nijhoff.

Stufflebeam, Daniel L., and William J. Webster. 1983. "An Analysis of Alternative Approaches to Evaluation." In *Evaluation Models. Viewpoints on Educational and Human Services Evaluation*, edited by George F. Madaus, M. Scriven, and Daniel L. Stufflebeam, 23–43. Boston: Kluwer-Nijhoff.

Sutherland, Gillian. 1973. *Elementary Education in the Nineteenth Century*. London: London Historical Association.

Taba, Hilda. 1962. *Curriculum Development. Theory and Practice*. New York: Harcourt Brace and World.

Terman, Lewis M. 1919. *The Intelligence of School Children*. Boston: Houghton Mifflin.

Thorndike, Edward L. 1918. "The Nature, Purposes and General Methods of Measurements of Educational Products." In *The Measurement of Educational Products*. Seventeenth Yearbook of the National Society for the Study of Education, Part II, edited by Guy M. Whipple, 16–24. Bloomington, IL: Public School Co.

Travers, Robert M. W. 1983. *How Research Has Changed American Schools: A History from 1840 to the Present*. Kalamazoo, MI: Mythos Press.

Turner, Glenn. 1984. "Assessment in the Comprehensive School: What Criteria Count?" In *Selection, Certification and Control*, edited by Patricia Broadfoot, 67–81. New York: Falmer.

Tyack, David, and Elizabeth Hansot. 1982. *Managers of Virtue: Public School Leadership in America*. New York: Basic Books.

Tyler, Ralph W. 1934. *Constructing Achievement Tests*. Columbus: Ohio State University.

Tyler, Ralph W. 1949. *Basic Principles of Curriculum and Instruction*. Chicago: University of Chicago Press.

Tyler, Ralph W. 1963. "The Impact of External Testing Programs." In *The Impact and Improvement of School Testing Programs*. Sixty-second Yearbook of the National Society for the Study of Education, Part II, edited by Warren G. Findley, 193–210. Chicago: University of Chicago Press.

Tyler, Ralph W., and Douglas Waples. 1930. *Research Methods and Teacher Problems*. New York: Macmillan.

Tynan, Michael. 1985. *Catholic Instruction in Ireland 1720–1950*. Dublin: Four Courts Press.

Walker, Decker, and Jon Schaffarzick. 1974. Comparing curricula. *Review of Educational Research* 44(1): 83–111.

Walkerdine, Valerie. 1988. *The Mastery of Reason: Cognitive Development and the Production of Rationality*. London: Routledge & Kegan Paul.

Wheeler, D. K. 1967. *Curriculum Process*. London: University of London Press.

Wheelock, Anne K., and Gayle Dorman. 1989. *Before It's Too Late: Dropout Prevention in the Middle Grades*. Boston: Massachusetts Advocacy Center.

White, E. E. 1888. Examinations and promotions. *Education* 8: 519–522.

Wiggins, Grant. 1989. A true test: Toward more authentic and equitable assessment. *Phi Delta Kappan* 70(9): 703–713.

Willems, Edwin P., and Harold L. Raush. 1969. *Naturalistic Viewpoints in Psychological Research*. New York: Holt, Rinehart and Winston.

Willis, Paul. 1977. *Learning to Labour: How Working Class Kids Get Working Class Jobs*. Farnborough, England: Saxon House.

Winner, Langdon. 1986. *The Whale and the Reactor: A Search for Limits in an Age of High Technology*. Chicago: University of Chicago Press.

Wise, Arthur E. 1979. *Legislated Learning: The Bureaucratization of the American Classroom*. Berkeley: University of California Press.

Wiseman, Stephen, ed. 1961. *Examinations and English Education*. Manchester, England: Manchester University Press.

Wodtke, K. H., Gregory F. Harper, Marlene Schommer, and P. Brunelli. 1985. "How Standardized Is School Testing? An Exploratory Observational Study of Standardized Group Testing in Kindergarten." Paper presented at the annual meeting, American Educational Research Association, Chicago.

Woody, Clifford, and Paul V. Sangren. 1933. *Administration of the Testing Program*. New York: World Book Co.

Worthen, Blaine R., and James R. Sanders. 1987. *Educational Evaluation, Alternative Approaches and Practical Guidelines*. White Plains, NY: Longman.

Wrightstone, Wayne J., Joseph Justman, and Irving Robbins. 1956. *Evaluation in Modern Education*. New York: American Book Co.

Part

2

HOW THE CURRICULUM IS SHAPED

6

CONSTRUCTING A HISTORY OF THE AMERICAN CURRICULUM

Herbert M. Kliebard
UNIVERSITY OF WISCONSIN-MADISON

Education, formal or otherwise, inevitably invites consideration of the question of what to teach, and efforts to chronicle and interpret why certain things have been taught in preference to others have followed naturally in the wake of those deliberations. In this sense, the history of curriculum is, practically speaking, as old as the history of education. As it has been traditionally practiced, history of education has generally included considerable attention to what was taught in schools. Since what we teach in schools is principally what we mean by the curriculum, the exact demarcation between the general domain of history of education and the presumably more restricted area of history of curriculum is difficult to establish. Rather than seeing those two areas in terms of firm boundary lines or one as encompassing the other, it may be more useful to delineate some of the controlling tendencies in curriculum history. The differences can probably be more productively expressed in terms of certain constituent properties associated with curriculum history than as a self-contained territory replete with borders and check-points.

Implicit in all the forms that curriculum history takes is the way in which social and political forces interact with both openly articulated and subtly intimated preferences as to school knowledge. One particular consideration that has given rise to history of curriculum as a more or less identified area of study and given it some legitimacy is the recognition that the knowledge that becomes embodied in the curriculum of schools is a significant social and cultural artifact. Seen in an archaeological sense, the curriculum in any period can be an invaluable relic of the forms of knowledge, social values, and beliefs that have achieved a special status in a given time and place. A curriculum is, after all, a selection of certain elements of a society's culture. Accordingly, when we know what areas of knowledge and belief have been consigned to schools for deliberate inculcation, it can help us understand what was consciously, or even unconsciously, valued in that society in particular periods. But reconstructing something of the values of a society from vestiges of its course of study is more difficult than it may seem. The established curriculum rarely, if ever, represents an explicit or even conscious consensus as to what knowledge is most valuable. While the curriculum is a product of a selective tradition, it is not always either conspicuous or calculated. Rather, its expression is the outcome of a complex interplay of competing values and traditions as signified by different interest groups and, at least in part, reflecting the meanings they attribute to social, political, and economic conditions.

Despite the fact that Herbert Spencer's question, "What knowledge is of most worth?" has, over time, taken on the status of the supreme curriculum question, the knowledge that schools actually purvey is not necessarily reflective of a society's consciously articulated hierarchy of knowledge tied to self-preservation (as Spencer would have wished) or to any other deliberately established criterion. Spencer's consciously directed emphasis on matters of self-preservation notwithstanding, decisions as to what gets taught in schools are often influenced by such factors as real or alleged economic considerations, national ideals, social change, the way in which schools are structured, gender, racial, and class distinctions, as well as symbol and ritual. Rather than representing an internally consistent and logically structured expression of a society's values, the curriculum is most likely to comprise a half-digested potpourri of knowledge and belief that in a given society has achieved sufficient status to be taught to its members or to subgroups thereof. A common problem in constructing curriculum history, therefore, is the tendency to assume that any curriculum is integral and coherent rather than the almost chaotic result of an interplay of forces, some rational and calculated, and a great deal that is instinctive or symbolic and ritualistic.

Just as the curriculum itself is unlikely to represent an internally consistent system of knowledge and belief, so the *process* of curriculum development is not necessarily a matter of reasoned deliberation. Walter Ong (1959, 103), for example, has suggested that the reasons offered as to why we teach certain things are not so much the product of careful premeditation as they are rationalized afterthoughts. Latin as part of the Renaissance curriculum, he argues, while it had a certain practical value, functioned principally as a puberty rite for boys. "Renaissance educators, like primitive peoples and like ourselves," according to Ong, "have no rationalized explanation for everything they do. They do certain things because they feel these things should be done, finding reasons for them afterwards if at all . . ." (122). In other words, we often make half-conscious decisions as to what knowledge is most appropriate to include in the curriculum and then afterwards devise the plausible-sounding reasons for so deciding. Those half-conscious decisions are tied in many instances to such matters as social class allegiances and to self-interest generally.

As such, curriculum history is not so much involved with traditional epistemological questions as with questions closely associated with sociology of knowledge. History of the curriculum, in other words, is critically concerned with what is *taken* to be knowledge in certain times and places rather than what is ultimately true or valid. In particular, it considers the factors that make certain forms of knowledge eligible for inclusion in the course of study in educational institutions as well as, in some cases, why other forms of knowledge are excluded (e.g., Hodson and Prophet 1983; Layton 1973; Teitelbaum 1987). In this respect, curriculum history is also concerned with curriculum efforts or curriculum movements that fail (or fail, relatively speaking) as well as those that succeed (or succeed, relatively speaking) in terms of implementation in schools. Why a curriculum fails, or succeeds only marginally, or becomes transformed over time can often tell us as much about social values and the relative power of social groups as those studies that focus on manifestly successful curriculum efforts.

While history of curriculum is closely tied to the question of why certain forms of knowledge are included in the course of study and others are excluded, it is also concerned with the effects, principally the social effects, that this inclusion or exclusion has. These consequences become particularly significant when certain social groups have access to certain forms of knowledge and gain special status through that access while others do not. A fundamental question imbedded in the history of curriculum, then, is not simply one of who went to school and who did not, but the way in which the social machinery may be constructed to differentiate access to certain forms of knowledge. What was the effect on women in Renaissance Europe, for example, of being excluded from the study of Latin, in particular as a rite of passage, even though they may have had access to schooling of some sort? Or, in a modern technological society such as the United States, what is the effect of segments of the school population being excluded from the study of algebra or highly regarded works of literature? Obviously, the answers to those questions are significant not just in a pedagogical sense but in terms of status attainment and social relations, if not social justice.

The history of curriculum as a field of study, therefore, is not only concerned with knowledge or even what is accepted as knowledge; it is also concerned with persons and with society generally. "The curriculum," as P. W. Musgrave (1988) contends, "is a major point of tension between the interests of the individual and society . . ." (11). Citing Karl Mannheim (1936, 45), Musgrave goes on to argue that this makes curriculum history necessarily social history in the sense that it deals with the relationship between social change and changing ideas. In this respect, it has the potential for organizing our understanding of curriculum issues by focusing on a range of interrelated elements. Among the most significant is why and under what circumstances certain forms of knowledge attain the standing necessary to be incorporated into a formal course of study while other knowledge configurations do not. But beyond that, it is concerned with the social ramifications and human consequences that accrue when certain segments of a given population have access to various forms of knowledge and belief that make their way into the curriculum of schools and others are denied it. Alluding to one social ramification, Terri Seddon (1989) argues that "Curriculum, the insitutionalized knowledge and beliefs transmitted to learners, appears as a key element in the 'selective tradition' which buttresses the existing social order" (5). Just as the curriculum is affected by social values and perceptions of social conditions, so too the curriculum can help reshape or preserve those values and conditions. The relationship between a society and its curriculum is reciprocal.

Another dilemma in the creation of a history of curriculum derives from the fact that school knowledge cannot be regarded as a fixed affair. What counts as knowledge in schools as well as in other contexts is fluid. In this sense, history of curriculum deals with the way school knowledge itself, as well as its status and significance, evolves over time. It is a mistake, as Raymond Williams (1961) once noted, to think of education as it if were "a fixed abstraction . . . a settled body of teaching and learning . . . as if the only problem it presents to us is that of distribution: this amount for this period of time, and to this or that group" (125). Seen in this light, the study of curriculum history requires going beyond access into those *evolving* structures of schooling that may lead to such significant social effects of schooling as the subordination of groups defined in terms of race, class, or gender, the school as a vehicle of social stratification, and the reproduction of inequality (Apple 1979). It also means giving considered attention to how that knowledge becomes transformed over time, as well as the different forms it may take for identified groups within even the same school population. This applies not simply to major upheavals in the curriculum such as those that tend to follow in the wake of significant political or social change; it also applies to the comparatively slow evolution of the course of study in periods of relative stability. The labels we attach to bodies of knowledge like science and English, because they are relatively fixed, are notoriously deceptive. It is true that what falls under the heading of science or English may indeed become embalmed as forms of knowledge in schools; but they are more likely to undergo internal transformations over the course of time as a consequence of evolving intellectual and social forces, as well as the actions and beliefs of those individuals and groups who are in a position to affect the curriculum. The seeming impenetrability of some aspects of the curriculum also presents a fascinating problem. Stability as well as change are highly critical factors to be reckoned with as historians try to make sense of why certain forms of knowledge are incorporated into the curriculum and others are not.

The fact that what does not achieve widespread acceptance in the curriculum can sometimes be as important as what does invites consideration of rival curriculum doctrines. Barring massive political and social upheaval, the dominant curriculum in any society is hardly ever subject to grand transformations. Rather, competing doctrines, drawing on fundamentally different social assumptions, are in a state of constant struggle for dominance. Since what becomes the curriculum is most likely to be the result of an unacknowledged compromise rather than a complete triumph (Kliebard 1986a; Williams 1961), the array of contending parties in the competition for acceptance in the school curriculum needs to be considered. Obviously, no curriculum doctrine should ever be confused with the day-to-day realities of the curriculum in schools. But the cumulative effect of small, frequently contradictory successes by opposing parties, against a backdrop of social trends and forces, is what the curriculum becomes.

Even such incomplete victories, however, are not achieved solely in the course of esoteric debates among the leaders of curriculum movements. Nor are they achieved by social and political events or trends alone. Neither the doctrine of social efficiency as expressed by its major leaders, for example, nor the orbiting of Sputnik *in and of themselves* had any effect on the curriculum. Rather, the drama of Sputnik made plausible or implausible certain ideas about the curriculum that had long been extant. It is in this sense that the history of curriculum focuses on the interaction between curriculum ideas and those political and social conditions that support or undermine their incorporation into the curriculum that is actually experienced at the school level.

CURRICULUM HISTORY AS AN IDENTIFIED AREA OF SCHOLARSHIP

The emergence of history of curriculum as a self-conscious area of scholarship is tied in certain respects to a serious reevaluation of historiography that began to take place in the 1950s within the framework of the history of education and which continued with even more vigor into the 1960s. A turning point was reached with the publication of Bernard Bailyn's historiographical essay in *Education in the Forming of American Society* (1960). One of Bailyn's major themes was that the writing of history of education generally had become imbued with a kind of missionary zeal and that the evangelism that had characterized the work of many chroniclers of American education had led eventually to a fatal parochialism. History of education, Bailyn argues, "grew in almost total isolation from the major influences and shaping minds of 20th-century historiography; and its isolation proved to be self-intensifying: the more parochial the subject became, the less capable it was of attracting the kinds of scholars who could give it broad relevance and bring it back into the public domain" (9). A significant concomitant of this parochialism is the standard interpretation of American history of education as an unremitting line of progress. For the budding teacher or school administrator, the study of the history of education had become a kind of initiation into a religion that proclaimed the triumph of the disciples of popular education over self-serving and heretical opposition. In a political sense, that achievement was commonly portrayed as the victory of democratic forces over the rule of entrenched aristocracy and elitism. In curriculum terms, the main battle lines were defined in terms of the adaptation and expansion of the American curriculum to the demands of a greatly expanded and also qualitatively different school population.

Bailyn's position was substantially endorsed in a subsequent historiographical essay by Lawrence Cremin (1965). Taking the widely read account of the history of education by Ellwood Cubberley (1919) as a case in point, Cremin agreed, at least in this case, that both parochialism and evangelism (among other "sins") are clearly evident (43). On one matter, however, Cremin takes issue with Bailyn, contending that the conflict in historical interpretation of American education was not so much opposition between historians and educationists but among historians generally. The widely read and patently sanguine account of the course of American education by the educationist, Cubberley, in other words, had counterparts in the work of Whiggish historians (43–45). Out of such self-criticism, a revivified history of education began to surface (Talbott 1971; Tyack 1970), and that new history included at least an implicit, if not an explicit, rejection of the celebratory history that had so long dominated the field.

As part of that reaction, some historians of education adopted a specific framework of class conflict in their interpretations. For Michael Katz (1968), for example, the crux of the new educational history became "the estrangement between the culture of the school and the working class community" (1–2). By 1976, however, Carl Kaestle (1976) suggests that, while the consensus view of the history of American education had some obvious deficiencies, the "Procrustean effort" to see all conflict as class-based has its limitations (394). It is possible, as Kaestle sees it, to be more precise in both the consensus and conflict formulations, as well as in finding an "elegant" rather than simply an eclectic way to combine the two. In particular, conflict in historical interpretation may take other forms than class conflict (395). It was within the context of this historiographic debate of the 1950s and 1960s and its aftermath that a specific identity for history of curriculum began to be forged. Born in the midst of factious controversy, the history of curriculum as a recognized area of historical scholarship has had a rather brief and somewhat shaky existence.

The writing of curriculum history, however, obviously predated its declared designation as an area of scholarship. Self-conscious attempts to chronicle the history of curriculum in particular, not just its incorporation into the broader area of history of education, obviously preceded its recognition as a subspecialty within history of education. One prominent example is Harold Rugg's (1926) long article (actually an entire section) on the subject in the 26th yearbook of the National Society for the Study of Education (NSSE). Rugg's account, while obviously exhibiting some of Bailyn's and Cremin's objections, has its merits. It is written with a rich gusto, and, at the least, provides in considerable detail some of the main events that characterized the development of the American curriculum between 1825 and 1925. A central theme is proclaimed in the opening sentence: "Not once in a century and a half of national history has the curriculum of the school caught up with the dynamic content of American life" (3). The curriculum, in general, is portrayed as constantly lagging behind significant social trends, such as the industrial revolution, and as a patchwork rather than a systematic organization of the cultural resources of American society. In ringing tones, Rugg calls for "prophetic leadership" especially through the curriculum (4), a "transformation of the individualistic order into a social one" (5), and ultimately "a generation of men and women . . . who settle matters of controversy on the basis of reflection rather than prejudice" (6). These were themes that Rugg sounded over the course of his long and productive career and marked the rise to prominence of a strain in curriculum thinking that emphasized the role of the curriculum in ameliorating the ills that beset social life, if not the actual reconstruction of society through a revitalized course of study.

If Franklin Bobbitt's *The Curriculum* (1918) marked the birth of curriculum as a professional field of specialization, NSSE's 26th yearbook, including Rugg's historical essay, marked its coming of age. There is hardly any question, however, that Rugg treats curriculum making in the past as a benighted prelude, if not to an enlightened present, at least to an auspicious future. What Cremin calls the "sin" of parochialism is present on almost every page of Rugg's essay (Walker 1975). According to Rugg (1926), the Committee of Ten approached its task "piecemeal—subject by subject"; its composition reflected a bias in the direction of subject matter; and its members represented the interest of colleges and private preparatory schools rather than public elementary and secondary schools (39). These were, of course, themes that dominated historical interpretations of the Committee of Ten for many years to come and were reflective of the mood in the burgeoning field of curriculum that the past stood as a kind of object lesson, something to be studied to be sure, but studied primarily as a justification for sweeping away the cobwebs of an unenlightened past. Rugg's conclusion proclaims a rejection of "unproved academic subject divisions of the past" and a movement in the direction of a what he called a "unified curriculum" (116). These again are the very directions that Rugg himself pursued in later years (Carbone 1977; Nelson 1978; Kliebard and Wegner 1987).

A notable exception to presentist interpretations of curriculum history is John Elbert Stout's (1921) *The Development of High-School Curricula in the North Central States from 1860 to 1918*. In fact, it is hard to extract from Stout's monograph any interpretive framework. It is a work, however, that is extraordinarily rich in detail and remains a valuable source of data on the development of the high school curriculum in the North Central region. There is, for example, documentation of the gradual shift in terminology from "Department" to "Course" as a way of designating a sequence of studies, as well as the early division of the curriculum into two courses of study, the Classical Course and the English Course. This bifurcation of the curriculum was a kind of forerunner of differentiation of the curriculum occurring first in the late 19th and then more elaborately in the 20th century. Stout's monograph also traces the disappearance or amalgamation of some of the early subjects, and, through an analysis of commonly used textbooks, is able to shed some light on what was probably taught under those subject labels. For example, over the period covered by the study, the teaching of grammar remained constant, but the teaching of literature went through rather significant transformations. The most radical changes in the course of study as a whole, however, occurred after around 1910. Of 60 high schools in the sample only 11 had more than four distinct courses of study in 1906–1911, while in the period 1915–1918 that number had already increased to about half (203–206). Although trends of this sort are noted, Stout almost studiously refrained from ascribing to them any social or even pedagogical significance.

In 1966, Mary Louise Seguel's *The Curriculum Field: Its Formative Years* was published as a kind of explicit recognition of the status that curriculum had achieved as a recognized subspecialty within the overall area of professional education in the period from 1895 to 1937. The book concentrates specifically on the work of certain major figures in the educational world—Charles and Frank McMurry, John Dewey, Franklin Bobbitt and W. W. Charters, Harold Rugg, and, finally, Hollis Caswell—and the way in which their efforts helped shape an established curriculum field. Each is seen as making a distinctive contribution, with these efforts advancing in a more or less incremental way the eventual emergence of curriculum as a professional field of study. Thus, for example, the work of the Herbartians, Charles and Frank McMurry, gave "needed order and system to the curriculum" (177), while Bobbitt and Charters "established the basic importance of a method of curriculum making" (178), and Caswell made curriculum an accepted field of study in colleges and universities (179). Seguel's work is patently a history of the development of an acknowledged professional field as opposed to a history of curriculum per se and reflects the pride that normally accompanies that recognition.

These historical works represent three examples of forerunners of curriculum history before history of curriculum began to be accepted as a scholarly enterprise in its own right. Perhaps the earliest explicit recognition of history of curriculum as a demarcated area of scholarship came in the form of a review of research on the history of curriculum in the *Review of Educational Research* by Arno A. Bellack (1969). Later signals of a specific identity include a yearbook on curriculum history sponsored by the Association of Supervision and Curriculum Development (Davis 1976), an entry written by Daniel Tanner (1981) in the *Encyclopedia of Educational Research*, and a chapter devoted to the history of curriculum (Kliebard and Franklin 1983) in the American Educational Research Association's publication, *Historical Inquiry in Education: A Research Agenda* (Best 1983). In addition, the Society for the Study of Curriculum History was founded in 1977 (L. Tanner 1989), and although its membership remains small, proceedings of some of its meetings have been published, and a 10th anniversary collection of papers delivered at its meetings has recently been issued (Kridel 1989). Craig Kridel has also initiated an archives collection at the University of South Carolina, and, in 1989 alone, two international conferences have been convened on the subject of the history of curriculum, one sponsored by the Institute für Pädagogische Wissenschaft in Kiel and the other by the Institute for Educational Research in Oslo.

A major theme in Bellack's (1969) review article is the ahistorical character of the curriculum field, and the sense in which the curriculum field is (or is not) ahistorical has been the subject of some debate. Part of the ahistoricism identified by Bellack was simply lack of knowledge of their past on the part of those associated with the curriculum field. John Goodlad (1966), for example, is cited as arguing that "a substantial number of the new crop of reformers have approached the persistent, recurring problems of curriculum construction in the naive belief that no one had looked at them before" (as quoted in Bellack 1969, 283). The implication, of course, is that those who are associated with the curriculum field lack an invaluable perspective on present issues by virtue of ignoring their past. One explanation for that form of ahistoricism was well expressed by O. L. Davis (1977). "The curriculum field," he says, "is an activist, largely nonreflective enterprise. Forward is the generally perceived direction of movement" (159). Born in the context of reform, the curriculum field tends to view the past as something to be gotten away from.

That stance, however, may lead to another, rather different, form of ahistoricism as well, which was also implied in Bellack's review. Reflecting concerns about presentism, Bellack refers to the position that "rallying cries and slogans" are treated "as if they had an immediacy they no longer possess" (Kliebard 1968, 69). Ahistoricism in this latter sense is represented by uncritical acceptance of fundamental ideas and ways of thought inherited from past curriculum leaders. The implication here is not that history of curriculum is simply being ignored, but that the presentism imbedded in what is actually a commonly cited history results in an obfuscating, rather than an illuminating, effect on curriculum issues. In a related criticism, J. Stephen Hazlett (1979) argues that the curriculum field is and perhaps always has been indeed "historically aware" but is nevertheless ahistorical. Like Davis, Hazlett maintains that this form of ahistoricism derives from the fact that curriculum is "a field of practical normative activity carried on with urgency in a crisis atmosphere" (131). Under these circumstances, the present almost inevitably intrudes on our understanding of the past, and the past becomes little more than a rationale for exhortations in behalf of urgent changes in the present.

Although no formal subspecialty in historical scholarship was actually being proposed by Bellack and others concerned with the evolution of the American curriculum, the emergence of history of curriculum was at least implicitly being justified on two grounds: One was simply that members of any professional group should know their past because it enlarges their understanding of fundamental issues and problems that characterize that field. The second, however, reflected the growing controversy within the larger framework of history of education as to whether what passed for history of curriculum manifested its ahistoricism, not so much in actually ignoring history, but in an explicitly Whiggish view of its past. That view, in turn, led to uncritical acceptance of recurring watchwords and slogans. In history of curriculum perhaps even more than in history of education, it appeared as if "the past," as Bailyn (1960) expresses the idea, "was simply the present writ small" (9), and that professional socialization in the field of curriculum included as one major ingredient an historical account of the modern curriculum as the unfolding of an inexorable march of progress. This issue of presentism still constitutes a serious form of tension between those historians of curriculum who take a consensual view of the evolution of the American curriculum and those who see it as the outgrowth of conflict among competing groups defined not simply in terms of class but in such other ways as ethnicity, ideology, race, and gender.

Ironically, the view of the history of curriculum as proceeding in a more or less orderly way in the direction of a grand consensus may itself have been a product of the historical setting and social milieu in which the curriculum field was born. Some historians have traced the emergence of curriculum as a field of professional identification to around 1918 (D. Tanner 1981; Kliebard 1968). As already mentioned, the first modern book on curriculum, Bobbitt's (1918) *The Curriculum*, appeared in that year, and it was also the year when the Commission on the Reorganization of Secondary Education issued its celebrated *Cardinal Principles of Secondary Education* (National Education Association 1918), long regarded as a milestone in a changed conception of the curriculum. The question of whether these and similar works in that period actually were influential or not in terms of school practice is only a minor aspect of their possible significance. Much of their significance lies in the way they reflected dominant intellectual and social ideas, whether in flux or relatively settled. Without benefit of critical historical reflection, the creeds they embodied were often passed on to subsequent generations as received doctrine.

Of at least equal importance to these reports themselves (as well as other historically significant events), therefore, is the way they have become part of the process of professional socialization. The earliest educational leaders to maintain an explicit identification with curriculum as a field of study, such as Bobbitt and Charters, regarded themselves as scientists, or at least engineers (Bobbitt 1912; Charters 1948). In broad terms, they saw their mission as bringing the light of science to the study of curriculum, a field that had been plagued in the past by vague speculation and imprecise formulations. Thus, the emphasis on science as the avenue to curriculum development at a time when the curriculum field was in its infancy may have helped shape the way the history of curriculum in modern times was perceived. In general, the modern curriculum was seen as the culmination of a succession of incremental scientific advances that had been made since the dark ages of the 19th century and before. In this respect, the predominant view of the history of curriculum, especially as it appeared in a variety of introductory textbooks (Schubert 1980), paralleled the more general victory of public education over various misguided opponents that Cubberley (1919) and others had proclaimed in the larger sphere of history of education (Cremin 1965). To the initiate into the field of curriculum, these interpretations were presented as part of professional holy writ.

Much of the work in history of curriculum over the past quarter century, in the United States at least, has taken the form of revising and reinterpreting the standard portrayals of what have been traditionally regarded as significant events or movements in curriculum over the course of recent history. The more frankly revisionist in tone have bluntly taken to task what they regard as biased and therefore unilluminating, if not self-serving, accounts of curriculum history. Certain heroes (and even classes of heroes) became villains, and celebrated victories were reinterpreted as setbacks. Others have subtly tried to shift the ground on which those debates take place. Class analysis and the role of racial minorities and women, either as agents or as victims, began to figure more prominently. In either case, these studies have had (at least here and there) a demythologizing effect on the way the evolution of the course of study is seen. The history of curriculum today is seen not so much in progressively incremental terms, but replete with false starts, wrong turns, and much backing and filling, as well as an advance here and there.

The sections that follow are not intended as a comprehensive history of the modern American curriculum, but as illustrations of how recent scholarship in the arena of curriculum history has sought to reconstruct earlier interpretations, as well as to indicate the status of certain current debates insofar as those interpretations are concerned. These sections reflect five different but related sources of controversy and concern within the domain of curriculum history: (1) the import of national trends in curriculum such as those as embodied in the recommendations of major curriculum committees; (2) the role and function of ideological movements in curriculum of broad scope, such as scientific curriculum making; (3) the validity or significance of basic ideas about curriculum as expressed by individuals (e.g., John Dewey); (4) methodological issues, especially the relationship of historical case studies to the overall question of historical inquiry into the curriculum; and, finally, (5) the particular focus on the evolution of school subjects as instances of the social construction of school knowledge.

INTERPRETING THE SIGNIFICANCE OF COMMITTEE REPORTS

A traditional but often criticized facet of curriculum history is the attention that has been lavished on such artifacts of curriculum as committee reports. It has been argued that attention to what this or that committee had to say on curriculum matters is hardly relevant to the curriculum as experienced in schools. That criticism obviously has merit, but it may also be overstated. If a report such as that issued by the Committee of Ten is indeed seen as an artifact, then it represents one form of evidence as to what at least one segment of the social and pedagogical community saw as legitimate or desirable knowledge. It is true that whether those recommendations were actually translated into school practice remains to be seen (Cohen 1987); but what does not get incorporated into the curriculum of schools is sometimes as important as what does. Moreover, the question of whether given recommendations were translated into practice may not even be the most important question one may raise about those reports. They may signal the waning or the arrival of certain particular fashions in curriculum, or even be a portent of what is to come.

A second area of interpretation tied to committee reports, as well as to curriculum movements and the work of individuals, lies in the process of myth making that often flows in the wake of historical interpretation. When presentism reigns, it becomes natural to hold up certain conspicuous events in the history of curriculum as representative either of an unenlightened past or of an uplifting future. Over time, these interpretations become petrified as the common wisdom within a professional field, and those standard accounts are rarely reexamined.

One of the earliest and most significant departures from predominant renditions of curriculum history can be illustrated by Edward A. Krug's (1964) reinterpretation of the recommendations of the Committee of Ten (National Education Association 1893), especially in relation to the *Cardinal Principles* report 25 years later. With remarkable consistency, the Committee of Ten, convened in 1892 under the leadership of Harvard University's illustrious president Charles W. Eliot, had been interpreted in curriculum textbooks, as well as in explicitly historical works, as an obstacle to be overcome in the American curriculum's procession of progress. Among the most damaging of the charges was that the committee reflected an elitist bias which took the form of imposing college domination on the high school curriculum. According to the standard interpretation, the committee simply failed to take into account the enormous variability within the high school student population. The academic bias that the Committee of Ten presumably reflected was commonly viewed as antagonistic to the needs, not simply of a growing student population, but one that was unable to cope with the rigors of subjects like algebra and foreign languages. For most of its existence, it should be recalled, the curriculum field has regarded the term "academic" as having clearly pejorative connotations (Hazlett 1979, 132). Therefore, from a presentist perspective, a committee report recommending a set of academic curricula would carry with it not only immense practical difficulties but antidemocratic overtones as well. It would represent the imposition of an unfair obstacle to the great mass of the student population and add an aristocratic cast to a school system struggling to extend opportunity to all.

Thus, in the traditional annals of curriculum history, the recommendations of the Committee of Ten were seen as an impediment to the procession of progress in curriculum making. By contrast, the *Cardinal Principles* report (National Education Association 1918), whose famous seven aims reflected a distinctly functional, rather than academic, orientation to curriculum making, was interpreted as representing an important corrective to the short-sighted and misguided views of the framers of the Committee of Ten report. The *Cardinal Principles* report was portrayed as declaring the independence of the high school curriculum from the academic yoke imposed by colleges and universities and, therefore, bringing the curriculum more closely in line with the real needs of adolescents. In this way, the artificial barrier between the curriculum of schools and the functions of daily living was being breached. According to the *Cardinal Principles* report, for example, each subject in the high school curriculum was enjoined to reorient itself in line with the functional aims that were being proposed. The venerated seven aims of the report actually represented categories of human activity (with the possible exception of "command of fundamental processes") to which the school subjects would be subordinate.

Diverging from the standard interpretation of the significance of committee reports, Krug (1964) advanced the view that the Committee of Ten sought such moderate reforms in the high school curriculum as enhancing the status of modern academic subjects in relation to classical ones, the principle of election of subjects (although not as explicitly enunciated in the report as Eliot himself would have liked), and that a high school education was primarily for "life" rather than for college admission. By contrast, the *Cardinal Principles* report is seen by Krug as recommending that the so-called academic subjects be "hauled before the bar of justice" and allowed to survive only "on the promise of good behavior" (376), that is, by demonstrating their efficacy in promoting those skills actually needed in the course of daily activity.

In essence, traditional interpretations of the two most significant committee reports in the modern history of curriculum were being stood on their head. Eliot and his colleagues on the Committee of Ten, long treated as elitist and tradition-bound, are portrayed as moderate reformers who were not yet ready to concede that "the children of the plain people" (Krug 1964, 169–189) then entering the high school were incapable of studying modern academic subjects. By contrast, the long-revered *Cardinal Principles* report is seen as recommending differentiated curricula tied to predicted social roles and thereby inhibiting access to significant forms of knowledge. Krug credits the chief architect of the *Cardinal Principles* report, Clarence Kingsley, however, with managing to avoid some of the extremes of vocationalism such as those being advocated by such prominent curriculum policymakers as David Snedden and Charles Prosser.

While the impact of committee or commission reports on the curriculum had long been the subject of inquiry, not just in the United States but in other countries as well, Krug had subtly changed the terms of those inquiries. Interpretations of curriculum policies, especially in the United States, had been most commonly framed in terms of the forces of "progressive" change versus "conservative" or "traditional" entrenchment. Krug raised the possibility, indeed the likelihood, that some change may be regressive in social as well as pedagogical terms and what had been regarded as conservative, especially when considered in the context of its time, may reflect desirable change. In particular, Krug revived the term "social efficiency," a term in common use in the early part of the 20th century, to describe the social and educational doctrine that lay behind reforms such as certain of the recommendations of the *Cardinal Principles* report. His use of that fundamental concept added new complexity to way the course of the modern American curriculum was perceived. Before Krug's reintroduction of the term, it had fallen into virtual disuse as a way of characterizing the ideology that lay behind many curriculum reforms in the 20th century.

Krug defines social efficiency as a blending of two forces for change in American education, education for social control and education for social service (249). Its widespread acceptance was not, in other words, simply a victory of "progressive" forces over the armies of tradition and reaction. Consistent with this interpretation, Krug also rejects the common assertion (Cremin 1961; Hofstadter 1963; May 1959) that John Dewey, long the symbol of progressive change in American education, had actually influenced the recommendations contained in the *Cardinal Principles* report. To be sure, the report included much of the language of democracy, but that in itself, according to Krug, is not sufficient as evidence of a direct influence. Significantly, contemporary arguments questioning the desirability of a differentiated curriculum for American schools now include, at least here and there, a more favorable interpretation of the long-denigrated Committee of Ten's recommendation of an academic curriculum for all (Oakes 1984).

Just as the significance of these reports cannot rest on the question of which was the more influential in terms of school practice, so is the matter of which was more pedagogically efficacious only part of the issue. As is the case with committee reports generally, none is likely to represent either an intellectual triumph or a major breakthrough in terms of school practice. Those reports are, however, reasonably representative of what passed for conventional wisdom about the curriculum in their respective periods. As such, the recommendations of the reports and the controversies they engendered can offer some clues as to the way in which certain forms of knowledge were being regarded relative to others. If nothing else, the fact that within a 25-year period the Committee of Ten (National Education Association 1893), the Committee on College-Entrance Requirements (National Education Association 1899), and the *Cardinal Principles* report (National Education Association 1918), all with increasing fervor, departed from the reigning classical curriculum in American secondary schools is a strong indication of how quickly status was being accorded to different forms of knowledge and new ideals of education generally were taking hold. By 1918, with the issuance of the *Cardinal Principles* report, the value not merely of classical subjects in particular, but of academic subjects generally, was brought into question.

If the curriculum in any period can indeed be seen as an artifact, then committee reports, as well as the formulated positions of various curriculum leaders (Carbone 1977; Drost 1967; Gutek 1970; Schubert 1980), can be seen as the pottery shards from which some notion of what passed for the curriculum in these periods can be at least partially reconstructed. To be sure, it would be a mistake to take documents of this sort to be the reality of the curriculum as implemented in schools or, most certainly, as the curriculum actually experienced by students in classrooms, but it would be equally erroneous to disregard such evidence as irrelevant to schools and classrooms. The four "programmes" recommended both for "life" and for college entrance by the Committee of Ten, for example, were drawn not merely from the imaginations of the committee members. In large measure, they were drawn from the secondary schools of that time and then idealized somewhat. Similarly, the *Cardinal Principles* report represents both an admittedly incomplete compendium of early 20th-century wisdom on the curriculum and a foreshadowing of major drives for curriculum change in the 20th century, such as vocationalism.

Considered as artifacts, even the late 19th-century committee reports offer substantial evidence of significant change and perhaps even revolution in the way the curriculum was perceived if not practiced (Burns 1987). In essence, the Committee of Ten report as well as its immediate successor, the report of the Committee on College-Entrance Requirements, signalled (but did not necessarily precipitate) a significant victory of the English curriculum or the "moderns," as the new subjects then bidding for entry into the secondary school curriculum were then called. The opposition between the English and the classical curriculum had, of course, been going on for some time. Benjamin Franklin's academy, especially that part known as the "English school," represented one of the most serious challenges to the old order in curriculum (Franklin 1749). Franklin's admixture of the two competing doctrines later met with some acceptance in 19th-century academies (Sizer 1964a) and fleeting success in an occasional high school such as the Cambridge, Massachusetts high school in the 1850s (Burns 1988), but for the most part, the English curriculum existed side by side with the classical curriculum in a kind of uneasy truce.

It is in this sense that the Committee of Ten report may be seen as a tentative but nevertheless significant sign of the integration of what had been two distinct curricular traditions—what Theodore Sizer (1964b) calls the "classical-humanist" and the "practical." The somewhat tentative nature of the final report was most probably a result of divisions within the committee as to the merits of two programs of study, with Eliot attempting a bolder move in the direction of the moderns and William Torrey Harris, the "great conservator" (Curti 1935, 334), leading those whose inclinations were more in the direction of classical subjects. Eliot, himself a scientist and advocate of electives, had so structured the subcommittees that the ultimate endorsement of the controversial doctrine of the equivalence of school subjects was almost a foregone conclusion. Nevertheless, the proclamation by the committee that a modern subject like French was the equivalent of Latin and Greek as a subject of study represented a considerable victory for the forces arrayed against the classical curriculum. Still more revolutionary (even in the context of present-day curriculum debates) was the unanimous recommendation on the part of all the subcommittees representing the different subjects that no curriculum distinction be made between the college-going and noncollege-going segments of the high school population.

The centerpiece of the report was, of course, the four "programmes" that the committee recommended both for college and for "life," and it is here that the compromises are most evident. Rather than recommending a curriculum that attempted an integration of the classical and modern subjects, the committee settled upon a set of four options. Even among those options, there were concessions to the modern subjects. Greek, for example, had long been the subject that was the hallmark of a college entrance program. But even in the classical program, the number of years of study required was reduced from the traditional three years to two as part of the committee's effort to postpone early "bifurcation," and Greek does not appear at all in the other recommended programs, even though they were all being recommended for entry into college. Even more dramatic was that both the modern languages and the English curricula did not even require the study of Latin, despite the fact that they were being recommended as the basis for admission for college as well as for "life."

Critics of the time as well as latter-day commentators charged the committee with hypocrisy, or at least inconsistency, and often for the same reasons. G. Stanley Hall, probably the most prominent and vociferous of the critics, objected to the recommendation that subjects should be taught the same way to all students, to the doctrine of the equivalence of school subjects, and to the idea that no distinction should be made between students preparing for college and those who were not. With particular vehemence, he referred to the latter group as "the great army of incapables, shading down to those who should be in schools for dullards or subnormal children" (Hall 1904, 510–515). The committee's hypocrisy, according to Hall, resided mainly in their effort to inflict the viewpoint of the colleges on secondary schools. As already indicated, in his historical review of curriculum in the NSSE's 26th yearbook, Rugg (1926) endorsed these criticisms in large measure. He declares, for example, that the committee "launched the era of *curriculum-making by college entrance*" (41, original italics) and strongly suggests that reformers since that time have been trying to remedy those ill effects. Modern interpretations of the committee's work are mixed on this point. Daniel and Laurel Tanner (1980), for example, interpret the Committee of Ten, its own protestations notwithstanding, as creating "superior and inferior tracks" (186). They point to the committee's statement that "the programs called respectively Modern Languages and English must in practice be distinctly inferior to the other two" (National Education Association 1893, 48).

Given the overall thrust of the report in the direction of the English curriculum, there are at least two explanations for this apparent inconsistency. In the first place, it may simply have been necessary for Eliot to compromise with the conservatives on the committee at that point in their deliberations. But Eliot, considered by many to be Harvard University's most eminent president, is unlikely to have been guilty of a blatant contradiction in the committee's main recommendations. It is more plausible to assume that, although an element of compromise may have been involved, the wording of the statement should simply be taken literally. It is very likely that "in practice" the classical and the Latin-scientific programs were in fact superior to the other two, at least in terms of such matters as the experience and competence of teachers and of textbooks and other materials associated with those programs. The committee was simply saying that there is no difference between the classical and the Latin-scientific programs on one hand and the modern languages and the English on the other in terms of some ultimate hierarchy of studies, but there is a real and practical difference between them in terms of the current state of educational practice.

Whether the Committee of Ten's controversial report actually impelled change in one direction or another is the subject of considerable debate. (Burns 1987; Kliebard 1986b; Krug 1964) At the least, it was the focus of a curriculum controversy that brought certain ideological differences into focus. Until recent times, the position espoused by the committee that all children and youth should be exposed to the same (or to a very similar) curriculum was taken to be an instance of failure on the part of educational conservatives to take into account the enormous variance within the school population (as Hall contended). The opposing position, that the curriculum should be differentiated according to the probable destination of the pupils, was generally regarded as the liberal view. In the light of current debate about the school as a vehicle of social mobility or of social stratification, there seems to be reason for a reappraisal of how that curriculum policy should be interpreted (Oakes 1984). In his response to his critics, for example, Eliot enunciated a position that resonates with the contemporary view that early differentiation in the curriculum can easily become a form of predestination. Who, he asks, gives the school the right to sort children according to dubious "prophecies" as to their future station in life? (Eliot 1905, 330–331).

No account of the significance of the Committee of Ten report would be complete without a consideration of Eliot's remarkable turnabout on the issue of a curriculum built on the foundation of the probable destination of students. In 1908, only three years after his impassioned defense of a curriculum for all in the interest of democratic values, Eliot (1908) announced unequivocally that even elementary schools had the duty "to sort the pupils and sort them by their evident or probable destinations" (12–13). Krug (1964) treats this proclamation as an "enigma," perhaps even something of an aberration, pointing out that Eliot in later speeches modified this position (226–227). Although he agrees with Krug that Eliot did indeed retreat on his new position within a year or so, Arthur Wirth (1972) offers the view that there were really "two Eliots," one that rejected determinisms of all sorts and urged a society as well as a school system based on free will (hence electivism), but also one who also recognized a kind of aristocracy of talent (101). Another interpretation sees Eliot's sharp reversal as related to the swiftly changing mood on the issue of curriculum differentiation, arguing that Eliot, at heart a committed defender of the liberal arts tradition, came to believe in the end that the curriculum he so long cherished, if it was to be preserved at all, had to be accorded to a small elite (Kliebard 1986a, 123–124). Stephen Preskill (1989) posits the view that Eliot's basic conservatism and social elitism, including hints of racism on some issues and concerns about waves of new immigrants from Southern and Eastern Europe, finally burst through in the end. Whatever may be the explanation, such a complete reversal on a fundamental issue of curriculum doctrine remains virtually unprecedented.

Eliot's retraction of his position on early bifurcation notwithstanding, the Committee of Ten report does indicate that, by the 1890s, the long-brewing controversy between the advocates of the classical and the English curriculum had reached a boiling point. The fact that the report conceded as much as it did in the direction of modern subjects is one indication that a major shift in the secondary school curriculum was taking place. For subjects like science, social sciences, and modern foreign languages even to be called the equivalent of Latin, Greek, and mathematics by such a prestigious committee (whether this was true in practice or not) represented a major advance in terms of their status as part of the school curriculum. That the report marked a shifting of a curricular balance that had long held sway is probably best indicated by the sometimes neglected report that was issued only six years later.

The Committee on College-Entrance Requirements (National Education Association 1899) was headed by Augustus F. Nightingale, a man who, in his own rapidly shifting positions, represents almost in miniature the radically changing direction of curriculum policy. As early as 1887, while principal of the Lake View Township High School, Nightingale staunchly held his ground against an assault on the status of Greek, arguing with some prescience that the next step would be the subverting of the status of Latin. Within 10 years, he lent his voice to the dismantling of those same subjects (Krug 1964, 34). In 1894, for example, he endorsed the recommendation of the Committee of Ten that no curricular distinction be made between the college-going and noncollege-going populations, further arguing that the Latin and Greek requirements by colleges represented an impediment to that policy. By the time he had been appointed to chair the Committee on College-Entrance Requirements in 1895, he had already moved beyond the position of moderate reformers like Eliot (Burns 1987). That Nightingale regarded his work as carrying forward the work of the Committee of Ten is clear. He even reported the work of the earlier committee as "admirable" in his own report (National Education Association 1899, 8). But a bare two years after they had begun their deliberations, Nightingale's rhetoric in one of the committee's progress reports became downright revolutionary: "One after another the old idols are broken. The giants that stood in the path and said to every student 'Let him who enters here' leave all behind but Latin, Greek, and mathematics, are growing limp and lifeless" (as quoted in Burns 1987, 31). In the end, the report managed to do away with one of the most controversial and cumbersome aspects of the Committee of Ten report, the four parallel courses of study.

The vehicle for effecting that dramatic transformation is now so widely accepted that it has, for all intents and purposes, lost its standing as a radical innovation. In its time, however, the change was regarded as nothing short of "Copernican" (Brown 1901, 449). Basically, Nightingale's committee recommended that the high school curriculum be represented as a 16-unit program of studies and divided into constants and electives. (A unit was defined essentially as a year of study.) The constants were represented by four units of foreign languages, two units of mathematics, two of English, one of history, and, finally, one in science. With 16 units needed for the high school diploma, this left four units available as electives. Two thirds of the high school curriculum, in other words, was conceived as common to the entire school population and one third left for choice among selected elective subjects.

As in the case of the Committee of Ten's recommendations, that course of study emphatically made no distinction between those students presumably destined for college and those who were not. Moreover, the distinction in terms of status between modern academic subjects and the classical was virtually obliterated. "The committee presents first the proposition," the report declared, "that the study of the English language and its literature is inferior in importance to no subject in the curriculum" (National Education Association 1899, 12–13). According to the committee, the study of English should incorporate both "the study of English literature and the cultivation of the art of expression" (13). Insofar as the crucial issue of the study of foreign languages was concerned, no distinction was made between modern and classical languages. What is more, in endorsing the principle of electivism, the committee went beyond a choice among predetermined programs of study, as was recommended by the Committee of Ten, making room instead for individual choice by subject.

In short, the report of the Committee on College-Entrance Requirements not only introduced the ingenious device of apportioning the high school curriculum according to a system of constants and electives; it translated into more explicit terms the doctrine of the equivalence of school subjects that the Committee of Ten had proclaimed. (Of course, the committee never envisioned the incredible range of courses that would one day find their way into the American high school curriculum. In *The Shopping Mall High School*, for example, Powell, Farrar, and Cohen [1985] found 400 courses not to be unusual.) It may be fruitless to argue whether those committee reports actually brought about the collapse of such subjects as Greek and Latin or whether the reports simply marked the time and articulated the already publicly held reasons why those changes were in the making. It is almost certainly the latter; but, in either case, despite the fact that far more radical proposals for change in the structure of the American curriculum were to follow in the course of the 20th century, the significance of the toppling of the classical subjects from the pinnacle they had occupied for about 300 years should not be underestimated.

Taken together, the reports of the Committee of Ten (1893), the Committee on College-Entrance Requirements (1899), and the Commission on the Reorganization of Secondary Education (1918) represent one sort of indicator as to how the curriculum was being perceived at a critical juncture in school affairs. By themselves, of course, they do not tell us very much about school practice; but the direction in which they point is consistent with other sorts of evidence. Nightingale's turnabout on the value of classical languages, for example, is mirrored in trends of high school enrollment in Latin. In 1900, about half of high school students enrolled in grades 9 through 12 were studying Latin. Half a century later, that figure had dipped to less than 8 percent. The precipitous decrease in enrollments in classical languages was accompanied by declines in such other subjects as algebra and physics. Even enrollments in modern foreign languages, for which Eliot sought equal status with the classical, have declined for most of the 20th century.

Another source of evidence consistent with what the committee reports recommended was the abrupt change in curriculum direction described by Robert and Helen Lynd in their classic study, *Middletown* (1929). As part of their effort to portray American life and values through an intensive investigation of one typical American city, the Lynds undertook a direct examination of the curriculum of the schools there. In particular, their contrast between the curriculum of Middletown schools in 1890 and in 1923–1924, when they were collecting their data, represents another kind of documentation of the trend to which the committee reports in question were pointing. In 1890, the curriculum of the Middletown schools bore a remarkable resemblance to what Eliot and his colleagues endorsed. By the early twenties, however, the functional direction which the *Cardinal Principles* report sanctioned was clearly in evidence. In particular, of 12 courses of study available in Middletown High School, all but 4 were distinctly vocational in character (192).

The evidence represented by data on enrollment by subject or by case studies of individual schools should not be interpreted as indicating the *influence* of committee reports. Rather they should be read as indicating one sort of consistency between different kinds of artifacts. While no one can assume that committee reports in themselves accurately convey the direction that the American curriculum took, neither can those reports be dismissed as irrelevant to constructing a history of the American curriculum.

Another sort of caveat also should be entered here, however. Whether they accurately reflect school practice or not, committee reports are themselves products of interactions with certain social and intellectual trends. Both the Industrial and the Darwinian revolutions, changes in the structure of the workplace, urbanization, demographic changes in schools, and immigration patterns all affected in varying degrees the way the committees, as well as their critics, perceived the role of school knowledge in American society. Neither committee reports nor the curriculum movements they frequently reflected were independent of the social milieu in which they were imbedded.

SCIENTIFIC CURRICULUM MAKING AND THE CHALLENGE TO ACADEMIC SUBJECTS

What has been said about the significance (or the lack thereof) of committee reports applies equally to curriculum movements, such as scientific curriculum making. As in the case of the *Cardinal Principles* report, old icons among curriculum movements became subject to reinterpretation. As the reexamination of the course of curriculum history proceeded into the 1970s, even the proud record of the early scientific curriculum makers, usually regarded as the progenitors of the curriculum field, came under critical scrutiny. The ideas of such formidable figures as Franklin Bobbitt, W. W. Charters, and David Snedden had not so much been openly revered as quietly, almost unconsciously, embraced. Such fundamental precepts in the curriculum world as the necessity for formulating explicit educational objectives as a prelude to curriculum planning, the emphasis on the relationship between what is studied in school and directly functional outcomes, and the stress on choosing a course of study on the basis of the student's probable role as an adult in the social order all derive from the formulations of the scientific curriculum makers. The absence of historical inquiry into the impact of their work and the relatively inconspicuous incorporation of their doctrines into modern curriculum thinking generally had left ideas such as those virtually bereft of critical scrutiny. They became simply the common wisdom within the professional world of curriculum making. Earlier reforms became regarded as at best timid and at worst retrenchment. Hardly a quarter of a century after the Committee on College-Entrance Requirements had laid such stress on English as opposed to the classical subjects, Rugg (1926), already a formidable figure in the curriculum world, characterized that emphasis as one where "formal discipline, memorization, literary dissection, held sway over vivid understanding" (43). Academic study itself was being identified with outmoded theoretical constructs such as mental discipline.

By the second decade of the 20th century, profound curricular changes were being proposed from a variety of sources, not all compatible; in fact, some were downright antagonistic to one another. William Heard Kilpatrick and the early leaders of the Progressive Education Association, for example, articulated the idea that the curriculum should be organized around the child's own needs and predilections. (The Progressive Education Association was organized in 1919 by Marietta Johnson, Stanwood Cobb, and others primarily associated with nonpublic, experimental schools [Graham 1967].) In particular, Kilpatrick (1918) challenged the very basis of the structure of the curriculum itself, the school subject. In place of the subject, he proposed what he called the project as the basic unit of the curriculum (Kilpatrick 1924). He identified the project with purposeful human activity and thus was able to claim that subject matter was not something set out to be learned, but a means to achieving human purposes. Mastery of subject matter was not the point of schooling as had been commonly supposed; subject matter was a means to something that lay beyond it. Although Kilpatrick attracted a devoted following in the educational world, and elements of his proposals were incorporated here and there, the impact of ideas that he promoted was not nearly as powerful as is commonly supposed (Cuban 1984).

By contrast, the scientific curriculum makers, while presenting ideas quite radical in their time, were not actually challenging the supremacy of subject matter itself as the basic stock-in-trade of the curriculum. Their challenge came in the form of attempting to substitute supremely functional subject matter for the academic subjects. The ultimate criterion for incorporation into the curriculum was not its status as a valuable resource of the culture, as was the case with the committee recommendations in the 1890s, nor with its compatibility with the child's own world, as Kilpatrick and his followers proposed, but with efficiency. Efficiency as it was endorsed by the scientific curriculum makers was a two-edged sword. In one blow, it promised to eliminate, first of all, the useless and the merely ornamental from the curriculum, thus creating a firm connection with what was learned in school and the actual duties that one needed to perform in life; and, second, it would make society itself more efficient by basing the curriculum on the probable destination of students. Supposedly, individuals benefit from not being burdened with subject matter of no use to them, and society benefits from citizens specifically trained for the social role for which they are destined.

Both child-centered educators, such as Kilpatrick, and scientific curriculum makers such as Bobbitt, Charters, and Snedden were deeply suspicious of academic subject matter as the basis for the American curriculum, but the reasons for that dissatisfaction were markedly disparate, and their proposals for reform were often conflicting. For Kilpatrick, academic subject matter was something merely set out to be learned with no connection to the child's world or way of thinking. Subject matter was the instrument for achieving human purposes. The curriculum, in his view, should be defined in relation to the child's own interests and with the full participation of children. For Bobbitt and other scientific curriculum makers, the curriculum was first and foremost a preparation for adult living. In their minds, academic subject matter was wasteful because, for the vast majority of adults, it did not function in any direct way in their roles as adults; large segments of the population were simply not destined to use it. More important, however, the knowledge that the various segments of the school population really needed in order to adapt to their future social role was being neglected. As scientific curriculum makers saw it, society did not need a population with their heads filled with academic subject matter as the late-19th-century committees recommended; society needed a school system that prepared future citizens specifically and directly for the social roles they would one day occupy. The school curriculum in this sense was perceived as the mechanism by which the social order maintained its stability and accorded each citizen his or her place in a smoothly running society.

It is this latter aspect of the efficiency criterion in curriculum that has attracted substantial criticism and controversy among historians of curriculum. It was becoming obvious to historians of the scientific curriculum movement that, imbedded in the seemingly innocuous, even beneficent, effort of scientific curriculum makers to streamline the curriculum was a controversial social ideal of great significance as well as considerable public appeal. That social ideal, "social efficiency," was a term in fairly common use by scientific curriculum makers themselves and their supporters but, as already indicated, had gone largely unrecognized by historians of the period until Krug (1964) revived the term. Certain key trends that had previously been characterized as progressive now more commonly were interpreted as falling under the far less favorable rubric of social efficiency.

For the most part, it was the social control component of the social efficiency movement, the schools' role in instilling values and standards of behavior, that raised grave social questions as to what were the nature and impact of many of the educational reforms in the first half of the 20th century, reforms that had casually been regarded as "progressive" by some historians of the period. The issue being debated was not whether social control should exist or not. As Krug expresses it, "No society, in fact, can exist without it" (250). Taken as society's mechanisms for instilling desired beliefs and behaviors in individuals, the issue becomes the fervor with which it is embraced, how it is used, what forms it takes, and with what effects. The great proselytizer for an emphatic emphasis on social control was the American sociologist, Edward A. Ross, whose series of articles on the subject in the *American Journal of Sociology* published between 1896 and 1898 were collected into one volume in 1901. In his *Social Control*, Ross (1901) is ardent in expressing the view that "the absence of hostile encounter is a mark of the social order" and that any individual's inclination to disturb that order "depends on their mental make-up" (2). Thus the "passive unambitious Hindu" presents a less serious problem than "the restless, striving, doing Aryan, with his personal ambition, his lust for power, his willingness to turn the world upside down to get the fame, or the fortune, or the woman, he wants . . ." (3). Those latter characteristics are what make the American more difficult to control even than the West European, hence the need for a conscious and concerted program to keep those characteristics in check.

Much of Ross's book comprises a registry of the mechanisms available to society that could accomplish that task. That responsibility was made particularly urgent by the decline of certain traditional institutions of social control, such as the family and organized religion, as well as the influx of immigrants with a motley set of characteristics. (A later book by Ross, *The Old World in the New* [1914], consists largely of a catalog of the desirable as well as the undesirable traits of a variety of immigrant groups. Thus, he avers that "The South Italian is volatile, unstable, soon hot, soon cool" [117] and reports that "Genial settlement residents who never tire of praising Italian and Greek, testify that no other immigrants are so noisy, pushing and disdainful of the rights of others as the Hebrews" [150].) When turning his attention to education as a means of social control, Ross (1901) admits that to think of education as "'an economical system of police' sounds rather brutal in this smooth spoken age," but he then goes on to cite as support for his position such sources of that belief as Swift, Napoleon, the Jesuits, and Webster, who, according to Ross, had no compunctions in so regarding the function of education. "The ebb of religion," Ross declares hopefully, "is only half a fact, the other half is the rising tide of education" (174–175). In this regard, Ross ruefully concedes that "the American common school had been given an intellectual bias" (176), with the result that it falls woefully short in its social control function. In his final chapter, Ross poses the question as to whether "humanity, having sown its wild oats, will now settle down and be good" (432). Ross finds some hope in what he called natural adaptation but, he concludes, "the more this adaptation is artificial, the less need it be natural" (437). It is clear to him that society's future could not rest alone on the operation of natural forces. Society's weapons against the natural aggressiveness of Americans, as well as immigrants with other undesirable traits in need of curbing, had to be employed. The schools, with the curriculum as their main instrument, could play a vital role in that task if only they could curtail their preoccupation with intellectual matters.

An early attack on modern manifestations of social control in the curriculum was launched by Joel Spring (1976), who argues that 19th-century forms of social control, by being so visible, made it obvious to the student that he or she was not free. The new socialized classrooms, however, gave the appearance of freedom, and this made them more dangerous (162–166). Later, Barry Franklin (1986), in a work devoted to the impact of the conception of social control on the American curriculum, traces the way in which Ross's conceptions of social control (as contrasted with Charles Horton Cooley's and George Herbert Mead's) made their way into the curriculum. While Ross was only indirectly involved in education, many who were influenced by his powerful arguments in behalf of social control worked directly in the curriculum field. Over the course of time, some of Ross's concepts became modified. The social visions of Bobbitt and Charters, for example, were not nearly as apocalyptic as was Ross's, and they tended to blend Ross's conception of social control with a strong emphasis on the same kind of sheer efficiency that Frederick Winslow Taylor had urged in the arena of scientific management.

Actually, it is rare to find in the work of Bobbitt and Charters any explicit expression of a social vision. Rather, they perceived their work as bringing the precision and rationality of science to a field that had been dominated by mere tradition and philosophical rumination. The social control function associated with their work was more implicit than openly proclaimed. When Charters, for example, undertook to develop a curriculum for women for Stephens College of Columbia, Missouri, he saw his work simply as tying the curriculum of that school to the actual work that the women students would perform as adults. If women's work consists of setting tables and caring for children, then it would be simply wasteful to teach them higher mathematics and science. Through the use of a questionnaire survey, in other words, Charters undertook to determine (scientifically of course) what the curriculum for women should be (Charters 1921, 1926). The social implications of a curriculum constructed according to such precepts are not explicitly drawn. As it emerged, social efficiency became a blending of a sometimes subterranean form of social control and the kind of scientific efficiency of production that Taylor envisioned in the industrial world.

Another segment of the social efficiency movement, primarily those who regarded themselves as sociologists, however, was much more explicit in enunciating the connection between a reconstructed curriculum and a rejuvenated social order. Probably the most celebrated and most productive of these was David Snedden. While a student at Stanford University, Snedden had become profoundly influenced by Ross (Drost 1967), and, throughout the course of his long career, he sought to promote the idea that a revitalized school curriculum could become a potent instrument in creating a society driven by the tenets of social efficiency. Like Bobbitt and Charters, Snedden's vision of a reformed curriculum was tied to directly functional outcomes, but for Snedden, the curriculum was a much more vital and potent instrument for achieving a stable and efficient social order. While this premise was mainly implicit in the work of scientific curriculum makers like Bobbitt and Charters, Snedden was unambiguous in the way his saw the curriculum as the medium by which each person learned to perform his or her social duties in line with a definitive social destiny. Snedden's (1924) "great community" foresaw the possibility of unity, to be sure, but the society he envisioned emphasized the distinct and diverse roles that were required for that society to succeed in maintaining itself:

> We make a good football team or submarine crew by picking men for the respective functions involved, training them intensively for their parts, and, incidentally, helping them to feel deeply the unity of the composite function in which they are collectively engaged. Dare we be guided by similar procedures in junior high school curriculum making? (11)

In practical terms, this meant a curriculum finely tuned to the needs of a modern industrial democracy (at least as Snedden perceived those needs). Since "not all minds are endowed with sufficient powers to make effective use of algebra," for example, only 2 percent need to study it in order to gain any degree of proficiency. Likewise, while "some of us" can derive satisfaction from reading Henry James, Conrad, and Meredith, "clearly, only Utopians (or aspirationists) can expect the rank and file of people to have similar interests" (11).

Like others who saw the curriculum as pivotal to their social vision, Snedden liked to engage in prophecies as to America's future, invariably inserting his own utopian fantasies into those conjectures. While Commissioner of Education in Massachusetts, Snedden (1914), at the Seventh Annual meeting of the American Home Economics Association in Cleveland, undertook to forecast the role of women by the end of the next half century. By 1964, he predicted, "[t]he great majority of married women will give their entire working time to home-making, with employed assistance as at present only at critical periods" (430). If a proper curriculum in home economics were to be achieved it must be recognized that "a large majority, approximating 100 percent of all women, must be expected eventually to become wives and mothers" (431). Snedden need hardly have added that the social economy of the future required that women be trained directly and specifically for the tasks involved in such an occupation. Snedden's unswerving principle in the education of homemakers—as in the case of other social roles—requires "that we decide for what vocations we are preparing; and that we unsparingly test the efficiency of the means which we adopt" (434). For Snedden and all those committed to the ideal of social efficiency, all education becomes an extension of vocational education.

In a more ambitious exercise in prognostication, Snedden (1931) undertook to describe, not just the secondary school as it would be in 1960, but a society according to Snedden. In that society, a National Production Apportionment Board keeps a watchful eye on the labor market, carefully apportioning workers to respective occupations so that none would become overcrowded. "Increasingly," according to Snedden, "the total range of outgoing constructive activities of civilized adults became *departmentalized*, and even *compartmentalized*, according to distinctive functional aspects" (72). The school curriculum, of course, reflects those compartments of functional activity. Familiar subject labels like English and mathematics give way to studies of a truly functional nature like Friendly Letter Writing, Business Letter Writing, and Reading to an Audience (87–88). Higher mathematics is reserved for those who were destined to put it to good use. Thus "a very few students in the eleventh and twelfth grades take a course in Pre-engineering mathematics . . . [and] not more than twenty percent of pupils take *any* mathematics in grades seven to twelve" (89). Subjects like algebra virtually disappear from the high school curriculum. Even Snedden's favorite subject, vocational education, loses its general and nonfunctional character: "Almost overnight the older nebulous conceptions of 'vocational education without vocations' were swept away . . . " (102). In its place are eight or nine hundred highly specific forms of vocational education.

Snedden's (1931) *Secondary Schools 1960*, obviously, is an exercise in wishful thinking, and some of Snedden's conjectures about a revitalized secondary school curriculum are patently outrageous. His immoderation, however, may serve to mask the extent to which the American school curriculum has crept almost imperceptibly in the direction he envisioned. Even the most fervid of contemporary defenders of academic subject matter seek their justification not in terms of their intellectual virtues or in terms intrinsic to their study but in the very utilitarian and functional ideals that Snedden so ardently sought for every subject in the school curriculum. What Snedden did not foresee was that the subjects he denounced so vigorously as nonfunctional would one day be perceived as a vital cog in the social machinery. Higher mathematics, for example, is being urged on every side, not because it opens new vistas of intellectual endeavor and insight but because our technological race with this or that country will be lost unless a reasonable number of American students make it part of their studies. This is not exactly the equivalent of a National Apportionment Production Board, but it smacks of a corresponding way of expressing the value of school subjects.

As in the case of committee reports, legitimate questions have been raised as to the extent to which utterances by major leaders in the curriculum field, such as Charters and Snedden, have any relationship to what was actually practiced in schools. Taken as an literal exercise in forecasting the future, for example, Snedden's (1931) *Secondary Schools 1960* is silly. Reading Snedden is no substitute for knowing what elements of the proposed curriculum actually became imbedded in schools; but the life adjustment movement of the 1940s and 1950s was in fact built on very much the same principles that Snedden enunciated. Academic subjects were either treated with disdain altogether or deemed to be appropriate only for a select few. Even life adjustment education, however, a curriculum movement with real adherents and a real constituency, and even some support from the Federal government, did not have nearly the effect envisioned by its most ardent proponents or by its spiritual ancestors such as Snedden. It did, however, have *some* effect (Broder 1977), and it still does. Social efficiency has survived very successfully as a doctrine, even if it is less conspicuous in its current incarnation than it was in Snedden's time and its language more muted.

Using the voices of major figures in the curriculum field to lay bare certain fundamental assumptions should not be taken as attributing to those leaders power and influence or even conceptual innovation. George Herbert Palmer (1905) once said that "The tendencies of an age appear more distinctly in its writers of inferior rank than in those of commanding genius. These latter tell of past and future as well as of the age in which they live. They are for all time. But on the sensitive responsive souls of less creative power, current ideals record themselves with clearness" (xii). Leading scientific curriculum makers such as Bobbitt and Charters were such responsive souls. They spoke not simply for themselves but for the age in which they lived, recording with reasonable accuracy certain prevailing social tendencies, as well as many of the extant hopes for the remediation of social ills through the vehicle of a reconstructed curriculum. While their voices may seem quaint, even foolish, to the modern ear, their role as articulaters of the most fundamental and even persistent curriculum ideas of our times should not be underestimated.

Examination of the doctrines of social efficiency as expressed by its archetypical leaders serves to cast in a dramatic new light the kinds of reforms that dominated the world of scientific curriculum makers. It serves as well to accentuate the extent to which their central doctrine of probable destiny as the key to curriculum design has become at least an unconscious, if not a quite deliberate, constituent of modern curriculum thought. The conception of education as preparation for adult living in all its manifestations has become so ingrained in modern curriculum making that one can hardly think of education in different terms. What else is the curriculum but a tribulation to be passively endured as a rehearsal for a remote but putatively predictable future? That question remained almost buried before historians began to lay bare its origins and development.

THE LEGACY OF JOHN DEWEY AND THE MEANING OF PROGRESSIVE EDUCATION

If Palmer was right in looking to people of "inferior rank" in order to characterize an age, then John Dewey will not serve that purpose in the way that Bobbitt, Charters, and Snedden do. Dewey was not only a product of his age; he also transcended it. In his case, it is the validity of the ideas themselves that occupies center stage. Some attention has been directed, however, to whether those ideas, valid or not, actually influenced the course of American education as is commonly supposed. In addition, given the complexity of those ideas, there is continuing debate as to what those ideas actually were or how they should be interpreted.

There is no question that Dewey has become a symbol at home and abroad of American education, but both his admirers and detractors disagree as to how successfully his ideas permeated what we actually teach in schools (Kliebard 1987; L. Tanner 1987). As already suggested, part of the problem with this sort of debate is that influence is in any case an extraordinarily difficult thing to trace. Dewey, to take one example, actively opposed the bifurcation of American secondary schools under two separate mechanisms of control, one academic and one vocational (Dewey 1915a, 1915b), as some major reformers of the period such as Charles Prosser and David Snedden had urged, and the comprehensive high school did indeed become the standard structure for American secondary education. But it would be extremely risky to attribute that significant turn of events to the influence of Dewey, since any number of other factors could have been more decisive either cumulatively or individually. The fact that Dewey or anyone else espoused a position that became accepted practice is no guarantee or even evidence of influence.

A commonly expressed version of the controversy over Dewey's influence is that, while his own ideas were not actually translated into visible practice, the easily contorted versions of his ideas promoted by his followers in fact were. Although the first part of that proposition has been challenged directly and indirectly here and there (Hirsch 1987; L. Tanner 1987), a comparison of what is undoubtedly the most detailed account of the curriculum of Dewey's own Laboratory School, which he directed between 1896 and 1904 (Mayhew and Edwards 1936), and contemporary accounts of the state of the American curriculum at both the elementary and secondary levels (e.g., Goodlad 1984; McNeil 1986; Powell, Farrar, and Cohen 1985; Sizer 1984), indicates a massive mismatch between the kind of curriculum Dewey sought to implement and what the American curriculum has become. We may take for granted that the account provided by two former teachers in Dewey's school would be somewhat idealized, especially after the passage of more than 30 years. Nevertheless, the contrast between active intellectual activity on the part of the children in the Dewey School with the passivity and disengagement of contemporary American pupils, the continual striving for unity in Dewey's curriculum as opposed to widespread fragmentation and specialization in contemporary schools, and the active and intelligent involvement of teachers in the development of the curriculum in Dewey's school, as compared to the bureaucratic imposition of "standards" as the currently most popular pattern of curriculum reform, offers little to substantiate the claims made by both Dewey's admirers and detractors that his work in fact influenced what is today the American curriculum.

Actually, some of the difficulty in assessing Dewey's impact at certain important junctures in the development of the American curriculum may be illustrated by his somewhat ambivalent or perhaps just complex position on the introduction of vocational education into the curriculum. As an active participant in what Morton White (1949) calls the "revolt against formalism," he had deep reservations about a curriculum that was guided principally by the imposition of society's inherited culture on its young. In this respect, Dewey could easily be seen as someone who would applaud the introduction of a note of practical skill training as a way of relieving the remoteness of the typical academic curriculum. But, as Charles Frankel (1960) points out, Dewey's "enemies," not simply in education but throughout the entire range of his philosophical thought, "were routine, drill, external dictation and the ready-made ideas; and the targets he attacked were social arrangements, educational methods or philosophical systems that seemed to promote such qualities" (320). It was not academic subject matter that Dewey rejected; it was externally imposed and externally directed routines of any sort.

In examining Dewey's position on vocational education, then, it becomes important not simply to ascertain whether vocational education represented for Dewey simply a welcome break from the monotony of academic drill, but whether it may also have served a social system that encouraged the imposition of external control and dulling routine on great masses of people. There is probably no philosopher who took the day-to-day experiences of individuals more seriously than Dewey did. In fact, contrary to popular belief, Dewey found his ideal form of experience, not in the precision and order of science but in the spontaneity, the personal involvement, and the delight that are associated with the arts (Frankel 1960). In this sense, it becomes all the more important in Dewey's case, therefore, to see his position in curriculum matters, as well as in other policy areas, as the outcome of a system of ideas rather than a point of emphasis here and there.

Frankel's point may be illustrated by Dewey's revealing interchange with one of the major proponents of vocational education as well as, of course, a leading exponent of social efficiency, David Snedden. To the casual observer and perhaps even to the general historian, Dewey and Snedden were "progressives," both seeking to overturn the established order in education. But from the viewpoint of *curriculum* history, the positions they espoused were not simply different; they were manifestly in opposition to one another.

In an article appearing on the subject of industrial education in *New Republic*, Dewey (1915a), concerned about pending legislation involving vocational education, refers to the reason that had thus far been advanced for integrating industrial education into the standard curriculum as "an undigested medley." He points to statistical evidence indicating that in Germany, often cited as the model for the new programs of vocational education, skilled workers received little more in wages than unskilled workers. The policy, in other words, rather than benefiting workers is "frankly nationalistic" in character (11). Dewey goes on to warn that schools should not be converted "into preliminary factories at public expense" and argues that the aim of any program of industrial education must be what he calls "industrial intelligence" rather than skill training. He also declares his concern that the proposed legislation would subordinate any educational interest to the interests of industry (12).

In his reply, Snedden (1915) first professes "profound respect" for Dewey but finds himself "somewhat bewildered" by Dewey's criticism (40). Expressing himself unequivocally, Snedden takes virtually the opposite position from Dewey's on this issue. "Vocational education," he declares flatly, "is irreducibly and without unnecessary mystification, education for pursuit of an occupation" (41). He goes on to call on the states to maintain vocational schools "for the various trades, for farming, for home-making, and for different commercial pursuits" (41). For Snedden, the issue of dual control, so important in Dewey's thinking, is simply a matter to be decided in terms of "the greatest efficiency," and he expresses the view that separate control of vocational schools may "prove absolutely essential" in "states where the academic tradition strongly persists" (42). Dewey's (1915b) short reply concludes the exchange. "I object," he says, "to regarding as vocational education any training which does not have as its supreme regard the development of . . . intelligent initiative, ingenuity and executive capacity as shall make workers, as far as may be, the masters of their own industrial fate" (42).

Alluding to his doubts about theological predestination, Dewey expresses no equivocation about its social counterpart. "I am utterly opposed," he states, "to giving the power of social predestination, by means of narrow trade-training, to any group of fallible men no matter how well-intentioned they may be." Dewey brought the interchange to an end by saying that he is forced to conclude that the differences between Snedden and him are not so much matters of narrow educational policy as they are "profoundly political and social," and he urges his readers to resist the policy that Snedden has so ardently promoted. He insists instead on "a kind of vocational education which will first alter the existing industrial system, and ultimately transform it" (1915b, 42). As is plainly evident, Dewey was once again swimming against the tide on this issue. Vocational education has become almost precisely what Snedden thought it should be ("education for pursuit of an occupation") and is patently far removed from Dewey's idea of industrial education as a vehicle for the promotion of an intelligent understanding of industrial democracy (to say nothing of workers as "masters of their own industrial fate").

There is an echo of the Dewey-Snedden exchange in Dewey's magnum opus in education, *Democracy and Education* (1916). At the conclusion of his chapter on "Labor and Leisure," Dewey tries to argue that subjects of study should not be regarded as either cultural or utilitarian but that, properly conceived, subjects of study may be both cultural and useful at one and the same time. He feels that by aiming so narrowly at the utilitarian, vocational subjects actually limit their potential use. "It will generally be found," he says, "that instruction which, in aiming at utilitarian results, sacrifices the development of imagination, the refining of taste and the deepening of intellectual insight—surely cultural values—also in the same degree renders what is learned limited in its use" (258). As in the case of his debate with Snedden, Dewey returns to the matter of the relation of the curriculum to the social and economic system:

> In the degree in which men have an active concern in the ends that control their activity, their activity becomes free or voluntary and loses its externally enforced and servile quality. . . . *In what is termed politics, democratic social organization makes provision for this direct participation in control: in the economic region, control remains external and autocratic.* (260; emphasis added)

Of particular significance here (I am indebted to my colleague, Daniel Pekarsky, for calling this passage to my attention) is the indication that Dewey is going beyond the question of workers' understanding of the workplace and thereby identifying with their work and its purposes, he wants them to share in the formulation of those purposes, just as all people share in the formulation of purposes in an ideal democracy.

The sharp interchange between Dewey and Snedden, as well as Dewey's subsequent observations in opposition to vocational education as commonly perceived, were not about an obscure point of curriculum doctrine; it boiled down to what the relationship between an educational system and the society in which it finds itself was all about. Vocational education, after all, went on to become the most far-reaching curriculum innovation of the 20th century, and the relationship between education and the workplace has become one of the most vexing and contentious issues of modern times. It is a matter of some irony that the widely celebrated philosopher, the once living symbol of American education, seemed curiously out of touch here with the social tenor of his time. It was Snedden, on the other hand, the now relatively obscure figure in the curriculum world, who was able to point in the direction that vocational education actually took in the 20th century.

Addressing the issue of Dewey's influence, then, requires going beyond the points of emphasis that abound in his writings on curriculum and turning instead to the question of whether the course that the American curriculum has actually followed in any way conforms to the *core* of Dewey's thinking in the areas of education and society and on the intellectual independence of individuals. It is the failure to focus on these very controlling ideas in Dewey that frequently leads to misconceptions, not simply about what he meant but what he supported or opposed, and this is what makes the second part of the claim, that Dewey's followers perpetrated distorted versions of his ideas on American schools, much more difficult to dismiss out of hand. While there were few who presumed actually to speak directly in Dewey's name, there were many who invoked it. Moreover, certain key terms that are commonly associated with Dewey have ordinary and familiar meanings besides the ones that he specifically assigned to them. (Dewey's [1902] use of the term "occupations" in *The Child and the Curriculum* is a case in point. It is obvious that

Dewey is using "occupations" in the sense of fundamental human activities rather than as a means of earning of living.)

Here and there, one may find Dewey explicitly rejecting an idea that came to be associated with him, but, much more often than not, Dewey spoke in generalities without specific attribution of ideas to real or alleged disciples. In *The Way Out of Educational Confusion*, to cite one exception, Dewey (1931) comes as close to rejecting the project method as a mode of curriculum organization as one could expect from someone of his scholarly habits. Yet, Kilpatrick's project method, at least by association, continues to be associated with Deweyan thought.

More typically, Dewey's *Experience and Education* (1938) may be read, almost literally, as a last-ditch effort to clarify misconceptions that had become associated with his name and ideas. On the need for authority in educational matters: "When external authority is rejected, it does not follow that all authority should be rejected, but rather that there is need to search for a more effective source of authority" (8). On the nature of freedom: "The only freedom that is of enduring importance is freedom of intelligence, that is to say freedom of observation and judgment exercised in behalf of purposes that are intrinsically worthwhile. The commonest mistake about freedom is, I think, to identify it with freedom of movement or the external or physical side of activity" (69). On the significance of subject matter: "[F]inding the material for learning with experience is only the first step. The next step is the progressive development of what is already experienced into a fuller and richer and also more organized form, a form that gradually approximates that in which subject-matter is presented to the skilled, mature person" (87). The list could be extended. The point is, however, that to this day Dewey's ideas on education remain associated with a rejection of authority, unbridled freedom amounting to license, and the renunciation of subject matter in the curriculum.

The most tempting and in the end perhaps the most promising explanation for this curious state of affairs is that Dewey's ideas on curriculum were not so much studied and carried forward into practice in a conscious and deliberate way as they were converted into a slogan system that served a variety of purposes according to the situation and the actors involved. This applies about equally to his proponents and his detractors. In other words, Dewey functioned in a symbolically political role much like the way history of curriculum itself functioned for so long. He, like the history of curriculum, became a convenient vehicle for pointing to existing evils, as well as to desired new directions. Where a change from traditional practices was the order of the day, Dewey's name could be invoked as the force behind it, and where a return to the status quo ante was being promoted, Dewey's spirit could be conjured as the source of the problem. Under those circumstances, the actual feasibility or validity of the ideas themselves became really beside the point. That question of validity is worth resurrecting.

If Dewey, long acknowledged as the embodiment of progressive education, has functioned largely as both a positive or negative symbol of what American education has become, rather than a source of specific practice, one cannot help but wonder how progressive education itself has functioned. Complicating that question is the fact that, while a persistent study of Dewey's ideas may yield some coherence, it is unlikely that anything like consistency could be found in progressive education. As the debate between two "progressives," Dewey and Snedden, indicates, progressive education as a concept is full not just of inconsistencies but of massive internal contradictions. Upon historical examination, these contradictions turn out to be not of a tangential nature, but of what the study of curriculum history is all about. If curriculum history is systemically concerned not just with what gets taught in schools but with the social ideals that lie behind those factors, as well as the effect on individuals and social relations, then progressive education can at best be regarded as a political symbol for what is good *or* bad about American schools. If social and political progressivism, as represented by Dewey or, say, Boyd Bode is thrown into the same hopper with ideas and ideals that point in virtually the opposite direction, such as those of Snedden and Bobbitt, then progressive education as an historical construct means practically nothing.

METHODOLOGICAL VARIANCE IN CURRICULUM HISTORY

Two complementary approaches to curriculum history now characterize its methodology. The still predominant form of historiography in curriculum focuses on efforts to transform the curriculum more or less as a whole through doctrines and ideologies that reflect both fundamental pedagogical and social beliefs. The strength of this approach lies in the fact that it opens debate on long-neglected issues and invites reconsideration of fundamental ideas that have long held sway in the curriculum world. Even assumptions that have long been hidden from view may be unearthed and subjected to scrutiny, especially as they may be related to social change and the struggle within society by different groups for status and recognition. The basic emphasis in this approach is most commonly on the worthiness or unworthiness of ideas about curriculum that have emerged over the course of time. As already indicated, the curriculum ideas of a John Dewey may be examined in terms of their merits or deficiencies, irrespective of whether those ideas were implemented or not.

Valid or not in a philosophical sense, however, political questions may also legitimately be raised as to whose interests would be served by the implementation of certain curriculum doctrines. There is considerable evidence that vocationalism as a national movement, to take one example, did in fact have a major impact, at least in certain areas of the country (Kantor 1988; Kean 1983); but, whether widely translated into practice or not, it would still be critical to know in what respects the target populations of that movement would be well served, however nobly intentioned the advocates. The appeal of dealing with global movements and fundamental ideas remains strong and can offer valuable insight into the course of curriculum history. In particular, the relationships that exist between the emergence and sanctioning of basic doctrines in curriculum and social transformations involving such matters as the distribution of power, the rise of professionalism, and changing conceptions of the state represent intriguing lines of further research (Cherryholmes 1987; Kliebard 1990; Popkewitz 1989).

Concentration on historically significant curriculum movements and national trends also has some obvious drawbacks. As already indicated, one of the most conspicuous but also most difficult to overcome is the potential discrepancy between the announced positions of curriculum commissions or the pronouncements of major curriculum leaders and what actually transpired in schools. It can be safely assumed, however, that such broad national movements as child-centered education, social reconstructionism, and life adjustment education had *some* effect on what was actually taught in schools; in each case, evidence can be adduced that documents the implementation or at least the adaptation of these doctrines here and there (Cuban 1984).

What remains, however, are unanswered questions of very considerable significance. One common tendency on the part of critics of American education is to point to certain doctrines as the root causes of real or alleged failures. Arthur Bestor, for example, one of the most potent of the critics of American education in the 1950s, based much of his condemnation of the American curriculum on the *enunciated* policies of the advocates of life adjustment education (Bestor 1953; Kliebard 1986a). But the evidence of implementation of life adjustment policies is quite scant (Broder 1977). Similarly, E. D. Hirsch, Jr. (1987) attributes the impoverished state of cultural literacy in the United States largely to the pervasive influence of John Dewey, but the extent and nature of Dewey's actual influence on American educational practice, as already has been seen, remains the subject of continuing debate and has even been cast into considerable doubt (Kliebard 1987; Schubert 1987).

The important question is not so much *whether* historically significant curriculum doctrines, such as those proclaimed by major curriculum commissions and by leaders in the curriculum field, were modified or even transformed when they reached school sites, but to what extent, how, and with what effect. One way of conceiving of the relation of ideology and practice is in terms of what has been called "hybridization" (Kliebard 1986a). This conception derives in part from the fact that curriculum doctrines rarely if ever succeed each other chronologically. Divergent and even competing doctrines almost invariably exist side by side. While at one level curriculum doctrines in their pure form may be examined and contrasted with some legitimacy as, for example, they are expressed by national spokespersons, their translation into curriculum practice is most likely to be an admixture of those doctrines. The rhetoric of reform is usually so persuasive that reforms of widely differing character and purpose often find their way into the same school curriculum. This highlights the significantly political character of what passes for curriculum change. At the school level, it is more expedient to satisfy influential interest groups or to appease a disgruntled clientele than to implement a coherent and internally consistent program of studies. In a contemporary context, for example, Powell, Farrar, and Cohen (1985) found the curriculum of American high schools to be governed by the idea that there should be something for everybody, with no sense of controlling purpose or direction.

Something of the process by which this hybridization process takes place may be revealed by historical case studies that focus on the relationship between national curriculum movements and changes in curriculum in particular school sites. Examination of some of these historical case studies can serve to bring into focus unresolved issues on the national level such as those already discussed. Franklin (1982a), for example, seeks to trace the influence of the social efficiency movement in the Minneapolis school district in the period 1917 to 1950, particularly as expressed in what was called the Common Learnings Program. He is thus attempting to examine the social efficiency movement in the light of empirical evidence (Jackson 1980) derived from an actual attempt to implement that doctrine. Franklin finds that, while the rhetoric of the local administrators of the program was unquestionably imbued with the language and ideas of social efficiency, local conditions made it difficult to translate that rhetoric into a fully functioning social efficiency program. The implementation of a full-blown social efficiency Common Learnings Program was thwarted to some extent, for example, by regulations emanating from the state department of education as well as opposition from the Parents Council. (The Common Learnings Program was an effort to integrate the curriculum around such functional rather than academic content as marriage and the family and community living.) While the presence of social efficiency doctrine was clearly evident and even dominant, the actual program that was implemented, according to Franklin, was so innocuous that it was unlikely that it acted to subjugate particular social groups as has frequently been charged by critics of the social efficiency movement.

In a critique of Franklin's Minneapolis study, Landon Beyer (1982) raises the question of whether mandated programs by state agencies could have been satisfied in conjunction with the social efficiency orientation of the administrators. He also argues that part of the collapse of the Common Learnings Program could be attributed to "resistance" (Apple 1979; Willis 1977) by groups such as the Parents Council and the teachers in the Minneapolis schools. He further maintains that the various groups that Franklin identified may have indeed been acting out of class interests contrary to Franklin's interpretation and, whether classbound or not in its development, a given curriculum change may still be so in its consequences. Finally, Beyer is disturbed by the implication that examination of practice can serve "as a check on theorizing" (312), thereby giving practice a higher ontological status than theory. In his rejoinder to Beyer, Franklin (1982b) argues against casting his study in a Marxist theoretical framework, which he finds could not adequately explain the ambiguities and complexities in the Minneapolis case. Rather, he suggests that his study exemplifies the kinds of compromises among competing interest groups that curriculum implementation requires.

The interchange between Franklin and Beyer is particularly illuminating in that it, first of all, illustrates how historical case studies in curriculum can serve to focus on issues of great theoretical significance. But, second, it illustrates how the historical case study, rather than settling matters of historical and theoretical concern, such as the issue of class domination through the curriculum, enhances the level of debate over those issues. Whatever the empirical evidence that case histories uncover, they do not vitiate the theoretical differences that lie behind those studies. Rather, they raise the debates about those differences to new levels.

Historical case studies of curriculum, then, can be seen as serving multiple functions. They can, as in the case of Franklin's Minneapolis study, direct attention to the relationship between broad movements in curriculum (such as social efficiency) and how or in what form those major curriculum doctrines made their way into the curriculum of some schools. It can be assumed without argument that none of the major curriculum ideologies rising to prominence in the 20th century was instituted in schools in its pristine form. What case studies illustrate are the kinds of resistance that emerge and the ways in which local conditions transmute the visions of the major exponents of those doctrines. Also, as the debate between Beyer and Franklin indicates, neglected or unacknowledged aspects of the doctrine can be brought into focus.

Yet another significant element that case studies may embody can be illustrated by Harvey A. Kantor's (1988) analysis of the way in which the national vocational education movement actually affected the curriculum of schools in California during the period between 1880 and 1930. Like the Franklin study, Kantor's deals in large measure with the way in which social control ideologies made their way in the curriculum of schools, in this case by illustrating how vocational education as a curriculum innovation was incorporated into the schools of one state. Kantor's purpose, however, is not to search for what he refers to as "good" or "evil" intentions (xii), but to focus on what those reformers perceived as the problem of schooling. By then examining the remedies they sought to apply to that problem, he seeks to arrive at an interpretation of what the consequences of the reform were. In this sense, whether the participants were seeking, by subterfuge or other means, to exercise a greater measure of social control on the mass of students then entering secondary schools, or whether they were humanitarians seeking to bring to that new population a curriculum more in tune with its real aptitudes and needs is really beside the point. What is important is how those programs functioned and with what effect.

As was the case with Franklin's Minneapolis study, Kantor concludes that the policies of national leaders were at least somewhat transformed when translated into practice. Particularly intriguing is Kantor's account of how and under what circumstances these mismatches occurred. Contrary to the claims of the proponents of vocational education, he concludes that, because those leaders proceeded from erroneous assumptions, the programs themselves "did little to keep young people in school longer; nor did they make industry more efficient" (168). Those programs and the campaigns that promoted them, however, did result in certain notable accomplishments. Although vocational education supported a gender-segregated labor market, for example, girls, in contrast with boys, were able to use vocational education as a vehicle for social mobility. One factor in this unexpected result was that the drive for vocational education in the curriculum happened to coincide with a growing discrepancy between blue-collar and white-collar occupations. While it can be argued that women were still being exploited in the labor force, entry into the world of commerce, even in its lowest echelons, was a distinct step up over its alternative in factory labor.

Perhaps the most far-reaching of the movement's successes, however, was in the way it shifted the standard justification for getting an education in the first place (Kliebard 1990). As Kantor puts it, "More than ever before, preparation for work became a standard rationale for secondary education, thereby institutionalizing the idea that educational reform was a key solution to the nation's economic ills" (168). That education is so viewed in the context of contemporary debates about the nature and function of schooling is evident in many of the recent critical reports on the state of American education.

Historical case studies, therefore, need not be limited to supporting or modifying existing theoretical constructs that have been engendered by studies of national curriculum movements. They may also generate theoretical constructs in their own right. One of the most compelling examples of what Kaestle calls "elegant" historical interpretations is framed in the context of a historical case study of a single high school: David Labaree's (1988) study of the Central High School of Philadelphia between 1838 and 1939. While Labaree's work is not confined specifically to the history of the curriculum in that school, its central interpretations revolve around the ebb and flow of the curriculum of the school in that 91-year period. That period, of course, includes the years when highly regarded national committees were seeking to determine the nature and direction of the American high school curriculum, and Labaree does intimate that the Committee of Ten report did indeed help shape the course of study in Central High School in the period around 1900. In particular, of the four programs of study that were instituted in Central High School, three, the classical, the Latin-scientific, and the modern languages courses were adopted either in whole or in part from the 1893 report. The commercial course obviously was not (153). The Committee on College-Entrance Requirements and the *Cardinal Principles* report are not mentioned.

Rather than seeking to confirm or disconfirm existing debates over the historical significance of those committee reports, Labaree's guiding theoretical framework is derived from historical data directly pertinent to Central High

School's own evolving curriculum. There appears to be no consciously predetermined theoretical framework. His interpretation of curriculum change, for example, is not particularly tied to class conflict. In fact, if high school graduation is taken as the criterion of success, Labaree indicates that academic performance rather than class was the most significant variable. While Central High School was far from a typical high school, the shifts in its curriculum structure as a response to the demands of the credentials market reflects in some ways how the high school curriculum evolved nationally.

Labaree's emphasis on the relationship between the curriculum and the shifting market for the high school diploma casts a different light on the extraordinary controversies surrounding the high school curriculum generally around the turn of the century. According to Labaree, two developments, market competition from another secondary school in Philadelphia and the professionalization of the middle class, culminated in a newly stratified curriculum by the beginning of the 20th century. Whatever may have been the merits of the debate between, say, Eliot and Hall over the future of the American curriculum, Hall's position triumphed, not so much because of the persuasiveness of his arguments or the validity of his ideas, but as a consequence of the fact that the "growing situation of the credentials market" (168) created a need in Central High School, and by extension other high schools, to establish a close bond with the university. Thus, as Labaree puts it,

> The new curriculum represented a major turning point in the perceived purpose of a high school education, from preparation for business to preparation for higher education and the professions. . . . A uniform course of study with no electives was transformed into a menu of choices arranged in a hierarchy. From the start, the academic courses occupied the top stratum. (169)

Seen in this light, whatever may have been the professed or genuine convictions of national leaders like Eliot and Nightingale about the equivalence of school subjects, the status of particular courses and programs of study arranged themselves into a hierarchy, and this stratification of the curriculum was a response to a saturated credentials market. The upper echelons of the new stratified curriculum was a way of protecting the value of the high school diploma for the high school's middle-class constituency. It did so in effect by arranging the curriculum so that all programs were equal but some were more equal than others. Thus, although the elementary school curriculum may still reflect something of the older values associated with republican virtues, the high school curriculum became dominated by the vagaries of the credentials market and the extent to which those credentials could be traded for things of value, such as professional status and high salaries.

Labaree's interpretations of the shifting state of the curriculum of Central High School is illustrative not simply of how historical case studies may illuminate persistent curriculum issues but also of the varied forms that conflict interpretations of the evolution of the American curriculum may take. Labaree's interpretation is not so much a matter of class conflict, or even conflict among competing curriculum ideologies, but of conflicts within the American ideal of education itself. According to that ideal, education, with the curriculum as the principal vehicle, is supposed to open access and promote equality and, at the same time, serve as a meritocratic sorting mechanism, thus providing advantages for certain individuals and not others (Spring 1976). The historical case study in this instance, then, serves neither as a way of determining whether national influences were indeed reflected in practice nor as a way of checking on claims by historians who have examined those national curriculum movements, but as a way of originating a conceptual framework for understanding curriculum change in a new light. Labaree's emphasis on market forces is grounded in his own data. If nothing else, his case study opens the possibility that there may be a legitimate alternative to a market structure of schools. Schools, in other words, may find their source of legitimacy in something other than a reaction to the marketplace.

Historical case studies also offer valuable insights into the way regional and local differences affect the implementation of the curriculum. In a study of curriculum change between 1890 and 1925 in Atlanta, for example, Wayne Urban (1981) indicates that while the promoters of change used similar arguments to those heard elsewhere and that, in fact, local leaders were actually pointing with admiration to changes that had already been instituted in other parts of the country, vocationalism as it emerged in the Atlanta schools was neither as pervasive nor as specialized in terms of occupational training as apparently was the case elsewhere. Although separate technical and commercial high schools were indeed created, they did not become educational dead ends. Even in these specialized high schools, a college preparatory function was consistently maintained. Of particular relevance in this outcome was the work of two of Atlanta's most prominent reformers, Hoke Smith and Robert Guinn. As leaders of the "progressive" faction of the Democratic party, they saw school reform as part of a larger struggle in the arena of local politics. Change in the sense of promoting coherent curriculum reform was relatively inconsequential. What was important was to give the appearance of change as a way of positioning oneself as a reformer within the political spectrum.

Urban indicates that beyond even the political motivations of the key reformers lay the matter of cost-consciousness on the part of the city council. (The sometimes overlooked significance of financial support as it relates to the question of which curriculum innovations achieve a measure of success also figures prominently in the case study of the Gary, Indiana schools by Lynn McKinney and Ian Westbury [1975].) As Urban interprets the conflict between the school board and the council in Atlanta, change was possible when the reform proposals of the board would result in adding new jobs in the system, a politically popular move; when reforms were proposed that did not incorporate that element, the cost-conscious council would be more likely to reject them. Thus, the reformers Smith and Guinn were thwarted in some of their more ambitious efforts by a fiscally conservative city council. In addition, key professionals within the system, such as the superintendent, were not ideologically in tune with those reforms and posed opposition of their own. Beyond that, the race issue, involving as it did segregated education for whites and blacks, played a significant role. Specific job-related vocational education proved to be more acceptable for blacks than it was for whites, which in effect served to maintain inferior status for the black population in Atlanta.

Urban's study constitutes an important reminder of the way in which local traditions, individual actors, racial divisions, and political contexts play an important role in the way curriculum change does or does not take place. As he puts it, "'Progressivism,' 'reform,' and 'innovation' did not carry the same automatic rhetorical loading in this New South city that they seemed to carry in other settings" (1981, 127). But beyond the question of regional variation, as Urban indicates, the penchant for focusing historical attention on the work of reformers may lead to an underestimation of the potency and the successes of their traditionalist opponents to curriculum change. In this respect, the restricted success of reformers may not have been as local a phenomenon as may appear on the surface.

Case study research, in other words, may not only be valuable in elucidating what may be significant regional and local differences by tracking the way in which curriculum reform was received and implemented in given times and places; it may also serve to clarify and exemplify what may have been happening at a national level. In a set of studies on curriculum change in Detroit, for example, Jeffrey Mirel and David Angus (1985, 1986) treat the Detroit school system not so much in terms of its regional or restricted conditions but as a "trendsetting district during a watershed era in educational history" (1986, 102). In one of these studies, the issue of youth unemployment during the period of the Great Depression is tied to changing pressures on secondary schools (Mirel and Angus 1985). With the entry of the federal government into the youth unemployment arena through such agencies as the National Youth Administration, professional educators reacted defensively in what, in Detroit at least, turned out to be a "jurisdictional dispute" (495).

In this context, curriculum reform took on a special urgency, particularly in view of the fact that many professional educators began to lose faith in vocational education as an vehicle for keeping youth in schools and as an instrument toward achieving the goal of universal attendance in secondary schools. The result, according to Mirel and Angus, was that the high school curriculum began to take on much more of a custodial character than one tied to future employment. It was in this context that national leaders such as Charles Prosser began to sow the seeds of what later became life adjustment education, a major curriculum movement of the 1940s and 1950s. The social and economic conditions of the Great Depression, in other words, particularly a growing confrontation between the federal government and the traditional guardians of America's youth, engendered new strategies for changing the curriculum. Over the course of the depression era, the number and type of courses offered expanded significantly (Mirel and Angus 1986, 108). In general, academic subjects such as English, mathematics, and science gave way to courses like industrial drawing and gymnastics, which were perceived as contributing to the holding power of the secondary school. In fact, by 1924, as part of a dramatic rise in the rate of failures in what was called the General Curriculum, Detroit school officials simply undertook to make that program easier. As one example, science courses were modified to eliminate laboratory work and new courses such as Personal Standards (grooming) were introduced as electives (110).

In the long run, however, Mirel and Angus's findings challenge one of the most widespread assumptions about the relationship between enrollments and course offerings. Despite retrenchments in terms of curriculum, high school enrollments soared, casting doubt on the common wisdom that the key to school retention lies in an expanded curriculum specifically designed "to meet the needs" of children and adolescents. Instead, their findings suggest that fluctuations in the labor market rather than curriculum change were most critical in that regard. In addition, the Detroit studies suggest that the movement toward custodialism (and with it a marked decline in academic emphasis) had its inception well before the formal proclamation of life adjustment education in 1945. These case studies by Mirel and Angus add still another dimension to what case studies can contribute to the creation of curriculum history. Widely held assumptions as to the effects of certain curriculum changes, going back in some cases to the turn of the century, can be cast in a new light. The idea, for example, that a less academic curriculum, one attuned to practical concerns of children and youth, would result in a marked increase in the holding power of the schools goes back at least to the Douglas Commission report of 1906 (Massachusetts Commission on Industrial and Technical Education 1906).

The range of historical case studies in curriculum chosen for illustration here is obviously not exhaustive. Nor is it possible for it be comprehensive even as to the kinds of findings that may accrue from such explorations. As illustrated, these studies can take as their focus the way particular programs of study were or were not influenced by national movements, sources of curriculum change within individual institutions, regional variance, and an interpretation of data from individual school districts as reflections of national trends. Their impact has been to modify more global interpretations of the evolution of the curriculum by focusing on specific school effects, generating new hypotheses as to why and under what circumstances curriculum changes tend to occur. Also, in some instances, their impact has been to attach new significance to the ways in which such matters as local politics and economic stringencies may affect the course the curriculum may take, and to challenge conventional wisdom as to what the effects of certain curriculum changes may be. As such, they have provided a welcome complement to the more traditional studies that center on national movements and the expressions of national leaders. While national studies provide a convenient and economical vehicle for contrasting competing curriculum ideologies and for interpreting the course that the curriculum has taken within broad social, political, and economic contexts, more restricted case studies provide much needed refinements to those studies. Even more significant, however, is that case studies have proven invaluable in engendering new interpretations of the course that the curriculum has taken.

THE CURRICULUM OF SCHOOL SUBJECTS

A further promising direction for research, actually another form of case history, especially reflected in the work of curriculum historians outside the United States, is the effort to interpret the direction that particular school subjects have taken over time and to tie these interpretations to the impact of class divisions, including the role of dominant elites. As Ivor Goodson (1984) has indicated, much of the significance of this work lies in the fact that, contrary to common belief, "subjects are not monolithic entities but shifting amalgams of subgroups and traditions" (28). Thus, over time, emphases and even subject boundary lines shift as interest groups struggle for status, public acceptance, and advantage in terms of access to resources. The study of particular school subjects, therefore, may reflect many of the issues that characterize studies of the curriculum as a whole. Some studies are celebratory; some are critical. Some concentrate on the impact or meaning of prestigious commissions, major leaders, or state-sponsored initiatives; some seek to gain access to the way subjects were actually taught in schools. Some are primarily concerned with the validity of certain conceptions of the subject field; some concentrate on the way a particular subject evolved in a particular time and place.

In contrast to Europe and other parts of the world, the history of school subjects in the United States is virtually in its infancy. This may be the case because what has most captured the imagination of curriculum leaders in the United States have been dramatically far-reaching proposals that have sought to transform the entire curriculum. For example, Kilpatrick, as has been indicated, sought to substitute the project for the subject as the unit element of the curriculum, with subject matter conceived as instrumental to the carrying forward of that activity rather than its focal point. In the case of social efficiency educators, what were sometimes called problems of living, actually categories of life activity, were sought as directly functional replacements for the traditional academic subjects. Those attempts rarely succeeded in actually replacing the subject; at best, in some cases, they were able to modify what was taught under the orthodox subject labels. Whatever has been the evolution of the curriculum over the course of the 20th century, subjects have remained, as McKinney and Westbury (1975) insists, "the pervasive and fundamental building blocks of the curriculum" (3).

One thing that sets the history of school subjects somewhat apart from the more general history of curriculum is that, since many of the school subjects retain their original names, there is a tendency to see them as static. On a common-sense level, English remains English and mathematics, mathematics. Beyond the subject labels, however, lie subtle and often not-so-subtle transformations of what we mean by those subjects. This has led certain scholars consciously to go beyond the subject labels and into the topics and activities that comprise those subjects. William Reid (1984), for example, sees much of what becomes the curriculum of schools, as emerging not from the educational system itself or from remote social forces but from a world external to schools. Drawing on the work of the sociologist, John W. Meyer, Reid explores the possibility that what survives as forms of knowledge in the schools is not so much what professionals determine but what "interested publics" (defined not so much as formal groups as loose constituencies) accept as having value and significance. The demise of the so-called "new math," for example, may be seen, at least in part, as the consequence of having departed too sharply from the way mathematics was perceived by the wider public. Innovations may succeed even when they are internally generated within an institution, but that innovation must mesh with public perceptions.

In this respect, schools subjects succeed, at least in terms of survival, only when the disjunctures between what is taught and what is publicly acceptable do not become too great. As Reid (1984) puts it, "successful rhetorics *are* realities" and, therefore, the history of school subjects may be seen as "the development and maintenance of legitimating rhetorics" (75). It becomes especially important in studying the history of school subjects, therefore, not to concentrate too heavily on the initiatives of professional educators but to take into account the way in which the institutional categories we call subjects or topics, as well as activities, gain or decline in terms of public acceptance.

A different but not necessarily contradictory view of how school subjects evolved is imbedded in David Layton's (1973) exemplary account of the origins of school science in England. Layton traces the evolution of science as a school subject from its humble beginnings as the "Science of Common Things" developed by Richard Dawes in a village school in Hampshire in 1842. As Dawes conceived his curriculum, it was to be "connected with the every-day concerns of common life" (41), such as the manufacture of clothing or the cultivation of food. Over time, the study of science took on the familiar academic trappings that it carries today. Essentially, that transformation took place in three stages (Goodson 1981): In the first stage, essentially an amateur (rather than a professional) educator finds a place for a given subject that is based on what is of interest to learners and their natural curiosity. In the second stage, an established scholarly tradition asserts itself and attracts students, not so much in terms of their interests but by virtue of its academic status. Finally, the teachers of the subject, no longer amateurs, become representatives of a professional body whose job it is to initiate students into the mysteries of the discipline. In this final stage, one finds growing passivity and disengagement on the part of the learner.

Science, however, is a relative newcomer in the panoply of established school subjects, and it is certainly possible that in the case of other subjects the progression from concern with everyday affairs to lofty academic status is not as linear as that model suggests, although Goodson (1981) proposes that the history of geography as a school subject followed a similar pattern. "The process of evolution for school Subjects," he says, "can be seen not as a pattern of disciplines 'translated' *down* or of 'domination' *downwards* but very much as a process of 'aspiration' *upwards*" (176). In the case of traditional subjects such as mathematics, classical languages, and history, however, their incorporation into the curriculum may have already been attended by the conventional academic trappings relatively unrelated to any interests on the part of the learner. In some of these cases, one can speculate, the climb has been from, say, revered and time-honored classics of literature "downward" toward works that more closely approximate the interests of learners in terms of literature.

It is likely also that, besides the differences that may accrue from the traditions within the subjects themselves, there are differences that derive from variations in the structure of schooling within as well as differences across national boundaries. In reformulating Goodson's theory of the development of school subjects, for example, Martyn Hammersley (1984) expressed it this way: "given an examination system controlled by the universities, resources and rewards within schools will tend to be distributed in such a way as to maximize or at least achieve a 'satisfactory' level of examination results; and to gain a place, or to expand its role, in the school curriculum a subject will have to take on an academic cast" (22). This makes perfect sense; but if there is no nationally recognized examination system and therefore no formal controls emanating from the universities who control the substance of those examinations, as is the case in the United States, then neither the academic cast itself nor its tenacity is likely to be as pronounced.

In the American context, Thomas S. Popkewitz (1987) has suggested that, whatever the intellectual claims of the conventional school subjects has been, their central thrust has been in the direction of moral uplift and adaptation to "a democratic, corporate, and Protestant nation" (6). Thus, early infant schools were intended to curtail vice (Bloch 1987), biology to instill appropriate hygiene habits (Rosenthal and Bybee 1987), and the art curriculum emerged as a vehicle for the practical purpose of decorating one's home (Friedman 1987). Another consideration in Kerry Friedman's interpretation of the rise of art as a school subject is the concern expressed in a variety of quarters as to how the masses were to spend their leisure time. In line with social efficiency doctrine, including its incorporation into the *Cardinal Principles* report as one of the aims of schooling, "worthy use of leisure" could be seen as a wholesome outlet for "a working class with free time on its hands" (70).

Critical to the way Popkewitz (1987) sees the development of school subjects is the rise of social science, ostensibly as a force for social amelioration, but actually as an instrument of social control. A decisive condition to the success of that movement was the rise of professionalism in social affairs. "Social science," he says, "became part of the social agenda itself," and the development of new subjects in the curriculum, as well as the transformation of existing ones, was the expression of a social gospel movement designed to achieve a kind of secular salvation for 20th-century Americans. While Goodson (1984) sees the early stages of school subjects (if we are to take geography as an example) as prefigured by "idiosyncratic local versions" (29) and only later falling under the control of formalized academic traditions, Popkewitz attributes much of the shifting of subject boundaries and their status to the emergence of professional classes with specific social agendas. Reid (1984), by contrast, ascribes primary significance in the emergence, amalgamation, or fluctuation of subjects to the interplay between academic conceptions of what topics or activities fall legitimately within a subject and that of the public. For him, public acceptance or rejection may be decisive when substantial revisions of existing subjects are undertaken.

Something of the complexity of tracking the twists of fortune within a school subject can be illustrated by George Stanek's (1984) approach to interpreting the unfolding of mathematics as a school subject. No clear line of development seems evident. Rather, mathematics seems subject to the same vagaries and shifts in ideological fashion as does the curriculum as a whole. By the early 20th century, the teaching of mathematics had already made its appearance in colleges and universities as an area of professional study. While its existence in the American school curriculum was justified in the 19th and early 20th centuries as a vehicle for training the mind, the American report of the International Commission on the Teaching of Mathematics (1912) was already incorporating elements of social efficiency. As the century progressed, other sometimes conflicting ideals influenced the way in which school mathematics was defined.

Stanek (1987) interprets the course of the teaching of mathematics as a consequence of "a network of related influences" (146), in much the same way that the curriculum as a whole was. At various times, not simply justifications but modifications in the mathematics curriculum appeared, reflecting not only its time-honored ability to develop reasoning power but also its value in the daily functioning of adults or its value in business and science. Moreover, since these justifications for the teaching of mathematics existed alongside each other, amalgams of different forms of mathematics reflecting different and sometimes contrasting interpretations of its value as a school subject were often incorporated into the same curriculum. Even the study of mathematics, then, for centuries considered a staple of any curriculum, had its periods of decline, not simply in status but in enrollments at the secondary level, and these declines in enrollments were interrelated with such factors as the labor market and a professional stake in keeping children in school for as long as possible (Mirel and Angus 1986).

A provocative offshoot of the study of school subjects has been the historical study of particular crusades that may not have had as their direct focus the introduction or remodeling of a school subject so much as the identification of a particular problem which could somehow be corrected through a particular curriculum reform. A prominent example would be the drive to Americanize immigrants in roughly the first quarter of the 20th century. To some extent that urgent concern actually did result in the creation of a new subject, community civics (Sivertson 1971), but its ramifications extended much further. Michael Olneck (1989), for example, argues the case that the transmutation of American culture rather than the actual reconstruction of the values of newly arrived immigrants was the most significant outcome of that campaign. According to Olneck's account, "organized efforts during the first two decades of the twentieth century to 'Americanize' immigrants must be counted as failures" (398), but the movement may have succeeded in a more significant sense.

Drawing on the work of the eminent political scientist Murray Edelman (1971) and the work of Joseph Gusfield (1963), Olneck interprets the movement as succeeding in defining a symbolic order, one in which "collective identity is depicted, status recognized, and normative orthodoxy expressed and sanctioned" (399). This kind of interpretation draws what may be exaggerated attention away from the instrumental efforts at curriculum change in the direction of how social definitions are reconstructed, as well as what constitutes legitimate action, in the course of debates about curriculum reform. As in the case of ritual or what Edelman (1988) calls "dramaturgy," the principal effect resides in the performance of the act itself rather than in what it purports to accomplish (Kliebard 1990). What emerged from this drive to reconstruct the curriculum in the interest of Americanizing immigrants, therefore, was not its effects on immigrants or their children in schools but a sanctioned view of what it meant to be an American. The primary effect was legitimation, not instrumental change.

It is apparent that the complexities involved in reconstructing the histories of school subjects parallel the complexities in interpreting the curriculum as a whole. As with case study research, the history of school subjects offers the prospect, not only of recounting the twists and turns that school subjects have taken over the course of their histories, but of generating interpretations that are not easily detectable when the broad sweep of the curriculum is the focus of the study. In some cases, obviously, the direction that a particular subject takes is intimately tied to national movements and broad ideological concerns. As Steven Selden (1988, 1989) has demonstrated, for example, the eugenics movement in the early part of this century affected not only the way biology was taught, but legitimated a particular view of human development through the way biological knowledge was purveyed in schools. In other studies, new theoretical constructs can be formulated in connection with the fortunes of particular efforts to introduce entire new components into the curriculum, such as sex education (Imber 1982), as well as efforts to reconstruct old ones such as science (Hodson and Prophet 1983).

Case studies and historical studies of school subjects need not be viewed as antagonistic to the more popular global studies of curriculum. On the contrary, since case studies may often challenge traditional interpretations drawn from a wider array of data, their impact is clearly salutary in terms of our historical understanding. As Harold Silver (1983) puts the matter, "Analytical history benefits from the tension between the case study and what is previously known or assumed in terms of the ability of historians not merely to pile narrative on narrative, data upon data, but to contribute to decisions about what is important to understand and how to shape the process of understanding" (303). The potentialities are limitless. A relatively neglected area of case study research, for example, is the recent (post-1958) era of curriculum history, during which the National Science Foundation, with a massive influx of money from the federal government, undertook a far-reaching program of curriculum reform in several school subjects. In the United States, there is nothing comparable to Brian Woolnough's (1988) interpretation of changes in physics or to Bob Moon's (1986) account of recent reform of the mathematics curriculum in England. It is also worth mentioning that there is a very regrettable dearth of good historical studies dealing with the curriculum, including school subjects, prior to the 19th century. Two notable exceptions are Emile Durkheim's (1977) *The Evolution of Educational Thought: Lectures on the Formation and Development of Secondary Education in France* and David Hamilton's (1989) *Towards a Theory of Schooling*.

It seems plausible that individual subjects may be even more sensitive to the winds of political and social change than the curriculum when seen in its entirety. Even in the contemporary context, new subjects or, as Reid would emphasize, topics and activities within subjects, emerge almost as soon as social problems are perceived and identified. AIDS, child abuse, drug addiction, alcohol dependency, and unwanted pregnancies as subjects, or as topics within the curriculum, have already made their way into courses of study across the United States. While the proclaimed purpose of the introduction of these subjects and topics is invariably instrumental, that is, to ameliorate the problem identified, parallel historical studies may reveal the extent to which the curriculum has been evolving as a repository for perplexing and even intractable social dilemmas. It is in this sense that new insights may emerge on the relationship of the curriculum to the symbolic order, rather than as an instrument to achieve a defined social purpose. The emergence, rise to ascendancy, decline, or disappearance of school subjects (or topics), in other words, may have as its principal significance not so much in the commonly assumed effect of instrumental efficacy but in the much more subtle, though perhaps more enduring, consequence of organizing perceptions in relation to staggering social problems.

DEFINING THE SCOPE AND DIRECTION OF CURRICULUM HISTORY

If there is a direction that the history of curriculum has taken in the course of its short history, it has been mainly toward a multiplicity, if not a new complexity, in its interpretations. This is especially true of the relationship between what is accepted as the knowledge that should be incorporated into the curriculum and the consequences for various social groups, as well as for society generally. Challenging its roots in a history of education for which the past was simply the present "writ small" (Bailyn 1960), there emerged a cadre of revisionists who saw in many of the "progressive" reforms of the 20th century the makings of domination by elites over oppressed racial and ethnic minorities, as well as the working class generally.

The effects of curriculum differentiation, to take one example, were perceived not so much as a noble attempt to adapt the curriculum to the extensive range of abilities and aspirations to be found in the new school population. In many of the new interpretations, curriculum differentiation, whether by ability grouping or tracking, began to be interpreted as an instrument for the maintenance of existing lines of social stratification. In this respect, the history of curriculum as it emerged as an identified area of study reflected those aspects of the "new" history of education which undertook a frontal attack on the celebratory historical scholarship that had been dominant for most of the 20th century and even before.

That skepticism as to the effects of what was once regarded as genuine curriculum reform remains a healthy manifestation of an emerging field. Over time, however, what had been a division between, say, Whig and revisionist history or between conflict and consensus interpretations has been both elaborated and amended considerably. As indicated, some of the newer interpretations of the rise and decline of curriculum doctrines and effects include fluctuations in the labor market, the rise of professionalism, symbolic action, the market value of school credentials, as well as the more established class conflict framework. The emergence of new conceptual frameworks through which historical data become interpreted serves to punctuate the significance of context in historical interpretations of curriculum.

If the history of curriculum contributes anything to the understanding of why and with what effect things are taught in school, it is by underscoring the significance of context. It is clear, as Seddon (1989) puts it, that the curriculum "appears as an historically specific pattern of knowledge which is selected, organised and then distributed to learners through educational institutions" (3). Moreover, these selections are made not by disembodied essences but by real people with social convictions, political creeds, professional aspirations, class allegiances, and economic motives. This holds just as true for those at the receiving end of the curriculum, those, in other words, on whom the curriculum is perpetrated, as it does for those who are in a position to validate it. Moreover, the effects of the inclusion or exclusion of elements of the culture in the curriculum may vary according to the social, political, and institutional contexts in which those selections are made.

This emphasis on context in the course of interpreting curriculum history has served (when heeded, of course) the vital role of turning attention away from a strictly technological approach to curriculum design, with its mask of neutrality, and placing it squarely within the social and political arena. The curriculum, in other words, becomes not the exclusive domain of putative expert knowledge and technological skill but emerges as a contested terrain. Given the predominant views of how curriculum construction proceeds, this is no mean accomplishment. The curriculum field, it should be recalled, was born in an era and was nourished in a milieu in which the beacon of science, usually equated with technical expertise, precision, and predictability, was supposed to replace the nebulous and untested sentiments of dilettantes. But when the design of the curriculum is seen as part of a configuration of factors that is time-bound and context-specific, then not the "one best system" (Tyack 1974), but a variety of trajectories may be plotted. Partially hidden behind each twist and turn that the curriculum took over the course of its history lay other trails, and historical studies of curriculum, rather than providing concrete object lessons, may help to clear the underbrush from those half-forgotten paths.

References

Apple, Michael W. 1971. The hidden curriculum and the nature of conflict. *Interchange* 2(4): 27–40.

Apple, Michael W. 1979. *Ideology and Curriculum*. London: Routledge & Kegan Paul.

Apple, Michael W. 1982. *Cultural and Economic Reproduction in Education*. London: Routledge & Kegan Paul

Bailyn, Bernard. 1960. *Education in the Forming of American Society*. New York: Vintage Books.

Bellack, Arno A. 1969. History of curriculum thought and practice. *Review of Educational Research* 39(3): 283–292.

Best, John Hardin, ed. 1983. *Historical Inquiry in Education: A Research Agenda*. Washington, DC: American Educational Research Association.

Bestor, Arthur E., Jr. 1953. *Educational Wastelands: The Retreat from Learning in Our Public Schools*. Urbana: University of Illinois Press.

Beyer, Landon E. 1982. Ideology, social efficiency, and curriculum inquiry: An essay response to Franklin's "The social efficiency movement reconsidered." *Curriculum Inquiry* 12(3): 305–316.

Bloch, Marianne N. 1987. "Becoming Scientific and Professional: An Historical Perspective on the Aims and Effects of Early Education." In *The Formation of Schools Subjects*, edited by Thomas S. Popkewitz, 25–62. London: Falmer.

Bobbitt, Franklin. 1912. The elimination of waste in education. *The Elementary School Teacher* 12: 259–271.

Bobbitt, Franklin. 1918. *The Curriculum*. Boston: Houghton Mifflin.

Broder, Dorothy E. 1977. "Life Adjustment Education: An Historical Study of a Program of the United States Office of Education." Unpublished doctoral dissertation, Teachers College, Columbia University, New York.

Brown, Elmer E. 1901. Present tendencies in secondary education. *School Review* 9(87 and 88): 446–458, 498–515.

Burns, Gerald T. 1987. "Revolution by Committee. The NEA and the Emergence of the Modern American Secondary Curriculum in the 1890s." Paper presented at the Annual Meeting of the History of Education Society, Teachers College, Columbia University, October 9–11, 1987.

Burns, Gerald T. 1988. Tradition and revolution in the American secondary curriculum: The Cambridge High School case. *Journal of Curriculum Studies* 20(2): 99–118.

Carbone, Frank, Jr. 1977. *The Social and Educational Thought of Harold Rugg*. Durham, NC: Duke University Press.

Charters, Werrett W. 1921. The reorganization of women's education. *Educational Review* 62(3): 224–231.

Charters, Werrett W. 1926. "Curriculum for Women." Proceedings of the High School Conference of November 19, 20, and 21, 1925. Edited and compiled by the High School Visitor, 327–330. Urbana: University of Illinois.

Charters, Werrett W. 1948. Ideas, men and engineers in education. *Educational Forum* 12: 399–406.

Cherryholmes, Cleo H. 1987. A social project for curriculum: Post-structural perspectives. *Journal of Curriculum Studies* 19(4): 295–316.

Cohen, Ronald D. 1987. The shaping of the American curriculum in the twentieth century: Do we know enough? *Journal of Curriculum Studies* 19(6): 568–573.

Cremin, Lawrence A. 1961. *The Transformation of the School*. New York: Knopf.

Cremin, Lawrence A. 1965. *The Wonderful World of Ellwood Patterson Cubberley: An Essay on the Historiography of American Education*. New York: Teachers College Press.

Cuban, Larry. 1984. *How Teachers Taught: Constancy and Change in American Classrooms 1890–1980*. New York: Longman.

Cubberley, Ellwood P. 1919. *Public Education in the United States*. Boston: Houghton Mifflin.

Curti, Merle. 1935. *The Social Ideas of American Educators*. New York: Scribners Sons.

Davis, O. L., Jr., ed. 1976. *Perspectives on Curriculum Development, 1776–1976*. Yearbook of the Association for Supervision and Curriculum Development. Washington, DC: Association for Supervision and Curriculum Development.

Davis, O. L., Jr. 1977. The nature and boundaries of curriculum history. *Curriculum Inquiry* 7(2): 157–168

Dewey, John. 1902. *The Child and the Curriculum*. Chicago: University of Chicago Press.

Dewey, John. 1915a. A policy of industrial education. *New Republic* 1(7): 11–12.

Dewey, John. 1915b. Education vs. trade training—Dr. Dewey's reply. *New Republic* 3(27): 42–43.

Dewey, John. 1916. *Democracy and Education*. New York: Macmillan.

Dewey John. 1931. *The Way Out of Educational Confusion*. Cambridge, MA: Harvard University Press.

Dewey, John. 1938. *Experience and Education*. New York: Macmillan.

Drost, Walter H. 1967. *David Snedden and Education for Social Efficiency*. Madison, WI: University of Wisconsin Press.

Durkheim, Emile. 1977. *The Evolution of Educational Thought: Lectures on the Formation and Development of Secondary Education in France*. Translated by Peter Collins. London: Routlege & Kegan Paul.

Edelman, Murray. 1971. *Politics as Symbolic Action*. New York: Academic Press.

Edelman, Murray. 1988. *Constructing the Political Spectacle*. Chicago: University of Chicago Press.

Eliot, Charles W. 1905. The fundamental assumptions in the report of the Committee of Ten. *Educational Review* 30: 325–343.

Frankel, Charles. 1960. John Dewey's legacy. *The American Scholar* 29(3): 313–331.

Franklin, Barry M. 1982a. The social efficiency movement reconsidered: Curriculum change in Minneapolis, 1917–1950. *Curriculum Inquiry* 12(1) 9–33.

Franklin, Barry M. 1982b. Reply to Landon Beyer's "Ideology, social efficiency, and curriculum inquiry." *Curriculum Inquiry* 12(4): 413–417.

Franklin, Barry M. 1986. *Building the American Community: The School Curiculum and the Search for Social Control*. London: Falmer.

Franklin, Benjamin. 1749. *Proposals Relating to the Education of Youth in Pennsylvania*. Philadelphia.

Friedman, Kerry. 1987. "Art education as social production: Culture, society and politics in the formation of curriculum." In *The Formation of School Subjects*, edited by Thomas S. Popkewitz, 63–84. London: Falmer.

Goodlad, John. 1966. *The Changing School Curriculum*. New York: Fund for the Advancement of Education.

Goodlad, John. 1984. *A Place Called School*. New York: McGraw-Hill.

Goodson, Ivor F. 1981. Becoming an academic subject: Patterns of explanation and evolution. *British Journal of Sociology of Education* 2(2): 163–180.

Goodson, Ivor F. 1984. "Subjects for study: Towards a social history of curriculum." In *Defining the Curriculum: Histories and Ethnographies*, edited by Ivor F. Goodson and Stephen J. Ball, 25–44. London: Falmer.

Graham, Patricia Albjerg. 1967. *Progressive Education: From Arcady to Academe*. New York: Teachers College Press.

Gusfield, Joseph R. 1963. *Symbolic Crusade: Status Politics and the American Temperance Movement*. Urbana: University of Illinois Press.

Gutek, Gerald L. 1970. *The Educational Theory of George S. Counts*. Columbus: Ohio State University Press.

Hall, G. Stanley. 1904. *Adolescence*. New York: Appleton-Century-Crofts.

Hamilton, David. 1989. *Towards a Theory of Schooling*. London: Falmer.

Hammersley, Martyn. 1984. "Making a Vice of our Virtues: Some Notes on Theory in Ethnography and History." In *Defining the Curriculum: Histories and Ethnographies*, edited by Ivor F. Goodson and Stephen J. Ball, 15–24. London: Falmer.

Hazlett, J. Stephen. 1979. Conceptions of curriculum history. *Curriculum Inquiry* 9(2): 129–135.

Hirsch, E. D., Jr. 1987. *Cultural Literacy: What Every American Needs to Know*. Boston: Houghton Mifflin.

Hodson, Derek, and Robert B. Prophet. 1983. Why the science curriculum changes—evolution or social control? *School Science Review* 65(230): 5–18.

Hofstadter, Richard. 1963. *Anti-Intellectualism in American Life*. New York: Knopf.

Imber, Michael. 1982. Toward a theory of curriculum reform: An analysis of the first campaign for sex education. *Curriculum Inquiry* 12(4): 339–362.

International Commission of the Teaching of Mathematics. 1912. *Report of the American Commissioners of the International Commission on the Teaching of Mathematics*. Washington, DC: U.S. Government Printing Office.

Jackson, Philip. 1980. Curriculum and its discontents. *Curriculum Inquiry* 10(2): 159–172.

Kaestle, Carl F. 1976. Conflict and consensus revisited: Notes toward a reinterpretation of American educational history. *Harvard Educational Review* 46(3): 390–396.

Kantor, Harvey A. 1988. *Learning to Earn: School, Work, and Vocational Reform in California, 1880–1930*. Madison: University of Wisconsin Press.

Katz, Michael B. 1968. *The Irony of Early School Reform: Educational Innovation in Mid-Nineteenth Century Massachusetts*. Cambridge, MA: Harvard University Press.

Kean, Carol Judy. 1983. "The Origins of Vocational Education in the Milwaukee Public Schools, 1870–1917: A Case Study in Curricular Change." Unpublished doctoral dissertation, University of Wisconsin, Madison.

Kilpatrick, William Heard. 1918. The project method. *Teachers College Record* 19(4): 319–335.

Kilpatrick, William Heard. 1924. How shall we select the subject matter of the elementary school curriculum? *Journal of Educational Method* 4(1): 3–10.

Kliebard, Herbert M. 1968. "The Curriculum Field in Retrospect." In *Technology and the Curriculum*, edited by Paul W. F. Witt, 69–84. New York: Teachers College Press.

Kliebard, Herbert M. 1986a. Bestor agonistes. *Educational Studies* 17(4): 542–549.

Kliebard, Herbert M. 1986b. *The Struggle for the American Curriculum, 1893–1958*. London: Routledge & Kegan Paul.

Kliebard, Herbert M. 1987. The question of John Dewey's impact on curriculum practice. *Teachers College Record* 87(1): 139–141.

Kliebard, Herbert M. 1989. Cultural literacy or the curate's egg. *Journal of Curriculum Studies* 21(1): 61–70.

Kliebard, Herbert M. 1990. Vocational education as symbolic action: Connecting schools with the workplace. *American Educational Research Journal* 26(1): 9–26.

Kliebard, Herbert M., and Barry M. Franklin. 1983. "The Course of the Course of Study: History of Curriculum." In *Historical Inquiry in Education: A Research Agenda*, edited by John Hardin Best, 138–157. Washington, DC: American Educational Research Association.

Kliebard, Herbert M., and Greg Wegner. 1987. "Harold Rugg and the Reconstruction of the Social Studies Curriculum: The Treatment of the 'Great War' in his Textbook Series." In *The Formation of School Subjects*, edited by Thomas S. Popkewitz, 268–287. New York: Falmer.

Kridel, Craig, ed. 1989. *Curriculum History: Conference Presentations from the Society for the Study of Curriculum History*. Lanham, MD: University Press of America.

Krug, Edward A. 1964. *The Shaping of the American High School*. New York: Harper & Row.

Labaree, David F. 1988. *The Making of an American High School: The Credentials Market and the Central High School of Philadelphia, 1838–1939*. New Haven, CT: Yale University Press.

Layton, David. 1973. *Science for the People*. London: Allen and Unwin.

Lynd, Robert S., and Helen M. Lynd. 1929. *Middletown: A Study in Contemporary American Culture*. New York: Harcourt, Brace.

Mannheim, Karl. 1936. *Ideology and Utopia*. London: Routledge & Kegan Paul.

Massachusetts Commission on Industrial and Technical Education. 1906. *Report of the Commission on Industrial and Technical Education*. Boston: Wright and Potter Printing

May, Henry F. 1959. *The End of American Innocence*. New York: Knopf.

Mayhew, Katherine Camp, and Anna Camp Edwards. 1936. *The Dewey School*. New York: D. Appleton-Century Company.

McKinney, W. Lynn, and Ian Westbury. 1975. "Stability and Change: The Public Schools of Gary, Indiana, 1940–1970." In *Case Studies in Curriculum Change*, edited by William A. Reid and Decker F. Walker, 1–53, London: Routledge & Kegan Paul.

McNeil, Linda. 1986. *Contradictions of Control*. New York: Routledge & Kegan Paul.

Mirel, Jeffrey E., and David L. Angus. 1985. Youth, work, and schooling in the Great Depression. *Journal of Early Adolescence* 5(4): 489–504.

Mirel, Jeffrey E., and David L. Angus. 1986. The rising tide of custodialism: Enrollment increases and curriculum reform in Detroit, 1928–1940. *Issues in Education* 4(2): 101–120.

Moon, Bob. 1986. *The "New Maths" Curriculum Controversy*. London: Falmer.

Musgrave, P. W. 1988. Curriculum history: Past, present, and future. *History of Education Review* 17(2): 1–14.

National Education Association. 1893. *Report of the Committee on Secondary School Studies*. Washington, DC: U.S. Government Printing Office.

National Education Association. 1899. *Report of the Committee on College-Entrance Requirements*. Washington, DC: The Association.

National Education Association. 1918. *Cardinal Principle of Secondary Education. A Report of the Commission on the Reorganization of Secondary Education*. Washington, DC: U.S. Government Printing Office.

Nelson, Murray R. 1978. Rugg on Rugg: His theories and his curriculum. *Curriculum Inquiry* 8(2): 119–132.

Oakes, Jeannie. 1984. *Keeping Track: How Schools Structure Inequality*. New Haven, CT: Yale University Press.

Olneck, Michael O. 1989. Americanization and the education of immigrants, 1900–1925: An analysis of symbolic action. *American Journal of Education* 97(4): 398–423.

Ong, Walter J. 1959. Latin language as a Renaissance puberty rite. *Studies in Philology* 56(2): 103–121.

Palmer, George Herbert. 1905. *The English Works of George Herbert Palmer*. Boston: Houghton Mifflin.

Popkewitz, Thomas S. 1987. "The Formation of School Subjects and the Political Context of Schooling." In *The Formation of School Subjects: The Struggle for Creating an American Institution*, edited by Thomas S. Popkewitz, 1–24. New York: Falmer.

Popkewitz, Thomas S. 1989. "A Political Sociology of Educational Reform and Change: Power, Knowledge, and the State." Paper presented at the annual meeting of the American Educational Research Association, San Francisco, California.

Powell, Arthur G., Eleanor Farrar, and David K. Cohen. 1985. *The Shopping Mall High School*. Boston: Houghton Mifflin.

Preskill, Stephen. 1989. Educating for democracy: Charles W. Eliot and the differentiated curriculum. *Educational Theory* 39(4): 351–358.

Prophet, Robert B. 1989. "Curriculum Policy Development and Social Control: Science Education in Nineteenth Century England." Paper presented at the 17th IPN Symposium on Comparative Curriculum History: The Social System of Curriculum Administration, July 1989.

Reid, William A. 1984. "Curricular Topics as Institutional Categories: Implications of Theory and Research in the History and Sociology of School Subjects." In *Defining the Curriculum: Histories and Ethnographies*, edited by Ivor F. Goodson and Stephen J. Ball, 67–75. London: Falmer.

Reid, William A., and Decker F. Walker, eds. 1975. *Case Studies in Curriculum Change: Great Britain and the United States*. London: Routledge & Kegan Paul.

Rosenthal, Dorothy B. and Roger W. Bybee. 1987. "Emergence of the Biology Curriculum." In *The Formation of School Subjects*, edited by Thomas S. Popkewitz, 123–144. London: Falmer.

Ross, Edward A. 1901. *Social Control*. New York: Macmillan.

Ross, Edward A. 1914. *The Old World in the New*. New York: Century.

Rugg, Harold O. 1926. "A Century of Curriculum-Construction in American Schools." In *Curriculum Making Past and Present. The Twenty-sixth Yearbook of the National Society for the Study of Education. Part I*, edited by Harold O. Rugg, 2–116. Bloomington, IL: Public School Publishing Co.

Schubert, William H. 1980. *Curriculum Books: The First Eighty Years*. Lanham, MD: University Press of America.

Schubert, William H. 1987. "Educationally Recovering Dewey in Curriculum." In *Current Issues in Education*. Normal, IL: College of Education, Northern Illinois University. 1–32.

Seddon, Terri L. 1989. Curriculum history: A map of key issues. *Curriculum Perspectives* 9(4): 1–16.

Seguel, Mary Louise. 1966. *The Curriculum Field: Its Formative Years*. New York: Teachers College Press.

Selden, Stephen. 1988. Resistance in school and society: Public and pedagogical debates about eugenics, 1900–1947. *Teachers College Record* 90(1): 61–84.

Selden, Stephen. 1989. "The use of biology to legitimate inequality; The eugenics movement within the high school biology textbook, 1914–1949." In *Equity in Education*, edited by Walter Secada, 118–145. London: Falmer.

Silver, Harold. 1983. *Education as History: Interpreting Nineteenth- and Twentieth-Century Education*. London: Methuen.

Sivertson, Sidney C. 1971. "Community Civics: Education for Social Efficiency." Unpublished doctoral dissertation, University of Wisconsin, Madison, WI.

Sizer, Theodore, ed. 1964a. *The Age of the Academies*. New York: Columbia University, Teachers College, Bureau of Publications.

Sizer, Theodore. 1964b. *Secondary Schools at the Turn of the Century*. New Haven, CT: Yale University Press.

Sizer, Theodore. 1984. *Horace's Compromise: The Dilemma of the American High School*. Boston: Houghton Mifflin.

Snedden, David. 1914. Current problems in home economics. *Journal of Home Economics* 6(5): 430–437.

Snedden, David. 1915. Vocational education. *New Republic* 3(27): 40–42.

Snedden, David. 1924. Education for a world of team-players and team-workers. *School and Society* 20(514): 552–557.

Snedden, David. 1931. *American Secondary Schools and Vocational Schools in 1960*. New York: Bureau of Publications, Teachers College, Columbia University.

Spring, Joel. 1976. *The Sorting Machine*. New York: Longman.

Stanek, George M. A. 1987. "Mathematics Education in the Beginnings of the Twentieth Century." In *The Formation of School Subjects*, edited by Thomas S. Popkewitz, 145–175. London: Falmer.

Stout, James Elbert. 1921. *The Development of High-School Curricula in the North Central State from 1860 to 1918*. Chicago: The University of Chicago.

Talbott, J. E. 1971. The history of education. *Daedalus* 100(1): 133–150.

Tanner, Daniel. 1981. "Curriculum History." In *Encyclopedia of Educational Research*, edited by Harold E. Mitzel, 412–420. New York: Free Press.

Tanner, Daniel, and Laurel N. Tanner. 1980. *Curriculum Development: Theory into Practice*. 2nd ed. New York: Macmillan.

Tanner, Laurel N. 1982. Curriculum history as usable knowledge. *Curriculum Inquiry* 12(4): 405–411.

Tanner, Laurel N. 1987. Events that happen—and "unhappen." *Teachers College Record* 87(1): 133–138.

Tanner, Laurel N. 1989. "The Tenth Anniversary!" In *Curriculum History: Conference Presentations from the Society for the Study of Curriculum History*, edited by Craig Kridel, 14–18. Lanham, MD: University Press of America.

Teitelbaum, Kenneth. 1987. "Outside the Selective Tradition: Socialist Curriculum for Children in the United States, 1900–1920." In *The Formation of School Subjects*, edited by Thomas S. Popkewitz, 238–267. New York: Falmer.

Tyack, David. 1970. "New Perspectives on the History of American Education." In *The State of American History*, edited by Herbert J. Bass. Chicago: Quadrangle Books.

Tyack, David. 1974. *The One Best System*. Cambridge, MA: Harvard University Press.

Urban, Wayne J. 1981. "Educational Reform in a New South City: Atlanta, 1890–1925." In *Education and the Rise of the New South*, edited by Ronald K. Goodenow and Arthur O. White, 114–130. Boston: G. K. Hall and Co.

Walker, Decker F. 1975. The curriculum field in formation: A review of the twenty-sixth yearbook of the National Society for the Study of Education. *Curriculum Theory Network* 4(4): 263–280.

White, Morton. 1949. *Social Thought in America: The Revolt Against Formalism*. New York: Viking.

Williams, Raymond. 1961. *The Long Revolution*. London: Chatto & Windus.

Willis, Paul. 1977. *Learning to Labour: How Working Class Kids Get Working Class Jobs*. Westmead: Saxon House.

Wirth, Arthur G. 1972. *Education in the Technological Society: The Vocational-Liberal Studies Controversy in the Early Twentieth Century*. Scranton, PA: Intext.

Woolnough, Brian E. 1988. *Physics Teaching in Schools, 1960–85: Of People, Policy and Power*. London: Falmer.

7

CURRICULUM POLICY

Richard Elmore
HARVARD UNIVERSITY

Gary Sykes
MICHIGAN STATE UNIVERSITY

In curriculum policy, as in most areas of public life, the government's presence has grown over the past few decades. Changes in state- and locally mandated course requirements, increased graduation standards, state involvement in the development and implementation of new curricula, and increased attention to the curricular impact of testing and textbook decisions have all figured in recent education reform efforts. As a result of its increasing visibility, curriculum has also entered the stream of education policy research. Over time, one would expect the curriculum concerns of policymakers and researchers to produce a relatively well-organized body of research.

In fact, research on curriculum policy is anything but a well-organized, distinctive field of inquiry. To be sure, a body of research—small by comparison with others in education—deals explicitly with government involvement in curriculum. But this literature is loosely organized, both topically and conceptually, and consists mainly of case studies of government-sponsored curriculum development and a few empirical analyses of curriculum decision making. Most of the research that bears on curriculum policy comes not from inquiry directed explicitly at curriculum policy but from a variety of other sources. One of these sources is disciplinary research applied to education—politics, sociology, history, and the like—that treats curriculum as an occasional topic of study. Another is the literature on evaluation of government-sponsored interventions that are thought to have curricular relevance. And a third, often overlooked, source is the literature on public policy generally, extended to the special problems of curriculum policy.

So, of necessity, "curriculum policy research" is an artificially constructed field. This chapter is less a review of research on curriculum policy, then, and more an essay on what various related bodies of research say about curriculum policy. To bound this chapter, we have grouped the relevant literature in two main categories. One covers studies of public policy that have some bearing on curriculum, either because they treat curriculum in some way or because they contribute directly to our understanding of curriculum policy. A second category includes studies of curriculum, based in the social sciences or humanities, that raise important policy issues. The chapter is organized around the two main topics of *public policy perspectives on curriculum* and *curriculum perspectives on public policy*. Part one is a selective review of research on public policy, the forms that government action takes, and the problems that typically arise in the formation and implementation of public policy, using curriculum as a topical focus. Part two deals with what existing research says about the nature of curriculum and the social and political problems that curriculum raises, using policy as a topical focus. By constructing the chapter in this way, we hope to underscore the importance of curriculum policy while acknowledging that this subject is something less than a well-defined, coherent field of inquiry. In the final section of this chapter, we look ahead to future research topics and to emerging opportunities for research on curriculum policy. We should enter a caveat at this point that we have chosen to limit the subject matter of this chapter in at least two other important ways. First, we focus our attention on policies that affect curriculum in public elementary and secondary schools, and we do not treat either the subject of public regulation of private schools or curriculum policy for post-secondary education. Second, we focus mainly on curriculum policy in the United States, with occasional contrasting references to other countries. We have chosen this latter focus both because an international frame of reference would require the development of a scheme for comparing different curriculum policy systems, which we felt was beyond the scope of this chapter, and because we felt that much of what we had to say about U.S. examples is relevant to other systems.

PUBLIC POLICY PERSPECTIVES ON CURRICULUM

The study of public policy has emerged in recent decades as a differentiated field with a core set of intellectual concerns. One approach to defining the subject matter of curriculum policy research is to start with these core concerns and apply them to curriculum. Four such issues make up our analysis: (1) the nature of policy and its consequences for how we think about curriculum policy; (2) the policy formation process and its impact on curriculum policy; (3) the forms of government action that influence individuals and institutions and how these forms relate to government involvement in curriculum; and (4) the relation of policy to practice in institutional settings, with emphasis on curriculum and instruction in schools.

What Is Curriculum Policy?

We may begin by defining "curriculum policy" as the formal body of law and regulation that pertains to what should be taught in schools. Research on curriculum policy, then, explores how official actions are determined, what these actions require of schools and teachers, and how they affect what is taught to particular students. Such research might examine, for example, how course requirements are set by governments, how these requirements are translated into policies at the local district and school level, and how policies from various levels affect the organization and delivery of academic content to specific types of students in schools. This simple identification of policy with formal law and regulation serves as a useful point of departure, but oversimplifies the meaning of both curriculum and policy while concealing much of what is interesting and important about their relationship.

Intent versus Action. The literature on public policy distinguishes between policies as statements of intent and policies as actions—policies as statements of what ought to be and policies as what actually happens. One formulation of this distinction defines "policy statements" as "declarations of intent on the part of government . . . to do something" and "policy actions" as "what government does as distinguished from what it says it is going to do, sometimes with many conflicting and unclear voices" (Ripley 1985, 40–41). This distinction between policy statements and policy actions suggests that policies are not simply made and then implemented (or not implemented). Rather, a constant tension develops between the intent of formal policies and the ensuing actions of people and institutions.

This tension surfaces in concrete ways. Seemingly straightforward policies—content requirements for specific grade levels, for example—are often implemented very differently across localities, schools, and classrooms. The relative emphasis given to particular topics, the materials used to present the topics, and the instructional strategies employed—could each produce significant variation in the curriculum delivered to students. Is the "policy" in this example the original statement of the curriculum content or the actual content the student receives? From the policymaker's or the bureaucrat's point of view, policy is usually stated in law or regulation. From the parent's, child's, or teacher's point of view, policy is likely to mean what is actually delivered in the classroom.

This tension arises from several sources. First, policy statements usually lack sufficient detail to prescribe actions fully, as when, for example, state curriculum guides describe a course of study in a specific subject but do not say anything about how to decide among the relative importance of the various subjects (e.g., "Do we spend two days or two weeks on probability in fourth-grade mathematics?"). Hence, policy statements usually require a high level of discretion and interpretation on the part of those who are supposed to carry them out. Second, policy statements often do not resolve important conflicts among political interests, as when, for example, creationist and evolutionist views of biology are both mentioned in state curriculum guides, leaving local districts to sort out these competing views. In these cases, political conflicts embedded in policy statements can drive disputes to lower levels and result in a myriad of adjustments, compromises, and continued periodic conflicts.

Even when policy statements are successful in resolving political conflicts, they often do so by pushing aside important practical issues, as when new textbook adoptions by state agencies fail to take account of the transitional problems of moving from one text to another. As local educators attempt to carry out policy statements, these practical issues emerge again, often resulting in significant adaptations of the initial policy.

Finally, policy actions often precede, rather than follow from, policy statements, as when a science curriculum, first developed and tried in a few schools, becomes the basis for district-wide curriculum and then state guidelines. So our conception of policy, as applied to curriculum, should include not just official statements of what is intended, but also the reciprocal relationship between intention and action. Practice makes policy, even as policy shapes practice.

Uncertainty. In a similar vein, policies are made with highly uncertain knowledge of their potential consequences. Most policies are more or less well-informed guesses, or hypotheses, about means-end relationships.

> The object of any policy proposal is to control and direct future courses of action—which is the only action that is subject to con-

> trol. Accordingly, [policies] are assertions of fact of the if-then form, and the one thing we know about them is that their truth value has not been determined. All policies, therefore, carry with them some probability of error and cannot be accepted as correct a priori. (Landau 1977, 425; see also Pressman and Wildavsky 1974)

While policies are typically uncertain predictions, policymakers usually regard them as simple assertions of fact. Policy making involves political advocacy, and advocacy blurs the distinction between fact and prediction. Hence, while policy advocates may see a given policy as transparently beneficial and feasible—as correct a priori—policy researchers are likely to see the same policy as a web of highly uncertain, interdependent events. While policy advocates may assign the causes of a policy's failure to bad motives on the part of implementors or political opponents, policy analysts are more likely to look for the causes of failure in faulty prediction and design. So, for example, advocates of increased high school graduation requirements, in the form of more academic courses, see the benefits as self-evident. Analysts or researchers would ask whether additional required courses actually result in additional learning; whether uniform course requirements affect all students equally or have a greater impact on some students; and whether additional required courses actually result in more academic content being offered by local school systems (they may simply relabel existing courses).

From the perspective of the advocate or policymaker, policies appear to be tightly connected assertions of value and fact. From the perspective of the researcher, policies are more or less uncertain predictions, never to be taken at face value.

Multiple Forms of Authority. In curriculum, as in many other areas of public policy, direct government intervention, in the form of law or regulation, is only one among many sources of influence on what gets taught. Governments influence curriculum in a variety of indirect ways—for example, by sponsoring research and development, by endorsing the curriculum ideas of professional organizations, and by the way they frame policies in related areas, such as teacher preparation and testing. Furthermore, governmental policy is not the only source of authoritative ideas about curriculum. Teachers and schools take their cues about curriculum from a number of authoritative sources, including their own professional judgment, professional reference groups, informal networks of colleagues, and higher education institutions. In many instances, these sources have authority equal to or greater than formal policy; indeed, policy often incorporates or capitalizes on these sources in order to influence curriculum. If direct governmental intervention is one among many sources of authority over curriculum decisions, then the study of policy effects must take account simultaneously of other sources of influence.

Policies as Symbolic Action. Policymakers and researchers alike often take an instrumental view of policy: policy making is purposeful behavior designed to accomplish tangible results by changing people and institutions. In fact, policy making often has little to do with instrumental action. Policymakers of all types—elected, appointed, and career officials—engage in a variety of behaviors designed to generate and solidify support of various constituencies. A major way of doing this is by taking positions on key issues (see, e.g., Mayhew 1974). When a legislator, school board member, or school administrator takes a position in favor of a specific approach to bilingual education, he or she is often articulating a particular constituency's interest on the issue or trying to gain the support of a constituency by articulating a position. On certain issues, the practical consequences of particular policies may be less important to policymakers than articulating positions and building alliances (Edelman 1967; Elder and Cobb 1983).

Policy making may have little to do with instrumental action because political circumstances often force policymakers to act even though they have no idea what the correct action is. Early cases of acquired immune deficiency syndrome (AIDS) in schools, for example, provoked a series of actions on the part of local school boards and administrators, some of which involved the introduction of new content to the curriculum. These early actions, one might argue, were based less on a considered understanding of the role that education would play in reducing the incidence of AIDS and more on the necessity for some public expression of concern about the problem, regardless of its instrumental value. Policies, then, often signal that certain public concerns are legitimate, even though the role that policy can play in these concerns may be unclear.

Most policies, of course, are combinations of instrumental and symbolic action. In the late 1960s and early 1970s, the National Science Foundation (NSF) invested nearly $5 million in the development of an upper elementary social studies curriculum called Man: A Course of Study (MACOS). MACOS provoked a major debate among educators and policymakers, in which its opponents argued that it indoctrinated students in ethical relativism and legitimated antisocial behavior. MACOS was conceived as a deliberate, instrumental use of public resources to develop a new approach to social studies. Its opponents saw it as an attempt to undermine the moral fiber of American youth (Schaffarzick 1979, 9–15; Boyd 1979, 91). This combination of the instrumental and symbolic pervades many curriculum policy decisions.

Policies as Ideologies for Organizing Authority. If policies serve symbolic functions, they also provide or reflect ideologies about the organization of authority in society. In the United States, for example, we have a long-running debate about the meaning of federalism in education policy (Elmore 1986). A consistent motif in this debate has been the ideology of local control. Most important decisions about what is taught in public schools, the story goes, should be made by elected officials at the local level, because local government is closest to the citizens. The ideology of local control is violated as often as it is honored, of course.

Federal and state governments routinely intervene in local policy decisions when broader interests are at stake. Private corporations—publishers, test makers, and the like—exercise significant influence over local decisions (Cohen 1978). Local control, in certain periods and places, has been synonymous with political patronage, corruption, and discrimination.

Similarly, the ideology of local control is inconsistent with other important ideologies. It is often contradicted, for example, by the doctrine that states exercise the formal constitutional authority over education, and by the doctrine that states are constitutionally accountable to the federal government for providing equal protection under the law for all citizens. Despite these contradictions, the ideology of local control persists, with powerful effects on the language of education policy, because it provides a relatively simple formula for making sense of the enormous diversity of local conditions in the United States. The ideology of local control in education is important, not for its accuracy in portraying how the system actually works, but for its utility in organizing complexity and acknowledging diversity in the face of homogenizing forces at the state and federal levels. Local control, that is, provides a way of organizing conceptions of authority in a complex system.

Policies operate on many levels to organize authority. They set norms for how levels of government deal with each other. They define relationships among key organizational and political interests, as when collective bargaining laws and contracts define relations among teachers and administrators. They structure interactions between schools and their clients, as, for example, when they define mechanisms for parent participation in school decision making or define rules for parent choice of schools. And they organize authority among parts of the education system when they provide separate finance and governance structures for elementary and secondary schools, community colleges, state colleges, and universities.

So the accumulation of policies around an area like curriculum carries with it an ideology—often more than one—for organizing authority. In U.S. public elementary and secondary education, the prevailing ideology is that authority for the formal curriculum resides largely with elected officials and administrative agencies at the local and state levels, while the authority for application of curriculum in the classroom and school largely resides with teachers and administrators in those settings (Kirst and Walker 1971). As we shall see later, this ideology considerably oversimplifies relationships among key influences on curriculum and instruction. But the ideology serves as a general organizing principle for policy making about curriculum. And changes in policy which challenge this ideology create conflict and uncertainty.

The answer to the question, "What is curriculum policy?" might begin from a concrete reference point in the body of law and regulation that prescribes what should be taught to whom. But this relatively simple definition does not capture the many dimensions of policy as it actually operates. Policy includes not just the intentions of policymakers embodied in law and regulation but the stream of actions that follow from those intentions. Policies are not simply authoritative edicts but also uncertain predictions about means and ends that can be subjected to test. Policies are not the sole determinants of official actions; rather, they work in concert with other influences. Policies operate not just as instruments for accomplishing tangible results but also as powerful symbols for mobilizing political interests and as ideologies that legitimate authority.

These complexities in the meaning of policy run parallel to complexities in the meaning of curriculum. Just as scholars of public policy see a tension between formal statements of intention and the actions that are associated with them, so too do scholars of curriculum see a tension between curriculum as stated in formal terms and the curriculum as enacted in the classroom. Attempts by researchers to separate "*what* is (or should be) taught," "*how* it is (or should be) taught," "and *to whom* it is taught"—to separate curriculum from instruction directed at particular students—have proven difficult to sustain. Just as scholars of public policy treat policies as hypotheses about government action and its effects (Pressman and Wildavsky 1974), so too do curriculum scholars often treat curriculum as a complex set of predictions about the relationship between content and student learning (e.g., Floden et al. 1988; Schwille et al. 1988; Walker 1990). Just as scholars of public policy are likely to see direct government intervention as only one among many sources of authority that operate on key decisions in society, so too do curriculum scholars see curriculum as emerging from a variety of sources in society. Just as scholars of public policy are likely to see policies not just as instruments but also as symbols and ideologies, so too do curriculum scholars often see curriculum as performing symbolic and ideological, as well as instrumental, purposes. So complexities in the meaning of policy and curriculum are parallel.

Agenda Formation: Where Do Curriculum Policies Come From?

Tracing the origins of policy and describing how policy is formed are important aspects of the study of public policy. In the most literal sense, this kind of study traces the path of decisions leading to a particular law or regulation. Authoritative decisions about what is taught to whom—changes in course requirements, textbook adoptions, the development of a new curriculum—are preceded by a process that can be subjected to scrutiny. Indeed, much of the literature that bears on curriculum policy involves some reconstruction of the processes by which authoritative curriculum decisions are made (see, e.g., Atkin and House 1981; Welch 1979), and frequently implicates larger issues than who decided what.

Decisions and Nondecisions, Conditions, and Problems. At any given time, some subjects are considered appropriate for public decision making and others are not

(Bachrach and Baratz 1962). The culture of public problems in the U.S., for example, features a general taboo against introducing religious subjects into the public school curriculum. Religion enters public discussions of curriculum on the margins of decision making—in the form of protests against the way textbooks treat sensitive religious topics, for example—rather than as a decision about, say, which religious topics should be included and how. Likewise, problems of curriculum and instruction associated with certain types of students—language minorities and handicapped students, for example—often do not surface as issues requiring public decision until advocacy groups bring these problems to the attention of school officials (Boyd 1979).

Research that focuses on formal decision making about curriculum tends to overlook the processes by which some problems are determined to be "public," whereas others are not. Behind formal decision making lie deeper processes through which ideas about social problems arise, take some coherent form, and are defined as appropriate subjects for public policy.

Students of public policy distinguish between conditions and problems. "Conditions become defined as problems when we come to believe that we should do something about them" (Kingdon 1984, 115; see also Wildavsky 1979, 42). High school graduates' knowledge of academic subjects, for example, was simply a condition until it was articulated as a problem requiring public action, first in the late 1950s and again in the early 1980s in the United States. The transition from a condition to a problem requires information about the condition, a focusing event or set of events, and some set of actors privy to decision making who can make a case for public action (Kingdon 1984). In the late 1950s, for example, the focusing event was the Soviet launch of Sputnik, which brought to light a torrent of information about the state of education. In the 1980s, the focusing event was a perceived decline in U.S. economic competitiveness together with publication of a presidential commission report, *A Nation at Risk* (National Commission on Excellence in Education 1983). This waxing and waning of attention to academic performance also illustrates how certain public problems can fade into the background, as others emerge (Walker 1990, 108–110). In the aftermath of the Sputnik era, the problem of mathematics and science education was displaced by a growing concern over racial equality in the 1960s, not because the initial problem had been "solved," but because a different set of focusing events raised the salience of a different set of problems.

By the time conditions become defined as problems appropriate for public decision making, they typically already contain the seeds of a solution. In the political decision making process, ideas become compelling reasons for public action

> to the extent that they distinguish heroes from villains, those who must act from those who need not, and to the extent that these distinctions fit with the aspirations of the parties so identified . . . If powerful people are made heroes and weaker ones villains, and if work is allocated to people who want it and away from people who do not, an idea has a greater chance of becoming powerful. (Moore 1988, 80)

Focusing on the state of mathematics and science knowledge among American high school students, for example, limits to a manageable level the universe of heroes and villains, those who must act and those who need not, and hence carries with it an implicit set of solutions to the problem of waning American competitiveness.

The ideas required to galvanize public action may contain the seeds of their own solutions, but they provide only vague and contradictory guidance for the design of specific policies. Definitions of academic achievement as a policy problem in the United States, for example, typically cast teachers as both villains and heroes, as both the root of the problem and as the source of the solution. Hence, policies that attempt to address academic achievement too often treat teachers punitively, by introducing external controls, and direct attention away from increases in knowledge and capacity that are required to make major changes in students' learning (Elmore and McLaughlin 1988).

The Conditions of Policy Making: Rational Actors or Garbage Cans? Until recently, analyses of policy making tended to take one of two broad views. The first, noted above, is an instrumental view in which policy making is purposeful, goal-directed behavior designed to accomplish tangible results by changing people and institutions. Policy, in this view, is a rational means for achieving collective social ends and for making improvements on a scale that cannot be achieved by even the most enlightened individual actions. This view characterizes much of the general literature on policy analysis (see, for example, Weimer and Vining 1989) and studies of curriculum policy that prescribe methods for making effective curriculum decisions (see, e.g., Walker 1990). A second view, pluralist in its orientation, depicts policy making as political bargaining. Policies emerge from interactions among actors, each with their own political interests, each exercising limited influence on specific decisions, the effect of which is to produce incremental changes in policy over time. This view characterizes much of the literature on political bargaining (see, for example, Lindblom and Braybrooke 1963) as well as studies that focus on the politics of curriculum decisions (see, e.g., Boyd 1979; Elboim-Dror 1970; Kirst and Walker 1971; and Merelman 1973).

Both of these views impute considerable rationality to policy making. Instrumental views see policy as rising out of well-defined social purposes, and policy making as the joining of purposes with means. Pluralist views see policy as rising out of the purposeful actions of diverse political interests, and policy making as the process of reconciling these competing interests. In each of these views, people are portrayed as acting rationally on their interests, and the resulting policy is seen as an expression of these interests.

An alternative to these views emerges from recent research on policy making. This alternative view relaxes certain assumptions of rationality embedded in earlier theories of policy making and paints a less deterministic picture of the conditions under which policy is made.

According to the alternative view, policy making is characterized by a constant flow of problems, solutions, participants, resources, and outcomes. The process is not a rational one, in which problems arise and solutions are deployed through the purposive actions of participants using their resources to produce desired outcomes. Rather, problems and solutions flow in more or less independent streams, and they converge, often in random ways, around critical events. Decision making is

> a garbage can into which various kinds of problems and solutions are dumped by participants as they are generated. The mix of garbage in a single can depends on the mix of cans available, on the labels attached to the alternative cans, on what garbage is currently being produced, and on the speed with which garbage is collected and removed. (Cohen, March, and Olsen 1972, 2)

Policy making is composed of three "process streams":

> First, various problems come to capture the attention of people in and around government. . . . Second, there is a policy community of specialists—bureaucrats [planners, evaluators, budget analysts, legislative staff], academics, interest groups, researchers—which concentrates on generating proposals. They each have their pet ideas or axes to grind; they float their ideas up and the ideas bubble around in these policy communities. . . .Third, the political stream is composed of things like swings of national mood, vagaries of public opinion, election results, changes of administration, shifts in partisan or ideological distributions [of decision makers], and interest group pressure campaigns. (Kingdon 1984, 92–93)

These three process streams operate more or less independently of one another: problems sometimes emerge without obvious solutions, solutions are argued without reference to particular problems, the policy community converges on particular problems or solutions independently of key political actors, or key political actors articulate interests and ideologies that are attached to no particular policy solutions. This "policy primeval soup" (Kingdon 1984, 122) of problems, solutions, advocates, decision makers, and resources work to form agendas of ideas in good currency, which, coupled with some set of precipitating events, creates an occasion for decision making. Problems and solutions get joined together in often unpredictable and opportunistic ways, and policies are set in motion.

This looser, less rational view of policy making has several important implications for research. First, rather than studying formal processes of decision making—the legislative process, for example—this view suggests that research should focus on the "policy communities" or "issue networks" (Heclo 1978) that form around certain concerns. School board decisions about the biology curriculum, the National Science Foundation's decision to invest in a particular new science or mathematics curriculum, or a state legislature's decision to change high school graduation requirements are formal processes embedded in a more complex set of relationships. By the time decisions arrive in these formal settings, they have already been influenced in important ways by a larger process of agenda formation. In order to understand how curriculum issues are decided, one must understand this process by which the agenda is formed, not just the process by which the formal decisions are made.

Second, this view suggests that research should treat relationships between problems, solutions, and political interests in policy making as problematic. Rather than assuming that policymakers act rationally on the basis of well-formed conceptions of problems and alternative solutions, one might examine the sources of problems and solutions and how they get joined in the actions of policymakers. Rather than assuming that interest groups have well-formed solutions aligned with their perceptions of problems that need solving, one might examine how interest groups make use of existing problems and solutions to enhance their influence in issue networks. Attention in state legislatures to academic standards for high school students, for example, might be less a function of the desire to increase performance in an internationally competitive economy, and more a function of the hope to find a quick, low-cost response to a pressing political problem in a period of limited revenue. A political upheaval about the teaching of evolution in the biology curriculum may have less to do with formal decision making about curriculum content, and more to do with the perception of certain interest groups that they are routinely excluded from networks in which key curricular issues are formed into an agenda.

Third, this view suggests that traditional notions of control and power need to be modified to reflect a more complex and elusive substructure of decision making. Rather than assuming that, at any given time, some collection of actors has the power to decide for others, one might examine the complex ecology by which actors cooperate around key problems and solutions to enhance their influence relative to others. Increased policy making activity at the state level, for example, does not necessarily mean decreased control at the local district level or the school level (see Cohen 1982; Fuhrman and Elmore 1990). Education professionals at the state, local, and school level may, in fact, be cooperating to increase their influence relative to other actors—business, elected officials, and so forth. Simple power relationships in which one side loses and the other side wins may not accurately portray the fluid structure of influence around issues like curriculum.

Studies of curriculum policy making typically take formal processes of decision making as their initial point of departure, overlooking the processes by which the agenda of decision making is formed. Agenda formation and decision making may not be as orderly or purposive as prevailing views of curriculum policy would suggest. The roots of curriculum policy run deeply into key policy communities—academic experts, commercial publishing and testing concerns, state and local policymakers, administrative elites, and religious and political interest groups. Understanding how curriculum policy decisions are made depends in part on understanding how these policy communities define problems and solutions and how they influence each other.

Forms of Government Action

Policy Instruments. Government involvement in curriculum, as in many other areas of public life, is not a simple matter of making and implementing rules. Government action takes a variety of direct and indirect forms, and it involves both the exercise of rule-making authority and the mobilization of authority from other sources. Curriculum policy represents the full variety of forms of government action. (This section draws on McDonnell and Elmore 1987; see also Elmore 1987, 1988; Ingraham 1987; Linder and Peters 1989; Salamon 1989.)

The most commonly recognizable forms of government action, are mandates and inducements. *Mandates* are rules governing the action of individuals and agencies that are intended to produce compliance. *Inducements* are transfers of money to individuals and agencies in return for certain actions. In curriculum policy, an example of a mandate might be a state requirement that all schools offer a specified number of courses in a given subject matter area. Failure to comply with the requirement might result in a loss of state accreditation. An example of an inducement might be a state grant program that supplies funds to school districts willing to adopt a curricular innovation.

Governments employ two other strategies as well. One is *capacity building*, or the transfer of money for investment in material, intellectual, or human resources directed to long-term production of desired results. An example of capacity building might be grants by government agencies, such as the National Science Foundation, to universities for the development of new curricula in math and science, which are then made available for voluntary adoption by schools and districts. The distinction between capacity building and *inducement* is the difference between transfers of money intended to produce immediate effects (inducements) and transfers intended to increase the long-term ability of individuals and agencies to produce desired results (capacity building).

A final form of government action is *systemic changes*, or transfers of authority among individuals and agencies in order to alter the nature of social relationships by which public goods and services are produced. An example might be the creation of teacher centers, independently chartered organizations to which teachers belong and from which they receive assistance and support in the development of new materials and teaching techniques.

Most policies combine these common instruments and strategies, but distinguishing among forms of government action at some elemental level is useful because each form of action raises a different type of problem.

Mandates raise the basic problem of enforcement, compliance, and variable capacity. When a state issues a regulation specifying what should be taught in a given subject, for example, it assumes responsibility for enforcing that regulation, and the resources that the state agency uses for enforcement are resources it cannot use for other purposes. And schools will vary in their capacity and inclination to comply with a given regulation. Some already will be in compliance, some will find compliance easy to manage; for others, compliance may be costly and difficult. Faced with variable capacity, the state then confronts the problem of whether to use enforcement to generate compliance or to use inducement or capacity building to assist schools or districts at the low end.

Inducements also raise problems of variable capacity. Some schools and districts are initially better prepared to respond to inducements than others. Hence, any grant program that attempts to get schools and districts to implement a particular curriculum will necessarily produce a range of responses. The state can attempt to reduce variability by using mandates or seek to increase the capacity of less well-prepared districts.

Capacity building raises problems of the uncertainty of long-term results. Governments investing in curriculum development, for example, have discovered that the development process may go awry; that few schools or districts may adopt the product without additional inducements; and that districts adopting new curricula may lack the capacity to implement them if they require ambitious new conceptions of teaching and learning. Faced with the uncertainties involved in capacity building, governments typically either reduce their risks by limiting their investments, or focus on short-term results rather than long-term improvements in capacity.

Systemic changes raise problems that accompany the disruption of any stable set of political and institutional relationships. When governments create new institutions and alter the distribution of authority for the production of public goods and services, they invite defensive reactions from established institutions. Authorizing teachers' centers to engage in curriculum and staff development activities might cause school systems and established staff development organizations to change their own activities and to use their political leverage with state and local policymakers to limit the influence of these new institutions. Faced with these political reactions, policymakers confront the problem of whether to protect the new institutions with mandates and capacity building or "domesticate" them by drawing them into a more formal relationship with existing institutions.

When policymakers enter a complex field like curriculum, they face an important threshold question about the form of government action most appropriate for the type of problem they are attempting to address. The "fit" between forms of government action and the problems that policymakers face should be a basic concern for research on curriculum policy. The type of issue that arises in the process of implementing curriculum policy is related to the type of action embedded in policies. An important part of policy research on curriculum issues, then, should be a more refined conception of the type of problems that follow from particular courses of action.

Institutional Choice. Embedded in the choice of government actions is a more basic issue of which institutions in society should be authorized to deal with collective problems, and how these institutions should be designed (Brandl 1988; Clune 1987; Gormley 1987). Policy researchers call this issue *institutional choice*.

At any given moment, policy is made within a fairly stable set of institutional relationships and these relationships represent an implicit division of authority and capacity. In curriculum, for example, the federal government focuses largely on research and development activities designed typically to increase the capacity of schools; states engage in some level of development and capacity building, but focus their curriculum involvement on regulation designed to ensure student access to certain types of subject matter; and localities engage mainly in the direct delivery of academic content. The full range of institutional actors that operate on curriculum decisions is, of course, much broader. Colleges and universities affect curriculum in elementary and secondary schools by the standards of admission they set and by the education they provide to teachers. Textbook publishers and testing firms have a proprietary interest in supplying materials and assessment instruments that fit with prevailing state and local views of curriculum. A variety of educational interest groups—associations of teachers, administrators, subject matter specialists, parents, and school boards—have a stake in curriculum decisions that are related to their spheres of influence.

Typically, the study of policy making and implementation holds these institutional relationships constant. Analyses of institutional choice ask the more fundamental questions of which institutions should perform which roles in a given area, what are the strengths and limits of particular institutions, what institutional roles seem to be lacking, and how new institutions should be designed to perform certain functions.

An example of an institutional choice issue is the development of the National Board for Professional Teaching Standards. The proposal for the board grew out of a blue ribbon report issued by a task force sponsored by the Carnegie Corporation (Carnegie Forum 1986). A majority of the membership of the board is teachers. When it becomes fully operational, the board will provide voluntary certification for teachers wishing to be distinguished in their field. This certification will be based on a broad battery of assessments that may include conventional examinations of subject matter, simulated problem-solving exercises, and evaluation of teacher-assembled portfolios. The board is a new institutional actor in the process of certifying teachers. The board's primary reference group is the profession of teaching, rather than institutions of higher education or state and local educational agencies. Board certification introduces a new type of credential into the educational system. The board's methods and criteria of assessing teachers for certification introduce a new standard for "what teachers should know and be able to do." The development of assessment techniques involves a major research and development activity that will influence prevailing views of good teaching. In other words, the deliberate introduction of a new institutional actor into an established set of institutions that operate on teacher preparation and certification alters the conditions for policy making and implementation in teacher preparation, certification, and—eventually, as new expectations percolate through the system—in curriculum.

Embedded in any set of curriculum policies, then, is a set of implicit or explicit assumptions about the allocation of public authority among institutions, public and private. Policy research typically holds these assumptions constant and studies the play of action around them. Another perspective on curriculum policy might be to expose these assumptions about institutional choice and examine their effect on how policies are formed and implemented. Still another perspective might be to suggest alternative institutional choices and predict their effects on policy formation and implementation.

The Relationship Between Curriculum Policy and Practice

As noted above, the complexities of policy run parallel to the complexities of curriculum. Understanding curriculum policy, then, involves understanding the parallel processes by which policy and curriculum are elaborated in teaching practice. In its simplest form, this policy-practice connection can be portrayed as a system in which curriculum emanates from authoritative sources, is influenced by the medium of school organization and established patterns of teaching practice, and results in certain effects on student learning. Central agencies—federal and state governments, and district offices—formulate policies that are designed to change teaching practice. For example, a state government concerned with math literacy among high school graduates might increase the number of years of mathematics required for graduation. Once developed, policy is carried through the system to the practitioner by one or more forms of government action. These implementation mechanisms reach practitioners through their immediate working environment and have some impact on teaching practice, which in turn has some impact on student learning.

Policy analysts offer a number of accounts of the influence of educational policy on classroom practice. Some argue that policy has a major impact on practice, while others see only modest effects. Still others argue that policy impact varies across classrooms and schools. Analysts also differ on the nature of the change in practice that results from policy. Some argue that educational policy has a negative impact on teaching. Others believe that policy can have a positive impact on teachers' content decisions. Finally, analysts offer contrasting explanations for the relationships they describe between educational policy and classroom practice. Some attribute the minimal influence of educational policy to the inherent conditions of practitioners' work, others to the nature of the educational organization. Still others suggest that the explanation for minimal impact lies in the nature of policy rather than in the nature of organization *or* work. The picture of the policy-practice relationship that emerges from these alternative views, then, supplies conjectures and explanations for research on curriculum policy.

Hyperrationalization of Learning. One view, expressed by Arthur Wise in *Legislated Learning* (1979), is that policy has had an ever-increasing impact on practice, constraining and regulating the work of teachers in the interest of efficiency and cost effectiveness. A myriad of new educational policies have been enacted over the past several decades through state and federal legislation and judicial decisions. These policies include minimum competency testing, state accountability laws, desegregation decisions, compensatory education laws, and finance equalization laws. These policies have aimed to increase the effectiveness of schools for disadvantaged students, but the result has been to centralize policy making. The increased external regulation of teaching Wise refers to as

> hyperrationalization . . . an effort to rationalize beyond the bounds of knowledge, [which] involves imposing means which do not result in the attainment of ends or the setting of ends which cannot be attained, given the available means—imposing unproven techniques, on the one hand, and setting unrealistic expectations on the other. (Wise 1979, 65)

When policies are based on logic, but divorced from the reality of teaching, the argument concludes, hyperrationalization results.

Underlying such misguided policy is a rationalistic model of schooling that demands measurable outputs but pays scant attention to the processes through which they are achieved. Attempts to legislate learning promote a simplistic conception of teaching that fails to acknowledge its complexities. Teaching is a highly uncertain activity with no agreed-upon technology (Jackson 1968; Lortie 1975). Teachers approach their work intuitively, relying on their own school experiences and the particulars of their classrooms. The rationalistic model, on which legislative and judicial policy is based, fits poorly with the fundamental, time-honored patterns of teaching and results in mischievous mandates that are harmful to the quality of teaching in the long run. Wise supplies no empirical support for his arguments but clearly views policy as having substantial, pernicious effects on teaching, learning, and curriculum.

Contradictions of Control. Closely related is Linda McNeil's (1986) view that externally initiated policies have a negative impact on teachers' curriculum practices, though her explanation is substantially different from that offered by Wise. Public schools embody a basic contradiction between social efficiency goals, represented in tracking and selection systems, and educational goals, which proclaim access to all children. This conflict is rooted historically in the evolution of a school system charged simultaneously with educating citizens and with selecting them for roles in a stratified economic system. The decline in educational quality is a result of the ongoing tension between these irreconcilable goals of schooling. Efficiency-oriented controls, designed to streamline selection, have combined over time to trivialize the school curriculum and to subvert the educational goals of schooling.

Current reforms, the argument continues, have misconstrued the problem of quality by failing to acknowledge this basic contradiction. These reforms have relied on policies that centralize control over the school curriculum—testing, graduation requirements, teacher certification, and the like—thereby increasing the pressure to control, select, and track, rather than to educate. "The language of control has become the language of education reform" (McNeil 1986, xvii).

McNeil notes a further contradiction between teachers' expressed goals and the teaching styles they employ. The ideals teachers expressed would require long-term, in-depth inquiry and open-ended discussion, but teachers instead taught defensively, oversimplifying knowledge, presenting fragmented information, and omitting controversial knowledge. Defensive teaching results from the administrative structure of schools, which places primary importance on classroom control. Teachers' "patterns of knowledge control were, according to their own statements in taped interviews, rooted in their desire for classroom control" (159). Furthermore, teachers' domination and control of knowledge is linked to their lack of control in the larger school organization. The deskilling of teachers results in teacher resistance in the form of defensive teaching. The administrative structure of schools also promotes the deskilling of students, transforming them into passive receptors of knowledge prepared to invest minimal effort in school work. An administrative structure that rewards teachers for controlling students rather than educating them ultimately undermines genuine teaching and learning. Policy, in this view, generally reinforces bureaucratic controls, trivializes teaching, and subverts the goal of providing access to knowledge for all students.

Street-Level Bureaucracy. In contrast to these interpretations emphasizing the high impact of policy on teaching practice, others argue that external policies have but modest effects. One version of this argument emerges from Michael Lipsky's *Street Level Bureaucracy* (1980), an exploration of work in public organizations where street-level workers engage in direct relationships with clients (teachers, policemen, and social workers, for example). Street-level work has a number of important attributes.

First, there is considerable uncertainty about outcomes. "Street level bureaucrats characteristically work in jobs with conflicting and ambiguous goals" (Lipsky 1980, 40). Not only are goals difficult to specify but they tend to be idealistic (e.g., equal justice, good health), and hence difficult to achieve. Furthermore, client-centered goals that focus on improving individual well-being often conflict with organizational and political goals that stress efficiency and cost control. Second, uncertainty also characterizes the means which street-level bureaucrats apply in their work settings to attain their goals. The speed with which new approaches to teaching appear and disappear in education illustrates a basic indecisiveness regarding the technology of teaching. Yet a third complication in street-level work is the unpredictability of social interactions with clients. Responding to clients' personal needs and to clients' reactions to *their* decisions involves a high degree of uncertainty for street-level workers. Finally, street-level bureaucrats struggle with limited resources, including lack of time, service restrictions, and heavy case loads. These constraints force human service workers to make quick decisions based on inadequate information.

Fundamental conditions of work, then, exert powerful influence relative to external policy. The effect is to increase the discretion that street-level bureaucrats must exercise to get their work done and to decrease the impact of external control. Vague goals, uncertain means, unpredictable client relations, and limited resources all force street-level bureaucrats to make frequent judgments in their dealings with clients, and these judgments have a large effect on service that clients receive. The nature of the work is such that it is difficult to supervise and control by direct inspection.

Street-level bureaucrats adopt a number of coping mechanisms to make their workloads manageable. They routinize interaction with clients to achieve greater efficiency, and to discourage deviations from their routines. And they modify task conceptions and client images to fit the constraints under which they operate. Clients are classified according to stereotypes to make interaction with them more manageable. Lipsky argues that, at times, these routines and simplifications of the task *are* the policies the public receives. A teacher's classification of students according to academic ability significantly influences the type of knowledge that those students receive. For those students, the teacher's coping mechanisms constitute the policy that governs access to knowledge.

This view suggests that policies in general, and curriculum policies in particular, have limited influence on what gets taught to whom. Teaching entails a high degree of uncertainty regarding what should be taught and how it should be taught, for which external policies provide only limited guidance to practitioners. Teachers' generally heavy workloads result in the modification of policies to suit the amount of time and expertise available in the workplace (see Weatherly and Lipsky 1977). Faced with a host of requirements designed to influence their work, teachers are forced to modify policies to fit the amount of time and energy available. Finally, the highly uncertain character of teaching, coupled with the administrative structure of schools, makes supervision of teachers' work difficult. Minimally affected by external controls, they enjoy considerable discretion over what is taught to whom.

Institutionalized Structures and Loose Coupling. Another version of the low-impact argument comes from Meyer and Rowan (1977, 1978). Drawing on Weick's (1976) notion of loose coupling, they argue that policy has little impact on practice because of the weak core technology of teaching and the lack of agreement about which instructional methods are most effective. Exposure of this weak core technology, by direct inspection of practitioners' teaching and direct control of instructional activities and school outputs, would damage public confidence in the school system. Consequently, citizens would question the legitimacy of the school system as the main mechanism for social stratification in society. Instead of direct inspection and control, external policies and regulations focus on the formal institutional structure that surrounds schools—teacher certification, student classification, and school classification, for example. Attention to the formal structure of the school organization buffers the weak technical core of teaching and thereby preserves public confidence in the school system.

In this view, educational policy has a minimal impact on teaching because it is not directed at this aspect of schooling. The function of external policies is not to standardize or change curriculum practice in classrooms. Rather, policy is directed at sustaining the confidence of society in schooling as an important social institution.

By extension, curriculum policy serves not to determine what gets taught to whom but to maintain public confidence in the institutional forms of schooling. Curriculum policy initiatives can be seen as signals to school constituents, to allay uncertainty that schools are failing. Policy, in other words, does not dramatically influence the curriculum, but functions instead to bolster public satisfaction with the school system.

Multiple Influences, Weakly Coordinated. Yet another version of the weak influence argument comes from research on the sources of influence on practitioners' content decisions—the "content determinants" literature (see below, pp. 204–205). This research argues that external policies exert limited influence on curriculum. Teachers' content decisions are affected by informal factors such as student and parental pressures and teachers' prior convictions and beliefs about what should be taught to whom (Porter et al. 1986, Schwille et al. 1983). External policies have an impact on teachers' content decisions, but they have not standardized teacher practice. "Perhaps because content policies are not as prescriptive as they might be, teachers interpret policies differently" (Porter et al. 1988, 102). As a result, teachers act as brokers between their own convictions about curriculum content and external curriculum policies.

The impact of local context (teachers' beliefs, etc.) on content decisions can be minimized, the content determinants research argues, if policy is more precise in its requirements and more directive in its implementation. Using multiple policies that are consistent, prescriptive, and supported by legal and expert authority will provide central policy makers with greater instructional leadership (Floden et al. 1986). Teachers demonstrate a willingness to make changes that break with their prior beliefs if they receive help in implementing changes directed from sources whose authority teachers perceive as legitimate (Floden, Porter, Schmidt, Freeman, and Schwille 1981; Schwille et al. 1983). Curriculum policy could have a more direct impact on teaching practice, the argument goes, if policies were more carefully designed and implemented.

These alternatives present a range of interpretations on the relationship between policy and practice. The high-impact views of Wise and McNeil suggest that external policies have a strong, negative influence on what is taught to whom because they impose an artificial structure on teaching and promote the stratification functions of schooling over the educative functions. The low-impact perspectives of Lipsky and of Meyer and Rowan suggest that the nature of teaching work and the institutional structure of schooling buffer teaching practice from the effects of external policies, so that teachers make authoritative decisions about what is taught to whom by default. Both the high- and low-impact portrayals regard teaching as a highly discretionary, judgmental activity which is difficult to influence positively via external controls. The content determinants research, on the other hand, suggests that external policy's limited impact is traceable neither to the nature of the work nor to the institutional structure of schooling, but to poorly designed and articulated policies.

These various perspectives lay bare the basic elements of existing research on the relationship of policy to teaching practice. First, they all entail assumptions about the nature of teaching, against which they contrast the influences of policy. Most characterize teaching as highly discretionary and difficult to influence through direct control. But the content determinants research suggests that teachers are influenced by what they regard as authoritative sources and will change their practice in response. Future research on the relationship of curriculum policy to teaching practice, then, should deal more systematically with the actual nature of teachers' work and its relationship to external influences. Second, these perspectives deal with a relatively narrow range of policies focused mainly on what we earlier called mandates and inducements. Future research might focus on a broader range of forms of government action, including attempts to influence teaching through changes in institutional capacity or the incentives under which teachers and students work. Finally, all these studies portray the relationship of policy and teaching practice more or less homogeneously, with little attention to how policy influences might vary across settings. Future research on curriculum policy might explore the variability in influence across settings that other research (e.g., Elmore and Mclaughlin 1988) has uncovered.

In this section, we have explored the relevance of the literature on public policy to curriculum. We treated the nature of policy, the nature of policy formation, the main forms of government action, and the range of portrayals of how policy might influence teaching practice. We now move the focus of our attention to the relevance of the literature on curriculum to public policy.

CURRICULUM PERSPECTIVES ON PUBLIC POLICY

Policy making provides an increasingly important arena for working out curriculum issues, and policy analysis provides a distinctive perspective on curriculum. From the other side, the field of curriculum sets certain problems for policy which we explore via four traditions of inquiry. Each sets problems for policy, raises particular questions, and points to forms of influence over curriculum.

The oldest, mainstream tradition regards *curriculum as worthwhile knowledge* and focuses on what knowledge is of most worth within a society, in order to set the criteria and grounds for developing a curriculum. The touchstones may be an intellectual heritage, or the characteristics of learners, or scientifically validated knowledge, or a conception of a good society, and the policy-related aim is to provide authoritative prescriptions for curriculum content that express the underlying orientation.

A second tradition sees *curriculum as a rational system*. Analysts here regard curriculum as an instrument to achieve large-scale change in educational practice, increased efficiency in the use of public funds for education, and greater consensus on the core values a nation promotes through its public education system (Walker 1990, chapter 12). Curriculum, in this view, is a rational means for achieving collective social ends and for making improvements on a scale that cannot be achieved by enlightened individual actions.

A third tradition emphasizes *curriculum as control* and includes two streams of analysis. One group of analysts seeks to determine who should and actually does exert influence over the curriculum. Within this stream, curriculum is treated not as a knowledge claim nor as a rational means of achieving collective ends, but as a product of pluralist political bargaining. Curriculum policies emerge from interactions within a complex web of political actors, representing diverse interests and points of view, exercising limited influence on specific decisions, and producing incremental changes in educational practice in response to pressing social problems (e.g., Boyd 1979; Elboim-Dror 1970; Kirst and Walker 1971; Merelman 1973).

A second stream of analysis regards curriculum as neither knowledge claim, rational instrument, nor political result, but as a means by which certain economic and political interests in a society assert dominance over others by defining what is legitimate knowledge and by controlling access to it. From this perspective, curriculum is an expression of the dominant interests in a society and of the fundamental values such interests use to determine the distribution of knowledge (e.g., Apple 1979; Bernstein 1975; Bourdieu 1971, 1973; Bourdieu and Passeron 1977).

A fourth perspective, related to the third, treats *curriculum as capital*. Hence, the curriculum becomes a commodity in a credentials market that enters transactions with other cultural valuables. Analysts within this tradition describe the properties and dynamics of the market, concentrating particularly on processes that determine the economic value of curriculum and on principles of distribution and access (e.g., Collins 1979; Green 1980; Labaree 1989). Curriculum is treated as an economic system, participation in which produces a distribution of benefits with various consequences for society and the individual.

These four perspectives represent complex ways of seeing the curriculum, each suggesting phenomena to observe, questions to ask, and modes of interpretation (see Tyack 1976). Other orientations are available, including, for example, a linguistic analogue—curriculum as a system of meaning, as dialogue, as language. But these four perspectives serve our purpose best, which is to illuminate the relationship between curriculum and policy.

We also attend to two cross-cutting issues. The first takes up the distinction between policy as intent and as action. Curriculum scholars have pursued both conceptions of policy, examining, in the first case, a range of evidence on policy statements, rationales, and conceptions; and in the second, looking at policy effects and at the actions of educators within districts, schools, and classrooms.

A second important issue is the relationship between curriculum and instruction. How policy construes this relation is critical to how knowledge is represented and to how learning is organized. To oversimplify for the moment, two alternatives are available. The modest policy alternative seeks to influence the content of the curriculum. The ambitious alternative encompasses pedagogy within curriculum and seeks to exercise joint influence. Each approach to curriculum policy creates distinctive problems in conceptualizing and conveying knowledge.

Consider first the modest alternative. Curriculum policy aims ultimately to influence what children learn in school. By requiring that certain subjects be included in the school curriculum and by setting learning standards for those subjects, policy can have powerful effects on learning. Common sense suggests that children are more likely to learn a subject that is in the curriculum than one that is not, and at this general level—presence versus absence of content—curriculum policy mandates are an effective means of promoting learning, and several potent considerations support the separation of content from method.

One is feasibility. Influencing the nature of instruction on a widespread basis is a complex, uncertain endeavor that cannot be managed easily in the face of large variability in the settings of practice. Another is political expediency. The political environment of policy making notoriously presses toward short-term, simple, low-cost solutions that produce visible signs of success. Efforts to influence instruction, however, are likely to develop slowly and fitfully, to be costly, and to produce few immediate political pay-offs. Specification of curriculum content comes much closer to meeting these political criteria than do efforts to influence instruction.

Yet a third reason for the predominance of the modest approach is legitimacy. Instruction is regarded as the teacher's professional province, the necessary kernel of autonomy within the shell of constraints imposed by policy and administration. Shulman (1983, 501–2) expresses the relationship in this fashion:

> . . . policies are very much like laws and teachers like judges. Educational systems are organized to permit the design of policies and their interaction in the court of the classroom. Teachers must understand the grounds for competing demands on their time, energy, and commitment. They must be free to make choices that will cumulate justly in the interests of their students, the society, and humanity.

Policy must formulate a balance of public-professional and central-local forms of authority over education in our society that gives play to multiple interests across overlapping spheres of influence.

Decoupling curriculum and instruction, then, provides a neat way to manage the political and jurisdictional problems. But logic of policy does not match the logic of pedagogy, for in the classroom curriculum and instruction interpenetrate. Because criticism of education typically involves both what is taught to whom and how it is taught, pressures to respond press toward more ambitious curriculum policies that include instruction, giving rise to more ambitious strategies of curriculum policy making.

As policy becomes more ambitious, however, difficulties arise, including dispute over knowledge claims and theories, conflicts of legitimacy and control, and problems of implementation and coordination among multiple policy instruments and actors. Pedagogy as a problem for curriculum policy, then, will be a focal concern.

Curriculum as Worthwhile Knowledge

One line of scholarship in the curriculum field seeks to identify the broad orientations to the school curriculum that have arisen over the years. This work portrays the curriculum as a battleground among contending ideas, each representing complex, distinctive answers to the question of worthwhile knowledge.

Orientations to Curriculum as a Policy Concern. Various students of the curriculum have attempted to categorize fundamental orientations to the curriculum, then study their interplay in policy and practice. Two illustrative attempts are Herbert Kliebard's (1987) history of the American curriculum from 1893 to 1958, and Eisner and Vallance's (1974) depiction of "conflicting conceptions of curriculum." Each analysis identifies four powerful, contending wellsprings for curriculum that include the tradition of the liberal arts, cognitive-developmentalist approaches to learning, efforts to create efficient systems of instruction, and social reconstruction (Eisner and Vallance add a fifth orientation they label "self-actualization").

Kliebard traces the "humanist" tradition to a seminal event in the history of American education, the 1893 Committee of Ten report that affirmed liberal education as the best preparation for college and for life. Kliebard characterizes the humanists as "the guardians of an ancient tradition tied to the power of reason and the finest elements of the Western cultural heritage" (1987, 27). Their strong influence on the curriculum extends from Harvard's President Eliot, who chaired the Committee of Ten, through Robert Maynard Hutchins' "Great Books" programs, together with other champions at the University of Chicago (e.g., Mortimer Adler, Allan Bloom), to William Bennett, Secretary of Education in the Reagan Administration. This tradition always has drawn its strongest proponents from higher education, and the argument, implicit or explicit, is that the liberal learning represented in the college curriculum is the best guide to the curriculum for secondary education, perhaps even for elementary education.

Recent scholarship has challenged the notion of a single, unitary liberal arts tradition. In his history of the idea of liberal education, Bruce Kimball (1986) draws attention to two contending traditions with origins in the ancient Greek: "orators," who stressed commitment to a body of traditional and civic knowledge, and "philosophers," who served as forerunners for today's university research specialists. This history alerts us to the continuing scholarly process of identifying distinctive curricular traditions.

Kliebard identifies the cognitive-developmentalist tradition with another towering educator in the late 19th century, the psychologist G. Stanley Hall, who helped originate the child study movement. "Although frequently infused with romantic ideas about childhood," Kliebard writes, "the developmentalists pursued with great dedication their sense that the curriculum riddle could be solved with ever more accurate scientific data, not only with respect to the different stages of child and adolescent development, but on the nature of learning" (28). This approach has echoed down the decades of the 20th century in the work of Jean Piaget and other developmentalists, and in the many-stranded inquiries pursued by today's cognitive psychologists.

Yet a third tradition has concentrated on developing techniques, procedures, and systems for smoothly and efficiently organizing the curriculum. Equal parts science and business, the ideology of social efficiency represents another powerful strain within the American curriculum, tracing its 20th-century Pilgrim's Progress from the muckraking of Joseph Mayer Rice at the century's turn, through the time and motion studies of Frederick Taylor, the "scientific" curriculum making of Franklin Bobbitt, the reliance on school surveys, and the rise of the psychometric movement under Edward Lee Thorndike, to today's policy-driven efforts from state and local levels to create an efficient system of curriculum alignment.

A fourth and final orientation encompasses the powerful impulse in American political culture to reform society through the schools. Quoting Kliebard again,

> . . . the social meliorists saw the schools as a major, perhaps the principal, force for social change and social justice. The corruption and vice in the cities, the inequalities of race and gender, and the abuse of privilege and power could all be addressed by a curriculum that focused directly on those very issues, thereby raising a new generation equipped to deal effectively with those abuses. (29)

The social crises provoked by urbanization and industrialization, the waves of immigration, the struggle for civil rights, the persistence of poverty amidst affluence, all have evoked curricular responses at various times.

Throughout our history, these competing efforts to identify worthwhile knowledge have served as the broad frameworks organizing policy responses to the curriculum. Humanists and social reconstructionists define the curriculum in terms of content, while cognitive-developmentalists and social efficiency reformers have advocated a process approach, based in the first case on ideas about human learning and development and in the second on ideas about systems of instruction.

Knowledge, Curriculum, and Instructional Practice. The orientations just described point to some of the conflicts among ideas that have surfaced in curricular discourse over the years. These conflicts have played out in the speeches, journal articles, conference proceedings, and books contributed by scholars and other influentials seeking to exercise broad influence on curriculum, and historians have consulted this literature in identifying the seminal figures and their ideas.

Another place to search for ideas informing the curriculum is within the classroom, where knowledge is transacted and constructed through student-teacher interchanges. Note that these two modes parallel the distinction between policy as intent and as action. When the search for conceptions of knowledge in curriculum turns to the classroom, then the intertwined nature of curriculum and pedagogy becomes apparent. As curriculum policy seeks to influence what knowledge is represented in the classroom, inquiry must pursue the rich, complicated business of teaching and learning, for the ideas that inform the operating level of the system simultaneously implicate what is taught and how.

Just as scholars have identified distinctive curricular traditions, so have they described orientations to teaching that involve curriculum decisions. The literature on models of teaching is large, varied, and beyond the scope of this chapter. Our purpose, though, is to explore how curriculum policy may influence the way knowledge is construed within the classroom. To illustrate this possibility, consider one contemporary portrayal of teaching as the management of multiple dilemmas, a perpetual balancing act among competing goods and competing conceptions of the good (Berlak and Berlak 1981; Lampert 1985). Teachers may resolve dilemmas by adopting an approach that favors one side or the other, or by attempting to hold together opposing tendencies within their practice—"embracing contraries" in Peter Elbow's (1986) phrase. What determines how teachers become aware of and manage dilemmas in teaching? One line of inquiry seeks to assess the relative influence of policy.

To illustrate the potential impact of policy, consider three curricular dilemmas noted by the Berlaks (1981). Teachers, they argue, may choose to represent *personal versus public knowledge*, a cleavage with roots deep in western philosophy over what is worthwhile knowledge. Many teachers believe that valuable knowledge resides in the accumulated traditions of the ages, external to and independent of the knower. Alternatively, however, teachers also believe knowledge acquires genuine value in relationship to the knower. A second and related tension poses *knowledge as given versus knowledge as problematical*. In their pedagogy, teachers may represent knowledge as immutable truth or treat it as constructed, provisional, and subject to political, social, and cultural influences. Finally, teachers may treat *learning as holistic or as molecular*. In the first instance, learning is the active construction of meaning, an understanding of the whole, a process that unfolds differently from learning as the accumulation of parts or elements. The second approach treats learning as the gradual mastery of discrete parts that add up to complete understanding or skillful performance. Within this perspective, learning depends on the proper division, sequence, and reinforcement of the parts.

Curriculum policy adjudicates (often unknowingly) among such dilemmas. Imagine, for example, a state or district policy implemented via a regimen of regular standardized testing linked to highly specified scope, sequence, and pacing guides and correlated with texts that organize learning to read as the accumulation of discrete skills best acquired through drillwork. Teachers working within such a regime will still vary considerably in their instruction (see Freeman and Schmidt 1982; Porter and Kuhs 1982; Schmidt et al. 1987), but the *tendency* of such a policy framework presses toward knowledge construed as public and given, and learning as molecular.

Policy and its implements are but a portion of the influences on instructional practice, whose relative strength is open to question. One important line of inquiry, though, might trace the connections among ideas about knowledge that inform curriculum, the policies that shape curriculum, and the practices that constitute curriculum within the classroom. Curriculum conceived as worthwhile knowledge directs attention to the epistemology of policy and practice, the ferment of ideas about knowledge, and this is its comparative advantage as a way of seeing curriculum policy.

Curriculum as Rational System

A second broad perspective treats curriculum policy making as the construction of a rational system, susceptible to efficient design. In a sense, this perspective takes up where the first leaves off, for what preoccupies analysts here is not knowledge questions and claims but design principles for organizing efficient systems of instruction once first principles concerning aims have been settled.

Sociotechnical approaches to curriculum have a long history, ably documented in Raymond Callahan's widely read critical study, *Education and the Cult of Efficiency* (1962). In the early decades of this century, many of the famous systematizing efforts arose at the district level, under the leadership of dynamic school superintendents and education professors, both imbued with principles of "scientific management" employed in business. In Newton, Massachusetts, for example, superintendent Frank Spaulding introduced a range of accounting procedures into the instructional system, while "scientific" curriculum makers such as Franklin Bobbitt and W. W. Charters conducted activity and job analyses to determine the content of the curriculum (Callahan 1962, chapter 5).

Also in this period, hundreds of school systems throughout the country hired university consultants to conduct "school surveys" that concentrated on financial and managerial aspects of schooling. These surveys assessed the costs of district operations, searching for ways to increase productivity. They constituted a defense for administrators in demonstrating their efficient management of school budgets and operations, much as businessmen were held accountable for profits and losses. The surveys infrequently took up matters of curriculum and instruction, but exerted an unmistakable influence on how administrators thought about such matters. The school survey became the talisman of scientific management, an indispensable device for demonstrating sound administrative practice. And, in Gary, Indiana, superintendent Willard Wirt introduced the platoon school in 1908, an efficiency measure designed to better utilize the school plant in processing children. By 1929, over 1,000 schools across the country had adopted this scheme, which declined and faded away in subsequent years. The devices employed by the business-minded efficiency reformers extended beyond but included curriculum in their systematizing embrace.

Traditions of local control have given way to increasing activism at state and federal levels, but as higher levels in the federal system have become more active, lower levels are not less so. Rather, the sources of initiative have multiplied and the level of complexity has increased: "Within the formal governance system, then, when policy expanded at higher levels, parallel and semi-autonomous centers of power and organization also grew at lower levels" (Cohen 1982, 478). The need arose to sort out roles, responsibilities, and relationships across a fragmented "system" that sometimes appears to be centralizing and decentralizing simultaneously on different dimensions.

Models of the System. The notion of a curriculum policy system is relatively recent, and Decker Walker (1979, 269) offers one helpful depiction of the elements of a broader system, when he indicates that

> the one term "curriculum development" covers at least three distinguishable enterprises: *curriculum policy making*, the establishment of limits, criteria, guidelines, and the like with which curricula must comply, without developing actual plans and material for use by students and teachers; *generic curriculum development*, the preparation of curriculum plans and material for use potentially by *any* students or teachers of a given description; and *site-specific curriculum development*, the many measures taken in a particular school or district to bring about curriculum change there.

The past 30 years have witnessed a range of initiatives that attempt to join these elements, and a review of the most prominent normative-descriptive models will suggest variations in the choice of institutions and implements configured into systematic approaches. Early in this period, a number of federal programs adopted a *Linear R & D model* (Wirt 1975) that sought to move the results of basic research into applications that could be tested, validated, and disseminated. Unhappiness with the results of this model led to several reconsiderations, including a *configurational perspective* (Guba and Clark 1974) that emphasized loosely coordinated, decentralized, and temporary systems that could capitalize swiftly on dispersed developments; and an *inductive policy model* (Schon 1971) that relied on networking among local units rather than center-periphery dissemination of innovations.

These various models largely rose out of federal efforts throughout the sixties and seventies to promote educational change and the adoption of innovative curricula. As the locus of activism shifted from the federal to the state level in the eighties, so too did the intervention strategy. States have relied more heavily on mandates whose implements include course requirements, curriculum guidelines, required texts and materials, and statewide systems of standardized tests. Initially, states adopted these instruments singly, with policy formation rising out of issue and influence networks around particular policy innovations (e.g., minimum-competency testing). A new model, however, often referred to as *curriculum alignment*, coordinates the use of multiple implements within a state policy system.

Early Approaches: The Linear R & D Model. In 1965, colleges and universities received 77 percent of federal funding for educational R & D. By 1974, their portion had declined to 29 percent. Federal funds by then were concentrated in 17 regional laboratories and centers, in 22 major contractors, and in 10 school districts (Orlich 1979). For the next 10 to 15 years, the federal government invested in a range of strategies designed to produce, test, and disseminate high-quality curricular materials. During this period, one powerful line of development sought to couple social science to an engineering model of curriculum reform that came to be known as Linear R & D.

We can briefly sketch features of this model by examining three federal initiatives: the National Science Foundation's (NSF) curriculum development projects; the effort to establish a system of regional labs and centers; and the early childhood program known as Follow Through, which led to the largest social experiment ever mounted by the federal government. (Each of these cases is an oft-told tale surrounded by a literature too large to summarize in detail; for general reviews of this history, see Atkin and House 1981; Elmore and McLaughlin 1988; Jackson 1983; and Welch 1979.)

The federal government does not possess constitutional authority over education, but has the power to sponsor and organize research and development. Exercising this power has led to inducement-oriented and capacity-building strategies whose effects have been well documented in a number of cases, including "the" curriculum development movement sponsored by the NSF from 1954 to 1975. This federal agency funded several dozen development projects in the areas of elementary and secondary mathematics and science in a far-reaching attempt to influence both content and pedagogy. Developers were distinguished university-based scientists and the results included high-quality curricular materials for single courses (e.g., high school physics) and for course sequences (e.g., elementary mathematics).

The NSF reforms aimed not only to produce *more* math and science in the schools but to encourage a *different kind* of instruction at all levels (Jackson 1983, 157). To accomplish this aim, the NSF also supported institutes to train teachers in use of the new materials, for the curricula were not self-implementing and the accompanying necessary changes in pedagogy were significant.

The evidence in three NSF studies conducted in the late seventies (Helgeson, Blosser, and Howe 1977; Stake and Easley 1978; Weiss 1977) suggests limited effects on curricular content: the materials produced found their way into some elementary and secondary classrooms, and had secondary effects on the contents of commercially produced textbooks, particularly in biology. But the effort to alter instructional practice in mathematics and science largely failed. For example, many of the science projects advocated "process" or inquiry approaches to science—conceiving science as a verb, rather than as a noun, in Paul Hurd's phrase (Jackson 1983, 151). Several of the elementary science projects, for example, produced complicated kits of materials to encourage "hands on" science rather than text-centered instruction. But many elementary teachers were not well-educated in the sciences, found the materials difficult to manage, and soon abandoned them for traditional practices.

In their heyday, the NSF projects captured the imagination of policymakers and appeared to be the wave of the future. Scientific knowledge and a scientific process of development would produce a dramatic breakthrough in the curriculum. The next step would be to move from a project mode to a capacity-building strategy that would institutionalize curriculum development. For this purpose the federal government envisioned a complete system of free-standing labs that would serve every region in the country. A parallel set of institutions, the university-based research centers, would supply basic research around such broad topics as learning and development, individualized instruction, and teaching.

The architects of the system held a simple model, often depicted as a straight line: a set of necessary and linear functions that could be linked to form a system of agencies and agents, with shared yet separate goals, assigned responsibilities in research, development, dissemination, and adoption (Guba and Clark 1974). This tendency emerged explicitly in the creation of the National Institute of Education (NIE) in 1972, one of whose four major objectives was "to build an effective educational research and development system" (NIE 1973, 1). The capacity to bend research and development to educational improvement would become institutionalized in a system that was responsive to federal priorities but that would serve local needs.

In the years since 1965, the number of labs and centers has fluctuated, but the full system never came to fruition. Over this period, a number of the labs engaged in full-scale, systematic development of curriculum materials which they sought to disseminate to schools, including, for example, the mathematics and aesthetic education programs developed through the St. Louis–based regional laboratory. Others went further in designing entire instructional systems that they sought to implement. Prominent examples included Individually Guided Education (IGE), developed at the Wisconsin Research and Development Center, Experience-Based Career Education, developed out of four regional labs, and Individually Prescribed Instruction, created at Pittsburgh's Learning Research and Development Center.

The record of adoption and use was dismal, however, relative to the investment. Some of the problems were political, as the fate of the MACOS curriculum indicates (see p. 187). Others were commercial. The linear development of materials did not include publishers, and the government had no business competing in the marketplace. Furthermore, there was often no market for the materials. As one lab director put it, "the government wanted something new, but the educators wanted something they knew how to use" (Atkin and House 1981, 15). Finally, projects that required changes in teacher knowledge and practice had no means to produce them; the mere introduction of new materials was not enough.

The Follow Through project also supported development and implementation of exemplary programs that enjoyed science's imprimatur. In this case, however, what began as a development project in early childhood education to continue the progress made in the successful Head Start program became a large-scale planned variation experiment. The project implemented 20 models in 180 sites, and involved extraordinarily expensive, complex, and protracted processes of packaging the models and training teachers. Alongside the project ran an evaluation intended to identify which models were most effective. Instead, the evaluation concluded that

> the effectiveness of instruction depends mainly on factors that were not controlled in the experiment. Variations in effects among classrooms, among schools, and among localities were larger than variations among models. . . . the success of teaching was mainly influenced by (undefined) attributes of the setting in which it was done, rather than the expensive expertise and social science methods brought to bear on teachers. (Elmore and McLaughlin 1988, 19)

Initiatives reflecting the Linear R & D model utilized scientists and their methods to create and validate programs that could be disseminated to schools. But the various federal efforts to create a system that would manage this enterprise largely came to nought. Few of the exemplary programs found their way into the schools, and most encountered difficulty around pedagogy, for these ambitious programs involved more than the introduction of new content. Many of the federal programs also ran into political difficulties, as local communities resented federal intrusions into the curriculum, and Congress regularly looked over the shoulders of the bureaucrats and program managers, questioning whether the investment was paying off. Almost from the outset, then, challenges to the Linear R & D model emerged.

The Configurational Perspective. One set of critics thought the model itself was flawed—perhaps doomed—from the very beginning. They noted that the rational system view did not correspond well with the messy, proliferating world of agencies and activities involved in R & D. The real world of "knowledge production and utilization" had few properties of a system. Analysts began to elaborate other conceptual models that had a number of features in common (see, for example, Guba and Clark 1974, and Havelock 1969, 1973). They challenged the root metaphor of "system," attempting to replace it with more organic, naturalistic metaphors including community, ecology, and social interaction. These models attempted to identify how agencies and individuals actually engaged in knowledge production, transfer, and use and to propose a new set of assumptions for government action.

For example, Guba and Clark (1974) characterized R & D as a decentralized "cottage industry" with emergent and idiosyncratic, not shared, goals, considerable overlap and duplication in functions, no principles of hierarchy, and a pattern of negotiated, not delegated, authority. Interaction across agencies was sporadic and temporary, and R & D was peripheral, not central, to all of the players involved, even universities, where teaching is the official mission.

This naturalistic model resonated with many R & D planners, but the implications for organizing such an enterprise were murky. The configurational perspective certainly offered a better description than the linear model, but generated no clear intervention strategy. In their paper, Guba and Clark (1974) advocated greater reliance on "field-initiated studies," long-term, stable support for existing agencies, including labs and centers, and coordinating mechanisms such as an "Educational Conference Board" to supply overall planning and direction. These hardly seemed to be dramatic departures, and in fact such initiatives were already present in the mix of federal strategies. Nevertheless, what this vein of analysis contributed was a more accurate description of the diffuse, far-flung, and *non*systematic R & D enterprise.

Inductive Policy Making and the Networking Strategy. Not all of the literature challenging Linear R & D failed to produce clear policy alternatives. In his critical analysis, for example, Donald Schon (1971) provides a framework that captures an alternative line of experience within federal curriculum policy making. Schon distinguishes "center-periphery" from "periphery-periphery" models of government R & D sponsorship. In the former, the center of the system, usually a federal agency, is the source of ideas in good currency which form the basis for policy and its implementation. This "propose-dispose" model then leads government to strategies for encouraging locals to adopt the center's policies and programs.

An alternative approach conceives of the center's role as detecting good ideas around the periphery of the system, then spreading these ideas to other units. Policy making proceeds by induction—locating many exemplary instances, then creating connections among units so that good practices may be shared laterally, rather than from the center outward. The strategy appropriate to this conception is networking—putting individual units in touch with one another for the mutual sharing of knowledge, support, and other resources. Practitioners are identified as the source of ideas about curriculum, and they share these ideas with other practitioners. There is no assumption here that ideas in good currency emanate only from elite sources such as government agencies or universities.

Networking as a dissemination and assistance strategy has been widely used in education (for a review of cases and principles, see Miles 1978 and Parker 1977), including a number of federal efforts that stand in contrast to the strategy represented by the NSF projects and the regional labs and centers. Two such instances are the National Diffusion Network and its association with Title III/IV C of the Elementary Secondary Education Act (ESEA) and the federal Teacher Center Program, which enjoyed a short life in the late seventies. These projects appear to overcome some of the problems associated with systematic, large-scale development, but they have encountered difficulties of their own.

Between 1965 and 1981, ESEA's Title III supported thousands of small projects on a wide range of curricular matters that were initiated by teachers in local school districts. The results, as documented in the "change agent" studies (Berman and McLaughlin 1975; Mann, Greenwood, and McLaughlin 1975), were highly variable, contingent on such local factors as the support of a committed administrator. Over time, Title III lost favor with Congress, developing a reputation as

> an unfocused source of "mad money" for states and localities, rather than as a program with a strategy and a clear identity. Because the money was distributed in fairly small grants across many local districts, and because the projects it funded were often not highly visible, the program failed to develop a strong political constituency. (Elmore and McLaughlin 1988, 22)

Congress eventually retooled this program, turning over dissemination of projects deemed exemplary to a federal initiative known as the National Diffusion Network (NDN), which provided assistance to adopting districts by linking them with expert consultants. The strategy shifted from encouraging local development to disseminating a limited number of projects approved by a federal panel of experts (the Joint Dissemination Review Panel) through a network organized from the federal level with state affiliates and local operators. The new strategy emphasized knowledge transfer and the adoption of innovations (McDonnell et al. 1980), with practitioners serving as both developers and adopters (for an evaluation of the NDN, see Emrick 1977). The NDN was eventually terminated under program consolidation and budget reductions in the early eighties.

A second networking strategy involved federal subsidies for teacher centers, awarded competitively. Originally a British import, teacher centers sprang up around the country to support informal or open education. The early grass roots centers championed by open education advocates served as places where teachers worked voluntarily on curriculum and teaching through workshops, seminars, and hands-on activities. The teacher center movement spread gradually as an effort through which teachers could control their own continuing education, sharing craft knowledge on a peer-to-peer basis. In 1976, Congress passed legislation establishing a federal program to fund teacher centers, and for the next four years this program provided support for over 100 centers nationally. It also fell victim to budget reductions and program consolidation.

The Teacher Center Program is an interesting contrast to the programmatic R & D of the labs and centers. It represented creation of a new set of institutions that were controlled by teachers, that conveyed local, craft knowledge from practitioner to practitioner, and that spread good practice through lateral connections fostered by the federal program office and by the Teachers' Centers Exchange, a separate, federally sponsored network operation (see Devaney 1982 for a history of this project).

Both the configurational perspective and the networking strategy challenge the assumptions of Linear R & D, but none of the models has successfully managed the problem of changing teachers' instructional practices to accommodate new programs. The ambitious NSF reforms and many of the lab and center projects sought unsuccessfully to introduce significant changes into practice. The grass roots programs attempted to stimulate many small-scale local innovations, then spread new practices through informal sharing (making changes from exchanges, as one observer put it), but had difficulty demonstrating that anything valuable was taking place. Eventually, the reform movement of the eighties signalled an end to federal programmatic activism, and a fourth model emerged from the state level.

Curriculum Alignment: The Emerging State Strategy. States possess authority to directly control the school curriculum, although traditions of local control are strong in many communities. However, a powerful trend beginning in the 1970s and extending to the present has been the increase in state control over the curriculum (Boyd 1979; van Geel 1976). Increased requirements are one indication, but states recently have begun to pursue more ambitious strategies that employ multiple policy instruments in concert to influence curriculum and instruction.

The time-honored state role is to set course requirements for advancement and graduation, and a body of evidence suggests that these curriculum content mandates produce the intended effects, at least in terms of student course-taking patterns. The first wave of educational reform in the 1980s serves as a broad case study. State after state increased course requirements for high school graduation, and often raised college entrance requirements as well. The general trend of these new mandates was toward a more uniform curriculum that replaced elective "frills" with core academic courses and toward common course requirements across high school tracks, so that more students would take the core courses. This state-level curriculum policy making was widely studied throughout the eighties and the various studies converged on a common set of findings (see, for example, Grossman et al. 1985; Hanson 1989; Rossman et al. 1987; Westat, Inc. 1988).

The new high school graduation requirements had relatively little effect on academically oriented students, for they already took the required courses. But the requirements did result in substantial increases among low- and middle-range students in academic courses, particularly mathematics and science, but also foreign languages, computer science, and English, at the expense of vocational and elective courses. The studies are inconclusive, however, on whether the new requirements increased the drop-out rate, as some feared, and on what the academic quality of the new courses was. On balance, however, it appears that this round of curriculum policy successfully encouraged more students to take academic courses.

Within limits, then, curriculum policy is an effective means for broadly specifying content. However, criticism of education typically involves both what is taught to whom, and how it is taught. More ambitious curriculum policies take shape that include instruction, and this mode of policy making has led to efforts to create a systematic *set* of policies to influence curriculum and instruction.

Interest in "curriculum alignment" emerged in the 1970s with the turn to minimum-competency testing as the backbone of the accountability movement. By the 1980s, states were beginning to coordinate instruments in the design of curriculum policy systems. One study (Freeman 1990), for example, surveyed the directors of elementary education in all 50 state departments of education to determine how states were encouraging teaching for conceptual understanding, problem-solving, and other aspects of higher-order thinking. Findings indicated that 43 states employed four policy initiatives to encourage more ambitious teaching: in-service programs, goals and objectives statements, guidelines for developing local curriculum, and statewide tests.

One half of these states used two of these implements, the most common pairing being teacher in-service with goals/objectives statements. However, seven states were moving aggressively to coordinate a wider range of instruments, with California on the leading edge of this trend. That state has sponsored the development and dissemination of curriculum guides, has intervened with textbook adoptions, and is revising the statewide testing program to reflect the new goals of instruction, changing the content and format of the tests, and adding tests in additional subjects at additional grade levels.

State curriculum policy in the period from the late 1960s to the early 1980s concentrated on basic skills and minimum competencies, which were relatively easy to assess via paper and pencil tests. Researchers contributed teaching technologies designed to convey basic skills, and many districts adopted computers as an instructional tool for conveying basic skills. But within policy circles, a new consensus began to form in the mid-1980s around a new agenda—advanced cognitive skills for all children, in-depth learning over superficial coverage, lively engagement with subject matter, and teaching for conceptual understanding. Simultaneously, states have become more active in influencing instruction, but the policy implements and instructional strategies in use so far match poorly with the new agenda for teaching and learning. The minimum-competency tests, the textbooks, the curriculum guidelines, the in-service programs, do not yet reflect the vanguard consensus, and states are beginning to reform the curriculum policy system, in some cases dramatically revising the policy instruments in use.

Public policy, as Thomas Green (1983, 322) notes, "is a crude instrument for securing social ideals. We would not use a drop-forge to quarter a pound of butter or an axe to perform heart surgery. Public policy is the drop-forge or the axe of social change." This brief review suggests that policy is reasonably effective in determining the broad content of the school curriculum. But as the aims of policy become more ambitious—to introduce new *conceptions* of content, to jointly influence curriculum and instruction, to change what teachers and students know, believe, and choose to work on together—then the limits of policy emerge.

The federal efforts reviewed relied on one set of institutions and instruments. The government consciously sought to create new institutions—labs and centers, national networks of developers and adopters, teacher centers—that might be coordinated into a system. These various efforts vested authority in the expertise of university-based social scientists, in the capacity of full-time curriculum developers, and in the craft knowledge and inventiveness of teachers. No set of strategies emerged as superior, and each of the approaches ran into implementation problems and political opposition.

The unfolding strategy at the state level relies on a different set of instruments to achieve systematic control over the curriculum. Tests, texts, guidelines, and in-service education are prescribed and coordinated to yield a powerful framework to direct the curriculum. Initial evidence from a study of California's new mathematics framework, however, suggests that the curriculum alignment strategy may encounter many of the difficulties uncovered through studies of the federal programs (see the case studies reported in the Fall 1990 issue of *Educational Evaluation and Policy Analysis*). Many California teachers are unaware of the new goals of teaching for conceptual understanding, and are unclear how to pursue them in their classrooms. Old ways of thinking about mathematics and traditional methods of math teaching have a strong hold on practice and do not give way easily to new ideas.

Returning to Walker's (1979) distinctions, we see that the federal efforts of the sixties and seventies supported both generic and site-specific development as modes for influencing curriculum. Labs and centers concentrated on generic projects, while the NDN and the teacher centers supported site-specific development. Federal agencies relied on inducements and capacity building in this period. In the eighties, curriculum policy making shifted dramatically from the federal to the state level, and from development projects to policy mandates. A new conception of the policy system emerged, stressing a state regulatory role in directing the mix of compliance versus assistance-oriented policies (Elmore and McLaughlin 1982). The curriculum alignment strategy, however, is not fully in place in any state and has yet to receive a strong test. The search continues for large-scale, powerful systems through which to influence curriculum.

Curriculum as Control

The third perspective that we consider directs attention to issues of control over and through curriculum. One line of inquiry explores the normative basis for asserting control over curriculum. Another body of empirical research attempts to estimate the strength of various influences over curriculum decision making. And yet another tradition of scholarship regards curriculum as one means through which social and cultural control is achieved within society. The element uniting this diverse literature, however, is an interest in the forms and uses of power and authority in relation to curriculum.

Principles for Allocating Authority: Who Should Control the Curriculum? Various analysts have noted the trend toward greater government involvement in the curriculum (see Boyd 1979; van Geel 1976). Within a fragmented federal system, conflicts of authority arise among the levels of government and between public and professional interests. While political scientists study the play of interests to determine who actually wields authority, political theorists explore the principles that legitimate patterns of authority, a concern as old as Plato's *Republic*, which proposed placing all children full time in state institutions, thereby denying parents any authority in raising children.

In his review of judicial opinions in court cases involving the curriculum, van Geel (1976, 7–12) derives 10 principles that come into play in justifying the allocation of authority. His list, a complex mix of political values and cultural traditions, substantive norms and procedural safeguards, includes: *paternalism*, the responsibility of adults to guide the education of children and to protect them from harm; *the right of parents* to control the upbringing of their children; *the interests of state and nation* in the education of the citizenry; reference to the core political values of *liberty and democracy* in support of local control and the protection of minorities; *the principle of affected interests*, which holds that everyone affected by a decision has a right to participate in the decision making; *no delegation of legislative power*, which prevents state legislatures from abandoning their constitutional responsibility to provide education; *community control*, which identifies geographic locales within which individuals construct social relations as meaningful units for preference formation; *equity*, another core political value often used to justify federal and judicial intervention in the school program; *efficiency and effectiveness*, principles used to place authority in the hands of experts and to create conditions that maximize learning while minimizing costs; and *keeping education out of politics*, a principle used to justify professional-bureaucratic control.

Curriculum policy discourse is filled with references to these principles and to the conflicts among them, typically along the twin axes of public versus professional authority and of local versus centralized control, but the patterns are complex. Teachers may be regarded as professionals who ought to have a strong role in determining curriculum, based on their expert knowledge and their understanding of local context. But the appeal to "professionalism" has ambiguous referents. It might refer to national organizations representing teachers, such as the National Council of Teachers of Mathematics, or to state-level curriculum review committees composed of teachers, or to district- or school-level committees. And, appeals to "the" profession might include discipline-based scholars, teacher educators and researchers who study pedagogy, or classroom teachers.

Public interests also involve conflicts among principles and patterns of aggregation. Localities assert their right to control curriculum based on the affected interests of parents and of the community, while higher levels of government intervene in the name of equity and of the national interest. In the sixties, the NSF justified its curriculum reforms on the basis of national defense, and drew as well on the involvement of experts—university-based scientists who would reform the curriculum. The federal rationale then shifted to equity considerations associated with compensatory education.

In the wake of community backlash against federal intrusions, as represented most sharply in the MACOS controversy (see Nelkin 1976; Schaffarzick 1979), the federal government largely withdrew from curriculum development, but states soon became more active in asserting control over curriculum through policy making. In the eighties, the rationale for government activism was to strengthen the U.S. economic position in an era of global competition. The federal role, however, was largely indirect: commission reports, the bully pulpit, and research and the gathering of statistics. The national interest in education for a strong economy would be pursued through state and local action, not direct federal initiatives.

An interplay has developed over the years among core values and the governmental units authorized to pursue those values. Governance conflicts have emerged around the values themselves, including academic excellence, equity, choice, and efficiency, the public-professional mix of authority, and the balance of powers within a federal system. The mix of educational values and federal principles has proven unstable over the years, with some broad trends evident, including increased central control, but with considerable variation across states and even localities within states. Inquiry on the normative basis for allocating authority traces the interplay of principles and values over time and their variation across jurisdictions (for an analysis of state political cultures that shape values, see Mitchell, Marshall, and Wirt in press; Wirt 1977; Wirt, Mitchell, and Marshall 1988; for a more specific comparison of state curriculum policy, see Schwille et al. 1988).

Pluralism and Control: The Distribution of Influence Over Curriculum. If one line of inquiry explores the evolution and interplay of principles used to justify control over curriculum, another studies the actual influence of various interests. Early work on the politics of curriculum making applied concepts of community power studies to school systems, focusing on the role of organized elites and interest groups (see Schwille, Porter, and Gant 1979; Scribner and Englert 1977; Ziegler, Jennings, and Peak 1974). With few exceptions, however, research in the politics of education tradition did not concentrate on control over curriculum per se. Kirst and Walker (1971) set forth a systematic account of agents and processes involved in curriculum policy making, while Boyd (1979) explored the balance of continuity and change in curriculum. His analysis pits a cadre of professional reformers, located in universities, foundations, and government agencies, against the forces for stability at the local level. The clash of professional reformers constantly agitating for change with local educators maintaining familiar practices produces the distinctive version of curriculum policy making that combines crises with incrementalism. The continuous surface turbulence created by the reformers seldom disturbs the depths, where teaching and learning go on as always (Cuban 1979). Policies are passed and projects started, this view proposes, but implementation does not exert much influence on practice.

More recently, a sustained program of empirical research has taken a fine-grained look at both who exerts influence on curriculum and on the mechanisms of influence. The Content Determinants Project initiated through the Institute for Research on Teaching at Michigan State University has contributed a decade's worth of conceptual and empirical analysis on factors influencing curriculum decisions in fourth grade mathematics (Floden et al. 1988; Freeman et al. 1983; Porter et al. 1986; Schwille et al. 1983, 1988). The research includes content analyses of elementary mathematics textbooks and tests in use, telephone and mail surveys of district and state policymakers in a sample of locales, and study of teacher content decision making, using rating tasks, semi-structured logs, and interviews.

What emerged gradually out of this research was a three-factor model that distinguished content decision making, the influence of various policy instruments, and the sources of policy strength for instruments in combination. The first dimension, curriculum content, was operationalized as four teacher decisions hypothesized to determine student learning opportunities: how much time to allocate to a subject (e.g., mathematics instruction in fourth grade); what topics to cover within the allocated time; whether or not to distinguish among students in topic coverage; and what standards of achievement to hold in making decisions about pacing (e.g., Schwille et al. 1983). The research then explored variation among teachers on these factors and the range of influences on teacher decision making.

The second dimension distinguished one set of influences, the policy instruments used to shape curriculum content. The typology included: (1) objectives, syllabi, and curriculum guides established at state and local levels; (2) student testing policies; (3) student placement policies, i.e., for promotion, mandatory remediation, and graduation; (4) textbook policies; (5) time allocation policies; and (6) teacher qualification policies. (Floden et al. 1988; Schwille et al. 1988) Studies then examined the relative influence of these instruments on the content decisions.

The third dimension sought to gauge the sources of policy strength. Following the conceptual lead of Spady and Mitchell (1979), the researchers identified four factors to characterize policy strength: *prescriptiveness*, how specific and explicit an external policy is in directing what is to be taught to what standard of achievement; *consistency*, the linkage among multiple policies in reinforcing messages sent to teachers about content; *authority*, the basis for a policy's legitimacy as grounded in law, in expert opinion, in prevailing social norms, or in charismatic leadership; and *power*, which refers to the sanctions or rewards attached to policy. These distinctions allowed the researchers to make judgments about the overall policy system that operates to influence curriculum through teacher decision making.

Findings from this research challenge a number of assumptions about both policy and practice. First, considerable variation emerges across teachers in their practices, and teachers are open to external influences they perceive to be authoritative. In particular, teachers are willing to add new content to their curriculum, but tend to resist eliminating topics (Porter et al. 1986; Schwille et al. 1983). Textbooks exert relatively weak influence, and teachers using the same text vary widely in their coverage of topics, pacing, and standards. The texts and tests in use also vary: what appears at a general level to define a common curriculum breaks down upon closer examination of text and test content by topics (Freeman et al. 1983).

The research also uncovered variable policy effects on teachers' content decision making. In general, the researchers found that policy exerts rather weak effects when judged against the four sources of policy strength. While teachers did not perceive inconsistencies across district and state policies, neither did they feel particularly constrained or directed by them. District policy appears neither to strengthen teacher autonomy through in-service education and other means nor to routinize teacher decision making through highly prescriptive use of multiple policies backed up by rewards and sanctions (Floden et al. 1988). However, policies supported by law and expert authority, particularly teacher involvement on state and district committees, do have influence on teachers. The picture emerging, then, is one of "weak policies, strong effects," in that teachers are open to policy influence, but the impact is not uniform across teachers, nor across the range of decisions that combine to produce the curriculum in use (Porter et al. 1988).

The project also examined variation across states in the policy instruments in use. The "zones of tolerance" created by policy around content decision making vary from direct-control states such as South Carolina and New York to indirect- and low-control states such as Ohio and Michigan. In general, the policy instruments having greatest impact included state guidelines and student testing policy. Few states relied on such potentially powerful policies as student placement directives, required time allocations, or teacher in-service, supported by consistent rewards and sanctions (Schwille et al. 1988). At the time of data collection, few states worked systematically to coordinate a powerful set of policies, but in the intervening years, this trend has emerged in several of these states, including California and South Carolina. The "curriculum alignment" strategy described above (see pp. 201–203) appears to be unfolding in several of the direct-control states around the country. Recent reports within this program of research have introduced another dimension for analysis: the broad aims of instruction in mathematics, distinguishing skills development, problem-solving abilities, and conceptual understanding. Employing these distinctions yields a depiction of the elementary mathematics curriculum as heavily oriented to basic skills, with superficial coverage of many topics, considerable overlap in content across grade levels, and wide variation across teachers in the amount of time devoted to mathematics (Porter 1989; see also Goodlad 1984, chapters 5 and 7). The policy framework in place, it appears, has helped create a curriculum "out of balance," and the new agenda calls for greater concentration on problem solving and understanding, fewer topics covered in greater depth, standard time allocations, and better coordination across grade levels to reduce the repetition.

Two limitations of this research are worth noting, each pointing to emerging work. One is the concentration on elementary mathematics. Perhaps subject matter mediates the influence of policy on curriculum so that another important dimension of variation is the subject. Other research suggests this may be the case. For example, in a careful comparative analysis of teachers' curriculum decision making in mathematics and social studies, Stodolsky (1989, 1988) found marked differences in the effects of texts and tests across these subject areas. Likewise, Roth, Anderson, and Smith (1987) detected wide variation in science instruction, suggesting the relatively weak influence of texts and tests, and conversely the potential impact of improved instructional materials in that field. It appears likely, then, that "the" policy framework surrounding curriculum may vary substantially by subject and perhaps by grade level. Future research may extend our understanding of such variation.

A second limitation is the restriction to curriculum conceived as content. When curriculum change pursued through policy implicates pedagogy, then research must examine the interplay of curriculum and instruction, and the implementation strategies aimed at influencing instructional practice. As indicated above, a test case for such curriculum change is California, where the newly developed state curriculum frameworks set forth ambitious teaching and learning goals that require significant changes in teachers' knowledge, beliefs, and patterns of practice. One study underway has begun to explore the impact of the new mathematics framework, relying on both interviews and classroom observation in a number of classrooms (see the case studies reported in the Fall 1990 issue of *Educational Evaluation and Policy Analysis*). Early results of this work indicate the difficulties in changing teaching practice, but point to the importance of classroom observation in assessing the impact of policy on practice when more than curricular content is at stake.

Curriculum as Control: Transmitting Privilege, Reproducing Inequality. The perspectives reviewed to this point fall within the mainstream American tradition of scholarship that is essentially *pragmatic* in experimenting with designs for systems of policy control, and *pluralist* in assuming the play of multiple interests in a fragmented federal system of governance. Yet another way of seeing the curriculum is essentially *critical* in identifying how education functions as an institution serving dominant interests to reproduce an unequal social order. Not surprisingly, this scholarly tradition traces its origins to a European cultural matrix and the sociological theories of Marx, Durkheim, Gramsci, and others, with contemporary extensions in the work of Jurgen Habermas, Raymond Williams, Pierre Bourdieu, and Basil Bernstein. In this chapter we cannot begin to do justice to this large, rich, intricately nuanced body of theory, but we can indicate the central questions and some main themes, particularly as reflected in the U.S. context (for overviews of this scholarship, see the volumes by Apple 1979, 1982, 1986; Young 1971).

Theorists within this tradition begin with society, more particularly with the divisions within society. What must be explained is the social order that subordinates some members of a society to others, and how that order is reproduced from generation to generation. Education emerges as a critical institution for perpetuating inequalities rooted in the cultural constituents of identity and consciousness: class, gender, race, ethnicity. Theory identifies the principles and mechanisms at several levels of analysis through which a social order is established and maintained, while inquiry explores how these mechanisms operate in particular historical eras and particular societies—for example, middle class efforts to dominate working class schools during the period of immigration and urbanization in the United States (see Kaestle 1973; Lazerson 1971; Wrigley 1982).

Scholars in this tradition seek to question the most elementary and settled assumptions of social life, and to make problematic what participants take for granted, their common sense appraisals and beliefs (see, for example, Bourdieu and Passeron 1977). Such inquiry is literally consciousness-raising, for its subject *is* consciousness and its production through social structure and social relations. "The difficult thing to explain about how middle class kids get middle class jobs is why others let them. The difficult thing to explain about how working class kids get working class jobs is why they let themselves," writes Paul Willis (1977, 1). Social and cultural control over meaning obviates recourse to more overt controls. How certain interests gain such control, securing the tacit acceptance of subordinate groups, is a complex process for study that includes attention to educational institutions.

Within this general perspective, a number of questions emerge that involve curriculum. One centers on how certain kinds of knowledge are legitimated within the school curriculum, and with what social consequences. "The *problem* of educational knowledge," writes Michael Apple (1979, 45),

> has to be considered as a form of the larger distribution of goods and services in a society. It is not merely an analytic problem (what shall be construed as knowledge?), nor simply a technical one (how do we organize and store knowledge so that children may have access to it and "master" it?), nor, finally, is it a purely psychological problem (how do we get students to learn x?). Rather, the study of educational knowledge is a study in ideology, the investigation of what is considered *legitimate* knowledge . . . by specific social groups and classes, in specific institutions, at specific historical moments.

Elite knowledge appears to be the property of certain classes that have greater access to it, not least through continuities across socialization settings. The way knowledge is organized and represented in curriculum, then, serves to advantage some classes before children even arrive at school. Conversely, cultural and linguistic discontinuities between home, community, and school put many children at a disadvantage, but this process, subtle and hidden from view, fails to challenge the meritocratic assumption that everyone has an equal chance at getting ahead through schooling (see, for example, Heath 1983). This perspective takes up the question of worthwhile knowledge, but situates it in relation to class interests and cultural conflict.

Interest in the legitimation of knowledge has produced several related inquiries, including attention to ideological bias in curricular materials, e.g., the prevalence of consensus versus conflict interpretations of history, the omission of topics and issues such as working class history or women's history (see Anyon 1978; Fitzgerald 1979); and to the social consequences of knowledge organization. Basil Bernstein (1977), for example, has contributed a provocative analysis that distinguishes collection from integrated codes, to indicate curricular organization featuring strong versus weak boundaries between subjects. He then proposes a range of hypotheses that link forms of curricular organization to authority relations, patterns of interaction in schools, degrees of consensus about teaching and learning, and other matters. Collection codes, he hypothesizes, strengthen hierarchical relationships among principals, teachers, and students, reduce collegial interaction, and render teaching isolated and invisible. His theory suggests that not only the content but also the organization of the curriculum convey powerful messages that tend to support the existing social order.

Linda McNeil's (1986) research, referred to earlier (see pp. 193), is another outstanding contribution within this tradition. Her work explores how curriculum becomes a weapon in the hands of educators intent on establishing social control. Whereas Bernstein locates the controlling aspects of curriculum in structure, McNeil contributes descriptions of teaching processes through which knowledge is made inaccessible to students. The common interest in both analyses is the latent functions of control, often referred to as "the hidden curriculum."

Another theme pursued by critical theorists takes up the stratification of knowledge within curriculum. Correspondence theories (e.g., Bowles and Gintis 1976) that posit parallels between economic and educational stratification have led to more subtle formulations, but the consistently widening theoretical perspective seeks to demonstrate how schools contribute to the cultural reproduction of class relations and to an economic order that involves little real mobility. Schools are trapped in contradictions between their manifest and latent functions. The ideology of liberal progressivism supports education for equal opportunity, common citizenship, and personal fulfillment ("meeting the needs of children"; "serving society and the economy"), yet these egalitarian aims conflict with the school's role in maintaining an unequal society and in supplying a compliant labor force for a stratified economy.

Empirical work within the critical perspective then explores how access to knowledge is controlled and allocated at multiple levels of analysis, through multiple processes. For example, studies examine how entering inequalities in "cultural capital"—middle class linguistic and social competencies—disadvantage certain groups (Bernstein 1977); how teachers within classrooms construct social reality and relationships that promote inequality through grouping strategies, expectation processes, and other means (Apple 1979, chapter 3; Keddie 1971; Rist 1970); how high schools stratify knowledge by tracks (see Gamoran and Berends 1987; Oakes 1985); how cultures of resistance form among working class youth (Everhart 1983; Willis 1977); and how the school milieu, associated with the social class of the surrounding community, produces systematic differences in access to elite knowledge (Anyon 1981; Sharp and Green 1975).

This larger body of critical scholarship poses a direct challenge to conventional policy analysis on curriculum by arguing that policy is highly limited in its capacity, and is itself likely to serve dominant interests. Henry Levin (1977, 26–27) reflects this point in writing,

> Educational policies that are aimed at resolving social dilemmas that arise out of the basic malfunctioning of the economic, social, and political institutions of the society are not amenable to solution through educational policy and reform. The leverage available to the most benevolent educational reformer and policy specialist is limited by the lack of a constituency for change and the overwhelm-

ing momentum of the educational process in the direction of social reproduction of the existing polity.

The critical theorists, then, raise questions and issues that seldom emerge within the more tightly focused pragmatic tradition, and that challenge the pluralist assumptions of mainstream scholarship on control of the curriculum. Their work suggests that incremental policy making is unlikely to achieve large-scale social reform and directs attention to yet larger spheres of action.

Curriculum as Capital

A final perspective on the curriculum has emerged in recent years and is related conceptually to the critical theories just reviewed. The critical theorists are interested in school knowledge as cultural capital that is distributed to reproduce the existing structure of social relations. In this interest, they seek to articulate the school curriculum with larger social and institutional patterns and to understand the broader functions of curriculum in relation to society. Analysts who employ the curriculum-as-capital metaphor also are interested in the relation between schooling and larger systems, concentrating on occupational and status attainment.

This economic view of the curriculum treats education as a commodity that may be exchanged within a marketplace for other educational and social goods. Thomas Green's (1980) analysis distinguishes three types of benefits distributed by the educational system: educational benefits including knowledge and skill, taste and manners, and civility; noneducational social benefits including occupational opportunity, income, and social status; and second-order educational benefits including certificates, diplomas, and licenses. The curriculum-as-capital perspective examines the relationship among these benefits and the principles that regulate their distribution.

Analysis in this mode tends to reverse fundamental assumptions about curriculum and its effects. The educational assumption is that the character of the curriculum affects society and the economy through the knowledge and skills conveyed to workers and citizens. The economic perspective proposed by the curriculum-as-capital theorists, however, regards the interaction between the educational, economic, and social systems as affecting the character of the curriculum, and this reverse perspective sheds new light on curriculum policy.

Viewing curriculum as a form of capital that may be accrued, exchanged, and distributed leads to certain questions. What is the medium of exchange? What determines the value of curriculum-as-capital? What is the nature of the market through which this capital flows? Working from a number of disciplines, including sociology (e.g., Collins 1979), history (e.g., Cohen and Neufeld 1981; Labaree 1989), and policy analysis (Green 1980), analysts have converged on an interpretation. Credentials emerge as the central medium of exchange, whose value derives from their scarcity. The high school diploma confers distinction and distributes social goods until a majority attain this credential. As high school graduation rates increase over time, the benefits shift in magnitude and kind. The marginal utility of a high school diploma decreases, and its significance shifts: "as the social value of second-order benefits declines for those who receive them, the social liabilities suffered by any individual as a consequence of not securing them will increase" (Green 1980, 97). The high school diploma's value decreases and is transformed from a benefit to the avoidance of a liability.

Other dynamics unfold as well. One is system growth on a number of dimensions (see Green 1980, chapters 5 and 6). First, when attainment becomes nearly universal at a certain level, pressures will mount to *expand* the system by adding levels whose attainment will confer benefits. Second, the system will *intensify* by shifting the focus from attainment to achievement, in order that selectivity may occur within existing levels of the system. Attention turns to standards and to measures of achievement as a basis for advancement. Finally, the system will *differentiate* by developing new institutions, programs, and pathways to desirable social goods so that more individuals and groups have access. Historical examples of this tendency include the rise of vocational and technical education, junior and community colleges, and multiple programs within high schools to serve the social spectrum.

A dialectic also develops between two principles within the educational system, to provide equal access and to confer selective benefits, to serve the public good and to distribute scarce private goods. Historians have documented the tensions between these principles. In his case study of Philadelphia's Central High School between 1838 and 1939, for example, Labaree (1989) demonstrates how the early emphasis on the virtues of republican community and Protestant morality gave way to competitive individualism and middle class striving to secure economic advantage. The public, egalitarian ideals of the common school collided with the demands of favorably situated classes to gain a leg up.

The curriculum has been strongly shaped by these dynamics. Utilitarian purposes have triumphed over the expressive and political purposes envisioned by the founders. The content of the curriculum has shifted toward vocationalism. And the curriculum has grown through expansion, intensification, and differentiation. Labaree (1989, 8) captures the dialectic:

> The high school's success in the credentials market brings political pressure for wider access; wider access lowers the market value of high school credentials for members of the middle class who already have access; this market situation puts pressure on the high school to stratify (both schools and curricula) in order to permit both wider access in the lower tracks and schools and exclusiveness at the upper end.

The emphasis on the credential value of education also undercuts intrinsic value. Second-order benefits come to matter more than the actual learning they are supposed to signify. Surrogate learning results, and bargaining processes ensue between teachers and students over what learning is expected in return for a diploma (Powell, Farrar, and Cohen 1985; Sedlak, Wheeler, Pullin, and Cusick 1986). A new dialectic emerges between external standard setting and informal bargaining that shapes the curriculum in use.

Theorists in this mode converge on an interpretative framework, but disagree over explanations. Green proposes that the educational system develops independent laws and has "a dynamic of its own not to be explained by the economic or social events surrounding it." (1980, 113) Sedlak, Wheeler, Pullin, and Cusick (1986) offer the more familiar explanation that schools are subject to external influences that determine the worth of educational credentials and that provoke developments in the system. It is difficult to test these rival hypotheses, but their import for curriculum policy is clear. What has shaped the curriculum in fundamental ways over the years are system dynamics, not rational design and policy.

Conceptual and empirical studies within the curriculum-as-capital frame have concentrated on the United States, but recent cross-national comparisons challenge these conclusions. Rather than regarding credential value as based strictly on educational system dynamics, this research proposes that the education-work connection is a critical, contingent link among student effort, credentials, and subsequent opportunity. In countries such as Japan (Rosenbaum 1989; Rosenbaum and Kariya 1989) and West Germany (Hamilton 1990), high school grades determine access to work, the high schools play a significant role in allocating students into the labor force, and a highly developed apprentice system supplies upper secondary education and vocational training. State systems that articulate school and work as a matter of public policy give students external incentive to work hard in school, for results in the form of grades, tests, scores, and credentials determine access not only to higher education but to occupations. This research suggests that student motivation to learn is not simply an instructional problem for teachers but a linkage issue in organizing the transition from school to work (see also Bishop 1989, 1990).

The economic analysis of curriculum as capital draws attention to, and supplies a provocative interpretation of, curriculum as a system of exchange and distribution. The system in motion has had profound, unanticipated effects, an understanding of which can inform policy analysis in relation to curriculum. In company with critical theory, this way of seeing curriculum is determinist in its orientation and skeptical of narrowly conceived policy efforts to exert much influence on the underlying processes. However, cross-national comparative work sheds a more hopeful light on the problems of the American system, pointing policy analysis beyond characteristics of schools to larger spheres of potential influence.

FUTURE RESEARCH ON CURRICULUM POLICY

As we noted in the introduction, curriculum policy is not a well-defined field of research with its own discrete literature and core concerns. It is, rather, an artificially constructed field composed of a few direct studies of curriculum policy and a large volume of collateral research on public policy and curriculum that provides insight into how curriculum is treated as a public issue. Our approach has been, first, to view curriculum from the perspective of public policy research and, second, to view public policy from the perspective of curriculum research. From these alternative views, we have attempted to distill some key ideas that might shape future research on curriculum policy. This section summarizes these ideas.

How Public Ideas About Curriculum Are Politically Constructed

Our discussion of public policy research suggested that the policy agenda at any given moment is constructed by the coincidence of problems, policy communities, and political events. Our discussion of curriculum research emphasized that the portrayal of the role of curriculum in public life depends on the perspective adopted. Combining these two observations, a reasonable question for future research might be how particular conceptions of curriculum come to influence political discourse at particular times.

For example, the current debate about the reform of public schooling involves two very different conceptions of the public role of curriculum. One view, represented largely by reform-oriented policymakers in state and local government, treats curriculum as a rational system to be used as a tool to accomplish collective ends. For these reformers, the dominant question is how to make public schools more responsive to the emerging demands of a competitive international economy. This view recurs in virtually all the education reform reports of the last decade. Another view in the current reform debate, expressed by what might be called academic traditionalists, treats curriculum as the repository of society's dominant values about worthwhile knowledge. This view is best represented by former U.S. Education Secretary William Bennett, Allan Bloom, and J. D. Hirsch. Largely absent from these policy debates are the other curriculum perspectives we noted above—curriculum as control of access to knowledge and curriculum as the production and distribution of knowledge. How do certain conceptions of the public role of curriculum come to dominate political discourse, while others recede into the background?

The answer probably lies, as we suggested earlier, in how policy communities appropriate and use ideas about the public role of curriculum in their attempts to influence policy. That is, certain ideas about the public use of curriculum have greater visibility and authority than others because certain actors occupy key positions in the agenda formation process, have the resources to influence others, and have access to key policymakers at opportune times. But we actually know very little about how the policy agenda of the current education reform movement was formed. Virtually all existing research on education reform starts from the point at which policies are set, and then examines the content of policy and its implementation. Our argument suggests that researchers might usefully focus their attention on the earlier stages of agenda formation and examine how ideas about the public role of curriculum are politically constructed.

Another implication is that relationships among problems, policy communities, and political events around curriculum policies are not just subjects for descriptive research; they are also amenable to analysis and prescription. When curriculum arises as a policy issue, as it has in the recent generation of educational reforms, policymakers seldom reflect on alternative conceptions of the problems they are trying to solve or on alternative approaches to the public use of curriculum. What sparked the current education reform debate was a rising concern about economic competitiveness articulated by business and government leaders. Policy communities—education interest groups, elected officials, and business interests—mobilized with competing solutions around various conceptions of the problem, but the view that came to dominate portrayed a gap between what schools teach and the emerging demands of society and the economy. Like flypaper, this problem definition attracted solutions that spanned a huge range: from increased graduation requirements to making welfare payments and drivers' licenses contingent on successful school performance to ambitious ideas about changing the structure and governance of schools. Throughout this debate, however, educational research contributed little to the discussion of whether representations of the problem were based on accurate information, whether the conceptions of curriculum that underlie design of policies are appropriate to the problem, and what light alternative conceptions of curriculum would shed on the political, economic, and social stakes of educational reform. In other words, a more thorough analysis of alternative conceptions of the problem and alternative solutions might influence the policy debate to move in other directions.

Conceptions of Teaching Embedded in Existing Curriculum Policy and the Design of New Policies

We have observed that research on the relationship between policy and practice contains assumptions about the nature of teaching and that alternative conceptions of curriculum contain different views of the relationship between content and instruction. A major theme cutting across both bodies of research is the important role that teachers play in determining what curriculum actually reaches students. Yet we know very little about the conceptions of teaching and teachers' work embedded in curriculum policies.

The dominant view of teachers' work in both the policy analysis and the curriculum literature depicts teaching as a highly judgmental activity that entails complex problem-solving skills and the ability to manage competing, often contradictory, tasks. Policy analysis tends to characterize teachers as "professionals," "policy brokers," and "street-level bureaucrats," exercising a high degree of influence through the orchestration of competing external demands. In the curriculum literature, a necessary condition of teaching is seen to be the ability to "embrace contraries" and "manage dilemmas." Policy*makers*, on the other hand, attempt to use influences external to teaching—rules, model curricula, tests, and so forth—to prescribe what should be taught, and sometimes how it should be taught, in what order, at what pace. The dominant view of teaching in most curriculum policies, then, is that teachers act as conduits for the delivery of socially approved knowledge.

A tension is evident between the dominant views of teaching expressed in research and those represented in policy. The existing literature deals with this tension either by stipulating a model of teaching and exploring its contradictions with policy, or by examining how teachers juggle the competing demands of policy. Future research could considerably deepen our understanding of the relationship between curriculum policy and teaching practice by examining the implied or express models of teaching embedded in existing policies and by examining the relationship between inquiry versus policy-based conceptions of teaching. If, as research on policy and curriculum suggest, curriculum policies typically embody simplified, often superficial, notions of teaching, then research can play a role in broadening these conceptions.

In this area, too, research might play a more prescriptive role. Many researchers and policymakers now believe that we must introduce more ambitious conceptions of teaching and learning into the curriculum of elementary and secondary schools. They argue that the economic and social well-being of future generations depends on a series of fundamental changes in teaching and learning: preparing students to manipulate complex bodies of information actively at a level beyond recitation of facts and algorithms, teaching students to solve problems in groups rather than in isolation, and evaluating student learning in terms of the application of abstract knowledge to concrete practical situations, rather than solely in terms of traditional paper and pencil tests. This view is often characterized as "higher-order thinking" or "teaching for understanding."

While we know something about the type of curriculum and classroom practice that corresponds to these more ambitious conceptions of teaching and learning, we know almost nothing about how to design policies that promote, enhance, or propagate these practices. Research can play a role in mapping the requirements of more ambitious conceptions of teaching and learning onto the policies that are designed to influence what is taught to whom. In terms of our earlier discussion of policy design, new policies will almost certainly involve a broader repertoire of policy instruments, relying less on traditional means of influencing curriculum—notably mandate-driven changes in curriculum requirements and inducements to schools and districts to adopt model curricula—and more on involving schools in the active development of new models and on changes in the incentives for schools and districts to adopt new practices. Curriculum policies designed to promote more ambitious conceptions of teaching and learning will probably also address the issue of consistency or coherence among multiple sources of influence on what is taught to whom. New policies, that is, will have to address the relationships among previously unrelated policies, such as content requirements, teacher preparation, testing and evaluation, and financial incentives. Influencing curriculum probably will not be seen solely as a problem of changing "curriculum policy" as traditionally defined: rules about what should be taught to whom. Rather, the curriculum that reaches the student will be seen as the product of a number of influences, including a variety of policies. The problem of policy design, then, is how to make these influences operate more coherently in the interest of more ambitious conceptions of teaching and learning. In terms of our earlier categories, then, there is a role for sustained analysis of curriculum as a rational system for achieving higher levels of understanding on a broader scale.

CURRICULUM ENACTMENT AS A POLICY CONCERN

Throughout this chapter, we have noted tensions in conceptualizing the connection between curriculum policy and classroom practice. The prevailing thrust of research presumes that policy shapes practice through implementation. Inquiry then aims to understand the process flowing from policy to practice. Analysts have modified this implicit framework in a number of respects by shifting the focus from policy effects to school and classroom practices (Clune 1990). This shift appears in several guises, including the distinction between policy as intent and as action, in the perspective of teachers as street-level workers whose discretionary actions *construct* policy, in the blurring of curriculum versus instruction, and in the emphasis on teacher decision making as a curriculum policy factor.

In light of the emerging interest in promoting higher-order thinking and learning for understanding, we believe that curriculum policy research should focus yet more strongly in the future on the enactment of curriculum in schools and classrooms.

One approach to this issue explores curriculum representation and enactment as fundamental dimensions of teaching in classrooms (see Carter 1984; Carter and Doyle 1987; Doyle 1983, 1987; Doyle et al. 1985). Central to this interest is the concept of *academic tasks* as defined by four elements: a student product, the operations to produce the product, the resources used, and the significance of the task in the classroom accountability system. From this theoretical perspective, the same content can be represented by fundamentally different tasks. For example, writing may involve combining sentences as practice in creating more complex compositions or as a composing task in which students struggle to express their own ideas.

In this scheme, curriculum is represented to students as work, and work dimensions within classrooms shape the enacted curriculum in fundamental ways. Commenting on the relative absence in classrooms of tasks that require students to struggle with meaning and understanding, Doyle (1986, 377) concludes that

> certain types of task are *suitable* for classrooms, that is, they fit the constraints of teacher and student work systems in these environments, and these tasks tend to represent the curriculum as discrete skills and procedures rather than as occasions for struggling with meaning.

This perspective combines attention to the management, instructional, and curriculum aspects of classrooms to illuminate teaching and learning. Constraints within the classroom emerge as a powerful determinant of knowledge representation and curriculum enactment.

A second, complementary perspective emerging from the study in progress of teacher responses to California's new mathematics framework emphasizes the impact of practice on policy. This research also concentrates on classroom teaching, but explores the difficulties inherent in efforts to dramatically change teaching practice. What constitutes a chief impediment to altered practice is the prior subject matter and pedagogical knowledge, skills, and beliefs of teachers as shaped by a variety of factors, including past policies. The classroom slate is never clean; teachers must work with residues of the past (Cohen and Ball 1990). Trained in direct instruction and Madeline Hunter-based lesson structures, California teachers must now fundamentally alter their teaching to reflect the spirit of the new framework. In the new regime, teachers would rely less on direct instruction and more on open-ended, exploratory discourse about mathematical ideas, on hands-on experiences in "doing math," on orchestrating exchanges among students, on cooperative learning projects, and the like. Policy as represented in frameworks, texts, tests, and in-service education can reach practice only by way of what teachers know and believe about subject matter and teaching. Not surprisingly, what emerges within classrooms from policy initiatives to change practice is a blend of the old and the new, direct instruction with teaching for understanding.

These studies converge in revealing the difficulties of introducing ambitious departures to prevailing patterns of classroom practice, but differ in their explanations. Doyle et al. stress the constraints of the classroom as a setting for ambitious teaching and learning, while the California study emphasizes the impediment of teachers' prior knowledge and beliefs as shaped by their history and the history of past reform. Neither project constitutes curriculum policy research narrowly construed, but they each point to promising work in the future. Such research should explore classroom processes up close, will accord teachers and students a pivotal role in enacting curriculum, and should map implications for policy from fine-grained understanding of curriculum in the classroom. Such work also will explore how contextual factors such as the subject taught, the students, and the setting interact with policy to shape student learning. Finally, future research should extend to the students and should incorporate their perspectives and experiences in interpreting the effects of policy and practice.

Curriculum Policy and Access to Knowledge

In our review of research on policy, we noted that a recurring theme is how policies act as ideologies for organizing and rationalizing authority in political systems. The accumulation of policies over time in a given area, such as curriculum, expresses a set of ideas about which institutions should exercise authority over what aspects of curriculum. These ideas, in turn, are expressed as relationships among levels of government, organized interest groups, and individuals in various social roles. In our review of curriculum research, we observed that a recurring theme is the use of curriculum to control access to knowledge. A major theme cutting across both policy perspectives on curriculum and curriculum perspectives on policy is that curriculum policy acts both as determinant of access to knowledge and as an expression of a society's ideas about how this access to knowledge should be manifested in institutional structures.

Most research on access to knowledge has taken the form either of fine-grained descriptions of how students from different social backgrounds are treated in classrooms and schools or criticism designed to raise social consciousness about how societies preferentially allocate knowledge to selected groups. Very little systematic research has been done on how specific policies related to curriculum influence the access of specific types of students to specific types of learning. We know something about how classroom practices and school-level organization differentiate among students, but we know little about how policies amplify or dampen this differentiation, nor do we know much about how policies specifically designed to redistribute access to knowledge actually work.

In elementary schools, for example, how much is differential access to knowledge explained by teachers' coping behaviors and beliefs about students, and how much is explained by school, district, and state policies on content, sequencing, and assessment of student learning? In secondary schools, how much is differential access to knowledge explained by tracking practices, and how much is explained by conceptions of student learning embedded in definitions of content, curriculum materials, and sequencing? In these settings, how effective are policies that seek to influence access to knowledge by changing teachers' ability to cope with student differences? redefining academic content? altering grouping or tracking practices? or revising the sequencing of subject matter to provide greater flexibility in access to content?

Changes in policy and practice designed to influence students' access to knowledge would clearly reverberate through the institutional structure that allocates authority over curriculum decisions. Questioning the role that curriculum structure and content play in determining access to knowledge is, in effect, to question the ideology used to organize authority within schools and between schools and their broader environment. Claiming that course content and sequencing in English, mathematics, or science has the effect of excluding certain students from access to certain types of knowledge is, in effect, to challenge how authority is allocated among teachers within schools, how decisions about content and sequencing are made, and how these decisions are embedded in broader structures at the community and state levels. Likewise, alternative structures require alternative solutions to the allocation of authority—solutions that existing research does not suggest.

Institutional Choice and Design Around Issues of Curriculum Policy

Policies, we have noted, entail decisions at two levels: what should be done and which institutions should be authorized to act. The first level is policy content, the second is institutional choice and design. Policy research typically focuses mainly on the former and seldom addresses the latter explicitly. We likewise noted that a variety of approaches to institutional choice and design were embodied in government efforts to influence the curriculum, ranging from a linear research and development model through a loosely articulated configurational model to an inductive model. These models offer various solutions to the problem of where to locate primary responsibility for the development of new knowledge about curriculum—with experts, with temporary collections of experts and practitioners, or with practitioners—and how to define relationships and incentives among key actors. Policymakers currently seem to be interested in an alignment model, which implies coordination among multiple policy implements around common objectives, but which carries no explicit solution to the problem of institutional choice and design. Both curriculum and policy research seem to argue for bringing issues of institutional choice and design more explicitly into the foreground.

Treating issues of institutional choice and design more explicitly in curriculum research might take at least two forms. One line of inquiry is simply to analyze more explicitly the nature of relationships among institutions in the present curriculum policy structure. We know a fair amount about how formal decisions affecting curriculum are made by state and local educational agencies, but have only the most sketchy and impressionistic accounts of how these formal decisions and agencies relate to other key actors, including academic experts, textbook publishers, professional groups, and other organized constituencies interested in influencing curriculum content. A basic point of departure for more explicit treatment of institutional choice and design would be a more systematic knowledge of how the existing institutional structure works, beyond the formal public institutions. A second line of inquiry would be to suggest new institutional designs, either from emerging forms, like curriculum alignment, or from an analysis of the shortcomings of the existing structure. These new institutional designs would have to address not just how authority should be distributed among various institutions but also how to design incentive structures that would bind these institutions together. That is, it is one thing to say that practicing teachers should be brought into a closer relationship with academic experts and curriculum developers, but it is quite another thing to define the structure of incentives that provides teachers with an opportunity to work on long-term curriculum development projects and still maintain their roots in teaching practice. It is one thing to define a structure that brings new conceptions of teaching and learning more immediately into the development and demonstration stage in schools, but it is quite another thing to define the incentive structure that moves these new developments into the broader system of dissemination, which is currently dominated by textbook publishers and textbook adoption procedures. In other words, solving problems of institutional design is not just saying what the best structure might be for a given set of objectives, but also providing the incentives that will hold it together.

References

Anyon, Jean. 1978. Elementary social studies textbooks and legitimating knowledge. *Theory and Research in Social Education* 6(3): 40–55.

Anyon, Jean. 1981. Social class and school knowledge. *Curriculum Inquiry* 11(1): 3–42.

Apple, Michael W. 1979. *Ideology and Curriculum*. London: Routledge & Kegan Paul.

Apple, Michael W. 1982. *Education and Power*. London: Routledge & Kegan Paul.

Apple, Michael W. 1986. *Teachers and Texts. A Political Economy of Gender and Class Relations in Education*. London: Routledge & Kegan Paul.

Atkin, Myron, and Ernest House. 1981. The federal role in curriculum development 1950–80. *Educational Evaluation and Policy Analysis* 3(5): 5–36.

Bachrach, Peter, and Morton Baratz. 1962. Two faces of power. *American Political Science Review* 56(4): 947–952.

Berlak, Harold, and Ann Berlak. 1981. *Dilemmas of Schooling. Teaching and Social Change*. London: Methuen.

Bernstein, Basil. 1977. *Class, Codes, and Control. Volume 3: Towards a Theory of Cultural Transmissions*, 2nd ed. London: Routledge & Kegan Paul.

Bishop, John. 1989. Why the apathy in American high schools? *Educational Researcher* 18(1): 6–10.

Bishop, John. 1990. "Docility and Apathy: Their Cause and Cure." In *Education Reform: Making Sense of It All*, edited by Samuel Bacharach, 234–258. Boston: Allyn & Bacon.

Bourdieu, Pierre. 1971. "Systems of Education and Systems of Thought." In *Knowledge and Control: New Directions for the Sociology of Education*, edited by Michael F. D. Young, 189–207. London: Collier-Macmillan.

Bourdieu, Pierre. 1973. "Cultural Reproduction and Social Reproduction." In *Knowledge, Education, and Cultural Change*, edited by Richard Brown, 71–112. London: Tavistock.

Bourdieu, Pierre, and Jean Passeron. 1977. *Reproduction: In Education, Society, and Culture*. Beverly Hills, CA: Sage.

Bowles, Samuel, and Herbert Gintis. 1976. *Schooling in Capitalist America*. New York: Basic Books.

Boyd, William. 1979. "The Changing Politics of Curriculum Policy Making for American Schools." In *Value Conflicts and Curriculum Issues: Lessons from Research and Experience*, edited by Jon Schaffarzick and Gary Sykes, 73–138. Berkeley, CA: McCutchan.

Brandl, John. 1988. On politics and policy analysis as the design and assessment of institutions. *Journal of Policy Analysis and Management* 7(3): 419–424.

Braybrooke, David, and Charles Lindblom. 1963. *A Strategy of Decision*. New York: Free Press.

Callahan, Raymond. 1962. *Education and the Cult of Efficiency*. Chicago: University of Chicago Press.

Carnegie Forum on Education and the Economy. 1986. *A Nation Prepared: Teachers for the 21st Century*. New York: Carnegie Forum on Education and the Economy.

Carter, Kathy. 1984. Academic tasks in classrooms. *Curriculum Inquiry* 14(2): 129–149.

Carter, Kathy, and Walter Doyle. 1987. "Teachers' Knowledge Structures and Comprehension Processes." In *Exploring Teachers' Thinking*, edited by James Calderhead, 147–160. London: Cassell.

Clune, William. 1987. Institutional choice as a framework for research on educational policy. *Educational Evaluation and Policy Analysis* 9(2): 117–132.

Clune, William. 1990. "Three Views of Curriculum Policy in the School Context: The School as Policy Mediator, Policy Critic, and Policy Constructor." In *The Contexts of Teaching in Secondary Schools: Teachers' Realities*, edited by Milbrey McLaughlin, Joan Talbert, and Nina Bascia. New York: Teachers College Press.

Clune, William, Paula White, and Janice Patterson. 1989. *The Implementation and Effects of High School Graduation Requirements: First Steps Toward Curricular Reform*. CPRE Research Series RR-011. New Brunswick, NJ: Rutgers University, Center for Policy Research in Education.

Cohen, David. 1978. Reforming school politics. *Harvard Educational Review* 48(4): 429–447.

Cohen, David. 1982. Policy and organization: The impact of state and federal education policy in school governance. *Harvard Educational Review* 52(4): 474–499.

Cohen, David, and Deborah Ball. 1990. Relations between policy and practice: A commentary. *Educational Evaluation and Policy Analysis*, 12(3): 249–256.

Cohen, David, and Barbara Neufeld. 1981. The failure of high school and the progress of education. *Daedalus* 110(3): 62–89.

Cohen, Michael, James March, and Johan Olsen. 1972. A garbage can theory of organizational choice. *Administrative Science Quarterly* 17(1): 1–25.

Collins, Randall. 1979. *The Credential Society: An Historical Sociology of Education and Stratification*. New York: Academic Press.

Cuban, Larry. 1979. "Determinants of Curriculum Stability and Change, 1870–1970." In *Value Conflicts and Curriculum Issues*, edited by Jon Schaffarzick and Gary Sykes, 139–196. Berkeley, CA: McCutchan.

Devaney, Kathleen. 1982. *Networking on Purpose*. San Francisco, CA: Far West Laboratory.

Doyle, Walter. 1983. Academic work. *Review of Educational Research* 53(2): 159–99.

Doyle, Walter, 1985. *Patterns of Academic Work in Junior High School Science, English, and Mathematics Classes: A Final Report*. Research and development report no. 6190. Austin: University of Texas, Research and Development Center for Teacher Education.

Doyle, Walter. 1986. Content representation in teachers' definitions of academic work. *Journal of Curriculum Studies* 18(4): 365–379.

Edelman, Murray. 1967. *The Symbolic Uses of Politics*. Urbana: University of Illinois Press.

Eisner, Elliot, and Elizabeth Vallance, eds. 1974. *Conflicting Conceptions of Curriculum*. Berkeley, CA: McCutchan.

Elboim-Dror, Rachael. 1970. Some characteristics of the education policy formation system. *Policy Science* 1(3): 231–253.

Elbow, Peter. 1986. *Embracing Contraries. Explorations in Learning and Teaching*. New York: Oxford University Press.

Elder, Charles, and Roger Cobb. 1983. *The Political Uses of Symbols*. New York: Longman.

Elmore, Richard. 1986. "Education and Federalism: Doctrinal, Functional, and Strategic Views." In *School Days, Rule Days: The Legalization and Regulation of Education*, edited by David Kirp and Donald Jensen, 166–186. Philadelphia, PA: Falmer Press.

Elmore, Richard. 1987. Instruments and strategy in public policy. *Policy Studies Review* 7(1):174–186.

Elmore, Richard. 1988. "Policy Analysis as the Study of Implements." In *Managing Disasters: Strategies and Policies*, edited by Louise Comfort, 315–329. Chapel Hill, NC: Duke University Press.

Elmore, Richard, and Milbrey McLaughlin. 1982. "Strategic Choice in Federal Education Policy: The Compliance Assistance Trade-Off." In *Policy-Making in Education: The Eighty-first Yearbook of the Society for the Study of Education*, Part I, edited by Ann Lieberman and Milbrey McLaughlin, 159–194. Chicago: University of Chicago Press.

Elmore, Richard, and Milbrey McLaughlin. 1988. *Steady Work: Policy, Practice, and the Reform of American Education*. Santa Monica, CA: Rand.

Emrick, John. 1977. *Evaluation of the National Diffusion Network*, Vols. 1–2. Menlo Park, CA: Stanford Research Institute.

Everhart, Robert. 1983. *Reading, Writing, and Resistance*. London: Routledge & Kegan Paul.

Fitzgerald, Francis. 1979. *America Revised*. Boston: Atlantic, Little, Brown.

Floden, Robert, Andrew Porter, William Schmidt, Donald Freeman, and John Schwille. 1981. Responses to curriculum pressures: A study of teacher decisions about content. *Journal of Educational Psychology* 73: 129–141.

Floden, Robert, et al. 1986. *Instructional Leadership at the District Level: A Framework for Research and Some Initial Results*. East Lansing: Institute for Research on Teaching, Michigan State University.

Floden, Robert, et al. 1988. Instructional leadership at the district level: A closer look at autonomy and control. *Educational Administration Quarterly* 24(2): 96–124.

Freeman, Donald. 1990. State guidelines promoting teaching for understanding and thinking in elementary schools: A fifty-state survey. *Educational Evaluation and Policy Analysis* 11(4): 417–430.

Freeman, Donald, and William Schmidt. 1982. "Textbooks: Their Messages and Their Effects." Paper presented at the annual meeting of the American Educational Research Association, New York.

Freeman, Donald, et al. 1983. Do textbooks and tests define a national curriculum in elementary school mathematics? *Elementary School Journal* 83(5): 501–513.

Fuhrman, Susan, and Richard Elmore. 1990. Understanding local control in the wake of state education reform. *Educational Evaluation and Policy Analysis* 12(1): 82–96.

Gamoran, Adam, and Mark Berends. 1987. The effects of stratification in secondary schools: Synthesis of survey and ethnographic research. *Review of Educational Research* 57(4): 415–435.

Goodlad, John. 1984. *A Place Called School*. New York: McGraw-Hill.

Gormley, William. 1987. Institutional policy analysis: A critical review. *Journal of Policy Analysis and Management* 6(2): 153–169.

Green, Thomas. 1980. *Predicting the Behavior of the Educational System*. Syracuse, NY: Syracuse University Press.

Green, Thomas. 1983. "Excellence, Equity, and Equality." In *Handbook of Teaching and Policy*, edited by Lee Shulman and Gary Sykes, 318–341. New York: Longman.

Grossman, Pamela, et al. 1985. *Curricular Change in California Comprehensive High School: 1982–83 to 1984–85* (PACE Policy Paper No. 85–7–4). Berkeley: Policy Analysis for California Education.

Guba, Egon, and David Clark. 1974. *The Configurational Perspective: A Challenge to the Systems View of Educational Knowledge Production and Utilization*. Bloomington: Indiana University.

Hamilton, Stephen. 1990. *Apprenticeship for Adulthood: Preparing Youth for the Future*. New York: Free Press.

Hanson, Thomas. 1989, September. *Curricular Change in Dade County, 1982–83 to 1986–87. A Replication of the PACE Study*. New Brunswick, NJ: Rutgers University, Center for Policy Research in Education.

Havelock, Ronald. 1969. *Planning for Innovation Through Dissemination and Utilization of Knowledge*. Ann Arbor, MI: Institute for Social Research, CRUSK.

Havelock, Ronald. 1973. *The Change Agent's Guide to Innovation in Education*. Englewood Cliffs, NJ: Educational Technology Publications.

Heath, Shirley. 1983. *Ways with Words*. Cambridge: Cambridge University Press.

Heclo, Hugh. 1978. "Issue Networks and the Executive Establishment." In *The New American Political System*, edited by Anthony King, chapter 3, 87–124. Washington, D.C.: American Enterprise Institute.

Helgeson, Stanley, Patricia Blosser, and Robert Howe. 1977. *The Status of Pre-College Science, Mathematics, and Social Science Education: 1955–1975, Vol. I, Science Education,* stock no. 038-00-00362-3. Washington, D.C.: U.S. Government Printing Office.

Ingraham, Patricia. 1987. Toward more systematic consideration of policy design. *Policy Studies Journal* 15(4): 611–628.

Jackson, Philip W., 1968. *Life in Classrooms.* New York: Holt, Rinehart and Winston.

Jackson, Philip W. 1983. The reform of science education: A cautionary tale. *Daedalus* 112(2): 143–166.

Kaestle, Carl. 1973. *The Evolution of an Urban School System.* Cambridge, MA: Harvard University Press.

Keddie, Nell. 1971. "Classroom Knowledge." In Michael F. D. Young, ed., *Knowledge and Control.* London: Collier & Macmillan.

Kimball, Bruce. 1986. *Orators and Philosophers. A History of the Idea of Liberal Education.* New York: Teachers College Press.

Kingdon, John. 1984. *Agendas, Alternatives, and Public Policies.* Boston: Little, Brown.

Kirst, Michael, and Decker Walker. An analysis of curriculum policy making. *Review of Educational Research* 41(4): 479–509.

Kliebard, Herbert. 1987. *The Struggle for the American Curriculum, 1893–1958.* London: Routledge & Kegan Paul.

Labaree, David. 1989. *The Making of an American High School. The Credentials Market and the Central High School of Philadelphia, 1838–1939.* New Haven, CT: Yale University Press.

Lampert, Magdalene. 1985. How do teachers manage to teach? Perspectives on problems in practice. *Harvard Educational Review* 55(2): 178–194.

Landau, Martin. 197. The proper domain of policy analysis. *American Journal of Political Science* 21(4): 424–427.

Lazerson, Marvin. 1971. *Origins of the Urban School.* Cambridge, MA: Harvard University Press.

Levin, Henry. 1977. "A Radical Critique of Educational Policy." Stanford, CA: Occasional Paper of the Stanford University Evaluation Consortium. mimeographed.

Lindblom, Charles, and David Braybrooke. 1963. *A Strategy of Decision.* Glencoe, IL: Free Press.

Linder, Stephen, and Guy Peters. 1989. Instruments of government: Perceptions and contexts. *Journal of Public Policy* 9(1): 35–58.

Lipsky, Michael. 1980. *Street Level Bureaucracy.* New York: Russell Sage Foundation.

Lortie, Dan. 1975. *Schoolteacher: A Sociological Study.* Chicago: University of Chicago Press.

Mann, Dale, Peter Greenwood, and Milbrey W. McLaughlin. 1975. *Federal Programs Supporting Educational Change: Vol. III, Appendix A: Innovations in Classroom Organization and Staff Development* (R-1589/3-HEW). Santa Monica, CA: Rand.

Mayhew, David. 1974. *Congress: The Electoral Connection.* New Haven, CT: Yale University Press.

McDonnell, Lorraine, et al. 1980. *Program Consolidation and the State Role in ESEA. Title IV* (R-2531-HEW). Santa Monica, CA: Rand.

McDonnell, Lorraine, and Richard Elmore. 1987. Getting the job done: Alternative policy instruments. *Educational Evaluation and Policy Analysis* 9: 133–152.

McNeil, Linda. 1986. *Contradictions of Control.* New York: Routledge & Kegan Paul.

Mereleman, Richard. 1973. Public education and social structure: Three modes of adjustment. *Journal of Politics* 35(4): 798–829.

Meyer, John, and Brian Rowan. 1977. Institutionalized organizations: Formal structure as myth and ceremony. *American Journal of Sociology* 83(2): 340–363.

Meyer, John, and Brian Rowan. 1978. "The Structure of Educational Organizations." In *Environments and Organizations,* edited by Marshall Meyer, 78–109. San Francisco, CA: Jossey-Bass.

Miles, Matthew. 1978. "On Networking." Unpublished manuscript, National Institute for Education, Washington, D.C.

Mitchell, Douglas, Catherine Marshall, and Frederick Wirt. In press. *Culture and Educational Policy in the American States.* New York: Falmer.

Moore, Mark. 1988. "What Makes Public Ideas Powerful?" In *The Power of Public Ideas,* edited by Robert Reich, 55–83. Cambridge, MA: Ballinger.

National Commission on Excellence in Education. 1983. *A Nation at Risk: The Imperative for Educational Reform.* Washington, DC: U.S. Department of Education.

National Institute of Education. 1973. *Building Capacity for Renewal and Reform.* Washington, DC: National Institute of Education.

Nelkin, Dorothy. 1976. The science-textbook controversies. *Scientific American* 234(4): 33–39.

Oakes, Jeannie. 1985. *Keeping Track: How Schools Structure Inequality.* New Haven, CT: Yale University Press.

Orlich, Donald. 1979. Federal educational policy: The paradox of innovation and centralization. *Educational Researcher* 8(7): 4–9.

Parker, Alan. 1977. "Networks for Innovation and Problem-solving and Their Use for Improving Education: A Comparative Overview." Unpublished manuscript, National Institute for Education, Washington, DC.

Policy Alternatives for California Education. 1988. *Conditions of Education in California 1988.* Policy Paper No. PP88-3-2. Berkeley: PACE.

Porter, Andrew, 1988. "Content Determinants in Elementary School Mathematics." In *Perspectives on Research on Effective Mathematics Teaching, Vol. 1,* edited by Douglas A. Grouws and Thomas J. Cooney, 96–113. Hillsdale, NJ: Erlbaum.

Porter, Andrew. 1989. A curriculum out of balance: The case of elementary school mathematics. *Educational Researcher* 18(5): 9–17.

Porter, Andrew, and Teresa Kuhs. 1982, April. "A District Management-by-Objectives System: Its Messages and Effects." Paper presented at the annual meeting of the American Educational Research Association, New York.

Porter, Andrew, et al. 1986. "Content Determinants." Research Series No. 179. East Lansing: Michigan State University, Institute for Research on Teaching.

Powell, Arthur, Eleanor Farrar, and David Cohen. 1985. *The Shopping Mall High School: Winners and Losers in the Educational Marketplace.* Boston: Houghton Mifflin.

Pressman, Jeffrey, and Aaron Wildavsky. 1974. *Implementation: How Great Expectations in Washington Are Dashed in Oakland.* Berkeley: University of California Press.

Ripley, Randall. 1985. *Policy Analysis and Political Science.* Chicago: Nelson Hall.

Rist, Ray. 1970. Student social class and teacher expectation: The self-fulfilling prophecy in ghetto education. *Harvard Educational Review* 40(3): 411–451.

Rosenbaum, James. 1989. What if good jobs depended on good grades? *American Educator* 13(4): 10–15, 40–43.

Rosenbaum, James, and Takehiko Kariya. 1989. From high school to work: Market and institutional mechanisms in Japan. *American Journal of Sociology* 94(6): 1334–1365.

Rossman, G., et al. 1987. *Pathways Through High School: Translat-*

ing the Effects of New Graduation Requirements. Report to the Office of Educational Research and Improvement, Department of Education. Annapolis, MD: Maryland Department of Education.

Roth, Kathleen, Charles Anderson, and Edward Smith. 1987. Curriculum material, teacher talk, and student learning: Case studies in fifth grade science teaching. *Journal of Curriculum Studies* 19(6): 527–548.

Salamon, Lester, ed. 1989. *Beyond Privatization: The Tools of Government Action*. Washington, DC: Urban Institute Press.

Schaffarzick, Jon. 1979. "Federal curriculum reform: A crucible for value conflict." In *Value Conflicts and Curriculum Issues: Lessons from Research and Experience*, edited by Jon Schaffarsick and Gary Sykes, 1–24. Berkeley, CA: McCutchan.

Schmidt, William, et al. 1987. Four patterns of teacher content decision making. *Journal of Curriculum Studies* 19(5): 439–455.

Schon, Donald. 1971. *Beyond the Stable State*. New York: Random House.

Schwille, John, et al. 1983. "Teachers as Policy Brokers in the Content of Elementary School Mathematics." In *Handbook of Teaching and Policy*, edited by Lee Shulman and Gary Sykes, 370–391. New York: Longman.

Schwille, John, et al. 1988. State policy and the control of curriculum decisions. *Educational Policy* 2(1): 29–50.

Schwille, John, Andrew Porter, and M. Gant. 1979. "Content Decision-Making and the Politics of Education." Research Series No. 52. East Lansing: Michigan State University, Institute for Research on Teaching.

Scribner, Jay, and R. M. Englert. 1977. "The politics of education: An introduction." In *The Politics of Education: The Seventy-sixth Yearbook of the National Society for the Study of Education*, Part II, edited by Jay Scribner, 1–29. Chicago: University of Chicago Press.

Sedlak, Michael, Christopher W. Wheeler, Diana C. Pullin, and Philip A. Cusick. 1986. *Selling Students Short*. New York: Teachers College Press.

Sharp, Rachel, and Anthony Green. 1975. *Education and Social Control*. London: Routledge & Kegan Paul.

Shulman, Lee. 1983. "Autonomy and Obligation: The Remote Control of Teaching." In *Handbook of Teaching and Policy*, edited by Lee Shulman and Gary Sykes, 484–504. New York: Longman.

Spady, William, and Douglas Mitchell. 1979. "Authority and the Management of Classroom Activities." In *Classroom Management: The Seventy-eighth Yearbook of the National Society for the Study of Education*, edited by Daniel Duke, 75–115. Chicago: University of Chicago Press.

Stake, Robert, et al. 1978. *Case Studies in Science Education, Vol. I, The Case Reports*, stock no. 038-000-00377-1. Washington, DC: U.S. Government Printing Office.

Stodolsky, Susan. 1988. *The Subject Matters: Classroom Activity in Math and Social Studies*. Chicago: University of Chicago Press.

Stodolsky, Susan. 1989. "Is Teaching Really by the Book?" In *From Socrates to Software: The Teacher as Text and the Text as Teacher. Eighty-ninth Yearbook of the National Society for the Study of Education*, edited by Philip Jackson and Sophie Haroutunian-Gordon, 159–184. Chicago: University of Chicago Press.

Tyack, David. 1976. Ways of seeing: An essay on the history of compulsory schooling. *Harvard Educational Review* 46(3): 355–389.

van Geel, Tyll. 1976. *Authority to Control the School Program*. Lexington, MA: Heath.

Walker, Decker. 1979. "Approaches to Curriculum Development." In *Value Conflicts and Curriculum Issues*, edited by Jon Schaffarzick and Gary Sykes, 263–290. Berkeley, CA: McCutchan.

Walker, Decker. 1990. *Fundamentals of Curriculum*. New York: Harcourt Brace Jovanovich.

Weatherly, Richard, and Michael Lipsky. 1977. Street-level bureaucrats and institutional innovation: Implementing special-education reform. *Harvard Educational Review* 47(2): 171–97.

Weick, Karl. 1976. Educational organizations as loosely coupled systems. *Administrative Science Quarterly* 21(1): 1–19.

Weimer, David, and Aidan Vining. 1989. *Policy Analysis: Concepts and Practice*. Englewood Cliffs, NJ: Prentice Hall.

Weiss, Iris. 1977. *Report of the 1977 National Survey of Science, Mathematics, and Social Studies Education*, stock no. 038–000-00364. Washington, DC: U.S. Government Printing Office.

Welch, Wayne. 1979. "Twenty Years of Science Curriculum Development: A Look Back." In *Review of Research in Education*, edited by David Berliner, Vol. 7, 282–306. Washington, DC: American Educational Research Association.

Westat, Inc. 1988, May. *Preliminary Tabulations: Nation at Risk Update Study as Part of the 1987 High School Transcript Study* (Report for the U.S. Department of Education, Center for Education Statistics). Rockville, MD: Westat, Inc.

Wildavsky, Aaron. 1979. *Speaking Truth to Power*. Boston: Little, Brown.

Willis, Paul. 1977. *Learning to Labor*. New York: Columbia University Press.

Wirt, Frederick. 1977. "State Policy Culture and State Decentralization." In *The Politics of Education: The Seventy-sixth Yearbook of the National Society for the Study of Education*, Part II, edited by Jay Scribner, 164–187. Chicago: University of Chicago Press.

Wirt, Frederick, Douglas Mitchell, and Catherine Marshall. 1988. Culture and education policy: Analyzing values in state policy systems. *Educational Evaluation and Policy Analysis* 104(4): 271–284.

Wirt, John. 1975. *R & D Management: Methods Used by Federal Agencies*. Lexington, MA: Lexington Books.

Wise, Arthur. 1979. *Legislated Learning*. Berkeley: University of California Press.

Wrigley, Julia. 1982. *Class Politics and Public Schools: Chicago 1900–1950*. New Brunswick, NJ: Rutgers University Press.

Young, Michael, ed. 1971. *Knowledge and Control*. London: Collier-Macmillan.

Ziegler, Harmon, M. Kent Jennings, and G. Wayne Peak. 1974. *Governing American Schools: Political Interaction in Local School Districts*. North Scituate, MA: Duxbury Press.

8

CURRICULUM STABILITY AND CHANGE

Larry Cuban
STANFORD UNIVERSITY

"The history of American education is a chronicle of fads."
W. W. Charters, 1922

"Changing schools is like moving a graveyard."
Hyman Rickover, 1983

It is so easy to probe at the apparent contradiction of frequent changes amidst inertia within public schools. One-liners underscore the acute vulnerability of public schools to social change: When society has an itch, the schools scratch. Yet the torpor of schools, their seeming indifference in adjusting to social change, is just as familiar: It is easier to get a man on the moon than to reform schools. To make sense out of curricular change and stability, a subset of the larger issue of change and stability in schooling (and in society), I explore in this chapter this apparent contradiction of faddism amidst rigidity within public schooling. The outline of that exploration follows.

To understand curricular change and stability, it is essential to question three common beliefs about change: planned change is good; change is divorced from stability; and once planned change is adopted, improvements occur. In questioning these beliefs, I lay a foundation for examining different forms of planned change (incremental and fundamental) and for exploring why districts, schools, and classrooms (the units of analysis used in this chapter) reflect both change and constancy. Since momentum for most reforms begins outside schools, I analyze the different ways that external pressures for change enter, stay, and often exit the schools. These reexamined beliefs and distinctions among planned changes become a framework for answering four questions about curricular change and persistence:

- To what extent has curriculum changed from 1870 to the present?
- To what extent has curriculum been marked by stability over these decades?
- What factors account for curricular change and stability in districts, schools, and classrooms?
- What are plausible explanations for both curricular change and stability?

In answering these questions, I first distinguish between the intended (or official) curriculum and the curriculum that teachers teach, and then between the taught curriculum and what students learn. While planned changes have occurred in the intended curriculum in districts and schools, there has been a remarkable durability in the taught curriculum. To explain these changes, I use a political perspective. Economic, demographic, political, social, and cultural changes

The author wishes to thank David Tyack and Laurel Tanner for their comments on this chapter.

mediated by groups and individuals reshape schooling inexorably and alter policies and practices at the district and school levels. Such interest group pressures at work in a decentralized system of school governance have produced a broad array of incremental, rather than fundamental, changes in the intended curriculum and much less modification in what teachers teach.

To explain the durability in curricula, I use an organizational perspective. Districts, schools, and classrooms as organizations absorb external pressures for change and convert them into routine add-ons compatible with existing practices. These organizations bend, deflect, and transform pressures for change to maintain curricular continuity. Thus, incremental changes are assimilated and reinforce continuity. There are, of course, other ways of interpreting curricular change and stability than these political and organizational explanations, and in the final section I explore those also.

A FRAMEWORK FOR UNDERSTANDING CHANGE IN SCHOOLS

Three common beliefs provide the underpinnings for a broad acceptance of planned change. They deserve examination. The first belief is that planned change is positive; it is growth, progress, and improvement wrapped into a shiny package. Anchored in evolutionary ideas which can be traced back to the Greeks and wedded to the historic values of the American culture, the idea of progress has been honed by generations of theorists, policymakers, and publicists (Nisbet 1980). Yet change may or may not be progress. The divorce that devastates one spouse finds the other relishing a new-found freedom. To some U.S. educators, the curricular changes that have been designed over the last century to accommodate millions of children from foreign lands, the poor off the farm, and others who had few advantages are clear signs of progress. As the nation enters the 21st century, the varied curricula, better textbooks, and a rich array of instructional materials provide solid evidence of improvement for the least advantaged in society. To other educators, the very same evidence is viewed as a poor education for those labeled at risk, those who speak English as a second language, and those who are barely attached to schooling (Carnegie Foundation 1988).

A second assumption is that change in districts and schools is divorced from stability: It is either undergoing change or static. Yet constancy and change coexist in an individual, group, organization, and culture. Psychologists point to the durability of personality traits over time, even as a child matures into a youth and adult. Sociologists stress the persistent features that mark organizations as they evolve from infancy to maturity. Anthropologists record how both distant and near cultures adapt traditions. Political scientists underscore the continuity of national impulses that endure through centuries of revolutionary changes in regimes. Stability and change are entangled in individuals and institutions, families and nations. Why not districts, schools, and classrooms? It is not wordplay to speak of stable forms of change or continuity amidst change (Getzels 1970; March 1981; Meyer and Rowan 1978; Moore 1963; Nisbet 1969; Shils 1981).

A third belief in need of reexamination is the assumption that once plans designed by educators are adopted, improvements occur. Indeed, while many changes are initiated and planned by school authorities, most designs are imposed upon schools or negotiated into existence. Educational policymakers often accommodate to these external impositions of planned change by trimming and tailoring routine activities. The journey from design to practice is far more zig-zag than a straight line.

Consider a continuum that stretches from externally imposed changes to those that are negotiated to voluntary changes in schools. At one end of the continuum would be demographic, cultural, political, social and economic changes that jolt districts and schools. Because the system of American public schools is decentralized into 50 states with over 15,000 school districts (it was over 100,000 a half century earlier), much looseness, variability, and contradiction pervade the many levels of schooling. Each level of schooling becomes the immediate environment of the next level (e.g., the school is the classroom's environment). These nested layers are characteristic of American schools. Within the informal national system of schooling, there are state systems; within those state systems, there are districts and, within them, there are schools which contain individual classrooms, each a system in and of itself. In analyzing different forms of change along this continuum, and, because of the diversity and looseness among these nested layers of systems, I do not assume that changes that affect one level of schooling automatically affect another (Bidwell 1965; Meyer and Rowan 1978; Smith, Dwyer, Prunty, and Kleine 1988; Weick 1976).

Economic downturns shrink dollars allocated to schooling; the civil rights movement's efforts widen student access to schools, liberalize hiring policies, and reshape textbook content; fears of the AIDS epidemic leads to curricular mandates and programs of instruction. Or recall the recurring passions that sweep across the society for particular school solutions to national social problems, such as compensatory education, instructional television, and the desktop computer.

Because of these powerful forces at work in the larger society, federal and state laws, new regulations, and policy mandates give state, district and school-site officials little choice but to adopt the imposed changes as they filter through the various nested layers. They accommodate in two ways. Some officials endorse the imposed changes and move swiftly to adopt the new policies. Other officials question the direction of the changes as well as the process. They also act, but try to keep things as they are. School boards, for example, may initiate novel compensatory programs for low-performing students, but keep them insulated from mainstream students. Or districts may purchase microcomputers, but place the machines in rooms open to students only a few hours a week. Such token or symbolic changes are tactical responses by the institution to conserve what already exists.

In the middle of the continuum is a form of change initiated by schools. It comes from the bargaining and compromises struck between individuals and groups. These changes result from natural conflicts that exist within state, district, and local systems over value differences in operating schools and the directions that schools should pursue with children. An obvious example is when school boards negotiate with teacher unions to create binding agreements on salaries and working conditions. Another instance of negotiated change would be when a superintendent persuades her board of education to align a board policy mandating computer literacy for every high school graduate with the recommendations of an ad hoc citizens' committee on technological illiteracy.

At the other end of the continuum are voluntary planned changes. These are designs and blueprints that school policymakers and practitioners elect to initiate, adopt, and implement. These are not tactical responses to social changes and organizational conflicts. The distinction I wish to draw is between planned changes that are directly traceable to external pressures—as those mentioned above—and uncoerced changes undertaken by policymakers and practitioners who anticipate emerging issues in the school and community or respond imaginatively to existing problems.

Obviously, no change is completely free of external influences, but there are instances of individuals and groups who voluntarily initiate, adopt, and implement designs for change without a sword of public furor or a threatening letter from the state department of education hanging over their heads. A school board that wants teachers to collaborate secures waivers from the state to permit teachers to both coach and evaluate peers. Or the principal decides with her staff to ungrade their elementary school because the teachers want smaller classes. Ungrading the school would permit those smaller classes and wider experimentation in teaching approaches with the school's diverse students. Or the high school social studies teacher who wants students to think critically redesigns his course for an in-depth examination of eight topics for the entire school year, rather than covering three dozen chapters in the textbook.

This continuum of change suggests that the sources of changes largely come from outside the schools, yet policymakers, administrators, and practitioners have some measure of influence over how they respond to these external forces (see Figure 8–1). Responses to change may be accommodating, tactical, or voluntary. Although the changes along the continuum are planned, it would be too easy to fall into the trap of viewing all planned change as the same. While I have distinguished among planned changes based upon their sources and responses, there is an additional distinction that needs to be drawn about the direction of the change. Toward what ends?

First- and Second-Order Changes

There are at least two types of planned change (Watzlawick, Weakland, and Fisch 1974). First-order, or incremental, changes are intentional efforts to enhance the existing system by correcting deficiencies in policies and practices. Such changes try to make what exists more efficient and effective without disturbing basic organizational features. Those who propose incremental changes, then, assume that the existing goals and structures of schooling are both adequate and desirable. Such changes are aimed essentially at improving the core features of the organization.

Examples of incremental school reform include raising salaries, selecting new texts, adding (or deleting) courses to (or from) the curriculum, lengthening the school day, and introducing more effective evaluation of teachers. The compensatory programs of the 1960s and since are instances of first-order reforms. The school effectiveness movement and its swift spread into state-driven reforms in the 1980s with its emphasis on more student time spent on academic tasks and tighter alignment with curricular goals, texts, and tests is another instance of incremental change.

Second-order, or fundamental, changes seek to alter the essential ways that organizations are put together because of major dissatisfaction with present arrangements. Fundamental changes introduce new goals, structures, and roles that transform familiar ways of performing duties into novel solutions to persistent problems.

For example, mid-19th-century U.S. school reformers imported from Prussia the innovation of the graded school. These reformers sought to restructure the then-current one-room schools in towns and cities to fit a new vision of social order, efficiency, and democracy. Moving from the one-room schoolhouse in the 1840s with one untrained, unsupervised teacher responsible for children ranging in age from 6 to 18, where each child would get a few minutes a day of the teacher's attention, to a graded elementary school with a principal, a separate classroom for each teacher, children grouped by age, a curriculum divided into grade-level pieces, and annual promotions was a fundamental change in schooling (Kaestle 1973; Tyack 1974).

Other, more recent, changes intended to alter schools and classrooms in fundamental ways are open-space buildings and open classrooms. In these settings, teachers and principals are expected to view children as individuals who need to make their own decisions, work together, and connect knowledge and skills learned in school with what occurs outside those walls. Such educators would have relationships with children quite unlike colleagues who view children as pupils who have to be filled with correct knowledge and trained to be adults (Barth 1972; Silberman 1971).

Consider also other proposals for fundamental change, such as vouchers or designs that delegate budgetary and staffing decisions to individual schools. In each instance, the intention is to alter a basic structure of schooling

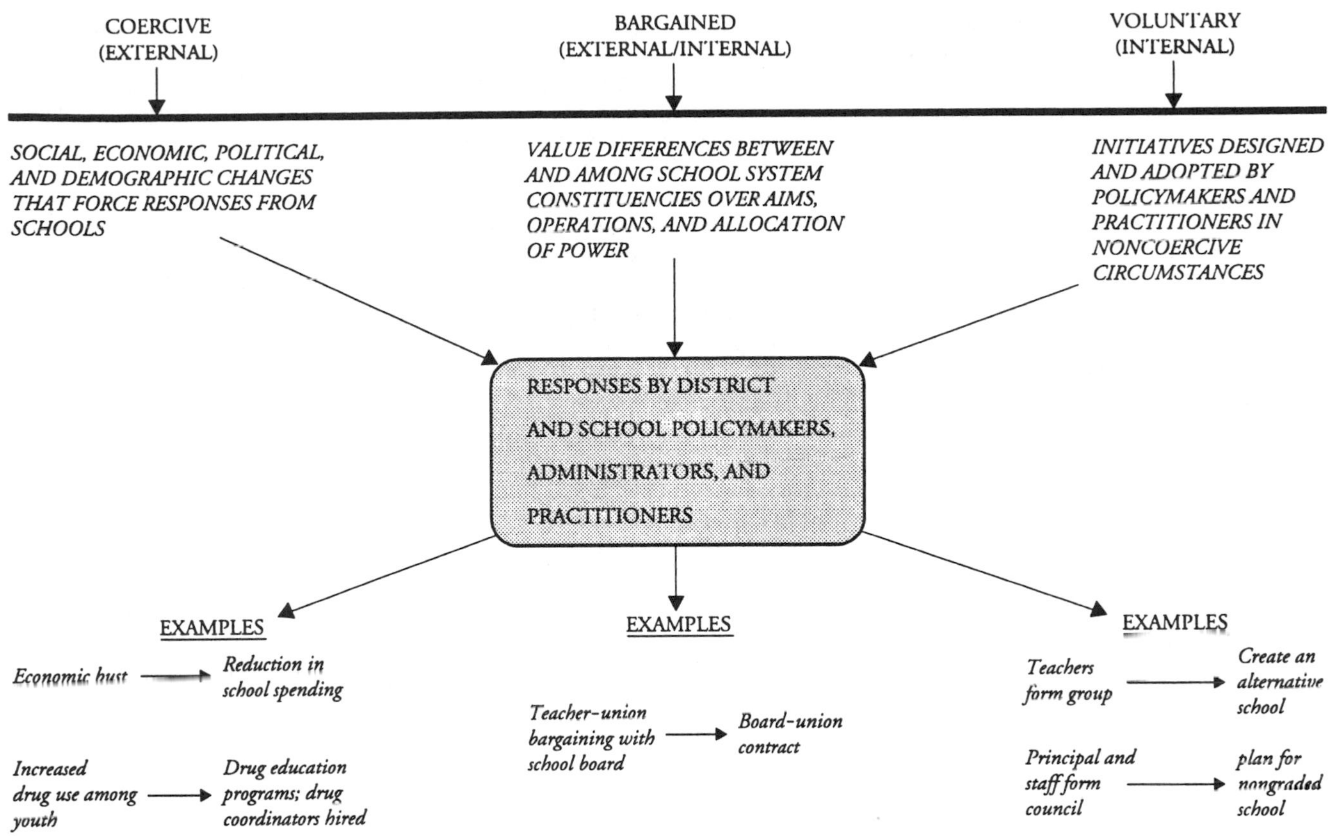

FIGURE 8–1. Sources of Planned Change and Responses by District and School Policymakers, Administrators, and Practitioners

through enlarging choice and autonomy or rearranging how schools are funded and operated. Frequently, these proposals aim at particular structures of schooling; seldom are they comprehensive, taking in both the formal structures of how schooling is organized and processes occurring in schools and classrooms.

By examining three common assumptions about change, constructing a tripartite continuum of different forms of change, and distinguishing between incremental and fundamental forms of planned change, a framework for understanding change in schools begins to emerge. No doubt I may have missed particular assumptions or omitted other types of change. Like others who have tried to pull together varied notions of social change embedded in equilibrium and conflict theories as they apply to schools, I recognize that much work remains to be done (Paulston 1976; Stevens 1976). Note that what appears here as pure versions of change is obviously presented in this manner for analytic purposes. Most changes are probably combinations and vary in degree. Yet as a beginning the framework suggests rough-hewn categories of change.

Of equal importance, this framework underscores that schooling is deeply embedded in the larger society. Many, but not all, of the impulses for changing public schools arise in the larger society. To a certain degree, when society has a cold, schools do much of the sneezing. Yet at the same time, what schools do is not wholly determined by impersonal, social forces. For schools do blunt, reshape, and sidestep changes imposed by external groups; they maintain their institutional stability. Moreover, at particular times and places, practitioners and policymakers have redefined and created classrooms, schools, and districts that respond to issues they have identified prior to the escalation of outside pressures. As institutions, schools are embedded in the culture, yet they have a life of their own (Hansot and Tyack 1988; March and Olsen 1984; Selznick 1949; Smith et al. 1988).

How Schools Maintain Their Continuity

Apart from handling externally imposed changes, either incremental or fundamental in intention, school organizations at each level have internal processes for preserving their stability, for making sure that what happens today will probably occur tomorrow (Stinchcombe 1965; Straw 1982).

Already mentioned above are the expedient changes introduced by those in schools who wish to preserve continuity (March 1981).

Districts, individual schools, and classroom teachers develop routines for detecting noise in their immediate surroundings and handling it. Early warning systems, for example, are embedded in procedures that many school boards follow in listening to parents at public meetings, superintendents informally meeting with students, teachers, and parents, and periodic surveys of citizen opinion. State departments of education hire lobbyists to work the legislature and signal the state board and superintendent about impending moves from the lawmakers.

There are even more complex ways that school organizations remain stable. Recall the butterflies of reform, beautifully present for a few spring days but gone not long after: programmed learning, talking typewriters, the Dalton Plan, the Initial Teaching Alphabet, differentiated staffing, open classrooms, flexible scheduling—the list extends indefinitely. The pattern of how most innovations and proposals get adopted as reforms, soar, plummet, and disappear is so familiar as to almost qualify as a ritual. The pattern itself is part of a stable process for sustaining the core structures of schooling (Dewey 1901).

First, revelations of terrible school conditions or unacceptable student performance appear. Influential public figures link these undesirable conditions in schools to national problems, suggesting that schools must improve. Then, a crisis is announced. Solutions to end the crisis spill forth. Public expectations soar. Reformers enlarge their vocabularies with new slogans and catch phrases. Finally, policies are adopted and new programs launched. Certain policymakers and practitioners get labeled as heroes and appear in the media. Optimism is at its height.

Then, information about the innovative programs begins to appear. Rumors circulate. Flashy stories of astounding results mix with dour accounts of inaction. Scientific studies are completed, but results are ambiguous; they can be interpreted as signs of either success or failure. Public interest begins to flag. A reassessment of whether the resources invested in the innovation are worth the effort gets underway. Public attention slides to another crisis elsewhere in society. Because the problems that originally sparked the reform still endure, seemingly unabated, experts pronounce the innovation a failure. Villains are sought. The highly publicized programs disappear. Disappointment spreads over the gap between what was expected and what happened. Pessimism about what the innovation can do seeps into policymakers' hearts.

As brief as a few years and as long as a decade, this pattern in the life cycle of an innovation leaves the basic structures of schooling largely untouched. The seizing of innovations in the early part of this sequence of events strengthens public loyalty to a system of schooling that is responsive and current with what is new and worthwhile. However, continuity reigns. This life cycle for many innovations shows the intersection between public expectations of schooling, the symbolic importance of reform talk, and political and bureaucratic processes at work both outside and inside schools (Brickell 1964; Downs 1972; Meyer 1986; Popkewitz 1988).

Some innovations are hardier, yet, over time, lapse into incremental changes. A familiar example is the curricular reforms of the 1950s and 1960s guided, in large part, by academic specialists and funded by the federal government. Aimed at revolutionizing teaching and learning in math, science, and social studies, millions of dollars were spent in producing textbooks, classroom materials, and training teachers. By the end of the 1970s, when researchers reported on what occurred in classrooms, they found conventional teaching aimed at imparting knowledge and little evidence of student involvement in critical thinking, although there was a different curricular residue left in textbooks (Atkin and House 1981; Stake and Easley 1978; Suydam 1977; Weiss 1978).

A more complicated way in which fundamental reforms become incremental changes is what George and Louise Spindler call "substitute change." They studied a small school in a southern German village called Schönhausen for over a decade. Initially a rural area, the villages were undergoing changes in land ownership and wine production, that is, the creation of larger plots and introduction of machines to till and harvest grapes; moreover, shifts in population were making the area urbanized.

For decades, the school curriculum had emphasized the land, the village community, and family values. The federal and provincial ministries of education, however, mandated a new curriculum and textbooks based upon life in cities, the importance of modernization, and high technology. The Spindlers studied the village and its school in 1968 and returned in 1977 after almost a decade of reform.

What surprised the Spindlers was that, in spite of this clear attempt by ministry officials to make a village school more modern and responsive to urban and cultural differences, children, teachers, and parents continued to make tradition-based and village-oriented choices. In the school, trips that once took classes for day-long strolls in the countryside gave way to role-playing a petition to the village council. Much of the earlier content about the beauty of the land was lost but the cultural goals and values nourishing the traditions of the village were maintained. How?

The Spindlers found that the way teachers taught and classroom order sustained village traditions in the face of curricular reforms. Teachers substituted a play about the village political process—recommended in the new curriculum—for a romantic folktale that was in the previous curriculum, but as it transpired in the class the core meaning of the importance of living in the village remained the same. An effort to fundamentally alter the values of villages in that part of Germany to make them more responsive to urban life got transformed into a reaffirmation of village values (Spindler and Spindler 1982).

Fundamental reforms sometimes became diluted by shunting the change to the periphery of the school. For example, innovative programs that reduce class size, reconceptualize the student-teacher relationship, integrate subject matter from diverse disciplines, and structure activities that involve students in their learning often begin in regular classrooms but, over the years, migrate to out-of-the-way rooms in the main building or far-away sites. The schools have, indeed, adopted and implemented programs fundamentally different from what mainstream students receive, yet it is the outsiders, students labeled as potential dropouts, vocational students, pregnant teenagers, those identified as gifted, at-risk students, and handicapped pupils who benefit from the innovative programs. Thus, some second-order changes get encapsulated, like a grain of sand in an oyster; they exist within the system but are often separated from mainstream programs (Powell, Farrar, and Cohen 1985).

These organizational strategies to retain continuity are seldom conspiratorial or even due to conscious acts on the part of top leaders. Such transformations occur as a consequence of bureaucratic and political processes deeply embedded in the different levels of schooling as they interact with external forces in the larger society. They occur as a result of deep-seated impulses within the organization to appear progressive, to convince those who support the schools that what happens in schools is up-to-date and responsive to the wishes of its patrons. Thus, pervasive and potent processes within the institution of schooling preserve independence to act even in the face of powerful outside forces intent upon altering what happens in schools and classrooms.

This framework of analysis suggests that an apparent contradiction in the opening epigraphs to this chapter is not misleading after all. Fads do occur repeatedly in educational history, and schools are, indeed, stable institutions, not easily changed.

CURRICULAR CHANGE AND STABILITY

Within a general framework of understanding school change and stability, I include curriculum. In making sense of both constancy and change in curriculum two issues have to be explored: First, what is meant by "curriculum" and, second, how that definition of curriculum connects to the multi-level system of policy and practice in American schooling. In short, to answer the question: Has curriculum changed? depends upon how one defines curriculum and at what level of schooling one looks for change and continuity.

Definitions of Curriculum

Over 1,100 curriculum books have been written since the turn of this century, each with different versions of what "curriculum" means; many of the definitions conflict (Schubert 1986, 26; Walker 1990, 4). "Images," "conceptualizations," and "orientations" are words researchers have used to get at the complex meaning of the term without slipping into the cul-de-sac of a narrow definition. Within this volume, there is a broad range of opinion concerning its meaning. It is probably best to simply assert that such diverse characterizations mirror the writers' different experiences with public schooling and their values about what public schooling should be. After all, at its core, the notion of a curriculum, however defined, tries to answer three questions fundamental to formal schooling: What knowledge, skills, and values are most worthwhile? Why are they so? How should the young acquire them? The "what," "why," and "how" have produced a rich variety of responses (and fierce debate) over the purposes, content, organization and implementation of curriculum for the last two millennia; they also help me frame the view of curriculum that I will use in this chapter.

A curriculum of a classroom, school, district, state (or nation) is a series of planned events intended for students to learn particular knowledge, skills, and values and organized to be carried out by administrators and teachers. This concept of curriculum stresses purposes, content, organization, relationships, and outcomes for students.

Levels of Curricular Policy and Practice

Policy decisions produce curriculum. Formally adopted at federal, state, and district levels in the decentralized system of U.S. educational governance, curricular policies are shaped by many forces. Curriculum materials developed in federally funded projects, statewide exams, and district mandates on graduation requirements are familiar instances of policy making at the different levels. These policies are expected to be put into practice in schools and classrooms. To the degree that principals and teachers reshape the adopted policies as they implement them in their sites, these practitioners can be considered policymakers also (Schwille et al. 1983).

Although these different levels of governance are separate, they are nested within one another, and much interplay between layers occurs (e.g., a local school board attacked by fundamentalist religious groups adopts a state-approved eighth grade science textbook which omits content on Charles Darwin and evolution). Thus, curricular policy making is primarily a political rather than technical process (Boyd 1979; Kirst and Walker 1971).

With a definition that stresses purposes, content, organization, and practice and a multilevel, decentralized policy system that includes a political process of both adoption and implementation, one remaining piece needs to be inserted.

Types of Curriculum

Curriculum can be differentiated among the intended, that is, content which is expected to be learned, the curriculum that is taught, and, finally, the curriculum that students learn. All three types are embedded in the historical curriculum, the residue of purposes, content, organization, and practice that existed prior to any proposed changes in curriculum (see Figure 8–2).

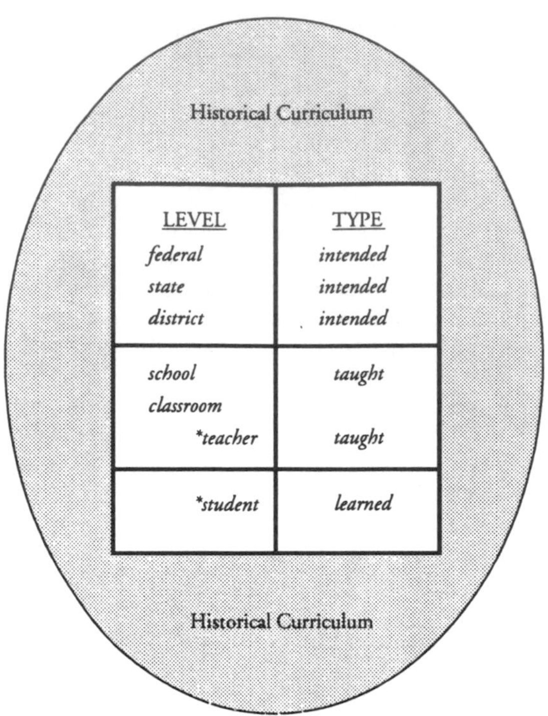

Historical Curriculum
LEVEL
TYPE
federal
intended
state
intended
district
intended
school
taught
classroom
*teacher
taught
*student
learned
Historical Curriculum

FIGURE 8–2. Levels and Types of Curriculum

Intended. Labeled variously as "recommended," "adopted," "official," "formal," or "explicit," the intended curriculum is that body of content contained in state frameworks, district courses of study, listings of courses taught in a school, and syllabi. It is written. It is the subject matter, skills, and values that policymakers expect to be taught (Goodlad 1984). It is the intended curriculum that federal, state, and district policymakers believe will convey core knowledge and values children absorb. Theories of schooling, teaching, learning, and knowledge are embedded deeply within the intended curriculum. To some specialists who have devoted their careers to constructing curriculum, it is equal in importance to, if not greater than, the teacher. Harold Rugg, a professor at Teachers College, Columbia University, and a leader in the movement to change the traditional curriculum in the decades prior to World War II, stated bluntly in 1926:

> Under proper conditions, of course, the true educational intermediary between the immature child and adult society is the teacher. If we had 750,000 teachers (or even, say, 300,000) who, like William Rainey Harper, 'could teach Hebrew as though it were a series of hair-breadth escapes,' the curriculum itself would stand merely as a subordinate element in the educational scheme. The teacher would occupy the important place of guidance we have given to the materials of instruction.
>
> But under the current hampering conditions (better, of course, than in earlier decades and improving slowly) of inadequately trained teachers of large and numerous classes, heavy teaching programs, insufficient facilities and lack of educational perspective—I fear we tend to reverse the process and teach hair-breadth escapes as though they were Hebrew. Hence, my allegiance to the curriculum rather than to the teacher as the effective educational intermediary between the child and society. (Rugg 1926, 3)

This view of the critical importance of the intended curriculum has seldom been stated as explicitly, save for the talk during the 1960s of "teacher-proof" materials. Thus, the intended curriculum is a map of theories, beliefs, and intentions about schooling, teaching, learning, and knowledge.

Taught. Included here are the formal and informal lessons taught in classrooms and in schools. Sometimes called the "implicit," "delivered," or "operational" curriculum, it is what teachers do (lecture, ask questions, listen, organize classes into groups, etc.) and use (chalk, texts, worksheets, machines, etc.) to present content, ideas, skills, and attitudes. Here is where teachers' beliefs begin altering the intended curriculum. There is also an informal side to the curriculum taught in a classroom. It is observed in a teacher's ad lib comments, handling of cheating on tests, and letting a pupil sleep in class. The informal side has been labeled the "hidden" curriculum (Goodlad 1984; Jackson 1968).

Similarly, at the school level there are formally and informally taught curricula. The school teaches in what it chooses to focus on in its courses of study. The school teaches in the way building space is organized and time scheduled for activities. The school teaches in its range of extracurricular choices and staffing. Consider the principal of an urban high school that is largely vocational in its course of study. The principal desires to make the school into a comprehensive high school stressing academics. Over a few years, the principal hires different staff, alters the course offerings, works hard at promoting higher student aspirations, and provides additional help for those students wishing to attend college. There are slow but steady changes in school rules, printed slogans in the corridors, and the opening of jobs for students in the community. Whether such changes mean that the new goal is being achieved misses the point that the school, like the teacher, teaches formal and informal lessons (Dreeben 1968; Jackson 1981; Lightfoot 1983).

Learned. Determining exactly what students have learned as a result of being in a classroom has been the dream of reformers, policymakers, and psychologists interested in testing and measurement since the turn of the century. Pediatrician and school reformer Joseph Mayer Rice collected data in 1897 from 33,000 children on how they spelled. He found virtually no link between the time they spent in school on spelling drills and their performance on a spelling test (Cremin 1961, 7–8). Since then, the expansion of the testing industry and concentration upon measuring student learning have produced myriad instruments. Still, complaints about testing in schools continue. Such tests inadequately plumb the depth of what knowledge, skills, and attitudes students acquire. As insufficient but available tools, they provide an incomplete portrait of student learning. Or as the Resnicks put it: "American school children are the most tested in the world and the least examined'' (Haney 1984; Madaus 1988; Resnick and Resnick 1985, 17).

The gap in knowledge between what is taught and what is learned—both intended and unintended—is large. One line of research has explored student thought processes during and after classroom lessons. One researcher listened to primary grade students talk about the seatwork their teacher assigned. What the students were most concerned about was finishing the work, not understanding it (Anderson 1984). Another researcher collected instances of students solving math word problems in a mechanical way, even when their answers did not make sense in the real world. ''I look through the problem and circle the numbers,'' one student said, ''Then I start reading from the back, because the key word is usually at the end.'' Students learn, the researcher argues, that school math is arbitrary and that you do not have to understand ''problems'' in the book to solve them (Schoenfeld 1990, 20). Research into students' misconceptions about science and math (e.g., the forces acting on a baseball after being hit by a bat), embedded in what these scholars call ''naive theories,'' directs attention to the importance of student thinking (Champagne, Klopfer, and Gunstone 1982, Romberg and Carpenter 1986; White and Tisher 1986).

Other researchers have begun to document unintended student learnings. For example, a number of researchers have studied high school classrooms and found that students negotiate covertly but insistently with their teachers over the rules, the amount of work, the level of performance, and acceptable classroom behavior. These ''treaties'' or bargains struck between students and teachers offer unintended lessons to the students about the nature of schooling, work, and their power (Cusick 1983; Powell, Farrar, and Cohen 1985). This is what I mean by the learned curriculum.

Historical. Every effort to alter the intended or taught curriculum has to contend with the past, that is, the formal purposes, official content, buried assumptions about knowledge, the organization and relationships within classrooms, schools, and districts that are inherited. It is the historical curriculum that contains the accumulated weight of previous innovations and mandates embedded in a district's or school's standard offerings of subject matter and activities. The weight and mass are sufficient to annoy each generation of curricular reformers eager to introduce new subjects, organizational innovations, and teaching strategies.

The historical curriculum is like coral, a mass of skeletons from millions of animals built up over time, that accumulates into reefs above and below the sea line, and gets battered and reshaped by that sea as it forms into islands. It is a presence that cannot be ignored either by ships or inhabitants.

Herbert Kliebard (1986) documents the shifting currents of curricular opinions in national commissions and diverse interest groups active since the turn of the century. He traces the fingerprints of these earlier efforts at curricular reform as they reappear in subsequent decades. Gerald Burns (1988) describes the enduring struggle between the academic and practical in the intended curriculum in Cambridge (Massachusetts) High School's revision of its courses of study in the 1850s. In analyzing curricular changes in Finnish schools since the 1880s, Risto Rinne (1988) notes the shifts in subjects offered, but also that schooling practices (the use of time, space, etc.) dating to the origins of the state system of schooling had a durable influence upon what happened in the schools. Tomas Englund (1986) points out the continuity of different conceptions of citizenship education in Sweden in the 20th century. Ian Westbury (1980), drawing from both British and U.S. examples, argues for the impact that the history of the classroom, curricular goals, and schools as institutions has had upon current practices. Ideas about teaching, curriculum, and schooling become things—organizational forms, he argues, and, over time, they shape what practitioners do daily.

In the next section of this chapter, I will identify the determinants of curricular change and stability. To do so, I need to identify which levels and types of curriculum I will examine and what period of time I will focus upon. Much attention has been given to the intended curriculum because sources are readily available in documents, speeches, reports, and articles. Far less attention has been paid to the core task of schooling: the transactions between teacher and student over content. What is taught and what is learned, particularly what students take away from their years in school, have received little examination. Yet it is the latter, for which very little research has been undertaken, that remains an area richly deserving of attention. Limited space, however, prevents my covering all areas.

Therefore, I will focus upon the intended and taught curricula in investigating the determinants of change and stability because the interaction between what is planned and what occurs is critical in coming to a deeper understanding about schooling. I will refer to the ''learned'' curriculum frequently but will not focus directly upon it. My reason is that the gap between what is intended and what is taught is already large, but some researchers have begun to map its terrain. It needs to be further laid out and understood clearly. The units of analysis for the intended curriculum will be the district and the school, and, for the taught curriculum, the classroom.

I will examine both curricula between the 1880s and the present. School reformers and practitioners had established by the 1880s a structure of schooling marked by diverse goals, funding mechanisms, governance, school organization, curricular variety, instructional repertoires, and bureaucratization that citizens and educators today would find familiar (Cremin 1988; Kaestle 1983; Katz 1971; Tyack 1974; Tyack and Hansot 1982). To view schooling over a century permits an analysis of factors that influenced both the intended and taught curricula within an organizational structure that has remained fundamentally constant, although it has undergone incremental changes.

Finally, a few words about the specific factors that I will identify. The list is incomplete. There are other determinants associated with change and stability that I have omitted for lack of evidence. One researcher noted: "Most of the studies cited failed to show a linkage . . . between forces affecting society as a whole, education as a field and curriculum as it is actually found in the classroom" (McNeil 1969, 299). I have included those factors that not only are associated with curricular change and stability, but also have some evidence to suggest a close linkage to the intended and taught curricula.

Note, however, that although the determinants of change and stability will be isolated and examined, the world is too complicated and untidy for me to argue that the factors I identify capture the way that things happen or that they are a complete explication of the complex interplay between schools and culture, or factors within schools, or even within classrooms.

Furthermore, no single theory informs the perspective offered here. Some researchers lean heavily upon theories of bureaucracy, political behavior, and culture. Others draw deeply from neo-Marxist theories. As a historian, I find various theories drawn from many disciplines more congenial than marriage to any single one. My affection for combining theories, based upon experience and research, colored the choices I made. I do have a point of view drawn from political and organizational perspectives. I use a political perspective to explain curricular changes and an organizational perspective to explain curricular stability.

DETERMINANTS OF CHANGE IN THE INTENDED AND TAUGHT CURRICULA

My view on the determinants of curricular change and how change occurs, particularly with the intended curriculum, is at its core political. Issues of curricular policy making involve power, control, coalitions, bargaining, and compromise among and between groups and individuals operating inside and outside a decentralized system of governing schools. A framework of political pluralism acknowledges the dispersal of power and the necessity of alliances among interest groups in such a fragmented policy system simply to insure financial and moral support of the institution. Within this view, it should come as no surprise that school boards and superintendents preside over changes in the intended curriculum to satisfy external demands and defuse pressure while enhancing the legitimacy of schooling. Others share versions of this view (Boyd 1979; Goodson 1983; House 1974; Kirst and Walker 1971; Kliebard 1986; Meyer and Rowan 1978; Popkewitz 1987; Smith et al. 1988; Walker 1990; Wirt and Kirst 1972).

Many researchers have identified different change factors they believe have influenced what teachers and administrators did in schools and classrooms. The typologies vary (Chase 1966; Counts 1926; Cuban 1979; Eisner 1979; Henry 1961; Kirst 1972; Kliebard 1988; Mackenzie 1964; McNeil 1969; Popkewitz 1987; Reid 1978).

Commonly, scholars divide determinants of curricular change into those external (e.g., social reform movements or interest groups outside school organizations) and those internal to the system (e.g., school board, teachers, students, parents). Although I do use these categories, note that there is a complex web of connections between external and internal determinants that cannot be easily isolated, examined, and assessed. While the individual factors are important, so are the visible and invisible linkages between them.

External Factors

Since the 1870s, the nation has experienced a number of social movements that have altered the fabric of society. Because schools are nested within the larger culture, social tremors reverberate within schools. I have selected just a few of the movements that have had documented influence upon both the intended and taught curricula to illustrate the potency of this factor. Virtually every commentator on curricular change has identified the two that I use as examples in reshaping curricula.

The Progressive Movement. A number of writers have documented the impact of post–Civil War industrialization, urban growth, and the consequences of immigration upon schooling in the late 19th and early 20th centuries, especially the growth of the progressive movement (Cremin 1961, 1988; Katz 1971; Krug 1964; Peterson 1985; Reese 1986; Tyack 1974). The movement was a political umbrella covering businessmen, foundation leaders, women's organizations, union advocates, social workers, school administrators, teachers and scores of others interested in alleviating the worst effects of unrestrained industrialism and urban poverty.

Historians Lawrence Cremin and David Tyack distinguished among groups of school reformers within the larger political movement. Tyack, for example, identified the administrative progressives (e.g., University of Chicago's Charles Judd, Stanford University's Ellwood P. Cubberley, and Superintendent Frank Spaulding) who used the latest concepts in corporate management and scholarly research to streamline a school district's organizational, curricular, and instructional machinery. This wing of the school progressives drew from the work of Frederick Taylor on managerial efficiency and from Clark University's G. Stanley Hall, Teachers College professor Edward Thorndike, and a growing legion of psychologists who used the model and tools of the natural sciences to convert education into a science. Tyack distinguished these progressives from social reformers (e.g., George Counts, John Childs, and Harold Rugg), who advocated using the schools as an instrument for national regeneration, and the pedagogical progressives (e.g., Francis Parker, Flora Cook, and William H. Kilpatrick), who saw the child as central to the school experience. Although substantial differences existed between, and among, progressive reformers, they all drew deeply from the well of John Dewey's ideas.

This political movement, enlisting a wide variety of school reformers, both elite and grass roots, still contained common themes in changing schools between the 1890s and 1940s. Cremin (1988) identifies four. Goals and functions expanded to include concern for a child's health, preparation for the workplace, family and community. A second theme was to apply to curricula and instruction more humane, active, and rational content and activities drawn from research. Another was to match curriculum and instruction to the large numbers and different kinds of children now entering public schools. Finally, there was the theme of using more efficient, rational tactics, drawn from industrial firms, to manage and govern schools (229).

While there is continuing disagreement among historians about why these themes emerged as they did among school reformers, there is consensus that the schools changed a great deal in the first three decades of the 20th century. New buildings included space for doctors and nurses, space for social workers to help children and their families, lunchrooms, and playgrounds. Curricula expanded to accommodate perceived ability and gender differences among children. Vocational schools were founded. The comprehensive high school took hold, encompassing multiple courses of study to match the different futures of youth. Kindergartens and junior high schools were added to the eight-grade grammar school. School governance changed from large, politically appointed school boards to smaller, elected boards composed of businessmen and professionals. The notion of an expanded role for schools in the lives of children and the better fitting of the school to the differences among children are concepts that have become embedded in the intended curricula and, for the most part, have persisted into the last decade of the 20th century.

Two of the themes identified by Cremin and other historians, however, are more difficult to assess when it comes to the impact upon the taught curricula: the application of rational techniques to the operation of schools and the introduction of a more active, humane student-centered instruction.

Historians have noted the strong affection among administrative progressives for the corporate organizational model with its passion for uniformity and managerial efficiency (Callahan 1962; Cronin 1973; Kantor 1986; Katz 1971; Kliebard 1986; Krug 1964; Tyack and Hansot 1982). While these writers disagree about why schools swiftly adopted the language, ideas, and approaches of the emerging corporate industrial community, effects upon the intended curriculum were readily observable.

Raymond Callahan (1962) recorded how school administrators' passion for standardization and efficiency in the early decades of the 20th century led many to convert curricular decisions into cost decisions. Frank Spaulding, Newton (Massachusetts) superintendent, explained to fellow school chiefs in 1913 that, in his district, "Of every dollar expended, 0.3 of one cent goes for Greek, while 15.6 goes for English. We buy 0.4 of one cent's worth of instruction in vocal music while buying 12.1 cents' worth of instruction in mathematics." He then pointed out: "Comparisons of the costs of the unit under different conditions is perhaps the best starting point for a campaign to reduce unit costs or to improve the quality of units of service" (74).

The influence of scientific management permeated the construction of the intended curriculum as well. Franklin Bobbitt of the University of Chicago used such phrases as "educational engineer" for the superintendent and "plant" for the school. According to Kliebard (1986), he applied the metaphor of the factory to curriculum as early as 1912:

> Work up the raw material into that finished product for which it is best adapted. Applied to education this means: Educate the individual according to his capabilities. This requires that the materials of the curriculum be sufficiently various to meet the needs of every class of individuals in the community; and that the course of training and study be sufficiently flexible that the individual can be given just the things that he needs. (98)

In various cities, when business executives felt strongly that the existing public school curriculum was too academic, they would endow private schools, as J. P. Morgan did in the New York Trade School with a $500,000 gift. They would also pressure school boards, as in Baltimore, to open a public manual-training school. By the early 20th century, many of these private schools were incorporated into public school systems and their vocational-technical curricula retained. The early distrust that existed between many labor unions and the National Association of Manufacturers, who endorsed vocational curricula in public schools, had evaporated by 1910. A survey completed in that year showed that 29 (of 46) states had mandated some form of industrial education. Even more revealing is that in one decade, 25 of those states had enacted their laws. "No other educational movement calling for large expenditures and involving sweeping changes in curriculum and method," the survey concluded, "has received such prompt legislative recognition" (Cremin 1961, 51; see also 32, 36, 38, 50). Even bastions of academic propriety, such as Philadelphia's selective Central High School, introduced between 1912 and 1939 a wide array of vocational courses so that, by 1920, almost two of every three students were enrolled in commercial, mechanic arts, or industrial arts courses of study. (Labaree 1988, 163–165) Other studies have similarly documented the triumph of vocational education in the early decades of the 20th century (Hogan 1985; Kliebard 1986; Lazerson and Grubb 1974).

If the presence of separate manual arts and vocational schools and the introduction of vocational curricula in previously academic high schools record the obvious penetration of business and industrial ideologies into the intended curriculum, how much of the movement for uniformity and efficiency shaped what teachers did in classrooms?

School administrators, for example, spent much time preparing curricular guides for teachers to standardize the content taught to students. By 1924, the New York City Board of Education had authorized 26 curricular bulletins and syllabi to be used by teachers. The next year, Superintendent William O'Shea ordered annual testing of elementary and junior high students in composition, arithmetic, spelling, and vocabulary. At the school level, principals and supervisors circulated rules for teachers to follow in their classes such as:

FOR ALL ELEMENTARY AND SECONDARY TEACHERS IN THE BRONX:

Size the children and assign seats. . . .

Make a seating plan of the class. . . .

Drill on standing and sitting; on putting the benches and desks up and down noiselessly. . . .

Place your daily plan, your time schedule on the desk where you can refer to them frequently. . . . (Cuban 1984a, 51–53)

While such evidence of the spillover from the spread of corporate industrialism and its enthusiasm for scientific efficiency suggests direct influence upon the taught curriculum, still there remains a gap between these rules and what occurred in the rooms once the door closed. Researchers have tried to reconstruct how teachers taught, but the elements of that reconstruction—what teachers did in classrooms, the content they taught, and student responses—are so entangled with other factors that shape pedagogy and subject matter (e.g., organizational pressures, prior socialization of teachers) that attributing teacher actions to be direct results of forces such as the application of rational management techniques to the curriculum is tenuous, at best (Cuban 1984a; Finkelstein 1989; Tyack, Lowe, and Hansot 1984; Zilversmit 1976).

There are researchers who have tried to make such linkages between the rationalizing of the taught (including the hidden) curriculum and dominant ideologies among the elite classes (Bowles and Gintis 1976; Carnoy and Levin 1985; Katz 1968; Spring 1972). Some have underscored the dominant ideologies but have also acknowledged that schools are not robotic agents of elite groups, nor are students empty containers to be filled with prevailing ideas and attitudes. Schools rework the dominant cultural knowledge into forms that students absorb (Apple 1982). Others have emphasized the clashes of lower and middle class values in schools and classrooms (Willis 1977; Woods 1979). Again, the question of whether what occurs in classrooms can be directly attributed to class-linked ideologies is paramount (Rubinson 1986). Stronger evidence might come from investigating what happened in vocational education classrooms. Few researchers have spent sufficient time in those classrooms or described in detail what occurred (Gaskell 1986).

Similarly, few historians have examined the record to determine if the efforts of the pedagogical progressives succeeded in introducing student-centered content and activities into the taught curriculum. Policy making stakes are high since such historical questions go to the heart of debates over whether federal, state, and district mandates to alter intended curriculum ever get past the classroom door.

Unfortunately, studies which examine the historical record have yet to still the policy debate over the efficacy of reforming schools in reordering what teachers do. David Hamilton (1989), for example, used teachers' manuals and debates among educators to argue that mainstream teaching practices such as the recitation weakened considerably in these decades in response to social and political changes in the larger society. Taking a stronger position, Diane Ravitch (1983) states that reformers transformed both the intended curriculum and how teachers taught (43, 45, and 58). Cremin (1961) had taken a similar position but has drawn back in his most recent volume (1988) to suggest that, while penetration of the classroom did occur in a substantial minority of classrooms and teachers did adopt specific practices, most teachers taught as they had before. Robert Hampel (1986) cites course-taking evidence during the high tide of progressivism in the 1930s and 1940s and notes that group guidance, hygiene, home management, consumer buying and family relationships—courses favored by pre–World War II progressives—attracted only 1 out of 10 students. Social science courses, such as problems of democracy economics, and psychology enrolled one third of upperclassmen, and core courses—combinations of English and history—captured just over 1 in 10 students. He concludes that such courses were indeed at the "edge" of the curriculum but, "at some point in his four years, a student might take one or another of the classes oriented to personal and social relations" (48).

Other scholars have challenged this triumph-of-progressivism view and argued that even though a major theme in progressivism, such as student involvement in activities and connections between the community and children, may have penetrated the intended curriculum, much in existing academic content and activities persisted (Sedlak and Schlossman 1985; O'Connor 1980; Franklin 1982; Cremin 1971; Bruner et al. 1941). In trying to figure out to what degree student-centeredness permeated the taught curriculum, a few researchers have concluded that while many teachers, especially elementary ones, have adopted specific progressive practices, most teachers did not (Cuban 1984a, Tyack, Lowe, and Hansot 1984, Zilversmit 1976).

The debate among historians will continue, but whether sufficient evidence will accumulate to persuade policymakers about the effectiveness of school reforms in the intended and taught curricula is another matter. Here, then, was a social and political movement sweeping up an unlikely coalition of school reformers in the early decades of this century that altered the talk about, if not the substance of, schooling.

Cold War and National Defense. Beginning in the early 1950s, national policymakers translated their growing unease about security threats into a concern over the public school's diminished role in producing scientists, mathematicians, and engineers. Origins of privately and federally funded efforts to toughen the math and science taught in public schools could be traced to the perceived insecure military position of the United States vis-à-vis Soviet Russia. That nation's production of the atomic and hydrogen bombs was not simply viewed, as one wag quipped, as "Their German scientists had gotten ahead of our German scientists'' (Silberman 1971, 169); the security gap was linked to deficiencies in the nation's technical and scientific schooling. That this emerging definition of a national defense problem coincided with attacks by public figures and academicians upon public schooling's alleged softness and intellectual decay made possible a vocal and prestigious coalition of critics (Goodlad 1964; Silberman 1971).

In the early 1950s, the National Science Foundation (NSF) and private groups underwrote several curriculum development projects headed by such well-known academics as Jerrold Zacharias and James Killens. In 1954, NSF spent $1,725 on curriculum development. Three years later expenditures jumped to $500,000. By 1959, they soared to $5.5 million (Jackson 1983, 148). These professors, professional reformers, and policymakers believed that the science taught in schools was anemic and antiquated. The Soviet launch of a satellite in 1957 accelerated criticism of schools and mobilized far more intensely the existing coalitions. The passage of the National Defense Education Act in 1958 marked the capstone of a movement to inject new scientific content and academic vigor into the classroom (Atkin and House 1981; Black 1967; Goodlad 1966).

By the mid-1960s, scholars had developed new biology, chemistry, and physics courses based upon notions of the structure of a discipline and inquiry methods of teaching. In a 1965 survey, 20 percent of the students taking introductory physics were using new curriculum materials; among the ablest college-bound teenagers, the totals reached 40 percent for physics, 25 percent for biology, and 20 percent for chemistry (Silberman 1971, 171). Seven years after the initiation of the project, the Biological Sciences Curriculum Study held 30 percent of that textbook market. These materials were markedly different from mainstream textbook content; the teacher manuals called for very different approaches in the classroom (Atkin and House 1981, 13). In 1976–1977, almost 60 percent of all school districts were using one or more of the federally funded science programs in grades 7 through 12; almost 30 percent of the elementary districts reported using at least one of the science curricula (Quick 1977). Peak interest in new science curricula, however, softened considerably after the mid-1970s (Jackson 1983). There is evidence, then, that the emerging federal presence introduced new content into the intended science curricula, expanded the information studied by students, and updated subject matter usually presented in commercially produced texts.

When the taught curriculum is examined, however, the initial glow of optimism generated by the above figures dims. In the new math, for example, teacher enthusiasm ran strong initially, but within a few years many teachers, along with parents, criticized the materials. After a decade of the new math, two researchers observed classrooms using the standard versions of the curriculum. They concluded that the new and old math were indistinguishable insofar as how they were taught and whether they encouraged students to continue the study of math (Sarason 1982).

In the mid-1970s, the National Science Foundation (NSF) commissioned a team of researchers to determine the extent to which NSF-funded projects had influenced what teachers taught and how they taught it. The researchers observed math, science, and social studies teachers in their rural and urban, elementary and secondary classrooms in 11 districts, interviewed key participants, and read materials. They found that the textbook was the primary source of information and teaching tool; they found that the methods the teachers used and the topics they chose to teach to students were largely unaffected by federal curriculum efforts. They found that the inquiry methods, central to many of the curricular materials developed under the aegis of NSF and other federally funded projects, seldom appeared in the classrooms that they observed. The usual sequence of classroom activities was for the teacher to assign pages in the text, conduct a question-answer recitation about the assigned pages, test, and discuss again (Stake and Easley 1978). As Paul Hurd, one of the authors of the new biology curriculum, concluded: ''For most teachers, science is still a noun, not a verb'' (Jackson 1983, 151).

The NSF also commissioned a survey of almost 5,000 teachers, asking them how they taught. The results of these self-reports corroborated the findings of researchers in the 11 case studies (Weiss 1978). More recent data from students suggest that the familiar content and approaches used by teachers persist into the mid-1980s. Recent data drawn from student reports of practices in U.S. history classrooms, for example, portray the familiar pattern of textbook use (89 percent of students reported weekly use), memorization of information (64 percent at least once a week), and teacher lecture (97 percent at least some of the time) (Applebee, Langer, and Mullis 1987). The taught curriculum largely remained the same after the dissemination of federally funded curriculum materials although the intended curriculum and commercially produced materials included different content for a substantial minority of classrooms.

There are other political and social movements that have penetrated the different levels of schooling and changed the intended and taught curricula. In selecting these two as instances of larger social forces impacting the different levels of curricula, I make no special case for these being the most important. I offer them as illustrations only.

Legislative and Legal Decisions. Another force for curricular change is state and federal laws and court decisions. Numerous researchers have identified the impact of these legislative and judicial acts (Boyd 1979; Eisner 1979; Geel 1979; Kirst and Walker 1971; Schwille et al. 1988; Short 1983; Tyack et al. 1987).

For over a century and a quarter, state laws have either mandated specific courses of study or the content that teachers must teach. Frequently, groups lobbied state legislatures to introduce into the formal curriculum subject matter that they believed essential for the moral health of children. By 1895, all states compelled local school districts to teach children about the evils of alcohol. By 1923, 43 states (90 percent) prescribed U.S. history as the vehicle for instruction in patriotism. By 1930, 11 states and the District of Columbia required the reading of the Bible in the classroom (Tyack, James, and Benavot 1987, 157–172). The trend toward specific mandates in subject matter, state-approved textbooks, assigning responsibility for making the content available to students, time allotments, and sanctions in withheld state aid for instruction was sufficiently clear by 1926 (Flanders 1926).

In other areas as well, the state legislature became an arena for conflicting interest groups to lobby for state intervention. Compensatory education and special education mandates touching the intended curriculum occurred throughout the 1960s and 1970s. The most recent surge of state intervention into curriculum occurred in the 1980s with an explosion of laws aimed at overhauling the secondary school curriculum. Legislatures prescribed graduation requirements. Stress on student performance generated a wide array of state achievement tests. Some states closely aligned their graduation requirements, curricular frameworks, textbook selections, and tests in order to directly influence what districts, schools, and teachers chose to teach (Wirt and Kirst 1989; Timar and Kirp 1988; Schwille et al. 1988).

Federal intervention in the intended curriculum also has a long, rich history. Vocational legislation dates back to the Smith Hughes Act (1917) with subsequent revisions over the next seven decades. The National Defense Education Act (1958) supported science, math, and foreign languages; in 1964, the law was extended to English, reading, history, and geography. The Economic Opportunity Act (1964) influenced preschool curricula with its Head Start programs. The Elementary and Secondary Education Act (1965) targeted low-income students, touching over 90 percent of the nation's school districts with classes for talented and underachieving youth, enrichment programs, and scores of other activities. The Education for All Handicapped Children Act (1975) established procedures for expanded access to schooling, the conduct of that schooling for disabled children (e.g., the Individualized Education Plan), and due process regulations. Federal monies flowed directly to school districts, through state agencies to districts, and through nonstate agencies (e.g., regional research and development centers) specifically established to assist local districts along a range of activities, including curricular improvement (Elmore and McLaughlin 1988; Fullan 1982; Kaestle and Smith 1982; Singer and Butler 1987; Wirt and Kirst 1989).

In addition, other federal legislation, aiming at different targets, contained curricular provisions that influenced existing courses of study or stimulated curriculum development, such as the Juvenile Delinquency and Youth Offenses Act (1961), International Education Act (1966), Ethnic Heritage Act (1972), and Title IX of the 1972 Education Amendments. Finally, federal agencies have sought to improve curriculum, particularly NSF, which has spent hundreds of millions of dollars to develop science, math, and other curricula. While there have been periods of intense federal activity (1960s and early 1970s) and clear efforts to shrink the federal presence (1980s), the United States Office of Education and its successor agencies, the National Institute of Education and the U.S. Department of Education's Office of Educational Research and Improvement, have seldom strayed far from trying to influence curricular content. Even though less than 10 percent of what states and local districts spend on education comes from the federal government, still the pattern of centralizing control of school programs, including the intended curriculum at both the state and federal levels, is apparent (Geel 1979; Kaestle and Smith 1982; Tiedt 1972; Wirt and Kirst 1989).

That centralizing pattern is made even more apparent by decisions rendered by federal and state courts since the early 1960s. If legislation influenced the curriculum, so did litigation. As Geel (1979) notes, "A whole new body of law has sprung up surrounding the school program. There are new doctrines and rules as to what may or may not be taught, how it must or must not be taught, and who has authority to decide curricular matters" (62).

Most of the federal laws cited above have had sections tested in court, and judges have reinterpreted portions of these laws and their agency regulations, thus making new law. Tyack, James, and Benavot (1987, 196) note that the total number of court cases involving education nearly doubled from 1957–1966 to 1967–1976. Cases involving only federal legislation went from 729 in 1957–1966 to 3,486 in the next decade.

While these judicial decisions seldom dealt directly with curriculum, there have been many decisions that indirectly shaped the intended and taught curriculum. In the decade following the *Brown v. Board of Education* decision (1954), for example, court decisions moved many desegregated school districts to modify their procedures for grouping students and adopting texts. A number of studies document the ripple of changes that ebbed and flowed through schools complying with desegregation decisions (Metz 1978; Orfield 1975; Mack 1968). One example of a judicial decision anchored in the earlier Brown mandate will illustrate how a case penetrates the curriculum.

In *Hobson v. Hansen* (1967), federal judge Skelly Wright ruled that the four-track system designed by Superintendent Carl Hansen in Washington, D.C. had been a conscious effort to segregate white from black students and must therefore be dismantled. In Washington and other school districts that were either ordered to or chose to end this form of ability grouping, the impact upon teachers was substantial. "College-bound," "general," "business," and "basic" courses of study, each containing an English class, for example, varied in content covered and methods used. With the four-track system abolished, teachers had to determine what content was appropriate for their mixed-ability classes and what methods would fit the range of student skills and abilities. More stress was placed on different curricular practices in the classroom. New buzz words entered practitioners' vocabularies: flexible grouping, individualized instruction, and prescriptive teaching (Orfield 1975).

Other *Brown*-related developments also influenced the intended and taught curricula. As the momentum of the civil rights movement quickened and attention turned to school practices, what content was taught came under examination. New courses, aimed at blacks, Hispanics, and other ethnic groups appeared in the curriculum, especially in secondary schools. Curriculum guides with new content and revised subject matter in history, English, and other content areas were published. By the 1970s, textbook publishers had produced schoolbooks and pamphlets that moved one critic of history texts to praise what publishers have "achieved in their treatment of black Americans" (Black 1967, 106–126). Frances Fitzgerald (1979) was less generous in her assessment and called the textbook changes an indigestible intellectual porridge.

Influential Groups

Already the cast of actors that shape the intended curriculum crowd the policy-making stage. Federal and state legislators join the judiciary. Other groups external to the formal system of schooling also exert influence: publishers, foundations, academics, and professional associations.

All of these groups mediate between the sharp probes of social change and schools, softening jagged edges, smoothing rough cusps, and selecting what is important that needs doing. Many of these groups lobby social impulses into legislation and translate national hopes into local practice. Many of these groups sell change.

Control over the intended curriculum, then, is splintered among many groups. The complexity of the interrelationships among and between internal and external participants is staggering. Some researchers have mapped the complexity and untidiness that mark curricular policy making in a decentralized system of schooling (Boyd 1979; Kirst and Walker 1971; Mackenzie 1964; Walker 1990). Examining a few of these influential groups will help make clear their role in shaping changes in the intended and taught curricula.

Publishers. Students spend a great deal of time reading and memorizing texts. Teachers spend a great deal of time using texts and other published materials. Pupils, according to Hillel Black, read at least 32,000 textbook pages in their 12 years of public schooling (Black 1967, 3 and 120). The Texas Governor's Commission on Public Education estimated that, in 1969, 75 percent of students' classroom and 90 percent of their homework time was spent using schoolbooks, a finding that was supported a decade later (Komoski 1978; Wirt and Kirst 1972, 212). While these patterns in textbook use apply to most secondary schools, basal readers dominate the choice of content and allocation of time in elementary schools (Barr and Dreeben 1983). What content that gets into books, then, has a captive audience of both teachers and students.

With teachers and students heavily reliant upon the content in instructional materials, there is much evidence that publishers respond to the marketplace of dollars and ideas. Already referred to have been the new science and mathematics texts that have replaced older, outdated ones (Quick 1977). New inquiry-based texts, softbound books, texts with worksheets and audio and videocassettes have penetrated the nation's schools. Shifts in content as a consequence of changing ideas in the larger culture have been documented in reading, language arts, and science (Chall, Conrad, and Harris-Sharples 1977) and social studies (Fitzgerald 1979; Kliebard and Wegner 1987; Voege 1975).

While teachers report using textbooks most of the time in classrooms, there is evidence that how they are used by teachers varies greatly, departing in many instances from what the publishers intended (Squire 1988, 143–145). One researcher observed teachers leading reading groups and spending little time on comprehension even though the teachers' manuals for the readers contained many suggestions and instructions (Durkin 1978, Schwille et al. 1983). Stodolsky (1989) reports a number of studies of math teaching in elementary schools where 80 percent of the instructional time was spent on topics covered in the texts, but teachers varied in their uses of the math texts. Publishers introduce changes into the intended curriculum through new content in texts, although the degree to which teachers use the materials as intended may vary.

Foundations. The Ford, Rockefeller, Carnegie, and Kettering foundations over the last half century have initiated projects, funded commissions to examine emerging issues, and filled gaps left from federal support of curriculum in such areas as the arts and social sciences. Ford's Fund for the Advancement of Education in the 1950s and 1960s spent $50 million, for example, over a decade and a half in team teaching, masters of arts in teaching programs, teacher use of technology, and other innovations. It was followed by a $30 million, decade-long, Comprehensive School Improvement Program that focused upon new staffing patterns, novel curriculum materials, and technology. Little evidence is available on the impact of these efforts on either the intended or taught curricula (Kiger 1972; Wirt and Kirst 1972, 214). The Carnegie Foundation subsidized secondary school studies by James B. Conant in the 1950s. In the 1980s, publically and privately funded commissions (e.g, the Carnegie Corporation and its many councils) at the state and national levels have been especially active in producing reports on teaching as a profession, the middle school, and deteriorating urban schools (Plank 1987).

Professional Associations. Beginning in the late 19th century, professional groups of teachers, superintendents, and university professors gathered together annually to confer on matters of schooling, including the curriculum. Frequently, these organizations established special commissions to study a particular issue and report back to the membership with recommendations. On many occasions, these commissions altered the intended curriculum. The National Educational Association's Committee of Ten (1893) and its later invention, the Committee for the Reorganization of Secondary Education (1918), exerted much influence on school boards and superintendents as they made curricular decisions (Sizer 1964, Kliebard 1986).

During the surge of curriculum change in the 1950s and 1960s, the American Association for Advancement of Science and the American Institute for Biological Sciences fought for the concept of evolution in biology texts. The American Mathematical Society sponsored the new math efforts until federal funds picked up the tab. Similarly, the American Council of Learned Societies helped revise social studies courses (Kiger 1972).

Because local school boards lack money to mount major curricular revisions, develop sophisticated instructional materials, or carry on even modest research, these external groups play a critical role in generating an array of curricular choices from which school boards and administrators can choose different content for teachers to give to students.

Organized teachers' groups such as the National Education Association (NEA) and the American Federation of Teachers (AFT) have focused their attention on salaries, working conditions, and protection of teachers' rights since the 1960s when the strike became a weapon that teachers used to secure collective bargaining. An earlier generation of union activists, such as Margaret Haley in Chicago, bred in the crucible of turn-of-the-century progressivism, pushed for teacher autonomy through Teacher Councils. The aims of the early unions and their successors were to secure basic economic rights for teachers and to protect, even enlarge, classroom autonomy (Hogan 1985; Tyack 1974).

By 1984, teacher unionization had swiftly spread and attained legal status in 33 states which required formal bargaining; 11 states permitted it and only 4 banned the process (Johnson 1988, 603). While some researchers have investigated the effects of unionism and collective bargaining on classroom practice, few have examined the influence of such groups on either the intended or taught curricula.

In a review of research on the effects of collective bargaining, Susan Johnson (1988) cites the few studies that have explored teachers' influence on curricular policy. One national study in 1979 found 31 percent of teacher-school board contracts provided for teacher involvement in curriculum decisions. In New York State, researchers in 1983 found such language in 39 percent of the contracts they examined. Similarly, in Connecticut, 35 percent of the contracts had clauses calling for teacher participation. In most cases, the involvement was advisory (Johnson 1989, 618). Little work has been done to determine the influence of such involvement on the intended curriculum.

Because the union movement has sought both increased teacher influence on curricular policy making and classroom autonomy, researchers will need to investigate the degree to which that influence and independence have occurred as a consequence of collective bargaining, and how that marginal increase has shaped the curriculum for the district and what teachers do in their classrooms.

Influential Individuals

Ask a crowd of historians of education to list the people who have had a pronounced effect upon intended and taught curricula, and my guess is that only a few names would turn up on all the lists. The reason would be found as much in the question as it would with the historians.

Half of the problem is getting historians to agree upon what is meant by curriculum, what would constitute change, and how the influence can be tracked. The other half of the problem would be located in the issue of determining an individual's impact upon events. With an acute awareness among social scientists and historians of organizational, political, bureaucratic, and demographic models, to suggest that change might be partially explained by the impact of individuals seems, at best, quaint. Doubts remain even in the minds of historians who acknowledge the possibility of individual impact upon events. Was the change the direct result of a person's effort? Or did the person happen to be in the right place at the choice moment and thereby influence the course of the change? Or was the person tossed upon the stage by powerful forces coincidentally as the change occurred and simply flowed with events that could hardly be controlled by anyone?

I offer no answer to these questions since I have my share of queries. But I do suggest that some individuals who wrote, spoke, taught, and worked in schools modified both the intended and taught curricula. Perhaps the influence was modest, even slight or indirect. Yet our lack of firm knowledge about individual effects on events and institutions should not be an excuse to dismiss the impact of particular people in reshaping curricula.

To make this point, I offer three people who might have showed up on many of those historians' lists: teacher, writer, and philosopher John Dewey; researcher and university professor Edward Thorndike; and researcher, professor, and writer Ralph Tyler. These men—and there could just as well be other names—affected theory, content, materials, and instruction through their research findings, consulting, speaking out in public life, and teaching. All were professors who exerted much influence on their students who, in turn, often became researchers, professors and administrators. All were prolific writers, producing research studies, textbooks, and essays. They were translators of social change; they mediated between political and social movements and school practices. They believed in education as a science and a basis for conducting educational practice. Because they wrote and taught, however, their direct effects upon each level of curriculum is difficult to disentangle.

Lawrence Cremin, for example, wrestled with assessing John Dewey's impact upon schooling. Dewey's disciples went their different pedagogical ways. As heirs to Dewey, they added, deleted, and shifted their own freight to their mentor's baggage. Every thinker, Cremin reminds us, must suffer from ardent disciples and Dewey was no exception. Is the mentor accountable for the distortions made not by one but by hundreds of followers? Cremin concluded that, until further studies are done of Dewey's work, studies that recognize the changing context in which he operated and sort out the changes he helped give birth to from those he explained and criticized, the precise nature of his influence will evade historians, although the frequent citations of his work and the ready acknowledgment by educators of the importance of his writings offer minor clues to his influence (Cremin 1961, 234–239; Shane 1980).

There seems to be less doubt about the long-term influence of Thorndike and Tyler. Thorndike's work on achievement testing and his prolific studies, including his influence on students who worked closely with him at Teachers College, penetrated all levels of schooling (Clifford 1968). One historian sees Thorndike's influence on research and practice as overwhelming that of Dewey's in the eventual victory of testing, precision in objectives, the passion for efficiency, and quantification of virtually every aspect of formal schooling (Lagemann 1989).

Tyler's influence on curriculum building, especially after 1950, when his book on curriculum and instruction appeared, has been asserted by many writers who connect him to earlier advocates of curriculum building, such as Franklin Bobbitt and W. W. Charters (Schubert 1986). What began as a syllabus for a course that Tyler taught at the University of Chicago went on to become a best seller among educators, be translated into 10 languages, and receive as high acclaim from educators as Dewey's *Democracy and Education* (Shane 1980). A proxy for influence may be the amount of critical attention that the "Tyler Rationale" for curriculum has received (Eisner 1979; Kliebard 1975).

Evidence of curricular change due directly to these men is scattered and impressionistic. The most conservative statement that can be supported is that these men have had an impact upon theory, ideas expressed, and the language of the intended curriculum. They clearly affected ideas as measured in the wealth of writings by them and about what they believed in. It was Dewey who captured the imagination of a generation of teachers, administrators, and reformers with the possibilities of a new teaching role and the redesign of schools for children. But it was Thorndike who resolutely shaped the dominant line of research on the nature and impact of schooling (Lagemann 1989), and Tyler who may have triumphed in shaping the form and mechanics of the intended curricula. What needs to be mapped out in detail are the intellectual threads that can be traced into content, materials, and pedagogy. Avid fly casters who lack rod, tackle, and bait on the bank of a stream abundant with trout do not say that fishing is unimportant. They seek different ways of fishing. So, too, should historians and social scientists search for diverse ways of assessing an individual's impact upon different levels of curricula.

Internal Factors

All of these factors have been ones outside the usual boundaries of districts and schools. Within these organizations, there are groups and individuals who influence curricular change.

Groups and Individuals Within the School System. Students, teachers, principals, curriculum specialists, and superintendents initiate curricular changes by choosing among the alternatives or generating their own. Because much has already been written about the formal role that the school board, superintendent, and principals play in shaping the intended curriculum, let me focus briefly upon three groups (students, teachers, and parents) that seldom receive attention in influencing the intended and taught curricula.

While there is evidence of students starting new programs (Birmingham 1970; Counts 1926; Gutowski 1988), their influence on the taught curriculum is largely confined to how they participate in the activities of a lesson and alter what happens (Doyle 1983; Mehan 1979), modifying what they study and negotiating academic demands with teachers (Cusick 1983; Powell et al. 1985; Sedlak et al. 1986; Tyler 1961). Some researchers, operating out of different theoretical perspectives and keenly aware of the teacher's role, see students as actors in reshaping and influencing what occurs in the classroom beyond the usual bargaining over content and procedures (Jones 1989; Willis 1977; Woods 1979). How socioeconomic status precisely influences the covert bargaining that occurs is largely unexplored, although the links between students' social class and content covered have been investigated (Anderson 1982; Bernstein 1977; Goodlad 1984; Oakes 1985; Rist 1970; Willis 1977).

The literature on teachers initiating curricular changes in their classroom includes personal accounts, newspaper and magazine articles, and books (Cuban 1984a; Kohl 1967; Macrorie 1984; Wigginton 1985). When the door closes, that private world within a public school is an arena for change worked through by teachers, who are often alone and without help. They revise the intended curriculum and produce the taught one (Schwille et al. 1983).

One group, unmentioned so far, that can change the intended and taught curricula by itself is aroused, angry parents. No superintendent or school board can safely ignore the sporadic flash flood of hot anger that sweeps over a school system when community values are ignored. Sex education, subversive content taught in a government class, the concept of evolution, and library books viewed as obscene are instances when parental groups charge into school board meetings and demand changes in what is taught.

Less aroused but just as insistent groups of parents, concerned about their native language being ignored in the schools, have worked slowly and steadily through political and bureaucratic channels to achieve instruction in German and other languages during the last quarter of the 19th century (Peterson 1985; Troen 1975; Tyack 1974). Parent-teacher associations and lay groups have campaigned quietly but persistently for curricular changes and gotten them over time. Other ad hoc parent groups, unhappy with the conventional program, have prodded school authorities to establish an alternative school or a new school-within-a-school. The Progressive Education Association's Commission on the Relation of School and College, for example, helped get the remarkable Eight Year Study underway in 1933 (Cremin 1961).

These influential groups are some of the top sergeants of curricular change. They mediate between national social movements, demographic shifts, and cultural changes and the local school system by selecting, promoting, and installing changes. These groups, in ever-changing, shifting coalitions, acting as filters, help determine changes in the intended and taught curricula.

Summary

These, then, are the primary forces that determined change with far more frequency and salience in the intended curriculum than in the taught curriculum over the last century. Social, political, economic, and other changes exerted the most influence, while the rest of the determinants acted as second- and third-level mediators—softening, selecting, modifying, and promoting different, less-potent versions of the larger changes jolting the society. Schools are vulnerable to each wave of social change because state and federal legislators, judges, special interest groups, professional educators, and a host of other groups and individuals fashioned a fit between the external pressures for change and the existing contours of a system of schooling.

Schools are institutions readily vulnerable to their surroundings. But they are not helpless. They reshape what an unpredictable environment tosses up. Through negotiation and bargaining between these various groups outside and inside the system of schooling, schools accommodated, reacted, sometimes responded in predictable, occasionally imaginative, ways, and in some instances, initiated programs and directions unprodded by external pressures.

Gender practices in schools, for example, both reflected and diverged from what occurred outside schools. Separate classes for boys and girls taking physical education, vocational curricula, and segregated sports were clear instances of schools mirroring the dominant norms of the larger society. Yet, as Elisabeth Hansot and David Tyack point out, schools also made no gender distinctions in admitting students, promoting them from grade to grade, instructional practices or school awards. Gender was less important in such matters. In other words, there were a variety of gender and gender-free policies and quiet practices in schools that demonstrate the school's embeddedness in the culture and its institutional independence (Hansot and Tyack 1988).

But the traces of such gender policies, particularly the less visible ones, cannot be easily recovered. It is the intended curriculum over time that most reveals the imprint of these erratic social impulses being transformed into curricular changes. State frameworks, courses of study, and syllabi to guide teachers leave signs of shifts in social attitudes, negotiated changes, and professional initiatives. Far less obvious are modifications in what teachers taught.

As the limited evidence and research suggest, schools are incapable of wholly turning aside such potent forces. Because schools are embedded within, and dependent upon, the culture, as the waves of social change sweep across the schools, each wave leaves a curricular residue. Just as marine biologists can tell from the rocks, tidal pools, and shore exactly what plants and animals inhabit each layer of the intertidal landscape by the life clinging to the rocks and shores as the tides ebb and flow, an alert eye can identify the residue in courses of study and instructional materials from earlier reform movements, population shifts, and political sea changes.

As noted earlier I have used a political pluralist framework to explain the changes in the intended curriculum. But this framework is limited in three ways: It does not explain fully why districts and schools are continually so vulnerable to externally driven pressures for change; nor does a pluralist perspective explain why the content and activities teachers use in their classrooms appear less vulnerable to those same externally driven pressures for change. There appears to be far more continuity in what teachers have done in their classrooms than in the intended curriculum. Finally, this perspective does not account for the voluntary initiatives launched by teachers and administrators to alter both the intended and taught curricula.

The strengths of this viewpoint in explaining mandated and negotiated changes are offset by its inability to explain an apparent stability in what teachers do in their classrooms and the voluntary changes that school professionals occasionally initiate. I need to make clear what I mean by stability.

Even though incremental changes do occur and variation in curricula exists, continuity in fundamental curricular beliefs, theories, organization, and delivery of content largely persists. For example, in one study, I found that a series of instructional approaches that I had labeled teacher-centered endured during and after major reform efforts to convert teaching into a more student-centered enterprise. Yet I also noted that a substantial minority of elementary teachers adopted specific student-centered methods and created hybrid versions of instruction in their classes. Moreover, there was variation among teachers who used the dominant mode of instruction. Finally, I pointed out that small numbers of teachers departed from the norm dramatically and instituted fundamental changes within their classrooms. All of these occurred, however, within a general framework of stability in the dominant beliefs, theories, organization, and delivery of content (Cuban 1984a).

Stability in the taught curriculum, then, encompasses both variation and incremental changes. There are limits to a political perspective in explaining continuity in the what and how of classroom teaching. Let me set aside for the moment these limitations. I will return to them after exploring the determinants of curricular stability and examine other perspectives to help explain issues that a political pluralist way of seeing could not.

DETERMINANTS OF STABILITY IN THE INTENDED AND TAUGHT CURRICULA

If many researchers have explored the factors that produced curricular changes, few have investigated regularities in these curricula (Counts 1926; Cuban 1984a; Englund 1986; McKinney and Westbury 1975; Reid 1978; Sarason

1982; Wayland 1964). As before, in examining those factors that have been identified, I will divide them into two categories: external and internal. The same caveats I raised above concerning the complexity of interactions among these determinants apply here.

Insofar as the perspectives that I will use, a political framework will also be applied here, in part, to explain curricular constancy. Harnessed to the political framework, however, will be an organizational perspective, that is, a view that sees schools and classrooms as organizations. If the political perspective looks outward for explanations of what occurs, an organizational perspective looks inward. Both are needed to understand stability in curricula.

External Factors

Anyone familiar with American schools and the tradition of local control is often amazed at the similarities in curriculum across a nation with about 15,000 school districts. The primary determinant for that similarity and also for curricular stability are the goals and functions of schooling.

Goals and the Functions of Schooling. What the public expects of its schools is frequently stated explicitly. As a consequence of attending school, the public expects students to:

- master basic skills;
- think rationally and independently;
- accumulate general knowledge in various subjects;
- possess sufficient skills to get a job;
- participate in the civic culture of the community;
- know what values are prized in the community and be able to live them.

Such formal goals come from state and district statements (Goodlad 1984). There are other goals that are implicit, that lie in the shadows but nonetheless weigh heavily in public expectations. Schools should:

- house students safely five to eight hours a day;
- shield the adult labor market from competition;
- sort students to fit different socioeconomic niches;
- equip students from low-income families with the means for moving into higher social classes;
- solve persistent national problems.

The public expects schools to change children into competent, economically useful citizens, while also performing other valuable social, political, symbolic, and economic duties in society. These multiple and conflicting goals are wired into the structures and processes of public schooling and account for the explicit and implicit socialization that occurs. If goals are intentions, functions are what happen in schools. While writers differ significantly in explaining why these functions have arisen and persist, they generally agree that the school, especially in the hidden curriculum, is a powerful agent in turning children into citizens (Bernstein 1977; Bidwell 1965; Dreeben 1968; Lynd and Lynd 1924; Waller 1965).

Teachers and administrators have absorbed the intentions and socializing functions into their ideologies and behaviors. Observations of schools and classrooms, especially elementary ones, yield many instances of teachers and administrators inculcating and consciously reinforcing punctuality, proper work habits, patriotism, and other adult expectations (Apple 1977; Finkelstein 1989; Jackson 1968; Lortie 1975).

How do these goals and functions help determine stability in the intended and taught curricula? Curricular innovations, particularly those that challenge the socializing functions, may get token attention from practitioners but, over time, seldom alter fundamentally what is offered. Dropping U.S. history or vocational education courses from the curriculum or stopping teachers from instructing little boys and girls on the values of honesty, cleanliness, and neatness seldom go far in a community. Because such functions are so much a part of who teachers are, what they do, and the organization of the intended curriculum, they account for much of the persistent continuity in content over the last century.

Providing concrete support for this stability are two studies completed at different times (1926 and 1940) during the ascendancy of the progressive movement. As part of a systematic effort to ascertain how much of the progressive ideals had penetrated mainstream practice, the National Society for the Study of Education commissioned a committee of its membership, chaired by Harold Rugg of Teachers College, Columbia University to investigate the current state of curriculum in the nation. Members of the committee were a virtual Who's Who of progressivism's various streams (child-centered, scientific, etc.). National surveys of curricular changes at elementary and secondary schools in towns and cities across the nation were completed. These local reports from superintendents and principals came in from hundreds of districts (132 for public elementary schools and 184 for public secondary schools out of 900 total sent out). The picture presented by these self-reports is varied and, depending upon one's biases, reveals an uneven penetration of progressive ideas upon the intended curriculum. In the summary chapter, Harold Rugg and George Counts (who completed the high school study) asked the central question at the heart of child-centered progressives' reform efforts: What influence has the new emphasis on pupil activities had on public school curricula?

> To this question no single answer can be given. In the high school, the movement has left no mark; in the elementary school, its influence may be traced here and there. Within the school subjects there is a marked tendency to make learning active rather than passive. . . . There is an increasing use of excursions, field trips, observation of the physical world, map and graph making, individual pupil research. . . . But practically all of this utilization of child activity is

> *within* [original emphasis] the confines of the established school subjects. . . . The chief outlines of the curriculum are still traced in terms of reading, arithmetic, language, nature study, history, geography, current events, etc . . . (Rugg 1926, 432–433)

A decade and a half later, an unusual survey of courses of study was undertaken by the Curriculum Laboratory of Teachers College. By 1940, the Laboratory had collected 28,500 courses of study, submitted by 7,000 districts, dealing with 17 subject matter areas from all grade levels. Researchers analyzed the curricular guides for science, social studies, and industrial arts in grades 4 through 12 produced between 1930–1940, years of intense district activity in revising curriculum. They looked for the frequency particular topics were offered in various subjects at different grades. The researchers, located at the citadel of progressive ideology, expressed fervor for curriculum improvement and found some evidence of what they sought in the novel ways that courses had been organized and new content introduced. Their disappointment, however, was also obvious:

> There is a persistent attempt in the majority of courses to utilize traditional subject matter to satisfy new needs. Part of the new content that had been introduced is in many instances not significant. It is as academic as is the remainder of the course. For example, . . . A unit on forms of government lists dictatorships without reference to the present world crisis. . . .
>
> There are glaring shortages in content in certain fields. . . . For example, in social studies there is little or no mention of advertising and its widespread influence, art, child labor, housing, insurance, installment buying, consumer education, social security, dictatorships, and many other vital problems today. . . . (Bruner, Evans, Hutchcroft, Wieting, and Wood 1941, 209)

Herbert Bruner, the academic who headed this study, became superintendent of the Minneapolis public schools in the late 1940s where he endorsed and expanded the progressive innovation of the Common Learnings Program begun in 1945. This required two-hour class in the junior and senior high schools that replaced the English and social studies courses came under intense criticism from small groups of parents deeply concerned about the perceived loss of academic rigor in the innovation. By 1950, the board of education, reeling under continuing criticism and rejecting the superintendent's recommendation, made the Common Learnings Program optional. Bruner resigned and returned to a university. Barry Franklin (1986) noted that this progressive innovation had never really taken hold within the schools in its short life and that the content usually taught in English and social studies—contrary to the parental criticism—persisted.

To put it another way, with all the apparent changes, many of which were intended to be fundamental in altering not only what subject matter teachers taught but how they taught it over all these decades in U.S. history, students still studied the Puritans.

Beyond the influence of formal goals and socializing functions, there are other external forces, such as state and federal policies, that reinforce curricular stability.

State and Federal Policies. State and federal policies initiated changes in curricula, as described in an earlier section of this chapter. Once in place, however, such changes took root and became difficult to budge. A clear instance of government policies strengthening existing structures by making incremental changes in the intended curriculum occurred in the 1980s. State and federal pressures for improved schooling, as measured by gains in standardized test scores, prodded districts toward more uniformity. Most of these incremental changes strengthened existing curricular and instructional practices. For example, Florida mandated a weekly written assignment; Mississippi expanded its testing program to include grades 4, 6, 8, and 11 (Timar and Kirp 1988). What was intended to be taught was increasingly prescribed by the state in mandated curricula, the content of required minimum competency exams and state-devised basic skills tests. Here, then, increasing state and federal centralization over schooling intensified curricular stability (Corbett and Wilson 1988; Darling-Hammond and Wise 1985; Geel 1979; Goodlad 1984; McNeil 1986; Plank 1987; Resnick and Resnick 1985; Wise 1979).

Beyond official state and federal policies there are unofficial regional and national nongovernment agencies that have exerted much informal pressure to alter curriculum; they have also enhanced its continuity.

Accrediting and Testing Agencies. Accreditation is viewed as an educational life or death issue. For example, high school graduates from an unaccredited school find college admission officers most reluctant even to consider them. Formal curriculum requirements of the Southern Association of Schools and Colleges (founded in 1895) and the North Central Association (1895), for instance, set local standards that are pursued religiously. Over half of all the high schools in the nation use authorized manuals produced by regional associations to evaluate their schools. Often a year of self-study is followed by a visiting team of educators to assess the school in relation to the criteria laid out in the evaluation manuals. While these agencies seldom levy sanctions, the threat of withdrawing accreditation is ever present, reinforcing their minimum requirements. Getting accredited certifies educational respectability (Jurkowitz 1981; Meyer and Rowan 1978; Wirt and Kirst 1972).

Fundamental curricular changes become most difficult to install in the face of these requirements. Drastic changes do occur in unaccredited schools anxious to secure certification. In those schools, changes are made to meet the regional accreditation association's requirements. Once a school is pronounced satisfactory, the boundaries for permissible change narrow. The implicit curricular model in these association manuals is subject-centered, weighs required and elective courses differentially to determine value, and requires a certain number of courses in specified areas to attain graduation. If anything, according to Carolyn Jurkowitz, "accreditation has operated as a mechanism of curriculum control" (Jurkowitz 1981, 111).

College admission standards also shape the intended curriculum, especially in the high school. Prior to the establishment of regional accrediting associations, colleges used a certificate system. Begun in 1871, college inspectors visited high schools and assessed the number and content of courses, what teachers did in their classrooms, the length of the periods, and the like. This attempt to standardize secondary school offerings lasted until the early decades of this century, when the accrediting associations took over the task. The Committee of Ten's report in 1893 sought also to secure a greater degree of uniformity in high school curricular offerings. In the surge of state reforms aimed at raising academic standards in the 1980s, a corresponding movement among colleges and universities to raise their admission requirements occurred, causing high schools to modify their offerings. Once changed, however, the feeder relationship between a high-status segment of the high school population and college admission requirements over the last century has had a stabilizing influence on the courses and subject matter taught in high schools (Counts 1926; Jurkowitz 1981).

National tests devised by the College Entrance Examination Board, the National Merit Scholarship system, and standardized ability and achievement tests are common. Many of these tests, such as the College Board's Scholastic Aptitude Test, were designed to assess individual performance and be divorced from mainstream curricula offered in secondary schools. Such tests, supposedly curriculum-free, act as crude monitoring instruments of overall student performance (Chapman 1980; Resnick and Resnick 1985; Wayland 1964).

Many other tests, however, are curriculum-based and seek to hold educators accountable for what is taught. Such tests serve to maintain what is being taught. Beginning in the late 19th century, state- or district-designed achievement tests aimed at finding out exactly how much of the curriculum had been learned by students (e.g., New York State Regents Examinations). Not until the expansion of testing in the 1960s for minimum competency and college credit (e.g., Advanced Placement) did testing for district and school accountability emerge as a clear trend, one that has carried through to the 1990s. Many states and districts have installed competency-based curricula married to examinations that determine how many of the skills and how much of the knowledge have been learned by students (Corbett and Wilson 1988; Haney 1984; Resnick and Resnick 1985).

Most of these curriculum-based tests and standard-setting groups have given a solid durability to particular courses of study, content, and instruction. Both accrediting associations and national tests have helped smooth out regional differences and brought more uniformity and stability to a quasi-national curriculum.

Over the last half century, this trend toward uniformity has seldom been challenged. The Eight Year Study, involving 30 secondary schools across the country from 1934 to 1941, secured a novel moratorium on college admission requirements for their graduates and on the taking of national tests in order to stimulate curricular changes (Thirty Schools 1942). Few recall this curricular experiment and unusual challenge to standardization.

A generation later, another challenge to curricular uniformity came with interdisciplinary efforts to introduce new subjects in the U.S. and abroad (Silberman 1971). Ivor Goodson studied the attempt to introduce environmental studies (involving the subjects of geography, biology, and rural studies) in one part of England. He found that the new subject lacked the required high-status knowledge derived from an academic discipline. Moreover, it had to be wired to a high-stakes test such as the "A" exam. Protracted political negotiations and bargaining among subject area specialists, university professors, and school officials delayed and eventually led to the slow demise of the new subject (Goodson 1983).

Textbooks. Enhancing the stabilizing function of accreditation and testing are textbooks. In the late 19th century, McGuffey Readers were a common school experience. Currently, with a national publishing industry, most school systems retain texts three to five or more years. With revisions, a popular text can last for more than a decade. In elementary schools, basal readers and series span the grades and give an internal continuity to reading, language arts, science, social studies, and math programs.

The content and organization of these books promote stability. Ruth Elson's (1964) study of schoolbooks in the 19th century is titled: *Guardians of Tradition*. The value judgments conveyed in these books, she concludes, are straightforward: "love of country, love of God, duty to parents, the necessity to develop habits of thrift, honesty, and hard work in order to accumulate property, the certainty of progress, the perfection of the United States." Unlike late-20th-century texts, these schoolbooks "made no pretense of neutrality" (338).

Judith Soltis studied American grammar texts used in schools between 1890 and 1984 and found both stability and change. What persisted in these popular grammar texts is the content (parts of speech, sentence construction, etc.), the methods of presentation (teachers offer models of proper form and students do the drills), and the consistency in presenting exemplars of what "good living" meant at the time the book was published (a sentence in a 1909 text: "George deserves the prize because he worked hard"). What changed were the exemplars of the "good life" used in sentences and essays in the late 19th century, the 1930s, post–World War II, and the present (Soltis 1987).

State-driven mandates in the 1980s aimed at raising academic standards and student performance brought accreditation, testing, and texts together into a holy alliance for reform. Formal curricular goals in a subject area were linked to what subject matter was expected to be taught at each grade level; the accompanying textbooks and instructional materials were analyzed to make sure that they matched the content teachers were expected to teach; all of the foregoing occurred to ensure that what was being taught was faithfully mirrored in standardized achievement tests administered by the state, district, or both. This tight coupling of a district's, and in some cases a state's, curricular and instructional systems to mandated tests occurred with increasing frequency throughout the 1980s, particularly in areas marked by undesirable academic performance as measured by standardized achievement tests (Cuban 1984b; Corbett and Wilson 1988; Madaus 1988). Again, what appears as curriculum reform actually reinforces the existing subject matter, the texts that convey that content, and the tests that assess how much has been absorbed by students.

Internal Factors

These external factors that work toward maintaining the intended and taught curricula interact with factors internal to the system of schooling, such as students, teachers, principals, the weight of the past in the historical curriculum, and the structures of classrooms and schools.

Students. Studies on students' thinking and actions within a classroom setting are few, indeed. Already mentioned are the classroom negotiations between teachers and students over content and academic demands. Such bargaining influences pedagogy, changing it in some instances, but largely reinforcing the existing repertoire that the teacher uses in other cases. Few researchers since Willard Waller (1965) have explored the conservative expectations that students bring to classrooms about how teachers should teach, what constitutes learning, and what content is appropriate for teachers to use. Such student beliefs may constrain teacher efforts to experiment with subject matter and pedagogy.

Some researchers, however, approach students and teachers as being engaged in reproducing within the classroom the social relationships that exist in the larger society. These researchers view teachers as unwitting agents of the larger culture. Students are seen as passive spectators unknowingly acquiring the values, attitudes, and skills that will ease their passage into social niches similar to their parents' (Anyon 1980, Carnoy and Levin 1985). These few studies reveal only the bare outline of an argument that students' views, however derived, and actions (or lack thereof) accept or, on occasion, mildly challenge the existing curriculum and pedagogy.

Teachers. More researchers, however, have investigated how teachers play a part in maintaining existing subject matter, classroom activities, and materials. In 1926, George Counts commented on the difficulties of altering the high school curriculum. "A great conservative force which must be overcome in achieving any radical change in the program of studies" is the "habits, attitudes, and dispositions of the members of the teaching staff." Trained by study and experience in a particular subject, "a teacher naturally objects to the abolition of procedures of which he is master" (Counts 1926, 129).

Numerous studies since Counts investigated high school curricula have documented a durable continuity in "habits, attitudes, and dispositions" among teachers. Both Lortie (1975) and Goodlad (1984) reached similar conclusions a half century later.

Other evidence accumulates. Researchers James Hoetker and William Ahlbrand (1969) summarized all the studies they could locate that documented how teachers have relied upon the question-answer format, often called the recitation, for over a century. J. T. Dillon (1988) found few changes two decades later. Judith Langer (1984) summarized the research on reading and writing instruction. She concluded that teachers, even those who were committed to students playing an active role in their learning and those who sought new ways of teaching writing, continued to use a "transmission" view of instruction. In English, Arthur Applebee reported the findings of studies done in 1932, 1936, and 1963–1965 about how English teachers taught their subject. In these studies, the researchers observed classrooms and found them "teacher-dominated." In 1,600 classes visited in the 1960s, recitation and lecture far outstripped discussion (used only 23 percent of the time). There was little evidence of teachers using group work or audiovisual aids (Applebee 1974, 211). In math, science, and social studies, the refrain is the same: "frontal" teaching, traditional instruction, teacher-centered instruction, conventional teaching—the value-charged code words differ, but the habits of teachers persist (Applebee, Langer, and Mullis 1987; Cuban 1990; Goodlad 1984; Stake and Easley 1978; Suydam 1977; White 1985).

From the attempt to introduce innovative science curricula in two Scottish schools (Hamilton 1975) and a school district in the U.S. (McKinney and Westbury 1975) to university consultants establishing a system of curricular accountability in a small Oregon district (Wolcott 1977) to the persistent reluctance of most U.S. teachers to adopt machine technologies (Cuban 1986), the evidence of teachers sticking to familiar tools, content, and activities mounts.

Some writers locate this conserving impulse within the occupational culture of teaching. This conservatism, they argue, is rooted in the people who are recruited into the profession, how they are informally socialized, and the school culture of which teaching itself is a primary ingredient. Serving an apprenticeship through observing teachers for over a decade and a half as students, those who enter the occupation absorbed lessons of how to teach as they watched their teachers. The ordeal of first-year teachers trying to survive drives many to use practices that were used by former teachers; they readily accept counsel from seasoned veterans. The folklore, norms, and beliefs about children, knowledge, and the nature of learning are reinforced by the daily grind; all strengthen the impulse to maintain stability rather than nourish skepticism or promote change (Grant and Sleeter 1985; Jackson 1968; Hargreaves 1980; Hargreaves 1984; Lortie 1975; Waller 1965).

Other writers locate the impulse to maintain teacher-centered instruction in teachers mirroring deep-seated historic and cultural beliefs about the nature of knowledge, teaching, and learning. These cultural beliefs, almost a folk wisdom shared by all, stretch back to antiquity and guide popular thinking about how school should be and what is proper for teachers to do in their classrooms. The ideas of Pestalozzi, Froebel, Dewey and neoprogressives concerning the role of the child in constructing and expressing knowledge and what such a concept means insofar as revising instruction are relatively new, that is, a few hundred years old, and have yet to seep into the cultural mainstream as accepted views appropriate for schooling. For teachers to embrace these "new" notions and teach contrary to accepted beliefs would be to invite criticism and even endanger the legitimacy of their work and that of the school (Cohen 1987, 1988, 1989).

Finally, some writers seek explanations in the school and classroom structures within which teachers work to explain the continuity of instruction across subject matter offerings and levels of schooling. I deal with this in a separate section below.

Principals. Principals are both bosses and bureaucrats. They are caught in the middle between a district office that requires policies to be implemented in schools and teachers upon whom they are utterly dependent. Moreover, the principal is expected to buffer teachers from intrusions by external constituencies (including the principal's bosses) while satisfying the demands of groups outside the school, such as parents and neighbors. The multiple and conflicting roles they play, their aversion to increasing conflict and drawing untoward attention to themselves, and the structures they inhabit combine to keep most principals focused on managing, that is, maintaining the existing arrangements—including the curriculum (Cuban 1988; Sarason 1982; Wolcott 1973). Those classroom and school structures within which the principals labor also maintain stability for teachers, students, and themselves.

School and Classroom Structures. By structures, I mean the way physical space is arranged in the school, how content and students are organized into grade levels, how time is allotted to tasks, and how school rules govern adult and student behavior. Less tangible are the beliefs and expectations shared by students, teachers, principals, and parents about what makes a school a school and how adults and children should act in such settings. These structures help shape the behavior of all inhabitants.

The classroom organization, nested within the school structures, is a crowded setting in which the teacher must manage 25 to 40 or more students of approximately the same age who involuntarily spend—depending upon their age—anywhere from 1 to 5 hours daily in the same space. The teacher is expected to maintain control, teach a prescribed content, capture student interest, vary levels of instruction according to student differences, and show tangible evidence that students have performed satisfactorily. Given these school and classroom structures and demands, teachers cope (Dreeben 1973; Jackson 1968; Meyer and Rowan 1978; Sarason 1982; Smith and Geoffrey 1968).

Coping means that teachers, even when they hold views about teaching and content inconsistent with what they do in the classroom, construct a pedagogy that will permit them to survive and extract satisfaction from an array of expectations impossible to fulfill within existing structures. Teaching the entire class at one time is an efficient and convenient use of a teacher's time to cover the mandated content and to maintain control. Lecturing, question-answer drills, seatwork, and homework drawn from texts are direct, uncomplicated ways of transmitting knowledge to a group. Given the limits placed upon teachers by the daily school schedule and the requirements that a course of study be completed by June, these instructional practices, sometimes inconsistent with beliefs buried in a student-centered tradition of teaching, permit the teacher in a timely, efficient manner to determine whether students have learned the material. Writers on both sides of the Atlantic Ocean have offered this view as explaining how teachers negotiate practical compromises to dilemmas wrought by these structures and display reluctance to alter substantially what they teach and how they teach it (Cuban 1984a; Cusick 1983; Denscombe 1982; McNeil 1986; Sosniak, Ethington and Varelas in press; Westbury 1973).

The Historical Curriculum. In addition to the school and classroom structures that have been in place for a century and a half since the introduction of the graded school is the long shadow of the historical curriculum: the deposits in the curriculum left by previous reform efforts. This residue rests unexamined in unrevised curriculum guides and policies. It is the content that survives every effort to remove it from the curriculum. It is the models of curriculum making and the beliefs about knowledge and teaching that were introduced decades, even centuries, earlier that continue as the ways of thinking and making curriculum (Englund 1986). In Gary (Indiana), Minneapolis (Minnesota), and Sweden scholars have shown how reformers changed course titles, adopted new courses of study, and produced scads of documents, but the previous models of thinking about subject matter and the content itself during and after these changes have endured (Englund 1986; Franklin 1986; McKinney and Westbury 1975).

Lawrence Cremin (1971) acknowledged the potency of the historical curriculum in maintaining stability when he examined how curriculum was made in the United States over the last century. Cremin had initially concluded that a radical change in curriculum and pedagogy had occurred between the 1893 report of the Committee of Ten and the 1918 report of the Commission on the Reorganization of Secondary Education. Both reports seemingly took opposite positions on the nature of subject matter and how important it was to weave together what happens outside the school with the school curriculum.

On reflection, however, he saw a basic continuity in the intended curriculum in the quarter century between the earlier decades and even with the curricular reform of the 1960s under the aegis of academic specialists. In referring to Jerrold Zacharias's work with high school physics, Cremin pointed out that the curriculum reformers of the 1950s and 1960s did expand the options within several subject fields and cracked the grip of nonacademics on curricular change. Nonetheless, he stresses that curricular reformers over the decades have "ended up accepting the paradigm of curriculum-making that had prevailed for three-quarters of a century" (Cremin 1971, 216).

Summary

These are the primary factors that determined stability in the intended and taught curricula over the last century. The regularities in both curricula are too obvious to be dismissed or ignored. The goals and functions of schooling, working in concert with school and classroom structures, are potent influences in maintaining curricular continuity. State and federal policies, accrediting and testing agencies, and textbooks enact the formal and informal goals desired by the various publics and the deeply held beliefs about what role schools should play in this society. In addition, internal actors strengthen the durability of the different curricula. Students, teachers, and principals, for very different reasons, buttress the existing curricula, keeping it more like it was than what it ought to be. All of these factors are anchored in an historical curriculum whose strong residual influence is shadowy but nonetheless felt. In this section of the chapter, the constancy in the intended curricula—even noting the many incremental changes and the inevitable variation among districts—has been highlighted. Even more pronounced, however, has been the durability in the taught curricula.

PERSPECTIVES ON CURRICULAR CHANGE AND STABILITY

In discussing the determinants of change earlier in the chapter, I pointed out that a political view acknowledged the embeddedness of schools in the culture and their dependence upon external constituencies for financial and moral support. Furthermore, I pointed out limits to the usefulness of this way of seeing in explaining certain patterns in the intended and taught curricula.

Pluralist Political Perspective

I find this pluralist framework useful in understanding important aspects of curricular change. In a tax-supported, lay-governed policy system of dispersed authorities, the impetus for most incremental and occasional fundamental curricular changes comes from outside the schools. Once the changes are incorporated into routine operations, external groups (e.g., federal and state policies, testing and accrediting agencies, etc.) also help to sustain the regularities that mark the intended curricula over time. New goals and functions are derived from political coalitions, bargaining between stakeholders, and social movements. Various government agencies and groups within the private sector interpret and enact the functions. Groups inside the school system also operate within a political arena. Tensions between students and adults in schools—between teachers and administrators, for example—are acted out and negotiated politically. The results of this political activity combine to maintain, rather than to alter in any fundamental way, what curriculum is intended or taught.

Yet while I find this conceptual framework useful, as I stated earlier, it is limited. If it explains why the intended curriculum in districts and schools is so vulnerable to externally driven pressures for change, mostly incremental, it fails to explain why the taught curriculum is seemingly so invulnerable to fundamental changes. Nor does it explain why groups and individual teachers, administrators, and district policymakers will voluntarily undertake changes without prodding from outside agencies or interest groups. These questions go beyond a pluralist perspective; they require another way of seeing.

Other Perspectives

Clearly, there are other perspectives. Some neo-Marxist scholars argue that the dominant capitalist classes, using the mantle of reform movements, reshaped schools during the mid-19th and 20th centuries as a way of controlling working class militancy and other threatening elements in the population (Anderson 1975; Bowles and Gintis 1976; Katz 1968; Spring 1972). Related but distinct from this view is one that sees schooling as a political dialectic between social classes. Not passive victims of the capitalists, the working classes struggled with both the middle and upper classes and, through the struggle, the nature of public schooling evolved over the last century and a half (Anderson 1982; Carnoy and Levin 1985; Hogan 1985; Katznelson and Weir 1985; Wrigley 1982). Another view anchored in a neo-Marxist framework, but more closely linked to notions of agency, argues that teachers and students can shape what happens in schools even though the dominant forms of cultural knowledge embedded in schools mirror elite norms and reproduce inequality (Apple 1982; Giroux 1981).

Those researchers who acknowledge the agency of groups and individuals within schools, yet adhere to the view that schools distribute cultural knowledge unequally and thereby reproduce the social inequality, still have to explain the puzzles of stability and change in both the intended and taught curricula suggested in this chapter. There have been many incremental changes in the intended curriculum not touching the fundamental beliefs, models, and content embedded in it; yet there have been fewer incremental changes within the taught curricula over the last century and an enduring stability in basic beliefs and practices. Moreover, there have been instances of novel approaches to both curricula in both public and private school communities, dominated by religious and ethnic groups such as Native Americans, rural blacks, the Nation of Islam and Hispanics. Such distinctions in curricula are infrequently made and the variety of curricular responses to external forces has been unexamined.

Finally, it is possible to argue that class interests or the struggles between classes in this nation have been exaggerated. Rubinson (1986) argues that political structures of this society—mass voting and legislative government—transformed what might have been class interests into state and federal policies, thereby weakening the formation of labor and capital as distinct classes. Other societies have political structures that more directly translate class interests than the United States. "Schooling," he concludes about the U.S., "has reflected the absence of class forces rather than their presence" (Rubinson 1986, 543). For these reasons, I find the various views within the neo-Marxist framework unsatisfying in responding to questions unanswered by a political point of view.

Equally unsatisfying is the perspective that the dissonance between intended and taught curricula is simply a lapse in rational behavior. If organizations had clear goals, crisp formal structures to achieve those goals, hierarchial roles distinctly defined to prevent duplication of responsibilities or errors in delegation of authority, and a technology tightly linked to the goals, structures, and roles, then districts and schools would be productive and satisfying places to work. The turbulent and unpredictable environment would seldom intrude. Such rational, bureaucratic organizations would make sensible curriculum choices, and the results would testify to the organization's efficiency and effectiveness. The task, according to this perspective, is to make the organization more rational and less vulnerable to its surroundings.

As applied to schooling, such technocratic views lean heavily upon policymakers committed to systems analysis as a technique of decision making and upon an academic community committed to research and development to produce scientifically respectable findings useful for improving organizational productivity. In the early decades of this century, a technical approach to curriculum making emerged in the work of Franklin Bobbitt, Charles Judd, W. W. Charters, David Snedden and others who saw a rational, systematic way of setting out objectives and designing curricular frameworks. That tradition was renewed with the publication and popular success of Ralph Tyler's *Principles of Curriculum and Instruction* (1950). Scientific construction of curriculum produced an intended curricula, but its penetration into the taught curriculum was suspect even then (Kliebard 1975, 1986; Rugg and Counts 1926). Myron Atkin and Ernest House (1981) point to the reassertion of the technical approach in both research and development under the largesse of the federal government during the 1960s. A large body of literature has shown that this rational perspective has definite limitations in explaining the behavior of most public and private organizations (March and Olsen 1976; Pfeffer 1982; Scott 1981; Smith 1973).

More recently, researchers, policymakers, and practitioners deeply interested in improving schools for large numbers of low-income, ethnic minorities have embraced certain portions of the effective schools movement that has at its core the notion of a rational, trim, and tightly coupled organization. These technocratic views have led to aligning instructional goals to the intended curriculum, textbooks, and tests. The outcomes of this alignment would be teachers teaching a curriculum wired to organizational goals. Such views of a rational, efficiently managed bureaucracy were ascendant during the first 2 decades of this century and have reappeared since the late-1970s with the effective schools movement and the state-driven school reforms of the 1980s (Callahan 1962; Cuban 1984b; Purkey and Smith 1983; Timar and Kirp 1988; Tyack and Hansot 1982).

The research cited thus far suggests strongly that a system of decentralized schooling within a democratic society is highly vulnerable to its environment and must come to terms with it in a series of accommodations and compromises. Schools have multiple and conflicting goals. Often these goals are vaguely stated and are difficult to measure with precision. Moreover, the nature of teaching is complex; it is highly personal and seemingly invulnerable to prescriptions imposed from outside the classroom. Given this evidence, the rational-organization perspective which aims for control and certainty in the face of an unpredictable environment is less than satisfying.

No doubt there are other perspectives. What I offer is both incomplete and limited. Two other viewpoints, briefly presented above, fail to account fully for the research findings on stability and change in the intended and taught curricula and the three questions I asked which the political framework failed to answer. To repeat:

Why are schools and the curricula they offer so vulnerable to externally driven change, most of which is incremental?

Why are the curricula that teachers teach seemingly so insulated from fundamental changes?

How can teacher, administrator, and school board initiatives to alter the intended and taught curricula, undertaken with little or no external pressure, be explained?

I will explore another way of seeing, not because I believe it is best, but because, in concert with the pluralist political framework, it seems to match more consistently the evidence I provided here and respond more fully to the three unanswered questions.

Organizational Perspective

While school organizations, a species of public service bureaucracies, are similar to nonpublic organizations in many respects, it is their differences that help answer the above questions. By schools, I mean both the individual sites and the district. The district organization includes a school board, superintendent, district office staff, and the varied constituencies inside and outside the district. The individual schools with their principal, teachers, students, parents and other groups are units within the system but are themselves organizations nested in the district. Obviously, the district organization is nested in a community itself containing groups interested in education and that community in a county and state.

What makes schools different from nonpublic organizations is that they are tax-supported and under lay governance. These two deep structural traits mark schools as unique organizations. To retain support from its constituencies who provide the children and dollars, school boards display multiple and conflicting goals, many of which are stated ambiguously, making them most difficult to measure. Individuals and groups enter and exit the organization, participating as voters, parents, volunteers, advocates and critics; the traffic in and out of the organization is constant. Without support from these participants and the constituent groups within its surroundings, a school district would lose its legitimacy and eventually lose its clientele (March and Olsen 1976; Meyer and Rowan 1978; Pincus 1972).

So school organizations try to satisfy what their constituencies believe is proper for schools. The public expects teachers to be certified to teach. The public expects mathematics offered in the eighth grade to prepare 14-year-olds for algebra in the ninth grade. The public expects transcripts of high school graduates to be considered by colleges. The public expects a principal to be qualified to supervise a staff of 50 teachers and a superintendent who can put a budget together for the school board. School system policymakers, in turn, retain the endorsement of their community by insuring that all of its personnel meet state requirements for their occupations, schools are accredited, textbooks come off the state-approved lists, and third graders practice cursive writing like other third graders in nearby districts. If many groups define a problem in schools as, for example, "too many teenagers take drugs," before too long school authorities will have introduced a special drug program or expanded its existing one and appointed a district office coordinator for drug education. In this manner, the school organization signals external groups that it is responsive to their concerns. If the public loses confidence in the school organization's capacity to act like a system with these rules and classifications, political support and funding shrink swiftly (Dowling and Pfeffer 1975; Meyer 1980; Meyer and Rowan 1978).

The unique organizational characteristics of this tax-supported public bureaucracy governed by lay policymakers, merged with its strong desire to retain the loyalty of the system's constituencies, help explain the permeability of the system, or what I labeled "vulnerability," to pressures for change from external groups. External pressure, then, merges with an organizational drive to retain the faith of critical supporters; such conditions prepare school districts to adopt innovations so as to be viewed as worthy of continued endorsement. The combined political and organizational perspectives also help to explain why districts in different parts of a state, region, and the nation resemble one another in structures, roles, and operations. To be too different from other districts risks questions about the credibility of the district or school. All of the findings cited in this chapter that portray an intended curriculum undergoing frequent incremental changes fit squarely within this combination of political and organizational perspectives (DiMaggio and Powell 1983; Pincus 1972; Rowan 1982).

But a school system is also responsible for maintaining order, instructing the young, and producing students who have learned. To ensure that the organization is both efficient and effective, the district has a bureaucracy to coordinate and control what occurs in classrooms and elsewhere in the system. If district policymakers face outward to their publics, administrators face inward. Managers ensure that there are tight linkages between external requirements and district rules in whether the staff meets state and local criteria for employment, the standards set by regional accreditation associations, and the proper courses necessary for students to attend prestigious colleges. District operations are also tightly coupled in meeting legal requirements for bids and purchases, avoiding conflicts of interest, and spending state and federal funds. To check that these linkages are intact, they are monitored. Any departures from policy and procedures are scrutinized. Because these categories signal the public that the schools are schools and doing what they are supposed to do, careful attention is paid to these items (Elmore and McLaughlin 1988; Meyer and Rowan 1978).

The tight coupling loosens considerably when it comes to the central core of the system's work: classroom instruction. The transaction between a teacher, students, and content is the basic reason for compelling parents to send their children to school. Those daily transactions are a mix of art and science subject to improvisation and unpredictability in outcomes. The structures of the graded school and segmented curriculum make the self-contained classroom a world unto itself. To cope with the unique nature of the classroom and its imperatives, teachers have devised a practical pedagogy that often goes uninspected by either district administrators or policymakers. While there are ties between classroom and school, and between school and district office, there is no tight coupling here (Bidwell 1965; Cuban 1984a; Elmore and McLaughlin 1988; Meyer and Rowan 1978; Westbury 1973).

The usual bureaucratic tools to control what teachers do in their classrooms are inspection and tests. But teachers, working as solo practitioners, teach for long periods of time without inspection from their supervisors. Principals who are utterly dependent upon teachers to achieve any degree of school effectiveness must rely upon their teachers' craft. This dependence makes evaluations of teacher performance seem ritualistic even when high stakes are involved. Similarly, superintendents who are dependent upon principals to achieve improved school performance have to trust principals' judgment and skills. Virtually the same lack of inspection by superintendents, evaluation of performance, and isolation mark the lot of the principal. The bureaucratic mechanism of inspection exists, but it functions more as a ritual than a tool for coordination and control (Bidwell 1965; Dornbusch and Scott 1975; Dreeben 1973; Elmore and McLaughlin 1988; Weick 1976).

Testing is the other bureaucratic means for controlling what occurs in classrooms. Teachers give their students tests frequently. Most of these are teacher-made or linked to textbook assignments. Seldom, if ever, are the results of these tests used to gauge teacher productivity. While standardized achievement tests are ubiquitous, it is infrequent that student scores are used to formally assess individual teacher performance. Student scores are aggregated at the school and district levels. Because the practice of publishing test scores school by school have become fairly common in cities and many suburbs, there have been growing pressures to hold principals responsible for the school's academic performance, as measured by standardized achievement tests. While there have been such pressures, and in particular locations such accountability may be formalized, it has yet to become general practice. So, without either the usual bureaucratic tools of inspection or tests to determine instructional productivity, the daily delivery of instruction is virtually decoupled from administration and policy making (Duke and Imber 1985; Meyer and Rowan 1978; Resnick and Resnick 1985).

Decoupling the practice of instruction from administration and policy making in the organization occurs because policymakers and administrators are deeply concerned about maintaining district credibility in the eyes of families that send children to school, citizens that pay taxes, and state and federal bureaucracies that monitor district actions. Without credibility, there is no chance of the schools being viewed as successful. Because obtaining teachers' support is critical, a bargain is struck over the degree of inspection and its consequences (often encased in a contract when unions are present); little inspection in return for teacher support of the school (Elmore and McLaughlin 1988; Meyer and Rowan 1978; Weick 1976).

Here, then, is an organizational perspective stitched together from the work of a number of researchers that begins to explain why the curriculum that teachers teach is insulated from externally driven pressures for fundamental changes. The decoupling of instruction from administration and policy making achieves an autonomy and isolation that teachers find satisfying. They can introduce innovative materials designed by outside consultants, especially if they see the value of their use in class. They can alter a mandated sequence of topics for students to cover if they believe that their choices will be in the students' best interest. They can initiate novel changes that bear their signature. There are limits, of course, on how much and how far teachers can change what occurs in the classroom, limits set by those very same constituencies whose support of the school is needed. Choice is situationally constrained.

This organizational perspective focuses upon the importance of administrators turning inward and policymakers facing outward to sustain the organization's credibility and the decoupling of instruction from administrative control. Harnessing this organizational perspective to a political one discussed above supplies, at the least, plausible answers to the three questions I asked earlier.

To the question about the vulnerability of schools and their curricula to externally driven change, both these perspectives offer an obvious answer; there are both political and unique organizational reasons for districts and schools to be as sensitive as radar to blips in their surroundings. Without sustained credibility and responsiveness as an organization to external groups, there is little chance of securing the budgetary and electoral support necessary to survive, much less get labeled as a success.

To the question of why the curricula that teachers teach is seemingly so insulated from pressures for fundamental change, the classroom and school structures that help shape teaching behavior and the decoupling of instruction from bureaucratic oversight offer plausible explanations for a durable classroom continuity punctuated by occasional teacher-designed innovations.

To the question of how could initiatives to alter the intended and taught curricula by teachers, administrators, and policymakers be explained, both perspectives are needed. First, decoupling instruction from inspection provides the discretionary room for individual teachers to design changes for their classrooms; second, decoupling enables an internal political process to achieve planned changes. A principal can negotiate with a faculty to introduce a new program that excites both parties; a superintendent can build a coalition of subordinates, principals, and teachers to adopt and implement a novel program. The decoupling creates a narrow zone of discretion and bargaining for voluntary changes to occur; it does not, however, guarantee that such changes will happen. Yet the capacity to initiate change, even at the risk of threatening credibility with constituencies, assures that districts, schools, and individual teachers are not merely captives of their surroundings; they can and do act.

Finally, in using both ways of seeing—what I come to call situationally constrained choice—frequent incremental changes in the history of public schooling and infrequent fundamental alterations in its goals, structures, and roles (including the intended and taught curricula) become understandable. The apparent contradiction of American education as a "chronicle of fads" and having the rock-hard durability of a graveyard dissolves with the application of these perspectives. Both statements are true.

Not all, however, is tidy. Is this perspective of situationally constrained choice bound by time and place? In this chapter, I do suggest that these combined political and organizational frameworks are generic to all settings and timeless in understanding curricular change and stability. House (1979), for example, used these and other perspectives to explain federal involvement in research since the 1950s. He shows how policymakers' shifts in strategies over a quarter century can be better illuminated by multiple perspectives. He applies a different perspective for different time periods. In doing so House suggests indirectly that generic perspectives that cut across place and time may be inappropriate.

Also, more perspectives are needed to explore and apply to the available evidence. I have already discussed neo-Marxist perspectives concerning the role of class interests embodied in schooling and how that schooling reproduces social inequalities. Whether or not one is convinced by these arguments and evidence, this framework does highlight the importance of social class as a category for understanding differences in what students receive in the intended and taught curricula. Scholars who are not Marxists have for decades identified class as a critical variable in schools. Sociologists have explored how class-linked beliefs and behaviors have permeated schooling (Havighurst 1961; Hollingshead 1949). More recently, researchers representing various ideologies have shown a connection between socioeconomic status and school organization, the content displayed for students to learn, and what is taught in classrooms (Anyon 1980; Goodlad 1984; Oakes 1985; Rist 1970; Willis 1977; Woods 1979). Separating this category from ethnicity, race, and religion is both difficult and necessary in any examination.

A cultural perspective that sees classrooms, schools, and districts as distinct entities with their shared beliefs, norms, rituals, and language also might be more fully explored to explain much teacher and administrator behavior (Feiman-Nemser and Floden 1986; Johnson 1985; Metz 1978; Sarason 1982; Smith and Geoffrey 1968; Spindler and Spindler 1982; Waller 1965; White 1984; Willis 1977; Wolcott 1973, 1977; Woods 1979). Or a social-psychological view that considers the role that boredom plays in swaying individual practitioners and policymakers to entertain novel initiatives deserves attention. Individual variation around attitudes toward stability and change and toleration of differences in a work setting are often noted by observers and participants. Whether such perspectives can also explain both stability and change in the intended and taught curricula merit investigation.

Why are more perspectives needed? Because public officials' eagerness to reform schools and their curricula has been unabated in this century, especially since World War II. Policymakers have ready-made explanations for why schools are so hard to change, why students learn what they do, why stability is so pervasive in classrooms and schools, and why previous curricular reforms failed. These instant explanations drawn from experience and biases may or may not be informed by alternative ways of seeing a situation or historical research.

The state-driven school reforms of the 1980s, for example, aimed at regenerating the American economy, were anchored in a view of the recent past (the 1960s and early 1970s), when educators supposedly permitted standards to slip and the intended and taught curricula failed to challenge students. In the 1950s, an earlier generation of school critics and policymakers argued that Deweyan ideologies had so permeated the public schools of the 1930s and 1940s that the curriculum had become virtually useless in providing the nation with scientists and engineers. Few critics, and even fewer researchers, knew what teachers had taught and children had learned in these schools. Reform visions rely upon a view of the past. The drumbeat of critics' assertions about what happened in schools in earlier decades and policymakers' assumptions about the past become a handy formula for taking action to reform schooling.

Thus, the stakes for policy making are high since such questions about whether or not past reforms succeeded go to the heart of present policy debates over whether federal, state, and district mandates to alter intended curriculum will ever get past the classroom door. If researchers could present conceptual frameworks elaborated with sufficient evidence that such intervention not only reshapes the intended curriculum but also directly affects what teachers do in the ways intended, policymakers would have even a stronger case for improving schools. If scholars could go beyond the meager research on how much of the taught curriculum is learned by students, such evidence would inform the directions that policymakers might pursue. So, too, if researchers could demonstrate convincingly that reform movements will decidedly affect the language, adopted policies, and the intended curriculum, but will seldom enter the toolkit that teachers use daily, then policymakers might reconsider both strategies and tactics.

To the degree that policy decisions can be informed by multiple perspectives and research, such findings can be useful. Finally, to the degree that policymakers and practitioners find relevance in conceptual frameworks that try to explain the pervasive patterns of curricular stability amidst change, such research may help scholars, policymakers, and practitioners both to understand and to act in ways that they had not before.

References

Anderson, James. 1975. "Education as a Vehicle for the Manipulation of Black Workers." In *Work, Technology, and Education: Dissenting Essays in the Intellectual Foundations of American Education*, edited by W. Feinberg and H. J. Rosemont. Urbana: University of Illinois Press.

Anderson, James. 1982. "The Historical Development of Black Vocational Education." In *Work, Youth, and Schooling*, edited by D. Tyack and H. Kantor. Stanford, CA: Stanford University Press.

Anderson, L. 1984. "The Environment of Instruction: The Function of Seatwork in a Commercially Developed Curriculum." In *Comprehensive Instruction: Perspectives and Suggestions*, edited by G. Duffy, L. Roehler and J. Mason. New York: Longman.

Anyon, Jean. 1980. Social class and the hidden curriculum of work. *Journal of Education* 162(1): 67–92.

Apple, Michael. 1977. What do schools teach? *Curriculum Inquiry* 6(4): 341–358.

Apple, Michael. 1982. "Curricular Form and the Logic of Technical Control." In *Cultural and Economic Reproduction in Education*, edited by M. Apple. London: Routledge & Kegan Paul.

Applebee, Arthur N. 1974. *Tradition and Reform in the Teaching of English: A History*. Urbana, IL: National Council of Teachers of English.

Applebee, A., J. Langer, and I. Mullis. 1987. *The Nation's Report Card: Literature and U.S. History*. Princeton, NJ: Educational Testing Service.

Atkin, J. Myron, and Ernest House. 1981. The federal role in curriculum development. *Educational Evaluation and Policy Analysis* 3(5): 5–36.

Barr, Rebecca, and Robert Dreeben. 1983. *How Schools Work*. Chicago: University of Chicago Press.

Barth, Roland. 1972. *Open Education and The American School*. New York: Agathon.

Bernstein, Basil. 1977. "Class and Pedagogies: Visible and Invisible." In *Power and Ideology in Education*, edited by J. Karabel and A. H. Halsey. New York: Oxford University Press.

Bidwell, Charles. 1965. "The School as a Formal Organization." In *Handbook of Organizations*, edited by J. March. Chicago: Rand McNally.

Bidwell, Charles, and J. D. Kasarda. 1980. Measuring the effects of school and schooling. *American Journal of Education* 88(4): 401–430.

Birmingham, John. 1970. *Our Time is Now*. New York: Bantam Books.

Black, Hillel. 1967. *The American School Book*. New York: Morrow.

Bowles, Samuel, and Herbert Gintis. 1976. *Schooling in Capitalist America*. New York: Basic Books.

Boyd, William L. 1979. "The Changing Politics of Curriculum Policy Making for American Schools." In *Value Conflicts and Curriculum Issues*, edited by J. Schaffarzick and G. Sykes. Berkeley, CA: McCutchan.

Brickell, Henry M. 1964. "State Organization for Educational Change." In *Innovation in Education*, edited by M. Miles. New York: Teachers College Press.

Bruner, Herbert B., Hubert M. Evans, Cecil R. Hutchcroft, Maurice C. Wieting, and Hugh B. Wood. 1941. *What Our Schools Are Teaching*. New York: Bureau of Publications, Teachers College, Columbia University.

Burns, Gerald. 1988. Traditions and revolution in the American secondary curriculum: The Cambridge High School case. *Journal of Curriculum Studies* 20(2): 99–118.

Callahan, Raymond. 1962. *Education And The Cult of Efficiency*. Chicago: University of Chicago Press.

Carnegie Foundation. 1988. *An Imperiled Generation: Saving Urban Schools*. New York: Carnegie Foundation for the Advancement of Teaching.

Carnoy, Martin, and Henry Levin. 1985. *Schooling and Work in the Democratic State*. Stanford, CA: Stanford University Press.

Chall, Jeanne, Sue Conrad, and Susan Harris-Sharples. 1977. *An Analysis of Textbooks in Relation to Declining SAT Scores*. New York: College Entrance Examination Board.

Champagne, A. B., L. E. Klopfer, and R. F. Gunstone. 1982. Cognitive research and the design of science instruction. *Educational Psychologist* 17: 31–53.

Chapman, Paul. 1980. Schools as Sorters: Lewis M. Terman and The Intelligence Testing Movement, 1890–1930. Unpublished doctoral dissertation, Stanford University, Stanford, CA.

Charters, W. W. 1922. Regulating the project. *Journal of Educational Research* 5:245.

Chase, Francis. 1966. "School Change in Perspective." In *The Changing American School*, edited by J. Goodlad, 271–306. Chicago: National Society for the Study of Education.

Clifford, Geraldine J. 1968. *The Sane Positivist: A Biography of Edward L. Thorndike*. Middletown, CT: Wesleyan University Press.

Cohen, David K. 1987. Educational technology, policy, and practice. *Educational Evaluation and Policy Analysis* 9(2): 153–170.

Cohen, David K. 1988. "Teaching Practice, Plus Que Ca Change. . . ." In *Contributing to Educational Change*, edited by P. Jackson. Berkeley, CA: McCutchan.

Cohen, David K. 1989. "Practice and Policy." In *History of Teaching, Teachers, and Teacher Education in the United States*, edited by D. Warren. New York: Macmillan.

Corbett, H. D. and B. L. Wilson. 1988. "Raising the Stakes in Statewide Mandatory Testing Programs." In *The Politics of Reforming School Administration*, edited by J. Hannaway and R. Crowson. New York: Falmer.

Counts, George S. 1926. *The Senior High School Curriculum*. Supplementary Educational Monographs. Chicago: University of Chicago.

Cremin, Lawrence. 1961. *The Transformation of The School*. New York: Vintage.

Cremin, Lawrence. 1971. Curriculum-making in the United States. *Teachers College Record* 73(2): 207–220.

Cremin, Lawrence. 1988. *American Education: The Metropolitan Experience, 1876–1980*. New York: Harper & Row.

Cronin, Joseph. 1973. *The Control of Urban Schools: Perspectives on The Power of Educational Reformers*. New York: Free Press.

Cuban, Larry. 1979. "Determinants of Curriculum Change and Stability, 1870–1970." In *Value Conflicts and Curriculum Issues*, edited by J. Schaffarzick and G. Sykes, 139–196. Berkeley, CA: McCutchan.

Cuban, Larry. 1984a. *How Teachers Taught: Constancy And Change in American Classrooms, 1890–1980*. New York: Longman.

Cuban, Larry. 1984b. Transforming the frog into a prince: Effective schools research, policy, and practice at the district level. *Harvard Educational Review* 54(2): 129–151.

Cuban, Larry. 1986. *Teachers and Machines*. New York: Teachers College Press.

Cuban, Larry. 1988. *The Managerial Imperative and the Practice of Leadership in Schools*. Albany, NY: State University of New York Press.

Cuban, Larry. 1990. "The History of Teaching in Social Studies." In *Handbook of Research on Social Studies*, edited by J. Shaver. New York: Macmillan.

Cusick, Philip. 1983. *The Egalitarian Ideal And The American High School*. New York: Longman.

Darling-Hammond, Linda, and Arthur Wise. 1985. Beyond standardization: State standards and school improvement. *Elementary School Journal* 85(3): 315–336.

Denscombe, Martin. 1982. The "hidden pedagogy" and its implications for teacher training. *British Journal of Sociology of Education* 3: 249–265.

Dewey, John. 1901. The situation as it regards the course of study. *Journal of Proceedings and Addresses of the Fortieth Annual Meeting of the National Education Association*, 332–348.

Dillon, J. T. 1988. The remedial status of student questioning. *Journal of Curriculum Studies* 20(3): 197–210.

DiMaggio, Paul J., and Walter W. Powell. 1983. The iron cage revisited: Institutional isomorphism and collective rationality in organizational fields. *American Sociological Review* 48(April): 147–160.

Dornbusch, Sanford M., and W. Richard Scott. 1975. *Evaluation and the Exercise of Authority*. San Francisco, CA: Jossey Bass.

Dowling, John, and Jeffrey Pfeffer. 1975. Organizational legitimacy, social values, and organizational behavior. *Pacific Sociological Review* 18: 122–136.

Downs, Anthony. 1972. Up and down with ecology—the issue attention cycle. *Public Interest* 28(Summer): 38–50.

Doyle, Walter. 1983. Academic work. *Review of Educational Research* 53(2): 159–199.

Dreeben, Robert. 1968. *On What Is Learned in School*. Reading, MA: Addison-Wesley.

Dreeben, Robert. 1973. "The School as a Workplace." In *Handbook of Research on Teaching*, edited by R. M. W. Travers. Chicago: Rand McNally.

Duke, Daniel L., and Michael Imber. 1985. Should principals be required to be effective? *School Organization* 5(2): 125–146.

Durkin, Dolores. 1978. *What Classroom Observations Reveal About Reading Comprehension Instruction*. Urbana: University of Illinois Center for The Study of Reading. NTIS, 106.

Eisner, Elliot. 1979. *The Educational Imagination*. New York: Macmillan.

Elmore, Richard F., and Milbrey W. McLaughlin. 1988. *Steady Work: Policy, Practice, and the Reform of American Education*. RAND Corporation. NTIS, R-3574-NIE/RC.

Elson, Ruth Miller. 1964. *Guardians of Tradition*. Lincoln: University of Nebraska Press.

Englund, Tomas. 1986. *Curriculum as a Political Problem*. Uppsala, Sweden: Chartwell-Bratt.

Feiman-Nemser, Sharon, and Robert E. Floden. 1986. "The Cultures of Teaching." In *Handbook of Research on Teaching*, edited by M. Wittrock. New York: Macmillan.

Finkelstein, Barbara. 1989. *Governing The Young: Teacher Behavior in Popular Primary Schools in 19th Century United States*. New York: Falmer.

Fitzgerald, F. 1979. *America Revised*. Boston: Little, Brown.

Flanders, J. K. 1926. "Curriculum-Making by the State Legislatures." In *The Foundations and Technique of Curriculum-Construction*, edited by G. M. Whipple. Bloomington, IL: Public School Co.

Franklin, Barry. 1982. The social efficiency movement reconsidered: Curriculum change in Minneapolis, 1917–1950. *Journal of Curriculum Inquiry* 12(1): 9–33.

Franklin, Barry. 1986. *Building the American Community: The School Curriculum and The Search for Social Control*. New York: Falmer.

Fullan, Michael. 1982. *The Meaning of Educational Change*. New York: Teachers College Press.

Gaskell, Jane. 1986. The changing organization of business education in the high school: Teachers respond to school and work. *Curriculum Inquiry* 16(4): 417–437.

Geel, Tyll van. 1979. "The New Law of The Curriculum." In *Value Conflicts and Curriculum Issues*, edited by J. Schaffarzick and G. Sykes. Berkeley, CA: McCutchan.

Getzels, J. W. 1970. "Creative Administration and Organizational Change: An Essay in Theory." In *Frontiers in School Leadership*, edited by L. Rubin. Chicago: Rand McNally.

Giroux, Henry A. 1981. *Ideology, Culture, and the Process of Schooling*. Philadelphia, PA: Temple University Press.

Goodlad, John. 1964 *School Curriculum Reform*. New York: Fund for the Advancement of Education.

Goodlad, John. 1966. "The Curriculum." In *The Changing American School*, edited by J. Goodlad. Chicago: National Society for the Study of Education.

Goodlad, John. 1984. *A Place Called School*. New York: McGraw-Hill.

Goodson, Ivor F. 1983. *School Subjects and Curriculum Change: Case Studies in Curriculum History*. London: Croom Helm.

Grant, Carl, and Christine Sleeter. 1985. Who determines teacher work: The teacher, the organization, or both? *Teaching and Teacher Education* 1(3): 209–220

Gutowski, Thomas W. 1988. Student initiative and the origin of the high school extracurriculum: Chicago, 1880–1915. *History of Education Quarterly* 28(1): 49–72.

Hamilton, David. 1975. "Handling Innovation in the Classroom: Two Scottish Examples." In *Case Studies in Curriculum Change*, edited by W. Reid and D. Walker. London: Routledge & Kegan Paul.

Hamilton, David. 1989. *Towards a Theory of Schooling*. London: Falmer.

Hampel, Robert. 1986. *The Last Little Citadel*. Boston: Houghton Mifflin.

Haney, Walt. 1984. Testing reasoning and reasoning about testing. *Review of Educational Research* 54(4): 597–654.

Hansot, Elisabeth, and David Tyack. 1988. Gender in American public schools: Thinking institutionally. *Signs* 13(4): 741–760.

Hargreaves, Andy. 1984. Experience counts, theory doesn't: How teachers talk about their work. *Sociology of Education* 57(October): 244–254.

Hargreaves, D. 1980. "The Occupational Culture of Teachers." In *Teacher Strategies*, edited by P. Woods. London: Croom Helm.

Havighurst, Robert. 1961. "Social Class Influences on American Education." In *Social Forces Influencing American Education*, edited by N. B. Henry. Chicago: National Society for the Study of Education.

Henry, Nelson. 1961. *Social Forces Influencing American Education*. Chicago: National Society for the Study of Education.

Hoetker, James, and William Ahlbrand. 1969. The persistence of the recitation. *American Educational Research Journal* 6(March): 145–167.

Hogan, David. 1985. *Class and Reform: School and Society in Chicago, 1880–1930*. Philadelphia: University of Pennsylvania Press.

Hollingshead, August. 1949. *Elmstown's Youth*. New York: Wiley.

House, Ernest. 1974. *The Politics of Educational Innovation*. Berkeley, CA: McCutchan.

House, Ernest. 1979. Technology versus craft: A ten year perspective on innovation. *Journal of Curriculum Studies* 11(1): 1–15.

Jackson, Philip. 1968. *Life in Classrooms*. New York: Holt, Rinehart and Winston.

Jackson, Philip. 1981. Secondary schooling for children of the poor. *Daedalus* 110(4): 39–58.

Jackson, Philip W. 1983. The reform of science: A cautionary tale. *Daedalus* 112(2): 143–166.

Johnson, Norris B. 1985. *West Haven: Classroom Culture and Society in a Rural Elementary School*. Chapel Hill: University of North Carolina Press.

Johnson, Susan M. 1988. "Unionism and Collective Bargaining in the Public Schools." In *Handbook of Research in Educational Administration*, edited by N. Boyan. New York: Longman.

Jones, Alison. 1989. The cultural production of classroom practice. *British Journal of Sociology of Education* 10(1): 19–31.

Jurkowitz, Carolyn M. 1981. Shaping the high school curriculum: The case of regional accreditation. *Journal of Curriculum Theorizing* 3(1): 103–113.

Kaestle, Carl. 1973. *The Evolution of an Urban School System: New York City, 1750–1850*. Cambridge, MA: Harvard University Press.

Kaestle, Carl. 1983. *Pillars of the Republic*. New York: Farrar, Straus.

Kaestle, Carl, and Marshall Smith. 1982. The federal role in elementary and secondary education, 1940–1980. *Harvard Educational Review* 52(4): 384–408.

Kantor, Harvey. 1986. Work, education, and vocational reform: The ideological origins of vocational education, 1890–1920. *American Journal of Education* 94(3): 401–426.

Katz, Michael. 1968. *The Irony of Early School Reform*. Cambridge, MA: Harvard University Press.

Katz, Michael. 1971. *Class, Bureaucracy, and Schools: The Illusion of Educational Change in America*. New York: Praeger.

Katznelson, Ira, and Margaret Weir. 1985. *Schooling for All: Class, Race, and the Decline of the Democratic Ideal*. New York: Basic Books.

Kiger, Joseph. 1972. "Foundation Support of Educational Innovations by Learned Societies, Councils, and Institutes." In *Innovation in Education: A Foundation Goes to School*, edited by M. Miles. New York: Ford Foundation.

Kirst, Michael, and Decker Walker. 1971. An analysis of curriculum policy-making. *Review of Educational Research* 41(5): 479–509.

Kliebard, Herbert M. 1975. "Reappraisal: The Tyler Rationale." In *Curriculum Theorizing: The Reconceptualists*, edited by W. F. Pinar. Berkeley, CA: McCutchan.

Kliebard, Herbert M. 1986. *The Struggle for The American Curriculum, 1893–1958*. Boston: Routledge & Kegan Paul.

Kliebard, Herbert M. 1988. "Fads, Fashions, and Rituals: The Instability of Curriculum Change." In *Critical Issues in the Curriclum*, edited by L. N. Tanner. Chicago: National Society for the Study of Education.

Kliebard, Herbert, and Greg Wegner. 1987. "Harold Rugg and The Reconstruction of the Social Studies Curriculum: The Treatment of the 'Great War' in His Textbook Series." In *The Formation of the School Subjects*, edited by T. S. Popkewitz. New York: Falmer.

Kohl, Herb. 1967. *36 Children*. New York: New American Library.

Komoski, Kenneth P. 1978. The realities of choosing and using instructional materials. *Educational Leadership* 36(October): 46–50.

Krug, Edward A. 1964. *The Shaping of The American High School*. New York: Harper & Row.

Labaree, David. 1988. *The Making of an American High School: The Credentials Market and the Central High School of Philadelphia, 1838–1939*. New Haven, CT: Yale University Press.

Lagemann, Ellen C. 1989. The plural worlds of educational research. *History of Education Quarterly* 29(2): 185–214.

Langer, Judith. 1984. Literacy instruction in American schools: Problems and perspectives. *American Journal of Education* 92(November): 107–132.

Lazerson, Marvin, and Norton Grubb. 1974. *American Education and Vocationalism: A Documentary History, 1870–1970*. New York: Teachers College Press.

Lightfoot, Sara L. 1983. *The Good High School*. New York: Basic Books.

Lortie, Dan. 1975. *Schoolteacher*. Chicago: University of Chicago Press.

Lynd, Robert, and Helen Lynd. 1924. *Middletown*. New York: Harcourt, Brace.

Mack, Raymond. 1968. *Our Children's Burden*. New York: Random House.

Mackenzie, Gordon. 1964. "Curricular Change: Participants, Power, and Processes." In *Innovation in Education*, edited by M. Miles 399–424. New York: Teachers College Press.

McKinney, W. Lynn, and Ian Westbury. 1975. "Stability and Change: The Public Schools of Gary, Indiana, 1940–1970." In *Case Studies in Curriculum Change*, edited by W. A. Reid and D. Walker. London: Routledge & Kegan Paul.

McNeil, John. 1969. Forces influencing curriculum. *Review of Educational Research* 39(3): 293–318.

McNeil, Linda. 1986. *Contradictions of Control: School Structure and School Knowledge*. New York: Routledge & Kegan Paul.

Macrorie, Ken. 1984. *Twenty Teachers*. New York: Oxford University Press.

Madaus, George. 1988. "The Influence of Testing on The Curriculum." In *Critical Issues in Curriculum*, edited by L. Tanner. Chicago: National Society for the Study of Education.

March, James. 1981. Footnotes to organizational change. *Administrative Science Quarterly* 26(December): 563–577.

March, James G., and Johan P. Olsen. 1976. *Ambiguity and Choice in Organizations*. Bergen, Norway: Universitetsforlaget.

March, James G., and Johan P. Olsen. 1984. The new institutionalism: Organizational factors in political life. *The American Political Science Review* 78: 734–749.

Mehan, Hugh. 1979. *Learning Lessons*. Cambridge, MA: Harvard University Press.

Metz, Mary. 1978. *Classrooms and Corridors: The Crisis of Authority in Desegregated Secondary Schools*. Berkeley, CA: University of California Press.

Meyer, John. 1986. "The Politics of Educational Crises in the United States." In *Educational Policies in Crisis*, edited by W. Cummings, E. R. Beauchamp, W. Ichikawa, Y. N. Kobayashi, and M. Ushiogi. New York: Praeger.

Meyer, John, and Brian Rowan. 1978. "The Structure of Educational Organizations." In *Environments and Organizations*, edited by M. Meyer. San Francisco, CA: Jossey-Bass.

Meyer, Marshall. 1980. Organizational structure as signaling. *Pacific Sociological Review* 23: 401–500.

Moore, W. E. 1963. *Social Change*. Englewood Cliffs, NJ: Prentice Hall.

Nisbet, Robert A. 1969. *Social Change and History*. London: Oxford University Press.

Nisbet, Robert A. 1980. *History of the Idea of Progress*. New York: Basic Books.

O'Connor, Carol A. 1980. Setting a standard for suburb innovation in the Scarsdale schools, 1920–1930. *History of Education Quarterly* 20(3): 295–311.

Oakes, Jeannie. 1985. *Keeping Track: How Schools Structure Inequality*. New Haven, CT: Yale University Press.

Orfield, Gary. 1975. How to make desegregation work: The adaptation of schools to their newly-integrated student bodies. *Law and Contemporary Problems* 39(Spring): 314–340.

Paulston, Rolland G. 1976. *Conflicting Theories of Social and Educational Change*. Pittsburgh, PA: University Center for International Studies, University of Pittsburgh.

Peterson, Paul E. 1985. *The Politics of School Reform*. Chicago: University of Chicago Press.

Pfeffer, Jeffrey. 1982. *Organizations and Organization Theory*. Boston: Pitman.

Pincus, John. 1972. Incentives for innovation in the public schools. *Review of Educational Research* 44(1): 113–144.

Plank, David. 1987. Why school reform doesn't change schools: Political and organizational perspectives. *Politics of Education Association Yearbook* 1987: 143–152.

Popkewitz, Thomas S. 1987. *The Formation of the School Subjects*. New York: Falmer.

Popkewitz, Thomas S. 1988. Educational reform: Rhetoric, ritual, and social interest. *Educational Theory* 38(1): 77–93.

Powell, Arthur, Eleanor Farrar, and David Cohen. 1985. *The Shopping Mall High School: Winners and Losers in the Educational Marketplace*. Boston: Houghton Mifflin.

Purkey, Stewart, and Marshall Smith. 1983. Effective schools: A review. *Elementary School Journal* 83(4): 427–452.

Quick, Suzanne. 1977. Secondary Impacts of the Curriculum Reform Movement: A Longitudinal Study of the Incorporation of Innovations in the Curriculum Reform Movement into Commercially Developed Curriculum Programs. Unpublished doctoral dissertation, Stanford University, Stanford, CA.

Ravitch, Diane. 1983. *The Troubled Crusade: American Education, 1945–1980*. New York: Basic Books.

Reese, William. 1986. *Power and the Promise of School Reform: Grassroots Movements during the Progressive Era*. Boston: Routledge & Kegan Paul.

Reid, William. 1978. *Thinking about the Curriculum*. London: Routledge & Kegan Paul.

Resnick, Daniel, and Lauren Resnick. 1985. Standards, curriculum, and performance: A historical and comparative perspective. *Educational Researcher* 14(3): 5–20.

Rickover, Hyman. 1983. *Statement on Education*. Richmond: Virginia State Board of Education.

Rinne, Risto. 1988. From ethos to habitus: The changing curriculum codes of Finnish schooling. *Journal of Curriculum Studies* 20(5): 423–435.

Rist, Ray. 1970. Student social class and teacher expectations. *Harvard Educational Review* 40: 411–451.

Romberg, Thomas A. and Thomas P. Carpenter. 1986. "Research on Teaching and Learning Mathematics: Two Disciplines of Scientific Inquiry." In *Handbook of Research on Teaching*, edited by M. Wittrock. New York: Macmillan.

Rowan, Brian. 1982. Organizational structure and the institutional environment: The case of public schools. *Administrative Science Quarterly* 27(June): 259–279.

Rubinson, Richard. 1986. Class formation, politics, and institutions: Schooling in the United States. *American Journal of Sociology* 92(3): 519–548.

Rugg, Harold. 1926. "The School Curriculum and the Drama of American Life." In *The Foundations and Techniques of Curriculum Construction*, edited by G. M. Whipple. Bloomington, IL: Public School Co.

Rugg, Harold, and George Counts. 1926. "A Critical Appraisal of Current Methods of Curriculum-Making." In *The Foundations and Technique of Curriculum-Construction*, edited by G. M. Whipple. Bloomington, IL: Public School Co.

Sarason, Seymour. 1982. *The Culture of the School and the Problem of Change*. Boston: Allyn & Bacon.

Schoenfeld, Alan. 1990. "On Mathematics As Sense-Making: An Informal Attack on the Unfortunate Divorce of Formal and Informal Mathematics." In *Informal Reasoning and Education*, edited by D. Perkins, J. Segal, and J. Voss. Hillsdale, NJ: Erlbaum.

Schubert, William H. 1986. *Curriculum: Perspective, Paradigm, and Possibility*. New York: Macmillan.

Schwille, J., A. Porter, L. Alford, R. Floden, D. Freeman, S. Irwin, and W. Schmidt. 1988. State policy and the control of curriculum decisions. *Educational Policy* 2(1): 29–50.

Schwille, J., A. Porter, G. Belli, R. Floden, D. Freeman, L. Kuhs, T. Knappen, and W. Schmidt. 1983. "Teachers as Policy Brokers in the Content of Elementary School Mathematics." In *Handbook of Teaching and Policy*, edited by G. Sykes and L. Shulman. New York: Longman.

Scott, W. Richard. 1981. *Organizations: Rational, Natural, and Open Systems*. Englewood Cliffs, NJ: Prentice Hall.

Sedlak, Michael, and Steven Schlossman. 1985. The public school and social services: Reassessing the progressive legacy. *Educational Theory* 35(4): 371–383.

Sedlak, Michael, Christopher Wheeler, Diana Pullin, and Philip Cusick. 1986. *Selling Students Short: Classroom Bargains and Academic Reform in the American High School*. New York: Teachers College Press.

Selznick, Philip. 1949. *TVA And The Grass Roots*. Berkeley, CA: University of California Press.

Shane, Harold. 1980. Significant writings that have influenced the curriculum. *Phi Delta Kappan* 62(5): 311–314.

Shils, Edward. 1981. *Tradition*. Chicago: University of Chicago Press.

Short, Edmund C. 1983. Authority and governance in curriculum development: A policy analysis in the United States context. *Educational Evaluation and Policy Analysis* 5(2): 195–205.

Silberman, Charles. 1971. *Crisis in The Classroom*. New York: Knopf.

Singer, Judith D. and John A. Butler. 1987. The Education for All Handicapped Children Act: Schools as Agents of Social Reform. *Harvard Educational Review* 57(2): 125–152.

Sizer, Theodore. 1964. *Secondary Schools at the Turn of the Century*. New Haven, CT: Yale University Press.

Smith, Anthony D. 1973. *The Concept of Social Change*. London: Routledge & Kegan Paul.

Smith, Louis, and William Geoffrey. 1968. *The Complexities of an Urban Classroom*. New York: Holt, Rinehart and Winston.

Smith, Louis, David Dwyer, John Prunty, and Paul Kleine. 1988. *Innovation And Change in Schooling*. New York: Falmer.

Soltis, Judith. 1987. "American Grammar Texts (1890–1984): Their Role in the Explicit, Operative, and Implicit Curricula of Schools." Paper presented at the annual meeting of the American Educational Research Association, Washington, DC.

Sosniak, Lauren A., Corinna A. Ethington, and Maria Varelas. In press. Teaching mathematics without a coherent point of view: Findings from the Second International Mathematics Study. *Journal of Curriculum Studies*.

Spindler, George, and Louise Spindler. 1982. "Roger Harker and Schönhausen: From Familiar to Strange and Back Again." In *Doing the Ethnography of Schooling*, edited by G. Spindler. New York: Holt, Rinehart and Winston.

Spring, Joel. 1972. Education and the Rise of the Corporate State. Boston, MA: Beacon Press.

Squire, James. 1988. "Studies of Textbooks." In *Contributions to Educational Change*, edited by P. Jackson. Berkeley, CA: McCutchan.

Stake, Robert, and Jack Easley. 1978. *Case Studies in Science Education*. Urbana, IL: Center for Instructional Research and Evaluation.

Stevens, L. B. 1976. The paradox of school reform: Are the schools impervious to redesign? *Phi Delta Kappan* 57(February): 371–374.

Stinchcombe, Arthur, L. 1965. "Social Structure and Organizations." In *Handbook of Organizations*, edited by J. G. March. Chicago: Rand McNally.

Stodolsky, Susan. 1988. *The Subject Matters*. Chicago: University of Chicago Press.

Stodolsky, Susan. 1989. "Is Teaching Really by the Book?" In *From Socrates to Software: The Teacher as Text and the Text as Teacher*, edited by P. W. Jackson. Chicago: National Society for the Study of Education.

Straw, Barry. 1982. "Counterforces to Change." In *Change in Organizations*, edited by P. A. A. Goodman. San Francisco, CA: Jossey-Bass.

Suydam, Marilyn. 1977. *The Status of Pre-College Science, Mathematics, and Social Science Education, 1955–1975: Mathematics Education*. Columbus, OH: Ohio State University, Center for Science and Mathematics Education.

Thirty Schools Tell Their Story. 1942. Volume 5. New York: Harper & Brothers.

Tiedt, Sidney. 1972. "Historical Development of Federal Aid Programs." In *What Should Be the Policy Toward Financing Elementary and Secondary Education in the United States?* Washington, DC: U.S. Government Printing Office.

Timar, Thomas B., and David L. Kirp. 1988. *Managing Educational Excellence*. New York: Falmer Press.

Troen, S. 1975. *The Public and the Schools: Shaping the St. Louis System 1838–1920*. Columbia: University of Missouri Press.

Tyack, David. 1974. *The One Best System*. Cambridge, MA: Harvard University Press.

Tyack, David, and Elisabeth Hansot. 1982. *Managers of Virtue: Public School Leadership in America, 1820–1980*. New York: Basic Books.

Tyack, David, Robert Lowe, and Elisabeth Hansot. 1984. *Public Schools in Hard Times*. Cambridge, MA: Harvard University Press.

Tyack, David, Thomas James, and Aaron Benavot. 1987. *Law And The Shaping of Public Education, 1785–1954*. Madison: University of Wisconsin Press.

Tyler, Ralph. 1950. *Basic Principles of Curriculum and Instruction*. Chicago: University of Chicago Press.

Tyler, Ralph. 1961. "The Impact of Students on Schools and Colleges." In *Social Forces Influencing American Education*, edited by N. B. Henry. Chicago: National Society for the Study of Education.

Voege, Herbert W. 1975. "The Diffusion of Keynesian Macroeconomics through American High School Textbooks, 1936–1970." In *Case Studies in Curriculum Change*, edited by W. A. Reid and D. Walker. London: Routledge & Kegan Paul.

Walker, Decker. 1990. *Fundamentals of Curriculum*. San Diego, CA: Harcourt Brace Jovanovich.

Waller, Willard. 1965. *The Sociology of Teaching*. New York: Wiley.

Watzlawick, Paul, John Weakland, and Richard Fisch. 1974. *Principles of Problem Formation and Problem Resolution*. New York: Norton.

Wayland, Sloan R. 1964. "Structural Features of American Education as Basic Factors in Innovation." In *Innovation in Education*, edited by M. Miles. New York: Teachers College Press.

Weick, Karl. 1976. Educational organizations as loosely coupled systems. *Administrative Science Quarterly* 21(March): 1–19.

Weiss, Iris. 1978. *Report of the 1977 National Survey of Science, Mathematics, and Social Science Education*. Washington, DC: National Science Foundation.

Westbury, Ian. 1973. Conventional classrooms, "open" classrooms and the technology of teaching. *Journal of Curriculum Studies* 5(2): 99–121.

Westbury, Ian. 1980. "Schooling as an Agency of Education: Some Implications for Curriculum Theory." In *Rethinking Educational Research*, edited by W. B. Dockrell and D. Hamilton. London: Hodden and Stoughton.

White, Jane J. 1985. "What Works for Teachers: A Review of Ethnographic Research Studies as They Inform Issues of Social Studies Curriculum and Instruction." In *Review of Research in Social Studies Education*, edited by W. B. Stanley. Washington, DC: National Council for the Social Studies.

White, Richard T., and Richard P. Tisher. 1986. "Research on Natural Sciences." In *Handbook of Research on Teaching*, edited by M. Wittrock. New York: Macmillan.

Wigginton, Eliot. 1985. *Sometimes a Shining Moment: The Foxfire Experience*. New York: Anchor Press.

Willis, Paul. 1977. *Learning to Labor*. Lexington, MA: Heath.

Wirt, Frederick, and Michael Kirst. 1972. *The Political Web of American Schools*. Boston: Little, Brown.

Wirt, Frederick M., and Michael Kirst. 1989. *Schools in Conflict*. Berkeley, CA: McCutchan.

Wise, Arthur. 1979. *Legislated Learning: The Bureaucratization of the American Classroom*. Berkeley, CA: University of California Press.

Wolcott, Harry. 1973. *The Man in the Principal's Office*. New York: Holt, Rinehart and Winston.

Wolcott, Harry. 1977. *Teachers and Technocrats*. Eugene, OR: Center for Educational Policy and Management, University of Oregon.

Woods, Peter. 1979. *The Divided School*. London: Routledge & Kegan Paul.

Wrigley, Julia. 1982. *Class Politics and Public Schools*. New Brunswick, NJ: Rutgers University Press.

Zilversmit, Arthur. 1976. "The Failure of Progressive Education, 1920–1940." In *Schooling and Society: Studies in the History of Education*, edited by L. Stone. Baltimore, MD: Johns Hopkins University Press.

9

THE RELATIONSHIP BETWEEN CULTURE AND CURRICULUM: A MANY FITTING THING

Alan Peshkin

UNIVERSITY OF ILLINOIS—URBANA-CHAMPAIGN

"Chief Poropot agrees that everyone must learn Portuguese. 'The language of the Kaiapo is very ancient and it will never end,' he says. 'But the women and the children need to learn Portuguese to defend themselves.' "

"Defend themselves?"

" 'If they go to shop in Redencao, they have to talk,' " he says. 'If they get sick, they cannot tell the doctor what they have.' "

Simons (1989,52)

Chief Poropot's words capture an issue of culture and curriculum at its most poignant level. The Kaiapo, a tribe of the once-remote Amazon River basin, now have frequent contact with non-Kaiapo Brazilian society. Mastering Portuguese, as did Chief Poropot and others of his tribe, facilitates informed access to the encompassing Brazilian culture; mastering Portuguese is a beginning for the Kaiapo to understand themselves in an extraordinarily different context than that of the jungle fastness which for centuries has sheltered and nurtured them. As Cheik Hamidou Kane (1972) dramatized in *Ambiguous Adventure*, his fine novel of a fictional Muslim society in French West Africa, once-isolated tribes cannot retreat from the overwhelmingly dominant societies which inevitably confront them. Thus, if the Kaiapo or Kane's Muslim tribe, the Diallobé, strive to pursue their traditional cultures, taking recourse in the "curriculum" of their traditional socializing institutions, they may sustain a close fit between culture and "curriculum." The resulting fit, however, may ultimately prove disastrous in the face of the encroaching alien culture of Portuguese and French speakers. Old fits, good for old times, prove inadequate to meet the challenges of dramatically different times. For better and worse, new languages fit students for the emergent new world in their lives.

In Robert Wellesley Cole's account (1960) of his school days in the Sierra Leone of the early 1920s, we learn of the new become salient. He describes the jolt he and his fellow students received when the colonial government announced that external examinations for secondary school students would be set in West Africa rather than in the United Kingdom. The government reasoned thus: Would not Africans "be better off with local examinations framed to suit 'the realities of local conditions?' " (1960, 185)

Cole, his classmates, their families, and the press rallied

The author is indebted for invaluable library research to Joel Judd and Denise Flowers, for much appreciated financial support to Russ Ames and the National Center for School Leadership, and for a useful external reading to Hope Jensen Leichter.

to resist what Western-educated Sierra Leoneans interpreted as an effort by their British rulers to keep them in their place. Cole knew that unless he and his classmates took school-leaving examinations set abroad, they could not attend Oxford or Cambridge and thereby gain access to occupational mobility. What colonial policymakers perceived as a fitting curriculum—of which tests surely are an integral aspect—Sierra Leoneans deemed unfitting and staunchly resisted. Clearly, one person's good fit is another person's crunched opportunities.

What curriculum suits what cultural orientation as seen by whom is the subject of this chapter. It is a complex topic because the culture of most contemporary nations is a tangled tapestry of subcultural variants. The variants have curricular ramifications. Different groups may agree about what language to conduct instruction in and whose history to teach, and disagree about what other languages to offer and what topics with what emphasis to include in the history course. The translation of some aspect of culture or subculture into its curricular terms is undertaken by persons who often have high stakes in what they support. Indeed, as we see with Chief Poropot and Portuguese, the Diallobe and French, and Sierra Leonean Cole and the setting of external examinations, what is at stake is no less than fundamental well-being and survival as some agent defines them. (I will use agent to designate who, in light of some cultural orientation, proposes or supports some curricular element.)

If the stakes are not always so high, they seldom are trivial because schooling is too intimately tied to perceptions of individual, group, national, and international fortune. And the tie is not confined to colonial or third-world circumstances. We can hear the sounds of urgency in Zuga's characterization of American industrialists—the agents—whose willingness to "cooperate with the schools may be fostered by an underlying desire to control the 'products' of the schools in order to have a better fit between the needs of the labor force and the graduates of educational institutions" (1989, 2). Labor force needs are far from trivial. The Business Higher Education Forum, "a group of about 80 corporate chief executives and university presidents," urges a "concerted national effort" to "revitalize American education" so that we can meet "the demands of the global marketplace" (Walsh 1988, 7). What this organization of executives has in mind is distant in cultural and curricular terms from the legislation Governor Thompson of Illinois approved. Illinois now requires all state schools to "determine a specific curriculum . . . on the historical significance, as well as the ethical and moral implications, of the Holocaust and other historical incidents of genocide" (Holmes 1989, 7–8; see also *Education Week*, October 4, 1989). The advocates of a curriculum suitable for meeting global marketplace demands compete with advocates of a curriculum suitable for comprehending genocide. Survival is at issue in both instances; neither would necessarily concede the priority of the other.

My intent in this chapter is to discuss the relationship between culture and curriculum within the concept of fit, but first I must explicate all three terms, identify the agents, and, finally, examine the linkage of culture and curriculum.

CULTURE, CURRICULUM, AND FIT

The concept of "culture" is having a heyday. The ubiquitous appearance of the term in social science and education literature testifies to its construal as necessary; in the process, it has become fashionable, as well. Such is the case in the field of educational scholarship, whose writers adopt established definitions of culture and construct definitions of their own. Notwithstanding that it is overdefined and that if one looks long enough one can find a conception to match any purpose, there is reasonable convergence on the referents of culture so that we borrowers need not feel that our choice of definitions is arbitrary.

Some writers prefer to state what culture is not. Metz, for example, writes that culture "is not a systematic set of logically interrelated propositions about values, norms and the nature of the empirical world," but, she adds at once, it is "a broad, diffuse, and potentially contradictory body of shared understanding about both what is and what ought to be" (1986, 54; see also Rossman, Corbett, and Firestone 1988, 5). I value Metz's reference to "what ought to be" because it captures a common aspect of the translation of culture into curriculum: the often imperative tone of the agents' curricular recommendations. This tone is implied in Goodenough's definition that "a society's culture consists of whatever one has to know or believe in order to operate in a manner acceptable to its members" (quoted in Mehan 1982, 64). When Goodenough speaks of what "one has to know and believe" he points to categories of curricular experience for which agents will have particular recommendations. Cazden and Mehan "think of culture as the normal, expected ways of perceiving, thinking, and behaving of large social groups" (1989, 49), nations, or communities; they exclude the smaller social groups whose "normal, expected ways" are those of a subculture. For my purposes, both culture and subculture are important for examining the culture-curriculum relationship.

Erickson picks up on the subcultural factor in his view of culture as "learned and shared standards for ways of thinking, feeling, and acting," so that he can identify the problem or misfit in the case of the classroom teachers' "learned ways of thinking and acting that have not yet been learned by their students" (1986, 117). An issue in culture-curriculum fit arises from the discrepancies among the involved subcultures, those of the teachers and students in Erickson's example. Based on her research on magnet middle schools, Metz identifies a teacher subculture. It develops by virtue of shared "meaning systems" (see also Maehr 1987, 295–96), and, she usefully adds, "has roots in the larger culture of the society" (1986, 221). Given the prospect of a range of subcultural "meaning systems" operating within the shared space of a school, and within the larger society where subcultures abound, we see the occasion for conflict over what curriculum should prevail.

In practice, what strictly speaking are subcultures writers often refer to as cultures. Thus, Rossman, Corbett, and Firestone (1988) refer to "teacher culture," Metz (1983) to "home culture," Shakeshaft (1987) to "female culture," and

Maehr (1987) to "organizational culture." It is well to bear in mind that subcultures are rooted in the "larger culture of the society" because this suggests the legitimacy of what is an inevitable fact of complex societies: To varying degrees, subcultures are in competition with each other as they try to enact their "meaning systems" in the curricula of their society's schools. It is, therefore, a matter of good guys doing battle with each other as they contend for the right to define what goes on in school.

Considerations of fit—what element of culture goes with what element of curriculum—arise from the concerns of agents of both culture and subculture. In this regard, some curriculum theorists adopt Linton's (1936) tripartite conception of culture. His three components of culture are universals and specialties, which roughly correspond to culture and subculture as noted above, and alternatives, which are departures from ordinary, accepted ways of doing and believing. Smith, Stanley, and Shores (1950) used Linton's conception in their classic *Fundamentals of Curriculum Development*. This entire book is a study of the culture-curriculum relationship (see also Reynolds and Skilbeck 1976), about which they have a particular point of view: ". . . in the core program [which contains the central aspects of culture that Linton calls universals], the social problems criterion . . . constitutes the primary measure of curriculum content" (1950, 743). They state unequivocally that that which "comprises the curriculum" of a school invariably derives from its host culture (10). I cannot imagine curriculum in any other sense; indeed, this is the premise of this chapter. What remains hereafter is to identify what the cultural and subcultural agents (Erickson 1986b; Smith, Stanley, and Shores 1950) believe ought to be (Metz 1986) in regard to perceiving, thinking, and behaving (Cazden and Mehan 1989).

Curriculum, like culture, also has a long history of being defined. Its referents can be as broad as an entire K–12 school system for an entire nation, or as narrow as a particular place, school, grade, or classroom. The planned or formal curriculum is one consideration, and the enacted curriculum, or what teachers actually do in their classrooms, is another. My sense is to stay out of the thicket of existing definitions of curriculum and leave the actual definition, for the purposes of this chapter, to emerge from the many culture-curriculum examples I will cite. Nonetheless, I find it useful to think of curriculum in the three manifestations—explicit, implicit, and null—that Eisner (1979, 74–92) explores. "Explicit" corresponds to the manifest, formal expression of a curriculum, to what can usually be found in plan books or filed manila folders. "Implicit" corresponds to the latent, informal expression of a curriculum, to what otherwise is known as the hidden curriculum (see Dreeben 1968; Jackson 1968; Turner 1983). Often no less important in its consequences than the explicit curriculum, we can infer the existence of the hidden curriculum from observing the conduct of teachers, students, and administrators, from studying tests and homework assignments, and the like. "Null" corresponds to what is untaught and thus not learned at school. The null curriculum is untaught because it reflects unvalued or undervalued aspects of culture for which there is an insufficient constituency, for which no agent or too few or too ineffectual agents have raised a banner and led a cause.

In any event, it is the relationship between culture and curriculum broadly conceived that is my focus, as when Smith, Stanley, and Shores say, "The curriculum is always a reflection of what people think, feel, believe, and do" (1950, 4), and when Reynolds and Skilbeck present curriculum as "a mediation or a bridge between the learner's experiences and the processes, forms and substances of contemporary culture" (1976, 100).

Those curricular specifications that agents endorse are meant to fit their culturally oriented sense of what is good in the curriculum that should be perpetuated, of what is missing and should be included, and of what is included but not in the right degree or right way and should be modified. These generalities get translated into decisions, for example, about what the language of instruction should be; whether and to what extent second languages should be taught; what subjects should be taught and what their relative emphasis and their contents should be; what emphasis should be given to an overall attribute of the school, such as moral instruction, discipline, patriotism, critical thinking, or civic participation in the community; and what should be the nature of and emphasis given to the extracurricular program.

As I discuss below, decisions applicable to curriculum are derived from culturally rooted premises about the nature and/or well-being of children, a particular group, the society, or the world. On behalf of some cultural commitment, someone, an agent, makes a judgment. As determined and absolutist as agents may sound, their outlook represents but one point of view. Accordingly, we must consider that any particular curricular rendering drawn from any particular cultural premise is but one of several judgments that could be made. Recall the case of Cole (1960) and the setting of external examinations in early 20th-century Sierra Leone: What was fitting to colonial masters was not to colonized students and parents. And both perspectives would likely have been rejected by local orthodox religious leaders to whom the Western-type education favored by students and colonialists was anathema in any form. Battiste makes clear that it makes a difference who decides what is fit when he calls literacy developed from within a group "cultural transmission" and literacy developed from outside the group "cultural imperialism" (1984, 3). From the agent's perspective, however, the judgment of fittingness is invariably positive.

The judgment of fittingness represents a point of view that something for some purpose is suitable or appropriate; seemly, proper, or prudent; ready or prepared; or healthy. One's socks or gloves can fit, but not perfectly. When a fit is less than perfect, there are costs and benefits to examine. Socks and gloves can serve their intended purposes, even if the fit is poor; the results may be uncomfortable but not disastrous. In the case of medication and sickness or curriculum and culture, a poor fit can be costly.

What we have seen so far about the concept of fit is that it always represents someone's point of view, and that it is a normative, relational term. Moreover, in modern nations the judgment of fittingness between culture and curriculum is inordinately complex because there is no clear relationship between what is valued, and therefore worthy of perpetuation, and what is done in schools in the name of perpetuation. Like the economist's basic problem of infinite wants with but finite resources to satisfy them, societies have a plethora of cultural claims that seek curricular representation. These claims not only resist translation into a single curricular form about which there is certain consensus, let alone unanimity, they also compete for a school's limited curricular space. Numerous cultural agents, as I discuss in the next section, are intent on adding to what already exists.

AGENTS OF FIT

Many agents are in the academic world, usually in the professional ranks of higher education. James Lynch, Dean of the Faculty of Education at Sunderland Polytechnic in England, is an example. His books (1986, 1987) and talks (1988) are forums for his advocacy of multicultural education. Reynolds and Skilbeck (1976) identify teachers and students as agents. Peterson (1988) alerts us to the role of principals as "culture builders" who "foster the development of norms, values, and beliefs"—the very stuff of culture. Peterson's referent point is the school's organization, but it seems that it could as well be the school's curriculum. He cites Schein (1985) to clarify that principals shape culture—and curriculum, as well—by what they pay attention to, measure, and control; by how they react to critical incidents; by their modeling, teaching, and coaching behavior; by their allocation of rewards and status; and by the criteria they use for selection and promotion of personnel (Peterson 1988, 254). This set of behaviors characterizes the conduct not only of principals but also of several types of individuals (superintendents of schools and other administrators) and groups (foundations and federal agencies, for example) as they play the role of agent.

It does not take much reflection to compose a list of agents. They abound in the United States, where legitimate agents are not confined to professionals in universities and centralized bureaucracies (e.g., state departments of education). Indeed, the more complex and open a society, and the stronger its tradition of local control of education, the more they abound. As a high school teacher, I got my share of materials from patriotic organizations—the American Legion and Daughters of the American Revolution; from business organizations—the Chamber of Commerce and the National Association of Manufacturers; from labor unions—the AFL-CIO; and from manufacturing companies which sent free "instructional" materials. Whether the organizations sponsored an essay contest, distributed materials, or sent out speakers, they had a cultural axe to grind: a way of seeing the citizen's response to country, the voter's selection of candidates, or the worker's relationship to production. In short, the organizations had ideas embodying values they deemed worthy of dissemination.

Following World War II, when the federal government found warrant to amplify its role in education, federal agents joined an already existing large crowd of: professional associations—the National Education Association, the National Council of Teachers of English, the American Federation of Teachers, and the National Association of Secondary School Principals; foundations—Ford, Carnegie, and Rockefeller; regional accrediting bodies; textbook publishers; and a multitude of special interest groups that identified a stake in education with curricular ramifications.

A limited but important group of federal government programs was the subject of a volume edited by Campbell and Bunnell (1963). They included chapters on the National Science Foundation (Mendelson 1963), whose expenditures on education rose in the period 1952–1962 from \$1.5 to 84.5 million; the National Defense Education Act (Kratzmann 1963), whose spending in the period 1959–1962 rose from \$115.3 to \$211.6 million; and the National Merit Scholarship Program (LaVigne 1963), whose participants in the period 1956–1961 rose from 58,158 to 586,813. In curricular terms, these several projects signified emphasis on certain students—the college-bound gifted—and on certain subjects—mathematics, science, and foreign languages. They exemplified the federal government's involvement as an active agent in school affairs, and disposed educators to expect that federal funds would be available to facilitate their response to societal pressures for change.

More so than anywhere else in the world, nonfederal and nonstate levels of government in the United States have significant prerogatives for controlling the operation—administratively and instructionally—of schools. These prerogatives are exemplified by the right of communities to select their administrators and teachers and to purchase their instructional materials in the absence (notwithstanding ACT and SAT tests) of an externally composed, nationally certified school-leaving examination. Which is to say that within local communities there are several types of agents—from parents, parent organizations, and school boards, to administrators, teachers, and counselors. But this is not news. What is news is the undermining of these prerogatives by the increasing role of state and federal agents. In 1947, public schools received 58.9 percent of their financial support from local sources, 39.8 percent from the state, and 1.3 percent from the federal government (Wahlquist et al. 1952, 33). By 1986–1987, the local contribution had declined to 43.7 percent, eclipsed by the state's 49.6 percent and the federal government's 6.4 percent; these are averages which belie much variability. For example, the state's share is 5.9 percent in New Hampshire and 75.1 percent in New Mexico (*Education Week* 1989, 3). In his study of school control, Kirst found that state governments believed local governments did not pay sufficient attention to "curriculum quality, teacher evaluation, and academic standards" to be able "to compete in a world economy" (1988, 7 and 14). Consequently, contrary to past recommendations for decentralized control (see Fein 1971; Levin 1972), and the current decentralizing efforts in Chicago (Designs for Change 1989), we are more likely to read about state initiatives in education. New York's Commissioner of Education, for example, proposes that "the state would set 'standards of excellence' that all schools could aspire to as well as minimum standards that could trigger state intervention" (Jennings 1988, 12).

My intent here is to produce neither a systematic picture nor a history of the expanding efforts of the federal government (see *Harvard Educational Review* 1984 and *Harvard Educational Review's* 1982 special issue on "Rethinking the Federal Role in Education"), or the continuing efforts of professional organizations, foundations, and private interest groups. The results of these several efforts produced an avalanche of words. Indeed, the year 1983 spawned a banner crop of words, as the Carnegie Foundation addressed the American high school (Boyer 1983); the U.S. Department of Education alerted us to reform so badly needed that we had become *A Nation at Risk* (National Commission on Excellence in Education 1983); the National Science Foundation looked, as reform-oriented reports often do, to the next century, focusing on mathematics, science, and technology (National Science Board 1983); and the Education Commission of the States highlighted "excellence," a soon-to-be overused word, as educators and politicians debated and brooded over school improvement (Task Force on Education for Economic Growth 1983).

My intention, rather, is to demonstrate the breadth of work undertaken by numerous agents. In one issue of *Education Week* (November 2, 1988, 10) readers got a page full of national organizations which sought a re-forming of the fit between culture and the curriculum of some level of schooling, a re-forming that incorporated each organization's particular cultural propensities. Several of them were associated with a certain founder—John Goodlad's National Network for Educational Renewal and Theodore Sizer's Coalition of Essential Schools. Others were the work of the rival teacher unions—the American Federation of Teachers' Center for Restructuring and the National Education Association's Mastery in Learning Project and Learning Laboratory Districts. Other groups in the *Education Week* review further suggest the range of agent groups at work: the Association for Supervision and Curriculum Development's Consortium on Restructuring, the Holmes Group's Work on Tomorrow's Schools, the National Association of State Boards of Education's school improvement projects in New Mexico and Washington, and the National Governors' Association's Restructuring Schools Project.

Any list of agents also must include the Supreme Court and its decisions; the impact of national test programs such as the Educational Testing Service's Scholastic Aptitude Test; the work of the various parent groups, notably the National Parent Teacher Association; the data collected by groups such as the National Assessment of Educational Progress; research conducted by groups such as the Rand Corporation; and the consequences of collaboration between a school district and an academic to create schools that incorporate a certain concept. An example is the new magnet school in Indianapolis based on the writing of psychologist Howard Gardner (*Teacher* 1989, 60–61).

We get an idea of a comparable list of agents operating in England from Ball's historical treatment of English in the school curriculum:

> The arenas in which English as a school subject was established—the Board of Education, the English Association conferences, the Newbolt Committee—and the interest groups involved—the universities and public schools, politicians and educational civil servants, and eminent writers and educationalists—clearly define curriculum change in terms of the influence and decision-making and conflicts of interests among a number of overlapping educational elites. (1983, 84)

Ball's colleagues Bowe and Whitty write in the same volume about the need to develop an agent, where now there is none, to express a preferred type of curricular response. Finding in their study of school-leaving examinations that capitalist forces had this important aspect of education to themselves (1983, 245), they urged "the Left to develop a position on curriculum and examinations as part of the broader political strategy of the labor movement" (1983, 246). Bowe and Whitty identify a national political entity—a political party—as the agent. Indeed, where education is centrally controlled, political parties may be crucial agents. Given the diffuse structures of control in American education, however, the educational platform of our political parties is of much less consequence.

The number and diversity of interests of American agents sets the stage for the broad-scale politics of the culture-curriculum fit. Thus, in addition to the direct politics of local school board elections, where the attention is on one particular school district, the politics of the many interested agents may well affect a particular school district but operate on state, regional, or national levels. The local district's school-board guardians contend with competing pressures from numerous other agents.

Having discussed the three concepts of culture, curriculum, and fit, and the variety of agents who advocate a particular relationship among the three, I turn next to illustrations of this relationship drawn primarily from a review of contemporary literature.

THE CULTURE-CURRICULUM RELATIONSHIP

In this section, I will suggest the varied ways that agents seek to have some aspect of culture become manifest in school activity. I consider agents as representatives of a subculture, with subculture conceived loosely as one of the numerous alternative expressions of cultural behavior that contemporary nations harbor. The previous section on agents of fit demonstrated the breadth of this group. In this section we will see the different ways they connect some aspect of culture and its curricular representation or means. The agents often appear as advocates of change. They perceive curriculum as the means to change some aspect of society. The particular change they advocate derives from their cultural orientation. Drawing upon this orientation, they frame a purpose or rationale for what they hope to achieve through schooling. In some of the following examples (see Kickbusch and Everhart [1985] below), however, no agent is present and no change is suggested; the authors depict a status quo which I presume to be the outcome of earlier work by some agent who established a culture-curriculum fit.

The many examples I cite below to explore the association of culture, curriculum, and fit contain, implicitly or explicitly, an if-then type of reasoning. *If* an agent desires that some state of affairs be introduced, improved, or sustained—the "if" term is drawn from the agent's cultural orientation—*then* the schools should do something—the "then" term is drawn from the agent's perception of curriculum. Thus Bennett opens her study with this statement (which has the form more of a rationale than a purpose): "Given that we live in a multicultural society and a world that is becoming increasingly interdependent, multicultural education is an imperative" (1988, 2). As Bennett reasons, if this type of society and world, then that type of schooling. She sees the success of her recommended curriculum in the capacity of teachers to "select texts and resource materials that present authentic images of diverse ethnic and socioeconomic groups" (1988, 2). From an array of possible characterizations of the world and American society, Bennett chose interdependent and multicultural, respectively. These are the cultural facts of consequence to her. Her choice of curriculum activity is meant to fit these facts.

As the forthcoming cases will clarify, there are many different bases that agents can draw upon in addition to the world and American society. In one set, macrolevel in nature, the agents refer to culture, community, society, marketplace, or the world. In another set, microlevel in nature, agents refer to one or several attributes either of a group or subculture, or of individuals. The former (not meant to be exhaustive) includes language, interaction style, cognitive style, interests and values, situational conditions, and ethnicity in general. The latter includes socioeconomic status (SES), gender, and intellectual ability, effort, or achievement. What cultural meaning and, therefore, what curricular consequences these attributes have is a matter of interpretation.

Before continuing with further examples, I will bring together the several new concepts from this section and relate them to culture, curriculum, agent, and fit, the concepts discussed in previous sections. We have seen that culture is "understanding about both what is and ought to be" (Metz 1986, 54); what "one has to know and believe" (Goodenough, quoted in Mehan 1982, 64); the "expected ways of perceiving, thinking, and behaving" (Cazden and Mehan 1989, 49); and "ways of thinking, feeling, and acting" (Erickson 1986a, 117). When I refer to an agent's cultural orientation, I have in mind these several characterizations of culture. The individuals, organizations, and groups I call agents act in behalf of cultures or subcultures to tie all or some manifestation of culture to curriculum. Their intention is to insure a fit at some point between curriculum and culture.

Agents may take large units as their charge, referring to an entire culture, society, or the world, as does Bennett in the above example. Bennett takes as the basis for her agency what she perceives as salient about American society—it is multicultural, and about the world—it is interdependent. Out of the numerous possible focal points of culture, Bennet, embedded in particular cultural and subcultural alternatives, gives voice to two expressions. The number of such expressions is unlimited. Bennett would not soon exhaust what she could say about American society and the world. Of the many possibilities she could identify, she chose two. They came not from out of the blue but, rather, from the complex of her personal cultural and subcultural orientations. They represent the cause she wants served by some aspect of curriculum; they are the warrant for the curricular means she endorses. Bennett did not focus on health, unemployment, or pollution. Had she done so, she would have tendered other bases for thinking about schools, offered warrant for endorsing other aspects of curriculum to fit other aspects of culture.

As I have discussed them, agents appear as conscious activists. This image misrepresents a whole set of agents—teachers, students, and parents, for example—whose behavior "makes" curriculum out of some cultural orientation, but not necessarily in a conscious way or with specified, articulated bases in mind. Their agency is performed in the normal course of playing their role as teacher, student, or parent, although each may join groups and organizations that have been formed to give them voice. Examples below that relate to resistance illustrate this point. When, say, students and parents resist what happens in school, their actions contribute to the null curriculum. They become agents for undoing some aspect of curriculum, such as tests—they should be fewer and easier; homework—there should be less of it; books—which ones are acceptable to read; and sex education—an unsuitable subject for classroom instruction.

Macrolevel Referents for Curriculum

A notably general premise, its breadth at once making it incontestable and not particularly useful, is that schools should transmit the culture of their society. Of course they should! This functionalist orientation (Reynolds and Skilbeck 1976, 32) can be expressed as schools should "prepare the young to take their place in the society of adults" (Kimball 1974, 257). Observers are rarely content to let matters stand at this global level, though where they go thereafter is highly variable.

Kimball (1974) looks at the social and cultural interests of the community in which a school is located. When a school draws upon these interests, for example, in shaping its extracurricular activities, it prepares students to participate in the social life of their community. Less personal than the community as a premise is the marketplace, a starting point of substantial weight for many agents. When Sewall (1983) takes career education and work study programs to task, his grounds are their failure to teach "industry and discipline" or to raise the "status of manual labor" (156–157). In what amounts to a combination of community and marketplace, Labaree (1988) describes Central High School in Philadelphia, a select public institution which for years admitted male students and only by examination. The result was a special group of students drawn largely from the self-employed middle class. When political pressure forced the school to admit more students, the school introduced a track (actually a sidetrack) system for the newcomers so it could be free to continue its special curriculum. The latter changed over the years in response to available job opportunities, but the changes also were in response to pressure from adult constituents that the school provide a moral education, a sense of a "republican community" (5), at one time, and a special economic credential, at another.

Writing in the spirit of the critical theorists, LaBelle observes the painful dilemma of nations with a dominant group and several large minority groups. Minority groups are subjected by the controlling force of the majority. LaBelle translates this dilemma into educational terms by arguing for a curriculum "that would naturally and effectively represent the ethnic-cultural identity of its subgroups while simultaneously deriving its legitimacy from a reflection of the needs and interests of the total population" (1979, 51). This deceptively simple, straightforward premise attracts attention from writer-agents who focus on the pluralist nature of societies throughout the world. Their protective instincts seek justice for subordinated cultural subgroups in danger of being overwhelmed. They often advocate some version of a multicultural curriculum. In this vein, Walkling (1980) wants a "transformationist" curriculum which, by its recognition of "the worthwhile features of any way of life" (94), would be appropriate for a multicultural society. He explicates his premise thus: a multicultural society must provide "a dynamic context [read "curriculum"] in which people's beliefs are exchanged, defended, argued about, converted, retained, assessed, ignored ostentatiously, and so on: all the reactions people have to the beliefs of other people whom they take seriously" (94).

With Walkling's concept of "transformation" we learn of another general function of schooling, the first type being "transmissionist," whereby the charge of schools is perceived as passing on something. Transformationists such as Walkling want to transform the learner's consciousness in schools that have assumed the role of social critic and cultural synthesizer (90). Those who, like Kimball (1974), write about transmission also realize that the pace of change in all nations necessitates curricular attunement to avoid the obsolete, the impractical, and the useless, while favoring knowledge and behavior that is up-to-date. Indeed, it is inconceivable that agents could hold an exclusively transmissionist conception; somewhere, somehow, they have transformationist views. They differ in regard to their conceptions of the rationale, substance, and instructional means to realize their preferred transformation.

Perhaps the most determined transformationists are the critical theorists. In my terms, they pass muster as agents. They oppose the perpetuation of inequality by the schools of capitalist societies. They focus directly on culture and curriculum in their explanations of the relationship between the material conditions of a society and the nature and impact of its schools (see, among others, Apple 1979; Bowles and Gintis 1976; Everhart 1983; Giroux 1981; Willis 1977). In their view, schools reproduce the inequalities inherent in social class distinctions. Accordingly, cultural transmission is the process of reproducing the ideologies, forms of knowledge, and skills that currently are the basis of and perpetuate class distinctions (Giroux 1983).

Critical theorists reject the status quo in the schools they study, often leaving implicit just what type of schools and curriculum could feasibly replace those they reject. To be sure, Giroux (1983) applauds the "resistance" to the ruling class's structures he and others see (Anyon 1979, 1980, for example, and many writers published in the *Journal of Education*). By their resistance, teachers, parents, and students mitigate and manage the adversity of the status quo. The often determined, but far from organized, efforts of students enhances their personal comfort and control in school. Their behavior can affect the pace, cognitive level, and volume of classwork; they also introduce classroom activities that are nonacademic and represent values they esteem. In examples from the United Kingdom, Willis refers to the use of "ignorance" as "a barrier to control" (1977, 192), Measor to "strategies to maintain a balance between the formal and informal pleasures and pressures of school" (1984, 211), and Player to students whose "couldn't care less attitude" was a "stylized form of resistance to alien cultural values" (1984, 222). In an example from the United States, Smith and Andrew refer to the strong antagonism nonstriving black students direct to modifying the behavior of striving black students, saying: "If you get good grades, the other kids'll just kill you" (1988, 26).

Kickbusch and Everhart explore two classrooms in a suburban American high school. They discuss how a "humanistic classroom" and teachers with a "critical perspective" (1985, 313) can mitigate the impact of inequality in these classrooms. The commentaries and insights of critical theorists do not amount to a curricular conception for schools that would replace the curriculum which nationwide reflects the dominant modes of production. Kickbusch and Everhart's notion seems to be of the sort that says, "Here's what to do until the revolution comes," as does Lather's (1986) empowering, emancipatory conception of research, Giroux' (1983) resistance, and Carlson's (1987) activist role for teachers. These and other critical theorists do not typically address the matter of revolution, curricular or otherwise. Their analyses and prescriptions have an in-the-meantime aspect to them, reflecting their antagonism to capitalism and its injustices, and their personal and professional embeddedness in the institutions they professedly abhor.

Broudy (1988), in the course of making a case for the high school's primary emphasis on general education, identifies four uses of schooling—associative, replicative (the most common usage), interpretive, and applicative. Broudy argues for interpretive and applicative because they provide students with the means to live as adults in a complex, changing society. Though Broudy does not use the term "liberatory" to characterize his recommended uses of the school, his emphasis on knowledge and skills congruent with interpretation and application would, in fact, be liberatory, though not as Paulo Freire (1985) imagines it. Freire's hope for the education of the dispossessed peasants of his Brazilian homeland is that learners would become so conscious of the conditions that stifle their lives that they would be motivated and enabled to alter them.

The particulars of transformation are not left to chance. Transformationists, accordingly, may be explicit about the nature of the future to which liberation is to be tied, or about the process for getting there. Beyer's writing is an example of the latter. Appalled by groups which reduce education to "private gain and an accountant's profit/loss sheet for public good" (1988, 3), he urges a restructuring of American schools so they can foster "participatory democracy." He is specific not about a product called "participatory democracy" but about a curricular process that will lead to such a society. His curriculum would encourage the exploration of controversial issues and alternative explanations for important events, as well as develop an appreciation of divergent opinions (1988, 323). Musgrove, reflecting what he sees as the conditions of his United Kingdom homeland, also emphasizes process. He visualizes a "third cultural" reality, arguing that there is need "not to preserve or transmit particular cultures but to transcend them; and the curriculum of any school in a multicultural society will be rooted in the unending dialectic of integration-pluralism" (1982, 183).

In their focus on teacher education, Giroux and McLaren highlight their commitment to the "critical democratic tradition." They seek teachers prepared "for the role of transformative intellectual," teachers who can rethink "the relationship of schooling to the social order" (1986, 237–238). Finally, in this set of process-oriented premises, Cazden and Mehan consider as fact that, given the demography of American society, "teachers and students will not share cultural and social experiences" (1989, 47). Therefore, they advise, teachers must "learn how to learn about students and their families," not as "solution" but as "general procedure" (1980, 55). The result, presumably, is an emergent curriculum and an emergent society.

Strongly contrasting with the process orientation of Beyer, Musgrove, and others is the ideologically specific future of fundamentalist Christians. Christian education leaders establish schools with a scriptural foundation (Peshkin 1986); they aspire to a society with the same foundation. In their schools, children acquire principles to direct what they should think and how they should act in the humanist world they condemn. Christian day school students learn about patriotism, the military, foreign policy, capitalism, and candidates for elected offices—all in the spirit of the sponsoring church's conservative doctrine. Fundamentalist Christians are apt to be transformationists with a vengeance, in strong contrast to the Amish and other small, insular groups (Hostetler 1971). The latter seek schools with a definite ideological thrust, but since they do not proselytize, they are content to perpetuate their own subgroup and leave the larger society to go its own way.

A final macrolevel premise is located in the transnational arena of global economies or multinational politics. The National Governors' Association (NGA), reflecting the contemporary phenomenon of high-level elected officials making their mark as education governor or president, issued a report calling for a curriculum with "foreign languages, international history, geography, and foreign cultures" (Flax 1989, 11). Their rationale, says NGA chairman Governor Bailes of Virginia, is the preparation of students able to do business "anywhere on earth" (Flax 1989, 11; see also Schmidt 1989). Sicinski (1985), similarly transnational but substantively divergent from the NGA, finds his curricular rationale in a "global village" where people need a solidarity as broad as humanity. His concern underscores interdependence and the necessity of mutual understanding; his issues are the need to live well together, not to compete effectively.

Microlevel Referents for Curriculum

Kickbusch and Everhart (1985) studied high school classrooms. They labeled students "conformists" or "nonconformists," which I take as designations of subcultures. Since the conformists saw their school experience as applicable to the valued outcomes of higher education and good jobs, they "affirmed the legitimacy of the dominant curriculum" (309) by their regular attendance, completion of assignments, and participation in class discussions. The curriculum they endorsed offered "formal, academic learning." Conformists affirmed their school experience because it fit them. As the children of college graduates, they were pleased with a school that was instrumental to their status maintenance. Kickbusch and Everhart do not identify an agent as such; I should think, however, they would attribute the prevalence of schools that conformists favor to the capitalist social structure that induces particular forms of reproduction (see also Bowles and Gintis 1977).

The fit between a curriculum, indeed an entire school, and a particular subculture is evident in a range of cases. Hart (1963) focuses on education in "primitive" societies where the curriculum in postpubertal initiation schools is precisely shaped to mold youth into fully fitting members of society. Interestingly, the schools emphasize proper belief and conduct, not how to make a living. The curriculum of the school rests on the undisputed cultural heritage of the tribe. If the ideological foundations of a group are undisputed, the curriculum of its schools is not subject to controversy. Such is the case in Amish and Hutterite communities as regards the conduct of informal education (Hostetler 1987). Their children often attend state schools with a standard public school curriculum. Under such circumstances, the Hutterites strive to control the teachers with lectures, admonitions, gifts, and the insistence that the schools contain no radios, films, or record player. "The English school [the public school taught in English] is encapsulated by the colony pattern, and ideally its influence cannot go beyond the bounds set by its culture" (Hostetler 1987, 132).

In a manner of speaking, Hutterite children already are encapsulated when they enter public school because of their home socialization and because they have attended a kindergarten whose medium of instruction is German, the language of the Hutterites, and that teaches them how to live in Hutterite terms. In contrast, the public school is conducted in English and teaches worldly facts. Valuing both orientations, the Hutterites endorse a form of biculturalism. They strive to maintain their subculture to a degree greater than do most minority subgroups other than the wealthy, whose cultural maintenance is served by carefully selected elite institutions, from nursery through university schooling.

Unlike the Hutterites and the wealthy, who, where they are the majority, can control their children's schools, other subgroups with a strong ideological focus do not successfully encapsulate the schools their children attend. The fundamentalist Christians in Kanawha County, West Virginia, are such a group. Since they did not control the school district their children attended, the district purchased books which they found objectionable. The new readers, they claimed, undermined their basic cultural values (see Hillocks 1978; Kincheloe 1983). What previously had been a fitting place for the education of their children, they condemned as unfitting when the new books entered the curriculum. With their sense of cultural fit violated, they resorted to violence. A group's inability to encapsulate and control a public school often inspires the establishment of private schools based on their particular ideological beliefs. Racial avoidance notwithstanding, many fundamentalist Christian schools arose from the wishes of parents and pastors to fashion schools containing teachers and instructional materials at the service of scripture (see Parsons 1987; Peshkin 1986).

In public school districts where the host community is generally homogeneous, as it tends to be in nonpublic schools, local control enables the development of schools quite fully reflective of prevailing values, beliefs, and behaviors. Teachers and administrators are selected by a school board which acts as the guardian agent of a close school-community fit (Peshkin 1978, 58–99). Supreme Court rulings which forbade religious expression in public schools can be viewed as the work of one agent countermanding the preferences of another, notably the school boards in these homogeneous communities which traditionally enjoyed, for example, daily prayer and the celebration of Christmas.

Judgments about the salubriousness of the close fit in private Christian schools and public rural schools reveal the uncertainty of outsiders about these schools. In the case of Christian schools, fundamentalist Christians enjoy and support the close fit; many nonfundamentalist Christians see the fit as misguided and excessive; while still others, of many different religious persuasions, fear the divisiveness they imagine such schools engender (Peshkin 1986). In the case of rural schools, insiders see the close fit as comfortable and comforting, while outsiders see their comparatively constricted academic opportunities as limiting the life chances of their graduates (Peshkin 1978).

Language, as I referred to above in the cases of the Kaiapo (Simons 1989) and the Diallobé (Kane 1972), becomes a matter of special consideration when the language of instruction differs from that which students learn at home and come to school speaking. Leaders of both the Kaiapo and the Diallobé advocate learning the foreign language which is the *lingua franca* of the schools their children would attend. They see mastery of a particular foreign language as instrumental to economic if not political opportunity. Or, put another way, the warrant for instruction in a particular language is an agent's interest in economic and political opportunity.

The language component of curriculum incites strong emotional responses because it draws upon cultural values relating to patriotism, citizenship, and group (tribe, nation, region, or state) perpetuation (see Friedrich 1968; Sayigh 1968). As a *sine qua non* for participation in their new social group, immigrant children turn readily to learning the new language and, in the process, may never master the language of most comfort to their parents and family elders. Judgments about the culture-curriculum fit for linguistic minorities may be clear-cut to some observers. Rodriguez (1981), for example, endorses learning the public over the private or home language of the student. Depending on the political context, judgments about language are a matter of considerable controversy to others. In the contemporary Soviet Union, the revitalization of local nationalisms engenders issues relating to the relative place of Russian and the languages of the non-Russian nationalities (Kramer 1990). Among other things, Russian is a robust means of social control in the Soviet Union; as such, it bears the stigma of its uninvited supremacy.

In a similar vein, Battiste identifies literacy as a factor in unwanted cultural assimilation, making his point from a study of the Micmac Indians of Northeastern Canada. Powerful colonial and national governments, as well as influential missionaries, have used the acquisition of literacy as a means to impose values of special interest to themselves. Battiste (1984), like the chiefs of the Kaiapo and the Diallobé, says literacy is indispensable for "underdeveloped" or "primitive" peoples to cope in today's world (4), but he wants a respectful literacy of the type advocated for bilingual-bicultural education (21). Literacy that is typically unfitting, and thus "cultural imperialism" is, however, fitting in government and missionary terms.

When the school is an important extension of the familiarities of home, as in the case of Kickbusch and Everhart's (1985) conformists, an ease exists between teachers and students in the many interactions that characterize their instructional relationship. Conversely, when the familiarity—and, thus, the ease—is not a given, then dysfunctions follow. At issue here is not, as above, the language of instruction or what is taught but the nature of student-teacher and student-student interaction. Bowles (1972b) applauds the success of postrevolutionary Cuban education for establishing cooperative relations among students and democratic relations between students and teachers in keeping with the socialist orientation of Cuban society. A world away in the South Pacific, Howard studied a group called the Rotuman and also found grounds for applause. Rotuman teachers "adapted the school to their [students'] community" in regard to "cooperation and competition, to various forms of punishment and reward, and to different teaching rhythms" (1970, 63). They do this notwithstanding that the purpose of education in Rotuma is to make people competent in the modern, urbanized world. This world, however, is remote from prevailing Rotuman tradition. Similar adaptations are reported by Dumont (1969) on the Cherokee, Erickson (1986a) on Native Americans in Alaska (Barnhart 1982) and native Hawaiians in Hawaii (Au and Jordan 1980; Au and Mason 1981), and Dillon (1990) on black Americans.

In the aforementioned cases, there are agents, most usually educators, who have responsibility for the instruction of children whose lives are rooted in a culture different from that of the teachers and the curriculum. The agents urge a curricular adaptation by teachers based on students' accustomed, out-of-school modes of interaction so that instruction can be effective. The warrant for this recommendation is pedagogical (see Epstein 1988) and personal well-being; ultimately, it is political and economic success. Should the adaptation be unsuccessful, incomplete, or untried, student resistance (see Erickson 1986b; Wolcott 1965) can forcibly remind teachers of the gulf between them. In a recent study (Peshkin 1991), a student conveyed his and his fellows' efforts to bring their teacher into line in interactional terms:

> In this one class, Mrs. Rolland, she walked in the first day and there she is. "My name is Mrs. Rolland." I'm this way, I'm that way. I don't do this, I don't do that, I don't take this. That lasted for about a week. We changed her. Where she was Adolf Hitler at the beginning, we turned her into something totally different. We became her friends, is what I feel. She wasn't trying to dominate us anymore. She was trying to be a part of us, is what I feel. She had to get used to us; we're kinda different.

Wolcott's (1982) Kwakiutl students were considerably less gentle with him than were Mrs. Rolland's, a measure, perhaps, of how culturally alien his American ways appeared to them.

At the high school level, an issue is played out in the tension and controversy between teachers of so-called academic and vocational subjects, with ramifications for the distribution of curricular time and resources. Within the academic arena, controversy exists between teachers who see their subject matter as an invitation for intellectual engagement and teachers who see it as an opportunity for developing "appropriate behavior" (Rossman, Corbett, and Firestone 1988). Clearly, the issue here relates to the instrumental outcomes of schooling. A related issue is what knowledge is of most worth. The answer may lie in teacher conceptions of the meaning of their subject. From his study of three high school American history teachers, Evans (1988) observed the influence of their conceptions of history on their selection of content. One teacher saw history as a "moral crusade," a second saw it as a means to develop cosmic awareness, and a third saw it as necessary background for educated citizens. Their common focus on some type of citizenship belies the curricular variations that follow from each teacher's cultural starting point.

The worth of a subject may be plainly conveyed when we see its location on timetables—mornings are reserved for worthier subjects—and the time per week allotted to different subjects; and it is also revealed by what we see designated as "examinable knowledge." To geographers in the United Kingdom, environmental studies did not prove to be sufficiently worthy as an A-level subject. They considered such studies to be watered-down knowledge (Goodson 1984, 35). Also in the United Kingdom, Measor (1984) found students' attentiveness remarkably different in English and mathematics, which students judged as necessary, compared to music, which they judged as not (202–205).

Shortly before Secretary of Education William Bennett left office in 1988 he issued a list of books as part of his model K–8 curriculum. The books, of course, are "classics"—*Great Expectations*, *Ivanhoe*, *The House of the Seven Gables*, and many more. "Classic" is the imprimatur of time-tested literary worthiness. Susan Ohanian (1988) rejects Bennett's choices. Reflecting her experience with minority children, she argues for *Nigger*, *Autobiography of Malcolm X*, and *Manchild in the Promised Land*. They connect with the life of children, says Ohanian, in ways that Ivanhoe never could. Ohanian's preferred books could facilitate "understanding . . . how power, resistance, and human agency can become central elements in the struggle for critical thinking and learning" (Giroux 1983, 293). Bennett and Ohanian, as agents, share an interest in what children read. Their disparate choices reveal the gulf between their views of what use literature should have in the lives of its readers, if not how schools should function in the lives of their students.

Varied cognitive bases selected from an infinite range of cultural possibilities lead to varied curricular circumstances. On the one hand, Heath (1982) demonstrates that black children may not answer teacher questions because they are set in unaccustomed forms which permit one-word answers, whereas the children come to school having learned to see and answer questions about things in context. On the other, Zec, in his examination of multicultural education, urges educators not to build their curriculum on the basis of what "'belongs' to a minority culture" but, rather, on the basis of universal criteria of rationality (1980, 83). His hope is to avoid the hazards of relativism which can result from focusing on the particularities of subcultures.

That children arrive at school having learned ways of thinking about and perceiving matters that the school also deals with is the point of Erickson's (1986) conceptualization of the relationship between culture and science education. Hewson and Hamlyn (1985) exemplify Erickson's point in their study of an African group, the Sotho, and how they use heat metaphors. Bishop (1988) extends the case to mathematics, claiming, in addition to our customarily sweeping view of its universality, that it also is a culture-specific phenomenon. For more examples relating to mathematics, see the symposium papers organized by Lave (1985, 171–213). And for the home culture-school culture point in general, see the work of Jordan (1985) and her associates in Hawaii.

In Jordan's applied anthropological project, her goal is the development of "a culturally compatible program" between home and school, rather than one that is "culturally isomorphic" or "culturally specific" (1985, 117). Efforts to develop culturally compatible programs can flounder when relevant actors in the shaping of curriculum disagree on fundamental matters. This is Erting's (1985) observation after studying deaf students. Teachers and parents of deaf children disagreed on the nature and function of communication and language. Both parents and teachers endorsed a child's fullest participation in society, but by not sharing perceptions of how a successful deaf person behaves in society, they also failed to share understandings about curriculum.

The warrant or purpose of the type of fit Erickson, Jordan, and others discuss is pedagogical, in that they want children who typically have been failures in school to be successes. Though not invariably mentioned, making it in the majority culture is an implied, if not explicit, interest (Harrison 1986). The pedagogical opportunities that culturally compatible programs enable are not meant merely for the students' cultural comfort. Under societal circumstances—such as those of the Australian Aborigines—which threaten a group's integrity, the warrant may be cultural maintenance. Liberman describes such a school in Western Australia. The premise of the school is that since all Aborigines are not and will not be city dwellers, the school's curriculum and teaching should be "consistent with the Aboriginal traditions of the community" (1981, 141). Aboriginal elders, as Liberman writes, vigilantly eliminate all that is European, but they overlook the most critical European curricular element in the school—its English literacy class. However much the indigenous culture shapes classroom texts and discussion, acquiring English proficiency is a powerfully countervailing force to the school's otherwise highly adapted curriculum.

Filipino parents living in Milwaukee recognize the importance of English-language competence. Lacking the Aborigine's sense of threat from the dominant culture, Filipino parents, according to Ammann (1983), enthusiastically promote their children's English-language skills. To be sure, they do not want to abandon all Filipino ways, but they view acquiring American ways as congruent with their sense of identity. Accordingly, they desire and seek no curricular adaptations. The most compatible curriculum for their children is the one available to children of successful white parents.

The matter of curricular compatibility is not confined to situations involving overtly different subgroups, for example, Aborigines in Australia or Filipino newcomers in Milwaukee. We see the concerns of groups for compatibility in the many Supreme Court cases that grow out of accusations of censorship (Flygare 1982; Kemerer and Hirsh 1982; *Time*, August 23, 1982). The incident (Hillocks 1978) created by the reaction of fundamentalist Christians to new textbooks in Kanawha County, West Virginia, reveals the extent to which people will go to insure compatibility.

Censorship epitomizes the extreme to which groups will go to correct curricular circumstances they deem culturally dangerous. Censorship (see Jenkinson 1979; Kemerer and Hirsh 1982) shapes a curriculum by dictating what should be excluded. The agents of censorship—community groups acting on their own or through their school board members—are the agents for suppressing unfitting books and teacher classroom conduct. The issue for educators, as Beezer (1982) frames it, is the extent of teacher authority. The issue otherwise stated is the intent of some subset of noneducators to shape curriculum for the purpose of maintaining ideological purity, personal well-being, or a sense of order or decorum. Rossman, Corbett, and Firestone are explicit on this point: "When the schools are no longer attuned to local culture, parents and other residents apply pressure to bring them back in line with local expectations" (1988, 96). Judging from the substantial increase in censorship attempts (Margolis 1989), individuals and groups (Eagle Forum, Concerned Women for America, and Christians for Excellence in Education) perceive much that is "out of line."

At different times in our national and educational history, race or ethnicity have been advanced as the basis for curriculum development. For a time in the 1960s and 1970s, many individuals and groups argued for the necessity of black or Hispanic studies (see Leslie and Bigelow 1970; Mackey 1970; National Council for the Social Studies 1976; Wagner 1972), the purpose varying from ethnic pride to national well-being: "the Black experience is more than just an important aspect of American life: *it is in fact central to understanding American history at all*. . . . Black studies are needed for everyone, and above all for Whites" (Ad Hoc Committee on the Social Studies 1968, 8–9).

Support for introducing black, Hispanic, or Asian studies arose at a time of intense emotion in American society when minorities rejected the prominence of white males in the conduct of social research, and as its major subjects, as well. Consequently, we saw the proliferation of studies that responded to a new awareness of who were "the people" in America. Examples of such studies are Ladner's *The Death of White Sociology* (1973), Ludwig and Santibanez' *The Chicanos: Mexican American Voices* (1971), TeSelle's *The Rediscovery of Ethnicity* (1973), Cahn's *Our Brother's Keeper: The Indian in White America* (1969), and Kozol's *Death at an Early Age: The Destruction of the Hearts and Minds of Negro Children in the Boston Public Schools* (1967).

The past outpouring of recommendations for ethnic courses in the curriculum has been more than matched by recent recommendations from British, Australian, and

American writers for a multicultural curriculum. Lynch (1983, 1986) is a leader in England, Bullivant (1981a, 1981b, 1984) in Australia, and Banks (1981a, 1981b) in the United States. Banks and Lynch (1986) joined forces to organize a book that explored multicultural education in the United States, Canada, United Kingdom, Australia, and Western Europe. The subtitle of Modgil, Verma, Mallick, and Modgil's (1986) edited volume—*The Interminable Debate*—captures the sense of years of advocating ideas that have not been translated into curricular practice. If the premises of the argument are not moot—that racism, ethnocentrism, invisibility, and inequality are awful—the curricular consequences to be drawn from them are. Despairingly, Banks concludes, "Its [multicultural education's] biggest problem is that we have not had the will and vision to give it a chance to succeed" (1986, 230). Nonetheless, the logic continues to find academic supporters. Ahlquist writes that "Multicultural education . . . should be reflected in every aspect of classroom and school life" (1989, 4). And, perhaps of more importance, it finds political supporters. Note the case of the state of Minnesota requiring all its school districts "to develop 'multicultural and gender fair' curricula" (Rothman 1988, 1). Here the state is the agent, but by leaving the curricular specifics to local districts, they make them agents, as well. The purpose is stated by a representative of Minnesota's board of education: to develop in students "greater understanding and respect for other people" (1).

Class, gender, and intellectual attributes are the bases of curricular formation in the remainder of this section. Their separate treatment here is essentially organizational; these attributes do not actually operate in isolation, either from each other or from the previously discussed bases. What must be understood about these several attributes is that, though they may be seen as sociological, biological, and psychological constructs, they are also cultural constructs. That is, how they are defined and what meaning they have are a matter of cultural construal. For educational purposes, that class differences exist is less an issue than how different agents perceive and act upon the prerogatives of class, the nature of equality, the function of schools, and the concomitant curricular implications.

Among the most extensive studies of the connection between SES and curriculum is Anyon's (1981) year-long investigation of elementary classrooms. Their students were distinguished by four social class levels—working class, middle class, affluent professional, and elite executive. Anyon examined the instructional materials, assignments, class discussions, and tests in these classrooms. She found a correlation: the higher the SES of the students in a classroom, the higher the cognitive level of its curricular elements. That this correlation is not inevitable Dillon (1990) demonstrates in her well-documented case study of low-reading-ability black students in a high school English classroom. The teacher used literature and asked questions that in other settings are associated with higher SES students. When cognitive styles are hierarchically arranged, so are students. Dillon's study provides some grounds for rejecting an invariable association between low SES and cognitive downgrading, but Wilcox concludes from her study of two suburban schools that the propensity to rank students and, therefore, curricular experiences, is located "in the wider society" (1982, 303). Thus, the capacity of educators to ameliorate the situation is limited.

Implicit in the cognitive hierarchy that varies by social class is the judgment that different texts are more appropriate for some than for other types of children. Anyon pursued this point in her study of 17 American history textbooks. She found that "the [textbooks'] historical interpretations provide ideological justification" for the "wealthy and powerful" (1979, 379). From her study of 19th-century England, Purvis (1984) confirms Anyon's finding, as does Thomas (1988) from his study of schooling in Buffalo during the period 1918–1931. And Rossman, Corbett, and Firestone (1988) provide corroborating text from their research in the pseudonymous working class neighborhood of Somerville, but without the ideological tones of Thomas and Anyon.

Somerville High School took pride in its large business education department and annual Business Graduates' Day "when graduates returned and told current students about their careers" (1988, 110). Somerville High graduates successfully found jobs. Thus, Somerville educators resisted the imposition by central administration of additional required academic courses because they reduced the time available for the favored business electives. Giroux argues "that there are complex and creative fields of resistance through which class-, race-, and gender-mediated practices often refuse, reject, and dismiss the central messages of the school" (1983, 260). However, the object of resistance by subordinate groups is not necessarily what Giroux anticipates. We infer from Rossman, Corbett, and Firestone's account that Somerville's working class parents preferred the opportunities provided by their school's commitment to "order and preparation for the world of work" (1988, 126) over those provided by a more academic-oriented curriculum.

The hierarchical arrangement of curricula by SES has a counterpart in what some investigators call "gendered knowledge." "Schools sort and select what knowledge to teach students; most often knowledge by and about nonwhites, and women, is selected out of school knowledge" (Sleeter and Grant 1985, 52). Sleeter and Grant drew this conclusion from their case study of a junior high school that intended to develop an "appreciation of human diversity" (38). Earlier, Anyon observed that what is taught at school—"school knowledge"—is a social product, that is, someone selects it. Those who traditionally made the selections—textbook writers, publishing companies, and educators—acted in terms of norms that did not grant full respect to women. Thus, women have been overlooked or demeaned, on the one hand, or channeled into certain curricular areas, on the other (1979, 382). Anyon's work in textbooks has been buttressed by that of other groups that, in pursuit of fairness and equity as they see it, documents the limitations of textbooks (see Baltimore Feminist Project 1976; Council on Interracial Books for Children 1977).

Instructional materials or courses that honor either males or females may promote limitations for one and opportunities for the other. Purvis (1984) describes the dame school in 19th-century England, which reflected a particular cultural view of females and SES. It offered girls a New Testament lesson, some reading, and a lot of knitting and sewing. With this same cultural view extant, Grafton et al. lament the disproportionate enrollment of English secondary school girls in a child care course. They note with strong approval Sweden's requirement—reflecting a different cultural view—that "home management, typing and technology are to be compulsory for both boys and girls at junior and senior level" (1983, 168).

Measor (1983) has another angle on the matter of gendered knowledge. Based on 18 months of observation of 11- to 13-year-olds in science courses, she identifies a "gender code of behavior." In science classes, girls liked work that involved baby chicks and disliked work that involved dissection, fire, getting dirty, and pyrotechnical displays with chemicals and electricity (173–177). Though Measor acknowledges the culture-based dispositions of female students, she does not unqualifiedly endorse a "feminine science" that would draw its experiments and examples from phenomena more closely allied to the world of females (190). What she, Purvis, Anyon, Grant, and Sleeter want is a curriculum that neither bars females from opportunities that schools may offer nor educates males and females with constricted views about their place in society.

Differential judgments about students that have bearing on curricular decisions derive not only from SES and gender but also from assessments of students' academic achievement, interest, and ability. An outcome of these assessments is the tracking of students into separate curricular channels distinguishable by instructional materials, pace of instruction, and, as Anyon (1981) has shown, the cognitive level of classroom discussions, assignments, and tests. Tracking is a widespread phenomenon (see Cusick 1986; Oakes 1985; Rosenbaum 1976). Teachers support tracking as a viable means to do academic justice to students of diverse intellectual abilities. Bowles sees an insidious motivation behind tracking: "Vocational schools and tracks were developed for the children of working families. The academic curriculum was preserved for those who would later have the opportunity to make use of book learning" (1972a, 44). In fact, in addition to the obvious, designated tracks, high schools contain many cubbyholes for students based on judgments of their ability, as well as of their conduct and emotional condition (see Peshkin 1991). The curriculum in each cubbyhole, as in each track, has the appearance of similarity, in that the subjects taught bear the same name—English, social studies, or mathematics, for example. Beyond the common names, there is little else that is common in the curriculum that students experience who are tucked away in one of a school's several academic resting places.

Cusick (1986) examined curriculum development in three American high schools and was struck by the proliferation of elective courses. Schools rationalize the resulting curricular elongation (see also Powell, Farrar, and Cohen 1985) as meeting students' interests and needs, if not the test of "relevance." The curricular pendulum, however, is swinging increasingly toward the expansion of the required curriculum, argued variably on pedagogical, economic, or military grounds. In this regard, see, for example, California's S.B. 813 (Loren 1985; Odden and Marsh 1988). It also is swinging toward concern for the lack of consensus about "what a proper high school education should be," say Powell, Farrar, and Cohen (1985, 65), a situation they analyze as inviting a greater empowerment of teachers as agents of curriculum development (1985, 309–321).

The most damaging grounds for establishing a fitting curriculum is one based on the judgment of an entire group's ability as inferior. For the most part, it no longer is socially acceptable to make such sweepingly condemning statements, though Jensen's (1969) work is presumed to provide warrant for them. At one time it was acceptable, however, as Ball (1984) reminds us in his study of the colonial curriculum in Africa. Europeans generally believed that Africans were genetically inferior; indeed, when they did well on external examinations, they were given credit not for intelligence but for possessing prodigious memories (136–137). The growth of trade schools in some parts of Africa, and also the limited availability of academic post-primary schooling, developed from judgments about African intelligence and the colonial government's need for low-level labor. Whatever the particular motivation of colonial governments as agents, the putative civilizing effect of the Western-based curriculum often added fervor to their efforts to educate colonized peoples (Sutton 1971).

Colonial settings are rife with attempts to establish a fitting curriculum for the "natives." "Adaptation" is the term most often applied to the movement to identify a curriculum drawn from some agent's assessment of what education the natives needed that would do justice to their home culture. In Africa, the British were the prime architects of adaptation (see Ball 1984; Foster 1965a), in contrast to the French, who thought that the education suitable for French children also was suitable for African children ("Reorganization of Education in French Equatorial Africa," 1965, 53–58). As we have already seen in the reactions of Cole (1960) and his compatriots to an indigenous rather than an external school-leaving examination, African parents and their children resisted the adapted curriculum. Foster (1965b) explained why: The more closely the curriculum for African children approximated that received by English children at home, the greater the economic promise it contained. In short, a fully academic, in contrast to an adapted, curriculum truly provided useful vocational education in the modern sectors of colonial society; the most prestigious, well-paying jobs were the reward for undergoing an education that was unadapted in traditional terms.

In the complex intersection of culture and curriculum, the purposes of ethnic maintenance, assimilation, economic opportunity, and political pride and nation-building often conflict. Variant curricula follow from each. The mix and priority given these purposes varies with the circumstances of colonialism, recent independence, and resurgent nationalism. South Africa's government framed the Bantu Education Act of 1953 in the language of opportunity for blacks and respect for preserving Bantu culture; in fact, behind a façade of ethnic maintenance was the reality of a white regime that precluded blacks from acquiring skills to compete with whites for jobs (LaBelle 1979). In contrast, New Zealand's 19th-century educational policy aimed to assimilate the Maori (Ogbu 1978); Maori schools were to resemble European schools in content and language. Today, the policy for Maori is neither adaptive nor assimilative but bicultural, which is intended as a nod in both, otherwise antagonistic, directions. Newly independent nations face a problem comparable to that of older nations with minority subgroups: how to abandon the vestiges of the colonial curriculum, which enjoyed considerable support among parents and children, while doing justice to the needs of national integration and cultural maintenance, which have the prestige of logic and policy behind them, but not the hearts of school clientele. It is ironic, but understandable, that newly independent nations urgently introduce curriculum changes—teaching in the vernacular and offering compulsory courses in agriculture—that resemble those of the rejected adaptation policies of colonial times (see Urch 1968 and the early five-year plans of nations in Africa and Asia).

RESEARCH PROSPECTS

It is overstatement to picture schools as battlefields for competing conceptions of culture and curriculum, though for brief, painful moments the battlefield image might not be an exaggeration. The sense of sides at war comes to mind in the Kanawha County textbook controversy, as it also does in censorship issues and in multilingual countries that try to establish one particular language, instead of some others, as the medium of instruction in school, unaware of how intimately the mother tongue is situated in the identity of its speakers (LePage 1964, 21). The honoring of one language and the perceived denigration of others can lead to bloodshed.

It is not overstatement to picture schools as arenas for contending views about what subjects to teach, the relative importance of each subject, what content to emphasize within a subject, the level of cognitive challenge at which to pitch a subject, as well as what is appropriate regarding instructional matter, pedagogical styles, types of tests, and so forth. Of the many contenders, or agents, as I have designated them, some are winners—their conceptions find a place in the curriculum. Many more are losers: That is, given a dearth of supporters and also the constraints of time and place, there is not room enough to contain most of what they press schools to do. Given, however, that curricula are subject to change, for agents to have lost at one moment does not condemn their perspective to oblivion. Education is in the political domain of society, and, accordingly, schooling is subject to change in response to new political alignments. This is true at a macrolevel in centralized systems and at both macro and microlevels in decentralized systems.

There is much to learn about the shaping of curriculum at the macro and microlevel from studies conducted within a single nation, as well as from comparative studies conducted simultaneously within several nations. Some agents, political parties and religious groups, for example, direct their efforts toward the curriculum as a whole, their ideology applicable as the basis for an entire curriculum. Learning about the educational commitments of political parties through single-nation and comparative studies would be useful, as would similar studies directed at other agents that have an ideology that is foundational to an entire curriculum.

Single-nation and comparative studies could address other agents—professional organizations within the field of education and interest groups—in order to understand the origin and nature of their conceptions, the means they use to get them enacted, and what success they have had. These agents may have an ideology, as does the Chamber of Commerce, the National Education Association, or the National Association of Secondary School Principals, but it is not likely to be as explicitly articulated or as fixed as that, say, of some religious and political groups. And these agents may address only one aspect of the curriculum, the science or social studies subjects, or one level of schooling, elementary rather than secondary. It would be instructive, moreover, to develop historical accounts of the agents, taking note of the nature and rationale of their changing curricular recommendations and cultural antecedents.

We have much to learn from single-nation, comparative, and historical studies that focus on the work of the agents. At a descriptive level, we know something of value about a society from learning about the number, type, budget, and operation of organizations that address issues of curriculum. Do they operate in an open market? What is the nature of the competition among agents? Are there groups with interests but no agents? Whose interests do the agents represent? Take the case of agents in Spain before and after Franco's regime. Witte (1986) identifies a number of organizations committed to educational development, such as the National Research Centre for Educational Development, Supreme Council for Scientific Research, Educational Science Institute, and the National Institute of Educational Science. It would be useful to learn if these organizations existed in Franco's time, and, if they did, how they worked before and after Franco's death.

Behind the facile expression that schools should serve all the children of all the people is the reality of some groups gaining more benefits than others. Stratifications of knowledge, by gender or social class, include some and exclude other types of students in terms of what they are taught and who is eligible to receive the instruction. There is need for continuing studies of the nature and effects of such stratification, focusing on Eisner's (1979) null curriculum—what is not taught, and on the null group—who is not invited or encouraged to learn. There also is need for studies directed at the consequences of curricula shaped by local control.

In rural and fundamentalist Christian schools, the close fit between a student's school experience and parental expectations clearly satisfied parents (Peshkin 1978 and 1986). However, since rural and Christian schools exist in a society in which other values prevail, paradoxes thereby arise. In the rural school, parents accepted levels of intellectual challenge that many other school systems would not tolerate. And the rural school, by omission, endorsed the racism that often prevails in its host community. It is easy to imagine a curriculum that the rural constituency would reject. By being responsive to other values, such a curriculum would alter the prevailing close fit between the culture of the rural subgroup and the school. Paradoxes also arise from the practices of many Christian schools, which, by their rigid commitment to doctrinal orthodoxy, denigrate other believers and nonbelievers alike. Though such schools exist because of our national commitment to the principle of pluralism, their curriculum may give no credence to this principle.

With regard to Christian and other types of nonpublic schools, both denominational and nondenominational, the concept of fit suggests the promise of several inquiries. Nonpublic schools may originate in the desire of a particular subgroup to establish a school that fits its own cultural orientation, a school formed in particular class, ideological, or pedagogical terms. Research that is either contemporary or historical, single- or multination, would reveal a great deal about subgroups themselves (see Musgrove 1982, 131) and the paradoxes they give rise to, as well as about the school and society in which rejection of public education is taking place.

It would be productive to examine the consequences of close culture-curriculum fits, asking whose interests, needs, and values do such close fits neglect or exclude, and what price may be paid by students who are being instructed by such curricula. One could get at the dynamics of maintaining a particular fit by a study of the hiring practices of school districts, attending to the details of what emphasis they give to the candidate's intellectual accomplishments, nonacademic activities, residential background, university attended, and so forth.

The issue of whom schools should serve is at least implicit in all considerations of fit. For while it may be very appealing to see one's children attending a school that in some sense was fashioned in one's own image, the results of this fashioning could be detrimental to other highly valued interests. This is a problem whether schools are controlled by a centralized ministry of education or by a decentralized system, such as that of the United States. The problem is damnably palpable in the latter instance because Americans are accustomed to thinking of schools as their own, of feeling a possessiveness and attendant prerogatives that belie the fact of broader societal interests. Thereby hangs another set of studies. They would examine the interplay of policies and pressures that arise from local, state, and federal interests, focusing on the particular types of curricular fits pursued by agents at each level.

A whole range of studies is possible under the conditions of centralized control. Such control tends to put schools at some distance from its users. The distance may be bridged by local-level bodies, such as school boards and school councils, that connect parents to their childrens' school. How do parents and other agents see their role in regard to curriculum? Are there channels through which protest can be registered short of the next national election? Is it the case, as Horio (1988) claims in Japan, that teachers have no freedom to determine the curriculum and parents have no freedom to affect what their children learn? What would diverse samples of Japanese and American parents say about whose values their schools should reflect and how responsive the curriculum should be to local subcultural variations?

The fact that one group's good fit is another group's misfit indicates the desirability of cost-benefit analyses that ask, What is lost in the course of gaining something else? Do the gains amply compensate the losses, and how can such estimations be made? Who is benefiting and who is losing? Since there is no curricular vacuum anywhere, something new always enters the curricular field with something old in its way, so to speak. Thus, curricular change involves trade-offs, something relinquished for something introduced. Perhaps no place more than in third world nations is the problem of trade-offs more painful. As long-colonized, newly independent states, they try to throw off the stigmatized vestiges of their colonial curriculum; indigenize their curriculum (see, e.g., Toure 1965) to give honor to their history, literature, art, and languages; and introduce courses that reflect their urgent need for survival in economic, political, and technological terms. The curriculum-making policies and practices of these nations provide unlimited opportunities for serious scholarship.

Curricular accommodations made to get teachers closer to the cultural affinities of their students (as in Au and Jordan 1980; Au and Mason 1981) are resisted by those who fear that such students might thereby remain overly attached to their home culture at the expense of the national or dominant culture. Such fears are manifest in the passage by state legislatures of laws that make English the official language and in the antagonism many lay persons and educators direct to bilingual education. What, in fact, are the outcomes of culturally accommodated classrooms? Are their students any less attached to national values and symbols? Are the pedagogical gains of such schools and classrooms acquired at the cost of lessened devotion to national well-being?

From another angle, one that supports the idea of curricular accommodations to students' subcultural distinctions, there is need for further examination of the broker function (Dillon 1990) that teachers play in such classrooms. How do they learn the broker role? Does the role differ with students from different subcultures? with the age of the children? with the subject being taught? with the larger cultural context within which the school and classroom are located? Are there circumstances in which such curricular accommodation is unsound? Is there an upper limit to the age and grade of the students when it should be stopped?

The premise underlying all curricular change is that educators can modify their usual practices. Yet most recommendations for redefining a prevailing culture-curriculum fit refer to schools where some such fit already prevails as the status quo, and where, therefore, educators, if not students and parents, have learned to work in the service of this fit. Moreover, Feiman-Nemser and Floden (1986) cite the findings of Doyle and Ponder (1977) to note that "teachers were most receptive to proposals for change that fit with current classroom procedures" and those of Cuban (1984) to note that "certain formats like the recitation persist because they fit the environmental demands of classrooms" (516). That educators are capable of modifying how they perform is far from reassuring. Can and will they make the modifications entailed by proposals for change? The energy, effort, emotion, and care different individuals invest in any extant fit dispose them to like things staying basically as they are. We do not understand sufficiently well what their cultural stakes are and how they attach students, teachers, parents, and school board members to a particular curricular state of affairs. The consequence of not being well understood is resistance (Giroux 1983), although resistance is made not only to proposals for change but also to existing states of affairs.

When superintendents, as agents, strive to change some aspect of curriculum, what are they up against? What is the magnitude of what must be relinquished by those who have been party to a particular fit? Do superintendents focus on the out-there of instructional materials or methods and fail to grasp the inertia of the in-here of cultural orientations, the personal antecedents of what goes on out there? Metz (1986) captures the complexity of the task of change as it pertains to teachers, but her point applies equally well to others:

> A principal who wants to change a faculty culture must try to understand it and its sources, and then try to find a way to change the circumstances which gave rise to it, to give currency to alternative interpretations of common events, and to offer other, more constructive, ways of meeting the needs it serves. (222)

Case studies of principals and others, both successes and failures, would provide much needed insight into curricular undertakings that are driven by education-oriented governors and state legislatures, as well as by the much publicized reports of high-status blue-ribbon committees. Promising insights also would result from studies of the fate of any report or conference that makes formal recommendations for curriculum changes. Such case histories could prove to be usefully sobering documents.

These many research possibilities may well founder, however, without increasingly sophisticated conceptualizations of fundamental matters, such as the question of whom the schools should serve, and the related one of what constitutes a fitting curriculum. The manifold perspectives that can be brought to bear on the determination of fit is a concomitant of an open, democratic society. These manifold perspectives emerge from the numerous subcultural variations that compose contemporary societies. While power may give precedence to the interests of the mighty, the ubiquity of voices speaking on behalf of equality and justice can leaven the impact of this precedence and appropriately complicate the establishment of the culture-curriculum relationship.

Confronted with an array of voices, and thus of divergent purposes—for assimilation, ethnic or community maintenance, economic competitiveness, status maintenance or reversal, citizenship, ad infinitum—professionals and laypersons alike are understandably confused, if not moved to avoidance, lethargy, and inaction. Would not agents of fit, from teachers in the classroom to bank presidents who chair blue-ribbon committees to would-be education presidents, be helped by knowing who their competition is? By knowing that the viability of their competition is testimony to the intellectual and moral strength of their society? And also by knowing that since wishes are not horses, beggars don't ride. Thus, making recommendations for curricular change is not tantamount to having a magic wand able to wave in tomorrow's new culture-curriculum fit. Which fact gives fits to the uninformed. We can never know enough about the cultural roots of curriculum, who is attached to these roots, and to what ends, if any, the elements of curriculum will relate.

Chief Poropot, speaking prophetically, reasoned that the antiquity of his tribe's language would ensure its survival. His prophecy may be wishful thinking. History better supports his assertion that learning Portuguese is necessary for his people to defend themselves. For this judgment he earns his spurs as an agent, although future generations of Kaipo could well construe the entry of the Portuguese language into Kaipo life as a major step toward the extinction of their traditional culture. The fitting of Kaipo children into modern Brazilian society by their access to Portuguese may simultaneously unfit them for sustaining a Kaipo society of any integrity, let alone the society of their parents and grandparents. Exploring the complications attending the many fits of culture and curriculum strike me as a worthy scholarly undertaking, one that bears heavily on critical issues of personal and collective identity, of who we are and who we can and mean to be.

References

Ad Hoc Committee on the Social Studies. 1968. *The Wingspread Report*. Racine, WI: National Association of Independent Schools.

Ahlquist, Roberta. 1989. "Developing Our Diverse Voices: Critical Pedagogy for the Multicultural Classroom." Paper presented at the annual meeting of the American Educational Research Association, San Francisco, CA.

Ammann, Richard. 1983. "Transmitting Filipino-American Ethnolinguistic Patterns." Paper presented at the annual meeting of the American Anthropological Association, Chicago. (ERIC Reports, ED245026. Microfiche.)

Anyon, Jean. 1979. Ideology and United States history textbooks. *Harvard Educational Review* 49(3): 361–386.

Anyon, Jean. 1980. Social class and the hidden curriculum of work. *Journal of Education* 162(1): 67–92.

Anyon, Jean. 1981. Social class and school knowledge. *Curriculum Inquiry* 11(1): 3–42.

Apple, Michael. 1979. *Ideology and Curriculum*. London: Routledge & Kegan Paul.

Au, Katheryn H., and Cathie Jordan. 1980. "Teaching Reading to Hawaiian Children: Finding a Culturally Appropriate Solution." In *Culture in the Bilingual Classroom*, edited by Henry Trueba, Grace P. Guthrie, and Kathryn H. Au. Rowley, MA: Newbury House.

Au, Kathryn H., and Jana Mason. 1981. Social organizational factors in learning to read: The balance of rights hypothesis. *Reading Research Quarterly* 17(1): 115–152.

Ball, Stephen J. 1983. "A Subject of Privilege: English and the School Curriculum." In *Curriculum Practice: Some Sociological Case Studies*, edited by Martyn Hammersley and Andy Hargreaves. London: Falmer.

Ball, Stephen J. 1984. "Imperialism, Social Control and the Colonial Curriculum in Africa." In *Defining the Curriculum: Histories and Ethnographies*, edited by Ivor F. Goodson and Stephen J. Ball. London: Falmer.

Baltimore Feminist Project. 1976. *Sexism and Racism in Popular Basal Readers*. New York: Racism and Sexism Resource Center for Educators.

Banks, James A., ed. 1981a. *Education in the 80's: Multiethnic Education*. Washington, DC: National Education Association.

Banks, James A. 1981b. *Multiethnic Education: Theory and Practice*. Boston: Allyn & Bacon.

Banks, James A. 1986. "Multicultural Education and its Critics: Britain and the United States." *In Multicultural Education: The Interminable Debate*, edited by Sohan Modgil, et al. London: Falmer.

Banks, James A., and James Lynch, eds. 1986. *Multicultural Education in Western Societies*. London: Holt, Rinehart and Winston.

Barnhart, Carol. 1982. "Tuning in: Athabaskan Students and Athabaskan Teachers." In *Crosscultural Issues in Alaskan Education*, vol. 2, edited by Ray Barnhart. Fairbanks: University of Alaska, Center for Crosscultural Studies.

Battiste, Marie. 1984. "Micmac Literacy and Cognitive Assimilation." Paper presented at the International Conference of the Mokakit Indian Education Research Association, London, Ontario, Canada. (*ERIC Reports*, ED267957. Microfiche.)

Beezer, Bruce. 1982. How extensive is teacher authority to determine classroom methodology? *Phi Delta Kappan* 63(9): 615–618.

Bennett, Christine. 1988. "The Effects of a Multicultural Education Course on Preservice Teachers' Attitudes, Knowledge, and Behavior." Paper presented at the annual meeting of the American Educational Research Association, New Orleans, LA.

Beyer, Landon. 1988. "Schooling for the Culture of Democracy." In *The Curriculum*, edited by Landon Beyer and Michael Apple. New York: State University Press.

Bishop, Alan J. 1988. The interactions of mathematics education with culture. *Cultural Dynamics* 1(2): 145–157.

Bowe, Richard, and Geoff Whitty. 1983. "A Question of Content and Control: Recent Conflicts over the Nature of School Examinations at 16+." In *Curriculum Practice: Some Sociological Case Studies*, edited by Martyn Hammersley and Andy Hargreaves. London: Falmer.

Bowles, Samuel. 1972a. "Unequal Education and the Reproduction of the Social Division of Labor." In *Schooling in a Corporate Society*, edited by Martin Carnoy. New York: McKay.

Bowles, Samuel. 1972b. "Cuban Education and the Revolutionary Ideology." In *Schooling in a Corporate Society*, edited by Martin Carnoy. New York: McKay.

Bowles, Samuel, and Herbert Gintis. 1976. *Schooling in Capitalist America*. London: Routledge & Kegan Paul.

Boyer, Ernest. 1983. *High School: A Report on Secondary Education in America*. Princeton, NJ: Carnegie Foundation for the Advancement of Teaching.

Broudy, Harry. 1988. *The Uses of Schooling*. New York: Routledge & Kegan Paul.

Bullivant, Brian M. 1981a. *The Pluralist Dilemma in Education: Six Case Studies*. Sydney: George Allen & Unwin.

Bullivant, Brian M. 1981b. *Race, Ethnicity and Curriculum*. Melbourne: Macmillan.

Bullivant, Brian M. 1984. *Pluralism: Cultural Maintenance and Evolution*. Clevedon, Australia: Macmillan.

Cahn, Edgar S., ed. 1969. *Our Brother's Keeper: The Indian in White America*. Washington, DC: New Community Press.

Campbell, Roald F., and Robert Bunnell, eds. 1963. *Nationalizing Influences on Secondary Education*. Chicago: Midwest Administration Center.

Carlson, Dennis. 1987. Teachers as political actors: From reproductive theory to the crisis of schooling. *Harvard Educational Review* 57(3): 283–307.

Cazden, Courney B., and Hugh Mehan. 1989. "Principles from Sociology and Anthropology: Context, Code, Classroom, and Culture." In *Knowledge Base for the Beginning Teacher*, edited by Maynard C. Reynolds. Oxford: Pergamon Press.

Cole, Robert W. 1960. *Kossoh Town Boy*. London: Cambridge University Press.

Council on Interracial Books for Children. 1977. *Stereotypes, Distortions and Omissions in U.S. History Textbooks*. New York: Racism and Sexism Resource Center for Educators.

Cuban, Larry. 1984. *How Teachers Taught: Constancy and Change in American Classrooms: 1890–1980*. New York: Longman.

Cusick, Philip. 1986. *The Egalitarian Ideal and the American High School*. New York: Longman.

Designs for Change. 1989. *The Chicago School Reform Act: Highlights of Public Act 85-1418*. Chicago.

Dillon, Deborah R. 1990. Showing them that I want them to learn and that I care about who they are: A microethnography of the social organization of a secondary low track English-reading classroom. *American Educational Research Journal* 26(2): 227–259.

Doyle, Walter, and Gerald Ponder. 1977. The practicality ethic in teacher decision making. *Interchange* 8(3): 1–12.

Dreeben, Robert. 1968. *On What Is Learned in School*. Reading, MA: Addison-Wesley.

Dumont, Robert V. 1969. Cherokee children and the teacher. *Social Education* 33(1): 70–72.

Education Week 1988. November 2: 10.

Education Week 1989. Diffusion network finally funds holocaust program. October 4: 20.

Education Week 1989. School dollars: Where they come from, where they go. October 12: 3.

Eisner, Eliot W. 1979. *The Educational Imagination*. New York: Macmillan.

Epstein, Joyce. 1988. "Effective Schools or Effective Students: Dealing with Diversity." In *Policies for America's Public Schools*, edited by Ron Haskins and Duncan Mac Rae. Norwood, NJ: Ablex.

Erickson, Frederick. 1980. Culture difference and science education. *The Urban Review* 18(2): 117–24.

Erickson, Frederick. 1986. "Qualitative Methods in Research on Teaching." In *Handbook of Research on Teaching*, 3rd ed., edited by Merlin C. Wittrock. New York: Macmillan.

Erting, Carol. 1985. Cultural conflict in a school for deaf children. *Anthropology and Education Quarterly* 16(3): 225–243.

Evans, Ronald W. 1988. Lessons from history: Teacher and student conceptions of the meaning of history. *Theory and Research in Social Education* 16(3): 203–225.

Everhart, Robert B. 1983. *Reading, Writing and Resistance: Adolescence and Labor in a Junior High School*. London: Routledge & Kegan Paul.

Feiman-Nemser, Sharon, and Robert E. Floden. 1986. "The Cultures of Teaching." In *Handbook of Research on Teaching*, 3rd ed., edited by Merlin C. Wittrock. New York: Macmillan.

Fein, Leonard J. 1971. *The Ecology of the Public Schools*. New York: Pegasus.

Flax, Ellen. 1989. Emphasis on international education essential to economy, governors say. *Education Week* March 8: 11.

Flygare, Thomas J. 1982. Supreme Court perpetuates confusion in school library censorship case. *Phi Delta Kappan* 64(3): 208–209.

Foster, Philip J. 1965a. *Education and Social Change in Ghana*. London: Routledge & Kegan Paul.

Foster, Philip J. 1965b. "The vocational school fallacy in development planning." In *Education and Economic Development*, edited by C. Arnold Anderson and Mary Jean Bowman. Chicago: Aldine.

Freire, Paolo. 1985. *The Politics of Education*. South Hadley, MA: Bergin and Garvey.

Friedrich, Paul. 1968. "Language and Politics in India." In *Schools in Transition: Essays in Comparative Education*, edited by Andrea M. Kazamias and Erwin H. Epstein. Boston: Allyn & Bacon.

Giroux, Henry A. 1981. *Ideology, Culture and the Process of Schooling*. Philadelphia, PA: Temple University Press.

Giroux, Henry A. 1983. Theories of reproduction and resistance in the new sociology of education. *Harvard Educational Review* 53(3): 257–293.

Giroux, Henry A., and Peter McLaren. 1986. Teacher education and the politics of engagement: The case for democratic schooling. *Harvard Educational Review* 56(3): 213–238.

Goodson, Ivor F. 1984. "Subjects for Study: Towards a Social History of Curriculum." In *Defining the Curriculum: Histories and Ethnographies*, edited by Ivor F. Goodson and Stephen J. Ball. London: Falmer.

Grafton, Teresa, et al. 1983. "Gender and Curriculum Choice." In *Curriculum Practice: Some Sociological Case Studies*, edited by Martyn Hammersley and Andy Hargreaves. London: Falmer.

Harrison, Barbara. 1986. Manokotak: A study of school adaptation. *Anthropology and Education Quarterly* 17(2): 100–110.

Hart, C. W. M. 1963. "Contrasts Between Prepubertal and Postpubertal Education." In *Education and Culture*, edited by George Spindler. New York: Holt, Rinehart and Winston.

Harvard Educational Review 1982. Rethinking the federal role in education. 52(4): 371–589.

Harvard Educational Review 1984. Symposium on the year of the reports: Responses from the educational community. 54(1): 1–31.

Heath, Shirley B. 1982. "Questioning at Home and at School: A Comparative Study." In *Doing the Ethnography of Schooling*, edited by George Spindler. New York: Holt, Rinehart and Winston.

Hewson, Mariana G., and Daryl Hamlyn. 1985. Cultural metaphors—Some conceptions for science education. *Anthropology and Education Quartery* 16(7): 31–46.

Hillocks, George. 1978. Books and bombs: Ideological conflict and the schools. *School Review* 86(4): 632–654.

Holmes, Cynthia. 1989. Illinois high schools to study holocaust. *Daily Illini* September 12: 7.

Horio, Teruhisa. 1988. *Educational Thought and Ideology in Modern Japan*. Tokyo: University of Tokyo Press.

Hostetler, John A. 1971. *Children in Amish Society: Socialization and Community Education*. New York: Holt, Rinehart and Winston.

Hostetler, John A. 1987. "Education and Communitarian Societies: The Old Order Amish and the Hutterian Brethren." In *Education and Cultural Process*, edited by George Spindler, 2nd ed. Prospect Heights, IL: Waveland Press.

Howard, Alan. 1970. *Learning to be Rotuman: Enculturation in the South Pacific*. New York: Teachers College Press.

Jackson, Philip W. 1968. *Life in Classrooms*. New York: Holt, Rinehart and Winston.

Jenkinson, Edward B. 1979. *Censors in the Classroom: The Mindbenders*. Carbondale, IL: Southern Illinois University Press.

Jennings, Lisa. 1988. New York plan: Parents may leave failing schools. *Education Week* October 12: 12.

Jensen, Arthur. 1969. How much can we boost I.Q. and scholastic achievement? *Harvard Educational Review* 39(7): 1–123.

Jordan, Cathie. 1985. Translating culture: From ethnographic information to educational programs. *Anthropology and Education Quartery* 16(2): 105–223.

Kane, Cheikh Hamidou. 1972. *Ambiguous Adventure*. London: Heinemann.

Kemerer, Frank R., and Stephanie A. Hirsch. 1982. School library censorship comes before the Supreme Court. *Phi Delta Kappan* 63(7): 444–447.

Kickbusch, Kenneth W., and Robert B. Everhart. 1985. Curriculum, practical ideology, and class contradiction. *Curriculum Inquiry* 15(3): 281–317.

Kimball, Solon T. 1974. *Culture and the Educative Process*. New York: Teachers College Press.

Kincheloe, Joe L. 1983. *Understanding the New Right and Its Impact on Education*. Bloomington, IN: Phi Delta Kappa Educational Foundation.

Kirst, Michael W. 1988. *Who Should Control Our Schools: Reassessing Current Policies*. Stanford, CA: CERAS, Stanford University.

Kozol, Jonathan. 1967. *Death at an Early Age: The Destruction of the Hearts and Minds of Negro Children in the Boston Public Schools*. New York: Bantam Books.

Kramer, Jane. 1990. Letter from Europe (The Soviet Union). *New Yorker* March 12: 74–90.

Kratzmann, Arthur. 1963. "The National Defense Education Act of 1958." In *Nationalizing Influences on Secondary Education*, edited by Roald F. Campbell and Robert A. Bunnell. Chicago: Midwest Administration Center.

Labaree, David F. 1988. *The Making of an American High School*. New Haven, CT: Yale University Press.

LaBelle, Thomas J. 1979. Schooling and intergroup relations: A comparative analysis. *Anthropology and Education Quarterly* 10(1): 43–60.

Ladner, Joyce, ed. 1973. *The Death of White Sociology*. New York: Random House.

Lather, Patti. 1986. Research as praxis. *Harvard Educational Review* 56(3): 257–277.

Lave, Jean. 1985. The social organization of knowledge and practice: A symposium. *Anthropology and Education Quarterly* 16(3): 171–213.

LaVigne, Lorraine. 1963. "The National Merit Scholarship Program." In *Nationalizing Influences on Secondary Education*, edited by Roald F. Campbell and Robert A. Bunnell. Chicago: Midwest Administration Center.

LePage, Robert B. 1964. *The National Language Question*. London: Oxford University Press.

Leslie, Larry L., and Ronald C. Bigelow. 1970. Black studies: A practical alternative. *Clearing House* 44(8): 479–482.

Levin, Henry M. 1972. "The Case for Community Control of the Schools." In *The Political Economy of Education in America*, edited by Martin Carnoy. New York: McKay.

Liberman, Kenneth. 1981. Aboriginal education: The school at Strelles, Western Australia. *Harvard Educational Review* 51(1): 139–144.

Linton, Ralph. 1936. *The Study of Man*. New York: Appleton-Century.

Loren, Kaye. 1985. *Making the Grade? Assessing School Districts' Progress on S.B. 813*. Sacramento, CA: Tax Foundation.

Ludwig, Ed, and James Santibanez, eds. 1971. *The Chicanos: Mexican American Voices*. Baltimore, MD: Penguin.

Lynch, James. 1983. *The Multicultural Curriculum*. London: Batsford.

Lynch, James. 1986. *Multicultural Education*. London: Routledge & Kegan Paul.

Lynch, James. 1987. *Prejudice Reduction and the Schools*. New York: Nichols.

Lynch, James. 1988. "Pedagogical Strategies to Reduce Prejudice: Towards Middle Range Theories." Paper presented at the annual meeting of the American Educational Research Association, New Orleans, LA.

Mackey, James. 1970. Rationale for black studies. *Social Studies* 61(7): 323–325.

Maehr, Martin L. 1987. "Managing Organizational Culture to Enhance Motivation." In *Advances in Motivation and Achievement: Enhancing Motivation*, edited by Martin L. Maehr and Douglas A. Kleiber. Greenwich, CT: JAI Press.

Margolis, Gary. 1989. Report reveals censorship in public schools on the rise. *The Daily Illini*. September 12: 3, 8.

Measor, Lynda. 1983. "Gender and the Sciences: Pupils' Gender-Based Conceptions of School Subjects." In *Curriculum Practice: Some Sociological Case Studies*, edited by Martyn Hammersley and Andy Hargreaves. London: Falmer.

Measor, Lynda. 1984. "Pupil Perceptions of Subject Status." In *Defining the Curriculum: Histories and Ethnographies*, edited by Ivor F. Goodson and Stephen J. Ball. London: Falmer.

Mehan, Hugh. 1982. "The Structure of Classroom Events and Their Consequences for Student Performance." In *Children In and Out of School: Ethnography and Education*, edited by Perry Gilmore and Allan A. Glatthorn. Washington, DC: Center for Applied Linguistics.

Mendelson, Lloyd J. 1963. "The National Science Foundation." In *Nationalizing Influences on Secondary Education*, edited by Roald F. Campbell and Robert A. Bunnell. Chicago: Midwest Administration Center.

Metz, Mary H. 1983. Sources of constructive social relationships in an urban magnet school. *American Journal of Education* 91(2): 202–245.

Metz, Mary H. 1986. *Different by Design: The Context and Character of Three Magnet Schools*. New York: Routledge & Kegan Paul.

Modgil, Sohan, et al., eds. 1986. *Multicultural Education: The Interminable Debate*. London: Falmer.

Musgrove, Frank. 1982. *Education and Anthropology: Other Cultures and the Teacher*. New York: Wiley.

National Commission on Excellence in Education. 1983. *A Nation at Risk: The Imperative for Educational Reform*. Washington, DC: U.S. Department of Education.

National Council for the Social Sciences. 1976. *The Taskforce on Ethnic Studies Curriculum Guidelines*. Arlington, VA: National Council for the Social Studies.

National Science Board Commission on Precollege Education in Mathematics, Science, and Technology. 1983. *Educating Americans for the 21st Century*, 4 vols. Washington, DC: National Science Foundation.

Oakes, Jeannie. 1985. *Keeping Track: How Schools Structure Inequality*. New Haven, CT: Yale University Press.

Odden, Allan, and David Marsh. 1988. How comprehensive reform legislation can improve secondary schools. *Phi Delta Kappan* 69(8): 593–598.

Ogbu, John. 1978. *Minority Education and Caste*. New York: Academic Press.

Ohanian, Susan. 1988. How to create a generation of "aliterates." *Education Week* October 12: 32.

Parsons, Paul F. 1987. *Inside America's Christian Schools*. Macon, GA.: Mercer University Press.

Peshkin, Alan. 1978. *Growing Up American: Schooling and the Survival of Community*. Chicago: University of Chicago Press.

Peshkin, Alan. 1986. *God's Choice: The Total World of a Fundamentalist Christian School*. Chicago: University of Chicago Press.

Peshkin, Alan. 1991. *The Color of Strangers, the Color of Friends: The Play of Ethnicity in School and Community*. Chicago: University of Chicago Press.

Peterson, Kent. 1988. Mechanisms of culture building and principals' work. *Education and Urban Society* 20(3): 250–261.

Player, John. 1984. "The Amorphous School." In *Defining the Curriculum: Histories and Ethnographies*, edited by Ivor F. Goodson and Stephen J. Ball. London: Falmer.

Powell, Arthur G., Eleanor Farrar, and David K. Cohen. 1985. *The Shopping Mall High School: Winners and Losers in the Educational Marketplace*. Boston: Houghton Mifflin.

Purvis, June. 1984. "The Experience of Schooling for Working-Class Boys and Girls in Nineteenth-Century England." In *Defining the Curriculum: Histories and Ethnographies*, edited by Ivor F. Goodson and Stephen J. Ball. London: Falmer.

"Reorganization of Education in French Equatorial Africa." 1965. In *Education and Nation Building in Africa*, edited by Laing G. Cowan, James O'Connell, and David G. Scanlon. New York: Praeger.

Reynolds, John, and Malcolm Skilbeck. 1976. *Culture and the Classroom*. London: Open Books.

Rodriguez, Richard. 1981. *Hunger of Memory*. Boston: Godine.

Rosenbaum, James. 1976. *Making Inequality: The Hidden Curriculum of High School Tracking*. New York: Wiley.

Rossman, Gretchen B., H. Dickinson Corbett, and William A. Firestone. 1988. *Change and Effectiveness in Schools: A Cultural Perspective*. Albany, NY: SUNY Press.

Rothman, Robert. 1988. Minnesota to mandate "multicultural and gender fair" curricula. *Education Week* December 14: 1.

Sayigh, Rosemary. 1968. "The Bilingualism Controversy in Lebanon." In *Schools in Transition: Essays in Comparative*

Education, edited by Andreas M. Kazamias and Erwin H. Epstein. Boston: Allyn & Bacon.

Schein, Edgar N. 1985. *Organizational Culture and Leadership*. San Francisco, CA: Jossey-Bass.

Schmidt, Peter. 1989. Governors stress curricular reforms as linchpin of restructuring efforts. *Education Week* September 27: 10.

Sedlak, Michael, et al. 1986. *Selling Students Short: Classroom Bargains and Academic Reform in the American High School*. New York: Teachers College Press.

Sewall, Gilbert T. 1983. *Necessary Lessons: Decline and Renewal in American Schools*. New York: Free Press.

Shakeshaft, Charol. 1987. *Women in Educational Administration*. Newbury Park, CA: Sage.

Sicinski, Andarzej. 1985. "Educational Objectives and Cultural Values." In *Reflections on the Future Development of Education*. Paris: UNESCO.

Simons, Marlise. 1989. Brazil's savvy Indians. *New York Times Magazine* February 26: 37, 48–52.

Sleeter, Christine E., and Carl A. Grant. 1985. Race, class and gender in an urban school: A case study. *Urban Education* 20(1): 37–60.

Smith, Bunnie O., William O. Stanley, and J. Harlan Shores. 1950. *Fundamentals of Curriculum Development*. New York: World Book.

Smith, Kitty L., and Loyd D. Andrew. 1988. "An Explanation of the Beliefs, Values and Attitudes of Black Students in Fairfax County." Paper presented at the annual meeting of the American Educational Research Association, New Orleans, LA.

Sutton, Francis X. 1971. "Western Education and Political Development in Africa." In *Education in Comparative and International Perspectives*, edited by Kalil I. Gezi. New York: Holt, Rinehart and Winston.

Task Force on Education for Economic Growth. 1983. *Action for Excellence: A Comprehensive Plan to Improve Our Nation's Schools*. Denver, CO: Education Commission of the States.

Teacher 1989. Creating schools from the ground up. (1): 60 61.

TeSelle, Sallie, ed. 1973. *The Rediscovery of Ethnicity: Its Implication for Culture and Politics in America*. New York: Harper & Row.

Thomas, William B. 1988. A quantitative study of differentiated school knowledge transmission in Buffalo 1918–1931. *Journal of Negro Education* 57(1): 66–80.

Time. 1982. Showdown in Texas. August 23: 47.

Toure, Sekou. 1965. "Education and Social Progress." In *Education and Nation Building in Africa*, edited by Laing G. Cowan, James O'Connell, and David G. Scanlon. New York: Praeger.

Turner, Glenn. 1983. "The Hidden Curriculum of Examinations." In *Curriculum Practice: Some Sociological Case Studies*, edited by Martyn Hammersley and Andy Hargreaves. London: Falmer.

Urch, George E. 1968. *The Africanization of the Curriculum in Kenya*. Comparative Education Dissertation Series, No. 13. Ann Arbor: University of Michigan Press.

Wagner, Jon J. 1972. Education and black education: Some remarks on cultural relevance. *School Review* 80(4): 591–602.

Wahlquist, John T. et al. 1952. *The Administration of Public Education*. New York: Ronald.

Walking, Philip H. 1980. The idea of a multicultural curriculum. *The Journal of Philosophy of Education* 14(1): 87–95.

Walsh, Mark. 1988. Group urges focus on U.S. "human capital." *Education Week* October 12: 7.

Wilcox, Kathleen. 1982. "Differential Socialization in the Classroom: Implications for Equal Opportunity." In *Doing the Ethnography of Schooling*, edited by George Spindler. New York: Holt, Rinehart and Winston.

Willis, P. 1977. *Learning to Labour*. Farnborough, England: Saxon House.

Witte, G. B. 1986. "Curriculum Research in Spain." In *Curriculum Research in Europe*, edited by Uwe Hameyer, et al. Berwyn: Swets North America.

Wolcott, Harry F. 1982. "The Teacher as an Enemy." In *Education and Cultural Process*, edited by George Spindler. Prospect Heights, IL: Waveland Press.

Zec, Paul. 1980. Multicultural education: What kind of relativism is possible? *Journal of Philosophy of Education* 14(1): 77–86.

Zuga, Karen F. 1989. "Influences of the Industrial Culture on a Partnership Program, Teachers, and Curriculum." Paper presented at the annual meeting of the American Educational Research Association, San Francisco, CA.

10

CONCEPTIONS OF KNOWLEDGE

Francis Schrag

UNIVERSITY OF WISCONSIN, MADISON

The title of this chapter does not denote any well-demarcated body of scholarship or set of concerns. No two scholars are likely to agree on the major issues or most important scholarly contributions. Such lack of consensus increases the probability that readers will feel that my choice of topics and emphases is eccentric, slighting work they consider important. Perhaps at the least, the chapter may help other scholars to organize the subject more fruitfully in the future. I have divided the chapter into four main sections. The first describes a number of educational traditions associated with different approaches to knowledge. The second focuses on the way in which curriculum documents reflect ideas about the nature and acquisition of knowledge. The third examines a variety of ways of classifying knowledge. The final section discusses the relationship between knowledge and politics. I should say at the outset that no single thread of argument runs through the four sections. If there is any general theme, it is that curriculum designers and researchers cannot sidestep issues concerning knowledge that are at root philosophical; yet curriculum scholars are likely to find standard philosophical approaches to epistemology less germane to their concerns than they might have hoped.

EDUCATIONAL TRADITIONS AND KNOWLEDGE

Education is centrally (though far from exclusively) concerned with the transmission of knowledge, not just of facts, of course, but of modes of inquiry, attitudes toward inquiry, and the like. It is therefore only natural to suppose that the stance one adopts toward educational issues will depend, in part, on the view one adopts toward the nature and sources of knowledge.

Since the identification and examination of diverse views concerning knowledge is the concern of that branch of philosophy called epistemology, it is not surprising that philosophers of education have appropriated the categories of epistemology to analyze the way in which conceptions of knowledge have influenced or ought to influence the educational process. *The Fifty-fourth Yearbook of the National Society for the Study of Education*, published in 1955, for example, canvases the positions of realism, Thomism, idealism, and experimentalism, among others (Henry 1955). As recently as 1986, William Schubert, in his synoptic text-

The author would like to acknowledge the help received from a number of quarters.

Before writing the chapter the writer canvassed the views of over two dozen philosophers and curriculum scholars about which topics and authors such a chapter should be sure to include. Not only was there no consensus, but also in many cases there was no overlap among the suggestions. Respondents included Michael Apple, Harry Broudy, Margaret Buchmann, Abraham Edel, Kieran Egan, Walter Feinberg, Noel Gough, D. Bob Gowin, David Hamilton, Peter Hewson, Herbert Kliebard, Magdalene Lampert, Daniel Liston, Max van Manen, Nel Noddings, Antoinette Oberg, Hugh Petrie, D. C. Phillips, Kingsley Price, William A. Reid, Thomas Romberg, Israel Scheffler, William Schubert, Hugh Sockett, Jonas Soltis, Kenneth Strike, Lawrence Thomas, and Ian Westbury.

During the process of collecting, digesting, and evaluating books, articles, and ideas, the author was fortunate to have the services of an outstanding graduate assistant, Hank Bromley. Hank also made incisive comments on the manuscript in its various versions. The editor assigned Emily Robertson to review the manuscript, and she gave it an exceptionally careful reading, forwarding many valuable criticisms and suggestions. Craig Cunningham and my wife, Sally, did likewise with respect to style. A number of friends and colleagues read the entire chapter in whole or in part, and the author is grateful for their criticisms and suggestions, not all of which could be incorporated. These include Michael Apple, Jürgen Herbst, Mariana Hewson, Carl Kaestle, Herbert Kliebard, James Ladwig, Richard Merelman, Michael Olneck, Terry Penner, and Elliott Sober.

book of curriculum, identifies these same "isms" as providing foundations for different approaches to curriculum and instruction (Schubert 1986, 127–131).

There is, to be sure, something right about the attempt to link divergent educational conceptions to diverse ideas about knowledge, but the conventional approach of deriving educational implications from traditional epistemological "isms" is, regrettably, neither philosophically current nor educationally illuminating. To begin with, epistemologists no longer employ the categories "realism," "idealism," and the like. In contemporary epistemology, the most discussed alternative accounts of the justification of knowledge are labeled "foundationalism" and "coherentism" (Bonjour 1985; Chisholm 1982; Goldman 1988; Pollock 1986; Tomberlin 1988). But there is no need to survey these positions because commitment to one or another of them carries no particular educational implications. The reason is this: Epistemology is largely concerned with the problem of how to justify apparently unassailable beliefs, such as my belief that there is a tree outside my window, that I have two hands, that the chair I am sitting on is brown, or that 2 + 2 = 4. But no sane person, whether teacher or not, can act as if such beliefs are open to question or doubt. Whatever one's pedagogical orientation, one must as a practicing educator assume the epistemological adequacy of beliefs such as these. There are legitimate questions about the nature and justification of assertions made in a large variety of fields, from physics to poetry, but these controversies all *presuppose* the adequacy of "commonsense" beliefs of the kind mentioned.

Moreover, the alleged link between fundamental metaphysical or epistemological positions and curricular or pedagogic policies is, in fact, difficult to discern. Consider, for example, that thinkers with such diverse views about knowledge as Plato, Rousseau, Piaget, and Dewey all appear to endorse a "discovery learning" approach to mathematics instruction. Conversely, the educational views of Paul Goodman (1964) and Sidney Hook (1946), two "experimentalist" disciples of John Dewey, diverge considerably. All this is not to say that fundamental epistemological issues can or should be avoided in a chapter on conceptions of knowledge in curriculum. On the contrary, they must be confronted honestly, but they are best raised within the context of educational issues and controversies. In the third and fourth sections, I shall discuss some of these controversies as I examine the issue of the objectivity of knowledge. (I shall even use the term "realism," which *is* frequently used these days to denote a point of view in the philosophy of science.)

A more satisfying way of discovering connections between educational ideas and practices, on the one hand, and ideas about knowledge, on the other, is to identify major educational traditions connected not to the epistemological views of philosophers but to views about *what knowledge is most worthy of transmission* and, more important, *where it is to be found* and *how it is to be transmitted*. The identification of such traditions is always arbitrary, to some extent, as there is no authoritative way of determining the boundaries of a tradition. And it is not hard to realize that any such exercise in schematic representation of complex phenomena risks the danger of oversimplication. Still, I believe it is possible and useful to identify six such traditions, each associated with a different view of knowledge. I label these the apprenticeship, philosophical, rhetorical, scientific, mystical, and psychotherapeutic traditions. I shall sketch out each one and say something about its relationship to the school, our primary educational institution. The purpose of this section is twofold: to adumbrate a history of educational practice as the embodiment of diverse ideas about knowledge and to show the extent to which contemporary schools are informed by some of these traditions more than by others. It is only fair to acknowledge that aside from a brief mention of Asian traditions in the section on the mystical, this section ignores the rich heritage of Jewish, Islamic, and other non-European traditions of learning.

The Apprenticeship Tradition

I shall begin with the apprenticeship tradition because it is surely the oldest and most universal. In simpler societies, as well as in our own, children learn to hunt, cook, weave, or repair cars primarily by watching, assisting, and imitating their elders, but apprenticeship as a vital legal institution is generally associated in the West with the rise of the guilds in the late Middle Ages (Dunlop 1912). Apprenticeship flourished in the United States as well, from the colonial period into the 19th century (Rorabaugh 1986). As a systematic approach to learning, apprenticeship is still vital, especially in Europe, where it is now organized in factories under government sponsorship (Organization for Economic Cooperation and Development 1979). Because of the dearth of philosophical formulations or justifications for apprenticeship as an educational mode, it is easy to overlook its importance. But it clearly is the principal means by which most people obtain technical know-how in fields as diverse as bricklaying, hairstyling, glassblowing, courtroom litigation, and neurosurgery.

Perhaps the principal mark of apprenticeship as a mode of education is its identification of knowledge with know-how. The only useful source of know-how is that of master practitioners, ideally those who not only can perform at a high level but also can explain the rationale for their performance. Under an apprenticeship system, the know-how of the master craftsperson is analyzed into subtasks. These tasks are then identified with various stages in the training. The apprentice first learns the most rudimentary and least rewarding parts of the occupation, moves on to the more engaging and skilled aspects, and ultimately acquires the secrets of the guild (Rorabaugh 1986). Traditionally, after seven years, the apprentice demonstrates his or her competence in the production of a "masterpiece."

A general feature of apprenticeship is its thoroughly utilitarian cast. It is normally a means of acquiring a livelihood. Some philosophers, for this reason, would be loathe to dignify apprenticeship with the label "education." Nevertheless, even though the transmission of know-how supplies its rationale, apprenticeship as an institution embraces much more—socialization into a way of life, with its heroes and villains, lore, songs, humor, and distinctive outlook on the world (Plummer 1972).

The traditional home of apprenticeship is the workplace, not the school. From the educational point of view, this is both a handicap and a principal asset. Since the teachers earn their livelihood through production rather than teaching, there is an incentive to exploit the labor of apprentices; to cut short the time devoted to demonstrating and explaining the craft; and to prevent them from making mistakes, hence depriving them of the opportunity to learn from those mistakes. On the credit side, the work and the setting are authentic; the work is not make-work, and students are not merely going through the motions to please teachers.

In the first decades of this century in the United States, the apprenticeship tradition, the training of young people for specific occupations, moved from the workplace into the secondary school, as Herbert Kliebard has so convincingly shown (Kliebard 1986, 128–152). Vocational tracks within comprehensive high schools and vocational high schools are still very much part of our educational landscape. In 1981, Philip Jackson reported on a visit to a vocational high school in Atlanta with a reputation for excellence. His portrait of the school points to aspects which justify that reputation as well to those that call it into question, not least of which is the mediocre teaching that he found.

> What is mediocre teaching? A "class discussion" where students copy answers from a textbook and then dutifully recite them back to the teacher, who is barely listening. A shop area where the students sit idly in groups for almost an entire period before the teacher shows up and excuses them because there is not enough time left to do anything. . . . Classroom after classroom in which the students (those who are doing anything) are laboring over workbooks while their teacher sits at a desk like some benign Buddha, nodding and smiling beatifically, but not otherwise engaged in what is going on. (52–53)

My purpose in citing this passage is not to pass judgment on vocational education but simply to illustrate the difficulty the school has in replicating the authenticity of the workplace when it tries to assimilate the apprenticeship tradition. Of course at advanced levels of training, the university is the workplace, and we may view the student in the archives or the biology laboratory as undergoing an apprenticeship that culminates in a scholarly "masterpiece," the dissertation (see Polanyi 1958).

We should recognize that American schools, or rather American educationalists, are the dubious beneficiaries of another feature of the apprenticeship tradition: the penchant for conceiving of education as the acquisition of a collection of discrete skills or, in the jargon of the behaviorists, "competencies" identified by "scientific" observation of adult living (Kliebard 1975).

The Philosophical Tradition

The second tradition, the philosophical, derives from Socrates, Plato, and their successors in ancient Greece. It originated, as we all know, in the public square and marketplace, where Socrates met young Athenian aristocrats and engaged them in conversation about the nature of holiness, justice, knowledge, pleasure, and the like. Plato founded the Academy, perhaps the first school of philosophy, in 387 B.C.E. (Marrou 1964 [1956], 99). It is important to understand that the dialogues recorded by Plato were at the same time pedagogic encounters and philosphical investigations. A key method of investigation Plato developed in the dialogues has been called the "method of hypothesis" by a recent interpreter (White 1976). Common opinion about the nature of something (like justice or holiness) provides the basis for someone to hazard a hypothesis, a definition of the true nature of that thing. This hypothesis is then tested to see whether it leads to any absurd or unacceptable consequences. As White puts it, "If it passes this test but disagreement nevertheless persists among those in the discussion, then a search is made by the proponent of the hypothesis for a 'higher hypothesis' which entails the original one, and this new hypothesis is tested in the same way" (77).

By the end of the process, it is hoped that agreement is reached, at least among those present on the question at issue. Of course there are many "methods" in contemporary philosophy, but this description would fit many seminars in philosophy more than two millennia later. As is well known, the pedagogic effect of this procedure on Socrates's interlocutors, as on generations of students since, was often to startle them into realizing that they had little or no understanding of matters they purported to find unproblematic at the outset of the investigation.

The most important assumption about knowledge made by Plato and his successors down to the present is that knowledge—that is, the most fundamental, general truths about the universe and human life—emerges from deep and sustained *reflection* on our beliefs and experiences. Such reflections can be and often are represented as unimpassioned arguments leading to conclusions. Within this tradition a conclusion is warranted only if it follows ineluctably from a chain of assertions, each link of which is designed to withstand the most intense scrutiny by those who hold contrary views.

The philosophical tradition had its original home in public places, where small groups of men (women were excluded) gathered for intense, sustained conversation. Conversation or dialectic provided the philosophical mode of investigation. No books and no experimental apparatus were needed. All the resources required to secure knowledge, insofar as it could be be secured, were contained between the ears of the participants. As Durkheim (1977 [1938] 152) perceptively notes, the exclusive reliance on debate as an approach to truth is made more understandable when we realize that only at the end of the 16th century was a viable alternative tradition to the discovery of truth developed, that of experimental science.

Plato was the first philosopher to write down his thoughts. He himself realized that the entire philosophical conversation could be internalized: One philosopher could play the role of two or more interlocutors. Much subsequent philosophical debate was carried on by correspondence rather than in person, but the debate format and spirit have persisted. The positions taken by others may provide support for one's views, a foil for one's own position, or just a point of entry to an investigation, but their provenance is no *guarantee* of their authority. In fact, throughout the philosophical tradition, the writings of previous authorities are often treated pejoratively. After all, Plato challenged the authority of Homer, regarded as the "educator of Hellas." And Descartes (1955 [1628]) in the 17th century, in one of his earliest works, stated the following among his rules for the direction of the mind:

> In the subjects we propose to investigate, our inquiries should be directed, not to what others have thought, nor to what we ourselves conjecture, but to what we can clearly and perspicuously behold and with certainty deduce; for knowledge is not won in any other way. (3)

The philosopher's stance implied that most questions with which we humans occupy ourselves, what to do with respect to *particular* problems facing *us*, in *this* place, *now*, are not worthy of investigation by lovers of truth, that is, by philosophers. It also implied the denigration of those forms of discourse that gain assent through appeal to the passions, through elegance, guile, and innuendo rather than through forthright, unadorned argumentation.

What did this tradition contribute to institutionalized education? The philosophical tradition penetrated the universities and to a lesser extent the grammar schools of the middle ages (Durkheim 1977 [1938]; Orme 1973). Vestiges of that tradition, such as exclusive reliance on the oral examination, existed in universities well into the 19th century. The first record of a written examination at Harvard was in 1833 (Smallwood 1935, 15).

The medieval university established the disputation as a method of teaching second in importance to the lecture (Piltz, 1981; see also Durkheim 1977 [1938]; Haskins 1957). Here students would vie with one another in oral debate on specific questions of theology and philosophy. In the early medieval university, until the beginning of the 16th century, disputations were the *sole* basis on which students were judged. Although often ignored, university regulations actually forbade dictation and even students' taking pen and ink into the classroom. The disputations were summarized by the professor, who provided the authoritative solution, the *determinatio*, as it was called in Latin (Ong 1958, 155). One of the great philosphical works of the Middle Ages, Thomas Aquinas's *Summa Theologica*, is written in disputation form, with Thomas's doctrine propounded in the solutions to 3,000 questions.

The medieval schoolmen were, then, the heirs of the pedagogical tradition founded by Socrates. By the 20th century, the oral defense of the doctoral thesis at the university level and the debate clubs that were a staple of extracurricular life in secondary schools and colleges are probably its only extant legacies. At lower levels, despite frequent lip-service paid to Socratic questioning, abundant evidence indicates that there is precious little of it (Sirotnik 1983). For one thing, the invention and spread of printed books in the Renaissance undermined reliance on the spoken word (Ong 1958, 1971). For another, the teacher's ability to control a large group of young people in a small space—whether by the kind of extended, open-ended questioning of individual students that Socratic questioning requires or by the more student-centered debate format, with the teacher acting only as moderator—is jeopardized (Schrag 1988). Rhetoric about schooling is full of praise for maieutic teaching and student participation in discussion, and recently there has been a renewal of interest in "critical thinking." But such rhetoric only reflects the inability of philosophically inspired pedagogy to penetrate most classrooms. The modern school is no more hospitable to the institutionalization of the philosophical tradition than it is to the apprenticeship tradition.

The Rhetorical Tradition

I turn next to the rhetorical tradition, which developed side by side and often in direct conflict with the philosophical tradition. (See the magnificent discussions of Bantock 1980b and Kimball 1986.) This tradition had its origin in the Athens of fourth century B.C.E. as well. Its founder was Isocrates, of whom Marrou (1964 [1956]) writes in his authoritative examination of education in ancient times:

> On the whole it was Isocrates, not Plato, who educated fourth century Greece and subsequently the Hellenistic and Roman worlds. . . .
>
> . . . In so far as the three Renaissances returned to the classical heritage, in so far as this tradition has been perpetuated in our own teaching methods, it is to Isocrates more than to any other person that the honour and responsibility belong of having inspired in our Western traditional education a predominantly literary tone. (120)

The rhetorical tradition, which began with Isocrates, included (among others) the Romans Cicero and Quintilian and was reinvigorated by the Renaissance humanists, of whom Erasmus was perhaps the most eminent. It has many contemporary defenders, of whom the former United States Secretary of Education William Bennett is perhaps the best known. This tradition aims at the nurture of civic leaders, cultivated people whose combination of eloquence and virtue would enable them to direct society through persuasion rather than force. The Roman exponents of the tradition emphasized oratory suited to the law courts and legislative arena. By the time of Erasmus and his associates, oratory was still valued, but persuasive and elegant writing had become indispensable to the prince and his courtier, secretary, or ambassador. It should not be forgotten that although the tradition aimed at the cultivation of the civic leader—not the specialist in a particular craft—the training was intended to be preparation for a career as a lawyer; public servant; or in the case of 18th-century England, country gentleman (Grafton and Jardine 1986; Rothblatt 1976).

What is most important, given this chapter's focus on knowledge, is that from the time of the Renaissance humanists on, exponents of the rhetorical tradition maintained that the only worthy source of knowledge was found in *texts* (though of course not just any text was suitable). Of course the philosophers studied texts as well, but whereas the philosophers' curriculum tends to be organized by questions and issues, that of the rhetoricians tends to be organized by texts and authors. The Renaissance humanists agreed that the greatest authors wrote in Greek and Latin, the dominant languages of learning from the Renaissance until our own century. Hence according to Erasmus, boys must learn Greek and Latin grammar "*because almost everything worth learning is set forth in these two languages*" (Erasmus 1978 [1511], 667; emphasis added).

This tradition asserts the centrality of human affairs, and here success requires a different kind of knowledge from the abstract generalities that occupy the philosophers. Giambattista Vico (1965 [1708]), a 17th-century critic of Descartes, contends,

> The learned but imprudent individual, traveling in a straight line from general truths to particular ones, bulls his way through the tortuous paths of life. . . .
>
> Therefore, it is an error to apply to the prudent conduct of life the abstract criterion of reasoning that obtains in the domain of science. (35)

Although circumstances change, men could still learn from the ancient Greeks and Romans because they provide models of probity, courage, and the other civic virtues that are never obsolete. (I deliberately employ the masculine noun here to indicate that this tradition, like the philosophical, was with some exceptions, limited to males.) Moreover, their deeds and wise opinions are recorded in works that, themselves, furnish models of eloquence for the young to emulate. Erasmus (1978 [1511]) contends that "true ability to speak correctly is best fostered both by conversing and consorting with those who speak correctly and by the habitual reading of the best stylists" (669).

Among the many kinds of writing exercises that humanists like Erasmus (1978 [1511]) recommend to students is that "From time to time they should imitate in vocabulary and style a letter of Pliny or Cicero" (679). Whereas Descartes and other philosophers often expressed disdain for their predecessors, the rhetoricians usually adopt a far different stance. Speaking here specifically of the arts but characteristic of the rhetorician's veneration of the ancient Greeks and Romans, Vico (1965 [1708]) says,

> Those who left us masterpieces of the arts, had before their eyes no model to imitate except the best that is in nature. But those who take as models, in order to imitate them, the highest masterpieces of art—let us say, the best paintings—are usually unable to create better ones. . . . To equal them is also impossible, since imitators are not endowed with the force of imagination of their predecessors. . . . Since imitators cannot surpass or even equal the innovators, they can only fall short of their achievement. (71)

Finally, the rhetorical tradition realizes the limitations of philosophical argument as a vehicle for persuasion, especially when addressed to those who lack the training to follow the arcane, arid argumentation relished by that tradition. The rhetorical tradition recognizes a fundamental fact, namely, that people are creatures of flesh and blood, of passionate desire and aversion.

> Two things only are capable of turning to good use the agitations of the soul, those evils of the inward man which spring from a single source: desire. One is philosophy, which acts to mitigate passions in the soul of the sage, so that those passions are transformed into virtues; the other is eloquence, which kindles these passions in the common sort, so that they perform the duties of virtue. (Vico 1965 [1708], 38–39)

Unlike the traditions so far described, the rhetorical tradition sank deep roots in the schools and universities in Europe and the United States. When liberal educators today speak of the importance of "the humanities" they speak more often as descendants of Quintilian and Erasmus than of Socrates and Descartes. This tradition identifies its prime mission as the inculcation of civic virtue through immersion in the "best that has been thought and said" (Arnold 1960 [1868], 6), but we must be careful not to confuse the aspiration with the reality. We must remember that access to this wisdom depended for 500 years on first mastering a second and usually a third language. Thus before the great works could be appreciated, an enormous amount of preliminary mastery of "dead" languages had to be absorbed. Much of the actual teaching, even in the most famous humanist schools of the Renaissance, was less than inspiring. Grafton and Jardine (1986) provide an account of Guarino Guarini's (1374–1460) famous humanist school in Verona, based on extensive documentation left by Guarino and his students.

The boys began with a course in elementary Latin. They "probably read in unison from a basic Latin text . . . which lists and analyzes the parts of speech as a series of questions and answers" (Grafton and Jardine 1986, 9–10). The second part of the course involved a section focused on the rules of grammar and syntax and another that exposed students to the background information needed to read and write classical Latin. All this information had to be committed to memory. "Memorisation, repetition, catechism—these are the activities on which Guarino's humane learning is firmly grounded" (11). The students had to learn to write a Latin "resembling as closely as possible that of the age of Cicero and Virgil" (11). Appreciation of Latin literature was predicated on a grasp not only of a wealth of background knowledge but also of the subtle connotations and allusions found in all great masters. Lectures and ingenious exercises were designed to help the student acquire this immense corpus of information. Once the student had achieved some facility in Latin, Greek was introduced.

Training in rhetoric followed the grammar course. Here the principal activity was Guarino's lecture and commentary on a rhetoric text widely (but falsely) believed at that time to have been composed by Cicero. The students tried to take down notes verbatim, and some have survived. About a page of notes record Guarino's commentary on a single sentence of the text.

> The notes convey an overwhelming preoccupation with a profusion of tiny detail. . . . The truth appears to be that the rhetoric course was simply a more elaborate introduction to the same sorts of material that had occupied the student of grammar: explanation of interesting words and constructions, very brief and sketchy discussions of historical points, bits of general information of the sort that a cultivated person should know and formal analysis of the rhetorical loci used by Cicero himself. There is little attention to Cicero's train of thought or line of argument—this is entirely lost in the scramble for detail. (Grafton and Jardine 1986, 20)

Despite the vast differences of subject matter and clientele, the realities of classroom life (especially the ethos of mindless routine, of tedious inauthenticity) in this famous Renaissance school for young aristocrats bears a depressing resemblance to those of the contemporary vocational school portrayed by Jackson.

The Scientific Tradition

We turn next to the second youngest educational tradition, that of experimental science, which began to bear fruit only at the end of the 16th century. This tradition might be considered a hybrid of the philosophical and apprenticeship traditions. Like many of the philosophers, the scientists sought fundamental truths about the nonhuman world, but the scientists' search depended on a new mode of discovery, experimentation, which could be learned only by apprenticeship.

In his introduction to *Chemical Manipulation*, written in 1830, Michael Faraday, who himself began his career as an apprentice to Sir Humphry Davy without having completed even a grammar school education, captures the essence of the experimental scientist's view of knowledge:

> Chemistry is necessarily an experimental science; its conclusions are drawn from data, and its principles supported by evidence derived from facts. A constant appeal to facts, therefore, is necessary; and yet so small, comparatively, is the number of these presented to us spontaneously by Nature, that were we to bound our knowledge by them, it would extend but to a very small distance, and in that limited state be exceedingly uncertain in its nature. To supply the deficiency, new facts have been created by experiment, the contrivance and hand of the philosopher having been employed in their production and variation. (1)

Unlike the great philosophical and humanist scholars, the pioneer scientists were not typically connected to universities (Randall 1962, 571). Fully one third of the eminent scientists—educated as late as the early part of the 19th century—whom Francis Galton sampled in his study of genius, had not even *attended* a university (Layton 1973, 29). Most of the innovators were associated informally in academies, of which perhaps the most famous was the Royal Society in Great Britain, which received its charter in 1662 (Randall 1962, 572). The society's motto, *Nullius in verba* ("Nothing in words"), captured the essence of its dedication to the discovery of truth by means of experimentation (Layton 1973).

Today the background prerequisites for original discovery in science presuppose years of schooling, but the art of discovery itself is, as in the past, only acquired directly by working closely with a master discoverer. For knowledge, as this tradition views it, is ultimately know-how, albeit know-how guided by theory (Polanyi 1958; Ravetz 1973). As in the apprenticeship tradition, the actual work demands manual as well as mental dexterity, and the master often assigns more rudimentary tasks to beginners. Only after several years of supervised work, culminating in the dissertation (equivalent to the medieval masterpiece), is the aspirant in a position to open an original line of inquiry in his or her own laboratory. More than any of the others, this tradition requires equipment and materials beyond mere books, pencils, and leisure. In the past, significant discoveries such as those made by Benjamin Franklin, another innovator who rose to great heights without benefit of a university education, required only a kite, a jar, and a key; but in today's era of big science, the equipment may carry a hefty price tag. For example, a high-resolution electron microscope may cost $1 million.

Although there is enormous variation and tension within the tradition, there is a strong commitment, originating with Francis Bacon, to the notion that the fruits of scientific discovery ought to issue in practical inventions that will improve the quality of life for all. The young Humphry Davy (Faraday's mentor), for example, upon assuming his post at the Royal Institution in 1801, was directed to acquaint himself with tanning and agriculture (Bud and Roberts 1984, 23).

Although the tradition has its great founders and heroes, current and potential experimentation can overturn the most venerable "truth." Galileo overturned Aristotle, Einstein superseded Newton, and even Einstein's formulations are not invulnerable to challenge. To an even greater extent than the philosophical tradition, this tradition is forward- rather than backward-looking. Finally, to a degree rarely matched even in philosophical communication, scientific rhetoric is pruned of those linguistic devices that persuade through intimation and connotation. Scientific communication is addressed, John Ziman notes, "to an actual sceptic, a potential critic; it must be convincing, it must be watertight. By a psychological inversion this rhetorical motive is best served by a very plain and modest style" (Ziman 1978, 12). This tradition penetrated the schools and universities only in the 19th century. To take two benchmarks, a small chemistry laboratory was installed in England's famous Rugby School in 1860 (Layton 1973); in the United States, the first high school science laboratory was installed in Boston in 1865 (Hounshell 1989).

Pioneer science educators such as England's John Henslow, who took charge of a rural village school in the 1830s, understood the need for a different kind of initiation into science than was found in conventional studies, an initiation that went beyond book knowledge and emphasized the usefulness of science in illuminating the everyday world.

> A prime consequence of Henslow's conception of the educational role of science was a stress on individual practical work by the learners. Accurate knowledge of the structure of plants, for example, required a devotion not to books, but to the specimens themselves. (Layton 1973, 60)

As with the philosophical and apprenticeship traditions, the scientific tradition was vulnerable to being assimilated to the rhetorical tradition at its least imaginative. Nineteenth-century British educational reformer Henry Mosely described a lesson typical of those he had observed:

> A teacher proposing to give an oral lesson on coal . . . holds up a piece of it before his class, and having secured their attention, he probably asks them to which kingdom it belongs, animal, vegetable, or mineral—a question in no case of much importance, and to be answered, in the case of coal, doubtfully. Having, however, extracted the answer which he intended to get from the children, he induces them by many ingenious devices, much circumlocution, and an extravagant expenditure of the time of the school, to say that it is a *solid*, that it is *heavy*, that it is *opaque*, that it is *black*, that it is *friable*, and that it is *combustible*. And then the time has probably transpired, and the lesson on the science of common things, assumed to be so useful to a child, is completed. (quoted in Layton 1973, 124)

As Layton (1973) notes, without an adequate knowledge of science on the part of the teacher, "lessons on the science of common things degenerated into barren exercises in 'observation' and 'classification' " (124).

The Psychotherapeutic Tradition

Since the psychotherapeutic tradition has had very little impact on schooling, I shall say only a very few words about it. The practice established by its founder, Sigmund Freud, of requiring novice therapists themselves to undergo psychoanalysis so that they might better understand their own psychodynamics gives us a reason to classify the psychoanalytic transaction as fundamentally an educational one (see Schrag 1972). The tradition is only about 100 years old; Alfred Adler, Carl Jung, Karen Horney, and other disciples of Freud number among its founders (see Mullahy 1955).

Almost all forms of psychotherapy except the behavioral derive from psychoanalysis, even if their proponents reject one or more of its assumptions (Enelow 1977). The psychotherapeutic tradition shares with the philosophical both a mode of inquiry based on conversation between a novice and a guide and a disdain for approaches to knowledge that require tools or texts. As in the philosophical tradition, initiates have a kind of knowledge that noninitiates not only lack but also do not even recognize that they lack. In contrast to the philosophical tradition, however, the psychotherapeutic tradition views adherence to rigorous canons of logic as an *impediment* to the discovery of personal truth (see Rieff, 1966, 1979). Unlike Socrates and his descendants, the psychotherapist is generally urged to be nonjudgmental. Even more than the rhetorical tradition, the psychotherapeutic takes seriously the nonrational, passionate side of human existence. Indeed, from the beginning the psychoanalytic technique required the analysand to "undertake to report to the analyst without exception whatever thoughts come into his mind and to refrain from exercising over them either conscious direction or censorship" (Brenner 1957, 8).

As originally conceived, psychoanalytic conversations serve two purposes: the search for general truths about the nature of the psyche and the discovery of personal truths that inter alia help the client alleviate the distress due to psychic conflict. These personal truths, although they may be formulable in propositions, reveal themselves in action. As with the apprenticeship tradition, knowledge is essentially know-how, knowing how to avoid self-destructive patterns in one's work and personal life (see Bellah, Madsen, Sullivan, Swidler, and Tipton 1985; Enelow 1977; Rieff 1966, 1979).

Although educational theory has been influenced by Freud's view of human development, the psychotherapeutic tradition's approach to the acquisition of personal knowledge has rarely found its way into the schools. Still, some of the activities recommended to elementary school teachers to help children feel good about themselves and the values clarification activities designed to facilitate students' discovery of their own values are clearly influenced by this tradition. In both cases, the teacher is urged, for example, to take a nonjudgmental role with respect to children's responses. It should not be forgotten, of course, that the psychotherapeutic tradition does enter the schools when guidance staff take on the role of therapist to help students experiencing distress.

The Mystical Tradition

Because it is a very minor tradition in Western civilization (except possibly among indigenous peoples) and because (unlike even the psychoanalytic tradition) it has had no influence on the schools, I shall speak only very briefly about the mystical tradition. Still, it is worth including because a few Westerners have been captivated from time to time by the notion that our failure to incorporate this tradition, indeed even to acknowledge its existence, constitutes a serious defect in our understanding. One of the purest exemplars of the mystical tradition is found not in the West at all, where religion and philosophy are closely intertwined, but in the education of the Zen monks in Asia. Knowledge in this tradition is identified with enlightenment (*Satori*), which is an intuitive comprehension beyond words and concepts yet which engenders a profound attunement with the rest of the universe. In meditating, the adherent aspires to "tranquilize the turbulence of self-assertive passions and to bring about a state of absolute identity in which the truth is realized in its inwardness" (Suzuki 1961, 83). Although a master is needed to assist the student in securing this kind of knowledge, there is no need for books, equipment, or other paraphernalia.

Even though the truth to be experienced lies beyond language, language is essential in the training. But the uses of language to which the disciple is exposed transcend the discursive and even the suggestive. Indeed, they border on the antirational. Sometimes the disciple is given mysterious challenges (*koans*), which defy rational solution (e.g., "Talk without using your tongue"). Sometimes the disciple's own questions are met with "nonsensical" answers. Sometimes the disciple is asked to concentrate on a meaningless syllable ("Mu") to the exclusion of all else (see Suzuki, Fromm, and DeMartino 1960, 43–58).

> The intellect may raise all kinds of questions—and it is perfectly right for it to do so—but to expect any final answer from the intellect is asking too much of it, for this is not in the nature of intellection. The answer lies deeply buried under the bedrock of our being. (48–49)

The knowledge acquired in this tradition is both the most and the least practical. What is meant by this paradoxical statement is that, on the one hand, the disciples are not equipped for performing a different role in the world or even for performing their normal roles more effectively; on the other hand, their every practical activity is infused with a profoundly altered consciousness.

The Traditions Compared

Having sketched out six educational traditions, each of which reflects a distinctive orientation to knowledge, let me highlight a few generalizations and points of comparison:

1. These traditions are *not* parallel to the conventional divisions of metaphysics or epistemology. We cannot identify the scientific tradition with the empiricist theory of knowledge, for example. Although they were apostles of the scientific tradition in education, neither Jean Piaget (a Kantian) nor John Dewey (a pragmatist) are "empiricists" as philosophers use the term.

2. The apprenticeship, rhetorical, and scientific traditions were originally closely connected to occupational training. Only the philosophical, the psychotherapeutic, and the mystical traditions may be said to seek knowledge in a way that is divorced from training for particular roles in society.

3. Education in any of the traditions entails more than acquisition of a specific corpus of knowledge or definite set of skills. It entails the assimilation of a worldview.

4. From their origins until well into the 19th century, the philosophical and rhetorical traditions were aimed at an elite: students drawn from the upper reaches of society, who were destined to become its leaders, or those freed from the need to labor, who had the time to pursue philosophical investigations. Both traditions evince a disdain for manual labor. The apprenticeship tradition was, of course, intended for those who would provide the goods and services the leisured classes needed to sustain themselves. The scientific tradition, since it did not *at its outset* depend on a university education or mastery of the classical languages, was not restricted to a social elite. Faraday's father was a blacksmith, for example; Franklin's, a candle and soap maker.

5. The rhetorical tradition, focused primarily on the text, has been the most influential tradition in European and American schools since the Renaissance. The centrality of the classical languages themselves lasted until almost our own times. For example, only in 1899 did the Committee on College Entrance Requirements in the United States drop Latin and Greek as requirements for college entrance (Burns 1987). In Britain, Latin remained an entrance requirement for study at Oxford and Cambridge until the late *1950s* (Stray 1985, 19). (When I say that the rhetorical tradition has profoundly influenced school practice, I do not, of course, imply that the primary goal of ancient or Renaissance education in rhetoric, the preparation of young people for civic leadership, informs our own practice.)

6. Although elements of the philosophical, scientific, and apprenticeship educational traditions are highly visible in educational discourse, they are not notably conspicuous in the day-to-day realities of most classrooms. Of course, some elements are there: the more active, "hands-on" learning found in the preschool and elementary years, in the arts and crafts, in the "shop" classes, in the science laboratory, and in the extracurriculum of the high school (see Cuban 1984). The discussion and debate format deriving from the philosophical tradition are sometimes found in high school classrooms. In some vocational programs or advanced high school science courses, the authenticity of the workshop and laboratory survives transplantation to the school, but all too often the vitality of the nonschool traditions is undermined when they are transplanted into the school. That legacy of the rhetorical tradition, the textbook, which provides the bedrock of curriculum, is often devoid of literary merit, and the teacher's presentation of its contents only too rarely excites the students' emotions or challenges their intellects.

KNOWLEDGE AND CURRICULUM

The discussion of teaching and learning to this point has not referred specifically to curriculum. It will be helpful to say a few words about the nature of curriculum before discussing the way it embodies ideas about knowledge. The term (deriving from the Latin for "race course") is first found in the 16th century, according to historian David Hamilton (1989). Originally, "curriculum" referred to "the entire multi-year course followed by each student, not to any shorter pedagogic unit'' (45). Today we still use it in that way but also to refer to the specification of subjects studied in a single year or even in a single course. Although the term is easily understood in ordinary usage, there have been lively debates among educational scholars about the best way to conceptualize it. Let me remind the reader that I have deliberately avoided canvasing alternative philosophical accounts of the nature and justification of knowledge claims because I do not believe that such accounts provide much illumination to the curriculum scholar. In subsequent sections, however, I shall be considering some philosophically inspired attempts to classify knowledge as well as some controversies surrounding the justification of knowledge claims in specific contexts as these bear on curricular disputes.

Defining the Curriculum

In an article discussing the meaning of curriculum, A. I. Oliver (1978) recognizes that more or less expansive meanings may be given, ranging from ''all the experiences the child has regardless of when or how they take place'' to ''the systematic arrangement of certain courses designed for certain pupil purposes'' (7–8). The issue of definition is not trivial because it carries implications for the scope of the curriculum worker's job and for the politics of curriculum as a field within educational scholarship.

There are disadvantages to both narrow and expansive definitions. If we limit ourselves to the narrow notion of the ''program of studies,'' we may overlook school characteristics that influence children significantly, characteristics that affect but do not derive from its published program of studies. On the other hand, if we adopt a broad definition, we are liable to lose a grip on just what features of schooling the curriculum worker (as distinct from the administrator, guidance counselor, or teacher) is responsible for.

Those who favor the more expansive definition want to make sure that it includes what is often called the ''hidden'' curriculum (Dreeben 1968, 1976; Eggleston 1977; Jackson 1970; Whitty 1985). The term ''hidden curriculum'' has been used variously over the last 20 years, and there is even controversy about whether such a thing exists (Gordon 1982; Lakomski 1988), but the notion is, I believe, one of the most important recent contributions to the discussion of schooling.

The idea derives from a sociological awareness that educational transactions involve more than interactions among teachers, students, and books; these interactions take place in institutional settings with distinctive characteristics and traditions, which cannot but influence students even though the precise nature and magnitude of the influence is often difficult to determine. To take a simple example, much schoolwork is graded, and grades are usually competitive—not every student can get an A. Judgments resulting in feelings of adequacy and inadequacy *in relation to others* are constantly being made. It is, of course, difficult to specify just what students individually and collectively actually learn from these cumulative experiences, but it is no easier to specify what they actually learn about arithmetic, geography, and the like. It is difficult to suppose that the former lessons are less deep and pervasive than the latter.

Some features of the hidden curriculum may not be the result of anyone's intentions; other features now ''hidden'' may have been introduced quite deliberately in an earlier era (Vallance 1973–1974). Consider this example: We may suppose that students learn much about our cultural attitude toward time and work by observing the way learning is regulated by the clock. But we may not be aware that clocks were once placed in classrooms for this very purpose:

> The habit of correct observation cannot be cultivated in a better way than by a constant reference to time. In school this is particularly the case. Every day has its appointed duties, and every hour its special exercise. To secure punctuality, regularity, harmony, and good order, a clock which may now be obtained for a small sum, should be placed in some conspicuous position in the schoolroom. (Hodgins 1858, 86)

I said at the outset that whatever else it embraces, education includes the transmission of knowledge, broadly conceived. Although the designation ''hidden'' may be misleading, I do not see how we can reject the notion that knowledge is transmitted by the school's structure and its routines—by its organization of time, for example—as well as by its teachers and textbooks.

Which ''lessons'' are learned from which organizational characteristics is easier to speculate about than to demonstrate with any confidence, partly because of the structural similarities among schools. We may note that the lessons that Dreeben (1968) identified with the hidden curriculum are quite different from those identified by Bowles and Gintis (1976). Here lies a rich field of research for those interested in the impact of the schools on students' understanding of the social world and their own place in it. It would, moreover, be highly desirable if curriculum designers paid more rather than less attention to those features.

Although all learning is acquired in some social environment and hence is accompanied by some kind of ''hidden curriculum,'' not all learning nor all teaching depends on a manifest curriculum. What is required for us to say that a particular set of educational experiences is guided by a curriculum? I shall stipulate two conditions that appear to me to be necessary and jointly sufficient: first, that the learning must take place in a *prepared* environment and, second, that there must be a *planned sequence* of experiences. Although much can be learned from a trip across the United States and although such a trip may be based on a carefully worked-out itinerary, I am reluctant to apply the word ''curriculum'' to such a set of learning experiences in which the environment is unprepared. Similarly, although a baby's playroom may be carefully designed for learning, since there is no prescribed sequence of experiences, I would not consider that learning to be guided by a curriculum.

But it is possible to speak of the "curriculum" of a Montessori preschool even though the *sequence* of concepts mastered is determined by no more than the way in which the instructional materials are designed and arranged in the environment (Standing 1962). And it is plausible to argue that the sequence of roles, each with its prescribed rights and responsibilities, that students in the 19th-century British public schools moved through from the time they entered to the time they graduated constitutes a curriculum for the formation of gentlemen (Honey 1977).

Most curriculum workers focus on the visible part of the curriculum, often called the "manifest curriculum." The sequences on which they focus are typically sequences of lessons or courses that identify what is to be learned. In contrast to the hidden curriculum, the manifest curriculum is often visible in *documents* such as textbooks and curriculum guides that describe (in order of magnitude) single lessons; course syllabi; sequences of courses to fulfill graduation requirements; and examinations that evaluate the success of students, teachers, and programs. Some documents merely enumerate or specify a sequence of courses or lessons. Others offer an explicit defense of their proposals. The principal role of most curriculum workers is the design, evaluation, and improvement of such documents.

Some will insist that these documents are far from the most important determiners of the educational experience. I do not know whether this is so. Even Michael Apple (1988), a curriculum scholar who favors an expansive conception of curriculum, notes, "Whether we like it or not, the curriculum in most American schools is not defined by courses of study or suggested programs, but by one particular artifact, the standardized, grade-level-specific text . . ." (85). Regardless of how influential the manifest curriculum is, unless we keep it conceptually separate from the myriad other influences on students, we will never be able to determine its importance.

How should we understand the relationship between the document and the educational experience it is intended to guide? I have found the following analogy useful in considering this question: Educational experiences are to curriculum documents as musical performances are to scores. The features of the analogy to which I wish to call attention are these:

1. Curriculum documents, like musical scores, must be *enacted*, and performance always involves *interpretation*. Two performances of the same score may be quite different.
2. Curriculum documents, like musical scores, may leave more or less to the discretion of those who will make use of them. As no curriculum is needed for learning to take place, so no score is needed for music to be performed.
3. Enactment of curriculum depends on available technology. The photocopier and computer open possibilities that did not exist in the era when information storage and transmission were limited to what could be printed in books. Musical performance likewise depends on instruments that depend on available technology. A Bach prelude, for example, can be performed on either a harpsichord or synthesizer.
4. Curriculum documents, like scores, can be evaluated to some extent apart from the characteristics of identifiable cohorts of students. But just as a brilliantly conceived lesson may be unsuited to a particular group of students, so a particular score may be inappropriate for a particular audience.

(Of course an analogy is just an analogy. The fit is not perfect. The students, for example, even when they do not have copies of the "score," have a decisive influence on the "performance." Indeed, some might consider them to be more like an orchestra, which coproduces the music, than like an audience, which passively listens.)

Curriculum Documents and Knowledge

Curriculum documents may be said to embody ideas concerning knowledge in a variety of ways: First, and most important, such documents prescribe a *selection*. From the infinitely large corpus of what is known, certain portions are identified as worthy of transmission in school. (By implication, other areas are considered less worthy or unworthy.) But such selection cannot be conceptualized as simply checking off a number of items from a longer list of possible choices because a variety of kinds of lists can be made, or to put it differently, the universe of knowledge lends itself to diverse modes of *conceptualization*.

Second, since the purpose of curriculum documents is to facilitate the transmission of knowledge, such documents, especially at the course or lesson level, reflect ideas about the acquisition of knowledge. Finally, since curriculum documents may prescribe one or several simultaneous sequences, they reflect ideas about how different areas of knowledge—both within and across subjects—are related to one another, ideas concerning the *organization* of knowledge.

Of course, curriculum documents, in reflecting a distinctive selection and conceptualization of subject matter, reflect more than ideas about knowledge and learning. They reflect ideas about educational aims that go beyond the transmission of knowledge narrowly conceived to include the development of attitudes toward self and others. These educational aims may, in turn, be the reflections of more general ideas about human flourishing. Although I touch on these normative aspects in places, I do not stress them since they are discussed in the chapter by Sockett in this *Handbook*.

The preceding, rather abstract formulations will be understood more readily if we discuss a few examples.

Conceptualization of Knowledge in Curriculum

Perhaps the most fundamental distinction in the way in which curriculum knowledge is conceptualized is reflected in a table found in Harold Rugg and Ann Shumaker's (1928,

69) *The Child-Centered School* contrasting "child-centered schools" and "conventional schools," which is partially reproduced below:

Child-Centered School	Conventional School
A food study—fruits and vegetables	Algebra
A knight study—making and giving a play	Arithmetic
A play city	English Composition
A study of milk	Geography
How man has made records	Latin
Care of a flock of chickens	Rhetoric
Story of the growth of Chicago	Science

To some, such as the influential British philosophers R. S. Peters (1967) and P. H. Hirst (1972), the disciplines are the most defensible basis for curriculum organization. (What we mean by a "discipline" is discussed in the following section.) But as Rugg's table demonstrates, the knowledge to be transmitted by the school need *not* be conceptualized in terms of academic disciplines. Educational scholars have been reminded of this point both explicitly by philosophers such as Jane R. Martin (1970, 1982) and implicitly through the attempt to introduce new school subjects not reducible to single disciplines such as women's studies or peace education, but it seems a point that is all too easy to forget.

Just because conceiving knowledge along disciplinary lines is virtually second nature to most students and teachers, John Dewey's critique of almost a hundred years ago has a contemporary ring:

> Custom and convention conceal from most of us the extreme intellectual poverty of the traditional course of study, as well as its lack of intellectual organization. It still consists, in large measure, of a number of disconnected subjects made up of more or less independent items. An experienced adult may supply connections and see the different studies and lessons in perspective in logical relationship to one another and to the world. To the pupil, they are likely to be curiously mysterious things which exist in school for some unknown purpose, and only in school. (Quoted in Mayhew and Edwards 1965 [1936], 468)

If one views schooling as a preparation for life, the school's virtually exclusive focus on the disciplines appears more, not less, puzzling since actual problems requiring resolution can never be confined to an academic discipline. A headline on the front page of a recent morning's paper reads, "High Ozone and Acid-Rain Levels Found Over African Rain Forests" (*New York Times*, June 19, 1989). The acid rain is reported to result from fires set by African herdsmen seeking to increase grazing ground for their flocks. The identification and solution to this problem, if it comes, will require contributions from scholars in atmospheric science (which itself depends on physics and chemistry), various branches of biology, economics, political science, and even history and anthropology.

Progressive educators in the 1920s tried to initiate a dramatic shift in curriculum conception in the direction indicated by Rugg and Shumaker's left-hand column. In 1926 a national committee of educational scholars, including such luminaries as Franklin Bobbitt, George Counts, Charles Judd, William Heard Kilpatrick, and chaired by Rugg himself, jointly promulgated a statement setting forth their views on the foundations of curriculum making. The statement criticized the existing subject divisions, noting,

> One of the chief intellectual purposes of the school is to develop understanding of the institutions, problems, and issues of contemporary life. Historically, whenever a rapid transformation of the conditions of living has taken place, the tendency has been for the curriculum to lag behind. Because of the great changes in modern life, there is at present a real need in certain fields for a new synthesis of knowledge and, correspondingly, for a new grouping of the materials of the school. (Rugg et al. 1926, 21–22)

The statement sounds just as timely to some contemporary critics of the school 60 years later. Attempts to conceptualize the curriculum along alternative lines are, indeed, not limited to long-dead progressive educators. But why have such efforts not taken hold? The reasons go beyond our purview here, but the weaknesses of the progressive alternative are perhaps best appreciated by considering the work of one of its contemporary exponents, Ira Shor.

In *Critical Teaching and Everyday Life*, Shor (1987, chap. 5) develops a five-step structure for organizing subject matter. The approach is illustrated by a unit on the hamburger, a unit he developed with his community college English class. In the first step, a theme or object is described in great detail. Subsequently the theme is related to its immediate social setting. The object is then placed in its global relations to discern its place in a much broader context. The time dimension is then introduced; the evolution of the object in the recent past is investigated, and projections for the future are attempted. The last step expands the time dimension into the distant past and future. It includes an avowedly "utopian" dimension, which "calls upon students to re-invent the thing being studied, so that the future will not reproduce the present" (166).

Admittedly, the extension of the theme in time and space will take students into history, geography, economics, and the like, but presumably the focus on the hamburger provides for both student interest and intellectual coherence. Even if there are still bits and pieces, their relevance to the theme can be easily appreciated by the students.

Assessing the relative power of "progressive" and conventional conceptualizations of subject matter is no easy matter. We cannot simply test matched groups to find out which has learned more because we cannot easily devise tests that are fair to both approaches. Shor's approach, let us suppose, is a less efficient way to provide an understanding of labor economics, capital markets, and multinational corporations than could be given in an introductory economics course, but Shor's units are not intended to be efficient vehicles for delivering conventional subject matter. Shor's (1987) own aims are implicit in his critique of the education his students have received in conventional schools: ". . . their education has not permitted them to find out who they are and what's been happening to them, and what they need to be free and whole" (195). The designers of a more conventional economics course may not share these ambitious aspirations for students. They should not be penalized for not helping their students to be "whole," but neither should Shor be penalized for not giving them as firm a grounding in economics. These difficulties are buried when we fail to remember that curriculum documents necessarily embody normative commitments concerning human and social welfare as well as ideas about knowledge.

As attractive as we might find the progressive way of conceptualizing subject matter, its limitations become apparent upon further thought, especially if we focus on its self-proclaimed concern for the students to find coherence in their schoolwork. Suppose that the unit on the hamburger has been completed; how is the next theme to be selected? Presumably, the teacher and students choose another "object" for investigation, the automobile, say, another of Shor's examples. The nature of capitalism may guarantee that the "automobile" unit and the "hamburger" unit do not form two "disconnected subjects made up of more or less independent items." Some overlap is assured since some of the concepts used in the first discussion (wage labor and capital markets) are also needed for the second. But there is no assurance that this overlap will effect a *cumulative* development of understanding.

It is just this kind of cumulative development that a disciplinary orientation may provide, at least in theory, for the continuing evolution of disciplines themselves provides an incentive to experts to organize them for effective transmission. If we take another look at Rugg and Shumaker's two lists, we can agree that there is probably little chance for a link between rhetoric and science. But equally, there is little reason to expect students to discern a link between "a knight study" and "care of a flock of chickens." Prima facie, it appears that what the child-centered approach may gain in the way of short-term coherence it stands to lose in long-range coherence (see Hirst 1972).

The choice between these two ways of organizing knowledge need not be an either/or affair. John Dewey (1938) proposed a gradual evolution. In the case of young children, learning must be "derived from materials which at the outset fall within the scope of ordinary life-experience" (87). But this is only the first step: "The next step is the progressive development of what is already experienced into a fuller and richer and also more organized form, a form that gradually approximates that in which subject-matter is presented to the skilled, mature person" (87).

Dewey's own experimental school at the University of Chicago centered each grade's activity on a particular theme, beginning with Household Occupations and including such themes as Progress Through Invention and Discovery, Local History, and Colonial History and the Revolution (Mayhew and Edwards 1966). Overall continuity derived from the requirement, adapted from the "culture epochs" notion of the Herbartians, that the curriculum must trace the growth of civilization through different stages of its evolution. A different kind of integration of the conventional and progressive approaches is found in Daniel Bell's *The Reforming of General Education* (1966). Bell proposes that at the culmination of the college experience, students should take a course that "would allow for a useful application of the social science disciplines to a set of problems that illustrate the need for a multidisciplinary approach" (263).

Even if a school subject is conceptualized along disciplinary lines, the questions facing curriculum designers are not merely those of deciding what information to include and exclude because the disciplines themselves can be conceptualized in diverse ways. Rather than treat a number of subjects superficially, I shall single one out for more extended treatment. I choose chemistry, in part on the assumption that the kinds of questions that need answering for one of the "hard sciences" would be even more difficult to answer for history or English. A college text, *Principles of Modern Chemistry* (Oxtoby and Nachtrieb 1986), provides a standard exposition in 22 chapters. Appended to each chapter is a problem set and a list of "Concepts and Skills" the student should have mastered by the end of that chapter. None of the "skills" describes the actual manipulation of chemicals or laboratory apparatus. *Laboratory Chemistry* (Carmichael, Haines, and Smoot 1975) comprises 38 *experiments*, which students are expected to perform, such as "The Gas Law: The Effect of Temperature on Volume." The text for each experiment includes a set of procedures and questions. The teacher's guide includes instructions on how to set up the experiments, which techniques to demonstrate, the background information students would need for each experiment, suggestions for what points to emphasize or pursue, and the correct answers to the questions.

A different approach to chemistry, one that dispenses with both teacher and laboratory, is found in a series of booklets called *Programmed Units in Chemistry*. A booklet entitled *Mass and Volume Relationships* (Powell 1977) consists of some 150 numbered questions and problems requiring calculation, each with a blank for the student to register his or her answer. Each question builds on the previous question and adds a bit of information. The *correct* answer to a question, which the student is to cover up while working, appears below the question so that it can be immediately checked. Each set of problems is preceded by a sample problem and solution that illustrate the correct procedures for solving that kind of problem.

What does it mean to be a "knower" of chemistry? Despite important differences, the approaches give a common answer: Knowing chemistry involves finding the correct solution to problems requiring calculations. Only in the laboratory approach are students expected to furnish their own data through hands-on experiments. Only in the college text are there questions that ask the student to *explain* why something happens or to *predict* what would happen were something to be done. None of the texts expects initiates to be able to *ask* questions themselves, to *design* experiments to answer questions, or to understand why certain problems are still outstanding or why certain ideas are currently controversial.

I am sure that the authors and teachers who use these and other texts are aware that science involves asking questions, defending controversial ideas, and designing experiments; they no doubt believe that such activities are the responsibility of advanced students, however, not of novices. When time is insufficient to transmit the settled, it would be wasteful, they could be expected to argue, to pursue matters that are still unresolved by experts or to expect novices to design their own experiments or to ask worthwhile questions.

Unfortunately, many, perhaps most, students will never reach the advanced levels; for these students, chemistry (like most school subjects) is represented essentially as a body of settled information and problem-solving procedures rather than as a living, often competitive social enterprise (see Apple 1979; Fensham 1985; Hull 1988). This representation of scientific subject matter as made up largely of "rote recall of a large number of facts, concepts and algorithms that are not obviously socially useful" (Fensham 1985, 418) is unfortunately reinforced by most examinations.

Because they are administered *after* a course or unit of study, the role of examinations in shaping student experience is not always recognized. Once again the words of the Rugg committee have a decidedly contemporary sound (see, e.g., Doyle 1983):

> One of the most potent forms of curriculum-control is measurement by means of uniform examinations and standardized tests. Teachers and pupils will inevitably work for the elements represented in the instruments by which their success is measured; therefore, it is of the utmost importance that changes in goals and methods be accompanied by the development and use of new tests and examinations. . . .
>
> This committeee condemns emphatically the evaluation of the product of educational effort solely by means of subject-matter types of examinations now prevalent in state and local systems. We have reference specifically to the rigid control over the school curriculum exercised by those administrative examinations which over-emphasize the memory of facts and principles and tend to neglect the more dynamic outcomes of instruction. (Rugg et al. 1926, 25)

The design of examinations, especially standardized examinations, has been largely the province of psychometricians, who are concerned primarily with the measurement characteristics of tests. Since tests are increasingly used to underpin decisions regarding not just students but also teachers, schools, and entire school systems, these concerns are certainly legitimate, but they obscure a fundamental tension, illuminated 40 years ago in a penetrating essay by Joseph Schwab (1978 [1950]), between the validity and educational usefulness of a test. A valid test of a particular curriculum aspires to perfect conformity with that curriculum, not testing material that the students had not been explicitly taught. But such a test would not be as educationally valuable as one that suggested to teachers alternative or additional aims and alerted them to the "unknown and unanticipated consequences (in addition to those intended) which any effective curriculum inevitably must produce upon its students" (277). A valid test is "sedative instead of stimulative to the teacher's search for better means of instruction and more adequate conceptions of his aims" (278).

Of course, as Schwab and many others have noted, the ambition of testing only what has been taught is never realizable. Most tests are, among other things, tests of reading, of working under time pressure, of contriving strategies to figure out what the teacher wants, and so on. Examinations which openly acknowledge this fact can include tasks that not only are more realistic and engaging to students but also represent a more dynamic conceptualization of what knowing a subject entails.

For illustrative purposes, contrast the following kinds of examination questions, taken again from science. The first, taken from *A Learning Program for Chemistry* (Demmin 1987), contains a list of words at the top of a page and a group of sentences with blanks. The instructions require the student to "choose words from the word list to fill in the blanks . . ." (11). The first sentence reads, "The properties of a substance are that set of specific __________ by which the substance is recognized." (The correct answer, "characteristics," could be correctly chosen simply on the basis of its syntactic features.)

Another kind of question is included as an illustration in a report prepared in connection with the design of the new national curriculum in Great Britain. This question is intended for 11-year-olds in the areas of science, mathematics, and language. It is administered orally to groups of three. The task requires the students to carry out (and record) an experiment designed to discover the most effective design of a boat, given a choice of two boats, and several sail shapes and sizes. The experiment involves apparatus including the boats, masts, meter ruler, timer, fan, and tray filled with water. The task proceeds in a series of steps, beginning with drawing the sails and determining their area by measurement and calculation, then discussing how to carry out the experiment, then making predictions, and finally conducting the experiment to test actual against predicted results (Black 1988, Appendix E, Example 21).

I think it fairly clear that the second question is much harder to administer and might be of doubtful value in assessing either a student's or a teacher's progress through a conventional curriculum. However, the second task requires students to do some science, whereas the first is more accurately labeled as a test of English reading and grammar. The point is that present tendencies to produce ever closer "alignment" between curricula and examinations are not just narrow-minded but may be educationally *harmful*, as Schwab suggested. Focusing on examinations as representations of what it means to be a knower in a particular subject area could be liberating for both test and curriculum developers (see Frederiksen 1984).

Selection of Knowledge to Be Studied

Once a curriculum writer has *conceptualized* a school subject along disciplinary lines, important questions still need addressing: What knowledge should be included or excluded? What are the fundamentals of the field and how should those be conceived? What is the best order of presentation? What is the relation of this subject to others in the curriculum? Issues of selection and organization, it will be obvious, are often inextricably linked to issues of conceptualization. Perhaps less obvious will be divergent normative ideas about the aims of education implicit in alternative construals.

In William Bennett's (1987, 31) blueprint for the American high school, the chemistry curriculum is identified with 15 *topics* such as chemical bonding, colloids and suspensions, and the like. A science curriculum project prepared in 1989 under the auspices of the American Association for the Advancement of Science (AAAS) identifies chemistry with a number of "Key *Concepts*," such as "Chemical Transformations of Atoms and Molecules Produce Materials Whose Properties Differ from Those of the Reactants" (Bugliarello 1989, 22; emphasis added)

A somewhat broader interpretation of chemistry is illustrated by *Chemistry, A Human Concern* (J. A. Young 1978). Some of its chapter headings are conventional, such as "Bonds and Structures," but included among its 15 chapters are one on "Energy: Current Usage and Future Limitations"; one on "Chemistry, Pollution and Environment"; another on "The Chemical Industry"; and a final chapter, "Science, and . . ." which compares science to other human endeavors such as religion and the arts.

Although the impact of science and technology on society is a theme of the AAAS report, the scope of chemistry and the other physical sciences is limited, so that science and society interactions are excluded from any of the "key concepts" of those disciplines. The panelists do appear to be concerned with the public's *image* of chemistry though, as shown by some comments on teaching the subject:

> The general public usually thinks of chemicals as being artificial substances that have societal benefits in some cases but are responsible for unpleasant smells, major health problems such as cancer and chronic respiratory diseases, and the destruction of the environment. This stereotyped image of chemistry and chemicals needs to be corrected by teaching (1) the pervasiveness of chemicals . . . (2) the need for caution in producing and using chemical materials, (3) the actual and potential contributions of chemistry to the solution of existing social and environmental problems . . . and (4) the other societal benefits of chemistry. (Bugliarello 1989, 23–24)

In Bennett's blueprint, even *technology* is seen exclusively in technical terms, isolated from any interactions with society. Whereas "Each Design Has Side Effects" is one of the "Key Concepts" in engineering acording to the AAAS report (Bugliarello 1989, 38), the Bennett (1987) report lists among its possible topics for a one-year course on "Principles of Technology" only items such as resonance, amplifiers, logic elements, torque, heat transfer, etc. (31).

Acquisition of Knowledge

Curriculum documents frequently reflect a view not just of what it is to know a subject but also of how that knowledge is acquired. The chemistry texts we have been examining, in other words, embody different ideas about learning. According to the authors of *Laboratory Chemistry*, actual experience in the chemistry lab is essential. "We observe the properties and changes of matter, using our senses and devices available in the modern chemistry laboratory" (Carmichael, Haines, and Smoot 1975, 7). Oxtoby and Nachtrieb (1986), however, declare that the "best way to master physical and chemical concepts is to solve problems" (vi). What they mean by "problems" is clear from their identification of difficulties students often experience in "the conversion from the words of the problem through formal statements of concepts to manipulable mathematical equations" (vi). Powell's (1977) programmed text is explicit about the value of the programmed approach, "a method to help you learn better and more easily. You proceed in small steps, check yourself at each step, make few errors, and work at your own speed" (1).

The theory of learning found in the programmed text was extremely popular in the 1960s and 1970s, an era when behaviorist psychology dominated the study of learning and educational psychology dominated educational research and development. Whereas the behaviorists aspired to learning that was error free, contemporary cognitive psychologists stress the importance of feedback from error for the development of understanding (Berkson and Wettersten 1984; Schrag 1988).

It is not hard to see how Powell's (1977) effort to protect students from error may limit their mastery of chemistry, at least as Oxtoby and Nachtrieb (1986) characterize it. Recall that according to them, one of the chief difficulties students have is converting the words in a problem to the appropriate concepts. This difficulty is finessed for students of the programmed text because they know at any point in the program what concepts are relevant to a problem. But once outside the program, where problems don't come correctly labeled, the student has no way of knowing which concepts are needed.

Organization of Knowledge in Curriculum

Curriculum documents may contain implicit or explicit ideas about the relationship of various school subjects to one another. The AAAS project, for example, identifies chemistry as part of a cluster, which can be integrated by means of "unifying concepts." Included in the cluster are physics; chemistry; earth, planetary, and astronomical sciences; information science; computer science; and engineering. Biology is located in a different cluster, with the "health sciences." In another reform effort, the Paideia Program, directed by Mortimer Adler, it is suggested that chemistry and biology be integrated at the high school level in a two-year course under the heading of "molecular studies" (Cowan and Puck 1984).

Let us consider the issue of organization a bit more fully in the context of yet another reform proposal authored by the executive director of the National Science Teachers Association (NSTA) (Aldridge 1989). The proposal is based on the notion that most U.S. students are not given a chance to understand science. This lack results not just in a limited pool from which future scientists may emerge but also in widespread scientific illiteracy.

Focusing on the high school, the proposal notes that although 60 percent of the students take a year of biology, only 40 percent go on to take chemistry, and only 20 percent take these two as well as physics. These low percentages result from the fact that the three high school science courses are taken in sequence and that physics and chemistry are (and are perceived to be) extremely demanding and highly abstract, largely because of the need to cram a substantial amount of material into a course that lasts just one year. In most other countries, science is less concentrated and the various sciences are studied over a four- or five-year period, which allows for better sequencing of material and permits coordination among the various scientific subjects.

I am not sure how the sequence of courses in American high schools got established, but a clue to its rationale is found in a report prepared by the National Education Association's Committee on Secondary School Studies at the end of the last century. All but one committee member accepted a resolution that the study of chemistry should *precede* physics, though the order is "plainly not a logical one" (Remsen et al. 1893, 119). The rationale provided is that more background in mathematics is needed for the study of physics, a rationale repeated by Cowan and Buck in 1984. A single dissenter to the 1893 report, W. J. Waggener, argued that physics ought to precede chemistry because the phenomena it studies are "directly perceptible to the senses" whereas chemical changes are "inferred—not observed" (Remsen et al. 1893, 122).

Aldridge (1989) proposes the elimination of the sequential pattern entirely. He urges all students to take all three subjects, biology, chemistry, and physics, simultaneously over a three- or even a six-year period. This practice would permit coordination of the three sciences, as exemplified by a course in the U.S.S.R., cited by Aldridge, in which students study the human heart and circulatory system in biology class, chemical reactions involving oxygen in chemistry, and the kinematics and dynamics of fluid flow in physics. Note here another way in which disciplines may be related: Some of the phenomena studied in one discipline are studied from a different perspective in another. Under Aldridge's proposal, the individual sciences would be sequenced in such a way that initial exposure would focus on the descriptive and phenomenological; the intermediate level would focus on empirical and semiquantitative aspects; and only in the last years would the sciences be presented in theoretical, abstract terms.

What I want to call attention to here is not the strengths or weaknesses of the NSTA proposal but rather the fact that as with any curriculum proposal, its justification depends on ideas about not just scientific knowledge and its acquisition but also children's development and, most important, the purposes of schooling. The proposal that the sequence of courses within each science should be arranged from the concrete and descriptive to the theoretical and abstract depends on an account of human cognitive development, familiar from Rousseau on, as proceeding from the concrete to the abstract. The proposal is based on our presumed need not only for a larger number of science professionals but also for a larger number from *underrepresented* groups. And the concern with science education is not limited to the training of science professionals but is aimed at nurturing people who are "sufficiently literate in science to participate effectively in our scientific and technological world" (Aldridge 1989, 1). Embodied here are notions about the need to develop a more democratic, more egalitarian polity.

Fundamental issues concerning the nature of human development, the flourishing life, and the just society are often given explicit attention in curriculum reform proposals and manifestos. But even when these issues are not broached directly, such documents often contain tacit assumptions of a fundamental kind, which may have far-reaching influence in the way a proposal is interpreted or implemented. One of the important tasks of the curriculum specialist is to discern and expose these tacit commitments.

Summary

I have argued that curriculum documents may impose or reflect various understandings about the nature and uses of knowledge. Does it really matter how knowledge is construed? How important are these documents in guiding the experience of students? Are such documents more like the scores classical musicians play from or more like the "fake books" that jazz musicians use as a basis for improvisation? Obviously curriculum documents are "filtered through the lived culture of teachers and students" (Apple 1989, 108), but what kind of a filter do they provide, and what opportunities are closed and what opened by different "filters"? I think these are important, researchable questions, which have not received much attention. (This subject is treated more fully in the chapter by Clandinin and Connelly, in this volume.)

I am struck by the high quality of thinking about this issue that characterizes the contributions to the 1926 Yearbook of the National Society for the Study of Education, edited by Rugg. The curriculum field appears to have neglected discussion of these more general issues, which transcend particular academic subjects, thus leaving the rhetorical and practical field open to the university experts in specific disciplines who have not thought deeply about education and to textbook publishers who are rewarded for thinking in terms of profits rather than reflectively about how knowledge should be represented for transmission.

KINDS OF KNOWLEDGE

We have already seen that curricular documents may conceptualize knowledge in different ways. In this section, I explicitly confront attempts to demarcate and classify varieties of knowledge with a view to assessing the curricular fruitfulness of such classification schemes. Since the disciplinary classification dominates, and since philosophers and philosophers of education have spent considerable effort attempting to distinguish among disciplines, I devote some space to assessing those efforts.

The task of demarcating kinds of knowledge is not unlike that of demarcating different territories on a map. As there are different kinds of maps of territory, so there are different kinds of maps of knowledge. Similar questions may be asked in both cases. Are the conventional divisions of knowledge into disciplines such as history and chemistry natural, like the representation of naturally occurring features (e.g., forests and mountain ranges), or simply conventional, like the representation of political jurisdictions, which exist in people's minds but are not visible from an airplane? As there are maps that represent different kinds of features, climatic, say, rather than political, so there are "maps" of knowledge that represent features different from those associated with the academic disciplines. Are such maps of importance to educators? Before discussing the nature of academic disciplines, it will be worthwhile to examine two alternative mappings. (I should note that space does not permit a discussion of many mappings based on identifying distinct cognitive processes, such as are found in Arnheim [1985] and Bruner [1985]. These are treated in the chapter by Bereiter, this volume.)

Alternative Mappings

In an effort to demolish the Cartesian doctrine concerning the relation between minds and bodies, Gilbert Ryle (1949), in *The Concept of Mind*, examined the distinction between knowing *how* and knowing *that*. Ryle, in an effort to discredit the "absurd assumption made by the intellectualist legend . . . that a performance of any sort inherits all its titles to intelligence from some anterior internal operation of planning what to do," argued that knowing how was not reducible to knowing that (31). When conceptual analysis as a mode of philosophizing was introduced into the educational community, primarily by Richard Peters in Great Britain and Israel Scheffler in the United States, the Rylean distinction received considerable attention (Soltis 1968). Ryle's chapter, "Knowing How and Knowing That," was included in an early anthology introducing the linguistic approach to American philosophers of education (Scheffler 1958).

(This is as good a place as any to insert a parenthetical remark: The view that philosophy is essentially a clarification of the language and concepts of ordinary speech was ascendant in the United States for only about a decade, from the mid-1950s to the mid-1960s. Today it has few adherents in the English-speaking world, although the concern for rigorous argumentation and lucidity, which marked its discourse, has been a hallmark of philosophy in English ever since.)

The search for fundamental, logically irreducible kinds of knowledge conducted by the new converts to conceptual analysis turned out to be surprisingly difficult. By the time Jonas Soltis (1968, 35–41) discussed the Rylean distinction in his judicious introduction to the analysis of educational concepts, he already sensed that philosophical interest and educational relevance were by no means coincident. Whatever its philosophical importance, the distinction appears somewhat artificial to practicing educators. It takes only common sense to realize that the demonstration of propositional knowledge requires skills, at least those required to speak and write intelligibly; by the same token, the mastery of most skills presupposes some propositional knowledge (e.g., skill in chess depends on the knowledge that a king may not remain in check). Some educators may have been attracted to Ryle's (1949) work because the focus on knowing how appeared to support the introduction of more active learning in classrooms, but "activity"-oriented reformers predated Ryle and could defend their position quite persuasively without reference to presumed defects in Cartesian dualism. Ryle's emphasis on knowing how served, at best, as a reminder to educators who identified learning with the passive assimilation of propositions of the incompleteness of their view. If the central curricular issues are the structures and traditions of the school as an organization and the conceptualization, selection, and organization of subject matter, it is hard to make a case that Ryle's analysis has much to offer the curriculum specialist.

Here we have another example of a phenomenon I mentioned at the outset: that of educational scholars adopting not just the tools but also the agendas of their philosophical colleagues, assuming that their importance to educators is somehow commensurate with their importance to scholars in the disciplines.

A more recent mapping, which expands Ryle's (1949) categories from two to five, is offered by Carl Bereiter and Marlene Scardamalia (in press). Because the authors are applied psychologists, their work is a more promising source of illumination for curriculum workers. Their mapping posits five kinds of knowledge required for the development of expertise in any field, be it physics, auto mechanics, or musical performance: formal knowledge, procedural knowledge, informal knowledge, impressionistic knowledge, and self-regulatory knowledge (chap. 4). The first two categories are basically descendants of the Rylean dichotomy, adopted and given new names by researchers in the artificial intelligence community. Informal knowledge, the third category, is intermediate between the two. It designates knowledge that we utilize in solving problems but normally cannot articulate in words or formulas. Unlike skills, informal knowledge depends on understanding, but understanding that is typically "represented" by qualitative mental models of phenomena rather than the quantitative, formal models that usually appear in textbooks. Some informal knowledge is widely shared and goes under the name of "common sense," whereas some is limited to particular, local contexts in which we have developed expertise.

Impressionistic knowledge derives from Harry Broudy's "knowing with" (Broudy 1977). It refers to amorphous background knowlege, which is also difficult to specify and formulate but which can exert a strong influence on the stances we adopt in confronting ourselves, our circumstances, and the world we read about and see depicted in the media. Impressionistic knowledge is what remains with us from our classroom encounters with Shakespeare, for example, when we have forgotten almost all of the lines, the plots, and even the names of most of the characters. For example, our encounters with *Macbeth* may influence the attitude we have toward people in high places who commit crimes. Finally, self-regulatory knowledge—which may include knowledge of each of the preceding kinds—is identified by its subject matter, a person's own intellectual functioning. Knowledge of one's strengths and weaknesses, of "what works for me" and "what I can't seem to get the hang of," are examples.

Does this mapping offer particular insight to the curriculum worker? The recognition of the importance of tacit knowledge, which owes a substantial but insufficiently acknowledged debt to Michael Polanyi (1958), need not undermine the case for the conventional curriculum, organized along disciplinary lines. In fact Broudy's intent in stressing its importance is precisely to offer a new defense of general education in the disciplines. According to Broudy (1977), general education "furnishes a context within which a particular situation is perceived, interpreted, and judged" (12; see also Broudy 1988).

I do not think Bereiter and Scardamalia (in press) would disagree, but their concern with the development of expertise leads me to draw a somewhat different inference about the import of their scheme. Bereiter and Scardamalia clearly recognize the importance of formal knowledge in the development of expertise. But they also recognize the limitations of formal knowledge. Informal knowledge in particular plays a critical role in effective problem solving. The conversion of formal knowledge into procedural is driven by the limitations of existing problem-solving procedures. The conversion of formal to informal knowledge arises in the quest for better understanding, but what stimulates this quest? Sometimes it is simple curiosity, but more often it is the challenge of authentic—which does not necessarily mean practical—problems. Here Bereiter and Scardamalia echo Dewey's conviction that perceived problems are the stimulus to inquiry. This realization seems to me to have implications for both the manifest and hidden curricula. In the former case, it suggests the need for giving children of all ages a chance to see how formal knowledge can become usable in the solution of authentic problems, which unlike many textbook problems, cannot be confined to a single discipline. Experiencing formal knowledge "in use" is likely to happen only when some of the challenges given the young are of the kind described earlier in the boat design task. But the conventional organization of schools does not favor that kind of activity. I think there is an intersection between tacit knowledge required for problem solving and the hidden curriculum. As applied psychologists better understand the way inaccessible knowledge operates, it is hoped that they will raise the consciousness of the curriculum worker concerning the barriers to the development of such knowledge posed by the hidden curriculum of schools.

The Disciplines

The most common mapping of knowledge is into territories now often called disciplines but formerly often called sciences or branches of philosophy. (This mapping is clearly not isomorphic with those just discussed.) We have seen that school subjects may but need not be conceived along disciplinary lines, but we have not asked the question, What are disciplines? We may be uncomfortable calling engineering or poetry disciplines, but earlier generations had no difficulty in including poetry and ethics among the sciences. Beginning with Aristotle, scholars have attempted to provide maps of the world of knowledge; among noteworthy attempts are those of Thomas Aquinas, Francis Bacon, and Thomas Hobbes (see Machlup 1982).

Demarcating Disciplines

Reproduced in Figure 10–1 is Hobbes's map of science (Hobbes 1966 [1651], 54–55).

We must realize, however, that science was for Hobbes only one kind of knowledge; the other kind he called absolute knowledge, which comprises the facts we bear witness to with our senses as well as the register of such knowledge, which is history. Three things are worth noting about this map: First, it is not simply an enumeration but a pattern derived from an analysis of the properties of the ultimate constituents of the universe. Second, it is not limited to those studies that we honor with the name "science." It includes music and poetry, which many might hesitate to call branches of knowledge at all, much less branches of science. It also includes architecture and navigation, which many might prefer to call "applied fields" rather than sciences, and it includes astrology, which most would now consider to be a pseudoscience. Third, it fails to include fields that many today do consider sciences: biology, economics, and the other social sciences, to name a few. The absence of biology may have been an oversight; it could easily be inserted. The absence of the social sciences was no oversight; they had not yet been invented. In fact, Hobbes's *Leviathan* is one of the foundations of the scientific study of society.

What can we learn from this 1651 map? First, we can learn that disciplines (in this section I use "science" and "discipline" interchangeably) need not be identified with narrow conceptions of scientific method. Music, poetry, and rhetoric appear to Hobbes to have equal standing with astronomy and geometry. Since Hobbes's willingness to include these disciplines corresponds to our inclinations as reflected in school curricula everywhere, I see no reason to exclude them.

Second, we can see that although some of our sciences have a venerable ancestry, others do not. Disciplines appear not to be eternal but seem, like species, to emerge at different times: Some, like meteorology, are destined to survive; others, like phrenology, to die (see Foucault 1972; Hull 1988). The analogy with species suggests that the enterprise

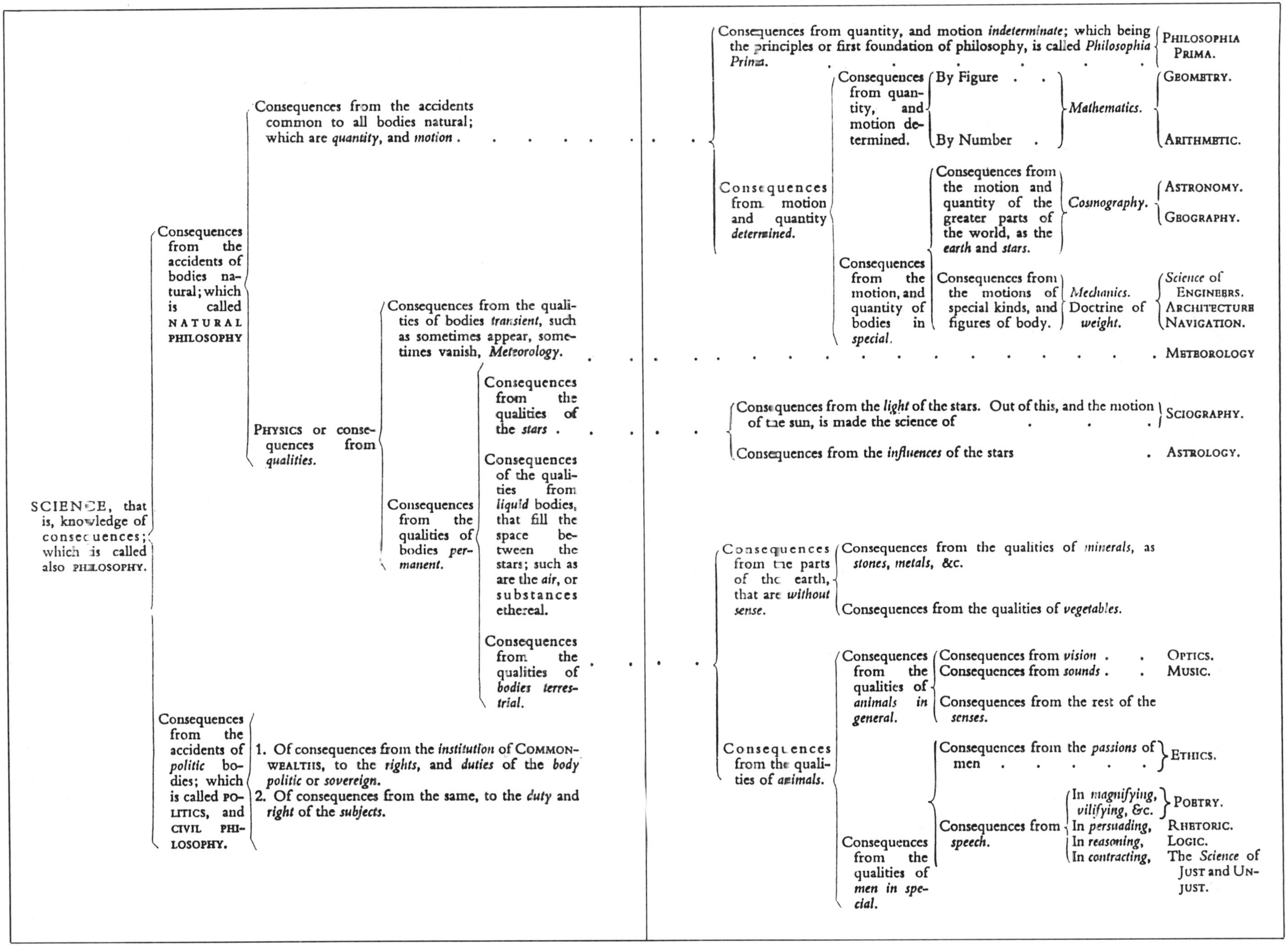

- SCIENCE, that is, knowledge of consequences; which is called also PHILOSOPHY.
  - Consequences from the accidents of bodies natural; which is called NATURAL PHILOSOPHY
    - Consequences from the accidents common to all bodies natural; which are *quantity*, and *motion*.
      - Consequences from quantity, and motion *indeterminate*; which being the principles or first foundation of philosophy, is called *Philosophia Prima*. — PHILOSOPHIA PRIMA.
      - Consequences from motion and quantity *determined*.
        - Consequences from quantity, and motion determined.
          - By Figure — *Mathematics*. — GEOMETRY.
          - By Number — *Mathematics*. — ARITHMETIC.
        - Consequences from the motion, and quantity of bodies in *special*.
          - Consequences from the motion and quantity of the greater parts of the world, as the *earth* and *stars*. — *Cosmography*. — ASTRONOMY. GEOGRAPHY.
          - Consequences from the motions of special kinds, and figures of body. — *Mechanics*. Doctrine of *weight*. — *Science of* ENGINEERS. ARCHITECTURE. NAVIGATION.
    - PHYSICS or consequences from *qualities*.
      - Consequences from the qualities of bodies *transient*, such as sometimes appear, sometimes vanish, *Meteorology*. — METEOROLOGY
      - Consequences from the qualities of bodies *permanent*.
        - Consequences from the qualities of the *stars*.
          - Consequences from the *light* of the stars. Out of this, and the motion of the sun, is made the science of — SCIOGRAPHY.
          - Consequences from the *influences* of the stars — ASTROLOGY.
        - Consequences of the qualities from *liquid* bodies, that fill the space between the stars; such as are the *air*, or substances ethereal.
        - Consequences from the qualities of *bodies terrestrial*.
          - Consequences from the parts of the earth, that are *without sense*.
            - Consequences from the qualities of *minerals*, as *stones, metals*, &c.
            - Consequences from the qualities of *vegetables*.
          - Consequences from the qualities of *animals*.
            - Consequences from the qualities of *animals in general*.
              - Consequences from *vision* — OPTICS.
              - Consequences from *sounds* — MUSIC.
              - Consequences from the rest of the *senses*.
            - Consequences from the qualities of *men in special*.
              - Consequences from the *passions* of men — ETHICS.
              - Consequences from *speech*.
                - In *magnifying, vilifying, &c.* — POETRY.
                - In *persuading*, — RHETORIC.
                - In *reasoning*, — LOGIC.
                - In *contracting*, — The *Science* of JUST and UNJUST.
  - Consequences from the accidents of *politic* bodies; which is called POLITICS, and CIVIL PHILOSOPHY.
    1. Of consequences from the *institution* of COMMONWEALTHS, to the *rights*, and *duties* of the *body politic* or *sovereign*.
    2. Of consequences from the same, to the *duty* and *right* of the *subjects*.

FIGURE 10–1. Thomas Hobbes's Map of Science

of trying to identify the properties that any entity must have if it is to be a science, or to demarcate boundary lines between disciplines, is no easy task.

Hobbes's method of demarcating where one science ends and another begins is ultimately in terms of the objects they study, surely a plausible way of proceeding. For us 300 years later, alas, this does not seem to be a very satisfactory principle of demarcation because several disciplines may study the same phenomena, as our earlier example from science education illustrated. There, we may recall, physicists, chemists, and biologists all studied the human heart, albeit focusing their attention on different aspects. To take another example, economists, geographers, and sociologists may all study immigration patterns.

But how else could we identify and demarcate (*individuate* in philosopher's jargon) disciplines? An obvious suggestion is by methodology, but anyone familiar with academic research knows that methods do not map onto disciplines in any neat way. Scholars from such different disciplines as ecology and economics may use the same models, such as optimization theory. Scholars within a single discipline like biology may use a vast variety of methodologies—think, for example, of the difference in the methods employed by ethologists and molecular biologists. Nor can we distinguish disciplines by the uses they make of certain tools, like mathematics or statistics. Some historians and literary scholars use statistical techniques that are vastly more arcane and complex than those used by ethologists.

But surely, it will be claimed, the methods of the literary critic are different from those of the scientist? Actually, this claim is not sure at all. The literary theorist E. D. Hirsch, Jr. (1987), argues that the interpretation of a poem follows the same logic as the validation of a scientific hypothesis, whereas from the other side numerous scholars contend that the sciences, including even so austere a discipline as mathematics, employ all manner of rhetorical devices to persuade readers (Nelson, Megill, and McCloskey 1987).

A third way of identifying disciplines is by the criteria of acceptability to which they subscribe and aspire. Granted, this approach might not be expected to distinguish each discipline from its neighbor, but it would certainly distinguish poetry and the visual arts from, say, physics. Regrettably, even this distinction is far from obvious; the search for beauty has inspired many scientists. The eminent physicist S. Chandrasekhar (1987), in an article on the role of aesthetic considerations in scientific work, quotes the French physicist and mathematician Poincaré: "The Scientist does not study nature because it is useful to do so. He studies it because he takes pleasure in it; and he takes pleasure in it because it is beautiful" (59).

In the same chapter, Chandrasekhar (1987) relays a story about the mathematician-physicist Hermann Weyl, who is quoted as saying, "My work always tried to unite the true with the beautiful; but when I had to choose one or the other, I usually chose the beautiful" (65). If the role of beauty in the search for truth is acknowledged, the view of the arts as disengaged from the disciplined pursuit of truth is also far from uncommon. As A. C. Crombie (1986) has shown, the artists of the Renaissance, drawing inspiration from Aristotle, saw themselves as partners of the scientists, engaged in the same fundamental enterprise:

> Experimental scientist and rational artist were then both exemplary men of *virtu*, achieving their objectives by a similar intellectual behavior, mastering their subject matters by an analytical anticipation of effects, and committed to an examined life of reasoned consistency in all things. (69)

This notion may sound a bit quaint, but a more modern version of it is found in the work of the philosopher Nelson Goodman, who also sees artists and scientists participating in a common enterprise, that of "worldmaking" (N. Goodman 1978; Goodman and Elgin 1988). Criteria for acceptability in the sciences are not substantially different from those found in the arts. Truth is neither a necessary nor a sufficient condition for the choice of a statement in science. Agreeing with Weyl, Nelson Goodman (1978) says,

> Not only may the choice often be of a statement that is the more nearly right in other respects over one that is the more nearly true, but where truth is too finicky, too uneven, or does not fit comfortably with other principles, we may choose the nearest amenable and illuminating lie. Most scientific laws are of this sort: not assiduous reports of detailed data but sweeping Procrustean simplifications. (121)

However, the concept of "rightness," which is central to science, applies legitimately to art, even to abstract art. According to Goodman, "Rightness of abstract works . . . is neither identical with nor utterly alien to truth; both are species of a more general notion of rightness" (133).

There is far from consensus on these matters. Indeed, there are persuasive attempts to identify fundamental differences between the fine arts and the sciences (see Bruner 1985; Cavell 1986; Gadamer 1988; Gass 1985). One apparent difference lies in the fact that the arts, unlike the sciences, do not appear to progress (Weiskopf 1986).

Another attempt to differentiate between families of disciplines is that of the German philosopher Jürgen Habermas (1971), who identifies three families of disciplines, each associated with a different "knowledge-constitutive interest." The natural sciences aim at control of nature, the historical studies aspire to extend mutual understanding, and the critical sciences—of which psychoanalysis provides an example—strive for enlightenment (see Geuss 1981). This scheme faces difficulty when subjected to careful scrutiny (see Miller 1975). It is difficult, for example, to subsume contemporary cosmology and evolutionary biology under the rubric of technical control, as that phrase would normally be understood. And Marx's historical materialism may be said to aim at the control of human destiny rather than at mutual understanding alone. My all too brief discussion is not intended to pass judgment on these efforts but to indicate the difficulty of producing convincing "natural demarcations" between disciplines or families of disciplines on the basis of their methods, aims, or criteria of validity.

A final approach to identifying and demarcating disciplines is to identify the distinctive *concepts* they employ. Now it is true that a concept used in molecular biology is not *likely* to be used in sociology or music; even if the same word is used, it is apt to have a different meaning, e.g., "free radical" as used by a chemist and a historian. The inability of scholars in one discipline to understand those of another reflects the esoteric vocabulary of specialized concepts each discipline has developed. Nevertheless, we learn no more about what makes disciplines distinctive by comparing vocabulary lists than we learn about what makes nations distinctive by comparing names of cities.

But couldn't we identify certain concepts as essentially connected to certain disciplines? This suggestion, though plausible, is likely to distort three important facts about disciplines or sciences. First, as with disciplines themselves, terms and concepts emerge at different times; those that are central at one time may fade out of use at a later time, as illustrated by "phlogiston" in physical science, for example. Concepts that are central now, like "field" in physics or "abstract" in art, would not have been central to those disciplines a hundred years ago. To assert that some small set of concepts is essential to any discipline is merely to freeze that discipline at its present state of development. Second, it denies familiar mechanisms by which concepts that emerged in one discipline are appropriated by others, concepts like "fitness" or "function" or "marginal utility," or by which new disciplines, like biophysics, are created through the amalgamation of concepts derived from their "parent" disciplines. Third, it denies what is all too obvious to scholars *within* the disciplines, that there is often disagreement, indeed, bitter conflict, over what the central concepts of a particular field ought to be (see Hull 1988; Phillips 1987; Schwab 1978).

Some attempts have been made to identify disciplines on the basis of a combination of several of the preceding factors. Philip Phenix's (1964) six "realms of meaning" is one such attempt; Paul Hirst's (1972) seven "forms" of knowledge is another. These have been subjected to rigorous scrutiny over the years; I will limit myself to a brief, general comment and refer the reader to some of the acute analyses made of them (Bailey 1984; De Leon 1987; Griffiths 1986; Phillips 1987; Vandenberg 1988).

Efforts to define and demarcate the disciplines assume that disciplines, even when they are acknowledged to evolve, are like Platonic forms in having timeless characteristics with distinct "natures." There are only a few "pure" forms (from which hybrids may develop), and these can be identified on the basis of a philosophical inspection of the various modes of inquiry. Recent investigations of the nature of science as a social process make such an assumption highly questionable (see Hull 1988). The territorial divisions, discovered at a single time, when reified, distort the complex processes resulting in the birth, evolution, and extinction of concepts, subject matters, techniques, and modes of inquiry and expression. This is true even for efforts like that of Habermas to identify disciplines with particular cognitive interests. Moreover, attempts to hold "disciplines" to some arbitrary standard, such as Hirst's testability against experience, nearly always turn out to legitimize certain disciplines (like physics) and disenfranchise others (like music).

However, the failure of existing efforts to demarcate disciplines in a philosophically convincing way is no great loss to educators because curriculum designers derive little benefit from such conceptual efforts beyond legitimation of the status quo. The reason is this: Whether the demarcations are those of Phenix, Hirst, or Bailey, it turns out that music, history, chemistry, and mathematics are distinct "nations." But this is precisely the set of demarcations that is *already* enshrined in the traditional curriculum map. The principal problem facing the curriculum designer who adopts the disciplinary perspective is not how to distinguish *between* disciplines; it is how to *select* which versions of which disciplines to impart at a time when not only the number of disciplines but also the number of *versions* of extant disciplines is constantly expanding. Here analyses like those of Phenix and Hirst offer no guidance.

Disciplines and Truth

My uncritical citation of Nelson Goodman may engender in the reader familiar with his work a suspicion that I align myself with him and others, such as Richard Rorty (1982, 1989) in philosophy and Elliott Eisner (1985) in education, against the idea of objective truth and of realism in the philosophy of science. Eisner echoes Goodman when he writes,

> Knowledge is considered by most in our culture as something that one discovers, not something that one makes. Knowledge is out there waiting to be found, and the most useful tool for finding it is science. If there were greater appreciation for the extent to which knowledge is constructed—something made—there might be a greater likelihood that its aesthetic dimensions would be appreciated. (32)

The question of the objectivity of scientific knowledge is too large and too deep for a full treatment here, but neither can it be entirely sidestepped. Some curriculum workers, like Eisner, have enlisted Nelson Goodman in the attempt to give the aesthetic dimension greater centrality. Others are attracted to the antiobjectivist, "constructivist" doctrine because it appears to justify the introduction of a more process-oriented pedagogy in which students participate in "making" math or science or music rather than in the "passive" assimilation of ready-made truths *about* these matters. But the defense of active learning has no need for an antiobjectivist view of the scientific enterprise. The 1960s curriculum reformers, as some may recall, were passionately devoted to "discovery learning" despite having a pre-Kuhnian understanding of scientific activity (Heath 1964).

Moreover, as Kenneth Strike (1987) has argued, the constructivist doctrine, where it is most plausible—e.g., in pointing out that scientific concepts such as "neutron" and "niche" are not perceptible features of or objects in our familiar world of tables and trees—is banal. However, according to Strike, more radical forms of constructivism lead not only to skepticism but also to idealism. To hold that not just neutrons and niches but also tables and trees themselves are nothing but "constructs" of the mind is to hold a version of idealism that is highly problematic. Suppose someone claims there is no tree where I see a tree outside my window? Is one of us right? Strike shows that the alternatives here are equally unpalatable to the constructivist: skepticism or the very empiricism that the constructivists set out to reject.

Some educational scholars are attracted to the antiobjectivist view because of its potential for undermining an unequal social order. The argument could be couched like this: Certain groups are "kept in their place" by their failure to master the "truths" enshrined in the disciplines. But once these disciplines are correctly seen to be human artifacts, their legitimacy is called into doubt, and with it the unequal society that fosters the appearance of that legitimacy.

Alluring though it is to the educational reformer, the antiobjectivist position has its dangers, not always recognized by those who fall under its spell. The motivation to adopt this position is almost always that of finding an intellectual lever to alter the way schooling (or some other aspect of society) is now carried on, but this view assumes that the way schooling is now carried on can be ascertained *objectively*. An illustration is provided by Cherryholmes (1988), who identifies himself with Richard Rorty's philosophy, yet contends, "Critical educators believe, as do I, that social oppression is an important characteristic and outcome of contemporary educational systems . . . " (164). But if all knowledge is made rather than found, then so is knowledge about the way the school (or society) operates. Thus, in their efforts to enlist the supporter of the status quo, the reformers cannot appeal to the unsatisfactory state of schooling *there for any disinterested investigator to discover*, only to the unsatisfactory state of schooling they (the *reformers*) have *made*—hardly a compelling appeal.

As a matter of fact, Nelson Goodman notwithstanding, scientists are generally quite comfortable speaking about discovery and truth. Recall that Hermann Weyl was quoted as choosing beauty over truth. Was the choice justified? In Weyl's case it apparently was. This is Chandrasekhar's (1987) contention: "We have evidence, then, that a theory developed by a scientist, with an exceptionally well-developed aesthetic sensibility, *can turn out to be true* even if, at the time of its formulation, it appeared not to be so" (66; emphasis added). If some theories can turn out to be true, others can turn out to be false. So in an appreciative essay about the astrophysicist Arthur Eddington, Chandrasekhar describes Eddington's cosmological model:

> It is now pertinent to ask what the present status of Eddington's cosmological model is. The advances in our knowledge since 1944 leave little doubt that *it is not the right one*. The evidences derive, principally, from the discovery of the universal 3 K black-body radiation and the fact that helium is of primordial origin (129; emphasis added).

Without any knowledge of astrophysics, we can appreciate what Chandrasekhar is saying: that evidence "out there" requires the rejection of Eddington's model. The locutions of a practicing scientist, even an eminent one, may be thought to be less than convincing almost 30 years after Thomas Kuhn's (1970) much discussed revision of the standard account of the history of science. Even though extended examination of Kuhn's work is impossible, no discussion of truth in science could fail to mention that contribution and the controversy it has given rise to. Kuhn's work did, indeed, overturn a popular view of the growth of science hinted at in a statement by Ernest Rutherford, quoted (without citation) by Chandrasekhar (1987): "Scientists are not dependent on the ideas of a single man, but on the combined wisdom of thousands of men, all thinking of the same problem and each doing his little bit to add to the great structure of knowledge which is gradually being erected" (14).

Kuhn's (1970) reflections on the history of science showed this depiction of the scientific enterprise to be mythical. Science does not proceed in this way at all. Far from being a gradual, cumulative building of a single structure, Kuhn showed scientific discovery to be the erection of a number of such diverse structures. A few exemplary scientists lay the foundations for the first building in some domain; then the more routine construction work is performed by "ordinary" scientists. But at some point, the foundations no longer bear the weight of the edifice; it is abandoned when a group of "revolutionary" scientists lay the foundations for a new structure, which is free of the defects found in the old. Eventually, however, the new structure meets the same fate, has to be replaced, and so on.

What is the relationship between the old and the new buildings (theories)? If each can be judged only on its own merits, there may be as many different truths as there are different theories. If, on the contrary, we can speak of later structures as improvements over earlier ones, the notion of cumulative, though discontinuous, progress can be maintained. This is a critical question, which has been debated ever since Kuhn's work first appeared. It would be naive and grandiose to think that I could in a few pages resolve a controversy that has stirred so many brilliant philosophers over several decades. I shall, therefore, once again content myself with a brief general discussion and a listing of some important references to discussions of the issue (Campbell 1974; Hull 1988; Lakatos and Musgrave 1970; Laudan 1977; Leplin 1984; Phillips 1987; Popper 1972; Suppe 1977; Toulmin 1972).

I believe I can provide an illustration that will do justice to the two contrary intuitions that generate and sustain the controversy: The first is the intuition reflected in the scientist's and often the artist's natural way of looking at the world—namely, that the truth exists, that it is the scientist's (or artist's) job to discover and communicate it, and that some attempts end in failure and others in success. The second intuition—the one that motivates not only philosophers of science like Kuhn but also those like Rorty, Nelson Goodman, and Hilary Putnam (1987), who meditate on realism in science and the arts—is that there is no ultimate standpoint, no ultimate theory or even vocabulary from which to view reality. There is always a variety of perspectives, frameworks, and stances available to the inquirers—whether they are artists or scientists.

Here is the illustration: *The Purloined Letter* by Edgar Allan Poe, the inventor of the detective story, consists primarily of the ingenious reasoning of the detective C. Auguste Dupin (the model for Sherlock Holmes) in discovering and retrieving an extremely valuable stolen letter from the apartment of the person who is known to have stolen it. (For purposes of my argument, please assume it is a true story.) On a visit to the thief, Dupin recognizes the letter because of its appearance even though that appearance differs markedly from the description given to him by the chief of police. Whereas the letter was described to him as clean, untorn, and carrying a small red seal, the letter he discovers is soiled and torn, with a large black seal, and so on. Dupin's ingenuity is revealed by the way he penetrates the mind of the thief, who, he correctly infers, has deliberately altered the document to mislead searchers.

Now, is there a correct account of how the letter came to exhibit the specific properties and location that it did? Most assuredly there is, one that alludes to the motives of the thief and the strategy he employed to conceal the letter's whereabouts. Notice that the fact that there is a correct account to be *discovered* in no way diminishes the brilliance, the artistry if you will, of M. Dupin, who succeeds where the most thorough police work has failed. But this does not settle the matter against pragmatists like Putnam and Rorty because a quite different account might have been given of the alteration of the letter's location and condition, one that made no mention of human plans and purposes at all. We could give another, *equally correct* account of the letter's change of appearance and location based exclusively on the principles of physics and chemistry. The stain on the letter would be explained in terms of the chemistry of liquids and paper; the tearing of the letter, in terms of the physics of paper; its change of location, on the basis of chemical processes originating in the thief's brain, leading to contraction of certain muscles in the fingers; and so on. To one who claimed that this explanation would explain nothing relevant to the case, Putnam (1978) and others would reply that this, precisely, demonstrates his point that explanation is always "interest-relative," that there is no such thing as an explanation that is true in some absolute sense.

The word "relative" raises the spectre of relativ*ism*, another huge topic of intense debate over the last couple of decades. I can touch on the subject only briefly. Almost everyone who has thought seriously about the issue wishes to avoid the claim that *the truth of an assertion about the world is relative to the person uttering it*. That the thief in our example tore and stained the letter to make it appear to be a worthless document either is or is not so—it is not "true for Dupin" and "false for the police." The alternative, namely, that the truth of an utterance is relative to the person uttering it, is on reflection one that is not only implausible but also difficult even to formulate coherently because the italicized portion of the sentence is itself an assertion that is intended not to depend on the person uttering it (see Krausz and Meiland 1982).

In acknowledging the legitimacy of two accounts of the stolen letter I am subscribing to a position that avoids the dangers of relativism, a position Putnam (1987) dubs "conceptual relativity." In neither of the two accounts of the letter's transformation is truth "just a name for what a bunch of people can agree on" (17–18). Still, the question "How did the letter get there in that condition?" is one that admits of two quite different kinds of answers. One appears "natural" only because of the interests we bring to the question. Given other interests, we might answer it within a different conceptual framework (see Hollis and Lukes 1982). (There are "educational interests" comparable to "cognitive interests." In certain contexts it may be valuable to give students clues and ask them to solve a problem; in other contexts, we may wish simply to provide the solution to a problem, without requiring them to discover it for themselves.) Is my position here consistent with what I said about the dependence of reformers on objectivity? I think so. The question of whether American schooling reduces or exacerbates existing social inequalities is one for which there is a *true* answer that is not "just a name for what a bunch of people can agree to." This is not to say that that answer is now available, that it is easy to find out, or that it is easy to agree on what evidence would be needed to answer with confidence, or even that we will ever be in a position to answer the question, only that its truth is independent of the number of people that can be gotten to subscribe to one or another answer. But consistent with Putnam's position I acknowledge that there is no "absolute" criterion against which the outcomes of schooling can and must be examined. Inquirers guided by other cognitive interests may wish to know, for example, how much American students know today relative to earlier generations or relative to their counterparts overseas.

This section is headed "Disciplines and Truth," but I have been speaking only about science, largely because philosphical discussions of science have generated so much excitement over the last couple of decades. Can we simply assume that the arts aim at truth and objectivity in the same way as the sciences? As I noted before, this is a topic about which no consensus is to be found. I shall limit myself here to identifying the principal alternatives and some of their exponents. Some, like Nelson Goodman (1978), would counsel against using "truth" to describe *either* the arts or the sciences; others, like Hans-Georg Gadamer (1986) and David Novitz (1987), wish to sustain the connection between art and truth while insisting that science and art pursue different paths to truth; finally, others, like Michael Oakeshott (1959), wish to maintain the separation of art and science and to deny that the former has any connection to truth at all.

Summary

Many important issues have been only barely touched on here, whereas others, such as the objectivity of social studies, have received no attention whatever. The issues touched on in this section are of fundamental philosophical importance, but it does not follow that this importance automatically transfers to the curricular arena. In the absence of substantial evidence about the relationship between teachers' conceptions of a field and their representations of it to students, it is difficult to pronounce on the matter. It is true that school subjects rarely represent disciplines as incomplete, evolving, contested, collective enterprises, but what is the reason for this: Is it that children are not in a position to countenance uncertainty and ambiguity? Is it that teachers hold philosophically naive views of the matter? Or is it simply that the hidden curriculum of schools precludes most teachers in most settings from transmitting the spirit of intellectual adventure that they, themselves, embrace? These are questions we cannot confidently answer at the present time.

KNOWLEDGE, POLITICS, AND CURRICULUM

Education has always been acknowledged to be political in the sense that it aims at promoting conditions favoring the good life, and there are many versions of what the good life is and hence of what conditions it requires. But recent debates in epistemology, raising doubts about the validity of methods and conclusions in almost every field of inquiry, have led many to assert that the processes of acquiring and transmitting knowledge are not as insulated from the political sphere as earlier generations had supposed. If political processes are involved in the very creation of knowledge, political and curricular issues must be closely intertwined, indeed. It is in fact difficult to discuss the relationship among knowledge, politics, and curriculum without alienating a section of the scholarly community because the very tone and mode of analysis might be said to reflect a political stance on the issue in question. My aim here is to be as clear and as fairminded as I can be.

Education and Politics

We are faced immediately with a somewhat paradoxical state of affairs. It is a basic tenet of the political and academic left that all educational systems are political through and through. Yet the role of politics in education in the United States appears to be minimal compared with that it plays in most European countries. There education is an avowedly partisan issue, and political parties have their educational platforms in the same way that they have their economic platforms. In the United States, in contrast, educational issues are rarely high on the political agenda at either state or national levels. It would be difficult to discern any clear differences between the educational policies of Republicans and Democrats, especially before the 1960s. Of course, there have been occasional politically inflammatory issues such as racial integration or prayer in the schools, but many Americans believe that the provision of education has been and should remain "above politics." The educational research community, modeling itself on other scientific communities, tends to reinforce this view.

Perhaps some of the air of paradox can be lifted by considering the meaning of "political," both to those who deny and to those who insist on the political character of education in the United States. Those who deny it mean primarily that education is considered to be a technical, consensual enterprise rather than a strongly partisan or ideological one. But those who claim education is fundamentally political are trying to express something different, namely, that the provision of education is closely linked to the determination of which groups have and do not have *power* in our society, regardless of whether educational issues find a prominent place on the official agenda.

Power is a notoriously difficult concept to conceptualize. Steven Lukes (1986) identifies a conception of "power" that is useful here: Assume a background of competitive and conflictual social relations. The question "Who can get what?" then presupposes that not all can get what they want or need. "Here the significant effects of power are the securing of mutually recognized advantages (material and social), in a context of relative scarcity and competing claims" (11).

Consider a popular educational manifesto by Mortimer Adler, an author not noted for his political radicalism, indeed a sometime target of the educational left (see Apple 1988). The basic argument of *The Paideia Proposal* is easily found (Adler 1982).

> We are politically a classless society. Our citizenry as a whole is our ruling class. We should, therefore, be an educationally classless society. . . . To give the same quality of schooling to all requires a program of study that is both liberal and general, and that is, in several crucial, overarching respects, one and the same for every child. (5, 21)

From this perspective, "At the very heart of a multitrack system of public schooling lies an abominable discrimination" (Adler 1982, 15). If we accept Adler's argument, public education has, indeed, been involved in an "abominable discrimination," hardly a location "above" politics. From the point of view of a subscriber to Adler's argument, the fact that educational issues rarely occupy center stage in our political debates —and that when they do, issues of effectiveness dominate—might be taken to illustrate the power of dominant interests and ideologies to configure the educational agenda and discourse in such a way as to obscure the political aspects of the debate. Perhaps we can agree on at least this: The question of the extent to which politics is necessarily embroiled in education is not easily settled by turning to the evidence because ideological opponents often disagree on what evidence is relevant and how it ought to be interpreted.

Although we may easily understand the way in which the sorting of students into different educational tracks is inescapably political, it is less easy to understand what is meant by the charge, explicit or implicit in many of the critiques made by the left, that schools reflect not only a stratification of groups and individuals but also a stratification of *knowledge*. Insofar as it concerns the role of knowledge, the critique of the academic left depends on discerning a connection among three highly plausible propositions: (1) The social world is stratified, that is, marked by inequalities of wealth, power, and prestige. (2) What was taken as knowledge in previous eras (as well as today) is marked by systematic biases, which underestimate and distort both the accomplishments and capacities of subordinate groups. (3) The distribution of knowledge is itself stratified; the knowledge transmitted to the privileged by the educational system is different in kind, amount, and organization from that which is transmitted to the less privileged. The alleged connection is that social stratification is sustained, if not created, by the school, with its stratified curricula, and is legitimized by what is taken for knowledge but is really ideology in the Marxist sense—that is, false belief, which reinforces the existing order.

I asserted that the three claims are highly plausible. I doubt that evidence on the first is needed. We might take as illustrative the relative power, both economic and political, of women vis-à-vis men or blacks vis-à-vis whites. The second proposition, to which I now turn, is the more controversial.

Science and Politics

I take it that no evidence is needed to convince readers that much which was taken to be knowledge in the past has subsequently been shown to be false. But the second claim goes beyond that: The mistakes and misinformation were not random; the distortions were systematic. Since the issue of gender bias has received the most thorough discussion, we shall take that issue as illustrative. It had been consistently maintained from the times of the Greeks that women lacked the capacities or temperament suited to roles of power and leadership. Such views were repeatedly reinforced by scientists. Barbara Ehrenreich and Deirdre English (1979) cite the characteristic warning of a physician, R. R. Coleman, writing at the end of the 19th century:

> Women beware. You are on the brink of destruction: you have hitherto been engaged in crushing your waists; now you are attempting to cultivate your mind: . . . now you are exerting your understanding to learn Greek, and solve propositions in Euclid. Beware! Science pronounces that the woman who studies is lost. (128)

Although such obviously outrageous statements rarely get into print today, the charge persists that even the most contemporary, "objective" studies contain subtle biases against women. After reviewing a number of sources of such biases in the social sciences, Sandra Harding (1986) concludes, "feminist criticisms do severely challenge social science's self-perceived attempts to be value-neutral, objective, and dispassionate" (91). The same may be said with respect to biological studies of gender differences, according to Harding. She charges that "biology and the social sciences have been key culprits in promulgating what we can now see as false and socially regressive understandings of women's and men's natures and 'proper' activities in social life" (106; see also Committee on the Status of Women in Sociology 1980). Even contemporary investigations of gender differences by biologists have been subject to cogent criticisms (Bleier 1984; O'Rand 1989). I have neither the space nor the competence to assess authoritatively the merits of such charges, but I do find the evidence persuasive.

More difficult to assess, even to understand, is the charge that science itself exhibits gender (and perhaps other) biases, not only in most of its branches but also at its very roots. It is plausible to suppose that many, perhaps most, studies that focus on the fundamental features of human biological and social life will contain subtle and not so subtle biases if they are carried out by men only or whites only. (Note that such accusations, if they are to be demonstrated, presuppose a realist rather than a "constructivist" view of science; the charge is that *mistaken* conclusions are based on partial evidence or tendentious argumentation.)

But it is not so easy to know what it would mean to say that Chandrasekhar's (1987) or Eddington's cosmological models (mentioned in the last section) were androcentric. The ideological critics of science are tempted to view all science as a reflection of the social position of the scientists. For this reason, some feminists appear to believe that only a feminist science can rectify the errors of androcentric science (see, e.g., Harding 1986, chap. 6; Rose 1983). But what would be the relationship between masculine and feminine science? One possibility is that they would complement each other, each capturing some aspect of reality. But as Harding herself has noted, the two sciences immediately proliferate into more (chap. 7), for there are points of view not represented by white heterosexuals—those of homosexuals or native Americans or Africans, for example. Is there to be a separate science for each social or cultural group?

A second possibility is that feminist science will replace androcentric science.

> The feminist standpoint epistemologies argue that because men are in the master's position vis-à-vis women, women's social experience—conceptualized through the lenses of feminist theory—can provide the grounds for a less distorted understanding of the world around us. (Harding 1986, 191)

Is there any reason whatever to think that women have a less distorted view of cosmology or immunology than men? Have the "standpoint epistemologists" heard about the Nazi campaign to discredit theoretical physics in the late 1930s when the theories of Einstein and others were labeled products of the "Jewish spirit" (Weiner 1969)?

Perhaps the feminist claim is that *feminist science*, not female scientists, will provide a less distorted view of the world. Feminist science, according to Evelyn Fox Keller (1982), would be science "less restrained by the impulse to dominate" (which she takes to be a typically masculine impulse), science guided by the impulse to "converse" with nature (601). I am not sure whether the dichotomy between conversing with and dominating nature is relevant to all fields of science. Does it apply to cosmology, the study of the origin and structure of the physical universe, for example? Is Einstein's theory of relativity illustrative of an attempt to dominate nature because it led to the making of the atomic bomb? Suppose Barbara McClintock's pioneer work in genetics (Keller's exemplar of the "conversational" stance) is used to develop biological weapons. Would that make McClintock an apostle of domination? I suspect that any wholesale attempt to link gender attitudes with scientific attitudes raises at least as many questions as it answers.

Perhaps the claim in the quote by Harding should be limited to an understanding of the social world. Even here, though, as feminist philosopher Claudia Card (1988) has courageously argued, the contention is hardly credible because whereas the master harbors a partial and distorted view of the social world, so does the slave. According to the Brazilian educational philosopher Paulo Freire (1970), they have, in fact, the same view; the slave internalizes the view of the master.

Despite the justified criticisms that may be lodged against the "standpoint epistemologies," they do contain, in my view, an important grain of truth. This truth can best be appreciated in the light of an illuminating discussion of subjectivity and objectivity by Thomas Nagel (1986):

> An objective standpoint is created by leaving a more subjective, individual, or even just human perspective behind; but there are things about the world and life and ourselves that cannot be adequately understood from a maximally objective standpoint. . . . A great deal is essentially connected to a particular point of view, or type of point of view, and the attempt to give a complete account of the world in objective terms detached from these perspectives inevitably leads to false reductions or to outright denial that certain patently real phenomena exist at all. (7)

There is, I believe, no strong reason for believing that either feminist science or female scientists have or will develop a better understanding of the biology of reproduction than conventional science or male scientists, to take an example. But it is quite likely that inquiries into the *significance* of children in the lives of their parents or into the *experience* of childbirth will overlook or distort important aspects of experience if the investigators are all male or if the questions they pose and the frameworks they employ to answer them are not informed by the contributions of feminist scholars. (Additional discussions of the relation between gender and science may also be found in Gergen 1988; Grimshaw 1986; Jaggar 1983; Keller 1982; Levin 1988; Martin 1988, 1989; Winant 1987).

The feminist critiques of gender relations in society and of science itself share a common assumption: that all human enterprises are ultimately social products whose malleability is limited not by nature but solely by ideology and convention based on power relations. It is only to be expected that most opponents of the status quo would embrace a position that underestimated the limits of such malleability. Since such limits may well exist—this is after all a question that cannot be answered a priori—I conclude this section with a quotation that although endorsing a realist view of science, acknowledges, even embraces, the biological contribution to human nature. What makes the quotation noteworthy is that it comes not from a political conservative but from Noam Chomsky (1988), a scholar with unimpeachable progressive credentials:

> Surely people differ in their biologically determined qualities. The world would be too horrible to contemplate if they did not. . . .
>
> Case by case it is difficult to take seriously the idea that environmentalism is somehow "progressive" and should therefore be adopted as doctrine. Furthermore, the issue is irrelevant, because the issue is one of truth, not doctrine. Questions of fact cannot be resolved on the basis of ideological commitment. As I have observed throughout, we should be delighted that environmentalism is utterly misconceived, but the question of truth or falsity is not resolved by our preference for one or another outcome of inquiry. (164–165)

Obviously, a quotation does not constitute an argument, but it may give pause to uncritical adherents of the view that "progressive" social views are incompatible with standard ideas about science and truth or with recognition of our biological inheritance.

Knowledge and Social Stratification

The third fundamental proposition in the radical critique, that knowledge is itself stratified, is difficult to challenge. Take the totality of knowledge to include everything from folk wisdom to common sense to expert knowledge, from popular culture to high culture. It is obvious that different branches of this knowledge have differential (though alterable) social prestige.

Consider a few illustrations: Knowing how to change a diaper has lower prestige than knowing how to change a heart valve. Knowing how to address an audience of elementary school teachers has less prestige than knowing how to address an audience of diplomats. It is also obvious that the totality of knowledge is not diffused equally throughout the population, nor is its distribution random. So, for example, more women than men know how to change a diaper; more men than women know how to change a heart valve. More people at the upper end of the social scale know how to address diplomats.

Differences in the social value and distribution of knowledge extend to the "subjective" realm of taste as well. Few lower-income people can identify a painting by Rembrandt, an aria from Mozart's *Magic Flute*, a performance by Artur Schnabel, or a film of Ingmar Bergman. As there are differences in economic assets, so we may say with the French sociologist Pierre Bourdieu (1984; Bourdieu and Passeron, 1977) that there are differences in the *cultural capital* owned by different "social classes." The subordinate groups do not lack culture, but the cultural capital they possess is accorded a lower value by those who have power and prestige. The distribution of economic capital does not completely coincide with cultural capital; but there is a considerable overlap both at the top, in what Bourdieu (1984, 114–125) calls the dominant class, and at the bottom, where semiskilled and unskilled workers have neither economic nor cultural capital. Bourdieu studied France, of course, but there is evidence that his general schema applies to the United States as well (DiMaggio 1982b, 1982c).

The delineation of our "common heritage" always reflects the interests of particular groups or classes to some extent, as Raymond Williams (1961) has persuasively argued. The corpus of that which is worthy of preservation and transmission constitutes an evolving "selective tradition" (chap. 2). Decisions about what to preserve and transmit, which imply decisions about how dominant groups wish to represent a society to itself and to the next generation, involve issues of power as well as merit. In any generation, some worthwhile works are neglected while other, less meritorious works are preserved. The interests of dominant groups in such decisions are often visible. An egregious illustration of the operation of the "selective tradition" is provided by the representation of native Americans in American history books (see, e.g., Fitzgerald 1979).

The evidence for each of the three propositions is, I believe, compelling. What has been and remains contentious, however, is the notion that the evolution of schooling has served to sustain rather than to undermine existing patterns of stratification. To what extent have and do educational institutions distribute knowledge unequally?

We need to begin with the fact that from the earliest schools in Roman times until well into the 20th century, the most prestigious knowledge was transmitted to men of the privileged classes alone. The philosophical tradition was closed to women until the last century. The rhetorical tradition in the Renaissance, though including an occasional woman, was fundamentally a male preserve (Grafton and Jardine 1986; Ong 1971). The scientific tradition remains dominated by males. Only the apprenticeship tradition embraced women and men of the less privileged classes.

The movement to educate students of all social classes, both men and women, is not much more than a hundred years old. But even this revolutionary movement did not seek to provide the same knowledge to men and women of all classes and races (Bryant 1979; Kaestle 1983; Muller, Ringer, and Simon 1987; Wardle 1970; Williams 1966).

The alignment of curriculum to social class was no secret. In an 1867 pamphlet, Robert Lowe stated the aims of the movement to expand public education in England:

> The lower classes ought to be educated to discharge the duties cast upon them. They should also be educated that they may appreciate and defer to a higher cultivation when they meet it, and the higher classes ought to be educated in a very different manner in order that they may exhibit to the lower classes, that higher education to which, if it were shown to them they would bow down and defer. (Quoted in Wardle 1970, 25)

To take another example, Victor Duruy, a mid-19th-century French educational reformer, proposed a new secondary track for those not expected to continue their studies in higher education:

> From the foundation provided by an enlarged and unified primary system, two parallel secondary programmes will rise: one classical, for the so-called liberal professions; the other vocational, for careers in commerce, industry and agriculture. . . . [Children] of different [social] origins and destinations will thus live together . . . and this contact will profit both groups. (Cited in Muller, Ringer, and Simon 1987, 73)

The new world was not as class conscious as the old. But here, too, the notion that different curricula were appropriate for different students became conventional wisdom in the early 20th century (Kliebard 1986). The influential educational reformer Edward Thorndike believed that the task of the high school was to prepare students for their future vocations. He described a majority of students entering high school who were not "efficient at dealing with ideas, but whose talent is for the manipulation of things" (quoted in Kliebard 1986, 109). These students would be better suited to curriculum tracks that emphasized practical subjects rather than the traditional academic subjects.

But even today, when such differentiation is much less acceptable, the knowledge distributed to students in different tracks under the same academic rubric is far from equivalent, as Jeannie Oakes (1985) has shown. So, for example, although all students are required to take English in high school, what is taught to students in different tracks is dissimilar. Those in the high tracks are exposed to standard works of literature, classic and modern. The lower-track students do not encounter these works.

> What literature they did encounter was so-called young-adult fiction—short novels with themes designed to appeal to teenagers . . . and written at a low level of difficulty. These novels constituted part of the focus of low-track novels on basic literacy skills. (76)

Of course, track placement need not coincide with social class, but it usually does. Oakes notes that in virtually every study that has been conducted, "poor and minority students have been found in disproportionately large percentages in the bottom groups" (64).

Although we tend to conceive of the selection and representation of knowledge to different groups of students in apolitical terms, many historically significant conflicts over curriculum were bound up with issues of power and justice in the larger society. The debate between Dewey and David Snedden over vocational education in the pages of the *New Republic* is one of many examples found in Kliebard's (1986, 145–149) history of curriculum in the United States. Numerous recent histories examining in detail the evolution of curriculum subjects in England and the United States attest to the importance of larger social and political conflicts in determining who is taught what (see Freedman and Popkewitz 1988; Goodson 1985; Johnson 1979; Layton 1973; Popkewitz 1987).

The "New" Sociology of Education

The study of the systematic connections between the stratification of knowledge in society and school curricula has been the dominant theme of the "new sociology of education" pioneered by French and British sociologists. Their original and primary emphasis has been on class rather than gender or other inequalities. The founders of this line of research include Bourdieu (1977) in France, Basil Bernstein in England (1971a, 1971b, 1972, 1975), Raymond Williams (1966), and M. F. D. Young (1971). In the United States, principal contemporary exponents of the approach are Michael Apple (1979, 1982, 1988) and Henry Giroux (1981; Anyon 1979; Wexler 1987). I shall offer a concise summary of only a few of the leading ideas, postponing my critique to the subsequent section.

Whereas some may view the spread of formal schooling as an attempt to liberate the unschooled classes from ignorance, Bourdieu sees it as a means of maintaining class domination. For him imposition is the essence of education, which does not imply that imposition is the motive of educators or that schooling is experienced as oppressive.

> In any given social formation, because the PW [pedagogic work] through which the dominant PA [pedagogic action] is carried on tends to impose recognition of the legitimacy of the dominant culture on the members of the dominated groups or classes, it tends at the same time to impose on them, by inculcation or exclusion, recognition of the illegitimacy of their own cultural arbitrary. (Bourdieu and Passeron 1977,41)

Bourdieu offers an illustration: "Home medicine" is implicitly delegitimized when scientific medicine and hygiene are taught, "providing a market for material and especially symbolic products . . . which . . . are virtually monopolized by the dominant classes (e.g., clinical diagnosis . . .)" (42).

What is striking about Bourdieu's formulation is his use of the adjective "arbitrary" to describe the culture of both dominant and subordinate classes. He provides his own definition:

> The selection of meanings which objectively defines a group's or a class's culture as a symbolic system is *arbitrary* insofar as the structure and functions of that culture cannot be deduced from any universal principle, whether physical, biological or spiritual, not being linked by any sort of internal relation to "the nature of things" or any "human nature." (Bourdieu and Passeron 1977, 8; italics in original)

The notion that the knowledge selected for transmission by the school is in an important sense arbitrary is fundamental to the "new sociology." It is implicit in M. F. D. Young's (1971) statement that sociologists ought to begin with the assumption that "those in positions of power will attempt to define what is to be *taken* as knowledge . . ." (32; emphasis added) and in his assertion that "academic curricula in this country involve assumptions that some kinds and areas of knowledge are much more 'worthwhile' than others" (34).

Bourdieu's definition is unimpeachable; a survey of other cultures would reveal that there is no cultural or human imperative that demands that Latin or physics even exist, much less that they be singled out for transmission in schools (Bourdieu and Passeron 1977). And Young's stance is necessary for the sociologist of knowledge who wishes to inquire into the mechanisms by which knowledge is stratified. When we look at the history of curriculum in the West, moreover, the notion that certain kinds of knowledge were privileged over others, on a basis that can only be considered arbitrary, becomes compelling. Take note, once again, of the fact that for about 700 years after their invention in the 13th century, universities granted admission only to those who had mastery of a language that barely anyone had spoken since the fall of the Roman Empire, a language that was rarely accessible to the vast masses of peasants and laborers, whose children had neither the resources nor the leisure to acquire it.

Bourdieu focuses on the way in which the rhetorical tradition, which dominates French secondary schooling, reproduces the ascendancy of the privileged classes (Bourdieu and Passeron 1977). Bernstein's (1971b) emphasis is less on the issue of knowledge selection and more on the issues of conceptualization and organization. In his important essay "On the Classification and Framing of Educational Knowledge," he introduces a number of alternative ways in which knowledge can be organized for transmission. His contrast between "collection codes" and "integrated codes" roughly parallels my earlier designation of "disciplinary" and "progressive" modes of conceptualizing knowledge (51–54). Bernstein suggests that the "collection code" prevalent in schools provides a view of knowledge as rigid and hierarchical, a view mirrored in the school's organizational characteristics.

In a subsequent article, Bernstein (1975) argues that the early socialization of middle-class children prepares them for initiation into the collection code whereas that of working-class children does not. The upshot is that the dominant collection code provides an advantage to the more privileged. Thus, "the less rigid social structure of the integrated code makes it a potential code for egalitarian education" (1971b, 67). The entire new sociology tradition may be said to be concerned with the conditions giving rise to domination and subordination. Instead of accepting the view that the differential political and economic resources mobilized by different groups depend either on differential genetic endowment, as conservatives might hold, or on distinctive parenting and cultural styles, as many liberals would maintain, this tradition looks at the way knowledge itself becomes stratified and to the processes whereby curriculum selection, conceptualization, and organization tend to favor those who already control the resources of the society.

Social Inequality and Curriculum Design

The new sociologists seek to explain the sources of continuing social inequality, not to provide remedies for it. What is the status of their explanations? Although Bourdieu's study included some empirical evidence about the relationship between schooling and social mobility, his contribution is primarily theoretical (Bourdieu and Passeron 1977). M. F. D. Young, in his 1971 paper, was essentially setting out a research agenda, and Bernstein (1971b) in his chapter in the same volume underlines the point that his scheme of knowledge classification "requires at every point empirical evidence" (68). There have, to be sure, been a number of excellent ethnographic studies such as the oft-cited study of working-class youths in England by Paul Willis (1977). Although suggestive, such work suffers from two weaknesses: Its practitioners often draw sweeping conclusions about the nature of schooling in Great Britain, the United States, or in other advanced capitalist societies, but the basis for such far-reaching generalizations is often quite meager. More regrettable is the fact that many studies employ modes of analysis that presuppose the validity of the theory at issue. Thus, starting from another perspective, one may view the same data in a quite different light (see, e.g., Hargreaves 1982).

In the United States, Bourdieu's ideas have furnished the basis for some careful empirical work by DiMaggio (1982b, 1982c; DiMaggio and Mohr 1985), although these studies are constrained by the lack of data. In a paper on the relation of cultural capital and school success, for example, DiMaggio (1982a) found that after controlling for family background and measured ability, cultural capital has a significant impact on grades in high school. The evolution of the distinction between high and popular culture in the United States is the focus of some of DiMaggio's work and also of Lawrence Levine's (1988) *Highbrow/Lowbrow*. The latter shows, for example, that in mid-19th-century America, Shakespeare's plays enjoyed wide popular appeal to audiences of every class and ethnic group. Only subsequently did the bard become the exclusive possession of the educated portions of society.

Although they do not derive directly from Bourdieu, some excellent studies of books written for the young explore the way in which the more powerful groups' depiction of the social world can serve purposes of domination. See Joel Taxel's (1986) study of the portrayal of the black experience in children's fiction and Linda Christian-Smith's (1987) analysis of the representation of women in adolescent romance fiction. The evolution and role of "cultural capital" in promoting social stratification remains, I believe, fertile ground for historians and sociologists of education.

A 1985 volume by Geoff Whitty, a student of Bernstein, which traces the evolution of the new sociology from the late 1960s to the early 1980s, provides a useful overview of its accomplishments. To this point, however, I can only conclude that despite some impressive individual studies inspired by the new sociology, a systematic body of evidence clearly supporting its assertions does not exist (see also Eggleston 1977; Lawton 1975).

The new sociologists make no secret of their distaste for social stratification, their commitment to a more egalitarian society. What curriculum proposals emanate from this position? Unfortunately, the majority of people identified with this position show an uncharacteristic reticence when it comes to providing models or blueprints of egalitarian curricula. There are, to be sure, general admonitions about "alternative curricular and teaching practices drawing on the students' own cultural and economic experiences of work and family, and grounded in their class, race, and gender realities . . ." (Apple 1988, 193). Cherryholmes (1988) gestures in the same direction when he asks what appears to him to be a rhetorical question: "Do we want to provide opportunities to learn a structure of the disciplines at the expense of teaching about the causes and consequences of racism, sexism, and social inequality and injustice?" (143). The Australian educational scholar Bob Connell also argues for the rejection of the "hegemonic curriculum."

> A . . . notion is now emerging. . . . It proposes that working-class kids get access to formal knowledge via learning which begins with their own experience and the circumstances which shape it, but does not stop there. This approach neither accepts the existing organization of academic knowledge nor simply inverts it. It draws on existing school knowledge and on what working-class people already know, and organizes this selection of information around problems such as economic survival and collective action . . . managing the problems of personal identity and association, understanding how schools work, and why. (Connell, Ashenden, Kessler, and Dowsett 1982, 199–200)

Much of this rhetoric is simply warmed-over progressivism dressed up in contemporary jargon. The disinclination to go beyond vague gestures can be traced, in part, to a reluctance to play the role of cultural imperialist, to legislate for others what they ought to study (see Apple 1986). I sympathize with such reluctance, but I see no reason why it precludes the proposal of perhaps a number of model curricula, at least for discussion purposes. The British scholar Raymond Williams (1966, 153–154) did just that in his widely and justifiably admired work, to which I have already alluded. Whatever the reason for their disinclination to publicize model curricula, the voice of the new sociologists is muted in national debates about curriculum.

A question that exponents of the new sociology are fond of asking when critiquing curricular proposals emanating from other sources is, Whose knowledge is it? The question generally presupposes a view, found explicitly in Bourdieu, as noted earlier, that what is "taken" for knowledge to be transmitted in school is largely arbitrary, a reflection of which class or group has power and which does not. This presupposition merits scrutiny. In some contexts it appears to me to be absolutely appropriate. Consider music, on the one hand: If a curriculum proposes the study of "classical" music and identifies composers to be studied, from Bach to Stravinsky, the question "*Whose* music is it?" is justified. The question implies that there are alternative traditions of music, equally rich, equally unfamiliar to most young people (otherwise why study them in school), and equally worthy of the designation "classical" if by that is meant music of lasting value. Are there such traditions? Indeed, there are. Jazz is one such tradition; folk music is another.

The choice of one tradition and the exclusion of the others is quite arbitrary. The explanation for the inclusion and exclusion must focus on the differential power of different groups to define what is taken to be "classical."

Consider chemistry, on the other hand: Take the periodic table of the elements, a staple of almost any chemistry course ever taught, and ask the question, Whose knowledge is it? Does music offer an analogy? Is Williams's notion of "selective tradition" applicable here? I think not. Of course, an understanding of the periodic table is more likely to be found in socially privileged groups, but the implication that there are equally rich, equally valid versions of chemistry that are the property of the dispossessed is simply unfounded. Of course, there are different versions of chemistry as we saw, some that emphasize and others that conceal its connections to society. But none of these is the "property" of any subordinate group. Whether particular versions of chemistry benefit or handicap particular groups is an important empirical question, which cannot be settled by pronouncement.

The inclusion of the periodic table, even the inclusion of chemistry itself, in a curriculum is still arbitrary in Bourdieu's sense; it cannot be "deduced from any universal principle," but it is far from arbitrary in the ordinary sense. Much of the human-made world depends on knowledge derived from chemistry, and as far as the survival of our industrial civilization is concerned, such knowledge is anything but arbitrary. G. A. Cohen (1978) makes this point about physics in his impressive defense of Marx's historical materialism:

> Destroy all steam engines but preserve knowledge of how to make and use them and, with a bit of luck in the matter of raw materials, you can soon return to the *status quo ante*. Destroy the knowledge and preserve the engine and you have a useless ensemble of metal, a material surd, a relic of the future (unless the producers have enough skill left to rediscover the engine's *modus operandi*, but that they could, with *sufficient* general knowledge, do so is a way of making our point). (41–42; italics in original)

We may imagine a spectrum: Music with a number of diverse, legitimate traditions tied to distinctive cultural groups lies at one end, and physics and chemistry, with no such legitimate diversity, lie at the other. Many disciplines, such as medicine and education, lie in between. It is in the middle of the spectrum that the relations between power and knowledge are especially intimate and difficult to disentangle (see Foucault 1972; Rabinow 1984; Rajchman 1985).

The fact that the knowledge of physics and chemistry underlies our civilization is not *sufficient* reason for including them in the curriculum. By the same token, the fact that the music of Bach to Stravinsky is not part of working-class culture is not sufficient reason to exclude it from the curriculum of the working class. Excluding physics and chemistry from such curricula because they form no part of working-class knowledge would appear to undermine the very equality the political left is committed to. Many decisions that affect the distribution of wealth and power depend on the conclusions of chemists and physicists; moreover, a modicum of understanding of those fields is part of the "cultural capital" of the dominant groups.

The case of "classical" music is more difficult. Its role in forming the cultural capital of the privileged could be said to provide a strong reason for those committed to equality to press for its inclusion. This is the burden of the argument in E. D. Hirsch, Jr.'s (1987) much discussed *Cultural Literacy*. Hirsch's opponents on the left—who often mistakenly label him an elitist—argue that the notion of "classical" needs to be broadened to include the other traditions. I agree, but I see no reason why the two projects have to be seen as mutually exclusive. It is disingenuous for Hirsch's critics to impugn the cultural literacy that makes it possible for them to participate in the conversation about the future of our educational system.

Summary

How, finally, do I assess the contribution of the new sociology and more generally the educational left? These scholars played an important role in challenging the "functionalist" paradigm that was dominant for a good part of the 1950s and 1960s, a paradigm that suggested that each component of the society was the way it was because of the particular role that it played in maintaining the equilibrium of the whole. In emphasizing the role of conflict and contestation in the evolution of school systems and curricula, the educational left demonstrated the way in which conflicts within the educational sphere mirror conflicts in the wider society, where issues of power cannot be overlooked. They correctly stressed the point well formulated by the British social theorist J. B. Thompson (1984):

> What may have seemed like a sphere of effective consensus must in many cases be seen as a realm of actual or potential conflict. Hence the meaning of what is said—what is asserted in spoken or written discourse as well as that about which one speaks or writes—is infused with forms of power; different individuals or groups have a differential capacity to make a meaning stick. (132)

M. F. D. Young, Bernstein, and Bourdieu, among others, have proposed some important issues for inquiry, and made some suggestive conjectures. Unfortunately despite some exemplary individual studies, educational scholars identified with the left have never investigated these conjectures as systematically as would have been required to convince scholars with a different ideological bent of the veracity of their assertions. Indeed, at times the educational left appears to exhibit a disdain for systematic empirical investigation, a disdain that makes it easy for scholars with different political allegiances to ignore their claims. At the same time, their reluctance to propose model curricula for elementary and high schools or to produce any equivalent to the popular manifestos of Adler, Bennett, Hirsch, or the AAAS (to name just those referred to) has restricted the public debate to centrist and neoconservative positions.

CONCLUSION

As I acknowledged at the outset, the four major themes I have treated do not carry forward a single line of argument. I hope the chapter as a whole does show that some of the debates among philosophers and some of the resources of philosophical argumentation are germane to curricular issues. But I also hope to have shown that the best entry to these debates is by way of the curricular issues themselves. Educational scholars can and should make use of what philosophy has to offer without allowing their agendas to be set by philosophers. The following brief conclusion, then, is not so much a summing up of what has gone before as a succinct overview of the immense challenges facing curriculum designers at the beginning of the 1990s.

The problem of curriculum design is twofold: the selection, conceptualization, and organization of content, and the design of institutional settings congruent with the educational aspirations that undergird that selection. In the hundred or so years since schooling for all became an agreed-upon goal, the task of curriculum design has become harder for several reasons. First, the increasing heterogeneity of students makes us uncertain whether the pursuit of democracy requires a single curriculum for all or a plurality of curricula. Hirsch, Bennett, and Adler argue that democracy requires a single curriculum. Conservatives such as G. H. Bantock (1980a) argue that a uniform curriculum serves the educational needs of neither the academically talented nor the slower learner. Some educators on the political left, such as Connell, also appear to be committed to offering diverse curricula to distinct cultural groups and classes.

Second, the explosion of knowledge and the growing heterogeneity of individual disciplines makes identification of what is basic or fundamental almost impossible. It also puts an increasingly severe strain on the aspiration to provide any coherence to the course of studies, a problem that already loomed large to Vico (1965 [1708]) at the beginning of the 18th century.

Third, as we become more sophisticated, we realize that even our most deeply held convictions about the development of understanding, those that form the basis for the way we think about curriculum, are far from immune to challenge. Take a notion we have adopted from Dewey and other progressive educators as illustration: Curriculum ought to begin with the familiar, with the life-world of the child, only gradually expanding horizons outward in time and space. This conventional wisdom has been powerfully challenged by an articulate minority who argue on various grounds that schools need to provide a sharp break with everyday experience rather than to build on it (Egan 1988; Floden, Buchmann, and Schwille 1987; Oakeshott, in Fuller 1989).

Finally, although the growth of choices about what and how to proceed seems to be overwhelming, at least in theory, the settings within which we could implement these choices has remained very stable for a century. Thus the power of the organizational "noise" may swamp whatever "signals" we might wish to send. This institutional stagnation is not just a source of frustration to curriculum reformers; it is a barrier to our finding out what the possibilities for educational revitalization might actually be.

References

Adler, Mortimer. 1982. *The Paideia Proposal: An Educational Manifesto*. New York: Macmillan.

Aldridge, Bill G. 1989. *Essential Changes in Secondary School Science: Scope, Sequence and Coordination* Washington, DC: National Science Teachers Association.

Althusser, Louis. 1971. *Lenin and Philosophy*, translated by Ben Brewster. New York: Monthly Review Press.

Anyon, Jean. 1979. Ideology and U.S. history textbooks. *Harvard Educational Review* 49(3): 361–386.

Apple, Michael W. 1979. *Ideology and Curriculum*. London: Routledge & Kegan Paul.

Apple, Michael W. 1982. *Education and Power*. Boston: Routledge & Kegan Paul.

Apple, Michael W. 1986. Curriculum, capitalism, and democracy: A response to Whitty's critics. *British Journal of Sociology of Education* 7(3): 319–327.

Apple, Michael W. 1988. *Teachers and Texts: A Political Economy of Class and Gender Relations in Education*. New York: Routledge.

Apple, Michael W. 1989. Regulating the text: The socio-historical roots of state control. *Educational Policy* 3(2): 107–123.

Arnheim, Rudolph. 1985. "The Double-Edged Mind: Intuition and the Intellect." In *Learning and Teaching the Ways of Knowing. Eighty-fourth Yearbook of the National Society for the Study of Education*, Part II, edited by Elliot Eisner, 77–96. Chicago: NSSE.

Arnold, Matthew. 1960 (1868). *Culture and Anarchy*. Cambridge: Cambridge University Press.

Bailey, Charles. 1984. *Beyond the Present and the Particular: A Theory of Liberal Education*. London: Routledge & Kegan Paul.

Bantock, George H. 1980a. *Dilemmas of the Curriculum*. Oxford: Martin Robertson.

Bantock, George H. 1980b. *Studies in the History of Educational Theory. Volume 1: Artifice and Nature, 1350–1765*. London: George Allen & Unwin.

Bantock, George H. 1984. *Studies in the History of Educational Theory. Volume 2: The Minds and the Masses, 1760–1980*. London: George Allen & Unwin.

Bell, Daniel. 1966. *The Reforming of General Education: The Columbia College Experience in its National Setting*. New York and London: Columbia University Press.

Bellah, Robert, R. Madsen, W. M. Sullivan, A. Swidler, and S. M. Tipton. 1985. *Habits of the Heart: Individualism and Commitment in American Life*. Berkeley: University of California Press.

Bennett, William J. 1987. *James Madison High School: A Curriculum for American Students*. Washington, DC: U.S. Department of Education.

Bereiter, Carl, and Marlene Scardamalia. In press. *Expertise as Process*. La Salle, IL: Open Court.

Berkson, William, and John Wettersten. 1984. *Learning from Error: Karl Popper's Psychology of Learning*. La Salle, IL: Open Court.

Bernstein, Basil. 1971a. *Class, Codes and Control. Volume 1: Theoretical Studies Towards a Sociology of Language*. London: Routledge & Kegan Paul.

Bernstein, Basil. 1971b. "On the Classification and Framing of Educational Knowledge." In *Knowledge and Control: New Directions for the Sociology of Education*, edited by Michael F. D. Young, 47–69. London: Collier-Macmillan.

Bernstein, Basil. 1972. *Class, Codes and Control. Volume 2: Applied Studies Towards a Sociology of Language*. London: Routledge & Kegan Paul.

Bernstein, Basil. 1975. *Class, Codes and Control. Volume 3: Towards a Theory of Educational Transmissions*. London: Routledge & Kegan Paul.

Black, P. J. 1988. *National Curriculum: Report of the Task Group on Assessment and Testing*. London: Department of Education and Science and the Welsh Office.

Bleier, Ruth. 1984. *Science and Gender: A Critique of Biology and Its Theories on Women*. New York: Pergamon.

Bonjour, Lawrence. 1985. *The Structure of Empirical Knowledge*. Cambridge, MA: Harvard University Press.

Bourdieu, Pierre. 1984. *Distinction: A Social Critique of the Judgment of Taste*, translated by Richard Nice. Cambridge, MA: Harvard University Press.

Bourdieu, Pierre, and Jean Claude Passeron. 1977. *Reproduction in Education, Society and Culture*, translated by Richard Nice. London and Beverly Hills, CA: Sage.

Bowles, Samuel, and Herbert Gintis. 1976. *Schooling in Capitalist America*. New York: Basic Books.

Brenner, Charles. 1957. *An Elementary Textbook of Psychoanalysis*. Garden City, NY: Doubleday Anchor.

Broudy, Harry S. 1977. "Types of Knowledge and Purposes of Education." In *Schooling and the Acquisition of Knowledge*, edited by Richard C. Anderson, Rand J. Spiro, and William E. Montague, 1–18. Hillsdale, NJ: Erlbaum.

Broudy, Harry S. 1988. *The Uses of Schooling*. New York and London: Routledge.

Bruner, Jerome. 1985. "Narrative and Paradigmatic Modes of Thought." In *Learning and Teaching the Ways of Knowing. Eighty-fourth Yearbook of the National Society for the Study of Education*, Part II, edited by Elliot Eisner, 97–115. Chicago: NSSE.

Bryant, Margaret. 1979. *The Unexpected Revolution: A Study in the History of the Education of Women and Girls in the Nineteenth Century*. London: University of London Institute of Education.

Bud, Robert, and Gerrylynn K. Roberts. 1984. *Science versus Practice: Chemistry in Victorian Britain*. Manchester, England: Manchester University Press.

Bugliarello, George. 1989. *Physical and Information Sciences and Engineering Report of the Project 2061: Phase I, Physical and Information Sciences and Engineering Panel*. Washington, DC: American Association for the Advancement of Science.

Burns, Gerald T. 1987. "Revolution by Committee: The NEA and the Emergence of the Modern American Secondary Curriculum in the 1890's." Paper presented at the Annual Meeting, History of Education Society, New York.

Campbell, Donald T. 1974. "Evolutionary Epistemology." In *The Philosophy of Karl Popper*, Book 1. La Salle, IL: Open Court.

Card, Claudia. 1988. Women's voices and ethical ideals: Must we mean what we say? *Ethics* 99(1): 125–135.

Carmichael, L. N., David F. Haines, and Robert C. Smoot. 1975. *Laboratory Chemistry: Teacher's Annotated Edition*. Columbus, OH: Charles E. Merrill.

Cavell, Stanley. 1986. Observations on art and science. *Daedalus* 115(3): 171–177.

Chandrasekhar, S. 1987. *Truth and Beauty: Aesthetics and Motivations in Science*. Chicago: University of Chicago Press.

Cherryholmes, Cleo. 1988. *Power and Criticism: Poststructural Investigations in Education*. New York: Teachers College Press.

Chisholm, Roderick. 1982. *The Foundations of Knowing*. Brighton, England: Harvester Press.

Chomsky, Noam. 1988. *Language and Problems of Knowledge: The Managua Lectures*. Cambridge, MA: MIT Press.

Christian-Smith, Linda. 1987. Gender, popular culture, and curriculum: Adolescent romance novels as gender text. *Curriculum Inquiry* 17(4): 365–406.

Cohen, G. A. 1978. *Karl Marx's Theory of History: A Defence*. Princeton, NJ: Princeton University Press.

Committee on the Status of Women in Sociology, American Sociology Association. 1980. *Sexist Biases in Sociological Research: Problems and Issues*. Washington, DC: Association of American Colleges.

Connell, R. W., D. J. Ashenden, S. Kessler, and G. W. Dowsett. 1982. *Making the Difference*. Sidney: George Allen & Unwin.

Cowan, Donald, and Theodore Puck. 1984. "Science." In *The Paideia Program: An Educational Syllabus*, edited by Mortimer Adler, 86–108. New York: Macmillan.

Crombie, Alistair C. 1986. Experimental science and the rational artist in early modern Europe. *Daedalus* 115(3): 49–74.

Cuban, Larry. 1984. *How Teachers Taught: Constancy and Change in American Classrooms 1890–1980*. White Plains, NY: Longman.

De Gonzales DeLeon, Corinne. 1987. Classifactory schemes and the justification of educational content: A reinterpretation of the Hirstian approach. *Journal of Philosophy of Education* 21(1): 103–111.

Demmin, Peter. 1987. *A Learning Program for Chemistry*. 2nd ed. Newton, MA: CEBCO-Allyn & Bacon.

Descartes, René. 1955 (1628). "Rules for the Direction of the Mind." In *Philosophical Works of Descartes*, vol. 1, edited by Elizabeth S. Haldane and G. R. T. Ross, 1–77. New York: Dover.

Dewey, John. 1938. *Experience and Education*. New York: Macmillan.

Dewey, John. 1966 (1936). "The Theory of the Chicago Experiment." In *The Dewey School: The Laboratory School of the University of Chicago, 1896–1903*, edited by Katherine C. Mayhew and Anna C. Edwards, 463–477. New York: Atherton Press.

DiMaggio, Paul. 1982a. Cultural capital and school success: The impact of status culture on the grades of U.S. high school students. *American Sociological Review* 47(2): 189–201.

DiMaggio, Paul. 1982b. Cultural enterpreneurship in nineteenth-century Boston: The creation of an organizational base for high culture in America, Part 1. *Media, Culture, and Society* 4(1): 33–50.

DiMaggio, Paul. 1982c. Cultural entrepreneurship in nineteenth-century Boston: The classification and framing of American art, Part 2. *Media, Culture, and Society* 4(4): 303–322.

DiMaggio, Paul, and John Mohr. 1985. Cultural capital, educational attainment, and marital selection. *American Journal of Sociology* 90(6): 1231–1261.

Doyle, Walter. 1983. Academic work. *Review of Educational Research* 53(2): 159–199.

Dreeben, Robert. 1968. *On What Is Learned in School*. Reading, MA: Addison-Wesley.

Dreeben, Robert. 1976. The unwritten curriculum and its relation to values. *Journal of Curriculum Studies* 8(2): 111–124.

Dunlop, Olive J. 1912. *English Apprenticeship and Child Labor: A History*. London: T. Fisher Unwin.

Durkheim, Emile. 1977 (1938). *The Evolution of Educational Thought: Lectures on the Formation and Development of Secondary Education in France*, translated by Peter Collins. London: Routledge & Kegan Paul.

Egan, Kieran. 1988. *Primary Understanding: Education in Early Childhood*. New York: Routledge & Kegan Paul.

Eggleston, John. 1977. *The Sociology of the School Curriculum*. London: Routledge & Kegan Paul.

Ehrenreich, Barbara, and Deirdre English. 1979. *For Her Own Good: 150 Years of the Experts' Advice to Women*. Garden City, NY: Doubleday.

Eisner, Elliot. 1985. "Modes of Knowing." In *Learning and Teaching the Ways of Knowing. Eighty-fourth Yearbook of the National Society for the Study of Education*, Part II, edited by Elliot Eisner, 23–36. Chicago: NSSE.

Enelow, Allen. 1977. *Elements of Psychotherapy*. New York: Oxford University Press.

Erasmus. 1978 (1511). *Collected Works: Literary and Educational Writings*, vol. 2, edited by Craig R. Thompson. Toronto: University of Toronto Press.

Faraday, Michael. 1830. *Chemical Manipulation, Being Instructions to Students in Chemistry, On the Methods of Performing Experiments of Demonstration or of Research, with Accuracy and Success*. London: John Murray.

Fensham, Peter. 1985. Science for all: A reflective essay. *Journal of Curriculum Studies* 17(4): 415–435.

Fitzgerald, Frances. 1979. *America Revised*. New York: Vintage Books.

Floden, Robert E., Margaret Buchmann, and John Schwille. 1987. Breaking with everyday experience. *Teachers College Record* 88(4): 485–506.

Foucault, Michel. 1972. *The Archaeology of Knowledge and the Discourse on Language*, translated by A. M. Sheridan Smith. New York: Pantheon Books.

Frederiksen, Norman. 1984. The real test bias: Influences of testing on teaching and learning. *American Psychologist* 39(3): 193–202.

Freedman, Kerry, and Thomas Popkewitz. 1988. Art education and social interests in the development of American schooling: Ideological origins of curriculum theory. *Journal of Curriculum Studies* 20(5): 387–405.

Freire, Paolo. 1970. *Pedagogy of the Oppressed*. New York: Seabury.

Fuller, Timothy, ed. 1989. *The Voice of Liberal Learning: Michael Oakeshott on Education*. New Haven CT, and London: Yale University Press.

Gadamer, Hans-Georg. 1986. *The Relevance of the Beautiful and Other Essays*. Cambridge: Cambridge University Press.

Gadamer, Hans-Georg. 1988. *Truth and Method*. New York: Crossroad.

Gass, William H. 1985. *Habitations of the Word*. New York: Simon & Schuster.

Gergen, Kenneth. 1988. "Feminist Critique of Science and the Challenge of Social Epistemology." In *Feminist Thought and the Structure of Knowledge*, edited by Mary Gergen, 27–47. New York and London: New York University Press.

Geuss, Raymond. 1981. *The Idea of Critical Theory: Habermas and the Frankfurt School*. Cambridge: Cambridge University Press.

Giroux, Henry. 1981. *Ideology, Culture and the Process of Schooling*. Philadelphia: Temple University Press.

Goldman, Alvin H. 1988. *Empirical Knowledge*. Berkeley: University of California Press.

Goodman, Nelson. 1978. *Ways of Worldmaking*. Indianapolis, IN: Hackett.

Goodman, Nelson, and Catherine Z. Elgin. 1988. *Reconceptions in Philosophy and Other Arts and Sciences*. Indianapolis, IN: Hackett.

Goodman, Paul. 1964. *Compulsory Mis-education and the Community of Scholars*. New York: Vintage Books.

Goodson, Ivor, ed. 1985. *Social Histories of the Secondary Curriculum: Subjects for Study*. London and Philadelphia: Falmer.

Gordon, David. 1982. The concept of the hidden curriculum. *Journal of Philosophy of Education* 16(2): 187–198.

Grafton, Anthony, and Lisa Jardine. 1986. *From Humanism to the Humanities: Education and the Liberal Arts in 15th and 16th Century Europe*. Cambridge, MA: Harvard University Press.

Griffiths, Morwena. 1986. Hirst's forms of knowledge and Körner's categorial frameworks. *Oxford Review of Education* 12(7): 17–30.

Grimshaw, Jean. 1986. *Philosophy and Feminist Thinking*. Minneapolis: University of Minnesota Press.

Habermas, Jürgen. 1971. *Knowledge and Human Interests*, translated by J. Shapiro. Boston: Beacon Press.

Hamilton, David. 1989. *Towards a Theory of Schooling*. London: Falmer.

Harding, Sandra. 1986. *The Science Question in Feminism*. Ithaca, NY: Cornell University Press.

Hargreaves, Andy. 1982. Resistance and relative autonomy theories: Problems of distortion and incoherence in recent Marxist analyses of education. *British Journal of Sociology of Education* 3(2): 107–126.

Haskins, Charles. 1957. *The Rise of Universities*. Ithaca, NY: Cornell University Press.

Heath, Robert W. 1964. *New Curricula*. New York: Harper & Row.

Henry, Nelson. 1955. *Modern Philosophies and Education: The Fifty-fourth Yearbook of the National Society for the Study of Education*, Part I. Chicago: University of Chicago Press.

Hirsch, E. D., Jr. 1987. *Cultural Literacy: What Every American Needs to Know*. Boston: Houghton Mifflin.

Hirst, Paul H. 1972. "Liberal Education and the Nature of Knowledge." In *Education and the Development of Reason*, edited by R. F. Dearden, Paul Hirst, and R. S. Peters, 391–414. London: Routledge & Kegan Paul.

Hobbes, Thomas. 1966 (1651). *Leviathan*. Oxford: Basil Blackwell.

Hodgins, J. G. 1858. *The School House: Its Architecture, Arrangements and Discipline*. Toronto: Lovell and Gibson.

Hollis, Martin, and Steven Lukes. 1982. *Rationality and Relativism*. Cambridge, MA: MIT Press.

Honey, J. R. 1977. *Tom Brown's Universe: The Development of the English Public School in the Nineteenth Century*. New York: Quadrangle/New York Times Book Co.

Hook, Sidney. 1946. *Education for Modern Man*. New York: Dial Press.

Hounshell, Paul. 1989. Labs off limits. *Science Teacher* 56(4): 31–32.

Hull, David L. 1988. *Science as a Process: An Evolutionary Account of the Social and Conceptual Development of Science*. Chicago: University of Chicago Press.

Jackson, Philip W. 1970. "The Consequences of Schooling." In *The Unstudied Curriculum*, edited by Norman Overly, 1–15. Washington, DC: Association for Curriculum Development, National Education Association.

Jackson, Philip W. 1981. Secondary schooling for children of the poor. *Daedalus* 110(4): 39–57.

Jaggar, A. M. 1983. *Feminist Politics and Human Nature*. Totowa, NJ: Rowman and Allanheld.

Johnson, Clifton. 1963. *Old-Time Schools and School Books*. New York: Dover.

Johnson, Richard. 1979. "'Really Useful Knowledge': Radical Education and Working-Class Culture, 1790–1848." In *Working-Class Culture: Studies in History and Theory*, edited by John Clarke, Chas Critcher, and Richard Johnson, 75–102. London: Hutchinson.

Kaestle, Carl. 1983. *Pillars of the Republic: Common Schools and American Society, 1780–1860*. New York: Hill & Wang.

Keller, Evelyn F. 1982. Feminism and science. *Signs: Journal of Women in Culture and Society* 7(3): 589–602.

Kimball, Bruce. 1986. *Orators and Philosophers: A History of the Idea of Liberal Education*. New York: Teachers College Press.

Kliebard, Herbert. 1975. The rise of scientific curriculum making and its aftermath. *Curriculum Theory Network* 5(1): 27–38.

Kliebard, Herbert. 1986. *The Struggle for the American Curriculum: 1893–1958*. Boston: Routledge & Kegan Paul.

Krausz, Michael, and Jack W. Meiland, eds. 1982. *Relativism: Cognitive and Moral*. Notre Dame, IN: University of Notre Dame Press.

Kuhn, Thomas. 1970. *The Structure of Scientific Revolutions*, 2nd ed. Chicago: University of Chicago Press.

Lakatos, Imre, and Alan Musgrave, eds. 1970. *Criticism and the Growth of Knowledge*. Cambridge: Cambridge University Press.

Lakomski, Gabriele. 1988. Witches, weather gods, and phlogiston: The demise of the hidden curriculum. *Curriculum Inquiry* 18(4): 453–463.

Laudan, Lawrence. 1977. *Progress and Its Problems: Towards a Theory of Scientific Growth*. Berkeley: University of California Press.

Lawton, Denis. 1975. *Class, Culture and the Curriculum*. London: Routledge & Kegan Paul.

Layton, David. 1973. *Science for the People: The Origins of the School Science Curriculum in England*. New York: Science History Publications.

Leplin, Jarrett. 1984. *Scientific Realism*. Berkeley: University of California Press.

Levin, Margarita. 1988, winter. Caring new world: Feminism and science. *American Scholar* 100–106.

Levine, Lawrence. 1988. *Highbrow/Lowbrow: The Emergence of Cultural Hierarchy in America*. Cambridge, MA: Harvard University Press.

Lukes, Steven, ed. 1986. *Power*. Oxford: Basil Blackwell.

Machlup, Fritz. 1982. *Knowledge: Its Creation, Distribution, and Economic Significance. Volume 2: The Branches of Learning*. Princeton, NJ: Princeton University Press.

Marrou, Henri I. 1964 (1956). *A History of Education in Antiquity*, translated by George Lamb. New York: Mentor Books.

Martin, Jane R. 1970. "The Disciplines and the Curriculum." In *Readings in the Philosophy of Education: A Study of Curriculum*, edited by J. R. Martin, 65–86. Boston: Allyn & Bacon.

Martin, J. R. 1982. Two dogmas of curriculum. *Synthese* 51(1): 5–20.

Martin, Jane R. 1988. Science in a different style. *American Philosophical Quarterly* 25(2): 129–140.

Martin, Jane R. 1989. Ideological critiques and the philosophy of science. *Philosophy of Science* 56(7): 1–22.

Mayhew, Katherine C., and Anna C. Edwards. 1965 (1936). *The Dewey School: The Laboratory School of the University of Chicago 1896–1903*. New York: Atherton Press.

Miller, Richard. 1975. Review of J. Habermas, *Knowledge and Human Interests*. *Philosophical Review* 84(2): 261–266.

Mullahy, Patrick. 1955. *Oedipus Myth and Complex: A Review of Psychoanalytic Theory*. New York: Grove.

Müller, Detlev K., Fritz Ringer, and Brian Simon. 1987. *The Rise of the Modern Educational System: Structural Change and Social Reproduction, 1870–1920*. Cambridge: Cambridge University Press.

Nagel, Thomas. 1986. *The View from Nowhere*. New York and Oxford: Oxford University Press.

Nelson, John, Allan Megill, and Donald McCloskey, eds. 1987. *The Rhetoric of the Human Sciences: Language and Argument in Scholarship and Public Affairs*. Madison: University of Wisconsin Press.

Novitz, David. 1987. *Knowledge, Fiction and Imagination*. Philadelphia: Temple University Press.

Oakes, Jeannie. 1985. *Keeping Track: How Schools Structure Inequality*. New Haven, CT: Yale University Press.

Oakeshott, Michael. 1959. *The Voice of Poetry in the Conversation of Mankind: An Essay*. London: Bowse and Bowse.

Oliver, A. I. 1978. "What Is the Meaning of 'Curriculum'?" In *Curriculum: An Introduction to the Field*, edited by James R. Gress and David E. Purpel, 6–16. Berkeley, CA: McCutchan.

Ong, Walter. 1958. *Ramus: Method, and the Decay of Dialogue*. Cambridge, MA: Harvard University Press.

Ong, Walter. 1971. *Rhetoric, Romance, and Technology*. Ithaca, NY: Cornell University Press.

O'Rand, Angela M. 1989. "Scientific Thought Style and the Construction of Gender Inequality." In *Women and a New Academy*, edited by J. F. O'Barr, 103–121. Madison: University of Wisconsin Press, 1989.

Organization for Economic Cooperation and Development. 1979. *Policies for Apprenticeship*. Paris: OECD.

Orme, Nicholas. 1973. *English Schools in the Middle Ages*. London: Methuen.

Oxtoby, David, and Norman Nachtrieb. 1986. *Principles of Modern Chemistry*. Philadelphia: Saunders.

Peters, R. S. 1967. *Ethics and Education*. Glenview, IL: Scott, Foresman.

Phenix, Philip H. 1964. *Realms of Meaning: A Philosophy of the Curriculum for General Education*. New York: McGraw-Hill.

Phillips, D. C. 1987. *Philosophy, Science and Social Inquiry: Contemporary Methodological Controversies in Social Science and Related Applied Fields of Research*. Oxford: Pergamon.

Piltz, Anders. 1981. *The World of Medieval Learning*, translated by David Jones. Totowa, NJ: Barnes & Noble.

Plummer, Alfred. 1972. *The London Weavers' Company 1600–1970*. London: Routledge & Kegan Paul.

Polanyi, Michael. 1958. *Personal Knowledge: Towards a Post-Critical Philosophy*. Chicago: University of Chicago Press.

Pollock, John. 1986. *Contemporary Theories of Knowledge*. Totowa, NJ: Rowman and Littlefield.

Popkewitz, Thomas, ed. 1987. *The Formation of School Subjects: The Struggle for Creating an American Institution*. New York: Falmer.

Popper, Karl R. 1972. *Objective Knowledge: An Evolutionary Approach*. Oxford: Clarendon Press.

Powell, V. 1977. *Programmed Unit in Chemistry: Mass and Volume Relationships*. Englewood Cliffs, NJ: Prentice Hall.

Putnam, Hilary. 1978. *Meaning and the Moral Sciences*. Boston and London: Routledge & Kegan Paul.

Putnam, Hilary. 1987. *The Many Faces of Realism*. Lasalle, IL: Open Court.

Rabinow, Paul, ed. 1984. *The Foucault Reader*. New York: Pantheon Books.

Rajchman, John. 1985. *Michel Foucault: The Freedom of Philosophy*. New York: Columbia University Press.

Randall, John H., Jr. 1962. *The Career of Philosophy: From the Middle Ages to the Enlightment*, vol. 1. New York: Columbia University Press.

Ravetz, Jerome. 1973. *Scientific Knowledge and Its Social Problems*. New York: Oxford University Press.

Remsen, Ira, et al. 1893. *Report of the Committee on Secondary School Studies*. Washington, DC: U.S. Government Printing Office.

Rieff, Philip. 1966. *Freud: The Mind of the Moralist*, 3rd ed. Chicago: University of Chicago Press.

Rieff, P. 1979. *The Triumph of the Therapeutic: Uses of Faith After Freud*. New York: Harper & Row.

Rorabaugh, W. J. 1986. *The Craft Apprentice*. New York: Oxford University Press.

Rorty, Richard. 1982. *Consequences of Pragmatism*. Minneapolis: University of Minnesota Press.

Rorty, Richard. 1989. *Contingency, Irony and Solidarity*. Cambridge: Cambridge University Press.

Rose, Hilary. 1983. Hand, brain, and heart: A feminist epistemology for the natural sciences. *Signs: Journal of Women in Culture and Society* 9(1): 73–90.

Rothblatt, Sheldon. 1976. *Tradition and Change in English Liberal Education: An Essay in History and Culture*. London: Faber & Faber.

Rugg, Harold, et al. 1926. "The Foundations of Curriculum-Making." In *Twenty-sixth Yearbook of the National Society for the Study of Education*, Part II, edited by Guy M. Whipple, 11–28. Bloomington, IL: Public School Co.

Rugg, Harold, and Ann Shumaker. 1928. *The Child-Centered School: An Appraisal of the New Education*. Yonkers-on-Hudson, NY: World Book Company.

Ryle, Gilbert. 1949. *The Concept of Mind*. London: Hutchinson.

Scheffler, Israel. 1958. *Philosophy and Education: Modern Readings*. Boston: Allyn & Bacon.

Scheffler, Israel. 1966. *Philosophy and Education: Modern Readings*, 2nd ed. Boston: Allyn & Bacon.

Schrag, Francis. 1972. "Psychoanalysis as an Educational Process." In *Philosophy of Education 1972*, edited by Mary A. Raywid, 289–297. Edwardsville, IL: Philosophy of Education Society.

Schrag, Francis. 1988. *Thinking in School and Society*. London: Routledge & Kegan Paul.

Schubert, William H. 1986. *Curriculum: Perspective, Paradigm, and Possibility*. New York: Macmillan.

Schwab, Joseph. 1978. "Education and the Structure of the Disciplines." In *Science, Curriculum and Liberal Education: Selected Essays*, edited by Ian Westbury and Neil Wilkof, 229–272. Chicago: University of Chicago Press.

Schwab, Joseph. 1978 (1950). "Testing and the Curriculum." In *Science, Curriculum and Liberal Education: Selected Essays*, edited by Ian Westbury and Neil Wilkof, 275–286. Chicago: University of Chicago Press.

Shor, Ira. 1987. *Critical Teaching and Everyday Life*. Chicago: University of Chicago Press.

Sirotnik, Kenneth. 1983. What you see is what you get—consistency, persistency, and mediocrity in classrooms. *Harvard Educational Review* 53(1): 16–31.

Smallwood, Mary L. 1935. *An Historical Study of Examinations and Grading Systems in Early American Universities*. Cambridge, MA: Harvard University Press.

Soltis, Jonas. 1968. *An Introduction to the Analysis of Educational Concepts*. Reading, MA: Addison-Wesley.

Standing, E. M. 1962. *Maria Montessori: Her Life and Work*. New York: Mentor-Omega.

Stray, Christopher. 1985. "From Monopoly to Marginality: Classics in English Education Since 1800." In *Social Histories of the Secondary Curriculum: Subjects for Study*, edited by Ivor Goodson. London: Falmer.

Strike, Kenneth. 1987. "Toward a Coherent Constructivism." In *Proceedings of the Second International Seminar: Misconceptions and Educational Strategies*, 480–489. Ithaca, NY: Cornell University Press.

Suppe, Frederick, ed. 1977. *The Structure of Scientific Theories*. Urbana: University of Illinois Press.

Suzuki, D. T. 1961. *Essays in Zen Buddhism*, First Series. New York: Grove.

Suzuki, D. T., Erich Fromm, and Richard DeMartino. 1960. *Zen Buddhism and Psychoanalysis*. New York: Grove.

Taxel, Joel. 1986. The black experience in children's fiction: Controversies surrounding award winning books. *Curriculum Inquiry* 16(3): 245–281.

Thompson, John B. 1984. *Studies in the Theory of Ideology*. Cambridge: Polity Press.

Tomberlin, J. E., ed. 1988. *Philosophical Perspectives and Epistemology*. Atascadero, CA: Ridgeview.

Toulmin, Stephen. 1972. *Human Understanding*. Princeton, NJ: Princeton University Press.

Vallance, Elizabeth. 1973–1974. Hiding the hidden curriculum: An interpretation of the language of justification in nineteenth-century educational reform. *Curriculum Theory Network* 4(1): 5–21.

Vandenberg, Donald. 1988. Knowledge in schooling. *Phenomenology and Pedagogy* 6 (2): 63–78.

Vico, Giambattista. 1975 (1708). *On the Study Methods of Our Time*, translated by Elio Gianturco. Indianapolis, IN: Library of Liberal Arts.

Wardle, David. 1970. *English Popular Education, 1780 1970*. Cambridge: Cambridge University Press.

Weiner, Charles. 1969. A new site for the seminar. In *The Intellectual Migration: Europe and America, 1930–1960*, edited by D. Fleming and B. Bailyn, 190–234. Cambridge, MA: Harvard University Press.

Weisskopf, Victor. 1986. Observations on art and science. *Daedalus* 115 (3): 186–189.

Wexler, Philip. 1987. *Social Analysis of Education: After the New Sociology*. London and New York: Routledge & Kegan Paul.

White, Nicholas. 1976. *Plato on Knowledge and Reality*. Indianapolis, IN: Hackett.

Whitty, Geoff. 1985. *Sociology and School Knowledge: Curriculum Theory, Research and Politics*. London: Methuen.

Williams, Raymond. 1961. *The Long Revolution*. New York: Harper Torchbooks.

Willis, Paul. 1977. *Learning to Labour*. Westmead, England: Saxon House.

Winant, Terry. 1987. The feminist standpoint: A matter of language. *Hypatia* 2(1): 123–148.

Young, Jay A. 1978. *Chemistry, A Human Concern*. New York: Macmillan.

Young, Michael F. D. 1971. "An Approach to the Study of Curricula as Socially Organized Knowledge." In *Knowledge and Control: New Directions for the Sociology of Education*, edited by Michael F. D. Young, 19–46. London: Collier-Macmillan.

Ziman, John. 1978. *Reliable Knowledge: An Exploration of the Grounds for Belief in Science*. Cambridge: Cambridge University Press.

11

CURRICULUM IDEOLOGIES

Elliot W. Eisner
STANFORD UNIVERSITY

Education is a normative enterprise. It is a process aimed at the achievement of certain virtues. The curriculum—that array of activities used by schools to achieve its ends—is one of its two major pedagogical resources. The other is teaching. Like the systole and diastole of the beating heart, curriculum and teaching reside at the center of education.

Because educational practice is concerned with the achievement of certain desired end states, it relies on a larger value matrix to secure and justify the directions in which it moves. That value matrix is the subject matter of this chapter: the ideologies that give direction to one of the school's major resources, the curriculum.

The term "ideolog*ies*," rather than "ideology," is used here to indicate that there is no single ideology that directs education. Values, particularly in America, proliferate, and these values find their educational expression in the ways in which schooling, curriculum, teaching, and evaluation are to occur. Curriculum ideologies are defined in this chapter as beliefs about what schools should teach, for what ends, and for what reasons. Insofar as an ideology can be tacit rather than explicit, it is fair to say that all schools have at least one ideology that provides direction to their functions.

THE SIGNIFICANCE OF IDEOLOGIES IN EDUCATION

Ideologies are belief systems that provide the value premises from which decisions about practical educational matters are made. For example, a conception of the aims of education as rooted in the desire to help students secure Christian salvation will emphasize the importance of developing in the young the ability to read, for without such literacy the scriptures are inaccessible, and if inaccessible, salvation is unlikely. A Christian ideology of the kind reflected in the laws of 1642 and 1647 (Cremin 1970a) in the Massachusetts Bay colonies provided the value premises both for educational policy—schools were legally mandated in towns with over 50 inhabitants—and for curricular goals: Biblical literacy, achieved through the ability to read, was of paramount importance.

In some ways, curricular ideologies derive from what might be regarded as *Weltanschauungen*—worldviews. Although religious ideologies, as they are played out in schooling, often provide the most visible forms of ideological influence, there are many important nonreligious ideologies that have long functioned in schooling. One of the aims of this chapter is to explore some of their most important features and to describe their implications for curriculum practice.

Ideologies in education also influence what is considered problematic and nonproblematic in the curriculum. The term "problematic" can be regarded in two ways. First, what is considered to be a given or believed to be axiomatic in education enjoys a kind of security that is seldom threatened by marginalization: there are few people today for whom the development of literacy is a questionable aim of schooling. In this sense, this particular aim is nonproblematic. How it ought to be achieved is another matter, but that it ought to be achieved is not. In contrast, whether subjects like the arts or courses in the psychology of child development should be an important part of the curriculum is another question. Given some educational ideologies, these areas of study are problematic in much the same way that for some, federal support to the National Endowment for the Arts is problematic. For some the government has no business supporting the arts, and for others the school has no business teaching adolescents about child development.

Second, when a curriculum ideology emphasizes the importance of a particular subject, that subject ineluctably becomes problematic. By "problematic" here I mean that since decisions about the best ways of achieving the aims of highly valued fields are almost always less than optimal, student performance in the subject is typically a source of discontent and, in this sense, problematic. The problematic character of the most valued subjects makes them continuous objects of attention, whereas those subjects that are marginalized or neglected altogether never achieve a problematic status. Anthropology, for example, is simply not a problem in the school's curriculum because it is seldom considered important enough to care about. The same holds true for the arts and a variety of other fields.

I suggested earlier that curricular ideologies emerge in religiouslike views of the world. Any orthodoxy attempts to make the world into its own image, especially the educational world. Walker (1979) has pointed out that curriculum policies are like political platforms; they present to the world a position on some array of curricular options. Beliefs about the importance of the neighborhood school or the self-contained classroom or a multicultural curriculum have similarities to the planks in a political platform. Ideologies also function in much subtler ways. They do not carry signs announcing their positions on important educational matters; rather, they manifest themselves in the kinds of language that imply or suggest rather than state explicitly what is educationally important and what the schools' curricula should address. For example, when the language of industrial competition is used to make a case for particular educational aims—"losing our competitive edge"—our conception of the mission of schools is gradually shaped in industrial terms. The school becomes viewed as an organization that turns out a product—a student—whose features are subject to the same quality control criteria that are applied to other industrial products. In contrast, if the child is viewed as a biological organism subject to natural laws of growth and atrophy, the kindergarten becomes an appropriate model for thinking about the kind of environment that is most suitable for young children. Getzels (1974) has described how models of the learner influence images of the classroom. When children are regarded as passive receptacles to be filled rather than active, stimulus-seeking organisms, bolting down desks in orderly rows makes sense. If they are thought of as stimulus-seeking organisms, the classroom is likely to have a very different look.

What is important about such educational practices is that they emanate from ideologies no less powerful than those directed by publicly expressed orthodox beliefs. Indeed, because the former practices may obscure their ideological sources, they may be especially difficult to change. Looked at this way, it becomes clear that at the broadest social level, acculturation itself can be regarded as a form of ideological induction. Consider, for example, the way in which political socialization occurs in nations that allow only one political party. Consider the ways in which the curriculum in schools in such countries is formulated and prescribed. Consider the restricted array of educational options students are allowed to entertain. In such nations the official ideology is often so pervasive that the absence of competing views may leave its citizens unable to think about alternatives. The ubiquity of a single ideological view renders them insensitive to the ways in which their own beliefs have been shaped; they are too close to the scene to recognize its features.

On a smaller scale there are subcultures—the Amish, for example—whose views of life ripple throughout the curriculum their schools provide. The congruence between their general view of the world and the worldview into which their children are initiated is virtually isomorphic. Curriculum ideology shaping Amish schools is essentially an extension of the relatively consistent worldview of Amish parents.

It is worth emphasizing that when a particular ideology becomes pervasive or has no competing alternative, it tends to become invisible. Another impediment to recognition emanates from the incorporation into our language of conceptions that so shape our view of curriculum, the aims of schooling, or human aptitude that we do not notice them as having this effect. For example, when we define intelligence as the ability to deal with abstraction and identify abstraction solely with the ability to use words and numbers, we impose on schools standards that reflect those conceptions and, thereby, limit other possibilities.

The foregoing conception of an ideology is neither fundamentally different from a constructivist perspective, pertaining to the function of theory in cognition, nor from one that Gruber (1981) calls "images of wide scope." The purported difference is that ideologies are typically regarded as value-laden commitments, whereas theories in the social sciences are frequently idealized as merely descriptions of the world rather than an expression of what is to be valued. Such a distinction, however, will not stand up to analysis. Language is constitutive of experience; it is not simply descriptive, and the way in which the world is parsed has significant value consequences for matters of educational practice. Gardner (1983) points out that Piaget's theory of cognitive structure is essentially an ascension from lower to higher forms of thought that has as its apotheosis a scientific model of mind. For Piaget (1973) the pinnacle of cognitive achievement is found in the scientist: A human as scientist, rather than a human as artist, is the end state of cognitive growth. Gardner writes,

> According to Piaget, a final stage of development comes into being during early adolescence. Now capable of *formal operations*, the youth is able to reason about the world not only through actions or single symbols, but rather by figuring out the implications that obtain among a set of related propositions. The adolescent becomes able to think in a completely logical fashion: now resembling a working scientist, he can express hypotheses in propositions, test them, and revise the propositions in the light of the results of such experimentation. These abilities in hand (or in head), the youth has achieved the end-state of adult human cognition. He is now capable of that form of logical-rational thought which is prized in the West and epitomized by mathematicians and scientists. (19)

It takes no huge imagination to recognize how a view as influential as Piaget's can reinforce a certain conception of knowledge and intelligence and how, in the process, it can limit other options. If we believe that Piaget's cognitive structures correctly define a hierarchy of human cognitive attainment, the works of a Mozart, Matisse, or Balanchine are likely to be diminished. If, however, we regarded artistic thought as the paramount cognitive achievement, the content of our curriculum and who receives rewards for success might look very different from the ones we provide today.

Recognition of the constitutive functions of language and the power of theory to shape perception has been fostered from several sources. First, that branch of psychology rooted in the world of psycholinguistics and represented early in the work of Edward Sapir (1962) and Benjamin Lee Whorf (1956), and more recently in the cognitively oriented work of Bruner (1964), Case (1984), Cole (1974), and Olsen (1988), has emphasized the complex nature of cognition in general and the function of what Bruner has called "structure" in the creation of understanding. To these researchers the mind is a cultural achievement influenced by biological predisposition but, nevertheless, shaped by the features of a culture. Second, there is that branch of philosophy that historically has emphasized the importance of symbol systems in creating different forms of consciousness. Ernst Cassirer (1961–1964), Nelson Goodman (1978), and Susanne Langer (1942) are scholars whose theories of knowledge are directly related to the ways in which the world is represented. Different symbol systems, they claim, perform different epistemic functions. Third, there are the deconstructivists (Culler 1982), who pay special attention to the impact of language on cognition and on the values tacit in the language that is used. Their aim has been to raise consciousness to the covert values residing deeply in the language we use by revealing these values through the techniques of deconstruction—substituting, for example, key terms with other terms representing opposing meanings. Their efforts are not only epistemologically motivated but also often motivated by particular political commitments (Eagleton 1983). "Emancipation" from the linguistic and cognitive fetters of the culture is for them an important political aim.

The extension of the concept of ideology into the general sphere of cognitive theory, linguistics, philosophy, and deconstruction is advanced here since it is an arguable case that the most influential ideologies are not those formally acknowledged and publicly articulated but rather those that are subliminally ingested as a part of general or professional socialization. We may be very much more ideological, given this broadened view, than we realize. Thus, understanding the covert ways in which ideologies operate becomes crucial if they are to be the subject of reflective examination. As long as we remain oblivious to the values that animate our intellectual life, we will be in no position to modify them.

Thus far I have described ideologies largely as a function of acculturation and as an inherent part of the psychological structures—language and theory—that we acquire as members of a culture. Although in some societies ideological commitments can be both uniform and powerful, it is not the case that in pluralistic societies uniformity among ideologies is the norm. More often than not, ideological positions pertaining to curriculum and to other aspects of education exist in a state of tension or conflict. In pluralistic societies a part of the pluralism emerges in competing views of what schools should teach and for what ends. These competing views prevail or succumb in a political marketplace. For example, the admonitions of evangelical Christians to exclude Darwinist explanatory constructs in the teaching of biology and to replace them, or at least to complement a Darwinian view, with a creationist revelation encountered sufficient resistance in California to make it possible for a scientific, Darwinian perspective to prevail. In this particular battle for ideological supremacy, evangelical fundamentalism lost.

My point here is that regardless of how powerful an ideological view may be in any individual's or even group's orientation to the world, it is seldom adequate to determine what the school curriculum shall be. There is a political process that inevitably must be employed to move from ideological commitment to practical action. When a society is characterized by value plurality and when the political strength of groups is comparable, the process almost always leads to certain compromises. As a result, the public school curriculum seldom reflects a pure form of any single ideological position. Indeed, the more public the school and the more heterogeneous the community, the less likely there will be ideological uniformity in schooling.

Where schools are private, and Christian fundamentalist schools are examples, it is much more likely that not only the curriculum of the school but also other aspects of school life will reflect the values of the group. Peshkin (1986) points out that in the Christian fundamentalist school he studied, virtually every aspect of the school—from the hiring of maintenance workers to the extracurricular life students led outside of school—was governed by religious values that went virtually unquestioned. Is such uniformity a virtue or a vice? Is the need to compromise values a necessary evil or something that represents a form of corporate wisdom? Answers to these questions depend, I think, on one's own degree of commitment to an ideological position. If one believes that the truth resides in a particular conception of humanity, compromising that conception for political expediency is not necessarily an asset. Perhaps the major virtue of a democracy is the instantiation of a process that allows individuals to exercise choice, even out of ignorance.

I have described curriculum ideologies as a set of beliefs about what should be taught, for what ends, and for what reasons. I pointed out that although such ideologies are most clearly visible in orthodox views of schooling, whether secular or sectarian, ideological commitments are expressed and developed through the processes of acculturation and professional socialization and are reflected in the tacit as well as the explicit assumptions we make about the nature of reality, knowledge, mind, and education. These ideological commitments reveal themselves in the kind of language we use to describe schools, teaching, and learning; metaphors count in creating a value valence in our attitudes and beliefs about curriculum. Hence, curriculum ideologies can be said to reside on a continuum from the most explicit forms—positions about education presented, for example, in manifestos about what should be taught—to the most implicit, delicate shadings of language about education, including language that is intended to be purely descriptive. Indeed, it was argued that the less visible an ideology is, the more insidious it can be, for in that form it often eludes scrutiny.

It should not be inferred from my remarks that ideologies are, somehow, a kind of infection in education that is to be cured by taking the proper medicine. Nor should it be inferred that ideologies somehow interfere with the exercise of "pure rationality." Because education is a normative enterprise, it cannot be approached value-free. Such a position would leave educators with neither rudder nor compass. Any normative enterprise is, by definition, guided by certain beliefs about what counts. These beliefs, in one form or another, constitute an ideological view. Finally, I pointed out that schools or school systems seldom develop their programs through the straightforward application of political decisions deduced from a codified array of value assumptions. The political process in democratic and pluralistic societies requires deliberation, debate, adjustment, and compromise. As a result, examples of "pure" ideologies in action in schools are rare.

One other point is worth making. Schools are not objects that once modified in a particular way, remain so. Because schools and school districts are subject to the vicissitudes of local and national expectations, changes in schools based on the prevalence of a particular ideological view may last for a short time. As the social and economic conditions of a community change, as its political climate alters, as staffs come and go, it becomes necessary for schools to make adjustments and to accommodate to these newly emerging conditions. What this means at the level of practice is the continual readjustment of programs and priorities, even if one wishes to maintain the direction the school has taken before those changed conditions. Educational practices and priorities reflecting ideological commitments need modification to survive, just as a tightrope walker must correct for movement in the wire to remain on it. Put another way, sustaining a direction in schooling or maintaining a set of priorities in the curriculum is much more like nurturing a friendship than installing a refrigerator in the kitchen. The latter requires virtually no attention after installation; the same cannot be said of friendship.

A COMMENT ON THE CURRENT STATE OF CURRICULAR IDEOLOGIES

Although I pointed out that ideologies in education can be located on a continuum from the most obvious, public, and articulate statement of purpose, content, and rationale to the most subtle, private, and latent view, there is a tendency among writers on particular topics—in this case, curricular ideologies—to succumb to the temptation to see the world in terms of the topic about which they write. As important as curricular or, more broadly, educational ideologies are for schools, they are rarely presented in a public and articulate form. This is not to say that values do not direct the enterprise; they do. It is to say that American schools, for example, are driven by a complex of values and traditions and by fairly uniform expectations for a shared way of life that is both long-standing and widespread, rather than by a manifesto-like, publicly available ideological doctrine. There are, to be sure, statements of philosophy that school districts dutifully formulate; they are seldom read, and what they have to do with the actual operations of schools is less than clear. In this sense most public schools in the United States, once one goes beyond general statements of philosophy, do not "stand" for anything. That is, they do not display a uniform, articulate, ideological position that allows citizens to say that this educational view is for me, that is not.

What most citizens want are good schools. Good schools mean teaching children basic skills, preparing them for the world of work or for college, helping them avoid the evil of drugs, and paying attention to those less central topics and issues that arise from time to time and from place to place in schools across the country (Gallup and Clark 1987). The major mission of schooling, however, remains largely the same, as does the structure and practice of schooling. Its use of time and space, what it offers, and what it requires of students are remarkably constant. If these features constitute what might be called the operational ideology of schooling, ideological uniformity more than ideological diversity prevails.

If we examine the schools from an operational perspective, as Dreeben (1968) and others have done, that is, from the way in which their day-to-day operations inculcate and tacitly express beliefs and values, and if we regard these beliefs and values as ideological, the following picture appears.

Schools teach children to be punctual. At the middle and secondary school levels, where departmentalization prevails, students must arrive and leave class on time, 16 times each day (Eisner 1985b). All of these arrivals and departures occur within 5-minute intervals between classes. Schools also teach children to be alone in a crowd (Jackson 1968) and to delay those gratifications that issue from providing the correct answer in order to allow classmates to have a chance to do so. To be in school is to acquire a worldview that appears in the form of largely disconnected subjects. Children learn to separate ways of knowing that reflect the different subjects they study because of the way those subjects are organized in the curriculum (Eisner 1985b). Being in school means learning how to complete assignments on time and how to accept such assignments from others rather than generating them for oneself (Apple 1982). It means regarding rationality as the need to have clear-cut goals in mind at the outset of any intellectual enterprise and to regard means related to those goals as a kind of experimental treatment; rationality is tacitly modeled after a scientistic or technological form rather than, for example, an intuitive one.

Schools also convey to students a need to compete. Resources—particularly rewards—are limited and the garlands go to the swiftest. Swiftness, in turn, is defined mainly through achievement in particular forms of cognition. Verbal and mathematical aptitudes are the most useful, given the tasks in which students compete, and the emphasis on these particular aptitudes teaches the young that intellectual ability is defined largely in terms of verbal and mathematical performance.

Because of the ways in which schools organize and sort children, opportunities to learn from other students, younger or older, are diminished. Schools organize children by "litter"—children of the same age are assigned to the same grade, and progression through the school keeps constant this form of age-grading (Goodlad and Anderson 1959). This form of school organization reinforces the idea that the task of being a successful student is to learn the content of the grade, a condition that results in promotion to the next. It also reinforces the idea that knowledge is fixed and tidy, that smart people possess it, that textbooks contain it, and that the aim of schooling is its orderly transmission (Jackson 1986).

The kinds of curricular tasks and subjects emphasized in the early grades are also instructive in ways well beyond their original intent. Reading, writing, and arithmetic at the early levels of schooling are subjects that are highly rule-governed in character. By rule-governed I mean that these so-called skill subjects emphasize the correct application or use of social conventions. Spelling and arithmetic are two examples of rule-governed tasks. Such tasks convey to children that their most important activities in school have single, correct answers; that those answers are known by the teacher; and that their primary responsibility as students is to provide the correct one. The school creates an environment that does not put much premium on imagination, personal spirit, or creative thinking. It emphasizes a form of rationality that seeks convergence on the known more than exploration of the unknown. It emphasizes the virtues of hard work. It limits the degree to which personal goal setting can occur, and it rewards conformity to correct outcome more than it rewards productive idiosyncrasy.

Can such practices be regarded collectively as a curricular ideology? The answer to this question is, at base, arbitrary. If an ideology is defined as a *public* statement of a value position regarding curriculum, the absence of such a statement would disqualify it as an ideology. If, however, an ideology also refers to a shared way of life that teaches a certain worldview or set of values through action, schools everywhere employ and convey an ideology because they all possess, in practice, a shared way of life or what may be called an operational ideology.

It needs to be said that the ideologies that make a difference for those in school—teachers and students—are those that permeate their activities on a daily basis. A written manifesto of educational beliefs that never infuses the day-to-day operations of schools has no practical import for either teachers or students; such beliefs are window dressing.

The view presented in this chapter is that it is useful to conceive of a curriculum ideology, or even more broadly an educational ideology, in two ways. That is, it is useful in comprehending educational practice, first, to understand how beliefs about what is valued influence what is taught, for what ends, and for what reasons. Shifts in those beliefs can have substantial consequences for how schools function. At the same time, it is the way in which schools actually function that, de facto, helps shape the way students come to view the world and the values they secure about it. Second, it is also useful to examine schools to uncover their tacit ideologies, their subtexts, as well as what they publicly espouse. Such inquiries have been undertaken by Dreeben (1968), Eisner (1985b), Jackson (1968), Smith and Geoffrey (1968), Waller (1932), and many others.

It is important to note that in the United States in recent years there has been a movement toward the creation of schools that *do* reflect particular educational ideologies. Magnet schools (Metz 1986) have been developed throughout the country that provide special programs, emphasizing particular kinds of educational values. For example, there are magnet schools that advertise an emphasis on traditional educational values: homework each day, achievement testing each week, and an emphasis on the three R's. Other schools advertise an experientially based program: individualization of the curriculum, hands-on activities, field trips, group projects, and cooperative learning. Such schools provide very different educational environments. Each is guided by a different image of its mission and what students ought to learn in the course of their education. Given their distinctive mission, they do what the typical public school does not do: They hoist an ideological flag that tells the community what they stand for and therefore give the public a choice.

SIX CURRICULUM IDEOLOGIES

Thus far I have provided a general description of the forms through which ideologies function in the schools. In this section I will identify six curriculum ideologies and describe their assumptions, core values, and views about curriculum, including their views of the mission of the school. Although these six ideological positions do not exhaust those that influence schools, they are among the most prominent. It should also be said that ideologies are never as definite or clear in practice as they are on paper. In addition, interpretations of any particular ideology differ, even among their adherents; hence what follows are, of necessity, general characterizations of ideological positions rather than unassailable descriptions of the particular views of individual adherents. Following this section, I will examine the research that has been done to trace the development of these ideologies and to describe their influence on practice. The six ideologies are referred to as religious orthodoxy, rational humanism, progressivism, critical theory, reconceptualism, and cognitive pluralism.

Religious Orthodoxy

One feature that all religious orthodox ideologies share is their certainty in the existence of God and the importance of God's message in defining the content, aims, and conditions of educational practice. In America, about 90 percent of all private elementary and secondary schools are Roman Catholic. The major aim of Roman Catholic schools is to induct the young into the Roman Catholic Church and, through the Church, to Christ. American Evangelical Christians have similar aims, though clearly not "the same" God. Orthodox Jews, whose schools serve less than 1 percent of the American school-age population, are similarly engaged. At the heart of the religious enterprise is a conception of how life ought to be lived and a clear conception of the kinds of habits and beliefs that will lead to its realization. How do religiously constituted groups with relatively clear opinions about the constituents of educational virtue go about realizing their educational aims in schools? How do their beliefs affect the experience of the young? Certain religious groups, the Jesuits, for example, have had a long-standing interest in social justice. This interest is displayed in their educational priorities and in their attention to this aspect of religious life in the curriculum. Kuntz (1986), himself a Jesuit and a student of Jesuit education, writes,

> In the Jesuit tradition, it is the teacher who must be responsible for the success or failure of education for justice. The teacher in the Jesuit school has a double purpose: to enable the students to appropriate Christian norms of morality even in the face of external cultural pressures, and to encourage the students to conduct their lives in accordance with those norms. Jesuit educators place the primary responsibility for moral education on the teacher. (113)

Convictions such as this are central to the Jesuits, but they are not as critical for other Catholic orders. Thus, Catholicism as one variant of Christianity is itself varied, even pluralistic, in its orientation to education. When it comes to other forms of Christian belief, evangelical Christianity, for example, the variability is just as wide within, not to speak of the differences between, evangelicals and Catholics.

Jews express their common faith in three major religious belief systems: orthodox, conservative, and reform. Members of each group embrace different ideas about what it means to be a Jew and therefore the kinds of personal attributes, beliefs, and behaviors children and adolescents ought to develop under the aegis of their schools. For orthodox Jews, only certain forms of adaptation to secular life are acceptable. For example, on the Sabbath it is not permitted to walk more than 2,000 "paces," a safeguard against using the Sabbath for purposes of work. The orthodox Jew must eat kosher food and keep a kosher home, meaning, among other things, that eating utensils for dairy and meat products must be kept separate. In addition, daily prayers are mandatory, and the Sabbath—the holiest day of the week—must also be observed.

For conservative and reform Jews, religious laws pertaining to daily life are less demanding and the relationship between religious and secular life more forgiving. Thus, even within the same religion, the meaning of what it means to be religious has considerable variance, and those differing views find their practical expression not only in how their adherents behave in general but also in what is emphasized in schools. For example, in orthodox Jewish religious schools, it is estimated that about 60 percent of the day is devoted to the study of religious texts. In reform Jewish schools, about 30 percent of the time is devoted to such materials. In orthodox schools, boys and girls are separated. In conservative and reform schools, the classes are mixed. Each group has a different view of what God requires, even though each of the three groups honors the "same" God.

At the upper reaches of secondary schooling, a special place of curriculum privilege is given to the interpretation of text. Religious texts are traditionally subject to various interpretations, and the ability to discover God's meaning has been the ultimate aim of biblical and Talmudic scholarship. As a result, hermeneutic analyses have been one of the important intellectual practices in the development of religious scholarship. In this process, conflicting interpretations among authorities are sometimes employed to stimulate readers into participating in the intellectual puzzlements that emanate from competing, but at the same time plausible, interpretations of text. Such practices, when they occur, have a paradoxical quality in the context of a dogmatically committed educational ideology.

As indicated earlier, the aim of an orthodoxy is to shape the views of others so that they match the views of those who have already discovered the truth contained in the orthodoxy. Orthodoxies are not essentially about doubts, but about certainties. Indeed, to become orthodox is to become a true believer. The exploration of competing views regarding biblical interpretation is, at the very least, an admission that truths, even biblical truths, are uncertain. Hence, the cultivation in the young of attitudes that seek and even reward the enjoyment of ambiguity—for interpretation always requires some ambiguity in order to have the space to function —seems paradoxical. True beliefs revealed through dogma appear antithetical to ambiguity, yet biblical interpretation as an intellectual process requires it.

It is clear that in the elementary grades the propensity of the young to question, doubt, and criticize the basic tenets of religious orthodoxy is strongly discouraged, particularly in evangelical schools, where the mission of the institution is to pass on God's word, not to question it (Peshkin 1986). In this environment the cultivation of a critical attitude is troublesome because it can undermine the very ideology directing the system and can erode the structure of authority it requires to maintain its intellectual hegemony.

In *Smith* v. *Board of School Commissioners of Mobile County* (Smith et al. [illegible]), the suit filed by evangelical parents alleged not only that the board omitted culturally appropriate Christian content from the curriculum but also that the attitudes fostered by instruction in the schools undermined parental authority by encouraging children to question critically their parents' traditions and conventional beliefs. Smith's attorneys argued in their brief to the court,

> Plaintiffs Smith now seek relief from this Court from (1) the unconstitutional advancement of the religion of Humanism in the curriculum used in the Mobile County school system; (2) the unconstitutional inhibition of Christianity caused by the curriculum used in the Mobile County school system; (3) the unconstitutional violation of the free exercise of religion rights of teachers and students by the exclusive teaching of Humanism and the systematic exclusion from the curriculum of the existence, history, contributions, and role of Christianity in the United States and the world; (4) the unconstitutional violations of the rights of students to receive information, of the rights of teachers to free speech, and of the prohibitions against governmental disapproval of religion, inhibition of religion, and discrimination against religion caused by the systematic exclusion from the curriculum used in the Mobile County school system of the existence, history, contributions, and role of Christianity in the United States and the world; and (5) the violation of the statutory mandate to teach the "established facts of American history, tradition and patriotism." (3)

What is clear is that the values embraced by the Mobile, Alabama, Board of Education were in direct conflict with the values held by evangelical parents. Parents embracing the evangelical ideology represented by their religion had no interest in developing in their children the kind of critical skepticism that is prized in rational or humanistic orientations to education. For them the development of such skills and attitudes could serve only to weaken the religious commitment that parents believed essential to salvation. In addition, parents argued that not only did the Mobile, Alabama, curriculum omit important factual content, such as attention to the influence of Christianity in the history of the United States, but also the curriculum advertently or inadvertently promoted an alternative religious doctrine. Rational humanism, they argued, constituted this doctrine, and the school board, therefore, violated students' rights by acts of omission as well as direct acts of commission. The parents went to the court to remedy what they believed to be a violation of their religious rights under the First Amendment to the Constitution.

In related cases, beliefs about the theory of evolution, which pertains directly to beliefs about the nature of human beings, have been subject to legal review, motivated by people whose religious convictions find evolutionary theory antithetical to their own certainty concerning genesis on earth. When religious groups create and manage their own schools, the presence of strong religious views and the virtual absence of more widely held secular views pose no significant, overt problem. The public schools do what state education codes and their trustees think best, and those directing religious schools follow their own path. To be sure, court cases and local pressures emerge from time to time and are resolved largely on an ad hoc basis. In general, though, secular and sectarian schools operate within their own sphere of influence and induct the young into the views their parents hold dear.

At first glance it seems that insulation and isolation from mainstream values is simply a form of benign neglect or a congenial way to cope with a problem of value conflict. One must, however, raise the question about how far a democratic nation can permit groups to inculcate into their children such a level of dogmatic belief that should their children achieve political saliency, they would restrict the very freedoms that have been afforded to them in their own schools. Peshkin (1986) raises this important question in his analysis of evangelical fundamentalist schooling in America. It is the issue that James Madison (1961 [1784]) raised in the Federalist Papers, where he struggled with creating a set of principles that would provide for minority protection and minority rights and that maintains a system of government "ruled" by the majority. The tensions that Madison identified in 1784 are still with us.

Although not itself a religious ideology, political belief structures can approximate some of the dogmatic features of religious views regarding the ways in which schools should function and the ends they should seek to attain. Teruhisa Horio (1988), a Japanese scholar, writes of the current tendencies of the Japanese Ministry of Education to promulgate educational policies for Japanese schools that are uncomfortably close to the militaristic policies promulgated by the Ministry of Education during the days of imperialist Japan prior to and during World War II. According to Horio, in Japan, local control of schools is being eroded and the scope of teacher authority is being diminished. In addition, textbooks have failed to provide Japanese children with the kind of balanced social view that Horio believes a viable democracy requires. As a result, the Japanese educational system is being guided by a subtle but influential array of authoritarian beliefs, which may in the long run undermine the democratic potential of modern Japan. In Horio's view, business interests now dominate educational policies, and traditional reliance on authority and status is being recultivated by the government. The same ideologies that led Japan astray in the early decades of the 20th century are, in Horio's opinion, reappearing today:

> At about the same time, the then Vice-President of the United States, Richard M. Nixon, declared on an official visit to Japan that the Peace Constitution represented a major "mistake" in America's postwar policy for the reconstruction of Japan. Thus peace education was conceived of by both American and Japanese leaders as an obstacle to constitutional revision and remilitarization. Patriotic education was strongly advocated as the most desirable way to correct what were then being spoken of as the "excesses of democratization." Through their calls for a new emphasis on patriotism the anti-pacifist, anti-socialist, pro-American elements in Japanese society had found a new way to revive the prewar *kokutai* ideology and reassert what were ultimately anti-democratic values. (148)

If one substitutes dogmatism for religious ideological views, the scope of the category increases considerably because under such an umbrella can fall all types of dogmatic positions, especially those advocated at either end of the political spectrum. Both the ultraleft and the ultraright are utterly convinced in the veracity of their own opinions and values.

Another example of ideological influence on curriculum can be found in the Waldorf schools. These schools, and more important the programs they provide, were initiated in 1919 by the German philosopher Rudolph Steiner. Asked by the owners of the Waldorf-Astoria Cigarette Company to create a school for the children of its employees, Steiner set about to design an educational program based on the principles of anthroposophy. Uhrmacher (1990) writes,

> Anthroposophy might be thought of in two ways. First, it is a path of self-development for those who wish to follow Steiner's direction toward spiritual cognition. According to Steiner, human beings can develop latent organs of cognition so that they may directly perceive the spirit world. Second, Anthroposophy is also the fruit born from Steiner's ideas and methods. Biodynamic farming, Anthroposophic medicine, eurythmy and Waldorf schools are a few of the results from Steiner's spiritual knowledge. (chap. 1)

It tries to connect life before birth to life after death, to conceive of human development in mystical, yet optimistic, terms. As an educational movement, it has had an impressive growth throughout the world. At present, there are about 330 Waldorf schools functioning in 40 countries throughout the globe. In America alone, there are over 80 such schools. What we have in Waldorf education is a stunning example of a nonevangelical movement growing slowly but surely over a 60-year period. Waldorf schools, largely neglected by mainstream educators and educational researchers, provide not only a curriculum based on philosophical and developmental principles, but also an organizational structure and teaching practices that reflect those principles. For example, it is the individual teacher who admits students to any particular Waldorf school. It is a teacher council that determines the educational policy for the school. Students remain with the same class teacher for an eight-year period rather than moving from teacher to teacher each year. Even the color of the classroom walls is determined by developmental principles that Rudolph Steiner articulated. These and other practices, such as a main lesson each day, an emphasis on myth and legend in the curriculum, and the keeping of a log by each child, are a part of the educational regimen of Waldorf schools. These schools, as much as any I know, attempt to transform philosophical beliefs into specific classroom and school practices, and judging by the growth they have enjoyed, they are apparently succeeding.

All of the foregoing ideological views, even Japanese imperialism, are in one way or another rooted in religious beliefs. They all share a belief in a supernatural being at the core of their philosophy, and some permit no critical analysis of their basic value assumptions. For some ideologies this prohibition of critical scrutiny of core beliefs leads to a form of dogmatism that could be regarded as the antithesis of an educational process. When the aim of an enterprise is directed toward the production of true believers, a tendency to prize rationality or the consideration of alternative sources of evidence in weighing beliefs is in jeopardy. Yet those who hold dogmatic beliefs believe that their first obligation to children is to induct them into their belief structure. For dogmatists a negative account of "nonrational" activity appears to be mistaken. They claim that human rationality at its best is incapable of fully understanding God's plan; only arrogance and ignorance would suppose otherwise. It is precisely our inability to comprehend God's ways fully that leads to faith, a central tenet of any religiously oriented ideology. The result is a kind of standoff between those who claim that orthodoxies of any kind lead to dogmatism, and that dogmatisms are inherently alien to education, and those who say that faith in God's word represents a higher form of human rationality and that it is our overblown sense of self, our inflated conception of our own limited powers, that leads us to believe that we can "test" God's word.

When ideological beliefs make no difference in the content of educational practice or the conditions within which such practices occur, these beliefs can make no difference in the lives of the young. The fact of the matter is, however, that such ideologies are hardly ever without consequences for the practice of education, and for Waldorf schools and private evangelical Christian schools with practical manifestations of beliefs, the consequences are likely to be substantial.

Rational Humanism

Now we turn to a second ideology bearing on schooling—rational humanism.

Rational humanism locates its modern roots in the Enlightenment and its ancient roots in Plato. Today, its most visible educational manifestation is found in Mortimer Adler's (1982) *Paideia Proposal* and, in the 1930s through the 1950s, in the Great Books program promulgated by Robert Maynard Hutchins and Mortimer Adler. There are some important distinctions to make regarding the aspirations of Enlightenment scholars such as Auguste Comte and modern-day rational humanists.

Comte and others believed that the universe in which we live is, in principle, understandable and that through rational methods, best exemplified in science, the workings of the clocklike character of the world could be discovered. Mysticism and religious revelation were practices that for them were ill suited to a human's rational nature and that rational nature, as Aristotle had indicated, was to know. With the Enlightenment, a new optimism was cultivated, and the promise of success was sufficiently attractive to lead scholars to believe that an orderly universe would someday be discovered by a rational mind. Scientific method was the procedure, par excellence, for achieving this enlightened status. With it came a new faith in the powers of humanity, particularly in a human's intelligence to guide and control his or her own future, to take control of his or her own life. The spirit that animated the rational humanism of Hutchins and Adler is broader than the methods of science. The laboratory was, according to Hutchins (1953), only *one* of the important resources for learning and knowing. There were others, and these were, at base, even more potentially powerful than science.

The pedagogical method that Hutchins (1953) espoused is based on his view that the distinctive feature of the human being is the capacity to exercise reason, and reason does not ultimately depend on empirical demonstration or on conditions necessary for science but on reflection and insight. Reflection and insight, in turn, could be cultivated, Hutchins argued, by providing two educational conditions in the classroom. First, the content of the curriculum needed to offer students old enough to reason the very best that humans have written and created. *The Great Books of the Western World*, the program that Hutchins and Adler began in 1938, reflected this belief. Hutchins reasoned that since not all human works were "created equal" and since time in school is limited, students should study the very best rather than the mediocre. Hence, decisions of content inclusion and exclusion were of paramount importance (Walker and Schaffarzick 1972).

Of equal importance was the method through which the great works were studied. In a great many schools there is a heavy emphasis on the memorization of information, a process that is reinforced through short-answer and multiple-choice tests (Cuban 1979). When teaching methods emphasize the transmission of information and testing methods assess the extent of its recall, pedagogical methods that develop rational powers are not likely to be used. To develop such powers it is necessary to employ what Adler (1982) calls mieutic processes, which engage students in in-depth reasoning about the material they study. Ideally, the teacher's behavior is dialectic rather than didactic. It is intended to enable students to provide reasons for their opinions and to find evidence and counterarguments to the views being expressed. For such matters the most useful pedagogical method is likely to be philosophical, literary, or artistic in character. It is likely to invite or stimulate analysis, even controversy. Rationality, according to Hutchins and Adler, is a part of human nature, but its cultivation is required for it to flourish.

The very principles that rational humanism advances—the centrality of human reason, human beings as the measure of all things, and the contextualized nature of knowledge as a human construction, while at the same time recognition of the existence of truth—are principles that religious dogmatists reject. If God exists and if God is truth, to conceive of education in terms that makes human beings the measure of all things is to lead children into spiritual damnation.

The practical educational implications of rational humanism center on curriculum content and teaching methods. As I already indicated, once students have learned how to read and cipher, they ought to be exposed to the best of the best. This, incidentally, does not mean reliance on secondary commentaries but, on the contrary, on the appropriate use of primary source material. It is much better to read Thomas Jefferson than to read about Thomas Jefferson. Indeed, from recent commentaries of contemporary critics of education regarding the vacuity and lifelessness of school textbooks, the admonition does not seem far off the mark. But in addition, discussion, analysis, and debate are to be among the critical methods of instruction. As long as the issues students address are not cut and dried, debate is possible. As long as debate is possible, the higher mental processes can be stimulated and practiced.

Rational humanism, as an educational ideology, is often accused of being culturally parochial—only Western content is offered—and elitist. The former accusation is, in my view, unjustified, certainly at the level of principle. There is no reason why the content of the curriculum must necessarily be derived from works of the Western world, even if traditionally they have been so derived. If the premise that goodness adheres unequally in different works is accepted, there is no reason within rational humanism to restrict goodness to works created in the West.

As far as elitism is concerned, there are several ways to respond to this charge. One is that the proper aim of education is to expand the elite, that is, to enable students to practice and to be informed by humans' best work. A second is that if the best work that has been produced is restricted to those now able to decode its meaning—the upper-middle and upper classes—then surely those in the lower socioeconomic classes will be consigned to a second-class intellectual status because of the second-rate curriculum that they will be offered. If it is argued that the quality of a human's work is simply determined by arbitrary judgment that has no possible justification or evidentiary base, the selection of content becomes not only arbitrary but also relativistic, and if relativistic, there can be no basis for the appraisal of educational development. If *all* works are of equal value, *any* selection is as good as any other.

The cornerstone of rational humanism is a belief in the primacy of reason and in a human's ability to make rational and defensible judgments about the goodness of things. As long as this cornerstone remains intact, relativism must be rejected as a basis for the selection of curriculum content.

Although rational humanism has received much fanfare, mainly from its critics, its implementation in American schools is not widespread. Except for some private schools and those public schools that have attempted to develop *Paideia* programs, the ideas of rational humanism are more like latent ideals than operating processes. The national penchant for evidence regarding educational attainment through measured performance does not sit comfortably with an orientation to educational attainment that celebrates reason, rationality, and extended explanation. Exegesis is difficult when the optical scanner must score student responses. In short, our assessment technology imposes its own practical values and limitations on the content and methods of schooling. Those practical values are often incongruent with the values that rational humanists hold dear.

A few recent developments in American education reflect some of the values found in rational humanism, although the match is far from perfect. The developments I speak of are the efforts among some to define a curricular canon and to use original source material, especially in literature and history, to provide curriculum content. Hirsch's (1987) *Cultural Literacy*, which in many ways is antithetical to rational humanism, nevertheless participates in the view that not all content is created equal. Knowing what counts matters, and Hirsch (1988) and his colleagues have endeavored to identify what every American should know. Their most egregious failure is their effort to create a dictionary that will provide what all Americans should know. However, rational humanism properly conceived places little emphasis on the idea of a dictionary of content; indeed such an emphasis, even tacitly, misconceives the meaning of content. Content is not to be construed as memorizing the facts but as the development of a critical understanding of the values and premises that underlie important human works. The implication of a fixed body of content to be found in Hirsch's "dictionary" runs counter to the spirit of the enterprise, even though it shares one of its important features.

Perhaps more closely identified with a rational humanistic ideology is the 1987 publication of the National Endowment for the Humanities, *American Memory* (Cheney 1987). This public policy statement does echo much of the spirit of rational humanism: the emphasis on great works and humanistic forms of understanding; the desire for a common core curriculum for all, regardless of ability; and the promulgation of the higher mental processes through critical analyses of primary source material. These features of sound curricula are quite congruent with the humanists' educational values.

It should be said that although some might feel that the prescription of a common curriculum for a nation of 250 million is utopian or naive or ethnocentric, the case rational humanists wish to make is that without such commonality some children—most likely those of the poor—will receive an inferior program of studies, thus condemning them to a further life of poverty. Rather than to differentiate educational quality on the basis of ethnic, social, or economic criteria, all children should be afforded the very best the culture has to offer. Where variability might be required is in method, not in content or educational aim. It is those who wish to accommodate group differences by differentiating content and aims that are the true elitists. Societies that differentiate the educational programs provided to the young on the basis of their economic or cultural roots deny opportunities to the less advantaged. As Hutchins (1953) has said, since in a democracy all who vote rule, all should have the education of rulers.

One other feature of rational humanistic ideology is important, that of curriculum electives and vocational specialization prior to graduate school. To those who share the values of Hutchins and Adler, both options are anathema. Electives are undesirable, they believe, because the child is not in a good position to know what will best serve his or her educational interests since to have that knowledge requires one to have an education, something the child in school does not yet have. As for vocational specialization, that option is appropriate only after the student's general education has been completed. Furthermore, it is inappropriate to attempt such specialized teaching in public schools since the public schools are notoriously out of date regarding vocational matters. In addition, Hutchins asserts, the good schoolmaster is known by the important subjects he or she refuses to teach. Not everything that is important—and vocational skills are important—is the responsibility of elementary and secondary schools. But even if this were not so, it would be premature to focus a student's attention on vocational concerns before the course of general education has been completed. It is the virtual absence of a common intellectual culture that weakens the nation's ability to communicate: We lack a common cultural context. This is one of the major problems that Hirsch's (1987) *Cultural Literacy* was intended to cure.

Given America's current romance with the world of commerce—regaining our "competitive edge" is the current catchword—it is unlikely that in the short term rational humanism will have much of a place in mainstream American schools. Where this idealized orientation is more likely to flourish is in those private schools that serve a social and economic elite, and perhaps in those schools serving a population that has had so long a history of failure that virtually any new approach promising success will be tried. Currently, the appetite for approaches to education that appear noninstrumental to practical ends measured in standardized ways is not very large. A nation that has little toleration for ambiguity and a need for happy endings is likely to regard rational humanism as a bit too intellectual to be appropriate for today's world.

Progressivisim

The third curricular ideology that I will examine, progressivism, is most forcefully expressed in the writings of John Dewey and the large group of followers he and his ideas attracted. As Cremin (1970b) and others have pointed out, progressivism in education has had two related but distinguishable streams. One of these was rooted in the nature of human experience and the development of intelligence, the other in social reform. Although Dewey addressed the romantic and reform side of his educational philosophy at different periods in his career, these two streams within American progressivism are perhaps most clearly represented in the works of Harold Rugg and Ann Shumacher (1928) and George Counts (1932). Rugg and Schumacher's *The Child-Centered School* was influenced by the desire to address the covert, emotional life of the child, a life that Freud paid so much attention to. George Counts, however, was concerned with the society at large and thought schools had a positive obligation to "change the social order." Some of the manifestations of Schumacher's orientation to education finds expression in the work of A. S. Neill (1960) and in the present-day work of curricular reconceptualists, particularly Grumet (1988) and Pinar (1988), whereas the legacy of Counts appears in the writings of critical theorists such as Apple (1982) and Giroux (1989).

In one sense, the streams within progressivism can be regarded as, on the one hand, emphasizing the personal and, on the other, the political. Dewey himself would never have made such a distinction since he believed the nature of the political process inevitably influenced the kind of personal life the individual led, and the kind of individual life an individual was able to lead was shaped by the kind of politics he or she was able to embrace.

Because Dewey's work is so central to any analysis of progressivism in American education, and because progressivism, writ large, has been such an important ideological strain in American educational thought, Dewey's works will be used to exemplify progressive ideology.

Dewey's work is rooted in a biological conception of the human being; by this I mean that he regards the human being as a growing organism whose major developmental task is to come to terms, through adaptation or transformation, with the environment in which he or she lives. Because the environment is not always hospitable to the comfort or even the survival of the organism, thinking is required. It is through the exercise and development of intelligence that the environment is reshaped. It is through the reshaping process that the individual learns and intelligence grows. In this sense, for Dewey, human life is a continuous process of constructive adaptation. Intelligence itself is not fixed; it grows. It is not a thing; it is a process. It is not restricted to a limited sphere of content—words or numbers—but it manifests itself wherever and in whatever material problems can be posed and solved.

The development of intelligence—what Dewey called "growth"—does not emerge from biology or genetics alone; it requires the resources of culture. Young humans are notoriously dependent on adults for survival. The early manifestations of dependency are largely physical, but later, as biological development occurs, cultural resources are provided and children begin to incorporate into their intellectual repertoire the variety of social skills and cultural tools—language, for example—made available to them. These cultural resources are, in a sense, intellectual amplifiers: They expand the individual's ability to cope with the objective conditions of the environment. Such coping includes the ability to conceptualize or pose problems through which constructive adaptation occurs. Indeed, one of the school's major tasks, according to Dewey (1902), is to create what he calls the educational situations through which a child becomes increasingly able to deal with ever more complex and demanding problems. What grows through this process of increasing competence is the child's intelligence.

The roots of Dewey's progressivism are found in Darwin's (1975 [1859]) evolutionary theory in biology and in Hegel's (1900) ideas concerning thesis and antithesis. They were also shaped by the temper of the time. The turn of the century was an intellectually exciting period in America, indeed in the world. In the young behavioral sciences, a new optimism was emerging: the possibility of creating a scientific understanding of human nature. In America, waves of immigrants were populating American cities, and workers were organizing to secure their rights in industry (Cremin 1970b). The schools were being criticized for their lack of productivity (Callahan 1962), while at the same time, they were expected to do more and to serve a wider and more diversified population. In addition, a more dynamic view of human development was appearing among American intellectuals. The climate was right for educational change.

> The same era that saw the rise of social Darwinism—both the conservative and the reform varieties—also witnessed the birth of a new psychology dedicated to the scientific study of human behavior in general and the phenomena of mind in particular. As with correlative developments in sociology, European influences were critical, but they were always tempered by the distinctive demands of the American scene. Thus, Edwin Boring has noted that the paternity of American psychology was German, deriving from the work of Gustav Fechner, Hermann von Helmholtz, and Wilhelm Wundt; while the maternity was English, and is to be found in the work of Darwin, Francis Galton, and of course, Spencer. The child, however, was much influenced by the environment in which it grew up; for the Americans, as usual, borrowed selectively, and ended up fashioning a psychology clearly designed to serve the practical needs of their own civilization. (Cremin 1962, 100)

The conditions Cremin described provided a fertile ground for the liberal ideas that Dewey advanced, particularly in that most optimistic of institutions, education. No longer was it appropriate to regard the child as a passive receptacle to be filled with curriculum content. No longer could mind and emotion be regarded as independent. No longer could the curriculum be thought of as a static, fixed body of content, created in administrative offices and handed down to teachers. The child acted on the environment, not simply digested it, and in the process that environment was personally transformed. Emotion could not be disregarded in dealing with intellectual matters since how children felt about what they studied influenced how they thought about what they studied. As for the curriculum, it could not be optimally developed by people who had never seen the child; hence teachers needed to play a fundamental role in its creation.

As familiar and reasonable as these ideas may seem today, their introduction in the late 1880s was innovative, indeed radical. As they began to transform and develop in the first four decades of the 20th century, they took a direction that Dewey himself felt compelled to caution against. Dewey's (1938) concerns about the excesses of American progressive education are most succinctly expressed in his *Experience and Education*. Simply stated, this small book is an effort to save his philosophy of education from his friends.

Despite Dewey's reservations concerning the ways in which his ideas were interpreted, his work provided then as it does today a powerful ideological view of what school, curricula, and teaching should be about. His conception of cognitive development—a term that he did not use—is consonant with the ideas of psychologists such as Piaget (1973) in France and Vygotsky (1962) in the Soviet Union. And his conception of the nature of intelligence as an active *process* rather than a static entity, as an event that is displayed differentially by individuals depending on the circumstances and the form of representation employed, is congruent with recent theoretical conceptions of intellectual ability (Olsen 1988). In short, Dewey's work adumbrated many of today's most advanced notions pertaining to the intellectual and social development of children.

Three points I wish to emphasize regarding Dewey's thought are central to a progressive educational ideology. These pertain to his conception of the school as a whole, his view of appropriate curriculum content, and his view of the teacher's professional duties.

For Dewey (1938), the "envelope" for the educational process was the school itself. Broader than the formal curriculum, it provided in its shared way of life the social conditions that themselves convey to the child the norms of social living. Although Dewey did not believe that there could be parity between adult and child in educational decision making—after all, the teacher did know more—he did believe that to the degree possible, the school and the classroom should reflect democratic principles. What this meant in practice was that schools and classrooms should offer children appropriate opportunities to formulate their own rules for social living, internal and personal needs should be respected in the creation of learning activities, and group processes should be fostered so that children learned how to use collective intelligence to cope with problems in which their peers had an equal interest. It would be fatal, Dewey believed, to espouse the virtues of democratic life and to impose on schools an authoritarian form of management. The school, in a sense, was to be what the society under the best of circumstances was to become. This lesson, alas, is one that is yet to be learned in most schools.

As far as the curriculum itself, it was to display several features. First and foremost, it was to be problem-centered. By problem-centered, Dewey meant that the art of teaching was one that enabled the teacher to so construct the environment that children would be motivated to formulate problems or, in other terms, to make their situations problematic. The instantiation of a problem, itself an act of intelligence, provided the conditions for the use of experimental thought in pursuit of resolution. For Dewey (1910), the "complete act of thought"—the movement from purpose to experimental treatment to assessment of results—so exquisitely exemplified in science, was a model toward which curricula should aspire.

To create such problematic situations, the teacher needed to understand not only the intellectual potential of a body of ideas but also the child. "Start from where the child is" became a familiar admonition to progressive teachers, an admonition that is not very distant from Vygotsky's (1962) notion of the zone of proximal development. The importance of starting from where the child is is directly related to the need to relate the problematic situation to the child's experience, as well as to his or her level of skill and understanding. The artistry in pedagogy is partly one of placement—finding the place within the child's experience that will enable the child to stretch intellectually while avoiding tasks so difficult that failure is assured. To achieve this placement, the teacher needed to know the child.

As for teaching the "progressive way," each child was to be treated as a distinct personality. This goal implies an approach that required teachers to appreciate the child's background, to deal with the "whole child." "Whole" here meant the child was to be seen as a social and emotional creature, not only as an academic or intellectual one. The progressives quite correctly recognized that children do not park their emotions on the threshold to the school as they enter. What a child had experienced and how the child was feeling was directly relevant to the teacher's professional aims.

It should be noted that such attitudes toward teaching practice were far distant from the efforts being made during the same period to run schools like factories and to manage the teacher's performance in ways similar to those used in industrial settings. The efficiency movement in education did not speak of the child's needs or of the child's wholeness (Callahan 1962). Teaching was not viewed as a matter of artistry but as a matter of efficiency. The outcomes of schooling were not thought of as the cultivation of unique talents but the achievement of standardized goals. In short, the images of educational virtue reflected in progressive educational ideology and those reflected in what Callahan has called "the cult of efficiency" were almost opposite. It requires no great insight to recognize that these polarities concerning the method and purpose of education are still salient today.

In addition to the artistry that progressives assigned to teaching at its best, the responsibilities of the teacher included in-context curriculum development. Thus although a school district or even a state might provide a framework for curriculum development, the primary responsibility for designing educational programs, often on the wing, resided with the teacher. Not only is the teacher the one who knows the child, but also events within the classroom cannot be predicted and the need to exploit the teachable moment is always present. It is precisely this kind of pedagogical adaptability that Dewey (1910) regarded as exemplifying what he called "flexible purposing."

It is of more than passing interest to note that much of the current debate concerning the improvement of schooling in both the United States and the United Kingdom is centered on the appropriateness of prescriptions by federal authorities of common national standards, or as is the case in the United Kingdom, a national curriculum. When the public becomes concerned about the quality of education, it tends to have two reactions. The first is to monitor more closely than it had in the past the performance of schools; this is called accountability. Second, it reiterates in the public forum its national (or state) goals for education. Through standardization of assessment and prescriptive curriculum, that is, by tightening up and reducing the professional discretionary space for teachers, political efforts are made to create more educationally productive schools. Ironically, at the same time that such standardization is occurring, policies are being promoted that urge that teachers, as the primary professional stakeholders, should have greater professional discretion in program planning and in monitoring and governing "their" schools (Holmes Group 1988).

These tensions are not unusual in nations that permit ideological pluralism. The efficiency movement in American education had its heyday during the very same period in which American progressive education was virtually at its peak. Perhaps one of the indexes of democracy is its tolerance for ideological pluralism. Yet pluralism in the name of democracy ensures neither the virtue nor the efficacy of the positions espoused. It seems to me unlikely that national standards, even national assessment, will be sufficient to improve American or British schools. The problems are more complex and the kind of investment needed much larger. If the public articulation of national goals were sufficient, *A Nation at Risk* (National Commission on Excellence in Education 1983), perhaps the most widely disseminated statement on education published in America during the 20th century, should have done the trick. But who today can remember the five "new basics" given such vast publicity in 1983?

One final comment on progressive education as a curricular ideology: Given the visibility that progressive education has had—some laudatory, some hostile—one might conclude that during its peak period, say from the end of the 1920s to the end of the 1940s, progressive education was a mainstream movement in American public schools. It was not. Where progressive education did flourish was in small independent schools. Indeed, the first eight presidents of the Progressive Education Association were principals of such schools (Cremin 1962). As in many other ideologically driven movements—the Plowden-oriented British primary schools of the 1960s, for example—there was more talk than practice. In England my search for progressive British primary schools in 1980 proved to be more difficult than I anticipated (Eisner 1974). I estimate that at the very most only 10 percent of the primary schools in Britain at that time could be said to reflect the spirit of the Plowden Report (1966).

Perhaps the important lesson to be learned here is that it is unwise to confuse the public visibility of an idea in professional journals and in the public media with its practical application in the schools. Schools are remarkably robust institutions, slow to change, and it is much easier to talk about innovation than to achieve it. Cuban (1979) describes the situation by making an analogy between the operations of the school and a storm at sea. Although the storm might wreak havoc on the surface of the water—waves of 30 or more feet might be blown about—at the bottom of the sea the waters remain calm and quiet. Similarly, although the press might have a heyday with new, even radical ideas about educational practice, teachers working alone in classrooms quietly go about business as usual; the most experienced have learned very well how to ride out the storm. Thus, if we want to know what schools are like, we need data closer to the phenomena than those described or promoted in print.

We turn now to the fourth ideology, one that has substantial visibility in scholarly circles: critical theory and its educational variants.

Critical Theory

With few exceptions, critical theorists have not developed a coherent public statement pertaining to the aims, content, and methods of education. In this sense, critical theory is less of an educational ideology than religious ideologies, rational humanism, or progressivism. Yet critical theory provides one of the most visible and articulate analyses of education found in the pages of educational journals and in books devoted to the state of the schools. It is for this reason—its salience in the intellectual community and its potential for reforming the current priorities of schools—that it is included here as an ideology affecting education in general and curriculum in particular.

What is critical theory and what is its "project"? Critical theory is an approach to the study of schools and society that has as its main function the revelation of the tacit values that underlie the enterprise. The approach has been influenced by a hermeneutic orientation to texts; critical theorists often regard themselves as revealing the covert assumptions and values in the *social* text.

In some sense this orientation to schooling may be thought of as a hermeneutics of suspicion, a search for invisible and sometimes nefarious motives. Critical theorists, almost always on the political left, are typically concerned with raising the consciousness of unsuspecting parents, students, and educators to the insidious and subtle ways in which an unequal and often unjust social order reproduces itself through the schools. In this sense critical theory is aimed at emancipating (their word) those affected by the schools from the school's debilitating practices.

The achievement of such ends typically requires careful attention to the structure of schooling, the ways in which roles are defined, the covert messages that are taught—in short, it requires an awareness of the school's "hidden curriculum" (Eisner 1985a). The term "hidden" is used intentionally in distinction to the "covert" or "implicit" curriculum. The hidden curriculum consists of the messages given to children by teachers, school structures, textbooks, and other school resources. These messages are often conveyed by teachers who themselves are unaware of their presence. "Hidden" implies a hider—someone or some group that intentionally conceals. Concealment, in turn, suggests a form of subterfuge to achieve some gain. Hence, the hidden curriculum is often believed to serve the interests of the power elite, which the school itself is covertly thought to serve.

One of the important questions children are taught to ask of practices and policies in schooling and elsewhere is, Whose interests are being served? They are taught a hermeneutics of suspicion. Although conspiracy theories are currently out of fashion—it is now more popular to conceive of schools in less deterministic ways and to emphasize more a philosophy of hope—the political gist of the views of critical theorists is that the covert functions of schooling are rooted deeply in their belief that a capitalistic economy cannot, in principle, provide for either an equitable society or an equitable school system. As Bourdieu (1977) has written, the school is essentially an institution whose mission is cultural reproduction. When the society is thought to be inherently unfair, cultural reproduction through schooling is thought to be no virtue.

The roots of these ideas are found in Marx (1987 [1859]), particularly his views about the alienation of labor. For Marx the objective conditions of work define the realities that workers experience, and when work is organized to provide profit to those who own the sources of production, the working class is inevitably exploited. The essential problem that must be addressed, therefore, is to help the working class assume control of the sources of production, that is, to socialize the economy so that each individual receives according to one's needs and contributes according to one's ability. Class and equality are essentially a function of economic conditions.

Although few critical theorists today would take such a doctrinaire view of the ills of the social order, the views they do embrace are descendants of Marx's views. As a result, they claim that the school alienates labor—the students—and "de-skills" them in the course of schooling by withholding opportunities for them to formulate their own aims and goals (Apple 1982). In this way schools develop a dependency on authority; foster one-way communication, from top to bottom; and in general provide a distorted view of American history, which in turn undermines the kind of social consciousness needed to bring about change. One critical theorist writing of the deleterious influence of industry on schools says,

> The industrial-capitalistic interests entertained a very different role of public schooling from that which had been thought good under agrarianism and mercantile capitalism. As industry became more complex, the school also had to change to meet its needs. Compulsory schooling became essential and more accepted by the working class, and the compulsory schooling age rose. The high school (an urban school) became a necessity as did industrial education: manual training, vocational guidance, the enactment of child labor and additional compulsory education laws. These developments in public schooling were aimed at striving for greater efficiency in preparing children for occupational roles in the expanding economy. (Pratte 1977, 99)

What is characteristic of this genre of writing is its half-empty character. Almost always the emphasis is on the negative aspects of schooling, and although pulling weeds is helpful, their elimination in a garden does not ensure the presence of flowers; flowers have to be planted. Most critical theorists do not plant flowers; they pull weeds.

It should be acknowledged that depending on one's set of values, there are many weeds to pull in schools. Indeed, it is the mark of any respectable academic to be critical. Yet the continually strident voices of so many critical theorists often become relentless and excessive. Consider, for example, the following comments on Bloom's (1988) *The Closing of the American Mind* and Hirsch's (1988) *Dictionary of Cultural Literacy*:

> Read against the recent legacy of a critical educational tradition, the perspectives advanced by both Bloom and Hirsch reflect those of the critic who fears the indeterminacy of the future and who, in an attempt to escape the messy web of everyday life, purges the past of its contradictions, its paradoxes, and ultimately, of its injustices. Hirsch and Bloom sidestep the disquieting, disrupting, interrupting problems of sexism, racism, class exploitation, and other social issues that bear down so heavily on the present. This is the discourse of pedagogues afraid of the future, strangled by the past, and refusing to address the complexity, terror, and possibilities of the present. Most important, it is a public philosophy informed by a crippling ethnocentrism and a contempt for the language and social relations fundamental to the ideals of a democratic society. It is, in the end, a desperate move by thinkers who would rather cling to a tradition forged by myth than work toward a collective future built on democratic possibilities. This is the philosophy and pedagogy of hegemonic intellectuals cloaked in the mantle of academic enlightenment and literacy. (Aronowitz and Giroux 1988, 194)

The tone of these remarks is not uncommon, nor are the code words that populate such texts: "emancipation," "valorize," "hegemony," and the like. It is almost as if an entire vocabulary had been developed to display to the world how capitalism has corrupted the schools.

As I have indicated, the major intellectual disposition of critical theorists is critical—in the negative sense. They are typically much more interested in displaying the shortcomings of schooling—raising consciousness, they say—than providing models toward which the schools should aspire. Nevertheless, some have described the sense of possibility they value. Giroux (1989), for example, emphasizes the importance of teachers and their potential role in defining the aims of schooling and in assessing its performance. Others speak of the potential coalition of teachers and parents as a way of creating a truly educational climate for their children, one free from the constraints of government bureaucracy. Others, such as Apple (1982), emphasize the importance of restoring to children a sense of personal meaning by allowing, indeed encouraging, them to define their own educational ends and to relate these ends to the community in which they live. In some ways the directions in which critical theorists would take the schools resemble the social side of the progressive educational ideology.

Perhaps because a positive agenda for school programs has been so underplayed in the writing of critical theorists, it is hard to say just where their implied agenda for educational reform has been implemented. Unlike the Christian evangelicals, who have created schools to reflect their ideology, or progressive educators, who have influenced school practice even in public schools, or rational humanists, who have a league of *Paideia* schools, there are no counterparts that I know of for the critical theorists. The primary locus of their writing is found in books and learned journals; their ideas have been timely, insightful, and useful, but they speak essentially to intellectuals. They tend not to be read or heeded by teachers or school administrators. As far as I know, they have had little or no impact on government educational agencies or on local school boards. My sense is that if their material were less strident, more hopeful, more generous, and more concretely constructive with respect to options, it would be much more likely to influence practice.

One example of a program that does share some of the values advanced by critical theorists, but is not itself associated with critical theory, is Lawrence Stenhouse's (1982) humanities curriculum, developed in the United Kingdom in the 1970s. Stenhouse was interested in providing adolescents with opportunities to study and debate closed or controversial issues: matters pertaining to race relations, sex, politics, and church and state relations. With foundation support he devised a humanities curriculum that invited students to debate sensitive issues; he did not take a position on these issues but prescribed a role for the teacher intended to deepen the students' level of discussion and through that their understanding of underlying value conflicts. Stenhouse wanted to help students develop a more complex view of controversial issues so that their own value structure would be less secure and more open to examination. As I understand Stenhouse's curriculum, it was not *formally* an example of critical theory in action, yet it had some of the features that critical theorists would, I believe, applaud.

Closer to critical theory in a formal sense is the work of Paulo Freire (1970). Working with illiterate peasants in Mexico, Freire devised an approach to the development of literacy that was based on the deep-seated and practical needs of his students. Reading materials were texts whose words and content were directly related to the world of work his students knew firsthand. But Freire did not stop with mere "literacy"; he also used his students' newly acquired ability to read as a base through which to help them understand the conditions of their labor and the interests being served by their work. In short, literacy was an instrument for political education.

What both Stenhouse and Freire have in common is their practical efforts to create and construct materials and relationships designed to enable their students to understand better the values and conditions that affect their lives. Each, so to speak, rolled up his sleeves to demonstrate an approach to educational practice that reflects his educational ideology. Critical theorists, in the main, reveal, often with much insight and eloquence, what the world of schooling suffers from, but they have a tendency to stop with criticism rather than with construction. As a result, the debate has mainly been limited to scholars rather than to the reshaping of practice.

Given this emphasis, is it appropriate to regard critical theory as an instance of an educational or curricular ideology? I believe it is. There is no group I know more ardent about its beliefs or as outspoken about the righteousness of its cause. It attracts adherents, it provides a common lexicon for its advocates, and it has a common canon. Its views of the ills of education are often exceedingly plausible; they are frequently both trenchant and accurate. What is missing is a positive agenda. Scholars who have directed their attention to practice, such as Adler (1982), Goodlad (1984), and Sizer (1984), have displayed the ways in which beliefs can be acted on, as did Dewey in his Laboratory School in 1896. This agenda, now absent in critical theory, is what is needed to move from text to action.

Reconceptualism

A fifth curriculum ideology is called by its advocates reconceptualism. Emerging on the educational scene in the early 1970s, this view is far from complete, nor do its adherents want it to be complete. It is more of an orientation than a dogma. That is, it is a way of thinking about education and the kind of programs that will serve its ends well.

The central ideas for reconceptualists are implicit in the work of James MacDonald (1975) and especially Dwayne Heubner (1963), but in the United States the major spokesperson for this view is William Pinar (1975). Writing of *currere*, the conception Pinar embraces, he says,

> The questions of *currere* are not Tyler's; they are ones like these: Why do I identify with Mrs. Dalloway and not with Mrs. Brown? What psychic dark spots does the one light, and what is the nature of "dark spots," and "light spots"? Why do I read Lessing and not Murdoch? Why do I read such works at all? Why not biology or ecology? Why are some drawn to the study of literature, some to physics, and some to law? Are phrases like "structures of the mind" usable and useful? If so, are these varying structures, and in what sense do they account for the form intellectual interests take or for their complete absence? What constitute "structures," and what are their sources?
>
> Such questions suggest the study of *currere*. The information our investigations bring us is the knowledge of *currere*. It is its own knowledge, and while its roots are elsewhere, its plant and flower are its own; it is another species, a discipline of its own. (401–402)

Those familiar with Pinar's publications and those of others whose views participate in its ideological orbit will recognize the importance that personal experience enjoys in their texts on education. What is missing from American schools, they argue, is a deep respect for personal purpose, lived experience, the life of imagination, and those forms of understanding that resist dissection and measurement. What is wrong with schools, among other things, is their industrialized format, their mechanistic attitudes toward students, their indifference to personal experience, and their emphasis on the instrumental and the out of reach. To provide children with a decent educational environment requires a reconceptualization of how we think about educational programs, who develops them, and what they are for. They are not primarily, in the views of reconceptualists, for learning how to earn a living but for learning how to live. To learn how to live the child must learn how to listen to his or her own personal drummer in an environment that makes such attention not only possible but also desirable. Like the critical theorists, reconceptualists tend to believe that American schools—perhaps most schools in Western industrialized societies—have been excessively influenced by a means-ends mentality modeled after a world that does not exist. Life is not like a scientific experiment or the operation of an assembly line. Schools that intend to prepare students for life mislead when they convey to them that all problems have solutions and that all questions have answers. What is even worse, the message given to students is that not only are answers to all questions and solutions to all problems available but also there is a correct one for each. The aim of schools for students becomes converted from the expansion of consciousness and the exploration of the possibilities of the imagination to successful adaptation to a technocratic routine.

For reconceptualists the dominant mode of curriculum theory, best represented perhaps in a narrow reading of Tyler's (1950) rationale, reinforces what is problematic and ill conceived in schools. Such a rationale urges educators to regard curriculum planning as a type of experimental treatment: Objectives are to be operationalized through measured procedures; treatment consists of the curriculum provided and is to be revised on the basis of its efficacy. After objectives are achieved, another set of objectives and curricular treatments are implemented. The entire enterprise is aimed at the achievement of specific, standardized goals. Convergence on what is common to all is the ideal that guides the enterprise.

Reconceptualists regard such aims as seriously misconceived and oversimplified. What is needed, especially in a culture already characterized by high levels of alienation and personal indifference, is an approach to teaching that does not exacerbate our culture's major problems but, on the contrary, compensates and helps students overcome its deficits. What is needed is not more of the same, only better, but a reconceptualization of the aims and processes of schooling. Rather than attending solely to the child's behavior, reconceptualists believe educators should try to understand the nature of his or her experience. In other words, the need is to turn from a behavioristic to a phenomenological attitude.

Although there are magnet schools and individual teachers that foster what might be called a phenomenological attitude, there is no unified, organized, or concerted program to create schools or teaching practices that develop or implement a reconceptualist approach. In many ways, the virtual absence of organized efforts to create teaching practices congenial to reconceptionalism is understandable. Ideologies that lead to specific, more or less routinized procedures are indeed implementable; behavioristic teaching practices are examples. Reconceptualism is partly an attitude and unless teachers have acquired a disposition congruent with it, no routinized prescriptions are likely to be effective.

How then can such an approach to education be promulgated? Mainly through persuasion, it seems. Whenever an approach to practice requires artistry, even craft, standardized routines will be found wanting. Reconceptualization, like critical theory, is an orientation to schooling, indeed to living, that functions through the use of particular perspectives rather than through the application of rules.

Given the fact that in the United States there are over 100,000 schools and more than 2.5 million teachers, is it likely that a nonprescriptive, nonstandardized approach to teaching will gain saliency? Probably not, unless there is an unforeseeable social change in the culture at large that supports its major tenets. The factors that drive schools—standardized testing and the maintenance of "our competitive edge"—are widely accepted. As long as they are, reconceptualists will have an uphill battle. After having said that, it also needs to be said that those associated with reconceptualism have not simply stood by waiting for a miracle to happen. They have sponsored a journal, *The Journal of Curriculum Theorizing*, that publishes articles related to their interests and hold an annual conference, the Bergamo Conference, that explores educational problems from their perspectives. Intellectual interest is there, and a community of scholars sympathetic to its ideological commitments has been formed. Whether these efforts will be sufficient to have a significant impact on schools is another question.

Cognitive Pluralism

The sixth curriculum ideology is called cognitive pluralism. Although this concept is at least as old as Aristotle's distinctions among three different forms of knowledge—theoretical, practical, and productive—it has only been in the last two decades that a genuinely pluralistic conception of knowledge and intelligence has been advanced in the field of education. Cognitive pluralism is a conception of mind and knowledge that has two different but related branches. As a conception of knowledge, cognitive pluralism argues that one of the human being's distinctive features is the capacity to create and manipulate symbols. These symbols are powerful cultural resources played out in mathematics, music, literature, science, dance, and visual arts, indeed in any area of human life in which action or form is used to give expression or to represent experience or intention. Language, in the narrow sense of the term, is only one of the means through which the private, personal life of the individual is given a public presence; the symbol systems previously identified constitute a few of the others.

Several functions that symbol systems or "forms of representation" perform make them particularly important (Eisner 1982). First, the ability to use a symbol system or form of representation makes it possible to stabilize evanescent thoughts and feelings: Nothing is more elusive than an idea. Second, such stabilization makes it possible to reflect on what has been represented and to edit one's thinking. Third, the public transformation from what is private into a public form makes its communication possible. Fourth, the opportunity to represent through some material or device provides the occasions for the invention or discovery of ideas, images, or feelings that were not necessarily present at the inception of the activity. Put another way, the act of representation is also an opportunity for creative thinking. Finally, and most important, the features of the particular symbol system or form of representation used both constrain and make possible particular types of meaning. Poetry, for example, allows one to represent or recover meanings inexpressible in mathematics or even in prose.

Since the quest for meaning, it is argued, is part of human nature, the ability to represent or recover meaning in the various forms in which it can be experienced should be a primary aim of schooling. Some philosophers go even further. Symbol systems are regarded as so significant that Goodman (1978) believes they are foundational in the construction of our personal worlds. "There are as many worlds," he tells us, "as there are ways to describe them."

The roots of cognitive pluralism go back to Aristotle's tripart distinction between the ways of knowing. Its modern variants can be found in the works of Ernst Cassirer (1961–1964), Nelson Goodman (1976), and Susanne Langer (1976). In the curriculum field, similar ideas have been found in the works of Paul Hirst (1974) and Richard Peters (1960) in England and Elliot Eisner (1985a) and Phillip Phenix (1964) in the United States. The latter four curriculum theorists have all, in one way or another, emphasized the plurality of knowledge and the unique functions of different cognitive forms. These conceptions have, in turn, served as foundations for their views of what school programs should teach and what educational ends should be prized.

Related to the emphasis on the plurality of meaning is that on the plurality of intelligence (Gardner 1983). The long psychometric tradition influencing American education has emphasized the identification and measurement of the "G" factor. What most psychometricians have sought is the essential property or function that makes intelligence possible. Further, they have eschewed the idea that intelligence is multiple, or that its presence depends on the context, material, or circumstances in which individuals function. Related to the disposition to find essences has been a tendency to emphasize genetic rather than environmental influences. In some ways it is understandable that those who seek essences should have little appetite for measuring a process subject to the vicissitudes of the environment. What kind of mental science can be built on such a tentative personal feature?

During the past 15 years, the pluralism that has accompanied our conception of the nature of knowledge has also appeared in the way in which intelligence itself is conceived. Its meaning has shifted from a noun to a verb; intelligence for more than a few cognitive psychologists is not merely something you have but something you do. Furthermore, these doings are precisely that—different ways of acting. Gardner (1983), one of the leading spokespersons for this idea, identifies seven intelligences that he believes individuals possess in varying degrees. For Gardner, these are not "simply" aptitudes or talents but socially important ways of solving problems. Furthermore, he argues that environmental conditions have something to do with the particular kind of intelligence that will be valued and practiced.

The relationship between knowledge types and forms of intelligence is an important one. If the kind of mind that children can come to own is, in part, influenced by the kinds of opportunities they have to think, and if these opportunities are themselves defined by the kind of curriculum schools provide, it could be argued that the curriculum itself is, as Bernstein (1971) has suggested, a kind of mind-altering device. In this view it is easy to see how decisions about content inclusion and exclusion are of fundamental importance. Eisner (1985a) has argued that what is omitted from the school curriculum—what he calls the null curriculum—is every bit as important as what is left in. The kinds of decisions that individuals make is influenced not only by what they know but also by what they do not know. Large areas of important but unexamined content can have a very significant influence on the kinds of decisions people make and the kinds of lives they lead. Thus, symbol systems have the potential to provide not only unique forms of meaning but also the opportunity to practice and develop particular mental skills. Without these skills, the meanings that constitute the various symbol systems will be unrecoverable.

The ramifications of cognitive pluralism extend beyond curriculum matters. They also pertain to research methodology and to evaluation practices. As the idea of multiple ways of knowing gains legitimacy, qualitative research and evaluation methods have become increasingly visible and programs in schools of education have been created to prepare students in their use. The literary as well as the literal, the metaphorical as well as the mathematical, are increasingly being acknowledged as ways of conveying to the world what has been learned. As such methods grow in use and legitimacy, they may contribute to or reinforce the cognitive pluralistic perspective advanced by philosophers and curriculum theorists and broaden the ways in which students are assessed in school, something that could have a very important impact on the priorities of schooling.

In some ways this practice is beginning to occur in teacher assessment. The widespread interest in teaching and the growing recognition that it is one half of the systole-diastole relationship described at the beginning of this chapter has led to the desire to develop what Bronfenbrenner (1979) has called "ecologically valid" assessment methods. These methods are intended to assess what Aristotle thought of as practical knowledge, or knowledge about what to do. It is knowledge that pertains to decision making in context. The growing recognition among cognitive psychologists that the simple possession of factual content, even when it is understood, does not ensure its utility in situations that matter has led to what they call "situated knowledge," a form of understanding that does have utility in real situations. The distinction between situated and what might be called nonsituated or theoretical knowledge echoes Aristotle's distinction between the theoretical and the practical; it harkens back to progressive thinking about the nature of practical intelligence; and it supports the cognitive pluralism of philosophers and curriculum theorists, who have paid particular attention to the various ways of knowing.

What one currently sees in looking at the broad field of education is less certainty about what in the 1930s was referred to as a unified theory of science and more receptivity to the idea that forms of knowledge differ, that symbol systems or forms of representation are not only descriptive but also constitutive of experience, and that the insights that are intuitively grasped and acted on in teaching far exceed in number and are different in character from the generalizations produced in laboratorylike settings. The practical world has reappeared in a cognitive countenance.

By opening the door to cognitive pluralism, a whole new array of *potential* consequences flow for curriculum. First, the concept of literacy must be expanded. Although the term "literacy" typically refers to the ability to read, it has been extended to include the encoding or decoding of information in any of the forms that humans use to convey meaning (Eisner 1982). At its broadest level, the concept merges with semiotics, the theory of signs. At a somewhat narrower level, it recognizes that each of the various cultural forms imposes its own requirements on representation as well as on interpretation. In Phenix's (1964) words, each form of representation provides its own "realm of meaning." Since the pursuit of meaning is a basic part of human nature and since meaning is in large measure achieved through the use of symbol systems, the ability to read symbol systems that mediate meaning is critical if meaning is to be secured. The kind of pluralism advocated in the curriculum writing of Phenix, Peters, Hirst, and Eisner leads to programs that intentionally provide for the development of multiple forms of literacy.

Another potential consequence of cognitive pluralism is the expansion of educational equity in the classroom. Given the fact that there are differences in aptitudes among children, the creation of programs that restrict the use of aptitudes for those dealing with curricular tasks provides an advantage to those children whose aptitudes are consonant with the tasks provided. Children whose aptitudes are not useful in dealing with the tasks schools emphasize are disadvantaged. By creating a wider array of curricular tasks, those that require the use of different forms of intelligence, for example, or depend on different aptitudes, opportunities for success in school are expanded. These opportunities are expanded *if* success on this wider array of tasks is regarded as having equal intellectual merit. If, for example, high-level ability in the arts is regarded as laudable, but nonintellectual in nature, and if the school gives its most highly prized awards to what it regards as intellectual achievements, children who shine in the arts will never shine as brightly as those excellent in mathematics; the arts, as the children attracted to them, will remain second-class citizens in the hierarchy of curricular values.

Thus far no consortium has been created to promote or implement programs reflecting a cognitively pluralistic orientation to curriculum, although individual schools can be found that do attempt to provide such an approach. The Key School in Indianapolis, Indiana, is currently attempting to develop a curriculum that is consistent with Gardner's theory of multiple intelligences, and Malkus, Feldman, and Gardner (1988) have been attempting to identify what they call proclivities among preschool children. Although their efforts are still too new to assess, they do represent a move into the practical world of schooling.

Each of the foregoing curricular ideologies has different degrees of implementability. Rational humanism and religious orthodoxy are two ideologies that have their counterparts in schools. Indeed, there are consortia and organizations whose primary mission is to expand and improve the practice of schools embracing these ideological positions. Progressivism is probably more prevalent in American schools than reconceptualism, cognitive pluralism, or critical theory. The programs needed to implement a cognitively pluralistic approach to curriculum are scarce, and critical theory and reconceptualism are, in some ways, more attitudinal in nature than methodologically prescriptive. In all, their ideological presence in curriculum is mixed.

As indicated earlier, in the public arena ideas about priorities, goals, and the allocation of resources must survive a tough array of competing proposals from those who feel equally convinced of the correctness of their views. Educational policies are modified not only behind the closed door of the classroom but also in the arena in which they are debated. With 50 states responsible for educational policy and 16,000 school districts making and interpreting policies, homogeneity in micropolicy terms is hard to find. It is, of course, this heterogeneity that comes with the local control of schools and, at the same time, complicates the utilization of research in schools and classrooms: One never knows if the conditions that existed when the research was undertaken in one educational experiment also prevail in the school district in which one wishes to implement the experimental practice. When national policy for schools is determined by a national ministry of education, the problem of implementating policy and the practices associated with it is not *quite* so complex, although it is very far from simple. Teachers still close the classroom door, and children seldom match the expectations formulated by educational policymakers and technicians working in government bureaucracies. In the end, ideological change motivated by alternative ideologies may be among the important changes that can be made in the field of education.

RESEARCH ON IDEOLOGIES AND THEIR SIGNIFICANCE IN CURRICULUM

There are three ways to consider research on curricular ideologies. First, one can identify the emergence of such ideologies from, say, the turn of the century and describe the social and intellectual conditions that gave rise to them. Second, one can try to determine through historical research the practical consequences of curriculum ideologies on the content and form of the curriculum. Third, one can try to assess the effects of curriculum ideologies on the processes and outcomes of schooling: Do children and adolescents subject to, say, specific, consciously shaped ideological forms acquire beliefs that reflect the content and values of those ideologies?

By far the most widely used approach to the study of curricular ideologies is historical. The reasons for this prevalance are not difficult to discern. Curriculum ideologies are typically regarded as broadly swept, normatively orientated, socioeducational movements, that is, generalized ways of thinking about education, particularly its content and aims in the context of schooling. As a part of intellectual history, such developments do not lend themselves to the more tightly controlled research forms of social scientists, particularly psychologists. It is difficult to control the variables that are thought to be required to provide meaningful scientific claims about something as nebulous as an ideology. In addition to what might be considered nebulousness is the problem of commensurability. In conventional approaches to experimental research in education, dependent variables for treatment groups are held constant. The basic question is, Are there any differences in measured outcomes, given differences in experimental treatment? The experiment is an effort to identify differential effects, given a common set of tasks or objectives. In comparing different curricular ideologies, the end states are not the same. When ends differ, the problem of making meaningful comparisons on the basis of different treatments (curricula) is particularly difficult. If outcomes are incommensurate—not comparable—making comparisons is odious. In other words, comparing educational programs based on different ideologies is at best difficult and at worst irrelevant. I believe social scientists have recognized this problem and have elected to direct their energies toward problems more suitable to their methods. There is, however, one exception to this practice. It resides in ethnographic-like studies of schooling.

Only recently have social scientists in education undertaken the task of examining the overall impact of schooling as a place to be—a kind of culture in which children spend so much of their childhood. This has not been the case for educational historians. Examining the ways in which social, intellectual, and economic changes influence schools has been a major preoccupation, as has been attention to those individuals whose force of personality or vision has significantly influenced the schools.

Research in Religious Orthodoxy

One of the major studies of schools embracing religious orthodox educational ideology is Coleman and Hoffer's (1987) comparative study of Catholic and public schools. Coleman and Hoffer conclude that on verbal skills and mathematics, Catholic schools achieve higher levels of educational attainment than public schools serving comparable populations.

> Both the comparisons of achievement growth across sectors for students who continued in school from the sophomore to senior year, and the comparisons of achievement growth between dropouts and those who remained in school in each sector show strong evidence of greater growth in Catholic schools than in public schools, in both verbal skills and mathematics. The magnitude of the differential effect is about one grade equivalent—with Catholic sector students showing an achievement growth over the two years of about three grade equivalents compared to the two grade equivalents of growth in the public sector. There is no evidence of greater growth in science knowledge or civics in the Catholic schools. (92)

What Coleman and Hoffer (1987) did not appraise, and this goes to the heart of the mission of any religiously oriented institution, is the degree to which Catholic schools succeed at their most important educational aim: the development of good Catholics. The primary educational mission of a religious institution is to promulgate the faith by inducting the young into its belief system. The "mere" development in the young of the ability to read, write, and cipher or to understand biology or history or music or art can be accomplished by the public schools. These are not distinctive missions; religious induction is. What the Coleman and Hoffer study does not provide are indexes that speak to such aims. Thus, ironically, what is most educationally important in Catholic schools is neglected in the study, whereas what is least educationally unique is attended to.

It must be recognized that if Coleman and Hoffer had addressed the religious effectiveness of Catholic schools, it would have been impossible to compare such schools *on that dimension* with public schools; public schools do not have a counterpart to the religious aims of Catholic schools. Thus the problem of commensurability becomes especially acute when there is no basis for comparison. What could have been assessed, however, is the efficacy of Catholic schools with respect to their own values. Do these schools succeed in achieving what they set out to accomplish?

One study that did try to determine such effects is James Kuntz's (1986) study of the teaching of social justice in two Jesuit high schools. As indicated earlier, the Jesuits have had a long-standing interest in social justice and regard its promulgation and achievement of central importance. As a result, many Jesuit high schools focus on issues of social justice in the curriculum, and some offer courses on the topic. Kuntz found a tension between the values pertaining to social justice that students brought with them from home and the values they encountered in their classes. The efforts of their teachers were not wholly successful, judging from the attitudes that students reflected in their comments about social issues and in their behavior. Yet one never knows what attitudes would have prevailed without attention to social issues by the teachers Kuntz observed. Further, one does not know how students function outside of their schools on matters that pertain to social justice. In short, the assessment of attitudes and behavior change outside of the school is what is needed to know whether curriculum and teaching make a significant difference in the lives of the young. Neither the Coleman and Hoffer (1987) study nor the Kuntz study has much to say about these matters.

Research in Rational Humanism

As far as I am able to determine, no empirical studies are available on the effects or practices of rational humanistic approaches to schooling. In some ways, this lack is not surprising. Rational humanists place little faith in the ability of behavioral scientists to measure what they care about the most: the development of human rationality through the study of great works. Those most steeped in such values are themselves not likely to have the inclination, let alone the empirical research skills, to undertake the studies. As a result, those most engaged in this orientation to education are least likely to study it, whereas those least engaged are least interested in doing so. It should also be said that the kinds of outcomes the rational humanists prize are not those that lend themselves to most of the testing procedures now used to assess school productivity. Rationality, in the terms in which it is usually described, is a notoriously slippery notion; it manifests itself in different ways in different materials. It requires perceptivity to recognize and it is impossible to standardize. It is much more likely to be described than measured, and it is likely to lead to incommensurability with respect to the outcomes described. Yet despite these difficulties, and they are formidable, it is unfortunate that efforts have not been made to describe and interpret what goes on in schools that reflects this ideology. Schools that embrace and function in the *Paideia* mode can, in principle, be studied in qualitative, critical, or ethnographic terms. Teaching practices can also be studied. As for outcomes, the appraisal of student work—the insight of ideas generated, the strength of arguments created, the subtlety of style, the level of intellectuality—is possible, despite its resistance to measurement. As yet, I have been unable to find studies of either the practices of schools that use *Paideia* programs or the effect of these programs on students. It seems to me that this is a research agenda waiting to be formulated and pursued.

Research on Progressivism

Progressive schools have not had much saliency in American education during the past 20 years. During the 1960s attitudes emerged toward schooling and community that were much in keeping with the spirit of educational progressivism: the conviction that schools should emphasize democratic processes, that the affective life of students should be taken into account as well as their cognitive development, that curricula should be designed to reflect and build on children's interests, that teaching methods should emphasize sensory experience and real-life problems, that educational outcomes were more complex and personalized than clear-cut and standardized, and that educational evaluation practices need to encompass what is personal and subtle. Hence, since the late 1960s public concerns about the quality of American education have grown, and as a result, interest in progressive practices, often seen as antithetical to what is truly educationally substantive, has decreased. As a result, there are relatively few schools that continue to promote progressive educational practices. The 1960s reflected in the eyes of many a kind of social anarchy, and John Dewey continues to receive "credit" for what many believe to be the sorry state of American education.

Therefore, opportunities to assess the effects of progressive schools are limited, and in any case, progressive educators tend not to place much faith in academic achievement measures that require students to respond to multiple-choice tests. Such modes of assessment seem to progressives of marginal importance in education. They are more concerned with complex forms of problem solving, with idiosyncratic outcomes, and with the development of positive dispositions toward learning and receptive attitudes toward schooling. Although it is possible to study the effects, for example, of discovery-oriented teaching, progressivism as an educational ideology is considerably wider. It is intended to permeate the school as a whole, its social character as well as its pedagogical techniques, its form of organization as well as the content it includes in its curriculum, and its modes of assessment as well as its relationship to the life students lead outside of school. In short, progressivism, writ large in education, is not an isolated form of educational practice but a shared form of educational life.

As far as I am able to determine there have been no studies undertaken in the past decade that have examined the effects of schools that reflect, as a whole, such an approach to education. To determine the educational consequences of such schools, they would need to have a consistent educational agenda reflecting the foregoing beliefs and practices. Such schools could not be "partially progressive."

Interestingly, one of the recent developments in the creation of such schools is the type that flies under the banner of "accelerated school." Levin (1990) and his colleagues at Stanford are employing many of Dewey's ideas in building schools that share most of the features described above. These schools are designed primarily for students at risk, that is, students who are likely to be unsuccessful in schools as they now typically function. Levin's notion is that at-risk students would profit from programs specifically designed for them, which did not emphasize drill and practice, depended on parental guidance and support, and provided a curriculum sufficiently problem-centered to challenge the higher mental processes that at-risk students are able to display and in fact do display in situations outside of school. It is, at present, too soon to determine the effectiveness of accelerated schools. Preliminary reports suggest that academic achievement, even on standard academic measures, is exceeding expected levels of performance. Yet these schools are only beginning, and it will take 5 to 10 years to determine if the progressive orientation that pervades them will have the hoped-for effects.

Research in Critical Theory

Research in critical theory is primarily of two kinds. First, there are studies of the climate and character of schooling such as those done by Giroux (1989), Willis (1977), and others. These studies, like the work of Bourdieu (1977), are essentially interpretive in character. Are they empirical studies? Although they do not emphasize or often use quantitative measures to secure information, the basis on which the interpretations are made is clearly empirical in nature. What typically results from these interpretations is a litany of inequities and other ills that schools display, often reflecting the problems and inequities of the society that created them.

A second kind of study is closer to the type of research typically emphasized in the educational research community. These do set out to investigate particular schools or classrooms and often formulate hypotheses derived from a theoretical view of the consequences of particular values and practices. Anyon (1981), for example, studied curriculum, pedagogy, and pupil evaluation practices in five elementary schools differentiated by social class. She concludes her study by saying,

> This study has suggested, as well, that there are class conflicts in educational knowledge and its distribution. We can see class conflict in the struggle to impose the knowledge of powerful groups on the working class and in student resistance to this class-based curriculum. We can see class conflict in the contradictions within and between school knowledge and its economic and personal values, and in attempts to impose liberal public attitudes on children of the rich.
>
> Class conflict in education is thus not dormant, nor a relic of an earlier era; nor is the outcome yet determined. No class is certain of victory, and ideological hegemony is not secure. Those who would struggle against ideological hegemony must not confuse working-class powerlessness with apathy, middle-class ideology with its inevitability, or ruling-class power and cultural capital with superior strength or intelligence. Just as blacks were not the happy-go-lucky fellows of former stereotypes, so the working class is not dull or acquiescent, and the rich are not complacent or secure. Indeed, perhaps the most important implication of the present study is that for those of us who are working to transform society, there is much to do, at all levels, in education. (38–39)

In Anyon's work there is also an emphasis on inequity rather than on the constructive features of educational practice in schools. It is almost as if those looking for trouble are able to find it, no matter where they look.

Some studies, such as those by Bowles and Gintis (1976), do make use of statistical data secured from a wide variety of sources to interpret the consequences of schooling in "capitalist America." Their work has been widely used and discussed and is a trenchant commentary on the state of American education, given their neo-Marxist orientation.

It should also be said that in spirit, critical pedagogy, which is derived from critical theory, is congruent with some aspects of feminism and multicultural education. I refer here to efforts in these areas to display critically the covert values of the social text: Feminists are quick to display the ways in which society and schools are gendered, often to their disadvantage, and minorities are quite articulate regarding the saliency of Anglo values and the cultural parochialism of schools. In their efforts to reveal what has become virtually unseen common fare, feminists and minorities share some of the methods, if not always the aims, of critical theorists.

Research in Reconceptualism

The work of William Pinar (1988) and his students has been the major locus of research into the phenomenological features of school experience. Their work has focused more on matters of interpretation than on the invention of teaching methods intended to yield particular forms of experience. This orientation is altogether in keeping with the assumptions that undergird their work. These assumptions include the belief, as already indicated, that technologically oriented, means-ends approaches to educational practice cannot be successfully employed to bring about the kind of experience that is both deep and personal; there can be no technology of teaching. There are ideas, sensibilities, a pedagogical imagination, and indeed an attitude that teachers need to possess that are conducive to the development of what they call "currere." In fact, the attempt to create a scientifically guided technology of teaching, and more broadly of schooling, has been, in this view, a source of most of the problems that schools confront. In a sense, many of these problems are caused by the school because of the misguided ways in which curriculum has been conceptualized and teaching pursued.

As a result of the disinclination to create experimental approaches to teaching, approaches that could be "packaged," transported, disseminated, and implemented, the availability of research of an interventionist character is very scarce. What is available are texts—texts interpreted or "deconstructed," analysis of logs and interviews, observations of practice, and the appeal to interpretive frameworks (psychoanalysis, e.g.) that are intended to provide insight into human experience. If there is an "experimental treatment," it resides in the effort to persuade readers embracing a more conventional ideology to reconsider, indeed to try to reconceptualize, curriculum and, even more broadly, the educational agenda. One way in which they believe this agenda can be rethought is by examining carefully one's own experience as a teacher or school administrator. For such purposes the writing of biography can be useful. The works of Connelly and Clandinin (1988) and Miller (1983, 1987) are examples of how the arts of exposition provide a way to induce change. This way is the closest thing to a method. Pinar (1988) describes the foundations of method as follows:

> Part of what we must do is reestablish contact with the preconceptual and describe the essences of both substances and situation as they disclose themselves to us. Such an absolute perspective or transcendental ego (to be distinguished from the natural ego, which is the predictable *persona* or public self that the behaviorists attempt to explain) is not a given, but a developmental possibility indicated by transpersonal psychology and Zen Buddhist psychology. It is hoped that this method carries with it beneficial developmental consequences.
>
> This approach, then, is grounded in existentialism, phenomenology, Jungian psychoanalysis, the radical psychiatry of Cooper and Laing, and aspects of literary and educational theory. The ambition is that it surpasses these roots and becomes an area in its own right, with its own boundaries, content, and research method. (423)

This orientation to change is in some ways like a therapeutic process: The teacher is invited to articulate and, through articulation and the writing of text, to stabilize what is evanescent so that a new consciousness is created. It is out of this new consciousness that schools have their most promising opportunity for being reconceptualized.

The virtues of the approach are also its liabilities. Attention to experience and to the meaning it has is surely important. What students and teachers make of their lives cannot be irrelevant to the aims of any educational process. Yet just how one fosters such awareness cannot be standardized in the ways in which other approaches to educational change can be. Can an approach to educational practice survive a nonstandardized format? Will teachers and administrators seeking "what works" be content with a method that in some ways is more of an attitude toward others and the situations in which they live than a procedure? Will a society that is meritocratic in character be willing to accept an approach to practice that is personal and that puts a high premium on productive idiosyncrasy? These are some of the questions that beleaguer reconceptualism and make it so difficult to disseminate. Nevertheless, encouraging educational practitioners and policymakers to pay attention to the covert experiential aspect of life in schools is no trivial accomplishment. If experimental treatments are conceptualized to include the results of such efforts, it might be said that reconceptualism as a curricular ideology has the potential to perform a very important educational function: It can remind those engaged in education that there is considerably more to practice than bringing about behavioral change.

Research in Cognitive Pluralism

Like several of the major curricular ideologies, cognitive pluralism has been advanced by theoreticians whose main interest is in conceptualizing possibilities for education rather than in developing programs designed to reflect the conceptualizations. The work of Paul Hirst (1974) and Richard Peters (1960) has been published in journals in the philosophy of education and in books that are philosophical in nature. These two leading British educational philosophers devoted their attention to the development of persuasive cases: Their interests are essentially epistemological in character.

Similarly, Phillip Phenix's (1964) work, as well as Eisner's (1982, 1985a, 1985b), is conceptual in orientation. Much has been written that urges educators to attend to aspects of cognition and to the range of symbol systems available in the culture, but as far as I can tell, no systematic efforts have been undertaken to develop the kinds of curricula that reflect such an orientation. As a result, there is a paucity of dependable empirical evidence to support the analyses and recommendations that have been made. As already indicated, the Key School in Indianapolis, Indiana, is engaged in implementing a program reflecting Gardner's (1983) theory of multiple intelligence. However, the school is too new, as of this writing, to determine whether the implementation of Gardner's ideas is indeed congruent with the ideas themselves and, if so, whether they make any difference in the kind of thinking that students are able to do.

One other study, a doctoral dissertation by Terrie Epstein (1989), which reflects Eisner's ideas about the utility of forms of representation, has been used in teaching a unit in social studies and is perhaps closest to the kind of assessment of cognitive pluralistic practices available. Epstein's study, a qualitative effort, was aimed at developing a unit built on the utilization of literary forms, video, music, and dance, as well as on historical text, for teaching the preslavery period in America. The goal of the study was to determine whether the provision of such forms of representation would enhance the students' understanding of this important period in American history. To achieve this goal, the music of the slaves was played, their folklore was read, videos such as *Roots* were viewed, stories and parables were discussed, and pictures that portrayed the life of the slaves were seen. These forms, in conjunction with historical text, provided much of the content of the unit. Students were then given the opportunity to represent in their own terms and in media that they selected ideas or feelings they had experienced in the course of studying these materials. The result was the production of a rich array of diverse forms: music reflecting the slavery period, pictures, stories, and the like. Epstein's view was that students should be given the opportunity to display what they have gotten out of such a unit in forms that are congruent with their own interests and aptitudes. The material they produced was judged by Epstein to be insightful and intellectually rich.

The problem, of course, that Epstein (1989) and anyone else who uses such an approach encounters is, again, the incommensurability of the material. When students are given the opportunity to choose the way in which they wish to display what they have learned, the ability to make comparisons across students is diminished. In addition, when students paint images stimulated by historical reading, for example, one can raise the question of whether or not what they are displaying is in fact historical knowledge or understanding. Nevertheless, such approaches, it seems to me, have substantial promise in pushing the boundaries of curriculum theory and educational evaluation. What is particularly impressive about Epstein's work is her willingness not only to entertain these notions at a conceptual or theoretical level but also to transform them into curricula, to teach them to children, and to assess the results. Her study is the only one I know of that makes use of such an approach within the social studies arena.

CONCLUSION

It is clear from examining the history of educational practice, and even more the history of curricular thought, that particular ideologies have emerged within the culture that have given direction to practitioners and to the aims of schools. In America, at least, such aims are seldom uniform, and the ideologies that buffet schools are often competitive. The result of these forces has been to create a political arena for educational policy; the directions that should be taken, at least for the "debatable" dimensions of schooling, are typically on the table as a matter of negotiation. Those areas that are not typically negotiated are those considered so central to schooling that there is no debate about them: the development of skills in the three R's, for example, as well as those subjects that are so marginalized that they never become problematic in schooling. Yet ideologies in education provide a broad frame that makes it possible for small decisions as well as large ones to be made according to certain philosophical lights. These small decisions collectively influence the kind of place that schools become for both teachers and students. In this sense educational ideologies, broadly speaking, and curricular ideologies, more specifically, fundamentally influence our deliberations about what the curriculum should become and what schools should be.

Penetrating the specific recommendations that are made for school improvement to their ideological core is one of the marks of competent educational scholarship. Such analysis does much to rationalize educational debate. Whether the rational analysis of starting points will alter ideological commitment is, of course, another matter. There may indeed be deep-seated commitments to visions of education that cannot be adequately addressed, even by the most articulate educational analysts. Yet the reasonable option is to try. This chapter has tried.

References

Adler, Mortimer. 1982. *The Paideia Proposal*. New York: Macmillan.

Albertini, John, and Bonnie Meath-Lang. 1986. An analysis of student-teacher exchanges in dialogue journal writing. *Journal of Curriculum Theorizing* 7 (1): 153–201.

Anyon, Jean. 1981. Social class and school knowledge. *Curriculum Inquiry* 11(1): 3–42.

Apple, Michael. 1982. *Education and Power*. Boston: Routledge & Kegan Paul.

Aronowitz, Stanley, and Henry Giroux. 1988. Schooling, culture, and literacy in the age of broken dreams: A review of Bloom and Hirsch. *Harvard Educational Review* 58(2): 172.

Atkin, Myron. 1989. Can educational research keep pace with education reform? *Phi Delta Kappan* 71(3): 200–205.

Atkin, Myron, Donald Kennedy, and Cynthia Patrick. 1989. *Inside Schools: A Collaborative View*. London: Falmer.

Bernstein, Basil. 1971. "On the Classification and Framing of Educational Knowledge." In *Knowledge and Control*, edited by Michael Young, 47–69. London: Collier-Macmillan.

Bloom, Allan. 1987. *The Closing of the American Mind: How Higher Education Has Failed Democracy and Impoverished the Souls of Today's Students*. New York: Simon & Schuster.

Bourdieu, Pierre. 1977. *Reproduction in Education's Society and Culture*. London: Sage.

Bronfonbrenner, Urie. 1979. *The Ecology of Human Development*. Cambridge, MA: Harvard University Press.

Bowles, Samuel, and Herbert Gintis. 1976. *Schooling in Capitalist America*. New York: Basic Books.

Boyer, Ernest. 1983. *High School*. New York: Harper & Row.

Bruner, Jerome. 1964. The course of cognitive growth. *American Psychologist* 19(1): 1–15.

Callahan, Raymond. 1962. *Education and the Cult of Efficiency*. Chicago: University of Chicago Press.

Case, Robbie. 1984. *Intellectual Development: Birth to Adulthood*. Orlando, FL: Academic Press.

Cassirer, Ernst. 1961–1964. *The Philosophy of Symbolic Forms*, 3 vols., translated by Ralph Manheim, Preface and Introduction by Charles W. Hendel. New Haven, CT: Yale University Press.

Cheney, Lynn. 1987. *American Memory*. Washington, DC: National Endowment for the Humanities.

Cole, Michael. 1974. *Culture and Thought*. New York: Wiley.

Coleman, James, and Thomas Hoffer. 1987. *Public and Private High Schools*. New York: Basic Books.

Connelly, F. M., and D. Jeanne Clandinin. 1988. *Teachers as Curriculum Planners: Narratives of Experience*. New York: Teachers College Press.

Counts, George. 1932. *Can the Schools Build a New Social Order?* New York: John Day.

Cremin, Lawrence. 1970a. *American Education*. New York: Harper & Row.

Cremin, Lawrence. 1970b. *The Transformation of the School*. New York: Knopf.

Cuban, Larry. 1979. "Determinants of Curriculum Change and Stability, 1870–1970." In *Value Conflicts and Curricular Issues*, edited by Jon Schaffarzick and Gary Sykes, 139–196. Berkeley, CA: McCutchan.

Cuban, Larry. 1988. *The Managerial Imperative and the Practice of Leadership in Schools*. Albany: State University of New York Press.

Culler, Jonathan. 1982. *On Deconstruction: Theory and Criticism After Structuralism*. Ithaca, NY: Cornell University.

Darwin, Charles. 1975 [1859]. *The Origin of Species*. New York: Norton.

Dewey, John. 1902. *The Educational Situation*. Chicago: University of Chicago Press.

Dewey, John. 1910. *How We Think*. Boston: Heath.

Dewey, John. 1938. *Experience and Education*. New York: Macmillan.

Dreeben, Robert. 1968. *On What Is Learned in School*. New York: Addison-Wesley.

Eagleton, Terry. 1983. *Literacy Theory*. Minneapolis: University of Minnesota Press.

Eisner, Elliot W. 1974. *English Primary Schools*. Washington, DC: National Association for the Education of Young Children.

Eisner, Elliot W. 1982. *Cognition and Curriculum: A Basis for Deciding What to Teach*. White Plains, NY: Longman.

Eisner, Elliot W. 1985a. "Aesthetic Modes of Knowing." In *Learning and Teaching the Ways of Knowing. Eighty-fourth Yearbook of the National Society for the Study of Education*, Part II, edited by Elliot W. Eisner, 23–36. Chicago: University of Chicago Press.

Eisner, Elliot W. 1985b. *The Educational Imagination*, 2nd ed. New York: Macmillan.

Eisner, Elliot W. 1985c. *What High Schools Are Like: Views from the Inside*. Stanford, CA: Stanford School of Education.

Epstein, Terry. 1989. "An Aesthetic Approach to the Teaching and Learning of the Social Studies." Ph.D. dissertation, Harvard University, Cambridge, MA.

Friere, Paulo. 1970. *Pedagogy of the Oppressed*. New York: Seabury.

Gallup, Alec, and David Clark. 1987. The 19th annual Gallup poll of the public's attitudes toward the public schools. *Phi Delta Kappan* 69(1): 17–30.

Gardner, Howard. 1983. *Frames of Mind: The Theory of Multiple Intelligences*. New York: Basic Books.

Geertz, Clifford. 1973. *The Interpretation of Cultures*. New York: Basic Books.

Getzels, Jacob. 1974. Images of the Classroom and Visions of the Learner. *School Review* 82(4): 527–540.

Giroux, Henry. 1989. *Critical Pedagogy, the State, and Cultural Struggle*. Albany: State University of New York Press.

Goodlad, John. 1984. *A Place Called School: Prospects for the Future*. New York: McGraw-Hill.

Goodlad, John, and Robert Anderson. 1959. *The Non-graded Elementary School*. New York: Harcourt, Brace.

Goodman, Nelson. 1976. *The Languages of Art: An Approach to a Theory of Symbols*, 2nd ed. Indianapolis, IN: Hackett.

Goodman, Nelson. 1978. *Ways of Worldmaking*. Indianapolis, IN: Hackett.

Gruber, Howard. 1981. *Darwin on Man*. Chicago: University of Chicago Press.

Grumet, Madeline. 1988. *Bitter Milk*. Amherst: University of Massachusetts Press.

Hegel, George W. 1900. *The Philosophy of History*. New York: Willey Book Co.

Heubner, Dwayne. 1963. "New Modes of Man's Relationship to Man." In *New Insights and the Curriculum*, edited by Alexander Frazier, 144–164. Washington, DC: Association for Supervision and Curriculum Development.

Hirsch, E. D. 1987. *Cultural Literacy*. Boston: Houghton Mifflin.

Hirsch, E. D. 1988. *Dictionary of Cultural Literacy*. Boston: Houghton Mifflin.

Hirst, Paul. 1974. *Knowledge and the Curriculum*. London and Boston: Routledge & Kegan Paul.

Holmes Group. 1986. *Tomorrow's Teachers: A Report of the Holmes Group*. East Lansing: Michigan State University Press.

Horio, Teruhisa. 1988. *Educational Thought and Ideology in Modern Japan*. Tokyo: University of Tokyo Press.

Hutchins, Robert. 1953. *The Conflict in Education in a Democratic Society*. New York: Harper.

Jackson, Phillip. 1968. *Life in Classrooms*. New York: Holt, Rinehart and Winston.

Jackson, Phillip. 1986. *The Practice of Teaching*. New York: Teachers College Press.

Kuntz, James F. 1986. "The Transmission of Values in Two Jesuit High School Classrooms." Ph.D. dissertation, Stanford University, Stanford, CA.

Langer, Suzanne. 1942. *Philosophy in a New Key*, Cambridge, MA: Harvard University Press.

Langer, Suzanne. 1976. *Problems of Art*. New York: Scribners.

Lepper, Mark, and David Greene, eds. 1978. *The Hidden Cost of Reward: New Perspectives on the Psychology of Human Motivation*. Hillsdale, NJ: Erlbaum.

Levin, Henry. 1990. *Accelerated Schools: A New Strategy for At-Risk Students*. Stanford, CA: Accelerated Schools Project, Stanford University.

MacDonald, James. 1975. "Curriculum Theory." In *Curriculum Theorizing*, edited by William Pinar, 5–18. Berkeley, CA: McCutchan.

McKeon, Robert, ed. 1941. *The Basic Works of Aristotle*. New York: Random House.

Madison, James. 1961 [1784]. *Federalist Papers*. New York: New American Library.

Malkus, U., D. Feldman, and H. Gardner. 1988. "Dimensions of Mind in Early Childhood." In *The Psychological Bases of Early Education*, edited by A. D. Pelligrini. Chichester: Wiley.

Marx, Karl. 1987 [1859]. *Manifesto of the Communist Party*. Chicago: Charles H. Kerr.

Metz, Mary. 1986. *Different by Design*. London: Routledge & Kegan Paul.

Miller, Janet. 1983. A search for congruence: Influence of past and present in future teachers' concepts about teaching writing. *English education* 15(1): 5–16.

Miller, Janet. 1987. "Teachers' Emerging Texts: The Empowering Potential of Writing In-service." In *Educating Teachers: Changing the Nature of Pedagogical Knowledge*, edited by John Smyth, 193–205. London: Falmer.

National Commission on Excellence in Education. 1983. *A Nation at Risk*. Washington, DC: U.S. Government Printing Office.

Neill, A. S. 1960. *Summerhill: A Radical Approach to Child Rearing*. New York: Hart Publishing Co.

Neisser, Ullrich. 1976. *Cognition and Reality: Principles and Implications of Cognitive Psychology*. San Francisco: Freeman.

Olsen, David. 1980. *The Social Foundations of Language and Thought*. New York: Norton.

Olsen, David. 1988. *Developing Theories of Mind*. Cambridge: Cambridge University Press.

Peshkin, Alan. 1986. *God's Choice: The Total World of a Fundamentalist Christian School*. Chicago: University of Chicago Press.

Peters, Richard. 1960. *Authority, Responsibility, and Education*. London: George Allen & Unwin.

Phenix, Phillip. 1964. *Realms of Meaning: A Philosophy of the Curriculum for General Education*. New York: McGraw-Hill.

Piaget, Jean. 1973. *The Child and Reality*, translated by Arnold Rosin. New York: Grossman.

Pinar, William, ed. 1975. *Curriculum Theorizing: The Reconceptualists*. Berkeley, CA: McCutchan.

Pinar, William. 1988. *Contemporary Curriculum Discourse*. Scottsdale, AZ: Gorsuch Scavisbrick.

Plowden Report. 1966. *Children and Their Primary Schools*. London: Her Majesty's Stationery Office.

Powell, Arthur G., Eleanor Farrar, and David K. Cohen. 1985. *The Shopping Mall High School*. Boston: Houghton Mifflin.

Pratte, Richard. 1977. *Ideology and Education*. New York: Mc Kay Co.

Rugg, Harold, and Ann Shumacher. 1928. *The Child-Centered School*. Yonkers-on-Hudson, NY: World Book Company.

Sapir, Edward. 1962. *Culture, Language and Personality*. Berkeley: University of California Press.

Schoen, Donald. 1983. *The Reflective Practitioner: How Professionals Think in Action*. New York: Basic Books.

Schwab, Joseph. 1969. The practical: A language for curriculum. *School Review* 78(5): 1–24.

Singer, Marcy. 1990. "Senses of History: An Inquiry Into Form, Meaning, and Understanding." Ph.D. dissertation, Stanford University, Stanford, CA.

Sizer, Theodore R. 1984. *Horace's Compromise: The Dilemma of the American High School*. Boston: Houghton Mifflin.

Smith, Douglas T., et al. (n.d.). *Douglas T. Smith, et al., Plaintiffs* v. *Board of School Commissioners of Mobile County, et al.* Consolidated with *Douglas T. Smith, et al., Plaintiffs* v. *George C. Wallace, Governor of Alabama, et al.*

Smith, Lewis, and William Geoffrey. 1968. *The Complexities of Education in an Urban Classroom*. New York: Holt, Rinehart and Winston

Stenhouse, Lawrence. 1982. *Teaching About Race Relations*. London: Routledge & Kegan Paul.

Sternberg, Robert. 1988. *The Triarchic Mind*. New York: Viking.

Tyler, Ralph. 1950. *Basic Principles of Curriculum and Instruction*. Chicago: University of Chicago Press.

Uhrmacher, Bruce. 1990. "Waldorf Schools Marching Quietly Unheard." Ph.D. dissertation, Stanford University, Stanford, CA.

USA Research. 1984. *A Nation at Risk: The Full Account.* Cambridge, MA: USA Research.

Vygotsky, Lev. 1962. *Thought and Language.* Cambridge, MA: M.I.T. Press.

Walker, Decker. 1979. "Approaches to Curriculum Development." In *Value Conflicts and Curriculum Issues*, edited by Jon Schaffarzick and Gary Sykes, 263–290. Berkeley, CA: McCutchan.

Walker, Decker, and Jon Schaffarzick. 1972. Comparing curricula. *Review of Educational Research* 4: 83–112.

Waller, Willard. 1932. *The Sociology of Teaching.* New York: Wiley.

Whorf, Benjamin L. 1956. *Language, Thought, and Reality.* Cambridge, MA: M.I.T. Press.

Willis, Paul. 1977. *Learning to Labor.* Lexington, MA: D. C. Heath.

12

ORGANIZATION OF THE CURRICULUM

John I. Goodlad
UNIVERSITY OF WASHINGTON

Zhixin Su
CALIFORNIA STATE UNIVERSITY, NORTHRIDGE

There is a vast body of writing on the organization of the curriculum but little of it reports research, if one defines "research" as studies seeking to demonstrate or describe a relationship between, for example, some pattern of organization and such outcomes as the understanding of subject matter. Most such research is confined to studies into school subjects—mathematics, reading, history, and so on—and is reported elsewhere in this *Handbook*. Most of the writing and reporting on curriculum organization is either conceptual or descriptive. The former depends for its validity on argument, usually from a foundation of values or principles believed to be sound. The latter describes work in progress or completed—work usually involving a shift in emphasis from, for example, primary attention to the nature of the subject matter to greater attention to learners' interests or stage of development. Rarely does either rest its case on experiments or on reporting effects beyond the opinions of persons involved or affected.

Most of the literature reviewed in what follows represents, then, a broad conception of research best viewed as inquiry—frequently, reasoned argument for a given approach to curriculum organization based on qualitative, contextual criteria. One argues for what one believes to be good and true and perhaps even beautiful and just: good for children and youths, good for society, true to the structure of the discipline, beautiful in its appeal to the senses, and just in that the organization of the curriculum denies no one access to first-class knowledge. One argues that the organizational pattern fits or follows from stated ends or values and may stop with an argument based on the face validity of this or that proposition or go on to provide data supporting correlational relationships. Or one argues that the curricular arrangements commonly assumed (in the experimental paradigm) to be means justified only by their relationship to ends must be viewed as ends in themselves, to be justified by the criteria of good, true, beautiful, and just. Eisner (1977) refers to part of this process of judgment and justification as educational connoisseurship.

Various ways of organizing the curriculum have enjoyed attention for a period of time and then largely disappeared. Sometimes, a little of what was proposed was absorbed into conventional practice; sometimes a pattern of organization returned to popularity later in new dress. Because of this evolutionary character of patterns of curriculum organization, in particular, our inquiry is in large part historical in nature.

Needless to say, reasoned argument leads to reasoned counterargument. Consequently, a portion of the literature on curriculum represents ongoing debate over competing positions. There is much of it. The various approaches wax and wane in popularity, appearing and reappearing in discourse. When the nation's welfare appears to be at stake because of the perceived condition of our schools, organizational arrangements that stay close to the academic disciplines tend to be in favor. Tough, subject-oriented approaches in subsequent eras of reform are perceived to be shortchanging the needs and interests of students and tend to be followed by approaches appearing to be softer and more tender.

We endeavor in what follows to sift through this voluminous body of literature in search of patterns of curriculum organization based on careful consideration of the range of variables to be taken into account if the curriculum is to be coherent. In particular, we attempt to locate the concepts and elements considered central or unique to a particular form of curriculum organization. Our critique focuses more on the underlying rationale than on the debate among competing positions. In this way, we limit ourselves rather sharply, eschewing what would otherwise be an exhaustive, exhausting review of a rather diffuse body of literature.

DEFINITIONS AND CONCEPTS

The primary purposes of seeking alternative ways to organize the curriculum are to increase human accessibility to knowledge and ways of knowing and to foster understanding. The perspective one brings to the task is heavily influenced by one's conception of knowledge (see Chapter 10 in this *Handbook*), however well or ill formed. Ideally, the way the curriculum is organized should enhance students' effectiveness as citizens, workers, parents, and participants in the whole of life—their ability to take part in the human conversation (Oakeshott 1962, 199). Curriculum organization is intended to render knowledge in such way that it is readily accessible to large numbers of people (Cremin 1971).

Curriculum and Curriculum Organization

Skilbeck (1985) defines curriculum organization as

> the manner in which the elements that constitute the curriculum of an educational system or institution are arranged, interrelated, and sequenced. These elements comprise such general factors as teaching plans and schemes, learning materials, equipment and plant, the professional expertise of the teaching force, and the requirements of assessment and examinations bodies. (1229)

It is clear from Skilbeck's definition that his unit of selection and analysis is an institution such as a school, college, or university or even the educational system of a district or state. The elements of curriculum to be arranged, consequently, are very general and lie outside of what some other definitions embrace. For example, if the unit of analysis is confined to a subject only, such as mathematics, the curriculum planner's concentration narrows to the sequencing of mathematical topics and operations, estimates of student time required for mastery, possible integrations with other subjects, and the like. Clearly, then, the problems and issues of organizing curricula are shaped by one's definition of curriculum.

The range in definitions is enormous: from that of a common dictionary—the courses offered by an educational institution—to much broader ones, such as "planned actions for instruction" and "all the experiences a learner has under the auspices of a school" (Foshay 1969, 275–276). Connelly and Lantz (1985) posed nine discrete definitions. However, over the years, definitions have tended to fall into four broad categories, each reflecting a different perspective and each having different implications for organizing curricula: (1) The curriculum is a design or plan of institutionalized education; (2) the curriculum consists of the actual learning opportunities provided at a given time and place; (3) the curriculum is an instrument for bringing about behavioral changes in learners as a result of their activities in an educational institution; (4) the curriculum is all the educational experiences that a learner has under the guidance of the school (Kearney and Cook 1960). The search for a single definition (occupying more than a little of the literature in the field of curriculum inquiry) is futile simply because widely differing phenomena are viewed—justifiably—as a curriculum or as curricula. Consequently, the phenomena of curriculum organization are not everywhere the same.

Goodlad (1966, 29–39; 1979, 33–37) attempted to sort out these different curricula according to their levels of remoteness from those for whom they were planned. He identified four: societal, institutional, instructional, and idealogical. The *societal level* is far removed from the intended learners and involves a sociopolitical process of determining goals and, usually, the subjects to be studied in schools. The country, province, or state often goes on to spell out in curriculum guides the topics to be studied, the time to be spent on them, and the books and other materials to be used (Klein and Goodlad 1978). In Denmark in 1986, for example, schools had on hand more than 40 guides for all of the subjects to be taught (Florander and Skov 1986, 173). The actors in determining goals, contents, and organization of the curriculum for children and youths in the schools are politicians, spokespersons for special interest groups and the general public, a variety of different kinds of administrators, and various professional specialists (van Bruggen 1986, 133).

The *institutional curriculum* is that of a school or college. This curriculum is constrained by the finite time limitations of year, week, and day, and it commonly is organized according to subjects derived from the major domains of knowledge and knowing, with the topics and themes to be studied specified for each of several grade levels. This curriculum is derived in large part from the societal curriculum specified by the state or province and modified by the school board, after varying degrees and kinds of input from school personnel and lay citizens. It is to this school curriculum that most curriculum reform is directed (Schaefer 1971, 15). Also, it is around this curriculum that most controversy swirls: How much of it should be commonly required for all? To what degree should students' interests be considered? Should each subject be taught as a separate discipline, or should efforts be made to combine those that are closely related? These are essentially questions of curriculum organization.

The *instructional curriculum* is the one that teachers

plan and endeavor to deliver to students. This one, too, is derived from specifications of the state but more directly from what has been determined necessary or desirable for each school by school authorities. In elementary and secondary schools—much, much more than in colleges and universities—how teachers organize this instructional curriculum is restrained by an array of regulations and expectations coming down from more remote levels of decision making (McNeil 1986). The instructional level of curriculum planning and organization is also the frequent target of reform and criticism. Experts of all stripes from outside the school hesitate not at all in prescribing for teachers the educational objectives they should seek and how to organize the curriculum to attain them.

The societal, institutional, and instructional domains of curriculum planning and delivery are affected significantly by human circumstances: immediately available resources, power struggles, issues of authority and responsibility, teachers' skills, and more. Good ideas frequently are pushed aside by social, political, economic, and technical realities. There is a curriculum of ideas, however—the *idealogical domain*—in which the decisions of curricular goals, content, and organization are addressed in their pure state, so to speak. Literally thousands of "curricula of ideas" have been proposed and almost as many abandoned, frequently to be resurrected later in some form. These are most frequently directed to the institutional level, especially during eras of intense attention to educational reform. For example, during the 1960s, millions of federal and private philanthropic dollars were poured into efforts to bring together the best ideas of subject matter specialists and learning theorists in new curricular configurations for high school students (Bruner 1960; Goodlad 1964). Later in this chapter, we discuss these and other examples.

The societal, institutional, and instructional levels of curriculum planning and organization devote attention to a curriculum of intentions for individuals other than those designing it. But there is, of course, that most important of all curricula—the one internalized and made personal (Tyler and Goodlad 1979; Tyler and Klein 1973). This is the *experiential level* that provides the final test of curriculum organization—how the individual learner is affected (L. L. Tyler 1978).

It is our intent to deal with curriculum organization as it gains increasing proximity to teachers teaching and students learning. Consequently, we focus on that technical-professional arena where specialized knowledge and skills are practiced. Here we have the domains of action in which scholars and teachers try to devise curricula of good ideas arranged according to their beliefs about how people learn, teachers and administrators endeavor to rearrange what they view as essential or important into finite periods of time, and teachers plan and carry out an instructional curriculum (Goodlad, Klein, and Tye 1979, 43–76). This chapter addresses the more traditional questions of curriculum organization as they apply to the institutional, instructional, and idealogical domains of curriculum inquiry.

Commonplaces of Curriculum Organization

Fields of inquiry are characterized by certain elements commonly addressed by individuals professing to be scholars in or of them. For example, learning theorists differ in their views on transfer of training, but they include this topic as a commonplace of their field.

> By "topics" or "commonplaces" I mean those foci of attention within an area of interest which fulfill two conditions: (a) They demand the attention of serious investigators; (b) their scrutiny generates diverse investigations and consequent diversities of definitions, doctrines, and emphases. (Schwab 1964, 5–6)

The curriculum field of inquiry is made up of a number of such commonplaces (Goodlad 1985). How each is addressed ultimately determines the curriculum resulting from inquiry, be it at the societal, institutional, or instructional level of discourse and action or strictly ideational. Some curriculum theorists simply reject the concept of organizing curricula around a framework or scaffolding designed to hold the pieces together in an organized way. For example, a teacher might begin with a social problem such as drug abuse and proceed to take a group of students through a process of inquiry designed to come to some conclusions regarding the nature of the problem and how it might be constructively addressed. But some theorists would argue that this approach still involves commonplaces of curriculum organization: The canons of inquiry constitute organizing elements; the problem of drug abuse, itself of significance, is the organizing center. (Organizing elements and centers are defined below.) Our perspective is that curriculum decisions and actions inescapably involve curriculum commonplaces—by both omission and commission.

Schwab (1973) identified four major curricular commonplaces: learners, teachers, subject matter, and milieu. According to Schwab, all curriculum development, including organization, must deal in some way with these elements since they are common to all curriculum discourse. In other words, they are "places" where curriculum theorists must commonly stand and address each one from his or her conceptions of education and curriculum. There are subcategories of each of these, which in turn have commonplaces of their own. Moreoever, there is not full agreement on commonplaces among curriculum theorists. For Ralph Tyler (1949, 1), for example, curriculum commonplaces presumably are purposes, experiences, organization, and evaluation. It is to the commonplaces of curriculum organization that we now turn.

The organization of the curriculum of a school or class, for example, represents decisions of scope, continuity, sequence, and integration—all commonplaces of curriculum organization. *Scope* refers to breadth: A school curriculum might be confined to mathematics, the natural sciences, the social sciences, and the humanities. The natural sciences might be confined to biology, and a course to human biology. Decisions of scope are designed to determine the breadth of a curriculum at a given time—that is, it is viewed horizontally across, for example, the array of courses offered by a secondary school in a given year or those taken or to be taken by a given student. *Continuity* and *sequence*, in contrast, are commonplaces of vertical organization; the school's or a student's curriculum is viewed over time—perhaps over the entire length of elementary and secondary education.

Continuity in the organization of the curriculum seeks to assure students' revisitation of a theme or skill; *sequence*, to build on what preceded: Students add two-digit numbers, for example, and use what they learn in moving on to the addition of three-digit numbers. Teachers' guides to series of reading textbooks identify skills of reading and seek to show how these are built up through step-by-step activities. The 1958 *Yearbook of the Association for Supervision and Curriculum Development* (ASCD) is a model effort to demonstrate continuity in school programs from level to level of schooling, with provision for broadening at each level to ensure sequence.

Sequence, one of the most complex commonplaces, is not just the recurrence and repetition of a skill or concept but the deepening of it, so that each successive encounter builds on the preceding one (Leonard 1950). Philosophers, psychologists, and curriculum theorists have stressed curricular sequences tied to successive stages of human development (Piaget 1926, 1962 [1928]; Whitehead 1957), to a combination of materials and increasing complexity of subject matter (Sullivan 1967), and to successive steps of subject matter complexity tested against experimental studies of students' successful progression through them (Gagné 1977; Klausmeier 1976). Bruner (1960) gave credibility to the discredited concept of intuition in proposing a curricular sequence based on the marriage of intuition and "the structure of the discipline." The massive curricular reform projects of the 1960s drew heavily on Bruner's ideas. Smith, Stanley, and Shores (1950, 233) identified four sequential approaches to the exposition of content: from the simple to the complex, the successive identification of prerequisites, from the whole to the part, and the chronological. From studies of curriculum practice, Leonard (1953) extracted the following approaches to effecting curricular sequence: time or chronological order, logical order, difficulty, geographical expansion, and the unfolding of the child.

Armstrong (1989) has summarized four of the most frequently used approaches to sequence in curriculum organization:

1. The chronological approach, in which content elements are sequenced in terms of calendar time. The sequence may be from past to present or from present to past. This approach makes sense only when the subject matter to be treated has some logical connection to chronological time (e.g., history and English literature).
2. The thematic approach, in which content elements first are organized under any one of several major themes. Decisions about which themes are to be taught first, second, third, and so forth may be left entirely to the discretion of the instructor (e.g., elementary school language arts programs may feature such thematic topics as short stories, creative writing, plays, and poetry—none of the topics necessarily builds on any of the others).
3. The part-to-whole approach, in which topics or units are sequenced so that basic elements of content precede more complex elements (e.g., math and foreign language programs).
4. The whole-to-part approach, which reverses the sequencing order used in part-to-whole course planning. In this design, general information is typically introduced first, providing class members with a broad overview of what they are to learn. Only after they have a good grasp of this overview is more specific information introduced that allows them to study smaller parts of this "whole" (e.g., geography). (78–80)

Integration of the curriculum is intended to bring into close relationship such elements as concepts, skills, and values so that they are mutually reinforcing (Aceland 1967). The ultimate integration is in the learner, of course; the process is aided presumably by the way in which the curriculum components are organized. This organization is more readily done in elementary schools, where teachers are responsible for all or most of the subjects. At the secondary and tertiary levels, however, collaborations among teachers are commonly required for curriculum integration. For many teachers, the time and energy involved in the logistics outweigh the perceived advantages. Universities such as Chicago, Michigan, and Western Washington have developed whole undergraduate curricula designed for optimal integration by students—in separate colleges in the case of the last two.

Although there have been many attempts to develop curricula in accordance with principles of continuity, sequence, and integration that include considerations of students' developmental and learning sequences (Dressel 1958), these have been confined almost exclusively to relatively short, vertical time periods (e.g., a few grade levels) and a few subjects (such as the visual arts and the social studies). Interesting exceptions are found in the work of Hilda Taba, who joined with schoolteachers (circa the mid-1940s) in her project on intergroup education (Taba, Brady, and Robinson 1952) and later in another project in Yolo and Contra Costa Counties, California. Her more theoretical work (Taba 1962) was deeply influenced by these and other experiences and is revealed particularly in her definitions and treatment of commonplaces of curricular organization. There is a clear overlap between her conceptualization of curriculum organization and that of Ralph Tyler's (1949) *Basic Principles of Curriculum and Instruction*, presumably resulting in part from their colleagueship during the earlier Eight Year Study (discussed later).

A somewhat less ambitious but nonetheless thorough effort is represented by the Annehurst Curriculum Classification System (Frymier 1977). Again, there is close attention to the commonplaces of curriculum organization; again, the integration is of learners and subject matter. The contributions of both Taba and Frymier represent close collaboration between university-based and school-based educators.

This discussion on organization of the curriculum is resurrecting, to a considerable degree, commonplaces that have received little attention in recent scholarly work beyond the domains of the school subjects. That is, whereas curriculum thought and practice in a field such as mathematics give a great deal of systematic attention to the commonplaces of vertical organization in particular (Gagné 1967), such approaches to entire institutional curricula are much less common. Two essentially related commonplaces—organizing element and organizing center—receive even less attention, whether at the institutional or the instructional level. Both receive a good deal of attention, however—much of it intuitive—in practice. Curriculum theorists would be well advised to observe practitioners carefully.

Organizing elements might be compared to steel fibers in a concrete tower—not seen but necessary to the tower's strength. An organizing element is what the curriculum maker or teacher has in mind in selecting the next topic or unit of work: a concept such as energy, a skill such as legible handwriting, or a value such as respect for one another. The experiment chosen, the exercise required, or the interpersonal anecdote to be analyzed constitutes the *organizing center* to be used in seeking to understand energy, advance the skill of handwriting, or increase awareness of and sensitivity to others. An inanimate book on a shelf in the classroom comes to life when the teacher chooses and reads an anecdote sharply highlighting the sad consequences of people's inhumanity. Organizing centers have been described as "curriculum carriages for our students to ride in" (Goodlad 1988, 180)—the curricles of the curriculum. The organizing element is the path they follow, sometimes a deepening rut from which there is no escape.

Ralph Tyler (1949) gives us a rather clear sense of the organizing element and its function in the organization of the curriculum in a quotation from a school's social studies curriculum committee:

> The Committee on the Social Studies has developed a list of common elements of the social studies curriculum that can serve as the threads running from the nursery-primary through the middle school and the high school to provide the basis for continuity, for sequence, and for integration in the curriculum. The Committee identified three kinds of common elements: concepts, values, and skills. (87)

A conference held at the University of Chicago over four decades ago was virtually summative in its conceptual treatment of generic principles of curriculum organization and the commonplaces discussed above (Herrick and Tyler 1950). At least three papers addressed organizing elements and the matter of obtaining sequence in their curricular development. It was here that Herrick (1950, 46) directed attention to the fact that justification of the organizing centers selected to foster sequence and integration on the basis of their relationship to ends alone is not sufficient. His paper suggests the genesis of work that was to occupy his attention later—the determination of factors to be taken into account in designing effective organizing centers, whatever the subject matter. This is a topic very much neglected in the general curriculum literature.

Subsequently, Herrick (1954, 1962, 1965) worked with teachers in developing the qualities most likely to characterize good organizing centers, that is, centers that would be "friendly" to both teachers and learners. The characteristics that emerged reinforced the importance of learners' interests but went far beyond them, into considerations of subject matter, relationships among subject matters, practical considerations of the accessibility of materials and other resources, the likelihood of the activities leading to others, and so on.

The effort to identify commonplaces of curriculum organization and inquire into different ways of addressing them has not extended far beyond the K–12 system. Colleges and universities rarely get beyond the construction of individual courses (and undoubtedly some professors do pay attention to such matters as sequence and integration) and the order in which they are to be taken. Usually, criteria for the arrangements decided on are not specified or clear. A notable exception was the complete redesign of the nursing education curriculum at the University of Washington, a five-year project that paid attention to all of the commonplaces discussed above (Sand 1958). The so-called Tyler rationale of curriculum questions and how to go about answering them (R. W. Tyler 1949) was used later by the National League for Nursing (1977) in a relatively long-term, continuing effort to develop accreditation criteria.

Viewed over several decades, the efforts of curriculum theorists, developers, and practitioners to organize curricula for effective student learning have been quite prodigious, resulting in an extraordinary array of patterns and accompanying analyses and categorizations. Much of this work has remained in the conceptual stage; some of it has been incorporated into textbooks and other learning materials, state and district curriculum guides, and courses of study, losing much in the translation process.

Before turning to this area, it is necessary to look at what might be called the roots or sources of the ideas that came to dominate in a given pattern of organization, setting it apart from another just enough to give it a different name or so much that it must be recognized as of another genre. Education is a normative enterprise, driven by values. Values are deeply embedded in patterns of curriculum organization. Ways of organizing survive because they consistently reflect values that come to dominate in our society's struggle over the curriculum. These ways are replaced—often only temporarily—by alternatives representing values that compete successfully with those prevailing previously (Kliebard 1986). We turn now to some ways of thinking, of viewing the world, that lie behind ways of organizing curricula.

INTELLECTUAL SOURCES OF CURRICULUM ORGANIZATION

We return to Schwab's (1973) major curricular commonplaces: learners, teachers, subject matter, and milieu. These are the components that come together to determine the nature of the learning—the experiential curriculum. They are also the components that provoke profound differences in regard to which pattern large numbers of people would prefer to be the dominant orientation. We will see that child-centered and subject-centered advocates, for example, have provided the major pull-and-tug debate over the organization of the curriculum. Consequently, it appears that Schwab's commonplaces reflect curriculum discourse—as they should if they are to meet Schwab's criteria of commonplaces cited earlier.

But Schwab's criteria differ from Ralph Tyler's (1949), if we assume that Tyler's selection of four critical topics—purposes, experiences, organization, and evaluation—infer that these, for him, are major curricular commonplaces. It is important to note that Tyler draws on the Schwab commonplaces (without identifying them as such) in seeking to answer his own questions regarding purposes, experiences, organization, and evaluation.

This is not the place to argue the relative significance or relevance of the two formulations, an exercise more appropriately left to their creators. There is a difference between the two, however, that helps to frame what follows. For Tyler, data are of paramount importance: Knowledge about learners, subject matter, and society are the sources consulted in determining purposes. The curriculum makers seek agreement on normative matters (their philosophy) to determine consistencies and inconsistencies among a preliminary list of objectives after these have been determined by examining the three sources. Their philosophy serves as a screen through which the list is sifted (R. W. Tyler 1949, 33). Once determined, these objectives guide the other curricular decisions, including organization. That is, objectives guide essentially analytical and technical operations; there is no further reference to philosophical considerations. Means are justified by their relevance to ends.

Schwab's (1973) formulation leaves open the flow of norms and philosophical orientations into all four of his commonplaces. Were he to address the selection and organization of learning activities in Tyler's rationale, for example, presumably he would raise questions about the moral meanings embedded in choices and not merely check relevance to stated purposes. In other words, the ends do not fully justify the means; the virtue of means must be determined quite apart from their efficacy in the attainment of objectives.

Ralph Tyler's (1949) four-step formulation of curriculum development is a reasonable reflection of the social, political, and technical processes that characterize the societal, institutional, and instructional levels of decision making. Schwab's (1973) four commonplaces identify the essential ingredients, almost invariably addressed from varying perspectives as these processes proceed—processes so charged with conflicting values that agreement is difficult to achieve and then is achieved only temporarily. The Tyler rationale becomes most useful after consensus has been reached and its implementation lies ahead.

We turn now to some of the differing conceptions that make the achievement of consensus in curriculum matters difficult to achieve and maintain (see Chapter 1 in this *Handbook*).

Sources Influencing Curriculum Thought

Schubert (1982, 421–422) identifies three general modes of thought having profound implications for curriculum organization that had emerged by the turn of the century: the intellectual traditionalist, the social behaviorist, and the experientialist. Each embodied certain assumptions about knowledge and their implications for the curriculum. Each persists today, although the labels may differ.

Intellectual traditionalism, the dominant mode of thought before 1900, was sometimes referred to as the "mental disciplines approach." This mode likened the mind to muscles that improved with the exercise of such faculties as reason or imagination, achieved through the study of subjects derived from the classical trivium (grammar, rhetoric, and dialectic) and quadrivium (arithmetic, geometry, astronomy, and music). It encouraged the development of a subject-oriented curriculum.

Although strong intellectual currents have buffeted the so-called separate subject pattern of organization, it has remained the rocklike structure at the center of the stream. All efforts to crack or crush it have been little more than eddies, accompanied by the cries of many birds, swirling around its edges. It is fair to say that the proposed alternatives, to the degree that they have survived at all, have developed apart—in a few private schools, occasionally a university-connected laboratory school, and today most of all in magnet or alternative schools. In higher education, experimental colleges with differing patterns of curriculum organization have operated side by side with the "regular" college, the latter often hardening itself against intrusions from its radical neighbor. Curricula organized around subjects and forwarded through topics remain alive and well today: In 1987, a book advocating a long list of topics for all people became a nonfiction best seller in the United States (Hirsch 1987).

Social behaviorism was a rather natural accompaniment of growth in business, industry, and science during the first quarter of the century. It combined precise explanation, technological efficiency, and social utility. Bobbitt (1924) pioneered the "activity analysis" through which the curriculum maker defined precise objectives, which virtually determined the selection and organization of everything in the curriculum. These objectives were reduced increasingly to smaller and smaller ones, to the point where each became the organizing center for learning—a process that was essentially the precursor of teaching machines and programmed instruction (Pressey 1960). Charters (1923) saw the whole as a nearly scientific process of first gathering data regarding human activities—such as what nurses and secretaries do—translating these into specific objectives, and organizing learning activities geared to mastering these operations. Both Bobbitt and Charters stayed largely away from normative questions about the goodness or rightness of these specifics. They assumed that the principles of engineering would remain the same regardless of ideology. Using these processes, the curriculum of a totalitarian regime and of a democratic one could be engineered with equal efficiency.

Ralph Tyler's later attention to stating desired behaviors in objectives earned for him the title "father of educational objectives"—a misnomer, given the earlier work of Bobbitt and Charters. Tyler was directly influenced by the latter, but he eschewed the elaborate process of reductionism, recommending that a dozen or so broad statements should suffice, each containing both a general behavior and the content or area of life in which that behavior was to be developed or to operate (R. W. Tyler 1949, 46–47). He saw the objective as a general guide to curriculum organization but a very precise guide to curriculum evaluation—a point he makes clear in discussing the procedures for developing the tests initially used in the National Assessment of Educational Progress (R. W. Tyler 1973, 109–110). It was to aid the process of evaluation that elaborate taxonomies of educational objectives were constructed (Bloom 1956; Krathwohl 1964).

It fell to Mager (1962) and Popham (Popham, Eisner, Sullivan, and Tyler 1969) to resuscitate the behavioral objective to the position of power in the organization of the curriculum given to it by Bobbitt and Charters. For both, it became the organizing element and a major component of the organizing center. In other words, it became the focal point and, therefore, both the ends and the means of the entire curriculum domain (Baker and Popham 1973; Popham and Baker 1970).

It is worth noting that this spur of behaviorism, which found rich soil in curriculum theory and development, departs rather markedly from the work of the noted behaviorist B. F. Skinner (1971), for example. Indeed, relatively late in his career, Skinner appeared to go out of his way to disassociate himself from the limitations of behavioral objectives, which appeared to him to fall short of providing the array of contingencies necessary to human conditioning.

Experientialism emphasized the notion of "apperceptive mass"—the accumulated results of a repertoire of experiences. Schubert (1982) concludes that this orientation marked the beginning of a science of teaching method based on interest. The task of curriculum development was to arrange knowledge to which students could relate systematically, building up their apperceptions and, therefore, the array of interests to which the teacher might respond. We see here the roots of a problems-oriented approach to curriculum organization that begins with problems already experienced by students (Dewey 1902). The scientific aspect of curriculum development becomes that of synthesizing different kinds of knowledge of learners, subject matter, and milieu so that a sequence of problem-solving experiences results.

There have been periods during the 20th century when the orientation to students' interests appeared to be the dominant approach to curriculum organization for and in the schools. Except in the primary grades and a few private and laboratory schools around the country (including the Dewey School at the University of Chicago and the Francis W. Parker school), the subject-oriented curriculum prevailed, however. Nonetheless, there has been throughout much of the century a debate between child-centered advocates and subject-centered advocates sufficient to suggest that the two positions are about equally represented in curricular and instructional theory, if not practice.

Cremin's (1990) depiction of the intellectual differences between John Dewey and Robert Hutchins nicely illustrates the fundamental differences between the traditionalist position and the experimentalist position (as it matured in the 20th century) and the curricular orientations that stemmed from them:

> For Dewey, education was a process of growth that had no end beyond itself, a process in which individuals were constantly extending their knowledge, informing their judgments, refining their sensibilities, and illuminating their moral choices. For Hutchins, education was nothing more or less than the cultivation of the intellect, the training of the mind, and there was a group of what he called "permanent studies" that had long been of proven value in achieving that end, namely, the arts of reading, writing, thinking, and speaking, together with mathematics, which he saw as "the best exemplar of the processes of human reason." (7–8)

Social reconstructionism must be added to Schubert's three modes of thought that have influenced curriculum organization. The experientialist position can be pushed to include this fourth orientation but not without doing considerable violence to the strong role of students' lives and interests in the position of many experientialists. Indeed, it was a perception of "a one-sided absorption in the individual pupil" that pushed some critics, already looking for alternatives to subject-centered perspectives, toward a curriculum oriented to the requirements of education in a democratic society (Bode 1938, 54).

Educational and curriculum theorists who found an intellectual home in curricula devoted to education for citizenship in a democratic society varied widely in their attitudes toward reconstruction. Positions ranged from advocating curricula to prepare children and youths to cope with American civilization (Rugg 1926) to advocacy of school programs addressed to reconstructing the social order (Counts 1932). There is little in Schwab's (1973) concept of curriculum commonplaces to suggest that "milieu" might be extended from the immediate circumstances of the learning environment to considerations of the social order as a whole, but neither does his formulation preclude them.

Critical inquiry (Habermas 1971, 1973, 1975) is not precluded in any of these intellectual orientations, either. Indeed, it is central in the thinking of reconstructionists, in particular. Consequently, as we shall see, some proposals for curriculum organization focus on a process that, like Dewey's process of inquiry, is imbued with moral choice (Giroux, Penna, and Pinar 1981). Moral issues in the social context are more likely to be the organizing centers of the curriculum than topics extracted from subject disciplines or students' interests.

Reflections in Curriculum Modes of Organization

Only rarely have real curricula in real schools reflected nearly sole dependence on one of these intellectual roots or any other. Most schools and colleges retain through successive eras of reform a curriculum organized around the subject disciplines, some rhetorically committed to breaking down the subject divisions in favor of patterns organized with more attention to human development or the social context, for example. Nonetheless, conceptual alternatives always attract a following, even when there is no great pressure resulting from public anxiety over the performance of our schools.

There follows a loose classification of patterns of curriculum organization, each of which retains a primary orientation to subject disciplines, students' interests and life experiences, problems of living posed by the environmental milieu, and reconceptualization or revision of the social order. This is a very arbitrary classification scheme, fuzzy around the edges. Indeed, some patterns classified at the margins of one category might well be classified at the margins of another that has different intellectual roots. Neither the classification scheme nor the patterns of curriculum organization encompassed by it is intended to be exhaustive.

PATTERNS OF CURRICULUM ORGANIZATION

Tanner and Tanner (1975, 10–19) have cut through a rather vast body of curriculum writing to remind us that only a very few conceptions of curriculum have prevailed to determine the various patterns of organization that have enjoyed recognition over the past 50 years or so. Their analysis provides a kind of bridge from the educational modes of thought presented by Schubert (1982) to the curricular modes of thought represented in the many patterns of organizing the curriculum that have enjoyed long or brief periods of attention.

Major Themes of Curriculum Organization

Curriculum as the cumulative tradition of organized knowledge continues to prevail, as it did during the early years of the century. The *perennialist* position holds that the curriculum should consist principally of the "permanent studies"—the rules of grammar, reading, rhetoric, logic, and mathematics and the greatest books of the Western world (Hutchins 1936). The *essentialist* position holds that the curriculum must consist essentially of disciplined study in the major domains of human conversation: command of the mother tongue and the systematic study of grammar, literature, and writing; mathematics; sciences; history; and foreign languages (Bestor 1956, 48–49). The *discipline* doctrine holds to the position that the mind is best disciplined in a school curriculum organized around the subject disciplines. The curriculum reform movement of the 1960s made much use of the term "the structures of the disciplines," but it made relatively little progress in determining precisely what these are and in organizing learning activities around them (Schwab 1962, 197).

The second persisting conception, according to Tanner and Tanner (1980, 10), is oriented to a *curriculum organized around modes of thought*. "The curriculum is considered to be the increasingly wide range of possible modes of thinking about men's experiences—not the conclusions, but the models from which conclusions derive, and in context of which these conclusions, these so-called truths, are grounded and validated" (Belth 1965, 262). Again, this conception emerges over and over, but there has been relatively little transfer from concept to practice. Because the demands on scholarship are high, it is not surprising that such approaches are sometimes found in experimental colleges inside of the traditional schools and colleges of the arts and sciences.

The concept of *curriculum as experience* never emerges as dominant in practice but always seems to have its advocates (Dewey 1938). It has sponsored controversy between the child-centered and the subject-centered rationales. The child-centered orientation has significantly contributed to a definition of curriculum as "all the experiences a learner has under the guidance of the school" (Foshay 1969, 275). This makes sense to a good many educators. But when practice turns to the organization of the curriculum, what comes out usually has little relationship to this definition but a great deal to the tradition of organized knowledge in a subject curriculum.

The field of curriculum has been described as moribund (Huebner 1982; Schwab 1970). This description is in some ways puzzling, in view of the degree to which differing conceptual orientations have clashed. Just as there has been a political struggle for the curriculum, there has been an idealogical one (Kliebard 1986). There appears to have been over the years considerable intellectual debate, with stagnation occurring at the points of implemention of a given conception. Eisner and Vallance (1974) have provided an interesting analysis of differing curricular orientations and their implications for tasks such as organization. But finding these implications in practice is more often than not a disappointing pursuit.

The development of cognitive processes is primarily concerned with the refinement of intellectual operations. It refers only rarely to curriculum content, focusing instead on the "how" rather than the "what" of education. The central task of the curriculum is to sharpen the intellectual processes and to develop a set of cognitive skills that can be applied to learning virtually anything. This orientation to curriculum focuses on the child and refers to the learning process per se rather than to the broader social context in which it occurs. The research and thinking of Piaget (1962 [1928]), in particular, had a tremendous impact on the organization of curricula worldwide, especially in elementary school science. Although the work of Piaget was slow to have an impact in the United States, it was beginning to influence the curriculum projects of the 1960s before these began to fade into obscurity (Goodlad 1964; Goodlad, von Stoephasius, and Klein 1966). The cognitive processes approach was a particularly salient orientation in curriculum thinking in the mid-1970s, when psychologists developed greater confidence in their ability to identify the mechanisms through which thinking proceeds and to translate them into curricular operations (Bruner 1960; Gagné 1967).

Curriculum as technology, like the cognitive processes approach, also focuses on process. It is concerned with the technology by which knowledge is communicated and learning is facilitated. Again, it is concerned with the "how" rather than the "what" of education. The function of curriculum is to find efficient means to a set of predefined and, usually, rather simple ends. The focus is on the practical problem of efficiently packaging and presenting the material to the learner but not on the individuality of the learner or the content. The technologists claim to be developing a value-free system.

This approach speaks the language of production; curriculum technologists see curriculum as an input to supply and demand systems. The impact on curriculum materials and their use as the basis for organizing the curriculum has been substantial. Tyler, Klein, and Michael (1971) and Tyler, Klein, and associates (1976) made an evaluative effort to develop criteria that would require a more comprehensive approach to the development of curriculum materials.

The self-actualizing curriculum is directed toward clarifying personal purpose and toward personal integration. The function of the curriculum is to provide personally satisfying experiences for each individual learner, leading to increased self-understanding (Association for Supervision and Curriculum Development 1962). It is child-centered, viewing education as an enabling process that provides the means to personal development and liberation (Greene 1969, 1971; Maslow 1968).

These conceptions of education and curriculum have found their way at various times and in various forms into rather specific patterns of curriculum organization that make claims of uniqueness. Some of them have barely taken form in curricular practice; some began and then faded; some faded and then came back, clothed in new rhetoric. We have endeavored to identify the various patterns with the descriptive words and phrases most commonly attached to them.

Organization Primarily Around Subject Disciplines

The *single-subject* pattern of organization emphasizes a presumed logical organization of each subject, with no deliberate attempt to interrelate several (Hunkins 1980). Each subject is treated as a discrete component of the curriculum. In the 1920s, attempts to make the subjects progress through the grades in orderly, sequential fashion were a natural extension of the growing interest in curriculum making as a kind of science. The work of Thorndike (1910, 1913) during the previous decade was becoming powerfully compelling in developing what might be referred to as "the new scientifically designed textbooks." Although Dewey is more often cited than Thorndike in discussions of influences on American schooling, it is probably fair to say that Thorndike's work much more determined the actual educational experiences of children and youths by virtue of its influence on textbooks. Later, textbooks in the separate subjects for teachers as well as for students became big business. Professors of education wrote them with considerable enthusiasm and often enjoyed substantial financial return. Books on the mathematics curriculum, the language arts curriculum, the social studies curriculum, and the science curriculum, for example, endeavored to join subject matter and suggestions for how to teach it.

Beginning in the 1950s (with roots in the 1940s for mathematics), curriculum developers in an array of subjects sought to select organizing centers around their elements and to combine their so-called structures with conceptions of how students might best understand and use them. What was meant by "structure of the discipline" was not always clear to those involved, let alone to the teachers who were to use the materials produced. Nonetheless, the curriculum reform movement that these ideas propelled represented a refreshing recognition of the fact that attention to subject matter alone is an insufficient basis for organizing an effective curriculum. Translating the interesting experimental patterns of curriculum organization into materials to be used by teachers and students proved to be a challenge that resulted in considerable loss of the fundamental concepts, some of them backed by research (Goodlad, von Stoephasius, and Klein 1966; Schaffarzick and Hampson 1975).

This approach faded away in the 1970s. Some critics argued that the programs were too heavily oriented toward the interests of the college-bound learner. Others found it difficult to find consensus among professionals in some fields about the nature of the structure of their discipline. Still others felt that the approach placed too much emphasis on academic disciplines and that other topics and subjects deserved more attention in school programs.

Fraser (1962) reviewed the special projects and studies dealing with the academic subjects in the school curriculum in the late 1950s and early 1960s. Her review covered more than 40 projects in science, mathematics, English, foreign languages, and social studies. Her recommendations from studying the projects included the need to maintain balance and continuity in the student's total school experience and to provide effective education for all children and youths. Educational reform, she concluded, ultimately rides on the back of the separate-subjects pattern of curriculum organization—a pattern to which teachers resonate most easily.

Some years later, Welch (1979) looked back on the precollege science curriculum development projects funded by the National Science Foundation—all discipline-oriented approaches to curriculum organization. His conclusion was that in spite of the expenditures of millions of dollars and the involvement of some of the most brilliant scientific minds, the science classroom in the late 1970s was little different from that of 20 years before. Although there may be new books on the shelves and clever gadgets in the storage cabinets, the day-to-day operations of classes are largely unchanged—curriculum and instruction are organized and conducted around the separate school subjects, a pattern of organization that remains little changed over the years.

Correlated-subject designs address the integration or relationship of learning experiences in two or more areas. These designs attempt to build on relationships between and among subject areas but continue to emphasize the identities of the individual subjects. For example, an English teacher and a social studies teacher might decide to develop part of the English program and part of the social studies program in a correlated manner. The intent is to broaden learners' understanding by providing a concurrent treatment of a common topic from the perspectives of two subjects (Armstrong 1989).

Klein (1985) describes this pattern as the multidisciplinary or correlated variation of the subject-oriented curriculum. It occurs when several subject areas are interrelated for study, but the separate subject's identity is protected to a considerable degree (Hunkins 1980). Through this approach, it is hoped that students will experience a greater degree of unity in knowledge derived from the content of the subject fields.

The *fused curriculum* is similar to correlated designs in that it attempts to build on relationships between and among two or more separate subjects. However, whereas correlation designs preserve the identities of the individual subjects, in fusion design these identities tend to disappear. Related content from several subjects is joined under a new label. For example, a course in Western civilization might well fuse such subjects as history, geography, music, and literature. Elementary school mathematics and science projects sometimes have represented an effort to fuse concepts from both subjects (Tanner and Tanner 1980, 472). Fusion designs are not common. A major barrier to their development has been the difficulty of achieving agreement on theoretical rationales to justify the blending of contents from disciplines commonly viewed as independent of each other.

The *broad-field* patterns of organization seek to create a unity that cuts across an entire domain of knowledge. The intent is somewhat the same as in fusion designs: to create a new unity from constituent subjects that lose their individual identities during the process of fusing them in the selected organizing center. However, the scope of broad-fields design is grander: All the domains of knowledge and knowing—not merely related subjects—are synthesized in class projects such as "westward migration in America during the 19th century." As Tanner and Tanner (1980) point out, there is not a broad-fields program when a department of social studies continues to offer separate courses in history, economics, and geography. To be a broad-fields program, these subject labels must disappear and content from many different sources must be integrated. It is intended that this design will assist the student in achieving a high degree of integration of the separate subjects so that the content is related to life. A commonly recognized limitation of this approach, however, according to critics, is the danger of a superficial encounter with content (Hunkins 1980).

We thus see a kind of progression from each well-established subject (such as history and geography) organized separately to two or more subjects deliberately related (as when the history and geography of a country are taught side by side or together) to the fusion of both and other subjects (such as composition and literature) so that the identity of each subject disappears. The organizing center used to involve students almost invariably grows larger and occupies increasingly longer periods of time in the school year. The increasing complexity of organizing the curriculum becomes intimidating. Patterns that go beyond single subjects require exceedingly competent teachers and considerable flexibility in the organization of the school as a whole to accommodate the demands created. Not surprisingly, there have been over the years relatively few ventures into correlated, fused, and broad-fields patterns of curriculum organization. Yet there seem always to be teachers who are intrigued by such arrangements and who are willing to spend the additional hours of planning with others that are invariably involved.

Patterns of Organization Oriented to Students' Interests and Development

There have been proposed at various times curricula organized around the present interests of students. Efforts to implement such proposals fall into three traps almost immediately. First, schools are agencies charged by society with quite specific educating functions. Any group of curriculum planners that abandons the specifications of the societal level of curriculum making crosses the bounds of convention, often to the point of being out of compliance with state requirements and in danger of loss of funds or accreditation. Second, the depth of students' interests is not easily identified; a student asked to state interests today may deny them tomorrow and substitute new ones. Third, it is unreasonable to expect students to express interest in something they know nothing about, and so the very learning most needed to broaden their perspectives goes by the board because they expressed no interest in it.

Most teachers conscientiously try to deliver the curriculum already specified. They depart from it at their risk.

Given the preceding traps and teachers' propensities, we should not be surprised to learn that curricula organized around students' interests are nonevents. This conclusion does not negate another conclusion: Many teachers do attempt to motivate learning by endeavoring to connect what they want to teach to students' expressed interests. However, such efforts are pedagogical devices designed to attract students to a prearranged (and usually subject-oriented) curriculum. They fall short of providing alternative patterns of organization.

It is fair to say that curriculum designs organized around students' interests represent a contradiction. Once designed, curricula are rarely redesigned as part of an ongoing interaction between teachers and students. Rather, students' interests, at best, become a component of an organizing center containing other components, including subject matter.

The activity curriculum represents one such pattern and the project method an approach to it. Kilpatrick (1918) identified the "purposeful act" as the building block for the curriculum and "child purposing" as the key to learning. The curriculum took the form of projects rather than formal school subjects; the school program resembled a series of workshops. Arithmetic, reading, history, science, and other subjects were brought in as needed to flesh out a given project. The idea behind this approach was that children would learn to think if they worked on problems of genuine interest to them.

Kilpatrick (1918) wanted to develop a pedagogical theory that would combine educational psychology and philosophy—Dewey's method of intelligence. For him, a project was "a wholehearted purposeful activity proceeding in a social environment" (320). The project method was proposed as a complete theory for curriculum development as well as a method. A series of projects was to constitute the curriculum—an arrangement almost directly opposite to a curriculum organized around behavioral objectives, for example.

Less ephemeral than patterns springing from students' interests have been those based on analyses of their general developmental sequences. Organization around the developmental tasks commonly confronted in growing up is somewhat more student-oriented than organization around the situations that one's culture presents, but both give priority attention to learners. The former is classified in the curriculum literature as organization around *developmental tasks*; the latter, as organization around *persistent life situations*.

Daniel Prescott (1938) had been deeply affected by his experiences in World War II, experiences that sensitized him to the need for educational programs to relate in constructive, supportive ways to the tasks young people face simply in growing up. Drawing on his prewar work, he devised an in-service, carefully sequenced educational program for teachers. During the first year, a teacher studied the progression of one child through the school year, carefully documenting classroom events (with that child as the unit of selection). During the second year, the teacher focused on that child's interactions and relationships with peers. The third year was devoted to observation of a small group of children. Teachers became sensitized in their analyses of these records in seminars with other teachers who were maintaining parallel accounts (all under the direction of a child-study leader trained by Prescott and his associates). By the late 1940s and early 1950s, thousands of teachers in all sectors of the United States were enrolled in the Prescott child-study program.

Educational research was not at the time a high priority of most schools of education, and there was little effort to document and evaluate the program. But it did contribute to an initiative designed not only to define the theoretical roots of an approach to curriculum organization based on the developmental tasks of children and youths but also to catalog the most frequently encountered developmental tasks. Tryon and others (1950), in the *1950 Yearbook* of the Association for Supervision and Curriculum Development, presented the results of an impressive analytical and documentary effort. There was in this work a close identification with Prescott's (1938) earlier explorations of the mental health and stress of children and youths in schools.

The yearbook represented a significant curricular breakthrough in that it provided a relatively orderly approach to curriculum development and implementation closely allied with sequences of human development—a pattern that ensures considerable security and direction for teachers. At any rate, large numbers of teachers resonated with the Prescott version. Nonetheless, what was once a near-national movement quickly faded into obscurity, to be remembered almost entirely and exclusively by those teachers, principals, and study-group leaders who participated in it.

Almost simultaneously, large numbers of teachers were influenced by the persistent life situations approach being developed by Florence Stratemeyer and her colleagues at Teachers College, Columbia University (Stratemeyer, Forkner, and McKim 1947). There were in this work echoes of earlier curriculum patterns based on life needs (Bonser 1932), especially on series of projects or student-oriented activities.

A tremendous amount of analysis went into the identification of these persistent life situations. A revised version of the 1947 volume that introduced and amply illustrated the concept provided page after page of practical illustrations of life situations emerging from individuals seeking to satisfy their physiological, emotional, and social needs; make moral choices; develop aesthetic expression and appreciation; establish person-to-person relationships, membership in groups, and intergroup relations; deal with natural phenomena; use technological resources; and so on (Stratemeyer, Forkner, McKim, and Passow 1957).

Although there may appear to be some kinship between the persistent life situations approach to curriculum organization and various patterns organized around goals and objectives, the connection ends quickly. Stratemeyer and her associates attempted no reductionism in regard to human drives. Rather, after defining them, they moved immediately to curricular situations derived from the life situations generally encountered in growing up. The kinship is much closer to the work of Tryon and her associates (1950) in attempting to define developmental tasks as the organizational foci.

Organization Around Major Social Issues

Whereas curricula organized around both developmental tasks and persistent life situations took their cue from analyses of human encounters in growing up—with individuals and groups as the units of selection—somewhat parallel kinds of patterns grew out of analyses of society's problems. Organizing the curriculum to prepare students to adjust to or improve the larger social context becomes the orientation. Content is derived from conditions and circumstances in a society, societies, or the world. Students study the characteristics of societies—particularly their own—the function of institutions, the major activities of social life, the persistent problems of students and humankind, and so on (Smith, Stanley, and Shores 1950).

Some advocates proposed a critical orientation and the need to develop a consciousness of dangers to the tenets of a democratic society, to the environment, to peace, and to world order (Counts 1934; Rugg 1931). The concepts underlying curricula organized around major social issues spawned proposals for reorganizing the high school and especially its social studies curriculum. Recognition of the need to orient local and national circumstances to the nature and common problems of humankind has emerged with increasing intensity in recent years (Becker 1979; Goodlad 1986; Goodlad, Klein, Novotney, Tye, and associates 1974).

The *reconceptualist* or *revisionist* movement in curriculum development does not fit nicely into the "social issues" pattern. Nonetheless, its attention to social problems such as inequality and to developing the power of critical inquiry in students establishes a kinship with earlier curriculum reformers in this mode. In the 1970s, in particular, a group of theorists played a significant role in reconceptualizing the major issues, concerns, and modes of inquiry to provide new foci for curriculum thought and practice (e.g., Apple 1979; Greene 1973; Huebner 1975; Macdonald 1975; Pinar 1975). Drawing selectively on such European intellectual traditions as existentialism, phenomenology, psychoanalysis, and neo-Marxism (Habermas 1971, 1973, 1975), these theorists attempted to counter the relatively apolitical, technological, and instrumental orientation they perceived to have characterized the curriculum field for at least 50 years. They were particularly critical of the Ralph Tyler (1949) rationale and of the mechanistic justification of means by their efficiency in attaining ends characterizing curriculum patterns organized around behavioral objectives.

In general, the reconceptualists represent a mode of theorizing whose supporters reject the positivistic and conservative nature of existing curriculum theory and practice. At its core is an attempt, which takes many forms, to make the human subject a primary focus of concern and to develop modes of criticism and social practices directed toward dismantling what these theorists refer to as forms of false consciousness and idealogically frozen social relations (Giroux, Penna, and Pinar 1981). Giroux (1981) attempted to sum up the views of these conceptualists as follows:

> The new sociology of curriculum group strongly argues that schools are part of a wider societal process and that they must be judged within a specific socioeconomic framework. In addition, the curriculum itself is viewed as a selection from the larger culture. From this perspective, the new critics argue for a thorough reexamination of the relationship between curriculum, school, and society. This reexamination focuses on two broad interrelationships. On the one hand, the focus is on the relationships between schools and the dominant society . . . on the other hand, the focus is on how the very texture of day-to-day classroom relationships generates different meanings, restraints, cultural values, and social relationships. Underlying both of these concerns is a deep-seated interest in the relationship between meaning and social control. (103)

For a decade beginning in the 1970s and extending into the 1980s, the views of the reconceptualists appeared to be the dominant theoretical position, virtually taking over the curriculum field and replacing the highly behaviorist-driven period that preceded. There was very little attention to the more traditional and conventional commonplaces of curriculum development and organization. Indeed, the reconceptualists eschewed these commonplaces in discourse dealing with the whole of education rather than with what large numbers of curriculum theorists had conventionally regarded as the domains of curriculum as a field of study; the reconceptualists were succeeding in their stated intent. The vigor appeared to go out of the movement during the 1980s, but the fundamental concepts are too powerful and have too long a history simply to fade away.

Hybrid Organizational Patterns

In practice, virtually all patterns of organizing curricula are hybrid, especially in the rhetoric of documents developed at the societal and institutional levels of planning. Patterns clearly oriented toward subjects stress the importance also of students' interests and motivation. Patterns organized around students' interests almost always move to considerations of relevant subject matter and how to join the two. One of the major contributions of the Ralph Tyler (1949) rationale is the degree to which it seeks a balance of attention among learners, subject matter, and society, all of which are considered legitimate sources of curriculum decisions.

The *core curriculum*, as commonly viewed today, fits solidly into the subject-oriented organizational patterns: a specification of those fields deemed essential for all students (usually geared to college admission requirements), most often mathematics, science, English, and social studies. Much contemporary debate over the secondary school curriculum focuses on the question of how much of this core should be required of all students (Adler 1982; Powell, Farrar, and Cohen 1985; Sizer 1984). In spite of specification of subjects in this version of the core curriculum, frequent stress on the importance of pedagogy in seeking to engage students supports once again the hybrid character of most patterns of curriculum organization. Nonetheless, the mode of educational thought brought initially to the process of curriculum organization slants the outcomes almost invariably toward emphasis on the subject, the learner, or society.

Whereas today's conception of a common core puts the subject first, the core curriculum of the 1940s and 1950s attempted to combine almost equally students' needs and society's problems (Alberty 1947; Harap 1952); students were to consult subject matter only after an organizing center directed to students and society had been selected—usually through a process in which students played a major role (Bossing 1949). The interplay between the concept of learners having common needs and that of recurrent social issues that should be addressed in the curriculum becomes apparent in the following series of quotes spread over a period of nearly 20 years:

> The emphasis upon the development of a unified program of studies . . . has resulted in the organizing of a common core of experiences drawing content from all the major areas of human living, a curriculum which disregards subject matter lines and which is generally required of all pupils a substantial part of each day. (Brown 1938, 210)
>
> The core program then is made up of those educational experiences which are thought to be important for each citizen in our democracy. Students and teachers do not consider subject matter to be important in itself. It becomes meaningful only as it helps the group to solve the problems which have been selected for study. (MacConnell 1940, 25)
>
> A core represents the sum total of personal youth problems and the problems of social significance encountered by youth. It exists without relation to subject lines and is organized around problems. (Smith 1945, 164)
>
> The term core has come to be applied in modern education to those types of experiences thought necessary for all learners in order to develop certain behavior competencies considered essential for effective living in our democratic society. (Bossing 1949, 394)
>
> A true core curriculum attacks the problems common to all youth. It is a functional approach to harmonizing the concerns of youth, on the one hand, with the demands of society, on the other, without unduly emphasizing one or neglecting the other. (Burnett 1951, 97)
>
> The core curriculum may be regarded as those learning experiences which are fundamental for all learners because they are drawn from their common individual and social needs as competent citizens of a democratic community. (Kessler 1956, 43)

All of these comments are a far cry from the core curriculum frequently proposed for high school students after publication of *A Nation at Risk* (National Commission on Excellence in Education 1983): a core of courses in the fields of the natural sciences, the social studies, mathematics, and English required for admission for college.

Perhaps the most hybrid patterns of all are those appearing to grow out of the experientialist mode of thought. The implementation of Dewey's (1897) pedagogical creed in the laboratory school of the University of Chicago fits this mode, as does Summerhill (Neill 1960). In more recent times, the high school in Rabun Gap, Georgia (commonly connected with the Foxfire Experience), comes to mind (Wigginton 1985). The critical assumption is that learning is part of living; the experiences one has in life should be brought into the school curriculum, where they become organizing centers for exploring these experiences and coming to understand them and one's life better (Dewey 1902).

Progressive educators have always wanted to design school curricula around the life experiences of their students. This design has seldom proved to be easy; consequently, the few reasonably successful efforts have attained considerable attention. Usually, however, the concepts are threatening to those who believe that curricula organized around anything other than the subject disciplines are "soft" and, in the long run, dangerous for students and society.

COMMENTARY ON RESEARCH

As stated at the outset, almost all the literature on curriculum organization is conceptual or prescriptive and rarely experimental. In this review, we have relied rather heavily on secondary materials that analyze the various approaches because the body of descriptive writing is so vast.

Needless to say, empirical studies have used almost exclusively the model that compares the effectiveness of differing curriculum designs in producing various student outcomes (Cronbach 1957, 1975). *Dissertation Abstract International* identifies a number of such studies conducted over the past two decades in particular. This paradigm enables doctoral students to conduct relatively tight studies within the time constraints of earning their degrees. More often than not, the differences in outcomes are relatively insignificant. Even when statistically significant differences are obtained, the results are not socially significant—that is, the gains do not compensate for the difficulties inherent in launching experimental programs or may not be significant enough to readdress major learning problems. As the problems addressed become more complex and of more social significance, the problems of controlling an increasing number of variables become more complex, place increasing demands on researchers, and almost invariably require substantial funds for research. The common limitation in this research is the necessity of using some kind of standard measure of achievement to determine the effectiveness of a given program. Other outcomes such as students' attitudes or students' mental health tend to be ignored.

The 1950s and 1960s saw the entry of psychologists into the field of curriculum organization. Work such as that of Gagné (1977) focused on the careful, sequential organization of "learning sets"—precise units of work designed to be cumulative over a period of time. This approach suited very well single-subject patterns of curriculum organization. Glaser (1966), in particular, engaged in extensive research to support the development of materials arranged in this sequential, orderly fashion—materials that encouraged individual progress and appeared to fit into extant research on individual differences and continuous pupil progress. This approach was most easily applied to mathematics and the sciences, but associates connected with the Learning Research and Development Center at the University of Pittsburgh pursued such other fields as reading and social studies. The materials developed included opportunities for branching, so that students who had completed part of a basic sequence could enrich their work by branching out into related areas. Glaser stressed the importance of learning processes being specific to subject fields (23).

Two practical problems emerge from this paradigm. First, the progression of students through very carefully organized sequential materials allows little opportunity for the intuitive leaps favored by some psychologists and others whose work undergirded the curriculum reform movement of the 1960s. Not surprisingly, although research showed significant advances in average achievement, the range between bottom and top students tended to narrow. It became necessary, therefore, in seeking to challenge all students, to enrich the program through discussion and inquiry sessions of various kinds. The second problem is related and grows out of the difficulty teachers have finding things to do for students who progress quickly through such material. Teachers often were negative toward the technology used to control progress through the sequences of subject matter (Jamison, Suppes, and Wells 1974). Students dealing with materials most competently quickly finished and sat idle while others were endeavoring to catch up. This is one of the many problems Bloom (1981) endeavored to address in "mastery learning." The most able students manage to extend their insights and competence by tutoring the slower ones.

It becomes clear that tightly organized curricular sequences tend to produce organizing centers characterized by a rather narrow range of difficulty. The presupposition is that all students who are ready will be tackling the same task at once. The handling of individual differences therefore becomes a highly individualized process governed by the materials themselves.

In contrast, the paradigm guiding efforts to organize curriculum around a core of developmental tasks, social problems, and the like tends to result in very large or broad organizing centers, often involving a diverse group of students over a period of several weeks. Students have an opportunity to read widely, take field trips, confer with resource people, prepare reports in the library, and so on (Herrick 1965). Under these circumstances, the range of individual accomplishments seems to widen without endangering the average of the whole group. The major difficulty encountered in such approaches, however, is that of justifying results on the basis of students' scores on standardized achievement tests. Because students in such programs have been spending their time in a good many areas, they often are not as well prepared for the narrow range of achievement measured by the tests. More sensitive evaluation would tap into the full range of their learnings.

One of the most massive and impressive efforts to use hybrid curricular approaches of this kind and to develop appropriate evaluative methods was demonstrated by the so-called Eight Year Study, extending from 1933 to 1941 (Aiken 1942; Thomas 1990). The study attempted to compare a group of secondary schools freed of the usual college subject matter entrance requirements for traditional secondary schools. The study and its results were presented in several volumes. In general, students in the experimental group performed about as well as those in the control group on achievement in the various subjects covered by standardized tests. However, the experimental group in general performed better on broader educational goals determined by the schools themselves—goals representing the stated goals of schooling in the United States (Boyer 1983; Goodlad 1984).

Revisiting and reflecting on the story of the Eight Year Study helps us to realize why there is so little research on major projects seeking to redesign institutional and instructional curricula. As stated, the demands on time, people, and money are high; university-based researchers can advance up the ladder toward tenure and other rewards more rapidly by doing individual, short-term, small-sample studies. We begin to understand how fads can run rampant, unchecked by research findings simply because the resources (and rewards) for large-scale studies are not readily obtained (Slavin 1989). Then, because policymakers and funding agencies often are skeptical of educational research and reluctant to support it, costly fads resurface in every educational reform movement and are tried and abandoned without a discovery of what might give sensible guidance the next time around.

If efforts to design better curricula must always be judged according to the results of narrowly focused studies based on standardized achievement tests of students coming through these programs, innovative and experimental efforts are likely to be stifled. Evaluations conducted must conform to the educational goals established in the first place, not be determined on the basis of other criteria simply because they are easily measured. Although conceptions of such evaluation are well developed, conventional policy and practice still hold to performance on standardized achievement tests as the sine qua non of excellence (Sirotnik and Goodlad 1985). Consequently, curricular patterns not organized around subjects tend to be eschewed or approached with great caution. The central dilemma of research to determine the effectiveness of various patterns of curriculum organization is a moral one—clearly confronted, for example, in the effort of Lois Nelson (1964) to compare two quite different patterns at the instructional level. Partway through her effort, she became convinced that one, much more than the other, was more compelling for students and for her. To continue would have contaminated the results because of her own conversion. She became convinced of the immorality of continuing with a pattern she regarded as inferior to the other and not in the best interests of the children. Consequently, she redesigned the study along the lines of a more naturalistic methodology and abandoned the experimental paradigm.

Alternative patterns of organizing the curriculum have built into them the alternative beliefs and values held by those individuals advocating them. These values and beliefs drive the energies of those engaged in developing a given alternative. It should not surprise us, then, that efforts so driven, probably more than attributes inherent in the alternative curricular mode, account for any advantages ultimately realized. That is, the alternative introduced does better what was intended for it than does the alternative with which it is placed in competition: "When curricula have different effects, the differences are roughly what we should expect to find if we simply compared, in a commonsense fashion, their content and objectives" (Walker 1976, 273). This conclusion does not negate, however, the proposition that some patterns of curriculum organization are more beautiful and more just than others.

References

Aceland, R. 1967. *A Move to the Integrated Curriculum*. Exeter, England: University of Exeter.

Adler, Mortimer J. 1982. *The Paideia Proposal*. New York: Macmillan.

Aiken, Wilford M. 1942. *The Story of the Eight-year Study*. New York: Harper & Row.

Alberty, Harold. 1947. *Reorganizing the High School Curriculum*. New York: Macmillan.

Apple, Michael. 1979. *Ideology and Curriculum*. Boston: Routledge & Kegan Paul.

Armstrong, David G. 1989. *Developing and Documenting the Curriculum*. Needham Heights, MA: Allyn & Bacon.

Association for Supervision and Curriculum Development. 1958. *A Look at Continuity in the School Program. Yearbook of the Association for Supervision and Curriculum Development*. Washington, DC: ASCD.

Association for Supervision and Curriculum Development. 1962. *Perceiving, Behaving, Becoming: A New Focus in Education. Yearbook of the Association for Supervision and Curriculum Development*. Washington, DC: ASCD.

Baker, Eva L., and W. James Popham. 1973. *Expanding Dimensions of Instructional Objectives*. Englewood Cliffs, NJ: Prentice Hall.

Becker, James M., ed. 1979. *Schooling for a Global Age*. New York: McGraw-Hill.

Belth, Marc. 1965. *Education as a Discipline*. Boston: Allyn & Bacon.

Bestor, Arthur. 1956. *The Restoration of Learning*. New York: Knopf.

Bloom, Benjamin S., ed. 1956. *Taxonomy of Educational Objectives: Cognitive Domain*. New York: McKay.

Bloom, Benjamin S. 1981. *All Our Children Learning: A Primer for Parents, Teachers, and Other Educators*. New York: McGraw-Hill.

Bobbitt, Franklin. 1924. *How to Make a Curriculum*. Boston: Houghton Mifflin.

Bode, Boyd H. 1938. *Progressive Education at the Crossroads*. New York: Newsom.

Bonser, Frederick G. 1932. *Life Needs and Education*. New York: Bureau of Publications, Teachers College, Columbia University.

Bossing, Nelson L. 1949. *Principles of Secondary Education*. Englewood Cliffs, NJ: Prentice Hall.

Boyer, Ernest L. 1983. *High School*. New York: Harper & Row.

Brown, William B. 1938, May. The core is not all of the curriculum. *Curriculum Journal* 9: 210.

Bruner, Jerome. 1960. *The Process of Education*. Cambridge, MA: Harvard University Press.

Burnett, Lewie W. 1951, February. Core programs in Washington State junior high schools. *The School Review* 59: 97–100.

Charters, W. W. 1923. *Curriculum Construction*. New York: Macmillan.

Connelly, F. Michael, and O. Lantz. 1985. "Curriculum, Definitions of." In *International Encyclopedia of Education*, edited by Torsten Husén and T. Neville Postlethwaite, 1160–1163. Oxford: Pergamon.

Counts, George A. 1932. *Dare the Schools Build a New Social Order?* New York: John Day.

Counts, George A. 1934. *The Social Foundations of Education. Part IX, Report of the Commission on the Social Studies, American Historical Association*. New York: Scribners.

Cremin, Lawrence A. 1971. Curriculum-making in the U.S. *Teachers College Record* 73:207–220.

Cremin, Lawrence A. 1990. *Popular Education and Its Discontents*. New York: Harper & Row.

Cronbach, Lee J. 1957. The two disciplines of scientific psychology. *The American Psychologist* 12:671–684.

Cronbach, Lee J. 1975. Beyond the two disciplines of scientific psychology. *The American Psychologist* 30: 116–127.

Dewey, John. 1897. My Pedagogical Creed. *The School Journal* 54: 77–80.

Dewey, John. 1902. *The Child and the Curriculum*. Chicago: University of Chicago Press.

Dewey, John. 1938. *Experience and Education*. New York: Macmillan.

Dressel, Paul L. 1958. *The Integration of Educational Experience. Fifty-seventh Yearbook of the National Society for the Study of Education*, Part III. Chicago: University of Chicago Press.

Eisner, Elliot W. 1977, February. On the use of educational connoisseurship and educational criticism for evaluating classroom life. *Teachers College Record* 78: 345–358.

Eisner, Elliot W., and Elizabeth Vallance. 1974. "Five Concepts of Curriculum." In *Conflicting Conceptions of Curriculum*, edited by Elliot W. Eisner and Elizabeth Vallance, 1–19. Berkeley, CA: McCutchan.

Florander, Jesper, and Paul Skov. 1986. "Curriculum Planning and Development in Denmark." *In Views on Core Curriculum*, edited by Rudd J. Gorter, 173–176. Enschede, The Netherlands: National Institute for Curriculum Development.

Foshay, Arthur W. 1969. "Curriculum." In *Encyclopedia of Educa-*

tional Research, edited by R. L. Ebel, 275–276. New York: Macmillan.

Fraser, Dorothy M., ed. 1962. *Current Curriculum Studies in Academic Subjects*. Washington, DC: National Education Association.

Frymier, Jack. 1977. *Annehurst Curriculum Classification System: A Practical Way to Individualize Instruction*. Bloomington, IN: Kappa Delta Pi.

Gagné, Robert M. 1967. "Curriculum Research and the Promotion of Learning." In *Perspectives of Curriculum Evaluation*, edited by Ralph W. Tyler, Robert M. Gagné, and Michael Scriven, 19–38. Chicago: Rand McNally.

Gagné, Robert M. 1977. *The Conditions of Learning*, 3rd ed. New York: Holt, Rinehart and Winston.

Giroux, Henry A. 1981. "Toward a New Sociology of Curriculum." In *Curriculum and Instruction*, edited by Henry A. Giroux, Anthony N. Penna, and William F. Pinar, 98–108. Berkeley, CA: McCutchan.

Giroux, Henry A., Anthony N. Penna, and William F. Pinar, eds. 1981. *Curriculum and Instruction*. Berkeley, CA: McCutchan.

Glaser, Robert. 1966. "Variables in Discovery Learning." In *Learning by Discovery: A Critical Appraisal*, edited by Lee S. Shulman and Evan R. Keislar, 13–26. Chicago: Rand McNally.

Goodlad, John I. 1964. *School Curriculum Reform in the United States*. New York: Fund for the Advancement of Education.

Goodlad, John I. (with Maurice N. Richter). 1966. *The Development of a Conceptual System for Dealing with Problems of Curriculum and Instruction*. Los Angeles: Institute for Development of Educational Activities, University of California.

Goodlad, John I. 1979. "The Scope of the Curriculum Field." In *Curriculum Inquiry: The Study of Curriculum Practice*, edited by John I. Goodlad and associates, 17–42. New York: McGraw-Hill.

Goodlad, John I. 1984. *A Place Called School*. New York: McGraw-Hill.

Goodlad, John I. 1985. "Curriculum as a Field of Study." In *International Encyclopedia of Education*, edited by Torsten Husén and T. Neville Postlethwaite, 1141–1144. Oxford: Pergamon.

Goodlad, John I. 1986, October. The learner at the world's center. *Social Education* 50: 424–436.

Goodlad, John I. 1988. "Coping with Curriculum." In *Contributing to Educational Change: Perspectives on Research and Practice*, edited by Philip W. Jackson, 179–190. Berkeley, CA: McCutchan.

Goodlad, John I., M. Frances Klein, Jerrold M. Novotney, Kenneth A. Tye, and associates. 1974. *Toward a Mankind School*. New York: McGraw-Hill.

Goodlad, John I., M. Frances Klein, and Kenneth A. Tye. 1979. "The Domains of Curriculum and Their Study." In *Curriculum Inquiry: The Study of Curriculum Practice*, edited by John I. Goodlad and associates, 43–76. New York: McGraw-Hill.

Goodlad, John I., Renata von Stoephasius, and M. Frances Klein. 1966. *The Changing School Curriculum*. New York: Fund for the Advancement of Education.

Greene, Maxine. 1969, fall. The arts in a global village. *Educational Leadership* 26: 439–446.

Greene, Maxine. 1971, December. Curriculum and consciousness. *Teachers College Record* 73: 253–269.

Greene, Maxine. 1973. *Teacher as Stranger*. Belmont, CA: Wadsworth.

Habermas, Jürgen. 1971. *Knowledge and Human Interests*. Boston: Beacon Press.

Habermas, Jürgen. 1973. *Theory and Practice*. Boston: Beacon Press.

Habermas, Jürgen. 1975. *Legitimation Crisis*. Boston: Beacon Press.

Harap, Henry. 1952. *Social Living in the Curriculum: A Critical Study of the Core in Action in Grades One Through Twelve*. Nashville, TN: George Peabody College for Teachers.

Herrick, Virgil E. 1950. "The Concept of Curriculum Design." In *Toward Improved Curriculum Theory*, edited by Virgil E. Herrick and Ralph W. Tyler, 37–50. Chicago: University of Chicago Press.

Herrick, Virgil E. 1954, December. Approaches to helping teachers improve their instructional practices. *School Review* 62: 533–534.

Herrick, Virgil E. 1962. *Collected Papers and Source Materials on Curriculum Operations and Structure*. Madison, WI: College Printing and Typing.

Herrick, Virgil E. 1965. "Organizing Centers." In *Strategies of Curriculum Development (Selected Writings of the Late V. E. Herrick)*, edited by James B. Macdonald, Dan W. Anderson, and Frank B. May, 107–113. Columbus, OH: Charles E. Merrill.

Herrick, Virgil E., and Ralph W. Tyler, eds. 1950. *Toward Improved Curriculum Theory*. Chicago: University of Chicago Press.

Hirsch, E. D., Jr. 1987. *Cultural Literacy*. Boston: Houghton Mifflin.

Huebner, Dwayne. 1975. "Curricular Language and Classroom Meanings." In *Curriculum Theorizing: The Reconceptualists*, edited by William F. Pinar, 217–236. Berkeley, CA: McCutchan.

Huebner, Dwayne. 1982. What is curriculum theorizing? What are its implications for practice? *Educational Leadership* 40: 290–294.

Hunkins, Francis P. 1980. *Curriculum Development: Program Improvement*. Columbus, OH: Charles E. Merrill.

Hutchins, Robert M. 1936. *The Higher Learning in America*. New Haven, CT: Yale University Press.

Jamison, Dean, Patrick Suppes, and Stuart Wells. 1974, winter. The effectiveness of alternative instructional media: A survey. *Review of Educational Research* 44: 1–67.

Kearney, Nolan C., and Walter W. Cook. 1960. "Curriculum." In *Encyclopedia of Educational Research*, edited by Chester W. Harris, 358–365. New York: Macmillan.

Kessler, Harry L. 1956, September. Why a core curriculum for a democratic community? *High Points* 38: 43.

Kilpatrick, William H. 1918. *The Project Method*, 10th series, vol. 3. New York: Teachers College, Columbia University.

Klausmeier, Herbert J. 1976. "Continuity in Learning: Long-range Effects." In *Learning: An Overview and Update*, edited by Kenneth H. Hansen, 15–42. Washington, DC: Council of Chief State School Officers.

Klein, M. Frances. 1985. "Curriculum Design." In *International Encyclopedia of Education*, edited by Torsten Husén and T. Neville Postlethwaite, 1163–1170. Oxford: Pergamon.

Klein, M. Frances, and John I. Goodlad. 1978. *A Study of Curriculum Decision Making in Eighteen Selected Countries*. Los Angeles: Research Division, Institute for the Development of Educational Activities.

Kliebard, Herbert M. 1986. *The Struggle for the American Curriculum 1893–1958*. Boston: Routledge & Kegan Paul.

Krathwohl, David R., ed. 1964. *Taxonomy of Educational Objectives: Affective Domain*. New York: McKay.

Leonard, J. Paul. 1950. "Some Reflections on the Meaning of Sequence." In *Toward Improved Curriculum Theory*, edited by Virgil E. Herrick and Ralph W. Tyler, 70–79. Chicago: University of Chicago Press.

Leonard, J. Paul. 1953. *Developing the Secondary School Curriculum*, rev. ed. New York: Holt, Rinehart and Winston.

MacConnell, Charles M., and others. 1940, March. The core curriculum. *Educational Trends* 8: 25.

Macdonald, James B. 1975. "Curriculum Theory." In *Curriculum Theorizing: The Reconceptualists*, edited by William F. Pinar, 5–14. Berkeley, CA: McCutchan.

McNeil, Linda M. 1986. *Contradictions of Control*. New York: Routledge.

Mager, Robert F. 1962. *Preparing Instructional Objectives*. Palo Alto, CA: Fearon.

Maslow, Abraham H. 1968, fall. Some educational implications of the humanistic psychology. *Harvard Educational Review* 38: 685–696.

National Commission on Excellence in Education. 1983. *A Nation At Risk*. Washington, DC: U.S. Government Printing Office.

National League for Nursing. 1977. *Criteria for the Appraisal of Baccalaureate and Higher Degree Programs in Nursing*. New York: National League for Nursing.

Neill, A. S. 1960. *Summerhill: A Radical Approach to Child Rearing*. New York: Hart.

Nelson, Lois N. 1964. "The Effect of Classroom Interaction on Pupil Linguistic Performance." Ed.D. dissertation, University of California, Los Angeles.

Oakeshott, Michael. 1962. *Rationalism in Politics and Other Essays*. London: Methuen.

Piaget, Jean. 1926. *The Language and Thought of the Child*. London: Kegan Paul, Trench, Trubner.

Piaget, Jean. 1962 [1928]. *Judgment and Reasoning in the Child*. New York: Humanities Press.

Pinar, William F. 1975. "Search for a Method." In *Curriculum Theorizing: The Reconceptualists*, edited by William F. Pinar, 415–424. Berkeley, CA: McCutchan.

Popham, W. James, and Eva L. Baker. 1970. *Systematic Instruction*. Englewood Cliffs, NJ: Prentice Hall.

Popham, W. James, Elliot W. Eisner, H. J. Sullivan, and Louise L. Tyler. 1969. *Instructional Objectives*. Chicago: Rand McNally.

Powell, Arthur G., Eleanor Farrar, and David K. Cohen. 1985. *The Shopping Mall High School*. Boston: Houghton Mifflin.

Prescott, Daniel. 1938. *Emotion and the Educative Process*. Washington, DC: American Council on Education.

Pressey, Sidney L. 1960. "A Simple Apparatus Which Gives Tests and Scores—and Teaches." In *Teaching Machines and Programmed Learning: A Source Book*, edited by Arthur A. Lumsdaine and Robert Glaser, 35–41. Washington, DC: Department of Audio-Visual Instruction, National Education Association.

Rugg, Harold O. 1926. "The School Curriculum and the Drama of American Life." In *Curriculum Making: Past and Present. Twenty-sixth Yearbook of the National Society for the Study of Education*, Part I, edited by Guy M. Whipple, 3–16. Bloomington, IL: Public School Co.

Rugg, Harold O. 1931. *Culture and Education in America*. New York: Harcourt, Brace.

Sand, Ole. 1958. *Curriculum Study in Basic Nursing*. New York: Putnam.

Schaefer, Robert J. 1971. "Retrospect and Prospect." In *The Curriculum: Retrospect and Prospect, Seventieth Yearbok of the National Society for the Study of Education*, Part I, edited by Robert M. McClure, 3–25. Chicago: University of Chicago Press.

Schaffarzick, Jon, and David H. Hampson, eds. 1975. *Strategies for Curriculum Development*. Berkeley, CA: McCutchan.

Schubert, William H. 1982. "Curriculum Research." In *Encyclopedia of Educational Research*, 5th ed., edited by Harold E. Mitzel, 420–431. New York: Free Press.

Schwab, Joseph J. 1962, July. The concept of the structure of a discipline. *The Educational Record* 43: 197–205.

Schwab, Joseph J. 1964. "Problems, Topics, and Issues." In *Education and the Structure of Knowledge. Fifth Annual Phi Delta Kappa Symposium on Educational Research*, edited by Stanley Elam, 4–42. Chicago: Rand McNally.

Schwab, Joseph J. 1970. *The Practical: A Language for Curriculum*. Washington, DC: National Education Association.

Schwab, Joseph J. 1973. The practical 3: Translation into curriculum. *School Review* 81: 501–522.

Sirotnik, Kenneth A., and John I. Goodlad. 1985. "The Quest for Reasons Amidst the Rhetoric of Reform: Improving Instead of Testing Our Schools." In *Education on Trial*, edited by William Johnston, 277–298. San Francisco, CA: Institute for Contemporary Studies.

Sizer, Theodore R. 1984. *Horace's Compromise: The Dilemma of the American High School*. Boston: Houghton Mifflin.

Skilbeck, Malcolm. 1985. "Curriculum Organization." In *International Encyclopedia of Education*, edited by Torsten Husén and T. Neville Postlethwaite, 1229–1233. Oxford: Pergamon.

Skinner, B. F. 1971. *Beyond Freedom and Dignity*. New York: Knopf.

Slavin, Robert E. 1989, June. PET and the pendulum: Fadism in education and how to stop it. *Phi Delta Kappan* 70: 752–758.

Smith, B. Othanel, William O. Stanley, and J. Harlan Shores. 1950. *Fundamentals of Curriculum Development*. New York: World Book Company.

Smith, Norville L. 1945, April. The core program. *Social Studies* 36: 164–168.

Stratemeyer, Florence B., Handen L. Forkner, and Margaret G. McKim. 1947. *Developing a Curriculum for Modern Living*. New York: Bureau of Publications, Teachers College, Columbia University.

Stratemeyer, Florence B., Handen L. Forkner, Margaret G. McKim, and A. Harry Passow. 1957. *Developing a Curriculum for Modern Living*, 2nd ed. New York: Teachers College, Columbia University.

Sullivan, Edmund V. 1967. *Piaget and the School Curriculum: A Critical Appraisal*, Bulletin no. 2. Ontario: Ontario Institute for Studies in Education.

Taba, Hilda. 1962. *Curriculum Development: Theory and Practice*. New York: Harcourt, Brace.

Taba, Hilda, Elizabeth H. Brady, and John T. Robinson. 1952. *Intergroup Education in Public Schools*. Washington, DC: American Council on Education.

Tanner, Daniel, and Laurel N. Tanner. 1975. *Curriculum Development*. New York: Macmillan.

Tanner, Daniel, and Laurel N. Tanner. 1980. *Curriculum Development: Theory Into Practice*, 2nd ed. New York: Macmillan.

Thomas, Bruce R. 1990. "The School as a Moral Learning Community." In *The Moral Dimensions of Teaching*, edited by John I. Goodlad, Roger Soder, and Kenneth A. Sirotnik, 266–295. San Francisco, CA: Jossey-Bass.

Thorndike, Edward L. 1910, January. The contributions of psychology to education. *The Journal of Educational Psychology* 1: 5–12.

Thorndike, Edward L. 1913. *Educational Psychology*. New York: Teachers College, Columbia University.

Tryon, Carolyn, ed. 1950. *Fostering Mental Health in Our Schools. Yearbook of the Association for Supervision and Curriculum Development*. Washington, DC: ASCD.

Tyler, Louise L. 1978. Evaluation and persons. *Educational Leadership* 35(4):275–279.

Tyler, Louise L., and John I. Goodlad. 1979. "The Personal Domain: Curricular Meaning." In *Curriculum Inquiry: The Study of Cur-*

riculum Practice, edited by John I. Goodlad and associates, 191–208. New York: McGraw-Hill.

Tyler, Louise L., and M. Frances Klein. 1973. "Not Either–Or." Paper read at annual meeting, American Educational Research Association, February 25, New Orleans.

Tyler, Louise L., M. Frances Klein, and associates. 1976. *Evaluating and Choosing Curriculum and Instructional Materials*. Los Angeles: Educational Research Associates.

Tyler, Louise L., M. Frances Klein, and William B. Michael. 1971. *Recommendations for Curriculum and Instructional Materials*. Los Angeles: Tyl Press.

Tyler, Ralph W. 1949. *Basic Principles of Curriculum and Instruction*. Chicago: University of Chicago Press.

Tyler, Ralph W. 1973. "Educational Evaluation in the Revolutionary Age." In *Educational Communication in a Revolutionary Age*, edited by I. Keith Tyler and Catharine M. Williams, 101–118. Worthington, OH: Charles A. Jones.

van Bruggen, Johan C. 1986. "Establishing a Modern Core Curriculum: A Tricky Business or a Political Art?" In *Views on Core Curriculum*, edited by Rudd J. Gorter, 131–150. Enschede, The Netherlands: Institute for Curriculum Development.

Walker, Decker F. 1976. "Toward Comprehension of Curricular Realities." In *Review of Research in Education*, edited by Lee S. Shulman, 268–308. Itasca, IL: Peacock and the American Educational Research Association.

Welch, Wayne W. 1979. "Twenty Years of Science Curriculum Development: A Look Back." In *Review of Research in Education*, edited by David C. Berliner, 282–306. Itasca, IL: Peacock and the American Educational Research Association.

Whitehead, Alfred N. 1957. *The Aims of Education and Other Essays*. New York: Free Press.

Wigginton, Eliot. 1985. *Sometimes a Shining Moment: The Foxfire Experience*. New York: Anchor Press/Doubleday.

13

SCHOOL ORGANIZATION AND CURRICULUM

Charles E. Bidwell

Robert Dreeben

UNIVERSITY OF CHICAGO

Relationships between school organization and curriculum are virtually unexplored research territory. Our purpose in this chapter is to venture into one part of this territory. We shall consider the processes of institutionalization through which the social structure and content of education become objectified as the formally organized school and as the curriculum. Once institutionalization has occurred, knowledge codes, embodied in curricula, themselves become organizational properties that help to define the structure of schools and of the larger educational systems that comprise them. When we discuss this relationship, we will in effect construe curriculum as an aspect of educational organization. This perspective has rarely been adopted.

Although the organization and content of education are intimately related, there is surprisingly little literature on the connection between school organization and curriculum. The works that have been produced focus almost entirely on the single theme of stratification and differentiation, showing how the schools of modern Western societies have adapted to socially and economically heterogeneous enrollments by streaming or tracking. This work is treated elsewhere in this *Handbook,* in the chapter by Oakes, Gamoran, and Page, and will not be dealt with here.

Prior to the institutionalization of education, changes in its forms and contents were crescive outcomes in whatever social institutions conducted educational activities, such as family, church, or workplace. However, once schools and curricula became objects of explicit social action, they became matters of both public debate and political action within the state. Then, change in the forms and content of education became primarily a matter of political initiative. One could argue that the institutionalization of education has itself been one salient aspect of the emergence of state and polity as distinctive of civil society.

Therefore, to the extent that one is interested in the dynamics of school organization and curriculum and in the processes by which the forms and contents of education change, adaptively or maladaptively, in relation to social and cultural changes in society, an understanding of the initiation, development, and outcomes of the institutionalization of education is necessary. To pursue this line of inquiry, one must ask what in a society's development stimulates the institutionalization of education and guides the evolution of school organization and curriculum into social objects. One must also ask how the evolving organizational and curricular forms act on one another to affect the course of institutionalization. Finally, as institutionalization proceeds, one must ask how state structures and political actors and interests become mobilized to affect the course of organizational and curricular change in the schools and about the relative vulnerability or invulnerability of school organization and curriculum to external influence. To what extent, for example, is organizational or curricular change led by the schools or responsive to initiatives that lie elsewhere?

These questions suggest that when we compare different societies or historical periods, we are likely to find differences in how curriculum and school organization are related to one another and to the society. These differences should result from variation in the course of institutionalization, in the interests and power of the actors who attempt to influence what is taught and to whom, and in political and state structures.

In this chapter, we shall examine relationships among school organization, curriculum, and environment, drawing illustratively on the historical course of American public, common education from the colonial period through 1865. The reader may wish to compare our approach with that taken many years earlier by Durkheim (1977 [1938]). Durkheim traced the institutionalization and subsequent evolution of secondary schools and curricula in France from medieval beginnings forward. He gave prime attention to both ideological and intellectual movements and to interest-driven group action as major sources of curricular and organizational change in French secondary education. However, he gave virtually no attention to the way the structures and contents of secondary schooling were connected, although the relationships that connect school organization and curriculum are at the center of educational institutionalization and change. In a similar vein, Goodson (1983) discussed the recent history of curricular change in Great Britain. He detailed how curricula may define intellectual and occupational territories that ground the interests and affect the occupational mobility strategies of teacher groups.

In the pages to follow, we shall see that in the American case, the colonial through the early national and pre-Civil War periods exemplify the movement toward objectifying curricula and organization that we think is generally characteristic of national histories of education. This national case provides a rich and reliable secondary literature that will let us specify our ideas about school organization and curriculum. Using only one national case, a case that is in many ways exceptional in comparison with the more general development of national educational systems, may strike the reader as limiting, perhaps distorting. However, our purpose is to illustrate a way of thinking about the formation and development of school organization and curriculum, not to advance or test propositions, and the U.S. case is suggestive. The comparative research remains to be done.

DEFINITIONS

Curriculum denotes the formal specification of what is taught in a school. From an organizational perspective, it is the content of the frontline work that schools conduct. Curricula are formally specified in such school entities as units, courses, clusters, or sequences of courses, and these specifications are represented by organizational arrangements that express their institutionalization.

What is taught to children and young people may be matters of informal understanding, at times codified in traditions and in the conventional understandings of educators, policymakers, or laypersons but at other times subject to substantial diversity, disagreement, uncertainty, or confusion. The point is that what is taught becomes curriculum when it is formally codified. Once in place, a curriculum may itself be subject to and influenced by various informal understandings.

School organization denotes the enacted social structural patterns characteristic of individual schools, the enacted structures that link schools into local school systems or districts, and the patterns of managerial doctrine and activity that characterize the persons who administer the work of schools and systems. The organizational patterns of individual schools include a division of teachers' labor and an arrangement of classrooms and other units for instruction. They may or may not include some explicit provision for the coordination of work.

We shall see that early in the United States schools developed organizational patterns that permitted highly flexible adaptations to the curricular changes that took place, and thus put few constraints on other forces that drove curricular evolution. As a result, it is not always easy to distinguish curricular from organizational innovation or change in the history of American schools. For example, the spread of schools graded by age is a story of the concurrent stratification of both classrooms and subjects.

OVERVIEW OF THE CHAPTER

In the United States, from the colonial era through the middle part of the 19th century, the content of education evolved in three principal stages of institutionalization. First, in the colonial and early federal periods, the content of what was to be taught to children and young persons was firmly grounded in conventional understandings about the aims and substance of education. These understandings centered on widely acknowledged conceptions of the personal requisites of citizenship and how to impart them through instruction. This educational content, though broadly accepted and understood, had not yet been objectified as a distinctive aspect of schooling.

Second, the early 19th century was marked by educational competition, especially at the secondary level. Different organizational forms of schooling sought niches in an expanding educational market, each to a degree claiming to provide distinctive instructional content. The result of this competition was reduced organizational diversity in educational provision and a corresponding convergence on a more uniform coverage and arrangement of subject matter. In this competitive context, the curriculum emerged as a distinctive object and aspect of school. Like the school organization in which it was embedded, it became a product of social processes that shaped what teachers and students encountered in the classroom.

Third, in the Jacksonian period, the traditional underpinnings of the implicit colonial agreement broke apart. Once again, a diverse array of subjects and courses appeared, variously offered in an equally diverse array of schools. By the time of the Civil War, this curricular and organizational diversity had substantially diminished. It gradually gave way to a far more common curriculum that once more sought to prepare for citizenship. However, this curriculum was directed toward a conception of citizenship more suited to a commercial and industrial age and to a student body that was rapidly growing in size and social and economic heterogeneity.

This decline of curricular diversity was accompanied by a commensurate decline of organizational diversity, especially at the secondary level. There, the comprehensive public high school preempted the enrollments that had sustained its precursors and competitors, the academy and various specialized private venture schools. Moreover, the comprehensive high school was incorporated into graded local school districts, so that in both organization and curriculum, it became part of a larger scheme of common education, funded at public expense. The stage was set for a new version of the curriculum, now in the formally codified form that was advanced by expanding local and state educational bureaucracies.

At the secondary level, this curriculum was subdivided rather intensively by subject matter and carefully graded by levels of difficulty to accommodate an increasingly heterogeneous student body. Although students of differing social and economic origins, aspirations, and likely destinations were incorporated within the single public high school, they studied different things and progressed at different rates through those subjects that they did have in common. The comprehensive high school added or expanded the coverage of subjects in its socially incorporative enterprise by adding courses. Each of these courses was taught as a separate offering by members of faculties that were increasingly specialized by subject.

Thus, the high school curriculum became more intensively differentiated into subject matter segments and, correspondingly, organized its teaching work into course and classroom segments: the course, the teacher of the course, and the classroom in which the course was taught. This dual curricular and organizational segmentation provided a frame that made it easy to add whatever new segments popular demand, student need, or professional judgment made desirable. One result of this process is the three-track structure (academic, general, and vocational) that remains with us today.

The institutionalization of education in all modern societies can be depicted as the emergence and elaboration of a fan-shaped structure for allocating students among subject matters and levels of measured attainment (Bidwell 1989). In this structure, the curriculum and the organizational pattern in which it is taught become progressively differentiated horizontally by areas of instruction and vertically by a combination of student age (e.g., school grades) and accomplishment (e.g., streams or tracks).

When schools gain institutional standing as distinct organizations for conducting education, what is taught develops into "a curriculum composed of blocks—courses of study of varying length and content specificity" (Bidwell 1989, 124). This process is responsive to both the ideas and initiatives of a professionalizing cadre of teachers and school administrators and the preference of lay interest groups and individual consumers of education. The case that we shall present will allow us to explore in a little detail one instance of this series of events.

THE COLONIAL YEARS

The American colonies displayed great differences of geography, population, religion, and aims of colonizing. However, the principal source materials on colonial education focus on the northern seaboard. For that reason, this section will rely more heavily on materials about these colonies, especially in New England, than on information about the middle and southern colonies. Fortunately, matters of organizational form and educational content, to which we shall attend, show considerable similarity from colony to colony (Cremin 1970, 235–243).

In formulating the relationship between the organization of schools and what they taught during the colonial period, it is essential to recognize that schools were not the principal institutional settings with responsibility for the education of children. Thus, relationships between school organization and curriculum are not, strictly speaking, a 17th-century American question.

In the colonial period, there was broad popular agreement about what the young citizen should be taught. In fact, this agreement rested on a conception of the moral, intellectual, and economic elements of citizenship, an amalgam of ideas about right thought and conduct in the family, community, and economy. These elements included the basics of reading and writing; civic and moral belief; and later in the period, figuring. This agreement was embodied in the work of parents, ministers, tutors, masters of trades, private venture schoolmasters, supervisors of the poor, and others who undertook to teach or to ensure that one or another category of children was taught. From the Puritan perspective, humankind, after the Fall, had at best an unclear understanding of right action in the conduct of life by God's law. According to Edmund Morgan (1966 [1944]), "Christians . . . had been given a priceless gift, by which the partial loss of their rational faculties was compensated—the Scriptures. Here God had set down his laws in black and white, and here every man could read them and learn how to act in every circumstance" (11).

From belief in the importance of knowing how to read God's law, it followed that parents should ensure that their children learned to read. This parental responsibility was of the same order as the responsibility for baptism, the preference for naming children after biblical figures whose characters exemplified laudable Puritan traits, and the practice during odd moments each day of teaching children religious lessons that would start them on lives devoted to their salvation and the glorification of God (Axtell 1974).

The religious purpose of learning to read was plain: Ignorance of scripture served the interests of Satan. "Where ignorance raigneth, there raines sinne: and where sinne raigns, there the divell rules: & where he rules, men are in a damnable case" (Axtell 1974, 12). Although John Cotton, exhorting parents to educate their children, urged, "Learn them to read the Scriptures," Morgan (1966 [1944]), indicates that it did not mean "Learn them to read" (12) in the sense simply of mastering a general skill. Rather, the injunction to teach children to read Scriptures had practical as well as religious significance. It was directed toward raising them for honest, industrious employment that would benefit themselves and the commonwealth and prevent them from becoming public charges. Samuel Morison (1936), for example, attacks a narrowly religious interpretation of the Puritan stress on education: "Education was conceived of as a training for citizenship and service in a civilized state, rather than as a vehicle for sectarian propaganda" (64–66). Morison means that the religious and secular components of education were inextricably tied together. The citizenship envisioned in early New England was in a religious commonwealth but one whose survival depended as much on its economic viability as on the conduct of its citizens, living their lives according to God's law (see also Cremin 1970; Demos 1970).

Several institutions at this time had diffuse and interconnected responsibilities for transforming children into adults. The family was the earliest in the life of the child to make its influence felt, an influence that continued through the years of preparation for citizenship in the commonwealth. The heavy educational burden assumed by the family in part represented an adaptation to colonial conditions of scarcity; schooling and teaching resources that were more plentiful in England were in short supply in the New England wilderness.

However, one must be careful to recognize that the Puritan family did not stand as a distinct social unit that prepared its younger members for entrance into a separate and remote social world. "What the family left undone by way of informal education," according to Bernard Bailyn (1960),

> the local community most often completed. It did so in entirely natural ways, for so elaborate was the architecture of family organization and so deeply founded was it in the soil of stable, slowly changing village and town communities in which intermarriage among the same groups had taken place generation after generation, that it was at times difficult for the child to know where the family left off and the greater society began. (17–18)

The boundary between church and family responsibilities was indistinct. Ministers told parents that their children would benefit more from public preaching if they prepared them for it at home through religious instruction and catechism (Axtell 1974, 14–15). Puritans harbored a deep suspicion of any religious education that was governed centrally by a church, as it had been in England under Bishop Laud. Axtell observes that "Puritan writers were describing the household as 'a little Church,' 'a little Common-wealth,' and a 'schoole' of obedience and religion" (20).

Whereas in Virginia catechizing was regarded primarily as a ministerial function, families in New England were entrusted with catechetical responsibility. When they failed to do their duty, the task reverted to the church, under the direction of the church teacher responsible for giving sermons, explaining Scripture, and catechizing (Axtell 1974).

> In that [dull and repetitive] practice [of catechizing] many a youngster must have found himself, willy-nilly, learning to read. . . . And since it was but a short step from catechizing to more general education, many a minister must have served from time to time as schoolmaster to the children of his congregation, moving from catechism and Scripture to sustained instruction in the arts and ancient languages. (Cremin 1970, 156–157)

The education of children, in short, was not a specialized social function in Puritan New England, nor was it in the other colonies (Cremin 1970; Kilpatrick 1912; Morgan 1966 [1944]). Rather, it was one among the many ordinary activities of family and church, institutions that performed overlapping functions.

Moreover, responsibility for children's education extended well beyond these two institutions. It was a key element in the rearing of young people through arrangements of servitude, particularly those of apprenticeship. Apprenticeship education was in a sense fundamental because of its significance in preparation for work. Morgan (1966 [1944]) states,

> Servitude in New England was not simply a device by which one class of men got work out of another class. It was also a school, where vocational training was combined with discipline in good manners and guidance in religion, a school of which all servants were the pupils and to which many respectable and godly men sent their children. (132)

Colonial apprenticeship took its form in a fairly direct application of the 1562 Statute of Artificers (Calhoun 1969, 12–15), a piece of English legislation originally designed to prevent local abuses in apprenticeship practices by establishing a national system of regulation. It stipulated the length of the term and obligated the apprentice to "serve diligently," obey reasonable commands, keep the master's secrets, and abstain from vice. For his part, the master was enjoined to instruct the apprentice in a trade; provide food, clothing, and lodging; and take responsibility for his moral welfare (Seybolt 1917, 13–14).

In the same way, apprenticeship figured into the rearing of the young by virtue of the colonial application of the provisions of the 1601 English Poor Law (Calhoun 1969, 15–16). It provided that church warders and overseers could have the children of the poor apprenticed. This law was essentially a welfare provision. Although it was not designed for training in the skilled trades, it nevertheless contributed to that end (Seybolt 1917, 20–21). According to Seybolt, "Not only was apprenticeship of fundamental social and economic importance, as in England, but it was the most fundamental educational institution of the period" (22), and it remained of such importance until late in the 18th century (Kaestle 1973, 8–9). The importance of both laws, as well as of later colonial legislation based on them, was that they provided, as matters of government responsibility, for the training of children and youths in skills that would enable them as adults to support themselves and their families and for conveying the principles of moral conduct that would make them upstanding members of a community.

There was chronic and deep concern in the colonies about those parents and masters who did not show proper care for the moral education of their children, particularly if they were illiterate or poor (Calhoun 1969, 21–22). Plymouth in 1671 legally required not only parents but also masters of apprentices to teach children to "read the Scriptures, and other profitable Books in the English tongue and the knowledge of the capital laws" (Seybolt 1917, 37), and selectmen were to visit homes to determine whether this was being done and to mete out sanctions accordingly.

When families were unequipped for the task of moral and religious training, of which teaching in reading was an important component, local authorities might send the children as apprentices to a master. Unfortunately, however competent the master was to teach his trade, he was not always literate or capable of teaching proper morality. To address this problem, children were remanded to literate masters who kept schools (Seybolt 1917, 41).

The school had a place in education, but even in light of the Puritan commitment to education, its place was limited. Schools did not proliferate in the early colonial period. In a sequence that reflected the Puritans' religious zeal, "The church preceded the school; the meetinghouse was the first public building, while the schoolhouse often waited for more than a generation before it was voted and longer before it was built" (Small 1969 [1914], 240). Schooling, in contrast, was carried on in kitchens, manses, churches, meetinghouses, and sheds "erected in fields, and shops erected in towns . . . by parents, tutors, clergymen, lay readers, precentors, physicians, lawyers, artisans, and shopkeepers" (Cremin 1970, 192–193) in addition to schoolmasters.

Economic and political functions had prior claims on the public purse. Only when schools became distinct institutions did they gain their own distinctive physical structures to house their activities. Education remained a highly diffused social function. Its institutionalization in schools would come later, and even though there was substantial agreement about what beliefs and knowledge education should impart to the young, this agreement was not yet embodied in what we have defined as a curriculum.

We can plausibly date the onset of the institutionalization of schooling to the year 1647, when the Massachusetts General Court passed a law that (1) established a state requirement for the support of teachers (though not necessarily of schools), (2) tied this requirement to population growth, and (3) made access to this education formally independent of family wealth. The law required townships, "after the Lord hath increased them to the number of fifty Householders" (Morison 1930, 186), to support a teacher for reading and writing. It required townships with 100 or more inhabitants to support a grammar school to prepare students for the university, with the schoolmaster's wages to be paid by parents, by masters of apprentices, or from the town rate (Calhoun 1969, 23–24; Seybolt 1917, 42). Finally, it obligated townships to subsidize families unable to pay tuition and otherwise to support the newly enacted educational provisions.

The sanction for noncompliance with the 1647 law was tough. A fine was paid not to the General Court but to the nearest town that was in compliance, a blow to civic pride as well as to the local public purse. Nonetheless, the financing of schoolmasters was no easy matter in the mid-17th century because land was plentiful and thus not a good source of income (Updegraff 1908, 20–29). Consequently, the 1647 law did not lead to a great profusion of schoolmasters or of school buildings to house them.

The passage of the 1647 law in Massachusetts and similar laws in Plymouth and New Haven (Axtell 1974) testified to a growing concern that families more and more were defaulting their responsibility for educating their children (Cremin 1970). At the same time, church control of schools (a principle rooted in European Puritan doctrine) was loosening (Updegraff 1908, 39). There was also a response to a perceived decline in adherence to religious standards of conduct, evidenced by the General Court's regulation of sabbath observance (Bridenbaugh 1964 [1938], 76). This pattern appeared in other East Coast port cities in addition to Boston.

As the state sought remedies for these ills, it turned to formal education. The schools were becoming civic institutions, matters of public surveillance and debate, as the state tried to improve them to find a way to strengthen civic and moral virtue. In effect, the improved school was to complement a family and church no longer equal to their educational tasks (Eggleston 1901, 228–231; Morison 1936; Updegraff 1908). Morison (1936) illustrates the symptoms of these inadequacies in the statements of contemporary observers:

> In 1672 the Reverend Thomas Shepard of Charlestown [Massachusetts] declared: "There is a great decay in Inferiour Schools, it were well if that also were examined, and the Cause thereof removed. . . . " [Cotton Mather in 1689] speaks of "the too general Want of Education in the Rising Generation; which if not prevented, will gradually but speedily dispose us, to [a] sort of Criolian Degeneracy. . . . " (72)

After the first generation of settlement, the secular interests of the Massachusetts colonists expanded and diversified. The passage of the Half Way Covenant by the Synod of 1662 reflected this change dramatically. The covenant allowed people to join the church who, though baptized, were earlier excluded because they did not fully conform to the Puritan faith. The covenant, as Updegraff (1908) explains, "indicates a loosening of the religious bonds—a weakening of the former rigor in preserving a unity of ideals and of life" (86).

Colonial Schools

Boston, initially a tightly knit religious community, developed into a small urban center of domestic manufacture, commerce, and foreign trade, surrounded by a hinterland of relatively isolated clusters of rural households, where children were needed for farm labor. An increasing and diversifying population; exposure to the urban problems of crime, pauperism, and vagrancy; the appearance of refugees from Indian wars; and problems of public health and safety all posed difficulties that drew the attention of civic authorities. Similar developments occurred in the port cities of Newport, New Amsterdam, Philadelphia, and Charles Town in Carolina (Bridenbaugh 1964 [1938]). There was increasing interest among householders in their economic advancement and in the settlement of readily available land and a growing preoccupation with things secular in their adaptation to changing conditions of life.

These economic, social, and cultural changes created slowly but steadily growing sentiments that reinforced the effect of perceived inadequacies in family, apprenticeship, and church provision for the education of children. At a commensurately slow rate, schools were founded. In 1635 or 1636, the Boston town meeting had agreed that "Mr. Philemon Pormont shalbe intreated to become scholemaster for the teaching and nourtering of children wth us," the funds to be pledged by "the richer inhabitants" (Seybolt 1935b, 1, 33). It is not clear whether Pormont actually took the job (Small 1969 [1914], 3). According to Seybolt, the date of the first school building is unknown, but a new one was apparently constructed in 1655; not until 1684 was another one opened by the town. In 1720, Boston had two grammar and three writing schools, an arrangement that lasted until 1789 (Seybolt 1935b, 10). Other colonies founded schools equally slowly.

The earliest public provision for schooling consisted of grammar schools, starting instruction at about age 7 in both Latin and English (Johnson 1904, 3), to prepare older boys for entrance into Harvard College.

In 1655, entrance to Harvard required an ability to read Cicero, Virgil, or "any such ordinary classical authors," to speak or write Latin in prose and verse, and "to construe and grammatically to resolve ordinary Greek, as in the Greek Testament, Isocrates, and the minor poets." (Cremin 1970, 185)

To the extent that grammar schools were public schools, in the sense that they were sanctioned and financially supported by a town, they were open to the boys of all town members. Admission to a grammar school required the ability of boys to "stand up and read words of two syllables and keep their places" (Small 1969 [1914], 162); girls were not admitted.

Preparation for entrance to a grammar school remained the responsibility of the households. Parents taught their own children or sent them to dame schools (petty schools in Virginia). These schools were conducted by mothers who prepared their own children and also taught neighbor children for a fee (Cremin 1970, 128–129). Learning to read remained at the heart of household teaching, based on various combinations of written materials such as the hornbook (containing syllables and the Lord's Prayer or Apostles' Creed); the catechism; the Bible; and such texts as Edmund Coote's *The English Schoole-Maister*, which "went systematically from letters, syllables, and words, to sentences, paragraphs, and colloquies" (Cremin 1970, 129). The religious and skill content were inextricably entwined.

As a result of changing social and economic conditions of the colonies toward the latter part of the 17th century and increased military activity as a result of the Indian wars, the kind of grammar school preparation that led to admission to Harvard became decreasingly appropriate to the interests of young men. Schoolmasters had to teach more and more students who were unprepared for the classical curriculum. The grammar schools by necessity also had to provide instruction in the rudiments of reading and writing because families and dame schools failed to do so.

New Englanders stuck to the traditions of England "to bring up theyer children in Learninge" so that the next generation "may attaine some proficiency, whereby they may com to bee fitt for service to god in church and common wealth." They were, [however,] beginning to define "Learninge" in a new way, just as their English contemporaries were doing, leaning toward the practical and that which was useful immediately. (Axtell 1974, 177)

The late 17th century witnessed the appearance of different kinds of schools, which began to serve an increasing demand for education in the basic components of literacy and in preparation for employment in the trades and commerce and which made provision for education in towns whose populations and areas were growing.

In New England, for example, the geographic expansion of towns in the early 18th century combined with difficulties of terrain and climate to exacerbate conflicts concerning access to school (as well as to church). The moving school, a device for shifting the location of a grammar school to different parts of a town for fractions of the year, was a solution to this problem (Updegraff 1908).

Malden, in 1702, voted the school "to be kept at four several places at four several times, one quarter of a year in a place"; Amesbury, in 1711, voted "that the school should be kept the first four months at the meetinghouse, the next four months at the Pond's Hill fort, and the last four months at Left. Foot's fort or thereabouts" (Small 1969 [1914], 66).

The great variety of such arrangements, designed to serve the interests of an increasingly dispersed population, meant considerable disparities in the availability of and exposure to schooling, depending on the wealth and political alignments of each town that adopted the scheme. The moving school provides evidence of a strong tendency to shift educational activity into schools and away from other agencies, but without clear agreement about who should be taught or for how long. Nevertheless, an organizational basis for the emergence of curriculum was beginning to develop.

The early 18th century also saw the rapid expansion of private venture education, which provided instruction in the skills required for the artisan trades and commerce and in their underlying principles. A sense of what these schools taught is provided in newspaper advertisements of the day:

Opposite to the Mitre Tavern in Fish-street near to Scarlets-Wharff, Boston, are Taught Writing, Arithmetick in all its parts; And also Geometry, Trigonometry, Plain and Sphaerical, Surveying, Dialling, Gauging, Navigation, Astronomy. . . . (Seybolt 1935a, 11).

At the house of Mr. George Brownell . . . is taught Writing, Cyphering, Dancing, Treble Violin, Flute, Spinnet, &c. Also English and French Quilting, Imbroidery, Flourishing, Plain Work. . . . (12)

To be taught . . . The Principles of Algebra, Sir Isaac Newton's incomparable Method of Fluxions, or any of Universal Methods of Investigation used by the Moderns, Conic Sections, the Doctrine of Curves; or any Part of Speculative Mathematicks. . . . (18)

These excerpts illustrate only a small fraction of the stunning array of private instruction offered by individual teachers and announced by public advertisement. This teaching was overwhelmingly practical in content, serving secular household and artistic interests, especially for females, as well as being oriented toward a labor market for males in which a multiplicity of trades and commercial activities were represented. Kaestle (1973), describing the situation in mid-18th-century New York City, referred to teaching as one of the trades, not as an occupation, in which individuals offered instruction in one or more skills for payment. The men who taught usually did other things for a living, and their schools lacked an institutionalized basis as places for learning.

The evening school was still another variety of private school. It came into being in mid-17th-century New Amsterdam in connection with apprenticeship. Seybolt (1925, 13) states, "One of the earliest references to an evening school in the English colonies occurs in a Harlem apprenticeship-indenture of November 25, 1690, in which the master promised that his apprentice 'shall have the privilege of going to the evening school.'" Courses of instruction resembled those of the private schools noted earlier. However, for the particular benefit of indentured servants, the evening schools also stressed reading, writing, and arithmetic, the last often distinguished into its elementary and more occupationally specialized components. For example, "Thomas Carroll . . . offered instruction in 'Writing and Arithmetick both Vulgar and Decimal, Interest and Annuities, Extraction of Roots of all Powers . . .'" (24).

Instruction in arithmetic and mathematics affords an illuminating example of the way in which the market for education expanded and diversified in the 18th-century colonies. We can see the gradual emergence of subject matters as topics of public discourse. In the early colonial period, arithmetic and mathematics were not included among the components of education. These subjects lacked the religious foundation that would have brought them into the education that first family, apprenticeship, and church and then the school and civil state conducted. Patricia Cohen (1982) observes that some colonies in the 18th century extended apprenticeship regulations to obligate masters "to include 'cyphering as far as the rule of three'" (124).

The impetus for instruction in arithmetic arose out of market demand for quantitative skills in a burgeoning commercial economy and in a society by now self-conscious about republican principles and those of civil society. In the late 18th century, a shift to a decimal from the English monetary system simplified calculations, a move understood and defended as a democratizing of commerce that would bring monetary calculation within the range of ordinary people. Arithmetic now was included with reading and writing as a basic skill. Here economic demand and ideology were closely linked. Rational mental capacities were deemed important for the citizen of a democracy and participant in a market economy. "Decimal money and arithmetic education were justified as fruits of republican ideology; numeracy was hailed as a cornerstone of free markets and a free society" (P. C. Cohen 1982, 127).

The case of arithmetic is especially instructive because it represents an attempt to justify the inclusion of a particular body of knowledge into the work of schools. Such an effort would have made little sense in the 17th century because schools had not yet emerged as organizations devoted to the dissemination of discrete bodies of knowledge. The latter part of the 18th century witnessed the early emergence of schools as repositories of knowledge and of subjects as discrete bodies of knowledge. In sum, only now did schools emerge as singular settings for the dissemination of specialized knowledge, providing growing reasons to justify and argue about the inclusion of incipient subjects into what was taught.

Curriculum and Educational Organization

To sum up, during the greater part of the colonial period, until roughly the middle of the 18th century, there was a broad popular and elite agreement about what a child and young person should learn. However, this agreement did not include an explicit understanding of curriculum, nor did it embrace beliefs about the way education should be organized to impart a curriculum. Learning and teaching were a part of life.

Trying to describe the nature of this agreement by reference to a connection between curriculum and school organization is clearly wrong. Until close to the end of the 17th century, the school as an organizational entity distinct from family, church, and apprenticeship scarcely existed. Although these social agencies imparted knowledge—skills, beliefs, and moral standards—that young people learned through daily participation, they did not exist primarily to convey knowledge. Learning how to read, to gain knowledge, to beat the devil, to gain salvation, to know how to live in the community were not tantamount to acquiring specialized skills; each was implicit in the world of the child or young person.

Concepts of curriculum or of what schools did with curricula do not capture the way in which knowledge spread into and among the colonies and their inhabitants. It is more appropriate to think about ideas related to religion, commerce, technology, agriculture, and manufacture spreading along networks formed by traders, relatives, missionaries, and immigrants and the circulation of written materials between England and the colonies, as well as within and between them (Cremin 1970). Education came about through traffic in ideas within and across generations, as well as across places, not primarily through specialized institutions that sponsored and conveyed standardized bodies of knowledge.

This period largely lacked distinct, uniform ideas about a class of young people that we would now call students. The invention of the moving school and the multiple uses of the term "free school," for example, testify to this lack of uniformity. "In Roxbury, the term 'free' meant free to the children of subscribers, in Salem free to all poor children, in Ipswich free to a limited number of children, and in Dedham free to all children . . ." (Cremin 1970, 193). The various senses in which a school was thought of as free meant variation in who was likely to attend and what knowledge they would be exposed to.

With the exception of rough notions about sufficient facility in reading and writing prior to entrance to grammar school, colonial education lacked a clear sense of the sequential acquisition of knowledge. In addition to the fact that responsibility for education was spread among several overlapping agencies, years of school attendance, bodies of knowledge to be mastered, the duration of school terms, the progression of subjects, and the qualifications of teachers were not fixed. In fact, there was no clear definition of which agencies were responsible for imparting different kinds of knowledge. The centrality of family, church, and apprenticeship in education and the coexistence of dame school, grammar school, moving school, and private venture school all provide evidence of this ambiguity and variety of definition.

Although at no period is the school the only educational institution, during the colonial period the notion of the school as an institution with a substantial specialized responsibility for education was largely absent. Modern ideas about curriculum and schools are essentially built around this latter conception. The late colonial period witnessed signs of the gradual emergence of differentiation in educational functions, such as the appearance of private entrepreneurial schools, to provide specialized training in skills necessary to earn a living and maintain a household.

Remember that arithmetic, mathematics, and related areas were not part of early colonial family, school, church, or apprenticeship instruction. These topics gradually entered the educational realm through private efforts of a utilitarian kind, not through any conception of mathematics (along with reading) as basic categories of knowledge that the schools had responsibility to impart. Although schools and other agencies, differing so much in organizational form, clearly transmitted knowledge and skills, it would distort reality to impute to them a curriculum, a term that suggests bodies of knowledge organized within an explicit educational agenda and designed for specified populations of students.

Important developments occurred during the late 18th and early 19th centuries that transformed these loose and dispersed educational efforts into prototypical forms of educational systems. Early in the colonial period, precedents had been set for dealing with educational matters through political means. Colonies and towns enacted laws that established the conditions under which schools of certain kinds were to be founded and financed. They also specified sanctions for failure to comply with the law. There were substantial differences from colony to colony and from town to town within colonies in access to the schools. Yet as Cremin (1951) has documented, a consensus was developing that foreshadowed the concept of a common school in which children from all social conditions would be welcome. This concept, with its implications for educational equality primarily in the students' early years, also represented an educational unit of roughly common organizational form, a departure from the highly diversified agencies of the colonial period.

During the transition from colonial education to the evolving school systems of the middle and late 19th century, educators addressed in both public and political arenas the question of what common schools would teach. As education became more systematically and explicitly organized in the 19th century, the public school system replaced the haphazard collection of colonial public and private educational ventures. What bodies of knowledge were to be taught, how long a school term should be, and how many terms would be offered or required became matters of explicit public policy.

FROM NATIONHOOD TO 1865

The transition began early in the 19th century. Cremin (1951), pointing up the contrast with the colonial period, states that by the early 19th century the question of what to teach was addressed

> in terms of subjects. When the educators of this period wanted the school to deal with this area or that, it was always regarded as a matter of the teacher *teaching* a given body of material to the student, and the student *learning* this material. Although there was much discussion about the cultivation of certain desirable attitudes, the means of cultivation always involved a certain body of content, the mastery of which would give rise to the desired values in the student. (62)

This development, the presentation of knowledge in a subject format that defines what common schools are supposed to convey, provides an ideational and organizational foundation for a modern conception of school curriculum, a conception that the earlier variegated forms of educational enterprise could not support. Evidence that supports the idea of subject matter schooling is found in New York State legislation of 1795 that appropriated a matching grant to counties "for the encouragement of [charity and 'other'] schools where the common subjects were taught." The law stated that the money should be used to maintain schools where children learned English, arithmetic, mathematics, "and other branches of knowledge as are most useful and necessary to complete a good English education." (Kaestle 1973, 65)

Nevertheless, as Kaestle (1973) reports, the disbursement of the funds got caught up in disputes over whether government or teacher groups should apportion them and which schools should qualify. At the same time, the notion of what a public school was also began to change from "places open to the public where children learned together . . . to places of education erected and maintained with governmental assistance and administered either by governmental representatives or a surrogate board acceptable to them" (69).

The institutionalization of school curriculum and organization was a principal educational fruit of the first half of the 19th century. In this process, three forces were principally at work:

1. The emergence of local communities as dynamic educational markets, especially in the years leading up to 1830;
2. The consolidation of individual, publicly supported schools into town or township districts, with resulting gains of territory and population size, diversity, and wealth (gaining force midway in the period);
3. A subsequent growth in the complexity and centralization of power within these districts.

We shall discuss these matters first in general terms and then illustrate how these forces worked themselves out in the evolving St. Louis public school district, which is a good example of the course of 19th-century school district development throughout the American North and West. We shall draw for this purpose on Troen's (1975) excellent study of public education in St. Louis.

As the American population came increasingly to settle in cities and towns, these communities became centers of demand for various kinds of schooling or training. They gained occupational and cultural diversity as the citizenry became more heterogeneous and as a developing economy created new jobs, especially in manufacturing and commerce. Industrial and commercial development sustained a growing middle class, which could afford the costs of educating sons and, on occasion, daughters.

As demand for an educated citizenry increased in response to nation building and economic growth, instruction in an explicit, subject-ordered curriculum became even more than in the preceding period the responsibility of schools and teachers. This development was a departure from the past, when such responsibility was more widely diffused among agencies other than the schools. This early stage of institutionalization is extremely important because it shaped all future developments of school organization and curriculum.

The 19th-century story, according to Cremin (1980), has two chief elements: the expansion and specification of demand for education, which was an outcome of competing interests consequent on growing population diversity and continuing economic growth, and a resulting differentiation of school organization and elaboration of what was taught to incorporate new subject matter or more advanced or extensive treatment of extant subjects. As schools became more complex and formalized, to accommodate larger and more heterogeneous numbers of students, they adapted to the presentation of the accepted subject matter as discrete blocks of time within the work of a single classroom, as separate courses within a student's school day, or as a sequence of subjects alternating or succeeding one another over a longer period. This subject-ordered curriculum also provided the base for curricular elaboration by adding new subjects and subject coverage in a linear process. This process meant that school organization would develop as a progressively segmented arrangement, with more subjects (or parts of them) embodied in each school day in a structure of courses and classrooms and extended in a temporal sequence.

These are matters of some import. One can argue that this curricular frame accelerated the transformation of the earlier common conception of citizenship education into diverse offerings for varieties of citizens. Yet this transformation took place within the formally unitary structure of the public school and school district, and it directed the development of American education toward a common rather than streamed national system. As we shall see, it was the emergence of the unitary system that led the public high school and the fee-charging academy to become competitors for the same body of students rather than components of an evolving system, each serving a distinct student pool (Grizzell 1923; Inglis 1911).

Markets and the Unitary System

Cremin (1980, especially 388–399) gives a fine account of the market-driven diversification of schools that characterized the first third of the 19th century. We shall draw heavily on his interpretation. In the process of diversification that Cremin describes, the expansion of numbers of schools and students that had begun in the later colonial years continued, so that schooling soon became widely available in the more settled places.

At first, the colonial diversity of schools remained—semiformal schools in rural kitchens and churches, charity schools in New York City and Philadelphia, town schools in New England, church-supported systems (Quaker, Episcopalian, and Presbyterian), academies, and special-purpose private venture schools. As before, the private venture schools were segregated by gender, offering useful commercial skills for boys and either economically useful skills like sewing or refined attainments like French or piano playing for girls.

At the elementary level, however, the various educators of colonial times, tradespersons, ministers, schoolmasters, and so on, gave way early in the federal period to the district school and its teachers. The district school succeeded the moving school and was produced by competition among expanding towns whose inhabitants wanted the schools for young children to be located near where they lived (Updegraff 1908).

Although the provision of common elementary education remained a responsibility and interest of local governments throughout the 19th century, how this provision was to be made became a matter of considerable debate and interest-driven conflict during the Jacksonian years. At first, responsibility for elementary education was dispersed to independently acting town and township districts (Grizzell 1923; Inglis 1911; Troen 1975). This arrangement was adapted to a dispersed population, often insufficient fiscal means, and in many localities a democratic ideology antithetical to the centralization of powers.

In a reaction by educational reformers, local elites, and Whig and more moderate Democratic political leaders to a common education they thought was inadequate in content and quality, the small districts were combined into town or township districts. This process had advanced considerably by the Civil War years in most of the northern and western parts of the country.

These districts were responsible for all the local common schools. Each operated numbers of elementary schools, providing the same subjects to pupils whatever the school they attended. Wherever town or township districts were established, efficiency and economy were the professed rationale of reformers and other public figures and educators who pressed for this program of organizational unification. However, a plausible case can also be made that in the larger number of American cities policy making was driven by such interests as those of teachers and administrators, employers, and ethnic communities. Very likely, similar though less well-documented events took place in the smaller towns and countryside. The emergence of the town- and township-wide district was an early stage of a trend toward both curricular and organizational rationalization within the frame of local government.

At the secondary level, despite the variety of sponsorship and the curricular diversity of private venture education, the schools of the federal period in fact had evolved into three principal curricular kinds: the English school, the Latin grammar school, and the academy. The Latin grammar school (mostly in the eastern cities and larger towns) accepted boys aged 9 or 10, on the often erroneous assumption that they could read and write English and knew some English grammar. It led them through a four- or five-year curriculum of Latin and Greek, with a modicum of history, geography, geometry, algebra, and trigonometry.

First established in Boston, the English school provided at public expense an alternative to the Latin grammar school for those who wanted to continue their schooling in English. The English school stressed reading, spelling, writing, arithmetic, and (somewhat less often) geography and history. In the colonial years, this school at first had provided both elementary and secondary education in one building, enrolling students between the ages of 2 and 14. Very soon, in more populous places, the English school was divided by age, so that primary and secondary students and subjects were located in separate buildings or departments. This division occurred at age 8 or 9. The elementary level of the English school was thereafter absorbed into the district school. The secondary level remained as one element of the array of secondary schools that was available during the federal years.

The academy, in turn, was a private venture, eclectic agglomeration of the English and Latin school curricula, shaped according to local demand. It was usually found away from the largest centers of population. To supply revenues sufficient to their operation, the greater number of the academies tried to attract students from a little distance by offering boarding arrangements.

Differences in organizational form and sponsorship proved to be critical elements in the further development of American secondary schools. Smaller communities soon sought to imitate the Boston model by providing an alternative to the classical course in a town-sponsored high school. However, in these places this public high school quickly became a comprehensive school that offered the choice of an English or a classical course. It charged at most a very small tuition and thus was a public counterpart to the more expensive academy.

Indeed, the principal story of secondary education between 1810 and 1830 is the spread of the comprehensive high school as a part of the graded local public school district. Graded classes, which outcompeted Lancasterian schooling by being more attractive to republican sentiment (Cremin 1980, 396), divided pupils into presumably more manageable and instructionally suitable groups and thus promoted efficient education. It did not otherwise divide the unified curriculum, and it made gradations of subject matter difficulty, content sequence, and coverage more formal. In effect, the public high school continued and intensified the student's primary school course of study, forming a rung on a unitary curricular and organizational ladder.

As the public high school rose, the academy declined, as did private venture schooling. Consequently, a segmental form of secondary school organization spread rapidly. In this pattern, discrete courses were taught within discrete classrooms. These curricular and organizational changes went hand in hand. The evolving segmental curriculum represented not only a structure of instructional content but also a structure of teachers' work, a division of instructional labor that increasingly characterized the public high schools.

This segmented structure allowed schools to assign students to courses according to ability, accomplishment, or preference. The evolving secondary system now could encompass a student population that was increasingly heterogeneous in social and economic origins, abilities, and interests. Had the public, comprehensive high school not supplanted the academy, the curricular and organizational ground would have been prepared for the development of a streamed national educational system in the United States.

District Expansion and the Unitary System

The town or township district provided a base for the establishment of graded, common education. Its primary schools provided the academic preparation that could make the district's public high school accessible to more students than before and to students of more heterogeneous social origins, interests, and expectations. In addition, these larger districts provided tax dollars to underwrite district-administered high schools, and the graded structure of common education could easily be extended upward to incorporate secondary education.

The rapid spread of the unitary system in the northern and western United States can be attributed in part to the growing supply (in variety and breadth of distribution) of inexpensive textbooks in virtually all subjects of the primary, high school, and (early in the process) grammar school curricula (Cremin 1980, 390–394). These texts allowed even relatively small communities to offer a comparatively full version of a standard curriculum, although even in the latter half of the 19th century many small rural districts relied principally on the books that children brought from home (Fuller 1982).

From the early 1800s onward, at the secondary level this standard curriculum had undergone continuing linear expansion—for example, the addition of French and sewing for girls; bookkeeping and science for boys; and elocution, physiology, drawing, and music for both. By about 1830, the core secondary school subjects of spelling, reading, writing, arithmetic, grammar, history, and geography were available in many settled places.

One might argue that this curricular differentiation both followed on and fostered an increasing diversity of enrollment in the secondary schools, but in either case school organization had to adapt to the diversity. It is probably true that in the less settled places, the core subjects at best were all that was available and were taught in one-room schools to students who attended only intermittently. Nevertheless, in its essentials what was taught in these schools by 1830 was cut from the same curricular cloth as were the public school offerings elsewhere.

The availability of texts was by no means the whole story of the rise of the public high school within the unitary curriculum and district. As these local districts grew, they provided a level of funding, a means of control, and a degree of curricular formalization that were no less important than access to texts. We have seen that through ready recruitment of students and a low price, the public high school soon became a feature of the larger number of school districts, outperforming its competitors in the provision of secondary education. However, the enlarged districts did still more. They provided local standardization of the content of elementary education, an organizational and fiscal base for the professionalization of teachers, and local centralization of instructional responsibility.

More specifically, these districts afforded the organizational means through which curricular content could be not only standardized by grade across schools but also integrated across grades school by school. Moreover, they provided a frame for and stimulus to the work of educational professionals in local settings that now often were free of such competitors as the academy or the private venture school. In this way, they fostered a professional consensus that transcended localities and was a means of local professional power (often near autonomy). Taken together, these consequences of district organization later led to the wide diffusion and consequent convergence of both curricular and organizational forms in the United States. This agreement was advanced further by the professional administrators who, in increasing numbers, were being hired to oversee the unitary districts. Some of them, like William Torrey Harris in St. Louis, by virtue of the prominence of their districts and the force of their arguments, became potent agents for disseminating ideas about best teaching practice.

The fruits of this convergence of professional curricular doctrines is well documented by Inglis (1911) for developments in Massachusetts and by Mann (1928) for a sample of 444 cities in the United States. The data that Inglis presents show clearly that by the 1860s in Massachusetts, the high school curriculum had developed into statewide, graded offerings, often departmentalized by broad field. These offerings embraced such relatively specialized fields as composition, rhetoric, declamation, and literature, within English; algebra, geometry, trigonometry, and surveying, within mathematics; French, Greek, and Latin, within foreign languages; ancient and modern European history and history of the United States, within history; natural philosophy, chemistry, astronomy, physiology, botany, and geology, within science; and such other subjects as bookkeeping, drawing, and music. Some high schools presented even more intensively specialized subjects, although some, almost certainly, offered less in practice than they promised.

Mann's (1928) data, reporting proportions of the high school day given to various subjects, are consistent with the picture drawn by Inglis (1911) for Massachusetts. However, they suggest a greater range of variation, perhaps commensurate with the greater range of school districts covered, and in general a modest rather than a highly intensive level of subject matter specialization. Nevertheless, these data provide good evidence of the concurrent specialization of curriculum and intensification of the division of teachers' labor.

Complexity and Centralization

From 1830 through the 1850s, local political structures generally became more complex and centralized in the North and West, and there was a parallel increase in complexity and centralization within the educational arena. As a result, the organizational structures through which school policies were made, and the more and more professional educators and administrators who made them, became increasingly significant elements and actors in curricular development. School organization now began to grow into specialized offices and distinct levels of authority and responsibility. It thereby gained the capacity to buffer or screen external political and intellectual influences and became to a degree less directly responsive to local preferences for schooling. As a result, school organization appeared not only as a structure of teachers' work but also as a structure of curricular decision making and control.

Once the public elementary and high schools were embraced by the unitary curricular and organizational system, they could be readily adapted to changing demand for subject matter by linear incorporation or elimination, the processes documented by Inglis (1911) and Mann (1928). The local centralization of curricular decision making and control could proceed without the restraining effects that might have resulted from a more interdependent structure of teachers' work. The segmental pattern of instructional organization allowed teachers to act independently of one another and to adapt their work to changes of curricular content or structure without serious effects on the work of other teachers. It could thereby accommodate subject matter of virtually any level of differentiation.

As a result, the key issue in the relationship between school organization and curriculum moved from the domain of teaching to the domain of administration and governance. There, professionalized high school principals and district superintendents, in bureaucratic offices that were oriented especially to local political events and broader occupational and professional intellectual movements, could alter school curricula by adding or subtracting subjects or programs, reasonably confident that the teaching force would adapt to these changes without much stress.

Consequences for Later Curricular Change

In sum, by about 1870 both elementary and high schools in the greater part of the United States approximated current curricular and organizational structures, namely, the "egg crate" form in which the elementary school class and the high school day are divided segmentally into a large number of subject-specific periods (Cremin 1980; Hogan 1985; Labaree 1988). This pattern now was to become more securely institutionalized, gaining legitimacy on a pedagogical base provided by faculty psychology; it was to become further entrenched in the educational system by virtue of the rise of the Carnegie unit (Kliebard 1986). However, the pattern had been set earlier. These later developments should therefore be seen as reinforcing rather than initiating forces. They are important, nonetheless.

By the early part of the 20th century, curricular reformers felt that their efforts were at best difficult and most likely doomed because the segmental structure of schooling was an intractable barrier to a curriculum set up on any other than a subject-intensive basis. In the reformers' view, the segmented school structure would be virtually impossible to dislodge because of widespread teacher acceptance, the systemic connection between school and college provided by the Carnegie unit, and an apparent consistency with lay and administrative preferences for businesslike efficiency in education.

In an address delivered while he was head of the University of Chicago Laboratory School, John Dewey (1901) described the more recent history of American education as a series of failed efforts at reform. He attributed this failure primarily to organizational features of the school that grouped students by grade and subject, recruited teachers to teach in this format, and rewarded them for doing so. Trying to temper the zeal of fellow reformers, Dewey reminded his audience "that it is precisely such things as these that really control the whole system, even on its distinctively educational side" (338).

St. Louis

The principal dimensions of change that we have identified in American 19th-century public school curricula and organization were clearly visible in St. Louis. (In this section, we draw heavily on Troen 1975, especially 5–54 and 141–156.) In 1838, the city established a public school district by opening two common schools that together enrolled 288 pupils. By that time, St. Louis was already on the way toward its standing as one of the great 19th-century American boom towns, favored by its location at the meeting of the Mississippi and Missouri rivers, the invention of the steamboat and the expansion of river transportation, and the flood of westward-bound immigrants. These forces combined to make the city a major entrepôt and transportation center for goods and people alike.

Keeping pace with the economic growth of St. Louis, its school district by the last decades of the century had become an important urban system, enrolling something like 80,000 elementary school students and an impressive number of high school students. For public education, the district had become a national curricular and organizational model, led by Superintendent William Torrey Harris. Harris was one of the period's great professional leaders in public education and one of its most articulate spokespersons on curricular policy.

In the years that preceded the opening of the district schools in St. Louis, those who could afford the fees enjoyed a considerable diversity of educational possibilities. St. Louis had been founded in 1764 and was already a major trading center by the beginning of the 19th century. This economic expansion was accompanied by a commensurate growth of demand for schooling, with a diversity that reflected the increasing variety of interests found in a nascent mercantile city. By the late 1700s, there were French classes for both boys and girls, and by 1808, the first English school. Soon there were also several academies and convent schools, operated by teaching orders in the heavily Roman Catholic settlement, and many private venture schools that catered to the sons and daughters of the wealthy. These schools tried to differentiate themselves in the market by offering training in one or another special skill or body of knowledge, extending to music and dancing classes and the services of fencing masters. Meanwhile, for those who could not afford schooling, there were mission schools operated by Catholic teaching orders and charity schools sponsored by the Protestant churches.

As the century advanced and St. Louis grew into a major industrial and commercial center, it acquired the specialized occupational structure, range of class interests, and rich mixture of native and immigrant population groups that characterize such places. Despite this increasing economic and demographic heterogeneity, St. Louis lost much of its earlier variety of schools and school sponsorship. From the outset in 1838, the St. Louis school district followed the organizational example set in the East and provided for professional administration: a superintendent and school principals. These professionals, along with business leaders and even some of the educational entrepreneurs, formed the leadership that brought the common school movement to St. Louis.

This leadership initially faced the not uncommon task of cleansing public education of a reputation as education for paupers. It accomplished this task successfully by building first-class buildings (including a central high school built in 1855 for the then very large sum of $50,000), hiring good teachers (for a time training them in the district's own normal school), and offering courses that attracted the sons of merchants and professionals by preparing them either directly for business or for college.

By 1860, the district's leaders were following a rationale of administrative and fiscal efficiency and were guided by a principle of curricular uniformity in a district that was steadily adding common schools and pupils. Consequently, the district adopted a graded, progressively differentiated curriculum in the elementary schools that led into a high school that exemplified fully the subject-specialized curriculum described by Inglis (1911) and Mann (1928). This curriculum could not be matched by any of the private venture schools of the city, and high school enrollment grew apace with population increase (the latter doubling, e.g., from 79,000 to 160,000 during the 1850s). Not every potential student in fact enrolled, and the high school drew most heavily from the more affluent wards in the city.

Although religious schools remained an important part of the educational scene in St. Louis and some secular private schools remained as well, the public high school dominated. It was firmly embedded in a district bureaucracy that could supply revenues, students who had experienced something like a uniform course of preparation, and teachers competent in its special subjects. At the same time, the segmentally structured St. Louis public high school, like its counterparts elsewhere, could easily adapt to changing student and parent demands. It was a formidable competitor.

IMPLICATIONS FOR UNDERSTANDING ORGANIZATIONS

The case of American common education, as we have sketched it, has interesting implications for current approaches to the study of formal organizations. These implications are worth considering in themselves and help us understand what the case materials mean. Four major strands in this literature deal variously with conditions that affect the emergence of formal organizations or with mechanisms involved in their structural development. Our story, in a highly schematic form, is this. Once education had become a matter of public awareness, a dynamic, expanding social and economic environment created local markets that stimulated a diversity of educational content and organizational forms. Subsequently, local elites, within a supporting context of republican ideology, belief in businesslike procedures, and popular economic and occupational ambitions, used the tools of government to bring something like the full spectrum of curriculum within a unified public organization. Once this organization was in place, its privileged access to the public purse allowed it to outcompete all other varieties of schooling.

This story is at variance with much of the organizational literature. First, with respect to organizational genesis or establishment, a principal line of argument (Williamson 1975) contends that organizations emerge when markets are less efficient coordinators of human activities than formal organizations (i.e., are more costly at the margin). However, the joint curricular and organizational evolution of American schools suggests that the way curriculum and institutional structure changed had very little to do with efficiency derived from coordination. Although the unitary school district was justified in part by assertions of its efficiency, both the curricular and organizational developments that we have described were powerfully motivated by elite and popular conceptions of the public interest.

For example, the public high school embodied a conception of the best ways to prepare productive citizens, initially articulated by educational reformers in the common school movement and then advocated by such professional leaders as W. T. Harris. These conceptions, endorsed by local voters, informed and motivated the way secondary schooling was incorporated into the curriculum and organization of the unitary districts. Thus, these districts emerged as instruments that could be used by local elites to ensure that common and secondary education, by virtue of content and cost, was widely accessible. The high school replaced the academy in large part because it cost less to attend, but this cost advantage was almost certainly more the result of public subvention than of administrative efficiency, whatever the claims of superintendents and school boards. The unit district was an organizational device that allowed the burden of this subvention to be spread among all or most of the local taxpayers.

Second, most students of organizations envision organizational change as a process of differentiation in which organizational functions or activities (e.g., school subjects) and corresponding organizational units (e.g., high school departments) accumulate in an organization through linear additions. In this process, the structure of organizations becomes progressively more complex and elaborate as a consequence of gains in the volume and complexity of work (e.g., Blau and Schoenherr 1971; M. W. Meyer 1985). In effect, this argument assumes that organizations are established with a certain set of activities and a structure made up of corresponding operating units, an administrative unit, and the relationships between these operating and administrative parts.

Although this formulation fits fairly well the curricular and organizational evolution of American public education after about 1830, it is not a reasonable summary of the events of the preceding two centuries. At the secondary level, what during the colonial period had been an agreed-upon set of subjects and instructional procedures in the Latin grammar schools became, early in the national period, increasingly diversified. However, this diversification did not take the form of a more complex grammar school curriculum. Rather, gains in the strength and heterogeneity of demand for schooling fostered an array of subject offerings, each distinctive of specific kinds of schools such as academies, public high schools, and various more specialized private venture schools. Each of these kinds of schools catered to a specific clientele.

At the elementary level, there was from the start an agreed-upon realm of rather undifferentiated knowledge, centered on literacy and morality, combined with some training in a trade. This realm of knowledge was gradually expanded, consolidated, and reexpanded in response to a growing preoccupation with secular considerations and a more and more diverse student body, as well as the ideas of an increasingly professionalized group of educators and school reformers. As we have seen, the emergence first of the district school and then of the elementary sector of the town and township districts was as much a matter of interest-driven politics and decision making as it was of reformist concern for efficiency.

So far as the secondary schools were concerned, the years leading up to the Civil War were a period in which the variety of schools diminished, and their several sets of offerings were gathered together into a comprehensive, public high school that catered to many different kinds of students—diverse in social origins, interests, and capabilities. The public, comprehensive high school replaced its chief competitor, the academy, and the other varieties of private venture schools, not because of greater organizational efficiency, as we have already noted, nor because its offerings were intrinsically more attractive to the greater number of students or families, but in large part because local public policy increasingly favored the public subvention of common school education, thereby giving the public high school a price advantage that few parents, whatever their means, could overlook.

In any event, these processes do not resemble very closely the conventional view of organizational change as chiefly a matter of the linear functional and structural differentiation within organizations. Rather, by about 1850, out of a complicated and somewhat shambling set of events in which organizations and their activities multiplied and recombined, there arose the two principal parts of what we now know as the public school system—the elementary school and the comprehensive high school. Only subsequently did they form within one coherent organizational frame—the school district, which then fostered their curricular integration into graded courses of study spanning the years from kindergarten or first grade through the senior year of high school.

Third, these events are no better depicted by another reigning argument in organizational studies—that organizations change in function and structure as a result of the capacity of certain social forms to outcompete others by virtue of greater fitness to environmental opportunity or constraint (e.g., Hannan and Freeman 1977; Stinchcombe 1965). On the surface, this argument might seem to square with the course of events that we have just summarized. However, note that the high school was at a competitive advantage with respect to the academy not because of its social or curricular form (since the two had become very much alike early in the 1800s) but simply because it cost the consumer less for essentially the same curricular product.

Indeed, the rise of the unitary district and the segmental curriculum and organization of the high school can be understood in institutional terms (J. W. Meyer 1977) as the consequence of a process of social construction in which both curriculum and school became objectified as symbols and instruments of the common school ideal. Curriculum and school were sufficiently flexible to embrace numerous local variants and approximations of this ideal without excessive, or at least unduly apparent, strain. However, social constructions alone were not sufficient to induce the changes that we have described. They provided a community of belief and interest among local elites and citizens that enabled political and civic leaders and school reformers to bring the fiscal and administrative resources of government into the arena of educational action. It was this action that created a form of curriculum and schooling that was at once highly adaptive to changing demand and enrollment, resistant to curricular and instructional doctrines at variance with its core structural elements, and secure in the prospect of continuing public subvention.

CONCLUSIONS

In this chapter we have argued that curriculum and the organization of schools are related aspects of educational institutions. Their relationship, however, is anything but simple and straightforward. The meaning of curriculum itself is far from self-evident. As an element of schooling, it is a phenomenon to be explained, not assumed. In the colonial period, by way of illustration, schools were not the primary agency of education. Their contributions to raising the next generation were shared with families, churches, and familylike apprenticeship arrangements for training in crafts and trades. And although there was substantial agreement about what education should comprise, what knowledge, skills, beliefs, and habits of mind it should impart, it would distort the picture of colonial education to speak of the curriculum of the school.

A most conspicuous characteristic of schools during the first two centuries of American history was their extraordinary variety, ranging from grammar schools that prepared students for entrance to Harvard College to the dame schools and to the private educational ventures that offered training in skilled trades, household activities, and leisure pursuits in a society becoming increasingly attentive to its economic viability, areal expansion, and population increase. The multiplicity of educational ventures in school settings represented a source of diverse institutional forms that in the course of time became assembled into structures that we now call school systems, one of whose key elements is an institutionalized curriculum consisting of bodies of subject matter knowledge the schools are responsible to impart.

Both the education of young people and the early formation of schools, even though few in number, were supported by the legislative action of governments (e.g., the General Court in Massachusetts and town governments). Early in American history both education and schooling became matters of government interest and the subject of public policy, including such questions as who was eligible to attend school, how schools should be supported financially, where they should be located, and how sanctions should be meted out when public law was violated (Updegraff 1908; Vinovskis 1985). Concerning knowledge conveyed in schools and other educational settings, an array of ideational influences came into play: Tudor and Stuart ideas about education; Puritan religious influences; nationalistic ideas pertaining to the nature of Americanism; and considerations related to the marketplace, where the demand for skilled tradespersons and commercial workers derived from an expanding economy. These secular influences expanded at the expense of dedication to building a Puritan commonwealth.

The key elements of early 19th-century educational development included the consolidation of publicly supported schools into districts, accompanied by the inclusion of subjects previously taught in both publicly supported and privately run schools. There was an increasing tendency for knowledge transmitted in a diversity of settings to become school subjects—mathematics being a case in point. This branch of knowledge was largely absent from the educational ventures of the colonial period but later became incorporated into school-based bodies of knowledge. With these developments we can refer to a phenomenon now recognizable as a curriculum located in a particular kind of school organization.

We can think about education in this period as becoming embodied in a form of school organization that enabled schools to offer subjects, to add them, and to remove them. In addition, the emergence of the classroom, the widely distributed textbook, and the gradation of knowledge by difficulty (the last derived from Lancasterian principles) represent the components that were developing into a set of curricular arrangements and became embodied in organizational structure and institutionalized as modern schools.

One of the last stages of this historical process was the emerging preeminence of the public high school over its competitors, a development that established continuity at the secondary level with common school principles that had become established at the elementary level as far back as the colonial period. Events leading to the emergence of the public high school, organized on a comprehensive basis, also inhibited the development of secondary schools specialized according to curriculum and to type or clientele, a pattern that predominated on the Continent. (See Clark 1983 for a discussion of the integration of American secondary schools with elementary schools and of European secondary schools with universities.)

In sum, we regard the structure of American schools as a particular kind of curricular organization that grew out of a diverse array of educational arrangements. The mature form of American schools emerged shortly after the middle of the 19th century. These schools were organized around a kind of curricular format in which graded subjects, treated as units and presented in classrooms, could be added to and subtracted from a school's offerings. Under this scheme, specialized teachers took independent responsibility for imparting subject matter knowledge, under the general direction of a professionalized district administration responsive to the interests of the citizens of local communities. Exceptions to this pattern, of course, were found in the late 19th and early 20th centuries in rural areas whose schools possessed some structural characteristics prevalent in the 18th century (Fuller 1982). Although historians have made much of the growth of school district management during this period and of the corresponding advance of school bureaucracy (Callahan 1962, Tyack 1974), in contrast we have focused on the centrality of curriculum in understanding the structure of schools. In no way does this emphasis gainsay the importance of bureaucratic development over the past century. Indeed, the development of curriculum in the form of unitized subjects long before the growth and diffusion of school bureaucracies undoubtedly facilitated the later bureaucratization of schools and school systems. These subjects provided standardized units of educational organization—subject matter, classrooms, and standard time units—stuff of a kind that bureaucracies thrive on.

In the American context, curricular content and the organizational form of schools have become linked and institutionalized in joint form. The most significant indication of their juncture was the fact that schools became the predominant repository of curricular knowledge, a phenomenon that occurred for the most part early in the 19th century.

In the beginning of this chapter, we observed that in modern societies, the institutionalization of education usually entails a process of curricular and organizational change, in which subject matter forms a sequential, differentiated block structure and school organization forms an arrangement of students, teachers, and material resources that is adapted to the curricular block structure in which instruction is embedded. Our case materials from the United States have provided a specific example of the working out of this process within the institutionalization of public education. They also allow us to suggest, in terms that may apply across the range of modern societies, both the elements and the conditions of the objectification of curriculum and school organization and their subsequent structural elaboration.

The elements include conceptions of

1. The consequences of learning (e.g., becoming an effective citizen or worker)
2. The bodies or items of knowledge and the skills that will have these consequences
3. The ways in which the knowledge and skill are to be ordered with respect to each other
4. How instruction is to be ordered in relation to this structure of knowledge and skill
5. The categories of persons to teach and to be taught
6. Relations among the duration of instruction, its structure, and its objectives.

As each of these elements comes within a community of public discourse, the objectification of curriculum and school organization proceeds and their connections as specific, differentiable components of social action develop.

The prime conditions that stimulate this process are to be found in those aspects of expansion and structural differentiation in societies that break down complexes of social action into their constituent activities; undermine their customary, taken-for-granted nature within the everyday round of life; and produce a sheer volume of social activity that tends to overwhelm the capacity of existing institutions. These conditions include

1. Increase in population size
2. Increase in population heterogeneity
3. Territorial expansion, which is likely to entail growth in the levels and diversity of economic and social circumstances and in the complexity and means of social action
4. Consequent gains in the specialization of social action, including the emergence of specialized organizations and occupations
5. A consequent increase in reliance on the state rather than civil society to administer and regulate the conduct of the emerging specialized institutions and their component organizations and occupations.

We have seen that as these processes advanced in the United States, curriculum became an organizational feature of schools through the linkage of classrooms directed by independent teachers and knowledge embodied in unitary subjects. Once this new educational arrangement became governed by local political agencies, schools became subject not only to local political and economic interests but also to the influence of national forces, originating in a growing industrial economy and in national debates about what the nature of education should be. Although local and regional differences in the nature of schooling continued, and to a certain extent remain through the present day, education through schooling nevertheless became increasingly influenced by the homogenizing forces of an urbanizing and industrializing nation.

Indeed, this pattern of educational homogenization has shaped the nature of schooling in all parts of the world that have undergone similar patterns of secular social change (J. W. Meyer 1987). All countries with modern industrial and commercial sectors are very much alike in the organizational form of their schools and their prevailing beliefs about what is legitimate curricular content—e.g., grades, classes, subjects, and subject sequences, on the organizational side; and stress on reading, writing, and arithmetic, as basic skills, and on mathematics, national and foreign languages, history, and science, as more advanced material. These curricular beliefs are associated with an emphasis on "rational" habits of mind.

These countries have differed primarily in what bodies of subject matter knowledge will be the responsibility of specific kinds of schools and what student populations each of these kinds of schools will serve. In brief, these differences are variations on a common organizational and curricular theme. They have arisen from particular demographic, social, economic, and political circumstances associated with the timing of educational change and the formation of policies that govern access to subject matter and courses of study.

If we were to carry our historical analysis of American school organization and curriculum into the 20th century and up to the present day, we would discuss the controversies about education geared to the psychological development of individuals, to the demands of the marketplace, and to the expectations of the colleges; we would address vocational education, testing, ability grouping, and high school tracking (see the discussions of these issues in D. K. Cohen 1985; Cremin 1988; Kliebard 1986). In each of these controversies, taken for granted are the forms of school organization and the principal content elements of curriculum that had been institutionalized by the mid-19th century. At issue are the organizational and curricular specifications and arrangements of these basic forms and elements—elaboration of the received curriculum and how its parts should be distributed among students of varying social origins and presumed social destinations.

In the United States and in virtually all modern societies, the relationship between curriculum and the organization of schools has been remarkably stable. In the United States, the results of the processes of institutionalization that we have discussed have been in place for about a century, and it is not easy to foresee substantial changes in them. Curricular forms and content, of course, have been subject to controversy throughout the past hundred years. To a lesser extent and of more recent vintage have been debates over school organization.

Curricular content is revised, new ways to teach are proposed, and different boundaries between levels of schools are established. Nevertheless, the basic structure of schools, as organized around interchangeable content-based subjects, has remained remarkably durable, even in the face of mass attendance through high school, the emergence of school-centered social movements, the rise of the federal government as an influence on local school policy, and the appearance of youth-oriented government agencies in competition with the public schools.

In this chapter, we have turned aside from the more

conventional lines of inquiry into the connection between curriculum and school organization. For example, we have not discussed the connection among curriculum, school organization, and theories of learning or the nature and outcomes of efforts at curricular reform.

Our line of argument leads us to a research agenda that poses a different range of questions. If curriculum is to be understood as an organization of knowledge in subject format, one needs to know how certain bodies of knowledge gain standing as legitimate school subjects, how extant school organization may facilitate or hamper this process, and how evolving organizational and curricular structures interact to affect the diffusion of new subjects and new organizational forms. This problem leads directly to questions about the allocation of various kinds of knowledge to different student populations and to the interplay in this knowledge distribution of types of schools; types of students; curricular structures like tracks, streams, and ability groups; and regional variation in conceptions of schooling and in the means of realizing these ideas about what is to be taught to whom.

One should not assume that even with the institutionalization of schooling, schools become the sole agents of education. Other public and private agencies (e.g., the military, public welfare organizations, youth groups and movements, apprenticeship, and on-the-job training) may be purveyors of knowledge with jurisdictions that overlap the jurisdiction of schools. How responsibility for education comes to be located in one institution or another at different times and in different places awaits treatment as a major analytical problem if we are to understand the connection between school organization and the curriculum.

References

Axtell, James. 1974. *The School Upon a Hill*. New Haven, CT: Yale University Press.

Bailyn, Bernard. 1960. *Education in the Forming of American Society*. Chapel Hill: University of North Carolina Press.

Bidwell, Charles E. 1989. "The Meaning of Educational Attainment." In *Research in the Sociology of Education and Socialization*, vol. 8, edited by Ronald G. Corwin and Krishnan Namboodiri, 117–138. Greenwich, CT: JAI Press.

Blau, Peter M., and Schoenherr, Richard. 1971. *The Structure of Organizations*. New York: Basic Books.

Bridenbaugh, Carl. 1964 [1938]. *Cities in the Wilderness: The First Century of Urban Life in America 1625-1742*. New York: Knopf.

Calhoun, Daniel, ed. 1969. *The Educating of Americans: A Documentary History*. Boston: Houghton Mifflin.

Callahan, Raymond E. 1962. *Education and the Cult of Efficiency*. Chicago: University of Chicago Press.

Clark, Burton R. 1983. *The Higher Education System*. Berkeley: University of California Press.

Cohen, David K. 1985. "Origins." In *The Shopping Mall High School*, edited by Arthur G. Powell, Eleanor Farrar, and David K. Cohen, 233–308. Boston: Houghton Mifflin.

Cohen, Patricia C. 1982. *A Calculating People: The Spread of Numeracy in Early America*. Chicago: University of Chicago Press.

Cremin, Lawrence A. 1951. *The American Common School*. New York: Teachers College.

Cremin, Lawrence A. 1970. *American Education: The Colonial Experience 1607–1783*. New York: Harper & Row.

Cremin, Lawrence A. 1980. *American Education: The National Experience 1783–1876*. New York: Harper & Row.

Cremin, Lawrence A. 1988. *American Education: The Metropolitan Experience 1876–1980*. New York: Harper & Row.

Demos, John. 1970. *A Little Commonwealth: Family Life in Plymouth Colony*. London: Oxford University Press.

Dewey, John. 1901. "The Situation as Regards the Course of Study." In *Journal of the Proceedings and Addresses of the Fortieth Annual Meeting of the National Education Association*, 332–348.

Durkheim, Émile. 1977 [1938]. *The Evolution of Educational Thought in France*. London: Routledge & Kegan Paul.

Eggleston, Edward. 1900. *The Transit of Civilization from England to America in the Seventeenth Century*. New York: Appleton.

Fuller, Wayne E. 1982. *The Old Country School*. Chicago: University of Chicago Press.

Goodson, Ivor F. 1983. *School Subjects and Curriculum Change*. London: Croom Helm.

Grizzell, Emit D. 1922. *Origin and Development of the High School in New England Before 1865*. Philadelphia, PA: Macmillan.

Hannan, Michael, and Freeman, John H. 1977. The population ecology of organizations. *American Journal of Sociology* 82(5): 929–964.

Hogan, David J. 1985. *Class and Reform: School and Society in Chicago, 1880–1930*. Philadelphia: University of Pennsylvania Press.

Inglis, Alexander J. 1911. *The Rise of the High School in Massachusetts*. New York: Teachers College.

Johnson, Clifton. 1904. *Old-Time Schools and School-Books*. New York: Macmillan.

Kaestle, Carl F. 1973. *The Evolution of an Urban School System: New York, 1750–1850*. Cambridge, MA: Harvard University Press.

Kilpatrick, William H. 1912. *The Dutch Schools of New Netherland and Colonial New York*. Washington, DC: U.S. Government Printing Office.

Kliebard, Herbert M. 1986. *The Struggle for the American Curriculum, 1893–1958*. Boston: Routledge & Kegan Paul.

Labaree, David F. 1988. *The Making of An American High School: The Credentials Market and the Central High School of Philadelphia, 1838–1939*. New Haven, CT: Yale University Press.

Mann, Carleton H. 1928. *How Schools Use Their Time: Time Allotment Practice in 444 Cities, Including a Study of Trends from 1826 to 1926*. New York: Bureau of Publications, Teachers College, Columbia University.

Meyer, John W. 1977. The effects of education as an institution, *American Journal of Sociology* 83(1): 55–77.

Meyer, John W. 1987. "Implications of an Institutional View of Education for the Study of Educational Effects." In *The Social Organization of Schools*, edited by Maureen T. Hallinan, 157–175. New York: Plenum.

Meyer, Marshall W. 1985. *Limits to Bureaucratic Growth*. New York: deGruyter.

Morgan, Edmund S. 1966 [1944]. *The Puritan Family*. New York: Harper & Row.

Morison, Samuel E. 1930. *Builders of the Bay Colony*. Boston: Houghton Mifflin.

Morison, Samuel E. 1936. *The Puritan Pronaos*. New York: New York University Press.

Seybolt, Robert F. 1917. *Apprenticeship and Apprenticeship Education in Colonial New England and New York*. New York: Teachers College.

Seybolt, Robert F. 1925. *The Evening School in Colonial America. Bureau of Educational Research Bulletin No. 24*. Urbana: University of Illinois.

Seybolt, Robert F. 1935a. *The Private Schools of Colonial Boston*. Cambridge, MA: Harvard University Press.

Seybolt, Robert F. 1935b. *The Public Schools of Colonial Boston, 1635–1775*. Cambridge, MA: Harvard University Press.

Small, Walter H. 1969 (1914). *Early New England Schools*. New York: Arno Press.

Stinchcombe, Arthur L. 1965. "Social Structure and Organizations." In *Handbook of Organizations*, edited by James G. March, 142–193. Chicago: Rand McNally.

Troen, Selwyn K. 1975. *The Public and the Schools: Shaping the St. Louis System, 1838–1920*. Columbia: University of Missouri Press.

Tyack, David. 1974. *The One Best System*. Cambridge, MA: Harvard University Press.

Updegraff, Harlan. 1908. *The Origin of the Moving School in Massachusetts*. New York: Teachers College.

Vinovskis, Maris A. 1985. *The Origins of Public High Schools*. Madison: University of Wisconsin Press.

Williamson, Oliver. 1975. *Markets and Hierarchies, Analysis and Antitrust Implications: A Study in the Economics of Internal Organization*. New York: Free Press.

14

TEACHER AS CURRICULUM MAKER

D. Jean Clandinin
UNIVERSITY OF ALBERTA

F. Michael Connelly
JOINT CENTRE FOR TEACHER DEVELOPMENT,
ONTARIO INSTITUTE FOR STUDIES IN EDUCATION/UNIVERSITY OF TORONTO

Writing a chapter on teachers as curriculum makers for the *Handbook of Research* series constitutes a special challenge. Three American Educational Research Association (AERA) volumes on teaching (*Handbook of Research on Teaching, HRT*) already exist, totaling 100 chapters and over 3,600 pages. In those volumes, one might imagine, any literature worth reviewing and anything worth saying about teachers would be found. Our first task, then, was to evaluate the potential of this topic, considering both the availability of an unreviewed literature on teachers and curriculum and the extent to which something important could still be said on teachers and teaching. Of the 100 chapters, only one, "Critical Value Questions and the Analysis of Objectives and Curricula" (MacDonald and Clark 1973), refers to curriculum in its title, and at eight pages it is the shortest of all. Each *Handbook* has a set of chapters on the teaching of school subjects; the emphasis in these tends to be on the organization of classrooms and the learning of subject matter, whereas the commonplace, the teacher, receives relatively scant notice. Two relevant, closely related topics, teacher lesson planning and teacher decision making, were treated (Clark and Peterson 1986), and we have not repeated this review. Otherwise, however, we were somewhat surprised to find that the literature we tended to consult on the teacher as curriculum maker was not referenced in the *HRT* volumes. We concluded that the literature on teachers as curriculum makers is not adequately covered by the literature on teaching. This conclusion is based partly on what we define as an appropriate literature for review in a chapter on teacher as curriculum maker. Our definition and, as becomes apparent later, our creation of an appropriate literature emerges from our view of the teacher in relation to curriculum—that the teacher is an integral part of the curriculum constructed and enacted in classrooms. This view led us to two literature sets, one reasonably well accepted—teachers' roles in curriculum development and reform—and the other not widely acknowledged—teachers' stories and stories of teachers.

The narrative literature of teachers' stories and stories of teachers is a kind of "research on teaching" literature that lies outside the scope of most reviews. We believe this forgotten literature has a great deal to contribute to an understanding of teachers as curriculum makers. Our attachment to it rests on our own professional lives and curriculum practice. We have taught in schools and universities and devote considerable time to thinking about our teaching. We regard ourselves primarily as school people working in a university setting rather than as university observers of schools. Our sympathies tend to lie with teachers: When we read research reports we frown when we imagine teachers

The authors are especially indebted to graduate students Marion Blake, Carola Conle, and Carol Mullen for their considerable assistance with the preparation of this chapter. They conducted library searches, reviewed and summarized articles, and edited chapter drafts. Blake collected and drafted materials on the Humanities Curriculum Project, Mullen did the same for the Eight Year Study and Project Follow Through, and Conle did likewise for European research. Gary Pyper, a text-processing specialist, organized the text and, along with the other text-processing specialist, Frances Tolnai, prepared the references; Vashty Hawkins and Lynn Austin supported the team. The authors also wish to thank Karen Zumwalt (Teachers College, Columbia University) for a thorough, helpful review of an early draft.

might frown and we smile when we think teachers might smile. Consequently, we have not followed this *Handbook*'s editorial rules precisely; we have reviewed the literature not so much as colleagues of the research authors but as we imagine it might be reviewed by practicing teachers. Although some may interpret our method as biased toward teachers, we see it as interpretation from their point of view.

Who reads research reports? Ordinarily, other researchers, but sometimes they are read by policymakers, administrators, and teachers. We believe that research texts are different when read by researchers than they are when read by classroom teachers with students to meet. Indeed, the comparison of research reports read as texts for further inquiry with the same reports read as texts for practice is important to an understanding of teachers as curriculum makers. Studies are needed on how teachers read and use research. Even more to the point of this chapter, we believe there is a need to work with teachers and their stories, lived and told, to create new interpretations. As the chapter develops, we draw in teachers' stories and stories of teachers and read them from the point of view of curriculum making.

For lack of a better term we think of the chapter as an "upside down" approach, somewhat in the way that some think of Dewey's writing as inverted Platonism. What may appear as a critical sentiment toward research is intended only as a teacher's reading. The "upside down" reading takes on a more positive tone in our accounts of teachers' stories and stories of teachers, presented later in the chapter. Accordingly, at different points in the chapter three things are happening: We read existing research through teachers' eyes; we draw in a new literature of teachers' stories and stories of teachers; and finally, we work with these stories to create a new literature of teachers as curriculum makers.

The Structure of the Chapter

The chapter is organized into two main sections. The first section outlines the various meanings of curriculum and examines how the teacher has come to be seen as separate from curriculum. This exploration leads to the literature of school reform, in which much work on the teacher as curriculum maker has occurred as an offshoot of the main research and development purposes. As we reviewed this literature, we became aware of a pervasive "conduit" metaphor of teachers in curriculum development and reform. A review of several projects provided insights into the ways this metaphor affected how teachers were perceived. In this respect, the Rand Corporation study of change (Berman and McLaughlin 1978) was particularly important; in this study a view of mutual adaptation between developer and teacher predominated. Still keeping in mind the conduit metaphor, we looked at what we called the teacher-proof literature. Finally, we examined a series of literature sets that took us from curriculum materials development to school-based curriculum development, staff development, and action research.

The second part of the chapter uses a narrative structure to review the Humanities Curriculum Project. By looking at this project from the perspective of how teachers experienced it, we attempt to understand the view of the teacher that governed the project. We then turn to a literature of teachers' stories and stories of teachers as a literature of the teacher as curriculum maker.

Finally we work with the texts of two teachers' stories, those of Robert Coles and Vivian Paley, in a preliminary attempt at creating a new research literature of the teacher as curriculum maker. The chapter concludes with an examination of the ways in which our review points to a collaborative agenda of work with teachers in their schools and classrooms.

IMAGES OF TEACHERS AS CURRICULUM MAKERS: IN THE CONDUIT

A Meaning for Curriculum. "Curriculum" has a tangled definitional history, as will be evident elsewhere in this *Handbook*. Despite our reluctance to introduce yet another discussion of definition, we find it necessary to do so both to suggest at the outset how we imagine the teacher is relative to curriculum and to see how this imagining fits in relation to education and educational reform generally. Our discussion is intended to help the reader understand how and why the chapter is structured as it is.

The *Oxford English Dictionary* (*OED*) defines "curriculum" as follows: "[L., = course, career (*lit.* and *fig.*)]; *specifically* a regular course of study or training, as at a school or university (the recognized term in the Scottish universities); curriculum vitae, the course of one's life; a brief account of one's career." In defining curriculum, educators have focused on the first part of the *OED* definition. Bussis, Chittenden, and Amarel (1976) describe how a variety of definitions have evolved from "course of study." They write that "over the years, however, educational research has gradually sapped curriculum of its content meaning and injected in its place a 'methods' and 'forms' emphasis. This metamorphosis has been achieved by the persisting preoccupation with questions about the formulation and use of educational objectives, the form and organization of curricular materials, and the methods of presenting material" (10).

These authors are undoubtedly correct in stating that research is partly responsible for the metamorphosis, but organizational and logical factors have also contributed to it. In Upper Canada and New France (long before the formation of Canada in 1867), there existed in the Jesuit colleges a "Ratio Studiorum," or plan of studies (Tomkins 1986, 5). In the United States the land grant colleges institutionalized a distinction between curriculum and instruction (C&I), either by creating C&I departments or separating the two by establishing instructional departments alongside elementary and secondary education departments. The logic of this distinction is summarized by Popham and Baker (1970) as follows: "There are basically two kinds of decisions that the educator must make. First, he must decide what the objectives (that is, the ends) of the instructional system should be, and second, he must decide on the procedures (that is, the means) for accomplishing those objectives" (82). They make clear that for them the distinction between curriculum and instruction is a distinction between ends and means.

From the point of view of a researcher studying classrooms, teachers, and curricula, these distinctions and terms may provide some grip on a complex, practical world. But from the point of view of practitioners the distinctions are largely irrelevant. As Bussis, Chittenden, and Amarel put it, "What is extraordinary is its indifference to the reality of education" (11), and as Goodlad (1969) adds, "If the abstract categories of research and discourse . . . bear no identifiable relationship to the existential phenomena called curricula, then there is, indeed, cause for concern" (369).

We recently attempted what we like to think of as a Deweyan view of the curriculum from a teacher's vantage point (Clandinin 1986; Connelly and Clandinin 1988). Dewey's (1938) notion of "situation" and "experience" enabled us to imagine the teacher not so much as a maker of curriculum but as a part of it and to imagine a place for context, culture (Dewey's notion of interaction), and temporality (both past and future contained in Dewey's notion of "continuity"). In this view, ends and means are so intertwined that designing curricula for teachers to implement for instructional purposes appears unreal, somewhat as if the cart were before the horse.

This point brings us back to the second half of the *OED* definition: "the course of one's life; a brief account of one's career." In our effort to examine the literature from the point of view of the teacher, this meaning takes precedence. Teachers and students live out a curriculum; teachers do not transmit, implement, or teach a curriculum and objectives; nor are they and their students carried forward in their work and studies by a curriculum of textbooks and content, instructional methodologies, and intentions. An account of teachers' and students' lives over time is the curriculum, although intentionality, objectives, and curriculum materials do play a part in it.

Following this line of thinking further, what researchers are inclined to call curriculum, i.e., the course of study, is more akin to the *OED*'s "curricle," defined as "a light, two-wheeled carriage for rapid movement." Curriculum packages, complete with intentions, instructional strategies, and materials, are rather like a carriage for the curriculum, and teachers become the curricle drivers. Admittedly, at this point our account is as abstract and distant from "reality" as are the "constructs" and distinctions between ends and means, but the matter will become more concrete as we proceed.

Educational Visions and Cycles of Reform

The Early History: "Curriculum" and "Teacher" as Separate Inquiries. Since its introduction into the English language in the 19th century, the word "curriculum" in an educational context emphasized formal courses and programs of study (Cremin 1971; Tomkins 1986). From the 1920s, when the term came into more frequent use (Bellack 1969; Cremin 1961; Kliebard 1968, 1971, 1975; Seguel 1966; Tyack 1974), "curriculum" linked the school course of study with disciplinary subject matter (Cremin 1971). The implicit linking of the idea of curriculum to subject matter instead of classroom practice embedded the means-end distinction that has characterized, and often plagued, the field since. Thus, a science curriculum meant science subject matter presented over a period of time, the high school years, for instance, or a grade or semester. The language that educators have come to associate with curriculum and that is found in virtually all curriculum textbooks and manuals, the most famous in North America being Tyler's (1949) *Basic Principles of Curriculum and Instruction*, has its basis in this meaning.

Thus, for curriculum developers, "objectives," "vertical integration," "horizontal integration," "sequence," "subject matter," "units," and "organization" became the functional language that defined curriculum in practice. This is not, following the *OED*, a language of "curriculum vitae." Nor did the unprecedented government and foundation-driven reform movement of the 1950s and afterward soften this technical means-ends language with personal and experiential terms. Consider the well-known Rand studies, in which Berman and McLaughlin (1978), in their discussion of "The Local Processes of Education," introduce the terms "mobilization," "implementation," and "institutionalization" to structure their discussion (26).

"Teacher" did not figure as a key term in that early curriculum literature (Lee 1966). The development of an association of "teacher" with "curriculum" appears to have been mostly a consequence of a working distinction between ends and means, which presumed that teachers and teaching mediate between the curriculum and its object, students. At the risk of venturing an oversimplified historical observation, it appears that ideas of the teacher and teaching generally originated in a philosophical literature on teaching that owed little to curriculum, at least as it came to be known by 20th-century educators. Examples include works such as Broudy's (1963) "Historic Exemplars of Teaching Method" (in the First *Handbook of Research on Teaching*, later expanded and published as a book, Broudy and Palmer's (1965) *Exemplars of Teaching Method*); Maxine Greene's "Philosophy and Teaching" (1986; in the Third *Handbook of Research on Teaching*) and her *Teacher as Stranger* (1973) and "The Teacher in John Dewey's Works" (1989); and Simpson and Jackson's (1984) *The Teacher as Philosopher*.

In general, concepts of the teacher and the teacher's role in such works arise from theories of knowledge, learning, human nature, social life, and combinations of these; the curriculum, if mentioned at all, is assumed to be derived from the concept of the teacher thereby generated. It is, we think, fair to say that the conceptual histories of the teacher and curriculum as seen in the research literature have been more or less independent. To say that their histories are incompatible would be too strong, although Rugg (1926) apparently had expectations that they might turn out this way when he concluded a footnote, "Hence my allegiance to the curriculum rather than to the teacher as the effective educational intermediary between child and society" (3). People writing in each field have tended to think of the work of the other as derivative: that teachers and teaching are means to curriculum ends and, conversely, that curriculum ought to be designed in part around certain concepts of the teacher and teaching.

Tyler and Schwab: The Making of an Idea of Teacher as Curriculum Maker. Curriculum writers have appeared to accept the prescriptions of those concerned with theories of the teacher and teaching and to have adopted such theories as part of the curriculum ends that teachers (as means) were expected to implement. Tyler (1949) more or less cast the die for the past 40 years when he wrote that philosophy and psychology ought to be resources for planning educational purposes. Tyler, of course, is not alone among key figures in his notion of teachers as curriculum implementors. Consider, for example, Bruner's (1977 [1960]) *The Process of Education*, in which it is said that "a curriculum is more for teachers than it is for pupils. If it cannot change, move, perturb, inform teachers, it will have no effect on those whom they teach" (xv). Although Tyler's examples of philosophy had more to do with the good life, values, society, and the relationship of school to society than with teachers and teaching, it is safe to say that "neo-Tylerians" interpreted Tyler's prescription broadly and adopted various philosophical theories of teaching. From the viewpoint of the classroom teacher, however, these theories were treated as part of a set of curriculum ends for translation during instruction. As Tyler wrote, "It is then possible to infer the kinds of activities which the instructor might carry on in an effort to obtain the objectives—that is, in an effort to bring about the desired changes in the student" (44).

This was only half of the "ends" picture for Tyler, which if not derived from Bobbit's *How to Make a Curriculum* (1924; see also 1913, 1918), owed much to it (Callahan 1962; Cuban 1976; Kliebard 1970). In addition, content was to be specified, and through the specification of both content and student behavior, appropriate teacher behavior could be imagined. In Tyler's (1949) view, "the teacher can provide an educational experience through setting up an environment and structuring the situation so as to stimulate the desired type of reaction" and "the teacher's method of controlling the learning experience is through the manipulation of the environment in such a way as to set up stimulating situations" (64).

Tyler (1949) appears to have been at odds with himself on the question of the significance of the teacher's role. Following a discussion of his content-behavior grid for the specification of objectives, he writes that "when objectives are formulated in a two-dimensional chart of this sort, it becomes a concise set of specifications to guide the further development of the course"; ". . . it should be clear that the kind of experience a student needs to have in order to get understanding of important facts and principles is . . ."; and ". . . similarly, the objectives implied by the third column set up certain specifications regarding the learning experiences to be provided" (51–52). These and phrases like them suggest that the hard work has been done; most of what is left up to the teacher is "concise," "clear," and "implied." In contrast, in a discussion of the selection of learning experiences, he writes that "this places considerable responsibility upon the teacher, both to set up situations that have so many facets that they are likely to evoke the desired experience from all students or else a teacher will vary the experiences so as to provide some that are likely to be significant to each of the students in the class" (65). Our interpretation of Tyler is that he appears to have thought of curriculum making (i.e., ends) as the primary intellectual, social, and educational challenge and that the means for realizing the curriculum through instruction was an important, though lesser, task.

Tyler's (1949) work is pivotal to an understanding of the teacher as curriculum maker because it is derived uneasily from both senses of the *OED* definition—course of study and course of life. His book has typically been misread as a curriculum book, which it is not. It is a curriculum and instruction book, and most of what is actually said in it, at least in terms of pages written (including those in which the teacher is referenced), are on instruction. Tyler maintained the distinction between curriculum as ends and instruction as means.

However, when the means-end distinction is ignored and Tyler's (1949) text is deliberately misread, as it often is, as a curriculum text, all that has been said about experience and the teacher's role in selecting and planning student experience becomes curriculum activity. By implication, then, the teacher becomes a curriculum maker rather than a curriculum transmitter or implementor. This reading helps make sense of our view that Tyler's work marks a key moment in the history of thought on the teacher as curriculum maker.

Tyler's colleague, Joseph Schwab (1960), essentially took the "curriculum misreading" of Tyler and advanced the claim that any account of curriculum, admitting there were many, entailed an account of four commonplaces, or "desiderata": teacher, learner, subject matter, and milieu. For Schwab and "neo-Schwabians," a statement that does not contain a direct or implied reference to "teacher" is not an "adequate" (Schwab's term) curriculum statement. Schwab, in the 1960 paper, was not arguing that the teacher was a curriculum maker, that is, that the teacher was the agent of curriculum with a set of commonplaces; teacher agency, and many other possible roles, might be imagined. The key point for us is that bringing Tyler's and Schwab's ideas together provides the makings of an image of the teacher as curriculum maker. Schwab provided the rationale, which was a kind of reinterpretation of Tyler, and Tyler provided the agency. In this view the teacher is a maker of only half a curriculum loaf, the half that often goes by the name of means.

School Reform and the Teacher in Curriculum Research. Most of what is known about "teacher as curriculum maker" is found in the literature of school reform through curriculum development. Although curriculum reform in the schools "became a kind of national pastime" (Kliebard 1968, 71) in the 1920s, our focus in this section is on the 1950s to the 1980s. This later literature of school reform—impressionistic overviews (e.g., Goodlad 1988), reviews, (e.g., Fullan 1972; Fullan and Pomfret 1977), and empirical studies (e.g., Smith, Dwyer, Prunty, and Kleine 1988; Smith and Keith 1971; Smith, Kleine, Prunty, and Dwyer 1986; Smith, Prunty, Dwyer, and Kleine 1987)—is too sweeping in scope for a comprehensive review here. In much of this literature either teachers are treated only incidentally or their presence is only implied. In our review of this literature we found few studies explicitly on teachers. The reform literature is a literature of ends and of the technology of arriving at ends; the teacher figures mostly in the discrepancies—anticipated and actual—between intended and achieved ends. In the reform movement there is no literature of the teacher as curriculum maker in the way that there is, for example, an identifiable literature of teaching as process-product.

Although peripheral to the main reform theses, nonetheless an idea of "teacher" has figured since the beginning of modern curriculum reform in the late 19th century. According to Cremin (1971), in the United States this movement can be traced to William Harris (1876, 1897), a "reformer . . . who laid out all of the pieces . . . for the game of curriculum-making that would be played over the next half-century" (208–210). According to Cremin's view of Harris, the teacher "encourages and mediates the process of instruction" (210). (Oddly enough, Harris says nothing about the teacher in his 1897 "My Pedagogical Creed," a striking omission for those familiar with the role of the teacher in Dewey's "My Pedagogic Creed" published in the same journal earlier that year.) In Canada, Tomkins (1986) attributes a similar influence to Egerton Ryerson, appointed chief superintendent of schools for Upper Canada in 1846. Ryerson's first effort was to devise programs for immigrant children, and he subsequently created a bureaucracy to supervise teachers, which, says Tomkins, has had lasting effects. Thus, while Harris set in motion a chess game of curriculum reform, Ryerson set in motion an administrative structure for its control. From the point of view of teachers as curriculum makers, the net effect seems to have been much the same.

Since its introduction into the English language, then, curriculum has been seen as an instrument of school reform and teachers as mediators between the curriculum and intended outcomes. Teachers were generally told what to do and, at least in Canada, supervised to make sure they did it. The continuous string of curriculum reformers, reforms, and innovations have, we believe, created a pervasive climate of antipathy to reform on the part of teachers. Ben-Peretz and Tamir (1981), for instance, found that Israeli teachers did not assign high priority to their own role in curriculum implementation. More to the point, in their National Institute of Education reports, Hodgkinson (1977) and Schaffarzick (1976) claimed that the question of who had control over curriculum decisions was taking precedence in stakeholders' eyes over the question of curriculum content. Phillips and Hawthorne (1976) argued that the reason for this development was that local communities view central government initiatives as an attempt to usurp local control.

When public charges are made that schools are not doing their job, teachers inevitably come in for a large share of the criticism (Spady 1977); when reformers try to do something in response to public concern, almost inevitably with disappointing results, teachers are usually seen as the principal impediment (Charters and Pellegrin 1973; Common 1981; Fullan, Eastabrook, and Biss 1977; Gross, Giacquinta, and Bernstein 1971; McLaughlin, Wallin, and Marsh 1978; Regan and Leithwood 1975). For teachers, then, curriculum reform is both potential master and source of retribution. School reformers and curriculum theorists (who are sometimes one and the same) have, perhaps unwittingly, conspired in this outcome.

What might have happened had a different sense of curriculum, one more related to the *OED*'s second meaning, taken root in professional and academic educators' minds? To play out an idealized scenario, there would have been no curricula to implement, no people as "means" to enact someone else's "ends," no hierarchy of curriculum thinkers over teacher doers, no experts to decide who the expert teachers are—indeed, no grand reforms to implement. Would the functional split between curriculum and teacher, now ingrained in the reform literature, have developed as it has?

Ideologies of Control: Centralization and Decentralization. It would be a mistake to give the impression that curriculum making is always thought of as the development of a set of ends, complete with materials and the like, to be introduced into the schools for teacher translation. Rather, since the turn of the century the pendulum has swung between centralization and decentralization of curriculum making, a pair of terms popular in the reform literature (Connelly 1972; Kirst 1983; Lawton 1980; Lortie 1975; MacKenzie 1970; Sirotnik 1983; Smith, Prunty, Dwyer, and Kleine 1987; Tyack, Kirst, and Hansot 1980; Westbury 1970). The swings no doubt reflect prevailing ideologies of social opinion as much as current knowledge about education or particular outlooks on schooling. Cremin (1961), for example, shows how the progressive education movement in the early decades of this century was an expression of a progressive social outlook. Since curriculum came, above all else, to be a kind of philosophical endeavor—the creation of purpose (ends)—it is perhaps not surprising that ideologies valued in society have tended to dominate the curriculum literature.

The various ideological appeals that seem to affect the pendulum swings are, however, often more an academic surface dressing with little application to curriculum practice. They appear in a literature that academics and policymakers tend to address to one another, with little reference to what is happening in the schools (Clifford 1988; Cuban 1976; Ramsey 1983). This is one of the literatures that Schwab (1970a, 1970b) had in mind when he wrote his practical series and observed that the literature was marked by flights from the field.

Interestingly, reformers have resisted these swings in their own practices of reform (Cremin 1971; Cuban 1976, 1986). Cremin's demonstration of this point is especially interesting because it is based on the humanistic, apparently decentralized claims of the progressive education movement (210). In his analysis of two key documents—the Committee of Ten (1893) and the Commission on the Reorganization of Secondary Education (1918)—Cremin (1955) concluded that there had been a "revolution in secondary education." But in 1971, following an analysis of the actual subject area recommendations of the later document, he revised his assessment, admitted he had been wrong, and concluded that "the Puritans remained in the curriculum" (212). (See also, below, our story of the British Humanities Curriculum Project, which demonstrates a similar point.)

Franklin (1982, 1984) found himself in academic hot water for challenging the "truths" academics tell themselves, unconstrained by school-based evidence. Franklin, like Cremin, altered his view of the American social efficiency movement of the early 20th century, a view he had derived from his historical document analysis of the Minneapolis schools from 1917 to 1950. Originally his views were similar to those of Egan (1983) and Greene (1983), both of whom lamented certain schooling defects they believed were caused by the movement. Egan laid the blame for the social studies curriculum at the feet of Deweyan progressivism, and Greene thought the progressive reformers such as Dewey and Horace had misread the American dream, which was, in part at least, a dream of efficiency. But Franklin found only small changes in school board documents over the time period when the efficiency movement was at its height. Following his review of other literature on the efficiency movement—the introduction of vocational education in Atlanta from 1890 to 1925 (Urban 1981); efficiency curriculum in Scarsdale (O'Connor 1980); and vocationalism in Fetchbury, Massachusetts, 1908 to 1928 (Ringel 1981)—Franklin (1984) concluded that "the impact of social efficiency ideas on North American educational practice has been at best ambiguous" (325). Both Greene (1984) and Egan (1984) took exception to Franklin's conclusions, although Egan "concedes" Franklin's point about practice (342).

The historical work of Cremin and Franklin underlines the uneasy and often blurred boundaries between research and reform. Educational research, it is often argued, should follow agendas set outside the research community (Dunkel 1972; Dunkel, Gowin, Thomas 1972; Gowin 1972). But it is one thing for researchers to engage in what amounts to policy research for social reform and quite another for researchers to be the reformers. Sometimes the transition from research to reform takes place with the creation by researchers of curriculum development projects to represent their own ideas of proper ends. The reforms of the 1950s and 1960s are littered with examples: Zacharia, Bruner, Glass, Schwab, Karplus, and so on. Sometimes researchers adopt a reform style based on their own or others' research, and at least one entire field of study—curriculum implementation—grew to support what Cremin (1971) might have called a "Puritan" ideology.

By using Cremin's term "Puritan," we intend to draw attention to three interrelated points. One is the faithfulness to original intentions with which change was made or not made. A second, related point is the sense in which "Puritan" has a particular ideological flavor. The third point concerns a sense of ideational clarity and perfection, unmarred by the messy reality of practice. Much of the recent literature of curriculum implementation is "Puritan" in the first sense. As Hall and Loucks (1977) put it, "it has been vital to know whether the innovation process or product is being implemented in the classroom. This research is based on the assumption that the primary unit of adoption is the individual classroom teacher or professor" (264–265).

Although we know of no historical study that makes the point, we think it probable that curriculum implementation originated in academic response to the curriculum developer's frustration over failed ends, combined with accountability concerns of funding agencies—governments, foundations, universities, and laboratories. In this literature the teacher performs a similar "means for the translation of ends" role to that seen in the curriculum-making literature, except that the teacher is now viewed as one of the many factors or forces that condition change (Fullan 1982; Leithwood 1982). Our point is that to the extent that research takes place in the context of curriculum reform, it contributes to the ends versus means outlook, thus limiting the idea of the teacher as curriculum maker.

Stability and Change. Legions of writers have affirmed that schools, perhaps like other organizations (Nisbet 1969, 1980), are remarkably stable amid an always fermenting climate of reform (e.g., Goodlad 1984; Goodlad and Klein 1970; McKinney and Westbury 1975; Sirotnik 1983; Smith, Dwyer, Prunty, and Kleine 1988). Grand schemes such as the Eight Year Study (Cuban 1976), the progressive education movement (Cremin 1961), the social efficiency movement (see above), the Humanities Curriculum Project (HCP) in England (see below), and the disciplines movement of the 1950s and 1960s (Kirst and Meister 1985) have largely passed from view, although not without leaving lasting "deposits when they pass" (Tyack, Kirst, and Hansot 1980, 255–256) (to which one might add, "at least among academic exchanges"; e.g., the HCP and the Eight Year Study were the topic of a 1988 AERA annual meeting symposium.)

Cuban (1976, 1986, 1988) in the United States and Tomkins (1986) in Canada have devoted considerable energy to understanding the dilemma of change and stability. Cuban's (1976) question is this: "Why in an institution so vulnerable to social change do classrooms seem so invulnerable to decades of curriculum change?" (57). Waves of immigration and changes in a community's socioeconomic status affect the way schools function and influence teacher attitudes, outlooks, and methods (Smith, Dwyer, Prunty, and Kleine 1988), but deliberate attempts to manipulate teachers and schools leave only marginal residue. Cuban's answer to his question is that "the teacher, and I wince that in 1976 it still has to be said, is the source of both curricular change and stability" (80). This observation embarrasses Cuban, probably because of its self-evidence, the fact that it has been repeated so often in the literature (recent case studies that make the point are Cusick 1983; Lightfoot 1983; Sizer 1984), and the fact that it has been mostly ignored in the reform and implementation literature. To take the teacher seriously, as Cuban insists, is to do more than design implementation strategies to minimize teacher effects on the curriculum while working to gain their commitment to its purposes.

Knowing More About Teacher Practice. About the time that Cuban's (1976) lesson was being relearned and it was becoming evident that the heavily funded "alphabet soup" curriculum reforms of the 1950s and 1960s were not taking hold in the schools, Schwab (1970a, 1970b, 1971, 1973) urged researchers to move their studies out of the lab and into schools and to start writing a different kind of literature for a different kind of journal. He argued that the improvement of schools should be based on knowledge of them rather than on (or perhaps in addition to) Tyler's philosophical, psychological, and socially derived ends, transmitted, as Schwab (1983) put it, as messages from Moscow. Many researchers, Cuban (1984, 1986) among them, have followed this advice; an exception, perhaps, is evident in the critical theory literature, although even here there is a tradition of school-based critical ethnography. But it is far from clear, at least to us, that doing so has provided much of an answer to the dilemma of stability and change. The implementation field is illustrative, as is the range of literature reported in the AERA *Handbooks of Research on Teaching*. In both of these "find-out-what-is-going-on-and-do-something-about-it" literatures, the dominant, "Puritan" ideology evident in the reform literature and confirmed since the times of Ryerson and Harris, is in evidence. Both literatures by and large remain founded on a distinction between ends and means.

Although some writers would disagree and could probably provide examples to the contrary (e.g., Berman and McLaughlin 1978; Brown and McIntyre 1982; Crandall et al. 1983; Fullan 1985; Getzels 1978; Huberman 1981; Loucks 1983), we believe it is fair to observe that the incredibly refined descriptions of the intricacies of curriculum implementation and the equally refined descriptions of those of teaching have made only marginal difference to the capacity to change schools (Fullan, Eastabrook, and Biss 1977; Good and Brophy 1986; Olson 1980). Phillips (1985) called some of the research "trivially true." Jackson (1987) and Doris Ryan (1986) claim we are still "ignorant." Furthermore, Jackson does not think more such research would lessen our ignorance. Given the means-ends distinction and the prevailing ideology, the proper thing to do, after all, may not be to go into the schools to understand more about teachers. We believe, and will argue later, that viewing means and ends as inextricably linked might lead to different ways of imagining the researcher's enterprise. The preeminent North American advocate of this view is John Dewey, and we shall tie this story to his. To foreshadow the point, knowing more about practice would no longer be the issue; for curriculum researchers the issue would be the mutual making of curriculum with teachers and other practitioners. To do so we shall not need to know more but, rather, to do more.

Metaphors of Reform, Teachers, and Teaching

Recent theories of metaphor (Johnson 1987; Lakoff 1987; Ortony 1979a; Schön 1979) put forward the view that metaphors are no mere "anomalies of language" (Schön 1979, 254) but are, instead, expressions of living (Lakoff and Johnson 1980). These theories are potentially illuminating for studies on the uses of metaphor in the literature of teachers and curriculum. Educators either use metaphors unconsciously or they are conscious of them and deliberately generate and identify them in the literature.

Not everyone, of course, would agree that metaphor plays the significant role in experience, as suggested here. Green (1979), in responding to an article by Petrie (1979) on metaphor and learning, wrote that "reason has a much larger role in ordinary life and in everyday teaching than Petrie is willing to acknowledge" (464) and that "metaphors are nice; sometimes they are needed; often times they are useful; but epistemologically necessary they are not" (472–473). Perhaps because we have spent many hours over the past 10 years with teachers and have listened to and read their stories and narratives of personal images and metaphors, we have a preference for the recently expanded theory of metaphor. For the teachers with whom we work—indeed for ourselves—it is not so much that images and metaphors are needed; rather we and other teachers are, in an important sense, living our images and metaphors.

The Conduit Metaphor in Education. Reddy (1979) argued that "the stories English speakers tell about communication are largely determined by semantic structures of the language itself" (285). The dominant "communication structure" for Reddy is the conduit metaphor, which Johnson (1987, 59) summarizes as follows:

1. Ideas or thoughts are objects.
2. Words and sentences are containers for these objects.
3. Communication consists in finding the right word-container for your idea-object, sending this filled container along a conduit or through space to the hearer, who must take the idea-object out of the word-container.

There could hardly be a clearer, more concise account of the roles of curriculum and teaching in the educational reform literature. The conduit metaphor was beautifully illustrated for us by a school board official in our Bay Street School study, who explained that there are so many board policies that "we hold the funnel over one school and pour in a few and hold it over another school and pour in a few others, but we never pour them all into one school." The emergence of fields like curriculum implementation and the uses to which curriculum implementation and studies of teaching are put are understandable in terms of the conduit metaphor. The lack of a curriculum-making role for teachers in the curriculum reform movement needs to be understood not only as a curiosity of educational thought but also as an expression of a communication metaphor.

On these grounds, the possibilities for change in our thinking about change are further beyond our current grasp than writers such as Tomkins, Cuban, Greene, Schwab, Eisner, and Jackson may have imagined. Raising the problem to the level of metaphor (understood in the "new" sense) may be seen by some as an argument against, rather than for, changing educational thinking about change. After all, it might be argued, if societal communication is dominated by a conduit why fight it in educational reform. Reddy's (1979) conclusion should, however, at least give pause to the formulation of that argument:

> The conduit metaphor is leading us down a technological and social blind alley. That blind alley is mass communications systems coupled with mass neglect of the internal, human systems responsible for nine-tenths of the work in communicating. We think we are "capturing ideas and words" and funnelling them out to the greatest public in the history of the world. But if there are no ideas "within" this endless flood of words, then all we are doing is replaying the myth of Babel—centering it, this time, around a broadcasting tower. (310)

This metaphor, too, conveys the reform movement and the relationship of teachers to curriculum, a relationship begun in the times of Ryerson and Harris, with waves of broadcasting ever since.

The Teacher Framed by the Conduit Metaphor. We recently wrote that the terms "teaching" and "teacher" carry an authoritarian overtone, so when educational writers with an egalitarian bent wish to describe roles for the teacher they often resort to metaphor; frequently they do not mention the word "teacher" at all (Connelly and Clandinin 1990, in press). At the time we wondered why "teacher" and "teaching" carried this connotation and why so many writers wanted to avoid using the terms. The conduit metaphor helps answer our query; since the teacher possesses what is moved through the conduit, teachers become, in our sense, the *OED*'s "curricle drivers." Metaphors consistent with the conduit metaphor are teacher as "worker" (Connell 1985), "machine" (as in the "teaching machine" literature, Grobman 1970), "manager" (Clegg 1973), and doubtless many more. Metaphors that attempt to run counter to the conduit metaphor and place the teacher in a "maker" role are "mentor" (Broudy and Palmer 1965, 6), "catalyst" (Sand 1971, 238), "learner" (Lightfoot and Martin 1988), "shop steward" (Parker 1982), "cheerleader" (Pearson 1985), and "student" (Harste, Woodward, and Burke 1984).

Some of these metaphors are perhaps, as Green (1979) suggested, merely linguistic devices used by authors as they try to communicate their personal sense of teaching. Reason and logic are needed to make detailed meanings of what is suggested by such metaphors. But the conduit metaphor is of a different order: It is in our bones; it shapes the world of curriculum and teachers and underlines the various metaphors for teachers mentioned above.

Looking at Teachers in Terms of the Conduit Metaphor. Since the surge of discipline-based curriculum development in the 1950s, much has been learned about the workings of reform-oriented curriculum projects. The largest projects have been conducted in the United States and United Kingdom, whereas countries such as Canada, Australia, and Israel tended to adopt previously developed projects (Tamir 1976; Tamir, Blum, Hofstein, and Sabar 1979; Tomkins 1986). The Centre for Educational Research and Innovation of the Organization for Economic and Cooperative Development, for instance, carried out a "curriculum adaptation project" for Ireland, Scotland, and several other European countries in which various curriculum projects of potential use to the host country were adopted. As a result of the concern for program effectiveness, curriculum development became one step in a set of reform processes variously called "needs assessment," "dissemination," "implementation," "diffusion," "development," "research," and "evaluation." Acronyms such as RD&I (Research, Development, and Implementation) and DD&D (Development, Dissemination, and Diffusion) became popular. Studies of these processes, many of which took place in the context of specific reform projects, are the source of a reasonably extensive, though primarily incidental, literature of the relationship of teachers to curriculum. It is that literature that we examine in this section.

Since at least the early 1970s, project descriptions have had a place in the journal literature. *Curriculum Theory Network* (now called *Curriculum Inquiry*) published a monograph of case studies (Connelly 1971), and *Curriculum Perspectives* has included a section on project descriptions off and on since its first issue in 1980. In addition, a number of books have been published containing sets of case studies (e.g., Reid and Walker 1975); detailed descriptions of a single case (e.g., Shipman 1974; Wooton 1965); or several books on one case, perhaps the most remarkable of all being the series by Smith et al. (1971, 1986, 1987, 1988) on Kensington School. We attempt to use this project literature to construct the relationship of teachers to curriculum and to build bridges to the themes developed earlier in this chapter. It should, at the outset, be borne in mind that this literature is almost exclusively one in which the distinction between ends and means is maintained and in which the conduit metaphor is a dominating intellectual structure. The literature of curriculum projects reports on either out-of-school reformers acting on school systems or in-school reformers acting on their school system.

Project Variation: An International Survey. Garry, Connelly, and Dittman (1975) reported a study conducted to describe and analyze the developmental characteristics of 12 curriculum projects in seven countries: 1 in Australia, 2 in Canada, 2 in France, 1 in Germany, 1 in Sweden, 3 in the United Kingdom, and 2 in the United States. Project directors or their designates were interviewed, and each completed a descriptive survey questionnaire; in addition, an analysis of project documents was undertaken.

One attitude was common across the projects: All developers saw themselves as reformers rather than "as producers of new materials." They saw "their main function as educational innovators" and defined their task as planning and implementing change. They felt "responsible that the proposed innovation be turned into actual behavior at the school or administrative level" (Garry, Connelly, and Dittman 1975, 101).

Despite the common reform orientation, however, the projects varied widely in origin, funding source, organization, scope, intended user, and procedure, including the role of teachers in the curriculum development process. Although this is not an exceptional observation, it is worth bearing in mind since abstract and theoretical criticisms of educational reform tend to give the impression that the reform "conduit" has only one track. It does not. The "reality" of the curriculum development conduit is as complex—in somewhat the same way, if not to the same degree—as is the "reality" of school.

Although all the projects were concerned with the teacher in one way or another, the sanctioning and control contexts varied widely. Some projects were largely independent of government or teacher group sanctions and control, whereas others were controlled and run by central governments in which teachers are civil servants. It is fair to say that all 12 projects were consistent with the conduit metaphor as far as rank-and-file teachers were concerned. Once in motion, the projects became somewhat insular, visible entities, often independent of the ongoing work of schooling. From the point of view of teachers not involved in a project, it matters little whether it is run by other teachers, government officials, or academics; the project itself is external to their classroom situations.

But although the conduit was clearly in place in these projects, there was a great deal of variation in the teachers' relationship to the proposed curriculum. This variation is evident in three projects in which teachers were involved in the writing of curriculum materials: the U.K. Geography 14–18 Project, the Austrian Learning Objectives for Vocational Schools Project, and the German Mathematics Project. As Garry, Connelly, and Dittman wrote, "The three projects represent a continuum, as ordered, in the degree of teacher responsibility for the ideas and materials developed" (105).

In jurisdictions with strong central administrations, projects generally have little status until becoming government policy, either (or both) through listing in a government document of approved texts or through being built into a curriculum guideline structure mandated by the government. For example, in Sweden, "teachers have great leeway in deciding how to organize their instruction" (107), provided they follow the national syllabus, which is outlined in general terms. In the United States and the United Kingdom, federal and state specification of curriculum policy is minimal. But in other settings where government policy directs the details of content and instruction, as it does in some Canadian provinces, the fitting in of projects unsanctioned by the central government is much more difficult. The potential for teacher initiative in the selection and adaptation of curriculum projects varies substantially, therefore, according to the role played by the central government in the specification of curriculum policy.

In the 12 projects studied, the most common role for teachers was to provide test sites for the formative evaluation of developers' materials. Here again, however, considerable variation is evident in teacher involvement. In the U.K. Geography 14–18 and the German Mathematics projects, "development and evaluation is an interwoven activity, since teachers are the principal writers as well as the testers" (106). In other projects, test teachers and sites were chosen independently and teachers provided various kinds of feedback to the developers.

Eventually project developers, regardless of the degree to which teachers are involved in the developmental process, almost inevitably turn to training them in the use of materials. Again there was a great deal of variation, from having the involved teachers serve as a network for informing and helping other interested teachers to the development of materials aimed at assisting teachers to help children in discovery methods. The most common in-service programs were teacher workshops, although other methods such as demonstration classrooms taught either by project personnel or by teachers trained by them were also used.

At the conclusion of their section on teacher involvement, Garry, Connelly, and Dittman observed that "an overemphasis on the purity of ideas as defined by project staff can lead to excellent but potentially useless materials" (108). The developers of these projects seem caught in a dilemma: the desire to create ideal materials, which teachers may find unusable, and the necessity to create less than perfect but workable materials that teachers can use. Since "Puritans" tend to favor purity, and therefore ideal but unworkable materials, it is not surprising that many curriculum projects lose their effectiveness once project control and involvement slacken. The U.K.'s Geography 14–18 Project appears to be an exception: Teacher usability seemed uppermost on the developers' agenda. The Schools Council Humanities Curriculum Project shared some of the school-based rhetoric of the geography project but was more concerned with achieving the widespread effects the project team wanted.

Teachers in and out of the Conduit. In a much more narrowly focused study, a team of researchers, made up of subteams in administration and curriculum, undertook a detailed interview, observation, and document analysis study of curriculum reform in one Ontario county school system (Greenfield et al. 1976). The diversity of forms of curriculum development seen in the international study reported by Garry, Connelly, and Dittman (1975) was magnified in this single school system. To begin with, there were seven formal curriculum decision-making groups: board, education committee, academic coordinating committee, principals' group, subject councils, curriculum council, and special committees. In addition, there were six types of curriculum and administration positions: senior administrators, principals, consultants, secondary school department heads, teachers, and trustees. A new curriculum idea might be initiated by anyone holding an administrative, curriculum, or teaching position as well as by any of the decision-making groups. The team identified nine general patterns or routes that might be followed (each with variations) once ideas were initiated.

It is reasonably evident that in this county school system, teachers and groups of teachers could initiate curriculum reforms that might receive board of education approval. At the same time, a given teacher might be on the receiving end of several curriculum reforms initiated in different parts of the system, each carrying different sanctions, derived from their origin and route of decision making and approval. There were considerable differences between the reforms in the elementary and secondary schools and in the extent to which they were focused on individual teachers or on the system as a whole. Thus, even in those projects that put teachers at the receiving end of the "conduit," there was considerable variation in the kinds of constraints imposed.

In a related study of the secondary school biology curriculum in metropolitan Toronto, Connelly, Ben-Peretz, and Enns (1978) found that roughly two thirds of the curriculum taught was outside the bounds of policy as specified in the provincial guidelines document and was therefore technically illegal. An amusing footnote to this study is that government officials were relieved at the teachers' failure to implement the curriculum policy since the document was dated 20 years earlier and mandated a curriculum that few officials wanted and fewer could defend. Sample biology programs written and taught by the teachers were obtained and analyzed and were, according to the analysis, at least as innovative as many popular, large-scale projects, and more so than the courses of study in the standard array of government-approved texts in Ontario's *Circular 14: Textbooks*.

What these studies suggest is consistent with findings, such as those of Cremin and Franklin, that the more closely one looks at schools, the more doubt is cast on the efficacy of the means-ends split between teachers and curriculum. The three studies described here raise doubts about the appropriateness of the accountability and fidelity concerns of curriculum reforms. From the point of view of teachers, the world of curriculum and teaching is much more flexible than one would imagine from reading the reform literature, the research that supports it, and the sometimes sophisticated analysis of reform ideologies such as those discussed earlier in this chapter. Indeed, studies such as these hint at the possibility that the conduit metaphor applies primarily to the attitudes of those outside the classroom. It justifies curriculum reform and the associated practical and academic studies of "impact"; "effect"; and degrees of implementation, dissemination, diffusion, and use. But if the studies reported here are indicative, "teachers as curriculum makers" is a more appropriate metaphor for describing *their* curriculum world than is the conduit metaphor.

Mutual Adaptation Within the Conduit: The Rand Corporation Study of Change. Perhaps the most widely quoted study of school change is *Federal Programs Supporting Educational Change*, the Rand Corporation's two-phase, four-year study of federally funded programs, reported in eight volumes. Our discussion is based on volumes V (Berman, Greenwood, McLaughlin, and Pincus 1975) and VIII (Berman and McLaughlin 1978). Volume VIII summarizes the findings and describes the processes of change based on the study at the local level.

The purpose of the Rand study was to examine and evaluate a national sample of educational innovations funded by federal programs of the U.S. government. Phase one "examined four federal change-agent programs (Elementary and Secondary Education Act Title III, Innovative Projects; Elementary and Secondary Education Act Title VII, Bilingual Projects; Vocational Education Act, 1968 Amendments, Part D, Exemplary Programs; and the [Right-to Read Program] . . . and . . . identified what kinds of strategies and conditions tend to promote change in the schools and what kinds do not" (Berman and McLaughlin 1978, iii). The second phase "examined what happened to local projects in the largest change-agent programs—ESEA Title III and ESEA Title VII—when federal funding stops . . . and analyzed the institutional and project factors that promote or deter the sustaining of Title III and Title VII projects" (iii).

This is not, therefore, a study of teachers and their relationship to curriculum, although a great deal is said, and more implied, about teachers. We have a double purpose in this section: to extract and summarize the various findings about and project positions on teachers and to imagine how this study might be seen from a teacher's point of view. The second task is difficult and academically risky since it is an attempt to read the study from a different point of view than governed the study's purpose. The Rand methodology was complex, using the following quantitative and qualitative procedures:

1. Literature review
2. National survey of 18 states using 293 change-agent projects; conducted for Rand by the National Opinion Research Center (NORC)
3. Interviews of 1,735 people at all professional levels in school districts; conducted by NORC
4. Observation and interview field studies of 29 projects drawn from the larger survey sample
5. Interviews, some by telephone and some face to face, with federal, state, and project officials

Phase one, designed to understand the fate of an innovation while a federal and project presence remains, was organized into three stages: "initiation," "implementation," and "incorporation." The distinction between implementation and incorporation is between the time the project "first confronts another reality" and "when the project is no longer an exotic plant, nurtured by special funding, but becomes part of the daily environment of the district" (Berman, Greenwood, McLaughlin, and Pincus 1975, 8–9).

With respect to implementation, "the interaction between project and setting" yielded three types of situations: "mutual adaptation," when both the project design and institutional setting changed; "non-implementation," when neither element changed, usually because of LEA (local education authority) indifference or lack of abilities; and "cooptation, where the LEA changed the project, usually emasculating it, to meet its needs, without any corresponding change in the institution" (Berman, Greenwood, McLaughlin, and Pincus, ii).

Program "fidelity," or what we earlier called faithfulness to original intentions, was not observed. The authors wrote, "no class of existing educational treatments has been found that consistently leads to improved student outcomes (when variations in the institutional setting and non-school factors are taken into account)" (Berman and McLaughlin 1978, v). Statistically, lack of fidelity results in teacher variation, which is as great or greater within programs than among them (Cohen 1970; Rosenshine 1970).

"Mutual adaptation" is the single most important academic term associated with the Rand study. It is a term that "practical" people are likely to consider a virtue since it balances centralized control over curriculum change in schools (which the authors believe characterized the intentions of government officials) with grass-roots notions of reform. But it is clear that the Rand authors think of "mutual adaptation" more as a practical trade-off than a desirable process. They write that "non implementation" was due to "indifference" or poor ability and that "cooptation" was "emasculating" the project. There is little sense that the teachers, schools, and districts might have had other, perhaps parallel, agendas of merit.

Let us examine "mutual adaptation" more closely. In a list of "factors affecting implementation and continuation" (Berman and McLaughlin 1978, vi–viii), implementation strategies "could determine whether teachers would assimilate and continue using project methods or allow them to fall into disuse" (vii). Six strategies are listed as ineffective and seven as effective. Of the latter, the first six bear directly on teachers:

- concrete, teacher-specific, and extended training
- classroom assistance from project or district staff
- teacher observation of similar projects in other classrooms, schools, or districts
- regular project meetings that focused on practical problems
- teacher participation in project designs
- local materials development
- principal participation in training (viii)

These strategies contain a mix of "teacher-proofing" workshops (Connelly and Clandinin 1988), with hints of what has lately become known as the "coaching" of skills (Hunter 1984; Joyce and Showers 1982).

In addition to "implementation strategies," another factor affecting "implementation and continuation" was "characteristics of schools and attributes of teachers" (Berman and McLaughlin 1978, viii). Here, three factors were in evidence: Secondary school teachers were less likely than elementary school teachers to change; the longer the teacher had taught, the more "negative effects" there were; the greater the teachers' sense of efficacy, i.e., their "belief that the teacher can help even the most difficult or unmotivated student," the more "positive effects" there were (viii).

Similar findings are postulated at the "incorporation stage." The assimilation of new practices was "more likely when the project replaced existing practices, when there was an emphasis on training, when teacher training focused on practical classroom issues, and when curriculum materials were developed by the project staff" (Berman, Greenwood, McLaughlin, and Pincus 1975, 11).

In a discussion of the "factors that affect project outcomes," the "nature and amount of teacher change required" (15) was considered important. However, the authors found themselves in a paradoxical situation. Teachers tended to perceive projects that required substantial change in behavior as unsuccessful. However, the authors noted that "unless the project required such changes in behavior, long-run effectiveness was suspect" (15), and finally, that "even when mutual adaptation and successful implementation outcomes were achieved, there were no guarantees of project continuation after federal funding stops" (16).

The authors believed that for projects to be successful, teachers must be changed: "Many analysts, ourselves included, believe that improved student outcomes cannot be obtained in the long-run without teacher change; accordingly, we consider teacher change to be a critical project outcome in its own right" (Berman and McLaughlin 1978, 5). In specifying project outcomes and effectiveness, "the type and extent of teacher change precipitated by the innovation" (5) are important. Thus, although the projects under study by the Rand team were aimed at improving student outcomes in some area, one of its major impacts was to lodge in the reform literature, and indeed, in the curriculum literature generally, the view that curriculum development is a form of imposed teacher development. Or to put it as reformers might, if teacher development did not occur, student development in the direction specified by the reform would not follow. Teachers, in this view, are as much the target of reform as are students.

This view suggests that teachers are students and therefore learners, a notion that might seem positive in educational circles. The idea that everyone learns in a collaborative situation has gained credence in recent years (e.g., Lieberman 1986c). But the notion of "teacher as learner" that emerges from the Rand studies is that teachers should not only change but also do so in directions specified by the reformers. The notion further holds that if these learnings, i.e., "changes," do not occur, then projects will be deemed "ineffective" and teachers will have had "negative effects." It would not be surprising, therefore, if the teaching profession did not wholeheartedly pick up on the recent "progressive educator" notion that teachers are learners and that teaching, learning, and curriculum making are reciprocal educational processes. The teacher as learner within the view suggested by the Rand studies and other implementation studies has negative overtones that may carry over to the more recent notions of the teacher learning through curriculum making.

Many statements in the Rand studies (Berman and McLaughlin 1978, 7, 13–15, 17, 18, 29) on teachers in the context of mutual adaptation support the view that the studies read from a teacher's viewpoint are ominously controlling. The following statement is representative: "At the classroom level, the crux of the matter is the extent to which teachers have 'assimilated' project methods or materials into their regular classroom practice; unless this assimilation takes place, continuation will amount to no more than ritual" (6). Other statements suggest that "good" teachers are those who commit themselves to project goals. There is also a sense that participation is not valued in itself or for the education of teachers but because it contributes to project goals (see particularly 29).

We can imagine how academics who may react positively to the Rand study might feel if someone were to apply these statements to them as teachers. They would probably think that the best among them would be offended if a Rand-like study were aimed at their teaching methods and responses to an imposed program of curriculum reform at the university level. Yet following Cohen's (1988) observations on academics as teachers, academics would appear to be no better as teachers, in general, than are the school system teachers referred to by the Rand studies.

Now that we have analyzed the Rand study from the point of view of teachers, we wish to remind readers that our reading was deliberately undertaken from a very different point of view than the one used to justify the study. Our reading, if interpreted as a criticism, is unfair because we changed the terms of reference. We believe that the study has been strongly influential in softening the excesses of means-end thinking in curriculum reform and has sensitized professionals at all levels of the educational system to the curriculum life of the classroom. Berman (1980), however, later implied that mutual adaptation is less acceptable for well-developed innovations and that a high degree of fidelity is possible and desirable. A more recent study of U.S. government projects (Crandall and associates 1983; Huberman and Crandall 1983) takes a less benign view of teacher influences, advising readers to expect, but try to limit, change of the innovation. Subtle ways of committing teachers to reform purposes by using other teachers for developer ends have been proposed, as the following example indicates:

> That the presenter of the new practice is another teacher, implicitly sharing similar experiences and a common collegial bond with other teachers, tends to increase credibility. This credibility is further enhanced by the fact that the teacher's practice has been formally evaluated, and then validated by an official federal or state panel. . . . A credible, dynamic, charismatic presenter armed with a validated exemplary practice consistent with the values and capabilities of the adopting teacher can be a compelling—and effective—force behind implementation. He or she can dissipate some of the well founded skepticism many teachers feel about new practices. (Crandall 1983, 9)

Once again, the purpose is to persuade teachers to fulfill the intentions of reformers. The tactic of having trained teachers intervene with untrained teachers on behalf of the developer changes nothing insofar as the role of teachers in the reform is concerned. Overall, from the point of view of schools, and especially of teachers, the Rand studies suggest that teachers should now be on guard when they are invited to collaborate in curriculum making. They would be wise to mistrust invitations to participate in curriculum reform projects that may end up labeling them impediments to change.

"Teacher-Proof" Curriculum Within the Conduit: From Teaching Machines to Distance Education. A simple model of the relationship of teachers to new reform curricula and to research results consists of three parts: "teacher-proof curricula," "teachers as active implementors," and "teachers as adaptors in development" (Connelly and Ben-Peretz 1980). These descriptions are organized along a continuum of decreasing intended control over the teacher's role. This section focuses on the literature often thought to be close to the "teacher-proofing" end.

We were unable to find specific descriptions of projects that set out to be "teacher-proof," although programs such as DISTAR and Elbow's (1973) *Writing Without Teachers* come close. The term was popular among some writers in the 1950s who were defending a role for teachers in curriculum planning (see the National Institute of Education conference transcript, edited by Noddings [1976], in which Gates, Taylor, Williams, Randolph, Cuban, and Davis, among others, argue against notions of teacher-proof curricula). It became fashionable to turn the term on itself with another, the "curriculum-proof" teacher (e.g., Olson 1976). As Grobman (1970) wrote, "Probably no materials are entirely teacher-proofed, even if the role of the teacher is limited to distributing materials and collecting completed work. However, some materials minimize the role of the teacher to a major extent" (122). Various programs have, over the years, attempted to limit the teacher's role either by constructing materials in such a way that teachers' screening influence between materials and students was minimized or by devising implementation strategies to ensure materials were used as intended.

We review four such programs, all from the field of machines in education: teaching machines, programmed learning, and programmed textbooks; computer-assisted instruction/computer-assisted learning; computer learning environments and computer-mediated communication systems; and correspondence education/distance education.

Teaching Machines, Programmed Learning, and Programmed Textbooks. Skinner (1958) claimed that teaching machines (by which he meant a wide variety of audiovisual aids) might "supplant lectures, demonstrations, and textbooks. In doing so they serve one function of the teacher: they present material to the student and, when successful, make it so clear and interesting that the student learns" (69). Skinner went on to argue that teachers were not to be replaced in this process but that machines would free them to engage in productive exchanges with students in small-class settings. Travers (1968) worried, however, that Skinner was promoting Pressey's (1932) idea of an "industrial revolution in education." Travers, and all the other participants in the conference on technology in the curriculum in which the work is reported (Witt 1968a), conceptualized and defended a role for teachers within educational technology. Still, although none of the authors viewed technology as replacing teachers, some wanted the materials to be teacher-proofed in the sense that teachers should be trained to use the new technology properly (e.g., Witt 1968b).

The idea of teaching machines was closely linked to the idea of programmed textbooks. For instance, Cram's (1961) *Explaining "Teaching Machines" and Programming* is a programmed book to teach the concept of the teaching machine. About the time of Cram's book, Mager's (1962) *Preparing Objectives for Programmed Instruction* was popular in Canadian and American faculties of education (Popham 1974). In a curious way, the preparation of behavioral objectives for programmed instruction and the design of instructional programs, including those for machines and programmed textbooks, demonstrated a *greater* sense of the teacher as curriculum maker than many of the curriculum packages under development at the time. If the prescriptions for teachers as writers of objectives and the preparation of programmed materials were to be taken seriously, the general impetus was to put teachers in the forefront of a technology of curriculum and instruction. Generally speaking, however, many educators saw this literature as diminishing the role of the teacher, and alternatives were suggested (e.g., Eisner 1969).

Computer-Assisted Instruction/Computer-Assisted Learning. Another development in the teaching machine literature was computer-assisted instruction (CAI), sometimes called computer-assisted learning (CAL). Many feel that CAI/CAL tends to utilize mediocre courseware with routine instructional procedures (Centre for Educational Research and Innovation 1983, 11). However, in 1973, McLean optimistically wrote that "new developments . . . are likely to change the field drastically" (35). The two major systems that captured McLean's imagination were the University of Illinois's PLATO system and the TICCIT (Time-Shared, Interactive Computer Controlled Information Television) systems. He also reviewed other programs, some of which were designed to replace teachers in part of the curriculum (Bunderson 1972). McLean's (1973) view was that "teachers will not be replaced, but their role will be substantially revised" (39). In CAI, as in the case of programmed textbook and earlier teaching machines, one role teachers could assume was to be an "author" of software (McLean 1973), a role that flourished with the advent of microcomputers (Kass and Kieren 1986; Kass and Nay in press).

The reports of major CAI enterprises suggest that although generally there was more fear of teacher-proofing associated with the teaching machine and programmed learning movements than with other curriculum reforms, they were intended to be neither more, and sometimes less, teacher-proof than many packaged curriculum reforms.

Computer Learning Environments and Computer-Mediated Communication Systems. The field of teaching machines now appears to have bypassed CAI language; the literature refers to "computer learning environments" and to "computer-mediated communication systems (CMC)" (Harasim in press). We believe it is fair to say that the state of the art in this field is muddled; the emphasis is on the design of learning environments to facilitate student learning, but the place of the teacher is unclear. Computer environments appear to allow a form of direct curriculum program interaction with students in which the teacher's role is similar to that projected for PLATO, TICCIT, and other programmed learning machines. The CMC design of interactive communication networks among teachers and students appears to be a more formal structure that permits interactions to evolve in various directions, depending on teachers, students, and content. Bates (1986) argued that the CMC approach gives "greater importance to teaching as two-way communication between teachers and learners than does CAI/CAL" (51).

For example, Burge (1988) points out that the "two-way communications technologies" of CMC are "helping distance educators develop their own kinds of interactive classrooms: small and large, local and regional group configurations of learners are created by a telephone, computer conferencing and face-to-face meetings and workshops" (6). Burge's interest is in androgogy, the education of adults, as opposed to pedagogy, the education of children. The teacher appears to be a significant curriculum maker in androgogynous CMC systems, although with a different role than imagined in pedagogy. In androgogy, curriculum making is conceived as a cooperative venture between teacher and student, and the key curriculum-making act is, then, a collaborative one in which the teacher plays a "facilitator" role (Knowles 1980).

Burge (1988) casts the problem of modern distance education practices in an interesting way. She describes the dilemma of a communication system that is well defined for the teacher but based on a philosophy of collaboration in curriculum making between student and teacher. She wonders how this system affects a distance adult educator "caught between a personal philosophical acceptance of a learner-centered view and the prevalence of highly directive, transmittal modes of distance education teaching?" (13). Burge maintains that the computer environment is able to facilitate a notion of the teacher as curriculum maker.

Correspondence Education/Distance Education. A useful though somewhat outdated review of this literature is given in Ruggles et al. (1982). According to Sewart (1982), "Most distance teaching systems use a package of attractively presented self-instructional materials" in which "a great deal of time and effort is put into producing the package" (27). The problem with this approach, says Sewart (1981), is that it does not take into account the student's frame of reference. To do so requires teacher mediation. If Sewart's assessment of the field of distance education is accurate, the teachers' curriculum-making role is to give students "individualized advice, support, interpretation, and mediation" (27). The curriculum package is a given, as is the student's self-direction in taking the course. Although authors such as Clennell, Peters, and Sewart (1983, 333) say that humane and encouraging commentary on student assignments is desirable, the curriculum role of the teacher is on the teacher-proof end of the continuum.

Although distance education in the 1980s is often written about as an adult activity of special interest to developing countries (Coldevin 1988; Daniel, Stroud, and Thompson 1982; Keegan 1986; Sewart, Keegan, and Holmberg 1983), it is also evident in school jurisdictions in developed countries (see, e.g., the Ontario Ministry of Education's Independent Learning Centre). Keegan (1982) points out that UNESCO's (1979) definition of correspondence education as "education conducted by the postal services without face-to-face contact between teacher and learner" cannot encompass the new forms of education in the 1980s: print, audio, video and computer-based possibilities. When one considers that CMC is a version of distance education, it becomes clear that a wide range of teacher roles in curriculum making are evident in correspondence education. In some cases teachers do little more than mark student assignments, never meeting their students, whereas in other cases, they may interact with them in the way described by Burge and Sewart. Keegan, from an Australian perspective, classifies correspondence education arrangements into four types: correspondence school, multimedia system, consultation model, and integrated mode. Each exhibits different teacher roles in curriculum making. The greatest degree of teacher-proofing probably occurs in correspondence-style programs, in which most of the instructors are part-time and women (Carr 1984; Markowitz 1983).

Davis (1983), in his review of distance education for small secondary schools in Canada, the United States, New Zealand, and Western Australia, points out that in all of these countries, although designed originally to provide a balanced curriculum for rural secondary school certification, distance education has been expanded to adult and urban environments (Davis and Ryan 1980; Edington 1976; McVeagh 1981; O'Neal and Beckner 1981; Sher 1981; Turney, Sinclair, and Cairns 1980). There is no intention to replace the teacher but rather to use distance education courses in conjunction with regular ones. In addition, the trend in distance education is to have the teacher's role be more than a supervisor of correspondence courses (Davis 1983; Gall 1983). Thus, this literature conveys a sense that teachers interacting with students are makers of curriculum.

More recent terms in the language of distance education are "on-line education," "electronic schoolhouse," and "computer learning networks" (Harasim 1986). Some observers see these developments as the promise of a teacher-proof era. Naisbitt (1984), for instance, predicted that "personal computers will turn living rooms into classrooms" (23). But a more creative curriculum-maker role for teachers is evident in the literature. Experimental projects are under way in various places (Gee 1988; Harasim 1986), many of them necessitating an active teacher role. For example, in some of them (Harasim 1986), in addition to the usual class role, there is a heavy "curriculum-making" emphasis in the interactions within groups and in teacher interaction with individual students. These projects place teachers well over on the side of curriculum makers, both with respect to the content of the communication and to the curriculum created in the interactions among participants—teachers and students.

From External Development to School-Based Development: From Materials Development to Staff Development

Studies of Teachers in Reform Settings. For many, Wolcott's (1973) view that "the real change agents of schools in modern societies are the young teachers, the young parents, and the pupils themselves" (321) is now accepted wisdom rather than idiosyncratic observation. In the research literature of the English-speaking world, one consistent finding is that teachers make the difference when it comes to realizing the intentions of external developers. This finding has generated a small body of literature focused on teacher attitudes toward, preferences about, and actions within curriculum development activities. Some of this work was done in the context of particular projects (e.g., Crandall 1983; Little 1981; Newton and Kinakin 1989; Olson 1980); some within school systems (e.g., Brady 1987; Finch 1981; Kimpston and Anderson 1982; Seddon 1981; Young 1979, 1985), and some in centralized government curriculum policy systems, either adopting or developing specific projects (e.g., Ben-Peretz and Kremer 1979; Ben-Peretz and Tamir 1981; Brown and McIntyre 1982; Kremer and Ben-Peretz 1980; Sabar, Silberstein, and Shafriri 1982). There is also, of course, classroom research in which some aspect of teachers and curriculum is under study; no particular reforms are being introduced, but the work is intended to be of use to policymakers (e.g., Ashton and Webb 1986).

Teachers' attitudes toward participation in external curriculum development appear to be mixed, some wanting to become involved and some not, for a wide variety of reasons (Kimpston 1985). This literature, combined with the literature on teachers in studies of implementation, has generated a plethora of factors and forces ranging over the political-social climate, policy, school structure, organizational factors and forces, administrative arrangements, disciplinary bodies of inquiry, career paths, and professionalism—all of which are seen to condition teachers' commitment to curriculum reforms (Fullan 1982, 1983; Leithwood 1982).

An interesting concept in this literature is "curriculum potential" (Ben-Peretz 1975), the idea that curriculum materials and packages are not embodiments of things for teachers to do but reservoirs of "potential" from which teachers and students may create a variety of classroom curricula. This idea has heuristic value. It helps resolve the dilemma created by social pressure for school reform through the curriculum set against the resistance of schools, classrooms, and teachers to externally directed change. With this concept it is possible to retain the hope, spirit, and intelligence of reformers without turning them into persons who demand fidelity to their cause or achieve their ends by deceptive means.

Staff Development and School-Based Curriculum Development. An expanded literature of school-based curriculum development and staff development has emerged in the past decade, encouraged perhaps by the research findings that some ***kinds*** of innovations were more readily implemented by teachers than others (e.g., Brown and McIntyre 1982), that it was possible to obtain a high degree of teacher ''fidelity'' to developer intentions if programs were sufficiently precise and teachers were carefully trained and supported (e.g., Crandall 1983), and that some such innovations had lasting effects (e.g., Kirst and Meister 1985). Some of this writing has an ''expressive'' quality (Eisner 1969); it focuses on the creation of situations rich in curriculum potential (e.g., Boomer 1982; Dow 1982; Eggleston 1980; Holly and Southworth 1989; Hopkins 1985; Jersild 1946; Lieberman 1986a; Miel 1952; Miller and Lieberman 1988; Munby 1986; Russell and Munby in press; Schostak and Logan 1984; Thiessen in press). However, there is much in the staff development and school-based curriculum development literature that suggests an alliance between reformers and researchers with policymakers and school administrators—that somehow if these groups could work together more closely, they would be able to force reform through the conduit into the classrooms.

Guskey (1986) writes that ''staff development programs vary widely in context and format, yet they generally share a common purpose'' (4). This purpose was defined by Griffin (1983) as ''to alter the professional practices, beliefs, and understanding of school persons toward an articulated end'' (Guskey 1986, 2). Young (1979) wrote in her study of teacher participation, ''School-based management, at its best, also includes built-in accountability'' (124). Even when ''considerable curriculum decision making is transferred from district to school the school staff is held accountable to the district for the outcomes of its decision making'' (124) through an evaluation process. ''Commitment'' for some teachers may be related to their desire for promotion to administrative or research posts (House 1974; Young 1985).

School Improvement. Another recent literature at the conduit-classroom interface concerns school improvement. Marsh (1988, 5) points out that it first became prominent in the United States in the 1960s with reference to federal and state programs for school improvement in specific areas.

An internationally known idea associated with the school improvement literature is the Concerns-Based Adoption Model (C-BAM) (Hall and Loucks 1977). The link between external reformers and C-BAM is illustrated in the following:

> Innovations were frequently not fully implemented and, therefore, not fairly tested. This situation led us to observe more closely the experiences of teachers and college professors as they adopted and implemented educational innovations. . . . We documented examples and began to describe these stages and levels, thereby contributing to the Concerns-Based Adoption Model. (Hall and Hord 1984, 7)

The C-BAM model allows reformers to analyze teachers' concerns in order to construct a profile of ''levels of use'' of innovation. The profile allows reformers to categorize the ways teachers respond to particular innovations and is used to enhance the level of classroom use by identifying and building on teachers' concerns. The current educational impulse for the coaching of teachers (Joyce and Showers 1982) and for ''direct teaching'' (Hunter 1984) are other school improvement strategies for shaping teachers to the intentions of reformers.

Action Research. In our discussion of the Humanities Curriculum Project we show that action research, as usually interpreted, is another, albeit subtle, example of treating teachers as the means to carry out others' ideas. This point is less obvious in the action research literature since researchers shift their reform ''intentions'' from students to teachers, claiming that teachers need to emancipate themselves and become the creators of curriculum purpose for themselves and students. Many writers in the action research movement are anxious to dissociate themselves from impositional ''reproductive'' ideologies and from ''big R Research'' (Boomer 1987, 13). The moral tone of their arguments differs from that of the ''technical rationality'' reform literature to which they object. For example, Elliott (1985) writes that Stenhouse's process model of curriculum development is built on a radically different ''view about the nature and development of teachers' professional knowledge and its relationship to educative practice'' (241) from ''the model of technical rationality. It is a view that gives teachers, rather than specialist researchers and theorists, responsibility for generating their own expert knowledge'' (242). In Elliot's view, the ''teachers as researchers movement'' emerged in the United Kingdom in the context of process-focused curriculum development projects (242).

Read from the teachers' viewpoint, however, this view merely replaces one set of reform intentions with another: Teachers are now required to develop knowledge, undertake research, change, grow, reflect, revolutionize their practice, become emancipated, emancipate their students, engage in group collaboration, assume power, and become politically active. Readers, teachers, and other reformers will exhibit various biases for and against such a view of what teachers should do, just as readers exhibit biases for and against the assumptions and content of more traditional reforms and what teachers should do with them. It is no accident that the present educational version of the action research movement grew out of a highly public, well-funded project led by a reformer with the energy and rhetoric to demand the attention of other researchers, policymakers, and teachers. Proponents of action research may see themselves as liberators in comparison with ''traditional'' reformers who, they claim, promote ''technical-rational,'' ''non-process'' curriculum reforms. It seems, however, that the action researchers are equally imbued with Cremin's (1961) spirit of ''puritanism'' and passionately wish teachers and schools to be something other than they are.

When one reads the action research literature in the context of other severe critics of ''top-down,'' ''hegemonic'' reform (e.g., Apple 1986; Giroux 1988), it is clear that the classroom has become a battleground for winning the hearts of teachers to a particular view about who they are and what they *should* become. It is a power struggle to replace one hegemony with another, to gain control of the messages within the conduit. Cuban's (1976) metaphor applies: It is all rather like the squalls that disturb the surface of the sea, which underneath remains calm.

IMAGES OF TEACHERS AS CURRICULUM MAKERS: STORIES OF TEACHERS

The Reconstruction of an Idea of Teacher as Curriculum Maker: Dewey with Jackson, Schwab, and Eisner

In this section we return to the historical origins of the idea of teacher as curriculum maker: Our purpose is to pick up threads not generally evident in the literature reviewed so far and almost wholly missing from the "research on teaching" and "teacher thinking" fields. From this process will emerge a reconstructed idea of the teacher as curriculum maker. This idea is intended to serve as a basis for reviewing literature that bears on our topic and to help us explore its implications for collaborative efforts of professors of curriculum and teachers.

John Dewey's writings and the work of Dewey's school—The Laboratory School of the University of Chicago—constitute the core of the idea. We have chosen to elaborate on Dewey's ideas with writings by Philip Jackson, Joseph Schwab, and Elliot Eisner. Each taught at the University of Chicago, and Jackson was director of the Laboratory School for a time; each acknowledges a debt to Dewey's thinking in his writings; each has made a career of writing on the link between teaching and curriculum; each is widely quoted in the literature on the teacher as curriculum maker. Other writers have made important contributions and meet some of these criteria; Maxine Greene, Lawrence Stenhouse, Ann Lieberman, Donald Schön, John Goodlad, Malcolm Skilbeck, George Tomkins, and Seymour Sarason come to mind. But no one known to us meets the criteria as fully as Jackson, Schwab, and Eisner do.

John Dewey and the Dewey School. Although Dewey did not directly concern himself with curriculum making (Seguel 1966, 4), he wrote works expressing a view of curriculum in which the teacher plays an active and creative role. These works include *The Child and the Curriculum* and *The School and Society*, both published in 1956 as a single volume with a joint title, and "My Pedagogic Creed" (1897). The time in which Dewey wrote has an ironic quality when regarded from the point of view adopted in this chapter. It was a period when teachers were thought not to be well educated, and the curriculum movement was just beginning. It was a period that current humanistic writers decry as an era of dehumanizing "scientific curriculum making" (Kliebard 1975). The irony is, first, that such a time was, it would appear, also one of high hopes for what the schools might accomplish; second, a time of confidence in teachers as curriculum makers (much more so than characterizes our current era); and, third, a time when it was accepted that the schools were places of social experiment and their participants had something to teach theoreticians and researchers.

With respect to the first and last of these three points, we note that the *Twenty-sixth Yearbook of the National Society for the Study of Education* (Whipple 1926) was built around descriptions of schools under the following five headings: Lincoln School of Teachers College, Columbia University; Current Practices in Curriculum-Making in Public Schools; Examples of Progressive Curriculum-Construction in Public School Systems; Curriculum-Making in Private Laboratory Schools; Miscellaneous Curriculum Studies.

Dewey found it necessary to develop his ideas in situ and was head of the University of Chicago Laboratory School (where his wife was principal) from 1894 to 1904. A detailed account of this period, authorized by Dewey, is given in *The Dewey School* (Mayhew and Edwards 1936). Furthermore, Dewey, with his daughter, wrote *Schools of To-Morrow* (Dewey and Dewey, 1915). The book describes, with photographs,

> what actually happens when schools start out to put into practice, each in its own way, some of the theories that have been pointed to as the soundest and best ever since Plato. . . . The schools we have used for purposes of illustration are all of them directed by sincere teachers trying earnestly to give their children the best they have by working out concretely what they consider the fundamental principles of education. More and more schools are growing up all over the country that are trying to work out definite educational ideas. (i–ii)

With respect to the second point—a time of confidence in teachers—our view is primarily based on Seguel's (1966) work and the historical sources discussed in other sections of this chapter. Following Seguel's trail, which begins with McMurry and proceeds through Bobbit, Charters, Rugg, and Cazwell, we can see that there was a working assumption during the early years of this century that whatever was thought about education would need to be thought out and developed in schools by teachers. Charles McMurry (1914) wrote, "The teacher is working at the very smelting process, the point of difficulty where new, uncomprehended knowledge meets this tumult of the child's mind" (258); and Rugg and Counts (1926) wrote, "There is a crucial need that the energies of both teachers and specialists be harnessed to the task of organizing the creative activities of the elementary and secondary schools" (446).

We are not historians and our account here reflects this fact. We believe that proper historical studies of this period would be illuminating; not only would they help us to understand the history of the teacher as curriculum maker but also they would provide a more balanced picture of the ways in which schools, colleges of education, faculties, consortia, and laboratories might work together. There was more to this period of time than scientific curriculum making. It was, after all, a progressive era (Cremin 1961). It is almost as if the massive injection of funds by governments and major foundations during the Sputnik era of the 1950s erased a part of our collective memory of schools. We do not remember, and cannot therefore imagine, how it was to think theoretically about schools at a time when practice and schooling were preeminent; when it was not assumed that schools and teachers were something like potter's clay, to be shaped by carefully constructed programs run by carefully designed implementation methods and supported by the latest in school improvement, staff development, research on teaching and teacher thinking, and action research strategies. What, one wonders, did it feel like for teachers and theoreticians to live in a mental landscape where theory and practice had a different shape from that which we have come to experience, living as we do in an age of the conduit?

Our sense of the period in which Dewey wrote is of a time when people of ideas felt mostly powerless to impose their ideas on others; they had a feeling in their bones that for their ideas to be developed and take root they needed to work with teachers and schools, in the teachers' terms and on the teachers' territory. We gained little sense of the conduit as we turned the pages of little-used books of the period (although the conduit is doubtlessly present in some form). The assumption that underlies modern educational literature, i.e., that the conduit is in place and that it is merely a question of making it work well or of unblocking the dam at the classroom end, is scarcely evident in this earlier literature. We sense the period as one of hope in the potential of schools to develop and work out ideas; today's hope by and large is that schools and teachers will learn to do well what the thinkers and policymakers tell them to do. In general, the more academics have come to know about teaching, curriculum development and reform, and implementation, the less trust we have placed in teachers and schools. Scientific knowledge of schooling appears inversely related to confidence in the schools as places of social growth and reform. We need historical studies to help us understand the effect on schools of our relatively newfound knowledge about teaching and curriculum reform. We anticipate that these studies would cast a shadow of doubt on our collective belief that the schools are somehow better places than they were 70 years ago because scholars have pursued their research and development projects and agendas.

Dewey (1897) wrote,

> I believe, finally, that the teacher is engaged, not simply in the training of individuals, but in the formation of the proper social life.
>
> I believe that every teacher should realize the dignity of his calling; that he is a social servant set apart for the maintenance of proper social order and the securing of the right social growth.
>
> I believe that in this way the teacher always is the prophet of the true God and the usherer in of the true kingdom of God. (80)

These lines appear in the fifth of five articles in his Creed, and when read in the context of Article I, Dewey is understood to be saying that in the laboratory of the school, teachers not only reproduce the "inherited cultural wisdom" of civilization but also reconstruct, with children, this wisdom through inquiry; inquiry is viewed as a social movement involving practical "conflicts" and theoretical and intellectual "controversies" (Dewey 1938, 5), thereby establishing visions of social growth.

When we also take into account other of Dewey's writings, in which we see that all philosophy is a philosophy of education, and life and education are two sides of the same coin, the teacher as curriculum maker means more than the reconstruction of social heritage and student experience for student growth. Through this reconstruction, it means the growth of society itself. Social and personal growth are intimately connected in an "organic" venture in which the teacher is the central curriculum maker. Here is a glimpse of the experience of two teachers—Mayhew and Edwards (1936)—in the Dewey school:

> The school felt and thought out its way as it went along. Its principles and practices were quite unlike those of contemporary method whether in the teaching or administrative area. The school was a social institution. Parents, teachers, administrators were joined in a search for a better way of schooling, where each individual, whether child or adult, could have his chance for normal, happy growth and the satisfactions of creative expression that was social in its character and purpose. In such a school, cooperation must replace competition, and the efforts of each must align, not vie, with one another in a search for a common end. All this meant new planning, new setting of the stage for daily activities which should permit and promote a socially motivated school life. (365–366)

In a footnote, George W. Myers, professor of mathematics in the Chicago Institute and later in the School of Education, is quoted as saying, "Mr. Dewey had the greatest real faith of any real educator I have ever known in the classroom teacher's judgment as to what children can and should do" (Mayhew and Edwards 1936, 366). The reconstructive quality of life in this school's classrooms, and the intermingling of theory and practice in the interactions of teachers, students, administrators, and parents, is seen in Mayhew and Edwards' remark,

> Although the immediate decision with regard to treatment of subject-matter and method was left to the individual teacher, each teacher's method was so checked and rechecked by cooperative discussion . . . that changes in viewpoint continually took place. Therefore, teachers and children, administrators and parents, as a result of sharing in the same social process, shared also in the educational benefits therefrom. (381–382)

Dewey's ideas have been kept alive and, indeed, reconstructed in the writings of Jackson, Schwab, and Eisner, among others. Instead of reviewing these authors' works, we propose only to identify a single idea in each of importance to our purpose and to suggest that a thorough historical review of this topic is needed.

Philip Jackson. Jackson has been a devastating, though sympathetic, critic of research on teaching. In 1966 he worried that "the moral cast of educational research" (8) was turning up in research work; researchers were more concerned with what "ought to be happening" in classrooms than with finding out "what actually happens in classrooms" (8). What especially troubled Jackson was the "undeniable fact that our search for the 'good' just doesn't seem to have paid off. Almost all of the noble crusades that have set out in search of the best teacher and the best method—or even the better teacher and the better method—have returned empty-handed. The few discoveries to date . . . are pitifully small in proportion to their cost and time and energy" (8–9).

Jackson's attitude was no more favorable in 1985, when he wrote of the time-on-task literature, "I have grave doubts about its yielding very much in the way of genuine new insights into either the teaching or the learning process" (305), nor in 1987 when, in an article entitled "Facing Our Ignorance," he referred to the Holmes Group report on teacher education as "boastful" in its claims about what is known about teaching. Indeed, he believed that the net effect of research on teaching is negative and that "we may even know less today than we once did about how to teach and particularly about why teaching is so important for the future of our society" (74). (We sensed the truth of this claim as we weighed the writings in the *Handbooks of Research on Teaching* and the "teacher thinking" literature against such writings as the *Twenty-sixth Yearbook* [Whipple 1926] and Dewey's works.)

Jackson (1987), like Eisner, asks the profession to step out of the conduit, "abandoning forever our dreams of a science of education" (78). His (1966) distinction between "preactive" and "interactive" teaching activities and what each portends for the study of teaching and curriculum is important to our purpose. He reminds readers of their own interactive moments of teaching to draw attention to its moral quality (something, curiously, rarely hinted at in research on teaching). His own *Life in Classrooms* (1968) was the kind of study he had in mind. This document is foundational to the literature we call "teachers' stories and stories of teachers."

Joseph Schwab. We have already remarked that through his notion of the commonplaces of curriculum, Schwab insisted that the ideas of curriculum and teacher implicate one another. Almost all of Schwab's writings may be read as autobiographical excursions. He prided himself on his teaching and twice won the University of Chicago's excellence in teaching award. "Teacher" is the vantage point for anyone wishing to understand the significance of Schwab's writing on curriculum. A collection of his writings, along with a complete bibliography of his works, is found in *Science, Curriculum, and Liberal Education* (Westbury and Wilkof 1978). Schwab wrote that "curriculum is brought to bear, not on ideal or abstract representations, but on the real thing, on the concrete case, in all its completeness and with all its differences from all other concrete cases, on a large body of fact concerning which the theoretic abstraction is silent" (quoted in Westbury and Wilkof 1978, 309–310). Schwab's point was not only that curriculum needed to deal with what goes on in practice—in schools—but also that once in schools, researchers needed to pay attention to specific curricular settings, not to statistically significant groups. As Westbury and Wilkof put it, "Instincts of this kind have through all of his career as a teacher and a scholar driven Schwab inward to *this* classroom, to a careful analysis of the characteristics of the students he had *this* semester and always to a concern to the here-and-now of the next class, in *this* course, in this program" (35).

In one of Schwab's (1954) most compelling essays, "Eros and Education," he explored eros, "the energy of wanting," as an affective bond between teacher and student in the search for truth. Successful education, he said, needed to tap this energy source. Only the teacher can do so, and the agency of a teacher in curriculum making rested in the capacity to enter into powerful relationships with particular students.

As we reflect on the literature of teachers' stories, on Dewey's work in a school to develop his ideas, and on Jackson and Schwab referencing *their own* teaching as a basis for their ideas about teaching, we marvel at the equanimity with which writers on curriculum reform, research on teaching, teacher thinking, and action research prescribe on the basis of images of research rather than of teaching, let alone on images of their own teaching put up for inspection.

Schwab's (1983) final paper before he died was entitled "The Practical 4: Something for Curriculum Professors to Do." This is a practical paper on the art of being a curriculum professor. He describes the curriculum planning process as a collaborative one in which the first members chosen for the team should be teachers: "The children of the school are learners . . . what they disdain and what they see as relevant to their present or future lives, are better known by no one than the teacher. It is he who tries to teach them. It is she who lives with them for the better part of the day and the better part of the year" (245). Here, again, we see a language of affect used to speak of the curriculum relationship established between teacher and child. Schwab also disdains the conduit:

> Teachers will not and cannot be merely told what to do. Subject specialists have tried it. Their attempts and failures I know at first hand. Administrators have tried it. Legislators have tried it. Teachers are not, however, assembly line operators, and will not so behave. Further, they have no need, except in rare instances, to fall back on defiance as a way of not heeding. There are thousands of ingenious ways in which commands on what and how to teach can, will, and must be modified or circumvented in the actual moments of teaching. Teachers practice an art. Moments of choice of what to do, how to do it, with whom and at what pace, arise hundreds of times a school day, and arise differently every day and with every group of students. No command or instruction can be so formulated as to control that kind of artistic judgment and behavior, with its demand for frequent, instant choices of ways to meet an ever varying situation (245).

Elliot Eisner. Eisner is another neo-Deweyan who is central to the idea of the teacher as curriculum maker. We use

Eisner's work later to construct what we consider to be a future agenda for writers on the teacher as curriculum maker and will therefore leave his important contributions for later discussion. One anecdote, however, makes a highly relevant point about the quality of his thought. In the early 1970s Eisner called together a group at the University of Illinois for no other purpose than to talk and, by that talk, to establish a sense of community. Behind his call for the meeting was a feeling of academic isolation. Although he was widely quoted in the literature and had numerous speaking engagements, he did not feel part of a developing research community. To varying degrees the others invited to the meeting also led isolated academic lives, apart from the mainstream. We believe this quality marks the academic lives of each of our neo-Deweyans and, indeed, of Dewey himself. Part of the "success" of certain lines of research is that they are defined by a relatively close community of scholars who trade citations, meet together, and vie for group influence in major academic organizations. But Eisner and his Illinois group were part of no research line. Eisner, along with Schwab and Jackson, swam against the theory and practice current, which generally flowed toward an increasingly refined definition of the conduit and increasing treatment of schooling and teacher actions as means for social purpose, theory, and curriculum reform. Academics who view *themselves* as means for social progress defined by schools and teachers, rather than as the source of social progress, inevitably have only the smallest of academic, collegial communities. Their community is their own classrooms and students and the teachers with whom they establish close working relationships.

In the next section we review in depth one curriculum development project to see, from a teacher's perspective, the place of the teacher as curriculum maker.

The Humanities Curriculum Project: Stories Within Stories of Teachers as Curriculum Makers

One kind of literature that allows us to explore teachers as curriculum makers is that on school-based curriculum projects. The Humanities Curriculum Project (HCP), initiated in the United Kingdom under the joint sponsorship of the Schools Council and the Nuffield Foundation and headed by Lawrence Stenhouse, specifically acknowledged the centrality of the teacher in the classroom and is frequently referenced in discussions of the teacher as researcher. It is an important project to explore because of its focus on the teacher, and on the teacher as an inquirer into the ways in which curriculum is shaped in the classroom. Thinking of school reform through the work of teachers as researchers represents a major shift in the field of curriculum; the work of Stenhouse and the HCP is frequently cited as the forerunner in this development.

Many books, papers, and articles have been written on various aspects of the project. Our task in this review is to reconstruct the story to portray the project's view of the teacher as curriculum maker, using discussions about the project, descriptions of project activities, and teachers' stories about their experience. The review is extensive, for we needed first to construct the project story in ways that would allow us to examine the teacher as curriculum maker.

Our intent in exploring this project is to go beyond the researchers' ways of thinking about it and to convey the teachers' stories as they lived out their practices in their classrooms. We trace different stories of the project. We begin by reconstructing the project story in broad brush strokes, sketching the setting, the characters, and the activities in which they engaged. The data on the teachers' stories are, for the most part, taken from *People in Classrooms: Teacher Evaluations of the Humanities Curriculum Project* (Elliott and MacDonald 1975), a collection of essays written for a symposium on the project. Stenhouse's story as project director is a narrative thread woven through the other stories.

Teachers at the Time of the HCP. Many teachers in England, at the time of the initiation of the HCP in the 1960s, came from two broad types of backgrounds. Some had been successful working-class children. In winning places in the grammar schools, they had lost or been forced to give up their home dialect to fit in and succeed. Others, such as Stenhouse, had been children of privilege. Their grammar school education had not disrupted their lives.

Patricia Sikes (1988) described the teachers in an innovatory humanities faculty of a West Riding (Yorkshire) comprehensive school as individuals who as students in the early 1960s had been politically to the left and who as teachers believed in education as a potent force for social change:

> Teachers such as these were ready to take up the philosophy and practice of the Humanities Curriculum Project in its dissemination phase and later. However, there were also teachers who had neither the experience nor the social conscience to question the assumption that only twenty per cent of eleven year olds were capable of academic work. (1)

The Setting of the Project. The HCP began in the mid-1960s in Britain at a time when students were streamed at age 11 at the end of primary school on the basis of what was termed the "11+ examinations." A policy change had just been instituted whereby students went to comprehensive schools called "secondary moderns," which housed the three "types" of students. Many students (about 40 percent) who attended the secondary modern schools wrote no secondary-level examinations, leaving school at age 15 with no official qualifications. These students were often referred to as the "4Zs," that is, the lowest stream of the fourth form. As in primary school, the curriculum for the school leavers was controlled within the school by the headmaster, department heads, and teachers.

Students who failed the 11+ examinations were committed to secondary modern schools until they could legally leave and seek work. Elliott (1988) described large numbers of these students as lacking "any interest in the subject-matter of the curriculum. Their slim chances of securing examination success meant that examinations were a poor extrinsic motivator. The alienation was particularly acute in those humanities subjects which students and their parents perceived to have little relevance to the world of work: namely, history, geography and religion'' (2).

Elliott (1988) pointed out that ''faced with passive resistance and active rebellion teachers in the Secondary Modern had two choices. The first was to develop and maintain a system of coercive control: to turn Secondary Moderns into 'concentration camps.' The second was to make the curriculum more intrinsically interesting for the students and transform the examination system to reflect such a change'' (2–3). Elliott described the secondary moderns of the 1960s as situated on a continuum: The ''concentration camps'' were at one end, at the other were the ''innovatory Secondary Moderns,'' and in between were the majority of schools struggling with the tension between these two climates.

The ways in which schools were administered by the government underwent change in the early 1960s. Under the Education Act of 1944, the Local Education Authorities (LEAs) prescribed curricula; in practice teachers largely controlled what they taught. In May 1964 the Schools Council for Curriculum and Examinations, a representative body of LEAs, teachers, and other relevant agencies, was formed. The council was supported by public funds, but its constitution was intended to prevent its control by the funders and, in some sense, to place it in the control of the teachers. The early assumption was that it would increase the freedom of teachers rather than impose direction. Manzer (1972) wrote that ''schools would retain the fullest possible measure of responsibility for their own work within a framework reflecting the general interests to the community in the educational process and taking account of requirements of further education and professional organizations'' (123). He concluded that it was ''an organization which can cock a snook at the Ministry any time it likes, yet has no powers of dictation over the man in the classroom'' (124). The original constitution of the council merely legitimized a long-established pattern of informal relationships among teachers and central and local administrators in the area of curricular development.

Between 1964 and 1976 the council initiated and supported more than 160 projects ''whose major concern had been to lend speed and quality to the ongoing process of curriculum change in the classroom by centralizing the functions of invention and production. The implicit model of planned change was thus centre-peripheral: innovation is accelerated at the centre, then disseminated to the outposts'' (MacDonald and Walker 1976b, 1).

The Emergence of the Humanities Curriculum Project. The following account is based on MacDonald's (1978) *The Experience of Curriculum Innovation*. A 1967 circular of the school council entitled ''The Raising of the School Leaving Age (ROSLA) and the Curriculum Programme of the Council'' announced two initiatives: the temporary assignment of a small group of head teachers to act as field officers for the council and the council's decision to set up a new national program in the area defined as ''society and the school leaver.'' The circular read, in part, ''The Project will be jointly supported by the Nuffield Foundation and the Council. The area of the curriculum on which the team will concentrate is mainly within the fields of History, Geography, English and Religious Education but it is hoped that account can also be taken of the contribution of those studies which can be defined as the social sciences'' (quoted by MacDonald 1978, 39). With this circular the stage was set for the project that eventually became the Humanities Curriculum Project. A second circular in 1967 stated that the project would supply free materials to the trial schools and stated the criteria for their selection.

In November 1967, 30 LEAs were chosen and were notified that Stenhouse, appointed project director in January 1967, would visit them in spring 1968 ''in order to get the precise schools which fit into the structure of the sample needed for the trials, which may in some cases mean finding alternatives to those schools which LEAs have put forward'' (MacDonald 1978, 51). In March 1968, Stenhouse ''began what was virtually a whistle-stop tour of participant LEAs, explaining the experimental design in some detail, finalizing the choice of school, talking to the headmasters concerned. His main aims were to secure a firm promise of support from each LEA and to make personal contact with the head of each school'' (51).

The 36 trial schools represented a range of secondary modern and comprehensive schools in suburban, urban, and rural settings. In individual schools the project teams ranged from two to eight members, three or four being the norm. To prepare for the beginning of the project in September 1968, the teachers were invited to a regional induction conference with the project team in July. For many teachers, this was their first encounter with the project. The LEAs were invited to a half-day conference in September, at which the development of the project and the progress of its trials were fully described.

Induction of Teachers into the HCP (Trial Phase). The teachers in the trial schools attended one of three 5-day regional induction conferences with the project team in July 1968 in preparation for a September start-up. Stenhouse (1983) spoke at each conference and later noted that as a result, ''the relationship towards which we looked was achieved with about a fifth of the teachers involved'' (70).

In his talk Stenhouse (MacDonald 1978) told the teachers who they were, or rather what the project team wanted them to become.

> We want colleagues to take part in an experiment with us. It isn't a situation in which we make something and you try it, but one in which we explore something together. . . . The kind of teaching we look towards has familiar elements. . . . But as a centre for this work there will, we hope, be a type of discussion which is quite unfamiliar in schools. We want to develop this type of discussion and to study it in a setting of the total pattern of teaching. (108)

Stenhouse listed what the project team asked of their teacher colleagues: that they accept the desirability of mounting free and open-ended discussions of controversial social and personal issues; that they realize that this is difficult work and that it will tax both them and their pupils; that they will press toward higher standards than thus far achieved; that they will work toward a relationship with school leavers that helps these students to grow up by stressing their maturity and responsibility rather than prolonging their childhood and dependence; that the rooms will be arranged for discussion rather than instruction; that resources will be used to supplement the teachers' packs; that wallboards will be used to display photographs and clippings; that they will become members of the project team, that is, that they will fully accept the aims and implications of what is being attempted; that they will be prepared to be studied, even filmed, and to study themselves in the classroom. The teacher was to assume the role of neutral leader in classroom discussions. Stenhouse said, "We want to work with teachers who care and who are tough minded and persistent. We do not expect to work with teachers who are virtuosos in discussion techniques" (112). In his explanation of the teachers' work in the project, it was clear that Stenhouse was presenting a comprehensive view of what the curriculum in each classroom should look like.

Stenhouse then explained what the project team would provide: clear and coherent hypotheses so that experimental teachers were in no doubt about what the project was trying to do; stimulus, support, and materials to the limits of time and ability; and responsiveness to the reports teachers gave and the needs they defined. All project handbooks and notes were to be regarded as drafts to be shaped by teachers' comments (MacDonald 1978, 115).

Stenhouse's view of the project in each classroom was clear. It specified the work of the teacher, learner, subject matter, and milieu and spelled out the ways in which one should relate to another. MacDonald and Walker (1976a) comment that

> the project held out to the teacher a vision of what schools and teaching could become if they started from different premises . . . . The promise was a future in which, through a process of redefinition of the relationship between teacher, taught, and knowledge, schools would be transformed into democratic institutions, teachers into research-based master craftsmen of a new professional tradition, and students into reflective scholars. (81)

Teachers were "to recast themselves in a research role in the classroom, to follow laid-down procedures, and to implement their findings subsequently" (81). Although Stenhouse said, "We have nothing to recommend" (81), it was clear from the formulation presented in these initial sessions that a great deal was being recommended.

Early Teacher Stories of the Project. Three visits with teachers, described by MacDonald (1978) after the initial training sessions, show the range of stories of teachers' involvement in the project. The teachers' early experiences ranged from accounts in which children were "mute" and teachers "stiff as boards and sweating anxiety" to teachers who "think they can do what they like. And they don't like what they think Stenhouse said" to schools "where the Project is going well, and where the HCP team leader demonstrates a grasp of Project theory at least equal to that of the central team members" (287, 288).

Training of Other Teachers in the HCP: (Dissemination Phase). Training of teachers continued after the first induction course in summer 1968. These sessions were designed as part of the dissemination phase of the project. Training began with the regional training courses run in weekly sessions by Jean Rudduck and Stenhouse in winter 1969–1970.

The central team planned training courses for future trainers within individual LEAs or groups of LEAs. The plan was to have local trainers engage in a six-stage dissemination cycle: mapping local interest, arranging local training courses, assessing final commitment, supporting work in local schools (materials and moral support), institutionalizing the process (establishing groups of teachers to do follow-up work and training more and more teachers), and evaluating. A year later the principle of training for trainers was abandoned and the courses were designed to respond to the needs of individuals (Humble and Simons 1978): "The form of training became more sophisticated and probably more effective as time went on. The team was able to call on more and more teachers . . . they compiled booklets about the difficulties of innovating. . . . They drew from evaluation data on the experience of diffusion . . . and played evaluation videotapes of classroom discussions" (14). Humble and Simons (14–16), in a quote from an interview with Rudduck, write that the team began to work with speakers because a "lot of LEAs have said they need speakers from outside of the project team to come in because anything from outside is the kind of authority that makes things go" (16).

When the project disbanded on August 31, 1972, training virtually ended. The publisher promised to help interested advisers set up exhibits of materials and possibly provide speakers. "It was a curious end, perhaps a fateful one, if one teacher was to be believed. He was asked, way back at the first central training course, what he thought would be the project's prime concern in diffusion. His reply? To survive" (Humble and Simons 1978, 18).

Teachers' Stories of Their Participation in the Project. *People in Classrooms: Teacher Evaluations of the Humanities Curriculum Project* (Elliott and MacDonald 1975) is a collection of essays by teachers about their participation in HCP, documenting their range of experiences. To convey a sense of the multiplicity of stories, we provide a few excerpts here.

The first is taken from Lawn (1975), of the Holy Family Catholic Secondary School. In this school the humanities group was "as typical a collection of slow-learning adolescents as any teacher of fourth-year pupils will recognize" (32). Among other things, Lawn wrote about his experience with the neutral chairmanship: "By listening with respect through procedural neutrality I allow pupils to come to their own conclusions . . . a neutral chairman is not neutered" (36). He found he "had no behavioral problems. . . . They have all had a turn at group chairman and they appreciate that they alone in the school have taken part in an experiment and so did something special. They have risen to my expectation of them in the discussion situation" (36–37).

Wenham (1975), another project participant, wrote, "Neutral or impartial chairmanship by the tutor is crucial to Humanities Curriculum Project strategy. It is a positive and demanding role for the teacher and by no means easy for the students to accept . . . the teacher/chairman is responsible for the quality of learning that takes place during discussion" (53). Wenham noted the need for "a belief in rationality, sensitivity, and imaginativeness" (53) and found "a working knowledge of the pack itself highly desirable but it takes considerable practice and judgement on the part of the chairman to sense the correct moment to introduce fresh evidence into the discussion" (55).

Soutter (1975), a teacher in a London school with a non-English population of 30 to 35 percent, wrote that "the printed material is too difficult for the below average child to read and understand" (27). In his experience "a lot of the evidence in the pack was not used because we felt that many of the issues raised were too unrelated to their own experience or too sophisticated for the pupils to do more than talk superficially about them" (30).

Other teachers who did not write essays told stories of frustration. One felt that pupils in other years "achieved more in half-an-hour than my present group has achieved in five hours. . . . This feeling naturally produces within me great frustration . . . my attitude becomes very unenthusiastic towards the whole project" (11). Another teacher questioned the maturity of the fourth-year pupils and the difficulty of the materials. He felt there were "other things and other ways of working with fourth and fifth year pupils which would be more to their benefit and far more comfortable to me" (11). He felt that "as chairman, when I've not been neutral or when I've been deliberately provocative, that a great deal more has come from the discussion group situation. . . . I think you are beginning to preach dangerous revolution" (12). A third group of teachers described the HCP as aimless. They noted that the "discussion is of a sporadic nature and at a very superficial level" (12). They questioned other practices such as divergence and the practice of not allowing the teacher to express personal views. They felt that the danger of an authoritarian teacher imposing his or her views could "be minimized by choosing the right type of teacher who will put forward his views modestly, yet sincerely and with conviction . . . there is an imbalance in the materials in favour of a humanistic viewpoint . . . a good teacher, like a good parent, must be, to quote a recent archbishop's statement on the subject, 'loving, devoted, and anything but neutral' " (13).

These fragments of teachers' stories highlight the range of their experiences as well as demonstrate how they were shaped by the research purposes. Requirements for practice, such as neutral discussion leaders, discussion groups, and use of materials, shaped teachers' stories in a variety of ways.

The Story of the Project's View of Teachers as Curriculum Makers. MacDonald and Walker (1976a) described the project as spelling out "quite explicitly a radical alternative to which established teacher practice was largely irrelevant. Because its 'subject,' values education, was, as a formal category, quite new, this was not seen by teachers as an attack on their existing professional identities but as an opportunity to acquire an additional identity" (75). They described the HCP as built "upon an assumption that teachers, provided with the right kind of support and encouragement, were capable of developing a high order of professional expertise" (75).

As we reconstructed a story of the teacher in the project, we understood the project as acknowledging the centrality of the teacher as an active participant in classroom curriculum and in research and development. Indeed, Stenhouse's language is very much the language of empowerment of teachers to act as professionals in their classrooms, to be reflective practitioners, and to view teaching as an inquiry process. When we probed beneath the language to the action, however, we saw something else. In the end we came to understand Stenhouse's lived story and the way the story was lived by teachers (at least as we understood it in our reconstruction from various records and writings) as no different from other stories of projects in which researchers' stories shape teachers' stories to the research purpose.

Stenhouse held an image of the teacher that he was living out in his practices of the project. It was an image in which teachers were to become researchers of their practice, including serving as neutral discussion leaders; learners would learn to question established practices and values in class discussions; the subject matter would be the ways people lived their lives in societies both local and distant. The immediate classroom milieu would allow informed discussion with both near and far milieux as sites from which problematic situations emerged. This image was the one presented to teachers at the first induction meeting. Teachers were allowed to shape the ways in which the image was lived out, but their stories were constructed in response to that of the researcher. In the end, the teachers' story of the HCP is one in which teachers were bent to another's purposes; they were to fulfill the researcher and developer's vision of what teachers should be in their classrooms.

Stenhouse's view of the teacher as expressed in project plans was one of the teacher as researcher. His intent was to have teachers learn to tell their stories of teaching practice as stories of research practice and as stories of inquiry. We can see this as an implicit message to teachers that they were not to value their teaching practice but to value research practice.

Reconceptualizing Teacher as Researcher. This view of the teacher as curriculum maker offers a particularly troubling insight into how we understand teachers as curriculum makers. Cohen (1988) described teachers' work as work over which they have little control, an inference from the low adoption rate of innovations and from teachers' resistance to change. He speculated that teachers who work in colleges, universities, and private schools might respond differently to innovation since their work conditions allow them more control. In these settings teachers are presumed to have much more influence over their work and course design and to undergo few, if any, evaluations of their teaching. Characteristically, however, teaching at this level is neither innovative nor highly valued by those who work in research universities (Lanier and Little 1986). Resistance to innovation marks teaching in both public and private schools as well as postsecondary institutions. Teachers at all levels resist innovations. Indeed, postsecondary teaching is marked by many practices deplored in public schools.

The recent calls in the literature, then, for teachers to become researchers takes on a new aspect. The calls are not to have teachers teach, as do academics in the research universities, but rather to become like researchers when they do their research. Once again, the message is for teachers not to value their practice as teachers but to value our practice as researchers. Teaching practice, in itself, is seen to be of little value except as it resembles research.

Teacher as Researcher Versus Teaching as Inquiry. A wide range of meanings has been ascribed to the term "teacher-researcher." For instance, teacher-researchers in the Calgary Listening Inquiry Project (Plattor 1988) identified needs (in cooperation with a university researcher) in the area of listening and then conducted a series of studies in their classrooms derived from these teacher-defined concerns. They developed activities and then implemented and assessed them in their classrooms. The teacher as researcher also comes under the heading of action research, which has been defined as "a form of self-reflective enquiry undertaken by participants in social situations in order to improve the rationality and justice of their own practices, their understanding of these practices, and the situations in which the practices are carried out" (Carr and Kemmis 1986, 162). They see "two essential aims of all action research: to improve and to involve. . . . those involved in the practice being considered are to be involved in the action research process in all its phases of planning, acting, observing and reflecting" (162–164). This view of teacher as researcher is necessarily collaborative in that "the research process is extended towards including all those involved in, or affected by, the action. Ultimately, the aim of action research is to involve all these participants in communication aimed at mutual understanding and consensus, in just and democratic decision-making, and common action towards achieving fulfillment for all" (199).

Much of what is written under the broad heading of teacher as researcher differs from the view of the teaching process itself as being a kind of inquiry, that is, "a process of engaging learners in trying to make sense" (Duckworth 1986, 494). Hawkins (1983) also writes about teaching as a kind of inquiry in which we "help children sort and rectify . . . observing and listening, of searching for clues, and of then providing that which may steady and further a budding curiosity, or failing may lead to further clues" (74). These writers offer a different conceptualization of teaching from one that views research as added to the work of teachers. The conception of teaching as a kind of inquiry fits comfortably into the literature we review in the following section.

Teachers' Stories and Stories of Teachers

If we ignore the calls to have teachers become researchers of their own practice, we need to understand how to work with teachers to hear their stories of themselves as curriculum makers. We need to look first in a body of literature that seems absent from the research on teaching. We have named this literature "teachers' stories and stories of teachers" (Connelly and Clandinin 1990).

These terms refer to first- and second-hand accounts of individual teachers, students, classrooms, and schools written by teachers and others. Some illustrations of teachers' stories are Armstrong 1980; Barzun 1944; Booth 1988; Calkins 1983; Coles 1989; Dennison 1969; Meek, Armstrong, Austerfield, Graham, and Placetter 1983; Natkins 1986; Paley 1981, 1986; Rieff 1972; Rowland 1984; Steedman 1982; and Urwin 1988. Examples of stories of teachers are Bullough 1989; Butt and Raymond 1987; Clandinin 1989; Clandinin and Connelly 1986; Conle in press; Elbaz 1981; Enns-Connolly in press; several chapters in Graff and Warner 1989; Kilbourn in press; Kroma 1983; Lightfoot and Martin 1988; Oberg and Blades, 1990; Ryan 1970; Smith et al. 1986, 1987, 1988; and Yonemura 1986. Jackson's (1968) *Life in Classrooms* plays an especially generative role for the literature of teachers' stories and stories of teachers.

This literature portrays the understanding of several tasks. One is the task of a researcher or a group of researchers working closely with a teacher or a group of teachers so that the teachers will serve one research purpose or another by telling their stories. These stories are, for the most part, constructed by researchers from teacher interviews. For example, Smith et al. (1986) undertake both tasks in the first book of their trilogy, *Educational Innovations: Then and Now*. The trilogy is based on a follow-up study of an innovative school. Their task was "to locate, observe, and interview the two dozen key administrators and teachers who originated the school" (19).

The researchers used their data to develop three broad themes, which became the organizing framework for the stories of the teachers. The first theme, "educational careers: people and positions over time," was a "more outside, behavioral view of what has happened to our innovators over the last fifteen years" (25). In the second theme, "true believers and educational innovations," the authors dealt with the relationships between belief systems and educational innovations. The final theme dealt with the relations between "people and issues" and their "organizational context" (26). The work as a whole described "this very unusual group of educators . . . from the outside perspective of their careers, positions over time. The inside perspective accents the conceptions of belief systems . . .

and we keep returning to the organizational context'' (26). Their account of the teachers' stories was framed by themes that emerged from the collective reading of all participants' stories and as they were interpreted within the broad context of educational innovation and change.

A second kind of task is the telling of teacher stories by teacher-researchers, who see their task as the detailed reconstruction of a teacher's work when teacher-researcher and teacher work together in a classroom. The story they tell is less the story of the teacher and more the story of the children. Armstrong (1980), for instance, worked as a researcher with a teacher, Stephen Rowland, for one year in a participant-observer role. He ''wanted to study, within the context of one particular school, the character and quality of children's intellectual understanding: the insights which they display and the problems which they encounter, their inventiveness and originality and their intellectual dependence'' (7). The story is mostly of the children, although we learn a great deal about Rowland from the kinds of work he prepares for his pupils.

Rowland (1984) subsequently left his classroom and worked with another teacher, Chris Harris, in a similar project. Once again, the purpose was ''to combine the roles of teacher and researcher and thereby to investigate the quality of children's intellectual understanding and its growth'' (5). Again, his was less the story of the teacher than of the children, although we gain a strong sense of both the teacher's and the researcher's stories as they describe how the classroom curriculum was constructed. Rowland writes, ''The ways in which we make sense of the actions of others are inextricably linked to the ways in which we see ourselves. For this reason, the process of reflecting upon children's understanding inevitably involves an element of introspection, a conscious attempt to perceive not only how the child views the world . . . but how we perceive this world too'' (10). Rowland calls for teachers to ''write about our experience in the classroom, our interpretations of the children's work, our educational values, with the confidence that we have something significant to say and that our experience is valid'' (159). Rowland suggests that ''a genuine sharing of ideas'' (159) is the major benefit of such projects.

A third task is the telling by teachers of their own stories as teachers. There is a reasonably long tradition of such work (e.g., Ashton-Warner 1963, 1972). Although this work is often not considered ''research'' but rather personal stories, we maintain that teachers' autobiographies are a critical part of the research literature of the teacher as curriculum maker. Two teachers' stories—by Coles and Paley—will be considered in detail later.

A fourth task undertaken in this literature is found in works such as Ayers (1989). His is a ''sustained inquiry into the work and lives of preschool teachers. The point of the study is to examine in detail the work of a few teachers, to construct with each a meaningful account of her life, and to consider how her own self-understanding has had an impact on her teaching practice'' (xi). The book attempts to ''capture descriptive accounts of teachers teaching as well as telling stories of teaching and of becoming teachers'' (1). This is a collaborative process, which ''involves classroom observations of teachers teaching, and pedagogical dialogues of teachers reflecting on their lives as they influence teaching practices'' (137). Teacher and observer collaborate in ''the production of a meaningful narrative text that describes and links together influences, events, people, and experiences that contribute to the creation of the teacher as she finds herself today. This text, assumed to be neither comprehensive nor complete, becomes the focus for the teacher to critically examine her teaching practices and to locate them in a continuum from past to future'' (137–138). The story that is eventually told becomes the story of both teacher and researcher, one that is mutually constructed and said by Ayers to be ''a story of six teachers, but it is also my own story'' (149).

This literature of teachers' stories and stories of teachers provides an important avenue for conceptualizing the work of teachers as curriculum makers. Learning to listen to the stories teachers tell of their practice is an important step toward creating an understanding of the teacher as curriculum maker. However, we see our task as researchers as moving beyond this step to a second: to create with teachers a story of teachers as curriculum makers. We see this task as a collaborative one in which we participate with teachers in their classrooms and together live out and construct a story of the teacher as curriculum maker and, in this endeavor, imagine the possibility of curriculum reform.

This way of working allows us to learn about the ways in which teachers are curriculum makers and, through such collaborative projects, to see ourselves as ''researchers as teachers'' rather than to have teachers see themselves as researchers. We come to know teaching practice as ''bred in our bones.'' We experience the cyclical nature of school time and place, understand how school events shape our stories as we live them and tell them in classrooms, and discover children's stories as they are lived out in relation to those of others. Practice becomes part of our personal knowledge. Our purpose is not to silence our own voices but to create a lived text of researcher, teacher, and learners in which a new story is lived and told.

In the next section we undertake a collaboration of sorts with the texts of two teachers' stories. We do this retelling to suggest how we might begin to give accounts of teachers' stories as stories of curriculum makers. Robert Coles and Vivian Paley both have told stories of themselves as teachers. Coles (1989), in his book *The Call of Stories: Teaching and Moral Imagination*, tells the story of his work as a teacher reconstructed from his experience as a child, medical student, intern, doctor, and later university teacher. Paley (1979, 1981, 1985, 1986, 1988), in a series of books, tells her story as a teacher. What we have tried to do in this collaboration is to create another story in which our voices as curriculum professors are also heard and to point the way to the kind of research that will help us to understand the teacher as maker of curriculum.

Robert Coles as Curriculum Maker. As he tells his story as teacher, Coles looks at phases in his life. He begins with his experiences as a learner both in school with his teachers and at home with his parents. The narrative threads of our reconstruction of him as a curriculum maker are found in these first stories.

One particularly telling account concerns Coles's (1989) childhood experience with a high school English teacher and a novel of Dickens. He and a friend discovered their teacher's copy of a "well-worn study guide of *A Tale of Two Cities*," which contained "a summary of the plot and a list of all the characters" (xiii). Coles borrowed a library copy of the guide, only to have it discovered by his parents. Coles's stories of his parents are of people who loved literature and who read to each other in the evenings. When his mother discovered the notes, she asked him why he had taken a shortcut. She explained that "Dickens was meant to "edify and entertain, not to become someone's 'fast study,' as she put it." She questioned whether the teacher had suggested such a resource. Coles responded that the teacher himself used the study guide. He then told how his parents had told "about *A Tale of Two Cities*, about their appreciation of the book, their delight in it. They gave us a flesh-and-blood account of the English and French history upon which the novel drew and we were impressed. That plot summary seemed skeletal in comparison" (xiii).

In our retelling we can see how Coles opens up the issue of the teacher's relationship to the subject matter in the contrasting responses of his English teacher and his parents. Teachers' knowledge of subject matter, their shaping of it, their methods of teaching, and the ways in which they learn subject matter in preservice and in-service education emerge as important questions.

Later, Coles (1989) tells stories about his experience as a medical intern, particularly about his relationship with his two supervising doctors, "senior psychoanalysts who were to help me make sense of what I was hearing" (3). His stories were of sharply contrasting experiences with the two teachers. Dr. Binger urged him to "read more in the psychiatric literature so that [Coles] might understand 'the nature of phobias' " (3). Coles describes Dr. Binger as giving him "words to grasp," a "strategy," a "purpose." Coles saw himself as "in possession of knowledge, maybe even wisdom: Dr. Binger, with distinctions galore, had given me an explanation, a suggestion" (4). He portrayed Dr. Binger as someone who "kept encouraging me to 'formulate the problems' I was trying to treat" (8). He found his talks with Dr. Binger "very helpful" (8) because he got "an intellectual fix from him" (8). He would present Dr. Binger with a "prepared speech, reading aloud notes I'd taken while the patient spoke, or thoughts set down afterward, and then waited while a learned, marvelously articulate and self-assured psychiatrist told me what was 'really' happening in those 'therapeutic sessions' " (8–9). He got from Dr. Binger what he saw as the answer and "often found myself feeling less afraid for myself, if not for the patient. I now 'knew' her, and I could look forward to yet another chance to listen, to inquire, to hear confirmed what I had been taught" (8–9).

Coles's (1989) other supervisor, Dr. Ludwig, encouraged him to listen to his patients' stories and to try to help them make sense of them. He saw his work as a supervisor to listen to Coles give his accounts of the patients' stories. Dr. Ludwig told him that "each patient will tell you a different story, and you're an all-day listener" (14). Coles was being encouraged to do something quite different from that which his other teachers advised. He was being told to stop forcing his patients (not to mention his own mind) "into a variety of theoretical constructs: He wanted me to hold off the rush to interpretation, to restrain myself from trying to get him to give me his interpretation, which for me would become the definitive one, at least until the next supervisor came along" (14).

Dr. Ludwig offered not only a different way of working with patients but also a different image of the teacher's role. Coles (1989) wrote that Dr. Ludwig saw supervision as a "meeting of two persons, a shared possibility for each of them" (8). He saw that physicians brought their own stories to the consultation room and also that "the teachers of physicians carry their stories into the consulting rooms where 'supervisory instruction' takes place. Sometimes our knowledge and our theories . . . interfere with or interrupt a patient's momentum; hence the need for caution as we listen and get ready to ask our questions. The same was true for the 'case presentations' I was making to my supervisors" (24).

In our retelling we interpret Coles's stories as questioning the nature of the relationship between teacher and learner, the ways in which the teacher's story shapes the curricular experience of the learner, the ways in which theory and practice interrelate, the relationship between teaching and political ideology, and the politics of curriculum research. These are issues explored in curriculum research centering on the teacher as curriculum maker; they touch on research areas as broad as theory-practice, implementation, political ideology, and the hidden curriculum.

In a second phase of his story, Coles (1989) talks about his work as a doctor with young polio patients. As his patients told him stories about their experiences with their teachers, Coles learned more about teaching. One story is about Phil, a 15-year-old who told Coles about a teacher who had come to visit him in the hospital. The second time the teacher had brought a book and left it. The teacher had not pushed the book on Phil but simply left it. Phil talked about how he felt: "I was really curious to see which book he'd brought. I looked and saw it was the Mark Twain one, *Adventures of Huckleberry Finn*. I started flipping through the pages. I wondered why he had brought it. I'd already read it—in his class, last year" (35). Phil had wondered about the teacher's purpose, felt annoyed, and did not read the book until a few days later. When he began reading the book, Phil did not want to stop, and when he finished it he described himself as feeling different. He could not explain what happened but knew his mind had changed after he had read *Huckleberry Finn*. Phil said, "I couldn't get my mind off the book, I forgot about myself—no, I didn't, actually" (36). He felt he had "joined up with Huck and Jim; we became a trio" (36). Phil described how he had "talked with those guys, and they straightened me out!" (36).

In a later conversation Phil wondered if Coles (1989) had ever read a book that "really made a difference to you—a book you couldn't get out of your mind and you didn't want to [get out of your mind]?" (36). Coles told him a story about William Carlos Williams, a doctor and poet he had known, and they talked about writers and their lives: "The reason for Phil's interest in pointing out the connection between art and life was not too hard for me to comprehend—or for him, either" (36). Phil began to read other books and became interested in other characters. He had been receiving tutoring in the hospital, but as Coles tells the story, Phil now began teaching himself. He wanted, through the books, to "leave this hospital, and find a friend or two, and a place where we could be happy, but I don't want to leave the whole world I know" (38). He began to "notice hypocrisy or deceit in the world as it came to him" (39) and to call what he saw phony; he told Coles that "both Twain and Salinger were warning the reader to take a hard, close look at the world" (39).

As we retell Coles's story of his experience with Phil, we see Coles opening up the issue of the relationship among teacher, learner, and subject matter. Coles raises questions that we interpret as being about the relationship among the three curriculum commonplaces. We see him asking questions about the narratives of experience of both learner and teacher and the ways they come together around a particular text, a particular subject matter. These are questions curriculum researchers have asked—about teachers as learners, the links between the personal and the professional, teacher-student interaction, and a concept of curriculum as experienced.

Later Coles (1989) tells a story about a student in his wife's grade 12 class who had read Elizabeth Bowen's *Death of the Heart* and Toni Morrison's *The Bluest Eye*. When the student talked about *The Bluest Eye*, she said she thought she would have trouble with it because she would "have to get into the scene, and it's a pretty sorry one" (59). She found, however, that when she "got into the story" (59) she "began to forget that Pecola . . . was black just as it didn't occur to me to think of Portia as white, or even rich, when I was reading about her life. To me, Pecola—well, she was someone who was caught in a terrible jam: a miserable family life" (59). She made links to her own life, in which she heard her mother tell her father, "If we could just get away, then I'll come back a new person, and life will be different" (59). The student continued to make links between her story and the young women in the novels. Her reading made her wonder "how you become the person you do become" (60). She saw the novels as making "you stop and look around so you don't get lost yourself" (60).

Coles focuses attention on how a high school student begins thinking about her own life "after giving thought to the lives storytellers tell about" (69). He credits his wife's teaching, in which she "read aloud portions of those novels and asked for volunteers among her students to do likewise. She showed the class slides of the Regent's Park neighborhood. She connected *The Bluest Eye* to the Olsen story 'O Yes,' and both of them to the self-discovery her students were experiencing as adolescents" (60). He talks about the ways in which his wife shared some of her own stories. In that story Coles showed how the "two young women in the novels, Pecola and Portia, took on a vivid and continuing life for many of the students through my wife's ability to connect their stories to her students' and her own" (60).

In our retelling, we wanted to emphasize the ways in which Coles as curriculum maker dealt with the relationship between teacher and learner and with the lives of both teachers and learners in and out of school. Questions of the ways in which curriculum connects to life are raised, and the special role of the subject matter in linking learners to teachers is highlighted.

In the next part of his story, Coles (1989) tells about learning how to use literature with college students, a task he saw as "an essentially psychological inquiry" (189) in which he could learn "the ways students respond to literature—there would be different ways, I speculated, for different kinds of students" (189). He thought students, depending on their career choice, would respond differently to different stories, that is, that some stories "would address particular audiences with special poignancy or persuasiveness" (189). He discerned that this was not the case. Rather, he "found an astonishing range of responsiveness in my classes—to the point that my stereotypes contributed very little" (190). He saw that the "decisive matter is how the teacher's imagination engages with the text—a prelude, naturally, to the students' engagement" (190). Coles learned from his students that "constructing a good reading list involves not so much matching student interest with author's subject matter (though there is no reason to ignore the pleasures such a correspondence can offer) as considering the degree of moral engagement a particular text seems able to make with any number of readers" (190).

This story opens up considerations of relationships between teaching as curriculum inquiry and the broader issues of the relationship of teaching to inquiry. Coles portrays himself as a learner, referring to a curriculum problem he created by trying to categorize students and subject matter. Other curricular questions apparent in our retelling of the story concern the relationship between teachers and language.

Coles's (1989) final story describes his involvement with Gordon, a student who "always asked a lot of himself" (199). He tells Gordon's stories of his early life and about choosing economics at college. Gordon became "bored with the numbers and the theories. I liked reading history, and I liked reading novels" (202). He was critical of "the way the professors used the books—zeroing in on 'the text,' raking and raking, sifting and sifting it through narrower and narrower filters. I'm not against learning about symbols and images and metaphors, but there was something missing in those tutorials" (202). He began to experience the texts as separate from his life, in "such a way that they're not stories anymore; and the characters in them aren't people anymore, like you and me, all caught up in contradictions, and fighting to stay above water morally" (202). Gordon wanted "to read stories and get lost in them, and some of the characters—they become buddies of mine, friends, people I think of" (202).

Coles (1989) describes how Gordon began working with a student volunteer organization, tutoring children in a poor neighborhood. He tried to interest them in reading "just enough so they could begin to get turned on" (202). Coles relates much more of Gordon's story, and it always shows Gordon concerned with phoniness in his life. At one point Gordon says, "I've tried to take courses in moral philosophy. I read the books. I become smarter in the analysis I do. But I leave the lecture hall and I can see myself as the same—the way I'll think of certain people, the way I'll behave. I guess this place is where your intellect changes. I guess it's no behavior-modification place" (203). Coles's narration of Gordon's story ends with a rhetorical question put to him by Gordon. Gordon counted

> among his friends characters in certain novels. He denies any distinctiveness or originality in that kind of friendship: many of his high school buddies, he reminded me, "would talk about Holden as if he was one of us." Having said that, he asked me a rhetorical question, well worth a pedagogical conference or two, I think: "Why don't you guys [college professors] teach that way?" Which way, I wanted to know. "As if Holden was—I mean is—as real as you or me." (204)

Coles (1989) finishes the story and the book with these thoughts: "So it goes, this immediacy that a story can possess, as it connects so persuasively with human experience" (205). In his story of his teaching, he wanted learners to consider the moral issues in life, good ways to "live this life: a person's moral conduct responding to the moral imagination of writers and the moral imperative of fellow human beings in need" (205).

Coles as a teacher explores the issues and themes that curriculum researchers explore. In our retelling of his story as curriculum maker, we raise questions about the ways in which the milieu shapes learners and teachers and the ways they shape the milieu, and questions about the ways learners at different times in their lives respond differently to subject matter. Our retelling sheds light on the question of dilemmas in teaching and curriculum and the ways in which curriculum is ultimately moral: It has to do with the ways in which we live our lives. That teachers are moral agents is important to our notion of the teacher as curriculum maker.

Vivian Gussin Paley as Curriculum Maker. Detailed accounts of one teacher's work written over a period of time are rare. Vivian Paley's work is an exception. She has, since 1979, documented her teaching and her attempts to understand what it means to work with young children in ways that develop their understanding of the world. Her work is found in a series of books: *White Teacher* (1979), *Wally's Stories* (1981), *Girls and Boys* (1985), *Molly Is Three* (1986), and *Bad Guys Don't Have Birthdays* (1988). The accounts make compelling reading. Our purpose here is to retell her story as one of the teacher as curriculum maker.

Paley's classroom curriculum is built around young children's experiences with stories of several kinds. Cazden, in her preface to *Wally's Stories* (Paley 1981), reports that some stories "are made up by Wally and his classmates, some are picture books and fairy tales . . . others are five-year-olds' discussions of very serious topics—like whether stones melt when they are boiled. When you are five, there is much in the world that needs to be accounted for, and these accounts are 'stories' to us adults when children prefer their magical explanations to those we call 'true.'" Paley writes, "we usually acted out stories as soon as they were written and books as soon as they were read" (9). The acting out of stories became theater-in-the-round: "The new stage was both necessary and symbolic; acting had become the major integrating factor of the day, encircling and extending every other interest. We dramatized three kind of stories: picture-story books, the children's own material, and fairy tales. Each served a different purpose, none was a substitute for the other" (66). The curriculum evolved over the course of each year from working with these kinds of stories.

Paley (1984) has found that "storytelling is easy to promote when there is a tangible connection to play" (2). Classroom situations are structured in ways that let children play and move from their play to stories based on it and to other stories. She writes, "A child feels competent when he takes part in a story-play. There is just enough plot to adapt a few lines of dialogue to several fragments of action. . . . The children feel they are playing together inside a story" (1981, 167). Paley notes that the child, in acting out the story, "must be more conscious of language than he is in free play. He cannot suddenly move to a parallel dialogue that has nothing to do with the plot. He can use his own words, but he must remain within the structure of the story. In addition, the stories must make sense, for they should provide directions that actors can follow. In this way a story often contributes academic lessons worthy of the best kindergarten curriculum" (167). In addition to their own story-plays, Paley says, "children need stories written by adults. The complex plots, larger vocabularies, and wide range of characters yield an endless supply of exercises in logical thinking" (170). We read in Paley's work how the children's own stories and the stories of other writers become the text of the lived curriculum in the classroom. From this lived text, Paley comes to know the lessons the children are learning.

The classroom situations involve free play in two environments: active social play on one side, and sedentary play on the other (Paley 1985, 30). Depending on the ages of the children, physical education and music are part of the program of studies. This program emerges from Paley's (1981) view of her work as a teacher. For her, "logical thinking and precise speech" are the "important precursors to formal schooling and the main business of the kindergarten teacher" (213). She sees her work as trying to find the child's point of view to help the child take a further step. Because much practice is required to learn the skills of rational discourse, the teacher "must use material that children want to discuss and dramatize" and she "must help the child see how one thing he knows relates to other things he knows'' (213). Her task ''is to keep the inquiry open long enough for the consequences of their ideas to become apparent to them'' (213). She describes herself as like ''the ancient Greek chorus, seeking connections and keeping track of events, but the decisions must come from the children'' (214). Her story of her work as teacher is to provide for ways in which ''Step by step, the children and I can follow a train of thought, giving those who need more time the opportunity to reflect. And the teacher is there to make connections'' (219).

Paley (1981) tells many stories about her days with children; she describes ''herself as teacher'' as one character in the unfolding daily story. Each day was ''tied together by a continuity of mutual purposes that transcended play, but wandered not far from it. For play is the natural response of children, with its own logic and consequences'' (223). She describes her relationship with the children as bound by a contract that ''reads more like this: if you will keep trying to explain yourselves I will keep showing you how to think about the problems you need to solve'' (223). The curriculum story is told as the children's stories and hers come together in play.

The classroom curriculum emerges from the children's stories, from their ways of making sense. In *Superheroes* Paley (1985) writes, ''In trying to sort out what is real from pretend, one looks through mirrors. I choose books that seem relevant, but it is the children who operate the mirrors and make connections'' (98). In her work with 4-year-olds (described in *Bad Guys Don't Have Birthdays*), Paley (1988), writes that the teacher who wants to study fantasy play finds the main threads ''by watching those who are watched. The group itself is the best judge of authenticity, choosing leaders who give voice to common concerns in the language and logic of their peers'' (viii). Paley knows that each year the children's ''stories reveal the same truths. Ideas and purposes must be processed through other children in social play if a child is to open to an ever larger picture and determine how the pieces fit together'' (viii). Her story is one of listening to ''the process by which the children think about a subject and follow a theme along the intertwining paths of discussion, play, and storytelling'' (viii–ix).

In watching and listening carefully to each child and to the mutually constructed play, we find the plot outlines of the experienced curriculum. Paley (1988) knows her own place in the story and describes herself in different ways as she thinks about herself as a character in the plots and subplots of the curriculum story. She differentiates herself from a researcher, who is able to stay outside the story. As a teacher she sees herself as part of the classroom curriculum story: ''The school teacher who studies and describes her own classroom cannot remove herself from the picture'' (44). Her work is to ''try to see it all, and may need to deal with my own feelings even as I decide what to do about the child's. Or what to do about the child's view of my feelings'' (44).

Paley's (1988) place in the classroom curriculum is a moral place; as a teacher she represents her culture and society. She becomes most aware of this situation at those moments of tension when she recognizes her own conventionality, which makes it difficult for her to listen to the voices of the children. She writes, ''When I care more about what the children say and think than about my own conventionality, those are the times I sense the beat and hear the unspoken lines. As I try to measure my response to the forms and ideas of this emerging society that inhabits my classroom, it becomes necessary to grasp its point of view'' (viii). She also acknowledges her work within the culture of schooling, particularly when she talks about her work with young girls. ''As in all areas of uncertainty'' Paley (1985) writes, ''I vacillate between the evidence continually provided by the children's behavior, and my need to conform to conventional standards and opinions'' (11).

Paley (1981) acknowledges the ways of knowing that emerge from listening to each character, to the children as they live out their stories: ''These kindergarten children are finding out they can make significant, lasting changes in their own social organization, and they are certain that absolute safety lies in absolute fairness. It is a heady feeling, encouraging the most advanced thinking and speaking skills in the cause of establishing rules of fairness'' (25). We see her as curriculum maker, listening very carefully to the stories that the children construct as they engage with one another and the materials in the classroom. After a particular story had been read and acted out, Paley reflected on her understanding of punishment as enacted in her relations with the children: ''No wonder punishment doesn't work. I would have punished the fox, and the children think the fox is right. I defend Tico, but the children say Tico is wrong. Now I understand why Wally has to ask me every day if he is good. Our definitions of goodness do not match'' (27).

We see Paley (1988) understanding herself as teacher as only one character in the making of the classroom curriculum. When she reflects on the children's stories as lived and told in her classroom, she learns about herself and about what it means for her to teach. As a teacher she sees herself as ''privileged to attend the daily performance of private drama and universal theatre that is called a preschool classroom'' (vii).

Children learn from one another's stories and see themselves as new characters both in their own stories and in the story being constructed in the classroom. As we reconstruct Paley's (1981) work as curriculum maker, we understand her sense of the journeys children are taking as they live out their lives in her class. She watches and gives accounts of the ways in which the children learn to tell their own stories and to make meaning from their experiences. She understands that ''An 'I know what she means' or an 'I changed my mind' says a child has recognized a truth and is stretching after the special meaning it may have for him. When children question each other, arguing or agreeing, it means they are listening carefully. They want to know about experiences they have in common with another child; they are curious about what has happened to someone else because it may also happen to them" (120). In her knowing of teaching she knows that when there is no such interaction, "the children do not understand the subject" (120). We can understand in this discussion how Paley is making sense of the curricular issues of the relationship among teacher, learners, and subject matter.

Some children more than others influence the classroom story. Wally is one such person, and Paley (1981) gives an account of him in one book. Other children watch Wally and Paley's response to make sense of the interaction. Wally, however, "seldom takes his cues from adults, bringing forth his own script for being a five-year-old" (6). Paley as curriculum maker knows that Wally's experience in the classroom is an important part of the ways in which the other children make sense of their classroom experience. "The children like Wally's explanations for events better than mine, so I give fewer and fewer interpretations each day and instead listen to Wally's. The familiar chord he strikes stimulates others to speak with candor, and I am the beneficiary. However, Wally does not always teach me what I want to learn" (6). She knows her own difficulty in acknowledging that the stories being lived out in the classroom are not always the stories she prefers.

Paley's writing documents her development as a teacher. She learns from the children by paying close attention to what they do and say. The books also detail her learning from year to year, from book to book. In a recent edition (1989) of her first book, *White Teacher* (1979), Paley has added an epilogue. She looks back to note, "The more I study this culture the children fashion as they learn to play out the rhythms and meaning of group fantasy, the more I see that the uniqueness of every person is an accepted premise from the very beginnings of social life. The children know they are each different in style and story" (141). She goes on to say that when she first began writing, she thought she knew "certain children best because our backgrounds were similar, and that it was my task to open up the classroom, to explore and welcome differences. I have since discovered that all the children have more in common with one another than any one of them has with me. The major source of incongruity is between their thinking and mine" (142). Paley acknowledges how she has learned as a teacher from the care she has given to her pupils: She has learned as she worked with them to create and re-create curricular situations.

As we did in our work with Coles's story, we have attempted to work with Paley's texts to create a reading that highlights ways of seeing teachers' stories as research on the teacher as curriculum maker. In the two remaining sections, we discuss the curricular significance of this reading and we develop these ideas as possible future research directions.

Coles and Paley Revisited. What do we learn from this reading of Coles and Paley? At one level their stories, and our reading of them, reveal the same sorts of things curriculum researchers and theorists working in a different mode have noted. For example, Coles's moral insights read as bits of curriculum knowledge are widely recognized in the curriculum literature. Although this is not the main reason for being attentive to teachers' stories, it is noteworthy that much of what is learned and understood by very different research methods may also be seen in their analysis. But stories, read as such rather than for what their analysis might reveal, yield things of importance to curriculum making not otherwise seen. Stories are temporal, and it is through the media of time and space that people, things, and events reflect, and are seen to reflect, one another. Dewey repeatedly made the point that experiential occurrences in existential situations reformed the participating elements. Stories are accounts of such transformations. The dynamics of a life story presses particular events and understandings into the background to become a context for the curriculum constructed and reconstructed by teachers and students. These participants live out intersecting lives with a combination of shared and independent story lines, all of which impinge on the curriculum constructed in the unfolding classroom story. These possibilities for seeing and recording curriculum in the making constitute the justification of our belief that the creation of a new literature is warranted.

Coles's and Paley's stories, as well as a curriculum reading of them, illustrate this literature's potential for curriculum studies. Our purpose in working with their stories is to demonstrate the embeddedness of teachers', students', and researchers' knowledge in the classroom making of curriculum. We understand Coles as curriculum maker, with high school and college students, using literature as the subject matter to create educative experiences. Literature is rooted in Coles's experience of his parents' way of relating to the world, to each other, and to him. As we read his story, education, life, and literature are interconnected. Literature is central to how he tells his own life and how his teaching relationship with students forms a connecting link between his own and his students' lives.

Paley makes curriculum in somewhat similar ways with preschool children when she helps them make connections between their play and how they are learning to live in the world as they move between the classroom community and society at large. The way Coles uses literature to help his students connect with life in his classroom and the way Paley helps children make connections between classroom life and life at large is remarkable: At the very least, the rich nuances of their stories of curriculum making are of vicarious value as their readers work through similar matters for their own curriculum making. But our main point here is not to demonstrate the remarkable teaching possibilities illustrated in these two teachers' stories but to show some of the potential of a new literature for bringing the general insights of curriculum theory and research together with the particularities of a teacher's practice.

We have not gone far with the writing of such a literature and we have relied on other sources for the stories. What we have done, we hope, will make some small contribution to wresting from obscurity the existing literature of teachers' stories and stories of teachers by encouraging readers to work with this literature in their own teaching and research. In so doing, teachers and students will be seen as curriculum makers in time, space, life, and person.

Future Directions: Learning to Tell a Collaborative Story of Teacher as Curriculum Maker

In this chapter we have reviewed the literature on the teacher as curriculum maker. We began by suggesting that curriculum might be viewed as an account of teachers' and students' lives together in schools and classrooms. We came to this view by erasing the distinction between curriculum and instruction, between ends and means. It is a view in which the teacher is seen as an integral part of the curricular process and in which teacher, learners, subject matter, and milieu are in dynamic interaction. Our view of curriculum drew attention to a conception that Zumwalt (1988) calls the enacted curriculum. We went on to examine the ways in which the teacher had been portrayed as a curriculum maker.

Much of the existing research literature on the teacher as curriculum maker arises from the literature of school reform. We characterized that literature as one in which the teacher generally figures in the discrepancy between intended and achieved ends; curriculum is seen as an instrument of reform, and teachers are regarded as mediators between the curriculum and intended outcomes. Attitudes to teachers have been dominated by a pervasive metaphor of communication as a conduit. This metaphor appears to be "bred in the bones" of researchers who work within the contexts of curriculum reform and development. These notions were explored through a review of the literature of school reform through curriculum development to see how certain reform projects were experienced by teachers. Even in the Humanities Curriculum Project, in which the teacher was central, researchers largely shaped teachers to researcher purposes and paid little attention to what stories the teachers were living and telling in their classrooms before and during the project.

When we began to search for a literature that portrayed the teacher as curriculum maker, we explored the literature of teachers' stories and stories of teachers. We heard teachers tell stories of their curriculum work in classrooms and we heard researchers tell teachers' stories of their work. We saw the potential for collaborative research between the researcher and teacher and, to begin to construct such a literature, worked collaboratively with stories relating the lived experience of two teachers, Vivian Paley and Robert Coles.

In our view, the future direction for the teacher as curriculum maker is an agenda shared with teachers. It has two parts: to listen to teachers' stories of their work and to construct together stories of teachers as curriculum makers. Both parts send us back to the classroom to listen to teachers' stories of their work. As Eisner (1988) wrote, researchers are increasingly

> beginning to go back to the schools, not to conduct commando raids, but to work with teachers as colleagues in a common quest and through such collaboration to rediscover the qualities, the complexities, and the richness of life in classrooms. We are beginning to talk with teachers, not only to teachers. We are beginning to ask ourselves how we can see and describe the minor miracles of stunning teaching instead of prescribing how teachers should go about their work. (19)

Our initial task, then, is the one described by Eisner (1988): to listen to teachers' stories as they are told and lived out in practice. These are the teachers' stories of themselves as they engage with learners and subject matter within both the immediate and larger social, political, and cultural milieux. Some researchers are beginning to undertake this task. Although their purposes are varied, their common intention is to listen to teachers' stories as they are lived and told and to retell them in "methods and languages that do justice to what we have seen" (20). We briefly outlined some of these studies. Other researchers, such as Atwell (1987), Bissex and Bullock (1987), Duckworth (1986), Erickson (1987), Goodman (1984); Grumet (1988), Kilbourn in press, Lampert (1985), Pinar (1981), Russell (1988), M. C. Thomas (1989), Woods (1984), have developed a tradition of listening to teachers' stories. The autobiographical tradition, in which teachers work to tell their own stories, is a powerful one. Grumet's work in empowering teachers to learn to hear their own stories is particularly insightful.

As we began our work on teachers' personal practical knowledge, we saw our task as described above. However, when we stilled our researchers' voices to hear the teachers recount stories of their lives in classrooms and schools, we sensed a need to have spaces in which both stories, those of researchers and teachers, could be heard. As we learned to listen to the teachers' stories and as we became aware of the ways in which our stories were lived out in the classroom, we saw that both stories could be told. Neither voice was silenced, nor did we seek to achieve a mere compromise or consensus between the stories. A new kind of story of the teacher as curriculum maker was being constructed, one in which both stories were told. This is the second part of the agenda, and it is a collaborative one. Kennard (1988) describes this collaborative relationship as "a mutual research, revisioning and restorying, a way of achieving voice within the exigencies of our narrative impulse" (31). This mutual construction of stories that arise from collaborative inquiry provides possibilities for change in the practices of teachers as curriculum makers and in the kind of research we envision. These possibilities spring from the close connection with the worlds in which teachers live out their stories. Without that connection to practice and without changing what is "bred in our bones" as curriculum researchers, developers, and reformers, we risk continuing to tell a story of curriculum reform dominated by the conduit metaphor.

The collaborative living out of researchers', teachers', and children's stories in the classroom changes the curriculum: It is not the same curriculum as it would be without the researcher. Inclusion of the researcher's story makes it possible to focus both researcher and teacher on the ways in which the curriculum is being lived as each learner constructs new meaning and learns to live a new but connected story. In their collaborative endeavor, researcher and teacher see the unfolding plots of the stories and observe them closely. When they tell their mutually constructed story of the teacher as curriculum maker to other teachers and researchers, it invites others to see and examine their stories' plots, scenes, and characters closely. Thus we see the potential for change and growth as other teachers work in their classrooms. To fulfill this agenda calls for not only the creation of a literature that records these stories but also the construction of a method of working with current and prospective teachers and researchers to educate them to the imaginative possibilities of reading this literature.

Lieberman (1986a, 1986b, 1986c), Noddings (1986), and Zumwalt (1988) also call for more collaborative relationships between researchers and practitioners to construct together an account of the teacher as curriculum maker. Some studies already indicate ways in which we might do so. Hogan (1988) worked with a group of teachers engaged in a collaborative study of their practices. She wrote that for a researcher working with teachers it was important to listen to teachers' voices, their telling of their stories, rather than turning "teachers into researchers" (26). In her work she constructed with them stories that were stories of teachers as curriculum makers in which she showed "how one group of teachers has engaged in working together to develop their own ways of making sense of practice" (26). Davies (1988), a teacher member of the same collaborative group with Hogan, wrote that "I am also aware of my need to be actively involved in teaching in order to think creatively. Questions arise and as answers are found my continuous spiral of knowing is constructed" (23).

Our purposes for work with teachers as curriculum makers are not well served by the currently accepted definitions of the words "curriculum" and "research." The word "curriculum" has come to mean only a course of study rather than, or as well as, a course of life. "Research" is taken to mean only searching and discovering, and a researcher is a searcher, discoverer, and investigator. At one time or another most of us have even been called "principal investigator" for a research grant. In their current use, "curriculum" and "research" fail to encompass what we see as our work as curriculum professors. Part of that work is the creation of a new language and thus a new way of seeing that situates us within the practical. The common usage of "research" and "curriculum" leaves us situated within the conduit, with theory separated from practice.

We want to return to a vision of curriculum as a course of life and develop a language of practice in which we think, talk, theorize, and act differently in relation to practice. When we construct the ways in which teachers have experienced our work as curriculum researchers, we realize that we have continued to act out the conduit metaphor, reinforcing the assumption that knowledge is conveyed from outside classrooms to the teachers inside them. This process disallows the use of knowledge that Dewey suggests is "a vehicle for change in our ever changing environment, in our understanding of the world" (Johnson 1989, 312). We wish to come to know teachers' knowledge as the "very way they construct their reality as they live it through their embodiment, with all its tempos, moods, patterns, and projections. No verbal and intellectualized account of the teacher's beliefs could ever do justice to the experienced reality of this web of experiential processes that constitute the teacher's knowledge-in-process" (312).

In our work as curriculum professors, we propose a new agenda based on a new metaphor—the teacher as curriculum maker. Not only should we listen closely to teachers and to the stories they live out in their classrooms, but also we need to learn to tell our own stories as we live them out in our work with teachers in their classrooms. Our work then becomes learning to tell and live a new, mutually constructed account of teachers as curriculum makers. What emerge from this relationship are stories of teachers as curriculum makers, stories that offer fresh possibilities for both professors and teachers to learn to live new stories in their practices.

References

Alderman, Donald L. 1978. *Evaluation of the TICCIT Computer-Assisted Instructional System in the Community College*, Final report, vol. I. Princeton, NJ: Educational Testing Service.

Apple, M. W. 1986. *Teachers and Texts: A Political Economy of Class and Gender Relations in Education*. London: Routledge & Kegan Paul.

Armstrong, M. 1980. *Closely Observed Children: Diary of a Primary Classroom*. London: Writers and Readers in association with Chameleon.

Ashton, P. T., and R. B. Webb. 1986. *Making a Difference: Teachers' Sense of Efficacy and Student Achievement*. New York/Toronto: Simon & Schuster/Bantam.

Ashton-Warner, Sylvia. 1963. *Teacher*. New York: Simon & Schuster.

Ashton-Warner, Sylvia. 1972. *Spearpoint: "Teacher" in America*. New York: Knopf.

Atwell, Nancie. 1987. *In the Middle: Writing, Reading, and Learning with Adolescents*. Upper Montclair, NJ: Boynton/Cook.

Ayers, William. 1989. *The Good Preschool Teacher: Six Teachers Reflect on Their Lives*. New York: Teachers College Press.

Barzun, Jacques. 1944. *Teacher in America*. New York: University Press of America.

Bates, Tony. 1986. Computer assisted learning or communications: Which way for information technology in distance education? *Journal of Distance Education* 1(1): 47–57.

Bellack, Arno A. 1969. History of curriculum thought and practice. *Review of Educational Research* 39(3): 283–292.

Ben-Peretz, Miriam. 1975. The concept of curriculum potential. *Curriculum Theory Network* 5(2):151–159.

Ben-Peretz, Miriam, and Lya Kremer. 1979. Curriculum implementation and the nature of curriculum materials. *Journal of Curriculum Studies* 11(3): 247–255.

Ben-Peretz, Miriam, and Pinchas Tamir. 1981. What teachers want to know about curriculum materials. *Journal of Curriculum Studies* 13(1): 45–54.

Berman, Paul. 1980. "Thinking about Programmed and Adaptive Implementation: Matching Strategies to Situations." In *Why Policies Succeed or Fail*, edited by H. Ingram and D. Mann. Beverly Hills, CA: Sage.

Berman, P., Peter W. Greenwood, Milbrey Wallin McLaughlin, and John Pincus. 1975. *Executive Summary. Volume 5 of Federal Programs Supporting Educational Change*. Prepared for the U.S. Office of Education, Department of Health, Education, and Welfare. Santa Monica, CA: Rand.

Berman, Paul, and Milbrey Wallin McLaughlin. 1978. *Implementing and Sustaining Innovations. Volume 3 of Federal Programs Supporting Educational Change*. Prepared for the U.S. Office of Education, Department of Health, Education, and Welfare. Santa Monica, CA: Rand.

Bissex, Glenda, and Richard Bullock, eds. 1987. *Seeing for Ourselves: Case-Study Research by Teachers of Writing*. London: Heinemann Educational Books.

Bobbit, Franklin. 1913. "Some General Principles of Management Applied to the Problems of City School Systems." In *The Supervision of City Schools. Twelfth Yearbook of the National Society for the Study of Education*, Part I, 7–96. Chicago: University of Chicago Press.

Bobbit, Franklin. 1918. *The Curriculum*. Boston: Houghton Mifflin.

Bobbit, Franklin. 1924. *How to Make a Curriculum*. Boston: Houghton Mifflin.

Boomer, Garth, ed. 1982. *Negotiating the Curriculum: A Teacher-Student Relationship*. Sydney: Ashton Scholastic.

Boomer, Garth. 1987. "Addressing the Problem of Elsewhereness." In *Reclaiming the Classroom: Teacher Research as an Agency for Change*, edited by D. Goswami and P. R. Stillman, 4–13. Upper Montclair, NJ: Boynton/Cook.

Booth, Wayne C. 1988. *The Vocation of a Teacher: Rhetorical Occasions 1967–1988*. Chicago: University of Chicago Press.

Brady, Laurie. 1987. The relationship between models and methods in school based curriculum development. *Curriculum Perspectives* 7(1): 47–52.

Breland, Hunter M., Marianne Amarel, and Spencer Swinton. 1974. *The Evaluation of PLATO: Educational Analysis of the Elementary School Components*. Washington, DC: Office of Experimental Projects and Programs, National Science Foundation.

Broudy, Harry S. 1963. "Historic Exemplars of Teaching Method." In *Handbook of Research on Teaching*, edited by N. L. Gage, 1–43. Chicago: Rand McNally.

Broudy, Harry S., and John R. Palmer. 1965. *Exemplars of Teaching Method*. Chicago: Rand McNally.

Brown, Sally, and Donald McIntyre. 1982. Influences upon teachers' attitudes to different types of innovation: A study of Scottish integrated science. *Curriculum Inquiry* 12(1): 35–51.

Bruner, Jerome. 1977 (1960). *The Process of Education*. Cambridge, MA: Harvard University Press.

Bullough, Robert V. 1989. *First-Year Teacher: A Case Study*. New York: Teachers College Press.

Bunderson, C. V. 1972. "Mainline CAI, Necessary but Not Oppressive." In *Proceedings of the American Federation of Information Processing Societies Spring Joint Computer Conference*, 399–405. Montvale, NJ: AFIPS.

Burge, Liz. 1988. Beyond androgogy: Some explorations for distance learning design. *Journal of Distance Education* 3(1): 5–23.

Bussis, Anne M., Edward A. Chittenden, and Marianne Amarel. 1976. *Beyond Surface Curriculum: An Interview Study of Teachers' Understandings*. Boulder, CO: Westview Press.

Butt, Richard L., and Danielle Raymond. 1987. Arguments for using qualitative approaches in understanding teacher thinking: The case for biography. *Journal of Curriculum Theorizing* 7(1): 62–93.

Calkins, Lucie McCormick. 1983. *Lessons from a Child: On the Teaching and Learning of Writing*. Melbourne: Heineman Educational Books.

Callahan, Raymond E. 1962. *Education and the Cult of Efficiency*. Chicago: University of Chicago Press.

Carr, R. 1984. Course development procedures. *ICDE Bulletin* 5:21–27.

Carr, Wilfred, and Stephen Kemmis. 1986. *Becoming Critical: Education, Knowledge, and Action Research*. London: Falmer.

Centre for Educational Research and Innovation. 1983. *Information Technology in Education and Training*. Paris: Organization for Economic Cooperation and Development.

Charters, W. W., and Roland J. Pellegrin. 1973. Barriers to the innovation process: Four case studies of differentiated staffing. *Educational Administration Quarterly* 9(1): 3–14.

Clandinin, D. Jean. 1986. *Classroom Practices: Teacher Images in Action*. London: Falmer.

Clandinin, D. Jean. 1989. Developing rhythm in teaching: The narrative study of a beginning teacher's personal practical knowledge of classrooms. *Curriculum Inquiry* 19(2): 121–141.

Clandinin, D. Jean, and F. Michael Connelly. 1986. Rhythms in teaching: The narrative study of teachers' personal practical knowledge of classrooms. *Teaching and Teacher Education* 2(4): 377–387.

Clandinin, D. Jean, and F. Michael Connelly. In press. "Narrative and Story in Practice and Research." In *The Reflective Turn: Case Studies of Reflective Practice*, edited by Donald Schön. New York: Teachers College Press.

Clark, Christopher M., and Penelope L. Peterson. 1986 "Teachers' Thought Processes." In *Handbook of Research on Teaching*, edited by M. C. Wittrock, 255–296. New York: Macmillan.

Clegg, Ambrose A. 1973. The teacher as a manager of the curriculum. *Educational Leadership* 30(4): 307–309.

Clennell, S., J. Peters, and D. Sewart. 1983. "Teaching for the Open University." In *Distance Education: International Perspectives*, edited by David Sewart, Desmond Keegan, and Borje Holmberg, 327–338. New York: St. Martin's Press.

Clifford, Geraldine Joncich. 1988. "The Professional School and Its Publics." In *Contributing to Educational Change: Perspectives on Research and Practice*, edited by Philip W. Jackson, 1–26. Berkeley, CA: McCutchan.

Cohen, David K. 1970. Politics and research: Evaluation of social action programs in education. *Review of Educational Research* 40:213–238.

Cohen, David K. 1988. "Teaching Practice: Plus Que Ca Change. . . ." In *Contributing to Educational Change: Perspectives on Re-*

search and Practice, edited by Philip W. Jackson, 27–84. Berkeley, CA: McCutchan.

Coldevin, Gary. 1988. Teacher training: The quick fix that stuck. *Development Communication Report* 4:5–15.

Coles, Robert. 1989. *The Call of Stories: Teaching and the Moral Imagination*. Boston: Houghton Mifflin.

Common, Dianne L. 1981. Two decades of curriculum innovation and so little change. *Education Canada* 21(3): 42–47.

Conle, Carola. In press. Language, experience, and negotiation. *Curriculum Inquiry*.

Connell, R. W. 1985. *Teachers' Work*. Sydney, London, Boston: George Allen & Unwin.

Connelly, F. Michael, ed. 1971. *Curriculum Theory Network*, vol. 7. CTN Monograph Supplement: Elements of Curriculum Development. Toronto: Ontario Institute for Studies in Education.

Connelly, F. Michael. 1972. The functions of curriculum development. *Interchange* 3(2/3): 161–177.

Connelly, F. Michael, and Miriam Ben-Peretz. 1980. Teachers' roles in the using and doing of research and curriculum development. *Journal of Curriculum Studies* 12(2): 95–107. Also published as Chapter 6.5 in James R. Gress and David E. Purpel, eds. 1978. *Curriculum: An Introduction to the Field*. Berkeley, CA: McCutchan.

Connelly, F. Michael, Miriam Ben-Peretz, and Robin Enns. 1978. *The York University Biology Achievement Test: A Case Study of the Relationship Between Curriculum Policy, School Program and External Testing*. Toronto: Ontario Ministry of Education.

Connelly, F. Michael, and D. Jean Clandinin. 1985. "Personal Practical Knowledge and the Modes of Knowing: Relevance for Teaching and Learning." In *Learning and Teaching the Ways of Knowing. Eighty-fourth Yearbook of the National Society for the Study of Education*, Part II, edited by Elliot W. Eisner, 174–198. Chicago: University of Chicago Press.

Connelly, F. Michael, and D. Jean Clandinin. 1988. *Teachers as Curriculum Planners: Narratives of Experience*. New York: Teachers College Press.

Connelly, F. Michael, and D. J. Clandinin. 1990. Stories of experience and narrative inquiry. *Educational Researcher* 19(5): 2–14.

Connelly, F. Michael, and D. Jean Clandinin. In press. "Teacher Preparation and Evaluation, Alternative Policies for." In *International Encyclopedia of Education: Research and Studies*, Supplementary vol. 2, edited by Torsten Husen and T. Neville Postlethwaite. Oxford: Pergamon.

Cram, David. 1961. *Explaining "Teaching Machines" in Programming*. San Francisco: Fearon Publishers.

Crandall, David P. 1983. The teacher's role in school improvement. *Educational Leadership* 41(3): 6–9.

Crandall, David P., and Associates. 1983. *People, Policies and Practices: Examining the Chain of School Improvement*, Vols. I–X. Andover, MA: Network.

Cremin, Lawrence A. 1955. The revolution in American secondary education, 1893–1918. *Teachers College Record* 56: 295–308.

Cremin, Lawrence A. 1961. *The Transformation of the School*. New York: Knopf.

Cremin, Lawrence A. 1971. Curriculum-making in the United States. *Teachers College Record* 73(2): 207–220.

Cuban, Larry. 1976. "Determinants of Curriculum Change and Stability, 1870–1970." Paper prepared for the U.S. Department of Health, Education and Welfare, National Institute of Education Curriculum Development Task Force, Washington, DC.

Cuban, Larry. 1984. *How Teachers Taught: Constancy and Change in American Classrooms, 1890–1980*. White Plains, NY: Longman.

Cuban, Larry. 1986. *Teachers and Machines*. New York: Teachers College Press.

Cuban, Larry. 1988. "Constancy and Change in Schools (1880s to the Present)." In *Contributing to Educational Change: Perspectives on Research and Practice*, edited by Philip W. Jackson, 85–105. Berkely, CA: McCutchan.

Cusick, P. 1983. *The Egalitarian Ideal and the American High School: Studies of Three High Schools*. White Plains, NY: Longman.

Daniel, John S., Martha A. Stroud, and John R. Thompson, eds. 1982. *Learning at a Distance: A World Perspective*. Edmonton: Athabasca University/International Council for Correspondence Education.

Davies, A. 1988. "Two Caring Communities: A Story of Connected Empowerment and Voice." Manuscript, University of Calgary, Alberta.

Davis, John E., 1983. Distance education courses: Re-discovered tools for small secondary schools. *Distance Education* 4(2): 195–202.

Davis, John E., and D. W. Ryan. 1980. *Constraints on Secondary School Programmes*. Toronto: Ontario Ministry of Education.

Dennison, George. 1969. *The Lives of Children*. New York: Vintage Books.

Dewey, John. 1897, January. My pedagogic creed. *School Journal* 54: 77–80.

Dewey, John. 1938. *Experience and Education; The Kappa Delta Pi Lecture Series*. New York: Collier Books.

Dewey, John. 1956. *The Child and the Curriculum* (1902) and *The School and Society* (1900, rev. 1915), 1st Phoenix ed. Chicago: University of Chicago Press.

Dewey, John, and Evelyn Dewey. 1915. *Schools of To-morrow*. New York: Dutton.

Dow, Gwyneth. 1982. *Teacher Learning*. London: Routledge & Kegan Paul.

Duckworth, Eleanor. 1986. Teaching as research. *Harvard Educational Review* 56(4). 481–495.

Dunkel, Harold B. 1972. "Wanted: New Paradigms and a Normative Base for Research." In *Philosophical Redirection of Educational Research. Seventy-first Yearbook of the National Society for the Study of Education*, Part I, edited by Lawrence G. Thomas, 77–93. Chicago: NSSE/University of Chicago Press.

Dunkel, Harold B., D. Bob Gowin, and Lawrence G. Thomas. 1972. "Introduction." In *Philosophical Redirection of Educational Research. Seventy-first Yearbook of the National Society for the Study of Education*, Part I. edited by Lawrence G. Thomas, 1–5. Chicago: NSSE/University of Chicago Press.

Edington, E. D. 1976. *Strengthening the Small School*. Austin, TX: National Educational Laboratory Publications.

Egan, Kieran. 1983. Social studies and the erosion of education. *Curriculum Inquiry* 13(2): 195–214.

Egan, Kieran. 1984. A rejoinder to Green, Franklin, Case, Daniels, and LaBar. *Curriculum Inquiry* 14(3): 341–345.

Eggleston, John. 1980. *School-based Curriculum Development in Britain*. London: Routledge & Kegan Paul.

Eisner, Elliot W. 1969. "Instructional and Expressive Objectives: Their Formulation and Use in Curriculum." In *AERA Monograph on Curriculum Evaluation: Instructional Objectives*, edited by W. J. Popham, 1–18. Chicago: Rand McNally.

Eisner, Elliot W. 1988, (June/July). The primacy of experience and the politics of method. *Educational Researcher*: 15–20.

Elbaz, Freema. 1981. The teacher's "practical knowledge": Report of a case study. *Curriculum Inquiry* 11(1): 43–71.

Elbow, Peter. 1973. *Writing Without Teachers*. London: Oxford University Press.

Elliott, John. 1985. "Educational Action-Research." In *Research, Policy and Practice*, edited by John Nisbet, Jacquetta Megarry, and Stanley Nisbet, 231–250. World Yearbook of Education. New York: Nichols.

Elliott, John. 1988, April 5–9. "Teachers as Researchers: Implications for Supervision and Teacher Education." Paper presented at the annual meeting, American Educational Research Association, New Orleans.

Elliott, John, and B. MacDonald, eds. 1975. *People in Classrooms: Teacher Evaluations of the Humanities Curriculum Project*, CARE Occasional Publication 2. Norwich, England: University of East Anglia, Centre for Applied Research in Education.

Enns-Connolly, Esther. In press. Translation and the translator: A narrative study of personal practical knowledge in the construction of meaning. *Curriculum Inquiry*.

Erickson, Gaalen L. 1987, April. "Constructivist Epistemology and the Professional Development of Teachers." Paper presented at the annual meeting, American Educational Research Association, Symposium on Educational Implications of Personal and Social Construction of Knowledge, Washington, DC.

Finch, Mary Ellen. 1981. Behind the teacher's desk: The teacher, the administrator, and the problem of change. *Curriculum Inquiry* 11(4): 321–342.

Franklin, Barry M. 1982. The social efficiency movement reconsidered: Curriculum change in Minneapolis, 1917–1950. *Curriculum Inquiry* 12(1): 9–33.

Franklin, Barry M. 1984. Educational ideas and school practice: A response to Kieran Egan and Maxine Greene. *Curriculum Inquiry* 14(3): 319–326.

Fullan, Michael. 1972. Overview of the innovative process and the user. *Interchange* 3(2–3): 1–46.

Fullan, Michael. 1982. *The Meaning of Educational Change*. Toronto: OISE Press.

Fullan, Michael. 1983. Evaluating program implementation: What can be learned from follow through. *Curriculum Inquiry* 13(2): 215–227.

Fullan, Michael. 1985. Change processes and strategies at the local level. *Elementary School Journal* 85(3): 391–421.

Fullan, Michael, Glenn Eastabrook, and John Biss. 1977. "Action Research in the School: Involving Students and Teachers in Classroom Change." In *Education, Change, and Society: A Sociology of Canadian Education*, edited by R. A. Carlton, L. A. Colley, and N. J. MacKinnon, 508–522. Toronto: Gage Educational.

Fullan, Michael, and A. Pomfret. 1977. Research on curriculum and instruction implementation. *Review of Educational Research* 47(1): 335–397.

Gall, Jan. 1983. "Home Tutors' Difficulties in Coping with Curriculum." In *Coping with Curriculum*, 58–64. Nedlands: University of Western Australia, National Workshop on Distance Education, Perth.

Garry, Ralph, F. Michael Connelly, and F. Dittman. 1975. "Interpretive Case Study of Selected Projects." In *Handbook on Curriculum Development*, edited by Per Dalin, 55–118. Paris: Organization for Economic Cooperation and Development, Centre for Educational Research and Innovation.

Gee, Tom. 1988. Alberta's distance learning in small schools project: 1988–89 update. *Small Schools Network Newsletter* 2(2): 3–4.

Getzels, Jacob W. 1978. "Theoretical Research and School Change." In *Research and Development and School Change*, edited by Robert Glaser, 27–45. Hillsdale, NJ: Erlbaum.

Giroux, Henry A. 1983. *Theory and Resistance in Education*. South Hadley, MA: Bergin and Garvey.

Giroux, Henry A. 1988. *Teachers as Intellectuals: Toward a Critical Pedagogy of Learning*. South Hadley, MA: Bergin and Garvey.

Glaser, Robert, ed. 1978. *Research and Development and School Change*. Hillsdale, NJ: Erlbaum.

Good, Thomas L., and Jere E. Brophy. 1986. *Looking in Classrooms* (3rd ed.). New York: Harper & Row.

Goodenow, Ronald, and Arthur O. White, eds. 1981. *Education and the Rise of the New South*. Boston: Hall.

Goodlad, John I. 1969. Curriculum: State of the field. *Review of Educational Research* 39(3): 367–375.

Goodlad, John I. 1984. *A Place Called School: Prospects for the Future*. Toronto: McGraw-Hill.

Goodlad, John I. 1988. "Coping with Curriculum." In *Contributing to Educational Change: Perspectives on Research and Practice*, edited by Philip W. Jackson, 179–190. Berkeley, CA: McCutchan.

Goodlad, John I., and M. Klein. 1970. *Behind the Classroom Door*. Worthington, OH: Jones.

Goodman, Jessie. 1984. "Masculinity, Feminism, and the Male Elementary School Teacher: A Case Study of Preservice Teachers' Perspectives." Paper presented at the annual Curriculum Theory and Practice Conference, Dayton, OH.

Gowin, D. Bob. 1972. "Is Educational Research Distinctive?" In *Philosophical Redirection of Educational Research. Seventy-first Yearbook of the National Society for the Study of Education*, Part I, edited by Lawrence G. Thomas, 9–25. Chicago: NSSE/University of Chicago Press.

Graff, Gerald, and Michael Warner, eds. 1989. *The Origins of Literacy Studies in America: A Documentary Anthology*. New York: Rutledge, Chapman & Hall.

Green, Thomas F. 1979. "Learning Without Metaphor." In *Metaphor and Thought*, edited by Andrew Ortony, 462–473. Cambridge: Cambridge University Press.

Greene, Maxine. 1973. *Teacher as Stranger*. Belmont, CA: Wadsworth.

Greene, Maxine. 1983. On the American dream: Equality, ambiguity, and the persistance of rage. *Curriculum Inquiry* 13(2): 179–193.

Greene, Maxine. 1984. A rejoinder to Green, Case, Daniels, LaBar, and Franklin. *Curriclum Inquiry* 14(3): 337–339.

Greene, Maxine. 1986. "Philosophy and Teaching." In *Handbook of Research on Teaching*, edited by Merlin C. Wittrock, 479–501. New York: Macmillan.

Greene, Maxine. 1989. "The Teacher in John Dewey's Works." In *From Socrates to Software: The Teacher as Text and the Text as Teacher. Eighty-ninth Yearbook of the National Society for the Study of Education*, Part I, edited by Philip W. Jackson and Sophie Haroutunian-Gordon, 24–35. NSSE/University of Chicago Press.

Greenfield, Thomas B., F. Michael Connelly, and John Davis (with Brendan Barnet, Chester Carlow, Ray Danley, David Ducharme, Richard G. Duffin, Faye Norsworthy, and John Ross). 1976. *Creating and Changing Curriculum in a School System: A Design for Development, Implementation and Evaluation*. Report to the Wellington County Board of Education, Guelph, Ontario. Toronto: Ontario Institute for Studies in Education, Department of Educational Administration.

Griffin, G. A. 1983. "Introduction: The Work of Staff Development." In *Staff Development. Eighty-second Yearbook of the National Society for the Study of Education*, edited by G. A. Griffin. Chicago: NSSE/University of Chicago Press.

Grobman, Hulda. 1970. *Developmental Curriculum Projects: Decision Points and Processes*. Hasca, IL: Peacock.

Gross, N., J. Giacquinta, and M. Bernstein. 1971. *Implementing Organizational Innovations*. New York: Basic Books.

Grumet, Madeleine R. 1988. *Bitter Milk: Women and Teaching*. Amherst: University of Massachusetts Press.

Guskey, Thomas R. 1986. Staff development and the process of teacher change. *Educational Researcher* 15(5): 5–12.

Hall, Gene E., and Shirley M. Hord. 1984. *Change in Schools: Facilitating the Process*. New York: State University of New York Press.

Hall, Gene E., and Susan F. Loucks. 1977. A developmental model for determining whether the treatment is actually implemented. *American Educational Research Journal* 14(3): 263–276.

Harasim, Linda M. 1986. Computer learning networks: Educational applications of computer conferencing. *Journal of Distance Education* 1(1): 59–70.

Harasim, Linda M. In press. "Bibliography on Educational CMC." In *Online Education: Perspectives on a New Environment*, edited by Linda M. Harasim. New York: Praeger.

Harris, William T. 1876. A course of study from primary school to university. *The Western* 2: 521–538, Reprinted in Carl Lester Byerly, *Contribution of William Torrey Harris to Public School Administration*. Chicago: n.p., 1946.

Harris, William T. 1897. My pedagogical creed. *School Journal* 54(26): 813–815.

Harste, J., V. Woodward, and C. Burke. 1984. *Language Stories and Literacy Lessons*. Portsmouth, NH: Heinemann.

Hawkins, D. 1983, spring. Nature closely observed. *Daedalus*: 65–89.

Hodgkinson, Harold L. 1977. *NIE's Role in Curriculum Development: Findings, Policy Options, and Recommendations*, prepared by Jon Schaffarzick and Gary Sykes. Washington, DC: National Institute of Education, Curriculum Development Task Force.

Hoffman, L. 1988. "Teacher Personal Practical Knowledge." Master's thesis, University of Calgary, Alberta.

Hogan, P. 1988. "A Community of Teacher Researchers: A Story of Empowerment and Voice." Manuscript, University of Calgary, Alberta.

Holly, Peter, and Geoff Southworth. 1989. *The Developing School*. London. Falmer.

Holmberg, B. 1982. *Distance Education: A Short Handbook*. Stockholm: Libertryck.

Hopkins, David. 1985. *School Based Review for School Improvement: A Preliminary State of the Art*. Leuver, Belg.: Academic Publishing.

House, Ernest R. 1974. *The Politics of Educational Innovation*. Berkeley, CA: McCutchan.

Huberman, Michael. 1981. *Emergency Care Research Institute, Masepa, North Plains: Case Study*. Andover, MA: Network.

Huberman, Michael, and D. Crandall. 1983. *People, Policies and Practices: Examining the Chain of School Improvement, Volume 9: Implications for Action, A Study of Dissemination Efforts Supporting School Improvement*. Andover, MA: Network.

Humble, S., and H. Simons. 1978. *From Council to Classroom: An Evaluation of the Diffusion of the Humanities Curriculum Project*. Schools Council Research Studies. London: Macmillan Education.

Hunter, M. 1984. "Knowing, Teaching and Supervising." In *Using What We Know About Teaching*, edited by P. Hosford, 169–192. Alexandria, VA: Association for Supervision and Curriculum Development.

Irwin, Rita. 1988. "The Practical Knowledge of a Fine Arts Supervisor in Educational Change: A Case Study." Ph.D. dissertation, University of British Columbia, Vancouver.

Jackson, Philip W. 1966. "The Way Teaching Is." In *The Way Teaching Is: Report on the Seminar on Teaching*, edited by Ole Sand and Leslee J. Bishop, 7–27. Washington, DC: Association for Supervision and Curriculum Development/National Education Association, Center for the Study of Instruction.

Jackson, Philip W. 1968. *Life in Classrooms*. New York: Holt, Rinehart and Winston.

Jackson, Philip W. 1985. "Chapter 17: Time-off-Task at a Time-on-Task Conference." In *Perspectives on Instructional Time*, edited by Charles W. Fisher and David C. Berliner, 301–308. White Plains, NY: Longman.

Jackson, Philip W. 1987. "Facing Our Ignorance." In *Reforming Teacher Education: The Impact of the Holmes Group Report*, edited by Jonas F. Soltis, 74–79. New York: Teachers College Press.

Jersild, Arthur T. 1946. *Child Development and the Curriculum*. New York: Teachers College Press.

Johnson, Mark. 1987. *The Body in the Mind: The Bodily Basis of Meaning, Imagination, and Reason*. Chicago: University of Chicago Press.

Johnson, Mark. 1989. Embodied knowledge. *Curriculum Inquiy* 19(4): 361–377.

Johnston, S. 1988. Focusing on the person in the study of curriculum in teacher education. *Journal of Education for Teaching* 14(3): 215–223.

Joyce, Bruce R., and Beverly Showers. 1982. The coaching of teaching. *Educational Leadership* 40(1): 4–10.

Kass, Heidi, and T. Kieren. 1986. "Computers and Canadian Youth." Final report, submitted to the Social Sciences and Humanities Research Council of Canada, University of Alberta, Edmonton.

Kass, Heidi, and M. Nay. In press. "The Use of Computers in Science Instruction." In *Second International Science Study, Canada*, edited by F. Michael Connelly, Robert Crocker, and Heidi Kass. Final report, submitted to the Social Sciences and Humanities Research Council of Canada.

Keegan, Desmond. 1982. "From New Delhi to Vancouver: Trends in Distance Education." In *Learning at a Distance: A World Perspective*, edited by John S. Daniel, Martha A. Stroud, and John R. Thompson, 40–43. Edmonton: Athabasca University/International Council for Correspondence Education.

Keegan, Desmond. 1986. *The Foundations of Distance Education*. London: Croom Helm.

Kennard, B. 1988. "Moments of Seeing: Parallel Stories of Narrative Change in Collaborative Relationships." Manuscript, University of Calgary, Alberta.

Kilbourn, Brent. In press. *Constructive Feedback: Learning the Art*. Toronto: OISE Press.

Kimpston, Richard D. 1985. Curriculum fidelity and the implementation tasks employed by teachers: A research study. *Journal of Curriculum Studies* 17(2): 185–195.

Kimpston, Richard D., and Douglas H. Anderson. 1982. A study of analyze curriculum decision making in school districts. *Educational Leadership* 40(2): 63–66.

Kirst, Michael W. 1983. "Policy Implications of Individual Differences and the Common Curriculum." In *Individual Differences and the Common Curriculum. Eighty-second Yearbook of the National Society for the Study of Education*, Part I, edited by G. D. Fenstermacher and John I. Goodlad, 282–299. Chicago: University of Chicago Press.

Kirst, Michael W., and Gail Meister. 1985. Turbulence in American secondary schools: What reforms last? *Curriculum Inquiry* 15(2): 169–186.

Kliebard, Herbert M. 1968. "The Curriculum Field in Retrospect." In *Technology and the Curriculum*, edited by Paul W. F. Witt, 69–84. New York: Teachers College Press.

Kliebard, Herbert M. 1970. Reappraisal: The Tyler rationale. *School Review* 78:259–272.

Kliebard, Herbert M. 1971. "Bureaucracy and Curriculum Theory." In *Freedom, Bureaucracy, and Schooling. Yearbook of the Association for Supervision and Curriculum Development*, edited by V. F. Haubrich, 51–69. Washington, DC: ASCD.

Kliebard, Herbert M. 1975. The rise of scientific curriculum making and its aftermath. *Curriculum Theory Network* 5(1): 27–38.

Knowles, M. S. 1980. *Modern Practice of Adult Education: From Pedagogy to Androgogy*, 2nd ed. New York: Cambridge Books.

Kremer, Lya, and Miriam Ben-Peretz. 1980. Teachers' characteristics and their reflection in curriculum implementation. *Studies in Educational Evaluation* 6:73–82.

Kroma, Siaka. 1983. "Personal Practical Knowledge of Language in Teaching." Ph.D. dissertation, University of Toronto, Toronto.

Lakoff, George. 1987. *Women, Fire, and Dangerous Things*. Chicago: University of Chicago Press.

Lakoff, George, and Mark Johnson. 1980. *Metaphors We Live by*. Chicago: University of Chicago Press.

Lampert, M. 1985. How do teachers manage to teach? Perspectives on problems in classrooms. *Harvard Eductional Review* 55(2): 178–194.

Lanier, Judith E., and Judith W. Little. 1986. "Chapter 19: Research on Teacher Education." In *Handbook of Research on Teaching*, edited by Merlin C. Wittrock, 527–569. New York: Macmillan.

Lawn, Noel. 1975. "A Study of the Family." In *People in Classrooms: Teacher Evaluations of the Humanities Curriculum Project*, edited by John Elliott and Barry MacDonald, 31–37. Norwich, England: University of East Anglia Centre for Applied Research in Education.

Lawton, D. 1980. *The Politics of the School Curriculum*. London: Routledge & Kegan Paul.

Lee, Gordon C. 1966. "The Changing Role of the Teacher." In *The Changing American School. Sixty-fifth Yearbook of the National Society for the Study of Education*, Part II, edited by John I. Goodlad, 9–31. Chicago: NSSE/University of Chicago Press.

Leithwood, Kenneth A. 1981. The dimensions of curriculum innovation. *Journal of Curriculum Studies* 13(1): 25–36.

Leithwood, Kenneth A. ed. 1982. *Studies in Curriculum Decision Making*. Toronto: OISE Press.

Leithwood, Kenneth A., and R. MacDonald. 1981. Decisions given by teachers for their curriculum choices. *Canadian Journal of Education* 6(2): 103–116.

Lieberman, Ann. 1986a. Collaborative research: Working with, not working on. . . . *Educational Leadership* 43(5): 28–32.

Lieberman, Ann. 1986b. Collaborative work. *Educational Leadership* 43(5): 4–8.

Lieberman, Ann. 1986c. *Rethinking School Improvement*. New York: Teachers College Press.

Lieberman, Ann. 1987. Teacher leadership. *Teachers College Record* 88(3): 400–405.

Lightfoot, Martin, and Nancy Martin, eds. 1988. *The Word for Teaching Is Learning: Essays for James Britton*. London: Heinemann Educational Books.

Lightfoot, Sarah Lawrence. 1983. *The Good High School: Portraits of Character and Culture*. New York: Basic Books.

Little, J. W. 1981. *School Success and Staff Development: The Role of Staff Development in Urban Desegrated Schools. Executive Summary*. Washington, DC: Institute of Education.

Lortie, Dan C. 1975. *School-teacher: A Sociological Study*. Chicago: University of Chicago Press.

Loucks, S. F. 1983. At last some good news from a study of school improvement. *Educational Leadership* 42:4–5.

MacDonald, B. 1978. *The Experience of Innovation. Volume 2. Towards Judgement*, rev. ed. Publications of the Evaluation Unit of the Humanities Curriculum Research Project, Occasional Research Paper 6. Norwich, England: University of East Anglia, Centre for Applied Research in Education.

MacDonald, B. 1988. April 5–9. "Evaluating the Humanities Curriculum Project: A retrospective." Paper presented at the annual meeting, American Educational Research Association, New Orleans, LA.

MacDonald, B., and R. Walker. 1976a. "The Alternative Error?—H.C.P.: The Dream Merchants." In *Changing the Curriculum*, edited by B. MacDonald and R. Walker, 75–84. London: Open Books.

MacDonald, B., and R. Walker. eds. 1976b. *Changing the Curriculum*. London: Open Books.

MacDonald, James B., and Dwight Clark. 1973. "Critical value Questions and the Analysis of Objectives and Curricula." In *Second Handbook of Research on Teaching*, edited by Robert M. W. Travers, 405–412. Chicago: Rand McNally.

MacKenzie, G. N. 1970. "Why a Strategy for Planned Curricular innovation?" In *Strategies for Planned Curricular Innovation*, edited by M. R. Lawler, 1–12. New York: Teachers College Press.

McKeon, Richard. 1952. Philosophy and action. *Ethics* 62(2): 79–100.

McKinney, W. Lynn, and Ian Westbury. 1975. "Stability and Change: The Public Schools of Gary, Indiana, 1940–70." In *Case Studies in Curriculum Change, Great Britain and the United States*, edited by William A. Reid and Decker F. Walker, 1–53. London: Routledge & Kegan Paul.

McLaughlin, Milbrey Wallin, and David D. Marsh. 1978. Staff development and school change. *Teacher's College Record* 80(1): 69–94.

McLean, Leslie D. 1973. It's almost time for CAI. *Interchange* 4(4): 35–47.

McMurry, Charles A. 1914. *Conflicting Principles in Teaching and How to Adjust to Them*. Boston: Houghton Mifflin.

McVeagh, H. E. 1981. "The New Zealand Correspondence School: A Pragmatic System for the Basic Schooling of Isolated Children." In *Rural Education in Urbanized Nations: Issues and Innovations*, edited by J. P. Sher. Boulder, CO: Westview Press.

Mager, Robert F. 1962. *Preparing Objectives for Programmed Instruction*. San Francisco: Fearon Publishers.

Manzer, R. A. 1972. "The Secret Garden of the Curriculum." In *Problems of Curriculum Innovation*, edited by Eric Hoyle and Robert Bell, 120–124. Bletchley, England: Open University Press.

Markowitz, Harold, Jr. 1983. Independent study by correspondence in American universities. *Distance Education* 4(2): 149–170.

Marsh, Colin J. 1988. *Spotlight on School Improvement*. Sydney: Allen & Unwin.

Mayhew, Katherine Camp, and Anna Camp Edwards. 1936. *The Dewey School*. New York: Atherton Press.

Meek, Margaret, Stephanie Armstrong, Vicky Austerfield, Judith Graham, and Elizabeth Placetter. 1983. *Achieving Literacy: Longitudinal Studies of Adolescents Learning to Read*. London: Routledge & Kegan Paul.

Miel, Alice. 1952. *Cooperative Procedures in Learning*. New York: Teachers College Press.

Miller, Lynne, and Ann Lieberman. 1988. School improvement in the United States: Nuance and numbers. *Qualitative Studies in Education* 1(1): 3–19.

Munby, Hugh. 1986. Metaphor in the thinking of teachers: An exploratory study. *Journal of Curriculum Studies* 18:197–209.

Naisbitt, J. 1984. *The Year Ahead: 1985*. Washington, DC: Naisbitt Group.

Natkins, Lucille G. 1986. *Our Last Term: A Teacher's Diary*. Lanham, MD: University Press of America.

Newton, Earle, and Debra Kinakin. 1989. "The Meaning of Curriculum Change: Views of Pilot Teachers." Working paper, University of Saskatchewan, College of Education, Saskatoon.

Nisbet, R. 1969. *Social Change and History*. New York: Oxford University Press.

Nisbet, R. 1980. *History of the Idea of Progress*. New York: Basic Books.

Noddings, Nel, ed. 1976. *A Report of the NIE Curriculum Development Conference*. Los Altos, CA: National Institute of Education.

Noddings, N. 1986. Fidelity in teaching, teacher education, and research for teaching. *Harvard Educational Review* 56(4): 496–510.

Oberg, A., and Corey Blades. 1990, June. "The Spoken and the Unspoken: The Story of an Educator." Paper presented at a meeting, Invitational International Pedagogy Conference, Banff, Alberta.

O'Connor, Carol A. 1980, fall. Setting a standard for suburbia: Innovation in the Scarsdale schools, 1920–1930. *History of Education Quarterly* 20: 295–311.

Olson, John K. 1976. The role of the teacher in curriculum development. *Science Education* 60(1): 61–67.

Olson, John K. 1980. Teacher constructs and curriculum change. *Journal of Curriculum Studies* 12(1): 1–11.

O'Neal, L., and W. Beckner. 1981. Rural education: Past and present. *Rural Educator* 5(1): 15–19.

Ontario Ministry of Education. 1989. *Circular 14: Textbooks*. Toronto: Ministry of Education.

Ortony, Andrew. 1979a. "Metaphor: A Multidimensional Problem." In *Metaphor and Thought*, edited by Andrew Ortony, 1–16. Cambridge: Cambridge University Press.

Ortony, Andrew, ed. 1979b. *Metaphor and Thought*. Cambridge: Cambridge University Press.

Paley, Vivian Gussin. 1979. *White Teacher*. Cambridge, MA: Harvard University Press.

Paley, Vivian Gussin. 1981. *Wally's Stories: Conversations in the Kindergarten*. Cambridge, MA: Harvard University Press.

Paley, Vivian Gussin. 1985. *Girls and Boys: Superheroes in the Doll Corner*. Chicago: University of Chicago Press.

Paley, Vivian Gussin. 1986. *Molly is Three: Growing up in School*. Chicago: University of Chicago Press.

Paley, Vivian Gussin. 1988. *Bad Guys Don't Have Birthdays: Fantasy Play at Four*. Chicago: University of Chicago Press.

Parker, J. 1982. *The Writer's Workshop*. Don Mills, Ontario: Addison-Wesley.

Pearson, D. 1985. Changing the face of reading comprehension instruction. *The Reading Teacher*: 724–738.

Petrie, Hugh G. 1979. "Metaphor and Learning." In *Metaphor and Thought*, edited by Andrew Ortony, 439–461. Cambridge: Cambridge University Press.

Phillips, Denis C. 1985. "The Uses and Abuses of Truisms." In *Perspectives on Instructional Time*, edited by Charles W. Fisher and David C. Berliner, 309–315. White Plains, NY: Longman.

Phillips, J. Arch, and Richard Hawthorne. 1976. Political dimensions of curriculum decision making. *Educational Leadership* 35:362–66.

Pinar, William F. 1981. Whole, bright, deep with understanding: Issues in qualitative research and autobiographical method. *Journal of Curriculum Studies* 13(3): 173–188.

Plattor, E. 1988. Assessing listening in elementary schools: An examination of four listening tests. *Journal of the International Listening Association* 2:33–44.

Popham, W. James. 1974. "Curriculum Design: The Problem of Specifying Intended Learning Outcomes." In *A Monograph on Program Development in Education*, edited by J. Blaney, I. Housego, and G. McIntosh, 76–88. Vancouver: University of British Columbia, Education-Extension, Centre for Continuing Education.

Popham, W. James, and E. L. Baker. 1970. *Establishing Instructional Goals*. Englewood Cliffs, NJ: Prentice Hall.

Pressey, Sidney L. 1932. A third and fourth contribution towards the coming "industrial revolution" in education. *School and Society* 36(934): 668–672.

Ramsey, Peter. D. K. 1983. Fresh perspectives on the school transformation-reproduction debate: A response to Anyon from the Antipodes. *Curriculum Inquiry* 13(3):295–320.

Reddy, Michael J. 1979. "The Conduit Metaphor: A Case of Frame Conflict in Our Language About Language." In *Metaphor and Thought*, edited by Andrew Ortony, 284–324. Cambridge: Cambridge University Press.

Regan, E., and K. Leithwood. 1975. *Effecting Curriculum Change*. Toronto: OISE Press.

Reid, W. A. and Walker, D. F., eds. 1975. *Case Studies in Curriculum Change, Great Britain and the United States*. London: Routledge & Kegan Paul.

Rieff, Philip. 1972. *Fellow Teachers: Of Culture and Its Second Death*. Chicago: University of Chicago Press.

Ringel, Paul J. 1981, April. "Cooperative Industrial Education: The Fitchburg Plan." Paper presented at the annual meeting, American Educational Research Association, Los Angeles.

Rosenshine, B. 1970. Evaluation of classroom instruction. *Review of Educational Research* 40:279–300.

Rowland, Stephen. 1984. *The Enquiring Classroom*. London: Falmer.

Rugg, Harold O. 1926. "The School Curriculum and the Drama of American Life." In *Curriculum-making: Past and Present. Part 1. The Foundations and Techniques of Curriculum-Construction. Twenty-sixth Yearbook of the National Society for the Study of Education*, edited by Guy M. Whipple, 3–16. Bloomington, IL: Public School Publishing.

Rugg, Harold O., and George S. Counts. 1926. "A Critical Appraisal of Current Methods of Curriculum Making." In *Curriculum-making: Past and Present. Part 1. The Foundations and Techniques of Curriculum-Construction. Twenty-sixth Yearbook of the National Society for the Study of Education*. edited by Guy M. Whipple 425–447. Bloomington, IL: Public School Publishing.

Ruggles, Robin H., John Anderson, David E. Blackmore, Clay Lafleur, J. Peter Rothe, and Terry Taerum. 1982. *Learning at a Distance and the New Technology*. Vancouver: Educational Research Institute of British Columbia.

Russell, H., ed. 1969. *Evaluation of Computer-assisted Instruction Program*. St. Ann, MO: Central Midwestern Regional Educational Laboratory.

Russell, Thomas L. 1988. "The Pressure to Cover the Curriculum: A Case Study." Paper presented at meeting, Canadian Society for the Study of Education, Windsor, Ontario.

Russell, Thomas L., and H. Munby. In press. "Reframing: The Role of Experience in Developing Teachers' Professional Knowledge." In *The Reflective Turn: Case Studies of Reflective Practice*, edited by Donald Schön. New York: Teachers College Press.

Ryan, Doris W. 1986. *Developing a New Model of Teacher Effectiveness: Lessons Learned from the IEA Classroom Environment Study*. Toronto: Ontario Ministry of Education.

Ryan, Kevin. 1970. *Don't Smile Until Christmas: Accounts of the First Year of Teaching*. Chicago: University of Chicago Press.

Sabar, Naama, Moshe Silberstein, and Nitza Shafriri. 1982. Needed: Curriculum coordinators for teachers developing learning materials: A systematic analysis of coordinators' characteristics for better planned training. *Curriculum Inquiry* 12(1): 53–67.

Sand, Ole. 1971. "Curriculum Change." In *The Curriculum: Retrospect and Prospect. Seventieth Yearbook of the National Society for the Study of Education*, edited by Robert M. McClure, 219–244. Chicago: University of Chicago Press.

Sarason, Seymour B. 1988. *The Making of an American Psychologist*. San Francisco: Jossey-Bass.

Schaffarzick, Jon. 1976. *Current Issues, Problems and Concerns in Curriculum Development*. Washington, DC: National Institute of Education, Curriculum Development Task Force.

Schön, Donald A. 1979. "Generative Metaphor: A Perspective on Problem-setting in Social Policy." In *Metaphor and Thought*, edited by Andrew Ortony, 254–283. Cambridge: Cambridge University Press.

Schön, Donald A. 1990. *The Reflective Turn: Case Studies in Reflective Practice*. New York: Teachers College Press.

Schostak, John F., and Tom Logan. 1984. *Pupil Experience*. London: Croom Helm.

Schwab, Joseph J. 1954. Eros and education: A discussion of one aspect of discussion. *Journal of General Education* 8:54–71.

Schwab, Joseph J. 1960. "What Do Scientists Do?" In *Science, Curriculum, and Liberal Education: Selected Essays*, edited by Ian Westbury and Neil J. Wilkof, 184–228. Chicago: University of Chicago Press.

Schwab, Joseph J. 1969. *College Curriculum and Student Protest*. Chicago: University of Chicago Press.

Schwab, Joseph J. 1970a. "The Practical: A Language for Curriculum." In *Science, Curriculum, and Liberal Education: Selected Essays*, edited by Ian Westbury and Neil J. Wilkof, 287–321. Chicago: University of Chicago Press.

Schwab, Joseph J. 1970b. *The Practical: A Language for Curriculum*. Washington, DC: National Education Association.

Schwab, Joseph J. 1971. The practical: Arts of eclectic. *School Review* 79:493–542.

Schwab, Joseph J. 1973. The practical: Translation into curriculum. *School Review* 81:501–522.

Schwab, Joseph J. 1983. The practical, 4: Something for curriculum professors to do. *Curriculum Inquiry* 13(3): 239–265.

Seddon, Teresa. 1981. Intention and reality of school-based curriculum development. *Curriculum Perspectives* 2(1): 9–16.

Seguel, Mary Louise. 1966. *The Curriculum Field: Its Formative Years*. New York: Teachers College Press.

Sewart, David. 1981, summer. Distance teaching: A contradiction in terms. *Teaching at a Distance*: 8–18.

Sewart, David. 1982. "Individualizing Support Services." In *Learning at a Distance: A World Perspective*, edited by John S. Daniel, Martha A. Stroud, and John R. Thompson, 27–29. Edmonton: Athabasca University/International Council for Correspondence Education.

Sewart, David, Desmond Keegan, and Borje Holmberg, eds. 1983. *Distance Education: International Perspectives*. London: Croom Helm.

Sher, J. P., ed. 1981. *Rural Education in Urbanized Nations: Issues and Innovations*. Boulder, CO: Westview Press.

Shipman, M. D. 1974. *Inside a Curriculum Project*. London: Methuen.

Sikes, Patricia K. 1988, September 1–3. "Fifteen Years Is a Long Time Ago: A Humanities Faculty Revisited." Paper presented at meeting, British Educational Research Association, Symposium on Teacher Development, University of East Anglia, Norwich, England.

Simpson, Douglas J., and Michael J. B. Jackson. 1984. *The Teacher as Philosopher*. Toronto: Methuen.

Sirotnik, Kenneth A. 1983. What you see is what you get: Consistency, persistency, and mediocrity in classrooms. *Harvard Educational Review* 53(1): 16–31.

Sizer, T. 1984. *Horace's Compromise: The Dilemma of the American High School*. Boston: Houghton Mifflin.

Skilbeck, Malcolm. 1984. *School-based Curriculum Development*. London: Harper & Row.

Skinner, B. F. 1958. Teaching machines. *Science* 128(3330): 969–977.

Smith, Louis M., David C. Dwyer, John J. Prunty, and Paul F. Kleine. 1988. *Innovation and Change in Schooling: History, Politics, and Agency. Book 3. Anatomy of Educational Innovation: A Mid to Long-term Re-study and Reconstrual*. Philadelphia, PA: Falmer.

Smith, Louis M., and Pat M. Keith. 1971. *Anatomy of Educational Innovation: An Organizational Analysis of an Elementary School*. New York: Wiley.

Smith, Louis M., Paul F. Kleine, John P. Prunty, and David C. Dwyer. 1986. *Educational Innovators: Then and Now. Book 1. Anatomy of Educational Innovation: A Mid to Long-term Re-study and Reconstrual*. Philadelphia, PA: Falmer.

Smith, Louis M., John P. Prunty, David C. Dwyer, and Paul F. Kleine. 1987. *The Fate of an Innovative School: The History and Present Status of the Kensington School. Book 2. Anatomy of Educational Innovation: A Mid to Long-term Re-study and Reconstrual*. Philadelphia, PA: Falmer.

Soutter, Desmond. 1975. "Exploring Relations Between the Sexes in a Boy's School." In *People in Classrooms: Teacher Evaluations of the Humanities Curriculum Project*, edited by John Elliott and Barry MacDonald, 27–30. Norwich, England: University of East Anglia, Centre for Applied Research in Education.

Spady, W. G. 1977. "Power, Authority and Empathy in Schooling." In *Education, Change, and Society: A Sociology of Canadian Education*, edited by Richard A. Carlton, Louise A. Colley, and Neil J. MacKinnon, 359–375. Toronto: Gage Educational.

Steedman, Carolyn. 1982. *The Tidy House*. London: Virago Press.

Stenhouse, Lawrence, ed. 1980a. *Curriculum Research and Development in Action*. London: Heinemann.

Stenhouse, Lawrence. 1980b. "Reflections." In *Curriculum Research and Development in Action*, edited by Lawrence Stenhouse, 244–262. London: Heinemann.

Stenhouse, Lawrence. 1983. *Authority, Education and Emancipation: A Collection of Papers by Lawrence Stenhouse*. London: Heinemann.

Tamir, Pinchas. 1976. The Israeli high school biology project: A case of adaptation. *Curriculum Theory Network* 5(4): 305–315.

Tamir, Pinchas, Abraham Blum, Avi Hofstein, and Naama Sabar, eds. 1979. *Curriculum Implementation and Its Relationship to Curriculum Development in Science*. Jerusalem: Hebrew University, Amos De Shalit Science Teaching Center.

Thiessen, Dennis. In press. "Classroom-based Teacher Development." In *Understanding Teacher Development*, edited by A. Hargreaves and M. Fullan. London: Cassell.

Thomas, L. G. ed. 1972. *Philosophical Redirection of Educational Research. Seventy-first Yearbook of the National Society for the Study of Education*, Part I. Chicago: NSSE/University of Chicago Press.

Thomas, M. Carey. 1989. "From 'The Making of a Feminist: Early Journals and Letters of M. Carey Thomas (1871–83).'" In *The Origins of Literary Studies in America: A Documentary Anthology*, edited by Gerald Graff and Michael Warner, 179–189. New York: Rutledge, Chapman & Hall.

Tomkins, George. 1986. *A Common Countenance: Stability and Change in the Canadian Curriculum*. Scarborough, Ont.: Prentice Hall.

Tomkins, George, F. Michael Connelly, and Jean-Jacques Bernier. 1981. *State of the Art Review of Research in Curriculum and Instruction*. Ottawa: State of the Art Review of Educational Research, Canadian Society for Study of Education.

Travers, Robert M. W. 1968. "Directions of the Development of an Educational Technology." In *Technology and the Curriculum*, edited by Paul W. F. Witt, 85–101. New York: Teachers College Press.

Turney, C., K. E. Sinclair, and L. G. Cairns. 1980. *Isolated Schools*. Sydney: Sydney University Press.

Tyack, David B. 1974. *The One Best System: A History of American Urban Education*. Cambridge, MA: Harvard University Press.

Tyack, David B., Michael W. Kirst, and Elizabeth Hansot. 1980. Educational reform: Retrospect and prospect. *Teachers College Record* 81(3): 253–269.

Tyler, Ralph W. 1949. *Basic Principles of Curriculum and Instruction*. Chicago: University of Chicago Press.

UNESCO. 1979. *Terminology of Adult Education/Terminologie de la educacion de adultos/Terminologie de l'éducation des adultes*. Paris: Ibedata.

Urban, Wayne. 1981. "Educational Reform in a New South City: Atlanta, 1890–1925." In *Education and the Rise of the New South*, edited by Ronald Goodenow and Arthur O. White. Boston: Hall.

Walberg, Herbert J. 1986. "Synthesis of Research on Teaching." In *Handbook of Research on Teaching*, edited by Merlin C. Wittrock, 214–229. New York: Macmillan.

Wenham, Peter. 1975. "Reflective Discussion: Its Problems and Possibilities." In *People in Classrooms: Teacher Evaluations of the Humanities Curriculum Project*, edited by John Elliott and Barry MacDonald, 52–57. Norwich, England: University of East Anglia, Centre for Applied Research in Education.

Westbury, Ian. 1970. Curriculum evaluation. *Review of Educational Research* 40(2): 239–260.

Westbury, Ian, and Neil J. Wilkof, eds. 1978. *Science, Curriculum, and Liberal Education: Selected Essays of Joseph Schwab*. Chicago: University of Chicago Press.

Western Australia Education Department. 1979. *Educational Provision in Sparsely Populated Areas of Western Australia*. Perth: Education Department.

Whipple, Guy M., ed. 1926. *Curriculum-making: Past and Present. Part 1. The Foundations and Techniques of Curriculum-Construction. Twenty-sixth Yearbook of the National Society for the Study of Education*. Bloomington, IL: Public School Publishing.

Witt, Paul W. F. 1968a. "Educational Technology: The Education of Teachers and the Development of Instructional Materials Specialists." In *Technology and the Curriculum*, edited by Paul W. F. Witt, 53–67. New York: Teachers College Press.

Witt, Paul W. F., ed. 1968b. *Technology and the Curriculum*. New York: Teachers College Press.

Wittrock, Merlin C., ed. 1986. *Handbook of Research on Teaching*, 3rd ed. New York: Macmillan.

Wolcott, Harry F. 1973. *The Man in the Principal's Office: An Ethnography*. New York: Holt, Rinehart and Winston.

Woods, P. 1984. "Teachers, Self and Curriculum." In *Defining the Curriculum: Histories and Ethnographies*, edited by Ivor F. Goodson and S. J. Ball. Lewes, England: Falmer.

Wooton, William. 1965. *School Mathematics Study Group: The Making of a Curriculum*. New Haven, CT: Yale University Press.

Yonemura, Margaret V. 1986. *A Teacher at Work: Professional Development and the Early Childhood Educator*. New York: Teachers College Press.

Young, Jean Helen. 1979. Teacher participation in curriculum decision making: An organizational dilemma. *Curriculum Inquiry* 9(2): 113–127.

Young, Jean Helen. 1985. Participation in curriculum development: An inquiry into the responses of teachers. *Curriculum Inquiry* 15(4): 387–414.

Zumwalt, Karen. 1988. "Are we Improving or Undermining Teaching?" In *Critical Issues in Curriculum. Eighty-seventh Yearbook of the National Society for the Study of Education*, edited by L. Tanner, 148–174. Chicago: University of Chicago Press.

15

CURRICULUM IMPLEMENTATION

Jon Snyder

Frances Bolin

Karen Zumwalt

TEACHERS COLLEGE, COLUMBIA UNIVERSITY

Research on curriculum implementation has yielded clear findings about the conditions that facilitate or inhibit the process of implementing a proposed curriculum. Yet the field of study, partially as a consequence of research findings, is undergoing change. Underlying assumptions about the nature of curriculum knowledge, change, and the role of the teacher in the process, are being questioned. While the term "implementation" is still widely used, some researchers are increasingly interested in studying how the curriculum has been enacted and experienced by teachers and students, rather than how a proposed curriculum is implemented or adapted by teachers.

The changing nature of the field has made drawing the parameters of this chapter entitled "Curriculum Implementation" somewhat problematic. As the field is evolving, the lines between this chapter and those by Clandinin and Connelly ("Teacher as Curriculum Maker"), Doyle ("Curriculum and Pedagogy"), and Erickson ("Students' Experience of the Curriculum") are blurred. We have chosen to recognize the changing nature of curriculum implementation research, but have left in-depth development of these areas to the designated authors. Separate chapters on curricular change (Cuban) and curriculum assessment and evaluation (Madaus and Kellaghan) have also delimited the scope of this chapter.

While the evolving nature of this field of study integrates many chapters, we have taken the conventional view of curriculum implementation research as our starting point because of the way the chapters in the *Handbook* have been delineated. Hence, the major focus of this chapter is on research describing how a proposed curriculum is put into action. Planned curricular changes are usually considered to involve changes in at least one of the following areas: goals, organization, role of the teacher, content, instructional strategies, classroom management, materials, or evaluation.

While general studies concerning school and curriculum improvement provide context, the focus of this chapter is on studying the process of implementing a proposed curricular change. As we will see, this working definition of curriculum implementation research serves us well as we look at the dominant approaches to research in this area (i.e., fidelity, mutual adaptation), but breaks down as we look at evolving conceptions of curriculum implementation. Nonetheless, since "curriculum implementation" has been a common designator for an area of curriculum research, we have chosen to use it as an initial working definition of the field and to indicate its problematic nature in our discussion of an evolving approach to curriculum implementation research, which we are calling "curriculum enactment."

After a brief historical overview, we review findings and describe some significant or exemplar studies illustrating three approaches to the study of curriculum implementation. This section is followed by a consideration of conceptual and methodological issues in studying curriculum implementation. The chapter concludes with some thoughts

All three authors contributed equally to the creation of this chapter. The order of names was chosen by lot. Also contributing to the chapter were Philip Panaritas, who worked with us in the summer of 1989, and doctoral students in the "Seminar in Supervision and Curriculum Improvement," Teachers College, Columbia University, Spring 1989.

about future directions for researchers interested in studying curriculum implementation, adaptation, and enactment.

HISTORICAL OVERVIEW

Research on curriculum implementation is a relatively recent phenomenon. "Implementation" is not a term found in the early curriculum literature. It appears that the process of curriculum implementation was not studied as a separate entity. During the formative years of the curriculum field, school curriculum was essentially the textbook. William Torrey Harris is credited with placing textbooks in the hands of teachers, who were expected to make decisions about how to use them.

According to Rugg (1926) the introduction of textbooks ushered in a era of "curriculum making by textbook writers," which gave way to a new era, "curriculum making by college entrance requirements," introduced by the Committee of Ten. In his opinion, neither of these was an acceptable approach to so highly demanding, technical, and complicated a task. Rugg is representative of those who struggled to translate what amounted to an explosion of knowledge in human growth and development, subject matter, and educational research into a curriculum that would prepare students for responsible citizenship in American society. He was acutely aware of the needs of a poorly prepared and largely unqualified teaching force challenged by a flood of children who appeared at school in compliance with compulsory education laws. "Lacking a half million dynamic teachers, are we not forced to put into our schools a dynamic curriculum?" Rugg reasoned (1926, 7). Apparently, implementation was assumed. Boards of education adopted courses of study which they *expected* teachers to follow. But implementation was not strictly prescribed. Courtis (1926), in a survey of elementary schools, found that teachers were allowed "considerable latitude" in methods. "The course of study provides rather definite general directions and standards, but after conforming to these, the teacher has freedom to adjust her work to meet the needs of individual classes and pupils (freedom under law)" (133).

As supervisors and administrators began to check on how well the course of study was being executed, they learned that teachers were too "free under law": courses of study were not being used effectively (Caswell 1950). The logical conclusion was that teachers did not relate to courses of study because they had been written by people who were too far removed from classroom practice. This is a viewpoint summarized in the 14th yearbook of the Department of Superintendence (1936). Yearbook authors noted that many courses of study collected dust because teachers had not been involved in their production. Too many superintendents had almost literally thrown materials at the teacher, failing to realize "the tremendous importance of thoroly [sic.] acquainting teachers with the aims, spirit, content, and proposed possible uses of these materials, in advance of the actual tryouts. . . . Little attention has been paid to the problem of proper installation" (356). "Production" and "installation" were the terms curriculum researchers and workers began to use to describe the process of development and implementation of curriuclum (Caswell 1950). More attention was placed on production—usually of courses of study—than installation because content was seen as more significant than methods (Counts 1926; Courtis 1926).

As it became apparent that installation could not be taken for granted, the role of the teacher became more prominent in the literature on curriculum change. Caswell (1946) observed that administrative order and modification of external factors had failed to significantly modify outcomes of education "except as they have led teachers to modify their points of view, purposes and procedures" (183).

By the 1940s many writers argued that curriculum development would be more effective if it involved teachers. The Forty-fourth Yearbook of the National Society for the Study of Education (NSSE) included a list of characteristics of good curriculum programs, compiled by Prudence Cutright (1945). Among the characteristics was "*Provide for wide participation on the part of teachers*" (274). Like Newlon, who declared that there was "no substitute possible for a maximum of teacher participation" (1926, 233), Cutright argued that teachers should be provided with release time from classroom teaching to develop and write curriculum materials. Despite confidence that school districts could "grow" by involving teachers in the development process, rather than by installing a curriculum, efforts to bring new curricula to classrooms remained problematic. Caswell (1950) observed that "teacher resistance to change, development of antagonism toward those who do move ahead, and discouragement and frustration are blocks to curriculum improvement very often encountered in the practical situation" (68). Drawing on new work being done in social psychology, particularly Lewin's notion of factors constraining and contributing to organizational change, Caswell and others began to speculate about the psychological factors, such as security and recognition, teachers needed in order to risk curriculum change.

While identified as a problem, research on the process of curriculum implementation did not become a major focus of researchers until the late sixties and early seventies. By this time it had become increasingly clear that assessment of planned outcomes was not an adequate way to evaluate many of the innovative programs initiated during this era. As John Goodlad notes, "Often innovations which are thought to have failed really have not; they really were never implemented" (Goodlad, as quoted in Basch and Sliepcevish 1983). Researchers began to question the assumptions that "the move from the drawing board to the school or classroom was unproblematic, that the innovation would be implemented or used more or less as planned, and that the actual use would eventually correspond to planned or intended use" (Fullan and Pomfret 1977). Thus, curriculum implementation emerged as an area of focus for researchers interested in measuring and understanding school change.

The rationale for initiation of curriculum implementation studies is described in Fullan and Pomfret's (1977) review of the first decade of research in this area. They suggest the following reasons why such studies became important:

1. To know what has changed, it must be conceptualized and measured directly;
2. To understand why so many proposed educational changes fail, it is necessary to study some of the most problematic aspects to bring about change;
3. To not do so may result in implementation being ignored or being confused with other aspects of change process such as adoption (the decision to use an innovation);
4. To interpret learning outcomes and to relate them to possible determinants, it is necessary to examine the implementation of an innovation separately.

In the past two decades of research on curriculum implementation, there have been three different approaches to the topic by researchers. The initial and most extensively documented approach to curriculum implementation research assumes a fidelity perspective. "The main intent is to determine the degree of implementation of an innovation in terms of the extent to which actual use of the innovation corresponds to intended or planned use and to determine factors which facilitate and inhibit such implementation" (Fullan and Pomfret 1977, 340). The second approach to implementation research, growing out of the fidelity perspective, is mutual adaptation (Berman and Pauley 1975; McLaughlin 1976). Researchers with this orientation are interested in studying how the innovation is adapted during the implementation process rather than in measuring the degree to which the innovation is implemented as planned. In the third approach, the focus shifts from studying the implementation and adaptation of proposed curriculum to studying curriculum enactment. Researchers with this orientation are interested in studying how curriculum is shaped through the evolving constructs of teachers and students.

THREE APPROACHES TO CURRICULUM IMPLEMENTATION

Fidelity Perspective

Most curriculum implementation has been studied from a fidelity perspective. The concerns of researchers have focused on (1) measuring the degree to which a particular innovation is implemented as planned and (2) identifying the factors which facilitate or hinder implemention as planned.

It is assumed that the desired outcome of curricular change is fidelity to the original plan. Underlying this perspective are certain assumptions about curriculum knowledge, change, and the role of the teacher. Curriculum knowledge is primarily created outside the classroom by the experts who design and develop the curriculum innovation. Change is conceived of as a linear process, with teachers implementing the innovation as developed in the classroom. The curriculum is evaluated to determine whether the planned outcomes have been achieved. Implementation is successful when the teachers carry out the curricular change as directed. If they do carry out the plan as intended, then the curricular change itself can be fairly evaluated. If they do not implement the innovation correctly or fully, then the change cannot be fairly evaluated because it was never really implemented.

Fidelity was the dominant perspective underlying the curriculum implementation research reviewed by Fullan and Pomfret in 1977. Twelve of the 15 studies reviewed were undertaken from this perspective, while 3 were oriented toward the emergent perspective at the time, mutual adaptation. Although the authors were clearly sympathetic to the mutual adaptation approach, the fidelity perspective, with its appealing logic, was difficult to escape. In fact, they opened their review using a legislative metaphor to make the point that implementation is a process worth studying in its own right. "If they (the members in charge of implementing the regulatory legislation) respond to influences other than the intentions of the law's advocates, then even the most carefully worded and strongly supported legislation is unlikely to be implemented as planned" (335). Although realistically often not achieved, regulatory legislation is intended to be carried out the way it is written. Similarly, many people have assumed that new curricula should be implemented as the developers intended, but recognize that this is often not the case. Hence, a major focus of researchers has been to attempt to measure the degree to which curriculum innovations have been implemented as planned and, subsequently, to try to figure out the factors that encourage or hinder full implementation of a particular curriculum innovation.

Measuring the degree of implementation became a critical factor in dealing with the seemingly disappointing results of the intervention programs of the sixties. Once innovations had been planned and adopted, evaluation of outcomes became the major focus of policymakers and researchers. "There [was] a singular lack of curiosity about what happened to an innovation between the time it was designed and various people agreed to carry it out, and the time that the consequences became evident" (Fullan and Pomfret 1977). While results from evaluations of multisite innovations often showed little or no change, differences between sites supposedly implementing the same innovation indicated some successes. The Project Follow-Through evaluation, for example, indicated that there was more variation within sites using the same program model than between sites using different models (Rivlin and Timpane 1975). It became clear that once an innovation was adopted, one could not assume that it would be implemented as planned. Leinhardt (as quoted in Fullan and Pomfret 1977,

339) has estimated that 35 percent of the variance in outcomes could be accounted for by differences in implementation. Before declaring a program a failure because the desired outcomes were not achieved, it is first necessary to determine whether the program was really implemented. To do so, the innovation needs to be clearly defined so that those charged with implementing it will know what to do. The properties of the innovation need to be clearly identified so that researchers can determine to what degree each characteristic is being implemented.

Typically, an implementation scale or checklist is developed to match desired practices, such as use of materials and activities, new roles/behavior, new understandings and attitudes. For some curricular changes, developing such a list is rather straightforward, but for other curricular changes, particularly those involving new roles for teachers, such as open education, developing the scale or checklist is more problematic since it is difficult to describe the desired curricular change in clear, unambiguous observable terms. Hence, defining the actual innovation is often the first step in developing a scale or checklist which is faithful to the intentions of the developers. The developers or a panel of experts are typically asked to judge the validity of the instrument being used to make sure it matches the intentions of those who developed the curriculum innovation.

Once the scale or checklist is developed and validated, it is used to assess the degree of implementation of a particular innovation. It can be administered as a self-report questionnaire, as an observation schedule, as an interview schedule, or serve as a content analysis guideline or any combination of these methods. Over time, the value of self-report questionnaire responses from teachers and/or administrators has been questioned, and the use of multiple means of assessment has become more common (Fullan and Pomfret 1977).

In reviewing studies dealing with measuring the degree of implementation, Fullan and Pomfret (1977) identified "virtually all the ones we could find that deal explicitly with measuring implementation" (340). All 12 of the studies conducted from a fidelity perspective attempted, with differing degrees of success, to measure the degree of implementation in some quantitative fashion. Since the aim of the researchers was to determine how close actual practice matched intended practice, such a quantitative approach seems logical. In a footnote, Fullan and Pomfret (1977) admit that "it should be said that there exist some participant observation studies that provide excellent qualitative data related to implementation" (e.g., Smith and Keith 1971, 340). That such studies were excluded from the review is indicative of the pervasiveness of the fidelity perspective and the positivistic tradition among educational researchers in defining the field of study.

To illustrate how studies from a fidelity perspective go about measuring the degree of implementation, we have chosen three studies to highlight. An early and often cited study is Gross, Giacquinta, and Bernstein's (1971) study of the implementation in an inner city elementary school of an innovation demanding "a radical redefinition of the role of the teacher." Work by Hall and Loucks (1976) represents, according to Fullan and Pomfret, "the most sophisticated and explicit conceptualization" of the fidelity orientation to assessing degree of implementation (335). More recently, the studies of the National Diffusion Network (NDN) represent a large-scale modified Research, Development, and Dissemination (RD&D) approach to studying the implementation of various curriculum products (Crandall et al. 1983; Huberman 1983).

Redefining the Role of the Teacher. Gross, Giacquinta, and Bernstein's study was initiated in the late 1960s amid reports of failed programs designed to provide equal educational opportunities for disadvantaged students. They felt that the actual implementation of compensatory programs had been inadequately measured. They asserted that social scientists had been wrongly focusing on introduction of an innovation (adoption) as the fundamental problem of change. Rather than just focusing on overcoming initial resistance, they speculated that the process of implementation should have been viewed as problematic as well. Hence, they decided to study implementation of an innovation in a school where the staff did not seem to be resistant to the change. Under these conditions, they argued, if previous writers were correct, the innovation should be fully implemented.

The staff of Cambire Elementary School, an inner city school designated as a laboratory school designed to improve the education of disadvantaged students, was introduced to the innovation in the fall and expected to implement it by late January. Five months later, at the end of the school year, Gross, Giacquinta, and Bernstein assessed the degree of implementation.

The innovation, labeled "catalytic role model," involved a change from teacher-directed, traditional instruction to child-centered instruction aimed at creating independent, responsible, thinking students.

> The new definition of the teacher's role viewed the teacher as assisting children to learn according to *their* interests throughout the day in self-contained classrooms. She was expected to emphasize the *process*, not the content, of learning. She was expected to allow pupils maximum freedom in choosing their own activities. (1971, 12)

In studying the implementation of the catalytic role model, Gross, Giaquinta, and Bernstein were interested in determining "the extent to which organizational members have changed their behavior so that it is congruent with the behavior patterns required by the innovation" (16). After analyzing documents describing the new catalytic role model and consulting with the developers, they developed an observation instrument which identified 12 teaching behaviors that should be present if the teachers were fully implementing the innovation:

- make the materials existing in the room available to pupils;
- allow or encourage pupils to interact with each other;
- allow pupils to move freely about the room;

- encourage or allow pupils to choose their own activities;
- allow pupils to decide whether they wanted to work individually, in pairs, or in groups;
- move about the room;
- have the room arranged into work areas;
- utilize the room according to these work areas;
- try to work with as many individual pupils or groups as possible;
- try to act as a guide, catalyst, or resource person between pupils;
- try to act as a guide, catalyst, or resource person between pupils and the materials. (96)

The researchers made it clear that these 12 behavioral criteria did "not provide a complete description of a teacher who would fully carry out the innovation" (96) but rather included indicators of some of the behavior which should be present if the teachers were carrying out the innovation as intended.

Teachers were observed at times in which *they reported* they would be attempting to implement the innovation. Using the checklist, observers rated teachers in terms of each item on a five-point scale ranging from "not at all" to "completely" (*quality of implementation*). All classes were also "spot checked" on a daily basis to see if the teachers were employing "traditional or innovative efforts" (*quantity of implementation*).

Gross, Giacquinta, and Bernstein found that both quantity and quality of implementation were low. Teachers displayed behavior congruent with the innovation about 16 percent of the time. Individual teachers ranged from 2 percent to 40 percent, with four of the six classes below 14 percent. In terms of quality of implementation, the average scores for the 12 criteria on a collapsed three-point scale ranged from 2.74 to 1.23. Ten of the 12 criteria averaged less than 2.00. (The criteria are listed above in descending order of implementation.) "Most engaged in activities that required them to expend little effort," and they did not try to act like a guide even when they were attempting to implement the innovation (117).

Gross, Giacquinta and Bernstein conclude that "the staff exhibited a minimal degree of implementation of the catalytic role model" (118). While there was variation among teachers, generally, the staff just gave "lip service" to the innovation. They gave little evidence of implementing the basic notion underlying the catalytic role model, despite initially expressing willingness to attempt to implement the innovation. The authors believe their findings support their contention that the process of implementation is not only worthy of study but also a precursor to evaluating an innovation.

In studying Cambire School, the authors also tried to address a deficiency in the implementation literature. Since "there has been little concern for testing theories or generating testable hypotheses about factors influencing degree of implementation" (35), they examined the barriers and obstacles to implementing the catalytic role model. The five factors found to inhibit implementation were:

1. Teachers' lack of *clarity* about the innovation;
2. Teachers' lack of *skills and knowledge* needed to conform to the new role model;
3. Unavailability of required instructional *materials;*
4. Incompatibility of *organizational arrangements* with the innovation;
5. Staff's lack of *motivation.*

The circumstances which contributed to these factors are described in great detail. For instance, the strain and fatigue resulting from role overload and the staff's uncertainty about being reappointed as teachers to Cambire the following year decreased their motivation to implement the innovation. The rigid scheduling of school time, the assignment of pupils according to age, and the use of subject-oriented report cards undermined the process-oriented, child-centered approach central to the innovation. Basically, the administration failed to recognize and cope with the problems because they themselves did not understand their own role in an expanded view of the implementation process. "It was assumed by the innovator (and other school administrators) that any professional teacher 'worth his salt' could read a document describing the innovation and then, on his own, radically change his behavior in ways that are congruent with the new role model" (211).

The Concerns Based Adoption Model. Following Frances Fuller's work on stages of teacher development (1969), a group of researchers at the Research and Development Center for Teacher Education at the University of Texas applied the same "concerns based" stage concept to teachers as they go through the "innovation-adoption process." The Concerns Based Adoption Model (CBAM) has been developed, validated, and expanded as new dimensions of the adoption and implementation of innovations in schools have become evident. Fullan and Pomfret (1977) call CBAM "the most sophisticated and explicit conceptualization of the fidelity orientation to assessing degree of implementation" (335).

The concept of "concerns" was developed to describe individuals' perceptions, feelings, motivations, frustrations, and satisfactions as they progress through different stages in the process of implementating an innovation (Hall and Loucks 1978). Seven stages of concerns progressing from unrelated concerns (stage 0) to self-concerns (stage 1 and 2) to task concerns (stage 3) to impact concerns (stages 4, 5, 6) have been verified through analysis of focused interviews in a series of cross-sectional and longitudinal studies. The seven specific stages are:

Stage 0 (AWARENESS): Little concern about or involvement with the innovation is indicated.

Stage 1 (INFORMATIONAL): A general awareness of the innovation and interest in learning more detail about it is indicated. The person seems to be unworried about himself/herself in relation to the innovation. She/he is interested in substantive aspects of the innovation in a selfless manner, such as general characteristics, effects, and requirements for use.

Stage 2 (PERSONAL): Individual is uncertain about the demands of the innovation, his/her adequacy to meet those demands, and his/her role with the innovation. This includes analysis of his/her role in relation to the reward structure of the organization, decision making and consideration of potential conflicts with existing structures or personal commitment. Financial or status implications of the program for self and colleagues may also be reflected.

Stage 3 (MANAGEMENT): Attention is focused on the processes and tasks of using the innovation and the best use of information and resources. Issues related to efficiency, organizing, managing, scheduling, and time demands are utmost.

Stage 4 (CONSEQUENCES): Attention focuses on impact of the innovation on students in his/her immediate sphere of influence. The focus is on relevance of the innovation for students, evaluation of student outcomes, including performance and competencies, and changes needed to increase student outcomes.

Stage 5 (COLLABORATION): The focus is on coordination and cooperation with others regarding use of the innovation.

Stage 6 (REFOCUSING): The focus is on exploration of more universal benefits from the innovation, including the possibility of major changes or replacement with a more powerful alternative. Individual has definite ideas about alternatives to the proposed or existing form of the innovation. (Hall, Wallace, and Dossett 1973)

Using the 35-item Stages of Concern (SoC) Questionnaire, an individual's concern profile can be generated. While an individual has concerns at several stages, generally certain concerns are dominant. Alternately, an open-ended question requesting the individual to write about his or her concerns can be coded with the SoC categories.

In validating the SoC concept, CBAM researchers noticed great variability in concerns about an innovation; concerns evolved in the hypothesized developmental fashion only under certain circumstances (Hall and Loucks 1982, 141). Progression through the stages depended on such factors as the appropriateness of the innovation, how facilitative line administrators were, and whether adequate time (3 to 5 years) had been given. Developmental progression was the exception, rather than the rule, because these conditions were often not met.

Early in their field work, it became apparent that just because an innovation had been adopted one could not assume it was being implemented in every classroom. As teachers were found to have different levels of concerns, they were also found to be using the innovation at different levels. After developing operational definitions of different levels of use, the researchers generated a list of behavioral indicators of each level of use. The eight levels are:

Level 0 (NONUSE): The user has little or no knowledge of the innovation, no involvement with the innovation, and is doing nothing toward becoming involved.

Level I (ORIENTATION): The user has recently acquired or is acquiring information about the innovation and/or has recently explored or is exploring its value orientation and its demands upon user and user system.

Level II (PREPARATION): The user is preparing for first use of the innovation.

Level III (MECHANICAL USE): The user focuses most effort on the short term, day-to-day use of the innovation with little time for reflection. Changes in use are made more to meet user needs than client needs. The user is primarily engaged in a stepwise attempt to master the tasks required to use the innovation, often resulting in disjointed and superficial use.

Level IVA (ROUTINE): Use of the innovation is stabilized. Few if any changes are being made in ongoing use. Little preparation or thought is being given to improving innovation use or its consequences.

Level IVB (REFINEMENT): The user varies the use of the innovation to increase the impact on clients within immediate sphere of influence. Variations are based on knowledge of both short- and long-term consequences for clients.

Level V (INTEGRATION): The user is combining own efforts to use the innovation with related activities of colleagues to achieve a collective impact on clients within their common sphere of influence.

Level VI (RENEWAL): The user reevaluates the quality of use of the innovation, seeks major modifications of, or alternatives to, present innovation to achieve increased impact on clients, examines new developments in the field, and explores new goals and the system. (Hall and Loucks 1977)

Assessment of levels of use (LoU) through a focused interview correlated .98 with direct observations (146). When, later, the initial implementation level (IV) was further differentiated into a routine (IVA) and refinement level (IVB), the level IV numeration was kept to preserve the theoretical parallelism between SoC and LoU (147).

Using LoU contributed to the realization that degree of implementation had to be measured before one could legitimately evaluate a new curriculum (147). Hall and Loucks believe that teachers should be using the innovation in a routine manner (level IVA) before one can say that the innovation has been implemented and before summative evaluations should take place. The user at level IVA is essentially implementing the innovation in the manner intended. It should be noted that such fidelity to the intent of the designers was viewed as developmentally necessary before any local refinements might take place.

A third dimension was added to CBAM framework: Innovation Configuration (I-C). In working on LoU, it became apparent that users had different ideas about what "doing the innovation" meant. In their experience, Hall and Loucks have found that a "persistent problem with developing and implementing new programs or improving existing ones is that they are rarely well defined or clearly communicated to the users. Furthermore, teachers frequently adapt the programs to their own needs, making changes that may leave out key components and can lead to decreased results" (Hall and Loucks 1981, 46–47). The I-C instrument was developed to measure the forms and patterns of the innovation in practice. It requires identifying the essential operational components of an innovation, as well as acceptable and unacceptable variations.

These essential components and acceptable variations are identified by the program developers and facilitators in the planning stages and through interviews and observation of early users of the innovation. Sometimes, as in the case of programs which have been "validated" to be effective, the resulting checklist of components matches the innovation as prescribed by the developer. At other times, a checklist of components is derived after initial use of the curriculum to obtain a better sense of variation in practice that might be deemed desirable, acceptable, or unacceptable. Having a good picture of current use makes it possible to make "data-based decisions about what the curriculum should look like" (56). For instance, one might want to define the acceptable components as what most teachers are doing, what exemplary teachers are doing, or what teachers who are producing the best outcomes are doing. Making such a decision may involve adapting the developers' original list of essential components and variations. For example, in one case, a configuration analysis might indicate higher math achievement in classrooms where the materials developed for the new mathematics program were integrated with other materials, rather than used as the sole means of instruction (George and Hord 1980, 57). Hence, integrated use might become an essential component. After such adjustments are made in the final form of the I-C instrument, descriptions of actual use of an innovation are available as a starting point for in-service work aimed at "facilitating the desired operational forms of the innovation" (54).

CBAM has provided researchers, policymakers, and users with a common language to talk about the implementation of innovations. It lends support to the notion that the implementation of curriculum itself is worthy of study and has consequences for staff development and program evaluation. CBAM and the instruments developed to measure concerns, use, and innovation configurations have provided helpful tools and served to reinforce a fidelity orientation to the implementation of innovation. Underlying this model is a valuing of a systematic rational change process (Hall and Loucks 1981, 47) and psychometrically rigorous research. Concepts must be operationally defined, measures developed and studies designed and undertaken. Validity is research-based and practitioner-reviewed (Hall and Loucks 1982, 152). According to Hall and Loucks, implementation problems often occur because designers and policymakers have not considered "implementation of their policies in an operational sense" (1982, 155). They suggest that, by combining traditional validation with validation by users of the products (consumers), some of the characteristics that are critical to putting a policy into operation can be identified prior to implementation:

> The identification of key teacher behaviors or particular organizational arrangements can help policy makers develop alternative operational descriptions to what a policy solution would look like when implemented. Such a practice would further alleviate the problem of policies that "evolve" in their definitions over the first several years of implementation. This evolution frequently punishes early adopters who in later years find themselves to be "out of compliance" with the revised operational definitions of acceptable practice. (155)

Although Hall and Loucks promote their "contour research," where concepts have traditional and consumer validity, as "linking practitioners and policy makers through continued and adaptive interaction," the feasibility and desirability of identifying operational characteristics of an innovation prior to implementation indicate an underlying commitment to the fidelity orientation to curriculum implementation. Acknowledging that "research indicates that some degree of adaptation is associated with sucessful implementation" (55), Hall and Loucks (1981) state that it is particularly important to clarify how much adaptation can be allowed—what essential components must be implemented. "How much and in what way teachers are free to vary use of the program should be determined by someone and communicated early in the inservice process" (55).

The Research, Development, and Dissemination Approach. Dissemination Efforts Supporting School Improvement (DESSI) describes efforts to study the implementation process of National Diffusion Network (NDN) programs. The NDN was a federally funded program for the dissemination of effective projects. Exemplary federal projects were brokered by state-level people who helped school districts find out about and adopt the best curriculum available—no matter where developed. It was a systematic attempt to: (1) identify locally developed programs that were educational successes, (2) create awareness about the programs, and (3) provide training so that programs could be replicated in other districts. The National Diffusion Network's development and implementation of curriculum products illustrates a modification of the fidelity orientation. The NDN used a modified Research, Development, and Dissemination (RD&D) model in which teachers and practicing educators were the experts doing the RD&D instead of the traditional academic-based researchers or professional curriculum developers. If practitioners wanted their curriculum product accepted into the NDN, they had to provide evidence that the program was effective with students and could be adopted effectively in another setting. The NDN was designed to tap into practitioner knowledge, narrow the gap between theory/research and practice, and provide materials and methods that were created by teachers for teacher use. NDN was to make effective products available for adoption by schools at a low cost, thus saving them the time and expense involved in looking for a solution that already existed.

While the developer of the curriculum products was no longer the outside expert, the other elements of the fidelity approach to implementation remained. The teachers who designed the curriculum products were also responsible for the training and monitoring of the implementation of the curriculum project. They had to specify the elements essential to the success of the program and then monitor it to ensure that those elements were in place. Since the curriculum product had already been "validated"—it had raised students' test scores—the adopting districts were evaluated on how closely their teachers followed the model as written. The fear was that if the fidelity model of implementation were not followed then teachers might "retreat into improvisation" (Huberman 1983), and, while harmony might be preserved, improvement would stymied (Crandall et al. 1983).

The method the NDN used to bring about change following adoption of an innovation involved four steps: (1) the teacher learned the technology of the new program in a short workshop; (2) teaching materials and other needed products for the program were provided; (3) help was offered by the principal or external change agents when needed; and (4) administrative personnel or external change agents continually monitored the fidelity with which the program was being implemented (Parish and Aguila 1983). In sites where the building administrator and the change agent fulfilled their respective roles, DESSI researchers discovered commitment developing after implementation, after teachers were actively engaged in using a new practice.

> We found that with clear, direct leadership from building and central office administrators, training by a credible person in the use of practice that was known to be effective, and continued support and assistance, teachers tried the new practice, mastered it, saw results with their students and developed a strong sense of ownership. And this with little or no early involvement in problem-solving, selection or decision making. (Crandall et al. 1983, 7)

Commitment of teachers usually developed through the actual use of materials, rather than being a prior condition. Other factors found to be the most important contributors to successful implementation included:

- curricular or instructional practices that were carefully developed, well-defined and determined to be effective;
- training by credible people, often former teachers, and follow-up support activities through the first 3 years;
- assistance and support by an array of players, including other teachers, principals, district staff, external trainers, and linkers;
- attention to factors contributing to institutionalization, including line items on budgets, orienting new or reassigned staff, and writing the changes into curriculum guidelines. (Loucks 1983)

Since fidelity remains an important criterion for sucessful implementation, it is not surprising that the role of the principal was revealed as being critical. As Huberman (1983) concludes from examining the DESSI data: "If one wants specific results as an administrator, one has to shape them, which entails some benevolent authoritarianism, a combination of muscle, tenderness and tutoring." This approach "works especially well and appears to be the most manageable in the dual sense of having the most control over the flow of events and of being the most buffered from environmental turbulence" (24).

The role of the successful administrator was aptly characterized in Huberman's four scenarios of decreasing effectiveness (Huberman 1983; Huberman and Miles 1984).

1. Enforcers: Administrators exert strong and continuous pressure on teachers to adopt the curriculum, but also provide substantial ongoing assistance. Teachers are allowed little latitude to make changes, but eventually, if the caliber of the curriculum is high, teachers are won over.
2. Overreachers: Teachers, with the help of career-motivated administrators, adopt a particular program. Original adoption results from acknowledgement of a local problem by teachers. The teachers then see and get administrative approval to make changes in the innovation so that it better meets their perceived local problem. Teachers work together to make the change work. This succeeds for a while, but then the administrator gets promoted and the teachers burn out. Institutionalization rarely occurs in this scenerio.
3. Program Blunting or Downsizing: The program was administratively pushed, but teachers are allowed to redo innovations as individuals. Generally, the program is unbundled and only those components that are congenial to personal teaching styles remain—thus trivalizing the change. Administrators who allow a lot of leeway, often in order to get the innovation accepted, and then turn their attention somewhere else are asking for a placebo—the appearance of change for public relations.
4. Indifference and Discouragement: A demanding and threatening change is pushed by opportunitistic administration. The change is resisted by teachers, which results in weak commitment to implementing the program. Poor leadership and feeble assistance lead to minimal mastery of necessary elements of the innovation, and the innovation withers away.

Huberman's conclusions are that administrators, at both the central office and building levels, have to go to center stage and stay there if school improvement efforts are to succeed. Administration must provide the initial impetus and continuing assistance necessary for teachers to be able to succeed at the new practice so that they will eventually be commited to the new program. "If administrators accomplish their list of tasks, teachers will be able to get theirs done" (1983, 27).

In the 1980s, many of the prescriptions for successful

curriculum implementation have been based on the data generated from the DESSI study. For example, Hord and Huling-Austin's (1986) recommendations involve developing supportive organizational arrangements, training, and follow-up activities focused on teachers' problems and concerns, and monitoring and evaluation used as a basis for designing future assistance for teachers. The variable most significantly related to successful implementation was how the principal viewed his/her role. In looking at schools implementing change, they classsified principals as initiators, managers, or responders. Initiators were principals who held a vision of what a school could become, who pushed their staff to improve practice, who supported their teachers and worked with them in these efforts. Managers maintained well-organized, smoothly running and efficient schools. They understood teachers, provided them assistance, and protected them from demands on their time and energy. Responders believed teachers were professionals who were responsible for instruction. They responded to teacher requests and were honestly interested in the happiness of teachers and students. The more a principal matched the initiator profile, the greater the number of interventions he/she made and the greater the degree to which the change was implemented.

In order to help principals become more of the initiator type, Huddle (1987) prescribes the following principles for principals. During adoption, the principal should: (1) increase staff concern about the need for improvements; (2) ensure the change is based in successful practice and consistent with the school's beliefs about good practice; (3) prevent too many programs from occurring simultaneously; (4) encourage collegial relationships; and (5) obtain community support. During implementation, the principal should: (1) ensure quality training and develop on-site and in-district experts; (2) ensure the program is essentially self-contained but flexible; (3) provide continuing technical assistance and peer support; (4) recognize and reward staff members; and (5) construct, use, and report measurement devices. During institutionalization, the principal should (1) change the reward and supervisory structures and (2) build technical assistance into the system.

While many recent studies emphasize the role of the principal, it should be remembered that successful implementation in the DESSI study involved more than support from the principal. DESSI concluded that leadership in school change must be shared and involve a variety of roles and functions. No single role or type of assistance is sufficient to bring about successful implementation of a new program. Since ongoing monitoring and follow-up activities (consultation and reinforcement) have often been the missing link in the past, DESSI-based prescriptions recommend greater emphasis on these types of interventions in implementation plans.

As this line of research has continued, critics by the mid-seventies were proclaiming that the dominant RD&D conception of educational innovation was not working the way it was supposed to work. There were "thousands of new products" created by the federal laboratories and centers, but they were "not widely used by teachers in the schools" (House 1979, 3). The RD&D approach assumed a rational sequence of activities—"massive planning, a division of labor, high development costs, and a passive consumer" at the end of the line (Havelock, as quoted in House 1979, 3). Despite disappointment and criticism, House wrote at the end of the seventies that "the technological perspective survives and flourishes, not only in subdued and camouflaged RD&D approaches, but in young and virulent forms," such as the competency-testing movement. "It is not likely that the technological perspective will disappear in such a strongly technological civilization." (4) In fact, some of its variants, such as the mutual adaptation model, which emerged from the findings that teachers were adapting, rather than adopting, curriculum, can be viewed as pragmatic modifications of a technological orientation rather than as new orientations to curriculum implementation.

Mutual Adaptation

Since we have chosen to organize our review of research on curriculum implementation by examining fidelity, mutual adaptation, and enactment approaches, logic suggests that we have in mind a continuum of research. In such a continuum mutual adaptation might represent a midpoint along a line that moves from complete fidelity in implementation of a curriculum to a polar opposite: curriculum enactment, or the ongoing, joint creation of curriculum by students and teachers.

The definition of mutual adaptation further suggests the notion of points along a continuum of implementation. Mutual adaptation is seen as that process whereby adjustments in a curriculum are made by curriculum developers and those who actually use it in the school or classroom context. This implies a certain amount of negotiation and flexibility on the part of both designers and practitioners. We are reluctant to speak of mutual adaptation research as representing a point or points along a continuum, however.

In examining research on fidelity of implementation and implementation as enactment, one can find clearly identifiable views on the curriculum, major research questions which are characteristic of the perspective, and a shared view of education. Mutual adaptation studies are not so easily classified. Even though a cluster of studies might be grouped together by their contribution to our understanding of mutual adaptation, it is difficult to argue that mutual adaptation is a discrete perspective on change in the way the fidelity and enactment studies denote a perspective.

Mutual adaptation research has not necessarily represented a commitment on the part of researchers to developer and user negotiations and collaboration in implementation. In fact, the initial research from which our understanding of mutual adaptation is drawn did not begin as an effort to study the adaptation phenomenon. It was the result of attempting to understand the practical realities of the change process and practices that did not lend themselves to strict models which could be replicated. We have also learned about mutual adaptation from studies concerned with the application of social science research methodologies and critical perspectives to educational problems, with curriculum implementation as a convenient example.

For this reason we have chosen to describe mutual adaptation research in terms of the practical or critical orientations of researchers in three studies that have contributed to our understanding of implementation. Mutual adaptation will be discussed in terms of the context from which the concept emerged. We will then consider the kinds of practical and critical questions with which mutual adaptation research is concerned. Studies examined will include: (1) the Rand Change Agent Study, which contributed the term "mutual adaptation" to the literature and provides an example of a practical orientation; (2) Smith and Keith's study of educational innovation, which brought social science theories and methodologies to the study of school problems and is both practical and critical in orientation; and (3) Popkewitz, Tabachnick, and Wehlage's documentation of the effect of ideology on implementation, which illustrates a critical perspective.

Emergence of Mutual Adaptation as a Concept. By the 1980s it had become apparent that more was known about how to fail at implementation of curriculum innovation than about how to succeed. The fidelity model had assumed that innovations were like technologies—by learning new behaviors and organizational patterns provided by the innovation, teachers and school systems would change. Legislators and policy makers, too, seemed to ignore the fact that "what people did and did not do was the crucial variable" (Fullan 1982a, 54). But research by Sarason (1971) pointed out that innovations adopted by a school district were not institutionalized in a significant way.

Numerous other studies pointed to implementation problems as the reason for failed change efforts (Bentzen 1974; Bredo and Bredo 1975; Charters and Pellegrin 1972; Goodlad and Klein 1970; Gross, Giaquinta, and Bernstein 1971; Sarason 1971; Smith and Keith 1971). Much of what appeared to happen in the actual implementation of an innovation was more akin to bargaining than a straightforward installation of a curriculum model. Those who were to use the curriculum insisted on shaping it in ways that suited their own purposes.

As researchers attempted to understand failures of the fidelity model they increasingly came to believe that "*change is a process, not an event*" (Fullan 1982a, 41). Many studies that shed light on the mutual adaption phenomena were initiated by researchers who wanted to understand change as a process. Other researchers began to reason that if modification of a curriculum by its users was inevitable, it was better to plan for it. Much of the literature reads as if mutual adaptation were the result of a reluctant concession to reality, rather than a commitment to a perspective on change.

The term "mutual adaptation" emerged from the Rand Study headed by researchers Berman and McLaughlin. Their research represented a departure from practices that were typical in fidelity research. Berman and McLaughlin were interested in studying practices that were based on different assumptions about children, teachers, and learning than those practices studied by fidelity researchers (McLaughlin 1976). "The very nature of these projects required that implementation be a *mutually adaptive process* between the user and the institutional setting—that specific project goals and methods be made concrete over time by the participants themselves" (McLaughlin 1976, 340).

Berman and McLaughlin appear to have been motivated by the desire to learn more about the implementation process. They recognized that the complexity of the programs they were to study required other than process-product research. Smith and Keith wanted to discover what happens when social science theory is applied to educational problems. At the outset of *Anatomy of an Educational Innovation*, a report of their study, Smith and Keith declared that their interest was in capturing the development of a new, uniquely designed school building, asking, "What happens in such a novel situation?" (1971, 6). Popkewitz, Tabachnick, and Wehlage (1981) were interested in the way a particular curriculum was affected by underlying ideological assumptions of those who implemented it.

These researchers were not motivated by the kind of clear commitment to a perspective on implementation that seems apparent in the fidelity perspective. Rather, they were committed to a way of studying educational problems. As a result of casting a wider net than could be cast by experimental designs appropriate to the fidelity perspective, these researchers happened upon mutual adaptation (Berman and McLaughlin 1975) and the effect of the context on innovation (Popkewitz, Tabachnick, and Wehlage 1981; Smith and Keith 1971).

Researchers holding the fidelity perspective are interested in measuring the degree to which a particular innovation is implemented as planned. Mutual adaptation researchers appear to be committed to (1) using new methodologies and theories from the social sciences to discover what intensive, descriptive data will yield about the various problems of education; and (2) identifying factors which facilitate or hinder implementation as planned, especially organizational variables. Identifying factors facilitating or hindering a planned innovation is a commitment shared with researchers holding the fidelity perspective and may be said to be more akin to goals of the Rand Study than those of Popkewitz, Tabachnick, and Wehlage or of Smith and Keith. This reflects the practical orientation of the Rand Study. Berman and McLaughlin were focused on change, sharing many assumptions about implementation that were compatible with a fidelity perspective. Popkewitz, Tabachnick, and Wehlage, on the other hand, brought a critical perspective to their research. This perspective challenged assumptions of fidelity researchers by focusing on what fidelity research had taken for granted—the values and assumptions of those implementing a curriculum, "Our intent is not only to describe the perceptions and actions of people in the schools; we are concerned with the underlying assumptions and social values implicit in school practices, and how they affect the realization of reform technologies'' (1981, 7). While their study may be considered a mutual adaptation study in that it yields new insight about the extent to which an innovation is revised in light of institutional style, beliefs about knowledge, and professional ideology, it is based on different beliefs and assumptions about schools than those held by Berman and McLaughlin.

The major research questions asked by those concerned with mutual adaptation depend upon whether the researcher is more practical or critical in orientation. A critical orientation is more concerned with ''the complex and profound relationships of reform, institutional life, and methodology'' (Popkewitz, Tabachnick, and Wehlage 1981, 7). A more practical orientation is concerned with the process of implementation itself. The more practical the orientation of the researchers, the more likely they are to ask (1) To what degree has a curriculum been implemented? (2) What factors facilitate or inhibit the implementation of a curriculum? and (3) What are the methodological issues in studying mutual adaptation? Practical research is concerned with the kinds of support adopters need for implementation and what might be considered minimum integrity of a program design. Researchers who share both practical and critical orientations will be likely to want to know the effect the program has on participants and how designers and users view the program. Critical researchers are more likely to deal with issues related to the meaning of perceptions and actions of all those involved with a program and its implementation.

The fidelity perspective sees curriculum knowledge as something created outside the school. Mutual adapation research, whether practical or critical in orientation, tends to see curriculum knowledge as one facet of a larger, complex social system that cannot be taken for granted. Who initiates curriculum knowledge is secondary in importance to understanding the constellation of factors that influence any innovation or change, whether from within or without the school.

Those with a more practical orientation are likely to see change as a linear process. Adaptation is a predictable phenomenon and can be expected to follow a consistent pattern. Those with a more critcial orientation are likely to see the change process as convoluted, nonlinear, and as unpredictable as it is complex. Researchers with the latter orientation focus on the social situation in which implementation will or will not take place. Detailed documention is made in order to discover more about the situation, which may include discovering what happened to the innovation (Popkewitz, Tabachnick, and Wehlage 1981; Smith and Keith 1971) or discovering what explains failure to implement along the lines of the original design (Berman and McLaughlin 1975).

In fidelity research, evaluation is tied to the degree of match between an implemented curriculum and an original design. Evaluation of an implementation in mutual adaptation studies is more likely to consist of reporting what has happened in the context that was studied and drawing conclusions in line with the perspectives that motivated the research. Educational change is seen as an implementation-driven process. Hence, how an innovation is implemented is equally significant to outcomes as its content (Berman 1981; Berman and McLaughlin 1974). Berman and McLaughlin reported on mutual adaptation. Smith and Keith, on the other hand, reported on the fact that the innovative vision or doctrine of the school they studied was incongruent with reality and what they called the ''true believer'' phenomenon, factors which are not incompatible with the idea of mutual adaptation. Nor are Popkewitz, Tabachnick, and Wehlage's findings incompatible with the idea of mutual adaptation—''faced with reform, insitutions exhibit remarkable resilience: innovations are first incorporated into existing patterns of beliefs, then used to legitimate ongoing educational conduct, while being identified in slogans to suggest reform'' (1981, 19–20). Their conclusion was that ''innovations cannot be treated apart from the uses to which they are put'' (1981, 20).

While assumptions underlying the perspectives that furnish us with the concept of mutual adaptation are often muddy, much of its discussion in the literature seems to parallel Fullan's concern with the ''fidelity-variation dilemma.'' Mutual adaptation is allowed with the hope that there will be as little contamination of the program goals and design as possible. Notable exceptions are the studies that are more critical in orientation. At the same time, there is merit in thinking about a position between fidelity and enactment perspectives on curriculum implementation. Such a perspective does seem to be emerging in the literature. This emerging perspective sees mutual adaptation as desirable. It is distinct from the perspective which supposes that implementation is a matter of installing an educational plan or technology. Building on the application of social science theories to education, this perspective on mutual adaptation assumes that implementation *should* involve adjustments in needs, interests, and skills of participants and organizations as well as in project goals and methods. Bird describes this emergent perspective: ''Mutual adaptation has an agreeable political and social flavor; it grants a measure of deserved respect both to the proponents and to the adopters of an innovation and therefore lets them meet on equal terms'' (Bird 1986, 46).

Interestingly enough, this is not a new approach to implementation, but one that can be found in earlier anecdotal literature on curriculum revision and installation. A notable example is that of the Denver schools curriculum developed under the leadership of Jesse Newlon in the 1920s. Later, as we discuss curriculum enactment, we will see how the lines between mutual adaptation and enactment were blurred as Denver teachers and students exerted more control over the curriculum.

The Process of Mutual Adaptation. The Rand Change Agent Study documented the ''*mutation* phenomenon'' (Berman 1981, 263). Examining implementation as a process of mutual adaptation, some of the problems related to identifying what might be referred to as a ''pure mutual adaptation'' perspective become apparent.

The Rand Change Agent Study of federal programs (*Federal Programs Supporting Educational Change,* a multiyear study from 1973 to 1977, was "perhaps the most comprehensive single study of a large number of educational innovations ever carried out" (Fullan and Pomfret 1977). Eight volumes report the study, primarily authored by Berman and McLaughlin. Researchers examined four federally funded programs designed to promote change in the structures or practices of schools and a variety of innovative practices including classroom organization, reading programs, bilingual and career development programs. There were two phases to the study. In Phase I (1973–1975) a national survey was made of 293 sites in 18 states. From among the survey sites, 29 were chosen for case studies to supplement data from participant questionnaires. In Phase II (1975–1977) researchers focused on the fate of innovations after "seed money" for the innovation ran out. Title III and Title VII, which were the two largest programs in the study, were targeted for Phase II. A sample of 100 Title III projects was surveyed, in addition to the field work and follow-up of Title VII projects studied in Phase I. Case studies, surveys of teachers, and interviews were analyzed (Berman 1981; McLaughlin 1976; for the report, see Berman and McLaughlin 1975, 1977, 1978, 1979). It was concluded that program sponsors did not adequately deal with local political and organizational circumstances, contributing to the failure of implementation and institutionalization of innovations.

The five measures of implementation used in the Rand Study that have been described as weak (Berman 1981; Fullan and Pomfret 1977) were:

1. Perceived success by teachers (related to goals achieved);
2. Perceived fidelity by teachers (related to implementation as described in the original proposal);
3. Reported changes in behavior by teachers;
4. Reported difficulty of implementation;
5. Expected continuation of the project once federal funds are withdrawn. (Fullan and Pomfret 1977, 360)

Fullan and Pomfret (1977) questioned these measures on grounds that they depended on changes that were *reported* or perceived and were too global. Self-reports by users were criticized as "often inaccurate and misleading" (360). Global measures did not "require specific knowledge of the dimensions of implementation" (360). The first criticism is one that can always be made of qualitative studies that examine perceptions of participants. The second, that global measures do not require knowledge of "the dimensions of implementation," may presuppose commitment to a fidelity perspective.

Berman and McLaughlin discovered that straightforward adoption and application of educational technology was not an effective way to bring about desired changes. Implementation dominated the change process and its outcomes. "Specifically, the change agent study concluded that *successful implementation is characterized by a process of mutual adaptation*" (McLaughlin 1976, 340).

The Rand Study points to a dynamic process that is "neither automatic nor certain" (McLaughlin 1976, 341) taking shape over time through interactions between a project's goals and methods and the institution and participants. In some cases, the innovation was *co-opted* by the institution and participants, who simply modified the innovation so that it conformed to their own ways of doing. They were essentially unchanged by it. In other cases, there was simply *nonimplementation* because the process either broke down or was ignored by the institution and participants (Berman 1981; McLaughlin 1976). All of the projects that were sucessfully implemented in the Rand Study were characterized, to some extent, by the process of mutual adaptation. Even so, effects of these programs diminished over time and were hard to replicate elsewhere (Berman and McLaughlin 1978).

Following Berman and McLaughlin, researchers have made use of the term *mutual adaptation* as they have focused on the problem of implementation. The Rand Change Agent Study has contributed greatly to our knowledge of factors that facilitate the implementation process. These are discussed later in this chapter along with major findings of fidelity and mutual adaptation studies (see pages 415–416).

Educational Innovation. Smith and Keith set out to describe the development of a new, uniquely designed school building that was characterized in substance and goals as "what might be called 'the new elementary education' of the 1960s" (1971, 23). Kensington was to be an experimental, open space school, released from constraints of a prescribed curriculum and policy. The faculty was to develop the curriculum and they were to find ways to promote individualization, humanization, dramatization, and socialization as methods (23). Team teaching, ungradedness, democratic pupil decision making, and a student-centered environment were to be included in the unique Kensington program. It was to be part of a district-wide plan for change, serving as a prototype program for establishment system wide.

Smith and Keith referred to their work as a "formulative, model building study" (9) that made use of participant observation, supplemented by interviews, analysis of documents and verbatim accounts of meetings. Observations were made of classroom interaction, facility use, faculty meetings, faculty teams, the curriculum committee, and parent school-council meetings.

Development of the school was followed through three main periods: (1) the four-week workshop prior to the opening of school, (2) the September to December location of the school's three academic divisions in separate facilities, (3) the December to June location of academic divisions in the building. Smith and Keith wanted to examine problems related to:

1. the development of the faculty social system;
2. the principal's role vis-à-vis the faculty social system;
3. the teachers' innovations in instruction; and
4. the development of the school-wide pupil social system. (6)

Subproblems of staff peer groups and administration decision making were of continued interest as the study developed. Additionally, organizational development and formal doctrine emerged as significant.

Two years after it began, the Kensington school ceased to exist as the experimental model. A quality of "true belief" was reflected in the selection and early socialization of the staff. That is, they were convinced of the rightness of the model from the beginning. But the principal and many of the staff left. Smith and Keith concluded that the innovation vision or doctrine of the school was incongruent with the reality of practice and led to a year characterized by staff conflict and struggle. Kensington was not as it was described to the public. A multiplicity of events had an impact on the Kensington outcome: "Perhaps, the most critical doctrinal outcome for the organization was the inability of a number of the individual conceptions to become merged into a common enough framework, an agreed on interpretation of the doctrine. . . . The staff was verbal and articulate in isolating and elaborating 'reasonable but incompatible' individual interpretations of what Kensington stood for" (37).

The departure of the principal to begin an open school in another state, the incongruence between values of a conservative community and an innovative school system, policy shifts within the school and at the district all contributed to the fate of the school.

The change strategy behind the Kensington program was described by Smith and Keith as the "alternative of grandeur." Complete and sweeping changes were to be made immediately. This brought "visibility and notoriety from being in the mainstream of educational innovation" along with some hard realities: "By concentrating on the alteration of multiple components, there was a higher level of uncertainty. In settings that are more variable and unpredictable, there is greater reliance on coordination by mutual adjustment. . . . Coordination by mutual adjustment is accompanied, in turn, by an increase in unintended outcomes" (370). The use of multiple temporary systems contributed to "ideas, tensions, and stress within and between the interacting units of Kensington" (389). As a consequence, characteristics of temporary systems invited the notion that anything was possible. "This facet in the instance of Kensington interacted with the dimension of true belief, with the extreme expenditures of time and effort, and with the strength of the commitment to ideas embodied in the doctrine" (391).

Smith and Keith observe that most innovators seem to assume that social structures are malleable and can be controlled and changed by decision makers. "Our data suggest limits to the modification of personality, at least, to subcomponents such as 'teacher personality' or teacher behaviors" (402).

In a later work, Smith (Smith et al. 1988) points out that the first study focused primarily on the Kensington school and those people and events directly connected with it. This focus is described as insufficient to explain what happened to Kensington. Instead there appear to be "multiple categories of antecedents" for change, "conflict, politics, and legal constraint" that affect the events that represented planned and unplanned innovation (270). "In summary, agency and context intermixed over time. Innovation took both a dynamic and politically interactive quality" (261).

A Critical Perspective on Implementation. Popkewitz, Tabachnick, and Wehlage (1981) report on the processes of adaptation and response of six schools implementing Individually Guided Education (IGE). Each of the schools studied had already been identified as exemplary in its succesful implementation of IGE. IGE was a curriculum developed in the 1960s by a government-sponsored research and development center. It proposed to make organizational, instructional, and curricular aspects of schools more responsive to individual variations in learning by providing a complete instructional system that was "believed to be a neutral, nonideological technology" (39).

The researchers intended "to make problematic the assumptions and procedures" of IGE through describing "the implicit as well as the explicit learning that occurs when students, administrators, and teachers respond to an educational reform" (4). In doing so they hoped to explain how the technologies of IGE receive meaning through their incorporation "into the continuing social and political context of schooling" (4). It is important to note that they did not ask what might be referred to as "mutual adaptation questions" about supports needed for adoption, minimum integrity of a design and the like.

Initially 17 model IGE schools were visited, and from this group 5 were selected for more intensive study. During the second year an additional school was added to the group. In the second year of the 4-year study, intensive case studies were developed. Each school was visited a minimum of three times. The last 2 years of the study were devoted to analysis and interpretation of data and writing.

In discussing the methodology chosen for this study, Popkewitz, Tabachnick, and Wehlage point out that choice of procedures should be more than a technical activity:

> Problems of methodology cannot be considered adequately without referring to the questions, theories, and intellectual traditions that make particular investigative strategies plausible. Data and descriptions of social conditions are not presented in a vacuum, but are inevitably tied to a theory. A study of educational reform, therefore, involves the complex and profound relationships of reform, institutional life, and methodology. (6–7)

One choice would have been to assume a fidelity perspective and measure the extent to which IGE had been successfully implemented. Another would have been to include perspectives of those using the program. Instead, the researchers chose to focus on describing the events, perceptions, and actions of both school people and the IGE developers and make explicit the effect of assumptions and values of both on the reform. Questions guiding the study were "How are school programs actually used? What social values and meanings do reforms and their technologies generate as they are used in schools? What are the assumptions behind and the implications and consequences of using reform technologies in day-to-day schooling?" (7).

During the course of the study, Popkewitz, Tabachnick, and Wehlage discovered "fundamental variations in the conditions and social implications in the six schools studied, as well as diferent institutional responses to the technologies of IGE" (6). Each school implemented IGA in a way that was responsive to its own unique social context. "Schools did not merely adapt the program, making modifications to reach the same goal; rather, they revised both the technology and its espoused goals" (4). These revisions conserved different work styles and conceptions of knowledge and maintained a "professional ideology" that reflected the social values and interests of the larger social context of the community. Often "the very school practices and values the program was intended to change" were conserved and legitimated in the process (5).

The categories that emerged as useful in describing variations in institutional responses to IGE and their significance were technical, constructive, and illusory schooling.

Technical schools were schools in which "techniques have become the ends of school activity rather than a means of instruction, and technology provides an independent value system that gives definition to curriculum, classroom activity, and professional responsibility" (61). Whereas all schools employ educational technology in a variety of ways, the *technical schools* here saw technology as a value. Schooling was conceptualized "through systems analysis, behavioral objectives, and criterion-referenced measures" (94). Knowledge was seen as something to be imparted to students. Curriculum planning was dominated by rational planning, efficiency, and standardization based on predetermined goals and outcomes. Learning experiences utilized sequential steps. Evaluation was based on objective measurement of outcomes. Routines and technical procedures were legitimized and sustained through every aspect of school life. Uncertain elements of school life and the curriculum that are characterized by "ambiguity, creativity, and nonstandardized learning" were given peripheral status. Each of these elements of technical schools was further sustained by a positive school climate described as "warm" and "supportive" of students and both professional and community support. The teacher's role was one of structuring and managing.

In constructive schools "problematic, aesthetic, and integrated knowledge were emphasized" in an environment that supported interpersonal skill and control (95). Multiple forms of knowledge were acknowledged and supported in instructional programs—children actively participated in learning through a variety of experiences in drama, art, music, and more traditional subject areas. Schooling was conceptualized in terms of constructivist psychology, consistent with a view of knowledge as something created, discovered, and experienced. Curriculum goals were open-ended, as were outcomes. Children had opportunities to take personal responsibility, exercise initiative, and be in control in the instructional setting through a variety of learning experiences. Children's growth and development, as well as many varied forms of evaluation, influenced teacher judgments about achievement. As in the case of the technical school, the constructivist school was supported by professional staff and community. The teacher's role was that of guide and facilitator.

The illusory school was characterized by "a series of anomalies, discontinuities and contradictions" (121). School activities seemed to be governed by the desire to create the image of a school that was rational, in control, and productive. Knowledge was secondary to socialization. Goals were explicitly stated in terms of basic skills. Implicit goals were control and respect for authority. Formal actions seemed to be unrelated to wider curriculum purposes. "There were facts and subjects to be taught, but the rituals and ceremonies of the formal curriculum were unrelated to this content and therefore could not produce success for most pupils" (121). Learning experiences depended on a controlled environment. Evaluation was based on objective measures of outcomes. School failures and shortcomings were attributed by teachers to "inadequacies of the poor and minority communities in which the schools were situated" (122). The teacher's role was that of authority. Teachers were expected to control students.

Factors Affecting Implementation. Berman and McLaughlin introduced the concept of mutual adaptation to the change literature. As a result, we know more about the local school district as an "infrastructure for change" (1979). We know more about the process of planned curriculum change and "what kinds of strategies and conditions tend to promote change in the schools and what kinds do not" (1978, iii).

The process of planned curriculum change is far more complex than researchers studying fidelity to program models had assumed. This is made clear in the Smith and Keith study. Their study of the Kensington School introduced social and organizational theory into the study of schooling. Smith and Keith pointed out that many critics of schooling were overly optimistic or romantic in assuming that an educational utopia would evolve, given a new institution that was dedicated to human purposes, provided flexibility in its curriculum, and individualized its procedures.

Open-mindedness and freedom to experiment are not sufficient, however. Conflicts between individual ideals and institutional goals, individual actions, and group process do not melt away in the presence of good will, nor does the "inordinate time demanded for invention," attitudes and values of the community, and skill in attending to the learning needs and styles of children. By documenting the realities of an innovation that ultimately failed, despite the fact that it was introduced with considerable support and dedication by participants, Smith and Keith made problematic the taken-for-granted. Implementation could no longer be seen as a straightforward process that would work with the introduction of right techonologies. Life and death of an innovation are not simply a matter of providing appropriate supports for the innovation and making mutual adjustments as it is being installed. Rather, life and death of an innovation depend on the unique configuration of social, historical, political, and ideological factors that make up the school and its social, community context.

Perhaps the most significant outcome of the Popkewitz, Tabachnick, and Wehlage study is that it highlights the fidelity perspective as problematic. Fidelity research takes for granted that schools transmit culture and knowledge, assuming that "the task of research and reform is to identify the most efficient procedures to accomplish this" (11). Fidelity research, by definition, has not been concerned with ideological commitments of either an innovation or its proposed installation site. Popkewitz, Tabachnick, and Wehlage point out that focusing on efficiency and effectiveness, without attention to the often-hidden issues of ideology of reformers and of the school and its community, misses the important point that "schooling does not just pass on culture, it modifies unanticipated and unintended consequences" (11). When these modifications are unexamined, the process of selection of content and practice is not exposed to critique. Not only does this risk social injustice but it perpetuates the notion that the superficial "ceremonies and slogans" of the school have meaning in themselves. Agreements at the superficial level mask real differences in understanding, values, and commitments of all of those involved.

It would appear that fidelity in implementation would require a match between the ideological commitments and values implicit in an innovation and the belief system of school and community into which it is introduced. The degree to which a match is absent will affect the extent of adaptation or its actual failure. In reality, the degree of fidelity may be a measure of the degree to which the context reflects an ideological perspective compatible with that of the innovation. Adaptation, then, would reflect varying degrees of departure from the innovation's ideological perspective.

Taken together, studies that have examined curriculum implementation have provided us with a great deal of information about factors which support and inhibit implementation. Fullan (1982a) has identified factors which influence implementation, listing "all those factors on which there is sufficient evidence to warrant generalizing about how and why the particular factor influences implementation" (55). Using Fullan's factors as a framework, examples of studies are presented with particular attention to those used in this chapter. Fidelity and mutual adaptation studies are grouped together because it is often difficult to distinguish between the two, particularly when studies have been driven by practical concerns.

Many factors are related to *characteristics of the change:*

1. Need and relevance of the change. Need and relevance refer to the perceived need on the part of implementors. It would seem that the greater the recognized need for change, the greater the degree of implementation. While Fullan cites the Rand Study as supportive of this factor, it may be said to be so in a very general sense since McLaughlin (1976) comments that institutional receptivity is necessary but not sufficient for implementation to occur satisfactorily. Innovations in the Rand Study involved strategies of open education and team teaching, for which it is difficult to find objective evidence that matters "to school boards, voters and anxious parents" (343). McLaughlin (1976) observes further that "change-agent policies would be well advised not only to address the user needs that are part of the implementation process *per se* but also to consider the developmental needs of local educational personnel" (350). The Rand Study also underscores the fact that what policymakers and district personnel think teachers need and what teachers perceive to be their needs are not always congruent. See Rosenblum and Louis (1979), Emrick and Peterson (1978), Louis and Sieber (1979).
2. Clarity. Clarity refers to understanding of goals and means of an innovation by users. The greater the understanding of goals and what is to be gained from their adoption, the greater the degree of implementation. Gross, Giacquinta, and Bernstein (1971) list lack of clarity as one of the five inhibitors of implementation. Popkewitz, Tabachnick, and Wehlage open this to question, however. Goals and means of IGE were clear and explicit. See Robinson (1982), Sarason and Doris (1979).
3. Complexity. Complexity has to do with the difficulty and extent of change required of users. The greater the complexity in innovations with differentiated components incrementally introduced, the greater the degree of implementation. McLaughlin (1976) notes that projects in the Rand Study were "complex, unspecified, and inherently difficult in nature" and were, therefore, seldom initiated without active district officials' and participants' support (343). See Bussis, Chittenden, and Amarel (1976), Crandall et al. (1983), Rosenblum and Louis (1979), Yin, Herald, and Vogel (1977).
4. Quality and practicality of program. This refers to the quality and availability of materials. Users must perceive that materials are going to meet important needs as well as be practical and usable. Gross, Giacquinta, and Bernstein include unavailability of required materials as an inhibitor of implementation. The DESSI data supports curricular or instructional practices that are carefully defined, well developed, and effective. McLaughlin (1976) points out that materials developed by staff on a local level produced a sense of ownership and provided an opportunity to learn underlying concepts of the project. See Doyle and Ponder (1978), Emrick and Peterson (1978), Louis and Rosenblum (1981).

Fullan identifies a number of *characteristics at the school district level as factors affecting implementation:*

5. The district's history of innovative attempts. The more positive the previous history with innovation the greater the degree of implementation. See Berman and McLaughlin (1979), Fullan (1982).
6. The adoption process. The higher the quality of plan-

ning to meet problems, the greater the degree of implementation. Routine, frequent staff planning provides for effective institutional feedback and a mechanism for dealing with unexpected consequences/events and was characteristic of projects studied by Rand. See Rosenblum and Louis (1979), Miles (1978), Giaquinta (1973).

7. District administrative support. The greater the "real" district-level support, the greater the degree of implementation. Berman and McLaughlin describe the positive effect of administrative support. DESSI researchers found clear, direct leadership from central office administrators to be a supporting factor. Gross, Giacquinta, and Bernstein list incompatibility of organizational arrangements as an inhibiting factor. See Emrick and Peterson (1978), Rosenblum and Louis (1979).
8. Staff development and participation. The greater the quality and quantity of sustained interaction and staff development, the greater the degree of implementation. Both Berman and McLaughlin and Smith and Keith note that pre-implementation training is not effective. DESSI researchers note the importance of training and continued support and assistance. Both Smith and Keith and Popkewitz, Tabachnick, and Wehlage offer what might be considered contrary evidence. Despite high participation, the Kensington project failed, and the degree of implementation of IGE is questionable. See Crandall et al. (1983), Fullan, Miles, and Taylor (1980), Hall and Loucks (1978), Herriott and Gross (1979), Hodges et al. (1980), Leithwood et al. (1978), Loucks (1978), Louis and Rosenblum (1981), Melle and Pratt (1981), Miles et al. (1978), Rosenblum and Louis (1979), Stallings (1979), Yin, Herald, and Vogel (1977).
9. Time-line and information systems (evaluation). There are two aspects of this factor. First, the greater the extent to which timing of events is guided by an understanding of implementation, the greater the degree of implementation. Studies by Cowden and Cohen (1979) and Yin et al. (1977) support this notion. Second, the greater the linkages between evaluation data and school/class level improvement needs, the greater the degree of implementation. Supporting studies include: Apling and Kennedy (1981), Cohen (1981), Edmonds (1982), Melle and Pratt (1981).
10. Board and community characteristics. The greater the board and community interest and support without controversy, the greater the degree of implementation. Smith and Keith point to initial support and the effect of withdrawal of that support. See Corwin (1973), Gold and Miles (1981), Miles (1980), Smith and Keith (1971).

School-level factors affect implementation as well.

11. The role of the principal. The greater the active support of the principal, the greater the degree of implementation. DESSI researchers call attention to the importance of building administrators. Berman and McLaughlin mention the leadership role of the principal. Supporting studies include Emrick and Peterson (1978), Galanter (1978), Hord and Huling-Austin (1986).
12. Teacher-teacher relationships. The more collegiality, trust, support, interaction, and open communication between teachers, the greater the degree of implementation. Innovations in the Rand Study required a great deal of teacher collaboration. Smith and Keith highlight the breakdown of teacher collaboration. See Little (1981), Miles et al. (1978), Rosenblum and Louis (1979), Rutter, Maughan, Mortimer, Ouston, and Smith (1979).
13. Teacher characteristics and orientations. The greater the sense of teacher efficacy, the greater the degree of implementation. Gross, Giacquinta, and Bernstein name lack of teacher knowledge and skill to conform to the new model as one inhibiting factor, with lack of staff motivation as another. McLaughlin (1976) and Berman and McLaughlin (1977) refer to attitudes of teachers as critical. Without "motivation by professional concerns," rather than tangible rewards, teachers will not make the extra effort required. See Cohen (1981), Edmonds (1979), Little (1981), McLaughlin (1976), Rutter, Maughan, Mortimer, Ouston, and Smith (1979).

The external environment affects implementation:

14. Government agencies. The greater the congruence between local needs and the reform and the greater the awareness of subjective realities, the greater the degree of implementation. See Cowden and Cohen (1979), Elmore (1980), Kirst (1979), Rosenblum and Louis (1979), Yin, Herald, and Vogel (1977).
15. External assistance. The greater the integration with local district, the greater the degree of implementation. See Crandall et al. (1983), Elmore (1980), Louis (1981), Louis and Rosenblum (1981).

Research on mutual adaptation has contributed greatly to our understanding of schools and of the change process. As a result of mutual adaptation research, we now accept that adaptation is an activity that goes on during implementation and that this process is viewed differently by the various participants in the process. Berman (1981) points out that, in addition to adaptation, clarification occurs as parts of the process. As adaptations are made, participants become clearer about philosophy and goals—both their own and those of the proposed change. Bird (1986) describes the effect this had on the Delinquency Prevention Research and Development Program (DPRD) as an instance of mutual adaptation where "the apparent inevitability of adaptation was a constant rationale for stretching the design a bit further" (47). He notes:

> While what happens to the innovation and to the school can be called mutual adaptation, what is required of the proponents and the adopters is mutual accomplishment. If the participants succeed, the product of their work is not just the remainder of a product of mutual attrition of innovation and school (in which the innovation is likely to lose), but is a new construction. (Bird 1986, 47)

The strategy central to DPRD was alteration of the social organization of teaching and learning by adoption of selected practices. It was assumed that implementation was not to be the adoption of strategies designed to protect a model from erosion, but rather that implementation was to be a process whereby the conditions in which the design could be realized would be created. "In this view, the problem of implementation is not to squeeze the most out of scarce possibilities but to organize an overabundance of them" (49), consistent with the findings from both mutual adaptation and fidelity studies that rich redundancy offers more likelihood that an innovation will be implemented.

The program design used a variety of methods to apply a "multivariable theory of social control and social learning bearing on juvenile delinquency" (56). Connecting methods and theory in ways that acknowledged the rationality of various viewpoints was a continuing challenge. "Turning 'just theory' into 'just common sense' will be important part of the mutual accomplishment of implementation" (56).

Through extensive interaction, the written DPRD program design came to have meaning that was specific and shared by participants—both national proponents and local participants. Bird (1986) describes how proponents and participants worked to discover what program and research designs meant: "Throughout, there was the constant choice between reducing the rigor of the program and finding the conditions under which its requirements could be attained" (49). Key to success of the program was providing support for experimentation. Without support, Bird concludes, teachers will be stingy with innovation; with support, they are likely to be generous. Organization of support should be the work of mutual adaptation, or the mutual accomplishment of proponent and adopters.

Bird's term "mutual accomplishment" invites consideration. It suggests how a research design itself can become part of the process of curriculum enactment. As teachers shape curriculum in response to their understanding of their context as Paris (1989) documents, whether this involves adapting or inventing new curricula, researchers studying the process are affected. As teachers learn more about the research and its goals, their practice is affected. While it is not our intent to provide a review of the DPRD, Bird's discussion of it suggests to us a thin line between mutual adaptation and the enacted curriculum.

Curriculum Enactment

Though it is sparse when compared to research using the fidelity and mutual adaptation perspectives, there is a curriculum enactment research tradition. From the enactment perspective, curriculum is viewed as the educational experiences jointly created by student and teacher. The externally created curricular materials and programmed instructional strategies at the heart of the fidelity and mutual adaptation perspectives are seen as tools for students and teacher to use as they construct the enacted experience of the classroom.

The major research questions revolve about such issues as: (1) What are the enacted experiences and how do students and teacher create them? (2) What effect do outside factors (e.g., curricular materials, programmed instructional strategies, school/district/state/federal policies, student and teacher characteristics) have on the curriculum as enacted? (3) What are the effects on students of the curriculum as actually enacted? These effects go beyond "planned outcomes" to other questions, such as: "Can teachers and students be trusted to enact a curriculum that produces socially desirable outcomes?" "How can teachers and students be empowered to enact such a curriculum?" and "What is the impact of the hidden curriculum?"

Underlying this perspective are assumptions about curriculum knowledge, the change process, and the role of the teacher that are different from the other two traditions. Curriculum knowledge is a personal construct which must answer to both personal and external standards. In this way, curriculum knowledge is "individualized" but not left floundering in a sea of relativity. The mind is seen as a fire to be kindled rather than as a vessel to be filled by the knowledge of external experts.

Change is not merely observable alterations in behavior, but rather a personal developmental process, both for the teacher and student. As Marris (quoted in Fullan 1982a) states:

> No one can resolve the crisis of reintegration on behalf of another. Every attempt to pre-empt conflict, argument, and protest by rational planning, can only be abortive; however reasonable the proposed changes, the process of implementing them must still allow the impulse of rejection to play itself out. When those who have power to manipulate changes act as if they have only to explain, and when their explanations are not at once accepted, shrug off opposition as ignorance or prejudice, they express a profound contempt for the meaning of lives other than their own. For the reformers have already assimilated these changes to their purposes, and worked out a reformulation which makes sense to them, perhaps through months or years of analysis and debate. If they deny others the chance to do the same, they treat them as puppets dangling by the threads of their own conceptions. (25)

Thus, successful implementation (the personal developmental change process) demands the understanding and acceptance of the subjective realities of the players undergoing the change process.

The role of the teacher, then, is as a curriculum developer who, together with his or her students, grows ever more competent in constructing positive educational experiences. The process of the enacted curriculum is one of continual growth for both teachers and student. If the mind is a fire to be kindled, the role of the external curriculum expert is a teacher of teachers—one who kindles the fire of teachers who then join their fire with those of their students, thus continually adding to the flame.

An early example of the enactment perspective in practice is the Denver Curriculum Project. In 1922, Jesse Newlon, Superintendent of Schools in Denver, Colorado, reported to the Board of Education that committees of teachers, cooperating with administrative and supervisory staff, had been appointed to begin reconstructing courses of study in subject areas at each of the three instructional levels: elementary, junior high, and high school. Not only were teachers represented on every committee but every committee was chaired by a teacher. Working after school, during the school year, the committees were to read and discuss the available professional literature. Newlon urged the Board to adopt a program that would support and provide a structure for their efforts. As adopted, the program included these main features:

1. An appropriation by the Board for the curriculum revision project and at the end of 2 years a permanent department was to be established and given a budget;
2. Relief of teachers who served as members or chairs of curriculum revision committees from regular classroom work, with a few days to a few months release time;
3. Employment of specialists, nationally known for their contribution to problems of teaching in their own fields;
4. Arrangements with the University of Colorado and State Teachers College for professors of education to devote weekly time to general supervision of the curriculum revision work of the more than 40 committees;
5. Provision of a clerical staff to support committee work (Caswell 1950; Hall and Lewis 1925; Newlon 1923)

Appropriations were made available for printing the courses of study completed by committees. By 1923 a professional library had been developed and received the services of a full-time librarian. Curriculum revision was to be a continuous process, drawing upon the latest educational research and experience. Teachers in word and in deed were essential to the process.

To Newlon, personal growth and morale of teachers were as important as any specific outcomes of their curriculum efforts. Development and enactment of the curriculum were simultaneous, as courses of study were shaped by teacher committees and in turn shaped by teachers and students who used them. This comment from Newlon's Twentieth Annual Report to the Board (1923) is illustrative:

> In organizing supervision the controlling principle is a consideration of ultimate rather than immediate results. The assumption is that the community can afford to wait two or three years in order to reap the results of this type of organization, rather than to attempt by more arbitrary methods to obtain rigid uniformity of practice at the expense of the teacher's initiative and resourcefulness. (22)

Later he was to argue that "unless the teacher engages in the thinking from which new policies eventuate, he can be only what he has so long been—at best, an artisan who can work only according to definite specifications and under close supervision" (1934, 218–219). Problems in cooperation within the school were to be seen as opportunities for individuals to learn more about problem-solving. The administrator was not to be a supervisor who required teachers to surrender principles of conduct and thinking if teachers were honest and professional about their work (Johnston, Newlon, and Pickwell 1922).

Caswell (1950) reported that the practice spread throughout the school system and became an accepted practice in the Denver schools. As a result of the Denver program, courses of study were produced in each of the subject areas at all three school levels. These materials were widely known, circulated, and used nationally. One wonders which implementation perspective was used by districts adopting Denver Curriculum Project materials. If adopting districts assumed a fidelity perspective, the parallels with the National Diffusion Network are uncanny, as in both instances materials were developed locally with an enactment perspective and then disseminated nationally with a fidelity perspective.

More significant for a research focus on implementation as enactment, however, is the fact that by 1933 the Denver high schools were selected to be participants in the Eight Year Study. What had emerged from the 10 years of teacher involvement in curriculum development and revision was involvement of students in the curriculum development process. "Where previously the course of study had been prepared by a committee of teachers for use by all, now teachers and pupils, planning in terms of their own situation and needs, developed units of study with a minimum of prescription by others" (Caswell 1950, 153).

We will discuss three studies that exemplify this perspective of curriculum implementation (1) *The Eight Year Study* (Aikin 1942); (2) *Beyond Surface Curriculum* (Bussis, Chittenden, and Amarel 1976); and (3) *Contexts of Curriculum Change: Conflict and Consonance* (Paris 1989).

The Eight Year Study. A heated item of discussion at the 1930 Progressive Education Association's (PEA) National Convention was how progressive education might be extended more effectively in secondary schools. While the PEA steadfastly refused to outline a single philosophy statement or to produce a set of curricular materials, they did "endorse by common consent, the obvious hypothesis that the child rather than what he studies should be the centre of all educational effort and that a scientific attitude toward new educational ideas is the best guarantee of progress" (Burton Frank, President of PEA, quoted in Cremin 1961, 258). Since there was so little evidence of the child-centered curriculum in secondary schools, the PEA conventioneers perceived the issue as a curriculum implementation problem. The best method to arrive at a solution was a "scientific attitude," which involved empirical investigation into the problem and rigorous evaluation of the proposed solution.

The problem was diagnosed as an overemphasis on externally prescribed input in the form of standardized and regulated courses of study. Colleges demanded specific courses for admission and those courses, rather than "learning," became the purpose of secondary schools. "The mold into which education was poured, rather than its essence and spirit became the goals of pupil and parents alike. This emphasis on 'credits' blinded even the teachers so that they could not see their real task" (Aikin 1942, 7). As a result, "Principals and teachers . . . knew what grades students made on tests of knowledge and skill, but few knew or seemed really to care whether other objectives such as understandings, appreciations, clear thinking, social sensitivity, genuine interests were being achieved," and "Teachers' lives were needlessly and unfortunately narrowed and impoverished" (Aikin 1942, 9–10). Essentially, "in spite of greater understanding of the ways in which human beings learn, teachers persisted in the discredited practice of assigning tasks meaningless to most pupils and of listening to re-citations" (Aiken 1942, 6).

Based on this analysis, the PEA's "solution" was an experiment in which 30 secondary schools would be invited to offer to their students whatever the local school people, students, and community felt would be best for their students. Meanwhile, colleges agreed to accept students from these experimental schools based upon recommendations from school staff and would not require specific credits or test results. The PEA's idea was to do away with externally prescribed courses of study and see what happened.

"Seeing what happened" was not, however, a haphazard affair. As a result of their analysis of the existing situation, the PEA noted:

> It is an amazing fact that our schools . . . know little of the results of their work. It is even more amazing that they seldom attempt seriously to find out what changes schooling brings about in students . . . . How can this lack of knowledge . . . be explained? There are doubtless many causes but one of the most obvious is the universal emphasis upon the accumulation of credits for promotion, graduation, and admission to college. (Smith and Tyler 1942, xvii)

What they discovered was the "what-gets-tested-is-what-gets-taught" syndrome.

> What goes on the school record becomes the real objective of the student, no matter what the school says its purposes are. . . . One of the major reasons for the over-emphasis upon these limited objectives is that results in these fields are more easily measured than in other less tangible areas. . . . Because such tests are at hand the teacher uses them. Because instruments of appraisal in other areas have not been available, the teacher tends to neglect other objectives and to strive only for results that can be ascertained with relative ease and objectivity. (Smith and Tyler 1942, xvii–xviii)

If traditional measurement tools were a cause of the problem, then new measurement tools would need to be created—not only to evaluate the effects of the curriculum change but also to allow the curriculum change to be implemented in the first place. "The available achievement tests did not provide measures of many of the more important achievements anticipated from these new courses" (Smith and Tyler 1942, 4), so new tools would need to be devised to evaluate the effects on students of the experimental curriculum. New tools would be needed not only to measure student growth but to measure teacher growth, curricular inputs, and processes as well. Each would need to be observed and measured in order to evaluate the implementation of a progressive curriculum.

The purposes for evaluating the implementation of the curriculum were to (1) provide periodic checks on the effectiveness of institutions and indicate necessary improvements; (2) validate the hypotheses on which the institutions operate; (3) provide information for guidance of students; (4) provide psychological security to staff, students, and parents; and (5) provide a sound basis for public relations (Smith and Tyler 1942).

Throughout these stated purposes the emphasis was on the needs of the local school rather than on the researchers or external policy-making bodies. Just as the schools were to be responsible for constructing the curriculum, so too would they be responsible for measuring, recording, and reporting the results of their work. The freedom to create, assess, and revise every aspect of a school's work was a daunting reponsibility. One participating principal noted, "My teachers and I do not know what to do with this freedom. It challenges and frightens us. I fear that we have come to love our chains" (quoted in Aikin 1942, 16). Now that schools were being provided freedom, many admitted that they had not used the freedom they possessed previously and that "college prescriptions were often only an excuse for stagnation and inaction. Now that these requirements were no longer binding for the thirty schools, they were under the necessity of proving that they could use freedom creatively and wisely" (Aikin 1942, 22).

The issue of whether or not teachers use freedom wisely to produce socially desirable outcomes is one of the key questions of all studies in the curriculum enactment tradition. The Eight Year Study first and foremost chose to answer that question by following the students from the experimental high schools through their college careers. The study's technique was to pair 1,475 experimental school college students with a graduate of another secondary school matched as closely as possible with respect to sex, age, race, scholastic aptitude scores, home and community background, and vocational and avocational interests. The following categories were measured:

1. intellectual competence (scholarship, intellectual curiosity and drive, scientific approach, study skills and habits);
2. cultural development, use of leisure time, appreciativeness and creativity (in the arts, athletics, other student activities, hobbies and social service/church work);
3. practical competence, common sense and judgment (financial competence, ability to obtain and keep a job, time management, and environmental adjustment);
4. philosophy of life (vocational and philosophical objectives);
5. character traits (integrity, responsibility, initiative);
6. emotional balance (self-control, confidence, sense of humor, independence, sensitivity, family relationships, religious outlook, adjustment to other students);
7. social fitness (ability to make and keep friends, poise, social accomplishments)
8. sensitivity to social problems (concern about campus issues, awareness of contemporary problems, ability to criticize intelligently, willingness to assume responsibilities of citizenship and make personal sacrifices); and
9. physical fitness (health habits, activities engaged in).

Such a listing reinforces the study's belief in the necessity to create and use measurement tools beyond standardized achievement tests and listings of courses taken. The measurement tools used for the subcategory intellectual curiosity and drive are representative of the efforts given to creating new methods of assessment (see Smith and Tyler 1942 for full account of the development of the entire evaluation process). Five descriptive categories were created, and each student was placed into one of the following five categories:

1. Habitually wonders about information which is new to him. Recognizes that much of knowledge is as yet (by him) unexplored. Goes to some trouble to find what lies under the surface. Not content to cease seeking information when the class hour ends or a chapter is finished. Wants to know how things work, what others have thought, which means cause which results;
2. Prefers to know a great deal about a few subjects rather than a little bit about a great many. Tenacious in seeking all information available about a specialized field;
3. Ordinarily content to do his work in routine fashion, but on occasion (because of a personal interest, stimulus of a provocative idea, etc.) will explore a subject further;
4. Becomes enthusiastic over a new idea, thinks how satisfying it would be to know more about it, intends to—but never gets around to it;
5. Apathetic, no intellectual interest, indifferent, incurious, not responsive to intellectual stimulus.

The placement was supported with "positive and valid evidence based on the student's performance in courses, interests expressed by the student, comments of teachers and fellow students, and examination of written work" (Chamberlin, Chamberlin, Drought, and Scott 1942, 45).

Using this wide array of criteria and measures, the study found that graduates of the experimental schools equaled or exceeded their counterparts from nonexperimental schools in every assessment area. "It is quite obvious from these data that the Thirty Schools graduates, as a group, have done a somewhat better job than the comparison group whether success is judged by college standards, by the students' contemporaries, or by the individual students" (Chamberlin et al. 1942, 208). Even Professor Gumere, the representative from Harvard (one of the five colleges that refused to drop the standardized test requirements for admission), joined in saying, "It looks as if the stimulus and the initiative which the less conventional approach to secondary school education affords sends on to college better human material than we have obtained in the past" (Aikin 1942, 150).

Schools and their personnel were also found to benefit greatly from participation in the experiment. "In all the schools many teachers have had a new birth of freedom. Their lives, professionally and personally, have been immeasurably enriched. Teaching has become a thrilling, absorbing experience" (Aikin 1942, 85). The study made it plain that teachers, like their students, are capable of continuous development, and as teachers become aware of their roles as learners they became better teachers as measured by positive student outcomes. In short, "Participation in the study has brought renewed vitality to every school. . . . Out of their attempts to meet a challenge, out of searching study of their own work, out of their struggle to serve youth better, the thirty schools have grown immeasurably in educational stature and wisdom" (Aikin 1942, 138).

Input and process findings from the study are difficult to separate because the curriculum as enacted was defined as being developed, not implemented. Schools that tried to replicate a curriculum created by the experts made

> a serious mistake and the results were unsatisfactory. Genuine reconstruction does not come that way. All teachers, all faculties must go through the hard experience of thinking their own problems through. The experiences of other teachers and schools can be useful in pointing the way, but no teacher or school can travel for others the hard road of reconstruction. Schools must find their own answers to their most puzzling questions. (Aikin 1942, 131–132)

Teachers were at the core of the reconstruction process. The teacher "does not merely play his assigned part; he helps select the play and is concerned with the whole production. . . . He no longer works in isolation. He shares with administrators and other teachers in determining the school's principles and purposes, in formulating policies and in putting them into practice, and in building the curriculum" (Aikin 1942, 41).

The teachers and administrators involved in the 30 schools reported they needed the following in the ways of "inputs" in order to build a curriculum successfully:

1. Time—especially for teachers to study and plan together;
2. As broad a base of participation as possible—including parents and students;
3. Cooperative coordination (comprehensiveness);
4. Research—both general findings and specific local conditions;
5. Planning—The amount of planning talk was not the problem. It was only if, after all the talk, no action was taken that problems began. Looking back, many schools felt they talked too much, but blamed it on inability to work in a group and lack of experience in "real" thinking. "The schools that plunged into change without taking time to think their problems through often found it necessary to go back to the beginning and start over" (Aikin 1942, 127). "The search for purpose and meaning was the turning point for many of the participating schools" (Aikin 1942, 133);
6. Continual internal evaluation—to record, report, and analyze what was happening;
7. Willingness to experiment and change;
8. Conviction and courage;
9. Collaborative leadership and teacher collaboration. The study was very strong on this point. Without teachers willing and able to collaborate, the rest of the preceding list was inadequate to the task;
10. Freedom *and* responsibility (Giles, McCutchen, and Zechiel 1942).

After determining that students from the experimental schools outperformed those from nonexperimental schools and examining the nature of the curriculum development process in experimental schools, the study did a forerunner of an effective-schools study, carefully examining two of the most successful schools to analyze what in particular about those schools correlated with their success. The schools were deliberately mismatched in size, setting, SES, and nature of the program offered.

It was discovered that the most effective schools were more experimental in nature. The connection was powerful and direct: The more experimental the school, the better the outcomes for both students and teachers. It is of considerable interest that one of these most experimental/most effective schools was located in an area characterized by poverty and predominantly populated by low socioeconomic students. Despite these disadvantages, students from this school outperformed students from more advantaged environments but less experimental schools.

As a result of their analysis, the study made two statements concerning the process of curriculum development:

1. "The important characteristics of both [of the more effective schools] were: their willingness to undertake a search for valid objectives; organizing curricula and techniques and setting them in motion in order to attain the objectives; and finally measuring the effectiveness of curricula and techniques by appropriate evaluation devices. These are basic processes; their utility in any type of school is proved." (Chamberlin, Chamberlin, Drought, and Scott 1942, 182)
2. "Uniformity would be neither necessary nor desirable in the work of the school." (Aikin 1942, 123)

Beyond Surface Curriculum. Bussis, Chittenden, and Amarel (1976) unabashedly acknowledge an enactment perspective: "The most significant educational variation exists at the level of the individual practitioner—not at the level of instructional materials, packaged programs, or the like" (1). It is the teacher and the child who hold the central role in decisions "that determine the nature and course of learning" (2). The authors' position on implementation research is that it needs to be directed away from methodological questions of how to measure degree of fidelity to a reconsideration of basic assumptions. The "engrossment with definition and method reflects an attempt to develop a science related not so much to crucial problems within its field as to its own refinement" (11). The problem is not insufficient technical sophistication, "it is the rationale underlying present data gathering and analysis—the basic research and evaluation paradigm—that needs rethinking" (8).

Bussis, Chittenden, and Amarel argue that if significant educational change is to take place, then teacher thinking, feeling and assumptions must change, not just content or materials. "Neither a stimulus nor a curriculum can be psychologically relevant entities apart from a person's interpretation of them" (13). Implementation of a program is construed as a change in teacher thinking. Thus, the study's "major emphasis is on a theoretical analysis of teachers' understandings" (3). "Understandings" are the meaning of behavior as described by the teachers, so the study concerns itself not with the specifics of behavior per se but rather with "what the described behaviors represent" (15).

The purpose of the study is not to provide prescriptions of what works when implementing an educational change, but rather to share "what is now available in the hope that it will stimulate alternative approaches to research and will strengthen a growing trend in American education that clearly recognizes the centrality of the teacher's role" (5).

The innovation studied was "open education." The choice is significant because the underlying assumptions of open education, as conceived by the authors, match the epistemological underpinnings of the study. "First, the school is viewed as a place where adults as well as children learn. Second, the very process of teaching is construed as a process of learning" (30). The open education movement eschewed prescribed plans and demanded that teachers accept the tasks of encouraging and guiding children's learning, which placed upon them the "key decisions as to whether, when, how, and for what purpose to intervene in a child's activity" (25). The lack of prescribed methods in open education accentuates what the authors feel is "a central feature of all educational programs—namely, the particular construct system of an individual teacher" (34).

The authors looked at three sets of understandings (construct systems) that are directly related to implementation: (1) understandings of curriculum; (2) understandings of children; and (3) understandings of the in-service component of the innovation (advisory groups). The study utilized in-depth, semistandardized interviews to define and analyze these construct systems. The validity of the interview data was not subjected to statistical manipulations nor to observations in the classroom because the purpose was not to determine the accuracy of teachers' statements about what they did in the classroom but rather to provide a general picture of their construct systems. The strength of the interview format was "its ability to elicit personal opinions, knowledge, and understandings—the type of evidence necessary to obtain a general picture of personal constructs and construct systems" (42). After completion of the study and numerous other administrations of the interview, the authors conclude "the evidence indicates that an interview methodology such as the one reported here is a sensitive approach to the study of underlying constructs about teaching and learning that have visible counterparts in the classroom and that have a traceable continuity over time" (171).

The sample for the study consisted of 60 teachers from five different centers. The organizing centers were in-service advisory groups rather than schools or districts. The teachers all volunteered to implement open education and also to be subjects in the study. While acknowledging that the volunteer factor perhaps makes the sample atypical, the authors point out that some teachers felt more "volunteered" than voluntary. The population varied in experience (2 to 29 years), class size (18 to 38 students) and were from four different urban areas (New York City; Boston; Burlington, Vermont; and Scranton, Pennsylvania). Forty-six of the teachers were participating in programs offering on-site advisory service and 14 were "boot strap" teachers who were attempting to implement open education without in-service advisory support and with varying degrees of institutional support. Fifty-four of the 60 taught in primary classrooms (K–3).

Following the interviews, categories were derived for coding the data. The final coding schemes were a theoretical/empirical blend. The general categories tended to be based upon what open education theory stipulates is integral to its philosophy (i.e., active learning). The subcategories representing teacher responses were the result of field-generated data that described the variety existing within the population. The organization of the subcategories of the coding scheme around the viewpoints of the teachers is essential to the study. "The teacher observes and learns about children from a vantage point that is necessarily distinct from those of the parent, the pediatrician, the test-maker or the research psychologist. Inherent in each of these points of view are constraints and responsibilities that affect how children are perceived and that shape ideas about learning and development" (111).

The coding of the interviews themselves was admittedly subjective and not subjected to statistical measures of intercoder reliability. Nevertheless, "concordance of judgement" in coding was typically established by two pairs of coders (four total people) comparing and refining their work over a 2-year period. The authors felt strongly enough about the value of the coding schemes to call them perhaps "the most important outcome of the study" (48).

The authors used a powerfully subtle distinction in describing and analyzing teacher curriculum construct systems: surface-structure curriculum versus deep-structure curriculum. Surface-structure curriculum refers to the "variety of encounters a teacher plans and provides for children—experiences that are actively encouraged, as well as those that are optional or perhaps merely tolerated . . . what an observer would see going on in the classroom" (50). The surface structure is the activities a teacher uses, the "what" of the curriculum. Deep-structure curriculum refers to the "*organizing content* that consists of the learning priorities and the concerns that a teacher holds for children . . . what does the teacher want children to know, do, feel, think, or care about" (50). The deep structure is the teacher's rationale for the activities selected, the "why" of the curriculum.

Specific teacher curriculum construct systems were developed by reconstructing both surface and deep curriculum as well as the connections the teacher made between the two. The resulting curriculum construct systems fell into four groups.

Group 1: (12 percent) Grade-level facts and skills were the dominant priority, along with socialization, construed as "good" school behavior. These teachers exhibited little experimentation or change from previous practices. In short, they were not even implementing open education at the surface level. One teacher, when asked about building on children's interests, replied, "I don't do that" (57). No connections were made between their surface and deep curriculum.

Group 2: (22 percent) Grade-level facts and skills remained a dominant priority, but student involvement replaced "good" behavior. This group experimented with and changed the surface curriculum but had difficulty seeing connections "between their innovations and their most deeply held priority" (57). "The surface curriculum tended to become organizing priorities in and of themselves" (58). The overriding characteristics of this group were confusion and low self-confidence captured by the plaintive plea "if they could only tell me *what exactly* has to be covered" (58).

Group 3: (39 percent) Grade-level facts and skills, though mentioned, are no longer the dominant priority of this group and have been replaced by student initiative, independence, and contentment. The surface curriculum here was potentially much richer than with the first two groups, and connections between surface and deep curriculum were, if not always eloquently made, at least implicit.

Group 4: (27 percent) Grade-level facts and skills were not even codable for this group; instead, reflectivity, intention, awareness, and acceptance of self were the organizing principles. "I want them to have a sense of self—to know that their ideas and feelings are okay, and that they have knowledge and their knowledge will grow. If they really know that, I don't give a damn what kind of education they run across later in life. I think they'll make it" (66). Again, the evidence suggested a rich surface curriculum. Connections between surface and deep currriculum were explicitly made, and these teachers had the ability "to go from organizing priorities to surface curriculum and back again—occasionally in the same breath" (69).

The teachers' value ratings of materials underscores the significance of these findings. The value of materials for groups 1 and 2 was based upon their ability to "teach specific outcomes," while teachers in groups 3 and 4 demanded "construing possibilities" and "experiential learning" for their materials. Additionally, "within each group it was the emphasis on construing possibilities or experiential learning that distinguished teachers who saw connections clearly from those who perceived them less clearly" (72). For teachers who could make connections between surface and deep curriculum, the use of materials matched the organizing priorities of the curriculum. Group 3 and 4 teachers used and valued materials in ways consistent with their thinking. Their surface and deep curriculum were congruent. Group 2 teachers, on the other hand, had adopted the "what" of open education (surface curriculum) while retaining the "why" of their traditional approaches (deep curriculum). No wonder they were uneasy and had trouble making connections—they were not there to be made.

Though the authors do not do so, it is possible to interpret groups 1 and 2's inability to make connections as a mismatch between the deep curriculum of open education and their personal deep curriculum. Given this interpretation, the fidelity-driven DESSI findings are somewhat more consistent with enactment driven findings than might at first be considered. DESSI found that some teachers who were forced into using new curricular materials and methods eventually became committed to them when they saw the materials "working" for their students. If the deep curriculum of the enforced program matched the deep curriculum of those teachers, then, after being coerced into using the new program, they became capable of seeing the connections between the program's surface-curriculum change and their own most deeply held priorities for their students. The implementation of the new program did not involve a change in the "why" component of their curriculum constructs but did involve a change in the "what" component and *in the teachers' ability to make connections between the two.* DESSI could identify that situation as a successful implementation because of the behavioral changes of a surface curricular program. *Beyond Surface Curriculum* might call it a semisuccessful implementation because the teachers' eventual ability to make connections between deep- and surface-curriculum levels indicates a change in their thinking even without a change in the deep curriculum.

In the area of teacher understandings of children, the teachers in the sample felt: (1) children expressed their needs and feelings more in open education; (2) the benefits of such expression outweighed the difficulties it might cause; (3) teachers more often expressed their own feelings; and (4) the general classroom climate was more personal, friendly, and satisfying (79–80). Thus, teachers were able to gather much more information about their students in the open setting, and the question the study decided to address was how the teachers organized this new information. The three general categories of the coding scheme (needs and feelings; interests and choice; social interaction) were generated by open education theory while the subcategories were products of teacher responses. For each of the three general categories, four teacher orientations (subcategories) were found.

Needs and Feelings: Orientation A teachers (20 percent) felt the main benefit of open education was that children were not afraid to speak out and state confusion about assignments. Orientation B teachers (15 percent) did not really know what to do with their new knowledge of their students' needs and feelings. They believed in the importance of children's feelings but were concerned with how to control those feelings so learning could proceed. The affective was viewed as at odds with the cognitive. "A child can't learn if he is 'upset', 'too excited' or even 'too interested' " (84). Orientation C teachers (32 percent) "perceived the expression of needs and feelings to be a natural condition, and welcomed . . . its contribution to . . . a warm and humane environment" (85). Orientation D teachers (33 percent) related the feelings and emotions of their students to learning and development. Unlike the other orientations, this group integrated thought and feeling.

Interest and Choice: Orientation A teachers (20 percent) were unlikely even to talk about children's interests and choices, and when they did it was to express concern that children could not be trusted to be interested in or to choose the basic skills they needed. "The program provided all these nice materials, but I can't use them. I have . . . math series to cover . . . I don't have the time" (92). Orientation B teachers (30 percent) believed worthwhile learning could result from student interest and choice but conceived the resulting learning as enrichment. Children were still not seen as capable of being interested in or choosing to learn the basics of their curriculum. Orientation C teachers (22 percent) used student interests and choice, but tended to take an interest or choice at face value and thus missed "the range of meanings it may hold for the child and will have difficulty in conceiving of the many directions in which the interest can be developed" (95). This group focused on the "what" of the student interest rather than the "why," and this limited applications of student interest to traditional subject matter activities (e.g., a child is interested in dinosaurs, the resulting activity is to measure one). Orientation D teachers (28 percent) saw children's interests as integral to learning. This group was "very concerned with the way in which children chose to investigate a particular matter, evaluating their choices along the way as indicating the real direction of their interests" (99).

Social Interaction: Orientation A teachers (18 percent) did not perceive peer interaction as an educative process. Orientation B teachers (5 percent) could perceive potential benefits for peer interaction, but were so focused on the "disruptive or interfering qualities of interaction" (105) they did not attempt to achieve those possibilities. Orientation C teachers (37 percent) considered peer interaction "a tremendous resource for instruction that previously had not been tapped nor even considered" (106). Yet they viewed social interaction mostly in the realm of peer tutoring: "Children can be very good teachers" (106). The process of interchange was not perceived as valuable, only the outcomes. Orientation D teachers (40 percent) conceived of learning as highly social in character and saw in the reciprocity of the social interchange a major resource for children's intellectual growth and development.

These four orientations were then analyzed in terms of three other important attributes of open education: (1) inquiry into the child's perspective; (2) permeability of constructs/understandings; and (3) children and adults as learning resources. Orientation D teachers were much more likely to inquire into and understand their students' perspective, which allowed more effective guidance of student learning. Orientation D teachers also had much greater permeability of their constructs—that is, they were much more likely to change both children and curriculum constructs based upon input from students than were the other three orientations. Finally, the teaching construct system of Orientation D teachers perceived and used both students and other adults as learning resources.

Though rich in describing an enacted curriculum based upon teachers' curriculum and children constructs, as an implementation study *Beyond Surface Curriculum* could have gone further by connecting those two construct systems. The findings regarding curriculum construct systems provide a wealth of information concerning level of implementation, while the teacher understandings of children provide an equal wealth of information concerning how and why the surface curriculum of classroom was constructed. Unfortunately, the authors did not explore the relationships between the two. Thus, the reader is left wondering, for instance, about the nature of the relationship between Group 4 curriculum constructs and Orientation D children constructs, about the relationships between implementation viewed as a change in thinking, and implementation viewed as classroom behavioral changes. If a purpose of inquiry, however, is viewed as more insightful inquiry in the future, then the research was a successful implementation study.

Finally, *Beyond Surface Curriculum* analyzed teacher understandings of the Advisory Groups (the in-service component of the innovation). The teachers found the support useful—82 percent of the comments were positive, with only 18 percent negative. As could be expected, what the teachers thought useful differed from teacher to teacher. What is perhaps more surprising was the chasm between what the advisers thought they were providing and what the teachers thought the advisers were providing. For instance, adviser visitations to classrooms were viewed by advisers as providing models of alternatives while teachers listed administrative service; helping hand; emotional support; respect of individuality; problem solver; provider of alternatives; theorist; modeling agent; demonstrator (differs from modeling in that the teacher's intent is to copy what the adviser does); appreciative critic; reflective agent; and leadership.

One quarter to one third of the positive comments at each site fit under the general category of emotional support. Yet the most discontent was expressed about the same category. This is not as contradictory as it may at first appear because what the teachers valued most highly they missed the most when it was lacking. Most of the discontent expressed concerning emotional support arose when comparing individual advisors. In general, in fact, the higher the teachers rated a benefit of the advisers, the greater the amount of discontent they expressed about the same area. The teachers' high valuing of emotional support stands in stark contrast to the fidelity-driven findings, which indicated the "pushy principal" (initiator) had more succesful implementation than the manager or the responder.

The second highest expressed discontent was in the area of demonstrator. Interestingly enough, the advisers, to a person, did not want to accept this role. They wanted to provide alternatives, not behaviors to be imitated. The least amount of teacher discontent was expressed in the providing alternatives function—the role the advisers most highly valued and chose for themselves.

The analysis of how teachers used the support was based upon "mediation." Mediation consisted of three hierarchical psychological processes: (1) internalization (e.g., the teacher could articulate a specific method received from the adviser, but showed no evidence of personally selecting what to "take in"); (2) selection (e.g., the teacher selected certain ideas and information to "take in," but there was no evidence that the selected information had been integrated with the teacher's personal deep structure curriculum); and (3) integration (e.g., the teacher gives a personal shape to the interaction with the adviser, evidence of conceptual reorganization of the teacher's deep structure).

The general finding regarding mediation was that "the advisors were highly successful in promoting and supporting a mediative stance among those teachers who were most receptive to them" (162). The more "mediated" the teacher, the greater the emotional, intellectual, and practical support the teacher reported receiving from the advisor. The authors argue that there are definite connections between teacher receptivity to advisers, teacher mediation, deep-structure connections to rich-surface structures (Curriculum Construct Groups 3 and 4), and implementation of an open education curriculum. In short, when teachers' deep constructs match the deep construct of open education, they will be more likely to create an open education surface curriculum, make deep and surface level connections, and be helped by in-service support.

From their data and analysis, the authors generate two conclusions:

> The general picture supports two major conclusions. First, commitment to the educational philosophy on the part of the teacher appears essential for the development of understandings that are necessary to implement an open approach. . . . The second conclusion we draw is that for teachers committed to an open education philosophy, the external adviser usually plays a critical role during the initial two or three years in helping them conceptualize an open approach to educating young children. (168)

The study thus seems to indicate that successful implementation of an innovation is possible only when there is no need for teachers to change their ordering priorities for education. If surface-structure curriculum changes are first-level implementation and deep-structure curriculum changes are second-level implementation and perhaps indicative of "real" educational change (doing "new things differently" rather than doing the "same thing better"), these findings beg the question of how to bring about second-level implementation. Is "real" education change possible?

Contexts of Curriculum Change: Conflict and Consonance. Cynthia Paris (1989) acknowledges an enactment perspective as the starting point for her research (see also Cochran-Smith, Kahn, and Paris 1990). She states her assumptions as:

1. Curriculum knowledge includes situated knowledge, created in practice when teachers engage in the ongoing processes of teaching and learning in classrooms.
2. Curriculum change is a process of individual growth and change in thinking and practice rather than an organizational procedure of design and implementation.

3. Teachers' work with curriculum, whether creating and adapting their own curricula or responding to curricula created and imposed by others, is shaped in response to their perceptions of their contexts. (2–3)

Paris' research locates the process of curriculum squarely "in the complex, and often conflicting historical, interpersonal, and ideological contexts of the individuals and organizations involved in the process of change" (3).

These types of assumptions led Paris to use an interpretive mode of research in order to understand curriculum change (as opposed to curriculum implementation, as the term itself indicates a fidelity perspective). She felt it necessary to examine curriculum as enacted by teachers in complex contexts over time and to interpret the process, outcomes, and contexts of the curriculum from the meaning perspective of teachers. Thus, methods of data collection and analysis were grounded in ethnographic assumptions and procedures. The data were drawn from a 2-year ethnographic study of five elementary teachers' work as they created and adapted a word processing curriculum. Equally, a perspective emphasizing teacher meaning making required a focus on the "process of curriculum change rather than technology in curriculum . . . the outcomes of a process of curriculum change in which teachers are the creators rather than receivers of curriculum knowledge; the nature of the process by which they achieve those outcomes; and the influences that contributed to the shape of both the outcomes and processes" (Paris 1989, 1). Paris embeds the process of curriculum change in the "multiple and often conflicting contexts that include ongoing practices, histories and dominant ideologies of organizations and individuals, and interprets the influence of these contexts from the meaning perspectives of the participants" (23).

A recently hired district-level administrative team in the studied district was in the midst of standardizing the curriculum in order to provide instruction of uniform quality. One of the few areas of discretion that remained in the teachers' work with the curriculum was the word processing curricula, which provided the entry point for the study. The teachers, however, were used to a somewhat more laissez-faire administrative approach that allowed greater teacher selection for appropriate instructional materials and strategies.

Essentially, what Paris studied then was the conflict and consonance resulting from a clash between the fidelity perspective of the district-level administrative team and the enactment perspective of the teachers. The building principal, while sharing the teachers' enactment perspective, encouraged a minimal level of compliance with district requirements in order to avoid closer scrutiny and thereby permitting teachers the freedom to continue their active engagement with the curriculum.

The teachers shared the enactment assumptions that teaching requires context-specific knowledge acquired through deliberative practice, which by definition cannot be the same static truth for all. To the teachers, the skills, talents, and knowledge necessary to enact a curriculum were context specific and had to be achieved "again and again by individual exploration" (13). The best way to enact a quality curriculum, then, was for teachers to pursue ideas through (1) classroom exploration; (2) discussions and observations with colleagues; and (3) formal instruction. These ideas are then "subjected to the teachers' ongoing evaluation and revision in practice in her own classroom. It was not expected that a particular teacher's knowledge would be imposed on others but that her knowledge would be a resource to others as they sought their own ways" (Paris 1989, 13–14).

It comes as no surprise, then, that the new standardizing policies of the district came in conflict with the teachers' assumptions. Teachers were offended by district-level identification and mandating of uniform curricula, as well as by the presentation of those curricula in mandated district-wide in-service meetings where teachers were passive receivers of truth. Such actions were interpreted by teachers to suggest that the administration believed that "(a) the teachers' context specific knowledge was invalid; (b) that curriculum knowledge generated by others was superior to and should replace their own; (c) that all teachers were deficient in this knowledge to the same degree; and (d) that all teachers would best acquire this knowledge through didactic instruction in inservice meetings" (14).

Thus, the beliefs and assumptions of the fidelity-perspective administrators, beliefs and assumptions that gave meaning to their policies and procedures, were in direct conflict with the beliefs, assumptions, and practices of the teachers. The fidelity-oriented administrators sincerely believed they were using the best change methods known to ensure that all teachers would use the best instructional methods and materials in order to help students based upon the historical and interpersonal contexts in which they conducted their day-to-day work—contexts that differed significantly from those of the enactment-oriented teachers. Teachers perceived the district as placing limits on their exercise of professional judgment. It was what those limits communicated to the teachers "about their professionalism and their individuality that caused the most persistent conflict" (24).

Paris found that the perspectival clash about the teacher's role in the creation of curriculum resulted in destructive conflict. Time, energy, and resources were expended in ways that moved away from the mutually held goals of the fidelity-oriented administrators and the enactment-oriented teachers. "At points of conflict, teachers' energies were needlessly wasted 'managing' to conduct their work within and around constraints and conflicts and to cope with the anger and frustration they engendered. Efforts were blocked, ideas sacrificed, and goals compromised at the points of conflict that could not be 'managed' or, in teachers' words, 'gotten around' " (2).

In a more positive vein, however, Paris also provides:

> a description of what is possible when teachers are the creators rather than receivers of curriculum knowledge and curriculum change. Without mandates to change, without uniform training and

standardized curriculum materials or timetables for implementation, the five teachers in the research project and many of their colleagues learned to use word processing, created their own curriculum for teaching word processing to their children and developed ways to use word processing to support and extend their ongoing curricula.(22)

Conclusion. While the three exemplar enactment studies do not provide prescriptions for successful enactment/implementation of a curriculum, all three do suggest remarkably consistent responses to the essential questions of this perspective.

All three studies suggest that the effect of outside influences (e.g., curricular materials, programmed instructional strategies, local/state/federal policies) differs depending upon their proposed function. When the outside influences are designed to control through attempting to standardize classroom experiences of teachers and students, these studies report a negative effect on students and teachers. When the outside influences are perceived and used as attempts to provide teachers with tools to collaboratively develop their skills, knowledge, and attitudes in context-specific environments, they have positive effects for teacher development, enriched curricular experiences, and student outcomes. In regard to the essential, if somewhat condescending, question, "Can teachers and students be trusted to enact a curriculum that results in socially desirable outcomes?" the three studies respond with a resounding affirmative.

When the question turns to, "What are the enacted experiences that result in desirable outcomes and how are they created?" the studies are a bit nebulous. All three agree on the methodological need to go to the source, to analyze and trust the perspectives of students and teachers on how curriculum is actually constructed and to determine curriculum outcomes of innovative practices. Yet all three seem equally wary of stating specifically what an enacted curriculum is.

This wariness may partially result from the enacted perspective's fear of fixing ever-evolving experience with a definition and thus coming in conflict with its own assumptions about the nature of teaching, learning, and change. For instance, The Eight Year Study refused to outline a philosophic statement or to produce a set of curriculum materials, yet its findings emphatically state that the more experimental a school, the more successful it is. What is experimental? Without providing more definitional and conceptual clarity, it is difficult to analyze what it is about the nature of the process or the products of experimentation that influence effective enacted experimental experiences for students and their teachers. One can question whether it is even possible to define what an experimental curriculum is without removing the experimental essence that made it effective in the first place.

Another contributing factor may be the concomitant fear that Bussis, Chittenden, and Amarel (1974) state concerning the vacuousness of research when it becomes engrossed with definition, method, and its own refinement. This seems to suggest that one cannot precisely pin down what an enacted curriculum is without: (1) wasting time, money, and intellect and (2) hindering teachers (Paris 1989), students (Aikin 1942), and researchers (Bussis, Chittenden, and Amarel 1976).

These definitional issues may nevertheless be a crucial line of research for the enactment perspective to address. Otherwise, researchers may be guilty of doing nothing more than discovering their own assumptions. The perspective is in need of a transcendent synthesis that would allow greater clarity of conceptualization without becoming mired in inappropriate attempts to standardize experience or chasing its own definitional tail.

CONCEPTUAL AND METHODOLOGICAL ISSUES IN STUDYING CURRICULUM IMPLEMENTATION

Viewing "curriculum implementation" from these three different perspectives provides some illuminating contrasts and illustrates the complexity of what might be viewed as a straightforward task: studying the implementation of curriculum. Labeling the field of study "curriculum implementation" is, in itself, problematic. The words not only have varied meanings, both in denotation and connotation, but the term "implementation" is more compatible with one perspective than with the others. As we have seen, the three perspectives also operate from different underlying assumptions about curriculum knowledge, curriculum change, and the role of the teacher. After providing an overview of these conceptual differences, we explore them in more depth by examining the major research questions asked about curriculum implementation from each perspective:

1. To what degree has a curriculum been implemented?
2. What factors facilitate or inhibit the implementation of a curriculum?
3. What are the methodological issues in studying the implementation, adaptation, or enactment of curriculum?

Conceptual Issues: Definitions and Underlying Assumptions

The term "curriculum" has taken on many meanings (Zumwalt 1989). Perhaps the most conventional meaning, both for the lay public and educational researchers, refers to the planned curriculum that may be embodied in a course of study, a textbook series, a guide, a set of teacher plans, or an innovative program. A curriculum is something concrete—something that can be pointed to—something that a teacher can implement and something that can be evaluated to see if its goals have been accomplished. This is the meaning of "curriculum" used by researchers with a fidelity perspective and by many oriented toward mutual adaptation. Some researchers studying the "mutual adaptation" of a curriculum extend their definition to include the constellation of contextual factors in school and community that help give shape to the curriculum. The study by Popkewitz, Tabachnick, and Wehlage (1981) is a good example of how the situational context shaped the same curriculum (IGE package), making it, in effect, a very different curriculum in technical, constructivist, and illusory settings. The curriculum becomes very different when adapted and enacted. A little further along the continuum, enactment takes on more idiosyncratic and personal meaning. The enacted curriculum becomes that which is jointly created and jointly and individually experienced by students and teacher. While many curriculum theorists are most comfortable with this sense of the experienced curriculum, it has not been the dominant conception of researchers operating from the more common behavioralist conception of schooling.

To speak of curriculum being "implemented" implies that there is something concrete (a plan, a program) to be carried out by teachers. The term owes its popularity to a fidelity perspective on curriculum improvement. Such "curriculum implementation" research is a relatively recent phenomenon, despite the existence of earlier studies. Part of the contribution such researchers have made is to demonstrate that implementation is worthy of study as a separate entity. It is seen as an event as important as "adoption." Earlier researchers focusing on overcoming initial resistance had assumed that adoption was the biggest barrier to educational change. Hence, studies of curriculum implementation added a new and significant dimension to studies of change.

A major modification to the curriculum implementation literature was made by researchers who discovered that, in reality, curriculum was never really implemented as planned but rather adapted by local users. While some researchers see this adaptation as a pragmatic compromise and might still feel comfortable with the term "implementation," others, who see adaptation as an essential feature not just a necessary concession, would probably feel more comfortable with eliminating the term "implementation" altogether. And those who view curriculum enactment as situationally and personally based outwardly reject the technological orientation of the entire adoption, implementation, and institutionalization change literature. To proclaim "implementation" as worthy of study as a separate entity makes little sense to them, not only because they reject the idea of a curriculum being implemented but because such constructs mean little apart from a person's interpretation of them.

Thus, we seem to have a continuum of shifting meanings, which is rather inaccurately called "research on curriculum implementation." The continuum might be characterized as moving through different phases of curriculum (i.e., planned, actual, and experienced) and processes (i.e., implementation, adaptation, and enactment).

Researchers from a fidelity perspective and those approaching mutual adaptation from a more practical perspective are interested in studying the degree to which a planned curriculum is implemented and in identifying factors that could explain why the curriculum was not implemented as intended. Researchers holding a more critical mutual adaptation perspective focus on how the planned curriculum is shaped by the adapters and the situational context. They may or may not also study the hidden curriculum—the unintended consequences of adopting a particular curriculum. Researchers who believe that mutual adaptation is an essential element of curriculum work, not just a necessary concession to reality, are interested in how the curriculum actually gets shaped as it is played out in the classroom. Their approach overlaps with researchers from an enactment perspective, who view the actual or enacted curriculum as their focus. Further on the continuum are those with an enactment perspective, who are interested in describing not just how the curriculum is shaped as it gets acted out in specific settings but also how it is experienced by the particular participants in the settings. For them, curriculum has meaning only in terms of individuals' interpretation of it.

While the three perspectives have been a useful heuristic tool in conceptualizing the field and organizing this review, we feel they are too precise in their categorization of the field. The continuum described above is a more accurate representation, although we know it oversimplifies some permutations, and various versions of "mutual adaptation" defy being placed along points on a continuum. While we continue to use the three orientations to help clarify differences, we hope the reader remembers that we see the divisions among the categorizations as fluid. Viewing them as distinct orientations allows us now to contrast, in a clearer manner, the different underlying assumptions about curriculum knowledge, change, and the role of the teacher.

Curriculum Knowledge. From the fidelity perspective, curriculum knowledge is primarily created outside the classroom by curriculum experts for teachers to implement in the way the experts have decided is best. The experts are usually curriculum specialists external to the school system (e.g., consultants, academicians, publishers, teachers) but can also be local experts (e.g., central office administrators, building administrators, curriculum committee). Practitioner knowledge may be one source of knowledge tapped by these experts, but it is used during the process of developing a curriculum (and the instrument to measure the curriculum, as in the case of CBAM), not in the process of implementing a curriculum. The curriculum to be implemented is a concrete manifestation of curriculum knowledge.

Since many mutual adaptation approaches can be viewed as variations of this fidelity approach, curriculum knowlege still primarily resides in the outside expert who develops the curriculum to be adapted by teachers to the local context. These adaptations are viewed as understandable adjustments to a product developed for more generic purposes. The concern with how much adaptation teachers can be permitted in the process of implementation before the integrity of the curriculum has been lost belies the underlying view that curriculum knowledge resides in the experts who designed the curriculum rather than in the teachers who can make minor adjustments.

People operating from a "purer" mutual adaptation perspective, rather than a fidelity variation, respect both the external source of curriculum knowledge and that which resides in practitioners, as a group or as individuals. They understand and are interested in the constellation of factors that interact to influence any curriculum. Wherever the curriculum was created, in the process of implementation there must be adjustments in the goals and methods, as well as in the needs, interests, and skills of the participants. Curriculum knowledge is reshaped in the process of adaptation, but that which is being reshaped still was created by those who are seen as possessing some specialized curriculum knowledge.

For those operating from a curriculum enactment perspective, curriculum knowledge is not viewed as a product or an event but rather as an ongoing process. It is the only perspective that is not dependent on an externally created piece of curriculum as the center of its study, although it is not excluded. An externally designed curriclum is viewed as a resource for teachers who create curriculum as they engage in the ongoing process of teaching and learning in the classroom. Context-specific curricular knowledge is acquired through deliberative practice. While teachers may use externally designed curriculum and benefit from the stimulation of an "outsider," it is they and their students who create the enacted curriculum and give meaning to it. They are creators rather than primarily receivers of curriculum knowledge.

Curriculum Change. Given these different views of curriculum knowledge, change is understandably viewed differently by people holding the three different perspectives. Whether in its "pure" or modified form, the fidelity perspective assumes a rational, systematic, linear change process that can be better managed the more we know about the factors that facilitate and hinder the smooth operation of the process. For those with a mutual adaptation perspective, change is viewed as a more unpredictable, less linear process with a more active "consumer" at the end of the process. The process of change needs to be understood to help explain what happens to the curriculum. There is a recognition that how a curriculum is implemented is as significant to its outcomes as it is to its content. From the enactment perspective, curriculum change is a process of growth for teachers and students—a change in thinking and practice—rather than an organized procedure for design and implementation of a new curriculum. It involves "genuine reconstruction": Thinking, feeling, and assumptions must change, not just content and materials. Studying this personal development process demands an understanding and acceptance of the subjective realities of the players undergoing the change process.

Role of the Teacher. The teacher's role also differs depending on one's perspective. From the fidelity perspective, the role of the implementing teacher is one of a consumer who should follow the directions and implement the curriculum as those possessing curriculum knowledge have designed it. Being the deliverer of the curriculum to students, the role of the teacher is recognized as being critical to the success of the curriculum. The curriculum cannot achieve its aims or be fairly evaluated unless the teacher implements it in the way in which it was intended to be implemented. Because curricula are not always faithfully implemented, adequate training prior to implementation, and support and monitoring during implementation, have become standard features of this approach to curriculum implementation. From the mutual adaptation perspective, the role of the teacher becomes more active in shaping the curriculum to meet the demands of the local context. For those with an underlying fidelity orientation, this is a role that is pragmatically necessitated, but which must be contained within certain parameters if curriculum integrity is to be maintained. For those with a "purer" mutual adaptation approach, the role of teachers becomes more central because their input in shaping the curriculum is required if the curriculum is to be successfully implemented in the particular settings.

From the enactment perspective, the role of the teacher is integral to the process, for there would be no curriculum without the teachers and students giving form to it in the classroom. Whether using an externally created and imposed curriculum, adapting a curriculum, or developing their own, teacher and students in the classroom create the curriculum that is worthy of study. It is teachers' and students' interpretations of what is happening in the classroom and changes in their ways of thinking and believing that are the focus of researchers who study curriculum enactment rather than curriculum implementation.

To What Degree Has a Curriculum Been Implemented?

This question has been a major research question for those with a fidelity view of curriculum implementation. Sometimes the question has been a starting point for researchers, while at other times the question stems from an evaluation study indicating that a particular innovation did not achieve its goals. Once it was realized that one cannot assume that an adopted curriculum automatically becomes a reality, studying the extent to which a particular curriculum has been implemented as intended became a major focus of researchers. It is the question that has to be addressed before the factors affecting implementation or evaluation of the curriculum change can be understood. As Fullan and Pomfret (1977, 336) state, "We simply do not know what has changed unless we attempt to conceptualize and measure it directly." Hence, researchers must first clarify the essential characteristics and acceptable adaptations, if any, of a curriculum in order to measure the degree to which the curriculum has been faithfully implemented.

From the mutual adaptation perspective, measuring the degree to which a curriculum has been implemented takes a different focus. While the fidelity researcher is interested in seeing how close the implemented curriculum is to the intended curriclum by matching the former to the latter, the mutual adaptation researcher assumes the implemented curriculum and the intended curriculum will not, or should not, match. So rather than measuring fidelity, studying the degree of implementation becomes studying the kinds of adaptations that occur in the process of implementing a particular curriculum.

From a curriculum enactment perspective, this question, as stated, is meaningless because the starting point is not a curriculum to be implemented or adapted but rather how a curriculum takes form through the evolving constructions of teachers and students. When studying teachers and students working with an externally designed and imposed curriculum, the interest is not in measuring how faithfully the curriculum is carried out, nor even so much how the original curriculum is adapted, but rather in describing and understanding the meaning given the evolving curriculum by those creating it—the teacher and students.

What Factors Facilitate or Inhibit the Implementation of a Curriculum?

This is a major question for reseachers operating from fidelity and mutual adaptation perspectives. The fidelity researcher is trying to discover the factors that will maximize faithful implementation, whereas the mutual adaptation researcher is trying to explain what happened to the curriculum in the process of implementation. Sometimes the latter is an attempt to understand a model gone awry and sometimes it is an attempt to understand the expected or desired process of adaptation. The factors summarized earlier represent the major substantive findings of this type of research. By identifying the factors affecting implementation, such research contributes to improving the effectiveness of future implementation efforts, both of the fidelity and mutual adaptation variety.

From the curriculum enactment perspective, this research question makes sense if reworded to state: What effects do outside factors (e.g., curricular materials, packaged curricula, school/district/state/federal policies, parental expectations, student and teacher characteristics) have on the curriculum as enacted? The question is asked not so much from the perspective of determining factors to improve the implementation of curriculum, as to describe and better understand how curriculum is enacted, providing insight to those who create and study curriculum.

Perhaps some of the contradictory findings about factors affecting curriculum implementation result not just from contextual differences but from different underlying rationales for studying "factors" and different valuing of outcomes. Principals as "enforcers" may be most effective at ensuring faithful implementation of curriculum, as Huberman (1983) concludes from the DESSI study. But what he devalues, teacher-initiated change ("overreaching") or teacher-reconstructed change ("program blunting or downsizing"), may be viewed as desirable by those holding a curriculum enactment perspective.

Although coming from research with very different underlying assumptions, factors identified by researchers with different perspectives can be useful to researchers and practitioners. They provide additional variables to be considered or additional commonplaces to help deliberate about or understand the adapted or evolving enacted curriculum. For instance, some of the factors Gross, Giacquinta, and Bernstein (1971) found to inhibit the implementation of the catalytic role model might be reinterpreted by teachers or researchers with other than a fidelity persuasion. One of the inhibiting factors was the teachers' lack of skills and knowledge needed to conform to the new role model. This might lead the fidelity-oriented researcher to recommend that the prerequisite skills and knowledge be identified more clearly and the teachers be provided adequate training and support in terms of the necessary skills and knowledge so that they can successfully implement the curriculum. The mutual adaptation researcher would conceptualize the necessary skills and knowledge differently because the question is not what skills/knowledge are necessary to faithfully implement the curriculum but what skills/knowledge are needed in order to successfully adapt the curriculum to the particular local context. The curriculum enactment researcher would turn the question back to the teacher and students: As the curriculum is evolving, what skills and knowledge have you found useful or would you find useful to make the curriculum more meaningful to you?

Methodological Issues in Studying Curriculum Implementation, Adaptation, and Enactment

Methodological issues in studying curriculum implementation from a fidelity perspective are the same as those found in traditional, psychometrically rigorous research. Concepts need to be operationally defined, valid and reliable measures need to be developed, and studies need to be designed and undertaken in a manner conforming to conventional standards. Developing and utilizing more technically sophisticated methods enable fidelity researchers more accurately to measure the degree of implementation and understand the factors that will eventually enable a more faithful implementation of curriculum. Accommodation to other points of view can be technically addressed. For instance, CBAM researchers, recognizing that adaptation seems to be a given, now find out what kinds of adaptations pilot teachers make and add acceptable adaptations to their list of essential characteristics of a curriculum innovation before the curriculum is implemented. Issues such as when it is fair to evaluate a newly implemented curriculum, likewise, represent a technical problem of determining when the curriculum has actually been implemented. Hall and Loucks (1982) have determined that it takes 3 to 5 years before teachers are routinely using a new curriculum at level IVA and a fair evaluation of the curriculum can take place.

The mutual adaptation perspective seems to have developed in two different ways: as one of the primary findings of fidelity-driven implementation studies and as a result of attempts to apply social science and/or critical theory and more qualitative methodologies to the study of school change. Not only is the initiating factor different but the value of existing research is viewed differently by those holding practical and critical orientations. As Fullan and Pomfret (1977) comment in their review of the newly emerging mutual adaptation perspective, the studies, including the Rand Study, are to be faulted for using "weak measures" of implementation. They are critical of the dependency on "self-reports" and the use of instruments that are too global (i.e., are not based on operationally defined characteristics of the curriculum). While mutual adaptation studies may be faulted for not being as psychometrically rigorous as fidelity studies, these researchers feel justified in using a wider range of methodologies because they want to capture the process of implementation, rather than measure the degree of implementation. Not only are other research methods needed to study how a curriculum is adapted rather than determining whether it has been implemented but the instruments used by the fidelity researchers, with their predetermined characteristics (and acceptable adaptations), lack validity if one has a mutual adaptation perspective because they deny the very process that is being studied. This is not to say that all researchers studying the mutual adaptation of curriculum are totally comfortable with the idea of adaptation. Hence, one of the questions such researchers often struggle with concerns what might be considered minimum integrity of the original curriculum plan: When does mutual adaptation become nonimplementation?

The instruments and methodology used in mutual adaptation studies that have been criticized as "weak" are the mainstay of the researchers who hold a curriculum enactment perspective. "Self-reports" are exactly the reality that one is trying to understand. Such researchers favor in-depth interviews in contrast to the "self-report" questionnaires seen in many mutual adaptation studies because they permit the participant's perspective to evolve in the interview rather than to be structured by a predetermined questionnaire items. To examine the enacted curriculum from the meaning perspective of the teacher and students requires a variety of methods of data collection and data analysis. Methodological concerns are similar to all research using a multimethods approach to studying educational phenomena. There are researchers who, out of their own conviction or the desire to gain legitimacy for their work, carefully design their studies to conform to standards of scientific acceptability; others are less concerned with traditional criteria if their purposes are being served. For instance, Bussis, Chittenden, and Amarel (1976) did not check the validity of their interview data by statistical manipulation, classroom observation, or triangulation because the purpose was not to determine the accuracy of teachers' statements about what they did in the classroom but rather to gain a general picture of their construct system. They had confidence in the well-described procedures they used. Since this perspective does not have as established a tradition as the other perspectives, many of the issues connected with the study of curriculum enactment are just emerging. Basic questions such as, "What exactly is a curriculum as enacted?" and "How can curriculum enactment be studied" are still legitimate questions.

Thus, research on curriculum implementation, adaptation, and enactment involves methodological concerns related to conceptualization and procedures which reflect different purposes and different research traditions. When researchers approach this field, they bring their own commitments and conceptions of curriculum, choose research approaches and methods that are compatible with these orientations, and in some senses can be said to discover their own assumptions.

Policymakers using research from the different perspectives also ask different questions that serve, in turn, to motivate researchers. While the fidelity policymaker is concerned with how variation can be minimized to ensure that validated curriculum is fully implemented, the mutual adaptation policymaker is asking how much variation should be permitted. The policymaker with a curriculum enactment perspective struggles with the question of whether or how teachers and students can be trusted and empowered to produce socially desirable outcomes.

THOUGHTS ABOUT FUTURE RESEARCH

We have identified a variety of studies in a continuously evolving line of work that focuses on how a proposed curriculum is put into practice. At one extreme we find studies that are concerned with the degree of fidelity to both goals and methods of an external curriculum design. Another extreme is represented by studies that document the process by which curriculum is constructed or reconstructed by those who are using it. As we have pointed out, identifying a continuum of studies between these two extremes is less easily accomplished. We have grappled with lack of clarity, referring to research in this in-between area as mutual adaptation research, suggesting that it might more nearly be divided into practical and critical orientations to research.

We have chosen to think of future research from a variety of conflicting perspectives. Various perspectives on curriculum knowledge, research, and practice exist because there are genuine differences in values and commitments that are represented in the way individuals understand and conceptualize the field. It seems reasonable that approaches to the study of the curriculum of schools in a pluralistic society would be characterized by pluralistic perspectives. Conceding that pluralism exists is less challenging than acknowledging the truth and rationality of conflicting perspectives, however.

We have not seen our role as ascertaining which is the more legitimate or useful perspective, but as reporting and asking what purposes are to be served by each. We have chosen to do this by imagining a dialogue among the three perspectives.

Future Research on the Fidelity of Implementation

Fidelity researchers would be likely to inform us of the need for increased sophistication in instruments of measurement in order to enable us to better determine the degree of implementation and to understand better those factors that facilitate and inhibit implementation.

While mutual adaptation researchers with a practical orientation to research would agree that degree of implementation is something worthy of measuring, they would argue that many innovations cannot be measured effectively by experimental designs. They would call for fidelity researchers to develop multiple approaches to research that allow for both developer and user perspectives on the degree and/or nature of implementation. Other mutual adaptation researchers would contend that important social, political, and contextual factors are completely missed by fidelity researchers. They would urge that fidelity researchers begin to look at the work that is being collected by researchers using qualitative methodologies and think about how the two approaches could be more complementary.

Researchers who share the value commitments implicit in an enactment perspective on the curriculum would criticize fidelity research for the subtle effect it has had on the erosion of the image and role of teacher as a thinking, knowing, and acting professional. They would add that it also has limiting and deadening effects on students and has provided a model of knowledge as fixed and static. They would urge that fidelity researchers spend some time with teachers and ask them what questions need to be answered by experimental work. They would point out, along with Dewey, that the real verification of the findings of experimental researcher on education is in the classroom, where teachers discover whether it is truly applicable in the "real world."

Future Research on Mutual Adaptation

Fidelity researchers would urge that documenting what is, even in exquisite detail, may add to our understanding of schools, but it does not tell us what ought to be or necessarily how to bring it to pass. From a fidelity perspective, more work needs to be done to sharpen the methodology used by mutual adaptation researchers, making it less subjective. Further, fidelity researchers would point out that future qualitative research is needed in order to furnish an ample supply of information from which to generate both theories and hypotheses that are testable and can be used to inform policymakers.

Mutual adaptation researchers who apply methodologies borrowed from the social sciences to study educational problems would hasten to point out that while we have a growing body of such research, we simply do not know enough about what happens in schools. They would call for more detailed, ethnographic work that captures the complexity of schools as social organizations. They would point out that the variation in implementation is not a dilemma, but is inevitable. Furthermore, ethnographic research provides an opportunity to ask new questions about what influences the kind and degree of variation.

The enactment perspective would applaud mutual adaptation research for beginning to furnish a mirror of schools and would urge these researchers to extend their mirroring by developing case studies of classrooms and teachers that are working effectively. They would contend that many teachers know a great deal about their craft, yet too often this knowledge is not shared with many who could benefit from it. Variation is not a dilemma but is necessary to account for the uniqueness of individuals.

Future Research on Enactment

Fidelity researchers would point out that the enactment perspective overlooks the fact that many teachers would like to know what works best. Not all teachers are motivated to invent curriculum with students, nor are they qualified. Enthusiasm, good will, and commitment do not compensate for lack of technical knowledge and expertise. They would urge teachers and researchers who are inclined to develop their own curriculum materials to both use and replicate findings from fidelity studies to strengthen their own implementation process. Many of the factors that facilitate or inhibit change have implications for classroom curriculum development. Mutual adaptation researchers would urge teachers to become participant observers, documenting their experiences in order to advance understanding of classroom practice from the teacher's perspective.

Enactment researchers would encourage teachers to engage in action research and assume more responsibility for development of the profession as well as their own development. They would point out that the key to successful implementation is successful invention.

Many questions remain. If each has a contribution to make, when is each appropriate? Who makes decisions about appropriateness? Fidelity researchers would argue that this is the role of policymakers and curriculum developers. Mutual adaptation researchers would say that, regardless of who makes the decision, a curriculum will be profoundly influenced by the context into which it is introduced. Enactment researchers would say that decisions must be made by those they most directly affect. Despite a plurality of perspectives that assume answers to this question, we see it as more complex and situational. For example, we can envision occasions when, for compelling social reasons, it would be highly desirable to have a curriculum designed by experts in content and methodology in order to disseminate information and skills necessary for the health or survival of a population. In this case, degree of implementation becomes exceptionally important.

In other cases, such a high degree of specificity is neither necessary nor desirable. It may, in fact, lead to deskilling of teachers and disenfranchisement of students. We envision situations in which multiple means of accomplishing curriculum goals are acknowledged by subject specialists and curriculum experts who design a curriculum with the assumptions that teachers will and should reshape it in light of their own circumstances and inclinations.

Between these two extremes are an infinite number of possibilities for mutual adaptation and accomplishment. Perhaps this is what Caswell referred to as the distinction between curriculum making and curriculum development—it is development that makes "curriculum ideas come alive in the classroom" (Foshay, 1989). In this sense, curriculum making belongs with the fidelity approach and curriculum development with enactment.

Yet the question of who determines appropriateness remains unanswered, except as it is answered from somewhat defended perspectives. Other questions and implications for future research are myriad: These include issues related to teacher preparation and accountability, such as ongoing efforts to "reform" teacher education, "restructure" schools, and "professionalize" teaching. The specific future research questions related to these issues depend upon whether one approaches "curriculum implementation" from a fidelity, mutual adaptation, or enactment perspective.

References

Aikin, Wilford. 1942. *Adventure in American Education, Vol. I: Story of the Eight Year Study*. New York: Harper & Brothers.

Apling, Richard N., and Mary Kennedy. 1981. *Providing Assistance to Improve the Utility of Information from Tests and Evaluations*. Cambridge, MA: Huron Institute.

Basch, Charles, and Elena Sliepcevich. 1983. Innovators, innovations and implementation: A framework for curricular research in school health education. *Health Education* (March–April): 20–24.

Bentzen, Mary M. 1974. *Changing Organizations: The Magic Feather Principle*. New York: McGraw-Hill.

Berman, Paul. 1981. "Toward an implementation paradigm." In *Improving Schools*, edited by R. Lehming and M. Kane. Beverly Hills, CA: Sage.

Berman, Paul, and Milbrey McLaughlin. 1974. *Federal Programs Supporting Educational Change. Vol. I: A Model of Educational Change*. Santa Monica, CA: Rand.

Berman, Paul, and Milbrey McLaughlin. 1975a. *Federal Programs Supporting Educational Change. Vol. III: The Process of Change, Appendix B: Innovations in Reading*. Santa Monica, CA: Rand.

Berman, Paul, and Edward Pauley. 1975b. *Federal Programs Supporting Educational Change. Vol. II: Factors Affecting Change Agent Projects*. Santa Monica, CA: Rand.

Berman, Paul, and Milbrey McLaughlin. 1975b. *Federal Programs Supporting Educational Change. Vol. IV: The Findings in Review*. Santa Monica, CA: Rand.

Berman, Paul, and Milbrey McLaughlin. 1976. Implementation of educational innovation. *Educational Forum* 40(3): 345–370.

Berman, Paul, and Milbrey McLaughlin. 1977. *Federal Programs Supporting Educational Change. Vol. VII: Factors Affecting Implementation and Continuation*. Santa Monica, CA: Rand.

Berman, Paul, and Milbrey McLaughlin. 1978. *Federal Programs Supporting Educational Change. Vol. VIII: Implementing and Sustaining Innovations*. Santa Monica, CA: Rand.

Berman, Paul, and Milbrey McLaughlin. 1979. *An Exploratory Study of School District Adaptations*. Santa Monica, CA: Rand.

Bird, Tom. 1986. "Mutual adaptation and mutual accomplishment: Images of change in a field experiment." In *Rethinking School Improvement: Research, Craft and Concept*, edited by A. Lieberman. New York: Teachers College Press.

Bredo, Anneke E., and Eric R. Bredo. 1975. "Effects of Environment and Structure on the Process of Innovation." In *Managing Change in Educational Organizations: Sociological Perspectives, Strategies and Case Studies*, edited by J. Victor Baldridge and Terrence E. Deal, 449–466. Berkeley, CA: McCutchan.

Bussis, Anne, Edward Chittenden, and Marianne Amarel. 1976. *Beyond Surface Curriculum: An Interview Study of Teachers' Understandings*. Boulder, CO: Westview Press.

Caswell, Hollis L. 1946. *The American High School: Its Responsibility and Opportunity*. Eighth Yearbook of the John Dewey Society. New York: Harper & Brothers.

Caswell, Hollis L. 1950. *Curriculum Improvement in the Public Schools*. New York: Teachers College Press.

Chamberlin, David, E. S. Chamberlin, N. Drought, and W. Scott. 1942. *Adventures in American Education. Vol. IV: Did They Succeed in College?* New York: Harper & Brothers.

Charters, W. W., and Roland J. Pellegrin. 1972. Barriers to the innovation process: Four case studies of differential staffing. *Educational Administration Quarterly* 9(1):3–14.

Cochran-Smith, Marilyn, Jessica L. Kahn, and Cynthia L. Paris. 1990. *Making Connections: Teachers, Children, and Word Processing*. New York: Ables.

Cohen, Elizabeth G. 1981. "Sociology Looks at Team Teaching." In *Research in Sociology of Education and Socialization*, Vol. 2, edited by Alan C. Kerckhoff and Ronald G. Corwin, 163–193. Greenwich, CT: JAI Press.

Cohen, Michael. 1981. Effective schools: What the research says. *Today's Education* (April–May): 466–506.

Corwin, Ronald. 1973. *Reform and Organizational Survival—The Teacher Corps as an Instrument of Educational Change*. New York: Wiley.

Counts, George S. 1926. "Some Notes on the Foundations of Curriculum-Making." In *The Twenty-sixth Yearbook of the National Society for the Study of Education*, edited by Guy M. Whipple. Bloomington, IL: Public School Co.

Courtis, Stuart A. 1926. "Reading Between the Lines." In *The Twenty-sixth Yearbook of the National Society for the Study of Education*, edited by Guy M. Whipple. Bloomington, IL: Public School Co.

Cowden, Peter, and David K. Cohen. 1979. *Divergent Worlds of Practice*. Cambridge, MA: Huron Institute.

Crandall David. 1983. The teacher's role in school improvement. *Educational Leadership* 14(3): 4–9.

Crandall, David P. et al. 1983. *People, Policies and Practices: Examining the Chain of School Improvement*. Andover, MA: The Network.

Cremin, Lawrence. 1961. *The Transformation of the School: Progressivism in American Education, 1876–1957*. New York: Vintage Books.

Cutright, Prudence. 1945. "Practice in Curriculum Development." In *Forty-fourth Yearbook of the National Society for the Study of*

Education, Part I, Sec. IV, *Curriculum Reconstruction,* edited by Nelson B. Henry, 267–288. Chicago: University of Chicago Press.

Department of Superintendence. 1936. *The Social Studies Curriculum*. Fourteenth Yearbook. Washington, DC: National Education Association.

Doyle, Walter, and Gerald A. Ponder. 1978. The practicality ethic in teacher decision-making. *Interchange* 8(3): 1–12.

Edmonds, Ronald. 1979. Effective schools for the urban poor. *Educational Leadership* 37(1): 15–24.

Edmonds, Ronald. 1982. "Programs of School Improvement: A 1982 Overview." Paper prepared for Conference on Implications of Research on Teaching for Practice. Washington, DC: National Institute of Education.

Elmore, Richard. 1980. *Complexity and Control: What Legislators and Administrators Can Do About Implementing Public Policy*. Washington, DC: National Institute of Education.

Emrick, John A., and Sonya M. Peterson. 1978. *A Synthesis of Findings Across Five Recent Studies in Educational Dissemination and Change*. San Francisco, CA: Far West Laboratory.

Foshay, Arthur W. 1989. Hollis Caswell: The legacy. *Curriculum Studies Newsletter*. AERA: Division B and the George Washington University, 3–4.

Fullan, Michael. 1982a. *The Meaning of Educational Change*. New York: Teachers College Press.

Fullan, Michael. 1982b. *The Use of External Resources for School Improvement by Local Education Agencies.* San Francisco, CA: Far West Laboratory.

Fullan, Michael, Matthew B. Miles, and G. Taylor. 1980. Organizational development in schools: The state of the art. *Review of Educational Research* 50(1): 121–183.

Fullan, Michael, and Alan Pomfret. 1977. Research on curriculum and instruction implementation. *Review of Educational Research* 47(1): 335–397.

Fuller, Frances F. 1969. Concerns for teachers: A developmental conceptualization. *American Educational Research Journal* 6: 207–226.

Galanter, Wynne L. 1978. "Elementary School Staff Support System Effects on Program Implementation and Job Satisfaction." Unpublished Ph.D. dissertation, Fordham University, New York.

George, Archie A., and Shiveley M. Hord. 1980. *Monitoring Curriculum Implementation: Mapping Teacher Behaviors on a Configuration Continuum*. Austin: Research and Development Center for Teacher Education, University of Texas.

Giacquinta, Joseph B. 1973. "The Process of Organizational Change in Schools." In *Review of Research in Education*, edited by F. B. Kerlinger. Itasca, IL: Peacock.

Giles, H., S. McCutchen, and A. Zechiel. 1942. *Adventures in American Education. Vol II: Exploring the Curriculum*. New York: Harper & Brothers.

Gold, Barry A., and Matthew B. Miles. 1981. "Change and Conflict: Educational Innovation in Community Context." In *Designing and Starting Innovative Schools: A Field Study of Social Architecture in Education*, Part III, edited by Matthew B. Miles et al. New York: Center for Policy Research.

Goodlad, John I., and M. Frances Klein. 1970. *Behind the Classroom Door*. Worthington, OH: Charles A. Jones.

Gross, Nelson, Joseph Giacquinta, and Marilyn Bernstein. 1971. *Implementing Organizational Innovations: A Sociological Analysis of Planned Educational Change*. New York: Basic Books.

Hall, Gene, and Susan Loucks. 1976. *A Developmental Model for Determining Whether or Not the Treatment Really Is Implemented*. Austin: Research and Development Center for Teacher Education, University of Texas.

Hall, Gene, and Susan Loucks. 1977. A developmental model for determining whether the treatment is actually implemented. *American Educational Research Journal* 14(3): 263–276.

Hall, Gene, and Susan Loucks. 1978. Teacher concerns as a basis for facilitating and personalizing staff development. *Teachers College Record* 80(1): 35–53.

Hall, Gene, and Susan Loucks. 1981. Program definition and adaptation. *Journal of Research and Development in Education* 14(2): 46–58.

Hall, Gene, and Susan Loucks. 1982. "Bridging the Gap: Policy Research Rooted in Practice." In *Policy Making in Education, Eighty-first Yearbook of the National Society of the Study of Education*, Part I, edited by A. Lieberman and M. McLaughlin, 133–158. Chicago: University of Chicago Press.

Hall, Gene, R. C. Wallace, Jr., and W. A. Dossett. 1973. *A Developmental Conceptualization of the Adoption Process Within Educational Institutions*. Austin: Research and Development Center for Teacher Education, University of Texas.

Hall, Janie L., and Arthur J. Lewis. 1925. "The Denver Program." National Education Association. Addresses and Proceedings. Washington, DC: National Education Association.

Havelock, Ronald G. 1971. *Planning for Innovation*. Ann Arbor: Center for Research on Utilization of Scientific Knowledge, Institute for Social Research, University of Michigan.

Herriot, Richard E., and Neal Gross. 1979. *The Dynamics of Planned Educational Change: An Analysis of the Rural Experimental Schools Program*. Berkeley, CA: McCutchan.

Hodges, Walter, et. al. 1980. *Follow Through: Forces for Change in the Primary Schools*. Ypsilanti, MI: High Scope Press.

Hord, Shirley M., and S. Huling-Austin. 1986. Effective curriculum implementation: Some promising new insights. *The Elementary School Journal* 87(1): 96–115.

House, Ernest R. 1979. Technology versus craft: A ten year perspective on innovation. *Journal of Curriculum Studies* 11(1): 1–15.

Huberman, A. Michael. 1983. School improvement strategies that work: Some scenarios. *Educational Leadership* 41(3): 23–27.

Huberman, A. Michael, and Matthew B. Miles. 1984. *Innovation Up Close: How School Improvement Works*. New York: Plenum.

Huddle, Eugene. 1987. All that glitters isn't gold—Four steps to school improvement. *NASSP Bulletin* 71(499): 80–86.

Johnston, Charles H., Jesse H. Newlon, and Frank G. Pickell. 1922. *Junior-Senior High School Administration*. New York: Scribners.

Kirst, Michael. 1979. "Strengthening Federal-Local Relationships Supporting Educational Change." In *The Dynamics of Planned Educational Change*, edited by R. Herriot and N. Gross. Berkeley, CA: McCutchan.

Lambright, W. Henry, et al. 1980. *Educational Innovations as a Process of Coalition Building: A Study of Organizational Decision-Making*. Washington, DC: National Institute of Education.

Leinhardt, Gaea. 1974. "Evaluation of the Implementation of a Program of Adaptive Education at the Second Grade (1972–1973)." Paper presented at the meeting of the American Educational Research Association, Chicago.

Leithwood, Ken, et al. 1978. "An Empirical Investigation of Teachers' Curriculum Decision-Making Processes and Strategies used by Curriculum Managers to Influence Such Decision-Making." Unpublished report, Ontario Institute for Studies in Education.

Little, Judith. 1981. "The Power of Organizational Setting: School Norms and Staff Development." Paper adapted from final report to National Institute of Education, *School Success and Staff Development: The Role of Staff Development in Urban Desegregated Schools*. Washington, DC: National Institute of Education.

The Lou Chart. 1976. *Operational Definitions of Levels of Use of the Innovation*. Austin: Research and Development Center for Teacher Education, University of Texas.

Loucks, Susan. 1983. At last: Some good news from a study of school improvement. *Educational Leadership* 41(3): 4–5.

Louis, Karen. 1981. "External Agents and Knowledge Utilization: Dimensions for Analysis and Action." In *Improving Schools*, edited by R. Lehming, and M. Kane. Beverly Hills, CA: Sage.

Louis, Karen S., and Sheila Rosenblum. 1981. *Linking R and D with Schools: A Program and Its Implications for Dissemination*. Washington, DC: National Institute of Education.

Louis, Karen S., and Sam D. Sieber. 1979. *Bureaucracy and the Dispersed Organization—The Educational Extension Agent Experiment*. Norwood, NJ: Ablex.

McLaughlin, Milbrey. 1976. Implementation of ESEA Title I: A problem of compliance. *Teachers College Record* 80(1): 69–94.

Melle, Marge, and Harold Pratt. 1981. "Documenting Program Adoption in a District-Wide Implementation Effort: The Three Year Evolution to an Instructional Improvement Plan." Paper presented at American Educational Research Association, annual meeting, Los Angeles.

Miles, Matthew B. 1980. School innovation from the ground up: Some dilemmas. *New York University Educational Quarterly* 11(2): 2–9.

Miles, Matthew B., et al. 1978. *Project on Social Architecture in Education*. New York: Center for Policy Research.

Newlon, Jesse H. 1923. *Twentieth Annual Report of School District Number One in the City and County of Denver and State of Colorado*. Denver: Denver School Press.

Newlon, Jesse H. 1934. *School Administration as Social Policy*. New York: Scribners.

Paris, Cynthia. 1989. "Contexts of Curriculum Change: Conflict and Consonance." Paper presented at the American Educational Research Association, San Francisco, CA.

Parish, Ralph, and Frank Aquila. 1983. Comments on the school improvement study: The whole is more than the sum of parts. *Educational Leadership* 41(3): 34–36.

Popkewitz, Thomas S., B. Robert Tabachnick, and Gary Wehlage. 1981. *The Myth of Educational Reform: A Study of School Responses to a Program of Change*. Madison: University of Wisconsin Press.

Rivlin, Alice M., and P. Michael Timpane, eds. 1975. *Planned Variation in Education: Should We Give Up or Try Harder?* Washington, DC: Brookings Studies in Social Experimentation.

Robinson, Floyd G. 1982. "Superordinate Curriculum Guidelines as Guides to Local Curriculum Decision-Making." In *Studies in Curriculum Decision-Making*, edited by Kenneth A. Leithwood. Toronto: OISE Press.

Rosenblum, Sheila, and Karen Louis. 1979. *Stability and Change: Innovation in an Educational Context*. Cambridge, MA: ABT Associates.

Rugg, Harold. 1926. "Curriculum-Making: Points of Emphasis." In *Twenty-sixth Yearbook of the National Society for the Study of Education*, edited by Guy M. Whipple. Bloomington, IL: Public School Co.

Rugg, Harold, and George S. Counts. 1926. "A Critical Appraisal of Current Methods of Curriculum-Making." In *The Foundations and Technique of Curriculum-Construction*, Twenty-sixth Yearbook of the National Society for the Study of Education, Part I, edited by Harold Rugg. Bloomington, IL: Public School Co.

Rutter, Michael B., Barbara Maughan, Peter Mortimer, Janet Ouston, and Alan Smith. 1979. *Fifteen Thousand Hours: Secondary Schools and Their Effects on Children*. Cambridge, MA: Harvard University Press.

Sarason, Seymour. 1971. *The Culture of the School and the Problem of Change*. Boston: Allyn & Bacon.

Sarason, Seymour, and John Doris. 1979. *Educational Handicap, Public Policy, and Social History*. New York: Free Press.

Smith, Eugene, and Ralph W. Tyler. 1942. *Adventures in American Education. Vol. III: Appraising and Recording Student Progress*. New York: Harper & Brothers.

Smith, Louis, and Pat Keith. 1971. *Anatomy of an Educational Innovation: An Organizational Analysis of an Elementary School*. New York: Wiley.

Smith, Louis, et al. 1988. *Innovation and Change in Schooling: History, Politics and Agency*. Philadelphia, PA: Falmer.

Stallings, Jane. 1979. Follow through: A model for in-service teacher training. *Curriculum Inquiry* 9(2): 163–181.

Taba, Hilda. 1945. "Problems of Curriculum and Reconstruction." In *American Education in the Postwar Period*, Section II, Forty-fourth Yearbook of the National Society for the Study of Education, Part I, edited by Nelson B. Henry. Chicago: University of Chicago Press, 80–138.

Yin, Robert K., Karen Herald, and Mary Vogel. 1977. *Tinkering with the System*. Lexington, MA: Heath.

Zumwalt, Karen. 1989. "Beginning Professional Teacher: The Need for a Curricular Vision of Teaching." In *Knowledge Base for the Beginning Teacher*, edited by Maynard C. Reynold. Oxford, England: Pergamon.

16

TEXTBOOKS IN SCHOOL AND SOCIETY

Richard L. Venezky
UNIVERSITY OF DELAWARE

School textbooks occupy a highly visible position in American life, situated where the paths of education, society, and commercialism cross. As part of an educative process, textbooks have assumed an ambiguous and often protean role. Rousseau, as expressed in *Émile*, saw no need for textbooks in the ideal education, withholding all exposure to books, save *Robinson Crusoe*, until the late teens, when the classics were to be first presented. Dewey also opposed prepared curricular materials, at least for the early stages of a child's education. At the Laboratory School at the University of Chicago, Dewey's curriculum was to be based on fundamental occupations, the socioindustrial arts of mankind, as they developed historically (Dewey 1902). Cronbach (1955a) refers to textbooks as tools in teaching, implying that the curriculum is defined outside the text itself. In contrast, Apple (1988) sees the textbook as the statement of curriculum. "Whether we like it or not, the curriculum in most American schools is not defined by courses of study or suggested programs, but by one particular artifact, the grade-level-specific text . . ." (85).

The image of the teacher as subservient to the text, slavishly following each command and cue from front to back, is presented in some semipopular works on teaching materials (e.g., Black 1967). Studies on textbook adoption that cite percentages of teachers who teach from textbooks (e.g., EPIE 1977; Porter 1981; Shaver, Davis, and Helburn 1979; Weiss 1987) tend to reinforce these images, yet few (if any) of these studies investigated what teachers actually do with textbooks in their classrooms. Stodolsky (1989, 180) analyzed data from 6 fifth-grade math and 6 fifth-grade social studies classes and found "little evidence . . . to support the idea that teachers teach strictly by the book." She also found little in the research literature to support this view. Instead, teachers vary within and across subject areas in the degree to which they supplement and complement the textbook content, follow the given suggestions for extensions and enrichment, and use the suggested pedagogical approaches.

To many educators, textbooks have been a barrier to educational progress, a millstone around the neck of educational reform. Charles Eliot, president of Harvard from 1869 to 1909 and forceful chairman of the Committee of Ten, called the school readers of his day "ineffable trash" and insisted that only novels with great literary value be admitted into the reading classroom (Eliot 1969 [1898], 185). More recently, history textbooks have been condemned as dull and inattentive to real social problems (FitzGerald 1979), favoring the interests of the wealthy and powerful while distorting labor history and socioeconomic change (Anyon 1979). Science and mathematics textbooks have also been heavily criticized, although primarily for their scientific failings (e.g., Flanders 1987; Porter 1989; Staver and Bay 1987).

For the public, textbooks are the visible manifestation of the school's beliefs and intentions, an open script that can be scrutinized by different segments of society for evidence of cultural dissonance. Watchdog organizations, ranging from the reactionary Educational Research Analysts in Longview, Texas, to civil rights organizations like People for the American Way, publish regularly on the content of school textbooks and exhort their followers to play active roles in local textbook adoptions. But beneath the sensationalism of the major textbook censorship cases that have been adjudicated in recent years lies a complex set of views about the role that compulsory schooling plays in the lives of children and how particular values can be maintained in a world in which parental and group authority has been seriously eroded. Although the content of actual teaching is sometimes attacked, as in the Scopes case in the 1920s (de Camp 1969), the latent or hidden curriculum as expressed by textbooks is more frequently the target of those dissatisfied with the school program.

To understand these various viewpoints and to locate textbooks accurately in the educational, cultural, and commercial worlds in which they are immersed is the goal of this chapter. Since no field of textbook analysis exists and methods for analyzing textbooks are rarely mentioned in methodology texts, one goal here is to define the territory over which the study of school textbooks has roamed, particularly in this century, with some attention to the methods commonly deployed in this effort. A second goal is to trace the evolution of school textbooks from their earliest importation into the American colonies up to the present day, emphasizing particularly the complex interrelationship that has developed between the textbook industry and the educational system.

The plan of this chapter is to develop first an orientation and a framework for situating and analyzing textbooks and then to focus on four basic issues: (1) Why are textbooks so commonly used? (2) Who controls textbook content? (3) What constitutes the latent (or hidden) content of textbooks? and (4) How did textbooks develop into what they are today? My focus is American elementary and secondary textbooks, which hereafter will be referred to simply as textbooks unless ambiguity might result. Other forms of printed materials will receive occasional mention, in particular workbooks and teacher guides, but except for computer courseware, only textbooks will be thoroughly examined. What is not covered, among other topics, are issues related to textbook adoptions, Third World development and use of textbooks, and the entire field of textbook comprehension and textbook design.

A FRAMEWORK FOR TEXTBOOK STUDIES

A textbook exists both as a *cultural artifact* and as a *surrogate curriculum*. It exists in relationship to various antecedent textbooks through its *intertextuality*, and it possesses, through a variety of mechanisms, a *validation*. As a cultural artifact it represents a particular state of the printing craft and a particular mode of production. Within the domain of craft, paper, binding, typography, and design are all insignias of the book's production, each creating a particular status within the culture of printing. In the middle 19th century a leather-bound textbook would have occupied a higher status than one bound with oak boards, and the latter would have been preferred over paper or cardboard. (Lowest in rank would have been unbound signatures.) For primers of the same period, numbered pages stood above unnumbered pages, and woodcuts by a recognized engraver like Alexander Anderson stood above those done by an unrecognized artist.

Mode of Production

A textbook's mode of production, viewed in terms of Williams' (1980) base and superstructure model for culture and society, refers to the various social, cultural, and technical conditions that were active in the production of the book. To determine these requires an understanding of the procedures through which publishers develop textbooks; select authors, writers, designers, and editors; and bring books to the market. The regular educational forces that activate the school curricula provide a focus for studying the dynamics of textbook creation. For completeness we must add to this framework a fuller description of the extraneous (i.e., noneducational) forces that function in this process, plus a feedback loop that defines the role that textbooks already on the market play in modifying the school curriculum.

Assessing mode of production also requires an understanding of market forces: the nature of textbook adoptions, sales techniques, competition, and economics. Each of these influences the nature of textbooks—their physical, visual, and educative content. Mode of production must be examined both synchronically and diachronically. Methods for developing and marketing secondary textbooks differ from those for elementary textbooks, and together these modes of production are radically different from those of the early 19th century, when printer and publisher were identical and large, organized school systems did not exist.

Cultural Artifact

A textbook's status as a cultural artifact was often validated by its publisher alone. Thus a product from Isaiah Thomas' press at the end of the 18th century, or from Mathew Carey's or Samuel Wood's at the beginning of the 19th century, would have been held in higher esteem at those times than almost any others. Validation today is sometimes promoted through identification (usually within the colophon) of the book's typographic and production insignias. "This text was designed, set in Times New Roman, and illustrated by x. It was printed by y on Glatfelder Smooth Antique, an acid-free paper, and bound by z." (However, such statements would not be as common for a modern textbook as they would be for a children's book.)

Surrogate Curriculum

A textbook is also a surrogate curriculum, that is, a reflection of a sometimes undocumented curriculum that may also be only partially specified. A curriculum is an abstraction, an amalgamation of goals and aspirations. From a single set of curriculum guidelines an infinite number of textbooks could be built, each with its own interpretation of the intent of the guidelines. Amount of coverage for specific topics, difficulty level, language of explanation, and the like, could differ and yet each text still be true to the original blueprint. As a surrogate curriculum, a textbook contains a *manifest curriculum* (Bierstedt 1955), which is its subject content; a *latent* or *hidden curriculum*; and a *pedagogical apparatus*.

Manifest and Latent Curricula

The manifest curriculum is what is most evident, both in the table of contents and in the index, if one exists. It is also found in the difficulty level of the material presented, for example in what Tufte (1983) calls "graphical sophistication"; that is, the number of variables represented in statistical graphs. The latent curriculum, on the other hand, is a series of secondary messages, transmitted on top of the manifest curriculum through commission and omission. It is not intentionally defined in either the table of contents or the index but can sometimes be abstracted from these. A literature anthology that has 80 percent British authors and 20 percent American transmits one type of message about the center of the literary world, while an anthology that reverses this ratio sends a different message. A primary school reader that shows only white, middle-class children in neatly trimmed suburban settings provides a different latent curriculum from a reader with the same stories that mixes races, shows women in traditional male roles, and exhibits a cross-section of housing forms. And a science text that presents knowledge as permanent and definitive suggests a different type of authority from one that views knowledge as tentative and open to questioning.

The latent curriculum, in part, reflects the selective tradition of society (Williams 1980). It displays meanings and values of the effective dominant culture, its practices and expectations. These are equivalent to the shared set of expectations and interpretations that define, from an anthropological perspective, any given culture. In Williams' (1980, 38) terms, they define the "ordinary understanding of the nature of man and his world," but they should not be viewed as an imposition of the upper or ruling class; the sense of reality they define is operative for most of society. Furthermore, alternative opinions, attitudes, and meanings can be accommodated within this dynamic system.

The latent curriculum also has a specialized component, as reflected, for example, in particular views of the function of science education. Textbooks of the 1950s and 1960s presented a "neutral" view of science, detached from moral or ethical constraints (Lynch and Strube 1985). Modern science is presented within a more value-laden framework wherein technological components like nuclear energy and industrial waste can be potentially harmful and require at least consideration of control. A number of studies that will be discussed in later sections have focused on the latent curriculum in textbooks (e.g., Ahier 1988; Luke 1988).

Pedagogical Apparatus

The pedagogical apparatus of a textbook is reflected by its arrangement of topics, its presentation techniques, its cohesive elements (Calfee and Chambliss 1987), and overt didactic mechanisms: quizzes, practices, metaphors, diagrams, and teaching suggestions. For elementary-level textbooks, the teaching suggestions are often bound into a separate volume, complete with black-line masters for tests and extra practices. Some teaching suggestions are meant for the teacher, but at the secondary level many are directed to the student, offering suggestions for study techniques and self-evaluation.

Validation

The manifest curriculum and to a lesser degree the pedagogical apparatus of a text are validated through several mechanisms. The authors and their affiliations often can provide one level of validation and are frequently chosen in part for this purpose. The publisher can provide another level, while engravers and designers can provide yet another. Certain labels, like "2nd ed., revised" both situate the textbook in an intertextual network and at the same time attempt to validate it through implication of improvement and currency. Nineteenth-century textbooks often attempted to validate themselves through testimonials to their virtues, reproduced in the beginnings or endings of the texts. For example, in the 1847 copyright of William Russell's *Primary Reader*, Rev. Joseph Allen, chairman of the School Committee of Northborough, Massachusetts, declares his affections for the text with an eloquence unfamiliar to most modern writers.

> We were much struck with the beautiful spirit which pervades the series, especially the parts designed for younger classes; and cannot doubt that the introduction of the whole series into our schools, will tend to nourish in the minds of our children, the love of nature, kindness to animals, benevolence to man, and piety to God. (4)

Other texts informed their readers of the numbers of copies already sold or the various locations where school adoptions had been secured.

Intertextuality

The intertextuality of a textbook is its lineage, its derivation from and relationship to other texts, both written and oral. This is often difficult to trace, due in part to the failure of most publishers to identify all successive editions. A third reader in a basal reading series relates to all of the other texts in the series and to its corresponding teacher's guide, if one exists as a separate entity. Then, this particular imprint might be a corrected version, not identified as such, of an earlier edition that bears the same edition number and copyright. It might also relate to an identified earlier edition. Finally, derivational linkages exist, connecting, for example, colonial primers and spelling books to early national primers and first readers and contents of particular readers to contents of source volumes. Spieseke (1938), as an example, has traced the origins of almost all of the passages in America's first history book, showing that most were copied without attribution from other American texts.

The Curricular Chain

Since textbooks occupy one of the intersection points of education, commerce, and culture, no single framework can adequately encompass the different interpretive structures, research methodologies, and even language sets that exist for the study of this object. Instead, multiple frameworks are needed, with cross connections specified. To begin, I will outline a framework for the area of most immediate concern of this present volume—that is, the educative function as represented by the manifest curriculum. The goal here is not to establish new theoretical positions but to draw upon what is available to establish at least a semblance of order for an inchoate field, one that has yet to be codified in any meaningful manner.

Needed Curriculum. To accommodate variations in textbook use, it is necessary to move backwards a step or two and view textbooks within the total process of curriculum design. Drawing on several models proposed for the development of textbooks (e.g., Raizen and Jones 1985; Venezky 1989), we can define five curricula for any subject area: the needed curriculum, the desired curriculum, the prescribed curriculum, the delivered curriculum, and finally the received curriculum. The needed curriculum is very often an amorphous entity, consisting of the more valued suggestions from philosophers of the discipline, curriculum specialists, politicians, blue-ribbon panels, and content area authorities. Its statements often take the form "We need more of x in the curriculum . . .," or "American children are failing to learn y," but occasionally more codified directives are issued, as, for example, in the National Commission on Excellence in Education's (1983) eight "Recommendations." The dicta of these authorities are usually presented without concern for the operational issues of classroom implementation—for example, time, cost, teacher training. This curriculum is more an aspiration than a statement of what realistically might be accomplished, a set of general goals to guide the specification of more specific curricula. (See "Conceptions of Curriculum," this volume.)

Desired Curriculum. The *desired curriculum* is the first place where operational issues are considered, but the influence of these issues is still weak. This curriculum is represented by various state and school district guidelines and by the suggested curricula and guidelines of professional organizations like the National Society for the Teaching of Mathematics and the International Reading Association. Typical state guidelines in science, for example, specify topics to be covered at each grade level and occasionally indicate instructional emphasis, such as the amount of hands-on experience that is desired. A few state science guidelines are organized by broader science themes—for example, change, cycles, cause and effect—but most focus almost exclusively on science content.

Although desired curricula tend to be developed by curriculum specialists, they are not totally independent of influence from publishers and politicians, particularly in social studies and science. The inclusion of evolution in the biology curriculum and the treatment of capitalism or racial inequality in social studies are rarely left to academic considerations alone. In some cases, state statutes and educational mandates bear directly on curriculum guidelines. A Wisconsin law, adopted in 1923, forbade the use of any textbook "which falsifies the facts regarding the War of Independence, or the War of 1812, or which defames our nation's founders or misrepresents the ideals for which they struggled and sacrificed, or which contains propaganda favorable to any foreign government" (cited in Schlesinger 1938, xviii). More recently (in 1982), the Texas state board of education proclaimed that "textbook content shall promote citizenship and the understanding of the free enterprise system, emphasize patriotism and respect for recognized authority. . . . Textbook content shall not encourage lifestyles deviating from generally accepted standards of society" (*Time* 1982). Other states have instituted similar regulations, including restrictions on the languages in which textbooks can be written.

The desired curriculum is influenced both directly and indirectly by the needed curriculum. Direct influence is usually evidenced by direct reference to specific authorities who are (or were) responsible for elements of the needed curriculum or to specific doctrines, such as blue-ribbon panel recommendations. Indirect influence is, by definition, more subtle, deriving from professional and general cultural diffusion. At present, for example, considerable concern is being expressed about the ability of American children to think critically and engage in complex problem solving. A recent comparison of American 13 year-olds to students of the same age in other industrialized nations showed American students to be last in mathematics ability and in the bottom quarter for science ability (LaPointe, Mead, and Phillips 1989). Several proposed curricula, including the AAAS 2061 science curriculum (AAAS 1989), have made higher-level thinking skills a top priority, as have a number of state guidelines for math, science, and reading/literature.

Prescribed Curriculum. Next in the chain running from general to specific is the *prescribed curriculum*, which is the textbooks and other curricular materials that define or prescribe not only the content of courses but also the sequence of topics and quite often the pedagogical strategies to employ in teaching them. The influences on publishers that lead to the contents of each text are a matter of considerable concern and will be discussed below. Clearly, in a society dedicated to capitalism, economic issues play a major role in the production and marketing of textbooks. But other factors are also present, influencing not only what Bierstedt (1955) labeled the *manifest* curriculum (i.e., the curricular content) but also the *latent* or cultural functions of the textbook. This ***hidden curriculum*** has also been the subject of a vast and interesting literature and will be discussed more fully below.

Delivered and Received Curricula. What teachers deliver in the classroom, with or without textbooks, is the *delivered curriculum*, and what students acquire as a result of classroom activity, although difficult to measure accurately, is the *received curriculum*. The received curriculum differs from the prescribed curriculum not only because of the mediation of the delivered curriculum but also because of the active interpretation of the student, based upon prior knowledge and upon cultural tendencies. To what degree students are influenced by textbooks and by teachers has not been extensively investigated. Some criticisms of textbooks (e.g., Luke 1988) assume that even 6-year-olds are sensitive to subtle differences between story forms and can be influenced by story images. Others (e.g., Ahier 1988) have questioned the extent to which either textbooks or classroom instruction can influence thinking patterns and attitudes of children. These arguments are not new, however. Sullivan (1927), for example, in discussing the influence of the McGuffey Readers, cites opinion on both sides of the issue.

Closing the loop from received curriculum back to needed curriculum are two threads. One derives from well-publicized test results, such as the science and mathematics comparisons cited above, which reveal some ostensible failing in the abilities of American youth. The other is the more amorphous attitude, revealed most poignantly by the reaction to the launching of Sputnik, that almost any fault in American society is an indicator of failure or malfeasance in the educational system. Sputnik led to a massive overhaul of the science and mathematics curriculum, the results of which are still being analyzed, while most of the newer problems, such as drugs and AIDS, are leading to demands to insert new material in the curriculum.

Educational Research. Educational research floats through this framework like a vaporous cloud, unanchored to any particular level and driven by the winds of chance and caprice. Clifford (1973) could find little evidence that educational research had a direct impact on curriculum; instead, she posited a cultural diffusion route. Nonetheless, evidence for a more complex relationship between research and curriculum materials exists. First, the educational research and development laboratories, funded since the middle 1960s by the U.S. Office of Education and its successors, engaged in research and in the direct translation of this research into curriculum practice, including textbooks and other curriculum materials (e.g., Klausmeier, Rossmiller, and Saily 1977). Although the thoroughness and quality of this work could in many instances be questioned, the possibility of forcing a direct translation of research into practice was demonstrated and continues to be used in a variety of government-sponsored centers today.

Why the products of these centers failed to gain wide support within the schools has not been thoroughly explored. Most products that entered the schools did so through textbook publishers, who were allowed to bid for publication rights for those products deemed ready for wider distribution. Therefore, the answer cannot be that the publishers conspired to eliminate them from the market. Many of these programs required extra resources for classroom use that were not generally available to schools after field tests were concluded. Still others required extensive record keeping that teachers found distasteful or too time-consuming to justify. But even with these problems, it is difficult to ignore totally the mechanisms through which modern textbooks are marketed and the role of surface features and price incentives in their attractiveness to teachers and other educational decision makers.

Few textbooks are marketed today on the basis of their effectiveness. Multicolor art, voluminous support components, scripted teacher guides, and in-service training incentives occupy a significantly larger portion of textbook promotion than does any attention to tested outcomes of their use. Textbook publishing houses will give lip service to field testing, but few have even the semblance of departments committed to this activity, and rarely, if ever, are objective postpublication studies commissioned. That school districts and states don't require such testing is more remarkable, however, than the failure of publishers to provide it.

A second form of evidence for a direct route for research into practice is evidenced by a number of recent textbooks in reading and mathematics that have attempted to implement the results of studies on metacognition and problem solving (e.g., Schoenfeld 1985). Although the designation of which research to implement is highly selective and tied as much to fads as to convincingly tested ideas, the publishers have shown, nevertheless, the capability of reacting quickly to research findings. The political culture that leads to the selection of one result while ignoring another of equal validity remains to be examined. Singer (1970) has written about this issue in reading instruction through an examination of studies that he felt should have had an impact on instruction but which did not. That educators often use research to validate firmly held opinion is not a secret, but this does not explain totally the selection process, particularly for practices whose popularity rises and falls like dress hemlines.

Although the desired and the prescribed curricula genuflect to research, the needed curriculum is most closely tied to it, but not exclusively so because, in the end, authority determines which ideas will be legitimated. Educational research centers, under the requirement of dissemination, are as apt as commercial institutions to propagandize their results, often suggesting directly to textbook publishers what they should be doing. Publishers, therefore, must be aware of the centers of power in the fields in which they publish, and to co-opt them whenever possible.

Implications. One implication of this framework is that textbook content, while immediately specified by textbook publishers, is heavily influenced by other factors, including the *needed* and the *desired* curricula. Textbook publishers are rarely free to select on their own the content of a textbook, and the more capital required for entry into a particular textbook field, the less willing are the publishers to take risks on either content or methodology. In part this explains why publishers tend to avoid controversial content.

Since the second quarter of the 19th century when improvements in transportation and in printing technology allowed well-capitalized publishing houses to sell to a national market, publishers have tended to avoid, particularly for the elementary school market, material that would limit sales to any appreciable subsector of that market. Thus, in revising the McGuffey Readers, the various firms that held the copyrights to these texts carefully avoided any mention of Abraham Lincoln and any reference to the Civil War beyond a single, innocuous poem (Westerhoff 1978). Even after Lincoln's assassination, the McGuffey Readers eschewed the Gettysburg Address, the Second Inaugural Address, and all of the memorial pieces that derived from the Lincoln presidency. McGuffey's main competitor in the 1880s, the Appleton Readers, authored by a team of distinguished scholars including William Torrey Harris, a former commissioner of education, removed the Gettysburg Address from one of his readers for fear of losing southern business (Carpenter 1963).

As a consequence of the corporate approach to textbook development, the term "authorship" has suffered inflation. For some high school texts, authors are well identified and generally represent the main intellectual input to the texts, although editorial modification may still be large. Most elementary textbooks, in contrast, are productions of writing houses, graphic designers, and in-house editors, where the authors play more of an advisory role. Some might develop model lessons or even write a segment for a teacher's guide, but the overall design of the books and their content are more the result of in-house than author decisions. Furthermore, most of those who actually write the texts are not credited for their true contributions.

This marketing committee approach to textbook development has produced a writing style that Barzun (1945) characterized as the "impersonal voice." "The Truth drones on with the muffled sound of one who is indeed speaking from a well" (66). Margolis (1965), in lamenting the rise of the author-team over the writer, saw textbooks not as *written* but *assembled*. Within this development process, the authors' names are as much a part of the sales promotion as are the posters, brochures, and flyers and are chosen to reflect a desired image.

Perhaps most telling of this situation is that when elementary textbooks are attacked for offending some group's sensibilities or political views, almost invariably the publishers are named as the culprits. Rarely is an author of an elementary text held responsible for its contents. The net result is that responsibility also becomes elusive. The publishers, as corporate entities, are not identical to authors. They claim to respond primarily to the needs of the schools so that whatever is contained in the books, or withheld, is a result of decisions made in the educational community, not in the publishing houses (Reid 1969).

In the 18th and 19th centuries, almost all readers were authored by a single individual or by at most two persons. A small number of series toward the end of the 19th century featured three authors (e.g., the Appleton readers, authored by William Torrey Harris, Andrew Rickoff, and Mark Bailey), but generally one of these authors was included for a speciality such as elocution or rhetoric. In the 1930s contributing authors were added to the title pages. By the 1950s up to four authors was not uncommon, but a major shift occurred in the 1970s when the total number of main authors, book authors, and instructional consultants could number up to eight (Woodward 1986). The Silver Burdett and Ginn reading series, copyrighted in 1989, lists eight main authors and two consulting authors.

A second implication of this framework is that what the student acquires from the textbook is mediated by the teacher, even though the student interacts directly with the text. By deciding how long to spend on specific subjects; by selecting, rejecting, and supplementing textbook material; and by presenting attitudes toward the text materials, teachers help frame student responses to textbooks. The manner in which the teacher helps to shape the student-textbook interaction is no different from the way some writers of fiction attempt to shape reader-text interactions or the way publishers of novels deal with this same relationship. Almost no research has been done on how student-textbook interactions are controlled, but the work done on reader interaction with fiction provides provisioning for such explorations (e.g., Davidson 1989; O'Brien 1989). Tests, whether teacher made or externally derived, also help shape student responses by suggesting what is most important to acquire from a text.

THE VALUE OF TEXTBOOKS

Three major attempts have been made in this century to explore the general nature of textbooks and their use. The first was the Thirtieth Yearbook of the National Society for the Study of Education, which chose to focus exclusively on the preparation and selection of textbooks (Whipple 1931). In this collection a handful of prominent American educators, including such senior figures as J. B. Edmonson of the University of Michigan, William C. Bagley of Teachers College, and Guy T. Buswell of the University of Chicago, stumbled over each other in a rush to glorify the American textbooks and their publishers. The costs of texts were found to be negligible compared with the total cost of public education, and higher costs were declared "fully warranted where necessary to secure better instructional material for pupils" (306f).

Opposition was expressed by the Society's Yearbook Committee on the Textbook to any barriers erected by states or local school districts to the rights of publishers to market textbooks as they wished; standards of practice within the industry for selection and marketing of textbooks were judged to be "at least as high as those prevailing in other businesses" (220); and the "critical trial of instructional materials in classrooms before publication in textbook form" was commended (307). The Committee remained totally silent on any issues related to textbook content, declaring that "too much praise cannot be given to the reputable publishers of the United States for the meticulous care with which manuscripts are examined and with which errors in form and content are detected and corrected" (308). In an era in which textbooks were openly sexist and racist (Zimet 1972), where immigrants from vast areas of Europe were portrayed as ignorant and unwashed (Saveth 1949), where state censorship of textbooks was increasing, and where topics like evolution were rarely treated in science texts, these were remarkable statements from educational researchers, almost all of whom, however, had vested interests in the health and well-being of the textbook industry.

A second and far more successful effort began at the University of Illinois as the Text Materials Study under the leadership of Lee Cronbach and resulted in an exceptionally insightful monograph, *Text Materials in Modern Society* (Cronbach 1955b). In explaining the goals and work plan of the Text Materials Study, Cronbach wrote,

> Very little research has examined the contribution of text materials; this work has been scattered, inconclusive, and often trivial. Philosophical study of texts has led to equally insubstantial results. . . . We have today no comprehensive modern view of what texts should try to do, what limitations they have, and how they might contribute more in school. (4)

We still have "no comprehensive modern view of what texts should try to do," but we do have a new body of work that reflects a deeper probing of the messages of textbooks and that relates the analysis of textbooks to studies of other aspects of schooling and society. Although these studies remain scattered and without a sense of central goals and paradigms, they indicate a maturing field that may be ready soon to assume a regular place in the study of education.

Equal in quality and significance to the University of Illinois study is the most recent yearbook of the National Society for the Study of Education, *Textbooks and Schooling in the United States* (Elliott and Woodward 1990). With contributions from researchers, educators, and representatives of the publishing industry, the 13 chapters of this collection probe a variety of issues related to textbooks and their usage, including who controls the contents of American textbooks. Of particular significance are the chapter by Caroline Cody on the politics of textbook publishing, adoption, and use, which explores the methods through which various groups in society have attempted in recent years to gain control of the school curriculum, and the chapter by David Elliott and Arthur Woodward that, among other topics, discusses how states and the federal government have attempted to influence textbook content.

Teacher Needs

Nevertheless, no clear consensus can be gained from existing studies on why textbooks are so popular in the classroom. Perhaps the answer is too logical to require articulation. Teachers, especially those at the elementary level, are trained to use textbooks rather than to develop their own curricula. Courses on instructional design are not particularly common in preservice training for elementary or secondary-level teachers, nor would a single course on this topic suffice for the design needs of the lower elementary grades. An elementary teacher in a self-contained classroom must teach reading, language arts (i.e., penmanship, spelling, grammar, writing, reference skills), mathematics, science, social studies, health education, and occasionally music, art, physical education, career awareness, environmental education, and human relations (Eisner 1987). Therefore, teachers choose to use textbooks (and workbooks and teacher guides) out of practical necessity rather than by compulsion of administrators, as suggested by Shannon (1982).

Even if teachers would be willing and able to design instruction across any or all of these topics, they would have to do so on their own time because their jobs are not structured to allow curriculum development. Few elementary teachers have free periods during the day that could be devoted to such work, and no supports are provided by the schools. In the average school there is neither space, nor sufficient reference and background materials, nor clerical and secretarial support for curriculum development. Conceivably, summer salary could be provided for talented teachers to develop new instructional materials, but such funds are not generally available, nor is it obvious that the provision of such funds would radically improve instruction.

Textbooks provide a limited content expertise for a topic, plus a logical sequencing and a variety of pedagogical supports: activities, questions, test items, and sometimes summaries of expected student difficulties and misconceptions. They may help make the curriculum content oriented and comprehensive while allowing more effective use of teacher time than might occur on the average without them (Westbury 1990). In Third World countries, textbooks are significantly more important and are often the only books that students encounter in their studies. In addition, they often show national policy and national will (Altbach 1987).

Textbooks and Knowledge

A textbook is considered to be a standard work, an instruction manual for a particular subject. This implies selectivity or gatekeeping for its content, but also sequencing and presentation. The role of a textbook in mediating knowledge differs by subject matter. Kuhn (1970) has offered a three-way classification of knowledge-text relationships, meant primarily for university-level teaching, but equally applicable to high school texts and partially applicable to elementary texts. For the graphic arts, music, and literature, textbooks assume a secondary role. Students generally interact directly with the artists' works, whether they be objects, musical works, or prose and poetry. Other print materials might be used, such as handbooks, but textbooks do not intercede between students and the primary objects of study.

In contrast, history, philosophy, and the social sciences are typically taught with textbooks, but with parallel readings in the original sources: the Declaration of Independence, Thomas Paine's *Common Sense*, an original article by Thorndike or Skinner, Rousseau on education, and so on. Finally, the natural sciences tend to use textbooks exclusively, at least through undergraduate work. "Why, after all, should the student of physics, for example, read the works of Newton, Faraday, Einstein, or Schrodinger, when everything he needs to know about these works is recapitulated in a far briefer, more precise, and systematic form in a number of up-to-date textbooks?" (Kuhn 1970, 165). Unfortunately, when a scientific community repudiates a past paradigm, it tends also to repudiate all of the texts and articles that are based upon that paradigm, thus distorting the discipline's past. Kuhn notes, not without some wit, that we have no equivalent of the art museum for literature, science, mathematics, and the like.

McMurray and Cronbach (1955) place primary emphasis on the knowledge transmission role of textbooks. They derived a four-way classification of textbook knowledge content, based upon types of verbal knowledge: narration and description, prescription and directive, generalization, and theory. "What determines the potential educative value of materials is the subordination, coordination, or superordination of one type with respect to the other" (58). They see the textmaker as a gatekeeper, regulating which knowledge gets through to the classroom, and optimistically portray this function as potentially useful for social reform. Apple (1988) also sees the knowledge provision role of textbooks as liberatory in part, but points out that textbooks often function as part of a system of social control.

CONTROL OF TEXTBOOK CONTENT

According to the model presented above, a textbook results from a sequence of decisions made from within and without the links represented by the needed, desired, and prescribed curricula. However, not all actors within this system have equal billing. Educational psychologists, philosophers of science, and content area specialists, as groups, perform at a great distance from the actual production of textbooks, influencing mainly the needed curriculum. Schools, although the primary users of textbooks and therefore the most important clients of the publishers, have no organized voice in promoting their educational needs. Because of lay control of school boards and widely varying textbook adoption practices, educational consensus on textbook quality is nearly impossible to obtain. The academic research community, furthermore, has failed to assist schools in deriving effective textbook analysis criteria (Westbury 1990).

Teachers are generally considered to have little direct influence over any of the various curricula in the model presented above. They are often represented on textbook selection committees, and sometimes on district and state curriculum guideline committees, and may, by contributing to the selection of a particular text or series, cause the unsuccessful suppliers to reconsider this or that feature of their wares. But other than through procedures that publishers sometimes institute to try out materials under development, teachers have no organized communication channels for expressing their instructional needs or wants.

In theory they could indirectly influence the desired curriculum through their effectiveness, or lack thereof, in teaching a particular topic, but relationships between textbooks and achievement are modulated by a variety of factors, many of which are difficult to measure accurately (e.g., teacher competence, out-of-school assistance). Furthermore, neither publishers nor school officials have ever shown an enduring interest in establishing such relationships. Thus, a loosely coupled system exists across the various curricula, with few mechanisms for evaluation.

What allows this state of affairs to exist is the lack of a national agency that regulates curricula and textbooks. American education is founded upon the principle of local control of schools and lay control of what is taught in the classroom (Cody 1990). Without a national consensus on educational goals and values, and with relatively weak expression of state goals and values, publishers, national social action organizations, and local parent groups are left with considerably more influence over curriculum and textbooks than they have in most other countries. Textbook editors may be more important than educational psychologists in influencing educational trends (Broudy 1975; Schramm 1955).

The federal government has at various points attempted to influence the curriculum, and therefore the textbooks, but generally without notable success. In the 1960s and early 1970s the principal avenue of federal involvement was through the funding of curriculum reform projects. PSSC Physics, BSCS Biology, CHemStudy, and several elementary kit-based programs (e.g., SCIS, S-APA,ESS) were produced during this era with federal funding and tried out in the schools. Most of these were influenced by the Woods Hole Conference of 1959, which strongly emphasized the need to introduce inquiry methods into the school curriculum (Bruner 1960). But in spite of generous funding and considerable fanfare, none of these programs achieved widespread adoption. Part of this failure was due to implementation difficulties and unrealistic user expectations (Marker 1980) or to neglect of teacher training (Elliott 1990).

But part of the failure may have derived from the radical shift that most, if not all, of these programs required in teacher-student relationships. Inquiry and hands-on discovery, which were central to the pedagogical approaches of the new programs, require encouragement of questioning, doubting, and testing of both text and teacher. For teachers who are experienced mainly in imparting facts and acting as authoritative sources of knowledge, this shift in roles is difficult. Many may have adopted the materials without changing teaching methods, thus negating the primary emphasis of the programs.

A second approach to federal influence over textbooks was demonstrated in the 1980s by Secretary of Education William Bennett, who, through direct funding of selected "research" on textbook content and through a "bully pulpit," attempted to impress his own ideas for curriculum on schools and publishers. Bennett's focus was on "excellence," which in the 1980s had come to imply a classical view of education, with explicit teaching of American values, traditional Western literature, and a heavy emphasis on American history (Cody 1990). How successful this effort was remains to be explored, but several of the mechanisms fostered by Bennett for his reforms remain in place and may yet achieve some of their goals.

Another actor in the curriculum chain is the states, who exert influence through their curriculum guidelines and through state-wide textbook adoption (which 23 states now require). In the past states have not taken an activist role in textbook development other than through limited attempts in the late 19th and early 20th centuries at state-developed textbooks. But in the 1980s the California Department of Education announced its intention to force major revisions in textbooks used within the state. Given the size of the textbook market in California, the possibility of this endeavor succeeding appeared to be large. Nevertheless, after three major adoptions (science, mathematics, reading), no revolution has occurred. The group that framed the state curriculum guidelines opted for tougher standards and new instructional approaches, not all of which were supported by empirical evidence. The textbook selection committees, in contrast, opted for fairly standard instructional fare (Woodward and Elliott 1990).

Almost by default, the primary influence over textbook content has been left to two groups: the publishers and society, as represented both by broad social movements and by special interest groups that act directly upon the schools and publishers. How these groups influence textbook content is the concern of the following sections.

Publishers

To the commercial sector, textbooks are a marketable commodity, grossing nearly $2 billion a year (Squire and Morgan 1990). With nearly 95 percent of classroom instruction in grades K–8 and 90 percent of homework time derived from printed materials (EPIE 1977), textbooks dominate the school day. Dewey (1976 [1901], 276) saw the textbook publishers as manipulators of the curriculum.

> Publishing companies affect not only the textbook and apparatus, the garb with which the curriculum clothes itself, but also and that directly the course of study itself. New studies are introduced because some publishing firm by a happy coincidence, has exactly the books which are needed to make that study successful. Old studies which should be entirely displaced . . . are retained because there is a vested interest behind them.

Curti (1978 [1935]) generally held that business's influence on education was indirect, resting upon a large overlap of interests and views with educators. "Educators accepted, in general, the business man's outlook and consciously or unconsciously molded the school system to accord with the canons of a profit-making economic system" (230). However, Curti also agreed with Dewey that business influenced the curriculum directly through textbooks, particularly in the introduction of new subjects or the retention of outdated ones. More recently, Goodlad (1979) has expressed an even stronger view.

> In fact, it is fair to say that the ends and means of curricula frequently are determined by publishers and not by the elected representatives of the people, although the process is a cyclical one, with the identification of who is influencing whom being exceedingly difficult. (34)

Due to a lack of empirical data on the development and marketing of textbooks, little is known about the decision-making procedures of the major textbook publishers. Some personal accounts of textbook publishing have been produced by retired executives of the industry (e.g., Exman 1967; Reid 1969), along with a few uncritical sketches of textbook publishers (e.g., Livengood 1953; Pulsifer 1921), and older, uncritical material on the textbook industry (e.g., Henry 1931; Jensen 1931a; see Buswell 1931 for a bibliography of material published prior to 1930). Recent speculative work on the publishing industry also exists (e.g., Apple 1988; Luke 1988), as does material on textbook adoptions (Jensen 1931b; Judd 1936; Squire 1985; Tully and Farr 1985; Weeks 1900), but legitimate information on the processes of modern textbook making and selling are exceedingly rare. It is striking how little has been revealed by the publishing companies about textbook development (one exception is Young 1990.) For example, we have no case studies on the design of new textbook series that would allow insights into the origins of textbook innovations or the decision-making processes that lead to the retention or rejection of specific content or design. DelFattore (1986) points out that publishers, under pressure from citizens groups, removed specific stories from high school literature anthologies (e.g., Shirley Jackson's "The Lottery") in the 1980s, yet we have no accounts of the discussions and debates within the industry that led to these decisions.

Another issue of vital concern for present-day schooling is the difficulty level of textbooks. Have they, as claimed by some, been "dumbed down" (e.g., Ravitch 1985), or is this conclusion an artifact of particular analysis methods? Should the difficulty level of a text be determined strictly from the text itself, or is the manner in which the text is used also a factor? The publishers have been singularly quiet about this issue, although they clearly are in a position to contribute to an understanding of how difficulty levels for textbooks are controlled. Most attempts to assess difficulty levels for textbooks have depended upon readability measures (e.g., Chall 1977); however, whatever utility these may have does not extend beyond narrative fiction. The complexity of a science text, for example, depends not just on its reading level but also on its vocabulary load, its conceptional structure, its organizational and rhetorical structures, and the quality of its explanations (Chambliss and Calfee in press; Raizen and Jones 1985; Strube 1989).

Textbook publishers claim to be market driven, yet little is known about the processes implied by this phrase beyond the assumption of focus groups, teacher surveys, and the like. Authors, as will be discussed below, are carefully chosen by elementary textbook publishers, both for their potential contributions to the eventual product and for the image they represent to the educational market. Once again, however, almost nothing on this topic has been published. The commercial framework for studying textbooks, that is, the modes of production, is mostly a series of placeholders, a recognition of the importance of the modern production and marketing of textbooks, but not much else. In contrast, a considerable amount has been found on the production of specific textbooks from the late 18th and middle 19th centuries (e.g., Monaghan 1983; Westerhoff 1978) and on the history of the trade up to the present time (Tebbel 1972–1981).

Publishers may be America's only national agency for curriculum development, but may also lack the capability and authority for this task (Westbury 1990). Without defined curricular leadership from the educational community, publishers lead by following, tracking market trends rather than devoting their resources to improving the quality of their materials. Lacking protection for textbook *ideas*, publishers have negative incentives for producing radically different texts from their competition. A high capital investment for most textbooks, coupled with a short product cycle and seemingly superficial criteria for adoption, further discourage major innovation.

Society

Social control of textbook content derives from two different mechanisms. First is the selective tradition of modern society, the superstructure of Williams' (1980) base and superstructure model. This tradition, manifest particularly in the latent curriculum, determines which meanings and practices will dominate in a society, which will be ignored, and which will be reinterpreted. Sex roles as reflected in reading textbooks exemplify this selective process. Prior to 1776, female characters were seldom portrayed in textbooks for children, mainly because boys, more so than girls, were sent to school or given academic training at home beyond introductory reading (Monaghan 1989; Zimet 1972). After the Revolution more girls were sent to school, and in time more females appeared in the textbooks.

In post–World War II America, as well as in Canada and England, sex-role stereotyping was common in textbooks, particularly readers, reflecting sex-role stereotyping in the societies involved (Lorimer and Long 1979–1980; Shirreffs 1975; Trecker 1971). As women's roles in the home, workplace, and society in general have moved closer to parity with men, textbook images of both women and men have changed accordingly (Bordelon 1985; Hahn and Blankenship 1981).

Throughout American history, textbooks have reflected mainstream, conservative interests. In part, this is to state that the means for producing and consuming textbooks have been in the hands of these sectors of society. Publishing has been an entrepreneurial activity since its inception; capitalism itself is sometimes traced to Benjamin Franklin's printshop and to its defining aphorism, "A penny saved is a penny earned." The common school system was promoted by upper-class Protestants who, according to Curti (1978 [1935]), were willing to promote the interests of the business class in return for their support. Christianity, as defined by Protestant precepts, and schooling were nearly synonymous almost to the Civil War. There were daily Bible readings in many schools, and textbooks were openly hostile to Catholics, Jews, and other religious minorities. This tradition dates at least to the beginning of the early national period (1783–1837), when Jedidiah Morse portrayed the Catholic inhabitants of Spain and Portugal as inferior to the denizens of Protestant Europe.

In the first half of this century this attitude was revealed most strongly in the treatment of immigrants in history texts. A typical textbook from the 1920s declares,

> Immigrants that came from the Northern countries of Europe are of a class that make good citizens. . . . But since the War of Succession most of the immigrants coming to this country have been from the lower classes of Eastern and Southern Europe, and they give much trouble. They are for the most part very ignorant. . . . They have no respect for law or government. In fact, many of them would like to see the government of the United States destroyed. (Waddy Thompson, *The First Book in United States History*; cited in Saveth 1949, 494f)

During the 1920s and 1930s racial and ethnic bias became respectable in the United States. Organizations like the Ku Klux Klan, the Daughters of the American Revolution, and the American Legion and individuals like Father Coughlin, Lothrop Stoddard, and Henry Ford all contributed, openly or more subtly, to American bigotry. The Great Depression and Hitler were further encouragements for this bigotry, which found expression in textbooks as outright hostility to blacks and Chinese and more subtle bias against Jews and, occasionally, Catholics (Saveth 1949).

Bierstedt (1955) notes that racial bias appears in textbooks in a number of forms, including language, stereotypes, and in the exclusion by schools of texts authored by individuals whose names are ethnically undesirable. It also appears negatively when textbook authors refuse to take a moral stand on such issues as segregation and other forms of discrimination. Similarly, Banks (1969), in analyzing discrimination toward blacks in a sample of 36 American history textbooks for grades 4–8, found that authors depicted racial violence as frequently as they did peaceful relations among races. The sufferings of American blacks under slavery and as a result of more recent segregation and discrimination were rarely discussed, and the masses in general were ignored in favor of a few selected black heroes. Discrimination was discussed without explaining or condemning it. Similar results are reported by FitzGerald (1979) for a wide range of American history textbooks. More extreme cases can be found in the South prior to desegregation, as in

Mississippi where the state Senate Education Committee "recommended that the civics texts provided for Negro schools contain no references to voting, elections, civic responsibility, or democracy" (cited in Bierstedt 1955, 112).

History texts in particular have been singled out as a reflection of majority control. Anyon (1979) analyzed 17 secondary school U.S. history texts and found the majority of the texts examined to be generally unsympathetic to the labor movement. Fourteen of the 17 texts mentioned the same three strikes, all major setbacks for the labor movement. The conditions of workers not represented by unions were ignored, and no attempt was made to promote a working-class identity. Inherent in this evaluation are a number of value judgments that would not be shared universally; nevertheless, the general results are supported by the work of others (e.g., FitzGerald 1979).

History texts have also been criticized for their extreme nationalism (American Council on Education 1949; Bagley and Rugg 1916; Bierstedt 1955; Walworth 1938), for their "drum and trumpet" school of history (Walworth 1938), and for their failure to apportion blame for any problems this country faces. "There are no polluters: there is only the pollution which we are all struggling against. And what I call the natural disaster theory of history" (FitzGerald 1979, 55). More recently, a panel selected by the People for the American Way to examine current U.S. history texts noted an improvement in objectivity.

> We happily note a reversal of an apparent trend to water down school history. . . . The United States of America is presented in a positive light by all of the textbooks studied. At the same time, these books do not tend to obscure recognizable blemishes on the story of our nation's continuing progress. (Davis, Ponder, Burlbaw, Garza-Lubeck, and Moss 1986, 9)

The second means of social control is represented by citizens' action groups and other socially based organizations that act within the curriculum chain to influence textbook content or more directly on schools to influence textbook use. Whether these are local groups or nationally based organizations like the Heritage Foundation, their effectiveness derives from the inherent vulnerability of schools and their openness to outside pressures (Sieber 1968). Although the role of such agencies is most often labeled censorship, they need to be seen in a wider context of power and control within the American social system. Within the context of textbooks and schooling, two different types of control are involved. In the first, exemplified by the plaintiffs in *Mozert v. Hawkins County Public Schools*, control is desired only over one's own. The parents who brought suit in 1983 in Greeneville, Tennessee, against the public schools asked only that their children not be required to read certain objectionable passages from the reading series that the schools were using at the elementary level. These passages concerned evolution, futurism, supernaturalism, magic, values clarification, and other topics the parents claimed conflicted with their religious beliefs. While objecting to the exposure of their own children to these materials, they did not sue to restrain others from reading them.

Similar positions have been taken by other groups throughout American history. At the beginning of the 19th century, for example, Quakers began to produce their own textbooks, particularly for reading instruction, because they objected to the inclusion of fiction, fairy tales, references to war, and certain other matters in the prevailing texts of the day. The Society of Friends started their own schools where they could afford to do so and used their own textbooks (Frost 1973). Similarly, the South, beginning in the 1850s, started to produce its own textbooks in reaction to northern-produced texts that expressed opposition to slavery. Although the particular reason advanced for desiring regional texts was objectionable, the right of the South to produce its own schoolbooks was no different from that claimed by the West, which expressed its individual interests through the early editions of the McGuffey Readers.

These separatist intentions, nevertheless, still exert an influence beyond the immediate context of their expression. In the Hawkins County case, although the U.S. Court of Appeals for the Sixth Circuit ruled against the plaintiffs, declaring that the school context does not involve "the critical element of compulsion to affirm or deny a religious belief," the publisher of the readers still chose to revise its series shortly afterwards to reduce its "humanistic" appearance (DelFattore 1986). Economic power is also censorship power, as demonstrated year after year by the textbook adoption policies of Texas and California. No textbook publisher is required to do what these states want, but not to do so is to foreclose on a significant portion of the American textbook market.

One approach to understanding these conflicts has been to view them as part of an effort to maintain social control in the face of cultural change. To the parents in Kanawha County, West Virginia, who in the middle 1970s fought successfully to keep humanism, socialism, and other threats to their beliefs out of the schools, most nationally produced textbooks represented an alien and frightful society from which they hoped to protect their children (Moffett 1988). But the net effect of such actions, once magnified in the media and threatened against other school systems by overzealous organizations, is control over textbooks and therefore over the content of schooling. It is important, nevertheless, to try to understand the motives and actions of these organizations and ad hoc collectives within the framework of their own (legitimate) beliefs (Carper and Weston 1990).

The second form of control is overt and is expressed by individual reformers or by such organizations as Norma and Mel Gabler's Educational Research Analysts, which lobbies throughout the United States against the inclusion in textbooks of a wide range of expressions that they oppose: profanity, sexual references, nonstandard English, women in nondomestic roles, socialism, criticism of the United States or its founders, criticism of religion, and more (DelFattore 1986). From the late 1940s until the early 1970s most individual school reform efforts ignored textbooks. The popular reform tracts of the 1940s and 1950s—Mortimer Smith's *And Madly Teach: A Layman Looks at Public School Education*, published in 1949; Arthur Bestor's *Educational Wastelands*, published in 1953; and Hyman Rickover's *Education and Freedom*, published in 1959—make almost no mention of textbooks, reserving their ammunition for the more visible markers of progressive education. Even the first edition of Rudolf Flesch's *Why Johnny Can't Read*, published in 1955, was tolerant of the prevailing reading textbooks. (It wasn't until the second edition that Flesch attacked what he called "the dirty dozen" for failing to give sufficient emphasis to phonics.)

In contrast, textbook attacks, at least until the 1970s, were generally devoid of any educational reform agenda. Particular texts were singled out, usually for a perceived (or real) deviation from some social or political norm. The attacks in the 1930s and 1940s against Harold Rugg's social studies texts were among the first of the national campaigns mounted by any group in this country outside of the educational community to influence textbook use. Rugg was a faculty member at Teachers College in the 1920s when he began a systematic analysis of the problems facing American society and the concepts that students in grades 3 through 12 held about these problems. A member of the Progressive Education Association and a social meliorist, Rugg favored a unified social studies curriculum constructed on social justice and social worth (Kleibard and Wegner 1987).

In the middle 1920s he signed a contract with Ginn & Company for a social studies series that was to be developed from his survey and assessment work. From the time that the first volume of *Man and His Changing Society* was published (1929) until 1939, 1,317,960 copies of the various texts were sold, along with 2,687,000 workbooks (Kliebard 1986). The series was one of the first to treat such topics as the slave trade, urban blight, and poverty with candor, but its restrained treatment of the free enterprise system was what fired the National Association of Manufacturers and the Hearst newspaper chain into national campaigns of opposition. Primarily through the efforts of these groups, the series was driven out of the schools by the early 1940s (Tanner 1988). Rugg's defense of the series in 1941 came too late and was read by too few to overcome the damage that already had been done (Rugg 1941).

At about the time that the battle over Rugg's program was concluding, conservative and right wing groups in America shifted their attention to a supplementary social studies series developed by the Society for Curriculum Study. *Building America* was an attempt by a group of leading educators during the depression to examine openly contemporary socioeconomic problems. Under the direction of the late Paul Hanna and with funding supplied primarily by the editorial board itself, 91 theme-based paperbacks were issued between 1935 and 1948. The texts were accused of being un-American, and the board members were attacked for being either Communist fronts or fooled by Communists (Tanner 1988). By the late 1940s the texts were forced out of most schools and the series discontinued publication. Like the Rugg case, no broad reform agenda was advocated by the textbook opponents; instead, their primary objective was to maintain the status quo.

A second battleground in the social control power struggle has been biology textbooks, especially in relation to evolution. At the end of *Descent of Man and Selection in Relation to Sex*, Darwin (1930 [1871], 633) stated "The main conclusion arrived at in this work, namely that man is descended from some lowly organized form, will, I regret to think, be highly distasteful to many." Just why it has been more distasteful to the conservative denizens of North America than it has to any others is not of immediate importance. But its importance to textbook publishing is difficult to ignore. Prior to 1920 little attention was given to evolution in high school biology texts and prior to 1959 the term "evolution" rarely appeared (Skoog 1979). A general biology text in 1895 was apparently the first school textbook to mention evolution, but several biology texts at the beginning of the 20th century totally excluded the topic (Rosenthal and Bybee 1987). (Human genetics also received disinterested treatment in high school biology texts in the first half of the 20th century.) Skoog (1979, 1984) reports that of eight texts commonly used from the period 1900 to 1919, only three had chapters on evolution, and of these, one did not mention the word "evolution," and one mentioned it only once. During the 1920s a number of authors strongly supported the teaching of evolution, but it was also during the 1920s that the first major reactions to its teaching in the schools occurred. In 1920 Oklahoma outlawed the use of textbooks that taught evolution, and a few years later Tennessee barred the teaching of evolution, whether from a textbook or any other source.

The Scopes trial, held in Dayton, Tennessee, in 1925, involved a high school teacher, John Thomas Scopes, who agreed to test the validity of the state law banning evolution from the schools. Besides bringing an all-star cast of legal aids to Dayton, including Clarence Darrow, Arthur Garfield Hays, and William Jennings Bryan, the case presented the first of a series of skirmishes between science and society. The prosecution won the case, only to be reversed at the state level on a technicality. But the statute against the teaching of evolution remained on the books in Tennessee.

Soon after the Scopes case was resolved, Mississippi and Arkansas passed similar laws barring the teaching of evolution. It was the Arkansas law, known as the Rotenberry Act, that reached the Supreme Court in 1968. The court then ruled that it was illegal to bar the teaching of evolution in public schools and colleges (De Camp 1969). Tennessee countered in 1973 with a law requiring equal time for special creation—that is, the Genesis version of how life began. The California Board of Education had adopted a similar position in 1969. "[The] Book of Genesis presents a reasonable explanation of the origin of life . . . special creation should be taught as an alternative to the theory of organic evolution" (cited in Nelkin 1976, 33). The Tennessee equal time law was declared unconstitutional by the Supreme Court and was repealed in 1975. The California Board of Education, in the meantime, also reversed itself and pressed publishers for a more extensive treatment of evolution in biology texts.

In viewing the evolution controversies, it is critical to understand the nature of the present-day objectors. They are not mainly the residents of rural Appalachia, but middle-class citizens from areas like southern California and urban Texas, many with technical training (Nelkin 1976). Fundamentalist movements grew rapidly in these areas in the late 1960s, perhaps as a response to the uncertainties of technology. Creation research centers were established, and creationism was pushed as a valid, scientific concept. In parallel, high school courses and texts that taught evolution or that appeared to give science a role greater than that of religion were attacked. Programs like MACOS suffered from these movements, as did a number of specific textbooks (Conlon and Dow 1975).

Opposing the right wing organizations (e.g., the Heritage Foundation, Save Our Children, Parents Who Care, Concerned Women for America) are a number of mostly left-of-center organizations that lobby for civil rights in relation to textbooks. People for the American Way, for example, has worked in defense of a number of school systems that were attacked by right wing groups. But the NAACP, NOW, the ACLU, and the People for the American Way also are part of the power struggle over control of textbook content in that they also lobby for or against specific content (e.g., fair treatment of minorities, portrayal of women in professional roles, omission of racial slurs). Although their tactics and immediate intentions may appear to be different in kind from the right wing organizations, these latter groups play an identical role in the framework of textbook production. Pressure from one side of the political spectrum results in censorship of *Romeo and Juliet*, while pressure from the other side results in censorship of *The Adventures of Huckleberry Finn*. From a structural standpoint the results are the same. But this is not the only valid perspective for treating this subject.

THE LATENT CONTENT OF TEXTBOOKS

Analysis of the latent content of textbooks, over which much of the turmoil just reviewed has occurred, provides a useful vantage point for examining both methods and outcomes in textbook studies. The majority of the studies of latent content have been done on reading texts, primarily because, in contrast to all other areas of the curriculum, reading has no specified content of its own. Ostensibly, what is taught during reading is procedural: how to extract meaning from different forms of texts. Unfortunately, for reasons based strongly in the evolution of the school curriculum, reading has come to mean literature, and therefore almost all reading instruction is based upon fiction, with limited attention to the skills required to gain meaning from expository texts (Venezky 1982). But as was described above, an important body of work on the latent curriculum has also focused on social studies and history texts and to a lesser degree on science texts.

Studies of reader content, at least up to the 1980s, involved analyses of stories for particular features, such as themes (Starch 1921), references to religion (Tingelstad 1913), or sex stereotyping (Zimet 1972). Generally, sampling was somewhat loose, depending particularly for pre-20th-century materials on the contents of specified libraries. Establishment of specific content was often done impressionistically without interrater reliability estimates, although more accurate methods of counting also occurred.

Exceptions to these cruder methodologies are found in the work of McClelland (1961) and de Charms and Moeller (1962), both dealing with images of achievement motivation in elementary-level readers. McClelland (1961) is an attempt to assess the relationship between *n* Achievement (i.e., need for achievement) and national economic growth. More specifically, McClelland hypothesized that high *n* Achievement would predispose a society to vigorous economic activity, and this predisposition would be revealed in the stories that children were given in their school readers. Stories from second- to fourth-grade readers of 23 countries for the period 1920–1929 and 40 countries for the period 1946–1955 were sampled, and those not in English were translated literally to English. An elaborate coding scheme for the characters in each story was developed, requiring ratings for an individualistic achievement value complex (e.g., status of ego, influences on ego, motives of ego) and an interaction value complex. Over 1,300 stories were collected and coded in this manner, with interrater reliabilities for coders ranging from .92 to .98.

Although the *n* Achievement ratings of 1925 readers correlated .46 with a combined economic gain measure, correlation of these two factors for 1950s readers was −.08. Furthermore, *n* Achievement scores for most of the underdeveloped countries were higher than those for the developed countries. McClelland concluded that "the reader stress on achievement may represent something more like 'national aspirations'—the tendency of people in public (e.g., in children's textbooks) to think about achievement" (79). McClelland also questioned whether the stories in readers were typical of the literate classes in a country, or of the government in power, or the educational philosophy of the current ministry of education, or perhaps of some other agency. He also speculated that the treatment of cultural values in elementary readers, rather than guiding and shaping the beliefs and attitudes of children, might only confuse them.

Using the McClelland results as a point of departure, de Charms and Moeller (1962) sampled American reading textbooks typical of 20-year periods from 1800 to 1960. Four popular texts from each period were selected and ratings done of every third page. Separate scores were given for (1) achievement imagery, (2) affiliation imagery, and (3) moral teaching (e.g., implicit or explicit judgments between right and wrong). Achievement imagery rises steadily from 1810 (the midpoint of the 1800–1820 interval) to 1890, and then drops just as rapidly thereafter. A curve for the number of patents issued per one million population for the same time period shows the same shape as the achievement imagery curve, but with a small time lag. Moral teaching drops steadily from 1810 to 1950, with the largest drops occurring in the periods 1850–1870 and 1910–1930.

The authors associated the shifts in achievement imagery with a shift in American culture from a Protestant ethic to a social ethic; that is, from an ethic based on thrift, hard work, and competition to one based upon a belief in the group as the primary source of creativity. With this latter belief belongingness is viewed as the ultimate need of individuals and is achieved through the application of science. Achievement motivation is associated with what Riesman labeled the inner-directed character type, while affiliation motivation is associated with the other-directed type (Riesman 1950).

Elson's Central Tendency Theory

A second type of analysis centers on what might be called the central tendency in textbook content, which has been summarized succinctly by Elson in her study of 19th-century textbooks.

> The schoolbooks delineated for [an American child] an idealized image both of himself and of the history that had produced the admitted American type. They were a compendium of ideas popularly approved at the time, and they offer an excellent index of concepts considered "proper" for the nineteenth century American. (Elson 1964, vii)

This view implies that we could predict the main thrust of textbook content at any point during the 19th century from those ideas that had popular approval then. Notice that the emphasis here is not upon accuracy or verisimilitude in any sense, but rather upon idealized images and folk mythologies, that is, upon those beliefs that had popular approval, including those about where as a nation we came from and what we were. The view of history and society that 19th-century textbooks presented was one in which the path of American history revealed God's scheme for moral government, where the heroes of American history were "exemplars of industriousness, honesty, and intelligence" and where hard work and clean thoughts were rewarded by both spiritual and material gains (Cremin 1980, 73).

Elson's 1964 study, *Guardians of Tradition*, is a study of themes, images, and attitudes in American textbooks of the 19th century, based upon a sample of over 1,000 readers, spellers, arithmetics, histories, and geographies. Only texts from grades 1 to 8 were included, and the basic methodology is impressionistic, involving no rating or counting of text features. Elson assumes that children accept school attitudes that are not contradicted by their immediate experience, for example, by parents or by others of primary importance, but admits that the degree of influence of textbooks on people cannot be easily determined.

Up to the early 19th century, the central tendency theory finds support in the heavy religious content of 17th- and early 18th-century New England school materials (e.g., hornbooks, *New-England Primer*, Bible) and in the admixture of religious, moral, and nationalistic selections that were evidenced after the Revolution. Theology was life's guide for the earliest settlers; it regulated not only their daily lives but also their views of how the young child advanced to adulthood. Original sin and predestination were the justification for continual inculcation of the catechism, with corporal punishment for deviations from expected behavior. The ideas the Puritans accepted and the society they expected to build were, in the earliest days, well represented by the *New-England Primer*. As church government gave way to civil government, and old country patterns of family and society changed, morality and good character gained equal footing with religion in the textbooks. With the American Revolution, nationalism was added.

Influence of Textbook Content

Elson's basic assumption is that schoolbooks provide insights into the ideas held by the common people in the 19th century by demonstrating the political, economic, social, cultural, and moral concepts to which they were exposed. While Elson leaves open the question of the extent to which an individual might be influenced by schoolbook concepts, she does point out that schoolbooks in the 19th century were probably more influential than those in the 20th century, due to the lack of competition from the media and from other reading material (Elson 1964, vii).

Cremin (1980) is more certain on this point, claiming that during the national period (1783–1876) textbooks "played a significant role in articulating and shaping the attitudes, values, tastes, and sensibilities of the American people" (70). Although we have no thorough study of this issue, the bulk of the evidence points to a maintenance role for textbooks, which often lagged by years behind the changes occurring in society itself. Schools usually reflected prevailing, established practices and beliefs about children and their care and training, rather than initiating these changes. In addition, during a large portion of the 19th century, textbooks were purchased by families and passed from child to child until lost, destroyed, or no longer needed. Since instruction, particularly in rural areas, was often based on whichever texts were brought from home, a textbook could continue to reflect attitudes and beliefs far beyond the time when the ideas it embodied held currency. Finally, as many recent studies have shown (e.g., Miles 1981), public schools, like most other public institutions, tend to be conservative. They provide continuity across generations rather than acting as agencies for change.

Alternative Views

Elson's (1964) analysis of textbook content covers concepts of nature, God and man, nationalism and its attendant concerns, and individualism. She also probes the prevailing textbook views on economic, social, and political concepts and values and attempts to demonstrate how content varied with changing social views. Both Garfinkle (1954) and Mosier (1947) present a less charitable view of the motivation for textbook content. Mosier writes exclusively of the McGuffey Readers, centering mainly on the period from their introduction in the 1830s until the last major revision in 1879. Garfinkle (1954) concentrates on textbooks spanning the period from the first publication of Webster's spelling book (1783) until the 1860s. Both conclude that after 1840 the economic ideas in readers reflected the conservative interests of merchants and industrialists rather than those of the common man. Garfinkle (1954) builds on Curti's suggestion that the promoters of the common school movement needed the support of the business class, which looked with some alarm on the expanding labor movement and the concomitant spread of radical ideas about property, voting rights, and the like (Curti 1959 [1935], 227ff and 583). Along with religion, education was seen as a force that could instill respect for the established order in the poorer classes; that is, it could promote social control.

Mosier (1947) makes a similar argument for the McGuffey Readers, but he sees the Hamiltonian tradition, as espoused by Alexander Hamilton, John Marshall, and Daniel Webster, as the guiding philosophy behind the compilers of these texts. Mixed with these politics are a strong Calvinist religious streak and a middle-class Protestant morality. "God made the poor man as well as the rich man" is a consistent theme, as is the need for religion and education to help reconcile republican institutions with "universal suffrage and the terrors of undisciplined democracy" (156). Nowhere do these readers show any faith in popular government nor any interest in strong individualism. While the beauty and solitude of the West is often compared to the overcrowded urban ugliness of the East, western folk heroes like Mike Fink and Davey Crockett are conspicuously absent.

As plausible as the arguments of both Garfinkle (1954) and Mosier (1947) might be, they need to be examined against a wider data base than either presents. Garfinkle based his views of early 19th-century American readers on only three texts, the 1826 and 1841 editions of Webster's spelling book and Murray's *English Reader*.

Webster's speller was originally issued in 1783, but underwent major revisions in 1804 and 1829 (Monaghan 1983, 51ff). Therefore, arguments about early 19th-century values cannot be readily derived from the two Webster texts Garfinkle cited. And while Webster's speller and Murray's reader were the most widely used texts for teaching reading in the late 18th and early 19th centuries, they faced increasing competition after the 1820s, particularly from Cobb's spellers and readers and Pierpont's readers. Lindley Murray, although born in the United States, moved to England in 1794 and remained there until his death in 1826 (Belok 1973). His reading texts were all written in England and contained nothing that could be mistaken for American nationalism. His work, therefore, has limited value as evidence for the attitudes of American textbook writers.

What Garfinkle (1954) interprets as the special interests of conservative businessmen and industrialists might also be attributed to the prevailing Protestant ethic, which found no fault in the doctrine of materialism. Supporting the cultural dynamic that transformed the early Puritan society well before the middle of the 18th century were personal responsibility for one's own actions and an unremitting stress on industry, activity, and spirit. What failed to mirror the true interests of the American character was not the materialism-based readers of the McGuffey era but the conservative, heaven-oriented readers of the generation before (see Kaestle 1983, 67f). Industry and thrift are persistent themes in readers throughout the 19th century, and the rewards of one's labors become more and more materialistic as the century progresses. With a focus on character that reaches almost to obsession, many 19th-century textbooks work to death what Commager (1962) called "the essential virtues": industry, sobriety, thrift, propriety, modesty, punctuality, and conformity.

Mosier's (1947) views are partially supported in Commager (1962) and Lindberg (1976), but his work suffers from a failure to consider separately the major editions of the McGuffey Readers. Few selections survived the entire course of changes that took place from 1836 until 1879 (Nietz 1964). For example, Mosier's depiction of the strong sectional bias of the readers, particularly toward the West, is based on two paeans to the glory of western settlers, western geography, and western literature in the first edition of the Fourth Reader, both written by Daniel Drake, a friend of the McGuffeys. But Mosier fails to point out that the most westerly, chauvinistic of these selections was deleted from the 1844 edition of the Fourth Reader, and the other was dropped in 1857, neither to reappear.

Westerhoff (1978) defines the viewpoint of the original editions of the first four McGuffey Readers, which were the only ones written by William Homes McGuffey, as early 19th-century Presbyterian Calvinism, permeated throughout with salvation, righteousness, and piety. This perspective was radically altered by the various publishers of the succeeding editions, so that by 1879 the series represented American middle-class attitudes, values, and beliefs, with their underpinning of civil religion. About 20 percent of the content of the 1844 Fourth Reader was religious, while only 3 percent of the 1901 edition of this text was (Nietz 1964, 122–123). Mosier seldom refers to the first four readers (8 percent of his references, according to Westerhoff 1978, 26), and few of these are to the editions published before 1850. Consequently, the views of William Holmes McGuffey were not representative of the second half of the 19th century but of an earlier time. His publishers were left with the task of catching up to prevailing social attitudes in subsequent editions.

The McGuffey Readers, like all others, were commercial ventures and were targeted toward a specific audience. For example, the southern market was important territory for the McGuffey Readers and was undoubtedly the reason for an almost total exclusion of readings on the Civil War, save for a single impartial piece. As was mentioned earlier, even in the 1879 edition, the name of Abraham Lincoln, already immortalized in myth and song in American literature, was missing. Similar deviations from ideas popularly approved at the time are found in the omission of Mark Twain, Walt Whitman, the California gold rush, the Oregon Trail, and, as mentioned, such backwoods heroes as Mike Fink and Davey Crockett (Commager 1962, xi).

The entrepreneurial element in reader content has not

been examined closely, yet is commonly assumed to be present, particularly in the 20th century (Anderson et al. 1985; Clifford 1984). Few modern publishers of reading series have included topics in reading selections that might displease the large adoption states, regardless of how popular these subjects might be elsewhere. By contrast, the degree to which Webster altered his content to compete with Lyman Cobb and others was probably small, given the limited amount of reading material in the revised Webster spelling book of 1829. But marketing considerations in the selection of reader content increased as single spellers and readers graduated to series of readers, as the school-age population multiplied, and as transportation to national markets became more efficient.

A second limitation on the central tendency notion occurred in the second quarter of the 19th century when primers and first readers began to stress nature themes and simple accounts of everyday observable objects and events. The progression in introductory material from the *New-England Primer* and the Webster spelling book of 1783 to the 1867 revision of McGuffey's *Pictorial Eclectic Primer* provides a case study for the spread of Pestalozzianism. *The New-England Primer* is almost totally devoid of secular matter, taking every opportunity to preach the gospel of true faith. Webster mixes moralism and religion but admits an occasional secular paragraph on a didactic topic. In contrast, McGuffey's revised *Pictorial Eclectic Primer* makes almost no mention of moralism and religion. A fly runs, a top hums, a boy hops, a cat gets out of a box, a bird is killed, and a little girl gets a new doll. Of 89 lessons in the text, at most 3 have any obvious religious or moralistic teaching. William Holmes McGuffey had no role in the 1867 revision of the primer (Westerhoff 1978). By the time that this revision was finished, Pestalozzian schooling principles were known throughout the United States. The object lesson had already begun to appear in textbooks and was described in various speeches before the American Institute of Instruction and in articles in the American Annals of Education. McGuffey began his moralizing in the original first reader, but by the 1870s even the second and third readers contained mostly nature and childhood stories.

Good Literature Arrives

Yet another deviation from what the central tendency theory would predict began to appear toward the end of the 19th century as college presidents and professors of educational administration began to join the educational reform movement. These administrative progressives, as Tyack (1974) calls them, attempted to apply the corporate model to school organization, with a stress on strong centralized control. Urban schooling was to be made socially efficient, with schooling differentiated according to the student's position in society. Associated peripherally with this movement was the desire to impose good literature on the language arts curriculum. N. B. Smith (1965) traces the origins of this cultural emphasis in reading instruction to the 1880s, with acceleration of the movement in the 1890s under the influence of Herbartianism. Herbart, like most other educators of the 19th century, saw the elementary school as a central agent in the development of character, but instead of using the Bible or explicit moral tales for achieving this end, Herbart encouraged the use of literary and historical stories. The new education of the 1880s and 1890s strongly stressed the needs and interests of the individual child, as the age-graded school was being institutionalized throughout the United States. From Froebel's influence on the spreading kindergarten movement, from the child study movement initiated by G. Stanley Hall, and from the Herbartians, the desire to appeal to the child's imagination became the watchword of textbook compilers.

By the end of the 19th century both schooling and society in the United States had matured to the point where culture had become an important concern. With the West settled, movement and opportunity were vertical rather than horizontal—rising up the social and industrial ladder rather than running westward to claim another patch of untamed countryside. A flood of immigrants, many from poor, rural areas of Europe, resulted in further pressures on the schools to homogenize and Americanize. The result was a reader content based on good literature, what one reading textbook called the "famous stories that are the rightful heritage of every English speaking child" (Fassett 1918, iii). This is not exactly what Charles W. Eliot had in mind when he called for the substitution of real literature for readers, but it was as close as reading programs were to come, even up to the present.

The total domination of literary selections in the upper-level readers, which came by the first decade of the 20th century, reduced the ability of the reader to convey "a compendium of ideas popularly approved at the time" (Elson 1964, vii). This literary emphasis has continued up to the present day, where real life and fantasy account for the majority of the reading selections (Willows, Borwick, and Hayvren 1981). Changes have occurred in the past 50 years, particularly in the portrayal of minorities and women, but the literary emphasis remains. Current reader content appears to be influenced less by popularly approved ideas than by the constraints of a long list of taboos, created in response to state adoption requirements and the pressures of special interest groups.

In summary, the latent content of textbooks from the middle of the 17th century until the last decade of the 19th century was, with some deviations, regulated by society's idealized image of itself, including its expected future and its ennobling past. This image was, however, primarily of a white, Protestant nation, in which men were strong and noble, and women supportive and caring. In early colonial times, society built its self-image around theological concepts, particularly salvation. With commercial expansion and the elevation of civil religion in the second half of the 19th century, mankind began to celebrate itself, and it presented its children with visions of tangible and immediate rewards for proper behavior. With the shift to silent reading for comprehension, and with the change in child psychology to a nurturing view, society's adult images were sublimated to the needs and interests of the child. Beginning readers built on fantasy and adventure, while more advanced readers explored good literature. With the introduction in the 20th century of a culturally diverse literature, a clear image of adult American society and of the child's role in it was no longer available and has not reappeared. But how these images, whether in readers, histories, or any other textbooks, affected the minds and worldviews of children remains to be explored.

EVOLUTION OF THE MODERN TEXTBOOK

Although the term "textbook" dates only from the fourth quarter of the 18th century in English writing, the use of particular texts as standard works for the study of a subject derives from the Middle Ages and possibly earlier. In the Middle Ages, for example, Boethius' *De Musica*, Cassiodorus' *On the Liberal Arts and Sciences*, and Alcuin's *Astronomy* were the standard texts used for instruction, alongside such classics as Aristotle's *Physica* (Cubberley 1920). Even before movable type printing became common in Europe, a network of scribal houses, centered primarily around the universities, had developed to make copies of manuscript books. By the beginning of the 13th century an active book trade existed outside the monasteries, supplying copies of both classical and modern works to university professors, students, and an emerging reading public. From the 13th and 14th centuries alone, over 2,000 copies of Aristotle's works have survived in manuscript form (Febvre and Martin 1976 [1958], 22.).

The modern schoolbook with pictures, pedagogical devices, and inviting graphical design evolved primarily from children's works produced in Germany and Italy at the end of the 15th and the beginning of the 16th centuries. Christopher Hueber, a Bavarian teacher, included pictures in an ABC book in 1477, as did the Florentine humanist Jacob Publicius in 1485 (Davies 1974). By the end of the 16th century, English schoolbooks, which were the models for almost all American textbooks until the early 19th century, were being adapted for the interests and abilities of children. Richard Mulcaster's *Elementary*, first issued in 1581, advocated simple language and familiar content in books for children. Fifteen years later Edmund Coote's *The English Schoolmaster* became the first English pedagogical text to contain graded vocabulary exercises. Later English textbooks were strongly influenced by John Amos Comenius' *Orbis Sensualium Pictus*, which first appeared in Germany in 1657 and was translated soon after into English by Charles Hoole (Bardeen 1887). Early school textbooks in America were primarily sources of received knowledge. Webster's blue-back speller and Morse's geographies contained few suggestions to the teacher on how to present the material. After the first quarter of the 19th century, however, as the common school movement began to spread, textbooks began to provide more substantial aids for teachers.

The earliest popular textbook in the American colonies, *The New-England Primer*, measured approximately 3 by 5 inches, had fewer than 80 pages, and could fit in a farmer's shirt pocket, no doubt by design. The modern reading textbook is actually a series of books, thousands of pages in length, printed in full color with accompanying teacher guides that, together with the books, weigh almost as much as the youngsters who are to acquire literacy through exposure to them. Between these two anchor points are not only almost 300 years in time but radical transformations of culture, education, and commerce. Where colonial printers produced for a local market, modern conglomerates produce for a national market. Where a journeyman in 1800 could expect to raise enough capital to buy his own press and print primers, readers, and arithmetics without paying royalties or permission fees, millions of dollars are now required for a single mathematics, reading, or social studies series (Rorabaugh 1986).

The evolution of the modern textbook is in part the history of American education and in part the history of American culture. No thorough text on this history exists, but various parts of it have been delimited. Nietz (1961, 1966) and Carpenter (1963) cover the general history of American textbooks, focusing on authors and textbook content. These are uncritical works, mostly archival and anecdotal, but useful as inventories. Also general in nature, but more limited in scope, are Littlefield (1904) and Johnson (1963 [1904]). Elson (1964), discussed above, is an important bibliographic source, but is not a textbook history. Reading textbooks have been more thoroughly examined than any other subject area (e.g., Lamport 1937; Reeder 1900; N. B. Smith 1965; Venezky 1986), and a variety of studies exist on specific reading texts; e.g., the Horn-book (Tuer 1897), *The New-England Primer* (Ford 1899; Watters 1985/1986), Noah Webster's blue-back speller (Monaghan 1983), McGuffey's Readers (Lindberg 1976; Minnich 1936; Westerhoff 1978), and the Dick and Jane readers (Luke 1988).

Children's books (i.e., children's trade books), which until almost the Civil War were difficult to distinguish from schoolbooks, have been cataloged by Rosenbach (1933), St. John (1958, 1975), and Welch (1972). The 20,000 plus collection of textbooks in the U.S. Department of Education Research Library has not been completely cataloged, but a sampler catalog of approximately 5,000 titles was issued recently (Svobodny 1985). Confederate textbooks have been thoroughly cataloged by Parrish and Willingham (1987). But in general, textbooks have been ignored by major libraries; the collections that exist are often uncataloged. Few libraries have attempted to collect complete series or editions, so that tracing even as popular a series as the Dick and Jane readers is exceedingly difficult. The Library of Congress and the American Antiquarian Society have extensive holdings of early American textbooks, as does the British Museum. Large, well-maintained collections can also be found at Trinity College in Hartford, Connecticut, New York University, Columbia University/Teachers College, Harvard University, the University of Pittsburgh, and selected public libraries, including the Philadelphia Free Library and the New York Public Library. Recent work at the American Antiquarian Society in cataloging into RLIN (Research Libraries Information Network) 19th-century children's books, including some textbooks, is providing a model for processing of textbooks, which in time other libraries may follow.

The Colonial Period

The evolution of the modern textbook can be traced through at least five distinct periods: Colonial (1639–1782), early national (1783–1837), pre-Civil War (1838–1865), early modern (1866–1920), and modern (1921–present). In the colonial period most textbooks were imported from England; what few were produced in the colonies (e.g., Cheever's *A Short Introduction to the Latin Tongue*, published in 1737) were based upon English models. Printing facilities and papermaking were limited in the colonies, and imported paper was expensive. The cost of shipping goods over land was also expensive, constraining the distribution of printed materials. Some writers even sent manuscripts to England for printing and then imported the books back into the colonies. Hugh Jones, for example, wrote a grammar for the colonies in 1724 but sent it to England for printing (Nietz 1961). (The first grammar to be written and printed in the colonies was done by Samuel Johnson, first president of Kings College in New York City.)

Although the basic tone of textbooks was highly religious throughout most of this period, the secularization of colonial society that began before the middle of the 18th century was reflected in particular in reader content. Primers less devotional than the *New-England Primer*, at first imported from England (e.g., *The Royal Primer*), began to appear. In addition, native arithmetics and grammars were produced, although sparingly. Nevertheless, *The New-England Primer*, which appeared in hundreds of editions, remained the dominant model for colonial textbooks and the most often produced reading text (Ford 1899). This text, however, was much less a guide to reading than it was a religious document in which the Calvinist views of the child and of human disobedience to the authority of God were expounded. "The text of the *Primer* developed at the time of a crisis of authority in New England, involving . . . the transition from colony to province, and in most general terms, much of the *Primer* defines for the child his or her place in relation to parental, civil and religious authority figures" (Watters 1985/1986, 193).

Although most writers date the *New-England Primer* to the end of the 17th century, no concrete evidence of pre-18th-century editions exists. The references to the *Primer* in the *Stationer's Registry* and in advertisements before 1700 may have been to a related text, John Cotton's *Spiritual Milk for American Babes*. Like Webster's *Speller* and the McGuffey Readers, the *New-England Primer* was radically revised during its lifetime, the most dramatic revision being in the 1750s, in response (perhaps) to the Great Awakening. The earliest surviving example of the *Primer* was printed in 1727; however, given the fragility of the text and the relatively low survival rate of colonial print materials, that date cannot be accepted with confidence as the first printing of the text. (See Heartman 1934 and 1935 for an inventory of New England and non-New England primers identified up to the mid-1930s.)

The Early National Period

With the American Revolution and independence began a period of American production of textbooks, almost all of which were infused with intense nationalism. Noah Webster's *Speller* (first published in 1783), Jedidiah Morse's *Geography* (also first published in 1783), and Caleb Bingham's *American Preceptor*, which was published a year later, were prominent examples of the new nationalism, but others followed. For example, Erastus Root, in the 1796 edition of his *Introduction to Arithmetic*, urged the replacement of the English money system with that of America's (Curti 1959 [1935]). Nevertheless, many textbooks continued to be imported from England and some, like Lindley Murray's readers, captured a major share of the American market. Packer (1954), drawing on *The Boston Booksellers' Catalogue* of 1804, concludes that, in the textbooks advertised for sale in 1804, 25 percent were by English authors. Without an international copyright law, however, American copies could be made of imported books without payment of royalties so that the popularity of an import nearly always guaranteed domestic printing.

The transition from religious to secular textbooks continued through the initial part of this period and was particularly evident in the sales of the *New-England Primer*, which was rapidly replaced by more secular primers that were devoted exclusively to reading instruction.

> This secularization [1790–1800] was an attack by its friends from which the book never quite recovered, for the printers having once found how much more saleable such primers were, and parents having found how much more readily their children learned, both united in encouraging more popular school-books, and very quickly illustrated primers, which aimed to please rather than to torture, were multiplied. (Ford 1899, 109ff)

Nevertheless, tradition held strong in the New England countryside, and as late as the period 1836–1850, over 50,000 copies of the *New-England Primer* were printed and sold (Tebbel 1972).

During the early national period, the content of many textbooks began to shift in emphasis from classical learning to more modern learning. Regional interests were more strongly expressed, especially in texts like the early editions of the McGuffey Readers, which were initially produced for western and southern markets, but with popularity shed their regional guise (Venezky 1907). Other popular regional texts included James Hall's *Western Reader*, published in Cincinnati, Ohio, in 1833; *The Western Primer*, published in Columbus, Ohio, in 1837; and *The Western Farmer's Almanac*, published in Lexington, Kentucky, in 1845.

The people who authored major textbooks during the early national period were mostly from New England, highly educated, overwhelmingly Protestant, and classically oriented (Belok 1973). Most were not authors but rather compilers who often gave no credit to the sources from which they borrowed extracts. John M'Culloch, for example, who compiled the first American history text (cited in Spieseke 1938), borrowed lengthy extracts without permission or attribution from Jedidiah Morse's *Geography Made Easy* (Spieseke 1938). Authors' attitudes toward religions other than their own was at best intolerant.

> It is not surprising to find these early school-books taking a very intolerant attitude toward Catholics and other major religions. The word "papist" was freely strewn throughout the books, and generally the references were in the pejorative sense. Most religions were divided into Christians and pagans. . . . The seeds of "know-nothingism" and America's fear of conspiracy were probably sown quite early. (Belok 1973, 64f).

Elson (1964) found this same attitude toward non-Protestant religions continuing throughout almost the entire 19th century.

Concern for the quality of textbooks was expressed early in the 19th century, particularly in the reform-oriented educational journals that began appearing at that time. An unidentified writer at the end of the 1820s (who may have been Henry Barnard) was one of several who pressed for more child-oriented texts through the pages of the *American Journal of Education*. "Our spelling books in general what are they? Fit for philosophers it may be—fit for those who already possess a liberal education, but evidently unfit for children" (*American Journal of Education* 1829, 482). The primary targets of the textbook reformers were spellers and readers, and their goal was the reduction of content complexity to a level appropriate for younger children.

The Pre-Civil War Period

With the spread of the common school movement in the 1830s and 1840s, textbook publishing moved from a staple of the printing press, akin to stationery and business forms, to a major independent business, complete with specialized publishing houses and separate sales forces. Truman, Smith & Company, incorporated in Cincinnati in 1833, was one of the first firms to make a major investment in schoolbooks and rose within 2½ decades to be the largest schoolbook publishing house in America (Sutton 1961). Two of its earliest products, Joseph Ray's *Arithmetic* and the McGuffey Readers, sold over 100 million copies each in their lifetimes and made millionaires out of a number of corporate executives. With increased markets, more publishing houses began to specialize in textbooks, and with many school systems establishing district-wide textbook adoptions, many of the forces that drive the current textbook trade were established.

Among the contributors to textbook publication during this period, and continuing throughout the 19th century, were various religious and missionary organizations, including the American Sunday School Union, whose publication archives are now housed at the Free Library of Philadelphia, the American Tract Society, the American Bible Society, and the Baptist Tract Society (Tebbel 1972). Most of these organizations published primers and readers, some of which were written in Native American languages. So far, however, no thorough treatment of this subject has been published, but works on specific denominational presses have appeared (e.g., Hostetler 1958; Pilkington 1968; Rice 1917). Another important publication source for textbooks, the southern press, particularly during the Confederacy, also has not been critically examined, although good bibliographic materials exist (Parrish and Willingham 1987). Even though the quality of southern printing was inferior to that of the North, due to the lack of both good press equipment and high-quality paper, southern textbooks remain important sources of regional expression.

The physical quality of textbooks improved markedly in the second quarter of the 19th century, due both to improved printing and papermaking technologies and to increased competition for the expanding common school market. But the content of many elementary school texts continued to reflect adult competencies rather than those of the children for whom they were intended. School readers in particular tended to offer complex and recondite selections to students whose feet could barely reach the floor from the benches on which they sat. Horace Mann, commenting in 1839 on the content of the popular school readers of the time, summarized much of the criticism of that period in characterizing them as containing "demonstrative arguments on the most abstruse and recondite subjects, tasking the acuteness of practised logicians, and applicable only by them . . ." (Mann 1839, 295).

The Early Modern Period

With the conclusion of the Civil War, textbook publishing expanded rapidly.

> The tremendous surge of education after the Civil War had created a record demand for textbooks, which had brought the new firms into being and compelled the older ones either to expand the sales forces or get out of the business. . . . Textbook companies had at least 300 agents in the field by 1868, and the number was growing every year. (Tebbel 1975, 560)

With fortunes to be made, corruption was rampant. Companies expanded, bought out other companies, and drove the smaller ones out of business through price cutting and bribery of school officials. Conditions within the trade deteriorated far enough by 1870 that 53 textbook publishing firms were willing to meet and form the Publishers' Board of Trade to regulate pricing.

> Aside from the fact of organization, the most important result was an agreement that after March 17 [1870] no schoolbook could be introduced at less than half the published retail prices for cash, paid

within ninety days after completion of the introduction. The board also agreed that publishers must issue a retail price list. (561)

Almost immediately the agreements that were made with the formation of the Board were diluted and by 1877, with the departure of two of the largest publishing firms from the organization, it finally collapsed. In response to the chaotic marketing conditions in the textbook trade, several states began to publish their own textbooks, led by California in 1883. In 1890 a number of the largest textbook publishers combined to form the American Book Company, which was capitalized at $5 million—a rather large sum for the time. Almost immediately the American Book Company was involved in litigation over charges both of bribery and of being an illegal trust. Although never convicted of either of these charges, the company remained a center of controversy for a number of decades.

The Modern Period

Following World War I, a further consolidation took place in the textbook trade as smaller companies continued to be bought up by larger ones. Publishing was centered primarily in New York in the East and Chicago in the Midwest, with a small number of firms still located in Philadelphia, Baltimore, and Cincinnati. The modern basal reading series assumed the form that is seen today, and mathematics, social studies, and science series followed.

The rapid expansion of the high school system, particularly after the beginning of the 20th century, provided a new market for textbooks, but not as appreciable as the elementary market. Secondary-level textbooks evolved more under the influence of college-level practices and state guidelines than did the elementary textbooks of the time. Secondary-level biology texts, which were discussed above in relation to the teaching of evolution, are representative of this pattern. General biology first entered the high school curriculum in the 1880s and was taught from college-level texts—for example, Thomas Huxley and Henry Martin's *A Course of Practical Instruction in Elementary Biology*. Texts developed specifically for high school instruction soon followed, but were concatenations of botany and zoology texts, presented side by side in what was called the "fern and worm" method. Some state syllabi (e.g., the New York Board of Regents syllabus of 1899) defined biology through a tripartite division of botany, zoology, and human physiology and thereby encouraged nonintegrated textbooks (Rosenthal and Bybee 1987). Other frameworks encouraged integration, leading to the first integrated biology textbook, James George Needham's *General Biology*, first issued in 1910.

With the expansion of the secondary school system, particularly around the time of World War I, and with an emphasis on making biology relevant to everyday living, a wide variety of new biology texts appeared. One of these was George W. Hunter's *Civic Biology*, published in 1914, the first high school textbook to discuss genetics and the state-approved text in Tennessee, which John Scopes was using when he was arrested for teaching evolution in 1923 (Tanner 1988). In the early 1920s a survey of biology courses in 69 large cities found 67 different texts and reference books in use (Richards 1923).

In the 1980s yet another consolidation of the textbook industry took place, with large conglomerates taking over groups of publishing houses, reminiscent of the formation of the American Book Company at the end of the 19th century. Although it may be too early to determine what influence this reduction in competition will have on the quality of textbooks, past experience gives little reason to expect increases in variety of texts or in the willingness of the surviving publishers to explore alternative approaches to pedagogical design.

Alternative Formats

Over the past 50 years several variations on the standard textbook have been proposed or tried, including programmed textbooks, computer-assisted instruction, and more recently, customized publishing. Each of these opens up a unique set of issues for the definitions and frameworks proposed earlier in this chapter and each holds a different promise for improvement of instruction.

Programmed Textbooks. Programmed textbooks were an attempt to realize programmed instruction in a print form, thereby gaining the supposed advantages of this method of instruction but without the need for expensive mechanical or electronic devices. Programmed instruction grew out of the work of Skinner and other behaviorists, who found that through appropriate feedback schedules rats, pigeons, and other animals could be trained to do quite complicated tasks. Skinner's theory of *operant conditioning*, extended to humans, was realized through decomposition of instruction into such small steps that failure was almost entirely eliminated (Skinner 1954, 1963). At first, mechanical teaching machines were used to present question-and-answer alternatives and to evaluate responses, building on devices first demonstrated by Pressey at Ohio State University (Benjamin 1988; Pressey 1926). But the idea of a programmed textbook emerged soon after the teaching machine business was established.

In 1958 Harcourt Brace Publishing Company entered into a contract with Skinner to jointly develop a marketable teaching machine, with Skinner taking major responsibility for the design of the device itself and Harcourt Brace the programmed materials it would deliver. An existing high school grammar text was reduced to programmed form and readied for transfer to punched paper tape. However, the teaching machine collaboration did not progress much beyond the initial ideas and was terminated in 1959. Harcourt Brace, left with the programmed grammar materials, decided to publish them as a programmed book entitled *English 2600*, where the 2600 represented the number of steps in the program (Reid 1969). The resulting text, first published in October 1960, went through at least three editions in the 1960s and sold over one million copies.

Although Harcourt Brace established a division of Programmed Instruction in its high school department and issued 16 programmed books over the next decade, the idea failed to catch on and the division was eventually phased out.

Programmed books were more expensive to write, edit, and print than conventional textbooks. In addition, they were also more boring and allowed less room for the author's style (Feldhusen 1963). Materials written to ensure a 90 to 95 percent correct response rate were so inherently simple that learners didn't need feedback to reassure them of giving correct responses. Beyond these practical matters, programmed books were an attempt to eliminate teacher mediation between text and student, making the prescribed curriculum and the delivered curriculum identical. Each step in a programmed book consisted of a short amount of text and, usually, a question with multiple choice answers. Depending upon the alternative selected, the reader was routed to another such frame, progressing thusly through the entire text. Both the physical problems with flipping back and forth frequently through the text and the rigidity of the programmed instruction approach brought a quick end to programmed books.

Computer-Assisted Instruction. Computer-assisted instruction (CAI) developed out of the same psychological paradigm as programmed instruction, but it has managed after almost 30 years of zigs and zags to shed most vestiges of its parenthood. Over this same period the delivery mechanism for CAI has changed from large, mainframe computers to minicomputers to microcomputers (Venezky and Osin 1991). A variety of modes of on-line instruction exist, ranging from test and drill for specific skills to complex simulations of chemistry laboratories, international relations, and the like. Of more immediate interest here, however, are the variations on the concept of a fixed text that CAI offers. One such deviation derives from the simple alternative of allowing the student to select topics to study from a menu, thus varying the order in which text units are encountered. Another variation derives from extra help sequences that are encountered by some students but not by others.

A far more sophisticated variation on a fixed, linear text, however, derives from hypermedia concepts. A hypertext is a text that has rich internal linkages so that traversal of the text is not limited to a single order (Conklin 1987). A novel, for example, might have linkages across all of the activities of each character so that a reader can view the story from the perspective of a single character rather than from the author's imposed order. Similarly, glossary, dictionary, and atlas entries can be linked to particular words and phrases, entire texts of bibliographic references linked to sentences and paragraphs, and corresponding passages from successive editions of the same text linked. Hypertext is both auto-deconstruction and auto-construction, allowing multiple definitions and traversals of the same text, but at the same time eliminating the concept of "text," other than as a reference to material issued in a set physical form. Hypertext is the most radical change yet attempted in the definition of a textbook, empowering readers and instructors with choices that have been closely guarded by authors and publishers in the past. Like customized publishing, discussed below, hypermedia changes the development procedure for the prescribed curriculum and potentially alters the relationship between the prescribed and delivered curriculum.

Customized Publishing. A textbook today, in spite of a variety of problems in the publishing industry, still represents an authoritative statement about a topic. A reference to a particular text and edition (e.g., John F. Stoddard, *The American Intellectual Arithmetic*, new revised edition, 1860) is a pointer to a definite, fixed text that can be examined equally by all who choose to do so. Customized publishing, now announced for college texts, and proposed for high school and elementary texts, may change that concept of a textbook (McDowell 1989). Using a new publishing and printing machine that allows convenient and inexpensive selection and editing of material for a book, publishers can now tailor textbooks for individual instructor needs, adding or deleting material, altering the difficulty level of problems, and the like. Even the instructor's name, institution, and course number can be imprinted on the cover and title page. A textbook with a single title may soon exist in a thousand different forms, thus altering the basic definition of a textbook.

Customized publishing also alters the relationships across needed, desired, and prescribed curricula by giving local control over a major part of the text content. Where today authors or editorial committees translate the desired curriculum into the prescribed curriculum, customized publishing allows a far more complex set of relationships. The textbook of the future might consist of a base or frame, plus a variety of options for inclusion within this frame. Schools, school districts, and states could then specify the particular configurations they desire, varying emphases, methods of presentation, and specific content. The machine that allows all of this to occur economically also generates indexes, paginates, prints, and binds. The result, if implemented on a wide scale, could be a revolution in the control of textbook content, giving to the customer not just a choice among the products of different publishers but also the ability to edit any existing text or potentially to configure a new text from available components. Textbook design would also need to change from a set of decisions on single choices for each text feature to selection of a range of options plus techniques for ensuring coherence and compatibility as options are selected by consumers.

CONCLUDING VIEWS

Textbooks occupy a dominant position in American education, perhaps because of problems in the selection and training of teachers. Ideally, textbooks would be resources for teachers to use in designing instruction rather than recipes for instruction itself. While much can be said about the limitations of modern textbooks and particularly about their bias toward the established order, it is difficult to construct an ideal role for these texts. The alternative to propagation of the values of the effective dominant culture is to incorporate values that challenge this domination. Yet probably few parents would agree that this is a legitimate role for textbooks. In addition, the impact of such clashes of values on youth would be uncertain. If Elson (1964) is correct, children accept only those school values that are not contradicted by their immediate out-of-school environment. Opposition of values, therefore, might confuse rather than redirect children.

For the study of textbooks, exact methods are lacking. In some instances, particularly in the study of content in science and mathematics texts, high interrater reliabilities indicate that reasonably uniform evaluation schemes are being applied. However, in many other studies only anecdotal evidence is offered with limited criteria for replication. Even with proposed reforms in teacher training, it is unlikely that textbooks will become any less important in the coming decade. Therefore, it is important that valid and reliable methods be used in their analysis, especially if both the manifest and the latent curricula are to be aligned with the needed curriculum.

Many issues in textbook development, adoption, and use remain to be explored. We know little about the decision making processes of publishers and editors and probably less about how textbook design directs the relationship between student and text. Teachers also direct the student's relationship with the textbook, but how effectively they do this and how their mediation is influenced by textbook appearance and promotion is open to debate. Control over textbook content is another broad area in need of further exploration. Why, for example, have teacher unions been so ineffective in giving teachers a voice in textbook content? And why have academics, other than through individual involvement, been so unsuccessful in developing acceptable adoption criteria for textbooks? Have federal and state policies been responsible for the lack of national educational leadership in curricular design? Have these policies favored entrepreneurs over educators by fostering fragmentation in the educational community?

These are some but not all of the issues that textbook studies could engage. This is a field waiting to be organized, to be inducted into the collective of educational science. Without a national agency for textbook development, the prescribed curriculum will continue to be instantiated by private enterprise. Whether for promotion of school reform or simply for understanding better a vital component of the schooling process, textbook studies should become a more active pursuit within educational research.

References

Ahier, John. 1988. *Industry, Children, and the Nation: An Analysis of National Identity in School Textbooks*. London: Falmer.

Altbach, Philip G. 1987. "Textbooks in Comparative Education." In *Educational Technology—Its Creation, Development and Cross-Cultural Transfer*, edited by R. Murray Thomas and Victor N. Kobayashi, 159–175. Oxford, England: Pergamon.

American Association for the Advancement of Science. 1989. *Science for All Americans*. Washington, DC: American Association for the Advancement of Science.

American Council on Education. 1949. *Intergroup Relations in Teaching Materials: A Survey and Appraisal*. Washington, DC: American Council on Education.

American Journal of Education. 1829. Thoughts on primary education. *American Journal of Education* 4: 61: 482–497.

Anderson, Richard C., Elfrieda H. Hiebert, Judith A. Scott, and Ian A. G. Wilkinson. 1985. *Becoming a Nation of Readers: The Report of the Commission on Reading*. Washington, DC: National Institute of Education.

Anyon, Jean. 1979. Ideology and United States history textbooks. *Harvard Educational Review* 49(3): 361–386.

Apple, Michael W. 1988. *Teachers and Texts: A Political Economy of Class and Gender Relations in Education*. New York: Routledge & Kegan Paul.

Bagley, William C., and Harold O. Rugg. 1916. The content of history as taught in the seventh and eighth grades: An analysis of typical school textbooks. *University of Illinois School of Education Bulletin* 16: 5–59.

Banks, James A. 1969. A content analysis of the black American in textbooks. *Social Education* 33: 954–957, 963.

Bardeen, C. W., ed. 1887. *The Orbis Pictus of John Amos Comenius*. Syracuse, NY: Bardeen.

Barzun, Jacques. 1945. *Teacher in America*. Boston: Little, Brown.

Belok, Michael V. 1973. *Forming the American Mind: Early Schoolbooks and Their Compilers (1783–1837)*. Moti Katra, Agra-U.P. (India): Satish Book Enterprise.

Benjamin, Ludy T., Jr. 1988. A history of teaching machines. *American Psychologist* 43(9): 703–712.

Bestor, Arthur E. 1953. *Educational Wastelands: The Retreat from Learning in our Public Schools*. Urbana: University of Illinois Press.

Bierstedt, Robert. 1955. "The Writers of Textbooks." In *Text Materials in Modern Education*, edited by Lee J. Cronbach, 96–126. Champaign: University of Illinois Press.

Black, Hillel. 1967. *The American Schoolbook*. New York: Morrow.

Bordelon, Kathleen W. 1985. Sexism in reading materials. *The Reading Teacher* 38: 791–797.

Broudy, Eric. 1975. The trouble with textbooks. *Teachers College Record* 77: 13–34, 38–43.

Bruner, Jerome S. 1960. *The Process of Education*. Cambridge, MA: Harvard University Press.

Buswell, Guy T. 1931. "A Selected and Annotated Bibliography of Literature Pertaining to Textbooks." In *Thirtieth Yearbook of the National Society for the Study of Education*, Part II *(The Textbook in American Education)*, edited by Guy Montrose Whipple, 309–323. Bloomington, IL.: Public School Co.

Calfee, Robert C., and Marilyn J. Chambliss. 1987. The structural design features of large texts. *Educational Psychologist* 22: 357–378.

Carpenter, Charles. 1963. *History of American Schoolbooks*. Philadelphia, PA: University of Pennsylvania Press.

Carper, James C., and William J. Weston. 1990. Conservative protestants in the new school wars. Essay review. *History of Education Quarterly* 30(1): 79–87.

Chall, Jeanne S. 1977. "An Analysis of Textbooks in Relation to Declining SAT Scores." Paper prepared for the Advisory Panel on the SAT Score Decline, jointly sponsored by the College Board and the Educational Testing Service, New York City.

Chambliss, Marilyn J., and Robert C. Calfee. In press. Designing science textbooks to enhance student understanding.

Clifford, Geraldine J. 1973. "A History of the Impact of Research on Teaching." In *Second Handbook of Research on Teaching*, edited by R. M. W. Travers, 1–46. Chicago: Rand McNally.

Clifford, Geraldine J. 1984. Buch und Lesen: Historical perspectives on literacy and schooling. *Review of Educational Research* 54: 472–500.

Cody, Caroline. 1990. "The Politics of Textbook Publishing, Adoption and Use." In *Eighty-ninth Yearbook of the National Society for the Study of Education*, Part I *(Textbooks and Schooling in the United States)*, edited by David L. Elliott and Arthur Woodward, 127–145. Chicago: National Society for the Study of Education.

Commager, Henry Steele. 1962. Foreword to *McGuffey's Fifth Eclectic Reader*, by Alexander Hamilton McGuffey. New York: New American Library.

Conklin, Jeff. 1987. Hypertext: An introduction and survey. *Computer* 20(9): 17–41.

Conlon, John B., and Peter B. Dow. 1975. Pro/con forum: The MACOS controversy. . . . *Social Education* 39: 388–396.

Cremin, Lawrence A. 1980. *American Education: The National Experience 1783–1876*. New York: Harper Colophon Books.

Cronbach, Lee J. 1955a. "The Text in Use." In *Text Materials in Modern Education*, edited by Lee J. Cronbach, 188–216. Champaign: University of Illinois Press.

Cronbach, Lee J., ed. 1955b. *Text Materials in Modern Education*. Champaign: University of Illinois Press.

Cubberley, Ellwood P. 1920. *The History of Education*. Boston: Houghton Mifflin.

Curti, Merle. 1978 [1935]. *The Social Ideas of American Educators*. Totowa, NJ: Littlefield, Adams.

Darwin, Charles. 1930 [1871]. *The Descent of Man and Selection in Relation to Sex*. 2nd ed., revised and augmented. New York: Appleton.

Davidson, Cathy. 1989. "The Life and Times of *Charlotte Temple*." In *Reading in America*, edited by Cathy Davidson, 157–179. Baltimore, MD: Johns Hopkins University Press.

Davies, W. J. Frank. 1974. *Teaching Reading in Early England*. New York: Harper & Row.

Davis, O. L., Jr., Gerald Ponder, Lynn M. Burlbaw, Maria Garza-Lubeck, and Alfred Moss. 1986. *Looking at History: A Review of Major U.S. History Textbooks*. Washington, DC: People for the American Way.

De Camp, L. S. 1969. End of the monkey war. *Scientific American* 220: 15–21.

de Charms, Richard, and Gerald H. Moeller. 1962. Values expressed in American children's readers: 1800–1950. *Journal of Abnormal and Social Psychology* 64: 136–142.

DelFattore, Joan. 1986. Contemporary censorship pressures and their effects on literature textbooks. *ADE Bulletin* 83: 35–40.

DelFattore, Joan. 1989. Religious implications of children's literature as viewed by religious fundamentalists: The Mozert case. *Children's Literature Association Quarterly* 14: 9–13.

Dewey, John. 1902. *The Child and the Curriculum*. Chicago: University of Chicago Press.

Dewey, John. 1976 [1901]. *The Educational Situation. John Dewey. The Middle Years, 1899–1924*, edited by Jo Ann Boydston, vol. 1, 257–313. Carbondale: Southern Illinois University Press.

Eisner, Elliot. 1987. Why the textbook influences curriculum. *Curriculum Review* 26(3): 11–13.

Eliot, Charles W. 1969 [1898]. *Educational Reform*. New York: Arno Press.

Elliott, David L. 1990. Textbooks and curriculum in the post war era, 1950–1980. In *Eighty-Ninth Yearbook of the National Society for the Study of Education*, Part I *(Textbooks and Schooling in the United States)*, edited by David L. Elliott and Arthur Woodward, 42–55. Chicago: National Society for the Study of Education.

Elliott, David L., and Arthur Woodward, eds. 1990. *Eighty-Ninth Yearbook of the National Society for the Study of Education*, Part I *(Textbooks and Schooling in the United States)*. Chicago: National Society for the Study of Education.

Elson, Ruth Miller. 1964. *Guardians of Tradition: American Schoolbooks of the Nineteenth Century*. Lincoln: University of Nebraska Press.

EPIE (Educational Products Information Exchange) Institute. 1977. *Report on a National Study of the Nature and Quality of Instructional Materials Most Used by Teachers and Learners*. Report No. 76. New York: EPIE.

Exman, Eugene. 1967. *The House of Harper: One Hundred and Fifty Years of Publishing*. New York: Harper & Row.

Farrell, Joseph P., and Stephen P. Heyneman. 1988. "Textbooks in Developing Countries: Economic and Pedagogical Choices." In *Textbooks in the Third World*, edited by Philip G. Altbach and Gail P. Kelly, 19–44. New York: Garland.

Fassett, James H. 1918. *The Beacon Readers*. Boston: Ginn.

Febvre, Lucien, and Henri-Jean Martin. 1984 [1958]. *The Coming of the Book: The Impact of Printing 1450–1800*. London: Verso.

Feldhusen, John F. 1963. Taps for teaching machines. *Phi Delta Kappan* 44: 265–267.

FitzGerald, Frances. 1979. *America Revised: History Schoolbooks in the Twentieth Century*. Boston: Little, Brown.

Flanders, James R. 1987. How much of the content in mathematics textbooks is new? *Arithmetic Teacher* 35 (September): 18–23.

Flesch, Rudolf. 1955. *Why Johnny Can't Read and What You Can Do About It*. New York: Harper & Brothers.

Ford, Paul Leicester. 1899. *The New-England Primer*. New York: Dodd, Mead.

Frost, Jerry William. 1973. *The Quaker Family in Colonial America: A Portrait of the Society of Friends*. New York: St. Martin's Press.

Garfinkle, Norton. 1954. Conservatism in American textbooks, 1800–1860. *New York History* 35: 49–63.

Goodlad, John. 1979. *Curriculum Inquiry: The Study of Curriculum Practice*. New York: McGraw-Hill.

Hahn, Carole L., and Glen Blankenship. 1981. Women and economics textbooks. *Theory and Research in Social Education* 11(3): 67–76.

Heartman, Charles F. 1934. *The New England Primer Printed in America Prior to 1830: A Bibliographic Checklist*. 3rd ed. New York: Bowker.

Heartman, Charles F. 1935. *American Primers, Indian Primers, Royal Primers, and Thirty-Seven Other Types of Non-New England Primers Issued Prior to 1830*. Highland Park, IL: Weiss.

Henry, Nelson B. 1931. "The Problem of Publishers in Making and Marketing Textbooks." In *Thirtieth Yearbook of the National Society for the Study of Education*, Part II *(The Textbook in American Education)*, edited by Guy Montrose Whipple, 175–198. Bloomington, IL: Public School Co.

Hostetler, John A. 1958. *God Uses Ink: The Heritage and Mission of the Mennonite Publishing House After Fifty Years*. Scottsdale, PA: Herald Press.

Jensen, Frank A. 1931a. "The Selection of Manuscripts by Publishers." In *The Thirtieth Yearbook of the National Society for the Study of Education*, Part II *(The Textbook in American Education)*, edited by Guy Montrose Whipple, 79–92. Bloomington, IL: Public School Co.

Jensen, Frank A. 1931b. "Current Practices in Selecting Textbooks for the Elementary Schools." In *The Thirtieth Yearbook of the National Society for the Study of Education* Part II (*The Textbook in American Education)*, 127–142. Bloomington, IL: Public School Co.

Johnson, Clifton. 1963 [1904]. *Old-Time Schools and School-Books*. New York: Dover.

Judd, Charles H. 1936. The significance for textbook-making of the newer concepts in education. *Elementary School Journal* 36: 575–582.

Kaestle, Carl F. 1983. *The Pillars of the Republic*. New York: Hill and Wang.

Klausmeier, Herbert J., Richard A. Rossmiller, and Mary Saily, eds. 1977. *Individually Guided Elementary Education*. New York: Academic Press.

Kliebard, Herbert M. 1986. *The Struggle for the American Curriculum 1893–1958*. Boston: Routledge & Kegan Paul.

Kleibard, Herbert M., and Greg Wegner. 1987. "Harold Rugg and the Reconstruction of the Social Studies Curriculum: The Treatment of the 'Great War' in his Textbook Series." In *The Formation of School Subjects: The Struggle for Creating an American Institution*, edited by Thomas S. Popkewitz, 268–287. London: Falmer.

Kuhn, Thomas S. 1970. *The Structure of Scientific Revolutions*. 2nd edition, enlarged. Chicago: University of Chicago Press.

Lamport, Harold B. 1937. *A History of the Teaching of Beginning Reading*. Chicago: private edition.

LaPointe, Archie E., Nancy Mead, and Gary W. Phillips. 1989. *A World of Differences. An International Assessment of Mathematics and Science*. Report No. 19-CAEP-01. Princeton, NJ: Educational Testing Service.

Lindberg, Stanley W. 1976. *The Annotated McGuffey*. New York: Van Nostrand Reinhold.

Littlefield, George Emery. 1904. *Early Schools and Schoolbooks of New England*. Boston: Club of Odd Volumes.

Livengood, William Winfred. 1953. *Our Textbooks, Yesterday and Today*. New York: American Institute of Graphic Arts.

Lorimer, Rowland, and Margaret Long. 1979–1980. Sex-role stereotyping in elementary readers. *Interchange* 10(2): 25–45.

Luke, Alan. 1988. *Literacy, Textbooks and Ideology: Postwar Literacy Instruction and the Mythology of Dick and Jane*. London: Falmer.

Lyman, Rollo La Verne. 1922. *English Grammar in American Schools Before 1850*. Chicago: Privately printed.

Lynch, Paddy P., and Paul D. Strube. 1985. Ten decades of the science textbook: A revealing mirror of science past and present. *Journal of Science and Mathematics Education in Southeast Asia* 8(2): 31–42.

Lynden, Frederick C. 1985. Reporting book prices. *Book Research Quarterly* 1(2): 87–89.

McClelland, David C. 1961. *The Achieving Society*. Princeton, NJ: Van Nostrand.

McDowell, Edwin. 1989. Facts to fit every fancy: Custom textbooks are here. *New York Times*, 23 October, D1, D11.

McMurray, Foster, and Lee J. Cronbach. 1955. "The Controversial Past and Present of the Text." In *Text Materials in Modern Education*, edited by Lee J.Cronbach. Champaign: University of Illinois Press.

Mann, Horace. 1839. Reading and reading books. *American Annals of Education* 9: 289–299.

Margolis, Richard J. 1965. The well-tempered textbook. *Teachers College Record* 66(8): 663–670.

Marker, Gerald W. 1980. Why schools abandon 'New Social Studies' materials. *Theory and Research in Social Education* 7: 35–56.

Miles, Matthew B. 1981. "Mapping the Common Properties of Schools." In *Improving Schools: Using What We Know*, edited by Rolf Lehming and Michael Kane, 42–114. Beverly Hills, CA: Sage.

Minnich, Harvey C. 1936. *William Holmes McGuffey and His Readers*. New York: American Book.

Moffett, James. 1988. *Storm in the Mountains: A Case Study of Censorship, Conflict, and Consciousness*. Carbondale: Southern Illinois University Press.

Monaghan, E. Jennifer. 1983. *A Common Heritage: Noah Webster's Blue-Back Speller*. Hamden, CT: Archon Books.

Monaghan, E. Jennifer. 1989. "Literary Instruction and Gender in Colonial New England." In *Reading in America*, edited by Cathy N. Davidson, 53–80. Baltimore, MD: Johns Hopkins University Press.

Mosier, Richard D. 1947. *Making the American Mind: Social and Moral Ideas in the McGuffey Readers*. New York: King's Crown Press.

National Commission on Excellence in Education. 1983. *A Nation at Risk: The Imperative for Educational Reform*. Washington, DC: U.S. Department of Education.

Nelkin, Dorothy. 1976. The science-textbook controversies. *Scientific American* 234: 33–39.

Nietz, John A. 1961. *Old Textbooks*. Pittsburgh, PA: University of Pittsburgh Press.

Nietz, John A. 1964. Why the longevity of the McGuffey readers? *History of Education Quarterly* 4: 119–125.

Nietz, John A. 1966. *The Evolution of American Secondary School Textbooks*. Rutland, VT: Tuttle.

O'Brien, Sharon. 1989. "The Case Against Willa Cather." In *Reading in America*, edited by Cathy N. Davidson, 240–258. Baltimore, MD: Johns Hopkins University Press.

Packer, Katherine H. 1954. *Early American School Books: A Bibliography Based on the Boston Booksellers' Catalogue of 1804*. University of Michigan Library Science Studies No. 1. Ann Arbor: Department of Library Science, University of Michigan.

Parrish, T. Michael, and Robert M. Willingham, Jr. 1987. *Confederate Imprints: A Bibliography of Southern Publications from Secession to Surrender*. Austin, TX: Jenkins.

Pilkington, James Penn. 1968. *The Methodist Publishing House: A History*. Nashville, TN: Abingdon Press.

Porter, Andrew C. 1981. "Elementary Mathematics Textbooks." In *The Textbook in American Society*, edited by John Y. Cole and Thomas G. Sticht, 19–20. Washington, DC: Library of Congress.

Porter, Andrew C. 1989. A curriculum out of balance: The case of elementary school mathematics. *Educational Researcher* 18(5): 9–15.

Pressey, Sidney L. 1926. A simple device for teaching, testing and research. *School and Society* 23: 373–376.

Pulsifer, William E. 1921. *A Brief Account of the Educational Publishing Business in the United States*. Atlantic City, NJ: Privately printed.

Raizen, Senta A., and Lyle V. Jones, eds. 1985. *Indicators of Precollege Education in Science and Mathematics: A Preliminary Review*. Washington, DC: National Academy Press.

Ravitch, Diane. 1985. *The Schools We Deserve: Reflections on the Educational Crisis of Our Times*. New York: Basic Books.

Reeder, Rudolph R. 1900. The historical development of school readers and of method in teaching reading. *Columbia University Contributions to Philosophy, Psychology and Education* 8(2).

Reid, James M. 1969. *An Adventure in Textbooks, 1924–1960*. New York: Bowker.

Rice, Edwin Wilbur. 1917. *The Sunday-School Movement, 1780–1917, and the American Sunday-School Union, 1780–1917*. Philadelphia, PA: American Sunday-School Union.

Richards, Oscar W. 1923. The present status of biology in the secondary schools. *School Review* 31(2): 143–146.

Rickover, Hyman G. 1959. *Education and Freedom*. New York: Dutton.

Riesman, David. 1950. *The Lonely Crowd: A Study of the Changing American Character*. New Haven, CT: Yale University Press.

Rorabaugh, William A. 1986. *The Craft Apprentice*. New York: Oxford University Press.

Rosenbach, Abraham Simon Wolf. 1933. *Early American Children's Books*. Portland, ME: Southworth Press.

Rosenthal, Dorothy B., and Rodger W. Bybee. 1987. "Emergence of the Biology Curriculum: A Science of Life or a Science of Living?" In *The Formation of the School Subjects*, edited by Thomas S. Popkewitz, 123–144. New York: Falmer.

Rugg, Harold O. 1941. *That Men May Understand: An American in the Long Armistice*. New York: Doubleday, Doran.

Russell, William. 1847. *Primary Reader: A Selection of Easy Reading Lessons, With Introductory Exercises in Articulation, for Young Classes*. Improved edition. Boston: Tappan and Whittemore.

Saveth, Edward N. 1949. Good stocks and lesser breeds: The immigrant in American textbooks. *Commentary* 7: 493–498.

Schlesinger, Arthur M. 1938. Introduction to *School Histories at War*, by Arthur Walworth. Cambridge, MA: Harvard University Press.

Schoenfeld, Alan H. 1985. *Mathematical Problem Solving*. New York: Academic Press.

Schramm, Wilbur. 1955. "The Publishing Process." In *Text Materials in Modern Education*, edited by Lee J. Cronbach, 129–165. Champaign: University of Illinois Press.

Shannon, Patrick. 1982. Some subjective reasons for teachers' reliance on commercial reading materials. *The Reading Teacher* 35: 884–889.

Shaver, James P., O. L. Davis, Jr., and Suzanne W. Helburn. 1979. The status of social studies education: Impressions from three NSF studies. *Social Education* 43(2): 150–153.

Shirreffs, Janet H. 1975. Sex role stereotyping in elementary school health education textbooks. *Journal of School Health* 45: 519–529.

Sieber, Sam D. 1968. "Organizational Influences on Innovative Roles." In *Knowledge Production and Utilization in Educational Administration*, edited by Terry L. Eidell and Jeanne M. Kitchel, 120–142. Eugene: Center for Advanced Study of Educational Administration, University of Oregon.

Singer, Harry. 1970. Research that should have made a difference. *Elementary English* 47: 27–34.

Skinner, Benjamin F. 1954. The science of learning and the art of teaching. *Harvard Educational Review* 24(2): 86–87.

Skinner, Benjamin F. 1963. Reflections on a decade of teaching machines. *Teachers College Record* 3: 168–177.

Skoog, Gerald. 1979. Topic of evolution in secondary school textbooks 1900–1977. *Science Education* 63(5): 621–640.

Skoog, Gerald. 1984. The coverage of evolution in high school biology textbooks published in the 1980s. *Science Education* 68(2): 117–128.

Smith, Mortimer B. 1949. *And Madly Teach: A Layman Looks at Public Schools*. Chicago: Regnery.

Smith, Nila B. 1965. *American Reading Instruction*. Newark, DE: International Reading Association.

Spieseke, Alice Winifred. 1938. *The First Textbooks in American History and Their Compiler John M'Culloch*. New York: Bureau of Publications, Teachers College, Columbia University.

Squire, James R. 1985. Textbooks to the forefront. *Book Research Quarterly* 1(2): 12–18.

Squire, James R., and Richard T. Morgan. 1990. "The Elementary and High School Textbook Market Today." In *Eighty-Ninth Yearbook of the National Society for the Study of Education*, Part 1 *(Textbooks and Schooling in the United States)*, edited by David L. Elliott and Arthur Woodward, 107–126. Chicago: National Society for the Study of Education.

St. John, Judith. 1958, vol. 1. *The Osborne Collection of Early Children's Books 1566–1910*. A Catalogue. Toronto: Toronto Public Library.

St. John, Judith. 1975, vol. 2. *The Osborne Collection of Early Children's Books 1476–1910*. A Catalogue. Toronto: Toronto Public Library.

Starch, Daniel. 1921. The content of readers. In *Twentieth Yearbook of the National Society for the Study of Education*, Part II *(Report of the Society's Committee on Silent Reading)*, 145–151. Bloomington, IL: Public School Co.

Staver, John R., and Mary Bay. 1987. Analysis of the Project Synthesis goal cluster orientation and inquiry emphasis of elementary science textbooks. *Journal of Research in Science Teaching* 24(7): 629–643.

Stodolsky, Susan. 1989. "Is Teaching Really by the Book?" In *Eighty-Ninth Yearbook of the National Society for the Study of Education*, Part I *(From Socrates to Software: The Teacher as Text and the Text as Teacher)*, edited by Philip W. Jackson and Sophia Haroutunian-Gordon, 159–184. Chicago: National Society for the Study of Education.

Strube, Paul. 1989. The notion of style in physics textbooks. *Journal of Research in Science Teaching* 26(4): 291–299.

Sullivan, Mark. 1927. *Our Times: The United States 1900–1925*. vol. 2, *America Finding Herself*. New York: Scribners.

Sutton, Walter. 1961. *The Western Book Trade: Cincinnati as a Nineteenth-Century Publishing and Book Trade Center*. Columbus: Ohio State University Press.

Svobodny, Dolly, ed. 1985. *Early American Textbooks 1775–1900*. Washington, DC: U.S. Department of Education.

Tanner, Daniel. 1988. "The Textbook Controversies." In *Eighty-Seventh Yearbook of the National Society for the Study of Education*, Part I *(Critical Issues in Curriculum)*, edited by Laurel N. Tanner, 122–147. Chicago: National Society for the Study of Education.

Tebbel, John. 1972. *A History of Book Publishing in the United States. Vol. 1: The Creation of an Industry 1630–1865*. New York: Bowker.

Tebbel, John. 1972–1981. *A History of Book Publishing in the United States*. 4 vols. New York: Bowker.

Tebbel, John. 1975. *A History of Book Publishing in the United States. Vol. 2. The Expansion of an Industry 1865–1919*. New York: Bowker.

Tingelstad, Oscar A. 1913. "The Religious Element in American School Readers." Unpublished master's thesis, University of Chicago.

Trecker, Janice Law. 1971. Women in U.S. history high school textbooks. *Social Education* 35: 249–260.

Tuer, Andrew W. 1897. *History of the Horn-Book*, 2 vols. New York: Arno Press.

Tufte, Edward R. 1983. *The Visual Display of Quantitative Information*. Cheshire, CT: Graphics Press.

Tully, Michael A., and Roger Farr. 1985. Textbook adoption: Insights, impact, and potential. *Book Research Quarterly* 1(2): 4–11.

Tyack, David B. 1974. *The One Best System*. Cambridge, MA: Harvard University Press.

Venezky, Richard L. 1982. The origins of the present-day chasm between adult literacy needs and school literacy instruction. *Visible Language* 16: 113–127.

Venezky, Richard L. 1986. Steps toward a modern history of American reading instruction. *Review of Research in Education* 13: 129–167.

Venezky, Richard L. 1987. A history of the American reading textbook. *The Elementary School Journal* 87(3): 247–265.

Venezky, Richard L. 1989. "Representation of the Content and Process of Science." Paper presented at the annual meeting of the American Educational Research Association, May 27–31, San Francisco, CA.

Venezky, Richard L., and Luis Osin. 1991. *The Intelligent Design of Computer-Assisted Instruction*. New York: Longman.

Walworth, Arthur. 1938. *School Histories at War*. Cambridge, MA: Harvard University Press.

Watters, David H. 1985/1986. "I spake as a child": Authority, metaphor and the *New-England Primer*. *Early American Literature* 20: 193–213.

Weeks, Stephen B. 1900. "Confederate Text-Books (1861–1865): A Preliminary Bibliography." In *Report of the Commissioner of Education for 1898–99*, 1139–1155. Washington, DC: U.S. Government Printing Office.

Weiss, Iris R. 1987. *Report of the 1985–86 National Survey of Science and Mathematics Education*. Research Triangle Park, NC: National Science Foundation.

Welch, d'Alte A. 1972. *A Bibliography of Children's Books Printed Prior to 1821*. Worcester, MA: American Antiquarian Society.

Westbury, Ian. 1990. "Textbooks, Textbook Publishers, and the Quality of Schooling. In *Eighty-ninth Yearbook of the National Society for the Study of Education*, Part I *(Textbooks and Schooling in the United States)*, edited by David L. Elliott and Arthur Woodward, 1–22. Chicago: National Society for the Study of Education.

Time. 1982. Showdown in Texas. *Time* (23 August): 47.

Westerhoff, John H., III. 1978. *McGuffey and his Readers*. Nashville, TN: Abingdon.

Whipple, Guy Montrose, ed. 1931. *The Thirtieth Yearbook of the National Society for the Study of Education*, Part II *(The Textbook in American Education)*. Bloomington, IL.: Public School Co.

Williams, Raymond. 1980. *Problems in Materialism and Culture*. London: Verso.

Willows, Dale M., Diane Borwick, and Maureen Hayvren. 1981. "The Content of School Readers." In *Reading Research: Advances in Theory and Practice*, edited by G. E. Mackinnon and T. Gary Waller, 100–175. New York: Academic Press.

Woodward, Arthur. 1986. Taking teaching out of teaching and reading out of learning to read: A historical survey of reading textbook teachers' guides, 1920–1980. *Book Research Quarterly* 2(1): 53–73.

Woodward, Arthur, and David L. Elliott. 1987. Evolution and creationism in high school textbooks. *American Biology Teacher* 49: 164–170.

Woodward, Arthur, and David L. Elliott. 1990. "Textbooks: Consensus and Controversy." In *Eighty-ninth Yearbook of the National Society for the Study of Education*, Part I *(Textbooks and Schooling in the United States)*, edited by David L. Elliott and Arthur Woodward, 146–161. Chicago: National Society for the Study of Education.

Woodward, Arthur, David L. Elliott, and Kathleen Nagel. 1988. *Textbooks in School and Society: An Annotated Bibliography and Guide to Research*. New York: Garland.

Young, M. Jean. 1990. "Writing and Editing Textbooks." In *Eighty-ninth Yearbook of the National Society for the Study of Education*, Part I *(Textbooks and Schooling in the United States)*, edited by David L. Elliott and Arthur Woodward, 71–85. Chicago: National Society for the Study of Education.

Zimet, Sara, ed. 1972. *What Children Read in School*. New York: Grune & Stratton.

Part

3

THE CURRICULUM AS A SHAPING FORCE

17

STUDENTS' EXPERIENCE OF THE CURRICULUM

Frederick Erickson
UNIVERSITY OF PENNSYLVANIA

Jeffrey Shultz
BEAVER COLLEGE

> The word "interaction". . . expresses [one of the] chief principles for interpreting an experience in its educational function and force. It assigns equal rights to both factors in experience—objective and internal conditions. . . . The immediate and direct concern of an educator is . . . with the situations in which interaction takes place. The individual, who enters as a factor into it is what he is at a given time. It is the other factor, that of objective conditions, which lies to some extent within the possibility of regulation by the educator. . . . [The notion of] "objective conditions" covers a wide range. It includes what is done by the educator and the way in which it is done, not only words spoken but the tone of voice in which they are spoken. It includes equipment, books, apparatus, toys, games played. It includes the materials with which an individual interacts, and, most important of all, the total *social* set-up of the situations in which a person is engaged. (Dewey 1963 [1938], 43 and 45)

Why would any educator need to know about student experience of the curriculum? We can test students to find out if they learned or not. If there is sufficient money and we are well organized enough we can reteach those who didn't learn the first time around and catch those who slipped through the cracks and somehow didn't get taught at all. But if we are concerned that a wide range of students learn judgment and reasoning, as well as facts, perhaps a clearer understanding by educators of students' subjectivity in school is required.

This chapter is an attempt to explore the notion of student experience of the manifest curriculum—that is, what the school and its personnel set out deliberately to teach students and what the learning is as seen and felt by students. While we were preparing the chapter it became increasingly apparent that student experience of curriculum

For editorial advice the authors thank reviewer Jay Featherstone of Michigan State University and their colleagues Janet S. Theophano and Joanne Straceski. The authors are grateful as well to Merridy Malin and Frances Riemer for their assistance in library research.

has not received much attention recently from educators. Neither in conceptual work, nor in empirical research, nor in the conventional wisdom and discourse of practice does the subjective experience of students as they are engaged in learning figure in any central way. There are intimations of student experience as a phenomenon in some perceptive classroom research and in some prescriptive talk about teaching and learning in schools. But in our judgment, student experience has been treated in partial and incidental ways, as researchers, teacher educators, and policy analysts consider relatively thin slices of classroom life, usually from a single perspectival angle. None of these slices have been multidimensional enough to capture students' subjective worlds as whole phenomena.

We assume that students' immediate educational experience consists of aspects that researchers usually hold analytically separate—the social, the emotional, and the cognitive. Because existing theory and methods presume such separation, it may be impossible to study student experience in an integrated way. But we have been surprised by the apparent lack of attempts at such study. In consequence, what is currently known about student experience seems at best to be fragmentary guesswork.

In this chapter we consider why so little is known currently by researchers and practitioners, how one might conceive of student experience and its possible diversity, what empirical work has already been done, and how and why one might conduct research that would better inform us about relations between students' and teachers' experience in learning situations and the kinds and amounts of learning that take place within such experience. We will approach the notion of student experience in successive stages. The chapter begins with a conceptual discussion, speculating about the nature of student experience and about some of the circumstances within which the subjective experience of learning tasks might be arising for students. Then, very briefly, we consider the origins of modern classroom life as a setting for student experience and will review a range of current research. Some of this work seems to us suggestive, but no particular stream of research treats student experience in a very direct or illuminating way. We then present recommendations for further study of student experience of curriculum. Given that this topic has been underconceptualized as well as underresearched, the chapter concludes with cautionary remarks and with speculations about the policy implications of such research.

TOWARD CONCEPTIONS OF STUDENT EXPERIENCE

A View from an Earlier Era

There seems to be no better way to begin than to consult a classic source. John Dewey was a philosopher of educational experience. As the material quoted in our epigraph suggests, he saw student experience as a transaction, constructed in interaction between the student and environing conditions which were themselves constituted (in part) by the subjectivity of the student. That subjectivity involved what we think of as the social and the cognitive (Dewey 1963 [1938], 43 and 45).

Thus to understand educative experience in the Deweyan sense, it would be necessary to pay close attention, first, to the needs, purposes, personality disposition, and intellectual capacities brought by the student to the scene of immediate curricular engagement and, second, to what is present in that scene to be engaged by the student, as she sees, hears, speaks, and otherwise acts among the persons, artifacts, and social relations in and through which "curriculum" is being encountered. The social relations and meanings within which a student confronts a book page, a bunsen burner, an utterance, or a glance by a teacher or fellow student were fundamental in Dewey's conception of educational experience. How students construed those social relations, what residues of social meaning were brought by the students to the scene of engagement as a result of past experience, and what new social/intellectual meanings and feelings were generated as students and teachers interacted with curriculum were crucial for the subjective experience of learning. Thought, action, motive, and emotion in school were social constructions, accomplishments that arose in the interaction of people, materials, and subject matter.

In more modern terms we might say that the relative richness and subjective meaning of student experience of curriculum makes for the difference between acquisition of lower-order and higher-order skills, between higher literacies and lower ones, or between learning to reason and learning to follow algorithms. But Dewey's notion of experience is richer than our current notions of skills, algorithms, or even of reasoning and literacy as we usually conceive it. Educational experience in his sense of the term, that which advanced the continuity of sustained growth in the student, was the *situs* not only of clear and dexterous thinking but of the passion, truthfulness to self, and commitment in the face of risk that is inherent in genuine learning. Such learning was intrinsically worthwhile, as distinct from the spurious learning into which students had to be coerced or bribed. Dewey saw the latter as false and miseducative experience.

In ordinary classroom life it is the "enacted curriculum" (Eisner 1985) rather than the stated one that is engaged by students and by teachers. How that engagement takes place in concrete interaction and what it becomes as subjective experience for the student is the topic of this chapter. The student's experience of enacted curriculum is significant, presumably, because it is within such experience that learning about self and the world takes place. What is or is not learned and how such learning, relearning, and unlearning are entailed in the unfolding constitution of students as persons can be presumed to vary with the differing kinds of educational experience that students have. Thus, for the proper conduct of teaching, of school organization, and of research in education, a clear understanding of the natures and conditions of student experiences would seem to be fundamental. Indeed we might do well to paraphrase William James and retitle this chapter "The Varieties of Student Experience." Let us try to consider more fully the possibilities of diverse subjective worlds that students could be inhabiting in schools.

The Absence of Student Experience in Current Discourse

Because so little empirical and conceptual work has directly considered student experience, we will begin to explore some issues indirectly, by means of a metaphor. (This characterization of normal educational practice, while whimsical, is generally warranted by the following descriptions of ordinary life in schools published over a number of years, especially over the last 3 decades. The list is as follows: Cuban, 1984; Cusick, 1973, 1983; Dreeben 1968; Eisner 1985; Goodlad 1984; Goodman 1962; Henry 1963; Holt 1964; Jackson 1968; Kohl 1967, McDermott 1974; Mehan et al. 1985; Metz 1978; Powell et al. 1968; Rist 1970, 1978; Rose 1990; Sizer 1985; and Waller 1932.) In ordinary classroom practice in American schools it appears that the reigning conception of curriculum and pedagogy is that of school lunch. It is as if the job of the teacher were to take packages of mind-food from the freezer (the curriculum), thaw them in a microwave (instruction), and see to it that the students eat it until it is finished (classroom management to maximize time on task). It is not the teacher's responsibility (nor that of the student) to decide what or how much should be eaten or when and how long mealtime should be. Not only is the food served entirely prepackaged but much of each student's daily portion is chopped into small bits, boiled, or mashed in an attempt at predigestion that lowers its basic nutritional content. Moreover, large amounts of sugar, salt, and fat are found in the food. Although these substances enhance palatability somewhat, they are deleterious for the students' long-term health and well-being.

The emphasis, both in preparing and serving the lunch, appears to be to stimulate consumption and monitor its short-term nutritional effects, which are called *outcomes*. If certain students repeatedly refuse to eat the normal lunch, or eat it very slowly, they are served specially wrapped packages of the same food, chopped a bit more finely (remedial instruction). The lunch room attendants monitor those students individually or in small groups to make sure that they eat what is set before them. If the students continue to be slow in consuming their lunch or refuse to eat it at all, they are taken away to another lunchroom (special education). A few students eat very quickly. These may be sent a few times a week to a small cafeteria where they can choose fresh vegetables and fruits to make their own salads and desserts (gifted and talented program). Especially when the students are young, they watch each other carefully during lunch. They are very aware of what, how much, and how fast one another eat and of how the attendants react to the various kinds of eaters.

It is in the nature of metaphor and analogy that they do not fit perfectly the cases to which they are applied. Here the relationship between ingestion and digestion differs from that between instruction and learning. Formal education thus seems to be a far more mysterious process than having lunch. Students can refuse to learn what the school claims to teach them, not only by not "eating"—by refusing to sit still for instruction—but by going through the appearance of learning without actually assimilating what was presented in the curricular "meal." Students can withhold assimilating what is being attempted to be taught by offering what Dewey called "outer attention," as distinct from "inner attention" (1965 [1904], 148).

In spite of a lack of fit between some particular aspects of school lunch in comparison with classroom teaching and learning, the metaphor of lunch, prepackaged and upon occasion force fed, appears to characterize all too well the ways in which contemporary educators conduct instruction as a means of getting the curriculum into students. Questions about students' inner attention go unasked in the typical pedagogical lunchroom.

It would make sense, then, that student experience and its possible diversity do not appear as a phenomenon of interest in current debates on educational policy and research. It is a nuisance, a distraction, to think that different students, together with their teachers and fellow students, might be inhabiting and constructing profoundly differing subjective worlds as they encounter what the school presents as a standardized curriculum with intendedly standardized methods of instruction and assessment.

During the past 30 years of educational practice there has been an attempt, which in some instances was certainly deliberate, to finesse the issue of the relation between student experience and student learning. Curriculum materials were developed to be "teacher-proof," and this can be seen as a move to make them "learner-proof" as well. Behavioristically oriented research on teacher effectiveness (see, for example, the review essays of Brophy and Good 1986 and Rosenshine 1979) has seen teaching as a "treatment," an independent variable. Observational coding systems that presume the teacher as agent and the student as recipient of action are unable to portray the mutual influence of students and teachers in the course of instructional interaction. Measures of student learning by tests administered after the fact of curricular engagement are unable to reveal the kinds and qualities of experiences students had during the course of learning.

In sum, virtually no research has been done that places student experience at the center of attention. We do not see student interests and their known and unknown fears. We do not see the mutual influence of students and teachers or see what the student or the teacher thinks or cares about during the course of that mutual influence. If the student is visible at all in a research study he is usually viewed from the perspective of adult educators' interests and ways of seeing, that is, as failing, succeeding, motivated, mastering, unmotivated, responding, or having a misconception. Rarely is the perspective of the student herself explored.

Classroom research typically does not ask what the student is up to, nor does it take a critical stance toward its own categories and assumptions so as to question whether "failing" or "mastering" or being "unmotivated" or "misconceiving" adequately captures what the student might be about in daily classroom encounters with curriculum.

A Perspective on Immediate Curricular Engagement and Student Experience

An essential condition of student engagement in classroom tasks is that it is done "on line," in real time. It is the moment-to-moment character of engaging the manifest curriculum that is perhaps least well understood by researchers, by teachers, and by students themselves. There are limits inherent in empirical study of real-time phenomena. Direct observation cannot reveal fully the student's experience in the midst of engagement with curriculum, although close observation can provide clues that point to the nature of the experience. Interviewing would seem to be a more appropriate means to uncover the subjective experience of a student within a classroom task. Yet interviewing after the fact of immediate experience produces retrospective accounts that tend not only to be overrationalized but that, because of their synoptic form, condense the story of engagement in a way that fails to convey the on-line character of the actual engagement.

Classroom tasks as experienced in real time are always sequential and are usually recursive as well. Whether one is writing an essay on the causes of the American Civil War or conducting an experiment on photosynthesis in plants or completing a page of problems in an arithmetic workbook or reciting the Pledge of Allegiance to the Flag, one does not engage the whole task at any single moment in time. Rather, one engages the task in a series of steps. These may be predetermined by the display of the task in the instructional materials or in the classroom interaction as led by the teacher. In some tasks the succession of steps may be sequentially ordered at the partial discretion of the individual learner, as in silent reading. Sequences may recur, as in repeated observations in the photosynthesis experiment, in a repeated set of mathematical operations as one completes a series of arithmetic problems assigned for practice, and in returning to the upper left-hand side of each new page in reading a novel.

When a student engages a classroom task, at any given moment within a connected sequence of steps there is always a social relational aspect and a subject matter aspect to the work at hand. What has come to be called "task analysis" of a sequence, as done by cognitive psychologists, can provide an interpretation of the state of the task at any moment in terms of the intellectual cognition that is required of the student at that point in the sequence. Such an analysis can uncover the logical operations required in the task as presented. It does not identify the problem space: the cognitive structure of the task as perceived (see the discussion in Posner 1982). But even that more sophisticated conception of an intellectual task, as seen through the eyes of the thinker who confronts it, sketches only the subject matter aspect of the task. This is only one of the two main aspects or dimensions of a classroom task as a student experiences it. The other aspect is that of social relations and social meaning. This bears on the overall cognitive difficulty of the task, on the feelings of the learner regarding it, and, often, on the interactional logistics and politics of accomplishing the particular step in a task that the student confronts in a given moment.

Issues of social relations are entailed in—indeed constitute—every step along a task's way, from its appearance on the scene to its completion. In the setting of the task there are issues of social relationship between the teacher and the student. Who chose the task and who chose the way of engaging it? Given the general tenor of relationship the student has with the teacher, how does the student feel about doing this particular step within the task? Does the student trust the teacher or not? Is the teacher of the same race or class as the student? Is the teacher male or female? How does this influence the way the student construes the task in its entirety and the particular step encountered at just this moment?

Is the student under the scrutiny of peers or of the teacher when doing the step? How do the peers regard and define the task? What is their race, class, and gender? Who among them are special enemies or friends, allies or competitors? If the student is not sure what to do in encountering a particular step in the task, how does he get help? From a peer who is a friend or one who is a competitor? From the teacher? Does seeking help affiliate the student with others, or is it a disgrace to ask for help? Is it a social set-up, to use Dewey's term, in which the teacher defines it a crime to offer assistance and peers define it an obligation? (We can define tests in social relational terms as a curricular task in which no other person is legitimately available for assistance. Tests are a qualitatively different kind of classroom task from review and practice work precisely because of the dimension of social organization. The subject matter content can be identical in practice and in a test—the same arithmetic problem or spelling word. What makes the test distinctive as a learning situation is its character as a particularly framed occasion of social interaction.)

How does a task relate to the trajectory of the student's purposes in learning? How have those purposes been influenced by immediate past experience with this classroom, teacher, and set of peers, by the influence and identification with, or disaffiliation from, parents and siblings, and by experience in the more distant past with other peers and other teachers? Consider the example of the photosynthesis experiment. If at some point in that work it becomes necessary to use long division as the student summarizes numerically a set of observations, how is her current experience of long division influenced by her prior experience with long division, by the teacher who originally taught it, by parents who urged the student to master it, or who mocked it as a useless skill? How is the student's experience affected by the immediate scene, if, for example, she is the only one in the group conducting the experiment who doesn't know how to do as rapidly and accurately as others in the group the kind of long division that is necessary at this point in the experiment? What issues of face become salient then, and how do these become part of the student's experience of learning about photosynthesis? How does all this affect the nature of classroom tasks as variously experienced by different students?

Recent work on the socially situated nature of everyday cognition (Brown, Collins, and Duguid 1989; Wertsch 1985, 1991) suggests that, depending upon the learner's purposes, the emotional content of relations with other persons in the scene, the cultural familiarity of oral discourse routines by which the task is being manifested in classroom talk, and a myriad of other features of social relations that can bear on accomplishing a classroom task successfully, the task itself becomes a fundamentally different entity depending upon its situation in social relations. Hence we can say more formally (see Erickson 1982a, 1982b; Erickson and Shultz 1981) that the overall academic task structure (ATS) as encountered by a student consists of a social participation task structure (SPTS) and a subject matter task structure (SMTS). Both aspects or dimensions of the task structure involve sequential steps, they call upon prior knowledge, and they evoke feelings about the sociocognitive activity at hand. It is not simply that affect is connected to the social aspects of the task and cognition to its subject matter aspects. Students do think work in dealing with issues of social relations ("How do I get a turn at talk appropriately?" "How can I display knowledge or ignorance without embarrassing myself or others?"), and they do feeling work in engaging issues of subject matter ("Aaargh! Long division again!").

The Classroom as a Scene for Student Experience of Curriculum

Classrooms are so familiar to us that we usually take for granted main features of their social organization. Yet the typical American school classroom is a very special kind of setting. As a social form the classroom institutionalizes certain patterns of social relations. Taken together these form a learning environment that, we can presume, is influencing student experience of curriculum in certain ways. What those influences are, more precisely, and how they actually contribute to the student's subjective experience of learning remain to be explored systematically in research. But perhaps if we consider the general nature of the classroom as a learning environment in the same speculative way in which we have just considered curricular engagement at the level of the individual student, we can shed further light on the initial conceptions and directions that formal research might take. Accordingly, we will step back a bit from the view of the student at his desk in order to think about classrooms in their normal organization as places that generate particular kinds of scenes of curricular engagement.

American classrooms in their social and intellectual ecology present distinct circumstances in which learners engage curriculum. Classroom instruction brings students and teachers together with subject matter. The immediate purposes of students and the teacher, the more distal aims behind the selection of certain contents and materials, and the even more general cultural frameworks—the ontological assumptions about proper ways of thinking and acting in teaching and learning—that influence the interaction of teachers and students with subject matter are, at the point of subjective experience, inseparable for the student and for the teacher as well.

The manifest aim of the normal classroom as a scene of life is that students are to be taught there and are to learn what they are assigned to learn by the teacher, who may or may not be acting in concert with the aims of some authority external to the classroom. Learning what is assigned may not take place, however, either because students withhold assent to learn or because the learning tasks set by the teacher are presented in such a form that they are impossible for the students to master.

Classrooms, as sites in which students act upon new knowledge and skills, are busy places in which much interaction occurs rapidly (Jackson 1968). It was apparent in our previous discussion of curricular engagement that students in classrooms do not encounter the manifest curriculum (what is officially and deliberately assigned to be learned) by working as isolated minds in solitary cells, as did Foucault's prisoners observed in a panopticon (Foucault 1979, 195–209). Rather, the engagement of students with curricular tasks is audienced. This is an essential feature of such engagement. Students are constantly aware of the potential attention of the teacher in the presence of other students, who potentially may also attend to what the student is doing in any given moment.

Thus classrooms are semipublic arenas for the display of interest and/or competence by students or for the display of student lack of interest and/or incompetence. In these arenas, competition frames the moments of display. Within various arenas, constructed anew in daily interaction, some students compete to show that they know and can do what they are supposed to be doing, others compete to show that they cannot or will not do what they are supposed to be doing, while still others withdraw from display and competition as much as possible, hiding out from both positive and negative attention from others (see McDermott 1974).

Classrooms are characterized by marked asymmetry of formal and informal rights and obligations among participants. Formally and informally the roles of teacher and student are asymmetric. In addition, there are often formal distinctions among students, who are "tracked" into separate instructional groupings according to their levels of academic performance. In elementary schools this tracking usually occurs within classrooms, as students are divided into so-called "ability groups" for instruction, often in reading and sometimes also in mathematics. In middle school and high school, tracking often occurs between classrooms, with separate sections of a subject offered at different levels of difficulty and with separate programs of study offered to different sets of students (Oakes 1985).

Informally as well as formally there are significant role distinctions among students who occupy statuses within pecking orders on various dimensions. Some of those rankings are defined by affiliation and approval between students and the teacher. Other rankings are defined by distancing and disapproval from the teacher. Still other rankings are more powerfully influenced by relations among differing subgroups of peers than they are by relations with teachers or other adults. Despite general and surface similarities among classrooms, the local social set-up of specific classrooms can differ markedly in the extent to which academic achievement and affiliation with the teacher and with peers varies systematically along lines of student social identity (e.g., race, ethnicity, language background, gender, and class). This variation contributes to the production of qualitatively different kinds of classroom ecologies within which students engage curriculum.

It should be apparent from the previous discussion that the teacher's attention, and the patterning by which it is directed in daily classroom life, is probably a powerful influence upon the generation of a routine classroom social system and culture, which, because of its ubiquity, makes life predictable for classroom participants. Thus, it is worth elaborating on the organization of teacher attention.

The objects of teacher attention are at least fourfold, with various weightings across differing loci of attention. Some teachers pay attention mainly to student deportment. For others, students' feelings are especially salient. Some teachers, especially in the early grades, are very aware of informal student identities and pecking orders, while others seem less aware of the informal casts (and, possibly, castes) of characters and dimensions of ranking in their rooms. Some teachers appear to attend mainly to student displays of knowledge and skill (in the form of oral answers and completed assignments as products), while others attend as closely as possible to the developing reasoning of the students—to the questions, emerging theories, inferences, and drafts that make up the production of finished work and understanding.

Because interaction in the full, busy classroom is so dense in texture, attention by the teacher to students and by students to one another is inherently incomplete from moment to moment, even though it is pervasive overall. The potential for scrutiny by the teacher of the subject matter knowledge and deportment of individual students is constant, even though that potential is actualized for the individual student only intermittently. The spotlight of teacher attention sweeps, fixes for an instant, and then moves on, as in the prison camps portrayed in war movies, or as in a Broadway stage production, depending upon how the student experiences the classroom scene and the play of teacher attention within it.

Classroom underlife (its informal social organization) seems to ebb and flow in the recurring periods of darkness and light as the spotlight of teacher attention sweeps around the room. This underlife can be thought of as continually organizing and reorganizing around the teacher's attention. It also appears to organize to some extent apart from relations with the teacher. It contains its own more covert spotlights and arenas for attention among peers. Students may seek out or avoid such forums depending upon their purposes and lines of affiliation. In elementary school, the student underlife seems to thrive in the interstices of classroom events (e.g., going to the pencil sharpener, turning in a paper, getting ready to leave the room), as well as on the playground, at the school assembly, on the way home. In the high school, underlife is carried on in glances across the aisles of desks and, to some extent, is played out in classroom discourse. But the underlife seems also especially vigorous as it walks out the classroom door and creates interstices in the hallways and on the school's approaches—its sidewalks, lawns, parking lots—and in various sports events and entertainment sponsored by the school, such as football games and the prom. Serious trouble can develop in a school in which class, race, and ethnicity are grounds for conflict over what kinds of music are played in the school cafeteria.

In ways we don't yet understand at all clearly, certain kinds of trouble in the school's underlife and hidden curriculum could be an index to variation in student experience with the manifest curriculum. Do students act out on the front steps because of intensely negative experiences in the classroom? Given the current state of knowledge, one can only guess about this. It is reasonable to assume that ordered kinds of relations between school and classroom underlife and overlife contribute to the subjective experience of students in engaging what the school is attempting to teach through its stated curriculum. But little attempt has been made, apparently, to link research on the hidden curriculum with research on the manifest curriculum as it is enacted in instruction.

Teacher attention is only one among a number of fundamental processes in classrooms that are likely to influence the educational experience of students. Another process, equally pervasive, is the social and cultural organization of classroom trust and legitimacy. This is an issue in relations among students, and it seems to be an especially fundamental issue in relations between teachers and students.

In classrooms in which student learning is taking place, trust is continually at stake because of the risk of embarrassment and loss of face. Learning places one at the edge of one's capacity to perform adequately, with or without assistance. This is the crux of Vygotsky's (1978, 84–91) notion of the zone of proximal development. When students confront curriculum that engages within their own zones of proximal development there is always the possibility that they will make mistakes—that is, they will act in ways that are incompetent or only partially competent. If because of the nature of the classroom social system (or because of ethnic cultural values regarding privacy and indirection or because of individual temperament) students do not consider it safe to be scrutinized while they are attempting to master new knowledge and skill, they may try to hide their incompetence or even to avoid attempting to learn altogether. Especially in situations in which students do not feel affiliated with their teacher, or in which their attempts to affiliate are not reciprocated by the teacher, it may seem safer to the student to try to maintain face by refusing to try to learn rather than to risk loss of face by trying to learn, failing, and being exposed in that unsuccessful attempt. Given the risks to self-image that are inherent in trying to learn, trust in the teacher especially and also in one's peers may be essential for the establishment of classroom learning environments that are maximally educative. Yet trust in the good intentions of the teacher and in the legitimacy and potential benefit of the exercise of teacherly authority cannot be taken for granted. It may not exist for students when instruction begins. It may need to be earned by the teacher before successful instruction can proceed. This seems especially likely when instructors and students come from groups in society that are in conflict across lines of gender, race and ethnicity, first language, and class. Student experience of curriculum can be assumed to vary under differing conditions of trust and legitimacy in the teacher-student relationship.

Another issue in the classroom social system involves the alienated or nonalienated character of student and teacher labor. When "curriculum" means in ordinary practice a mandate to the teacher by someone else regarding what should be taught and what the student should learn, there may be little sense of the ownership of work by the teacher or by the student. It is not simply that for a student the assigned academic task may be seen as irrelevant or boring. It is that in some kinds of classrooms student work is never complete in itself; its aims are never clear to students; it is never self-initiated, and never owned. In certain classrooms presided over by warm or charismatic teachers, affiliation with the teacher as an attractive figure appears to justify or ameliorate in some way the structurally alienated character of the students' work. If those students like and trust the teacher they may do the work assigned even if they do not understand or own its purposes. But if the students have not bonded with the teacher and the assigned work lacks intrinsic interest for them, they may withhold effort on the tasks assigned or go through the mere motions of learning. Collusion develops, in which teachers do not press students to learn what may be meaningless or face-threatening for them and students do not press the teacher by disrupting the class (see especially McDermott 1974; Powell et al. 1986; Sizer 1985).

When student labor is alienated in the classroom and when teacher labor is alienated in relation to student labor, one could reasonably infer that this alienation must somehow affect student experience of curriculum. Classroom conditions of trust and legitimacy and patterns of attention from peers and from the teacher are also likely to affect student experience, as are the prior educational experience of the student and the student's personality, temperament, and ability. The social participation structure and the subject matter structure of curricular tasks, as assigned and as perceived, are likely to affect the experience of the student in addressing the tasks. Yet how any or all of these phenomena actually work in the daily construction of student experience is not presently understood in any systematic way. Adept and empathic teachers may make effective guesses about the roles of such matters as attention, trust, and legitimacy in their teaching. They even may be able to make fairly accurate "seat of the pants" judgments about the fit of particular tasks with particular students and about the varieties of student experience in their classrooms. But if this is so, their inferences are for the most part intuitive and transparent to themselves. Hence, their hunches are not available to others with a stake in their teaching—administrators, researchers, parents, and students. Moreover, key aspects of their own understanding are not available to them for critical reflection. Teachers themselves need to know more about varieties of student experience if they are to educate a wide variety of students really well.

RECENT RESEARCH

Perspectives from the Anthropology and History of Education

Let us begin to consider current research by looking briefly to work that reviews the emergence of the classroom as a social form. This will provide a context within which the relationships among teaching, learning, and curriculum in contemporary classrooms can be better understood. An important feature of classrooms as they now exist is that instruction is provided to many students by one teacher at the same time. This has not always been the case. In many traditional societies, individual instruction has been the norm. The emphasis in such groups has been on *learning* as contrasted with *teaching*. Parents wishing to provide a child with training in a particular skill sought out another adult in the community who could teach the child what she needed to learn. Okakok (1989) describes this situation as it still occurs among the Inupiat on the North Slope of Alaska.

> Parents often stand back and let a child explore and experience things, observing the child's inclinations. If a child shows an aptitude for skills that the parents don't possess, they might arrange for their child to spend time with an expert, or an adult may ask to participate in the education of the child. Thus, many adults in the community have a role in the education of our children. (414)

This is not to say that no alienation or difficulty can be presumed to have existed in traditional, nonliterate societies or that there were no differences in educational experiences across them. But apparently several assumptions about learning and teaching frame education in nonliterate societies, and some of these assumptions stand in sharp contrast to mass education in modern societies. First, there is a generally agreed upon body of knowledge that is necessary for the student to learn. This "curriculum" is understood by all involved: the student, the teacher, and other members of the society, including parents. Second, learning takes place in and around the activities of everyday life. It is not set apart either in time or in space from what people ordinarily do. Third, adults regard most children as capable of learning everything that needs to be learned. It is assumed that children will be interested in learning what adults know, and they can be brought along in adult daily life to observe and occasionally receive didactic instruction on how and why adults do what they do. Finally, what is taught to each child is tailored to his or her particular talents. There is therefore no "standardized curriculum" for all children (Okakok 1989). Learning is not forced, and its purposes and "relevance" need not be rejustified continually to the learner.

> There are several striking differences between our concept of education today and that of any contemporary traditional society; but perhaps the most important one is the shift from the need for an individual to learn something which everyone agrees he would wish to know, to the will of some individual to teach something which it is not agreed that anyone has any desire to know. (Mead 1970, 3)

The shift from individual to whole group instruction that characterizes modern educational practice occurred in part as a result of a number of factors: (1) the development of schools from those included in medieval monasteries to those established separately in the 15th and 16th centuries; (2) the rise of capitalism in the late 17th and early 18th centuries; (3) an end to the apprenticeship system that resulted from the new market economy; (4) children leaving the work force in large numbers due to new compulsory attendance laws that resulted from the influence of trade unions and their working-class constituencies; and (5) innovations in social policy that led to a great deal of emphasis being placed on formal institutions to deal with and ameliorate social problems. (See discussions by Hogan 1989; Katz 1987; Katznelson and Weir 1985; Zelizer 1985.)

> Shapers of social policy had embodied in concrete form the notion that rehabilitation, therapy, medical treatment, and education should take place within large, formal, and often residential institutions. In the process, they created the institutional state that governs and regulates our lives today. (Katz 1987, 9)

These forces combined to create a need for models to provide schooling to large numbers of pupils at one time. The delivery systems that resulted, precursors of the modern-day classroom, were grounded in bourgeois social relations, "characterized by competition, isomorphic contractual commitments, individual achievement, meritocratic mobility, and free markets in land, commodities, and labor" (Hogan 1988, 383, note 6).

Among these models were those developed by Joseph Lancaster in Britain around the year 1800. Lancaster's framework for schooling has influenced greatly the structures of classrooms and teaching that exist today. In an attempt to educate large numbers of poor children at one time, Lancaster's model included the following features:

1. "classing" of students by ability;
2. whole class instruction, which replaced the more prevalent individual instruction; and
3. promotion of individual students from one graded class to the next, based on their performance on examinations.

Inherent, as well, in this model was a system of prizes and awards that rewarded exceptional achievement. Students competed with each other for these visible acknowledgments of their superior performance. Essentially, anyone, no matter how humble his social rank upon entering school, could achieve success through hard work and perseverance.

One of the results of the necessity of teaching many students at one time was the homogenizing of curriculum. The granting of awards and prizes necessitated the development of a system of comparative evaluation, where the performance of each student could be measured in relation to all others. This led to a situation in which "all students were exposed to the same content and instructed with the same materials, at the same time by the same monitor" (Hogan 1988, 389). The Lancaster model, and others that also attempted to deal with the issue of instructing large numbers of students, effected great changes in both curriculum and instruction, thus bringing about dramatic modifications in classroom social relations.

While the basic features of general public education have been implemented in this country and elsewhere, there is some dispute about whether or not the results have produced opportunities for meritocratic mobility for all students. At least in the United States and other "first world" countries, there are strong beliefs that talent and motivation are, at best, distributed in the total student population along a bell-shaped curve. Based on this belief, it can be expected that close to one half of the students in a given classroom, due to their limited capacity, will have trouble learning what the school curriculum presents in their best interest as low-level, factual knowledge. (This may be a secular survival of Calvinism—one expects that some of the students will be "damned," and only some will be the "elect." The educator's task in such a situation is to work to keep the elect saved and let the rest suffer their justly deserved punishments, now and hereafter.)

For low socioeconomic status and minority populations the belief is that the distribution of talent and motivation is skewed in a negative direction. Thus it becomes reasonable for educators to assume that more than half of the students in an inner city school will have trouble learning school knowledge, framed as "right answers." If many of these students do poorly academically and evidence alienation from school, that is not shocking but to be expected. The impartiality inherent in Lancaster's model has thus been transformed into a system in which rewards are unequally distributed, in fact a system of fictive meritocracy.

Such expectations and inequities, together with the scene of teaching being one in which large numbers of students are involuntarily gathered in a setting apart from everyday life, frame an essentially adversarial relationship between teacher and students. This stands in direct contrast to the individualized nature of instruction found in many traditional societies, from which we can infer that for the vast preponderance of human history adults did not approach the next generation with the belief that most children could not learn, and children did not approach adults doubting that the adult could be trusted to teach what was in the child's best interests.

Other changes were occurring in American society during the latter part of the 19th century that affected the creation of the social form of the modern-day classroom. Immigrant workers were politically influential in this. Not only had they been involved in the movement to enact mandatory school attendance laws but as members of linguistic minority groups, these workers exerted pressure on schools to offer language instruction in their native tongues. Through their involvement in trade unions, immigrant workers also advocated the establishment of manual training programs. There is considerable evidence to suggest that working people were actively involved in helping form schools and were not "simply the objects of policymakers" (Katznelson, Gille, and Weir 1982).

The changing roles of women at this time had a profound impact on what happened in schools. During the latter part of the 19th and the early part of the 20th centuries, the role of women in society changed, first for those in middle-class families, and later for working-class women as well. Women became the "moral guardians and spiritual saviors of an increasingly corrupt and irreligious society" (Katz 1987, 11). Their role shifted from economic providers to a focus on domestic life, in which it was their responsibility to provide a safe and loving home for their husbands and children. The "Cult of True Womanhood" championed by women's magazines and religious literature of the era promoted this ideal of the woman as nurturer and caretaker of the needs of her family (Welter 1978, 313).

As schooling on a large scale became a necessity and social policymakers created the institution of public schooling, it was expected that these large-scale institutions would resemble homes. As such, they should be presided over by "wise and loving mothers" (Katz 1987, 12). Women therefore took over the responsibilities of educating children, particularly in the earlier grades. The "feminization of teaching" became a reality (Katz 1987).

This change in gender of primary school teachers was aided by another factor. The need for educating large numbers of children was increasing, and the concomitant need for additional teachers placed great economic burdens on local communities. This problem was solved by hiring women as schoolteachers, as they commanded approximately one half the wages paid to men (Katz 1987, 12). Primary school classrooms thus became settings for women to nurture and care for younger children.

During the early part of the 20th century, the growth of cities, the accompanying rise in urban poverty, large-scale immigration, and the removal of many adolescents from the work force created problems for social planners. One of the results of their efforts was the creation of public secondary schools as places where these unemployed adolescents could be trained to be good citizens and productive workers.

As described above, the focus of all schooling during these years was on the social and emotional needs of students, as opposed to the development of their intellectual capacities. The teacher's role as nurturer, social worker, and disciplinarian was paramount. "Public school systems existed to shape behavior and attitudes, alleviate social and family problems, and reinforce a social structure under stress. The character of pupils was a much greater concern than their minds" (Katz 1987, 23).

In Lancaster's models for the organization of curriculum and instruction, in the adoption by the society of bourgeois values brought about by the rise of capitalism, in workers' interests in manual training, language instruction, and compulsory schooling, and in the concern for the caretaking, nurturing, and "civilizing" of students, we see the seeds of the form of the modern-day classroom, with its typical patterns of relationships among teachers and students. We turn now to research that examines aspects of life in contemporary classrooms.

There appears to have been a separation in the literature that at least impinges on the issue of student experience of curriculum. Research focused on subject matter in various fields has treated the manifest curriculum as the central phenomenon of research interest, often to the exclusion of consideration of the hidden curriculum that students encounter at the same time they are encountering the manifest curriculum. Research focused on the hidden curriculum has tended to take the subject matter, the academic content of instruction at any particular time, as a vehicle for analyzing the social relationships among the various participants, both teachers and students. What is being studied or talked about in most cases does not matter. We have found very little in the research literature that does both, combining what is learned academically with the ways in which the various actors play out their parts as it is learned. Our review of research here is brief. We have reported on a selected set of studies to stand as exemplars for the broader streams of work that have been done.

Studies of Manifest Curriculum

Research on subject matter, the manifest curriculum, takes on two forms in the literature: (1) studies of student attitudes toward particular subjects; and (2) studies of student conceptions of subject matter, particularly in the sciences. Studies of student attitudes toward particular subjects are based primarily on questionnaires filled out by the students and, in some cases, on follow-up interviews with some of the students. (See, for example, Shaughnessy and Haladyna 1985 for a study of student attitudes toward social studies; Shaughnessy, Haladyna, and Shaughnessy 1983 for student attitudes toward mathematics; Johnston 1987 for an analysis of attitudes toward microcomputers in language learning.) In these cases, what is being tapped does not seem to be how the students experience curriculum. Rather, the collective responses of the students provide a retrospective account of how they felt about a particular subject at the time the surveys were done. There are attempts at connecting these attitudes with particular features of teachers, learners, and the learning environment. However, these connections are made in the absence of information on how the students actually experienced curriculum in real time.

The attitude surveys attempt most often to describe how students feel about a particular subject and not what they have learned in that area. As one researcher put it,

> An open-ended question asked pupils to reflect on what they thought they had learned while using the microcomputer. Nearly one-third (31 percent) were unable to comment on the learning outcomes, possibly because they rarely consciously articulate this to themselves or others, since they are neither used to controlling their own learning activities nor to subsequently reviewing what they have done and achieved. (Johnston 1987, 50)

Measor's study (1984) of gender differences in attitudes toward the sciences differs from those described above in that it was based on observations of students actually engaged in learning science, as opposed to surveys of their attitudes. Measor used the way girls respond to the physical and natural sciences and boys respond to the domestic sciences as a comparative frame for discussing the development of gender identity in relation to the curriculum. The curricular subject matter, the sciences, and students' engagement with it in schools were not studied as ends in themselves; rather, the way students acted during the science classes was used as a means for studying aspects of their gender identities.

Most of the research on student response to science is concerned with their "misconceptions" regarding scientific phenomena (see Shymansky and Kyle 1988 for an extensive review of this literature; see also Chapter 19, "Cognition and Curriculum," in this *Handbook*). There is some disagreement among science educators regarding what these erroneous notions of scientific theory should be called, ranging from misconceptions to alternative conceptions (Abimbola 1988). However, they are studied not as a way of understanding how students perceive and experience the subject matter they are encountering but rather as a way of improving science instruction.

> The practical problem facing science teachers and educators is to get the student, who uses a certain alternative conception to interpret a certain phenomenon, to use the scientifically accepted conception in interpreting that particular phenomenon and, possibly, other phenomenon [sic] as well. . . .
>
> An analysis of the nature and patterns of student errors is potentially useful for devising more effective teaching strategies, especially when this information is used with a powerful model of cognitive functioning. (Shymansky and Kyle 1988, 304)

The major foci of this research, then, are initial states and changes in student cognitive functioning and *not* the ways in which these alternative conceptions of scientific phenomena come to be, what role they play in the students' lives, or how they function in classroom interaction between students and their teachers and among the students themselves. Thus these studies, while providing interesting information regarding differences between adult and child conceptions of science, are not enlightening regarding student experience of subject matter.

Studies of the Implicit Curriculum

Research on the hidden curriculum has focused on the nature of social relationships among participants in the everyday lives of classrooms and schools. In some cases, descriptions of subject matter lessons are used as a vehicle for analyzing the relationships among the various participants. These studies have been conducted primarily by critical theorists and ethnographers of educational settings.

A main theme in this literature is the myriad ways in which students manipulate the system of schooling to accomplish their own ends (see, among others, D'Amato 1988; Everhart 1983; Furlong 1984; Mehan 1980; Willis 1977). In many of these studies, the behavior of students is seen as oppositional to that of teachers. The interaction between students and teachers and among groups of students is described in detail as a way of demonstrating the negotiated nature of social interaction in classrooms. While there may be mention of subject matter in the various descriptions, it serves mainly as a backdrop for the execution of relationships among the various participants. Students are not seen as primarily engaging with and experiencing subject matter. Rather, they are portrayed mainly as acting to create and negotiate the social relationships of which they are a part.

These studies form a subset of a larger set that focuses on student responses to school as an alienating experience. A major emphasis in this regard by critical theorists is student resistance to schooling (for an extensive review of this issue, see Giroux 1983).

Educational anthropologists have also studied resistance, conflict, and alienation in schools. Among the issues examined in these studies are students dropping out and tuning out because they are bored by school work and abused by the professional staff (Delgado-Gaitan 1988); the differential success rate of males and females in school resulting from culturally specific gender expectations (Gibson 1982); the strategies used by students with learning disabilities to manage their identities to appear as though they know what they are doing (Rueda and Mehan 1986); the negative reactions of some students to African-American peers who performed well academically and spoke relatively standard English in their classes in a Washington, D.C. high school (Fordham 1988); and the use of non-school-sanctioned activities that allow students to gain recognition from peers when they are failing to be successful in the "official" work of school (Deyhle 1986; Gilmore 1983).

Sociolinguistic research on classrooms seems to suggest that student experience with curriculum is culturally relative (see Cazden 1988 and Cazden, John, and Hymes 1972 for surveys of this work). Au (1980) has found that when ethnic Hawaiian students in early grades discuss a reading text in culturally appropriate ways interactionally (with overlapping speech permitted among members of the reading group), the students participate more actively and learn more than when the interaction patterns in conversation follow the "one speaker at a time rule" of culturally mainstream classroom practice. The work of Dumont (1972), Erickson and Mohatt (1982), and Philips (1983) suggests that

Native American students and their teachers find inappropriate and embarrassing the teacher's public reinforcement of the actions of individual students. This appears to be so whether the teacher's attention is positive or negative. Even teacher praise is experienced as an undesirable spotlight. It singles out an individual for comparison with others, holding that person's action as worthy of emulation by others. That is seen, in many Native American communities, as inappropriate, as a kind of coercion that is improper.

Related to the research cited above, additional literature focuses on the ways in which schools have responded to student dissatisfaction and alienation. As with the literature on students' alternative conceptions of science, the emphasis here is on changing the routine organization of classrooms by understanding something about the perspectives of the students. Approaches termed "culturally responsive pedagogy" are thus perceived to be better able to meet the needs of students by being more congruent with the cultural values and interactional styles of the students (see the reviews by Cazden 1986 and 1988). Included in this work is research on programs developed for Hawaiian children (Au and Mason 1983; Weisner, Gallimore, and Jordan 1988), for Spanish-speaking working-class students (Moll and Diaz 1987), and for rural African-American and white Appalachian students (Heath 1983).

Sociolinguistic analysis of classroom discourse, and of interaction patterns in schools more generally, is suggestive and evocative. It raises the strong possibility that for some students, especially for those who fare least well in schools organized according to current standard practice, the medium of cultural interactional style is strongly implicated in the messages of subject matter content and of personal identity work that students interpret and manifest as they experience school and classrooms on a daily basis. Yet we still know relatively little about how aspects of ethnic and class culture relate to school and classroom culture, especially as this relationship concerns student engagement with manifest curriculum. Moreover, there is controversy over the policy significance of the role of cultural communication style in classroom pedagogy (see Erickson 1987 and Ogbu 1987 for one version of this debate).

Although there are glimpses of student engagement with specific curricular tasks in the work cited above, this must often be inferred from what the authors say globally about classroom interaction. The most promising arena we have found for examining student engagement with curriculum is in the curricular area of literacy in general and writing in particular. Specifically, this work has examined the different understandings of writing, written work, and written assignments of teachers and students at different grade levels (Dyson 1984; Nespor 1987; Sperling and Freedman 1987). Unlike the literature on student misconceptions in science, studies of writing do not label students' alternative understandings as deviant or deficient. Moreover, the understandings are shown descriptively as occurring in actual written assignments the students are required to complete and to which the teachers respond. Thus, by monitoring naturally occurring student writing through analytic narrative description, these researchers have given us some insight into the specific ways in which students engage curriculum. While not providing the interactional detail available in microethnographic studies of the hidden curriculum, this research comes closer than any other work we have discovered to an account of student engagement with curriculum as we have defined it in this chapter.

RESEARCH AGENDAS

Substantive Questions About Student Experience

One line of possible inquiry concerns the development of student experience across time. This could reveal ways in which earlier and later experience in school may be connected. It could also shed light on the possibility that the subjective experience of curriculum might be developing across time at differing rates and in qualitatively differing ways among differing kinds of students in school. It may be that across their entire school careers students become more and more different from each other in the ways they experience curricular tasks. Knowing more about this could inform the reorganization of school teaching and learning. That might benefit especially those students who are least well served by our current approaches to curriculum and instruction.

Is there a relationship between the experience of flash card addition problems in first grade and being asked to go to the chalkboard in introductory algebra class? Presumably there are issues of mathematical knowledge, of audienced performance, and of the student's feelings about self that are involved, as the 6-year-old enters engagement with arithmetic and as that same child, as a 13-year-old, enters engagement with algebra. There may be issues of the cultural organization of classroom discourse involved for the child as well. Presently it is not at all clear how social relations with the teacher and with fellow students become part of the math problem the student encounters, nor do we know how the student's "archaeology" of past experience with mathematics in both its social and intellectual aspects enters into the experience of the academic task structure of the moment at hand.

For some students who experienced early success in arithmetic, or who were not frightened by such arrangements of social participation structure as flash cards, going to the board, or being asked to call out an answer in front of other children, the later school experience of algebra within a scene of going to the chalkboard may be one of conceptual clarity and emotional ease. Yet for other students, who had aversive experiences with arithmetic in the early grades that were perhaps compounded by embarrassment when called to demonstrate arithmetic calculation at the chalkboard, the introductory algebra experience might be cognitively confusing or emotionally threatening, or both. And this would be the case not simply because of the *algebra* of the curricular task, but because of the combination of *algebra* with *going to the board*.

Knowing more about the evolution of experience with curriculum for students across the school years might help explain the increasing distance in school performance across the elementary school years between students who are doing well (or better and better) and poorly (or worse and worse). By fourth-grade, lower-class minority children have begun to fall farther and farther behind middle-class white children in test scores and other indices of school performance and affiliation. This may be due in part to a quantum leap in the difficulty of academic subject matter between, say, late second grade and early fourth-grade. But it may not simply be that the fourth-grade academic work is more complex, in a strictly cognitive sense. It may be that the African-American or Latino student who starts early in the fall of fourth grade to accelerate in a downward spiral of achievement is not simply confused by the intellectual demands of the classroom tasks. Perhaps the student understands some of the subject matter task structure he confronts but is sick at heart in being displayed before other students as only partially competent. Perhaps by fourth grade he just can't bear it, one more time in one more year, to be held up for public scrutiny in lessons whose social participation structures magnify before others the flaws in his performance. Perhaps then he stops trying. In such a case the way of teaching—the social interactional road to a student's encounter with curricular content—would be reinforcing the student's distancing and resistance to engaging academic tasks. Or perhaps the student was both embarrassed and intellectually confused, and then stopped trying. The two cases would involve two distinct varieties of student experience of curriculum. Those different subjective experiences for students, each of which led to giving up on learning, might require differing strategies of prevention and remedy by teachers. Are there crucial turning points that appear in various school years for different kinds of students as their experience of curriculum accumulates and evolves in various ways across time? We know very little about this.

Another line of inquiry involves questions about the variation that may obtain in student experience across subject matters. If you have trouble learning to read in first grade, how does this relate to your experience of first-grade arithmetic? (And, to make it a bit more complex, does your experience of reading in first grade relate in any ways to your experience of arithmetic in later grades?)

Teacher and parent folk wisdom, as well as some formal research and psychological testing, supports the notion that individuals differ in the ways in which they process and remember information. Thus, it is believed, some students are better at language-related learning, while others are better at numerical or spatial reasoning tasks. It would seem likely that student experience of curricular tasks would differ with the degree of fit between the student's preferred information processing styles and modalities and the requirements of differing kinds of subject matter tasks.

New research could address issues of variation in kinds of student experience across subject matters. Again there is the question of the relative influence upon student experience of the cognitive ordering and demands of the subject matter task structure and the interactional ordering and demands of the social participation task structure within the overall academic task structure at a given moment of curricular engagement.

It is reasonable to assume that differences in cognitive capacities, propensities, and histories of intellectual development among students would make what on the surface appeared to be the "same" classroom task very different experientially for different students. What is less obvious is that the social organizational structure of a task as engaged might be an important source of variation in student experience. This involves what Dewey called the "social set-up." If a student were comfortable or uncomfortable with the social participation structure of an academic task, that might well affect the way in which the task was experienced cognitively. Some students may be more willing to endure the stress attendant upon cognitive difficulty—indeed to regard that stress as stimulating—when the social participation structure is experienced as appropriate by the student than they are when the social participation structure is experienced as inappropriate and alienating.

There appear to be at least three reasons that the social participation structure of academic tasks might be experienced as inappropriate by students. Each of these might be explored in future research. One reason involves the fit between the culturally learned assumptions about appropriateness in communication and in social relationships that the student has learned from family and peers. Sociolinguistic research in education that we have reviewed in this chapter, and broader sociolinguistic research, has identified systematic differences in cultural assumptions about the proper and expectable conduct of interaction that run along lines of race and ethnicity, gender, class, age, and religion.

A second source of influence on the experience of certain modes of social relations in learning may be the individual's temperament or personality. (Here a caveat. Culturally learned assumptions about interaction style often are interpreted as uniquely individual characteristics by educators—as having to do with traits such as personality, field dependence/independence, and locus of control. What often gets "read" clinically in schools as an emotional or developmental problem, for example, hyperactivity or inadequate capacity for social role taking, may be due more to ethnic or class cultural style than to a diagnostic entity that resides inside the individual student. Because of this we think it wise to consider carefully the temperament and personality explanations for student experience and to conduct research that is cross-culturally informed and interculturally sensitive.)

A third source of influence over the learner's experience of social relations as appropriate or inappropriate concerns the power relations inherent in the classroom social system and in the curriculum as a cultural system. Certain classroom participation structures may be experienced by students as unjust, and certain contents of learning may be experienced as demeaning to the self, family, or community, or as totally detached from the student's life experience. In such situations the curricular tasks assigned can be alienating for students. To recall our concern about personality explanations in the previous paragraph, if a student is in an alienating classroom situation because of power asymmetry and says things that could be interpreted as indicating a low sense of fate control, it may be because she is in a situation that objectively can be characterized as oppressive. Consequently, her sense that she has little control over her destiny is realistic within the situation in which she finds herself. There seems often to be a local politics of social relations and subject matter content in the classroom that repeats, in the local patterns of engagement between learners, teachers, and subject matter, the wider politics of interest group relations in society as a whole. This should not be overlooked in considering student experience of curriculum.

Yet another way in which classroom social relations and curriculum intertwine and thus may influence student experience is found in customary associations between certain subject areas and the social participation structures teachers employ in teaching those subjects. There appear to be strong associations between certain patterns of classroom interaction and certain subject matters. For example, students usually do not "go to the chalkboard" to demonstrate writing. That is a social arena more commonly used for the display of arithmetic calculation by students. Conversely, students do not usually write dialog journals in arithmetic or in science. If dialog journals are used in the classroom at all, they tend to focus around language arts instruction. Group projects are more common in social studies, and sometimes in science, than they are in plane geometry, algebra, or arithmetic. Allowing students to help one another complete an assignment in writing is increasingly being seen by teachers as editing rather than as cheating. Helping one another may be more likely to be perceived as cheating or disruption by teachers during arithmetic practice than it would be during essay-writing time. Thus differing social frameworks for engaging curriculum tend to run along subject matter lines. This may affect student experience of curriculum, but little work appears to have been done on this issue.

The typical tendency to use restricted ranges of interactional frameworks for engaging various subject matters is contrasted with more innovative approaches to pedagogy, such as the whole language movement in literacy instruction and inquiry methods in science. In those approaches the social arrangements for engaging learning blur across subject matters. What is usually thought of as distinctly different subject matter contents can also blur across boundaries, as in the case of laboratory notebooks in an inquiry approach to science instruction becoming in some classrooms a rich source of experience in expository writing.

Given that there are usual associations between kinds of subject matter and kinds of social participation structures used in accomplishing subject matter engagement, it is possible that positive or negative reactions by students to subject matter may not simply be a question of their intellectual tendencies and prior mastery of subject matter skill and knowledge. Certain students may not be "good at math," not because of inherent lack of aptness in cognizing mathematical operations but because they experience as unfamiliar or as alienating the participation structures by which mathematics is customarily engaged in the classroom. If mathematics as social experience changes from a matter of doing careful work and getting the right answer in elementary school to argumentation and risk-taking in higher mathematics in high school and college, this could explain in part the tendency of women students to avoid advanced study in mathematics. To these students as girls, arithmetic may have appeared appropriately girl-like, but to the same individuals as young women, higher mathematics may not appear to be appropriately womanly, despite cultural changes in the current generation in definition of women's roles.

In addition, there is the matter of variation in the ways in which students conceptualize the subject matter structure of classroom tasks. We have mentioned a growing literature in science and mathematics instruction on the implicit conceptions students bring to subject matter. Students, for example, may bring Aristotelian conceptions of dynamics and force to problems in physics, and they may have invented algorithms for solving mathematical problems that "worked" at one level of mathematical operations but are no longer appropriate as the student confronts the next level of problems. Those students who do not recognize that their conceptions of the subject matter differ from those required for successful work on an assigned task may experience curricular engagement in a particular subject area as a mine field or as a computer program with bugs in it—things blow up or break down inexplicably. It may be that such students have a kind of experience with curriculum in such moments which differs from that of students whose initial subject matter conceptions upon engaging a task were more congruent with the task requirements.

Student conceptions of academic task structure can involve notions of the hidden curriculum as well as that of the manifest. Students in the early grades can develop a sense that it is more important to finish their seatwork before other students do than it is to complete the work carefully. Easeley has claimed (1979) that typical school mathematics instruction influences students to conceive of mathematics as a process of applying the right procedures with effort in order to get the right answer. The emphasis is on correctness of algorithm and of result rather than on understanding. Easeley is not alone in pointing out the tendency of students to transform all mathematics into a search for a right answer (see the review by Putnam, Lampert, and Peterson 1990). A special contribution of Easeley has been to argue that mathematics as ordinarily taught may be more a matter of moral discipline, from the student point of view, than of intellectual discipline and growth. Lampert provides a poignant and analytically powerful account (1990) of the resistance she encountered from fifth-grade students when she insisted that they learn mathematics by generating alternative solutions and comparing them rather than by seeking the right answer from her. Her description and analysis of classroom discourse appears to confirm Easeley's hunch about mathematics engagement defined by students as a situation of moral choice. Analogous issues arise in the language arts, where students, teachers, administrators, and parents may place more emphasis on putting the correct punctuation mark at the end of the sentence than on the substance of the sentence written or on the relation of authenticity or inauthenticity between writer and audience.

One wonders about the ways in which engagement with various subject matters is transmuted in student experience of hidden curricular issues into a set of perceived problems which differ from those that were assigned. To what extent in such transformations do codes of honor and of fairness, as well as of moral discipline, apply? Do curricular tasks in any school subject matter, besides physical education, become tests of courage or machismo for some students? This seems to happen occasionally in graduate education, within specialized study of a particular discipline. To our knowledge such issues have not been studied directly.

More broadly speaking, there is a need to combine studies of the manifest and hidden curricula in schools. We have discussed an extreme separation in the research literature that has been unfortunate in limiting our insight into student experience.

Thus, for example, there are studies of reading pedagogy that may point to some aspects of student experience but that treat reading as if it were the only thing being taught and learned. There is often no mention of the lessons about self and society that are being taught in the same time as reading and writing. Different ways of teaching can present literacy in alternative ways—as a job of identifying symbols correctly, of learning how to speak and write correctly, or as a matter of making sense of text, having inferences, going beyond the information given, acquiring authorial voice. Such conceptions of literacy are built into instructional materials and pedagogy. They define the role of the reader and writer and, in so doing, speak to issues of selfhood and agency in the world. Recent research on literacy considers the authority of writers more deeply than earlier research did, but we have yet to see the assumption of authority which asks what that is like as it is subjectively experienced by student writers. Developing an author's voice appears not merely to be a matter of learning inscriptive technique but of claiming entitlement to speak and write and taking an expository and descriptive stance of one's own as a writer. Different ways of teaching would seem to be related to differing subjective experience of students as writers, fostering or inhibiting authorial voice.

Similar issues may obtain with other subject matters. It is difficult to imagine students learning to inquire into science in a classroom in which right answers are held up as the main purpose of learning. If students encounter the manifest and the hidden curricular aspects of classroom tasks simultaneously in daily experience, then study of that experience would lead us necessarily to treat the two aspects of curriculum together analytically rather than to treat them separately, as has been the case for most of the research we have reviewed.

We have noted that the separation cuts both ways. Just as the specialists in subject matter have tended to ignore the hidden curriculum as they study curriculum and instruction, so the specialists in the study of hidden curriculum—anthropologists, sociologists, critical theorists—have tended to ignore the manifest curriculum, or at least to place it in the background of research attention. Seminal empirical and conceptual works on hidden curriculum, such as those of Anyon (1980), Apple and Weis (1983), Bernstein (1975), Bourdieu and Passeron (1977), Dreeben (1968), Henry (1963), Willis (1977), and Young (1971), illustrate this tendency.

It is understandable that those with primary research interest in issues of hidden curriculum would not place manifest curriculum in the foreground of their research attention. Yet if their analyses are well founded, it is in and through what teachers think they are trying to teach deliberately—reading, mathematics, science—that implicit messages about self and one's place in society reach the student. Schools may indeed be teaching powerful framing definitions of individual and group identity. Students may in fact be learning in school to be docile workers for an external authority or active and entitled owners of their own lives. If so, that needs to be shown as it arises in their experience in the midst of the details of such activities as doing arithmetic or reading a Shakespeare play, as well as in such activities as saying the Pledge of Allegiance to the Flag in elementary school or carrying hall passes and taking examinations in high school. Research that takes a unified approach to student experience of the manifest curricula in relation to the implicit ones can make the relations between the two aspects of what is assigned to be learned in school more clear than empirical research has done in the recent past.

In sum, for various reasons which this chapter could only begin to consider, student experience of curriculum may be far more diverse than previously contemplated. That variation may for the most part go unseen and unheard by educators. Much further research needs to be done to uncover the kinds of variations in student experience that may obtain within and across subject matters and within and across grade levels. Indeed, we have suggested here that the evolution of student experience with curriculum should be studied across the entire student career in school. We know relatively little about the social and cognitive ecology of student experience of curriculum. How does this vary with the social backgrounds of students and teachers, and by the types of schools in which they learn and teach? Presently we do not understand at all clearly how intellect, will, culture, and politics meet at the intersection of curricular materials, classroom arrangements, pedagogical approaches, and students, within whose subjective experience learning presumably takes place.

Focus and Methods in the Conduct of Research

Major polarities in choice of research approaches are those of depth and breadth, of synchronic and diachronic perspective, and of insider and outsider accounts of student experience. We will treat each of these polarities in turn, beginning with the tension between the depth and richness of data collected and the breadth of generalization that is possible from those data.

Depth and Breadth of Focus. An ideal would be to maximize both the scope of information that is sought and the specificity of focus in any particular data set collected. This could be done by linking longitudinal case studies of individuals in a limited number of classrooms with wider ranging surveys (cross-sectional as well as longitudinal) of sets of students across a large number of classrooms in order to check the generalization of what was being found in the case studies. One would want to look across differing kinds of preschool and K–12 school populations, across different streams of curricula and students within the schools, and across different subject matters. One would want, as well, to consider the relations between experience of the hidden and manifest curricula.

Personal experience, by its very nature, is evanescent and transitory. Capturing glimpses of it on the wing, as it were, requires rich and detailed inquiry and reporting. Because such ethnographic, interpretive case study work is so labor intensive, it can involve only a limited number of sites and researchers. Yet detailed investigation is necessary, for without it one cannot develop a coherent theoretical picture of the natures and varieties of student experience. We need to understand better the range of variation in kinds of experience that students have in engaging curriculum. The scope of the direct observation and interviewing that is required to study that variation empirically can be extended somewhat without sacrificing depth if classroom teachers, principals, and students were to become actively engaged in articulating student experience by reflecting and writing on it.

This suggests multiple approaches and mixtures of approaches in case study work that portray student experience through analytic narrative description. One is the standard approach of participant observation by means of long-term visiting done by outsiders. Such visitors watch recurrent events and ask questions of those involved in the events, in an attempt not only to document the specifics of what happens in a particular setting but also to identify and reflect upon what those happenings mean to the persons engaged in them.

Another approach to case study is to ask teachers and principals, those already close to students on a long-term basis, to become more observant of student experience, paying systematic attention to and reporting explicitly upon the thoughts and feelings of students as they engage curriculum (see the review of teacher research by Cochran-Smith and Lytle 1990). A more innovative approach, an extension of effort in the spirit of the previous two approaches, would be to engage students themselves in the work of becoming more observant participants in their own experience, asking them to reflect and report on their experience through deliberate conversation (by means of dialog journals, interviews, focus group discussions, student newsletter projects) with fellow students, with teachers, and/or with intermittently visiting principals or researchers. (Inviting students as partners in research on their own experience raises questions of the inherent tensions between insiders and outsiders in social research. We will mention these below. Research by students on their own educational practice also has implications for the reorganization of teaching and learning in classrooms and for issues of student voice in the educational process. We will allude to these briefly in the concluding remarks at the end of this chapter.)

Case study particularizes. It can report detailed information on the palpable texture of experience in a specific setting. But contrary to conventional assumptions in social research, case studies are not antithetical to generalization. They do stimulate and enable generalizing of a special and important kind. At its best, case study always involves theory construction. Through narrative description a case study proposes (actually or in effect) a model or theory of the organization of the phenomena that were observed and reported. The generality of the theory or model so proposed must be tested empirically by further observation.

In case study the locus of generality testing differs from that which obtains in studies involving statistical generalization from a sample to a larger population. In case study, demonstration of generalization is a process that resides in the judgment of the reader of the study rather than in the operations of the author in amassing data and analyzing it (sampling and statistical generalization). Readers of a case study that is well constructed and reported look to their own situation and ask, "How well does this fit our own experience? Is anything like what was reported in the case study happening here where we are?" (See Hamilton 1981 for a discussion of theoretical generalization in contrast to statistical generalization.)

In spite of the theoretical generalization that can come from narrative reports, one still is interested in formal evidence that speaks to the issue of how typical are the thoughts, feelings, and actions of persons that are reported in case studies. One wants small amounts of information about many individuals across many settings to better determine a case study's generalizability, in the traditional sense. Survey, demographic, and economic data—from questionnaires and testing and monitoring school attendance, streaming, graduation rates, and school income and expenditures—are the usual means of amassing evidence across many sites.

Surveys are the most direct means of learning about broad patterns of distribution. Yet the survey research on student opinions that we have seen (a subset of which was discussed in this chapter) has tended to be thin on substance. When it approached issues of student experience at all, it tended to do so obliquely rather than directly. For example, student opinion, when sought, was usually treated as a summative judgment rather than as an ongoing phenomenon in the midst of curricular engagement. Less static conceptions of student experience need to inform the construction of new kinds of survey instruments.

The simplest approach to changing a questionnaire is to add open-ended items to the forced-choice ones. Surveys can be adapted more radically to elicit information on the texture of experience as perceived by students. Lambert (1968), for example, collected information on students in English boarding schools by visiting selected schools and designating students who would write narrative diary entries on their school experience, mailing them periodically to the researcher. By this means Lambert collected information on 66 schools and 10,181 students during a 2-year period.

A more complex approach would be to try to monitor student experience directly through new approaches in educational testing, a form of survey research. Portfolio assessment, the analysis of student work by means of computer simulation of classroom tasks, and other new possibilities for alternative assessment of student learning can potentially collect information, not only on the processes by which students produce final outcomes but also on their subjective experience in the midst of those processes. Written or dictated protocols, perhaps in the form of diarylike entries or intellectual autobiographies, as well as new kinds of forced-choice items could, if included in alternative assessment instruments and procedures, enable researchers to amass over time extensive data that would point to students' subjective experience of curriculum.

Ideally, survey data should be collected by the study teams who are also doing case studies so as to ensure that the substantive focus of the survey research would be congruent with that of the participant observation and interviewing. If the two types of evidence were to be collected by separate study teams, it is likely that the theorectical constructs regarding student experience contained in the surveys would differ substantially from the constructs guiding the case studies. The result would be two distinct kinds of data sets that would be incongruent and incommensurable. This is a difficult problem for the practical conduct of research and for the organization of its funding. All too often, even in studies that attempted to combine survey and narrative observational data, the two different kinds of evidence have not fit well together.

Synchronic and Diachronic Approaches. It seems to us that a crucial issue is the question of whether and how student experience evolves across the school years. Change happens not only in the development of the child across time but also in the organization of curriculum and instruction the child encounters. This should mean that student experience differs qualitatively across differing points in the life cycle of the school career.

Ultimately longitudinal (diachronic) study, research that monitors school experience across time with the individual as the unit of analysis, is necessary to determine this. Ideally, such research should be done both by case study and by survey methods, for the reasons discussed above. Cross-sectional (synchronic) research could also be employed, especially at the outset, to provide clues that would guide subsequent longitudinal study of selected cohorts of students of different backgrounds in differing types of schools. This synchronic research should also combine survey and case study means of data collection and analysis.

We need longitudinal work on individual students. For example, if we could see even a few of the same children in first, third, fourth, sixth, eighth, and tenth grades, we could begin to determine the evolution of student experience as both the classroom scene and the child changed. Cross-sectional data would be logistically easier to collect, but longitudinal data would be better scientifically. How to commission and fund such study is a major issue the research community would have to address in order for such work to be undertaken.

Insider and Outsider Perspectives. What has been most conspicuously absent from the recent research literature, a body of work that only partially approaches the phenomena of student experience of curriculum in a concrete and direct way, is the first-person voice of the student. On the topic of student experience, students themselves are the ultimate insiders and experts. Yet interview studies that probe student experience are rare, and, in richly descriptive narrative accounts of classrooms authored by participant observers or by teachers themselves, it is the teacher's thoughts and feelings that are centrally represented. Only in some of that work is the teacher's subjective world even portrayed directly. Students, for the most part, are shown as *doing* in the classroom rather than as *thinking*, *intending*, and *caring*.

We looked beyond research literature to the ways students' school experience has been represented in general popular culture through fiction, autobiography, and cinema, which are accounts by adults that presumably draw on memory and empathy in an attempt to represent an Other, someone else's reality. Interestingly, in the representations in popular culture it is the social relational aspects of school experience that figure most centrally, with academic study appearing only very peripherally, if at all. This is especially true in recent American films that represent students' school experience—for example, *The Breakfast Club* and *Heathers*. The same pattern can be seen in fiction and autobiography. Apparently what resonates most for adult authors are the struggles and joys of students with one another rather than with curricular tasks. Even in an autobiography that aims to report educational experience centrally, such as that of Waugh (1964), it is family life and peer relationships in school that are represented narratively. Waugh says virtually nothing about the actual study of subject matter in the two private schools he attended before college. A recent autobiographical account by Rose (1990) is notable in that it describes his engagement with subject matter as a high school student, then as a college student, and finally as a college teacher. Interestingly, his subject field is the teaching of writing, the same field in which our literature search had revealed research that came closer than any other to representing student experience with curriculum.

Students as authors appear only rarely. Perry (1988) wrote an account comparing her experience as an African-American student in public and private high schools. A major point of comparison was the difference in attitudes between mathematics teachers. She reports that the public school mathematics teacher's stated goal was to teach mathematics as computation, while the private school teacher's goal was to teach students "how to become 'theoretical mathematicians'" (Perry 1988, 332). Those attitudes by teachers influenced Perry's experience of mathematics in the two schools. Another example of student writing on school experience is *Letter to a Teacher*, which was authored by Italian working-class schoolboys from a mountain village in Tuscany (Schoolboys of Barbiana 1970). The students described a special academy started for students who were having difficulty in the public schools. They also presented a critique of the effects of public schooling on the poor.

Given this paucity of first-person accounts by students of their own experience, the development of ways in which students themselves can reflect upon and represent their experience seems a first priority for future research. The next closest view of student experience could come from teachers who are unusually attentive to students and who write about their practice, for example, Kohl (1967), Lampert (1990), Paley (1979), Rose (1990), and Strieb (1985). But the teacher may or may not be aware of student experience, or may reconstrue it through the eyes of the adult stance and teacherly role in ways that obscure rather than illuminate the subjective experience of the student. It seems significant that in Kohl's account of a year of teaching (1967), the experience and voice of students did not emerge until he began to teach them by asking them to write about their own lives. By the end of the book, and the end of the school year, the experience of students figured prominently. That was because Kohl changed his approach to teaching. By asking students to write he was altering role relationships in the classroom. Out of that change in social organization the experience of students emerged as a phenomenon of interest—to the teacher and to the pupils as well.

Given the limits of teachers' roles and of the social organization of traditional pedagogy, sensitive participant observation by outsiders who visit a class only intermittently can also play a part in making visible the immediate experience of students with curriculum. We have noted the tendency of narrative reporting on classroom life by outsiders to focus on the hidden curriculum at the expense of the manifest. If participant observation were to focus more directly on subject matter, as in the recent astute work of Florio-Ruane and Dunn (1987) and Stodolsky (1988), we could learn more about student experience in engaging it.

Problems and tradeoffs are inherent in the roles of distal and proximal observers. The distal, intermittent observer may not get close enough to the routines of daily classroom life to be able to see and hear student experience, which, in its aspects as an interior phenomenon, is not immediately apparent to observation. Yet the proximal observer—in this instance the teacher or the student—may be too close to immediate experience to be able to see it until, through time and an intellectual stance for critical reflection, it can become apparent to the self. Just because one is an insider one is not automatically able to articulate the implicit ordering of daily life. On this point anthropologists quote a proverb about ethnography that is attributed, perhaps apocryphally, to the American anthropologist Clyde Kluckhohn: "The fish would be the last creature to discover water." There is a certain truth to this. Yet there is a danger in taking such a notion too far, for that would be to adopt uncritically an implicitly colonialist assumption that only the outsider can validly understand and define an Other. This is a position that is increasingly being questioned as anthropology turns toward critical scrutiny of its own customary ways of seeing (see Clifford 1988 and Rosaldo 1989). Somehow the perspectives and voices of students themselves need to appear more prominently in research on teaching, learning, and curriculum if students' experience of curriculum is to become an object of serious attention by researchers.

CONCLUSION

This chapter has considered possible varieties of student experience and possible ways of learning more about them. Currently we know little. That seems due in part to theoretical orientations about teaching and learning that have guided major streams of empirical research in education. Immediate student experience, especially in the sense of a combination of its sociocultural, emotional, and cognitive aspects, has not been a central construct in those orientations and assumptions. We also know little about student experience because it is technically difficult to study. It must be probed for in ways that are not yet fully conceived and that seem likely to be labor intensive and costly if they were to be developed further.

But the task may be difficult for deeper reasons. The absence of student experience from current educational discourse seems to be a consequence of systematic silencing of the student voice. Most fundamentally, student experience goes unheard and unseen for what appear to be ideological reasons. The commonsense view of educational practice, of what is most important to pay attention to in and about schools, has left little room indeed for the points of view of the very persons who are the first-level consumers of educational services. Especially when one considers that student-proof curriculum characterizes remedial instruction and that such instruction is delivered to those most in trouble academically—the children of the poor generally and ethnic and linguistic minority students in particular—the transparency and inaudibility of student experience in our research and in our root conceptions of teaching and curriculum can reasonably be seen as the result of silencing. Much of classroom life is a monologue followed by a test. In the absence of interchange, of genuine conversation in the ways we usually teach, students are prevented from developing voice—a critical awareness of their own ends, means, and capacities in learning.

If our analysis is correct, it spells trouble for the study of student experience. Silencing is a profound process that is not readily remedied. Olsen (1978) observes that silencing among authors has both external and internal aspects. Writing becomes more difficult when, because of the necessity to earn a living, the author cannot devote full energy and attention to creative endeavor. Economic circumstances are an external press limiting the options of a writer; they silence voice by exerting outside influence on choice and action. But there are internal constraints on voices as well, especially self-doubt, which inhibits "conviction as to the importance of what one has to say, one's right to say it" (Olsen 1978, 27). Olsen decries these limits, especially as they apply to women writers. She locates the ontogeny of the internal limits on voice in women's routine life experience: "The leeching of belief, of will, the damaging of capacity begin so early" (27). Without using the term, Olsen alludes to the workings of hegemony. This is the social process by which we are so easily persuaded that what we see around us as customary is entirely reasonable. If we never encounter new possibility for thought and action, we never question the lack of development of those possibilities in ourselves.

Students in schools are in a one-down position relative to adults which structurally resembles that which usually obtains between women and men in society more generally. Perhaps their voices are absent from contemporary discourse in education because they have not been asked to speak. But if they were to be asked about their experience they might well not be able to answer immediately. To be more articulate about their experience, external and internal conditions might have to change. They would need to be educated in ways that build time for critical reflection into ordinary classroom tasks. They would also need more social and intellectual space in school if reflection were to occur there, the authority to be reflective and to participate in defining and choosing what they learn, and a critically analytic framework from which to consider and reconsider their experience in learning. As Giroux (1988), among others, has observed, education for critical reflection would require fundamental change in the ways curriculum, teaching, and learning are organized in schools. Giroux (1987) also speculates that this may be what happens in whole language approaches to literacy instruction. Because those ways of teaching subject matter redefine relationships between students, teachers, and school knowledge, students may become more reflective through their classroom learning. This may be why, as our review of current research suggests, research on new approaches to literacy makes student experience more visible. Those changes in the content of instruction involve basic changes in classroom social relations as well, out of which student experience becomes both more articulate and more salient, for students and teachers alike.

The absence of student experience from current educational discourse limits the insight of educators as well as that of students. In the ordinary practice of their craft teachers are deskilled in listening. They lack experience in noticing and making sense of what student voices might be saying, had students developed their capacities to speak. If student voices were to be more articulate, more room would need to be made for them in the ordinary conduct of classroom life.

We can speculate that student experience may differ markedly according to such aspects of student identity and general life experience as race, first language, social class, gender, and handicapping conditions. Questions then arise about equity in access to instruction and in the outcomes of instruction. Research and policy debates occur about whether or not schooling is a fair arena of access to opportunity; whether or not students receive different kinds of benefits or confront different kinds of handicaps because of their social background. Most concretely this involves equity of access to opportunity to learn. We have argued here that student experience is intimately related to that opportunity. It seems not simply a matter of providing students with time to learn. Rather, we need to consider the quality of student experience, as subjectively defined by the student, during the time of engagement in learning. Opportunity, then, has an internal and subjective aspect, as well as a more external and objective one.

Current research and policy debates also focus on the relative desirability of public or private schools. In our view, this debate hinges on the nature of student experience: whether or not public and private schools tend to generate quite different qualities of student experience and thus differing environments for subjective opportunity to learn.

Moreover, there is considerable discussion currently of whether schools can or should offer intellectually richer learning environments to a wide variety of students. In the past, reasoning and high literacy in the humanities, sciences, and mathematics have been offered only to the most talented students, as talent has been conventionally defined in schools. But some authorities are recommending that richer learning should become more widely available (see, for example, Cole and Griffin 1987; Goodlad and Keating 1990; National Research Council 1985; Resnick 1987). To deliver such instruction successfully requires not only that we come to know more about the nature of rich learning environments as occasions of social and cognitive interaction but also that we come to know more about the subjective experience of students within that interaction.

If we really want to improve the quality of education for the nation it may be necessary to broaden access to high-quality learning time. That is a point made by Anrig and Lapointe (1989) in their recent review of data on overall educational progress of American students. For richer learning to occur, "What students generally experience as learners in our schools must change first . . . high quality supervision and curriculum development should [help educators to examine] what is assigned and taught from the perspective of what an individual student experiences" (Anrig and Lapointe 1989, 8). Writing in a similar vein, Cole argues (1990, 2–7) that we need to change our conceptions of educational achievement from those informed by behavioral psychology and by the attempt to design instruction that would improve basic skills. We may have come as far as we can in improving basic skills by the use of existing educational practices, she contends. To foster higher-order thinking and more advanced kinds of knowledge among students, we need to turn to cognitive psychology and educational philosophy in redefining what achievement means and rethinking how to organize curriculum and instruction to foster it (Cole 1990, 3–4). It is apparent that new ways of conducting assessment are also necessary if learning and teaching are to change fundamentally. We presume that researchers in the tests and measurement community would be confronting the need to monitor how students are learning and how they experience that subjectively, as well as to monitor the outcomes of that learning in more sophisticated ways.

We may be at a watershed moment. Which way will the water flow—toward more emphasis on the outcomes of schools or toward integrated emphases on processes and outcomes, more richly conceived and more sensitively monitored? It is quite possible that the school experience of students as an object of research attention may play an important role in the general improvement of learning in America's schools. If that is the case, then research agendas and research support should follow.

One must remember that fundamental change in American school practice has proved elusive in the past. For students' experience of curriculum to become generally visible to researchers, we have argued, it must first appear as salient in classrooms. We wonder if that will happen. Yet the power of past custom is not absolute. As Apple and Weis have observed (1983, 22), "if schools (and people) are not passive mirrors of an economy, but instead are active agents in the processes of reproduction and contestation of dominant social relations, then understanding what they do and acting upon them become of no small moment. For if schools are part of a 'contested terrain,' . . . then the hard and continuous day to day struggle at the level of curriculum and teaching practice is part of these larger conflicts as well." So too for student struggles and voices as they experience curriculum in schools.

References

Abimbola, I. O. 1988. The problem of terminology in the study of student conceptions in science. *Science Education* 72(2): 175–184.

Anrig, Gregory R., and Archie E. Lapointe. 1989. What we know about what students don't know. *Educational Leadership* 47(3): 4–5, 7–9.

Anyon, Jean. 1980. Social class and the hidden curriculum of work. *Journal of Education* 162(1): 67–92.

Apple, Michael W., and Lois Weis, eds. 1983. *Ideology and Practice in Schooling*. Philadelphia, PA: Temple University Press.

Au, Kathryn H. 1980. Participation structures in a reading lesson with Hawaiian children: Analysis of a culturally appropriate instructional event. *Anthropology and Education Quarterly* 11(2): 91–115.

Au, Kathryn H., and Jana M. Mason. 1983. Cultural congruence in classroom participation structures: Achieving a balance of rights. *Discourse Processes* 6(2): 145–167.

Bernstein, Basil. 1975. *Class, Codes, and Control: Toward a Theory of Education Transmissions* (vol. 3). London: Routledge & Kegan Paul.

Bourdieu, Pierre, and Jean-Claude Passeron. 1977. *Reproduction in Education, Society and Culture*. Beverly Hills, CA: Sage.

Brophy, Jere, and Thomas L. Good. 1986. "Teacher Behavior and Student Achievement." In *Handbook of Research on Teaching*, 3rd ed., edited by Merlin C. Wittrock, 328–375. New York: Macmillan.

Brown, John S., Allan Collins, and Paul Duguid. 1989. Situated cognition and the culture of learning. *Educational Researcher* 18(1): 32–42.

Cazden, Courtney B. 1986. "Classroom discourse." In *Handbook of Research on Teaching*, 3rd ed., edited by Merlin C. Wittrock, 432–463. New York: Macmillan.

Cazden, Courtney B. 1988. *Classroom Discourse: The Language of Teaching and Learning*. Portsmouth, NH: Heinemann.

Cazden, Courtney B., Vera P. John, and Dell Hymes. 1972. *Functions of Language in the Classroom*. New York: Teachers College Press. (Reprinted by Waveland Press, 1982.)

Christie, Michael J. 1984. "The Classroom World of the Aboriginal Child." Unpublished doctoral thesis, University of Queensland (Australia).

Clifford, James. 1988. *The Predicament of Culture: Twentieth-Century Ethnography, Literature, and Art*. Cambridge, MA: Harvard University Press.

Cochran-Smith, Marilyn, and Susan L. Lytle. 1990. Research on teaching and teacher research: The issues that divide. *Educational Researcher* 19(2): 2–11.

Cole, Michael, and Peg Griffin, eds. 1987. *Contextual Factors in Education: Improving Science and Mathematics Education for Minorities and Women*. Madison: Wisconsin Center for Education Research, University of Wisconsin.

Cole, Nancy. 1990. Conceptions of educational achievement. *Educational Researcher* 19(3): 2–7.

Cuban, Larry. 1984. *How Teachers Taught: Constancy and Change in American Classrooms: 1890–1980*. New York: Longman.

Cusick, Philip. 1973. *Inside High School: The Student's World*. New York: Holt, Rinehart and Winston.

Cusick, Philip. 1983. *The Egalitarian Ideal and the American High School: Studies in Three Schools*. New York: Longman.

D'Amato, John. 1988. Acting: Hawaiian children's resistance to teachers. *The Elementary School Journal* 88(5): 529–544.

Delgado-Gaitan, Concha. 1988. The value of conformity: Learning to stay in school. *Anthropology and Education Quarterly* 19(4): 354–381.

Dewey, John. 1963 [1938]. *Experience and Education*. London: Collier.

Dewey, John. 1965 [1904]. "The Relation of Theory to Practice in Education." In *Teacher Education in America: A Documentary History*, edited by Merle L. Borrowman, 140–171. New York: Teachers College Press.

Deyhle, Donna. 1986. Break dancing and breaking out: Anglos, Utes, and Navajos in a border reservation high school. *Anthropology and Education Quarterly* 17(3): 111–127.

Dreeben, Robert. 1968. *On What Is Learned in School*. Reading, MA: Addison-Wesley.

Dumont, Robert V., Jr. 1972. "Learning English and How to be Silent: Studies in Sioux and Cherokee Classrooms." In *Functions of Language in the Classroom*, edited by Courtney B. Cazden, Vera P. John, and Dell Hymes, 344–369. New York: Teachers College Press. (Reprinted by Waveland Press, 1985.)

Dyson, Anne Haas. 1984. Emerging alphabetic literacy in school contexts: Toward defining the gap between school curriculum and child mind. *Written Communication* 1(1): 5–55.

Easeley, J. 1979. A portrayal of traditional teachers of mathematics in American schools. *Critical Reviews in Mathematics in Education* 9: 84–108. Bielefeld: Institut für Didaktik der Mathematik der Universität Bielefeld.

Eder, Donna. 1982. "Differences in Communicative Styles Across Ability Groups." In *Communicating in the Classroom*, edited by Louise Cherry Wilkinson, 245–264. New York: Academic Press.

Eisner, Elliot W. 1985. *The Educational Imagination: On the Design and Evaluation of School Programs*, 2nd ed. New York: Macmillan.

Erickson, Frederick. 1982a. Taught cognitive learning in its immediate environment: A neglected topic in the anthropology of education. *Anthropology and Education Quarterly* 13(2): 149–180.

Erickson, Frederick. 1982b. "Classroom Discourse as Improvisation: Relationships Between Academic Task Structure and Social Participation Structure in Lessons." In *Communicating in the Classroom*, edited by Louise Cherry Wilkinson, 153–181. New York: Academic Press.

Erickson, Frederick. 1987. Transformation and school success: The politics and culture of educational achievement. *Anthropology and Education Quarterly* 18(4): 335–356.

Erickson, Frederick, and Gerald Mohatt. 1982. "The Cultural Organization of Participation Structures in Two Classrooms of Indian Students." In *Doing the Ethnography of Schooling*, edited by George Spindler, 132–174. New York: Holt, Rinehart and Winston.

Erickson, Frederick, and Jeffrey Shultz. 1981. "When is a Context? Some Issues and Methods in the Analysis of Social Competence." In *Ethnography and Language in Educational Settings*, edited by Judith L. Green and Cynthia Wallat, 147–160. Norwood, NJ: Ablex.

Everhart, Robert B. 1983. "Classroom Management, Student Opposition, and the Labor Process." In *Ideology and Practice in Schooling*, edited by Michael W. Apple and Lois Weis, 169–192. Philadelphia, PA: Temple University Press.

Florio-Ruane, Susan, and Saundra Dunn. 1987. "Teaching Writing: Some Perennial Questions and Some Possible Answers." In *Educators' Handbook: A Research Perspective*, edited by V. Richardson-Koehler, 50–83. New York: Longman.

Fordham, Signithia. 1988. Racelessness as a factor in black students' school success: Pragmatic strategy or pyrrhic victory? *Harvard Educational Review* 58(1): 54–84.

Foucault, Michel. 1979. *Discipline and Punish: The Birth of the Prison*. New York: Random House (Vintage Books).

Freire, Paulo. 1971. *Pedagogy of the Oppressed*. Translated by M. Berman Ramos. New York: Herder and Herder.

Furlong, Virginia. 1984. "Interaction Sets in the Classroom: Towards a Study of Pupil Knowledge." In *Life in School: The Sociology of Pupil Culture*, edited by Martyn Hammersley and Peter Woods, 145–160. Milton Keynes, England: Open University Press.

Gibson, Margaret. 1982. Reputation and respectability: How competing cultural systems affect students' performance in school. *Anthropology and Education Quarterly* 13(1): 3–28.

Gilmore, Perry. 1983. Spelling "Mississippi": Recontextualizing a literacy-related speech event. *Anthropology and Education Quarterly* 14(4): 235–256.

Giroux, Henry A. 1983. Theories of reproduction and resistance in the new sociology of education: A critical analysis. *Harvard Educational Review* 53(3): 257–293.

Giroux, Henry A. 1987. Critical literacy and student experience: Donald Graves' Approach to Literacy. *Language Arts* 64(2): 175–181.

Giroux, Henry A. 1988. *Schooling and the Struggle for Public Life: Critical Pedagogy in the Modern Age*. Minneapolis: University of Minnesota Press.

Goodlad, John I. 1984. *A Place Called School*. New York: McGraw-Hill.

Goodlad, John I., and Pamela Keating, eds. 1990. *Access to Knowledge: An Agenda for Our Nation's Schools*. New York: College Entrance Examination Board.

Goodman, Paul. 1962. *Growing Up Absurd*. New York: Random House.

Hamilton, David. 1981. "Generalization in the Educational Sciences: Problems and Purposes." In *The Study of Schooling: Field-Based Methodologies in Education Research*, edited by T. Popkewitz and R. Tabachnick, 227–241. New York: Praeger.

Heath, Shirley B. 1983. *Ways with Words: Language, Life, and Work in Community and Classrooms*. Cambridge: Cambridge University Press.

Henry, Jules. 1963. *Culture Against Man*. New York: Random House.

Hogan, David. 1988. The market revolution and disciplinary power: Joseph Lancaster and the psychology of the early classroom system. *History of Education Quarterly* 29(3): 381–417.

Holt, John. 1964. *How Children Fail*. New York: Dell.

Jackson, Philip W. 1968. *Life in Classrooms*. New York: Holt, Rinehart and Winston.

Johnston, Vivien M. 1987. Attitudes towards microcomputers in learning: 1. Pupils and software for language development. *Educational Research* 29(1): 47–55.

Katz, Michael B. 1987. *Reconstructing American Education*. Cambridge, MA: Harvard University Press.

Katznelson, Ira, Kathleen Gille, and Margaret Weir. 1982. Public schooling and working-class formation: The case of the United States. *American Journal of Education* 90(2): 111–143.

Katznelson, Ira, and Margaret Weir. 1985. *Schooling for All: Class, Race and the Decline of the Democratic Ideal*. New York: Basic Books.

Kohl, Herbert. 1967. *36 Children*. New York: New American Library.

Lambert, Royston, with Spencer Millham. 1968. *The Hothouse Society: An Exploration of Boarding-School Life Through the Boys' and Girls' Own Writings*. London: Weidenfeld and Nicholson.

Lampert, Magdalene. 1990. When the problem is not the question and the solution is not the answer: Mathematical knowing and teaching. *American Educational Research Journal* 27(1): 29–63.

McDermott, R. P. 1974. "Achieving School Failure: An Anthropological Approach to Literacy and Social Stratification." In *Education and Cultural Process*, edited by George D. Spindler, 173–209. New York: Holt, Rinehart and Winston. (Reprinted by Waveland Press, 1987.)

McDermott, R. P. 1976. "Kids Make Sense: An Ethnographic Account of the Interactional Management of Success and Failure in One First Grade Classroom." Unpublished doctoral dissertation, Stanford University, Stanford, CA.

Mead, Margaret. 1970. "Our Educational Emphasis in Primitive Perspective." In *From Child to Adult: Studies in the Anthropology of Education*, edited by John Middleton, 1–13. Garden City, NY: National History Press.

Measor, L. 1984. "Gender and the Sciences: Pupils' Gender-Based Conceptions of School Subjects." In *Life in School: The Sociology of Pupil Culture*, edited by Martyn Hammersley and Peter Woods, 89–105. Milton Keynes, England: Open University Press.

Mehan, Hugh. 1980. The competent student. *Anthropology and Education Quarterly* 11(3): 131–152.

Mehan, Hugh, A. Hertweck, and J. L. Meihls. 1986. *Handicapping the Handicapped: Decision Making in Students' Careers*. Stanford, CA: Stanford University Press.

Metz, Mary Haywood. 1978. *Classrooms and Corridors: The Crisis of Authority in Desegregated Secondary Schools*. Berkeley: University of California Press.

Moll, Luis C., and Stephen Diaz. 1987. Change as the goal of education research. *Anthropology and Education Quarterly* 18(4): 300–311.

National Research Council. 1985. *Mathematics, Science and Technology Education: A Research Agenda*. Washington, DC: National Academy Press.

Nespor, Jan. 1987. Academic tasks in a high school English class. *Curriculum Inquiry* 17(2): 203–228.

Oakes, Jeannie. 1985. *Keeping Track: How Schools Structure Inequality*. New Haven, CT: Yale University Press.

Ogbu, John. 1987. Variability in minority school performance: A problem in search of an explanation. *Anthropology and Education Quarterly* 18(4): 312–334.

Okakok, Leona. 1989. Serving the purpose of education. *Harvard Educational Review* 59(4): 405–422.

Olsen, Tillie. 1978. *Silences*. New York: Delacorte Press/Seymour Lawrence.

Paley, Vivian, 1979. *White Teacher*. Cambridge, MA: Harvard University Press.

Perry, Imani. 1988. A black student's reflection on public and private school. *Harvard Educational Review* 58: 332–336.

Philips, Susan U. 1983. *The Invisible Culture: Communication in the Classroom and Community on the Warm Springs Indian Reservation*. New York: Longman.

Posner, George J. 1982. A cognitive science conception of curriculum and instruction. *Journal of Curriculum Studies* 14(4): 343–351.

Powell, Arthur G., et al. 1986. *The Shopping Mall High School: Winners and Losers in the Educational Market Place*. Boston: Houghton Mifflin.

Putnam, Ralph T., Madgalene Lampert, and Penelope L. Peterson. 1990. "Alternative Perspectives on Knowing Mathematics in Elementary Schools." In *Review of Research in Education*, edited by Courtney B. Cazden, Vol. 16, 57–150. Washington, DC: American Educational Research Association.

Resnick, Lauren B. 1987. *Education and Learning to Think*. Washington, DC: National Academy Press.

Rist, Ray C. 1970. Student social class and teacher self-fulfilling prophecy in ghetto education. *Harvard Educational Review* 40(3): 411–450.

Rist, Ray C. 1978. *The Invisible Children*. Cambridge, MA: Harvard University Press.

Rosaldo, Renato. 1989. *Culture and Truth: The Remaking of Social Analysis*. Boston: Beacon Press.

Rose, Mike. 1990. *Lives on the Boundary: A Moving Account of the Struggles and Achievements of America's Educational Underclass*. New York: Penguin Books.

Rosenshine, Barak. 1979. "Content, Time, and Direct Instruction." In *Research on Teaching: Concepts, Findings and Implications*, edited by Penelope Peterson and Herbert Walberg, 28–56. Berkeley, CA: McCutchan.

Rueda, Robert, and Hugh Mehan. 1986. Metacognition and passing: Strategic interactions in the lives of students with learning disabilities. *Anthropology and Education Quarterly* 17(3): 145–165.

Schoolboys of Barbiana. 1970. *Letter to a Teacher*. New York: Random House (Vintage Books).

Shaughnessy, Joan M., and Thomas M. Haladyna. 1985. Research on student attitudes toward social studies. *Social Education* 49(8): 692–695.

Shaughnessy, Joan M., Tom Haladyna, and J. Michael Shaughnessy. 1983. Relations of student, teacher, and learning environment variables to attitude toward mathematics. *School Science and Mathematics* 83(1): 21–37.

Shymansky, James A., and William C. Kyle, Jr. 1988. A summary of research in science education—1986. *Science Education* 72(3): 249–402.

Sizer, Theodore R. 1985. *Horace's Compromise: The Dilemma of the American High School*. Boston: Houghton Mifflin.

Sperling, Melaine, and Sarah Warshauer Freedman. 1987. A good girl writes like a good girl: Written response to student writing. *Written Communication* 4(4): 343–369.

Stodolsky, Susan S. 1988. *The Subject Matters: Classroom Activity in Math and Social Studies*. Chicago: University of Chicago Press.

Strieb, Lynne. 1985. *A Philadelphia Teacher's Journal*. Grand Forks, ND: North Dakota Study Group Center for Teaching and Learning.

Vygotsky, Lev S. 1978. *Mind in Society: The Development of Higher Psychological Processes*, edited by Michael Cole, Vera John-Steiner, Sylvia Scribner, and Ellen Sonberman. Cambridge, MA: Harvard University Press.

Walker, Rob, and Clem Adelman. 1975. *A Guide to Classroom Observation*. London: Methuen.

Waller, Willard. 1932. *The Sociology of Teaching*. New York: Wiley.

Waugh, Evelyn. 1964. *A Little Learning; An Autobiography: The Early Years*. Boston: Little, Brown.

Weis, Lois. 1985. *Between Two Worlds: Black Students in an Urban Community College*. New York: Routledge, Chapman and Hall.

Weisner, Thomas S., Ronald Gallimore, and Cathie Jordan. 1988. Unpackaging cultural effects on classroom learning: Native Hawaiian peer assistance and child-generated activity. *Anthropology and Education Quarterly* 19(4): 327–353.

Welter, Barbara. 1978. "The Cult of True Womanhood: 1820–1860." In *The American Family in Social-Historical Perspective*, edited by Michael Gordon, 372 392. New York: St. Martin's Press.

Wertsch, James V., ed. 1985. *Culture, Communication, and Cognition: Vygotskian Perspectives*. Cambridge: Cambridge University Press.

Wertsch, James V. 1991. *Voices of the Mind*. Cambridge, MA: Harvard University Press.

Willis, Paul. 1977. *Learning to Labour: How Working Class Kids Get Working Class Jobs*. Farnborough, England: Saxon House.

Young, Michael F. D., ed. 1971. *Knowledge and Control: New Directions for the Sociology of Education*. London: Collier Macmillan.

Zelizer, Viviana A. 1985. *Pricing the Priceless Child: The Changing Social Value of Children*. New York: Basic Books.

18

CURRICULUM AND PEDAGOGY

Walter Doyle
UNIVERSITY OF ARIZONA

This chapter is about the theoretical, empirical, and practical issues surrounding the intersection of curriculum and pedagogy. The meeting point between these two domains has always been somewhat fuzzy, in part because the terms denote separate but interrelated phenomena (see Beauchamp 1981; Johnson 1967; Macdonald 1965). As usually understood, curriculum refers to the substance or content of schooling, the course of study (literally, a "racecourse") that specifies what is to be taught. Discussions of curriculum typically focus on issues of content selection and arrangement that float well above the surface of particular classrooms. Pedagogy, on the other hand, refers largely to the processes or the "how" of schooling, the human interactions that occur during actual teaching episodes. Central topics in pedagogical discussions are motivation, communication, engagement, feedback, and the like. Given this distinctiveness, it is not surprising that a considerable amount of work in each domain has gone on as if the other did not exist. At the same time, a curriculum is intended to frame or guide teaching practice and cannot be achieved except during acts of teaching. Similarly, teaching is always about something so it cannot escape curriculum, and teaching practices, in themselves, imply curricular assumptions and consequences. It is difficult, therefore, to avoid stumbling on curriculum when one is trying to understand teaching, or commenting on pedagogy when one is deliberating about curriculum.

The chapter can be described as an attempt to stand between curriculum and pedagogy in order to examine theory and research that have a bearing on understanding how these areas intersect. The chapter begins with a focus on conceptual and historical matters, that is, on the factors that have shaped concepts of curriculum and pedagogy, and the development of ideas and practices around these domains. Attention then turns to research programs that address, in one way or another, the relationships between curriculum and pedagogy. Research on curriculum implementation, which represents an important body of work on how curriculum becomes teaching practice, is summarized here only as necessary. A more complete treatment of this literature can be found in Chapter 15 in this volume, "Curriculum Implementation" by Snyder, Bolin, and Zumwalt. In addition, attention in the present chapter is directed to general curriculum issues. Although reference is made to the teaching of particular subjects (e.g., reading, writing, mathematics, and science), no systematic attempt is made to treat at length issues of curriculum and pedagogy within various content domains. These areas are covered in separate chapters in this volume. Finally, for another view of the mutuality of curriculum and pedagogy, one that focuses primarily on teachers, see Chapter 14 in this volume, "Teacher as Curriculum Maker" by Clandinin and Connelly.

A systematic discussion of curriculum and pedagogy is quite timely. Interest in curriculum is spreading rapidly among researchers who have traditionally studied teaching (see, e.g., Brophy 1990; Carter and Doyle 1989; Doyle 1986b; Shulman 1986a). Similarly, curriculum scholars are moving into the classroom to examine more closely the curriculum that is taught and learned and the knowledge teachers and students use to achieve these enactments (e.g., Anyon 1980; Cornbleth 1988; Elbaz 1983; Posner 1988; Zumwalt 1989). At the same time, the emergence of cognitive science and qualitative-interpretive research perspectives has given rise to a fundamental reformulation of the disciplinary foundations of educational inquiry. This reformulation is opening exciting new theoretical and empirical corridors for research framed around issues of learning, teaching, and curriculum (see, e.g., Brown, Collins, and Duguird 1989; Connelly and Clandinin 1986; Golden 1989; Marton 1989).

CURRICULUM AND THE CONTROL OF TEACHING

To convey the complexity of the relationship between curriculum and pedagogy, it is necessary to sketch broadly the intellectual and empirical traditions that have grown up around these two domains. In this section, the curriculum field is surveyed with special attention to how matters of pedagogy are treated, and research on teaching is examined with particular attention to curriculum issues. In addition, some of the underlying themes that have shaped growth in these two research domains are explored.

The term "curriculum" has multiple definitions or images, no one of which completely captures the scope of meaning associated with its use (see Beauchamp 1981; Schubert 1986; Zais 1976). As suggested above, curriculum refers in a broad sense to the substance or content of schooling, that is, to the knowledges, methodologies, and dispositions that constitute the experiences and the outcomes of schooling. Problems in defining the term more specifically occur in part because curriculum discourse operates at both institutional and experiential levels. There is a formal curriculum that defines the core substance of schooling and an experienced curriculum that is taught and learned in classrooms. For reasons that will become apparent, formal knowledge about curriculum has centered on the institutional curriculum, a tradition that has fundamentally shaped understanding of the relationship between curriculum and pedagogy. It is necessary, therefore, to begin the discussion at the institutional level.

The Institutional Curriculum

At an institutional level, curriculum discourse serves primarily to define or typify schooling (on typification, see Berger and Luckmann 1967). If one were to ask what goes on in a school or school system, the answer is likely to be framed in terms of broad goals and general experiences (e.g., a process approach to science or a whole-language emphasis in reading) rather than the multiplicity of particular incidents occurring daily. Schooling is often typified, in other words, through a relatively abstract model of what a school or school system is and does. This abstract model is the institutional curriculum. It is important to underscore that the institutional curriculum is not equivalent to the formal or written curriculum. At its core, the institutional curriculum is a tacitly understood and shared conception or paradigm of schooling. The written curriculum often captures much of this conception and the document itself has important political and managerial functions (as will be seen), but the operating form of the curriculum is the shared social conception that is used to judge the adequacy of discourse about schooling and teaching.

Curriculum at an institutional level has closely related external and internal functions. Externally, curriculum discourse operates at the intersection of schooling and society to translate the community's definitions and expectations for schools into concrete programs and, in turn, to represent the forms and procedures of schooling as responses to these expectations (see Lazerson, McLaughlin, McPherson, and Bailey 1985; Reid 1984). Underlying this process is a set of explicit and implied arguments that rationalize the selection and arrangement of content (knowledge, skills, and dispositions) and the transformation of that content into school subjects, that is, into a form suitable for use in classrooms (see Fenstermacher 1984). Important historical studies of the formation of school subjects have recently appeared (see Goodson 1987; Goodson and Ball 1984; Popkewitz 1987a). These analyses provide insight into the intellectual and political processes through which bodies of knowledge are defined and transformed into curriculum.

Because social demands and political circumstances often change rapidly, the institutional curriculum becomes a convenient instrument for school systems to convey responsiveness to external communities. Buildings, instructional materials, and teachers are difficult and expensive to change, but the curriculum, that is, the language for talking about schooling, can be changed with relative ease. It is not surprising, then, that the curriculum field is preoccupied with the themes of innovation and change. In addition, it is not surprising that a variety of voices are heard representing personal, social, moral, and political perspectives or platforms on curriculum (Eisner and Vallance 1974). At an operational level, these multiple voices within the curriculum field provide a pool of alternative typifications that administrators can use to redefine quickly the way schooling is portrayed in the face of changing social and political circumstances.

Internally, the institutional curriculum serves as a normative framework for defining and managing the work of teachers. In one-room schools, practical questions of scope and sequence could be resolved by individual teachers. As enrollments grew, however, the need to organize levels of schooling and synchronize the work of several teachers within and across these levels increased. In became necessary, in other words, to define more precisely what teachers within a "graded" system were supposed to do in their separate classrooms (see Tyack 1974). The curriculum became a useful tool for constructing these definitions and, thus, for controlling teaching. To this end, curriculum guides sometimes include concrete specifications for teaching practice in an effort to "teacher-proof" the curriculum.

From an institutional perspective, then, curriculum is an abstract model that defines the essential character, that is, the experiences and outcomes, of a school or school system. This model is sometimes instantiated in a document but, more broadly, it exists in the shared perceptions of the participants in schooling and their relevant communities. This model defines both an arena within which tensions between school and society are resolved and a set of norms for controlling teaching.

At an institutional level, curriculum and pedagogy easily become separate domains, and the relationship between them is construed as linear. In simple terms, the curriculum defines the substance of schooling and perhaps its pedagogical implications. Then comes pedagogy to deliver the curriculum faithfully and effectively (Beauchamp 1981; Foshay and Foshay 1980). It can be noted that the view of curriculum and pedagogy as separate domains is common among academics, whose vision has dominated American schooling (see Kliebard 1986). As guardians of the disciplines, academics concentrate on subject matter, with a view toward defining the latest content of a field. For them, pedagogy is largely a matter of motivation and style.

The Professionalization of Schooling

In the United States the institutional meanings and functions of curriculum, as well as understandings of pedagogical theory and research, were deeply entrenched in the professionalization of schooling which occurred in the late 19th and early 20th centuries. A brief discussion of this extraordinary period in the history of schooling will clarify the nature of inquiry related to curriculum and pedagogy (for greater detail, see Doyle 1976). Two features of this discussion need to be clear at the beginning. First, the analysis is seen to apply primarily to developments in the United States. Different social patterns and intellectual traditions are likely to be found in other countries. Second, the focus is largely on themes and issues related to the study of curriculum and pedagogy (that is, the character of thought in the research community) rather than what actually took place in schools and classrooms (see Franklin 1986).

A profession is conventionally defined as an occupation whose members are reputed to possess high levels of knowledge, skill, commitment, and trustworthiness and whose practices are based on a body of specialized technical knowledge (see Lieberman 1956). Freidson (1970) notes, however, that an emphasis on the competence and moral dispositions of members of a profession misses an important aspect of the professionalization process. Professionals may or may not be morally superior or more technically proficient than members of other occupations, but a profession enjoys a preeminence in a division of labor to the extent that it "gains control over the determination of the substance of its own work" (Freidson 1970, xvii). A profession, in other words, monopolizes its sphere of practice.

This dominance is achieved and maintained through social and political processes designed to secure wide acceptance of an occupation's claims to technical and moral superiority. All occupations make such claims; a profession is an occupation whose claims are in fact believed by the general public, or at least by influential segments of that public, and supported by government policy. The key to professional status is not simply the existence or even the validity of such claims, but rather acceptance of the legitimacy of what the occupation asserts about itself. The public must believe, in other words, that the occupation seeking professional status has special control over the means necessary to achieve solutions to problems in a domain. The professional ethic of exemplary knowledge and virtue serves, therefore, not to define a profession but to aid in the processes of "establishing, maintaining, defending, and expanding the legal or otherwise political advantage of the occupation" (Freidson 1970, 200).

Achieving professional dominance also depends upon three additional beliefs. First, the work of the occupation must be seen as having significant and far-reaching social consequences. Second, the occupation must be seen as having control over the means by which the problems confronting its members can be solved. Finally, the public must perceive that it is unable to conduct this work on its own or to evaluate adequately the available options within this sphere. These beliefs set the conditions for identifying an occupational group that appears to have the moral and technical qualities necessary to handle the public interest in a particular domain. Occupational groups, in turn, bid for this special status by claiming to possess these qualities.

Discussions of professionalization in education typically focus on the relative status of teachers (Dreeben 1970; Etzioni 1969). This conventional habit diverts attention away from an extraordinary event in the history of American education: During the late 19th and early 20th centuries, schooling professionalized in response to perceived threats to social order and community from industrialization, urbanization, and immigration (see Doyle 1976; Franklin 1986; Wiebe 1969). That is, public elementary and secondary schools came to monopolize the domain of education. Schooling came to be seen as an important symbol of education and was increasingly linked to social mobility, vocational success, and equality of opportunity. Schools, in addition, were viewed as key instruments for eradicating social ills and securing national prestige, defense, and economic security.

It is also important to underscore that the key actors in this professionalizing process in the United States were school superintendents rather than teachers (for this argument, see Doyle 1976; see also Tyack and Hansot 1980). Because schooling rather than teaching was professionalized, administrators were the focal group around which the issues of power and control in the education of American youth were to be resolved. Teachers, in turn, were often depicted as instruments to be controlled rather than as agents who made the basic decisions about how schooling was to be conducted (see Clandinin 1986; Elbaz 1983). This image of teachers and teaching shaped developing conceptions of curriculum and pedagogy.

Curriculum, as an instrument for connecting schooling to social expectations and for regulating teaching, obviously played a key role in the professionalizing of schooling. Through curriculum, professionals could define how schooling should address the public interest in education and promise its accomplishment by regulating pedagogical practice. They could claim, in other words, to control the means of education (see Franklin 1986; Kliebard 1986).

As a normative system, however, curriculum is a weak force for regulating teaching. Individual teachers may or may not see the pedagogical implications or follow the specifications contained in curriculum guides or even accept the paradigm around which they are constructed. Indeed, it is not easy to teacher-proof a curriculum. Even in highly specified curricula such as Distar and the science initiatives of the 1960s, variations in teaching practice occurred across sites (see R. B. Anderson 1977; Rosenshine 1970). These possibilities are problematic from the administrators' perspective because the strength of administrators' claims to control the means of schooling rests on perceptions that the curriculum is delivered faithfully. This problem was addressed, of course, through supervision, a function that was traditionally exercised by school boards and eventually delegated to county and local superintendents (see Gwynn 1961, 3–17; Payne 1875). If supervision procedures were in place and made sufficiently visible through a rhetoric of accountability, then administrators could project an image of control, and the blame for school failure could easily be shifted to teachers.

A Science of Education

Traditionally, knowledge about curriculum was grounded in academic subjects, philosophical speculation about the mind or about children, conventional wisdom about teaching, and conceptions of society. Pedagogical knowledge, in turn, was rooted in methods, that is, in philosophical and curricular arguments about the nature of knowledge, the character of learners and the learning process, and the impact of teaching activities. During the 19th century, the intellectual climate in the United States regarding methods was especially rich (see Bayles and Hood 1966; Kliebard 1986; Seguel 1978), and university appointments in methods were made (see Woodring 1975). Mental disciplinarians argued for rigorous teaching of difficult subjects to train mental faculties. Pestalozzi's methods for teaching young children based on ideas of sense impression, experience, and development were promoted by such leading educational figures as Horace Mann and Henry Barnard. Froebel's kindergarten based on the educative value of play was a popular movement. And the Herbartian concepts of apperception, correlation, concentration, culture epochs, and the five-step plan for teaching were widely discussed. In this era, methods were integrated frameworks within which curriculum and pedagogy were closely tied.

In keeping with the practices of other professional groups striving for social power in the late 19th and early 20th centuries, there was a move in schooling to ground curriculum and supervision in science (see Hays 1972; Lagemann 1989). A science of education promised an objective means to settle arguments among various proponents of different approaches and thus provide a decisive authority for judgments about school subjects or teachers. Given the framework of professionalization, quality control and effectiveness became the driving themes in the search for and development of this science.

Lagemann (1989, 185) has argued that "one cannot understand the history of education in the United States during the twentieth century unless one realizes that Edward L. Thorndike won and John Dewey lost." This assertion calls attention to the fact that the emerging field of educational psychology (as expounded in the early decades of this century by such leading figures as Edward Thorndike at Teachers College and Charles Judd, Dewey's successor at the University of Chicago) became the foundational discipline for educational thought and research. This psychology, intentionally designed to mirror the forms of the physical sciences, was behavioral, experimental, and atomistic. The focus was on precise measurement of specific behaviors and the use of controlled conditions to verify scientific laws. These laws, in turn, were intended to be prescriptive, that is, they would define precisely what teachers must do in order to cause student learning. It was a science dedicated to control rather than to making sense of the forms and processes of schooling and teaching (see Bayles and Hood 1966; Joncich 1968; Lagemann 1989; Popkewitz 1987b).

Dewey's view of science and the relationship between science and practice stood in sharp contrast to that of Judd and Thorndike (see Kliebard 1986; Lagemann 1989; White 1982). Dewey saw science as means of gaining an understanding of the social complexities of education in its concrete forms. Experimentation was thus a collaborative process in which teachers and researchers (from a variety of academic disciplines) jointly explored forms of schooling to understand better how to bring the child and the curriculum together in natural settings. The style of this inquiry was naturalistic and observational, and the product was knowledge teachers could use in solving practical problems rather than laws or prescriptions for controlling teachers' practice. Moreover, Dewey's root metaphors were ecological rather than chemical or mechanical. As a result, he rejected the narrow stimulus-response conceptions of behavioral psychology and found much greater affiliation with sociological and anthropological formulations of the day.

Dewey's conceptions, as well as the rich intellectual heritage of teaching methods, were swept aside in the academic community by the rapidly growing prestige of behavioral psychology. A psychology of this type was intended to provide the necessary scientific authority for the social efficiency movement that had, through the efforts of Rice and Taylor, already begun to influence schooling and business (see Kliebard 1986). In addition, it served well the ends of professionalization. As Lagemann (1989, 212) notes, "Judd and Thorndike produced authoritative school surveys, curricula, tests, and laws of learning. They offered the kind of educational science that many educators needed and wanted as aids in explaining their actions and policies, successes and failures."

Issues of status within the academic world helped shape the substance and character of educational science. To enhance their academic standing, educationists such as Judd sought to emulate the science laboratory and to move away from teacher education and the study of classrooms, areas dominated largely by women, to the preparation of men for advanced degrees as administrators and researchers. As Lagemann notes:

> Judd believed that the professionalization of education, and therefore, the improvement of education required that teachers and researchers fulfill distinct functions. Teachers should teach, in the process transmitting subject matter, organizing classrooms, and approaching children according to knowledge generated by researchers. In accord with the differences of function, Judd believed there should also be differences of gender—teachers should be

> female, researchers, male; and differences in levels of education—teachers should not be required to pursue graduate training, researchers should possess the Ph.D. [even the Ed.D. was not good enough]. (Lagemann 1989, 205)

Educational psychology was the best candidate to provide the foundation for the research that would direct teaching. But to compete for academic status, the study of classrooms was excluded from educational science:

> The scorn of many pure psychologists against brethren in the applied sciences forced educational psychologists to create research settings that appeared unrelated to application. The most successful educational scientists tended to withdraw into a laboratory setting, often substituting animals for children, as did Edward Thorndike. Examining life in the natural setting of the classroom was scientifically unnecessary. (White 1982, 154–155)

The framing of educational science, then, clearly reflected the themes of power and quality control embedded in the professionalization of schooling. This affiliation of educational research with institutional themes meant that inquiry moved away from teachers and the complexities of classroom learning and toward the simplicity and precision of the experimental laboratory. This definition of the character of educational research had substantial consequences for the study of curriculum and pedagogy.

The Curriculum Field

A behavioral version of psychological science had an enormous impact on the development of the curriculum field, that is, a school- and university-based group who proclaimed specialized knowledge about curriculum and the processes associated with its planning and management. This field was framed initially by a social efficiency spirit and a commitment to using the methods of science for defining the character of school subjects, specifying the procedures for curriculum making, and settling arguments about effective pedagogical practice (see Bobbitt 1913, 1918, 1924 and commentaries by Franklin 1986; Kliebard 1986; and Seguel 1966).

This image of science manifested itself in several ways. With respect to the curriculum itself, educational psychologists generated a psychology of school subjects that consisted largely in the reduction of curriculum content to the categories and processes studied in psychological laboratories (see Joncich 1968; White 1982). Judd, for instance, helped to develop methods for studying eye movements to improve reading and handwriting, and Thorndike worked on frequency counts of words and the psychological processes involved in learning arithmetic. Bobbitt and Charters extended this framework by developing a method called "activity analysis" in which the domestic, social, and occupational activities of adults were meticulously recorded (Bobbitt 1924; Charters 1923). As Kliebard (1986, 108) notes, "Thorndike's image of mind as consisting of innumerable tiny functions, and Bobbitt's scientific curriculum drawn from a laborious analysis of the multitudinous tasks that comprise human life were all of one conceptual piece." Activity analysis was intended to provide a specialized scientific foundation for defining curriculum content to replace the traditional academic disciplines as sources of school subjects.

Along similar lines, a scientific procedure for curriculum construction was proposed. This procedure—which eventually came to be known as the Tyler Rationale (Tyler 1949)—consisted of a linear model for transforming content into a design or plan for teaching. Curriculum planners were to begin with specific behavioral objectives, assess entering performance of students, design instructional experiences, and evaluate learning outcomes to determine if instruction worked. The teacher's role in this scheme was to implement the instructional design.

Standardized testing, which developed rapidly in the early decades of this century and embodied the new psychology at its core, was an especially powerful symbol of objectivity and rationality (Buros 1977). In 1917, for example, Cubberley, an influential professor of educational administration who studied at Teachers College under Thorndike, saw in standardized tests a valuable tool for both teachers and superintendents:

> To the teacher it cannot help but eventually mean not only concise and definite statements as to what she is expected to do in the different subjects of the course of study, but the reduction of instruction to those items which can be proved to be of importance in preparation for intelligent living and future usefulness in life. . . . For the superintendent it means the changing of school supervision from guesswork to scientific accuracy, and the establishment of standards of work by which he may defend what he is doing." (Cubberley 1917, vii-viii)

Curriculum, it can be noted, played a key role in the development of testing to the extent that the construction of standardized achievement tests depended upon the standardizing of curriculum.

Pedagogical Research

In addition to the potential benefits of testing for regulating teaching, supervision needed to be grounded in pedagogical knowledge that would validate judgments about observed classroom practice (see, e.g., Sears 1921). The result was research on pedagogy driven by the theme of effectiveness, that is, a search for the best way to teach or the criteria for identifying the best teachers. The impact of the new psychology on knowledge about teaching was especially strong since pedagogy was historically viewed as a branch of philosophical psychology. As a result, pedagogical knowledge was fundamentally transformed.

The experiment, a hallmark of scientific method, was expected to provide the necessary tool to settle disputes about methods by testing the relative effectiveness of different teaching approaches. Under controlled conditions, two or more methods or "treatments" could be compared in terms of their consequences for students' learning. If all worked well, the most effective method would be discovered, and this method would then define uniform practice for classrooms. Rice (1893) began this tradition in the 1890s with studies of different methods of teaching spelling, and Bobbitt (1913), who received his degree in psychology from Clark University and was hired at the University of Chicago by Judd, was a vocal advocate for this experimental approach (see also the discussion in Barr 1931, 167–181). Although these "horse races" seldom produced clear winners, numerous methods experiments were conducted throughout this century (see Walker and Schaffarzick 1974; Wallen and Travers 1963), and the tradition of proposing and testing methods or teaching models remains vigorous, especially within specific subject areas (see Easley 1977; Joyce and Weil 1972; Nuthall and Snook 1973).

Efforts by Barr (1926, 1929, 1931) and others in the 1920s to put instructional supervision on a scientific basis gave rise to a separate tradition of pedagogical inquiry known as "teacher effectiveness research." In this tradition, the teacher rather than the method was the primary unit of analysis. The logic of teacher effectiveness research is compelling: Some teachers are clearly better than others, so, if the qualities that cause these differences can be discovered, then all teachers can be improved, or at least the good can be sorted from the bad. The form of this research reflected the character of the supervisory processes: direct observation of teachers and judgments about the quality of observed performance. The goal was to identify indicators—features of teachers—that reliably predicted effectiveness, that is, scores on a measure of valued outcomes or consequences (Gage 1963). Studies in this tradition were of two major types. The first type consisted of research on personal qualities of teachers, such as personality dimensions, attitudes, intelligence, preparation, academic achievement, and the like (see Getzels and Jackson 1963). The second type—now popularly known as "process-product research"—consisted of studies of dimensions of classroom performance measured by either high-inference rating scales (e.g., clarity, enthusiasm, warmth) or low-inference categories (e.g., frequency of praise, number of processes questions) (see Gage 1978; Rosenshine 1976). Outcomes of instruction in teacher effectiveness studies were measured either by subjective ratings from principals or supervisors or by objective tests of student achievement or attitude.

Studies of personal qualities and their relationship to criteria of effectiveness were designed to produce information useful primarily in selecting teachers either for preparation programs or for teaching positions (see Schalock 1979). Studies of classroom dimensions were intended to produce information useful in selecting content for teacher preparation or evaluating classroom performance (Gage 1978). The argument in teacher effectiveness research, in other words, was grounded in issues of personnel administration and training rather than curriculum.

The framing of pedagogical research as a question about teacher effectiveness and the grounding of this research in behavioral psychology led to an increasingly generic view of pedagogy. The language of behavioral psychology focused on overt actions and the effectiveness question focused on teachers or teaching methods as the direct causes of outcomes. Taken together, these frameworks excluded students and curriculum from the analysis. Methods became treatments, for example, lecture versus discussion, devoid of the rich theoretical propositions about the nature of content and its acquisition that had characterized 19th-century discussions of method. In process-product research, behaviors rather than content were measured during classroom observations. In one study, for instance, the percent of time teachers spent smiling was the sole teaching variable used to account for effectiveness (Harrington 1955). Questions of what was being taught to whom slipped into the background.

A generic view of teaching was quite compatible, however, with the administrative uses of effectiveness research for the remote control of teaching through evaluation and training. If one is making decisions about a large number of teachers for an entire school system, then indicators of effectiveness need to be few in number, easily applied, and highly generalizable across teaching situations. If indicators must be specific to each teaching area, it becomes impossible to find a common metric to judge teachers. Moreover, if each teacher must be evaluated within each curricular area, the task of teacher evaluation would become enormous. The press, therefore, was for the identification of a few context-free indicators of teaching effectiveness that could be easily observed. The new behavioral psychology of Thorndike and Judd promised to establish just such a set of scientifically derived standards for teaching quality that could empower supervisors (largely men) to decide on supposedly disinterested, rational grounds the qualifications of teachers (mostly women).

The fact that the search for generalizable indicators of quality was not always successful did not diminish the importance of effectiveness as a theme in research. Then as now, professions, in the absence of scientific solutions, justify their claims by calling attention to the amount of effort expended to solve problems (Burnham 1972). Activity with a recognizable scientific character became, in this way, a proxy for possessing a validated answer to a crucial question. The very existence of research on teaching effectiveness—that is, the fact that a scientific answer to the question was being sought—became an important element in legitimizing the claims of schooling professionals. Research had value, then, primarily "as an activity expected of an expert group and not for its substantive contribution to either theory or practice" (Joncich 1968, 559).

Summary

This analysis suggests that knowledge about the processes of schooling—administration, supervision, curriculum, and teaching—grew as a resource for substantiating administrators' claims to have control over the means of educating America's children. So the knowledge of most worth—that is, practical knowledge—tended to be that which administrators could use to control how schooling was conducted.

In this context, the separation between curriculum and pedagogy—between substance and delivery—was quite dramatic, and distinct research programs in curriculum and in pedagogy evolved. Indeed, much of the work in pedagogy went on as if curriculum did not exist and vice versa. In addition, by the time of World War I, behavioral psychology became the core or mainstream discipline for educational research, providing both the central constructs and the methodological standards for a science of education. This dominance can be seen, for example, in the commitment to measurement among the founders of the American Educational Research Association in 1915 (see Lagemann 1989, 210).

Curriculum theory evolved in two directions. The first domain consisted of propositions about the core content or substance of the curriculum, propositions organized around the general question of "What knowledge is of most worth?" This area came under the traditional purview of philosophers and specialists in academic disciplines, who, Kliebard (1986) argues, eventually held sway against the scientific curriculum making of educationists in the control of curriculum content. The second domain of theory in the curriculum field consisted of knowledge related to curriculum administration or engineering: how to structure the curriculum to achieve balance, articulation, and integration; how to evaluate its consequences; how to formulate curriculum committees, establish priorities, set agendas, and guide the interaction among various constituencies; how to monitor and supervise teaching practice; and how to manage innovation and change (see Beauchamp 1981; Glatthorn 1987).

In contrast to curriculum, pedagogy was traditionally and conceptually closer to psychology. As a result, research on teaching became thoroughly infused by the new behavioral psychology of Thorndike and Judd. Pedagogical research participated, therefore, in the growing prestige of psychology as the core discipline of educational science. At the same time, curriculum and the classroom context were stripped from the study of teaching in its psychologized version. In the end, findings from research on teaching became a source of authority independent from curriculum for controlling quality in teaching practice. It is not surprising, therefore, that findings from process-product research were widely celebrated in the 1980s as a triumph for educational research (see Gage 1985) and have played a significant role in state and school district policies concerning teacher education and evaluation (see Zumwalt 1988).

Within the dominant institutionalized view of curriculum as an instrument for controlling teaching, little direct work on the experienced curriculum emerged. Most who proposed curriculum models showed little interest in the details of implementation in classrooms, except as discrepancies from the model became apparent. Similarly, pedagogical researchers paid little attention to curriculum as a classroom experience or to the situational factors that might shape teaching practice. The search was for features of teachers or teaching that were independent of local circumstances, including curriculum.

As a result, most research at the juncture of curriculum and pedagogy has focused on curriculum implementation (for a review of this work see Chapter 15 in this volume, "Curriculum Implementation" by Snyder, Bolin, and Zumwalt). Implementation research rests on concepts and methods borrowed from social psychological studies of general processes of innovation, adoption, and change (e.g., Bennis et al. 1976; Fullan 1982). In this work, which represents a central preoccupation in the curriculum field, attention is focused on attitudes of teachers toward innovations and change (e.g., resistors or promoters) and the design of interventions (e.g., group discussions) for promoting and managing change (e.g., Loucks and Hall 1979; Loucks and Pratt 1979). As Richardson (1990) notes, the underlying theme of much of this literature is how to get teachers to follow the wishes of others. In instances in which observed practice is not aligned with institutional specifications—not an uncommon circumstance—attention is directed to improving the effectiveness of implementation strategies rather than understanding classroom contingencies.

From an institutional perspective, curriculum stands outside classrooms as a definition of the purposes and contents of schooling. This definition specifies what is to happen in classrooms, that is, what teachers are to teach. Within classrooms, attention shifts from curriculum issues which were resolved at the institutional level to teaching techniques and behaviors and to interpersonal processes between teacher and student. Teaching is seen largely as a process of directing and controlling or praising and encouraging students so that they can learn. The curriculum becomes invisible in the standard generic view of pedagogical theory (see, for example, Dunkin and Biddle 1974, 31–52).

The Experienced Curriculum

In recent years a growing number of scholars have challenged the production system conception of education and the technical rationality that underlies the professionalizing and scientizing of schooling. In particular, these scholars reject the fractionization of curriculum and pedagogy that seems inherent in these perspectives, as well as the practice of defining curriculum and teaching practice out of context. In their place, they have emphasized a view of curriculum as a "contextualized social process" (Cornbleth 1988), as "events" (Posner 1988), as "what students have an opportunity to learn" (McCutcheon 1988), or as "an evolving construction" resulting from the interaction of teacher and students (Zumwalt 1989, 175). They argue that the curriculum exists not as a document but as a set of enacted events in which teachers and students jointly negotiate content and meaning (Elbaz 1983). Similarly, pedagogy is seen not simply as a neutral pipeline for delivering content, but as a social context that has fundamental curricular effects (see Doyle 1986b). As Zumwalt (1989, 175) states, "Choices of 'how' are more than instrumental, they influence the curriculum, often in profound ways." These socially embedded notions blur the distinction between curriculum and pedagogy. The curriculum is what teachers and students experience, and, thus, the relevant unit of analysis is, in Weade's (1987, 15) term, "curriculum'n'instruction."

Interest in the experienced curriculum is not new. Many 19th-century pedagogical theorists, such as Pestalozzi and Froebel, focused on the immediate experiences of children and the meanings (i.e., curriculum) that emerged from these experiences (see Adelman 1984; Bayles and Hood 1966). The experienced curriculum was also a central feature of Dewey's thinking (see Kliebard 1986, especially 59–88). Dewey rejected both a disciplinary view in which the child is shaped to fit the content and an extreme child-centered view in which the child's interests become the only curriculum. In contrast, Dewey sought to bring the child and the curriculum together in settings or contexts—what he called "occupations"—in which content became a tool children and teachers shared in thinking and problem solving around familiar objects and events. Experiences in such contexts, Dewey argued, would lead progressively to organized knowledge of subject matter and to a capacity for living democratically.

The modern surge of interest in the experienced curriculum signals fundamental changes in educational discourse. The emphasis on technical rationality and the remote control of teaching are increasingly being interpreted as strategies for creating and sustaining power over a largely female teaching force (Garrison 1988; McDonald 1988; Smyth 1987). This analysis has given prominence to the legitimacy of teachers' personal practical knowledge, their control of the substance and use of inquiry (Carr and Kemmis 1986), and their role as curriculum makers (Clandinin 1986; Connelly and Clandinin 1986; Zumwalt 1988; see also "The Teacher as Curriculum Maker" by Connelly and Clandinin, this volume). At the same time, the conceptual and methodological authority of behavioral psychology has been successfully challenged. Teaching is no longer seen simply as applied psychology. This depsychologizing of pedagogy has opened doors to studies of teaching grounded in anthropological, social, linguistic, and literary ways of knowing (see Cazden 1986; Doyle 1978; Erickson 1986). Moreover, curriculum has become a necessary feature of pedagogical inquiry (see Shulman 1986a). This ferment appears to be leading to fundamentally different conceptions of the character of educational science and of the relationship between research findings and classroom practice.

The remainder of this chapter is devoted to a general survey of research programs in which issues of curriculum and pedagogy are converging. The survey is divided into five sections. The first section is devoted to research on textbooks and their use by teachers. The second section contains a brief summary of emerging work in which subject matter or content is a basic element in the study of pedagogy. The third section includes investigations of the social context of curriculum, with special emphasis on the extent to which the taught curriculum appears to reflect broader social and economic forces. Attention in the fourth section turns to research on curriculum and pedagogy within classrooms, beginning with the burgeoning work in the sociolinguistic tradition on lesson structures and processes and extending to emerging studies of knowledge production processes in classrooms. In the fifth section the discussion is focused on research on classroom tasks. Given the range of programs covered in these sections, the literature cited is only representative of much larger bodies of work. The overall purpose is to give readers a sense of the available domains of inquiry rather than an exhaustive review.

TEXTS AND TEACHERS

Students spend a great deal of their time in classrooms exposed to and working with prepared materials: texts, worksheets, tests, posters, videotapes, films, recordings, and computer programs. It is reasonable to argue, therefore, that such materials are an important means by which the curriculum is made manifest in teaching episodes (for an analysis of the relation of text, curriculum, and instruction, see Cherryholmes 1988). In fact, most formal curricula specify scope and sequence, but instructional materials, especially textbooks, often supply the actual content that students encounter.

Not all texts used in classrooms are textbooks. Nevertheless, textbooks are an important instrument for connecting knowledge domains to school subjects, that is, for transforming content into curriculum (see Cooper 1984; Goodson 1987; Popkewitz 1987a). Noah Webster's spellers and the McGuffey Readers stand, for example, as major historical symbols of the school curriculum (see Monaghan and Saul 1987, 94). Moreover, it is commonly believed that textbooks and text programs with accompanying teacher's guides are the primary sources for the content covered and the pedagogical strategies used in most classrooms. It is not surprising, then, that considerable attention has focused on textbooks (see Squire 1988), including the economic and political circumstances of their production (Apple 1986; FitzGerald 1979), their content and their linguistic and pedagogical features (Anderson and Armbruster 1984; Beck and McCaslin 1978; Beck, McKeown, and Gromoll 1989; Durkin 1981; Meyer, Greer, and Crummey 1987; Osborn 1984), and their correspondence to the tested curriculum (Armbruster, Stevens, and Rosenshine 1977; Freeman et al. 1983).

It is not possible or appropriate to review all of this literature here. The focus, rather, is on selected studies that illuminate the curricular and the pedagogical aspects of textbooks and their use in classrooms.

The Character of Textbooks

Empirical studies suggest a complex picture of text quality and use (for an overview, see Squire 1988). Investigations indicate that there are significant variations in content covered among standard textbooks. Beck, McKeown, and Gromoll (1989) examined the content covered in four major fourth- through seventh-grade textbook programs. Although at a broad topic level all texts followed the common "expanding environments" organization of the social studies curriculum, there was substantial variation across programs in the interpretation of a particular topic. For instance, region, the organizing fourth-grade topic, was defined by topography and climate in two of the programs and by geography in the other two. Moreover, even when programs used the same definition of region, the content covered varied across programs. As a result, the range of regions covered differed significantly among the programs, and only one region—the Sahara—was common to all programs. Even in the case of the Sahara, differences in the treatment of this region across programs were large. Although content similarity was greater for U.S. history in fifth-grade texts than for regions in fourth-grade, there were wide variations across programs in the amount of space devoted to topics.

Similar variations were found across textbooks and standardized tests in fourth-grade mathematics by Freeman and his colleagues (1983). A total of 385 topics were covered by at least 20 items in one of the four texts or five tests analyzed. Only 9 topics were common to all standardized tests and 19 topics were common to all four texts. Of 22 specific core topics identified (i.e., topics covered by at least 20 items in all four texts), only six were common to all textbooks and tests analyzed. In fact, "The proportion of topics covered on a standardized test that received more than cursory treatment in a textbook was never more than 50%" (Freeman et al. 1983, 511). For a related study of textbook and test overlap in third-grade reading, see Armbruster, Stevens, and Rosenshine (1977).

The overall impression left by these studies is that textbooks do not represent a common curriculum. Moreover, studies indicate that textbooks appear to have substantial pedagogical deficiencies. Beck, McKeown, and Gromoll (1989), for example, used recent cognitive research on comprehension to analyze in considerable detail the way information was presented in fourth- and fifth-grade social studies texts. Their analysis focused primarily on the extent to which the texts developed clear goals and arranged content to meet these goals. They found that content goals were unclear, that is, the major issue of a segment of content (paragraph, section, or chapter) was often not stated or was made obscure by the presentation. Further, even when a goal was implied, the presentation of information did not seem to be designed to bring about understanding. Deficiencies in presentation included both poor choices in the selecting and ordering of information and the making of unwarranted assumptions about the background knowledge of the students.

In an earlier study of eight beginning reading programs for low-achieving students, Beck and McCaslin (1978) found similar results: The texts often presented information to students in ways that were likely to confuse, and the instructional procedures recommended to teachers were often unnecessarily complicated. For related studies of the considerateness and the pedagogical features of textbooks, see Anderson and Armbruster (1984), Durkin (1981), Gammon (1973), MacGinitie (1976), and Meyer, Greer, and Crummey (1987). Experiments in which students are given texts redesigned to correct many of these problems have demonstrated improved comprehension (see Beck, McKeown, and Gromoll 1989).

These studies of the way textbooks represent the curriculum and shape pedagogy would seem to have clear implications for redesign of these materials. At the same time, they provide little insight into the factors that shape textbook production (see Cherryholmes 1988, 58–59). Why are textbooks written the way they are? That is, what drives reasonably intelligent adults to produce texts that are so inconsiderate? One compelling hypothesis is that text writing is governed by the demands of seatwork exercises and tests. Sentences such as "Copper comes from the Atacama Desert in Northern Chile" (Beck, McKeown, and Gromoll 1989, 118) would seem to lend themselves easily to the construction of true-false or fill-in-the-blank exercise or test items. In addition, studies of textbook characteristics provide little insight into how teachers and students cope with texts in classrooms. That is, how do teachers embellish the texts for students and what sense do students make of what they read in these books? It may well be that teachers' explanations serve to disentangle the presentations of content available in textbooks. Studies reviewed in the next section suggest that texts are used in a variety of ways by teachers. Furthermore, work summarized in subsequent sections of the chapter suggests that textbooks and other materials are experienced in a context that shapes interpretation and comprehension in fundamental ways.

Teaching by the Book

Stodolsky (1989) has argued that, despite the powerful image it conveys, the apparently simple phrase "teaching by the book" is fundamentally ambiguous. What does it mean to say that a teacher is teaching by the book? To explore this question, two research projects are summarized here.

The first project was reported by Barr and Sadow (1989). This project was framed within an organizational analysis of classroom instruction in which district and school level decisions about curriculum, materials, time schedules, and student placements are seen to determine the resources and conditions available to teachers (Barr and Dreeben 1983; for a similar emphasis on "frame factors" in teaching, see Lundgren 1977). Barr and Sadow examined basal materials as resources that provide readings tasks for students as well as recommendations to teachers for instructional activities. They studied 7 fourth-grade classes from two school districts in the Chicago area which represented a broad range of socioeconomic differences. Features of two basal reading programs were analyzed, and data on teaching were collected in the form of daily teacher logs kept throughout the year, interviews with the teachers, and eight observations to verify logs and determine how instructional time was used. The two programs were quite similar in the number and types of reading selections and skill lessons with two notable differences. Series A supplemented the text with 64 ditto sheets for students' practice and bound fiction and nonfiction separately, with skill lessons attached to the nonfiction selections only. Series B did not have these features and placed less emphasis on vocabulary in reading lessons than the first program.

In classes using Series B in which fiction and nonfiction selections were combined and both framed in skill lessons, Barr and Sadow found that teachers used nearly all of the reading selections (82 to 99 percent) and the practice materials (95 to 100 percent). The selections omitted tended to be short. Teachers using Series A, in which fiction was bound separately and did not contain skill lessons, used nearly all of the nonfiction selections but omitted many fiction selections and many of the practice materials. In fact, the separate fiction book was used after the nonfiction volume was almost finished, even though the publishers recommend they be used simultaneously. The teachers using this series apparently saw fiction as separate from the core of reading instruction. Teachers using Series A varied in their use of practice materials, and none used more than 86 percent of these materials.

In the classroom, teachers varied considerably in the length and the use of time for reading lessons. Across groups, however, teachers spent one half or more of their time on practice materials (skills), with correspondingly less time on contextual reading. The teacher's guides emphasized a directed lesson sequence of developing background, reading of the selection, and discussion after. Teachers generally did not follow this sequence for a single lesson but rather extended it over several days. Prereading segments were routinized and uniform across lessons for most teachers. Consistent with the design of the programs, teachers using Series A included vocabulary practice in prereading sessions and, with one exception, teachers using Series B did not. Discussions of background and purpose before reading often reflected information contained in the guides. Only one teacher encouraged students' speculation about text content as part of prereading. Discussion was the main postreading activity, although teachers differed in the extent to which postreading segments occurred at all and showed little consistency in focus (e.g., text-based versus interpretation or personal reaction) across lessons. Teachers varied widely in the use of questions from the guide. The researchers concluded that instruction reflects the orientations and activities of the teacher's guides and noted that teachers typically did not include practices (e.g., student speculation) not included in the guides.

In the second project summarized here, Stodolsky (1989) reviewed studies and presented original evidence to suggest that there is considerable variation in the classroom use of textbooks in most subject areas. Investigators have focused on the extent to which textbooks influence the topics selected and the content covered by teachers. Evidence is especially strong in reading that textbooks influence topical content, especially in the use of basal readers in the primary grades (Barr and Dreeben 1983). In elementary mathematics, Freeman and Porter (1989) found that textbooks influenced most the choice of topics but had little impact on time allocations, standards of achievement, and instructional procedures. They also found variations among teachers in their reliance on texts for topical content and order of presentation. The general conclusion seems to be that teachers covered the topics that were in the textbooks, but exercised considerable latitude in deciding how topics were to be covered. Stodolsky also noted that the degree of overlap seemed to depend on how broadly topics are defined. When broad definitions were used, more congruence between texts and teachers were noted than when topics were defined narrowly.

Stodolsky also reviewed studies of how the content of particular sections and pages of textbooks (e.g., reading passages, comprehension questions, skill development problems, and vocabulary exercises) are used by teachers. Again, reading data at the primary level suggest close adherence to materials in the books (Barr and Dreeben 1983). Durkin (1984) found that teachers used the reading passages from basal readers but did not consistently follow the suggestions in the teachers' manuals. In math, exercises and review sections are commonly used, whereas there is wide variation in the use of developmental and enrichment sections. Moreover, students report not reading much of their math books, teachers typically do not cover nearly the last third of the textbooks, and there was wide variation in use of individual lessons across teachers (see Freeman and Porter 1989). Outside of reading and math, researchers have documented that textbooks are used in various content fields, but little has been done to trace how these books are used in classroom situations.

Finally, Stodolsky reported her own research on the use of textbooks by experienced teachers in fifth-grade math and social studies. This analysis was part of a larger study of math and social studies classes taught by fifth-grade teachers from 11 school districts in the Chicago area (Stodolsky 1988). In the textbook study, Stodolsky and her colleagues examined textbook use by six math and six social studies teachers. Observers spent 2 consecutive weeks during midyear in each class writing detailed narrative accounts of activity structures and student involvement. Attention was given to whether topics taught were from the book, what sections of the book or other materials were used, and whether suggestions in the teacher's editions were followed.

These investigators found wide variation among teachers in their use of textbooks and differences across subject matter domains. In math, what the teachers taught was typically in the textbooks (e.g., manipulation of fractions), but they seldom followed the textbook sequence, did not cover all of the topics, and did not necessarily use the book itself as the primary basis for teaching. Only one of the teachers followed the text and the teacher's guide closely and directed the students to the text during teaching. The other teachers, to varying degrees, departed from the text by bringing in their own explanations and exercises from other sources. One teacher emphasized mastery of basic arithmetical operations but appeared not to use the textbook at all. All teachers were selective in their use of the book and accompanying materials. They skipped sections (usually maintenance, test, and enrichment sections) and sometimes entire topics, supplemented the text with their own explanations and materials (but not topics) or with those obtained from sources other than the textbook series, and seldom used suggestions from the teacher's editions. They tended to be consistent, however, in using the practice exercises from texts as seatwork and homework assignments. Finally, the texts in math seem to define the scope of the taught curriculum: What teachers taught was in the books, but they did not teach everything that was in the books.

In social studies, the picture of textbook use was slightly different. Texts did not define the range of topics that were taught, although when texts were used the topic sequence was generally followed. However, teachers often simultaneously introduced topics not contained in the text at all. In fact, the diversity of topics within a class in a given week was sometimes quite dramatic, and the text seemed to be only one of several sources of content or instructional material. Teachers in innovative programs (e.g., MACOS, Man: A Course of Study) seemed to follow the texts more closely, although the sample was quite small.

Overall, there was a general emphasis in math and social studies on mastery of computational algorithms and knowledge of the content, and a tendency to ignore text sections and suggestions for teachers involving activity-based curricular experiences, such as group projects, enrichment, manipulatives, and exploratory activities. Teachers, therefore, often made instruction more traditional and teacher centered than the textbooks were designed to be. Pedagogically, the emphasis was not, as Cherryholmes (1988) would have it, on deconstruction of text meaning but rather on mastery of curriculum content.

These results strongly suggest that textbooks, even highly structured basal reading programs, do not define the experienced curriculum but, rather, are used by teachers as resources in service of their own curricula. The implications of this finding on text use are ambivalent. Should teachers be required to follow texts more closely? In other words, should texts become curriculum so that curricular ideas will not be blunted at the classroom door by teachers? Or is text independence the pedagogical ideal? This ambivalence is reflected in the way textbooks are treated in preservice teacher education. Ball and Feiman-Nemser (1988) found that elementary teacher education students in a large midwestern U.S. university gained the impression in their preservice courses that, to be good teachers, they should avoid following textbooks and teacher's guides and create their own lessons and materials. In student teaching, these students discovered that texts were widely used and often required and that they lacked the necessary knowledge and experience to create their own curricula. Indeed, some of the lessons they created contained major flaws in content interpretation and pedagogy. In the process, the students did not receive much instruction in how to use textbooks effectively.

Summary

Research reviewed in this section raises important questions about textbooks as representations of the curriculum and about their role as a link between curriculum and pedagogy. Content itself is transformed in major and sometimes illogical ways in the design of textbooks. Teachers, in turn, appear to exercise independent control over the curriculum as it is enacted by using texts and other materials selectively in the service of their own curricula. Because this research is focused primarily on the extent to which teachers' practices match the textbooks, little insight is offered concerning what teachers' conceptions of curriculum are, how curricula are used by teachers and students in classroom contexts, and what pedagogical factors shape the experienced curriculum. As will be seen, these topics have been addressed in other research programs.

CONTENT DIMENSIONS IN CONCEPTIONS OF PEDAGOGY

Conventionally, conceptions of teaching have been constructed around a set of psychological processes—learning, memory, motivation, rehearsal, reinforcement—that presumably (1) are independent of specific topics or subject matters and (2) define techniques or treatments that teachers can use to accomplish their work. One of the ironies of classroom studies of teaching, however, is that content variables appear to be quite robust. Coverage, that is, the extent to which the content covered in class matches the content of achievement tests, is, for example, a commonly found predictor of effectiveness (see Brophy and Good 1986). This variable, and its proxies, such as opportunity to learn and academic learning time, suggest that content plays a substantial role in effectiveness. Regardless of what a teacher does, little connection between classroom events and measures of student outcomes can be expected if content is not common across these two domains.

Considerable attention has focused recently on the pedagogy of content, that is, the processes involved in teaching subjects such as mathematics and history or particular topics such as subtraction or DNA to particular students. Much of this work has roots in the psychology of school subjects, a specialization that emerged early in this century in the works of Judd and Thorndike (see Shulman 1974). At the same time, the field is being infused currently with insights from cognitive science concerning knowledge structures and interpretive processes in such areas as reading, writing, math, science, and social studies. As a result, emphasis is being placed on the transformations of content for use in teaching situations and the design of experiences for bringing students in contact with the content. These issues of transformation and design are, of course, close to the hearts of curriculum specialists and they define an arena in which curriculum and pedagogy intersect.

A great deal of the work in this domain is treated in other chapters in this volume, especially in Bereiter's discussion of "Cognition and Curriculum" (Chapter 19) and in the chapters devoted to particular subject matter areas. Nevertheless, this work is appropriately discussed here from the perspectives of the intersection of curriculum and pedagogy. For these purposes, two areas are examined: (1) selected examples of developments based on learners' perspectives on content and (2) recent work on teachers' pedagogical content knowledge.

Content Pedagogy

Recent attempts by cognitive scientists to understand knowledge representations and comprehension processes in various subject matter domains have, as one might expect, stimulated widespread interest among specialists in instruction. A journal, *Cognition and Instruction*, has been established, and major reviews have appeared (Calfee and Drum 1986; Putnam, Lampert, and Peterson 1990; Scardamalia and Bereiter 1986). Resnick (1987) has provided a clear and informative general summary of much of this field.

As Marton (1989) points out, this work is grounded in a fundamental consideration of the learner's perspectives or paradigms as these relate to understanding a particular unit of content. The ultimate aim of such research is to generate content-specific theories of how people handle particular contents, rather than general psychological theory applicable across content domains. Marton further argues that this research enterprise has a kinship with the much earlier work of Comenius (1592–1670) and Pestalozzi (1746–1827) on teaching method, and it differs markedly from the search for content-neutral quantitative predictors, a perspective that dominated inquiry for most of this century and led to what he calls "five dead decades" of educational research.

Considerable attention in cognitive science has been given to comprehension processes in reading (Calfee and Drum 1986) and text production processes in writing (Scardamalia and Bereiter 1986). Resnick (1987) emphasized that higher-order processes are involved at the very basic levels of school learning and performance. Reading, as a task of comprehending text, requires the simultaneous use of complex processes of symbol manipulation, prediction, and inference that cannot be reduced to a set of simple skills. Pedagogical strategies have been designed and tested by several investigators in this area. Palinscar and Brown (1984), for example, have devised reciprocal teaching, a scaffolding procedure for developing comprehension-fostering and comprehension-monitoring abilities in low-achieving middle school students. In reciprocal teaching sessions, the teacher read a passage and modeled interpretive processes such as asking questions, summarizing, and predicting. The students took turns performing these activities and commenting on one another's performances. Gradually, responsibility for the comprehension activities were assumed by the students as they learned to monitor their own comprehension.

Reading and writing are, however, special curricular cases in that they are tool subjects without disciplinary content of their own. In school subjects such as mathematics, science, history, and English, one must account for the theoretical content of the parent disciplines. Thus, much of the work in mathematics and the sciences has focused on conceptual change, that is, the theoretical work students must do to move from their preconceptions (i.e., naive representations or theories) to mature understandings of natural phenomena (see Confrey 1990; Posner et al. 1982; Resnick 1983).

The pedagogical issue in discipline-related subjects is how to construct instructional simplifications that accurately represent the content (i.e., do not introduce misconceptions), make contact with the students' own theories of the content, and motivate students to engage in the theoretical work necessary to learn new representations (see Kirsch 1977; Putnam, Lampert, and Peterson 1990). Some illustrative attempts have been made to design such pedagogies. Schoenfeld (1987), for example, has developed teaching approaches with secondary school and college students in which he made explicit the mathematical reasoning and the mathematical belief systems that underlie problem solving. Lampert (1986a, 1986b) has demonstrated methods for teaching mathematical operations that start from elementary students' implicit understandings of their worlds. For example, she posed problems involving a combination of coins to reach a set amount. The class members then created stories about these problems and discussed or "decomposed" these versions to discover their utility in solving the problem.

One of the central purposes of these methods is to represent content to students in "authentic" ways. Authentic representation is a fundamental theme in the cognitive apprenticeship framework proposed by Brown, Collins, and Duguid (1989). They argue, along with Lave (1988), that all cognition is situated: "Situations might be said to co-produce knowledge through activity" (Brown, Collins, and Duguid 1989, 32). Knowledge, in turn, is a tool embedded in a community of those who use the tool for specific purposes. Learning, then, is a process of enculturation into a knowledge community. Cognitive apprenticeship is a method of enculturation into a discipline through activity which involves authentic tasks worked on collaboratively. Such an approach, they argue, stands in sharp contrast to typical classroom tasks which are isolated from a community of practitioners and seldom involve the ordinary and authentic practices of a culture.

Comments

In many respects the body of work on content pedagogy mirrors the traditions of educational psychology in that knowledge about psychological processes is used as a basis for thinking about and designing instructional procedures and for psychologizing the content to be taught. But the differences between the past and the present are quite important. The work today reflects richer conceptions of subject matter and its representations (e.g., mathematical relationships or scientific propositions rather than noun-pair lists) and much richer descriptions of learners' perspectives or paradigms with respect to that subject matter. Indeed, subject matter and learners' paradigms have become the focus of research rather than the objects one extrapolates to from studies of more elementary processes in learning and memory. Because of this fundamental shift in the target of research, psychology is no longer the sole discipline upon which to ground inquiry. Linguistics, philosophy, anthropology, artificial intelligence, and, to an increasing extent, the disciplines themselves, are essential to the study of cognition and instruction. One sign of this change is the diminishing centrality of the concept of "learning" and the ascendancy of such constructs as "interpretation" and even "enculturation" in the language used to discuss cognition and instruction.

Nevertheless, the emphasis in this work is largely pedagogical, rather than curricular. In most cases only small pieces of content are selected for attention, for example, particular misconceptions or topics, with little attention to the curriculum context in which the pieces fit. Moreover, content is usually taken to mean discipline rather than school subject. Issues of content (mathematics, science, social studies), in other words, are viewed almost exclusively as matters within the academic disciplines rather than within the school curriculum. Thus, little mention is made of the goals and functions of schools which frame content decisions or, importantly, of the transformations of content that have occurred as it is incorporated into school curriculum. There are important differences, for example, between science as a discipline and science as a school subject and as a component of a school curriculum. And it is not altogether clear that elementary and secondary schools exist solely or even primarily to enculturate students into disciplinary communities.

Of equal significance is the almost complete lack of a classroom perspective in the research on content pedagogy. Investigators have concentrated on content representation but, with the exception of Lampert (1986a, 1986b), have given little attention to the enactment of lessons under ordinary school conditions. At the same time, research and theory related to content pedagogy have suggested a striking contrast between the culture of the experienced curriculum in classrooms and the culture of a discipline or even of the everyday applications of content knowledge (Brown, Collins, and Duguid 1989; Lave 1990; Stigler and Baranes 1988). This issue of the distinctiveness of the classroom curriculum obviously needs further investigation.

Pedagogical Content Knowledge

One seemingly obvious impact of curriculum on teaching is in the area of planning and teacher knowledge. Teachers presumably use the curriculum as a tool or guide during the preactive phase of teaching (Jackson 1968) to decide what should be taught and how lessons should be structured and conducted. There was little curriculum focus, however, in early studies of teacher planning (see Clark and Peterson 1986 for a comprehensive review).

In recent years there has been a substantial increase in attention to the subject matter knowledge of teachers and, in particular, the knowledge teachers need to represent and convey subject matter to students (see C. W. Anderson 1989; Ball and McDiarmid 1990; Grossman, Wilson, and Shulman 1989; Leinhardt and Smith 1985; Shulman 1986b, 1987; Wilson, Shulman, and Richert 1987). To teach at all, Shulman (1987) argues, a teacher must

> understand the structures of subject matter, the principles of conceptual organization, and the principles of inquiry that help answer two kinds of questions in each field: What are the important ideas and skills in this domain? and How are new ideas added and deficient ones dropped by those who produce knowledge in this area? That is, what are the rules and procedures of good scholarship or inquiry? (9)

In addition, a teacher needs "pedagogical content knowledge," that is, the capacity "to transform the content knowledge he or she possesses into forms that are pedagogically powerful and yet adaptive to the variations in ability and background presented by the students" (Shulman 1987, 15). This capacity distinguishes a teacher from a nonteaching specialist. Knowing biology is necessary, but certainly not sufficient, to know how to represent biological content to students in a teaching situation.

> What is also needed is knowledge of the most useful forms of representation of those ideas, the most powerful analogies, illustrations, examples, explanations, and demonstrations—in a word, the ways of representing and formulating the subject that make it comprehensible to others. . . . Pedagogical content knowledge also includes an understanding of what makes the learning of specific topics easy or difficult: the conceptions and preconceptions that students of different ages and backgrounds bring with them to the learning of those most frequently taught topics and lessons. If those preconceptions are misconceptions, which they so often are, teachers need knowledge of the strategies most likely to be fruitful in reorganizing the understanding of learners. . . . (Shulman 1986b, 9–10)

The study of teachers' pedagogical content knowledge is based, for the most part, on richly detailed cases of beginning and experienced teachers, with a focus on how they use their knowledge of the content and of pedagogy, learners, materials, and educational aims, to create representations (demonstrations, analogies, explanations) of particular pieces of subject matter and carry these out in classrooms (see Grossman 1987, 1989; Grossman and Gudmundsdottir 1987; Gudmundsdottir 1989, in press; Hashweh 1987; Wilson, Shulman, and Richert 1987; Wilson and Wineburg 1988). Special attention in this work is given to secondary school teaching candidates who are making the transition from expert student to novice teacher, a research site that allows investigators to study how teachers struggle with the task of transforming their content knowledge for use in teaching episodes. This research site also reflects the interest these investigators have in teacher education.

One major aim of this research program is to map, and eventually understand better, the processes involved in the development of pedagogical reasoning, particularly with respect to the transformation of content into classroom representations. The work so far indicates that teachers have content orientations or perspectives (i.e., personal curricula) that have a fundamental impact on their decisions about how to represent that content to students and how to use available texts and instructional materials (see Grossman 1990; Gudmundsdottir 1989). Social studies teachers with strong anthropology backgrounds, for example, emphasize very different aspects of historical events than those prepared in political science or in history (Wilson and Wineburg 1988). An English teacher with a person orientation will often stress connections between literature and students' personal realities, whereas a teacher with an orientation to literary interpretation will stress attention to details of the text itself (Grossman and Gudmundsdottir 1987). The character of a teacher's content orientation, in other words, affects the potential for content representation in classrooms. The nature of teachers representations have consequences for students' achievement. Peterson et al. (1989) found, for instance, that first-grade teachers with a strong cognitively based orientation to mathematics, in contrast to those with less cognitive orientation, made extensive use of word problems and sought knowledge of their students' problem-solving strategies through direct observation rather than formal assessments. In addition, students of cognitive-oriented teachers were better at problem solving than students of teachers with less cognitive orientation to the content.

In addition, it appears that, as teachers gain experience, they develop integrated pedagogical content models that fuse subject matter and pedagogy around common teaching phenomena, such as the school schedules, the format of textbooks, and the reactions of students (Gudmundsdottir in press). They begin to see content, in other words, as a discipline with its own rules and demands, but also as a medium for engaging students' interests and values (Elbaz 1983; Grossman 1989). An important implication of this finding is that teachers' content knowledge itself becomes transformed into a unified framework or theory of the content as school curriculum. A teacher's theory of the content facilitates planning and enables him or her eventually to lift the curriculum away from texts and materials to give it independent existence. This finding is similar to that emerging from studies of textbook use: Teachers have their own curriculum theories which influence in profound ways the experienced curriculum. More attention needs to be given to these theories of content and how they are shaped by classroom experiences.

THE SOCIAL CONTEXT OF CURRICULUM

Several curriculum theorists have focused on ways in which the taught curriculum or the curriculum in use is shaped by broader social forces and, in turn, serves as an instrument of social reproduction (see Cornbleth 1990). Critical theorists, in particular, have focused attention on the analysis of knowledge distribution in schooling and its connection to political and economic inequalities that exist in the larger society (see Apple 1979, 1986; Everhart 1983). They argue that the curriculum in use defines what counts as school knowledge in a particular situation, as well as the cultural norms for having access to that knowledge (e.g., high literacy skills, tolerance for abstraction). Thus, the curriculum in use creates the symbolic cultural capital that is the medium of exchange between teachers and students. Students differ in the extent to which they possess and/or accept this capital or have access to it in schools.

Studies by Keddie (1971) and by Anyon (1980) are often cited as examples of the unequal distribution of school knowledge across social class categories. Keddie examined the forms of school knowledge represented in the same course taught across ability tracks in the same British secondary school. She found that the emphasis in the curriculum of the A track was on higher-level thinking and expressiveness, whereas the C track focused on memorization and routinized learning. Keddie also examined the attitudes of the teachers and students that appeared to sustain these differences. For a similar argument, see Oakes (1985).

Anyon (1980) studied 5 fifth-grade teachers in five schools that differed in social class composition of the students. Observations were conducted for ten 3-hour periods through the year in each classroom. She found that in the two working-class schools in her sample, the curriculum in use consisted largely of procedures and mechanics, with little choice or decision making. In the middle-class school, the emphasis was on getting the right answer to get a good grade and on following the textbook with little creativity or critical perspective. In the affluent professional school, work was creative activity carried out independently. The students' products—typically essays, stories, and crafts rather than worksheets—often reflected expressiveness and choice. Finally, in the executive elite school, the emphasis was on developing analytical intellectual capabilities of a very high academic quality and a large range of discretion and decision making. Anyon concludes by arguing that these curricular emphases reflect hidden social expectations for the occupational roles students in these different social classes will achieve. In this matter, schools participate in sustaining the distribution of social power and privilege.

These and other investigators have examined the extent to which students' practical ideologies conflict with the definitions of school knowledge and the norms that surround the curriculum in use (Everhart 1983; Kickbusch and Everhart 1985; Willis 1981). Some students appear to reject or resist the legitimacy of the school's norms and framing of knowledge, and this resistance often takes the form of misbehavior, absences, or refusal to do the work. Thus, students are seen as active participants in the generation of school effects.

Critical theorists give primary attention to linking curriculum to political and economic forces and, in the process, often focus on the students' dispositions toward the curriculum. As a result, they bypass the intricate details of curricular and pedagogical processes in classrooms. In other words, critical theorists often keep their distance from teachers, who are sometimes portrayed as accomplices to the forces reproducing social and cultural inequities.

LESSON STRUCTURES AND PROCESSES

Knowledge about the actual curriculum in use has grown as investigators with ethnographic, sociolinguistic, and ecological perspectives have begun to study classrooms more intensively (see Cazden 1986; Doyle 1978; Erickson 1986). This very large literature cannot be covered comprehensively here. An effort is made, however, to represent major bodies of work in this domain that contribute to an understanding of the relationship between curriculum and pedagogy in classrooms. Particular attention is given to studies that focus on (1) communication structures and processes in classrooms and (2) lesson construction processes.

Communication Processes in Classrooms

Investigators from ethnographic and sociolinguistic traditions have directed considerable attention to the communication processes that affect students' access to teaching and to the analysis of classroom events as occasions for the development of children's literacy. A selective review of this work will indicate its contributions to knowledge about how curricular and pedagogical processes work.

In one line of inquiry in this tradition, investigators have noted the constricted and vague character of student talk within the formal structure of lessons (see Alvermann and Hayes 1989; Barnes 1976; Bellack et al. 1966; Dillon and Searle 1981; Edwards and Furlong 1978; Harrod 1977; Searle 1975). Most public talk by students consists of short comments that are tightly indexed to texts, teacher questions, or gestures. Indeed, some students appear to develop strategies of hesitating or offering provisional answers so that fellow students will answer for them or the teacher will "pilot" them to the correct response (MacLure and French 1978; Mehan 1974; Lundgren 1977), and teachers sometimes reformulate students' responses so that they fit the teacher's agenda (Cazden 1988). In contrast, student talk in other, less formal settings (e.g., at home or during sharing time or playground activities at school) is animated, elaborated, and expressive (Cazden 1988; Michaels 1981).

Similar results have been reported for written literacy. Studies suggest that students typically are not required to write frequently, that most assignments require only brief responses or answers, that the teacher is usually the sole audience for students' written products, and that students produce more text and more expressive text for their own writing than they do for school assignments (Applebee 1981; Florio and Clark 1982; Graves 1975).

These findings concerning the quality of classroom language use are sometimes given pedagogical interpretations (see Cazden 1986). It is argued that classroom lessons and assignments provide limited opportunity for students to practice or display literacy competencies. As Dillon and Searle (1981, 327) note, "the limited code required in school fails to utilize children's full range of language and learning abilities" (italics removed). As a result, researchers often suggest ways for improving the communicative richness and authenticity of literacy occasions in classrooms (see, e.g., Cazden 1988; Florio-Ruane and Dunn 1987; Mehan 1979).

Substantial attention in the study of classroom discourse has also been given to the structures, rules, and processes that govern participation in public talk. Several investigators have identified a three-phase structure of lesson exchanges in which the teacher initiates a contact by soliciting a response from a student (usually with a known-answer question), the student responds, and the teacher evaluates the response (see Bellack et al. 1966; McHoul 1978; Mehan 1979; Philips 1983). Within this structure the teacher has considerable power to select who will speak when, and individual response times are protected from interruption. It is argued that a great deal of interpretive work is needed by students to participate in lessons, that is, to read the cues that indicate when speaking is appropriate (Green and Weade 1985). Students must learn, in other words, to know what context they are in. Successful bids for turns, for instance, must typically be thematically relevant to the topic on the floor and occur at appropriate junctures in the initiation-response-evaluation sequence (see Erickson and Shultz 1981; Green and Harker 1982; McHoul 1978; Mehan 1979).

Analyses that focus on the organizational routines, communication rules, and social knowledge requirements of classrooms are often used to argue that there is a "hidden" curriculum in classrooms (Jackson 1968; Cazden 1986; for a discussion of the problems with the concept of hidden curriculum, see Gordon 1988; Lakomski 1988). To be successful in school, a student must not only be able to do the academic work required, but also master the social participation rules that afford access to resources and enable appropriate display of competence (Erickson 1982). Moreover, this interpretive skill and social knowledge is unevenly distributed among students because of their ethnic, socioeconomic, and cultural backgrounds. As a result, some students, and most often minority students, fail to establish and maintain functional relationships with teachers in lessons and are unable to express their own identity and competence adequately (Cazden 1988). These factors often combine, it appears, to produce differential treatment of students by teachers and different curricula across ability and cultural groups (see Eder 1982; McDermott 1976). Low-achieving students and students in low-achieving groups often experience more delays, interruptions, and social disorder; have less opportunity to respond, especially to higher-order questions; and spend less time reading than students in higher-achieving groups. Similarly, the cultural knowledge of students from various ethnic minorities does not always match the social and conversational norms of the dominant social group. Thus school demands may conflict with tacit understandings of how one interacts and learns so that students become alienated from school (Au 1980; Florio and Shultz 1979; Philips 1983). As a result, these students do not have access to the curriculum.

Although providing valuable insights into the factors that shape and surround the experienced curriculum, much of the early sociolinguistic research in classrooms was only weakly tied to academic events and curriculum processes. By concentrating on speech acts and language use, sociolinguists often focused on the management of social structures and processes within a multicultural context and bypassed the substance of classroom exchanges (i.e., the formal curriculum). The emphasis, in other words, was on the structures and processes that govern students' access to the classroom conversation. Results, in turn, were seen to have pedagogical implications: If the quality of social and cultural interaction could be improved, then access to curriculum would be more direct and teaching more effective. The curriculum itself was not studied.

Lesson Construction

Recently some investigators in the sociolinguistic tradition have begun to move closer to curriculum by focusing on how teachers frame schoolwork. Central to these analyses is the distinction between social tasks defined by the requirements for appropriate participation in a lesson (e.g., knowing how to get the floor, when to speak, and what topics are relevant) and academic tasks defined by the requirements of the content students are to learn (e.g., what a term means or how to apply an algorithm correctly; see Erickson 1982; Lemke 1989b).

One particularly important line of work in this area is being conducted by Green and her colleagues on lesson construction (see Green, Harker, and Golden 1987; Green, Weade, and Graham 1988; see also Bloome and Theodorou 1988). In this work, lessons are viewed as socially constructed classroom events in which teachers and students work together to meet curriculum goals. "Lessons, then, are defined by what occurs, with whom, in what ways, for what purpose, under what conditions, and with what outcome" (Green, Weade, and Graham 1988, 13). Although lessons often have familiar structures, the form and processes of a particular lesson cannot be predicted exactly. Lessons, in other words, have evolving social and academic "texts," that is, spoken and written information about expectations, content, and procedures. To gain access to information and participate appropriately, teachers and students must "read" these texts as they unfold.

Lesson construction, then, can be likened to the construction of a group composition that is simultaneously being written, read, and revised. In order to contribute to the developing lesson, participants must interpret both the information to be presented (academic text) and the appropriate form for presentation or addition of information (social text). The text construction process in lessons, like construction of a written composition, involves consideration of factors such as content, form, author intention, and audience. Viewed in this way, lesson construction is a creative process in which teacher and students construct text through their actions and interactions (Green, Weade, and Graham 1988, 13–14).

Green and her colleagues argue that interpretation of lessons depends on both the personal frames of reference which participants bring to situations, as well as lesson-specific frames that evolve within a particular context. Lesson-specific frames include local frames to interpret a message or action at a particular point, an academic frame related to what is emphasized and accepted, a social frame related to norms and expectations for participation, and an instructional-pedagogical frame related to the nature of the task at a given point in a lesson (e.g., interpreting directions to underline a word). Finally, there is a materials frame contributed by the textbooks and other instructional materials used in lessons.

The analysis of lessons by these investigators begins with a detailed mapping of verbal and nonverbal messages of teachers and students in lessons. Sequences of conversational-tied message units are designated as interaction units, and a series of thematically coherent interaction units are called instructional sequence units. Instructional sequence units that are tied together pedagogically form lesson phase units marked by changes in tasks or in participants' rights and obligations.

Weade (1985; see also Weade and Evertson 1988) used this method to examine how teachers construct academic content demands within lessons. The study focused on lessons recorded in mid-November in four junior high school English classes taught by teachers who differed in ratings of classroom management effectiveness. Three of the lessons dealt with identifying verbs and verb forms and one dealt with spelling. However, demands and participation structures were similar across lessons. The analysis was concentrated on social and academic participation demands and the sequence of development of topical themes. Weade found that more shifts in demands, especially in social expectations, were required of students in less effectively managed classes in contrast to those of more effective teachers. The analysis of themes (i.e., how teachers conveyed academic content and demands) in single lesson phases (approximately 6 to 11 minute segments) further suggested that less-effective managers provided fewer cues and opportunities for students to understand their work and sometimes presented contradictory information about how work was to be accomplished.

Green and her colleagues (Green, Harker, and Golden 1987; Green, Weade, and Graham 1988) applied the lesson construction framework to the analysis of storytelling lessons of approximately 21 minutes each taught by two teachers whose students differed in performance on a story recall test. Teacher G, whose students remembered more of the story, used a two-phase lesson structure in which she first introduced students to the story book itself (title, author, dedication, pages, pictures) and then read the story and asked students questions about the text. Teacher S, whose students remembered less, introduced the lesson by asking students what they knew about animals (the topic of the story), moved into a reading of the story and a continuing discussion of students' knowledge about animals, and then a general discussion of the story. The lessons differed not only in structure but also in task and coherence. Teacher G focused students' attention on the story itself and ran a smooth-flowing and consistently focused lesson. Teacher S focused on students' knowledge about animals and generated divergent comments and reactions as well as multiple bidding for turns as the lesson proceeded. This analysis suggested that the two lessons, despite similarities in content and duration, were very different experiences for students. It is also possible that these teachers had very different curricular ideologies concerning what constitutes reading comprehension (see Mosenthal 1983).

Knowledge Production in Lessons

Although the work on lesson construction captures aspects of lesson content and suggests ways in which that content is played out in classroom settings, the emphasis is primarily pedagogical, that is, on the generic teaching and learning processes that occur in classrooms and on how teaching practices might be changed to increase achievement. A more specific focus on the content being taught is reflected in recent studies of knowledge production in classrooms.

Heap (1985) has concentrated on the analysis of how knowledge is produced collectively by teachers and students through discourse in lessons. At one level, the initiation-response-feedback structure of classroom discussion can be seen as a format for the co-production of propositional knowledge. The teacher asks a question (''Why was the boy angry?''), a student supplies an answer (''Because he lost the game''). The proposition to be learned includes both the content of the question and the content of the answer. The teacher's feedback verifies the answer as correct and, thus, that the student knows the lesson content and that his or her answer counts as knowledge for the group. In this way the curriculum is produced as knowledge in a particular situation.

Heap also argues, however, that propositional knowledge is not the only kind produced in lessons. He extends the analysis by examining closely the comprehension phase of lessons in which the teacher asks students questions about the text just read. He contends that some elicitations in the comprehension phase serve to introduce the method of text consulting as the source of information needed to complete propositions. Other elicitations require students to generate inferences based on, but not contained in, the text (e.g., what would happen if . . . ?). To answer such elicitations, students must bring cultural logic and knowledge to bear on a text. ''In this sense, reading comprehension is comprehension of culture and the logic of its organization and possibilities. The text is simply the site for launching that comprehension'' (Heap 1985, 265). The point, then, of the comprehension phase is not merely to transmit propositional knowledge, but also to acculturate students, that is, to teach them ''how the story can and is to be understood as part of the culture, hence governed by its logic'' (Heap 1985, 266).

Golden (1988, 1989), using reader-response criticism from literary theory and text analytic procedures, has demonstrated ways in which the meaning of the text itself is constructed by students in lessons. ''The text, from this view, is seen as a highly organized arrangement of cues which evoke a range of cognitive operations resulting in the formulation [by the reader] of the aesthetic work'' (Golden 1988, 71). In one study, Golden (1988) used this perspective to analyze the story-reading lessons by Teacher G and Teacher S discussed above in reference to Green's research. Golden described the episodic structure of the text itself and then the structures of the instructional texts (instructional moves and themes) produced by the two teachers in reading the story and asking questions. Both teachers appeared to be sensitive to the episodic structure of the story text but differed in their emphasis on themes. Teacher G focused on episodic information from the text itself as a central point of reference, whereas Teacher S emphasized text-related themes (i.e., relevant to the text but not referenced to information in an episode). Golden then examined students' recall texts. Recall patterns appeared to be related both to features of the story text itself and to the teachers' instructional texts, particularly the differential emphasis on episodic versus text-related themes.

In a second study, Golden (1989) analyzed a 5-day lesson in a sixth-grade class in which the principal text was an excerpt from an autobiography focusing on a Mexican-American's acculturation experience upon entering school. The basal reader also provided a biographical sketch of the writer. The structure of the text itself, as an excerpt from a larger text, was complicated because of the absence of the larger text and lack of clarity about its purpose and genre. The teacher mediated this text in three ways. First, she emphasized oral reading performance (e.g., intonation, enunciation) as students read the text aloud. Second, she focused on word identification strategies as students had difficulty with pronunciation. Finally, she interpreted the text and related it to life experience. Although the teacher elicited personal reactions to the narrator's feelings, she maintained tight control over which interpretations were acceptable. When students' responses did not move in the direction the teacher wanted, she drew on her own experiences to model the appropriate interpretation. The teacher was the primary interpreter of the text and she used the text as a convenient way to present text-based lessons about patriotic behavior.

Michaels (1987) studied how selected students accomplished a writing assignment—a composition about a visit to the circus—in a sixth-grade class. In contrast to most investigators in this tradition, she argued that texts written in the class were part of a classroom writing system consisting of the activities and norms related to all the writing students did in the classroom. The individual assignment was analyzed within this broader system of organization.

The events related to the circus composition lasted for 3 days and consisted of a whole-group brainstorming session in which the teacher explained the assignment, writing sessions during which the students wrote drafts, and conferences with the teacher. In studying these events closely, Michaels found that the teacher had a schema for how the composition should be structured, although this schema was never explicitly stated to the students. Some students' compositions matched the teacher's schema from the beginning and others did not. During conferences with mismatched students, the teacher suggested deletions and substitutions that brought the students' compositions more in line with her schema and, in many instances, changed the meaning that the students intended. Interviews and analyses of successive drafts suggested that students preferred their own schemata but generally tried to conform to the teacher's version and adopted her rhetorical strategies. Michaels concludes by raising several questions about what students learned about writing and what factors shape the teacher's expectations for written texts.

Lemke (1989a, 1989b) is one of the few in this research tradition who has focused on disciplinary knowledge in lessons, what he calls the "thematic patterns" of a subject. His particular interest is in how the formal language of science becomes part of the students' language capabilities. To study this problem, he has analyzed classroom conversations to ascertain how teachers attempt to bridge the formal language or register of textbooks and the customary language of students. He found that in many instances students received little opportunity to practice the language of the subject and tended to use it cautiously and hesitantly. "Even when given the opportunity, students are reluctant to try speaking the language of the subject"(Lemke 1989b, 138). He argues, therefore, that students need multiple opportunities to speak the language of science in order to master the thematic patterns of the curriculum.

Lemke (1989a) also found tension between the formal register of the subject and the everyday register of students with respect to activity flow in classrooms. Students were more responsive to informal talk, thus encouraging teachers to simplify the content and avoid the formal language patterns. In addition, teachers sometimes had to sacrifice the orderliness of the interaction pattern to preserve the integrity of the thematic content. Finally, students' questions can be difficult to interpret (i.e., the student's "theory" may not be clear) or can appear as challenges to teacher authority and, thus, do not receive appropriate pedagogical attention. These findings suggest that providing opportunities for students to practice the formal language of science is sometimes difficult.

These studies by Heap, Golden, Michaels, and Lemke are important for at least two reasons. First, they demonstrate ways of examining content itself rather than simply the processes surrounding the use of that content. This is a significant breakthrough for classroom research on curriculum. Second, they show that texts read and written in classrooms are embedded in interpretive structures created and governed by teachers as they struggle to transform and represent the curriculum to students in a complex social setting. More needs to be known about these structures and how they function over time to affect the range of realizations of curriculum in classrooms.

Comments

The sociolinguistic research reviewed in this section provides rich portrayals of processes in classrooms. These portrayals suggest that a considerable amount of interpretive work is necessary for students and teachers to navigate classroom life and participate in lessons. Moreover, the social and curricular aspects of classrooms are jointly constructed and evolve over time. As a result, curriculum experiences and products of assignments are deeply embedded in classroom events. At the same time, with the exception of Michaels (1987), the lessons selected for analysis are typically single occurrences isolated from their curricular contexts. Weade, for example, selected brief lessons conducted in mid-November and provided no information about the surrounding activity or task structures established in the classes. Green and her colleagues asked teachers to conduct storyreading lessons outside their regular classes and curricula. This focus on single lessons narrows the range of attention to curriculum issues and, ultimately, strips content and context from the analysis.

CLASSROOM TASK STRUCTURES

Recently, attempts have been made to analyze academic task structures as the central organizing frameworks in classroom settings (see Doyle 1983). In these studies the focus is directly on curriculum events and processes in classroom environments, that is, on the curriculum in motion. The concept of "task" has roots in anthropology, sociology, and cognitive psychology (see Bossert 1979; Dawes 1975; Erickson 1982; Laboratory of Comparative Human Cognition 1978) and is used to refer to the way in which work, and thus cognition, is organized or structured in a particular setting. Tasks provide, in other words, situational instructions for thinking and acting. If someone is asked, for example, to count the number of times the letter "t" appears in a paragraph, it is unlikely that this person will acquire much information about the substance of the text.

The conception of task in this research program differs substantially from that used in many of the ethnographic and sociolinguistic studies reviewed in the previous section. In those studies, the term "task" appears to refer primarily to immediate interpretive demands (i.e., what does a specific message mean?) or the immediate requirements of a direction or request at a particular moment in a lesson (i.e., what is the answer the teacher wants?). The unit of analysis, in other words, is very small (at the individual message level), and tasks change frequently as lessons evolve (Michaels 1987 is an exception to this pattern).

In the work being discussed in this section, "task" is defined as a broad interpretive framework that integrates entire lessons or sequences of lessons. Doyle and Carter (1984), for example, identified 14 tasks accomplished over 2½ weeks in a junior high school English class. One task was a two-paragraph assignment in which student were required to compare Christmas in Capote's story "A Christmas Memory" with Christmas today. In addition, students were to use five active verbs and one compound sentence in each paragraph, and circle transition words. A total of 105 minutes of class time across 3 separate days were devoted to introducing and working on this task. From this perspective, a task is not a message within a lesson or a feature of a lesson, but a context that frames the interpretation of events, texts, and episodes (see Mosenthal 1983).

In describing tasks at this level of analysis, investigators focus on three essential components: (1) a goal or end state to be accomplished; (2) a problem space or set of conditions and resources (e.g., information, tools) available to accomplish the task; and (3) the operations (thoughts and actions) involved in assembling and using resources to reach the goal state (Doyle 1983; see also Marx and Walsh 1988). In classrooms, goal states for curriculum tasks are usually embedded in a product—such as words inserted into blanks on a worksheet, answers to a set of test questions, or an original essay—that must be generated to complete an assignment. Resources in classrooms vary widely. For some tasks, students can consult peers and for others they must work strictly alone. The nature of a writing task depends upon whether a student can complete the assignment by following a standard format or must compose an original text unaided. The operations students are to use to accomplish work are not always clearly specified by teachers (Durkin 1978–1979) and sometimes are difficult to communicate (Groen and Resnick 1977). Moreover, students often circumvent task demands or invent their own strategies for getting work done.

It is important to emphasize that these components are not separate dimensions to be rated but rather features to be considered in constructing a description of a task. For example, completing a worksheet may require that students select the appropriate word form (e.g., singular or plural forms of verbs) in practice sentences. Typically, the work is to be done alone and students are expected to apply to rule to determine the appropriate option. When students are finished, the teacher might grade papers privately or go over the answers in class, sometimes calling on students to supply the correct items publicly. A worksheet assignment usually counts as a daily grade, but might also be direct practice on items that will appear on a more heavily weighted unit test. In contrast, an essay assignment (e.g., write a description of a character in a story) is often less clearly structured and specified, students are sometimes allowed to consult with peers or the teacher for comments and feedback on drafts, and grading criteria are more loosely applied. As these examples suggest, tasks are not variables to be scored but events to be described. And since the life history of a task may extend from several minutes to several days, the burden of description can be substantial, often requiring close and continuous observation over several weeks (see Doyle and Carter 1984).

In addition, a task cannot be adequately described in isolation from the task system in which it is embedded in a particular class. Products in classrooms, for example, are often weighted according to their importance in the grading system (Doyle and Carter 1984; Sanford 1987). A daily journal entry in language arts, for instance, may have only minimal effect on a student's grade for a term, whereas an assignment to write a three-paragraph description of a native American tribe may count 15 percent of the final grade. The significance of a task is thus determined by its relationship to other tasks.

A fundamental premise of task investigators is that tasks organize students' cognitions and, therefore, have powerful treatment effects in classrooms (see Doyle 1983; Posner 1982). Students learn from the information they process to accomplish the tasks they encounter. As a result, tasks frame both pedagogy and curriculum. The significance of a teacher's actions in explaining, questioning, and praising students depends upon their relationships to the task system in a classroom. If, for instance, a teacher asks higher-order questions during class discussions but holds students accountable in written work only for knowing definitions of key terms, it is unlikely that students will, over time, pay much attention to classroom questions. To capture the curriculum in use, then, one must describe the tasks enacted with respect to that curriculum. From this perspective, issues of content representation are examined, not simply in the explanations teachers provide for students but also in the work teachers design for students to accomplish (see Doyle 1986b; Grant 1987).

Finally, tasks do not exist as intellectual entities only. Rather, tasks occur in the complex activity systems of classrooms and thus are deeply entwined with the structure and flow of action in these environments. As Blumenfeld, Mergendoller, and Swarthout (1987) note, it is possible to distinguish between task content (learning objectives and the perceived appeal, familiarity, and difficulty of subject matter) and task form (the nature and procedural complexity of activities, products, and social organization). They also argue that task form has important consequences for motivation and task completion. Because of these social dimensions, tasks have an inherently dynamic quality that requires participants to do a considerable amount of interpretive work to ascertain what a particular task is and how it can be accomplished. This dynamism also complicates description and analysis for researchers. Indeed, many tasks can be understood only retrospectively after work on the task is completed.

Varieties of Task Research

Not all task studies are curricular in character. Major attention has been given, for instance, to issues of pedagogy and motivation, that is, to questions of students' dispositions toward tasks and the management of tasks by teachers to increase achievement (see Blumenfeld, Mergendoller, and Swarthout 1987; Rohrkemper and Corno 1988). In task studies without a curricular emphasis, task themselves are not described in any detail. Rather, the features or characteristics of inferred or announced tasks are coded, and these variables are related to students' responses on questionnaires or tests (see L. M. Anderson et al. 1988; Blumenfeld and Meece 1988). Although these studies provide useful information about pedagogy and lesson design, they contain little information about the curriculum in use.

Studies of particular relevance to an understanding of curriculum and pedagogy fall into two broad categories: (1) students' versions of tasks; and (2) the types of tasks occurring in classrooms. Work in each of these areas is surveyed in the following sections.

Students' Versions of Tasks. In most studies, tasks are conceptualized at a class level. This level of description is usually achieved by positing, explicitly or implicitly, an ideal student who is attentive to publicly available information and seeks to interpret this information. This device makes it possible to define tasks, insofar as possible, as classroom entities. Some authors argue, however, that this approach ignores important information about individual differences in the interpretation of tasks and the role of students' prior experience in formulating these interpretations (e.g., Posner 1982). Nespor (1986), in particular, argues that meaning inheres not in classroom structures but in the fit of these structures to students' existing schemata. As a result, students' learning and cognition in class cannot be understood solely in terms of intrinsic properties of that setting. He urges a focus, therefore, on how students construct their own versions of tasks and on how academic experience accumulates across the grades.

Not a great deal of task research has been done at the individual student level, but, as might be expected, existing work suggests wide variations in students' interpretations and success rates. Both Nespor (1987) and Doyle (1986b), for example, have described instances in which secondary school students differed dramatically in their interpretations of the same writing tasks and how they could be accomplished.

Alton-Lee and Nuthall (1989) have developed, through observations, interviews, and broadcast microphones, detailed records of individual students' (three 9-year-olds and four 11-year-olds) involvement with specific items in the curriculum and the relationship of this involvement to performance on corresponding test items. Descriptions included the nature of the lesson in which the content was introduced, what the student said during the lesson and at other times, what the student wrote on assignments and notes to himself or herself. Students sometimes forgot what they appeared to have learned, learned items that they did not apparently process in the classroom, and rehearsed items to be learned in several different situations outside of the immediate lesson context. These analyses suggest that students' paths through the curriculum are influenced by a variety of background and situational factors. The investigators also found that traditional on-task behaviors such as reading and writing were inconsistently related to learning, with effects mediated by the quality of the content presentation. On the other hand, behaviors such as moving during group work, "fiddling around," and erasing were positively related to learning. The latter behaviors signaled that students were seeking resources, alert to conceptual difficulties, or reformulating their ideas.

Murphy (1987) studied closely how 4 fifth-grade students in one class defined and accomplished reading tasks. Murphy found variations in task understanding and success among the students on the same tasks, variations that were attributable to students' previous experiences and perceptions of themselves as learners. She also found that the difficulties students had with tasks stemmed not from a lack of attention but from a failure to understand what the teacher wanted them to do. Failure to understand, in turn, seemed to result from ambiguity in the presentation of tasks within the complex social circumstances of classrooms. High-achieving students often helped each other interpret task demands, but low achievers usually struggled alone to make sense of their assignments. Finally, Murphy found that the high level of public accountability in the class increased risk, which had a negative impact on students' persistence, flexibility, and self-perceptions.

Bennett and his colleagues (1984) have studied the matching of task demands to children's attainments. They examined over 600 language and mathematics tasks assigned throughout the year to six target students in each of 16 second grade and 24 third-grade classes in England. They found that, overall, approximately 40 percent of all tasks were matched, 28 percent were too difficult, and 26 percent were too easy. In addition, high attainers were underestimated 41 percent of the time and low attainers were overestimated 44 percent of the time. In a subsequent study of 500 mathematics, language, and social studies tasks in grades three through six, greater mismatching was found (see Bennett and Desforges 1988).

Bennett et al. (1984) observed and interviewed individual students as they struggled to interpret and accomplish tasks. Low-attaining students worked diligently on overestimated tasks, focusing on procedures, but seldom understanding the work. High attainers were also industrious, but were not challenged by many tasks. Overall, the students were happy and satisfied, and teachers frequently praised them for following procedures correctly. During interviews, teachers reported that they recognized overestimation when students had difficulty following routines. However, because teachers attended primarily to completed work, they seldom noticed underestimation. Moreover, teachers appeared to spend little time diagnosing students' level of attainment so that tasks could be matched more appropriately.

An intensive in-service course for a sample of 17 second- and third-grade teachers had little effect on diagnostic practice. Teachers found it difficult to conduct individual diagnostic interviews in classroom settings and often focused on correcting errors so that students could complete assignments, rather than helping students understand the content. The researchers concluded that the problem of matching was as much one of classroom management as it was teacher knowledge and skill. In a follow-up study, Desforges and Cockburn (1987) interviewed experienced teachers concerning task assignments in math. The teachers perceived that matching was a problem, but that it was embedded in a larger set of problems related to sustaining classroom activities, dealing with the wide diversity of interests and personalities in a class, and moving through the math curriculum in concert with other teachers in the building. The investigators conclude that the problem of matching involves matters of curriculum policy as well as pedagogical practice.

The studies by Bennett and his colleagues (1984) provide an interesting perspective on how students might come into contact with the curriculum and what factors appear to shape such encounters. Further discussion of this topic can be found in Chapter 17 in this volume, "Students' Experience of the Curriculum" by Erickson and Schultz.

Types of Tasks in Classrooms. A major portion of task research has focused on the types of tasks that occur in classrooms (see, for example, Aulls 1990; Doyle and Carter 1984; Sanford 1987; Tobin and Gallagher 1987). Typologies of tasks are usually constructed around the presumed cognitive processes or operations that are required to accomplish tasks. Doyle (1983), for instance, distinguished between tasks involving (1) memory or the reproduction or recognition of information previously encountered (e.g., spelling tests); (2) routines or algorithms that reliably generate answers (e.g., arithmetic or grammar exercises); (3) opinion or the expression of a disposition toward content (e.g., reactions to a poem); and (4) understanding, including recognizing transformed versions of text, selecting appropriate procedures to solve complex problems, and drawing inferences or making predictions from information given (e.g., solving word problems in math, performing science experiments, or reading a new passage with comprehension). Bennett and his colleagues (1984) classified tasks as (1) incremental if they involved introduction of a new idea, procedure, or skill and demanded recognition or discrimination; (2) restructuring if they demanded invention or discovery of an idea, process, or pattern; (3) enrichment if they involved application of familiar skills to new problems; and (4) practice if they involved tuning of new skills on familiar problems.

Several investigators have commented on the preponderance of lower-order, procedural tasks in classrooms. Korth and Cornbleth (1982) reported that nearly 80 percent of the tasks observed in English, science, and social studies classes in a suburban middle school required information acquisition and memory rather than comprehension or reasoning. In a follow-up study of how tasks were established at the beginning of the year, Cornbleth, Korth, and Dorow (1983) found that teachers emphasized order, procedures, and grades. Academic demands were minimal, skills were often separated from subject matter issues and problems, and few opportunities were provided for divergent thinking or reasoning. Mergendoller et al. (1988) examined the level of cognitive demand and accountability practices for 31 laboratory activities, 45 worksheets, and 31 exams in 11 seventh-grade life science classes during two instructional units. In general, the tasks represented in these assignments made minimal cognitive demands on students. Most tasks could be accomplished by following simple procedures or reproducing information previously encountered.

Doyle and his colleagues (Doyle 1986b; Doyle and Carter 1984; Doyle et al. 1985; Sanford 1987) reported that many of the tasks observed in secondary school science, mathematics, and English classes consisted of familiar work which could be accomplished by reproducing information or using reliable formulas or routines. Moreover, tasks with potentially high cognitive demands (e.g., word problems, essays, or research papers) were often proceduralized so that the actual work students did was simplified. Sanford (1987) found that teachers managed comprehension-level tasks in secondary science classes by maintaining high demands for accountability and then supplying "safety nets" in the form of group work, peer and teacher assistance, opportunities for revision of products, access to extra credit, and flexible grading standards. Some of these task management strategies appeared to lower the cognitive demands of the work.

Similar observations on the simplification and proceduralization of school work have been made by investigators from a wide range of perspectives (e.g., Bloome, Puro, and Theodorou 1989; Cusick 1983; Goodlad 1984; McNeil 1986; Schoenfeld 1988). Blumenfeld and Meece (1988) reported that the elementary school students interviewed in their study tended to describe work in terms of procedures and products rather than ideas or concepts even though they were aware of the point of the lessons.

Several attempts have been made to account for these patterns of classroom tasks. Cornbleth (1990) argues on the basis of her own studies and those of McNeil (1986) and Popkewitz, Tabachnick, and Wehlage (1982) that classroom patterns are shaped in fundamental ways by administrative and community priorities and practices. Teachers act "defensively" in simplifying demands on students to achieve order and compliance and thus meet administrative and community expectations for discipline and smooth operation. Moreover, curriculum changes that involve modification of school work are often superficial. The language changes to match the change effort, but underlying patterns of teaching and school work persist.

Doyle and Carter (1984; see also Doyle 1986b and Doyle et al. 1985), on the other hand, argue that there are powerful forces within classrooms that shape curriculum tasks. Their efforts to trace the life histories of tasks have revealed that when academic work is routinized and familiar to students (e.g., spelling tests or recurring worksheet exercises), the flow of classroom activity is typically smooth and well ordered. When work is problem-centered, that is, students are required to interpret situations and make decisions to accomplish tasks, activity flow is frequently slow and bumpy.

From the students' perspectives, problem-centered work involves high levels of ambiguity concerning the precise character of the product and risk that they will not be successful. Students often respond to the ambiguity and risk involved in such work by negotiating directly with teachers to increase the explicitness of product specifications or reduce the strictness of grading standards. Or, more passively, error rates go up and engagement and completion rates go down, creating pressures on work flow and order in classrooms. Teachers sometimes respond to these pressures by excluding higher-level tasks from the classroom altogether. More often, however, they revise or simplify task demands by defining specifications clearly, emphasizing procedures for completing assignments, providing prompts and resources, and adjusting accountability for work (Sanford 1987). When this happens, students' attention shifts from meaning and the underlying operations with content to obtaining correct answers and completing the work. As a result, the basic academic purposes of the curriculum are circumvented. In sum, novel or problem-centered work stretches the limits of classroom management and intensifies the complexity of the teacher's tasks of orchestrating classroom events. This analysis ties curriculum and classroom management together in a common system (see Doyle 1986a).

Summary

The research on tasks and task structures is beginning to provide useful insights into the fate of curriculum within classrooms. The curriculum that individual students encounter is represented in tasks to be accomplished. A student must interpret what the task means and struggle with the work itself. The degree of difficulty a student encounters depends upon the way the task is presented and the fit between the task and the student's preconceptions and level of competence. At a classroom level, tasks are pushed around by intrinsic factors related to management, activity flow, and direct student negotiation. It often appears that the classroom environment is quite robust and that only certain types of tasks, for example, familiar and routinized work, fit the social demand structures of these settings. In addition, tasks appear to be shaped by perceptions and expectations that operate within schools and the larger society.

TOWARD AN INTEGRATED CONCEPTION OF CURRICULUM AND PEDAGOGY

The lines of inquiry that have been reviewed in this chapter demonstrate that it is possible to study the curriculum in motion and to understand better the structures and processes by which knowledge is experienced and constructed by teachers and students in classroom settings. The survey also suggests, however, that it is quite difficult to keep both curriculum and pedagogy simultaneously in focus. When investigators try to capture the curriculum, pedagogy slips into the background, and when their attention turns to pedagogy, curriculum easily becomes invisible. In this concluding section, an attempt is made to construct an integrated conception of curriculum and pedagogy to hold both in place at the same time. In addition, it is hoped that this conception will serve as a vehicle for summarizing the diversity of topics treated in the chapter and provide a framework for expanding and directing future research.

Transformation: A Curricular and a Pedagogical Process

A major theme permeating this chapter is that the doing of both curriculum and pedagogy involves transforming content in some way. At the institutional level, the curriculum as a whole expresses a conception or a paradigm of what schooling should be with respect to a society, and content is selected and defined in the service of this expression. Similarly, at intermediate levels between the institution and the classroom, curriculum writing (in the form of textbooks, guides, and the like) involves the transforming of content with the intention of making it suitable for use by teachers and students (see Fenstermacher 1984). Finally, to teach is to simplify content to make it accessible to novices (see Kirsch 1977). Thus, transformations are inescapable in teaching.

A central issue for inquiry at the intersection of curriculum and pedagogy is the grounds on which such transformations, especially at the classroom level, are made. Attention has begun to focus, in other words, on the theories of the content that drive the pedagogical and curricular decisions teachers make. Indeed, a curriculum is not simply content, but a theory of content, that is, a conception of what the content is, what it means to know that content, and what goals one is accomplishing when one is teaching the content.

Traditionally, psychological conceptions of learning and motivation played a key role in defining the basis for pedagogical transformations, but this domination has been challenged recently by developments in cognitive science and in disciplinary pedagogy (see Putnam, Lampert, and Peterson 1990). In addition, classroom studies reveal that teachers fundamentally transform content as they teach (see Doyle and Carter 1984; Lemke 1989a; Michaels 1987). What is needed is a framework for understanding these pedagogical transformations of curriculum.

Teaching as a Curriculum Process

An integrated conception of curriculum and pedagogy requires that teaching be understood as a curriculum process, rather than simply as interpersonal exchange. This formulation means that classrooms are contexts in which students encounter curriculum events, that is, occasions in which they must act with respect to some content. These events can be thought of as consisting of written, oral, and behavioral "texts" that must be interpreted and acted upon toward some purpose. Teachers "author" curriculum events to achieve one or more effects on students. In this sense, teachers are like other authors except that they are present while their works are being read. Teachers can therefore frame their works during enactment in classroom situations by guiding students through the texts, shaping the interpretations that are allowed on the floor, and, importantly, by creating tasks that students are to accomplish with respect to these texts. At the same time, students contribute to the authoring of curriculum events as they participate in these enactments. (More will be said on this point shortly.) The authoring of curriculum events is, therefore, a dynamic process in which content is produced and transformed continuously. Moreover, the curriculum, at the level of enactment, is a "working space" (Stella 1986) in which teachers and students struggle with meaning.

The relationship between the institutional curriculum and curriculum events in classrooms is quite indirect for at least two reasons. First, the language of curriculum policy is discontinuous with the demands of conceptualizing and managing classroom events. As Reynolds and Saunders (1987, 212–213) argue, there is a basic

> dissociation between curriculum discourse and curriculum practice: . . . [a] lack of mesh between, on the one hand, the (planning-derived) protocols . . . by means of which curricular matters are formally addressed, and, on the other hand, the idioms of everyday conduct through which the teachers of particular schools reconcile their own satisfactions, capabilities, and circumstances with external requirements and support.

As a result, it is difficult to translate curriculum policy into actual curriculum events. Second, as the research reviewed in this chapter indicates, the curriculum is shaped in powerful ways by local factors in classrooms, including teachers' own curriculum perspectives.

The major external governing device for the classroom curriculum appears to be visibility. Students, who often share the broader social norms embodied in the institutional curriculum, witness classroom curriculum events and judge them as "proper" or not (see Burgess 1984; Reid 1984). These definitions and judgments would seem to play an important role in sustaining curriculum events within classrooms. At the same time, as curriculum events become visible in various ways to administrators, parents, and citizens, forces can be brought to bear on at the classroom level. Through these mechanisms, the classroom curriculum is connected indirectly back to the institutional curriculum and, thus, to social conceptions of schooling.

Students' Interpretations and the Classroom Culture

Reader-response critics maintain that the meaning of a text lies with the reader (see Culler 1981, 1982; Golden 1988; Schauber and Spolsky 1986). All texts are inherently indeterminant and, thus, the reader must write the unwritten part of the text, that is, construct the meaning of the text. At the same time, texts contain codes and conventions that the reader uses in producing meaning. The study of interpretation, then, becomes the study of the structures and signs that make a work intelligible. An interpretation of a work is, in other words, an account of "the reader's attempt to bring to bear on the text the codes and conventions deemed relevant and the text's resistance to or compliance with particular interpretive operations. The structure and meaning of the work emerge through an account of the reader's activity" (Culler 1982, 35).

The same can be said of curriculum events. Meaning in classrooms lies with the student. Students construct meaning by interpreting curriculum events and accomplishing tasks within these events. What is missing in research on curriculum and pedagogy is an analysis of the codes and conventions that make curriculum events intelligible. Individual students' interpretations and misconceptions have been recorded, but little effort has been made to situate these interpretations within specific curriculum events. By focusing on codes and conventions, the reader-response framework situates interpretation within a community of norms, expectations, and preferences that readers share.

This analysis highlights at least two important aspects of teaching. First, interpretation and knowledge are placed at the center of pedagogy. These constructs are likely to be much more powerful than "learning" and "behavior" for understanding teaching. Because of its behaviorist heritage, the study of learning tends to focus attention on performance and outcomes. Interpretation, on the other hand, directs the analysis to the frameworks of meaning that students bring to situations and how these frameworks interact with the curriculum contexts in which they find themselves. Since interpretation cannot easily be reduced to a test score, curriculum will likely remain a focus in the study of pedagogy if interpretation rather than learning is the target of analysis. This perspective also suggests that moving through the curriculum successfully involves a large amount of basic theoretical work by students as categories are reformulated, propositions understood, and interpretations revised. The work on conceptual change indicates that such theoretical work is central to schooling and takes a great deal of energy and time (see Confrey 1990; Posner et al. 1982). One can hardly expect significant knowledge acquisition to result from the mastery of a specific operation or behavior at the end of a single lesson, as implied by many behaviorist principles of instructional design.

Second, the analysis underscores a theme that emerges in several lines of inquiry: Students' curricular knowledge is deeply embedded in the fabric and culture of a classroom. Indeed, there is evidence to suggest that curriculum is locally produced and jointly constructed as teachers and students go about enacting and accomplishing tasks. Attempts at remote control of this process, especially through a small set of generic indicators of implementation fidelity, teaching effectiveness, or standardized achievement, are likely to distort the process itself (see Madaus 1988). Moreover, studying curriculum processes and students' knowledge would seem to require a much more thorough description of event structures in classroom settings than has characterized previous research.

Teachers' Theories and Knowledge

Research on textbook use, pedagogical content knowledge, and knowledge production processes in classrooms suggests that teachers have very robust theories of content that they use to author and direct curriculum events in their classrooms. We are only beginning to understand the nature of these content theories and how they are acquired and shaped by experience. Clearly, such theories are grounded in knowledge of and beliefs about content and in conceptions of students' learning and motivation. But such knowledge becomes situated with classroom experience. As a result, teachers' knowledge is likely to be event-structured (Carter and Doyle 1989; Nelson 1986), that is, organized around the real world events (e.g., activities, assignments, student reactions and typical mistakes, and time allocations) that occur when particular topics are treated. Teachers' knowledge structures also appear to include (1) situational cues, such as steering group performance (Lundgren 1977), that teachers use to pace the curriculum; and (2) a curriculum script (Putnam 1987) that teachers use to monitor progress over time and judge the performance of individual students. Since different curricular topics are associated with different classroom events, knowledge in this form is quite valuable to teachers in selecting curriculum items and predicting the course of classroom action.

Nelson (1986, 12) argues that events "involve people in purposeful activities" which consist of "acting on objects and interacting with each other to achieve some result." This argument suggests that knowledge structures are formulated around efforts to achieve purposes within the circumstances in which teachers and students find themselves. Thus, transformations of content occur in the service of solving practical problems of authoring and enacting curriculum events. It would seem to follow that teachers' content theories grow, in part, out of their experience of curriculum events in classrooms. To study teachers' content theories, then, it is necessary to examine such events closely.

From this perspective, learning to teach can be understood as a process of learning the curriculum as a set of classroom events (see Carter 1990; Carter and Gonzalez 1990). The core problem in learning to teach, in other words, is learning how to enact curriculum with students in complex instructional settings. On the surface, this problem looks easy: Teachers teach and students learn. But in its enacted form a curriculum is an intricate social event shaped by the understandings, dispositions, resources, and goals of the teacher and students. Reading in an elementary classroom is a complex event in which students struggle with the demands of text, their knowledge of the content, their understanding of language, and the social rules for interacting with peers and the teacher. DNA is an important topic in life science, but accomplishing classroom tasks associated with this topic requires students to understand and interpret very complex information. To initiate and sustain these curricula it is necessary to have a rich store of situated knowledge of curriculum content, classroom social processes, academic tasks, and students' understandings and intentions. Novices, who lack this situated knowledge, often struggle to make sense of classroom events and in this struggle their knowledge of curriculum is shaped in fundamental ways. Experienced teachers have a foundation of situated knowledge but must continually expand that store as new knowledge and new pedagogy become available to them through classroom experience, reading, or other modes.

This approach suggests a reconceptualization of the relationship between a science of education and teaching practice. Traditionally it has been assumed that research has utility to the extent that findings can be translated into prescriptions for practice or criteria for judging the quality of teaching performance. If one accepts the view that achievement is constructed locally in classroom environments, then attention shifts from isolated variables and predictors of success as abstractions of the complex life of classrooms (see Freedman 1988) to knowledge that is descriptive and theoretical, that is, a representation and explanation of the events that occur in classroom settings.

Conclusion

The central message of this chapter is that the study of teaching and curriculum must be grounded much more deeply than it has been in the events that students and teachers jointly construct in classroom settings. We must understand more fully the structure and operating processes of these events and the ways in which interpretations of students and teachers contribute to and are shaped by their participation in these events.

Realization of the embedded nature of curriculum and pedagogy for both teachers and students also points to a need to reformulate notions of classroom realities. Researchers tend to assume that classrooms are artificial, that they are staged performances that can be changed easily by rewriting the script or redesigning the stage. Clearly, this assumption has not served the educational community well. Prescriptions typically crash into powerful forces within classrooms. But if classrooms are believed to have their own inherent structures, then much can be learned by trying to understand classroom events as they are constructed by students and teachers. Fortunately, useful theoretical and methodological tools are emerging for studying the curriculum as a pedagogical event in classroom settings.

References

Adelman, Clem. 1984. "The Play House and the Sand Tray." In *Defining the Curriculum: Histories and Ethnographies*, edited by Ivor F. Goodson and Stephen J. Ball, 77–88. London: Falmer.

Alton-Lee, Adrienne, and Graham Nuthall. 1989. "Pupil Experiences and Pupil Learning in the Elementary Classroom." Paper presented at the annual meeting of the American Educational Research Association, San Francisco, CA.

Alvermann, Donna E., and David H. Hayes. 1989. Classroom discussion of content area reading assignments: An intervention study. *Reading Research Quarterly* 24(3): 305–335.

Anderson, Charles W. 1989. "The Role of Education in the Academic Disciplines in Teacher Preparation." In *Research Perspectives on the Graduate Preparation of Teachers*, edited by Anita E. Woolfolk, 88–107. Englewood Cliffs, NJ: Prentice Hall.

Anderson, Linda M., Dannelle D. Stevens, Richard S. Prawat, and Jacquelyn Nickerson. 1988. Classroom task environments and students' task-related beliefs. *Elementary School Journal* 88(3): 281–295.

Anderson, Richard B. 1977. "The Effectiveness of Follow Through: What Have We Learned." Paper presented at the annual meeting of the American Educational Research Association, New York.

Anderson, Thomas H., and Bonnie B. Armbruster. 1984. "Content Area Textbooks." In *Learning to Read in American Schools: Readers and Content Texts*, edited by Richard C. Anderson, Jean Osborn, and Robert J. Tierney, 193–226. Hillsdale, NJ: Erlbaum.

Anyon, Jean. 1980. Social class and the hidden curriculum of work. *Journal of Education* 162(1): 67–92.

Apple, Michael W. 1979. *Ideology and Curriculum*. Boston: Routledge & Kegan Paul.

Apple, Michael W. 1986. *Teachers and Texts: A Political Economy of Class and Gender Relations in Education*. New York: Routledge & Kegan Paul.

Applebee, Arthur N. 1981. *Writing in the Secondary School: English and the Content Areas*. Urbana, IL: National Council of Teachers of English.

Armbruster, Bonnie B., Robert J. Stevens, and Barak Rosenshine. 1977. *Analyzing Content Coverage and Emphasis: A Study of Three Curricula and Two Tests*. Technical Report No. 26. Urbana: Center for the Study of Reading, University of Illinois.

Au, Katherine H. 1980. Participation structures in a reading lesson with Hawaiian children: Analysis of a culturally appropriate instruction event. *Anthropology and Education Quarterly* 11(2): 91-115.

Aulls, Mark W. 1990. "The Relationship Among Co-occurring Academic Tasks and Teacher-class Discourse, Teachers' Unit Goals and Student Learning in Social Studies." Paper presented at the annual meeting of the American Educational Research Association, Boston.

Ball, Deborah L., and Sharon Feiman-Nemser. 1988. Using textbooks and teachers' guides: A dilemma for beginning teachers and teacher educators. *Curriculum Inquiry* 18(4): 401–423.

Ball, Deborah L., and G. William McDiarmid. 1990. "The Subject-Matter Preparation of Teachers." In *Handbook of Research on Teacher Education*, edited by W. Robert Houston, 437–449. New York: Macmillan.

Barnes, Douglas. 1976. *From Communication to Curriculum*. Harmondsworth: Penguin Books.

Barr, A. S. 1926. *Elementary School Standards for the Improvement of Teaching*. Ann Arbor, MI: Edwards Brothers.

Barr, A. S. 1929. *Characteristic Differences in the Teaching Performance of Good and Poor Teachers of the Social Studies*. Bloomington, IL: Public School Co.

Barr, A. S. 1931. *An Introduction to the Scientific Study of Classroom Supervision*. New York: Appleton.

Barr, Rebecca. 1987. "Classroom Interaction and Curricular Content." In *Literacy and Schooling*, edited by David Bloome, 150–168. Norwood, NJ: Ablex.

Barr, Rebecca, and Robert Dreeben. 1983. *How Schools Work*. Chicago: University of Chicago Press.

Barr, Rebecca, and Marilyn W. Sadow. 1989. Influence of basal programs on fourth-grade reading instruction. *Reading Research Quarterly* 24(1): 44–71.

Bayles, Ernest E., and Bruce L. Hood. 1966. *Growth of American Educational Thought and Practice*. New York: Harper & Row.

Beauchamp, George S. 1981. *Curriculum Theory*. 4th ed. Itasca, IL: Peacock.

Beck, Isabel L., and Ellen S. McCaslin. 1978. *An Analysis of Dimensions that Affect the Development of Code-Breaking Ability in Eight Beginning Reading Programs*. Pittsburgh: Learning Research and Development Center, University of Pittsburgh.

Beck, Isabel L., Margaret G. McKeown, and Erika W. Gromoll. 1989. Learning from social studies texts. *Cognition and Instruction* 6(2): 99–158.

Bellack, Arno A., Herbert M. Kliebard, Ronald T. Hyman, and Frank L. Smith, Jr. 1966. *The Language of the Classroom*. New York: Teachers College Press.

Bennett, Neville, and Charles Desforges. 1988. Matching classroom tasks to students' attainments. *Elementary School Journal* 88(3): 221–234.

Bennett, Neville, Charles A. Desforges, Anne Cockburn, and Betty Wilkinson. 1984. *The Quality of Pupil Learning Experiences*. Hillsdale, NJ: Erlbaum.

Bennis, Warren G., Kenneth D. Benne, Robert Chin, and Kenneth E. Corey, eds. 1976. *The Planning of Change*, 3d ed. New York: Holt, Rinehart and Winston.

Berger, Peter L., and Thomas Luckmann. 1967. *The Social Construction of Reality*. New York: Doubleday.

Beyer, Landon E. 1987. "What Knowledge Is of Most Worth in Teacher Education?" In *Educating Teachers: Changing the Nature of Pedagogical Knowledge*, edited by John Smyth, 19–34. London: Falmer.

Bloome, David, Pamela Puro, and Erine Theodorou. 1989. Procedural display and classroom lessons. *Curriculum Inquiry* 19(3): 265–291.

Bloome, David, and Erine Theodorou. 1988. "Analyzing Teacher-Student and Student-Student Discourse." In *Multiple Perspective Analyses of Classroom Discourse*, edited by Judith L. Green and Judith O. Harker, 217–248. Norwood, NJ: Ablex.

Blumenfeld, Phyllis C., and Judith L. Meece. 1988. Task factors, teacher behavior, and students' involvement and use of learning strategies in science. *Elementary School Journal* 88(3): 235–250.

Blumenfeld, Phyllis C., John R. Mergendoller, and Donald W. Swarthout. 1987. Task as a heuristic for understanding student learning and motivation. *Journal of Curriculum Studies* 19(2): 135–148.

Blumenfeld, Phyllis C., Paul R. Pintrich, Judith Meece, and Kathleen Wessels. 1982. "The Formation and Role of Self Perceptions of Ability in Elementary Classrooms." In *Focus on Teaching*, edited by Walter Doyle and Thomas L. Good, 182–201. Chicago: University of Chicago Press.

Bobbitt, Franklin. 1913. *The Supervision of City Schools.* Twelfth Yearbook of the National Society for the Study of Education, Part 1. Bloomington, IL: Public School Co.

Bobbitt, Franklin. 1918. *The Curriculum.* Boston: Houghton Mifflin.

Bobbitt, Franklin. 1924. *How to Make a Curriculum.* Boston: Houghton Mifflin.

Bossert, Steven. 1979. *Tasks and Social Relationships in Classrooms: A Study of Instructional Organization and its Consequences.* Cambridge: Cambridge University Press.

Brophy, Jere. 1990. Teaching social studies for understanding and higher-order applications. *Elementary School Journal* 90(4): 351–417.

Brophy, Jere, and Thomas L. Good. 1986. "Teacher Behavior and Student Achievement." In *Handbook of Research on Teaching.* 3d ed., edited by Merlin C. Wittrock, 328–375. New York: Macmillan.

Brown, John S., Allan Collins, and Paul Duguid. 1989. Situated cognition and the culture of learning. *Educational Researcher* 18(1): 32–42.

Burgess, Robert G. 1984. "'It's Not a Proper Subject: It's Just Newsom.'" In *Defining the Curriculum: Histories and Ethnographies*, edited by Ivor F. Goodson and Stephen J. Ball, 181–200. London: Falmer.

Burnham, John C. 1972. "Medical Specialists and Movement Toward Social Control in the Progressive Era: Three Examples." In *Building the Organizational Society: Essays on Associational Activities in Modern America*, edited by Jerry Israel, 19–30. New York: Free Press.

Buros, Oscar K. 1977. Fifty years in testing: Some reminiscences, criticisms, and suggestions. *Educational Researcher* 6(7): 9–15.

Calderhead, James, and Eddie Miller. 1985. "The Integration of Subject Matter Knowledge in Student Teachers' Classroom Practice." Paper presented at the annual meeting of the British Educational Research Association, Sheffield, England.

Calfee, Robert, and Priscilla Drum. 1986. "Research on Teaching Reading." In *Handbook of Research on Teaching.* 3d ed., edited by Merlin C. Wittrock, 804–849. New York: Macmillan.

Carr, Wilfred, and Stephen Kemmis. 1986. *Becoming Critical: Education, Knowledge and Action Research.* London: Falmer.

Carter, Kathy. 1990. "Teachers' Knowledge and Learning to Teach." In *Handbook of Research on Teacher Education*, edited by W. Robert Houston, 291–310. New York: Macmillan.

Carter, Kathy. In press. Teacher comprehension of classroom processes: A new direction in classroom management research. *Elementary School Journal.*

Carter, Kathy, and Walter Doyle. 1987. "Teachers' Knowledge Structures and Comprehension Processes." In *Exploring Teachers' Thinking*, edited by James Calderhead, 147–160. London: Cassell.

Carter, Kathy, and Walter Doyle. 1989. "Classroom Research as a Resource for the Graduate Preparation of Teachers." In *Research Perspectives on the Graduate Preparation of Teachers*, edited by Anita E. Woolfolk, 51–68. Englewood Cliffs, NJ: Prentice Hall.

Carter, Kathy, and Luz Gonzalez. 1990. "Teachers' Knowledge of Classrooms and Classroom Events." Paper presented at the annual meeting of the American Educational Research Association, Boston, MA.

Cazden, Courtney B. 1986. "Classroom Discourse." In *Handbook of Research on Teaching.* 3rd ed., edited by Merlin C. Wittrock, 432–463. New York: Macmillan.

Cazden, Courtney B. 1988. *Classroom Discourse: The Language of Teaching and Learning.* Portsmouth, NH: Heinemann.

Charters, W. W. 1923. *Curriculum Construction.* New York: Macmillan.

Cherryholmes, Cleo H. 1988. *Power and Criticism: Poststructural Investigations in Education.* Advances in Contemporary Educational Thought, vol. 2. New York: Teachers College Press.

Clandinin, D. Jean. 1986. *Classroom Practice: Teacher Images in Action.* London: Falmer.

Clark, Christopher M., and Penelope L. Peterson. 1986. "Teachers' Thought Processes." In *Handbook of Research on Teaching.* 3rd ed., edited by Merlin C. Wittrock, 255–296. New York: Macmillan.

Confrey, Jere. 1990. "A Review of the Research on Student Conceptions in Mathematics, Science, and Programming." In *Review of Research in Education*, edited by Courtney B. Cazden, vol. 16, 3–56. Washington, DC: American Educational Research Association.

Connelly, F. Michael, and D. Jean Clandinin. 1986. On narrative method, personal philosophy, and the story of teaching. *Journal of Research in Science Teaching* 23(4): 293–310.

Cooper, Barry. 1984. "On Explaining Change in School Subjects." In *Defining the Curriculum: Histories and Ethnographies*, edited by Ivor F. Goodson and Stephen J. Ball, 45–63. London: Falmer.

Cornbleth, Catherine. 1988. Curriculum in and out of context. *Journal of Curriculum and Supervision* 3(2): 85–96.

Cornbleth, Catherine. 1990. *Curriculum in Context.* London: Falmer.

Cornbleth, Catherine, Willard Korth, and E. B. Dorow. 1983. "Creating the Curriculum: Beginning the Year in a Middle School." Paper presented at the annual meeting of the American Educational Research Association, Montreal.

Cubberley, Ellwood P. 1917. Editor's introduction. In *Educational Tests and Measurements*, edited by Walter S. Monroe, James C. DeVoss, and Frederick J. Kelley, v–ix. Boston: Houghton Mifflin.

Culler, Jonathan. 1981. *The Pursuit of Signs: Semiotics, Literature, Deconstruction.* Ithaca, NY: Cornell University Press.

Culler, Jonathan. 1982. *On Deconstruction.* Ithaca, NY: Cornell University Press.

Cusick, Philip A. 1983. *The Egalitarian Ideal and the American High School: Studies of Three Schools.* New York: Longman.

Dawes, Robyn M. 1975. "The Mind, the Model, and the Task." In *Cognitive Theory*, edited by Frank Restle, Richard M. Shifrin, N. John Castellan, Harold R. Lindman, and David B. Pisoni, vol. 1, 119–129. Hillsdale, NJ: Erlbaum.

Desforges, Charles, and Anne Cockburn. 1987. *Understanding the Mathematics Teacher.* Basingstoke, England: Falmer.

Dillon, David, and Dennis Searle. 1981. The role of language in one first grade classroom. *Research in the Teaching of English* 15(4): 311–328.

Doyle, Walter. 1976. "Educational for All: The Triumph of Professionalism." In *Perspectives on Curriculum Development: 1776–1976*, 1976 Yearbook, edited by O. L. Davis, Jr., 17–75. Washington, DC: Association for Supervision and Curriculum Development.

Doyle, Walter. 1978. "Paradigms for Research on Teacher Effectiveness." In *Review of Research in Education*, edited by L. S. Shulman, vol. 5, 163–198. Itasca, IL: Peacock.

Doyle, Walter. 1983. Academic work. *Review of Educational Research* 53(2): 159–199.

Doyle, Walter. 1986a. "Classroom Organization and Management." In *Handbook of Research on Teaching.* 3rd ed., edited by Merlin C. Wittrock, 392-431. New York: Macmillan.

Doyle, Walter. 1986b. Content representation in teachers' definitions of academic work. *Journal of Curriculum Studies* 18(4): 365–379.

Doyle, Walter, and Kathy Carter. 1984. Academic tasks in classrooms. *Curriculum Inquiry* 14(2): 129–149.

Doyle, Walter, Julie P. Sanford, Barbara S. French, Edmund T. Emmer, and Barbara S. Clements. 1985. *Patterns of Academic Work in Junior High School Science, English, and Mathematics Classes: A Final Report* (R&D Report 6190). Austin, TX: University of Texas, Research and Development Center for Teacher Education.

Dreeben, Robert. 1970. *The Nature of Teaching*. Glenview, IL: Scott, Foresman.

Dunkin, Michael J., and Bruce J. Biddle. 1974. *The Study of Teaching*. New York: Holt, Rinehart and Winston.

Durkin, Dolores. 1978–1979. What classroom observations reveal about reading comprehension instruction. *Reading Research Quarterly* 14(4): 481–533.

Durkin, Dolores. 1981. Reading comprehension instruction in five basal reader series. *Reading Research Quarterly* 16(4): 515–544.

Durkin, Dolores. 1984. Is there a match between what elementary school teachers do and what basal reader manuals recommend? *The Reading Teacher* 37(8): 734–749.

Easley, J. A., Jr. 1977. Seven modeling perspectives on teaching and learning: Some interrelations and cognitive effects. *Instructional Science* 6(4): 319–367.

Eder, Donna. 1982. "Differences in Communicative Styles Across Ability Groups." In *Communicating in the Classroom*, edited by Louise C. Wilkinson, 245–264. New York: Academic Press.

Edwards, A. D., and V. J. Furlong. 1978. *The Language of Teaching*. London: Heinemann.

Eisner, Elliot W., and Elizabeth Vallance, eds. 1974. *Conflicting Conceptions of Curriculum*. Berkeley, CA: McCutchan.

Elbaz, Freema. 1983. *Teacher Thinking: A Study of Practical Knowledge*. London: Croom Helm.

Erickson, Frederick. 1982. Taught cognitive learning in its immediate environment: A neglected topic in the anthropology of education. *Anthropology and Education Quarterly* 13(2): 149–180.

Erickson, Frederick. 1986. "Qualitative Methods in Research on Teaching." In *Handbook of Research on Teaching*. 3rd ed., edited by Merlin C. Wittrock, 119–161. New York: Macmillan.

Erickson, Frederick, and Jeffrey Shultz. 1981. "When Is a Context? Some Issues and Methods in the Analysis of Social Competence." In *Ethnography and Language in Educational Settings*, edited by Judith L. Green and Cynthia Wallat, 147–160. Norwood, NJ: Ablex.

Etzioni, Amatai, ed. 1969. *The Semi-Professions and Their Organization*. New York: Free Press.

Everhart, Robert B. 1983. *Reading, Writing, and Resistance: Adolescence and Labor in a Junior High School*. London: Routledge & Kegan Paul.

Fenstermacher, Gary D. 1984. "Some Superficial Thoughts on a Profound Problem." Paper prepared for the Conference on the Study of Curriculum in Graduate Education, College of Education, Michigan State University.

FitzGerald, Frances. 1979. *America Revised: What History Textbooks Have Taught Our Children About Their Country, and How and Why These Textbooks Have Changed in Different Decades*. New York: Vintage.

Florio, Susan, and Christopher M. Clark. 1982. The functions of writing in an elementary classroom. *Research in the Teaching of English* 16(2): 115–130.

Florio, Susan, and Jeffrey Shultz. 1979. Social competence at home and at school. *Theory into Practice* 18(4): 234–243.

Florio-Ruane, Susan, and Saundra Dunn. 1987. "Teaching Writing: Some Perennial Questions and Some Possible Answers." In *Educators' Handbook: A Research Perspective*, edited by Virginia Richardson-Koehler, 50–83. New York: Longman.

Foshay, Wellesley R., and Arthur S. Foshay. 1980. Curriculum development and instructional development. *Educational Leadership* 38(8): 621–626.

Franklin, Barry M. 1986. *Building the American Community: The School Curriculum and the Search for Social Control*. London: Falmer.

Freedman, Sara E. 1988. "Teaching, Gender, and Curriculum." In *The Curriculum: Problems, Politics, and Possibilities*, edited by Landon E. Beyer and Michael W. Apple, 204–218. Albany: State University of New York Press.

Freeman, Donald J., Therese M. Kuhs, Andrew C. Porter, Robert E. Floden, William H. Schmidt, and John R. Schwille. 1983. Do textbooks and tests define a national curriculum in elementary school mathematics? *Elementary School Journal* 83(5): 501–513.

Freeman, Donald J., and Porter, Andrew C. 1989. Do textbooks dictate the content of mathematics instruction in elementary schools? *American Educational Research Journal* 26(3): 403–421.

Freidson, Eliot. 1970. *Profession of Medicine: A Study in the Sociology of Applied Knowledge*. New York: Dodd, Mead.

Fullan, Michael. 1982. *The Meaning of Educational Change*. New York: Teachers College Press.

Gage, N. L. 1963. "Paradigms for Research on Teaching." In *Handbook of Research on Teaching*, edited by N. L. Gage, 94–141. Chicago: Rand McNally.

Gage, N. L. 1978. *The Scientific Basis of the Art of Teaching*. New York: Teachers College Press.

Gage, N. L. 1985. *Hard Gains in the Soft Sciences: The Case of Pedagogy*. Bloomington, IN: Center on Evaluation, Development, and Research, Phi Delta Kappa.

Gammon, Elizabeth M. 1973. "Syntactical Analysis of Some First-Grade Readers." In *Approaches to Natural Language*, edited by K. J. J. Hintikka, J. M. Moravcsik, and P. Suppes, 85–133. Dordrecht, Holland: D. Reidel.

Garrison, James W. 1988. Democracy, Scientific Knowledge, and Teacher Empowerment. *Teachers College Record* 89(4): 487–504.

Getzels, J. W., and P. W. Jackson. 1963. "The Teacher's Personality and Characteristics." In *Handbook of Research on Teaching*, edited by N. L. Gage 506–582. Chicago: Rand McNally.

Glatthorn, Allan A. 1987. *Curriculum Leadership*. Glenview, IL: Scott, Foresman.

Golden, Joanne M. 1988. "The Construction of a Literary Text in a Story-Reading Lesson." In *Multiple Perspective Analyses of Classroom Discourse*, edited by Judith L. Green and Judith O. Harker, 71–106. Norwood, NJ: Ablex.

Golden, Joanne M. 1989. Reading in the classroom context: A semiotic event. *Semiotica* 73(1/2): 67–84.

Goodlad, John I. 1984. *A Place Called School*. New York: McGraw-Hill.

Goodson, Ivor. 1987. *School Subjects and Curriculum Change*. London: Falmer.

Goodson, Ivor F., and Stephen J. Ball, eds. 1984. *Defining the Curriculum: Histories and Ethnographies*. London: Falmer.

Gordon, David. 1988. Education as Text: The Varieties of Educational Hiddenness. *Curriculum Inquiry* 18(4): 425–449.

Grant, Grace E. 1987. "Transforming Content Knowledge into Work Tasks: Teaching Reasoning in Four Subject Areas." Paper presented at the annual meeting of the American Educational Research Association, Washington, DC.

Graves, Donald H. 1975. An examination of the writing processes of seven-year-old children. *Research in the Teaching of English* 9(3): 227–241.

Green, Judith L., and Judith O. Harker. 1982. "Gaining Access to

Learning: Conversational, Social, and Cognitive Demands of Group Participation." In *Communicating in the Classroom*, edited by Louise C. Wilkinson, 183–222. New York: Academic Press.

Green, Judith L., Judith O. Harker, and Joanne M. Golden. 1987. "Lesson Construction: Differing views." In *Schooling in Social Context: Qualitative Studies*, edited by George W. Noblitt and William T. Pink, 46–77. Norwood, NJ: Ablex.

Green, Judith, and Regina Weade. 1985. Reading between the words: Social cues to lesson participation. *Theory into Practice* 24(1): 14–21.

Green, Judith L., Regina Weade, and Kathy Graham. 1988. "Lesson Construction and Student Participation: A Sociolinguistic Analysis." In *Multiple Perspective Analyses of Classroom Discourse*, edited by Judith L. Green and Judith O. Harker, 11–47. Norwood, NJ: Ablex.

Groen, Guy, and Lauren B. Resnick. 1977. Can preschool children invent addition algorithms? *Journal of Educational Psychology* 69(6): 645–652.

Grossman, Pamela L. 1987. "The Tale of Two Teachers: The Role of Subject Matter Orientation in Teaching." Paper presented at the annual meeting of the American Educational Research Association, Washington, DC.

Grossman, Pamela L. 1989. A study in contrast: Sources of pedagogical content knowledge for secondary English. *Journal of Teacher Education* 40(5): 24–32.

Grossman, Pamela L. 1990. "Knowing, Believing, and Valuing: The Role of Subject Matter." Paper presented at the annual meeting of the American Educational Research Association, Boston, MA.

Grossman, Pamela L., and Sigrun Gudmundsdottir. 1987. "Teachers and Texts: An Expert/Novice Comparison in English." Paper presented at the annual meeting of the American Educational Research Association, Washington, DC.

Grossman, Pamela L., Suzanne M. Wilson, and Lee S. Shulman. 1989. "Teachers of Substance: Subject Matter Knowledge for Teaching." In *Knowledge Base for the Beginning Teacher*, edited by Maynard C. Reynolds, 23–36. Oxford: Pergamon.

Gudmundsdottir, Sigrun. 1989. "Values in Pedagogical Content Knowledge." Paper presented at the annual meeting of the American Educational Research Association, San Francisco.

Gudmundsdottir, Sigrun. In press. "Pedagogical Models of Subject Matter." In *Advances in Research on Teaching*, edited by Jere Brophy, vol. 2. Greenwich, CT: JAI Press.

Gwynn, J. Minor. 1961. *Theory and Practice of Supervision*. New York: Dodd, Mead.

Harrington, Gordon M. 1955. Smiling as a measure of teacher effectiveness. *Journal of Educational Research* 48(9): 715–717.

Harrod, P. M. F. 1977. Talk in junior and middle school classrooms: An exploratory investigation. *Educational Review* 29(2): 97–106.

Hashweh, Maher Z. 1987. Effects of subject matter knowledge in teaching biology and physics. *Teaching and Teacher Education* 3(2): 109–120.

Hays, Samuel P. 1972. "The New Organizational Society." In *Building the Organizational Society: Essays on Associational Activities in Modern America*, edited by Jerry Israel 1–15. New York: Free Press.

Heap, James L. 1985. Discourse in the production of classroom knowledge: Reading lessons. *Curriculum Inquiry* 15(3): 245–279.

Jackson, Philip W. 1968. *Life in Classrooms*. New York: Holt, Rinehart and Winston.

Johnson, Mauritz, Jr. 1967. Definitions and models in curriculum theory. *Educational Theory* 17(2): 127–140.

Joncich, Geraldine M. 1968. *The Sane Positivist: A Biography of Edward L. Thorndike*. Middletown, CT: Wesleyan University Press.

Joyce, Bruce, and Marsha Weil. 1972. *Models of Teaching*. Englewood Cliffs, NJ: Prentice Hall.

Keddie, Nell. 1971. "Classroom Knowledge." In *Knowledge and Control*, edited by Michael F. D. Young, 133–159. London: Collier-Macmillan.

Kickbusch, Kenneth W., and Robert B. Everhart. 1985. Curriculum, practical ideology, and class contradiction. *Curriculum Inquiry* 15(3): 281–317.

Kirsch, Arnold. 1977. "Aspects of Simplification in Mathematics Teaching." In *Proceedings of the Third International Congress on Mathematics Education*, edited by H. Athen and H. Kunle, 98–120. Karlsruhe, West Germany: University of Karlsruhe.

Kliebard, Herbert M. 1986. *The Struggle for the American Curriculum: 1893–1958*. Boston, MA: Routledge & Kegan Paul.

Korth, Willard, and Catherine Cornbleth. 1982. "Classroom Activities as Settings for Cognitive Learning Opportunity and Instruction." Paper presented at the annual meeting of the American Educational Research Association, New York.

Kounin, Jacob S. 1970. *Discipline and Group Management in Classrooms*. New York: Holt, Rinehart and Winston.

Kounin, Jacob S., and Paul V. Gump. 1974. Signal systems of lesson settings and the task related behavior of preschool children. *Journal of Educational Psychology* 66(4): 554–562.

Laboratory of Comparative Human Cognition. 1978. "Cognition as a Residual Category in Anthropology." In *Annual Review of Anthropology*, edited by Bernard J. Siegel, Alan R. Beals, and Stephen A. Tyler, vol. 7, 51–69. Palo Alto, CA: Annual Reviews.

Lagemann, Ellen C. 1989. The plural worlds of educational research. *History of Education Quarterly* 29(2): 185–214.

Lakomski, Gabriele. 1988. Witches, weather gods, and phlogiston: The demise of the hidden curriculum. *Curriculum Inquiry* 18(4): 451–463.

Lampert, Magdalene. 1986a. Knowing, doing, and teaching multiplication. *Cognition and Instruction* 3(4): 305–342.

Lampert, Magdalene. 1986b. Teaching multiplication. *Journal of Mathematical Behavior* 5(3): 241–280.

Lave, Jean. 1988. *Cognition in Practice: Mind, Mathematics, and Culture in Everyday Life*. New York: Cambridge University Press.

Lave, Jean. 1990. "The Culture of Acquisition and the Practice of Understanding." In *Cultural Psychology: Essays on Comparative Human Development*, edited by James W. Stigler, Richard A. Shweder, and Gilbert Herdt, 309–327. New York: Cambridge University Press.

Lazerson, Marvin, Judith B. McLaughlin, Bruce McPherson, and Stephen Bailey. 1985. *An Education of Value: The Purposes and Practices of Schools*. Cambridge: Cambridge University Press.

Leinhardt, Gaea, and Donald A. Smith. 1985. Expertise in mathematics instruction: Subject-matter knowledge. *Journal of Educational Psychology* 77(3): 247–271.

Lemke, Jay L. 1989a. "The Language of Science Teaching." In *Locating Learning: Ethnographic Perspectives on Classroom Research*, edited by Catherine Emihovick, 216–239. Norwood, NJ: Ablex Publishing Company.

Lemke, Jay L. 1989b. Making text talk. *Theory into Practice* 28(2): 136–141.

Lieberman, Myron. 1956. *Education as a Profession*. Englewood Cliffs, NJ: Prentice Hall.

Loucks, Susan F., and Gene E. Hall. 1979. "Implementing Innovations in Schools: A Concerns-Based Approach." Paper presented at the annual meeting of the American Educational Research Association, San Francisco. ED 206 109.

Loucks, Susan, and Harold Pratt. 1979. A concerns-based approach to curriculum change. *Educational Leadership* 37(3): 212–215.

Lundgren, Ulf P. 1977. *Model Analysis of Pedagogical Processes*. Studies in Education and Psychology 2. Stockholm: CWK Gleerup.

McCutcheon, Gail. 1988. "Curriculum and the Work of Teachers." In *The Curriculum: Problems, Politics, and Possibilities*, edited by Landon E. Beyer and Michael W. Apple. Albany: State University of New York Press.

McDermott, Raymond P. 1976. "Kids Make Sense: An Ethnographic Account of Interactional Management of Success and Failure in One First-Grade Classroom." Unpublished Ph.D. dissertation, Stanford University, Stanford, CA.

Macdonald, James B. 1965. "Educational Models for Instruction: Introduction." In *Theories of Instruction*, edited by James B. Macdonald and Robert R. Leeper, 1–7. Washington, DC: Association for Supervision and Curriculum Development.

McDonald, Joseph P. 1988. The emergence of the teacher's voice: Implications for the new reform. *Teachers College Record* 89(4): 471–486.

MacGinitie, Walter H. 1976. Difficulty with logical operations. *The Reading Teacher* 29(4): 371–375.

McHoul, Alexander. 1978. The organization of turns at formal talk in the classroom. *Language in Society* 7(2): 183–213.

MacLure, Margaret, and Peter French. 1978. "Route to Right Answers: On Pupils' Strategies for Answering Teachers' Questions." Paper presented at the Conference on Teacher and Pupil Strategies, St. Hilda's College, Oxford.

McNeil, Linda M. 1986. *Contradictions of Control: School Structure and School Knowledge*. New York: Routledge & Kegan Paul.

Madaus, George F. 1988. "The Influence of Testing on the Curriculum." In *Critical Issues in Curriculum*. The Eighty-Seventh Yearbook of the National Society for the Study of Education, edited by Laurel N. Tanner, Part 1, 83–121. Chicago: University of Chicago Press.

Marton, Ference. 1989. Towards a pedagogy of content. *Educational Psychologist* 24(1):1–23.

Marx, Ronald W., and John Walsh. 1988. Learning from academic tasks. *Elementary School Journal* 88(3):207–219.

Mehan, Hugh. 1974. "Accomplishing Classroom Lessons." In *Language Use and School Performance*, edited by Aaron C. Cicourel, Kenneth H. Jennings, Sybillen H. M. Jennings, Kenneth C. W. Leiter, Robert MacKay, Hugh Mehan, and David R. Roth, 76–142. New York: Academic Press.

Mehan, Hugh. 1979. *Learning Lessons: Social Organization in the Classroom*. Cambridge, MA: Harvard University Press.

Mergendoller, John R., Virginia A. Marchman, Alexis L. Mitman, and Martin J. Packer. 1988. Task demands and accountability in middle-grade science classes. *Elementary School Journal* 88(3): 251–265.

Meyer, Linda A., Eunice A. Greer, and Lorraine Crummey. 1987. An analysis of decoding, comprehension, and story text comprehensibility in four first-grade reading programs. *Journal of Reading Behavior* 19(1): 69–98.

Michaels, Sarah. 1981. "Sharing time": Children's narrative styles and differential access to literacy. *Language in Society* 10(3): 423–442.

Michaels, Sarah. 1987. Text and context: A new approach to the study of classroom writing. *Discourse Processes* 10(4): 321–346.

Monaghan, E. Jennifer, and E. Wendy Saul. 1987. "The Reader, the Scribe, the Thinker: A Critical Look at the History of American Reading and Writing Instruction." In *The Formation of School Subjects: The Struggle for Creating an American Institution*, edited by Thomas S. Popkewitz, 85–122. London: Falmer.

Mosenthal, Peter. 1983. The influence of social situation on children's classroom comprehension of text. *Elementary School Journal* 83(5): 537–547.

Murphy, Susan B. 1987. "Making Sense of School: An Ecological Examination of Students' Definitions of Reading Tasks." Unpublished doctoral dissertation, Virginia Polytechnic Institute and State University, Blacksburg.

Nelson, Katherine. 1986. *Event Knowledge: Structure and Function in Development*. Hillsdale, NJ: Erlbaum.

Nespor, Jan. 1986. Theoretical note: On students' experiences across the grade levels. *Anthropology and Education Quarterly* 17(4): 203–216.

Nespor, Jan. 1987. Academic tasks in a high school English class. *Curriculum Inquiry* 17(2): 203–228.

Nuthall, Graham, and I. Snook. 1973. "Contemporary Models of Teaching." In *Second Handbook of Research on Teaching*, edited by Robert M. W. Travers, 47–76. Chicago: Rand McNally.

Oakes, Jeannie. 1985. *Keeping Track: How Schools Structure Inequality*. New Haven, CT: Yale University Press.

Osborn, Jean. 1984. "The Purposes, Uses, and Contents of Workbooks and Some Guidelines for Publishers." In *Learning to Read in American Schools: Readers and Content Texts*, edited by Richard C. Anderson, Jean Osborn, and Robert J. Tierney, 45–111. Hillsdale, NJ: Earlbaum.

Palinscar, Annemarie S., and Ann L. Brown. 1984. Reciprocal teaching of comprehension-fostering and monitoring activities. *Cognition and Instruction* 1(2): 117–175.

Payne, William H. 1875. *Chapters on School Supervision*. Cincinnati: Van Antwerp, Bragg.

Peterson, Penelope L., Elizabeth Fennema, Thomas P. Carpenter, and Megan Loef. 1989. Teachers' pedagogical content beliefs in mathematics. *Cognition and Instruction* 6(1): 1–40.

Philips, Susan. 1983. *The Invisible Culture: Communication in the Classroom and Community on the Warm Springs Indian Reservation*. New York: Longman.

Popkewitz, Thomas S. 1987a. *The Formation of School Subjects: The Struggle for Creating an American Institution*. London: Falmer.

Popkewitz, Thomas S. 1987b. "The Formation of School Subjects and the Political Context of Schooling." In *The Formation of School Subjects: The Struggle for Creating an American Institution*, edited by Thomas S. Popkewitz, 1–24. London: Falmer.

Popkewitz, Thomas S., B. Robert Tabachnick, and Gary Wehlage. 1982. *The Myth of Educational Reform*. Madison: University of Wisconsin Press.

Posner, George J. 1982. A cognitive science conception of curriculum and instruction. *Journal of Curriculum Studies* 14(4): 343–351.

Posner, George J. 1988. "Models of Curriculum Planning." In *The Curriculum: Problems, Politics, and Possibilities*, edited by Landon E. Beyer and Michael W. Apple, 77–97. Albany: State University of New York Press.

Posner, George J., Kenneth A. Strike, Peter W. Hewson, and William A. Gertzog. 1982. Accommodation of a scientific conception: Toward a theory of conceptual change. *Science Education* 66(2): 211–227.

Putnam, Ralph T. 1987. Structuring and adjusting content for students: A study of live and simulated tutoring of addition. *American Educational Research Journal* 24(1): 13–48.

Putnam, Ralph T., Magdalene Lampert, and Penelope L. Peterson. 1990. "Alternative Perspectives on Knowing Mathematics in Elementary Schools." In *Review of Research in Education*, edited by Courtney B. Cazden, vol. 16, 57–150. Washington, DC: American Educational Research Association.

Reid, William. A. 1984. "Curricular Topics as Institutional Categories: Implications for Theory and Research in the History and Sociology of School Subjects." In *Defining the Curriculum: Histories and Ethnographies*, edited by Ivor F. Goodson and Stephen J. Ball, 67–75. London: Falmer.

Resnick, Lauren B. 1983. Mathematics and science learning: A new conception. *Science* 220(4596): 447–478.

Resnick, Lauren B. 1987. *Education and Learning to Think*. Washington, DC: National Academy Press.

Reynolds, John, and Murray Saunders. 1987. "Teacher Responses to Curriculum Policy: Beyond the 'Delivery' Metaphor." In *Exploring Teachers' Thinking*, edited by James Calderhead, 195–214. London: Cassell.

Rice, Joseph M. 1893. *The Public School System of the United States*. New York: Century.

Richardson, Virginia. 1990. Significant and worthwhile change in teaching practice. *Educational Researcher* 19(7): 10–18.

Rohrkemper, Mary, and Lyn Corno. 1988. Success and failure on classroom tasks: Adaptive learning and classroom teaching. *Elementary School Journal* 88(3): 297–312.

Rosenshine, Barak. 1970. Evaluation of instruction. *Review of Educational Research* 40(2): 279–301.

Rosenshine, Barak. 1976. "Classroom Instruction." In *The Psychology of Teaching Methods*. Seventy-Seventh Yearbook of the National Society for the Study of Education, edited by N. L. Gage, Part 1, 335–371. Chicago: University of Chicago Press.

Sanford, Julie P. 1987. Management of science classroom tasks and effects on students' learning opportunities. *Journal of Research in Science Teaching* 24(3): 249–265.

Scardamalia, Marlene, and Carl Bereiter. 1986. "Research on Written Composition." In *Handbook of Research on Teaching*. 3rd ed., edited by Merlin C. Wittrock, 778–803. New York: Macmillan.

Schalock, Del. 1979. "Research on Teacher Selection." In *Review of Research in Education*, edited by David C. Berliner, vol. 7, 364–417. Washington, DC: American Educational Research Association.

Schauber, Ellen, and Ellen Spolsky. 1986. *The Bounds of Interpretation: Linguistic Theory and Literary Text*. Stanford, CA: Stanford University Press.

Schoenfeld, Alan H. 1987. *Cognitive Science and Mathematics Education*. Hillsdale, NJ: Erlbaum.

Schoenfeld, Alan H. 1988. When good teaching leads to bad results: The disasters of "well-taught" mathematics courses. *Educational Psychologist* 23(2): 145–166.

Schubert, William H. 1986. *Curriculum: Perspective, Paradigm, and Possibility*. New York: Macmillan.

Searle, Dennis J. 1975. A study of the classroom language activity of five selected high school students. *Research in the Teaching of English* 9(3): 267–286.

Sears, Jesse B. 1921. The measurement of teaching efficiency. *Journal of Educational Research* 4(2): 82–96.

Seguel, Mary L. 1966. *The Curriculum Field: Its Formative Years*. New York: Teachers College Press.

Seguel, Mary L. 1978. "Conceptualizing Method: A History." Paper prepared for the Society for the Study of Curriculum History, Toronto.

Shulman, Lee S. 1974. The psychology of school subjects: A premature obituary? *Journal of Research in Science Teaching* 11(4): 319–339.

Shulman, Lee S. 1986a. "Paradigms and Research Programs in the Study of Teaching: A Contemporary Perspective." In *Handbook of Research on Teaching*. 3rd ed., edited by Merlin C. Wittrock, 3–36. New York: Macmillan.

Shulman, Lee S. 1986b. Those who understand: Knowledge growth in teaching. *Educational Researcher* 15(2): 4–14.

Shulman, Lee S. 1987. Knowledge and teaching: Foundations of the new reform. *Harvard Educational Review* 57(1): 1–22.

Smyth, John, ed. 1987. *Educating Teachers: Changing the Nature of Pedagogical Knowledge*. London: Falmer.

Squire, James R. 1988. "Studies of Textbooks: Are We Asking the Right Questions?" In *Contributing to Educational Change*, edited by Philip W. Jackson, 127–169. Berkeley, CA: McCutchan.

Stella, Frank. 1986. *Working Space*. Cambridge, MA: Harvard University Press.

Stigler, James W., and Ruth Baranes. 1988. "Culture and Mathematics Learning." In *Review of Research in Education*, edited by Ernest Z. Rothkopf, vol. 15, 253–306. Washington, DC: American Educational Research Association.

Stodolsky, Susan S. 1988. *The Subject Matters: Classroom Activity in Math and Social Studies*. Chicago: University of Chicago Press.

Stodolsky, Susan S. 1989. "Is Teaching Really by the Book?" In *From Socrates to Software: The Teacher as Text and the Text as Teacher*. Eighty-Ninth Yearbook of the National Society for the Study of Education, edited by Philip W. Jackson and Sophie Haroutunian Gordon, Part 1, 159–184. Chicago: University of Chicago Press.

Tobin, Kenneth, and James J. Gallagher. 1987. What happens in high school science classrooms? *Journal of Curriculum Studies* 19(6): 549–560.

Tyack, David B. 1974. *The One Best System: A History of American Urban Education*. Cambridge, MA: Harvard University Press.

Tyack, David B., and Elisabeth Hansot. 1980. From social movement to professional management: An inquiry into the changing character of leadership in public education. *American Journal of Education* 88(3): 291–319.

Tyler, Ralph W. 1949. *Basic Principles of Curriculum and Instruction*. Chicago: University of Chicago Press.

Walker, Decker F., and Jon Schaffarzick. 1974. Comparing curricula. *Review of Educational Research* 44(1): 83–111.

Wallen, Norman E., and Robert M. W. Travers. 1963. "Analysis and Investigation of Teaching Methods." In *Handbook of Research on Teaching*, edited by N. L. Gage, 448–505. Chicago: Rand McNally.

Weade, Regina. 1985. "Lesson Construction and Instructional Management: An Exploration of Social and Academic Content Demands Within Lessons." Paper presented at the annual meeting of the American Educational Research Association, Chicago.

Weade, Regina. 1987. Curriculum'n'instruction: The construction of meaning. *Theory into Practice* 26(1): 15–25.

Weade, Regina, and Carolyn M. Evertson. 1988. The construction of lessons in effective and less effective classrooms. *Teaching and Teacher Education* 4(3): 189–213.

White, Woodie T., Jr. 1982. The decline of the classroom and the Chicago study of education, 1909–1929. *American Journal of Education* 90(2): 144–174.

Wiebe, Robert H. 1969. The social functions of public education. *American Quarterly* 21(2, part 1): 147–164.

Willis, Paul E. 1981. *Learning to Labor: How Working Class Kids Get Working Class Jobs*. New York: Columbia University Press.

Wilson, Suzanne M., Lee S. Shulman, and Anna E. Richert. 1987. "'150 Different Ways' of Knowing: Representations of Knowledge in Teaching." In *Exploring Teachers' Thinking*, edited by J. Calderhead, 104–124. London: Cassell.

Wilson, Suzanne M., and Samuel S. Wineburg. 1988. Peering at American history through different lenses: The role of disciplinary perspective in teaching history. *Teachers College Record* 84(4): 525–539.

Woodring, Paul. 1975. "The Development of Teacher Education." In *Teacher Education*. Seventy-Fourth Yearbook of the National Society for the Study of Education, edited by Kevin Ryan, Part 2, 1–24. Chicago: University of Chicago Press.

Yinger, Robert J. 1982. "A Study of Teacher Planning." In *Focus on Teaching*, edited by Walter Doyle and Thomas L. Good, 239–259. Chicago: University of Chicago Press.

Zais, Robert S. 1976. *Curriculum: Principles and Foundations*. New York: Harper & Row.

Zumwalt, Karen K. 1982. "Research on Teaching: Policy Implications for Teacher Education." In *Policy Making in Education*. Eighty-First Yearbook of the National Society for the Study of Education, edited by Ann Lieberman and Milbrey W. McLaughlin, Part 1, 215–248. Chicago: University of Chicago Press.

Zumwalt, Karen K. 1988. "Are We Improving or Undermining Teaching?" In *Critical Issues in Curriculum*. Eighty-Seventh Yearbook of the National Society for the Study of Education, edited by Laurel N. Tanner, Part 1, 148–174. Chicago: University of Chicago Press.

Zumwalt, Karen K. 1989. "Beginning Professional Teachers: The Need for a Curricular Vision of Teaching." In *Knowledge Base for the Beginning Teacher*, edited by Maynard C. Reynolds, 173–184. Oxford, England: Pergamon.

19

COGNITION AND CURRICULUM

Carl Bereiter and Marlene Scardamalia

CENTRE FOR APPLIED COGNITIVE SCIENCE
ONTARIO INSTITUTE FOR STUDIES IN EDUCATION

The so-called "cognitive revolution" is much in evidence in education. It appears in both direct and indirect form. The direct form is educational research actually done by cognitive scientists. Glaser and Bassok (1989) review several strands of such research, which they see as becoming an increasingly integral part of mainstream cognitive science. But the cognitive revolution is also represented in the work of many educational researchers who are not explicitly doing cognitive science. Their work reflects more broadly the increasing interest of educators in finding out what is going on in the minds of students and teachers and using such knowledge to shape curriculum and instruction. No one could claim this is a new interest. Educational decisions always involve, at least implicitly, notions about what goes on in the mind. What is new is the explicitness of the interest and the effort to give mentalistic notions an empirical and scientific basis.

By way of illustration, we may cite three areas in which cognitive concerns have come to prominence. Each of these will be treated in more detail later. At present, the point we want to bring out in each case is how an educational concern with cognitive processes or outcomes inevitably forces a confrontation with more basic theoretical issues of cognition.

1. *Conceptual change*. Science education journals now burgeon with studies of student misconceptions and experimental efforts to change them (a representative selection is published in West and Pines 1985). Around 1980, independent groups of cognitive scientists and science educators began publishing findings that a large proportion of university students, including ones who had studied physics, responded to questions about falling or propelled objects in a way that was more consistent with medieval than Newtonian physics (Champagne, Klopfer, and Anderson 1980; McCloskey, Caramazza, and Green 1980; Viennot 1979). Struck by evidence of the ineffectuality of conventional science instruction, particularly by the indications that science learning can be layered on top of naive beliefs without significantly affecting them, science educators have begun developing curriculum designs in which the changing of students' conceptions becomes a central goal (e.g., Ben-Zvi, Eylon, and Silberstein 1986). A problem arises, however, as to what constitutes a concept and, by extension, a misconception. We have seen some (mercifully, unpublished) studies in which every multiple-choice test response erroneously selected by a certain number of students was classed as a misconception. The problem is more than definitional. A growing body of research supports the proposition that all concepts are grounded in implicit theories (Murphy and Medin 1985). If this is true, then dealing effectively with students' misconceptions is likely always to require digging beyond the manifest errors to the underlying system of beliefs that gives rise to them. Since such belief systems are almost always tacit—thus, not directly reportable by the student—identifying them entails developing and testing a theory about them, which is a task that puts the researcher squarely in the mainstream of cognitive science research.

2. *Process-tracing research*. Having people think aloud as a way of gaining access to what is going on in their minds came to prominence in Newell and Simon's influential study of problem solving (1972). Educational researchers had occasionally made use of the technique earlier, however (e.g., Bloom and Broder 1950). Whereas psychologists have mainly used the technique as a first stage in creating models or simulations of cognitive processes, educational researchers have been interested in using the technique comparatively. The result has been to identify many apparent differences in the processes that lie be-

hind more obvious differences in achievement (Garner 1987). The use of thinking-aloud protocols has caused much concern among educational researchers, however. There is concern that it gives only a partial or distorted picture of what is going on in the mind, and that the task of thinking aloud may itself alter what is going on (Black, Galambos, and Reiser 1984; Cooper and Holzman 1983). These concerns are legitimate and perhaps unresolvable so long as one is obliged to use thinking-aloud protocols descriptively, as literal records of mental activity. In the context of cognitive science research, however, these protocols play a different and less problematic role. They are simply data (Ericsson and Simon 1980), and like any other kind of data their interpretation is theory-bound (J. R. Anderson 1987a). One does not try to read nature from them directly but rather from theories that purport to account for them. It is the validity of the whole theory that is at issue rather than the validity of pictures suggested by the protocol material; one of the ways a theory may be tested, however, is by making predictions from it about protocol data. It would seem that process-tracing research as a whole is constrained to a descriptive level that is either superficial or dangerously speculative, unless it remains in close contact with more theoretically grounded cognitive research.

3. *Research on expertise*. Research aimed at understanding the bases of expert performance has been an important part of cognitive science for the past two decades. Comparisons of experts and novices have begun increasingly to appear in such school-related areas as reading (Garner and Reis 1981), writing (Flower and Hayes 1980), science problem solving (Chi, Feltovich, and Glaser 1981), and teaching (Berliner 1986). As Ericsson and Smith (1991) note, however, the acquisition of expertise is its least understood aspect. It seems that this may be a matter in which applied and theoretical research may proceed hand-in-hand. For people concerned with elementary and secondary education, educating for expertise presents the formidable question of what kind of early experience will be most conducive to expertise later in life. Since an empirical answer to that question will be a long time in coming, predictions will have to be based on conjecture. Good conjectures will require good theory, but the development of good theory in this area is likely to require collaborative efforts from several basic sciences as well as from educational studies.

These examples point to a conclusion that will take on added weight as the chapter proceeds. Educators cannot safely appropriate the tools and findings of cognitive research while ignoring the theoretical questions that lie behind them. This is not to say that present-day cognitive science has answers to those questions or even that it is on the right track. It is to say, however, that now that there is a vigorous science devoted to understanding the mind, the stakes have gone up for playing at the cognitive table.

WHAT IS COGNITIVE SCIENCE?

Briefly put, cognitive science is the scientific study of the mind. Although cognitive science includes people from a wide range of sciences and disciplines, this short definition serves to sort out those who pursue cognitive science from others who, in philosophy and the humanities, may study the mind but from nonscientific perspectives, or who, in the behavioral or biological sciences, may pursue related kinds of scientific study but in ways that exclude concepts of mind (e.g., behaviorists, many economists and neuroscientists). We will not dwell on what "scientific" means in this definition, because, of course, it means different things to different researchers. It is a sufficiently challenging idea that the mind can be studied scientifically at all, in any of the ordinary senses of scientific. Behaviorists, as is well known, deny this; it is also denied by many people who take a humanistic, holistic, or hermeneutic view of cognition (Erickson 1986). Despite these widespread doubts, the "cognitive revolution" has been a peaceful one. It seems that a great many behavioral scientists, behaviorists included, were quite ready to come over to take up cognitive research as soon as they could be convinced that it was possible to do some kind of decent science involving mental phenomena.

The Mental Level of Description

Although (or perhaps because) mental terms pervade ordinary language, it has been a significant challenge to clarify what it means to formulate scientific theory at a mental level of description (Dennett 1978, 1987; Pylyshyn 1984). Perhaps the easiest way to grasp what a mental level of description means is to start by working with a nonhuman example. Consider a spelling checker, of the kind often found in word processing software. (For readers who find this example unpromising, either because of unfamiliarity with spelling checkers or because of an aversion to machine analogies, a livelier example, involving communication in vervet monkeys, is elaborated by Dennett [1983].) You could describe what it does at a behavioral level, in terms of what appears on the computer screen. For instance, the spelling checker announces that it does not recognize a certain word and presents a list of alternatives. You also know that behind this behavior is a program that controls the hardware in such a way as to produce the behavior. Describing the program at that level would correspond to describing human behavior at a neural level. But if you use a spelling checker often enough, you are likely to wonder and form hypotheses about how it selects the list of words it presents as alternatives. You are, in effect, speculating about how the program "thinks." If you formulate your hypotheses clearly enough, you may be able to test them—for instance, by inserting words that you predict will "fool" the spelling checker in a certain way. You could now claim to be doing cognitive science, with the spelling checker as a subject. You have created a model of the spelling checker's "mind" and refine it by testing it against actual behavior.

Your model of the spelling checker's "mind" is likely to consist of rules that you believe the program follows. This is much different from describing the machine-level code, about which you may have no idea whatever. But is it any different from a detailed description of input-output behavior, similar to the descriptions a behaviorist would give of a trained pigeon? There is this difference: Your description consists of rules that you believe are actually represented somehow in the program. You could be wrong. The rules you have devised may simply account for what you have observed and may be quite different from the rules actually embodied in the program, but the purpose of your experimenting is to reduce such discrepancies. The crucial difference between cognitivists and behaviorists turns out to be quite subtle. The issue is whether the rules that describe the behavior of a subject are represented within the subject. To the behaviorist this is a pointless or unanswerable question. To the cognitivist the distinction is critical (Fodor 1975).

One important qualification to the spelling checker analogy must be registered. Conceiving of the spelling checker's mind as a system of rules is a good idea because that is probably how the people who created the spelling checker conceived of it. We cannot be so confident about the human mind. Theories formulated as systems of rules (often taking the technical form of production systems), have predominated in cognitive science (J. R. Anderson 1983; Klahr, Langley, and Neches 1987). They are also the foundation of expert systems and intelligent tutoring systems (e.g., Clancey 1987). But, as we will discuss in the final section of this chapter, rule based or symbolic models of human cognition are being seriously challenged and alternatives are emerging.

Thus, cognitive science is not committed to the belief that rules or anything else in particular constitute the mind. Such issues are open. The beliefs cognitive scientists do seem to share are that there is a mental level of description at which useful statements can be made, that there are important problems to be solved at that level, and that advances on those problems can be made scientifically (Pylyshyn 1984). The relevance of cognitive science to education depends on the fact that many of those mental-level problems can be recognized as important to education as well.

A Thumbnail History

Anglophobes may need to be reminded that continental European psychology has been mainly cognitive in its orientation right along. Piaget, in his *Psychology of Intelligence* (1966), gives a nice historical sketch of the psychological tradition leading up to his own work, with nary a mention of Watson or Skinner, and Thorndike introduced only as a forerunner of Clarapede, whom he credits with relegating trial-and-error learning to its proper place on the margins of intelligence (94–95). Piaget does not mention Freud either (in this context), although Freud must also be counted a cognitivist, because his theorizing was at the mental, as distinct from the neurological or behavioral, level.

Traditional European cognitive psychology remained close to philosophy, however, and tended to produce what one European colleague has aptly termed "verbal theories." Such theories differ from one another more in how they talk about things than in what they claim to be true, and thus they have lacked the falsifiability necessary for progressive science (Lakatos 1970). In *Insights and Illusions of Philosophy*, Piaget (1971) gives a devastating, though sympathetic, critique of this philosophizing tradition, from which his own theoretical and empirical work marked an important departure.

The beginning of modern cognitive science is sometimes given the precise date of 1956 (Gardner 1985). That was the year of a symposium at which Newell and Simon reported on their *Logic Theorist*, the first artificial intelligence endeavor that could be seriously claimed to simulate a human level of intelligence (Newell, Shaw, and Simon 1958); Chomsky introduced transformational grammar (Chomsky 1957); and Miller (1956) introduced the powerful idea that human cognition is constrained by a limited short-term memory. Also appearing in that year was Bruner, Goodnow, and Austin's *A Study of Thinking* (1956), which gave impetus to the experimental study of cognitive strategies. Although differing in practically everything else, these four contributions shared the at-that-time unusual characteristic that their subject matter was mental events. Moreover, they departed from the verbal theorizing that had typified cognitive psychology in the past. Instead, they formulated explanations in terms of explicit rules. This gave their work a certain scientific boldness. They advanced daring hypotheses that were vulnerable to evidence. Thus, they served as proofs by example that the mind could be studied scientifically.

Over the next two decades, cognitive research grew steadily, not only in quantity but also in the level of problems it tackled. Cognitive research has tended to start with "toy" problems—problems that have a formal resemblance to the problems human intelligence typically struggles with but that are freer of real-world complications. By the 1970s, however, basic cognitive science had begun to move toward problems on the order of those faced by the normal human learner. The understanding of natural discourse, for instance, became a major focus both in artificial intelligence and in experimental cognitive research (Just and Carpenter 1977; Schank and Abelson 1977).

Something that became strikingly clear as cognitive researchers shifted from toy problems to more realistic problems was the tremendous amount of knowledge required to deal with the latter. Common sense might say, "Of course," but the quantity and diversity of knowledge that proved necessary in order for an artificial system to handle even the most mundane of real-life tasks intelligently was well beyond anything that had previously been suggested in the educational literature. The curriculum implications of this expanded conception of the role of knowledge will be discussed in a later section. Historically, however, it might be said to be the idea that changed the landscape of instructional research.

The cognitive educational research that began to gain momentum in the early 1970s was mainly focused on students' thought processes. It is summarized by Wittrock (1986a), whose own research (e.g., "Learning as a Generative Process," 1974) was seminal. The main practical outcome of this work has been an emphasis on the teaching of cognitive strategies, particularly strategies for comprehension and learning (Pressley and Levin 1983; Weinstein and Mayer 1986). An emerging emphasis on knowledge became evident, however, with the appearance of *Schooling and the Acquisition of Knowledge* (R. C. Anderson, Spiro, and Montague 1977). In the study of reading, evidence began to accumulate suggesting that the key to reading comprehension does not lie in readers' thought processes, but rather in their background knowledge, represented in "schemata" that are activated by the text being read (R. C. Anderson 1978). Today most cognitive instructional researchers would probably acknowledge the importance of both cognitive strategies or skills and background knowledge. Many, however, would argue for the primacy of knowledge, rejecting the idea that cognitive skills are general capacities that generate learning wherever they are applied, claiming instead that such skills themselves are developed within domains where the learner has ample knowledge and are only later extended to other domains (Glaser 1984). As we shall see in later sections of this chapter, knowledge has become a pervasive theme, playing a part in the consideration of nearly every cognitive issue. It is also, of course, a theme that links cognitive science to the traditional concerns of curriculum research.

Problems in Understanding What Cognitive Science Is About

The cognitive revolution has taken place not only without bloodshed but also without a manifesto. The absence of the militant self-justification that has characterized many other contemporary movements in the human sciences has, however, made it difficult for outsiders to gain a clear grasp of what cognitive science is. In this section we will address three issues in understanding the nature of cognitive science that have particular relevance to its educational applications: computers, culture, and emotion.

The Role of Computers in Cognitive Science. Because computers play a large role in cognitive science and are often used to simulate cognitive processes, it is easy to fall into the misconception that cognitive scientists believe that the computer is an adequate model of the mind. Taken literally, such a statement does not correspond to any known belief. Computer modeling is common in many different kinds of science and technology. Using a computer to model cognition does not imply a belief that computers are similar to human minds, any more than using a computer to model weather patterns implies a belief that computers are similar to air masses. It is the model, not the medium in which it is represented, that is supposed to have a correspondence to the real thing. This may seem obvious, but once it is acknowledged, it should then be clear that questions such as "Can computers really think?" although perhaps interesting in their own right, have no particular relevance to the use of computers in cognitive science. Pylyshyn (1984) distinguishes between "computation," which he argues that the mind literally does, and "computers," which are able to simulate cognition because they also carry out computation, although not necessarily in any comparable way.

A word should be added about educational computing. Some of it has a relation to cognitive science, but most of it does not. In the section on "Educational Envisionments" we discuss developments in educational computing that do relate closely to cognitive research.

Does Cognitive Science Ignore Culture? It is sometimes charged that focusing on the mental level of description represents a kind of tunnel vision that makes cognitive science blind to culture, history, economics, the environment, and all those other forces that shape our lives (Engeström 1987; Sampson 1989). Piaget, who was often criticized along these lines, responded: "As for the role of culture in the education of the individual, one would have to be very naive not to take it into consideration, but the psychological problem is to establish how culture acts" (Piaget 1980, 281). What we take Piaget to be saying is that the great cultural forces, if they are to have an effect on human behavior, must somehow be represented at the mental level, in individual minds.

In the atheoretical, functionalist tradition (Hilgard and Bower 1974, chapter 9) that characterizes much of educational research, there is no problem in throwing cognitive, social, and any other sorts of variables together in the same functional expression. This works fine if one's object is to predict one set of variables from the others (Mosenthal 1983) or perhaps just to talk about them. Cognitive scientists, however, generally share the commitment of natural scientists to press beyond the identification of causal factors toward process theories (Cassirer 1950, chapter 10), theories that try to explain how things work. Process explanations that connect the individual and the social planes are exceedingly difficult and close to nonexistent (see Harré 1984; Lumsden and Wilson 1981). In the final section of this chapter we note developments within cognitive science that are attempting to move in this direction.

Cognition and Emotion. Everyone knows that emotions influence thoughts, just as thoughts influence emotions. It therefore seems wrong to have cognitive theories that do not deal with emotions. Yet, as Iran-Nejad, Clore, and Vondruska (1984) document, that is the norm. It is not that cognitive science as a whole ignores emotion. Iran-Nejad's own work, which relates to the role of affect in school learning, is a counterexample, but there are many others. There is a journal called *Cognition and Emotion*, and there are a number of strong research programs, such as those reported in a volume edited by Plutchik and Kellerman (1980). But the grand architectural efforts at cognitive theory, such as those of John Anderson (1983), Holland et al. (1986), and Laird, Newell, and Rosenbloom (1987) do tend almost totally to ignore emotion.

We could speculate on why general theories of cognition tend to ignore emotion. It may have much to do with their reliance on rules as a representational form, rules perhaps being inappropriate for representing affective processes (see, however, Colby 1981). If this is true, we may expect things to change with the advance of alternatives to rule-based models, some of which are discussed in the final section of this chapter. Perhaps the most that can be claimed at present is this: Cognitive scientists recognize the challenge of explaining the relationship between cognition and emotion, some of them are addressing it, and hardly anyone outside cognitive science is doing so. The challenge is to go beyond empirical generalizations that say, for instance, that an increase in anxiety has such-and-such effect on cognition or that such-and-such beliefs cause people to feel depressed, and to explicate the processes that mediate such effects. The test, and practical value, of such a theory would be that it could predict cognitive-emotional effects beyond those that we already know.

The Scope of Cognitive Science

The preceding points have argued against several limiting conceptions of what cognitive science is about. What, then, is cognitive science about? As far as we can judge, there are no phenomena of human behavior categorically outside the scope of cognitive science. The only recognizable boundary, and it is a fuzzy one, is the boundary determined by a mental level of description, variously conceived, and by constraints of the scientific enterprise, which are also variously conceived.

KEY IDEAS RELEVANT TO CURRICULUM PROBLEMS

One effect of the cognitive revolution has been to restore the scientific status of ordinary mentalistic terms like "believe," "think," and "desire." Such terms form the vocabulary of "folk psychology"—the psychology according to which most of us (behaviorists included) conduct our daily course through the social world (Stich 1983). This is also the psychology on which teaching is ordinarily based—what Carroll (1976) has called, without any intended disparagement, "naive learning theory." Consequently, as Carroll points out, many of the educational implications of cognitive science simply reaffirm what has long been common belief among educators—the importance of students' own desires and intentions, for instance, and the importance of learning with understanding. Contemporary cognitive science should not be looked to for radical new ways of thinking about curriculum issues but rather for clarifying concepts and for insight into the workings of factors whose importance is already recognized.

The ideas to be discussed in this section are ones that applied cognitive scientists have found important in linking cognitive research to educational issues. Essentially the same set of key ideas is used, for instance, by Glaser, Lesgold, and Lajoie (1987) in discussing implications of cognitive science for achievement testing. Absent from the present discussion are a number of topics that are mainly relevant to classroom processes rather than to curriculum issues—topics such as motivation, student and teacher thought processes, and classroom discourse. Cognitive research has made contributions to all of these, which are treated in appropriate chapters of the *Handbook of Research on Teaching* (Wittrock 1986b). It should also be noted that the ideas discussed here are at least one level of abstraction removed from the core theoretical ideas of cognitive science. As entry points to the theoretical literature, we recommend either philosophical treatments, such as Dennett (1978, 1987), or Howard Gardner's historical interpretation, *The Mind's New Science* (1985).

The Centrality of Knowledge

Common sense recognizes both reason and knowledge as contributors to the success of human actions. Cognitive research has by no means repudiated the role of reason, as subsequent items in this "Key Ideas" section will show, but, as we indicated in the preceding discussion, it has greatly shifted the balance in favor of the role of knowledge. Three major strands of research converge in this effect: research on discourse comprehension, research on expert-novice differences, and artificial intelligence research.

1. Discourse Comprehension: The Role of Schemata. Childhood memory: listening to the Lone Ranger on radio, hearing talk of the "stage" leaving town with passengers and a shipment of gold on board, the clatter of the horse-drawn "stage" in motion, then the bandits shouting for the passengers to get down from it—all the while picturing the "stage" as a platform mounted on wheels. This is an example of schema-based comprehension (Rumelhart and Ortony 1977). Two competing schemata were evoked by the Lone Ranger episodes—one a *stage* schema, representing a platform on which actors strut, the other a *horse-drawn vehicle* schema, with the traditional horse-and-buggy as its prototypic representation. "The process of understanding discourse," said Rumelhart (1980, 47), "is the process of finding a configuration of schemata that offers an adequate account of the passage in question." In this case the configuration arrived at was a modification of the *stage* schema to incorporate essential elements of the *horse-drawn vehicle* schema—hence, a stage on wheels, with horses pulling it. Although the result produced rather bizarre imagery, it was adequate for understanding and experiencing the drama of the radio show. It was certainly better than would have been achieved by a child who had no knowledge of stages or horse-drawn buggies.

Commonsense or "folk" psychology (Stich 1983) would treat this as an instance of reasoning and problem solving in the service of comprehension. That is also how Thorndike (1917) treated comprehension in his classic paper on reading. But was there actually any effort to figure out what "stage" referred to? Schema-directed processes can be, and most often are, unconscious and automatic. Richard Anderson et al. (1977) found that most readers interpret the following passage as being about a convict planning a prison escape:

> Rocky slowly got up from the mat, planning his escape. He hesitated a moment and thought. Things were not going well. What bothered him most was being held, especially since the charge against him had been weak. He considered his present situation. The lock that held him was strong but he thought he could break it. He knew, however, that his timing would have to be perfect. Rocky was aware that it was because of his early roughness that he had been penalized so severely—much too severely from his point of view. The situation was becoming frustrating; the pressure had been grinding on him for too long. He was being ridden unmercifully. Rocky was getting angry now. He felt he was ready to make his move. He knew that his success or failure would depend on what he did in the next few seconds. (372)

When it was presented to students in a weight-lifting class, however, most of them interpreted it as being about a wrestler trying to break a hold. Regardless of how people interpreted the passage, fewer than 20 percent of them reported being aware of another possible interpretation while reading. It seems that the opening lines automatically evoke a readily available schema, which continues to direct comprehension unless some serious mismatch is perceived.

Background knowledge, in the form of hierarchically structured schemata, does more than provide meanings. Richard Anderson (1978) reviews evidence that such knowledge affects how new information is encoded or registered, by determining what elements are attended to as significant, that it affects remembering, by providing plans used in searching memory, and that it provides a basis for inferential elaboration and gap-filling. (See also Voss 1984, for another line of research that demonstrates profound effects of prior knowledge on the kind of new knowledge constructed from texts.)

2. Expertise as Knowledge. The studies of chess experts by deGroot (1965) and Chase and Simon (1973) have had a resounding effect on cognitive scientists' approach to human abilities. Their conclusions were that chess grand masters do not think more deeply or cleverly than lesser players, consider more possibilities, or plan further ahead. Instead, they are distinguished by a remarkable ability to take in and remember chessboard configurations at a glance. This ability, the studies showed, could not be attributed to generally superior perception or memory because it held only for meaningful arrangements of chess pieces. In remembering random arrangements, the experts were no better than lesser players. Performance on the memory tasks was better accounted for by attributing to the grand masters a repertoire of learned patterns running into the tens of thousands. Subsequent research has required some moderation of the original findings, but on the whole it has further emphasized the importance of stored knowledge, especially in distinguishing among players at an advanced level (Charness 1991). The advantage due to a repertoire of stored patterns has been substantiated not only in chess but in other fields, such as team sports (Allard and Burnett 1985) and electronics (Egan and Schwartz 1979).

Chess-playing computers, the best of which now compete at master levels, offer a clue as to why stored knowledge plays such a dominant role in human expertise. The currently most powerful chess automata do not emulate human chess masters. Instead, they use brute-force reasoning, considering more possibilities and searching farther ahead than human players do in order to discover the best move. Computers can do this flawlessly, and powerful ones can do it fast enough to keep up with the regulation pace of tournament play. Human beings, however, as John Anderson (1985) notes, are quite poor at extended chains of reasoning, whereas they are very good (in comparison to present-day machines) at pattern recognition. Thus, Anderson speculates, becoming an expert involves shifting the burden of performance from processes we are poorly equipped for to processes that we are well equipped for. This means, in general, shifting the burden on to stored knowledge and away from inferential reasoning. (Apropos of the earlier remarks about whether cognitive scientists assume a close resemblance between mind and computer, note that this insight into human intelligence derives from well-recognized differences between mind and computer.) A large variety of expert-novice comparisons (Chi, Glaser, and Farr 1988) can be summarized by this simple but paradoxical formula: Novices think; experts know. (See the section on "Education for Expertise" later in this chapter, however, for a discussion of the limitations of this formula.)

3. Lessons Learned from Intelligent Systems. The lore of computerized discourse understanding is full of examples of bizarre misunderstandings resulting from the system designer's failure to anticipate all of the knowledge required for comprehension. Given the sentence, "The doorbell rang. It was Constable Murphy," a discourse understanding system equipped with rules for interpreting anaphoric references but devoid of world knowledge would infer that the doorbell was Constable Murphy. Even a moderately knowledgeable system would know enough to avoid that error, but it might well lack the complex and subtle knowledge required to infer that Constable Murphy rang the doorbell, that someone probably went to the door, and that that person was on one side of the door and Constable Murphy was on the other. As became apparent to designers of discourse understanding systems, huge amounts of world knowledge are required to achieve even the most pedestrian level of text comprehension. Even more is required for text composition (Black 1982).

Expert systems attempt to reproduce the competence of expert medical diagnosticians, repair technicians, and the like. A typical system consists of a thinking part, the inference engine, and a knowledge base, usually a set of if-then rules. Folk psychology would situate much of the expertise in the inference engine, for it is what does the Sherlock Holmesian work. But expert system developers have found they get best results by having a relatively simple inference engine—one might say "simple minded"—and putting all the expertise into the knowledge base (Davis 1984).

A whole technology of "knowledge engineering" has evolved for observing and questioning experts so as to dig out the information to put into the expert system's knowledge base. The reason such a technology is needed is that experts generally are not able to state directly the knowledge that guides their practice, and it is not to be found in textbooks either. Lying behind the formal knowledge that gets put into textbooks is, evidently, a vast sea of expert knowledge, at least some of which can be formulated into explicit statements, although it normally is not. Dreyfus and Dreyfus (1986) have emphasized the limitations of the rule-like knowledge that goes into expert systems, and how it pales before the tacit knowledge of the human expert. But from a curriculum standpoint, it may be equally important to heed Minsky's remarks (1984) about how remarkably well artificial systems have been able to do with the superficial knowledge built into them. Knowledge that can be built into an expert system is, by its nature, teachable. Even though it may represent only one part of expert competence, it is a demonstrably significant part, and one that is not usually taught. Knowledge engineering thus has potential as a technology for use in curriculum development.

Curriculum Implications. An often repeated saw is that instead of filling students' heads with information, we should teach them the skills of finding information when they need it. The three lines of research just discussed all suggest that this notion is somewhat worse than plain wrong. It implies a choice that does not actually exist. Any conceivable design for an effective knowledge-finding system would have to incorporate a rich fund of knowledge for the system to use in directing its search. In human terms, it takes knowledge to get knowledge, even to know what it is that one needs to know. A system that was all process, that had no knowledge to build on, could never understand anything.

One educator who has taken seriously the need for knowledge in order to get knowledge is E. D. Hirsch. His listing, in *Cultural Literacy* (1987), of hundreds of discrete items of information that he says students ought to acquire, has caused considerable outrage among educationists (e.g., Estes, Gutman, and Estes 1989). From a cognitive psychologist's standpoint, however, it is not the value of such knowledge that is questionable so much as its teachability. Drawing on research on text comprehension, Hirsch makes a convincing argument for the value of even the most superficial knowledge of culturally important names and events. Although of little value in its own right, it makes it possible to comprehend ordinary texts sufficiently to build knowledge that is valuable. However, Hirsch's proposal brings us face to face with an enormous unsolved problem. Evidence has been available for years about the mind's poor ability to retain isolated items of information and the need for meaningful connections in order to preserve information in memory (Tyler 1930; Ausubel 1963). Recent research on mnemonic devices, such as the Key Word method (Pressley, Levin, and Delaney 1982), has identified techniques that can be helpful for situations that do require rote memorization (for instance, memorizing the counting numbers in a foreign language), but they do not quite answer to the need for cultural literacy. The problem is how to build coherent, meaningful knowledge when one does not already possess a suitable schema for assimilating it (Bereiter 1990). A few leads toward solving this problem are discussed in subsequent sections on "Metacognition" and "Learning as Problem Solving."

Mental Models, Formal Knowledge, and Skill

It is perhaps obvious to everyone that knowledge in the head is different from formal knowledge (as represented in textbooks, handbooks, and the like), but the differences have not been articulated well enough to be helpful in designing instruction or in restructuring textbooks to make them more compatible with what gets represented in the mind. Philosophical analyses suggest that knowledge in the head is more subjective, whereas textbook knowledge is more readily treated as an object (Popper 1972); that it is more concerned with "knowing how" than with "knowing that" (Ryle 1949); and that it contains much that is tacit or implicit (Polanyi 1964). Such analyses, however, tend to make knowledge in the head appear mysterious and inaccessible to direct treatment, thus perhaps encouraging the essentially anti-intellectual belief that "real" knowledge must inevitably be acquired through means other than the formal curriculum.

Recent research and theorizing in cognitive science offer, on the one hand, more substantive ideas about how personal knowledge differs from formal knowledge, and on the other, a coherent account of how formal knowledge can play a part in the development of know-how.

Mental Models. Two important books of the same name, *Mental Models*, appeared in the same year (Gentner and Stevens 1983; Johnson-Laird 1983). Johnson-Laird's particular target is the idea implicit in most psychologizing, that there is a little logician in the head who generates inferences according to a set of rules. Johnson-Laird proposes that this is not how human reasoning works at all. Instead, people create models of situations and use those models to generate possible outcomes. He shows, through simulation experiments, how models account for both the general logicality of human thinking and also the deviations from it that are predictable on certain kinds of problems. A models theory makes it obvious, for instance, why people usually reason more accurately about familiar situations: They are better able to construct mental models that capture critical structural features of those situations.

The Gentner and Stevens (1983) volume contains contributions from investigators more concerned with people's knowledge of substantive domains. Physics provides the most instructive domain, because formal knowledge can often be precisely described by sets of equations. Expert physicists, of course, have such formal knowledge, but for practical reasons it cannot be the knowledge that guides most of their thinking. In order to think on their feet, as it were, when working in the laboratory or engaging in discussions with colleagues, they need models that can be run mentally, at reasonable speed, and that apply more directly to concrete situations than do the formalisms of their discipline. Protocol studies of live physicists, as well as computer simulations, suggest that physicists' informal thinking is carried out with models that are consistent with the formal models, but that differ from them in fundamental ways (Bobrow 1985). The informal models are causal and dynamic, whereas the formal models represent equilibrium states. The informal models are only weakly quantified, involving conditions of increase, decrease, or no change, rather than specific quantities. The informal models incorporate pragmatic and concrete knowledge (e.g., under sufficient pressure a valve will leak) missing from the idealized formal models.

Although mental models presumably develop informally, it does not follow that formal education could not contribute to their development. Larkin et al. (1980) found that naive physics students represented textbook problems in ways that corresponded to their roles in everyday life rather than to the relevant physical principles, thus making it difficult for them to apply their formal knowledge. Larkin (1985) criticizes science textbooks for reinforcing students' naive models and failing to show how situations can be modeled in ways that facilitate the applications of formal principles.

A growing research literature documents the kinds of naive mental models that students bring to school with them—naive in the sense that they are developed through everyday experience and are little influenced by formal knowledge. This research, as it relates to science curriculum issues, is discussed in Chapter 28, "Science and Technology," in this *Handbook*. Here we will deal more generally with the issue of naive models as they relate to formal knowledge. Investigators of children's cosmographies find that children's early models reflect, as might be expected, the phenomenal world: flat earth, sun and moon as medium-sized objects passing over it, stars as tiny objects in the background. Under the impact of formal instruction, naive models are revised but not abandoned. Children may adopt a heliocentric model of the solar system, yet still believe stars are tiny, and they may devise wondrous models to account for people's not falling off a spherical earth (Nussbaum 1979; Vosniadou and Brewer 1987). Perhaps the most ingenious model has people in the northern hemisphere living on the outer surface of the globe while people in the southern hemisphere are safely ensconced inside it.

A currently unsettled question is the extent to which naive models are theorylike (Vosniadou and Brewer 1987). Are the mental models people employ stable structures in memory or are they constructed ad hoc in response to problems? Various answers are conceivable, such as that some are stable and some ad hoc, or that models are created ad hoc but under constraints imposed by stable beliefs. The question is of educational consequence. If naive models are theorylike in their stability and coherence, then changing them may involve something like a Kuhnian paradigm shift (Carey 1985). If they are more transitory but are constrained by stable beliefs, then identifying and changing those constraining beliefs might be the educational focus.

From Formal to Procedural Knowledge. John Anderson (1982, 1987b) has produced a workable theory of how what he calls "declarative" knowledge gets translated into "procedural" knowledge or skill. In the initial stage of skill learning, declarative knowledge provides goals. The eggplant recipe says "Sauté until nicely browned." This is a goal that can be pursued directly, provided one knows how to sauté. If not, more declarative knowledge is required. A cookbook section on sautéing says, among other things, "Agitate the pan constantly," with no further advice on how this is to be accomplished. Achieving the goal of a constantly agitated pan may therefore require problem solving—trial and error, hypothesis testing, and so on. Perplexed, one may decide to substitute the goal of turning the food over frequently, a more readily achieved goal that, according to one's understanding of cookery, may be judged to have the same function as agitating the pan. In this way, additional declarative knowledge of a more general sort is brought to bear on the establishment of goals. The point is that declarative knowledge, whatever its nature, is not translated directly into actions but is translated into goals, which are then pursued using available procedures or new procedures devised through problem solving. Progress from this early "cognitive" or problem-solving stage to the smooth and automatic functioning of a well-learned skill usually involves the dropping out of steps that involve declarative knowledge. Such knowledge becomes implicit in the procedures themselves, and the declarative knowledge itself may even be forgotten (as physicians, for instance, may discover if they relocate in midcareer and have to take medical qualifying examinations over again). Since declarative knowledge no longer plays an active role, skilled practitioners may tend to discount its importance, overlooking its part in the initial construction of procedures.

Perspective on the Role of Formal Knowledge. Although formal knowledge, of the kinds that can be presented in textbooks or lectures, has been a mainstay of education, it has been viewed with misgivings by educational thinkers from Plato to Whitehead. By identifying mental models and procedural knowledge as the really functional forms, cognitive research might be seen to fall in with the many other criticisms of formalism that continue to occur in discussions of curriculum. The question of how expertlike mental models can be fostered in students will be discussed in a later section on "Education for Expertise." At this point, we want merely to emphasize that the pursuit of mental models does not imply a rejection of formal knowledge.

In contrast to Whitehead (1929), who was concerned that students acquired formal knowledge without a sense of how to use it, John Anderson (1987b) claims that a virtue of formal knowledge is precisely that it can be learned and retained without having to know what it will be used for. Expert mental models tend to be fully consistent with the experts' formal knowledge, unlike naive mental models. Resnick (1987a), speaking with reference to mathematics learning, suggests that growth in understanding requires the continual transformation of formal knowledge into intuitive understanding in order that it may support the further growth of formal knowledge. How that might be accomplished raises issues of metacognition, to which we now turn.

Metacognition

The easily recognized parts of a historian's knowledge are knowledge of content—facts and ideas—and knowledge of methods of historical inquiry. There is, however, a whole other layer of knowledge that competent historians would be expected to have. This layer includes knowledge of the point and value of studying history and of their personal interests and goals as historians. It includes self-assessments of strengths and weaknesses, awareness of what areas they know well or poorly, and an awareness of their own questions, perplexities, hunches, and doubts. It also includes ways of managing themselves as historians—styles of work, ways of coping with flagging attention or overload of data, ways of getting around conceptual roadblocks and of thinking through questions, ways of orienting themselves to an unfamiliar body of material. None of this quite counts as knowledge of history. It is a kind of second-order or *meta*knowledge. Much of it is actually self-knowledge, but self-knowledge closely related to knowledge of history. Although having this kind of knowledge does not make one a historian, it is hard to imagine being a competent historian without it. Yet this kind of knowledge is seldom touched on in curricula.

The layer of knowledge we have been describing has of late been given the name "metacognitive" (Flavell 1979). Studies motivated by the idea of metacognition have spread into many different areas of interest, so that it has become difficult to say what the boundaries of the concept are (Brown et al. 1983). Indeed, to speak of teaching or fostering metacognition, as educators sometimes do, is hopelessly vague. Some more specific description is invariably required. Nevertheless, we believe the term "metacognition" remains useful for referring to a very broad class of knowledge and skills that has suffered neglect in educational practice.

One kind of metacognitive research that has already begun to have an impact on practice is that concerned with self-regulatory strategies for reading, writing, memorizing, and mathematics problem solving (Pressley and Levin 1983; Garner 1987; Scardamalia, Bereiter, and Steinbach 1984; Schoenfeld 1985). Generally, these efforts involve taking strategies that have been identified in able performers (an application of expert-novice comparisons) and formulating them as principles that can be taught through some combination of explaining, modeling, and coaching. Recently attention has shifted from demonstrating the efficacy of strategy instruction to investigating its shortcomings. Students may learn self-regulatory procedures but not know when or for what purpose to apply them (Garner 1990). There seems to be some confusion in the educational literature, embodied in the expression, "learning when to apply strategies." Strategies just are conditional rules or systems of such rules. If students have not learned the conditions, they have learned not strategies but only procedures. Looking back in the text is often included among reading strategies that are taught, but in fact all students look back on occasion (Garner and Reis 1981). The whole strategy is in knowing when to look back and where. Teaching genuine functional strategies that are not just slogans or isolated bits of behavior may require a substantial restructuring of the teaching-learning context (Collins, Brown, and Newman 1989). This notion will be elaborated in the section titled "Cognitive Teaching."

There is more to metacognition than self-regulatory strategies, however. The following points deal with four areas in which the metacognitive layer of knowledge seems important but has received considerably less attention:

1. Nature and Purpose of What Is Being Learned. Students are often little aware of the nature and purpose of what they are learning. Many children, especially the poorer readers, define reading as "saying the words" and seem unaware of its communicative function (Myers and Paris 1978). Bettelheim and Zelan (1982) observed that in Polish primers, before any actual reading is introduced, there are pictures of people reading in various contexts, and these are used by teachers to discuss with the children what reading is and what it is for. This simple and commonsensical metacognitive teaching seems to find no place in American curricula. It should be emphasized that more is involved here than teaching children the utility (if any) of what they are learning. More fundamentally, it is helping students to become aware that they are learning something and to understand what the nature of that something is. To teach such things would mean incorporating a certain amount of epistemology into curricula at all levels.

2. Students' Implicit Theories of Learning. Schools are often criticized for encouraging rote learning, but there is evidence that students themselves (including university students) often equate memorization with learning and neglect comprehension, even when examinations clearly require it (Biggs 1984). In short, students are often unaware of the cognitive demands and expectations being placed on them and tend to assume that these are of a lower order than they actually are (Winne and Marx 1982). There is some evidence that teaching students a more elaborated concept of learning can help them approach learning more intelligently (Biggs and Rihn 1984). This is not the same as teaching students how to learn, about which we will say more later, but it is a kind of conceptual learning that may be worthy of curricular attention in its own right.

*3. **Teachers' Preempting of Metacognitive Activity.*** Because metacognition is not recognized as a part of competence, teachers often do most of the metacognitive work themselves, thus taking it out of the hands of the students. This is the case, for instance, with the traditional reading lesson, institutionalized in conventional basal reading programs: The teacher takes all the responsibility for setting objectives, activating relevant knowledge, judging what is important, evaluating understanding, and identifying difficulties, even though these are all important metacognitive aspects of competent reading (Bereiter and Scardamalia 1987a). The problem here seems to be a conception of reading that is limited to its surface manifestations. A similar criticism may be made with respect to the teaching of arithmetic, when the focus is on observable computational procedures rather than on underlying meaning (Lampert 1986); of science, when the process is seen in terms of overt messing around rather than in terms of an underlying inquiry (Roth 1988); and of writing, when the process is seen as overt activities of prewriting, writing, and rewriting rather than as mental activities of planning, translating, and reviewing or rethinking, that do not necessarily coincide with the overt sequence of behaviors (Flower and Hayes 1981). It seems unlikely that merely instructing teachers in deeper theories of reading, mathematical understanding, and the like, would have much effect, but it might be a necessary foundation for building metacognitively more sophisticated practice.

*4. **Metacognition During Teacher-Directed Learning.*** Although it is easy to appreciate that metacognitive abilities are needed for independent learning, their importance is less well recognized in teacher-directed learning. Yet there is evidence of large and consequential differences in metacognitive activity among students while they are listening (Bereiter and Scardamalia 1989), reading assigned texts (Garner 1987; Scardamalia and Bereiter 1984), working textbook problems (Chi et al. 1989), and carrying out tasks using mathematics manipulatives (Resnick and Neches 1984). Perhaps the most graphic example comes from Corbeil (1989), who tape-recorded thinking-aloud protocols from English-speaking students during actual sessions of a French class. When the teacher was calling on individual students to respond, the more successful students monitored every interchange, covertly responded themselves, and tried to learn from the feedback provided by the teacher to the student who was called on. Less successful students thought only about their own turns to perform. Thus, in the same situation, the more successful students received an order of magnitude more practice with feedback than did the more metacognitively inert students. Perhaps none of this is surprising, but its implications are nonetheless radical: There may not be any such thing as passive receptive learning, or, at any rate, not such that it can be a factor in educational planning. It may be that none of the major cognitive objectives of a curriculum can be achieved unless the students are trying to achieve them—which is quite a different thing from trying to do well in the overt activities. This would suggest that intentional learning, that is, effort directed toward cognitive goals over and above effort directed toward task performance, ought itself to become a goal of instruction (Bereiter and Scardamalia 1989).

Three Faces of Problem Solving

The term "problem solving" is applied more broadly in cognitive science than it is in ordinary language. One encounters titles like "Reading as Problem Solving" (Olshavsky 1977) and "Writing as Problem Solving" (Hayes and Flower 1980), which sound metaphorical but are intended literally. Educators often distinguish "problem finding" from problem solving, and point out that finding and formulating a problem can be a more significant accomplishment than solving the problem once it has been formulated (Getzels 1979). Cognitive scientists, however, usually treat problem finding as a part of the problem-solving process (Hayes 1981, 1). The concept of problem solving has indeed been extended so far that Newell (1980, 697) has proposed that "the fundamental organizational unit of all human goal-oriented symbolic activity is the *problem space*."

What seems to have happened is this: Newell and Simon (1972) developed a general model of problem solving that has proved useful enough as a conceptual tool that cognitive scientists began applying it to a widening range of phenomena beyond what is ordinarily thought of as problem solving. The central—and, unfortunately, hardest to grasp—concept in Newell and Simon's theory is the *problem space*. Problem spaces are abstract. They do not exist in the environment and are not necessarily explicitly represented in the mind. However, problem spaces are populated by *knowledge states*, which do correspond to mental representations. They are mental representations of possible states of the *problem environment*. One such knowledge state corresponds to the initial state of the problem environment. One or more other knowledge states correspond to *goal states*. *Operators* are possible actions or moves that get from one state to another. Problem solving is conceived of as search through a problem space for a path which can be traversed, by the application of operators, that leads from the initial state to a goal state. *Search control knowledge* (Newell 1980) consists of strategies, heuristics, and the like that are used to direct the search. If one already knows how to get from the initial state to the goal, of course, search is unnecessary and no problem exists. In a well-structured problem like winning at tic-tac-toe, the problem space can potentially be fully specified in advance. In the ill-structured problems of real life, such as finding a job, the goal state and intermediate states may be only partially or vaguely known in advance. (Dustin Hoffman, in *The Graduate*, has little idea of what he wants in a career, but he recognizes that the single word, "plastics," reduces the problem space in a way that he cannot accept.) New operators (for instance, new questions to ask during a job interview) may be discovered during the search. Thus the problem space itself keeps being reconstructed during problem solving.

Among the virtues of the Newell and Simon model are that it provides a principled way of comparing one problem with another (problems are isomorphic to the extent that the states and operators of one can be matched with the states and operators of the other), of comparing one person's problem representation with another's, and of explicating the nature and function of problem-solving strategies. Means-end analysis, for instance, is a general strategy that can be precisely described in terms of movement in a problem space. Working backward from the goal, you may see a state from which the goal can be reached by a known path. This intermediate state may then be taken as a subgoal and the process repeated to find a still earlier state from which you can see a path to that subgoal—and so on until a subgoal is located that can be reached from the present state. Certain classic problems such as the Tower of Hanoi and the game of Nim can be solved easily in this way. Others take a more groping search that works forward from the present state and backward from the goal state until a hook-up can be found.

Voss (1988) provides a wide-ranging review of problem solving as it relates to instruction. He notes two different ways in which problem solving connects with educational issues: learning to solve problems and learning through problem solving. We have proposed a third: learning itself being treated as problem solving (Bereiter and Scardamalia 1989). Since this is the least obvious face of problem solving in education, we will discuss it first.

Learning as Problem Solving. The difference between learning *through* problem solving and learning *as* problem solving is brought out in a study by Ng and Bereiter (in press), who obtained thinking-aloud protocols from adults as they worked their way through a short course in computer programming. As is typical, much of the course work consisted of solving programming problems intended to teach the use of particular commands in the programming language. About half the students concentrated exclusively on accomplishing the programming tasks, with hardly any attention to what they were supposed to be learning from the tasks. That is learning through problem solving—in other words, learning as a by-product of solving problems. The other half of the students, however, to varying extents, focused on the learning itself as problematic. In this group one could find students saying things like, "I got the PRINT command to work right, but I still don't think I understand it." These students, not surprisingly, showed superior learning. Much, perhaps most, of everyday learning goes on automatically, as an incidental consequence of activities carried out for other purposes. But learning can be problematic, which is to say that one has a learning goal but no clear path for achieving it, so that searching through a problem space is required. Reading comprehension, as was noted earlier, is normally an automatic process. But when a difficult passage is encountered, skilled readers will invoke problem-solving strategies to achieve comprehension (Johnston and Afflerbach 1985). Problematic learning is liable to occur frequently in schools just because, in a large sense, schools exist in order to promote kinds of learning that do not come naturally from experience (Bereiter 1990). Problematic learning will also occur when instruction is indirect or incomplete or, as must often occur, imperfectly matched to the knowledge of the learner (Resnick and Glaser 1976).

A curious disjunction appears between conventional school wisdom and the view afforded by cognitive research. Typically, students who find learning problematic are considered to lack learning skills or to be otherwise in need of remediation. Interview studies indicate, by contrast, that it is the more able students who approach learning and comprehension as problematic and the weaker or less mature ones who approach it as a matter of executing routines (Bereiter and Scardamalia 1989; Biggs 1984). It would be interesting to examine the extent to which school curricula encourage students to confront learning problems as opposed to encouraging them to focus on tasks and activities, with learning left to occur as a by-product.

Learning Through Problem Solving. Anzai and Simon (1979) developed a theory of "learning by doing" that accounts for people's ability, starting with a crude initial problem space and only weak methods of search, to discover profitable subgoals and more effective strategies, and in the process to acquire causal knowledge applicable to the problem environment (see also Anzai 1991). However, it does not address the larger expectations that educators often hold for "learning by doing"—namely, that it will contribute to learning concepts and principles of the domain that apply beyond the problem-solving tasks themselves.

These larger expectations have been addressed by Sweller and his associates in a series of studies summarized by Sweller (1988). These studies indicate, in a variety of mathematics and science contexts, that textbook problems of the usual kind are a poor vehicle for learning generalizable concepts and principles. They induce students to use means-end methods in which they focus on answer-generating formulas and devote little attention to the concepts to which the formulas refer. Indeed, Sweller has been able to simulate student solving of physics problems with a simple program that has access to a list of formulas but has no knowledge of physics whatever.

Chi et al. (1989) obtained thinking-aloud protocols from high-achieving and low-achieving students as they attempted to solve physics problems by the common method of referring to a worked example. The low-achieving students proceeded in a manner consistent with Sweller's simulation, transporting procedures from example to problem without thought to meaning. The high-achieving students, however, spent time studying the example and referring back to the expository text in an effort to understand why the modeled procedures worked and how they related to underlying laws. It would seem, therefore, that the high-achieving students were setting problems for themselves over and above the assigned problems—problems of learning and understanding. Thus they were engaged in learning *as* problem solving, in addition to learning *through* problem solving.

In a number of the Sweller studies, better learning was achieved by a modified problem-solving task. The situations described in textbook problems were presented, but instead of ending with "Find such-and-such," they ended with the instruction to find out everything that could be inferred from the givens of the problem. This instruction eliminates the need for means-end analysis and encourages students to work forward from what they know, accumulating findings as they go. Information processing load is reduced and attention is directed toward possible implications, rather than toward finding a path to a specific goal. Putting together the several lines of research cited here, we arrive at the provisional conclusion that what people learn through problem solving is how to achieve the manifest object of the problem. Where this object is itself a worthwhile objective, such as learning to steer a ship, learning through problem solving can be effective. But when the hope is that learning of a more general conceptual sort will result, these hopes are likely to be disappointed unless the students, either through their own efforts or through the structure of the problem, actually pay attention to those more general ideas.

Learning to Solve Problems. Most cognitive scientists, it appears, are skeptical about the teachability of problem solving. Even those who are optimistic, who may even teach courses in problem solving, tend to have very circumscribed expectations about teachability (e.g., Hayes 1985). A monograph by Resnick (1987b) is a personal distillation of views emerging from a working group organized under the auspices of the National Research Council to consider "higher-order skills." The tone is charitable and positive, but Resnick concludes, "we have less evidence than would be desirable, and less than the proliferation of programs would suggest, on whether thinking abilities that are integrated and usable can actually be cultivated" (47).

A common distinction in the cognitive literature on problem solving is between "weak" and "strong" methods (Newell 1980). Weak methods are very general methods, like trial-and-error and means-end analysis, that apply across many domains. Strong methods are domain- or task-specific. Examples would be the method of least squares in statistics, the method of loci in mnemonics, and the method of carbon dating in paleontology. No one questions the value of teaching strong methods, but that is not what is usually meant by teaching problem solving. What is usually meant is the teaching of general strategies or skills, applicable to problems regardless of domain—in other words, weak methods. No disparagement should be read into the term "weak." They are obviously chancier and less straightforward in application than methods engineered for a specific job, and that is all "weak" means. In novel situations, where no strong methods have been devised, weak methods are all anyone has. We use them all the time, whenever we are stumped. But just because everyone uses them, could hardly survive without doing so, and therefore practices them extensively, there is reason to question the value of teaching them. Teaching problem-solving skills may be an illusion, like teaching babies to talk.

Another important source of skepticism about the teachability of problem solving, emphasized by Resnick and also by Voss (1988), is the overwhelming evidence of the importance of domain-specific knowledge. To see why the latter evidence casts doubt on the teachability of problem solving, we may consider the findings from expert-novice studies of physics problem solving.

1. Experts spend more time developing a representation of the problem, whereas novices go directly for a solution (Chi, Feltovich, and Glaser 1981).
2. Novices tend to work backward from the goal, whereas experts work forward from the givens (Larkin et al. 1980).
3. Novices look for applicable formulas whereas experts look for applicable laws (Larkin 1985).

In each of these instances, it is questionable whether novices could adopt the expert approach or would profit from trying to do so. Developing a cogent problem representation, working forward in an orderly manner, and looking for underlying laws all depend on a deep knowledge of physics and familiarity with the kinds of problems presented.

But surely there must be something to being a good problem solver besides knowing one's subject. Resnick (1987b) points to what she calls "enabling skills" of learning and thinking: "These include a wide range of oral and written communication skills, mathematization and representational abilities, principles of reasoning, and skills of argument construction and evaluation" (46).

More generally, the range of metacognitive knowledge and skills discussed in the preceding section could be expected to facilitate problem solving in the domains where they are applicable. Both Resnick (1987a) and Voss (1988) also note evidence of possible attitudinal effects of training in problem solving. Since problem solving, especially for novices, often requires perseverance through a succession of impasses and failed attempts, confidence in one's ability might well be an important factor in success. Confidence in problem-solving ability seems likely, however, to be domain-specific, which suggests that even for attitudinal purposes it might be best to teach problem solving within students' chosen fields rather than in all-purpose courses.

Automaticity and Processing Load

One of the formative ideas in cognitive science has been the limited processing capacity of the human cognitive system (Miller 1956). We are equipped with long-term memories providing us quick, flexible access to prodigious amounts of information, but only a tiny amount of this information can be activated at any one time. This information-processing bottleneck is variously referred to as limited processing capacity, working memory capacity, short-term memory capacity, or attentional capacity. It forces us, in inductive learning situations, to consider only one or two hypotheses at a time, when ideally it would be more efficient to consider a multitude of hypotheses simultaneously. We have already noted how it forces human chess masters to rely on stored knowledge of patterns (in long-term memory) rather than on brute-force reasoning, as a computer can do. The idea of *processing load*, the amount of processing capacity required by a task or concept, gives psychological meaning to the idea of complexity.

In practical terms, limited information processing capacity means that we cannot pay attention to very many things at once. Four is the currently favored approximate number (Simon 1974). Even handling that many is experienced as mental exertion. There are three related ways that we overcome this major limitation:

1. *Using long-term memory for look-up.* Children invent ways of adding single-digit numbers by mental counting. This is a mentally demanding task because of the need to hold one number in mind while doing something with the other. Eventually the burden is alleviated by storing addition results in long-term memory as data that can be looked up when needed (Siegler 1988). The school term, "number facts," accords well with their status, from the standpoint of cognitive theory, as items of declarative knowledge. Children who fail to exploit long-term memory in this way have a serious problem with more advanced arithmetic, because having to devote attention to figuring out single-digit sums while at the same time trying to cope with a novel multidigit procedure overloads short-term memory. Lack of well-memorized number facts has been found to be the single outstanding feature of children classified as having a mathematical learning disability (Russell and Ginsburg 1984).
2. *Chunking* (Miller 1956; Rosenbloom and Newell 1987). Chunking means combining several ideas or actions so that they are treated as a single unit in working memory. An important thing to realize about chunking is its subjectivity. You cannot objectively define the chunks in a situation; they depend on the perceiver. "Squeeze play" may be a single chunk to an experienced baseball player but a combination of separately remembered actions to a novice.
3. *Automaticity.* Decoding print, at one time a laborious process, becomes so automatic that we are no longer aware of doing it. It no longer demands appreciable use of information processing capacity; hence most of our capacity is free to devote to problems of meaning. Try reading with a mirror, and decoding again becomes resource-demanding, and comprehension is likely to suffer as a result. Although reading disabilities take various forms, a common result is that decoding does not become automatic and so poor readers have to devote attentional capacity to figuring out what the words are, thus having less attention available to devote to meaning (Stanovich 1980).

To this list could be added a fourth, using external aids—scratchpads, counters, and just the natural structure of things in the environment—which make information perceptually available, rather than having to be held in working memory (Pascual-Leone and Smith 1969). However, the reason for highlighting the first three is that they form a constellation of psychological means about which educators often have misgivings. They bespeak rote memorization and drill, which many educators see as the enemies of meaningful learning.

To cognitive scientists, the relation between rote and meaningful or—more technically—between automatic and controlled processes (Shiffrin and Schneider 1977) is almost always seen as reciprocal rather than antagonistic. Automatic processes are indeed "mindless," but therein lies their value for freeing the cognitive system for more mindful activity. Furthermore, meaningful knowledge plays an essential role in the initial stages of acquiring a skill that eventually becomes automatic (J. R. Anderson 1987b). Accordingly, in the perennial battle between phonics and wholistic methods in reading instruction, cognitive researchers are nearly unanimous in favoring direct teaching of phonic decoding skills to achieve automaticity, but with the skills being exercised in the service of comprehension (Adams 1990).

Adapting Instruction to Limited Processing Capacity. Cognitive researchers make a sharp distinction between the initial acquisition of a skill, which often involves problem solving, and its subsequent development through practice (J. R. Anderson 1982). These often appear to be confounded in school instruction. Teachers will claim to be teaching reading comprehension when all they are doing is providing practice (Durkin 1979). Information processing load is a problem mainly in the initial, cognitive stage of acquiring a skill, before chunking and automaticity have had a chance to develop. The problem is compounded when learners are young. Whether or not there are maturational changes in information processing capacity is a thorny question, many sides of which are aired in a volume edited by Siegler (1978). Fortunately, educational implications do not appear to depend on resolving the underlying biological issue. There is plenty of evidence that younger children act as if they cannot handle as much complexity as older ones, and Case

(1985b) has argued persuasively that, regardless of whether the age effect is due to neural maturation or to functional gains resulting from chunking and automaticity, it is general across the full range of cognitive behavior. It therefore becomes something for school curricula to take into account—but how?

The behaviorist dictum that instruction should proceed in small steps may be seen as a rule-of-thumb way to cope with this processing load problem. Behaviorist psychology, however, provides no way, except after the fact, to judge the size of a step (Case and Bereiter 1984). A method of cognitive task analysis developed by Case (1985b) provides a systematic, albeit far from algorithmic, way to estimate processing load. The kind of analysis that Case and his students have found necessary in order to gauge and reduce processing load requires, in effect, a good mental model of how a student of a certain age is likely to think. In that way it is possible to think through a task from the student's point of view, using the kinds of chunks and interpretive schemes the child is likely to have available rather than those available to the adult. Only in this way is it possible to count the number of units that will have to be held in mind at points of peak load in a task and thus recognize what simplifications may be required. In one way this presents a discouraging prospect for educators and curriculum designers, because it indicates there is no principled way of dealing directly with subject matter so as to estimate and adjust its difficulty. But such an expectation is unrealistic in any event. The hopeful sign is that, to judge from the work of Case and his associates, cognitive task analysis can be done with some precision, thus providing a way of improving on unguided intuition in adapting the curriculum to limited processing capacity.

Training for Automaticity. Parents of our acquaintance received a form letter from their daughter's third-grade teacher asking them to drill the child on multiplication facts. When asked what was being done at school in this regard, the teacher replied that it was against her educational philosophy to use rote drill. Ambivalence about skill training is not usually so blatant, but seems to be pervasive. It is probably fair to say that both the advocates and the opponents of skill training in the schools make it out to be a much simpler matter than it actually is.

Cognitive psychologists are generally agreed that automaticity is essential to free information-processing capacity for further learning, and that automaticity requires extensive practice. Beyond that, however, matters become complex. Schneider (1985) discusses a number of commonly held fallacies about skill learning. One is the simple belief that practice makes perfect; instead it may entrench faulty procedures. Another is the belief that practice of the whole task is always to be preferred over practice of isolated components. Designing training that selectively strengthens skill components that are not adequately practiced in performing the whole task is a major challenge faced by trainers of high-level skills. This is well recognized and developed to a high art in championship sports, but neglected in the design of school instruction. A typical basal reading program is likely to include exercises purporting to train skills whose very existence as skills is questionable (e.g., "classification skills") or ones that are not components of the intended skill (e.g., selecting titles for reading passages or identifying words that contain a particular sound, neither of which occur as parts of the reading process). The most common and deplorable thing we have observed about skill exercises in schools is that they are assigned to students who have not yet learned the skills they are supposed to practice—and, when these students perform badly, the prescription is often more exercises.

A model of a cognitive approach to training for automaticity is provided by the work of Frederiksen (1982; Frederiksen, Warren, and Rosebery 1985a, 1985b) on component reading skills. Frederiksen began with basic research to identify components of reading skill that were particularly deficient in poor readers. He then designed computer games that would provide motivating practice of these component skills. One component was rapid recognition of familiar parts in unfamiliar long words. The game was a speed game in which a short word and a long word were flashed on the screen and the task was to decide as quickly as possible whether the short word was included in the long word. A second component was automaticity in phonological decoding. Here the game was to respond orally as quickly as possible to words flashed on the screen. Since the computer could not judge the correctness of the oral response, however, this game ran the risk of providing practice in inaccurate decoding, and so a discrimination task was built in that provided a check on accuracy. Noteworthy in this approach are (a) that the isolated skills are actual components of the reading process; (b) that the training is aimed at automaticity of skills that the students can already perform; and (c) that the contribution of componential training to performance on the whole task is not taken for granted but is treated as an empirical question.

Intermediate Knowledge States

Folk psychology provides few concepts for dealing with the intermediate states that may exist between total ignorance and full mastery of a domain. Intermediate states are typically thought of as partial knowledge, a subset of the elements composing complete knowledge, possibly with some incorrect elements that will need to be replaced. Among developers of intelligent tutoring systems, such descriptions are referred to as "overlay models," and are recognized as the weakest sort of model of student competence (VanLehn 1988). In ordinary education the overlay model has been enshrined in the practice of representing individual students' levels of attainment as percentages of items correct on mastery tests.

The idea that intermediate states of knowledge could have a structure and integrity of their own was advanced by Piaget and embodied in his theory of cognitive stages (Piaget 1970). Perhaps the most extensively studied of intermediate structures are those that occur in the course of language development. Child language shows two properties: (1) it follows consistent rules that are not just a subset of adult rules; and (2) it works—that is, it functions in one way or other to meet the child's communication needs (Bruner 1983).

An understanding of intermediate states of competence has two applications to curriculum. One is to the traditional problem of curriculum sequencing. The other is to the more adventurous possibility of designing new subject matter to serve transitional functions.

Curriculum Sequencing. Some of the common principles of curriculum sequencing are *easy-to-hard*, as in basal readers graded according to reading difficulty; *familiar-to-unfamiliar*, as in the "widening horizons" sequence in social studies, which moves from a focus on home and neighborhood to increasingly large or remote social entities; and *concrete-to-abstract*, as in approaches to science and mathematics that emphasize manipulations and direct experience before formal principles are introduced. Despite some rule-of-thumb validity, all of these principles have been seriously challenged. A number of studies have shown that efforts to simplify school texts commonly make them harder to understand (Davison 1984). Simplified history texts tend to cut back to bare narrative, with the result that, although students may understand what happened, they have no idea of its significance (Beck, McKeown, and Gromoll 1989). At a more basic level, Pascual-Leone et al. (1979) argue that making everything easy to learn deprives students of opportunities to develop cognitive structures for dealing with difficult material.

The familiar-to-unfamiliar sequence of the "widening horizons" curriculum has been severely criticized by Ravitch (1987) as having no basis in research, theory, or common knowledge about children's interests. The familiar-to-unfamiliar principle does, in fact, run contrary to a well-established psychological generalization, that interest is highest at an intermediate level that is neither too familiar nor too unfamiliar, too predictable nor too unpredictable (Berlyne 1962; Hidi 1990). The concrete-to-abstract principle, often wrongly attributed to Piaget, is challenged by any number of studies that have shown advantages of presenting "advance organizers" (Ausubel 1963) at a high level of abstraction prior to instruction (Hartley and Davies 1976). A more basic challenge is offered by Case and Griffin (1990), who provide evidence that in the initial acquisition of fundamental conceptual structures like that of counting, students learn best with representations that minimize interference from real-life contexts.

Almost all of the cognitive research relevant to curriculum sequencing comes from cognitive developmental studies. We still run into educationists, some even within cognitive science, who believe that developmental psychology only offers a set of "Thou canst not" strictures to the curriculum planner. Since the mid-1970s, cognitive developmentalists have been tracing many different kinds of knowledge and competence from their earliest (often extremely early) appearances through successive restructurings toward their mature forms. A systematic textbook treatment that pays special attention to school-related knowledge is Siegler (1986). The result of this enterprise is that there now exist detailed descriptions of naturally occurring sequences of knowledge states in virtually every area that childhood educators might be interested in. Knowledge development in adolescence and beyond has not been nearly so extensively studied, and it may be that by then the formal curriculum exerts such a strong influence that developmental studies would only reflect it back. In childhood, however, that appears not to be the case. Children's development in basic arithmetic, story comprehension, and scientific understanding appear to go through stages that are only incidentally affected by school inputs (Mandler et al. 1980; Nussbaum 1979; Siegler 1988). Even with such a school-bound topic as ratios and proportions, students have been found to acquire the concepts in an order that reflects their complexity rather than the order in which they have been taught (Case 1985a).

Two contemporary applications of developmental research are worth pointing out, if only by way of contrast to the rather floundering attempts to apply developmental findings during the Head Start era (see, for instance, the descriptions in Stanley 1972). Careful studies of children's undirected efforts at writing by Clay (1975), Ferreiro and Teberosky (1982), and others formed the basis of the "emergent literacy" curriculum, one of the few radical innovations in recent curriculum practice that looks as if it may stick (Mason and Allen 1986). By basing a time-telling program on the sequence by which normal children actually learned to tell time, Case and Sandieson (1986) were able to achieve remarkable success in teaching severely retarded children. Case and Sandieson (1986) advance a general argument for basing curriculum sequences on naturally occurring sequences rather than solely on analysis of expert or target performance. The result could be a general methodology for developing "emergent" curricula.

Designing Transitional Forms. In the realm of motor skills there are many examples of skills that serve transitional functions and are eventually superseded by other skills: learning to ride a bicycle with training wheels and to ski with short skis; the underhand serve in tennis and the frog kick in swimming. In the school curriculum, however, transitional forms are rare, and when introduced they often inflame opposition—as exemplified in the response of American educators to the Initial Teaching Alphabet (Downing 1965).

Kieran Egan (1988) has argued in effect that myth functions as a transitional knowledge form in children's learning. It represents historical and social knowledge of a type compatible with the way young children are prepared to understand the world. Characteristically, the schools, if they have not completely banished myth, have reduced it to a vestige, retaining some of its form but hardly any of its function. Interestingly, they have done exactly the same with phonics, another transitional form relevant to beginning literacy (Adams 1990).

It would seem that, in order to be acceptable in schools, transitional knowledge forms must not only accommodate the needs of the learner but must also have respectability. They must not be too incongruous with the final or adult form, either in substance or in appearance. Students appear spontaneously to construct a Lamarckian notion of evolution, believing that traits develop in response to experienced needs of the organism (Deadman and Kelly 1978). As a transitional knowledge form, Lamarckism could serve nicely as a framework within which to develop and elaborate knowledge about adaptation, in advance of learning about evolutionary mechanisms. But it seems unlikely that educators would ever knowingly accede to such a curriculum strategy. Meeting the dual requirements of pedagogical usefulness and respectability presents a formidable problem of invention, but one that may be surmountable.

An example of such invention is the intermediate models devised by White and Frederiksen (1990) for understanding electronic circuitry. Naive models of how electrical circuits work use analogies such as water flow, which are useful up to a point but are not adequate for solving problems. On the other hand, the formal models normally taught in courses on electronics are beyond the grasp of many students. Guided by research on the nature of qualitative mental models, as discussed previously, White and Frederiksen created sequences of causal models, each capable of handling more of the complexity of real electronic circuits. In effect, they had to invent a series of electronic theories, differing in complexity, but all "respectable" in the sense that they were congruent with the accepted formal theory.

If the White and Frederiksen effort is taken as representative, then it is clear that the creation of intermediate knowledge forms where they are currently lacking would constitute a curriculum writing agenda more formidable than that of the last great wave of curriculum reform. It would require deep analysis not only of the discipline but also of mental models relevant to functioning in the discipline.

EDUCATIONAL ENVISIONMENTS

In the preceding section, curricular implications of cognitive research were organized around particular ideas from cognitive science. That organization gave little opportunity for more global implications of cognitive research to emerge. In this section we shift to a more global perspective by considering three areas of education in which cognitive research seems to be converging on one or two coherent envisionments, on things that might be called "cognitive approaches" to education.

Cognitive Teaching

A considerable amount of instructional experimentation is being carried out under the umbrella of cognitive research. Representative work appears in the journal, *Cognition and Instruction*. It is reviewed in the series, *Advances in Instructional Psychology* (Glaser 1978, 1982, 1987) and by Glaser and Bassok (1989). It is the substance of Ellen Gagné's textbook, *The Cognitive Psychology of School Learning* (1985).

Do these instructional research efforts converge on anything that could be called a cognitive approach to teaching? Collins, Brown, and Newman (1989) propose "cognitive apprenticeship" as a unifying concept to embrace what is distinctive about the emerging cognitive approaches to teaching.

> The differences between formal schooling and apprenticeship methods are many, but for our purposes, one is most important. Perhaps as a by-product of the relegation of learning to schools, skills and knowledge have become abstracted from their uses in the world. In apprenticeship learning, on the other hand, target skills are not only continually in use by skilled practitioners, but are instrumental to the accomplishment of meaningful tasks. (453)

From an analysis of exemplary models, they identify six teaching methods characteristic of cognitive apprenticeship:

1. Modeling—particularly cognitive modeling, which demonstrates to students the thought processes involved in expert performance.
2. Coaching—which focuses on events and problems arising while students are in the process of attempting target tasks.
3. Scaffolding—external support from the teacher or from artifacts, which helps students achieve early success but that can be withdrawn as students are able to function independently.
4. Articulation—getting students to demonstrate or verbalize their own knowledge and cognitive processes in a domain.
5. Reflection—especially reflection that compares students' processes with each other's, with those of the expert, or with an ideal model.
6. Exploration—in which students not only solve problems independently but seek them out independently.

As the first attempt to synthesize the instructional implications of the recent wave of cognitive research, "cognitive apprenticeship" has deservedly received much attention. The six methods identified by Collins, Brown, and Newman (1989) do appear to be characteristic of the instructional approaches emerging from cognitive research. Although, taken individually, none of the methods are radically new, when taken together, they seem to have a distinctive emphasis incorporating several of the key ideas discussed in preceding sections: mental models, shared metacognitive activity, problem solving with its several faces, and the active cultivation of intermediate states of competence.

An itemization of methods, however, tends to miss essentials. One essential of emerging approaches is principled understanding, as exemplified in the work on mathematics teaching by Lampert (1986). Another is an increased emphasis on the student's role as agent in the learning process (a role that does not fit well with the apprenticeship metaphor). Bereiter and Scardamalia (1987a) explicate this new emphasis by identifying three idealized models of teaching. The Teacher A model is an exercise model, in which the emphasis is on having students do work believed to be of educational benefit. The Teacher B model is the one most widely endorsed in teachers' manuals and the like; it has the teacher assuming responsibility for a variety of metacognitive activities—setting goals, activating prior knowledge, asking thought-provoking questions, evaluating understanding, and so on. The Teacher C model, identified with the emerging cognitive approach to teaching, is concerned with developing in students the ability to take over these metacognitive aspects themselves. The effort to find a unifying metaphor or model reflects a growing sense among cognitive instructional researchers that their work is starting to add up to something distinctive. Undoubtedly there will be many more efforts to define what that distinctive something is.

Computer Environments

Two distinct lines of development in educational computing have close ties with cognitive science—intelligent tutoring systems (Polson and Richardson 1988) and media educational systems (Pea and Sheingold 1987). These roughly align with the two broad approaches traditionally at odds in education: the one instructional, with its emphasis on close monitoring and guidance of the learner; the other environmental, with its emphasis on varied resources and rather open activity structures in which students can exercise personal options in the pursuit of goals. Much of what can be said about these developments in educational computing simply restates what has been said countless times about the traditional approaches to which they are related—the pros and cons, the possibilities of synthesis, and so on. Of greater interest is the possibility that, through cognitively based design, each approach may be able to capture some of the advantages of the other and overcome its own typical disadvantages. Thus, there are envisionments of intelligent tutoring systems that support independent inquiry and media systems that support rigorous study in the disciplines.

The incorporation of artificial intelligence (AI) into computer-assisted instruction (CAI) represents a more profound shift than may be apparent from the outward performance of the programs. Fundamentally, it is a shift from programs that store and consult answers to exercises to programs that actually represent the knowledge required to do the exercises (Clancey 1987, 244). In conventional CAI, there is no reasonable sense in which the program can be claimed to "know" the subject it is intended to teach (any more than a geometry textbook can be said to know geometry). But with intelligent tutoring systems, such claims can be made, at least in the controversial sense that they are made for expert systems, to which they are closely allied. Thus, Anderson's geometry tutoring program (J. R. Anderson, Boyle, and Yost 1985; see also Glaser and Bassok 1989) "knows" geometry in the sense that it contains representations of principles and procedures that enable it to prove theorems that have not been presented to it before. Provided with such knowledge, AI-based teaching programs are no longer bound to predetermined questions and answers. They have the potential to interact more flexibly with the learner and even to turn much of the initiative over to the learner. These potentialities have scarcely begun to be explored, however. Because of the stupefying amount of labor required, few knowledge-based tutoring programs have been produced, and all stop well short of what is envisioned as desirable. Clancey (1987), whose GUIDON program (discussed further in the next section) is perhaps the most advanced of existing programs in its flexibility of interaction with the learner, opined that "it may be another five years before questions about completeness, usefulness, and reliability of AI-based instructional programs are even meaningful" (245).

Intelligent tutoring systems make the computer a highly active agent in the educational process. There are other approaches, however, that assign a passive (though sometimes intelligent) role to the computer. It is conceived as providing an environment or a medium for educational activity (Burton 1988; Scardamalia et al. 1989). In a provocative paper titled "The Next Knowledge Medium," Stefik (1986) remarks, "AI technology, as it now exists, does not function in an important way as a knowledge medium in our society. Its influence has been far less important to the creation and propagation of knowledge than the secondary roads in France" (40). He envisions "an information network with semi-automated services for the generation, distribution, and consumption of knowledge" (34–35) that would be somewhat like a road system in its cultural impact—aiding in cultural diffusion and stimulating a variety of unforeseeable initiatives by virtue of the increased flow and interaction of knowledge.

The current educational uses of computer-based communication networks (e.g., Newman and Goldman 1987) may be seen as a move in the direction of a knowledge medium. A premise of the knowledge media idea, as advanced by Stefik, is that facilitating the distribution of knowledge contributes to its overall growth, somewhat in the manner that facilitating the distribution of goods contributes to overall economic growth (hence the analogy to a road system). A full-blown educational medium could be conceived as one that exchanges information among and between students, teachers, and outside experts. To be practical, however, such a medium must be designed so as to take account of the varying informational needs, competencies, and time resources of the parties involved, and provide the necessary scaffolding for productive interactions. Thus, quite serious cognitive, and not just engineering issues, are involved. For a discussion of these issues as they relate to a prototype effort to implement Stefik's vision, see Scardamalia et al. (1989) and Scardamalia and Bereiter (in press).

Education for Expertise

The study of expertise represents one of those occasional dramatic instances where a theoretically motivated line of research intersects with an urgent social need. Most of the recent calls for "excellence" can be read as calls for higher levels of competence, often motivated by evidence suggesting that other nations have gained an edge in scientific and technical expertise.

The principal finding of research on expertise in knowledge-rich fields is, as we have noted earlier, the astonishing quantity of knowledge found to underlie expert performance. This is knowledge consistent with and influenced by formal knowledge, but it is different in character from and much vaster than the knowledge to be found in textbooks. The obvious conclusion from current research is that the way to promote expertise is to promote development of the kinds of tacit knowledge experts have. But how is this to be done?

The literature on expertise, it must be recognized, is largely silent on the question of educational means. Two handy words, "experience" and "practice," paper over the large gap that should be filled by a theory of acquisition. The literature does, however, offer pointers to kinds of research that should yield educationally useful knowledge:

1. *Fuller descriptions of experts' tacit knowledge*. As suggested earlier, knowledge engineering is a potentially valuable technology for expanding curriculum content to incorporate more of experts' knowledge. It is an artful combination of observing, questioning, and analyzing thinking-aloud protocols of experts at work. As used in the development of expert systems, knowledge engineering focuses on knowledge that can be made explicit, but for curriculum development purposes there is no reason why it could not be usefully extended to provide descriptions of more elusive, less clearly specifiable components of expert knowledge.
2. *Identification of teachable components of tacit knowledge*. Expert systems embody experts' knowledge in rules, which, since they have in a sense been taught to a machine, can potentially be taught to human learners. Just such a possibility has been pursued by Clancey (1987), who started with an expert system for diagnosis of infectious diseases, reconfigured the knowledge base to give it a more coherent and teachable structure, and turned it into a teaching system that could convey to students the knowledge and thinking that lay behind its diagnoses. The qualitative physics of deKleer and Brown (1985), derived from studies of physicists' informal understanding of physical systems, has been systematized into a real physics with a vocabulary, notational system, and laws that could be taught like any other physics. Whether it would be a good physics to teach is another question; what their work does show is that informal knowledge can be formulated as teachable subject matter. Even when expert knowledge lies beyond the immediate reach of the curriculum, it may still be possible to build toward such knowledge, provided it is well enough understood. A repeated finding in expert-novice comparisons is that novices represent the surface appearance of problems whereas experts represent their underlying structure (Glaser and Chi 1988). Novices cannot really be expected to do otherwise, since they lack the requisite knowledge; but if representing the deep structure of problems is recognized as a long-range goal, it may be possible to fashion instruction and problem-solving activities from the earliest stages so as to lead in that direction (Mestre et al. 1988).
3. *Identification of functionally important conceptions*. Although expert-novice studies generally emphasize the role of informal knowledge, they also often point to formal concepts that have particular functional importance. One such is the idea of static forces. Naive common sense associates force with motion and thus does not consider the book and the table it is resting on to be exerting force on one another. But working successfully with Newtonian mechanics requires such a notion. Once the concept of static forces is recognized as problematic, ways can be developed to make it more intuitively appealing to students (Clement 1986). But it is through studying expert-novice differences in functional contexts, rather than studying only the structure of formal knowledge, that such concepts can be singled out for attention.
4. *Expanding the scope of problem solving in the curriculum*. We have already cited reasons for questioning the value of the textbook problems that make up a large part of mathematics and science curricula. Yet it is also evident that much of expertise is developed through problem solving (Scardamalia and Bereiter 1989). Curricula might include (at appropriate levels of difficulty) more of the kinds of problems experts actually deal with. Examples are (a) problems that call for finding lawful relationships in data or open-ended problems of the "Find-out-what-you-can" type (Sweller 1988), (b) metaprocedural problems ("Is there an easier way?" "Is this move legal?"), and (c) problems of explanation ("Why is it that . . . ?").
5. *Study of experts' ways of learning*. In knowledge-rich fields, experts often invest substantial effort in continued learning, apart from the effort put into productive work or performance. Studying experts as learners, and comparing their approaches to learning with those of novices, could provide valuable insights into the kind of learning conducive to expertise. A prototype for such research is provided by Ghent (1989). She collected thinking-aloud protocols from a professional concert pianist and two advanced piano students as they went about learning the same unfamiliar piece of music. The expert took a problem-solving approach, made deliberate but cautious use of his background knowledge, engaged in considerable metacognitive monitoring, and tried to shape new skills to meet the novel requirements of the music. One student approached the task in essentially the same way as the expert, despite great differences in background

knowledge and skill. The other minimized the need for learning, adopting already-familiar procedures wherever they seemed to fit. The differences in learning approaches resulted in performance differences that were immediately recognizable by a musicologist. Such a small study can only be suggestive, of course, but it does indicate that studying how experts in various fields learn may lead to identifying kinds of learning essential to the acquisition of expert competence.

The preceding is more of a research agenda than a coherent vision of what education for expertise might be like. From what is currently known about expertise, however, it seems likely that carrying out this research agenda could lead to radical transformations in curriculum content and curriculum organization, in the kinds of learning activities pursued, and in the approaches to learning that students are encouraged to take.

A LOOK TO THE FUTURE

Cognitive science may be in the early stages of a revolution—a revolution in the Lakatosian sense of a change in core belief (Lakatos 1970). Cognitive theories have been variations of what Fodor and Pylyshyn (1988) label RTM, the representational theory of mind. The core belief of RTM is that the mind does not operate directly on the world but on symbolic representations of it. This seemingly self-evident and necessary belief is being challenged from two sides, which are giving rise respectively to (1) a new connectionism; and (2) a resurgence of ecological perspectives on cognition. Most cognitive models presume, furthermore, that mental representations are built up by an inductive learning process. This belief is being challenged by a third development, a kind of new biologism. All three movements have potential significance for curriculum studies, although only in the second of the three have educational implications been made explicit. We will sketch these movements only broadly, since our intent is merely to alert readers to keep an eye on their further development.

Connectionism

If the mind only operates on representations of the world, then the only way it can achieve new representations is by operating on existing ones. If this is true, it leads to vexing problems concerning the initial state of the organism (Fodor 1975, 1983) and the possibility of ever learning something more complex than what one already knows (Bereiter 1985). In the emerging connectionist approach to cognitive modeling, the system does not start with symbols. It starts with units that, like neurons, have no symbolic properties. Symbolic or representational value is an emergent property of the network of interconnections that develops among these in-themselves meaningless units.

At present, connectionist theorizing is not very accessible to the nonspecialist, especially to the nonmathematical nonspecialist. A basic treatise, in two volumes (Rumelhart et al. 1986; McClelland et al. 1986), contains many readable sections, however, and is generally more intelligible than magazine efforts to popularize the subject. Hofstadter (1985, especially chapter 26) provides a good orientation to the kind of thinking that leads up to connectionism, but does not present connectionist theory as such. A nonmathematical explanation of how connectionist networks are able to learn patterns without learning rules is provided by Bereiter (1991).

Although we make no attempt to explain connectionism here, we offer a few pointers that may be helpful to curriculum researchers who wish to tackle the literature on the topic:

- Contemporary connectionism does bear some relation to the Thorndikean connectionism of old (Thorndike 1949), but it is probably best to subdue that thought when first approaching the contemporary literature. There is no evidence of direct influence, and the basic theoretical motivation is entirely different.
- It is important to separate connectionist theory from connectionist technology. The situation is much like that with factor analysis, which grew out of a certain theoretical orientation in psychology (e.g., Thurstone 1934), but also developed as a technology that acquired many uses unrelated to its original conception. Connectionist technology, familiarly called PDP (parallel distributed processing), in fact is mathematically related to factor analysis and has found application in such far-flung areas as organic chemistry. PDP technology is likely to have applications in education that have no relation to connectionist theorizing. For instance, in current research in our laboratory it is being used to select statements that maximally agree or disagree with students' expressed beliefs on science topics.
- The term "neural modeling" applies to some but not most connectionist AI work. Consequently, unless they explicitly claim to be doing so, one should not assume that connectionists are basing their work on assumed similarities between PDP networks and brain anatomy (Smolensky 1988).

Among the hopes for connectionist models are that they will better capture the intuitive and spontaneous character of human thought, the role of emotion in cognition and vice versa, and the gradual progression from vagueness to clarity that often characterizes concept learning. What any of this might mean for education it is too early to tell, but any theory that could accomplish such things would surely be significant for educational thought. It should be recognized that no theories do this now with any degree of power, so that, if connectionist modeling succeeds, it will not displace existing theories in these regards but will break new ground.

Ecological Cognitive Science and Situated Learning

Because it treats cognition as operating only on mental representations, RTM has difficulty dealing with the very complex and dynamic interaction between the person and the external world, particularly the social world. Vygotsky's idea (1962, 1978) that cognition originates in social activity and only later is reconstructed ("internalized") in the individual mind has attracted many educators, including cognitive instructional researchers (Brown and Palincsar 1989; Davydov and Radzikhovskii 1985; Zinchenko 1985). Nothing in RTM denies this idea, but at the same time there is not much RTM can do with it.

What we are calling "ecological cognitive science" does not refer to one coherent movement, but rather to a variety of efforts to work with an expanded notion of cognition, which sees cognitive processes as including external as well as inside-the-head events. Among the influences that can be recognized in current movements are (1) Vygotsky, who in addition to the idea of internalization, also provided the idea of externalization—the creation of artifacts and changes in the environment that support and thus become a part of cognitive processes; (2) J. J. Gibson (1979), who held that our cognitive systems have evolved in such a way that critical features of the environment and their pragmatic implications are perceived directly, without the need for mediating symbolic processes—interpretations, concepts, and the like (Neisser 1988); and (3) a variety of ethnographic studies which indicate that in ordinary life, unlike school life, people do not rely on context-free principles such as those of mathematics, but instead learn ways of interacting with their environment that result in the effective handling of such things as quantities and distances (Rogoff and Lave 1984).

One group of researchers is explicitly concerned with educational implications of what they term "situated cognition" (Brown, Collins, and Duguid 1989b). Mainly connected with the Center for the Study of Learning in Palo Alto, members of the group are undertaking an ambitious program of research that ranges from studies of learning in work settings to developing an environmentally situated approach to artificial intelligence. In an earlier section (Cognitive Teaching) we discussed "cognitive apprenticeship," one of the key educational ideas emerging from this group. To what extent situated cognition represents a new conception and to what extent it is a restatement of ideas already articulated by John Dewey, with a dash of Ivan Illich, is a matter of current dispute (Brown, Collins, and Duguid 1989a; Palincsar 1989; Wineburg 1989). Although the intuitions motivating ecological approaches to cognitive science are easy enough to resonate to, these intuitions have yet to be formulated in a way that makes it possible to "situate" them philosophically (see, however, Harré 1984).

The Rediscovery of Human Nature

This half century may well be seen in retrospect as a time when the social sciences were blinkered by a massive denial of humanity's biological nature. There is, for instance, scarcely a single conclusion about the effects of home environment on behavior that is not put in doubt as soon as it is acknowledged that the home environment may partly reflect genetic dispositions of the household members (Plomin, DeFries, and Loehlin 1977; Scarr and McCartney 1983). Cognitive science, as a child of this era, has tended to share in the denial of biology, although only in part. As far as the architecture of the cognitive system is concerned, it is assumed that this is genetically given. Thus, as we discussed earlier, an important aspect of cognitive research has been working out the implications of our limited information processing capacity. But as for what is in the mind, cognitive scientists—like behavioral scientists in general—have tended to attribute that solely to experience.

Since the 1970s, however, a strong element of nativism has been making its way into cognitive science, largely through the influence of Noam Chomsky (1975, 1980), who has argued that the universals of human language and language acquisition cannot be accounted for simply by positing innate capabilities or dispositions, that it is necessary to posit something on the order of an innate grammar as well. This version of the nature/nurture controversy reached a head in an important debate featuring Chomsky and Piaget (Piattelli-Palmarini 1980), with Piaget—perhaps to the surprise of some educators—emerging as the die-hard environmentalist.

Child development research, in the meantime, has been turning up evidence of basic concepts at earlier and earlier ages, making it seem increasingly unlikely that they are wholly learned (Gelman 1990). There is strong evidence for innateness of some counting number concepts (Gelman and Gallistel 1978; Starkey, Spelke, and Gelman 1983), and at least suggestive evidence for innateness of causal reasoning (Brown 1990), story grammar (Mandler et al. 1980), and the sorting of the world into classes of discrete objects (Spelke 1982). Equally important, however, is the identification of culturally important concepts that appear not to be innately supported—such as proportionality and related concepts dependent on multiplicative structures (Resnick 1987a).

Lumsden and Wilson (1981) raise the question of how it is that most societies developed brother-sister incest taboos long before they could have had empirical knowledge of the genetic disadvantages of sibling inbreeding. They develop a complex but plausible theory that involves an interaction of individual cognition, social norms, and natural selection, such that an individual cognitive bias that has material benefits results in natural selection with respect to that bias. The resulting small shifts in frequency are magnified through their effects on social norms, which results in larger selection effects, and so on until something functionally equivalent to knowledge can become established, even if it lacks an epistemic basis. The theory has generated much criticism (see the peer commentaries following Lumsden and Wilson 1982), and it is not for us to evaluate it here. We point to it, rather, as the precursor of a kind of theorizing that unites the several lines of development we have been discussing. It is theorizing that treats individual cognitive processes, the physical and social environment, and evolved species traits as components of a coherent process theory.

This kind of theorizing can have curricular implications. Cosmides (1989), for instance, hypothesizes that social exchange ("I do this for you; you do that for me") has been an "evolutionarily crucial domain," with the result that special cognitive skills have evolved for determining whether other people are holding up their end of the social contract. She produces experimental support for this hypothesis by showing that logically identical tasks are handled differently, depending on whether or not a look-for-cheaters theme is involved, with people generally showing more acute logical abilities when it is. The earlier cited work on children's mathematical understanding may similarly be interpreted as pointing to number as an evolutionarily crucial or, as Ann Brown (1990) puts it, a "privileged domain" (and a domain not, of course, unrelated to the detection of cheaters, as any parent knows who has mediated children's disputes over sharing). If, in fact, the intellect is not all of a piece, but is adapted differently to certain domains in ways that reflect the long-term interaction of culture and biology, then the design of curricula adapted to the learner becomes not only much more complicated but also much more interesting.

Advocates of open education, natural education, and the like often put forth children's learning of their mother tongue as the model for all learning (Goodman and Goodman 1979). But if evolution has specifically prepared us for acquiring language, number, and a few other basic competencies, these may be altogether inappropriate as exemplars of the kinds of learning schools were created to promote—namely, kinds of learning that do not come about naturally through ordinary experience (Bereiter and Scardamalia 1987b, chapter 1). Emerging insights into the cognitive complexity of human nature pose several challenges to curriculum research: to distinguish culturally important learning which comes naturally from that which does not; to perfect ways of teaching those things that are not supported by nature or that perhaps even go against natural intuitions (for instance, the counter-intuitive parts of Newtonian mechanics); and, perhaps most challenging of all, to find ways to exploit natural knowledge endowments in the service of more advanced learning (cf. Resnick 1987a)

References

Adams, Marilyn J. 1990. *Beginning to Read: Thinking and Learning about Print*. Cambridge, MA: MIT Press.

Allard, Fran, and Neil Burnett. 1985. Skill in sport. *Canadian Journal of Psychology* 39(2): 294–312.

Anderson, John R. 1982. Acquisition of cognitive skill. *Psychological Review* 89(4): 369–406.

Anderson, John R. 1983. *The Architecture of Cognition*. Cambridge, MA: Harvard University Press.

Anderson, John R. 1985. *Cognitive Psychology and its Implications*. 2d ed. San Francisco, CA: Freeman.

Anderson, John R. 1987a. Methodologics for studying human knowledge. *Behavioral and Brain Sciences* 10(3): 467–505.

Anderson, John R. 1987b. Skill acquisition: Compilation of weak-method problem solutions. *Psychological Review* 94(2): 192–210.

Anderson, John R., Charles F. Boyle, and G. Yost. 1985. "The Geometry Tutor." In *Proceedings of the Ninth International Conference on Artificial Intelligence*, edited by Aravind K. Joshi, 1–7. Los Altos, CA: Morgan Kaufman.

Anderson, Richard C. 1978. "Schema-directed Processes in Language Comprehension." In *Cognitive Psychology and Instruction*, edited by Alan M. Lesgold, James W. Pellegrino, Sipke D. Fokkema, and Robert Glaser, 67–82. New York: Plenum.

Anderson, Richard C., Ralph E. Reynolds, Diane L. Schallert, and Ernest T. Goetz. 1977. Frameworks for comprehending discourse. *American Educational Research Journal* 14(4): 367–381.

Anderson, Richard C., Rand J. Spiro, and William E. Montague, eds. 1977. *Schooling and the Acquisition of Knowledge*. Hillsdale, NJ: Erlbaum.

Anzai, Yuichiro. 1991. "Learning and Use of Representations for Physics Expertise." In *Toward a General Theory of Expertise: Prospects and Limits*, edited by K. Anders Ericsson and Jacqui Smith, 64–92. Cambridge: Cambridge University Press.

Anzai, Yuichiro, and Herbert A. Simon. 1979. The theory of learning by doing. *Psychological Review* 86(2): 124–140.

Ausubel, David P. 1963. *The Psychology of Meaningful Verbal Learning* New York: Grune & Stratton.

Beck, Isabel L., Margaret G. McKeown, and Erika W. Gromoll. 1989. Learning from social studies texts. *Cognition and Instruction* 6(2): 99–158.

Ben-Zvi, Ruth, Bat-Sheva Eylon, and Judith Silberstein. 1986. Revision of course materials on the basis of research on conceptual difficulties. *Studies in Educational Evaluation* 12(2): 213–223.

Bereiter, Carl. 1985. Toward a solution of the learning paradox. *Review of Educational Research* 55: 201–226.

Bereiter, Carl. 1990. Aspects of an educational learning theory. *Review of Educational Research* 60 (4): 603–624.

Bereiter, Carl. 1991. Implications of connectionism for thinking about rules. *Educational Researcher* 20(3): 10–16.

Bereiter, Carl, and Marlene Scardamalia. 1987a. An attainable version of high literacy: Approaches to teaching higher-order skills in reading and writing. *Curriculum Inquiry* 17(1): 9–30.

Bereiter, Carl, and Marlene Scardamalia. 1987b. *The Psychology of Written Composition*. Hillsdale, NJ: Erlbaum.

Bereiter, Carl, and Marlene Scardamalia. 1989. "Intentional Learning as a Goal of Instruction." In *Knowing, Learning, and Instruction: Essays in Honor of Robert Glaser*, edited by Lauren B. Resnick, 361–392. Hillsdale, NJ: Erlbaum.

Berlyne, Daniel E. 1962. Uncertainty and epistemic curiosity. *British Journal of Psychology* 53(1): 27–34.

Berliner, David C. 1986. In pursuit of the expert pedagogue. *Educational Researcher* 15(7): 5–13.

Bettelheim, Bruno, and Karen Zelan. 1982. *On Learning to Read: The Child's Fascination with Meaning*. New York: Knopf.

Biggs, John B. 1984. "Learning Strategies, Student Motivation Patterns and Subjectively Perceived Success." In *Cognitive Strat-*

egies and Educational Performance, edited by John R. Kirby, 111–134. Orlando, FL: Academic Press.

Biggs, John B., and Bernard A. Rihn. 1984. "The Effects of Intervention on Deep and Surface Approaches to Learning." In *Cognitive Strategies and Educational Performance*, edited by John R. Kirby, 279–293. Orlando, FL: Academic Press.

Black, John B. 1982. "Psycholinguistic Processes in Writing." In *Handbook of Applied Psycholinguistics*, edited by Sheldon Rosenberg, 199–216. Hillsdale, NJ: Erlbaum.

Black, John B., James A. Galambos, and Brian J. Reiser. 1984. "Coordinating Discovery and Verification Research." In *New Methods in Reading Comprehension Research*, edited by David E. Kieras and Marcel A. Just, 287–297. Hillsdale, NJ: Erlbaum.

Bloom, Benjamin S., and Lois J. Broder. 1950. *Problem-Solving Processes of College Students*. Chicago: University of Chicago Press.

Bobrow, Daniel G., ed. 1985. *Qualitative Reasoning About Physical Systems*. Cambridge, MA: MIT Press.

Brown, Ann L. 1990. Domain-specific principles affect learning and transfer in children. *Cognitive Science* 14(1): 107–133.

Brown, Ann L., John D. Bransford, Roberta A. Ferrara, and Joseph C. Campione. 1983. "Learning, Remembering, and Understanding." In *Handbook of Child Psychology*. Vol. 3, *Cognitive Development*. 4th ed., edited by John H. Flavell and Ellen M. Markman, 77–166. New York: Wiley.

Brown, Ann L., and Annemarie S. Palincsar. 1989. "Guided, Cooperative Learning and Individual Knowledge Acquisition." In *Knowing, Learning, and Instruction: Essays in Honor of Robert Glaser*, edited by Lauren B. Resnick, 393–451. Hillsdale, NJ: Erlbaum.

Brown, John Seely, Allan Collins, and Paul Duguid. 1989a. Debating the situation: A rejoinder to Palincsar and Wineburg. *Educational Researcher* 18(4): 10–12, 62.

Brown, John Seely, Allan Collins, and Paul Duguid. 1989b. Situated cognition and the culture of learning. *Educational Researcher* 18(1): 32–42.

Bruner, Jerome S. 1983. *Child's Talk: Learning to Use Language*. New York: Norton.

Bruner, Jerome S., Jacqueline J. Goodnow, and George A. Austin. 1956. *A Study of Thinking*. New York: Wiley.

Burton, Richard R. 1988. "The Environment Module of Intelligent Tutoring Systems." In *Foundations of Intelligent Tutoring Systems*, edited by Martha C. Polson and J. Jeffrey Richardson, 109–142. Hillsdale, NJ: Erlbaum.

Carey, Susan. 1985. *Conceptual Change in Childhood*. Cambridge, MA: MIT Press.

Carroll, John B. 1976. "Promoting Language Skills: The Role of Instruction." In *Cognition and Instruction*, edited by David Klahr, 3–22. Hillsdale, NJ: Erlbaum.

Case, Robbie. 1985a. "A Developmentally Based Approach to the Problem of Instructional Design." In *Thinking and Learning Skills*. Vol. 2, *Research and Open Questions*, edited by Susan F. Chipman, Judith W. Segal, and Robert Glaser, 545–562. Hillsdale, NJ: Erlbaum.

Case, Robbie. 1985b. *Intellectual Development: Birth to Adulthood*. Orlando, FL: Academic Press.

Case, Robbie, and Carl Bereiter. 1984. From Behaviourism to Cognitive Behaviourism to Cognitive Development: Steps in the Evolution of Instructional Design. *Instructional Science* 13(2): 141–158.

Case, Robbie, and Sharon Griffin. 1990. "Child Cognitive Development: The Role of Central Conceptual Structures in the Development of Scientific and Social Thought." In *Developmental Psychology: Cognitive, Perceptuo-motor, and Neurological Perspectives*, edited by Claude-Alain Hauert, 193–230. North-Holland: Elsevier Science Publishers B.V.

Case, Robbie, and Robert Sandieson. 1986. Two cognitive-developmental approaches to the design of remedial instruction. *Cognitive Development* 1(4): 293–333.

Cassirer, Ernst. 1950. *The Problem of Knowledge: Philosophy, Science, and History Since Hegel*. New Haven, CT: Yale University Press.

Champagne, Audrey B., Leopold E. Klopfer, and John H. Anderson. 1980. Factors influencing the learning of classical mechanics. *American Journal of Physics* 48(12): 1074–1079.

Charness, Neil. 1991. "Expertise in Chess: The Balance Between Knowledge and Search." In *Toward a General Theory of Expertise: Prospect and Limits*, edited by K. Anders Ericsson and Jacqui Smith, 39–63. Cambridge: Cambridge University Press.

Chase, William G., and Herbert A. Simon. 1973. Perception in chess. *Cognitive Psychology* 4(1): 55–81.

Chi, Michelene T. H., Miriam Bassok, Matthew W. Lewis, Peter Reimann, and Robert Glaser. 1989. Self-explanations: How students study and use examples in learning to solve problems. *Cognitive Science* 13(2): 145–182.

Chi, Michelene T. H., Paul J. Feltovich, and Robert Glaser. 1981. Categorization and representation of physics problems by experts and novices. *Cognitive Science* 5(2): 121–152.

Chi, Michelene T. H., Robert Glaser, and M. J. Farr, eds. 1988. *The Nature of Expertise*. Hillsdale, NJ: Erlbaum.

Chomsky, Noam. 1957. *Syntactic Structures*. The Hague: Mouton.

Chomsky, Noam. 1975. *Reflections on Language*. New York: Pantheon Books.

Chomsky, Noam. 1980. *Rules and Representations*. New York: Columbia University Press.

Clancey, William J. 1987. *Knowledge-Based Tutoring: The GUIDON Program*. Cambridge, MA: MIT Press.

Clay, Marie M. 1975. *What Did I Write: Beginning Writing Behaviour*. Auckland, New Zealand: Heinemann.

Clement, John. 1986. "Methods for Evaluating the Validity of Hypothesized Analogies." In *Program of the Eighth Annual Conference of the Cognitive Science Society*, 223–234. Hillsdale, NJ: Erlbaum.

Colby, Kenneth Mark. 1981. Modeling a paranoid mind. *Behavioral and Brain Sciences* 4(4): 515–534.

Collins, Allan, John Seely Brown, and Susan E. Newman. 1989. "Cognitive Apprenticeship: Teaching the Crafts of Reading, Writing, and Mathematics." In *Knowing, Learning, and Instruction: Essays in Honor of Robert Glaser*, edited by Lauren B. Resnick, 453–494. Hillsdale, NJ: Erlbaum.

Cooper, Marilyn, and Michael Holzman. 1983. Talking about protocols. *College Composition and Communication* 34(3): 284–293.

Corbeil, Giselle. 1989. "Adult Second Language Learners: Fostering High Levels of Constructive Processes in Response to Corrective Feedback." Unpublished doctoral dissertation, University of Toronto, Ontario.

Cosmides, Leda. 1989. The logic of social exchange: Has natural selection shaped how humans reason? Studies with the Wason selection task. *Cognition* 31(3): 187–276.

Davis, Randall. 1984. "Amplifying Expertise with Expert Systems." In *The AI business: Commercial Uses of Artificial Intelligence*, edited by Patrick H. Winston and Karen A. Prendergast, 17–40. Cambridge, MA: MIT Press.

Davison, Alice. 1984. "Readability: Appraising Text Difficulty." In *Learning to Read in American Schools: Basal Readers and Content Texts*, edited by Richard C. Anderson, Jean Osborn, and Robert J. Tierney, 121–151. Hillsdale, NJ: Erlbaum.

Davydov, V. V., and L. A. Radzikhovskii. 1985. "Vygotsky's Theory and the Activity-Oriented Approach in Psychology." In *Culture, Communication, and Cognition: Vygotskian Perspectives*, edited by James V. Wertsch, 35–65. Cambridge: Cambridge University Press.

Deadman, J. A., and P. J. Kelly. 1978. What do secondary school boys understand about evolution and heredity before they are taught the topics? *Journal of Biological Education* 12(1): 7–15.

deGroot, Adrien D. 1965. *Thought and Choice in Chess*. The Hague: Mouton.

deKleer, Johan, and John Seely Brown. 1985. "A Qualitative Physics Based on Confluences." In *Qualitative Reasoning About Physical Systems*, edited by Daniel G. Bobrow, 7–84. Cambridge, MA: MIT Press.

Dennett, Daniel C. 1978. *Brainstorms*. Montgomery, VT: Bradford Books.

Dennett, Daniel C. 1983. Intentional systems in cognitive ethology: The "Panglossian paradigm" defended. *Behavioral and Brain Sciences* 6(3): 343–390.

Dennett, Daniel C. 1987. *The Intentional Stance*. Cambridge, MA: MIT Press.

Downing, John A. 1965. *The Initial Teaching Alphabet: Reading Experiment*. Chicago: Scott, Foresman.

Dreyfus, Hubert L., and Stuart E. Dreyfus. 1986. *Mind Over Machine*. New York: Free Press.

Durkin, Dolores. 1979. What classroom observations reveal about reading comprehension instruction. *Reading Research Quarterly* 14(4): 481–533.

Egan, Dennis E., and Barry J. Schwartz. 1979. Chunking in recall of symbolic drawings. *Memory and Cognition* 7(2): 149–158.

Egan, Kieran. 1988. *Primary Understanding: Education in Early Childhood*. New York: Routledge.

Engeström, Yrjö. 1987. *Learning by Expanding: An Activity-Theoretical Approach to Developmental Research*. Helsinki. Orienta-Konsultit Oy.

Erickson, Frederick. 1986. "Qualitative Methods in Research on Teaching." In *Handbook of Research on Teaching*, 3d ed., edited by Merlin C. Wittrock, 119–161. New York: Macmillan.

Ericsson, K. Anders, and Herbert A. Simon. 1980. Verbal reports as data. *Psychological Review* 87(3): 215–251.

Ericsson, K. Anders, and Jacqui Smith, eds. 1991. *Toward a General Theory of Expertise: Prospects and Limits*. Cambridge: Cambridge University Press.

Estes, Thomas H., Carol J. Gutman, and Julie J. Estes. 1989. Cultural literacy: Another view from the University of Virginia. *Curriculum Inquiry* 19(3): 309–325.

Ferreiro, Emilia, and Ana Teberosky. 1982. *Literacy Before Schooling*. Translated by Karen Goodman Castro. Exeter, NH: Heinemann.

Flavell, John H. 1979. Metacognition and cognitive monitoring: A new area of cognitive-developmental inquiry. *American Psychologist* 34(10): 906–911.

Flower, Linda S., and John R. Hayes. 1980. The cognition of discovery: Defining a rhetorical problem. *College Composition and Communication* 31(1): 21–32.

Flower, Linda S., and John R. Hayes. 1981. A cognitive process theory of writing. *College Composition and Communication* 32(4): 365–387.

Fodor, Jerry A. 1975. *The Language of Thought*. New York: Crowell.

Fodor, Jerry. A. 1983. *The Modular Theory of Mind: An Essay on Faculty Psychology*. Lexington, VT: Bradford Books.

Fodor, Jerry A., and Zenon Pylyshyn. 1988. "Connectionism and Cognitive Architecture: A Critical Analysis." In *Connections and Symbols*, edited by Steven Pinker and Jacques Mehler, 3–71. Cambridge, MA: MIT Press/Bradford Books.

Frederiksen, John R. 1982. "A Componential Theory of Reading Skills and their Interactions." In *Advances in the Psychology of Human Intelligence*. Vol. 1, edited by Robert J. Sternberg, 125–180. Hillsdale, NJ: Erlbaum.

Frederiksen, John R., Beth M. Warren, and Ann S. Rosebery. 1985a. A componential approach to training reading skills: Part I. Perceptual units training. *Cognition and Instruction* 2(2): 91–130.

Frederiksen, John R., Beth M. Warren, and Ann S. Rosebery. 1985b. A componential approach to training reading skills: Part II. Decoding and use of context. *Cognition and Instruction* 2(3 & 4): 271–338.

Gagné, Ellen D. 1985. *The Cognitive Psychology of School Learning*. Boston: Little, Brown.

Gardner, Howard. 1985. *The Mind's New Science: A History of the Cognitive Revolution*. New York: Basic Books.

Garner, Ruth. 1987. *Metacognition and Reading Comprehension*. Norwood, NJ: Ablex.

Garner, Ruth. 1990. When children and adults do not use learning strategies: Toward a theory of settings. *Review of Educational Research* 60(4): 517–529.

Garner, Ruth, and Ron Reis. 1981. Monitoring and resolving comprehension obstacles: An investigation of spontaneous text lookbacks among upper-grade good and poor comprehenders. *Reading Research Quarterly* 16(4): 569–582.

Gelman, Rochel S., ed. 1990. Structural constraints on cognitive development. *Cognitive Science* 14(1). Special issue.

Gelman, Rochel S., and Charles R. Gallistel. 1978. *The Child's Understanding of Number*. Cambridge, MA: Harvard University Press.

Gentner, Dedre, and Albert L. Stevens. 1983. *Mental Models*. Hillsdale, NJ: Erlbaum.

Getzels, Jacob W. 1979. Problem-finding: A theoretical note. *Cognitive Science* 3(2): 167–171.

Ghent, Pam'la. 1989. "Expert Learning in Music." Master's thesis, University of Toronto, Ontario.

Gibson, James J. 1979. *The Ecological Approach to Visual Perception*. Boston: Houghton Mifflin.

Glaser, Robert, ed. 1978. *Advances in Instructional Psychology*. Vol. 1. Hillsdale, NJ: Erlbaum.

Glaser, Robert, ed. 1982. *Advances in Instructional Psychology*. Vol. 2. Hillsdale, NJ: Erlbaum.

Glaser, Robert. 1984. Education and thinking: The role of knowledge. *American Psychologist* 39(2): 93–104.

Glaser, Robert, ed. 1987. *Advances in Instructional Psychology*. Vol. 3. Hillsdale, NJ: Erlbaum.

Glaser, Robert, and Miriam Bassok. 1989. Learning theory and the study of instruction. *Annual Review of Psychology* 40: 631–666.

Glaser, Robert, and Michelene T. H. Chi. 1988. "Overview." In *The Nature of Expertise*, edited by Michelene T. H. Chi, Robert Glaser, and M. J. Farr, xv–xxvii. Hillsdale, NJ: Erlbaum.

Glaser, Robert, Alan M. Lesgold, and Susan Lajoie. 1987. "Toward a Cognitive Theory for the Measurement of Achievement." In *The Influence of Cognitive Psychology on Testing*, edited by Royce R. Ronning, John A. Glover, Jane C. Conoley, and Joseph C. Witt, 41–85. Hillsdale, NJ: Erlbaum.

Goodman, Kenneth S., and Yetta M. Goodman. 1979. "Learning to Read is Natural." In *Theory and Practice of Early Reading*. Vol. 1, edited by Lauren B. Resnick and Phyllis A. Weaver, 137–154. Hillsdale, NJ: Erlbaum .

Harré, Rom. 1984. *Personal Being: A Theory for Individual Psychology*. Cambridge, MA: Harvard University Press.

Hartley, James, and Ivor K. Davies. 1976. Preinstructional strategies:

The role of pretests, behavioral objectives, overviews and advance organizers. *Review of Educational Research* 46(2): 239–265.

Hayes, John R. 1981. *The Complete Problem Solver*. Philadelphia, PA: Franklin Institute Press.

Hayes, John R. 1985. "Three Problems in Teaching General Skills." In *Thinking and Learning Skills*. Vol. 2, *Research and Open Questions*, edited by Susan F. Chipman, Judith W. Segal, and Robert Glaser, 391–405. Hillsdale, NJ: Erlbaum.

Hayes, John R., and Linda S. Flower. 1980. Writing as problem solving. *Visible Language* 14(4): 388–399.

Hidi, Suzanne E. 1990. Interest and its contribution as a mental resource for learning. *Review of Educational Research* 60(4): 549–571.

Hilgard, Ernest R., and Gordon H. Bower. 1974. *Theories of Learning*, 4th ed. Englewood Cliffs, NJ: Prentice Hall.

Hirsch, Eric D., Jr. 1987. *Cultural Literacy: What Every American Needs to Know*. Boston, MA: Houghton Mifflin.

Hofstadter, Douglas R. 1985. *Metamagical Themas: Questing for the Essence of Mind and Pattern*. New York: Basic Books.

Holland, John H., Keith J. Holyoak, Richard E. Nisbett, and Paul R. Thagard. 1986. *Induction: Processes of Inference, Learning, and Discovery*. Cambridge, MA: MIT Press.

Iran-Nejad, Asghar, Gerald L. Clore, and Richard J. Vondruska. 1984. Affect: A functional perspective. *Journal of Mind and Behavior* 5(3): 279–310.

Johnson-Laird, Philip N. 1983. *Mental Models: Toward a Cognitive Science of Language, Inference and Consciousness*. Cambridge: Cambridge University Press.

Johnston, Peter, and Peter Afflerbach. 1985. The process of constructing main ideas from text. *Cognition and Instruction* 2(3 and 4): 207–232.

Just, Marcel A., and Patricia A. Carpenter. 1977. *Cognitive Processes in Comprehension*. Hillsdale, NJ: Erlbaum.

Klahr, David, Pat Langley, and Robert Neches, eds. 1987. *Production System Models of Learning and Development*. Cambridge, MA: MIT Press.

Laird, John E., Allen Newell, and Paul S. Rosenbloom. 1987. SOAR: An architecture for general intelligence. *Artificial Intelligence* 33(1): 1–64.

Lakatos, Imre. 1970. "The Methodology of Scientific Research Programmes." In *Criticism and the Growth of Knowledge*, edited by Imre Lakatos and Alan Musgrave 91–195. Cambridge: Cambridge University Press.

Lampert, Magdalene. 1986. Knowing, doing, and teaching multiplication. *Cognition and Instruction* 3(4): 305–342.

Larkin, Jill. 1985. "Problem Representations in Physics." In *Thinking and Learning Skills*. Vol. 2, *Research and Open Questions*, edited by Susan F. Chipman, Judith W. Segal, and Robert Glaser, 141–159. Hillsdale, NJ: Erlbaum .

Larkin, Jill, John McDermott, Dorothea P. Simon, and Herbert A. Simon. 1980. Expert and novice performance in solving physics problems. *Science* 208(4450): 1335–1342.

Lumsden, Charles J., and Edward O. Wilson. 1981. *Genes, Mind, and Culture*. Cambridge, MA: Harvard University Press.

Lumsden, Charles J., and Edward O. Wilson. 1982. Precis of "Genes, mind, and culture." *Behavioral and Brain Sciences* 5(1): 1–38.

McClelland, James L., David E. Rumelhart, and the PDP Research Group. 1986. *Parallel Distributed Processing: Experiments in the Microstructure of Cognition:* Vol. 2. *Psychological and Biological Models*. Cambridge, MA: MIT Press.

McCloskey, Michael, Alfonso Caramazza, and Bert F. Green. 1980. Curvilinear motion in the absence of external forces: Naive beliefs about the motion of objects. *Science* 210(4474): 1139–1141.

Mandler, Jean M., Sylvia Scribner, Michael Cole, and Marsha DeForest. 1980. Cross-cultural invariance in story recall. *Child Development* 51(1): 19–26.

Mason, Jana M., and Jobeth Allen. 1986. A review of emergent literacy with implications for research and practice in reading. *Review of Research in Education* 13: 3–47.

Mestre, Jose P., Robert Dufresne, William Gerace, and Pamela T. Hardiman. 1988. "Hierarchical Problem Solving as a Means of Promoting Expertise." In *Program of the Tenth Annual Conference of the Cognitive Science Society*, 312–318. Hillsdale, NJ: Erlbaum.

Miller, George A. 1956. The magical number seven, plus or minus two: Some limits on our capacity for processing information. *Psychological Review* 63(2): 81–97.

Minsky, Marvin L. 1984. "The Problems and the Promise." In *The AI Business: Commercial Uses of Artificial Intelligence*, edited by Patrick H. Winston and Karen A. Prendergast, 243–254. Cambridge, MA: MIT Press.

Mosenthal, Peter. 1983. Defining classroom writing competence: A paradigmatic perspective. *Review of Educational Research* 53(2): 217–251.

Murphy, Gregory L., and Douglas L. Medin. 1985. The role of theories in conceptual coherence. *Psychological Review* 92(3): 289–316.

Myers, Meyer, II, and Scott G. Paris. 1978. Children's metacognitive knowledge about reading. *Journal of Educational Psychology* 70(5): 680–690.

Neisser, Ulric. 1988. The ecological approach to perception and memory. *New Trends in Experimental and Clinical Psychiatry* 4(3): 153–166.

Newell, Allen. 1980. "Reasoning, Problem Solving, and Decision Processes: The Problem Space as a Fundamental Category." In *Attention and Performance VIII*, edited by Raymond S. Nickerson, 693–718. Hillsdale, NJ: Erlbaum.

Newell, Allen, J. C. Shaw, and Herbert A. Simon. 1958. Elements of a theory of human problem solving. *Psychological Review* 65(3): 151–166.

Newell, Allen, and Herbert A. Simon. 1972. *Human Problem Solving*. Englewood Cliffs, NJ: Prentice Hall.

Newman, Denis, and Shelley V. Goldman. 1987. Earth Lab: A local network for collaborative classroom science. *Journal of Educational Technology Systems* 15(3): 237–247.

Ng, K., L. Evelyn, and Carl Bereiter. In press. Three levels of goal orientation in learning. *The Journal of the Learning Sciences*.

Nussbaum, Joseph. 1979. Children's conceptions of the earth as a cosmic body: A cross-age study. *Science Education* 63(1): 83–93.

Olshavsky, Jill E. 1977. Reading as problem solving: An investigation of strategies. *Reading Research Quarterly* 12(4): 654–674.

Palincsar, Annemarie S. 1989. Less charted waters. *Educational Researcher* 18(4): 5–7.

Pascual-Leone, Juan, Doba Goodman, Paul R. Ammon, and Irene Subelman. 1979. "Piagetian Theory and Neo-Piagetian Analysis as Psychological Guides in Education." In *Knowledge and Development*. Vol. 2, *Piaget and Education*, edited by Jeanette M. Gallagher and Jack Easley, 243–289. New York: Plenum.

Pascual-Leone, Juan, and June Smith. 1969. The encoding and decoding of symbols by children: A new experimental paradigm and a neo-Piagetian model. *Journal of Experimental Child Psychology* 8(2): 328–355.

Pea, Roy D., and Karen Sheingold, eds. 1987. *Mirrors of Minds: Patterns of Expertise in Educational Computing*. Norwood, NJ: Ablex.

Piaget, Jean. 1960. *The Psychology of Intelligence*. Paterson, NJ: Littlefield, Adams.

Piaget, Jean. 1970. *Science of Education and the Psychology of the Child*. New York: Orion Press.

Piaget, Jean. 1971. *Insights and Illusions of Philosophy*. New York: New American Library.

Piaget, Jean. 1980. "Afterthoughts." In *Language and Learning: The Debate Between Jean Piaget and Noam Chomsky*, edited by Massimo Piattelli-Palmarini, 278–284. Cambridge, MA: Harvard University Press.

Piattelli-Palmarini, Massimo, ed. 1980. *Language and Learning: The Debate Between Jean Piaget and Noam Chomsky*. Cambridge, MA: Harvard University Press.

Plomin, Robert, John C. DeFries, and John C. Loehlin. 1977. Genotype-environment interaction and correlation in the analysis of human behavior. *Psychological Bulletin* 84(2): 309–322.

Plutchik, Robert, and Henry Kellerman. 1980. *Emotion: Theory, Research, and Experience*. Vol. 1. *Theories of Emotion*. New York: Academic Press.

Polanyi, Michael. 1964. *Personal Knowledge: Towards a Post-Critical Philosophy*. New York: Harper & Row.

Polson, Martha C., and J. Jeffrey Richardson, eds. 1988. *Intelligent Tutoring Systems*. Hillsdale, NJ: Erlbaum.

Popper, Karl R. 1972. *Objective Knowledge*. Oxford: Clarendon Press.

Pressley, Michael, and Joel R. Levin, eds. 1983. *Cognitive Strategy Research: Educational Applications*. New York: Springer-Verlag.

Pressley, Michael, Joel R. Levin, and Harold D. Delaney. 1982. The mnemonic keyword method. *Review of Educational Research* 52(1): 61–92.

Pylyshyn, Zenon W. 1984. *Computation and Cognition: Toward a Foundation for Cognitive Science*. Cambridge, MA: MIT Press.

Ravitch, Diane. 1987. Tot sociology: Or what happened to history in the grade schools. *American Scholar* 56(3): 343–354.

Resnick, Lauren B. 1987a. "The Development of Mathematical Intuition." In *Minnesota Symposium on Child Psychology*. Vol. 19, edited by Marion Perlmutter, 159–194. Hillsdale, NJ: Erlbaum.

Resnick, Lauren B. 1987b. *Education and Learning to Think*. Washington, DC: National Academy Press.

Resnick, Lauren B., and Robert Glaser. 1976. "Problem Solving and Intelligence." In *The Nature of Intelligence*, edited by Lauren B. Resnick, 205–230. Hillsdale, NJ: Erlbaum.

Resnick, Lauren B., and Robert Neches. 1984. "Factors Affecting Individual Differences in Learning Ability." In *Advances in the Psychology of Human Intelligence*, edited by Robert J. Sternberg, 275–323. Hillsdale, NJ: Erlbaum.

Rogoff, Barbara, and Jean Lave, eds. 1984. *Everyday Cognition: Its Development in Social Context*. Cambridge, MA: Harvard University Press.

Rosenbloom, Paul S., and Allen Newell. 1987. "Learning by Chunking: A Production System Model of Practice." In *Production System Models of Learning and Development*, edited by David Klahr, Pat Langley, and Robert Neches, 221–286. Cambridge, MA: MIT Press.

Roth, Kathleen J. 1988. *Conceptual Understanding and Higher Level Thinking in the Elementary Science Curriculum: Three Perspectives*. East Lansing, MI: Center for the Learning and Teaching of Elementary Subjects. Mimeographed.

Rumelhart, David E. 1980. "Schemata: The Building Blocks of Cognition." In *Theoretical Issues in Reading Comprehension*, edited by Rand J. Spiro, Bertram C. Bruce, and William F. Brewer, 33–58. Hillsdale, NJ: Erlbaum.

Rumelhart, David E., James L. McClelland, and the PDP Research Group. 1986. *Parallel Distributed Processing: Experiments in the Microstructure of Cognition*. Vol. 1. *Foundations*. Cambridge, MA: MIT Press.

Rumelhart, David E., and Andrew Ortony. 1977. "The Representation of Knowledge in Memory." In *Schooling and the Acquisition of Knowledge*, edited by Richard C. Anderson, Rand J. Spiro, and William E. Montague, 99–135. Hillsdale, NJ: Erlbaum.

Russell, Robert L., and Herbert P. Ginsburg. 1984. Cognitive analysis of children's mathematics difficulties. *Cognition and Instruction* 1(2): 217–244.

Ryle, Gilbert. 1949. *The Concept of Mind*. London: Hutchinson.

Sampson, Edward E. 1989. The challenge of social change for psychology: Globalization and psychology's theory of the person. *American Psychologist* 44(6): 914–921.

Scardamalia, Marlene, and Carl Bereiter. 1984. "Development of Strategies in Text Processing." In *Learning and Comprehension of Text*, edited by Heinz Mandl, Nancy L. Stein, and Tom Trabasso, 379–406. Hillsdale, NJ: Erlbaum .

Scardamalia, Marlene, and Carl Bereiter. 1989. "Conceptions of Teaching and Approaches to Core Problems." In *Knowledge Base for the Beginning Teacher*, edited by Maynard C. Reynolds, 37–46. New York: Pergamon.

Scardamalia, Marlene, and Carl Bereiter. In press. "Schools as Knowledge-Building Communities." In *Human Development: The Tel Aviv Annual Workshop*. Vol. 7. *Development and Learning Environments*, edited by Sidney Strauss. Norwood, NJ: Ablex.

Scardamalia, Marlene, Carl Bereiter, Robert S. McLean, Jonathan Swallow, and Earl Woodruff. 1989. Computer-supported intentional learning environments. *Journal of Educational Computing Research* 5(1): 51–68.

Scardamalia, Marlene, Carl Bereiter, and Rosanne Steinbach. 1984. Teachability of reflective processes in written composition. *Cognitive Science* 8: 173–190.

Scarr, Sandra, and Kathleen McCartney. 1983. How people make their own environments: A theory of genotype-environment effects. *Child Development* 54(2): 424–435.

Schank, Roger C., and Robert P. Abelson. 1977. *Scripts, Plans, Goals, and Understanding*. Hillsdale, NJ: Erlbaum.

Schneider, Walter. 1985. Training high performance skills: Fallacies and guidelines. *Human Factors* 27(3): 285–300.

Schoenfeld, Alan H. 1985. *Mathematical Problem Solving*. Orlando, FL: Academic Press.

Shiffrin, Richard M., and Walter Schneider. 1977. Controlled and automatic human information processing: II. Perceptual learning, automatic attending, and a general theory. *Psychological Review* 84(2): 127–190.

Siegler, Robert S., ed. 1978. *Children's Thinking: What Develops?* Hillsdale, NJ: Erlbaum.

Siegler, Robert S. 1986. *Children's Thinking*. Englewood Cliffs, NJ: Prentice Hall.

Siegler, Robert S. 1988. The perils of averaging data over strategies: An example from children's addition. *Journal of Experimental Psychology: General* 116(3): 250–264.

Simon, Herbert A. 1974. How big is a chunk? *Science* 183: 482–488.

Smolensky, Paul. 1988. On the proper treatment of connectionism. *Behavioral and Brain Sciences* 11(1): 1–74.

Spelke, Elizabeth S. 1982. "Perceptual Knowledge of Objects in Infancy." In *Perspectives in Mental Representation: Experimental and Theoretical Studies of Cognitive Processes and Capacities*, edited by Jacques Mehler, Edward C. T. Walker, and Merrill Garrett, 409–430. Hillsdale, NJ: Erlbaum.

Stanley, Julian C., ed. 1972. *Preschool Programs for the Disadvantaged*. Baltimore, MD: Johns Hopkins University Press.

Stanovich, Keith E. 1980. Toward an interactive-compensatory model of individual differences in the development of reading fluency. *Reading Research Quarterly* 16(1): 32–71.

Starkey, Prentice, Elizabeth S. Spelke, and Rochel S. Gelman. 1983. Detection of intermodal numerical correspondences by human infants. *Science* 222(4620): 179–181.

Stefik, Mark. 1986. The next knowledge medium. *AI Magazine* 7(2): 34–46.

Stich, Stephen P. 1983. *From Folk Psychology to Cognitive Science: The Case Against Belief*. Cambridge, MA: MIT Press.

Sweller, John. 1988. Cognitive load during problem solving: Effects on learning. *Cognitive Science* 12(2): 257–285.

Thorndike, Edward L. 1917. Reading as reasoning: A study of mistakes in paragraph reading. *Journal of Educational Psychology* 8(6): 323–332.

Thorndike, Edward L. 1949. *Selected Writings from a Connectionist's Psychology*. New York: Appleton-Century-Crofts.

Thurstone, Louis L. 1934. The vectors of mind. *Psychological Review* 41(1): 1–32.

Tyler, Ralph W. 1930. What high-school pupils forget. *Educational Research Bulletin* 9(17): 490–492.

VanLehn, Kurt. 1988. "Student Modeling." In *Intelligent Tutoring Systems*, edited by Martha C. Polson and J. Jeffrey Richardson, 55–78. Hillsdale, NJ: Erlbaum.

Viennot, L. 1979. Spontaneous reasoning in elementary dynamics. *European Journal of Science Education* 1(2): 205–221.

Vosniadou, Stella, and William F. Brewer. 1987. Theories of knowledge restructuring in development. *Review of Educational Research* 57(1): 51–67.

Voss, James F. 1984. "On Learning and Learning from Text." In *Learning and Comprehension of Text*, edited by Heinz Mandl, Nancy L. Stein, and Tom Trabasso, 193–212. Hillsdale, NJ: Erlbaum.

Voss, James F. 1988. "Problem Solving and the Educational Process." In *Foundations for a Psychology of Education*, edited by Alan M. Lesgold and Robert Glaser, 251–294. Hillsdale, NJ: Erlbaum.

Vygotsky, Lev S. 1962. *Thought and Language*. Translated from the Russian by G. Vakar and edited by E. Haufmann. Cambridge, MA: MIT Press.

Vygotsky, Lev S. 1978. *Mind in Society: The Development of Higher Psychological Processes*. Translated and edited by Michael Cole, Vera John-Steiner, Sylvia Scribner, and Ellen Souberman. Cambridge, MA: Harvard University Press.

Weinstein, Claire E., and Richard E. Mayer. 1986. "The Teaching of Learning Strategies." In *Handbook of Research on Teaching*. 3d ed., edited by Merlin C. Wittrock, 315–327. New York: Macmillan.

West, Leo H. T., and A. Leon Pines, eds. 1985. *Cognitive Structure and Conceptual Change*. Orlando, FL: Academic Press.

White, Barbara Y., and John R. Frederiksen. 1990. Causal model progressions as a foundation for intelligent learning environments. *Artificial Intelligence* 42(1): 99–157.

Whitehead, Alfred N. 1929. *The Aims of Education*. New York: Macmillan.

Wineburg, Samuel S. 1989. Remembrance of theories past. *Educational Researcher* 18(4): 7–10.

Winne, Philip H., and Ronald W. Marx. 1982. Students' and teachers' views of thinking processes for classroom learning. *Elementary School Journal* 82(5): 493–518.

Wittrock, Merlin C. 1974. Learning as a generative process. *Educational Psychologist* 11(2): 87–95.

Wittrock, Merlin C. 1986a. "Students' Thought Processes." In *Handbook of Research on Teaching*. 3d ed., edited by Merlin C. Wittrock, 297–314. New York: Macmillan.

Wittrock, Merlin C., ed. 1986b. *Handbook of Research on Teaching*. 3d ed. New York: Macmillan.

Zinchenko, Vladimir P. 1985. "Vygotsky's Ideas about Units for the Analysis of Mind." In *Culture, Communication, and Cognition: Vygotskian Perspectives*, edited by James V. Wertsch, 94–118. Cambridge: Cambridge University Press.

20

THE MORAL ASPECTS OF THE CURRICULUM

Hugh Sockett

GEORGE MASON UNIVERSITY

"What schools do, consciously and unconsciously, to help the young think about issues of right and wrong, to desire the social good, and to help them behave in an ethical manner" defines the moral in the conduct of educational institutions (Ryan 1985, 3406). Such moral education "comes with the territory": It is found in every aspect of school life, whether or not that fact is recognized by parents, teachers, students, or researchers (Purpel and Ryan 1976).

THE PERVASIVENESS OF THE MORAL

The pervasiveness of the moral in schooling provides continuing opportunities, for "morality is a custodian. Wherever one goes, in or out, whatever decision is made, there is a moral dimension to it. The moral gate is always open" (Oser 1986, 917). Within the moral realm, however, there is a vast range of diverse, contradictory, and competing understandings. Differing philosophical views of the moral, Mill's utilitarianism, Stevenson's emotivism, James's pragmatism, Sartre's existentialism, Kant's objectivism, and others imply contradictory conceptions of moral education. Similarly, different sociological perspectives, from Talcott Parsons' functionalism to the critical approach of Habermas and Althusser, must be taken into account alongside the differing views of man implicit in Skinnerian behaviorism, Freudian and neo-Freudian psychoanalysis, and Piaget's developmentalism. For the general public, the curriculum form and content of moral education is seen as subjective or objective, religious or humanist, relativist or absolutist. Whatever this panoply of perspectives, the individual parent and the teacher are still faced with the "most fundamental moral decisions" if they are to answer one moral philosopher's question: "How shall I bring up my children?" (Hare 1961)

The Politics of Moral Education

Lawrence Kohlberg daringly declared in 1978 that "liberalism will probably not be replaced by a new ideology of the West but will continue to be the dominant ideology for the next century" (Kohlberg 1980a, 56), but the 1980s were marked by a resurgent conservatism in the West and strong views on moral and values education. The agenda of the Reagan presidency as expressed through Secretary William Bennett (1980) contained a strong appeal to the schools to teach traditional moral values with conviction, example, pride, and discipline. This agenda retains considerable support from religious fundamentalists, who, as the new radicals or moral majority, sustain a vociferous reluctance to allow the schools a place in matters that are seen as the responsibility of the family—while simultaneously advocating school prayer.

The moral function of the school is profoundly uncertain and is subject to greater political surveillance at a time of major social dilemmas and controversies. Teachers are frequently subject to state or local mandates on moral teaching. Their role has shifted since 1965 from in loco parentis (with its moral implications) to one governed by due process. The political paradox of moral education is that while few (Bereiter 1973 and Welton 1977) deny that schools have a moral function of some kind, and public opinion polls consistently reveal widespread support for moral education in schools, there is little agreement on what that should be.

Contemporary Issues and Moral Education

The most dramatic and far-reaching of the dilemmas for educators in the 1990s is encapsulated in the phenomenon of AIDS. Expert opinion held world-wide stresses that only through changes in behavior, brought about through education, can the spread of AIDS be curtailed.

In 1982, 75 percent of junior and senior high schools and two thirds of all elementary schools offered sex education as part of their curriculum. Programs ranged from a unit in general and life science classes to year-long courses in which decision making and behavioral changes, in addition to the biological processes, were course objectives. Sex education programs result in improved scores on tests assessing factual knowledge concerning sexual processes. However, no statistically significant differences have been found between control and experimental groups in attitudinal and behavioral changes or decision-making ability when these objectives are included in the curriculum (Kirby 1984). Sex education seems simply a failure in terms of its influence on students' attitudes and behavior, if sexual restraint is seen as a primary objective. That the connection between education and behavioral change is negligible is a devastating conclusion in the face of AIDS. Yet failure has been a common theme in the history of moral education in schools (Scriven 1975, 689).

Sex education is only one aspect of the range of formidable issues confronting schools. Public debate on abortion and homosexuality influences the development of family life curricula, which raises wider issues of the responsibilities, rights, and duties of parents in relation to the schools. Drug abuse, along with its causes and effects, is increasingly seen within a framework of children's mutual responsibility and care. The incidence of violence in families highlights both the character of sexual relations and the rights of women. Environmental problems of many different kinds incorporate issues of humanity's responsibility to nature (Passmore 1975). Social life forces a crisis of early adulthood on teenagers (Elkind 1984). Too little research on the curriculum implications of these factors is being conducted.

The Education of Teachers

Durkheim argued for the school as a critical link between family and state for the young (Durkheim 1973 [1961]). The process of schooling provides for moral learning, discipline for life in society, loyalty to a nation learned through attachments to school communities, and the moral climate of the school in which serious thought on moral matters may be engendered. Tom (1984) provides the most forceful recent statement of teaching as a moral craft, yet descriptions of teacher knowledge and the standards set by the National Professional Teaching Standards Board pay limited attention to the teacher's role as a moral educator (National Board for Professional Teaching Standards 1989). Ryan argues fervently that the education of teachers needs to be a moral education to redress the skills orientation of contemporary teacher education reform (Ryan 1987, 358–380), but the political and social constraints within which teachers operate make this unlikely in preservice education. Yet without moral education for teachers, it is argued that teachers cannot face up to the problems of their role, the work of the institutions they serve, and the pervasiveness of the moral in their professional role.

MORAL EDUCATION, MORAL LEARNING, AND MORAL DEVELOPMENT: HISTORY AND THEORY

Moral Education since 1914

Children living in America are brought up as Americans. In the 19th century the American public school was seen as the context of enculturation for diverse immigrant groups and for all levels of society: It was the place in which the generally accepted morality of the new society would be built into the minds of its new citizens. Demeanor, duty, character, good behavior, manners, and morals of an avowedly Christian kind should characterize this endeavor. McGuffey's Readers were the language arts curriculum vehicles for the ideas that Horace Mann, as the architect of the common school, had laid out (Filler 1965).

In keeping with the freedom of conscience principle immanent in the idea of America, this philosophy of a common school was marked in practice by diverse religious denominations founding their own institutions and by new elites who, like their predecessors and contemporaries, established private schools for the common education of their young. The ideal was therefore undermined by issues of class, race, and religion (Bowles and Gintis 1976). The "array of institutions and principles [has] rested upon a cultural foundation comprising a limited theological and/or metaphysical consensus and a much more explicit moral consensus rooted in a natural law ethic" (Johnson 1987, 59–67). In keeping, too, with the pioneering individualism that defined America, entrepreneurial competition, and the virtues of character which would promote it, "the school gave everyone a chance to become hard-working, literate, temperate, frugal and a good planner" (Tyack and Hansot 1982, 28). The development of a particular character became the way in which the "American" could be defined.

At the turn of the 20th century, public education underwent severe reexamination: Johnson's comprehensive account defines the change as the introduction of the belief in functions and utilitarian outcomes replacing the rhetoric of "imitation" and "virtue" (Johnson 1982). The belief that schools should be morally educative institutions persisted; in 1918 the National Educational Association took ethical character to be paramount among the objectives of the school (National Education Association 1918). Moral instruction continued to be direct, detailed attention to moral character in the general curriculum and the life of the school. "Character," as a term, avoided the difficulties of a religious-secular conflict over the words "moral" and "ethical." Yet this conflict, along with the moral relativism inevitable in a pluralist society, made consensus difficult to find.

The practice of character education was theoretically, if not practically, undermined by the Hartshorne and May inquiries of 1928–1930. These studies showed that conventional didactic ethical instruction has little effect on moral character and conduct as objectively measured by experimental tests of honesty, service, altruism, and self-control, though the data is constantly subject to reassessment (Burton 1976). The common practice of American schools, in other words, was an abject failure. From this Hartshorne and May were led to conclude that there was no such thing as character or conscience as individual traits, as had been argued by Charters (1927); rather, that concepts of good and bad conduct could be understood, like other conduct, only in terms of children's needs, the group's values, and the demands of the situation (Kohlberg 1971). While the impact of this research, as usual, took time to permeate to the classroom, there was a notable shift through the 1940s to an emphasis on citizenship education (always a strong presence in conceptions of character education), and that found a place particularly in social studies curricula.

The curriculum reform movement of the 1960s brought a much broader range of academic interest to public education. Yet the social context of the times was profoundly influential on schooling and curricula: The rise of a dynamic youth culture, the profound public issues of race and civil rights, the bitter controversy over the Vietnam War, and the development of the feminist movement each contributed to a belief in the inevitability of moral relativism, or, at least, in the impracticability of a school teaching moral values with any certitude. Young and old, black and white, women and men seemed embroiled in unresolvable disputes. The very idea of seeking objectivity as an educational principle, as, for example, in the social studies curriculum *Man: A Course of Study* (MACOS), was publicly assailed (Shaver 1987).

The public demand that the schools take some responsibility for moral education has not diminished in the 30 years since 1960. Against this background it is not surprising that the two dominating conceptions of moral education avoided a prescription of content, at least in their initial development. They focused, respectively, on moral dilemmas and on a pedagogy of process. The first, the cognitive developmental approach of Kohlberg, was built on Piaget, a Kantian view of justice, and, to a lesser degree, on Dewey. It sketched the ways in which children (predominantly male) use reason when faced with hypothetical dilemmas. The second, values clarification, was a movement that described the process. Apparently empty of moral content, this matched the relativism of the times in the procedures it devised for assisting children to sort out what they valued.

Whatever leading status these ideas had, it is important not to neglect the continuing interest of some educators in psychoanalytic theory and, with it, the belief that character is a reflection of deep emotional forces in the personality rather than a reflection of educational experiences as such. While making judgments on the basis of reason was the defining characteristic of the rational morality underpinning cognitive developmental theory, coming to terms with guilt and other feelings is critical in psychoanalytic theories. Social learning theory too, while not prevalent in classroom practice, focused on outcomes in behavior. Both pay great attention to developments in early childhood rather than to the stage development through adolescence as set out by Piaget and Kohlberg.

Alongside these differing approaches, three factors are worth noting. First, the philosophical interest in moral education expanded dramatically, prompted not merely by Kohlberg's Kantianism but by a revitalization of philosophy of education in the 1960s. Second, there has been the development of a corpus of ideas that a woman's perspective on morality is distinctive in its primary focus on caring relationships, rather than on justice embedded in rules (Gilligan 1982; Noddings 1984). Third, in the 1980s, there was a resurgence of interest in character education coming out of a philosophy of virtue rather than a psychology of trait.

How much this intellectual effort has changed the curriculum of schools is another matter. Values-clarification texts sold more than a half million copies each. Kohlberg participated in the development of various curricula to change the character of schools through the "cluster" and the "just community" school projects (Mosher 1980). Is it correct, then, to label moral education as a failure? Far from from being a failure, some critics see present practice as perniciously successful. In a biting attack on both values-clarification theorists and Kohlberg for their neglect of the Western tradition of moral thought, Hoff Sommers (1984) indicates that many college freshmen in her experience are in a complete moral stupor, needing to be shown that there is an important distinction between moral and nonmoral decisions. On this account, the college student as a product of schooling is a mix of psychological egoism, moral relativism, radical tolerance, and a profound sense that moral responsibility exists in society, not in individuals. The very idea of individual virtue is foreign to them, a view expressed at greater length by Allan Bloom (1987).

Apart from values clarification, there is not much sign that relativistic pluralism has undermined moral educational thought. Yet, at the same time, few are searching for any thoroughgoing theoretical eclecticism, even in the face of a sociomoral crisis. Only Peters (1974) and Hoffman (1980) have argued that the differing positions found in Piaget and Kohlberg, Skinner and Freud, and their respective heirs are not competing explanations but rather address different aspects of the growth of the human person. Tobin (1989) suggests that, although Peters seems to see himself as in broad sympathy with Kohlberg, an overview of his writing in moral education yields a quite distinctive, comprehensive, and broad based view of moral development, moral learning, and moral education, which needs to be recognized as such.

Is such a broad-based view possible or coherent? Kurtines and Gewirtz (1984) suggest that theoretical syntheses of psychological models may not be possible in a pluralist society, an argument that, if it is correct, effectively rules out any notion of value-free psychological science. While Kohlberg's school-based work in the 1980s has led to a rapprochement with reinterpretations of character education (Nucci 1989), there are few signs of a comprehensive account of differing aspects of moral development emerging in America.

For curriculum, only Pring's work is a sophisticated attempt to draw on a wide range of philosophical and psychological positions to construct a view of *Personal and Social Education in the Curriculum* that is also comprehensible to teachers (Pring 1984). While the purity of different theoretical stances can be valuable and productive, the fact that there is a national crisis of moral upbringing must raise questions about the myopia and the social responsibility of the research community. The zeal of the character education movement is a response to that vacuum in academic responsibility.

This chapter therefore pictures educational thought in 1990 as lacking an established view of moral development and moral learning. It is divided into an account of differing perspectives that influence curriculum.

Social Learning, Social Interaction, and Moral Education

Pavlov, Watson, Hull, and Skinner laid the foundations for the development of social learning theory. While there are critical differences among behaviorists, the fundamental methodology is an approach to human behavior through what can be observed objectively, rather than what individuals may report on what they think, feel, or do. Crudely, they look to movements (however complex) of the body and either deny the existence of the human mind or remain agnostic about its existence.

Skinner, however, carried the principles of behaviorism directly into curriculum and instructional proposals, believing that social equilibrium demanded certain (perspicuously desirable) kinds of behavior from members of a society and that the techniques for the development of desirable behaviors were known but not implemented (Skinner 1971). But social learning theorists began to emphasize the cognitive, drawing particularly on the work of Tolman, Mead, and Sullivan. Rotter (1984 [1954]) integrated both motivational and cognitive variables in a theory of personality with an emphasis on performance.

What marks off these writers as social learning theorists? Social learning theory places emphasis on social situations as the context in which both the basic and the major modes of behaving are learned in social situations. The mediation of other people is a crucial requirement for needs satisfaction. Thus Bandura (1971), while acknowledging the significance of reinforcement, emphasizes modeling, observation, imitation, and the extent of motivation. He concludes that behavioral changes that occur through classical and instrumental conditioning, as well as extinction and punishment, are actively mediated by cognition and processes of self-regulation, a view that is indicative of the broad development of social learning theory away from the simple notions of stimulus-response mechanisms.

Mischel (1973) articulated five major factors of human personality and learning. People differ, so there are variables of personality. They have different competencies or repertoires that influence their thought and action. They use decoding strategies and thus react to environmental stimulation in different ways. Their predictions of behavior and their expectancies also differ. They give differential affective weight to outcomes; their values are subjective. Finally, they use self-imposed standards, so their systems and plans are self-regulating.

Little of this work has found its way directly into curriculum in recent years. However, social interaction theory appears more relevant (Argyle 1969). Social life, in this view, is construed as a set of interactions for which individuals need mastery of the different patterns. Most people perform competently and unthinkingly, but the failures of social competence can reveal critical aspects of social skill—for example, the inability to see another person's point of view. On social interaction theory are built a wide range of techniques for the improvement of social skills, including role-play, simulation, coaching, and modeling, which may be used in a variety of teaching or therapeutic contexts.

Moral Education 13–16 was a British project rooted in social interaction theory: It began not with hypothetical dilemmas but with the existing interpersonal problems children face in adolescence (McPhail 1982; McPhail, Middleton, and Ingram 1978). They found that children wanted practical help, for example, in a situation in which an individual had been treated badly and didn't know how to respond. Three types of curriculum material were produced ("In Other People's Shoes"; "Proving the Rule"; and "What Would You Have Done?") using role play, simulation, discussion, and art with the aim of giving this practical help and getting children to take *care* in their social interactions and thereby to develop what is called "a considerate style of life." A second project on this basis was developed for use with elementary children (Ungoed-Thomas 1978), which is not dissimilar to a project on children's social adjustment (Spivak and Shure 1974). The curricular significance of these projects is their emphasis on behavior (through role play) and on the attention to the affective, the motivational aspect of morality, to which Bandura and others drew attention.

Psychoanalytic Theories and Education

The central aims of psychoanalysis are twofold: to strengthen the ego by making unconscious conflicts conscious and to help people to make decisions with full understanding of the irrational sources of what they feel forced to do or of what they use as guides to conduct (Peters 1974). In terms of moral education, psychoanalytic theory provides an account of the importance of the formation of conscience, within which feelings of guilt and shame are located. This is based on a view of infantile sexuality. Young children experience frustrations that, whatever their source, generate hostility toward parents. But the child wants to sustain as much bodily contact with his (rarely her) mother because of the erotic feelings this engenders. The father is thus a rival, and the child is often "punished" for seeking to sustain that contact. To avoid being rejected, the (usually male) child curbs the erotic desire and the anger that very hostility generates: He adopts the rules and regulations parents impose. The child thus copies the parents, but also imposes the rules on him (or her) self. With this self-punishment, the child experiences guilt intensely and seeks to avoid that by always following the rules. The child thus has erected internally a conscience, that is, an internal system of guilt and shame as a guide to action. Psychoanalysis is therefore curative rather than educational: It has focused primarily on persons who are impaired, judged by a somewhat arbitrary standard of common sense, and also, in Adelson's view, by "an insular theory and tired, overemployed concepts" (Adelson 1986).

It also has a continuing focus on males. Erikson's classic statement of the "Eight Ages of Man" (*sic*) matches eight stages of physical change and development with eight psychic conflicts in human development:

1	Oral Sensory	Basic Trust v. Mistrust
2	Muscular-Anal	Autonomy v. Shame, Doubt
3	Locomotor-Genital	Initiative v. Guilt
4	Latency	Industry v. Inferiority
5	Puberty and Adolescence	Identity v. Role Confusion
6	Young Adulthood	Intimacy v. Isolation
7	Adulthood	Generativity v. Stagnation
8	Maturity	Ego Integrity v. Despair

This is a picture of the development of the autonomous ego. Drawing on a variety of cases, Erikson (1963) has set out conditions for the success of developments at each stage.

Two main lines of work of special significance to contemporary curriculum and moral education are maternal deprivation and the importance of myth. Work on empathy in adolescence also demonstrates ways in which psychoanalytic theory can be integrated with other views of moral development.

First, in a context in which day-care centers for very young children are providing facilities that enable mothers to pursue full-time careers, psychoanalytic theorists provide evidence that there is a strong causal relationship between a child's experience with his or her parents and his or her capacity, as an adolescent or an adult, to make what Bowlby calls "affectional bonds" (Bowlby 1979, 1966). The claim is that personality disorders and many symptoms of neurosis are attributable to the variety of ways in which parents perform their roles. Central is (1) the provision of a secure base; (2) the extent to which parents develop their ability to sympathize with a child and understand that the child's frustrations must be met with love and care; and (3) their time that they make themselves available to the child—critical in present-day life. If "all children have contact only with their age mates, there is no possibility for learning culturally established patterns of cooperation and mutual concern" (Bronfenbrenner 1970).

Second, in the context of media influence on children's imagination and a "back to basics" movement influencing the curriculum of the elementary school, Bettelheim draws attention to the significance of the fairy tale:

> A child needs to understand what is going on within his conscious self so that he can also cope with that which goes on in his unconscious. He can achieve this understanding, and with it the ability to cope, not through rational comprehension of the nature and content of his unconscious, but by becoming familiar with it through spinning out daydreams—ruminating, rearranging, and fantasizing about suitable story elements in response to unconscious pressures.

Fairy tales have immense value in enabling a child to "structure his daydreams and with them give better direction to his life" (Bettelheim 1977, 7; see also Bettelheim 1970). The curriculum implication of this account also strengthens Egan's argument on the importance of myth (Egan 1986).

Finally, Hoffman acknowledges that there are more hypotheses than facts about the moral development of adolescents. He has sketched an important account of the development of altruism that is both critical and receptive of psychoanalytic theories (Hoffman 1976). He has also stressed the significance of the process of moral internalization, the way in which the adolescent takes on moral values as his or her own. He suggests that apparently competing theories of moral development yield three component (not staged) processes in a person's moral orientation. First, a primitive view of internalization is anxiety-based inhibition. In a mature society this would be minimal, but it may continue to be influential in moral action, as is the relationship of the child to parental authority. A second contributor to moral maturity, however, is an empathy-based concern for others, provided there is appropriate curriculum and socializing experience. A third is the experience of cognitive disequilibrium and the need for equilibration. Here one has to process information at variance with one's beliefs, for example, in considering dilemmas in class (Hoffman 1980).

Cognitive Development Theory: Lawrence Kohlberg

His intellectual debt to Kant, Piaget, and Dewey is one aspect of the immense volume of literature devoted to the work of Lawrence Kohlberg. Not only are his published and unpublished works extensive but the work of his colleagues—Turiel, Boyd, Gilligan, Power, Berkowitz, Mosher, Nucci, Colby, and others—as well as that of his various critics (Modgil and Modgil 1986; Sichel 1988, 310), make Kohlberg's work dominant in the research literature of moral education since 1965. An early assessment of his intellectual and human legacy on those who worked with him provides interesting insights, particularly on his personality and political motivations. (See Kohlberg 1981 and Kohlberg 1984 for the most comprehensive statements of his work.)

The Development of Kohlberg's Work on Moral Education. Kohlberg's work is framed by three succeeding but overlapping foci of interest: the development of a stage model of morality and procedures for its assessment, the construction of a model of moral education in general, and the interventive school-based work characterized in "cluster" schools and schools as just communities. The fundamental intellectual direction of the Center for Moral Education at Harvard under Kohlberg can be characterized as phenomenological, structuralist, and constructivist; phenomenological, because the actor's interpretation of the situation and the behavior is critical since the moral quality of the behavior is determined by that interpretation; structuralist because the focus follows Piaget's concern with the form of thinking rather than its content; and constructivist because human beings actively construct reality as they interact with the world (Colby et al. 1987). Other central features are the primacy of justice and the making of moral judgment, and the invariance of sequence in the model.

From Kohlberg's initial description in his 1958 Ph.D dissertation at the University of Chicago, the stage model of morality based on Piaget has been progressively developed and changed. Of critical importance is the fact that the model claims to fit psychological experience but is also a map that must embody a specific "conceptual (logical) cogency" (Kung 1985). There are three levels: I Preconventional, II Conventional, and III Postconventional or Principled. Each level has two stages. The stages are also descriptive of views of the moral world:

1. Heteronomous morality (morality of obedience and punishment)
2. Individualism, instrumental purpose, and exchange (morality of instrumental hedonism)
3. Mutual interpersonal expectations, relationships, and interpersonal conformity (the "good-boy–nice-girl" morality)
4. Social system and conscience (a morality of maintaining law and order)
5. Social contract or utility and individual rights (a morality of contract, law, and individual rights)
6. Universal ethical principles (a morality of individual principles of conscience).

Sichel believes the fact that Kohlberg's theory has retained its "intellectual stranglehold" in the face of considerable valid and important criticism deserves further investigation (Sichel 1988, 311). It is, however, critical to realize the major developments in Kohlbergian theory and their relation to practice, particularly as they began to appear in print in the 1980s. Moreover, these developments are of particular significance for curriculum theorists, as opposed to psychologists or philosophers.

In a paper of seminal importance to understanding Kohlberg's development, he writes:

> A psychologist takes a theory, developed and tested . . . and then starts to apply the theory and make prescriptions from theory to classroom practice. . . . I had never really felt that was a viable way of relating research to practice in moral education. I rather believed that you had to be in reciprocal collaboration with teachers. (Kohlberg 1985, 33)

Kohlberg goes on to describe the failure of the "one-way street model" and the need to take seriously the teachers' "concerns for action." The self-avowed practical inadequacy of the research model, with its focus on hypothetical dilemmas, led to reconsideration of the problem of content, the previously despised "bag of virtues." In 1990, Kohlberg is being described posthumously as an action researcher.

Criticisms of Kohlberg's Theory of Moral Development. The range of issues on which Kohlberg's views of moral development have been criticized is formidable, three of which may be noted here.

First, there has been concern about the status of stage six. Its central importance for Kohlberg is that "a terminal stage, with the principle of justice as its organizing principle, helps us to define the area of human activity under study" (Kohlberg, Levines, and Hewer 1983). It provides the link to Kant and to Rawls. Gibbs argues that stages five and six are not structural, as Piaget would understand it, but refer to metaethical matters (Gibbs 1977). Gilligan and Murphy deny the existence of a developmental path from stage five to stage six: We can postulate people with differing views of ultimate principles, for example, utilitarian, and six cannot thus be a sequential stage (Gilligan and Murphy 1979; see also Peters 1981). That matches criticism that Kohlberg's theory of moral development "is either implicitly prescriptive or so formal that it is of only limited significance for those who are interested in moral education . . . in a concrete way" (Peters 1974, 332). The studies of individuals at stage six are also extremely limited, weakening the empirical base. Concern of a different kind about stages five and six arises from Kohlberg's claim that for moral communications ("cognitive stimulations") to be effective, the developmental level of the teacher's verbalizations must be one step above that of the child (Fraenkel 1976).

Second, Kohlberg also insisted on the separation of the form or structure within which people make moral judgments from the content of those judgments. The rationale for this, as in the critique of the "bag of virtues," was that selected content would be arbitrary and thus indoctrinative. Critics such as Hamm (1977) and Peters argued that Kohlberg was either smuggling in content to his theory of moral development or that he failed to recognize, particularly in the early socialization of the child, the need for basic rules of content (e.g., not stealing, keeping your promises), without which social life could not be maintained. Kohlberg retreated from a no-content position (mistakenly viewed by some critics as one of neutrality) to one in which the "teacher is and should be an advocate for certain moral content" (Kohlberg 1985, 33). Advocacy was tenable, however, only on the basis of participatory democracy, not through any reliance on the teacher's authority or power. Lickona (1985) implicitly demonstrates the weaknesses of mere advocacy in establishing, at least, respect for other persons, care, and self-control as necessary content in the upbringing of children by their parents. Kohlberg's cavalier attitude to the problem is illustrated by such remarks as "teacher advocacy of a phase of enforcing a norm against stealing . . . seems to us non-controversial because respect for property rights is a basic norm of justice" (Kohlberg 1985, 60). What else, it may be asked, is packed into the norms of justice?

Third, Kohlberg's development toward school-based work left on one side various unanswered philosophical complaints. Critics have fastened particularly on the absence of a explicit relationship between moral judgment and moral action. Where moral development is conceived as one aspect of intellectual judgment, moral judgments reflect the level of intellectual reasoning (Sichel 1988, 195–197). The higher the stage of reasoning achieved, the greater the likelihood, in Kohlberg's account, that a moral judgment will be followed by a moral action, perhaps because

> "upper" levels reasons (e.g. "I couldn't live with myself if I did that") are unavoidable in a way which those associated with the "lower" levels (e.g. "I'll get a good hiding for doing that if my father finds out") are not. (Straughan 1982, 184; see also Suttle 1987)

But no account is offered of the relation between judgment and action within the Stage Theory (Blasi 1980). Kohlberg admitted that the development of justice reasoning stages through moral dilemma discussion was insufficient to affect moral actions. The just community approach aimed "to change individual action by changing the moral atmosphere of the school" (Kohlberg 1985, 61). The focus had shifted from judgment to action.

Experiments in Moral Education Practice

> As this situational atmosphere interacts with individual moral judgment and action, it influences not only judgments of rightness or justice but also individual judgments of the self's moral responsibility which mediate between deontological judgments of the rightness or justice of an action and the felt necessity or responsibility of acting in accordance with the judgment of rightness in a specific situation. (Kohlberg 1985, 61)

This "situational atmosphere" approach was supported by specific curriculum interventions in different schools.

Kohlberg was led into the shift from hypothetical dilemmas discussed in classrooms to an interventionist policy by the work of Blatt showing that one third to one half of students moved significantly toward the next stage in a year (Blatt and Kohlberg 1975). The cumulative record of these first school-based projects includes an account (Sperber and Milton 1980) of the Brookline Moral Education Project (1974–1979), curricular developments in history (Ladenburg 1980), race and ethnic prejudice (Alexander 1980), sex education (di Stefano 1980), the Holocaust (Strom 1980), and moral education in the elementary school (Stuhr and Rundle 1980), all of which are rich descriptions of classroom activity based on curricula planned on the developmental model. The pedagogy of moral discussion, its problems and effects, is discussed by Berkowitz (1985).

The shift into the "situational atmosphere" of the school, as it has been characterized here, is an espousal of the Durkheimian notion of developing the habit of common life as an alternative to prescribing particular virtues (Kohlberg 1980b, 37–43). This shift of approach is seen as a corrective to the moral discussion approach, an acknowledgment of the importance of cultivating feelings of social attachment and concern, as well as basic dispositions or habits of common living (Power, Higgins, and Kohlberg 1989). (Issues of gender and the just community are further discussed below.)

Assessment of Moral Progress. Wilson chastised educational research for what he defined as the failure to integrate normative and nonnormative research in the assessment of moral progress. He argued that moral development was a name for nothing clear, that we do not know which aspects of child development are relevant to moral development, and that we have no clear picture of the causal interactions of different views of development (Wilson 1973). However, Kohlberg and his followers, notably Colby, have developed a highly sophisticated set of scoring procedures for the measurement of moral judgment that has consistently informed the development of these curriculum practices (Colby et al. 1987).

Yet whatever the weaknesses, the work of Kohlberg and his followers is an intellectual benchmark in moral education and moral development. The rigorous intellectual quality of most of the literature produced by cognitive developmentalists is in sharp contrast with the writing of values-clarification theorists.

An Atheoretical Approach to Moral Education: Values Clarification

Raths, Harmin, and Simon first expounded the values-clarification approach in their 1966 book *Values and Teaching* and, partly as a response to their critics, published a second edition in 1978. As a movement, values clarification gained considerable popularity among teachers and has attracted, particularly in the 1980s, a sustained barrage of theoretical and political attack.

The Approach. Values clarification is a process. Its authors argue that teachers cannot be certain what values, what style of life, would be suitable for any person, and, therefore, they focus on the process of valuing. Seven criteria define this process: choosing freely, choosing from among alternatives, choosing after thoughtful consideration of the consequences of each alternative, prizing and cherishing, affirming, acting, upon choices, and repeating. Valuing is thus a process of choosing, prizing, and acting, and the results of that process are values. At least eight categories of behavior are values indicators, and the teacher's task is to help those children who choose to do so to raise these indicators to the level of values. A value is seen as the result of the valuing process.

The process of choosing has particular significance. To choose (properly) a child requires knowledge of alternatives that have meaning for the child and the consequences of that choice. He or she must also be free to choose. Each has implications for teaching. Teachers ensure that children have the knowledge relevant to choosing by asking questions: Children cannot be free to choose if they are coerced in classrooms by grades or punishments. To respect a child's life, teachers must respect the child's experience and his or her right to help in examining it for values.

While acknowledging the significance of other educational purposes, the cornerstone of a free society is claimed to be one in which every individual is entitled to the views that he has and to the values that he holds, especially where these have been examined and affirmed. By definition and by social right, values are personal things different from questions of truth and falsity where teachers can be authoritative. A major part of bringing up children is enabling them to clarify their value choices.

The Popularity of Values Clarification. By 1975 it was claimed that values clarification was one of the most popular and commercially successful educational fads of our generation and perhaps of all time (Stewart 1975). Teachers' classroom needs were satisfied in a series of publications from the National Humanistic Education Center. Teachers were able to claim neutrality in their teaching and thus resist parental criticism. Simultaneously, they could open up for classroom discussion major social issues without having to have a didactic or indoctrinative style for which they were then under attack or, for that matter, having to develop reasoned argument in complex areas for which they had no training (Postman and Weingartner 1969). Finally, as its authors hoped, teachers found the techniques positively engaged their students, although empirical studies of students' values and self-concepts do not bear out this enthusiasm (Leming 1981; Lockwood 1978).

The success of the values-clarification movement in the late 1960s and early 1970s can be partly explained in terms of the turbulent social context. Teachers as citizens were caught up in this social confusion. The volume of criticism in the 1980s reflects in part the conservative agenda with its wish to return to the "old" values launched from an attack on the moral bankruptcy of schools.

Values Clarification and Its Critics. This highly successful curriculum in moral education has attracted applause and criticism. Its success indicates that teachers want help in grappling with moral issues in their classrooms, but it has exposed them to severe political attack. Its success also may be due precisely to its implicit articulation of what is conceived as secular moral behavior and attitude in contemporary America, as opposed to a moral behavior guided by religious beliefs or other objective principles. Values clarification as a strategy has influenced teaching in other subjects, for example, literary or art appreciation, and the movement to critical thinking. Its techniques provide space for students to develop understanding rather than being instructed in the right interpretations.

Its strengths lie not just in its ease of practical application or wider curriculum influence. Moral development implies the development of personal autonomy; that is, individuals grow up able to decide between alternatives. Choice is of great significance for the moral agent: Indeed the process of determining principles on which an individual leads his or her life has been stressed by Hare (1961). The unexamined life, too, as Aristotle put it, is not worth living: Critical reflection on one's own moral views is crucial for the rational man (Simpson 1986). It is doubtful, however, whether the theorists would relish identification with either Aristotle or Hare.

The first major criticism can be summarized as the claim that values clarification is atheoretical as a practice in moral education. Kohlberg drew attention to the fact that it lacks any substantive theory of morality, as opposed to a reliance on a philosophy of value which draws on John Dewey (Dewey 1939; Kohlberg 1975). In the second edition of *Values and Teaching* the authors attempted to respond to the criticism that talk of values does not distinguish the moral from the nonmoral. In values clarification, it has been suggested, values become mere preferences (Boyd and Bogdan 1984). The movement also takes little notice of Peck and Havighurst's (1960) work on the problem of developmental stages or Peters' detailed analysis of the paradox of freedom: that is, that children can become choosers only on the basis of being "forced" to learn to follow rules (Peters 1974, 336–360).

Alongside this undergirding value of choosing lies a psychological (and valuable) account of man. The literature of the movement portrays psychological types: Those with confused values are portrayed as apathetic, uncertain, inconsistent, drifting, and overconforming, whereas those with clarity of values are portrayed as positive, purposeful, enthusiastic, and proud (Raths et al. 1966, 5–6). Lockwood (1977), the movement's most acute critic, and Elliott (1986) characterize values clarification as a form of client-centered therapy derived from Carl Rogers. The attacks on the weakness of the psychological theory underlying values clarification led its exponents to define it as an untested theory, one to be tested empirically and personally: "Try the theory and see if it works for you" (Raths et al. 1978, 6). That inadequate response suggests that the "theory" of values clarification is only honorifically theory, and the movement is atheoretical.

Second, the movement's definition of a value is that it is the endpoint of a process. Lockwood (1977, 37) points out that this rules out a person being said to value his religion (because he was brought up in it and didn't "freely choose" it) or those value choices on which a person does not act (for example, approving of the execution of Nazi war criminals).

Third, values clarification as a method of moral education has difficulty in characterizing the relation between a (moral) value and action. "[While] individuals may feel their actions are consistent with their values, it is an open question as to what actions, if any, are entailed by commitment to particular values" (Lockwood 1977, 39). On the ancient problem of weakness of will, values clarification is silent.

Other major criticisms of the movement include its lack of sophistication in matters of critical thinking (Boyd and Bogdan 1984), its failure to portray the discourse of moral choice and the connection with reason (Oser 1986), and the crudity with which it presents values education as a choice between relativism and authoritarianism (Lockwood 1977). But perhaps the most severe internal paradox of the movement is that it appears to assume a thoroughgoing ethical relativism while simultaneously claiming that the ethical value of freedom of choice that underpins the process is, in some sense, universal. In that, it may be said to reflect the moral confusion in pluralist American society (Bellah et al. 1985).

Moral Philosophy and Moral Education

Philosophy of education constitutes a major theoretical resource for a range of complex problems about moral education. Moral philosophy and the philosophy of mind are particularly significant for moral education. Any psychological theory or educational theory presupposes a view of man, and moral philosophers, in particular (see Rawls 1971 on justice; Bok 1979 on honesty), work on critical sociopolitical issues that are central to moral education. Second, as Piaget's term "genetic epistemology" indicates, critical questions in education are both philosophical and psychological in character (Mischel 1971), and theories of moral development are consistently open to philosophical critique (Rich and DeVitis 1985). Third, the debates in philosophy of education have not just been theoretical: Philosophers (Wilson, Beck, Pring, and others) have been involved in practical curriculum development, as indeed was Kohlberg. Fourth, issues at the heart of moral education controversies have been consistently addressed in the philosophical literature, even if these have not permeated curriculum thinking in general: for example, indoctrination, the relationship between morality and religion, the nature of the teacher's authority, definitions of morality, moral relativism, and so on. This chapter will be limited to a discussion of issues of indoctrination, and two utterly differing approaches to moral education from a philosophical standpoint.

Indoctrination. Kohlberg and values-clarification theorists were greatly concerned with the problem of indoctrination. For most philosophers, education is centrally concerned with the development of rationality (Dearden, Hirst, and Peters 1973). Problems are therefore raised for any form of teaching that seeks to prevent children raising critical questions by instilling in them beliefs which, for whatever reason, they are then unable to examine critically (Kazipedes 1982; Raywid 1984; Shermis and Barth 1985).

Discussions of indoctrination take two paths: First, there are the critical discussions of the notion of the neutral teacher. Second, there are more formal debates as to whether indoctrination is conceptually marked out by the teacher's intentions, the method used, or the content of what is taught, that is, the beliefs that the child comes to hold and how he or she holds them. Both of these main issues are important for curriculum and pedagogy.

The argument that schools or teachers be neutral in dealing with controversial moral problems or dilemmas arises because of the popular claim that, in morals, there is no right answer, hence the complicated matter of the teacher's legitimate authority in matters of knowledge. Yet schools can never be neutral, because values pervade the enterprise. The question then shifts to the stance schools take toward complex issues (Ennis 1959). Snook (1972) argues that modeling neutrality may well be a sensible stance for a teacher as a model of rational thought in the approach to a problem; indeed it may be necessary for the development of reason, but Bricker (1972) and Warnock (1977) claim that a teacher must be a model, notably in the display of an affective concern with moral problems. On a thoroughgoing neutrality, highly prejudiced student beliefs will be left unchallenged (Bailey 1971). Some of the controversy is based on conflicting conceptions of neutrality (Kleinig 1976), but Stenhouse (1983) argued vehemently that philosophical criticism neglected the empirical data on the growth of rationality that the highly specific "neutral teacher" pedagogy produced in the work of the Humanities Curriculum Project.

Whether aim, content, or method marks off indoctrination has provoked philosophers. The primary areas for curriculum concerns about indoctrination are political (which could include historical and social) beliefs and religious and moral beliefs. Kilpatrick (1975), Hare (1973), and White (1967) suggest that the indoctrinative teacher is distinguished by what he or she aims or intends to do. Crittenden (1980) suggests that intentions are insignificant compared to what is taught and the pedagogy used, while Flew (1975), in discussing religious beliefs, argues that the verifiability of content is the distinctive factor. Smart (1973) attacks the subject argument and indicates that a teacher indoctrinates, methodologically, by teaching half-truths as truths. Green (1964) construes indoctrination within a broad analysis of the concept of teaching as the process by which a teacher gets children to hold beliefs "non-evidentially" (i.e., without having the proper evidence for them): As far as the subject content is concerned, he indicates also that where a teacher seeks to instill in a child beliefs that are not open to change, this is a case of indoctrination. Suttle (1981), in examining these contrasting views, suggests that indoctrination is pernicious only where it is avoidable, and Casement (1983) suggests the argument is empty because of its failure to examine learner experience. The intricacies of this kind of debate are not superfluous for curriculum theory (Downey and Kelly 1978). They reveal the importance of examining each aspect within a given curriculum strategy of moral education, as Kohlberg (1985) does in explaining the basis of the just community approach. They provide one kind of philosophical contribution that can be made to the moral aspects of the curriculum.

The Components of the Morally Educated Person. An unusual attempt to link moral philosophy and moral education has been pursued by John Wilson, who, in a major British project, sought to tackle questions of moral education by defining what a morally educated person would be like. This work was based, philosophically, on Hare's account of the moral agent as a decider of principles. Since the project's first publication (Wilson, Sugarman, and Williams 1967), Wilson has continued to construct the logical components of "what it means" to be "educated in morality." (Wilson 1982) Wilson's central claim is for moral philosophy as the premier agent in defining what moral education is.

The project defined morality as prescriptive, rational, impartial, overriding, freely adopted, and concerned with the interests of others, an analysis which contemporary character education theorists would call "horizontal" development. The critical elements, with the abbreviated quasi-Greek identifiers used by the project, are:

having a concept, and an attitude, of respect toward others as persons (PHIL);
having an understanding of how others think and feel (EMP);
knowing other facts relevant to practical decisions in relation to other people (GIG);
formulating a system of values or prescriptions as a result of PHIL, EMP and GIG;
relating these formulations to oneself, who needs to be valued (PHRON); and
putting these principles into practice (KRAT).

Wilson (1973) proposed a set of curriculum strategies to assist teachers in helping students cross the gap between making judgments and acting. The emphasis on making decisions for oneself differs from the choices advocated in values clarification in that these are decisions of (moral) principle. The project was not simply philosophical. It included extensive statements of the psychological and sociological considerations relevant to this account of the morally educated man (Wilson, Williams, and Sugarman 1967).

Personal and Social Education

Wilson's project seems to have strength in its theoretical interconnections with other relevant disciplines of education. It contains a sincere attempt to contribute to curriculum. However its failure to influence schools indicates that, unlike Kohlbergian theory, values clarificationism, and others, it had no real roots in schooling, and thus made no impact.

Personal and social education, on the other hand, became a significant phrase in the United Kingdom in the 1980s. Its roots lie in the anxiety of British government agencies, concerned with children likely to go straight from school to work, to ensure the development of personal and social skills in such students. The work has great relevance outside the United Kingdom. Pring (1984) builds on his concerns with these educational proposals to outline an account of personal and social education that contains an eclectic view of moral learning, an antidote to arguments that an all-embracing view is impossible. Although his target is to get teachers to deliberate about the wide-ranging implications of this endeavor, he deploys both different philosophical and different psychological theories in support of articulated curriculum goals and instructional methodologies.

The conclusions toward which he builds are that personal and social education is not identifiable with a discrete curriculum subject; that there is an integral relation between the effect of the school as an institution and what individual respect for students as persons implies; that the cognitive developmental stages are sufficiently well established for us to take these as critical and to see them as governed by the way in which those with authority (in and out of school) see this development and how they exercise it; that the ethos of a school has to reach down into individual classroom practice by teachers; that developmental stages demand early acquisition of habits and rule-following behavior upon which concepts and attitudes can be established; that the central importance of the acquisition of moral agency makes it essential for "teachers to be ever more vigilant of the gradual destruction . . . of humanistic values" in a pragmatic utilitarian society (1984, 169); and, finally, that schools and teachers need to be highly conscious of the need to coordinate their work and subject it to constant critical appraisal. Pring, therefore, demonstrates that, from apparently competing theories, a framework of moral education and moral development can be built that would not leave teachers exposed to the prevailing winds of theoretical argument and the harsher storms of political pressures.

CONTEMPORARY ISSUES IN THE MORAL EDUCATION CURRICULUM

Four major topics confront curriculum research in moral education as it seeks to address some of the social predicaments of the day: the rebirth of character education, gender, family life curricula, and the problem of subjects as vehicles for moral education.

Character Education

That the Office of Educational Research and Improvement of the U.S. Department of Education published a comprehensive paper by Pritchard on character education is a reflection of the stimulus given to discussion of values education by Secretary William Bennett (Pritchard 1988). It is too early to assess properly the causes of its renaissance. Kohlberg's continuing attacks on a "bag-of-virtues" approach, particularly in the 1960s, no doubt inhibited its reemergence, although Peck and Havighurst, Reisman (1950), and Peters produced significant work from different disciplines on character and character development in this shadow period.

We can appreciate the paradox that Martin Luther King, Jr. (who had a special place as the model for stage six in Kohlberg's schema) declared in the famous Washington speech of 1963 that he looked forward to the time when "the negro would be judged not by the color of his skin, but by the content of his character." King's audience knew what he meant: For Kohlberg, that kind of talk was "bag-of-virtues" stuff. "Character," as a term, has a clear meaning in common sense, whatever theorists may do with it. However, a precise definition of "character" in theoretical terms seems elusive. Clearly it can be used descriptively or as a term of approbation referring to a batch of personal qualities that are relatively stable (Pritchard 1988, 3).

Typically, character education advocates a specific set of moral virtues: It concentrates on developing in children actions that embody these values and emphasizes aspects of personality that motivate the child to act. Its primary significance for writers in the contemporary movement is its "reconstructive" stance to what are seen as the visible cracks in the moral foundations of democracy, its view of the moral person as "integrated," and its emphasis on the significance of cultural norms and the role of institutions (Ryan and Lickona 1987). Unlike other recent movements, character education addresses the relationship of moral and religious education. In this section, those theorists who share these concerns are labeled as a movement.

The Character Education Movement as Reconstructive. The movement is based on a diagnosis of present moral ills, particularly among young people. Wynne and Hess (1988, 56) claim a "gross correlation . . . ; the abandonment of traditional values and their replacement with new, more individualistic ones, has been associated with the spread of youth disorder." They cite figures for homicides, suicides, out-of-wedlock births, premarital sex, illegal drug use, delinquent conduct, and the long-term decline in levels of measured cognitive learning in students. They admit the difficulty of detailed interpretation but note that, on their account, these developments are not connected to such causes as underfunded education or social welfare programs, oppression of the young, the spread of poverty, or general political stress. The pervasive, debilitating influence of television and other media (Sullivan 1987), the change in family structures (Coleman 1981), and the breakdown of strong relationships between schools and communities (Prakash 1988) are features in this framework of disintegration on the movement's diagnosis. The problems of rampant individualism it addresses are raised in Bellah et al. (1985). A major philosophical argument that seeks to reinstate a philosophy of virtue is contained in MacIntyre (1984), whose Aristotelianism appears central to the movement's thinking and influences some recent work among cognitive-developmentalists.

The movement thus seeks ambitiously to "reconstruct" the role of the teacher as moral educator, instructor, and exemplar. It sees the school as a moral community rather than a technical apparatus for learning subjects. It stresses the significance of relationships between the school and its constituent communities, families, and churches. It urges the revitalization of moral education in universities to improve the foundations of the democracy. Pritchard (1988) identifies the claims on which the movement bases its practical philosophy: that character education instills virtues that contribute to higher academic performance (Ginsburg and Hanson 1986) and that making good character educationally important introduces a noncompetitive goal into education (Kagan 1981).

The Moral Person. The movement supports an "integrative view of the moral agent" (Ryan and Lickona 1987), and its account may be compared with Wilson's atomic view of the morally educated person. First, human character is said to involve the interplay of three components: knowing, affect, and action. Second, it puts alongside Kohlberg's (vertical) view of moral development what it labels horizontal development—that is, the extension or application of a person's most mature capacities over a wider and wider range of life situations. Finally, it emphasizes community: Each community to which the child belongs must be interactive, participatory, supporting, and challenging, emphasizing interdependence and mutual responsibility.

Moral knowing includes becoming informed, having a moral imagination, having cognitive strategies for making decisions systematically, acquiring knowledge of moral content, and being able to make moral judgments. Of these elements, content proves the most controversial, as it is intended to describe the virtues handed on through a person's moral heritage. Different lists of virtues are propounded (Pritchard 1988, 3), often through the claim that these are universal or American values, a position which is clearly contentious (Lockwood 1985). Character education advocates need to examine these different virtues for justification on the model given by Bok (1979). The possibility of distinguishing different types of virtues in terms of their relationship to action and judgment would also defuse a debate over the virtues (Peters 1973; Sockett 1988) if it were not overlain with the problems of indoctrination.

Moral affect, identity, attraction to the good, commitment, compassion, and the like, are viewed as necessary components of character, bridging knowledge to action. Thus far, the movement has taken little account of the significance of guilt and remorse (Alston 1971). Moral action, which includes will, competence, and habit, addresses the gap in Kohlberg's theory. The notion of horizontal development emphasizes that moral personality is rounded, that morality applies across the range of a person's behavior, and it is matched by the emphasis on community as the social context of that behavior. The philosophical and psychological support for the movement is set out in two volumes (Knowles, Mann, and Ellrod 1986; Schindler, Mann, and Ellrod 1986).

Character Education in Classroom and School. This new breed of character education has yet to find widespread practical focus, and the social and political obstacles it faces are considerable. Wynne and Walberg (1989), noting the difficulty of philosophical and psychological consensus, bravely look to "educational consensus" on character education, and their proposals are reminiscent of best practice in traditional private schools in the United States and the United Kingdom: group and individual responsibilities with emphasis on accomplishment, school and community service projects, continuity of teachers through graaes to provide an unchanging supportive adult, a stress on academic activities, frequent and high-quality ceremonial activities, and a policy for including character in a school's judgment of a student.

The Child Development Project in North California is rooted in traditional socialization, cognitive development, and character education perspectives. Its focus is with significant adults outside the school on developmental disciplines, cooperative learning, helping, understanding others, and highlighting prosocial values (Watson et al. 1989). The emphasis on self-esteem and community, cooperative learning, helping, and friendship is established in Lickona's (1987) model of moral education in an elementary school. Beck's project in a junior high school within the broad framework of the movement offers challenging study units, topics, and themes for the study of morals as a curriculum activity not dissociated from the life of the school (Beck 1989). Starratt (1980) identifies 10 principles and a variety of classroom scenarios for work in any class in a high school. Throughout this so far exiguous literature on school practice, rather than theory, the emphasis is on the quality of the school and relationships within it. Whether schools, particularly high schools, can reconcile the sense of mutual responsibility, cooperation, and respect with their primary social function of stratifying children is a further question. Nevertheless, the underpinning philosophical claim, namely, that social pluralism does not imply moral relativism, is a significant claim in contemporary America, marking this movement off from values clarification.

Gender: The Moral Identity of the Child

One of George Eliot's characters remarks that anatomy is destiny. In the past 25 years women's struggles for equality and the social and political changes wrought by the feminist movement have influenced every public institution. Sadly, physical abuse of women and the prevalence of subtle discrimination remain major social evils. No other social issue is so enmeshed in the warp and woof of moral education because man-woman relationships are at the heart of human existence in most people's lives. Yet gender research is largely ignored in other work in education, for example, on restructuring schools (Tetreault and Schmuck 1985).

The predominant gender issue in moral education research may be framed thus: Women construe moral issues and dilemmas in terms of conflicts of responsibilities; men see them in terms of conflicts of rights. Compassion and care, it is claimed, matter to women more than abstract notions of equality and justice. Is this a claim that the affective has primacy over the cognitive? And/or is it a claim that a person's voice (the moral language one uses) and a person's orientation (one's focus in moral situations) are rooted in gender differences? And/or is this an alternative ethical theory with an ultimate moral "principle" based on care (rooted in gender) rather than justice (in the liberal tradition) or agapeistic love (in the Christian tradition)? Each claim has significant implications for moral education, particularly for the character of the school as a community.

Gilligan critiques the scientific methodology of psychoanalytic and developmental theorists. She argues that they are invariably based on male samples and with males as the formal subject, as in the work of Erikson, Piaget, and Kohlberg. Such theorists (and their followers) are thus deaf to a different voice. Piaget's marbles jurisprudence, for example, was constructed on a male sample and then applied to females. Kohlbergian theory describes only men's moral language. Hypothetical dilemmas (on which stages of reasoning are constructed) ignore the power of actual experience: the personal emotional involvement in the situation. Kohlbergian stages are thus related not to how people act but to what they say. A different development pattern could emerge from real-life dilemmas where thinking is "contextual and inductive rather than formal and abstract" (Gilligan 1979).

Walker (1984) interprets Gilligan's claims as implying that Kohlberg's theory and scoring are insensitive to women, that female patterns of thought are typically consigned to lower stages, and that the stage theory is androcentric. In an analysis of 108 research inquiries, he found only 8 (some of which were flawed) that gave Gilligan empirical support, and these were on adult rather than children's moral reasoning. Lack of stage disparity does not preclude differences in content (see also Nails 1983). Perhaps Brabeck (1987) is right: Only multiple methodologies are appropriate for moral education research.

Gilligan's claims are powerful indeed. She argues that the moral domain has been limited by attention only to the language of rights and justice (the natural language of men), but that another language of care and response (the natural language of women) is prevalent. These natural languages are basic gender differences. In reply to Vasudex (1988), Gilligan and Attanucci (1989) modify the totality of gender difference by indicating that concerns about care and justice are represented in people's thinking about real-life moral dilemmas, but people tend to focus upon one set of concerns and minimally respect the other. Men and women use both care and justice, but women emphasize care and men justice: The problem becomes one of both voice and orientation.

Moral thought, in a tradition stretching from Kant to Rawls, emphasizes the importance of universal principles, respect for persons and justice, and the formal character of putting oneself in another's situation. The feminist response from Gilligan is neither a generalized claim for the affective as against the cognitive nor for a new ethical theory. Rather, the claim is that moral situations can be construed from a base of caring and response characterized by unique situations, the relationship between actual persons, and in a concrete place and time.

Perhaps, as Pateman (1980) suggests, love and justice are antagonistic virtues, the one particularist, the other universalist. Sichel (1988), in a sympathetic and wide-ranging treatment of Gilligan, argues that she has neglected the logical properties of moral language (which includes sacrifice and hardship) and that the polarization of two languages leaves the public realm of rights discourse uninfluenced by the language of care. The collection of papers about work on female adolescent relationships at Emma Willard School is a major source of empirical data about differences in relationships and perspectives (Gilligan, Lyons, and Hammer 1990).

Noddings (1984) argues for a radical reconstruction in ethical thought, the central focus of which is "how to meet the other morally." Relationship (in the practice of being moral) is ontologically basic, for a person's individuality is defined in a set of relations that is the basic reality. Ethical maturity is defined as participating responsibly in caring relationships: It demands the development of a sense of "engrossment," of feeling with another person rather than simply analyzing their situation. We experience motivational displacement, where our own commitment to act is diverted in the service of another person. Caring, rather than contest, is the primary goal of education. No teacher can simply reason about this relational ethic with children: He or she must live it (Diller 1988). For Noddings this implies radically different instructional arrangements in schools, with an emphasis on dialog, modeling, and the institutionalization of caring relationships, such as "caring apprenticeships" (Noddings 1988), within differing views of good and evil (Noddings 1987). A "narrative" approach to moral development, whereby autobiography contributes to understanding, appears particularly congruent with an ethic of care (Tappan and Brown 1989).

For many of these writers the curriculum must be a journey from one that is male defined to one that is gender balanced (Tetreault 1986a). Gender issues affecting moral education have to be rethought in social studies and history textbooks (Tetreault 1987), in political education (Davies 1984), and in literature (Christian-Smith 1987; Kazemek 1986). Hypothetical dilemmas can contain sex equity issues to inform children's moral judgments (Styer 1988). Miller (1982) indicates how curriculum theorizing itself has failed to take sufficient cognizance of gender issues, and there are important arguments (Allen 1988; Klein 1988) for this perspective to influence family life courses. (For further study of gender issues, see Chapter 24, "Gender Issues and the Curriculum," in this *Handbook*.)

Family Life: The Sexual Identity of the Child

Some proponents of sex education programs seem to have taken too literally King Lear's mad outburst: "Let copulation thrive!" Sex education curricula, Diorio (1985) maintains, ignore other precious aspects of human sexuality.

Four fifths of states now require or encourage the teaching of sex education in the public schools, and nearly 9 in 10 large school districts support such instruction (Kenney, Guardado, and Brown 1989). Only four states do not support the provision of AIDS education, and support for instruction about sexually transmitted disease and abstinence is equally widespread. Pregnancy-prevention programs are less widespread but still apparent in the curricula of the majority of states. The large school districts seem to be bolder in the topics they teach, and they also offer more sophisticated support for teachers.

In the five teaching subjects selected as germane to sex education, 93 percent of teachers surveyed report that their schools offer sex education or AIDS education in some form, and almost all of them believed that a wide range of topics in sex education should be covered—by grades 7 or 8 at the latest. Sex education, however, does not usually occur primarily until the 9th or 10th grade. More important, there is a critical gap between what teachers think ought to be taught and what they teach. For instance, whereas most teachers believe that sex education in schools should cover sexual decision making, abstinence, and birth control, only 80 percent work in schools that provide it. Again, though teachers believe that birth control programs should include instructions on where to go to select a method, less than 50 percent of schools provide the opportunity (Forrest and Silverman 1989).

Teachers also believe strongly in programs that teach responsibility in sexual relationships and parenthood, the importance of abstinence, and resisting pressures to become sexually active, in addition to teaching about disease. But teachers are less supportive of programs that deal with such controversial topics as homosexuality and "safer sex" practices. The problems teachers see themselves facing in the implementation of such programs are parental, community, and administrative pressures: They also see problems in the lack of appropriate materials on the subject and in student reactions.

Family life programs are predominantly sex education programs, although expert practitioners in this field see them as an all-embracing opportunity to deal with interfamily relationships. Sex education is predominantly a prophylactic activity, replete with information and injunction about what not to do. Curriculum research has almost entirely neglected this part of the school curriculum, so that, while there are detailed curricula available from state departments of education and numerous curricula proposals, nationally and internationally (cited in ERIC), there is no great wealth of substantial critical appraisal available, apart from ASCD papers (Molnar 1987). Moral education research in general, where it focuses on hypothetical or real dilemmas or character development, rarely uses interpersonal sexual examples. Only Stafford (1988) has attempted to take seriously the problems of sexual identity in his work on homosexuality. The issue of parental rights has been addressed in general (Schrag 1971, 1977), but not in matters of sex education. At one level this lack of attention by curriculum researchers is understandable: At another, it is a sad reflection on the gap between school practice and the support needed by teachers in a socially volatile curriculum area.

Moral Development and Curriculum Subjects

C. P. Snow and F. R. Leavis conducted a major debate in the 1960s about the two cultures of science and the humanities. Both claimed that their area had particular value as a moral enterprise, science because it was concerned with truth proper (Snow 1959) and literature because it was concerned with understanding and insight into the human condition (Leavis 1963). The value of curriculum subjects as vehicles for moral education has been a consistent theme in educational thought. History was seen as such by Rousseau (Owen 1982) and Thomas Arnold, literature by Adam Smith (Court 1985), and art by John Ruskin (Stankiewicz 1984). Mead and Dewey saw moral education permeating the curriculum through subject teaching (Dennis and Stickel 1981). Teaching ethics as such to schoolchildren commands little support as an independent school subject. Although subject teachers may be often reluctant to admit any moral significance (Craig 1983), understanding in the humanities demands the development of imagination and intuition that can enhance moral and intellectual sensitivity (Gambell 1988).

The Humanities and Moral Education. The teaching of literature still lays claim to providing curriculum opportunities for explicit teaching of moral values, labeled by Casement (1987) as didacticism. Literature also provides a significant resource for moral education, even through figurative language (Hannabus 1987), and teachers need to use quality literature with values-clarification exercises (Mackey 1987). Kohlbergian stages can be related to fictional characters to generate student's insights on their own development (Readence 1982). Novels provide an opportunity for the identification of moral dilemmas, identified acts, moral reasoning, and moral decision making as elements in the relation between the adolescent novel and moral development (Yeazell and Cole 1986); for facing different moral codes in adolescence (Frangedis 1988); and (with young children) for the development of empathy (Wolf 1975). Adolescent romantic novels can provide a gender text (Christian-Smith 1987). Political novels provide complexity and moral ambiguity for students to grapple with (Endres 1984), although whether a literature teacher should be engaged or detached (Bogdan 1984) raises significant questions about the interrelation of the moral and the aesthetic. A series of ethical dilemmas for teachers arise where English teachers are expected to develop children's moral sensibility (Yeazell 1986). Fairness and equality have been cited as moral values appearing in drama and theater education. Young children can acquire concepts of friendship, property, obedience, and truth through values education materials (Schunke and Krogh 1982).

Historians and history teachers no longer have any confidence in their role as moral educators. Diorio (1985b) attributes the decline of history as a tool of moral training both to the development of relativism and the quest for objectivity in history (instanced by covering law theory). Historical claims have become contentious, and the subject has become primarily intellectual, rather a vehicle for patriotic sentiment. Historians have withdrawn from any instrumentalist claims for their discipline, which is not to say that they no longer have any confidence in its value (Hamerow 1985). Furthermore, its quasi-incorporation in social studies has left the subject without a firm base of its own in all levels of schooling.

The history teacher is caught between pressures to teach national values, for example, through teaching children the basis of liberty and sacrifice (Bauer 1984), and trying to instill objectivity, for example, by examining moral assumptions in such politicized areas as nuclear warfare (Carman and Kneeshaw 1985). Less controversial are the ways in which a history teacher might confront the Holocaust, where patriotic values as such are not under scrutiny directly, and the opportunity for moral indignation is, to say the least, proper (Farnham 1982; Strom and Parsons 1982). However, teachers also face critics who see in history textbooks the strong presence of class-based ideology (Anyon 1979), a bias against women (Tetreault 1986b), and a legion of critics of both content and pedagogy (Engle and Ocha 1988, 104–107). Indeed, it also remains unclear whether history in schools is part of social studies or part of humanities.

Social Studies Education and Moral Education. Merelman argues that a moral education approach to social studies is both pedagogically and politically unsound because political decision making is quite different from moral decision making (Merelman 1979). Yet, in seven doctoral dissertations cited by Leming (Leming 1983), value material in social studies was not an important factor in its content. Shaver (1987) sees the problem of the social studies as being one of clarity of purpose: Social studies may move toward greater objectivity, for example, by reinstating history proper and the defunct "New Social Studies" pioneered by Bruner, influenced perhaps by critical theorists. Alternatively it could move toward citizenship education, that is, to political socialization, in which case it will be picking up the historical link with character education gradually lost after Hartshorne and May. Shaver suggests that, on the latter view, the link with character education is an internal one and also that many of the issues or problems within social studies content in this mode have a moral flavor. Issues of race, prejudice, and human rights, common themes in the journal *Social Education*, are manifestly moral issues, but any definition of "citizen" leaves open the question of what counts as a good citizen.

Engle and Ocha (1988, 117–122) explain that those forms of social studies which neglect values are inadequate, that social studies should be conceived as citizenship education, and that examination of value issues is intellectually highly demanding. For citizenship education to be effective, values have to be taught, but it is claimed that the teacher's role is more that of a political theorist with a dialectic pedagogy (Battistoni 1985). Beyer (1979, 269–300), who approaches social studies as a form of reflective inquiry, embraces values clarification and developmentalist theories, seeing the informal, trusting, nonthreatening classroom atmosphere as necessary to both moral education and social studies.

Shaver's analysis strikes at the root of problems in social studies and its presently highly ambiguous position as a vehicle of moral education. Insofar as it moves toward citizenship, then, all the issues of character education are in play. But they are complicated by two questions. First, how can a distinction be made for the developing child between his or her moral personhood and his or her citizenship, and, therefore, between private wants and the public interest? Second, how can teachers be prepared to grapple with political controversy within a classroom, which is inevitable where political socialization is set within the democracy entailed by the U.S. Constitution (Shaver 1985)? Descriptive studies of exemplary practice are called for (Leming 1986). (For more on issues of social studies education, see Chapter 29, "Social Studies," in this *Handbook*.)

Physical Education and Moral Education. A little known but significant piece of social history was the movement, in cities, to supervise playgrounds of children whose street behavior was regarded as unorganized and unfettered and whose circumstances of poverty and degradation, a result of the moral corruption of capitalism, threatened their lives. Cavallo (1981) records how play was seen by such pioneers as Addams at the turn of the 20th century as a vital medium for shaping moral and cognitive development in deprived young people. Taking part in team games or sports offered opportunities for cooperation, group loyalty, and the subordination of the self to the social whole. Such movements as Young Life are a contemporary equivalent.

The development of moral virtue through physical education is what separates it from physical training. This has been a common theme in the history of education in the West and has also been marked by a sense of concern for the interrelation of mind and body. Children should be taught the use of their bodies, with their inborn sense of moral goodness (Levin 1982). Physical education is worthwhile only within a concept of the whole person (Oberteuffer 1977, 146–161). Moral development, self-confidence, and spiritual development are among the challenges offered by outdoor education (Knapp 1983–1984). Frost (1975) seems to be influenced by moral relativism, but somewhat contradictorily insists on physical education as a provider of participation values: self-discovery (particularly in outdoor education), cooperation, fighting "to the last ditch," courage, and mutual trust. Indeed, he writes of a full integration between the moral and the physical in physical education. Each of these perspectives are set within curriculum prescriptions.

Barrow and Brown, in their influential textbooks for physical education teachers and coaches (1988), bring together the work of the cognitive developmentalists, the character education movement, and character development theorists such as Peck and Havighurst. They claim that situations in physical education are "real life," not hypothetical; that physical education is a major forum for the development of self-esteem and self-concept; that teachers should be charismatic and models of developed character and personality; and they cite the American Academy for Physical Education's statement of moral and ethical values as the professional authority. Barrow and Brown see physical education as providing pedagogical opportunities for concept development and discussion techniques: They also retain a faith in transfer of training and sport for pleasure.

These kinds of rationales and prescriptions may be absent from contemporary practice where discipline mastery (the techniques for individual games, sports, or activities) overwhelms any commitment to student self-actualization (Jewett and Bain 1985). There is no firm quantitative data on the relation between physical education and values acquisition. Some teachers are committed to sets of perceived values that include such diverse values as adaptability, self-concept development, and a responsibility for nature (Ford and Blanshard 1985).

Physical education is one area in which moral education might be conducted without public controversy. School teams, too, may foster a certain ethos. However, the commercialization and hard competitiveness of sport, with its heroes as models for students, may tarnish such ideals. Participation by children in games, including Little League, and parental fanaticism may be influenced more by the concept of the hero than by moral ideals, which provides yet another example of the mismatch of educational and contemporary social values. (For more on issues of moral and physical education see Chapter 33, "Physical Education," in this *Handbook*.)

Science and Moral Education. Scientific literacy demands an interdisciplinary curriculum (Zeidler 1984), which must include ethical components for the analysis of policy issues with which science is irredeemably connected. Traditional didactic pedagogies are antipathetic to such a conception (Rolls 1984), and discussion methods must be used. But the content-free openness of value-clarification strategies (Thelen 1987) is in direct conflict with the importance given to firmly grounded knowledge. Martin (1986) argues for a close connection: Moral education and science education are mutually relevant, both developing virtues and propositional knowledge as moral decision making is developed within science, without indoctrination. The Middle Grade Reform of curricula (including science) in California schools has been built around character and ethical struggles (Honig 1988).

Two major moral problems presently affect science education, apart from the esoteric battle with creationism (Alexander 1985): the environment and the nuclear debate. Environmental education is not just an interdisciplinary study but demands the acquisition by students of a code of behavior for different ecosystems (Yambert and Donow 1986). Caduto (1983) uses Piaget and Kohlberg in a developed strategy for environmental education, though Simmons (1988) sees major dilemmas for the teacher in the presentation of values in environmental education. The nuclear debate, since it is at the heart of U.S. defense and foreign policy, is as problematic: Brians (1988) complains that children are not getting realistic accounts which honestly confront their fears, though there is no indication that nuclear education increases students' worries (Christie and Nelson 1988). That may be because it is taught in such a way as to invite acceptance of nuclear policy (Hamm and Adams 1988; La Farge 1988).

Controversial Issues and Moral Education. With the exception of physical education, all the school subjects cited, literature, history, social studies, and science, contain potential for controversial issues in the classroom. Their treatment may be legally sanctioned or taught within the uncertain climate of convention and public opinion in a given school district. What counts as controversial in a pluralist democratic society cannot merely be defined by what controversy exists but also by the epistemic character of the problem (Gardner 1981). Provoking controversy within the context of debate in classrooms is held by cooperative learning theorists to be important for intellectual development (Johnson and Johnson 1985). But different social movements (e.g., Prohibition) have always tried to legislate their views for schooling, and in that sense to treat the formally controversial as not so (Tyack and James 1985). Legally, however, states only have the right to mandate what is in line with the Constitution: The Constitution, on this argument, would be the noncontroversial given (Gordon 1984). Neutrality, impartiality, and commitment are all possible pedagogical approaches (Kelly 1986) that mesh the stance of the moral educator with that of the subject teacher.

Controversial issues in areas of major human concern in a society are necessarily moral in character, and the contemporary literature reveals a considerable range: issues of nuclear policy, Vietnam, apartheid, and political terrorism; issues of biotechnology and the environment; and issues of sexual behavior, smoking, and alcohol. These are not "hypothetical dilemmas," but they are inescapable issues for a child growing up to be an autonomous moral person and citizen. The risks of not examining the critical issues of citizenship, on which persons of goodwill may disagree profoundly, are severe. Cerjak (1987) suggests that we must confront the possibility that, like Abigail in *The Crucible*, children will develop no conscience or social conscience. They will then not be able to see controversial issues as moral issues. Green (1985), considering moral education in an age of technology, redefines moral development as the formation of conscience, concerned with more than moral conduct per se. In particular, with Abbs (1982), he stresses the significance of an ethical imagination, which can be developed as students are helped to face the human controversies of their generation.

Religious Education and Moral Education: A Note. Religious education in public schools is politically unacceptable, and it rarely surfaces in curriculum discussions. Perhaps it is a dormant volcano in moral education, but Cremin's identification of a movement of ethnoreligiosity in the 1980s finds expression in debates about citizenship education, not religious education in public schools (Cremin 1990). Peshkin's (1986) excellent account of a fundamentalist Christian school serves to confirm prejudices about religious education. Schools and teachers, for the most part, avoid anything that looks like religion.

There are, nevertheless, a variety of pressure groups advocating, for instance, school prayer or the teaching of religious liberty. This brief note focuses on the relation between religious and moral education, not between religion and other aspects of schooling, for example, history teaching. There are major questions to be studied philosophically on the relationship between religion and morality in the context of education discussed by British authors (Felderhof 1985; Hirst 1974). British literature, appropriate for a country with a tradition of religious education, is philosophically interesting to a comparative educator, rather than to a curriculum specialist, since the issue is of little relevance to American public schooling.

But contemporary American research does ignore three issues that are critical to curriculum, since they speak to the interface of the individual's religious experience and any attempt the school might make to develop a program of moral education. First, how does a religious person, who is a teacher, confront or undertake moral education in a secular school? Second, can a child's view of the moral life be developed properly where the child is totally ignorant of the perspectives religious believers hold on that morality? Third, how do children growing up in religious homes, particularly of a dogmatic kind, benefit from moral education in schools?

SCHOOLS AS MORAL INSTITUTIONS

The moral life of schools gradually came to dominate the agenda in the late 1980s, partly because of the general interest in the structure of schools. The detailed attention previously given to the individual and his or her moral development waned, so that even in the Emma Willard work (Gilligan, Lyons, and Hammer 1990), the school as an institution is very much present in the analysis of moral development in 12-year-old girls. From an institutional perspective, four topics can be discerned as of immediate interest: the development of an ethos for a school, the role of the teacher as a moral educator, the specific attempt by Kohlberg and his followers to develop a "just community" in a school (perhaps the only significant institutional innovation in moral education recently), and the attention devoted to the "hidden curriculum" since its presence was first articulated by Jackson in 1968.

Chazan (1985) describes a range of approaches to moral education, but provides a concluding chapter mentioning Illich, Neill, and Bereiter as examples of those who are "against" moral education. The difficulty for each of these thinkers, who in one way or another say that schools should not get involved in morals, is as follows: Schools, as presently constructed, cannot help delivering some moral education, even if they do it outstandingly badly. For, to take the simplest example, contexts arise daily in which children either are or are not taught that they ought to tell the truth. If the teacher treats honesty as if it were a problem of etiquette, say, like picking one's nose, then the teacher is adopting some kind of moral position (however incoherent), even if etiquette is interpreted as being morally "neutral." The issue itself also becomes a moral one. Bereiter, for example, has to use a moral argument to say that schools ought not to be in the moral arena, which is itself a moral statement. Moral education does indeed come with the territory, and those who say it should not (or ought not) must define what such a "free" institution would look like and also defend positively these radical institutional solutions intended presumably to protect children from the adult impositions they apparently abhor.

The Ethos of Schools

The institutional pervasiveness of moral education has recently been confirmed in only a few studies that need further development. Good and Brophy (1986) believe these studies are necessary to help us to understand qualitative aspects of schools. They regard Rutter's study (Rutter et al. 1979) as important in providing a link among a range of factors about school process and student outcomes. The cumulative effect of these social factors is the creation of a school ethos, or set of values, attitudes, and behaviors that characterize the school, although the study itself was not specifically a search for issues of moral education.

Issues of ethos, or what we might call "what the school stands for," are examined and described by Cusick (1983), Grant (1988), and, more briefly, Cusick and Wheeler (1988). These major studies are important because they indicate that the academic and social organization of a school itself is based ultimately on moral principles, for example, equality of opportunity. Schools also provide opportunities for choice. That carries with it an implicit view of a person and his or her development to adulthood. Codes of order, or even school rules, may not be seen by the students as moral, yet students complain (on the grounds of fairness) about patterns of discipline. Grant's study portrays the loss of a moral stance within a school. The portrait is devastating because it reveals the final incoherence of legalistic proceduralism in a school without any shared moral base. That is not to sigh for a golden age before Hamilton High broke down; for there, moral values were unreflectively held and conventional. Once again, the implication is clear: Schools, as we presently understand them, cannot help being moral institutions. The central determinants of an ethos include, based on these studies, personal relationships at all levels, a clear and consistent ideological and moral framework, a view of how children develop morally through their education, an understanding of how the different epistemological characters of taught subjects interweaves with moral matters, and what might be described as the moral balance among autonomy, discipline, and leadership.

Feiman-Nemser and Floden (1986), however, point to an immediate obstacle. They conclude that, although cultures in schools are not uniform, teachers still prefer to be left to themselves, and they do not see their rewards coming from interaction with administrators, parents, and colleagues, including the difficult arena of moral teaching. Teachers see only trouble in moral education. The same is apparently true for researchers in general. The 1986 *Handbook of Research on Teaching* reflects that focus on classroom learning (and the predominant interests of contemporary research) by dealing almost entirely with a "mimetic" rather than a "transformative" view of the practice of teaching. The "transformative" view, in Jackson's (1986) account, springs from a tradition that seeks to change the person in terms of character, ideals, and virtue, rather than merely giving them knowledge. It is this tradition of teaching that fits with the notion of a school's ethos to which all teachers contribute, even, for example, in a Montessorian preschool democracy (Krogh 1984).

In the early 1990s the discussion of school ethos has to be framed against the movement for educational reform in the 1980s and against the strong literature of sociomoral crisis (Bellah et al. 1985; Bloom 1987). That reform movement itself has also to be understood within a context of some political attention to values (e.g., former Secretary of Education William Bennett) and an increasing interest in a philosophy of virtue, particularly in the work of MacIntyre describing institutions in terms of their virtues. At the chalkface rather than at the top of the ivory tower, what could all this mean? What is it for a school to become "effective" or "restructured" without attention to the moral values which define its purpose (Bryk 1988)?

Lightfoot's study of six schools encourages reflection on questions of the goodness of a school, which she defines "as whole, changing and imperfect. It is in articulating and confronting each one of these dimensions that one moves closer and closer to the institutional supports of good education" (Lightfoot 1983, 311). She illustrates how sound leadership can produce strong ideological/moral stances, for example, in the institution emphasizing the significance of caring for its weak. She shows in her study of six high schools how "ideology, authority and order combine to produce a coherent institution that supports human interaction and growth" (350).

Yet such issues cannot be detached and viewed alone. Pincoffs (1986) presents a picture of the human moral character as a kind of network; Sichel (1988) writes of the complex configurations of moral education. Sichel makes the most distinctive contribution to issues of school ethos by connecting the existence of communities to the problems of character development. She analyzes institutions as being of three types: instrumental, sentimental, and constitutive. In the constitutive community there are common purposes, attitudes, and feelings that contribute to the identity of each individual, and schools have to develop in this way, as moral institutions, without indoctrination. Proefriedt (1989) suggests that this powerful argument could lead to redefining purposes in the kindergarten and elementary school for children to have a primary community upon which a constitutive community can be built, for many children simply do not have such a community in their own family.

For curriculum research the 1980s have brought the moral aspects of institutions right into the study of the curriculum. Just as Shulman (1987) and others have conceded that virtue must be considered alongside wisdom in the pedagogical development of a teacher, so too, it seems, issues of the ethos of the institution, must be considered in what counts as the "good" (or effective) school.

Teachers as Moral Educators

The delicacy of confronting moral issues with children has spawned a number of pedagogies based on different rationales, including values clarification, the "neutral" teacher, advocacy, and discussion methods; yet what teachers are supposed to do is far from clear (Ryan and Thompson 1975). What individual teachers actually do may in fact be more closely related to prevailing values in the rich diversity of particular communities they serve, and whose values they may share, than to prescriptive conclusions drawn from theory. Teachers are more comfortable with a focus on an intellectual, rather than a practical, approach to moral education (Kutnick 1988), but Goodlad's (1984) studies show only rare evidence that instruction in American schools goes much beyond mere possession of information to higher levels of intellectual activity.

Ryan's 1987 articulation of the teacher's role as (transformative) moral educator is in striking contrast to Raths, Harmin, and Simon's views in the 1960s. A teacher must be a positive model of good character and the moral person, seeing the development of the student's moral life and character as a responsibility and a priority. He or she must be able to engage the student in moral discourse, be able to articulate his or her own moral viewpoint, and help students empathize with others. Additionally a teacher must establish a positive moral climate in the classroom and provide support for school and community experience, thereby giving opportunities for ethical behavior and altruism (Ryan 1985).

These forthright claims are more complex, if not more controversial, than they appear. Sichel (1988, 225–245), for example, urges a distinction between those virtues that describe a person as a moral agent and those that are intrinsically a part of teaching. Stallings and Stipek (1986) record that cooperative activities in classrooms yield mutual concern and cross-racial friendships, but this is due in part to the diminution of interindividual competition, which suggests a role for teachers in conflict with a prevailing ethos of social competition. The extent to which school values clash with those of parents, as in family life curricula, raises profound issues about the legitimacy of the teacher's moral interventions (Schrag 1971). Finally, Duck's (1981) five alternative styles of "teaching with charisma" (essentialist, experimentalist, reconstructionist, existentialist, and perennialist) each contain a different set of problems about the relation between teaching style (and belief and ideology) and the teacher's moral role within the generality of Ryan's prescriptions.

One major lacuna in recent research descriptions of teachers as moral educators is any in-depth eclectic treatment of the teacher as a "model." The term is often used, by Noddings, for example, to indicate how teachers act as examples of intellectual or moral virtue in the expectation that students will catch on. Adelson (1986) locates the description (in discussion of college teaching) in the notion of identity, rather than identification. The distinction between skill (which a student may copy) and style (which a student may emulate) is critical: "We may speak of a progression from skill to style. The student is gradually changed and by accretion; as he acquires skills, these become part of the ego repertoire and, finally, of the ego identity" (101–119). Duck's epistemic categories of teachers are in marked contrast to Adelson's portraits of teachers as shamans, priests, and mystic healers. This varied set of classifications indicates that the notion of a teacher as a model (or as adopting a model) is seen as important, but has not been closely examined. It needs much more profound philosophical and psychological examination than has been attempted, because unintentional modeling will be a significant part of a hidden moral education curriculum. Moreover, the community within which a teacher works, as a Ryan-type moral educator, demands greater unanimity of purpose than individualist pictures of teachers suggest. If teachers are to be models, or are to be told they ought to be models either by others or by their colleagues, they ought to be able to look to the research community for some guidance on just what that means.

The Just Community

The just community is only one segment of a mainstream public school. In conception, it is a sophisticated theoretical and practical attempt to influence existing educational arrangements. It is a major development of the familiar common school and its culture, and it is substantially different from progressive schools established with a "moral" purpose. It does not go so far as A. S. Neill's *Summerhill*, which was ideologically rooted in the work of William Reich (Neill 1982). It owes nothing to the confused, even sentimental, Freudianism of Homer Lane's Little Commonwealth (Lane 1928). Bertrand Russell's school at Beacon Hill, another radical attempt at a break with traditional schooling, did not measure up to the sophistication of his philosophy (Perry 1967). Nor was the radical school-reform movement any influence on Kohlberg (Gross and Gross 1969).

Rather, the radical character of the Harvard intervention in schooling led by Kohlberg evolved from initial experimental secondary school programs. As an experiment in moral education, the just community may have very important lessons for those schools seeking to follow the approach of the Carnegie Council on Adolescent Development, which recommends the breaking down of large schooling units into "houses," precisely to provide the atmosphere of quality care and mutual concern that the just community idea claims is possible (Carnegie 1989).

The responsibility for character education, as seen by the just community approach, is that of every adult within the institution (Power 1987). A just community is a cluster of 60 to 90 students with 4 to 8 staff members within a conventional high school to which students and staff return for usual schooling purposes. It is a participatory democracy on issues of community living. This prevents the teacher from becoming an indoctrinator, allowing only advocacy, and is dependent on strong unity of purpose (Kohlberg 1985; Power, Higgins, and Kohlberg 1989; for an observer's critique, see Hoff Sommers 1984).

In the most recent theoretical explanation of the just community, Power, Higgins, and Kohlberg (1989) rely on Aristotle's view of moral development, particularly his emphasis on habituation, and Durkheim's notion of developing the habit of the common life. Students become members of the moral community by practicing the communal moral life within the institutional framework of a community meeting. In particular, the approach emphasizes the significance of students' examining and taking responsibility for rules and sanctions as part of that life, for example, on cheating. In contrast to those who would argue that moral behavior emerges through authority and discipline, the just community stresses responsibility and reasoning. It relies on the "master virtues of community": caring, trust, collective responsibility, and participation.

The Hidden Curriculum

What a school community does is not perspicuous because of the distinction between the curriculum as a planned experience and what, as a matter of fact, students actually experience. Where moral education is concerned, much of the curriculum may be hidden, even where control systems are apparent (McNeil 1986). Gress and Purpel state that the hidden curriculum refers to the discrepancy between what is planned and what is experienced, especially where what is hidden is inconsistent with, or detrimental to, the written or official curriculum (Gress and Purpel 1988). For Martin, whatever is hidden, qua curriculum, must necessarily have value transmission of some kind built into it, whether hidden because it is undiscovered or by someone with pernicious intent. But "it makes no sense to explain a hidden curriculum by means of a conspiracy theory . . . and at the same time describe its learning states as the unintended by-products of schooling" (Martin 1983, 131). Little attention has been given in the United States to the lore, language, and mores of students and the "unofficial" student curriculum, hidden from teacher authority, which on Hargreaves' account may be a counterculture from which students gain their perspective on schools. For some children this is the only way to preserve their dignity, whatever the school's rhetoric (Hargreaves 1967). Nor have school sporting activities been examined in relation either to the ethos of the school or to its hidden curriculum.

Vallance (1983) sees the term "hidden curriculum" as carrying a set of connotations that can be seen in the three dimensions of context, process, and degrees of intentionality. The ways in which these dimensions of the hidden curriculum are then analyzed are dependent on the academic discipline and political orientation of the investigator. Jackson's original argument (1968) was that "the crowds, the praise and the power" are the factors that combine to give the life in any classroom its distinctive flavor. These collectively form the hidden curriculum that teacher and students have to master. Jackson drew attention to the power of institutional expectations that, among other things, demanded the exercise of particular virtues, notably patience. Moreover while there may be common features across schools, institutional variety could make them very different. Kohlberg (1970) claimed that a hidden curriculum was institutionally inevitable and that it needed to be set within an atmosphere of justice.

Discussion on the hidden curriculum has, however, been pursued in a much wider framework of the social and the political than the particular moral aspects of the curriculum. For critical sociologists such as Giroux, Apple, and Illich, more significant questions about the relationship among ideology, instruction, and curriculum demanded exploration, because the hidden curriculum of political socialization is much more effective, particularly as an instrument of social control, than the official curriculum is as an instrument of liberation. Getting at the hidden curriculum and its effects is seen as a matter of comprehending the dialectic of school and society and in the syntax and concepts we use in discussing it. The ethos of schools, on this account, must be viewed within the economic framework of capitalism and the differential treatments students from different class backgrounds receive (Stevens and Wood 1987).

RESEARCH DIRECTIONS AND QUESTIONS

The panoply of perspectives on human beings as moral persons set against the pervasiveness of the moral in educational institutions must lead us to conclude that the notion of a common moral education for American children seems an unlikely eventuality, whatever its desirability (Johnson 1981). Yet the evidence remains of many young people growing up in a moral vacuum and schools and teachers reluctant, by neglect or by design, to pursue any course which would create public controversy. What is mandated by state or locality now defines the limits for a teacher's moral teaching.

The prevailing mood is for the development of a form of moral education that is school-wide. That will demand some practical and theoretical agreement and it will influence both the overt and the hidden curriculum. The plight of teachers faced with the complexity of interpersonal behavior (e.g., in sex education) and the forked tongues of competition versus cooperation and freedom versus political socialization makes the challenge of moral education immensely formidable. The traditional distance of research from practice, particularly in moral education, demands reassessment, and the following account of the agenda for curriculum research in moral education is wide-ranging and unavoidably prescriptive. (For accounts of recent doctoral dissertations, see Cochrane 1987 and 1988; for a bibliography, see Leming 1983.)

Moral Education and the Disciplines

In the heyday of the curriculum reform movement, curriculum research eagerly embraced experts from the subject disciplines in curriculum construction and design. This is a direction that deserves reexamination in curriculum research in moral education (see Chapter 1 of this *Handbook*.) Many current issues (for example, the influence of MacIntyre on talk of virtue) are philosophical in character. Urgently needed is the sophistication of a teacher's understanding, particularly in the discrimination of different virtues and their implications for school practice (Sockett 1988). What moral teaching is appropriate in the context of curriculum subjects, for example, science and history, could be deepened by the perspectives of specialist academics, particularly in such political-moral issues as the nuclear debate and environmental education. Of overriding importance is the fact that both school curricula and subject perspectives need a framework that addresses the issue of moral relativism and a more sophisticated vocabulary of morality (see Stout 1988). Most school subjects constantly wrestle with the pervasiveness of the moral, as major issues of public policy and private life have a direct location in different disciplines. The language required would be appropriate to Jackson's "transformative" curriculum and the role Ryan and others see for teachers as moral educators. One view of the curriculum task is to search for a common ground and a common language across disciplines as a basis for schooling in moral education, and a range of specialist academic insights would promote that development. That attempt must be grounded in the fact that teachers and students may well come from particular religious backgrounds (see above).

The Teacher as Moral Educator

Surprisingly we do not know what teachers now do by way of moral education in their classrooms, except in interventive projects (Ryan and Thompson 1976). We do not know the ways in which teachers generally confront such basic issues as racial prejudice and sexism or what their curriculum strategies look like. We do not know the extent to which teachers are more or less influenced by their religious persuasions when they teach, nor the precise extent to which state mandates or local community values inhibit moral teaching. Nor do we know to what extent teachers feel their integrity is compromised by any conflict between their world view in moral terms and the practices of the schools in which they work. Wynne's claim that there is an educational consensus may be correct. It may even be seen as desirable by teachers, but that does not mean it can be practicably embodied in a school, given the sirens of dissenting minorities.

Ryan's concern for the preservice moral education of teachers must also be matched by practice and research on work done in in-service programs. But traditional types of research inquiry on teachers will not necessarily contribute to the various quandaries in which teachers find themselves. The problem for curriculum research is, therefore, to use methodologies that both contribute to teaching knowledge and simultaneously assist practice, especially within a framework of school-wide approaches.

Research Methodology in Moral Education: A Focus on Schools

The framework in which educational research has been conducted seems to leave the "school curriculum" as a focus of study as far too large (and far too expensive) a target for traditional methodologies. For curriculum research to bring about change, a collaborative research model will be necessary, as Kohlberg suggested, such as is now usual in early education (White and Buka 1987). Action research and, particularly, reflective practice provides that opportunity. Without collaboration in research, without teachers being engaged in researching their own schools, as much as their own classrooms, researchers may replicate Kohlberg and Fenton's conclusion that the research may be a success but the patient dies. Collaborative reflective practice also opens up the possibility of sustained rigorous discussion for school faculty on issues of controversy. With the character education movement's concern for whole schools (Wynne, Ryan), and Kohlberg's legacy (whatever its merits) of a research-teaching partnership, a combined assault looks possible and desirable.

Curriculum researchers and their colleagues in educational disciplines must therefore reject the force of institutional tradition which keeps them at a distance from work with (as opposed to on) teachers (Lanier and Little 1986). Research itself must take a caring stance to the situations in which work is pursued (Noddings 1988). Some suggest that the notions of neutrality and objectivity must be abandoned and that research must stop evasion of issues of central human dignity as they affect the schools (Giroux and Purpel 1983).

A Focus on Students

While what students learn has been a primary focus of educational research, the student as a moral initiate has not been seen by research as a person with a life outside and between schools. In all curriculum subjects there is a complex transition as the child moves from elementary to secondary education. Yet, much more significant for the child's moral education is the difference in mores between schools, the effect of this transition on the child's moral development, and what schools might do to ease that transition. The transition is not merely a move from one set of official school mores to another but also a shift to the mores of a youth culture, the dimensions of which seem unexplored as a curriculum phenomenon. Researchers and teachers seem to know very little about the other cultures within which the child is growing up, particularly those inside the school building, and thus how far friendships, for example, would provide a more appropriate basis for group teaching than a class in a particular grade.

Finally the politically volatile character of all issues connected with "family life" curricula, particularly with the changes in *Roe v. Wade*, is highly unlikely to evaporate and presents to curriculum researchers a major challenge. The question is not whether the schools need help from curriculum research, but how within a complex political framework that support can best be delivered.

References

Abbs, Peter. 1982. Teachers, ethical imagination and world disarmament. *Teachers College Record* 84(1): 174–183.

Adelson, Joseph. 1986. *Inventing Adolescence. The Political Psychology of Everyday School*. New Brunswick, NJ: Transaction Books.

Alexander, Gary. 1985. Science, religion and the myth of creation. *Journal of Curriculum and Supervision* 1(4): 294–304.

Alexander, Robert. 1980. "Moral Education to Reduce Racial and Ethnic Prejudice." In *Moral Education: A First Generation of Research and Development*, edited by Ralph L. Mosher, 126–145. New York: Praeger.

Allen, Katherine R. 1988. Integrating a feminist perspective into family studies courses. *Family Relations* 37(1): 29–35.

Alston, William G. 1971. "Comments on Kohlberg's 'From Is to Ought.'" In *Cognitive Development and Epistemology*, edited by Theodore Mischel, 269–284. New York: Academic Press.

Anyon, Jean. 1979. Ideology and United States history textbooks. *Harvard Educational Review* 49(3): 361–386.

Argyle, Michael. 1969. *Social Interaction*. London: Methuen.

Bailey, Charles. 1971. Rationality, democracy and the neutral teacher. *Cambridge Journal of Education* 2: 68–76.

Bandura, A. 1971. *Social Learning Theory*. New York: General Learning.

Barrow, Harold M., and Janice P. Brown. 1988. *Man and Movement: Principles of Physical Education*, 4th ed. Philadelphia, PA: Lea and Ferbiger.

Battistoni, Richard M. 1985. *Public Education and the Education of Democratic Citizens*. Jackson: University of Mississippi Press.

Bauer, Gary L. 1984. Educating for liberty. *American Education* 20(10): 2–3.

Beck, Clive. 1989. "Moral Education in the Junior High School." In *Moral Development and Character Education: A Dialogue*, edited by Larry Nucci, 206–227 Berkeley, CA: McCutchan.

Bellah, Robert N., Richard Madsden, William M. Sullivan, Ann Swidler, and Steven N. Tipton. 1985. *Habits of the Heart*. New York: Harper & Row.

Bennett, William J. 1980. The teacher, the curriculum and values education development. *New Directions for Higher Education* 31:27–34.

Bereiter, Carl. 1973. *Must We Educate?* Englewood Cliffs, NJ: Prentice Hall.

Berkowitz, Marvin W. 1985. "The Role of Discussion in Moral Education." In *Moral Education: Theory and Application*, edited by Marvin W. Berkowitz and Fritz Oser, 197–219 London: Erlbaum.

Berkowitz, Marvin W., and Fritz Oser, eds. 1985. *Moral Education: Theory and Application*. London: Erlbaum.

Bettelheim, Bruno. 1970. "Moral Education." In *Moral Education*, edited by Theodore and Nancy Sizer, 85–109 Cambridge, MA: Harvard University Press.

Bettelheim, Bruno. 1977. *The Uses of Enchantment*. New York: Vintage.

Beyer, Barry. 1979. *Teaching Thinking in Social Studies: Using Inquiry in the Classroom,* rev. ed. Columbus, OH: Merrill.

Blasi, Augusti. 1980. Bridging moral cognition and moral action. A critical review of the literature. *Psychological Bulletin*. 88(1): 1–45.

Blatt, Moshe, and Lawrence Kohlberg. 1975. Effects of classroom moral discussions upon children's levels of moral judgment. *Journal of Moral Education* 4: 129–162.

Bloom, Allan. 1987. *The Closing of the American Mind*. New York: Simon & Schuster.

Bogdan, Deanne. 1984. Pygmalion as pedagague: Subjectivist bias in the teaching of literature. *English Education* 16(2): 67–75.

Bok, Sisella. 1979. *Lying: Moral Choice in Public and Private Life*. New York: Vintage.

Bowlby, John. 1966. *Maternal Care and Mental Heath*. New York: Shocken.

Bowlby, John. 1979. *The Making and Breaking of Affectional Bonds*. New York: Methuen.

Bowles, Samuel, and Herbert Gintis. 1976. *Schooling in Capitalist America: Educational Reform and the Contradictions of Economic Life*. New York: Basic Books.

Boyd, Dwight, and Deanne Bogdan. 1984. "Something" clarified, nothing of "value": A rhetorical critique of values clarification. *Educational Theory* 34(3): 297–300.

Brabeck, Mary M. 1987. Feminist perspectives on moral education and development. *Journal of Moral Education* 18(3): 163–166.

Brians, Paul. 1988. Nuclear fiction for children. *Bulletin of the Atomic Scientists* 44(6): 24–27.

Bricker, David C. 1972. Moral education and teacher neutrality. *School Review* 80(4): 619–627.

Bronfenbrenner, Urie. 1970. *Two Worlds of Childhood: US and USSR*. New York: Sage.

Bryk, Anthony S. 1988. Musings on the moral life of schools. *American Journal of Education* 96(2): 256–290.

Burton, Roger V. 1976. "Honesty and Dishonesty." In *Moral Development and Behavior: Theory, Research and Social Issues*. edited by Thomas Lickona, 173–198. New York: Holt, Rinehart and Winston.

Caduto, Michael. 1983. Towards a comprehensive strategy for environmental values education. *Journal of Environmental Education* 14(4): 12–18.

Carman, Philip, and Stephen Kneeshaw. 1985. Teaching "The Nuclear Predicament." *The History and Social Science Teacher*. 22(4): 216–220.

Carnegie Council on Adolescent Development. 1989. *Turning Points: Preparing American Youth for the 21st Century*. New York: Carnegie.

Casement, William. 1983. Another look at indoctrination. *Journal of Educational Thought* 17(3): 230–239.

Casement, William. 1987. Literature and didacticism: Examining some popularly held ideas. *Journal of Aesthetic Education* 21(1): 101–111.

Cavallo, Dominick. 1981. *Muscles and Morals: Organized Playgrounds and Urban Reform 1880–1920*. Philadelphia, PA: University of Pennsylvania Press.

Cerjak, Judith. 1987. Beware the loss of conscience: "The Crucible" as warning for today. *English Journal* 76(5): 55–57.

Charters, W. W. 1927. *The Teaching of Ideals*. New York: Macmillan.

Chazan, Barry I. 1985. *Contemporary Approaches to Moral Education: Analyzing Alternative Theories*. New York: Teachers College Press.

Chazan, Barry I., and Jonas F. Soltis, eds. 1973. *Moral Education*. New York: Teachers College Press.

Christian-Smith, Linda K. 1987. Gender, popular culture and curriculum: Adolescent romantic novels as gender text. *Curriculum Inquiry* 17(4): 365–406.

Christie, Daniel, and Linden Nelson. 1988. Student reactions to nuclear education. *Bulletin of the Atomic Scientists* 44(6): 22–23.

Cochrane, Donald. 1987. Doctoral dissertations in review. *Moral Education Forum* 13(1): 21–30.

Cochrane, Donald. 1988. Bibliography on moral development, values education and character development. *Moral Education Forum* 13(1): 14–30.

Colby, Anne, Lawrence Kohlberg, and collaborators. 1987. *The Measurement of Moral Judgment*, Vols. I, II and III. Cambridge: Cambridge University Press.

Coleman, James S. 1981. "How Do the Young Become Adults?" In *Cream of the Kappan*, edited by Stanley Elam, 344–351. Bloomington, IN: Phi Delta Kappa Society.

Court, Franklin E. 1985. Adam Smith and the teaching of English literature. *History of Education Quarterly* 25(3): 325–340

Craig, Donald. 1983. Teaching ethics: Not an impossible dream. *The Humanist* 43(3): 24–25, 36.

Cremin, Lawrence A. 1990. *Popular Education and Its Discontents*. New York: Harper & Row.

Crittenden, Brian S. 1980. Neutrality in education. *Educational Philosophy and Theory* 12(June): 1–18.

Cusick, Philip. 1983. *The Egalitarian School and the American High School*. New York: Longman.

Cusick, Philip, and Christopher W. Wheeler. 1988. Educational morality and organizational reform. *American Journal of Education* 96(2): 231–255.

Davies, Lynn. 1984. Political education, gender and the art of the possible. *Educational Review* 38(2): 187–195.

Dearden, Robert F., Paul H. Hirst, and Richard S. Peters, eds. 1973. *Education and the Development of Reason*. London: Routledge & Kegan Paul.

Dennis, Lawrence, and George Stickel. 1981. Mead and Dewey: Thematic connections on educational topics. *Educational Theory* 31(3–4): 319–331.

Dewey, John. 1939. *Theory of Valuation*. Chicago: University of Chicago Press.

Diller, Ann. 1988. The ethics of care and education: A new paradigm, its critics, and its educational significance. *Curriculum Inquiry* 18(3): 325–342.

Diorio, Joseph A. 1985a. Contraception, copulation domination and the theoretical barrenness of sex education literature. *Educational Theory* 35(3): 239–254.

Diorio, Joseph A. 1985b. The decline of history as a tool of moral training. *History of Education Quarterly* 25(1–2): 71–101.

di Stefano, Ann. 1980. "Adolescent Moral Reasoning About Sexual and Interpersonal Dilemmas." In *Moral Education: A First Generation of Research and Development*, edited by Ralph L. Mosher, 146–164. New York: Praeger.

Downey, Meriel E., and A. Victor Kelly. 1978. *Moral Education: Theory and Practice*. London: Harper & Row.

Duck, Lloyd. 1981. *Teaching with Charisma*. Boston, MA: Allyn & Bacon.

Durkheim, Émile. 1973 [1961]. *Moral Education*. New York: Free Press.

Egan, Kieran. 1986. *Individual Development and the Curriculum*. London: Hutchinson.

Elkind, David. 1984. *All Grown Up and No Place to Go: Teenagers in Crisis*. Reading, MA: Addison-Wesley.

Elliott, Robert. 1986. Making children moral. *Educational Theory* 36(3): 289–301.

Endres, William B. 1984. Teaching Vietnam: Reflections beyond the immediate. *English Journal* 73(8): 28–30.

Engle, Shirley H., and Anna S. Ocha. 1988. *Education for Democratic Citizenship: Decision-Making in the Social Studies*. New York: Teachers College Press.

Ennis, R. H. 1959. The "impossibility" of neutrality. *Harvard Educational Review* 29(2): 128–136.

Erikson, Erik H. 1963. *Childhood and Society*, 2nd ed. New York: Norton.

Farnham, James F. 1982. Teaching the holocaust: A rationale for dealing with the absurd. *Journal of General Education* 33(4): 273–283.

Feiman-Nemser, Sharon, and Robert E. Folden. 1986. "The Cultures of Teaching." In *Handbook of Research on Teaching*, edited by Merlin C. Wittrock, 505–526. New York: Macmillan.

Felderhof, Martin C., ed. 1985. *Religious Education in a Pluralistic Society*. London: Hodder and Stoughton.

Filler, Louis. 1965. *Horace Mann: On the Crisis in Education*. Yellow Springs, OH: Antioch Press.

Flew, Anthony. 1975. "Indoctrination and Religion." In *Concepts of Indoctrination*, edited by Ivan Snook, 89–101. Routledge & Kegan Paul.

Ford, Phyllis, M. and James Blanshard. 1985. *Leadership and Administration of Outdoor Pursuits*. State College, PA: Venture.

Forrest, Jacqueline D., and Jane Silverman. 1989. What public school teachers teach about preventing pregnancy, AIDS and sexually transmitted diseases. *Family Planning Perspectives* 21(2): 65–72.

Fraenkel, Jack R. 1976. The Kohlberg bandwagon: Some reservations. *Social Education* 40(April): 216–222.

Frangedis, Helen. 1988. Dealing with the controversial elements in "The Catcher in the Rye." *English Journal* 77(7): 72–75.

Frost, Reuben. 1975. *Physical Education Foundations, Practice and Principles*. New York, Addison-Wesley.

Gambell, Trevor. 1988. Literature: Why we teach it. *The English Quarterly* 19(2): 85–91.

Gardner, Peter. 1981. Another look at controversial issues and the curriculum. *Journal of Curriculum Studies* 16(1): 379–385.

Gibbs, James C. 1977. Kohlberg's stages of moral judgment: A constructive critique. *Harvard Educational Review*. 47(1): 43–61.

Gilligan, Carol. 1979. Woman's place in man's life cycle. *Harvard Educational Review* 49(1): 431–446.

Gilligan, Carol. 1982. *In a Different Voice: Psychological Theory and Women's Development*. Cambridge, MA: Harvard University Press.

Gilligan, Carol, and Jane Attanucci. 1989. Two moral orientations: Gender differences and similarities. *Merrill-Palmer Quarterly* 34(3): 223–237.

Gilligan, Carol, Nona P. Lyons, and Trudy Hammer. 1990. *Making Connections: The Relational Worlds of Adolescents at Emma Willard School*. Cambridge, MA: Harvard University Press.

Gilligan, Carol, and Jane E. Murphy. 1979. "Development from Adolescence to Adulthood: The Philosopher and the Dilemma of the Fact." In *Intellectual Development Beyond Childhood: New Directions for Child Development*. Vol. 5: 85–99. San Francisco, CA: Jossey-Bass.

Ginsburg, Alan, and Sandra Hanson. 1986. *Gaining Ground: Values and High School Success* Report to the U.S. Department of Education. Washington DC: U.S. Department of Education.

Giroux, Henry, and David Purpel, eds. 1983. *The Hidden Curriculum and Moral Education*. Berkeley, CA: McCutchan.

Good, Thomas L., and Jere E. Brophy. 1986. "School Effects." In *Handbook of Research on Teaching*, edited by Merlin C. Wittrock, 570–601. New York: Macmillan.

Goodlad, John S. 1984. *A Place Called School*. New York: McGraw-Hill.

Gordon, Robert M. 1984. Freedom of expression and values in education in the public school curriculum. *Journal of Law and Education*, 13(4): 523–579.

Grant, Gerald. 1988. *The World We Created at Hamilton High*. Cambridge, MA: Harvard University Press.

Green, Thomas F. 1964. A topology of the teaching concept. *Studies in Philosophy and Education* 3(4): 284–319.

Green, Thomas F. 1985. The formation of conscience in an age of technology. *American Journal of Education* 94(1): 1–32.

Gress, James R., and David E. Purpel, eds. 1988. *Curriculum: An Introduction to the Field*. Berkeley, CA: McCutchan.

Gross, B., and R. Gross, eds. 1969. *Radical School Reform*. New York: Simon & Schuster.

Hamerow, Theodore S. 1987. *Reflections on History and Historians*. Madison: University of Wisconsin Press.

Hamm, Cornel M. 1977. The content of moral education, or in defense of the "bag of virtues." *School Review* 85(2): 218–228.

Hamm, Mary, and Dennis Adams. 1988. What research says about teaching nuclear war. *Science and Children* 25(6): 37–38.

Hannabus, Stuart. 1987. Metaphors, morality and children's books. *Use of English* 38(3): 51–58.

Hare, Richard M. 1961. *The Language of Morals*. Oxford: Clarendon Press.

Hare, Richard M. 1973. "Adolescents into Adults." In *Moral Education*, edited by Barry I. Chazan and Jonas F. Soltis, 116–124. New York: Teachers College Pres.

Hargreaves, David. 1967. *Social Relations in a Secondary School*. London: Routledge & Kegan Paul.

Hartshorne, Hugh, and Mark A. May. 1928–1930. *Studies in the Nature of Character*. Vols I, II, and III. New York: Macmillan.

Hirst, Paul H. 1974. *Moral Education in a Secular Society*. London: University of London Press.

Hoff Sommers, Christina. 1984. Ethics without virtue. *The American Scholar* 53(3): 81–89.

Hoffman, Marvin. 1976. "Empathy, Role-Taking, Guilt and Development of Altruistic Motives." In *Moral Development and Behavior: Theory, Research and Social Issues*, edited by Thomas Lickona, 124–144. New York: Holt, Rinehart and Winston.

Hoffman, Marvin. 1980. "Moral Development in Adolescence." In *Handbook of Adolescent Psychology*, edited by Joseph Adelson, 295–344. New York: Wiley.

Honig, Bill. 1988. Middle grade reform. *Social Education* 52(2): 119–120.

Jackson, Philip W. 1968. *Life in Classrooms*. New York: Holt, Rinehart and Winston.

Jackson, Philip W. 1986. *The Practice of Teaching*. Columbia: Teachers College Press.

Jewett, Ann E., and Linda L. Bain. 1985. *The Curriculum in Physical Education*. Dubuque, IA: Brown.

Johnson, Conrad D. 1981. The morally educated person in a pluralistic society. *Educational Theory* 31(3 and 4): 237–251.

Johnson, David W., and Roger Johnson. 1985. Classroom conflict: Controversy versus debate in learning groups. *American Educational Research Journal* 22(2): 237–256.

Johnson, Henry C., Jr. 1982. "Moral Education." In *Encyclopedia of Educational Research*, 5th ed., Vol. III, 1241–1255. New York: Free Press.

Johnson, Henry C., Jr. 1987. "Society, Culture and Character Development." In *Character Development in Schools and Beyond*, edited by Kevin Ryan and George F. Mclean, 59–97. Westport, CT: Praeger.

Kagan, Jerome. 1981. The moral function of the school. *Daedalus* 110(3): 151–165.

Kazemek, Frances E. 1986. Literature and moral development from a feminine perspective. *Language Arts* 63(3): 64–72.

Kazipedis, Tasos. 1982. Educating, socializing and indoctrinating. *Journal of Philosophy of Education* 16(2): 155–167.

Kelly, Thomas E. 1986. Discussing controversial issues: Four perspectives on the teacher's role. *Theory and Research in Social Education* 14(2): 113–138.

Kenney, Asta M., Sandra Guardado, and Lisanne Brown. 1989. Sex education and AIDS education in the schools: What states and large school districts are doing. *Family Planning Perspectives* 21(2): 56–64.

Kilpatrick, William H. 1975. "Indoctrination and Respect for Persons." In *Concepts of Indoctrination*, edited by Ivan Snook, 47–54. London: Routledge & Kegan Paul.

Kirby, D., 1984. *Sexuality Education: An Evaluation of Programs and Their Effects*. Washington, DC: Center for Population Options.

Klein, Susan S. 1988. Sex education and gender equity. *Educational Leadership* 45(6): 69–75.

Kleinig, John. 1976. Principles of neutrality in education. *Educational Philosophy and Practice* 8(1): 1–16.

Knapp, Clifford E. 1983–1984. Ten more challenges in outdoor education. *Journal of Outdoor Education* 18: 22–24.

Knowles, Richard T., Jesse A. Mann, and Frederick A. Ellrod. 1986. *Psychological Foundations of Moral Education and Character Development*. Washington, DC: University Press of America.

Kohlberg, Lawrence. 1970a. "Education for Justice: A Modern Statement of the Platonic View." In *Moral Education*, edited by Theodore R. and Nancy F. Sizer, 57–85. Cambridge, MA: Harvard University Press.

Kohlberg, Lawrence. 1970b. "The moral Atmosphere of the Schools." In *The Unstudied Curriculum*, edited by Normal Overley, 109–127. Alexandria, VA: Association for Supervision and Curriculum Development.

Kohlberg, Lawrence. 1971. "Moral Education, the Psychological view." In *Encyclopedia of Education* Vol. VI, 399–406. New York: Macmillan.

Kohlberg, Lawrence. 1975. "The Relationship of Moral Education to the Broader Field of Values Education." In *Values Education: Theory, Practice, Problems and Prospects*, edited by J. R. Meyer, B. Burnham, and J. Cholvat, 79–86. Waterloo, Ontario: Wilfred Laurier University Press.

Kohlberg, Lawrence. 1980a. "The Future of Liberalism as the Dominant Ideology of the West." In *Moral Development and Politics*, edited by Richard W. Wilson and Gordon J. Schochet, 55–68. New York: Praeger.

Kohlberg, Lawrence. 1980b. "High School Democracy and Educating for a Just Society." In *Moral Education: A First Generation of Research and Development*, edited by Ralph L. Mosher, 20–49. New York: Praeger.

Kohlberg, Lawrence. 1981. *Essays on Moral Development*. Vol. One: *The Philosophy of Moral Development*. San Francisco, CA: Harper & Row.

Kohlberg, Lawrence, Charles Levines, and Alexandra Hewer. 1983. *Moral Stages: A Current Formulation and a Response to Critics* Basel, Switzerland: Karger.

Kohlberg, Lawrence. 1984. *Essays on Moral Development*. Vol. Two: *The Psychology of Moral Development*. San Francisco: Harper & Row.

Kohlberg, Lawrence. 1985. "The Just Community Approach to Moral Education." In *Moral Education: Theory and Application*, edited by Marvin W. Berkowitz and Fritz Oser, 27–87. London: Erlbaum.

Krogh, Suzanne L. 1984. Pre-school democracy—ideas from Montessori. *Social Studies* 75(4): 178–181.

Kung, Guido. 1985. "The Post-Conventional Level of Moral Development: Psychology or Philosophy?" In *Moral Education: Theory and Application*, edited by Marvin Berkowitz and Fritz Oser, 421–433. London: Erlbaum.

Kurtines, W. M., and J. L. Gewirtz. 1984. *Morality, Moral Behavior and Moral Development*. New York: Wiley.

Kutnick, Peter. 1988. "I'll teach you!": Primary school teachers' attitudes to and use of moral education in the classroom. *Journal of Moral Education* 17(1): 61–70.

La Farge, Phyllis. 1988. Nuclear teaching: Propaganda or problem solving? *Bulletin of the Atomic Scientists* 44(6): 14–20.

Ladenberg, Thomas. 1980. "Cognitive Development and Moral Reasoning in the Teaching of History." In *Moral Education: A First Generation of Research and Development*, edited by Ralph L. Mosher, 113–125. New York: Praeger.

Lane, Homer. 1928. *Talks to Parents and Teachers*. London: George Allen & Unwin.

Lanier, Judith E., and Judith W. Little. 1986. "Research on Teacher Education." In *Handbook of Research on Teaching*, edited by Merlin C. Wittrock, 527–570. New York: Macmillan.

Leavis, F. R. 1963. *Two Cultures? The Significance of C. P. Snow* London: Putnam Books.

Leming, James S. 1981. Curricular effectiveness in moral/values education. *Journal of Moral Education* 10(3): 147–164.

Leming, James S. 1983. *Foundations of Moral Education: An Annotated Bibliography*. Westport, CT: Greenwood.

Leming, James S. 1986. Rethinking social studies research and the goals of social education. *Theory and Research in Social Education* 14(2): 139–152.

Levin, David M. 1982. Moral education: The body's felt sense of value. *Teachers College Record* 84(2): 283–300.

Lickona, Thomas, ed. 1976. *Moral Development and Behavior: Theory, Research and Social Issues*. New York: Holt, Rinehart and Winston.

Lickona, Thomas. 1985. "Parents as Moral Educators." In *Moral Education: Theory and Application*, edited by Marvin Berkowitz and Fritz Oser, 127–146. London: Erlbaum.

Lickona, Thomas. 1987. "Character Development in the Elementary School Classroom." In *Character Development in Schools and Beyond*, edited by Kevin Ryan and George F. Maclean, 177–206. Westport, CT: Praeger.

Lightfoot, Sara Lawrence. 1983. *The Good High School: Portraits of Character and Culture*. New York: Basic Books.

Lockwood, Alan L. 1977. A critical view of values clarification. *Teachers College Record* 77(1): 5–50.

Lockwood, Alan L. 1978. The effects of values clarification and moral development curricula on school-age subjects: A critical review of recent research. *Review of Educational Research* 48 (3): 9–11.

Lockwood, Alan L. 1985. Keeping them in the courtyard: A response to Wynne. *Educational Leadership* 43(4): 9–11.

Lovin, Robin W. 1988. The schools and the articulation of value. *American Journal of Education* 96(2): 143–162.

MacIntyre, Alasdair. 1984. *After Virtue*, 2nd ed. Notre Dame, IN: University of Notre Dame Press.

McNeil, Linda. 1986. *Contradictions of Control: School Structure and School Knowledge*. New York: Routledge & Kegan Paul.

McPhail, Peter. 1982. *Social and Moral Education* Oxford: Basil Blackwell.

McPhail, Peter, Donald Middleton, and David Ingram. 1978. *Startline: Moral Education in the Middle Years* and *Moral Education 8 to 13*. Harlow, England: Longman.

Mackey, Gerald. 1987. Teaching values and values clarification in the English classroom. *Exercise Exchange* 32(2): 39–41.

Martin, Jane R. 1983. "What Should We Do with a Hidden Curriculum When We Find One?" In *The Hidden Curriculum and Moral Education*, edited by Henry Giroux and David Purpel, 122–143. Berkeley, CA: McCutchan.

Martin, Michael. 1986. Science education and moral education. *Journal of Moral Education* 15(2): 99–108.

Merelman, Richard M. 1979. A critique of moral education in the social studies. *Journal of Moral Education* 8(3): 182–192.

Miller, Janet L. 1982. Feminism and curriculum theory. *Journal of Curriculum Theorizing* 4(2): 181–186.

Mischel, Theodore, ed. 1971. *Cognitive Development and Epistemology*. New York: Academic Press.

Mischel, Walter. 1973. Toward a cognitive social learning reconceptualization of personality. *Psychological Review* 80(4): 252–283.

Modgil, S., and C. Modgil, eds. 1986. *Lawrence Kohlberg—Consensus and Controversy*. Philadelphia, PA: Falmer.

Molnar, Alex, ed. 1987. *Social Issues and Education: Challenge and Responsibility*. Alexandria, VA: Association for Supervision and Curriculum Development.

Mosher, Ralph L., ed. 1980. *Moral Education: A First Generation of Research and Development*. New York: Praeger.

Nails, Debra. 1983. Social-scientific sexism: Gilligan's mismeasure of man. *Social Research* 50(3): 643–664.

National Board for Professional Teaching Standards. 1989. *Towards High and Rigorous Standards for the Teaching Profession*. Washington, DC: National Board for Professional Teaching Standards.

National Education Association. 1918. *Cardinal Principles of Secondary Education: A Report of the Commission on the Reorganization of Secondary Education*: Bulletin 35. Washington, DC: National Education Association.

Neill, A. S. 1982. *Summerhill*. Harmondsworth, England: Penguin.

Noddings, Nel. 1984. *Caring: A Feminine Approach to Ethics and Moral Education*. Berkeley: University of California Press.

Noddings, Nel. 1987. Do we really want to produce good people? *Journal of Moral Education* 16(3): 177–188.

Noddings, Nel. 1988. An ethic of caring and its implications for instructional arrangements. *American Journal of Education* 86(2): 215–230.

Noddings, Nel, and Paul J. Shore. 1984. *Awakening the Inner Eye: Intuition in Education*. New York: Teachers College Press.

Nucci, Larry P., ed. 1989. *Moral Development and Character Education: A Dialogue*. Berkeley, CA: McCutchan.

Oberteuffer, Delbert. 1977. *Concepts and Convictions*. Washington, DC: American Alliance for Health, Physical Education and Recreation.

Oser, Fritz K. 1986. "Moral Education and Values Education: The Discourse Perspective." In *Handbook of Research on Teaching*, edited by Merlin C. Wittrock, 917–942. New York: Macmillan.

Owen, David B. 1982. History and the curriculum in Rousseau's *Emile*. *Educational Theory* 32(3–4): 117–129.

Passmore, John. 1975. *Man's Responsibility to Nature*. London: Duckworth.

Pateman, Carol. 1980. The disorder of Women: Women, love and the sense of justice. *Ethics* 91(1): 20–35.

Paul, Richard W. 1988. Ethics without indoctrination. *Educational Leadership* 45(8): 10–19.

Peck, R. F., and R. J. Havighurst. 1960. *The Psychology of Character Development*. New York: Wiley.

Perry, Leslie R. 1967. *Bertrand Russell, A. S. Neill, Homer Lane and W. H. Kilpatrick: Four Progressive Educators*. London: Collier-Macmillan.

Peshkin, Alan. 1986. *God's Choice: The Total World of a Fundamentalist Christian School*. Chicago: University of Chicago Press.

Peters, Richard S. 1973. *Reason and Compassion*. London: Routledge & Kegan Paul.

Peters, Richard S. 1974. *Psychology and Ethical Development* London: Allen & Unwin.

Peters, Richard S. 1981a. *Moral Development and Moral Education* London: Allen & Unwin.

Peters, Richard S. 1981b. "The Place of Kohlberg's Theory in Moral Education." In *Essays on Educators*, edited by Richard S. Peters, 113–128. London: Allen & Unwin.

Pincoffs, Edmund. 1986. *Quandaries and Virtues: Against Reductivism in Ethics*. Lawrence: University of Kansas Press.

Postman, Neil, and Carl Weingartner. 1969. *Teaching as a Subversive Activity*. New York: Delacorte.

Power, Clark, Ann Higgins, and Lawrence Kohlberg. 1989. "The Habit of the Common Life: Building Character Through Democratic Community Schools." In *Moral Development and Character Education: A Dialogue*, edited by Larry P. Nucci, 125–145. Berkeley, CA: McCutchan.

Power, Clark. 1985. "Democratic Moral Education in the Large Public High School." In *Moral Education: Theory and Application*, edited by Marvin Berkowitz and Fritz Oser, 219–241. London: Erlbaum.

Power, Clark. 1987. "School Climate and Character Development." In *Character Development in Schools and Beyond*, edited by Kevin Ryan and George F. McLean, 145–177. Westport, CT: Praeger.

Prakash, Madhu S. 1987. "Partners in Moral Education: Communities and Their Public Schools." In *Character Development in Schools and Beyond*, edited by Kevin Ryan and George F. McLean, 119–145. Westport, CT: Praeger.

Pring, Richard A. 1984. *Personal and Social Education in the Curriculum*. London: Hodder and Stoughton.

Pritchard, Ivor. 1988. *Character Education: Research Prospects and Problems*. Washington, DC: Office of Educational Research and Improvement, U.S. Department of Education.

Proefriedt, William A. 1989. Review article: Moral education. *Educational Theory* 39(1): [illegible].

Purpel, David, and Kevin Ryan, eds. 1976. *Moral Education . . . It Comes with the Territory*. Berkeley, CA: McCutchan.

Raths, Louis, Merrill Harmin, and Sidney B. Simon. 1966. *Values and Teaching: Working with Values in the Classroom*. Columbus, OH: Merrill.

Raths, Louis, Merrill Harmin, and Sidney B. Simon. 1978. *Values and Teaching: Working with Values in the Classroom*, 2nd ed. Columbus, OH: Merrill.

Rawls, John. 1971. *A Theory of Justice*. Cambridge, MA: Harvard University Press.

Raywid, Mary-Anne. 1984. Perspectives on the struggle against indoctrination. *Educational Forum* 48(2): 137–164.

Readence, John E. 1982. Kohlberg in the classroom: Responding to literature. *Journal of Reading* 26(2): 104–108.

Reisman, David. 1950. *The Lonely Crowd*. New Haven, CT: Yale University Press.

Rich, John M., and Joseph L. DeVitis. 1985. *Theories of Moral Development*. Springfield, IL: Charles C Thomas.

Rotter, J. B. 1984 [1954]. *Social Learning and Clinical Psychology*. Englewood Cliffs, NJ: Prentice Hall; New York: Johnson Reprint.

Rolls, Ian F. 1984. The future of science education: An alternative perspective. *School Science Review* 65(232): 429–439.

Rutter, Michael, B. Maughan, Peter Mortimore, John Ouston, and A. Smith, 1979. *Fifteen Thousand Hours: Secondary Schools and Their Effects on Children*. Cambridge, MA: Harvard University Press.

Ryan, Kevin. 1985. "Moral and Values Education." In *International Encyclopedia of Education*, Vol. 6, 3406–3413. New York: Pergamon.

Ryan, Kevin, and Michael G. Thompson. 1975. "Moral Education's Muddled Mandate." In *Moral Education . . . It Comes with the Territory*, edited by David Purpel and Kevin Ryan, 405–411. Berkeley, CA: McCutchan.

Ryan, Kevin. 1987. "The Moral Education of Teachers." In *Character Development in Schools and Beyond*, edited by Kevin Ryan and George F. McLean, 358–380. Westport, CT: Praeger.

Ryan, Kevin, and Thomas Lickona. 1987. "Character Development: the Challenge and the Model." In *Character Development in Schools and Beyond*, edited by Kevin Ryan and George F. McLean, 3–36. Westport, CT: Praeger.

Ryan Kevin, and George F. McLean. 1987. *Character Development in Schools and Beyond*. Westport, CT: Praeger.

Schindler, David, Jesse A. Mann, and Frederick E. Ellrod. 1986. *Act and Agent: Philosophical Foundations of Moral Education and Character Development*. Washington, DC: University Press of America.

Schrag, Francis. 1971. The right to educate. *School Review* 79(3): 359–379.

Schrag, Francis. 1977. The child in the moral order. *Philosophy* 52(200): 166–177.

Schunke, George M., and Suzanne L. Krogh. 1982. Values concepts of younger children. *Social Studies* 73(6): 268–272.

Scriven, Michael. 1975. "Cognitive Moral Education." In *Moral Education . . . It Comes With the Territory*, edited by David Purpel and Kevin Ryan, 313–329. Berkeley. CA: McCutchan.

Shaver, James P. 1985. Commitment to values and the study of social problems in citizenship education. *Social Education* 48(3): 194–197.

Shaver, James P. 1987. "Implications for Research: What Should be Taught in Social Studies?" In *Educators' Handbook: A Research Perspective*, edited by Virginia Richardson-Koehler, 112–130. New York: Longman.

Shermis, Samuel S., and James L. Barth. 1985. Indoctrination and the study of social problems: A re-examination of the 1930s debate in "The Social Frontier." *Social Education* 49(3): 190–193.

Shulman, Lee. 1987. Sounding the alarm: A reply to Sockett. *Harvard Educational Review* 57(4): 473–481.

Sichel, Betty. 1988. *Moral Education*. Philadelphia, PA: Temple University Press.

Simmons, Deborah. 1988. Environmental education and environmental ethics: Theory, practice and mixed messages. *Environmental Education and Information* 7(2): 52–61.

Simpson, Evan. 1986. A values-clarification retrospective. *Educational Theory* 36(3): 271–287.

Sizer, Nancy F., and Theodore R. Sizer, eds. 1970. *Moral Education*. Cambridge, MA: Harvard University Press.

Skinner, B. F. 1971. *Beyond Freedom and Dignity*. New York: Knopf.

Smart, Patricia. 1973. "The Concept of Indoctrination." In *New Essays in Philosophy of Education*, edited by Daniel J. O'Connor and Glenn Langford, 33–46. London: Routledge & Kegan Paul.

Snook, Ivan A. 1972a. Neutrality and the schools. *Educational Theory* 22(3): 278–285.

Snook, Ivan A. 1972b. *Indoctrination and Education*. London: Routledge & Kegan Paul

Snook, Ivan A. 1975. *Concepts of Indoctrination*. London: Routledge & Kegan Paul.

Snow, C. P. 1959. *The Two Cultures and the Scientific Revolution* Cambridge: Cambridge University Press.

Sockett, Hugh T. 1988. Education and will: Aspects of personal capability. *American Journal of Education* 96(2): 195–214.

Sperber, Robert and David Milton. 1980. "Organizing a School System for Ethics Education." In *Moral Education: A First Generation of Research and Development*, edited by Ralph L. Mosher, 58–83. New York: Praeger.

Spivak, G., and M. B. Shure, 1974. *The Social Adjustment of Young Children*. San Francisco, CA: Jossey-Bass.

Stafford, J. Martin. 1988. In defence of gay lessons. *Journal of Moral Education* 17(1): 11–20.

Stallings, Jane A., and Deborah Stipek. 1986. "Research on Early Childhood and Elementary School Teaching Programs." In *Handbook of Research on Teaching*, edited by Merlin C. Wittrock, 727–753. New York: Macmillan.

Stankiewicz, Mary-Ann. 1984. "The eye is a nobler organ": Ruskin and American art education. *Journal of Aesthetic Education* 18(2): 51–64.

Starratt, Robert J. 1980. "Moral Education in the High School Classroom." In *Moral Education: A First Generation of Research and Development*, edited by Ralph L. Mosher, 227–253. New York: Praeger.

Stenhouse, Lawrence. 1983. *Authority, Education and Emancipation*. London: Heinemann.

Stevens, Edgar, and George H. Wood, eds. 1987. *Justice, Ideology and Education*. New York: Random House.

Stewart, John S. 1975. "Problems and Contradictions of Values Clarification." In *Moral Education . . . It Comes with the Territory*, edited by David Purpel and Kevin Ryan, 136–151. Berkeley, CA: McCutchan.

Stout, Jeffrey W. 1988. *Ethics after Babel*. Boston, MA: Beacon Press.

Straughan, Roger. 1982. *"I Ought To, But . . . ." A Philosophical Approach to the Problem of Weakness of Will in Education*. Windsor, England: National Foundation for Educational Research.

Strom, Margot S. 1980. "Facing History and Ourselves: The Holocaust and Human Behavior." In *Moral Education: A First Generation of Research and Development*, edited by Ralph L. Mosher, 216–233. New York: Praeger.

Strom, Margot S., and William Parsons. 1982. *Facing History and Ourselves: Holocaust and Human Behavior*. Watertown, MA: Intentional Education.

Stuhr, David, and Louise Rundle. 1980. "Moral Education in an Elementary School: Unconventional Methods for Conventional Goals." In *Moral Education: A First Generation of Research and Development*, edited by Ralph L. Mosher, 237–249. New York: Praeger.

Styer, Sandra. 1988. Sex equity: A moral development approach. *Social Education* 52(3): 173–175.

Sullivan, Edmund V. 1987. "Television as a Moral Educator." In *Character Development in Schools and Beyond*, edited by Kevin Ryan and George F. McLean, 299–328. Westport, CT: Praeger.

Suttle, Bruce. 1981. The need and inevitability of moral indoctrination. *Educational Studies* 12(2): 151–161.

Suttle, Bruce B. 1987. Review article—"I Ought to, But . . ." *Educational Theory* 37(4): 477–486.

Tappan, Mark B., and Lyn Mikel Brown. 1989. Stories told and lessons learned: Toward a narrative approach to moral development and moral education. *Harvard Educational Review* 59(2): 182–205.

Thelen, Louis J. 1987. Values clarification: Science or nonscience. *Science Education* 71(2): 201–221.

Tetreault, Mary-Kay T. 1986a. The journey from male-defined to gender-balanced education. *Theory into Practice* 25(4): 227–234.

Tetreault, Mary-Kay T. 1986b. Integrating women's history: The case of the United States history high school textbooks. *History Teacher* 19(2): 211–262.

Tetreault, Mary-Kay T. 1987. Rethinking women, gender and the social studies. *Social Education* 51(3): 170–178.

Tetreault, Mary-Kay T., and Patricia Schmuck. 1985. Equity, educational reform and gender. *Issues in Education* 3(1): 45–67.

Tobin, Bernadette M. 1989. Richard Peters' theory of moral development. *Journal of Philosophy of Education* 23(1): 15–28.

Tom, Alan. 1984. *Teaching as a Moral Craft*. New York: Longman.

Tyack, David B., and Elizabeth Hansot. 1982. *Managers of Virtue*. New York: Basic Books.

Tyack, David B., and Thomas James. 1985. Moral majorities and the school curriculum: Historical perspectives on the legalization of virtue. *Teachers College Record* 86(4): 513–537.

Ungoed-Thomas, John R. 1978. *The Moral Situation of Children*. London: Macmillan.

Vallance, Elizabeth. 1983. "Hiding the Hidden Curriculum: An Interpretation of the Language of Justification in Nineteenth-Century Educational Reform." In *The Hidden Curriculum and Moral Education*, edited by Henry Giroux and David Purpel, 9–25. Berkeley, CA: McCutchan.

Vasudex, Jyotona. 1988. Sex differences in morality and moral orientation: A discussion of the Gilligan and Attanucci study. *Merrill-Palmer Quarterly* 43(3): 239–244.

Walker, Lawrence J. 1984. Sex differences in the development of moral reasoning: A critical review. *Child Development* 55(3): 677–691.

Warnock, Mary. 1977. *Schools of Thought*. London: Faber & Faber.

Watson, Marilyn, Daniel Solomon, Victor Battistich, Eric Schaps, and Judith Solomon. 1989. "The Child Development Project: Combining Traditional and Developmental Approaches to Values Education." In *Moral Development and Character Education: A Dialogue*, edited by Larry P. Nucci, 51–93. Berkeley, CA: McCutchan.

Welton, M. 1977. Is moral education possible in advanced capitalist societies? *The History and Social Science Teacher* 13(1): 9–22.

White, John P., 1967. "Indoctrination." In *The Concept of Education,* edited by Richard S. Peters, 171–191. London, Routledge & Kegan Paul.

White, Sheldon H., and Stephen L. Buka. 1987. "Early Education: Programs, Traditions and Policies." In *Review of Research in Education 14,* edited by Ernst Z. Rothkopf, 43–93. Washington, DC: American Educational Research Association.

Wilson, John. 1973. *A Teacher's Guide to Moral Education.* London: Chapman.

Wilson, John. 1982. "First Steps in Moral Education." In *The Ethical Dimensions of the School Curriculum,* edited by Lionel O. Ward, 116–132. Swansea, England: University College Press.

Wilson, John, Barry Sugarman, and Norman Williams. 1967. *An Introduction to Moral Education.* Harmondsworth, England: Penguin.

Wittrock, Merlin C., ed. 1986. *Handbook of Research on Teaching.* New York: Macmillan.

Wolf, Louis C. 1975. Children's literature and the development of empathy in young children. *Journal of Moral Education* 5: 45–49.

Wynne, Edward A., and Mary Hess. 1988. "Trends in American Youth Character Development." In *Character Development in Schools and Beyond,* edited by Kevin Ryan and George F. McLean, 36–57. Westport, CT: Praeger.

Wynne, Edward, and Herbert J. Wallberg. 1989. "Character Education: Toward a Preliminary Consensus." In *Moral Development and Character Education: A Dialogue,* edited by Larry P. Nucci, 37–50. Berkeley, CA: McCutchan.

Yambert, Paul A., and Carolyn Donow. 1986. Are we ready for ecological commandments? *Journal of Environmental Education* 17(4): 13–16.

Yeazell, Mary I. 1986. The neglected competency—moral sensibility. *Contemporary Education* 57(4): 173–176.

Yeazell, Mary I., and Robyn R. Cole. 1986. The adolescent novel and moral development: A demurrer. *Journal of Reading* 29(4): 292–298.

Zeidler, Dana L. 1984. Moral issues and social policy in science education: Closing the literacy gap. *Science Education* 68(4): 411–419.

21

CURRICULUM DIFFERENTIATION: OPPORTUNITIES, OUTCOMES, AND MEANINGS

Jeannie Oakes
UNIVERSITY OF CALIFORNIA, LOS ANGELES

Adam Gamoran
UNIVERSITY OF WISCONSIN, MADISON

Reba N. Page
UNIVERSITY OF CALIFORNIA, RIVERSIDE

The school curriculum represents choices made to ensure a culture's continuation: School knowledge is that which older generations accumulate, deem worthy, and make accessible to younger generations. It is of "double aspect," as John Dewey (1956 [1902]) noted in commenting on the school's task of establishing an interaction between the knowledge of the child and the knowledge of the human race. The curriculum combines a common core of knowledge, which a society enjoins all youth to learn, with the differentiated knowledge that prompts the intellectual engagement of diverse individuals. In U.S. schools, the "double aspect" of the school curriculum is represented in a distinctive pattern: Provisions for common, traditional, and required coursework compete with provisions for differentiated, innovative, and elective coursework (Kliebard 1986; Varenne 1974; Westbury 1988b).

WHAT IS CURRICULUM DIFFERENTIATION?

When educators differentiate the curriculum, they make different knowledge available to different groups of students. They organize school systems so that students who appear to vary in their educational needs and abilities can be taught separately, either in specialized schools or in the same school in distinct programs, classes, or instructional groups within classrooms. Within schools, these organizational arrangements are known variously as ability grouping, tracking, and streaming, and they are often thought to be synonymous with curriculum differentiation. In fact, they are only one part of a larger curricular dynamic that includes

- Beliefs about students' needs and abilities, the purposes of schooling, and a broad consensus about what school practices best accommodate these factors
- Alternative clusters of knowledge and skills, emphases, or modes of presentation in subject areas (e.g., courses of study identified as college preparatory or vocational; reading programs divided into "levels" that vary in quantity and type of content)
- Criteria for determining the appropriate curricula for particular students (e.g., ability, prior achievement, student or parent preference, completion of prerequisites)
- A process whereby students are identified as needing a

particular curriculum (teacher judgment, counselor guidance, survey of grades and test scores, student requests)

- An organizational structure that allows the delivery of alternative curricula to different students (e.g., within-class grouping, intact "grouped" classes, tracks)
- Purposes and meanings that are attached to various curricula by those in the setting

Curriculum differentiation cannot be well understood apart from two contexts in which it is embedded. The first is the schooling context, that is, the specific characteristics of schools and classrooms that affect and are affected by the decision to differentiate the knowledge to which students are exposed. This schooling context includes the ways in which schools organize curriculum and instruction generally and the impact of being a part of a particular curriculum on students' school and classroom experiences. When we look at the schooling context of curriculum differentiation, we find broad patterns of similarities as well as interesting variations in U.S. schools and around the world—for example, in students' course-taking patterns, the presentation of curricular content, the use of various instructional strategies, the creation of classroom environments, and the development of peer relationships.

Curriculum differentiation also exists within a wider social milieu, in which the members of the particular culture acknowledge norms and expectations about what schools ought to accomplish—the beliefs, values, and circumstances that originally influenced the institution of differentiation and those that continue to shape current practice. Examining this broader societal context provides a richer understanding of why a particular form of curriculum differentiation—or lack thereof—was adopted as a response to the multiple expectations modern cultures invariably have of schools. Most of this chapter will be devoted to understanding the American context of curriculum differentation, and our understanding will be enhanced by some initial attention to the contexts of differentiation in other countries.

Curriculum Differentiation in Selected Countries

In the United States, differentiation begins early, with most elementary schools employing between-class ability grouping for the entire day, between-class grouping for specific subjects, and/or within-class grouping for specific subjects. Differentiation continues with between-class grouping in the secondary years, and many comprehensive high schools also divide students into broader programs such as academic, general, and vocational (though this practice may be waning). Nonetheless, American schools rarely achieve the complete curricular separation found in most other nations because differentiated classes and tracks within comprehensive schools provide students with some common, overlapping experiences.

In striking contrast to the United States and many European countries, researchers report virtually no curriculum differentiation within grade levels in Japanese elementary and junior high schools (Cummings 1980; Rohlen 1983), although White (1987) describes considerable informal differentiation through private schooling in the *juku*. A standardized curriculum is delivered nationwide, without regard to student characteristics. But as Rohlen says,

> All of this is reversed at the high school level, where entire schools are differentiated by the presumed ability of their students, where tracking is the essential ingredient in the overall structure of schools, and where instead of offering equal education, high school offerings are responsive to and limited by the specific abilities of their students. From lumping, the system shifts to splitting. (121)

Students are sorted into several different types of schools for secondary education, including public, academically oriented high schools; public vocational schools; private academic high schools, whose status is generally lower than those of the public schools; and public, night high schools, for students working during the day (Rohlen 1983). These school types represent distinct missions, or "charters," which clearly indicate what their graduates can expect to attain (Kariya and Rosenbaum 1987). Within the academic and vocational categories, moreover, schools are ranked by reputations, which derive from their success at securing university admissions or job placement, depending on their charters (Rohlen 1983). Which high school a student attends matters a great deal for subsequent attainment, for the academic schools offer differential preparation for university entrance exams, and vocational schools often have direct links to employers (Rohlen 1983; Rosenbaum and Kariya 1989).

In American schools, students are typically sorted within schools at both the elementary and secondary levels. In Japan, there is no differentiation through eighth grade and then a great deal of differentiation afterward, all of which is between schools. Such formalized between-school divisions have been minimized in the United States, although recent years have seen a rise in magnet and specialty schools (Blank 1989; Metz 1986; Moore and Davenport 1988). In the United States, options for students tend to remain open through the later years of high school: Even a vocational-track student can attend a community college and ultimately a four-year college, although this is not the usual route (Velez 1985). In Japan, though, the nature of one's high school dictates the kind of academic future one can expect (Rosenbaum and Kariya 1989). Using Sorensen's (1970) framework, the difference can be seen as one of greater inclusiveness in the American system. However, by providing greater clarity, the Japanese system permits students to plan for the future more easily (Kariya and Rosenbaum 1987).

Despite these major differences, there are important similarities among the systems that evolved in quite different cultures. Like the classic form of American tracking, the Japanese system at the secondary level provides for finely tuned, permanent homogeneous groups (Kariya and Rosenbaum 1987). Both systems result in a high degree of academic segregation during high school. Curriculum differentiation during high school may turn out to be very similar at the level of the classroom, even though Japanese students are sorted between schools and American students, within.

Between-school differentiation at the secondary level has also been important in Europe. For example, German schools, like those in Japan, bear distinct charters: The *Gymnasium* has an academic curriculum that prepares students for university entrance; the curriculum of the *Realschule* mixes academic and vocational skills, ends at grade 10, and often leads to a full-time vocational school; and the *Hauptschule*, whose students generally do not go on after grade 10, presents a strictly vocational curriculum (Hamilton 1987; Oswald, Baker, and Stevenson 1988). This differentiation occurs earlier than in Japan, usually after grade 6 and sometimes even after grade 4. Although educational reforms have led to the opening of some comprehensive schools and wider access to universities for those outside the *Gymnasium*, the vast majority of students follow these differentiated paths (Hamilton 1987).

The move toward comprehensive high schools has taken hold in Britain, which now contains a variety of school types, including comprehensive schools, aiming to include a cross section of students; grammar schools, which have traditionally provided a classical academic curriculum to students selected for their academic skills; and secondary modern schools, for students not selected to the grammar schools. Unlike Japan, all four of these school types are sometimes internally stratified as well (Ball 1981; Kerckhoff 1986).

Outside Europe, the Israeli educational system has much in common with that of Britain. Both comprehensive and specialized schools are common, and the curriculum may be divided both between and within schools. Vocational high schools are much more common in Israel, though. In Britain and Israel researchers can study within- and between-school stratification simultaneously (e.g., Kerckhoff 1986; Shavit and Featherman 1988; Shavit and Williams 1985; Yogev 1981). This possibility has allowed comparisons between students in grouped and ungrouped schools, which has not been possible with U.S. national survey data.

With these cross-national contrasts and similarities in mind, we now provide a closer look at the practice of curriculum differentiation as it has been revealed through decades of research. In this literature, certain questions seem to persist through the years, and we raise these questions at this point in the hope of responding to them by the chapter's end.

Persistent Questions and Debates

In complex cultures, the issue of curriculum differentiation—whether different groups of children should be given different courses of study—prompts ambiguous school practices; voluminous but sometimes confusing research findings; and most certainly, persistent and partisan debate. The research and public debate have centered on three questions that go to the heart of what democratic cultures want for their schools. First, does curriculum differentiation work? Although there are multiple views about what "work" means, a complex issue that we will tackle later in the chapter, most debate focuses on whether curriculum differentiation enables schools to produce greater student learning. Second, is curriculum differentiation fair? Again, although there are a host of definitions of "fair," here the debate usually centers on whether curriculum differentiation affects all students in similar ways or helps some students at the expense of others—particularly whether it benefits advantaged white students at the expense of disadvantaged minority students. Third, does curriculum differentiation affect our ability to construct the curriculum and schools we want? That is, does it enhance or compromise our efforts to transmit the knowledge and values we most want the young of our culture to learn?

Since the 1920s, curriculum theorists, social scientists, and policy analysts have examined these questions to understand how curriculum differentiation affects what schools teach and why and to illuminate the consequences of the practice. Continuing today, they focus on the curricular purposes that rationalize differentiation; the grouping practices that make differentiation possible; the links between students' participation in various curricula and their schooling outcomes; and curriculum differentiation's connection to larger social processes, such as social stratification and mobility, work force participation, and cultural transmission. Most conclude that curriculum differentiation has created as many or more schooling problems as it has solved—although most also agree that efforts to move toward an undifferentiated curriculum generate other sorts of problems.

For most practitioners, curriculum differentiation is simply "how schools work." Most support differentiation, claiming that it benefits most students and that the organizational structures that support it (ability grouping and tracking) ease the instructional problems posed by individual differences. At the same time, others lament what they see as an ineffective, undemocratic practice that relegates the least advantaged students to diminished chances for school success.

Despite more than 70 years of research and discussion, the United States, in particular, remains perplexed about curriculum differentiation. Although the bulk of empirical evidence casts doubt on their efficacy, differentiated curricula are nearly universal in schools and remain astonishingly resistant to change. In this chapter, we review the research on differentiation with this tension uppermost in our minds.

Chapter Overview

The remainder of this chapter is divided into sections that reflect the primary aspects of curriculum differentiation as curriculum theorists, social scientists, and policy analysts have explored them. First, we review work that has added to our understanding of how U.S. schools go about the practice of differentiating curricula. Here, weaving work from various disciplinary perspectives together under the substantive questions that have stimulated researchers' interest, we deal with the explicit, articulated policies that drive school practices in three areas, as well as with some of their implicit dimensions: (1) differentiating content for various groups of students, (2) organizing an array of classes of various types that provide the structure in which different content is offered to different groups of students, and (3) determining which students belong in various curricula and ability-grouped classes. We also consider what these practices mean to schools and to students. Second, we take a step back to consider the broader societal context of tracking, i.e., various historical interpretations of the development of curriculum differentiation, tracking, and ability grouping in the United States. These historical studies attempt to explain why the particular form of curriculum differentiation makes sense in this culture.

Third, we turn to research that has explored the consequences of curriculum differentiation for schools and their participants. Although this review is dominated by U.S. studies, we also include here some findings from research done in other nations. We consider four types of intended and unintended consequences: (1) access to knowledge; (2) the dynamics of classrooms; (3) race and social class stratification; and (4) students' achievement, attitudes, peer relationships, and life chances.

Fourth, we turn to a discussion of how scholars have dealt with the three persistent debates noted earlier: Does curriculum differentiation work? Is it fair? Does it affect the nature of curriculum and schooling? The chapter concludes with our thoughts about promising directions for new research.

THE SCHOOLING CONTEXT—POLICIES AND PRACTICES FOR DIFFERENTIATING CURRICULA

In U.S. schools the differentiated curriculum is enacted in content that is both common and different, in organizational patterns that establish separate groupings of students for instruction, and in elaborate mechanisms for matching students to groups.

Differentiating Content

Curriculum content follows a persistent pattern: Provisions for common, traditionally academic, required coursework coexist and compete with provisions for differentiated, innovative, and elective coursework (Kliebard 1986; Varenne 1974; Westbury 1988b). The balance between common and differentiated coursework distinguishes the elementary from the secondary school curriculum; its dynamic takes on particular force in distinguishing among secondary curricula as well.

The elementary school curriculum is marked by relatively limited content and limited choice. Virtually all children study only a few predominantly academic subjects. Whole-class activities are common; individual differences are accommodated largely within classrooms through instructional variations, such as grouping by ability for the whole day or, more commonly, for particular subjects (Good and Brophy 1987). In a comprehensive survey (Goodlad 1984), elementary school teachers reported that more than half of each week's instructional time was devoted to only three subjects: reading, language arts, and mathematics. The other "central academic subjects," science and social studies, were pale competitors to the three R's, particularly in the first three grades. Even less instructional time was allocated to the arts and physical education. This allocation of a common academic curriculum for all young children is remarkably stable and virtually taken for granted by policymakers, practitioners, parents, and citizens (Goodlad 1984). To question its predominance is culturally heretical (Sarason 1982), although specific allocations of content vary between and within schools and classrooms, often as a consequence of curriculum pacing in which some classes or groups cover more material (Barr and Dreeben 1983; Gamoran 1986; Hanson and Schultz 1978; McDermott and Aron 1978; Rist 1973).

In contrast to the wide acceptance of required academic coursework for all elementary children is the heated debate about the differentiated curriculum offered to older students (see recent and past considerations of the high school, such as Adler 1982; Bellack, Kliebard, Hyman, and Smith 1966; Boyer 1983; Conant 1967; Dewey 1964 [1902]; Goodlad 1984; Krug 1960; Passow 1975; Sizer 1985; Westbury 1988a). At the secondary school level, the curriculum proliferates, as vocational and general subjects are added to the academic subjects (Conant 1967; Kliebard 1986; Krug 1964), along with a fourth, "special" curriculum for handicapped or socially troubled students (Powell, Farrar, and Cohen 1985). Furthermore, secondary schools match horizontal with vertical differentiation through ability grouping (Powell, Farrar, and Cohen 1985; Sorensen 1970). Finally, the curriculum is differentiated because secondary schools allow considerable student choice, with elective courses about evenly balanced in number with high school graduation requirements (Jackson 1981; Murphy, Hull, and Walker 1987; Westbury 1988b).

Junior high and middle schools introduce the characteristic pattern of alternation: They are institutions invented in part for the express purpose of offering young adolescents the chance to choose among a more diverse set of courses while continuing with traditionally academic, required instruction (Noblit 1987). "Practical" or "relevant" subjects appear, which infringe on the strictly "bookish" elementary school courses: Students "explore" vocational courses (home economics and industrial arts), the fine arts, and foreign languages. As a result, where 76 percent of the elementary school's instructional time is spent on the "central academic subjects," only 66 percent of the average junior high school day is occupied with academics (Goodlad 1984). Simultaneously, time is allocated more equally among the traditional academic subjects, so that science and social studies, for example, compete on a par with mathematics. Interclass tracking by ability in core subjects replaces the interclass groups of the elementary school.

Differentiation of the curriculum proceeds apace in U.S. high schools, which offer older adolescents even more choice and more varied subject matter than do junior high schools. About half of the student's coursework becomes elective, in explicit recognition of differences in individual students' abilities, interests, and aspirations. Nevertheless, the "double aspect" of the curriculum remains, with common parameters provided by graduation requirements. Historical accounts (Conant 1967; Jackson 1981; Kliebard 1986; Krug 1964; Westbury 1988b) confirm the stability of the present allocation, in which, on the average, about 55 percent of the secondary school's instructional time is devoted to "the central academic subjects": 3 to 4 years of English, 1 year of mathematics and of science, and 2 to 3 years of social studies.

However stable the nearly equal allocation between common requirements and individual electives, and between "central academic" and "practical" specialized subjects, the significance of the 50–50 curriculum is ambiguous and hotly debated. For example, the junior high "exploration" of diverse subjects may not be as free as explicit rationales suggest: Enrolling in a seventh-grade foreign language (Rosenbaum 1976) or in eighth-grade algebra (Oakes 1990b) can be scholastically consequential, as the choice predicts later placement in high-track classes in senior high school. Moreover, although high schools share statewide, usually academic, graduation requirements, because schools are often split internally into different tracks, students may earn equivalent credits but learn very different knowledge: advanced placement English, business English, science-fiction, and remedial English all provide the Carnegie unit in English that students need to graduate, but their contents are not equivalent. Finally, secondary schools differ from one another in the knowledge to which they award status and resources, so that there are many different versions of a "high school education," even though schools and diplomas are formally equivalent (Metz 1990; Page 1990a). For instance, schools in wealthy communities often allocate more teaching and material resources to academic subjects required for college preparation than do schools in poor communities (Hemmings and Metz 1990; Oakes 1990b; Sanders, Stone, and LaFollette 1987).

Practices such as these reflect knowledge's regular differentiation within and among schools, but they also raise provocative questions. Is the differentiated curriculum determined by socioeconomic differences among communities? Does differentiation signify unequal opportunity or responsiveness to students' and communities' choices, or both? In a democratic polity, what functions—vocational, intellectual, social, or personal—shall the curriculum be expected to meet (Krug 1960)? Such questions point to the differentiated school curriculum as a cultural amalgamation: school knowledge that is common as well as individualized, traditional as well as modern, and required as well as specialized. Modern cultures may find the "double aspect" of curriculum particularly complicated because new knowledge accumulates exponentially; student populations are increasingly inclusive and diverse; and complex societies face multiple, often contradictory, imperatives (Collins 1977; Dewey 1964 [1902]; Spindler and Spindler 1982).

In U.S. schools, curricular ambivalence is also pronounced. Historical accounts and analyses of contemporary practice suggest that the current U.S. pattern expresses the culture's drive for the equally cherished, but contradictory, values of individualism and community (Bellah, Madsen, Sullivan, Swidler, and Tipton 1985; Kammen 1974; Varenne 1977). Accordingly, as children grow, they experience individualism and community concretely as they are presented with the opportunity and the requirement to choose among school subjects. American educators also voice cultural and curricular paradoxes as they proclaim the need of all children for schooling yet express profound doubts about whether all can benefit from "bookish" education (Kliebard 1986; Powell, Farrar, and Cohen 1985). Ambivalence echoes as well through debates that juxtapose national curriculum standards with local control and individual electives, the abolition of tracking with increasingly individualized curriculum for the "special," or general education with early and efficient specialization (National Commission on Excellence in Education 1983; Westbury and Purves 1988).

Organizational Patterns

One can view the curriculum as a resource that is distributed by administrators and teachers to students within schools (Dreeben and Barr 1987). It is not distributed randomly or evenly, though; instead, it is "differentiated" according to the organizational structure of the school and the functions that correspond to different structural subunits. Organizational structure—the arrangement of roles within the school system—constitutes one mechanism through which curriculum is differentiated.

Today, much curriculum differentiation is formal, easily visible, and noncontroversial. As described, school subjects and their contents are typically divided by levels of the school system—elementary, middle, and secondary—and by grades within schools. Such differentiation is usually thought necessary to avoid redundancy and for students to accumulate knowledge in a progressive fashion. Within schools and grades, however, students are also frequently distributed to instructional settings on such criteria as perceived aptitude or achievement level. These divisions, which are as likely to be informal and obscured as formal and obvious, constitute equally important dimensions for differentiating the curriculum. In the United States they are known as ability groups and curricular tracks, and their use has engendered much controversy (see, e.g., Oakes 1985; Rosenbaum 1976; Wilson and Schmits 1978). The curriculum may also be formally differentiated between schools within districts, a practice that is relatively uncommon in the United States (in contrast to many other countries), even with the recent growth of magnet schools organized around content areas (e.g., only about 2 percent of the schools in the 1980 *High School and Beyond* sample were identified as vocational high schools, and another 5 percent were identified as "other specialized," a category that included anything from public magnet schools to private military academies).

Curriculum differentiation in the United States varies across levels of the school system, with important differences in the dominant patterns between elementary and secondary schools, and across schools within levels as well. Sorensen (1970) proposes four structural dimensions along which these patterns of organization may vary: (1) "selectivity," the extent of homogeneity within instructional settings; (2) "inclusiveness," the extent to which assignment to a position leaves options open for future educational placement; (3) "electivity," the extent to which students choose their own group or track assignments; and (4) "scope," the range and permanence of assignments.

Forms of Differentiation in Elementary Schools. In a synthesis of research on ability grouping, Slavin (1987b) identifies the main types of elementary school grouping as between-class for the entire day; between-class for specific subjects (such as reading and math), sometimes in combination with cross-grade grouping (the "Joplin plan"); and within-class for specific subjects. Structurally, the first type differs substantially from the others in its wide scope, lasting for the entire day and encompassing all subjects instead of being confined to one or two subjects and class periods. This difference turns out to be important, for Slavin shows that whereas between-class grouping for all subjects gives no advantage in achievement over heterogeneous grouping, some of the narrow-scoped grouping arrangements tend to produce higher achievement. Slavin attributes the poor performance of permanent between-class grouping to two factors. First, its permanence and rigidity makes grouping especially salient, which may heighten the negative psychological consequences of low-group assignment. Second, dividing students for all subjects at once results in classes that are not really homogeneous for any one subject. Consequently, any advantages of teaching in a homogeneous setting are minimized. Wide scope appears to hinder effective curriculum differentiation.

Forms of Differentiation in Secondary Schools. Secondary school grouping arrangements may be even more diverse. The classic form of differentiation, high school tracking, is one of wide scope, high selectivity, and low inclusiveness: Students enroll in programs of study—such as college preparatory, general, or vocational—that dictate their entire array of courses. In recent decades, American high schools have moved away from formal tracking to a system in which students enroll in courses on a subject-by-subject basis. Although this change is supposed to reduce the scope of tracking, it is not clear that it actually results in less rigid tracks. For example, in a case study of four American cities—New York, Chicago, Philadelphia, and Boston—Moore and Davenport (1988) report,

> In 1965, all four school systems had a rigid tracking process in which most students were assigned to a track that defined all of their courses. Subsequently, such formal tracks were abolished, but the reality of tracking has been preserved in many schools through a variety of new mechanisms. (11–12)

Instead of formal curricular tracking, schools in these districts assigned students to ability groups for academic subjects. But because students assigned to a high-level class for one subject tended to be assigned to a similar level in other subjects, the end result was a set of curricular tracks as distinct as in the past. Sometimes students were actually assigned to sets of classes at the same ability level all at once ("block-rostering"), even though official policy called for assigning them to one subject at a time. Other case studies report similar degrees of consistency in assignment patterns (e.g., Finley 1984). National survey data indicate that 60 to 70 percent of 10th graders who were in honors math also enrolled in honors English, and the data reveal a similar degree of overlap between remedial math and English (Gamoran 1988). Still, these tracking systems are probably less rigid than in the past.

Secondary schools differ further in the inclusiveness of their tracking systems. For example, some schools divide students into three levels of roughly equal size, with labels such as "advanced," "regular," and "basic" (Gamoran 1989c; Moore and Davenport 1988; Sanders, Stone, and LaFollette 1987). Elsewhere, most students are assigned to classes at the "regular" level, with single classes assigned for a few students skimmed off the top or bottom. A study of eighth-grade English classes in 16 schools in the Midwest found 6 schools with no homogeneous grouping in English, 7 that divided students more or less evenly, and 3 whose only divisions in English were special classes for the strongest or weakest students or both (Gamoran 1989c). These sorts of ability grouping occur in schools that have no formal curricular tracking as well as within tracks in schools that employ distinct curricular programs (Cicourel and Kitsuse 1963; Oakes 1985; Rosenbaum 1976).

Sometimes the curriculum is differentiated less by ability level than by course topic, so that what matters is not the ability level of a course but its position in the curricular hierarchy. This is particularly true for high school math: Students are divided in ninth grade by assigning them to general math, prealgebra, algebra, or geometry; and because the courses follow a sequence, students' initial assignments set a maximum on how far they can progress (DeLany 1986; Garet and DeLany 1988).

Student Assignment Practices

Formally at least, differentiation in high schools permits a high degree of electivity. About two thirds of American sophomores report having selected their own high school programs (Lee and Bryk 1988), and some schools report that in disputes over placement, students' and parents' wishes prevail (Camarena 1990; Oakes, Selvin, Karoly, and Guiton 1991; Selvin, Oakes, Hare, Ramsey, and Schoeff 1990). However, researchers have been skeptical of the extent to which students have actually chosen their tracks even when they say they have (Jencks 1972; Rosenbaum 1976; Selvin, Oakes, Hare, Ramsey, and Schoeff 1990). In England, Ball (1981) describes a process of assignment in which students have the final say but almost always follow the recommendations of school staff. Moreover, U.S. educators consistently report that a combination of criteria determine placements: standardized test scores, teacher and counselor recommendations, prior placements and grades, and (for some junior and senior high school students) student choice (Moore and Davenport 1988; Oakes 1985; Rosenbaum 1980a; Selvin, Oakes, Hare, Ramsey, and Schoeff 1990).

Measuring Curriculum Placements. Recent work has called attention to other conceptual and methodological issues that confound our understanding of students' assignments to various curricula and caution against an overreliance on analyses of existing large-scale survey data bases. Those issues are embodied in the assumption (on which most surveys have depended) that the differentiated high school curriculum is easily and accurately captured by the terms "academic," "general," and "vocational" and that students can be classified or can identify themselves as participants in one of these curricula.

These categories grossly oversimplify curriculum differentiation (Gamoran and Berends 1987; Garet and DeLany 1988; Kerckhoff 1986; Moore and Davenport 1988; Oakes 1985, 1987b). As noted earlier, although schools typically offer courses of different types or different ability levels (e.g., some of which satisfy college entrance requirements and others that do not), often they do not neatly fall into discrete, easily identifiable programs called academic, general, and vocational tracks. Even more troublesome for researchers is the fact that secondary school tracking systems differ from one another in important ways: the number of subjects tracked, the number of levels of courses in each subject that are offered, the placement criteria used for assigning students, and whether students are placed separately subject by subject or a single decision about all subjects is made (Oakes 1985; Rosenbaum 1976; Sanders, Stone, and LaFollette 1984). Consequently, the standardized, three-track categorization of student assignments found in much survey research provides only a crude proxy for the curriculum students actually experience. Given this mismatch of measurement strategy and school practice, it is not surprising that students' reported track assignments differ, depending on the data source used. For example, Rosenbaum (1980a) found that 20 percent of the students in the National Longitudinal Study's 1972 sample of high school seniors reported track placements that differed from those reported for them by school officials.

Evidence of variation in curriculum differentiation among U.S. schools also suggests that the effects of various student characteristics on assignment to particular curricula are moderated by school characteristics (Garet and DeLany 1988; Jones, Vanfossen, and Spade 1986; Metz 1978; Page 1987b; Selvin, Karoly, and Oakes 1990; Sorensen 1987). That is, variations among curriculum structures and policies will influence how any particular student is classified and placed. For example, placement criteria (e.g., cutoff scores on standardized tests, prerequisite course requirements, and considerations of students' aspirations) differ from place to place. That such differences can result in comparable students being placed differently at different schools is evidenced in recent studies contrasting tracking in public and Catholic high schools (Camarena 1990; Lee 1985; Valli 1990). For example, Lee found that student background characteristics are less influential in Catholic than in public schools and that Catholic school placement practices result in about 20 percent more students in the college preparatory track, even after student background characteristics are controlled. And as noted in the previous section, other track policy variations, such as "block-scheduling" or "block-rostering" (students staying together at a particular level for classes in several subjects), result in student assignments that are different from class-by-class placement.

Moreover, characteristics of the school population as a whole may influence an individual's placement since a student's relative standing at the school may affect which classes are made available to him or her (Hallinan and Sorensen 1986; Sorensen 1987). Students' chances for placement in the college preparatory curriculum are greater in schools with larger proportions of students enrolled in that track (Gamoran and Mare 1989). It is difficult, however, to disentangle the relative effects of school policy and characteristics of the school population on the proportion of students in academic programs. For example, in a study of what determines the placement of students in math and science courses at the individual school and departmental levels at four high schools, Garet and DeLany (1988) found that background characteristics had quite different effects on placements at different schools. These differences were related both to the schools' curriculum structures and tracking policies and to the composition of the schools' student bodies.

What Student Characteristics Affect Placement? Although little work has focused on the process whereby students are placed or the schooling context of those placements, a number of studies have examined how individual student characteristics relate to placement in particular classes and tracks. Because of the widespread concern about fair and equitable placements, ability, race, and social class have garnered the most attention. A few studies have also looked at the effects of gender.

Rist (1970) argued that elementary teachers were biased against poor children when they assigned students to within-class ability groups. However, quantitative studies have failed to support this claim. Studies by Gamoran (1989c), Haller (1985), Haller and Davis (1980), and Sorensen and Hallinan (1984) uncovered no direct effects of race or social class on assignment to ability groups at the elementary level.

Secondary analyses of large survey data bases investigating the relative effects of various characteristics on placement in academic, general, and vocational tracks make up the bulk of the studies at the secondary level (Alexander and Cook 1982; Alexander, Cook, and McDill 1978; Alexander and McDill 1976; Gamoran and Mare 1989; Heyns 1974; Jones, Vanfossen, and Spade 1986; Rehberg and Rosenthal 1978; Rosenbaum 1980b). Although such studies may be marred by the measurement difficulties noted above, their results have been reasonably consistent. Students' prior achievement is the strongest predictor of track placement, but family background characteristics are important as well. Moreover, whereas nearly all studies find proportionately fewer students of lower socioeconomic positions and minority status in college preparatory curricula, a number of researchers have found positive effects of being black, regardless of background and prior achievement (Alexander and Cook 1982; Alexander, Cook, and McDill 1978; Rosenbaum 1980b). For example, Gamoran and Mare (1989) recently found that those black students in the *High School and Beyond* sample with prior achievement, social backgrounds, and schools comparable to whites had a 10 percent greater chance of being placed in college tracks.

Using a slightly different approach (including a focus on placements in courses rather than in tracks) and new data from the *Second International Math Study*, Kifer (in press; see also McKnight et al. 1987) found that the distribution of U.S. students with comparable past achievement among four types of eighth-grade mathematics courses (algebra, prealgebra, general, and remedial) varied with students' social background. Girls, whites, and students whose fathers held high- rather than low-level occupations were more likely to be placed in algebra than were other students.

Although little case study or ethnographic work has considered the relative importance of ability and background to student placements, available studies do suggest that secondary students from different backgrounds are given different types of information, advice, and counselor attention and that social, class-based placements are produced in the advising process (Ball 1981; Cicourel and Kitsuse 1963; Erickson 1975; Oakes, Selvin, Karloy, and Guiton 1991; Rosenbaum 1976; Schafer and Olexa 1971; Selvin, Oakes, Hare, Ramsey, and Schoeff 1990; see also Mehan 1981 and Moll and Diaz 1987 on the placement of bilingual students). For example, Cicourel and Kitsuse found that although counselors consistently assigned low-income students with low grades and test scores to low-ability classes, similar students from middle- or higher-income families were sometimes placed in higher groups, particularly when parents intervened. They also found that although low-income students with low grades but test scores that qualified them for average groups were placed in low classes, comparable middle-income students were placed in the middle-level track. Some case study work has found that school counselors and teachers respond to comparable achievement scores of Asian and Hispanic students quite differently, with Asians far more likely to be placed in advanced classes than Hispanics with equivalent test scores (Oakes, Selvin, Karoly, and Guiton 1991).

However, other researchers have come to quite different conclusions. For example, examining the placement decisions about eighth graders in five school districts, Davis and Haller (1981) found that students chose their track levels based on their aspirations and that these aspirations were closely linked to ability. What resulted was a strong association between track level and student ability and a much weaker link between social class and assignment. Consequently, Davis and Haller inferred that little social class bias exists in the counseling and placement process.

Findings relating to gender effects on track placement are also mixed. Earlier studies found either no significant gender relationship or that track placements favored boys; that is, among boys and girls with comparable past achievement and family background, boys were more likely to be found in higher tracks (Alexander and Cook 1982; Alexander, Cook, and McDill 1978; Alexander, and McDill 1978; Rehberg and Rosenthal 1978). However, more recent work suggests a small but significant advantage for girls (Gamoran and Mare 1989). Some ethnographies (e.g., Page 1990b) note that some teachers permit girls who do not cause trouble to stay in regular classes but shift more difficult, equally able girls to a lower track.

Findings about students' assignments to ability-grouped classes and curriculum tracks not only are contradictory but also have been variously interpreted. Although most analysts agree that ability and background characteristics have independent effects on track placement, considerable controversy still exists about what these findings mean. Analyses of large survey data bases that have found larger direct effects for ability than for socioeconomic status are sometimes interpreted to mean that placements are unbiased and meritocratic (e.g., Heyns 1974; Rehberg and Rosenthal 1978). However, other analysts argue that issues of class and merit cannot be disentangled easily since race and class biases are embedded in measures of ability, prior achievement, and students' choices (e.g., Cicourel and Mehan 1984; Oakes 1985; Persell 1977; Rosenbaum 1980a).

THE SOCIETAL CONTEXT—HISTORICAL PERSPECTIVES

Present-day features of curriculum differentiation as well as enduring questions about the practice's efficacy and equity reflect historical patterns that developed between 1890 and 1925—a period of tumultuous social and economic as well as educational change. By the end of this period, ability grouping had emerged as a mechanism for differentiating the elementary school curriculum. But even more dramatic was the transformation of the character and purpose of the secondary school curriculum. What in 1890 was a rather haphazard assortment of courses of study taught in a handful of secondary schools to a small and privileged segment of the nation's youths became by the late 1920s a firmly entrenched and widely approved set of curriculum tracks meant to accommodate the diverse group of students attending a new mass institution—the public high school.

New forms of differentiation have continued to develop since the 1920s, in special programs for the gifted and talented, the educationally handicapped, and language minority students (Kleibard 1979a, 1979b, 1986; Powell, Farrar, and Cohen 1985).

The turn-of-the-century social and political events that capture historians' interest include the topsylike growth of public secondary schools, changes in the nation's economic base and industrial structure, the influx of southern and eastern European immigrants, and the shift from a largely rural to an increasingly urban society. Against the backdrop of these larger changes, the classical set of studies typically found in Latin grammar schools and the array of modern and practical courses in secondary academies were amalgamated in a new, comprehensive public high school curriculum.

The modern curriculum comprised three tracks: an academic track, which blended modern academic subjects (e.g., mathematics, science, and modern foreign languages) with the older classical course of Latin and Greek; a general track, which combined the academic and the practical courses from the academies; and a newly fashioned, strictly vocational track. As this growth and diversification took place, the academic curriculum enrolled increasing numbers of middle- and upper-class students, and the vocational programs enrolled a disproportionate share of those from working-class families, immigrants, and the poor (Lazerson and Grubb 1974). What resulted, then, by 1930 was a fairly distinct and well-organized set of curricular alternatives intended to prepare different groups of adolescents for informed citizenship in the commonwealth and for differentiation in the economy.

Two documents stand as bookends on either side of this curricular transformation (Cremin 1964; Kliebard 1979a, 1979b; Krug 1964). The first was issued in 1893 by the National Education Association's (NEA) Committee of Ten on Secondary Studies. The committee's charge was to recommend ways to bring order and standardization to the curriculum that prepared secondary school students for college. The committee, headed by Charles Eliot, president of Harvard University, issued a set of proposals for restructuring the whole of secondary education. The report advocated four courses of study, all acceptable for college admission or for work: (1) classical, (2) Latin-scientific, (3) modern languages, and (4) English. The committee went on record as a proponent of curriculum differentiation, but it unequivocally opposed the designation of some curricula for students going to college and other curricula for those who would go directly to work. These positions were supported by Eliot's optimism about the ability of most secondary school students to master a rigorous curriculum.

> It is a curious fact that we Americans habitually underestimate the capacity of pupils at almost every stage of education from the primary school through the university. . . . It seems to me probable that the proportion of grammar school children incapable of pursuing geometry, algebra, and a foreign language would turn out to be much smaller than we now imagine. (Cited in Krug 1964, 52–53)

At the other end of the curricular transformation stands *The Cardinal Principles of Secondary Education*, the 1918 report of the NEA's Commission on the Reorganization of Secondary Education. The report endorsed the addition to the high school curriculum of nonacademic programs and a clear delineation between academic and more practical curricula. "Differentiation should be, in the broad sense of the term, vocational . . . such as agriculture, clerical, industrial, fine-arts, and household-arts curriculums" (Commission for the Reorganization of Secondary Education 1918). The principle undergirding the recommendations was that schools should help ensure two necessary components of a democratic society—unification and specialization. Schools could help promote unification, i.e., the acquisition of those "common ideas, common ideals, and common modes of thought, feeling, and action that made for cooperation, social cohesion, and social solidarity" by having all students attend the same high schools. Some learnings would be common (the "mother tongue" and social studies), and students could experience "social mingling" with those of different backgrounds. Specialization would occur through a curriculum differentiated to meet students' different future vocational needs. "Education in a democracy," the report stated, "should develop in each individual the knowledge, interests, ideals, habits, and powers whereby he will find his place and use that place to shape both himself and society toward ever nobler ends." In the decade to follow, the report stimulated a flurry of reorganization as high schools sought to become comprehensive, with specialized programs for college preparation, vocational preparation, and general preparation.

Historians have scrutinized these curricular events in the context of the social ideas and movements that permeated this 35-year period: scientific management and industrial efficiency, social Darwinism, IQ, the Americanization of immigrants, the psychology of adolescence, and an apparent shift in the popular conception of a democratic education. That shift was clearly articulated in 1908 by the superintendent of Boston schools: "Until very recently [the schools] have offered equal opportunity for all to receive one kind of education, but what will make them democratic is to provide opportunity for all to receive education as will fit them equally well for their particular life work" (Boston School Committee 1908, 53). Among historians, there is little disagreement about the sequence of events that led to curriculum differentiation in 20th-century high schools; however, there exists considerable diversity in historians' interpretation of why and how these events came about and in their assessment of the consequences for schools and students.

Historical Interpretations

From the wide array of historical accounts, we can identify three fairly distinct perspectives on the institutionalization of curriculum differentiation: (1) generally optimistic analyses that focus on consensus and compromise as the processes underlying curriculum change; (2) more critical and pessimistic revisionist views that emphasize curricular change as a process of class conflict; and (3) cautiously pluralist accounts that see curricular change as an uneasy, unstable accommodation of disparate interests and ideas.

Curriculum Differentiation as Progress. Optimistic, even self-congratulatory historical accounts of turn-of-the-century curriculum reforms began early in the century with writings by such eminent educators as Ellwood Cubberly (1919) and others (Rugg 1926; Stout 1921; Uhl 1927). These commentators interpreted curriculum differentiation as both necessary and desirable if secondary schooling was to be relevant to its 20th-century constituency—a school population increasingly diverse in ability, social class, and ethnic background. For example, Cubberly (1947) wrote of the compelling need for differentiation:

> To enable our schools to meet these new problems of our changing democratic life we have been forced to change their direction and to adapt the instruction given to the new needs and conditions of society. A new educational theory has evolved, adjustments and differentiations in school work have had to be worked out. (viii)

Cubberly also lauded the efficiency of a differentiated curriculum: "The effect of the introduction of these specialized classes has been to reduce waste, speed up the rate of production, and increase the value of the output of our schools" (527). The democratic effects of providing separate curricula that meet the needs of various groups of students were also touted:

> As the children of these new classes have crowded into our public schools, our school systems have been compelled to pay more attention to the needs of these new elements in our population, and to direct their attention less exclusively to satisfying the needs of the well-to-do classes. Education has in consequence recently turned away still more from its aristocratic nature, and has become more and more democratic in character. (505)

In a similar vein, Uhl (1927) concluded that the "conventional curriculum of the past provided adequately for only a small proportion of the adolescents in most communities" (524). Accordingly,

> principals of such [secondary] schools before 1850 took great interest in enrolling children of unskilled and semi-skilled parents . . . still the prevailing purpose of the schools, as far as their programs indicate, was that of providing a sound training in a restricted group of general subjects, and not that of providing courses which might benefit particularly the members of unskilled and artisan groups. . . . At the present time it is not unusual to find that more than 75 per cent of the pupils are from the nonprofessional and noncommercial groups. This change in the character of the largest groups of secondary-school pupils, together with the organization of the curricula for groups not formerly well represented in schools, indicates that the broadened purposes of early high schools are now exhibited in practice as they were only in theory during the nineteenth century. (512)

Although this unabashedly optimistic view of curriculum differentiation as a democratic response has been less popular among historians in the second half of the century, its underlying sentiments are echoed in some recent analyses of the development of the comprehensive high school. For example, Daniel Tanner (1972) characterizes the diversified curriculum endorsed in the *Cardinal Principles* report as pointing "to the comprehensive role of the secondary school in its mission to educate all citizens for complete living in a democratic society. Of great significance was the recognition of the responsibility of the high school to serve all youth, not just the college bound" (94). Indeed, the "ideal of universal education . . . led to an expanding secondary school curriculum to meet the needs of all the children of all the people" (110).

Moreover, beginning in the 1950s and 1960s, prominent educational historians have posited essentially progressive assessments of curricular changes, including curriculum differentiation, even as they have eschewed earlier writers' naive and simplistic faith in schooling's goodness. In doing so, they have framed more sophisticated analyses of how curricular change came about. These historians—probably best represented by Lawrence Cremin (e.g., 1964) and Diane Ravitch (e.g., 1978)—suggest that schools have become more open, inclusive, and democratic during the course of the 20th century as a result of two forces: (1) a widespread consensus about the value of public schooling and (2) the considerable efforts of political actors who fought, negotiated, and compromised about the particular character of public schooling in a democracy. These historians root specific schooling changes in political, social, and economic forces that cause one set of curricular ideas to catch hold while others are ignored.

Cremin (1964) describes the incorporation of vocational education into comprehensive schooling as the result of a gradual coalescence of disparate interest groups—idealists who saw manual training as a means of invigorating more intellectual subjects; businesspersons who wanted practical trade training freed from union regulation; unions interested in wresting private trade schools from the influence of the National Association of Manufacturers; rural agricultural leaders interested in promoting more scientific farming methods and preventing the flight of rural youths to the cities; students who sought upward mobility by acquiring skills for technical occupations; and finally, those educators concerned about the potentially stratifying effects of separate vocational schools. In short, "Groups that were at best strange bedfellows found themselves lobbying together in Congress toward the common goal of a federal vocational education bill" (Cremin 1964, 50). Thus, through a give-and-take process of democratic politics, coalitions were built and the curriculum was differentiated in a way that satisfied most interests somewhat, even if it satisfied none completely. Although Cremin does not conclude that this decision (or any other specific decision) is ideally democratic, he suggests strongly that the process by which school reform occurs allows a gradual, if bumpy, progression toward that end.

Curriculum Differentiation as Domination. Diverging sharply from progressive, consensus-oriented perspectives is the work of radical revisionist historians, who in the early 1970s began reinterpreting the causes and consequences of changes in American schooling (see, e.g., Apple 1979; Bowles and Gintis 1976; Franklin 1986; Nasaw 1979; Selden 1977; Spring 1972). Essentially, the revisionist perspective asserts that school reforms—including curriculum differentiation—emerged as a part of social class conflict in which the dominant class prevailed over less advantaged groups. Such changes, the revisionists claim, have made schooling a more potent instrument for preserving social stability and economic inequality. Key to the revisionist argument are theories of social control and cultural reproduction (Bourdieu 1977; Bourdieu and Passeron 1977; Williams 1973), according to which the content and structure of the curriculum reflect and legitimate dominant class values; devalue working-class culture; and by doing so, help reproduce inequalities in the larger society.

Revisionists argue that curriculum differentiation arose in response to the widespread fear among whites of the middle and upper classes that eastern and southern European immigrants and poor, urban populations threatened the economic order and social stability. Accordingly, schools were expected to provide lower-class, immigrant children, who were considered of lower intelligence and diminished moral capacity, with specific and direct training for responsible citizenship and work: what Finney (1929) called "followership for the duller intellects" (387). The effect of curriculum differentiation, then, was to channel poor children into subordinate school curricula, which would lead to subordinate economic and political roles and to restricted social mobility.

For example, with regard to the class bias in curriculum assignments, Apple (1979) asserts that, "although they talked about differentiating the curriculum in terms of intelligence, both [Franklin] Bobbitt and David Snedden . . . suggested that the differentiation should also be made in terms of differences in social class and ethnic background" (76). Selden (1977), citing evidence of the explicit use of social class criteria in sorting students, concludes, "The class and race biases apparent in the planning and articulation of schools in the first decades of the twentieth century . . . must be considered as implied educational goals" (214). Similarly, David Nasaw (1979) writes, "This, then, was the new educational democracy. The school was to assume the reality and inheritability of social class. Democracy meant offering every student the opportunity for an education equally adjusted to what school officials assumed would be his or her future vocation" (132). In the view of the revisionists, then, curriculum differentiation was created and continues to exist in order to mirror the hierarchical economic order and to maintain the existing social class structure.

That the goal of curriculum differentiation was social control emerges as a theme in many revisionist accounts. For example, Apple (1979) argues that "by controlling and differentiating school curricula, so could people and classes be controlled" (77).

> Those of high intelligence were to be educated to lead the nation by being taught to understand the needs of society. They would also learn to define appropriate beliefs and standards of behavior to meet those needs. The mass of the population was to be taught to accept these beliefs and standards whether or not they understood or agreed with them. (75)

As Kliebard and Franklin (1983) note in their review of curriculum histories, revisionists differ in the extent to which they find a conscious purpose behind these goals. Some suggest that reforms like curriculum differentiation were prompted by sincere if misguided humanitarianism rather than by the conscious desire for class domination. Apple (1979) writes that "many of the arguments . . . about curriculum put forth by some of the early educators, curriculum workers, and intellectuals . . . were based on the best intentions of 'helping people' "(64). Although not directly contradictory, Nasaw (1979) intimates a less benign intent:

> The carrot and stick were used to direct the working-class students away from the academic courses into the new vocational curriculum. Students were promised that the industrial training, commercial, and domestic science courses would lead to more useful lives with more secure wages and warned that the academic subjects would lead nowhere but to frustration and unemployment. (138)

Curriculum Differentiation as Uneasy Accommodation. A third, and currently the most prominent interpretation, is that curriculum differentiation represents an uneasy accommodation of a disparate set of interests, ideas, and values—educational, social, political, and economic (see, e.g., D. K. Cohen 1985; Kliebard 1979a, 1979b, 1986; Krug 1964; Labaree 1986). Historians of this bent explore the various dimensions of the accommodation, how it came about, and its consequences for schools and students. Like the revisionists, most ground their explanations of curriculum differentiation on an accommodation in the complex interactions between precepts of curriculum and perceptions of social differentiation from wider ideological, social, and economic contexts. And most agree that curriculum differentiation has served a stratifying function—one that largely reinforces or reproduces social and economic inequalities.

However, this group of historians takes issue with the revisionist view that the specific character of schooling processes such as differentiation is mechanistically determined by external ideologies and economic forces. And they disagree that social control and reproduction of the economic structure stand out as curriculum differentiation's most significant consequences. Rather, this group sees schools as shaped by both their acquiescence and their resistance to a wide variety of pressures from their many constituencies. For example, Krug (1964) writes of the 1890 to 1920 period,

> The high school struggled through this period like a bewildered giant, accommodating itself as it could to a staggering degree to

pure growth, shaking off, for the most part, as it still does today, the barbs of its critics and the free advice of its many well wishers. As the image of the high school was a composite one derived from institutions varying much in size and environment, so were the causes of its development multitudinous and complex. (xiv)

Kliebard (1986) analyzes the interaction between competing curriculum ideologies and perceptions of sociohistorical events as it affected curriculum policy throughout the first half of the century. He concludes that curricular developments such as differentiation and tracking evolved from considerable jockeying by divergent interest groups and an uneasy juxtaposition of four educational claims on schooling: (1) a humanist goal of transmitting the traditional values and culture of Western civilization, (2) a child development aim of matching the curriculum with children's developing interests and abilities, (3) the desire for socially efficient schools that prepared children for their likely adult occupational roles, and (4) a social reconstructionist hope that schools would help create a just society. In the view of this formulation, curriculum differentiation came about and persists because it embodies an accommodation of these competing positions—for example, the reconstructionists' ideal of social equality (universal access to a high school education), the child development advocates' interest in providing students with curricula suited to their differing needs and abilities, and the social efficiency goal of preparing students for different adult roles. Moreover, Kliebard suggests that the waxing and waning of the popularity of a differentiated curriculum has been a part of a more general movement toward and away from these curriculum ideologies as they interact with perceptions of particular social events and ideas.

Other recent analyses take a similar view. However, some give greater attention than Kliebard to the links between competing curricular interests and more fundamental American ideological contradictions. For example, both David Cohen (Cohen and Neufeld 1981; Powell, Farrar, and Cohen 1985) and David Labaree (1986, 1988) have recently argued that the accommodation required of schools is one that balances conflicting but highly valued ideas about the good society—namely, a democratic political ideology that demands equality and the common good, and a competitive, capitalist economic ideology that emphasizes individual initiative and choice and leads to inequality.

David Cohen's work suggests that more than anything else, the differentiated high school curriculum has been shaped by its own success in providing nearly universal access to elementary and secondary schooling—"an achievement quite distinct in human history" (Cohen and Neufeld 1981, 69). In a model similar to Kliebard's competing claims, Cohen and Neufeld note paradoxes brought about by the provision of educational equality in a competitive society:

In the schools America seeks to foster equality—and individual Americans seek to realize it. But in the market, Americans seek to maintain or improve their economic and social position, thereby contributing to inequality even if they individually wish the reverse. (70)

Cohen and Neufeld (1981) trace the origins of this paradox to the growth of industrial capitalism and, with it, beliefs about the central role of schools in modernizing the nation. One belief was that schools could impart the special technical knowledge critical to economic development. A second was that ambitious people could attain rags-to-riches success through competition in the marketplace and that even ordinary families could gain a competitive advantage with more education for their children. With these beliefs, a competitive, "human capital" function was superimposed on the schools' more traditional role as "an agent of moral cohesion and political equality" (72). Widespread conviction that schooling was critical to economic and social mobility quickly changed the high school from an elite to a mass institution (see also Kantor 1986 for an elaboration of this argument related specifically to the rise of vocational education).

However, universal access to high schools required a new rhetoric and a different organization if the dual goals of equality and human capital development were to be accommodated. The new rhetoric gradually redefined educational equality: A common education available to all became an equal opportunity to take differentiated courses to prepare for differentiated adult roles. The new organization was curriculum tracking. That inequality of economic and social position would result was justified by the fairness of students' chances to compete for the most advantaged positions—a fairness undergirded by the science of testing. Curriculum differentiation, then, became the vehicle for gaining competitive advantage within an institution providing equal access for all.

But David Cohen (1985) sees the school itself as playing a central role in this curriculum paradox. Educators both responded to and promoted the paradoxes of equality and competitiveness. They acceded to the wishes of the expanded student and family clientele. Cohen cites work by Hollingshead (1975) and Lynd and Lynd (1929) showing how schools responded to parents' and students' valuing of and press for nonacademic activities with a watered-down, undemanding curriculum for most students. Moreover, the school's response was also shaped by the widespread belief among educators (supported by emerging psychological theories of intelligence) that most students lacked the abilities to pursue intellectually rigorous studies: "American educators quickly built a system around the assumption that most students didn't have what it took to be serious about the great issues of human life, and that, even if they had the wit, they had neither the will nor the futures that would support heavy-duty study" (Cohen 1985, 245).

At the same time, Cohen (1985) cautions against a narrowly cynical interpretation of this accommodation since it also encompassed educators' beliefs that they could serve democracy by providing practical, useful studies to the masses of less capable students. With this analysis, Cohen hints that the school's response to the competing demands of equality and economic competitiveness in high schools might have been quite different had educators' interpretations of social and curricular differentiation been different—had they believed that schools that provide universal access can also foster academic excellence and that a rigorous and demanding education is possible for all students.

David Labaree's (1986, 1988) analysis of the transformation of the secondary curriculum at Central High in Philadelphia leads him to argue, like Cohen, that curriculum differentiation embodies schools' accommodation to competing claims, i.e., to the fundamental tension between widely held, if contradictory, ideologies of democratic politics (equality and participation) and liberal, capitalist economics (liberty and free markets). Labaree (1987) also suggests that this accommodation has led to contradictory practices, constant reconsideration, and debates "that have severely compromised the integrity, stability, and effectiveness of the curriculum" (490). However, he places greater emphasis than does Cohen on the links between the structure of the economy and curriculum differentiation. Consequently, he suggests less latitude in the range of accommodations schools might have forged.

Labaree (1986) argues that although the common schools were founded by those interested in reducing inequality, promoting citizenship, and preserving morality, and thus embodied democratic ideals, common schools also functioned in an environment "dominated by markets and the ideology of possessive individualism" (40). Consequently, selective 19th-century high schools (through the credentials they provided to students) accommodated this environment by giving a competitive market advantage to a small segment of middle-class students. From their inception, then, American schools were used to promote both equality and individual advantage.

It is in this context that Labaree (1986) sees the rise of curriculum differentiation as a turn-of-the-century accommodation of diverse interest groups to both an increasing demand for universal access to a high school education and the continuing interest in providing credentials to an elite stratum of students. The democratization of the high school diploma created the need for a differentiated program of studies leading to diplomas that carried with them different exchange values in the marketplace. This analysis suggests less flexibility in the school's response than Cohen's since it gives greater weight to the connection between schooling and the demands of the marketplace than to educators' beliefs about students. However, unlike more radical revisionist historians, Labaree argues that the school curriculum is not simply determined by these outside pressures. Rather, curriculum evolves as the school accommodates marketplace demands in ways educators think are consistent with its traditionally academic mission. Labaree argues that through this process schools shape the American class structure just as they are shaped by it.

Following Kliebard, Labaree (1986) points to the diverse educational perspectives that resulted in a differentiated curriculum. However, whereas Kliebard suggests that curricular and social perspectives are in interaction, Labaree sees curriculum perspectives as being more directly shaped by social ideologies. Thus, the child-study movement provided the intellectual (the notion of individual differences) and technical (testing) bases for sorting students. At the same time, advocates for child-centered instruction provided a means for designing differentiated curriculum around the needs and interests of various groups, and in doing so, they helped democratize schools. On the one hand, the ideal of giving each student access to high school and a curriculum suited to his or her needs was consistent with egalitarian and participatory values. On the other hand, social efficiency educators helped establish the adult-oriented nature of different curricula—vocational and college preparatory—and in doing so, helped satisfy the needs of the competitive marketplace. Moreover, the meritocratic placement of students into different curricula (placements based on past performance or ability rather than on social class, race, etc.) meshed nicely with the value of competitive striving in entrepreneurial capitalism.

All three of these historians (Kliebard, Cohen, and Labaree) suggest that the uneasy tension inherent in the differentiated curriculum accounts for both its persistence and the recurring dissatisfaction with it. As Labaree (1987) concludes,

> The compromise curriculum, over the years, has pleased no one. Its great advantage, and the reason for its durability, is that it offers a viable defense against the charge of being either undemocratic or impractical. Yet this largely negative accomplishment leaves both sides unsatisfied. Those who seek democratic outcomes from schooling are not likely to be happy with a stratified and vocational curriculum; those who seek status attainment through schooling are not likely to be happy when schools provide the same diploma to students from all tracks. . . . One result of this vague and chronic dissatisfaction is that American education has been subjected to a continuing series of reform efforts, as interest groups have persisted in trying to bring it closer to one pole or the other in an attempt to provide the curriculum with a clear identity and a coherent structure. (482)

THE CONSEQUENCES OF CURRICULUM DIFFERENTIATION

In this section we consider the consequences of the quite remarkable history of curriculum differentiation. We review research from studies in the United States and other countries about its effects on five dimensions of the educational process: distribution of teachers, distribution of knowledge, dynamics of classroom life, sorting of students along race and social class lines, and educational and social outcomes of schooling. We then use the final section of the chapter to assess fundamental questions about curriculum differentiation in light of these consequences.

The Distribution of Teachers

One outcome of curriculum differentiation is that the resulting classes may not be equally desirable from the standpoint of teachers. Both U.S. and British researchers have noted that teachers often prefer instructing high-ability classes because they find those students more willing to go along with demands for academic work (Ball 1981; Hargreaves 1967; Lacey 1970; Metz 1978). However, occasionally teachers prefer not to teach high tracks, finding it threatening to work with students who challenge their authority (Metz 1978) or who are of higher social status (Lortie 1975).

Although some schools rotate the teaching of low- and high-ability classes among teachers, it is not uncommon for principals to use class assignment as a reward for teachers judged more powerful or more successful and as a sanction against those deemed weaker or undeserving (Becker 1953; Hargreaves 1967; McPartland and Crain 1987). In Finley's (1984) case study of a high school, teachers competed with one another for the right to teach advanced classes, and those who had that prerogative tended to keep it as long as they could. This process may well result in a vicious cycle for low tracks: Repeated assignment to the bottom of the school's status hierarchy may demoralize teachers, hindering their improvement and perhaps even reducing their competency over time (Finley 1984; Gamoran and Berends 1987; Hargreaves 1967).

Recent work analyzing the distribution of teachers among different types of math and science classes in a nationally representative sample of U.S. schools has found few differences in the backgrounds and qualifications of teachers at the elementary level but significant discrepancies among teachers assigned to various classes in secondary schools (Oakes 1990b). Teachers of low-ability, secondary science and mathematics classes are consistently less experienced, less likely to be certified in math or science, hold fewer degrees in these subjects, have less training in the use of computers, and less often report themselves to be "master teachers." These differences remain even when qualification differences for teachers among various types of schools (e.g., schools serving various racial and socioeconomic student populations) are controlled.

Access to Knowledge

As with the distribution of teachers, curriculum differentiation also affects the distribution of knowledge. Students assigned to different groups and tracks are not exposed to the same academic content. Like various teaching assignments, different types of knowledge have different statuses.

***Curricular Pace and Content*.** In within-class ability grouping in elementary schools, the groups in a class are all taught by the same teacher. Nevertheless (as is intended), they do not receive the same instruction. Several studies have shown that high-ability groups progress farther in the curriculum over the course of the year (Barr and Dreeben 1983; Gamoran 1986; Hanson and Schultz 1978; Rist 1973; Rowan and Miracle 1983). Although the curriculum for any one level may vary across schools and classrooms, the high-group advantage presumably cumulates as the years pass. As a result, in the typical case, students with a history of membership in high-ability groups are likely to have covered considerably more material by the end of elementary school. Differences in the instructional pace and quantity of coverage have also been detected at junior and senior high school levels (Ball 1981; McKnight et al. 1987; Metz 1978; Page 1987a).

Curriculum differentiation entails distinctions in the content as well as in the pace of instruction. Organizational patterns at the junior and senior high school level affect students' access to various course offerings and shape the paths they take through the school curriculum. In most schools, fewer mathematics and science courses are available to lower-track students, who are nearly always required to take fewer academic courses (Guthrie and Leventhal 1985; Sanders, Stone, and LaFollette 1987; Vanfossen, Jones, and Spade 1987).

Moreover, students who report that they are in non-college-preparatory curricula participate less often in honors or advanced classes. For example, Gamoran (1987b) found that about 15 percent of vocational- or general-track students in the *High School and Beyond* sample took honors English classes, compared with nearly half of the students in the academic track. Similarly, students in the academic track took three to five times as many advanced courses in math and science. In contrast, low-track students have greater access to elective courses in the arts and vocational subjects than most college-preparatory students, whose schedule of required courses allows little time for electives. However, the extent of access to courses and course taking for various tracks varies among schools with different tracking policies (Oakes 1985; Page and Valli 1990; Rosenbaum 1986). For example, Catholic high school students enrolled in non-academic tracks typically take more academic courses and fewer electives than do their counterparts in public schools (Lee and Bryk 1988; Valli 1990).

***Types of Knowledge*.** American researchers (as well as their British counterparts) have found track-related differences in the types of knowledge presented to students. At the elementary level, low reading groups spend relatively more time on decoding activities, whereas more emphasis is placed on the meanings of stories in high groups (Alpert 1974; Hiebert 1983; McDermott 1987; Wilcox 1982). High-group students do more silent reading and, when reading aloud, are less often interrupted (Allington 1980; Eder 1981). In secondary schools, low-track classes consistently offer greater exposure to less demanding topics and skills, whereas high-track classes typically include more complex material and more difficult thinking and problem-solving tasks (Burgess 1983, 1984; Hargreaves 1967; Keddie 1971; Metz 1978; Oakes 1985; Page 1989; Powell, Farrar, and Cohen 1985; Sanders, Stone, and LaFollette 1987; Squires

1966; Trimble and Sinclair 1986). These findings have been documented in quite different ways in survey and interpretative research.

For example, using cross-sectional survey data from 6,000 math and science classes in 1,200 U.S. elementary, junior high, and senior high schools, Oakes (1990b) found that a variety of curricular goals were emphasized less in classes in which students were classified as of lower ability than in higher-level classes. At both the elementary and secondary levels, teachers of low-ability classes reported giving less emphasis than teachers of other classes to such matters as students' interest in math and science, basic science concepts, inquiry skills and problem solving, mathematics and science ideas, and to preparing students for further study in these subjects. Secondary teachers of low-ability classes reported giving greater weight to making students aware of the importance of math and science and learning math computations than did teachers of high-ability classes. These track-level differences were consistently found across schools whose student bodies differed considerably.

Studies combining quantitative and qualitative methods have considered type and depth of coverage as well as amount. For example, in a study of 300 junior and senior high school English and mathematics classes, Oakes (1985) examined data from teacher and student questionnaires, teacher interviews, classroom observations, and content analyses of curriculum packages prepared by teachers. Together, quantitative and qualitative analyses revealed that high-track students were more often presented with traditional academic topics and intellectually challenging skills. Additionally, these teachers more often included among their most important curricular goals that students would learn to be competent and autonomous thinkers. In contrast, teachers of low-track classes more often emphasized basic literacy and computation skills and presented topics commonly associated with everyday life and work. These teachers' most important curricular goals placed greater emphasis on conformity to rules and expectations.

Nystrand and Gamoran (1988) measured differences in the type of curriculum coverage in eighth- and ninth-grade English and social studies classes through teacher and student questionnaires and classroom observations. Their data collection focused on such issues as the authenticity of the curriculum—the extent to which questions and assignments request information that is new to the teacher rather than requiring a prespecified answer; the curriculum source—the extent to which students ask questions and have a say in their assignments; the cognitive level of questions and tasks required of students; and curriculum contiguity—the ways that different aspects of classroom work interrelate. Their cross-sectional analyses indicate that higher-quality instruction more often occurred in classes designated "high ability" since high-level classes were more often characterized by authentic assignments, student control over work, and higher-order cognitive tasks.

Finally, a number of interpretive studies have provided rich descriptions and considerable understanding of differences in knowledge exposure in a wide range of schools and classrooms (e.g., Ball 1981; Keddie 1971; Metz 1978; Page 1989, in press; Powell, Farrar, and Cohen 1985). These studies are particularly useful since they include analyses of the dynamic processes in classrooms (including teachers' beliefs and expectations and students' responses to instruction) that help shape access to knowledge in classes at different curriculum levels.

Keddie's (1971) pioneering study of teaching and learning in A, B, and C "stream" humanities classes in a large British socially heterogeneous, comprehensive secondary school in the late 1960s illustrates how teachers differentiated the curriculum in ways they thought met the needs of students in the various groups. For example, teachers' prior expectations coupled with their interpretations of students' classroom questions about the meaning of concepts led to the conclusion that C-stream (lower-ability) students needed material that was more concrete, experiential, and supported by illustrative stories. Because A-stream students rarely asked teachers about meanings, teachers thought that they already knew them and that they needed more abstract or "intellectual" content. These perceptions of students' needs, interests, and aptitudes, Keddie notes, led teachers to differentiate content in ways that gave students in different streams access to markedly different types of knowledge. Keddie concludes that such differentiation led teachers to provide high-status knowledge to A-stream pupils and far more restricted content to the lower group.

Ball's (1981) ethnography of Beachside Comprehensive documents both course- and classroom-level curriculum differences related to streaming in the British secondary school. Stream placement led to differences in students' access to courses in some subjects; e.g., upper-stream students had earlier exposure to foreign language instruction. It also led to differences in the knowledge presented within subjects that all students took, such as mathematics, music, and chemistry. Because courses in different streams were governed by different texts and syllabi, classes at different levels had different goals and covered different content. Further, Ball notes that differences in students' exposure to content were affected by differences in teachers' pedagogical styles and interaction patterns with classes at different levels. Like Keddie, Ball concludes that these differences reflect teachers' assumptions about students' abilities and their expectations for students' learning.

Similarly, Page's (in press) ethnographic account of the differentiated English and social studies curricula at two large, midwestern high schools documents differences between the formal and the experienced curricula in regular- and lower-track classes as well as differences between lower-track curricula. Teachers provided classes with three forms of a lower-track curriculum: a skeletal curriculum, in which academic topics from regular classes were covered in less depth; a basic skills curriculum, in which academic subjects, such as history and literature, were reduced to reading, largely to decoding; and a therapeutic curriculum, in which practical or "relevant" topics, such as drug or law education, replaced traditional academic topics. Thus, in these schools, even when lower-track classes appeared from syllabi and teacher descriptions to study high-status, academic knowledge, teachers reduced the topics to sketchy lists, outlines, and elementary-school-like exercises. The "relevant" curriculum was equally reductive. For example, because teachers considered students unwilling or incapable of taking more academic work seriously, they often asked them to play entertaining games or to work puzzles. Page concludes that lower-track knowledge is highly ambiguous: neither individualized according to students' needs nor determined by students' sociocultural characteristics. Rather, it reflects teachers' perceptions of students' sociocultural and intellectual characteristics in interaction with each school's notion of valued knowledge.

Classroom Dynamics

One of the most distinctive dynamics in classrooms is the balance participants establish between education and order. Because classrooms are crowded, public places (Cusick 1973; Jackson 1968), groups of students must behave if individuals are to learn. Because lessons are often far from youths' heart-felt concerns, teachers must insist on attention. And because schools are social institutions designed to translate a culture to uninitiated generations, classrooms are "despotisms" (Waller 1932, 10). Thus, the balance between educative and instrumental concerns is both delicate and critical—a "perilous equilibrium," according to Waller. It varies with context, of which tracking is an important one.

Accommodating Education and Order. Oakes (1985) documents an overemphasis on control processes and a concomitant deemphasis on educative processes in lower-track as opposed to upper-track classes in 25 secondary schools. Teachers spent more time disciplining than teaching in lower-track than in upper-track classes. The climate in lower-track classes was more estranged. Furthermore, school knowledge contributed to tracking's dynamic. Schools allocated to lower-track classes a dull, isolating curriculum of passive drill and practice with trivial bits of information, whereas the upper-track curriculum encompassed imaginative, engaging assignments with "high-status knowledge" such as Shakespeare or calculus. The study concludes that "systematic" differences in academic and social relations between and among teachers and students are "institutionally created and perpetuated" (94) through tracking, and because students who are poor or who are racial minorities are disproportionately represented in lower-track classes, curriculum differentiation reflects rather than removes social inequities.

Using a national survey data set, Vanfossen, Jones, and Spade (1987) also note a pattern of between-track differentiation in the United States. College-track students were more likely than other students to describe their teachers as patient, respectful, clear in their presentations, and enjoying their work. Similarly, in another national survey, Oakes (1990b) finds differences in tracked math and science classes. In low-track classes, in contrast to regular- and high-track classes, teachers spent more time on routines; more frequently provided seat work and worksheet activities; and introduced technology, such as computers, in conjunction with low-level tasks, such as computation.

Other studies describe a similarly differentiated balance between education and order in regular- and lower-track classes, in the United States and other industrialized nations, and at the elementary as well as secondary school level (Ball 1981; Eder 1981; Furlong 1977; Gilmore 1985; Goodlad 1984; Hargreaves 1967; Keddie 1971; Lacey 1970; Leacock 1969; Lightfoot 1981, 1983; Metz 1978; Oakes 1990b; Page 1987a; Powell, Farrar, and Cohen 1985; Schwartz 1981; Vanfossen, Jones, and Spade 1987). Moreover, the conclusion that tracking provides less educational value to lower-track classes (often populated by lower-class students) is echoed in several comprehensive reviews (Gamoran and Berends 1987; Good and Brophy 1987; Murphy and Hallinger 1989; Persell 1977; Slavin 1987a).

Nevertheless, although a straightforward match between the school order and the social order is compelling in its simplicity, data about classroom processes and interpretations of their significance are neither unanimous nor so easily predicted. For example, a few qualitative studies find that the climate in lower-track classes is decidedly caring rather than conflictual (Camarena 1990; Valli 1990); that lower track classes are highly structured, although for academics rather than for behavioral compliance (Metz 1978; Wehlage, Stone, and Kliebard 1980); and that the lower-track climate is an ambiguous (and for precisely that reason, powerful) mixture of academic purpose and behavioral indulgence rather than a clearly negative or positive phenomenon (Page 1987a, 1990a). Other work suggests the significance of local variations in what is presented as "college-preparatory curriculum" or as "lower-status knowledge." Examining two high schools in a diverse school district, Hanson (1990) finds the upper-track curriculum at one school to be highly routinized, skills-based, drill and practice but at the other, liberal, 1960s-style discussion and debate. Surprisingly, the liberal curriculum is provided in a poor, urban school, whereas the routinized curriculum is provided in an upper-middle-class suburb.

Interpretations of the data are also mixed. For example, the greater emphasis on discipline rather than on education in lower-track classes may be interpreted as a prejudicial response in which teachers (not necessarily consciously) socialize lower-class students for futures in which intellectual acumen will be less important than following orders. The classroom dynamics thereby contribute to the reproduction of an unequal social order (Anyon 1981; Apple 1979, 1983; Bowles and Gintis 1976; Oakes 1985; Rosenbaum 1976; Sharp and Green 1975). Alternatively, the greater emphasis on order can also be interpreted as a realistic or necessary, if not beneficent, response to the obstreperousness of unskilled, unruly, uninterested students (Good and Brophy 1987, 365).

Making Sense of Ambiguities. A third interpretation moves beyond the realistic/revisionist dualism to examine contradictions in tracking practices and uses these as evidence of curriculum differentiation's ambiguity. The ambiguity inheres in part in lower-track classes being similar to as well as different from regular-track classes, rather than one or the other (Page in press). Because schools can configure differences and similarities in a variety of combinations, many renditions of "lower-track" classes are possible. Moreover, because regular education varies between schools (Metz 1978; Page 1987b, 1990a; Rutter, Maughan, Mortimore, and Ouston 1979), even more variants of a lower-track class are possible. In short, curriculum differentiation's meaning arises in a complex interaction of differentiation within a school and differences between schools (Gamoran 1989a; Goodlad 1984; Metz 1978; Page 1987b).

Even very small or infrequently manifested aspects of the disparity between lower- and regular-track classes may have a powerful impact. For example, some lower-track classes are caricatures of regular classes. Just as a political cartoonist presents a recognizable portrait of Nixon but slightly elongates his nose to make it a ski jump, so subtle differences may transform the usual rules of classroom discourse to an ambiguous parody. Lower-track teachers' questions, although recognizably teacher questions, present students with a situation in which no answer is provided for or expected (Page 1987a). The "punch" of such inauthentic questions derives precisely from the play between their similarity to and difference from regular teacher questions. Occasionally, however, lower-track classes are parallel rather than caricatured versions of a school's regular classes (Valli 1990). Dimensions in such classes may "count" as very similar to other lower-track secondary classes: the use of "low-ability/high-interest" reading materials rather than Shakespeare; of basic math, rather than calculus. However, even though students read remedial texts rather than literary classics, they are not treated as "slow," elementary-level students. Rather, even with remedial texts, teachers lead students to discuss important ideas of interest to adolescents, just as they do in regular tracks.

When lower-track classes are seen as versions of regular classes, the roles of lower-track teachers and students and the nature of the lower-track curriculum also emerge as ambiguous. For example, contradictory characterizations of adolescent, lower-track students abound: They are either unskilled, immature kids who need a slower pace, manageable competition, and a strict hand (Schwartz 1981), or they are "troublesome" school resistors who disdain academic endeavors because the effort schools require will not pay off for them (Ogbu 1978; Willis 1977), does not incorporate the knowledge they value (Connell, Ashenden, Keller, and Dowsett 1982), or is not as interesting as socializing (Cusick 1973).

These seemingly conflicting findings make sense only if lower-track students are not simply seen as either appreciative of or resistant to schooling but as ambivalent about it (Metz 1983). That is, they may understand schooling's importance in modern societies but also recognize the limits of their school success. Some may not question the goodness of their school experiences but their own competence (Oakes 1985). Hence the mixed reports in which lower-track students put on a good face about schooling but refuse to exert sustained, serious effort in the classroom (Furlong 1977).

If lower-track students are ambivalent about schooling, they may be particularly vulnerable to curricular arrangements: Lessons may exacerbate or assuage their uncertain engagement. For example, recitations and reading circles can be places for public failure (McDermott and Aron 1978). Consequently, less-successful students may prefer, rather than be alienated by, individualized worksheets, which allow them to work privately, at their own pace, on unambiguous questions with one right answer (Metz 1978). However, the curriculum nuances are subtle and contextualized. Academically unsuccessful students may also accept mindless assignments because they offer an easy way to beat the credentialling system (Furlong 1977; Page in press). Or in cases in which teachers direct even easy school lessons uncertainly, students may face conflicting demands, so that they are unable to act competently because they are unsure what is expected of them (Page 1987a).

Teachers may be as ambivalent about tracking as students are. As with characterizations of students, the literature describes lower-track teachers in contradictory terms: either as prejudiced, incompetent, negatively expectant taskmasters (Rist 1973; Wilcox 1982) or as efficient, often caring pedagogues who provide for students' exceptional needs (see review in Goldberg, Passow, and Justman 1966). However, some studies note both the positive and negative expectations of teachers. Accordingly, lower-track classes pose, or at least accentuate, teaching's irreducible paradoxes (Lampert 1985; Page 1989; Varenne 1974), and teachers oscillate in their responses to students. On the one hand, they expect academically unsuccessful students to "try," to enjoy educational opportunities, and to achieve scholastic success. On the other hand, they expect them to cause "trouble," to devalue educational endeavors, and to fail. Thus, Keddie's (1971) humanities teachers regard C-stream students as troublesome anomalies: They are not simply achievers or dullards.

Lower-track teachers make the ambivalence visible to students in their direction and design of lessons, to which students react in turn. Hence, rather than being onerously regimented or scrupulously academic, the lower-track curriculum can be seen as combining a remedial curriculum with elements of regular-track education in a curious, ambiguous mixture. For example, teachers may retain a regular-track syllabus but translate its academic topics into radically simplified lists of facts or into "busywork" that principally occupies lower-track students. Thus, the sinking of the *Titanic* presented in an entertaining crossword puzzle that uses key terms, such as "iceberg" or "ocean liner," may leave students uncertain about the importance of studying the historical event: Is the *Titanic* worthy of serious contemplation or is it merely a detail in Trivial Pursuit? Repeated daily, "fun" and "easy" lessons may play on academically unsuccessful students' ambivalence about school by suggesting that school knowledge is so trivial students need not worry about it; yet at the same time, because the trivia is school knowledge and students are graded on it, its mastery is crucial (Page 1990a).

Tracking, Classroom Dynamics, and School Production. American studies of school production shed light on the nature of track differences in classroom life. This line of research takes seriously the manifest function of schools: It demonstrates that student achievement hinges on schools providing the opportunity to learn (Barr and Dreeben 1983; Bidwell and Kasarda 1980; Sorensen and Hallinan 1986). By concentrating on theoretically informed formulations and careful measurement of classrooms' academically productive aspects, studies show that learning depends on curriculum and instruction, not solely or simply on individual ability, ability group or track placement, or inherent self-fulfilling prophecies associated with hierarchical school or social structures.

For example, elementary school teachers in a study by Barr and Dreeben (1983) grouped students for reading instruction based on their perceptions of diversity in students' readiness to read. However, they then used, or instructed, the groups in a variety of ways. Because grouping and group instruction were distinct activities, significant differences emerged in achievement among high-aptitude groups or among low-aptitude groups (Barr and Dreeben 1983; Dreeben and Barr 1988; Gamoran 1986). Although high-aptitude groups learned more overall, differences among high groups occurred because different teachers provided them with appropriate (or inappropriate) amounts and kinds of curricular materials. When the curriculum was paced briskly and at a high level, high-aptitude students covered more material and learned more vocabulary than comparable students given a slowed curriculum. Similarly, low-aptitude students learned more when teachers provided manageable curricular materials and sufficient time for mastery, rather than when teachers raced to meet high standards or relied simply on positive expectations.

Furthermore, studies of school production emphasize the multiple contexts that influence tracking's impact on instructional processes and achievement in classrooms. For example, Barr and Dreeben (1983) and Dreeben and Barr (1988) show that a teacher's particular arrangement of intraclass instructional groups is responsive to the number of low-aptitude students in the class. When the number of low-aptitude students is high, the teacher is constrained in the kinds of groups formed because low-aptitude children require more instructional time and support. However, the particular configuration of any class reflects wider influences as well: Teachers' grouping decisions are shaped by how a school distributes diverse students among classes as well as by the intellectual and socioeconomic conditions of a school community. Similarly, teachers' decisions about curriculum coverage are not unidimensional but can be constrained by the materials and plans adopted at a district level.

Measures of school production elucidate tracking's intended, formal, educative functions. Production theorists acknowledge but have given less attention to its tacit, unintended processes or to the possibly contradictory purposes and specific meanings of school participants. For instance, Dreeben and Barr (1988, 58) note that variation in teachers' instructional practices with similar groups of students flows from differences in teachers' notions about a wide variety of phenomena, but they do not explore the phenomenological differences, how they impinge on teachers' practices, or how students react to them. Such considerations are the main focus of interpretive studies, which assume that school practices are not inert facts or rationalized procedures but are constituted in participants' specific, if often inexplicit, contextualized interpretations of them. In this perspective, how teachers and students think about curriculum differentiation—its meaning—is inseparable from curriculum differentiation's inputs and effects.

Interpreting Track Differences in Classroom Dynamics. In "Classroom Knowledge," Keddie (1971) describes how teachers and students define and negotiate their respective roles and school knowledge. She notes that in their talk together in lessons, teachers and students intertwine tacit sociocultural and political precepts with explicit scholastic considerations. In Keddie's portrait, education is largely a matter of teachers maintaining their definition of the classroom situation, but because this often involves rendering students' definitions invalid, education is always in tension with control. Thus, curricular content and processes are serious power struggles, not necessarily neutral distributions of beneficial knowledge.

For example, good order and academic progress characterized A-stream (high-track) humanities classes in the British secondary school Keddie (1971) studied. Teachers attributed the easy classroom relations to positive student characteristics: Students were "independent" and able to think "abstractly." However, by examining the unfolding curriculum in use, Keddie documents instead the A-stream students' pliancy and docile acceptance of the teacher's right to define knowledge. Because upper-track students trusted that the teacher's frame of knowledge, if not immediately clear, would become meaningful eventually, they worked diligently through sets of exercises whose technical jargon and practical application they did not understand but did not question. As a result, Keddie concludes that A-stream students moved into the teacher's meaning system and gained access to a discipline's defining questions, concepts, and language.

In contrast to the taken-for-granted quality of the upper-track atmosphere, C-stream classes were "problematic." Teachers explained the uncertain atmosphere and the consequent need for heavier measures of control by citing lower-track students' lack of academic ability, aspirations, and interest. However, again through an examination of the curriculum in use, Keddie (1971) conveys the seriousness rather than superciliousness of C-stream students' regard for academic endeavors. These students were attentive and insightful but unlike "good" students in the A-stream, they raised rather than repressed questions about academic abstractions they did not understand. However, the humanities teachers "read" students' often apt queries negatively, discounting them as "thick" or "dull" or as undisciplined, off-topic malingering. At the same time, teachers differentiated curricular knowledge: They replaced the abstract concepts that provide entrance to further schooling with "concrete" examples and "stories"; lower-track discussions, if allowed, were rigorously limited to what the teacher had in mind.

Thus, Keddie (1971) delineates the symbolic interactions in which lower-track "trouble" was jointly, ongoingly constructed by teachers and students who came together at cross-purposes. From teachers' perspectives, C-stream students challenged both the academic and the social order of the classroom. They contradicted the abstract knowledge teachers presented as valuable when they raised questions based on practical experiences; their disagreements, in contrast to A-stream docility, disrupted the easy, orderly, Ping-Pong rhythm of recitations. However, from the C-stream students' perspectives, school knowledge appeared inane precisely because it contradicted what they knew experientially. Furthermore, when they introduced experiential knowledge into classroom discussions, it was discounted, so that students also experienced the teacher's coercive control of the curriculum.

Keddie (1971) explains the teachers' emphasis on control rather than education in lower-track classes by describing two facets of their perceptions of lower-track students. In a professional, "educationist context," the humanities teachers laid out positive, or liberal, theoretical assertions about tracking and C-stream students: "Ability" was an environmental artifact, accounted for as much by motivation, which reflected social-class antecedents, as by innate intelligence; streaming further disadvantaged the already socially disadvantaged by fixing teachers' expectations of low-stream students; students from all backgrounds, if given an undifferentiated, inquiry-based curriculum, would be motivated to work independently and rationally.

However, in the "teacher context" of the classroom, teachers acted in ways that were discrepant with their theoretical views (for other studies of ambiguities in teacher behavior, see Cusick 1973; Metz 1978; Page 1989; Rosenbaum 1976; Varenne and Kelly 1976; Wilcox 1982): There, they mixed notions of students' initiative, intelligence, and social class to explain variability in school success. That is, well-intentioned professionals, with high expectations and commitment to an undifferentiated curriculum, nevertheless deemed the predominantly working-class, C-stream students to be not only academically unskilled but also uninterested, "immature," and "unstable." As a result, teachers confounded moral, social, and intellectual categories and made them visible and consequential to students in daily lessons. Students rejected such judgments as not within the teacher's realm of prerogatives (for comparative descriptions of the "moralistic" nature of the lower-track curriculum and students' adverse reactions to it, see Henry 1963; Leacock 1969; Page 1990a, 1990b; Werthman 1963).

Keddie (1971) argues that teachers were blind to the contradictions between what they did and said and that they misinterpreted lower-track students' curricular reactions because they did not realize that the hypothetical "ideal" pupil they posed in the theoretical, "educationist context" already existed in fact in the "teacher context" in the persons of A-stream, middle-class students. That is, teachers had one kind of pupil in mind as they planned an undifferentiated curriculum for all. Their blindness to the controlling coerciveness of the ideal student definition and the knowledge appropriate to such a student led to the unintended conflict in lower-track lessons with students who did not match the ideal type.

Because Keddie (1971) examined only one school, tracking's influence on classroom dynamics is difficult to sort out from idiosyncrasies of the particular school or from antagonisms that might arise between middle-class teachers and working-class students. Other interpretive studies elaborate on the wider contexts, or frame factors, that prompt and limit tracking's impact on local classroom dynamics. In particular, they focus on the tacit, often contradictory dimensions of schools and communities as they influence (and are themselves influenced by) classroom participants.

For example, Metz's (1978) *Classrooms and Corridors: The Crisis of Authority in Desegregated Secondary Schools* examines how the informal, distinctive cultures or meaning systems of schools interact with formal organizational structures to shape the balance between education and order in tracked classes. In two demographically and structurally similar junior high schools, tracking desegregated students, lower-track classes were distinguished from regular classes by the emphasis teachers placed on control. This is the familiar balance: an emphasis on control and a deemphasis on education in lower-track classes populated by poor, minority children. However, despite apparent similarities in tracking, its meaning for participants differed in the contexts of the two institutions. In one school, lower-track placement was stigmatizing, exacerbated racial divisions, and provoked uneasy truces or classroom mayhem. At the other school, lessons proceeded and there were more positive relations between and among teachers and students. Worksheets predominated in both schools' lower-track curriculum, but in one context they signified the teachers' distance from and control of students, whereas in the second, they signified the provision of manageable assignments, shelter from public failure, and a reassuring routine.

Metz's (1978) analysis links the differences in tracking's meaning for classroom participants to each school's wider, distinctive culture. Where students were deemed disorderly and teachers were principally taskmasters, instrumental goals usurped educational goals and even upper-track classes were markedly regimented (see also Page 1987b, and contrast Hanson 1990). Where similar students were nevertheless defined by school norms as able to engage in education, teachers asserted greater control in lower-track classes, but their purposes were academic, not simply controlling (see also Valli 1990; Wehlage, Stone and Kliebard 1980). In other words, school cultures, built around acknowledged if informal norms of who teachers and students are, shape different enactments of tracking (Goldstein 1990;

Hymes 1980; Metz 1986; Page 1987b, 1990a; Rutter, Maughan, Mortimore, and Ousten 1979; Sarason 1982; Schlechty 1976; Valli 1990; Waller 1932).

Attention to the influence of contexts and meaning recasts thinking about the complicated relationship between education and control and between curricular and social differentiation. Accordingly, curriculum differentiation is not unconnected to social differences, such as race or class, despite ideologies about its neutrality. However, neither is curriculum differentiation necessitated by or mechanically related to social differentiation. As Metz and others working from an interpretivist research perspective (Erickson 1986; Jacob and Jordan 1987; Page 1987a; Varenne 1974) document, in particular circumstances institutions may define differently objectively similar student bodies. The institutional definitions influence (and are influenced by) classroom dynamics. Tracking may put students and teachers "at risk" of trouble (Erickson 1986) by confounding schooling's educative and instrumental purposes. However, studies of tracking's contexts show us that the practice is not uniformly or inherently negative in its effects nor unilaterally causal.

Thus, contextual elements that influence the classroom's "perilous despotism" are institutional: The oft-reported harmony in high-track classes may reflect the allocation of high status in an institution with limited rewards (Ball 1981; Hargreaves 1967; Lacey 1970; Schwartz 1981; but see also Bettelheim 1958 and Metz 1978 for negative effects of tracking on high-track participants). These contextual elements are also broadly sociocultural. Categories that may function as proxies for academic ability include race (Furlong 1977; Gilmore 1983; Goldstein 1990; Metz 1978; Rist 1973), ethnicity (Moll and Diaz 1987), social class (Anyon 1981; Willis 1977), gender (Cazden 1986; Davies 1984; Page in press), age (Hargreaves 1967; Page 1990b, in press; Valli 1990), intelligence (McDermott 1987), and appearance (Cicourel and Kitsuse 1963). Contextual influences also include those classroom participants furnish to one another in their face-to-face interactions: Some students are not skilled at academic work (Furlong 1977; Metz 1978), romanticized versions of student underdogs to the contrary; some teachers are incompetent (Finley 1984); and some lessons are insipid (Boyer 1983; Sizer 1985). In sum, research about curriculum differentiation's meaning, as that which measures the practice, augments our understanding of general patterns of curriculum differentiation with evidence about diverse settings and about the complexity with which humans can choose to act.

Race and Class Stratification in the United States

Disproportionate percentages of poor and minority students (principally black and Hispanic) are found in curricula designed for low-ability or non-college-bound students (e.g., Gamoran and Mare 1989; Moore and Davenport 1988; National Center for Educational Statistics 1985b; Oakes 1990b; Rosenbaum 1980a). Further, minority students are consistently underrepresented in programs for the gifted and talented (Darling-Hammond 1985). These race and social class placement differences seem to occur whether test scores, counselor and teacher recommendations, or student and parent choices are the basis for placement.

The connection between tracking and sociodemographic stratification seems to have two sources. First, tracking systems vary among schools serving different types of students, and second, different types of students vary consistently in their ability to satisfy requirements for entry into higher tracks. The proportion of advanced courses schools offer, the classification of specific classes at various ability levels, and criteria used to guide individual placements within schools are all associated with a disproportionate placement of non-Asian minority students in nonacademic curricula and low-ability classes. Schools serving predominantly poor and minority populations offer fewer advanced and more remedial courses in academic subjects, and they have smaller academic tracks and larger vocational programs (National Center for Educational Statistics 1985a; Rock et al. 1985). The number, size, and substance of tracks differ with the composition of schools' student populations—the greater the percentage of minorities, the larger the low-track program; the poorer the students, the less rigorous the college preparatory program (Hanson 1990; Oakes 1990b; Sanders, Stone, and LaFollette 1987).

In a recent study, Oakes (1990b) found that in the schools in the National Science Foundation's (NSF) National Survey of Science and Mathematics, the percentage of minorities in the student body strongly related to the availability of both standard college preparatory courses and more advanced courses in science and mathematics and to the distribution of classes at different ability levels. For example, 36 percent of the grouped classes in secondary schools enrolling 90 percent or more minority students were low-ability classes, whereas only 16 percent of the classes were high-ability classes. In contrast, schools enrolling fewer than 10 percent minority students had, on the average, only 16 percent low-ability science and math classes and 43 percent high-ability classes. Consequently, minority students' opportunities to take high-ability classes may be constrained by the types of courses their schools offer.

Why this distribution occurs is not clear. Small numbers of advanced courses may result from a shortage of students who "qualify," according to standard criteria—e.g., test scores. Indeed, there is some evidence that all other things being equal, a student's chances of getting into a high-status class are better at a low-SES (socionomic status) school (even if the number of such classes is small) because the competition is weaker and there is pressure to fill these classes (Garet and DeLany 1988). At the same time, more global decisions about what types of courses (and how many) to offer may reflect broad assumptions about what kind of curriculum various groups of students need, such decisions restrict or enhance the access of various groups (Selvin, Oakes, Hare, Ramsey, and Schoeff 1989).

Placement decisions within racially mixed schools result in the disproportionate placement of minority students in low-level classes. For example, Oakes (1990b) found that in the NSF secondary schools, 66 percent of the math and science classes with disproportionately large minority enrollments (i.e., minority enrollment was more than 10 percent greater than in the school as a whole) were identified as low-ability classes. Only 9 percent of the disproportionately minority classes in these schools were high-ability classes. Similar, if less pronounced, patterns were found in elementary schools. Moore and Davenport's 1988 study of four large urban school districts revealed a similar pattern of low-ability classes being disproportionately made up of poor and minority students. Although it seems clear that the consistently lower performance on tests by non-Asian minorities undergirds this pattern, the result is that curriculum differentiation leads to considerable race and class separation and race- and class-linked differences in opportunities to learn.

Other evidence indicates that not only do race and social class disparities occur among tracks but some stratification occurs within vocational tracks as well, with blacks and Hispanics more frequently enrolled in programs that train for the lowest-level occupations (National Center for Educational Statistics 1985b; Oakes 1983). As a part of Goodlad's 1984 study, Oakes found both the content and the format of vocational programs to differ for white and minority students. For example, at the junior high level, white students typically were enrolled in typing, home economics, and general industrial arts courses; minorities were far more frequently enrolled in classes preparing for specific jobs. One junior high with a mixed Hispanic-Anglo population had two-hour off-campus courses including building maintenance, duplicating skills, and home and community services (institutional and domestic work). Course enrollments were overwhelmingly Hispanic.

At the senior high schools in the study, even greater differences were found. Schools enrolling predominately white students provided more business and general industrial arts courses, and at racially mixed schools, white students more frequently enrolled in them. Minorities' modal patterns included specific preparation for trades such as cosmetology, building construction, institutional care, needle trades, housekeeping, and food services. The formats of courses differed as well, with minority students more often leaving campus for extended class periods. At one high school in the Southwest, low-SES Hispanic students received this low-level training 3 hours per day over a 3-year period. White students, in contrast, far more often took vocational courses (e.g., regular classroom home economics) as a part of their regular school schedule. The differences found in these schools were such that nonwhite students were enrolled earlier and more extensively in programs offering specific training for low-status jobs (e.g., poor and minority girls were more often enrolled in cosmetology, professional caretaking, and commercial cooking and sewing courses). Oakes (1983) concludes that the hours consumed by these courses and their off-campus location were likely to distance poor and minority students from academic learning and the schooling mainstream.

Outcomes for Students

Divisions among students, coupled with corresponding differentiation of curriculum and instruction, result in striking differences as students pass through the school system and on into postsecondary experiences. In terms of easily measured outcomes, one can think about the effects of curriculum differentiation in two ways: as having an impact on the *overall levels* of educational outcomes, such as test scores or years of schooling attained, and as influencing the *dispersion* of outcomes, to the extent that students in one group or track are affected differently than students elsewhere. Effects on levels of outcomes may be referred to as educational *productivity*; effects on the dispersion of outcomes involve educational *inequality* (Gamoran and Mare 1989). Writers vary in their attention to these two sorts of outcomes, with advocates of differentiation emphasizing what they see as its potential for productivity and critics focusing primarily on inequality (see Gamoran 1989b; Slavin 1990). Few empirical studies provide evidence on both counts.

The Effects of Differentiation on Student Achievement in U.S. Elementary Schools. The outcome that has drawn the most attention from researchers is the impact of grouping and tracking on cognitive skills. At the elementary level, reviewers report inconsistent findings for the effects of grouping on overall achievement, and the evidence has seemed somewhat muddled (compare, e.g., Cornell 1936; Ekstrom 1961; Esposito 1973; Good and Marshall 1984; Heathers 1969; Miller and Otto 1930). In an attempt to bring some order to the literature, Slavin (1987b) examined studies of elementary school grouping in four different categories: (1) classes grouped by ability for the entire day; (2) classes regrouped by ability only for certain subjects, such as reading and math; (3) regrouping by ability in combination with cross-grade grouping (Joplin plan); and (4) within-class ability grouping for mathematics. The first type—ability-grouped class assignment—revealed essentially no achievement difference between grouped and ungrouped students. In contrast, the three other types—those that regrouped elementary students in heterogeneous classrooms for instruction in selected subjects—tended to show an achievement advantage to students involved in these more limited grouping schemes. However, their effectiveness depends on teachers' adaptation of the pace or level of instruction to students' needs and the limits placed on the amount of regrouping (no more than two subjects). Slavin is most positive about the effects of the Joplin plan, attributing its success to the limited amount of grouping (reading only) and the increased flexibility and student mobility afforded by its multigrade structure. Slavin argues that part of the reason for the inconsistencies reported by previous reviewers is their failure to distinguish among the different forms of ability grouping.

Slavin's (1987b) review examined mainly studies that were carried out before 1970; only two studies occurred after 1972 (Hiebert 1987). The social contexts of American schools may be very different now, and patterns that held in the 1950s and 1960s may not hold in the 1990s. Further, none of the studies reviewed paid much attention to what happened to students after they were assigned to the different classes and groups, other than to measure their achievement. Essentially, then, Slavin's review (like those of others) concerns instructional organization but has much less to offer about curriculum differentiation (Gamoran 1987a; Hiebert 1987). It describes the outcomes of arranging students in different ways but, for the most part, fails to provide information about the curriculum and its implementation in the varied settings. This limitation has been recognized by Slavin, as well as by earlier reviewers of tracking (e.g., Cornell 1936; Ekstrom 1961; Esposito 1973): Ability grouping affects achievement when it occurs in combination with variations in curriculum and instruction. Because few studies have linked elementary school grouping, instruction, and achievement quantitatively, this conclusion rests mainly on logic, speculation, and anecdotal accounts.

Another important point about Slavin's (1987b) review is that it shows that the positive effects on average achievement of regrouping schemes occurred in the context of increasing inequality of achievement across group levels. Although students at all levels—high, average, and low—tended on the whole to do better than similar students who were not regrouped for selected subjects, students in high groups more often benefited the most, and those in low groups, the least. Not all studies reported results separately for the different levels, but of those that did, by our count, nine found the greatest gains for high-group students, and five observed larger gains in low groups (combining regrouping for specific subjects, Joplin plan, and within-class grouping systems). These results are consistent with other studies that did not examine the average effect of grouping but only showed its differentiating effects, finding that over time, the gap between high- and low-group students widens (Barr and Dreeben 1983; Gamoran 1986; Weinstein 1976).

To gain a clearer notion of the effectiveness of differentiated and undifferentiated curricula at the elementary level, the research on ability grouping (the predominant mechanism for differentiation in U.S. elementary schools) must be set next to the growing body of research on cooperative small-group learning. Cooperative learning—an alternative to ability grouping—includes a number of strategies that place groups of students together to work interdependently on learning tasks. In contrast to ability groups, in which teachers try to form the most homogeneous groups possible, teachers usually attempt to mix students of various abilities in cooperative groups. Hetereogeneity is seen as desirable, partly because an underlying principle of cooperative learning is that students' individual differences can be accommodated with an undifferentiated curriculum if the social organization of the classroom encourages children to help one another learn (e.g., E. G. Cohen 1986; Johnson and Johnson 1989; Slavin 1983).

Considerable evidence supports the achievement gains of students at all ability levels in cooperative settings that reward students for both individual and group performance above that which similar students achieve in traditional settings (E. G. Cohen 1984; Johnson and Johnson 1989; Slavin 1987a; Webb 1982). We know of no studies that directly compare the various forms of ability grouping to cooperative learning strategies. However, the efficacy of the latter suggests that undifferentiated settings that include specific strategies for accommodating students' diverse abilities may be as or more effective than ability grouping in increasing educational productivity while at the same time reducing outcome inequalities.

The Effects of Differentiation on Student Achievement in U.S. Secondary Schools. Paralleling findings about whole-class ability grouping at the elementary level, research at the secondary level has failed to show much overall advantage in achievement to ability-grouped class assignment and tracking. A meta-analysis by Kulik and Kulik (1982) indicates a small positive effect on average achievement. Additionally, there is some evidence from both U.S. and British studies that students in high tracks gain from grouping at the expense of low achievers (Gamoran and Mare 1989; Kerckhoff 1986). However, most experimental and correlational studies comparing grouped and undifferentiated settings do not observe these trends (Kulik and Kulik 1982; Slavin 1987a, 1990). Slavin (1990) concludes that ability grouping per se has no effect on the achievement of any group, although when curriculum tracking is combined with differences in course taking it may widen the gaps between high and low achievers.

Numerous studies comparing gains made by students in different tracks in secondary schools provide evidence of the increasing disparity between high- and low-track students as time goes by. Although some have questioned the presence of such an effect (Alexander and Cook 1982; Jencks and Brown 1975; Slavin 1990), the balance of the evidence supports it (for recent reviews, see Gamoran and Berends 1987; Murphy and Hallinger 1989). Of particular interest are studies using national survey data with good controls for initial conditions such as background and prior achievement. These include, from the United States, work by Gamoran (1987a); Gamoran and Mare (1989); Hotchkiss and Dorsten (1987); Lee and Bryk (1988); and Vanfossen, Jones, and Spade (1987). From Britain is work by Kerckhoff (1986), and from Israel analyses by Shavit and Featherman (1988). To counter claims that apparent track effects were inflated by selection bias (e.g., Slavin 1990), Gamoran and Mare used a statistical model that detects the influence of unmeasured variables on track placement and outcomes. Track effects remained strong even with this technique.

How large are these effects? Upon discovering that in most subjects, the academic-track advantage was larger than the gap between students in school and dropouts, Gamoran (1987a) argued that the effects must be viewed as substantively important (although see Slavin 1990 for a counterargument). They have consistently appeared largest in math achievement (Alexander and Cook 1982; Gamoran 1987a; see further Lee and Bryk 1988). For example, Gamoran estimated that the advantage to being in the academic track was about $2^1/_2$ times the gain of the average student between grades 10 and 12, whereas in reading, the track difference was about equal to the average 10th-to-12th-grade growth. Thus, we find considerable increases in the inequality of achievement at the secondary level that occur *without* the slight gain in productivity that may occur at the elementary level.

Effects on Peer Groups and Attitudes Toward School. Researchers at all levels of the school system have pointed out that grouping and tracking tend to divide schools socially as well as academically. Hallinan and Sorensen (1985), for example, show that within-class grouping in elementary schools may lead to friendship networks that result in part from students' positions in the grouping system. In grouped classes, students were more likely to choose someone in the same ability group as a "best friend"; as the year went by, the overlap between ability group membership and friendship networks increased. These findings are consistent with work done many years earlier by Petty (1953), who also found a tendency for students to list others in the same group as friends. Further, studies at the secondary level in Britain and the United States indicate that students' friendship networks tend to be centered within their own ability group levels (Abraham 1989; Ball 1981; Hallinan and Williams 1989; Hargreaves 1967; Lacey 1970; Rosenbaum 1976).

According to the British literature, when students reach secondary school, these social distinctions lead to a "polarization" of attitudes toward school: High-stream students develop proschool attitudes, whereas low-stream students resist the schools' demands (Abraham 1989; Ball 1981; Hargreaves 1967; Lacey 1970). Several American observational studies are consistent with this argument, finding that high-track students exhibit greater enthusiasm for school, whereas low-track students are more resistant (Metz 1978; Rosenbaum 1976; Schafer and Olexa 1971; Schwartz 1981; Stinchcombe 1964). It is unclear, however, whether curriculum differentiation actually causes the differentiation of attitudes toward school or reflects a distribution of attitudes that is already in place (Gamoran and Berends 1987). Attitudes and motivation, after all, may be among the criteria of track assignment. Moreover, attitudes are complex. At school, students' attitudes interact with the norms of the school culture (Grant 1988; Lightfoot 1983; Metz 1978, 1986; Page 1990b; Willis 1977).

In limited ways, this question has been addressed by ethnographers and survey researchers, who offer conflicting results. On the one hand, Ball (1981) and Lacey (1970) conclude from observations that the distinction in attitudes is greater under streaming than mixed-ability grouping. On the other hand, Waitrowski, Hansell, Massey, and Wilson's (1982) analyses of longitudinal survey data reveal no influence of track assignment on "attachment to school" (an attitude scale) or on delinquent behavior.

Effects on Educational Careers and Attainment. One of the most important criticisms of curriculum differentiation is that a placement, once made, tends to take on a life of its own, symbolizing a student's rank and capabilities and influencing his or her future chances independently of subsequent performance. The few studies that have examined this issue at the elementary school level are mainly consistent with the claim, and a substantial body of research supports it at the secondary level.

Several authors have decried the lack of mobility between primary school ability group levels during the course of a school year (Eder 1981; Groff 1962; Hawkins 1966; Rist 1973). Movement that does occur seems to respond to variations in student performance: Barr and Dreeben (1983) observed that 30 percent of the first graders they studied changed group levels during the year, and those who moved up tended to be above their groups' means in achievement, whereas those who moved down were below. In a study of ability group mobility between first and second grade, Gamoran (1989b) found that in some schools, second-grade group assignment corresponded to first-grade achievement, but in others, second-grade assignment followed first-grade group level regardless of students' performance levels at the end of first grade. To our knowledge, no American work has examined this issue in the later years of elementary school, but two British studies indicate little change in students' streams through the primary grades (Barker Lunn 1970; Daniels 1961).

Students' enrollments in high school curricular programs appear to be influenced by curricular experiences prior to high school. Alexander and Cook (1982) and Rosenbaum (1976) documented that students who had taken a foreign language in eighth grade were more likely to end up in a college preparatory program in high school. In Alexander and Cook's case, this finding held even after controlling for background and prior achievement. Both studies interpreted this result to mean that tracking at the junior high level feeds into the high school tracking system. This pattern is documented more clearly by studies outside the United States: In Israel, eighth-grade ability group position exerts a significant impact on ninth-grade track assignment (Yogev 1981); and in Taiwan, students in high-ability classes in eighth grade were more likely to attend high-status high schools in the following year (Hsieh 1987).

Once enrolled in a college preparatory program, students are more likely to graduate from high school—despite the hopes of educators that curriculum differentiation would allow students to thrive in high school programs that were suited to their skills and interests (see Mirel and Angus 1986). Gamoran and Mare (1989) showed that other things being equal, college-track students are about 10 percent more likely to graduate, which they consider "a substantial advantage considering the high average rates of graduation overall" (1172–1173). This finding occurred despite a statistical approach that was explicitly designed to reveal differences among students that would make some more suited to noncollege programs. And in a study of Irish secondary schools, Hannan (1987) discovered that schools with more differentiated curricula (i.e., those with fewer elective, more selective, and wider-scoped stratification systems) had lower graduation rates.

Other studies cast doubt on the efficacy of vocational-track enrollment. With data from Israel, Shavit and Williams (1985) indicate that except for very low-achieving students, vocational education programs failed to keep students in school longer than if they had been assigned to academic programs. American studies find that participation in vocational education does not enhance students' chances for securing employment related to training, avoiding unemployment, or securing higher wages than those of nonvocational high school graduates (Berg 1970; Berryman 1980; Grasso and Shea 1979; Rubens 1975; Stern, Hoachlander, Choy, and Benson 1985). California data, in fact, show high school dropouts faring as well in the workplace as vocational graduates (Stern, Hoachlander, Choy, and Benson 1985). Moreover, participation in vocational education is particularly detrimental to the work outcomes of poor and minority students (Berryman 1980; Stern, Hoachlander, Choy, and Benson 1985).

Finally, a broad set of studies documents the connection between high school curricular programs and postsecondary educational careers. Students enrolled in the college track are more likely to aspire to college and more likely actually to enroll (Alexander and Cook 1982; Alexander, Cook, and McDill 1978; Alexander and McDill 1976; Heyns 1974; Hotchkiss and Dorsten 1987; Jencks and Brown 1975; Rehberg and Rosenthal 1978; Rosenbaum 1980a; Vanfossen, Jones, and Spade 1987; Waitrowski, Hansell, Massey, and Wilson 1982). The advantage of college-track students holds even when compared to students with otherwise similar high school performance records (Hotchkiss and Dorsten 1987; Jencks and Brown 1975; Rosenbaum 1980a). These effects persist even through college, with those who had been in an academic track in high school more likely to graduate from college, controlling precollege plans and test scores, early college grades, and type of college attended (Velez 1985; see also Wolfle 1985).

Clearly, high school track position exerts a long-lasting impact on educational attainment and, indirectly, on the life chances of American students. It is worth recalling, however, that U.S. tracking programs are far less restrictive than between-school stratification systems found elsewhere. In countries such as Japan and Germany, the type of high school one attends virtually determines the kind of postsecondary experience one can expect (Kariya and Rosenbaum 1987; Oswald, Baker, and Stevenson 1988; Rohlen 1983). Turner (1960) described the difference as one of "contest mobility" in the United States, where students compete for access to higher education right up until the time of admission, in contrast to "sponsored mobility" systems, in which such decisions are made much earlier in life.

QUESTIONS, DEBATES, TENSIONS

Curriculum differentiation lies at the heart of perennially unsettled, unsettling debates. The practice is widespread, but school personnel vary in their regard for it (Rosenbaum 1976; Sanders 1990). Hundreds of research projects have studied tracking's effects, but in addition to their broad patterns, they are noteworthy for their unanswered questions and mixed interpretations (Goldberg, Passow, and Justman 1966; Passow 1988; Persell 1977).

Policy debates about curriculum differentiation recur with great regularity, but they almost always deadlock. Even when they do not, educators find the practice astonishingly difficult to change. Curriculum differentiation is a volatile, potentially divisive issue, not the kind bureaucracies relish. Particularly because curriculum differentiation raises issues of race and social class differentiation, in addition to notions about valued knowledge and its distribution, it unsettles: We ponder whether tracking fulfills (or foils) individual talents and aspirations and thereby contributes to the incorporation (or alienation) of thoughtful participants in school and society. One can appreciate that schools, rather than risk the complex, heated, good guy–bad guy debates that tracking typically evokes, might decide simply to forgo any discussion at all. (Anderson and Barr [1990] discuss the multiple, hidden agendas in a district that did not forgo discussion.)

Here, we tackle three fundamental issues that have dominated scholarly and policy discussions of curriculum differentiation throughout the century. First, does curriculum differentiation work? That is, does it help schools meet the diverse set of expectations society holds for them? Second, is curriculum differentiation fair? And third, does curriculum differentiation affect the quality of schooling and the curriculum? As we tackle these issues, however, we are mindful of important cautions that readers, too, should keep in mind. First, even though tracking is a very pressing, practical question about which people want answers, research (no matter how reviewed or undertaken) relates only indirectly to policy—it cannot tell us directly what to do. Policy decisions are value-laden matters appropriately settled in public debate. Second, although research can inform debate with regard to the empirical aspects and general concepts and patterns of tracking, it cannot provide certain knowledge about any particular school. Readers have to determine whether research generalizes in fact to their specific school. The forms and effects of grouping and tracking are not everywhere the same. Consequently, although our review to this point has attempted to identify factors, concepts, and facts that readers should consider when contemplating such questions as tracking's efficacy or equity, global answers are impossible. Moreover, we must bear in mind that to some, the dualistic formulation of these questions—does it work or doesn't it?—can be misleading and partly responsible for tracking's perennial opacity.

Nevertheless, we believe that it is important to address these questions—noting how curriculum differentiation usually works and what its typical consequences are. Schools must make daily and yearly decisions about whether and how to group students and differentiate curriculum, and through their impact on curriculum and instruction, these decisions have important consequences. Thus, with the cautions noted above, we point out in the following sections the broad patterns that characterize the operation of curriculum differentiation; and we summarize what most researchers have concluded are the most likely answers to these questions—at least in the typical case.

Does Curriculum Differentiation Work?

Perhaps the most frequently asked question is whether curriculum differentiation works. As we have noted, there are two broad patterns: one that suggests that tracking is generally ineffective, and a second that suggests advantages for upper-track students and disadvantages for others, especially at the secondary level. But as noted throughout, schools differ in the ways they use differentiation to distribute students' sociocultural characteristics and school knowledge (Barr and Dreeben 1983; Metz 1978; Page and Valli 1990). Catholic schools, for example, may produce less between-track inequality by making greater academic demands on students in noncollege tracks (Gamoran and Berends 1987; Valli 1990). As noted earlier, some schools have rigid tracking systems, whereas others are more flexible; some track students for all subjects; others differentiate in a more limited fashion (Oakes 1985; Sorensen 1970). Gamoran (1988) reports that high schools with more rigid curricular tracks produce larger achievement gaps between college- and non-college-bound students. These variations may lead to different kinds of outcomes for students, not all of which are limited to test scores. Moreover, the issue is further confounded by deeply held and often conflicting values about curricular and social differentiation. It is not surprising, then, that a final answer about whether tracking "works" is difficult to provide.

Does Tracking Create Homogeneous Groups? The explicit justification for grouping is the need to decrease classroom heterogeneity to facilitate curricular appropriateness, instructional efficacy, and academic achievement (Barr and Dreeben 1983; Strike 1983). Empirical studies suggest significant qualifications to the term "homogeneous" group. Grouping's effect on reducing even cognitive diversity may be very small. Goodlad (1960) estimated that dividing elementary students into two ability levels (based on IQ) results in only about a 7 percent reduction in the total variability in each class and that forming three groups results in a 17 percent reduction. Goodlad further suggests that because students' performance in one domain is imperfectly correlated with performance in other areas, dividing students on any single criterion produces classes quite heterogeneous in other respects (see also Passow 1988). Other studies document considerable overlap of students' skills and abilities among groups (Balow 1964; Oakes, Selvin, and Karoly 1990; Rosenbaum 1976; West 1933). Thus, the degree to which tracking reduces heterogeneity may be far less than we typically assume.

Does Tracking Raise Achievement? For many, the bottom-line question is whether grouping and tracking lead to higher achievement. The straight answer is, sometimes. At the elementary level, Slavin's (1987b) synthesis shows that, although the popular pattern of whole-class ability grouping is ineffective, more limited within-class grouping for mathematics and between-class grouping for specific subjects combined with cross-grade grouping produce higher overall achievement than traditional heterogeneous arrangements. In contrast to the mixed findings about elementary school grouping, secondary school tracking has little or no effect on overall mean achievement (Kerckhoff 1986; Kulik and Kulik 1982; Slavin 1990). Where tracking exists, however, it may raise achievement for high-track students; but because those in low tracks tend to suffer a corresponding loss, the net result is approximately the same (Kerckhoff 1986; however, see Slavin 1990, for a contrasting view).

Does Tracking Inhibit Equality of Opportunity? Differentiation often exacerbates initial differences between high and low achievers. Even though students at all levels may gain in some forms of elementary school grouping, students in high-ranked groups tend to gain the most. At the secondary level, the contribution to inequality appears even greater. As grouping is coupled with differential course taking, high-track students gain and low-track students lose. Another concern at the secondary level is the polarization of student attitudes, which at least to some extent, correspond to track assignment. Although the evidence is ambiguous on whether tracking is causally implicated in race and social class differentiation, assigning students to programs according to their purported talents and interests fails to mitigate the problem.

Multiple Functions of Curriculum Differentiation. If the success of differentiation in raising overall achievement has been limited, it seems to raise achievement fairly consistently for students in high-status positions. Thus, it increases productivity in the top segment of the population, and it may also be said to "work" in sorting and allocating students for future roles—if by "working" we mean to designate the pool of students who are eligible for high-status positions. Whether these effects are positive or negative depends on one's broader perspective.

The evidence noted above indicates that tracking's most consistent effects are in directing students toward differentiated future educational and occupational careers. Conflict theorists argue that this process restricts social mobility, especially in light of the correlation between track positions and social class backgrounds (e.g., Bowles and Gintis 1976; Carnoy and Levin 1986; Spring 1976). From a human capital perspective, however, this sorting serves a critical function by developing the skills of the most promising students and allocating them to suitable positions (e.g., Conant 1967). The sorting is deemed meritocratic since the connection between track assignment and social background is far from direct. Furthermore, to avoid judging the issue too simplistically, one must recall that the production of high achievement for the strongest students is as serious a matter for most schools as the injunction for equity. With only limited evidence that undifferentiated arrangements can provide the same level of success for students at the top, schools face great pressures to continue curriculum differentiation.

As these conflicting interpretations of tracking's effects suggest, the question "Does curriculum differentiation work" may be viewed as an oversimplistic (if very American) formulation of the issue (Varenne 1974). By its very nature, the question must be followed by "for what ends?" The question is problematic since, as with many complex social issues (Edelman 1977; Riesman 1950; Varenne 1982, 1983), it isolates curriculum differentiation in a plain either-or, good-bad fashion. However, curriculum differentiation (like schooling generally) serves multiple goals in a culture that is paradoxical, even contradictory. For example, a fundamental tension juxtaposes individualism and community (Bellah, Madsen, Sullivan, Swidler, and Tipton 1985). Members of the culture acknowledge choice as an important symbol of all persons' freedom to define themselves, but they also acknowledge community and enduring social relationships. Ironically, each value constrains the other. Alternatively, the paradox can be framed as tensions between widely held, if contradictory, ideologies of democratic politics and captitalist economics (Powell, Farrar, and Cohen 1985; Labaree 1986, 1987, 1988). Members of the culture cherish both the equality demanded by political democracy and the competition for individual advantage in the marketplace inherent in the economy. Here, too, competing values constrain each other.

However one frames these cultural tensions, curriculum differentiation can be seen as an enactment of them. Thus, on the one hand, the public expects virtually all American youths to attend school and to learn there a shared intellectual heritage, democratic processes, and the prerogatives and responsibilities of adult society. Embodying democratic ideology and the common good, school is presumed to be an equivalent, standardized, egalitarian setting. Yet on the other hand, invoking a contradictory set of individualistic, competitive norms, the public also expects the school to respond to local, regional values; to each individual's abilities, needs, and aspirations; and to the requirements of the economy. In short, schools must provide both "equal educational opportunities" for all and meet each student's "individual educational needs." Rather than one or the other, as the "Does it work?" question implies, schools are pressed not to discriminate at the same time that they must differentiate.

From this perspective, the partisanship and persistence of debate about tracking are understandable as a paradoxical cultural process in which we cannot choose between strongly held, contradictory values because choice would contravene one or the other. Thus, we find ambivalent sponsorship of and ambiguous enactments of tracking. Moreover, variation in curriculum differentiation's enactments is also promoted because in different historical periods and locales, and with semiautonomous institutions such as schools, people forge various locally sensible amalgamations of these multiple, conflicting goals.

Consequently, to ascertain whether, for whom, and how curriculum differentiation "works" requires examination of specific schools, specific practices, and specific purposes—as well as scrutiny of national patterns of practices and consequences. The research literature indicates that curriculum differentiation does not "work" neutrally, self-evidently, or linearly, explicit rationales to the contrary. At the same time, neither does tracking "work" determinately. Rather, "curriculum [works] in interaction with social trends. . . . [Social] beliefs and events [are] filtered through certain fundamental beliefs about the nature and function of the curriculum [to] pervade our consciousness" (Kliebard 1988a, 27). Simply asking "Does it work?" may deflect attention from broader, more useful questions: How does curriculum differentiation work in various settings? How does it serve various local and national purposes? Why does it persist? What alternatives are possible?

Is Differentiation Fair and Socially Just?

Closely related and as complex as the matter of whether curriculum differentiation works is the question of its fairness. Debate about this issue is heated since assessments of individual differences and appropriate curricula are not racially or socially neutral. For example, differences in curricular offerings and in the curriculum in use usually correspond to the socioeconomic status of school communities. In analyses of a large survey data base, school types (categorized by socioeconomic and racial characteristics) correlated with the extensiveness of offerings in math and science (Oakes 1990b). Scrutiny of the school culture indicates its base in educators' perceptions of communities' socioeconomic status and the knowledge they need (Hemmings and Metz 1990; Oakes 1987b).

Furthermore, within-school criteria for placement in ability groups and curriculum tracks consistently result in the disproportionate representation of poor and non-Asian minority students in lower groups and their consistent underrepresentation in programs for the gifted and talented. Thus, these students are most often found in those classes and tracks in which the quality of curriculum and instruction is typically lower and grouping effects on achievement are most likely to be negative. Blacks and Hispanics are more frequently enrolled in vocational programs that train for the lowest-level occupations (e.g., building maintenance, commercial sewing, and institutional care), whereas vocational opportunities for white children from wealthier families are those that translate into higher-income and higher-status positions in the work force (e.g., accounting, computers, and business law).

Track placements are defended as fair because they are meritorious—i.e., determined by prior school achievement rather than by race and class directly—or because they are self-imposed through students' own choices (e.g., Rehberg and Rosenthal 1978). Often elaborate procedures are designed to ensure that group placements are made accurately and fairly—such as providing culturally fair criteria. Little evidence can be found of explicit teacher bias (Haller 1985; Haller and Davis 1980, 1981), and substantial efforts have been made to eliminate vestiges of bias in standardized tests. The common conclusion is that as long as ability or choice explains most of the variance in curriculum placements, the concomitant existence of class and race relationships is less troublesome.

However, there is little consensus about the fairness of either placement criteria or choice. Differences in intelligence and school aptitude, a foundation on which grouping and tracking practices are based, are hotly debated. For example, rather than an objective assessment of intellectual aptitude or a tool for social mobility, some social scientists posit intelligence as a sociocultural construct that modern societies reify and embed in school practices, such as readiness and aptitude tests and tracking, to legitimate the present social order (Gould 1981; McDermott 1987). More specifically, some maintain that schools' assessments of students' abilities are conclusions produced as students and schools interact and that they may bear little relation to learning potential (Goodlad and Oakes 1988; Oakes and Lipton 1990; Rosenholtz and Simpson 1984).

For example, Goodlad and Oakes point to the fact that first-grade children are organized into subgroups, usually three, for reading and some other subjects, each group presumably different from the others on estimates of ability. However, since these estimates are made early in the year and since there is much confusion regarding the difference between ability and prior learning, the estimates often reflect home and family circumstances, especially the level of schooling attained by mothers and fathers. Children in the lowest groups are rarely moved to the highest groups; the disparity between the attainment and abilities of the highest and lowest groups grows greater over time. Thus, each subsequent assessment of ability is, in part, a product of the assessments that preceded it.

Reservations are also voiced about the claims that older students freely choose their track placements and postsecondary destinations. Although these choices are made by students (and their parents), they may not be free of influence. They are informed by the school judgments and placements made over eight years of schooling—by test scores and teacher recommendations (Oakes 1987a; Rosenbaum 1980a). By the time they reach senior high, students may have learned all too well their "appropriate" place in the school hierarchy. Consequently, their choices may be no more fair or accurate than the earlier choices made for them.

For many, these contemporary concerns are rooted in curriculum differentiation's historic links with race and class. As noted in our discussion of historical accounts, tracking students into academic and vocational curricula became standard practice in turn-of-the-century America with the spread of compulsory schooling laws, the proliferation of publicly supported high schools, and the influx of immigrants and newly freed blacks into northern cities. Debates among school leaders and boards of education, university presidents, industrialists, labor union leaders, and social scientists about how to organize high schools for this new clientele centered in part on the nature of human abilities (particularly of non-English-speaking immigrants and blacks) and on the functions of schooling (Tyack 1974). For example, some thought the intellectual, moral, and even biological differences among turn-of-the-century adolescents to be vast and immutable. A misguided social Darwinism posited that darker-skinned, recently arrived immigrant youths were on a fundamentally lower rung of the evolutionary ladder.

Since potential for school learning was seen to differ enormously among students from different social and ethnic groups, curriculum for more advanced groups (white, native-stock Protestants, for the most part) was not seen as appropriate for the less capable (predominantly southern and eastern European immigrants). Lewis Terman (1923), intelligence testing pioneer, wrote about immigrants, Mexicans, and blacks: "Their dullness seems to be racial. . . . Children of this group should be segregated in special classes. . . . They cannot master abstractions, but they can often be made efficient workers" (28). These views did not go uncontested, but the emerging school organizational pattern, curriculum differentiation, reflected their salience, and the distribution of scores on the newly developed ability tests reflected their assumptions.

Because the development of standardized tests of ability and achievement was intimately connected with this history (Gould 1981), many analysts view with considerable caution the claim that placements based on such tests are strictly neutral and meritocratic (e.g., Oakes 1985; Rosenbaum 1976). Some argue that we could judge appropriate the disproportionate placements of poor and minority students in low-track classes only if these children were known to be innately less capable of learning than middle- and upper-middle-class whites, but that is not the case (see, e.g., Cicourel and Mehan 1984; Oakes 1990a).

Moreover, scholars and policymakers have become increasingly troubled by the effects of tracking on students' access to learning opportunities: Course-taking patterns, exposure to curriculum content, instructional strategies, classroom environments, and peer relationships all appear to be influenced by tracking—so that the most educationally impoverished programs are offered to the least able students, particularly at the secondary level (see, e.g., reports by the Achievement Council 1985; Carnegie Council on Adolescent Development 1989; Council for Basic Education 1989; Massachusetts Advocacy Center 1990). With evidence that opportunities are quite different in various tracks, many educators no longer consider tracking as simply a neutral or passive conduit through which students' characteristics "take their natural course" toward high-, average-, or low-achievement outcomes, aspirations, and attitudes. Many suspect that when schools react to individual differences with tracking, they begin an interactive process that diminishes the educational success of children not in the "top" groups.

Findings about curriculum paths, course offerings, and track-related classroom differences suggest that the differentiated structure of schools erects barriers to achievement and participation of poor and minority students. Measures of ability work against them, which leads to minimal course offerings at their schools and their disproportionate placement in groups identified as slow. Once in these classes, their success seems to be further inhibited by the type of knowledge they are taught and by the quality of the learning experiences they are afforded. In schools where the overall quality of the curriculum is poor, low-income and ethnic minority students (by virtue of their disproportionate placement in low tracks) are further disadvantaged by their restricted access to knowledge and to the most highly valued educational credentials that the school has to offer. As a consequence, tracking appears to jeopardize equal educational opportunity.

Nevertheless, on the average, minority and low-SES students score lower on achievement tests, and schools respond with programs they see as educationally appropriate. But what is of particular interest here is that the prevailing view of appropriate schooling for these students appears to continue a cycle of restricted opportunities, diminished outcomes, and exacerbated differences between low-track students and their counterparts in higher tracks. These placements do not appear either to overcome students' academic deficiencies or to provide access to high-quality learning opportunities.

Thus, ethical and pedagogical arguments have been mounted for a common curriculum, even if individual differences among students prevent them from benefiting equally. For example, Fenstermacher (1983) has argued that

> using individual differences in aptitude, ability, or interest as the basis for curricular variation denies students equal access to the knowledge and understanding available to humankind. . . . It is possible that some students may not benefit equally from unrestricted access to knowledge, but this fact does not entitle us to control access in ways that effectively prohibit all students from encountering what Dewey called "the funded capital of civilization."(3)

With tracking, educators prejudge how much children will benefit, with the result that some children are not taught knowledge that provides access to future academic and social opportunity. Those who see tracking as unfair do so largely because their assessment of the empirical evidence about tracking's outcomes is that "it doesn't work"—i.e., that tracking and rigid ability grouping are generally ineffective means for addressing individual differences and, for many children, harmful. If being in the low track remediated the educational deficiencies that many poor and minority students exhibit or prepared children for success in higher tracks and opened up future career or school opportunities, tracking could be seen as fair. That this event rarely occurs is used as evidence supporting tracking's unfairness (e.g., Goodlad and Oakes 1988; Oakes 1987b; Slavin 1987a, 1990).

How Does Curriculum Differentiation Affect the Quality of Schooling?

As we have seen, curriculum differentiation emerged during the early decades of the century as the prepotent response of educators to an increasingly diverse student population and to perceptions of crucial social changes. Although every student was deemed able to benefit from schooling, not all were thought capable of benefiting from the traditional classical curriculum. Therefore, fairness, democracy, efficiency, and instructional efficacy demanded a differentiated curriculum. Most schools make such claims and thereby demonstrate their responsiveness to cultural norms (Meyer and Rowan 1978; Sanders 1990).

Yet such claims also have their critics. They suggest that curriculum differentiation has ominous consequences, and not just for students but also for schooling and the curriculum themselves. Especially with the increased use of accountability measures, prescribed curriculum and instructional strategies, and direct examination of curriculum, schooling's legitimacy may be undermined by revealing instances in which grouping entails no curriculum differentiation at all or, alternatively, in which differentiation occurs but is invidious. In other words, in contrast to the rhetoric, some tracked classes may be nothing but "dumping grounds," wherein the differentiated curriculum provides inequitable access to valued knowledge. Thus, in the long run, tracking may undermine both curriculum practices and public schooling's legitimacy. As John Goodlad asserts (1984, 297; quoted by Passow 1988, 220), "Tracking serves as an organizational device for hiding awareness of the problem [of how to respond to wide differences in students' academic achievement], rather than an educative means for correcting it."

Even with such criticisms, however—because the structures of tracking are in place, because tracking's salience fluctuates with the times, and because the norms to differentiate nondiscriminatorily are compelling yet paradoxical—curriculum differentiation is often not only unquestioned, as Goodlad remarks, but also unquestionable. An ingrained part of the school's culture (Sarason 1982), tracking may seem so taken for granted to school participants as to be virtually invisible. Only fools, children, or uncivilized barbarians would question its presuppositions: Tracking is commonsensical (Geertz 1983). Thus, tracking may confuse rather than clarify educative principles and practices. That is, it may screen from discussion fundamental questions of curriculum, pedagogy, and purpose. For example, practitioners typically assert the effectiveness of "homogeneous grouping," but as noted above, the assumed homogeneity afforded by tracking may be largely illusory.

According to labeling theorists (Hargreaves, Hester, and Mellor 1975; Rist 1977), not only may tracking conceal "homogeneity's" practical and theoretical complexity but also its commonsensical logic may promote divisive, largely implicit, typifications that take on lives of their own. Thus, as we described in regard to Keddie's (1971) investigation, well-intentioned teachers' perceptions of students and knowledge may nevertheless be predetermined by track typifications, such as that low-track students are "thick" or high-track students are "sharp." Using such typifications to interpret the behavior of individual students or to characterize whole groups, teachers may see an obstreperous high-track class as creative, whereas a lower-track class that exhibits objectively similar behaviors may be read as unpredictable, academically uninterested, or disorderly. Enacted in lessons and in particular distributions of knowledge, such typifications may become self-fulfilling prophecies: Ironically, they provide the conditions that prompt the very student behaviors teachers see as troublesome and want to avoid. In such scenarios, tracking may be enacted to contradict schooling's educative functions. Where curricular distributions correspond to invidious sociocultural characterizations, they may also run counter to the school's social functions, such as promoting equal educational opportunity and social mobility.

Tracking may prompt similarly unexamined, unexaminable understandings about "individual differences." Explicitly, tracking promises individualized instruction, a highly valued goal in American society and in American education. However, as with "homogeneity," empirical studies document that lower-track lessons, even though they are designated "individualized," may not be individualized in fact. Rather, students may complete work cards alone and at their own pace, but all confront the same work cards. Yet teachers may pass over assessments of the value of this "common curriculum" because they perceive lessons as "individualized." As an organizational procedure, tracking may preclude serious consideration or practice of individualized instruction.

Tracking may also divert serious dialogue about "school knowledge" by providing stereotypical, ranked categorizations of knowledge. It juxtaposes alternative curricula against the "traditional [academic] shape of the . . . school program" (Krug 1960) in a series of handy dualisms: low- versus high-status knowledge, easy versus hard, practical versus academic, headed versus handed, mental versus manual, and vocational versus college preparatory. From one perspective, the "hegemony" (Westbury 1988b), or predominance, of the academic standard is deemed paramount: It not only dominates formal graduation requirements but also, possibly more negatively, elevates "knowing that" over "knowing how," thereby depriving all students of a sense of the value of general or experiential knowledge (Boyer 1983; Goodlad 1984; Westbury 1988b). In comparison, practical, innovative, alternative curricula appear lacking in coherence, stability, and serious stature.

The weakness of alternative curricula (e.g., emphasizing knowing how) has been attributed to the high status of the liberal arts (Martin 1981), their articulation with the university, and the traditional casting of schooling as an academic endeavor (Westbury 1988b). In addition, the low status of alternatives may reflect a lack of thoughtful curriculum design, possibly tracking's most important potential diversion. That is, mere placement in a tracked class constitutes some schools' alternative curriculum—even if little curricular variation takes place. In other schools, a trivial, controlling curriculum of worksheets is presented, based on unexamined assumptions about how and what lower-track students need to learn (Moll and Diaz 1987; Oakes 1985). Sometimes lower-track lessons involve academic, presumably high-status topics, but they are skeletonized as they are "covered in less depth" (Page 1987a).

From a different perspective, not academic hegemony but utilitarian hegemony is the problem with "school knowledge." Practical subjects displace academic courses: Whereas high schools at the turn of the century debated the addition of other academic subjects such as modern languages and science to the classical trivium of Greek, Latin, and mathematics, 20th-century debate has concerned the addition of beekeeping, home management, and marketing (Commission on National Aid to Vocational Education 1914) and more recently of driver, drug, and sex education (Powell, Farrar, and Cohen 1985). Thus, the rationale undergirding some lower-track curricula is "relevance" (Page 1990b). At the same time, academic courses are reconstructed to be practical (Kliebard 1986, 1988a). In an empiricist milieu in which education is conceived increasingly as a means rather than as of intrinsic value, even upper-track history or English has to justify its place in the school curriculum by demonstrating its "relevance," not because it represents an intrinsically valuable and distinctive mode of inquiry into fundamental human concerns.

The school curriculum proliferates through differentiation. Particularly at the secondary level, an amorphous curriculum seriously erodes the institution's intellectual character and muddies its sense of purpose. What are schools for when the curriculum ranges from aeronautical engineering to cosmetology to Teen Al-Anon to synchronized swimming? Further, tracking's common sense often precludes serious dialogue about these complex issues.

One response to such concerns is national reports and national standards. For example, the dualism between the academic and the alternative curricula is visible in the "higher standards" invoked in the report by the National Commission on Excellence in Education (1983) on the state of the American high school. The report recommends tougher graduation requirements, including an additional year of math and of science, to stem the "tide of mediocrity" that overwhelms American education. However, although many states have responded by adding requirements for these "hard," "high-status," academic subjects, the courses students actually take may be watered down rather than "real" math or science. And the watered-down courses may displace art and vocational courses with far more curricular integrity (Clune, White, and Pattenson 1989).

Often lost in large-scale, frequently doctrinaire debates are examples of curriculum design in which the culture's paradoxes are creatively resolved, at least momentarily. In them, teachers respond imaginatively to both students' differences and their curricular implications: They "restore [academic] knowledge which appears at first to be so remote and obscure back to its origins in human experience" (Kliebard 1977, discussing Dewey's curriculum theory).

For example, Heath (1982) worked with first-grade teachers who were puzzled by the disproportionate failure of black children in their classes: Students seemed unable to answer even the simplest of recall questions. First, Heath used her expertise as an anthropologist to study and delineate the different types of questions black children answered at home and in school. Then, with the teachers, she designed curriculum materials that were culturally congruent, that is, that took into account the questions black children competently answered and the topics they knew about. Gradually, as students became comfortable in the classroom, the teachers used students' questions and topics to form a bridge to school questions and topics. At the same time, white children could use the special curriculum materials to expand their own repertoires of question answering. In short, Heath and the teachers acknowledged differences but did not interpret them as problems needing remediation to a univocal, white middle-class school standard or, alternatively, as evidence that black children could only succeed with and deserve a separate, black curriculum. Rather the curriculum acknowledged differences but interpreted them, practically and theoretically, as enrichments: The culturally congruent curriculum was not reserved for the "special" or the "different" but enriched the language and lives of all classroom participants.

Equally pluralistic curricula have been developed in writing for high school students (Heath and Branscombe 1985), for reading (Au, 1980; Jordan 1985), and for bilingual students (Cohen and DeAvila 1983; Moll and Diaz 1987). Such examples allow us to interpret differentiation's effects on schooling and the curriculum less deterministically and pessimistically than some of tracking's critics, as well as less glibly and optimistically than some of tracking's proponents.

DIRECTIONS FOR FUTURE RESEARCH

Although tentative answers are available for some of the central questions about curriculum differentiation, we have much to learn. Our knowledge remains at a most basic level: We know that curriculum differentiation promotes inequality of educational outcomes, but we have not documented how that occurs; and we have observed different sorts of attitudes and behavior among students in different curricular programs, but we lack information on the causal role of tracking in this process. There are many areas that need more work, but four stand out as particularly pressing: We need to know more about (1) the mechanisms through which the effects of tracking occur; (2) how curriculum differentiation affects educationally disadvantaged students; (3) international comparisons of curriculum differentiation; and (4) alternative curricular arrangements.

How Do the Effects of Differentiation Occur?

We now have some knowledge about the effects of curriculum differentiation: At all levels of schooling, it leads to greater inequality of results; students in high-status groups and tracks often benefit from differentiation; a few types of elementary school grouping may benefit low-group students, but others do not; and low-track students appear to suffer at the high school level. With these findings as a starting point, the next question must be, How do these effects come about?

Although we have yet to document the precise mechanisms through which differentiation affects student outcomes, there are some strong clues. We suspect that variation in the content and processes of curriculum and instruction serves as a key connection between the distribution of students and their unequal outcomes. One body of work, mainly qualitative in nature, has explored the differences in curriculum and instruction that correspond to the division of students; another set of studies, mainly quantitative, has examined the effects of differentiation on learning; but few writers have demonstrated empirically the links between the two. Thus we conclude that the relationship between differential classroom processes and student outcomes warrants considerable further inquiry.

Many of the findings we report in this chapter pertain to organizational differentiation, that is, the way students are sorted in schools. What we need, though, are studies of curriculum and instructional differentiation—works that examine the knowledge and instructional conditions around which students and teachers interact—and their connection with student outcomes. For example, Gamoran, Berends, and Nystrand (1990) show that between-track achievement differences in eighth-grade English could be attributed in part to more discussion and open-ended questions in high-track classes and more fragmentation of lessons and off-task behavior in low-track classes. Further studies of this sort would serve three critical purposes: (1) They would help show just how grouping and tracking lead to variation in achievement; (2) they would assess the claim, found in many reviews, that ability grouping has an impact on students when it is associated with modification of curriculum and instruction; and (3) they would allow one to examine whether or not, depending on how curriculum and instruction vary across groups, differentiation is beneficial to students in some schools and classes even though the usual effects are minimal or worse.

Another important connection that needs to be drawn is that between curriculum differentiation and the polarization of attitudes toward school. Whether this relation is a causal one or merely an association that results from selecting disaffected students into low tracks is a pressing question. One complication in such an endeavor is that the relation between tracking and attitudes may vary across schools. The greater the stigma attached to low-track assignment, the more likely that tracking contributes to antischool attitudes. In schools whose cultures emphasize academic seriousness in all tracks, the stigma of low-track assignment, and thus the polarization process, may be less salient. Again, such studies may show how to mitigate the harmful effects of differentiation, if possible.

Curriculum Differentiation and Disadvantaged Groups

Curriculum differentiation works against the success of academically deficient students: By the end of the year, they tend to fall even further behind. Even in the best of cases, in which ability grouping benefited low-ability as well as high-ability students in certain elementary school studies, high-group students tended to gain more, so that the gaps still widened. Thus, it would be simple to conclude that curriculum differentiation is harmful to disadvantaged students.

Yet there are complications to this issue that demand further research. First is the question of whether differentiation can remediate, even if it does not currently do so in the usual case. This question is acute at both the elementary and secondary levels. Also at issue is the legitimacy of the concern that when a school is largely made up of economically disadvantaged students, the needs of those at the top of the hierarchy take on special importance: the "triage" approach.

In the typical case, curriculum differentiation not only fails to remediate low-track students—that is, to catch them up to their higher-achieving peers—but also causes them to fall further and further behind. As noted, it is very likely that this outcome results from deficiencies in the curriculum and instruction provided to low-track classes. Is this an inevitable result of sorting students? Are there any exceptions to this general pattern? This question is critical because schools face strong pressures to differentiate, including the difficulties of instructing diverse groups of students, the desires of parents of high-achieving students for elite classes, and the more general cultural value placed on individualizing.

In theory, one might argue, as Keddie's (1971) teachers did, that it should be possible to provide equally challenging lessons to students at all ability levels, even if the lessons are not identical across classes. In practice, however, as our review suggests, this system appears difficult to implement: Low expectations, inadequate curricula, impoverished contexts, conflicting imperatives, and students' resistance all mitigate against it. This issue needs to be addressed directly, however, by studies seeking cases of successful remediation in low-track curricula. On the basis of previous study, it appears that Catholic schools (see Lee 1985; Valli 1990), alternative schools, dropout programs (Wehlage, Stone, Lesko, Nauman, and Page 1982); and magnet programs (Mitchell, Verney, and Benson 1989) might be places to explore this possibility.

A second concern is that schools with high proportions of economically disadvantaged students may feel a special pressure to differentiate among students and curricula. With limited resources and high failure rates, some report being compelled to "save a few" (Moore and Davenport 1988). To what extent can honors classes in inner-city schools attain the quality of results found in schools with more advantaged populations? Does the "triage" work? Research is needed that addresses the question of whether the use of ability grouping in disadvantaged schools is helpful or harmful to students at all performance levels.

At the secondary level, the impact of grouping and tracking varies for students from different sociodemographic backgrounds. Low-SES students end up in low tracks considerably more often than their more advantaged peers, thus increasing the achievement and attainment gaps between students from rich families and those from poor ones. Other things being equal, though, black students are more likely to be assigned to college-bound programs than whites, and tracking produces a smaller black-white achievement gap than would occur in its absence (Gamoran and Mare 1989; these findings on SES and race are consistent with several earlier studies as well). Thus, the connection between tracking and the education of the disadvantaged deserves closer scrutiny than it has been given in the past.

International Comparisons

Given the widespread international interest in educational stratification, it is surprising that no cross-national comparisons of tracking systems and their effects have been conducted. Because there are striking differences in the uses of curriculum differentiation, international comparisons would seem to be a key source of information on the limits and possibilities of the practice.

For example, Japanese elementary schools do not differentiate their curricula. One might expect this system to result in less inequality of results than one that uses ability grouping at the elementary level. Yet Japanese students vary widely in their performance levels by the transition to high school. How is this variation produced? What are the implications of this finding for American schools that are currently attempting to reduce their levels of differentiation?

Another subject needing international comparison is vocational education. In both Japan and Germany, for example, vocational training in schools is much more closely tied to the labor market than that found in the United States, and it appears to be much more effective in promoting noncognitive skills and labor market success. How does vocational and academic differentiation compare across nations? What accounts for cross-national differences in its success? In the United States, vocational programs produce lower cognitive outcomes than either college preparatory or noncollege, general programs. How well do vocational programs promote cognitive outcomes in other countries?

As Meyer (1980, 1987) has argued, for many kinds of "school effects" the essential source of variation occurs at the societal level. American schools have certain basic similarities, and insufficient variation inhibits our ability to detect what really matters. By placing American systems of curriculum differentiation in an international context, we would be better able to illuminate the problems and possibilities of our own system.

Alternative Curricular Arrangements

Better understanding of how differentiation's effects occur and how U.S. differentiation compares with that in other nations would pave the way for comparisons of alternative curricula and instructional organizations: whole-class instruction, tracking and ability grouping, and less conventional approaches to teaching in heterogeneous classes. One important alternative is cooperative learning. Much evidence at the elementary school level shows the advantage of this technique over traditional arrangements (e.g., Slavin 1983). Moreover, unlike differentiation, cooperative learning helps to reduce educational inequality. We also need to know how its effects on productivity compare to those of ability grouping. Cooperative learning may also be effective at the secondary level, although less research exists and the findings are less secure (Newmann and Thompson 1987). Research is needed to see if cooperative learning can bring the same advantage to high-ability students as curriculum differentiation, without the damaging effects on low-ability students. Another alternative, only recently conceived and as yet unexamined, is curricula that attempt to integrate academic and vocational topics and incorporate learning principles from research in cognitive science (Mitchell, Verney, and Benson 1989; Oakes 1986; Raizen 1989).

In addition to comparisons of alternative curricula and organizational patterns, we also need information about the policy conditions under which effective alternatives, should they be found, might be implemented. Given what we know about curriculum differentiation's history and close connections with deeply held cultural values, schools' efforts to implement alternatives will undoubtedly involve rethinking and restructuring many aspects that are now taken for granted. Such efforts will require more than traditional implementation strategies, namely, mandates from policymakers or administrators, adoption of curricular arrangements developed by experts or imported from other settings, or conventional teacher in-service activities (Elmore and McLaughlin 1989; Fullan 1982). It would be useful to have qualitative studies that shed light on how long-standing traditions, community and parental pressure, school and district guidelines, standards of common practice, and beliefs about students' abilities translate into specific curriculum differentiation policies in a variety of settings. We could also benefit from research on how investigations by teachers, administrators, and local policymakers into how curriculum differentiation works and the values and interests it represents in their own settings affect efforts to change curricular arrangements (Sirotnik and Oakes 1986). Such research would complement knowledge of the technical and managerial aspects of curriculum differentiation and its alternatives. It would add information about how beliefs, traditions, and values in the school culture; the participation of teachers and administrators; and conditions in the larger policy environments are likely to facilitate or impede curricular change.

References

Abraham, John. 1989. Testing Hargreaves' and Lacey's differentiation-polarisation theory in a setted comprehensive. *British Journal of Sociology* 40(1): 46–81.

Achievement Council. 1985. *Excellence for Whom?* San Francisco: Achievement Council.

Adler, Mortimer. 1982. *The Paideia Proposal*. New York: Macmillan.

Alexander, Karl L., and Martha Cook. 1982. Curricula and coursework: A surprise ending to a familiar story. *American Sociological Review* 47(5): 626–640.

Alexander, Karl L., Martha A. Cook, and Edward L. McDill. 1978, February. Curriculum tracking and educational stratification. *American Sociological Review* 43: 47–66.

Alexander, Karl L., and Edward L. McDill. 1976, December. Selection and and allocation within schools: Some causes and consequences of curriculum placement. *American Sociological Review* 41: 963–980.

Allington, Richard L. 1980. Teacher interruption behaviors during primary-grade oral reading. *Journal of Educational Psychology* 72(3): 371–374.

Alpert, J. L. 1974. Teacher behavior across ability groups: A consideration of the mediation of pygmalion effects. *Journal of Educational Psychology* 66(3): 348–353.

Anderson, Caroline, and Rebecca Barr. 1990. "Modifying Values and Behaviors About Tracking: A Case Study." In *Curriculum Differentiation: Interpretive Studies in U.S. Secondary Schools*, edited by Reba Page and Linda Valli. Albany: State University of New York Press.

Anyon, Jean. 1981. Social class and school knowledge. *Curriculum Inquiry* 11(1): 3–42.

Apple, Michael W. 1979. *Ideology and Curriculum*. Boston: Routledge & Kegan Paul.

Apple, Michael W. 1983. "Curriculum Reform and the Logic of Technical Control." In *Ideology and Practice in Schooling*, edited by Michael Apple and Lois Weis, 143–166. Philadelphia, PA: Temple University Press.

Au, Katheryn. 1980. Participation structures in a reading lesson with Hawaiian children: Analysis of a culturally appropriate instructional event. *Anthropology and Education Quarterly* 11(2): 91–115.

Ball, Stephen J. 1981. *Beachside Comprehensive: A Case-study of Secondary Schooling*. Cambridge, MA: Cambridge University Press.

Balow, J. H. 1964. The effect of homogeneous grouping in seventh-grade arithmetic. *Arithmetic Teacher* 11(3): 186–191.

Barker Lunn, J. C. 1970. *Streaming in the Primary School*. London: National Foundation for Educational Research in England and Wales.

Barr, Rebecca, and Robert Dreeben. 1983. *How Schools Work*. Chicago: University of Chicago Press.

Becker, Henry S. 1953. The teacher in the authority system of the school. *Journal of Educational Sociology* 27(3): 128–141.

Bellack, Arno, Hebert Kliebard, R. Hyman, and F. F. Smith, Jr. 1966. *The Language of the Classroom*. New York: Teachers College Press.

Bellah, Robert, R. Madsen, W. Sullivan, A. Swidler, and S. Tipton. 1985. *Habits of the Heart: Individualism and Commitment in American Life*. New York: Harper & Row.

Berg, Ivan. 1970. *Education and Jobs: The Great Training Robbery*. Boston: Beacon Press.

Berryman, Sue E. 1980. *Vocational Education and the Work Establishment of Youth: Equity and Effectiveness Issues*. Santa Monica, CA: Rand.

Bettelheim, Bruno. 1958. Sputnik and segregation: Should the gifted be educated separately? *Commentary* 26: 332–339.

Bidwell, Charles, and J. Kasarda. 1980. Conceptualizing and measuring the effects of school and schooling. *American Journal of Education* 88(4): 401–430.

Blank, Rolf. 1989. *Educational Effects of Magnet High Schools*. Madison, WI: National Center on Effective Secondary Schools.

Boston School Committee. 1908. *Documents of the School Committee* 7: 48–53.

Bourdieu, Pierre. 1977. "Cultural Reproduction and Social Reproduction." In *Power and Ideology in Education*, edited by J. Karabel and A. Halsey, 487–511. New York: Oxford University Press.

Bourdieu, Pierre, and Carl Passeron. 1977. *Reproduction in Education, Society and Culture*. Beverly Hills, CA: Sage.

Bowles, Samuel, and Hebert Gintis. 1976. *Schooling in Capitalist America: Educational Reform and the Contradictions of Economic Life*. New York: Basic Books.

Boyer, Ernest. 1983. *High School: A Report on Secondary Education in America*. New York: Harper & Row.

Burgess, Robert G. 1983. *Experiencing Comprehensive Education: A Study of Bishop McGregor School*. London: Methuen.

Burgess, Robert G. 1984. "It's Not a Proper Subject: It's Just Newsom." In *Defining the Curriculum*, edited by Ivor Goodson and Stephen Ball, 181–200. London: Falmer.

Camarena, Margaret. 1990. "Following the Right Track: A Comparison of Tracking Practices in Public and Catholic Schools." In *Curriculum Differentiation in U.S. Secondary Schools: Interpretive Studies*, edited by Reba Page and Linda Valli. Albany: State University of New York Press.

Carnegie Council on Adolescent Development. 1989. *Turning Points: Preparing American Youth for the 21st Century*. Washington, DC: CCAD.

Carnoy, Martin, and Henry Levin. 1985. *Schooling and Work in the Democratic State*. Stanford, CA: Stanford University Press.

Cazden, Courtney. 1986. "Classroom Discourse." In *The Handbook of Research on Teaching*, 3rd ed., edited by Merlin C. Wittrock, 432–463. New York: Macmillan.

Cicourel, Aaron V., and J. I. Kitsuse. 1963. *The Educational Decision-makers*. Indianapolis, IN: Bobbs Merrill.

Cicourel, Aaron V., and Hugh Mehan. 1985. Universal development, stratifying practices, and status attainment. *Research in Social Stratification and Mobility* 4: 3–27.

Clune, William, P. White, and Janice Pattenson. 1989. *The Implementation and Effects of High School Graduation Requirements*. Madison: Center for Policy Research in Education, University of Wisconsin.

Cohen, David K. 1985. "Origins." In *The Shopping Mall High School*, by Arthur Powell, Eleanor Farrar, and David K. Cohen, 233–308. Boston: Houghton Mifflin.

Cohen, David, and Barbara Neufeld. 1981, summer. The failure of high schools and the progress of education. *Daedalus* 110: 69–89.

Cohen, Elizabeth G. 1984. "Talking and Working Together: Status, Interaction, and Learning." In *Instructional Groups in the Classroom: Organization and Processes*, edited by P. Peterson and L. C. Wilkenson, 171–187. New York: Academic Press.

Cohen, Elizabeth G. 1986. *Designing Groupwork: Strategies for the Heterogeneous Classroom*. New York: Teachers College Press.

Cohen, Elizabeth G., and E. DeAvila. 1983. *Learning to Think in Math and Science: Improving Local Education for Minority Children*. Stanford, CA: Stanford University.

Coleman, James. 1961. *The Adolescent Society*. New York: Free Press.

Coleman, James. 1966. *Equality of Educational Opportunity*. Washington, DC: U.S. Department of Health, Education, and Welfare.

Collins, Randall. 1977. Some comparative principles of educational stratification. *Harvard Educational Review* 47(1): 1–29.

Commission on National Aid to Vocational Education. 1914. *Report of the Commission on National Aid for Vocational Education*. Washington, DC: U.S. Government Printing Office.

Commission on the Reorganization of Secondary Education, National Education Association. 1918. *Cardinal Principles of Secondary Education*. Washington, DC: Bureau of Education.

Conant, James. 1967. *The Comprehensive High School: A Second Report to Interested Citizens*. New York: McGraw-Hill.

Connell, R. W., D. J. Ashenden, S. Keller, and G. W. Dowsett. 1982. *Making the Difference*. Boston: George Allen & Unwin.

Cornell, E. R. 1936. "Effects of Ability Grouping Determinable from Published Studies." In *The Grouping of Pupils. Thirty-fifth Yearbook of the National Society for the Study of Education*, Part I, edited by G. M. Whipple, 289–304. Bloomington, IL: Public School Publishing.

Council for Basic Education. 1989, summer. Off the tracks. *Perspective* 1: 1–17.

Cremin, Lawrence A. 1964. *The Transformation of the School: Progressivism in American Education 1876–1957*. New York: Knopf.

Cubberly, Ellwood P. 1919. *Public Education in the United States: A Study and Interpretation of American Educational History*, rev. 1925, 1947. Boston: Houghton Mifflin.

Cummings, W. 1980. *Education and Equality in Japan*. Princeton, NJ: Princeton University Press.

Cusick, Philip. 1973. *Inside High School*. New York: Holt, Rinehart and Winston.

Daniels, B. 1961, June. The effects of streaming in the primary school: A comparison of streamed and unstreamed schools. *British Journal of Educational Psychology* 31: 119–127.

Dar, Y., and N. Resh. 1986. Classroom intellectual composition and academic achievement. *American Educational Research Journal* 23(3): 357–374.

Darling-Hammond, Linda. 1985. *Equality and Excellence: The Educational Status of Black Americans*. New York: College Entrance Examination Board.

Davies, Lynn. 1984. *Pupil Power: Deviance and Gender in School*. London: Falmer.

Davis, Sharon A., and Emil J. Haller. 1981, May. Tracking ability and SES: Further evidence on the "revisionist-meritocratic debate." *American Journal of Education* 89(3): 283–304.

DeLany, Brian. 1986. "Choices and Chances: The Matching of Students and Courses in High School." Ph.D. dissertation, Stanford University, Stanford, CA.

Dewey, John. 1956 (1902). *The Child and the Curriculum*. Chicago: University of Chicago Press.

Dewey, John. 1964. (1902). "The Educational Situation: As Concerns Secondary Education." In *John Dewey on Education*, edited by Reginald Archambault, 404–421. Chicago: University of Chicago Press.

Dreeben, Robert, and Rebecca Barr. 1987. "An Organizational Analysis of Curriculum and Instruction." In *The Social Organization of Schools: New Conceptualization of the Learning Process*, edited by Maureen Hallinan, 13–39. New York: Plenum.

Dreeben, Robert, and Rebecca Barr. 1988. The formation and instruction of ability groups. *American Journal of Education* 97(1): 34–64.

Edelman, Murray. 1977. *Political Language: Words that Succeed and Policies that Fail*. New York: Academic Press.

Eder, Donna. 1981, July. Ability grouping as a self-fulfilling prophecy: A microanalysis of teacher-student interaction. *Sociology of Education* 54: 151–161.

Ekstrom, Ruth B. 1961, summer. Experimental studies of homogeneous grouping: A critical review. *School Review* 69: 216–226.

Eliot, Charles W. 1960. "Status of Education at Close of Century." In *Addresses and Proceedings of the Annual Meeting of the NEA*, vol. 98, 196–199. Washington, DC: National Education Association.

Eliot, Charles W. 1961. "Shortening and Enriching the Grammar School Course. In *Charles W. Eliot and Popular Education*, edited by Edward A. Krug, 29–166. New York: Teachers College Press.

Elmore, Richard F., and Milbry W. McLaughlin. 1988. *Steady Work: Policy, Practice, and Reform of American Education*. Santa Monica, CA: Rand.

Erickson, Frederick. 1975. Gatekeeping the melting pot. *Harvard Educational Review* 45(1): 44–70.

Erickson, Frederick. 1984. School literacy, reasoning and civility: An anthropologist's perspective. *Review of Educational Research* 54(4): 525–546.

Erickson, Frederick. 1986. "Qualitative Methods in Research on Teaching." In *The Handbook of Research on Teaching*, 3rd ed., edited by Merlin C. Wittrock, 119–161. New York: Macmillan.

Esposito, Dominick. 1973. Homogeneous and heterogeneous ability grouping: Principal findings and implications for evaluating and designing more effective educational environments. *Review of Educational Research* 43(2): 163–179.

Fenstermacher, Gary. 1983. "Introduction." In *Individual Differences and the Common Curriculum. Eighty-second Yearbook of the National Society for the Study of Education*, Part I, edited by Gary Fenstermacher and John Goodlad. Chicago: University of Chicago Press.

Finley, Marilee K. 1984, October. Teachers and tracking in a comprehensive high school. *Sociology of Education* 57: 233–243.

Finney, R. 1929. *A Sociological Philosophy of Education*. New York: Macmillan.

Franklin, Barry M. 1986. *Building the American Community*. New York: Falmer.

Fullan, Michael. 1982. *The Meaning of Educational Change*. New York: Teachers College Press.

Furlong, Viv. 1977. "Anancy Goes to School: A Case Study of Pupils' Knowledge of Their Teachers." In *School Experience*, edited by Peter Woods and Michael Hammersley, 162–185. London: Croom Helm.

Gamoran, Adam. 1986. Instructional and institutional effects of ability grouping. *Sociology of Education* 59(4): 185–198.

Gamoran, Adam. 1987a. Organization, instruction, and the effects of ability grouping: Comment on Slavin's best-evidence synthesis. *Review of Educational Research* 57(3): 341–345.

Gamoran, Adam. 1987b, July. The stratification of high school learning opportunities. *Sociology of Education* 60: 135–155.

Gamoran, Adam. 1988. "A Multi-level Analysis of the Effects of Tracking." Paper presented at the annual meeting, American Sociological Association, Atlanta, GA.

Gamoran, Adam. 1989a, February. Measuring curriculum differentiation. *American Journal of Education* 97: 129–143.

Gamoran, Adam. 1989b. Rank, performance, and mobility in elementary school grouping. *Sociological Quarterly* 30(1): 109–123.

Gamoran, Adam. 1989c. "Tracking and the Distribution of Status in Secondary Schools." Paper presented at the annual meeting, American Sociological Association, San Francisco, CA.

Gamoran, Adam. 1990. "Instructional Organizational Practices That Affect Equity." In *Leadership, Equity, and School Effectiveness*, edited by H. P. Baptiste, Jr., H. C. Waxman, J. W. de Felix, and J. E. Anderson, 155–172. Newbury Park, CA: Sage.

Gamoran, Adam, and Mark Berends. 1987. The effects of stratification in secondary schools: Synthesis of survey and ethnographic research. *Review of Education Research* 57(4):415–435.

Gamoran, Adam, Mark Berends, and Martin Nystrand. 1990. Classroom instruction and the effects of ability grouping: A structural model. Paper presented at the annual meeting, American Educational Research Association, Boston.

Gamoran, Adam, and R. D. Mare. 1989. Secondary school tracking and educational inequality: Compensation, reinforcement, or neutrality? *American Journal of Sociology* 94(5): 1146–1183.

Garet, Michael, and Brian DeLany. 1988, April. Students, courses, and stratification. *Sociology of Education* 61: 61–77.

Geertz, Clifford. 1983. "Common Sense as a Cultural System." In *Local Knowledge: Further Essays in Interpretive Anthropology*, edited by Clifford Geertz. New York: Basic Books.

Gilmore, Perry. 1983. Spelling "Mississippi": Recontextualizing a literacy-related speech event. *Anthropology and Education Quarterly* 14(4) :235–255.

Gilmore, Perry. 1985. "Silence and Sulking: Emotional Displays in the Classroom." In *Perspectives on Silence*, edited by Deborah Tannen and Muriel Saville-Troika, 139–162. New York: Ablex.

Goldberg, Miriam, Harold Passow, and J. Justman. 1966. *The Effects of Ability Grouping*. New York: Teachers College Press.

Goldstein, Beth. 1990. "Refugee Students' Perceptions of Curriculum Differentiation." In *Curriculum Differentiation: Interpretive Studies in U.S. Secondary Schools*, edited by Reba Page and Linda Valli, 137–158. Albany: State Univeristy of New York Press.

Good, Thomas, and Jere Brophy. 1987. *Looking in Classrooms*, 4th ed. New York: Harper & Row.

Good, Thomas, and S. Marshall. 1984. "Do Students Learn More in Heterogeneous or Homogeneous Groups?" In *The Social Context of Instruction*, edited by Penelope L. Peterson, L. C. Wilkinson, and Maureen T. Hallinan, 15–38. Orlando, FL: Academic Press.

Goodlad, John I. 1960. "Classroom Organization." In *Encyclopedia of Educational Research*, 3rd ed., edited by C. W. Harris, 221–226. New York: Macmillan.

Goodlad, John I. 1984. *A Place Called School: Prospects for the Future*. New York: McGraw-Hill.

Goodlad, John I., and Jeannie Oakes. 1988, March. We must offer equal access to knowledge. *Educational Leadership* 45: 16–22.

Gould, Stephen J. 1981. *The Mismeasure of Man*. New York: Norton.

Graham, Patricia A. 1974. *Community and Class in American Education, 1865–1918*. New York: Wiley.

Grant, Gerald. 1988. *The World We Created at Hamilton High*. Cambridge, MA: Harvard University Press.

Grasso, J., and J. Shea. 1979. *Vocational Education and Training: Impact on Youth*. Berkeley, CA: Carnegie Council on Policy Studies in Higher Education.

Groff, Patrick. 1962, January. A survey of basal reading practices. *Reading Teacher* 15: 232–235.

Guthrie, Larry F., and Constance Leventhal. 1985. "Opportunities for Scientific Literacy for High School Students." Paper presented at the annual meeting, American Educational Research Association, Chicago.

Haller, Emil J. 1985. Pupil race and elementary school ability grouping: Are teachers biased against black children? *American Educational Research Journal* 22(4): 465–483.

Haller, Emil J., and Sharon A. Davis. 1980. Does socioeconomic status bias the assignment of elementary school students to reading groups? *American Educational Research Journal* 17(4): 409–418.

Haller, Emil J., and Sharon A. Davis. 1981, July. Teachers' perceptions, parental social status and grouping for reading instruction. *Sociology of Education* 54: 162–173.

Hallinan, Maureen T. 1984. "Summary and Implications." In *The Social Context of Instruction*, edited by Penelope Peterson, L. Wilkinson, and Maureen Hallinan, 229–240. Orlando, FL: Academic Press.

Hallinan, Maureen T., and Aagie B. Sorensen. 1985. Ability grouping and student friendships. *American Educational Research Journal* 22(4): 485–499.

Hallinan, Maureen T., and Aagie B. Sorensen. 1986. Student characteristics and assignment to ability groups: Two conceptual formulations. *Sociological Quarterly* 27(1): 1–13.

Hallinan, Maureen T., and R. A. Williams. 1989, February. Interracial friendship choices in secondary schools. *American Sociological Review* 54: 67–78.

Hamilton, Stephen F. 1987. Apprenticeship as a transition to adulthood in West Germany. *American Journal of Education* 95(2): 314–345.

Hammack, D. C. 1969. "The Centralization of New York City's Public School System." M.A. thesis, Columbia University, New York.

Hannan, D. F. 1987. *Schooling Decisions: The Origins and Consequences of Selection and Streaming in Irish Post-primary Schools*. Dublin: Economic and Social Research Institute.

Hanson, R. A., and R. E. Schultz. 1978. "A New Look at Schooling Effects from Programmatic Research and Development." In *Making Change Happen*, edited by D. Mann, 120–149. New York: Teachers College Press.

Hanson, Susan. 1990. "The College-Preparatory Curriculum Across Schools: Access to Similar Learning Opportunities?" In *Curriculum Differentiation: Interpretive Studies in U.S. Secondary Schools*, edited by Reba Page and Linda Valli, 67–90. Albany: State University of New York Press.

Hargreaves, David H. 1967. *Social Relations in a Secondary School*. London: C. Tinling.

Hargreaves, David H., S. Hester, and F. Mellor. 1975. *Deviance in Classrooms*. London: Routledge & Kegan Paul.

Hawkins, M. 1966, November. Mobility of students in reading groups. *Reading Teacher* 20: 136–140.

Heath, Shirley. 1982. "Questioning at Home and at School: A Comparative Study." In *Doing the Ethnography of Schooling*, edited by George Spindler, 103–127. New York: Holt, Rinehart and Winston.

Heath, Shirley, and Amanda Branscombe. 1985. "'Intelligent Writing' in an Audience Community: Teacher, Students and Researcher." In *The Acquisition of Written Language: Response and Revision*, edited by Susan Freedman, 3–32. Norwood, NJ: Ablex.

Heathers, Glen. 1969. "Grouping." In *Encyclopedia of Educational Research*, 4th ed., edited by R. L. Ebel, 559–570. New York: Macmillan.

Hemmings, Annette, and Mary Metz. 1990. "Real Teaching: How High School Teachers Negotiate Societal, Local Community, and Student Pressures When They Define Their Work." In *Curriculum Differentiation: Interpretive Studies in U.S. Secondary Schools*, edited by Reba Page and Linda Valli, 91–112. Albany: State University of New York Press.

Henry, Jules. 1963. *Culture Against Man*. New York: Random House.

Heyns, Barbara. 1974. Social selection and stratification within schools. *American Journal of Sociology* 79(6): 1434–1451.

Hiebert, Elfreda H. 1983. An examination of ability grouping for reading instruction. *Reading Research Quarterly* 18(2): 231–255.

Hiebert, Elfreda H. 1987. The context of instruction and student learning: An examination of Slavin's assumptions. *Review of Educational Research* 57(3): 337–340.

Hollingshead, A. 1975. *Elmstown's Youth, and Elmstown Revisited*. New York: Wiley.

Hotchkiss, Lawrence, and Linda Dorsten. 1987. "Curriculum Effects on Early Post High School Outcomes." In *Sociology of Education and Socialization*, edited by R. G. Corwin, 191–219. Greenwich, CT: JAI Press.

Hsieh, H-C. 1987. "Who Goes Where? The Determinants of Post-Compulsory Educational Placement in Urban Taiwan." Ph.D. dissertation, University of Wisconsin, Madison.

Hymes, Dell. 1980. "Educational Ethnology." In *Language in Education*, edited by Dell Hymes, 119–125. Washington, DC: Center for Applied Linguistics.

Jackson, Philip W. 1968. *Life in Classrooms*. New York: Holt, Rinehart and Winston.

Jackson, Philip W. 1981. Comprehending a well-run comprehensive: A report on a visit to a large suburban high school. *Daedalus* 110(4): 81–96.

Jacob, Evelyn, and Cathy Jordan, eds. 1987. Explaining the school performance of minority students. *Anthropology and Education Quarterly* (special issue) 18(4): 257–382.

Jencks, Christopher L., and Marcia Brown. 1975. The effects of high schools on their students. *Harvard Educational Review* 45(3): 273–324.

Jencks, Christopher L., Marshall Smith, Henry Adand, Mary J. Bane, David Cohen, Herbert Gintis, Barbara Heyns, and Stephan Michelson. 1972. *Inequality: A Reassessment of the Effects of Family and Schooling in America*. New York: Basic Books.

Johnson, David, and Roger Johnson. 1989. *Cooperation and Competition: Theory and Research*. Edina, MN: Interaction Book Co.

Jones, J. D., B. E. Vanfossen, and J. Z. Spade. 1986. "Curriculum Placement: Individual and School Effects Using the *High School and Beyond* Data." Paper presented at the annual meeting, American Sociological Association, Washington, DC.

Jordan, Cathy. 1985. Translating culture: From ethnographic information to educational program. *Anthropology and Education Quarterly* 16(2): 105–123.

Kammen, Michael. 1974. *People of Paradox: A Contrapuntal Civilization*. New York: Knopf.

Kantor, Harvey. 1986, August. Work, education, and vocational reform: The ideological origins of vocational education, 1890–1920. *American Journal of Education* 94(4): 401–426.

Kariya, Takehito, and James E. Rosenbaum. 1987. Self-selection in Japanese junior high schools. *Sociology of Education* 60(3): 168–180.

Keddie, Nell. 1971. "Classroom Knowledge." In *Knowledge and Control*, edited by M. F. D. Young, 133–150. London: Collier-Macmillan.

Kehliher, A. 1931. *A Critical Study of Homogeneous Grouping*. New York: Teachers College Press.

Kerckhoff, Alan C. 1986. Effects of ability grouping in British secondary schools. *American Sociological Review* 51(6): 842–858.

Kifer, Edward. In press. "Opportunities, Talents and Participation." In *Second International Mathematics Study: Student Growth and Classroom Process in the Lower Secondary Schools*, edited by Leigh Burstein. London: Pergamon.

Kliebard, Herbert M. 1975. "Persistent Curriculum Issues in Historical Perspective." In *Curriculum Theorizing: The Reconceptualists*, edited by William Pinar, 39–50. Berkeley, CA: McCutchan.

Kliebard, Herbert M. 1977. Curriculum theory: Give me a "for instance." *Curriculum Inquiry* 6(4): 257–269.

Kliebard, Herbert M. 1979a. The drive for curriculum change in the

United States, 1890–1958. I—The ideological roots of curriculum as a field of specialization. *Curriculum Studies* 11(3): 191–202.

Kliebard, Herbert M. 1979b. The drive for curriculum change in the United States, 1890–1958. II—From local reform to a national preoccupation. *Curriculum Studies* 11(4): 273–286.

Kliebard, Herbert M. 1986. *The Struggle for the American Curriculum*. London: Routledge & Kegan Paul.

Kliebard, Herbert M. 1988a. "Fads, Fashions, and Rituals: The Instability of Curriculum Change." In *Critical Issues in Curriculum. Eighty-seventh Yearbook of the National Society for the Study of Education*, Part I, edited by Laurel Tanner, 16–34. Chicago: University of Chicago Press.

Kliebard, Herbert M. 1988b. "The Liberal Arts Curriculum and Its Enemies: The Effort to Redefine General Education." In *Cultural Literacy and the Idea of General Education. Eighty-seventh Yearbook of the National Society for the Study of Education*, Part II, Westbury, edited by Ian Westbury and Alan Purves, 29–61. Chicago: University of Chicago Press.

Kliebard, Herbert M., and B. M. Franklin. 1983. "The course of the course of study history of curriculum." In *Historical Inquiry in Education: A Research Agenda*, edited by J. H. Best, 138–157. Washington, DC: American Educational Research Association.

Krug, Edward A. 1960. *The Secondary School Curriculum*. New York: Harper & Brothers.

Krug, Edward A. 1964. *The Shaping of the American High School*. New York: Harper & Row.

Kulik, Chu-Lin, and James Kulik. 1982. Effects of ability grouping on secondary school students: A meta-analysis of evaluation findings. *American Educational Research Journal* 19(3): 415–428.

Labaree, David F. 1986, January. Curriculum, credentials, and the middle class: A case study of a nineteenth-century high school. *Sociology of Education* 59: 42–57.

Labaree, David F. 1987. Politics, markets, and the compromised curriculum. *Harvard Educational Review* 57(4): 483–494.

Labaree, David F. 1988. *The Making of an American High School: The Credentials Market and the Central High School of Philadelphia, 1838–1939*. New Haven, CT: Yale University Press.

Lacey, Colin. 1970. *Hightown Grammar: The School as a Social System*. Manchester, England: Manchester University Press.

Lampert, Margaret. 1985. How do teachers manage to teach? Perspectives on problems in practice. *Harvard Educational Review* 55: 178–194.

Lazerson, Marvin, and W. Norton Grubb. 1974. *American Education and Vocationalism: A Documentary History, 1870–1970*. New York: Teachers College Press, Columbia University.

Leacock, Eleanor. 1969. *Teaching and Learning in City Schools: A Comparative Study*. New York: Basic Books.

Lee, Valerie E. 1985. "Investigating the Relationship Between Social Class and Academic Achievement in Public and Catholic Schools: The Role of the Academic Organization of the School." Ph.D. dissertation, Harvard University, Cambridge, MA.

Lee, Valerie E., and Anthony S. Bryk. 1988, April. Curriculum tracking as mediating the social distribution of high school achievement. *Sociology of Education* 62: 78–94.

Lightfoot, Sarah. 1981. Portraits of exemplary secondary schools: Highland Park. *Daedalus* 110(4): 59–80.

Lightfoot, Sarah. 1983. *The Good High School: Portraits of Character and Culture*. New York: Basic Books.

Lortie, Daniel. 1975. *Schoolteachers: A Sociological Study*. Chicago: University of Chicago Press.

Lynd, Robert, and Helen Lynd. 1929. *Middletown: A Study in American Culture*. New York: Harcourt Brace and World.

McDermott, Ray P. 1987. The explanation of minority school failure, again. *Anthropology and Education Quarterly* 18(4): 361–364.

McDermott, Ray P., and J. Aron. 1978. "Pirandello in the Classroom: On the Possibility of Equal Educational Opportunity in American Culture." In *Futures of Education for Exceptional Children: Emerging Structures*, edited by Maynard Reynolds, 41–64. Minneapolis, MN: National Support Systems Project.

McKnight, Curtis C., F. J. Crosswhite, J. A. Dossey, Edward Kifer, J. O. Swafford, Kenneth J. Travers, and T. J. Cooney. 1987. *The Underachieving Curriculum: Assessing U.S. School Mathematics from an International Perspective*. Champaign, IL: Stipes Publishing.

McPartland, James M., and Robert L. Crain. 1987. "Evaluating the Trade-offs in Student Outcomes from Alternative School Organization Policies." In *The Social Organization of Schools: New Conceptualizations of the Learning Process*, edited by Maureen T. Hallinan, 131–156. New York: Plenum.

Martin, Jane R. 1981. "Needed: A New Paradigm for Liberal Education." In *Philosophy and Education. Eightieth Yearbook of the National Society for the Study of Education*, Part I, edited by Jonas Soltis, 37–59. Chicago: University of Chicago Press.

Massachusetts Advocacy Center. 1990. *Locked In; Locked Out*. Boston: Massachusetts Advocacy Center.

Mehan, Hugh. 1981. "The Ethnography of Bilingual Education." In *Culture and the Bilingual Classroom: Studies in Classroom Ethnography*, edited by H. Trueba, G. Guthrie, and K. Au, 36–55. Rowley, MA: Newbury House.

Metz, Mary H. 1978. *Classrooms and Corridors: The Crisis of Authority in Desegregated Secondary Schools*. Berkeley: University of California Press.

Metz, Mary H. 1983, February. Sources of constructive social relations in an urban magnet school. *American Journal of Education* 91: 202–245.

Metz, Mary H. 1986. *Different by Design: The Context and Character of Three Magnet Schools*. New York: Routledge & Kegan Paul.

Metz, Mary H. 1990. "Real school: A Universal Drama Amid Disparate Experiences." In *Education Politics for the New Century*, edited by Douglas E. Mitchell and Margaret E. Goertz, 75–92. London: Falmer.

Meyer, John W. 1980. "Levels of the Educational System and Schooling Effects." In *The Analysis of Educational Productivity*. Vol. 2, *Issues in Macroanalysis*, edited by C. E. Bidwell and D. M. Windham, 15–63. Cambridge, MA: Ballinger.

Meyer, John W. 1987. "Implications of an Institutional View of Education for the Study of Educational Effects." In *The Social Organization of Schools: New Conceptualizations of the Learning Process*, edited by Maureen T. Hallinan, 157–175. New York: Plenum.

Meyer, John W., and Brian Rowan. 1978. "The Structure of Educational Organizations." In *Environments and Organizations*, edited by Marshall Meyer, 233–263. San Francisco, CA: Jossey-Bass.

Miller, W. S., and H. J. Otto. 1930. Analysis of experimental studies of homogeneous grouping. *Journal of Educational Research* 21(2): 95–102.

Mirel, J. E., and D. L. Angus. 1986. The rising tide of custodialism: Enrollment increases and curriculum reform in Detroit, 1928–1940. *Issues in Education* 4(2): 101–120.

Mitchell, Verney, and Charles Benson. 1989. *Exemplary Urban Career-oriented High Schools*. Berkeley, CA: National Center for Research in Vocational Education.

Moll, Luis, and Stephen Diaz. 1987. Change as the goal of educational research. *Anthropology and Education Quarterly* 18(4): 300–311.

Moore, Don, and Suzanne Davenport. 1988. *The New Improved Sorting Machine*. Madison, WI: National Center on Effective Secondary Schools.

Murphy, Joseph, and P. Hallinger. 1989. Equity as access to learning: Curricular and instructional treatment differences. *Journal of Curriculum Studies* 21(2): 129–149.

Murphy, Joseph, T. Hull, and A. Walker. 1987. Academic drift and curricular debris: An analysis of course-taking patterns in high school with implications for local policy makers. *Journal of Curriculum Studies* 19(4): 341–360.

Nasaw, David 1979. *Schooled to Order: A Social History of Public Schooling in the United States*. New York: Oxford University Press.

National Center for Educational Statistics. 1985a. *Analysis of Course Offerings and Enrollments as Related to School Characteristics*. Washington, DC: U.S. Government Printing Office.

National Center for Educational Statistics. 1985b. *High School and Beyond: An Analysis of Course-taking Patterns in Secondary Schools as Related to Student Characteristics*. Washington, DC: U.S. Government Printing Office.

National Commission on Excellence in Education. 1983. *A Nation at Risk*. Washington, DC: U.S. Government Printing Office.

Nevi, C. 1987, March. In defense of tracking. *Educational Leadership* 44: 24–26.

Newmann, Fred M., and J. A. Thompson. 1987. *Effects of Cooperative Learning in Secondary Schools*. Madison: Wisconsin Center for Education Research.

Noblit, George 1987. "Ideological Purity and Variety in Effective Middle Schools." In *Schooling in Social Context: Qualitative Studies*, edited by George Noblit and William Pink, 203–217. Norwood, NJ: Ablex.

Nystrand, Martin, and Adam Gamoran. 1988. *A Study of Instruction as Discourse*. Madison: Wisconsin Center for Education Research.

Oakes, Jeannie. 1983. Limiting opportunity: Student race and curricular differences in secondary vocational education. *American Journal of Education* 91(3): 801–820.

Oakes, Jeannie. 1985. *Keeping Track: How Schools Structure Inequality*. New Haven, CT: Yale University Press.

Oakes, Jeannie. 1986. "Beyond Tinkering: The Reconstruction of Vocational Education." In *Re-visioning Vocational Education in the Secondary School*, edited by G. Copa, J. Plihal, and M. Johnson, 65–84. St. Paul: University of Minnesota Press.

Oakes, Jeannie. 1987a. "Tracking: Beliefs, Practices, and Consequences." In *Social Issues and Education: Challenge and Responsibility*, edited by A. Molnar, 15–29. Arlington, VA: Association for Supervision and Curriculum Development.

Oakes, Jeannie. 1987b. Tracking in secondary schools: A contextual perspective. *Educational Psychologist* 22(2): 129–153.

Oakes, Jeannie. 1990a. *Lost Talent: The Underparticipation of Women, Minorities, and Disabled Persons in Science*. Santa Monica, CA: Rand.

Oakes, Jeannie. 1990b. *Multiplying Inequalities: The Effects of Race, Social Class, and Tracking on Opportunities to Learn Math and Science*. Santa Monica, CA: Rand.

Oakes, Jeannie, and Martin Lipton. 1990. "Tracking and Ability Grouping: A Structural Barrier to Access to Knowledge." In *Access to Knowledge*, edited by John I. Goodlad, 187–204. New York: College Entrance Examination Board.

Oakes, Jeannie, Molly J. Selvin, Lynn Karoly, and Gretchen Guiton. 1991. *Educational Matchmaking: Toward a Better Understanding of Curriculum and Tracking Decisions*. Santa Monica, CA: Rand.

Ogbu, John. 1978. *Minority Education and Caste: The American System in Cross-cultural Perspective*. New York: Academic Press.

Oswald, Hans, David P. Baker, and David L. Stevenson. 1988. School charter and parental management in West Germany. *Sociology of Education* 61(4): 255–265.

Page, Reba. 1987a. "Lower-Track Classes at a College-Preparatory School: A Caricature of Educational Encounters." In *Interpretive Ethnography of Education: At Home and Abroad*, edited by G. Spindler and L. Spindler, 447–472. Hillsdale, NJ: Erlbaum.

Page, Reba. 1987b. Teachers' perceptions of students: A link between classrooms, school cultures, and the social order. *Anthropology and Education Quarterly* 18(2): 77–99.

Page, Reba. 1989. The lower-track curriculum at a "heavenly" high school: "cycles of prejudice." *Journal of Curriculum Studies* 21(3): 197–221.

Page, Reba. 1990a. Cultures and curricula: Differences between and within schools. *Educational Foundations* 4(1): 49–76.

Page, Reba. 1990b. "A 'Relevant' Lesson: Defining the Lower-Track Student." In *Curriculum Differentiation: Interpretive Studies in U.S. Secondary Schools*, edited by Reba Page and Linda Valli, 17–44. Albany: State University of New York Press.

Page, Reba. In press. *Ambiguous Customs: An Ethnography of Lower-track Classrooms: An Educational Ethnography*. New York: Teachers College Press.

Page, Reba, and Linda Valli, eds. 1990. *Curriculum Differentiation: Interpretive Studies in U.S. Secondary Schools*. Albany: State University of New York Press.

Passow, A. Harold. 1975. Once again: Reforming secondary education. *Teachers College Record* 77(2): 161–187.

Passow, A. Harold. 1988. "Issues of Access to Knowledge: Grouping and Tracking." In *Critical Issues in Curriculum. Eighty-seventh Yearbook of the National Society for the Study of Education*, Part I, edited by Laurel Tanner, 205–225. Chicago: University of Chicago Press.

Persell, Caroline. 1977. *Education and Inequality: A Theoretical Synthesis*. New York: Free Press.

Petty, M. C. 1953. *Intraclass Grouping in the Elementary School*. Austin: University of Texas Press.

Powell, Arthur, Eleanor Farrar, and David K. Cohen. 1985. *The Shopping Mall High School*. Boston: Houghton Mifflin.

Raizen, Senta. 1989. *Reforming Education for Work: A Cognitive Science Perspective*. Berkeley, CA: National Center for Research in Vocational Education.

Ravitch, Diane. 1978. *The Revisionists Revised*. New York: Basic Books.

Rehberg, R. A., and E. R. Rosenthal. 1978. *Class and Merit in the American High School*. White Plains, NY: Longman.

Reid, William. In press. "The Ideology of Access in Comparative Perspective." In *Access and Achievement at Sixteen-plus*, edited by Clyde Chitty.

Riesman, David. 1950. *The Lonely Crowd: A Study of the Changing American Character*. New Haven, CT: Yale University Press.

Rist, Ray. 1970. Student social class and teacher expectations: The self-fulfilling prophecy in ghetto education. *Harvard Educational Review* 40(3): 411–451.

Rist, Ray. 1973. *The Urban School: Factory for Failure*. Cambridge, MA: MIT Press.

Rist, Ray. 1977. "On Understanding the Processes of Schooling: The Contributions of Labeling Theory." In *Power and Ideology in Education*, edited by Jerome Karabel and A. H. Halsey, 292–305. New York: Oxford University Press.

Rock, Donald A., H. I. Braun, Ruth B. Ekstrom, Margaret E. Goertz, J. Pollack, and P. R. Rosenbaum. 1985. *Study of Excellence in*

High School Education: Longitudinal Study, 1980–82. Final Report. Princeton, NJ: Educational Testing Service.

Rohlen, T. P. 1983. *Japan's High Schools*. Berkeley: University of California Press.

Rosenbaum, James E. 1976. *Making Inequality: The Hidden Curriculum of High School Tracking*. New York: Wiley.

Rosenbaum, James E. 1980a. "Social Implications of Educational Grouping." In *Review of Research in Education*, Vol. 8, edited by D. C. Berliner, 361–401. Washington, DC: American Educational Research Association.

Rosenbaum, James E. 1980b, April. Track misperceptions and frustrated college plans: An analysis of the effects of tracks and track perceptions in the National Longitudinal Survey. *Sociology of Education* 53: 74–88.

Rosenbaum, James E. 1986. "Institutional Career Structures and the Social Construction of Ability." In *Handbook of Theory and Research for the Sociology of Education*, edited by J. G. Richardson, 139–171. New York: Greenwood Press.

Rosenbaum, James E., and Takehiko Kariya. 1989. From high school to work: Market and institutional mechanisms in Japan. *American Journal of Sociology* 94(6): 1334–1365.

Rosenholtz, Susan, and C. Simpson. 1984. The formation of ability conceptions: Developmental trend or social construction. *Review of Educational Research* 54(1): 31–63.

Rowan, Brian, and A.W. Miracle, Jr. 1983, July. Systems of ability grouping and the stratification of achievement in elementary schools. *Sociology of Education* 56: 133–144.

Reubens, Beatrice G. 1975. "Vocational Education for All in High School?" In *Work and the Quality of Life*, edited by J. O'Toole, 299–337. Cambridge, MA: MIT Press.

Rugg, Harold. 1926. "A Century of Curriculum Construction in American Schools." In *Curriculum-making Past and Present. Twenty-sixth Yearbook of the National Society for the Study of Education*, Part I, edited by H. Rugg, 3–116. Bloomington, IN: Public Schools Publishing.

Rutter, Michael, B. Maughan, P. Mortimore, and J. Ouston. 1979. *Fifteen Thousand Hours: Secondary Schools and their Effects on Children*. Cambridge, MA: Harvard University Press.

Sanders, Nancy. 1990. "Tracking and Organizational Structure." In *Curriculum Differentiation: Interpretive Studies in U.S. Secondary Schools*, edited by Reba Page and Linda Valli, 207–230. Albany: State University of New York Press.

Sanders, Nancy, N. Stone, and J. LaFollette. 1987. *The California Curriculum Study: Paths through High School*. Sacramento: California State Department of Education.

Sarason, Seymour. 1982. *The Culture of the School and the Problem of Change*, 2nd ed. Boston: Allyn & Bacon.

Schafer, Walter E., and Carol Olexa. 1971. *Tracking and Opportunity*. Scranton, PA: Chandler.

Schlechty, Philip. 1976. *Teaching and Social Behavior: Toward an Organizational Theory of Instruction*. Boston: Allyn & Bacon.

Schneider, David. 1968. *American Kinship: A Cultural Account*. Englewood Cliffs, NJ: Prentice Hall.

Schwartz, Frances. 1981. Supporting or subverting learning: Peer group patterns in four tracked schools. *Anthropology and Education Quarterly* 12(2): 99–121.

Selden, Stephen. 1977. Conservative ideology and curriculum. *Educational Theory* 27(3): 205–222.

Selvin, Molly J., Jeannie Oakes, Sharon Hare, Kimberly Ramsey, and Diane Schoeff. 1990. *Who Gets What and Why: Curriculum Decisionmaking at 3 Comprehensive High Schools*. Santa Monica, CA: Rand.

Sharp, Rachel, and A. Green. 1975. *Education and Social Control: A Study in Progressive Primary Education*. London: Routledge & Kegan Paul.

Shavit, Y., and D. L. Featherman. 1988, January. Schooling, tracking, and teenage intelligence. *Sociology of Education* 61: 42–51.

Shavit, Y., and R. Williams. 1985, February. Ability grouping and contextual determinants of educational expectations in Israel. *American Sociological Review* 50: 62–73.

Sirotnik, Kenneth A., and Jeannie Oakes. 1986. "Critical Inquiry for School Renewal: Liberating Theory and Practice." In *Critical Perspectives on the Organization and Improvement of Schooling*, edited by K. Sirotnik and J. Oakes, 3–94. Bingham, MA: Kluwer-Nijhoff.

Sizer, Theodore. 1985. *Horace's Compromise: The Dilemma of the American High School*. Boston: Houghton Mifflin.

Slavin, Robert E. 1983. *Cooperative Learning*. White Plains, NY: Longman.

Slavin, Robert E. 1987a. Ability grouping and its alternatives: Must we track? *American Educator* 11(2): 32–36, 46–48.

Slavin, Robert E. 1987b. Ability grouping and student achievement in elementary schools: A best-evidence synthesis. *Review of Educational Research* 57(3): 293–336.

Slavin, Robert E. 1990. Achievement effects in ability grouping in secondary schools: A best evidence synthesis. *Review of Educational Research* 60(3): 471–499.

Sorensen, Aagee B. 1970, fall. Organizational differentiation of students and educational opportunity. *Sociology of Education* 43: 355–376.

Sorensen, Aagee B. 1987. "The Organizational Differentiation of Students in Schools as an Opportunity Structure." In *The Social Organization of Schools: New Conceptualizations of the Learning Process*, edited by Maureen T. Hallinan, 103–129. New York: Plenum.

Sorensen, Aagee B., and Maureen T. Hallinan. 1984. "Race Effects on the Assignment to Ability Groups." In *The Social Context of Instruction*, edited by Penelope L. Peterson, L. C. Wilkerson, and Maureen T. Hallinan, 85–103. Orlando, FL: Academic Press.

Sorensen, Aagee B., and Maureen T. Hallinan. 1986. Effects of ability grouping on growth in academic achievement. *American Educational Research Journal* 23(4): 519–542.

Spindler, Louise, and George Spindler. 1982. "Roger Harker and Schonhausen: From Familiar to Strange and Back Again." In *Doing the Ethnography of Schooling*, edited by George Spindler, 20–46. New York: Holt, Rinehart and Winston.

Spring, Joel. 1972. *Education and the Rise of the Corporate State*. Boston: Beacon Press.

Spring, Joel. 1976. *The Sorting Machine: National Educational Policy Since 1945*. New York: McKay.

Squires, James R. 1966. National study of high school English programs: A school for all seasons. *English Journal* 55(2): 282–290.

Stern, David, E. Gareth Hoachlander, Susan Choy, and Charles Benson. 1985. *One Million Hours a Day: Vocational Education in California Public Secondary Schools*. Berkeley: University of California School of Education.

Stinchcombe, Alan L. 1964. *Rebellion in a High School*. Chicago: Quadrangle Books.

Stout, J. E. 1921. *The Development of High School Curriculum in the North Central States from 1860 to 1918*. Chicago: University of Chicago.

Strike, Kenneth. 1983. Fairness and ability grouping. *Educational Theory* 33(3–4): 125–134.

Tanner, Daniel. 1972. *Secondary Education: Perspectives and Prospects*. New York: Macmillan.

Terman, Lewis. 1923. *Intelligence Tests and School Reorganization*. New York: World Book Company.

Trimble, Kim, and Robert L. Sinclair. 1986. *Ability Grouping and Differing Conditions for Learning: An Analysis of Content and*

Instruction in Ability-grouped Classes. Amherst: University of Massachusetts Center for Curriculum Studies.

Turner, Ralph. 1960. Modes of social ascent through education: Sponsored and contest mobility. *American Sociological Review* 25(6): 855–867.

Tyack, David. 1974. *The One Best System*. Cambridge, MA: Harvard University Press.

Uhl, W. 1927. *Secondary School Curriculum*, part 1. New York: Macmillan.

Valli, Linda. 1986. *Becoming Clerical Workers*. London: Routledge & Kegan Paul.

Valli, Linda. In press. "A Curriculum of Effort: Tracking Students in a Catholic High School." In *Curriculum Differentiation: Interpretive Studies in U.S. Secondary Schools*, edited by Reba Page and Linda Valli, 43–66. Albany: State University of New York Press.

Vanfossen, Beth E., J. D. Jones, and J. Z. Spade. 1987. Curriculum tracking and status maintenance. *Sociology of Education* 60(2): 104–122.

Varenne, Hervé. 1974. From grading and freedom of choice to ranking and segregation in an American high school. *Anthropology and Education Quarterly* 5(2): 9–15.

Varenne, Hervé. 1977. *Americans Together: Structured Diversity in a Midwestern Town*. New York: Teachers College Press.

Varenne, Hervé. 1982. "Jocks and Freaks: Social Interaction Among American Senior High School Students." In *Doing the Ethnography of Schooling*, edited by George Spindler, 210–235. New York: Holt, Rinehart and Winston.

Varenne, Hervé. 1983. *American School Language: Culturally Patterned Conflicts in a Suburban High School*. New York: Irvington.

Varenne, Hervé, and M. Kelly. 1976. Friendship and fairness: Ideological tensions in an American high school. *Teachers College Record* 77(4): 601–614.

Velez, W. 1985. Finishing college: The effects of college type. *Sociology of Education* 58(3): 191–200.

Vogel, E. 1965. *Japan's New Middle Class*. Berkeley: University of California Press.

Waitrowski, M. D., S. Hansell, C. R. Massey, and D. L. Wilson. 1982, February. Curriculum tracking and delinquency. *American Sociological Review* 47: 151–160.

Waller, Willard. 1932. *The Sociology of Teaching*. New York: Wiley.

Webb, Noreen M. 1982. Interaction and learning in small groups. *Review of Educational Research* 52(3): 421–455.

Wehlage, Gary. 1982. "The Purpose of Generalization in Field Study Research." In *The Myth of Educational Reform: A Study of School Response to a Program of Change*, edited by Thomas Popkewitz, Robert Tabachnick, and Gary Wehlage, 211–226. Madison: University of Wisconsin Press.

Wehlage, Gary, Calvin Stone, and Hebert Kliebard. 1980. *Dropouts and Schools: Case Studies of the Dilemmas Educators Face*. Madison: Wisconsin Governor's Employment and Training Office.

Wehlage, Gary, Calvin Stone, Nancy Lesko, Craig Nauman, and Reba Page. 1982. *Effective Programs for the Marginal High School Student*. Madison: Wisconsin Center for Educational Research.

Weick, Karl. 1976. Educational organizations as loosely coupled systems. *Administrative Science Quarterly* 21(1): 1–18.

Weinstein, Rhona S. 1976. Reading group membership in first grade: Teacher behaviors and pupil experience over time. *Journal of Educational Psychology* 68(1): 103–116.

Werthman, Carl. 1963. Delinquents in schools: A test for the legitimacy of authority. *Berkeley Journal of Sociology* 8: 39–60.

West, Parl. 1933. *A Study of Ability Grouping in the Elementary School*. New York: Teachers College Bureau of Publication.

Westbury, Ian. 1988a. How should we be judging the American high school? *Journal of Curriculum Studies* 20(4): 291–315.

Westbury, Ian. 1988b. "Who Can Be Taught What? General Education in the Secondary School." In *Cultural Literacy and the Idea of General Education. Eighty-seventh Yearbook of the National Society for the Study of Education*, Part II, edited by Ian Westbury and Alan Purves, 171–197. Chicago: University of Chicago Press.

Westbury, Ian, and Alan Purves, eds. 1988. *Cultural Literacy and the Idea of General Education. Eighty-seventh Yearbook of the National Society for the Study of Education*, Part II. Chicago: University of Chicago Press.

White, Mary. 1987. *The Japanese Educational Challenge*. New York: Free Press.

Wilcox, Kathleen. 1982. "Differential Socialization in the Classroom: Implications for Equal Opportunity." In *Doing the Ethnography of Schooling*, edited by George Spindler, 268–309. New York: Holt, Rinehart and Winston.

Williams, Raymond. 1973. *The Country and the City*. New York: Oxford University Press.

Willis, Paul. 1977. *Learning to Labor: How Working Class Kids Get Working Class Jobs*. Westmeed, England: Saxon House.

Wilson, Barry J., and Donald W. Schmits. 1978. What's new in ability grouping? *Phi Delta Kappan* 59(8): 535–536.

Wolfle, Lee. 1985. Postsecondary educational attainment among whites and blacks. *American Educational Research Journal* 22(4): 501–525.

Yogev, A. 1981, July. Determinants of early educational career in Israel: Further evidence for the sponsorship thesis. *Sociology of Education* 54: 181–195.

22

LOW-INCOME AFRICAN-AMERICAN CHILDREN AND PUBLIC SCHOOLING

Dorothy S. Strickland
RUTGERS UNIVERSITY

Carol Ascher
TEACHERS COLLEGE, COLUMBIA UNIVERSITY

Like all Americans, those of African-American descent place enormous faith in schooling as the road out of powerlessness and economic trouble and into mainstream jobs, political participation, and middle-class comforts. This belief holds despite their awareness that for black Americans, schooling does not yield economic well-being at the same rate as it does for whites. (The terms "African-American" and "black" are used interchangeably in this chapter.) And it holds despite a growing suspicion about the capacity of public education to teach them what they need to know, particularly if they are poor. Despite the promise of education as the great equalizer, schooling has generally not equalized opportunities for African-Americans. Though these same families are unlikely to be reassured by the fact that educators themselves have increasingly felt the pain of their failure to serve low-income black children, the fact is that for many, the school achievement of these children has become a template for the effectiveness of the public school system.

Despite the common use of the phrases "black children" or "African-American students" and the fact that data are often aggregated by race, not class, we must be clear at the outset that those black students who experience severe and enduring educational difficulties are the ones with little or no money, who most often live in neighborhoods with a high concentration of other poor families. Whatever differences in learning there may be among racial or ethnic groups, black middle-class children living in good neighborhoods do not have significantly more difficulty achieving in school than do white middle-class children. Standardized test scores, for example, show that there are substantial increases in performance for every $10,000 increase in family income (FairTest 1989). In fact, as the economic circumstances of middle-class blacks have improved and those of poor blacks have worsened, so the difference between the educational achievement of these two economic groups of African-Americans has increased. We do not deny the problems of middle-class black children living in good neighborhoods, who may be subjected to racism and to curricula that deny the contributions of African-Americans. We have, however, decided to focus our attention primarily on poor black children living in urban areas.

We therefore begin by describing briefly who these poor and low-income black children are, analyzing aspects of their economic and social backgrounds as well as their public schools, which may place them at educational risk. Then we survey some of the alternative explanations that have evolved for black students' strengths and difficulties in school. Finally, we offer a review of current educational reforms and pedagogical experiments affecting low-income black students and make recommendations for change.

BLACK CHILDREN IN PERIL

More than any other ethnic group, African-Americans have become an urban population—about 60 percent lived in central cities in 1980 (Bureau of the Census 1987). The concentration of blacks in urban areas has had several consequences. First, a number of cities have acquired large black populations: In 1980, 17 cities had black populations of 50 percent or more (Bureau of the Census 1987). This high density of urban blacks, combined with rapidly growing urban Hispanic populations, has resulted in highly segregated, largely poor neighborhoods, making schools difficult to desegregate.

There are approximately 9.7 million black children in this country, of which nearly 1 in 2 are poor—or 3 times the proportion among white children. Between 1973 and 1986, the poverty rate for young black families with parents under age 25 rose from 44 to 62 percent. And among single-parent black families—usually female-headed—⅔ of the children live in poverty (National Black Child Development Institute 1989).

Poverty among black children also tends to be more severe and longer-lasting than it is among white children. Although white children in one survey were poor on an average of less than a year during their first 15 years of life, black children were poor 5.4 years of their first 15 years. In all, roughly 1 in 4 black children were poor for 10 years or more, whereas only 1 in 200 white children were poor for that long (Orland 1989).

In contrast to poor white children, who often live in mixed neighborhoods, black children who are poor also tend to live in high-poverty urban ghettoes. Between 1970 and 1980, the percentage of people living in such high-poverty areas increased among both whites and blacks. However, an analysis of five cities shows that although the proportion of poor whites living in such neighborhoods increased 24 percent in this period, the percentage of blacks increased by 164 percent. Thus, as of 1980, only 7 percent of the nation's poor white population but 39 percent of all poor blacks lived in high-poverty areas (Wilson 1987, 46, 58).

In fact, these high-poverty areas do not merely house the poor; a significant number of nonpoor, low-status minorities also live there, and so their life chances are deeply affected as well. Nationwide, as the Children's Defense Fund (1985, 104) reports, "Black households are more likely than white households to live in neighborhoods inflicted with crime, trash, and abandoned buildings, and to live with unsatisfactory police protection, health services, public elementary schools, and outdoor recreational facilities." An analysis of housing patterns in Chicago makes clear that the afflictions of poor neighborhoods are not only the bane of poor blacks: Although 42 percent of Chicago's black children are poor, 71 percent of Chicago's black children live in high-poverty areas (Neckerman and Wilson 1988). Since attending school in a high-poverty neighborhood is more detrimental to learning than being poor but attending school in a nonpoverty area, even nonpoor black ghetto dwellers are still placed at serious educational risk (Orland 1989).

The dual plight of poverty and discrimination that exists for many black families can also be seen in housing. Black children, according to a study of housing in Michigan, are twice as likely as white children to live in inadequate conditions. Their housing, which is much more likely to be rented, tends also to be older, more crowded, and more deteriorated than that of whites. Poor insulation and faulty wiring lead to many fire-related accidents and deaths. And three times as many black as white families live without cars or telephones (Michigan Interagency Committee on the Black Child 1987).

The Black Underclass

Both educators and social critics have recently argued that demographic and employment shifts have created a new, more severe poverty in the high-poverty areas of inner cities. Because both the circumstances and the prospects of many who live in these high-poverty neighborhoods are significantly bleaker than those of previous generations, they have been called an underclass. For economic, sociological, and psychological reasons, individuals who are part of this underclass have little chance of sustained employment and often live on welfare and nonlegal means; moreover, without a significant change in our country's economy, public policy, or system of public education, their children are likely to be condemned to the same fate.

Along with the decline in our urban, industrial economy and the removal of many unskilled jobs from the cities, one of the most important of the demographic shifts to cause this new underclass has been the depletion of middle- and working-class black families from inner-city neighborhoods. This shift has deprived those remaining families of contact with regularly employed families, job networks, other middle-class resources, and models for diligence and mobility—in a word, realistic hope. As Wilson (1987) writes,

> in such neighborhoods the chances are overwhelming that children will seldom interact on a sustained basis with people who are employed or with families that have a steady breadwinner. The net effect is that joblessness, as a way of life, takes on a different social meaning; the relationship between schooling and postschool employment takes on a different meaning. (57)

Obviously, the social isolation of such neighborhoods generates behavior, such as tardiness and absenteeism, that is conducive to neither school success nor good work histories. Moreover, the absence of models who might show the benefits of disciplined studying means that schoolwork too often takes place amid many distractions but very little reinforcement.

Other demographic characteristics are associated with the pathology and dislocations of these high-poverty, inner-city neighborhoods. One interesting characteristic is the disproportionate numbers of young people, particularly among minorities, which is caused partly by in-migration and partly by higher birth rates than in middle-class areas. As Wilson (1987) notes, "The fact that only 58 percent of all black young adult males, 34 percent of all black males aged eighteen to nineteen, and 16 percent of those aged sixteen to seventeen were employed in 1984 reveals a problem of joblessness for young black men that has reached catastrophic proportions'' (43). This predominance of unemployed youths in itself sets off sudden and substantial increases in such problems as crime, addiction, and welfare dependency. Not surprisingly, although African-Americans constitute 13 percent of the population in cities, they account for over half of all city arrests for violent crimes. Clearly, the highest rates of violent crimes occur in underclass communities (22).

Black Men, Low Wages, and Joblessness

In 1986, for the first time, the number of employed black men was less than the number of employed black women; in contrast, there were over 12 million more white male than white female workers (Edelman 1987).

The transformation of urban economies is largely responsible for this serious disjuncture between the skills of black men and their employment possibilities. Although black males have steadily increased their educational attainment over the past two decades, those with high school degrees are concentrated in northern and midwestern cities, where employment opportunities have declined the fastest, and are least concentrated in those cities that have experienced economic expansion (Center on Budget and Policy Priorities 1988; Wilson 1987). Despite substantial increases in lower-skilled, entry-level jobs, these have occurred largely in the suburbs, exurbs, and nonmetropolitan areas, far removed from the urban ghettoes (Kasarda 1986). As a result, even when black males are employed, their wages tend to be extremely depressed. Table 22–1 shows the enormous loss in earnings experienced by young blacks since 1973, particularly those with minimum education, compared with other groups.

As both Edelman (1987) and Wilson (1987) have pointed out, there is a strong relationship between black male joblessness and the declining marriage rates among blacks. For example, in 1974 nearly 29.2 percent of all black men aged 20 to 24 were married and living with their spouses, but by 1984 only 8.6 percent of men in that age group were married. Among whites, although the percentages of young married men had also gone down, the decline was from 40.5 percent to 23.9 percent (Berlin and Sum 1988, 15). This significantly lower marriage rate among black males has two correlates: Fewer single black women become pregnant with a child that they intend to bear, and fewer black pregnant women, intent on bearing their child, marry before giving birth (Edelman 1987).

Poverty and the Female-Headed Family

The bleak prospects faced by single-parent families is the other side of the increasingly important second income in maintaining a decent family standard of living. Black children are 3 times as likely as white children to live in female-headed families. This statistic is important because black children in young female-headed households are the poorest in the nation (Edelman 1987).

Despite being the sole wage earners, black women workers aged 20 to 24 experienced major losses in wages between 1973 and 1984 (Witt 1988). In 1982, over 55 percent of all black female-headed families were poor (Wilson 1987), and the percentage was significantly higher among young black female-headed families: Over 85 percent of all black female-headed families in which the woman was under 25 were poor in 1983 (Edelman 1987). In an analysis of homeless families in several Boston shelters, almost 90 percent of the families were headed by a single mother; about 50 percent were receiving Aid to Families with Dependent Children (AFDC) (Bassuk and Rubin 1987).

Partly because the tendency to become pregnant as a teenager is related to being poor, black teenagers are 5 times as likely as white teengers to become unwed mothers (Edelman 1987, 57). Moreover, the problems of poverty stemming from adolescent pregnancy and parenting among black females are particularly severe. In the short run, adolescent parenting makes it more difficult for the black mother and child to move out of poverty: 65 percent of teen hourly workers and 29 percent of hourly workers in their early 20s could not earn sufficient wages to raise an intact, one-income family with a child out of poverty in 1984 (57). Although teenage pregnancy need not condemn black women to poverty, particularly if they later marry, samples suggest that these women are less likely to achieve educationally, more likely to receive welfare, and less likely to be married than later childbearers (Furstenberg, Brooks-Gunn, and Morgan 1987, 133). Over the long run, teenage mothers have children who become teenage mothers, and women

TABLE 22–1. Trends in Real Mean Annual Earnings of 20- to 24-Year-Old Males, 1973–84, by Educational Attainment and Race/Ethnic Group, in 1984 Dollars (Berlin and Sum 1988, 9)

Level of Education	Real Mean Earnings ($) of All (20–24) 1973	1984	% Change in Earnings, 1974–84 All	White	Black	Hispanic
No diploma	11,210	6,552	−41.6	−38.7	−61.3	−38.6
H.s. graduate	14,242	10,020	−30.1	−26.1	−52.2	−28.1
Some college	12,386	9,153	−26.1	−22.0	−50.3	−31.6
College grad.	12,970	12,443	−11.0	−12.2	+16.3	−14.9

who were on welfare as a child are more likely to go on welfare in their childbearing years, thus perpetuating the underclass phenomenon (Edelman 1987; Furstenberg, Brooks-Gunn, and Morgan 1987).

Ironically, in a period of declining wages and growing joblessness, there has also been decreasing government support in both cash and noncash benefit programs. Whereas in 1979 cash benefit programs lifted out of poverty 14.7 percent of the black female-headed families with children who would otherwise have been poor, by 1987 only 7.3 percent of these families were being rescued from poverty by such programs. If these programs had continued to have the same antipoverty impact in 1987 as they had had in 1979, 143,000 fewer black families with children would have been poor in 1987 (Center on Budget and Policy Priorities 1988, A–3). Not only have there been cuts in specific benefit programs such as food stamps and unemployment insurance, but also AFDC has lagged behind inflation. "In 1986, combined AFDC and food-stamp benefits were below the poverty level in every state and less than 75 percent of the poverty level in forty states" (Edelman 1987, 69).

SCHOOLING IN HIGH-POVERTY NEIGHBORHOODS

State fiscal equity cases have changed the ways in which schools are financed and have tended to reassure educators and the general public that the vast differences that once existed among schools in funding, physical facilities, equipment, and professional staff have been resolved. At the same time, our period of decreasing federal funds, widening pressure on state monies, and declining urban budgets has generally made the question of fiscal improvement appear to be moot. Yet a variety of structural and economic constraints continue to cause grave differences between the funding of urban public schools and that of public schools in suburban and other nonurban areas. To take one of the most obvious examples, state aid to school districts is generally calculated by average daily attendance (ADA) data, which tend to discriminate against urban districts with their high absentee rates. The New York City Board of Education calculates that the ADA formula excludes approximately 15 percent of its students from state aid (Ascher 1989). Moreover, recent court cases, most notably in Los Angeles and Miami–Dade County, suggest that even within urban school districts, schools serving poor, minority neighborhoods have fewer resources, poorer facilities, and less-well-trained teachers than those serving middle-class neighborhoods.

Combined with the loss of hope among many black educators in attaining the goals of desegregation, the economic straits of low-income schools have caused a shift in the focus of discussion to what, if anything, ghetto schools—as they exist—can do for black students. The tendency has been to identify those schools in poor neighborhoods that have made a difference—often because the principal was active, the teachers committed and caring, and the school climate improved. That is, as the effective-schools people have claimed, achievement for black students can be increased without real changes in school financing or school composition (Edmonds 1982).

Although we later suggest that some school management and pedagogical strategies appear more effective than others, here it is important to establish the very real and severe differences between the achievement that can be anticipated in schools in high-poverty, urban areas and in schools in middle-class neighborhoods. For instance, new research indicates the strong relationship between poverty and achievement at the school-building level. In other words, a nonpoor student in a poor school is actually more likely to be a low achiever than is a poor student in a low-poverty school, and this difference is not explained solely by the different types of students attending these schools but must be understood as a "unique school effect" on achievement (Orland 1989).

Because of the severe problems of urban school financing, schools in poor, inner-city neighborhoods are not as pleasant either to teach in or to learn in as are schools in middle-class neighborhoods (Ascher 1989; Corcoran, Walker, and White 1988). The former are often deteriorated, poorly maintained, and unclean; facilities such as laboratories, libraries, and auditoriums are meager or even absent (Carnegie Foundation for the Advancement of Teaching 1988). Black and Hispanic schools in urban school districts not only serve very disproportionate numbers of poor children but also continue to do much worse than white schools in academic achievement and graduation rates, which are as much measures of academic opportunity as of student success (Orfield and Monford 1988). Since the same students who experience long-term poverty also tend to attend high-poverty schools, these students are in effect faced with a double liability. Moreover, because many nonpoor blacks live in high-poverty areas, these students are also suffering from severe disadvantages in low-income schools. As Berlin and Sum (1988) point out, "American rhetoric continues its slogans about education as the great equalizer. But so long as severe race and class segregation continues to characterize living patterns, inequities will persist in American schooling, from lower expectations for student performance to unequal school finance" (26).

Black Educational Isolation

Because blacks remain less suburbanized than other minority groups, and because even in the suburbs their segregation remains quite high, the vast majority of blacks attending school tend to be very highly segregated from non-Hispanic whites (Massey and Denton 1988). Although the level of desegregation in metropolitan areas can differ within a state, state levels of desegregation reflect the level of desegregation in the states' major cities. States with the greatest desegregation of black students are not those with the smallest black population but rather those that have had extensive court-ordered busing, exchanging metropolitan and suburban area students. These more successfully desegregated districts are generally in the South. Nevertheless, in the South and border regions, where a substantial proportion of black students live, racial segregation increased in the 1980s in several cities, including Atlanta, Augusta, Little Rock, San Antonio, Tampa, and Baltimore, largely because of the growth of black inner-city populations.

Among the states remaining most segregated are those with large urban populations, fragmented school districts, and large losses in white enrollment. The Northeast is currently the most segregated region, and New York is the most segregated state in the region—a state whose schools have, in fact, become more racially segregated in the 1980s. Black students in New York City, which has never had a significant busing or city-suburban plan, are in schools that are on the average 89 percent nonwhite; and black students in Newark, Chicago, and Detroit are in schools that are 91 percent nonwhite. In the West, both San Francisco and Los Angeles became more segregated for black students in the 1980s (Orfield, Monford, and George 1987).

Thus, as of 1986–1987, about 1/5 of the large urban districts nationally had ¾ or more of their black students in intensely segregated schools, with 90 to 100 percent minority students; at the other end, only 1/6 of these districts had as many as ½ of their black students in schools with a white majority (Orfield and Monford 1988).

Even in legally desegrated schools, a number of school management practices often resegregate black students along racial and economic lines and re-create the advantages of white middle-class students in the school (Moore and Iadicola 1978; Oakes 1985). Among these practices are testing procedures aimed at sorting students into homogeneous ability groups, the tracking of students into upper and lower tracks, the inequitable funneling of black students into "special education classes," and suspension and expulsion policies that are used most heavily with black, male students. Although black students start school at only a slight academic disadvantage in comparison to whites, by the third grade there are beginning to be serious differences, and the average reading scores of black students decline slightly with age. Black children are more than 3 times as likely as white children to be placed in classes for the educably mentally retarded and only ⅓ as likely to be admitted to classes for the gifted and talented. Black students, particularly black females, are more likely than whites to end their high school careers in vocational rather than academic programs; and black males are almost twice as likely as white students to be suspended or corporally punished (Children's Defense Fund 1985). Finally, as we shall indicate more fully, black children tend to fill the compensatory education programs, whose modest achievement gains are often at the expense of stigma and further segregation (Ascher 1987a).

In reality, testing, tracking, and disciplinary policies are all interrelated, and all reinforce class and race divisions. Standardized tests often result in the disproportionate placement of minorities in lower-track classes, in part because these tests produce scores that reflect social class and were designed to serve the tracking model, which in itself can be seen simultaneously as a reflection of society's class structure and a means of socializing students into that structure (Oakes 1985). In fact, in their study of resegregation practices, Cook, Eyler, and Ward (1981) found evidence that educators' use of tracking and rigid ability grouping reflected their attitudes toward integration: "While the use of tracking and grouping is an approach to dealing with diversity that antedates desegregation, there is reason to believe that its resegregative effects are not entirely accidental" (20). Oakes also argues that the pattern of white students disproportionately assigned to high-track classes and minority students disproportionately assigned to low-track classes is most consistent in schools where minority students are also poor. Finally, it is well established that black males are disproportionately suspended and expelled from schools (Bickel 1980; Moody 1980). Not surprisingly, schools that discipline a high proportion of black males with suspensions and expulsions share a number of characteristics, including low administrative support for school desegregation, poor interracial environment, and the predominance of whites in the school (Bennett and Harris 1982).

"Barriers to Excellence": Academic Evaluation and Placement

Educators and researchers who are advocates for black children increasingly argue that testing and other evaluative practices are not geared toward improving learning. Instead, they perpetuate inequality by "actively contributing to the very problems experienced by minority students" since they are "the vehicle by which differential opportunity and reward can be explained and justified" (Hurtado and Haney 1989, 172). Standardized tests serve a number of bureaucratic functions: They make schools and districts "accountable" to the state, they provide a mechanism to sort students into homogeneous groupings within schools, and they point to academic priorities and so increasingly drive curriculum. Although standardized intelligence and achievement tests may assess students' knowledge in a narrow range of areas or their ability to perform certain basic skills and tasks, these tests are no better at predicting future performance than are grades, and they are generally not good diagnostic devices for eliciting what students need to learn (Ascher 1990). In fact, an entirely different system of testing is currently being evolved by researchers who want to understand how different students learn best or how instruction can be designed to meet varied approaches to understanding or different learning styles (Brown, Campione, Webber, and McGilly 1989; Resnick and Resnick 1989).

A recent national survey of testing suggests that standardized tests play a more powerful role in low-socioeconomic schools than in high-socioeconomic schools and that the use of such tests tends to limit instruction to a "measurement-driven" curriculum in schools serving poor students (Dorr-Bremme and Herman 1986). Moreover, testing has a particularly narrowing effect on curriculum in the lower tracks, so that students learn "the basics" through rote, fragmented, and decontextualized instruction (Oakes 1985).

Thus, African-American children are disproportionately labeled academically inadequate by the tests, which in turn justify placement in ability groupings that both stigmatize and deprive these children of rich learning experiences. In a study of literacy practices in kindergarten classrooms, black, urban children were more likely to receive instruction through drill on workbooks and worksheets than were their counterparts in suburban and rural settings. Experiences with children's literature, language experience charts, and opportunities to use writing materials independently were characteristic of suburban and rural classrooms. Because literacy was so well integrated throughout the curriculum, children in the suburban and rural classrooms actually spent more time on reading and writing than did the urban children. Equally important, the instruction was meaningful and appropriate to the age level (Strickland and Ogle 1990). "Barriers to excellence" has become a general term for the critique of structures and practices such as testing and tracking that obstruct, rather than promote, learning (National Coalition of Advocates for Students 1985).

Despite the nearly universal use of tracking in U.S. schools today, a number of strong, by now well-known, pedagogical arguments have been made against it. Most important, tracking is not a pedagogically sound practice. Instead of effectively matching instruction and resources with students' needs, tracking places students in rigid streams that rarely offer instruction directly related to the skills that need remediation and that have few options for changing tracks, should the students show improvement. Not surprisingly, students who are confined to lower tracks have more negative self-perceptions and lower educational aspirations. Lower-track students are also more alienated from school, misbehave more in classes, are more delinquent outside of school, and have higher dropout rates (Oakes 1985). These are all hazards, of course, for which low-income black students are particularly at risk—in large measure because of their tendency to be placed in low tracks. For a complete discussion of the problems associated with tracking, see the chapter by Jeannie Oakes, Adam Gamoran, and Reba Page in this *Handbook*.

WHY LOW-INCOME BLACK CHILDREN ARE AT RISK—SOME ALTERNATE EXPLANATIONS

Over the years, several dominant lines of explanation have emerged for the trouble low-income black children apparently experience in school: These can be characterized as genetic endowment, linguistic differences, cultural dissonance, societal racism, the effects of poverty, and inferior education.

Genetic Differences

The theory of genetic differences, which surfaces from time to time, especially in conservative circles, causes great distress in the African-American community as well as among liberal educators. In fact, the fear that surrounds this explanation makes it difficult to discuss. However, despite a minority of scholars who believe that they have found IQ differences between blacks and whites to be linked to heredity (see, e.g., Jensen 1985), the evidence in this direction is insupportable. No research shows that specific genes linked to lower IQ are found in higher proportion among blacks than among whites. Nor do any studies show that specific genes controlling conceptual skills, abstract reasoning, or problem solving are found in higher proportion among whites than blacks (Ogbu 1986).

Whatever its origins, however, its use is clear: A genetic explanation justifies decreasing educational services and continuing a stratified educational system. The belief that little can be done for black students because of their inferior heredity leads, in fact, to a position not unlike that of those who argue that little can be done for those "disadvantaged" by too disastrous an environment. For hereditarians, as for conservative environmentalists, educational standards are "diluted" only when the schools attempt to deal with students "on the margins."

Linguistic Differences

Differences between the language black children speak at home and in their neighborhood and the standard English they are required to use at school has been proposed as a possible cause of school failure (Dillard 1972; Fasold and Wolfram 1970; Labov 1966). The argument here has several strands. One is that black children are punished and stigmatized for using nonstandard English because teachers do not understand them, believe their language is inferior, or simply want to enforce the dominance of standard English. Orr (1987) even suggests that the use of Black English Vernacular affects the way black children think, inhibiting their ability to understand relationships in math and science. Certainly, for many years Black English was considered a haphazard, substandard language system, and it is only in the past two decades that research has shown it to be a systematic and highly predictable form of language that can accommodate all levels of thought (Cullinan 1974, 7). Another line of argument is that Black English interferes cognitively with black students' grasp of standard English grammar, making it even more difficult for them to learn to read and write in standard English than for students who come from entirely different language backgrounds.

For a brief period, a number of educators tried to develop curriculum materials and to offer instruction in black English. However, the method did not lead to significant improvements in black children's achievement; moreover, the concensus was that these students need to master standard English to succeed in mainstream society. Currently, few educators promote teaching in Black English, although most advocate respect for Black English as a dialect (Williams, Hopper, and Natalicio 1977).

Cultural Dissonance

There are two theories of cultural dissonance, one that ascribes black students' learning problems to the deprivations of black culture, and another that simply speaks of differences in cultural styles. According to the former, African-American children, particularly from low-income families, do not receive adequate stimulation from their parents (usually their mothers) during their early preschool years (Hess and Shipman 1965). This deprivation can be seen most dramatically when compared with the child-rearing styles of middle-class mothers. This deprivation model was instrumental in establishing Head Start and continues to be the rationale for various preschool efforts, which attempt early remediation in cognitive and social skills. Whether or not the theory is correct, preschool programs tend to have positive effects.

A second line of argument is that black children are culturally different, not deprived. Here, the reasoning is that on the one hand, standardized tests, grades, and other academic evaluations are "biased" against the culture of the black child, and on the other, blacks' "cultural style" negatively affects how they perform on tests and in other school situations that are geared to the middle-class child (Kochman 1989).

For a time, "culture-fair" tests were tried, but they were very hard to create and score. Moreover, since they do not predict students' performance in our current schools, they were given up as useless. Currently, the more modest goal is simply to decrease race and class bias in standardized tests.

At the same time, the concept of different learning styles continues to generate a good deal of interest and speculation, although research is still needed to inform educational practice. It is now well accepted that individuals have many different learning styles and that the most successful individuals are those who are able to work in their preferred styles. Although most academic instruction is said to value an analytical learning style, there is some research suggesting that black children are more at ease with a rational learning style that emphasizes visual and audio stimuli (Lee 1985). It is also said that because black students are accustomed to intense interaction at home, they are more comfortable with highly interactive learning styles (Hale 1982). Finally, some researchers have shown that black students learn more easily when provided with "hands-on" experiences. What this means, of course, is that incompatibilities between the learning styles that predominate in most classrooms and those with which many black students do best may be partly responsible for their lower achievement.

Societal Racism

The argument that there can be no educational equality while black students learn in segregated schools formed the moral energy behind *Brown* v. *Topeka Board of Education* 35 years ago. Despite important desegregation legislation and three decades of programmatic change to make schooling for all students integrated and equitable, it is not hard to see continuing instances of both personal and institutional racism in education. Nor is education the only sphere in which blacks continue to fight for equal treatment. Ogbu (1986) uses the phrase "castelike minorities" to distinguish blacks, Hispanics, and Native Americans, who historically were, he says, forcefully removed from their native homes or taken over by conquest, from immigrant or "autonomous minorities" such as Jews or Asians, who have exercised some choice in emigrating to this country. Whereas castelike minorities are treated as "less desirable neighbors, employees, workmates, and schoolmates" and so face a segmented job market, low wages, and more stringent rules for employment than whites, immigrant and autonomous minorities are not forced across the board to play specialized or denigrated social roles.

Not surprisingly, the objective situation of segregation and inequality has its subjective correlates: The perception of societal racism on the part of blacks and other castelike minorities has led to certain beliefs that may in themselves now work against them. For example, the reality of discrimination in education and employment fosters the view that efforts at self-betterment will not necessarily be worth it. In education, the fact that black school relations are "riddled with conflicts and suspicion, make it difficult for blacks to internalize the schools' goals, standards, and teaching and learning approaches" (Ogbu 1986, 49).

In fact, as Fordham and Ogbu (1986, 176) have discovered, black students often do poorly in school because of a complicated, self-imposed "anti-achievement ethic." This ethic results from a complicated source: White refusal to acknowledge their intellectual ability over the years has led to self-doubt and a sense that achievement is the province of whites. This belief in turn generates peer pressure that discourages black students from "acting white." Those black students who do achieve must take on a persona of "racelessness," detaching themselves from their own culture.

Effects of Poverty

A common explanation given for existing problems in black student achievement is simply the long grind of poverty, which as we have seen affects African-Americans more severely than other groups. This poverty is both separate from and tied to societal racism. For whites as well as blacks, poverty goes along with such factors as single-parent households, low educational level of mother, and little parental participation in schooling, which are also associated with low achievement (Myers, Milne, Ellman, and Ginsburg 1983). The argument for the negative effects of poverty becomes more powerful when one considers both that standardized achievement test scores rise with every additional $10,000 of annual income (FairTest 1989) and that every form of educational disadvantage experienced by black students, including high dropout rates, is predominantly a function of social class (Ascher 1987b).

Inferior Education

We have already shown a number of ways in which the education of low-income black students compares negatively to that of middle-class white students. Less experienced teachers, older facilities, and poorer equipment are the concrete manifestations that seem most directly linked to differences in financial support. They are also aspects of school quality that tend to decline in segregated schools. And as we have seen, school management practices such as testing, tracking, and homogeneous groupings also help to create an inferior education for poor black students. Curriculum tends to be taught in a more rote, fragmented, and measurement-driven manner in low-income schools. Moreover, even compensatory programs such as Chapter I, as we will see, have in no way equalized education for African-American students.

Clearly each of these explanations offers an incomplete understanding of the problems of black students. Together, however, they provide a compelling and rich insight into the variety of difficulties black students face both in and outside of school. What is surprising, in fact, is that some low-income black students do break through the many objective and subjective barriers finally to succeed in school and enter into the mainstream in work, politics, and private lives.

In the following section, we look at a variety of school efforts to improve education for low-income African-American students. Some of these efforts appear to be sadly misguided, others to be based on little research, and still others to offer some hope for real change. What is lacking in many of these efforts, however, is a conscious link between the reasons believed to be causing academic problems for black students and the educational remediations offered.

CURRICULUM REFORM AND INNOVATION

Just as the last decade has been a particularly hard period economically and socially for African-American children and youths, it has also been a difficult time educationally. The reform reports of the 1980s aimed to raise educational standards for all students. The result of some of these reports, however, has been twofold: They intentionally raised academic requirements and increased the use of standardized testing for promotion and graduation; they also unintentionally caused a greater educational precariousness for those students who were already at risk, partly because the intentional changes have not been accompanied by adequate support for students with academic difficulties. Also, the pressure to increase standards has created teaching to the tests, particularly in low socioeconomic schools; has increased the pressure to sort by homogeneous ability groupings; and has even accelerated the suspension, failure, and dropout rates as schools attempt to get rid of "troublesome" students (Dorr-Bremme and Herman 1986; National Coalition of Advocates for Students 1985).

However, there are public school programs in place, both large and small, national and local, that focus on low-income black children. It is these to which we now turn.

Poverty and Schooling

The largest, most far-reaching educational programs for black children have been under the federally funded Title I of the Elementary and Secondary Education Act (ESEA), initiated in 1965 and revised in 1981 as Chapter I of the Education, Consolidation and Improvement Act (ECIA). Intended to equalize educational opportunity by offering additional services to children from "disadvantaged backgrounds," low-income black children have received a variety of services as a result of this legislation. Recently, because of research showing the power of long-term poverty and of poverty concentration at the school level, there has been pressure to revise Chapter I to take these factors into consideration in the allocations formula (Ascher 1987a).

Unfortunately, whereas the need for special educational aid to low-income students (both black and white) is clear, the sense of what this assistance should be remains hazy nearly 3 decades after the inception of the ESEA. Although Title I/Chapter I has been the most widely researched effort of its type, there is little real consensus about the pedagogy needed to "compensate" for poverty or early signs of cognitive disadvantages. Even the belief in early childhood intervention is not accompanied by any agreed-upon curriculum. Nevertheless, because Chapter I illustrates some of the problems and possibilities of educating low-income black children, we devote considerable attention to this large-scale program.

Instructional Organization. Chapter I programs typically employ one of four basic organizational strategies: pull-out programs, add-on programs, in-class programs, and replacement programs, each of which has been evaluated by numerous investigations (Ascher 1987a). In addition, recent research suggests that more or less successful instructional strategies are being used within each.

Pull-out programs, providing instruction outside the classroom, are by far the most prevalent of the four organizational strategies. Used primarily for remedial reading, pull-out programs make use of small-group instruction by reading or compensatory education specialists. Early research on Title I suggested that pull-out programs offer a positive learning environment, largely because they allow smaller instructional groups; higher staff-to-student ratios; more student on-task behavior; less teacher time in behavioral management; a more harmonious classroom atmosphere; fewer negative comments by teachers; and a higher quality of cognitive monitoring, on-task monitoring, and organization of activities (Carter 1985, 5).

Unfortunately, several unintended negative effects also result from pull-out programs. First, total instructional time is decreased because of time spent moving to the location of the compensatory services. Second, students often experience fragmentation and discongruity between the material covered in the compensatory setting and that of the regular classroom. Compensatory education teachers and classroom teachers rarely plan cooperatively for the students they share. In most cases, neither is aware of what methods and materials the other is using, and few conferences, formal or informal, are held regarding student needs and progress. The result merely serves to exacerbate existing learning problems rather than to ameliorate them. Third, students who are pulled out of regular classes are often stigmatized and experience lowered expectations by their regular teacher. Fourth, segregation is increased as minority students move out of less segregated classrooms to receive Chapter I services in more segregated pull-out classrooms (Carter 1985, 5). And fifth, pull-out programs create homogeneous groupings, which have been shown to have negative effects on low achievers (Johnston, Allington, and Afflerback 1989; Wilkinson 1986).

In the most recent review of the instructional effects of pull-out programs, Madden and Slavin (1987) found that the more common programs, which evaluate students and then provide remedial instruction (individually or in small groups), showed minimum effectiveness, with many children's instructional needs going unmet. However, tutoring and computer-assisted instruction (CAI), which tailor instruction to each child's needs, had a greater impact on learning.

Here and there around the nation specific programs do manage to avoid some of these problems, for example, Reading Recovery, a program originally developed in New Zealand by Marie M. Clay (1979, 1985, 1987). Reading Recovery teachers are specially trained to help children be more strategic in their learning. The teaching of isolated skills and the use of passive, rote-learning methodology are avoided. Children read interesting storybooks, and they are actively involved in the instructional process. Swift progress and release from the program are key goals. Although children are pulled out for daily one-to-one work, the program is designed to release them to work competently and independently at the average level of instruction in their classrooms after 12 to 20 weeks. The program was first piloted in this country with urban, poor, black and white first graders in Columbus, Ohio, through a project based at Ohio State University. Having achieved very positive results, the program was expanded throughout Ohio and beyond. Ongoing research continues to focus on such problems as reexamining classroom curricula and improving teacher decision-making skills through continuing contact even after the training (Pinnell, Short, Lyons, and Young 1986).

Add-on programs are most commonly used to provide prekindergarten instruction or to extend the kindergarten day. Spurred by reports of significant, long-term achievement gains among poor minority children in early enrichment programs (Lazar and Darlington 1982), early childhood programs have been considered the potentially most powerful compensatory education intervention, and many urban school districts have allocated additional resources for that purpose. In a review of some 96 studies of early childhood intervention programs, Brown (1978, 179) concluded that there is "compelling evidence that early intervention works, that the adverse impact of a poverty environment can be overcome by appropriate treatment." However, it is important to note that although these early intervention programs were based on the general theory of early childhood maleability, they stemmed from an enormous variety of pedagogical theories and included both academically driven programs and programs that focused on social learning.

One extensive study of early childhood compensatory education, the Planned Variations Study of the Follow Through Program is a good example of the complexity and difficulty that has surrounded even this most positive aspect of compensatory education. Although all of the classrooms in the study aimed at increasing poor children's in-school academic achievement, each used a very different curricular model based on differing programmatic outcomes. Structured classrooms with teachers using systematic instruction resulted in higher mathematics and reading scores, and flexible classrooms that provided options and choices for children resulted in higher scores on a nonverbal reasoning test and willingness to work independently (Stallings 1975). Although some educators might opt for a curriculum that will produce high test scores among these young learners, many others would suggest that improving reasoning skills and fostering independent work habits are more likely to yield long-term academic competence; still others have argued that social learning must be the basis for later academic competence, even though it does not show immediate increases in test scores.

Summer school, before- and after-school programs, and weekend programs are common applications of compensatory add-on programs in the elementary grades. The assumption here is that simply spending more time in an instructional setting will improve students' achievement. The goal of summer school, by far the most often-used add-on program, is either to help make up for academic deficits or to reduce the summer losses thought to be greater among low-achieving students. However, there is little evidence that summer school programs are successful in reaching either of these goals (Ascher 1987a). According to Carter (1985), elementary students who attended Title I summer schools did not differ in achievement from their peers who did not attend. Problems associated with such programs include the excessive amount of time spent testing and the fact that teachers and students who are new to one another and sometimes new to the physical plant simply need more time to become acclimated before effective instruction can begin. Moreover, as Heyns (1978) points out, there are variations in students' efforts over time, as well as spurts and hiatuses in learning, that have not yet been differentiated from apparent results of different school schedules or increased time spent in school.

In-class programs, although relatively rare, may in fact be the best solution. Reduced transportation time, reduced stigma and the attendant problems of lowered expectations, less fragmentation, and the avoidance of increased segregation would theoretically be brought about by shifting the locale of compensatory education to the child's regular classroom (Archambault 1986). Because there has been relatively little research on in-class programs, however, the possibilities for successful innovative practice along these lines have yet to be explored. Holley (1986) reports that when the Chapter I teacher is a specialist, in-class programs create territorial uneasiness on the part of both the regular teacher and the specialist. Moreover, the press for time means that there is little planning and coordination, and fragmentation can take place in in-class as well as in pull-out programs.

Nevertheless, there is evidence that smaller classrooms, combined with better cooperation between the teacher and the specialist, could bring much improved conditions. In their review of organizational and grouping practices in poverty areas of big cities, Eubanks and Levine (1987) stress the need for a low average class size that allows for heterogeneous groupings and individualized and small-group instruction.

An important area of research might be to determine the best use of the specialist as support for teacher and student, as well as more effective ways to help teachers give more individualized attention to students in either pull-out or in-class situations. Perhaps the answer lies in allowing the specialist to act, to a greater extent, as a resource for classroom teachers, offering ongoing assistance with methods and materials aimed at working with students with diverse abilities. This kind of cooperative effort between specialist and classroom teacher could provide much needed continuity of effort and a reduction in wasted time.

Replacement programs are extremely rare, perhaps because a district must contribute its own resources to such programs. In a review of the research on Title I/Chapter I organizational strategies, Ascher (1987a) notes that only one such program has been evaluated, a school-wide program in Austin, Texas. According to an educator in the school district, this project was successful because it not only reduced class size but also eliminated the problem of "outside interferences in one teacher's responsibility for the learning of each student. There were no Title I teachers, there were no Title I aides, there was no Title I curriculum, there were no Title I supervisors" (cited in Ascher 1987a, 14).

Regardless of the type of instructional organization offered, the student's need for instructional continuity is crucial. One innovative attempt is a preteaching compensatory education program at the Willard Junior High School in the Berkeley, California, Unified School District. This program for slower-achieving students offers extra help in a manner that supports the requirements of the regular classroom. Compensatory education students remain in the regular classroom but receive help in the supplementary class, where they work on the reading materials before they are assigned in the regular class. In this way the students are prepared to read the assignment when the regular class begins studying the work. Once the work is assigned in the regular class, however, the students receive no further help in the supplementary class. According to Honig (1987), this preteaching program is effective because it reinforces the regular program rather than providing extra work that does not relate to the core curriculum. In addition to enabling students to do the regular work, it empowers them by helping them *before* they have had a chance to fail.

Obviously, however, all these management strategies still leave open the pedagogical questions. They leave untouched the issues of what African-American children may need to learn or how they ought to be taught it.

Curriculum Content

Sadly, curriculum has been a weak aspect of compensatory education, often being no more than the regular curriculum repeated, broken into meaningless segments, or "dumbed down." Because compensatory education programs are located in low-socioeconomic schools and are aimed at low-track students, the problems of a narrow, fragmented, measurement-driven curriculum that plague these schools also threaten the pedagogical utility of compensatory education. Finally, there is generally little relationship in compensatory curriculum to any perceived reasons for why low-income black students are having difficulty.

Reading and Mathematics. In the reading and mathematics compensatory education programs for poor black children, emphasis has been placed on the mastery of basic or foundational skills. This has occurred partly because reading and mathematics are more likely than other subjects to be targeted for standardized testing programs at the district or state levels, which in turn stems from their supposed predictability for skills in other subjects. (Obviously, however, if time is stripped from other subjects to be devoted to reading or math, this predictability is lost!) The emphasis on improving test scores has also created Chapter I programs that rely heavily on programmed instruction and teaching to tests (so that being able to give the right answers does not necessarily mean understanding the subject), and at a deeper level, reveal a lack of clarity by teachers and administrators about what students really need to know (Carter 1985).

Mastery learning, which dovetails with standardized testing, has been sold as being able to help those students with the greatest educational disadvantages, and it has resulted in raised test scores (Doyle 1986). However, its emphasis on skills arrays and small incremental learning patterns fosters a piecemeal, regimented approach to learning. Even the least capable learners often manage accurately to give back the bits and pieces of information fed to them in such programs. When the tests used to measure the learning make use of similar strategies, as is generally the case, these students appear to be achieving well. Unfortunately, this kind of learning is least likely to enable students to apply skills independently and purposefully—a true test of learning.

Focusing attention on reading and mathematics as foundation skills is crucial to academic achievement. However, separating these areas from their content strips them of interest and importance to students and renders them meaningless and dull. For students at any age, literacy and numeracy are processes that are best learned within a meaningful context. The use of manipulatives and the creation of interesting topical frameworks that students are curious about and care about not only helps students to understand but also helps them to apply what they have learned.

The Children's School Project, a cooperative venture of Lehman College of the City University of New York and Public School District 10, is designed to provide low-income minority children with a curriculum that focuses on process and helps students develop strategies that will be useful as they move on to independent reading and writing. Although mastery learning is used by having teachers create assignments and then correct them (often apart from the students), the Children's School Project allows students to become conscious of their own learning process, and "assessment" is a collaboration between teachers and students. Although the project has not been evaluated in traditional terms—children's achievement on tests—the curriculum is recognized as valid for young children. It has been selected as one of the three models for replication by New York City's Project Child, a major effort directed at high-risk students (Delisle 1989).

Higher-order Thinking Skills. Chapter I programs have been pressured to include higher-order thinking skills in the curriculum. However, a survey of 2,200 districts revealed uncertainty about what these skills are or how their inclusion into the curriculum is to be accomplished. The survey also showed that many teachers believe that Chapter I children are incapable of handling such skills (Reported in Ascher 1987a).

Unfortunately, this uncertainty about teaching thinking skills is not unique to Chapter I but permeates public schooling in general—in part because of the fragmentation of learning during the past decade or more. Not surprisingly, one controversy has been whether these higher-order skills are best taught through programs expressly designed for that purpose. However, as Resnick (1987), among others, has argued, thinking is always embedded in disciplines, and reasoning and judgment improve along with increased knowledge in a particular domain. At the same time, even reading and mathematics when taught correctly use higher-order thinking skills from the very beginning, as students construct meaning and use interpretive skills. Although reasoning and problem solving have been successfully taught as isolated skills, it is not clear how applicable students find these skills when faced with changed contexts. Thus educators and researchers increasingly understand that thinking must be woven into every area of the curriculum. Thus, tests must be changed so that they reflect these higher-order skills and do not encourage the view that these skills can be taught only after students have mastered "the basics."

An example of a literacy program based on the premise that language competence is far more than proficiency in the mechanics of grammar and punctuation and that thinking critically and independently is a key goal for all learners is the *Foundations for Learning: Language*. Created by a black scholar, Arthur E. Thomas, to be used with black inner-city youths, the program incorporates "the findings of linguistics research and current thinking on curriculum requirements" (Poussaint 1987, 52). The program integrates a content and process-based approach in all language domains: reading, writing, speaking, and listening. It emphasizes aspects of reasoning, problem solving, and critical thinking; employment of the vast fund of experience and knowledge students bring to the classroom, offering them a share of control over their own learning environment; and use of collaborative learning to provide feedback and to provide the basis for socialization and development of the art of constructive criticism.

Computers. Virtually all compensatory education program have begun to include instruction in the use of computers. A survey of 2,200 Chapter I districts revealed several factors contributing to the growing use of computers in these programs. Most important, since Chapter I money is available for them, hardware and software manufacturers have discovered that these programs are a "viable marketplace." A number of other influences are also at work, however, including state-mandated testing programs that incorporate computer literacy, state education agencies that promote computer usage through workshops and conferences, district efforts to standardize the instructional services provided, and innovation by individual district and school staffs. Unfortunately, in many urban areas, despite all the pressure for computer use, the only money available for computers is through compensatory education funds. This has had a narrowing effect on their use, since Chapter I money stipulates that computers can be used only for remediation.

Not surprisingly, findings on the use of computers in Chapter I programs is consistent with previous research on the use of computers with low-socioeconomic students. Although computers are a minor addition to the materials at a teacher's disposal in some schools and a central curricular feature in others, in all compensatory education programs computers are used primarily for rote learning activities such as CAI and drill and practice. They are rarely used for word processing or developing higher-order thinking skills as they are in upper tracks or in middle-class schools (Tucker 1983).

The educational assumptions that underlie the stratified use of computers need careful examination. The emphasis on drill and practice, which permeates so much of the teaching for low-socioeconomic students, results in less instruction in comprehension and meaning than advantaged students receive and severely curtails the former's chances for learning.

In their discussion of the role of computers in the teaching of reading, Strickland, Feeley, and Wepner (1987, 9–11) offer the following guidelines for equitable use: Computer instruction in reading for *all* students should (1) focus on meaning and reading comprehension, (2) foster active involvement and stimulate thinking, (3) support and extend knowledge of text structures, (4) make use of content from a wide range of subject areas, and (5) link reading to writing.

Multicultural Education. When curriculum content and materials are monocultural, they send forth a subtle message that other groups are not worthy of being included. Thus, for those who believe that the difficulties of African-American students arise largely out of identity problems, cultural dissonance, or conflicts over whether entering the mainstream culture implies racial disloyalty, multicultural education is a critical strategy. The proponents of multicultural education agree that students have a right to see themselves in, and to learn about themselves from, respectful and undistorted curriculum materials and that they have a right to see their great men and women so acknowledged (Brooks 1987).

In 1969, during a conference on multiethnic education, the Association for Supervision and Curriculum Development recommended that American curriculum be restructured to have a more meaningful, honest, and adequate "ethnic emphasis." This change would take place in all schools so that all children would grow up with a sense of their specific identity, develop a deeper understanding of people of other cultural and ethnic groups, and acquire the cultural diversity that characterizes our nation (Dunfee, cited in Baker 1983).

Aspects of multicultural education include teachers who understand and respect the interests and cultural background of the children they teach, materials that reflect the diversity of our pluralistic society, and a curriculum that integrates ethnic and cultural experiences throughout. Yet multicultural education does not mean the same thing for all children, classrooms, and schools. If a school is predominantly black, instruction should be structured to reflect the cultural base of the African-American experience. And the same holds true for classrooms that are predominantly Hispanic, Asian, Indian, or white. This does not mean that the instructional content should be confined to informing students only about their own ethnic group but rather that the instruction should be geared from that perspective (Baker 1983, 48). As Brooks (1987) points out, all learners must know about both the majority and minority cultures.

An excellent resource on literature for black learners is *Shadow and Substance: Afro-American Experience in Contemporary Children's Fiction* by Sims (1982), which offers teachers publications written and published by blacks as well as those written about them. Brooks (1987, 61) cautions, however, that no matter how good the materials, the key elements in the learning are determined by how they are handled—the attitudes, interpretations, and extensions of them made by the teachers themselves.

Hilliard (1988) also reports a good example of content equity. The Portland (Oregon) Public School Multiethnic Curriculum Project was developed by international experts (with appropriate multiethnic backgrounds) in five academic disciplines, working with diverse ethnic community groups. The content areas were science, mathematics, language arts, art, and music. The result was a massive multiethnic curriculum change in which all vestiges of racism, sexism, or any other kind of "ism" were removed (206–207).

Instructional Strategies

Despite only loose linkages with any theory of specific deficiencies or differences, several instructional strategies, tried both in and outside Chapter I, have been shown to be particularly effective with poor black students. Active instruction, cooperative learning, peer tutoring, and various approaches recommended for dealing with issues related to language diversity and cognitive style have been given particular attention.

Active instruction has been identified as a key link to the achievement gains of Chapter I students. Characterized by the teacher's strong personal involvement in instruction in a businesslike and task-oriented manner, active instruction focuses primarily on academic objectives rather than personal adjustment and group dynamics. Although recognizing that social and affective goals contribute to cognitive and academic achievement, care is taken that they do not replace academic objectives (Brophy 1986).

Active instruction, combined with a subtle understanding of psychological and social issues, is well demonstrated in the Yale Child Study Center School Development Program's Social Skills Curriculum for Inner-City Children, which successfully couples affective needs with a strong academic thrust. Designed to give low-income black children the experiences that many middle-income children gain simply by growing up with their parents, the program combines the teaching of basic skills, social skills, and appreciation for the arts through four units—politics and government, business and economics, health and nutrition, and spiritual and leisure time. This approach has promoted social development among the students, which has led to improved academic performance and set in motion a circular and reciprocal action that has gradually improved the quality of living and learning in the schools (Comer 1988).

Cooperative learning strategies have been found to be highly effective in improving achievement among black students (Slavin 1986). For some researchers, this finding is directly linked to the fact that black culture supports cooperation rather than competition. Moreover, researchers associate the improvements with the finding that heterogeneous groupings have a salutary effect, especially with low-income students (Ascher 1987a). Based on the principles of team sports, cooperative learning rewards helpfulness and sharing. The teams are heterogeneous, made up of high, average, and low achievers; boys and girls; and students of any ethnic groups represented in the class. For example, in the model called Student Teams-Achievement Divisions (STAD), developed at Johns Hopkins University, a teacher may present a lesson on map reading and then give students time to work with maps and answer questions about them in their teams. Afterward, students take individual quizzes on map reading. When the quiz scores are added up, however, the individual scores become part of the team scores, and all teams whose average scores meet a high criterion receive special recognition. Thus, rewards for achievement in cooperative learning are not limited to high or low achievers. In one rural Maryland study, black students started out significantly behind whites in language arts achievement; after 12 weeks of STAD, the achievement gap was gone (Slavin 1987).

Research on cooperative learning methods has taken place in grades 2 through 12; in urban, suburban, and rural schools; and in a range of subjects—mathematics, language arts, social studies, and science. Certain forms of cooperative learning are consistently effective in increasing student achievement as measured by standardized tests. Two elements appear critical: First, a group must be rewarded for doing well as a group. Second, the group's success must depend on the individual learning of each group member (Slavin 1987).

Peer tutoring has been found to be an unusually effective approach for disadvantaged students (Madden and Slavin 1987). Explanations for this phenomena include the fact that authority figures are minimized and that there is flexibility in allowing older children to tutor younger ones or more advanced students at the same level to tutor their peers. Peer tutoring is an ideal strategy for heterogeneous student groupings since those who are more knowledgeable are tutors for those who need to master the material. In addition, the tutors often learn as much as those whom they are tutoring.

Language Development. Attempts to deal with the range of dialects spoken in school have ranged all the way from trying to extinguish or prohibit nonstandard English in the classroom to the use of nonstandard Black English as a medium of reading instruction (see Steward 1969). Most educators agree, however, that on the one hand, attempts to subjugate or deny the child the use of his or her home language can cause confusion and resentment and may even inhibit language development. It would also be a blatant departure from what has become widely recognized as a need to foster pride in the child's cultural and linguistic background. On the other hand, the use of dialect materials has been viewed as impractical and insulting to the very population for whom they are intended. Generally speaking, black parents (including those who speak nonstandard dialect) do not want their children to be taught with special materials, using what they consider to be "bad" or "inferior" language. Furthermore, these parents are concerned that the use of such materials may impede their children's mastery of standard English, something that they consider important for success in mainstream society.

The use of traditional standard English materials, along with acceptance of the child's own dialectic renderings of standard English materials, is widely accepted, at least theoretically. Goodman and Buck (1973) explain that no special materials need to be constructed, but children must be permitted, actually encouraged, to read the way they speak. There is also evidence that the use of literature as a base for daily oral language activities increases the language development of black, nonstandard-English-speaking children (Cullinan, Jaggar, and Strickland 1974; Strickland 1973). Strickland and Feeley (1991) offer several guidelines to help make instructional decisions in the classroom:

1. Virtually all children come to school with a viable system of communication—their language. Although different from that which the school expects, it is not necessarily deficient.
2. Competence is not tied to the use of a dialect. Language competence is more likely to be affected by the quality of verbal interaction at home, general intelligence, and the range of background experiences than the dialect spoken.
3. Teachers need to know something about the language of the children they teach. Knowing the source of divergence when children make errors in speech or reading will help the teacher know what, if any, corrective measures should be taken.
4. Black children need not have mastery of standard English to any specific degree prior to reading instruction. Many varied experiences in listening and responding to literature, coupled with the use of predictable stories, chants, and rhymes as beginning reading materials, give these children a good start.

Parental Involvement

A final aspect of curriculum for black children on which educators and researchers agree is parental involvement. For a time, after the turbulence of the late 1960s and early 1970s, this aspect of schooling was somewhat downplayed. Its recent comeback as part of most programmatic recommendations is in a more restricted, less politicized form.

The object of parental involvement is obvious: narrowing the gap between the home and the school and creating a sense that both families and school personnel are working together in the students' behalf. For some, this involvement has the aim of showing parents how to do their job better, better to prepare students for school. For those who take a cultural dissonance point of view, however, parental involvement is a way of getting mothers or fathers to teach teachers how their children learn best (Heath 1983).

Recent programs in parental involvement, in fact, tend to focus more directly on parents as teachers and provide learning activities that parents and their children can do at home. The point is that the schools have students for a relatively small proportion of their time; if education is to improve, some of this work must be shared by parents.

DEVELOPING CURRICULUM FOR LOW-INCOME BLACK CHILDREN

Americans, perhaps more than citizens of any other country, believe that schools have the power to solve fundamental societal problems. Our schools are regarded as a major force in combating the problems associated with drugs, AIDS, racial and religious prejudice, and a host of other ills. Despite their ambivalence and conflicts about schooling, low-income black Americans view the schools as the key to a better life. According to the National Alliance of Black School Educators (1984),

> While public education will be the most productive when the environments for both living and learning are mutually supportive of human growth and development, we believe that effective educational leadership and "good teaching" will save large numbers of African American students from experiencing twelve or thirteen years of inconsequential public education. (13)

The report goes on boldly to affirm a somewhat controversial premise: "The educability of students derives far more from the nature of the school in which they are sent than it derives from the nature of the family from which they come." Whether or not one supports such strong faith in the public schools, the fact that this abiding trust remains strong among many black scholars and laypersons presents an extraordinary challenge, especially since it is clear that many of the educational reforms of the past may have unintentionally hurt rather than helped poor and minority children. Most recently, reforms inspired by a generally conservative political climate—such as the back-to-basics movement, the simplistic application of the effective schools research, and the overreliance on test scores as a means of setting academic standards—have all raised rather than lowered the barriers to educational advancement for low-income African-American students.

Although educators cannot rectify all of the social and economic problems associated with the poor academic performance of poor black children, they can work toward enlightened policy both within and outside the schools. As Futrell (1987) eloquently phrases it, "As classroom teachers, we have seen thousands of students succeed despite countless disadvantages. We know that many of the brightest students in public school are poor. These children want to learn. They can learn. They will learn" (108).

Recommendations

During the past few years, the notion of quality has often been offered in opposition to that of equality. Yet many of the strategies that have been tried in low-income schools and with minority students have worked against both equality and quality. Thus, to make schooling suit more closely the needs of low-income black students, a number of strategies should be tried. These strategies do not dilute education. Instead, they attempt to restructure schooling so that black students, as well as all other students, receive the best education for our current and future society.

1. School and social service intervention should be coordinated, occur as early as possible, and be ongoing. Its purpose should be to prevent failure and accelerate achievement rather than merely to remediate problems. Early intervention has lasting effects and has been demonstrated in the long run to be highly cost-effective.

2. Schools should be small enough or divided into manageable units so that individual students can feel known and recognized as participants of a community and closer student-teacher relationships are more likely to develop. At the upper levels of instruction, scheduling larger blocks of time rather than the usual periods of less than one hour help to promote the teacher's ability to function as coach and facilitator of learning rather than knowledge dispenser and materials manager.

3. Heterogeneity across race, ethnicity, class, gender, and ability should be encouraged. Hess and Lauber (1985) warn that schools that are dumping grounds for those who are considered "misfits" or filled with students who are leftovers from magnet and academically elite schools must not be tolerated. The school should place a high value on diversity of language, culture, and cognitive style and learn to capitalize and build on what children bring to the learning situation rather than ignore or attempt to eradicate it.

4. Curriculum development should be planned and monitored by empowered teachers in conjunction with administrative staff. Attempts should be made to achieve curricular programs that have built-in flexibility, with the freedom to adjust and refine practice according to the needs of specific groups within a system, rather than made teacher-proof, rigidly standardized, and paced. Hilliard (1988) states, "Many public policy efforts maintain a mission control mentality. This means that the management of day-to-day instructional decision-making often tends to be centralized outside the school site" (205).

5. Given incentives to attract the best teachers available, schools should provide ongoing staff development focused on empowering teachers to make instructional decisions. Classroom observation—how to assess what the student is learning and to use it to plan appropriately—should be emphasized. Teacher networks should be encouraged and supported by the administration. Operating as voluntary support groups, teacher networks allow teachers to organize their own staff development efforts so that ideas close to the classroom may be discussed in a risk-free atmosphere of mutual support.

6. Instruction should reflect the application of research on learning to classroom strategies. For example, classroom practice should be characterized by active involvement on the part of students. Collaborative group learning and peer teaching methods should play a major role in the instructional process. Mastery learning approaches, with their heavy emphasis on worksheet and workbook-type materials—where the only attempt to individualize is by the rate with which a student progresses through the materials and where teachers are largely reduced to managing materials—should be severely curtailed or eliminated.

7. The teaching of thinking should be stressed throughout the curriculum, not as a separate subject but as an integral part of everything students do. Critical, analytical, and organizational skills should be incorporated into every aspect of instruction in language and literacy and into

every content area. The focus should be on helping children learn how to learn for themselves.

8. Great care and caution should be exercised in the use of categories and labels designating children as "learning disabled" or "educable mentally retarded" or even Chapter I. Too often, placement in such programs is the result of dysfunctional instruction rather than dysfunctional learning. Unfortunately, the funding provided for these categories often makes them extremely attractive as placements for students the school simply has not found the means to instruct in mainstream classrooms. The overuse and legitimization of false categories leads ultimately to instant institutionalization of poor practice. More attention needs to be paid to the quality of educational services offered in regular classrooms and to the fact that the instructional needs of students in various categorical groups may indeed be similar.

9. Secondary programs should be linked to meaningful and nontraditional volunteer and vocational opportunities. Fine (1983) suggests that whenever possible, students who wish to drop out should be given serious informed consent options and that follow-up and second chance programs, with specially designed curricula, should be provided for those who nevertheless leave. The school must reach out in an attempt to work with and help revitalize whatever resources may be available in the local community to help these youths in particular.

10. Reliance on standardized tests should be drastically reduced and greater emphasis placed on informal classroom assessment and varied means of demonstrating achievement, such as systematic teacher observation and the collection and analysis of work samples. Past reliance on standardized tests as the primary indicators of academic performance has led to what has been termed a self-fulfilling prophecy. As Shepard (1989, 4) has noted, "Tests predicted how children would perform certain school tasks, and teachers taught in ways that confirmed those predictions." In addition, standardized tests often include material that is unfamiliar to low-income black children. Finally, standardized tests as currently constituted require them to work within a format that is the antithesis of the collaborative, socially interactive learning that has been demonstrated to be successful with these children.

The setting of academic standards solely on the basis of standardized tests must be eliminated. School districts must oppose schemes being advanced by state government officials and legislators, local boards of education, bureaucrats, and others who in the absence of needed fundamental changes, propose to improve achievement by simply "tightening up" on standards or testing the minimal competence of disadvantaged students (Eubanks and Levine 1987, 31). Day-to-day informal assessment that is linked to instruction and involves the student in the process should be emphasized.

References

Archambault, Frank X., Jr. 1986. "Instructional Setting: Key Issue or Bogus Concern." In *Designs for Compensatory Education: Conference Proceedings and Papers*, edited by Barbara I. Williams, Peggy A. Richardson, and Beverly J. Mason, 2–27. Washington, DC: Research and Evaluation Associates.

Ascher, Carol. 1987a. *Chapter 1 Programs: New Guides from the Research*. ED 289 947. New York: ERIC Clearinghouse on Urban Education, Institute for Urban and Minority Education, Teachers College, Columbia University.

Ascher, Carol. 1987b. *Trends and Issues in Minority Education*. ERIC/CUE Trends and Issues Series no. 6. New York: ERIC Clearinghouse on Urban Education, Teachers College, Columbia University.

Ascher, Carol. 1989. *Urban School Finance: The Quest for Equal Educational Opportunity*. New York: ERIC Clearinghouse on Urban Education Digest no. 55.

Ascher, Carol. 1990. *The Influence of Standardized Testing on Opportunity and Learning*. New York: ERIC Clearinghouse on Urban Education, Institute for Urban and Minority Education, Teachers College, Columbia University.

Baker, Gwendolyn. 1983. *Planning and Organizing for Multicultural Instruction*. Reading, MA: Addison-Wesley.

Bassuk, Ellen, and Lenore Rubin. 1987. Homeless children: A neglected population. *American Journal of Orthopsychiatry* 57(2): 279–285.

Bennett, Christine, and J. John Harris III. 1982. Suspension and expulsions of male and black students: A study of the causes of disproportionality. *Urban Education* 16(4): 399–423.

Berlin, Gordon, and Andrew Sum. 1988. *Toward a More Perfect Union: Basic Skills, Poor Families, and Our Economic Future*. New York: Ford Foundation.

Bickel, Frank. 1980. *Project Student Concerns: A Study of Minority Student Suspensions*. Interim report. ED 178–636. Washington, DC: Educational Research and Improvement Center.

Brooks, Charlotte. 1987. "Teachers: Potent Forces in the Learning Lives of Black Students." In *Educating Black Children: America's Challenge*, edited by Dorothy Strickland and Eric Cooper, 55–62. Washington, DC: Bureau of Educational Research, School of Education, Howard University.

Brophy, Jere. 1986. "Research Linking Teacher Behavior to Student Achievement: Potential Implications for Instruction of Chapter 1 Students." In *Designs for Compensatory Education: Conference Proceedings and Papers*, edited by Barbara I. Williams, Peggy A. Richardson, and Beverly J. Mason, 28–46. Washington, DC: Research and Evaluation Associates.

Brown, Ann, Joseph Campione, Lynne S. Webber, and Kate McGilly. 1989. *Interactive Learning Environments: A New Look at Assessment and Instruction*. Paper prepared for the National Commission on Testing and Public Policy. Berkeley, CA: UCLA Berkeley Graduate School of Education.

Brown, Bernard. 1978. *Found: Long-Term Gains from Early Intervention*. Boulder, CO: Westview Press.

Bureau of the Census. 1987. *We, the Black Americans: Booklet No. 3*. Washington, DC: U.S. Department of Commerce.

Carnegie Foundation for the Advancement of Teaching. 1988. *An Imperiled Generation: Saving Urban Schools*. Princeton, NJ: Princeton University Press.

Carter, Launor F. 1985. The sustaining effects study of compensatory and elementary education. *Educational Researcher* 13(7): 4-13.

Center on Budget and Policy Priorities. 1988. *Still Far from the Dream: Recent Developments in Black Income, Employment and Poverty.* Washington, DC: Center on Budget and Policy Priorities.

Children's Defense Fund. 1985. *Black and White Children in America: Key Facts.* Washington, DC: Children's Defense Fund.

Clay, Marie M. 1979. *Observing Young Readers.* Portsmouth, NH: Heinemann.

Clay, Marie M. 1985. *The Early Detection of Reading Difficulties.* Portsmouth, NH: Heinemann.

Clay, Marie M. 1987. Implementing reading recovery: Systematic adaptations to an educational innovation. *New Zealand Journal of Educational Studies* 22(1): 35–58.

Comer, James P. 1988. "Effective Schools: Why They Rarely Exist for At-Risk Elementary-School and Adolescent Students." In *School Success for Students at Risk,* 72–88. Orlando, FL: Harcourt Brace Jovanovich.

Cook, Valerie, Janet Eyler, and Leslie Ward. 1981. *Effective Strategies for Avoiding Within School Segregation.* ERIC 245 023. Nashville, TN: Vanderbilt University Center for Education and Human Policy Development.

Corcoran, Thomas B., Lisa J. Walker, and J. Lynne White. 1988. *Working in Urban Schools.* Washington, DC: Institute for Educational Leadership.

Cullinan, Bernice. 1974. *Black Dialects and Reading.* Urbana, IL: ERIC Clearinghouse on Reading and Communication Skills, National Council of Teachers of English.

Cullinan, Bernice, Angela Jaggar, and Dorothy Strickland. 1974. Language expansion for black children in the primary grades: A research report. *Young Children* 24(2): 98–113.

Delisle, Robert G. 1989. "The Children's School." In *Risk Makers, Risk Takers, Risk Breakers,* edited by Jo Beth Allen and Jana M. Mason, 83–92. Portsmouth, NH: Heinemann.

Dillard, Joey Lee. 1972. *Black English: Its History and Usage in the United States.* New York: Random House.

Dorr-Bremme, Donald W., and Joan L. Herman. 1986. *Assessing Student Achievement: A Profile of Classroom Practices.* Los Angeles: UCLA Graduate School of Education, Center for the Study of Evaluation.

Doyle, Dennis. 1986. "Vison and Reality: A Reaction to Issues in Curriculum and Instruction for Compensatory Education." In *Designs for Compensatory Education: Conference Proceedings and Papers,* edited by Barbara I. Williams, Peggy A. Richardson, and Beverly J. Mason, 125–140. Washington, DC: Research and Evaluation Associates.

Edelman, Marian Wright. 1987. *Families in Peril: An Agenda for Social Change.* Cambridge, MA: Harvard University Press.

Edmonds, Ronald. 1982. Program of school improvement: An overview. *Educational Leadership* 40(3): 4–11.

Eubanks, Eugene E., and Daniel U. Levine. 1987. "Administrative and Organizational Arrangements and Considerations." In *Educating Black Children: America's Challenge,* edited by Dorothy S. Strickland and Eric J. Cooper, 19–32. Washington, DC: Bureau of Educational Research, School of Education, Howard University.

FairTest. 1989. *Annual SAT and ACT Scores Share Continued Flaws.* Cambridge, MA: National Center for Fair and Open Testing.

Fasold, Ralph W., and Walter Wolfram. 1970. "Some Linguistic Features of Negro Dialect." In *Teaching Standard English in the Inner City,* edited by Ralph W. Fasold and Roger W. Shuy, 41–86. Washington, DC: Center for Applied Linguistics.

Fine, Michelle. 1983. "Perspectives on Inequity: Voices from Urban Schools." In *Applied Social Psychology Annual IV ,* edited by Leonard Bickman, 26–42. Beverly Hills, CA: Sage.

Fordham, Signithia, and John U. Ogbu. 1986. Black students' school success: Coping with the burden of "acting white." *Urban Review* 18(1): 1-31.

Furstenberg, Frank F., Jeanne Brooks-Gunn, and S. Philip Morgan. 1987. *Adolescent Mothers in Later Life.* Cambridge, MA: Cambridge University Press.

Futrell, Mary H. 1987. "Opening Remarks to the Conference on Educating Black Children." In *Educating Black Children: America's Challenge,* Dorothy S. Strickland and Eric J. Cooper, 106–112. Washington, DC: Bureau of Educational Research, School of Education, Howard University.

Goodman, Kenneth S., and Catherine Buck. 1973. Dialect barriers to reading comprehension revisited. *The Reading Teacher* 27(1): 6–12.

Hale, Janice. 1982. *Black Children: Their Roots, Culture, and Learning Styles.* Provo, UT: Brigham Young Press.

Heath, Shirley Brice. 1983. "Questioning at Home and at School: A Comparative Study." In *Doing the Ethnography of Schooling: Educational Anthropology in Action,* edited by George Spindler, 102–131. New York: Holt, Rinehart and Winston.

Hess, George A., Jr., and David Lauber. 1985. *Dropouts from the Chicago Public Schools: An Analysis of the Classes of 1982–1983–1984.* Chicago: Chicago Panel on Public School Finance.

Hess, Robert D., and Virginia C. Shipman. 1965. Early experience and the socialization of cognitive modes in children. *Child Development* 36(4): 869–886.

Heyns, B. 1978. *Summer Learning and the Effects of Achievement.* New York: Academic Press.

Hilliard, Asa. 1988. "Public Support for Successful Instructional Practices for At-Risk Students." In *Scholl Success for Students at Risk: Analysis and Recommendations of the Council of Chief State School Officers,* 195–208. Orlando, FL: Harcourt Brace Jovanovich.

Holley, Freda M. "Program Staffing and Structures Reactions from a Quarter-Century in Compensatory Education." 1986. In *Designs for Compensatory Education: Conference Proceedings and Papers,* edited by Barbara I. Williams, Peggy A. Richardson, and Beverly J. Mason, 76–99. Washington, DC: Research and Evaluation Associates.

Honig, Bill. 1987. "High Standards and Great Expectations: The Foundations for Student Achievement." In *Educating Black Children: America's Challenge,* edited by Dorothy S. Strickland and Eric J. Cooper, 11–18. Washington, DC: Bureau of Educational Research, School of Education, Howard University.

Hurtado, Aida, and Craig Haney. 1989. *Standardized Error: Testing and Employment Discrimination.* Paper commissioned by the National Commission on Testing and Public Policy. Berkeley: University of California Graduate School of Education.

Jensen, Arthur R. 1985. The black-white difference in G: A phenomenon in search of a theory. *Behavioral and Brain Sciences.* 8(4): 246–263.

Johnston, Peter, Richard Allington, and Peter Afflerback. 1989. The congruence of classroom and remedial reading instruction. *Elementary School Journal* 85(4):513–528.

Kasarda, John D. 1986. "The Regional and Urban Redistribution of People and Jobs in the U.S." Paper prepared for the National Research Council Committee on National Urban Policy, Washington, DC: National Academy of Science.

Kochman, Thomas. 1989. "Black and White Cultural Styles in Pluralistic Perspective." In *Test Policy and Test Performance: Education, Language, and Culture,* edited by Bernard Gifford, 259–296. Boston: Kluwer Academic Publishers.

Labov, William. 1966. *The Social Stratification of English in New York City.* Washington, DC: Center for Applied Linguistics.

Lazar, Irving, and Richard Darlington. 1982. *Lasting Effects of Early Education: A Report from the Consortium for Longitudinal Studies.* Monographs of the Society for Research in Child Development. Washington, DC: U.S. Government Printing Office.

Lee, Courtland C. 1985. An investigation of psychosocial variables related to academic success for rural black adolescents. *Journal of Negro Education* 53(4): 424–434.

Madden, Nancy A., and Robert Slavin. 1987. "Effective Pull-out Programs for Students at Risk." Paper presented at the annual convention, American Educational Research Association, Washington, DC.

Massey, Douglas S., and Nancy A. Denton. 1988. Suburbanization and segregation in U.S. metropolitan areas. *American Journal of Sociology* 94(3): 592–626.

Michigan Interagency Committee on the Black Child. 1987. *Black Child in Crisis.* Lansing: Michigan Interagency Committee.

Moody, Charles D. 1980. *Student Rights and Discipline: Policies, Programs and Procedures.* ED 160 926. Washington, DC: Educational Research and Improvement Center.

Moore, Helen, and Peter Iadicola. 1978. *Resegregation Process in Desegregated Elementary Schools and Status Relationships Among Anglo, Hispanic and Black Students.* Riverside: Department of Sociology, University of California.

Myers, David E., Ann M. Milne, Fran Ellman, and Alan Ginsburg. 1983. *Single Parent, Working Mothers, and the Educational Achievement of Elementary School Age Children.* ED 234–092. Washington, DC: Educational Research and Improvement Center.

National Alliance of Black School Educators. 1984. *Saving the African American Child.* Washington, DC: National Alliance of Black School Educators.

National Black Child Development Institute. 1989. Status of black children. *The Black Child Advocate* 15(4): 1–12.

National Coalition of Advocates for Students. 1985. *Barriers to Excellence: Our Children at Risk.* Boston: National Coalition of Advocates for Students.

Neckerman, Kathryn M., and William Julius Wilson. 1988. "Schools and Poor Communities." In *School Success for Students at Risk,* edited by Council of Chief State School Officers, 25–44. Orlando, FL: Harcourt Brace Jovanovich.

Oakes, Jeannie. 1985. *Keeping Track: How Schools Structure Inequality.* New Haven, CT: Yale University Press.

Ogbu, John. 1986. "Consequences of the American Caste System." In *The School Achievement of Minority Children: New Perspectives,* edited by Ulric Neisser, 22–25, 26. Hillsdale, NJ: Erlbaum.

Orfield, Gary, and Franklin Monford. 1988. *Racial Change and Desegregation in Large School Districts: Trends Through the 1986–1987 School Year.* A Report of the Council of Urban Boards of Education and the National School Desegregation Project of the University of Chicago. Alexandria, VA: National School Boards Association.

Orfield, Gary, Franklin Monfort, and Rosemary George. 1987. *School Segregation in the 1980's: Trends in the United States and Metropolitan Areas.* ED 285 946. Chicago: National School Desegregation Project.

Orland, Martin E. 1989. "The Demographics of Disadvantage: Intensity of Childhood Poverty and Its Relationship to Educational Achievement." In *Access to Knowledge,* 14–21. New York: College Board.

Orr, Eleanor W. 1987. *Twice as Less: Black English and the Performance of Black Students in Mathematics and Science.* New York: Norton.

Pinnell, Gay S., Kathy Short, Carol A. Lyons, and P. Young. 1986. *The Reading Recovery Project in Columbus, Ohio: 1985–1986.* Columbus: Ohio State University.

Poussaint, Alvin. 1987. "It Ain't No Consolation." In *Educating Black Children: America's Challenge,* edited by Dorothy S. Strickland and Eric J. Cooper, 44–54. Washington, DC: Bureau of Educational Research, School of Education, Howard University.

Resnick, Lauren. 1987. *Education and Learning to Think.* Washington, DC: National Academy Press.

Resnick, Lauren B., and Daniel P. Resnick. 1989. *Assessing the Thinking Curriculum: New Tools for Educational Reform.* Paper prepared for the National Commission on Testing and Public Policy. Berkeley: University of California Graduate School of Education.

Shepard, Lorrie A. 1989. Why we need better assessments. *Educational Leadership* 46(2): 4–9.

Sims, Rudine. 1982. *Shadow and Substance: Afro-American Experience in Contemporary Children's Fiction.* Urbana, IL: National Council of Teachers of English.

Slavin, Robert. 1986. *Using Student Team Learning.* Baltimore: Johns Hopkins Team Learning Project.

Slavin, Robert. 1987. "Cooperative Learning and the Education of Black Students." In *Educating Black Children: America's Challenge,* edited by Dorothy S. Strickland and Eric J. Cooper, 63–68. Washington, DC: Bureau of Educational Research, School of Education, Howard University.

Stallings, Jane. 1975. Implementation and child effects of teaching practices in follow-through classrooms. *Monographs of the Society of Child Development,* Serial no. 163, 40. Chicago: University of Chicago.

Steward, William. 1969. "On the Use of Negro Dialect in the Teaching of Reading." In *Teaching Black Children to Read,* edited by Joan C. Baratz and Roger W. Shuy, 156–219. Washington, DC: Center for Applied Linguistics.

Strickland, Dorothy. 1973. A program for linguistically different black children. *Research in the Teaching of English.* 7(1): 79–114.

Strickland, Dorothy, and Joan Feeley. 1991. "Research on Language Learners: Development in the Elementary School Years." In *Handbook of Research on Teaching the English Language Arts,* edited by James Flood, Julie Jensen, Diane Lapp, and James R. Squire. New York: Macmillan.

Strickland, Dorothy, Joan Feeley, and Shelley Wepner. 1987. *Using Computers in the Teaching of Reading.* New York: Teachers College Press.

Strickland, Dorothy S., and Donna Ogle. 1990. "Teachers Coping with Change: Assessing the Early Literacy Curriculum." In *The Role of Assessment in Early Literacy,* edited by Lesley M. Morrow and Jeffrey K. Smith, 160–165. Englewood Cliffs, NJ: Prentice Hall.

Tucker, Marc. 1983. Computers in schools: A plan in time saves nine. *Theory Into Practice* 22(4): 313–320.

Wilkinson, Louise C. 1986. "Grouping Low-Achieving Students for Instruction." In *Designs for Compensatory Education: Conference Proceedings and Papers,* 150–165, edited by Barbara I. Williams, Peggy A. Richardson, and Beverly J. Mason, 212–229. Washington DC: Research and Evaluation Associates.

Williams, Frederick, Robert Hopper, and Diana S. Natalicio. 1977. *The Sounds of Children.* Englewood Cliffs, NJ: Prentice Hall.

Wilson, William Julius. 1987. *The Truly Disadvantaged: The Inner City, the Underclass, and Public Policy.* Chicago: University of Chicago Press.

Witt, Virginia. 1988. *A Children's Defense Budget: FY 1989. An Analysis of Our Nation's Investment in Children.* Washington, DC: Children's Defense Fund.

23

THE CURRICULUM AND LINGUISTIC MINORITIES

Lily Wong Fillmore
UNIVERSITY OF CALIFORNIA, BERKELEY

Lois M. Meyer
SAN FRANCISCO STATE UNIVERSITY

In this chapter, we consider research issues related to curricular decision making and design for language minority students. Who are these students, and what are their special needs? How have schools adapted or failed to adapt curricula for the sake of students who come from linguistic and cultural backgrounds that are different from the one assumed by the school? What kinds of adjustments to the curriculum are appropriate and needed, and what kinds are not? It should be noted from the outset that although there has been considerable activity over the past two decades in the development of curriculum materials for language minority students, there is little formal research either evaluating their effectiveness or investigating the underlying issues in this area. Much of the curricula for language minority students has been developed through bilingual education projects in local school districts supported by Title VII funds under the Elementary and Secondary Education Act (ESEA). As a consequence, the materials that have been produced have tended to be quite local in their orientation, and whatever evaluations were conducted on them were largely subsumed under the evaluations of overall projects rather than on the curricular materials specifically. This body of work has not been easy to assess since it is neither readily available nor particularly informative. In our examination of the research issues, we will describe some of these curriculum development efforts and comment on the practical problems of assessing their value. Given this situation, the focus in this chapter is on research issues rather than on the state of the art of the present research on the curriculum for language minority students.

The next section begins with a brief historical overview of the educational treatment of language minority students in the society's schools as background to the discussion of the present situation. We then discuss the problems facing these students in getting access to the curricular content taught in school as well as the problems facing the schools in providing access. In the following section, we discuss some philosophical issues that are relevant to curricular decision making for students from diverse language and cultural backgrounds. The decision-making process of how best to educate such students has become so highly politicized over the past several decades that the philosophical issues that should figure in any discussion of curricular values and goals tend to get lost. What kind of political and philosophical commitments are reflected in the decisions we make about educating students from diverse backgrounds? In the following sections we consider the need for and some efforts toward adjusting content, pedagogy, language use, and instructional activity structure. Finally, we present a research agenda for future work on this topic.

BACKGROUND

As a nation of immigrants, the United States has always been a diverse society, but never before in its history has the diversity been quite so great. Over the past 15 or 20 years, 1 million new immigrants each year (½ million documented and up to ½ million undocumented, by some estimates) have been added to American society (National Coalition of Advocates for Students 1988). Whereas earlier migrations originated principally from Europe, the new immigrants are largely from Latin America, the Caribbean region, and Asia. They represent a diversity of languages, cultures, and experiences. These demographic changes are reflected in American schools: At present, the student population is one of the most diverse in the world. Although student diversity is not a new problem for American schools, the question of how (or whether) the school's curriculum should be adjusted for the sake of students who come from diverse linguistic and cultural backgrounds has been a matter of concern only in recent years.

The problems these students encounter in school are daunting. Many of them know no English when they enter school, although English is the main language of instruction in most American classrooms. How do they learn it, and how can they learn subject matter while they are in the process of learning English? Their prior experience with formal education may or may not prepare them to deal with the mainstream American educational system. They may or may not have had much, or any, formal education at all. How can they discover what is expected in the new situation when they do not understand what their teachers and classmates are saying? Minority students born in this country may come to school equally limited in English but with a history of alienation, confusion, and fear as they and their parents approach a public institution.

Looked at from the school's perspective, the problems of the language minority students, especially the newcomers, are just as daunting for the teachers and administrators who receive them. Few teachers are prepared to meet the complex educational needs of these students. They know how to teach subject matter at the grade levels at which they work, but few of them have much experience or background in language teaching. They are unlikely to know even one of the languages spoken by their non-English-speaking students, and therefore they lack any easy means of communicating with their students or of teaching them. In most places, the greatest influx of new immigrant students is at schools that are already crowded and diverse. Fear, mistrust, and antagonism among students as they encounter one another's languages and customs call for teachers to deal with a new set of problems that they may or may not be willing to take on. At present the society's schools and educators are ill prepared to deal with the student diversity they are encountering as a result of these demographic changes.

The problems that the schools now have in educating these students are nothing new. As noted earlier, Americans have always been a diverse people, and yet our schools have never found ways to handle diversity successfully. There is ample evidence that students—whether they are recent immigrants or natives—who come from nonmainstream language and cultural backgrounds do not fare as well educationally as do students who are from English-speaking or mainstream backgrounds. Statistics on school dropout rates have been available for just one language minority group, Hispanics, and those only since 1975. The most recent figures indicate that 31.8 percent of young Hispanic adults (ages 20 to 24) did not complete high school (U.S. Department of Education 1988). In the State of California, the attrition rate for Hispanics is even higher, 45 percent (Haycock and Navarro 1988).

The dropout rate for Hispanic students reflects the difficulty of making progress in a school system that has not been especially friendly to them. They, along with black students, score consistently lower than whites in tests of academic achievement in reading, writing, and mathematics. Their performance on tests of literacy skills indicates that the differences between them and white students are the greatest at the highest levels of reading (U.S. Department of Education 1988). By age 17, 40.6 percent of all white students are "adept readers": They are able not only to search for specific information and to interrelate ideas but also to make generalizations about and to explain relatively complicated literary, science, and social science materials. In contrast, only 12.9 percent of Hispanics and 7.1 percent of blacks are reading at that level. The differences begin early and increase as the students continue in school (Haycock and Navarro 1988). Hispanics and blacks are 6 months behind whites in their scores at the end of 1st grade. By the 12th grade, they are 3 years behind.

The patterns of underachievement for language and cultural minority students that are so familiar to us have been documented since the beginning of the century. David Cohen (1970), in an analysis of school achievement data from the early decades of this century, found that immigrant children from non-English-speaking countries were more likely to experience school retardation than those from English-speaking countries and that children from immigrant families tended to drop out of school earlier and at higher rates than American-born children. According to Cohen, it was not simply language differences that affected the school performance of these immigrant children but also differences in cultural and social background.

There is little evidence, however, of any large-scale efforts to adjust school programs to fit the needs of non-English-speaking immigrant children until rather recently. The notable exceptions were the early bilingual education efforts in a few French and Spanish communities in Louisiana and New Mexico and a number of midwestern communities with large concentrations of German-speaking families during the 1800s. The German immigrant communities in cities such as Milwaukee, Cincinnati, and Cleveland managed to establish bilingual education programs in both parochial and public schools. These programs were authorized by state law in a few states such as Ohio, Nebraska, and Pennsylvania (Andersson and Boyer 1970; Kloss 1966, 1977). In other states the decisions to establish bilingual programs were local ones, no doubt in response to practical necessity. A few of these programs lasted until the beginning of World War I, but many others were abandoned much earlier when groups protested the use of languages other than English in American schools (Leibowitz 1970).

Much of the opposition to bilingual education during that period stemmed from a xenophobic reaction to what was then regarded as "foreign influences" in the society. Immigrants were expected to adjust themselves to their adopted society, rather than the other way around. It would take a half century before bilingual education would be reconsidered as an option for educating language minority students. Bilingual education was unacceptable then as it is now to many Americans because it represented an intolerable accommodation on the part of society's institutions to the special needs of new Americans and to those who had not yet melted into the mainstream. To these early opponents of bilingual education, English was the only acceptable medium of instruction in the schools. If the children of immigrant and other linguistic minority groups did not understand it, they had better learn it. What such people feared was that any linguistic accommodation on the part of the school, for example, by permitting the use of languages such as Spanish for instructional purposes, would lead to the disintegration of the society. There has been in recent years a resurgence of such views. The U.S. English movement, a group lobbying for the passage of a constitutional amendment that would effectively ban the use of languages other than English from public life (Hayakawa 1985), has campaigned actively against bilingual education (Crawford 1986a, 1986b, 1989). It has charged that society would be "torn apart" by unassimilated linguistic subgroups if bilingual education were permitted to flourish in this country.

There is virtually no immigrant group that does not assimilate linguistically within two or three generations, but it can be a painful process. That it might facilitate the difficult linguistic, social, and cultural transitions the newcomers must make to life in their adopted society is not reason enough for these hardliners to support even small adjustments in the school's methods. If the educational problems of minority students are believed to stem from language and cultural differences, it is up to them to remove those differences rather than to expect any special allowances from the schools. This has been the attitude whether the group in question is immigrant or native.

The educational treatment of American natives over the past hundred years shows how greatly our attitudes toward minority groups in the society, acted upon, can harm children and their families. In a recent historical analysis Adams (1988) describes the motives and beliefs supporting the assimilationist efforts that were pursued aggressively throughout the 19th century and which continue today, although in a considerably less overt manner. Through a system of federal Indian schools, the U.S. government worked relentlessly at undermining the cultural integrity and tribal cohesion of the native peoples of America. Adams argues that the motive behind the campaign to assimilate the natives into the larger society, although rationalized on humanitarian grounds as an effort to "civilize" the Indians and save them from their own "savagery," was considerably less benevolent. What was at stake was land—land set aside as Indian reservations throughout the country—that others coveted. As long as the Indians maintained a tribal identity, it would not be easy to dispossess them of tribal lands, which were theirs by right of various treaties negotiated with the U.S. government. Adams characterizes the prevalent attitude in the following way:

> Indians possessed the land and needed civilization; whites on the other hand, had civilization but needed land. The philanthropic solution to the Indian question was now clear: a fair exchange whereby whites would give the Indians civilization in return for land cessions—land the Indians would no longer require once they were civilized. This was the basis for an Indian policy characterized by one historian as "expansion with honor." (17)

The means by which the Native Americans were to be civilized were educational. By 1891, Adams (1988) notes, Congress had made school attendance compulsory for Indian children. Parents who resisted sending their children to the system of boarding schools established by the federal government were treated punitively by the withholding of services and support to which they were entitled. Paul Blatchford (1977), a descendent of Manuelito, a revered chief of the Navajo people, described his education in such a boarding school beginning in 1921 at the age of 5:

> The general curriculum in the schools was history, arithmetic, English and penmanship, which were taught the first half of each day; while the other half was used to clean up dormitories and perform other jobs if the person was one of the younger students. The school offered vocational training in the early days for the older students, and it was taught the last half of the school day. The memories of how children were treated—and punished for every little thing they did—made me want my children to live at home. I felt that they could attend school nearby, but not a boarding school or a mission school away from home. Parents in those days, however, had nothing to say about the schools, although they did gripe and complain regarding how the kids were punished. The police forced those kids to go to school, and I know many parents whose teardrops fell—but they couldn't do anything about it. If the parents resisted the policemen, they [the parents] were put in jail; so there was really nothing they could do. (Blatchford 1977, 175–177)

The worst schools were located at great distances from the reservations, and children were kept for uninterrupted periods of up to 5 years before they were permitted to visit their parents and families. The isolation from families was justified on the grounds that as long as the children could go home, even for summer vacations or holidays, they were susceptible to relapses—regressions to the "savage ways" of their parents. The effects of such an educational treatment were considerable. In exchange for the education they received, many native Americans paid the price of language, culture, tribal integrity, and closeness with family and clan.

The foregoing account might suggest that our educational policies toward Native Americans were unique because of the ulterior motives supporting them, but they were actually not so different from policies toward other minority groups. Although no immigrant group has had its children forcibly taken away to be educated in boarding schools, the situation for many of them has been equally alienating. The major objective in the schooling of minority groups historically has been to assimilate them into the larger society, away from the family and the influence of the primary cultural group. Despite our legacy of diversity, Americans have never been comfortable with a heterogeneous society. We have endeavored to homogenize ourselves at all costs and to assume a homogeneity of background even when it does not exist (Greenbaum 1974).

The "melting pot" has long been a self-defining idealization for the society (Mann 1979), as well as a rationalization for our educational practices. For most minority groups, the classroom has been the melting pot, the place where they have been stripped of their old cultural identities as they take on a new one. For many language minority students, it has been the place where they have learned English but lost the language of their parents. For many immigrants and natives alike, the alienation from parents and primary community that Richard Rodriguez (1982) describes as he shifted from Spanish to English after beginning school is a familiar story:

> Matching the silence I started hearing in public was a new quiet at home. The family's quiet was partly due to the fact that, as we children learned more and more English, we shared fewer and fewer words with our parents. Sentences needed to be spoken slowly when a child addressed his mother or father. [Often the parent would not understand.] The child would need to repeat himself. [Still the parent misunderstood.] The young voice, frustrated, would end up saying, "Never mind"—the subject was closed. Dinner would be noisy with the clinking of knives and forks against dishes. My mother would smile softly between her remarks; my father at the other end of the table would chew and chew at his food, while he stared over the heads of his children. (23)

This loss of familial closeness in language minority families is not an inevitable part of the assimilation process, but it is nevertheless a common outcome of the usual way of educating language minority students. Bilingual education represents a major effort on the part of policymakers to make it possible for such students to gain an education and English language proficiency without losing their native languages and cultures, their personal identities.

Until 1968, when Title VII of the Elementary and Secondary Education Act (ESEA) was established, providing federal funds for the development of bilingual education programs for language minority students, the major accommodations made for them were compensatory in nature. The operating assumption was that these students did not thrive in school because they were deficient in foundational skills and experiences for academic learning. Their parents had not prepared them appropriately for school: They had taught them neither English nor the ways of learning that the school values. Until they acquired those basic skills, they could not be expected to handle the regular curriculum. Compensatory education was supposed to provide such basic skills, and such programs generally offered that and little else. Few, if any, of these programs made a lasting difference for the students who went through them.

Advocates for bilingual education argued that these compensatory programs were ineffective because they were based on a fundamental misassumption about what was needed. Language minority students such as the many Spanish speakers have done poorly academically not because they are deficient in their preparation but because they are different. Their parents have provided them with legitimate ways of speaking and learning, although they are different from the patterns expected in school. The proposal to provide instruction in the language of the home in addition to English and to make accommodations for different ways of learning through the adaptation of materials and instructional methods was a revolutionary idea in 1968, and it is a largely unrealized ideal today.

Bilingual education, as it was presented in the 1968 Bilingual Education Act, was fundamentally a compensatory education program in its aims. Although the maintenance of the mother tongue and cultural heritage were two of its three stated purposes, it nevertheless gave greater emphasis to the third—increasing English-language skills. It served students exclusively from low-income homes in which English was not the dominant language, and they could remain in the program only for as long as they were limited in their English skills (S880b–1). Its primary aim was clear, and that was to provide assistance to children who because they lacked English were at an educational disadvantage. Many of the earliest programs funded by Title VII were little more than compensatory English-language and basic skills programs based on a deficiency model of the educational needs of language minority students. Revisions in the program in 1974 and later in 1978 mitigated the compensatory orientation somewhat, but Title VII has nonetheless maintained that focus to the present. The educators who had originally proposed the funding of bilingual education had envisioned a program that considered the students' linguistic and cultural backgrounds as resources that could be developed.

How bilingual education has developed, what it has gone through in the past two decades, is far too complex a story to be told here. The story begins with the development and implementation of the Canadian immersion education programs (Cummins and Swain 1986; Lambert & Tucker 1972; Swain 1974; Swain and Barik 1976), continues with the Dade County bilingual schools for the children of Cuban refugees (Mackey and Beebe 1977), picks up the pace with the early Title VII projects (Troike 1978), and becomes a major educational issue with the *Lau* v. *Nichols* decision of 1974 (Teitlebaum and Hiller 1977). The story takes on complex undertones following the Lau decision, when in response to the Supreme Court ruling requiring schools to provide assistance for language minority students, many states adopted legislation mandating bilingual education for those who needed it. Once bilingual education was required, the opponents of any kind of departure from the assimilationist goals of American education attacked it, with predictable results (Epstein 1977; Glazer 1980). It is simply beyond the scope of this chapter to do justice to this complex story, this courageous and embattled attempt to adjust the school to fit the student, and we refer the reader to several recent examinations of bilingual education: James Crawford's (1989) *Bilingual Education: History, Politics, Theory and Practice*, Jim Cummins's (1989) *Empowering Minority Students*, his and Merrill Swain's (1986) *Bilingual-*

ism in Education: Aspects of Theory, Research and Practice, and Kenji Hakuta's (1986) *Mirror of Language: The Debate on Bilingualism*.

PHILOSOPHICAL ISSUES

Should public schools adapt to meet the special needs of language and cultural minority students, or should the students change—or be changed—to adapt to the school? That is, when Mexican-American or Salvadoran or Chinese or Vietnamese or Hmong students enter school and find that there is little match between their language and culture and those of the school, which side should be required to change, the school or the scholar? Is cultural contact necessarily a zero-sum game, in which one group must lose for the other to win? Are there other options, in which there are no winners or losers? When it comes to diversity in public education, where do individual needs and rights end and social or civic unity begin? Is it possible to imagine a middle ground, where the two extremes blur without being erased? What is the role and responsibility of the school in a diverse society? What goals should it seek to attain?

Tyler (1949) proposed an examination of the purposes of schooling as the first of his four fundamental questions to be considered in curriculum planning since "all aspects of the education program are really means to accomplish basic educational purposes" (3). His classic work laid out a process for curriculum planning in which the determination of appropriate goals was foundational to the selection of "a group of highly important, consistent objectives" (33) on which the selection, organization, and evaluation of learning activities depended. In Tyler's model, without appropriate goals the process of curriculum development is directionless.

In this section we will consider the goals and values that determine the direction of the educational experience of language and culture minority students in the public schools. If the outcomes of school programs and curricula targeted for minority students too often seem illusive or disappointing, it is not so much because of the lack of goals as because of the often unarticulated conflict between two competing goals: *cultural assimilation* and *cultural pluralism*. In subtle and not so subtle ways, these competing convictions have colored the national debate concerning excellence and equality in American education. We will consider here how excellence and equality are perceived and pursued by very disparate voices in this public debate, those of school reformers and critical education theorists. Their differing agendas for achieving minority student empowerment, a recent addition to the list of nationally lauded goals for schooling, will also be compared. Throughout the section, we will analyze the public rhetoric concerning the goals of excellence, equality, and empowerment to reveal the contrasting futures that are promised (though not always delivered) to language and culture minority students: melting and merging into one common American cultural amalgam (assimilation) or maintaining and manifesting cultural diversity in an environment of mutual respect (pluralism).

The necessary direction and goals of American schooling are self-evident to the authors of the school reform reports of the 1980s. There is a united call for a recommitment to the traditional goals that suffuse our national identity—economic competitiveness, social stability, equality of opportunity, preservation of democracy, national prosperity, and a shared national vision (Carnegie Foundation for the Advancement of Teaching 1988; Carnegie Task Force on Teaching as a Profession 1986). These goals represent a sacred public trust, for "without good schools none of America's hopes can be fulfilled" (Carnegie Foundation for the Advancement of Teaching 1988, xi). According to the reformers, our schools have largely betrayed this trust. At a time when higher and more rigorous standards are required if the traditional goals are to be achieved in a rapidly changing society, public schools are unable to succeed in meeting even the old standards. The consequences are dire: "The educational foundations of our society are presently being eroded by a rising tide of mediocrity that threatens our very future as a Nation and as a people" (National Commission on Excellence in Education 1983, 5). Public schooling must be massively overhauled, and American schools must be made "excellent" by new standards if the traditional goals are to be realized in this technologically sophisticated and globally competitive age.

> If our standard of living is to be maintained, if the growth of a permanent underclass is to be averted, if democracy is to function effectively into the next century, our schools must graduate the vast majority of their students with achievement levels long thought possible for only the privileged few. The American mass education system, designed in the early part of the century for a mass-production economy, will not succeed unless it not only raises but redefines the essential standards of excellence and strives to make quality and equality of opportunity compatible with each other. (Carnegie Task Force on Teaching as a Profession 1986, 3)

Although the issues of quality and equality have plagued the U.S. system of public schooling throughout the century, they have become more pressing now that classrooms across the nation display the demographics of diversity. In a *Wall Street Journal* article, Nazario (1989, R21–22) describes teachers in Los Angeles who cope with a student population speaking 81 primary languages. As many as 20 different languages are reportedly spoken by the students in a single classroom. Although some of these immigrant children come prepared culturally and linguistically to succeed in school, the situation for many others is "something out of Dickens" (R22): Many are poor, unable to speak or understand English, often uneducated, malnourished, ill, traumatized by violence in their home countries, and often undocumented and terrified of discovery. According to this article, nearly half the immigrant children in the Los Angeles School District drop out, but there is a steady stream of new arrivals to take their places.

The educational situation in large urban centers like Los

Angeles has reached crisis proportions throughout the country, but the challenge both to quality and equality in public education posed by minority students is not confined to large cities or to any specific region (National Coalition of Advocates for Students 1988). In large and small communities throughout the country, the influx of large numbers of language minority students over the past 10 or 15 years has strained the capacity of local school districts to serve them properly. There are disturbing signs that the minority student population is being missed—or even worse, misserved—by the school reform movement. Claims that positive change is occurring for this student population could be made only by employing narrow and impoverished definitions of excellence and equality:

> All indications are that the current reform movement will produce success defined in its own terms: Children will spend more hours and days in school, more coursework will be taken in mathematics, science, and technology, and mean achievement test scores will probably rise. But beyond indicators of movement toward "excellence" [higher numbers] lies evidence of an ominous side of reform. We can already see a declining college attendance rate for minorities, increased underrepresentation of minorities in postgraduate and professional education, limited access of minority students to computers in schools and to instruction in programming, disproportionately large enrollment of minority students in low-track classes and high enrollment of whites in programs for the gifted, and disproportionately high failure rates on minimum competency tests for minority students. (Oakes 1986, 77)

The noticeable inequality created by well-intentioned efforts toward excellence is increasingly being brought to public awareness. In a special report on urban schooling called *An Imperiled Generation* (Carnegie Foundation for the Advancement of Teaching 1988), the Carnegie trustees declare themselves to be "deeply troubled that the reform movement launched to upgrade the education of *all* students is irrelevant to many children—largely black and Hispanic—in our urban schools" (xi). They express the conviction that "equity and excellence cannot be divided" (4) and conclude that "saving the urban schools is perhaps the most urgent educational challenge this nation confronts" (xix).

> Equality of opportunity, along with the support to make it real and not merely rhetorical, must be seen as the unfinished agenda for the nation's schools. To expand access without upgrading urban schools is simply to perpetuate discrimination in a more subtle form. But to push for excellence in ways that ignore the needs of less privileged students is to undermine the future of the nation.(4)

The report lays out a comprehensive program for saving urban schools that retains the traditional goals despite an overwhelmingly diverse and nontraditional, urban student population. Carnegie's program includes the commitment to educate *all* children toward the same ends; the development of new governance procedures; a call for an educational renewal program for schools at the local level; and partnerships that link the school to a network of local, state, and federal support. Within the school itself, five priorities for renewal are established: priority to early schooling, which focuses on English-language development; a clearly defined core curriculum; flexible scheduling arrangements; a program of coordinated services; and safe and attractive facilities.

Related to equality and excellence in the Carnegie report is the goal of student empowerment, brought about through enriched English-language ability and the dominance of a standard core of knowledge. The report acknowledges in passing the existence of bilingual instruction while remaining essentially noncommittal on the issue of native language usage in the education of linguistic minority students (20). The importance of developing English-language skills, however, is declared to be a top priority, especially in the ungraded kindergarten through grade 4, which it calls Basic School:

> Children in the Basic School would, from the first, be speaking, writing, reading and talking about words, listening to stories, become linguistically empowered in an environment that the foreign language people like to call the "saturation method." No child should leave fourth grade without good command of English. (19)

The core curriculum, a "basic curriculum for all students" (26), which would be "based on those consequential ideas, experiences, and traditions common to all by virtue of our membership in the human family at a particular moment in history" (26), would be explored through studies in English, history, mathematics, science, and the arts. In its chapter entitled "The Mandate: Excellence for All," the report again speaks of empowerment as a goal that applies equally to all students: "Different approaches to learning are required, but all students, regardless of background, should be given the tools and encouragement they need to be socially and economically empowered" (1). The Carnegie message is clear, and clearly assimilationist: Empowering minority students means making them equal to, and indistinguishable from, majority students in mainstream-relevant competencies so that they can compete for the social and economic rewards that the system has to offer. Major tools of that empowerment process are mainstream cultural knowledge and fluency and facility with English. Equality appears to be synonymous with homogeneity, and empowerment seems to be achieved by encouraging diverse routes to a uniform end: cultural sameness.

Agreeing that the empowerment of students should indeed be the goal of education, Cummins (1989) argues that the tools and encouragement that would truly empower minority students look very different from those described in the Carnegie agenda. After an extensive review of the literature, Cummins contends that programs that succeed in promoting minority students' academic growth promote cultural plurality rather than cultural uniformity. Such programs develop students' native linguistic talents, foster a secure sense of personal and cultural identity, and promote confidence in the students' ability to learn. Cummins' review of the research refutes the hypothesis that minority students' academic failures are primarily caused by language differences or lack of English. Instead, says Cummins, disempowerment of minority students is the result of discrimination against them because of their differentness.

Bilingual education programs, although providing a vital opportunity for minority student empowerment, are only one aspect of a much broader change process required to reverse minority students' educational failure. Students are disempowered as a result of institutionalized racism that permeates the structure of schools and mediates the interactions between educators and students. According to Cummins (1989), "It is in the interactions with individual educators that minority students are either empowered, or alternatively, disabled, personally and academically" (4). Individual and well-intentioned educators empower or disable minority students in school by personally promoting or inhibiting (1) the incorporation of the minority students' language and culture into the school program, (2) the minority community's participation in the school as an integral component of children's education, (3) a pedagogy that motivates students to use language actively to generate their own knowledge, and (4) advocacy for minority students in issues of assessment by focusing primarily on the ways in which students' academic difficulty is a function of interactions within the school context rather than by legitimizing the location of the "problem" within students (58).

Cummins's and the Carnegie agendas for educating minority students express the same goals—equal access to quality education and student empowerment. Yet, point by point, the agendas are crucially different in each of the characteristics identified by Cummins. In stark contrast to Cummins's proposals, the agenda presented in *An Imperiled Generation* (Carnegie Foundation for the Advancement of Teaching 1988) makes no mention of the child's cultural identity; and in its one fleeting and noncommittal reference to bilingual programs, it remains neutral regarding the use of the native language (20). English-language development is given first priority, and standards of English performance are recommended for children before they have completed the early grades. The Carnegie agenda calls for parents to be collaborators with the educational system, "involved in schools, consulting with teachers and monitoring the progress of their children" (xviii), but there is no request that they be agents for change within the school system and society at large. There is no mention of the process of critical reflection, which Cummins seeks, in which parents, educators, and students deepen their awareness of institutional racism and discrimination by reflecting on their own interactions with schools, thereby empowering themselves to act to bring about significant change for minority children and communities.

An Imperiled Generation says little about pedagogy and nothing about a pedagogy in which students and educators together determine what is important to learn, construct their critical understanding of their world, and act to change and improve it. The imperiled students of the Carnegie report will experience the core curriculum through diverse and unspecified teaching approaches, but the basic content and purposes are predetermined and are presumably the same for all. Further, the minority students' academic difficulties are seen as stemming from their linguistic and cultural characteristics, not from the disabling interactions they have with educators within the school. Instead of reflecting on its own role in perpetuating minority students' failure, the school's task as laid out in the Carnegie agenda is to remediate students' "deficiencies" through health programs; Head Start; English-language development; diverse teaching approaches; and involvement and support in the schools by the community, business, and government.

Thus, we can see that although both of these educational agendas claim to empower minority students, they are based on contradictory goals: *cultural assimilation* versus *cultural pluralism*. Cummins's (1989) call for empowerment through cultural pluralism is clearly the more radical and troubling proposal in that it is profoundly at odds with traditional American educational goals. As was noted earlier, the United States throughout its history has dealt with the reality of a diverse society by positing a melting-pot ideal, which ultimately requires the complete assimilation of all of its constituent groups. Oakes (1986) contends that despite this ideal, "in reality only certain people were to be melted" (65). Historically, according to Oakes, efforts to Americanize immigrants have attempted not only to provide them with a common culture but also to make them conform to the society's dominant ways and values. The various school reform efforts, including *An Imperiled Generation*, are in the assimilationist tradition, though they rarely say so directly.

Hirsch (1987), in his *Cultural Literacy*, grants that cultural diversity in the form of multicultural education may indeed be valuable, but he maintains that it "should not be allowed to supplant or interfere with our schools' responsibility to ensure our children's mastery of American literate culture" (18), by which he means a culture that is, or ought to be, common to all. Hirsch is much more outspoken about his opposition to linguistic diversity or multilingualism: He avers that such a goal is "contrary to our traditions and extremely unrealistic" (93) and would foment "cultural fragmentation, civil antagonism, illiteracy, and economic-technological ineffectualness" (92).

To protect the belief that academic excellence for minority students will be achieved through cultural absorption into the mainstream, voices that call for cultural pluralism, social empowerment, and affirmation of diversity are frequently silenced (Fine 1987; Giroux 1984). According to Fine, "Simple, seamless pronouncements of equal opportunity and educational credentials as the primary mode of mobility are woven through the curriculum and pedagogy of urban high school classes. Silencing constitutes the process by which contradictory evidence, ideologies, and experiences find themselves buried, camouflaged, and discredited" (157). So pervasive at school is the lack of talk about instances of social, economic, and educational discrimination in the lives of minority and poverty students, according to Fine, that "the very voices of students and their communities that public education claims to nurture, shut down" (158). School as it now functions is far from a place that empowers students from minority or poverty backgrounds, according to Giroux (1984), for it "disconfirms rather than confirms their histories, experiences, and dreams" (189). Minority students who attempt to express their personal realities in their classrooms and schoolwork speak of their "struggle for voice" (Sola and Bennett 1985) and their "struggle for a speaking consciousness" (Walsh 1987).

Grant (1988) documents the disturbing, deepening silence in recent educational research concerning minorities and education. In a comparison of published articles in seven widely read journals in education, sociology, and anthropology, she found that the proportion of articles on race and schooling across the decade had declined overall from 12.7 percent in 1975 to 6.9 percent in 1985. Four other journals had substantially larger proportions of articles on this topic, with no decline across the decade, but these journals are less familiar and less frequently cited than the others. Grant suggests that there is a "ghettoization" (443) in research about minorities: "Articles on minorities in schools appear most frequently in sources where they are least likely to be seen by a broad spectrum of researchers and educators and hence are less likely to influence subsequent scholarship or educational practice" (443). The academic silence about racial and ethnic issues in schools, Grant maintains, has contributed to "colorblindness" (443), the inability of educators and researchers alike to see the effects of subtle racial and ethnic discrimination in schools because of their belief in their own and the institution's unbiased commitment to equality and nonprejudicial behaviors and attitudes.

Oakes (1986) implicates the school reform reports in the silencing subterfuge: The view of equality that they present—"mostly by omission" (72)—conveys the image of school as a neutral factor in the maintenance of social and economic inequalities; promotes the idea of a common culture that is Anglo-conformist in perspective; and quantifies excellence by using a single standard, one that is "undeniably white and middle-class" (74). Though school reform efforts come and go, Oakes contends that American schools do not change in their commitment to differentiated and, in practice, unequal treatment of poor and minority students. Tracking, the most prevalent form of differentiated schooling, has been justified as an effort to equalize opportunity by giving differently endowed students an equal opportunity to succeed; in reality, Oakes contends, it has maintained or increased the inequalities in the larger society. Even during the 1960s and 1970s, when costly investments in programs were supposed to have equalized educational opportunity in the schools, generous funding was given to programs that did not upset (1) the control of education, (2) the content or organization of schooling, (3) the pattern of distribution of educational resources, or (4) the eventual social and economic payoff for differing educational credentials (67). Few reforms, then or now, have questioned the very principles of equality of opportunity, according to Oakes, although affirmative action, minority community control of schools, and multicultural and bilingual education are examples of reforms that have raised such questions. Bilingual education, in fact, has "threatened the Anglo-conformity content and process of schooling" (67).

Oakes's analysis provides a background against which to assess Cummins's (1989) claim about public opposition to bilingual education: "The strong opposition to programs that promote bilingual students' linguistic talents and foster a secure sense of identity is because these programs challenge a division of power and status in the society that has been established over centuries" (viii). According to Cummins, "Schools historically have reflected the societal power structure by eradicating minority students' language and identity and by attributing their school failure to inherent deficiencies (viii).

The contradictory convictions concerning what constitutes the appropriate goal of minority education, cultural assimilation or cultural pluralism, have confounded efforts at curriculum and program evaluation:

> This perennial disagreement over whether bilingual education should promote assimilation or cultural pluralism makes it extremely difficult to compare the merits of different educational outcomes for LEP [limited English proficient] and NEP [non-English proficient] children. If assimilation is the relevant goal, LEP and NEP students succeed to the extent that they become largely indistinguishable from their English-speaking classmates. By contrast, if cultural pluralism is the objective, LEP and NEP children who emerge from the educational process identical to their English-speaking peers are failures; they succeed only by acknowledging their linguistic and cultural differences and taking pride in them. Clearly, this unresolved value dispute hobbles efforts to define positive educational outcomes for LEP children. (Moran 1986, 205)

Since goals and values (according to Tyler 1949) generate all other aspects of the educational program, the discrepancies between the assimilationist and pluralistic perspectives are especially troublesome. These differences not only hobble efforts to define and evaluate the outcomes of schooling but also confound the entire educational and curricular process. The selection, organization, implementation, and evaluation of instructional activities will communicate one or the other of these conflicting purposes, either by design or by default.

Cummins (1989) identifies three pedagogical approaches that are both consistent with his agenda for empowerment through proactive cultural pluralism and necessary for its practical implementation: critical literacy (Ada 1986, 1988; Ada and de Olave 1986; Freire 1973b), cooperative learning (Kagan 1986), and process writing (Graves 1978, 1983). All teaching strategies, these and others, are embued with value commitments. But in most other cases, the value commitments and cultural purposes of a specific pedagogical approach or curricular program for minority students are not so clearly set out, and they are left to districts or individual teachers to discover or to overlook.

The obvious and pervasive influence of conflicting values behind the competing goals of American schooling reveals a troublesome blind spot in Tyler's (1949) curricular model, what we might call a value blindness. Tyler periodically acknowledges the interpretive judgments inherent in various steps of his process for selecting appropriate goals. However, the technical efficiency and product orientation of his planning process mask and seemingly neutralize the value-laden choices and decisions that it continually requires. To gather information to help in the selection of appropriate educational goals, Tyler suggests assessing the learners' needs and interests, the needs and demands of contemporary life, and the recommendations of subject matter specialists.

Monette (1979) points out the value decisions that are glossed over in these processes: "It becomes apparent that the concept of need has no meaning without a set of norms and that it is therefore impossible even to identify needs without them. Needs are not mere empirically determinable facts; they are complex value judgments" (84). Moran (1986) raises the same objection to the idea that subject matter specialists might provide objective data for consideration:

> The myth of the unbiased expert may sometimes serve as a convenient crutch that spares decisionmakers from confronting the deep-seated value disputes that underlie a policy dilemma. By leaving problems to the experts, decisionmakers can understate the need for discussion of community values to achieve optimal social policies. (208)

Tyler (1949) himself acknowledges that in the end, the planning process is dependent on value-based decisions: "It is certainly true that in the final analysis objectives are matters of choice, and they must therefore be the considered value judgements of those responsible for the school" (4). But he does not acknowledge the iterative circle of judgments this dependency seems to require. Even the decision to consider this set of "facts" or to consult that group of "experts" is colored by the values of the one who decides.

The final question we will consider here, although Tyler does not discuss it, is exactly this: Who should decide? The question of whose values are to set the vision and determine the selection of goals for the education of linguistic minority students is a crucially important one. Should it be those of the well-intentioned educator whose mainstream commitments promote an assimilationist goal, or should it be the pluralistic goals of the reflective educator who criticizes and challenges the system? How much influence or control should the students themselves or their parents have in determining the purposes of their own or their children's educational lives? Confronting the pervasive practice of silencing minority student and community voices, Simon (1987) calls for a "pedagogy of possibility," in which such voices are not only heard but also are encouraged to diverge and to "interrogate each other" (379) and the cultural, moral, and political assumptions we hold:

> A curriculum and its supporting pedagogy are a version of our own dreams for ourselves, our children, and our communities. But such dreams are never neutral; they are always someone's dreams and to the degree that they are implicated in organizing the future for others they always have a moral and political dimension. (372)

So again the question, Who decides? The fate, not only of the many minority students in our schools, but indeed of our society, may well depend on how this question is answered over the next few decades and on the willingness of the educational establishment to reflect critically and to take risks in making its response.

ADAPTATIONS

A teacher in a suburban Los Angeles school, remembering the days before large numbers of immigrant children came into the school district, comments wistfully, "Everyone used to be on the same page of the reading book. That is no longer possible" (Nazario 1989). Whether covering the same content with all students in the same materials at the same time was ever advisable or even possible, teachers are increasingly realizing that content instruction must be different in classrooms in which language and culture minority students are present. Teaching today, according to Oakes (1986), is being shaped by "the central struggle of contemporary schooling practice—the development of curriculum and instruction suited to the wide range of abilities and future needs of American children" (62). Given the presence of growing numbers of linguistic minority students in the schools, this struggle includes the development of curriculum and instruction suited for a diversity of cultural backgrounds as well as a diversity in primary languages and in English-language proficiency.

It is clear that children are unlikely to "be on the same page of the book," but the alternatives are far from obvious. Should they be on different pages of the same book? Should they be in different books according to some assessment of their different levels of language proficiency or content mastery? Should the book be used at all or abandoned? Would books written in the students' home languages work better? Can textbooks written in English be adapted, and if so, how and by whom? Whose responsibility is it to make certain that the school's curriculum is taught in meaningful ways to all students, including those from diverse language and cultural backgrounds?

Before we examine some of the efforts to adapt the school's curriculum for language minority students, let us consider ways in which materials and methods can be adjusted as well as arguments for and against various kinds of adjustments. The first way materials and methods can be adjusted is linguistic. If the students do not know the school's language, what kind of adjustments can be made to give them access to the curricular content, and how can they be helped to learn English?

The second kind of adaptation to consider is pedagogical and structural: The modes of learning promoted in the home and the way activities are structured there may be quite different from the way things are done at school. How do sociocultural factors influence the way individuals approach the learning of subject matter? What kind of adjustments in structure and methods are necessary to ensure that all children, regardless of background, are able to participate in instructional activities and to learn the materials that are being taught?

The third type of adaptation is in content. How appropriate for minority students are the materials that are taught in school? Is the diversity of experience represented by the students reflected in the curriculum? Do curricular materials promote the level of subject matter learning that is expected of all students at each grade level?

Many of the curricular innovations discussed in the next section have been made in the context of bilingual programs, whether or not they were supported by Title VII funds. As noted earlier, descriptions of these innovations are not readily obtainable, although there are a number of important efforts over the past 20 years to collect and disseminate information on this work. A look at the checkered history of the Title VII materials development centers over the past 15 years will help the reader understand why curricular research for language minority students is in its present state.

In 1975, Title VII provided funds for the establishment of a network of national and regional centers to give general assistance to local and state school districts that were developing bilingual education programs, to collect and disseminate instructional materials that were being developed through these programs, and to provide assistance in the assessment of the programs. The most relevant to the present chapter were the Materials Development Centers (MDC), 19 of which were located throughout the country over the years, designing materials for many different language groups. The MDC in Anchorage, for example, produced materials in a variety of Alaskan native languages. The one in Albuquerque produced Navaho materials only. The Dallas and Tucson MDCs both specialized in Spanish and English, and those in Honolulu, Berkeley, Los Angeles, and San Francisco produced materials in a variety of Asian and Pacific languages. The materials that were developed were published and disseminated through 20 or so Bilingual Education Service Centers (BESC), which were regional, as well as through 3 national centers, known as the Evaluation, Dissemination, and Assistance Centers (EDAC), located in Texas, California, and Massachussetts.

The EDACs have long since disappeared; all that remains of these important efforts in collecting, evaluating, and disseminating the curricular materials produced in connection with the various Title VII developmental projects is the National Dissemination Center (NDC), which is sponsored by the Fall River Public Schools in Massachussetts. The NDC is no longer supported by federal funds but continues to disseminate at cost English- and native-language materials in Cape Verdean, Khmer (Cambodian), Chinese, English, French, Greek, Haitian Creole, Hmong, Italian, Korean, Portuguese, Spanish, and Vietnamese.

In addition to the EDACs, a Refugee Materials Center was funded by the U.S. Department of Education and located in Kansas City, Missouri. Its purpose was to develop and disseminate curricular and supplementary materials in support of programs for the education and resettlement of refugees and immigrants. Like the EDACs, the Refugee Materials Center no longer exists, and the materials that it prepared or collected have been archived at the Center for Applied Linguistics in Washington, DC. In 1984, the BESCs were transformed into 16 Bilingual Education Multifunctional Support Centers (BEMSC), which assumed the responsibilities of most of the MDCs, the BESCs, and the EDACs. More recently, the BEMSCs were transformed into 16 regional Multifunctional Resource Centers. The many transformations these centers have undergone over the past 15 years have greatly affected the progress in the creation and evaluation of curriculum materials for bilingual programs.

The National Clearinghouse for Bilingual Education (NCBE) was established in 1977 for the purpose of collecting, analyzing, and disseminating information on bilingual education; but although this task has included some of the curriculum materials that have been produced over the years, it has not been the clearinghouse's job to manage or circulate this massive collection. NCBE, too, has had problems over the years, given the way projects like it are funded. Over the course of its 12 years of operation, it has changed hands—gone from one contractor to another—three times. Each time it has moved, it has lost momentum and its scope of work has been redefined. At present, it is located at the Center for Applied Linguistics and is jointly operated by the center and George Washington University. Among its various functions, it maintains a computerized data base on bilingual education and a resource collection in its library, provides reference and referral services, and creates and disseminates a variety of information products such as bibliographies.

In addition to this important body of work collected over the years through the auspices of Title VII, there was established a National Center for Bilingual Research (NCBR), which was originally contracted to the Southwest Regional Education Laboratory and later to the University of California at Los Angeles and the Center for Applied Linguistics in Washington, DC. NCBR, which no longer exists, did not develop curriculum, although it conducted research on issues related to bilingual instruction over the course of both of its manifestations.

LANGUAGE ADAPTATIONS

What language adaptations are needed in curriculum for language minority students? We will consider research and development of three types of language adaptations: choice of language for subject matter instruction, how language is used for instructional purposes, and level of difficulty of the language used in materials. Curricular adjustments related to language teaching and learning are taken up in the section concerning pedagogical and structural adaptations.

Language Choice

Since English is the most apparent obstacle to subject matter learning for language minority students, it is not surprising that much of the curricular research related to their needs has focused on language choice. A relatively advanced level of English is required to understand even simple texts or a teacher's discussion of, say, mathematical concepts. In bilingual programs in which both the students' home language (HL) and English are used for instructional purposes, the question of how the two languages are to be distributed is an obvious issue. Should subject matter be taught in both languages, and if so, how should it be done? Should written materials be prepared in both languages? Can materials be taught effectively in a language the students do not understand fully? If adjustments are needed, should they be in the level of the language used or in the level of materials that are taught?

Our examination of the literature on bilingual education reveals that the answers to these questions are not obvious, at least to many practitioners. For some, bilingual instruction means that virtually every subject taught in school should be taught "bilingually," switching between the two languages as needed. The concurrent method, as this strategy is called, involves alternating between the two languages of instruction. In practice, this usually means that everything is taught in English, and the HL, when it is used, is to help the student understand what has been said or written in English.

Valdés-Fallis (1978) offers a comprehensive functional typology of code-switching patterns, in which she distinguishes between alternations made in response to external factors (e.g., contextual and situational switches) and internal ones (e.g., stylistic or random switches that reflect lexical need). In classrooms, one finds virtually all of Valdés-Fallis's patterns being used to one extent or another, but not all of them figure as centrally in instructional discourse. In the present discussion of the so-called concurrent method, the focus is on alternations that are made during instructional activities and are based on the teachers' beliefs about what is needed and appropriate, given their instructional objectives and the students' presumed language needs. Thus, the types of alternations are described here in terms of their instructional discourse functions rather than their more general communicative functions.

These alternations between languages can be of several distinct types. The first is direct translation, in which near exact translations of instructional discourse expressed first in English (typically) are provided in the students' HL. The assumption is that translations are needed because the students do not understand what is said directly in English. A variation of this method can be found in classrooms where there are both limited English speakers (LES) and fluent English speakers (FES). In such situations, teachers sometimes address each group in turn, using the language the students understand most easily; and in this case, the alternations depend on the group the teacher is addressing. Each group hears both versions, but in essence, each is addressed in just one language.

The second type of language alternation involves explanations or additional information: What has been said in English, say, is developed further in the other language. The instructional point made first in the language the students may or may not understand fully is expanded on and discussed in the language they do know. In this kind of alternation, the information is distributed between the two languages, but what is said in the HL generally builds on what is presented first in English.

A third type of language alternation can be described as dynamic: Teachers spontaneously alternate between the two languages for rhetorical or social reasons. English is the primary mode of instructional discourse, but switches to the HL are made for emphasis, for establishing rapport with the students, or whenever the social situation seems to call for it. This kind of language alternation is difficult to characterize because it is somewhat random and unpredictable: A language switch may reflect, as Valdés-Fallis (1978) has found, ease of lexical retrieval at the moment of speaking because of differences in language dominance, memory or automaticity, or speech habits in which the speaker switches languages for linguistic routines (e.g., "y'know"; "*que hay de nuevo*") or discourse markers (e.g., "moving right along"; "now then"; "as I was saying"; "*porque*"). Valdés-Fallis notes that most such switches are either at the lexical or phrasal level and are motivated principally by factors internal to the speaker.

Although the concurrent method is widely used, it is not without controversy. Andrew Cohen (1973, 1975), in an early study of bilingual education practices, found teachers in a Spanish-English bilingual program alternating between Spanish and English in offering "concept by concept" translations of the materials they were covering. Cohen (1975) notes that the teachers used "simultaneous translations" in the belief that this constituted teaching the "same content in both languages." Legaretta (1977, 1979), in a study of the effects of different patterns of language usage in six kindergarten classrooms, found that concurrent methods were far less effective instructionally than was an "alternate-days" approach, in which the teachers kept the two languages of instruction clearly separated by using just one of them during a given day, alternating between them from one day to the next. Children in the class in which the two languages of instruction were kept completely separate made greater gains both in English and in Spanish language development than did the children in classes that used translations.

Concurrent methods have been found to be ineffective in two important ways. First, alternations appear to affect the extent to which the students can use the language of instruction as input or as a foundation for language development, whether it is the HL or English. Students may eventually favor English over the HL (see, e.g., González and Maez 1980). In a bilingual program that attempted to promote two-way bilingualism (the goal being that the Spanish-speaking students would learn English and the English speakers would learn Spanish), Andrew Cohen (1973) found the concurrent method to be largely ineffective. The English speakers tended to ignore the Spanish, and the Spanish speakers mixed languages rather than keeping them separate.

Wong Fillmore (1982, 1985a) has shown how language alternation works against second language learning. For many LEP students, the language used by teachers and peers in classroom instructional activities constitutes their main exposure to English, the language they must learn in school. This language serves as "linguistic input"—the basis on which learners can acquire English—provided the social setting and activity allow the learners to figure out how it is being used. Language that serves as language learning input is not ordinary language. It is carefully adjusted for the sake of the learners (Hatch 1983; Long 1981) and is used in ways that allow attentive and motivated individuals to comprehend at some level what has been said (Krashen 1980) and to discover how it is patterned and used for various communicative purposes. The adjustments in form and usage that make language work as linguistic input are made when the speaker is trying to communicate directly with the learners in the target language (Wong Fillmore 1985a; Wong Fillmore and Swain 1984). When the speaker provides access to meaning through translations, such adjustments are not made in the target language, and the learners do not need to pay attention to the language they are supposed to be learning, as Andrew Cohen (1973) and Legaretta (1977) found. Further, even if learners were attentive to the mode of communication, the language used in such situations is generally not usable as input since the adjustments that would make it so are deemed to be unnecessary and tend not to be made (Wong Fillmore 1982, 1985b).

The second way in which concurrent methods are counterproductive is that the use of the two languages is rarely equivalent. The tendency is to put greater emphasis on one than on the other or for the two languages to become differentiated in undesirable ways. Valdés-Fallis (1978) argues that in bilingual programs the HL of the students is used primarily to maintain classroom control and order, whereas English is used for instruction. Such differential usages reflect the teachers' attitudes about the two language, she argues, and can influence the students' own language attitudes.

Other researchers and practioners have argued for various versions of concurrent methods, suggesting that language alternations, carried out judiciously, constitute an effective strategy for bilingual instruction. A concurrent method that Jacobson (1981) promotes as a solution to the problems associated with previous language alternation plans involves nontranslational switches for the reinforcement and review of materials previously presented in the other language. Language switches are permissible to achieve pedagogically sound objectives, provided a balance between the two languages can be maintained. Tikunoff (1983) in a nationwide study of instructional practices in successful bilingual classrooms (Significant Bilingual Instructional Features Study, or SBIF) found that teachers made just that kind of language alternation to the extent that they used the HL of the students for instruction at all. He found that the teachers tended to use English predominantly for instructional purposes, switching to the HL when individual students appeared not to understand or needed additional information or help. Tikunoff concludes that language alternation constitutes a significant feature of successful bilingual instructional practices.

Wong Fillmore (1983) in a critique of that conclusion, argues that language alternations of the type found by Tikunoff and his colleagues in the SBIF are effective from one perspective only: They enable LEP students to comprehend materials that they would not otherwise understand because they are presented in English, a language the students do not fully understand. However, the strategy seems to short-circuit the learning of English since, as noted above, English is not being used by the teachers in ways that invite or require the learners to figure out for themselves what is being said. Further, the HL, when it is used, is not sufficiently rich or full to serve as the basis for further development in that language either.

Language adjustments can also be related to subject matter. Most bilingual education theorists are persuaded that the best way to distribute the two languages of instruction is by teaching some subjects in the HL and others in English. But can LEP students handle subject matter taught entirely in English? And if they can be taught some subjects in English, why not teach them all subjects in English? Cummins (1981, 1984, 1989) has long argued that the educational problems of LEP students do not stem simply from the mismatch between home and school language. The Canadian immersion programs have provided ample evidence that students are able to learn subject matter taught in a language they do not know, and they can learn the language of instruction in the process as well (Lambert and Tucker 1972). Not knowing the language of instruction, however, does greatly increase the cognitive complexity of many kinds of learning.

It should be noted that there are two reasons why evidence from the Canadian immersion program should not be regarded as an argument against bilingual education. First, immersion education is, in fact, bilingual education and not a target-language-only instructional approach. Children are taught exclusively in a language they do not speak (French) during the first years of school, but gradually their HL is added as a language of instruction until it reaches parity of use around the third or fourth year. The Canadian programs are conceptualized as maintenance programs; that is, after the short initial period in which the nonnative language is used exclusively in school, instruction is offered bilingually, with the goal of producing fully bilingual individuals. Second, students in the Canadian immersion programs have largely been speakers of the majority language (English) being educated in a minority language (French). The comparable situation in the United States would be native English speakers being educated in Spanish, and indeed such immersion programs exist in this country. Educating minority Spanish speakers through the majority language, English, is not comparable to Canadian immersion and should not be claimed to be supported by Canadian immersion findings.

Cummins (1981) argues that academic development that takes place in the students' primary language both increases and strengthens their underlying cognitive capacity to learn and to function intellectually. He states that a common higher-order cognitive and linguistic proficiency serves as a foundation for whatever is learned in the separate languages of the bilingual, and what is learned in one language transfers easily to the other: "Experiences with either language can promote development of the proficiency underlying both languages" (25). Nonetheless, the more cognitively complex the task, the better the learners' chances of dealing with it successfully if it is conducted in a language the learners already understand and with which they do not need to struggle.

This seems to be the assumption, at any rate, in decisions concerning language choice for subject matter instruction. In general, the most widely accepted principle is that any subject that is especially demanding cognitively (e.g., science and math) or is highly dependent on language knowledge (reading and writing) should be taught initially in a language the student already knows. Subjects that are less linguistically dependent and cognitively demanding (art, music, crafts, etc.) can be taught in the language the students are just learning.

This was not the case in the earliest Title VII programs, in which the tendency was to teach all subjects "bilingually," as described earlier. In Blanco's (1977) discussion of the program models adopted by the early Title VII projects, we see that in some cases the HL and English components covered essentially parallel curricula. In other words, all subjects were taught bilingually, even if the languages were presumably being kept separate. In the early San Francisco Chinese program, for example, there were both an English-language arts component and a parallel Cantonese-language arts component. Typically, however, subjects like math and reading were taught in the students' dominant language during the earliest years of school, and after a time, they were taught either in English or bilingually. How long the initial period lasted, in which instruction was offered more or less exclusively in the HL, depended ultimately on the judgment of individual teachers, who followed their own dictates and beliefs about what was needed and possible. Since bilingual programs from the beginning held the goal to "transition" LEP students into all-English instruction, the question was not only which subjects should be taught in the HL and which in English but also how long any subject was likely to be offered in the students' HL before instruction switched to English.

There has been relatively little research on the issue of what subjects should be taught in which language and for how long. What research has been done has focused on the cognitive or academic benefits of subject matter learning in the HL, primarily in literacy development. In reading, the rationale for teaching students to read, initially at least, in a language they understand seems to be simple enough: Reading is a language dependent skill, so it makes sense to develop it first in the learner's dominant language. As sensible as this course might seem, many teachers nevertheless do the opposite. In fact, English reading is often taken to be English instruction—how else would one teach a language but with the basic elements, namely, the alphabet? English phonics instruction serves as the first exposure to English for many language minority children, and if they are attentive and motivated they can actually learn to decode English quite nicely with virtually no understanding of what they are "reading." Any real understanding of texts, no matter how simple, requires a working knowledge of the grammatical structure of the language they are written in, a vocabulary that includes at the very least the words used in a given text together with an understanding of what they mean in context, and some knowledge of the text conventions and features that figure in the text. Only then can students do what is necessary to reconstruct from the words on the page the meaning the writer of the text intended to convey (Fillmore 1982), which to most of us is what reading minimally involves. Learning to read, in this sense, calls for a relatively well-developed knowledge of the language of the text as well as considerable cognitive effort in discovering the relationships between text and meaning.

It is not surprising that most educators who are concerned with improving education for language minorities have argued for beginning literacy development in the dominant language. The UNESCO (1953) declaration that literacy and education should be provided in the vernacular languages has had an important impact on the thinking of educators. It is often cited in subsequent efforts to investigate the effects of language choice in reading instruction. An early study conducted by Modiano (1973) in Mexico investigated the effects of initial reading instruction in the students' primary language versus in their second language. Some of the subjects—Mayan Indian children—were taught to read in their primary language, whereas others were taught to read in their second language, Spanish. Modiano found that the former had an easier time learning to read than the latter. When Spanish reading was taught to the native-language readers several years later, they soon surpassed the second-language readers. These children had in the meantime learned Spanish and were able to transfer the reading skills they had developed in the native language to their new language without difficulty. The children who were taught to read in Spanish before they knew it well enough to make sense of what they were reading were overburdened cognitively, it appeared, and therefore were not able to make as much progress as they might otherwise have made. Modiano's research provided convincing support for teaching reading in the students' strongest language.

Engle (1975), in a comparison of the findings of studies of reading development in vernacular languages versus societal or second languages, found that overall the results were quite consistent. Students who learned to read in their native languages were generally more successful both in reading and in subject matter understanding than were students who had learned to read in a second language in which they were not fully proficient.

Rosier (1977), in a frequently cited study comparing native-language and second-language reading instruction, found that Navajo children who were taught to read in their native language learned to read more successfully than did comparable children who were taught to read in English, even though the latter were given additional help with English. These benefits were not immediately apparent, however. During the first two years, there was little difference between the two groups, and the English readers were actually reading somewhat better than the native-language readers. At the end of the third year, however, the children who had been taught to read in Navajo initially were scoring significantly higher in tests of English reading than those who had been taught to read directly in English. Rosier's research shows that the benefits of initial reading instruction in the child's native language are cumulative and may take several years to be manifested.

Cummins (1984, 158) reports similar results for Mexican-American children who were given Spanish reading 1 hour per day in a McAllen, Texas, bilingual-immersion program. The students, who were otherwise immersed in English, profited from even the small amount of the native-language instruction they received. They performed significantly better both in Spanish and English reading than did comparison students who were enrolled in a "transitional" program. In studies investigating the relationship between first-language (L1) and second-language (L2) proficiency and academic development of Canadian immigrant students, Cummins and his colleagues (Cummins, Swain, Nakayama, Handscombe, Green, and Tran 1981) found that students with well-developed L1 literacy skills learned English considerably faster and better than did students with less developed L1 skills. The evidence that instructional development in the student's native language does readily transfer to a second language is sufficiently convincing that the Association for Supervision and Curriculum Development (1987), in its review of bilingual education, declared that "it is clear that the ability to transfer to English what is learned in the native language applies not only to content-area subjects like science and math, but also to skills in reading and writing—even when the orthographic system is quite different from the Roman alphabet."

The available research clearly supports this statement: Reading instruction in the students' native language not only results in more successful literacy development in that language but also facilitates second-language literacy development once the skills acquired in the native language are transferred to the second language. Goldman, Reyes, and Varnhagen (1984) found that bilingual children were able to apply their knowledge of story structure acquired in their first language, Spanish, to story comprehension in their second language, English, once they were proficient in that language. Their conclusion is that information and skills that children gain, no matter in what language it is acquired, are transferable.

The question of when to "transition" students who have received reading instruction in their native languages to English reading is particularly vexing in programs for language minority students. Teachers who are not fully committed to bilingual instruction often attempt to move them out of native language reading too soon or to teach initial reading in both languages. The results of such practices are predictable. Andrew Cohen (1975) found that the students in the bilingual program he studied who were taught to read in both English and Spanish simultaneously did not learn to read as well as they might have had they been taught initially only in Spanish. There is no advantage to being taught to read in the native language if it is not done long enough to make a difference. Teaching children to read in two languages, one of which they do not know, is both confusing and counterproductive.

Most reading experts who have considered the problem have argued that oral proficiency in any language is a crucial prerequisite to successful reading in that language, at least where young readers are concerned. Thonis (1981) argues that in addition to second-language proficiency, students need to have achieved an effective level of reading as well as an adequate level of cognitive functioning in the native language before they should be switched to English reading. She argues that practitioners must "recognize that only *strong* skills transfer" (153); a transfer before students are ready for it or "violations of learning principles" that guide language choice in reading instruction can lead to the "reading failure presently found among language minority students" (153).

Goodman, Goodman, and Flores (1979) take a similar position, arguing that it is less critical for the students to have achieved a full oral command of English than a high enough level of reading competence in their native language. They acknowledge that a certain level of English-language proficiency is critical to being able to read in that language, but students can nevertheless profit from reading instruction if they know how to read well in their native language. In fact, the texts students read in a second language can serve as the basis for developing further their knowledge of English, as long as they receive appropriate instructional support. The authors report on a study conducted by Goodman and Goodman (1978) with four groups of bilingual children (Spanish, Arabic, Samoan, and Navaho bilinguals) who were learning to read in English. More important than language proficiency, they argue, is cultural appropriateness, the relevance of school tasks, and experiential differences. The children all read better than one might have predicted, given their linguistic backgrounds. The authors note that receptive skills in a language are more important than productive skills and that teachers often judge the receptive competence of students by their productive behavior.

Goodman, Goodman, and Flores (1979) advocate the adoption of a "comprehension centered curriculum" for second-language readers, through which receptive rather than productive skills are developed first and children are helped to acquire strategies for reading comprehension. The authors argue that children should be read to daily before they are required to read for themselves. They should be helped to become aware of the functions of written language through their own writing and to discover the communicative possibilities of texts. Reading instruction itself should focus on the development of interpretive strategies such as making predictions, confirming them, and rereading or self-correcting when necessary.

The issue of what kind of instruction is needed for successful transition to English reading is examined in just a few studies. Research by Díaz, Moll, and Mehan (1986) in San Diego examined the influence of the linguistic and pedagogical contexts in reading instruction. In this important investigation, the authors studied students in third- and fourth-grade classrooms who were receiving reading instruction in Spanish during a part of the day and later in English. The researchers found major differences in reading behavior and in performance in the two settings that were directly related to differences in the focus of instruction. The children in these classes were divided into high, middle, and low reading groups. In Spanish reading, all three groups received instruction that emphasized comprehension development, making sense of the texts, and how to extract information. Only in the low group was much emphasis placed on developing the mechanical skills of decoding. In English reading, the emphasis was almost exclusively on decoding, on grammar, and on words. Only in the high group was there any concern with comprehension, and the focus there was on recall of information contained in the text. Otherwise, the instruction had no relationship to that which the students were receiving in Spanish reading, and as a consequence there was little relationship between their performance in Spanish and English reading. Whereas in Spanish reading, the children were encouraged to interpret and to communicate their understanding of the texts to one another, there was a total absence of such activities in English reading. The English-speaking teachers tended to underassess the children's abilities and therefore to underestimate their ability to handle a higher level of instruction in their second language, despite the fact that the students, especially in the higher reading groups, were actually "conversationally fluent" in English.

Aside from the lack of coordination between the English and Spanish reading programs observed in these classes, the researchers point to other sources of difficulties. The teachers tended to group the students for English reading instruction on the basis of their English proficiency, despite the fact that they were actually performing at quite different levels of first-language reading proficiency. As a result, some children who were reading at high levels in Spanish were placed in the low reading group simply because they were not fully proficient in English, and vice versa. As a consequence, the students experienced considerable difficulty in English reading, some because they were placed too low, and others because they were placed too high. Overall, the English reading lessons were considerably lower than the work the children were handling competently in Spanish. The other problem identified by Díaz, Moll, and Mehan (1986) was the English teachers' tendency to confuse pronunciation problems with decoding problems. They emphasized phonics instruction in the mistaken belief that unless the students were achieving native-speaker-like levels of English pronunciation in decoding, they were not reading in English.

The work reported by Díaz, Moll, and Mehan (1986) was particularly important because they then went on to reorganize the English reading program, bringing it more in line with the Spanish reading program, to see whether or not changes in the interactional context as well as in the assumptions underlying the program might not make a difference in the students' English reading. The researchers began by considering the students' Spanish reading, assuming that if the children were able to perform at whatever level they were at in Spanish, they could with help make the shift to an equivalent level in English. The researchers selected English materials that were similar in level to the materials the children were reading in Spanish. Next, they shifted the emphasis in the program from the development of low-level decoding skills to the development of text comprehension skills. These shifts resulted in a 3-year increase in the performance of the students in English reading.

Research on language choice in the teaching of writing has been similar to that in reading. In a major review of the writing research, Valdés (1988) concluded that there has been little study of the development of native-language writing skills by Hispanic students. Much of the research on language minority students has focused on the development of English-language writing skills (see, e.g., Diaz, Moll, and Mehan 1986; Hudelson 1984; Kreeft-Peyton and Mackinson-Smyth 1989; Moll 1989). Some important exceptions have been the work of Carlisle (1986) on the development of rhetorical effectiveness in the first- and second-language writing of Hispanic students and of Edelsky (1986) on the development of writing skills by Mexican-American children in a bilingual program.

Edelsky (1986), who studied in considerable detail the process by which children learned how to write, their use of invented spellings, their developing sense of audience in their writings, and their discovery of genre features of various kinds of written texts, found that what the children learned in their first language transferred readily and successfully to their second. This was the case whether the children were speakers of a "standard" variety of Spanish or a "nonstandard" one. The children used complex forms and structures in their writing quite spontaneously, and it appeared that their developing bilingual skills did not generally interfere with their native-language skills. There was some native-language transfer or "interference" as well, but even that appeared to be in the end a positive process.

Ammon (1985), in a study of the second-language writing development of bilingual students, found that what interference could be found in the writing of Hispanic students was largely in confusion over orthographic conventions. Carlisle (1986) compared rhetorical effectiveness in the English writings of Hispanic middle school students (fourth and sixth graders) in a bilingual program with that of comparison students in an English submersion program. The students in the bilingual program outperformed the submersion students in comparisons of written language effectiveness, syntactic development, and overall productivity. The study strongly supports the argument that academic skills developed in the students' native language are transferable to a second language.

In studies of the influence of native-language development on English writing by bilingual students, Moll (1989) found that the outstanding teachers of Hispanic bilingual students he observed followed the so-called "whole-language approach," in which they develop reading and writing together as a means for the communication and understanding of meaning. The teachers set up collaborative activities in which children can practice, develop, and make use of their written-language skills. Bilingual students were grouped with students who spoke no English, characterized in this study as "ESL students," as a way of structuring activities in which bilingual peers could help the ESL students complete their written assignments. ESL students, provided they were competent in Spanish writing, were able to develop English writing skills, Moll observed.

Hudelson (1989), in a case study of two young, Hispanic, bilingual children, found substantial differences in their second-language writing development that were related to their personal styles. One of the children was serious, quiet, and a perfectionist. He was clearly hampered by his limited proficiency in English as he learned to write and was quite reluctant to express himself in writing. The other child was outgoing, talkative, and more relaxed about her performance in school. Although she knew no more English than the other child, she was soon producing written texts, using whatever means she could find. From this research, we can conclude that there may be no easy guidelines concerning when children should be encouraged to transfer their L1 writing skills to a second language.

In science and math, discussions of language choice for instruction generally support using the students' HL, although in practice such subjects are most usually presented in English, with some native-language support at best. This appears to be the case despite evidence of a relationship between English proficiency and achievement in mathematics taught in English (Crandall, Dale, Rhodes, and Spanos 1987). Cuevas (1984) reviews research findings regarding mathematics instruction for the second-language learner and the complications of assessing the mathematics skills of LEP students through English. He presents an instructional model for dealing with English as a second language in the mathematics classroom, incorporating language skills within the context of mastering mathematics skills and concepts.

A recent study by Secada (1989), in which he looked at patterns of performance in the solution of word problems relative to language proficiency, suggests that the relationship between language and problem solving is not a simple one. The subjects, some 50 first graders in a bilingual program, were given word problems to solve in English and Spanish. Secada found that the children's performance on the English problems was predicted by their "bilingual" language proficiency, but their performance on the Spanish problems was not. The children performed significantly better on the English problems than they did on the Spanish problems. A possible explanation for these findings is that given the emphasis on English instruction even in bilingual programs, the children were more familiar with word problems in English than they were with Spanish word problems.

In an extensive review of the literature on student diversity and mathematics learning, Secada (in press) reminds us that language is important, but it is just one of many factors to consider. It is equally important to consider curricular appropriateness, teaching strategies, and assumptions underlying instruction. When minority students are given educational experiences that develop little more than basic computational skills, they are unlikely to develop the competencies in mathematics that are being promoted in current attempts to reform instruction in this area.

In science education, there has been relatively little work investigating the issue of language choice directly, which is not to say that that there has not been important curricular research for language minority students. In the following sections, the developmental studies on the Finding Out/Descubrimiento (FO/D) program and the Cheche Konnen model will be discussed in relation to content adaptation, and although language figures in these programs, the question of language choice was not central. One study in which the language of instruction was the critical issue was conducted by Doebler and Mardis (1980–1981), who investigated the effects of bilingual and English-only instruction on the academic achievement of American Indian children (Choctaw speakers). They found that children who were instructed bilingually performed significantly better in science and social studies than children who received English-only instruction. In no other subject was a statistically significant difference found between the two conditions.

In an important bilingual developmental project sponsored by the California State Department of Education (Tempes 1986), a curriculum was designed calling for limited English speakers to be taught subjects such as language arts, math, science, health, and social studies in the children's HL during kindergarten and first grade. Only art, music, physical education, and English as a second language (ESL) were taught in English during those grades. By grades 2 and 3, however, the curriculum shifted radically to English. Children who were limited in English skills nevertheless received the bulk of their instructional program in English. At those levels, only language arts and social studies were taught in the native language of the students. Math, science, ESL, and health were taught through the "sheltered English" approach (discussed below), and the remaining subjects were taken in "mainstream" classes. By the third and fourth grades and thereafter, all but Spanish-language arts was taught in English, with most of the instruction being held in regular classes.

This is clearly a transitional model of bilingual instruction, and there obviously would be problems for students who enter the program with no English after the first grade. The results of this project appear to be highly favorable, although the students had not met all of the performance goals that had been set for it when the project ended after 3 years. Nonetheless, 60 percent of the children between grades 2 and 6 were scoring at or above state norms in math, and by the fourth grade, nearly all of the children were proficient in English. A study by Krashen and Biber (1988) on the outcome of this project found that in general, the children were achieving at levels close to grade norms and were outperforming comparable students in English-only programs.

Modifications in Language Use

The second major kind of language adaptation for limited-English-speaking students is in the language of instruction itself. In which language or languages should a given subject be taught? This question must be resolved by deciding whether to use English or the HL or both.

If the choice is the HL, it is then necessary to consider the issue of language variety or dialect. Such considerations are never simple: There are many layers of sociolinguistic and political concerns to sort through. Is the HL of the students the same as the standard variety (presumably) used in the school? If it is different, are the two varieties mutually intelligible? That is, can speakers of the two varieties understand one another easily? If they do not, the use of the standard variety of the HL in school may prove to be no help at all to the students since it means that instead of dealing with one language (English) they do not understand, they must deal with two (English and the school variety of the HL). In that case, the schools must decide whether they should teach the children in the HL variety or in English only.

The decision, however, is not a simple one. If the HL is a regional or national dialect (say, Moroccan Arabic versus Egyptian Arabic or Puerto Rican Spanish versus Mexican Spanish), there is no particular sense in which one could be regarded as "standard" and the other as "nonstandard." The question is rather, which variety should be taken as the standard to be used in school? It is usually resolved, provided the varieties are mutually intelligible, by the teacher—the variety to be used in school is whatever variety the teacher happens to speak. Even then, the teacher must confront a plethora of issues in using the non-English language in school. In which varieties of the language are instructional materials prepared and available? What adjustments are needed, say, in vocabulary, language structure, and content to render the materials appropriate for the students, given their HL variety? The problem differs from language to language, but it must be considered and dealt with thoughtfully.

If, however, the dialect is regarded as a social class dialect or if the HL regional variety happens to be viewed as a debased form of the standard, the problem of deciding whether or not to use the HL variety in school is much more complicated. This is a difficult problem confronting bilingual educators in many places. Taishan Cantonese (a variety of Cantonese spoken by many Chinese immigrants), for example, is regarded by speakers of "standard" Cantonese (the variety spoken by Chinese immigrants from Hong Kong) as a rural, low-status variety. The two varieties are not mutually intelligible. Should Taishan-Cantonese speakers be instructed in "standard" Cantonese, which is the one used in most Cantonese-English bilingual programs, or should they be taught in Taishan Cantonese, their HL? In this case, it turns out that given a choice, Taishanese parents prefer their children to be educated in "standard" Cantonese (even if it means they will have to grapple with two new languages in school) since that has been the traditional practice. Even in the prerevolutionary period in China, long before Mandarin was established as the national language, children in Taishan district schools were schooled in the regional language, Kwangtung Cantonese, which happens to be the one spoken in Hong Kong now. Because there has been no tradition of the local variety, Taishan Cantonese, being used in schools, members of this immigrant group largely regard it as inappropriate for academic purposes. Similar situations exist for the Hmong people and other related groups of Southeast Asian refugees and immigrants.

The problem is an especially painful one and is even more complicated when it is applied to the Spanish-language situation. In many places in the United States, the varieties of Spanish spoken by the Hispanic students are Hispanic-American dialects; they are indeed Spanish, but they have been modified by the immigrant experience and differ in many ways from the standard varieties spoken in their forebears' places of origin (say, Puerto Rico, northern Mexico, or Chile). Speakers of so-called standard varieties of Spanish often regard these dialects as "degenerate," "bastardized," or "uneducated" varieties—unworthy of consideration as authentic instances of Spanish. It should be noted that such attitudes are not always held solely by speakers of the standard varieties. Although some speakers of stigmatized varieties take considerable pride in their languages, others tend to deny the validity of their own languages.

In such situations, should the students' HL be used in school for instructional purposes, or should a standard variety be used, assuming that there is agreement on what constitutes the standard? If the decision is to use the HL variety, how should it be used since, in most cases, curricular materials are written in standard varieties of Spanish? The problem is difficult to resolve, whether the teachers speak the same variety of Spanish as do the students or a different one. Those who speak the HL variety may be reluctant to use it for instructional purposes, particularly if they themselves regard it as an invalid version of the language. This situation is especially common when fellow teachers who speak standard varieties of Spanish hold and make known their elitist attitudes towards the "nonstandard" variety. When teachers are able and willing to use the students' HL variety for instructional purposes, they then must decide whether or not they will teach the children a standard variety of Spanish in addition to English, just as teachers of nonstandard-English speakers try to teach standard English to their students.

These sociolinguistic dilemmas are not easy to resolve since almost always political overtones complicate the decision-making process. They must be confronted, however, in all but the simplest situation, in which both students and teachers speak a variety that is commonly acknowledged to be a standard variety and in which ample educational materials are available. In such idealized situations, there is no need to consider further language adaptation since presumably the students understand the variety used in school well enough to deal with subject matter instruction given in that language.

The choice of English as the language of instruction for any subject matter raises an equally complex set of concerns in relation to language adaptation. If the choice is English or both languages, the critical question is how to present the subject matter so that it can be understood and learned by the students. Much depends on how the language (or languages) of instruction is used for instructional purposes. It was noted that in many bilingual education programs, the choice is to teach most subjects bilingually, in both the students' HL and in English. Unadjusted English, when it is used by teachers and classmates during instructional activities, may be incomprehensible to LEP students. One kind of accommodation discussed earlier was language switching, whereby access to meaning is provided through the students' HL. It was noted that such adjustments enable learners to deal with content, but they seem to work against second language learning. Another kind of bilingual accommodation is to differentiate the uses of the two languages in instruction: For example, in the so-called preview-review method, teachers use the HL to give access to the subject matter before teaching it in English and then review the materials in the HL after they have been presented in English (González and Lezama 1976). In this section, we discuss the language adjustments that are needed when subjects are taught to LEP students exclusively in English.

Aside from those situations in which the teachers do not know the LEP students' HL and can therefore teach them only in English, there are important reasons for teaching some subject matter in English. Instructional activities conducted in English offer LEP students opportunities to hear and use English in ways that permit them to learn it as a second language. However, this exposure to English promotes language learning only if the learners can figure out how the language is being used and only if they can recover, from context, the meaning of what has been said. Modifications to the language of instruction that make it possible for learners to get direct access to the curriculum being taught are equally important.

The methods for teaching subject matter in a nonnative language have been explored and developed most fully in immersion education programs (Lambert and Tucker 1972; Swain and Lapkin 1982). The immersion approach, a bilingual education model pioneered in Canada, from the earliest period teaches subject matter entirely in the language children are to learn. English-speaking first graders, for example, are taught entirely in French from the time they enter school, and only gradually are they taught some of the curriculum in their native language. By the third grade, they may be receiving a third of their total program in their primary language, English, and the amount is gradually increased until the two languages are used in equal amounts.

Evaluation studies of these programs generally show that the students in the Canadian immersion programs who are being taught in French, a language they are in the process of learning, perform as well as comparison students who are instructed solely in their HL, English. Swain and Lapkin (1982) in a review of the 9 years of immersion education in Ontario, found that the students in these programs performed as well as or better than other students in mathematics from grades 1 through 8 and in science from grades 5 through 8. Further, the students had achieved high levels of competence in French as a second language, even if it was far from nativelike.

To have satisfied both the academic and linguistic aims, immersion education had to develop techniques involving considerable modification of language use. Lambert (1984) points out that the underlying assumption of the method is that children will learn a new language in much the same way as they learn their primary language—in contexts in which the language is being used for genuine communicative purposes:

> [Teachers] clearly, patiently and repetitively focus on the development of a basic vocabulary in the new language, relying, with the youngest age groups, on plastic art materials, songs, and animated stories. But from the start, the learning of language per se is made quite incidental to learning how to make and do interesting things. The new language becomes a constant verbal accompaniment rather than the focus. Later, new ideas of a scientific, mathematical, or problem solving nature are given the main focus, but even then the accumulation of skill in the new language appears to be incidental. (12)

In the immersion method, instructional activities that make heavy use of concrete, hands-on experiences, demonstrations, and enactment permit students to grasp the curricular content even though they do not initially understand what their teachers are saying. Gradually, however, the students are able to put together the language with what they are learning experientially, and they are on their way to learning the language itself. The use of language for instructional purposes in ways that give access both to the content and to the language itself has been variously described by researchers and practitioners (see, e.g., Gass and Madden 1985; Krashen 1980, 1981; Long 1981; Meyer Precup 1981; Terrell 1981; Wong Fillmore 1982, 1985b). Krashen argues that language used in ways that make meaning more or less recoverable to learners constitutes "comprehensible input," the critical condition for language learning. Together with Krashen, Terrell (Terrell and Krashen, 1983) characterizes this way of providing access to second-language learning the "natural approach." The teaching of subject matter through English that LEP students can understand is also described as "language sheltering," whereby teachers avoid using language in instruction that they believe the students will find difficult and are unlikely to understand. This kind of modification requires considerable thought and planning to work well since it must be made with constant reference to the students' current levels of developing English proficiency.

PEDAGOGICAL AND STRUCTURAL ADAPTATIONS

Adaptations in pedagogy as well as in the ways instruction is organized constitute the second major category of curricular adaptation for language minority students. The underlying assumption for such adaptations is that cultural differences in early experiences can mean substantial differences in learning patterns. Children who have been socialized in homes where parents and other caretakers emphasize learning through independent exploration and problem solving will be more inclined to learn independently than children who have been socialized by parents who believe in tightly supervising and manipulating their children's experiences in learning. Howard Gardner (1989) describes a situation that reveals just that difference between American and Chinese socialization patterns. The hotel where he and his family were staying in China encouraged guests to deposit their room keys in a box before leaving the hotel. Their 18-month-old son had observed his parents dropping the key through a narrow slot in the box and was attempting to do so on his own, to his parents' obvious delight. Given his age, he had not yet figured out that the key had to be properly oriented to fit into the narrow slot. The parents were pleased about their son's efforts, however, seeing it as "exploratory behavior," which would in good time lead to the child's independent solution of the problem. Gardner noted, however, that the Chinese attendants and guests at the hotel took a dim view of such parental behavior:

> Any Chinese attendant nearby—and sometimes even a mere Chinese passer-by—would come over to watch Benjamin. As soon as the observer saw what our child was doing, and noted his lack of initial success at the appointed task, she (or, less often, he) attempted to intervene. In general, she would hold onto his hand and, gently but firmly, guide it directly toward the slot, reorient it as necessary, and help Benjamin to insert the key. She would then smile somewhat expectantly at Ellen or me, as if awaiting a thank you—and on occasion, would frown slightly, as if to admonish the negligent parent. . . . We were dealing with markedly divergent attitudes about the preferred behavior for children and the proper role of adults in their socialization. (3–4)

These differences in the way children are socialized can profoundly influence the development of preferred modes of learning. Over the past 20 years, some important cross-cultural studies of language socialization have shown us what great differences exist across groups in how they structure and orient the socialization of their children (e.g., Boggs 1985; Gallimore, Boggs, and Jordan 1974; Heath 1982, 1983; Phillips 1972, 1983; Schiefflin and Ochs 1986; Tharp and Gallimore 1988.) Some of this work has shown quite persuasively that these differences can and do affect the way children participate in school as well as the way their teachers instruct them. Although there is by no means agreement among researchers about the extent to which a cultural mismatch between the patterns of learning promoted in the home and school explains differential patterns of school adjustment and learning, it seems clear that this is a factor that must be considered.

Ogbu and Matute-Bianchi (1986) object to such simple explanations for group differences in academic achievement. They argue that although differences can certainly be found across groups in learning patterns and preferences, such differences can be overcome easily enough. Even more important than cultural congruence between the socialization patterns of home and school, they say, is how real the opportunities are for academic and social advancement in the larger society for the members of different groups. If the chances for successful participation in the society are limited for a group, the children will see as limited their chances to succeed in school. More important, members of the groups that historically have been subordinated in the society (e.g., Hispanics, African-Americans, and Native Americans) develop "secondary cultural features," which have considerable consequences on their school performance.

The researchers explore these questions in a comparison of the school performance of Chinese and Mexican students. Both groups have experienced substantial discrimination as minority groups in the United States. However, a major difference between them is the conditions under which they came to the United States. The Chinese have been voluntary immigrants. They came to the United States in the hope of having a better life for themselves and their children, and they have reason to believe that school success will lead to economic success eventually. They are able to overcome the cultural and linguistic barriers to their participation in school by adapting to the linguistic and behavioral norms because they see the possibility that such adaptations will lead to school success.

Mexican-Americans, in contrast, were "involuntary" immigrants. They became Americans through the conquest and annexation of their territories. According to Ogbu and Matute-Bianchi, this historical factor has led to the subordination of this group to a castelike minority status. Not only have they experienced considerable discrimination, but also there have been clear ceilings on their social and economic mobility, which have led to "bitterness, frustration, resentment, and mistrust" (92). The response has been a low-academic-effort syndrome, in which members of castelike minority groups simply do not put as much effort into school as they might otherwise. For Ogbu and Matute-Bianchi (1986), the answer is not in any simple-minded tinkering with the curriculum to match the cultural styles of the various groups served by the school but in making substantial changes in how we conceptualize and contextualize schooling for minority group students. It is necessary to consider the many ways in which the structure and content of school reflects and reifies the social realities of the society and to make changes in it, even as we work at changing the society itself.

We will discuss a number of important investigations of pedagogy and curricular structure in programs for language minorities. The most important of these is the Kamehameha Early Education Project (KEEP), in which some 15 years of continuous research into every aspect of teaching and learning in native Hawaiian homes and at school led ultimately to a "redefinition of teaching and schooling" not only for native Hawaiian children but for all children (see Tharp and Gallimore 1988 for a review of the voluminous research that KEEP has conducted over the years). KEEP's basic premise was that the mismatch between the culture of the home and school was the underlying cause of the difficulties native Hawaiian children were having in school. Until quite recently, these children, like most other American native groups, performed well below national norms in every area of academic achievement. In trying to determine what they had to change to make the educational program at school culturally compatible with the children it served, the KEEP researchers considered the match not only between the socialization patterns of native Hawaiian homes and of the schools they attended (Boggs 1985; Gallimore, Boggs, and Jordan 1974) but also between home and school patterns of discourse, activity and participant structures, social structures, and patterns of beliefs and expectations. This research resulted in substantial changes in the structure and pedagogy followed at school as well as a major reconsideration of what should be taught.

In the area of literacy development, the project resulted in the design of a pedagogical model based on "instructional conversations"—small-group conversations in which students and teachers jointly engage in discourse on activities, ideas, and materials that enable the children to arrive at higher levels of competency in both the language of instruction and in the subject matter being learned. These group discussions begin with shared experiences and gradually move to higher levels of discussions on texts through the teacher's use of questions, feedback, and modeling (Au 1979; Au et al. 1986; Mason and Au 1986). The evaluation data for the KEEP reading program are impressive: In the experimental phase, children in the KEEP classes were scoring at about the 50th percentile in reading achievement tests, whereas children in control classes were at the 30th percentile.

A major aim of the KEEP researchers was to create instructional settings and activities in which children are actively engaged in learning in ways that are compatible with their own cultural patterns. In the native Hawaiian culture, children take an active and independent role in defining their own activities and in taking responsibility for the management of both their environment and activities. They were accustomed to a high degree of peer collaboration and cooperation in the achievement of whatever work they were engaged in. The usual inclination of teachers to maintain control over the environment and over the children's activities conflicted with the children's expectations of self-management and made it difficult for them to participate in classroom activities. They had considerable difficulty adjusting to instructional activities that were teacher-oriented and -structured. The development of independent peer learning centers, which enabled the children to regulate their own learning activities and to work collaboratively on whatever they were learning, consituted a major breakthrough for this group (Tharp and Gallimore 1988).

Other major investigations of peer and collaborative learning can be seen in the efforts to adapt the structure of instructional activities for language minority students. Kagan (1986) has argued that cooperative learning in which classrooms are structured so that students can work together in teams is especially important for language minority students. The problems of academic achievement for many minority groups, he argues, reflect a failure to find ways to provide meaningful and involving instruction and opportunities for prosocial development. The competitive and individualistic modes of learning promoted in school, as well as the autocratic models of teaching that are commonplace, are antithetical to learning and to prosocial development. Kagan argues for the adoption of cooperative learning strategies, in which students learn about interdependence and how to solve problems and to learn together as an alternative to current inappropriate and ineffective instructional models for language minority students. He reports substantial research support for the benefits of such structural changes in instructional programs for students from a variety of backgrounds.

Other researchers who have examined the effects of cultural differences in learning style would argue, however, that special attention needs to be paid to group characteristics in adopting instructional approaches such as cooperative learning. Wong Fillmore, McLaughlin, Ammon, and Ammon (1985) found that although Hispanic students profited from opportunities to work with peers in instructional activities, Asian students had difficulty dealing with such activities until they had achieved a level of comfort in their new surroundings and had reached an intermediate level of proficiency in the language they were learning. Until then, the Asians seemed to prefer working independently at assigned learning tasks or in teacher-directed and -structured instructional activities. Whereas the Hispanic students preferred and needed to work with their peers, the Asian students seemed to do their best work on their own or under the reassuring guidance of their teachers. This is not to suggest, however, that cooperative learning is inappropriate for Asian students. They can and should be helped to learn and work cooperatively with one another. Instructional activities structured as cooperative learning tasks need to be carefully adapted and designed to take into account their apparent preference for individual or teacher-directed instruction.

Group learning has also been the focus of research by Elizabeth Cohen and her colleagues at Stanford University (Cohen 1986; Cohen and De Avila 1983; Cohen and Intili 1981) in which they explored the question of whether or not group work can be used for developing language competence and subject matter learning. In research that gave children the opportunity to work in small groups on science and mathematics activities that were part of the Finding Out/Descubrimiento curriculum (De Avila and Duncan 1980), Cohen (1986) found dramatic gains in language and content learning. When both teachers and students were trained for cooperative learning, the children were prepared to deal with the many roles they had to play in group learning, and the teachers knew how to delegate authority to the children to take charge of their own learning activities, the children became independent and motivated learners. Through this program, the children learned to rely on one another as resources and to solve problems as a group. Cohen and her associates found that Spanish-speaking second through fourth graders made significantly greater gains in both content and language than comparison children who were not involved in the program. The children in the program with the lowest levels of English-language proficiency did generally better when compared with comparable children who had not been in the program than did children in the program who were more fluent in English when compared with comparable children who were not in the program.

Adjustments in pedagogy and in instruction are currently being explored through the development of an intriguing model in a project in Massachussetts (Warren, Rosebery, and Conant 1989). The Cheche Konnen (Haitian Creole for "search for knowledge") model seeks to reform the usual school science model, in which information is told to students rather than constructed by them out of their own investigations. In this model, language is regarded to be as essential a tool for learning science as mathematics is. That being the case, the students' knowledge of the language of classroom discourse in which they construct a shared understanding of the topics of inquiry is critical to their participation. The relationship between science learning and language is one of the topics of inquiry in the development of a model of science education that emphasizes inquiry, collaboration, and interdisciplinary learning. During the first year of the study, the Cheche Konnen model was pilot-tested in two quite different classes in an urban school. One was a combined seventh- and eighth-grade Haitian Creole bilingual classroom; the other was a high school "basic skills" ESL science class serving students from a variety of language backgrounds including Haitian Creole. The seventh- and eighth-grade students in the Cheche Konnen program conducted a number of studies in which they learned how to formulate research questions to guide their investigations (e.g., on the quality of tap water in the school), how to gather data, how to interpret the data, and finally, how to report their findings.

Warren, Rosebery, and Conant (1989) note that after one year of engaging in the collaborative discourse and group work that are key features of the Cheche Konnen model, students in the seventh- and eighth-grade pilot program were not only developing considerable sophistication and enthusiasm in conducting science investigations but also producing highly competent written reports. These reports, which were jointly produced, were considerably more detailed and accurate than any individual student could have produced.

The students in the high school did not profit much from the experience, not because the program was ineffective but because the teachers' goals and expectations were not congruent with the goals of the Cheche Konnen model. In this class, the teachers rejected the kind of structural and pedagogical change represented by the model because they could not get beyond their own self-defined limitations of what could be done with language minority students. For them, the language limitations of their students were barriers to the kind of learning promoted in the model, and their goals were to give the students the basic skills they needed to survive in school. Warren, Rosebery, and Conant (1989) report,

> One effect of the teachers' goals was to transform the Cheche Konnen model into its opposite, the very kind of science and language development against which the model had been defined, namely, school science dominated by teacher-led lecture and discussion by rote memorization and recitation of vocabulary and procedures. In this form of science, experiments are reduced to procedures, the execution of which leads to answers already known (e.g., to the teacher, the culture). Students learn about science more than they learn science. This model of science learning (or of learning in any discipline, for that matter) is ubiquitous throughout American education. . . . It is, in fact, the archetypal model for American education, and in many places, it is the desired model. Interestingly, it is often most prevalent in contexts where its failure is most conspicuous, namely, in inner city schools, special education classes or, in this case, language minority classrooms. Nevertheless, it persists and conditions the way teachers and students alike think about school, its purposes and its methods. (24)

Adaptations in pedagogy and curricular structure are needed for language minority students, but it may be that if we look at curriculum more generally, the question of more general reforms ought to be considered. Inappropriate and ineffective curriculum and instruction are much more conspicuous where students are at risk, as Warren and her colleagues remind us, but they should not be acceptable even where the students are not at any particular risk.

CONTENT ADAPTATIONS

As noted earlier, the academic problems of linguistic minority students are too often attributed to "deficiencies" in the child. Increasingly, however, the inappropriateness and inadequacies of instructional practices have been cited as being at least partly to blame for the unacceptably high rates of school failure for these students, and the need for adaptations in the forms and modes of teaching has been recognized. Only recently has attention turned to the possibility that the content of the curriculum itself might pose learning barriers for minority students.

In this section, we will consider issues involved in the adaptation of the content of the curriculum for linguistic minority students. First, we discuss the content of the mainstream curriculum and its role in isolating and alienating minority students from their own histories and life experiences. Second, adaptations to the scope or coverage of the mainstream content are discussed. These adaptations do not revise the substance of the content but rather selectively expose language minority students to concepts or aspects of the curriculum that are believed to be the most important or the least language-dependent. Finally, we will consider adaptations to the substance of the content itself and how they relate to assimilation, pluralism, control, and student empowerment in curriculum planning.

Why Adjust the Content?

What constitutes the appropriate content of the mainstream curriculum is itself a disputed issue. Eisner (1985) identifies five major orientations to schooling that have very different implications for deciding what content should be included in the curriculum. Depending on which orientation is predominant among curriculum decision makers, content priorities may focus on (1) the development of cognitive processes and thinking skills that are believed to be universal; (2) the great issues, thoughts, and thinkers of humanity; (3) personally meaningful learning and the dynamic emergence of learning goals through teacher-student interaction; (4) critical assessment of the ills of society in order to improve the social order or massively to reform it; and (5) the alignment of learning tasks and outcomes through a means-ends technological procedure, with outcomes operationalized through observable behaviors. Each of these orientations serves as a value-laden force in prioritizing certain content and in favoring certain instructional designs. Within specific subject matter areas the goals of learning are disputed, as well. For example, Ovando and Collier (1985) cite Lemlech's discussion of "three potentially conflicting social studies traditions" (153–154): social studies as the top-down transmission of the "right values" to be held by a good citizen; social studies as the study of "the structure, concepts, problems, and processes of both the separate and the integrated social science disciplines" (154); and social studies as reflective inquiry and critical analysis toward the goal of individual and informed citizenship decision making.

Student diversity in American schools has traditionally been addressed by tracking and differentiated curriculum (Oakes 1986). At any given time, the mainstream curriculum represents the decision makers' vision of what the typical student should learn and therefore provides the baseline against which curricular options for "special students" are determined. Hirsch (1987) argues that the mainstream curriculum is culturally specific and should transmit vital background knowledge on which competent literacy in our society depends. He claims that "cultural literacy" should be taught to all children since it comprises the society's common culture—"what every American needs to know."

It appears, however, that the mainstream curriculum is not only culturally specific but also far less common and more biased than Hirsch would admit. Pappademos (1989) charges that the mainstream content of schooling both excludes and negates the personal and cultural histories of minority students. In a survey of 17 textbooks of physics and physical science published by leading U.S. publishing houses since 1970 and currently used in schools, Pappademos found that the history of physics portrayed is far from neutral or objective; indeed, it "tends to reinforce racial stereotypes" (178):

> A whole continent [Africa] is deleted from the history of physics: in all 17 books surveyed, not once is a scientific discovery or discoverer identified as being of African origin. No Black scientist is pictured in any of the books, nor is a single Black scientist credited with any contribution. The picture of science in general and physics in particular that emerges from these books without exception is that the cradle of physics was in Europe and that it owes its present development entirely to scientists of the U.S. and Europe (rarely other than white males). (178)

Pappademos found the exclusion of minorities in these textbooks to be both textual and visual:

> Another mark of respect is the inclusion of a picture or a portrait of a scientist. As shown in my survey, out of the 17 books surveyed, although there were 94 different scientists appearing in 186 pictures of scientists, Asian scientists were pictured only eight times. . . . There was not a single Black or Latino scientist pictured in any of the books. (177–179)

Pappademos concludes that these contemporary U.S. textbooks "effectively promote the view that the progress of physics owes little or nothing to the intellectual ability and labor of other than whites" (179).

When given the opportunity, immigrant students often speak of their feelings of being alienated from their own cultural backgrounds and histories in U.S. schools. Immigrant students quoted by Olsen (1988) reveal feelings of loneliness, confusion, frustration, inadequacy, and defeat. In addition to the barrier of an unfamiliar language, they face content that is both alien and exclusive. A Vietnamese student who was interviewed on videotape by Macbeth and Meyer (1988b) comments, "The difficulty for me is history. I study history very difficult, I think very difficult. I study in Vietnam my history. Is different in America." Connections to their own past within the mainstream curriculum are few and brief but memorable: "I was so excited when my history teacher talked about the Vietnam War. Now at last, I thought, now we will study about my country. We didn't really study it. Just for one day, though, my country was real again" (11th-grade Vietnamese girl, quoted in Olsen, 68). Not only the student's past experiences but also her present ones are ignored by the traditional curriculum. Olsen records numerous accounts by immigrant students of racism and violence inflicted on them by their American classmates. Countless incidents of jeering, spitting, profanity, ridicule, pushing, and physical violence at school were tersely summarized by a Mexican tenth grader: "Everyone hates" (38).

This level of discrimination and prejudice ought to trigger a substantial educational effort on the part of the schools to reduce intergroup conflict. However, as Ovando and Collier (1985) write, few educators are willing to use the teaching curriculum to confront these disturbing issues directly.

Teachers, parents, and administrators often prefer to avoid such culturally sensitive issues as racism, prejudice, stereotypes, desegregation, interracial mixing, social exclusion, ethnocentrism, or cross-cultural conflicts. With the increased pressure to return to basics in the curriculum, educators often question whether imbuing the teaching-learning process with culture- and language-related themes would in fact distract from the perceived business of the schools, that is, to maintain the children at grade level and have them compete favorably with national norms in the principal content areas (Ovando and Collier 1985, 159).

In stark contrast to this view of the appropriate "business of school" is the view espoused by critical theorists: Although skill development is important, "schooling for self and social empowerment is ethically prior to a mastery of technical skills" (McLaren 1989, 162). Minority students are empowered, McLaren argues, as they learn to appreciate and love themselves and as they gain "knowledge and social relations that dignify rather than demean their own history, language, and cultural traditions" (186). Educators who are committed to empowerment must accept the responsibility to display and nurture what Giroux (1984) calls "critical literacy and civic courage" (190). This is the notion that true critical thinking, on which democratic processes depend, involves "the acquisition of a critical culture and social practices that allow students and others to view society with an analytical eye" (193). Critical theorists contrast Hirsch's static model of culturally transmitted literacy with a concept of critical, transformative literacy. As students learn to retain and value their own cultural strengths and "to question and selectively appropriate those aspects of the dominant culture that will provide them with the basis for defining and transforming, rather than merely serving, the wider social order" (McLaren 1989, 187), they begin a process of empowerment referred to by one student as "taking control of our own lives" (McLeod 1986).

Most efforts to adapt content for the sake of language minority students have been directed toward reducing the language barrier in instruction, rather than toward lowering the barrier caused by culturally inappropriate or alienating content and instructional experiences. The focus on linguistic barriers is a result of legal action. Subject matter instruction that is completely unadapted to the linguistic needs of language minority children, the so-called sink-or-swim method of instruction, has been found to be a violation of these students' civil rights. In the 1974 ruling in *Lau* v. *Nichols* (U.S. Supreme Court, 414 U.S. 563), the Supreme Court determined that schools must provide linguistic help to LEP students that will give them better access to the content of the school's instructional program.

To accommodate limitations in English, various types of adaptations have attempted to lighten the content learning load while students are in the process of acquiring English. Most of these adaptations involve a reduction in the amount of content covered. They include (1) reduction in the number of subjects covered, (2) reduction in the breadth or sophistication of the content covered, (3) use of selected content as a means of teaching English as a second language, and (4) content instruction "sheltered" for the needs of second-language learners. Some adjustments have maintained the complete scope of the grade-level content, adjusting instead the linguistic complexity of the instructional language and of the expectations for student participation.

Adaptations in the Scope or Coverage of the Curriculum

The first type of adaptation in the scope of the curriculum involves the reduction in the number of subjects covered. It is probably true that there are more subjects taught in school than are necessary or even wise, and not every subject needs to be treated separately. In schools without bilingual programs, educators generally decide what can and should be taught to LEP students and what must be eliminated altogether or put aside until the students have learned enough English to handle the challenge. Such decisions are sometimes based on what is deemed to be most critical to the academic development of the students and on what can be successfully and meaningfully taught to LEP students while they are learning English. One instance of this kind of planning can be seen in the program of studies at Newcomer High School in San Francisco (San Francisco Unified School District 1988). Newly arrived immigrant students spend a year at Newcomer to learn enough English to survive academically in other high schools, where they eventually will be mainstreamed. During that year, their program of studies includes three required classes of English as a second language (ESL), one mathematics course, and a history/social studies course. Whenever possible, the subject matter courses use the students' native languages for content instruction or native-language support. There is, in addition, a small number of elective courses for the students to choose from.

When content courses are pruned from the LEP students' curriculum, too often what remains is an instructional program that teaches English as a second language and little else. The danger here, as with any skills instruction, is that instruction becomes an attempt to teach students how to speak, read, and write English in a learning situation in which there is little of substance worth talking about. In observations in many schools serving language minority students, we have found it a common instructional coping strategy to delay challenging LEP students with much content until they have been taught basic English, on the grounds that English is the requisite skill they must have before they can learn anything else. In some cases the students' schedules are reduced to several courses of English as a second language, supplemented only by "nonacademic" courses that are less linguistically demanding (i.e., physical education, woodwork, or arts and crafts). In other cases, especially in elementary classrooms, LEP children may be physically present in the classroom when content instruction occurs but set apart to work in separate groupings or on individual tasks or seat work focused on ESL. The problem with such arrangements is that the students receive little more than formal language instruction; the other courses or activities add little intellectual substance to their program of studies.

A second type of adaptation to the scope of the curriculum is to reduce the breadth or sophistication of the subjects that are taught to LEP students. There are various ways such reductions are made. One is simply to reduce the amount of material covered in a course. When course materials are being taught in English to LEP students, teachers have to make special efforts to ensure their understanding and mastery of the materials. That takes extra time, meaning that fewer materials can be covered thoroughly. This is true even when the native language is used to support instruction that is given primarily in English. The "preview-review" method (González and Lezama 1976) takes more time than instruction would otherwise take, say, if the materials were taught directly in the language the students understood well. The materials are presented as many as three times: in a preview session, which is usually given in the home language; during the lesson itself, which is conducted in English; and in a review session, which is either in the home language or in English. The repetition or review of instruction means that less material can be covered, or it may mean that the materials have to be given a more superficial treatment since less time can be spent on each topic.

A second modification to the level of content is to reduce the sophistication of the treatment. If not planned and justified carefully, such reductions can be grossly inappropriate. The worst of them are based on the wrong-headed view that students' intellectual capabilities can be assessed by the level, or the limitations, of their English-language competence. These efforts inappropriately assume that what the LEP students can (or cannot) say in English represents intellectually "all they could handle" (Carnegie Foundation for the Advancement of Teaching 1988, 1).

In many schools, LEP students in the upper grades are given instructional materials taken from the lower grades. For example, it is not unusual to find middle school or even high school students working on phonics work papers that are used in kindergarten and first-grade classes. Neither the content nor the language is appropriate for them. Such practices grossly underestimate the students' cognitive capabilities and life experiences and seem to serve the institution rather than the student: "'It's a game we play,' said a teacher in Houston. 'If we held them all back, the system would get clogged up. So we water down the curriculum and move them along'" (Carnegie Foundation for the Advancement of Teaching 1988, 1).

In many schools, LEP students receive a steady diet of basic skills instruction in place of the regular curricular content. Reading instruction focuses on the development of decoding skills—phonics and more phonics. The students are given few opportunities to discuss the materials at hand or to consider what they mean. In mathematics instruction, they are taught computational skills and procedures for solving problems, but they are not offered any opportunity to discover the principles that figure in these problems or the reason for believing that there is any real purpose for what they are learning. As Resnick (1989) notes, "Educators typically treat mathematics, especially at primary levels, as a field with no open questions and no arguments" (1). Where language minority students are concerned, it is often even less than that: Mathematics is often taught in ways that suggest that it is a field of endeavor that has no relevance to them. Seldom are there instructional activities, whether in math or in any other subject, that are meant to develop higher-order thinking skills, problem-solving strategies, independent learning, or communicative competence. Science and even social studies, if they are covered at all, are given only the most superficial treatment, on the ground that LEP students would be unable to deal with a more thorough or higher-level coverage of the materials in the curriculum. In high school English classes for newcomers, for example, the usual curriculum consisting of literary works such as *Romeo and Juliet* or *A Tale of Two Cities* is often put aside, and in its place, teachers offer drills on English phonics, vocabulary, and structure.

Such drastic reductions are unnessary and self-defeating. Basic skills instruction may be necessary, but it is neither exciting nor motivating, nor should it be taught in isolation. Some students are greatly affected by instruction that has been inappropriately stripped of curricular content. Wong Fillmore, McLaughlin, Ammon, and Ammon (1985) found that Hispanic students in particular tended not to participate with much interest or enthusiasm in instruction that was meaningless or devoid of interest. When their programs provided little substance, they tended to do poorly in school. When the materials they were learning were challenging, interesting, and even difficult, the students were more inspired to learn and to participate enthusiastically.

Another basis for making adjustments in the content to be covered is that content instruction can provide the means for teaching the new language. Short (1989) distinguishes two ways in which integrated language and content programs may function: language-sensitive content or "sheltered English" instruction, and what might be described as content-sensitive ESL instruction. The two are contrasted according to whether mainstream content instruction or second-language instruction is given a higher priority. In content-sensitive ESL instruction, selected subject matter concepts are used as a vehicle for teaching the skills and functions of English. According to Short, "The language teachers' primary goal is still to help students develop language competence, but their secondary goals are to introduce terminology, content reading and writing skills, and study skills; and to reinforce content area information taught in other classes" (1). For example, Chamot and O'Malley (1987) describe their Cognitive Academic Language Learning Approach (CALLA) as providing a transition or bridge between special language programs and mainstream education. The primary intent of CALLA is to teach the language skills required to succeed in mainstream content classes: "CALLA is not intended to substitute for mainstream content-area instruction or to teach the basic content expertise required in school district curricula" (229).

Macbeth and Meyer (1988a, 1988b, 1989a, 1989b, 1989c) have documented the work of teachers who are highly skilled in integrating content and language instruction. One of them, ninth-grade ESL teacher Gil Sánchez, teaches the required Shakespeare classic *Romeo and Juliet* to his class of LEP immigrant students. He refuses to strip his course of meaningful content or of Shakespeare's powerful themes just because his students are at the very beginning stages of learning English. Nor is Sánchez willing to accept the argument that materials such as *Romeo and Juliet* are irrelevant to his students, many of whom have recently come from a variety of Latin American and Asian countries and are now working full time to support themselves while they attend school in San Francisco.

To Sánchez, *Romeo and Juliet*, which deals with the misunderstandings between people that sometimes become destructive and divisive, is just what his students need to think about and understand. Many of them come from societies that have been torn apart by civil strife, and they now live in barrios and ghettos where youth gangs are constantly at war with one another over misunderstandings of one kind or another. The Montagues and the Capulets, played by Sanchez's students, feud by kung fu instead of swords to express their theatrical rage in more culturally familiar ways. Many of his students do not read, so Sánchez reads the work with them. They do not understand academic English, let alone Elizabethan literary language, so in everyday, simple English, he explains, demonstrates, and dramatizes the work, bit by bit, until they get the gist of it. They have to learn to speak English, so he creates with them an ESL version of the drama, which gives them practice with simple English grammatical patterns and English pronunciation. They do not have much knowledge of English vocabulary, so he discusses and clarifies the meanings of words that are used during the rehearsal sessions and in the play.

Obviously, it takes time for Sánchez to teach materials like *Romeo and Juliet* well, and therefore he may end up covering fewer of the works included in the ninth-grade English curriculum than he might if the students were not learning the language of instruction while they were dealing with the content. Furthermore, Sánchez does not cover everything that he might otherwise include in a treatment of *Romeo and Juliet* if the students were fully proficient in English. He has to be selective about the concepts and topics he works on since, after all, the students are extremely limited in their understanding of English. Even then, Sánchez's students get considerably more from his class than they would from other English classes. Sánchez's focus is primarily on his students' acquisition of basic English-language and literacy skills, but he finds that great theater, with its drama and human pathos, captivates his students, provides a basis of pain and humanity with which they can identify, and thereby provides a meaningful context for learning and using their new English skills.

In language-sensitive content or sheltered English instruction, the learning of content concepts, rather than English-language skills, is the primary goal; "content teachers adapt their instructional techniques to meet the needs of LEP students, for whom traditional approaches may not be appropriate" (Short 1989, 1). Methods and teaching strategies are employed that simplify and reduce the amount of oral and written language used in instruction. The purpose of these adjustments, however, is to ensure effective instruction of content concepts, not English-language skills, for LEP students.

It is often felt that the scope of content that can be covered must be reduced for effective instruction to second-language learners. Mohan (1986) passes along the following recommendation to subject matter teachers of LEP students: "Cut down your teaching objectives by half, concentrating on the most important ones" (25). Mohan provides a framework for deciding how information on a topic might be selected, reduced, and organized for effective content instruction. The key to Mohan's integrated approach is to "find the main structure of topic information" (35) and to focus discussion and learning on that structure. Mohan's framework, "a guide to the structure of knowledge across the curriculum" (25), has two aspects: the specific, practical side, made up of the elements of description, sequence, and choice, and the general, theoretical side, constituted by concepts and classification, principles, and evaluation.

The Finding Out/Descubrimiento program (DeAvila and Duncan 1980), discussed earlier, represents one effort to select content that should be given special emphasis and that lends itself to the kind of structural adaptations that are felt to be needed. The program consists of a set of activity cards and worksheets used with cooperative learning techniques to achieve multiple goals: development of thinking skills, and oral proficiency, remediation of basic skills, development of grade-level concepts in math, experience with cooperative group work, and trust building and improvement of interracial relations in desegregated classrooms (E. G. Cohen 1986, 135–142). "Key concepts" of math and science have been selected for embedding in the task activities, though how extensively the selected concepts cover the full scope of the grade-level curriculum is not specified. However, Cohen reports that Finding Out/Descubrimiento has been documented to affect positively minority children's mastery of academic content: Working-class children attending predominantly Hispanic schools where the program is in use have consistently displayed significant gains in language arts, reading, and mathematics on nationally normed tests. Further, the degree to which children talked and worked together to complete the materials influenced their development of math concepts and problem-solving skills, with higher average gains achieved by those who spent most time talking and working together to complete the activities.

Decisions about how content should be reduced, and by how much, must be made with care and thought, and they need to be thoroughly evaluated. Adjustments in what is taught may actually be unnecessary if the ways of teaching through the new language and the context of instruction are sensitively adapted to LEP students' needs. Lapkin and Cummins (1984) report that Canadian immersion students "study the same curriculum content as their peers in the regular program" (58); they are, however, supported by an array of possible program alternatives, instructional approaches, curriculum materials development efforts, language use strategies that ensure the presence of both the home language (English) and the new language (French), instructional grouping arrangements, school and staffing organizational plans, and special support services that enable unreduced content instruction through the immersion language to be effective.

Tough (1977, 1985) developed a framework for instructional language usage based on an examination of the purposes for which children need to use language to participate in classroom and instructional activities. In dialogue with the student about his or her learning activities, the teacher targets the talk to the learner's level of second-language development rather than reducing the conceptual content of the task on which the dialogue is based. Meyer (1985; Meyer Precup 1981, 1982), influenced by both the Canadian immersion findings and Tough's work, describes the development of integrated thematic units of instruction for linguistic minority students that retain the scope of the grade-level content curriculum while adapting the language expectations and forms of instructional delivery. Because of the language barrier, it takes more time, thought, planning, and effort to teach grade-level subject matter effectively to students who do not fully understand the language of instruction, but the effort has been documented to be both possible and effective.

Adaptations to the Actual Content of the Curriculum

Over the years, there have been various efforts to adapt or completely reconstruct the content of the mainstream curriculum rather than merely retaining or reducing the existing content for language minority students. These efforts are generally motivated by the recognition that the unadapted curriculum is an exclusionary one for language minority students: The situations, events, people, ideas, concepts, and values represented in the instructional materials are not relevant to the students, so they are changed to make them "more appropriate" or less alienating.

Some of these changes are merely cosmetic—they are well-intentioned but superficial. A cursory examination of most published textbooks will reveal such well-meant but cosmetic efforts. The situations and characters in basal reader stories are no longer only in white, middle-class, nuclear family homes in the suburbs. Dick and Jane have been transformed into Ricardo and Juana, who now live in a barrio with their working, single parent, Mrs. Rodríguez. The illustrations depict a multiethnic world—Asian and Hispanic teachers, white mail delivery persons, African-American doctors, and the like. The materials and the messages and values they convey, however, are otherwise the same as before. Students are given a glimpse of their own realities, often sanitized, and a peek at realities other than their own, equally laundered. The look of the curriculum may be multicultural, but the focus is unidirectional—assimilation into the values and goals of the mainstream.

Some recent attempts have been made to adapt the content of the school curriculum seriously to include the experiences and perspectives of linguistic minority students. The best known of these is multicultural education, "an alternative, less ethnocentric lens with which to focus on an old subject—people and how they interact with one another and with nature" (Ovando and Collier 1985, 160). As the name suggests, multicultural efforts attempt to provide students with content and materials drawn from and reflective of several cultural perspectives, especially their own. Increasingly, for example, commercially produced, literature-based reading programs include poetry and reading selections written by international and minority authors. Banks (1984) and Saville-Troike (1978) suggest questions that teachers can ask about their subject matter and about their students to discover ways in which the mainstream content can be infused with cultural and multicultural understandings relevant to their students' lives. One effort of multicultural education is to display to students—all students, not just minority students—that although cultures and cultural life patterns vary greatly, beneath the obvious diversity is a humanity that is shared by all.

Several curriculum development projects are attempting to produce classroom curricular materials with multicultural and global perspectives. The Stanford Program on International and Cross-Cultural Education (SPICE) has produced about 60 units of instruction to improve international and cross-cultural education in elementary and secondary schools. Each unit is based on an experiential look at another culture or culture contrast. SPICE includes special projects focused on China, Japan, Africa, Latin America, international security and arms control, geography, and foreign-language services. In 1979, SPICE joined with two other organizations—the World Affairs Council of Northern California and Global Educators—to form the Bay Area Global Education Program (BAGEP), an international studies resource consortium serving K–12 school districts in northern California. Among other activities, including staff development and the planning of international study tours, BAGEP collects and disseminates curricular materials on global issues, including the SPICE units. In 1989, its 10th anniversary, BAGEP had spawned 60 similar teams in California alone and at least 40 teams in six other states that are based on the BAGEP model (World Affairs Council of Northern California 1989).

The students themselves, in their cultural diversity, can be the source of multicultural content if their own voices are celebrated rather than silenced. When creative and sensitive teachers create an environment in class in which minority students are free and comfortable to speak about their lives and their pains, the result can be a very special kind of understanding. In an urban high school creative writing class in San Francisco, teacher Judy Bebelaar and poet Kathryn Harer create a safe environment, where inner-city students of a variety of ethnic and racial backgrounds and grade point averages pour out the reality of their lives through poetry and creative writing (Mullen and Olsen 1990). There is the conviction that academic writing skills will be learned as they become relevant and important to the students through writing and editing their own work for oral presentation and publication. Other course objectives are equally important: "teaching students to write honestly and deeply 'from the heart' about their lives and feelings; helping students learn to share their work and to 'take responsibility for supporting each other,' and arousing the humanity in each student and helping them see self-expression as an avenue to making a difference in the world" (28).

In one class session documented on videotape (Macbeth and Meyer 1988a), black, Asian, Hispanic, and white inner-city students transformed their daily experiences (gang warfare, invalid mother, loneliness, prejudice against Asians, homelessness, parental suicide, and immigration) into artistic cries through poetry. Listening to one another's poems, the students felt their awarenesses were transformed, too: "We get a better understanding of the people, our classmates. It's like that's part of them, and that builds their character of who they are. I see them for who they are more than before" (white, female student). Their learning, according to the teacher, goes far beyond skills:

> They learn in the process of sharing. They share those basic experiences, and they begin to learn that they're not alone, which I think is another part of the class which gives them some strength and some courage to keep on struggling. And in the process, I think they and we discover our own humanity, which to me is what literature and writing and poetry is all about anyway. So I think we get sorta into the guts of what it's all about.

The course gives back to the students not only their voices but also themselves: "We feel comfortable and free about who we are. I feel all myself here, not like other classes where I only feel my body but not my heart" (Mullen and Olsen 1990, 30).

Critical educators such as McLeod (1986) call for a pedagogy that not only enables minority students to "see each other for who they are" but also empowers them to create actively what they might become. This is Simon's (1987) pedagogy of possibility, which intends to provide "the possibility for students to understand who they are in ways that are different from identities in-formed by the dominant culture" (378). Influenced by Freirian "conscientization" (Freire 1985), critical educators seek ways to "encourage students to think they can [and will succeed] by involving them in using language to serve their own purposes, and to interpret the events and institutions and power structures that determine their existence" (McLeod 1986, 40). Through their efforts to encourage in students the ability to analyze critically and interpret the social, political, and economic structures that influence their lives, McLeod and others have embarked on what might be called critical multicultural education.

The effort engaged in by critical educators is that of empowering minority students, and all students, to possess the skills and insights to use language and learning for their own purposes rather than for the purposes of even an enlightened educator. Part of the empowerment they seek through their teaching strategies is to unleash the silenced voices, to reunify bodies and hearts, and to share with minority students control over the content they learn and create in school. To pursue seriously with minority students a pedagogy of possibility would require us, as Simon (1987, 373) indicates, to allow differences to be expressed differently. In a pedagogy of possibility, the mainstream might become many streams rather than melting into one, cultural literacy might mean celebrating the multitude of ways that Americans know differently, and schools might be places where students and teachers discover together a curriculum that empowers rather than silences.

SUMMARY AND RESEARCH AGENDA

From our examination of the work in curricular reforms for language minority students, a number of issues have surfaced on which there has been little study. We present these issues as an agenda for future research in this important area.

Over the years a lot of money and effort have been spent in developing curriculum for use in bilingual education programs. Much of that work has been lost or forgotten, largely because of the vagaries of federal funding. Curriculum is designed, used, and then forgotten as fundings for programs run out. Some of these materials were collected, evaluated, and disseminated, but as funding for the Title VII–supported dissemination centers disappeared, so did much of the materials they handled. It has been extremely difficult to locate or access the materials that were produced, but they must surely still exist. It would take a major effort to find them, but they should be evaluated and studied. What is the nature of these materials? Are they just regular curriculum produced in various ethnic languages, or were there special adaptations that make them especially useful? How effective are they? Do any of these materials offer better ways to teach LEP students the subject matter of school? Are there curricular innovations among the warehoused materials that should be revived?

A major area of concern in programs for language minority students relates to instructional language: Should subject matter instruction be provided in the language the students understand or in the language they have to learn? This question has been enormously controversial. Critics of bilingual education argue that children cannot possibly learn English if they are being taught subject matter in their primary languages. Bilingual educators contend that students will not have access to the subject matter they are supposed to learn in school unless it is taught in a language they understand. They agree, however, that LEP students need some subject matter instruction in English in order to learn it. They point out that there is ample research evidence showing that LEP children do not have to be taught exclusively in English to learn it well; they can learn English with far less exposure to it than they get in an English-only program. But how much is enough? How much of the curriculum should be taught in English to provide the exposure children need to ensure their learning it as a second language? What subjects can be taught most readily and effectively in a language that is just being learned? What kind of adaptations to content are needed when it is being used as a vehicle for teaching English as a second language? How thoroughly can children understand instruction when it is taught in a language they are in the process of learning?

In looking at structural and pedagogical adjustments in curriculum, some major issues surfaced as we considered the work of researchers such as Ronald Gallimore and Roland Tharp, Spencer Kagan, and Elizabeth Cohen and her associates. According to KEEP researchers, modifications in pedagogy and structure need to be tailored to the cultural group being served by the school. The KEEP success was due in large part to the fact that the researchers have discovered just how the school environment and activity structures needed to be modified to make them more appropriate for the native Hawaiian children served by the program. Researchers such as Kagan and Cohen and her associates argue that there are structural modifications in learning environments and activities that are beneficial for all children. Both sides may be right, but we need to consider more carefully what works with whom and why. To what extent must pedagogical strategies and curricular structure be adapted for specific groups? How effective are strategies such as group work, collaborative learning, and peer teaching for all children? Are there group differences that must be considered, and how should children be prepared for such changes in the structure of activities? Are there intergroup differences in preferred learning styles that need to be considered when teachers use strategies that require children from diverse backgrounds to work together collaboratively? Are some activities more or less effective with students at certain second-language proficiency levels?

Teachers in today's schools have to be prepared to work with children with diverse needs. The kind of curricular decisions and planning they must do requires special preparation and understanding. Few teachers are prepared to make the adjustments and modifications in the curriculum that are required for students who do not speak English and who are unfamiliar with the culture of the school. They clearly need to learn more about curriculum planning and development and to realize the extent to which values and cultural attitudes figure in such work. What do teachers of LEP students need to know about curriculum design and philosophy to adjust and develop materials appropriately for students from diverse backgrounds? How much do teachers need to know about specific cultures to plan culturally sensitive materials? Are there ways short of doing research in the homes of their students to learn about the worlds from which these students come? Should teachers be engaged in curriculum development work, or should there be specialists in schools to take care of such activities? How much do teachers have to know about the processes of language learning to develop materials and strategies for teaching English through content instruction?

Where curricular adjustments have been made on behalf of language minority students, they have mainly focused on the student as an English-language learner or a "deficient" English speaker. Certainly the barrier that English presents to the academic and social success of students in school should not be underestimated and efforts to identify strategies for enabling students to succeed with English acquisition should be supported. Among these efforts, the role of the native language should be further investigated and the findings taken seriously and implemented in practice. Beyond these linguistic concerns, however, the concern for substantive evaluation of the content of the curriculum to identify and eliminate the ethnocentric aspects that exclude and alienate minority students must receive serious attention. Much of the pain and fear expressed by immigrant and minority students in school will disappear, not when the "surface structures" of their English syntax and morphology have improved, but rather when there has been a significant transformation in the "deep structures" of racism and ethnocentrism in our schools and society. Identifying and documenting the ways that curricula might equip students to analyze critically, confront, and transform the fears and hatreds that we harbor against one another in our society are some of the most crucial tasks confronting us in the decade ahead.

How might educators approach these complex and knotty curricular issues in the education of language minority students? In an important sense, the approach we should be taking is to consider these students' curricular needs in relation to the needs of all students rather than as special ones. We need to start with an examination of the role schools play, or ought to play, in the intellectual socialization of all of the society's children. This, at heart, is a philosophical issue. It requires us to engage in a philosophical consideration of what an educated person is. What do we expect our schools to do for all children? What kind of people does the society expect its schools to produce?

Most Americans believe that our society is both egalitarian and democratic, at least in the opportunities it offers for social and economic mobility: We believe that our schools offer every child, without regard for race or economic background, the means to rise without limit. And yet most Americans are aware that not all groups have the same opportunities for changing their social and economic circumstances and that this lack of mobility for certain groups in the society has something to do with what happens or does not happen in the schools. The notion that some groups do not succeed in the society because they are not well served by the schools, whereas others do because they are especially favored, is anathema to most Americans since it violates the belief that our society is egalitarian. Many people prefer the explanation that some groups are inherently less capable than others in the first place and are therefore less able to take advantage of what the school and society have to offer. Such an explanation absolves the society and the schools of the responsibility for serving all students equally. Our schools, instead of offering everyone the basis for unlimited mobility, have done the opposite by steering and channeling people into ability tracks that lead to predetermined places in a fixed social and economic hierarchy according to beliefs about who is capable and who is not. The danger is that what is believed gets incorporated into policy, which in turn supports practice, and so we perpetuate a version of the society that is fundamentally opposed to our own best interests. A major challenge facing the society's educators in the next century is to find appropriate ways of educating all of our society's children. A thoughtful consideration of our values and beliefs as expressed in the curriculum of our schools is the first step.

References

Ada, Alma F. 1986. Creative education for bilingual teachers. *Harvard Educational Review* 56 (4): 386–394.

Ada, Alma F. 1988. "Creative Reading: A Relevant Methodology for Language Minority Children." In *NABE '87. Theory, Research and Application: Selected Papers*, edited by Lillian M. Malave. Buffalo: State University of New York.

Ada, Alma F., and Maria de Pilar de Olave. 1986. *Hagamos Caminos*. Reading, MA: Addison-Wesley.

Adams, David W. 1988. Fundamental considerations: The deep meaning of native American schooling, 1880–1900. *Harvard Educational Review* 58 (1): 1–28.

Ammon, Paul. 1985. "Helping Children Learn to Write in English as a Second Language: Some Observations and Hypotheses." In *The Acquisition of Written Language: Response and Revision*, edited by Sarah Freedman, 65–84. Norwood, NJ: Ablex.

Andersson, Theodore, and Mildred Boyer. 1970. *Bilingual Schooling in the United States*. Washington, DC: U.S. Government Printing Office. Southwest Educational Development Laboratory, Austin, TX.

Association for Supervision and Curriculum Development. 1987. *Building an Indivisible Nation: Bilingual Education in Context*. Alexandria, VA: ASCD.

Au, Kathryn H. 1979. Using the experience-text-relationship method with minority children. *Reading Teacher* 32(6): 677–679.

Au, Kathryn H., Doris C. Crowell, Cathie Jordan, Kim C. Sloat, Gisela Speidel, Thomas W. Klein, and Roland G. Tharp. 1986. "Development and Implementation of the KEEP Reading Program." In *Reading Comprehension: From Research to Practice*, edited by Judith Orasanu, 235–252. Hillsdale, NJ: Erlbaum.

Banks, James A. 1984. *Teaching Strategies for Ethnic Studies*, 3rd ed. Boston: Allyn & Bacon.

Blanco, George. 1977. "The Education Perspective." In *Bilingual Education: Current Perspectives*, vol. 4, 1–63. Arlington, VA: Center for Applied Linguistics.

Blatchford, Paul. 1977. "Paul Blatchford." In *Stories of Traditional Navajo Life and Culture by Twenty-two Navajo Men and Women*, edited by Broderick H. Johnson, 173–181. Tsaile, Navajo Nation, AZ: Navajo Community College Press.

Boggs, Stephen T. 1985. *Speaking, Relating, and Learning: A Study of Hawaiian Children at Home and at School*. New York: Ablex.

Carlisle, R. S. 1986. "The Writing of Anglo and Hispanic Fourth and Sixth Graders in Regular, Submersion and Bilingual Programs." Ph.D. dissertation, University of Illinois, Champaign-Urbana. Dissertation Abstracts International 47 (9), 1987.

Carnegie Foundation for the Advancement of Teaching. 1988. *An Imperiled Generation: Saving Urban Schools*. Princeton, NJ: Carnegie Foundation.

Carnegie Task Force on Teaching as a Profession. 1986. *A Nation Prepared: Teachers for the 21st Century*. New York: Carnegie Forum on Education and the Economy.

Chamot, Ana U., and J. Michael O'Malley. 1987. The cognitive academic language learning approach: A bridge to the mainstream. *TESOL Quarterly* 21 (2): 227–249.

Cohen, Andrew D. 1973. "Innovative Education for La Raza: A Sociolinguistic Assessment of a Bilingual Program." Ph.D. dissertation, Stanford University, Palo Alto, CA.

Cohen, Andrew D. 1975. *A Sociolinguistic Approach to Bilingual Education*. Rowley, MA: Newbury House.

Cohen, David K. 1970. Immigrants and the schools. *Review of Educational Research* 40 (1): 13–27.

Cohen, Elizabeth G. 1986. *Designing Groupwork: Strategies for the Heterogeneous Classroom*. New York and London: Teachers College Press.

Cohen, Elizabeth G., and Edward A. De Avila. 1983. *Learning to Think in Math and Science: Improving Local Education for Minority Children. Final report to the Walter S. Johnson Foundation*. Palo Alto, CA: Stanford University Program for Complex Instruction.

Cohen, Elizabeth G., and Joanne K. Intili. 1981. *Interdependence and Management in Bilingual Classrooms. Final Report to the National Institute for Studies in Education*. Palo Alto, CA: Center for Educational Research.

Crandall, JoAnn, Theresa C. Dale, Nancy C. Rhodes, and George Spanos. 1987. *English Language Skills for Basic Algebra*. Englewood Cliffs, NJ: Prentice Hall.

Crawford, James. 1986a. Conservative groups take aim at bilingual-education programs. *Education Week* 5 (27): 1, 14.

Crawford, James. 1986b. Supporting comments reveal animosity toward ethnic groups. *Education Week* 5 (22): 23.

Crawford, James. 1989. *Bilingual Education: History, Politics, Theory and Practice*. Trenton, NJ: Crane Books.

Cuevas, Gilbert J. 1984. Mathematics learning in English as a second language. *Journal for Research in Mathematics Education* 15 (2): 134–144.

Cummins, James. 1981. "The Role of Primary Language Development in Promoting Educational Success for Language Minority Students." In *Schooling and Language Minority Students: A Theoretical Framework*, edited by California State Department of Education, Office of Bilingual Bicultural Education, 3–50. Los Angeles: Evaluation, Dissemination and Assessment Center, California State Department of Education.

Cummins, James. 1984. *Bilingualism and Special Education: Issues in Assessment and Pedagogy*. Clevedon, Eng.: Multilingual Matters.

Cummins, James. 1989. *Empowering Minority Students*. Sacramento: California Association for Bilingual Education.

Cummins, James, and Merrill Swain. 1986. *Bilingualism in Education: Aspects of Theory, Research and Practice*. London: Longman.

Cummins, James, Merril Swain, Kazuhiko Nakayama, Jean Handscombe, David Green, and Cho Tran. 1981. "Linguistic Interdependence Among Japanese and Vietnamese Immigrant Students." In *Communicative Competence Approaches to Language Proficiency Assessment: Research and Application*, edited by Charlene Rivera, 60–81. Clevedon, Eng.: Multilingual Matters.

De Avila, Edward A., and Sharon E. Duncan. 1980. *Finding Out/ Descubrimiento*. Corte Madera, CA: Linguametrics Group.

Díaz, Stephen, Luis Moll, and Hugh Mehan. 1986. "Sociocultural Resources in Instruction: A Context-Specific Approach." In *Beyond Language: Social and Cultural Factors in Schooling Language Minority Students*, edited by California State Department of Education, Office of Bilingual Bicultural Education, 187–230. Los Angeles: Evaluation, Dissemination and Assessment Center, California State Department of Education.

Doebler, Leland K., and Larry J. Mardis. 1980–1981. Effects of a bilingual education program for Native American children. *NABE Journal* 5 (2): 23–28.

Edelsky, Carol. 1986. *Writing in a Bilingual Program: Había Una Vez*. Norwood, NJ: Ablex.

Eisner, Elliot W. 1985. *The Educational Imagination: On the Design and Evaluation of School Programs*. New York: Macmillan.

Engle, Patricia. 1975. *The Use of Vernacular Languages in Education*. Arlington, VA: Center for Applied Linguistics.

Epstein, Noel. 1977. *Language, Ethnicity, and the Schools: Policy Alternatives for Bilingual-Bicultural Education*. Washington, DC: George Washington University, Institute for Educational Leadership.

Fillmore, Charles J. 1982. "Ideal Readers and Real Readers." In *Analyzing Discourse: Text and Talk*, edited by Deborah Tannen, Georgetown Round Table on Language and Linguistics 1981, 248–270. Washington, DC: Georgetown University Press.

Fine, Michelle. 1987. Silencing in public schools. *Language Arts* 64 (2): 157–174.

Freire, Paulo. 1970. *Pedagogia del Oprimido*. Mexico, D.F.: Siglo Veintiuno Editores, S.A.

Freire, Paulo. 1973a. *Education for Critical Consciousness*. New York: Continuum.

Freire, Paulo. 1973b. *The Politics of Education: Culture, Power and Liberation*. South Hadley, MA: Bergin and Garvey.

Freire, Paulo. 1985. Reading the world and reading the word. *Language Arts* 62 (1): 15–21.

Gallimore, Ronald, Stephen Boggs, and Cathie Jordan. 1974. *Culture, Behavior and Education: A Study of Hawaiian-Americans*. Beverly Hills, CA: Sage.

Gardner, Howard. 1989. *To Open Minds: Chinese Clues to the Dilemma of Contemporary Education*. New York: Basic Books.

Gass, Susan, and Carolyn Madden, eds. 1985. *Input in Second Language Acquisition*. Rowley, MA: Newbury House.

Giroux, Henry A. 1984. Public philosophy and the crisis in education. *Harvard Educational Review* 54 (2): 186–194.

Glazer, Nathan. 1980. "Pluralism and Ethnicity." In *Proceedings of "The New Bilingualism." Conference Sponsored by the Center for the Study of the American Experience*. Los Angeles: Annenberg School of Communication, University of Southern California.

Goldman, Susan, Maria Reyes, and Connie Varnhagen. 1984. Understanding fables in first and second languages. *NABE Journal* 3 (2): 35–66.

González, Eileen, and Juan Lezama. 1976. "The Dual Language Model: A Practical Approach to Bilingual Education." In *English as a Second Language in Bilingual Education*, edited by James E. Alatis and Kristie Twaddell, 105–112. Washington, DC: Teachers of English to Speakers of Other Languages.

González, Gustavo, and Lento F. Maez. 1980. "To Switch or Not to Switch: The Role of Code-Switching in the Elementary Bilingual Classroom." In *Ethnoperspectives in Bilingual Education Research, Volume 2: Theory in Bilingual Education*, edited by Raymond V. Padilla, 125–135. Ypsilanti: Eastern Michigan University.

Goodman, Kenneth, and Yetta Goodman. 1978. "Reading of American Children Whose Language Is a Stable Rural Dialect of English or a Language Other than English." Final report to NIE, Project NIE G-003-0087.

Goodman, Kenneth, Yetta Goodman, and Barbara Flores. 1979. *Reading in the Bilingual Classroom: Literacy and Biliteracy*. Rosslyn, VA: National Clearinghouse for Bilingual Education.

Grant, Linda. 1988. Introduction: Regenerating and refocusing research on minorities and education. *The Elementary School Journal* 88 (5): 441–448.

Graves, Donald. 1978. "Balance the Basics: Let Them Write." Report to the Ford Foundation.

Graves, Donald. 1983. *Writing: Children and Teachers at Work*. Exeter, NH: Heinemann.

Greenbaum, William. 1974. American in search of a new ideal: An essay on the rise of pluralism. *Harvard Educational Review* 44 (3): 411–440.

Hakuta, Kenji. 1986. *Mirror of Language: The Debate on Bilingualism*. New York: Basic Books.

Hatch, Evelyn M. 1983. *Psycholinguistics: A Second Language Perspective*. Rowley, MA: Newbury House.

Hayakawa, Sessue I. 1985. *The English Language Amendment: One Nation . . . Indivisible?* Washington, DC: Washington Institute for Values in Public Policy.

Haycock, Katie, and M. Susana Navarro. 1988. *Unfinished Business: Fulfilling Our Children's Promise*. Oakland and Los Angeles: Achievement Council.

Heath, Shirley B. 1982. What no bedtime story means: Narrative skills at home and school. *Language and Society* 11 (2): 49–76.

Heath, Shirley B. 1983. *Ways with Words: Language, Life, and Work in Communities and Classrooms*. Cambridge: Cambridge University Press.

Hirsch, Edward D., Jr. 1987. *Cultural Literacy: What Every American Needs to Know*. Boston: Houghton Mifflin.

Hudelson, Sarah. 1984. Kan yu ret and rayt en ingles? Children become literate in English as a second language. *TESOL Quarterly* 18 (2): 221–238.

Hudelson, Sarah. 1989. "A Tale of Two Children: Individual Differences in ESL Children's Writing." In *Richness in Writing: Empowering ESL Students*, edited by Donna M. Johnson and Duane H. Roen, 84–99. New York and London: Longman.

Jacobson, Rodolfo. 1981, June 12. "The Implementation of a Bilingual Education Model: The Concurrent Approach." Paper presented at the Ethnoperspectives in Bilingual Education Conference, Eastern Michigan University, Ypsilanti.

Kagan, Spencer. 1986. "Cooperative Learning and Sociocultural Factors in Schooling." In *Beyond Language: Social and Cultural Factors in Schooling Language Minority Students*, edited by California State Department of Education, Office of Bilingual Bicultural Education, 231–298. Los Angeles: Evaluation, Dissemination and Assessment Center, California State Department of Education.

Kessler, Carolyn, and Mary E. Quinn. 1980. "Positive Effects of Bilingualism on Science Problem-Solving Abilities." In *Current Issues in Bilingual Education. Georgetown University Round Table on Languages and Linguistics 1980*, edited by James E. Alatis, 295–308. Washington, DC: Georgetown University Press.

Kloss, Heinz. 1966. "German-American Language Maintenance Efforts." In *Language Loyalty in the United States*, edited by Joshua A. Fishman, 206–252. The Hague: Mouton.

Kloss, Heinz. 1977. *The American Bilingual Education Tradition*. Rowley, MA: Newbury House.

Krashen, Stephen D. 1980. "The Input Hypothesis." In *Current Issues in Bilingual Education. Georgetown University Round Table on Languages and Linguistics 1980*, edited by James E. Alatis, 168–180. Washington, DC: Georgetown University Press.

Krashen, Stephen D. 1981. "Bilingual Education and Second Language Acquisition Theory." In *Schooling and Language Minority Students: A Theoretical Framework*, edited by California State Department of Education, Office of Bilingual Bicultural Education, 51–79. Los Angeles: Evaluation, Dissemination and Assessment Center, California State Department of Education.

Krashen, Stephen D., and Douglas Biber. 1988. *On Course: Bilingual Education's Success in California*. Sacramento: California Association of Bilingual Education.

Kreeft-Peyton, Joy, and JoAnn Mackinson-Smyth. 1989. "Writing and Talking About Writing: Computer Networking with Elementary Students." In *Richness in Writing: Empowering ESL Students*, edited by Donna M. Johnson and Duane H. Roen, 100–119. New York and London: Longman.

Lambert, Wallace E. 1984. "An Overview of Issues in Immersion Education." In *Studies on Immersion Education*, edited by California State Department of Education, Office of Bilingual Bicultural Education, 8–30. Sacramento: California State Department of Education.

Lambert, Wallace E., and G. Richard Tucker. 1972. *Bilingual Education of Children: The St. Lambert Experiment*. Rowley, MA: Newbury House.

Lapkin, Sharon, and James Cummins. 1984. "Current Administrative Arrangements and Instructional Practices." In *Studies on Immersion Education*, edited by California State Department of Education, Office of Bilingual Bicultural Education, 58–86. Sacramento: California State Department of Education.

Legaretta, Dorothy M. 1977. Language choice in bilingual classrooms. *TESOL Quarterly* 11 (1): 9–16.

Legaretta, Dorothy M. 1979. The effects of program models on language acquisition by Spanish speaking children. *TESOL Quarterly* 13 (4): 521–534.

Leibowitz, Arnold H. 1970. *Educational Policy and Political Acceptance: The Imposition of English as the Language of Instruction in American Schools*. Washington, DC: Center for Applied Linguistics.

Leibowitz, Arnold H. 1982. *Federal Recognition of the Rights of Minority Groups*. Rosslyn, VA: National Clearinghouse for Bilingual Education.

Long, Michael H. 1981. "Input, Interaction, and Second Language Acquisition." In *Annals of the New York Academy of Sciences*, vol. 379, edited by Harry Winitz, 259–278. New York: New York Academy of Sciences.

Macbeth, Douglas, and Lois M. Meyer. 1988a. *Creative Writing Class, Galileo High School: Videotape of Judy Bebelaar's Creative Writing Classroom Instruction and Student Interviews with Five of Her Galileo High School Students*. San Francisco: HERALD Project, San Francisco Education Fund.

Macbeth, Douglas, and Lois M. Meyer. 1988b. *Teaching ESL to Newcomer Students through a Theater Production of Romeo and Juliet: Videotape of Gilbert Sanchez's Classroom Instruction and Student Interviews with Six of His Newcomer High School Students*. San Francisco: HERALD Project, San Francisco Education Fund.

Macbeth, Douglas, and Lois M. Meyer. 1989a. *Navajo School Day and Social Studies Instruction, Naschitti, NM: Videotape of a Day at Naschitti Elementary School on the Navajo Reservation, and Grace Henry's Social Studies Instruction*. Santa Fe: New Mexico State Department of Education, Title VII, ESEA, Bilingual Education Technical Assistance Unit.

Macbeth, Douglas, and Lois M. Meyer. 1989b. *Sheltered Science Instruction in West Las Vegas, NM: Videotape of Mary Jane Manzanares' Sheltered Science Lesson*. Santa Fe: New Mexico State Department of Education, Title VII, ESEA, Bilingual Education Technical Assistance Unit.

Macbeth, Douglas, and Lois M. Meyer. 1989c. *Spanish Reading Instruction in West Las Vegas, NM: Videotape of Elisia Bustamante's Spanish Reading Instruction*. Santa Fe: New Mexico State Department of Education, Title VII, ESEA, Bilingual Education Technical Assistance Unit.

Mackey, William F., and Von Nieda Beebe. 1977. *Bilingual Schools for a Bilingual Community: Miami's Adaptation to the Cuban Refugees*. Rowley, MA: Newbury House.

McLaren, Peter. 1989. *Life in Schools*. New York and London: Longman.

McLeod, Alex, 1986. Critical literacy: Taking control of our own lives. *Language Arts* 63 (1): 37–50.

Mann, Arthur. 1979. *The One and the Many: Reflections on the American Identity*. Chicago: University of Chicago Press.

Mason, Jana M., and Kathryn H. Au. 1986. *Reading Instruction for Today*. Glenview, IL: Scott, Foresman.

Meyer, Lois. 1985. *Excellence in Leadership and Implementation: Programs for Limited English Proficient Students*. San Francisco: San Francisco Unified School District.

Meyer Precup, Lois. 1981. Integrating second language learning into the elementary school curriculum. *MEXTESOL Journal* 5 (1): 1–15.

Meyer Precup, Lois. 1982. *You, Too, Tobui? A Preschool Program for English as a Second Language Instruction*. Mexico, D.F.: Editorial Educativa, S.A.

Modiano, Nancy. 1973. *Indian Education in the Chiapas Highlands*. New York: Holt, Rinehart & Winston.

Mohan, Bernard A. 1986. *Language and Content*. Reading, MA: Addison-Wesley.

Moll, Luis. 1989. "Teaching Second Language Students: A Vygotskian Perspective." In *Richness in Writing: Empowering ESL Students*, edited by Donna M. Johnson and Duane H. Roen, 55–69. White Plains, NY: Longman.

Monette, Maurice L. 1979. Need assessment: A critique of philosophical assumptions. *Adult Education* 29 (2): 83–95.

Moran, Rachel F. 1986. Forward—The lesson of Keyes: How do you translate "the American dream"? *La Raza Law Journal* 1 (3): 195–212.

Mullen, Nina A., and Laurie Olsen. 1990. You and I are the same. *California Tomorrow* 5 (1): 26–34.

National Coalition of Advocates for Students. 1988. *New Voices: Immigrant Students in U.S. Public Schools*. Boston: NCAS Immigrant Student Project.

National Commission on Excellence in Education. 1983. *A Nation at Risk: The Imperative for Educational Reform*. Washington, DC: U.S. Government Printing Office.

Nazario, Sonia L. 1989, March 31. Failing in 81 languages: Los

Angeles's huge immigrant community puts colossal stress on its school system. *Wall Street Journal*: R21–22.

Oakes, Jeannie. 1986. Tracking, inequality, and the rhetoric of reform: Why schools don't change. *Journal of Education* 168 (1): 60–80.

Ogbu, John U., and Maria Eugenia Matute-Bianchi. 1986. "Understanding Soiocultural Factors: Knowledge, Identity and School Adjustment." In *Beyond Language: Social and Cultural Factors in Schooling Language Minority Students*, edited by California State Department of Education, Office of Bilingual Bicultural Education, 73–143. Los Angeles: Evaluation, Dissemination and Assessment Center, California State Department of Education.

Olsen, Laurie. 1988. *Crossing the Schoolhouse Border: Immigrant Students and the California Public Schools*. San Francisco: California Tomorrow.

Ovando, Carlos J., and Virgina P. Collier. 1985. *Bilingual and ESL Classrooms: Teaching in Multicultural Contexts*. New York: McGraw-Hill.

Pappademos, John. 1989. "An Outline of Africa's Role in the History of Physics." In *Blacks in Science*, edited by Ivan Van Sertima, 177–196. New Brunswick, NJ: Transaction Books.

Phillips, Susan U. 1972. "Participant Structure and Communicative Competence: Warm Springs Children in Community and Classroom." In *Functions of Language in the Classroom*, edited by Courtney Cazden, Vera P. John, and Dell Hymes, 370–394. New York: Teachers College Press.

Phillips, Susan U. 1983. *The Invisible Culture: Communication and Community on the Warm Springs Indian Reservation*. White Plains, NY: Longman.

Resnick, Lauren B. 1989, September 4–7. "Developing Thinking Abilities in Arithmetic Class." Paper presented at the Third European Conference for Research on Research on Learning and Instruction, Madrid.

Rodriguez, Richard. 1982. *Hunger of Memory: The Education of Richard Rodriguez*. Boston: David R. Godinc.

Rosier, Paul. 1977. "A Comparative Study of Two Approaches of Introducing Initial Reading to Navaho Children: The Direct Method and the Native Language Method." Ph.D. dissertation, Northern Arizona University, Flagstaff.

San Francisco Unified School District. 1988. *Newcomer High School: Program Description*. San Francisco: Unified School District.

Saville-Troike, Muriel. 1978. *A Guide to Culture in the Classroom*. Rosslyn, VA: National Clearinghouse for Bilingual Education.

Schiefflin, Bambi, and Eleanor Ochs, eds. 1986. *Language Socialization Across Cultures*. Cambridge: Cambridge University Press.

Schlossman, Steven L. 1983. Is there an American tradition of bilingual education? German in the public elementary schools, 1840–1919. *American Journal of Education* 91 (2): 139–186.

Secada, Walter G. 1989. "The Relationship Between Degree of Bilingualism and Arithmetic Problem Solving Performance in First-Grade Hispanic Children." Paper presented at the annual meeting, American Educational Research Association, San Francisco.

Secada, Walter G. In press. "Student Diversity and Mathematics Education Reform." In *Dimensions of Thinking and Cognitive Instruction*, edited by B. F. Jones and L. Idols. Hillsdale, NJ: Erlbaum.

Short, Donna J. 1989. Adapting materials for content-based language instruction. *ERIC/CLL News Bulletin* 13 (1): 1–8.

Simon, Roger I. 1987. Empowerment as a pedagogy of possibility. *Language Arts* 64 (4): 370–382.

Sola, Michele, and Adrian T. Bennett. 1985. The struggle for voice: Narrative, literacy and consciousness in an East Harlem school. *Journal of Education* 167 (1): 88–110.

Swain, Merrill. 1974. French immersion programs across Canada: Research findings. *Canadian Modern Language Review* 31 (2): 117–129.

Swain, Merrill. 1985. "Communicative Competence: Some Roles of Comprehensible Input and Comprehensible Output in its Development." In *Input in Second Language Acquisition*, edited by Susan Gass and Carolyn Madden, 235–256. Rowley, MA: Newbury House.

Swain, Merrill, and Henry C. Barik. 1976. A large scale program in French immersion: The Ottawa study through grade three. *ITL, Review of Applied Linguistics* 33 (1): 1–25.

Swain, Merrill, and Sharon Lapkin. 1982. *Evaluating Bilingual Education: A Canadian Case Study*. Clevedon, Eng.: Multilingual Matters.

Teitlebaum, Herbert, and Richard J. Hiller. 1977. "The Legal Perspective." In *Bilingual Education: Current Perspectives*, vol. 3. Arlington, VA: Center for Applied Linguistics.

Tempes, Fred. 1986. *Case Studies in Bilingual Education: Second Year Report, 1984–85*. A report to the U.S. Office of Bilingual Education and Minority Language Affairs. Sacramento: California State Department of Education.

Terrell, Tracy. 1981. "The Natural Approach in Bilingual Education." In *Schooling and Language Minority Students: A Theoretical Framework*, edited by California State Department of Education, Office of Bilingual Bicultural Education, 117–146. Los Angeles: Evaluation, Dissemination and Assessment Center, California State Department of Education.

Terrell, Tracy, and Stephen Krashen. 1983. *The Natural Approach: Language Acquisition in the Classroom*. Oxford: Pergamon Press.

Tharp, Roland, and Ronald Gallimore. 1988. *Rousing Minds to Life: Teaching, Learning and Schooling in Social Context*. Cambridge: Cambridge University Press.

Thonis, Eleanor W. 1981. "Reading Instruction for Language Minority Students." In *Schooling and Language Minority Students: A Theoretical Framework*, edited by California State Department of Education, Office of Bilingual Bicultural Education, 147–182. Los Angeles: Evaluation, Dissemination and Assessment Center, California State Department of Education.

Tikunoff, William. 1983. *An Emerging Description of Successful Bilingual Instruction: An Executive Summary of Part 1 of the SBIF Descriptive Study*. San Francisco: Far West Regional Laboratory.

Tough, Joan. 1977. *Talking and Learning: A Guide to Fostering Communication Skills in Nursery and Infant Schools*. Glasgow: Ward Lock Educational with Drake Education Associates.

Tough, Joan. 1985. *Talk Two: Children Using English as a Second Language*. London: Onyx Press.

Troike, Rudolph. 1978. Research evidence for the effectiveness of bilingual education. *NABE Journal* 3 (1): 13–24.

Tyler, Ralph W. 1949. *Basic Principles of Curriculum and Instruction*. Chicago: University of Chicago Press.

UNESCO. 1953. *The Use of Vernacular Languages in Education*. Paris: UNESCO.

U.S. Department of Education. 1988. *Youth Indicators, 1988: Trends in the Well-Being of American Youth*. Washington, DC: U.S. Government Printing Office.

Valdés, Guadalupe. 1988. *Identifying Priorities in the Study of Hispanic Background Students: A Synthesis and Interpretation of Available Research*. Final report to the Center for the Study of Writing. Berkeley, CA: CSW.

Valdés-Fallis, Guadalupe. 1978. *Code Switching and the Classroom*

Teacher. Language in Education Series, no. 4. Arlington, VA: Center for Applied Linguistics.

Walsh, Catherine. 1987. Language, meaning, and voice: Puerto Rican students' struggle for a speaking consciousness. *Language Arts* 64 (2) :196–205.

Warren, Beth, Ann S. Rosebery, and Faith R. Conant. 1989. "Cheche Konnen: Science and Literacy in Language Minority Classrooms." Manuscript.

Wong Fillmore, Lily. 1982. "Instructional Language as Linguistic Input: Second Language Learning in Classrooms." In *Communicating in the Classroom*, edited by Louise Cherry Wilkinson, 283–296. New York: Academic Press.

Wong Fillmore, Lily. 1983. "Effective Language Use in Bilingual Classes." In *Compatibility of the SBIF Features with other Research on Instruction for LEP Students*, edited by William J. Tikunoff, 41–59. San Francisco: Far West Laboratory for Educational Research and Development.

Wong Fillmore, Lily. 1985a. "Second Language Acquisition: A Research Model." In *Issues in English Language Development*, edited by Ruth Eshch and Johanna Provenzano, 33–44. Rosslyn, VA: National Clearinghouse for Bilingual Education.

Wong Fillmore, Lily. 1985b. "Teacher Talk as Input." In *Input in Second Language Acquisition*, edited by Susan Gass and Carolyn Madden, 17–50. Rowley, MA: Newbury House.

Wong Fillmore, Lily, Barry McLaughlin, Paul Ammon, and Mary Sue Ammon. 1985. *Learning English through Bilingual Instruction*. Final report to the National Institute for Studies in Education. Berkeley: University of California.

Wong Fillmore, Lily, and Merrill Swain. 1984, March. "Second Language Acquisition in Children: Theoretical Perspectives from the Field." Paper presented at the Research Symposium of the annual conference of Teachers of English to Speakers of Other Languages, Houston, TX.

World Affairs Council of Northern California. 1989, fall. *Colloquy on Teaching World Affairs*. San Francisco: World Affairs Council.

24

GENDER AND THE CURRICULUM

Nel Noddings
STANFORD UNIVERSITY

Historically, issues concerning gender and the curriculum have clustered around a few main questions: Should females be educated at all? If they should be educated, should they have the same education as males? Is the presence of female teachers and students educationally harmful for boys? This chapter will treat all of these questions. In addition it will examine a recent feminist movement that raises questions about the adequacy of traditional male education even for men. This new movement reflects a radical shift from the liberal feminist tradition that has accepted the male model as one to be emulated—one through which to gain equality not only in schooling but in life chances as well.

Before starting the historical overview, major analytical themes should be described. Three major perspectives (or models) can be identified: segregation models, assimilation models, and transformational models. All three form interesting combinations. For example, a writer may recommend segregated education on the grounds that men and women perform different functions in life; that is, because men and women are segregated occupationally, their education should be separate and substantially different. This strict (or double) segregation model has been traditionally important. Now, however, a segregation-assimilation model is sometimes advocated. In this model, single-sex schooling is recommended, but both sexes receive roughly similar educations, and the objective is to prepare girls and boys for the kinds of adult lives traditionally reserved for men. This is a relatively new model.

Assimilation models may, similarly, be double or mixed. One may recommend, for example, that boys and girls receive identical educations and that they have access to the same professional futures, or one may argue (as Mary Wollstonecraft did) that boys and girls should receive the same education even though their "duties" in life would remain different or segregated.

Finally, transformational perspectives are now being explored and articulated. Transformational theorists usually reject both segregation and assimilation in education and occupational life. They want new forms of education that incorporate significant aspects of female experience in the curriculum for all students, and they want public and professional life to be transformed in the light of this experience. Assimilation-transformation perspectives also exist. In these, the main premise is that women should be educated as men are and that their equitable distribution in occupational life will itself tend to transform public and private life.

HISTORICAL OVERVIEW

The main purpose of this section is to provide a synopsis of Western women's educational history. In doing so I have tried to select prominent periods of Western culture and topics of particular interest to contemporary scholars in women's studies.

The Greeks and Romans

Plato stands out for feminist scholars not only because, as Alfred North Whitehead said, "The European philosophical tradition . . . consists in a series of footnotes to Plato" (see Okin 1979, 233) but, more important, because his discussion of women was so controversial. In the *Republic,* Book V, Socrates argues that women as well as men have the capacities to be guardians. Acknowledging differences in physical strength between men and women, Socrates insists that there are no significant intellectual male-female dif-

The author would like to thank David Tyack and Karen Kepler-Zumwalt for helpful suggestions on earlier drafts.

ferences; that is, there are no differences relevant to the duties of governing. Plato, through Socrates, seems to have made an early argument for assimilation in both education and public life.

There are several fascinating issues arising from analyses of Plato's writing. First, Plato may have represented the historical Socrates faithfully without embracing the view enthusiastically himself. Socrates is quoted in both Xenophon's *Symposium* and the *Meno* as a believer in women's moral and intellectual equality (Okin 1979, 21). In the *Symposium* Socrates argues that women's apparent inferiority stems from lack of education and experience, not from natural deficits. Further, the historical Socrates engaged in philosophical discussion with some women and confessed a particular intellectual debt to Aspasia, a remarkable woman, who some even say taught Socrates the Socratic method (Cantarella 1987). Unfortunately, it is not possible to isolate the historical Socrates. We hear him only through disciples, and his pronouncements on women are not consistently egalitarian.

Second, if the view expressed by Socrates in the *Republic* were shared by Plato, we would expect to find it repeated in other writings. Here, again, the evidence is ambiguous: In the *Laws*, Plato argues even more strenuously at a theoretical level against the waste of female talent and for equality of education and vocation, but he does not advocate an actual political change in the status of women. Further, in many places, he uses denigrating language in referring to women, and he even portrays Socrates as using such language (see Okin 1979). Hence the debate over Plato's "true" position is likely to continue.

A third aspect of the controversy is the traditional treatment of Plato's statements on women. Christine Pierce (1973) shows how Plato scholars have evaded his arguments for female equality by interpreting his recommendations as unfortunate byproducts of method—of abstracting from physical bodies to a world of immaterial forms. Although this interpretation is farfetched when examined closely, it can be used to explain how Plato could give a strong theoretical argument and yet leave the real political world intact.

What interests feminists in these arguments is the series of convoluted attempts to rescue Plato from the alleged foolishness of advocating women's equality. Not only 19th- and early 20th-century scholars argue this way. Susan Okin criticizes Allan Bloom's (1968) commentary on sections 449a–473c of the *Republic*, in which he labels Plato's remarks on women "absurd conceits" that "have never existed in reality or in the thoughts of serious men" (380; quoted in Okin 1979, 305). Bloom argues that Socrates's objective was to induce ridicule, to write a funnier comedy than Aristophanes (306). Okin asserts that Bloom "is a latter-day example of a series of scholars who have found Plato's arguments about women in *Republic V* both incredible and intolerable" (308).

This is not the place for a detailed analysis of Plato and contemporary commentators like Bloom and Okin. What is important for educators is that the early statements of Socrates (or Plato) are the first known comments on an assimilation model. But Plato's assimilation model is itself problematic for many current feminists. Avoiding the extreme misogyny of Athenian society, Plato nevertheless advocates a model that would have assimilated women to a male mode of life. Governing, contemplating, and waging war were the major elements of elite male life. Nowhere does Plato consider (except in disparaging side comments) the activities central to female life: bearing and raising one's children, maintaining a home, and nursing the ill and elderly. Plato would give women opportunities to be like men—if they were "up" to it (Martin 1985).

It is fascinating that the first outlines of an assimilation model arose in Athens, the most misogynist of all Greek states. There is reason to believe that other parts of the classical world were considerably more congenial to women. Aspasia, companion of Pericles and Socrates, was born in Miletus, in Asia Minor. Hipparchia worked with Crates of Thebes; Sappho spent most of her life at Mytilene (Cantarella 1987). Female poets gained renown in Boeotia (Corinna), Argos (Telesilla), Sicyon (Praxilla), Telas (Erinna), Sparta (Cleitagora), and Magna Graecia (Nossis), but the only intellectual associated with Athens was Aspasia, and of course, she was a foreigner (Cantarella 1987). The culture that bred Socrates and Plato outshone all its neighbors in its contempt for women.

The writings of Plato, however, provide proof that some thought was given early on to the status and education of women. Men, through their religious and political institutions, could have built on Plato's ideas. But Aristotle was far more influential than Plato in his writings on women. Believing firmly in the intellectual and moral inferiority of women, Aristotle described women as permanently handicapped by their anatomy. As we will see, this is the view that was adopted by the early Church fathers. It was more attractive to male thinkers than the "absurd conceits" of Plato and Socrates and would lead, first, to an odd version of the assimilation model in the patristic age and, second, to a segregation model that would persist into the 20th century. I will return to Aristotle's legacy in the next section.

Life did improve some for women in the Hellenistic age (323–30 B.C.) in both Greece and Rome. Cantarella (1987) says that in some areas, "women received the same education as men" (97), and a few women exercised considerable intellectual and political power. However, the vast majority of women in both Greece and Rome remained in subjugation, and indeed the liberation of women was often taken as a sign of cultural and political degeneration. The only educated women belonged to the aristocracy. Often they were educated so that they could be more interesting companions to their husbands. Occasionally, individual rebellion resulted, and an educated woman seized opportunities to exercise real power.

For contemporary curricularists the classical period should be of prime interest. Because so much of liberal education is built on the foundation laid in classical times, it is especially important to understand its horrors as well as its achievements. For example, the great literary themes that originated in classical times are defined from a masculine perspective, and the intellectual power of classical philosophical analysis is admired even though it sustained institutionalized violence and overt racism, classism, and sexism. An important task for the present is to critique traditional themes and to add new ones that arise from current feminist theory (Martin 1985, 1987; Noddings 1987).

The Age of the Church

From the earliest days of Christianity through the heights of the Catholic church in the 14th century, Christian theorists tended to follow Aristotle's, rather than Plato's, view of women. The Aristotelian view, combined with the Judaic legend of Eve, ensured a subordinate position for women. Aristotle, in *Generation of Animals* (IV, 2), had pronounced woman a "misbegotten male," a creature inferior both intellectually and morally, and the Church fathers largely accepted this assessment. The attitudes of religious institutions are, of course, central to issues of education because these institutions were for the most part the keepers and providers of education. Whereas Plato had traced women's alleged inferiority to a lack of education, Aristotle attributed it to nature—to female bodies themselves. From this perspective, the education of women in anything more than the rudiments needed to run a household was sheer waste.

The first wave of Christianity brought with it a new hope of equality. Arguments abound in feminist literature over the role of St. Paul. On the one hand, Paul accepted and encouraged an active role for women in the Church (McLaughlin 1974; Parvey 1974; Prusak 1974); on the other, he often defended and promulgated traditional positions on women. Again men were presented with a choice and, overwhelmingly, opted for the teachings that would keep women powerless. Thanks to St. Paul (or perhaps more accurately, his interpreters), women could not learn in the active, questioning pattern of men; nor could they teach. A much quoted text ensured their intellectual subordination:

> As in all the churches of the saints, the women should keep silence in the churches. For they are not permitted to speak, but should be subordinate, even as the law says. If there is anything they desire to know, let them ask their husbands at home. For it is shameful for a woman to speak in church. (I Corinthians 14: 34–35)

This passage seems to be a direct inheritance from Judaism, but the Greek tradition also contributed to its acceptance. Both the Jews with the Adam and Eve myth and the Greeks with the myth of Pandora (Cantarella 1987; Phillips 1984) held on to the notion of woman as the source of man's downfall. It was "shameful" for a woman to speak because she had once enticed men and angels to transgress against God; to allow her to speak in church would be to increase the possibility that she might do it again.

Thus Christianity was no more successful than Plato in bringing equality to women. However, an odd and interesting new possibility did arise. Women who were willing to forsake their sexuality could approximate the status of men. By the 4th century A.D. the Virgin Mary was venerated as the new Eve, and she became a model for women who sought status in the Church (Ruether 1974). Virginity was extolled, and women who gave up marriage for the Church were often more greatly admired than male religious. This phenomenon appears even in the early Church fathers—men notorious for their woman-hating attitudes. Jerome, for example, formed deep and lasting friendships with women ascetics. Indeed, Ruether writes, "Jerome is generous to the point of extravagance in his praise of these ascetic women" (173). By rejecting worldly and bodily interests, women could become more like men—that is, less sensual and more rational.

Another facet of Mary-worship is revealed in the tradition of courtly love (Warner 1976). In the late Middle Ages, knights pledged their love and devotion to a lady, often the wife of their lord. This lady was a surrogate of sorts for Mary, and she was supposed to embody many of her admirable traits. Troubadours, both male and female, sang her praises.

Aristocratic girls were trained in the image of a wifely Mary. Unless they entered an order, these girls would become wives and mothers, and they were taught to please men. In direct contradiction of Jerome's insistence that cleanliness of body implied dirtiness of mind and soul, these girls were taught to be clean, beautiful, and sweet-smelling. Several texts instructed male teachers how to train young women. Most counseled against teaching women to read, for it was thought that reading would lead to mischief. Girls should learn how to be pleasing, to be silent (especially at mealtime), and above all to be faithful and obedient (McLaughlin 1974). The Chevalier de la Tour Landry instructed his daughters to obey and support their husbands even if the husbands were evil! Evil husbands, he said, have greater need for good wives. Attitudes such as these necessitated a segregation model of education, and training for women had almost nothing to do with intellectual matters.

There was a way for women to receive an education more nearly like that of men. (We must keep in mind here that education was rare for men, too.) Even though the early Christian promise of equality was not fulfilled, women could follow in the footsteps of Jerome's female ascetics, and many did. In the 7th and 8th centuries, women often headed double monasteries, institutions in which male and female religious united their organizations to achieve a more efficient division of labor. McLaughlin (1974) says, "These women were learned in scripture; they taught; they administered great religious houses; they missionized alongside the men, and without any hint in the sources that these public roles were improper for women" (237).

By the late Middle Ages, however, the traditional ambivalence about women gave rise to a renewed emphasis on the weak and evil side of womankind. This is another fascinating and mysterious turn of events. Women religious had responded enthusiastically to the *vita apostolica*, a reform of monastic life that brought with it rigors reminiscent of Jerome's asceticism. Some writers suggest that female fervor helped to shape the reform movement (Grundmann 1961; McLaughlin 1974). Bynum (1987) even suggests that female religious were seen as a threat to the spiritual superiority of their male colleagues precisely because they went to such extremes in self-deprivation. Clare of Assisi, Mary of Oignies, Christina the Astonishing, Margery Kempe, Catherine of Siena, Ida of Louvain, and Elizabeth of Hungary all distinguished themselves by extraordinary fasting.

Many reasons have been given for the decline of female status in monasteries from the early 10th to the late 12th centuries (see McLaughlin 1974). For whatever reason, men began to react angrily and resentfully to the great influx of devout women to monastic life. Ultimately, the old "woman as devil's gateway" argument was used. A Premonstratensian statute argued that

> the iniquity of women surpasses all iniquities . . . and that there is no greater wrath than the wrath of a woman, that the poisons of vipers and dragons are healthier and less harmful for men than familiarity with women . . . to provide our descendants with things necessary for the well-being of their souls as well as their bodies, we shall receive under no condition . . . any more sisters for the increase of our perdition, but rather we shall avoid accepting them as if poisonous beasts. (Quoted in McLaughlin 1974, 243)

As a result of such attitudes, women religious were confined to more and more restricted roles. Cloistering increased, and the public life of women religious was severely curtailed. Even under these conditions, some argue that women maintained a keen sense of agency, interpreting their femaleness as a special form of suffering—a spiritual gift of sorts—that would ensure the return to oneness in heaven (Bynum 1987).

In these accounts, only now being explored in a concentrated, scholarly fashion, we find a new feminist emphasis on female agency in contrast to the earlier emphasis on female oppression. Contemporary historians of women have, indeed, argued over which facet of women's experience should be emphasized—oppression or agency. Mary Beard (1946) was an early advocate of the focus on women's agency, but the feminist movement of the 1960s and 1970s drew heavily on Simone de Beauvoir (1961) and her focus on woman as victim. Current historians seek a balance in the two orientations (DuBois, Kelly, Kennedy, Korsmeyer, and Robinson 1985).

In this very brief look at the influence of the Church in patristic times and the Middle Ages on the education of women, we see evidence of both segregation and assimilation models. The vast majority of women were, like the vast majority of men, not educated at all in a formal sense. Of those who were, most were urged to be Mary-like wives. Others exercised considerable agency as religious.

The importance of these times for contemporary curricularists is not merely historical; that is, the period would not be fully exploited educationally by its mere inclusion in the curriculum. More important is the recognition of sympathetic cooperation between religious and social systems to keep tight control over women's lives; equally important is the broken record of women's continual effort to exert influence in public life.

The Renaissance and Reformation

It seems right to question whether there was a Renaissance for women (Kinnear 1982). Certainly the political and martial activities that men embraced were not open to women. During this great revival of interest in classical times and arts, women were almost as deprived politically as they had been earlier. But now women were essential to social life, especially to life at court, and questions arose about their education.

Texts were produced to describe appropriate court behavior, and at least some writers defended the notion that women could be men's intellectual equals if they were properly educated (see Kinnear 1982). An assimilation-segregation model became the ideal for noble and wealthy women. They were taught many of the topics that men were taught, but with a different purpose. Whereas men were educated to lead productive public lives, women were educated to be stimulating companions to men. This mixed assimilation-segregation model would persist (with intermittent demands for either gender-sensitive segregation or full assimilation) well into the 20th century.

An assimilation-segregation model was easy to adapt to changing societal attitudes—provided they did not take revolutionary leaps. For example, during the Reformation, motherhood became more respectable than it had been in the high days of the Church. This enhanced respectability eventually became another argument for the liberal education of women. To be good mothers, women needed to have educations similar to their husbands'. And when women were granted voting rights ("full citizenship"), it could be argued again that women should be educated for citizenship. It was not necessary to make a double assimilationist argument; that is, one could argue for "equal" education without recommending that women should be able to use their education in productive occupations. Subjects that were clearly oriented toward professional life remained inaccessible to women.

During the Renaissance and Reformation, however, few women were educated, and women had not yet been given the task of supervising the education of children. The Reformation's tolerance of physical life—allowing priests to marry and elevating motherhood—is sometimes interpreted as an advance over the older, body-hating attitude of Catholicism (Douglass 1974). But the picture is ambiguous. Protestant women no longer had the option of "being like a man" by renouncing sexuality and entering a religious vocation. The assimilationist model of the Middle Ages was not available for non-Catholic women. The Reformation provided male religious with respectable release from celibacy but imprisoned women in the job of wife and mother.

There is another feature of this period that must be discussed although it is difficult to assess from an educational perspective. From the 14th through the 17th centuries, women were often accused of witchcraft. The witch craze was an enormously complex phenomenon (Klaits 1985), but it is clear that one of its messages to women was to resist any attempt at independence or autonomous power. Some feminists emphasize the drive to wipe out female healers and midwives (Ehrenreich and English 1973); some concentrate on the desire to destroy the last vestiges of older, female religions (Daly 1973). Descriptions of the social, religious, and political conflicts of the times (Klaits 1985) leave little doubt that these explanations are too simplistic. But that does not mean that they are totally wrong. If women had special areas of knowledge and spiritual gifts, these were effectively destroyed or coopted during these terrible centuries. What resulted was a model of almost total female subordination—of agency gone underground to survive in unpublicized circles and activities.

The Enlightenment

Neither the Renaissance nor the Age of Reason (Enlightenment) affected women in the positive ways men were touched. As feminist historians have learned, women worked in these times, and some produced art, literature, and even mathematics (Perl 1978). But most educated women were still not allowed to exercise their talents outside the home or salon. For present purposes, the conflict of the age can be captured in three figures: Rousseau, Kant, and Wollstonecraft. In both Rousseau and Kant we find strong emphasis on a segregation model; in Wollstonecraft we hear an eloquent argument for an assimilation-segregation model.

As the power of the Church waned, it would have been reasonable for the old arguments on women's inferiority to wane also. What actually happened was that the premise was retained and new arguments concocted to uphold it. Whereas the Church fathers, following Aristotle, had declared women morally inferior by nature and under the rule of men as punishment for the Fall, Kant and other philosophers began to talk about an innate female goodness. This goodness was not really moral virtue because such virtue requires the application of rational discipline, but rather it was a form of innocence combined with a well-trained aesthetic sense.

Kant argued that women, more often than men, did the "right" thing naturally—out of an instinctive sense of beauty. Whereas men struggle intellectually with moral problems, women head straight for the beautiful and so behave kindly, gently, amiably, and helpfully. Women are nice, Kant said. (Echoes of this belief are found in later claims that women are "stuck" in Kohlberg's stage 3 of moral development—the "good boy–nice girl" stage.)

Kant's description of women brings a smile to today's reader, coming as it does from a punctilious old bachelor. But his argument is pernicious, for he follows many earlier thinkers—including the witch prosecutors—in supposing that intellectual activity ruins a woman's natural grace and goodness: "A woman with a head full of Greek . . . or . . . mechanics . . . " says Kant, "might as well even have a beard; for perhaps that would express more obviously the mien of profundity for which she strives" (Kant 1983 [1764]). His attitude toward women is reflected (although not explicitly articulated) in his moral philosophy, in which we find that "good" acts done out of love or inclination have no moral worth. Current feminist criticism of Kant concentrates on his overemphasis on reason and the denigration of feeling rather than his naive and condescending statements on female nature (J. Grimshaw 1986; Noddings 1990a).

Kant's attitude toward women is echoed in Rousseau, who built such thinking into a model of female education—a full-blown model of segregated education and life. He took for granted that men and women were "essentially different in character and temperament" (quoted in Mahowald 1983, 181). Women were designed for reproduction and home life, men for freedom and, given the constraints of unnatural societies, for reasoned participation in public life.

Book 5 of Rousseau's *Émile* is a horror for women, particularly for women educators who may have revered Rousseau as the philosopher of freedom and an early advocate of educational plans resembling open education. Rousseau, in introducing his plan for the education of Sophie, wrote,

> Men and women are made for each other but they differ in the measure of their dependence on each other. We could get on better without women than women could get on without us. To play their part in life they must earn our esteem. By the very law of nature women are at the mercy of men's judgments both for themselves and for their children. It is not enough that they should be estimable: they must be esteemed. It is not enough that they should be beautiful: they must be pleasing. It is not enough that they should be wise: their wisdom must be recognized. Their honour does not rest on their conduct but on their reputation. Hence the kind of education they get should be the very opposite of men's in this respect. Public opinion is the tomb of a man's virtue but the throne of a woman's. (Mahowald 1983, 182)

This passage makes clear that, for Rousseau, men and women are essentially different beings. Women are created for men and should, therefore, be agreeable and pleasing. They ought not to think things through for themselves and behave "honorably," but rather they should be obedient and act to bring credit on themselves and their households. Whereas Emile must think for himself, Sophie must decide where public opinion lies and act accordingly. Rousseau did have second thoughts on making women entirely subservient to public opinion (Okin 1979). He admitted that "conscience" had to be the final arbiter for both men and women. But since women's education had to be directed toward the production of pleasing and obedient wives, the remedy for any possible conflict had to lie in perfecting public opinion. Men, that is, had the responsibility for constructing a moral society, one that would not tax the weak female by inducing conflicts between her conscience and public opinion.

Jane Roland Martin (1985) has used Book 5 of *Émile* to argue that Rousseau—far from deserving credit as a philosopher-educator of freedom—actually employed a production model similar to Plato's. She argues that Rousseau wanted to educate people for particular functions in life. But Martin's scheme, clever as it is, does not work. Rousseau, unlike

Plato, rejected the major inequalities among men; he did not plan to educate philosopher-kings, warriors, and artisans. He planned to educate all men, even ordinary boys, for a citizenship that would compensate, at least in part, for the loss of natural freedom. Women are to be trained but not really educated. It is hard to avoid the conclusion that Rousseau really regarded women as a class different from fully human beings. They are not to be educated for either themselves or for the state but only for the men who will rule their lives (Okin 1979).

Rousseau's model is important because it is a thoroughgoing segregation model and stands in opposition to all we usually regard as education. Mary Wollstonecraft (1975 [1792]) was thoroughly familiar with Rousseau's work and argued strenuously against his prescriptions for women's education. In *A Vindication of the Rights of Woman*, she argued that women were not naturally sentimental, intellectually vacuous, and in possession of virtues entirely different from those of men. Such qualities, if they appeared, and Wollstonecraft agreed that they did, were attributable to lack of education and experience. Wollstonecraft implored men to give women a chance to prove themselves. If they failed, she said, then men would at least be justified in assigning them a secondary and inferior education.

Wollstonecraft wanted women to have the same education as men. In this sense, she was an assimilationist. But she did not go so far as Plato. Instead she acknowledged that women and men had "different duties" in life; she made no argument for professional opportunities for women, although such an argument can be inferred from the body of her thought. Rather, she argued that women needed and deserved an education for self-actualization and to perform their assigned tasks effectively. Her main argument—astonishing that it needed to be made—was that women are fully rational human beings. In this assertion, she was responding to both Rousseau and Edmund Burke, who had claimed that "a woman *is* but an animal, and an animal not of the highest order" (Mahowald 1983, 204).

Wollstonecraft's life illustrates the themes of today's feminist historians. In it we find oppression and the acknowledgment of oppression but, also, agency and the courage to live independently and productively. The Enlightenment, for intelligent women, merely pointed up the enormous gap between reality and possibility.

The 19th and Early 20th Centuries

Several factors contributed to the advancement of women in the 19th century. One was the greater availability of reading material and the gradual increase in literacy. Another was the growth of public education and its widening mission to educate the masses. A third factor was the socially conscious interest in environmentalism that reached its pinnacle in the middle decades of the century.

Environmentalism had been preceded by an evangelical and reform trend in Calvinism (Brenzel 1983). This trend in itself called forth the effort and compassion of Christian women to turn wrongdoers and ne'er-do-wells toward a life of devotion and industry. But environmentalism held a special promise for women. Not only did it provide hope for the prevention of various forms of delinquency, but it also implied that the condition of women could be vastly improved through education. Indeed, education was sometimes seen as a panacea for social ills. Stephen Simpson wrote that it would "change the whole face of society into one radiant smile of contentment and enjoyment" (Brenzel 1983, 24).

Perhaps the call for women to play an active role in reform was even more influential for women's education than the mere fact of more schooling. Women were urged to take responsibility for the education of their children and to conduct their households in a way that would enhance the moral goodness of husbands, children, and visitors. Women now needed to be educated for their role as moral leaders in the private domain and willing helpers in the public program of social reform.

These were heady days for segregation models, even though elementary and secondary education were increasingly coeducational. It is almost as though women had decided to make the most of what nature and an oppressive culture had granted them. Catherine Beecher (1977 [1842]) argued for the importance of homemaking and wrote a widely used text not only explaining techniques and skills but also laying out a philosophy of womanhood. Women were to remain subordinate to their husbands and inactive politically (except as they influenced their husbands, and this they were to do diligently), but they were to be in charge of the domestic scene. Beecher saw women as domestic economists, scientists, educators, and religious leaders. For such roles they were to be educated primarily in "domestic employments" and only secondarily in traditional academic matters. But this education was nonetheless intellectual. Indeed, Beecher sounds very like many of today's educational theorists when she writes on the purpose of intellectual education: "Many persons seem to suppose that the chief object of an intellectual education is the acquisition of knowledge, but . . . it is the formation of habits of investigation, of correct reasoning, of persevering attention, of regular system, of accurate analysis, and of vigorous mental acts, that are the primary objects to be sought" (1977, 34; quoted in Martin 1985, 113). Beecher clearly saw domestic activity as rational and significant.

Another component of Beecher's curriculum is worth mentioning because of the nasty twist it was given later in the century. Beecher advocated lots of fresh air and physical activity for girls and young women. Given the generally sorry state of health in middle- and upper-class women, this was sound advice. But in the fin-de-siècle era, male theorists would claim that intellectual activity was injurious to women, particularly to their reproductive functions, and that well-balanced physical regimens were essential for females, who were once again described as primarily physical creatures.

Emphasis on environmentalism and women's domestic and moral leadership led to the creation of reform schools

(Brenzel 1983), which early on emphasized a philosophy very like Beecher's. Girls were to be reformed and reclaimed for full participation in womanhood. To accomplish this, families were recruited to work with the girls in a thoroughgoing attempt at education. As environmentalism gave way to social Darwinism later in the century, reform schools rejected the earlier model of education and settled on a narrow form of domestic training that relied on gainful work to keep their girls honest and unsullied. Efforts at full education for womanhood were abandoned.

Environmentalism and evangelism combined to increase missionary activity. Young women who wanted an education often trained as teachers and sometimes continued a form of liberal education in female seminaries. Many of these young women dreamed of becoming missionaries. No young woman would be sent to the field alone, however, and so her only chance was to marry a man headed for the missions. (Mission boards were also reluctant to send unmarried men into the field lest they be tempted to fraternize with indigenous females, so it was not too difficult to find a husband if one's priority was to be a missionary.) These gallant women headed to the field with the full intention of establishing schools and teaching beside their husbands, but this intention was usually quickly and completely frustrated. In the Hawaiian Islands, for example, women found that almost all their time was occupied in bearing and educating their own children (P. Grimshaw 1983). The perceived need to keep their children from "going heathen" restricted women's educational efforts to the home.

The great promises of environmentalism, reform, widespread common schooling, and evangelical fervor were dampened considerably by the rise and adaptation of Darwinism. Misogyny in intellectual circles increased dramatically. Bram Dijkstra (1986) says that the fin-de-siècle was characterized by a "war on woman—for to say 'women' would contradict a major premise of the period's antifeminine thought. If this was a war largely fought on the battlefield of words and images, where the dead and wounded fell without notice into the mass grave of lost human creativity, it was no less destructive than many real wars" (vii). Women were once again interchangeable biological entities.

In this era, science took the place of the Church in defending the doctrine of women's inferiority. Darwin (1871) himself had made remarks about women's childishness and the inevitability of greater intellectual gaps between women and men as evolution proceeded. Misogyny was rife in science, literature, the arts, politics, and education. Commenting on psychoanalysis (Freud) and romantic literature, Nina Auerbach (1982) writes,

> In these two popular romances [*Trilby* and *Dracula*] and the romantic beginnings of a modern science we see the image of prone womanhood at its most dispiriting. Personal and cultural disinheritance, we feel, could go no further than these tabulae rasae, all selfhood suspended as they were invaded by the hyperconscious and culturally fraught male/master/monster. But when we actually read *Trilby*, *Dracula*, or *Studies in Hysteria* we are struck by the kinds of powers that are granted to the women: the victim of paralysis possesses seemingly infinite capacities of regenerative being that turn on her triumphant mesmerizer and paralyze him in turn. (17)

Thus we hear an ambiguous story once again, and feminists are now uncovering agency and oppression in literature as in life. Education for women became even more problematic as well-known professors worried over the effects of intellectual activity on women. In Europe Paul Mobius (1908), a pathologist, declared women to be spiritually inferior, childlike, and incapable of reasoned thought. Forced to engage in intellectual activity, they would be incapacitated for breeding and turn into "useless hybrids." The views he expressed were not confined to Europe but were widely debated in American educational circles as well (Clarke 1873). Even when the notion that intellectual activity would shrivel a woman's ovaries was abandoned, prominent American psychologists held to the "variability thesis" of male superiority. According to this thesis, women were mediocre, rarely exhibiting traits of genius. Among its proponents were G. Stanley Hall, Edward Thorndike, and James M. Cattell (Rossiter 1982). Some women psychologists strongly opposed the variability thesis (Tyack and Hansot 1990), but their work did not achieve the prominence of the proponents'.

Nevertheless more and more women were being educated. Emma Hart Willard (1918 [1819]) had earlier led the campaign for women's academies and seminaries by arguing that women needed an excellent education to be the best possible mothers. Hers was an assimilation-segregation argument that would remain popular into the middle of the 20th century, but it was also an intelligent political rationale when Willard made it. Many of the women's academies and seminaries eventually became women's colleges, and groups of schools such as the Seven Sisters produced many illustrious graduates.

Under an assimilation-segregation model, even the brightest women graduates could not look forward to full professional and personal lives. They were employed mainly by the women's colleges and academies, and when they married, they were expected to resign and turn their full attention to housekeeping and motherhood. Nevertheless, the story of women's colleges is a fascinating one, and these schools clearly gave women a foothold in academe. (For a detailed and interesting account of the role of these schools in producing women scientists, see Rossiter 1982; for a biographical account of eastern and western schools—single-sex and coeducational—see the biography of Lucy Sprague Mitchell by Joyce Antler 1987.) Further, even though the dominant argument for women's education was the needs of motherhood, many women resisted occupational segregation and fought their way into professional life as nurses and nurse superintendents (Reverby 1987), educators and reformers (Addams 1905), scientists (Rossiter 1982), and writers.

Writing was a field particularly congenial to women. There was resistance, of course. Nathaniel Hawthorne, for example, had earlier grumbled about the "damned mob of scribbling women," but the "scribbling women" achieved considerable popularity. It is ironic that women writers and writers of color gradually lost places in the literary canon after 1920 (Lauter 1983). Writers who appeared in earlier anthologies—Willa Cather, Edith Wharton, Sarah Orne Jewett, Helen Hunt Jackson, Harriet Beecher Stowe, Ellen Glasgow, Zona Gale—all disappeared. Lauter attributes the loss to the professionalization of teaching literature, the growth of a formalist aesthetic theory, and the historiographic organization of texts into periods and themes.

Clearly the first of these—the professionalization of teaching literature—had an impact not only on women writers but also on women students and on all women who wanted to participate in literary discussion. Literary societies, previously dominated by women, were greatly reduced in number, and literature became the domain of professors. Further, the professoriate itself became more male. The Darwinian arguments and talk of "race suicide" so popular in the fin-de-siècle now bore fruit to condemn female college professors as "odd." Male professors publicly bemoaned the dominance of women in the literary field and blamed that dominance for the field's lack of prestige. In the early 1920s women earned 16 percent of all doctorates, many in the literary field. By the 1950s, they earned only 10 percent. Similar cuts occurred to women administrators at both colleges and public schools.

By the time of World War II and until the new wave of feminism in the 1960s, an assimilation-segregation model was firmly in place. Young women from economically comfortable families could receive an education comparable to men's, but they were expected to use it only in domestic life. Young women who might need to earn a living could be educated—"just in case"—as teachers, nurses, or librarians.

Since the days of Plato, progress for women has been uneven, gains have sometimes proved temporary, and we know now that what has been gained can be lost. This realization, together with a new appreciation for women's history, has led some contemporary feminists to reject both assimilation and segregation models. The new perspective, a transformational view, will be introduced in the next section and more thoroughly discussed in the final part of the chapter.

Summary

A few basic models of education have appeared and reappeared since the days of classical Greece. Plato suggested a double assimilation model; from such a perspective women and men should be educated in the same way, and both should be eligible for the full range of public activities. Even today many scholars cannot believe that Plato (or Socrates) was serious, and most later recommendations grew out of segregation models or combinations such as the popular model of the 19th and earlier 20th centuries—an assimilation-segregation model.

Besides illustrating the basic models, this brief historical overview has stressed two themes that feminist theorists often use to organize their work: women's oppression and women's agency. The latter is a relatively new theme—one that brings pride and hope to women's education—and it provides a background for the development of the transformational models that are now arousing considerable interest.

GENDER AND THE STANDARD CURRICULUM

In this section I will consider research that treats gender and the curriculum without challenging the basic structure of curriculum and schooling. In one sense, of course, all research on gender has the potential to challenge something about curriculum, and much of the research reviewed here raises questions that suggest changes: introducing women into standard history texts, facilitating women's study of mathematics and science, and curtailing sexist activities in the primary grades. But critiques that raise serious questions about the whole enterprise of schooling as we have come to know it will be reserved for the final third of the chapter.

Early 20th-Century Research

For many centuries the Church used its authority to keep women in subordinate roles. In the early 20th century, science took on the task of proving that women were, if not actually inferior intellectually, at least so different from men that they should not be educated in the male mode and certainly not prepared for typical male occupations. It was not unusual for men to express romantic admiration for women—often in flowery Victorian language—and at the same time to insist that these marvelous creatures be kept at home, where presumably they would remain innocent and unspoiled. Science undertook the task of showing the desirability of segregation models.

G. Stanley Hall (1904) argued vigorously against David Starr Jordan, president of Stanford University, for a segregation model of education. Jordan was not a feminist, and his opinions on women's intellectual capacities were neither high nor carefully reasoned, but he argued that women were properly challenged and men better behaved in coeducational settings. Hall admitted that women were not intellectually inferior to men, but he feared that women educated like men would have fewer children. He recommended an education "that fits her own nature," preparation for the roles of wife and mother. "We should respect the law of sexual differences," said Hall, and he referred to "at least eight good and independent statistical studies which show that the ideals of boys from ten years on are almost always those of their own sex, while girls' ideals are increasingly of the opposite sex, or also those of men" (Bell and Offen 1983, 160). Hall deplored this trend, feeling strongly that women should hold ideals of womanhood. It seems not to have occurred to him that women's only real option for independence lay in adopting male ideals. Finally, Hall expressed the belief that women trained in coeducational institutions would be "agamic or even agenic," fearing childbearing and dreading the limitations of married life. He therefore recommended a segregation model that would "educate [women] primarily and chiefly for motherhood" (162).

In response, M. Carey Thomas (1908), president of Bryn Mawr, wrote of her personal agony growing up terrorized by the account of Adam and Eve, the Pauline epistles, Milton's and Shakespeare's depiction of women, and—most horrible of all—Michelet's *La Femme*.

> Although during those thirty years [after reading Michelet] I had read in every language every book on women that I could obtain, I had never chanced again upon a book that seemed to me so to degrade me in my womanhood as the seventh and seventeenth chapters on women and women's education of President Stanley Hall's *Adolescence*. Michelet's sickening sentimentality and horrible over-sexuality seemed to me to breathe again from every pseudo-scientific page. (Bell and Offen 1983, 164)

Thomas countered Hall's science with surveys of her own and reports from coeducational colleges and segregated colleges with strong intellectual programs that showed women's high aptitude for intellectual work, their academic success despite little hope of eventual careers, and a persistent good health that contradicted all the dour warnings. She staunchly argued against special education for women, against "hygiene, and sanitary drainage, and domestic science, and child study . . . " (Bell and Offen 1983, 167). Thomas wanted and worked all her life for a double assimilation model. Women, like men, she argued, "must be prepared for some form of public service" (168).

The opposing positions of Hall and Thomas illustrate the perspectives that guided (and resisted) research. To this day there is a persistent interest in sex (or gender) differences on a host of variables, the effects of male or female teachers on the opposite sex, and the benefits of single-sex education. More recently interest has grown in the representation of gender in the curriculum and the effects of language in maintaining sex stereotypes.

Sex or Gender Differences

The words "sex" and "gender" are often used interchangeably in research on "differences." When they are distinguished, "sex" usually points to biological causation (Finn 1980; Maccoby and Jacklin 1974) and "gender" to cultural causation, but either can be—and has been—used to discuss both biological and social or cultural factors. Thus one cannot judge merely from the language used whether a study will concentrate on one set of factors or the other. I will use "gender" unless the work under review explicitly uses "sex."

Educational researchers have long been interested in gender issues (Tyack and Hansot 1988), and this interest has often focused on gender differences. Are males or females better at subject *X*? How much better? Why? Who has the greater aptitude for *Y*? Indeed the topic of gender differences, remarks Susan Chipman (1988), has been "far too sexy a topic." Researchers and policymakers have concentrated on sex or gender differences for over a century, and most of the differences uncovered have been small and/or unimportant. Years ago sociologist Arlie Hochschild (1973) raised questions about the usefulness of research on gender differences in the cognitive domain; more recently, Hyde (1981) has shown that the variance thus accounted for runs between 1 percent and 5 percent. Yet such differences continue to intrigue professional educators, and some accounts even make front-page newspaper stories (Benbow and Stanley 1980).

Because this research is voluminous, only a small part of it can be discussed here. Research particularly relevant to the curriculum field includes work on intelligence and aptitudes, motivation, and achievement. Gender differences in intelligence as measured by standardized tests have been shown to be minimal, and similarly, tests of achievement even in mathematics have shown minimal differences when other factors are controlled (Chipman and Thomas 1985).

Issues on women and mathematics, however, are still hotly debated. Because more boys than girls tend to excel on tests such as the Scholastic Aptitude Test (SAT), some researchers have suggested that there may be a gene favoring mathematical development in males (Benbow and Stanley 1980), but these studies have concentrated on highly talented students who have chosen to demonstrate their interest and proficiency in mathematics (Armstrong 1985; Chipman and Thomas 1985). As many researchers have pointed out, factors other than genetic predisposition are almost certainly operating by the time children enter junior high school, and many of these factors press young women to reject mathematical activity (Brush 1985; Casserly and Rock 1985). Many researchers now are more interested in women's participation in mathematics than in elusive, and for the most part insignificant, gender differences in mathematical aptitude.

The search for cognitive explanations of gender differences in participation in various mathematical fields goes on. The idea seems to be that cognitive differences simply must be involved and that they can explain the visible differences in participation. Visual and spatial aptitudes have long been considered good possibilities for explaining differences in participation (Linn and Petersen 1985). However, two developments have cast doubt on spatial ability as an explanation for the higher achievement and participation demonstrated by males. First, spatial ability is no longer considered a unitary aptitude; it has several components, and little gender difference is found in the most common components (Hyde and Linn 1986). Second, there is considerable uncertainty about the connection between spatial ability and general mathematics ability; that is, it is not clear that spatial ability is an independent contributor to mathematical ability. Even in spatial tests such as mental rotation—in which gender differences are fairly large (Chipman and Wilson 1985)—the question of relevance makes the results somewhat uninteresting for educators.

Researchers who believe that cognitive differences must underlie gender differences in participation are in direct conflict with those who believe that the differences can be explained by patterns of socialization or even overt discrimination. Similarly, research on gender differences in motivation also runs into value conflicts. The question of why women do not often choose careers requiring mathematics remains central. But as some feminists (Noddings 1988b) have pointed out, the current "problem of women and mathematics" reflects a particular social bias. Mathematical activity is highly valued, whereas the fields often chosen by women are not. Researchers rarely ask, for example, why men lag behind women in participation in nursing, elementary school teaching, child care, or full-time housekeeping. Thus the formulation of the "problem" is itself problematic for those who judge the question to be tainted by patriarchal values.

Other research on gender differences in motivation is similarly guided by stereotypical masculine values. For example, Matina Horner (1972) found that women's lack of achievement could be explained in part by something called "fear of success." Recognizing what they would have to give up, her female subjects preferred not to be first in their class or to rush off to professional school after graduating from college. Horner's way of casting the problem tends to blame women for their own condition and to suggest that the solution lies in psychological therapy of some sort. It also overlooks the possibility that women hold an alternative (and perhaps healthier) view of what it means to succeed in life (Gilligan 1982; Sassen 1980).

Closely related to Horner's study is a long line of research in education. As reviewed by Biklen (1987), this line suggests that women persist in teaching because they have been passed over for higher positions or marriage (Lortie 1975), that women's occupations appeal more to the heart than the to head (Dreeben 1970), that women lack motivation for intellectual mastery (Simpson and Simpson 1969), that they accept the rightness of deferring to men (Simpson and Simpson 1969), that they have a low professional commitment to teaching (Dreeben 1970), and that generally women see their occupations as "fillers" or adjuncts to their domestic lives (Grambs 1957; O. Hall 1966; Mason, Dressel, and Bain 1959). This research has provided a ready tool to explain the absence of women in educational administration.

The new scholarship on women starts with different assumptions and, not surprisingly, produces results that challenge those just discussed (Biklen and Shakeshaft 1985; Stimpson 1980). Gender differences in occupational commitment seem to be minimal (Epstein 1976; Grandjean and Bernal 1979; Marrett 1972). There do seem to be some differences, however, in the focus of commitment (Biklen 1987). Many female elementary teachers, for example, define their professional commitment in terms of devotion to children (Boston Women's Teachers' Group 1983). This finding does not necessarily confirm earlier conclusions about appeals of the heart over those of the head. Rather, it discloses a different locus of intellectual interest and, perhaps, a more appropriate balance between thinking and feeling in teaching.

In summary, although mainline research continues to pursue gender differences and explanations for those differences that are uncovered, feminist research on aptitudes, motivation, and achievement tends today to downplay gender differences. It often also tends to accept somewhat uncritically a double assimilation model; that is, it assumes that full participation in the male-constructed public world is a good to be won. Those differences recognized by feminist researchers center on perspective, values, and emphasis. Women do seem more concerned than men with interpersonal relations, direct care of the ill and elderly, and social problems in general (Bebeau and Brabeck 1987; Okin 1990; Sommers and Shields 1987). But even this well-documented difference may be as much a product of stereotypical expectations as the earlier findings on women's attitudes toward professional life. Women do take major responsibility for the tasks of caring, but whether they do so out of natural inclination, powerful socialization, or careful deliberation remains an open question.

Single-Sex Schooling

When segregation models have been propounded in education, they have usually been accompanied by occupational segregation in the society. Males are prepared for men's work; females, for women's work. Even educational assimilation models have often accepted occupational segregation. Today, however, some educators advocate single-sex schooling for women as the best preparation for occupational assimilation. In one sense, of course, the curriculum in these settings is still an assimilation curriculum since it is almost a duplicate of that offered to males, but the pedagogy and the climate are sensitive to the needs of girls and women.

Present research findings suggest that single-sex schooling has advantages for females: Such schools engender greater student satisfaction and higher educational aspirations (Lee and Marks 1988), a stronger sense of community, and more desirable attitudes toward intellectual and social life (Gilroy 1989; Jiminez and Lockheed 1988; Lee and Bryk 1986). However, most studies show that the positive effects of single-sex schooling are confined to females; coeducation seems better for many males (Jiminez and Lockheed 1988). Apparently boys are often spurred on by the presence of girls (as David Starr Jordan contended), whereas girls are impeded, intimidated, and silenced by the presence of boys. This result is consistent with the gender stereotyping that is by now familiar to everyone.

It is sometimes suggested that the positive effects of single-sex schools for girls are in part due to their dominantly female faculties, but this suggestion can be challenged. A majority of women in public coeducational schools does not seem to produce the same effects. It is possible, of course, that the substantial presence of male students affects women teachers in roughly the same way that female students are affected. If this is so, all-female schools may be healthier for teachers as well as students. It seems more likely, however, that the atmosphere is affected by power relations. Even if female teachers are a majority—perhaps, especially if they are a majority—their effect can be negative if they are obviously subordinate to male administrators. Positive effects in single-sex education may, then, be a result of perceived female efficacy.

Controversy over the effects of male or female teachers on students is perennial. James M. Cattell (1909), in his more misogynist period (before 1911), laid the blame for many of education's ills on the "horde of female teachers" who "subvert both the school and the family." He felt that both boys and girls needed male teachers and was particularly outraged at the large number of "celibate females" in teaching. These females, he thought, would have an adverse effect on both girls and boys, but especially on boys. When educators worried at all about the gender effects of coeducation and female teachers, they usually expressed concern that boys were adversely affected. Boys were more often held back and more often required remedial reading (Tyack and Hansot 1990). Boys looked on schooling as feminine and were "feminized" by the domination of female teachers. More recently this argument has been made by researchers who think that female teachers are especially damaging to black and Hispanic males (Levine 1964; Sexton 1969). Hence, although coeducation seems to favor middle- and upper-class white males, single-sex schooling with male teachers might have advantages for poor and minority males. Here, again, educational segregation is recommended in the interest of occupational and social assimilation.

It is paradoxical to hear segregation touted as a means to assimilation. Most 19th-century feminists felt strongly that coeducation was the route to equality in life after school. (For a comprehensive discussion of the campaign for full coeducation, see Tyack and Hansot 1990). Now so many evils have been associated with coeducation that its dominance is under scrutiny. Possibly both 19th-century writers and present-day researchers have captured practical, if somewhat different, wisdoms. Earlier, segregated education was, by its very nature, unequal—in the distribution of resources, prestige, opportunities, and pedagogy. Now that the curricula typical of male education are firmly entrenched everywhere, advantages in pedagogy and climate make single-sex schooling attractive again. But the reasons for renewed interest are entirely different from those of men like Hall and women like Beecher, who glorified the different social lives of women and men.

Gender in Regular School Subjects

So far, broad topics and trends in education have been discussed, and the curriculum has been treated at a very general level—whether, for example, it is designed for assimilation or segregation in school and life roles. Now the content of curriculum will be considered. Here the discussion will still be confined to the more or less standard curriculum and familiar disciplines. Women's studies will be explored in the final section of the chapter with transformational feminist critiques.

The first opportunity for educators to intervene in sex role development occurs in early childhood education or kindergarten. By age 2, most children know their own sex, and by 3 they are usually able to label others by sex (Brooks-Gunn and Schnapp-Matthews 1979; S. K. Thompson 1975). Thus children come to their first experiences in school with considerable knowledge about what is appropriate for males and females (Block 1979). Schools can reinforce gender stereotypes or try to break them down.

Teachers of young children have been aware for some time of the dangers of segregating girls in the doll corner and boys in the area with blocks and trucks (Paley 1973). Besides inculcating in boys the pernicious notion that caring for children is "women's work," such an arrangement deprives girls of experience with the toys that serve as an early introduction to science (Block 1979; Greenberg 1970). But there is another side to the problem. Because boys are even stricter than girls in monitoring their own sex-appropriate behavior (Greenberg 1985; Serbin, Connor, and Lipman 1977), it is especially important for them to learn that child care is men's work, too, and that playing with dolls is appropriate male behavior.

Children's early acceptance and understanding of sex roles are so pronounced that some theorists attribute them to biology. Although biological lines of research are interesting, they may be relatively useless for educators. Whether sex role identification is "natural" or not, educators still have to decide which of its features are to be valued and enhanced by education and which are deemed pernicious and, therefore, to be overcome by education. As philosophers have long preached, what *is* is not necessarily what *ought* to be.

Girls and boys come to kindergarten with somewhat different capacities already developed. For example, girls have had more opportunities to develop small muscles, and boys have had more opportunities to develop large muscles (Medrich, Roisen, Rubin, and Buckley 1982). If we value both forms of development, we will be sure to include both kinds of opportunities for girls and boys, paying particular attention to the needs of the underdeveloped sex. Similarly, the old arguments about the feminization of early schooling can be rethought in light of what we value for both sexes. A better balance between activities already attractive to boys and those with which they need more experience would reduce the boys' disadvantage. More active modes of learning might also be valuable for both girls and boys. Such modes are attractive to boys and, it can be argued, may be necessary for the continued success of girls. The so-called advantage of girls in early schooling may amount to early reinforcement of passivity and subordination. Thus, more active modes of learning might accommodate *what is* for boys and *what ought to be* for girls.

From preschool through graduate school, literature is the main subject that presents gender images and provides concrete models of manhood and womanhood. Research in the last two decades has revealed considerable gender bias in the reading materials used in schools: "(1) females appear as main characters and in illustrations far less frequently than males; (2) females and males are overwhelmingly portrayed in sex-stereotypical roles; (3) females appear more often than males in derogatory roles; and/or (4) male generic language is used" (Scott and Schau 1985, 219).

Publishers have reacted positively (if not always wisely) to demands for an end to gender bias in school materials. Most reading books now include both female and male main characters, sexist language is much reduced, and males and females are portrayed in nonstereotypical activities. From a feminist perspective, this reform is by no means complete (Bailey and Smith 1982; Tetreault 1986b), but the revisions already accomplished have not gone unnoticed by the opposition. Some conservatives object strongly to the loss of traditional values in revised texts (Vitz 1986), and more than one law case has challenged reading material that portrays boys and girls in nonstereotypical ways (Tyack and Hansot 1990).

Although substantial changes have been made in elementary reading texts, it is not clear that great changes have been made at the high school level. Recommendations have been made (National Council of Teachers of English 1976; Showalter 1974), but most high school curricula remain largely traditional. Although the high school canon has not changed greatly, considerable literature has grown up on language and language use with respect to gender. Feminist researchers have produced a huge amount of work on women and language (Thorne, Kramarae, and Henley 1983), which attacks not only the generic use of male terms but also the denigrating custom of tacking suffixes onto terms that should be gender-neutral—as in poet*ess*, suffrag*ette*, hero*ine*. It also deplores the monopoly men have enjoyed in the area of naming (Daly 1973, 1984; Spender 1980). Further, it documents women's silence (Olsen 1978) and begins to recover women's voices in a host of areas (Annas 1987).

There has also been much work on sex differences in language (Scott, Dwyer, and Lieb-Brilhart 1985). This work represents another chapter in the program that has long fascinated educational researchers: differences in vocabulary, decoding skill, patterns of communication (females are less direct and aggressive), and syntax and usage.

By far the most powerful curriculum work is being done at the college and university level. Here literary criticism, women's studies, and new methods in the teaching of writing have produced exciting developments. Writing teachers now use women writers as models to free women's "voice" (Goulston 1987). Virginia Woolf, Adrienne Rich, Simone de Beauvoir, Tillie Olsen, Alice Walker, and Doris Lessing are all prominent in writing as well as literature courses. Indeed, writing teachers anticipated feminists by several years in their emphasis on voice and its importance in writing (Frey 1987).

A prominent theme in contemporary literary criticism is women's agency. Nina Auerbach (1982) has described the remarkable agency and resilience of female characters in Victorian literature. Adrienne Rich (1979) has connected women's writing to the important notion of taking women students seriously. Judith Fetterley (1978) has analyzed representative American fiction to reveal its pervasive tendency to define both males and females from a male perspective. French feminists, working in the psychoanalytic tradition and the deconstructionist mode, have opened new vistas on literary criticism (Moi 1987), finding women working, loving, and living in the gaps and silences.

Teachers of literature have begun to construct new interpretations of the canonical literature in addition to their continuing attempts to change it. For example, Jerrold Hogle (1988) has presented a detailed analysis of *Hamlet* from a feminist perspective; Sandra Gilbert and Susan Gubar (1979) have analyzed the feminine presence in *Wuthering Heights*; Margaret Homans (1986) has reinterpreted female experience in 19th-century women's writing. Other significant contributors to the literary reconstruction of women's lives include de Beauvoir, Marilyn French (1981), Nancy Miller (1980), and Kate Millett (1970). All this work has a close relationship to the material on feminist criticism in the final section. It is included here because it affects the undergraduate curriculum in literature and has the potential to transform the secondary curriculum as well.

Perhaps most promising for the secondary school curriculum is the current emphasis on the writing process (Caywood and Overing 1987) because this approach requires a sense of self—of voice, audience, purpose, and style. Even here, although writing projects have sprung up all over the country and many involve discussion, peer cooperation, and emphasis on process rather than product, direct attention to women's lives is found mainly at the college level. Discussing the school writing curriculum, Scardamalia and Bereiter (1986) review research on writing processes and products but say nothing about the connection between writing and gendered experience.

Turning to social studies, we find many of the same problems. Even though feminist historians and social scientists have produced much fascinating material (DuBois, Kelly, Kennedy, Korsemeyer, and Robinson 1985; Smith 1987), the high school curriculum remains largely traditional, with slightly revised textbooks as the dominant tool of instruction (Shaver, Helburn, and Davis 1979). Revisions include the reduction of sexist language, better balance in the portrayal of males and females in nonstereotypical activities, and the inclusion of more famous women in history (Hahn and Bernard-Powers 1985). Social studies research has also documented the positive effects of many revised materials (see Hahn and Bernard-Powers 1985). However, Mary Kay Tetreault (1986a, 1986b) has shown dramatically just how limited the improvements are. Although 30 to 58 percent of illustrations in the new materials include women, only 5 percent of the text is about women. Further, discussions of women concentrate overwhelmingly on their contributions to male political activities. Some mention of women's oppression has been included in the new texts but very little on women's agency in the domain of female experience. Clearly, Tetreault would prefer a transformational model rather than the currently dominant assimilationist one.

The trend in precollegiate social studies research, like that in other subject areas, comes largely out of the liberal tradition. Emphasis is on gender differences in aptitudes and interests, equality of opportunity, equitable representation in texts, and the development of nonstereotypical curriculum materials (Hahn 1980). The exciting new material on women's contributions to the elimination of slavery, the reform of hospitals and mental institutions (Reverby 1987), the labor movement (Day 1952), the betterment of immigrants (Addams 1985), and a host of other social programs has not yet found its way into a prominent place in the school curriculum. Work on the lives and contributions of black women is also growing (Davis 1972; Lerner 1972; Steady 1981), and this material, too, holds promise for eventual transformation instead of mere assimilation.

Researchers in science education, like those in mathematics, have focused on gender differences and the "problem" of women and science. The resulting studies are replete with statistics documenting women's absence from science and whatever recent increases in participation can be documented (Stage, Kreinberg, Eccles, and Becker 1985). Although this material can be criticized for its lack of attention to feminist science and feminist theory generally, it provides useful information to educators who want to promote the participation of women in science.

For high school educators it is especially important to know that secondary school mathematics serves as a "critical filter" for later participation in science courses and for eventual work in science-related occupations (Sells 1975). However, taking the requisite math courses does not ensure success in science. There are too few women scientists to serve as models for young women, and the handful who have achieved success are so extraordinary that they hardly inspire realistic hope in average girls for careers in science or engineering (Kundsin 1974). Indeed, existing instruments to predict the choice of science-related careers are entirely based on males because too few females are actually working in science (Gilmartin, McLaughlin, Wise, and Rossi 1976).

This picture is changing, however, and many vigorous intervention programs have sprung up around the country (Aldrich and Hall 1980). The Math/Science Network involves over 1,000 scientists and educators in promoting the participation of girls in math and science; it regularly sponsors Expanding Your Horizons Conferences across the nation (Koltnow 1979). Special courses are offered for girls in mathematics by, for example, the Lawrence Hall of Science at Berkeley (Downie, Slesnick, and Stenmark 1981), Johns Hopkins University (Brody and Fox 1980), the University of Missouri–Kansas City (MacDonald 1980), and Purdue (Heckert et al. 1978). In addition, reentry programs have been designed for women who have dropped out of science careers (Shaw and Bulkin 1981), and a large amount of research has been aimed at understanding and conquering math anxiety (Tobias 1978).

Teacher education programs also aim to prepare teachers to work with girls in math and science. Among the most popular and successful is EQUALS (Kreinberg 1981), which supplies materials and provides workshops to a large number of districts in many states. Many states and cities have also established special programs to assist teachers in their work with girls (see Stage, Kreinberg, Eccles, and Becker 1985).

The work just reviewed assumes the desirability of occupational assimilation, and it has made great strides in reducing the stereotypes that have long impeded women's participation in science. However, it rarely refers to the work of feminist theorists in science (Bleier 1988; Harding 1986; Harding and Hintikka 1983; E. F. Keller 1983, 1985). A reviewer is necessarily struck by the apparent dichotomy between the two sets of literature—one so obviously guided by the liberal and assimilationist model, the other, by critical and transformational theories. Each might be considerably enriched by the other.

One area that seems to provide an exception to the separation between school curriculum and feminist theory is art. In the *Handbook for Achieving Sex Equity Through Education* (Klein 1985), the only chapter on school subjects that does not begin with a discussion of sex or gender differences is the one on art (Sandell, Collins, and Sherman 1985). It tackles instead the "status of women in art and art education"; reviews historical bias; and notes the reduction of blatant discrimination in "selection, admission, treatment, condition, and reward" (Glueck 1980). It is striking that many of the references cited in this chapter appear also in feminist art critiques outside education: Harris (1972), Nemser (1973), Nochlin (1974), and Petersen and Wilson (1976). One of the most useful tools developed by feminist art theorists for art classes is the collection of slides of women's art (Wilson and Petersen 1976). Interestingly, Sandell, Collins, and Sherman also recommend the preparation and teaching of women's studies courses in art education.

Finally, in this brief summary of gender and specific subjects, something should be said about physical education and vocational education. Before the 1970s both had been segregated by sex. With the sex equity provisions of Title IX in 1973 and its regulations in 1975, separate classes in physical education and vocational education were abandoned, and schools were instructed to reduce the disparity of expenditures between women's and men's athletics. As has happened so often in past attempts at legislating equity, Title IX has had mixed effects. The gap in expenditures between men's and women's athletics has closed considerably—"from a difference of 22 times in 1973–74 to a difference of five times in 1980" (Geadelmann 1985, 324)—and many more sports are now open to women. But women have lost coaching jobs. Indeed, as teams and classes were integrated, the number of male coaches increased by 182 percent and the number of female coaches fell by 20 percent.

In vocational education, segregation remains high (Wells 1983). Women are still segregated in lower-paying jobs, men in higher-paying ones. According to Wells, continued segregation at the occupational level is due at least in part to lack of commitment at the educational level. Farmer and Sidney (1985) comment that active recruitment and support services are necessary if this picture is to change. As in mathematics, science, and social studies, specific curricula are available that seem to make a difference. (See Farmer and Sidney for a list and description.)

Summary

In this section, I have considered research on gender differences thought to be relevant to education, single-sex schooling, and gender in the standard school subjects. Most contemporary work reviewed here proceeds from an assimilationist perspective; that is, it assumes that female education should be assimilated to the standard male model and that women should have equal access to formerly male-dominated occupations. Arguments for single-sex schooling seem, on the surface at least, to be examples of a segregation-assimilation model, but at bottom they usually accept the basic assimilationist premise—namely, that girls should be taught the subjects that have traditionally been taught to boys. Advocates argue that girls can learn these subjects better and retain higher levels of confidence if they are taught in gender-segregated classes.

Similarly, most of the research on gender and specific subjects is assimilationist. The aim is to increase the visibility of women in textual materials and the participation of women in subjects in which they have long been underrepresented. This aim has, to some degree, been met, but feminists have begun to raise issues that go further and deeper than questions of equity and assimilation.

TRANSFORMATIONAL PERSPECTIVES

Much of the research examined so far proceeds from a liberal perspective and accepts either a double assimilation or a segregation-assimilation model. Liberals usually identify the good life with some existing standard—e.g., a white, middle-class male model—and commit themselves politically to providing access to this pattern for all. In contrast, transformationists see the system containing the liberal ideal as itself implicated in the exploitation of some people for the benefit of others. From this perspective, it is not a matter of getting an essentially good system to work better but of changing the system in important ways.

Marxist and Critical Theories

Marxists, neo-Marxists, critical theorists, and transformational feminists agree that existing social and political structures support the oppression of workers, women, and various minorities. A hallmark of all these theories is their emphasis on oppression—its causes, manifestations, and possible cures. Although feminists agree with Marxists and critical theorists on this crucial theoretical focus, they have identified many difficulties in both of these perspectives. Feminist theorists are particularly concerned about the neglect of female experience and resultant theoretical and practical inadequacies in these positions.

Marxists put production at the center of their theorizing. However, as Linda Nicholson (1987) has pointed out, "production" is an ambiguous concept. Marx himself sometimes used it to refer to all the activities through which humans reproduce themselves and their culture. At other times he used it more narrowly to refer to the process of making products. The second emphasis entirely ignores what some feminists have called "reproductive functions" (Martin 1985)—bearing and rearing children, caring for the ill and elderly, and teaching the young. Even in the broader use of "production," women's traditional activities are ignored because they have not been wage-earning occupations.

As several writers have argued (Nicholson 1987; Polanyi 1957; Sahling 1976), narrow concentration on economic factors projects the features of capitalism on all societies and, thus, represents an inadequacy in cross-cultural analysis. But the problem is even more serious in a discussion of education. Neo-Marxists working in the curriculum field tend to connect symbolic and economic production (Apple 1979, 1982, 1986; Bowles and Gintis 1976; Carnoy and Levin 1985; Giroux 1983), and although this connection produces many useful insights, it also overlooks forms of life that are rich in symbolism and prominent in daily activity. In particular, such analysis entirely ignores the love and the social and ethical sense of relatedness that inspire and sustain so much of human activity (Noddings 1989). It further separates the "natural" and the "historical," omitting biological reproduction from the historical account of how "men" reproduce themselves (O'Brien 1981).

These omissions have a tremendous, if invisible, impact on schooling. The curriculum is constructed to prepare people for productivity, and the school day is organized in segments devoted to the acquisition of well-defined skills. Whereas neo-Marxists rightly deplore the fact that some children are systematically prepared for lives of alienated labor and others for professional or managerial work, feminists criticize the neglect of education for relatedness. Several feminist writers have suggested that we need to rethink what it means to be educated (Martin 1981, 1984; Noddings 1987, 1989).

A similar controversy is stirring in legal education, where feminists have often found allies in Critical Legal Studies (CLS). But just as feminists in education have found important problems in Marxist theory, feminist legal scholars have accused CLS theorists of overabstracting and detaching their arguments from the actual experience of oppression (Menkel-Meadow 1988). In both cases, the basic problem seems to be a theoretical failure to consider the roots of patriarchal oppression. CLS theorists attack hierarchy and domination (and even the language of rights—making their analysis interesting to enthusiasts of Gilligan's [1982] work on moral voices), but they fail to see that the traditional male-female relation is the most basic form of domination. In education some feminists argue that neo-Marxists err by using "the very terms and prejudices of the system that they [attempt] to criticize" (Grumet 1988, xiv). Their solutions, these feminists argue, tend to tinker with surface manifestations, leaving the basic evil intact.

Critical theorists such as Jürgen Habermas have been criticized in similar ways. For example, Nancy Fraser (1987) argues that Habermas has made a serious error in sharply separating the state-run economy and the male-headed family into two distinct categories. This separation tends to obscure the pernicious similarities between the two. For Fraser, as for other feminist critics, the basic evil is domination, and Habermas's analysis misses the most elementary form. For example, Habermas tends to associate family life with communicatively achieved consensus, whereas much of what goes on in families is actually directed by long-standing and unquestioned norms that reinforce the subordination of women. Thus, although the distinction between system-integrated and socially integrated action contexts is useful because it vividly reveals the limitations of individual agency, it is also problematic because it assumes a purity in family life that does not exist.

In general, the primary problem with Marxist and critical theorists' analyses is that the peculiar features of women's oppression and agency are lost in the focus on economic and symbolic oppression. Not all women are economically oppressed, but all women have suffered patriarchal oppression. Feminists are understandably skeptical about assurances that race, class, and gender can be studied effectively together simply because they are all forms of oppression. Just as feminist legal theorists had to break away from CLS to focus on the experience of women (Menkel-Meadow 1988), so feminist theorists in education feel the need to draw more heavily on feminist theory and the life experience of women than on critical theory in education. A main objection of feminist criticism in this area is the scarcity of feminist literature cited by Marxist and critical theorists.

Closely related to the objections directed at critical theory is a complaint against all forms of educational theory that retain man—white, middle-class, liberally educated man—as the standard against whom all others are evaluated. Whether theorists regard themselves as liberal, critical, or radical, they are viewed with some suspicion by transformational feminists as long as this standard is uncritically accepted.

Psychoanalytic Perspectives

Feminists have multiple reasons for analyzing psychoanalytic perspectives. First, Freudian insights are often named, along with Marxist thought, as revolutionary and fundamental to modern thought (Becker 1975). Second, psychoanalytic theory is notorious for its peculiarly male-centered ways of defining and describing female nature. Third, psychoanalytic theories have been influential in the literature on marriage, self-identity, and child rearing; as a result, many women totally ignorant of the theories have nevertheless felt their impact. Indeed, psychoanalytic thought has been so powerful and pernicious that Betty Friedan (1963) identified it as instrumental in the modern subjugation of women. Following Friedan, Alice Rossi (1964) felt it necessary to show that many psychoanalytic premises and predictions are wrong; for example, there is little empirical support for the notion that mothers' involvement in careers ruins the emotional lives of their children.

One line of attack on psychoanalytic ideas concentrates on identifying the premises that act against equality for women, tracing the connections between these premises and predictions of various social consequences and demonstrating that the predicted consequences do not occur. This is the line Rossi (1964) took in her influential "Immodest Proposal."

A second line of attack attempts to revise psychoanalytic theory from a feminist perspective. In the Freudian heritage, revision usually centers on pre-Oedipal life because it is, supposedly, resolution of the Oedipal conflict that introduces and solidifies the male ego and superego. Freud claimed that because girls do not have to fear castration (that dreaded event having occurred a priori), they do not internalize the voice of the father in the compelling way that boys do. Hence women were for Freud necessarily—biologically—morally inferior to men.

Nancy Chodorow (1978) launched a sociological attack on the biological premises of psychoanalysis. Concentrating on the pre-Oedipal period, she attempted to show that many of the differences between female and male psychological structures could be traced to child-rearing patterns. Because little girls can construct their gender identities in direct relation with their primary caregiver, they grow to maturity with an intact sense of relatedness. In contrast, little boys must separate themselves from their mothers to identify with the largely absent father. Such a critique accepts Freudian insights on the centrality of early childhood for the development of psychological deep structures, but it denies the inevitability of certain fundamental gender differences. Chodorow's work falls into a category called "object-relations" theory, which will be further discussed with feminist epistemology.

Chodorow (1978) introduces another notion that is attractive even to feminists who reject psychoanalytic theory entirely. She describes the relational structures of female personality as a strength rather than a weakness. Acknowledging the difficulties women experience in the public and professional arena, Chodorow insists that men suffer even greater emotional deprivation as a result of traditional child-rearing patterns. With more nearly equal involvement of males in child care, both boys and girls might develop healthy egos and moral commitment without abandoning relational structures and attitudes.

Chodorow's work could have considerable impact on education. As Madeleine Grumet (1988) has pointed out, children are placed almost entirely in the care of women for the first seven or eight years of their lives. They are then wrenched away from the fluid, relational existence of early childhood into a world dominated by masculine aims and structures. Grumet does not deny the need to teach children the "games and names of the fathers," but, like Chodorow, she questions the need for such sharp separation and denies the inferiority of female relatedness. For Grumet, no mere tinkering with curriculum can transform education, nor can the professionalization of teaching have the desired effects. From this perspective, a genuine transformation of education requires a fundamental change in our ways of thinking and living. Living together in appreciative and critical relation must be valued; it cannot be displaced by fragments of abstract knowledge, nor is it sufficient to provide all students with opportunities to acquire the knowledge considered important by privileged males. This last denial forms the ground for Grumet's criticism of Marxists and also her (1986) criticism of current advocates of *Paideia* such as Mortimer Adler (1982).

Despite the pervasive influence of psychoanalysis on modern life and especially on the lives of women, educational theorists have often neglected it. In reviewing feminist scholarship in education, Grumet (1987b) complains that it is "excessively empirical" and either neglects or devalues significant work in philosophy, literature, and psychoanalysis. Whereas feminist theorists are constructing and debating dramatic revisions of male-made psychoanalytic theories, educational theorists fail to appreciate the influence these theories have had on life in general and schooling in particular.

Freud, Erikson (1964), and Lacan (1977) put tremendous emphasis on sexual life and symbolism. All create an abstraction—Woman —from which they extrapolate to real, individual women. Woman is described as the Other, as the Unknowable, as Negativity, as non-Existent (see Cornell and Thurschwell 1987). Even feminists, in attempting to revise psychoanalytic descriptions, sometimes conflate this abstraction, Woman, with actual women (Kristeva 1980). Giving the name "Woman" to a longing that cannot be filled, and locating this longing in language that destroys our connection to the abstract, archaic Mother, exacerbates the voiceless condition of women. It also tends to obscure the practical, social, and political norms that enforce or encourage women's silence.

Feminists are, understandably, often more attracted to the work of Carl Jung than that of Freud, Erikson, or Lacan. Jung and his disciples describe the feminine in positive terms, but they still rely on a notion of feminine essence; that is, Jungians subscribe to the idea that there is a feminine nature that precedes and provides guidance for female experience. Many feminists find the emphasis on nature problematic because it is often accompanied by prescriptions for "true womanhood" and restrictions on women's activities and social attitudes. Jungian feminists, of course, try to retain Jung's central ideas, even the archetype (Lauter and Rupprecht 1985), without falling into dogmas that limit women's potential.

Possibly the most interesting features of Jung's (1959, 1973) work from an educational perspective are his discussions of polytheism and a morality of evil. Polytheism gives women an opportunity to find a deity in their own image (Christ 1982; Downing 1984), and feminist theologians and other theorists have uncovered a substantial female longing for such a deity (Spretnak 1982). Widespread interest in polytheism would threaten patriarchal values, and its widespread embrace would shake the very foundations of patriarchy. Further, feminists with intellectual interests in polytheism sometimes recommend the inclusion of religious studies in the school curriculum, and they would like to see all forms of spirituality subjected to critical and appreciative scrutiny (Noddings 1987, 1989). From this perspective, the constitutional separation of church and state not only protects the religious freedom of individuals and groups but also provides a protective armor around religious dogma and shelters religion from the critical inquiry educators are perennially trying to promote in other areas.

Jung's (1973) call for the development of a morality of evil rattles the foundations of both religious and political traditions. First, Jung posits a fallible deity—an idea attractive to some Jewish thinkers but very few Christian groups. Second, he recommends intensive and extensive study of the individual and group shadow. The "shadow" is a cluster of attributes that an individual or group prefers to deny in itself. Ignorance of the shadow often leads to projection of one's own hated traits onto others and a resulting attempt to destroy an exteriorized evil that remains nevertheless firmly in residence in its original psyche. Building on Jung's ideas in education would establish a new and perhaps healthier approach to civic education and patriotism. This new approach would require the study of a nation's shadow as well as that of individuals and groups. However, little has been done so far with Jung's ideas in educational circles.

Unfortunately the most influential forms of psychoanalysis have been those that attribute an essential nature to women. Freud, with his emphasis on the Oedipal conflict and its centrality in moral development; Erikson, with his notion of inner space; and Jung, with his separation of logos and eros, all have contributed to a "scientific" rationale for the continued subordination of women. It is enlightening (but not heartening) to read again Erikson's "Reflections on Womanhood" and Rossi's "Equality Between the Sexes" back to back in *Daedalus*, 1964. The difference between even an appreciative male view of "womanhood" and a description of actual female experience is dramatic.

Epistemological Transformations

With constructivists, pragmatists, and some hermeneuticists, feminist epistemologists reject the sharp separation of knowers from what they know. Feminists argue, further, that social movements such as feminism actually tend to increase the "objectivity" of science by drawing the attention of scientists to problems and perspectives that would not arise within science-as-usual. "It is movements for social liberation that have most increased the objectivity of science, not the norms of science as they have in fact been practiced, or as philosophers have rationally reconstructed them" (Harding 1986, 25). Harding means that a wider range of problems fall under public scrutiny. Feminists seek grounding for beliefs in social experience, not solely in the internal rules of scientific practice.

Object-relations theorists, working in the psychoanalytic tradition, have made important contributions to feminist epistemology. Their work describes and explains how patterns of early child care influence the way girls and boys look at themselves, the opposite sex, and nature itself (Chodorow 1978; Flax 1983; E. F. Keller 1985; J. B. Miller 1976). Keller critiques both the name "object-relations" and the failure of nonfeminist theorists to recognize the autonomy of mothers. (Mother is construed as the first "object" with which the child forms a relation.) The big error here is in assuming "that autonomy can be bought only at the price of unrelatedness" (E. F. Keller 1985, 72). This faulty way of looking at the world creates a sharp separation of subject and object, of knower and known, of nature and culture, and it also tends toward ideals of control and domination. The subject, knower, or scientist stands outside of what he or she studies and exerts control over the objects of study. It is not by accident, feminists note, that masculine scientists have so often referred to nature as "she"—something to be dominated and brought into submission. Feminist object-relations theorists conclude that a pattern of child rearing that requires females to be the primary caregivers leads to faulty epistemological premises and dangerous reliance on "universal" principles in ethics.

Sandra Harding (1986) identifies three programs of feminist epistemology in the sciences: feminist empiricism, feminist standpoints, and feminist postmodernism. Of the three positions, feminist empiricism is judged least radical because it leaves the standard methods of science in place. However, as Harding points out, it is radical in the sense discussed above: It asserts that problems arise out of investigators' social experience as well as scientific experience. How problems are defined, where they are sought, and how results are interpreted are all colored by social experience. Hence the absence of women in a scientific field is likely to reduce its objectivity since only a fragment of social experience is considered.

Standpoint epistemologies begin with the premise that investigators' standpoints influence what they see. This claim in itself is a currently acceptable one. But traditionally scientists are taught to fight against this influence, to dissociate and disinterest themselves as nearly as possible in order to be objective. However, feminist standpoint epistemologists, as identified by Harding (Flax 1983; Hartsock 1983; Rose 1983; Smith 1974, 1987), argue that the acceptance of standpoints *increases* objectivity. From this perspective, investigators who accept social experience as a valuable guide and build their science on well-defined social purposes are likely to produce more objective results, in the sense that their work is genuine and coherent from inception through interpretation. It is not distorted by the pretense of neutrality.

A complaint against standpoint epistemology is that the credibility of a finding seems to be judged by the status of the investigator; for example, a feminist scientist (female or male) is, on this account, more likely to produce a reliable study on women than a nonfeminist. Critics ask, then, whether we are to judge knowledge claims by the authority of those making them.

This criticism may arise from a misinterpretation of standpoint epistemology. Feminists working from this perspective do not make claims for absolute truth; neither are they relativists. They argue that all scientists want to accomplish something (often a social good), that identifying and accepting that goal and the experience from which it arises make it possible to launch a coherent program of research—one in which ends and means are not artificially separated. As Dorothy Smith (1974, 1987) asserts of sociology, science can be and should be intersubjective; it should be *for* its "subjects," not merely about them. Objectivity is construed as truthfulness or fidelity to situated subjects, not as disinterest, separation, or aloofness.

A more important objection to standpoint epistemology is that it too easily assumes that there is a woman's standpoint or a black standpoint or a worker's standpoint. It may, that is, deny the variety of viewpoints held by individual women, blacks, or workers. This danger can, perhaps, be overcome by cooperative social science. The investigator does not assume that a standpoint represents the perspective of all subject-participants but stands willing to construct a standpoint with them. What results is an honest picture painted from a particular viewpoint. One does not claim universality, but if universality is embraced as a regulative mechanism or ideal, an investigator would carefully invite a variety of views and a multitude of studies from different perspectives.

A controversy has arisen over Harding's (1986) categories and her labeling of some researchers as "standpoint epistemologists." Smith (1989), for example, has objected to being called an epistemologist. She considers herself a feminist sociologist and a standpoint theorist. The root of this controversy probably lies in feminist distrust of philosophy, particularly the traditional philosophy characterized by appeals to universality, loss of detail in theoretical abstraction, and separation from ordinary life experience. Naomi Scheman (1989) makes this view clear in her response to Harding's work. Feminists reject what Mary Daly (1973) has called "methodolatry"—the dominance of method and the search for one pure and universal method. In a few well-stated paragraphs, Scheman captures the feminist critique of method and provides a succinct history of the problem. It may well be that Smith rejects the label "epistemologist" because it carries with it so much of the baggage of methodolatry.

Feminist postmodernism avoids many of the problems of the other two schools; it simply gives up the pursuit of objectivity and universality. Instead of trying to redefine them, it recognizes the inevitable workings of power and authority, of multiple selves masquerading as individuals. It urges us to understand the power of language and ritual in which we are immersed. Although it avoids some of the obvious difficulties of the other two approaches, it often induces a feeling of personal helplessness and cynicism. It holds little hope for nonviolent and loving transformation.

Properly, it is not an epistemology at all but a position that rejects epistemology's traditional questions and methods. It is postepistemological as well as postmodern.

Ethical Transformations

Like those in epistemology, feminist critiques in ethics attack methodolatry. Feminist ethicists and theologians find the traditional emphasis on detached moral agency (method) particularly offensive (Cooey, Farmer, and Ross 1987; C. Keller 1986; Noddings 1984, 1989), and they urge consideration of human relatedness, bodily existence, and feeling. Naomi Scheman (1989) sums up the traditional attitude found so offensive:

> Thus, replicability became the hallmark of reputable experimentation, as universalizability became the hallmark of reputable moral thought: who you were in particular, to whom you were particularly connected, where you were particularly placed, was supposed to make no difference to how things seemed to you—provided, of course, that you were following the prescribed method, the main features of which were designed precisely to insulate your judgment from all these particularities. (41)

Feminist moral theory was enormously invigorated by the work of Carol Gilligan (1982). Her empirical studies cast some doubt on the universality of Lawrence Kohlberg's (1981) stages of moral development. Gilligan suggested that many women approach moral problems without relying on the rational method described (and prescribed) by Kohlberg. Instead of detaching themselves from their situations and relations, women tend to focus on them in making their moral decisions. Gilligan found an emphasis on needs, response, and responsibility rather than rights and justice.

A host of controversies has sprung up in response to Gilligan's (1982) work. Some researchers attacked Gilligan's methods, the thinness of her data, or the validity of her interpretations. Others concentrated on gender differences. Do women really score less well on Kohlberg's scale? Is the different voice described by Gilligan necessarily female? Is a needs-response framework as adequate as a justice-rights one? Whether or not an ethic of care turns out to be a valid description of female morality, the avalanche of positive female response to Gilligan's work is a phenomenon that in itself merits study. Obviously, many women recognized themselves in Gilligan's descriptions.

As some philosophers and feminist theorists began to describe caring, maternal thinking, and related concepts as possible alternatives to rights-based theories (Benhabib 1987; Held 1987; Noddings 1984, 1989; Ruddick 1980, 1989; Whitbeck 1983; Young 1981, 1987), other feminist theorists expressed alarm that an emphasis on affect and caring—especially if opposed to rational deliberation—would play into the hands of those who continue to judge women unable or unwilling to think rationally (J. Grimshaw 1986; Okin 1989; Tronto 1987). These critics and others also objected to particular components or arguments in ethics of caring or maternal thinking (Flanagan and Jackson 1987; Sichel 1988). Both sets of literature—the alternative analyses and their often sympathetic critics—are growing rapidly, and it is not possible to review them comprehensively here. Clumping names together as a means of economy also has its faults because the writers mentioned take different positions and emphasize different aspects of moral theory; so, too, their critics differ in how deeply they object and where they concentrate their objections.

Feminist thinkers in moral theory, like those in epistemology, express considerable agreement with other ethical theorists who question the validity of universality; method-based deliberation; and rejection of affect, personal relations, and projects (Blum 1980; MacIntyre 1981; Maguire 1978; Williams 1985). Again one hesitates to string these writers together because their positions vary greatly. But they have at least one interest in common with feminist moral theorists: They would all reembed ethics in social life. They reject the disavowal of bodily existence that has characterized Kantian (and often utilitarian) ethics. For each, who we are, the position we hold in our community, whom we love, what our projects are—all matter in moral life. However, despite the commonalities, feminists (and Blum and Maguire should be included here) may object to the elitism of MacIntyre's Aristotelian approach and the individualistic tone of Williams's argument.

Besides its influence on moral theory generally, feminist ethical theory has had considerable impact on feminist thinking in some professions (Noddings 1990b). Feminist legal theorists, for example, have invoked an ethic of care to augment other attacks on rights language, hierarchy, negative duties, and gender discrimination. (For a comprehensive review of the feminist program in law, see the *Journal of Legal Education* 1988.) In nursing, theorists have claimed a model of caring as central to nursing practice (Watson 1979, 1985) and have begun to use this model to challenge weaknesses in the medical science model and to build a new curriculum. The traditional concept of care in nursing has been enhanced by the new emphasis on caring in ethics, and nursing theorists have contributed extensively to both programs ("Caring and Nursing: Explorations in the Feminist Perspectives" 1988). Finally, feminist theologians share many of the interests found in ethics of care: a rejection of methodolatry (Daly 1973), the identification of separation as an evil (C. Keller 1986), the primacy of social experience (Welch 1985), an emphasis on relation (Maguire 1978), and the restoration of interest in bodily existence (Cooey, Farmer, and Ross 1987).

Transformational thinking in ethics has had some impact on both curriculum and instruction at the level of college and professional school. Its direct effects on curriculum, curriculum theory, and moral education will be discussed in the next section.

Transformations in Curriculum

Feminist transformations in curriculum may be discussed in two broad categories: actual changes in curriculum and significant works in curriculum theory. Changes in the standard curriculum, most of which represent assimilationist efforts, have already been discussed. One important change in the college curriculum, the addition of women's studies, will be discussed here. The rest of this section will be devoted to feminist curriculum theory and moral education.

During the 1960s and 1970s there was an enormous growth in women's studies. Florence Howe (1984) writes that

> women engaged in developing 452 women's studies programs, 40 centers for research on women, 30,000 women's studies courses, more than 500 women's centers, hundreds of centers for re-entry women, rape-crisis centers, committees on sexual harassment, committees on the status of women, not to mention the conferences, literary and arts festivals, special theatre and film programs, and musical celebrations. (x)

Women's Studies Quarterly (1989) lists some 500 women's studies programs, most at the undergraduate level but an impressive number at the graduate level as well. Virtually all of these programs are interdisciplinary; that is, their courses and topics draw on existing disciplines and represent significant modifications of those disciplines through feminist perspectives (see DuBois, Kelly, Kennedy, Korsemeyer, and Robinson 1985; Langland and Gove 1981).

Feminists remain concerned that despite the vigor of women's studies, changes in the mainstream curriculum are slow. The liberal arts still dominate the undergraduate curriculum, and as Howe (1984) points out, "The liberal arts curriculum still tells college students about their fathers, not their mothers" (274). It is paradoxical for feminist scholars in education that the leading educational reforms (Carnegie Task Force on Teaching as a Profession 1986; Holmes Group 1986) recommend a renewed emphasis on the liberal arts, whereas feminist scholars distrust and reject that tradition (Rich 1979). Howe gives counsel that she hopes will be heeded by professional educators:

> A return to the old masters does not forward the search for truth which has traditionally been at least part of the liberal arts mission. St. Augustine, Aristotle, Erasmus—these men return us to the monstrous misogyny of the past, which we must of course understand, but which, as the mainstay of the curriculum, is hardly sufficient. In short, then, if the traditional liberal arts curriculum won't do, what will? Nothing short of transformation, the major source for which is women's studies. (274)

Women's studies as a program aims to transform the curriculum and all of social life. Its proponents do not suggest women's studies courses as mere additions to the standard curriculum. Their hope is that young women well versed in the misogynist writings of Aristotle, Augustine, Rousseau, and Kant will raise questions in their mainstream liberal arts courses and that professors newly educated through feminist scholarship will insist on including appropriate critiques to misogynist classics in their syllabi. Only if this transformational process is endorsed can feminist educators in good conscience accede to a greater emphasis on the liberal arts.

Feminist scholarship has grown so prolifically that it threatens to overturn one of its chief goals—the interdisciplinary study of human experience and problems. Howe (1984) notes that "to gain an understanding of the new scholarship on women—whatever one's discipline—is comparable to beginning to earn a new doctorate" (275). To remain well informed in feminist philosophy, for example, requires not only reading in one's branch of philosophy but also in all the related fields of feminist inquiry. As the material grows, a temptation arises to read more narrowly in order to retain one's "expertise," but this is one of the tendencies in traditional scholarship that feminists have most heatedly criticized because it distorts human experience and makes the identification and solution of human problems more difficult. It separates scholars from other women and from one another.

Most of the transformational work in curriculum theory is directed at the college and university level, and the theoretical and methodological concerns discussed so far are prominent in that arena. But feminist professional educators are also concerned with the school curriculum and with problems of applying and extending feminist theory at the precollegiate level.

In a series of significant essays, Jane Roland Martin (1981, 1982a, 1982b, 1984, 1985, 1987) argues that the school curriculum has been constructed around the public and productive interests of males. The experience of women in bearing and raising children, maintaining homes, and caring for the ill and aged is entirely omitted from the disciplines traditionally offered in precollegiate education. Martin calls for a "new ideal" of the educated person, one that will "bring women into educational thought" and include female values, skills, and ways of relating.

Martin is a thoroughgoing transformationist. She wants to include women in educational thought not merely to balance the curriculum and do justice to women. Rather, her concern is with a dramatic transformation of social life. To balance cognition with affect, thinking with intelligent doing, judging with receptive perception, and control with harmony is part of a transformation that may be necessary for human survival. Hence her work has implications for liberal education, parenting, moral education, peace education, and environmental education.

Working along similar lines Patricia Thompson (1985, 1986a, 1986b, 1986c) suggests a Hestian ethic to guide curriculum building, moral education, and civic life. As a home economics educator, Thompson criticizes both the male-dominated tradition in curriculum and the frequent feminist rejection of home and life skills. Arguing that the separation of *oikos* and *polis* in Greek thought should be reconciled in contemporary life, Thompson would put renewed emphasis on the ethics of family life (Hestian ethics) and use it to transform life in schools and society generally. The alienation of feminists from home economics especially disturbs Thompson, who sees the difficulty clearly but rejects an escapist solution. Home economics has long been the special domain of women. As such it has been consistently devalued in the school curriculum and the occupational hierarchy. A feminist-escapist solution is to accept the devaluation and enter more prestigious fields. A transformationist solution, Thompson advises, is to teach all of our children to cherish circles of intimacy and affection, to acquire competence in the basic activities of everyday life, and to use the sympathies and understandings gained in family life to transform political life.

The work of Mary Kay Tetreault (1986a, 1986b) was discussed earlier in connection with the standard curriculum. It, too, has a transformationist flavor in that inclusion of women's traditional experience in the curriculum should raise the value of that experience and encourage boys and girls to study and emulate nurses, reformers, volunteers in public service, teachers, and child-care workers as well as kings, warriors, orators, and lawmakers. History would become more nearly the story of humankind and thus more honest and, perhaps, more interesting to learners.

My own recent work also falls into the transformationist category. Beginning with an analysis of caring and its place in ethics (Noddings 1984), I have argued for a curriculum aimed at producing people who will not intentionally harm others (1987); a transformed structure of schooling that will encourage the development of caring relations (1988a); a moral education that emphasizes maternal interests in preserving life, enhancing growth, and shaping acceptable children (in press); and the development of a morality of evil (1989) that should help all of us understand and control our own tendencies toward evil.

Feminist transformational theorists often advocate the use of narrative in education. Madeleine Grumet (1987a, 1987c, 1988) draws on fiction, poetry, biography, and autobiography to restore women's experience to both the purposes and practices of education. She argues—rather, *shows* dramatically and poetically—how the feminine is lost in education, how we forget that the desire for education is bound up with a desire to live with love, wonder, tenderness, and appreciation of everyday events. Women and their experience cannot be included in the curriculum by any standard method of addition because that method destroys the experience she urges us to preserve. Yet women are there—in schools, with children, in unexpressed thoughts and purposes, in a host of contradictory concepts and phenomena that Grumet analyzes and describes.

Jo Anne Pagano (1988) has also contributed to the growing transformational literature in feminist curriculum theory. Arguing for the primacy of friendship and mutual relations in teaching, she describes the growth of both students and teachers in classrooms where the traditional silence of women is broken.

Feminist emphasis on women's experience in curriculum contributes to a way of thinking that has recently been described by a number of theorists. The uses of personal experience in learning, of storytelling in teaching, and of narrative forms in curriculum making are all gaining attention (Bruner 1986, 1987; Greene 1975, 1978, 1986; Pinar 1975, 1988; Witherell and Noddings, 1991). Feminists are especially interested in employing such methods because they seem compatible with women's ways of knowing (Belenky, Clinchy, Goldberger, and Tarule 1986), but the methods also hold promise for a universal transformation of educational experience.

CONCLUSION

This chapter has described three large models of thought on the education of women, the place of women in curriculum, and the role of women in society. Assimilation models advocate identical educations for women and men. At times theorists have coupled educational assimilation models with occupational segregation models; that is, both assimilation-assimilation models and assimilation-segregation models have been discussed and used. Segregation models have been suggested by some theorists to accommodate the special and different needs of women and men. Usually, educational segregation models assume occupational segregation, but today educational segregation is sometimes advocated in the interests of occupational and social assimilation. Each of these models of thought and representative current research has been discussed in some depth.

Finally, transformation models were described. Feminist transformational thought rejects both assimilation and segregation models. Transformationists seek a radical change in education for both males and females. They want both sexes to participate fully in domestic and public life and to acquire a deep appreciation for the contributions of women as well as those of men. Further, they hope that such a transformed education will allow men to live less aggressively and all of us to live more harmoniously with one another and the planet that is our common home.

References

Addams, Jane. 1985. *Jane Addams on Education*, edited by Ellen Condliffe Lagemann. New York: Teachers College Press.

Adler, Mortimer. 1982. *The Paideia Proposal*. New York: Macmillan.

Aldrich, M. L., and P. W. Hall. 1980. *Programs in Science, Mathematics, and Engineering for Women and Girls in the United States: 1976–1978*. Washington, DC: American Association for the Advancement of Science.

Annas, Pamela J. 1987. "Silences: Feminist Language Research and the Teaching of Writing." In *Teaching and Writing: Pedagogy, Gender, and Equity*, edited by Cynthia L. Caywood and Gillian R. Overing, 3–18. Albany: State University of New York Press.

Antler, Joyce. 1987. *Lucy Sprague Mitchell: The Making of a Modern Woman*. New Haven, CT, and London: Yale University Press.

Apple, Michael W. 1979. *Ideology and Curriculum*. Boston: Routledge & Kegan Paul.

Apple, Michael W. 1982. *Education and Power*. Boston: Routledge & Kegan Paul.

Apple, Michael W. 1986. *Teachers and Texts: A Political Economy of Class and Gender Relations in Education*. Boston: Routledge & Kegan Paul.

Armstrong, Jane M. 1985. "A National Assessment of Participation and Achievement of Women in Mathematics." In *Women and Mathematics: Balancing the Equation*, edited by Susan F. Chipman, Lorelei R. Brush, and Donna M. Wilson, 59–64. Hillsdale, NJ: Erlbaum.

Auerbach, Nina. 1982. *Woman and the Demon: The Life of a Victorian Myth*. Cambridge, MA: Harvard University Press.

Bailey, Susan, and Rebecca Smith. 1982. *Policies for the Future: State Policies, Regulations, and Resources Related to the Achievement of Educational Equity for Females and Males*. Washington, DC: Resource Center for Sex Equity, Council of Chief State School Officers.

Beard, Mary. 1946. *Woman as Force in History: A Study in Tradition and Realities*. New York: Macmillan.

Beauvoir, Simone de. 1961. *The Second Sex*, translated and edited by H. M. Parshley. New York: Bantam Books.

Bebeau, Muriel L., and Mary M. Brabeck. 1987. Integrating care and justice issues in professional moral education: A gender perspective. *Journal of Moral Education* 16(3): 189–203.

Becker, Ernest. 1975. *Escape from Evil*. New York: Free Press.

Beecher, Catherine. 1977 (1842). *A Treatise on Domestic Economy*. New York: Schocken Books.

Belenky, Mary Field, Blythe McVicker Clinchy, Nancy Rule Goldberger, and Jill Mattock Tarule. 1986. *Women's Ways of Knowing*. New York: Basic Books.

Bell, Susan Groag, and Karen M. Offen, eds. 1983. *Women, the Family, and Freedom*, vol. 2. Stanford, CA: Stanford University Press.

Benbow, Camilla P., and Julian C. Stanley. 1980, December. Sex differences in mathematical ability: Fact or artifact. *Science* 210(4475): 1262–1264.

Benhabib, Seyla. 1987. "The Generalized and the Concrete Other." In *Feminism as Critique*, edited by Seyla Benhabib and Drucilla Cornell, 77–95. Minneapolis: University of Minnesota Press.

Biklen, Sari Knopp. 1987. "Women in American Elementary School Teaching: A Case Study." In *Women Educators: Employees of Schools in Western Countries*, edited by Patricia A. Schmuck, 223–242. Albany: State University of New York Press.

Biklen, Sari Knopp, and Charol Shakeshaft. 1985. "The New Scholarship on Women." In *Handbook for Achieving Sex Equity Through Education*, edited by Susan S. Klein, 44–52. Baltimore, MD: Johns Hopkins University Press.

Bleier, Ruth, ed. 1988. *Feminist Approaches to Science*. New York: Pergamon.

Block, James H. 1979. "Personality Development in Males and Females: The Influence of Differential Socialization." Paper presented in the Master Lecture Series at the annual meeting, American Psychological Association, New York.

Bloom, Allan, trans. 1968. "Interpretive Essay." In *The Republic of Plato*. New York: Basic Books.

Blum, Lawrence A. 1980. *Friendship, Altruism, and Morality*. London: Routledge & Kegan Paul.

Boston Women's Teachers' Group. 1983. "Teaching: An Imperilled Profession." In *Handbook of Teaching and Policy*, edited by Lee S. Shulman and Gary Sykes, 261–299. White Plains, NY: Longman.

Bowles, Samuel, and Herbert Gintis. 1976. *Schooling in Capitalist America*. New York: Basic Books.

Brenzel, Barbara M. 1983. *Daughters of the State: A Social Portrait of the First Reform School for Girls in North America, 1856–1905*. Cambridge, MA: M.I.T Press.

Brody, Linda, and Lynn H. Fox. 1980. "An Accelerative Intervention Program for Mathematically Gifted Girls." In *Women and the Mathematical Mystique*, edited by Lynn H. Fox, Linda Brody, and Dianne Tobin, 164–178. Baltimore, MD: Johns Hopkins University Press.

Brooks-Gunn, Jeanne, and Wendy Schnapp-Matthews. 1979. *He and She: How Children Develop Their Sex Role Identity*. Englewood Cliffs, NJ: Prentice Hall.

Bruner, Jerome. 1986. *Actual Minds, Possible Worlds*. Cambridge, MA: Harvard University Press.

Bruner, Jerome. 1987. Life as narrative. *Social Research* 54 (1): 11–32.

Brush, Lorelei R. 1985. "Cognitive and Affective Determinants of Course Preferences and Plans." In *Women and Mathematics: Balancing the Equation*, edited by Susan F. Chipman, Lorelei R. Brush, and Donna M. Wilson, 123–150. Hillsdale, NJ: Erlbaum.

Bynum, Carolyn Walker. 1987. *Holy Feast and Holy Fast: The Religious Significance of Food to Medieval Women*. Berkeley: University of California Press.

Cantarella, Eva. 1987. *Pandora's Daughters*, translated by Maureen B. Fant. Baltimore, MD, and London: Johns Hopkins University Press.

"Caring and Nursing: Explorations in the Feminist Perspectives." 1988, June 17–18. Presentations at a conference sponsored by the Doctoral Student Group and Center for Human Caring, Denver, CO.

Carnegie Task Force on Teaching as a Profession. 1986. *A Nation Prepared*. New York: Carnegie Forum on Education and the Economy.

Carnoy, Martin, and Henry Levin. 1985. *Schooling and Work in the Democratic State*. Stanford, CA: Stanford University Press.

Casserly, Patricia, and Donald Rock. 1985. "Factors Related to Young Women's Persistence and Achievement in Advanced Placement Mathematics." In *Women and Mathematics: Balancing the Equation*, edited by Susan F. Chipman, Lorelei R. Brush, and Donna M. Wilson, 225–248. Hillsdale, NJ: Erlbaum.

Cattell, James McKeen. 1909, January–June. The school and the family. *Popular Science Monthly* 74: 84–104.

Caywood, Cynthia L., and Gillian R. Overing, eds. 1987. *Teaching Writing: Pedagogy, Gender and Equity*. Albany: State University of New York Press.

Chipman, Susan F. 1988. Far too sexy a topic. *Educational Researcher* 17(3): 46–49.

Chipman, Susan F., and Veronica G. Thomas. 1985. "Women's Participation in Mathematics: Outlining the Problem." In *Women and Mathematics: Balancing the Equation*, edited by Susan F. Chipman, Lorelei R. Brush, and Donna M. Wilson, 275–328. Hillsdale, NJ: Erlbaum.

Chipman, Susan F., and Donna M. Wilson. 1985. "Understanding Mathematics Course Enrollment and Mathematics Achievement: A Synthesis of the Research." In *Women and Mathematics: Balancing the Equation*, edited by Susan F. Chipman, Lorelei R. Brush, and Donna M. Wilson, 275–328. Hillsdale, NJ: Erlbaum.

Chodorow, Nancy. 1978. *The Reproduction of Mothering*. Berkeley: University of California Press.

Christ, Carol P. 1982. "Why Women Need the Goddess: Phenomenological, Psychological, and Political Reflections." In *The Politics of Women's Spirituality*, edited by Charlene Spretnak, 71–86. Garden City, NY: Anchor Books.

Clarke, Edward. 1873. *Sex in Education: Or, A Fair Chance for the Girls*. Boston: J. R. Osgood.

Cooey, Paula M., Sharon A. Farmer, and Mary Ellen Ross, eds. 1987.

Embodied Love: Sensuality and Relationship as Feminist Values. San Francisco, CA: Harper & Row.

Cornell, Drucilla, and Adam Thurschwell. 1987. "Feminism, Negativity, Intersubjectivity." In *Feminism as Critique*, edited by Seyla Benhabib and Drucilla Cornell, 143–162. Minneapolis: University of Minnesota Press.

Daly, Mary. 1973. *Beyond God the Father*. Boston: Beacon Press.

Daly, Mary. 1984. *Pure Lust*. Boston: Beacon Press.

Darwin, Charles. 1871. *The Descent of Man, and Selection in Relation to Sex*. New York: D. Appleton.

Davis, Angela. 1972. Reflections on the black woman's role in the community of slaves. *Massachusetts Review* 13(1 & 2): 81–100.

Day, Dorothy. 1952. *The Long Loneliness*. San Francisco, CA: Harper & Row.

Dijkstra, Bram. 1986. *Idols of Perversity: Fantasies of Feminine Evil in Fin-de-siècle Culture*. New York and Oxford: Oxford University Press.

Douglass, Jane Dempsey. 1974. "Women and the Continental Reformation." In *Religion and Sexism*, edited by Rosemary Radford Ruether, 292–318. New York: Simon & Schuster.

Downie, D., T. Slesnick, and J. K. Stenmark. 1981. *Math for Girls and Other Problem Solvers*. Berkeley: University of California, Lawrence Hall of Science.

Downing, Christine. 1984. *The Goddess*. New York: Crossroad.

Dreeben, Robert. 1970. *The Nature of Teaching*. Glenview, IL: Scott, Foresman.

DuBois, Ellen C., Gail Paradise Kelly, Elizabeth Lapovsky Kennedy, Carolyn W. Korsmeyer, and Lillian S. Robinson. 1985. *Feminist Scholarship: Kindling in the Groves of Academe*. Urbana and Chicago: University of Illinois Press.

Ehrenreich, Barbara, and Deirdre English. 1973. *Witches, Midwives, and Nurses*. Old Westbury, NY: Feminist Press.

Epstein, Cynthia Fuchs. 1976. Sex role stereotyping, occupations, and social exchange. *Women's Studies* 3(2): 185–194.

Erikson, Erik H. 1964, Spring. Inner and outer space: Reflections on womanhood. *Daedalus* 92: 582–606.

Farmer, Helen S., and Joan Seliger Sidney. 1985. "Sex Equity in Career and Vocational Education." In *Handbook for Achieving Sex Equity Through Education*, edited by Susan S. Klein, 338–359. Baltimore, MD: Johns Hopkins University Press.

Fetterley, Judith. 1978. *The Resisting Reader*. Bloomington: Indiana University Press.

Finn, Jeremy D. 1980. Sex differences in educational outcomes: A cross-national study. *Sex Roles* 6(1): 9–26.

Flanagan, Owen, and Kathryn Jackson. 1987. Justice, care, and gender: The Kohlberg-Gilligan debate revisited. *Ethics* 97(3): 622–637.

Flax, Jane. 1983. "Political Philosophy and the Patriarchal Unconscious: A Psychoanalytic Perspective on Epistemology and Metaphysics." In *Discovering Reality: Feminist Perspectives on Epistemology, Metaphysics, Methodology, and Philosophy of Science*, edited by Sandra S. Harding and Merrill B. Hintikka, 245–281. Dordrecht, The Netherlands: Reidel.

Fraser, Nancy. 1987. "What's Critical About Critical Theory? The Case of Habermas and Gender." In *Feminism as Critique*, edited by Seyla Benhabib and Drucilla Cornell, 31–55. Minneapolis: University of Minnesota Press.

French, Marilyn. 1981. *Shakespeare's Division of Experience*. New York: Summit.

Frey, Olivia. 1987. "Equity and Peace in the New Writing Class." In *Teaching Writing: Pedagogy, Gender, and Equity*, edited by Cynthia L. Caywood and Gillian R. Overing, 93–106. Albany: State University of New York Press.

Friedan, Betty. 1963. *The Feminine Mystique*. New York: Norton.

Geadelmann, Patricia L. 1985. "Sex Equity in Physical Education and Athletics." In *Handbook for Achieving Sex Equity Through Education*, edited by Susan S. Klein, 319–337. Baltimore, MD: Johns Hopkins University Press.

Gilbert, Sandra, and Susan Gubar. 1979. *The Madwoman in the Attic: The Woman Writer and the Nineteenth-Century Literary Imagination*. New Haven, CT: Yale University Press.

Gilligan, Carol. 1982. *In a Different Voice*. Cambridge, MA: Harvard University Press.

Gilmartin, Kevin J., D. H. McLaughlin, L. L. Wise, and R. J. Rossi. 1976. *The Development of Scientific Careers: The High School Years*. Palo Alto, CA: American Institutes for Research.

Gilroy, Marcia K. 1989. *The Effects of Single-sex Secondary Schooling: Student Achievement, Behavior, and Attitudes*. Ann Arbor: University of Michigan Press.

Giroux, Henry H. 1983. *Theory and Resistance in Education: A Pedagogy for the Opposition*. South Hadley, MA: Bergin & Garvey.

Glueck, Grace. 1980. Women artists '80. *Art News* 79(8): 58–63.

Goulston, Wendy. 1987. "Women Writing." In *Teaching and Writing: Pedagogy, Gender, and Equity*, edited by Cynthia L. Caywood and Gillian R. Overing, 19–30. Albany: State University of New York Press.

Grambs, Jean D. 1957. "The Role of the Teachers." In *The Teacher's Role in American Society. Fourteenth Yearbook of the John Dewey Society*, edited by L. Stiles. New York: John Dewey Society.

Grandjean, Burke D., and Helen H. Bernal. 1979. Sex and centralization in a semi-profession. *Sociology of Work and Occupations* 6(1): 84–102.

Greenberg, Selma. 1978. *Right from the Start: A Guide to Nonsexist Child Rearing*. Boston: Houghton Mifflin.

Greenberg, Selma. 1985. "Educational Equity in Early Education Environments." In *Handbook for Achieving Sex Equity Through Education*, edited by Susan S. Klein, 457–469. Baltimore, MD: Johns Hopkins University Press.

Greene, Maxine. 1975. "Curriculum and Consciousness." In *Curriculum Theorizing: The Reconceptualists*, edited by William F. Pinar, 299–317. Berkeley, CA: McCutchan.

Greene, Maxine. 1978. *Landscapes of Learning*. New York: Teachers College Press.

Greene, Maxine. 1986. "Philosophy and Teaching." In *Handbook for Research on Teaching*, edited by Merlin C. Wittrock, 479–501. New York: Macmillan.

Grimshaw, Jean. 1986. *Philosophy and Feminist Thinking*. Minneapolis: University of Minnesota Press.

Grimshaw, Patricia. 1983. "Christian woman, pious wife, faithful mother, devoted missionary": Conflicts in roles of American missionary women in nineteenth-century Hawaii. *Feminist Studies* 9(3): 489–522.

Grumet, Madeleine. 1986. The Paideia proposal: A thankless child replies. *Curriculum Inquiry* 16(3): 335–344.

Grumet, Madeleine. 1987a. The politics of personal knowledge. *Curriculum Inquiry* 17(3): 319–329.

Grumet, Madeleine. 1987b. Review of *Feminist scholarship: Kindling in the Groves of Academe* by DuBois et al. *Teachers College Record* 88(3): 474–478.

Grumet, Madeleine. 1987c. Women and teaching: Homeless at home. *Teacher Education Quarterly* 14(2): 39–46.

Grumet, Madeleine R. 1988. *Bitter Milk*. Amherst: University of Massachusetts Press.

Grundmann, Herbert. 1961. *Religiose Bewegungen im Mittelalter*. Darmstadt, Germany: Wissenschaftliche Buchgesellschaft.

Hahn, Carole L. 1980, Winter. Social studies with equality and justice for all: Toward the elimination of sexism. *Journal of Research and Development in Education* 13: 103–112.

Hahn, Carole L., and Jane Bernard-Powers. 1985. "Sex Equity in Social Studies." In *Handbook for Achieving Sex Equity Through Education*, edited by Susan F. Klein, 280–297. Baltimore, MD: Johns Hopkins University Press.

Hall, G. Stanley. 1904. *Adolescence: Its Psychology and Its Relations to Physiology, Anthropology, Sociology, Sex, Crime, Religion, and Education*, 2 vols. New York: D. Appleton.

Hall, O. 1966. "The Social Structure of the Teaching Profession." In *Struggle for Power in Education*, edited by Frank W. Lutz and Joseph S. Azzarelli, 35–48. New York: Center for Applied Research in Education.

Harding, Sandra S. 1986. *The Science Question in Feminism*. Ithaca, NY: Cornell University Press.

Harding, Sandra, and Merrill Hintikka, eds. 1983. *Discovering Reality: Feminist Perspectives on Epistemology, Metaphysics, Methodology, and Philosophy of Science*. Dordrecht, The Netherlands: Reidel.

Harris, A. S. 1972. The second sex in academe, fine art division. *Art in America* 60(3): 18–19.

Hartsock, Nancy. 1983. "The Feminist Standpoint: Developing the Ground for a Specifically Feminist Historical Materialism." In *Discovering Reality: Feminist Perspectives on Epistemology, Metaphysics, Methodology, and Philosophy of Science*, edited by Sandra S. Harding and Merrill B. Hintikka, 283–310. Dordrecht, The Netherlands: Reidel.

Heckert, B. L., W. K. Le Bold, B. Butler, M. Knigga, C. D. Smith, M. Blalock, and E. Hoover. 1978. "A Model Research Program to Provide Equity for Women Entering Engineering." Paper presented at the annual meeting, American Educational Research Association, Toronto.

Held, Virginia. 1987. "Feminism and Moral Theory." In *Women and Moral Theory*, edited by Eva Feder Kittay and Diana T. Meyers, 111–128. Totowa, NJ: Rowman & Littlefield.

Hochschild, Arlie. 1973. "A Review of Sex Role Research." In *Changing Women in a Changing Society*, edited by Joan Huber, 249–267. Chicago: University of Chicago Press.

Hogle, Jerrold E. 1988. "Teaching the Politics of Gender in Literature: Two Proposals for Reform, with a Reading of *Hamlet*." In *Changing Our Minds*, edited by Susan Hardy Aiken, Karen Anderson, Myra Dinnerstein, J. N. Lensink, and Patricia MacCorquodale, 98–133. Albany: State University of New York Press.

Holmes Group. 1986. *Tomorrow's Teachers*. East Lansing, MI: Holmes Group.

Homans, Margaret. 1986. *Bearing the Word: Language and Female Experience in Nineteenth-century Women's Writing*. Chicago: University of Chicago Press.

Horner, Matina. 1972. Toward an understanding of achievement-related conflicts in women. *Journal of Social Issues* 28(2): 157–175.

Howe, Florence. 1984. *Myths of Coeducation*. Bloomington: Indiana University Press.

Hyde, Janet Shibley. 1981, August. How large are cognitive gender differences? A meta-analysis using omega squared. *American Psychologist* 36: 892–901.

Hyde, Janet Shibley, and Marcia C. Linn, eds. 1986. *The Psychology of Gender: Advances through Meta-analysis*. Baltimore, MD: Johns Hopkins University Press.

Jiminez, Emmanuel, and Marlaine E. Lockheed 1988. "The Relative Effectiveness of Single-sex and Coeducational Schools in Thailand." Working paper for Policy, Planning and Research. Washington, DC: World Bank.

Journal of Legal Education. 1988. Special issues. 38(1 and 2).

Jung, Carl G. 1959. *Collected works*. Bollingen Series. Princeton, NJ: Princeton University Press.

Jung, Carl G. 1973. *Answer to Job*, translated by R. F. C. Hull. Bollingen Series. Princeton, NJ: Princeton University Press.

Kant, Immanuel. 1983 (1764). "Of the Distinction Between the Beautiful and the Sublime in the Interrelations of the Two Sexes." In *Philosophy of Woman*, edited by Mary Briody Mahowald, 193–203. Indianapolis, IN: Hackett.

Keller, Catherine. 1986. *From a Broken Web*. Boston: Beacon Press.

Keller, Evelyn Fox. 1983. *A Feeling for the Organism: The Life and Work of Barbara McClintock*. New York: W. H. Freeman.

Keller, Evelyn Fox. 1985. *Reflections on Gender and Science*. New Haven, CT: Yale University Press.

Kinnear, Mary. 1982. *Daughters of Time: Women in the Western Tradition*. Ann Arbor: University of Michigan Press.

Klaits, Joseph. 1985. *Servants of Satan*. Bloomington: Indiana University Press.

Klein, Susan S., ed. 1985. *Handbook for Achieving Sex Equity Through Education*. Baltimore, MD: Johns Hopkins University Press.

Kohlberg, Lawrence. 1981. *The Philosophy of Moral Development*. San Francisco, CA: Harper & Row.

Koltnow, J. 1979. *Expanding Your Horizons: Conferences for Young Women Interested in New Career Options*. Washington, DC: U.S. Department of Education.

Kreinberg, Nancy. 1981. 1000 teachers later: Women, mathematics, and the components of change. *Public Affairs Report* 22(4): 1–7.

Kristeva, Julia. 1980. *Desire in Language: A Semiotic Approach to Literature and Art*, translated by Thomas Gara, Alice Jardine, and Leon S. Roudiez. New York: Columbia University Press.

Kundsin, Ruth B., ed. 1974. *Women and Success: The Anatomy of Achievement*. New York: Morrow.

Lacan, Jacques. 1977. *Ecrits*, translated by Alan Sheridan. New York: Norton.

Langland, Elizabeth, and Walter Gove, eds. 1981. *A Feminist Perspective in the Academy*. Chicago: University of Chicago Press.

Lauter, Estella, and Carol Schrier Rupprecht, eds. 1985. *Feminist Archetypal Theory*. Knoxville: University of Tennessee Press.

Lauter, Paul. 1983. Race and gender in the shaping of the American literary canon: A case study of the twenties. *Feminist Studies* 9(3): 435–464.

Lee, Valerie E., and Anthony S. Bryk. 1986. Effects of single-sex secondary schools on student achievement and attitude. *Journal of Educational Psychology* 78(5): 381–395.

Lee, Valerie E., and Helen M. Marks. 1988. *Sustained Effects of the Single-sex Secondary School Experience on Attitudes, Behavior, and Values in College*. Ann Arbor: Center for the Study of Higher and Postsecondary Education, University of Michigan.

Lerner, Gerda, ed. 1972. *Black Women in White America: A Documentary History*. New York: Random House.

Levine, Daniel. 1964. Coeducation—A contributing factor in miseducation of the disadvantaged. *Phi Delta Kappan* 46(3): 126–128.

Linn, Marcia C., and Anne C. Petersen. 1985, December. Emergence and characterization of sex differences in spatial ability: A meta-analysis. *Child Development* 56: 1479–1498.

Lortie, [illegible] 1975. [illegible] Chicago: [illegible] Press.

Maccoby, Eleanor E., and Carolyn N. Jacklin. 1974. *The Psychology of Sex Differences*. Stanford, CA: Stanford University Press.

MacDonald, C. T. 1980. "An Experiment in Mathematics Education at the College Level." In *Women and the Mathematical Mys-*

tique, edited by Lynn H. Fox, Linda Brody, and Dianne Tobin, 115–137. Baltimore, MD: Johns Hopkins University Press.

MacIntyre, Alasdair. 1981. *After Virtue*. Notre Dame, IN: University of Notre Dame Press.

McLaughlin, Eleanor Commo. 1974. "Equality of Souls, Inequality of Sexes: Women in Medieval Theology." In *Religion and Sexism*, edited by Rosemary Radford Ruether, 213–266. New York: Simon & Schuster.

Maguire, Daniel C. 1978. *The Moral Choice*. Garden City, NY: Doubleday.

Mahowald, Mary Briody, ed. 1983. *Philosophy of Woman*. Indianapolis, IN: Hackett.

Marrett, Cora B. 1972, winter. Centralization in female organizations: Reassessing the evidence. *Social Problems* 19: 348–357.

Martin, Jane Roland. 1981, August. Sophie and Émile: A case study of sex bias in the history of educational thought. *Harvard Educational Review* 51: 357–372.

Martin, Jane Roland. 1982a. Excluding women from the educational realm. *Harvard Educational Review* 52(2): 133–148.

Martin, Jane Roland. 1982b. Two dogmas of curriculum. *Synthese* 51: 5–20.

Martin, Jane Roland. 1984. Bringing women into educational thought. *Educational Theory* 34(4): 341–354.

Martin, Jane Roland. 1985. *Reclaiming a Conversation*. New Haven, CT: Yale University Press.

Martin, Jane Roland. 1987. Transforming moral education. *Journal of Moral Education* 16(3): 204–213.

Mason, Ward S., R. J. Dressel, and Robert K. Bain. 1959, fall. Sex roles and the career orientations of beginning teachers. *Harvard Educational Review* 29: 70–383.

Medrich, Elliott A., J. Roisen, V. Rubin, and S. Buckley. 1982. *The Serious Business of Growing Up: A Study of Children's Lives Outside of School*. Berkeley and Los Angeles: University of California Press.

Menkel-Meadow, Carrie J. 1988. Feminist legal theory, critical legal studies, and legal education or "The fem-crits go to law school." *Journal of Legal Education* 38(142): 61–86.

Miller, Jean Baker. 1976. *Toward a New Psychology of Women*. Boston: Beacon Press.

Miller, Nancy. 1980. *The Heroine's Text: Readings in the French and English Novel, 1772–1782*. New York: Columbia University Press.

Millett, Kate. 1970. *Sexual Politics*. Garden City, NY: Doubleday.

Mobius, Paul. 1908. *Ueber den Physiologischen Schwachsinn des Weibes*. Halle, Germany: Carl Marholm.

Moi, Toril, 1987. *French Feminist Thought: A Reader*. Oxford: Basil Blackwell.

National Council of Teachers of English. 1976. *Responses to Sexism: Class Practices in Teaching English*. Urbana, IL: NCTE.

Nemser, Cindy. 1973, July. Art criticism and women artists. *Journal of Aesthetic Education* 7: 73–83.

Nicholson, Linda. 1987. "Feminism and Marx: Integrating Kinship with the Economic." In *Feminism as Critique*, edited by Seyla Benhabib and Drucilla Cornell, 16–30. Minneapolis: University of Minnesota Press.

Nochlin, L. 1974. How feminism in the arts can implement cultural change. *Art in Society* 2(1): 80–89.

Noddings, Nel. 1984. *Caring: A Feminine Approach to Ethics and Moral Education*. Berkeley and Los Angeles: University of California Press.

Noddings, Nel. 1987. Do we really want to produce good people? *Journal of Moral Education* 16(3): 177–188.

Noddings, Nel. 1988a. An ethic of caring and its implications for instructional arrangements. *American Journal of Education* 96(2): 215–230.

Noddings, Nel. 1988b. "Preparing Teachers to Teach Mathematical Problem Solving." In *The Teaching and Assessing of Mathematical Problem Solving*, vol. 3, edited by Randall I. Charles and Edward A. Silver, 244–258. Reston, VA: National Council of Teachers of Mathematics and Erlbaum.

Noddings, Nel. 1989. *Women and Evil*. Berkeley: University of California Press.

Noddings, Nel. 1990a. "Ethics from the Standpoint of Women." In *Theoretical Perspectives on Sexual Difference*, edited by Deborah L. Rhode, 160–173. New Haven, CT: Yale University Press.

Noddings, Nel. 1990b. "Feminist Critiques in the Professions." In *Annual Review of Research*, edited by Courtney B. Cazden, 393–424. Washington, D.C.: American Educational Research Association.

Noddings, Nel. In press. "Shaping an Acceptable Child." In *Learning for a Lifetime: Moral Education in Perspective and Practice*, edited by Andrew Garrod. New York: Praeger.

O'Brien, Mary M. 1981. *The Politics of Reproduction*. Boston: Routledge & Kegan Paul.

Okin, Susan Moller. 1979. *Women in Western Political Thought*. Princeton, NJ: Princeton University Press.

Okin, Susan Moller. 1989. Reason and feeling in thinking about justice. *Ethics* 99(2): 229–249.

Okin, Susan Moller. 1990. "Thinking Like a Woman." In *Theoretical Perspectives on Sexual Difference*, edited by Deborah L. Rhode. New Haven, CT: Yale University Press.

Olsen, Tillie. 1978. *Silences*. New York: Delacorte Press/Seymour Lawrence.

Pagano, Jo Anne. 1988. "The Claim of Philia." In *Curriculum Theory Discourses*, edited by William F. Pinar, 414–420. Scottsdale, AZ: Gorsuch Skarisbrick.

Paley, Vivian. 1973, August. Is the doll corner a sexist institution? *School Review* 81: 569–576.

Parvey, Constance F. 1974. "The Theology and Leadership of Women in the New Testament." In *Religion and Sexism*, edited by Rosemary Radford Ruether, 117–149. New York: Simon & Schuster.

Perl, Teri. 1978. *Math Equals: Biographies of Women Mathematicians and Related Activities*. Menlo Park, CA: Addison-Wesley.

Petersen, Karen, and J. J. Wilson. 1976. *Women Artists: Recognition and Reappraisal from the Early Middle Ages to the 20th Century*. New York: Harper.

Phillips, John Anthony. 1984. *Eve: The History of an Idea*. San Francisco, CA: Harper & Row.

Pierce, Christine. 1973. Equality: Republic V. *Monist* 57(1): 1–11.

Pinar, William F., ed. 1975. *Curriculum Theorizing: The Reconceptualists*. Berkeley, CA: McCutchan.

Pinar, William F., ed. 1988. *Curriculum Theory Discourses*. Scottsdale, AZ: Gorsuch Skarisbrick.

Polanyi, Karl. 1957. *The Great Transformation*. Boston: Beacon Press.

Prusak, Bernard P. 1974. "Woman: Seductive Siren and Source of Sin?" In *Religion and Sexism*, edited by Rosemary Radford Ruether, 89–116. New York: Simon & Schuster.

Reverby, Susan. 1987. *Ordered to Care*. Cambridge: Cambridge University Press.

Rich, Adrienne. 1979. *On Lies, Secrets, and Silence*. New York: Norton.

Rose, Hilary. 1983. Hand, brain, and heart: A feminist epistemology for the natural sciences. *Signs* 9(1): 73–90.

Rossi, Alice S. 1964, Spring. Equality between the sexes: An immodest proposal. *Daedalus* 93: 607–652.

Rossiter, Margaret W. 1982. *Women Scientists in America: Struggles and Strategies to 1940*. Baltimore, MD, and London: Johns Hopkins University Press.

Ruddick, Sara. 1980. Maternal thinking. *Feminist Studies* 6(2): 342–367.

Ruddick, Sara. 1989. *Maternal Thinking: Towards a Politics of Peace*. Boston: Beacon Press.

Ruether, Rosemary Radford. 1974. "Misogynism and Virginal Feminism in the Fathers of the Church." In *Religion and Sexism*, edited by Rosemary Radford Ruether, 150–183. New York: Simon & Schuster.

Sahling, Marshall. 1976. *Culture and Practical Reason*. Chicago: University of Chicago Press.

Sandell, Renee, Georgia C. Collins, and Ann Sherman. 1985. "Sex Equity in Visual Arts Education." In *Handbook for Achieving Sex Equity Through Education*, edited by Susan S. Klein, 298–318. Baltimore, MD: Johns Hopkins University Press.

Sassen, Georgia, 1980, fall. Success anxiety in women: A constructivist interpretation of its sources and its significance. *Harvard Educational Review* 50: 13–25.

Scardamalia, Marlene, and Carl Bereiter. 1986. "Research on Written Composition." In *Handbook of Research on Teaching*, edited by Merlin C. Wittrock, 778–803. New York: Macmillan.

Scheman, Naomi. 1989. Commentary on Sandra Harding's "The method question." *Newsletter on Feminism and Philosophy* 88(3): 40–44. Newark, DE: American Philosophical Association.

Scott, Kathryn P., Carol Anne Dwyer, and Barbara Lieb-Brilhart. 1985. "Sex Equity in Reading and Communication Skills." In *Handbook for Achieving Sex Equity Through Education*, edited by Susan S. Klein, 269–279. Baltimore, MD: Johns Hopkins University Press.

Scott, Kathryn P., and Candace Garrett Schau. 1985. "Sex Equity and Sex Bias in Instructional Materials." In *Handbook for Achieving Sex Equity through Education*, edited by Susan S. Klein, 218–232. Baltimore, MD: Johns Hopkins University Press.

Sells, Lucy. 1975. "Sex, Ethnic, and Field Differences in Doctoral Outcomes." Ph.D. dissertation, University of California, Berkeley.

Serbin, L., J. Connor, and I. Lipman. 1977. Sex stereotyping and non-stereotyped introduction of new toys in the preschool classroom: An observational study of teacher behavior and its effects. *Psychology of Women Quarterly* 4(2): 261–265.

Sexton, Patricia Cayo. 1969. *The Feminized Male: Classrooms, White Collars, and the Decline of Manliness*. New York: Random House.

Shaver, James P., Suzanne Helburn, and O. L. Davis, Jr. 1979. The status of social studies education: Impressions from three NSF studies. *Social Education* 43(2): 150–153.

Shaw, C. M., and B. J. Bulkin. 1981. "Reentry Programs: Their Design and Impact." Manuscript, University of Dayton, Dayton, OH.

Showalter, Elaine, ed. 1974. *Women's Liberation and Literature*. New York: Harcourt Brace Jovanovich.

Sichel, Betty A. 1988. *Moral Education: Character, Community, and Ideals*. Philadelphia, PA: Temple University Press.

Simpson, Richard L., and Ida Harper Simpson. 1969. "Women and Bureaucracy in the Semi-Professions." In *The Semi-professions and Their Organization*, edited by Amitai Etzioni, 196–265. New York: Free Press.

Smith, Dorothy E. 1974. Women's perspective as a radical critique of sociology. *Sociological Inquiry* 44(1): 7–13.

Smith, Dorothy E. 1987. *The Everyday World as Problematic: A Feminist Sociology*. Boston: Northeastern University Press.

Smith, Dorothy E. 1989. A comment on Sandra Harding's "The Method Question." *Newsletter on Feminism and Philosophy* 88(3): 44–46. Newark, DE: American Philosophical Association.

Sommers, Tish, and Laurie Shields. 1987. *Women Take Care*. Gainesville, FL: Triad.

Spender, Dale. 1980. *Man Made Language*. London: Routledge & Kegan Paul.

Spretnak, Charlene, ed. 1982. *The Politics of Women's Spirituality*. Garden City, NY: Anchor Books.

Stage, Elizabeth K., Nancy Kreinberg, Jacquelynne Eccles, and Joanne Rossi Becker. 1985. "Increasing the Participation and Achievement of Girls and Women in Mathematics, Science, and Engineering." In *Handbook for Achieving Sex Equity through Education*, edited by Susan S. Klein, 237–268. Baltimore, MD: Johns Hopkins University Press.

Steady, Filomina Chioma, 1981. *The Black Woman Cross Culturally*. Cambridge, MA: Schenkman.

Stimpson, Catherine. 1980. The new scholarship about women: The state of the art. *Annals of Scholarship* 1(2): 2–14.

Tetreault, Mary Kay Thompson. 1986a. Integrating women's history: The case of United States history high school textbooks. *The History Teacher* 19(2): 211–262.

Tetreault, Mary Kay Thompson. 1986b, autumn. The journey from male-defined to gender-balanced education. *Theory into Practice* 25: 227–234.

Thomas, M. Carey. 1908. Present tendencies in women's college and university education. *Publications of the Association of Collegiate Alumnae* 3(17): 45–47, 49–51, 54–58.

Thompson, Patricia J. 1985. "Clio's Stepdaughters: Reclaiming Our Heritage." Paper presented at a symposium on Home Economics: The Meeting Place of Disciplines. Annual meeting, American Home Economics Association, Philadelphia, PA.

Thompson, Patricia J. 1986a, autumn. Beyond gender: Equity issues in home economics education. *Theory into Practice* 25: 276–283.

Thompson, Patricia J. 1986b. "Hestian Hermeneutics." In *The Conversation and Company of Educated Women*, edited by Linda Peterat, 79–87. Urbana Champaign: University of Illinois.

Thompson, Patricia J. 1986c. Home economics and the Hestian mode. *Illinois Teacher of Home Economics* 29(3): 87–91.

Thompson, Spencer K. 1975, June. Gender labels and early sex-role development. *Child Development* 46: 339–347.

Thorne, Barrie, Cheris Kramarae, and Nancy Henley, eds. 1983. *Language, Gender and Society*. Rowley, MA: Newbury House.

Tobias, Sheila. 1978. *Overcoming Math Anxiety*. New York: Norton.

Tronto, Joan. 1987. Beyond gender difference to a theory of care. *Signs* 12(4): 644–663.

Tyack, David, and Elizabeth Hansot. 1988. Silence and policy talk: Historical puzzles about gender and education. *Educational Researcher* 17(3): 33–41.

Tyack, David, and Elizabeth Hansot. 1990. *Learning Together: A History of Gender in American Public Schools*. New Haven, CT: Yale University Press and Russell Sage Foundation.

Vitz, Paul C. 1986, summer. Religion and traditional values in public school textbooks. *The Public Interest* 84: 79–90.

[illegible]. 1976. *Alone of All Her Sex*. New York: Knopf

Watson, Jean. 1979. *Nursing: The Philosophy and Science of Caring*. Boston: Little, Brown.

Watson, Jean. 1985. *Nursing: Human Science and Human Care*. Norwalk, CT: Appleton-Century-Crofts.

Welch, Sharon D. 1985. *Communities of Resistance and Solidarity*. Maryknoll, NY: Orbis Books.

Wells, J. 1983. *Statement of the National Coalition for Women and Girls in Education*. Washington, DC: National Coalition for Women and Girls in Education.

Whitbeck, Caroline. 1983. "A Different Reality: Feminist Ontology." In *Beyond Domination*, edited by Carol Gould, 64–88. Totowa, NJ: Rowman & Allenheld.

Willard, Emma. 1918 (1819). *A Plan for Improving Female Education*. Middlebury, VT: Middlebury College.

Williams, Bernard. 1985. *Ethics and the Limits of Philosophy*. Cambridge, MA: Harvard University Press.

Wilson, J. S., and Karen Petersen. 1976. *Women Artists* (slide program and notes). New York: Harper & Row.

Witherell, Carol, and Nel Noddings, eds. 1991. *Stories Lives Tell: Narrative and Dialogue in Education*. New York: Teachers College Press.

Wittrock, Merlin C., ed. 1986. *Handbook of Research on Teaching*, 3rd ed. New York: Macmillan.

Wollstonecraft, Mary. 1975 (1792). *A Vindication of the Rights of Woman*, edited by Carol H. Poston. New York: Norton.

Women's Studies Quarterly. 1989. Special issue 17(1–2).

Young, Iris Marion. 1981, fall. Toward a critical theory of justice. *Social Theory and Practice* 7: 279–302.

Young, Iris Marion. 1987. "Impartiality and the Civic Public." In *Feminism as Critique*, edited by Seyla Benhabib and Drucilla Cornell, 56–76. Minneapolis: University of Minnesota Press.

Part

4

TOPICS AND ISSUES WITHIN CURRICULAR CATEGORIES

25

CURRICULUM RESEARCH IN WRITING AND READING

Judith A. Langer and Richard L. Allington

UNIVERSITY AT ALBANY
STATE UNIVERSITY OF NEW YORK

A web of related issues has dominated both the research and the pedagogical literature on reading and writing curriculum throughout the 20th century. These issues focus on a range of topics, among them the role of reading and writing in the total curriculum (e.g., as separate from or integral to content learning), what to include as components of the reading and writing curriculum (e.g., grammar, structure, style, and interpretation), the unit of meaning on which the curriculum should focus (e.g., sounds, sentences, words, and whole textual meanings), the source of curriculum goals (e.g., student-centered or rule-based), and the underlying purpose of the curriculum itself (e.g., mastery of predetermined skills, demonstration of societally functional abilities, and acquisition of "high" literacy).

Although each of these topics has been of concern during the century, it is too simplistic to assume that either the particular issues or their theoretical sources have remained the same; few issues that were voiced in the past have entirely disappeared from current scholarly concerns. However, new concerns about old issues continue to be voiced. In some cases, the language used to refer to related issues has remained the same but has taken on new or broader meanings while in others the language has changed but the underlying concern remains the same. Echoes of today's concerns abound in the theoretical and pedagogical past, but because theoretical as well as pragmatic knowledge has grown, substantive differences in the underlying [illegible] and recommendations for action are evident.

For example, in both reading and writing, the desirability of producing complete messages for meaningful purposes and the related issue of reading and writing across the curriculum have been voiced at least through this century and remain current concerns today. Similarly, a focus on the mechanics of writing and reading apart from the larger meaning of a text has been negatively reviewed throughout the century. In some sense, these concerns have not changed. However, a theoretical focus on interrelationships among context, purpose, and cognition that has permeated the literacy literature since the mid-1970s has added new dimensions of concern—leading to new understandings of ways in which purposeful and complete literacy activities across the curriculum support the development of higher levels of literacy.

Along with shifting theoretical understanding, curriculum concerns about particular age groups have also shifted. Although concerns about relationships among literacy curricula at the elementary, secondary, and college levels have been voiced across the century, theory and research in particular eras have focused on particular grade levels. For example, at the turn of the 19th century, concerns focused almost exclusively on writing at the college level and on reading at the primary level. However, across time, the focus on reading and writing as functionally enabling activities for all students contributed to new concerns with their role in the curriculum across the grades. Thus although reading and writing research have been guided by some similar concerns, they have followed quite different trajectories in both research and practice.

A review of curriculum research in writing and reading indicates that although there have been important developments in theory and pedagogy, through the 1980s there was relatively little essential change in the received curriculum—

in the curriculum the students experience on a day-to-day basis in their classrooms. To tease apart what little has changed and what has not and why, to reflect on what we know and what to study, and to set a research agenda for literacy research, it is necessary to consider research in a number of areas: theoretical concerns that inform pedagogy, major curriculum recommendations and curriculum materials (their foci and shifts across time), and curriculum-in-action (status studies of what schools are doing). This chapter will provide such a review, using historical reflection to identify major themes and identify needed research directions.

THE ORIGINS OF CURRICULUM RESEARCH

Writing Through the 1930s

During the 19th century, conceptualizations of a curriculum for writing grew from existing course work in rhetoric. In the latter half of that century and the early part of the 20th century, these conceptions came to be challenged by functional and progressive ideas.

Theoretical Bases for Curriculum Research in Writing. In the 19th century, curriculum concerns in writing focused almost entirely on the college level, with minimal attention to its high school antecedents and almost no concern with elementary education. Three distinct movements informed conceptualizations of the college and, later, the high school writing curriculum and helped shape the notions of what should be taught in high school, as opposed to college: (1) classical rhetoric based on Aristotle, Cicero, and Quintilian; (2) belles-lettres rhetoric with a focus on literature, as evident in the work of Blair and Campbell; and (3) experience-based writing as training in the democratic process, based on Dewey (see Berlin 1984 and 1987 for a substantive review of this era).

Classical rhetoric, which emphasized the logical development of a work through application of rhetorical principles, dominated coursework in American colleges during the 18th century and was modeled after the curriculum already taught in English universities. The classical rhetoricians, beginning with Aristotle, were concerned with both the form and the process of composition (though their concern was with oratory rather than writing). The arts of classical rhetoric included invention, arrangement, style, memory, and delivery, and the first three of these became important elements in later theories of written composition. Invention, for example, was based on a set of heuristic procedures—the *topoi*, or topics—that could be used to explore exhaustively and deductively the possible grounds for argument. They include such procedures as definition, comparison and contrast, tracing of causal relationships, moving from parts to the whole, and formulating alternative courses of action. Arrangement was concerned with the order of discourse, an awareness of the proper parts of a formal presentation and the order in which they should occur. Such concerns continue to the present day in such prescriptions as beginning each paragraph with a topic sentence and in the formulaic structure of the five-paragraph theme. The third art, style, was concerned with the presentation of ideas, the clothing of ideas in words. Though clearly of subordinate concern to the classical rhetoricians, the elements of style were exhaustively analyzed. They included not simply correctness but also diction and word choice, varieties of sentence structure, and the various tropes and figures of speech that continue to flourish in the analysis of style in literature as well as in composition instruction.

Aristotelian rhetoric was elitist, oriented toward the educated few. In contrast, the merger of rhetoric and belles lettres was based on respect for individual consciousness and the development of "good taste," bringing appreciation of the art of writing into the commonplace tradition. In this tradition, excerpts from a wide variety of authors were studied and analyzed in terms of their adherence to rhetorical principles, all in the service of students' own writing abilities. French and English authors were included, as well as Latin and Greek. The belles-lettres view of rhetoric developed in Scotland in the 18th century and became the dominant paradigm for writing in America by the early 1800s.

One of the first of the Scottish rhetorics to be widely influential, Campbell's (1963 [1776]) *Philosophy of Rhetoric* was written against a background of faculty psychology; it described four functional modes of discourse that were associated with different mental faculties: to enlighten understanding, to please the imagination, to move the passions, and to influence the will. Like classical rhetoric, it also focused on diction, grammar, and language use. Campbell's four categories were the precursors of the division of discourse into four forms (narration, description, exposition, and argument), a codification that was completed by Bain in the 19th century.

Blair's (1965 [1783]) *Lectures on Rhetoric and Belles Lettres* was eventually to become the most widely used of the Scottish rhetorics. Its 130th edition was published in 1911. Blair was particularly notable for his focus on literary models drawn from a wide variety of authors, both classic and contemporary, though his approach to rhetorical analysis was somewhat mechanistic and prescriptive. Whately's (1963 [1826]) *Elements of Rhetoric*, another text that became popular in America, represented a melding of Aristotelian logic with Campbell's and Blair's attention to emotional appeal. In these rhetorics, students were expected to study the ways in which people write, using established works as models. However, they were not expected to create pieces of their own.

Toward the end of the 19th century, rhetoric was divided into three more or less discrete parts: persuasive discourse (primarily Aristotelian) was relegated to speech departments; imaginative discourse, including writing about literature (belles lettres), became the concern of literature departments; and writing courses (when they were offered) focused on practical reason. The college writing curriculum focused on the copying of models, drill, and exercises dealing with the mechanics of language. In fact, the curricula of the 19th century did not require students to write much on their own; the emphasis was on memorization and recitation of material from their textbooks and lectures.

During the second half of the 19th century, the Romantic movement in literature and the arts placed writing (and speaking) at the center of knowing, with the individual discovering reality through experience and interpretation. What is discovered, according to the Romantics, involves a holistic response that is not necessarily grounded only in the rational mode of interpretation; the moral and aesthetic have their place as well. Because the writer must appeal to the audience at all levels of awareness (not only through logic), a dialectic is developed in the act of composing. Emerson, himself a Romantic, drew the implications of this philosophy for the role of discourse in society; he argued that each person in a democracy has both the capacity and purpose to write and speak out, and thus that rhetoric involves a dialectic between writer and audience. During the last decade of the 19th century, Scott, Denny, and Buck applied a similar view of rhetoric to composition instruction at the college level in America. However, Berlin's (1984) historical research finds no indication of Emerson's influence on their work, despite the similarities in their concerns. He notes, instead, that Scott was a colleague of John Dewey at the University of Michigan, and it is likely they influenced each other in the development of an experience-based pedagogy.

In *English Composition as a Mode of Behavior,* Scott (1922) discussed the approach to curriculum he had used in his own textbook writing since the turn of the century. Scott focused on the act of communicating and the role of language in social construction and human consciousness. He emphasized a curriculum grounded in the social experiences of the student, calling for self-expression, since aspects of the student's reality cannot be expressed by teachers or texts (Scott and Denny 1900).

Based on this approach, Carpenter, Baker, and Scott (1903), in their early textbook on the teaching of English, developed a view of curriculum based on the belief that the vernacular is the instrument of communication with others, the instrument by which aesthetic needs are met, and the means by which an individual arrives at intellectual consciousness. Effective written expression is mainly a matter of intellectual skill and knowledge and depends on knowledge of the vocabulary and grammar of the language. This aspect, they believed, could be learned independent of the study of literature.

Carpenter, Baker, and Scott (1903) were among the first writing theorists to address the curriculum for the elementary as well as higher grades. They suggested that writing curriculum in the elementary grades needs to focus primarily on the acquisition and expression of ideas, and only secondarily on the facts and principles of language that underlie successful expression. (In this they are reversing the emphasis of the composition course based on classical rhetoric.) Across the grades, they call for attention to the meaning of the text as a whole and to the process of writing, by which they mean observation, inference, and expression. They also place great emphasis on matching curriculum goals with the child's experiences, knowledge, and interests and also on the teaching of writing in the total school curriculum. Their work promoted student writing of paragraphs (as opposed to merely studying models), and their work on the development of the paragraph continues to influence writing curriculum. In *The Teaching of English in the Elementary and Secondary Schools*, Carpenter, Baker, and Scott delineated a developmental curriculum based on their views; many of the writing reforms of the 1980s have antecedents in their student-centered curriculum suggestions.

Shifts in educational theory after the Civil War, largely in response to the industrial revolution, focused on educating all citizens and encouraged more open inquiry (Berlin 1984). Thus, education was conceptualized in more functional ways, with job preparation in a rapidly growing economy becoming a primary goal. Elective programs were adopted to permit students to specialize in particular areas, and classical studies with their focus on training of the mind were gradually abandoned in favor of a more functional curriculum. Led by Harvard's president Charles W. Eliot, the movement from the ancient to the modern curriculum affected the high schools as well as the colleges.

For most of the 19th century, rhetorical theory *was* the curriculum in writing. By the end of the century, however, as American colleges responded to the emphasis on more practical preparation for business and industry (Berlin 1984), these changes began to affect the teaching of writing. Faced with growing numbers of students in their freshman English A course, Harvard University in 1891 appointed a committee to study the situation and make recommendations (Berlin 1984). The report had a major impact, influencing the writing curriculum at the college and high school levels for at least the next 50 years. The study concluded that college freshmen were not prepared for the demands of college writing and recommended that college entrance requirements in writing be increased and that high schools (primarily preparatory schools) assume responsibility for writing instruction. Further, they highlighted the need for a focus on spelling, grammar, usage, and handwriting. These recommendations were particularly influential because they came at a time when the English course—and hence the first widely established curriculum in writing—was being institutionalized at the high school level. The *Report of the Committee of Ten*, sponsored by the National Education Association (1894) and chaired by Harvard's Eliot, echoed these goals, calling for "language and composition, and formal and systematic grammar" (86) as part of the focus on English curriculum in the elementary and high school levels. Thus by the beginning of the 20th century, writing instruction had taken on a concern with correctness, as well as a legacy of emphasis on the forms of classical rhetoric.

Between 1900 and 1930, there was a related movement

in favor of writing instruction across the grades and subjects being studied (Russell 1989). Foreshadowing the curriculum movement of the 1980s, the *Report of the Committee of Ten* also argued that "every lesson in geography or physics or mathematics may and should become a part of the pupil's training in English. There can be no more appropriate moment for a brief lesson in expression than the moment when the pupil has something which he is trying to express" (National Education Association 1894, 87).

The cooperative movement, as it was called, extended into the college as well (Russell 1989). As early as 1907, for example, the Massachusetts Institute of Technology offered writing instruction in subject classes with the cooperation of English faculty (Connors 1982). Compositions were assigned, conferences conducted, and journals kept. Similarly at Ohio State University, at the turn of the century a professor of English developed discipline-specific writing courses. At the school level, Vose (1925) surveyed schools that reported having writing across the curriculum programs at the beginning of the century and found that by the mid-1920s many of the programs had been abandoned because of increased enrollments, teacher turnover, or "administrative complexities." However, attempts at writing across the curriculum continued and were an important part of a report by the Curriculum Commission of the National Council of Teachers of English. *A Correlated Curriculum* (Weeks et al. 1936) provided suggestions for developing an integrated curriculum at the elementary through college levels.

Shifts in emphasis continued through the 20th century, with elitist, popular, and functional theories competing for dominance in curriculum development. The concerns of the 19th century continued (primarily in colleges), leading to an emphasis on education either for the elite or for the professions. At the same time, a student-centered view, based on John Dewey's notions of experiential education leading to self-development and societal and economic progress, became influential at the high school and, particularly, at the elementary school level. Until this time, attention to traditional rhetoric dominated at the college level. However, Dewey's work had some influence even in the colleges, leading some scholars to see writing as a means of self-expression, a part of individual development. Scott, Denny, and Buck were among the most influential scholars to develop and set new directions for a student-centered pedagogy, with an experiential curriculum as the basis for language and communication as its foundation. Influenced by Dewey's notions of learning as a process, Buck's work (1899, 1901) in particular foreshadowed present-day writing agendas, calling for a focus on the process of writing rather than simple reliance on the product.

Curriculum Recommendations in Writing. The first major attempt to define the teaching of writing and set curriculum standards and goals across the grades was undertaken by the National Education Association in 1894. It appointed what came to be known as the Committee of Ten (consisting of six college presidents, the commissioner of education, and principals or headmasters from three secondary schools), chaired by Harvard's president Charles W. Eliot, to recommend uniformity in school programs and college admissions. Its recommendations had a deep and lasting impact on writing curricula and therefore are a critical reference point for any serious study of change; the recommendations, based on a student-centered approach, set new standards, rejecting many traditional roots.

Despite the then current prevalence of analysis and recitation as the basis of the curriculum, the committee strongly suggested a curriculum based on first-hand writing experiences. Among its recommendations were that primary grade children acquire some fluency of expression by retelling in their own words stories read or told to them and by creating stories of their own. However, children should begin composing by third grade—copying short passages and writing them from memory and dictation as well as writing narratives and descriptions. Written exercises in correct form and usage were to be taught in grades 3 through 6. It was recommended that formal grammar not begin before age 13, and then it should be only incidental and related to the student's own reading and writing experiences because "although the study of formal grammar is valuable training in thought, it has only an indirect bearing on learning to write" (National Education Association 1894, 89). The teaching of rhetoric was suggested at the high school level, to connect the study of writing to the study of literature and also to provide students with principles of effective discourse. Although the committee recommended that elementary rhetoric be taught as part of preparation for college, it cautioned that it be connected to the students' own writing. The report states, "The power to write a language can be obtained only through unremitting practice." This report, in contrast with the Harvard reports, discouraged mechanical drills in grammar and language usage. The two views (rules *then* meaning versus rules *through* meaning) continued to underlie arguments about writing curricula throughout the century.

The effects of the work of the Committee of Ten (National Education Association 1894) can be seen in the New York State syllabi in English (New York State Department of Education 1905, 1910), both of which reflect similar emphases. The sections on composition and rhetoric listed the types of writing to be done, suggesting that writing should represent the students' best efforts on subjects within their grasp and experience. Students were encouraged to make an outline before writing and were to learn to correct their own mistakes. Attention was given to sentence structure; paragraph structure; and the principles of unity, coherence, and diction. Familiarity with the elements and terminology of rhetoric were suggested, to be identified in literature and put to use in compositions.

By 1917, in response to rapidly growing high school enrollments, changes in the mission and structure of the high school led to the need for another major report on the curriculum in English. *The Reorganization of English in the Secondary Schools* (Hosic 1917) was issued by the Joint Committee of Thirty, appointed by the National Education

Association and the National Council of Teachers of English. The first aim of the curriculum in writing in this report was to give students command of the art of communicating in writing. The report took a functional approach, arguing that the student must write to or for somebody, with a consciously conceived purpose to inform, convince, inspire, or entertain. Further, it recommended a separation in the teaching of literature and the teaching of composition, with equal time (a semester or shorter period) devoted to each. The curriculum aims (grades 7–12), first distributed in preliminary form and reiterated in the final report, were consonant with the recommendations of the Committee of Ten but went further in their focus on the social needs and experiential basis for writing. It too recommended development of the sentence and paragraph as well as principles of grammar, but these appeared lower in the lists of aims than attention to experience, interest, and thinking.

The New York State English Syllabus issued in 1917 (New York State Department of Education 1917) reflected many of the emphases of the new report. Continuing a concern with expression and communication, it stated that communication is the primary purpose of all writing and that to be interesting is a close second. Since each purpose presupposes something to convey and someone to receive, the committee recommended that an adequate motive be created for every assignment. The syllabus also suggested that all forms of discourse written in classes conform to the way they exist in real life. The uses of models were recommended as well as the presentation of principles and rules, but it was suggested that students be required to apply the rules.

Comments in the *Twenty-second Yearbook of the National Society for the Study of Education* (Hosic 1923) present a similar view. In discussing issues in evaluation, Hosic (the former secretary/treasurer of the National Council of Teachers of English [NCTE] and chair of the Committee of Thirty) argues that scales for measuring writing should focus on content, not mechanics: "Attention to mechanical and grammatical errors amounts to proofreading." He also attempts to link product with purpose, calling for a focus on two aspects of a composition: its practical aims and its literary or communicative end.

The Montana State syllabus of 1923 (Montana State Department of Public Education 1925) followed the recommendations of the Committee of Thirty (Hosic 1917), as did those of New York State and North Carolina in 1926 (each described in Bernhardt 1963). In general, the focus was on students' experiences with a variety of types of writing (both functional, such as letters, and academic, such as reports). The study of the sentence and paragraph was recommended, and correctness was still a goal. However, originality, creativity, and the development of ideas in writing were high on each list of goals.

By the 1930s, Dewey's emphasis on education as experience led to efforts to structure the curriculum around carefully selected experiences as well as to calls for team-taught courses and interdisciplinary approaches (Applebee 1974) to achieve a more integrated curriculum. Toward this end, the Curriculum Commission of NCTE offered *An Experience Curriculum in English* (Hatfield 1935). The report proclaimed that the ideal curriculum consists of well-selected experiences and went on to present a variety of "experience strands" for each area of the curriculum, kindergarten through grade 12. In the elementary school, writing objectives were functional, emphasizing such tasks as writing letters, filling out forms, making signs, and the like. In the high school, a fifth of the space also dealt with letters, moving on to news stories, reports, and (for senior high school only) opinions. The opinions section stressed familiar rhetorical techniques, such as logical organization, use of examples, and vivid verbs and specific adjectives. Creative expression, done primarily for its own sake, was treated separately from written communication. It reflected the widespread interest in creativity spurred by Mearns's *Creative Youth* and *Creative Power* (Hook 1979). Believing that formal grammar was useful only as an elective for high school seniors, the commission also devoted attention to the teaching of grammar and usage in context.

Thus, the Committee of Ten initiated a wave of curriculum recommendations that moved composition from literary and rhetorical analysis to functional use. It also legitimized a K–12 writing curriculum in its own right, with sequenced instruction to support students' growing ability to express themselves in writing, instead of merely as preparation to meet college requirements.

Curriculum Materials in Writing. Through the late 1800s, college texts were the primary tool for the teaching of rhetoric (Berlin 1984). They were written as treatises on the particular type of rhetoric the author favored, and students were expected to memorize and recite the principles presented in the texts. Grammar and usage exercises appeared in rhetoric textbooks, and separate publication of college grammar handbooks began during the latter part of the 19th century. Sentence diagraming, borrowed from the study of classical languages (Kelly 1969), became popular at that time, appearing, for example, in Reed and Kellogg's (1878) *Higher Lessons in English*. Although the Committee of Ten (National Education Association 1894) recommended that the teaching of grammar be relegated to the lower grade "grammar" schools, it remained a focus in college texts. Student papers were judged by standards of correctness, and correction symbols were developed to facilitate error correction (Berlin 1984).

The inclusion of grammar exercises became so prevalent in writing texts that when Scott, Denny, and Buck (leading proponents of a more progressive, experience-centered approach) jointly authored college textbooks, their publishers insisted that emphasis be given to diction, sentence structure, style, paragraphs, and forms of discourse—all traditional components of the curriculum of the era (Berlin 1984).

Lyman (1932) summarizes several studies of school textbooks conducted in the late 1920s and early 1930s. In general, his review points to an increase in attention to grammar, with relatively little room for development of the students' ideas. Marye's 1928 study (see Lyman 1932) of composition teachers' ratings of six currently used textbooks, for example, indicated that the major component they valued was attention to mechanics and grammar. In a comparison of seventh-grade texts in 1929, Dawson (see Lyman 1932) found that vocabulary, attention to audience, and mechanics were mentioned most frequently and treated most intensively. In the same study, a comparison of the amount of space devoted to different topics in textbooks published between 1920 and 1924 with that of the same topics in books published between 1925 and 1928 indicated an increase in attention to grammar, from 50 to 58 percent of the total. At the same time, study helps in writing decreased from 38 to 34 percent, and the inclusion of literature models decreased from 11 to 8 percent. Hatley in 1929 (see Lyman 1932) analyzed 32 textbooks and 40 courses of study in order to describe their attention to reflective thinking, but he found such attention generally lacking.

Gere (1986), in a review of writing instruction at the college level, traces the evolution of the focus on mechanics, decontextualized from the student' own writing, to the lack of theoretical conceptualization of its relationship to rhetoric. The first composition courses met with faculty resistance, with the study of rhetoric and the study of writing being treated antagonistically. A popular text by Adams Sherman Hill (1878), *The Principles of Rhetoric and Their Application*, continued this schism. In use in composition courses through the 1930s, it provided for a study of usage apart from the students' own work. Gere suggests that writing textbooks such as Hill's were particularly influential in the evolution of the writing curriculum because until the 1980s, teachers of composition received no formal training. Thus, throughout the century, with no articulated philosophy to guide them, textbooks served as their guides, and the focus on mechanics as separate from the students' own writing prevailed.

Donsky (1984) indicates that elementary school texts published between 1900 and 1959 took a different direction from high school and college texts; a student-centered focus appeared in elementary grade texts throughout the 60-year period she studied. She concludes that many present-day concerns have appeared as issues throughout the century. For example, concern with reading and writing relationships, teaching reading through writing, and revision appeared in elementary textbooks as early as 1932; conferencing appeared in texts published in the 1920s and 1930s; and peer interaction, with children talking to other children about their work, were included in texts published in the 1930s.

In contrast, Bernhardt's (1963) study of secondary school texts published from 1900 to 1960 identified threads of both the traditional and the progressive approaches. She reports her findings by decade: Texts in the first decade emphasized correctness, grammar, and the study of written composition as mental training (e.g., Emerson and Bender 1905). Texts in the second decade shifted the emphasis to utilitarian elements of composition through the communication of ideas in social situations (e.g., Lewis and Hosic 1916). Texts in the third decade continued to focus on writing in practical situations but some gave formal treatment to written composition (e.g., Ward 1920); composition was considered the practical side of rhetoric. Textbooks in the 1930s continued a focus on functional approaches to writing, adding emphases on creativity but also on correctness and on a return to the more formal principles of rhetoric (e.g., Hitchcock 1939). Bernhardt concludes that there remained a tension between two basic approaches: a traditional approach, focusing on the study of traditional modes of discourse and on applying general rules of correctness, and a student-centered approach, in which assignments were based on a student's interests or needs as an active member of a democratic society.

Writing Curriculum in Action. Until 1870, the goal of the college writing curriculum was to provide mental discipline through drill and exercises and to teach general principles needed for later use in the professions. The study of rhetoric involved little speaking or writing; students studied and memorized the principles of discourse presented in their texts, and classwork involved recitation. Neither teachers nor students presented their own ideas.

Berlin (1984) reports that in college classrooms at the turn of the century, the composing process was severely restricted: Objectivity was the goal, and interpretation was to be avoided. Composing was seen as finding the right language to capture observed phenomena. In response to the Harvard reports in 1892, 1895, and 1897, which were concerned about students' knowledge of grammar and usage, learning to write and learning grammar came to be seen as one—which had a profound effect on writing curriculum. Berlin (1894) posits that these reports encouraged a mechanistic view of writing, which found its way into the textbooks of influential Harvard faculty (e.g., Genung 1888; A. S. Hill 1878; Wendell 1891), and their ideas affected instruction at all levels.

Until 1876, there was no well-defined curriculum or system for the teaching of writing; the elements affecting the writing curriculum were borrowed from oratory, although instruction in rhetoric and English composition were established in several colleges by mid-century (Carpenter, Baker, and Scott 1903).

Elementary grade instruction in the mid-1800s was similarly rule-based; it emphasized grammatical rules, word meanings, spelling, and general "preparation" for the writing of composition (Carpenter, Baker, and Scott 1903). The correct forms were practiced by transcription of copybook sentences, dictation, letter writing, and paraphrasing. Instruction moved from the parts to the whole, with emphasis on the details before considering the entire composition; the writer's ideas were not considered. Carpenter, Baker, and Scott suggest that lacking ideas, the curriculum lacked interest and dignity, and instruction relied on spelling and formal grammar because these studies were definite and tangible. They decry that there was no training in thought, in gathering and ordering material, or in the process of writing. It was their goal, through their textbooks and pedagogical writings, to change this practice to a focus on the training of the mind through the expression of ideas.

By the 1890s, the daily theme was a common activity in the college classroom, largely in response to the Harvard reports (Berlin 1984). Composition topics were assigned, and although they were purported to appeal to student interest, they were developed for practice in the modes of writing (description, narration, exposition, and argumentation) as codified by Bain in 1866. The paragraph, also codified by Bain (1866) in his *English Composition and Rhetoric*, became a major focus of the curriculum, with the principles of unity, coherence, and emphasis of central importance. Like daily themes, these were first articulated by Harvard's Barrett Wendell.

To trace changes in instruction, particularly in response to the recommendations of the Committee of Ten (National Education Association 1894), Dexter (1906) conducted a nationwide study of the curricula of 80 high schools 1 year before the report and a replication study 10 years later. He found a 16 percent increase in the number of schools teaching composition from 1894 to 1904, from 68 percent to 84 percent. The time devoted to composition also increased, from 16 percent in 1894 to 80 percent in 1904. However, a good deal more rhetoric was taught than had been recommended by the committee.

A related study in 1906 of the writing curriculum in grades 4 through 12 focused on the teaching of grammar and correctness, one of the recommendations of the Committee of Ten. Colvin and Meyer (cited in Edmund 1960–1961) report that across the grades, schools emphasized mechanical exactness and correctness of form and "ignored or actually hindered the expression of the 'deeper' self" (27). Their comments suggest that although grammar in the context of student writing had been recommended by the committee and was well established among curriculum theorists, it had had little effect on the schools.

A number of survey studies indicates that an integrated curriculum with attention to both correctness and self-expression was important to teachers. In 1912, the English Round Table of the National Education Association, chaired by James Hosic, reported the results of a survey of the views of 700 teachers, administrators, and state officials about high school English preparation and college entrance requirements in English (Hosic 1912). The following were listed among the major concerns: (1) Little integration existed between elementary school and secondary coursework, (2) college entrants were poorly prepared to write about their everyday ideas, (3) an excessive amount of time was spent on definitions and rules, (4) school writing was too far removed from the actual linguistic needs of everyday life, and (5) little attention was being placed on writing in other subjects.

Although teachers voiced support for student expression, one can speculate that they may have solved the tensions between a writing-centered curriculum and a focus on grammar and usage by continuing to teach grammar apart from student writing, rather than in response to student writing. The Committee on Types of Organization of High School English of the National Council of Teachers of English (1913) published the results of a survey on composition instruction in 307 high schools. The results suggest that students were required to write one or two themes a week in their English classes, and theme writing was often replaced by writing based on literature during the final year. About half the schools regarded grammar as part of the writing course, and nearly all the composition books in use in these schools contained chapters on grammar. The movement seemed to be away from literary subjects for themes (although this was still prevalent) toward topics drawn from the students' own experiences. Grammar at the secondary school was generally taught as a review, with the assumption that the basics had been taught in the elementary grades. Although the problem of writing in other subjects was noted, the report cited some evidence of cooperation across subject areas.

This dual focus, direct instruction in grammar and usage coupled with an emphasis on student-based writing, seems to have continued for many years, with experiments in more progressive approaches being added to this divided curriculum. Hudelson (1923), in a survey of writing in 165 high schools, reports that in general rhetorical principles received the most emphasis. However, university-based high schools, small-city schools, and rural schools also emphasized interest and originality of thought, whereas large-city schools did so less often. Student writing as well as literature selections were used as models of good writing, and the use of class discussions and conferences was reported. Neatness and mechanical errors were of concern, but Hudelson suggests these were not necessarily corrected unless they involved matters of taste, judgment, or unfamiliar practices.

Counts (1926) also investigated the high school curriculum, but he focused on schools representing progressive orientations. Data were collected from high schools in 15 cities, and some visits were made to classrooms. He found that formal grammar received attention about 9 percent of the time, with another 5 to 7 percent of the time devoted to drills and exercises. Writing topics were drawn from personal experience, literature, current events, recreational interests, and the life of the school (in descending order of frequency), although he noted some movement away from writing about literary topics.

He also noted cooperation across subject areas. Subject teachers recommended themes for writing assignments, and some subject teachers graded their students' English. In addition, English departments furnished models for written work in other departments, and content teachers sent written work to be reviewed by the English teachers. Building principals also checked on written work in the subject areas. Classes in journalism, story writing, and composition for low-achieving students were offered.

Thus, there is indication that although the teaching of grammar and the focus on student experiences continued to be posed against each other in the theoretical and pedagogical debate, in the daily working of schools they had both become well-established components of the received curriculum.

However, the focus on students' experiences was only one aspect of the progressive movement, and other aspects of a student-based and meaning-based curriculum fared less well. Vose (1925) reports that English teachers used subject area topics and texts as the basis of their writing assignments and commonly corrected papers written in content courses. However, her survey of schools reported to have instituted successful cooperation between writing and subject departments during 1908 through 1915 found that by 1924 many of the enterprises were moribund or had been abandoned.

Dora V. Smith (1933) studied 156 courses of study from 125 cities in 35 states and visited 70 schools that presented "unique features of content or method." She found few progressive methodologies, with teacher-dominated classrooms and student recitation rather than inquiry as the norm. "Attention to individual need had little place in the classrooms visited. General regimentation of pupils was the rule; individualization, the exception," Smith commented. More time was devoted to grammar than to any other phase of instruction in American high schools. She concluded that instructional approaches at this time reflected a mix of traditional and progressive practices, with some provision for individual interests and differences.

Smith's (1933) findings suggest that there was a long-lived effect of the progressive movement on concern for experience-based topics; however, her work also suggests that despite prevailing theory and recommended pedagogy, the essential focus on developing the thought underlying the student's message, and on the role of instruction in supporting its development, seems not to have survived (if it had ever been embraced in practice at all).

Reading Through the 1930s

Whereas conceptualizations of writing curriculum grew from existing coursework in rhetoric and were challenged by emerging functional and progressive ideas, curriculum concerns in reading emanated from very different roots. Tradition in reading curriculum relied on British notions of primary instruction (for method), on religion (for content), and by the later 1800s on scientific experiments (for theory). Progressive views were put forward, but the major impetus for change came from elsewhere.

Theoretical Bases for Curriculum Research in Reading. Colonial times through the 1800s marked the era of the rise of the common school reader and the emergence of commercial publishers as important arbiters of the curriculum that guided reading instruction. The focus was on primary grade schooling and the rudiments of reading. Few theoretical issues were debated; most instruction emphasized an alphabetic method, and the materials often presented syllabaries for study. The instruction called for repetition and recitation, primarily of material with religious concerns. The *New England Primer*, first published in 1683 (N. B. Smith 1965 [1934]), was guided as much by the Puritan notions that linked literacy to salvation as by any theory of curriculum or instruction. Calvinism, as Venezky (1987) notes, provided a view of humankind as innately evil and God as wrathfully omnipotent. The introductory materials for developing literacy were codifications of religious creed. Since children received little formal schooling, the earliest reading teachers were parents, who through the middle of the 18th century were often bound by religious or commonwealth laws requiring them to develop the reading abilities of their children (Kaestle 1983).

Prior to the Revolutionary War few readers were published in the colonies, and students were likely to read from texts imported from Great Britain. However, the war brought nationalism to the foreground and American publishers to the marketplace. During the postrevolutionary era, the reading curriculum continued to be governed by particular religious and regional allegiances of the publisher and by the ethic of nationalism throughout the United States. Nila B. Smith (1965 [1934]) quotes from the introduction to Cobb's (1835) *North American Readers*: "The pieces in this work are chiefly American. The English Reader so largely used in this country does not contain a single piece or paragraph written by an American citizen. Is this good policy? Is it patriotism?" (38).

Since textbooks tended to include excerpts or specially written passages that were meant to serve a specific instructional goal, a small but continuing concern about the content of the material was also voiced, focusing on the authenticity, quality, and literary merit of the works students were asked to read. For example, as early as 1891 Charles Eliot, then president of Harvard University, decried the use of excerpts and stories, calling the content of reading textbooks "ineffable trash." He argued that classic literary texts in unabridged form were more appropriate materials for reading instruction. This debate has been resurrected periodically, with disagreement on the proportion of the curriculum that should involve the reading of original literary works.

Philosophy and pedagogy from around the world affected American educational thought, focusing on more student-centered and meaning-based views of curriculum. For example, Rousseau's beliefs about learning influenced views of childhood, regarding the young as developing individuals in their own right rather than as small-sized adults. In 1693, John Locke suggested that learning to read could be made playful—an almost heretical stance for the era (Kaestle and Vinovkis 1980). His influence, however, is seen more in shifts in content than in method.

Whereas progressive views and their focus on the child were debated by educators in general, reading specialists were more concerned with the text—the size of the unit to be taught and learned. Between 1798 and 1830, Friedrich Gedike and Philip Wackernagel in Germany developed a word method of reading, and the Frenchman Jean Joseph Jacotot wrote of his belief that learning proceeded from whole to part (Mathews 1966). By 1828 Samuel Worcester had published his primer in Massachusetts, the first curricular material to move away from the traditional alphabetic method. Worcester stated, "It is not, perhaps, very important that a child should know the letters before he begins to read. It may learn first to read words by seeing them, hearing them pronounced, and having their meanings illustrated . . .'' (quoted in N. B. Smith 1965 [1934], 86). Soon after, several new readers based on a whole-word approach appeared, and the dominant debate of the next 100 years began.

Before the turn of the century, J. Russell Webb extended these views to include his sentence, or ''mother nature,'' method. The use of whole sentences is called for, he argued, because words by themselves obscure meaning, and letters and sounds by themselves have no meaning. It is, he wrote, with the sentence method that true reading proficiency can be fostered (Allington 1975). His introduction presaged the central issue that next arose, which was inextricably linked to the issue of the unit of text to be emphasized in instruction.

The late 1800s to early 1900s was also the era of the emergence of the psychological study of reading processes—the roots of the rational/empirical science of education. In reading, this work tended to study eye movements, automaticity, and single-letter and letter-combination learning. Though not one of the early pioneers, Huey (1968 [1908]) provided the most comprehensive summary of the theoretical arguments of the day, reviewing the scientific research and arguing for a meaning-based view of reading. Three separate movements influenced the debates about reading curriculum and pedagogy: The scientific movement established the roots of empirical research in education; the management movement sought to organize schools into increasingly efficient producers of knowledge; the progressive movement attempted to reshape the view of the learner and of schooling. Each influenced the nature of American education and each influenced reading curriculum. However, in the long run the combined effects of the expanding scientific research base and the application of management principles to the organization of schools seemed to overwhelm the influence of the progressive reading educators.

Shortly after Huey's (1968 [1908]) text appeared there was an expansion of research on reading processes and their relation to curriculum that has continued largely unabated today. Early research focused on attempts to describe the basic psychological processes of reading. The child-study movement of G. Stanley Hall had acquainted educational researchers with the idea of attempting the precise measurement of physiological traits. This research tradition was applied to the study of reading by a number of investigators before Thorndike (1917) published his classic study illustrating that proficient oral reading did not ensure comprehension. Because recitation was still a predominant part of reading instruction, these studies led to calls for curriculum reform on a large scale, with William S. Gray (1917) the most prominent voice.

The development of standardized tests, especially tests of intelligence and reading ability, provided a way to assess large numbers of children or adults efficiently. It became apparent to researchers that many students in school and adults who had attended school could not read well, especially if recall or understanding of the material was required. With the advent of World War I and large-scale testing of military recruits, it became clear to an even larger community that school reading programs were failing to develop even minimal reading comprehension abilities in large numbers of students. At the same time it was also becoming clear that the fundamental nature of American society was changing with increasing urbanization, industrialization, and mechanization. All this resulted in calls for the reform of American education, beginning with the elementary school and, not surprisingly, with beginning reading instruction.

With most reading educators aligning themselves with the scientific movement, empirical research between 1900 and 1930 caused broad changes in reading curricula. Studies that assessed individual traits and abilities produced concern about using an identical standard of reading progress for all children; with the newly developed intelligence tests came calls for differentiated curriculum offerings. The move away from whole-class instruction called for by those who wished to consider individual differences fit well with the views of both the empiricists and progressives. Attention to individual needs became a password in the reading literature, and a concern for ''slow learners'' was established (Dolch 1931). The roots of reading diagnosis were also established in this era (Johnston and Allington in press), as tests and procedures for identifying various reading maladies were developed and implemented.

By 1920, curriculum informed by the scientific movement was widespread. As Shannon (1989) suggests, American educational psychology, led by E. L. Thorndike particularly, was now well established and was being applied to both curriculum development and instructional technique. Thorndike's Laws of Learning shaped the development of curriculum generally and reading especially. His Law of Readiness reflected the notion that learning was an ordered process and that the sequence of introduction of material to be learned mattered. His Law of Exercise indicated that practice led to habituated responses by strengthening the link between stimulus and response. The Law of Effect reflected the notion that reward increased the frequency of response. The Law of Identical Elements suggested that learning was largely specific and that little transfer occurred across learning tasks. This law was also used to argue that tests of learning had to be specific, that tests should present tasks and conditions identical, or at least similar, to the learning situation. Thorndike's laws served as the foundation for the development of the modern reading series. Whereas the progressive movement, led by Dewey, would have small influence on curriculum and instruction, the rise of the commercial reader series signaled the rise of the influence of the scientific movement.

Curriculum Recommendations in Reading. Near the end of the 19th century the National Education Association (1895) released its report on elementary schools, including a suggested elementary school curriculum. This was the first truly national report offering curriculum recommendations for reading. The Committee of Fifteen on Elementary Education noted that the word method was generally favored and that "Modern educational thought emphasizes the opinion that the child, not the subject of study, is the guide to the teacher's efforts" (24). However, the group also argued the need for graded reading materials, noting that almost all available series provided such selections. Curriculum plans at that time reflected a similar emphasis—the relegation of curriculum design to the creators of commercially available readers. For instance, the elementary course of study for the New York State Department of Education (1901) provides the following plan for first-grade reading: "Blackboard work. First reader begun" (6).

The recommendations of the Committee of Fifteen noted the need for beginning reading materials to emphasize colloquial vocabulary, thus creating a need for specially written texts. It was only after the patterns of words were learned that curriculum materials should include the works of established authors. For this more advanced instruction, it recommended a reading curriculum that emphasized the role of literary works in shaping thinking and aesthetic development. The suggested authors included Shakespeare, Tennyson, Bryant, Longfellow, Webster, Emerson, Swift, Milton, Wordsworth, and Irving. Thus, the committee reflected prevailing practice but raised the argument of whether curriculum should follow the "logical development of the subject" or the child's interests and development.

Because the Committee of Fifteen produced its report at the beginning of the scientific movement, it contained few references to research or to the theory of reading acquisition. Twenty-five years later, Gray (1919) summarized the research he felt most relevant to improved curriculum and instruction, focusing on issues "concerning economy and efficiency in teaching reading" (26). He also presented rudimentary curriculum goals for reading rate, comprehension, and phonics, as well as a series of pedagogical recommendations for different grades in the elementary school. In addition, he reported on an examination of curriculum materials that had been shown to produce the greatest reading gains and concluded that factors other than curriculum must be considered in such comparisons: Comprehension was also influenced by the reader's motive for reading, knowledge of the topic of the material, and the number of difficult words. These findings were later reflected in the reading curriculum he developed. However, almost none of the concern for the role of literature that dominated the report of the Committee of Fifteen is to be found in his review.

A concern of Gray's that did mirror one of the Committee of Fifteen was the difficulty of reading material, beginning reading texts in particular. The compilation of the *Teacher's Word Book* by Thorndike (1921) set the stage for readability research and the measurement of the relative difficulty of student texts. Klare (1984) has traced the history of procedures for estimating text difficulty; the findings concerning text variables such as word frequency and sentence length were seen as major advances in the scientific development of curriculum. With these new procedures and the recently developed standardized tests, it was thought that materials could be ordered in ideal sequences of difficulty.

The effects of this work are easily observed in the organization and content of children's readers produced after 1910. Although debates about method in beginning reading did not subside, the most popular commercial curricula adopted a rather eclectic approach, reflecting the influences of the competing positions, but all these curricula attempted to organize texts in a progression of difficulty. By 1920 reader series followed the accumulating evidence about word frequency, repetition, silent reading, and children's interests. By 1930 the modern basal reader series had been well formulated and included comprehensive teacher guides and practice books. The practice of reading curriculum construction has been little altered in the intervening era.

The concerns that had dominated early calls for curriculum reform in reading instruction—improvement in content, emphasis on silent reading and comprehension, and differentiated curriculum goals for learners of different aptitudes—were now accepted as conventional wisdom. The series of reports published in the yearbooks of the National Society for the Study of Education (Gray 1925; Horn 1919; Wilson 1915, 1917)—first by the Committee on Minimal Essentials in Elementary School Subjects, then by the Committee on the Economy of Time in Learning, and finally by the National Committee on Reading—reshaped the curriculum substantially. Reading was now a separate curriculum area, with blocks of time set aside for reading instruction each day; classrooms were organized by grade levels and readers by levels of difficulty; and silent reading comprehension was established as the ultimate goal. The influence of William S. Gray is inarguable; he chaired many of the committees and authored reports in each of the yearbooks noted. He also became senior author of what was to become the most popular commercial reading series of succeeding eras. Gray was firmly entrenched in the scientific research establishment, publishing original studies and annual reviews of research on the reading process from his laboratory at the University of Chicago.

Curriculum recommendations came to reflect calls for the efficient use of the new scientifically constructed basal readers. For instance, Bagley and Kyte (1926), in the *California Curriculum Study*, recommended that early reading should begin with primers developed from common words, and they prescribed a single basal series for grades 1–4. By grade 5, literature should become the curriculum material. They also recommended more detailed curriculum guides for teachers based on their evaluation of over 3,000 daily lesson plans.

Shannon (1989) notes the alliances developed between reading authorities and commercial publishers, especially after 1915. These reading authorities were typically university professors who generally were engaged in reading research. The reading curriculum materials produced began to reflect these research findings, especially those concerned with beginning reading issues. Basal series began to offer larger numbers of easy books, and the number of new vocabulary words began to decline. With each report of the inadequacies of current practice came an expansion of directions to the teacher, in the form of an ever-growing teacher's manual.

Curriculum Materials in Reading. Although the earliest curriculum materials reflected concern for literacy and salvation, there was little variation in method. These materials were purchased by parents, and children took the books their family owned to school. Such books were popular; Venezky (1987) reports that half the books imported from England at the end of the 17th century were schoolbooks. In 1830 schoolbooks represented about a third of all books published in the United States. After the Civil War, he notes, series of readers for use across the elementary grades began to appear and were labeled by level. (N. B. Smith 1965 [1934] and Gray 1948 both provide abundant reproductions of early materials as well as extensive quotations from the introductory remarks.)

Webster's Speller was the dominant reading curriculum material in the early 18th century, though it contained rather little to read. Nila B. Smith (1965 [1934]) reports that 74 of the 158 pages were devoted to lists of words and syllables, with another 39 pages providing rules for appropriate elocution while speaking and reading. Only about a third of the pages provided text to be read, and these were mostly brief, moralistic admonitions (e.g., "Play not with bad boys").

The McGuffey Readers were first published between 1836 and 1844 and remained continuously available well past 1900, though in revised editions. No other curriculum material was so widely used in American schools, though Venezky (1987) credits this popularity more to shrewd marketing by the publisher than to any noteworthy feature that would have set the series apart from its competitors. Nila B. Smith (1965 [1934]) credits McGuffey with originating the practice of limiting the vocabulary in beginning readers and of providing repetition of the new vocabulary in stories, though as Venezky (1987) notes, these practices became quite common in all readers of the era. The readers continued the nationalistic and moralistic emphasis but also included text obviously written for the series and excerpts drawn from literary works. Mosier (1965) reports that the focus of the McGuffey Readers was on building character, values, and cultural knowledge. He identified several recurrent themes, including respect for private property; the view of men as thrifty, industrious, and charitable and women as tidy and submissive; and the religious bases for current class structure. He also noted that the characters in the stories provided models for deportment and development.

The research on the content of school readers of this era is summarized by Venezky (1986, 1987). He delineates several limitations of the various analyses but provides documentation of the declining role religious and nationalistic content played during the period. For instance, about one third of the content of the 1844 edition of *McGuffey's Fourth Reader* was of religious nature, and this dropped to only 3 percent in the 1901 edition. However, virtues such as industry, thrift, intelligence, fair play, and charity remained central to the content.

In the latter half of the 19th century there were calls for changes in the content of the readers, calls to include content of interest to children. These calls reflected the growing interest in Pestalozzian principles of nurturance and child-centeredness in educating the young. Horace Mann was strident in his criticism of the available readers, arguing that they contained "demonstrative arguments on the most abstruse and recondite subjects, tasking the acuteness of practiced logicians" (quoted in Venezky 1987, 261). The content of readers shifted and came to include fairy tales, adventure stories, and classic tales with color illustrations. During this period an increased emphasis on reading beyond the reader emerged, with curriculum guidelines often suggesting other collections of stories or books for each grade level (N. B. Smith 1965 [1934]).

Beginning reading curriculum materials were designed to be used with the traditional alphabetic method, though the popularity of this method, with the spelling of each word before reading, was in decline, and materials with the word method were being emphasized. The additions to the array of beginning teaching methods included the sentence and story methods. These methods were derived from the same principles as the word method but increased the size of the unit of text that was initially focused on. For example, the Aldine Readers (published in 1906; described in Gray 1948) stressed rhymes for development of a sight vocabulary and teacher-pupil stories. The story method appeared just before the turn of the century, but by 1915 this was the dominant curriculum approach, appearing in readers published by Scott, Foresman; Macmillan; Silver-Burdett; Merrill; American Book; and Longmans and Green. Nila B. Smith (1965 [1934]) summarizes this method as presented in the Story Hour Readers of 1913. First, students hear and dramatize the story, then analyze it for meaning and structure (at the sentence, phrase, word, and phonetic level), and finally read the piece alone. The analysis phase was presented through activities that involved arranging sentences in order, rearranging words into sentences, and so on.

In contrast, the Pollard Synthetic Method, published in 1899, notes in the introduction,

> Instead of teaching the word as a whole and afterword subjecting it to phonic analysis, is it not infinitely better to take the sounds of the letters for our starting point . . . ? It has been proved . . . that first grade pupils are delighted with the busywork afforded by marking and sounding of letters. . . . Let no attempt be made to read until every word . . . has been marked and sounded. (quoted in Gray 1948, 10)

Other readers presented variations on the phonic method, including some, such as the Rational Method of Reading published in 1894, which presented diacritical marking systems that were designed to facilitate learning to read.

Thus, shortly after the turn of the century, reader series emphasized units of text from the letter to the story and virtually all units in between. In his historical review of these curricular developments, Gray (1948) laments the fact that these early reading materials, by and large, ignored the issue of vocabulary—both the quantity and the quality of the words used. He casts his interpretation on what evolved: "The newer reading programs boldly introduced vocabulary control, giving significant recognition to the problem of mastering words. . . . The interest content of reading series for the lower grades was greatly improved along with the introduction of controlled vocabularies" (27).

The problem of determining text difficulty was thought to have been resolved with the advent of readability formulas around 1925. The promise these techniques held for ordering stories and textbooks by difficulty was viewed as a significant scientific advance (Gray and Leary 1935). Likewise, word-learning experiments were now providing information on the number of repetitions needed to ensure learning, and estimates were being made of how many words could be learned in a standard lesson. This information was quickly incorporated into the design of reading curriculum, resulting in formulaic construction of the initial readers.

Chall (1967) reported the result of Gray's enthusiasm for vocabulary control: The readers produced by Scott, Foresman in 1920, the Elson Readers, included about twice as many words in the primer and first reader as did later editions for which Gray was the senior author. Similarly, the activity-based seat work of the earlier series, pages that presented sentences to be cut up into constituent words and reordered, for instance, were replaced with the *Silent Reading Workbook* and then with the *Think and Do Book*, both of which present letter and word practice exercises in a paper-and-pencil format.

It became common for a reading series to provide other components, especially workbooks with practice exercises to accompany each lesson. The earliest workbooks were an attempt to assist teachers, who were shifting curriculum emphasis to silent reading and comprehension (N. B. Smith 1965 [1934]). The workbooks contained questions to follow the reading of the story, sentence completion and word classification tasks, and suggestions for dramatizing or drawing elements of the story. These were seen as appropriate activities for extending attention to comprehension after silent reading, and the workbooks were viewed as components that were likely to facilitate change in teacher behavior and thus produce changes in the received curriculum. The scientific evidence from which Thorndike had derived his Laws of Learning was now the central contributor to the reshaping of the reading curriculum.

One other component of commercial reading materials was also being dramatically altered. The directions to the teacher that had previously occupied a few pages of introductory matter now became the teacher guidebook, complete with plans for each lesson. Several forces influenced the development of these teachers' manuals. First, the shift in emphasis from oral to silent reading required a change in teacher behavior. Second, reports of instructional practice typically suggested that teachers were uninformed about the emerging science of instruction. Third, proponents of the scientific rationale emphasized the need to order the curriculum to increase the efficiency of instruction. Finally, rising concern with limited reading abilities of school-age children raised doubts about the ability of teachers to provide adequate reading instruction, especially with the advent of new methods and materials. These combined forces led to the rise of the separate teachers' manual, wholly incorporated into the series published from about 1920 onward (H. A. Robinson 1977; Venezky 1987).

Reading Curriculum in Action. Only diaries, autobiographies, retrospective accounts, and school and town reports are available to provide information on the nature of the curriculum in reading during the pre- and postrevolutionary era (Kaestle 1983). These accounts provide little evidence that reading class was a time that children would look forward to. Given the limited material to read—limited in terms of available books for children and in the restricted content of the readers—the evidence suggests that children, especially the youngest, spent little time actually reading. Reading instruction at the elementary levels emphasized oral reading, with elocution emphasized in the upper grades through the end of the 19th century (Venezky 1986).

Finkelstein (cited in Shannon 1989) analyzed in 1970 the diaries, reports, and journals of nearly 1,000 teachers working between 1820 and 1880. Although Matthews (1966) and Nila B. Smith (1965 [1934]) both suggest that the word method was popular by 1850, Finkelstein found no mention of it until the 1870s. She noted that "reading instruction emphasized word identification over meaning, required oral reading rather than discussion, and was largely directed by the available textbooks" (Shannon 1989, 26).

When Joseph Rice (1893) surveyed elementary schools in 36 cities, visiting classrooms in each city and interviewing 1,200 teachers, he was not impressed with what he saw. Rice classified the reading curricula into three types based on his analysis of how well reading instruction was integrated into other subjects and the degree to which student interests were incorporated into the lessons. Most schools seemed to fit his category of "mechanical reading instruction." A second, and smaller, group he labeled "transition" schools, where change was underway but not yet "satisfactory." Schools in four cities were found to be "scientific" schools, where the principles espoused by Pestalozzi, Herbart, and Froebel were reflected. In these schools Rice found what he felt was a more unified curriculum, one that responded to the needs and interests of children.

Although the general characterizations of Rice and Finkelstein are similar, their reports are at odds with Kellogg's 1900 survey of reading in 10 large cities (cited in Venezky 1986). His report suggests that silent reading was more common, even in the primary grades. Perhaps, as was the case in the Bagley and Kyte (1926) study, rural and urban schools differed in the conduct of reading instruction. Urban schools seemed more likely to have incorporated the recommendations offered for modernizing reading instruction.

This was the era of the initial emphasis on silent reading

practice, and various authorities were recommending transforming reading instruction from oral rendition to silent comprehension (Allington 1984). Key participants in the scientific movement were developing an interest in schools, with scholars studying silent reading processes and making recommendations for changes in practice (McDade 1928; Pintner 1913). This was also the era of the emergence of the progressive movement in America (based on John Dewey's work) and the era of increasing bureaucratization of schools, especially in and around urban centers.

Three forces, the empiricists, the management specialists, and the progressive reformers, all set out to alter the nature of reading curriculum and instruction in American schools near the turn of the 20th century. Each had influence, but the combined efforts of the empiricists and management specialists seemed ultimately to carry the day, both in the organization of schools and in the modification of reading curriculum materials. The bureaucratization of schools and the ordering of the reading curriculum by difficulty and by skills were largely accomplished between 1880 and 1930. In addition, a general consensus held silent reading and comprehension as the primary curricular goals. The position statements of the Committee on Reading (Gray 1925, 1937) emphasized that reading instruction would be improved by the careful implementation of the new basal reader programs, and these, in turn, would continue to improve through targeted research.

As we have seen, reading curriculum and writing curriculum each has a strong link with its past, each gaining its early conceptualization from distinctly different sources, and each primarily concerned with a different stage in the schooling process. However, by the late 1800s, both the fields of reading and of writing were affected by progressive ideas. This change can be seen in the reports of the Committee of Ten (National Education Association 1894) and the Committee of Fifteen (National Education Association 1895), in which calls for attention to students' interests and understandings were placed side by side with those for a focus on mechanics and skills. Through the early 1900s, the experience-based curriculum seems to have been given more lip service than reality, with recitation and grammar practice receiving the primary focus; however, rhetoric was no longer at the heart of the curriculum. Reading curriculum at this time was strongly influenced by the scientific movement, particularly where the focus on individual differences seemed to coincide with progressive notions of a focus on students' reality. However, modernization of the reading curriculum involved a greater focus on mechanics, word recognition, and levels of difficulty than on meaning.

THE BEGINNINGS OF ECLECTICISM

Writing in the 1940s Through the 1960s

Theoretical Bases of Curriculum Research in Writing. It was not until the 1940s that the college curriculum returned to traditional rhetoric for its theoretical roots. This shift was influenced by the resurgence of interest in Aristotelian logic, advanced by the establishment of the Conference on College Composition and Communication as part of the National Council of Teachers of English (see Berlin 1984, 1987), and followed by growing competition among three theoretical views at the college level. The classical view, represented by the work of Edward Corbett (1965), is based on classical rhetoric. In this view, persuasion, in Aristotelian terms, is restored to the center of discourse. The expressionist view, represented by the work of Michael Halloran (1982), focuses on discourse as part of political reality and personal identity. The new rhetoric, represented by Peter Elbow (1971); Ann Berthoff (1981); and Young, Becker, and Pike (1970), places language at the center of the search for and creation of meaning.

By the 1960s rhetorical form had again become a prominent concern of the high schools, but with a new emphasis. Jerome Bruner's (1960) ideas of learning and cognition and their relation to the structure of the discipline influenced conceptualizations of what should be taught and learned. Instead of studying models and forms, students needed to engage in writing activities in which these forms would be important, learning the structures in the process of putting them to productive use under the guidance of a constructively critical teacher (see also Vygotsky 1962, 1978, whose views seem to have influenced Bruner during this period). Rather than a curriculum that proceeded sequentially through a body of knowledge, this practice would lead to a "spiral curriculum," which would return to essential concepts in cycles at ever more sophisticated levels of awareness and understanding.

The process-oriented writing research of the 1970s was shaped by a number of related influences, including Piaget's (e.g., Inhelder and Piaget 1958) and Bruner's (e.g., Bruner, Goodnow, and Austin 1956) studies of conceptual development as well as work on language acquisition (e.g., Brown 1973; Menyuk 1969; Weir 1962) that describes language development as a process of appropriate rule setting. Guided by the child's sense of language and the world at that particular time, the rule setting shifts to increasingly more complex forms as the child matures. This new understanding (related to but substantively different from the arguments underlying Dewey's experiential approach) led to an understanding of the student as an active problem solver whose topical, structural, and pragmatic knowledge affects the processes as well as the products of writing (Berlin 1987; Langer 1984a).

The 1940s were also a time of increased attention to democratic ideals and citizenship training, and writing was seen as a tool for communication and social development. Increasing enrollments and compulsory attendance laws fanned interest in the education of students of varying abilities and cultural and linguistic origins. During the 1950s attention shifted to the student as an individual and composition as a medium of self-expression, although a focus on the individual within a larger society continued.

At the same time, interest in usage continued. Partly in

response to a growing interest in the development of curriculum to benefit traditionally underachieving minority learners, the National Council of Teachers of English (NCTE) funded a study by Charles Fries (1940) on grammatical structures and social differences. His book made an important contribution toward the growing acceptance that conventional use and practice rather than prescriptions based on an inherited grammar or rhetoric are the basis of correctness in language. Fries himself suggested that the writing curriculum focus on the teaching of informal, standard usage.

This work was followed by a series of studies pointing to the rule-based systems underlying minority dialects (e.g., Fishman 1977; Labov 1966; Shuy 1967; Wolfram 1974) and their legitimacy as complex linguistic systems. The 1952 report of NCTE's Commission on the English Curriculum reflected the work of Fries and others in its recommendation regarding usage, stating that teachers must shift their emphasis from negative rules to the development of positive insights. Instead of teaching rules for the avoidance of error, students should be taught to observe and understand the way in which their language operates—its variety for communicative purposes.

During the 1960s, curriculum theory in general shifted toward the structure of the subject matter rather than the needs of the student. In the teaching of writing, concerns tended to move toward a new rhetoric (Evans and Walker 1966), which placed greater emphasis on the ideas that are explored in the process of composing and that affect the structure the piece will take (Braddock, Lloyd-Jones, and Schoer 1965). In the 1960s language study, including grammar, became a separate theoretical concern in response to Noam Chomsky's (1965) work on transformational grammar and the studies on sentence combining (e.g., Bateman and Zidonis 1966; Mellon 1964; O'Hare 1973). Further, there was a widespread movement toward language study, including grammar as a separate part of the English curriculum. (This subject is discussed in greater detail in the chapter by Arthur Applebee and Alan Purves in this *Handbook*.)

Thus, during the 1940s through the 1960s, theoretical concerns focused on writing as a process of active understanding, and the student was seen as an active language learner—one who set rules and gained conceptual understanding through firsthand experience. This view was consonant with the growing theory on learning written as well as oral language, and it provided impetus for extending broad curriculum goals of thought and language to all students.

Curriculum Recommendations in Writing. In the mid-1960s, the U.S. Office of Education made available new funds for curriculum development, some of which filtered into writing curriculum efforts. Funded by the National Defense Education Act, Project English Demonstration and Curriculum Centers were developed, several of which based their language study strands on transformational grammar or structural linguistics. In response to the emphasis on social and linguistic dimensions of language learning, the National Council of Teachers of English once again undertook a nationwide reevaluation of the prescribed curriculum. This extensive body of work was published in three separate volumes (Commission on the English Curriculum of the National Council of Teachers of English 1952, 1954, 1956), which unlike the prior NCTE reports, present few clear-cut, new directions. (Two further volumes in the series, on teacher education [1963] and college instruction [1965], were delayed so long that they represent a different era and emphases; by the time they were published they had little influence.)

The first report recommends curriculum from preschool through graduate school. The stated theoretical underpinnings build on those of the earlier eras but were strongly influenced by then current work in educational psychology, linguistics, sociology, and post-World War II social movements. It cites the need to reexamine the curriculum in response to changing concepts of learning as a result of research on human development, the recognition of language learning as part of human growth, and the idea that social as well as linguistic factors contribute to learning to write.

The curriculum guidelines suggest that written expression begins in the primary grades, based on the personal need to communicate. Copying, spelling, punctuation, and capitalization are also to be taught in the primary grades. In the intermediate grades, students are to write longer papers in a greater variety of functional situations, varying from copying from dictation to creative writing to selecting the best word. Although attention is given to handwriting and correctness, getting thoughts down on paper is the primary goal.

At the junior high school level, correlation of writing with the other language arts is suggested, but the teaching of grammar is discredited because of the lack of relationship between such study and effectiveness in writing. Recommendations for the high school include a continuing focus on writing activities that grow from the school's life, with attention to a range of forms (e.g., letters, personal accounts, exposition, and opinions), while encouraging writing about out-of-school interests.

The second volume from the Commission on the English Curriculum focused specifically on the elementary school. It emphasized the need for purposeful and genuine uses for writing about topics that students know about and are interested in. Suggestions that support the process of writing were provided, including thinking, drafting, revising, and self-evaluation. Grammar and mechanics instruction were to be taught through the students' own speaking and writing, not through the labeling and classification of forms.

The third volume focused on secondary school programs and stated as its goal the need to base a language arts curriculum on an understanding of students and the world in which they live. Self-expression and emotional release through writing were emphasized. It was suggested that students learn to be keen observers and to write about their experiences and the world around them. Ideas developed in written work could be shared with the class and in this way help students come to share opinions and respect the opinions of others.

Though reflecting a major effort on the part of many teachers and researchers, these reports offered little that seemed new or innovative. New theories and research in a variety of efforts were cited, but either the implications for curriculum were insufficiently well developed or sufficient consensus had not been reached to permit a national committee to reach agreement on new directions.

As the reports from the Commission on the English Curriculum showed little development, so did state syllabi between the 1930s and 1960s. Six editions of the New York State syllabi in English during this period (New York State Department of Education 1934, 1935, 1941, 1945, 1948, 1960) presented essentially the same views in revised booklets. During these 26 years, the stated goals and recommended curriculum in writing sought to enable students to say things as well as possible and also to write about their own interests. Correlation of writing with other subjects was encouraged, although considered a difficult task. For example, the 1934 report states that since it has been difficult to induce teachers of other subjects to insist on good habits of spoken and written English, the English teacher would do well to take the initiative and focus on the English students use in their history, science, and foreign language classes.

Although there had been changes in the social conditions of schools and society (changes that in part led the National Council of Teachers of English to undertake its major curriculum reevaluation effort), these concerns do not appear to have effected substantive changes in curriculum recommendations.

Change was in the air by 1960, however, and its shape was apparent a few years later with the publication of *Freedom and Discipline in English*. Sponsored by the Commission on English (1965) of the College Entrance Examination Board, the report was part of a widespread rejection of progressive education in the wake of Sputnik in 1957 and a reassertion of English as an academic discipline with its own subject matter, represented by the teaching of language, literature, and composition. As the report described its mission, it "reflected widespread concern that secondary school English, through a long process of diffusion, of trying to meet many needs not met elsewhere in the school, was in danger of losing its identity altogether" (1).

In discussing the curriculum in writing, the Commission on English (1965) outlined a three-part cycle: Early in the grades, and early in every grade, the emphasis would be on expression, "on what, in the best sense, is creative writing . . . discovery of the self and the world." The next stage "might concentrate on the discipline of form—on matters of arrangement, logic, and conventional correctness that make up the body of most books on composition." Finally, the third stage "should witness the development of style, as the first stage witnesses the development of invention, and the second of methods of arrangement and form" (90). The return to the classical arts of rhetoric was explicit, though in the commission's report they are linked with Bruner's (1960) spiral curriculum to suggest a cycle of instruction that will recur throughout the curriculum. The commission was unequivocal, too, about the necessity for high standards, including standards of correctness. In discussing the teacher's role, it notes that even "the most cursory reading should be accompanied by marking of errors in spelling, punctuation, grammar, and diction" (98). Fully aware that usage is relative, it concludes that this admission "exacts more, not less, discipline from the writer, and the teacher must be constantly alert to indict and require correction of faults in form and failures of taste" (99).

The Commission on English (1965) was not blind, however, to the advances that had been made by student-oriented pedagogies. It pointed to the importance of audience, the need for assignments that evoke "the best from the writer," the importance of revision, and the need to be able to take what students write seriously. As stated at the end of the discussion, "The pedagogical truth about instruction in writing lies somewhere between twentieth-century emphasis on the joy of learning and the classical emphasis on disciplined thought and precise expression. On that middle ground the teacher of composition must take his stand" (106).

When the New York State Department of Education (1969) reissued its syllabus in English, it seemed caught between the new emphasis on the discipline and its previous concerns. The syllabus represents a change in both goals and guidelines from the ones before, but the underlying rationale is more reflective of earlier curriculum movements than those of its time. In the forward, notice is given that memorization of rules and drills will not develop competencies, that all rules should be taught functionally, and that instruction should be based on students' writing. It also suggests that generalizations should be taught by discovery, as the result of personal experiences, and that creative expression should not be inhibited by overemphasis on skills. However, the curriculum that follows includes specific suggestions for the organization of entire texts as well as for the development of the sentence.

Curriculum Materials in Writing. A move toward traditionalism can be seen in the texts that appeared during the 1940s through 1960s. At the college level, this movement reflects an attempt to formulate a theoretical perspective on which college writing programs could build a pedagogy. The reappearance of rhetoric in college writing during the 1940s may have been part of such a move; it soon began to influence the writing texts that were published. Gere (1986) suggests that *Composition* by Richard Weaver (1957) brought classical rhetoric's enthymeme and topics to the teaching of writing, and Edward Corbett's (1965) *Classical Rhetoric for the Modern Student* attempted to integrate classical rhetoric and composition pedagogy. In doing so, they challenged the traditional model. However, in part because few new teachers of writing were hired during this period, textbooks following the traditional model continued to dominate in college writing classes throughout the 1960s.

The tension between traditional and progressive approaches in the curriculum also appeared in high school texts. In 1963, Lynch and Evans published the results of a study of 14 grammar and composition textbooks used in high school English classes. All were published between 1953 and 1961. In general, the texts assigned topics that pertained to the students' interests and adolescent worlds. With few exceptions, all the series presented instruction in usage (e.g., concrete and specific nouns, action verbs, and figurative language), writing skills (topic selection, gathering material, outlining, and proofreading), and organization and form (e.g., unity, coherence, and particular forms). The fullest and most explicit instruction was given to the paragraph, to the extent that "the presentation of instruction in the principles of the paragraph may be considered to stand generally for instruction in composition" (315). Lynch and Evans concluded that writing instruction was treated as a series of exercises in the mechanics of writing rather than in the development of ideas because although students were given practice with devices, the absence of essential purpose in the assignment reduced the practice of composition to mere exercise.

Bernhardt's (1963) review of two textbooks in each decade from 1900 to 1960 corroborates Lynch and Evans's (1963) larger study. She reports that although texts of this era attempted to present writing tasks relevant to the students' lives, all stressed the structure of the paragraph. Further, she found a great deal of similarity in the ways paragraphs were taught across the century. Unity and coherence were stressed.

Textbook publishers of this era seem to have been aware of the tension between traditional and progressive goals for the writing curriculum, and they resolved dissension by compromise.

Writing Curriculum in Action. The tension between traditional and progressive approaches to curriculum and texts seems to have worked itself through in different ways at the classroom level. Although there is some evidence of progressive approaches to instruction at the primary level, studies of intermediate and secondary classrooms leave little doubt that traditional teaching and traditional texts dominated the curriculum.

In her study of trends in primary grade writing instruction between 1940 and 1960, Parke (1960–1961) found an increase in young children's opportunities to express themselves in writing. She attributes this change to progressive curriculum changes that stressed firsthand experiences, student interests, and the view that writing is essentially a thinking process. Although she states her view that the mechanics of writing should be subordinated to content, no evidence is provided that this practice was actually occurring in primary classrooms.

Although primary classrooms may have begun to embrace more progressive approaches to the writing curriculum during the 1940s to 1960s, such was not the case in the higher elementary grades. Results of two 1957 surveys of intermediate grade writing support the contention that student-centered approaches were fading from use. Edmund (1960–1961) reports that fewer than half the students in his study had an opportunity to select writing topics, and fewer than four stories were written during one year.

Strickland's report (1960–1961) also reflects the tensions between traditional and progressive approaches to elementary grade writing. Although she reported utilitarian or functional writing assignments to be an integral part of classwork, she found that many teachers focused on form and correctness rather than on students' ideas. Although personal and creative writing were encouraged from the early grades, and critical writing from the intermediate grades, Strickland also found an excessive emphasis on formal grammar. She reported that in secondary schools there was also a heavy emphasis on grammar in the composition program but little agreement on the value and weight it should carry.

Squire and Applebee (1968) undertook the most sophisticated and comprehensive study of the English curriculum to their time—a four-year study of English programs in 158 high schools (selected largely for their reputations for excellence in English) in 45 states. Data included classroom observations; individual interviews with students and teachers; and analysis of curricula, examinations, and student papers. Their findings confirm, with greater detail, the continuing restrictions on the writing curriculum in American schools. They found that only 17 percent of class time was devoted to writing instruction, although as early as 1903 Carpenter, Baker, and Scott had called for class time to be split equally between literature and writing, and as late as 1965 the Commission on English was calling for equal attention to language, literature, and composition.

Their observations also indicated that the weight of instruction in composition occurred after papers had been written rather than before or during the writing. Despite the movement toward student-based writing earlier in the century, they reported that assignments generally presented "manufactured" topics, with primary attention going to mechanics and form rather than to substance. Experiences with various types of writing were restricted: Compositions were based primarily on literature, and topics dealing with personal experience, social issues, or imaginative and creative writing were assigned much less frequently.

Squire and Applebee (1968) described the usual "instructional" sequence as being one of writing, error correction, and revision; most teachers viewed correcting papers as teaching writing. In response to questions about student conferences, the teachers interviewed agreed that such conferences would be useful but that there was not enough time for them. In contrast to the results from class observations and teacher interviews, the department chairs maintained that the writing curriculum had a strong focus on clear thinking and organization of ideas.

With few exceptions, standards and requirements within departments were set in terms of the number of assignments rather than student growth in writing or a broader notion of process or sequence in learning to write. Most programs suffered from redundancy or fragmentation. A number of schools prepared their own spiral curricula, often based in part on the four traditional modes of writing. Literary models continued to be used in some classrooms, particularly in schools with sequential programs (Squire and Applebee 1968).

Thus, although theory moved the focus toward viewing all students as active language learners and users who learn rules through experience, the curriculum recommendations, materials, and activities in writing remained traditional, with few substantive changes and a consistent concern for correctness. Meanwhile, curriculum research in reading underwent extensive change in this period.

Reading in the 1940s Through the 1960s

Theoretical Bases of Curriculum Research in Reading. Whereas research of educational psychologists strongly influenced the development of reading curriculum after the turn of the century, later in the century researchers from other disciplines began exploring language learning, and some focused on reading acquisition. Linguists such as Leonard Bloomfield (1942) and Charles Fries (1963) focused on curriculum implications primarily for beginning readers, based on their structural linguistic analyses of the English language. In response to the work on language and concept acquisition during the 1950s (e.g., Bruner, Goodnow, and Austin 1956; Inhelder and Piaget 1958), with its focus on children's efforts to make sense of both language and the world, the long-standing debate about the appropriate unit for focus in initial reading instruction reemerged. Once again advocates of the letter, the word, and the story issued their arguments, while the most influential reading authorities continued to recommend an eclectic (or balanced, in their view) approach to reading curriculum, as represented by basal readers primarily although other recommendations were now included.

Textbooks on the teaching of reading relied heavily on evidence from psychological studies to inform their curriculum recommendations. For example, Anderson and Dearborn (1952) introduce *The Psychology of Teaching Reading* by stating, "Our principle purpose has been to review the psychological evidence which provides the very basis of method." They review a wide body of research on such varied topics as eye movements, legibility, mental development, cultural background, and self-selection, and they conclude by recommending an eclectic method based on basal reader series. Their text marks a new genre of texts on the teaching of reading; their comprehensive review, citing over 350 studies as foundation to their conclusions, was unique, as most previous works had cited few studies to buttress conclusions. The research they cited, however, was largely experimental and focused on skills development.

Cold war tensions and the launching of Sputnik led to general concern about the quality of American schooling (Spring 1989), thus initiating a reexamination of the curriculum, generally, and the reading curriculum, particularly. Efforts to return the curriculum to lost standards (and develop earlier and stronger readers) led to a series of popular books advocating a phonics approach (Chall 1967; Flesch 1955; Terman and Walcutt 1958; Walcutt 1961). At the same time, concerns about the rigid organization of reading instruction and the reading performance of children of poverty and color spurred other criticisms of the reading curriculum.

The work of Olson (1949), Veatch (1959), and Zirbes (1951) emphasized the role of "self-selection" in the development of literacy. Each supported an "individualized" reading curriculum with tradebooks that children elected to read. Veatch noted, "The development of individualized reading since its national recognition in 1952 has been nothing short of amazing. Educators everywhere have come to find an unsuspected community of interest in the matter, an interest being fed by a growing criticism of the traditional approach with its formalized ability-groups and omnipresent basal texts" (xii).

Shannon (1989), Veatch (1986), and others have argued that the demise of an individual-based curriculum was due in part to concerted efforts of basal publishers to maintain the status quo, in part to the continuing belief in the efficacy of the scientific method, and also in part to the lack of teachers' professional voices in the shaping of curriculum. The individualized reading movement reflected a historical tension between those who sought a logical ordering of reading curricula based on adult analysis and supported by empirical investigation and those who sought a curriculum derived from the needs and interests of children, which had also been subject to a lengthy history of empirical investigation. After a half century of scientific research into reading acquisition and its application to curriculum development, resistance to the lockstep and formalized approach resurfaced.

Basal readers were the primary outlet for the standardized curriculum, but their eclectic format had developed in response to specific calls for reform. The development of workbooks was part of the attempt to shift the emphasis of instruction from oral rendition to comprehension. The development of primers and preprimers was the result of concern that beginning readers posed too large a leap for entering first-grade children. The use of controlled vocabulary reflected attempts to reduce failure in beginning reading. Recommendations for reading beyond the basal were a response to calls for self-selection and independent reading. Teachers' manuals were developed out of concerns with current pedagogy and the limited training available to many elementary teachers. Nonetheless, these developments had standardized the curricula to the point where both teacher and learner were removed from the decision-making process in terms of the received curriculum.

Herrick, Anderson, and Pierstorff (1961) summarized the primary debate about reading curriculum during this era, concluding that a curriculum that combined the organizational strengths of basal programs with the child-centered strengths of the individualized approach was the most desirable. However, because of public concerns, the rising pressures from phonics advocates, the seeming benefits of tracking individualized progress, and the increasing calls for accountability, the next 10 years (1960 to 1970) produced tightly sequenced reading materials and skills management systems that prescribed curriculum and monitored mastery. Thus, the notion of individualization shifted to a reading skills framework, with self-selection, self-pacing, and wide reading from literature replaced by skills acquisition, preselected exercises, and mastery tests. Motivation was seen as critical but subordinated to success in the skills lessons, with attempts to design error-free learning and positive feedback as the keys.

Theories derived from the original associationist psychology guided the development of many of these new beginning reading curriculum frameworks (Della-Piana and Endo 1973). The work of Skinner (1957) shaped the design of several programmed learning schemes and other beginning reading materials. These were based on the perceived need for specific skills hierarchies for word recognition and comprehension. Criterion-referenced assessment of progress through these hierarchies was typically included. At approximately the same time, a psycholinguistic view of reading (K. S. Goodman 1967), derived from the developments in transformational-generative grammar (Goodman and Fleming 1969), developed. This position rejected the tradition of both a word- and phonic-centered beginning reading curriculum and focused attention on the language capabilities of children, with special attention given to the influence of syntactic and semantic knowledge that readers bring to the reading situation.

Curriculum Recommendations in Reading. Although the importance of comprehension in the reading curriculum had been the focus of concern a half century earlier, describing comprehension and translating it into curriculum goals remained an issue. The efforts of Gray and others to ease comprehension in primary grade materials resulted in new versions of beginning reading curricula, and it was in the upper grades that comprehension now produced concern. The adage "First you learn to read and then you read to learn" necessitated a reading curriculum that enabled proficiency in comprehending content area material (Moore, Readance, and Rickelman 1983). In the past, based on the recommendations of the Committee on Reading (Gray 1925), "study" questions were used to prepare students for the reading-to-learn experience. However, Artley (1944) reported that attention to specific reading comprehension processes was needed. Comprehension had long been considered a unitary process, but Artley's work and that of Davis (1944), whose factor-analytic studies had identified two major components of comprehension—word knowledge and reasoning—spurred further investigation in this area.

These concerns led to renewed focus on the secondary curriculum. Francis P. Robinson (1946) developed the SQ3R (survey, question, read, respond, review) study skills technique. Nila B. Smith (1964) focused on the need to develop fluency based on the knowledge of content-specific vocabulary and concepts. Harold Herber (1970) focused on secondary reading, with a view to helping students learn successful strategies for dealing with subject texts; his work suggests the use of study guides to support comprehension, discussion of alternative interpretations, and strategies such as prediction. H. Alan Robinson (1975, 1977, 1983) focused on the subject-specific nature of reading and writing and the need to help students develop expectations about the vocabulary, content, and structure of the particular course texts they would read. His later work, responsive to the process view of instruction, also focused on the support of comprehension and the development of flexible strategies available for use before, during, and after the actual reading of the text (see the chapter in this *Handbook* by Carl Bereiter and Marlene Scardamalia for more information). Much of this work was responsive to recent findings in applied cognitive psychology. Reading was treated as subject-specific, with the need to help students gain proficiency in comprehending across the various subjects, and this view served as the recommended basis of the secondary reading curriculum.

In response to psychological research on concept development (e.g., Bloom 1956), various schemes for delineating comprehension processes, skills, strategies, and levels of abstraction emerged (e.g., Barrett, 1968). These schemes typically presented three levels of comprehension: literal, inferential, and critical, with some breakdown of skills within each. These schemes continued the use of questions in comprehension development, but the questions were to be of different types in order to foster the acquisition of the various comprehension levels.

The tradition of relying on commercially produced materials had been long established, and reading in school was often limited to textbooks. Beust and Foster (1945; cited in Whipple 1949) reported only 16 percent of schools had central libraries, and the median number of volumes per pupil was far below recommended levels. Thus, basal reader series continued to dominate the experienced curriculum, especially in the early grades.

State curriculum guides generally reflected the longstanding tradition of using especially written texts in early reading instruction, with literature incorporated in the upper grades. For instance, a New York State curriculum guide (New York State Department of Education 1941) recommended beginning with experience charts and then using primers and readers through grade 3, noting that then "as soon as possible, the teacher tries to have the children read books that are not readers" (118). Almost 15 years later, the Commission on the English Curriculum of the National Council of Teachers of English (1954) offered similar recommendations but also provided a graded bibliography of recommended tradebooks. This increase in recommendations for reading outside the basal was reflected even in the basal series themselves during the beginning of the period (Woodward 1986). Such recommendations enhanced concern about the availability of satisfactory library facilities in schools, and federal support was provided later to expand and upgrade them.

The availability of a variety of content texts and opportunities for students to develop adequate study skills became a topic of concern (DeBoer and Whipple 1961; Gray 1949; McKee 1949). Specialized skills practice was recommended for upper elementary instruction as well as for secondary school reading instruction (primarily remedial instruction), along with content area texts (Bond and Kegler 1961). The contribution of content-specific reading instruction to students' general reading development was considered essential in the secondary reading curriculum, and thus the idea of reading across the curriculum, of every teacher as a teacher of reading, became a key goal.

Still, at the primary level, word recognition concerns were widely evident and much attention was given to the sequence of instruction. As with many other textbooks, Gray (1948) devoted one half of his book, *On their Own in Reading*, to a five-stage word recognition program. The text provides no such listing or guidelines for comprehension, although there are a few word-level activities for developing or deriving word meanings in context. Even 20 years later, the New York State Department of Education (1968) curriculum guide for reading presented 37 pages of objectives and activities for word attack, word study, and vocabulary but only 16 pages of comprehension objectives and activities. The pressure from the phonics and back-to-basics advocates was undoubtedly influential, but the advent of linguistic studies of phonology and phonetics and the application of these findings to reading curriculum development also played a role in focusing attention on word recognition.

Throughout this era there was a resurgence of interest in decoding, though at times the argument was recast from earlier eras. For instance, Bloomfield (1942) noted,

> There is always something artificial about reducing a problem to simple mechanical terms, but the whole history of science shows that simple mechanical terms are the only terms in which our limited human capacity can solve a problem. The authors of books on reading methods devote much space to telling why reading is worthwhile. The authors of these books would have done far better to stress the fact that the practical and cultural values of reading can play no part in the elementary stages. (126)

Thus began the argument for the "linguistic" approach, so called because Bloomfield, its major proponent and developer of curricula, was a linguist and based his plan on his analysis of the reading process. These series focused on vowel-consonant patterns, attempting to control text difficulty through restricted sets of words with the same consonant-vowel pattern (e.g., "Dan," "can," "fan," "Nan").

It was in 1955 that Rudolph Flesch published *Why Johnny Can't Read*, the only educational book to top the best-seller list in a half century. Flesch argued that "in every single research study ever made phonics was shown to be superior to the word method" (61). Thus began the great debate about phonics versus whole-word curricula, which has persisted for 35 years. Flesch's attack moved the issue into the public arena; no longer was the concern about the appropriate curriculum focus the province solely of educational authorities (McGill-Franzen 1987).

Finally, concerns about the performance of minority groups, the disadvantaged, and linguistically different children emerged as a national concern. Prior to Sputnik, federal involvement in education was minimal, primarily defined within the role of providing foodstuffs for lunch programs. With the national concern for educational performance, the National Defense Education Act of 1954 (NDEA) and the Elementary and Secondary Education Act of 1965 (ESEA) were passed. This legislation provided for substantial federal involvement through the funding of instructional programs for the disadvantaged, school libraries, research on curriculum and instruction in basic skills, teacher training, and innovative curriculum development projects. Calls for more research to improve the reading curriculum (there were similar calls in science and mathematics) appeared with some regularity, and regional, federally supported educational research and development centers were instituted (Spring 1989).

The Cooperative Research Program funded a massive effort to determine which approach to beginning reading was most effective (Bond and Dykstra 1967). Multiple studies were conducted across the nation comparing basal reader curricula with virtually every other curriculum approach then available. Although these studies were widely read, the conclusion that the teacher was more important than the curriculum material did little to resolve the debate. Proponents of every approach found some support for their preference.

The ESEA of 1965 also created the federally funded Title I remedial programs, which were soon evident in virtually every school district in the nation. This program created a vast new need for refinement of the reading curriculum (and instructional materials), with a focus on underachieving students. Largely through misunderstanding of the federal guidelines, school districts sought curriculum materials for Title I programs that were different from those used in the regular classroom program (Allington 1986). With the curriculum focus on basic skills development and with new sources of funds, small specialty publishers emerged and produced an array of curriculum materials. These were most often skill-based and concerned with developing rudimentary word recognition and comprehension skills, which were the focus of the remedial curriculum.

In response to the concern for individual differences, the diagnostic-presciptive methodology, long a staple in remedial classes, expanded into the general reading curriculum arena. Beck and Bolvin (1969) and Otto (1968) offered curriculum plans that emphasized individual monitoring of skills acquisition. These pretest-teach-posttest curriculum recommendations went beyond the existing curriculum sequences in specificity.

As the era came to a close, new philosophies about learning and instruction and concerns about the achievement of American students had altered curriculum possibilities and provided alternatives. The subskills of reading had been defined, with thousands of specific objectives delineated and organized by grade level. The "back to basics" movement was in full swing, and learning to read was largely depicted as adequate progress through a sequence of skills objectives.

Curriculum Materials in Reading. During this period there was a constriction in the number of basal series produced, even as new publishers entered the market. In 1927, Harris, Donovan, and Alexander had listed 52 different series that they felt were acceptable, whereas almost 40 years later the NSSE yearbook committee chose to review only 10 "acceptable" series (Herrick, Anderson, and Pierstorff 1961). Each of the 3 most popular series of this era (Scott, Foresman; Macmillan; and Houghton Mifflin) provided an eclectic curriculum focus—one that combined whole-word instruction with decoding support lessons. This period also saw the rise of several new code-emphasis reading series, based primarily on the linguistic principles of Bloomfield (1942) and the diagnostic-prescriptive curriculum guidelines.

Hildreth (1949) summarizes the perceived improvements in reading series early in this period. She notes such features as vocabulary control and the gradation of units, scientific checking of readability, provision of workbooks for systematic practice, multigraphing for reproducing practice materials, and easy-to-read storybooks. The use of readability estimates was widely praised by the authors of several chapters in the *Forty-eighth Yearbook of the National Society for the Study of Education* (Henry 1949), and teachers were admonished to use the manuals that accompanied the reading series. Hildreth notes, "Teachers are advised to make full use of the manuals accompanying the basic series which give suggestions for deriving the greatest value from the books. Failure to use the materials as the authors intended may destroy much of the value inherent in carefully prepared series of readers" (78; see also comments by McKee [131] and Whipple [152] in the same volume).

Herrick, Anderson, and Pierstorff (1961) analyzed the common features of 10 basal reading series. All provided readiness, preprimer, and primer books and graded series of texts through grade 6 (some through grade 8). They noted that each used vocabulary control strategies and repetition of words to control readability and foster initial learning. All basals provided teachers' manuals with extensive teaching plans and activities; all provided workbooks; and most included tests, audio-visual materials, word cards, and other supplementary materials. In terms of content, they note,

> As would be expected, the stories and reading activities of the primary grades deal with the lives of children of primary age in their home, school, and community relationships. . . . The sequence in the stories is from immediate and personal experiences in the home and community to the farm and more remote centers of interest—the zoo, firehouse, post office, or store. . . . The intermediate-grade materials extend these same themes to include people throughout the United States, the world, or other days. (177)

Basals attempted to reflect the progressive movement's concern for topic relevance and student comprehension. For beginning readers, learning was thought to be facilitated by widening the scope of content slowly and by limiting the new vocabulary to a few familiar words, as children's awareness of the world expanded through schooling.

Chall (1967) compared two traditional basal readers (Scott, Foresman's 1956 reader and Ginn's 1962 reader) and a new decoding-emphasis series (Lippincott's 1963 reader). The traditional and decoding-emphasis series differed on a number of features, including the introduction of decoding skills, use and length of stories, and dramatically different rates of introductions of new words. Both traditional readers introduced new words at the rate of approximately 2 per 100 running words. The introduction rate in the decoding-emphasis series, in contrast, was 37 per 100 running words. Chall reports that most other aspects of the series were similar, and she argues that the increased rate of word introduction is an advantage of the emphasis on decoding skills acquisition.

Chall (1967) also presented a historical analysis of first-grade readers produced by Scott, Foresman between 1920 and 1962. She noted that the most dramatic change had occurred in the vocabulary introduced in grade 1. The number of words introduced per book had been more than halved (from 425 to 153) during this period (though a small upward trend was observed in the newer series), and the number of pictures had doubled. Her report is better known for its advocacy of code-emphasis programs, but the curriculum analyses and the interviews with basal developers provide informative insights into the nature of reading curriculum development in that era.

Luke (1988) provides a detailed analysis of the reading curricula in British Columbia between 1945 and 1960, the predominantly used Gage Curriculum Foundation Series (a version of the Scott, Foresman Curriculum Foundation Series, known popularly as Dick and Jane, published and also widely used in the United States). Unlike Chall, who concentrates on the physical attributes of the series, Luke attempts to identify the "dominant assumptions of the authors and publishers of the curriculum regarding literacy, the role of literature in the curriculum and the optimal conditions for learning to read" (64). He begins by noting the effect that the scientific movement had on the production and marketing of reading series, suggesting that the new science of market research identified the wants and needs of schools and recommended an appropriate advertising strategy to announce that those needs were being met. Thus, the curriculum (as presented in textbooks) is the product of consensus, and the need to produce further "identical" materials is increased. Luke argues that beginning readers were total curricular creations, written just for the series and rarely reflecting the traditional stories and tales of earlier readers.

> What emerged was an altogether unprecedented genre of literature: the short literary passages consisting of fables and tales of the previous century had been superseded by the lexically, syntactically and semantically controlled texts about modern inter- and postwar life in an industrial democracy. These tales were fabricated solely for the purposes of teaching the "skills" and "habits" of

reading. The application of scientific theories of reading and linguistic development to the engineering of basal readers completed the shift from traditional literary content. (71)

These readers were developed from the point of "familiar experiences," stories set in a family, a neighborhood, and the modern era. What was produced, however, were series in which the story content reflected a single orientation to a particular segment of postwar society—characters who spoke in a language unique to reading series, who played out cultural stereotypical roles, and who exhibited no memory or learning across episodes. Luke (1988) calls these stories "closed" texts, texts that allow little or no interpretation; comprehension is recall of the text, as structured.

Teachers' manuals accompanying the series also changed, reflecting the belief that the materials needed to be used according to particular principles. The manuals presented a fairly standard plan: Each lesson began with a vocabulary list; a story summary for the teacher; questions to establish a story motivation; and in departure from earlier manuals, guided reading questions to be asked during the reading of the story. Scripts for teachers to follow in skill instruction, lesson introductions, and questioning were now standard (Woodward 1986).

As this era drew to a close, new curriculum materials, following the diagnostic-prescriptive skills development framework, began to appear. The SRA Skill Builders (published by Science Research Associates in 1966), Sullivan Programmed Readers (published in 1967), Individually Prescribed Instruction (Beck and Bolvin 1969), DISTAR (Science Research Associates 1969), and computer-assisted instruction (Atkinson 1968) were the result of a combination of federally supported research and development and the press for improved achievement and greater accountability. At the secondary school level, the use of various reading skill kits was attributable to similar influences.

Reading Curriculum in Action. Although reading curriculum had been largely standardized in the various basal series, schools were diverse and in some ways different from today. Whipple (1949) reports on a rural, one-room elementary school; a small urban school; and a large suburban school, demonstrating the needed variety of curriculum organization. Her analysis of the problems faced in providing appropriate curriculum for children of the poor presages many of the concerns that emerged more vocally a decade or two later.

Herrick, Anderson, and Pierstorff (1961) summarize several surveys of reading curriculum and instruction, reporting that at least 90 percent of the schools or teachers used a basal reader series, the majority using a single basal series and the others using a different series for different grades or groups of children. Likewise, over 90 percent of the respondents felt that workbooks were critical or essential elements of the curricular plan and that teacher manuals were essential. These results were mirrored in a national survey reported by Austin and Morrison (1963), who noted that the basal reader series was the dominant instructional tool in most of the 795 districts studied. Nearly two thirds of the districts reported predominant or exclusive use of a single series, and another third reported use of multiple series. They also reported that children spent the majority of their reading period completing workbook pages and that teachers followed the manuals "slavishly." In a similar vein, Barton and Wilder (1964) reported that 98 percent of first-grade teachers and 92 to 94 percent of second- and third-grade teachers used basals all or most days. In addition, about three quarters of the reading professionals in school districts felt that basal readers were essential for reading instruction and were scientifically constructed.

The use of commercial materials was pervasive, and publishers had a virtual lock on defining the received reading curriculum. Publishers hired authors, usually university professors and public school curriculum specialists, to advise in the production of the series; but as Luke (1988) and Shannon (1989) both note, marketing concerns played at least as influential a role as theories or research in the development of the readers. Although few school systems employed curriculum specialists when most school districts were small and rural, the consolidation of rural districts and the urbanization of the citizenry created larger schools and school systems and, ultimately, curriculum specialist positions and bureaus. In the Austin and Morrison (1963) survey, two thirds of the districts reported having curriculum guides for reading and language arts, but field study demonstrated that these played virtually no role in the instruction offered: Almost no teacher reported using them in planning instruction. Instead, teachers used the basal manuals and materials. At the end of the era, basal materials were already shifting to meet the new accountability demands and the increasing competition from curricula that emphasized mastery of individual skills.

Thus, the 1940s through 1960s was a period of social concern for underachieving students and language-based research (predominantly by linguists and psychologists). Although the concerns and new knowledge were known to writing and reading specialists alike, each field responded differently, taking a somewhat different theoretical as well as pragmatic course. Scientific investigators focused on reading, not writing, which is probably the reason progressive psychology and notions of individual differences took a different path in each field. For somewhat different reasons, during this period the curriculum focus in both writing and reading moved away from concerns with student engagement in relevant activities and from support for the learning of skills through meaningful experience.

CURRENT THEORY IN WRITING: THE 1970S THROUGH 1990

Theoretical Bases of Curriculum Research in Writing. Until the 20th century, the theories that informed curriculum in writing focused primarily on form and presentation, and the pedagogical approaches that were based on these views have had a continuing effect on writing curriculum. By the early 20th century these text-based theories were challenged by the experientially driven, student-centered views of Dewey; later, they were also challenged by the socially oriented views of language development emerging during the 1960s. However, even as these theoretical battles were emerging, notions of learning moved away from either a focus on product or a simple focus on experience (Kinneavy 1971). During the 1970s and 1980s, new scholarly views of language and cognition emphasized the relationships among the processes of writing, the cognitive experiences invoked by the writer, and the emerging text (e.g., Bereiter and Scardamalia 1982; Emig 1971; Flower and Hayes 1980; Hillocks 1972). This focus grew in part from work on language and cognition, with particular attention to the structure of language and memory (e.g., Anderson and Bower 1973; Chafe 1970; N. Chomsky 1965; Fillmore 1968; Lakoff 1970; Rumelhart 1975; Schank and Abelson 1977; Searle 1969; Tulving 1972; Winograd 1972).

Further, a rapidly growing body of work in sociolinguistics (see Cazden, John, and Hymes 1972; Cicourel et al. 1974; Halliday 1976; Shuy 1967; Sinclair and Coulthard 1975) helped change the focus from the individual as a language learner to the language learner in context. However, it was not until sociolinguistic and anthropological research methodologies were incorporated into literacy research (e.g., Cook-Gumperz, Gumperz, and Simon 1982; Heath 1983; McDermott 1977) that notions of context were reintroduced into studies of learning. This body of work provided a more comprehensive framework from which to understand relationships among the curriculum, the participants (both teachers and students), and the social settings that affect their interactions.

Building on these frameworks, the 1980s were particularly fruitful years for writing research, with growing bodies of work on the early school years (e.g., Dyson 1984; Florio and Clark 1982; Sulzby 1983), the middle and secondary grades (e.g., Applebee 1981; Cooper, Cherry, Copley, Fleischer, Pollard, and Sortiskey 1984; Freedman 1987; Hillocks 1979), and the college years and beyond (e.g., Bartholomae 1986; Faigley 1979; Kroll 1981; Odell and Goswami 1982).

However, during much of the 1980s, most researchers aligned themselves with cognitive or social approaches to research, rarely using the knowledge of one approach to inform the work of the other. Langer (1985, 1987, 1991), pointing to the contributions of both approaches toward a theory-based view of writing curriculum (and the limitations of either view alone), calls for a sociocognitive perspective on literacy that would combine social and cognitive perspectives in addressing issues of curriculum and schooling.

Gere (1986), in a review of the teaching of writing, points to the lack of a guiding theoretical base as a continuing problem in writing curriculum, suggesting that this void has contributed to the dominance of mechanical features. She describes four theoretical approaches to writing popular in the 1970s and 1980s: a formalist approach (Fulkerson 1979) focusing primarily on forms; discipline (Woods 1981), focusing on style and usage; current traditional (Fogarty 1959; Young 1978), drawing on Aristotle; and positivist current-traditional (Berlin 1984), focusing on the need for an objective message without including the personal or social forces that are also present. Gere sees the concomitant focus on writing process as having been grafted onto these various models of writing but generally lacking a conceptual base.

Applebee (1984), Langer (1984c), and Langer and Applebee (1987) argue on the basis of historical analyses as well as several large-scale studies that the lack of a theoretical reconceptualization of the process of learning to write and the role of the teacher—what to teach, how to teach it, and why—has limited the effectiveness of the reforms in writing curriculum introduced during the 1970s and 1980s. Instead, older conceptualizations have continued to influence work on writing curriculum.

Although few changes in writing curriculum seem to have occurred in the 1940s through 1960s, the 1970s and 1980s witnessed many changes, particularly as "writing process" approaches to instruction grew in popularity (e.g., Calkins 1983; Cooper 1985; Fortune 1986 [on the Bay Area Writing Project]; Graves 1983; Moffett 1968). Advocates of process-oriented approaches to writing take purposeful communication as their focus, developing specific suggestions for ways in which the teacher can support the processes of thinking and writing. Suggestions have included generating ideas through brainstorming and freewriting, a focus on successive drafts as necessary stages in the thinking process, opportunities for in-progress conferences with classmates as well as the teacher, and postponed attention to mechanics and presentation until the final draft.

A new emphasis on writing across the curriculum accompanied these concerns (Applebee 1981; Britton, Burgess, Martin, and Rosen 1975), including an awareness of the role thoughtful writing could play in the learning of academic coursework (Langer and Applebee 1987). In addition, in response to the focus of Bazerman (1981), Bleich (1978), and Toulmin (1976) on social purposes for communicating, a number of studies (e.g., Berkenkotter, Huckin, and Ackerman 1988; Herrington 1985; McCarthy 1987) began to investigate the role of writing in learning the social conventions of the discipline. Examination of large-scale curriculum recommendations will reveal whether and in which ways these theoretical concerns found their ways into actual curriculum statements as well as ways in which obvious theoretical conflicts were treated.

Curriculum Recommendations in Writing. In contrast with and perhaps in response to the lack of substantive changes in writing instruction during the previous 30 years, during the 1970s and 1980s attempts were made to involve teachers in understanding the instructional and curriculum implications of a process approach. As early as 1962, Kitzhaber, reporting on summer workshops conducted by the College Entrance Examination Board's Commission on English, described a widespread attempt to familiarize teachers with the process of writing—the premise being that they would come to understand the process better if they engaged in writing experiences themselves. (This approach is also a major ingredient of the writing workshops conducted by the National Writing Project and its more than 150 affiliates in the United States and other parts of the world.) A second premise is that writing is not simply a mechanical skill but a way to order experience, and thus involves the discovery of knowledge rather than simply the presentation of ideas.

The concern with a process-oriented curriculum has strongly influenced state syllabi in English. Both the California *Handbook for Planning an Effective Writing Program* (California State Department of Education 1982) and the New York State *Composition in the English Language Arts Curriculum* (New York State Department of Education 1986) were strongly influenced by the writing process movement, in intent as well as in a wide variety of curriculum suggestions. The California syllabus encourages programs that include writing as a means of learning, through a wide range of writing experiences in all curriculum areas. Integration of the language arts is recommended. The curriculum guidelines build on students' interests but treat writing as a process that includes prewriting, writing, responding, revising, editing, developing skills with writing conventions, evaluating, and postwriting. Instruction is integrated into the writing process. Grammar and usage are not to be taught in isolation.

The New York State syllabus marks a similar change in focus, also based on the view of writing as a process. It argues that "whole piece" writing should be emphasized as opposed to isolated subskills, suggesting that writing is more accurately termed the "writing process" and involves prewriting, composing, and revision. Students are encouraged to write from their own experiences and to develop several drafts, followed by individual mini-conferences or by instruction in grammar and mechanics. The specific foci of the K–12 writing curriculum are built around products the students might produce and the skills instruction they might need.

Similarly, a report on *Writing Achievement of California Eighth Graders* (Cooper and Breneman 1988) includes the following recommendations (among others) for writing curriculum: Elementary and junior high school students should be offered more direct instruction in writing and thinking strategies required for different types of writing; students should read widely and analyze the same types of texts they are writing; and sustained literacy programs should be extended to all students, including the disadvantaged, the bilingual, and low achievers.

The New York State syllabus in English (New York State Department of Education 1988) recognizes the importance of basic skills and competencies but places them within an integrated program of the language arts and their inseparable relationship to communication. It links the learning of content to language and thought and views writing as a vehicle for learning.

In addition, the National Council of Teachers of English, the Modern Language Association, and six other organizations concerned with the teaching of English held a joint 3-week meeting during the summer of 1987 to assess the language needs of students and discuss new directions for education. The conference report, *The English Coalition Conference: Democracy Through Language* (Lloyd-Jones and Lunsford 1989), called for a major effort to transform English education (including the teaching of writing) into an interactive experience in which teachers help students learn to use language to ponder meaningful topics and communicate what they think and know.

Thus, the "process" approach to writing instruction easily made its way into curriculum recommendations and guidelines. But to establish whether the guidelines followed rather than led changes in the experienced curriculum, it is necessary to include a brief review of research on the nature of the materials used to teach writing.

Curriculum Materials in Writing. Keroes (1983) conducted a study of college anthologies that used prose models to teach composition. Her findings indicate that in the treatment of the selections, most textbooks adhere to the traditional paradigm and do not reflect the changes in perspective suggested by recent work on the composing process.

A decade and a half after the Squire and Applebee (1968) report, Arthur Applebee (1984) analyzed the writing assignments and activities in the three most popular textbooks in seven high school subjects (composition/grammar, literature, Spanish, social science, science, mathematics, and business education) for evidence of the kinds of writing students were being asked to do. He concluded that the writing experiences in high school textbooks were narrow as well as limited. To an overwhelming extent, writing assignments were evaluative, seeking correct answers rather than engaging students in using writing to express their views or explore ideas. The types of writing requested were also limited, primarily calling for brief responses and placing the student in a passive, recitation role. The grammar and composition textbooks in particular provided little opportunity for extended writing, with 88 percent of the writing tasks prompting restricted writing (multiple choice, fill in the blank, and short answers) and the primary focus being on grammar and usage.

Thus, at the beginning of the 1980s, no appreciable change had occurred in textbooks' presentation of writing experiences. This is a pattern that weaves across the century: Although a growing body of research and theory has provided an increasingly rich knowledge base with potential to spur curriculum reform in writing, the closer to the classroom the focus, the more inertia is found. Pedagogical movements have followed research and theory fairly rapidly, but calls for changes in curriculum have lagged much further behind, and changes in textbooks seem minuscule. A review of the received curriculum from 1970 to 1990 will suggest that this is also the case in classrooms.

Writing Curriculum in Action. Despite efforts to involve teachers in the process movement, studies conducted in the late 1970s and early 1980s provide little evidence that such approaches have been carried into the classroom. For example, Graves (1983), in a report to the Ford Foundation about the status of writing in elementary schools, noted that elementary school children are seldom asked to write. The little writing they do consists of workbook exercises and drills emphasizing traditional subskills such as capitalization, punctuation, and grammar. There is also little emphasis on writing instruction; instead, teachers talk about writing rather than guiding students actually to write; nor do students write on their own. Graves suggests that teachers are ill prepared to teach writing and proposes a process-conference approach, in which the focus is on helping students discover their own ideas and ways to present them.

Bridge and Hiebert (1985) observed two students in each of six classrooms (grades 1, 3, and 5) for 3 full days and gathered additional data from a survey of 233 teachers in the same grades. Like Graves, they concluded that elementary children spend little time writing; they do more transcription than composition. Few assignments involved writing more than a sentence, and much of the writing was for fill-in-the-blank workbooks and worksheets. Emphasis was on the word and sentence level, with little focus on whole messages. Prewriting activities were seldom used, and little connection was made between writing and other content studies.

This pattern of a thoughtless writing curriculum continued throughout the 1980s, despite a century of progressive thought and large-scale reform efforts on behalf of process-oriented approaches. Applebee (1981) conducted the most comprehensive survey of writing undertaken at the high school level, in content as well as in English classes. Data were collected by observations and interviews in two schools for a full academic year, followed by a national survey. He reported that 44 percent of class time involved students in some sort of written work. However, 24 percent of that time was devoted to mechanical writing and 17 percent involved note taking; only 3 percent of the time was devoted to writing of paragraph length or longer. Although the writing of longer pieces occurred more frequently in English than in other classes, even there writing over a paragraph in length occurred only 10 percent of the time. Writing was found most frequently in math, science, and social science classes, but these activities generally involved short-answer or fill-in responses.

Across subjects, writing was most frequently used as a testing activity, with a right answer to a predetermined issue; rarely was it used as a means to explore ideas. Routine marking of grammar and usage errors was done by 71 percent of the teachers, and 47 percent rated error correction as one of the most important kinds of instruction they provided to their students. Fewer than one fifth of the teachers responding to the survey reported directly responding to their students' ideas on a routine basis.

In an attempt to learn more about the role of writing in the high school curriculum, Langer and Applebee (1987) studied subject teachers (English, history, biology, chemistry, survival skills, and world culture) for a period of from 6 months to 2 years. They also conducted a series of experimental studies with more than 400 students to examine the effects of writing on content learning. The results provide strong support for writing in subject classes: Activities involving writing (rather than reading or studying alone) led to better content learning than when no writing took place. However, the researchers found that teachers' traditional notions of learning facts before thinking about them limited extended writing. On the other hand, when teachers changed their views of writing to include thoughtful exploration of the content, both the use of writing and the complexity of the concepts the students focused on increased dramatically.

As part of its large-scale assessment of student achievement, the National Assessment of Educational Progress (1986) report, *Writing Trends Across the Decade: 1974–1984*, examined shifts in writing in the classrooms of 13- and 17-year-olds in 1974, 1979, and 1984. The results indicate that the number of students reporting little or no instruction in writing decreased significantly, from 48 percent to 35 percent, during these 10 years. However, one third of the 17-year-olds and two fifths of the 13-year-olds reported receiving no writing instruction. The 17-year-olds reported writing about the same number of papers during the decade, about four papers across all subjects over a 6-week period. Students were also asked about the frequency with which they revised and the frequency with which their teachers responded to their papers. Teachers' suggestions showed a clear increase during the decade for 17-year-olds, from 32 percent to 56 percent. Attention to drafting and encouragement to jot down ideas showed a less dramatic increase for both 13- and 17-year-olds. Thus, some changes in writing instruction clearly took place. However, these trends did not have an appreciable affect on students' writing performance as measured by the National Assessment. The report concludes that although the data are insufficient to reject recent attempts at reform, they do suggest the need to study the manner in which process activities are being carried out.

Thus, although the 1940s through 1960s was a period of quiescence in writing, the following 2 decades were unusually active, with much school-based as well as theoretical support for process-oriented approaches to both curriculum and instruction. In reading, shifts in orientation were also dramatic, emanating from different bodies of research but reflecting related concerns.

CURRENT THEORY IN READING: THE 1970S THROUGH 1990

Theoretical Bases of Curriculum Research in Reading. Since the beginning of the 20th century, much effort has been spent in the development of psychological theories of the reading process. The earliest efforts were confined primarily to associationist theories represented by the work of E. L. Thorndike. B. F. Skinner shaped much of the effort through the 1960s, though the fields of linguistics and artificial intelligence also began to exert an influence on the psychological models. Theoretical model building through the 1960s concentrated more on the word-recognition processes (Massaro 1984), although comprehension was not wholly neglected.

In the early 1970s several new curricula were developed and disseminated by federally funded research and development centers. These tended to reflect the diagnostic-prescriptive approach and emphasized both the early development of word-recognition skills and the close monitoring of skill acquisition (Della-Piana and Endo 1973; Quilling 1971; Schutz 1970). Coleman's (1970) research-based educational engineering included experimental scaling of word difficulty, letter-sound associations, and other phonic elements. His work and the similar work of others were directed at determining empirically the ideal curriculum sequence. Fueled by federal support, the new curriculum products were hailed as the solution to problems of basal readers, materials based more on tradition, it was argued, than on good experimental evidence.

Several factors converged in the early 1970s, and the nature of research on the reading process began to shift so that comprehension processes became the primary focus of many efforts. Bartlett (1932), whose gestalt views on comprehension included the notion of schema, was rediscovered and stimulated a substantial body of research and curriculum development (Anderson and Pearson 1984). At the same time, research in language acquisition and sociolinguistics influenced research on the reading process, again with a focus on the construction of meaning during the reading process (Bernstein 1972; Britton 1970; Brown and Belugi 1964; C. Chomsky 1970; Gumperz and Hymes 1972; Labov 1966; McDermott 1977). Finally, research in writing and shifts in that curriculum provided an impetus for reconsidering the reading curriculum (Fortune 1986; Graves 1978). From these diverse sources emerged a substantial body of research on learning from text with a constructivist view of comprehension (F. Smith 1971). This "cognitive psychology of reading" differed dramatically from the earlier associationist psychology that had dominated reading research from the turn of the century. This new view of reading as an interaction between the reader and the text altered earlier schemes for depicting comprehension. Similarly, the traditional views of levels of comprehension were modified to reflect the role of the reader (Langer 1985; Pearson and Johnson 1978).

Notions about text difficulty also shifted, as did procedures for estimating the difficulty of textual materials. The limitations of readability formulas that had served as the standard predicting comprehensibility of text became clearer and new procedures emerged (Bormuth 1966; Klare 1984). Cloze was touted both as a procedure for estimating text difficulty and, later, as a useful instructional tool for fostering or assessing comprehension. Topic familiarity, or prior knowledge, was viewed as necessary in estimating text difficulty (Langer 1984b) and reading comprehension (Johnston 1983). This body of research influenced both the development of curriculum materials and the design of instruction. Renewed emphasis on prereading activity resulted from studies of the effects of prior knowledge and schema activation on reading processes (Beck, Omanson, and McKeown 1982; Langer 1981; Pearson, Hansen, and Gordon 1979).

At the same time, models of learning, particularly Carroll's (1963), stimulated a number of classroom-based studies of teaching and learning and studies of reading instruction in elementary schools (Anderson, Evertson, and Brophy 1979; Berliner 1981; Carter 1984; Cooley and Leinhardt 1980; Duffy and McIntyre 1982; Quirk, Trisman, Nalin, and Weinberg 1975). The reports focused on a variety of features of classrooms that were positively correlated with reading achievement, but instructional time allocated to reading and the time students spent on academic tasks seemed to receive the greatest attention.

The classroom-based research, when combined with the emerging constructivist notions of the reading process, fostered new possibilities for curriculum reform. During the 1980s traditional curriculum frameworks were attacked for failing to focus on students' thinking and reasoning. Two lines of research and theorizing were carried out simultaneously, one dominated by cognitivist views of learning and the other by sociolinguistic understanding. The former continued the experimental research tradition, studying basic mental processes and textual features (e.g., Adams and Collins 1979; Palincsar and Brown 1984; Stein and Trabasso 1982). The latter, using qualitative research methods drawn from anthropology and linguistics, focused on the social organization of classrooms, the social nature of reading lessons, and teacher-child interactions (e.g., Au and Jordan 1981; Cazden 1988; Cicourel et al. 1974; Gumperz 1982; Heath 1983; McDermott 1977). Most researchers aligned themselves with one position or the other, although Langer (1987) called for a sociocognitive perspective that would merge the two camps.

Although much classroom research was conducted between 1970 and 1990, few studies investigated the intersection of curriculum and instruction. The classroom studies focused on student engagement with curriculum materials but offered little comment on the materials themselves. However, the findings led to calls for increased allocations of time to reading instruction and to reading itself (Allington 1983). Later studies focused on the interplay between teachers and students, but again the role of curriculum in the instructional enterprise was not studied.

The 1980s witnessed the renewal of concerns about (1) the content of the reading curriculum, especially the role of literature (Walmsley and Walp 1990); (2) the integration of reading and writing curriculum and instruction (Pearson and Tierney 1984); and (3) whether curriculum should reflect a predetermined and adult-driven organizational scheme or be child-centered. Attention to curriculum issues became particularly critical in this era when large-scale accountability for instructional programs became more widespread, with most states conducting statewide assessments of reading and the states' chief school officers and the federal government calling for increased national assessment efforts.

Curriculum Recommendations in Reading. Concerns about academic achievement, especially in urban areas, precipitated Edmonds's (1975, 1979) study of effective schools, and a national movement emerged that emphasized the productivity of classroom instruction and guidelines for enhancing learning. Edmond reported several factors associated with high academic achievement (usually reading): time spent on academic work, raising performance standards, and monitoring of performance. In practice, these were translated into longer reading periods, more difficult curriculum materials, heightened curriculum performance standards, and more frequent testing of progress.

The report of the National Academy of Education's Committee on Reading reflected a similar emphasis (Carroll and Chall 1975). Attention to the reading program, high expectations for success, regular assessment of progress, and flexibility in methods and materials are recommended (29). Later the committee argues for more comprehensive assessment tools and instructional systems, both recommended to alleviate the inappropriate teaching it perceived in the nation's schools. Finally, the report includes a chapter on the need to implement a token reward system for correct responses. The influence of associationist-behaviorist psychology is much evident throughout this report. Less evident is the influence of theories that incorporate cognitive-constructivist views drawing from the expanding literature on language acquisition and psycholinguistic theories of the reading process.

During this same period many states implemented competency testing for reading, and districts implemented reading performance standards for grade-level promotion. The combined effect of these actions was to narrow the curriculum goals and activities (Johnson and Pearson 1975) and increase rates of retention (Shepard and Smith 1989). Ten years later, the National Academy of Education released another report, *Becoming a Nation of Readers* (Anderson, Hiebert, Scott, and Wilkinson 1984), which more often reflected the findings of cognitive as well as associationist psychology. Like the earlier report, there were recommendations for more and better tests of reading progress, increased time for reading, well-designed phonics instruction, and better-designed early reading materials. The report also called for more and better comprehension instruction, less time on skill sheets, more actual reading and writing, better school libraries, and continued education for teachers.

Recently, the Reading Commission of the National Council of Teachers of English released the *Report Card on Basal Readers* (Goodman, Shannon, Freeman, and Murphy 1988). The preface notes, "It is the absolute dominance of basal readers that led . . . to this study into basal reading programs." Much like the earlier criticisms of basal readers (e.g., Boney 1938; Veatch 1959), the authors focus on alternative conceptualizations of reading curriculum, particularly trade books. This report goes beyond those prepared earlier, echoing the progressive movement in presenting a rationale for the empowerment of teachers and children to select appropriate curriculum materials and instructional organization. The criticisms of existing curriculum incorporate much of the research on reading processes and reading instruction from outside the associationist and cognitivist tradition, calling on sociolinguistic and anthropological studies for their evidence. The report includes a variety of recommendations that call for deemphasizing the role of basal readers, standardized tests, and a reconsideration of mandated programs of instruction.

Finally, Education Secretary William Bennett (1988) issued his model elementary school curriculum with a heavy emphasis on classic literature during reading. His criticisms of the content of school readers are strongly reminiscent of Eliot's at the turn of the century (National Education Association 1984). His other recommendations reflect the conservative back-to-basics movement that held sway in the 1960s. Although Bennett's recommendations differ markedly from those of the Reading Commission and the National Academy of Education, there are, however, several common points in the series of recommendations. Though their political and theoretical bases differ, each emphasizes the need for teachers who are better trained. There is a tendency to decry the heavy reliance on commercial reading materials, yet each report calls for improvements in their design. All point to changes in American society that make higher levels of literacy a requisite goal of reading education and call for a curriculum that ensures the development of such abilities. Only the *Report Card on Basals* (Goodman, Shannon, Freeman, and Murphy 1988) and Secretary Bennett's proposal raised serious questions about the essential goals as well as the design of the reading curriculum.

None of the reports actually addresses reading in the secondary school, and only an occasional mention is made of reading in content area classes. This is surprising given the increased accountability requirements that deny high school diplomas unless certain reading standards are met. During this period, much research in reading focused on the adolescent reader (for a comprehensive review see Alvermann and Moore in press) and on reading across the subject areas. Recommendations for altering the nature of secondary reading curricula are less common than the calls for change in elementary schools, but the few recommendations that do exist call for fundamental shifts in the conceptualization as well as the organization of secondary school curriculum and instruction (Langer and Applebee 1987; Sizer 1986).

During the 1980s, many states revised their existing reading curricula. Four populous states (California, Florida, New York, and Texas) developed curricula for reading that include many of the suggestions recommended by the various reports. California's *Framework for the Language Arts* (California State Department of Education 1987) presents a curriculum plan that departs measurably from the long-dominant skills approach, and one can observe a similar shift in New York's *Reading and Literature in the English Language Arts Curriculum* (New York State Department of Education 1988b). Nonetheless, California, although recommending a literature focus, elected to implement the state plan with a basal reader adoption, and New York explained the role of basal readers in fulfilling the curriculum requirements. Texas and Florida, in contrast, retained a traditional focus on the essential skills to be included at each grade level and also implemented their curriculum plans through statewide basal reader adoptions.

Tyson-Bernstein (1988) studied the effects of state curriculum guidelines on the development of commercial reading curricula and concludes that the harder state officials work at regulating the content of textbooks, the less useful textbooks become for students. Her recommendations begin with a call for states to cease the practice of issuing detailed, skill-oriented specifications for reading curriculum: "Authors and editors do not willingly chop and flatten sentences . . . [the] source of the writing problem is not the publishing house, but in the public agency. Legislators, educational policymakers, and administrative regulators have unintentionally drained the life out of children's textbooks" (1). Tyson-Bernstein gives a number of examples of such influence, but the case of readability formulas in the production of reading material may be the best. She notes that although readability formulas have been substantially criticized, their use is mandated in the production of readers and other textbooks in most states: Publishers must conform to be allowed in the market. Similarly, many states have guidelines for story content that publishers must adhere to as well as mandates for worksheets, chapter or unit tests, and of course comprehensive teacher's guides.

As the nation enters the 1990s, the basal reader is still the dominant curriculum. There are calls for other conceptualizations of the received curriculum, and some schools are implementing curricula that rely less on basal readers and more on literature, with an integration of reading and writing instruction (e.g., Hansen 1987; Routman 1988; Walmsley and Walp 1989). Some states are revising their curriculum standards and assessment procedures in an attempt to reflect developing conceptions of the reading process. The National Assessment of Educational Progress also is shifting assessment procedures and providing state-by-state comparisons for the first time. The tensions between "scientifically" organized curriculum and the "child-centered" curriculum have reemerged, as in previous eras (Y. Goodman 1989). And once again the debate about the appropriate unit of text on which to focus in beginning reading instruction has surfaced (Adams 1990; Stahl, Osburn, and Lehr 1990), and this historic debate is again vigorous (Rothman 1990).

Curriculum Materials in Reading. New theoretical models of the reading process, especially developments in cognitive models of comprehension processes, stimulated a variety of studies examining various facets of basal reader programs. Most of these studies were of relatively small scale, examining a limited number of basal materials or only limited features of these programs.

Willows, Borwick, and Hayvren (1981) studied the first-grade materials of four basal programs published in the 1970s. They report substantial variation in the series on virtually every feature examined, lending some doubt to the common notion that such materials are very similar. For instance, the number of words introduced in the first-grade readers ranged from 300 to over 1,000, suggesting that the decline in vocabulary load, which had been dropping since 1920 (Chall 1967), had been reversed. Some series contained twice as much reading material as others; the average number of repetitions of new words ranged from 10.2 to 44.2; and the rate of introduction of new words varied just as widely. They note that arguments for the use of "literary wholes" had no obvious effect since text averaged between 77 and 143 words. From half to all of the stories fit into their "real-life" content category.

Popp (1975) reviewed 13 basal series published in the late 1960s and early 1970s and reported that there was substantial evidence that many of them had been influenced by the calls for increased attention to decoding skills (Chall 1967; Flesch 1955). The organization of the decoding component reflected several perspectives. Some were more traditional phonics programs with an early emphasis on letter-sound relationships; others offered decoding skills following the linguistic method of vowel-consonant patterns, restricting initial material to the patterns previously taught. Only three of the programs were not considered to have a decoding emphasis. Popp concludes that the available curriculum materials reflect the lack of agreement about the nature of the reading process and the appropriate procedure for initiating reading instruction.

Other researchers examined specific aspects of basal reader curriculum. Some concluded that the word-recognition and decoding components are not well designed (e.g., Barnard and DeGracie 1976; Beck and Block 1979; Stotsky 1981); others reviewed comprehension features of lessons (e.g., Beck and Block 1979; Durkin 1981; Johnson and Barrett 1980), and some analyzed the content of the readers from a variety of perspectives (e.g., Butterfield, Demos, Grant, Moy, and Perez 1979; Flood and Lapp 1987; Kyle 1978; Schmidt, Caul, Byers, and Buchmann 1984; Taylor 1973); Osborn (1984), particularly, analyzed the workbooks that accompanied the basal series. These reports suggest that vocabulary load is increasing in the primary materials, that characters and illustrations better reflect the diversity of American society but still could be improved, and that the comprehension components of the curriculum have much room for improvement.

These studies of curriculum materials often reveal as much about the educational ideologies of the authors as about the materials themselves. Curriculum analysis has always been theory-driven; different views of the world, of the ideal society, and of the role of schools as agents of change or stability result in different analyses and conclusions. That said, it is interesting to see the continuing changes in basals as attempts to keep pace with strong but dissenting views of curriculum and instruction.

Reading Curriculum in Action. Studies of classroom reading instruction make little mention of the curriculum, except in the broadest sense. We know that basal readers are widely used (Education Products Information Exchange 1977), that students spend little of their scheduled reading period actually reading, that students do spend the majority of their time working alone at their seats on skill sheets, and that an individual student's progress through a basal reader series is well correlated with achievement test scores (Barr and Sadow 1989; Cooley and Leinhardt 1980; Gambrell 1984; Gamoran 1986; Howlett and Weintraub 1979; Rosenshine and Stevens 1984). But little is known about how curriculum interacts with instruction to facilitate learning except that beginning reading curricula with different emphases produce different reading strategies (Barr 1975; Calfee and Piontkowski 1981; Johnston and Allington in press).

Studies conducted during this period (Barr and Sadow 1989; Borko, Shavelson, and Stern 1981; Durkin 1984; Stodolsky 1989) suggest that even though basal materials are widely used, teachers may not adhere to the planned program quite as "slavishly" as had been depicted earlier (e.g., Austin and Morrison 1963); teachers routinely omit some segments of the lesson plan in the basal reader. Durkin (1984), for instance, expresses surprise that teachers ignore prereading activities designed to tap prior knowledge and set purpose, especially since a wealth of studies have demonstrated the value of such procedures. Barr and Sadow (1989) note that the organizational format of basal readers influences which components are used and that teachers make conscious choices about which activities to include or omit.

Other studies depict the variability of time allocated for reading instruction within and between schools and districts (e.g., Allington and McGill-Franzen 1989; Barr and Sadow 1989; Berliner 1984; Birman 1988; Gambrell 1984; Rowan and Guthrie 1989) and the time spent reading outside of school (Anderson, Wilson, and Fielding 1988). The most dismaying findings, perhaps, are that schools with large numbers of poor children scheduled substantially less time for reading than schools with few poor children and that children with the lowest reading achievements routinely receive the least reading instruction and engage in the least reading.

It is teachers who ultimately interpret and deliver curriculum to children in the form of lessons, assigned tasks, and evaluative responses. However, few studies examine the interaction of teachers and curriculum. One exception is a study by Bussis, Chittenden, and Amarel (1976) of primary grade teachers' attempts to move from a more traditional, teacher-centered curriculum to a more child-centered one. After extensive interviews, the authors identified several types of teachers, differentiated by the priorities they set. One group set narrow priorities for learning, speaking of the importance of acquiring grade-level facts and skills and showing little interest in changing the organization of the curriculum. Another group fell into a middle range of priorities, speaking of the need to develop independence and promote personal initiative among students, wanting the students to assume responsibility for their own learning, but showing concern for grade-level facts and skills. The comprehensive teachers were concerned with children's reflectivity, initiative, and independence. These teachers had dramatically altered the surface curriculum, evidenced little concern for grade-level facts and skills, and were engaged in substantial personal experimentation in their teaching. This last group was in the minority.

SUMMARY AND NEW DIRECTIONS FOR RESEARCH

Overall, reading and writing curriculum theory and research have both overlapping and also very different histories. It is clear that through the 1960s the two were not typically conceptualized as being related or integrated in any way. Yet, although each had its own very different tradition (one borrowing from the British university and one from the British primary curriculum), they were both affected by the global impact of progressive theory. Each also had cultural realities to contend with, be they the patriotism of a new nation or the pragmatic needs of a growing and changing society. Throughout the century each field also faced internal tension: Calls for grammar exercises and a student-centered curriculum competed in writing, and calls for reading mechanics and a meaning-based curriculum competed in reading.

These tensions became more obvious in the 1950s and 1960s, when research in concept development, language acquisition, and dialect described the rich language-learning abilities of children and the distinctions between child and adult rule setting and performance. The tensions became even more exacerbated during the 1970s and 1980s, when sociolinguistic and anthropological research methodologies focused on the implications of communication, context, and culture for learning.

In each field, while the theorists warred, the pragmatists compromised. No one studied the relative contribution each might make to a theoretically sound and largely reconceptualized curriculum, one that would need to undergo essential change in response to new knowledge, whatever its genesis.

There are continuing issues that the next generation of research needs to address in making substantive changes.

Immobility of the Received Curriculum. "As in other areas, theory and pedagogy do not necessarily coincide with practice" (Dexter 1906). This review of writing curriculum research provides no reason to think differently today. There has been a continuing tension between traditional and progressive ideologies, and the seeds of today's arguments can be found in those voiced more than 100 years ago, when writing became part of the academic curriculum. By the late 1800s tensions between the teaching of writing for functional purposes as opposed to "high" literacy were already in place, as were arguments about the merit (or folly) of exercises in grammar and usage. And despite continuing scholarly debates, a compromise seems to have been made long ago in practice. One can only speculate on why this has occurred, but at least part of the immobility has stemmed from the measures that have been used as indicators of learning. Strategies for content-based thinking seem to have vied with the demonstration of decontextualized knowledge as evidence of "knowing" (with display of skills and content being more easily tested), yet research has just begun to tease the two apart. A move toward open-ended questions designed to invite students to communicate their ideas in their own language, combined with a function-based notion of performance (e.g., primary trait scoring), is clearly in the right direction. But further research is needed in how these notions can best contribute to substantial reform of curriculum as well as assessment.

As in writing curriculum research, the received reading curriculum has experienced only subtle shifts during the last 100 years. These shifts are seen more in the content of the material read than in the nature of the organization of the curriculum. Unlike the writing curriculum, reading curriculum has been defined by commercially produced materials, typically basal reader series, with only infrequent and modest inroads achieved by other materials or curriculum plans. Reading is still more likely to be taught as a separate area than integrated with the other language arts or with other content area subjects.

The recent concern about cultural literacy (Hirsch 1987), with its emphasis on knowledge of classical tales and authors, is strikingly reminiscent of Eliot's strident argument before the turn of the century (National Education Association 1894). Although the use of "authentic literature" has been recommended during the several eras reviewed, there is little evidence that such literature has ever played a dominant role in many schools. Similarly, although basal reader series have been roundly and frequently criticized, they have dominated the received curriculum throughout the history of American schooling. Many use the basal series as the whipping post, attributing the various perceived ills of schools to their use. Less often have scholars studied why American society has perpetuated the basal series as the curriculum of choice. Shannon's (1987, 1989) work is the rare exception to this trend, but he stops at the point of acknowledging the existence of powerful institutional and individual belief systems that underlie the perpetuation of basal readers.

When children's books were rare and teachers largely untrained, the reader series served an obviously critical function. Today, however, these series seem somewhat anachronistic but still play a role at least as important as that played over a century ago. Perhaps basal series still serve because schools and instruction have not changed nearly as much as other institutions in society (Cuban 1984). Perhaps the received curriculum envisioned by some cannot be changed until schools do.

Although no other area of learning has been studied so well, we still have calls to provide research and development for effective reading instruction (National Governors Association 1986). We need, perhaps, research into the purposes of reading instruction and the goals of the reading curriculum. The most recent reports from the National Assessment of Educational Progress (1988) suggest that schools have enhanced the acquisition of basic reading skills, but these programs have not succeeded in improving the ability of students to reflect on what they read or interpret or to critique texts. Some have argued that this is good evidence that the "basic skills" emphasis of the past 2 decades has achieved its goal (Shor 1986). Recent debates about the teaching of reading have only infrequently addressed the question of the political purposes of schooling, generally, or reading instruction, particularly. Likewise, those involved in reading curriculum research have only rarely addressed such issues.

Recent calls for the reform of education leave little doubt that schools are seen as a central institution in the perpetuation of American society. Schools are depicted as failing to provide workers of appropriate aptitude and attitude for success in the global economy. If, as Spring (1989) argues, we continue to confuse the "thinkable" with the "doable," little will probably change in our schools or in our reading curriculum. Schools reflect the society in which they exist but are often viewed as important vehicles for change. Current literacy curricula perpetuate the sorting function—channeling students into one category or another, ordering by achievement. Given that schools were designed to fill this function, it is not surprising that literacy curricula have not been changed. Although some would like schools to lead society toward change, it is not at all clear that there is any common vision of what that change should be nor of how to achieve it. Research into the thinkable curriculum and its relationship to learning is needed.

The Unit of Focus in Instruction. During the century, the most basic and long-lived differences between proponents of traditional and progressive views of reading and writing are based on the unit of focus. In writing, the Harvard reports and the Committee of Ten contradicted each other within a few years. The first, concerned with an influx of college students who did not write as well as was expected, called for exercises in superficial correctness (spelling, grammar, usage, and handwriting), whereas the latter stated that attention to these areas separate from a student's own writing was ineffective. However, the focus on the student's writing versus the decontextualized practice of language skills became polarized, becoming the primary dividing lines between the traditional and progressive voices in writing throughout the century. In reading, the debate since the turn of the century has been on whether letters or words or meanings are the mainstay of the curriculum. What is most interesting in both reading and writing is that the issues are so long-lived.

Part of the issue was the teachability of the materials and the suggestions that were provided. Pedagogical suggestions in support of grammar and mechanics exercises were easily turned into an additive curriculum—with less complex skills and structures leading to more complex ones, and all parts building to "mature" writing or reading ability. Curriculum guidelines included specific skills and structures to be taught, and the sequences in which to teach them were codified in ways that could easily be "lifted" by materials developers and teachers. In contrast, experienced-based pedagogy had no such prescriptive plan to codify; it was the inappropriateness of such a plan that was at the heart of its theory. Thus, its suggestions to the field lacked the specificity and examples to teachers and textbook writers for carrying them out. The ways in which teachers could help students learn skills, strategies, and structures in the context of their own work (while giving them room to be creative and critical thinkers) seem to have escaped codification, making it a less specifiable (and less stable) part of the curriculum. Perhaps this need not be so; future research needs to explore ways in which the principles that underlie activity-based instruction can best be articulated; some of the most promising current work in this direction has been based on the ideas of Vygotsky (e.g., Griffin and Cole 1987; Moll and Diaz 1987).

Writing and Reading Across the Curriculum. Proposals for writing and reading across the curriculum have been in existence at least since the late 1800s. However, unlike the stability of instruction in grammar and usage, reading and writing across the curriculum seems to have moved in and out of favor depending on the theoretical leanings of the era. It is possible that such curricula require large-scale changes in the conceptualization of writing and reading instruction (and their goals), and therefore could never become part of a "compromise curriculum." Further research is needed to address the roles of reading and writing in subject area curricula—their effect on learning the subject and the effect of authentic uses of written language in subject coursework on students' growing ability to read and write. For example, Cooper and Breneman (1988), Hillocks (1986), Langer (1984a), Langer and Applebee (1987), Lloyd-Jones and Lunsford (1989), and National Assessment of Educational Progress (1986) all call for helping writers learn the kinds of thinking skills required by specific tasks in specific subjects. Attention to the range of discipline-specific literacy tasks and purposes and the particular kinds of thinking and learning they involve would make an important contribution to literacy curricula, and to educational reform in general.

Process and Product. It is quite clear that recent calls for process-oriented instruction also have a long history, dating at least to the early works of Buck (1901), Dewey (1915), and Huey (1968 [1908]). The experiential curriculum called for a focus on the experience itself, with instructional support provided along the way. However, during the century, writing and reading curricula seem to have focused on ways to provide student-centered experiences more so than on ways in which teachers could support the process, thus leaving classroom connections between process and product unspecified.

Since the 1970s, the focus on process in both reading and writing has led to important understanding of the processes involved. However, research has yet to put the parts together, exploring ways in which the knowledge of process and experience affect the product (what is understood or written) and the concomitant implications for curriculum.

There is actually rather little in the way of research findings to guide curriculum development. Most available research has attempted to describe methods, materials, or instruction. There are old method A versus method B studies, but these did not investigate the fidelity of implementation (of the received curriculum) nor the kinds of thinking and learning invoked by the particular methods, only superficial outcome indicators. What little experiential research on curriculum is available is short term, not longitudinal. Although certain approaches seem to have positive effects on short-term learning, the long-term effects of particular curricula on learning and use are little understood.

Reading and Writing as Curriculum. Although the major focus of this chapter has been on the lack of curriculum change during the 20th century, the chapter's very existence stands as evidence of the deep theoretical changes that have been taking place in reading and writing. Ten years ago, no one would have suggested that a combined chapter on reading and writing be written; the two domains were perceived as distinctly separate parts of the curriculum, involving different activities and goals. And this is no surprise since the history of their incorporation into the educational agenda is so different.

Yet there is clearly intellectual movement toward a unification of reading and writing in the curriculum. This movement recognizes the different functions that reading and writing serve in any particular activity (Florio and Clark 1982; Heath 1983) as well as the different kinds of thinking (often about somewhat different content) that are invoked by different kinds of reading and writing tasks (Hillocks 1986; Langer 1984a, 1984b; Langer and Applebee 1987). It also values the deeply related cognitive and linguistic contributions of reading and writing toward thought, learning, and communication of knowledge—seeing each as a tool that helps us gain, contemplate, and use ideas (Bissex 1980; Chall and Jacobs 1984; Harste, Burke, and Woodward 1983; Shanahan 1984; Teale 1982; Tierney and Pearson 1983).

This unified view of reading and writing can already be seen in curriculum recommendations that accentuate the ways in which the two embody the thinking skills that underlie performance in each of the subject areas (see Cooper and Breneman 1988; Lloyd-Jones and Lunsford 1989). The implication of these changes is nontrivial, involving the dismantling of long-lived, separated bodies of curricular study and replacing them with a new one. Such change will involve research into the ways in which reading and writing interplay on a day-to-day basis in academic learning, the contexts that support their development, and the implications for the shape of academic coursework.

Literate Thinking. Broad educational goals always aim for literate thinkers, students who not only can read and write but also can think and reason about what they are learning. However, curriculum disagreements throughout the century have centered on the best ways in which to help students become literate thinkers. Taking a sociocognitive view of literacy (e.g., Griffin and Cole 1984, 1987; Langer 1987, 1991), recent theory and research suggest that the classroom is a social community, with its own values, behaviors, and ways of thinking, and that literacy involves learning to read, write, and think in ways that are appropriate to that community. Underlying these ideas is the belief that use shapes thinking and learning and that the contribution of context and culture cannot be overstated in terms of the effects of what is learned. Although these notions are critical to schooling in a diverse society, much research is needed before they are incorporated into conceptualizations of curriculum.

At this juncture reading and writing curriculum researchers are faced with tension among historical relevance, disciplinary vision, and reality. Institutional and societal uses of and demands concerning reading and writing have changed, scholarly knowledge has changed, understanding about how reading and writing are learned has changed, and conceptualizations about how they can best be taught have changed. Yet this knowledge has not been applied in a research agenda bringing together issues of literate ways of thinking and the classroom experience in a manner that can lead to a new framework for describing the effects of restructured classroom values, goals, and interactions. Longitudinal research into the effects of different reading and writing instructional environments on the development of literate thought is essential.

Finally, few studies have looked at the effects of alternative literacy environments on the learning of traditionally underachieving students or on that of students of diverse linguistic or ethnic origins. These studies will require thorough examinations of relationships between expressed and received curricula and between new programs and long-term effects on thinking, learning, and use. Knowledge of such effects will be necessary to move educators and publishers away from their long-standing compromise.

CONCLUDING REMARKS

In the works reviewed in this chapter we have seen that although the major issues of concern today are reverberations of earlier ones, the breadth of knowledge that is currently available results from multidisciplinary research efforts to understand issues of reading, writing, and schooling. Although it might be easy to conclude that research is on the right track and that more similar work is needed, this is not at all the case. We know a good deal about reading and writing in general, but the paucity of *curriculum* research in these domains is astounding. The kinds of studies that address what needs to be taught to whom, under what conditions, and in response to what impetus or sequence have yet to be undertaken. Such studies will need to be complex, taking into account all we know about the social and contextual and cognitive factors that interact with curriculum. They will also need to rethink dramatically what curriculum means—as well as what it looks like—when these issues are addressed.

What little research on curriculum exists is thin, in part because of the enormity of the problem; literacy curriculum research of today must pioneer new directions, reconceiving the role as well as the structure of reading and writing instruction in schools. Many basic questions that underlie the teaching and learning of literacy remain to be answered. Many of these focus on the relative roles of content, skills, discipline-specific thinking, and the student in the instructional agenda. The limited amount of curriculum research is also due to the fragmentation of knowledge that has been used to guide existing research. Although the historical gap between reading and writing as distinct areas of specialization is narrowing and the overt antagonism between literacy cognitivists and contextualists that dominated the 1980s seems to have abated, many researchers in the critical areas are still not reading one another's work and are asking less comprehensive questions as a result. To some degree, then, we researchers share responsibility for the immobility of the literacy curriculum. There is much work yet to be done.

References

Adams, Marilyn J. 1990. *Beginning to Read: Thinking and Learning About Print.* Cambridge, MA: M.I.T. Press.

Adams, Marilyn J., and Alan M. Collins. 1979. "A Schema-theoretic View of Reading." In *Discourse Processing: Multidisciplinary Perspectives*, edited by Roy O. Freedle. Norwood, NJ: Ablex.

Allington, Richard L. 1975. One hundred years of progress. *The New England Reading Association Journal* 10(1): 24–27.

Allington, Richard L. 1983. The reading instruction provided readers of differing ability. *Elementary School Journal* 83(5): 548–559.

Allington, Richard L. 1984. "Oral Reading." In *Handbook of Reading Research*, edited by P. David Pearson, 829–864. White Plains, NY: Longman.

Allington, Richard L. 1986. "Policy Constraints and Effective Compensatory Reading Instruction." In *Effective Teaching of Reading: Research and Practice*, edited by James Hoffman, 261–289. Newark, DE: International Reading Association.

Allington, Richard L., and Anne McGill-Franzen. 1989. School response to reading failure of Chapter I and special education students in grades 2, 4, and 8. *Elementary School Journal* 89(5): 529–542.

Alvermann, Donna, and David Moore. In press. "Secondary School Reading." In *Handbook of Reading Research*, 2nd ed., edited by P. David Pearson, Rebecca Barr, Michael Kamil, and Peter Mosenthal. White Plains, NY: Longman.

Anderson, Irving H., and Walter F. Dearborn. 1952. *The Psychology of Reading*. New York: Ronald Press.

Anderson, John, and Gordon Bower. 1973. *Human Associative Memory*. Washington, DC: Winston.

Anderson, Linda M. 1984. "The Environment of Instruction: The Function of Seatwork in a Commercially Developed Curriculum." In *Comprehension Instruction: Perspectives and Suggestions*, edited by Gerald Duffy, Laura Roehler, and Jana Mason, 93–103. White Plains, NY: Longman.

Anderson, Linda M., Carolyn Evertson, and Jere Brophy. 1979. An experimental study of effective teaching in first grade reading groups. *Elementary School Journal* 79(4): 193–223.

Anderson, Richard C., Elfrieda H. Hiebert, Judith Scott, and Ian A. Wilkinson. 1984. *Becoming a Nation of Readers: A Report of the Commission on Reading*. Washington, DC: National Institute of Education.

Anderson, Richard C., and P. David Pearson. 1984. "A Schema-theoretic View of Basic Processes in Reading." In *Handbook of Reading Research*, edited by P. David Pearson, 255–292. White Plains, NY: Longman.

Anderson, Richard C., Paul Wilson, and Linda Fielding. 1988. Growth in reading and how children spend their time outside of school. *Reading Research Quarterly* 23(3): 285–303.

Applebee, Arthur N. 1974. *Tradition and Reform in the Teaching of English*. Urbana, IL: National Council of Teachers of English.

Applebee, Arthur N. 1981. *Writing in the Secondary School: English and the Content Areas*. Urbana, IL: National Council of Teachers of English.

Applebee, Arthur N. 1984. *Contexts for Learning to Write: Studies of Secondary School Instruction*. Norwood, NJ: Ablex.

Artley, A. Sterl. 1944. A study of certain relationships existing between general reading comprehension and reading comprehension in a specific subject matter area. *Journal of Educational Research* 37(6): 464-473.

Atkinson, Richard C. 1968. Computerized instruction and the learning process. *American Psychologist* 23(4): 225–239.

Au, Kathy H., and Cathie Jordan. 1981. "Teaching Reading to Hawaiian Children: Finding a Culturally Appropriate Solution." In *Culture and Bilingual Classrooms: Studies in Classroom Ethnography*, edited by Henry Trueba, Grace P. Guthrie, and Kathy H. Au. Rowley, MA: Newbury House.

Austin, Mary C., and Coleman Morrison. 1963. *The First R: The Harvard Report on Reading in Elementary Schools*. New York: Macmillan.

Bagley, William C., and George C. Kyte. 1926. *The California Curriculum Study*. Berkeley: University of California.

Bain, Alexander. 1866. *English Composition and Rhetoric: A Manual*. London: Longmans, Green.

Barnard, Douglas P., and James DeGracie. 1976. Vocabulary analysis of new primary reading series. *Reading Teacher* 30(2): 177–180.

Barr, Rebecca. 1975. The effect of instruction on pupil reading strategies. *Reading Research Quarterly* 10(4): 555–582.

Barr, Rebecca, and Marilyn W. Sadow. 1989. Influence of basal programs on fourth-grade reading instruction. *Reading Research Quarterly* 24(1): 44–71.

Barrett, Thomas C. 1968. "Taxonomy of Cognitive and Affective Dimensions of Reading Comprehension." In *Innovation and Change in Reading Instruction. Sixty-seventh Yearbook of the National Society for the Study of Education*, Part II, edited by Helen M. Robinson, 7–29. Chicago: University of Chicago Press.

Bartholomae, David. 1986. "Inventing the University." In *When a Writer Can't Write: Research on Writer's Block and Other Writing Process Problems*, edited by Mike Rose. New York: Guilford.

Bartlett, Frederic C. 1932. *Remembering*. Cambridge: Cambridge University Press.

Barton, Allen, and David E. Wilder. 1964. "Research and Practice in the Teaching of Reading." In *Innovations in Education*, edited by M. Miles. New York: Teachers College Press.

Bateman, Donald, and Frank Zidonis. 1966. *The Effect of a Study of Transformational Grammar on the Writing of 9th and 10th Graders*. Champaign, IL: National Council of Teachers of English.

Bazerman, Charles. 1981. What written knowledge does: Three examples of academic discourse. *Philosophy of the Social Sciences* 11(3): 361–387.

Beck, Isabel L., and K. K. Block. 1979. "An Analysis of Two Beginning Reading Programs: Some Facts and Some Opinions." In *Theory and Practice of Early Reading*, vol. 1, edited by Lauren B. Resnick and Phyllis A. Weaver, 279–318. Hillsdale, NJ: Erlbaum.

Beck, Isabel L., and John O. Bolvin. 1969. A model for non-gradedness: The reading program for individually prescribed instruction. *Elementary English* 46(2): 130–135.

Beck, Isabel L., Richard C. Omanson, and Margaret G. McKeown. 1982. An instructional redesign of reading lessons: Effects on comprehension. *Reading Research Quarterly* 17(4): 462–481.

Bennett, William J. 1988. *James Madison Elementary School: A Curriculum for American Students*. Washington DC: U.S. Department of Education.

Bereiter, Carl, and Marlene Scardamalia. 1982. "From Conversation to Composition." In *Advances in Instructional Psychology*, vol. 2, edited by Robert Glaser. Hillsdale, NJ: Erlbaum.

Berkenkotter, Carol, Thomas Huckin, and John Ackerman. 1988. Conventions, conversations, and the writer: Case study of a student in a rhetoric Ph.D. program. *Research in the Teaching of English* 22(1): 9–44.

Berlin, James. 1984. *Writing Instruction in Nineteenth-century American Colleges*. Carbondale: Southern Illinois University Press.

Berlin, James. 1987. *Rhetoric and Reality: Writing In American Colleges, 1900–1985*. Carbondale: Southern Illinois University Press.

Berliner, David C. 1981. "Academic Learning Time and Reading Achievement." In *Comprehension and Teaching: Research Review*, edited by John Guthrie. Newark, DE: International Reading Association.

Bernhardt, Norma W. 1963. *Trends in the Teaching of English Written Composition in the Secondary Schools of the United States*. Ann Arbor, MI: University Microfilms.

Bernstein, Basil. 1972. "Social Class, Language, and Socialization." In *Language and Social Context*, edited by P. Giglioli. Middlesex, England: Penguin Books.

Berthoff, Ann E. 1981. *The Making of Meaning*. Upper Montclair, NJ: Boynton/Cook.

Beust, Nora E., and Emery M. Foster. 1945. *Statistics of Public-School Libraries, 1941–42*. Washington, DC: Federal Security Agency, U.S. Office of Education.

Birman, Beatrice F. 1988. How to improve a successful program. *American Education* 12: 22–29.

Bissex, Glenda. 1980. *Gnys at Wrk*. Cambridge, MA: Harvard University Press.

Blair, Hugh. 1965 (1783). *Lectures on Rhetoric and Belles Lettres*, edited by Harold F. Harding. Carbondale: Southern Illinois University Press.

Bleich, David. 1978. *Subjective Criticism*. Baltimore, MD: Johns Hopkins University Press.

Bloom, Benjamin. 1956. *Taxonomy of Educational Objectives: Cognitive Domain*. New York: McKay.

Bloomfield, Leonard J. 1942. Linguistics in reading. *Elementary English Review* 19(4): 125–130, 183–186.

Bond, Guy L., and Robert Dykstra. 1967. The cooperative research program in first-grade reading instruction. *Reading Research Quarterly* 2(4): 5–142.

Bond, Guy L., and Stanley B. Kegler. 1961. "Reading Instruction in the Senior High School." In *Development in and Through Reading. Sixtieth Yearbook of the National Society for the Study of*

Education, Part I, edited by N. B. Henry, 320–335. Chicago: University of Chicago Press.

Boney, Charles. 1938. Basal readers. *Elementary English Review* 15(3): 133–137.

Borko, Hilda, Richard J. Shavelson, and Paula Stern. 1981. Teachers' decisions in the planning of reading instruction. *Reading Research Quarterly* 16(3): 449–466.

Bormuth, John R. 1966. Readability: A new approach. *Reading Research Quarterly* 1(3): 79–132.

Braddock, Richard, Richard Lloyd-Jones, and Lowell Schoer. 1963. *Research in Written Composition*. Urbana, IL: National Council of Teachers of English.

Bridge, Constance, and Elfrieda H. Hiebert. 1985. A comparison of classroom writing practices, teachers' perceptions of their writing instruction, and text book recommendations on writing practices. *The Elementary School Journal* 86(2): 155–172.

Britton, James. 1970. *Language and Learning*. London: Penguin Books.

Britton, James, Tony Burgess, Nancy Martin, and Harold Rosen. 1975. *The Development of Writing Abilities*, 11–18. London: Macmillan.

Brown, Roger. 1973. *A First Language*. Cambridge, MA: Harvard University Press.

Brown, Roger W., and Ursula Bellugi. 1964. Three processes in the child's acquisition of syntax. *Harvard Educational Review* 34(2): 133–151.

Bruner, Jerome S. 1960. *The Process of Education*. Cambridge, MA: Harvard University Press.

Bruner, Jerome S. 1966. *Toward a Theory of Instruction*. Cambridge, MA: Belknap-Harvard University Press.

Bruner, Jerome S., Jacqueline L. Goodnow, and G. A. Austin. 1956. *A Study of Thinking*. New York: Wiley.

Buck, Gertrude. 1899. *A Course in Argumentative Writing*. New York: Henry Holt and Company.

Buck, Gertrude. 1901. Recent tendencies in the teaching of English composition. *Educational Review* 22: 371–382.

Bussis, Ann M., Edward A. Chittenden, and Marianne Amarel. 1976. *Beyond Surface Curriculum: An Interview Study of Teachers' Understandings*. Boulder, CO: Westview.

Butterfield, Robin A., Elene S. Demos, Gloria W. Grant, Peter S. Moy, and Anna L. Perez. 1979. A multicultural analysis of a popular basal reading series in the International Year of the Child. *Journal of Negro Education* 48(3): 382–389.

Calfee, Robert C., and Dorothy C. Piontkowski. 1981. The reading diary: Acquisition of decoding. *Reading Research Quarterly* 16(3): 346–373.

California State Department of Education. 1982. *Handbook for Planning an Effective Writing Program K–12*. Sacramento: California State Department of Education.

California State Department of Education. 1986. *Handbook for Planning an Effective Writing Program: Kindergarten Through Grade Twelve*. Sacramento: California State Department of Education.

California State Department of Education. 1987. *English-Language Arts Framework for California Public Schools, Kindergarten Through Grade 12*. Sacramento: California State Department of Education.

Calkins, Lucille. 1983. *Lessons from a Child*. Exeter, NH: Heinemann.

Campbell, George. 1963 (1776). *The Philosophy of Rhetoric*, edited by Lloyd F. Bitzer. Carbondale: Southern Illinois University Press.

Carpenter, George R., Franklin T. Baker, and Fred N. Scott. 1903. *The Teaching of English in the Elementary and Secondary Schools*. New York: Longmans, Green.

Carroll, John B. 1963. A model for school learning. *Teachers College Record* 64(8): 723–733.

Carroll, John B., and Jeanne S. Chall. 1975. *Toward a Literate Society: A Report from the National Academy of Education*. New York: McGraw-Hill.

Carter, Launor F. 1984. The sustaining effects study of compensatory and elementary education. *Educational Researcher* 12(7): 4–13.

Cazden, Courtney B. 1988. *Classroom Discourse: The Language of Teaching and Learning*. Portsmouth, NH: Heinemann.

Cazden, Courtney B., Vera P. John, and Dell Hymes, eds. 1972. *Functions of Language in the Classroom*. New York: Teachers College Press.

Chafe, Wallace. 1970. *The Meaning and Structure of Language*. Chicago: University of Chicago Press.

Chall, Jeanne S. 1967. *Learning to Read: The Great Debate*. New York: McGraw-Hill.

Chall, Jeanne S., and Vicki A. Jacobs. 1984. "Writing and Reading in the Elementary Grades: Developmental Trends Among Low SES Children." In *Composing and Comprehending*, edited by Julie M. Jensen. Urbana, IL: ERIC Clearinghouse for Reading and Communication Skills.

Chomsky, Carol. 1970. Reading, writing, and phonology. *Harvard Educational Review* 40(2): 287–309.

Chomsky, Noam. 1965. *Aspects of a Theory of Syntax*. Cambridge, MA: M.I.T. Press.

Cicourel, Aaron V., Sybillyn H. M. Jennings, Kenneth H. Jennings, Kenneth C. Leither, Robert McKay, Hugh Mehan, and David R. Roth. 1974. *Language Use and School Performance*. New York: Academic Press.

Cobb, Lyman. 1835. *The North American Readers*, New York: B. S. Colins.

Coleman, Edmund B. 1970. Collecting a data base for a reading technology. *Journal of Educational Psychology Monographs* (4), part 2: 1–23.

Commission on English. 1965. *Freedom and Discipline in English*. New York: College Entrance Examination Board.

Commission on the English Curriculum of the National Council of Teachers of English. 1952. *The English Language Arts*. New York: Appleton-Century-Crofts.

Commission on the English Curriculum of the National Council of Teachers of English. 1954. *Language Arts for Today's Children*. New York: Appleton-Century-Crofts.

Commission on the English Curriculum of the National Council of Teachers of English. 1956. *The English Language Arts in the Secondary School*. New York: Appleton-Century-Crofts.

Commission on the English Curriculum of the National Council of Teachers of English. 1963. *The Education of Teachers of English for American Schools and Colleges*. New York: Appleton-Century-Crofts.

Commission on the English Curriculum of the National Council of Teachers of English. 1965. *The College Teaching of English*. New York: Appleton-Century-Crofts.

Committee on Types of Organization of High School English. 1913. Types of organization of high school English. *English Journal* 2(1): 575–595.

Connors, Robert J. 1982. The rise of technical writing instruction in America. *Journal of Technical Writing and Communication* 12(4): 329–352.

Cook-Gumperz, Jenny, John J. Gumperz, and Herbert D. Simons. 1982. "Final Report on School/Home Ethnography Project." Berkeley: University of California.

Cooley, William W., and Gaea Leinhardt. 1980. The instructional dimensions study. *Educational Evaluation and Policy Analysis* 2(1): 7–25.

Cooper, Charles, ed. 1985. *Researching Response to Literature and the Teaching of Literature*. Norwood, NJ: Ablex.

Cooper, Charles, and Beth Breneman. 1988. *Writing Achievement of California Eighth Graders: A First Look (Preliminary)*. Sacramento: California State Department of Education.

Cooper, Charles R., Roger Cherry, Barbara Copley, Stefan Fleischer, Rita Pollard, and Michael Sortisky. 1984. "Studying the Writing Abilities of a University Freshman Class: Strategies from a Case Study." In *New Directions in Composition Research*, edited by Richard Beach and Lillian S. Bridwell. New York: Guilford.

Corbett, Edward. 1965. *Classical Rhetoric for the Modern Student*. New York: Oxford University Press.

Counts, George S. 1926. *The Senior High School Curriculum*. Chicago: University of Chicago Press.

Cuban, Lawrence. 1984. *How Teachers Taught: Constancy and Change in American Classrooms, 1890–1980*. White Plains, NY: Longman.

Davis, Frederick B. 1944. Fundamental factors of comprehension in reading. *Psychometrika* 9(3): 185–197.

DeBoer, John J., and Gertrude Whipple. 1961. "Reading Development in Other Curricular Areas." In *Development in and Through Reading. Sixtieth Yearbook of the National Society for the Study of Education*, Part I, edited by Nelson B. Henry. Chicago: University of Chicago Press.

Della-Piana, Gabriel M., and George T. Endo. 1973. "Reading Research." In *Handbook of Research on Teaching*, 2nd ed., edited by Robert M. Travers, 883–925. Chicago: Rand McNally.

Dewey, John. 1915. *The School and Society*. Chicago: University of Chicago Press.

Dexter, Edwin G. 1906. Ten years influence of the report of the Committee of Ten. *The School Review* 14(4): 254–269.

Dolch, Edward. 1931. *The Psychology and Teaching of Reading*. Champaign, IL: Garrard.

Donsky, Barbara von Bracht. 1984. Trends in elementary writing instruction, 1900–1959. *Language Arts* 6(8): 795–803.

Duffy, Gerald G., and Lonnie D. McIntyre. 1982. A naturalistic study of instructional assistance in primary-grade reading. *Elementary School Journal* 83(1): 15–23.

Durkin, Dolores. 1981. Reading comprehension instruction in five basal reader series. *Reading Research Quarterly* 16(4): 515–544.

Durkin, Dolores. 1984. Is there a match between what elementary teachers do and what basal reader manuals recommend? *Reading Teacher* 3(8): 734–745.

Dyson, Ann. 1984. Learning to write/Learning to do school. *Research in the Teaching of English* 18(3): 233–264.

Edmonds, Ronald. 1975. Some schools work and more can. *Social Policy* 9(5): 28–32.

Edmonds, Ronald. 1979. *A Discussion of the Literature and Issues Related to Effective Schooling*. St. Louis, MO: CEMREL.

Edmund, N. R. 1960–1961. "Writing in the Intermediate Grades." In *Children's Writing: Research in Composition and Related Skills*, edited by Alvina T. Burrows, Champaign, IL: National Council of Teachers of English.

Education Product Information Exchange. 1977. *Report on a National Survey of the Nature and Quality of Instructional Materials Not Used by Teachers and Learners*. Technical report no. 76. New York: EPIE Institute.

Elbow, Peter. 1971. Exploring my teaching. *College English* 32(7): 743–753.

Emerson, Henry P., and Ida C. Bender. 1905. *Modern English: A Practical English Grammar with Exercises in Composition*. New York: Macmillan.

Emig, Janet. 1971. *The Composing Process of Twelfth Graders*. Research report no. 13. Urbana, IL: National Council of Teachers of English.

Evans, William H., and Jerry L. Walker. 1966. *New Trends in the Teaching of English in Secondary Schools*. Chicago: Rand McNally.

Faigley, L. 1979. The influence of generative factors on the syntactic fluency and writing effectiveness of college freshmen. *Research in the Teaching of English* 13(3): 197–206.

Fillmore, Charles J. 1968. *The Case for Case: Universals in Linguistic Theory*, edited by Edmund Bach and Robert T. Harms. New York: Holt, Rinehart and Winston.

Fishman, Joshua. 1977. *Bilingual Education: Current Perspectives, Social Science*. Arlington, VA: Center for Applied Linguistics.

Flesch, Rudolph. 1955. *Why Johnny Can't Read: And What You Can Do About It*. New York: Harper.

Flood, James, and Diane Lapp. 1987. Forms of discourse in basal readers. *Elementary School Journal* 87(3): 299–306.

Florio, Susan, and Christopher Clark. 1982. Functions of writing in the classroom. *Research in the Teaching of English* 16: 115–130.

Flower, Linda S., and John R. Hayes. 1980. The cognition of discovery: Defining a rhetorical problem. *College Composition and Communication* 31(1): 21–32.

Fogarty, Daniel. 1959. *Roots for a New Rhetoric*. New York: Russell & Russell.

Fortune, Ron, ed. 1986. *School-College Collaborative Program in English*. New York: Modern Language Association.

Freedman, Sarah W. 1987. *Response to Student Writing*. Urbana, IL: National Council of Teachers of English.

Fries, Charles C. 1940. *American English Grammar: The Grammatical Structure of Present-day American English with Especial Reference to Social Differences or Class Dialects*. New York: Appleton.

Fries, Charles C. 1963. *Linguistics and Reading*. New York: Holt, Rinehart and Winston.

Fulkerson, Richardson. 1979. Four philosophies of composition. *College Composition and Communication* 30(4): 343–348.

Gambrell, Linda. 1984. "How Much Time Do Children Spend Reading During Reading Instruction?" In *Changing Perspectives on Research in Reading/Language Processing and Instruction*, edited by Jerome A. Niles and L. A. Harris, 193–198. Rochester, NY: National Reading Conference.

Gamoran, Adam. 1986. Instructional and institutional effects of ability grouping. *Sociology of Education* 59(4): 185–198.

Genung, John F. 1888. *Handbook of Rhetorical Analysis: Studies in Style and Invention*. Boston: Ginn.

Gere, Ann R. 1986. "Teaching Writing: The Major Theories." In *The Teaching of Writing. Eighty-fifth Yearbook of the National Society for the Study of Education*, Part II, edited by Anthony R. Petrosky and David Bartholomae. Chicago: University of Chicago Press.

Goodman, Kenneth S. 1967. Reading: A psycholinguistic guessing game. *Journal of the Reading Specialist* 6(4): 126–135.

Goodman, Kenneth S., and James T. Fleming. 1969. *Psycholinguistics and the Teaching of Reading*. Newark, DE: International Reading Association.

Goodman, Kenneth S., Patrick Shannon, Yvonne Freeman, and Sharon Murphy. 1988. *Report Card on Basal Readers*. Katonah, NY: Richard C. Owen.

Goodman, Yetta. 1989. Roots of the whole-language movement. *Elementary School Journal* 90(2): 113–128.

Graves, Donald H. 1978. *Balance the Basics: Let Them Write*. New York: Ford Foundation.

Graves, Donald H. 1983. *Writing: Teachers and Children at Work*. Exeter, NH: Heinemann.

Gray, William S. 1917. "The Relation of Silent Reading to Economy in Education." In *Second Report of the Committee on Minimal Essentials in Elementary School Subjects. Sixteenth Yearbook of the National Society for the Study of Education*, Part I, edited by H. B. Wilson. Bloomington, IL: Public School Publishing.

Gray, William S. 1919. "Principles of Method in Teaching Reading as Derived from Scientific Investigations." In *Report of the Committee on Economy of Time and Learning. Eighteenth Yearbook of the National Society for the Study of Education*, Part II, edited by Ernest Horn. Bloomington, IL: Public School Publishing.

Gray, William S. 1925. *Report of the National Committee on Reading. Twenty-fourth Yearbook of the National Society for the Study of Education*, Part I. Bloomington, IL: Public School Publishing.

Gray, William S. 1937. "The Nature and Organization of Basic Instruction in Reading." In *The Teaching of Reading: A Second Report. Thirty-sixth Yearbook of the National Society for the Study of Education*, Part I, edited by William S. Gray. Bloomington, IL: Public School Co.

Gray, William S. 1948. *On Their Own in Reading*. Glenview, IL: Scott, Foresman.

Gray, William S. 1949. "Reading as an Aid in Learning." In *Reading in the Elementary School. Forty-eighth Yearbook of the National Society for the Study of Education*, Part II, edited by Nelson B. Henry, 233–253. Chicago: University of Chicago Press.

Gray, William S., and Bernice Leary. 1935. *What Makes a Book Readable?* Chicago: University of Chicago Press.

Griffin, Peg, and Michael Cole. 1984. "Current Activity for the Future: The ZOPED." In *Children Learning in the Zone of Proximal Development*, edited by Barbara Rogoff and James Wertsch. San Francisco, CA: Jossey-Bass.

Griffin, Peg, and Michael Cole. 1987. "New Technologies, Basic Skills, and the Underside of Education." In *Language, Literacy and Culture: Issues of Society and Schooling*, edited by Judith Langer. Norwood, NJ: Ablex.

Gumperz, John. 1982. *Discourse Strategies*. London: Cambridge University Press.

Gumperz, John, and Dell Hymes eds. 1972. *Directions in Sociolinguistics*. New York: Holt, Rinehart and Winston.

Halliday, Michael A. K. 1976. *Cohesion in English*. London: Longmans.

Halloran, Michael. 1982. Rhetoric in the American college curriculum. *Pre/Text 3*: 245–269.

Hansen, Jane. 1987. *When Writers Read*. Portsmouth, NH: Heinemann.

Harste, Jerome, Caroline Burke, and Virginia Woodward. 1983. *The Young Child as Writer-Reader, and Informant*. Final report to the National Institute of Education NIE-G-80-0121. Washington, DC: U.S. Department of Education.

Hatfield, Wilbur W. 1935. *An Experience Curriculum in English*. A report of the curriculum commission of the National Council of Teachers of English. New York: Appleton-Century Company.

Heath, Shirley B. 1983. *Ways with Words: Language, Life and Work in Communities and Classrooms*. New York: Cambridge University Press.

Henry, Nelson B., ed. 1949. *Reading in the Elementary School. Forty-eighth Yearbook of the National Society for the Study of Education*, Chicago: University of Chicago Press.

Herber, Harold. 1970. *Teaching Reading in the Content Areas*. Englewood Cliffs, NJ: Prentice Hall.

Herrick, Virgil E., Dan Anderson, and Lola Pierstorff. 1961. "Basal Instruction Materials in Reading." In *Developments in and Through Reading. Sixtieth Yearbook of the National Society for the Study of Education*, Part I, edited by Nelson B. Henry, 165–188. Chicago: University of Chicago Press.

Herrington, Ann J. 1985. Writing in academic settings. *Research in the Teaching of English* 19(4): 331–361.

Hildreth, Gertrude. 1949. "Reading Programs in the Early Primary Grades." In *Reading in the Elementary School. Forty-eighth Yearbook of the National Society for the Study of Education*, edited by Nelson B. Henry, 54–92. Chicago: University of Chicago Press.

Hill, A. S. 1878. *The Principles of Rhetoric and Their Application*. New York: Harper.

Hill, D. J. 1878. *The Elements of Rhetoric and Composition*. New York: Sheldon & Company.

Hillocks, George. 1972. *Alternatives in English*. Urbana, IL: ERIC.

Hillocks, George. 1979. The effects of observational activities on student writing. *Research in the Teaching of English* 13(1): 21–25.

Hillocks, George. 1986. *Research on Written Composition*. Urbana, IL: ERIC/NCRE.

Hirsch, E. Donald. 1987. *Cultural Literacy. What Every American Needs to Know*. Boston: Houghton Mifflin.

Hitchcock, A. M. 1939. *High School English Book*. New York: Henry Holt and Company.

Hook, Julius N. 1979. *A Long Way Together: A Personal View of NCTE's First Sixty-seven Years*. Urbana, IL: National Council of Teachers of English.

Horn, Ernest. 1919. *Fourth report of the Committee on the Economy of Time in Education. Eighteenth Yearbook of the National Society for the Study of Education*, Part II. Bloomington, IL: Public School Publishing.

Hosick, James F. 1912. "Progress in Articulating School and College English." In *National Education Association Addresses and Proceedings, 1912*. Chicago: University of Chicago Press.

Hosic, James F., ed. 1917. *Reorganization of English in Secondary Schools. Report of the Joint Committee on English*. Commission on the English Curriculum. Washington, DC: U.S. Government Printing Office.

Hosic, James F. 1923. "The Aims of English Composition Teaching." In *English Composition: Its Aims, Methods and Measurement. Twenty-second Yearbook of the National Society for the Study of Education*, part I, edited by Earl Hudelson. Bloomington, IL: Public School Co.

Howlett, Nancy, and Samuel Weintraub. 1979. "Instructional Procedures." In *Teaching Reading in Compensatory Classes*, edited by R. Calfee and P. Drum, 87–100. Newark, DE: Instructional Reading Association.

Hudelson, Earl. 1923. *English Composition: Its Aims, Methods, and Measurement. Twenty-second Yearbook of the National Society for the Study of Education*, Part I. Bloomington, IL: Public School Company.

Huey, Edmund B. 1968 (1908). *The Psychology and Pedagogy of Reading*. Cambridge, MA: M.I.T. Press.

Inhelder, Barbel, and Jean Piaget. 1958. *The Growth of Logical Thinking from Childhood to Adolescence*. London: Routledge & Kegan Paul.

Johnson, Dale D., and Thomas C. Barrett. 1980. "Prose Comprehension: A Descriptive Analysis of Instructional Practices." In *Children's Prose Comprehension: Research and Practice*, edited by Carol M. Santa and B. L. Hayes, 72–102. Newark, DE: International Reading Association.

Johnson, Dale D., and P. David Pearson. 1975. Skills management systems: A critique. *Reading Teacher* 28(8): 757–764.

Johnston, Peter A. 1983. *Reading Comprehension Assessment: A Cognitive Basis*. Newark, DE: International Reading Association.

Johnston, Peter A., and Richard L. Allington. In press. "Remediation." In *Handbook of Reading Research*, vol. 2, edited by P. David Pearson. White Plains, NY: Longman.

Kaestle, Carl F. 1983. *Pillars of the Republic: Common Schools and American Society, 1780–1860*. New York: Wang.

Kaestle, Carl F., and Mavis Vinovkis. 1980. *Education and Social Change in Nineteenth Century Massachusetts*. Cambridge: Cambridge University Press.

Kelly, Louis G. 1969. *Centuries of Language Teaching*. Rowley, MA: Harvard University Press.

Keroes, Jo. 1983. "Anthologies of Prose Models and the Teaching of Composition." Dissertation Abstracts International, 44.

Kinneavy, James. 1971. *A Theory of Discourse: The Aims of Discourse*. New York: Norton.

Kitzhaber, Albert. 1953. "Rhetoric in American Colleges, 1850–1900." Ph.D. dissertation, University of Washington, Seattle.

Kitzhaber, Albert. 1962. New perspectives on teaching composition. *College English* 23(6): 440–444.

Klare, George R. 1984. "Readability." In *Handbook of Reading Research*. White Plains, NY: Longman.

Kroll, Barry. 1981. "Developmental Relationships Between Speaking and Writing." In *Exploring Speaking-Writing Relationships*, edited by B. Kroll and R. J. Vann. Urbana, IL: National Council of Teachers of English.

Kyle, Diane W. 1978. Changes in basal reader content: Has anyone been listening? *Elementary School Journal* 78(5): 305–312.

Labov, William. 1966. *The Social Stratification of English in New York City*. Washington, DC: Center for Applied Linguistics.

Lakoff, George. 1970. *Irregularity in Syntax*. New York: Holt, Rinehart and Winston.

Langer, Judith A. 1981. From theory to practice: A pre-reading plan. *Journal of Reading* 25(2): 152–157.

Langer, Judith A. 1984a. The effects of available information on responses to school writing tasks. *Research in the Teaching of English* 18(1): 27–44.

Langer, Judith A. 1984b. Examining background knowledge and text comprehension. *Reading Research Quarterly* 14(4): 468–481.

Langer, Judith A. 1984c. Literacy instruction in American schools. *American Journal of Education* 93(1): 107–131.

Langer, Judith A. 1985. Levels of questioning: An alternative view. *Reading Research Quarterly* 20(5): 586–602.

Langer, Judith A. 1986. *Children Reading and Writing: Structures and Strategies*. Norwood, NJ: Ablex.

Langer, Judith A. 1987. "Sociocognitive Perspective on Literacy Learning." In *Language, Literacy and Culture*, edited by Judith Langer. Norwood, NJ: Ablex.

Langer, Judith A. 1991. "Literacy and Schooling: A Sociocognitive Perspective." In *Literacy for a Diverse Society*, edited by Elfrieda Hiebert. New York: Teachers College Press.

Langer, Judith A., and Arthur Applebee. 1987. *How Writing Shapes Thinking: Studies of Teaching and Learning*. Urbana, IL: National Council of Teachers of English.

Lewis, W. D. and James Hosic. 1916. *Practical English for High Schools*. New York: American Book Company.

Lloyd-Jones, Richard, and Andrea Lunsford. 1989. *English Coalition Conference: Democracy Through Language*. Urbana, IL: National Council of Teachers of English.

Luke, Alan. 1988. *Literacy, Textbooks and Ideology*. Philadelphia, PA: Falmer.

Lyman, Richard L. 1932. *Summary of Investigations Relating to Grammar, Language and Composition (January 1929 to January 1931)*. Chicago: University of Chicago Press.

Lynch, James J., and Bertrand Evans. 1963. *High School English Textbooks: A Critical Examination*. Boston: Little, Brown.

McCarthy, Lucille. 1987. A stranger in strange lands: A college student writing across the curriculum. *Research in the Teaching of English* 21(3): 233–265.

McDade, James E. 1928. *Essentials of Non-oral Reading*. Chicago: Plymouth Press.

McDermott, Ray P. 1977. Social relations as context for learning in schools. *Harvard Educational Review* 47: 198–213.

McGill-Franzen, Anne M. 1987. Failure to learn to read: Formulating a policy problem. *Reading Research Quarterly* 22(4): 475–490.

McGill-Franzen, Anne M. In press. *Shaping the Preschool Agenda: Early Literacy, Public Policy, and Professional Beliefs*. Albany: State University of New York Press.

McKee, Paul. 1949. "Reading Programs in Grades I Through VIII." In *Reading in the Elementary School. Forty-eighth Yearbook of the Society for the Study of Education*, Part II, edited by N. B. Henry, 127–146. Chicago: University of Chicago Press.

Massaro, Dominic W. 1984. Building and testing models of the reading process. *Handbook of Reading Research*, 111–146. White Plains, NY: Longman.

Mathews, Mitford M. 1966. *Teaching to Read: Historically Considered*. Chicago: University of Chicago Press.

Mearns, Hughes. 1929. *Creative Power*. Garden City, NY: Doubleday, Doran.

Mellon, John. 1964. *Transformational Sentence Combining for Enhancing the Development of Syntactic Fluency in English Composition*. Champaign, IL: National Council of Teachers of English.

Menyuk, Paula. 1969. *Sentences Children Use*. Cambridge, MA: M.I.T. Press.

Moffett, James. 1968. *Teaching the Universe of Discourse*. Boston: Houghton Mifflin.

Moll, Luis, and Rosa Diaz. 1987. Teaching writing as communication. In *Literacy and Schooling*, edited by David Bloome. Norwood, NJ: Ablex.

Montana State Department of Public Instruction. 1925. *Course of Study in English for Montana High Schools*. Helena, MT: State Department of Public Instruction.

Moore, David W., John E. Readance, and Robert J. Rickelman. 1983. An historical exploration of content area reading instruction. *Reading Research Quarterly* 18(4): 419–438.

Mosier, Richard D. 1965. *Making the American Mind: Social and Moral Ideas in the McGuffey Readers*, 26–43. New York: King's Crown Press.

National Assessment of Educational Progress. 1986. *Writing Trends Across the Decade: 1974–1984*. Princeton, NJ: Educational Testing Service.

National Assessment of Educational Progress. 1988. *Who Reads Best?* Princeton, NJ: Educational Testing Service.

National Council of Teachers of English. 1913. Types of Organization in high school English: Report of a committee of the NCTE. *English Journal* 2(8): 18–24.

National Education Association. 1894. *Report of the Commitee of Ten. On Secondary School Studies with the Reports of the Conferences Arranged by the Committee*. New York: American Books.

National Education Association. 1895. *Report of the Committee of Fifteen on Elementary Education*. New York: American Books.

National Governors Association. 1986. *A Time for Results*. Washington, DC: Center for Policy Research and Analysis.

New York State Department of Education. 1901. *Elementary Course of Study*. Albany: New York State Department of Education.

New York State Department of Education. 1905. *Syllabus for Secondary Schools*. Albany: New York State Department of Education.

New York State Department of Education. 1910. *Syllabus for Secondary Schools*. Albany: New York State Department of Education.

New York State Department of Education. 1917. *Syllabus for Secondary Schools*, Bulletin no. 640. Albany: New York State Department of Education.

New York State Department of Education. 1934. *Syllabus in English for Secondary Schools, Grade 7–12*. Albany: New York State Department of Education.

New York State Department of Education. 1935. *Syllabus in English for Secondary Schools, Grades 7–12*. Albany: New York State Department of Education.

New York State Department of Education. 1941. *Syllabus in English for Secondary Schools, Grades 7–12*. Albany: New York State Department of Education.

New York State Department of Education. 1945. *Syllabus in English for Secondary Schools, Grades 7–12*. Albany: New York State Department of Education.

New York State Department of Education. 1948. *Syllabus in English for Secondary Schools, Grades 7–12*. Albany: New York State Department of Education.

New York State Department of Education. 1960. *Syllabus in English for Secondary Schools, Grades 7–12*. Albany: New York State Department of Education, Bureau of Secondary Curriculum Development.

New York State Department of Education. 1968. *English Language Arts: Reading K–12*. Albany: New York State Department of Education, Curriculum Development Center.

New York State Department of Education. 1969. *English Language Arts: Composition K–12*. Albany: New York State Department of Education, Curriculum Development Center.

New York State Department of Education. 1986. *Composition in the English Language Arts Curriculum: K–12*. Albany: New York State Department of Education.

New York State Department of Education. 1988a. *English Language Arts Syllabus K–12: A Publication for Curriculum Developers*. Albany: New York State Department of Education.

New York State Department of Education. 1988b. *Reading and Literature in the Language Arts Curriculum*. Albany: New York State Department of Education.

Odell, Lee, and Dixie Goswami. 1982. Writing in a non-academic setting. *Research in the Teaching of English* 16(3): 201–223.

O'Hare, Frank. 1973. *Sentence Combining: Improving Student Writing Without Formal Grammar Instruction*. Urbana, IL: National Council of Teachers of English.

Olson, Willard C. 1949. *Child Development*. Boston: Heath.

Osborn, Jean. 1984. "The purposes, Uses and Content of Workbooks and Some Guidelines for Publishers." In *Learning to Read in American Schools: Basal Readers and Content Texts*, edited by Richard C. Anderson, Jean Osborn, and Robert Tierney, 45–112. Hillsdale, NJ: Erlbaum.

Otto, Wayne. 1969. *Overview of the Wisconsin Prototype System of Reading Instruction in the Elementary School*. Practical paper no. 5. Madison: Wisconsin Research and Development Center for Cognitive Learning.

Palincsar, Ann, and Ann Brown. 1984. Reciprocal teaching of comprehension-fostering and comprehension-monitoring activities. *Cognition and Instruction* 1(2): 117–175.

Parke, M. 1960–1961. "Composition in Primary Grades." In *Children's Writing: Research in Composition and Related Skills*. Champaign, IL: National Council of Teachers of English.

Pearson, P. David, Jane Hansen, and Christine Gordon. 1979. The effect of background knowledge on young children's comprehension of explicit and implicit information. *Journal of Reading Behavior* 11(3): 201–209.

Pearson, P. David, and Dale Johnson. 1978. *Reading Comprehension*. New York: Holt, Rinehart, and Winston.

Pearson, P. David, and Robert J. Tierney. 1984. "On Becoming a Thoughtful Reader: Learning to Read Like a Writer." In *Becoming Readers in a Complex Society. Eighty-third Yearbook of the National Society for the Study of Education*, edited by Alan C. Purves and Olive Niles, 144–173. Chicago: University of Chicago Press.

Pintner, Rudolf. 1913. Oral and silent reading of fourth grade pupils. *Journal of Educational Psychology* 4(6): 330–337.

Popp, Helen M. 1975. "Current Practices in the Teaching of Beginning Reading." In *Toward a Literate Society*, edited by John B. Carroll and Jeanne S. Chall. New York: McGraw-Hill.

Quilling, M. R. 1971. "The Reading Achievement of Primary Age Pupils Using the Wisconsin Design for Reading Skill Development: A Comparative Study." Paper presented at a meeting of the American Educational Research Association, New York.

Quirk, Thomas J., Donald A. Trisman, Katherine Nalin, and Susan Weinberg. 1975. Classroom behavior of teachers during compensatory reading instruction. *Journal of Educational Research* 68(5): 185–192.

Reed, A., and B. Kellogg. 1878. *Higher Lessons in English*. New York: Clark & Maynard.

Rice, Joseph M. 1893. *The Public School System of the United States*. New York: Century.

Robinson, Francis P. 1946. *Effective Study*. New York: Harper & Row.

Robinson, H. Alan. 1975. *Teaching Reading and Study Strategies: The Content Areas*, 1st ed. Boston: Allyn & Bacon.

Rosenshine, Barak, and Robert Stevens. 1984. "Classroom Instruction in Reading." In *Handbook of Reading Research*, edited by P. David Pearson, 745–798. White Plains, NY: Longman.

Rothman, Robert. 1990. From "Great Debate" to a full-scale war: Dispute over teaching reading heats up. *Education Week* 9(26): 1, 10–11.

Routman, Regie. 1988. *Transitions*. Portsmouth, NH: Heinemann.

Rowan, Brian, and Larry F. Guthrie. 1989. "The Quality of Chapter 1 Instruction: A Study of Twenty-Four Schools." In *Effective Programs for Students at Risk*, edited by Robert Slavin, Nancy Karweit, and Nancy Madden, 195–219. Boston: Allyn & Bacon.

Rumelhart, David E. 1975. "Notes on Schema for Stories." In *Representation and Understanding: Studies in Cognitive Science*, edited by D. B. Bobrow and Alan M. Collins. New York: Academic Press.

Russell, David. 1989. The cooperation movement: Language across the curriculum and mass education, 1900–1930. *Research in the Teaching of English* 24(4).

Scanlon, Robert G. 1970. Individually presented instruction. *Educational Technology* 10: 44–46.

Schank, Roger, and Robert Abelson. 1977. *Scripts, Plans, Goals and Understandings*. Hillsdale, NJ: Erlbaum.

Schmidt, William H., Jacqueline Caul, Joe L. Byers, and Margaret Buchmann. 1984. "Content of Basal Text Selections: Implications for Comprehension Instruction." In *Comprehension Instruction: Perspectives and Suggestions*, edited by Gerald G.

Duffy, Laura R. Roehler, and Jana Mason, 144–162. White Plains, NY: Longman.

Schutz, Richard E. 1970. The nature of educational development. *Journal of Research and Development in Education* 3(2): 39–64.

Science Research Associates. 1969. *What Is the Proof? The Distar Reading System*. Chicago: Science Research Associates.

Scott, Fred N. 1922. English composition as a mode of behavior. *English Journal* 11(7): 463–473.

Scott, Fred N., and Joseph V. Denney. 1900. *Elementary English Composition*. Boston: Allyn & Bacon.

Searle, John. 1969. *Speech Acts: An Essay on the Philosophy of Language*. London: Cambridge University Press.

Shanahan, Timothy. 1984. The nature of the reading-writing relation: An exploratory multivariate analysis. *Journal of Educational Psychology* 76: 466–477.

Shannon, Patrick. 1987. Commercial reading materials, a technological ideology, and the deskilling of teachers. *Elementary School Journal* 87(3): 307–329.

Shannon, Patrick. 1989. *Broken Promises: Reading Instruction in Twentieth-Century America*. Granby, MA: Bergin & Garvey.

Shepard, Lorrie, and Mary L. Smith. 1989. *Flunking Grades*. Philadelphia, PA: Falmer.

Shor, Ira. 1986. *Culture Wars*. Garden City, NY: Doubleday.

Shuy, Roger. 1967. *Discovering American Dialects*. Champaign, IL: National Council of Teachers of English.

Sinclair, J. McH., and R. M. Coulthard. 1975. *Towards an Analysis of Discourse*. London: Oxford University Press.

Sizer, Theodore. 1986. *Horace's Compromise: The Dilemma of the American High School*. Boston: Houghton Mifflin.

Skinner, B. F. 1957. The experimental analysis of behavior. *American Scientist* 45(4): 343–371.

Smith, Dora V. 1933. *Instruction in English: National Survey of Secondary Education*. Monograph No. 20. Washington, DC: U.S. Government Printing Office.

Smith, Frank. 1971. *Understanding Reading*. New York: Holt, Rinehart and Winston.

Smith, Nila B. 1964. Patterns of writing in different subject areas. *Journal of Reading* 13(1): 31–37.

Smith, Nila B. 1965 (1934). *American Reading Instruction*. Newark, DE: International Reading Association.

Smith, Nila B. 1966. *Be a Better Reader*. Englewood Cliffs, NJ: Prentice Hall.

Spring, Joel. 1989. *The Sorting Machine Revisited*. White Plains, NY: Longman.

Squire, James R., and Roger K. Applebee. 1968. *High School English Instruction Today*. New York: Appleton-Century-Crofts.

Stahl, Steven A., Jean Osborn, and Fran Lehr. 1990. *Beginning to Read: Thinking and Learning About Print, A Summary*. Champaign: Center for the Study of Reading, University of Illinois.

Stein, Nancy L., and Thomas Trabasso. 1982. "What's in a Story: Critical Issues in Comprehension and Instruction." In *Advances in Instructional Psychology*, vol. 2, edited by Robert Glaser. Hillsdale, NJ: Erlbaum.

Stodolsky, Susan S. 1989. "Is Teaching Really by the Book?" In *From Socrates to Software: The Teacher as Text and the Text as Teacher. Eighty-ninth Yearbook of the National Society for the Study of Education*, edited by P. Jackson and S. Haroutunian-Gordon, 159–184. Chicago: University of Chicago Press.

Stotsky, Susan. 1981. "Toward Reassessment of the Principles Underlying the Choice of Vocabulary and Teaching of Word Analysis Skills in Reading Instructional Materials." In *Directions in Reading: Research and Instruction*, edited by Michael L. Kamil. Washington, DC: National Reading Conference.

Strickland, Ruth G. 1960–1961. "Evaluating Children's Composition." In *Children's Writing: Research in Composition and Related Skills*, edited by Alvina T. Burrows. Champaign, IL: National Council of Teachers of English.

Sulzby, Elizabeth. 1983. *Beginning Readers' Developing Knowledges About Written Language*. Final report NIE G–80–0176. Evanston, IL: Northwestern University.

Taylor, Marjorie E. 1973. Sex-role stereotypes in children's readers. *Elementary English* 50(7): 1045–1047.

Teale, William T. 1982. Toward a theory of how children learn to read and write naturally. *Language Arts* 59: 555–570.

Terman, S., and C. C. Walcott. 1958. *Reading: Chaos and Cure*. New York: McGraw-Hill.

Thorndike, Edward L. 1917. Reading as reasoning: Mistakes in paragraph reading. *Journal of Educational Psychology* 8: 323–332.

Thorndike, Edward L. 1921. *The Teacher's Word Book*. New York: Teachers College Press.

Tierney, Robert J., and P. David Pearson. 1983. Toward a composing model of reading. *Language Arts* 60: 568–580.

Toulmin, Stephen. 1976. *Knowing and Acting*. New York: Macmillan.

Tulving, Ernest. 1972. "Episodic and Semantic Memory." In *Organization of Memory*, edited by Ernest Tulving and W. Donaldson. New York: Academic Press.

Tyson-Bernstein, Harriet. 1988. *A Conspiracy of Good Intentions: America's Textbook Fiasco*. Washington, DC: Council for Basic Education.

Veatch, Jeanette. 1959. *Individualizing Your Reading Program: Self Selection in Action*. New York: Putnam.

Veatch, Jeanette. 1986. Individualizing reading: A personal memoir. *Language Arts* 63(6): 586–593.

Venezky, Richard L. 1986. "Steps Toward a Modern History of American Reading Instruction." In *Review of Research in Education* vol. 13, edited by Erast Z. Rothkopf, 129–167. Washington, DC: American Educational Research Association.

Venezky, Richard L. 1987. A history of the American reading textbook. *Elementary School Journal* 87(3): 247–265.

Vose, R. M. 1925. "Co-operative Teaching of English in Secondary Schools." Master's thesis, University of Illinois, Urbana.

Vygotsky, Lev S. 1962. *Thought and Language*. Cambridge, MA: M.I.T. Press.

Vygotsky, Lev S. 1978. *Mind in Society*. Cambridge, MA: Harvard University Press.

Walcott, Charles C. 1961. *Tomorrow's Illiterates*. Boston: Little, Brown.

Walmsley, Sean A., and Trudy P. Walp. 1989. *Literature in the Elementary School*. Center for the Learning and Teaching of Literature, report series 1.3. Albany: State University of New York.

Walmsley, Sean A., and Trudy P. Walp. 1990. Integrating literature and composing into the language arts curriculum: Theory and practice. *Elementary School Journal* 90(3): 251–274.

Ward, C. H. 1920. *Theme-building*. Chicago: Scott, Foresman.

Weaver, R. 1957. *Composition: A Course in Writing and Rhetoric*. New York: Holt.

Weeks, Ruth M., et al. 1936. *A Correlated Curriculum. A Report of the Committee on Correlation of the National Council of Teachers of English*. New York: D. Appleton-Century.

Weir, Ruth. 1962. *Language in the Crib*. The Hague: Mouton.

Wendell, Barrett. 1891. *English Composition*. New York: Scribner.

Whately, Richard. 1963 (1826). *Elements of Rhetoric*, edited by Douglas Ehninger. Carbondale: Southern Illinois University Press.

Whipple, Gertrude. 1949. "Desirable Materials, Facilities, and Resources for Reading." In *Reading in Elementary School. Forty-eighth Yearbook of the National Society for the Study of Education*, Part II, edited by Nelson B. Henry, 147–171. Chicago: University of Chicago Press.

Willows, Dale M., Diane Borwick, and Maureen Hayvren. 1981. "The Content of School Readers." In *Reading Research Advances in Theory and Practice*, no. 2, edited by T. Gary Wallins and G. E. MacKinnon. New York: Academic Press.

Wilson, H. B. 1915. *Minimum Essentials in Elementary School Subjects—Standards and Current Practices. Fourteenth Yearbook of the National Society for the Study of Education*, Part I. Bloomington, IL: Public School Co.

Wilson, H. B. 1917. *Second Report of the Committee on Minimum Essentials in Elementary School Subjects. Sixteenth Yearbook of the National Society for the Study of Education*, Part I. Bloomington, IL: Public School Publishing.

Winograd, Terry. 1972. *Understanding Natural Language*. Edinburgh: Edinburgh University Press.

Wolfram, Walt. 1974. *Sociolinguistic Aspects of Association: Puerto Rican English in New York City*. Arlington, VA: Center for Applied Linguistics.

Worcester, Samuel. 1828. *Primer of the English Language*. Gloucester, MA.

Woods, W. 1981. Composition textbooks and pedagogical theory, 1960–1980. *College English* 43: 396–406.

Woodward, Arthur. 1986. Taking teaching out of teaching and reading out of learning to read. *Book Research Quarterly* 2(1): 53–73.

Young, Richard. 1978. "Paradigms and Problems: Needed Research in Rhetorical Invention." In *Research on Composing: Points of Departure*, edited by Charles Cooper and Lee Odell. Urbana, IL: National Council of Teachers of English.

Young, Richard, Alton Becker, and Kenneth Pike. 1970. *Rhetoric: Discovery and Change.* New York: Harcourt, Brace.

Zirbes, Laura. 1951. The experience approach in reading. *Reading Teacher* 5: 1–2, 15–16.

26

LITERATURE AND THE ENGLISH LANGUAGE ARTS

Arthur N. Applebee and
Alan C. Purves

NATIONAL RESEARCH CENTER ON LITERATURE TEACHING AND LEARNING

UNIVERSITY AT ALBANY

Since English emerged as a school subject at the end of the 19th century, literature has been at the center of the English curriculum. This chapter will explore the relationships among conceptions of English, literature, language, curriculum theory, and research on curriculum as they have evolved over the past century, ending with a discussion of the major issues in curriculum that remain to be addressed in the next decade. Since the teaching of writing and reading are addressed fully in Chapter 25 of this *Handbook*, they will not be addressed here. Similarly, because the language arts in the elementary school are dominated by reading and writing, the emphasis will be largely, though not exclusively, on secondary school curriculum.

Throughout history, the teaching of the English language arts has been influenced—and in some aspects determined—by forces that lie outside of the schools. Political, social, and economic forces in society at large have influenced not only broadly stated goals for schooling but also the specific content and approaches in the teaching of the English language arts. These forces will emerge repeatedly in the discussions that follow, for much of the existing research on the language arts curriculum has been concerned with tracing its historical roots.

THE EMERGENCE OF THE ENGLISH LANGUAGE ARTS AS A CURRICULUM AREA IN AMERICAN SCHOOLS

In 1800, English was not taught as a subject in American schools; by 1900, it was almost universally offered and well on its way to being universally required. Research during the past 20 years has clarified the emergence of English as a school subject as well as the forces that influenced the nature of the English curriculum during the ensuing decades. In reviewing the historical development of theory and research in curriculum in this subject, we will draw heavily on recent analyses (Applebee 1974; 1982; Hook 1979; Judy and England 1979; Piche 1977).

For most of the 18th and 19th centuries, the English language arts found their way into the curriculum through separate emphases on such subjects as spelling, grammar, rhetoric, literary history, reading, oratory, and elocution (Stout 1921; Witt 1968). Literary works, to the extent that they appeared at all, were used as material for other studies, particularly as texts for grammatical analysis. In an educational context that valued the classical languages, such sporadic and diffuse attention to the vernacular was all that could be expected—supplemented in the colleges by a vigorous extracurriculum in Shakespeare and other major English authors (Rudolph 1962).

Three early traditions shaped the newly emerging subject of English and continue to influence the curriculum of the present day. One was an ethical tradition, which placed its emphasis on moral and cultural development; the second was the tradition of instruction that governed the teaching of the classical languages, Latin and Greek; and the third was a nonacademic tradition of practical language skills and literary "appreciation," which developed outside of the traditional curriculum (Applebee 1974).

The Ethical Tradition

The ethical tradition began as part of the history of reading instruction, with its roots in biblical studies and its reliance on overtly moral or religious texts. (On the early history of reading instruction, see Johnson 1963; Reeder 1900; N. B. Smith 1934.) In this tradition, the development of a curriculum for the English language arts was determined by the ethical value of the selections for study: The morally right was the pedagogically appropriate, as well as the aesthetically beautiful. In the American colonies, this emphasis on particular religious doctrine was evident in *The New England Primer* (c. 1686). Combining an alphabet, syllabarium, and selections for reading, *The New England Primer* was really the first integrated textbook in the English language arts; it dominated elementary school instruction for some 100 years (Ford 1962).

With the plurality of cultural and religious values in the young United States, however, the emphasis on religious doctrine was eventually replaced by the new goal of promoting unity and a common American culture, a goal that contributed to the structure and content of the next series of texts to dominate instruction in the vernacular: Webster's *Grammatical Institute of the English Language*, published in 1783. The *Grammatical Institute* had three parts: a speller, a grammar, and lessons "in reading and speaking." The first part, the *Blue Backed Speller*, was the direct descendent of the earlier primers and was the most widely used. In addition to promoting a common American English language through the speller and grammar, the selections in these books were chosen for patriotic content, ethical emphasis, and usefulness in the development of the speaking voice.

McGuffey's Readers, published in 1836, were the final set of texts to dominate the early teaching of the vernacular. The books were graded by level of difficulty, with selections of real literary value predominating in the fifth and sixth readers. Even in McGuffey, however, the selections were short—usually a page or two at most—and reflected a stern Protestant ethic. Although the emphasis had changed, the underlying belief in the power of the materials for study to promote good or evil continued unabated, just as it continues to the present day (Purves 1987).

The belief in the power of reading selections was a mixed blessing in the early history of the English curriculum: Once literature was granted the power to do good, it also earned the power to do evil. Whereas nonfiction of various sorts was usually acceptable, imaginative literature in all of its forms was often suspect. Echoing Plato's arguments for banning poetry from his Republic, Horace Mann was typical of many influential educators when he argued that novels should not be taught because they appealed to emotions rather than to reason. Drama was even more suspect: In 1828 a Boston teacher was dismissed for reading to his class from one of Shakespeare's plays; and as late as 1893, the *New England Journal of Education* gave editorial support to a high school class that refused to read *Hamlet* (Witt 1968).

Before imaginative literature could benefit from the ethical tradition, the poets and critics of the Romantic era had to provide a new justification for it as a reservoir of cultural values and a source of moral strength. Writing against a background of political and industrial revolution, the Romantics turned the vision of art from that of a reflection of the world to that which creates worlds. Art became imaginative, creative, and ethical rather than a "rational" copy of the world and subject to the marketplace (Williams 1958). The knowledge of the artist was seen as a higher kind of knowledge than the rationalism to which it was opposed. The cumulative products of this artistic imagination came to be identified with a nation's culture, in the process transforming this culture into a body of knowledge to be consciously valued and studied. Formulated most fully in Matthew Arnold's *Culture and Anarchy*, the Romantic view of culture expanded the ethical tradition into a major justification for the study of imaginative literature (Katz 1968; Witt 1968). It also had the effect of transforming the great authors from objects of popular culture into a literary and artistic elite. The great works became the objects of serious study and interpretation, in the process being transformed into something difficult and inaccessible to the general populace (Levine 1988).

The Classical Analogy

The second early tradition that shaped the curriculum of the English language arts was the model offered by the study of classical languages and literatures. Though support for the teaching of the English vernacular developed gradually after 1800, the classical curriculum (Latin and Greek) continued to dominate until late in the century. The hegemony of the classics was fostered by the prevailing curricular theories of the time, which held that the educational value of any subject was directly proportional to the degree of internal structure that the subject exhibited, the apparatus of rules and knowledge that a student would be required to master and through which students would train their faculties of reason and memory (Lull 1913). The complex vocabularies, grammar, syntax, and rhetoric of the classical languages offered fertile ground for such training. English, at least from the classicist's point of view, was simply too easy: It had no substance, no organized body of knowledge, to promote the rigorous mental discipline that lay at the heart of education. Only by developing such a body of content could the English language arts move beyond the "mere chatter about Shelley" that the classicists ridiculed. (The quote is from E. A. Freeman, Regius Professor of History at Oxford, talking in 1887, cited in Palmer 1965, 96). As late as 1903, Carpenter, Baker, and Scott, in their early and influential textbook on the teaching of English, argued that the slow start for English lay "not so much in the lack of desire for instruction as in the general feeling that there was no general body of instruction to give" (45).

The development of a rigorous content for the curriculum in the English language arts took place in stages. Grammar was the first formal study of English to become a widespread part of the curriculum, and it did so by taking up the methods and approaches that had dominated in the teaching of the classical languages. Grammatical studies in the classical languages had traditionally emphasized two parts: the learning of rules and their "use" or practical application. An extensive methodology had grown up around both aspects, and this was transferred more or less intact to studies of English grammar. "Parsing" and analysis of sentences, diagraming, the learning of paradigms, and the correction of errors in usage all entered the curriculum through this tradition, together with rote memorization of definitions and rules for the various grammatical categories. Even the grammar itself was borrowed, representing a rough-and-ready application of Latin grammar to English syntax and usage. Indeed, the shift of grammatical studies from the classics to English involved a shift from the *teaching* of a foreign language to one of *correcting* a native one, the beginnings of a prescriptive tradition in the English curriculum that continues to the present day. (On traditions in the teaching of grammar in English and the classical languages, see Kelly 1969; Leonard 1929; Sherwin 1969. On changing attitudes toward usage and their reflections in school grammars, see Finegan 1980).

With its borrowed content and methodology, English grammar was widely taught in American schools by 1810; by 1819, the need to be "well acquainted" with English grammar was added to the admissions requirements of the College of New Jersey (later to become Princeton University). This was the first college entrance requirement for competence in any aspect of the vernacular language.

The second aspect of the classical curriculum to influence the emerging curriculum in English language arts was rhetoric and oratory (this history has been recounted by Hollingsworth 1973; Meikle 1945; Palmer 1965; and Parker 1967). Originally conceived of as part of the curriculum in grammar, rhetoric and oratory were divorced from their roots by a group of educators at the University of Edinburgh at about the same time that grammar was emerging as a school subject. These early rhetoricians included John Stevenson, Adam Smith, Robert Watson, and Hugh Blair, the last of whom gathered his lectures together into an influential text, *Lectures on Rhetoric and Belles Lettres*, published in 1783. Like the grammarians, who were their professional colleagues, the early rhetoricians were prescriptive, filling their texts with rules to be followed and with examples of errors of expression as well as of the successes of the best writers. The main point of reference was the Latin and Greek tradition, presented in English but with extensive classical illustrations from Vergil, Cicero, Aristophanes, Tasso, and many others. At the same time, and this is the significant departure that took place at Edinburgh, these rhetoricians argued that the principles were universal: They applied to written texts as well as to oratory and to English and French as well as to Latin and Greek. Favorite examples included Addison, Pope, Swift, Dryden, Milton, and Shakespeare, though the last violated many of the rhetorical "laws." It is interesting to note that although the "greats" of English literature were acknowledged, many of the most thoroughly discussed authors were contemporaries or near contemporaries of the rhetoricians.

In practice, the study of grammar and the study of rhetoric merged with each other and with the study of literature. Throughout the 19th century, rhetoric, analysis, and criticism usually indicated much the same course of study, in which literary passages would be critically examined to ensure that they conformed with the prescriptive rules of grammar and rhetoric, all in the ultimate service of students' speaking and writing skills. Though the rhetorical approach of Blair and his colleagues did not require any literature to be read at all, by the 1840s some schools were supplementing rhetoric handbooks with individual texts for parsing and analysis. Such texts were few in number until the end of the 19th century and were approached with the exhaustive line-by-line analysis that had characterized the grammar and rhetoric handbooks. *Paradise Lost* and Pope's *Essay on Man* were particularly popular; their Latinate style provided an excellent exercise ground for the Latinate grammars and rhetorics of the time (Applebee 1974).

Rhetoric and oratory were the first of the English language arts to become part of the college curriculum, though they were generally thought of as minor aspects of preparation for the clergy. In spite of occasional experiments with English or American literature, before 1860 these rhetoric and oratory courses represented the full extent of English studies in most American colleges.

The next aspect of the English language arts to enter the curriculum as part of the classical tradition was literary history (see Applebee 1974; Witt 1968). This subject took as its model studies of ancient civilization, themselves a well-established part of the classical curriculum. Though both the classical course and its English translation began with broad and humanistic goals, the curriculum was quickly dominated by an emphasis on rote memorization of names, dates, and places. Thomas Budge Shaw's *Outlines of English Literature* was the first textbook in this tradition to be widely used in America. Published in England in 1848, it was reprinted in America during the following year. The book was a simple narrative and included no selections from the authors at all, but it was very popular and went through many editions. By the end of the century, such histories often included brief extracts from the authors (sometimes as brief as a line, rarely more than a paragraph or stanza) for students to memorize; as Westlake (1898), the author of one such text, explained, such memorization of extracts had "long been recognized by educators as one of the most efficient means of culture" (iii). Westlake's justification of the use of extracts is an interesting precursor of contemporary arguments about the importance of knowledge of our literary or cultural heritage, of "cultural literacy," as E. D. Hirsch (1987) has termed it. (Like Westlake's, Hirsch's approach can easily degenerate into a literature curriculum that involves no literature at all.)

The final aspect of the study of English to enter the curriculum from the classical tradition was philology. Philological study began as a study of classical civilizations, transposed by the German Romantics to the study of German and later of English (on the history of philology, see K. Malone 1958). The goals of the German philologists were ambitious—nothing less than providing the biography of a nation, including attention to grammar, criticism, geography, political history, customs, mythology, literature, art, and ideas. In the hands of a few, Jacob Grimm and the editors of the *Oxford English Dictionary* among them, such studies came close to realizing their lofty goals, but in the hands of many they quickly degenerated into a kind of mechanical, pedantic textual criticism. Nonetheless, philology offered the fledgling study of English the justification it needed in the colleges of the second half of the 19th century. For the first time, it had a methodology and a subject matter, a substance to allow it to claim a legitimate place alongside of the other areas of university scholarship. With the sanction of philology, the teaching of literature spread quickly through the American college and university system (Allen 1968).

The Nonacademic Tradition

While an ethical tradition was emerging in elementary school reading materials and a classical one in secondary schools and colleges, a more amorphous but equally important tradition of the development of practical language skills and literary "appreciation" was emerging outside of the academic curriculum.

The "appreciative" aspect of this tradition flourished in the extracurriculum of the 19th-century preparatory schools and colleges, particularly in the literary and debating societies (Rudolph 1962; Sizer 1964). These societies provided forums for dealing with the political and philosophical issues of the times—issues more or less ruled out of the classical curriculum. The society libraries were also the only place for students to read contemporary fiction, poetry, biography, or drama; on most college campuses the libraries of the literary societies surpassed those of the colleges themselves in both quality and number of volumes. Through these societies, English literature became an important part of the college experience of most students, though not a part of their college curriculum.

In the high schools of the 19th century, English studies worked their way first into the "English" course that arose in opposition to the Latin or classical program of studies (Carpenter, Baker, and Scott 1903; Stout 1921). The most important step in this movement was the founding of Boston English High School in 1821. Established specifically to provide the non-college-bound child with "an education that shall fit him for active life, and . . . serve as a foundation for eminence in his profession, whether Mercantile or Mechanical," Boston English embraced instruction in the vernacular as the way to provide the necessary language skills (Hollingsworth 1973). The model was widely imitated, and by 1870 high schools modeled on Boston's English High School could be found in most American cities.

Blair's *Rhetoric* was included in the first course of study at Boston English High School, though it was never used at Boston Latin School. Lacking a classical cachet, these practical studies of English carried a certain stigma, an air of being a second-best choice for those who could not handle the rigors of classical studies. Thus English studies worked their way at a relatively early date into girls' finishing schools, and many of the early English textbooks were for "Young Ladies." Reflecting the classical bias, the U.S. commissioner of education in his annual report was, as late as 1889, tallying students taking English in business schools and in schools for the blind, deaf, and feebleminded, but not in public or private secondary schools (Applebee 1974).

Institutionalization of the English Curriculum

The influence of the ethical, classical, and nonacademic traditions converged to ensure that the English language arts had a place of sorts in the curriculum of American schools during the second half of the 19th century. But it took the influence of college entrance requirements to change the English language arts from a series of unrelated minor studies of the vernacular into a major curriculum area. As already noted, the first requirements were for knowledge of English grammar, which became quite widespread by the middle of the 19th century. These were followed by a Harvard requirement in "reading English aloud" in 1865 and finally, in 1873–1874, by a requirement for writing about literature, the subject to be "taken from one of the following works: Shakespeare's *Tempest*, *Julius Caesar*, and *Merchant of Venice*; Goldsmith's *Vicar of Wakefield*; Scott's *Ivanhoe*, and *Lay of the Last Minstrel*" (Harvard University 1896, 55). This requirement institutionalized the study of standard authors and set in motion a process that culminated in the widespread teaching of the English language arts as a unified curriculum (see Grommon 1968; Harvard University 1896; Hayes 1936).

The two decades following the Harvard requirement of 1874 saw a proliferation of similar requirements at other colleges, each with its own list of required authors that changed yearly. With multiple colleges producing multiple lists, the problem for schools was obvious, and it led by 1894 to the formation of the National Conference on Uniform Entrance Requirements in English, whose lists succeeded those of Harvard in shaping the secondary school English curriculum.

As schools and colleges turned their attention to complete works of English literature, a new kind of textbook began to emerge—the annotated classic. Edited by distinguished teachers and scholars, these editions of standard authors contained copious (and sometimes irrelevant) notes and guidelines; the study apparatus usually reflected a mix of historical and philological concerns. One early edition of *Julius Caesar* (1867) was typical of those that followed: In addition to 102 pages of text for the play itself, the edition contained an Introduction, The History of the Play, The Sources of the Plot, Critical Comments on the Play (26 pages), Notes (82 pages), and an Index of Words and Phrases Explained. This edition was edited by William Rolfe of Cambridge (Massachusetts) High School, who is usually credited with introducing the first regular high school instruction in literature (D. Malone 1935; Mersand 1960).

The final impetus for a unified curriculum in the English language arts came from the Committee of Ten, chaired by Harvard's president Charles W. Eliot. Appointed by the National Education Association (1894) to consider the whole of the secondary school curriculum, the committee chose English as one of nine fields of study. The subcommittee on English sought to summarize and reconcile conflicting views on the teaching of English, beginning with a statement of the purpose of such studies:

> The main objects of the teaching of English in schools seem to be two: (1) to enable the pupil to understand the expressed thoughts of others and to give expression to thoughts of his own; and (2) to cultivate a taste for reading, to give the pupil some acquaintance with good literature, and to furnish him with the means of extending that acquaintance. (86)

This statement of purpose forged the synthesis that became the English language arts.

Reflecting Eliot's own views on the importance of the vernacular, in the final committee report English is the only curriculum area recommended for all students during each of the four high school years. As both a summation of trends already well underway in the schools and a final authoritative sanctioning of the value of an English rather than a classical course of study, the report of the Committee of Ten marks the birth of the English language arts as a major area of the school curriculum. In the wake of the report, the issue for curriculum became not whether there should be a course in English but what such a curriculum should contain. The new subject could claim the intellectual strength of the classical tradition, the moral strength of the ethical tradition, and the utilitarian strength of the nonacademic tradition. It was to prove a fruitful alliance, if sometimes an uneasy one: The belief in the central curricular role of the language arts continues to the present day as one of the few points of agreement among scholars, educators, and members of the public, who otherwise split into diverse camps about the appropriate structure and content of the curriculum in English.

American Curriculum in an International Perspective

What we have outlined about the foundations of English education in the United States is not unique to this country. There have recently been a number of studies of mother-tongue curriculum history in Europe and in Asia. The patterns and movements show remarkable parallels across language systems, and they appear at nearly the same historical periods. The international patterns of development of vernacular instruction are outlined in Van de Ven (1987), who suggests a parallel development across systems of education as they move from a literary-religious rationale to a technical rationale in the 19th century to a social rationale that flowered in the 20th century. Van de Ven argues convincingly that these shifts emerge less from internal pressures on the curriculum (coming from new discoveries concerning the subject) than from external pressures on the schools. The 19th century saw a secularization of education and the influence of the industrial revolution on the demands for an urbanized work force. The 20th century saw an increased awareness of social injustice and the demand for more egalitarian schools.

The literary-religious tradition that Van de Ven (1987) describes sets forth a view that language should be studied from the perspective of the "true" or the "good" or the "beautiful." This can be seen as an elitist view, which focuses on the classics and takes an aristocratic or academic approach to style and composition. The technical rationale sees the curriculum in terms of technology and science and aims at producing people who can use the language in "everyday life." It can be seen as a bourgeois or meritocratic view, which considers literature and art of secondary importance. The social view provides an alternative to the technical by examining the relationships among social institutions with the view to changing them. It is a view that assumes the curriculum can "emancipate," or at least help people "understand" the social reality of their language. It aims to help students by making them more reflective, emotional, and expressive and better able to communicate competently within varied social situations.

These approaches can be related to broader approaches to cultural education: The technical approach focuses on cultural communication, the literary-religious approach on cultural loyalty, and the social approach on individual expression. Each of these is a matter of emphasis, of course, and most national curricula are hybrids of the three views. Historically, most systems appear to have adopted the technical approach during the past 50 years, and in many systems it appears to be the dominant one for it is attacked by the literary-religious group on the right and the social group on the left. The secondary school system, in particular, is seen as an opportunity to broaden cultural communication for most people, to allow an elite the "luxury" of the literary-religious heritage, and to foster a social underground for the less able. Such is the common critique of literacy education, although it has been challenged by some (Delpit 1988) who wonder why the poor and the cultural minorities are given a social message that effectively prevents them from access to the skills fostered by the technical approach.

Just as the roots of these various orientations were evident in the emergence of an English curriculum in the United States, their interactions over the following decades continue to shape the teaching of the English language arts.

THE SEARCH FOR A BASIS FOR THE CURRICULUM

Research in curriculum in the English language arts has been for the most part a search for a stable base for determining an appropriate content and structure for the curriculum as a whole. As in most subject areas, the field has been shaped by a succession of governing metaphors; a few empirical studies; and a variety of consensual summaries, usually sponsored by one of the major professional organizations.

A School for the People

The emergence of English as a school subject was brought about in large part by the needs of the college bound. The uniform lists of required readings that determined much of the content of the curriculum were themselves college entrance requirements; the definition of the curriculum in English by the Committee of Ten was the work of a committee chaired by the president of Harvard University. Perhaps inevitably, the decades immediately following the report became a period in which the high school sought to free itself from the domination of the college.

The uniform lists became an immediate focus of discontent: Why should titles chosen because of their appropriateness for the small proportion of students who went on to college determine the curriculum for all students? A series of studies published in *School Review* in 1907 made clear that in all sections of the country, the uniform lists had been elevated into a course of study, "a place for which those requirements were never designed and never adapted" (Applebee 1974, 49–50). Although Eliot and his colleagues had argued that in fact preparation for college was the best preparation for life, strong voices were soon heard urging that the curriculum be tailored more closely to the real needs and interests of the students. In 1911, dissatisfaction with the uniform lists led to the establishment of the National Council of Teachers of English (NCTE) as a means to focus and direct teachers' protests. The young organization proposed a more open examination system, leading by 1916 to a two-track system, with a "restricted" examination based on the uniform lists and an alternative "comprehensive" examination that included no lists of required titles; by 1931, the restricted examination, and with it the National Conference on Uniform Entrance Requirements in English, disappeared altogether (Applebee 1974; on the history of NCTE, see Hook 1979; Mason 1962).

The revolt against college domination of the curriculum in English had no clearly worked out principles for restructuring the program. "A school for the people" was a good rallying cry, but it was singularly vague in its specific implications. The result was a period of vigorous experimentation with alternative approaches, many of them tied at least loosely to the presumed needs and interests of students. Contemporary literature, appreciation rather than mental discipline, drama, ethical development, vocational education—all had their proponents and their embodiments in curricula during the first 2 decades of the 20th century. (These curricular movements and their origins are discussed in Applebee 1974.)

This period also marked the beginning of a continuing tradition of empirical studies seeking to determine the curriculum content that students would find both manageable and interesting. G. Stanley Hall addressed such problems as early as 1886 in a pamphlet entitled *How to Teach Reading, and What to Read in School*. In the program he outlined, selections were to be organized and sequenced on the basis of the interests and abilities of the students. This organization was coupled with a belief that individual development was a recapitulation of the historical development of a culture, and hence that the most effective sequence of materials (that most closely aligned with students' developing needs and interests) would recapitulate major stages in cultural history. Building on this argument in his later volumes on *Adolescence*, Hall (1904) suggested that myth and legend were the "best expression of the adolescent stage of our race." His specific suggestions, many of which were taken up by teachers of English, included "the literature of the Arthuriad and the Sangrail, the stories of Parsifal, Tristram, Isolde, Galahad, Geraint, Siegfried, Brunhilde, Roland, the Cid, Orlando, Tannhauser, Beowulf, Lohengrin, Robin Hood, and Rolando" (442–444). This concern with fitting the material to the child led directly to the first statistical studies of reading interests, many of which Hall published in his journal, *Pedagogical Seminary* (Applebee 1974).

The Reorganization Reports. The movement to develop a "school for the people" culminated in a series of reports sponsored by the National Education Association. The subject of English was dealt with in detail in *Reorganization of English in Secondary Schools* (Hosic 1917). Cosponsored by NCTE, the report was the culmination of the revolt against college domination. (On the reorganization movement, see Fay 1968.)

The report began by affirming the independence of the high school and rejecting the argument that preparation for college was the best preparation for life. Instead, the committee asked for a "considerable range" of course content to meet the varying backgrounds of students, while at the same time preserving "a reasonable uniformity of aims and a body of common culture" (Hosic 1917, 26). The report was very specific about the works to be studied, providing two lists at each grade level, one of books "for class work," the other of books "for individual reading." The grade-by-grade distribution of works echoed Hall's concerns with stages in the emotional and intellectual development of students. For the 8th and 9th grades, they urged "stirring narrative, full of movement and manly virtue"; for the 10th grade, "serious questions of right and wrong"; 11th grade would be the time "frankly to discuss the relations of men and women to each other" in the context of the "high ideality of *Idylls of the King* and *Silas Marner*." Finally, the 12th grade would offer a "literary" course, organized chronologically and including both American and English literature (69–70).

Although born in a rejection of college domination, the *Reorganization* report embraced much of the content that the colleges had required. Of the authors on the college entrance lists before 1900, all but three were part of the report's suggestions. Only Johnson, Dryden, and Burke fell completely from favor. The concerns with contemporary writing, with more closely aligning literature with the life of the students, were generously reflected, but their place was in the lists for individual reading rather than for class study.

The Progressive Era

The concerns shaping the *Reorganization of English in Secondary Schools* (Hosic 1917) were part of the first stages of the progressive era in education. Progressive principles, emphasizing a child-centered curriculum, the importance of learning by doing, and the value of scientific study, influenced the teaching of English language arts in two stages. During the first stage, culminating in the late 1930s, the curriculum was defined around the metaphors of "experience" and "exploration"; during the second stage, culminating in the middle 1950s, the boundaries of the curriculum were narrowed around the more pragmatic goals of "communication" and "life adjustment."

During the period between the wars, two broad movements shaped this evolution of the curriculum in English language arts. One was the application of science to the problems of curriculum definition; the other was the movement toward "experience" as the central metaphor guiding the educational process.

The Functional Curriculum. The scientific study of the curriculum in English began as part of a general concern with efficiency and economy of time (see Callahan 1962 on the general movement and Applebee 1974 on the movement in English). Impressed with the effectiveness of scientific management in industry, educators and (particularly) administrators sought to apply similar principles to the schools. A Committee on Economy of Time in Education, appointed by the Department of Superintendence of the National Education Association, issued four reports between 1915 and 1919. Their approach to minimal essentials of the school curriculum was rigidly empirical: Studies of life in the school and in society would show what knowledge and skills were needed; studies of child development would show how this content should be sequenced in the curriculum. NCTE sponsored its own Committee on Economy of Time, guided by similar principles, and a later Committee on Minimal Essentials.

In general, the English language arts came off quite well in these and similar studies. On the one hand, instruction in English was cheap compared with other subjects; on the other hand, language in its variety of uses inevitably surfaced high on any list of "universal needs." Even literary studies, much harder to justify in terms of concrete life activities, were protected by the widespread belief in the importance of literature for character development and ethics. The same justification appeared in the Carnegie Report on the high school (Boyer 1983). Finally, English studies as they had been brought together by the Committee of Ten were broad enough to allow an exceedingly wide array of functional activities to be included as part of the language arts curriculum.

Though English fared well in attempts to specify a curriculum based on minimal essentials, pressures from other subjects seeking to expand their place in the curriculum eventually forced English to defend itself as a functional study. This task fell to the NCTE Committee on the Place and Function of English in American Life. The committee conducted an extensive survey of the uses of English by 22,000 people in a range of social positions; the summary tables in the final report (Clapp 1926) provided a profile for the English curriculum to follow. As the committee summarized their recommendations,

> The schools might well devote more attention to a number of the language activities which according to the returns are widely used by persons of the many callings and social groups reporting, and which are reported as giving much difficulty. These activities in particular are: Interviewing: word of mouth inquiries; reports to a superior; instructions for subordinates; conferences. Conversation: with casual acquaintances; at social gatherings; over the telephone. Public Speaking: informal discussion; preparing addresses. Writing: informal notes and memos for one's self; formal notes of invitation, introduction, etc. Reading: legal documents. Listening: to an interview, a conference, or a public meeting. (46)

All of these concerns were taken up as part of the English language arts in the decades that followed, though the central problem with such attempts to specify the curriculum through an analysis of life is obvious even in this brief excerpt: The results of such surveys provide no organizing structure for separating the trivial from the important, reducing the curriculum to its least common denominator. Though the Clapp (1926) report was prompted by concerns with efficiency and functionality, one of the results was the expansion of the English curriculum to include a wide variety of relatively trivial studies.

Of the other attempts to define the curriculum scientifically at this time, the best known was Charles S. Pendleton's (1924) *The Social Objectives of School English.* In Pendleton's list of 1,581 separate "social goals," ranked in order of the frequency with which they had been cited, correct spelling ranked first and the ability to speak in complete sentences ranked second. A curriculum structured around such surveys could easily become preoccupied with minor concerns; few would argue that accurate spelling was *not* useful, but few would want to elevate it as the central goal of the English language arts. The products of such early attempts at providing an empirical basis for the curriculum were exhaustive lists of specific objectives, without a coherent organizing structure.

The greatest impact of the scientific approach to the specification of a functional curriculum was in language studies. S. A. Leonard's *Current English Usage*, published by NCTE in 1932, was the first of a series of publications that emphasized the functional study of language and usage rather than the prescriptive study of formal grammar that had been the legacy of the classical curriculum. Leonard's monograph, begun as part of the work of the NCTE Committee on Minimal Essentials, gathered judges' opinions on acceptable usage in punctuation and grammar, arriving at the conclusion that "it is not formal rules but the principle of clarity" (76) that governs usage in both grammar and punctuation. The study came complete with the recommendation from NCTE that it be used for "Building courses of study" and "Compiling bulletins on minimum essentials" (vi).

The curriculum in literature, on the other hand, remained largely untouched, if only because the cultural and ethical values that it was presumed to impart were so hard to specify in functional terms. At the same time, a variety of studies sought to determine a more efficient placement of literary works on the basis of the reading interests and comprehension difficulties posed by standard selections. These studies were descendants of Hall's (1886, 1904) earlier work on reading interests, now elevated into a criterion for the selection and placement of the works studied (see Applebee 1974). Studies of standard titles revealed a wide range of interest in response to individual works and considerable variability, depending on the reference group chosen to evaluate a work's "appropriateness." Though widely cited, none of the results led to major changes in the curriculum in literature (Applebee 1974).

Studies of reading interests have continued, though usually with a less overt concern with curriculum change than was the case in the early work (Purves and Beach 1972). Taken together, these studies revealed patterns of preference and solidified the choices made by curriculum planners and anthology editors. The studies clearly showed gender and age differences, for example, and selections were often weighted toward boys' interests and easier works (on the rationale that required texts should appeal to the interests of those who were seen as less able or less engaged). Such studies also supported the rise of adolescent or young adult titles, many of which were very popular with students.

English as Experience. If the functional movement sought to define the content of the English language arts curriculum, teachers had to look elsewhere for the principles on which to organize that content. In the 1920s, English teachers built on the methodological suggestions of progressives such as Kilpatrick (1925) to organize and justify the English curriculum in terms of a "broadening" of experience. As Kilpatrick explained it,

> The subject-matter of the curriculum is race experience, the picked winnings of the race, the best ways mankind has yet devised of meetings its problems. . . . The best way in which I can now conceive the curriculum itself is as a series of experiences in which by guided induction the child makes his own formulations. Then they are his to use. (274, 310)

English teachers responded well to this metaphor for their curriculum and to the later, related metaphor of "exploration" (Rosenblatt 1938). Under its guidance, they experimented with a variety of ways to stimulate student interest and searched for overall structures to guide students' experiences and explorations (see Applebee 1974; Bernd 1957; Ehrenpreis 1945). In this search for new structures, the project method as well as a curriculum organized around themes or topics all had strong proponents, but no clear consensus emerged as it had in the periods prior to the Committee of Ten or the *Reorganization* report.

Against such a background, NCTE appointed a Curriculum Commission in 1929 to develop a "pattern curriculum" that would provide the missing synthesis of the best of current practice. The final report, *An Experience Curriculum in English* (Hatfield 1935), began with the premise that "*The ideal curriculum consists of well-selected experiences*." Echoing the concern with functionalism, the commission turned to "life, noting what experiences most people have" as well as "desirable possible experiences they miss" (3). The real contribution of the commission, however, was not in deriving the experiences but in weaving the selected experiences into a coherent curriculum stretching from kindergarten to college.

To build this curriculum, the commission organized experiences into units, each of which was itself part of a larger "experience strand," "arranged like broad easy stair steps in a reasonably steady progression of intellectual difficulty and social maturity" (viii). The report divided the experience strands into several sets, including Literature Experiences, Reading Experiences, Creative Expression Experiences, Speech Experiences, Writing Experiences, Instrumental Grammar Experiences, Corrective Teaching, and Electives. The most radical, and most widely attacked, stand taken in *An Experience Curriculum* was the abandonment of formal grammar in favor of functional instruction. The only concession made at all was the inclusion of the study of grammar as a formal system among the suggested electives for high school seniors.

The curriculum in literature was equally liberal in conception, though disappointing in execution. The goals emphasized pupils' experiences, informal discussion, broadening horizons, and refining perception. The commission had no clear principles for attaining these goals, however, and the units themselves became an eclectic conglomeration of not necessarily compatible approaches. In the end, the concept of experience degenerated into primary objectives such as "To observe the effects of widening trade horizons on our daily lives" (Unit 6 in Exploring the Social World). Such objectives, however important in themselves, could be realized in many ways and missed any unique contribution that might be attained through study of the English language arts.

Much more successful was Louise Rosenblatt's (1938) *Literature as Exploration*. Rosenblatt argued that readers come to texts with a variety of human concerns and experiences that are an important and necessary part of reading. The idea of the active use of prior knowledge in reading literature, a main theme of *Literature as Exploration*, is the point of later reader-response critics, whom Rosenblatt anticipated by some 30 years. The reading of the text is an active event; it necessarily entails the bringing of prior knowledge to bear on what is read. What is in the mind cannot be the object of censure or praise: It results from prior experience, prior reading, and prior teaching. Readers cannot avoid using this knowledge and cannot avoid entering into a transaction with the text that makes the result peculiarly theirs. To say this is not to deny the possibility of general perceptions and readings but to assert that these general readings are always modified by human individuality.

Rosenblatt's (1938) volume provided the most complete

rationale for the teaching of literature as an important part of individual and social development. It also successfully transcended the limited vision of "experience" that hampered other curriculum statements of the time. It was, however, largely a theoretical work, with little explication of implications for practice and with no practical teaching suggestions. The potential for a new approach to the curriculum in literature remained unrealized for many years (for a recent attempt to apply Rosenblatt to the classroom, see Probst 1988).

Two studies by Dora V. Smith (1933, 1941), one national and the other focusing on New York State, provide some indication of the limited extent to which evolving theories of the curriculum were being carried over into classroom practice. The findings from both studies were similar and indicated that although conditions had changed considerably since the beginning of the century, a large gap remained between classroom practice and the discussions in professional journals or committee reports. Specifically, she found that although detailed rhetorical or grammatical analysis of single texts was no longer common, too much time continued to be devoted to reading single works and too little to reading more widely. Teacher-led recitations involving the whole class predominated over any sort of individualized or child-centered instruction.

In the 1933 study, Smith also found that anthologies of literary selections were widely used as the basis of the course in the junior high school and as a supplement to the classics in the senior high years. By 1941, the intervening years of the Depression had moved the anthology to the center of the course at all levels.

Anthologies of literary selections had become increasingly important as the progressives placed more emphasis on wide reading and moved the schools away from the uniform lists. Usually edited by leaders of the teaching profession, the anthologies themselves were at least a moderately progressive influence throughout this period. They were responsive to the broader movements for reform and provided teachers with a set of materials arranged in a coherent order. The early anthologies tended to be organized by genre or chronology, but by the mid-1930s thematic units organized around important personal or social goals dominated the 7th- to 10th-grade anthologies, and formal and historical studies continued to dominate the last two years. During this period the anthologies also reached a compromise between depth and breadth: Most included full-length selections from the classics as well as a broad range of classic and contemporary short stories, poems, and exposition. (On the development of the anthologies, see Bibb 1965 and Olson 1969.)

Narrowed Goals

Ultimately the metaphor of experience proved too broad for most teachers of English; during the ensuing decades they retreated toward narrower definitions of English as "life adjustment," "communication skills," "general education," or "adolescent needs." Whereas earlier approaches had stressed the broadening, liberating power of the English language arts, the narrower view saw them as a way to solve immediate problems and prepare students for the adult world.

Life Adjustment. *English for Social Living* (Roberts, Kaulfers, and Kefauver 1943) was one of the first attempts to provide a narrowly needs-oriented curriculum in English. Carried out under the guidance of the Stanford University education faculty with support from the General Education Board, the program sought to replace the traditional curriculum with one "designed and tested to meet specific personal and social needs" (11–12). Like other attempts at curriculum reformulation during this period, however, the guiding philosophy was so oriented toward the immediate school situation that it provided no guidelines for scope or sequence. Rather than an outline of a new curriculum, *English for Social Living* was really a collection of activities that had been undertaken in different schools by different teachers, grouped together under such general areas of concern as "building personality" and the need to "study and serve the community." Lacking external principles by which to determine scope and sequence, accepted practice deteriorated into a "multiple approach," in which the only criterion was that students be kept interested.

Matching selections to specific problems of pupils was especially important in this approach and took several forms. One was simply a reinterpretation of the values of the classic texts. *Silas Marner*, for example, was taught as a "storehouse of information necessary for understanding friends, family, and one's self" (Applebee 1974, 152). Teachers more fully committed to general education and life adjustment provided bibliographies organized around the major focuses of adolescent needs. Lenrow's (1940) *Reader's Guide to Prose Fiction* was the earliest and most extensive, though its frankness and willingness to deal with topics like homosexuality, birth control, and sex kept it from being widely used. As the basis of a curriculum in literature, all it lacked was sequence; but that was deliberate since the sequence was to come from the problems of each student at a given time.

More influential was a later bibliography, *Reading Ladders for Human Relations* (Taba et al. 1947). The selections were standard school texts and hence accessible to a majority of teachers. They were also organized in "ladders" of ascending difficulty that would provide a cumulative program, achieving its purposes through reconstructing experience at ever more advanced levels. The reading ladders, though they involved relatively few selections, implied that a curriculum could be constructed out of familiar materials that would be relevant to the new demands *and* be coherent and sequential.

Another approach to matching students' needs and interests was the development of an extensive body of literature dealing with specific developmental problems. Although teachers had long been concerned with good books suitable for children, the 1940s and 1950s saw the development of a new literary genre with its own authors and highly specialized audiences of adolescent readers (Applebee 1974). Although some good books entered the curriculum through this avenue, the genre also produced a flood of formula novels. As Martinec (1971) pointed out in a later analysis, the formula plots had a number of questionable implications: (1) Immaturity is somehow to be equated with isolation from the group, (2) all problems can be solved and will be solved successfully, (3) adults cannot help you much, and (4) maturity entails conformity. Such implications, which were shared by many of the other activities suggested at this time, eventually engendered a violent reaction against "life adjustment" and, indeed, against the progressive movement as a whole.

Language and Communication. If one aspect of the narrowing of goals was a concern with adjustment, a second sought to ensure that the general student would have "competence" to carry out the varied demands of life. The focus on language skills was highlighted in *Language in General Education* (Commission on Secondary School Curriculum 1940), sponsored by the Progressive Education Association. Although the rhetoric of the report was fully in harmony with the concerns of the life adjustment movement, for this committee it meant that children must be given the tools for successful living—and the prime tool was language. The report proposed the careful study of language as a symbolic system, drawing heavily on the work of I. A. Richards and the general semantics movement. Such study would not only give students control over their own language and the ability to resist the propaganda of others but also teach them to think: "Teaching language is teaching the technique of classifying, sorting, ordering, clarifying experiences—the technique of thinking straight" (63).

The concern with language skills was reinforced by the exigencies of war. When an NCTE committee just before World War II prepared a list of "Basic Aims for English Instruction in American Schools," its first point was that language "is a basic instrument in the maintenance of the democratic way of life." Instruction must emphasize the "four fundamental language arts: reading, writing, speaking, and listening" (Basic Aims Committee 1942).

After the war, NCTE again organized a Commission on the English Curriculum (1952, 1954, 1956, 1963, 1965) to outline the form and substance of the English Curriculum. The first three volumes of the report, issued between 1952 and 1956, illustrate the implications of life adjustment for instruction in English and the continuing inability of the movement to find a coherent set of principles to give order and structure to the curriculum. In these volumes, the language arts seemed to include virtually any activity with which the teacher might feel comfortable, with few guidelines about what would be "significant." In planning a sequence of activities, the commission turned to the concept of "growth," which involved "a definite sequential pattern" (1952, 31) of increasing maturity and complexity. But any number of activities could be justified as more difficult, more complex, or meeting a need, and all kinds of activities were offered. Eventually reaching five volumes (with the addition of one in 1963 on teacher education and another in 1965 on college teaching), the work of the Commission on the English Curriculum is by far the most extensive of the major historical statements on the scope and sequence of the English language arts. But it is also the least successful in providing a clear pattern for the curriculum to follow and as a result had little influence.

The Academic Resurgence

As the NCTE Commission on the English Curriculum was publishing its volumes, the progressive movement as a whole was under attack for its lack of intellectual discipline and its narrow focus on life adjustment. Even when the influence of the Progressive Education Association was at its height, a strong countermovement stressing a traditional "liberal education" was reflected in works such as Mortimer Adler's (1940) *How to Read a Book* and Hutchins's (1936) *The Higher Learning in America*. Unconvinced by the arguments of the "educationists," scholars in this tradition stressed the values of the classical texts, not just for the college bound but for all students. The Great Books program at St. Johns College and the Junior Great Books program in many schools are among the curricular legacies of these concerns (Bell 1966).

By the late 1950s, and particularly after Sputnik shocked the American consciousness in 1957, the objections to the trivialization of the curriculum led teachers and their professional associations to search for a new basis for the curriculum. Rather than continuing with the metaphor of experience or with the study of child development, the profession turned instead to recent scholarship in the field of English for a new set of structuring principles. They found their general model in the report of the Woods Hole Conference, chaired by Jerome Bruner (1960), which argued for a "spiral curriculum" based on the idea that any subject could be taught to children if its basic structure were made clear. The structure could then be presented in progressively more complex forms (see Applebee 1974; Shugrue 1968).

In searching for a new content in literary studies, the profession turned to structuralist approaches, including the work of Northrup Frye (1957) and of the "New Critics," who had come to dominate university scholarship; in language studies, the profession turned to the work of the structural and the transformational linguists. (There were attempts to find similar structural principles for rhetoric as well, mostly derived from communication theory and general semantics.) In particular, the New Criticism offered a discipline-based body of knowledge about how to read literature, while transformational grammar offered a discipline-based body of knowledge to reinvigorate the study of formal grammar.

The New Criticism was heralded by the work of I. A. Richards (1929) in England, whose *Practical Criticism* showed that university students had difficulty comprehending poetry. One of Richards's major findings was that his student readers tended to approach the works they read with what he called "stock responses," "mnemonic irrelevancies," "doctrinal adhesions," "technical preconceptions," or "general critical preconceptions." Half of the typologies of "failure in reading and judging poetry" came from the fact that readers were not blank slates when they read a poem. This was a matter of some concern to Richards, particularly because his students' filled slates did not match his. They tended not to be the "objective" readers that he had hoped the universities were training.

It took several years for the New Criticism to be translated into a teaching approach and many more years for this approach to have much influence on the schools. The first and classic book in the field was a college text, *Understanding Poetry*, by Cleanth Brooks and Robert Penn Warren (1938). Their concern was to shift the focus of instruction toward close readings of the texts themselves rather than to focus on the "irrelevancies" that distracted Richards's readers. They proceeded to demonstrate this concern by following each poem with a series of questions that could lead students to become dispassionate analysts of literary texts. The initial work with poetry was followed by work on fiction and drama, and close textual analysis divorced from historical or thematic emphases became a standard part of academic criticism and instruction. This approach had little effect on the school curriculum, however, for another 20 years; the New Critics were not even cited in the NCTE curriculum studies that appeared in the 1950s. By the 1960s, however, with curriculum reform focusing again on the academic disciplines, this critical approach was being recommended enthusiastically by scholars and teachers who sought to redefine the curriculum in literature (e.g., Squire and Applebee 1968).

The first attempt to define a new, academic curriculum for English grew out of a 1958 conference cosponsored by NCTE, the Modern Language Association, and the College English Association. The widely distributed conference report, *The Basic Issues in the Teaching of English*, asserted that English is a "fundamental liberal discipline" with a body of specific knowledge to be preserved and transmitted. By identifying this subject matter as the core of English, the conference also rejected the needs of the child and the accompanying metaphors of experience and exploration as the basis of the English curriculum. Instead, the attention of the profession turned to identifying the specific knowledge that best reflected the "core" of the discipline of English in each of its three components: language, literature, and composition (Applebee 1974; Shugrue 1968).

As part of the focus on a discipline-based curriculum, James Lynch and Bertrand Evans (1963), with sponsorship from the recently organized Council for Basic Education, undertook an analysis of literature anthologies and language textbooks. Lynch and Evans offered a trenchant critique, based on a painstakingly exhaustive analysis of the content and sequence of the textbooks. In examining the literature anthologies, they championed the reading of literature "for its own sake" (22), complaining vigorously about selections, units, and study apparatus that placed the emphasis elsewhere—on themes, on student interests, on enjoyment as an end in itself rather than a byproduct of careful study. They berated the anthology editors for the inclusion of ephemeral pieces, translations, and nonliterature (exposition and biographical narrative) and for editing and adapting selections, often without any indication that the text had been changed.

Their analysis of textbook treatments of grammar, usage, and mechanics was similarly unflattering. After tracing how various points of grammar and usage were treated across the high school years, they attacked the textbooks for excessive emphasis on exercise and drill materials and for senseless repetition of the same material from year to year. In the end, they recommended that the standard four-volume course be reduced to a single, one-volume handbook that would present the necessary concepts in a coherent, concise, and unrepetitive format.

Much of what Lynch and Evans (1963) found and attacked in their analyses of both types of textbook series reflected the success of earlier waves of educational reform. In particular, literature was being made relevant, and grammar and usage were being treated as functional. Neither of these goals was compatible with a treatment of the language arts as comprised of coherent academic disciplines (language, literature, and composition). Many of Lynch and Evans's criticisms were applicable whatever view of the curriculum was adopted: Excessive repetition, overemphasis on format and appearance that might catch the eye but distracted the mind, carelessness in attributions and editing of texts, and the uncomfortable size of the textbooks were problems no matter what the philosophy of education. Other criticisms interacted directly with the nature of the high school curriculum: Abandoning the chronological treatment of British and American literature, eliminating the four-year sequence in grammar and usage, and reducing the curriculum to a smaller core of works of "high literary distinction"—such suggestions mark the beginning of the reinvolvement of university professors in the school curriculum rather than obvious solutions that were quickly endorsed by the teachers who would be most affected.

If Lynch and Evans's (1963) suggestions were not quickly built on, other collaborations between school and college flourished in their aftermath. The mid-1960s was a time of great excitement in the English language arts, with renewed involvement of college professors in issues of curriculum and new funds for curriculum development through an expansion of the National Defense Education Act. Over two dozen curriculum study centers were eventually funded by the U.S. Office of Education, bringing together teachers and scholars to restructure the English curriculum. With a few exceptions, the centers built (of necessity) on work already underway at the sponsoring institutions, but they did provide concrete examples of discipline-based curricula in English. Bruner's (1960) theory of a spiral curriculum pervaded most of the curricula. Frye's (1957) "pregeneric modes" and "archetypes" could be found in the Nebraska curriculum, Chomsky's (1957) notions of transformational grammar appeared most notably in the Oregon curriculum, the Georgia curriculum used structural linguistics, and recent developments in rhetoric found their way into the curriculum at one or another of the centers (see Shugrue 1968). Though teachers were involved in the curriculum development centers, the driving force behind the new curricula was contemporary scholarship in literature, language, and composition. Although such curricula may have been workable for the college-bound student, there was little attention to the issue of how to make them work with the majority of students.

Interestingly, the two most innovative and influential projects—Smiley's *Gateway English*, developed at Hunter College and eventually published by Macmillan, and Fader's English in Every Classroom at the University of Michigan—were the least oriented toward the new academic emphasis. *Gateway English* was specifically designed for the urban disadvantaged; English in Every Classroom (better known under its published title, *Hooked on Books*) was designed for the students in a boys' reform school (Fader and Shaevitz 1966). Although a few of the other centers produced materials or reports that were widely used, they mainly influenced the individuals directly involved in the process of curriculum development.

The fullest statement of the rationale for a discipline-based curriculum in English was *Freedom and Discipline in English*. Written by the Commission on English (1965) of the College Entrance Examination Board, the report showed little development beyond the principles enunciated earlier in the basic issues conference. The commission continued to use the tripod of language, literature, and composition as the basis of the curriculum, with separate discussions and recommendations for each of the three areas. These discussions were firmly grounded on current scholarship in each of the disciplines. The New Criticism figured prominently in the discussion of literature, transformational grammar in the discussion of language. While stressing the disciplines of English as the source of the curriculum, however, the report offered little guidance on the shape that that curriculum would take. Instead, the specific shape of the curriculum was to be developed in each local school district, where it would reflect the professional judgment of the teachers who had been trained in commission-sponsored institutes. To hone teachers' professional judgment, the commission did offer two publications that included extensive samples of student writing and commentary indicating how each sample should be evaluated (Commission on English 1963, 1968).

Also influential during the academic resurgence was James Squire and Roger Applebee's (1968) study of instruction in high school English programs, published as *High School English Instruction Today*. Funded by the U.S. Office of Education, the study provided both an overview of current practice and specific recommendations that were framed from within a discipline-based perspective on the language arts curriculum. Squire and Applebee found exciting and well-developed programs for higher-achieving students and a nationwide neglect of the lower tracks. Literary studies accounted for some 52 percent of class time, language study for some 14 percent. As in Dora V. Smith's (1933, 1941) earlier studies, lecture, recitation, and whole-class discussion dominated most classrooms, with little group work and little in the way of innovative approaches to organizing the curriculum. Close study of individual texts, in the tradition of the New Criticism, was lauded when it was found but was used extensively by only about one quarter of the teachers. The programs singled out for praise, however, were built around careful study and close reading of individual texts, supported by a broadly based program of guided individual reading.

The teaching of language was largely functional, though this was hardly a point in its favor. Summarizing "functional" approaches, the authors concluded, "Whichever method is actually applied in the classroom, it is clearly accidental if a student is presented with lessons so complete and so ordered that he is able to develop any large conception of the basic structure of English" (Squire and Applebee 1968, 144). Again, the programs singled out for praise were those that took an academic, discipline oriented approach, emphasizing formal study of the history of language, dialectology, lexicography, or syntax.

Social Issues

The academic resurgence was relatively short-lived. By the late 1960s, attention in curriculum had shifted toward more socially relevant programs. The shift had many causes, including the general social upheaval generated by the civil rights movement and the Vietnam War as well as new views of the nature of schooling. In the English language arts, major changes occurred through acquaintance with child-centered models of teaching that had been developed in British schools, where the emphasis was on personal and linguistic "growth through English" (Dixon 1967) and where Piaget rather than Chomsky dominated the view of structuralism. The Dartmouth Conference, an international gathering of educators from Australia, Canada, the United Kingdom, and the United States, was particularly influential, both through its influence on the participants, many of whom had been leaders in the development of the academic model, and through its widely distributed conference reports (Dixon 1967; Muller 1967).

At about the same time, Squire and Applebee (1969) extended their studies of the English curriculum from American to British schools, with very different results. Overall, literary studies occupied only 39 percent of class time and language only 6 percent (compared with 52 and 14 percent, respectively, in the United States). Speech, on the other hand, was emphasized in 14 percent of the classes observed, compared with only 5 percent in the United States. Drama activities (17 percent of class time), small-group work, and project work all impressed the observers, although they had rarely been seen in American classrooms. Distressed by the lack of sequence and structure in some British programs and by the willingness of some teachers to abandon the literary tradition completely in favor of contemporary works, the observers nonetheless concluded that some British practices would prove useful in American programs. The most important of these involved more emphasis on the development of a personal response to literature; a focus on the traditional distinction between teaching about language (which was rarely observed in British schools) and teaching the use of language (which these schools seemed to be doing effectively); and more emphasis on speech, drama, and other oral-language activities.

These reports and the studies that followed returned the child to the center of the curriculum, though in doing so they based their analysis of curriculum on more powerful models of language development and language learning than had been the case in earlier cycles of curriculum reform (Barnes 1974; Britton 1970). These models, "when formulated clearly and incisively," offered "the conception of a dynamic interplay of speaking, writing, and personal thought as a basis for language learning (itself conceived as a developing ability to perceive and express relationships)" (Squire and Applebee 1969, 195). Squire and Applebee cited Dixon's (1967) Dartmouth Conference report, *Growth Through English*, as an example of such a clear and incisive formulation. James Moffett's (1968a, 1968b) "student-centered language arts curriculum" was the most carefully constructed implementation of the curriculum principles that the Dartmouth Conference espoused.

In developing programs that were more relevant, one of the most significant curriculum innovations was the widespread adoption of elective or phase-elective programs in the high school program. Taking many forms, these programs effectively broke with traditional patterns of content and organization, allowing teachers to determine what they would teach and students to select what they would learn. Free from the strictures of English I, II, III, and IV, elective programs opened the English language arts to contemporary materials, popular culture, film, and other media, as well as to experiments in team teaching, independent study, and interdisciplinary configurations of courses (Christenbury 1980).

Defended as a response to student needs and interests, elective programs in the English language arts nonetheless became in many schools a reflection of teachers' special interests, fragmenting the language arts into separate studies in a way that echoed the separate and unrelated English studies of the 18th and early 19th centuries. Analyzing elective programs in 1972, Hillocks concluded that rather than widespread improvements on traditional programs, elective curricula as they were being implemented carried over many of the faults of traditional programs and destroyed whatever sequence and coherence the traditional curriculum had had. (For a detailed evaluation of a specific elective program, see Hillocks 1971.) The timing of elective programs was also inopportune, for they soon ran afoul of trends toward assessment and accountability as well as of the back-to-basics movement.

Competing Models

Since the mid-1970s, the curriculum in the English language arts has been buffeted by a series of competing models. Some of these models have come largely from outside the profession. The excesses of the student-centered curricula, for example, generated a call for more "basic" studies and with it a return to a concern with minimal essentials, now accompanied by widespread state-level testing of minimum competencies. The emphasis on basic skills, which generated its own concern that schools might abandon the pursuit of excellence in the attempt to ensure that all students reached at least minimal goals, was followed by a reassertion of the values of a classical "liberal" curriculum (Adler 1982; Bennett 1988), bolstered by the new educational goal of cultural literacy (Hirsch 1987).

Even as these external calls have been shaping the teaching of English, leaders of the profession have been searching for a new basis for the curriculum. The difficulty of that process was evident in the next volume to emerge from the NCTE Commission on the English Curriculum. *Three Language Arts Curriculum Models* (Mandell 1980) did not even attempt a reconciliation, but instead presented three competing, comprehensive curriculum models for prekindergarten through college. The three models represent long-standing traditions in the English language arts: One was based on personal growth, one on cultural heritage, and one on the development of specific language competencies.

The most fully developed models to be offered for language arts instruction in recent years have been based on constructivist theories of language use and language development. Constructivist approaches have a variety of roots, with related frameworks emerging in fields as seemingly diverse as linguistics, psychology, history of science, sociology, and philosophy (on constructivist theories and their application to the language arts, see Applebee 1991a; Langer and Applebee 1986). What scholars in this tradition share is a view of knowledge as an active construction built up by the individual acting within a social context that shapes and constrains that knowledge but does not determine it in an absolute sense.

Constructivist theory involves an important shift in what counts as knowledge, and by implication in what should be taught in schools. From a constructivist perspective, notions of "objectivity" and "factuality" lose their preeminence, being replaced by notions of the central role of the individual learner in the "construction of reality" (Berger and Luckmann 1967). Instruction becomes less a matter of transmittal of an objective and culturally sanctioned body of knowledge and more a matter of helping individuals learn to construct and interpret for themselves. There is a shift in emphasis from content knowledge to processes of understanding. The challenge for educators is how in turn to embed this new emphasis into the curricula they develop and implement.

In the English language arts, constructivist frameworks have been particularly appealing to scholars who have emphasized the skills and strategies that contribute to ongoing processes of language use. During the 1970s and early 1980s, process-oriented approaches to instruction dominated writing instruction and affected literature instruction as well. In their early versions, these approaches differed from the constructivist framework in that they sought to find a universal mental process regardless of content. The constructivist framework takes a broader sociocultural view of mental acts and their relation to language and tends to see reading, writing, and the other language arts as an activity—using the terms of Soviet psychology as adapted by such American psychologists as Sylvia Scribner and Michael Cole (1981). Although process-oriented approaches developed first in the teaching of writing and reading and have been slower to develop in the teaching of literature, the constructivist framework suggests powerful models for these parts of the curriculum as well (Barr 1988; Langer 1989). At the same time, teachers who have been convinced of the value of process-oriented approaches to the teaching of writing have begun to look for ways to extend those approaches to other areas of the curriculum (Applebee 1989a; Langer 1984; Purves 1990; Purves, Rogers, and Soter 1990).

Responding to the tension between external calls for basic skills and a traditional liberal curriculum and the emerging focus within the profession on process-oriented approaches, the Modern Language Association, NCTE, and five other organizations concerned with the teaching of English as a first or second language formed an English Coalition to consider common problems and issues. As one part of their activities, they jointly sponsored a 3-week conference during which some 60 educators met daily to find common ground for their teaching of the language arts. Their report, *The English Coalition Conference: Democracy Through Language* (Lloyd-Jones and Lunsford 1989), is firmly within the constructivist tradition. The conference emphasized the role of students as "active learners" and argued, as the introduction to the report explained, that learning "inevitably unites skills and content in a dynamic process of practice and assimilation" (xxiii).

Although the conference participants, who represented a mix of elementary, secondary, and college teachers, found themselves in a surprising degree of agreement about goals and directions for the teaching of the English language arts, the report itself fails to capture the freshness of the dialogue or to offer clear guidelines for curriculum. Caught in a reaction against prescriptive "lists"—whether of texts to read or skills to learn—the conference found no broader structuring principles to offer. Instead of a unifying framework, the reports of the elementary, secondary, and college "strands" present a variety of alternatives and options, each of which is valuable in itself but the total of which do not provide a sense of unity and direction. In this respect, the coalition report is plagued by many of the same problems that plagued the earlier curriculum series from the Commission on the English Curriculum.

The status of the English curriculum in the 1980s has been examined in a series of studies (Applebee 1981, 1989a, 1989b; 1990; 1991b; Applebee, Langer, and Mullis 1987; Ravitch and Finn 1987). These reports suggest that the curriculum as a whole remains teacher-centered and traditional, with literary study guided by the New Criticism's close readings that Squire and Applebee (1968, 1969) had advocated in the 1960s. Literature continues to dominate some 50 percent of English class time at the secondary school level, with language study diminished to some 10 percent. The literature curriculum itself has broadened, including the addition of a wide variety of short stories, poems, and short nonfiction works by women and minority authors. However, the traditions represented by the book-length works that define the literary canon have remained remarkably stable since the turn of the century.

During the 1970s and 1980s, constructivist approaches revitalized theories of language learning, and process-oriented approaches to instruction generated considerable excitement and reshaping of the curriculum in writing, at least in many schools. The teaching of literature, however, stagnated while educators focused on other issues. Throughout this period, there was little research on the literature curriculum and little debate about what the implications of constructivist theories might be for elementary and secondary school literature programs. This situation occurred partly because scholarship and pedagogy in writing were so exciting, drawing attention away from other areas, and also partly because the importance of literature instruction was harder to defend to beleagered administrators and the general public in an era of back-to-basics and minimal competency. It was only late in the decade of the 1980s, as concern with reasoning and higher-order skills began to reemerge in the public debate, that teachers and scholars began a serious reexamination of the literature curriculum and of the coherence (or lack of it) in approaches to the various parts of the English language arts curriculum.

CURRENT AND CONTINUING ISSUES IN CURRICULUM

Whether or not they accept the constructivist principles underlying the coalition report, teachers in the coming decades will face a variety of new and continuing issues that will have to be addressed in the practical context of building a curriculum in the English language arts. Whether they turn to past experience, current enthusiasms, or careful scholarship to find their answers will depend in large part on the relevance, cohesiveness, and comprehensiveness of the next generation of curriculum theory and research. What will be the most productive avenues for such research? Several areas seem particularly important and will be discussed further here: the investigation of the current state of the curriculum, the specification of general principles to guide day-to-day curriculum decisions as well as overall curriculum guidelines, the extent to which the curriculum should be differentiated for diverse groups of students, the uses of assessment, the role of nonprint media, and the decision about which content to teach (which literature, which grammar, which criticism).

Status Studies

One of the continuing strands of research in the English language arts curriculum has involved studies of current practice as reflected in curriculum materials, textbooks, and day-to-day classroom teaching. Such studies have a dual interest: They serve as convenient historical reference points in examining the evolving curriculum, and they often play a significant role in defining the issues that will be considered important and the directions that reform will take. Thus the studies of the course of study published in *School Review* in 1907 became an important reference point and rallying cry in the subsequent movement to reform and reject the uniform lists. Similarly, Dora Smith's studies of instruction in the 1930s and Squire and Applebee's studies in the 1960s did more than simply chronicle current practice; at their best, they embodied a strong vision of an effective curriculum and thus served to define the direction for the next generations of curriculum reform. Because they play such a direct role in the evolution of the curriculum in the English language arts, such studies have been discussed in the context of the historical evolution of the subject. Their continuing importance, however, should not be minimized: They remain one of our primary ways of attaining enough perspective to see how our various professional enthusiasms interact to form a total curricular experience—a total experience that has often looked quite different than the sum of its parts.

General Principles for the Curriculum

As we have seen, the history of curriculum theory in the English language arts has in part been a history of changing reference points in determining scope and sequence in the curriculum. Whether guided by G. Stanley Hall's recapitulation theories, by the analysis of minimal essentials of the functionalists, or by the explication of the structure of the discipline, teachers and researchers have relied on a succession of external criteria to help them select what to teach and when to teach it. Such criteria are necessary, for the boundaries of the English language arts are easily extended outward: Almost any activity can be justified as having at least some relationship to the use of language. When the criteria for scope and sequence in the curriculum have become weakened, as they were when English was governed by the metaphor of experience and again during the search for personal and social relevance, the curriculum ultimately lost direction and strong countermovements began.

The current period in curriculum for the English language arts is a particularly vulnerable one. When the curriculum is defined in terms of process-related cognitive and linguistic skills, the task of laying out an orderly, sequential curriculum takes on a new complexity. It is no longer possible to refer to an external standard based on the subject matter, life needs, or normal patterns of growth. Instead, the curriculum has to be structured to foster the growth of problem-solving skills that may develop quite differently from student to student, depending on background, particularly linguistic and cultural background, interests, and previous experiences. The issue for curriculum theory becomes one of providing an orderly, coherent set of experiences, each of which is flexible enough to provide the appropriate degrees of challenge and support to students whose knowledge and skills may differ widely from one another.

In practice, this structuring is likely to mean that the external curriculum is highly indeterminate (as in fact it appears in the report of the English Coalition), with few constraints on school-level decisions about materials and activities assigned to various grades and classes. These decisions can be guided by local considerations, such as the ethnic background of the community, concerns of parents, and preferences of the teachers involved. Though arbitrary, these decisions are still important because the curriculum framework that results provides stability to the program and guidance to teachers and students, ensuring a necessary sense of order and coherence.

One critical area for curriculum research will be in providing guiding principles to shape the teacher's day-to-day decisions about teaching and learning that take place within these broad and arbitrary frameworks. These are decisions about the individual assignments that are constructed and the structure of the environment for teaching and learning that surrounds the assignments (on the influences on teacher decision making in English, see Barnes and Barnes in press; Barnes, Barnes, and Clark 1984; Grossman 1988; Hawthorne 1988). The principles that might govern this structure in a constructivist-oriented instructional environment are just beginning to be explored (e.g., Applebee 1991a; Langer 1984; Langer and Applebee 1986; Purves 1990), but clearly they will look very different from the scope-and-sequence charts that they will replace. Indeed, they are likely to be principles that rely for their implementation on the day-to-day judgment of the professional teacher rather than on the prescriptions of an external curriculum. There is as yet, however, little consensus about what such ordering principles should look like.

Differentiation of the Curriculum

Like the problem of scope and sequence, the issue of differentiation of the curriculum has been long-standing. The Committee of Ten argued strongly that preparation for college was the best preparation for life, the *Reorganization* report 20 years later argued just as strongly that different groups of students had different needs, and both sides of the argument have reasserted themselves over the ensuing decades. Adler's *Paideia Proposal* (1982), for example, argues trenchantly that "To give the same quality of schooling to all requires a program of study that is both liberal and general, and that is, in several, crucial, overarching respects, one and the same for every child" (21). The English Coalition (Lloyd-Jones and Lunsford 1989) argues just as trenchantly that the curriculum must vary with every classroom, so much so that no overall curriculum can be specified at all. In the decades to come, these issues will be aggravated by major shifts in the student population, with ever-larger numbers of students from minority cultures, including many who speak languages other than English.

The existence of a body of agreed-upon texts at the center of the high school English curriculum dates to the late 19th century, when the English language arts emerged as a major curriculum area. A series of factors shaped the body of agreed-upon texts (Applebee 1974, 1989b), including the prestige of Milton and the Augustan poets (whose Latinate styles made them especially suitable for parsing and analysis), a strong tradition of Shakespearean criticism, the influence of earlier traditions in the teaching of Latin and Greek, and a concern with contemporary literature (though "contemporary" has shifted over time from Dickens and Addison to Frost and Golding).

How central this body of agreed-upon texts should be has been a matter of continuing debate within the English language arts. On one side have been those who argue that the Great Books, and only the Great Books, are worthy of inclusion in the school curriculum. On the other have been those who argue that there are many other good books for children and adolescents, that the Great Books perpetuate a narrow and biased cultural hegemony, or that the only route to appreciation of the Great Books is by beginning with simpler and more accessible ones.

There has been no clear consensus about any of these issues. The Great Books have repeatedly been criticized by teachers of English for their inaccessibility and irrelevance just as often as they have been praised for their cultural importance. Efforts to find alternative selections have led many teachers to emphasize the genre of "adolescent" or "young adult" fiction, but just as many others have rejected such books for their shallowness and superficiality.

For all the debate that has occurred, a variety of studies have shown that the curriculum in literature has remained surprisingly stable over the years. The traditions represented by the college entrance lists before the turn of the century continue to dominate the contemporary curriculum. Minority authors and women have been marginalized, finding their way into the short stories and poetry selections but not into the book-length works that make up the high school canon.

The issues for curriculum theory and research continue unabated: To what extent is the lack of differentiation appropriate, that is, necessary to ensure a common national culture? In what ways can we ensure that the curriculum provides an effective education to all students—college-bound and vocational, men and women, majority and minority alike?

Assessment of Learning

As in other subjects, the curriculum in English language arts has been affected by assessment (Valentine 1987). Indeed, as was noted earlier, the very emergence of "English" as a unified subject within the school curriculum was closely tied to the influence of college entrance examination requirements during the late 19th century. And these requirements in turn led to a variety of curriculum studies that sought to provide an alternative to the examination-bound curriculum in the early 20th century (e.g., Hosic 1917).

In addition to college entrance examinations, the early part of the 20th century saw the development of school and district examinations and a few state-wide assessments, most notably the New York State Regents examinations. These examinations were used to determine matriculation, and they tended to follow European models (Purves 1973). The early examinations covered knowledge of particular texts, grammatical and rhetorical principles, or the history of language and literature. Set texts with a directly linked syllabus and examination were common throughout the first half of the century.

As the century progressed, the influence of the College Entrance Examination Board (CEEB) grew. Initially relying on written essays, the examinations of the CEEB were gradually replaced by machine-scorable, multiple-choice formats. Partly in response to criticisms of the influence of the examinations on the curriculum, the content of the examinations shifted from specific knowledge (such as that of set texts in literature) to aptitude or skill in reading and writing. The only major exception to this shift appeared in the advanced placement program during the 1950s, which had (and continues to have) a very direct influence on curriculum content.

For the literature curriculum, the result of these changes was to help drive instruction toward a New Criticism approach, which could be misinterpreted as allowing testing for a single main idea—a popular concept in the field of reading and one that now dominates the testing of literature nationally (Brody, DeMilo, and Purves 1989). For the language curriculum, the result has been a neglect of linguistic knowledge for an emphasis on standard usage.

The limitations inherent in such emphases are real and highlight a continuing challenge for research in curriculum: How can assessment programs be constructed so that they reinforce teachers' subject matter goals rather than constraining curriculum content or narrowing the definition of what counts as "knowing" the subject matter (Langer and Applebee 1988)? The development of innovative approaches to assessment is increasingly important in an era when assessment results at local, state, and national levels have become media events and the subject of political debate.

The Role of Nonprint Media and Technology

As we have demonstrated throughout this chapter, the English language arts curriculum in the United States has had a generally conservative character; it has embraced a content that has remained consistent since the rise of vernacular language studies: "classical" literature, oral and written composition, and study of the language itself. At the same time, the world outside the school has continuously added new literary forms and genres, new words and language structures, and new modes of presentation. How has the curriculum accommodated these intrusions into an orderly world?

One answer might be that it has not. The time period that we have tracked has witnessed the advent of film, radio, and television as modes of art and the typewriter, photocopier, and computer as modes of preparing and presenting text. Each of these has had a profound influence on literature, but the effect on teaching literature in the United States would appear to be surprisingly negligible. Drama has suffered a similar fate because, although it has long been seen as a legitimate art form, it has seldom been part of the curriculum except as the script of a play. Other minor players in the curriculum have been mass print media and popular culture, which are periodically given attention and then lie dormant.

The reason for this general neglect lies in the history that we have traced; the language arts curriculum has aristocratic and elitist roots and to allow popular culture to intrude too far would be to deny that heritage. A perennial solution for what to do with the media and popular arts has been to suggest that they are best suited for the poor students or as "motivators" before engaging in serious study, solutions that are not unique to the United States (Purves 1973).

Drama and Theater. The texts of plays, particularly Shakespeare, have long been a staple of the curriculum, but dramatic performance has played a secondary role. One of the problems, of course, is the logistical one of fitting the performance into the curriculum—either bringing the students to the theater or the players to the classroom. Over the years there have been many attempts to overcome this problem, and many states and communities have effected some sort of partnership. One research study showed the positive effects of such a project on the learning about and interest in drama by secondary school students in Los Angeles, New Orleans, and Rhode Island (Hoetker 1970), but the whole enterprise was complicated and the results about the effectiveness of alternative classroom arrangements were ambiguous.

Alternatives to live performances have included recorded versions—popular since the 1930s—and filmed or videotaped versions of plays. These have formed a staple of the curriculum, but there has been little study of their effectiveness as a means of presentation or of how they have been related to the study of the text.

If drama is an art form presented to students, dramatization is a means whereby students can display their understanding of literature. Drama in this form has its antecedents in memorization and oratory, but it has been most popular when student-centered curricula were in favor. In particular, dramatization and creative dramatics were prominent in the progressive experiments in the 1920s and 1930s and again in the post-Dartmouth curricula of the 1970s. This movement received support from James Moffett (1968a, 1968b), who argued for its centrality in the "student-centered curriculum," and from the Squire and Applebee (1969) study of British schools, which cited in particular the influence of the educator Dorothy Heathcote. Drama, particularly improvisation, became a popular instructional tool in the early 1970s. At best, however, dramatization, improvisation, reader's theater, and oral interpretation have remained minor aspects of the literature curriculum.

Film, Radio, and Video. If drama has an ancient history, film, radio, and video are new modes of presentation that have incorporated literary texts as a part of their content and have also created their own distinct art forms. During the course of this century, there have been regular attempts to incorporate the study of these forms into the curriculum in English language arts, but such attempts have never had a great impact. Rather than being widely accepted, studies of popular culture have always been somewhat suspect. Sometimes the curriculum has treated popular culture as the enemy, with the goal of teaching students the poor quality of popular works. Sometimes popular culture has been used as a motivator for the study of "real" literature. And sometimes it has been relegated to the curriculum for nonacademic and remedial tracks. Even film study, with relatively well-established credentials as an academic field at the college level, has remained on the fringes of the school curriculum.

Some teachers do argue that it is important to include film in the literature classroom and that it should be studied as an art form in its own right. To study film and examine students' responses to film is to acknowledge the legitimacy of the art form and the interplay of film and literature in the 20th century. In such a curriculum, film is not used as a substitute for teaching literature or for reading a written work; it becomes a literary work in its own right, something that provokes a response and that is worthy of discussion and study. Such an argument, however, has tended to fall on deaf ears, and there is little research on the role of film and video in the English language arts curriculum.

Computers in the Classroom. In the language arts, computers were first used in teaching grammar, which appeared to be a natural subject for programmed instruction and later for computer-assisted instruction. Programmed grammar materials abounded in the early 1960s and some were quite successful in the marketplace. They were followed by programmed vocabulary lessons and spellers.

There have been many attempts to use programmed and computer-assisted instruction in literature as well, but the indeterminate nature of textual interpretations has not lent itself to programmed instruction in its more determinate form. There has been a recent resurgence of such instruction at least at the experimental level, particularly with the teaching of poetry and metaphor. One of the most promising new approaches uses "hypertext," which unlike earlier programming is not sequential but allows for multiple alternatives. Hypertext allows the reader of a poem to draw on other materials—histories, criticisms, maps, illustrations, and other readers' commentaries—to shape an understanding of the poem. The computer helps the reader gain access to many perspectives and engage in a form of discussion with others. At this point such approaches to the curriculum are still new, but the possibilities for teaching literature seem exciting (Purves, Rogers, and Soter 1990).

Whether the computer will have an impact on the language arts curriculum apart from its use as a word processor is unclear. Like the other new media, its possibilities exceed the practice to which it has been put. New technologies have not yet replaced the old in language and literature, and the text remains paramount.

Language Study and the Curriculum

Another continuing issue in the English language arts curriculum concerns the role and content of the formal study of language. As was noted earlier, the English language arts curriculum has its roots in classical and philosophical study. Stemming from this tradition, one part of language instruction in the United States (as well as in virtually every educational system in the world) has been devoted to the study of language as a formal system and as a part of the cultural and social heritage of the society. This study normally includes such topics as phonology, morphology, grammar, and semantics. In different decades, preferred approaches to the study of language have been historical, descriptive, social, or psychological. Increasingly the tools of scientific investigation have been applied to language at an academic level, but when these topics become a part of the elementary and secondary curriculum, they are often confused with instruction in "proper" or "good" usage and with something called "study skills." A language arts curriculum, for example, may recast phonology as phonics or spelling as opposed to descriptive phonology or dialectology. Morphology is usually translated as "dictionary skills," grammar is taught as prescriptive rules, and semantics may be taught as vocabulary.

Because early instruction in the vernacular imitated the study of classical languages, particularly Latin, a set of grammatical terms and instructional approaches derived from the classical curriculum in Latin grammar was commonly used in instruction until the 1950s (Sherwin 1969). This included work on parsing and the diagraming of sentences as well as on matters of proper usage. During the 1950s, work in descriptive linguistics advanced to the point that its influence spread into the school curriculum (Gleason 1961), for the first time providing an alternative to the existing Latinate school grammars. These new approaches were followed swiftly by Noam Chomsky's (1957) work on transformational grammar. The curriculum projects of the 1960s, following on the idea of a tripod of language, literature, and composition, incorporated extensive introductions to transformational grammar, particularly evident in the materials from the Oregon curriculum study center. The exercises that were developed were not unlike the parsing and diagraming exercises of the earlier prescriptive grammars, but the terminology was different and was seen as "scientific" and rigorous. Many argued that the new linguistics gave English study a true body of learning, which it had hitherto lacked (e.g., Mellon 1964).

Research on the effects of the linguistic curriculum is sparse; the Project English curriculum projects did not undertake summative evaluations of their language programs. The only study of the effects of the language strand of the Oregon curriculum was conducted in New Zealand (Elley, Barham, Lamb, and Wyllie 1976), and that study focused less on the learning of grammar and more on the effects of grammar study on writing performance.

One aspect of transformational grammar did have a continuing impact on the language curriculum. Transformational-generative grammar provided a set of rules for generating sentences, as opposed to the rules for analyzing sentences, which had been the hallmark of traditional grammar and sentence analysis. Transformational grammar suggests that complex sentences are generated through a set of combinatory algorithms, which can be used to combine a finite number of sentence elements into an infinite number of actual sentences. Beginning in the early 1960s, a series of research studies (Bateman and Zidonis 1964; Mellon 1964; O'Hare 1973) demonstrated that students could learn these rules and apply them through a series of exercises in what came to be known as sentence combining. These studies also found that as a result of such study, students appeared to develop a more mature writing style, which then positively affected their grades in composition. Sentence combining has now become a staple of the language arts curriculum, although it is usually divorced from a formal study of language.

This effect of linguistics on the language curriculum has not been followed by other effects deriving from work in phonology, morphology, or sociolinguistics. Little of that knowledge appears to have entered into the school curriculum, although there was an attempt in the late 1960s to implement a rigorous language curriculum based on the work of the British linguist Michael Halliday. The British version, *Language in Use*, was imported and copied in the United States, though it was never widely used (Doughty, Pearce, and Thornton 1971).

If there was no direct effect of the work in language on the school curriculum, one indirect effect needs to be noted. Beginning in the 1960s, linguists began to rethink social dialects and to recognize that they were indeed highly rule-governed rather than aberrations from a standard dialect. One of the major results of this work was the gradual elucidation of Black English as a distinct dialect (Labov 1966). During the course of the late 1960s and early 1970s there were attempts to teach it as a language or to provide textbooks in the dialect. In general these specific curriculum efforts were abandoned, but they created a new awareness among language teachers of the nature of Black English as well as of other dialects and sociolects. This awareness became policy when NCTE promulgated a position paper on "The Students Right to Their Own Language." The document and the position it espoused became the object of a great deal of controversy; it declared that dialects were part of an individual's culture and could not be declared "wrong" or "bad English." Although teachers had the obligation to teach students the standard dialect, they should not do so in a manner that denigrated the self-worth of the students.

Another major work dealing with the teaching of language comes from Russia. *The Teaching and Mastery of Language* (Markova 1979) reports on efforts to transform the teaching of language in the middle school to a program based solidly on contemporary thinking about the nature of language and language learning. The model for Markova's work is found in the work of the psychologist Vygotsky, which led the research team to base the curriculum on the nature of "utterance" as the building block of discourse. The approach begins with the functions of utterances in the world and shows how form follows function. The curriculum treats language use as a social activity and deals with the specific acts of speaking, listening, reading, and writing as well as the analysis of morphology, grammar, and syntax in terms of the functional nature of the activity. The study is complex, and the evaluation of the curriculum suggests that it worked well with trained teachers in a laboratory school. There is no indication of how widely it was adopted in Soviet schools.

An examination of language study in the schools today, as reflected in textbooks on language arts and English, suggests that some of what has been learned in linguistics appears in the curriculum but that the traditional grammatical terms have generally survived, as has the traditional confounding of language study and "language etiquette." There is little research on the role of formal language study in the curriculum, except in the context of the relationship of such study to writing performance. The advocates of the study of language or linguistics in the elementary and secondary schools have yet to develop a strong argument for it and to demonstrate its value. Until then, the language curriculum will be at the mercy of the "pop grammarians" who continually decry the sorry state of usage by American speakers and writers.

Literary Criticism and the Curriculum

Another continuing issue in the English language arts concerns the relationship between scholarship in literature and the content of the school curriculum. During the first third of the century, the approach to literature instruction was historical and moral both in schools and in the university. The philological approach, which led to an immense body of scholarship in early texts, place names, regional dialects, and the like, provided the schools with an approach to literary study that shaped several generations of annotated editions of school texts. These approaches were challenged in the 1930s by the group that came to be known as the New Critics, led by such people as Cleanth Brooks, Allen Tate, R. P. Blackmur, and Robert Penn Warren. After their emphasis on the integrity of the text was translated into a practical pedagogy in Brooks and Warren's (1938) *Understanding Poetry*, the New Criticism soon came to dominate university scholarship. Yet these approaches had little effect on the school curriculum for another 20 years. Only in the 1960s, when curriculum reform again focused on the academic disciplines, was this approach taken up enthusiastically in the schools.

A second influence on the curriculum in criticism also appeared in 1938 with the publication of *Literature as Exploration* by Louise Rosenblatt. Her focus on the human concerns of the texts and the readers was an important reversal of the New Critics' emphasis on issues of style, language, and structure. What is in the reader's head is not erroneous but a necessary part of reading. It becomes a given of her definition of "reader."

The influence of Rosenblatt (1938) on the curriculum is difficult to trace directly, but clearly her suggestion that it is the theme rather than the structure and style that are important gave credence to what came to be known as the thematic approach to literature, an approach that was consonant with the general tenets of progressive education. Thematic units and thematic interpretations came to be a standard part of the secondary literature curriculum from the 1930s to the present.

Purves and his colleagues (Purves 1973; Purves, Bauer, and Quirk 1981) examined literature education in 10 countries in a 1970 study undertaken under the auspices of the International Association for the Evaluation of Educational Achievement (IEA). Compared to students in other countries, those in U.S. secondary schools generally favored a content-oriented or thematic approach to literature, and the critical questions preferred by students tended to deal with the moral content of the literary work. This approach differed from that favored by students in other systems of education, and in nearly all the countries the approach selected by students at the end of secondary school matched that selected by their teachers. The study suggested clearly that students do indeed learn critical approaches but that teachers are often unaware of the approaches they are teaching.

Since the IEA study, critical theory has gone through a number of twists and turns, led by various European critics and their English and American counterparts. Some of these are known by such terms as "reader response," "poststructuralist," "neo-Freudian," "neo-Marxist," and the like. Some of these movements have had an effect on the curriculum in literature, as did the early Freudian and myth critics in their focus on theme and symbol. More recently, articles and texts for teachers have begun to refer to semiotics, to neo-Marxist, and (particularly) to feminist criticism. In general these approaches have adopted the principle that the literary text is not a fixed and knowable entity but is constructed by its readers either individually or as participants in a social group. Such a position is clearly consonant with both the early and the later work of Rosenblatt.

Rosenblatt's (1978) *The Reader, the Text, the Poem* (1978) appeared at about the time that schema theory (Anderson and Pearson 1984), with its emphasis on readers' familiarity with content domains, became ubiquitous in the psychological literature concerning reading. In it, Rosenblatt set forth the idea that when readers read, they are indeed bringing various preconceptions to bear on the text, including preconceptions about the form, structure, or style of the text as well as about the content. In addition, the reader can choose to read a text aesthetically, thus pausing to consider the art of the writer and the nature of the experience rather than simply educing a meaning. Just as Rosenblatt's (1938) earlier work offered a corrective to the formalist tendencies of Brooks and Warren (1938), her 1978 volume offered a corrective to the content emphases of the schema theorists. Her work tends to support and make available to teachers the critical theorics that fall under the general heading of "reader response" and that can be supported by the constructivist view of language and language learning discussed earlier.

The issue for curriculum research remains the extent to which current scholarship in literary criticism can and should be translated into the school curriculum. Rosenblatt's (1978) work, though the most accessible to teachers, offers little help with the details of day-to-day curriculum decisions, nor does it provide practical guidelines for the overall shape the curriculum should take. Instead (like much contemporary scholarship) it offers broad principles about the nature and purpose of literary study against which the details of any new curriculum can be evaluated. It is clear that a curriculum that was consistent with Rosenblatt's arguments, however, would look little like the traditional curriculum that is deeply entrenched in American schools (Applebee 1989b; Brody, DeMilo, and Purves 1989; Langer 1984). A related issue for curriculum research is the role of background knowledge—including that represented by "cultural literacy" and by critical terminology and theory—in the secondary school curriculum. The stress on such knowledge has always been high, though its justification has tended to rely on its value in its own right rather than its usefulness in understanding literature.

CONCLUSION

In 1974, Applebee wrote a volume entitled *Tradition and Reform in the Teaching of English*. That title, viewed from the perspective of 1989, could be interpreted as ironic. What we have outlined in this chapter is a history of the English language arts curriculum in the United States, in which tradition has continually bested reform. Tradition has prevailed because it has been able to encompass the various tides of reform, whether that reform emphasized new content for the curriculum or new approaches to that content. Often, curriculum research has demonstrated the efficacy of particular new approaches, and it has also often demonstrated the lack of effect of many time-honored practices. Yet the fruits of this research are not apparent in the schools of the United States, and some promising practices have died of inattention.

To say this is less to be pessimistic than to acknowledge that curricular change in the English language arts, as in other parts of the common curriculum, is easy to prescribe but hard to implement. Many forces in the educational system are resistant to change through inertia rather than through ill will, and often the reformers have made their case poorly. Whether this situation will continue may well depend on how well the next generation of curriculum theory and research addresses the complexities of the classroom as well as the discoveries of the underlying academic disciplines.

References

Adler, Mortimer. 1940. *How to Read a Book: The Art of Getting a Liberal Education*. New York: Simon & Schuster.

Adler, Mortimer. 1982. *The Paideia Proposal: An Educational Manifesto*. New York: Collier Books.

Allen, Don C. 1968. *The Ph.D. in English and American Literature*. New York: Holt, Rinehart and Winston.

Anderson, Richard C., and P. David Pearson. (1984). "A Schema-Theoretic View of Basic Processes in Reading." In *Handbook of Reading Research*, edited by P. David Pearson, 255–292. White Plains, NY: Longman.

Applebee, Arthur N. 1974. *Tradition and Reform in the Teaching of English: A History*. Urbana, IL: National Council of Teachers of English.

Applebee, Arthur N. 1981. *Writing in the Secondary School: English and the Content Areas*. Urbana, IL: National Council of Teachers of English.

Applebee, Arthur N. 1982. "Literature." In *Encylopedia of Educational Research*, vol. 3, 5th ed., edited by H. Mitzel, 1105–1108. New York: Macmillan.

Applebee, Arthur N. 1989a. *A Study of Book-Length Works Taught in High School English Courses*. Report 1.2. Albany, NY: Center for the Learning and Teaching of Literature.

Applebee, Arthur N. 1989b. *The Teaching of Literature in Programs with Reputations for Excellence in English*. Report 1.1. Albany, NY: Center for the Learning and Teaching of Literature.

Applebee, Arthur N. 1990. *Literature Instruction in American Schools*. Report 1.4. Albany, NY: Center for the Learning and Teaching of Literature.

Applebee, Arthur N. 1991a. "Environments for Language Learning." In *Handbook of Research in the English Language Arts*, edited by James Flood, Julie Jensen, and James R. Squire. New York: Macmillan.

Applebee, Arthur N. 1991b. *A Study of High School Literature Anthologies*. Report 1.5. Albany, NY: Center for the Learning and Teaching of Literature.

Applebee, Arthur N., Judith A. Langer, and Ina V. S. Mullis. 1987. *Literature and U.S. History*. Princeton, NJ: Educational Testing Service for the National Assessment of Educational Progress.

Barnes, Douglas. 1974. *From Communication to Curriculum*. Harmondsworth, England: Penguin Books.

Barnes, Douglas, and Dorothy Barnes. In press. "Reading and Writing as Social Action." In *Developing Discourse Practices in Adolescence and Adulthood*, edited by Richard Beach and Susan Hynds. Norwood, NJ: Ablex.

Barnes, Douglas, Dorothy Barnes, and S. R. Clark. 1984. *Versions of English*. London: Heinemann.

Barr, Mary A. 1988. *Implementing a Research-based Curriculum in English-Language Arts, K–12*. Sacramento: California State Department of Education.

Basic Aims Committee. 1942. Basic aims for English instruction in American schools. *English Journal* 31(1): 40–55.

Bateman, Donald R., and Frank Zidonis. 1964. *The Effect of a Study of Transformational Grammar on the Writing of Ninth and Tenth Graders*. Champaign, IL: National Council of Teachers of English.

Bell, Daniel. 1966. *The Reforming of General Education*. New York: Columbia University Press.

Bennett, William J. 1988. *American Education: Making It Work*. Washington, DC: U.S. Government Printing Office.

Berger, Peter L., and Thomas Luckmann. 1967. *The Social Construction of Reality: A Treatise in the Sociology of Knowledge*. New York: Anchor Books.

Bernd, John M. 1957. "Approaches to the Teaching of Literature in Secondary Schools, 1900–1956." Ph.D. dissertation, University of Wisconsin, Madison. University Microfilms no. 24,264.

Bibb, Evelyn R. 1965. "Anthologies of American Literature, 1787–1964." Ph.D. dissertation, Columbia University, New York. University Microfilms no. 66–1728.

Boyer, Ernest L. 1983. *High School: A Report on Secondary Education in America*. New York: Harper & Row.

Britton, James N. 1970. *Language and Learning*. London: Allen Lane, Penguin Press.

Brody, Pamela, Carol DeMilo, and Alan C. Purves. 1989. *The Current State of Assessment in Literature*. Report 3.1. Albany NY: Center for the Learning and Teaching of Literature.

Brooks, Cleanth, and Robert Penn Warren. 1938. *Understanding Poetry: An Anthology for College Students*. New York: Henry Holt and Co.

Bruner, Jerome. 1960. *The Process of Education*. Cambridge, MA: Harvard University Press.

Callahan, Raymond. 1962. *Education and the Cult of Efficiency*. Chicago: University of Chicago Press.

Carpenter, George R., Frank L. Baker, and Fred N. Scott. 1903. *The Teaching of English in the Elementary and the Secondary School*. New York: Longmans, Green.

Chomsky, Noam. 1957. *Syntactics Structures*. The Hague: Mouton.

Christenbury, Leila. 1980. "The Origin, Development, and Decline of the Secondary English Elective Curriculum." Ph.D. dissertation, Virginia Polytechnic Institute and State University, Blacksburg.

Clapp, John M. 1926. *The Place of English in American Life*. Chicago: National Council of Teachers of English.

Commission on English. 1963. *End of Year Examinations in English for College-Bound Students Grades 9–12*. Princeton, NJ: College Entrance Examination Board.

Commission on English. 1965. *Freedom and Discipline in English*. New York: College Entrance Examination Board.

Commission on English. 1968. *12,000 Students and Their English Teachers*. Princeton, NJ: College Entrance Examination Board.

Commission on Secondary School Curriculum. 1940. *Language in General Education*. A Report of the Committee on the Function of English in General Education. New York: D. Appleton-Century.

Commission on the English Curriculum. 1952. *The English Language Arts*. New York: Appleton-Century-Crofts.

Commission on the English Curriculum. 1954. *Language Arts for Today's Children*. New York: Appleton-Century-Crofts.

Commission on the English Curriculum. 1956. *The English language Arts in the Secondary School*. New York: Appleton-Century-Crofts.

Commission on the English Curriculum. 1963. *The Education of Teachers of English for American Schools and Colleges*. New York: Appleton-Century-Crofts.

Commission on the English Curriculum. 1965. *The College Teaching of English*. New York: Appleton-Century-Crofts.

Delpit, Lisa. 1988. The silenced dialogue: Power and pedagogy in educating other people's children. *Harvard Educational Review* 58(3): 280–300.

Dixon, John. 1967. *Growth Through English*. Reading, England: National Association for the Teaching of English.

Doughty, Peter, John Pearce, and Geoffrey Thornton. 1971. *Language in Use*. London: Edward Arnold for the Schools Council.

Ehrenpreis, Ervin. 1945. *The "Types Approach" to Literature*. New York: King's Crown Press.

Elley, Warwick B., I. H. Barham, H. Lamb, and M. Wyllie. 1976. The role of grammar in a secondary school English curriculum. *Research in the Teaching of English* 10(1): 5–21.

Fader, Daniel N., and Morton H. Shaevitz. 1966. *Hooked on Books*. New York: Berkley Publishing Co.

Fay, Robert S. 1968. "The Reorganization Movement in English Teaching, 1910–1917." Ph.D dissertation, Harvard University, Cambridge, MA. University Microfilms no. 68–12,068.

Finegan, Edward. 1980. *Attitudes Toward English Usage: The History of a War of Words*. New York: Teachers College Press.

Ford, Paul L. 1962. *The New England Primer*. New York: Teachers College, Columbia University.

Frye, Northrup. 1957. *The Anatomy of Criticism*. Princeton, NJ: Princeton University Press.

Gleason, A. 1961. *An Introduction to Descriptive Linguistics*. New York: Holt, Rinehart and Winston.

Grommon, Alfred H. 1968. A History of the Preparation of Teachers of English. *English Journal* 57(4): 484–524.

Grossman, Pamela L. 1988. "A Study in Contrast: Sources of Pedagogical Content Knowledge for Secondary English." Ph.D. dissertation, Stanford University, Stanford, CA.

Hall, G. Stanley. 1886. *How to Teach Reading, and What to Read in School*. Boston: Heath.

Hall, G. Stanley. 1904. *Adolescence: Its Psychology and its Relation to Physiology, Anthropology, Sociology, Sex, Crime, Religion, and Education*. New York: D. Appleton and Co.

Harvard University. 1896. *Twenty Years of School and College English*. Cambridge, MA: Harvard University.

Hatfield, W. Wilbur. 1935. *An Experience Curriculum in English*. A report of the Curriculum Commission of the National Council of Teachers of English. New York: D. Appleton-Century.

Hawthorne, Rebecca. 1988. "Classroom Curriculum: Educational Criticisms of Teacher Choice." Ph.D. dissertation, Stanford University, Stanford, CA.

Hayes, Edna. 1936. *College Entrance Requirements in English: Their Effects on the High Schools*. New York: Teachers College, Columbia University.

Hillocks, George, Jr. 1971. *An Evaluation of Project APEX: A Nongraded Phase-Elective English Program*. Trenton, MI: Trenton Public Schools.

Hillocks, George, Jr. 1972. *Alternatives in English: A Critical Appraisal of Elective Programs*. Urbana, IL: National Council of Teachers of English and the ERIC Clearinghouse on Reading and Communication Skills.

Hirsch, E. D., Jr. 1987. *Cultural Literacy*. Boston: Houghton Mifflin.

Hoetker, James. 1970. *Students as Audience: An Experimental Study of the Relationships Between Classroom Study of Drama and Attendance at the Theater*. Champaign, IL.: National Council of Teachers of English.

Hollingsworth, Alan M. 1973. Beyond literacy. *ADE Bulletin* 36: 3–10.

Hook, J. N. 1979. *A Long Way Together: A Personal View of the National Council of Teachers of English's First Sixty-seven Years*. Urbana, IL: National Council of Teachers of English.

Hosic, James F. 1917. *Reorganization of English in Secondary Schools*. Bureau of Education Bulletin 1917, no. 2. Washington, DC: U.S. Government Printing Office.

Hutchins, Robert M. 1936. *The Higher Learning in America*. New Haven, CT: Yale University Press.

Johnson, Clifton. 1963. *Old-time Schools and School Books*. New York: Dover.

Judy, Steven N., and David A. England, eds. 1979. An historical primer in the teaching of English. *English Journal* 64 (entire issue).

Katz, Michael. 1968. *The Irony of Early School Reform: Educational Innovation in Mid-nineteenth Century Massachusetts*. Cambridge, MA: Harvard University Press.

Kelly, Louis G. 1969. *25 Centuries of Language Teaching*. Rowley, MA: Newbury House.

Kilpatrick, William H. 1925. *The Foundations of Method*. New York: Macmillan.

Labov, William. 1966. *The Social Stratification of English in New York City*. Washington, DC: Center for Applied Linguistics.

Langer, Judith A. 1984. Literacy instruction in American schools: Problems and perspectives. *American Journal of Education* 93(1): 107–132.

Langer, Judith A. 1989. *The Process of Understanding Literature*. Report 2.1. Albany, NY: Center for the Learning and Teaching of Literature.

Langer, Judith A., and Arthur N. Applebee. 1986. "Reading and Writing Instruction: Toward a Theory of Teaching and Learning." In *Review of Research in Education*, vol. 13, edited by Ernst Z. Rothkopf, 171–194. Washington, DC: American Educational Research Association.

Langer, Judith A., and Arthur N. Applebee. 1987. *How Writing Shapes Thinking: A Study of Teaching and Learning*. Research Monograph no. 22. Urbana, IL: National Council of Teachers of English.

Langer, Judith A., and Arthur N. Applebee. 1988. *Speaking of Knowing: Conceptions of Learning in Academic Subjects*. Final report to the U.S. Department of Education. Albany: State University of New York at Albany.

Lenrow, Elbert. 1940. *Reader's Guide to Prose Fiction: An Introductory Essay, with Bibliographies of 1500 Novels Selected, Topically Classified, and Annotated for Use in Meeting the Needs of Individuals in General Education*. For the Commission on Secondary School Curriculum. New York: D. Appleton-Century.

Leonard, Sterling A. 1929. *The Doctrine of Correctness in English Usage 1700–1800*. University of Wisconsin Studies in Language and Literature no. 25. Madison: University of Wisconsin.

Leonard, Sterling A. 1932. *Current English Usage*. Chicago: Inland Press for the National Council of Teachers of English.

Levine, Lawrence W. 1988. *Highbrow, Lowbrow: The Emergence of Cultural Hierarchy in America*. Cambridge, MA: Harvard University Press.

Lloyd-Jones, Richard, and Andrea Lunsford. 1989. *The English Coalition Conference: Democracy Through Language*. Urbana, IL: National Council of Teachers of English.

Lull, Herbert G. 1913. *Inherited Tendencies of Secondary School Instruction in the United States*, vol. 3, no. 3. Berkeley: University of California Publications in Education.

Lynch, James J., and Bertrand Evans. 1963. *High School English Textbooks: A Critical Examination*. Boston: Little, Brown.

Malone, Dumas, ed. 1935. *Dictionary of American Biography*. New York: Scribner.

Malone, Kemp. 1958. The rise of modern philology. *Annual Bulletin of the Modern Humanities Research Association* 30: 19–31.

Mandell, Barrett J. 1980. *Three Language Arts Curriculum Models: Prekindergarten Through College*. Urbana, IL: National Council of Teachers of English.

Markova, A. K. 1979. *The Teaching and Mastery of Language*. White Plains, NY: M. B. Sharpe.

Martinec, Barbara. 1971. Popular—but not just a part of the crowd: Implications of formula fiction for teenagers. *English Journal* 60(3): 339–344.

Mason, James H. 1962. "The National Council of Teachers of English—1911–1926." Ph.D. dissertation, George Peabody College for Teachers, Nashville. University Microfilms no. 62–5681.

Meikle, Henry W. 1945. The chair of rhetoric and belles lettres. *University of Edinburgh Journal* 13(1): 89–103.

Mellon, John. 1964. *Transformational Sentence Combining: A Method for Enhancing the Development of Syntactic Fluency in English Composition*. Champaign, IL: National Council of Teachers of English.

Mersand, Joseph. 1960. "The Teaching of Literature in American High Schools: 1865–1900." In *Perspectives on English*, edited by Robert C. Pooley, 269–302. New York: Appleton-Century-Crofts.

Moffett, James. 1968a. *A Student-Centered Language Arts Curriculum, Grades K–13*. Boston, MA: Houghton Mifflin.

Moffett, James. 1968b. *Teaching the Universe of Discourse*. Boston, MA: Houghton Mifflin.

Muller, Herbert J. 1967. *The Uses of English*. New York: Holt, Rinehart and Winston.

National Education Association. 1894. *Report of the Committee of Ten on Secondary School Studies, with the Reports of the Conferences Arranged by the Committee*. New York: American Book Company for the NEA.

O'Hare, Frank. 1973. *Sentence Combining: Improving Student Writing Without Formal Grammar Instruction*. Urbana, IL: National Council of Teachers of English.

Olson, James W. 1969. "The Nature of Literature Anthologies Used in the Teaching of High School English 1917–1957." Ph.D. dissertation, University of Wisconsin, Madison. University Microfilms no. 69–22,454.

Palmer, D. J. 1965. *The Rise of English Studies*. London: Oxford University Press.

Parker, William R. 1967. Where do English departments come from? *College English* 28(5): 339–351.

Pendleton, Charles S. 1924. *The Social Objectives of School English*. Nashville, TN: Charles S. Pendleton.

Piche, Gene L. 1977. Class and culture in the development of the high school English curriculum, 1880–1900. *Research in the Teaching of English* 11(1): 17–27.

Probst, Robert. 1988. *Response and Analysis: Teaching Literature in Junior and Senior High School*. Portsmouth, NH: Boynton/Cook Heinemann.

Purves, Alan C. 1973. *Literature Education in Ten Countries: An Empirical Study*. New York: Wiley.

Purves, Alan C. 1987. "Literacy, Culture and Community." In *The Future of Literacy in a Changing World*, edited by Daniel Wagner. Oxford: Pergamon.

Purves, Alan C. 1990. *The Scribal Society: an Essay on Litera-*

ture and Schooling in the Information Age. White Plains, NY: Longman.

Purves, Alan C., Barbara Bauer, and Donald L. Quirk. 1981. *Reading and Literature: American Achievement in International Perspective*. Urbana, IL.: National Council of Teachers of English.

Purves, Alan C., and Richard Beach. 1972. *Literature and the Reader*. Urbana, IL: National Council of Teachers of English.

Purves, Alan C., Theresa Rogers, and Anna Soter. 1990. *How Porcupines Make Love II: Teaching a Response-Centered Literature Curriculum*. White Plains, NY: Longman.

Ravitch, Diane, and Chester E. Finn, Jr. 1987. *What Do Our 17-Year-Olds Know?* New York: Harper & Row.

Reeder, Rudolph R. 1900. *The Historical Development of School Readers and of Methods of Teaching Reading*. New York: Macmillan.

Richards, I. A. 1929. *Practical Criticism*. London: Kegan Paul, Trench, Trubner, and Co.

Roberts, Holland D., Walter V. Kaulfers, and Grayson N. Kefauver. 1943. *English for Social Living*. New York: McGraw-Hill.

Rosenblatt, Louise M. 1938. *Literature as Exploration*. For the Commission on Human Relations of the Progressive Education Association. New York: D. Appleton-Century.

Rosenblatt, Louise M. 1978. *The Reader, the Text, the Poem*. Carbondale: Southern Illinois University Press.

Rudolph, Frederick. 1962. *The American College and University: A History*. New York: Vintage Books.

Scribner, Sylvia, and Michael Cole. 1981. *The Psychology of Literacy*. Cambridge, MA: Harvard University Press.

Sherwin, J. Stephen. 1969. *Four Problems in Teaching English: A Critique of Research*. Scranton, PA: International Textbook Co. for the National Council of Teachers of English.

Shugrue, Michael F. 1968. *English in a Decade of Change*. New York: Pegasus.

Sizer, Theodore, ed. 1964. *The Age of the Academies*. New York: Teachers College, Columbia University.

Smith, Dora V. 1933. *Instruction in English*. Bureau of Education Bulletin 1932, no. 17. National Survey of Secondary Education Monograph no. 20. Washington, DC: U.S. Government Printing Office.

Smith, Dora V. 1941. *Evaluating Instruction in Secondary School English*. A report of a division of the New York regents' inquiry into the character and cost of public education in New York State. Chicago: National Council of Teachers of English.

Smith, Nila B. 1934. *American Reading Instruction*. New York: Silver, Burdett.

Squire, James R., and Roger K. Applebee. 1968. *High School English Instruction Today*. New York: Appleton-Century-Crofts.

Squire, James R., and Roger K. Applebee. 1969. *Teaching English in the United Kingdom*. Urbana, IL: National Council of Teachers of English.

Stout, John E. 1921. *The Development of High-School Curricula in the North Central States from 1860 to 1918*. Supplementary Educational Monographs, vol. 3, no. 3. Chicago: University of Chicago Press.

Taba, Hilda, et al. 1947. *Reading Ladders for Human Relations*. Washington, DC: American Council on Education.

Valentine, John A. 1987. *The College Board and the School Curriculum: 1900–1980*. New York: College Entrance Examination Board.

Ven, Piet Van de. 1987. Some history of mother tongue teaching in western Europe: A comparative framework. *Mother Tongue Education Bulletin* 2(1): 40–50.

Welleck, René. 1953. "Literary Scholarship." In *American Scholarship in the Twentieth Century*, edited by Merle Curti, 111–145. Cambridge. MA: Harvard University Press.

Westlake, Professor. 1898. *Common School Literature*. Philadelphia, PA: Christoper Sower Co.

Williams, Raymond. 1958. *Culture and Society, 1780–1950*. London: Chatto & Windus.

Witt, Peter D. 1968. "The Beginnings of the Teaching of the Vernacular Literature in the Secondary Schools of Massachusetts." Ph.D. dissertation, Harvard University. Cambridge, MA. University Microfilms no. 69–11,507.

27

PROBLEMATIC FEATURES OF THE SCHOOL MATHEMATICS CURRICULUM

Thomas A. Romberg
UNIVERSITY OF WISCONSIN

The curriculum problem for any discipline, including mathematics, is that "deliberate teaching requires choices as to what to teach" (Kliebard 1977, 20). Of course, in general, choices must be made at two levels: first, at the level of determining whether a specific discipline will be chosen as a school subject; and second, if it is selected, what aspects should be included in the curriculum. For mathematics, the first decision is rarely considered because "There can be no doubt that there is general agreement that every child should study mathematics in schools" (Committee of Inquiry into the Teaching of Mathematics in Schools 1982, 1). This belief has been widely held by most societies since the creation of schools. While I affirm this belief in this chapter, I argue that the second issue reflects one's answers to the question: What is mathematics really about? Different answers, in turn, are based on different philosophic perspectives about mathematics. Following these choices, then, a number of organizational decisions need to be made regarding how to segment and sequence the mathematical topics and what kinds of student activities to suggest, among other issues.

The past decade has been dominated by public concern over the content and quality of school mathematics. These concerns have led to calls for radical reform throughout the world. In light of these concerns, the purpose of this chapter is to (1) examine four questions about the school mathematics curriculum related to these choices and decisions and (2) to consider the place of research in responding to those questions. The questions are:

1. What is mathematics?
2. Why should mathematics be taught in schools?
3. What is the structure of the current mathematics curriculum and why is it organized in this manner?
4. What is an authentic mathematics curriculum?

The first question is raised because there has been a philosophic shift in the discipline of mathematics in the past quarter century. In turn, this shift in view leads to the second question because a different justification for teaching mathematics leads to different choices about the aspects of mathematics children should study. The third question is about the past: "What has been . . . ?" and about the present: "What is . . . ?" The final question is about the future: "What should be . . . ?" To examine these four questions, I have gathered evidence from research and scholarly writings. Today, it is particularly important to consider these questions because of the social pressures to reform the school mathematics curriculum. However, before attempting to organize the evidence with respect to these questions, I define the key term "curriculum" and make explicit the framework I use to organize the evidence.

Curriculum

In the development of this chapter the term "curriculum" is defined as an "operational plan" for instruction that details what mathematics students need to know, how students are to achieve the identified curricular goals, what teachers are to do to help students develop their mathematical knowledge, and the context in which learning and teaching occur (National Council of Teachers of Mathematics 1989, 1).

As used here the term refers to what many would call the "intended curriculum" or a "curriculum plan" or the "preactive curriculum" (Jackson 1968) or even the "curriculum as fact" (Young 1977). These terms are used by different authors to distinguish the social decision-making process about what to teach from the interactive realization of the curriculum in practice. In this chapter the preactive notions will be emphasized; however, in developing any operational plan, expectations about student interactions and institutional problems and expectations must be considered.

Framework

The starting point for organizing the evidence to answer the questions raised about the school mathematics curriculum is an adaptation of E. G. Begle's (1961) description of problems in school mathematics. He presented four basic points: (1) School mathematics occurs within a *social context*, (2) *authentic* mathematics instruction is approached from a concern over what mathematics is taught, (3) mathematics instruction can be *effective* if the way in which students encounter and learn mathematics is considered, and (4) *efficient* mathematics instruction can be accomplished through the consideration of aspects of schooling.

To highlight the problematic features that can be derived from this general perspective about curriculum planning, four characteristics of instruction adapted from those used by Popkewitz, Tabachnick, and Wehlage (1982) are considered:

Schools are *goal* directed. Schools for all children are historically recent and were created to transmit aspects of the culture to the young and to direct students toward and provide them an opportunity for self-fulfillment.

Schools are places where conceptions of *knowledge* are distributed and maintained. One important decision that must be made by those who organize schools is to select what to teach. This decision must grow out of a consensus on what it is important for the young to know.

School is a place of *work*, where students, teachers, and administrators act to alter and improve their world; produce positive social relations; and realize specific human purposes. For example, it is assumed that knowledge will be acquired by the young via some deliberately created activities organized and managed by the teacher.

The work in schools is carried out by using an established *technology*.

The sections that follow address each of the four questions that have been raised. Furthermore, in each section the problematic features (issues or dilemmas) that make research on the question important—how appropriate research might be conducted and the implications for curricular reform in school mathematics—are presented.

WHAT IS MATHEMATICS?

This question is more easily asked than answered, nor is this the place for a lengthy answer. Nevertheless, it is a question that needs to be addressed for three reasons. First, many nonmathematicians such as sociologists, psychologists, school administrators, and even curriculum generalists see mathematics as a static, bounded discipline. Indeed, according to Edward Barbeau (1989), "Most of the population perceive mathematics as a fixed body of knowledge long set into final form. Its subject matter is the manipulation of numbers and the proving of geometrical deductions. It is a cold and austere discipline which provides no scope for judgment or creativity" (2). These views reflect an absolutist perspective about mathematics and are undoubtedly a reflection of the mathematics studied in school rather than an insight into the discipline itself. That these views are limiting is a serious problem since persons with such views often influence the decisions about school mathematics.

Second, during the past two decades there has been a growing awareness of the need to represent better what mathematics is about, to illustrate what mathematicians do, and to attempt to popularize the discipline. This does not mean that good books about the discipline did not exist before the 1970s. Classics such as *Mathematics: Its Content, Methods, and Meaning* (Aleksandrov, Kolmogorov, and Lavrent'ev 1956), *Mathematical Thought from Ancient to Modern Times* (Kline 1972), and *The World of Mathematics* (Newman 1956) have been available. Unfortunately, these books were really written for readers well trained in mathematics and science, although a large number of books about mathematics have recently been published for a nontechnically educated audience, for example, *The Mathematical Experience* (Davis and Hersh 1981), *Descartes' Dream* (Davis and Hersh 1986), *Mathematics and the Unexpected* (Ekeland 1988), *Innumeracy* (Paulos 1988), and *Speaking Mathematically* (Pimm 1987).

In addition, there have been several books about mathematics written for policymakers, general educators, and administrators in response to the current calls for reform in mathematics teaching and learning: *Mathematics Tomorrow* (Steen 1981); *Mathematics Counts* (Committee of Inquiry into the Teaching of Mathematics 1982); *Renewing US Mathematics: Critical Resource for the Future* (Commission on Physical Sciences, Mathematics, and Resources 1984); *Perspectives on Mathematics Education* (Christiansen, Howson, and Otte 1986); *Mathematics, Insight, and Meaning* (de Lange 1987); *Cognitive Science and Mathematics Education* (Schoenfeld 1987); *Everybody Counts* (MSEB 1989); *Curriculum and Evaluation Standards for School Mathematics* (NCTM 1989); *On the Shoulders of Giants* (MSEB, 1990a); *Reshaping School Mathematics* (MSEB 1990b); and *The Philosophy of Mathematics Education* (Ernest 1991).

The importance of this awareness of mathematicians and mathematics educators to do a better job of presenting their discipline to the public and to policymakers and other educators is demonstrated by the fact that a conference on the "popularization of mathematics" was organized by the International Commission on Mathematical Instruction and held at the University of Leeds, England, in 1989.

Third, to answer this question one must realize that the subject has many facets. One can define mathematics "as a language, as a particular kind of logical structure, as a body of knowledge about numbers and space, as a series of methods for deriving conclusions, as the essence of our knowledge of the physical world, or as an amusing intellectual activity" (Kline 1962, 2). Understanding these variations is important because different features have been emphasized in school mathematics programs at different times and by different authors. Furthermore, proponents of the current reform movement argue for a particular perspective that is different from that held by individuals, including the perspective of many (if not most) working mathematicians (Wheeler 1991). To understand the importance of this question, I have chosen to examine four problematic features: the difference between "absolutist" philosophies of mathematics and a "social constructivist" philosophy of mathematics, the distinction between "knowledge" and "the record of knowledge," mathematics as a cultural phenomenon, and the "doing" of mathematics.

Philosophy of Mathematics

For over two thousand years, mathematics has been viewed as a body of infallible truth far removed from the affairs and values of humanity. These views are being challenged by a growing number of philosophers of mathematics (e.g., Davis and Hersh 1981; Kitcher 1988; Lakatos 1976; Tymoczko 1986). They argue that mathematics is "fallible, changing, and like any other body of knowledge, the product of human inventiveness" (Ernest 1991, xi; Ernest includes as absolutist philosophies of mathematics logicism, formalism, and constructivism).

This philosophic shift has a significance that goes far beyond mathematics. In particular, it is significant to education, for if absolutist views of mathematics are taken, mathematics can bear no social responsibility for underrepresentation of women or minority groups of students in the field or for its relationship to social and political values.

On the other hand, if it is acknowledged that mathematics is a fallible social construct, then it is to be considered a process of inquiry and coming to know, a continually expanding field of human creation and invention, not a finished product. Such a dynamic view of mathematics has powerful educational consequences. The aims of teaching mathematics need to include the empowerment of learners to create their own mathematical knowledge; mathematics can be reshaped, at least in school, to give all groups more access to its concepts and to the wealth and power its knowledge brings; and the social contexts of the uses and practices of mathematics can no longer be legitimately pushed aside—the implicit values of mathematics need to be squarely faced. When mathematics is seen in this way, it needs to be studied in living contexts that are meaningful and relevant to the learners, including their languages, cultures, and everyday lives, as well as their school-based experiences. This view of mathematics provides a rationale as well as a foundation for multicultural and girl-friendly approaches to mathematics. Overall, mathematics becomes responsible for its uses and consequences, in education and in society. Those of us in education have a special reason for advocating this more human view of mathematics. Anything else alienates and disempowers learners.

This later philosophy of mathematics has been labeled by Ernest as "social constructivism," which, he argues, is based on three premises:

(i) The basis of mathematical knowledge is linguistic knowledge, conventions, and rules, and language is a social construction.
(ii) Interpersonal social processes are required to turn an individual's subjective mathematical knowledge, after publication, into accepted objective mathematical knowledge.
(iii) Objectivity itself will be understood to be social. (p. 42)

It is these differences in philosophic perspectives about mathematics that give rise to the following problematic features.

Mathematical Knowledge

The decisions about what mathematics society wants students to acquire in schools and the assumptions made about how students come to know that mathematics in classrooms constitute one problematic area. The choice of what mathematics to teach has varied with cultures. In classical Greek society, geometry and the logic of deductive arguments were emphasized (Heath 1956); arithmetic calculations became important in 15th-century Italy for commercial accounting (Swetz 1987); algebra and calculus, for engineering in the 19th century in Western countries (Freudenthal 1973); and now mathematical modeling and computer-based computational and graphical procedures for our emerging information age (Steen 1981). However, what is important is not what different aspects of mathematics are emphasized but the difference between absolutist views of knowledge and a social constructivist view. John Dewey (1916) described this as the difference between "knowledge" and "the record of knowledge." For an absolutist, "to know" means to identify the artifacts of the discipline (its record). For social constructivists, "to know" is "to do" mathematics. Mathematics as a "record of knowledge" has grown into a stupendous amount of subject matter. The largest branch builds on what is collectively called the real number system, which includes the ordinary whole numbers, fractions, and the irrational numbers. Arithmetic, algebra, elementary functions, calculus, differential equations, and other subjects that follow calculus are all developments of the real number system. Similarly, projective geometry and the several non-Euclidean geometries are branches of mathematics, as are various other arithmetics and their algebras. Unfortunately, too often this massive "record of knowledge, independent of its place as an outcome of inquiry and a resource in further inquiry, is taken to be knowledge" (186–187). In fact, Hans Jahnke (1986) has argued that for school mathematics, the separation of mathematics from its applications and the emphasis on the formal aspects of what is known developed as a consequence of the pressures for mass education in early 19th-century Germany.

On the other hand, social constructivists see knowing as "doing." This implies that a person gathers, discovers, or creates knowledge in the course of some activity that has a purpose: This active process is not the same as the absorption of the record of knowledge—the fruits of past activities. When the record of knowledge is taken to be knowledge, the acquisition of information becomes an end in itself, and the student spends his or her time absorbing what other people have done rather than experiencing knowledge as an individual. As I have argued elsewhere (Romberg 1983), this is not to imply that informational knowledge has no value. Information has value indeed to the extent that it is needed in the course of some activity having a purpose and to the extent that it furthers the course of the activity. "Informational knowledge" is material that can be fallen back upon as given, settled, established, or assured in a doubtful situation. The concepts and processes from certain branches of mathematics undoubtedly should be known by students.

This distinction between absolutist and social constructivist views about mathematics is more than just the difference between "knowing that" and "knowing how." Each makes different assumptions about the learning process. If "knowing that" is stressed, the student is treated as a "piece of registering apparatus, which stores up information isolated from action and purpose" (Dewey 1916, 147). And if "knowing how" is emphasized, the student is seen as an active constructor of knowledge "operating in important ways on his environment" (Bourne 1966, 36). These different psychological views about how one learns are important and are addressed more fully later in this chapter. However, it must be noted that instruction in most current classrooms emphasizes "knowing that," and the reform proposals emphasize "knowing how."

Culture and Mathematics

The social constructivist philosophy shows that mathematics, like all disciplines, is a social product. The current reform movement seeks to make this view a central feature of school mathematics. Research from the sociology of knowledge makes five aspects of mathematics' ties to culture obvious. First, mathematics has been created by humans over the past 6,000 years. During this evolution, mathematical objects were created in response to social problems and have contributed to the development of contemporary society. In fact, "next to the invention of language itself, . . . mathematics is without doubt the most subtle, powerful, and significant achievement of the human mind" (Schaaf 1966, iii). The primary objective of all mathematical work is to help humans make sense of the world around them. There is no question that during its development, mathematics has had reciprocal relationships with the sociocultural context of the times. It has grown as mathematicians have tackled societal problems, contributed to the understanding of those problems, and even been a source for some of the problems (Keitel, 1987). Today it is impossible to determine the overall impact of mathematics on contemporary culture because quantification and mathematical modeling permeate almost all aspects of society, and its influence is growing.

To illustrate this interdependence, Frank Swetz (1987) traced the development of capitalism in Western society to the adoption of Hindu-Arabic arithmetic by the merchants of Venice in the 15th century. From the interaction of this set of mathematical symbols and the rules for their use in confronting the growing problems faced by commercial entrepreneurs, modern mercantile capitalism evolved. However, the adoption of Arabic arithmetic was gained at a cost. Ray Nickerson (1988) provided an illustration of this fact when he compared several ancient systems of representing numbers with the Arabic system now in common use throughout the world. He suggests that "the Arabic system is a superior vehicle for computing . . . bought at the cost of greater abstractness. Numbers in the Arabic system bear a less obvious relationship to the quantities they represent than do numbers in many earlier systems" (181). Hence, for many, the computational algorithms we now use are mysterious routines only to be memorized.

Second, from an examination of several cross-cultural studies, Alan Bishop (1988) concluded that historically all cultures develop some mathematics in order to communicate. He classified the similar activities across cultures as counting, locating, measuring, designing, playing, and explaining. He argues that these are the "key 'universal' activities [which] are the foundations for the development of mathematics in culture" (59).

This point is important because it shows that mathematics has been an important development in all societies. In fact, the mathematical objects created by different societies, although often similar, are not all alike. For example, space in Western mathematics is described from a static perspective. In contrast, Navajo notions about space are dynamic (Pinxten, van Dooren, and Harvey 1983). To illustrate this point, note that in Western culture, boundaries are fixed relations between objects established naturally (e.g., between land and water) or by persons (e.g., fences on roads). For Navajos, boundaries are delineated by flexible relationships between objects of differential privileged status. This contrast demonstrates that mathematics is humanly created in response to social views of the world and not to a platonic set of artifacts uncovered over time.

Also, the differences in perspectives between cultures have rarely been considered. In particular, there are a few studies that make clear the extent to which Western mathematics has been imposed on children of different cultures.

For example, Gordon Knight (1989) found that the Maori of New Zealand regarded mathematics as non-Maori knowledge, and for that reason not worthy of study or mastery. Traders and educators who have attempted to teach them calculation skills have attributed their failure to intelligence rather than to culture. Only if mathematics were considered "Maori knowledge" would it have status in that society. Another example comes from Geoffrey Saxe's (1981) study on arithmetic instruction with children of the Oksapmin tribe in Papua, New Guinea. The number system of that culture uses 27 body parts as numerals. His study showed that Oksapmin mediated the effects of instruction spontaneously, using their indigenous counting system.

Third, as Ubriatan D'Ambrosio (1985), Jean Lave and her colleagues (Lave, Smith, and Butler 1988), Analucia Schliemann and Nadja Acioly (1989), and many others point out, even in contemporary culture there are several mathematical cultures. Schools emphasize the formal mathematics of collegiate mathematicians, but not the mathematics developed and used by farmers, carpenters, tailors, and others. Each of these social groups has of necessity developed its own mathematical language and procedures.

Fourth, students bring to the mathematics classroom their own culture. We are a multicultural society, and each student is a product of a particular cultural group.

Fifth, mathematicians operate within their own culture. From the social constructivist perspective, to appreciate what it means "to do" mathematics, one must recognize that mathematicians argue among themselves about what mathematics is acceptable, what methods of proof are to be countenanced, and so forth. Phillip Kitcher (1988) claims that

> mathematical practice has five components: a language employed by the mathematicians whose practice it is, a set of statements accepted by those mathematicians, a set of questions that they regard as important and as currently unsolved, a set of reasonings that they use to justify the statements they accept, and a set of mathematical views embodying their ideas about how mathematics should be done, the ordering of mathematical disciplines, and so forth. (299)

From this perspective, doing mathematics cannot be viewed as a mechanical performance, an activity that individuals engage in solely by following predetermined rules. Thus, mathematical activity can be seen more as embodying the elements of an art or craft than as a purely technical discipline. This is not to say that mathematicians are free to do anything that comes to mind. As in all crafts, as Kitcher (1988) argues, there will be agreement, in a broad sense, about what procedures are to be followed and what is to be countenanced as acceptable work. These agreements arise from the day-to-day intercourse among mathematicians. Thus, a mathematician engages in mathematics as a member of a learned community that creates the context in which the individual mathematician works. The members of that community have a shared way of "seeing" mathematical activity. Their mutual discourse will reinforce preferred forms and a sense of appropriateness, elegance, and acceptable conceptual structures (Kuhn 1970). Furthermore, the community promotes and reinforces its own standards of acceptable work, and as Hagstrom (1965) suggests, a major characteristic of a mathematical/scientific community is the continued evolution of its standards. Not only does the range of acceptable methods vary but in mathematics especially the standards of rigor have themselves been subject to continued modification and refinement, a point well illustrated by Eric Bell (1945):

> How did the master analysts of the eighteenth century—the Bernoullis, Euler, Lagrange, Laplace—contrive to get consistently right results in by far the greater part of their work in both pure and applied mathematics? What these great mathematicians mistook for valid reasoning at the very beginning of the calculus is now universally regarded as unsound. (153)

Nor did Bell have the last word, for during the 1970s, mathematical logicians such as Keisler (1971) and Robinson (1974) found a way to make rigorous the intuitively attractive infinitesimal calculus that was developed by Newton and Leibniz and extended by those master analysts to whom Bell refers.

One problem that grows out of communal activity is that the language of the discipline transforms its practices into a crystallized form (Popkewitz 1988). Although every discipline develops its own terms to communicate ideas, too often the terms become objects that students internalize and the reason for their use in inquiry is ignored.

Finally, there is a growing awareness that there are conflicts between the absolutist culture of school mathematics and the social constructivist culture of mathematics. Jahnke (1986) argues that although most teachers believe that "school mathematics and scientific mathematics are essentially identical, and that they differ merely with regard to the level and degree of difficulty" (85), this is a naive and false belief. He argues that schools have a social responsibility to educate, which is expressed in terms of societal goals described "in terms of methodological attitudes and philosophical beliefs" (85). School mathematics, as currently practiced, is based on absolutist premises. The consequence is that school mathematics bears little resemblance to what mathematicians do or to how mathematics is used. The awareness of the conflicts between these cultures was further made apparent with the publication in 1989 of a special issue of *The Journal of Mathematical Behavior* (Vol. 8, No. 2) on the two cultures.

In summary, mathematics is more than a vast collection of fixed and infallible concepts and skills. It is fallible, growing, and changing, and it is something that has been created by groups of persons in all cultures. Furthermore, mathematicians do it as members of a craft group who respond to and contribute to an evolving culture. And finally, at present, the cultures of mathematics and school mathematics are not identical. The implications for research on these cultural notions for education should be apparent. We know too little about the cultural ideas about mathematical objects students bring to classrooms or about the relationships and conflicts between what mathematicians do and what students do in mathematics classrooms. In fact, it is unlikely that the current curriculum reform efforts will be successful if such cultural notions are not considered and used.

Doing Mathematics

If mathematics is a social product, then what does a mathematician do? Simply recognizing that mathematics is a cultural product created by people does not answer this question. In fact, since mathematicians are human beings, many of the things they do are quite uninteresting. What are important are mathematics' essential activities. Identifying and describing these features for educators have been the focus of the work of several scholars. Even though in each of the following examples a different feature has been emphasized, all should be seen as different themes from essentially the same philosophic perspective.

The most influential scholar in the United States has been the noted mathematician George Polya. His writings stressed the importance of mathematical problem solving. His major books describe, through examples, the way in which mathematicians examine nonroutine problems. These books are *Mathematics and Plausible Reasoning* (1954), *How to Solve It* (1957), and *Mathematical Discovery* (1967). His emphasis has been on the elements of plausible reasoning that lead to the discovery of mathematical assertions. Polya called this kind of reasoning "heuristics," or the mental operations typically useful in the process of solving mathematical problems. His influence on mathematics education is reflected in such documents as *An Agenda for Action* (NCTM 1980) and *Curriculum and Evaluation Standards for School Mathematics* (NCTM 1989). In these (and many other) documents, problem solving is highlighted as the major activity of mathematicians. In fact, solving nonroutine problems is the central theme of the current reform movement in school mathematics in the United States.

Lynn Steen, a past president of the Mathematical Association of America, has written several papers that have stressed mathematics as "the science of patterns." His writings include *Mathematics Tomorrow* (1981), "Forces for Change in the Mathematics Curriculum" (1988a), "A 'New Agenda' for Mathematics Education" (1988b), "Out from Underachievement" (1988c), and "The Science of Patterns" (1988d). In addition, he is the principal author of the recent report of the Mathematical Sciences Education Board, *Everybody Counts* (1989), and is editor of two other MSEB reports, *On the Shoulders of Giants* (1990a), and *Reshaping School Mathematics: A Philosophy and Framework of Curriculum* (1990b). Steen's emphasis is on the fact that mathematics is at its roots an empirical science. As he states:

> The mathematician seeks patterns in number, in space, in science, and in computers, and in imagination. Mathematical theories explain the relations among patterns; functions and maps, operators and morphisms bind one type of pattern to another to yield lasting mathematical structures. . . . Patterns suggest other patterns, often yielding patterns of patterns. In this way, mathematics follows its own logic, beginning with patterns from science and completing the portrait by adding all patterns that derive from the initial ones. (1988a, 616)

Thus, he sees that all students need to experience the search for patterns at all levels. Mathematics is not a fixed set of concepts and skills to be mastered but an empirical science.

The most prolific and influential European scholar has been the Dutch mathematician Hans Freudenthal. He is the founding editor of the international journal *Educational Studies in Mathematics*, and his major books on mathematics education are *Mathematics as an Educational Task* (1973), *Weeding and Sowing* (1978), and *Didactical Phenomenology of Mathematical Structures* (1984). Central to Freudenthal's work are "the strategies of mathematizing." Mathematizing involves representing relationships within a complex situation in such a way as to make it possible to put them into quantitative relationship with one another. The basic components of mathematizing are shown in Figure 27–1.

Mathematicians must first decide which variables and relationships between variables are important and which do

FIGURE 27–1. The Basic Components in Model Building.

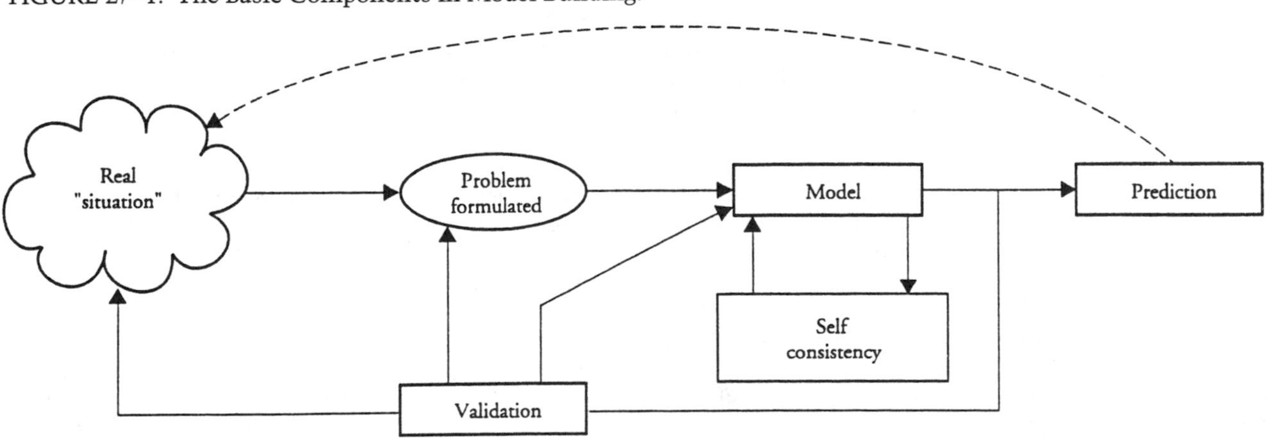

not matter when confronting a complex problem situation. Second, they make mathematical models, assign numbers to variables, and use numerical procedures to make predictions. Then they examine the results. It is this way of approaching nonmathematical phenomena that has enabled researchers to make such wise use of computers as tools. The computer does not mathematize, but once a model is created for a situation and quantified, the computer can quickly perform extensive computations to produce predictions for complex situations. Freudenthal (1984) believes that learning these strategies should be the central focus of all mathematics curricula. From this perspective, "mathematics for all and everyone" is the motto he chose to define the work of the research and development institute he founded at the University of Utrecht. His argument is that all students can and must experience mathematics in this manner. The complexity of the problems and the sophistication of the mathematical models may vary, but all can build mathematical models.

Finally, as a mathematics education researcher, I have presented still another complementary view. My works on the issue of "doing" mathematics include "Activities Basic to Learning Mathematics" (1975), *Individually Guided Mathematics* (1976), "A Common Curriculum for Mathematics" (1983), *School Mathematics: Options for the 1990s* (1984), with Deborah M. Stewart, *The Monitoring of School Mathematics: Background Papers* (1987), and *Changes in School Mathematics* (1988b). In addition, I was the chair of the writing group that produced *Curriculum and Evaluation Standards for School Mathematics* (NCTM, 1989). I argue that even with a superficial knowledge of mathematics, it is easy to recognize four related activities common to all of mathematics: abstracting, inventing, proving, and applying.

The *abstractness* of mathematics is easy to see. Mathematicians operate with abstract numbers without worrying about how to relate them in each case to concrete objects. The process of abstracting is characteristic of each branch of mathematics. The concept of a whole number and of a geometric figure are only two of the earliest and most elementary concepts of mathematics. They have been followed by a mass of others, too numerous to describe, extending to such abstractions as complex numbers, functions, integrals, differentials, functionals, n-dimensional spaces, infinite-dimensional spaces, and so forth. These abstractions, piled as it were on one another, have reached such a degree of generalization that they have apparently lost all connection with daily life, and the "ordinary mortal" understands nothing about them beyond the mere fact that "all this is incomprehensible." In reality, of course, such is not at all the case. Although the concept of n-dimensional space is no doubt extremely abstract, it does have a completely real content, which is not difficult to understand.

The abstractions of mathematics are distinguished by three features. First, as Steen has argued, they deal above all else with patterns. Second, they occur in a sequence of increasing degrees of abstraction, going very much further in this direction than the abstractions of other sciences. As John von Neumann said (in Newman [1956, 2063]), "It is a relatively good approximation to truth—that mathematical ideas originate in empirics, although the genealogy is sometimes long and obscure. But, once they are conceived, the subject begins to live a peculiar life of its own and is better compared to a creative one, governed by almost entirely aesthetical motivations." In fact, it is common for branches of mathematics to feed on one another, yielding ever more abstract notions. Third, mathematics as such moves almost wholly in the field of abstract concepts and their interrelations. Whereas the natural scientist turns constantly to the experiment for proof of his or her assertions, the mathematician employs only logical arguments.

Inventing involves creating a law or relationship. There are two aspects to all mathematical inventions: the conjecture (or guess) about a relationship, followed by the demonstration of the logical validity of that assertion. All mathematical ideas—even new abstractions—are inventions (like irrational numbers). Also, to assist them in the invention of their abstractions, mathematicians make constant use of theorems, mathematical models, methods, and physical analogues, and they have recourse to various completely concrete examples. These examples often serve as the actual source of the invention.

No proposition is considered to be a mathematical product until it has been rigorously *proved* by a logical argument. The demand for a proof of a theorem pervades the whole of mathematics. We could measure the angles at the base of a thousand isosceles triangles with extreme accuracy, but such a procedure would never provide a mathematical proof of the theorem that the base angles of an isosceles triangle are congruent. Mathematics demands that this result be deduced from the fundamental concepts of geometry, which are precisely formulated in the axioms. And so it is in every case. To prove a theorem means that the mathematician deduces it by a logical argument from the fundamental properties of the concepts related to that theorem. Approached in this way, not only the concepts but also the methods of mathematics are seen as abstract and theoretical. The importance of building mathematical arguments about assertions can not be underestimated: They are central to all mathematical discourse (Putnam, Lampert, and Peterson 1989).

Another characteristic feature of mathematics is the exceptional breadth of its *applications*. First, we make constant use, almost every hour, in industry and in private and social life, of the most varied concepts and results of mathematics, without thinking about them at all. For example, we use arithmetic to compute our expenses or geometry to describe the floor plan of an apartment. Second, modern technology would be impossible without mathematics. Scarcely any technical process could be carried through without building an abstract mathematical model as a basis for a sequence of more or less complicated calculations; and mathematics plays a very important role in the development of new branches of technology. Finally, it is true that every science, to a greater or lesser degree, makes essential use of mathematics. The progress of the sciences would have been completely impossible without mathematics. For this reason, the requirements of mechanics, astronomy, and physics have always exercised a direct and decisive influence on the development of mathematics. In other sciences (including the social sciences), mathematics plays a smaller role, but here, too, it finds important applications.

In summary, for each of these authors, mathematics is seen as a rational human creation. It is a vast collection of ideas derived as a consequence of searching for solutions to social problems. The abstractions and inventions help us make sense of our world and ourselves. This is true whether one emphasizes problem solving, searching for patterns, mathematizing, abstracting, inventing, proving, or applying. These are merely descriptions of what mathematicians do. Note also that neither the acquisition of concepts nor of skills has been emphasized by these authors. This is not to imply that concepts and skills are unimportant; however, it does imply that their acquisition is vacuous unless they are used in doing mathematics.

Given that these social constructivist descriptions of doing mathematics bear little resemblance to the doing of mathematics in classrooms, several researchable questions are apparent: Is it feasible to teach students to solve nonroutine problems, search for patterns, build mathematical models, and so forth? If so, when and how can this be done? Can important concepts and skills be developed from student work on mathematical projects that simulate what mathematicians do? These questions are addressed in a later section of this chapter.

WHY TEACH MATHEMATICS?

Given the importance of mathematics to society, it is no surprise that mathematics is so universally accepted as a part of the school curriculum. In fact, it is quite easy to give little or no thought to its justification. This is not to say that the question of justification has been entirely neglected. In fact, many authors have given different reasons for the study of mathematics. Authors who have addressed this question tend to be historians of mathematics education (e.g., DeVault and Weaver 1970; Freudenthal 1973; Jones 1970; Kline 1962; Stanic 1984b), reformers who are presenting an argument for curricular change (e.g., College Entrance Examination Board 1959, Committee of Inquiry into the Teaching of Mathematics in Schools 1982; Mathematical Sciences Education Board 1989; National Council of Teachers of Mathematics 1989), or reactors to curricular changes (e.g., Howson 1982; Kline 1966). Rarely is justification the topic of a scholarly paper. A notable exception is the recent chapter "Mathematics as a School Subject" by Christiansen, Howson, and Otte (1986). They argue that "there is a general feeling that to live a 'normal life' in many parts of the world at the close of the twentieth century requires everyday use of mathematics of some kind" (49). However, they go on to claim that there is "no real consensus from society, generally, on what it wants from mathematics education from the average pupil" (50). Yet all parents want their children to do well in mathematics. The lack of public consensus, coupled with a feeling that doing well in mathematics is important, leads to much general criticism. In fact, the answers given by most authors to the question, Why teach mathematics? are presented in relation to three other questions: What mathematics should we teach? How should we organize and sequence the mathematics we teach? How should we organize and implement instruction? Unfortunately, until recently most authors have spent more effort answering the last two questions than they have in providing reasons why mathematics should be included in the school curriculum. Furthermore, most authors have tacitly assumed absolutist perspectives about mathematics.

Functional Justification

The most commonly stated goal for teaching mathematics is that for both students and society mathematics will fulfill a "long-term functional need." This belief is congruent with the "functionalist" perspective on schooling (e.g., Dreeben 1968). These scholars believe that "schools are the essential transformation mechanism between life in the family and life as an adult in a modern, urban, industrial society" (Feinberg and Soltis 1985, 18). The argument is that schools should prepare students so that they can be productive citizens in society. For example, Paul Trafton (1980) argues, "We know the need for arithmetic to govern one's personal affairs and the requirements of many vocations using only a modest amount of mathematics" (11). He then states, "specialized training in mathematics is prerequisite for study in a wide range of fields. . . . A careful study of a large number of careers and their mathematical requirements leads one to see the importance of the substantial amounts of mathematics by all students" (11). Although there is no doubt that many occupations depend on mathematical training, it is also true that those who finally apply a relatively sophisticated mathematics will be a small minority among those who will apply mathematics at all. Furthermore, most such justifications assume that all students need to have mastered a specific set of concepts and skills (the absolutist's notions of basic skills).

Even if one accepts the functional rationale, the question is then, "How much mathematics is enough for all?" One could view this as the central issue in an ongoing curricular debate. Even if all were to agree that current mathematics programs need to be changed, one could argue that the debate concerns what parts of mathematics need to be covered. For example, the National Council of Teachers of Mathematics (1989) advocates more mathematics for all students:

> Traditional notions of basic mathematical competence have been outstripped by ever-higher expectations of the skills and knowledge of workers; new methods of production demand a technologically competent work force. The U.S. Congressional Office of Technology Assessment (1988) claims that employees must be prepared to understand the complexities and technologies of communication,

to ask questions, to assimilate unfamiliar information, and to work cooperatively in teams. Businesses no longer seek workers with strong backs, clever hands, and "shopkeeper" arithmetic skills. In fact, it is claimed that the "most significant growth in new jobs between now and the year 2000 will be in fields requiring the most education." (3–4)

This statement implies that all students should have the opportunity to study more and somewhat different mathematics than they do in the current curriculum. This side of the argument is central to a call for mathematics for everyone (Freudenthal 1984). What is implied in these calls for reform is that the "different" mathematics being referred to involves the social constructivist view about doing mathematics.

On the other hand, some absolutists believe that since algorithmic procedures (e.g., arithmetic and algebra) can now be done efficiently by machine, most children will not need to study very much mathematics (e.g., Burke 1989, Finn 1989). Furthermore, they see recommendations for change as a selective assault on drudgery and failure—two important lessons of life (Nelson 1989). They also argue that only a few talented students will need instruction on advanced mathematical topics.

Central to this debate are three issues. The first involves differences in the philosophic visions of mathematics and of what will be useful for citizens in the future. The "more" group sees socially constructed mathematics as becoming more important for all students; the other group sees absolutist pieces as either more or less important. The second issue involves the beliefs in individual differences and talents. The "more" group downplays the importance of such differences for schools. For example, NCTM (1989) has argued that

The social injustices of past schooling practices can no longer be tolerated. Current statistics indicate that those who study advanced mathematics are most often white males. Women and most minorities study less mathematics and are seriously underrepresented in careers using science and technology. Creating a just society in which women and various ethnic groups enjoy equal opportunities and equitable treatment is no longer an issue. Mathematics has become a critical filter for employment and full participation in our society. We cannot afford to have the majority of our population mathematically illiterate. Equity has become an economic necessity. (4)

The "less" group sees that a student's performance needs to be compared against that of others. In fact, "students must learn to cope with failure and to acknowledge the greater skills of others in certain areas of performance" (Feinberg and Soltis 1985). They conclude that a differentiated curriculum is efficient and that differentiation should be based on capability, interest, and societal need. The difficulty with this perspective, though, is that "If all students do not have the opportunity to learn this mathematics, we face the danger of creating an intellectual elite and a polarized society. The image of a society in which a few have the mathematical knowledge needed for the control of economic and scientific development is not consistent either with the values of a just democratic system or with its economic needs" (NCTM 1989, 9).

The third, and more salient issue involves the arguments put forward by those interested in the history of educational reform. These scholars argue that calls for reform insisting that all students learn more and somewhat different mathematics are not new. In the past, the results of such reform efforts have floundered in a web of problems. For example, Peter Damerow and Ian Westbury (1985) argue that the difficulties stem from "a need to find ways of changing the contents and conditions of general education as part of a larger concern for changing the fit between the work of schools and the rapidly changing scientific and social demand for qualifications, but how this is to be done is totally elusive" (175).

At issue is the fact that school mathematics evolved during the past century and a half into a particular absolutist social form. As Jahnke (1986) points out, "Schools exist to educate; school mathematics is, therefore, subject to particular forces which decisively distinguish it from mathematics as a scientific discipline" (85). Although all students begin the study of mathematics, the heart of school mathematics is for the able. Thus, the study of mathematics is reserved for a privileged elite. The difficulty in advocating that all students should study mathematics is that to make this happen, school mathematics must either give up its privileged position in the school curriculum or find a way to teach the subject to all (Damerow and Westbury 1985).

Jan de Lange has written two papers on this topic: "Geometry for All: No Geometry at All?" (1984) and "Mathematics for All Is No Mathematics at All" (1986). The issue he raises is whether it is possible to create a mathematics curriculum for all that does not surrender mathematics to other subjects so that mathematics is seen only as a tool in those subjects and is not studied as a discipline. Christine Keitel (1987) carries the argument further by raising the question: "What are the goals of mathematics for all?" She calls for a careful analysis of intentions so that the distinctions between instructional activities that foster the use of mathematics or the development of mathematical concepts and procedures can be distinguished from doing mathematics. Jahnke (1986) is more pessimistic. He argues that the problem arises because of "the *specific* compromise between everyday knowledge and scientific mathematics which was developed in the early nineteenth century and which resulted in a view of mathematics as a closed unified system and *not* as a method of analyzing and understanding our world. To restore the latter conception of mathematics one has to give up the former" (93).

Damerow and Westbury (1985) have summarized this concern in terms of three different levels of analysis of the mathematics curriculum:

(a) *The distribution of knowledge*. . . . The idea of mathematics for all involves issues of cultural exchange and intercultural understanding—within and between social groups and geopolitical communities.

(b) *The school system and its integration into society*. The idea of mathematics for all poses the issue of general education rather than elite education. At this level the idea of mathematics for all involves us in a rethinking of the traditional concerns of mathematics education—away from the "needs" of elites and towards the needs of both elites and average students; our sense of crowning achievements would not come from the achievements of the few but from the achievements of the many. Our index of accomplishment would be the overall *yield* of the school system (i.e., the percentage of a cohort mastering given bodies of content and skill), rather than the content and skill achievement of the most able alone.

(c) *Classroom interaction*. Mathematics for all is a problem of opportunities to learn and their relationship to the dynamics of the learning process. This level of concern must include an analysis of the assumptions, patterns, and practices of the within-school division of students into ability groups, sets and streams—for setting/streaming is ubiquitous in mathematics education from the early secondary years. (182)

In summary, the functional justification for the study of mathematics has long been assumed. Furthermore, the current debate could be viewed only as an argument within an absolutist perspective given the technological revolution. "More" mathematics or "less" could be seen as a debate about which and how many parts of mathematics should be learned. Such a view is simplistic and fails to appreciate the philosophic shift to doing mathematics.

Other Justifications

Although almost all authors initially justify having mathematics in the school curriculum on functional grounds, other reasons are also often given. A second justification is based on the notion that mathematics should be taught because, in some general way, it improves people's "thinking." "Correctness in thinking," said Robert Maynard Hutchins (1936), "may be more directly and impressively taught through mathematics than in any other way" (84). This goal has its roots in the writings of Plato: "Those who are by nature good at calculation are, as one might say, naturally sharp in every other study, and . . . those who are slow at it, if they are educated and exercised in this study, nevertheless improve and become sharper than they were" (Grube 1974, 178). Today this view is reflected in the emphasis placed on higher-order thinking skills (e.g., Resnick 1987) and is central to the new, social constructivist goals for students expressed in the *Curriculum and Evaluation Standards for School Mathematics* (NCTM 1989):

> We are convinced that if students are exposed to the kinds of experiences outlined in the *Standards*, they will gain *mathematical power*. This term denotes an individual's abilities to explore, conjecture, and reason logically, as well as the ability to use a variety of mathematical methods effectively to solve nonroutine problems. This notion is based on the recognition of mathematics as more than a collection of concepts and skills to be mastered; it includes methods of investigating and reasoning, means of communication, and notions of context. In addition, for each individual, mathematical power involves the development of personal self-confidence. (5)

A third justification, the "utility of effort," also comes from the *Republic* and posits that "calculation" is "not to be neglected" because "I do not think that you will easily find studies which give more trouble to the practicing pupil" (Grube 1978, 178). The belief in practice and effort also persists today. In their *Case Studies in Science Education*, Stake and Easley (1978) summarize the absolutist views of teachers they interviewed:

> Teachers said they could not change the fact that life is going to require youngsters to do a lot of things that do not make sense at the time, and that seem very difficult. Therefore, they argued that there should be a significant body of learning at every grade level which is difficult, which may not make sense at the time, but which has to be learned by every student. (16)

Mathematics is thought of as a major part of the "significant body of learning" mentioned above. This justification gained prominence in the 19th century during the era of faculty psychology and was a central theme of Thorndike's (1922) absolutist views about the teaching of arithmetic. Although the image of the "mind as a muscle which needs exercise" is no longer viewed as pedagogically valid, exercise and effort are still valued.

A fourth rationale for teaching mathematics is provided by Harold Jacobs (1970) in the "Letter to the Student" with which he introduces his text *Mathematics: A Human Endeavor*:

> You may come across topics in this book that would seem to be of little use to you in later life, but although mathematics is indispensable to most activities of the modern world, its true significance does not depend on its practical use. Don't be like the woman flying over the Grand Canyon who asked, "What good is it?" It was many years before some mathematics created in the past was discovered to apply to any useful problem. Some mathematics of today may never have any applications to other subjects. But, like the Grand Canyon, mathematics has its own kind of beauty and appeal to the person who is willing to look. (xii)

A fifth rationale for teaching mathematics is to replenish the supply of mathematicians. Hans Freudenthal (1973) pointed out the obvious fact that "a mathematician's natural inclination is to train mathematicians" (69). This inclination is deeply rooted in the way many mathematics professors approach their courses and lessons. Furthermore, since there is a considerable demand for mathematically trained persons and a very limited supply, this justification has some merit. Unfortunately, it is not a valid one for teaching all students mathematics since "one thing can be predicted with near certainty, that is, that [the *average* pupil] will not become a mathematician" (68).

A final rationale, which is rarely stated, involves getting students to understand and appreciate mathematics for its contribution to our Western democratic culture. Freudenthal puts this social constructivist view of mathematics very succinctly: "[Students] should learn mathematics because they need it as one aspect of their being human beings" (69). Trafton (1980) states the case in terms of general literacy.

Mathematics is a component of general educational goals. Thus, the curriculum must include "the level of mathematical knowledge needed to comprehend and interpret events in the world. . . . Even a casual reading of newspapers and periodicals reveals much mathematics that is a part of current issues and general news. Many aspects of good consumer awareness require a fairly sophisticated knowledge and understanding" (11).

Problems with Justifications

These quotes reflect only a sample of the rationales that have been given to justify the inclusion of mathematics in the school curriculum. Taken independently, each fails to explain the universal support given to the teaching of mathematics. Taken together, they make it clear that mathematics is viewed as an important school subject. However, most authors seem to give limited thought to the justification issue. In fact, most authors follow an absolutist view of mathematics. Hence, though authors feel compelled to list one or more rationales for teaching mathematics, the leap between rationale and curriculum recommendations is often carelessly made. In fact, there are many problems with the justifications that have been offered in the past. First, different rationales are likely to imply different subsets of mathematics to be included or emphasized in the curriculum. Second, the same rationale may be used by different groups to justify quite different mathematics. Third, even if goals are agreed upon, often there is a big gap between goal and actuality. And finally, until recently a justification based on mathematics as a part of culture has been neither common nor well developed.

Different Rationales Implying Different Mathematics. If one concedes that it is important to include mathematics in the school curriculum, the fact that mathematics is a dynamic, growing discipline too vast for any one individual to be cognizant of its full potential means that some subset needs to be chosen for inclusion in the school curriculum. Furthermore, those persons making the selection should base their choice in part on which philosophic rationale is used to justify mathematics in the curriculum. For example, if the inherent "beauty" of mathematics has been used to justify mathematics, applications may be ignored (or downplayed). This was precisely the problem faced in school mathematics in the "modern math" era of the 1960s. Such an approach to the mathematics curriculum has been characterized as "a systematic description of mathematics reorganized so as to emphasize structural considerations and presented in a uniform language with great precision" (Howson, Keitel, and Kilpatrick 1981, 100). This absolutist idea was to present the structure of mathematics in its pristine, logical elegance so that all could appreciate its stark beauty. Mathematics was to be seen as a "rich fabric of creative theory, which is often inspired by observations in the phenomenal world but is also inspired often by a creative insight that recognized identical mathematical structures in dissimilar realizations by stripping the realizations of their substance and concerning itself only with undefined objects and the rules governing their relations" (Rees 1966, 4).

The problem of this approach is, as Freudenthal (1973) has commented, that "[the goal was] to introduce children into a system of mathematics, a system that irradiates undeniably aesthetic charm, which, however, cannot be apprehended by people who have not profound knowledge of mathematics. The system of mathematics as a final aim is an aim for future mathematicians . . . but it can never be the aim of a general mathematical education" (69). The failure of "modern math" programs was in part due to that fact. Beauty to the eye of the mathematician could not be seen by students, teachers, or parents.

Similarly, if "work and effort" are emphasized in mastering arithmetic procedures, as has been the case in many programs for the elementary schools, the application of those procedures to unfamiliar problems may not receive much attention. In fact, teaching students to be fast, precise calculators is no longer an important goal for school mathematics. Just a half century ago, the situation was different. At that time a teacher who had drilled students to perform arithmetic calculations could still believe that this was a very important skill and was proud of it. In a way the teacher was right, for then a skilled calculator could earn a livelihood. Today this is not the case. No human can match the computer in speed or precision in carrying out calculations.

In addition, it should be noted that brilliant performance by students on arithmetic calculation is often an illusion. Data from a variety of sources make it clear that "performance for all ages was high on recall of basic facts and on simple calculations . . . [and at the same time] performance on nonroutine problems and on multistep problems was generally poor" (Carpenter, Corbitt, Kepner, Lindquist, and Reys 1981, 13). The difficulty, as Erlwanger (1975) has pointed out, is that students often have learned rules that enable them to perform operations that yield correct answers to sets of exercises without understanding the principles on which those rules are based. The teachers who think that mastery of arithmetic calculations is an educational aim in itself now need to ask themselves, "Is it all worthwhile?"

In summary, without belaboring the issue, it should be clear that different philosophic rationales imply different goals and, in turn, lead to different emphases in school mathematics programs.

Same Justification Leading to Different Mathematics. However, it should be no surprise that the same general justification for teaching mathematics can also lead to different goals and, in turn, different mathematical emphases in school programs. The prime example is that the knowledge of mathematics should be "functional" for students. One difficulty is, as George Stanic (1984b) has pointed out,

> One can conceive of a continuum on which rationales might be placed, with endpoints representing direct (or specific) utility and

indirect (or general) utility. The idea that mathematics should be taught because it improves students' "thinking" would fit on the "indirect utility" side of the continuum; that is, according to this rationale, the value of mathematics study lies not so much in the specific bits of information that are acquired, but in the general training of the mind which it provides. On the other hand, the idea that mathematics should be taught because it provides students with certain skills which are obviously, directly, and immediately applicable to the "real world" would fit on the "direct utility" side of the continuum. (6)

The situation is complicated, since different authors have different views about "direct utility." For example, NCTM (1980) claims that problem solving should be taught because it is directly functional in vocational and nonvocational life situations and in scientific applications: "Problem solving encompasses a multitude of routine and commonplace as well as nonroutine functions considered to be essential to the day-to-day living of every citizen. But it must also prepare individuals to deal with the special problems they will face in their individual careers" (2). More generally, this statement implies that the "directly functional" rationale is the justification for including mathematics in the school curriculum. Exactly the same claim has been made by those advocating "back to basics." In general, when people talk about basic skills in mathematics, they refer to computational skills with whole numbers, fractions, and decimals (not problem solving). Evidence for this view is found in the fact that most of the minimum competency testing programs around the country have operationally defined basic skills in mathematics in this way (see Pipho 1980).

These differences are more than a semantic issue concerning what constitutes "basic skills." NCTM (1980) states that the primary reason for focusing on problem solving is that it is directly applicable to "real-world" problems. The Council then classifies problem solving as one of 10 basic skill areas. In contrast, Thomas Good (1979), using a limited definition of basic skills, states, "The first step may be to improve basic skills. There is no reason to be excessively defensive about increasing students' performance on national achievement tests" (6). If problem solving is only one of 10 basic skill areas and if it is to be taught because it is directly functional, people have every right to say, "Maybe problem solving is important, but kids have to know how to add, subtract, multiply and divide *first*."

The significance of this attitude may not be easy to understand. After all, there is nothing wrong with wanting students to be able to perform fundamental operations with whole numbers, fractions, and decimals. But the way these skills are taught is crucial. As John Dewey (1933) said, a real danger exists when there is a limited focus on skill acquisition:

> The tendency is to take the shortest cuts possible to gain the required end. This makes the . . . [subject] *mechanical*, and thus restrictive of intellectual power. In the mastery of . . . [skills], the need for economy of time and material, for neatness and accuracy, for promptness and uniformity, is so great that these things tend to become ends in themselves, irrespective of their influence upon general mental attitude. Sheer imitation, dictation of steps to be taken, mechanical drill, may give results most quickly and yet strengthen traits likely to be fatal to reflective power. . . . Practical skills, modes of effective technique, can be intelligently, non-mechanically *used* only when intelligence has played a part in their *acquisition*. (62–63)

In summary, the reasons given by different authors to justify the teaching of mathematics in schools or for emphasizing some aspect of mathematics may on the surface seem similar when in fact the similarity may mask quite different philosophic positions.

The Gap Between Aims and Practices. "In no other field is the distance between aim and aimless use so great" (Freudenthal 1973, 64). That there is a gap between what is implied in given rationales and what occurs in classrooms is not surprising. The contrast between "preactive" and "interactive" notions about curricula is a central theme in the field (e.g., Greene 1971; Jackson 1968; Young 1977). The causes for this gap in school mathematics are many. First, there is often a gap between stated rationales and what appears in curriculum guidelines and textbooks based on those rationales. Invoking a particular rationale for teaching mathematics should mean that the assumptions behind the rationale and the implications are recognized and accepted. That is, for any particular mathematics curriculum, there should be a direct relationship between the reasons given for teaching mathematics and the form and content of the curriculum. Unfortunately, this vital connection does not always exist. For example, George Polya (1966) argued that texts based on the rationale of "thinking" rarely emphasized "active learning":

> Mathematics is not a spectator sport; it cannot be enjoyed and it cannot be learned without active participation, and so the principle of active learning is particularly important for us mathematics teachers, especially if we regard as our principal aim, or one of our major aims, to teach the students to think.
>
> If we wish to develop the student's mentality we must be careful to let first things come first. Some activities come to him more easily and more naturally than others: guesses more easily than proofs, solving concrete problems more naturally than building up conceptual structures. In general, the concrete comes before the abstract, action and perception before words and concepts, concepts before symbols, and so on.
>
> As the student should learn not passively, but by his own effort, let us start there where the effort is less and the goal of the effort more understandable from the student's standpoint: the student should become familiar with the concrete before the abstract, with the variety of experience before the unifying concept, and so on. (125)

Unfortunately, the weakest aspect of mathematics texts ostensibly written to foster "thinking" is that "almost all of their problems are one-rule-under-your-nose problems" (Polya 1966, 126). Routine exercises may be useful or even necessary if administered at the right time in the right dose. However, too often there are overdoses of routine exercises, which can only bore students. A specific rationale for teaching mathematics should be more than mere rhetoric. M. Frances Klein (1989) has identified one of the reasons for this gap between rationale and curriculum plans. When examining curriculum guides in many school districts, she found that many of the subject matter goals were translated into behavioral objectives. The strong emphasis on behavioral objectives in the curriculum literature and in current practice was reflected very clearly in the guides. Any controversy about their desirability and usefulness, although present in the research literature, was not acknowledged. Indeed, the desirability of behavioral objectives was clearly endorsed and never questioned. These two examples make it clear that the implications of stated rationales should be reflected in curricular plans and materials.

Second, the gap between rationale and curricular materials can be magnified by another gap between the materials and classroom instruction. For example, in an analysis of "modern" mathematics programs of the 1960s, the Conference Board of the Mathematical Sciences (1975) found that

> [One] argument for including set concepts and terminology in school curricula rests on the role that these ideas can play in organizing other mathematical facts and methods—in demonstrating connections between apparently different mathematical tools so that acquisition, retention, and transfer can be enhanced. Set theoretic ideas offer another vehicle for explaining, illustrating, and practicing basic mathematical concepts and skills. A similar argument supports inclusion of algebraic field properties in the study of number systems.
>
> The subtle function of these unifying concepts was often poorly incorporated by new curriculum materials and by classroom teachers. Early modern textbooks began with chapters on set concepts, language, and operations; but the balance of these books used little more than the notation of sets. For example, some teachers began "taking off points" for answers not enclosed in curly brackets. They drilled young children in correct spelling of the "commutative," "associative," and "distributive" terms rather than useful application of the concepts in computation. The proposed means to deepen understanding of useful mathematics became ends in themselves. (16)

Third, even if the materials reflect a rationale, teachers may change activities in ways that distort aims. For example, in 1988, I reported such distortions when studying the implementation of *Developing Mathematical Processes* (Romberg, Harvey, Moser, and Montgomery 1974, 1975, 1976). Numerous teachers were observed adapting activities that had been carefully developed.

> The adaptations were made for a variety of reasons. Often when interviewed, teachers justified the changes in terms of management (the class would be noisy) or perceived ability of their students (I have the low group of students). On other occasions the changes that were made drastically altered the mathematical intent of the lessons. For example, a sequence of activities on measuring length was designed to have first-grade children measure a variety of objects in their room with arbitrary units such as pencils, cards, and links. Then the teacher was to conduct a discussion on the objectives of the topic, including the iteration process used to count the number of units, the fact that small units yielded a large number for the measure while large units yielded a small number, and that there always is some error when measuring that needs to be resolved. The discussion eventually was to lead to children seeing the need for a common unit. One teacher changed the activity so that instead of measuring real objects with arbitrary units that required iterating and counting, the children measured line segments on a work sheet with a ruler marked in inches. Furthermore, the line segments were drawn so that the measures were nearly exact. The teacher justified the changes in terms of her view of mathematics: It was wrong to give children the impression that a math problem could have several right answers or that mathematics was ever imprecise (Stephens 1982). A lawyer who interpreted a law incorrectly would soon have few clients. Why is it assumed to be acceptable for teachers to modify and distort lessons so that the knowledge being transmitted is wrong? (Romberg 1988a, 228)

In a similar manner, Brian Donovan (1983) found that even when an innovative measurement program was implemented to supplement the primary syllabus, teachers relegated its exploratory activities to an aide and gave it no emphasis in assessment or grading, thus creating an illusion of expanding the children's opportunities to learn.

Finally, there is also a gap between what is taught and what is learned. Too often, teachers see their role as covering the content of the text. The curriculum in this perspective, as Kliebard (1972) has argued, is a route over which students are to travel under the leadership of an experienced guide and companion. Thus, the job of teaching is seen as analogous to being a "tour guide." This gap is created when one treats pupils only as "students" and not as "learners," as Yves Chevallard (1988) has described:

> A student is one who studies; a learner, one who learns. . . . Studying refers to the official role ascribed to the pupil in the teaching process: whenever a person comes to participate in such a process as a pupil, he or she will be made into a student. But an even subtler distinction should be posited at this point: I shall discriminate between "the student" and "the taught." "The taught" would point to the pupil in so far as he is *subjected* to the "teaching treatment"; "the student" refers to the pupil as someone who *reacts* to this treatment, by taking some definite course of action. In mentioning the taught, we really denote the pupil; but, at the same time, however surreptitiously, we connote the teacher or, more abstractly, whatever condition or constraint is being imposed upon the pupil by the teacher. (1)

In particular, this problem is endemic to most "preactive" notions about school mathematics programs because the "teaching treatment" is constrained by various political and administrative decisions, called "frame factors" by Lundgren (1979). Teachers are expected to teach certain content units so that students achieve particular objectives in a given time period. These factors constrain the teaching process by limiting instructional flexibility.

In summary, it is not surprising that there is a gap between rationales and practice. When statements of intent are often no more than rhetoric, and the pedagogical assumptions that should relate rationales with practice are neither explicit nor considered, gaps are inevitable.

Culture: The Other Rationale. During the past decade there has been a gradual philosophic shift in perspective about mathematics and the rationale for its inclusion in the school curriculum. The shift is an outgrowth of several forces. One has been from studies on the sociocultural nature of both mathematics and school mathematics (see Bishop 1988; D'Ambrosio 1985, 1987; Mellin-Olsen 1987). The consequences of such studies make it clear that mathematics is a social process in that choices of what mathematics to include in the school curriculum are culturally determined; further, the mathematics developed and used in various cultures may not resemble that taught in schools.

This sociocultural perspective has not been used very often to justify the teaching of mathematics, partly because mathematical knowledge for many persons has, as Bishop (1988) argued, "attributes of clarity, universality and truth" (117). Although admitting that mathematical developments grow out of sociocultural contexts, these same scholars believe that the social perspective is "at best an unnecessary diversion from the real tasks, and at worst an undesirable confounding of an already complicated field" (117). In a sense, they believe that school mathematics should be treated as a "culture-free" subject. Thus, many educators shun this rationale for others—particularly the "directly functional" rationale.

A second, more compelling, reason for the lack of a cultural justification for school mathematics is that the implications for curricular choice and instruction have not been well worked out. This failure is in part due to inadequate conceptualization. As C. Wright Mills (1959) pointed out, "the conception of 'culture' is more often a loose reference to social milieux plus 'tradition' than an adequate idea of social structure" (160). It is also in part due to the roots of cultural concern, as Chevallard (in press) argues:

> Interest in the socio-cultural aspects of mathematics education has been steadily gaining ground for the past fifteen years or so. This growing concern among mathematics educators is linked with the aftermath of colonization and the "enforcement" of Western-type ways of life—a world-wide process that has brought peoples and nations into contact with Western technology and culture, including mathematics education. (1)

He points out that this concern can lead to "cultural sentimentality" and in any case "tends to focus on symptoms, and easily ignores the root of the evil" (2).

What needs to be done is to reflect on the cultural aspects of mathematics described earlier: its history, its use in different cultures, the different mathematics within our culture, the cultural group of mathematicians, and the conflicts between the culture of school mathematics and scientific mathematics. Each of these aspects sheds light on the fact that mathematics has been created by humans to help make sense of the world. In other words, the cultural perspective for justifying the teaching of mathematics should be based on a belief that mathematical knowledge is a historical and social constructivist product. This leads to the following points articulated by Ernest (1991, 265):

1. Mathematics consists primarily of human mathematical problem posing and solving, an activity that is accessible to all. Consequently, school mathematics for all should be centrally concerned with human mathematical problem posing and solving, and should reflect its fallibility.
2. Mathematics is a part of human culture, and the mathematics of each culture serves its own unique purposes, and is equally valuable. Consequently, school mathematics should acknowledge the diverse cultural and historical origins and purposes of mathematics, and the real contributions of all, including women and non-European countries.
3. Mathematics is not neutral, but laden with the values of its makers and their cultural contexts, and users and creators of mathematics have a responsibility to consider it effects on the social and natural worlds.

> Consequently, school mathematics should explicitly acknowledge the values associated with mathematics, and its social uses. Learners should be aware of implicit social messages in the mathematics curriculum and should have the confidence, knowledge, and skills to be able to understand the social uses of mathematics.

These changes in perspective are critical. Since our society is undergoing a transformation from an industrial society to an information society, understanding the role of mathematics in both society's development and its transformation is ample justification for including mathematics in the school curriculum.

Summary

Few scholars have adequately justified the inclusion of mathematics in the school curriculum. The specific justifications are often shallow, fail to reflect actual recommendations or gaps between rationales and practices, and do not reflect the connections between formal mathematical procedures and their sociocultural roots. Based on these factors, there are three implications to note. First, educators need to be aware of these inadequacies; second, scholars need to consider seriously the basis for any justification of teaching mathematics in schools; and third, the social constructivist cultural perspective needs to be well developed. Nevertheless, all justifications reflect an underlying belief that mathematics is so important that aspects of the discipline must be included in the school curriculum.

WHAT MATHEMATICS IS CURRENTLY BEING TAUGHT AND WHY?

This question is being raised since some understanding of present curricular practices in school mathematics and how they have come about is essential so that the arguments about change and reform can be understood. The answer to this question involves describing current mathematics programs as they exist in American schools. Following a brief description, two problematic features are addressed: the traditions on which these programs are based and a contrast of these programs with those in other countries. Also, it should be apparent that current curricular practices are based on absolutist views of mathematics.

Describing the mathematics programs in American schools is not easy because of the complexity of the public school systems, although there are many similarities among schools. To portray this complexity, current practices and the typical features of the mathematics curriculum are discussed.

Current Schooling Practices

Any description must situate the teaching of mathematics within schools as they actually operate. One of the most striking features of American schools to foreign visitors is the diversity of schooling practices, particularly with respect to governance and how policy decisions are made, a result of the fact that educational policy is *not* national. In fact, the Constitution of the United States, by omitting any reference to education, left decisions about education to the states. Then, with the exception of one state, Hawaii, the states have, in varying degrees, turned over the control of schools to local communities with locally elected school boards. These district boards, in turn, hire administrators and teachers and approve programs. In 1985, there were 15,248 school districts in the United States. They contained 50,926 elementary schools, 9,785 junior high schools, and 13,837 senior high schools (Feistritzer 1985). As a consequence of shared state and local control and shared state and local taxes to support schools, there are vast differences in the quality of programs, facilities, staff, and teachers both across and within states. There is no national curriculum, no national set of standards for the licensing or retention of teachers, no common policies for student assessment of progress or admission to higher education, and so forth.

Nevertheless, in spite of this diversity in school governance, there is considerable similarity in practice. The most common pattern of schooling from the late 19th century until the 1950s was the requirement that all students attend elementary school for 8 years (ages 6–14). Each school housed some 200 students, grouped by age (grades 1–8) and further grouped into classes of 20 to 30 students, who then were taught all subjects for the school year by the same teacher. School lasted some 6 to 7 hours a day, 5 days a week for 9 months (September to June), with 2 weeks' vacation at Christmas and a week off at Easter. The long summer vacation was deemed necessary so that both students and teachers could help on the farms.

Secondary schools followed the same basic schedule, except they housed some 1,000 to 2,000 students for 4 years (grades 9–12). Attendance was not mandatory. Thus, many students never went to high school, and many who started did not graduate. Classes were organized around subject disciplines (English, science, social studies, and mathematics). Each class met 5 days a week for a semester (half a year) or for the school year. Each class was taught by a teacher who had been trained to teach that subject. Thus, a student would take 5 or 6 different classes a day from different teachers. Also, mathematics classes played a privileged role in school programs. Only if students did well in entry-level mathematics classes were they allowed to take later courses.

During the past 60 years, there have been many changes in the common pattern of schooling in the United States. Three aspects need to be mentioned. First, kindergartens have been almost universally added to the elementary schools. They require a half day (or full day) of schooling for 5-year-olds to acquaint them with the routines of schools so that they become familiar with the distinctions between work and play, among other things (King 1981). Second, compulsory schooling has been extended from age 14 to 16 (18 in some states). This rule has changed the clientele of secondary schools from that of college-bound, middle-class youths to all persons in these age groups. In turn, this factor has changed the course offerings from strictly academic subjects to a vast melange. In fact, although schools continue to require academic courses for high school graduation, the requirements have become minimal, and the course content modified and less demanding. Third, to accommodate problems of emerging adolescence, the transition to high school for the masses, and appropriate facilities, a new school (called junior high or middle school) has become common. These schools are for 400 to 600 students for 3 years (grades 6–8 or 7–9) and have features of both elementary and secondary schools.

Another feature of American schools that strikes foreign scholars as strange is the emphasis on athletics, drama, marching bands, and other activities that are emphasized in the rituals of our secondary schools. This emphasis grew with the development of schools in the isolated villages and small towns of many states in the century before War World II. Schools in these communities were, and often still are, the focus of the social life of the communities. Football games, school plays, or musical programs are attended by the entire community. Thus, schools in the United States have a broader social function within local communities than just to educate the young.

The schools in America are diverse. The reasons for this diversity are historic, economic, and political. Nevertheless, what has evolved in the later half of this century is a comprehensive schooling pattern that characterizes the majority of schools in America. It is this common pattern that is important with respect to mathematics instruction.

Typical Features of the Mathematics Curriculum

To understand the features common to the mathematics curriculum, the notions of knowledge, work of teachers and students, and technology are examined in some detail.

Knowledge. Mathematics in American schools is a large collection of hierarchically arranged (Romberg 1983) concepts and skills. Again, the distinction between the constructivist view of "knowledge" and the absolutist view of "record of knowledge," pointed out earlier, is important. The acquisition of information and the ability to demonstrate proficiency at a few skills have become ends in themselves, and students spend their time absorbing what others have done.

Scientific management has resulted in hierarchical classification and taxonomies of mathematical knowledge. To develop a curriculum, one needs to segment and sequence the mathematical ideas for instruction. Scope and sequence charts that specify procedural objectives to be mastered by students at each grade level are commonly produced. In fact, the use of behavioral objectives and learning hierarchies has separated mathematics into literally thousands of segments, each taught independently of the others.

The goal for students is that they sequentially master one concept or skill after another. Furthermore, the student's task is to get correct answers to well-defined problems or exercises. This method of segmenting and sequencing school mathematics has led to an assumption that there is a strict partial ordering to the discipline. Thus, in U.S. schools, you cannot study geometry unless you can solve linear equations or do algebra unless you have mastered arithmetic. Furthermore, the curriculum reflects the 19th-century compromise, described by Jahnke (1986), to formalize school mathematics as a closed unified system rather than as a sequence of methods for analyzing and understanding our world.

Another way of describing what mathematics is taught to students in these schools is to describe the topics that are covered in various grades. The emphasis in the elementary school is on computational proficiency in arithmetic. The standard topics include addition, subtraction, multiplication, and division of whole numbers, fractions, and decimals; some experience-based geometry; and a few word problems. In fact, the arithmetic content differs little from that used to train Italian merchants in the 15th century (Swetz 1987). Furthermore, instruction on each topic is repeated for several years. For example, in a recent study by Flanders (1986), the percentage of new content was calculated for three commonly used text series. He found an average of 72 percent new content in grade 1, and 30 percent new content in grade 8. Thus, for the majority of students, mathematics is really arithmetic, and even then the emphasis is on mastering a set of common paper-and-pencil calculation routines. However, this picture is somewhat deceiving. In actuality, although the mathematical content in curriculum guides, textbooks, and tests may exhibit common topics, the actual classroom emphasis and the amount of time spent on a topic often vary considerably (Jones and Romberg 1979).

At the secondary school level, the picture is quite different. First, for the college-bound math-science student, there is a 4-year mathematics sequence. The sequence includes a year of algebra at grade 9 (little changed since the 17th century), followed by a year of Euclidean geometry at grade 10 (little changed since the 3rd century B.C.), another year of algebra at grade 11, and a year of precalculus at grade 12. Students who are planning to go to college but not planning to study mathematics or the sciences are expected to take 2 or 3 years of the same sequence of courses. Then, for students who are not college bound, another year of arithmetic (general math) is usually required. Finally, a few students accelerate by starting algebra in grade 8 and taking a calculus course in grade 12.

Also, it should be pointed out that enrollment in mathematics courses declines dramatically at each grade level. Estimates of the percentage of enrollment in each course show that by the time an age group of students has reached high school graduation, about 79 percent have taken an algebra course, 56 percent a geometry course, 30 percent an advanced algebra course, and 6 percent a calculus course (Usiskin 1984). Another way of summarizing enrollment is by age group: 10 percent in an accelerated mathematics track, 20 percent in the science track, 20 percent in the college-preparatory track, and 50 percent in the general track (Weiss 1978).

The actual topics taught in classrooms are those that appear in the textbooks that are used, with the emphasis on those concepts and skills that appear on tests. The usual pattern of curriculum planning involves a school district adopting a curriculum framework, then selecting a set of texts and tests that can be shown to cover the topics in the framework. Of course, although there are over 500 producers of educational materials in the United States, only a few texts and tests gain wide acceptance. In fact, because of state adoption policies in a few large states, in particular California (elementary only), Texas, and Florida—where if districts select texts from the state-approved list, the state will pay for their purchase—only a few texts dominate the market. Thus, in actuality, the decisions about what is included in a mathematics program are influenced by curriculum developers, administrators, political pressure groups, publishers, and others interested in what is taught in schools.

A major difficulty with this approach is that, although an individual objective might be reasonable, it is not seen as part of a larger network. It is the network, the connections between objectives, that is important. Fragmentation and a corresponding emphasis on low-level objectives are reinforced by the testing procedures often associated with curricula based on behavioral objectives. Multiple-choice questions on concepts and skills emphasize the independence rather than the interdependence of ideas and reward right answers rather than the use of reasonable procedures.

Stress on isolated parts essentially trains students in a series of routines, without educating them to grasp an overall picture that will ensure the use of appropriate ideas for given purposes. Mathematics as a discipline has not only internal structure but also integral and reciprocal relationships with other disciplines, especially science and increasingly with the social sciences and humanities. The complexities of these relationships are challenging the traditional hierarchical taxonomies of content.

Work of Teachers. The work roles of teachers and students are complementary; some teach, the others learn. However, since the goals of schools are directed toward student learning, the role of the teacher should complement that of the student rather than vice versa. Unfortunately, when knowledge is regarded as knowing that rather than knowing how, the vocabulary reflects a reversal of emphasis. In traditional classrooms, the work of the teacher is to "transmit" knowledge, and the job of the student is to receive it, regurgitating it on demand. In fact, the real work of the student is often that of a passive routine, meeting expectations sufficiently to pass through the system (Skemp 1979). Clarke (1984) quoted a student's description of a mathematics classroom as follows: "She tells us what we're gonna do. And she'll probably write up a few examples and notes on the board. Then we'll either get sheets handed out or she'll write up questions on the board. Not very often. We mainly get a textbook. We'll get pages. She'll write up what work to do, page number and exercise. And that's about what happens" (22). The traditional situation described is organized, routine, controlled, and predictable—an unlikely environment for the creation of knowledge. In fact, traditional instruction is based on a metaphor of production in which students are seen as "raw material" to be transformed by "skilled technicians" (Kliebard 1972).

The job of teaching involves managing the production line and maintaining order and control (Romberg and Carpenter 1986). There is an inexorably logical sequence when the acknowledged work of teachers is to transmit the record of knowledge. The most cost-effective way to transmit such a record is through exposition to a captive audience. Theoretically, the child could read and cover the same ground, but that would require a voluntary act, which is unlikely as long as children are not setting their own goals. Consequently, exposition is not possible unless there is control, which is easier if children talk as little as possible and stay in one place. It is essentially a system for "delivering" knowledge to the group by controlling the individual. This simple sequence has dictated work, furniture arrangement, architecture, and so on, for the last 100 years. The result is that the traditional classroom focuses on competition, management, and group aptitudes; the mathematics taught is assumed to be a fixed body of knowledge, and it is taught under the assumption that learners absorb what has been covered (868). Additional evidence comes from three studies commissioned by the National Science Foundation (NSF), including a national survey of current practices (Weiss 1978), a review of literature (Suydam and Osborne 1977), and a set of case studies (Stake and Easley 1978). A synthesis of all three studies was prepared by a committee of the National Council of Teachers of Mathematics (Fey 1979a, 1979b). Although the profile and interpretation of mathematics teaching that emerge from these studies are neither simple nor consistent, the predominant pattern is "extensive teacher-directed explanation and questioning followed by student seatwork on paper-and-pencil assignments" (1979a, 494). The following remarks from one of the NSF case studies of mathematics teaching describe a typical day of instruction in secondary schools.

> In all math classes I visited, the sequence of activities was the same. First, answers were given for the previous day's assignment. The more difficult problems were worked by the teacher or a student at the chalkboard. A brief explanation, sometimes none at all, was given of the new material, and problems were assigned for the next day. The remainder of the class was devoted to working on the homework while the teacher moved about the room answering questions. The most noticeable thing about math classes was the repetition of this routine. (Welsh 1978, 6)

During the past quarter-century, because of concerns about trying to get teachers to adopt and use new programs, there has been a tendency to overspecify instructions for teachers. Both the detailed individualized programs and highly structured group programs deprive teachers of the opportunity to develop important teaching skills. Often there are no longer decisions to make about what activities to employ. Control of the instructional process is shifted from the teacher to the methods of assessment and rules for judgment. Taken to an extreme, the teacher becomes only a conduit in a system, covering the pages of a text without thinking or consideration.

The emphasis of teaching is on curricular content and the management of individual progress. The teacher is a supply sergeant (Jackson 1968) and a manager of resources and personnel (Berliner 1982). Today, teachers are not encouraged to adapt or change to meet local needs or conditions. They are not encouraged to relate the ideas of one lesson to another. Their task is to get students to complete pages or do sets of exercises with little relationship between ideas, and teachers are to reinforce this perspective. There are teachers and educators who will rightly object to this picture of mathematics instruction. Some teachers provide a different form of mathematics instruction. However, according to recent studies of "expert" versus "novice" teachers (e.g., Leinhardt 1986), the experts are only more efficient in carrying out the standard pattern of instruction.

Even though there have been changes, in 1975 the National Advisory Committee on Mathematical Education (NACOME) commissioned a study of elementary school mathematics instruction. The picture drawn from that survey is as follows:

> The "median" classroom is self-contained. The mathematics period is about 43 minutes long and about half of this time is written work. A single text is used in whole-class instruction. The text is followed fairly closely, but students are likely to read at most one or two pages out of five pages of textual materials other than problems. It seems likely that the text, at least as far as the students are concerned, is primarily a source of problem lists. Teachers are essentially teaching the same way they were taught in school. Almost none of the concepts, methods or big ideas of modern mathematics programs have appeared in this median classroom. (Conference Board of Mathematical Sciences 1975, 77)

In summary, the teaching of mathematics in the United States is viewed as a trade, involving personal management skills.

Work of Students. Most current mathematics programs in the United States have conceived of the learner as being a passive absorber of information, storing it in memory in small bits that are easily retrievable. Note that this view of learning is consistent with the fragmentation of mathematical content.

This conception of learning is based on the tenets of "behaviorism," a theory that evolved during the early part of this century. This is not the place for a lengthy discussion of the psychology of mathematics learning. Elsewhere, I have presented an overview of seven general psychological theories and their implications for mathematics instruction

(Romberg 1988d). The origins, general assumptions, and implications of behaviorism for instruction are well summarized by Gagné (1965). The relationships of behaviorism to other psychological theories have been summarized by Langer (1969) and Phillips and Soltis (1985). And the implications for instruction, from the fields of psychology to those of mathematics, have been presented by Resnick and Ford (1981). What is clear is that current instruction in most classrooms reflects the assumptions of behavioral psychology. This theory focuses on the outcomes of learning (behaviors) rather than on how learning occurs. It assumes that learning occurs by passively, but rationally, reflecting on stimuli from the environment. And it has been used by scholars to study how desired responses to stimuli (outcomes) become fixed by practice and praise (reinforcement). Learning is viewed as change in behavior (or performance) and change scores (pretest-posttest differences) on some measure of performance are often used as evidence for learning. This theory, in its many forms, has strongly influenced all education in the United States and, in particular, school mathematics. Its strength lies in what Schrag (1981) has called its "generative" characteristics. He means that the theory has generated a number of practical procedures that can be used in schools.

Technology. The technology of traditional instruction includes a basal text, which is a repository of problem lists, a mass of paper-and-pencil worksheets, and a set of performance tests. Although a few of the books include things to read, very little of it is interesting. Thus, workbook mathematics gives students little reason to connect ideas in today's lesson with those of past lessons or with the real world. The tests currently used ask for answers that are judged right or wrong, but the strategies and reasoning used to derive answers are not evaluated.

In summary, this picture of "what is" in mathematics instruction in school classrooms should make it clear that the current curriculum, although coherent, reflects the dominant absolutist perspective which is consistent neither with the reform perspectives about the discipline nor with the reform justifications given for its inclusion in schools. This state leads to the scrutiny of two provocative issues: the traditions that have given rise to current practice and the realization that practices are different in other countries.

Traditions Underlying School Mathematics

The current American school mathematics curriculum reflects established cultural traditions. As Karl Popper (1949) has argued, the role of traditions in society is twofold: First, traditions create a certain social structure; and second, traditions are something we can criticize and change. Curricular traditions, such as teaching a year of geometry to 15-year-olds, provide regularities in the social structure of schools. The mere existence of these regularities is more important than their merits or demerits. They bring order and rational predictability into the social world of schools. But as satirically narrated by Peddiwell (1939) in his classic *The Saber-Tooth Curriculum*, traditions—such as a course on "saber-tooth-scaring-with-fire"—sometimes outlive their usefulness (for example, continuing to teach "scaring-with-fire" even after saber-tooth tigers have become extinct). Today, interpolation by using logarithmic and trigonometric tables is still being taught in many classes even though hand-held calculators have replaced them in all practical situations; and elementary statistics is often still taught using precomputer computational approximations.

Traditions, in a sense, have a role similar to theories. They provide scholars with a framework to be critically examined and to be altered over and over again. For example, the "modern mathematics" movement changed few of our traditions in the teaching of mathematics. Geometry in "modern math" programs was still a year-long course for 15-year-olds; it still covered the basic propositions of Euclid's 3rd century B.C. treatise; it was still taught by a teacher to approximately 30 students for 45 to 55 minutes a day, 5 days a week. The only real change involved replacing Legendre's 19th-century adaptation of Euclid's assumptions with Birkhoff's (1932) adaptation, which reflects modern ideas of mathematical structure. Now, some 50 years later, further modifications in content, approaching geometry from plane transformations (Coxford and Usiskin 1971) or as an experimental subject on a computer (Schwartz and Yerushalmy 1985, 1986, 1987) have been proposed, texts written, or materials prepared and tried with classes. Alterations continue on some curriculum features, whereas other traditions remain virtually intact. Note that these changes fail to challenge the tradition of teaching a year of geometry in grade 10.

There are several reasons for the emergence of such traditions. Two themes are used to summarize these reasons: the "dual" educational system and the ideological conflict and compromise over the curriculum in the past 2 centuries.

Dual Educational System. In the industrial society of the past century, people were educated to maintain their places in the structure of the economy. A small, highly educated group established policy, led the government, managed industry, and advanced the scientific and technological base. The remainder of the population provided the physical labor for production and services and was educated to the level required for reliable performance. The educational system that evolved reflected this duality. In fact, as Freudenthal (1973) has argued, in Western Europe and the United States, when

> we talk about mathematical education, we usually mean the education of an often socially determined elite, and we do not care about the others. . . . Up until now education in Western Europe has been elite education, that is to say education of an elite or at least for an elite. This tendency alas has been reinforced by most of the innovation movements. As for mathematics, I am afraid that its educational programmes and methods are influenced by a belief which is natural for every mathematician, that mathematical education is education to become a mathematician—those who cannot keep pace are

left behind. And for those who were left behind or who never even embarked, they serve up a second infusion of this mathematics for the elite. . . . [There is] no convincing image of a new mathematics for all. There is one thing we need most badly, whether it be mathematics for an elite or for all—an image of mathematics for the totality of education. (63)

In a similar view, Lauren Resnick (1987) has described American schools as the inheritors of two quite distinct educational traditions—one aimed at the education of an elite, the other concerned with mass education. These traditions conceived of schooling in different terms, had different clienteles, and held different goals for their students. Only in the past 60 years have the two traditions merged (5). These two types of schools have been labeled "high literacy" and "low literacy" (Resnick and Resnick 1977). The high-literacy schools were, and still are, for the elite. They are private, religious, or special academic facilities in states or large cities or in affluent communities. Only a minority of young people attend, or are admitted, to such schools. The curriculum is strictly academic, aiming toward university entrance at the "best" universities in the country.

Schools for the "masses" arose from different roots and were aimed at producing minimal levels of competence in the general population. When the United States as a nation was formed, village schools were established that reflected the notions about a literate citizenship appropriate to the new nation. The educational system that then evolved during the 19th century focused largely on elementary schooling. This focus produced a sharp distinction between elementary and secondary education that still persists. Almost everyone went to school for up to 8 years, but few went on to high school. The low-literacy curriculum focused on the basic skills of reading, writing, and computation. Teachers in elementary schools were expected to teach all students all of the curriculum, whereas secondary teachers were subject matter specialists.

In summary, the structure of current schooling still reflects this duality: Teachers are generalists in elementary schools and subject matter specialists in secondary schools; all students are taught the same mathematics for several years before they are grouped and taught different mathematics; and so forth.

Ideological Conflict. School practices historically have evolved as a consequence of compromises between groups holding different ideological views about educating the young of a particular society. For example, Swetz (1987) has pointed out how in the 15th century, when merchants created schools to teach accountants Arabic arithmetic, many scholars considered this to be "vulgar" commercialism, unworthy of serious study. The model of academic mathematics was the austere and pristine Greek geometry. Arithmetic had none of these virtues but was useful. The compromise was to teach young children some arithmetic and to teach the able older children formal mathematics. Similarly, Jahnke (1986) has described how in the early 19th century in Germany, the school mathematics curriculum evolved through compromises that resulted in a curriculum divorced from its uses so that students would see mathematics as a formal, closed system.

In the 20th century in the United States, Herbert Kliebard (1985) has argued that the content and organization of the school curriculum that emerged during the first half of the century was "a feeble compromise" between the ideological positions of four groups (41). Kliebard labels these four groups the humanists, developmentalists, social meliorists, and social efficiency educators. Unfortunately, rather than seriously dealing with the conflicts, "most school curricula center around consensus" (Apple 1979, 7). Furthermore, all viewed mathematics more or less from absolutist perspectives. None saw mathematical knowledge as being socially constructed.

The humanists emphasized the importance of the traditional disciplines of knowledge as embodiments of the Western cultural heritage (a very strict form of absolutism). They represented the curriculum orthodoxy of the 19th century. Against them were pitted three reform groups. The developmentalists argued that the curriculum should be based on the natural order of development in the child. The social meliorists saw the school as an important instrument for improving society in general and the plight of suffering individuals in particular. Finally, the social efficiency educators advocated a "scientific" approach to developing a curriculum that would contribute to a smoothly functioning, efficient society, a curriculum that would prepare each person for his or her predetermined place in that society.

Depending on the social and political climate, each of these approaches made its mark on the American curriculum of today. Neither the traditional curriculum nor any of the three reform movements ever won a clear-cut victory. What passes for the contemporary American curriculum represents an agglomeration of all of them. Yet, all saw mathematics as a fixed infallible system. Since there is no unanimity of opinion at any given time on what is most worthwhile in a culture, it should not be surprising that each of these main currents of curriculum reform would find its adherents. The curriculum, after all, as a selection of elements from the culture reflects to some extent the diversity that exists within the culture. What emerged as a dominant strain in the curriculum was not a function of the force of a particular proposal alone but the interaction of curriculum ideas and sympathetic or antagonistic social conditions. Each doctrine had an appeal and a constituency.

However, the mathematics curriculum of today does not clearly reflect the compromises and ameliorative changes to the traditional humanist curriculum of the past century, as Kliebard (1985) claims. The humanist influence is apparent in maintaining Euclidean geometry as a separate course at the secondary level in spite of the calls for inclusion in the curriculum of the more modern notions from analytic and transformational geometry. The developmental influence on the mathematics curriculum has been minimal except in the early grades. The general influence of the work of scholars such as Jean Piaget and Jerome Bruner on initial learning has had an impact on the creation of instructional programs that emphasize manipulatives and small-group activities (e.g., Romberg et al. 1974, 1975, 1976). The influence of social meliorists has been negligible in mathematics, in large part because they failed to see mathematics as a socially constructed discipline. There are scholars who argue for realistic mathematics for slow learning students (e.g., Biggs 1986) or present arguments against tracking. Unfortunately, the mathematics curriculum, overall, remains a filter for separating an elite group (most often white males) that will continue the study of mathematics (MSEB 1989).

However, the impact of the social efficiency perspective on the mathematics curriculum has been profound. The political conditions under which education developed in the early part of this century encouraged the routinization of basic skills and standardized testing, among other changes. Standardization became a means of social control in diverse settings by ensuring that at least minimal curriculum standards would be met, that teachers would be hired on the basis of competency for the job rather than political or familial affiliation, and that those responsible for the expenditure of public funds would exercise orderly oversight on the process of education. This standardization was a consequence of the notions about efficiency and the effectiveness of routinization that grew out of the Industrial Revolution of the 19th century (Bobbitt 1924; Charters 1923; Rice 1913). These notions were limited to the machine-age thinking of the industrial revolution of the past century.

The intellectual contents of the machine age rested on three fundamental ideas. The first was reductionism. The idea was that to deal with anything, you had to *take it apart* until you reached its ultimate components. The second fundamental idea was that the most powerful mode in thinking is a process called analysis. Once you have broken something down to simple components, then you build it up again. The third basic idea of the machine age has been called "mechanism." Mechanism is based on the theory that all phenomena in the world can be explained by stating their cause-effect relationships. The primary effort of science is to break the world up into parts that can be studied to determine cause-effect relationships. The world was thought of as a machine operating in accordance with unchanging laws. These notions were all consistent with absolutist views of mathematics.

This whole process is clearly reflected in what has happened in school mathematics during the last half century. Mathematics was segmented into subjects and topics, eventually down to small parts—behavioral objectives. At this point, a hierarchy was created to show how these objectives were related to produce eventually a finished product. Next, the steps by which one traveled that hierarchy were mechanized via textbooks, worksheets, and tests. Furthermore, teaching was dehumanized to the point that the teacher had little to do but manage the production line. Businesses, industry, and in particular the school mathematics curricula have been based on this mechanical view of the world. Like the Model T Ford assembly line, current models of schooling were considered an example of the application of modern, scientific techniques. Today, we ought to be able to develop better school mathematics programs.

In summary, the general features of current school mathematics in the United States are as follows. Mathematics instruction is directed by *goals*, which prescribe under competitive conditions and time pressures the amount of procedural knowledge to be acquired. Furthermore, current programs provide differential opportunities for different populations of students to learn mathematics.

The current intent is that students develop a structured *knowledge* of mathematics based on absolutist views about the discipline. This approach, which has resulted in hierarchical classification and taxonomies of knowledge, means that mathematics to most students has been and still is the sequential mastery of one concept and skill after another. Thus, to most students, mathematics is a fixed collection of concepts and skills to be mastered one by one. Furthermore, the student's task is to get correct answers to well-defined problems or exercises.

The *work roles of students and teachers* are complementary; some teach, the others learn. The work of the teacher is to "transmit" knowledge, and the job of the student is to receive and regurgitate it on demand. In fact, the real work of the student is often a passive routine, meeting expectations sufficiently to pass through the system. This traditional situation, organized, routine, controlled, and predictable, represents an unlikely environment for the creation of knowledge. Most current mathematics programs conceive of the learner as being a passive absorber of information, one who stores in memory little pieces of information that are easily retrievable.

The teacher is primarily a manager of resources and personnel. Teachers are not encouraged to adapt or change to meet local needs or conditions. They are not encouraged to relate ideas of one lesson to another. Their task is to get students to complete pages or do sets of exercises, making little effort to establish relationships between ideas.

Finally, for most current programs, the *technology* includes a text, which is a repository of problem lists; a mass of paper-and-pencil worksheets; and a set of performance tests.

Furthermore, this picture must be seen as a product of the social, cultural, and economic conditions of the past century that were rooted in absolutist philosophies of mathematics and of the compromises that yielded a bland consensus curriculum. The current curriculum fails to reflect an authentic social constructivist view of mathematics.

Different Curriculum in Other Countries

American educators who have attended conferences at which mathematics programs of other countries are described, who have examined those countries' textbooks, who have visited their schools and mathematics classes, or who even have merely read excerpts about those countries' programs in *The International Encyclopaedia of Education: Research and Studies* (1985), *The IEA Study of Mathe-*

matics I: Analysis of Mathematics Curricula (Travers and Westbury 1989), or *National Curricula in Mathematics* (Howson 1991) are struck by the differences between what is taught and what is emphasized when compared with common practices in the United States. From my personal experience, when one visits a school, whether it be in Leningrad in the U.S.S.R., in Hobart in Australia, or in Merida in Venezuela, there is an immediate, institutional similarity. School buildings look like one another, with rooms and corridors; groups of children congregate in classrooms at desks facing one way; the teacher is in the front of the class directing work; rooms have blackboards and a bulletin board; students have books, paper, and pencils; and so forth. These surface features are familiar to all who have spent their professional lives in schools; they make one immediately comfortable. Furthermore, all industrialized countries have developed some form of a dual system. Students are sorted into those who are being prepared for university studies and those who are being prepared for trades (Freudenthal 1973). Although there are distinct differences in how this sorting is accomplished and in the final form of the groupings, differentiation of the mathematics curriculum for groups of students occurs in all countries. In addition, in all schools, mathematics is taught to all students as a separate subject according to a specific schedule.

However, beneath these surface similarities lurk profound differences. Unfortunately, the actual differences are hard to document, although a picture can be gleaned from three sources: comparative studies of mathematics achievement, studies that have compared mathematics curriculum outlines and textbooks, and reports given at conferences or following international visits.

Comparisons of Achievement. One way of comparing the curricula of different countries is to have educators and teachers judge the appropriateness of test items for their students and also to reflect on the performance of their students in light of those judgments. In this manner, the test items become a proxy for the curriculum. In 1964, 12 nations administered a common achievement test in mathematics (Husen 1967). This was the first international comparison involving several countries of student achievement in any discipline. In organizing the study, the international committee drafted an outline of topics that might be covered in a mathematics curriculum. This topical outline was sent to the national centers with instructions to judge whether the topic was covered in that country. The results made it very clear that topical coverage varied dramatically across countries (Husen 1967). The committee also added to the final test an item that required all teachers to rate whether the students had had the opportunity to learn each item of the test. One conclusion of the study was that reported achievement was virtually synonymous with coverage across countries.

A second international study of mathematics achievement was conducted in 1981 and 1982 in 20 countries (14 industrialized and 6 emerging nations) (Robitaille and Garden 1989). In preparing the tests again, each nation was asked to judge the validity of the items for its curriculum. Travers and Westbury (1989) reported the difficulties in making coherent judgments because of the lack of similarity of content coverage. Information was collected for each item from each country, both from experts at the National Centers, as an indication of the intended curriculum, and from teachers, as an indication of the implemented curriculum. Thus, this approach captured big differences between national curricula (e.g., whether calculus or statistics is included). However, it was not designed to capture subtle, but important, differences. For example, the extent of the use of realistic problems in the teaching of a topic or of calculators could be determined only if such items were part of the pool. Since the format and matrix precluded the inclusion of such items, any such differences remain to be detected. Again, there was considerable variation in coverage across studies.

The difficulties in making comparisons between the mathematics curricula of different countries by examining test items is apparent. For example, in the United States, most students do not study algebra until grade 9, they do not study transformational geometry, and few study calculus in grade 12. On the other hand, statistics is part of the curriculum in Israel. The real problem with the test analysis approach of comparing mathematical curricula is evaluating the appropriateness of the items, the format in which they are presented, and in these studies, the content-by-behavior matrix used to create the items. In a report to the National Academy of Sciences on the validity of the tests for American students, I found that although there were many very valid items, the validity of the scales and subscales was questionable (Romberg 1985a).

More recently, in 1988, the Educational Testing Service administered to 13-year-old students from five countries and four Canadian provinces tests consisting of mathematics and science items selected from the 1986 U.S. National Assessment of Educational Progress (1988). Teachers also rated students' exposure to the concepts tested by the items. Again, there was considerable variability in the opportunity for students to learn the mathematics tested by many items.

One can only conclude from these studies that the mathematics curricula across the variety of countries included in these studies differ widely. The topics covered or emphasized vary. Furthermore, the variations are reflected in the differences in achievement. However, on a different plane the curricula in almost all countries still picture mathematics as a closed, formal system. The differences are in sequencing, amount of review, and so forth. Students are still expected to learn a formal set of concepts and procedures divorced from their history and their uses. There are two possible exceptions. The first is in the primary grades in Bulgaria where Penkov and Sendov (1987) reported that in an experimental program, mathematics lessons are integrated with all other subjects via investigations. The second is in the Netherlands (de Lange 1987) where there has been a serious attempt to teach mathematics as something one does to make sense of the world.

Differences in National Curriculum Outlines and Textbooks. A more detailed picture of the differences in coverage across countries can be gathered by comparing curriculum outlines and textbooks.

Although sample texts from many countries are available, only three studies were located in which any systematic comparison was actually made. The first was written in 1959 by Schutter and Spreckelmeyer and published by the Council for Basic Education. In this study, 23 American arithmetic textbooks were compared with 36 books from 21 European countries. Although their findings are now undoubtedly dated, it is interesting to note that the authors found that European schools spent more time on the study of arithmetic than American schools, gave students a wider variety of problem types, stressed mental computation, gave more challenging tasks, and began instruction on various topics as much as 2 years earlier. In fact, the pace of instruction made it possible for much of arithmetic instruction to be completed by the sixth grade, so that other mathematical topics such as algebra and geometry could be introduced in grades 7 and 8.

In two more recent studies, Karen Fuson and her colleagues first compared U.S. and Soviet elementary textbooks in addition and subtraction word problems (Stigler, Fuson, Ham, and Kim 1986). Although very limited in scope, their findings indicate that in this comparison American textbooks appear to be haphazardly constructed, to be limited in coverage of the types of problems, to stress repetition rather than variation in problem types, and to contain fewer two-step problems. This same research group has also compared texts from Japan, China, the U.S.S.R., Taiwan, and the United States on the grade placement of addition and subtraction topics (Fuson, Stigler, and Bartsch 1988). Although limited to aspects of calculation, there was remarkable uniformity in grade placement except for the U.S. texts. In every case, the topics in the U.S. texts were covered 1 to 3 years later than others.

Finally, in the United States, there has been a growing interest in the "realistic" curriculum materials developed in the Netherlands. Hans Freudenthal's (1987) social constructivist plea that for children mathematics must be grounded in reality initiated the interest because it fit into the considerations of the reformers. This work was followed by Jan de Lange's (1987) description of the development and use of the *Hewet* project materials and the publication of some of the units in English. The structure and organization of these units, for example, *Shadow and Depth* (Goddijn 1980), is more like a story book than a typical text chapter. The implications of this approach to the American scene are, at present, not clear. However, a study by de Lange, van Reeuwijk, Burrill, and Romberg (in press), who prepared a realistic statistics unit that was then used in an American school in 1989, should provide evidence about the feasibility of such an approach in our schools.

Impressions from Conferences and Trips. The validity of the claims that the mathematical content covered and the methods of instruction used are different in other countries is bolstered by the numerous observations of scholars. Reports from international meetings are one important source. Examples include the summary reports of the meetings held by the International Congress on Mathematical Education, for example, at Berkeley in 1980 (Zweng et al. 1983), at Adelaide in 1984 (Carss 1986), and at Budapest in 1988 (Hirst and Hirst 1989). In each report, there are summaries of reports on a variety of issues, and the differences in practices are apparent in most summaries. Another example is the conference hosted in 1985 by the University of Chicago School Mathematics Project on Developments in School Mathematics Education Around the World (Wirszup and Streit 1985).

A second important source is reports prepared by American scholars after an extensive visit to a particular country. Two good examples are *An Analysis of Mathematics Education in the Union of Soviet Socialist Republics* (Davis, Romberg, Rachlin, and Kantowski 1979) and *Mathematics Education in Japan* (Becker 1989). Each report details, from an American perspective, the structure of the curriculum, the professional lives of teachers, preservice and in-service education, and other issues regarding mathematics education in the two countries.

Thus, although the picture about the real differences in what and how mathematics is taught in other countries is somewhat clouded because of the few scholarly comparative studies, all the evidence indicates that what is done in American schools is different. We spend less time teaching mathematics, emphasize paper-and-pencil routines, segment and sequence topics differently, and so forth.

Summary

The school mathematics curriculum in the United States is a coherent system that has evolved as a consequence of the restructuring of education in response to the pressures of the Industrial Revolution. What is taught reflects an absolutist perspective about mathematics, the goals of the dual educational system of that era, and the compromises made in an attempt to accommodate the conflicting views of educational reformers. Also, the curriculum is a product of our society. It differs in significant ways from the mathematics programs in other countries. The question currently being faced is whether or not the system of schooling in this country and the mathematics curriculum are still functional.

WHAT IS AN AUTHENTIC MATHEMATICS CURRICULUM?

The problem being faced by schools today is that during the past decade there has been a radical shift in what the mathematical sciences community considers to be "authentic" academic mathematical goals for students. The term "authentic" is used here as a label for a curriculum based on a social constructivist philosophy of mathematics. Thus, the shift is from a consistent absolutist perspective about mathematics to a social constructivist perspective. In one sense, the shift in emphasis is not new, because many of the aspects of the reform movement have been proposed since the formalization of school mathematics. However, what is new is the growing consensus on new mathematical goals for all students based on social constructivist notions. The dilemma now being addressed is that these goals cannot be achieved by the current absolutist curriculum and instructional practices in most schools.

To articulate the import of this dilemma and the problems now being posed, it is important first to address the need for schools to respond to a new social order. Then a brief outline of the features of the consensual vision of an authentic school mathematics curriculum is presented. Finally, five problems that must be faced in developing and implementing such a curriculum are discussed.

The Need for a New, Authentic Mathematics Curriculum

Americans have long believed that no other people ever demanded so much of their schools nor were so well served by their schools and educators. Unfortunately, as Colin Greer (1972) has argued, this legend is not now true nor has it ever been true for most Americans. To serve society well, schools and school mathematics must be redesigned to reflect a different social order. Upheavals in industry and the economy have spurred public awareness that we are moving into a new industrial age, variously called "the information age" (D. Bell 1973; Naisbitt 1982; Toffler 1985), "the postindustrial age" (D. Bell 1973), or "the super-industrial age" (Toffler 1985). Integration of the telephone, television, and computer now permits nearly instant transfer of information among people anywhere in the world. This factor, in combination with the exponential growth of knowledge, particularly in the mathematical sciences, is at the heart of this revolution, whose impact promises to be as dramatic as the shift from an agrarian society in the 1800s to an industrial society in the 20th century. Economically, the consequences of the revolution are only now being realized as market rivalries evolve from within-country to between-country competition. American auto manufacturing is a case in point: Today, individual manufacturers compete not only with their American counterparts but also with manufacturers from a variety of countries (e.g., Japan, Germany, Korea, and Yugoslavia) in a world market. Jennings (1987) has recently argued that this economic competitiveness represents "the Sputnik of the 80s" in educational reform.

Like urbanization, which is defined as a population shift that brought more than 50 percent of Americans to urban areas, identification of a predominantly information-based economy usually is linked to the time at which more than 50 percent of the population was earning its living through the sensible linking and exchanging of information. In the United States, this shift occurred in 1985 (Toffler 1985). The validity of this statistical definition is open to question; the concept is not (Naisbitt 1982).

The works of several authors (Naisbitt 1982; Provenzo 1986; Shane and Tabler 1981; Toffler 1985; Yevennes 1985) suggest the attributes of the new age. Naisbitt's key points characterize the shift to an information society:

1. It is an economic reality, not merely an intellectual abstraction.
2. The pace of change will be accelerated by continued innovation in communications and computer technology.
3. New technologies, which will be applied first to traditional industrial tasks, will soon generate new processes and products.
4. Basic communication skills will become more important than ever before, necessitating a literacy-intensive society.
5. Concurrent with the move from an industrial society to a society based on information is awareness of the change from a national economy to a global economy.

Information has value only if it can be controlled and organized for a purpose. To tap the power of computers, it is obligatory first to communicate efficiently and effectively, to be both literate and numerate. In addition, in an environment of accelerating change, the approach of training for a lifetime occupation must be replaced by learning power, which also depends on the abilities to understand and to communicate. This change is accompanied by the perception that the United States and other advanced societies of the West are losing their industrial supremacy. Mass production is more cheaply accomplished in the less developed parts of the world. Toffler (1985) envisioned the change as a series of waves, in much the same framework as Frederick Jackson Turner characterized the westward movement of the frontier in North America. Thus, just as industrial society replaced agrarian society and then began to push out, so the new postindustrial age will replace industrial society in the West and gradually expand.

The Mathematical Sciences Education Board (1990b) has summarized the impact of these changing conditions for school mathematics in terms of six points. First, as the economy adapts to information-age needs, workers in every sector—from hotel clerks to secretaries, from automobile mechanics to travel agents—must learn to interpret intelligent, computer-controlled processes. Most jobs now require analytical rather than merely mechanical skills, so most students need more mathematics in school as preparation for routine jobs. Similarly, the extensive use of graphical, financial, and statistical data in daily newspapers and in public policy discussions suggests a higher standard of quantitative literacy for the necessary duties of citizenship.

Second, in the past quarter of a century, significant changes have occurred in the nature of mathematics and the way it is used. In part, it is because of the nature and rapidity of these changes that the social constructivist philosophy of mathematics has emerged. Not only has much new mathematics been discovered but also the types and variety of problems to which mathematics is applied have grown at an unprecedented rate. Most visible, of course, has been the development of computers and the explosive growth of computer applications. Most of these applications have required the development of new mathematics in areas infeasible before the advent of computers (Howson and Kahane 1986).

Third, computers and calculators have changed the world of mathematics profoundly. They have affected not only what mathematics is important but also how mathematics is done (Rheinboldt 1985). It is now possible to execute almost all of the mathematical techniques taught from kindergarten through the first 2 years of college on hand-held calculators. This fact alone must have significant effects on the mathematics curriculum (Pea 1987). Although most developments at the forefront of a discipline cannot generally be expected to have a major effect on the early years of education, the changes in mathematics brought about by computers and calculators are so profound as to require readjustment in the balance and approach to virtually every topic in school mathematics. What is now being argued is that the emphasis must be on the social nature of mathematics.

Fourth, as mathematics has changed, so has American society. The changing demographics of the country and the changing demands of the workplace are not reflected in similar changes in school mathematics (MSEB 1989). In the early years of the next century, when today's school children will enter the work force, most jobs will require greater mathematical skills (Johnston and Packer 1987). At the same time, white males—the traditional base of mathematically trained workers in the United States—will represent a significantly smaller fraction of new workers (Oaxaca and Reynolds 1988). Society's need for an approach to mathematics education that ensures achievement across the demographic spectrum is both compelling and urgent.

Fifth, learning is not a process of passively absorbing information and storing it in easily retrievable fragments as a result of repeated practice and reinforcement. Instead, students approach each new task with some prior knowledge, assimilate new information, and construct their own meanings (Resnick 1987). Furthermore, ideas are not isolated in memory but are organized and associated with the natural language that one uses and the situations one has encountered in the past. This constructive, active view of learning is obviously consistent with the social or cultural view of mathematics and must be reflected in the way mathematics is taught.

And sixth, just as recognition of the global economy is emerging as a dominant force in American society, many recent reports have shown that U.S. students do not measure up in their mathematical accomplishments to students in other countries (e.g., Lapointe, Mead, and Phillips 1989; McKnight et al. 1987; Stevenson, Lee, and Stigler 1986; Stigler and Perry 1988). The implications of such data for employers is that the American work force will not be competitive with workers from other countries.

These points make the argument that a complete redesign of the content of school mathematics and the way it is taught is urgent. Unfortunately, schools and the mathematics taught in their classrooms are products of the past industrial age. The vision in this section describes an authentic curriculum—based on a social constructivist philosophy—in which students have an opportunity to learn the practical mathematical concepts and skills needed for everyday life, for intelligent citizenship, for vocations, and for human culture in an age centered on information rather than on industrialization. As Michael Apple (1979) has argued, what we now need is

> To hold our day-to-day activities as educators up to political and economic scrutiny, to see the school as part of a system of mechanisms for cultural and economic reproduction. . . . [T]he kinds of critical scrutiny I have argued for challenges a whole assemblage of values and actions "outside" of the institution of schooling. And this is exactly the point, for if taken seriously, it must lead to a set of commitments that may be wholly different than those many of us commonsensically accept. It requires the progressive articulation of and commitment to a [different] social order. (11)

Features of an Authentic School Mathematics Curriculum

During the past quarter century, the mathematical sciences education community has been struggling to redefine school mathematics and outline the features of a curriculum that would reflect societal needs. To summarize this effort, goals, knowledge, the work of teachers and students, and a technology for this vision are outlined.

Goal Statements. Three sets of goal statements have been chosen to reflect the thinking of the mathematical community. The first set of goals was written in 1965 by the mathematician R. Creighton Buck. He was trying to respond to the question, "Aside from its technological importance, what are the educational values of mathematics?" His answer was stated in terms of goals, as follows:

> Goal 1: To provide understanding of the interaction between mathematics and reality.
> Goal 2: To convey the fact that mathematics, like everything else, is built on intuitive understandings and agreed conventions, and that these are not eternally fixed.
> Goal 3: To demonstrate that mathematics is a human activity and that its history is marked by inventions, discoveries, guesses, both good and bad, and that the frontier of its growth is covered by interesting unanswered problems.
> Goal 4: To contrast "argument by authority" and "argument by evidence and proof"; to explain the difference between "not proved" and "disproved," and between a constructive proof and a nonconstructive proof.
> Goal 5: To demonstrate that the question "Why?" is important to ask, and that in mathematics, an answer is not always supplied by merely giving a detailed proof.
> Goal 6: To show that complex things are sometimes simple, and that simple things are sometimes complex; and that, in mathematics as well as in other fields, it pays to subject a familiar thing to detailed study, and to study something that seems hopelessly intricate. (949–955)

By stating and illustrating these goals, he hoped that educators would see that "mathematics need be neither austere nor remote, that it has relevance for almost all human activities, and that it can be of value to any sincerely interested person" (956). Although this tentative but socially constructive set of goals was prepared as a response to those advocating a formal school mathematics curriculum during the 1960s, they foreshadow the more aggressive goals of the current decade.

The second set of goals was stated by the British Committee of Inquiry into the Teaching of Mathematics in Schools in 1982. The committee's report, *Mathematics Counts* (popularly known as the Cockcroft report), lists four goals stated as responsibilities of the teacher:

- [E]nabling each pupil to develop, within his [and her] capabilities, the mathematical skills and understanding required for adult life, for employment and for further study and training, while remaining aware of the difficulties which some pupils will experience in trying to gain such an appropriate understanding.
- [P]roviding each pupil with such mathematics as may be needed for his study of other subjects.
- [H]elping each pupil to develop so far as is possible his appreciation and enjoyment of mathematics itself and his realisation of the role which it has played and will continue to play both in the development of science and technology and of our civilisation.
- [A]bove all, making each pupil aware that mathematics provides him with a powerful means of communication. (4)

The third set of goals was prepared by the Commission on Standards for School Mathematics of the National Council of Teachers of Mathematics in 1989. Its report, *Curriculum and Evaluation Standards for School Mathematics*, lists nine goals: four societal goals and five goals for students.

The four general social goals for education in the area of mathematics are:

1. *Mathematically literate workers*. The technologically demanding workplace of today and the future will require mathematical understanding and the ability to formulate and solve complex problems, often with others. "Businesses no longer seek workers with strong backs, clever hands, and 'shopkeeper' arithmetic skills" (3).
2. *Lifelong learning*. Most workers will change jobs frequently and so need flexibility and problem-solving ability to enable them to "explore, create, accommodate to changed conditions, and actively create new knowledge over the course of their lives" (4).
3. *Opportunity for all*. Because mathematics has become "a critical filter for employment and full participation in our society" (4), it must be made accessible to all students, not just the white males, the group that currently studies the most advanced mathematics.
4. *An informed electorate*. Because of the increasingly technical and complex nature of current issues, participation by citizens requires technical knowledge and understanding, especially skills in reading and interpreting complex information.

These social goals require students to become "mathematically powerful," a key phrase used by the NCTM authors to describe desired outcomes of schooling. "Mathematical power . . . denotes an individual's abilities to explore, conjecture, and reason logically, as well as the ability to use a variety of mathematical methods effectively to solve nonroutine problems" (5). The authors emphasize that mathematical literacy includes much more than familiarity with numbers and arithmetic: "To cope confidently with the demands of today's society, one must be able to grasp the implications of many mathematical concepts—for example, chance, logic, and graphs—that permeate daily news and routine decisions" (7–8).

The NCTM authors articulate the notion of mathematical literacy by proposing five general goals for students:

1. *Learning to value mathematics*. Understanding its evolution and its role in society and the sciences.
2. *Becoming confident of one's own ability*. Coming to trust one's own mathematical thinking and having the ability to make sense of situations and solve problems.
3. *Becoming a mathematical problem solver*. This is essential to becoming a productive citizen and requires experience in solving a variety of extended and nonroutine problems.
4. *Learning to communicate mathematically*. Learning the signs, symbols, and terms of mathematics.
5. *Learning to reason mathematically*. Making conjectures, gathering evidence, and building mathematical arguments.

These goals imply that students should be exposed to numerous and varied interrelated experiences that encourage them to value the mathematical enterprise, to develop mathematical habits of mind, and to understand and appreciate the role of mathematics in human affairs; that they are encouraged to explore, to guess, and even to make errors so that they gain confidence in their ability to solve complex problems; that they read, write, and discuss mathematics; and that they conjecture, test, and build arguments about a conjecture's validity. . . . The opportunity for all students to experience these components of mathematical training is at the heart of our vision of a quality mathematics program. The curriculum should be permeated with these goals and experiences such that they become commonplace in the lives of students. (5)

These goals reflect a shift away from the traditional practice of summarizing desired mathematical outcomes as knowledge of *skills*, *concepts*, and *applications* to an emphasis on broader *dispositions*, *attitudes*, and *beliefs* about the nature of mathematical knowledge and about one's own mathematical thinking. The traditional skills, concepts, and applications are subsumed under the more general goals for problem solving and communication. Throughout the *Standards*, the authors deemphasize the view that knowledge consists of distinct parts that should be treated separately. Rather, they emphasize providing students with experiences through which they can build rich connections among the various kinds of knowledge. These three sets of goals all implicitly reflect a social constructivist philosophy of mathematics.

Knowledge. The content of school mathematics is of necessity restricted. This factor leads to the controversy discussed earlier, between mathematics as a science and mathematics as a school subject. To develop a curriculum, one needs to segment and sequence the mathematical ideas for instruction. Mathematical knowledge, in the current view, means learning to do mathematics rather than knowing about mathematics. Such knowledge is both personal and communal, in the sense that although it may originate with an individual, it is validated by the community. Thus, the process of adding to mathematical knowledge through communicating is an integral part of knowing mathematics.

To decide on what is fundamental in so vast and dynamic a discipline as mathematics is no easy task. Yet this decision must be made. In fact, what is being called for is covering fewer topics, each in more depth. The rationale for this assertion comes from many sources, the most important source being psychologists who have studied mathematical cognition (e.g., Greeno 1987; Vergnaud 1983). Their premise is that the power of mathematics lies in the fact that a small number of symbols and symbolic statements can be used to represent a vast array of different problems. The identification and use of symbols can be organized into domains, which include the symbolic statements that characterize the domain; the implied tasks to be carried out; the rules that are to be followed to represent, transform, and carry out procedures; and the set of situations that commonly have been used to make the symbols, the relationships between symbols, and the rules meaningful (Romberg 1988b). For example, learning to measure basically involves procedures for assigning numbers to continuous attributes (properties of the attribute, choice of unit, iteration, precision and error, and instrumentation). Thus, rather than teaching students to measure length, weight, area, volume, time, and so on, as separate topics in the curriculum, what is being argued is to teach the process of measuring with one attribute, such as length, and then extend the process to other attributes as needed.

In the NCTM *Standards* (1989), most of the content is still on familiar topics. However, they are approached with a different emphasis because the issue is not solely that of what mathematical content should be included but also what it means for students to know that content and how they come to know it. The distinction between the constructivist notion of "doing" and the absolutist notion of "knowledge about" perhaps can be made clear by an analogy with other things people do (such as play basketball, fly a plane, or learn to play a musical instrument). For example, music, like mathematics, has numerous branches categorized in a variety of ways (classical, jazz, rock; instrumental or vocal); it has a sparse notational system for preserving information (notes, time signatures, and clefs) and theories that describe the structure of compositions (scales and patterns). However, no matter how many of the artifacts of music one has learned, it is not the same as "doing" music. It is only when one performs that one knows music. Similarly, in mathematics, one can learn the concepts about numbers, how to solve equations, and so on, but that is not "doing" mathematics. Doing mathematics involves solving problems, building mathematical models, abstracting, inventing, proving, and so forth.

Obviously, it is important to learn some mathematical concepts and practice some procedures so that one becomes a reasonably skilled performer (as learning to read musical notation and practice scales), but it is also important for all students to have an opportunity to solve problems (perform) at their level of capability. Too often, students find arithmetic, algebra, and sometimes calculus to be senseless, dull, and even intimidating. After all, who can enjoy routinely multiplying one 4-digit number by another or solving a system of simultaneous linear equations (analogous to playing scales on a piano forever)? As a result of such limited experiences, many students are prejudiced against the broader, more interesting aspects of mathematics. The objective, then, is to develop sequences of activities that should both interest students and give them an opportunity to develop "mathematical power."

The Work of Students and Teachers. Since the goals of schools are directed toward student learning, the role of the teacher should complement that of the student rather than vice versa. Unfortunately, when knowledge is regarded as knowing about rather than doing, the vocabulary reflects a reversal of emphasis.

The activities that need to be created should reflect the fact that learning does not need to occur through passive reflection. Instead, psychological research indicates that individuals approach each new task with prior knowledge. They assimilate new information and construct their own meanings. Ideas are not isolated in memory but are organized in collections in what Anderson (1983) has called "loosely structured schemas." Such schemas are associated with the natural language that one uses and the situations that one has encountered in the past. This constructive notion of learning must be reflected in the new instructional programs.

Briefly, then, the new program should expect students to be active and should constantly extend the structure of the mathematics that they know by having them make, test, and validate conjectures. As long as students are making the conjectures, their mathematical knowledge will always be structured, consciously or unconsciously, because conjecture cannot be created from nothing.

Verbal and written communication is a crucial part of the process for several reasons. First, communication in the form of logical argument is central to mathematical discourse. Second, communication is the means whereby personal knowledge is systematized into a domain and, thus, accepted as new knowledge (Rescher 1979). Third, developing competence in the categories and structures of the language system both structures the child's understanding and advances it toward a public mode of consciousness (Russell 1978). Clearly, the work of students should no longer be a matter of acting within somebody else's structures, answering somebody's else's questions, and waiting for the teacher to check the response. Nor should it be a matter of evaluating knowledge according to right or wrong answers. In the creation of knowledge, there are only that which fits the structure of mathematical knowledge already created by the student and that which does not and should, therefore, prompt conjecture.

The work of teachers is to support, promote, encourage, and in every way facilitate the creation of knowledge by students. Furthermore, they must create a collaborative learning environment in which the students can explore and investigate problems. Thus, they must guide, listen, discuss, prompt, question, and clarify the work of students. To do this, they must orchestrate appropriate and interesting activities as they attend to each student's needs. The National Council of Teachers of Mathematics has recently published *Professional Standards for Teaching Mathematics* (1991), in which an image of teaching in the manner implied has been detailed. This image sees teachers as being proficient in:

- selecting mathematical tasks to engage students' interests and intellect;
- providing opportunities to deepen their understanding of the mathematics being studied and its applications;
- orchestrating classroom discourse in ways that promote the investigation and growth of mathematical ideas;
- using, and helping students use, technology and other tools to pursue mathematical investigations;
- seeking, and helping students seek, connections to previous and developing knowledge;
- guiding individual, small-group, and whole-class work.

Technology. Rather than providing paper-and-pencil activities for students to do independently at desks, some activities should involve group problem solving. The technology used in problem solving may include video recordings, calculators, and computers as tools for students. Evaluation should involve judgments by students and their teachers of the coherence of presentations, the reasoning given, and so on.

In summary, there is general agreement within the mathematical sciences education community on the goals of the reform movement and on a vision of the curriculum that is needed. The belief that there is widespread agreement is based on the discussions, recommendations, and activities of several professional groups during the past decade. In fact, Henry Pollak (1986) commented, when concluding an MSEB conference on reform in school mathematics, "One of the first points that struck me . . . was the degree of agreement about mathematics education the outside world perceives in the mathematics education community" (1).

The argument is that a new school mathematics program must be based on a vision of the mathematics all students should have an opportunity to learn and of the way in which instruction should occur. Classrooms should be places where interesting problems are explored through important mathematical ideas. For example, in various classrooms, one could expect to see students recording measurements of real objects, collecting information and describing the properties of objects by using statistics, or exploring the properties of a function by examining its graph. According to this vision, students will study much of the same mathematics currently taught but with quite a different emphasis.

Given this agreement and vision, the question to be raised is, Is it possible that a school mathematics program can be developed and implemented that reflects this vision? To respond to this question, one must understand the challenge to current practice being advocated.

Attempts to change schooling practices must be viewed as natural. The impetus for change comes from personal, professional, community, and other social sources. Educational programs that respond to the reform movement in school mathematics need to be developed and implemented. However, the successful implementation of such programs will not just happen. Many scholars have studied the implementation process. For example, Romberg and Price (1983) have analyzed innovation in terms of its effect on school life. As described earlier, this study is based on the need to consider the culture of schools. An adopted program is not necessarily a used program, for it is rarely assimilated into the school in the manner intended by the developer.

The difficulty of implementing a particular innovation depends on many factors, ranging from the characteristics of the innovation itself to the structure of the culture affected by the change (see Chapter 15, "Curriculum Implementation" by Snyder, Bolin, and Zumwalt, in this *Handbook*). McClelland (1968) discusses how effective implementation may involve different levels of cultural restructuring. The simplest level is the substitution of one isolated component of a system for another, such as a change in the textbook. If this simplest of changes causes further systemic alterations, such as the purchase of manipulative materials for the classroom, a higher level of change is involved. The most complex of all changes deals with values, such as asking teachers to value an active classroom over a quiet one.

This way of characterizing innovations focuses on the degree of restructuring they involve. Romberg and Price (1983) labeled the poles of this dimension "ameliorative innovation" and "radical innovation." Ameliorative innovations are designed (or perceived as designed) to make some ongoing schooling practice better or more efficient, but they do not challenge the traditions associated with the school culture. At the other extreme, radical innovations are designed and perceived as challenging the cultural traditions of the school.

Given this definition and the earlier description of the goals of the reform movement, it should be apparent that what the mathematical sciences education community is calling for is radical change. Four challenges to the current culture of school mathematics seem apparent.

First, as pointed out earlier, the expectations that "all students will study considerably more and somewhat different mathematics" involve quite a different set of goals. Damerow and Westbury (1985) make it clear that however laudable these expectations may be, they challenge the accepted position of mathematics courses in the current programs of schools. What is being proposed is significantly different from current practice.

Second, the notion that students should learn to do mathematics so that all students see that "mathematics makes sense" is quite different. Mathematics should make sense to them, and they can use it to make sense of the world. Michael Young (1971) has characterized schools as institutions that distribute and maintain certain types of knowledge. He argues that the relationship between teachers and students is essentially a reality-sharing, worldview-building enterprise. As teachers and students interact, they develop a shared vocabulary and shared ways of reasoning, which give sense to one another's actions and provide a framework applicable to future experiences. This shared understanding is based on an implicit value structure that defines "being educated." The most important change expected from the reform movement involves change in the knowledge distributed by schools.

Third, to have teachers and students engaging in the kind of sense-making enterprise envisioned, a different kind of discourse community will need to be developed (NCTM 1991). The assumption being made is that it can be accomplished by creating a set of problems (activities) that can be periodically worked on by groups of students in a manner similar to that employed by mathematicians.

Fourth, the technological environment in which such work by both students and teachers will need to be done is different. The vision of students working in groups, collecting data, using calculators and computers, and so forth is quite different from the classroom of desks neatly arranged in rows, with quiet students working alone on collections of exercises with paper and pencil (Young 1971, 251).

> The change strategy for responding to these four challenges that is being advocated by NCTM (1989) is based on professional development rather than administrative directives. Professional development implies the direct involvement of professional organizations and their members. The vision of the mathematics curriculum and the goals in the *Standards* are offered by NCTM without a prescription for achieving them. The approach taken is one that will empower teachers and other educators, through their professional organizations, to make the changes. (251)

Given this set of challenges to current traditions of school mathematics, a number of questions could be raised. However, I have chosen to examine four specific questions about the possibility of radical change, the reasonableness of finding "real" activities to employ in the classroom, the feasibility of getting teachers to teach such activities, and finally whether or not a theory can be developed.

Is Radical Change Possible?

Although any change is possible, this question has been raised because, in the United States, education has been characterized by massive efforts, sponsored by foundations or the federal government, to engineer and implement such changes as team teaching, programmed learning, individualized curriculum programs, or open multi-graded schools. But as Bellack and Kliebard (1977), the Conference Board of the Mathematical Sciences (1975), and Goodlad (1976) have argued, it has been very difficult to find evidence that what teachers and pupils do in schools has significantly changed. Goodlad, in his review of several attempts to change teaching practices, concluded that schools are very stable institutions inherently resistant to such changes. Jeremy Kilpatrick (1989), describing some of the reasons for such resistance, argues that schools operate within a system of rules that are often invisible but heavily constrain teaching.

> Various laws and administrative regulations operate to insure that the power structure in schools reflects the dominant social ideology. The system of rules concerns the allocation and organization of time, instructional materials, assessment procedures, and human resources, all of which enable education to occur in a socially acceptable way. The teacher is not free to defy these rules with impunity.
>
> Traditional views of what instruction is and how it should be managed are deeply rooted and serve as stronger barriers to change than most reformers are prepared to acknowledge. In our "scholastic inheritance" (Cohen 1988), academic knowledge consists of facts established by authority, not ideas constructed by students or teachers. The teacher's job is knowledge transmission. The source of the teacher's authority is her or his access to legitimate knowledge. The student's job is to accumulate a store of the knowledge passed on by the teacher; learners are neither mature enough nor authoritative enough to construct their own valid knowledge. These views are widespread not only outside the school among parents and other citizens but inside the school as well as among teachers, administrators, and students. (2)

Furthermore, the reform movement in school mathematics is not congruent with the notions about school reform held by many educational policymakers. Too often, innovators fail to consider the persons who are involved. Coming from a "top-down" management perspective, many policymakers assume that reforms must be geared to making the current system more efficient and/or more effective (Carnoy and Levin 1976). Thus, increased course requirements for graduation, rising test scores, and higher percentages of students demonstrating minimal competency are seen as goals. Challenges to the traditions of schooling fail to meet the expectation of too many administrators, who assume that any challenge will affect only discrete decisions (Cohen and Garet 1975). As argued earlier, this would then produce only "ameliorative" change. This is not to imply that discrete changes are not warranted; they often need to be made. Again, the danger is that they may perpetuate practices that are no longer warranted. If radical change is needed, the sources of current traditions must be identified and challenged directly.

Finally, when presenting challenges to long-held traditions, one must be ready for what Eugene Provenzo (1986) calls a "neo-Luddite" reaction. The workers who destroyed machines during the early phases of the Industrial Revolution in England were called Luddites (after the pseudonym "Ned Ludd" used by the protestors). Provenzo argues that there will always be a group of reactors to any proposed change who will be united only in their opposition.

Taken together, the evidence is that schools are complex social institutions that are not easily altered. The faltering implementation of an innovation into school culture can be examined in terms of its effects on the knowledge dispensed, the work of teachers and children, the technology used, and the professional position of teachers. Institutional resistance to innovation can also be better understood by considering the perspectives held by the persons involved. Their perspectives are important because they govern the way innovations are ultimately used. Innovations are introduced into social situations in which people have beliefs, hopes, desires, and interests and into institutional contexts that structure actions. The net effect of an innovation can easily be a surface change consistent with existing values and assumptions. Innovations tend to be assimilated into existing patterns of behavior and belief, frequently coming to function as little more than slogan systems that legitimize the values and assumptions underlying the status quo.

In summary, although reformers are confident that change is possible, it will not be easy. Reformers must be cognizant of the barriers that need to be acknowledged and challenged.

Can "Real" Activities Be Found or Created?

One of the assumptions in the NCTM *Standards* (1989) is that "students need to experience genuine problems regularly" (10). In fact, "instruction should be developed from problem situations" (11). There are two parts to this assumption: first, that work on such problems will enhance learning and, second, that suitable activities will be found or created that will "connect ideas and procedures both among different mathematical topics and with other content areas" (11). The first part of this assumption seems warranted; the second is more problematic.

Learning by active participation implies that a mathematics program must be a program of activities from which knowledge or skills can be developed. However, simply developing a collection of interesting activities is not sufficient. The knowledge gained must lead somewhere. Thus, what is constructed by any individual depends to some extent on what is brought to the situation, where the current *activity* fits in a sequence leading toward a goal, and how it relates to mathematical knowledge. The suitability and effectiveness of selected learning activities are, therefore, empirical problems. They depend on both the student's prior knowledge and the student's expectations. Because these factors can be determined only by teachers, curriculum development cannot be an exact science. The "intended" curriculum can only include one's best guesses about what will both interest students and lead them all toward the development of mathematical power. At the same time, the "actual" curriculum depends on teacher choice, and the "achieved" curriculum depends on each student's interests and prior knowledge.

The potential utility of any curricular activity can be determined with respect to two criteria. First, it must reflect the intended mathematical objects and, second, it should reflect what we know about student learning.

Psychologists claim that knowledge about related concepts, skills, and contexts is organized in a student's memory in "schema." These schema develop over long periods of time and by continual exposure to related contextual events. Their development promotes both problem-solving skill and recall of textual material. James Greeno (1991) has argued that students develop schema with respect to specific mathematical domains where a

> domain may be thought of as an environment, with resources at various places in the domain. In this metaphor, knowing is knowing your way around in the environment and knowing how to use its resources. This includes knowing what resources are available in the environment as well as being able to find and use those resources for understanding and reasoning. Knowing includes interaction with the environment in its own terms—exploring the territory, appreciating its scenery, and understanding how its various components interact. Knowing the domain also includes knowing what resources are in the environment that can be used to support your individual and social activities and the ability to recognize, find, and use those resources productively. Learning the domain, in this view, is analogous to learning to live in an environment: learning your way around, learning what resources are available, and learning how to use those resources in conducting your activities productively and enjoyably. (175)

It is important to know what knowledge students bring to such activities. It is also argued that the encoding, comprehension, and retrieval of new information are aided when material is presented in a form that has structure and when the student is cognizant of that structure. In particular, these processes are facilitated when the information can be assimilated into an existing schema of the learner. Thus, when information is presented in a familiar contextual setting, the transitions and the concepts and procedures are likely to be remembered. Psychologists call this a generic story shell for the schema. They also claim that although students appear to make use of cause-effect relations in encoding information from problems, they have difficulty with conditions regulating the use of specific mathematical procedures. Failure to recognize these conditions often results in the development of buggy algorithms. For example, students who say that 43 – 17 = 34 have overgeneralized the statement "always take the smaller number from the larger" so that "3 from 7 is 4" and "10 from 40 is 30."

Next, it is believed that problem-solving ability and encoding of information are enhanced when schema are interrelated and form a hierarchical arrangement analogous to the way knowledge is used. For example, if multiplication is often used to solve proportion problems, the relationship between multiplication as repeated addition and proportion needs to be carefully developed and connected. Finally, some scholars liken the process of conceptual change in individuals to that of the scientific community and draw on recent developments in the philosophy of science to gain insight into conceptual change. For the radical reorganization of central concepts to occur, it is claimed that specific conditions must be met. There must be some sense of dissatisfaction with the existing conceptual framework; there must be alternate conceptions that are both intelligible and initially plausible; and the alternate conception must be seen as fruitful, useful, or valuable. In fact, Nussbaum and Novick (1982) suggest a three-part instructional sequence designed to encourage students to make desired conceptual changes. They propose the use of an *exposing event*, which encourages students to use and explore their own conceptions in an effort to understand it. This event is followed by a *discrepant event*, which serves as an anomaly and produces cognitive conflict. It is hoped that it will lead the students to a state of dissatisfaction with current conceptions. A period of *resolution* follows, in which the alternative conceptions are made plausible and intelligible to students and they are encouraged to make the desired conceptual shift.

These psychological views are important because mathematical knowledge must develop simultaneously in two distinct dimensions. The first is a symbolic dimension and includes the signs, symbols, and rules for the use of these symbols in specific mathematical domains. The second is the set of problem situations for which those symbols are used and give meaning. Jan de Lange (1987) portrayed the curriculum engineering problem in a manner shown in Figure 27–2. The first illustration shows the development of a mathematical domain in most traditional programs. The domain is first introduced through some problems; then most of the time is spent on mastering the use of the symbols, with an occasional applied activity. The second illustration portrays an activity program that is rich in a variety of things for students to do but never has the students step back from the situations to develop the connections, symbols, and rules for the domain in a coherent manner. Ideally, what is being advocated is a program that does both, as in the third illustration.

Jan de Lange's (1987) engineering problem, as illustrated in Figure 27–2, highlights the second problematic feature of this assumption. Although there is no doubt that many interesting activities exist or can be created, "Do they lead anywhere?" is a serious question. An activity approach could lead to "no mathematics at all." Christine Keitel (1987) has argued that the problem is one of relevance. Too often a problem is judged to be relevant through the eyes of adults, not children. Also, this perception is undoubtedly a Western, middle-class, static vision. Concrete situations, by themselves, do not guarantee that students will see relevance to their worlds; they may not be relevant for *all* students nor prepare them to deal with a changing, dynamic world.

In response to this concern, Ubriatan D'Ambrosio (1987) argues that the "emphasis should be shifted to 'really real' situations" (141). By this he means that projects of a global nature, "such as building a cabin, mapping a town or assessing the water consumption of a community" (141), should be taught since they require modeling and problem solving. However, Herbert Greenberg (1987) states, "It is hard for me to imagine that the system of mathematics education advocated by D'Ambrosio, ideal though it might be, could ever 'prepare our young for the future advancement and betterment of the socio-economic and political framework of society'" (217). His skepticism comes from his answer to the question, "Aren't we talking about the same teachers, the same students, the same schools and the same society that are today failing in mathematics?" (219). He assumes these are the people and institutions that must develop and implement this kind of program, and he can envision only failure leading to more failure. In essence, to paraphrase Damerow and Westbury (1985) again, there may be a need to change the contents and conditions of the school mathematics curriculum so that all students can study more and somewhat different mathematics, but how to do this is totally elusive.

Can Teachers Teach the Reform Curriculum?

In light of Greenberg's (1987) skepticism and because it seems apparent that change will occur only if teachers make it occur, this is an important question to address. Elsewhere

FIGURE 27–2. Three Types of Instruction Programs. (Adapted from de Lange 1987)

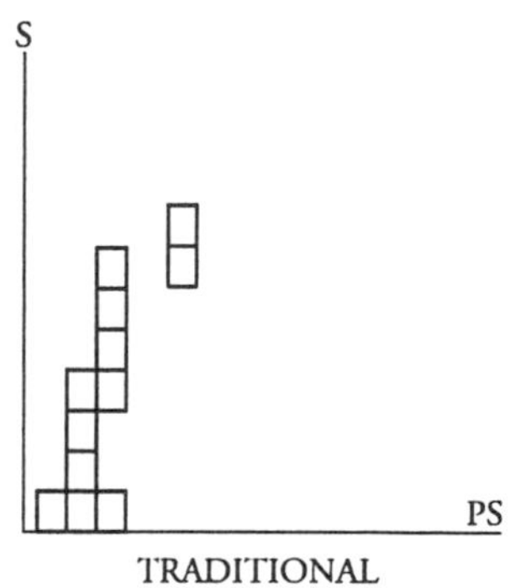

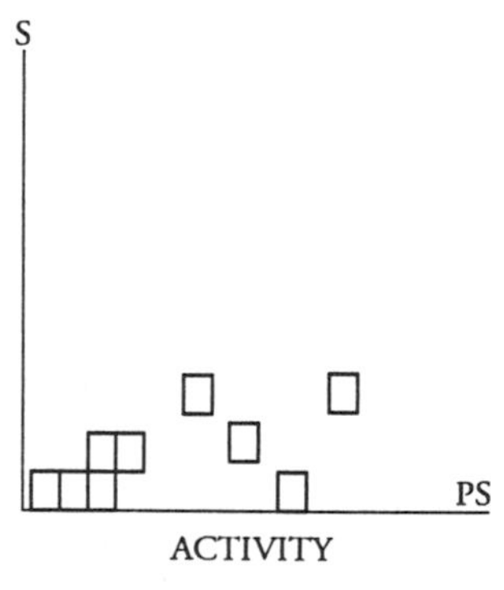

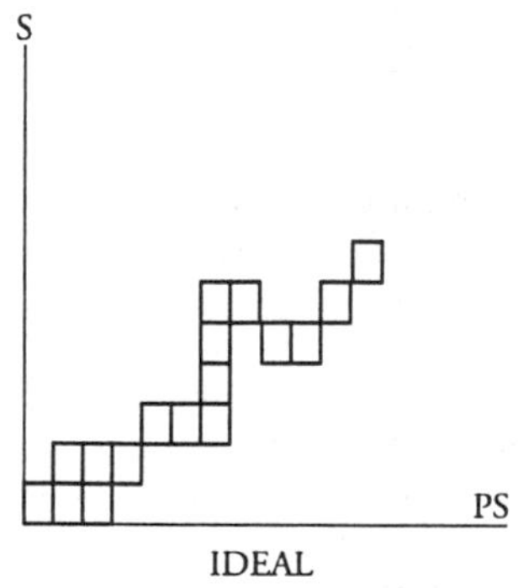

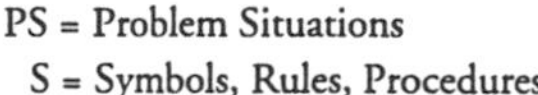

I have pointed out that the job of teaching in most schools "is to assign lessons to a class of students, start and stop lessons according to some schedule, explain the rules and procedures of each lesson, judge the actions of students during the lesson, and maintain order and control throughout" (Romberg 1985b, 5). In such situations, the teaching of mathematics becomes a procedural or managerial routine, often performed without care or reflection. In the context described, too many teachers feel obligated to cover the book and too few see student learning and the use of mathematics as the primary goal. Furthermore, many teachers have an inadequate academic background in mathematics and insufficient opportunity for sharing information with colleagues. Under these conditions,

> it is hard to argue that teaching is really a profession. The teacher's job is related neither to a conception of mathematical knowledge . . . nor to an understanding of how learning occurs, nor to knowing the likely outcomes of various instructional actions. [Thus,] research on learning and teaching has little relevance because the judgments and decisions being made are not about learning but about management. (5)

A typical assumption is that to improve teaching, one must improve teachers. In fact, Boyer (1986) states, "To improve the quality of education in the United States, we will need more 'outstanding new teachers in the years to come'" (xviii). An alternative view is that to improve teachers, one must improve teaching. This is to redefine the job of teaching.

Teachers, however, are not the sole answer to reform. The educational system in a society is the means whereby expectations, values, knowledge, and standards of behavior—the vehicles for the perpetuation of the society are instilled in the young. "Education isn't something that any *individual* does. Education is a *process*, an organic process that involves the complex, dynamic interaction of multiple components" (Futrell 1986, 6). Nevertheless, teachers are vital intermediaries in the process, and the current reform movement attaches great importance to the crucial role of teachers in the education of children. Society now needs teachers who are sufficiently independent in their thinking to adapt, innovate, and invent. Therefore, as Futrell has stated,

> restructuring teaching requires, before all else, reflection on the purpose of that reconstruction. . . . The imperative for reconstruction derives from the need to better prepare students to adapt and improvise successfully in the face of relentless change, and relentless . . . retreat from established orthodoxies. We must help students become mentally agile, emotionally resilient, and intellectually adventurous. We must help them to learn to be learners. (5)

The Holmes Group (1986) described the naive view of teaching as "'passing on' a substantive body of knowledge . . . 'planning, presenting, and keeping order.' . . . The teachers' responsibility basically ends when they have told students what they must remember to know and do" (27–28). This succinct, if simplistic, characterization described a perception of the role and work of teachers at the height of the industrial age; since then, values have changed, and, consequently, notions of effective teaching have also changed.

> Competent teachers are careful not to bore, confuse, or demean students, pushing them instead to interact with important knowledge and skill. Such teachers interpret the understandings students bring to and develop during lessons; they identify students' misconceptions, and question their surface responses that mask true learning. (Holmes Group 1986, 29)

The Holmes Group addressed the importance of the affective aspect of teaching, especially as it contributes to motivation and cognition as a secure context for the intellectual risk taking of conjecture.

Given the goal of long-term understanding in support of lifelong learning, a radically different but strongly supported picture of school mathematics teaching emerges. Succinctly, teaching for long-term learning and the development of knowledge structures requires teachers to create epistemic situations in which children can explore problems, create structures, generate questions, and reflect on patterns. It requires teachers with the academic and pedagogical knowledge to provide flexible approaches, encouraging informal and multiple representation while fostering the gradual growth of mathematical language. It requires teachers who can diagnose difficulties and devise questions to promote progress through cognitive conflict and teachers who, while having everything else expected of them, can maintain a collaborative atmosphere leading to students' increasing independence, careful reflection on strategies for cognitive motivation, and recognition of the epistemic, cognitive, and social commonalities of teaching and learning.

The intrinsic difficulties of mathematics and the problems created by neglecting meaning for notation—coupled with the demand for knowledge that will transfer to new situations—have made it essential to teach in such a way as to encourage long-term understanding based on well-founded knowledge structures. The capability to resume learning at any time to adapt to change requires a framework of support from which an understanding can be reconstructed, even though the details of its first introduction may have been forgotten (Bell and Purdy 1985). Such frameworks underlie both further understanding and the crucially important ability to transfer knowledge and strategies to new situations (Greeno 1983).

Reviewing the literature, Zarinnia, Lamon, and Romberg (1987) found a strong consensus that the following are intrinsic to teaching the construction of readily accessible mathematical knowledge structures capable of supporting further learning.

1. A didactic situation in which structures are developed or reinvented in the course of realistic involvement with phenomena. The situation serves as both a source of conceptual structures and a field of application.
2. Diversity of expression, using different representational notations, formal and informal, according to preference and purpose.

3. Dialogue, essential to the processes of knowledge construction and teaching and learning.
4. Diagnosis, a means to ascertain obstacles to learning and to plan tactics for teaching.
5. Devolution, deliberate transfer of control to the student.
6. Dissimilarity rather than homogeneity in the size and composition of student groupings.

Although a new description of the job of teaching is now emerging, a few researchers are working in school classrooms to explore instruction based on these assumptions about teaching and learning. That is, they are trying in various ways to bring these assumptions about knowing and learning mathematics into the classroom. In cognitively guided instruction, Carpenter, Fennema, and Peterson (1987) help first-grade teachers change their underlying views of learning. They do so by sharing their cognitive research with teachers on individual children's solving of addition and subtraction word problems. Cobb, Yackel, and Wood (1988) have worked with second-grade teachers to alter their teaching to be consistent with a constructivist view of learning. They began with the fundamental assumption that mathematics learning occurs as "individuals each construct *their* individual mathematical worlds by recognizing *their* experiences in an attempt to resolve *their* problems" (93).

In a classroom, Lampert (1988, 1990) is also exploring alternatives to pervasive views of knowing and learning mathematics, "in which doing mathematics means remembering and applying the correct rule when the teacher asks a question, and mathematical truth is determined when the answer is ratified by the teacher" (135). But rather than taking as her primary starting point a particular view of learning from psychological research on the individual learner, Lampert begins with assumptions about the nature of knowledge and knowledge growth within the discipline of mathematics. She argues, following Kramer (1970), that "in mathematics, authority comes from agreeing on shared assumptions and reasoning about their consequences" (Lampert 1988, 135). Thus, according to this view, the discourse in classrooms should be more like the discourse of argument and conjecturing that takes place within the discipline of mathematics, with a shift in authority of what constitutes valid mathematical knowledge from teacher decree to the sense-making and reasoning of the individual.

Martha Stone Wiske (1990) studied the experiences of a group of geometry teachers using *The Geometric Supposers* (Schwartz and Yerushalmy 1985, 1986, 1987). This is a software package that allows students to explore the properties of certain geometric figures, to make conjectures, and to have the computer verify or falsify those conjectures. What she found was that in order to use the new technology, teachers needed more traditional materials that connected the innovation with their accustomed curriculum and technologies. They needed problem sets to assign to students. As teachers became more experienced with the *Supposer*, they recognized a difference between "discovery" problems and "application" problems. Discovery problems were designed to lead students to discover a finding that played a central role in the teacher's agenda. Application problems were more open-ended; they allowed students to apply and consolidate knowledge they had already developed and build new knowledge in ways that teachers had not so clearly anticipated. These problems were often more fun for both teachers and students. Teachers found that their preferences for the balance in these two kinds of problems evolved over time and depended partly on their assessment of their students' ability.

In addition, teachers needed learning aids to help students organize their inquiry activities. For example, they needed to provide samples of data collection charts that helped students gradually learn the need for such displays to facilitate data analysis and the skills for developing their own. Teachers needed a repertoire of lesson plans organized into curricular units that build connections between *Supposer*-based empirical inquiry exercises and the logico-deductive structure of the text-based geometry that formed the backbone of their usual curriculum. These lesson plans were accompanied by teaching aids, such as diagrams and data display charts, that might be reproduced on overhead projection slides to facilitate whole-class presentations. Also, teachers needed assessment materials and exercises that enabled students to employ a range of tools, including the *Supposer*, to demonstrate their mastery of the broad curriculum described above.

Finally, given the calls for reform, there are a number of studies now underway that are examining the problems of both teachers and students in making the classroom a place where students can work with and acquire the powerful cognitive tools of mathematics. It is clear that the teacher must be one who uses these tools himself or herself. To grow in these ways, teachers need educational experiences that resemble in many ways the kind of guided inquiry they seek to conduct with their students. That is, teachers need guidance from people experienced in these kinds of teaching. They also need opportunities to try out new approaches, to modify and adapt materials, to invent their own materials and strategies, to share these with colleagues, and to learn through collegial exchange how to understand, explain, and expand their new knowledge, skills, and beliefs. The educational experience must address all three components because the changes teachers make involve intellectual, practical, and emotional challenges. At heart, the questions raised by shifting toward this kind of teaching are moral ones—questions about the basis for intellectual authority in the classroom and the allocation of rights and responsibilities for making knowledge among members of a community. Wrestling with these questions takes time, courage, and thought.

Toward a Theory of Curriculum Change

The final problematic feature related to the reform movement in school mathematics I want to discuss is the need for a new theory to interpret the vast quantities of information now being gathered in light of the shift from an absolutist philosophy of mathematics to a social constructivist philosophy. Today there is a lot of action in school mathematics. Policymakers are changing graduation and credentialing requirements; developers are creating new texts, tests, and software; researchers are conducting a variety of learning and teaching studies; and so forth. The data about the current reform movement are both vast and rich. Unfortunately, as Linda Flower (1989) reminds us, data is only data: "All data can do is provide the foundation for interpretation" (15). The problem is how one can use the data to make sense of the complex social situation of curriculum reform.

What is needed is a theory that can be used to understand the current system, the reform efforts, and the data being gathered. The term "theory" in scientific epistemology refers to statements about causal relationships between variables (Walker 1963). Such statements are produced by persons about complex phenomena in the world to explain their puzzling aspects. However, theories differ from most causal statements (speculations, hypotheses, etc.) in two ways. First, there is a group of persons who finds the causal statements useful; and second, they have been put to test several times and have survived. From this description, five related ingredients are apparent: (1) Theories are social constructs built by a group of persons. Thus, the existence of a scholarly group with common interests is the first ingredient. (2) The common interest of the group is in relationship to some real world phenomena. This is the second ingredient since the purpose of the theory is to explain some puzzling aspects of those phenomena. (3) The explanations given by the theory are in the form of statements. Such statements are classificatory for descriptive purposes, conjectures about relations or about causality, so that predictions can be made about the phenomena. The set of statements is the third ingredient. (4) The statements use an agreed-upon vocabulary and syntax; the fourth ingredient. (5) Finally, the statements are tested by gathering evidence using agreed-upon procedures to verify, falsify, or, with respect to predictions, either to confirm or reject the propositions. These procedures are the fifth ingredient.

At present, although there is general agreement on the puzzling, problematic phenomena of the school mathematics reform movement, there is no scholarly group with an agreed-upon ideology, syntax, and vocabulary ready to build, model, and test these phenomena in light of the philosophic shift so that a theory might emerge. This does not mean that curriculum theories do not exist. Many have been developed during the past half century (Lawton [1973] provides a good summary of this history). However, they tend to be static rather than dynamic. They may be adequate for describing current practice from absolutist perspectives, but fail to treat social constructivism adequately.

An adequate theory needs to be developed that considers some of the following. First, the conflicts arising from the shift in philosophies that influence curriculum decision making, although now acknowledged, have not been extensively examined and evaluated. Second, several years ago Arno Bellack (1963) suggested that it was a major task for curriculum theorists to find a way in which the curriculum could be developed so that the autonomy of the parts did not result in complete anarchy for the whole. This task needs to be accomplished from the social constructivist position. Third, as Linda Flower (1989) points out, today's theories must "examine how cognition and context interact" (4). Since the mathematics reform movement advocates instruction based on problems (context) and the belief that all students will construct knowledge from activity by working on those problems (cognition), her arguments need to be considered. Finally, the distinctions among the various actors in the curriculum field (planners, developers, teachers, etc.) need articulation (Chevallard 1987).

Thus, although curriculum reform in school mathematics is currently underway, there is no reason to believe that we will learn from this activity. Our understanding of the dynamic process of change, the barriers to change, and the consequences of the work of many scholars and educators will be minimal because of the lack of a framework to make sense of what is happening.

CONCLUSIONS

At the beginning of this chapter, four questions were raised to identify some of the problematic features of the school mathematics curriculum that must be examined in light of the reform movement that is now underway.

What Is Mathematics?

There is no easy answer to this question. However, what is clear is that there has been a shift from absolutist philosophies of mathematics to a social constructivist philosophy. Too many people still view the subject as a large collection of concepts and skills to be mastered. Not enough people see mathematics as a human activity or a cultural product. As Art Jaffe (1984) has said,

> Mathematics is an ancient art, and from the outset it has been both the most highly esoteric and the most intensely practical of human endeavors. As long ago as 1800 B.C., the Babylonians investigated the abstract properties of numbers, and in Athenian Greece, geometry attained the highest intellectual status. Alongside this theoretical understanding, mathematics blossomed as a day-to-day tool for surveying lands, for navigation, and for the engineering of public works. The practical problems and theoretical pursuits stimulated one another, it would be impossible to disentangle these two strands. (117)

Also, mathematics is both a body of knowledge and something people do. Curricular reformers are now advocating a shift so that all students learn to do mathematics.

Why Should Mathematics Be Taught in Schools?

Many reasons have been given. Because of the importance of mathematics in our society, many people clearly have a functional need to know mathematics. Also, given that the information revolution in our society is not a myth but a reality, it is claimed that the fundamental concepts and procedures that students should learn also have changed. A consequence is that it is now assumed that all students should learn more and somewhat different mathematics.

What Is the Structure of the Current Mathematics Curriculum, and Why Is It Organized in This Manner?

There is no question that the current system of schooling is a coherent one based on absolutist notions. It may be out of date and inappropriate for today's world, but all participants (students, teachers, administrators, and parents) understand their roles and responsibilities. Traditions have evolved over several decades that define the rules and regulations of the system. The overall system is still the dual system of the industrial period (common skills for all workers and specialized knowledge and skills for the elite). Current course offerings, credentialing requirements, testing procedures, and so forth reflect this history.

Reformers must be aware that their rhetoric and logic will not be enough unless they challenge the entire system as it exists. Change will occur only if the current system can be changed systemically. This shift will require a fundamental restructuring of the educational environment from the current "transmission of knowledge" model based on absolutist notions into one based on "stimulation of learning" growing out of social constructivist notions of mathematics. The transition will involve fundamental changes in content, modes of instruction, teacher education, and methods of assessing student progress.

What Is an Authentic Mathematics Curriculum?

The authentic teaching of mathematics began with the vision of school mathematics presented in NCTM's *Curriculum and Evaluation Standards for School Mathematics* (1989). This vision includes

- mathematical power for all in a technological society;
- mathematics as something one does—solve problems, communicate, reason;
- a curriculum for all that includes a broad range of content, a variety of contexts, and deliberate connections;
- the learning of mathematics as an active, constructive process;
- instruction based on real problems;
- evaluation as a means of improving instruction, learning, and programs (255).

This utopian vision assumes that the authentic teaching of mathematics has an inescapable social context that requires the redefinition of mass literacy from basic training to the universal empowerment of human potential. Thus, a radically different, but strongly supported, picture of mathematics teaching is envisioned. Succinctly, the vision requires teachers to create situations in which students can explore problems, generate questions, and reflect on patterns. It requires teachers with their academic and pedagogical knowledge to provide flexible approaches, encouraging informal and multiple representation while fostering the gradual growth of mathematical language. In order to improve schooling, "the public must offer teachers a professional work environment. That means a better salary, but more to the point, it means more resources to do the job. It means giving teachers a real voice in educational decisions . . . and more control over their time" (National Governors' Association Center for Policy Research and Analysis 1986, 36). "Schools as they currently exist must change both in physical and social structure if this kind of environment is to be created" (Romberg 1988a, 240).

In conclusion, the quality of instruction in the classrooms of this nation has always been a reflection of society at large. Change will occur only if society adopts a different perception of mathematics, of appropriate student activities, and of teacher roles and if it incorporates the different expectations of the many segments of society. However, the changes being proposed by the mathematical sciences education community will not be easy to implement. There are many reasons to anticipate probable difficulties, some of which have been discussed in detail in this chapter. Whether the proposed changes will come to pass is problematic. If so, it will take time, considerable resources, and the concerted effort and commitment of a large number of persons during the coming decade. In particular, curriculum theorists and researchers need to examine this reform movement in detail.

Throughout this chapter, there have been references to both theory and research. In fact, the prior sections are based on a large body of research, which has documented current deficiencies of the schooling system, and barriers to reform and suggested alternatives to current practices related to the teaching and learning of mathematics. However, in conclusion, I want to emphasize the development of new research agendas. This is a necessary component of the education community's response to the reform movement. The primary purpose of any research program is to try to make sense out of a complex phenomenon. The first step is to develop some theory (framework, model, or metaphor) designed to capture what are believed to be important features of the phenomenon. All such theories are of necessity incomplete. Nevertheless, they are fundamental to the investigations that follow, for it is from the theory that conjectures are derived. Second, a research program is established to gather and report evidence systematically to substantiate or refute those conjectures. In this sense, all research results are descriptive since the findings are about the model. Only in this manner will research eventually provide an understanding of the reform movement.

It must be noted that most of the body of past and contemporary research addresses the past vision of schooling and literacy. Such research does not support the pursuit of reliable knowledge about the new vision of mathematical literacy. The research agendas for the future must address questions in light of the reform.

References

Aleksandrov, A. D., A. N. Kolmogorov, and M. A. Lavrent'ev, 1956. *Mathematics: Its Content, Methods, and Meaning*. Cambridge, MA: M.I.T. Press.

Anderson, J. R. 1983. *The Architecture of Cognition*. Cambridge, MA: Harvard University Press.

Apple, M. W. 1979. *Ideology and Curriculum*. London: Routledge & Kegan Paul.

Barbeau, E. J. 1989, September. "Mathematics for the Public." Paper presented at the meeting of the International Commission on Mathematical Instruction, Leeds University, Leeds, England.

Becker, J. P. 1989. *Mathematics Education in Japan*. Carbondale: Southern Illinois University.

Begle, E. G. 1961. "Seminar in Mathematics Education: Class Notes." Manuscript.

Bell, A. W., and Purdy, D. 1985. *Diagnostic Teaching: Some Problems of Directionality*. Nottingham, England: Shell Centre for Mathematical Education, University of Nottingham.

Bell, D. 1973. *The Coming of Post-Industrial Society: A Venture in Social Forecasting*. New York: Basic Books.

Bell, E. T. 1945. *The Development of Mathematics*, 2nd ed. New York: McGraw-Hill.

Bellack, A. 1963. *Theory and Research in Teaching*. New York: Teachers College, Columbia University.

Bellack, A., and H. M. Kliebard 1977. *Curriculum and Evaluation*. Berkeley, CA: McCutchan.

Berliner, D. C. 1982, April. "The Executive Functions of Teaching." Paper given at the meeting of the American Educational Research Association, New York.

Biggs, E. 1986. *Teaching Mathematics 7–13: Slow Learning and Able Pupils*. Windsor, England: Nfer-Nelson Publishing Co.

Birkhoff, G. 1932. A set of postulates for plane geometry, based on scale and protractor. *Annals of Mathematics* 33: 57–81.

Bishop, A. J. 1988. *Mathematical Enculturation: A Cultural Perspective on Mathematics Education*. Dordrecht, The Netherlands: Kluwer Academic Publishers.

Bobbitt, F. 1924. *How to Make a Curriculum*. Boston: Houghton Mifflin.

Bourne, L. E., Jr., 1966. *Human Conceptual Behavior*. Boston, MA: Allyn & Bacon.

Boyer, E. L. 1986. "Foreword." In *The Condition of Teaching: A State-by-State Analysis*, edited by C. E. Feistritzer, xiii-xviii. Princeton, NJ: Carnegie Foundation for the Advancement of Teaching.

Buck, R. C. 1965. Goals for mathematics instruction. *American Mathematical Monthly* 72 (9): 949–956.

Burke, P. E. 1989, March 15. Quoted in W. Raspberry, "Math Isn't for Everyone." *Washington Post*.

Carnoy, M., and H. M. Levin. 1976. *The Limits of Educational Reform*. New York: McKay.

Carpenter, T. P., M. K. Corbitt, H. S. Kepner, Jr., M. M. Lindquist, and R. E. Reys 1981. *Results from the Second Mathematics Assessment of the National Assessment of Educational Progress*. Reston, VA: National Council of Teachers of Mathematics.

Carpenter, T. P., E. Fennema, and P. L. Peterson. 1987. "Cognitively Guided Instruction: The Application of Cognitive and Instructional Science to Mathematics Curriculum Development." In *Developments in School Mathematics Education Around the World. Proceedings of the University of Chicago School Mathematics Project International Conference on Mathematics Education*, edited by I. Wirzup and R. Streit, 397–417. Reston, VA: National Council of Teachers of Mathematics.

Carss, M. 1986. *Proceedings of the Fifth International Congress on Mathematical Education*. Boston, MA: Birkhauser.

Charters, W. W. 1923. *Curriculum Construction*. New York: Macmillan.

Chevallard, Y. 1987, May. "A Theoretical Approach to Curricula." Paper presented at the TME meeting, Frascate, Italy.

Chevallard, Y. 1988. "The Student-Learner Gap." In *Proceedings of the Third International Conference on the Theory of Mathematics Education*, edited by A. Vermandel, 1–6. Antwerp, Belgium: Universitaire Instelling Antwerpen.

Chevallard, Y. In press. On mathematics education and culture: Critical afterthoughts. *Educational Studies in Mathematics*.

Christiansen, B., A. G. Howson, and M. Otte. 1986. *Perspectives on Mathematics Education*. Dordrecht, The Netherlands: Reidel.

Clarke, D. 1984. Secondary mathematics teaching: Towards a critical appraisal of current practice. *Vinculum* 21(4): 1–22.

Cobb, P., E. Yackel, and T. Wood, 1988. "Curriculum and Teacher Development: Psychological and Anthropological Perspectives." In *Integrating Research on Teaching and Learning Mathematics: Papers from the First Wisconsin Symposium for Research on Teaching and Learning Mathematics*, edited by E. Fennema, T. P. Carpenter, and S. J. Lamon, 92–130. Madison: Wisconsin Center for Education Research.

Cockcroft, W. H. 1982. "Mathematics Counts: Report of the Committee of Inquiry into the Teaching of Mathematics in Schools." London: Her Majesty's Stationery Office.

Cohen, D. K. 1988. "Educational Technology and School Organization." In *Technology in Education: Looking Toward 2020*, edited by R. S. Nickerson and P. P. Zodhiates, 231–264. Hillsdale, NJ: Erlbaum.

Cohen, D. K., and M. S. Garet. 1975. Reforming educational policy with applied social research. *Harvard Educational Review* 45(1): 293–316.

College Entrance Examination Board. 1959. *Program for College Preparatory Mathematics*. Princeton, NJ: Commission on Mathematics.

Commission on Physical Sciences, Mathematics, and Resources. 1984. *Renewing United States Mathematics: Critical Resource for the Future. Report of the Ad Hoc Committee on Resources for the Mathematical Sciences*. Washington, DC: National Academy Press.

Committee of Inquiry into the Teaching of Mathematics in Schools. 1982. *Mathematics Counts*. London: Her Majesty's Stationery Office.

Conference Board of the Mathematical Sciences. 1975. "Overview and Analysis of School Mathematics, Grades K–12." Washington, DC: CBMS.

Coxford, A. F., and Z. P. Usiskin. 1971. *Geometry: A Transformational Approach*. River Forest, IL: Laidlaw.

D'Ambrosio, U. 1985. *Socio-Cultural Bases for Mathematics Education*. Boston, MA: Birkhauser.

D'Ambrosio, U. 1987. "New Fundamentals of Mathematics for Schools." In *The Monitoring of School Mathematics: Background Papers. Volume I. The Monitoring Project and Mathematics Curriculum*, edited by T. A. Romberg and D. M. Stewart, 135–148. Madison: Wisconsin Center for Education Research.

Damerow, P., and I. Westbury. 1985. Mathematics for all: Problems and implications. *Journal of Curriculum Studies* 17(2): 175–186.

Davis, P. J., and R. Hersh. 1981. *The Mathematical Experience*. Boston, MA: Birkhauser.

Davis, P. J., and R. Hersh. 1986. *Descartes' Dream*. New York: Harcourt Brace Jovanovich.

Davis, R. B. 1989. The culture of mathematics and the culture of schools. *The Journal of Mathematical Behavior* 8(2): 141–166.

Davis, R. B., T. A. Romberg, S. Rachlin, and M. G. Kantowski. 1979. *An Analysis of Mathematics Education in the Union of Soviet Socialist Republics*. Columbus, OH: ERIC Clearinghouse for Science, Mathematics, and Environmental Education.

de Lange, J. 1984. Geometry for all: No geometry at all? *Zentralblatt für Didaktik der Mathematik* 16(3): 90–98.

de Lange, J. 1986. "Mathematics for All Is No Mathematics At All." In *Mathematics for All. Document Series No. 20*, edited by P. Damerow et al., 66–71. Paris: UNESCO, Division of Science, Technical, and Environmental Education.

de Lange, J. 1987. *Mathematics, Insight, and Meaning*. Utrecht, The Netherlands: University Utrecht.

de Lange, J., M. van Reeuwijk, and G. Burrill. In press. *Learning and Testing Mathematics in Context—The Case: Data Visualization*. Madison, WI: National Center for Research in Mathematical Sciences Education.

DeVault, M. V., and J. F. Weaver. 1970. "Forces and Issues Related to Curriculum and Instruction, K–6." In *The National Council of Teachers of Mathematics: A History of Mathematics Education in the United States*, 93–152. Washington, DC: NCTM.

Dewey, J. 1916. *Democracy and Education*. New York: Macmillan.

Dewey, J. 1933. *How We Think: A Restatement of the Relation of Reflective Thinking to the Educative Process*. New York: Heath.

Donovan, B. F. 1983. "Power and Curriculum Implementation: A Case Study of an Innovatory Mathematics Program." Ph.D. dissertation, University of Wisconsin, Madison.

Dreeben, R. 1968. *On What Is Learned in School*. Reading, MA: Addison-Wesley.

Egan, K. 1978. What is curriculum? *Curriculum Inquiry* 8(1): 65–72.

Ekeland, I. 1988. *Mathematics and the Unexpected*. Chicago: University of Chicago Press.

Erlwanger, S. 1975. Case studies of children's conceptions of mathematics. *Journal of Children's Mathematical Behavior* 1(2): 157–281.

Ernest, P. 1991. *The Philosophy of Mathematics Education*. London: Falmer.

Feinberg, W., and J. Soltis. 1985. *School and Society*. New York: Teachers College Press.

Feistritzer, C. E. 1985. "The Condition of Teaching: A State-by-State Analysis." Carnegie Foundation for the Advancement of Teaching.

Fey, J. 1979a, October. Mathematics teaching today: Perspectives from three national surveys. *The Mathematics Teacher* 72: 490–504.

Fey, J. 1979b, October. Mathematics teaching today: Perspectives from three national surveys (for the elementary grades). *The Arithmetic Teacher* 27: 10–14.

Finn, C. E., Jr. 1989. A nation still at risk. *Commentary* 87(5): 17–23.

Flanders, J. 1986. How much of the content in mathematics textbooks is new? *The Arithmetic Teacher* 31(1): 18–23.

Flower, L. 1989. *Cognition, Context, and Theory Building*. Berkeley: Center for the Study of Writing, University of California.

Freudenthal, H. 1973. *Mathematics as an Educational Task*. Dordrecht, The Netherlands: Reidel.

Freudenthal. H. 1978. *Weeding and Sowing*. Dordrecht, The Netherlands: Reidel

Freudenthal, H. 1984. *Didactical Phenomenology of Mathematical Structures*. Dordrecht, The Netherlands: Reidel.

Freudenthal, H. 1987. "Mathematics Starting and Staying in Reality." In *Proceedings of the USCMP International Conference on Mathematics Education on Development in School Mathematics Education Around the World: Applications-Oriented Curricula and Technology-Supported Learning for All Students*, edited by I. Wirszup and R. Streit, 279–295. Reston, VA: National Council of Teachers of Mathematics.

Fuson, K. C., J. W. Stigler, and K. Bartsch. 1988. Grade placement of addition and subtraction topics in Japan, Mainland China, the Soviet Union, Taiwan, and the United States. *Journal for Research in Mathematics Education* 19(5): 449–456.

Futrell, M. H. 1986. Restructuring teaching: A call for research. *Educational Researcher* 15(10): 5–8.

Gagné, R. M. 1965. *The Conditions of Learning*. New York: Holt, Rinehart and Winston.

Gamoran, A., and R. D. Mare. 1989. Secondary school tracking and educational inequality: Compensation, reinforcement, or neutrality? *American Journal of Sociology* 94(5): 1146–1183.

Garden, R. A. n.d. "Validation of the Cognitive Items." Manuscript.

Goddijn, A. 1980. *Shadow and Depth*. Utrecht, The Netherlands: Wiskivon Department of the IOWO.

Good, T. L. 1979. Teacher effectiveness in the elementary school. *Journal of Teacher Education* 30(2): 52–64.

Goodlad, J. I. 1976. Schooling and education. In *The Great Ideas Today*, edited by R. Hutchins. New York: Encyclopedia Britannica.

Greenberg, H. J. 1987. "Mathematics Education: A Really, Real, Real World Problem: Reactions to Chapters 6–10." In *The Monitoring of School Mathematics: Background Papers. Volume 1: The Monitoring Project and Mathematics Curriculum*, edited by T. A. Romberg and D. M. Stewart, 213–221. Madison: Wisconsin Center for Education Research.

Greene, M. 1971. Curriculum and consciousness. *Teachers College Record* 3(2): 253–269.

Greeno, J. 1983. "Research on Cognition and Behavior Relevant to Education in Mathematics, Science, and Technology." In *Educating Americans for the 21st Century: A Plan of Action for Improving Mathematics, Science, and Technology Education for All American Elementary and Secondary Students So That Their Achievement Is the Best in the World by 1995. Source Materials*. National Science Board Commission on Precollege Education in Mathematics, Science, and Technology, 107–140. Washington, DC: National Science Foundation.

Greeno, J. 1987. Mathematical cognition: Accomplishments and challenges in research. In *The Monitoring of School Mathematics: Background Papers. Volume 2: Implications from Psychology; Outcomes of Instruction*, edited by T. A. Romberg and D. M. Stewart, 3–26. Madison: Wisconsin Center for Education Research.

Greeno, J. 1991. Number sense as situated knowing in a conceptual domain. *Journal for Research in Mathematics Education* 22(3): 170–218.

Greer, C. 1972. *The Great School Legend: A Revisionist Interpretation of American Public Education*. New York: Viking.

Grube, G. M. A., trans. 1974. Trans. *Plato's Republic*. Indianapolis, IN: Hackett.

Hagstrom, W. O. 1965. *The Scientific Community*. New York: Basic Books.

Heath, T. L. 1956. *The Thirteen Books of Euclid's Elements,* vol. 1, 2nd ed. New York: Dover.

Hirst, A., and K. Hirst. 1989. *Proceedings of the Sixth International Congress on Mathematical Education*. Budapest, Hungary: MALEV.

Holmes Group. 1986. *Tomorrow's Teachers: A Report of the Holmes Group*. East Lansing, MI: Holmes Group.

Howson, A. G. 1982. "The Aims of Mathematics Education." In

Mathematics Education: The Report of the Second Anglo-Soviet Seminar Held in Moscow at the Institute for Scientific Research into Content and Methods of Instruction, Academy of Pedagogical Sciences of the USSR, edited by B. Wilson, 40–50. London: British Council.

Howson, A. G. 1991. *National Curricula in Mathematics*. London: The Mathematical Association.

Howson, A. G., and J.-P. Kahane. 1986. *The Influence of Computers and Informatics on Mathematics and Its Teaching*. Cambridge: Cambridge University Press.

Howson, A. G., C. Keitel, and J. Kilpatrick. 1981. *Curriculum Development in Mathematics*. Cambridge: Cambridge University Press.

Husen, T. 1967. *International Study of Achievement in Mathematics: A Comparison of Twelve Countries*, vol. I. New York: Wiley.

Hutchins, R. M. 1936. *The Higher Learning in America*. New Haven, CT: Yale University Press.

The International Encyclopedia of Education: Research and Studies. 1985. Oxford: Pergamon.

Jackson, P. W. 1968. *Life in Classrooms*. New York: Holt, Rinehart and Winston.

Jacobs, H. 1970. *Mathematics: A Human Endeavor (Letter to the Student)*. San Francisco, CA: Freeman.

Jaffe, A. 1984. "Appendix C. Ordering the Universe: The Role of Mathematics." In *Renewing U.S. Mathematics: Critical Resources for the Future. Report of the Ad Hoc Committee on Resources for the Mathematical Sciences*, edited by the Commission on Physical Sciences, Mathematics, and Resources, 117–162. Washington, DC: National Academy Press.

Jahnke, H. N. 1986. Origins of school mathematics in early nineteenth-century Germany. *Journal of Curriculum Studies* 18(1): 85–94.

Jennings, J. F. 1987. The Sputnik of the eighties. *Phi Delta Kappan* 82 (2): 104–109.

Johnston, W. B., and A. E. Packer. 1987. *Workforce 2000: Work and Workers for the Twenty-first Century*. Indianapolis, IN: Hudson Institute.

Jones, G. A., and T. A. Romberg. 1979. "Three 'Time on Task' Studies and Their Implications for Teaching and Teacher Education." Project paper 79–6. Madison: Wisconsin Research and Development Center for Individualized Schooling.

Jones, P. S. 1970. "Present-day Issues and Forces." In *National Council of Teachers of Mathematics: A History of Mathematics Education in the United States and Canada*, 453–465. Washington, DC: NCTM.

Keisler, H. J. 1971. *Elementary Calculus: An Approach Using Infinitesimals*. Boston, MA: Prindle, Weber, & Schmidt.

Keitel, C. 1987. What are the goals of mathematics for all? *Journal of Curriculum Studies* 19(5): 393–407.

Kilpatrick, J. 1989. "Technology as Reform." Paper presented at the BACOMET III Conference, Berlin.

King, A. R., Jr., and J. A. Brownell. 1966. *The Curriculum and the Disciplines of Knowledge: A Theory of Curriculum Practice*. New York: Wiley.

King, N. R. 1981. "The Kindergarteners' Perspective." In *Focus on Teaching*, edited by W. Doyle and T. L. Good, 221–227. Chicago: University of Chicago Press.

Kitcher, P. 1988. "Mathematical Naturalism." In *History and Philosophy of Modern Mathematics. Minnesota Studies in the Philosophy of Science*, vol. XI, edited by W. Aspray and P. Kitcher, 293–325. Minneapolis: University of Minnesota Press.

Klein, M. F. 1989. *Curriculum Reform in the Elementary School: Creating Your Own Agenda*. New York: Teachers College Press.

Kliebard, H. M. 1972. Metaphorical roots of curriculum design. *Teachers College Record* 73(3): 403–404.

Kliebard, H. M. 1977, April. "Problems of Definition in Curriculum." Paper delivered at the annual meeting, American Educational Research Association, New York.

Kliebard, H. M. 1985. "Three Currents of American Curriculum Thought." In *Current Thought on Curriculum: 1985 ASCD Yearbook*, 31–44. Alexandria, VA: Association for Supervision and Curriculum Development.

Kline, M. 1962. *Mathematics: A Cultural Approach*. Reading, MA: Addison-Wesley.

Kline, M. 1966. "Mathematics and Axiomatics." In *The Role of Axiomatics and Problem Solving in Mathematics*, edited by E. G. Begle, 57–62. Boston, MA: Ginn.

Kline, M. 1972. *Mathematical Thought from Ancient to Modern Times*. New York: Oxford University Press.

Knight, G. 1989, September. "Cultural Alienation and Mathematics." Paper presented at the meeting of the International Commission on Mathematical Instruction, Leeds University, Leeds, England.

Kramer, E. E. 1970. *The Nature and Growth of Modern Mathematics*. Princeton, NJ: Princeton University Press.

Kuhn, T. S. 1970. *The Structure of Scientific Revolutions*, 2nd ed. Chicago: University of Chicago Press.

Lakatos, I. 1976. *Proofs and Refutations*. Cambridge: Cambridge University Press.

Lampert, M. 1988. "Connecting Mathematical Teaching and Learning." In *Integrating Research on Teaching and Learning Mathematics: Papers from the First Wisconsin Symposium for Research on Teaching and Learning Mathematics*, edited by E. Fennema, T. P. Carpenter, and S. J. Lamon, 132–165. Madison: Wisconsin Center for Education Research.

Lampert, M. 1990. When the problem is not the question and the solution is not the answer: Mathematical knowing and teaching. *American Educational Research Journal* 27(1): 29–64.

Langer, J. 1969. *Theories of Development*. New York: Holt, Rinehart and Winston.

Lapointe, A. E., N. A. Mead, and G. W. Phillips. 1989. *A World of Difference: An International Assessment of Science and Mathematics*. Princeton, NJ: Educational Testing Service.

Lave, J., S. Smith, and M. Butler. 1988. "Problem Solving as an Everyday Practice." In *The Teaching and Assessing of Mathematical Problem Solving*, vol. 3, edited by R. Charles and E. Silver, 61–81. Reston, VA: National Council of Teachers of Mathematics.

Lawton, D. 1973. *Social Change, Educational Theory, and Curriculum Planning*. London: Hodder & Stoughton.

Leinhardt, G. 1986. "Math Lessons: A Contrast of Novice and Expert Competence." In *Proceedings of the Eighth Annual Meeting of the North American Chapter of the International Group for the Psychology of Mathematics Education: Plenary Speeches and Symposium*, 1–42. East Lansing, MI: Psychology of Mathematics Education–North America.

Lundgren, U. P. 1979. "Background: The Conceptual Framework." In *Studies in Curriculum Theory and Cultural Reproduction. vol. 3: Code, Context, and Curriculum Processes*, edited by U. P. Lundgren and S. Pettersson, 5–35. Stockholm: Stockholm Institute of Education, Department of Educational Research.

McClelland, W. A. 1968. *The Process of Effecting Change*. Professional paper 32–68. Alexandria, VA: Human Resources Research Office.

McKnight, C. C., F. J. Crosswhite, J. A. Dossey, E. Kifer, J. O. Swafford, K. J. Travers, and T. J. Cooney, 1987. *The Underachieving Curriculum: Assessing United States School Mathe-*

matics from an International Perspective. Champaign, IL: Stipes Publishing.

Mathematical Sciences Education Board. 1989. *Everybody Counts: A Report to the Nation on the Future of Mathematics Education*. Washington, DC: National Academy Press.

Mathematical Sciences Education Board. 1990a. *On the Shoulders of Giants*. Washington, DC: National Academy Press.

Mathematical Sciences Education Board (MSEB). 1990b. *Reshaping School Mathematics: A Philosophy and Framework of Curriculum*. Washington, DC: National Academy Press.

Mellin-Olsen, S. 1987. *The Politics of Mathematics Education*. Dordrecht, The Netherlands: Reidel.

Mills, C. W. 1959. *The Sociological Imagination*. New York: Oxford University Press.

Naisbitt, J. 1982. *Megatrends: Ten New Directions Transforming Our Lives*. New York: Warner Books.

National Assessment of Educational Progress. 1988. *A World of Differences: An International Assessment of Mathematics and Science*. Princeton, NJ: NAEP.

National Commission on Excellence in Education. 1983. *A Nation at Risk: The Imperative for Educational Reform*. Washington, DC: U.S. Government Printing Office.

National Council of Teachers of Mathematics. 1980. *An Agenda for Action: Recommendations for School Mathematics of the 1980s*. Reston, VA: NCTM.

National Council of Teachers of Mathematics. 1989. *Curriculum and Evaluation Standards for School Mathematics*. Reston, VA: NCTM.

National Council of Teachers of Mathematics. 1991. *Professional Standards for Teaching Mathematics*. Reston, VA: National Governors Association Center.

National Governors' Association Center for Policy Research and Analysis. 1986. *Time for Results: The Governors' 1991 Report on Education*. Washington, DC: National Governors Association Center.

National Science Board Commission on Precollege Education in Mathematics, Science, and Technology. 1983. *Educating Americans for the Twenty-first Century: A Plan of Action for Improving the Mathematics, Science, and Technology Education for All American Elementary and Secondary Students So That Their Achievement Is the Best in the World by 1995*. Washington, DC: U.S. Government Printing Office.

Nelson, C. 1989. November. Bring back the old math. *The American Spectator*: 36–37.

Newman, J. R. 1956. *The World of Mathematics*. New York: Simon & Schuster.

Nickerson, R. 1988. Counting, computing, and the representation of numbers. *Human Factors* 30(2): 181–199.

Nussbaum, J., and S. Novick. 1982, March. Alternative frameworks, conceptual conflict, and accommodation: Toward a principled teaching strategy. *Instructional Science* 11:183–200.

Oaxaca, J., and A. W. Reynolds. 1988. *Changing America: The New Face of Science and Engineering*. (Interim report). Washington, DC: Task Force on Women, Minorities, and the Handicapped in Science and Technology.

Paulos, J. A. 1988. *Innumeracy: Mathematical Illiteracy and Its Consequences*. New York: Hill & Wang.

Pea, R. D. 1987. "Cognitive Technologies for Mathematics Education." In *Cognitive Science and Mathematics Education*, edited by A. H. Schoenfeld, 89–122. Hillsdale, NJ: Erlbaum.

Peddiwell, J. A. (pseudonym). 1939. *The Saber-Tooth Curriculum*. New York: McGraw-Hill.

Penkov, B., and B. Sendov. 1987. "The Bulgarian Academy of Sciences Research Group on Education Project." In *Proceedings of the USCMP International Conference on Mathematics Education on Development in School Mathematics Education Around the World: Applications-Oriented Curricula and Technology-Supported Learning for All Students*, edited by I. Wirszup and R. Streit, 98–108. Reston, VA: National Council of Teachers of Mathematics.

Philips, D. C., and J. F. Soltis. 1985. *Perspectives on Learning*. New York: Teachers College Press.

Pimm, D. 1987. *Speaking Mathematically: Communication in Mathematics Classrooms*. London: Routledge & Kegan Paul.

Pinxten, R., I. van Dooren, and F. R. Harvey. 1983. *The Anthropology of Space*. Philadelphia, PA: University of Pennsylvania Press.

Pipho, C. 1980. *Analysis of State Minimum Competency Testing Programs*. Report for the National Institute of Education by Education Commission of the States.

Pollak, H. 1986. *Summary Comments Given at the MSEB Conference on the School Mathematics Curriculum*. Los Angeles: University of California.

Polya, G. 1954. *Mathematics and Plausible Reasoning. Volume 1: Induction and Analogy in Mathematics*. Princeton, NJ: Princeton University Press.

Polya, G. 1957. *How to Solve It*. New York: Doubleday/Anchor Books.

Polya, G. 1966. "On Teaching Problem Solving." In *The Role of Axiomatics and Problem Solving in Mathematics*, edited by E. G. Begle, 123–129. Boston, MA: Ginn.

Polya, G. 1967. *Mathematical Discovery*. New York: Wiley.

Popkewitz, T. S. 1988. "Instructional Issues in the Study of School Mathematics: Curriculum Research." In *Mathematical Enculturation: A Cultural Perspective on Mathematics Education*, edited by A. J. Bishop, 221–249. Dordrecht, The Netherlands: Kluwer Academic Publishers.

Popkewitz, T. S., B. R. Tabachnick, and G. G. Wehlage. 1982. *The Myth of Educational Reform: A Study of School Responses to a Program of Change*. Madison: University of Wisconsin Press.

Popper, K. 1949. *Conjectures and Refutations: The Growth of Scientific Knowledge*. London: Routledge & Kegan Paul.

Provenzo, E. F. 1986. *Beyond the Gutenberg Galaxy: Microcomputers and the Emergence of Post-Typographic Culture*. New York: Teachers College, Columbia University.

Putnam, R. T., M. Lampert, and P. L. Peterson. 1989. *Alternative Perspectives on Knowing Mathematics in Elementary Schools*. East Lansing: Michigan State University.

Rees, M. 1966. "The Nature of Mathematics: Both Constructive Intuition and the Study of Abstract Structures Characterize the Growth of Mathematics." In *What Is Contemporary Mathematics?* edited by W. L. Schaaf, 3–10. Stanford, CA: School Mathematics Study Group.

Rescher, N. 1979. *Cognitive Systematization: A Systems-Theoretic Approach to a Coherentist Theory of Knowledge*. Totowa, NJ: Rowman & Littlefield.

Resnick, D. P., and L. B. Resnick. 1977. The nature of literacy: An historical exploration. *Harvard Educational Review* 47: 370–385.

Resnick, L. B. 1987. *Education and Learning to Think*. Washington, DC: National Academy Press.

Resnick, L. B., and W. W. Ford. 1981. *The Psychology of Mathematics for Instruction*. Hillsdale, NJ: Erlbaum.

Rheinboldt, W. C. 1985. *Future Directions in Computational Mathematics, Algorithms, and Scientific Software*. Philadelphia, PA: Society for Industrial and Applied Mathematics.

Rice, J. M. 1913. *Scientific Management in Education*. New York: Hinds, Noble, & Eldredge.

Robinson, A. 1974. *Non-Standard Analysis*. Amsterdam: North-Holland.

Robitaille, D. F., and R. A. Garden. 1989. *The IEA Study of Mathe-*

matics II: Contexts and Outcomes of School Mathematics. Oxford: Pergamon.

Romberg, T. A. 1975, October. "Activities Basic to Learning Mathematics: A Perspective." *The NIE Conference on Basic Mathematical Skills and Learning. Volume I: Contributed Position Papers*. Washington, DC: National Institute of Education.

Romberg, T. A. 1976. *Individually Guided Mathematics*. Reading, MA: Addison-Wesley.

Romberg, T. A. 1983. "A Common Curriculum for Mathematics." In *Individual Differences and the Common Curriculum*, edited by G. D. Fenstermacher and J. I. Goodlad, 121–159. Chicago: University of Chicago Press.

Romberg, T. A. 1984. *School Mathematics: Options for the 1990s. Chairman's Report of a Conference*. Washington, DC: U.S. Government Printing Office.

Romberg, T. A. 1985a. *The Content Validity of the Mathematics Subscores and Items for the Second International Mathematics Study*. Washington, DC: Committee on National Statistics, National Research Council of the National Academy of Sciences.

Romberg, T. A. 1985b. "Research and the Job of Teaching." In *Using Research in the Professional Life of Mathematics Education*, edited by T. A. Romberg, 2–7. Madison: Wisconsin Center for Education Research.

Romberg, T. A. 1988a. "Can Teachers Be Professionals?" In *Perspectives on Research on Effective Mathematics Training*, edited by D. A. Grouws, T. J. Cooney, and D. Jones, 224–244. Reston, VA: National Council of Teachers of Mathematics.

Romberg, T. A. 1988b. *Changes in School Mathematics: Curricular Changes, Instructional Changes, and Indicators of Changes*. New Brunswick, NJ: Center for Policy Research in Education.

Romberg, T. A. 1988c. "Necessary Ingredients for a Theory of Mathematics Education." In *Proceedings of the Second TME Conference: Foundations and Methodology of the Discipline Mathematics Education*, edited by H. G. Steiner and A. Vermandel, 97–112. Bielefeld, Antwerp: IDM Publications.

Romberg, T. A. 1988d. "The Theories of Mathematical Learning." In *Mathematics Education in Secondary Schools and Two-Year Colleges* by P. J. Campbell and L. S. Grinstein. New York: Garland Publishing.

Romberg, T. A., and T. P. Carpenter. 1986. "Research on Teaching and Learning Mathematics: Two Disciplines of Scientific Inquiry." In *The Third Handbook of Research on Teaching*, edited by M. C. Wittrock, 850–873. New York: Macmillan.

Romberg, T. A., J. G. Harvey, J. Moser, and M. Montgomery. 1974, 1975, 1976. *Developing Mathematical Processes*. Chicago: Rand McNally.

Romberg, T. A. and G. G. Price. 1983. "Curriculum Implementation and Staff Development as Cultural Change." In *Staff Development: Eighty-second Yearbook of the National Society for the Study of Education*, edited by G. Griffin, 154–184. Chicago: University of Chicago Press.

Romberg, T. A., and D. M. Stewart, 1987. *The Monitoring of School Mathematics: Background Papers. Volume 1: The Monitoring Project and Mathematics Curriculum*. Madison: Wisconsin Center for Education Research.

Romberg, T. A., and F. W. Tufte. 1987. "Mathematics Curriculum Engineering: Some Suggestions from Cognitive Science." In *The Monitoring of School Mathematics: Background Papers. Volume 2: Implications from Psychology; Outcomes of Instruction*, edited by T. A. Romberg and D. M. Stewart, 71–108. Madison: Wisconsin Center for Education Research.

Russell, J. 1978. *The Acquisition of Knowledge*. New York: St. Martin's Press.

Saxe, G. B. 1981. Body parts as numerals: A developmental analysis of numeration among remote Oksapmin village populations in Papua, New Guinea. *Child Development* 52(1): 306–316.

Schaaf, W. L. 1966. *What Is Contemporary Mathematics*? Stanford, CA: School Mathematics Study Group.

Schliemann, A. D., and N. M. Acioly. 1989. Mathematical knowledge developed at work: The contribution of practice versus the contribution of schooling. *Cognition and Instruction* 6(3): 185–221.

Schoenfeld, A. H. 1987. *Cognitive Science and Mathematics Education*. Hillsdale, NJ: Erlbaum.

Schrag, F. 1981. Knowing and doing. *American Journal of Education* 89(3): 253–282.

Schutter, C. H., and R. L. Spreckelmeyer. 1959. *Teaching the Third R: A Comparative Study of American and European Textbooks in Arithemtic*. Washington, DC: Council for Basic Education.

Schwartz, J. L., and M. Yerushalmy. 1985, 1986, 1987. *The Geometric Supposers*. Pleasantville, NY: Sunburst Communications.

Shane, H. I., and M. B. Tabler. 1981. *Educating for a New Millennium: Views of 132 International Scholars*. Bloomington, IN: Phi Delta Kappa Educational Foundation.

Skemp, R. R. 1979. *Intelligence, Learning, and Action*. New York: Wiley.

Stake, R., and J. Easley, eds. 1978. *Case Studies in Science Education*. Urbana: University of Illinois.

Stanic, G. M. A. 1984a, April. "The Growing 'Crisis' in Mathematics Education in the Years Leading Up to World War II." Paper presented at the annual meeting, American Educational Research Association, New Orleans, LA.

Stanic, G. M. A. 1984b. "Why Teach Mathematics? A Historical Study of the Justification Question." Ph.D. dissertation, University of Wisconsin, Madison.

Steen, L. A. 1981. *Mathematics Tomorrow*. New York: Springer-Verlag.

Steen, L. A. 1988a. Forces for change in the mathematics curriculum. *Wisconsin Teachers of Mathematics* 34(1): 3–7.

Steen, L. A. 1988b, May 11. A "new agenda" for mathematics education. *Education Week* 28: 21.

Steen, L. A. 1988c, Fall. Out from underachievement. *Issues in Science and Technology*: 88–93.

Steen, L. A. 1988d. The science of patterns. *Science* 240: 611–616.

Steen, L. A. 1989. *Achieving Standards in School Mathematics*. Northfield, MN: St. Olaf College.

Stephens, W. M. 1982. "Mathematical Knowledge and School Work: A Case Study of the Teaching of Developing Mathematical Processes." Ph.D. dissertation, University of Wisconsin, Madison.

Stevenson, H. W., S. Y. Lee, and J. W. Stigler. 1986, February. Mathematics achievement of Chinese, Japanese, and American children. *Science* 231: 693–699.

Stigler, J. W., K. C. Fuson, M. Ham, and M. S. Kim. 1986. *An Analysis of Addition and Subtraction Word Problems in United States and Soviet Elementary Mathematics Textbooks*.

Stigler, J. W., and M. Perry. 1988. "Cross-cultural Studies of Mathematics Teaching and Learning: Recent Findings and New Directions." In *Perspectives on Research on Effective Mathematics Teaching*, edited by D. A. Grouws, T. J. Cooney, and D. Jones, 194–223. Reston, VA: National Council of Teachers of Mathematics.

Suydam, M., and A. Osborne. 1977. *The Status of Pre-College Science, Mathematics, and Social Studies Education: 1955–1975*. Columbus: Ohio State University Center for Science and Mathematics Education.

Swetz, F. J. 1987. *Capitalism and Arithmetic: The New Math of the 15th Century*. LaSalle, IL: Open Court.

Thorndike, E. L. 1922. *The Psychology of Arithmetic*. New York: Macmillan.

Toffler, A. 1985. *The Adaptive Corporation*. New York: McGraw-Hill.

Trafton, P. R. 1980. "Assessing the Mathematics Curriculum Today." In *Selected Issues in Mathematics Education*, edited by M. M. Lindquist, 9–26. Berkeley, CA: McCutchan.

Travers, K. J., and I. Westbury, eds. 1989. *The IEA Study of Mathematics I: Analysis of Mathematics Curricula*. Oxford: Pergamon.

Tymoczko, T. 1986. *New Directions in the Philosophy of Mathematics*. Boston, MA: Birkhauser.

U.S. Congressional Office of Technology Assessment. 1988. *Technology and the American Transition*. Washington, DC: U.S. Government Printing Office.

Usiskin, Z. 1984. "Needed Changes in Mathematics Curricula." In *School Mathematics: Options for the 1990s*, edited by T. A. Romberg and D. M. Stewart. Madison: Wisconsin Center for Education Research.

Vergnaud, G. 1983. "Multiplicative Structures." In *Acquisition of Mathematics Concepts and Processes*, edited by R. Lesh and M. Landau, 127–174. London: Academic Press.

Walker, M. 1963. *The Nature of Scientific Thought*. Englewood Cliffs, NJ: Prentice Hall.

Weiss, I. 1978. *Report of the 1977 National Survey of Science, Mathematics, and Social Studies Education*. Research Triangle Park, NC: Research Triangle Institute.

Welsh, W. 1978. "Science Education in Urbanville: A Case Study." In *Case Studies in Science Education*, edited by R. Stake and J. Easley, 515–533. Urbana: University of Illinois.

Wheeler, D. 1991, April 12. "What Does It Mean to Know Mathematics?" Paper presented at the International Commission on Mathematics Instructors' Study Conference on Assessment in Mathematics and Its Effects on Instruction. Calonge, Spain.

Wirszup, I., and R. Streit. 1985. *Proceedings of the USCMP International Conference on Mathematics Education on Development in School Mathematics Education Around the World: Applications-Oriented Curricula and Technology-Supported Learning for All Students*. Reston, VA: National Council of Teachers of Mathematics.

Wiske, M. S. 1990. *Teaching Geometry Through Guided Inquiry. Part I. A Case of Changing Mathematics Instruction with New Technologies*. Madison, WI: National Center for Research in Mathematical Sciences Education.

Yevennes, M. 1985, March. The world political economy and the future of the United States labor market. *World Futures* 21: 147–157.

Young, M. 1971. *Knowledge and Control: New Directions for the Sociology of Education*. London: Collier-Macmillan.

Young, M. 1977. "Curriculum Change: Limits and Possibilities." In *Society, State and Schooling*, edited by M. Young and G. Whitty. London: Falmer.

Zarinnia, E. A., S. J. Lamon, and T. A. Romberg, 1987. "Epistemic Teaching of School Mathematics." In *The Monitoring of School Mathematics: Background Paper. Volume 3: Schooling, Teachers, and Teaching*, edited by T. A. Romberg and D. M. Stewart. Madison: Wisconsin Center for Education Research.

Zweng, M., T. Green, J. Kilpatrick, H. Pollak, and M. Suydam. 1983. *Proceedings of the Fourth International Congress on Mathematical Education*. Boston, MA: Birkhauser.

28

SCIENCE AND TECHNOLOGY

Peter J. Fensham
MONASH UNIVERSITY

During the 1980s there has been a quite novel coupling of the words "science" and "technology" in the curriculum field. An association of science education (or its curriculum in schools) with the technological nature of society is not new and was certainly present in the societal discussions that preceded and paralleled the major reforms of science curriculum that occurred on both sides of the Atlantic in the 1950s and 1960s. The current novelty lies, however, in the very widespread belief by politicians and other leading figures in society that technology itself should now be part of the curriculum of schooling and not just be, as it was earlier, a characteristic of the society for which learning science in school was, in various ways, a preparation.

An example of this belief is the enthusiasm with which Boyer (1983), in the report *High School* for the Carnegie Foundation, states that "technological literacy" is the first priority of education. He quotes Bernstein in his advocacy of educating students about technology and its relationship with science.

> We live in a complex, dangerous and fascinating world. Science has played a role in creating the dangers, and one hopes that it will aid in creating ways of dealing with these dangers. But most of these problems cannot, and will not, be dealt with by scientists alone. We need all the help we can get, and this help has got to come from a scientifically literate general public. Ignorance of science and technology is becoming the ultimate self-indulgent word. (Boyer 1983, 111)

Comments like this have been repeated by societal leaders so regularly through the 1980s in many countries that they are not without influence on thinking about the curriculum of schooling. Their translation into curriculum practice is, of course, proving to be a much more tortuous matter.

One result has been the emergence of technology education as a component of the curriculum of schooling. Thus, the National Science Board's Commission on Precollege Education in Mathematics, Science and Technology, in its report to the American people and to the National Science Foundation (1983), calls for a plan of action for improving mathematics, science, and technology education for all elementary and secondary students. Likewise, the Commonwealth Secretariat (1985) in London presented a report, *Interrelating Science, Mathematics and Technology Education*, as a basis for the general education of all students.

Instead of the traditional curriculum partnership of science and mathematics being schooling's contribution to meet the needs of the technological aspects of society, the new tripartite possibility that is indicated in these two reports is now a reality in a number of countries. As a consequence, in March 1989 the Organization for Economic Cooperation and Development (OECD 1989) felt it appropriate to convene a working group from 12 of its member countries to plan a major project in the 1990s to share experiences that are being gained in science, technology, and mathematics curriculum as part of its current overall emphasis on the curriculum of schooling. The United Nations Educational, Scientific and Cultural Organization (UNESCO), with its very much wider clientele of countries in all sorts of stages of industrialization, has also already published two volumes of *Innovations in Science and Technology Education*, indicating that the coupling is not simply a feature of the most industrialized countries (UNESCO 1986, 1988).

The International Council of Scientific Unions (ICSU) also adopted the coupling for the fourth conference its Science Teaching Committee has sponsored. The three

The author wishes to thank Professor Rosalind Driver and Professor David Layton of the University of Leeds for their critical comments and helpful suggestions in the preparation of this chapter.

earlier conferences—Varna 1968, Maryland 1973, and Nijmegen 1978—used "Integrated Science" as their identifying theme. In Bangalore in 1985 this was replaced by "Science and Technology and Future Human Needs," and the conference involved working parties linking education, science, and technology to human needs in relation to water, communication, food and agriculture, industry, and the environment (Lewis and Kelly 1987).

It is, thus, not surprising nor inappropriate for this chapter to be devoted to both science and technology. The relationship of these two components of the school curriculum is, however, problematic. A number of alternative forms of this relationship have already emerged, while in several other countries the problem is clearly recognized but unresolved. Quite different historical antecedents and contemporary forces are usually involved in the determination of the curriculum for science education and for technology education. Thus, variations in the relationship are both inevitable and full of interest. Indeed, they help to make clear just which forces are influential in a given social context.

Since science and technology are now autonomous curriculum areas in many school systems, they are discussed separately in this chapter. Their interrelationship has, however, been kept in mind and is taken up explicitly.

THE CURRICULUM OF SCIENCE

Science education, and particularly the way its curriculum was conceived, underwent a major reformation in the period from the late 1950s to the early 1970s. The early initiatives of what was to become an unprecedented concentration of human and other resources on curriculum development began in the United States, largely under sponsorship of the National Science Foundation, and in Britain, where the Nuffield Foundation played a similar role.

Many other countries followed these leads, sometimes slavishly by simply importing these curricula under a new form of educational imperialism. In most cases they have, some years later, developed indigenous responses to their own particular national demands for up-to-date and better science education in school. Thailand is an example of a country that entered this remarkable phenomenon of curriculum activity more than a decade after it began. In the early 1970s, a special curriculum Institute for the Promotion of Science and Technology Teaching (IPST) was established. Its staff, with relatively large resources and excellent leadership, has produced in a quite remarkable way many major curriculum innovations. These have been supported by student texts, science equipment, teachers' guides, and an extensive program for the professional development of teachers (UNESCO 1984).

Apart from these later starters in the reformation, most of the initial energy and resources had been dissipated by the late 1960s, and the products from the various projects—mainly curriculum materials but also many teachers who, with varying degrees of thoroughness, had been initiated into their intended use—were in or had been offered to schools.

The 1970s was a quiescent period as far as curriculum development in science was concerned and, indeed, increasingly became a decade of malaise and disappointment as evidence accumulated that many or most of the hopes and good intentions of the reformers were not being achieved in schools. Three major studies in the United States (CSSE 1978; Hegelson, Blosser, and Howe 1977; and Research Triangle Institute 1977) documented the shortfall in a particularly thorough way. An international conference in Israel in 1978 provided a forum for similar sobering reports on the problems of curriculum implementation in science (Tamir et al. 1979).

The last of the three U.S. studies under the direction of Stake and Easley at Illinois was a series of case studies that revealed, particularly for the United States, where more atomistic research designs had held sway in science education, how much what happens in science is a reflection of the whole contextual and curricular situation a school is facing. These case studies also set a trend for new ways of researching and evaluating the curriculum of schools and classrooms. As these qualitative forms of research were used more widely they began to tell stories of schools and classrooms (see Delamont 1989; Shapiro 1988), providing glimpses of why learning occurred for some students and not for others.

Beginning in New Zealand in 1979, and spreading to more and more countries as the 1980s proceeded, there is now a new wave of science curriculum reform. While not on quite the same profligate scale as the previous reforms, the resources being put into the current interest in school science are sufficiently large for it to be compared with the earlier efforts.

Accordingly, in order to discuss this more contemporary state of science curriculum it will be useful to review briefly some of the major influences that shaped the earlier reforms, which will be referred to henceforth as the "1950/1960s," although, as just indicated, in some countries this reform period embraced the 1970s as well.

Some of these earlier influences in their contemporary form are still very obvious in the present situation, but a number of new influences now exist that were not part of the scene in the 1950/1960s.

INFLUENCES ON THE CURRICULUM OF SCIENCE (1950/1960S)

From the debates and discussions that preceded the establishment of the projects of the 1950/1960s and from analysis of the project teams and their products, it is possible to identify at least five major influences. These are concerned science teachers, academic scientists, political and economic comparisons, psychological theories of teaching and learning, and philosophical ideas about science and science education.

Concerned Science Teachers

The interest and concern of leaders in the science teaching profession was very evident in Britain through their professional body, the Association for Science Education (Layton 1984), and many of these teachers then played leading roles in the projects themselves. Indeed, these Nuffield projects are still largely associated with names of persons who were grammar school science teachers until they joined the projects.

Science teacher concern was also strongly expressed in the United States, but science teachers never assumed, in the project phase itself, the prominence and influence of their counterparts on the other side of the Atlantic.

Academic Scientists

The National Science Foundation projects are associated with names like Pimentel (chemistry), Zacharias (physics), Glass and Grobman (biology), and Karplus (physics and elementary science)—all academic scientists who were encouraged to take the leading roles in the design and oversight of the curriculum development projects. Leading academic scientists, such as Mott, the director of the Cavendish Laboratory at Cambridge, and Nyholm, a chemist at University College, London, were also prominent and influential in Britain (Layton 1984). The latter's name is always associated with the early Nuffield projects, although neither he nor Mott was involved in the details of developing the projects or their writings. Rogers, an academic physicist, did, however, have a very strong influence on the physics project. In other countries, the extent of practical involvement of academic scientists varied between these two patterns of legitimating patronage and close direction.

In all cases, however, it is now clear that academic scientists exerted a crucial influence on the sort of science content that was included as worthy of learning. They were important legitimators of what topics and what sort of account of them were appropriate for school science. Their exercise of this role did vary in relation to different sciences (Fensham 1980a), being more constraining in the physical sciences than in the biological and earth sciences. Although they were more directly concerned with the curriculum for the later years of secondary schooling, the strong sequential assumptions about scientific knowledge and the preparatory role that one year of schooling plays for the next ensured that this influence had effect at all levels of science curriculum.

Political and Economic Comparisons

The onset of the reforms of the 1950/1960s in the United States and in Britain is often ascribed to the cold war and the launching of the first Sputnik by the Soviet Union in 1957. In fact, the significant lobbying for the reforms had already occurred, so that it was more general aspects of international comparisons that were influential in the decisions to reform. Nevertheless, the belief by politicians, military leaders and business and other societal leaders that scientific progress and technological development, in some senses, were ahead in other competing countries (politically and economically) contributed to the level of support that these reforms enjoyed.

Since at the time there were no significant data that linked achievements of schooling to these wider community requirements, and little that could be used to compare school systems, the assumption of cause and effect was a big one. There is, however, a recurring pattern for schooling to be seen as both the panacea for the problems societies face and the reason for the various ills of society that burst into prominence at various times.

Psychological Theories of Teaching and Learning

Conceptions of teaching and learning as psychological processes have been recurrent influences on curriculum reforms. They were certainly prominent in the projects of the 1950/1960s. Piaget's name is associated with a number of the British projects and with some elementary school projects in the United States. Gagné's more behaviorist views were overtly influential in other American elementary and junior high school projects, and in Britain's Integrated Science project, while Bruner's ideas of discovery learning, generalizing concepts, and readiness to learn were espoused by a number of senior secondary projects. Chaffe-Stenger (1986), for example, reviewed the very substantial influence of Bruner at the Woods Hole Conference conducted in late 1957.

It is interesting to note that the translation of such general theories of teaching and learning into curriculum materials for the teaching of science always resulted in considerable slippage. Between the theory and the preparation of materials for learning there were many opportunities for the influence to weaken, and even more between the materials and classroom practice. These theories were also developed largely from experimental studies in psychology that were divorced both from social contexts like classrooms and from the content of science.

As an illustration of slippage, the role of intuition in science learning—the third of Bruner's (1965) four great themes in *The Process of Education*, his report from the Woods Hole Conference—was virtually ignored by all the major curriculum projects. Many of their developers acknowledged influence from this book, but quite often subsequent practice has subverted potential influence into a role of legitimation.

Philosophical Ideas of Science and Science Education

Philosophical influences were also prominent. In Britain the heuristic ideas of Armstrong at the turn of the century were often referred to in the Nuffield projects (Jenkins 1979). Dewey's ideas of "learning by doing" had a parallel historical influence in North America. Especially in relation to the successful biology projects, Schwab (1962) provided a direct and powerful input from the philosophy of science to the project teams of the Biological Sciences Curriculum Study (BSCS). He argued that the nature of science itself is a process of inquiry—a search for cause and effect. To teach science as inquiry, he suggested that two changes were needed in the role of the laboratory. First, a substantial part of the laboratory work should be made to lead rather than lag the classroom phase of science teaching. Second, the demonstration function of the laboratory should be subordinated to two other functions, namely, to provide a tangible experience of some of the problems of acquiring data dealt with in science and to provide occasions for an invitation to conduct miniature but exemplary programs of inquiry.

A different influence from the philosophy of science, the role of models in science to explain physical phenomena, appeared in the Physical Science Study Committee (PSSC) and several other projects. One other influence from this same source will be discussed again later in the chapter. It was the definition of science processes as objectives for learning (i.e., as the things to be learned) in school science. The so-called process approach to science, with its atomized components of the investigative methods scientists employ, became strongly associated with elementary or primary education. Initially, and in the recommendations in *The Process of Education*, they had been advocated as essential components of the content of science to complement and to give a dynamic to the otherwise potentially sterile body of facts and conceptual knowledge that was now being seen as appropriate for school learners. Bruner also advocated that engagement in these processes was a good way to learn science.

In the struggle, however, to apportion the new ideas about what the content of school science might be in its traditional place in secondary education, and the pressure for it also to be part of the curriculum of the earlier years, a quite unphilosophical dissection occurred. Stated a little crudely but without much exaggeration, the elementary or primary curriculum got the processes, and the secondary curriculum retained the content of science, which was now much more conceptual and less factual and descriptive.

In the 1950/1960s these five influences were generally seen to be cooperative. This spirit of partnership can be summarized in a somewhat simplistic way as follows. The concern of science teachers for the state of their part of the school curriculum gained support from the political and economic comparisons so that decisions for serious reform were made. Academic scientists provided prestige and interest to the curriculum projects and worked with science teachers (usually the more academically well qualified) to produce new curriculum materials. The nature of science and its contemporary forms of expression in academic disciplinary science became the intended learning content of these new materials, and it was presented in ways that tried to be faithful to ideas about how learning occurs.

INFLUENCES ON THE CURRICULUM OF SCIENCE (1980S AND ONWARD)

The five influences that have just been described can all be identified in the spate of discussions, curriculum decisions, and curriculum projects that have been occurring since a revival of interest and concern about science education began in the early 1980s. There are, however, a number of major influences in the present situation that were not part of the 1950/1960s scene. Some of these result from changes within the educational scene itself, and others are more the result of new political and social realities that do not primarily have to do with education systems, but inevitably interact with them.

The influences that are used as a framework for the discussion of the contemporary curriculum trends in science are the following:

Concerned science teachers
Science educators and their research
Academic scientists
Evaluations of the 1950/1960s curricula
Political and economic comparisons
Historical and sociological analyses of curriculum
Theories of teaching and learning
New groups of learners
Philosophical ideas about science
Measurements of educational achievement and science education
Major social changes and international movements
Technologies for learning

It will be noted that the number of recognizable influences has more than doubled, and with such an increase in complexity the earlier sense of complementarity and co-achievement has not been sustained. Competition and tension are now much more the characteristics of the science curriculum scene. In each debate and in each new curriculum project it is clear that not all the interests and needs that these many sources of influence represent can be met. Some will be more successful than others and in that sense more influential.

In retrospect, it is possible to see that there was competition of interest and internal contradictions in what went on in the 1950/1960s. But that period of curriculum reform in science had no obvious previous precedent to analyze and learn from. It was, in a sense, a new phenomenon in education, the establishment of curriculum development as a new educational industry. It had quite new sorts of products, curriculum materials, workers, science educators, and curriculum developers. Together they redefined, in various ways, the idea of curriculum itself.

Historical and Sociological Analyses of the Curriculum

It is not surprising, therefore, that science curriculum became a major new object of study by educational scholars. Historians began to look at the antecedents of such an interesting phenomenon (Layton 1972, 1973) and, as the early projects were completed, they also began to be subjected to historical and social analysis (Fawns 1987; Jenkins 1979; Rowell and Gaskell 1987).

Sociologists of knowledge (Young 1971), sociologists of curriculum (Apple 1979; Bourdieu and Passerou 1977; Gintis 1972), and social analysts of the curriculum projects (Fensham 1980a; Waring 1979) have provided considerable evidence of the way in which an influence turns out to be both a resource for the development of a curriculum and a control of its particular form, its knowledge of worth, the styles of teaching it actually encourages, and the learners it will benefit.

It has been said that the curriculum movement of the 1950/1960s took place as if science and science classrooms were in a historical and social vacuum. With the array of results of historical and social analysis that is now available, it is impossible to excuse any such action in the contemporary scene. This is not to suggest that all the eager science teachers one now finds engaged in curriculum development are aware of these sorts of analyses. The lack of excuse applies to those now making decisions about science curriculum or giving leadership in its new projects. Most of them were part of at least the implementation phases of the efforts of the 1950/1960s and have had opportunities to become acquainted with the rich background of literature available about that period.

Social analysts like those above point out that schools are established by societies in which there are various social groups with interests that such an institutional form of education can serve. The curriculum, in its parts and in its totality, is the instrument to serve these interests, as well as being the field in which the competition between these societal interests in schooling is resolved.

A number of interests that compete for priority in the shape of the science curriculum have been identified. The sciences, particularly the physical sciences, in many societies are gateway subjects that filter the relatively few students who are allowed to move into certain professions of high status, societal influence, and economic security. Because of the societal power associated with these positions, we can call this a *political* interest in schooling. Again, industrial interests need a limited but definite number of persons with scientific skills and expertise to maintain and expand a variety of aspects of a society's economy. This is an *economic* interest. Scientists, particularly in research institutions and universities, are now a power faction in society with a major interest in *maintaining their discipline* as an elite and important field. They are thus keenly interested in having the schools begin the process of reproduction of the sciences as those in higher education define them. In addition, there are clearly many ways in which the *cultural* and *social life* of groups in society are now influenced by technology and by knowledge and applications from the sciences. Science education can assist these groups to have a sense of control rather than of subservience and to take advantage of what science in these various ways has to offer them. The fascination of scientific phenomena and the role of human inventiveness in relation to them offer much potential for school science education to meet the interests of its learners for *individual* growth and satisfaction.

If there are, as has just been indicated, a number of different societal interests in the science education that schools provide, it is not surprising that not all will be equally well met. Indeed, the probability is that the curriculum of a science education that meets one or several of these interests will not serve the others. Recognition of this probability, unfortunately, is still quite rare in the reports and policies of the 1980s, as it was in the 1960s. Without it, some critical implications for science curriculum are likely to be missed in decision making for the current reforms in science education, just as they so largely were in the development and implementations of the 1960s reforms. Hodson (1987) has suggested that each proposal should be subjected to a scrutiny that reveals the underlying sociopolitical motivation of the interest groups. Whose views of science, whose interests, and whose view of society are being advanced?

Curriculum Competition in Action. An example of this competition for the curriculum of science education at school is how it relates to two distinct targets: first, a scientifically based work force; and, second, a more scientifically literate citizenry. The former, related to interests like the political, the economic, and the maintenance of the discipline, is needed so that societies and economies can keep pace in a world in which scientific knowledge and technology are being exploited in a rapidly increasing way. The latter, more related to the other three interests above, consists of those who should benefit from the personal and social applications of science and who will be prepared to respond appropriately to the changes with a scientific or technological character that increasingly confront the society.

At first sight it can appear that the achievement of either of these two targets—a scientifically based work force or a scientifically literate citizenry—will also be a contribution to the other. That is, as the first target is met and exceeded, school science education is on the way to meeting the second. Or, if the second is met to any significant extent, the first will then follow. Just such a simplistic cooperative view of the interactions of societal demands and the curriculum of schooling operated in the reforms of the 1960s. Under the advice and guidance of well-meaning university scientists and encouraged by some slogans about the nature of learning that were current at the time, the 1960s projects did aim at inducting all learners in school into the world of the scientist. Not surprisingly, it was the research scientist they chose as their *model scientist*. There was, it seems, a genuine belief that both targets would be met if all children, in appropriate ways for their level of schooling, were to learn some of the ideas and some of the ways these sorts of scientists use to describe and explore the world. All (or as many as learned successfully) would thus have gained a degree of scientific literacy, and enough of them would be interested to continue on to become the specialist work force of tomorrow.

From the start, however, it became clear that the apparent even-handedness in the statements of intent gave way in practice to the interests the first target represents. The first curricula to be redesigned in, for example, the United States, Britain, Australia, Canada, Sweden, Thailand, and Malaysia were either for the upper secondary school or for elite secondary students—the very levels and streams that contained those from whom the specialist work force would be drawn. By giving priority to the curricula for these students, the projects were explicitly rejecting the interests of the larger target group in scientific literacy. Few countries in the early 1960s had even a majority of each age cohort still at school in these privileged sectors.

Both these target groups and the distinct goals they represent are again referred to in all the rhetoric of the contemporary scene. The rhetoric of "Science for All," that is, for the second goal, is, however, much stronger and clearer than it was in the 1950/60s, and the societal pressures for it to be achieved are much more substantial. Many countries now have a majority of each age group still in school (or are aiming to achieve this state) in the later years of secondary school, and most will not go on to become scientific professionals. Problems of the environment are now inescapable concerns for all citizens, and this world-wide situation is a critical difference between the 1980/1990s and the 1950/1960s that adds strength to the claims for "Science for All."

Roberts (1980) in Canada has contributed greatly to the topic of how competing interest groups in science education perceive the idea of scientific literacy and respond to its curriculum concerns. His notion of *curriculum emphases*, which was exemplified in a curriculum guide for teaching the common science topic properties of matter (Roberts and Orpwood 1979), has proved to be very helpful for discussing the curriculum of science education (Orpwood and Souque 1984) and in a number of curriculum development projects (e.g., Aikenhead 1985; Jenkins et al. 1989).

Roberts (1982) argues that seven curriculum emphases can be found in the history of science education practice in elementary and secondary schools in North America. These are "Everyday Coping, Structure of Science, Science Technology and Decisions, Scientific Skill Development, Correct Explanations, Self as Explainer and Solid Foundation." It is not difficult to associate most of these with one or more of the societal interests that have been described above.

These outcomes of the historical and sociological analyses of science curriculum have been presented before the other influences just described, because they provide the broad framework I wish to use in this chapter in discussing the trends and developments in the curriculum of both science and technology education. Knowledge of the outcomes (and of these sorts of analyses), of course, is also now a not inconsiderable influence on how curricula develop.

Evaluations of the 1950/1960s Curricula

Reference has already been made to summative evaluations carried out in the United States in 1976–1977 to see what impact the projects of the 1950/1960s have had on science curricula. What was found in these studies was also commonly found in other countries when summative evaluations were done (Tamir et al. 1979). First, these summative evaluations were very different from the essentially positive reports that most formative evaluations of the projects in their trial schools had produced. Second, the prestigious names of the National Science Foundation, the Nuffield Foundation, and their counterparts elsewhere helped systems or schools make the decisions to adopt this or that set of curriculum ideas and materials. They had much less effect on how they were implemented in schools and classrooms (e.g., Welch 1979).

The general view that emerges from this implementation literature is that educational innovations usually fail because the intentions of the curriculum developers are not reflected in the teachers' actions. Connelly (1972) has argued persuasively that it is wrong to conclude that this indicates necessarily a deficit on the part of teachers. The teacher's first responsibility is to a particular classroom. Teachers have to interpret the images the curriculum conjures up to them in order to translate these images into a *curriculum-in-classroom-use*. Ben-Peretz (1975) used the term "curriculum potential" to describe the creative but unintended (by the developers) uses by teachers of some project materials.

In terms of the curriculum content, the conceptual emphasis of the 1950/1960s had been widely adopted at the expense of much of the descriptive knowledge and the historical and applied aspects of science (Fensham 1984). The intentions for the understanding of the role of concepts in science have not, however, been successfully included. Many current curricula are now overpacked with the sterile or rote learning of concepts in the absence of an appreciation of how these concepts originated in the data of science or of their usefulness in applications of science in the real world. The national curricula in Japan provide one example of this sort of science content. Shimozawa (1989) has described this curriculum content, which has been in place since 1972 for the various science disciplines. Revisions are planned for 1993 that will add a more applied dimension to the disciplinary sciences and introduce an environmentally oriented integrated science at the senior secondary level.

New Groups of Learners

In the 1950/1960s few countries in the world had a majority of each age group at school for much of secondary education. Indeed, in many Third World countries, a number of which were just beginning as independent states, universal elementary education was, and for some still is, a target to achieve.

Full secondary schooling in most countries was an elite phenomenon, and these few students were headed for a university or other advanced studies that would lead to careers that fairly sharply divided into scientifically based or humanities-based ones. Thus, science education in these later years of schooling was essentially preparatory in its purpose for these further professional studies. For the other group of students, science at this level was not seen as necessary, nor even particularly desirable, since they were bound for the other sorts of professional careers. The curriculum issues at these levels of schooling were thus clear and uncomplicated, and essentially only the societal goal of a scientifically based work force was involved.

In country after country in the intervening years, secondary education has become a right and a reality for an increasing number of each year's cohort of youth. The "reality" meant that many more students were appearing in science classes, and the "right" meant, in the social climate of the later 1960s and 1970s, that selective groupings with different science programs were unacceptable. Science teachers found that their curricula, albeit quite recently designed but with only a minority of these students in mind, were hardly appropriate for the "mixed-ability" classes they now increasingly faced as secondary schooling became "comprehensive."

In the 1980s these changes reached the critical (for science) levels of upper secondary schooling. In many industrialized countries more than 70 percent of students now complete secondary education. The presence of these much greater and more socially representative numbers of students in the final years of secondary schooling, when science education has had its clearest definition and purpose, has meant that very new curriculum questions are being asked of science. Curricula that were designed for the preparation of future scientific professionals have not proven attractive or appropriate for students who are not likely to enter such professions. On the other hand, that the majority of students should cease to study the sciences in their last two or three years at school is also an inadequate response to the importance now claimed for science. What sort of science curriculum is appropriate for these new breeds of secondary students beyond what might be regarded as their basic years of schooling is one of the most pressing contemporary issues in science education. It highlights the competitive demands on its curriculum in a quite new way.

As secondary education becomes more universal, new subgroups of students become identified as in need of science education. In many countries some of these new subgroups can be culturally or ethnically defined. In all countries such an expansion means that there are increasing numbers of students from socioeconomic groupings who have not previously participated. Each new group potentially raises the question, How should or can the curriculum of science be designed so that it will optimally meet the needs of these students? The substantial research findings on how existing science curricula interact with the social and cultural contexts of students (see Wilson 1981) underline the difficulties curriculum designers face in trying to provide clear answers to these questions.

Boeha (1989) provided two examples that dramatically portray these problems. In his study of the difficulties students in Papua New Guinea have in learning physics, he describes the traditional procedures to produce fire and a personal experience as a child of getting a canoe into the water from the beach. The former procedure, which involves the selection of branches from two different sorts of trees, their preparation, and then the functional process of spinning the harder one rapidly against the other until the soft one begins to smoulder, is described in his first language by a single phrase. In the latter, the canoe was "too heavy" for him to pull into the water until his father showed him how to clear some of the sand and put round logs under the bow so that it would roll on them. The canoe was then "light"!

So far some research attention has been given to the language problems that obviously arise when the language of instruction for science is, say, English (as in the Philippines) and the language of the home (and perhaps for other areas of the curriculum) is another one. Much less attention has been given to the less tangible but very pervasive problems that traditional cultures can present to the curriculum of science. Modern science has been largely the product of European culture. Its thought forms and verbal descriptions inevitably are influenced by world views and ways of describing nature that are or were part of those nations. Kulkarni (1988) has referred to the tip of this iceberg of unexplored problems for science curricula in other cultures in an interesting paper on language and science education in India.

The one new group of students that has been fairly widely recognized and for whom there has been considerable curriculum response is *girls*. Girls have, of course, been present in schools in a number of countries alongside boys for many years, although in some they still participate less in school less than do their brothers. In the period since the 1950/1960s there has been a growing awareness in almost all countries that females' participation and achievement in science is less than males'. Because this awareness has been associated with social developments beyond schooling, it will be taken up in more detail later in the chapter in the discussion of the influence of social and international movements.

Measurement of Educational Achievement

Examinations or tests that are used to assess students' learning are powerful influences on the content of worth in any curriculum. In science, with its particular forms of knowledge and its own specific sets of concepts, such testing can critically determine how a curriculum will be interpreted in practice by both teachers and students.

An example of how assessment can be used to reinforce and support a science curriculum's intentions has been provided by Wilson (1987). In this outcome of the Secondary Science Curriculum Review in Britain, the potential of testing as a formative process is stressed. It reflects a view in which the student is an active partner and the form of the assessment is carefully chosen to encourage and motivate learning. It stresses the need for tests to cover the total nature of the science in the curriculum and for their results to be seen as evaluations of the curriculum itself and of the teaching as much as they are evaluations of the students.

Accountability became increasingly important in education throughout the 1970s and 1980s. In large part, this was a response to the evaluations of the many expensive educational projects of the 1960s and early 1970s that, like the science projects described at the beginning of this chapter, promised much but delivered considerably less. As the economies of countries have changed, with more demands on the public purse, it is not surprising that more hard-headed approaches to educational expenditure are now expected.

Although a number of constructive alternatives, such as the one described by Wilson (1987), exist to show how "account" could be given, the use of external tests of students' learning is the most prominent and common manifestation. This use is, in most cases, effectively summative in nature. Such tests do not have the same intimate relationship to the curriculum of a classroom or a course of study as do the assessments, oral, written, and practical, that a teacher or course examination board may construct and use. Particularly in countries in which the science curriculum is decentralized, this means that tests have a "curriculum" of their own that can match or mismatch the chosen curriculum of the school or school system.

In England and Wales, the Assessment of Performance Unit (APU), a national monitoring agency in the 1970s, set up a science team as one of its first areas of focus. The general tasks of the APU teams have been the development of methods of assessment, the monitoring of children's achievement at school, and the identification of under-achievement. The science team developed tests for students aged 11, 13, and 15. It argued successfully for light sampling and for an assessment framework that covered general methods of science inquiry and the application of a body of knowledge. The framework included written tests of "symbolic representation, interpretation and application"; "planning investigations"; and practical hands-on tests of "the use of apparatus and measuring instruments" (in groups), "observation" (in groups), and "performance of investigation" (individual).

Such wide-ranging tests of science learning, with their potential to give reinforcement and new emphases to the school science curriculum, have as yet been used in the United States only on a pilot scale (National Assessment of Education Performance [NAEP] 1987). State-wide and national testing is now so widespread in the United States that the luxury of light sampling seems to be reserved for research studies. Multiple-choice forms of written tests of science learning are much more economical to use than those developed by Blumberg et al. (1986), which involved more complex presentations and responses and hands-on operation of laboratory equipment.

Womer (1981) and Popham (1983) have pointed to the increasing pressure on teachers to *teach for test results*, and this situation has its supporters and detractors. Supporters argue that the national or state-prepared tests can, and often do, present a richer science curriculum than many of the tests constructed by teachers, with their emphasis on rote recall (Bloom 1984). Resnick and Resnick (1985), on the contrary, argue that the range is still very narrow when the richness of science is considered.

Supporters of testing have argued that it is useful to identify gender aspects of learning science, to identify exemplary schools and low-achieving ones, and to show gaps between the achievements of social groups of learners (Carlson 1981). It is not nearly so evident how the commonly used tests assist teachers to implement their curriculum's intentions. Indeed, it is likely that the use of state-wide testing has reduced the confidence and competence of teachers to design and choose their own assessment procedures (Calfee 1987).

Murnane and Raizen (1986) reported on an investigation of indicators of quality in science and mathematics education. Although the project revealed many weaknesses in present testing practices, and a number of negative effects on the science curriculum, its authors still recommended that external testing on a wide scale should continue and that more tests, other than multiple choice, be developed to measure other learning outcomes in science.

International Comparisons

Because of the prominence of science as a major focus of the curriculum movement in the 1950/1960s, it was natural that it should be one of the first curriculum fields to be studied by the International Association for the Evaluation of Educational Achievement (IEA).

Nineteen countries took part in the first science study, which was reported in 1973 by Comber and Keeves (1973). Science was again studied a decade later (IEA 1988), and 17 countries this time participated.

Random samples of students at various stages of elementary and secondary schooling are assessed in these studies for their knowledge of disciplinary and interdisciplinary science. A great deal of data are also collected about the conditions in which the students study, their schools, their teachers, and their school systems. The tests of knowledge achievement are cooperatively developed, and the design allows for particular items relevant to the content of each nation's courses of study to be included.

The International Association is very conscious of the interaction of the contextual variables and the learning achievements and thus takes care in all its publications to indicate the caution with which comparative judgments should be made about the national scores. Journalists do not always heed such warnings, and it was common in the later 1980s for media reports to simply refer to the IEA results as if they were definitive league tables. Politicians and other public figures, who usually see summarized versions of the IEA findings, also often tend to respond to them as if they were direct evidence of the worth of a school system. The extent to which comparative IEA findings have been quoted in the curriculum debates in various countries suggests that they have added substance or complacency to the international comparisons that stem from less direct educational measures of the comparative state of nations, such as unemployment, balance of payments, and technological competitiveness.

Despite the potential that these studies have, from their multivariate design, to provide some detailed findings of relevance to curriculum planning, there is surprisingly little evidence that this has occurred. Canada's participation in the second IEA science study has been linked to the Science Council of Canada's review of science education earlier in the 1980s. This may help to extend the influence of these sorts of data. Connelly, Crocker, and Kass (1985a, 1985b), who were responsible, were certainly very conscious of the complexity of interpreting the achievement data in the federal education system situation of Canada. They decided, therefore, to investigate the context of Canadian science education in a depth that went far beyond the independent variables collected in the IEA survey itself. Their chapters on the history of science education in Canada, and on science education in a changing society, are outstanding contributions that set standards for similar work elsewhere. Their description of contemporary Canadian science curricula portrays the confusing reality of federal systems that persons living in countries with unified national systems cannot begin to understand.

Against such a context they have discussed the achievement results and their correlates. The authors claim that their two volumes offer a solid body of descriptive data that can shed light on the relation between policy and practice and serve as a basis for needed curriculum reform. The extent to which the reforms that are now in process in a number of Canadian provinces draw on their data will be interesting to monitor.

Political and Economic Comparisons

In country after country the 1980s were punctuated by statements by prominent societal spokespersons and by reports on the state of the nation that urge more and better science education. These reports almost always include a research element that presents new data or a reworking of existing data. Some of them, like the Canadian one described below, represent major contributions to research on the curriculum. In this sense they differ from the more polemic comparative statements in the 1950/1960s discussed earlier. The research the reports present or represent is, however, constrained by the terms of reference of the review and/or the biases of those responsible. To command attention, these reports often make use of sweeping rhetoric: "Our children could be stragglers in a world of technology in which technological skills and sophistication are the basic capital of tomorrow's society" (National Science Foundation 1983) is a not untypical example.

The best efforts of the 1950/1960s reforms are acknowledged by such groups as impressive curricula for the more able and committed students, but by the 1980s this was not seen as being enough. Science and technology education, they argue in report after report, can no longer ignore the cultural and economic milieu of modern society or the great mass of the students who are now in school.

The two broad aims that were referred to in the curriculum reforms of the 1950/1960s—a scientifically based work force and a scientifically literate citizenry—are both now regular targets of these reports. They tend to assess the former as having been met with varying degrees of quantitative success, but see the *quantity* of the technological work force as a necessary but not sufficient condition for a healthy society. Equally important and not being achieved is the *quality* of this work force to address problems of national significance and to incorporate science and technology into the life of society without destroying its culture. They assess the second target as having been addressed thus far only incidentally and accordingly now give it a much greater priority.

The four-year study by the Science Council of Canada (1984), as an example, was reported as *Science for Every Citizen*, an indication of its priority for the second target. Four objectives for school science were stated as follows:

1. Develop citizens able to participate fully in political and social choices facing a technological society.
2. Train those with special interest in science and technology education for further study.
3. Provide an appropriate preparation for modern fields of work.
4. Stimulate intellectual and moral growth of students.

The first and second objectives identify the two target groups. The third objective acknowledges the changing nature of work for all in technological societies, and the fourth provides a link between the qualities in individuals and their corporate actions referred to in the first objective.

The Asian and Pacific regions of the world are made up of member states that are in many ways culturally, economically, industrially, and politically different from the countries in the Western world where these sorts of reports are easily accessible. Nevertheless, it was for these countries that their ministers of education, as a group in 1984, endorsed the report *Science for All* (UNESCO 1983) as a priority project for development. This is probably the first official use of this phrase, which in various guises epitomizes the new priorities for school science curricula. The tortuous task of shifting the relative position of these two priorities in the school science curriculum is the practical agenda for the contemporary situation across the world.

Concerned Science Teachers

The concern of the professional associations of science teachers has been a major factor in many countries in the revival of interest in science education and in the shape its curriculum might take. The quality of the input they can make to their local situations has increased since the 1950/1960s because they are now more informed about the problems that are being faced and the solutions being tried by their colleagues in other countries. In 1973 an International Council of Associations for Science Education was formed to link these national professional bodies. It has been active in promoting exchanges of teachers and curriculum information through large international conferences and newsletters and through sponsorship of smaller regional workshops where the problems and situations facing the participants are often more similar. Many of these science teacher associations now regularly produce or espouse policy statements on the science curriculum that can have considerable influence on their members, paving the way for their reception and response to curriculum decisions and to new projects and their products—areas of activity from which most teachers are excluded.

In their everyday experience in schools, teachers are the ones who experience the successes and failures of existing science curricula. They are the ones who are most aware of the extent to which and the way in which a science curriculum appeals to or repels the "new groups" of students that politicians and the administrators of educational systems are urging should be studying and benefiting from science learning.

In many countries, secondary science teachers have tended to polarize in the face of the new demands that "Science for All" is asking of them. Science usually has quite a high status in the community and almost invariably does in schools. The very concern in society about it is evidence of its importance. Traditionally, science has drawn an academically rather elite and unusual group of students who continue with science throughout secondary school. Teaching these students has been rewarding and professionally satisfying, and schools maintain these classes even though they may have fewer students than other subjects.

Teaching the majority of students science for their sake and not because they are also looking to scientific professions is a new challenge for many of these teachers, who find it a daunting social prospect and an educational task that is far from easy.

In general, the professional associations have taken a stand in the 1980s on the side of "Science for All," but many of their members are more hesitant and comfortable with the traditional types of elite curricula for which their own socialization in science has equipped them. There is considerable evidence of this conservatism among science teachers, and it is a definite brake on the prospects for curriculum reforms. Teachers well trained in one discipline of science are usually loath to teach across the disciplines. Science teachers have not usually been among those who respond to opportunities to innovate as schools have tried to be more responsive to their widening range of secondary students. Relatively few alternate science curricula have been devised in systems that allow such curriculum options and teacher initiatives to occur.

This tension among teachers was exemplified in the relatively conservative policy statement on science curriculum by the Association for Science Education (Association for Science Education 1981) in Britain. It resulted from what must have been a number of negative responses to the quite radical discussion paper (Association for Science Education 1979) prepared by a subgroup of teachers who had taken up the Science, Technology and Society (STS) and environmental challenges, encapsulating them in their startling suggestion that the loci for school science education should be *the laboratory*, *the workshop*, and *the field*. Very similar advances and partial retreats have been reported among science teachers in a number of countries through the 1980s.

Science Educators

Science educators as a professional group, distinct from science teachers or educational researchers more generally, can almost be said to have been created by the curriculum reforms of the 1950/1960s. Certainly before that time few persons had the characteristics that now mark this key group of persons in relation to science curricula. The projects of that period were staffed by experienced science teachers and academic scientists. Many of these teachers, after their experience as curriculum developers, moved into academic or advisory positions in science education where they were able to continue in curriculum development work, in professional development of teachers, or in research. Their substantive positions usually involved them in the initial education of science teachers, but they were different from the persons who had held these posts in the past and who had still been essentially teachers sharing with neonate teachers "how I did it" or "how I would do it."

The new breed of science educators had quite other perspectives to share and other questions to ask and answer. The first association for such professionals, the National Association for Research in Science Teaching, began in the early 1960s, and its pioneering journal in the field has now been joined by 6 to 10 other national and international journals devoted to research and development that relates to aspects of science curriculum.

These professionals have had the responsibility, time, and access to resources to develop a number of new, well-formulated bases for use in science curriculum. They carry out research studies on many aspects of science education, including those on its teaching and learning (discussed further in the section on the curriculum as construction of meaning). They have identified with a number of social movements and have worked to understand them and to translate them into terms that enable them to influence science curricula. These professionals and the many results of their research and other professional work were simply not available in the 1950/1960s. They now occupy many key positions in the curriculum discussions, decisions, and developments that are at present in progress. They are a very significant new source of influence, standing between the academic scientists and the science teachers.

In some countries, such as Britain, Canada, the United States, Malaysia, and Australia, science educators are grouped under the academic heading "education." On the continent of Europe and in China, Thailand, and Latin countries, science educators are usually grouped with the scientists whose disciplinary background they share. In general, they have been significant in the priorities now being given to "Science for All" in many countries. Those in education have tended to support a more general view of science and its relation to other subjects and to students' lives. Those in the science departments have tended to push for the emphases of the Science, Technology and Society movement (described later) in each science discipline.

Posner (1982) opened up an avenue of influence for more cognitively oriented science educators when he related a number of new developments in cognitive science to curriculum studies by using the idea of "tasks" as a central conception that indicates how the curriculum is viewed. If we want to understand what a student's experience of the process of learning is, and the reasons why some learning outcomes are occurring and not others, we must understand the tasks in which she or he is actually engaging and not just the tasks the teachers think they are "giving" to the student. Tasker's work in New Zealand classroom settings (Tasker and Freyberg 1985) supports this point very strongly.

Some science educators who have set out to gain this understanding are those involved in the Project to Enhance Effective Learning (PEEL) in Australia. The project had its origins in several studies of metacognition in science learning by Baird and White of Monash University, which were reported at the annual meeting of the American Education Research Association (AERA) in 1984 (see also Baird 1986; Baird and White 1982a, 1982b). These science educators then joined forces with Mitchell, a chemistry teacher in a local high school. Together they persuaded a group of 10 teachers in the school, who shared a number of junior high classes, to join a cooperative attempt to improve learning in their classrooms, an educational purpose these teachers understood and saw as needed and desirable. The research findings with which the PEEL group (the committed teachers and the Monash researchers) began were about children's conceptions and methods of gathering these (like those referred to in the section on theories of teaching and learning) and the metacognitive findings of Baird and White. The terms of the project for both teachers and researchers were to be committed to it for two years and to support each other in the innovations the teachers wished to try when they were ready. By halfway through the second year the group produced a book with 10 of its 14 chapters written by teachers and a student (Baird and Mitchell 1986). A number of other schools now have PEEL projects based on the same collaborative action research model, and their teachers are now inventing and trying out in their science classrooms many new strategies for teaching and learning. In briefly reporting this exciting curriculum development it would be unbalanced not to refer to the tensions that arose in these classrooms as teachers and students both began to realize that the "tasks," in Posner's sense, on which they were together engaged, did not follow their thinking, or even were not those they wanted. Conceptual change in what teaching and learning science is about is as stubbornly resistant to change as are conceptions of science. Shapiro (1988) has recently reported a delightful series of vignettes from elementary school science lessons that show all too clearly how these metacognitive conceptions begin to be shaped.

The very considerable teacher wisdom or professional knowledge that the PEEL project has unleashed is related to the ideas of Schon (1983, 1987) about professionals as reflective practitioners, which have caught the imagination of many groups involved in science and other curriculum fields. Shulman (1986) referred to the content of teaching as the missing paradigm in research on teaching. In the case of science curriculum the questions he raised are, What kind of science knowledge do teachers need? and Is the science knowledge for teaching different from the knowledge held by scientists in the field? His large project at Stanford on teacher knowledge has set out to answer these sorts of questions. Wilson and Shulman (1987) have reported some of their interesting findings and pointed to the implications they can have for curriculum implementation. These studies can be related to the shift in research focus occurring at that time, from children's conceptions of science to teachers' conceptions of science (e.g., Arzi 1988).

One of the important influences that the work of these science educators has had on the present curriculum scene has been to move its priorities from centrally produced curriculum materials for students to professional development of teachers. The evaluations of the 1950/1960s projects almost invariably indicated insufficient attention had been given to developing teachers to use the elaborate materials that were produced. Many contemporary science educators remember the way the pressure to produce the tangible products, such as texts, films, laboratory manuals, and teachers' guides, excluded those professional development features they knew were necessary.

Academic Scientists

Unlike the concerns and very considerable interest expressed by leading figures in the community of academic scientists during the reforms of the 1950/1960s, there was a more muted contribution from this source in the 1980s. The most general concerns expressed by university scientists in the 1980s were quantitative ones. There was concern that not enough students were coming out of schools to continue advanced studies in scientific and technological fields. There was concern that fewer of the high achievers in school science were choosing to continue studies in science. There was concern that the proposals to reshape and redefine the science curricula in schools in ways that suit "Science for All" would devote less time to traditional studies in basic chemical and physical content.

These sorts of concerns, on the whole, have acted as brakes on reform of science curricula rather than spurs for it. The first two concerns could result in spurs for reform if the scientific community could be convinced that many more students would study science and wish to continue with it if its curriculum in schooling were very different. However, this would not resolve the third concern, and, in general, the academic scientific communities have made a priority of maintaining this now-traditional content (Fensham 1988a; Gaskell 1987).

It is interesting to note that the very conceptualized

content for science is an emphasis that came into school science courses as a result of the 1950/1960s reforms and as part of a general push encouraged by the academic scientific community to bring the curricula of school science up-to-date. At that time, as a result of world-wide depression and World War II, it had been a long time since the science curricula in many countries had been seriously revised. In hindsight, however, it can be seen that what the push to "update" the curriculum achieved—particularly in physics and chemistry—was to include for learners in school the conceptual and more theoretical approach to well-established basic science topics that was the language and approach used in universities. This, rather than the inclusion of the many new topics and fields of science that had been developed during the war and in the 15 years before and after it, was what updating meant. Biological and earth science curricula proved more amenable to the inclusion of these sorts of topics. Fensham (1980a) has discussed the significant differences between the expectations academic scientists have for physics and chemistry in schools compared with those for other natural sciences.

Academic voices have expressed concern about the content of school chemistry and physics. Gillespie (1976) in Canada and Bucat and Cole (1988) in Australia are typical of one set of these voices. However, they are not calling for teaching about the many exciting new substances chemists have made and discovered in recent years. They are concerned about the emphasis on general concepts and abstract principles to the exclusion of familiarity with chemical reactions and with field and laboratory experiences. They do encourage knowledge and experience of the role of chemicals in applied areas like foods, building materials, and consumer products, but on the whole they seem to conceive of these applications in terms of simple and basic chemicals that have long been part of school chemistry rather than in terms of newer substances with quite novel properties.

A few exceptions can be noted to the claim mentioned earlier that there has been a lack of a coherent voice for new science and new approaches from the scientific community. The Royal Society (1985) in Britain produced a short and startling manifesto, *Science Is for Everybody*, in a report on the public understanding of science. A proper science education at school, it states, must provide the basis for an adequate understanding of science, which is then to be added to throughout life. This understanding includes not just facts but the methods of science and its limitations, as well as an appreciation of the practical and social implications of science. Some understanding of statistics, including ideas of risk, uncertainty, ratios, and variability, are so intrinsic to the method of science and to understanding many personal and public issues, the manifesto claims, that they should be goals of all science curricula.

This manifesto calls for a very different sort of curriculum for the whole school population. It is thus strong support for "Science for All." By not addressing the tension this creates for the elite and extended studies of individual science disciplines that still characterized British elite science education in 1985, it is not clear whether the tension was recognized. It seems likely that the manifesto from such a prestigious body was helpful in the subsequent moves that established a core curriculum of "balanced science" for all students up to the age of 16.

In the United States one curriculum project that has given singular prominence to scientists is Project 2061. With its title drawn from the year Halley's Comet will next appear, this project of the American Association for the Advancement of Science (AAAS) has recently reported on its first phase. In this phase nearly 60 scientists have been engaged in panels for biological and health sciences; mathematics; physical, information and engineering sciences; social and behavioral sciences; and technology to answer the question, What are the components your sciences offer to scientific literacy? Panels were asked, in answering this question, to list (and briefly explain) the scientific knowledge, skills, and attitudes all American students should acquire as a consequences of their total school experience from kindergarten to high school graduation. From these separate panel reports a composite report, *Science for All Americans* (AAAS 1989), was developed by the project team, advised by a large number (about 200) of reviewers.

The design of this project deliberately identifies school teachers with the later phases of the project. No panel in the first phase had any school teacher, consultant, or parent members, and among the host of reviewers, there were eight identifiable school persons and one parent representative. No students were asked to act as reviewers.

Reversing the trend to add more and more to school science curricula is a major goal of Project 2061. Accordingly, in preparing the composite report, the recommendations of its scientific panels that do include many new topics were subjected to educational criteria of "utility, social responsibility, intrinsic value of knowledge, philosophical value and childhood enrichment." The outcome of this process seems to be the elimination of a number of the more complex topics in the panel reports, but what remains will require a ruthless pruning of many current topics if the goal of reducing the quantity of knowledge and increasing the quality of learning is to be achieved.

Educators (including many school teachers, it is to be hoped) and scientists are to form teams in Phase II that will transfer the science content from Phase I into blueprints for action—a variety of curriculum models to become educational practice in schools and school districts in Phase III.

The project is avowedly top-down, with scientists at the top. Even in Phase II, in which the alternative curriculum models are to be worked out, there is talk of creating "a cadre of committed knowledgeable and experienced leaders" to translate the recommendations of Phase I into actual curricula and to act as "experts in school curriculum reform" (AAAS 1989, 162).

Some of the recommendations contrast strongly with those in many of the other approaches that are aimed at "Science for All." The content recommended by the scientific panels is very conceptual and is largely confined to the concepts science uses to describe the various scientific phenomena of importance. An experiential emphasis is recommended but underplayed as a goal.

The report commends the use of a historical perspective in teaching science for two reasons. It suggests that such an approach can exemplify the way ideas are products of their historical time and place, springing often from unexpected findings and growing slowly as many scientists contribute. Second, it wishes the cultural salience of some of the great episodes of scientific endeavor to be appreciated by students. Most science teachers are now, however, quite unfamiliar with this sort of a perspective, and it is largely absent from the socialization they receive in their own tertiary education in science. In such hands it seems unlikely that the potential of this suggestion is going to be realized for students. A major conference in Florida late in 1989 brought philosophers of science together with historians and science educators to address the issues these suggestions raise.

With respect to girls and other underparticipating groups, *Science for All Americans* takes a rather hard line. Teachers should select materials that illustrate the contributions of women and minorities. They should bring in role models, but they should make it quite clear to girls and minority students that they are expected to study the same subjects, at the same level, as everyone else and to perform as well.

It is interesting to see how technology is faring in Project 2061. Not surprisingly, technology was a panel in its own right. Quite surprisingly, however, engineering was not part of it but was grouped with the physical sciences—an alliance that is consistent with academic engineering's rejection of technology in schools (see below).

The technology panel identified eight basic areas of technology that collectively it describes as "the designed world." These are "agriculture, materials, manufacturing, energy sources, energy use, communications, information processing, and health technology." How technology works in these areas within the social, cultural, economic, and ecological systems in which students live was seen as what the focus of technology education in schools should be.

The science panels tended to see technology as an object of study. Students should learn about the nature of technology, its connections with science, its principles, and its connections with society. Technology draws on science and contributes to it. Engineering combines scientific inquiry with practical values. All technologies involve control. The essence of engineering is design under constraint. Technologies have side effects and they can fail. Technological and social systems interact strongly, and decisions about the use of technology are complex.

The social and behavioral sciences panel did not come up with either technology or the environment as central themes. The academic disciplinary threads that still run strongly through this project were very evident in the familiar and traditional social themes this panel identified as key sources for learning.

There is obviously a long way to go in this project before it can impinge as curricula on American classrooms generally. Its progress along this road will be very interesting to study in the 1990s because it is more like a 1950/1960s project in design than like most other recent curriculum projects. It seems to envisage school science as a steady induction *into* the sciences rather than the sciences being seen as an important set of sources *from which* knowledge and experiences relevant to the students' lives and futures can be drawn.

Theories of Teaching and Learning

Of the theories that were influential in the 1950/1960s, only that of Piaget still has much explicit currency. In the sense of the association between thinking and experience, the idea of emphasizing concrete, hands-on experiences with younger learners has widespread recognition in science curricula and in its practice. In the sense of how these experiences can be used to develop logical thinking about natural phenomena, only a few curricula are consistently maintaining and exploiting this emphasis.

Shayer and Adey (1981) in Britain and Lawson (1985) and Case (1989) in North America have for many years strongly advocated the importance of Piagetian ideas in the science curriculum. In Europe the curriculum emphases of *correct explanation* and *solid foundations* in disciplinary sciences have tended until recently to inhibit Piagetian influences compared with situations in which a *process approach* has been more espoused.

The most conspicuous psychological influence on curriculum thinking in science since 1980 has been the constructivist view of learning. In the 1970s, research studies in science education began from several different directions to explore how students in school conceived of various scientific phenomena and of concepts (such as force, life, electric current, and solution) that science uses to describe and explain these phenomena. Borrowing a type of clinical interviewing from the work of Piaget and Inhelder, a number of different probing techniques were used by Driver (1983), Gunstone and White (1981), Novak (1978), Osborne and Freyberg (1985a); and Pines et al. (1978).

The establishment of a new curriculum project in science in New Zealand in 1979 led to a concentration of effort there that rapidly refined some of these methods and produced many findings on the views that students across a wide age range have of many biological, chemical, and physical phenomena (Osborne and Freyberg 1985b). Champagne, Gunstone, and Klopfer (1985), and a number of other science education researchers who have followed them, have shown that conceptual change in students at a fundamental level is not easy. They have, however, found that certain conditions do encourage and facilitate it.

The expansion of these studies led to a number of reviews of the field (Driver and Ericksen 1983, Driver, Guesne, and Tiberghien 1985; Gilbert and Watts 1983) and to the establishment of a Special Interest Group (SIG) within the AERA for "Subject Matter Knowledge and Conceptual Change," which has a newsletter and an established record for lively sessions in the annual meeting and at a premeeting workshop. The appearance of a substantial monograph edited by West and Pines (1985) was also an important step in establishing constructivist ideas as an important base in science education.

The SIG now brings together on a regular basis scholars with this orientation toward science education. There had, however, already been a conference in Leeds in 1980, which, while not so exclusively concerned with conceptions studies, did lead to two further conferences on this field that have been held in Paris, at Cornell University (twice), and in Dortmund, Germany. Pfundt and Duit (1987) at the IPN in Kiel, Germany, have acted as a clearinghouse for studies in the conceptions field, and their most recent bibliography now contains more than 1,000 reports of studies.

The late Roger Osborne of New Zealand, a significant pioneer in this field, collaborated with Wittrock (1974), whose generative theory of learning had been published earlier, to produce an account of how this theory could be married to the science conceptions findings and thus be related to the curriculum of science education (Osborne and Wittrock 1985).

Under the more familiar title of a "constructivist approach to learning," these ideas have now been elaborated in considerable detail (Driver and Bell 1986; Driver and Oldham 1986; Fensham 1989). They are based on the idea that the learner is the constructor of her or his own knowledge and that nobody else can do this. Others, like teachers, can stimulate, elicit, challenge, facilitate, and guide this process of learning. The learner's own views and ability are respected in this sort of teaching, and the students' views become topics of explicit social discourse with peers and the teacher.

A basic difference between the case of this constructivist approach to learning as an influence on science curriculum and the theories of learning in the 1950/1960s described earlier is that so much of its development has been rooted in studies of young persons interacting with scientific phenomena. Another is that these studies have been done by science education researchers and not by psychologists, and they are increasingly being done in collaboration with teachers. It is thus not so much a general learning theory to be related to a science curriculum, but knowledge about the way learners interpret scientific phenomena and form concepts about them and about how teachers find they can facilitate such learning.

As an illustration of how these science educators interact and influence curricula, the work of the lively group of French science educators can be cited (Martinand and Giordan 1989). Between 1972 and 1980 the group at the National Institute for Pedagogical Research published six volumes of *Activités d'Éveil Scientifiques à l'École Élémentaire* (Consciousness Raising Activities in Science in Elementary School). These volumes have defined topics for investigation and drawn attention to conceptual frameworks for many teachers. Giordan in Geneva and Martinand in Paris together coedit *Actes des Journées Internationales sur l'Éducation Scientifique*, which annually reports the work of researchers and science teachers from countries with the Latin tradition.

Approaches to learning based on information processing models have also been evident in relation to science curriculum in the 1980s. For example, Greeno (1978) and Larkin (1983), from research on problem solving, have suggested that a learner first constructs a representation of a "problem space" that governs the way encoding of information then occurs.

Eylon and Linn (1988) and Linn (1986, 1987) have reviewed many of the more recent studies of science learning under four broad approaches. These have a concept-learning focus, a development focus, a differential focus that seeks to explain why some students learn science and others fail, and a focus on problem solving in science. The authors point out that these studies all concentrate on the learner, recognize the initial state of her or his knowledge as important, and show how difficult it is to bring about change. The four approaches together provide a detailed view of science learners that also emphasizes the complexity of science education and the many factors that contribute to its effectiveness. With respect to curriculum, research from these approaches would support "in-depth" coverage of a few science topics. Since this conflicts with the usual "in-breadth" coverage of many topics in most curricula, these authors suggest a few should be deliberately chosen for systematic coverage and the rest should be dealt with in less detail.

Philosophical and Sociological Views of Classroom Science

Reference has already been made to the broader perspectives on science curriculum as a whole that are available from historical, philosophical, and sociological studies now, as compared with the 1950/1960s. At the more tangible level of the classroom these sorts of perspectives have also been influential on the way curricula are and can be interpreted.

For example, Hodson (1988) has refined Schwab's earlier work on *Science as Enquiry* by pointing out differences among the inquiries in science. Each one arises in relation to specific subject matter, and the essence lies in the sorts of concepts, data, and questions that are employed. It is this interweaving of phenomena, concept, and process that Millar and Driver (1987) express in their concerns about the predominant place many junior science curricula have given to science processes over science content. Lybeck (1981), in his study of the teaching and learning of the Archimedes principle, has provided a splendid example of the point Hodson is making. Earlier Hodson (1985) used a philosophical basis to identify a number of distinct learnings in science education. If these distinctions are not to be blurred or lost, he argues, each needs a definite "space" in the curriculum so that students recognize it for what it is and have enough practice with it. Horwood (1982) makes a similar case using Robert's idea of curriculum emphasis discussed earlier.

Jenkins et al. (1989) in their STSC Chemistry set out to provide this sort of curriculum space for each of their emphases: "science, technology, society and communication."

Fewer contributions have been made at this classroom level by those with sociological orientations, as Delamont (1989), one of the exceptions, points out. She laments that many science teachers fall back on unthinking replications of classrooms from the past, despite the considerable, albeit fragmentary, evidence that other sorts of classroom environments they could create would have a profound effect on a curriculum's outcomes.

Some of the case studies in Stake and Easley's evaluation (CSSE 1978) of science education in the United States describe these sorts of environmental effects, although often these were not recognized by the teachers or used by them in a positive curricular sense. Shapiro (1988), in her intensive case study of elementary school children in science lessons, paints vivid portraits of a teacher unaware of the effect her classroom environment is having.

Driver (1989) and French (1989) have very recently provided examples of the sort of research Delamont is urging and of positive curricular responses to it. There is a tremendous scope for more studies and more active exploration of this potentially powerful aspect of curriculum. Fraser and Northfield (1981) found that the very different classroom environments that the Australian Science Education Project (ASEP) encouraged in the 1970s correlated well with those students' enjoyment of science. It was the only learning outcome, in fact, to do so, but this link is one that should not be underestimated. Suan (1976), in an evaluative study of the use of these ASEP materials in class, provided ethnographic data of the conversations among eighth grade students in practical activities. A decade later Wallace (1986) analyzed similar data into its functional roles and emphasized how essential these varieties of talk are to the success of the social operations of science practical work. Edwards and Marland (1984), in studies of more teacher-centered science lessons, has found ways students take "time out" as an essential aspect of their participation—an interesting subtlety on what previously had been interpreted as "time-on-task."

The science conceptions research has so far largely concentrated on the outcomes in learners of what are obviously a very complex array of social influences in and out of school. It needs to begin to tease out this complexity, and particularly the role that classroom experiences play, since these are the curriculum aspect most amenable to change.

Kulkarni (1988), Lemke (1982), and Sutton (1989), with quite different emphases and methodologies, have all reported on aspects of the influence of language. Solomon (1987) reviewed the scattered literature on a number of social influences on science learning. In each area she found evidence of pervasive influences that make the teaching of a rigidly insulated science, which has no contact with everyday contexts, nonsense for any group of students and a quite untenable option if the curriculum's intentions are widespread learning.

Major Social Changes and International Movements

Four major changes in society and on the international scene since the 1950/1960s have been direct influences on the curriculum of science. These stem from the movements for social responsibility of science, the environmental movement, and the women's movement.

In the 1950s the international Pugwash movement, established by the Nobel Laureate Bertrand Russell and associations like that of Atomic Scientists in the United States, while they involved some very distinguished scientists, were regarded with suspicion by governments and by the scientific communities. Their focus of concern was the threat of nuclear war, and inevitably this associated these scientists with the polarizations of such a politically charged agenda. Their concerns were certainly ignored by the curriculum reforms of the 1950/1960s.

During the 1960s governments of all sorts began to work more closely with Pugwash and these scientists. As some progress began to be made on nuclear disarmament, this group of scientists widened the area of their concerns to include a number of less obviously political issues. An organization actually called "Social Responsibility of Science" emerged in the late 1960s in a number of countries, and it attracted the support and interest of scientists from many disciplines. These interests have outlasted the formal organization, and many scientists are now concerned and involved in specific aspects of the interaction between science and technology and society.

Because these broader societal issues had many facets that were not solely scientific, they were also of concern to many others in society. In 1972 the United Nations conference on the Human Environment was held in Stockholm, and very quickly the environment became a focus for concern, action, and education across the world. An international program for developing environmental education at all levels of formal and nonformal education was launched (see UNESCO 1978).

Scientists have been prominent in the environmental movement through bodies such as the International Union for the Conservation of Nature and programs such as Man and the Biosphere. More and more resources of a scientific and technological kind are having to be diverted to try to stem the impacts that human society, particularly in its more technologically developed forms, has and is still having on the well-being of planet Earth. Much of this environmental damage is the direct result of the way scientific knowledge and technology have been practiced. Repair of this damage will certainly, however, involve more science and technology, as well as massive changes in social behavior on the part of many people. Scientists and technologists are in the environmental movement as both villains and saviors. At the end of the 1980s the political importance of the environment was on the increase, and governments of all sorts were recognizing that a response to the concern about it was essential if they were to retain office.

The 1960s also saw the emergence, in increasingly organized and effective ways, of women's movements in many countries. These have had, and continue to have, major consequences for the relations between men and women and for the places women occupy in society. Among the latter was the very evident fact that females, through the education system or because of social expectations, have been very low participators in those sectors of society that directly employ those who have studied in science and technology.

Educational responses to environmental concern began to be organized and defined from the mid-1970s. These, in turn, began to ask a number of new questions of the science curricula in schools, such as what emphasis was being given to topics like energy use, resource availability, agricultural efficiency, acid rain, and ecology systems where humans are major interactors. Not only were these topics usually absent from school science curricula but also many of these curricula did not include pedagogies that were as action oriented or as concerned with values as the environmental movement was urging.

Fensham and May (1979) summarized these environmental characteristics and presented a model whereby they could be incorporated into the curriculum as deliberate, though not the only, emphases of science education.

On the whole the educational responses both to the social responsibility of science and to the environmental movement have, in the 1980s, been subsumed into a movement known as "Science, Technology and Society (STS)," a trilogy of ideas that has increasing potency for science curricula. In a similar manner to that described earlier for the scientific community as a whole, the more general, and hence less focused, STS movement has provided a more neutral forum for concerned science teachers and educators than the primarily environmental one that has so sharply polarized societies over so many issues in the 1970s and 1980s.

Science, Technology, and Society. STS, as a moderate manifestation of two major social movements, is undoubtedly now a well-established source of new challenges and ideas for science education. It is an organized movement among teachers in several countries. For example, Science through Science, Technology and Society (SSTS) is a society of science educators in the United States that has a regular newsletter (*SSTS Reporter*), sponsors conferences and workshops, gains support for curriculum projects, and publicizes curriculum materials with an STS character. The International Organisation for Science and Technology Education (IOSTE) held biennial conferences throughout the 1980s and has provided a means for the interchange and spread of STS ideas among the science education community. This organization brings together educators whose interests are in science and technology as separate entities and those whose interests are in the interfaces of science, technology, and society. It has a special interest group for the latter, the STS Research Network, with a lively and regular newsletter called *Missives*. The basis in research of this newsletter has enabled it to provide a different and complementary set of stimuli for curriculum development from those in the *SSTS Reporter*.

The *Missives* of the STS Research Network draws attention to research studies on (1) conceptions various curriculum stakeholders have about STS topics; (2) methods for evaluating student learning in STS education; and (3) critical analyses of STS curriculum development. The *SSTS Reporter*, on the other hand, draws attention to resources for STS curricula and indicates both the connections each makes across the curriculum from science and technology and the STS features each contains. The set of features that are used in this content analysis is "societal relevance, mutual influence of S,T, & S, self and society, balance of views," and "broadens S-T interest to societal values issues, develops students' decision skills, encourages student action and introduces some science content or quantification."

Solomon (1988) has pointed out that the considerable influence the STS movement has had on school science curricula has been initially largely independent of the parallel and more intellectually vigorous debate about science and society at the level of university education. Under the name of "Science, Technology and Society," Spiegel-Rosing and Price (1977) published an influential series of papers, and Ziman (1980) identified seven different possible approaches to the teaching of STS at the tertiary level. More recently the academic community concerned with "social studies of science" has begun to be an influence on the curriculum of school science.

Aikenhead (1986) drew on Ziman's analysis at the tertiary level to propose a framework for STS content as follows: (1) science discipline, (2) technology discipline, (3) characteristics and limitations of science and technology, (4) interactions of science and technology in society, and (5) skills in communication and mathematics. He acknowledges that such a content-based framework has limitations, and he points to several alternatives. Waks and Prakash (1985) found four conceptions—"cognitive competency, rational/academic (epistemology and sociology of science), personal relevance, and social action"—in the STS literature of the United States. The "Cinderella" allusion in the title of their paper refers to the much lower profile the fourth level, "social action," has yet had in science curricula. Bybee's (1985) more conservative perspective on "Scientific and Technological Literacy" sets out to relate the familiar triad of "knowledge, skills, and attitudes" to the fields of science in its interactions with technology and society.

Solomon identified four approaches to STS in school science curricula—"the cultural, the political education for action, the interdisciplinary and problematic, and the vocational or technocratic." The first of these approaches was heralded by the Association for Science Education (1979, 1981) in Britain and by Hufstedler and Langenburg (1982) in a report to the National Science Foundation in the United States. The nature of science at school, these authors argued, needed to change as its purpose moved from preparation of the next generation of scientists to the scientific education of the citizen.

Aikenhead and Fleming (1975), in one of the early STS curriculas, used philosophical and historical approaches to enable 10th grade students in Canada make sense of their rapidly changing society. At about the same time Hall (1973), in the Schools Council Integrated Science Project, was encouraging students to practice using the search for patterns in data—a process basic to science—when they were deciding about applications of science and adding economic and social data to the science information to be so assessed.

Solomon (1983) was influential herself in promoting the use of historical preambles in a curriculum to foster interest and understanding of contemporary issues involving science. In Science in a Social Context (SISCON), an 11th grade course of study, this historical approach is used to show how similar issues in the past were dealt with or how the present issues arose.

In the second, more political, approach there is more obvious influence from the environmental concerns in society. Hines and Hungerford (1984) argued for a curriculum that develops citizens who are both willing and able to engage in environmental action. The introduction of nuclear power in Holland, Austria, and Sweden, the destruction of forests in North America and Europe by acid rain, and the mining of uranium in Australia have all contributed to curriculum changes in the 1980s that fall within this approach.

Aikenhead (1985) discussed how decisions are made about these complex socioscientific issues and later evaluated the extent to which theories about making decisions applied to the way students responded to a curriculum that explicitly set out to develop such capacities concerning alcohol and driving (Aikenhead 1989). Eijkelhof and Kortland (1988) described a fascinating study they have undertaken as a consequence of the Chernobyl disaster. In it they have sought answers, in the specific case of risks from ionizing radiations, to the important questions curriculum developers should ask about what facts, applications concepts, and processes need to be included in these STS-type curricula.

The "interdisciplinary and problematic" approach leads to a curriculum in which a series of issues or socioscientific topics are studied. These issues do not have sharp scientific boundaries that coincide with the scientific disciplines, and their ethical, economic, social, and political aspects are very real, whether or not such curricula include them or not. Zoller (1985) has illustrated the power and attractiveness of such curriculum packages, but unless they are substantial in study time and are carefully chosen, there is a danger that their topicality and specific interest will exclude the learning of more general lessons about the interactions of "Science, Technology and Society" and of a coherent body of scientific knowledge and skills.

The "vocational or technocratic approach" comes from the more instrumental view of science as the fuel of industry. In such courses (e.g., *Science and Society*, developed in England by Lewis 1980) the structure of industry and how science relates to its operation are included in the curriculum as topics for their own sake and not to reveal industry as a one of the factions in the overall concerns that face technological societies. Many industries have since the mid-1970s contributed substantially to the development of curriculum materials for science courses that make these approaches to STS accessible to science teachers. The lack of industrial experience of most science teachers, and the fact that they have not usually had the chance to study the critical aspects of other approaches to STS in their own scientific education, make them rather susceptible to this approach.

The Science and Technology in Society (SATIS) project in Britain has chosen to develop modules that are limited in the time of study required because its authors believe that adding on such brief learnings to the relevant science topic in existing curricula is the most feasible way to get wide-scale inclusion of some STS emphases in science curricula (Holman 1987). SATIS has had the independence as a project to draw on industries for technical information and to set this information in a wider scientific and social context.

To get a feel for the extent to which 23 topics with obvious STS or environmental potential were appearing in school science curricula, Fensham (1987) surveyed 33 countries, all but one of which reported some increases in learning experiences in relation to a number of the topics during the decade 1974–1984. Using the tough criterion of two thirds of the countries, 6 topics were now stronger in primary curricula, 11 in lower secondary, and 10 in upper secondary. The topics to emerge at all levels with increased attention are "more efficient use of energy," "alternative renewable sources of energy," "consumption and conservation of living resources," and "consumption and conservation of non-living resources." The lowest penetration was for "scientific aspects of armaments and the risk of nuclear war," "preservation of buildings of human historic heritage," "effective use of water in agriculture," and "water as a key ingredient for human health." Overall, these findings were, from the environmental/STS viewpoint, indicative of both encouraging gains and some real disappointments when the importance of the last four topics to the quality of life in many countries is considered.

Fensham (1988b) and Holman (1987) describe two very different ways of developing curricular materials for STS science education. The first is to take the existing topics and concepts of a science course of study and prepare some preamble or follow-up material that illustrates how this topic is important or relevant to society and to the individual student. The second is to identify a major application, topic, or issue in society and develop material that presents both the science of it as well as other societal aspects of it.

The scale of the STS components and the likelihood of their becoming part of the "knowledge of worth" in the curriculum in these two ways are obviously different. Fensham (1989) has pointed to a number of other differences that are more radical challenges to traditional views of science curricula. One of these differences is probed by the question, What determines the science to be studied? The first or "add-on" way mentioned earlier accepts as given the existing science in the curriculum, its place in the sequence of topics, and that the science content is the real knowledge of worth. The second or "central" way has the chance to allow quite different science(s) to be included in the curricula and for the order or conjunction of these topics and concepts to be quite radically different from the way they have usually been arranged. *The science of an application is quite different from science with applications,* to paraphrase a profound comment made by Fehr (1968) about mathematical curricula. The properties of any substances involved, their uniqueness or the alternatives that could also be suitable, and the way energy is involved are regular science aspects that would always appear in a curriculum based on the central way, whereas these would almost always be excluded in one using the add-on way unless it is the particular substance or energy that is the topic being illustrated.

The second difference relates to the questions, What concepts are used to describe the issue? and What content is expected to be learned? This is a critical check to apply to the numerous curricula that are now being developed with a structure commonly described as "Concepts in Contexts," such as the *Salters Chemistry* in Britain and *Chemistry in the Community* (CHEMCOM) in the United States (see below). If their knowledge of worth involves only science concepts of a traditional sort, these curricula, despite their apparent affinity with the second way, are more like the add-on materials of the first way. If the knowledge of worth includes technological concepts such as "strength of materials," "reverberation time," and "in vitro fertilization" and socioscientific ones such as "social risk," "available resource," "shelf life," "toxic level," and "waste," then these curricula genuinely belong to the central way and hence to a more substantial type of STS education. In other words, they have redefined the knowledge of worth in the conceptual terms that science now uses to value the knowledge of its own disciplines.

The Environmental Movement in the 1990s. Mikelskis (1988, 1989) argues cogently that environmental education in science curricula should not be subsumed in STS education. Rather, he sees them as needing to be in symbiotic relationship, or as two sides of a coin. STS aspects in science curricula should be informed by the environmental crisis, and environmental studies in science must recognize all three of the STS components. Although he assesses the impact of STS on environmental education on science curricula in Germany as small, he does cite examples of curriculum materials for studies of energy (grades 5 to 10) and of renewable energy (grades 10 to 11) that have the perspectives he has presented. These perspectives, as "Ecotechnology," have also been the basis he and other colleagues at IPN have used when developing a *Youth Dictionary of Technology—Humane and Ecological Technologies* (Bunder et al. 1987).

The very recent political realities, in which the environment is now looming in many countries as an issue comparable with the economy, suggests that the environmental movement may, in the 1990s, as Mikelskis is arguing, regain a more independent influence on science curricula.

STS Links with Gender. The personal aspects of STS have been espoused by some educators who are concerned with the problem of making science more attractive to girls and more accessible for their learning. Fleming (1986), Harding (1986), Sjøberg (1986), and Solomon (1988) have pointed out, however, that the gender concern should not mask the declining popularity of science among many boys at school and have suggested that the potential of STS science is that it could have positive effects for all students.

Jorg and Wubbels (1987) took this possibility for science curriculum designers a major step further when they explored the differential appeal of various applications of science that have been included in the physics curriculum of the Netherlands. In other words, they recognized that it is not just a matter of adding an STS dimension, because there are a number of possible STS dimensions. They found reason to question the widespread assumption that boys are more likely than girls, because they often already have technological careers in mind, to find technological topics of science satisfying. They found gender differences in the positive responses they received to a number of topics but found that "weather," "traffic," and "music" were satisfying to both boys and girls. Lazonby (1987) has also pointed to negative responses from students to indiscriminate use of industrial applications of science as STS and has argued for an approach more akin to Solomon's "cultural" one described earlier rather than one that is "instrumental" ("implicit industrial recruitment" is his term). Grant and Harding (1987) have pointed out another subtle aspect of STS. If "doubt" about the applications of science can be seen to be an accepted and integral part of their place in a science curriculum, then that type of STS curriculum is likely to have a receptive response from a wide cross section of students.

The Women's Movement. In the second half of the 1970s gender issues in education began to emerge in a number of countries, and the concerns about the unequal participation of boys and girls in science in school and, hence, in their career opportunities were expressed. There has been an increasing recognition of these gender issues in school systems and education ministries. Pressure for this recognition has come from a number of sources within the women's movement and from women science teachers and interested others within the science education community (e.g., Harding 1983).

The publication in Britain of the *The Missing Half: Girls and Science Education* (Kelly 1981) and in the United States of *Women in Science* (Kahle 1985) provided more substantive bases for concern and response. These two collections of essays and research papers present a great deal of national and comparative international data on the extent and depth of the bias that exists against girls in relation to the physical sciences in schools in most countries and in scientific and technological careers more generally.

In 1981 a small conference in the Netherlands established an international body known as GASAT (Girls and Science and Technology). There have now been six such international GASAT conferences (1983 in Oslo; 1985 in London; 1987 in Ann Arbor, Michigan; 1989 in Haifa; 1991 in Melbourne), and the publication of their proceedings has meant added documentation of the problems, as well as a number of reports of interesting innovations in curricula that seek to redress the biases. The existence of this international body has been important in strengthening the resolve and influence of the pressure groups in individual countries for these changes, since international comparisons can often be used to engender response and action in uninterested local contexts.

Governments and other bodies concerned with national economic issues in industrialized countries have taken up the concept of the "missing half" as the traditional supply of young males into science and technology continues to fall short of societal demands. The National Science Foundation is now required by Congress to report biennially on Women and Minorities in Science and Engineering. The National Research Council (1987) in the United States reported a workshop that addressed these serious gaps in human potential for careers in science and engineering, and the Royal Society and the Institute of Physics (1982) in Britain have similarly addressed these problems.

Several curriculum approaches have been taken as responses to the problem. The first was to begin to remedy the often quite blatant bias in the existing textbooks and other curriculum materials for science. Kelly (1985, 67) summarized the reported predominance of males in existing science textbooks as "between two and ten times as many illustrations of and references to men and boys as there are for women and girls" (see Heikkinen 1978 [U.S.]; Hilmo 1983 [Norway]; Kelly, Whyte, and Smail 1984 [Britain]; Walford 1983 [U.S.S.R.]).

During the 1980s some progress has been made in the removal of the more blatant biases (language, illustrations, the contexts in which phenomena are presented, and the applications chosen to illustrate concepts). Where school districts or ministries provide these curriculum materials, considerable pressure can be exerted on authors and publishers, but there are long time lags as schools turn over this stock slowly. Furthermore, as one set of biases are attacked, other, more subtle biases are being recognized. The meaning of the terms "gender neutral," "gender friendly," or, more important, "gender-inclusive" are still being uncovered as far as curriculum materials are concerned.

The second approach is to examine and change the way option and choice are built into the curriculum of schooling, particularly but not only in the later secondary years. There are three levels of these options and choices—the classroom, the school, and the wider educational system. At the classroom level, a number of studies (e.g., Spender 1978; Whyte 1984) have shown that teachers in Western classrooms allow and even encourage optional or differential participation in coeducational classrooms that favor boys. Participation in class discussion, opportunities or requirements to answer questions, and active roles in laboratory or experimental work (Whyte 1984) are examples of how learner options and teachers' choices can produce gender bias. Linn and Hyde (1989), from their meta-analysis of the literature, suggest that the redesign of learning and learning environments is likely to lead to greater gender equity. Teachers need training and support if they are to remedy these gender-stereotypic patterns of classroom interaction. Rennie, Parker, and Hutchinson (1985) and Kelly, Whyte, and Smail (1984) report encouraging outcomes from such intervention studies in primary and secondary classrooms, respectively.

An alternative that shifts this problem to the school level is to reorganize the classes for science at a given level of schooling so that they are single sex for the study of this subject. This eliminates the gender competition for classroom "space and domination" and obviously enables more girls to be active. More studies of this sort, involving the structural manipulation of classrooms, have been reported in mathematics than in science, and schools have generally been reluctant to use this approach even though, in some senses, it seems simpler than changing the established attitudes and patterns of interaction of teachers more generally.

Another example of the influence of choice at the school level is the way choices of optional subjects are presented, particularly when there are interactions with other interests of girls (e.g., languages) if they choose science.

At the system level the range of studies that is required or expected of students to be successful can have a profound bearing on how the sexes participate in the science curriculum. For example, in a number of Western countries, including Britain, the United States, Australia, and the Netherlands, there has been encouragement, but not requirements, for both girls and boys to continue studies in science in the later levels of secondary education. In addition, in these countries the choice of biology alone has been regarded as a choice for science, although the scientific outcomes or career prospects beyond school are so markedly different from those that are open if chemistry or physics (or commonly both) are chosen. Japan, a number of European countries, and Thailand do not allow such open or spurious choice and require students studying science (or even all students) at these levels to include both biological and physical sciences in their overall curriculum of learning. Klainin and Fensham (1987) and Klainin, Fensham, and West (1989) reported the spectacular outcomes of this pattern of enforced study in the Bangkok area of Thailand. They found that girls and boys were naturally participating in all three sciences equally. Furthermore, girls were outperforming boys in chemistry and performing equally with them in physics on a range of cognitive, practical, and attitudinal aspects of learning.

The third approach is to change the content of science learning. The work of Gilligan (1982), Head (1979), and Sjøberg and Imsen (1988) on the different interests and attitudes of boys and girls have been helpful foundations for these changes. Their studies are consistent with two sets of characteristics about the ways learners can interact with the content of science curricula. These have been labeled "analytical/instrumental" and "nurturative" by Smail (1987), picking up such juxtaposed pairs as "interest in rules/interest in relationships" and "interest in controlling inanimate things/interest in nurturing living things." Boys and girls are not neatly distinguished by these two sets of characteristics. The evidence indicates overlapping distributions, with more boys on the "analytical/instrumental" side and more girls on the "nurturative" one. Curriculum projects like Career Oriented Modules to Explore Technology and Science, COMETS (Smith 1987), Girls into Science and Technology, GIST (Kelly, Whyte, and Smail 1984), and Chemistry from Issues (Harding and Donaldson 1986) have in their own ways all tried to include more of the nurturative characteristics.

These curriculum approaches, however, are essentially a means to an end: to induce girls into a science that is essentially unchanged. Manthorpe (1982) has argued for going further and replacing current school science, with its established reputation as a masculine subject. To do this the curriculum of science, she argues, should feature:

- a holistic view in which social, ethical, and moral questions are unquestionably involved;
- a scientific community based on cooperation;
- respect for and equal valuation of different forms of knowledge—including the irrational and the subjective;
- a placement of emphasis on a rewriting of the intellect and emotion; and
- a reevaluation of the belief that the quality of life has priority over economics.

Such a "feminine" curriculum would certainly be different from present curricula and from the "girl-friendly" ones that have been advocated. In a similar but more extreme vein, Bentley and Watts (1986) have argued for a feminist science curriculum that they claim would also be more humanist. No examples of such a curriculum seem to have yet been reported.

The McClintock Collective (1987) in Australia has produced curriculum materials and conducted many curriculum workshops for science teachers that would be consistent with the "feminine" science curriculum of Manthorpe. Lewis and Davies (1988) combined these and similar initiatives into a curriculum manual. Some of the innovations reported at the GASAT conferences from Europe are also of this type.

As a result of further analysis of the data about young persons' interests, Harding (1985) has suggested that much of the bias between boys and girls in the physical sciences in upper secondary school is due to a minority group of boys who, for intrinsic and extrinsic reasons, persist with and learn these sciences at school. The majority of boys are much less dissimilar in their interests from the even larger majority of girls than had been thought earlier. There is also evidence that a number of topics in science that appeal to girls also appeal to many of these boys. These findings are important pointers to the sorts of science curricula that can serve the needs of the "Science for All" demand if they can be developed to differentiate between the sorts of applications of science to include in these curricula.

Technologies for Learning

Science involves the empirical investigation of nature. Its success and its progress has depended very much on the skill and ingenuity of human beings to design and make an amazing variety of equipment, large and small, to extend these investigations. Each of these is also in fact an application of science, or technology.

Although school systems can and do vary considerably in the extent to which they enable this empirical aspect of science to be part of the school curriculum, most of them acknowledge its importance and argue for more resources for these practical aspects of science. UNESCO (1979) has consistently supported the quest for low-cost equipment and encouraged its development and use.

Klainin (1988), from one of the newly emerging industrial countries, Thailand, provides some encouraging indications of one attempt to incorporate practical science into the curriculum with low-cost equipment. Hofstein and Lunetta (1982) have reviewed the role of the laboratory in science teaching. This review was timely because it was both an appraisal of part of the 1950/1960s reform that had gone particularly astray and an analysis that led to suggestions for recovery. Many of the curricula from the 1950/1960s were based on the assumption that practical investigations could have a central place in the learning experiences of students in school. They were launched in school systems that were simply unable or unwilling to provide the sorts of supports (laboratories, laboratory assistants, equipment storage, repair and renewal, and in-service training of teachers) that could have realized this assumption.

Many of these problems remain, as Hofstein and Lunetta point out, but some, naively overlooked in the 1950/1960s, have seen considerable progress. These are the issues of how practical work can be given status and worth through assessment and how it can, accordingly, better contribute to students' learning by reinforcing the intentions of the curriculum of which it is a part. Tamir in Israel, Yager in the United States, and Kempa in Britain have been leading figures in this revival of the potential of the laboratory for science curricula. Together with their graduate students they have laid a sound basis for its use (see Kempa 1986; Lunetta and Tamir 1979; Tamir 1972; Tamir et al. 1982; Yager 1981).

The Assessment of Performance Unit (APU) in England has also provided important support for hands-on activity in science curricula in England by insisting on the inclusion of such situations among its range of assessment tasks (APU 1980). Few other national testing programs seem to have been bold enough to do this. Gott, Welford, and Foulds (1988) have very recently combined these developments and some of their own into an excellent manual for the assessment of practical work in school science.

In addition to these technologies of science itself, the contemporary scene in schools in a number of countries is dramatically different now because of the presence of numbers of computers. This particular technology has meant very big differences in the way in which society is organized. It has also changed science in the way it is conducted and in the sorts of questions that can be asked and answered by scientists.

Rather strangely, the computer's impact on school science education is relatively minor, and there is little evidence to suggest it is likely to be a major influence in the next few years. Some enthusiastic science teachers are using computers to implement the curriculum in their own classrooms, but there is not yet much indication that state-wide or other regional curricula for science will require such action. Three different uses can be described. The first is the interfacing of computers with other pieces of equipment—for example, with the technical model kits that are now available and being used in elementary classes to simulate real-world ways of harnessing and operating scientific principles. This use could expand as the computer costs go down. The second is the use of computers to reinforce the teaching and learning of traditional science topics, the main thrust of the considerable effort that has so far gone into software design. The third makes use of other software, which can enable quite new aspects of science, such as modeling, to be taught and learned.

It would appear from several evaluative studies of the use of computers in schools and from several very recently designed science curricula that little general use of these available technologies is occurring or expected. Use by science teachers has not been as high as among some other subject-area teachers.

The new science curriculum to be part of the national curriculum of England and Wales does include one attainment target or broad topic (out of 17), Information Transfer, that will require students to engage with computers (National Curriculum Council 1988). It is also the stated intention of that curriculum that the use of information technology should pervade the students' normal work in the other broad topics, but none of their exemplary learnings listed for the other attainment targets have been written in a way that would require this to happen. By themselves, the exemplary learnings within Information Transfer are ones that are now quite commonly being included in school curricula in a number of countries. Usually they are not, however, part of science, and, indeed, they are essentially independent of the traditional content of science.

EXAMPLES OF SCIENCE CURRICULA

In the next sections of this chapter a number of recently developed curricula and some current projects are described. They are not intended to be representative but are chosen because they exemplify some of the influences described in the earlier sections or because they portray interesting and different ways in which the curriculum of science is now being interpreted.

The developments in curriculum that are now described contrast in an interesting way with the developments in research on curriculum that are included by White and Tisher (1986) in the third *Handbook of Research on Teaching*. Their discussions of curriculum stereotypes and the nature of curriculum and of curriculum procedures are heavily governed by research literature addressing the science curricula of what this chapter calls the 1950/1960s era. White and Tisher did identify some emerging areas of curriculum research, such as those that are responses to social forces, historical studies, and the presentation of science in a social context, which are now included in this review as major fields of activity in research and curriculum development. They also provide a substantial account of the sequence through the 1970s and into the 1980s of the research into prior knowledge, cognitive structure, and the probing of understanding that, a decade later, now warrants major discussion in this chapter as an influence on curriculum.

Curriculum as Teachers' Competence

The Secondary Science Curriculum Review in Britain, which extended from 1982 to 1986, was a major project that saw the curriculum for science primarily and essentially in terms of the expertise of science teachers (SSCR 1987). It used a rolling and decentralized network approach, coordinated by a small central team, to involve hundreds of teachers in the tasks of defining the weaknesses in their present teaching and setting quite new goals for what "Science for All" in a school might mean. The networks sought to use the many resources (human and materials) in Britain to work out approaches to curriculum decision making and to try new pedagogies that would move them in their desired directions.

The Review has been a means of professional development through the exchange of ideas, materials, and good practice. As a byproduct of its central purpose, the Review has produced a series of 12 curriculum guides, which will remind those teachers who were part of the Review and inform others of the collective wisdom that was gathered. The titles of these guides speak for themselves of the concerns and emphases of this project: *Better Science—Key Proposals; Choosing Content; Making It Relevant to Young People; Approaches to Teaching and Learning; How to Plan and Manage the Curriculum; For Both Girls and Boys; Working in a Multicultural Society; For Young People with Special Educational Needs; Health and Science Education; Building Primary/Secondary Links; Assessing Progress;* and *Learning How to Teach It.*

Another product is aimed at the reality that the science staff in a school is limited in the changes it can make unilaterally. *Better Science—Making It Happen* seeks to set the science curriculum of a school in the context of the whole school curriculum and, thus, to make not just the science staff responsible for its good health but the whole school community.

This approach to a science curriculum is particularly appropriate in educational systems in which the central prescription of the content of the science curriculum is low. Most countries of this sort have not yet deliberately put such major resources into professional development, although the need for it has been recognized by their science teachers.

Countries in which the curriculum content is more tightly specified have different sorts of priorities for professional development. Thailand is an excellent example of a country that gave a major priority in its science curriculum development to teacher expertise. Wongthonglour (1979) has described and evaluated, for one of the many curricula that the Institute for the Promotion of Science and Technology (IPST) has developed since 1972, the extremely thorough and extended in-service education that was provided for large numbers of teachers in Thailand. In this sort of situation, as well as in lifting the general pedagogical competence of teachers, there are the clearly defined curricular tasks of assisting teachers to gain the background knowledge needed to teach novel topics in the curriculum and to share with the curriculum developers and decision makers the meaning of its new intentions.

Curriculum as Construction of Meaning

It is not surprising, given the prominence in research that constructivist approaches to science education have had over the last decade, that some attention is now being paid to these approaches in developing curriculum. Champagne, Gunstone, and Klopfer (1985) were among the first science educators to show how hard it is to achieve conceptual change in students. They, and a number of others who have followed them, found, however, that certain conditions encourage and facilitate these changes.

The easier and more developed form of this attention is in projects where curriculum is seen as closely related to the expertise of teachers. In England, Canada, Australia, and New Zealand, substantial resources have been put into this curricular approach since 1985, and generally the results have been most encouraging. This statement needs to be qualified, however, by noting that relatively small numbers of teachers have been involved so far, a consequence of the sustained support that research has shown to be necessary if effective change in teachers is to be brought about.

Just as the research has shown that neither children nor adults change their conceptions of natural phenomena easily or quickly, so science teachers need time and support to reconstruct their views of their role so that it becomes consistent with a more constructivist view of learning. Nevertheless, where networks of teachers have worked with each other and with constructivist science educators over extended periods (compared with the usual single "events" that are a common but ineffective form of professional development), very positive changes have been observed in classrooms. White (1992) reported that in one such network the group of teachers had over a few years come up with more than 50 novel (for them and for most science teachers) pedagogies that had been mutually tried and refined. The Children's Learning in Science (CLIS) project in England has used its experience with these networks of teachers (both primary and secondary) to produce a set of in-service education modules that attempt to package the rather experiential and spontaneous discussions and arguments that characterize constructivist teacher development (Johnston 1989).

A second and more difficult form of giving attention to constructivist ideas is to develop a student textbook. As yet there are very few examples to review, and this task is certainly one for the 1990s. McFadden et al. (1986) claim that the texts in the series *Science Plus* (developed by Atlantic Science Curriculum Project) are constructivist as well as being STS (McFadden was a founder of IOSTE). *Science Plus* certainly has a number of features that are consistent with conceptions research and constructivist learning. First, it begins some of its topics with acknowledgment of the sorts of ideas students commonly present when asked about the difference between living and nonliving things. Second, it asks many questions of its readers that are not answered in the book (not even at the end of the text!) in an attempt to stimulate students to produce possible answers. Third, it contains many novel exercises (set in contexts of the students' world outside school) that seek and respect the opinions and reasoning of the students. Fourth, its range of activities is much less stereotyped than usual. Fifth, it asks "trivia" questions that are cleverly chosen to appeal to and engage the students in active questioning of others or searching of library resources to get answers. Sixth, it challenges the students to investigate novel, everyday situations involving the various science topics.

Berkheimer et al. (1988) have produced *Matter and Molecules* (MAM), a student text for 12-year-olds and a teacher's guide that are deliberate attempts to use the findings of their own and others' conceptions research on change of state and solution and also to be constructivist. The text supports an extended study over many weeks of these topics, and there is also an activity book with questions, problems, and experiments. The existence of alternative conceptions with regard to both the macroscopic phenomena being considered and the counterpart behavior on the atomic level is emphasized. The need for correct (scientific) conceptions of the observable world is the approach taken before a particulate theory at the atomic level is used to explain them. The text regularly lists conceptual learning goals (the scientific ones) and contrasts them with commonly held alternative ways of thinking. The constraint of using such brief statements to present the conceptual goals leads on a number of occasions to oversimplified presentations of the contemporary scientific views (are they still correct?). The authors try to solve the question of how to provide experiential evidence that will definitely support the conceptual goal, but the findings of Andersson (1984) and many others suggest the students of MAM will not be so easily convinced.

The CLIS group also developed *Properties of Matter*, a teacher's guide for 10 double lessons (a recognition of the need for time for reflection by students) for 13- and 14-year-olds. This guide draws on the same body of research as the MAM materials do. Andersson (1990) has compared these two sets of materials. The content goals of the CLIS curriculum are stated in broader terms than those in MAM, and it has as another primary goal introducing students to how theories are made in science. The teaching/learning sequences that are recommended differ markedly in the status they give to students' views. In MAM, the various views are elicited to establish their differences as a problem. CLIS elicits them because they are the basis from which reconstruction of meaning may occur. In MAM, the teacher next models the conceptual goal and then coaches the students in its use until the students appear to have mastered it, whereupon the teacher's role becomes one of maintenance. In CLIS, the teacher provides experiences that may lead to restructuring of the students' views as they discuss and compare their efficacy. Situations are then provided in which these views can be applied and hence tested by the students, who are encouraged to reflect on how well their views fit these experiences.

The CLIS sequence does not mean that the teacher cannot inject her view or the contemporary scientific view into the second and third steps in the CLIS sequence. These views should, however, simply take their place alongside the student views in the processes of evaluation and review in which students are encouraged to engage in reflection. In the CLIS contexts there is no certainty that the scientific views will gain the most credibility—a prospect Fensham (1983) foreshadowed as one that may need to be more commonly accepted in curriculum at this level of science education if the long-term interests of "Science for All" are to be served.

MAM provides the formal conceptual views of contemporary science as the goal targets for learning. In this way it is in danger of ceasing to be constructivist if students simply learn these stated conceptual goals by rote. MAM uses two criteria for a good explanation. The first asks, What substance is changing, and how is it changing? The second is about molecules: What is happening to the molecules of the substance? CLIS tries to communicate, using the analogies of detective work, that science can "tidy up" piles of apparently unconnected data, that making theories in science often involves searching for a pattern in data, and that "imaginative leaps" from data to proposed theory can be a fruitful way to proceed.

A student text and a teacher's guide for a first course in chemistry, *Chemistry in a Thousand Questions*, has been prepared for 14- and 15-year-olds in the Netherlands. A series of articles by the authors (de Vos and Verdonk 1985, 1986, 1987) describe its essential experiences and indicate the research rationale for its content. Much of the learning is in small groups who conduct experiments and work out together how the set questions can be answered. This curriculum is the outcome of several revisions, each of which has built on the increasing knowledge research is providing about alternative conceptions students hold about these phenomena and their descriptions in chemistry.

The Curriculum as a Set of Guidelines

A number of education systems have moved in recent years from a view of curriculum as syllabus—a detailed list of topics and content—to one that sees it much more as a set of intentions or guidelines that are concerned with aspects other than just the content to be learned. Indeed, as these other aspects of the teaching and learning situation are given more prominence in the curriculum, the detailed specification of content tends to becomes less.

One reason for this shift is the evidence from the 1950/1960s that statements of content for learning, and elegant materials that set it out in detail for teachers and students, were not sufficient to ensure effective teaching and learning as intended. Another is the recognition that as systems endeavor to educate all students in science, more flexibility is needed in what examples to use and what topics to include to achieve the sorts of understandings that future citizens, as distinct from future scientists, require.

This guidelines approach to curriculum is appearing at several levels of generality. An example at a very broad level is *Frameworks* in Victoria, Australia (Malcolm et al. 1987). In essence, *Frameworks* says that science education from grade 1 to grade 10, the compulsory years in that state, is (1) for all students; (2) learning science as science, as technology, as society, and as personal development; (3) learning and teaching that begins with and takes seriously the learner's perceptions and conceptions; (4) a course of study, the details of which are developed and implemented by its teachers; and (5) a sampling only of the possible content, and this sampling should depend on local resources, needs, and interests and be sufficiently limited so that real engagement occurs with ideas in science rather than superficial coverage of many.

At a much more detailed level the new National Curriculum in England and Wales is an example (National Curriculum Council 1988). At first sight its level of detail seems like a syllabus, since it lists 10 levels of learning for each of its 17 broad Attainment Targets. Closer examination, however, shows that an Attainment Target is not a topic area in the traditional syllabus sense. First, it is more like a statement of a very general learning intention than a topic; for example, the seventh one is "Pupils should develop their knowledge and understanding of the process of changing materials by chemical reactions and the way this is used in the manufacture of new materials." Second, this learning is intended to be developed progressively over 10 or so years from age 5 to 16, and a number of graded subtargets are suggested covering these primary and secondary years. Third, suggestions are given for the sorts of activities learners need to engage in at these various age levels if they are to have real opportunity to gain these learnings. All these statements and suggestions avoid the specificity and limiting detail that traditional syllabi as the statements of a curriculum's content have usually contained.

Curriculum as Science, Technology, and Society

The most pervasive features of new science curricula everywhere since the late 1970s has been their acknowledgment of the concerns of the STS movement and their willingness in a variety of ways to include applications of science in society. Some examples of this variety are now described.

Structural Requirements. A number of countries have begun to use assessment procedures in science as a means of ensuring some STS presence. In England and Wales since 1988 there has been a requirement in the assessments for the later secondary levels of science learning that at least 15 percent of the total marks be allocated to "technological applications, and social, economic and environmental issues." Such a requirement will undoubtedly encourage the curriculum intention to help students understand the relationship of their science studies to other areas of studies and their relevance to their own lives. However, it is in danger of being seen as an "extra" of no great significance, since no guidance has yet been provided as to what learning about these societal issues in science could involve. This contrasts poorly with the 85 percent of assessment for which very specific traditional content criteria in each science were defined. The new National Curriculum will strengthen the situation because a graded set of learnings, originally proposed for a separate Attainment Target entitled "Science in Action: Technological and Social Aspects," have now been worked into the other 17 Attainment Targets. Thomas (1987), from a decade of experience in Australia, has reported on the use of items in state-wide examinations to test quite sophisticated aspects of STS interactions, thus demonstrating that this type of learning can be taken seriously as knowledge of worth.

Whole Courses. *Chemistry in the Community* (CHEMCOM) is an American example of STS-influenced curriculum that has been sufficiently developed so that the nature of the influence is clear (Ware, Heikkinen, and Lippincott 1987). As its full title suggests, this is a chemistry curriculum that has made central the need the citizen has to understand issues at the chemistry-technology-society interfaces. It is also guided in its choice of content and experiences by the aim of helping students to realize the important role chemistry will play in their personal and working lives. It consists of studies of sociochemical issues, each occupying about one month. The issues are "supplying our water needs, conserving chemical resources, petroleum: to build or to burn?, understanding foods, chemistry—air and climate, chemistry and health, and the chemical industry: promise and challenge."

The course is quite definitely of the second STS type described earlier, in that the issues or contexts are part of the serious study, but considerable care has been taken to maintain the integrity of the chemistry that is included. The units are to be studied in sequence as later units build on chemical knowledge, skills, and ideas introduced previously. Social science concepts are part of this curriculum, and they are introduced in a way that enables students (and their teachers in this novel area) to proceed from the comparatively simple to the more complex.

Given the support this project has from the American Chemical Society and the chemical rigor its authors have sought to maintain, it is unfortunate that, in the present climate of *Science for All Americans* (AAAS 1989) they have succumbed to pressure to state so clearly that this curriculum is intended only for students who do not intend to become science majors. Many students may not be clear about such choices and so may avoid this curriculum in order to hold more options open.

A rather similar but bolder project is *Salters Chemistry* in Britain (Smith 1988). This project accepted the set of chemical concepts and criteria that had been laid down there as required study for students who may wish to continue with scientific studies beyond school. It then set out to develop a curriculum approach to the study of chemistry that would be attractive and worthwhile for a much wider cross section of British young people in the 13–16 age range. The required concepts would be studied by including them in carefully chosen contexts or themes, but much else is also intended to be learned concerning the contexts themselves. In grade 9, the units are "clothing, drinks, food, metals and warmth," in grade 10 "buildings, food processing, growing food, keeping clean, minerals, plastics, and transplanting chemicals," and in grade 11, "burning and bonding energy today and tomorrow, and making and using electricity."

The authors interpret "Science for All" in their curriculum approach by starting with material and phenomena familiar to 13–16-year-olds from their own experiences or from television or books and by introducing chemical concepts and explanations only when they are needed in working on these everyday things. Industrial, technological, economic, and social examples and their implications are integrated throughout the units and are thus obviously part of the learning in this curriculum. Teachers who wish to take the add-on approach mentioned earlier to the structural requirement for the STS component in Britain would find these materials difficult to use because the project has been so committed, as Smith (1988) argues, to the second or central way of developing curriculum materials.

The Physics Curriculum Development Project (PLON) was a physics curriculum project in the Netherlands throughout the late 1970s and 1980s. Over its years of existence its understanding of what STS means in a curriculum has evolved, but from its beginning it had a view of a curriculum that would contain:

- physics (basic concepts and skills) that is (1) useful in everyday life regarding decision-making situations of a personal and societal type, *and—at the same time*—(2) essential for those who continue studying physics in tertiary education;
- an authentic view of physics by paying attention to the history, nature, and methods of physics;
- ways of recognizing differences of interests, abilities, and plans among students; and
- a variety of activities that attract students to be involved.

Forty thematic units have been developed, and five or six are normally studied in each year as students move through the last 4 or 5 years of secondary school. Their titles are similar to those in the numerous science curricula that are now organized in this thematic way, for example, ***Living in Air*** and ***Working with Water*** in grade 8, ***Bridges*** and ***Reproducing Sound*** (grade 9), ***Music*** and ***Traffic*** (grade 10), and ***Sports***, ***Ionizing Radiation***, and ***Satellites*** (grade 11).

The earlier materials tended to present the physics and applications in the add-on way, and the societal aspects were a diverse and rather indiscriminate set of references to societal aspects of the physics and its technology. The later materials are perhaps the most sophisticated, yet developed for science curriculum that is not just STS-influenced but STS in character. Eijkelhof and Kortland (1988) have provided a description of this evolution. The general format of the later units is exemplified by the materials for *Ionizing Radiation*. It starts with an "orientation" introducing a number of everyday situations in which ionizing radiation is involved and raising the nature of the "risk" as a concept. The next part contains "basic information and skills" about the nature, effects, and sources of x-rays and radioactivity. Along with the relevant physics concepts, concepts important in risk assessment, such as half-life, dose, and somatic and genetic damage, are introduced. Students then work in groups on one of several options, such as nuclear energy, nuclear weapons, and the use of radiation in medicine, in each of which the socioscientific concept of risk is as central as are the more specifically physical ones. In the final part, "broadening and deepening," procedures that deal with the analysis and evaluation of the personal and societal risk in having a brain scan or in dumping nuclear waste at sea are studied. In addition to this general format, the role that physics plays in answering the variety of scientific and socioscientific questions appearing in these units is repeatedly raised for the students and their teacher to consider.

This way of integrating STS in a curriculum and of studying its interfaces with the same sort of rigor that has been the practice in more traditional science curricula are major contributions to science curriculum thinking.

STSC—Chemistry in Alberta (Jenkins et al. 1989) is the closest North American counterpart to the PLON physics materials and is of considerable interest because its texts show ways teachers can give a substantial STS dimension within the constraints of a traditional curriculum.

McConnell (1982) presented the prospects for teaching about STS in secondary schools as a dilemma for science education in the United States. At that early stage of the current developments in science curriculum, she rather pessimistically concluded that there was little prospect of three important questions being answered. Can we do such a type of education? Should we do it? (What effect would it really have on citizens?) How can it be done? She could not have anticipated the changes in the support climate for STS science and hence the current conclusion that a positive response should be the answer to all three questions. It is, however, sobering to remember that the curriculum materials of an STS type to which she had access when she wrote were those produced by the BSCS project in Colorado under the title *Innovations: The Social Consequences of Science and Technology*. The evaluation of their use in classrooms since that time would hardly support a widespread "yes" from schools and teachers. The new projects that have been established in the more enthusiastic recent climate have yet to be so widely tested by the marketplace of schools, and McConnell's questions should be asked again and again throughout the 1990s. Less gloomily, Brumby (1984) in Australia developed STS materials, *Issues in Biology*, that covered some very controversial and topical issues in human biology, such as life support technologies, organ transplants, genetic screening, and reproductive technologies. Within a year of publication, more than one third of Australian students taking biology were studying this option (about 25 percent of their studies), with very positive reactions from them and their teachers.

Isolated Modules. A great deal of effort in the last decade in a number of countries has been devoted to developing modular materials that deal with single topics. Most of these have been influenced by STS, and the spate of materials on energy use is a typical example. Many of them have been the outcome of joint projects between industry and teachers, but others have been produced by project teams that are set up to produce a series of these modules without the sense that the sum of them is to be a course of study, as is the case with the units produced by PLON, Salters Chemistry, or CHEMCOM.

The Chemicals in Public Places project (CEPUP) has ensured that its content emphases are associated with scientific literacy. It has done this by preparing materials and programs that are suitable for use with both secondary students and citizen groups—a challenging criterion that could well be used more widely during the 1990s (Thier and Hill 1988).

Usually the isolated modules are for quite short, flexible periods of study. The use of these modules in a science curriculum is to add an STS dimension, usually by illustrating an application of a science concept, to the normal sequence of conceptual teaching. Hunt (1988) provides a useful account of how one large project set about producing its modules. Holman (1987), director of the Science and Technology in Society (SATIS) project in Britain, pointed out that few centrally determined science curricula (the commonest type, world-wide) had formally adopted a redefinition that has a substantial STS character. Accordingly, the best a teacher in these circumstances can do is to add to his or her teaching of the official science topics a bit of STS character. Most teachers need help in what this means, and these modules provide such support.

An epistemological rationale for these curriculum materials is the view that the pure science content is what is important and the sequence of its disciplinary logic should not be disturbed. Pedagogically, moreover, it is argued that this science will be learned better by more students if it is presented by means of these brief sorts of encounters with its applications. This approach to the curriculum of learning science through its applications does, however, reduce what may seem to have been a significant STS curriculum to one that is less.

Curriculum for Primary or Elementary Education

The participants at an international meeting in 1980 on the incorporation of science and technology in the primary school curriculum found it easy to agree on seven general reasons why this was important for the education of young children (Harlen 1982). They also agreed that relatively little science is being taught at this level in most countries.

This group favored the continuation of science processes as the central learning goals of primary science, but they recognized that some science content was necessary to achieve these goals and agreed on two criteria for its selection: its richness in developing children's intellectual skills and its relevance to the social and environmental context of children. Harlen (1985), the editor of the report from this meeting, has been a leading proponent of what is known as the "process view" of a science curriculum. This is the contemporary successor to the *Process Approach to Science* that was a prominent alternative among several elementary science curriculum projects in the 1950/1960s.

In this view the learning of science process skills can be emphasized to such an extent that they are elevated above, and hence become separated from the phenomena with which they are dealing, and from the conceptual ways in which they are described. When such an approach becomes dominant in an elementary science curriculum, there will be a discontinuity as the learner moves into secondary schooling where conceptual views of science are paramount. Barber and Michell (1987) have identified this as a problem and used the outcomes of a number of mini-curriculum projects as the source of ways to build better links between these two levels of science education.

The predominantly process view of primary science has recently been attacked on a number of other grounds by Millar and Driver (1987). These include current understandings of the philospphy of science, which, they argue, denies a special connection between these processes and science. Furthermore, they point out that the process view does not correspond to the way science knowledge is learned and stored.

Another international meeting of curriculum experts in Cyprus in 1982 gave primacy of place to knowledge and practical experience of science and to its applications in society (Commonwealth Secretariat 1985). They listed 10 broad content areas within which they were all able to identify topics for learning in their own very different cultural and economic contexts that met two criteria. These were (1) that knowledge of this topic could be put to use by most of the learners outside the school context in the short-term future and (2) that the topic had a high potential for exciting the children's interest and sense of wonder (Fensham 1985). This meeting, however, was convened largely because of the absence or poor quality of such science in elementary schooling, the level that is, in a number of the African countries represented, still the only level in which a significant proportion of each youth age cohort participates (see Eisemon 1989; King 1989).

The projects of the 1950/1960s did not ignore these early years of schooling, and many curriculum projects were developed and enjoyed variable degrees of success in implementation. Even the most successful, however, rarely spread very far across whole school systems except where there was central determination and control, and even in these cases there are few reports of what could be called successful implementation on a wide scale.

There are many reasons for these failures, not the least among them the weak backgrounds and lack of confidence about science among primary teachers. A more fundamental reason is, however, needed to explain the failures of science in primary education. The same weaknesses in teachers are present with respect to mathematics, and yet number and mathematical skills are always taught extensively in the primary years, albeit not as well as its curriculum designers would want.

Despite all the recent rhetoric about the importance of primary science, most societies (parents, teachers, school authorities, etc.) remain unconvinced about the worth of science at this level compared with language and mathematics. In other words, those responsible for the curriculum of science and technology at this level have not yet come up with convincing content for learning. A simplistic comparison with mathematics helps to pose the great curriculum problem of primary science. Secondary school teachers of mathematics are very keen for primary teachers to succeed in teaching the basic number operations since they do not want to teach them. Many other secondary subject teachers also need this learning to be successful. Communities expect it and, as parents know very well, it will be hard for their children to cope with society without this knowledge. The science suggested thus far for the primary curriculum has not commanded this sort of widespread support.

Secondary science curricula are such that their teachers do not need to draw on science process skills for its learning. The more conceptually based primary science curricula included topics that were and are regularly part of secondary science. Communities see science as a body of knowledge, most of which is not readily applicable to everyday life, and most parents did not study it themselves in primary school and have survived without its knowledge.

Nevertheless, there has been renewed activity in the 1980s in relation to primary science curricula. Processes of science are still prominent in most of these projects, but there is evidence that content is being given greater priority in some and is being chosen on new grounds that are STS-influenced.

Construction kits that are based on familiar toys and that simulate technologies common in society are increasingly appearing in primary classrooms. These are used to illustrate scientific principles in an experiential sense that links them directly to social purposes. In this way the curricula of primary science are more closely linked to some aspects of technology education, such as experience of using technologies, than are the developments in secondary science.

There are still two major structural approaches. The first is to set science in a discrete component of the primary curriculum, and the second is to set it in a broader context for learning called by a variety of names—for example, "General Studies," "Environmental Studies," "Life Experiences," "Domestics."

Lauterbach and Frey (1987) described the community

curriculum introduced in 1985 in Nordrhein-Westfalen, the largest state in West Germany. It typifies a swing in that country away from the concept-oriented curricula of the early 1970s to an action-oriented and technology-oriented one within the frame of "General Studies." The potential for the new orientation is illustrated for two topics that are studied by children aged 8 and 9: "Natural and Created Environments" encourages finding out about the dependency of human beings, animals, and plants on environmental conditions (water, soil, heat, light,etc.); identifying the possibilities and limitations for plants and animals to adapt to different enviroments; getting to know how human beings intervene in environmental processes and how this affects human life, animals, and plants; and taking action to improve environmental conditions. "Materials and Machines" encourages assessing quality and usefulness of materials for certain purposes; getting to know the purposes of simple machines and how they function; finding solutions to simple technical problems; and developing handcraft skills.

This German situation stems from a general consensus there that the priority in elementary education is to be given to pedagogical methods that enhance the development of the child. Content is chosen with this in mind. The science and technology are to come in the curriculum of "Community Studies" as the children come to grips with their world in the pragmatic sense—that is, by experiencing their own constructive power in making things by themselves and in making sense of their experiences in the world.

A recent curriculum in New Zealand gives rather more priority to the development of knowledge and concepts of science; it has been strongly influenced by the many results on alternative conceptions (or children's science) from the Learning in Science Project in that country. Its five objectives, acquiring knowledge and developing concepts, process skills, communication skills, and interests and attitudes are not so unusual, but the emphases for its teaching and learning are. None of the objectives in this curriculum, it is stressed, can be achieved in isolation. The interdependence of knowledge and observation is used as one illustration of this important understanding about science. What a child already knows about a topic will influence what that child is capable of observing as well what she or he will actually observe. Again, in relation to the development of concepts, it is pointed out the children will interpret a new experience in a way that fits in with ideas they already have.

This curriculum recognizes that much of the children's learning about science occurs before and outside their experiences in school with science. The ideas they acquire from this extraschool learning need to be taken very seriously in school if the intended school learning is to be successful. In summary, this curriculum accepts that children need to understand the world in their own terms. This does not mean a blind acceptance by either the teacher or the child of the ideas the children have. Their present ideas can be challenged in a sensitive manner by the teacher and other children, thus enabling each child to achieve a richer understanding of her or his world (Department of Education 1985).

THE CURRICULUM OF TECHNOLOGY

Technology education as a component of the curriculum in its own right is far too new for its major influences to be identified in any adequate way. This account of it will thus take a less systematic and more discursive form.

The situation with technology education at the moment is still very fluid; for example, the form it will actually take in England and Wales, the Netherlands, and some Australian states, which have all moved to make it a compulsory part of the core curriculum of secondary schooling, will become evident only in the next few years. In Sweden, where it has been mandated for several years as part of the curriculum, it still has an uncharacteristically (for that country) ill-defined content and pedagogical emphasis.

A major reason for this uncertainty is that there is a very real interest in a number of countries in trying to define something new in the curriculum field. To do this, technology education needs to avoid simply being an evolution of those parts of the total curriculum that variously were, until very recently, called "Technical Education," "Industrial Arts," "Craft Education," "General Techniques," and so forth. A second and very important reason is the uncertainty in all these countries about who will, in fact, be its teachers, particularly its trend-setting teachers.

The National Commission on Secondary Vocational Education (1984) in the United States called for the school curriculum to include programs and experiences that bridge the gap between the so-called academic and vocational courses. It spoke of the urgent need to develop a more *practical* curriculum. McNett (1984), reflecting on a year that was marked by an unprecedented number of expert reports on the state of education in the United States, pointed out the concern the members of these reviews repeatedly expressed that a more practical curriculum should also be perceived as what a society means by excellence in education—clearly not a traditional perception.

In Britain the Royal Society for the encouragement of Arts, Manufacturing and Commerce (RSA), a very widely representative body, provided *Education for Capability*, a serious and detailed commentary on British education at all levels, to support a manifesto it launched under the same title. In the Foreword the RSA's concern is summarized as: "Young people acquire knowledge of particular subjects but are not equipped to use knowledge in ways that are relevant to the world outside the education system" (RSA 1986, ix).

The continuing reference to "capability" by curriculum writers in Britain and elsewhere is indicative that this slogan has become a movement of influence. Its demand is for a new definition of the "practical" in education. Instead of "practical" being associated with manual skills and arts only, it is now extended to include the "use of knowledge" in society. In this way it is not inferior to the traditional knowledge of schooling as it so often has been perceived to be. Rather, it is to go beyond this knowledge to something else.

It is clear that the moves to identify a new and distinct meaning for technology in the curriculum of schooling are responses to this widespread unease about the nature of schooling and, particularly, of secondary schooling. A brief scanning of reports, newspaper articles, and other sources of public debate throughout the 1980s provides ample evidence of the number of groups who are urging that technology be included in the curriculum, but which of these groups, in the end, will influence its form and details is much more uncertain. Spokespersons for industry want technology in schools so that more able young people will wish to enter industry. Professional engineers want it to persuade more bright young people to become engineers. Academic engineers are confused, since they may say they want it but not in any way that will deflect their future students from being prepared fully in the traditional studies of mathematics and the physical sciences. Environmental groups want technology in schools if it will teach children the wicked effects of much existing technology and the need for alternatives. Some teachers of science see it as part of their preserve. Other science teachers see it as nothing to do with them.

If gender balance or minority participation is a problem in science, it is much worse in technology in most school systems. In Britain, for example, it was found in one survey in the early 1980s that more than 65 percent of schools were practicing what amounted to quite differentiated craft studies for boys and girls. The move to a new curriculum subject—"Craft, Design and Technology"—did little to ease the problem because fewer than 1 in 10 of its students were girls. Home economics as a subject was just the reverse and was not part of this move.

In most countries, the practical subjects boys have taken in school can, without too much difficulty, be related to what is now being discussed as technology education. The practical subjects for girls, however, have never been seen as related to technology. Boben (1985) and Buffer and Scott (1986) set out guidelines and a special needs guide, respectively, as contributions to more equity in technology education. In England, the Girls and Technology Education (GATE) project produced a series of pamphlets on the conditions it found in schools that facilitate and constrain more gender-balanced participation.

There are signs that some quick fixes or sleight of hand may be the immediate curriculum responses to the gender concerns. If, for example, the term "technology education" is used as an umbrella title for the range of more practical studies that have been traditionally associated with boys and girls (e.g., industrial arts plus home economics and secretarial studies), then for this umbrella there is no gender imbalance in participation. This curriculum approach already exists in a number of countries in which technology education is being simply defined by a range of optional studies without a core or common component. Some of the options being included can share as little and as much as do history and geography. Some of the more distinctive approaches to a curriculum for technology education will now be described.

Curriculum Models from Industrial Arts

The Jackson's Mill Industrial Arts Curriculum Symposium met in the United States from 1979 to 1981. Its members tried to translate the debate about the future of their field into new curriculum action. The Symposium attempted to appropriate *technology* by defining it as one of two central objects of study for industrial arts programs—industry being the other one. "Technology is considered as the knowledge and study of human endeavors in creating and using tools, techniques, resources, and systems to manage the human-made and natural environments, to extend human potential, and the relationship of these to individuals, society and the civilization process" (Hales and Snyder 1982).

The cognitive knowledge base for technology education, the Symposium concluded, includes two familiar domains—the *sciences* and *humanities*—and a third made up of some compounding of individual *technologies*. These three are set within a fourth and very rational domain called *formal knowledge*. This cognitive knowledge base interacts mutually with three sorts of human *adaptive systems*—an ideological one, a technological one, and a sociological one. These are seen to be the ways that the social and technical orders of humanity evolve historically.

The symposium, in developing this model, assumed that as people discover more knowledge it helps them to adapt, and as people develop improved ways of adapting so their domains of relevant knowledge expand. These interactions should therefore become the curriculum base for the study of technology. Four particular societal areas of endeavor were also defined as fundamental contexts for study because they have been important throughout history—"manufactured goods, constructed structures, communicated ideas, and transported goods and people" (Hales and Snyder 1982, Part 2).

Such a definition of a curriculum for technology education certainly distinguishes it from the sciences, since the knowledge domains of the sciences relate to only one part of the content components and scientific processes have no particularly special significance in the process components. It also presents a curriculum for technology education that is radically different from those with which industrial arts teachers have been familiar. Knowledge domains that are new for them are very prominent, and the whole of the adaptive systems component is quite novel, as are three of the exemplary contexts.

The interests of the industrial arts education community in the United States to change its traditional orientation and role in schooling is evident in the new name of its professional association—the International Technology Education Association. Throughout the 1980s, the Association made many contributions to the debate on what form technology should take in the curriculum of schooling. It has published annually since 1984 *Resources in Technology*—which includes background information, topic papers, and summarized accounts of contemporary developments in technology and applied science. The titles in Number

4, "Satellite Communication," "Careers in Technology," "New Developments in Printing," "Composite Materials," "Check the Ceramics," "PRT—The Way to Go," indicate the sorts of topics this organization believes should become part of the technology curriculum (ITEA 1987). There have also been annual symposia on particular themes within the general topic, Technology Education, and the proceedings of these are also published. Explicit discussion, however, of the relationship between science education and technology does not appear to have been central among the issues for discussion.

In Britain, at the same time science was being reformed in the 1950/1960s, the Association for Technology Education in Schools and the Institution of Engineers were pressing for technology in the school curriculum.

As a result, a curriculum project, Project Technology, was set up. It was responsible for another of the commonly used definitions in the curricular debates about technology. "Technology is the purposeful application of man's knowledge of materials, sources of energy and natural phenomena" (Schools Council 1968, 2). This definition sees technology as a process, but the reference to the particular knowledge involved relates technology in schools to science, and the "purposeful application" maintains a relationship with the making of products, which was emphasized in craft subjects. Project Technology was the addition of ideas from applied science to craft education, but the science it drew on was almost exclusively physics.

By the time its materials were becoming available, craft as a subject in the curriculum had become "Craft, Design and Technology" (CDT)—a spectrum of studies with Project Technology's ideas of essentially applied physics at one end and design and communication at the other, with very little science explicitly involved. The traditional craft and practical subjects for girls were not involved in these very male-oriented, CDT developments, even though *design* was a familiar idea that a number of craft subjects for boys and girls shared.

Project Technology was criticized for its concentration on curriculum materials for able students at the higher levels of secondary education and for ignoring gender concerns. Its leaders recognized the importance of gaining status for technology, and its emphases on physics and on high-level cognitive processes like *design* and *problem solving* were obvious contributions to this end.

As crafts for boys became "Craft, Design and Technology," they retained a strong practical skills character, but the addition of design encouraged new sorts of artifacts to be constructed in schools from a range of materials. The "T" of CDT tended to be associated with knowledge of the properties of these materials (plastics, ceramics, and wood and metal) and of the physical principles of structures, pneumatics, electronics, and energy transfer. Sometimes physics teachers joined the CDT teacher in the class when these "T" topics were involved.

In the later 1980s, the curriculum committee in the Netherlands charged with developing the learning aims and objectives for the new technology education listed five characteristics as its basic description of technology:

1. a human activity for both men and women;
2. involves matter, energy, and information as inputs;
3. related to science (but conceived very much in physical terms);
4. a process of designing, making, and using products; and
5. interrelated with society.

These characteristics are drawn from the extensive research into conceptions and attitudes to technology that have been undertaken in the Pupils' Attitudes Towards Technology (PATT) project by the group in Eindhoven (de Vries 1988). Their projects and workshops have attracted a great deal of international interest, and much comparative data are now available for junior secondary students in countries with very different economic, political, and technological conditions. The draft recommendations of 1989 of the committee, however, suggest that the new curriculum will be less different from the present General Techniques subject of the 1980s—itself an evolution from technical subjects for less academically oriented students in the Netherlands than these five characteristics suggest. Design is likely to be much less prominent than it is to be in England and Wales, and the interrelationships with society may not be studied in very much depth.

Ziefuss (1980) reviewed the historical situation in Germany with respect to technical education and the various efforts to safeguard it as part of general education in the more radical social climate in the early years of the 1970s. Two approaches have emerged at the curriculum level. The first introduces *prevocation education* as a subject field, and the second involves an independent subject called *technology instruction*. Despite the long and strong philosophical tradition in Germany of the relationship of productive work and education and the strong recent support from unions, employers, and industrial associations for it, there has been reluctance to include such studies in the curriculum for all students and, particularly, to include them at the higher levels of secondary schooling.

A variety of curricula have been tried, however, in the different states, and the following objectives are commonly found:

- practical experience through production of technical instruments;
- recognition of technological realities (such as materials, machines, processes, required product characteristics) in situations of work, professions, home, leisure, etc.;
- introduction to forms of thought and problem solving that are typical of technology;
- formation of opinions about technical products/procedures;
- instruction that exemplifies the sorts of cooperative and individual work that occur in manual and industrial manufacture; and
- information that facilitates entry to the world of work.

The link with science is implicit here rather than explicit and is most likely to emerge as part of the technological realities when the properties of materials are linked through processes of manufacture to the social uses for which the product is being produced.

Emerging curricula for technology education in the states of Australia, where it is being defined as a distinctive component of the core of the general curriculum, tend to emphasize several of these objectives and to be as implicit about science as is this summary of the German scene. The major contributors in Australia seem to be people from the technical education field together with some interested persons with strong physics backgrounds—a combination very similar to those in England in the late 1970s and early 1980s.

The Senior Secondary Assessment Board of South Australia (SSABSA) has developed Technology Studies in upper secondary education as a curriculum umbrella within which there are a number of options, each of which is concerned with the application of knowledge relating to such things as materials, systems, tools, and equipment to meet a need or solve practical social problems (SSABSA 1989). The existence among these options of "Creative Woodwork," "Concrete and Masonry," and "Metal Machining" indicates the compromised and evolutionary nature of this curriculum. The presence of "Technology and Society," "Energy Technology," and "Control Technology" indicate more novel aspects. Physics seems to be the most evident science involved in terms of properties of materials and electronic systems, and little use appears to be made of chemical and biological sciences.

This and some other Australian developments suggest an emphasis on the relationship between human needs, human values, and technology. These curricula set out to encourage students to use problem-solving processes, but still appear to encourage their involvement in the extensive practice and wide range of activities that are needed to develop skills associated with correct and safe use of materials, tools, equipment, and machines.

Social Theorists of Curriculum

Scriven (1987), in a radical and eloquently argued paper, put a case for the development of a technology education independent of science and draws on historical, epistemological, pedagogical, and equity grounds for support. He goes considerably further than most other analysts of this curriculum field by identifying the *use*, *adaptation*, and *evaluation* of technologies as the central targets for technology education. In doing so, he has forsaken the traditional making of artifacts, with their tedious and difficult practical skills, and not replaced them with design as the major intellectual component, as is occurring in England (see below). Highly developed practical skills and original design are both, he would argue, minority human requirements and activities in modern postindustrial society. What most citizens need is knowledge, confidence, and experience of using a wide range of modern technologies, the ability to adapt them to their own particular purposes, and to compare (that is, evaluate) those that claim to be competitors for the same basic tasks. The problem solving in such adaptations and in the evaluative aspects provide new and important high-level intellectual targets for the curriculum of schooling. It is these in combination that can, he argues, provide answers to the groping for the "more practical" referred to at the beginning of this section.

Layton (1987) takes a less radical position, which derives from the substantial work he has done on the history of both technology and science. He too is in favor of the recognition of technology as an autonomous field that is coequal to a branch of science but not subordinate to it. There is a uniqueness, he argues, about technological knowledge that is characterized by its structural orientation to concrete praxis. He sees sharp distinctions between both the constitutive and contextual values of science and technology. Technology is so fundamentally linked to human and social behavior that Layton sees a moral component as an essential element of the curriculum of technology education.

The report of the Technology Panel of Project 2061 very largely exemplifies Layton's claim that technology is autonomous (AAAS 1989). Its members, however, see the interface with society in terms that are much more instrumental (successes and failures) than the moral ones of Layton (Johnson 1989).

The Australian Education Council set up a task force on education and technology. In its report it presented a view of curriculum generally that fostered essential competencies (including those of literacy and numeracy) by using the experiences of gathering, analyzing, and synthesizing information, encouraging flexibility and creativity, engaging students in making sound judgments, and working alone and in groups. It refers to understanding the role of technology in society and calls for more emphasis in mathematics and science on applications in everyday life. It recognizes a need humans have for frameworks so that they can understand the physical and social world and for practice in modifying them (Scriven's idea of adaptation). In an attempt to summarize these wide-ranging expectations for technology education, it refers to "learning to learn, learning about technology, learning to co-operate and learning to create" (Education and Technology Task Force 1986).

Technology as Work

There is a strong strand in both the Canadian and U.S. approaches to technology education that is about industry. Industry is that part of a society's economic sector where products are manufactured, and its companies and factories are the places where the traditional human skills of working with wood, metals, and other materials are practiced. These views of industry provide a new meaning and purpose for the craft skills that make up the curricula of industrial arts or technical studies. (See Chapter 31, "Vocational Education," in this *Handbook*.)

The very major changes that have occurred in manufacturing procedures in recent times mean that schools can no longer mirror these processes in their curriculum, quite apart from the shortage of time they now have to develop these personal skills. Industry, as a sector of society that is worthy of study, is, however, now more widely included in curricula for technology education.

Arbeitslehre (learning about work) in the Federal Republic of Germany has a well-developed structure as a curriculum for study, and some excellent supporting materials exist (e.g., a text by Ziefuss 1987). Students are introduced to the historical progression from traditional crafts to the counterparts (usually highly automated) in today's industrial scene. With this historical sense of meaning their own practice with tools and materials is encouraged in these curricula.

A series of key questions are addressed as industries that involve such things as "print, plants and animals, wood, metal, glass, textiles and leather, and ceramics" are studied:

- Under what conditions was and is this sort of work carried out?
- How have the work activities, objects, tools, and forms of organization changed in the course of time?
- What effects do these changes have on the satisfaction of the needs of individuals and society?
- To what extent are there changes in the scope that workers themselves have to influence their work and make decisions about it?

This curriculum is one of only a few among the emerging ones for technology education that so explicitly includes critical approaches to technology, although a number of them (e.g., the new one in England and Wales) include the idea of critique as part of technological literacy in their general aims.

A Novel Definition of the Curriculum for Technology Education

At the time of this writing, the curriculum developments for technology education in England and Wales seem to be more coherently argued and detailed than most. They are also rather novel in emphasis and, for these reasons, are interesting to present.

The Education Reform Act of 1988 designated technology as one of seven foundation subjects in the curriculum that all students must study (in addition to mathematics, English, and science—the core subjects) from age 5 to age 16—that is, the compulsory years. This very new view, for England and Wales, of a common national curriculum takes the form (as described above for science), in each of the above subjects, of a series of learning "Attainment Targets" within which the progression of learning over the years is also spelled out. National monitoring of this is planned to occur at 7, 11, 14, and 16 years of age. Technology thus has a status it has never had before, since the most able students in this country have not traditionally studied the craft or practical subjects that can be seen as the historical precursors of technology.

In 1985, the Assessment of Performance Unit (APU), a national body carrying out light national sampling of learning in a number of subject fields, established a project in the design and technology field. While it was not acknowledged as a major influence on the Working Group for technology in the National Curriculum, this project had paved the way for a radically different view of technology education to emerge. The APU project team saw a number of educationally desirable features in the curriculum of "Craft, Design, and Technology" (see earlier), but some of these they saw as similar to learnings associated with subjects such as home economics, textiles, art, and design, and others were shared by science, mathematics, and humanities.

One of the shared features in the first group of subjects is the idea of a *product* (or a *system*). Another is a *set of processes* that lead to this product. In society, the "manufacture" of an *effective* and *economic* product involves for each of the emphasized words such a set of processes. In education, students need the idea of a product to ensure, in its interplay with design, that they will engage in a set of learning processes that can lead them to both *understanding* and *capability*.

This interdependence of design and capability, and the importance of the idea of a product, had already been referred to by Black and Harrison (1985) in a small book entitled *In Place of Confusion: Technology and Science in the School Curriculum*. A product is still evident in the views of technology education that are now very influential in England, but inevitably there has been a decline in the importance accorded it and to the acquisition of high levels of performance of the skills associated with its making. These skills take time to acquire and repeated practice to master. As other processes such as task identification, design, evaluation, and decision making gained recognition, the time available for skill acquisition became shorter.

The APU team still describes "making" as one of the six processes in their models of design and technological activity. However, in the framework for their survey instruments with which they aim to catch the interplay in students between thought and action, they identify only four "intentions" that they see as integral to overall technological capability. These are "task identification, investigation, generation and development, and evaluation." The third of these, "generation and development," subsumes the making processes.

The APU test instruments include a content dimension that covers "materials, energy, and control systems." Other dimensions in these instruments are an affective one, one about consideration of people, one about communication skills, and one that is about the confidence demonstrated by the pupil. The items strongly emphasize meeting human needs. The project team argues that the in-school situation has a freedom from the more economic sense of social recognition that pertains to real technological products. In schools, "meeting human needs" can thus be used to develop critical dimensions in the students' understanding and in their design ideas. Findings from APU studies indicated the students' abilities at the tasks do not always transfer across contexts. The project, accordingly, takes context very seriously and includes test tasks concerning *People* (old and young), the *Environment* (built and botanical), and *Industry* (large and small). These interesting perspectives on technology had been worked out in England and Wales by the time a Working Group was established in 1988 to advise on learning attainment targets and programs of study for technology in the new National Curriculum. The Working Group, after a short period of intensive work, was able to set out in an interim report an educational rationale for technology in the curriculum and to explain in some detail a number of new ideas it had embraced (Department of Education and Science and the Welsh Office 1988).

"Design and Technology" (D&T) was seen as a unitary concept to attest to the intimate connection between the learnings implied in these two words and to emphasize that it is their combination that has the potential to provide valuable learning. It describes the value of this learning as the capability to operate effectively and creatively in the world—certainly an exciting educational aim in the face of the widespread concern about so much of schooling having failed to provide just this sort of capability.

D&T is always purposeful—a response to a perceived social need or societal opportunity. It will, the Working Group's report argues, thus be attractive to students. D&T should foster a competence in the "indeterminate zones of practice" and a concern with what might be a "visionary activity." Development in students of this competence through doodles, drawings, models, prototypes, and computer displays, *before* the realization of a product (an artifact, system, or environment), is a distinctive contribution technology education can make. D&T can also contribute to "communication skills, economics and career awareness, business understanding, persistence to follow a job, effective team work, and interpersonal skills."

The sorts of learning experiences (and hence the teaching to encourage them) that are essential for these ambitious learning outcomes include active engagement and practical involvement, together with critical reflection upon, and appraisal of, the social and economic results of technological activities beyond the school.

- D&T tasks will involve materials, energy, and information as media, and knowledge of these will need to be acquired because it will be both a needed resource and a constraint.
- D&T will lead students naturally to learn about the application and the effects of technological products.
- D&T tasks are about products that are subject to aesthetic, business, and production constraints.
- D&T tasks can develop general professional values, such as efficiency of resource use, value for money, and fitness for purpose, and specific values that relate to the contexts of production and use, such as health and safety, user preferences, and ecological benignity.

The Working Group's final report (NCC 1989) and its official outcome in the subsequent statutory orders set out a novel curriculum challenge to schools in England and Wales. The equivalent of four periods per week has been suggested for technology education as a regular subject, and already schools are exhibiting a variety of ways of providing and using this time, including extended blocks, such as a week or regular whole days, that enable the combination of learning experiences that are provided by a wide range of subjects to be brought together in a corporate learning project. It acknowledges that CDT and science have obvious contributions, but calls on humanities, art, mathematics, home economics, and so on, to all contribute to the new sorts of practical learning it defines for technology under four broad attainment targets (compared with 17 for science):

1. *Identifying needs and opportunities*. Pupils should be able to identify and state clearly needs and opportunities for design and technological activities through investigation of the contexts of home, school, recreation, community, business, and industry.
2. *Generating a design proposal*. Pupils should be able to generate a design specification, explore ideas to produce a design proposal, and develop it into a realistic, appropriate, and achievable design.
3. *Planning and making*. Pupils should be able to work to a plan derived from their previously developed design and be able to identify, manage, and use appropriate resources, including both knowledge and processes, in order to make an artifact, system, or environment.
4. *Evaluating*. Pupils should be able to develop, communicate, and act upon an evaluation of the processes, products, and effects of their design and technological activities and those of others, including those from other times and cultures.

Specific examples appropriate for ages 7, 11, 14, and 16 are given under each of the targets. This requirement for all these components of the curriculum to contribute to this new sort of practical learning is a call for a coordinated approach to a school's whole curriculum, not an amendment to one or other of its components. In this way both boys and girls are to have the opportunity to learn *technological capability* in a wide range of contexts that not only command their interest but also lead to progressive enhancement of their confidence in performance.

The implementation of such a curriculum will obviously require considerable support for its teachers. This is recognized, and various ways of providing it to both primary and secondary teachers and to whole school communities are now being tried. Whether these efforts will be sufficient to bring about the curriculum revolution just described will be a question of great interest throughout the 1990s.

It is important to note that the English decisions to espouse D&T as the essential concept for technology education is also a decision against technology education being primarily about existing technologies—the position that characterizes a number of the developments in other countries. It is also a decision against Scriven's (1987) plea above that technology education be essentially the use, adaptation, and evaluation of existing technologies.

A Curriculum about Technology

A curriculum with a different emphasis has been introduced in New York State under the much more modest mandate of all girls and boys completing one unit (5 days for 42 minutes a week for 1 year) before the end of grade 8 (Todd 1987).

The 10 curriculum modules for use in grades 7 or 8 are listed as:

1. Getting to know technology
2. What is needed for technology
3. How people use technology to solve problems
4. What must be known about systems and subsystems
5. How technology affects people and the environment
6. Choosing appropriate resources for technological systems
7. How resources are processed by technological systems
8. Controlling technological systems
9. Using systems to solve problems
10. Technology and you: Interests, decisions, and choices

The first five modules introduce "development, resources, problem solving, systems, and impacts of technology" as features of technology, and the second five return to these key ideas in more depth.

Advice to teachers about the pedagogy of this curriculum has been through Technology Learning Activities (TLAs) and a program of in-service education. Each TLA includes (1) the essential knowledge for the module; (2) the major concepts to be addressed; (3) a list of student objectives and competencies; (4) some instructional procedures; (5) the set of "constants" to be infused into this (and each unit), for example, the technological systems, the mathematics, the science, the creative problem solving, and the links to transfer learning; (6) a list of references and resources; and (7) examples of how to assess and evaluate learning.

This curriculum for technology education is clearly of the "learning *about* technology" type. It has a defined and coherent structure and a level of detail for its knowledge content that lends itself to a form of presentation that is consistent with traditional textbooks. Indeed, a number of such texts have recently appeared on the market in the United States. *Technology and You* (Goetsch and Nelson 1987) is an example of such a text that is aimed at students in the lower secondary levels, and *Technology in Your World* (Hacker and Barden 1987) covers a comparable set of topics but at a level more suited for older students. Although both the curriculum for New York State and the two exemplary texts refer to the importance of practical activities, the body of content knowledge included is so vast and diverse in topics that it seems likely that it will become dominant. Practical skill development or extended experience of using technologies are unlikely to be priorities in this approach to technology education. Its formalized and analytical approach to problem solving and decision making are also far removed from the more holistic and open-ended approach that is both the pedagogy and the learning targets being encouraged in England.

Fensham (1980b), in a search for comparative imperatives in the 1950/1960s curriculum development in science, suggested that the textbook had been a much more required element in the United States than in Britain and continental Europe, where the teacher is accorded much more authority in curriculum matters. The two examples of very different approaches to technology education 30 years later that have just been described are consistent with this hypothesis.

The example in the United States is also very much a definition of technology as a subject field in its own right that is very largely independent of the other subjects a student is studying. It fits an overall school curriculum that is seen as the sum of many parts. The English curriculum sees technology not as an independent autonomous field, but as concepts that can have expression in and, indeed, need the other components of the total curriculum. It encourages and requires schools to coordinate the learnings that they are seeking to provide to students through technology and science (and other subject areas).

RELATIONS BETWEEN SCIENCE AND TECHNOLOGY

In this final section I return to the issue of the relationship between science and technology education raised in the introductory section. Science educators and curriculum developers have been much more concerned with the issue than their counterparts in technology education. One attempt involving expertise from both camps is that by Black and Harrison (1985). They produced a model for the relationship when science is the source of the *resources* in it. These authors intend the model to be applied more generally, including other subject areas as *resources* in like manner.

Their model includes "capability" as the learning outcome from an interactive interplay between a person undertaking a "technological task" and the "resources" he or she has to use in the task. The need for resources, such as the knowledge, concepts, and skills to construct a solution to a personal or societal problem (that is, the technological task), generates the purpose and motivation to learn these skills. The practice of using these acquired learnings in the task shows their application and relevance.

When science is the subject field to be drawn on for the resources, science teachers may be familiar enough with its factual and conceptual knowledge and have competence in some of its skills. They are much less likely to be familiar with the concepts Black and Harrison (1985) include as resources from the science/society interface, such as ones having to do with "the nature of society and its values" and "the ethics of choice." Many teachers of technology education would likewise find such concepts strange ones to include in their set of resources because, in their own but different way, they tend to isolate production from the society for which it is intended.

The "task" part of the model will also still be strange to many science teachers, although in Britain, where the model was generated, it was present in a policy statement from its professional association in the 1980s: "The utilization of scientific knowledge and processes in the pursuit of further knowledge and deeper understanding and the development of an ability to function autonomously in an area of science studies, to solve practical problems and to communicate that inference to others."

For many science teachers and for the purposes of most current science curricula, it would be the first half of this long sentence that refers to what is meant by "problem solving" in science. For Black and Harrison (1985) their idea of "task" is characterized by key words like "problem solving, practical communication, and function autonomously." The distinctions between going deeper into science and going out from science to the society at large are so great that it is unfortunate they are combined into the one policy statement. These important distinctions are all too often overlooked in science curricula and by science teachers.

In their description of the model, its authors say that it is essential that neither "task" nor "resources" be master or servant of the other. Although, as just indicated, science is an essential element of this view of technological capability as a major "resource" for use and as a constraint to indicate what is possible, it is necessary to look at the sorts of scientific knowledge needed before we can conclude that science curricula as they exist can provide it.

Harrison (1989) himself raised a doubt about this when he referred to needing "to invert" the usual science concepts and having them in "multiple form" rather than in the singular form in which they are usually taught and learned in science. Layton (1987) used an allegorical approach to the culture of science and technology to discuss the nature of technological knowledge. He argued, from substantial historical studies of technology in the United States and elsewhere, that this is knowledge of how to do or make things. Science has a more general form of knowing. Technologists, he points out, value "design" so highly because it is "the cognitive bridge between the abstract, idealized conceptions of science to the concrete, highly complex products of technology in the real world" (Layton 1987, 604). These distinctions can be neatly summarized by describing the scientist as *homo sapiens* and the technologist as *homo faber*.

On the other side of the Atlantic another Layton (1988), also a historian of technology, examined the cultures of science and technology in seeking for common ground they might share in education. Instead, he found a number of very definite differences between scientists and technologists. The scientist is the understanding human; the technologist, the working or making human. Science is primarily about knowing that; technology about knowing how. Science is interested in propositional knowledge; technology in action knowledge. Understanding for its own sake in science contrasts with technology, which is always purposeful. Breaking up nature into parts is science's main route to understanding; technology seeks to put nature together to achieve a synthetic or artificial product. Science aims at a consensus view as close to truth as possible; technology always recognizes a set of possible solutions and requires value judgments to be made between them.

Layton concludes that these differences in culture are so great that science curricula would have to change considerably if they are to service technology education with the "action knowledge" it needs as one of its resources. In the light of these sorts of differences, what then is happening in science curricula that are so obviously being influenced by technology in the form of STS?

A way to understand this paradox is to see technology education as made up of rather distinct strands or possible areas of learning. "Technological awareness, understanding, capability, literacy, critique" are all labels to be found in the literature, although often they are not always used only for component strands and often not consistently to describe the same strand.

Black and Harrison's (1985) model is for an ability to complete a task, to find a solution to a technological problem. This is what they mean by *technological capability*. There is not much indication that science curricula are moving in directions that will lead them to contribute much to the practice by students of this ability component of technology education.

The two approaches to including STS in science curricula do, however, seem to be very relevant to "technological awareness" and to "technological understanding," respectively. The add-on approach, where applications of science are regularly pointed out, is likely to increase students' awareness of technology and of the fact that science does impinge on society in the form of many technologies. The study-of-an-application approach has the potential to provide students with a substantial understanding of the sort of scientific knowledge on which a technology is based and the sorts of limitations it thus has as far as science is concerned. This sort of understanding can be developed from science knowledge as it is normally learned in science because the learning is not to make the student competent to actually operate the technology.

As discussed earlier, these two approaches represent the now common meanings of the science-technology interface in science curricula. Both are concerned with science knowledge *about* a technology. For example, an examination of the very detailed learning targets in the new English National Curriculum confirms this science view of technology. "To be able to describe cloning methods and their use in agriculture" (Genetics Attainment Target) is a common sort of statement among the many listed targets of "knowledge and understanding." There are very few targets that encourage actual practical capability; nor is there the same sense of progression for these few practical skills as there is in the targets for knowledge and understanding. As part of the Electricity and Magnetism Attainment Target, students are "to be able to construct simple electrical circuits" at about age 11. This skill is, however, not referred to again among the learning targets for the next 5 years of study of these topics in science.

Although so few technology educators address this relationship issue, it is possible to see, from the sorts of examples and topics they give the sort of science knowledge they commonly see as important. Some of it turns out to be content that was not uncommon in science curricula before the 1950/1960s, while a number of the topics have never been part of science curricula. Examples of the former are Bernoulli's principle and other aspects and concepts of fluid flow, photography, pneumatics, elasticity, strength of materials, acoustics, chemical analysis, hydrostatics, machines, and efficiency. In the latter category are properties of alloys, ceramics and composites, systems theory, electronic control, adhesion, fiber optics, lasers, semiconductors, and holography.

It is hard to explain these two sorts of gaps in science curricula. Some of the topics are probably seen as insufficiently conceptual or quantitative, but others are quite as quantitative and conceptual as many topics in today's science curricula. There are traditions and fashions in science as in any other field, and it is probable that many of the science topics that technology education wants in its knowledge resources are not in fashion. Some would be regarded as too context specific to warrant inclusion in science. Others, like the anisotropic strength of supports of rectangular cross section, could be rejected for being too algorithmic, but then, much acceptable content in science is also merely algorithmic.

Until more systematic work is done on the difference between what Layton called "propositional knowledge" and "action knowledge," science education and technology education are likely to miss each other at the very point where they should overlap. Sjöberg (1990) has begun this task by providing a background resource text containing a number of examples that relate these two sorts of science knowledge.

Whether science educators and those who educate science teachers have enough interest in this task will determine very much whether the curricula in these two fields progress toward or away from each other in the next decade.

References

AAAS. 1989. *Science for All Americans*. A summary report of Phase I of Project 2061. Washington, DC: American Association for the Advancement of Science.

Aikenhead, Glen. 1985. Collective decision making in the social context of science. *Science Education* 69(4): 453–475.

Aikenhead, Glen. 1986. The content of STS education. *A Missive to the Science-Technology-Society Research Network* 2(3): 18–23. Saskatoon, Canada: STSRN Secretariat.

Aikenhead, Glen. 1989. Decision making theories as tools for interpreting student behaviour during a scientific inquiry simulation. *Journal for Research in Science Teaching* 26(3): 189 203.

Aikenhead, Glen, and Reg Fleming. 1975. *Science, a Way of Knowing*. Saskatoon, Canada: Department of Curriculum Studies, University of Saskatchewan.

Andersson, Björn. 1984. *Chemical Reactions*. Report *Elevperspektiv*, No. 12. Goteborg: Department of Education, University of Goteborg, Sweden.

Andersson, Björn. 1990. Pupils' conceptions of matter and its transformations (age 12–16). *Studies in Science Education* (in press).

Apple, Michael. 1979. *Ideology and the Curriculum*. London: Routledge & Kegan Paul.

APU. 1980. *Science in Schools: Report No. 1 (age 11), Report No. 2 (age 13), Report No. 3 (age 15)*. London: Assessment of Performance Unit.

Arzi, Hanna. 1988. "On Energy in Chocolate and Yoghurt or: On the Applicability of School Science Concepts to Real Life and Their Integration Across the Curriculum." Paper presented at the AERA annual meeting, New Orleans, LA.

Association for Science Education. 1979. *Alternatives for Science Education*. A discussion paper. Hatfield, Hertfordshire, England: Association for Science Education.

Association for Science Education. 1981. *Education through Science*. Policy Document. Hatfield, Hertfordshire, England.: Association for Science Education.

Baird, John. 1986. Improving learning through enhanced metacognition: A classroom study. *European Journal of Science Education* 8(3): 263–282.

Baird, John, and Ian Mitchell, eds. 1986. *Improving the Quality of Teaching and Learning: An Australian Case Study—the PEEL Project*. Melbourne, Victoria, Australia: Monash University Printery.

Baird, John, and Richard White. 1982a. Promoting self-control of learning. *Instructional Science* 11(3): 227–247.

Baird, John, and Richard White. 1982b. A case study of learning styles in biology. *European Journal of Science Education* 4(3): 325–337.

Barber, Brenda, and Mick Michell. 1987. *Building Primary-Secondary Links*. Better Science, Curriculum Guide 10. London: Heinemann Educational Books/Association for Science Education.

Ben-Peretz, Miriam. 1975. The concept of curriculum potential. *Curriculum Theory Network* 5(2): 151–159.

Bentley, Diane, and Michael Watts. 1986. Courting the positive virtues: A case for feminist science. *European Journal of Science Education* 8(2): 121–134.

Berkheimer, Glenn, et al. 1988. *Matter and Molecules, Teacher's Guide: Science Book*. Occasional paper no. 121. East Lansing: Institute for Research on Teaching Michigan State University

Black, Paul, and Geoffrey Harrison. 1985. *In Place of Confusion: Technology and Science in the School Curriculum*. London: Nuffield-Chelsea Curriculum Trust and the National Centre for School Technology, Trent Polytechnic.

Bloom, Benjamin. 1984. The 2 sigma problem: The search for

methods of group instruction as effective as one-to-one tutoring. *Education Research* 13(6): 4–16.

Blumberg, Fran, Marion Epstein, Walter MacDonald, and Ina Mullis. 1986. *A Pilot Study of Higher Order Thinking Skills Assessment Techniques in Science and Mathematics: Final Report, Parts 1 and 2*. ME-G-84-2006-P4, Princeton, NJ: National Assessment of Educational Performance.

Boben, Donna. 1985. *Guidelines for Equity Issues in Technology Education*. Reston, VA: International Technology Education Association.

Boeha, Beno. 1989. "Students' Beliefs and the Outcomes of Physics Instruction." Ph.D dissertation, Monash University, Clayton, Victoria, Australia.

Bourdieu, Pierre, and Jean Passerou. 1977. *Reproduction in Education, Society and Culture*. London: Sage.

Boyer, Ernest. 1983. *High School: A Report for the Carnegie Foundation on Secondary Education in America*. New York: Harper & Row.

Brumby, Margaret. 1984. *Issues in Biology*. Melbourne. Australia: Nelson.

Bruner, Jerome. 1965. *The Process of Education*. Cambridge, MA: Harvard University Press.

Bucat, Robert, and Andrew Cole. 1988. The Australian Academy of Science School Chemistry Project. *Journal of Chemical Education* 65(9): 777–779.

Buffer, James, and Michael Scott. 1986. *Special Needs Guide for Technology Education*. Reston, VA: International Technology Education Association.

Bunder, Wolfgang, et al. 1987. *Youth Dictionary Technology—Humane and Ecological Technologies*. Reinbeck bei Hamburg: Rowohlt Taschenbuch Verlag.

Butler Kahle, Jane. 1985. *Women in Science*. Sussex, England: Falmer.

Bybee, Rodger. 1977. The new transformation of science education. *Science Education* 61(1): 85–97.

Bybee, Rodger. 1985. "The Sisyphean Question in Science Education: What Should the Scientifically and Technologically Literate Person Know, Value and Do—as a Citizen?" In *Science-Technology-Society*, edited by Rodger Bybee. NSTA Yearbook, Washington, DC: National Science Teachers Association.

Calfee, Robert. 1987. The school as a context for assessment of literacy. *The Reading Teacher* 40(8):738–743.

Carlson, Dale, ed. 1981. *New Directions for Testing and Measurement: Testing in the States: Beyond Accountability*. San Francisco, CA: Jossey-Bass.

Case, Robert. 1989. "Science Teaching from a Developmental Perspective: The Importance of Central Conceptual Skills." In *Adolescent Development and School Science,* edited by Philip Adey, 125–149. London: Falmer.

Chaffe-Stengel, Priscilla. 1986. "The Impact of Bruner's Directorship of the Woods Hole Conference on the Curriculum Reform Movement in Science." Paper presented at AERA annual meeting, San Francisco, CA.

Champagne, Audrey, Richard Gunstone, and Leon Klopfer. 1985. "Effecting Changes in Cognitive Structures among Physics Students." In *Cognitive Structure and Conceptual Change*, edited by Leo West and Leon Pines, 163–186. Orlando, FL: Academic Press.

CLIS. 1987. *Approaches to Teaching the Particulate Theory of Matter*. Leeds, England: Centre for Studies in Science and Mathematics Education, University of Leeds.

Comber, Leslie, and John Keeves. 1973. *Science Education in Nineteen Countries*. International Studies in Evaluation 1, International Association for the Evaluation of Educational Achievement. New York: Wiley.

Commonwealth Secretariat. 1985. *Interrelating Science, Mathematics and Technology Education*. London: Commonwealth Secretariat.

Connelly, Michael. 1972. The functions of curriculum development. *Interchange* 3(2–3): 161–177.

Connelly, Michael, Robert Crocker, and Heidi Kass. 1985a. *Science Education in Canada, Vol. 1. Politicies, Practices and Perceptions*. Toronto, Canada: OISE.

Connelly, Michael, Robert Crocker, and Heidi Kass. 1985b. *Science Education in Canada, Vol. 2. Achievement and its Correlates*. Toronto, Canada: OISE.

CSSE. 1978. *Case Studies in Science Education*. Urbana-Champaign: CIRCE and CCE, University of Illinois.

Delamont, Sara. 1989. The fingernail on the blackboard?: A sociological perspective on science education. *Studies in Science Education* 16: 25–46.

Department of Education. 1985. *Science Primary: To Standard Four, Syllabus and Guide*. Wellington, New Zealand: Department of Education.

Department of Education and Science and the Welsh Office. 1988. *Interim Report, Design and Technology Working Group, National Curriculum*. London: Department of Education and Science and Welsh Office.

de Vos, Wobbie, and Adri Verdonk. 1985. A new road to reactions, part 1 and 2. *Journal of Chemical Education* 62(3): 238–240 and 62(8): 648–649.

de Vos, Wobbie, and Adri Verdonk. 1986. A new word to reactions, part 3. *Journal of Chemical Education* 63(11): 972–974.

de Vos, Wobbie, and Adri Verdonk. 1987. A new road to reactions, part 4, The substance and its molecules; and part 5, The elements and their atoms. *Journal of Chemical Education* 64(8): 692–694 and 64(12): 1010–1013.

de Vries, Marc. 1988. "What Should and Can Pupils Learn in Technology Education?" In *Basic Principles of School Technology*, edited by Jan Raat et al. Report of PATT-3 conference, vol.1. Framework for technology education. Eindhoven, the Netherlands: University of Technology.

Driver, Rosalind. 1983. *The Pupil as Scientist*. Milton Keynes, England: Open University Press.

Driver, Rosalind. 1989. "The Construction of Scientific Knowledge in School Classrooms." In *Doing Science: Images of Science in Science Classrooms*, edited by R. Millar, 83–106. London: Falmer.

Driver, Rosalind, and Beverley Bell. 1986. Students' thinking and the learning of science: A constructivist view. *School Science Review* 67(240): 443–456.

Driver, Rosalind, and Gaalen Erickson. 1983. Theories-in-action. Some theoretical and empirical issues in the study of students' conceptual frameworks in science. *Studies in Science Education* 70: 473–496.

Driver, Rosalind, Edith Guesne, and Andrée Tiberghien, eds. 1985. *Children's Ideas in Science*. Milton Keynes, England: Open University Press.

Driver, Rosalind, and Valerie Oldham. 1986. A constructivist approach to curriculum development in science. *Studies in Science Education* 13: 105–122.

Education and Technology Task Force. 1986. *Making Things Work: Learning for Competence and Enterprise*. A report to the Minister of Education and Technology. Adelaide, South Australia: Ministry of Technology.

Edwards, John, and Percival Marland. 1984. A comparison of student thinking in a mathematics and a science classroom. *Research in Science Education* 14: 29–38.

Eijkelhof, Harrie, and Koos Kortland. 1988. "Broadening the Aims of Physics Education." In *Developments and Dilemmas in Sci-*

ence Education, edited by Peter Fensham, 282–305. London: Falmer.

Eisemon, Thomas. 1989. The impact of primary schooling on agricultural thinking and practices in Kenya and Burundi. *Studies in Science Education* 17: 5–28.

Eylon, Bat-Sheva, and Marcia Linn. 1988. Learning on instruction: An examination of four research perspectives in science education. *Review of Educational Research* 58(3): 251–301.

Fawns, Roderick. 1987. "The Maintenance and Transformation of School Science, Parts 1 & 2." Ph.D. dissertation, Monash University, Clayton, Victoria, Australia.

Fehr, Howard. 1968. Contemporary mathematics and its intervention in the sciences. *Educational Studies in Mathematics* 1(3): 347–351.

Fensham, Peter. 1980a. Constraint and autonomy in Australian secondary science education. *Journal of Curriculum Studies* 12(3): 189–206.

Fensham, Peter. 1980b. Books, teachers and committees—A comparative essay on authority in science education. *European Journal of Science Education* 2(3): 245–252.

Fensham, Peter. 1983. A research base for new objectives of science teaching. *Science Education* 67(1): 3–12.

Fensham, Peter. 1984. Conceptions, misconceptions and alternative frameworks in chemical education. *Chemical Society Reviews* 13(2): 199–217.

Fensham, Peter. 1985. Science for all. *Journal of Curriculum Studies* 17(4): 415–435.

Fensham, Peter. 1987. "Changing to a Science, Society and Technology Approach." In *Science and Technology and Future Human Needs*, edited by John Lewis and Peter Kelly, 67–80. Oxford, England: ICSU/Pergamon.

Fensham, Peter. 1988a. Physical science, society and technology. *Australian Journal of Education* 32(3): 375–386.

Fensham, Peter. 1988b. Approaches to the teaching of STS in science education. *International Journal of Science Education*. 10(4): 346–356.

Fensham, Peter. 1989. "Theory in Practice: How to Assist Science Teachers to Teach Constructively." In *Adolescent Development and School Science*, edited by Philip Adey, 61–77. London: Falmer.

Fensham, Peter, and John May. 1979. Servant not master—a new role for science in a core of environmental education. *The Australian Science Teachers Journal* 25(2): 15–24.

Fleming, Reg. 1986. Adolescent reasoning in socio-scientific issues, part 1. *Journal of Research in Science Teaching* 23(8): 677–688.

Fleming, Reg. 1989. Literacy for a technological age. *Science Education* 73(4): 391–404.

Fraser, Barry, and Jeffrey Northfield. 1981. *A Study of Some Aspects of ASEP During its First Year of Availability*. Canberra, Australia: Curriculum Development Centre.

French, Jane. 1989. "Accomplishing Scientific Instruction." In *Doing Science: Images of Science in Science Education*, edited by Robin Millar, 10–37. London: Falmer.

Gaskell, P. James. 1987. "Science and Technology in British Columbia." Paper presented to the 4th International Symposium on World Trends in Science and Technology Education, Kiel, West Germany, I.P.N.

Gilbert, John, and Michael Watts. 1983. Concepts, misconceptions and alternative conceptions: Changing perspectives in science education. *Studies in Science Education* 10: 61–98.

Gilbert, John, Michael Watts, and Roger Osborne. 1985. "Eliciting Students' Views—Using an Interview—About Instances Technique." In *Cognitive Structure and Conceptual Change*, edited by Leo West and Leon Pines, 11–26. Orlando, FL: Academic Press.

Gillespie, Ronald. 1976. Chemistry—fact or fiction? Some reflections on the teaching of chemistry. *Chemistry Canada* 28(11): 23–28.

Gilligan, Carol. 1982. *In a Different Voice*. Cambridge, MA: Harvard University Press.

Gintis, Herbert. 1972. Towards a political economy of education. *Harvard Educational Review* 42(1): 70–96.

Goetsch, David, and John Nelson. 1987. *Technology and You*. Albany, NY: Delmar.

Gott, Richard, Geoff Welford, and Ken Foulds. 1988. *The Assessment of Practical Work in Science*. Oxford, England: Blackwells.

Grant, Martin, and Jan Harding. 1987. Changing the polarity. *International Journal of Science Education* 9(3): 335–342.

Greeno, James. 1978. "A Study of Problem Solving." In *Advances in Instructional Psychology*, edited by Robert Glaser. Hillsdale, NJ: Erlbaum.

Gunstone, Richard, and Richard White. 1981. Understanding gravity. *Science Education* 65(3): 291–299.

Hacker, Michael, and Robert Barden. 1987. *Technology and Your World*. Albany, NY: Delmar.

Hales, James, and James Snyder. 1982. Jackson's Mill industrial arts curriculum theory: A base for curriculum derivation. Parts 1 & 2. *Man, Society, Technology*, Feb. 6–10 and Mar. 6–9.

Hall, William. 1973. *Patterns: Teachers' Handbook*. London: Longman/Penguin.

Harding, Jan. 1983. *Switched Off: The Science Education of Girls*. York, England: Longmans for the Schools Council.

Harding, Jan. 1985. "Values, Cognitive Style and the Curriculum." In *Contributions to the Third GASAT Conference*, 159–166. London: Chelsea College.

Harding, Jan. 1986. "The Making of a Scientist?" In *Perspectives of Gender and Science*, edited by Jan Harding. Lewes, England: Falmer.

Harding, Jan, and Jim Donaldson. 1986. Chemistry from issues. *School Science Review* 68(242): 49–59.

Harlen, Wynne, ed. 1982. *New Trends in Primary School Science Education*, Vol 1. Paris: UNESCO.

Harlen, Wynne. 1985. *Primary Science: Taking the Plunge*. Oxford, England: Heinemann.

Harrison, Geoffrey. 1989. *Design and Technology*. Nottingham, England: Trent Consultancy, Trent Polytechnic.

Head, John. 1979. Personality and the pursuit of science. *Studies in Science Education* 3: 23–44.

Hegelson, Stanley, Patricia Blosser, and Robert Howe. 1977. *The Status of Pre-College Science, Mathematics, and Social Science Education 1955–1975, vol. 1. Science Education*. Washington, DC: National Science Foundation.

Heikkinen, Henry. 1978. Sex bias in chemistry tests: Where is women's place? *The Science Teacher* 45(1): 16–21.

Hilmo, Inger. 1983. "An Analysis of Norwegian Textbooks in Science." Paper presented at the 2nd GASAT Conference, Oslo, Norway.

Hines, Jodi, and Harold Hungerford. 1984. "Environmental Education Research Related to Environmental Action Skills." In *Monographs in Environmental Education and Environmental Studies* (1971–1982), 113–120. Columbus: ERIC, Ohio State University.

Hodson, Derek. 1985. Philosophy of science, science and science education. *Studies in Science Education* 12: 25–37.

Hodson, Derek. 1987. Social control as a factor in science curriculum change. *International Journal of Science Education* 9(5): 529–540.

Hodson, Derek. 1988. Towards a philosophically more valid science curriculum. *Science Education* 72(1): 19–40.

Hofstein, Arvi, and Vincent Lunetta. 1982. The role of the laboratory in science education. *Reviews of Educational Research* 52: 201–217.

Holman, John. 1986. *Science and Technology in Society, General Guide for Teachers*. Hatfield, Hertfordshire, England: Association for Science Education.

Holman, John. 1987. Resources or courses? Contrasting approaches to the introduction of industry and technology to the secondary curriculum. *School Science Review* 68(244): 432–438.

Horwood, R. Herbert. 1982. Explanations and descriptions in science teaching. *Science Education* 72(1): 41–50.

Hufstedler, Shirley, and D. N. Langenburg. 1982. *Science Education for the 1980s and Beyond*. Washington, DC: National Science Foundation and the Department of Education.

Hunt, Andrew. 1988. SATIS approach to STS. *International Journal of Science Education* 10(4): 409.20.

ICSU. 1987. *Science and Technology Education and Future Human Needs*, Vols. 1–9. London: Pergamon.

ITEA. 1987. *Resources in Technology 4*. Reston, VA: International Technology Education Association.

Jenkins, Edgar. 1979. *From Armstrong to Nuffield*. London: Murray.

Jenkins, Frank, et al. 1989. *Science, Technology, Society, Communication. CHEMISTRY*. Edmonton, Canada: Author Group, Karitann Publications.

Johnson, James. 1989. *Technology*. The report of the Project 2061 Phase 1 Technology Panel. Washington, DC: American Association for the Advancement of Science.

Johnston, Katherine. 1989. *Learning and Teaching the Particulate Theory of Matter: A Report on a Teaching Scheme in Action*. Leeds, England: Children's Learning in Science Project, University of Leeds.

Jorg, Ton, and Theo Wubbels. 1987. Girls and physics. *International Journal of Science Education* 9(3): 296–307.

Kelly, Alison. 1981. *The Missing Half: Girls and Science Education*. Manchester, England: Manchester University Press.

Kelly, Alison. 1985. The construction of masculine science. *British Journal of Sociology of Education* 6(2): 133–154.

Kelly, Alison, Judith Whyte, and Barbara Smail. 1984. *Girls into Science and Technology, Final Report*. Manchester, England: Department of Sociology, University of Manchester.

Kempa, Richard. 1986. *Assessment in Science*. Cambridge Science Education Series, Cambridge, England: Cambridge University Press.

King, Kenneth. 1989. Primary schooling and developmental knowledge in Africa. *Studies in Science Education* 17: 29–56.

Klainin, Sunee. 1988. "Practical Work and Science Education 1." In *Developments and Dilemmas in Science Education*, edited by Peter Fensham, 169–188. London: Falmer.

Klainin, Sunee, and Peter Fensham. 1987. Learning achievements in upper secondary school chemistry in Thailand: Some remarkable sex reversals. *International Journal of Science Education* 9(2): 217–227.

Klainin, Sunee, Peter Fensham, and Leo West. 1989. Successful achievements by girls in physics learning. *International Journal of Science Education* 11(1): 101–112.

Kulkarni, Vinoo. 1988. "Role of Language in Science Education." In *Developments and Dilemmas in Science Education*, edited by Peter Fensham, 150–168. London: Falmer.

Larkin, Jill. 1983. "The Role of Problem Representation in Physics." In *Mental Models*, edited by Dedre Gentner and Albert Stevens. Hillsdale, NJ: Erlbaum.

Lauterbach, Roland, and Karl Frey. 1987. *Primary Science Education in the Federal Republic of Germany*. Kiel, West Germany: I.P.N.

Lawson, Anton. 1985. A review of research on formal reasoning and science teaching. *Journal of Research in Science Teaching* 22(7): 569–617.

Layton, David. 1972. Science as general education. *Trends in Education* No.25: 12.

Layton, David. 1973. *Science for the People*. London: Allen & Unwin.

Layton, David. 1984. *Interpreters of Science: A History of the Association of Science Education*. Hatfield, Hertfordshire, England: Association for Science Education.

Layton, David. 1988. Revaluing the T in STS. *International Journal of Science Education* 10(4): 367–378.

Layton, Edwin, Jr. 1987. Through the looking glass from Lake Mirror Image. *Technology and Culture* 28(3): 594–607.

Lazonby, John. 1987. "Do Students Want to Learn About Industry?" In *Education, Industry and Technology*, edited by David Waddington, 39–40. London: Pergamon.

Lemke, Jay. 1982. *Classroom Communication of Science*. Report to NSF/RISE:SED R79-18967, (ERIC ED222-346).

Lewis, John. 1980. *Science in Society. Readers and Teacher's Guide*. Hatfield, Hertfordshire, England: Association for Science Education and London: Heinemann.

Lewis, John, and Peter Kelly, eds. 1987. *Science and Technology and Future Human Needs*. Oxford, England: ICSU/Pergamon.

Lewis, Susan, and Anne Davies. 1988. *Gender Equity in Maths and Science*. GAMAST Professional Development Manual, Canberra, Australia: Curriculum Development Centre.

Linn, Marcia. 1986. "Science." In *Cognition and Instruction*, edited by Ronna Dillon and Robert Steinberg. Orlando, FL: Academic Press.

Linn, Marcia. 1987. Establishing a research base for science education challenges, trends and recommendations. *Journal of Research in Science Education* 24(3): 191–216.

Linn, Marcia, and Janet Hyde. 1989. Gender, mathematics and science. *Educational Researcher* 18(8): 17–19, 22–27.

Lunetta, Vincent, and Pinchas Tamir. 1979. Matching lab activities with teaching goals. *The Science Teacher* 46(5): 22–24.

Lybeck, Leif. 1981. *Archimedes in the classroom: A subject educational narrative*. Goteborg Studies in Educational Sciences No. 37. Goteborg: Department of Educational Research, University of Goteborg, Sweden.

McClintock Collective 1987. *The Fascinating Sky*. Melbourne, Victoria, Australia: Ministry of Education.

McConnell, Mary. 1982. Teaching about science technology and society at the secondary school level in the United States. *Studies in Science Education* 9: 1–32.

McFadden, Charles, et al. 1986. *Science Plus*. Vols 1, 2, & 3 and Teacher's Guide of the Atlantic Science Curriculum Project. Toronto, Canada: Academic Press.

McNett, Ian. 1984. *A Guide to the Excellence Movement in Education*. Washington, DC: Council for Basic Education.

Malcolm, Clifford, et al. 1987. *The Science Framework P-10*. Melbourne, Victoria, Australia: Ministry of Education.

Manthorpe, Catherine. 1982. Men's science, women's science or science: Some issues related to the study of girls' science education. *Studies in Science Education* 9: 65–80.

Martinand, Jean-Louis, and André Giordan. 1989. French Research in Science Education. *Studies in Science Education* 16: 209–217.

Mikelskis, Helmut. 1988. Ecological education. The structuring of the man-nature relationship as the guiding theme of a pedagogical quest. *Ricerca Educativa* V(4): 48–60.

Mikelskis, Helmut. 1989. "Two Sides of One Coin—'STS Education' and 'Environmental Education.'" Paper presented in Torino, Italy. Kiel, West Germany: I.P.N.

Millar, Robin, and Rosalind Driver. 1987. Beyond processes. *Studies in Science Education* 14: 33–62.

Murnane, Richard, and Senta Raizen, eds. 1988. *Improving Indicators of the Quality of Science and Mathematics Education in Grades K-12*. Washington, DC: National Academy Press.

National Assessment of Educational Performance. 1987. *Learning by Doing*. A manual for teaching and assessing higher order thinking in science and mathematics. Princeton, NJ: National Assessment of Educational Performance.

National Commission on Secondary Vocational Education. 1984. *The Unfinished Agenda*. Washington, DC: National Board of Education.

National Curriculum Council. 1988. *Science for Ages 5 to 16*. London: Department of Education and Science and the Welsh Office.

National Curriculum Council. 1989. *Design and Technology for Ages 5 to 16*. York, England: National Curriculum Council.

National Research Council. 1987. *Women: Their Underrepresentation and Career Differentials in Science and Engineering*. Washington, DC: National Academy Press.

National Science Foundation. 1983. *Educating Americans for the 21st Century*. Report of the National Science Board Commission on Precollege Education in Mathematics, Science and Technology. Washington, DC: National Science Foundation.

Novak, Joseph. 1978. An alternative for Piagetian psychology for science education. *Studies in Science Education* 5: 1–30.

OECD. 1989. *Report of the Florida Workship on Mathematics, Science and Technology Curriculum*. Paris: CERI, OECD.

Orpwood, Graham, and Jean-Pascal Souque. 1984. *Science Education in Canadian Schools. Vol 1, Introduction and Curriculum Analysis*. Ottawa: Science Council of Canada.

Osborne, Roger, and Peter Freyberg. 1985a. "Children's Science." In *Learning in Science*, edited by Roger Osborne and Peter Freyberg, 5–14. Auckland, New Zealand: Heinemann.

Osborne, Roger, and Peter Freyberg. 1985b. *Learning in Science: The Implications of Children's Science*. Auckland, New Zealand: Heinemann.

Osborne, Roger, and Merle Wittrock. 1985. The generative learning model and its implications for science education. *Studies in Science Education* 12: 59–87.

Pfundt, Helga, and Reinders Duit. 1987. *Bibliography: Students' Alternative Frameworks and Science Education*, 2nd ed. Kiel, West Germany: I.P.N.

Pines, Leon, Joseph Novak, George Posner, and Judy Van Kirk. 1978. *The Clinical Interview: A Method for Evaluating Cognitive Structure*. Research Report no. 6. Ithaca, NY: Department of Education, Cornell University.

Popham, W. James. 1983. "Measurement as an Instructional Catalyst." In *New Directions for Testing and Measurement No. 13: Measurement, Technology, and Individuality in Education*, edited by Ruth Ekstrom, 19–30. San Francisco, CA: Jossey-Bass.

Posner, George. 1982. A cognitive science conception of curriculum and instruction. *Journal of Curriculum Studies* 14(4): 343–351.

Rennie, Leonie, Lesley Parker, and Pauline Hutchinson. 1985. *The effects of inservice training attitudes and primary school science classroom climates*. Research Report no.12, Perth, Western Australia: Measurement and Statistics Laboratory, University of Western Australia.

Research Triangle Institute. 1977. *National Survey of Science Education Curriculum Usage*. Research Triangle Park, NY: Research Triangle Institute.

Resnick, Daniel, and Lauren Resnick. 1985. Standards, curriculum and performance: A historical and comparative perspective. *Educational Researcher* 14(4): 5–20.

Roberts, Douglas. 1980. "Theory, Curriculum Development and the Unique Events of Practice." In *See Curriculum in a New Light: Essays from Science Education*, edited by Hugh Munby et al. Toronto, Canada: OISE Press.

Roberts, Douglas. 1982. Developing the concept of "curriculum emphases" in science education. *Science Education* 66(2): 243–260.

Roberts, Douglas. 1988. "What Counts as Science Education?" In *Developments and Dilemmas in Science Education*, edited by Peter Fensham, 27–54. London: Falmer.

Roberts, Douglas, and Graham Orpwood. 1979. *Properties of Matter: A Teacher's Guide to Alternative Versions*. Toronto, Canada: OISE Press.

Rowell, Patricia, and P. James Gaskell. 1987. "Tensions and Realignments: School Physics in British Columbia 1955–80." In *International Perspectives in Curriculum History*, edited by Ivor Goodson, 74–106. Beckenham, Surrey, England: Croom Helm.

RSA. 1986. *Education for Capability*. edited by Tyrrell Burgess. Windsor, England: NFER-Nelson.

Schon, Donald. 1983. *The Reflective Practitioner*. New York: Basic Books.

Schon, Donald. 1987. *Educating the Reflective Practitioner*. San Francisco, CA: Jossey-Bass.

Schools Council. 1968. *Technology and the School*, Working Paper 18. London: Schools Council.

Schwab, Joseph. 1962. "The Teaching of Science as Enquiry." In *The Teaching of Science*, edited by Joseph Schwab and Paul Brandwein. Cambridge, MA: Harvard University Press.

Science Council of Canada. 1984. *Science for Every Student: Educating Canadians for Tomorrow's World*. Ottawa: Supply and Service.

Scriven, Michael. 1987. "The Rights of Technology in Education: The Need for Consciousness Raising." A paper for the Education and Technology Task Force. Adelaide, South Australia: Ministry of Education and Technology.

Shapiro, Bonnie. 1988. "What Children Bring to Light: Towards Understanding What the Primary School Science Learner Is Trying to Do." In *Developments and Dilemmas in Science Education*, edited by Peter Fensham, 96–120. London: Falmer.

Shayer, Michael, and Philip Adey. 1981. *Towards a Science of Science Teaching*. London: Heinemann.

Shimozawa, John. 1989. Objectives of the revised edition of the course of study—Science courses for pre-university schools. *Journal Science Education of Japan* 13(2): 57–62.

Shulman, Lee. 1986. "Paradigms and Research Programs in the Study of Teaching: A Contemporary Perspective." In *Handbook of Research on Teaching*, 3rd ed., edited by Merle Wittrock, 3–36. New York: Macmillan.

Sjöberg, Stefan. 1990. *Tekniklara*. Stockholm: Biblioteksforlaget.

Sjøberg, Svein. 1986. *Science and Norwegian Schools: Pupils and teachers express their opinions*. Oslo: Universitetsforlaget.

Sjøberg, Svein, and Gunn Imsen. 1988. "Gender and Science Education I." In *Developments and Dilemmas in Science Education*, edited by Peter Fensham, 218–248. London: Falmer.

Smail, Barbara. 1984. *Girl-Friendly Science: Avoiding Sex Bias in the Curriculum*. London: Schools Council/Longman.

Smail, Barbara. 1987. "Organizing the Curriculum to Fit Girls' Interests." In *Science for Girls*, edited by Alison Kelly, 80–88. Milton Keynes, England: Open University Press.

Smith, Neil. 1988. In support of an application—first chemistry course: Some reflections on the Salter's GCSE scheme. *School Science Review* 70(250): 108–114.

Smith, Walter. 1987. "COMETS: Career Oriented Modules to Explore Topics in Science." In *Science and Technology Education and the Quality of Life*, edited by Kurt Riquarts. 1: 279–285. Kiel, West Germany: I.P.N.

Solomon, Joan. 1983. *Eight titles in the* SISCON in Schools *series and a Teacher's Guide*. Hatfield, Hertfordshire, England: Association for Science Education and Oxford, England: Blackwell.

Solomon, Joan. 1987. Social influences on the construction of pupils' understanding of science. *Studies in Science Education* 14: 63–82.

Solomon, Joan. 1988. "The Dilemma of Science, Technology, and Society Education." In *Developments and Dilemmas in Science Education*, edited by Peter Fensham, 266–281. London: Falmer.

Spender, Dale. 1978. "Don't talk, listen." *Times Educational Supplement*, Nov. 3.

Spiegel-Rosing, Ina, and Derek de S. Price. 1977. *Science, Technology and Society*. Beverly Hills, CA: Sage.

SSABSA. 1989. *Operating Guidelines, Technology Curriculum Area*. Rose Park, South Australia: Senior Secondary Assessment Board of South Australia.

SSCR. 1987. *Better Science: Making It Happen*. London: Heinemann/A.S.E.

Suan, Mang Za. 1976. *An Evaluation of ASEP—A Case Study Approach*. M.Ed. thesis, Monash University, Clayton, Victoria, Australia.

Sutton, Clive. 1989. "Writing and Reading in Science: The Hidden Messages." In *Doing Science: Images of Science in Science Education*, edited by Robin Millar, 137–159. London: Falmer.

Tamir, Pinchas. 1972. The practical mode: A distinct mode of performance. *Journal of Biological Education* 6(3): 175–182.

Tamir, Pinchas, et al. 1979. *Curriculum Implementation and Its Relationship to Curriculum Development in Science*. Jerusalem: Science Teaching Centre.

Tamir, Pinchas, et al. 1982. The design and use of a practical test inventory. *Journal of Biological Education* 16(1): 42–50.

Tasker, Ross, and Peter Freyberg. 1985. "Facing the Mismatches in the Classroom." In *Learning in Science*, edited by Roger Osborne and Peter Freyberg, 66–80. Auckland, New Zealand: Heinemann.

The Royal Society. 1985. *The Public Understanding of Science*. London: The Royal Society.

The Royal Society and the Institute of Physics. 1982. *Girls and Physics*. London: Institute of Physics.

Thier, Herbert, and Tricia Hill. 1988. Chemical education in schools and the community: The CEPUP project. *International Journal of Science Education* 10(4): 421–430.

Thomas, Ian. 1987. "Assessing Understanding of Science, Technology and Society Interactions in a Public Examination." In *Education, Industry and Technology*. Vol. 3. *Science and Technology Education and Future Human Needs*, edited by David Waddington, 199–220. Oxford, England: ICSO and Pergamon.

Todd, Ronald. 1987. "Technology Education in the United States: A Case Study of a State in Transition." In *Science and Technology Education and the Quality of Life*, edited by Kurt Riquarts. Kiel, Germany: F.D.R.-I.P.N.

UNESCO. 1978. Elements for a dossier: Educating for a better environment, a series of papers in *Prospects* 8: 421–522.

UNESCO. 1979. *New UNESCO Source Book for Science Teaching*. Paris: UNESCO.

UNESCO. 1983. *Science for All*. Bangkok: UNESCO Regional Office for Education in Asia and the Pacific.

UNESCO. 1984. "Science Education in Thailand—A National Report." In *Science Education Bulletin No. 25*. Bangkok: UNESCO Regional Office for Education.

UNESCO. 1986. *Innovations in Science and Technology Education*, Vol. 1. Paris: UNESCO.

UNESCO. 1988. *Innovations in Science and Technology Education*, Vol. 2. Paris: UNESCO.

Waks, Leonard, and Madhu Prakash. 1985. STS education and its three stepsisters. *Bulletin of Science, Technology and Society* 5(2): 105–116.

Walford, Geoffrey. 1983. Science education and sexism in the Soviet Union. *School Science Review* 65(231): 213–224.

Wallace, June. 1986. *Social interaction within second year groups doing practical science*. Thesis, University of Oxford, England.

Ware, Sylvia, Henry Heikkinen, and William Lippincott. 1987. "Industry and Technology: The CHEMCOM Philosophy and Approach." In *Education, Industry and Technology*, edited by David Waddington, 145–150. London: Pergamon.

Waring, Mary. 1979. *Social Pressures on Curriculum Innovations: A Study of the Nuffield Foundation Science Teaching Project*. London: Methuen.

Welch, Wayne. 1979. "Twenty Years of Science Curriculum Development: A Look Back." In *Review of Research in Education*, edited by David Berliner, Vol. 7, 282–308. Washington, DC: American Education Research Association.

West, Leo, and Leon Pines. 1985. *Cognitive Structure and Conceptual Change*. Orlando, FL: Academic Press.

White, Richard. 1992. "Improving the Teaching and Learning of Science." In *Science and Technology Education in Australia*, edited by Peter Fensham. Hawthorn, Victoria, Australia: Australian Council for Educational Research.

White, Richard, and Richard Tisher. 1986. "Research on Natural Sciences." In *Handbook of Research on Teaching*, edited by Merle Wittrock, 874–905. New York: Macmillan.

Whyte, Judith. 1984. Observing sex stereotypes and interactions in the school lab and workshop. *Education Review* 36(1): 75–86.

Wilson, Brian. 1981. *Cultural Contexts of Science and Mathematics Education*. Leeds, England: Centre for Studies in Science Education, University of Leeds.

Wilson, Cathy. 1987. *Assessing Progress*. Better Science, Curriculum Guide 11. London: Heinemann/Association for Science Education.

Wilson, Susanne, and Lee Shulman. 1987. "150 Different Ways of Knowing: Representations of Knowledge in Teaching." In *Exploring Teacher Thinking*, edited by James Calderhead. Sussex, England: Castle Educational.

Wittrock, Merle. 1974. Learning as a generative process. *Educational Psychologist* 11(2): 87–95.

Womer, Frank. 1981. "State-Level Testing: Where We Have Been May Not Tell Us Where We Are Going." In *New Directions for Teaching and Measurement No. 10: Testing in the States: Beyond Accountability*, edited by Dale Carlson, 1–12. San Francisco, CA: Jossey-Bass.

Wongthonglour, Sobhi. 1979. "Diffusion of IPST Physical Science Curricula: An Evaluation of Its Inservice Education Component." Ph.D thesis, Monash University, Clayton, Victoria, Australia.

Working Group. 1988. *Interim Report on Design and Technology for the National Curriculum*. London: Department of Education and Science.

Yager, Robert. 1981. "The Laboratory in Science Teaching—Main Course or Dessert?" In *Becoming a Secondary School Science Teacher*, edited by Leslie Trowbridge et al. Columbus, OH: Merrill.

Young, Michael. 1971. "An Approach to the Study of Curricula as

Socially Organized Knowledge." In *Knowledge and Control*, edited by Michael Young, 19–46. London: Collier/Macmillan.

Ziefuss, Horst. 1980. *Technical Education as a Part of General Education in the Federal Republic of Germany*. I.P.N. Report in Brief no. 23. Kiel, West Germany: I.P.N.

Ziefuss, Horst. 1987. *Vom Handwerk zur industreefacharbeit*. Kiel, West Germany: KN-Druck GmbH.

Ziman, John. 1980. *Teaching and Learning about Science and Society*. Cambridge, England: Cambridge University Press.

Zoller, Uri. 1985. "Interdisciplinary Decision-Making in the Science Curricula in the Modern Social Context." In *World Trends in Science and Technology Conference*, edited by Geoffrey Harrison, 76–88. Report on second international symposium, Nottingham, England: Trent Polytechnic.

29

SOCIAL STUDIES

Gerald Marker and
Howard Mehlinger
INDIANA UNIVERSITY

Imagine the following situation. The setting is a conference room in the Department of Education in one of the 50 states. Ten people are present: the Commissioner of Education, the state social studies consultant, a professor of social studies education, a historian, a political scientist, a geographer, a high school social studies department chairperson, an elementary school teacher, a businessperson, and a legislator. They have been called to the meeting by the Commissioner of Education, who wishes them to become the nucleus of a state-wide task force to prepare recommendations on the future of the social studies curriculum. Here is a portion of their discussion:

Commissioner: I want to thank you for agreeing to participate on this task force. I believe there is no more important challenge before us than to improve the social studies curriculum in our schools. While we do not have data on the academic performance of our students in social studies, I believe that their performance would be similar to students who have been studied nationally. And, if that is true, we should be alarmed. Students are ignorant of history, geography, American government, and the free enterprise system. It is hard to imagine how democracy can survive in the presence of such ignorance.

Historian: I couldn't agree more. I don't know what students study in high school, but at my university we assume that they know very little history when they arrive as freshmen.

Businessperson: I'm less concerned about their knowledge of history and geography than I am about their attitudes and skills. I want to employ high school graduates who can think, speak clearly, write cogently, meet the public, have good work habits, and possess sound character. The social studies should prepare students to assume adult responsibilities—those of parent, law-abiding citizen, and worker.

Geographer: I agree that schools should help develop these skills and values; but I don't agree that these are the responsibility of social studies. They can learn to be parents by growing up in good homes, but they will only learn geography in school. How can one be a good citizen without a firm understanding of geography? I don't agree that geography is important for only those continuing their education in college. Geographic knowledge is required of everyone.

Social Studies Consultant: My job will be to provide you with any information you require. We have already gathered courses of study from all of the other states. We have also assembled recommendations from various national commissions, indicating what they believe the social studies should be. We have assembled a bibliography of research in the area of social studies. We want to base our recommendations on research findings. We can provide data on nearly any topic that concerns you.

Elementary Teacher: I hope there is some research that will tell us what children are ready to learn in the primary grades. In the past, our elementary school curriculum has been based upon the "expanding environment" approach. Now, some people are recommending we teach history, fables, and myths in the primary grades. I don't know if it can be done. See if you can find research to answer this question.

Political Scientist: There is another kind of research that interests me. Each of the academic disciplines produces research that advances knowledge in their domains. Yet, I have the impression that the transfer of this knowledge to school subjects is a very slow process. If we accomplished nothing else by this task force, it would be a great achievement simply to have teachers instruct their students in up-to-date academic information based upon careful research. How such information is to be taught is a question I will cheerfully leave to others, but I'm certain it can be done. The important issue, however, is to make certain that what is taught has the respect of scholars.

High School Chairperson: Let's remember that whatever we decide should be taught must be relevant to schools as they are now and it must be able to be implemented. If we create a curriculum that differs greatly from other states, we will not find textbooks for our students. While we have many good teachers, most have not enrolled in graduate courses for many years. We cannot expect them to teach topics they don't understand, with textbooks that lack new information and approaches. We will have very little influence if teachers are unable to implement our recommendations.

Professor of Social Studies Education: I'm becoming very uncomfortable. The Commissioner is giving us the best opportunity we have ever had to design an ideal social studies curriculum—*social studies*, not history, geography, political science, economics, or whatever. The purpose of social studies is to provide children and youth with the knowledge, values, skills, and experiences they require to become active participants in our society. The K–12 curriculum we design should be directed toward that purpose only. Certainly, students will have to possess knowledge from all of the social science disciplines, but social studies is not limited to these academic fields as defined by their advocates. Social studies is an interdisciplinary field of study; it is an academic field in its own right. I also do not think we should be encouraging a blind socialization into what our society was and has become. We should prepare youth who are thoughtful critics of current traditions, practices, and institutions. Nor am I willing to be bound by the content of existing textbooks. I'm not sanguine about our ability to change textbooks, but we can discourage teachers from relying on them exclusively.

Legislator: Before students can become thoughtful critics they must understand the institutions and practices they are criticizing. I see an appalling amount of ignorance coupled with strong opinions about our political and economic system. If war came and we had to depend upon the average citizen to put our society back together, I doubt that we would recognize the results. I also suspect that many of the academic disciplines are merely protecting their own jobs and academic "turf." Frankly, I find that most of the advice I receive from academic scholars to be of marginal utility—all too theoretical—for the daily operation of government. Let's make certain that students learn how the American political and economic system operates; if we accomplish this, I will be completely satisfied.

Commissioner: It appears that we have already begun, and I am convinced I chose the right group to lead this effort. You do not agree, but you are bright, articulate people, and I know you will find common ground; our schools will be better because of your work.

Before I leave, I want you to know that the Governor and I would also appreciate your giving thought to how your recommendations might take into consideration such other state priorities as reducing the school dropout rate, attracting new industry to the state, reducing the number of people on welfare, discouraging teenage pregnancy, and eliminating drug and alcohol abuse by school-age youth. I think social studies can contribute to the amelioration of each of these problems. Good luck!

Research matters! What we eat, how we exercise, what we buy, and where we invest our money is based on the research of others. Policymakers use research to appraise policy options; they seek evidence of how similar policies have worked in the past, how likely new policy options will be accepted by the public and judged credible by experts, and what the new policies will cost to implement. The hypothetical curriculum "task force" described above also needs research findings. They need to know what people believe to be the purpose of social studies instruction and, therefore, what should be taught in schools; they must also learn what is actually taught, to whom, by whom, in what ways; who decides what is taught in social studies and what the obstacles to change may be; and what children learn now, what they are capable of learning, and what they are likely to learn about social studies without taking courses in the subject. Does social studies curriculum research provide answers to these questions? We shall see in the pages that follow.

PURPOSE OF SOCIAL STUDIES

In general, the reason why a particular subject is included in the curriculum seems self-evident. While not unique to social studies, its advocates seem driven to explain and to justify the place of social studies in schools. With the exception of articles on teaching methods (articles that lie outside the scope of this chapter and handbook), more is written about the "nature" of the social studies, its purpose, what it is, is not, and must become than about any other social studies topic.

With regard to the purpose of social studies, the term "research" must be used broadly. The vast majority of published articles and books employ philosophical analyses and model building. Typically, the authors set forth some assumptions about society, clarify their own values, and then present arguments for a particular approach to social studies that seems consistent with their values and social analysis. Some researchers have conducted historical research on the origins of the social studies and its purpose over time (Dougan 1988). Some have reported the contributions of individual social studies leaders to social studies philosophy (Davis 1989; Keels 1989; Laughlin 1989; Longstreet 1989; Metcalf 1989; Nelson 1989). Still others have compared American social studies to social studies approaches in other countries (Shafer 1981). But in the main, the "research" that authors use in publications on the purpose of social studies is reasoned argument, or what Stanley (1985) has referred to as "normative debates."

It is difficult to explain why so much attention is devoted to the nature and purpose of social studies in the curriculum. There is little evidence that classroom teachers use such statements; for them a curricular rationale seems to be something you employ after you have decided what you want to teach—if you articulate one at all. But for college professors the justification for social studies is of highest priority. They believe that one cannot possibly know what to teach before deciding why to teach it. Until the rationale is clear, it is pointless to proceed. Because philosophical arguments stimulate philosophical debates, each statement stipulating what social studies is, or should be, leads to further rounds of discussion about purpose. The effect of these debates is to postpone decisions about what the actual content of the curriculum should be and, as Leming (1989) suggests, perhaps to reinforce the development of two cultures so foreign to one another that they seldom communicate.

At the highest level of abstraction, there is general agreement about the purpose of social studies. It is to prepare youth so that they possess the knowledge, values, and skills needed for active participation in society. Few social studies leaders disagree with this proposal. Nearly all of the stated rationales begin with an analysis of society; without exception the researchers value democracy and republican forms of government over other forms; therefore, nearly all agree that citizenship education is the ultimate justification for the social studies (Hahn 1985b; Leming 1986; Stanley 1985). The few who disagree do so because they believe that such a purpose overlaps with the primary purpose of schools generally and, therefore, obfuscates the contribution of social studies; or they believe that the definition of a good citizen is so vague and the knowledge one requires to perform as citizen so freely interpreted that nearly any point of view can be folded into that noble purpose (Longstreet 1985; Lengel and Superka 1982); or they question whether more active participation by all citizens is even healthy for the society and thus a desirable goal (Leming 1986). Despite these few disclaimers, citizenship education is the primary justification for the social studies.

However, the apparent consensus on behalf of citizenship education is almost meaningless. Behind that totem to which nearly all social studies researchers pay homage lies continuous and rancorous debate about the purposes of social studies. Some believe that social studies should focus primarily on history and geography; others have argued that social studies should examine "closed areas," topics that are more or less taboo in polite society (Hunt and Metcalf 1955), decision making (Engle 1963), public policy (Oliver and Shaver 1966), environmental competence (Newmann 1975), moral development (Kohlberg 1973, 1975), and adult social roles (Superka and Hawke 1982). While a few think that the purpose of social studies is to make students astute critics of American society (Engle and Ochoa 1988), others believe, like the "businessperson" described earlier, that the purpose of social studies is mainly socialization into the values, habits, and beliefs that permit youth to find a niche in adult society.

Several attempts have been made to categorize these wide-ranging and apparently conflicting purposes. One study grouped these various positions into three main themes: citizenship transmission, social science, and reflective inquiry (Barr, Barth, and Shermis 1977). Another pair of researchers used these categories: conservative cultural continuity, the process of thinking reflectively, and the intellectual aspects of history and the social sciences (Morrissett and Haas 1982). While different titles are used, the two schemes are substantially the same. Both sets of researchers believe that social studies tends to be used for one of three purposes: socialization into society's norms; transmission of facts, concepts, and generalizations from the academic disciplines; and promotion of critical thinking. Research bias is hard to control in such studies. Barr, Barth, and Shermis clearly come down on the side of "reflective inquiry," while Morrissett and Haas favor teaching the "intellectual aspects of history and the social sciences." The researchers agree that "citizenship transmission" or "conservative cultural continuity" is the approach practiced most in the schools. This latter perspective tends to be confirmed by others who have examined school practices in the social studies (Shaver, Davis, and Helburn 1979; Stake and Easley 1978).

Despite years of work and hundreds of articles and books on the topic, social studies researchers seem no closer to finding a solution to the problem of divided purpose in social studies than they were decades ago. Why this is true seems fairly obvious. First, proclaiming citizenship education as the overarching purpose for the social studies contributes little or nothing to the debate. Few resist it, but the citizenship education label does nothing to discriminate among possible content proposals. Nearly every proposed topic can be justified by that label; indeed people who hold diametrically opposed views march together under the citizenship flag (Nelson 1980). Second, one goal of schooling itself is citizenship education; therefore, there is no simple way to distinguish easily the contributions social studies is to make to the education of youth that is separate from the broad socialization role of schools generally. This means there is no way to hold social studies accountable for success or failure in the citizenship education mission. Third, there is no organized, agreed-upon body of knowledge for citizenship education; until there is a "discipline" of citizenship, the term is devoid of meaning for curricular purposes (Longstreet 1985).

There is little hope that the various positions that characterize the social studies will be resolved. They are mainly assertions of personal bias and preference, and are not easily compromised. One person believes that children must know history to become a good citizen; another asserts that students must study current problems facing the society. It is unlikely that research will resolve these differences.

Some have called for a "national commission on the social studies" to decide the purpose of social studies and to recommend curriculum content for each grade level (Gross and Dynneson 1983; Mehlinger 1981). There is such a national commission; its first report appeared in November 1989 (Curriculum Task Force 1989). On the basis of preliminary reactions, it appears likely that its recommendations will not end the debate but merely add further fuel to the fire. In summary, the agreed-upon purpose of social studies is stated at such an abstract level as to make it virtually useless for curricular purposes. At a point where choices among goals and content are required, the leaders engage in endless debate about purpose. This has made the topic of purpose an interesting arena for scholarly writing, but researchers have largely added to the confusion and debate rather than brought resolution.

WHAT IS THE SOCIAL STUDIES CURRICULUM?

The answer to the question, "What is the social studies curriculum" depends upon one's perspective. A state social studies consultant might point to the approved state curriculum guide with its carefully drafted "scope and sequence" and individual grade-level or course-specific handbooks. A school superintendent or local school board member might refer to a locally approved sequence of courses. A school principal may present the textbooks that have been adopted for each social studies course. A teacher may offer his course syllabus, unit outlines, and daily lesson plans as evidence for what actually occurs in class. And the students enrolled in the course, having little or no knowledge of what others use as evidence, may mention things they or the teachers did in class that were memorable. What the social studies curriculum is depends upon perspective.

Multiple Perspectives

There should be some relationship among these various perspectives. It seems logical that what occurs in class should be related to the adopted textbook for the course, the school district's course of study, and the state's approved syllabus. There should be such a relationship, but several studies have made clear that the relationship is a tenuous one. Deciding what the social studies curriculum is, therefore, requires answering the question at multiple levels.

State Frameworks. Every state publishes an approved curriculum framework for social studies. These are frequently the subject of considerable discussion and debate, sparking controversy within the profession and sometimes beyond to the lay community. Occasionally, a state will break new ground and change its pattern of course offerings from previous experience and from other states. But even in such instances the pattern of course offerings are much more the same than they are different from state to state and from past to present (Gagnon 1988).

For most of this century the most frequent pattern of topics or courses has been:

K Self, school, community, home
1 Families
2 Neighborhoods
3 Communities
4 State history, geographic regions
5 United States history
6 World cultures, Western hemisphere
7 World geography or world history
8 American history
9 Civics or world cultures
10 World history
11 American history
12 American government

Typical deviations from this pattern are the inclusion of state histories that are unique to each state, the placement of American history, and emphasis upon world culture as opposed to world history or world geography. The use of electives permits each state to respond to interest groups that wish treatment on its topic to be included in the curriculum without forcing all students to study it. The one course that is universally offered and required is United States history (Lengel and Superka 1982).

The fact that courses can be moved from one grade level to another or be listed as electives rather than requirements underlines another feature of the social studies curriculum. There is no agreement within the profession regarding knowledge that is basic or fundamental to other knowledge (Gross and Dynneson 1983). Provided the classroom presentation is pitched to a cognitive level appropriate to the age of the student, practically any content can be justified and taught legitimately at any grade level. For a time, during the period of the "new social studies," this idea was made a virtue.

If there is no necessary pattern for sequencing course content, how has the current pattern become so institutionalized? As Ehman and Hahn (1981) observed, it is not because the pattern is well-grounded in research documenting its effectiveness. For the most part the current pattern of topics and courses has been influenced by the state of the academic disciplines, school attendance patterns, demographic trends, and the impact of the "progressive education movement" during the first quarter of this century. The term "social studies" itself was officially adopted as a curriculum area in 1916 by the Committee on the Social Studies of the Commission on the Reorganization of Secondary Education of the National Education Association (1916). It is significant that the Commission was sponsored by the National Education Association, an organization of teachers, school administrators, and teacher educators. The Commission's recommendations overturned a curriculum dominated by history and geography, one favored by academic scholars, especially history professors. Those who were dealing directly with the schools were sensitive to the onrush of immigrant children into the schools and the need to socialize them into American customs, traditions, and beliefs. Preparation for life and education for citizenship seemed more important then than preparation for college studies. New academic disciplines such as sociology and political science were also beginning to become important. Educators found their approaches compatible with school goals, and sociologists and political scientists had little interest in having history regain lost turf in the school curriculum.

The progressive education movement also had an impact upon the social studies curriculum, especially in the elementary grades. According to progressive educators, "education was not merely preparation for life; it *was* life" (Jarolimek 1981). Social studies teachers were encouraged to focus instruction on resolving social problems. Knowledge was to be used for the practical benefit of the community; therefore, having students do something through organized activity became an instructional goal.

Social studies began to blur the boundaries between academic disciplines, although this was more obvious in the elementary grades than in the secondary grades. Secondary school teachers pursued college majors in history or one of the social science disciplines while elementary school teachers did not, leaving the latter more willing to experiment with content reorganization. Over time, it became legitimate to use history or geography content for worthy social purposes: for example, to promote world peace, reduce racial intolerance, promote environmentalism, serve the poor. Historians were often horrified by how history content was employed; social studies educators responded by asserting that it was not the job of the schools to teach "history for history's sake." Instead, history should be included only to the extent that it served the goals of citizenship education.

The pattern of course offerings also reflects a time when few children completed high school. Thus, it seemed appropriate to segment social studies so as to provide a basic education for the many who would not continue schooling beyond grade 5, a more complete education for those who would remain through grade 8, and a college preparatory curriculum for the few who would complete high school. This is mainly why U.S. history is repeated in grades 5, 8, and 11. Although the proportions who finish high school have changed dramatically since 1916, the pattern of courses, invented to respond to the concerns of a different age, has remained frozen in time.

There is an ascendence of research on what the existence of a course in the state framework actually means in terms of the proportions and capability of students who actually enroll in it. When a state recommends world history as a grade 10 course but does not require it, the course may or may not be "elected" by a majority of students. The options available to students within a particular school also make a difference. For example, world history may be an elective course that competes with foreign language study for student enrollments. In such cases, those students planning to attend college may elect language study, leaving world history for those who do not have post-secondary school education aspirations. Or an elective course in world history may compete for enrollments with a vocational educational course, ensuring the more academically able students will take world history.

There is some research on whether electives are increasing or decreasing across states. The findings show that, almost without exception, the 1970s was a period in which course requirements were relaxed, and the number and range of elective courses grew. The 1980s has reversed that trend. One state after another has increased the requirements for social studies, and elective courses have waned (Hahn 1985b).

However, knowing what a particular state requires as a pattern of course offerings is only a partial indicator of the actual social studies content students receive. A more thorough study requires careful research in individual schools and classrooms.

***Social Studies in Individual Classrooms*.** The first observation to be made is that very few large-scale studies of social studies classrooms have been undertaken. It is not that such studies are judged to be unimportant; they are not conducted mainly because they are unmanageable and unfundable. By far the largest proportion of classroom studies are conducted on very few classrooms—a dozen or less—and involve an investigation of a limited number of variables. A common study is to investigate the impact of new content into the curriculum—political science concepts, ideas from economics, and so on. Large-scale studies such as those directed by John Goodlad (1984) or Ernest Boyer (1983) are exceptional. While some knowledge of the curriculum is gained from their reports, the tendency in these studies is to focus on *how* teachers present material (methods of teaching) rather than *what* they teach (social studies curriculum). The National Science Foundation supported a large-scale study of social studies classrooms in the late 1970s (Shaver, Davis, and Helburn 1979; Project SPAN Staff and Consultants 1982). This study found that despite the enormous investments by the federal government in promoting new curriculum materials and new approaches to instruction, little had changed.

These studies, however limited they may be in scope, document important facts. There is an enormous difference between the publicly declared formal curriculum and the actual curriculum confronted by the students. Different teachers—teaching the same subject in adjacent rooms to similar students and ostensibly using identical textbooks—teach different courses. Cornbleth (1985) argues that there are actually two curricula at work: the "technical curriculum" consisting of the published course of study, the textbook, teacher aids, and tests, and the "social process" curriculum which "is not a tangible product but the actual day-to-day classroom interactions of teachers, students, and ideas." This "social process curriculum" is different from the teaching method employed by the teacher, although they clearly interact. It is the way that the teacher confirms or creates doubt about assertions of knowledge, whether some opinions are treated as facts while other opinions are discounted as unworthy of consideration. One teacher may proclaim that one of democracy's virtues is a tolerance for many points of view, but in the classroom choke off views inconsistent with his or her own. Another teacher may offer no assertions about the value of democracy, while exhibiting its virtues in his or her own behavior. Both are engaged in subtle forms of instruction about democracy; the latter may prove the more successful although one could not assume so from an examination of lesson plans.

The inability of investigators to study what is actually taught in classrooms by way of large-scale, in-depth studies over time has led them to focus on the next best indicator: the textbooks used by teachers (Larkins, Hawkins, and Gilmore 1987; Thomas and Parsons 1984). While teachers are urged by teacher educators and supervisors to refrain from relying too heavily on textbooks (Alder and Downey 1985), one investigation after another has shown that textbooks do comprise the majority of the instructional material used in class and that teachers rest much of their instruction on textbooks, drawing upon them for recitation, or clarifying the information provided by textbooks (Hertzberg 1985; Shaver, Davis, and Helburn 1979).

Textbooks occupy a central place in American schools. In the absence of a national curriculum they are the nearest equivalent. Textbook publishers seek to sell their books nationally; thus they attempt to provide a consensus across the individual requirements of each state. They aspire to provide teachers with all that they need to teach their courses: reading materials for students, lecture and recitation notes for teachers, tests, supplementary teaching aids, workbooks, computer software, and so on. In the elementary grades, they go even further by providing an entire curricular approach across all grade levels from K to 8. They provide the scope and sequence, indicate the knowledge, skills, and values to be taught at each grade level, and correlate the social studies content with instruction in English, science, and other disciplines. They even may provide materials to help explain the program to parents and school administrators. Because textbook publishers try to provide everything a teacher needs to teach his course, it is tempting for researchers to conclude that the publisher's curricular package *is* the program students receive.

One study (Larkins, Hawkins, and Gilmore 1987) uncovered 154 articles that dealt with one or more aspects of textbooks: 18 dealt with readability of texts, 12 with procedures for evaluating them, 37 with topics other than their content, 32 focused on such biases as gender and race, 17 looked at the treatment awarded other countries, and 22 discussed the way values were handled in the books. Thomas and Parsons (1984) reviewed research reported in *Social Education*, *Theory and Research in Social Education*, and *Dissertation Abstracts International* for the period 1977–1984—a total of 159 studies—and also found that textbooks were the most common objects of study. Clearly, a very large proportion of social studies research on curriculum is directed toward the textbooks teachers use in school.

What do these studies reveal? First, they focus on social concerns of the times. For example, during the last two decades, minorities and sex roles have received increased attention (Leming 1985; Patrick and Hawke 1982); other topics given attention were the Vietnam War (Fleming 1984), propaganda (Fleming 1985), terrorism (Fleming 1986), global interdependence (Michigan State Board of Education 1984), and heroes and heroines (Broadbelt and Wall 1985). Alternately, topics such as social class bias have been ignored. (Anyon 1979; Leming 1985; Wilcox 1982). Second, the textbooks usually fall short of the investigator's beliefs regarding what they should contain. There is no mystery in why this occurs. A typical study may explore the way women are presented in textbooks. Generally, the investigator begins with a bias—for example, that textbooks should provide an "appropriate" level of content relating to the role of women in American society. It is surely predictable that the textbook will fail to measure up to the standards held by the investigator and the groups he or she represents. (Incidentally, textbook publishers give considerable attention to such studies, especially if they are highly publicized. The result is that subsequent editions will likely give more attention to women and attempt to resolve the issues raised by the study.) Textbook studies almost always conclude that social studies textbooks are bland, lack controversy, cover too much material superficially, and are written too simplistically (Hertzberg 1985; Larkins, Hawkins, and Gilmore 1987). These conclusions can be explained as the result of prior studies where books were found wanting, and in response the editors deleted material that offended some group, added names and events to placate groups that were not mentioned in earlier editions, and reduced the complexity of the language of textbooks to be adopted by teachers who had children with learning deficiencies. It should be noted that while researchers are often critical of textbooks for reasons noted earlier, teachers seem generally satisfied (Hertzberg 1985). Perhaps, this is why the books continue to be produced and purchased despite sharp criticism from researchers.

In short, social studies investigators conduct research on textbooks to find out what is taught in classrooms, recognizing that the textbooks are only a portion of the curriculum. Investigators also study textbooks primarily to uncover their weaknesses, not to discover how they may be actually used.

The Goals of Social Studies

If there is consensus that the purpose of social studies is to prepare youth for citizenship, there is also general agreement that the elements of a sound citizenship education are *knowledge, skills, values, and participation* (National Council for the Social Studies 1979, 1981). If students are to perform their citizen roles adequately, they presumably need facts and data, concepts and generalizations, and explanatory theories. They also require skills for acquiring, judging, and processing information, as well as skill in employing it to advantage through writing and oral argumentation. Democracy also requires citizens who hold democratic values—for example, a commitment to free and open debate, a willingness to accept majority decisions coupled with a respect for minority rights, and a devotion to democratic processes and the rule of law. And, finally, social studies must provide opportunities for participation so that youths can gain experience in the practice of democratic citizenship in order that they do it well. Bragaw and Hartoonian (1988) even call for a year of public service for all students.

Knowledge. As noted earlier there is little agreement regarding what knowledge is fundamental for citizenship education. Each of the relevant academic disciplines is quick to make a case for its knowledge domain; the most aggressive have been historians and geographers. Pressure for inclusion of economics in the curriculum has come mainly from the business community, who believe knowledge of the free enterprise system is fundamental to citizenship, rather than from university-based economists, although the latter have cooperated with the business community in encouraging greater study of economic principles. Lawyers and judges, concerned about the breakdown of law and order and a perceived growing disrespect for the American legal system, have promoted "law-related education." While other groups lobbying for peace education, environmental education, global education, and so on, promote their interests, none has either the resources or the political clout possessed by lawyers and businessmen (Alder and Downey 1985; Anyon 1979; Armento 1986a; Farmer 1988).

The lack of agreement about what knowledge is fundamental makes social studies, more than any other curricular area, susceptible to topical fads promoted by well-intentioned advocates. If there is a surge nation-wide in teenage violence and crime, for example, then social studies will be called upon to reverse the trend by teaching about the legal system. The belief among social studies educators that social studies should focus on problems confronting the society, and that the job of a citizen in a democratic society is to resolve problems through the political process, makes the social studies susceptible to the inclusion of any topic that can be termed "a problem."

There is no easy way to measure the impact that current topics and social problems have on the social studies curriculum. Relatively few of these gain sufficient support to acquire a course of their own; even in these rare cases, they are likely to become elective courses taken by few students. More commonly the strategy used by advocates is to "infuse" the existing curriculum by developing curricular components that can be inserted into existing courses of study. Thus, global educators look for ways to provide "a global perspective" within existing geography, world history, American government, economics, and American history courses by providing teachers with materials that complement existing textbooks. If a theme catches on, a textbook publisher may try to incorporate the theme into a basal textbook and feature the new emphasis in its promotion. Thus, a publisher may change the title of its textbook *U.S. History* to *U.S. History: A Global Perspective* in order to draw attention to its new emphasis. While the content may be fundamentally the same as other U.S. history textbooks, by adding statements and illustrations that connect developments in the United States with those of other countries, the book gains market advantage by appealing to teachers who want to incorporate global studies into their American history courses.

Perhaps most disturbing to social studies educators is that social studies is not given status equal to other subjects in the primary grades (Cawelti and Adkisson 1985; Gross 1977; Hahn 1985b). While debate rages among social studies leaders over whether a focus on "expanding environments" is the best approach in the primary grades (Egan 1983; LeRiche 1987) or whether children ought to be confronted with fairy tales, myths, and history in these grades (Ravitch 1987), it is apparent that many elementary school teachers believe that social studies can be ignored entirely. While textbooks for grades K–3 are produced and sold, apparently they are sometimes not adopted and when purchased are little used. Several explanations, based upon research, have surfaced. First, many primary school teachers believe their first priority is to teach reading and basic math skills (Atwood and Finkelstein 1987). Decades ago, the social studies books were one way that primary school teachers taught reading. The appearance of basal readers shoved social studies books aside as the main contributors to reading. Second, there seems to be little value placed on the content of social studies in the primary grades (Atwood 1986; Lengel and Superka 1982). Studies that have asked teachers, administrators, and scholars what topics they believe should be taught in social studies and the grades in which they should be taught reveal that the topics judged most important to teach are reserved for upper elementary grades, junior high school, and high school (Herman 1983). Third, some critics believe that the emphasis upon family, school, neighborhood, and local community in grades K–3 provides little knowledge that children do not already possess or will acquire easily and more rapidly later (Egan 1983; Larkins, Hawkins, and Gilmore 1987). And, finally, primary school teachers report feeling less competent in teaching social studies than they do in other subjects, except perhaps science (Eslinger and Superka 1982). More of their preparation has been focused on teaching reading and mathematics. Lacking knowledge in depth of history and the social sciences, they deal with the social studies curriculum in a superficial manner. Therefore, they may neglect the textbooks altogether. There is another aspect of the social studies in primary grades, largely unconnected with "expanding environments" or the textbooks, that appears to remain firmly in place; that is the observance of seasons, holidays, and the birthdays of American heroes (Lengel and Superka 1982). These provide occasions for decorating the classroom and for promoting children's artistic and literary proclivities. Thus, multiple purposes are being served.

Something resembling formal academic study begins with grade 4—usually devoted to either the history of the state or geography (Lengel and Superka 1982). It is also a time when in some schools there may be some subject matter specialization among teachers. Grade 5 provides the first introduction to U.S. history. Because U.S. history will be taken again in grades 8 and 11, fifth-grade textbooks tend to emphasize the colonial and national period, junior high texts the period from 1776–1900, and senior high school books give greatest attention to the period after 1860 (Alder and Downey 1985). Grades 6 and 7 have been somewhat less predictable, although world cultures, world geography, and world history in some form or another have tended to dominate this level. In some states there has been a tendency to focus on Latin America in one grade and to emphasize Asia or the Middle East at another grade level. In general, a chronologically organized world history has been more commonly left for senior high study. The fact that these courses are taught in junior high or middle school settings, where there can be a mix of subject matter specialization and core curriculum approaches, has lent a sense of uncertainty regarding what actually occurs in these classrooms.

The senior high school grades feature subject matter courses more like survey courses in their parent disciplines offered by colleges and universities. U.S. history is required for graduation in nearly all high schools. A semester or a two-semester requirement in American government is common; world history, taken by fewer and fewer students in the 1970s, is experiencing a resurgence and is increasingly required, although it is still taken by less than one half of all high school students.

Despite a strong ideology opposed to tracking by social studies leaders, the realities are that separate social studies courses are designed to appeal to students with varying interests and abilities. In many high schools, academically motivated students can both meet high school graduation requirements and earn college credits by taking "advanced placement" courses in U.S. history and European history. Meanwhile, courses in African-American history or "Women in American History" may be offered both to meet the American history graduation requirements as well as possibly appeal to students who are not otherwise interested in history. All three might be labeled American history; all can be offered to high school juniors; but they are likely to be three fundamentally different courses.

Skills. Skill development is an important goal of the social studies curriculum. State curriculum guides, teacher handbooks that accompany textbooks, and teacher-developed units indicate skills students will acquire from social studies courses. The range of skills extend from those that may be covered in several subjects—for example, study skills, critical thinking skills—to skills that may be unique to social studies—for example, geographic skills or interpreting economic data from tables and graphs. Very little research has been conducted on skill acquisition in the social studies. The considerable rhetoric about the importance of skills is not coupled with research on whether or how skills are learned. Perhaps the skills most commonly evaluated are map and globe skills. Whether recent emphasis on proficiency tests at various grade levels will affect the current situation is unclear.

Decision making is a widely proclaimed "skill" goal in the social studies. Given the purpose of social studies to prepare citizens, helping youth to acquire skills in reaching well-grounded decisions would appear to be an important responsibility for the social studies. However, the little research that has been conducted on decision making is not very encouraging. Shaver and Knight (1986) reviewed studies of decision making and concluded that models of decision making touted in the social studies were overly simplistic and did not conform to the real experiences of people confronting complex decisions. More complex models of decision making that take contextual factors into account seem impractical and require levels of knowledge beyond that possessed by most teenagers. The goal of helping students to acquire a capacity to make well-grounded decisions has not lost its appeal, but the results achieved to date on the basis of existing research are discouraging.

Values. Social studies educators have traditionally been of two minds with regard to values. On the one hand social studies is expected to contribute to the values vital for democratic citizenship—for example, respect for law, deciding issues by will of the majority, protecting the rights of minorities, and defense of expression of opinion. On the other hand, social studies educators have often encouraged teachers to promote critical inquiry in which few, if any, values were judged to be sacred and unassailable (Oliver and Shaver 1966). Whether social studies teachers are to socialize students into particular core values, whether they are to help students "clarify" their values, whether they are to nurture children's "moral development" (Kohlberg 1973, 1975; Lockwood 1988), or whether they are to promote critical inquiry of all values has been a divisive issue in the social studies.

Considerable research has focused on when children acquire their values and beliefs, what values and beliefs are promoted by curriculum materials and teachers, and what the consequences have been. Leming's (1985) conclusion following a review of the literature on values education was that teaching values did not figure prominently "in the planning and practice of the vast majority of social studies teachers" (185). Imparting knowledge is more important to teachers than promoting values. Furthermore, Leming concluded after reviewing a couple hundred pieces of research that "the standard social studies curriculum has no discernible impact on the socio-moral development of youth" (176).

Participation. If skill development and values receive mainly token attention from social studies educators, participation suffers even more. In theory, the knowledge, skills, and values imparted in a sound social studies program should be reinforced through experience in participating in concrete activities. In general, social studies educators favor activities that impact on national issues and concerns, whereas practice in helping resolve community and school concerns are more easily at hand (Newmann 1977, 1981; Newmann, Bertocci, and Landsness 1977). Some experimental efforts to focus social studies instruction on school and community participation have proved interesting, but have not been adopted by others, mainly because of the time and energy demands they place on teachers and the school system as a whole. Furthermore, Leming (1986) has argued that if educators were successful in increasing participation, it is likely that they would find the ensuing social results distasteful.

Trends in Social Studies Curriculum

The social studies curriculum changes over time, but these changes have not been sufficient to alter the overall purpose of social studies (i.e., citizenship education) or to change the typical pattern of courses. But changes in society and intellectual developments require that the purpose of social studies undergo reinterpretation and the content within course labels be altered; new skills are emphasized while older skills recede; the role of values is reinterpreted; and the importance and types of participation are reexamined. Thus a field that seems superficially stable over most of this century is constantly dealing with change below the surface as new ideas and approaches compete with the reigning ones.

Since 1950, at least three major movements have influenced the social studies. They are (1) the new social studies, (2) the affective revolution, and (3) back to basics.

New Social Studies. The "new social studies" was mainly a product of the same forces that led to "new math," "new physics," and so on. The perceived threat from the Soviet Union, highlighted by the launching of Sputnik in 1957, led American politicians and academic leaders to seek improvements in all aspects of the elementary and secondary school curriculum. While mathematics, science, and foreign languages were given attention first, social studies advocates claimed that they too were part of "national defense" and deserved study.

The primary focus was the effort to make courses more rigorous and academically respectable. "Advanced placement" courses that made it possible for students to enroll in college-like courses in American history and European history while in high school spread across the nation; they appeared as elective courses in high schools that served high proportions of students with college-attendance aspirations. Of greater significance, however, was the effort to redesign existing social studies courses or to create new courses that would serve most, if not all, students. Unlike advanced placement courses, these courses were not intended to be reflections of currently offered college survey courses; rather they were to capture the main ideas and current approaches to knowledge represented by academic research. In the social studies this meant cutting edge research by historians, geographers, sociologists, anthropologists, political scientists, psychologists, philosophers, and economists. The National Science Foundation provided leadership through funds for special curriculum development projects, mostly sponsored by scholarly associations. Soon the U.S. Office of Education and later the National Endowment for the Humanities provided grants to colleges and universities to support curriculum research and the development of experimental curriculum materials.

The major intellectual influence was Jerome Bruner, a Harvard University psychologist, who argued that any idea could be presented authentically to children and youth regardless of their level of cognitive development and who believed that to fully understand a field it is necessary to get at its underlying structure. His views encouraged curriculum developers to conclude that they could teach quite sophisticated academic content to young children provided they could identify the "structure" of each academic discipline. The structure was defined as a field's central concepts and generalizations as well as the mode of inquiry used by scholars in that field. To prove his point, Jerome Bruner became the principal designer of a new social studies course intended for fifth-grade students, called "Man: A Course of Study" (MACOS) that incorporated elements from many academic disciplines but mainly embodied ideas from anthropology. This course was intended to compete against the well-entrenched fifth-grade course in American history.

Seeking the "structure" of each academic discipline became a preoccupation among curriculum theorists and developers throughout most of the 1960s. Lawrence Senesh (1964), an economist with an interest in elementary schools, began work on an elementary school sequence in which he attempted to identify the structures of each academic discipline in order to provide all of the knowledge children would require. Edwin Fenton (1967) became the leading exponent of Bruner's ideas for the secondary grades. Special projects in geography, anthropology, sociology, political science, economics, and history appeared—each challenging the existing curriculum by inserting new content, new approaches to content, and new teaching techniques for existing courses and, in some cases, calling for new courses to replace what then existed.

If the academic disciplines appeared to be in charge, they did not have a monopoly on the reform agenda. While in the minority, social studies specialists who favored a problem-centered social studies had their champions as well—most notably Donald Oliver, James Shaver, and Fred Newmann, who developed materials for a Harvard-based program on public issues (Newmann 1970; Oliver and Shaver 1966). Unlike most of the other new social studies projects that sought mainly to represent the academic disciplines, the Harvard materials tried to introduce a "jurisprudential approach," a way of thinking about past and current problems that could be incorporated within existing social studies courses.

Millions of dollars and centuries of person-years were invested in the new social studies. "If measured by sheer output of new materials, the period of 1964 to 1972 is unequaled in the history of social studies education in this country" (Haas 1986, 62). Yet, little remains to show for the effort (Agostine and Barone 1985). Most of the projects failed to find commercial publishers; those materials that were published were promoted to an alternative market, rather than for the mainline market the publishers were accustomed to serving. While a few projects enjoyed early success through school adoptions, few went through second editions and enjoyed long-term commercial success (Hahn 1985b). Some of the ideas promoted by the projects—use of original documents, inquiry lessons drawing upon statistical data, case studies, and employment of overhead transparencies—were later incorporated within mainline narrative textbooks.

The new social studies failed because it challenged the existing curriculum, because it demanded too much of teachers and students, because the curricular products were expensive, and because it roused the ire of certain conservative groups. MACOS, the leading example of the new social studies, also contributed to the movement's demise. It had all of the faults cited above. It tried to dislodge American history with anthropology; it would not let schools adopt the program unless teachers were specially trained; its multimedia materials were many times more expensive than a typical fifth-grade textbook, and it dared to ask such questions as what constitutes a human being. Concerned parents attacked the materials for being antireligious and anti-American. Their opposition reached even the floor of Congress, where speeches denouncing MACOS ultimately contributed to cutting funds for the National Science Foundation and eliminating its support for curriculum development in the social studies. Changing public priorities also undermined this enormous public investment to make social studies a more rigorous academic enterprise.

Affective Revolution. If the new social studies were prompted by a fear of the Soviet Union, the affective revolution was inspired by domestic turmoil. The assassinations of President John F. Kennedy, and later Robert Kennedy and Martin Luther King, Jr., stunned the nation. Peaceful, nonviolent civil rights marches, as well as violent riots in such cities as Los Angeles, Detroit, and Washington, D.C., brought racism to the surface and led to charges that the United States was a racist nation. The conflicts that accompanied the rock and drug cultures plus the deep divisions over the Vietnam War pitted old against young, conservative against liberal, black against white, rich against poor. For a time, it seemed that the United States would literally tear itself apart.

American society was changing in other ways. Women, entering the work force in ever larger numbers, were no longer satisfied with "women's work." They demanded to be treated equally with men. The American economy, jolted by the actions of an oil cartel, inflation, loss in the value of the dollar, growing Federal deficits, and reversals in foreign trade, was no longer dominant. Meanwhile, new immigrants moved to the United States, legally and illegally—changing the face and voice of American cities. The nation was changing, and the American people were profoundly aware of the changes.

The social studies curriculum responded. It no longer seemed very important to promote the "structure" of academic disciplines; overcoming racism, sexism, ethnocentrism, and national chauvinism were more critical than whipping communism. Evidence for this change can be found by examining articles published by *Social Education* from 1968 to 1972 (Haas 1977). Teachers grew less certain about which knowledge was most important and deserved priority. Courses were judged according to their *relevance*—defined by whether they captured student interest, responded to social changes, and helped students reexamine their belief structures. Topical, elective courses were created to meet the need. Herman in 1983 listed 23 courses/topics as current in the social studies curriculum. Traditional textbooks were scrutinized to see if they were guilty of promoting one or more of the "isms" noted above. Nowhere is the reverse in tendencies so visible as in the content of charges made against textbooks in the late 1950s and early 1960s for promoting communism and in the late 1970s for defending American society (Anyon 1979).

But the affective revolution was mainly aimed at changing attitudes. If the new social studies tried to develop the mind, the new, new social studies tried to cultivate the heart. Overcoming injustice and acting morally became important. In the 1960s values were treated as variables to be taken into account, but largely "controlled" in analyses of society. In the 1970s values were of paramount importance. The only issue was how to treat them—value analysis, value clarification, moral development? The debates raged over what values should be taught in school, at what age, and by what methods.

What was the impact of the "affective revolution" on the social studies curriculum? Confusion, doubt, and loss in public credibility. An inability to set priorities over what knowledge was most important led to the conclusion it did not matter much what was taught. Electives undermined required courses; when electives failed to attract students, total social studies course enrollments sagged. Nor did the emphasis in social studies on the *process* for acquiring and judging values, rather than reaching closure on what values were important for all children to acquire, earn respect from the public.

By 1981, one social studies observer wrote that the social studies might actually be *dead* as an important part of the curriculum (Mehlinger 1981). The field was in such disarray and its credibility so low that it might be hanging on merely as a result of such "life support" systems as state or local course requirements and institutional inertia. He was wrong; the social studies did not die, but that surely was a time when its influence was low.

Back to Basics. Although few social studies authorities would wish to admit it, social studies as a curriculum field may have been saved by Ronald Reagan. Not that President Reagan personally, nor the various people he appointed to high office, had much regard for the social studies. Quite the opposite. But the conservative revolution represented by President Reagan raised fundamental questions about the effectiveness of American schools. And the impression that American students lacked knowledge of their culture, that they didn't possess the most elementary forms of historical knowledge, and that they couldn't even locate major American cities on a map led to a public outcry that something must be done to strengthen the teaching of history and geography in the schools. The result has been a renewed emphasis upon the importance of social studies in the curriculum and a restoration of course requirements.

Despite the renewed importance given to the place of social studies in the curriculum, many social studies advocates are unhappy with the results. To many, the back-to-basics movement is aimed at turning social studies back to an earlier time and replacing the existing social studies curriculum with updated versions of content, approaches, and values more characteristic of the beginning of the 20th century. Indeed, one of the current opinion leaders has proposed discarding the dominant "expanding environment" scheme for elementary school social studies and returning to the recommendations of the 1909 Committee of Eight of the American Historical Association (Ravitch 1987). The recently approved California framework for the social studies, for which Ravitch served as consultant, adopted many of the ideas from the 1909 Committee of Eight report (Gagnon 1988). To the degree that California is a trend setter for other states, it is possible to imagine that many of the ideas that have characterized social studies during most of the 20th century will be replaced by ideas that preceded even the idea of social studies.

The movement can be called "back to basics," not only because it signals a return to earlier approaches, but because it also emphasizes knowledge of facts and commitment to fundamental values (Taylor and Birchell 1983). The proponents are annoyed by problem-centered interdisciplinary studies, oppose progressive education with its concern for "life adjustment," are appalled by the lack of student knowledge of specific facts about American culture and its antecedents in Western European history, and are angered by what they judge to be the neo-Marxist critiques of American society that find their way into social studies textbooks.

In one sense, the back-to-basics movement has elements of the new social studies in that it is primarily academic in its orientation. Unlike the new social studies movement, however, it favors history over the social sciences, is traditional in its style, and makes no pretense to introduce children to advanced methods in helping them to analyze their society. It appears to be more devoted to passing on knowledge and values that its advocates judge to be central to American culture. It is more concerned with cultivating mainstream American values than with assisting students to develop their own value systems, despite the paucity of evidence that mastery of social studies content contributes to moral development (Leming 1985).

Hidden Curriculum

There is another social studies curriculum that is much more difficult to identify. It is "hidden" in the sense that it is less overt and more difficult to discover. It lurks in teacher biases and their expectations for students. For example, all students may be required to take a course in American government, but the course and its impact may vary across social classes. Upper-middle-class students may be taught how the American system actually operates and what they must do if they are to exercise leadership, while lower-class children may take a course that emphasizes the virtues of the American political system and the importance of obeying laws. The first group has been educated to govern, the second to be governed (Leming 1985; Wilcox 1982).

Teachers may include books and other readings to supplement adopted textbooks. These materials may substantially alter the message of the course. Teachers may choose to ignore topics altogether because they find them distasteful or difficult to handle. Thus, one teacher may choose to pass over the Vietnam War or the Watergate affair because of anxiety regarding what students may conclude about American government, because of his own loyalty to a President or a political party, or because of the controversy such discussions might provoke in the community.

Ethnographic studies such as those reviewed by White (1985) are beginning to document the substance and impact of the hidden curriculum. Because it seldom appears in formal curriculum documents, the hidden curriculum may be even more resistant to change than the formal curriculum.

WHO CONTROLS THE SOCIAL STUDIES CURRICULUM?

Social studies is a field about which one might say: "The more things change, the more they stay the same." As was described earlier, the pattern of social studies course titles has changed little since 1916. At the same time social studies seems to be in a constant state of siege from one group or another recommending changes in the curriculum as a whole or in specific courses. At times, dramatic changes—for example, the new social studies—seem to be making headway, but they don't survive long and have little lasting impact.

The topic of curricular innovation—how it begins, who determines its success, and why innovations succeed or fail—has drawn the attention of many social studies researchers. In part this research seems to stem from the frustration of curriculum innovators who have been disappointed with the lack of implementation of curriculum innovations and have attempted to discover why they were thwarted. Findings described below are organized around the roles played by six groups: textbook publishers, social studies teachers, state authorities, college and university faculty, special interest groups, and federal officials.

Textbook Publishers

Textbook publishers have been a popular target for those who are dissatisfied with the current state of social studies and who believe that the textbook publishers inhibit change (Gagnon 1987; Sewell 1988; Tyson-Bernstein 1988). Textbooks are judged to have a controlling impact on what is taught in schools. (The interested reader will find a more extensive treatment of the role of textbooks in Chapter 16 of this *Handbook*.) Some researchers believe that curriculum materials, including textbooks, are the primary influence on classroom instruction (Patrick and Hawke 1982, 119). They appear to be more influential than state—and locally—produced curriculum guides that are largely ignored by teachers (Stake and Easley 1978). Teachers organize their instruction around the textbook; indeed, Patrick and Hawke (1982) argue that the most important curriculum decision a teacher makes is the selection of a textbook. About half of all social studies teachers depend upon a single textbook; about 90 percent use no more than three textbooks (Wiley 1977).

What do social studies teachers think about their textbooks? It appears that teachers like their textbooks much more than textbooks critics believe they should. Numerous studies have found that teachers are generally satisfied with textbooks, have confidence in the knowledge they provide, and believe they support the kind of teaching they want to do (Hertzberg 1985; Patrick and Hawke 1982).

Textbook critics believe textbooks to be bland and uninteresting, but this may account partially for their success. Textbook publishers seek to make their books as widely acceptable as possible—to offend no one, if it can be done. In the process, they eliminate much of the controversy that would polarize potential customers. Bland though they may be, social studies textbooks may provide good indicators of the compromises that have been struck within American society at various points over time.

The influence of textbook publishers on social studies classrooms, however great, merely begs another question: Who influences textbooks? We shall examine those influences next.

Teachers

Regardless of the best efforts of national commissions, state departments of education, and textbook authors, the formal curriculum is what each teacher decides it will be. It is the teacher's role to connect the ideas in the textbooks to students' own experience. Through the judgments teachers make about what students already know and can understand to how to explain new information so it can be readily understood, teachers create a curriculum distinctly different from what the authors had anticipated (Marker 1980). Thus, to imagine a teacher-proof curriculum is unrealistic (White 1985).

Teachers act as cultural mediators, deciding which ideas will be allowed to enter the classroom and slamming the door on those they view as discordant (White 1985). Some view this as a kind of self-censorship, permitting the teacher to avoid controversy, thereby reducing stress and assuring job security (Nelson and Stanley 1985). This may be true, but that view is merely a negative way of describing what teachers perceive their role to be: to apply new knowledge and beliefs to augment locally held values and to pursue locally determined goals (White 1985). Thus, teachers reshape materials to fit their purposes. For example, a teacher using materials that draw distinctions among various cultures and ethnic groups may blunt the distinctions and stress the similarities so as to avoid offending representatives of the groups who may be enrolled in the course. Being nice or polite may be an important value to the teacher, while this value may seem irrelevant to the developer (White 1985).

While most teachers do not control which textbooks their students read, they control how the textbooks will be used. One study found that only 27.1 percent of 500 grade 7–12 teachers surveyed believed they were in control of textbook selection, but 89.7 percent said they controlled methods of instruction and 79.6 percent determined how the students would be tested and evaluated (Fontana 1980). The frustration experienced by curriculum developers is easy to explain. They devise a curricular product that calls for radically different teaching procedures. A school adopts the materials, but when the developer visits the classroom, the materials are used very differently than intended. The teacher, who may have had no role in adopting the new materials, is in control of how they will be used. Each teacher will modify the materials to fit his personal style and what he judges to be acceptable practice in the school and community (McKee 1988). It is unlikely that teachers deliberately sabotage the developer's intention; indeed they may believe they are fulfilling it (Jantz and Klawiller 1985). Yet, by their modifications, they have effectively created a course of their own, drawing upon the developer's ideas but fitting them to their purposes.

There is another way in which teachers play a major role in determining the content of their courses. Teachers supplement textbooks with topics they choose using materials they develop (Hahn 1985a). This is particularly noticeable in the kindergarten curriculum where teachers are more likely to use their own materials than those provided by the publishers (Atwood and Finkelstein 1987), but use of teacher-developed materials is common at other grades as well. These materials may range from a study of a local historical event that would be judged too specialized to be included in a textbook to a topic of current public interest that might appear in a subsequent text edition to a topic judged too controversial for a publisher to handle but is important to a particular teacher or community. Examples of the latter kind might be about a major environmental case, such as Three Mile Island, that would be treated by teachers in Pennsylvania but not elsewhere or the plight of a Congressman who might be forced to resign his seat because of his constituents' anger over his sexual affairs. Such topics may be too hot for national use but hard to avoid locally. Rather than offer entirely new courses on such topics, teachers find ways to "infuse" the topic into existing instruction (Hahn 1985b).

What factors influence teachers' decisions about the social studies curriculum? First, teachers want to teach what they know, and they know history more than they do other subjects. While social studies specialists may urge teachers to employ an interdisciplinary approach, "in the hearts of most social studies teachers history is still the king/queen of the social sciences" (Farmer 1988, 29). Second, they are greatly influenced by their school culture (McKee 1988; Popkewitz, Tabachnick, and Wehlege 1982). Fellow teachers, the school principal, even students and parents set an ethos regarding what is desirable and undesirable. Whether the school has high expectations for its students to attend college, whether forced busing and racial integration are important, whether extracurricular programs are given high priority: These and other factors influence judgments teachers make.

Decisions about the curriculum are affected by the demands the course may make on classroom management (Cornbleth 1985). The use of inquiry method teaching strategies were affected negatively by teachers' judgments that inquiry teaching required more class preparation time (Jantz and Klawiller 1985). Teachers lecture and engage in directed recitation because to place students into less-structured situations (e.g., small group discussions) is to risk loss of classroom control; recitation and lecture also ensure that material is covered, if not necessarily learned (Hertzberg 1985).

Of course, it would be foolish to pretend teachers are alike and respond in identical ways. Studies have shown, for example, that differences exist between elementary school teachers and secondary teachers, and between beginning teachers and more experienced ones. Elementary teachers are not likely to have pursued a major in one of the history or social science disciplines and thus feel less prepared to teach social studies (Eslinger and Superka 1982). They look upon social studies not as a separate subject but as part of citizen enculturation, as an integrative core of the elementary school curriculum, and as education for social action (Goodman and Adler 1985). Secondary teachers typically view themselves as subject matter specialists, pledged to teach history, American government, or some other subject to youth.

There are also differences among teachers according to their age and levels of experience. Beginning secondary school teachers seem more concerned about whether they know enough about their subjects to transmit knowledge accurately and successfully to their students. More experienced teachers seem more concerned about student motivation, classroom management, and teaching methods (Ross 1987). Experienced teachers are also more likely to favor a common curriculum for all students, to hold students accountable to common standards, and to allow students greater responsibility (Brousseau, Book, and Byers 1988).

State government influences the social studies curriculum in several ways. It may establish courses required for high school graduation; it may approve and fund textbooks for each course; it may prepare and distribute curriculum guides; it may mandate the inclusion of such topics as the study of religion or free enterprise in existing courses; and it may support in-service programs to provide training for teachers in new content and methodology. The general trend in the 1980s was for the states to become more prescriptive rather than less so (Hahn 1985b; Morrissett 1986). In addition to the techniques described above, states have begun to mandate tests for both teachers and students. The teacher exams are to ensure that teachers have an adequate knowledge of their subjects and teaching skills before they are granted licenses; student tests are designed to ensure that all students are acquiring the knowledge that is implied by the state curricula.

Relatively little research has been done on the impact of state requirements and mandates. Stake and Easley (1978) found that the influence of state curriculum guides is minimal; teachers pay little attention to them. State textbook adoption certainly influences the course agenda, but, as was shown earlier, teachers negotiate their own course of study, drawing upon but not impeded by the textbook. What is unknown is the impact that state achievement tests will have on instruction. Common opinion holds that teachers will "teach for the test" as best they can so as to avoid embarrassment and censure should their students perform badly. But as Stodolsky (1988) pointed out, a subject gains in priority when it becomes a part of the accountability system. Thus basic subjects are accorded more time and attention, while enrichment subjects like social studies are taken less seriously by teachers who are therefore less concerned by low student achievement. But until more studies are done, we shall not know whether the tests are enjoying the influence their advocates desire or their critics fear.

Colleges and Universities

Colleges and universities may have an impact on social studies instruction in several ways. Perhaps the most significant influence is through establishing admission standards for entering freshmen. For example, insisting that high school graduates must show 2 or 3 years of history and social science will affect the programs of at least those students who expect to attend college. Occasionally, college faculty attempt to influence the content of instruction within courses (Kingston and Bennett 1986), although there is little evidence that their efforts have much influence.

College curricula for those preparing to teach social studies are presumably influential. However, here also very little evidence exists regarding such impact. One problem is that there is little consistency among universities or within a particular university regarding preparation programs for social studies teachers. State departments of education, the National Council for the Social Studies, and the National Council for the Accreditation of Teacher Education provide broad guidelines for accrediting programs to prepare elementary, middle, and secondary school teachers; but these guidelines tend to be broad—for example, every elementary school teacher must have a course in world civilization. The result is that each college or university is free to decide what a course in "world civilization" means. Where a state grants licenses to secondary school teachers according to specific subjects they wish to teach—for example, world history, American history, American government—rather than by broad categories, such as secondary school social science, they ensure that teachers will have more focused preparation within a discipline rather than a broad survey of many disciplines. However, such priorities do not guarantee consistency within a subject area such as world history.

Colleges and universities also vary regarding how teaching methods and supervised practice are administered. In some colleges, the faculty of each discipline provides a course on the methods of teaching its discipline and supervises majors during their practice teaching in schools. In large universities this function may be assumed by colleges/schools of education. In such cases a general methods course on "teaching social studies" is substituted for specific courses on teaching history, government, economics, geography, and so on. Supervision of student teachers may be performed by the "methods professor" from the education department or school or by graduate students. In still other cases methods courses and supervision of practice are performed by classroom teachers employed on a part-time basis by the university or college for this purpose.

The lack of consistency in the preparation program is one issue; the problem is exacerbated when professors within the academic disciplines and the professors of social studies education disagree strongly about the purpose of the teacher education program. If the history department believes it is preparing a person to teach a secondary school course in history, while the professor of social studies education is discounting the importance of teaching history while urging interdisciplinary social studies, the opportunity for confusion is great for those preparing to teach (Mehlinger 1981). Elementary school teachers are less likely to be trapped in such a conflict. They typically major in education and have only a few hours within each academic discipline, thereby avoiding the socialization the disciplines provide secondary school teachers. If proposals such as those of the Holmes Group (1986), calling for academic majors for elementary school teachers, are realized, they too will likely experience the same conflict and confusion secondary school teachers are offered. In general, studies have shown years of classroom experience are a greater influence on teacher belief and practice than teacher training programs (Brousseau, Book, and Byers 1988).

College professors individually influence social studies through their roles as textbook authors. Magruder's influence on American government was significant and long lasting. Professors may be used as school consultants; they also provide in-service instruction. There is no research on their role as consultants. Evidence of the impact of in-service programs is mixed. One study explored the impact of in-service education on the ability of teachers to engage in inquiry teaching. The judgment was that instruction failed, largely because it remained too theoretical and failed to come to grips with the practical problems teachers confronted in implementing inquiry materials (Jantz and Klawiller 1985).

Special Interests

Special interests are of various kinds. They can be professional associations lobbying on behalf of their particular discipline, commercial enterprises such as electric power companies hoping to influence instruction about the environment, topical interest groups such as the National Rifle Association, the Population Council, or the John Birch Society, and national commissions organized for a broad purpose to strengthen the teaching of social studies. Little is known about the relative impact such groups have.

Newmann (1985) studied the content of six national reports on the social studies and discussed their potential impact at the time of his study. Armento (1986b) studied the impact the Joint Council for Economic Education has had on the social studies curriculum and judged it to be substantial. Its success is a result of the degree, scope, and continuity of influence. It provides the largest nongovernmental teacher training system in the nation, supports Economic Education Councils in each of the 50 states and at least 260 University Centers for Economic Education, and has produced tests and instructional materials for use in classrooms. No other special interest group has maintained the level and scope of activity to match the Joint Council for Economic Education; no other organization can match the money it invests in its work.

Some impacts may be so subtle that they pass unnoticed to many. Anyon (1979) argued that the social studies has served corporate interests since its very inception (Anyon 1979). She believes that such courses as American history have been biased to favor the interests of management over labor and to provide ideological support for practices that would provide compliant workers.

It is difficult to know on what basis teachers elect to use materials and ideas promoted by various interest groups. Studies have been done of "light house schools," those that follow closely and respond swiftly to ideas of national commissions and professional associations (Hahn 1977; Hahn, Marker, Switzer, and Turner 1976; Superka 1977). In general, such schools are quick to "adopt" new ideas and practices, and quick to change when new ideas appear to displace them. Being on the cutting edge seems as important to such schools as making deep and lasting change (Slavin 1989).

Federal Government

In general the popular view is that the federal government has no role in promoting school curricula. In fact, the federal government has had considerable influence at various times. During the period of the "new social studies" it provided most of the money needed for curriculum development and for conducting the in-service training teachers required to use the new materials. During that era, commercial publishers began to judge the federal government as an unwelcome and unfair competitor. Lobbying efforts by commercial publishers successfully halted congressional support for curriculum development by the federal government in the 1970s.

The federal government influences the social studies curriculum in less obvious ways as well. Since social studies attempts to deal with past and current problems affecting the society, the federal government influences the instructional agenda. Summit conferences and congressional hearings often provide grist for social studies content.

Conclusion

Who controls the social studies curriculum? Clearly, no single person or institution. Influence is interactive; any effort to effect change must take into account the multiple and competing levels of action and anticipate that any innovation is unlikely to be implemented unchanged. It is not merely that new ideas are resisted; it is also that multiple ideas and agendas are competing for attention. Propelling a social studies notion into action is akin to entering a contest where three sports are being played simultaneously, and no time out is called to admit the new player.

WHAT DO STUDENTS LEARN FROM SOCIAL STUDIES?

What are the effects on students of having taken courses in social studies? What do they know and believe? Do they behave differently from those who have not studied social studies? Does the social studies curriculum have any discernible effect? These are valid questions. Unfortunately, there are few dependable answers.

First of all, what does it mean to learn social studies? If a student learns certain information for an examination and then cannot recall the same information months or years later, was it learned? If a student acquires knowledge, skills, and values and fails to act on them when the appropriate occasion arises, have they been truly learned?

The overarching purpose of social studies is to prepare youth to be constructive members of American society. Two performance indicators of learning social studies might be respect for law and voting in elections. Less than 42 percent of the eligible 18–24-year-old voters cast votes in the 1984 presidential election (U.S. Office of Educational Research and Improvement 1988). In general, participation by 18–24 year old voters has declined since 1972, when they first gained the right to vote. Those who have most recently completed high school vote with less frequency than older voters; Miller (1985) was unable to find a relationship between exposure to social studies courses and levels of actual political participation. In 1985, about 62 percent of serious crimes committed in the United States were by youth 24 years old or younger. "The number of arrests per 1000 of young adults 18–24 years old more than doubled between 1965–1985" (U.S. Office of Educational Research and Improvement 1988). If social studies is intended to increase voter participation and respect for law, it appears to be failing.

Of course, defenders of social studies may argue that it is unrealistic to hold social studies accountable for these deficiencies. Various other factors affect voter participation and criminal activity by youth. Furthermore, they point to the fact that American society is the most stable and democratic in the world; social studies may be able to take some credit for that status. Yet, one cannot escape the conclusion that social studies cannot properly take the credit or blame for the performance of adult citizens. There are too many intervening variables. Thus, a reasonable question is whether social studies should adopt purposes for which it cannot be held accountable (Leming 1986).

Children are more likely to learn what they are taught than what they are not. Many studies have compared the knowledge, skills, and values of students who have participated in an experimental social studies course with control group students who were denied access to the experimental treatment. In most cases the experimental group has outperformed control groups when the evaluation instruments measured gains on knowledge and skills promoted by the experiment. However, all of these studies focus on short-term gains; no one has done longitudinal studies to measure long-term results.

Several reports have documented youth and adult knowledge of American and world history, geography, economics, and government. Inevitably, these studies point to relative degrees of ignorance of American youth and adults about these domains of knowledge (Finn and Ravitch 1988). Many Americans cannot locate major countries on a map; they cannot locate historical events in time; they cannot name current political leaders. Such studies do not make clear whether their respondents once knew the information and have forgotten it, which of the respondents had taken key social studies courses and who did not, and whether occupation and social class were key variables affecting what one knows or does not know from the social studies. In general, while the total numbers and percentages of youth completing high school and entering college have increased over the last 3 decades, the average SAT verbal scores for college-bound high school seniors has declined over the same period (U.S. Office of Educational Research and Improvement 1988). Some portion of the verbal section of the SAT test employs social studies items.

Nor does social studies seem to have a major impact on student values and their moral development. After reviewing a couple of hundred pieces of research, Leming concluded, "Standard social studies curriculum has no discernible impact on the socio-moral development of youth" (Leming 1985, 176). He attributes this result to the emphasis by teachers on the mastery of subject matter content.

These results point to the weaknesses of previous and current research as well as to any implied failures of the social studies curriculum. The researchers must make assumptions about what students actually studied in social studies on the basis of prescribed curricula, but, as has been noted earlier, course titles are insufficient indicators of the actual course content. Furthermore, social studies knowledge is acquired outside of school as well as from formal instruction. Student impressions of World War II, for example, may be influenced more by television and movies than by social studies textbooks; these impressions affect both those who have studied World War II in class and those who have not, for good or for ill. Nor do most studies reach beyond factual recall of social studies topics. Just as knowledge of science is more than recall of chemical formulas, so knowledge of momentous events—for example, the Holocaust—should require more than exact recall of the names of German concentration camps and the estimated number of people who perished in them.

Finally, there is something else students learn with regard to social studies. Many learn to dislike it. Social studies is seen by students as less important and less interesting than other subjects (Schug 1982). Negative attitudes toward social studies increase over time; the higher the grade level, the more negative students seem to be (Crawley 1988). In general, students with negative views of social studies find the content boring, unrelated to their experience, excessively detailed, and overly repetitious (Schug 1982). Those who have studied student attitudes toward social studies believe that the way the content is presented may be the most important variable. The kind of classroom environment created by teachers and their attitudes toward the subject appear to influence how their students react to the subject (Haladyna, Shaughnessy, and Redsun 1982). Diverse teaching strategies and routines, active student participation in the lesson, cooperative learning activities among students, and positive interpersonal relationships between the teacher and student have been shown to foster student interest in the social studies (Fouts 1987, 1989).

CONCLUSION

Social studies curriculum research is affected by the nature of the field, by the talent, interests, and time of the people who conduct research, and by available resources.

Nature of the Field

As noted earlier, social studies researchers devote an inordinate amount of attention to the purpose of social studies (Wallen and Fraenkel 1988). What accounts for this emphasis? Perhaps, it is because social studies, more than other areas of the school curriculum, is expected to carry out the socialization mission of schooling. Social studies educators must respond to political/social agendas advanced by public officials, interest groups, and the lay public. At the same time the curriculum is expected to reflect knowledge respected by academic scholars. It is not enough to teach sound American history in schools; it is also vital to teach a history that helps black children develop a strong self-concept, respects the traditions of ethnic Americans, advances the changing career aspirations of women, glorifies American heroes, preaches distrust of communism, and strengthens devotion to the free enterprise system, while avoiding political partisanship. The fact that these and other pressures vary over time merely adds to the complexity. Social studies provides the primary place in the curriculum where American children are taught what it means to be an American, with all the complexity that it implies. The tension between promoting propaganda leading to blind socialization and promoting knowledge and values leading to enlightenment and a student's ability to choose freely and wisely is one the social studies field experiences each day in school.

It is therefore not surprising how much energy is devoted to articulating the purpose of social studies. Should it promote certain values or prepare children to analyze values critically? Should it choose its content from the academic disciplines or according to social problems and individual student concerns? Should it stress local, national, or global perspectives? Should it focus on cognitive development, affective growth, or social participation? Or if all of the above, what proportions of each are most desirable? Finding an appropriate balance among these factors—all desirable if properly balanced—drives the search for purpose in the social studies.

Citizenship education has provided the label for social studies' purpose throughout most of the 20th century. It survives, despite occasional criticism, because it works. Citizenship education is broadly interpreted and can therefore justify widely divergent content and practices. Its meaning can also be redefined over time. What citizenship education meant during World War II is something different from its meaning during an era of global interdependence.

The fact that citizenship education provides a cover for widely divergent practices does not mean that individual social studies experts are content with what is permitted to exist under that label. The constant stream of books and articles on the "nature of social studies," on the purpose and goals of social studies, and on citizenship education are attempts to define and redefine citizenship education according to terms congenial to the authors and to persuade others to accept their formulations. The energy that drives this scholarship stems from the view that the field cannot advance until it defines itself properly and its aims correctly.

Promoting citizenship education may also accommodate the motivations of people who are attracted to social studies—people with interest and training in history and the social sciences who also have a desire to improve society. From their perspective it is less important that an individual child know more history, or geography, or economics; what is vital is that a child acquire the knowledge, values, skills, and participation experiences that will enable him or her to improve—perhaps even radically transform—American and world society. If the curriculum can so empower one child, perhaps it can be successful with many, even a majority; in this way social studies educators can affect society (Nelson and Shaver 1985).

In a perverse way the exceptional importance devoted to rationale and purpose may partially account for another characteristic of social studies research: the relative lack of sound research on school practice. Except for studies that evaluate a particular curricular innovation—typically a unit within a course or a semester-long course—to determine if the experimental group performed differently from the control group, there is little research on ways that broad curricular practices affect student outcomes. Studies that would examine the relationship of particular theoretical frameworks on school curricula or the impact of alternative theoretical approaches on student performances are glaringly absent. Indeed, Fred Newmann may be the only social studies researcher of note who has attempted over many years to investigate how his ideas relating to citizen participation can be practiced in schools and to what effects.

One result of ignoring practice is that social studies research has little credence among practitioners (Leming 1989). While teachers may admire the eloquence employed to describe social studies goals, existing research fails to answer the fundamental curriculum questions faced by classroom teachers, supervisors, and administrators: What should I teach? in what sequence? to whom? and in what ways?

The inability of social studies research to provide guidance on what to teach also leaves the field vulnerable when demands for student and teacher accountability are voiced. Few expect social studies to be held accountable for the actual behavior of adult citizens, regardless of the stated purpose of social studies with regard to citizen education. However, when public officials or the community at large ask what students know about history, geography, American government, economics, and so on, it is not helpful for social studies researchers to respond that these outcomes are trivial given the overall purpose of social studies. The social studies loses credibility when it posits goals for which it cannot be held accountable and refuses to accept goals that might be reasonably and legitimately pursued by social studies teachers and students.

The emphasis upon citizenship education may have other consequences. Social studies is expected to provide the classroom experience where boys and girls, rich and poor, across all ethnic and cultural backgrounds, regardless of intelligence, can meet as equals to gain experience in solving social problems. In this way social studies classes are expected to reflect a cross-section of American society. Tracking is discouraged as elitist and undemocratic. Except for elective courses, students attend the same classes and receive the same instruction. This may account for the decline in student interest in social studies as they proceed in school and why many students find social studies instruction boring, repetitious, and undemanding.

People

Social studies curriculum research is conducted primarily by college/university professors of social studies education and their doctoral students (Nelson and Shaver 1985). With few exceptions research in social studies is not performed by professors from other fields of professional education, professors of history and the social sciences, state department of education officials, school administrators, and social studies teachers. Social studies research engages a relatively small subgroup of educational researchers.

Research by doctoral students has contributed only marginally to the development of a body of research-based knowledge in the social studies. However worthy particular dissertations may be, they tend as a group to treat very limited issues, where variables are tightly controlled, and are largely unconnected to previous research. The purpose of a dissertation is mainly to demonstrate the candidate's ability to do research; candidates typically choose topics that can be managed with limited time and resources. There is no effort to have each dissertation build upon another so that in time the accumulated weight of evidence might lead to substantial and useful knowledge. Small-scale empirical studies of curricular innovations and textbook analyses have been chosen for many doctoral dissertations because they are manageable and can demonstrate the candidate's research capacities.

College professors also conduct small-scale empirical studies and textbook analyses, but professors are also the ones, primarily, who supply the field with books and articles on the rationale and purpose of social studies. It is not clear why this more philosophical writing holds greater appeal than empirical studies of actual practice. Perhaps, the philosophical writing fits professors' teaching roles best. Many teach undergraduate and graduate courses for social studies teachers where explaining and justifying the role of social studies—as contrasted to the separate academic disciplines—is a prominent feature. Perhaps there is something about the culture of higher education, which shows respect to ideas that are articulated powerfully, that influences professors of social studies. Perhaps professors are driven by many of the same forces confronting doctoral students; large-scale empirical studies that require years to complete are not so easily counted and recognized for salary, promotion, and tenure purposes and are difficult to finance.

One must wonder if social studies research were conducted by practitioners or by teams of practitioners and professors whether the research topics would be more closely related to practice and whether the research results would be used more often by those who are responsible for curriculum decisions.

Resources

The kind and quality of social studies research has been greatly affected by available resources. For the most part social studies research has been conducted by doctoral students and college professors, who have relied upon personal or institutional resources. Except for evaluation studies conducted in conjunction with major curriculum development projects and the SPAN study supported by the National Science Foundation, there have been few foundation or government investments in social studies research.

Most social studies research is performed in the library, by use of the mail, or through experimental studies with local groups near to home or campus. More extensive studies that would require travel, relocation, employment of assistants, and gathering data over several years require funds not easily available to social studies researchers. One reason textbook analysis studies are popular is that the research can assume—correctly or not—that a textbook provides evidence regarding what students will be taught and learn. Using the textbook as the source of data is less expensive and more manageable than spending time observing instruction in classes. If social studies research is less powerful than it should be, it may also be as good as can be expected, given the resources invested.

Needed Research

Fraenkel (1987) and others have discussed various ways in which social studies research could be improved and have suggested topical areas that need special study. Following are some types of curriculum research that are rarely done in social studies; they could add significantly to the field if resources and investigators could be found to support the investigations.

Longitudinal Studies. At the present time little can be said about the nature or consequences of a social studies education as experienced by individual students. Researchers have provided descriptions of social studies offerings; they have also conducted small-scale studies of particular curricular innovations. Longitudinal studies that follow a cohort of students through the curriculum from grade level to grade level and course to course, evaluating the impact of instruction at each stage in the process, would provide much richer data than currently exists about the meaning and significance of the social studies curriculum. Such studies would also permit the testing of the claims made for the many K-12 curriculum frameworks that continue to be advanced.

Case Studies. Social studies could profit from in-depth case studies focused on specific classrooms. It is not enough to know the name of the course and the textbook a teacher uses. It is important to observe systematically over an extended period of time how the course is mediated by a teacher. Such studies should include not only the formal curricula but the informal and "hidden" ones as well. Such studies are needed in order to gain more exact understanding of how social studies varies across grade levels, across schools serving different social classes and student abilities, across urban and rural schools, and by subject areas.

Cross-National Studies. American social studies research is rather ethnocentric. Until recently there have been relatively few studies of social studies in other countries. Where studies exist they provide unique glimpses of the way citizenship education is interpreted (Tucker and Mehlinger 1979), how textbooks are employed (Becker 1981), and the purpose of social studies in various countries (Lawton 1981). American researchers who are currently exploring the utility of "critical theory" for American social studies could profit from the extensive discussion of these ideas that occurred in the Federal Republic of Germany in the 1970s (Sussmuth 1980; Rusen and Sussmuth, 1980).

Building Knowledge, Values, and Skills Sequentially. In the elementary grades it is customary for textbook publishers to call for linkages of concepts, skills, and values across grade levels. Typically these are organized logically, or one suspects arbitrarily; there is little or no empirical support for the sequence provided.

Social studies teachers have little research support for their content choices. The common assumption is that one can teach almost anything, at any age, provided that the material is pitched appropriately to the child's level of development. The result is little or no foundation for deciding what to teach, when, and what content should be linked to other content to obtain maximum impact.

Alternative approaches and schemes should be carefully tested, so that the social studies is no longer held hostage to tradition or to the most appealing new rationale.

Studies of Power and Influence. For a period during the 1960s and 1970s, some researchers were interested in how social studies decisions were made, in how various groups exerted their influence on the curriculum (Center for Educational Field Studies 1970; Hahn, Marker, Switzer, and Turner 1977; Pincus 1974; Richburg 1969; Superka 1977). Since then, such studies have declined; yet, we still know very little about the influence of special interest groups or state mandates, or the impact of state testing programs and federal projects such as the celebrations of the ratification of the U.S. Constitution, or the power of test-based teacher certification programs. Such events appear to influence the social studies curriculum, but a much richer set of studies is needed if we are to know the extent of the power and influence of such factors.

The Tradition of Replication. The tradition of replicating research studies is well established in both the sciences and social sciences. Such studies are not, however, common in the social studies area (Fraenkel 1987). There are few standard measures of the effectiveness of different curriculum models, whether the desired outcomes are knowledge, skills, or values. Instead, researchers are likely to employ locally developed measures of curriculum success, not a surprising development given the diversity of models which have been proposed. The result makes the comparison of results virtually impossible. Editorial boards of journals could do a service to the field if they encouraged research that replicated important studies rather than publishing yet another theoretical curriculum model or framework.

If these kinds of research were undertaken, the knowledge necessary for sound curriculum choices would be much richer than it is today. And designing a proper social studies curriculum would become more a science and less a folk art (Ehman and Hahn 1981).

References

Agostine, V. Robert, and William P. Barone. 1985. A decade of change: Elementary social studies texts. *Social Studies Journal* 14(Spring): 20–29.

Alder, Douglas D., and Matthew T. Downey. 1985. "Problem Areas in the History Curriculum." In *History in the Schools, Bulletin no. 74*, edited by Matthew T. Downey, 13–24. Washington, DC: National Council for the Social Studies.

Anyon, Jean. 1979. Ideology and United States history textbooks. *Harvard Educational Review* 49(August): 361–385.

Armento, Beverly J. 1986a. "Promoting Economic Literacy." In *Social Studies and Social Sciences: A Fifty-Year Perspective, Bulletin no. 78*, edited by Stanley P. Wronski and Donald H. Bragaw, 97–110. Washington, DC: National Council for the Social Studies.

Armento, Beverly J. 1986b. "Research on Teaching Social Studies." In *Handbook of Research on Teaching*, 3rd ed., edited by Merlin C. Wittrock, 942–951. New York: Macmillan.

Atwood, Virginia A. 1986. "Elementary Social Studies: Cornerstone or Crumbling Mortar?" In *Elementary Social Studies: Research as a Guide to Practice, Bulletin no. 79*, edited by Virginia A. Atwood, 1–13. Washington, DC: National Council for the Social Studies.

Atwood, Virginia A., and Judith M. Finkelstein. 1987. Social studies in kindergartens: A status report. *Social Education* 5(November–December): 526–532.

Barr, Robert, James Barth, and Samuel Shermis. 1977. *Defining The Social Studies*. Arlington, VA: National Council for the Social Studies.

Becker, James. 1981. The Japan/U.S. textbook project: In search of mutual understanding. *Social Education* 46(7): 494–497.

Boyer, Ernest. 1983. *High School: A Report on Secondary Education in America*. New York: Harper & Row.

Bragaw, Donald H., and Michael H. Hartoonian. 1988. "Social Studies: The Study of People in Society." In *Content of the Curriculum*, edited by Ronald S. Brandt, 9–30. Washington, DC: Association for Supervision and Curriculum Development.

Brodbelt, Samuel, and Robert E. Wall. 1985. "An Examination of the Presentation of Heroes and Heroines in Current (1974–1984) Secondary Level Social Studies Textbooks." Paper presented at the Eastern Educational Research Association Conference, February 7–9, Virginia Beach, VA.

Brousseau, Bruce A., Casandra Book, and Joe L. Byers. 1988. Teacher beliefs and the cultures of teaching. *Journal of Teacher Education* 39(6): 33–39.

Butts, R. Freeman. 1978. *Public Education in the United States: From Revolution to Reform*. New York: Holt, Rinehart and Winston.

Cawelti, Gordon, and Janice Adkisson. 1985. ASCD study reveals elementary school time allocations for subject areas: Other trends noted. *ASCD Curriculum Update* (April): 1.

Center for Educational Field Studies. 1970. *An Evaluation of a Project for the Analysis, Development, Implementation, and Diffusion of the New Social Studies Curricula*. St. Louis, MO: Center for Educational Field Studies, Washington University.

Committee on Social Studies of the Commission on the Reorganization of Secondary Education. 1916. *The Social Studies in Secondary Education*. Washington, DC: Government Printing Office.

Cornbleth, Catherine. 1985. Social studies curriculum construction and reconstruction. *Social Education* 49(September): 554–556.

Crawley, Sharon J. 1988. What students think about social studies. *Southern Social Studies Quarterly* 13(Spring): 8–17.

Curriculum Task Force. 1989. *Charting a Course: Social Studies for the 21st Century*. Washington, DC: National Commission on Social Studies in the Schools.

Davis, O.L. 1989. Harold D. Drummond and social education: The practitioner and the practical. *The International Journal of Social Education* 3(3): 84–90.

Dougan, Alberta Macke. 1988. The search for a definition of the social studies: A historical overview. *The International Journal of Social Education* 3(Winter): 13–36.

Egan, Kieran. 1983. Social studies and the erosion of education. *Curriculum Inquiry* 13(Summer): 195–214.

Ehman, Lee H., and Carole L. Hahn. 1981. "Contributions of Research to Social Studies Education." In *The Social Studies: Eightieth Yearbook of the National Society for the Study of Education*, edited by Howard D. Mehlinger and O. L. Davis, Jr., 60–81. Chicago: University of Chicago Press.

Engle, Shirley. 1963. Decision making: The heart of social studies instruction. *Social Education* 24(7): 301–304, 306.

Engle, Shirley, and Anna Ochoa. 1988. *Education for Democratic Citizenship: Decision Making in the Social Studies*. New York: Teachers College Press.

Eslinger, M. V., and Donald P. Superka. 1982. "Teachers." In *Social Studies in the 1980s: A Report on Project SPAN*, edited by Irving Morrissett, 51–60. Alexandria, VA: Association for Supervision and Curriculum Development.

Farmer, Rod. 1988. Social studies teachers and the curriculum: A report from a national survey. *Journal of Social Studies Research* 11(2): 24–42.

Fenton. Edwin. 1967. *The New Social Studies*. New York: Holt, Rinehart and Winston.

Finn, Chester, and Diane Ravitch. 1988. No trivial pursuit. *Phi Delta Kappan* 69(8): 559–564.

Fleming, Dan B. 1984. "The Treatment of Peace and Security Issues in Social Studies Textbooks in the United States." Paper presented at the joint meeting of the Social Science Education Consortium and the Bundeszentrale für politisch Bildung, Irsee, Bavaria, West Germany.

Fleming, Dan B. 1985. The treatment of propaganda in selected social studies texts. *Social Education* 49(January): 53–57.

Fleming, Dan B. 1986. The treatment of terrorism in social studies texts. *Social Science Record* 24(1): 20–22.

Fontana, Lynn. 1980. *Status of Social Studies Teaching Practices in Secondary Schools*. Bloomington, IN: Agency for Instructional Television.

Fouts, Jeffrey T. 1987. High school social studies classroom environments and attitudes: A cluster analysis approach. *Theory and Research in Social Education* 15(Spring): 105–114.

Fouts, Jeffrey T. 1989. Classroom environments and student views of social studies: The middle grades. *Theory and Research in Social Education* 17(Spring): 136–147.

Fraenkel, Jack R. 1987. Toward improving research in social studies education. *Theory and Research in Social Education* 15(3): 203–222.

Gagnon, Paul. 1987. *Democracy's Untold Story: What World History Textbooks Neglect*. Washington, DC: American Federation of Teachers.

Gagnon, Paul. 1988. A look at the new California framework: Turning point for social studies reform? *American Educator* 12(Fall): 36–40.

Goodlad, John I. 1984. *A Place Called School*. New York: McGraw-Hill.

Goodman, Jesse, and Susan Adler. 1985. Becoming an elementary social studies teacher: A study of perspectives. *Theory and Research in Social Education* 13(2): 1–20.

Gross, Richard E. 1977. The status of the social studies in the public school of the United States: Fact and impressions of a national survey. *Social Education* 41(3): 194–200.

Gross, Richard E., and Thomas L. Dynneson. 1983. *What Should We Be Teaching in the Social Studies?* Bloomington, IN: Phi Delta Kappa.

Haas, John D. 1977. *The Era of the New Social Studies*. Boulder, CO: Social Science Education Consortium.

Haas, John D. 1986. Is the social studies curriculum impervious to change? *The Social Studies* 77(2): 61–65.

Hahn, Carole L. 1977. "Research on the Diffusion of Social Studies Innovations." In *Review of Research in Social Studies Education: 1970–75*, edited by F. P. Hawkins, 137–178. Washington, DC: National Council for the Social Studies.

Hahn, Carole L. 1985a. The status of nuclear education in social studies: Report of a survey. *The Social Studies* 76(6): 247–253.

Hahn, Carole L. 1985b. The status of the social studies in the public schools of the United States: Another look. *Social Education* 49(3): 220–223.

Hahn, Carole L., Gerald W. Marker, Thomas J. Switzer, and Mary Jane Turner. 1977. *Three Studies on Perceptions and Utilization of "New Social Studies" Materials*. Boulder, CO: Social Science Education Consortium.

Haladyna, T. M., J. Shaughnessy, and A. Redsun. 1982. Correlates of attitudes toward social studies. *Theory and Research in Social Education* 10(1): 1–26.

Herman, Wayne L., Jr. 1983. Scope and sequence in social studies education: What should be taught where? *Social Education* 47(2): 94–100.

Hertzberg, Hazel W. 1985. "Students, Methods and Materials of Instruction." In *History in the Schools, Bulletin no. 74*, edited by Matthew T. Downey, 25–40. Washington, DC: National Council for the Social Studies.

Holmes Group. 1986. *Tomorrow's Teachers: A Report of the Holmes Group*. East Lansing, MI: Holmes Group.

Hunt, Maurice P., and Lawrence E. Metcalf. 1955. *Teaching High School Social Studies: Problems in Reflective Thinking and Social Understanding*. New York: Harper & Brothers.

Jantz, R. K., and K. Klawiller. 1985. "Early Childhood/Elementary Social Studies: A Review of Research in Social Studies Education: 1976–1983." In *Review of Research in Social Studies Education: 1976–1983, Bulletin no. 75*, edited by William B. Stanley, 65–121. Washington, DC: National Council for the Social Studies.

Jarolimek, John. 1981. "The Social Studies: An Overview." In *The Social Studies: Eightieth Yearbook of the National Society for the Study of Education*, edited by Howard D. Mehlinger and O. L. Davis, Jr., 3–18. Chicago: University of Chicago Press.

Keels, Oliver M., Jr. 1989. Herbert Baxter Adams and the influence on the early social studies curriculum: A reassessment of the role of historians. *Theory and Research in Social Education* 8(3): 37–49.

Kingston, Paul W., and Clifford T. Bennett. 1986. Improving high school social studies: [illegible] colleges. *Theory and Research in Social Education* 14(1): 35–49.

Kohlberg, Lawrence. 1973. Moral development and the new social studies. *Social Education* 37(5): 369–375.

Kohlberg, Lawrence. 1975. The cognitive-developmental approach to moral education. *Phi Delta Kappan* 56(10): 670–677.

Larkins, A. Guy, Michael L. Hawkins, and Allison Gilmore. 1987. Trivial and noninformative content of elementary social studies: A review of primary texts in four series. *Theory and Research in Social Education* 15(4): 299–317.

Laughlin, M. A. 1989. Norris Sanders: From classroom questions to the information age. *The International Journal of Social Education* 3(3): 107–114.

Lawton, D. 1981. "Foundations for the Social Studies." In *UNESCO Handbook for the Teaching of Social Studies*, edited by Howard D. Mehlinger, 36–58. London: Croom Helm and UNESCO.

Leming, James S. 1985. "Research on Social Studies Curriculum and Instruction: Interventions and Outcomes in the Socio-Moral Domain." In *Review of Research in Social Studies Education: 1976–1983, Bulletin no. 73*, edited by William B. Stanley, 123–213. Washington, DC: National Council for the Social Studies.

Leming, James S. 1986. Rethinking social studies research and the goals of social education. *Theory and Research in Social Education* 14(2): 139–152.

Leming, James S. 1989. The two cultures of social studies education. *Social Education* 53(6): 404–408.

Lengel, James G., and Douglas P. Superka. 1982. "Curriculum Organization in Social Studies." In *The Current State of Social Studies: A Report of Project SPAN*, 81–104. Boulder, CO: Social Science Education Consortium.

LeRiche, Leo W. 1987. The expanding environments sequence in elementary social studies: The origins. *Theory and Research in Social Education* 15(3): 137–154.

Lockwood, Alan L. 1988. Moral education: Why not in public secondary schools? *National Center on Effective Secondary Schools Newsletters* 3(1): 3–5.

Longstreet, Wilma S. 1985. Citizenship: The phantom core of social studies curriculum. *Theory and Research in Social Education* 13(2): 21–30.

Longstreet, Wilma S. 1989. Boyd H. Bode: Quintessential Deweyan. *The International Journal of Social Education* 3(3): 55–62.

McKee, Saundra J. 1988. Impediments to implementing critical thinking. *Social Education* 52(6): 444–446.

Marker, Gerald W. 1980. Why schools abandon new social studies materials. *Theory and Research in Social Education* 7(4): 35–47.

Mehlinger, Howard D. 1981. "Social Studies: Some Gulfs and Priorities." In *The Social Studies: Eightieth Yearbook of the National Society for the Study of Education*, edited by Howard D. Mehlinger and O. L. Davis, Jr., 244–270. Chicago: University of Chicago Press.

Metcalf, Lawrence E. 1989. An overview of the Deweyan influence on social studies education. *The International Journal of Social Education* 3(3): 50–54.

Michigan State Board of Education. 1984. *A Study of Selected Eighth Grade United States History Textbooks: 1982–83 Michigan Textbook Study, vol. 1, Overview, Summary of Findings, Appendices*. Lansing: Michigan State Board of Education.

Miller, Jon D. 1985. "Effective Participation: A Standard for Social Science Education." Paper presented at the annual meeting of the Social Science Education Consortium, Racine, WI.

Morrissett, Irving. 1986. Status of social studies: The mid-1980s. *Social Education* 50(4): 303–310.

Morrissett, Irving, and John D. Haas. 1982. "Rationales, Goals, and Objectives in Social Studies." In *The Current State of Social Studies: A Report of Project SPAN*, 1–80. Boulder, CO: Social Science Education Consortium.

National Council for the Social Studies. 1979. A revision of the NCSS social studies curriculum guidelines. *Social Education* 43(4): 268.

National Council for the Social Studies. 1981. The essentials of the social studies curriculum guidelines. *Social Education* 45(3): 163.

Nelson, Jack L. 1980. "The Uncomfortable Relationship Between Moral Education and Citizenship Instruction." In *Moral Development and Politics*, edited by Richard W. Wilson and Gordon J. Schochet, 256–285. New York: Praeger.

Nelson, Jack L., and James P. Shaver. 1985. "On Research in Social Education." In *Review of Research in Social Studies Education: 1976–1983, Bulletin no. 75*, edited by William B. Stanley, 401–433. Washington, DC: National Council for the Social Studies.

Nelson, Jack L., and William B. Stanley. 1985. Academic freedom: 50 years of standing still. *Social Education* 49(8): 662–666.

Nelson, Murry R. 1989. Merl R. Eppse and studies of blacks in American history textbooks. *The International Journal of Social Education* 3(3): 84–90.

Newmann, Fred. 1970. *Clarifying Public Controversy: An Approach to Teaching Social Studies.* Boston: Little, Brown.

Newmann, Fred. 1975. *Education for Citizen Action: Challenge for Secondary Curriculum.* Berkeley, CA: McCutchan.

Newmann, Fred. 1977. "Building a Rationale for Civic Education." In *Building Rationales for Citizenship Education*, edited by James P. Shaver, 1–33. Arlington, VA: National Council for the Social Studies.

Newmann, Fred. 1981. "Political Participation: An Analytic Review and Proposal." In *Political Education in Flux*, edited by Derek B. Heater and Judith A. Gillespie, 149–180. Beverly Hills, CA: Sage.

Newmann, Fred. 1985. *Educational Reform and Social Studies: Implications of Six Reports.* Boulder, CO: ERIC Clearinghouse for Social Studies/Social Science Education.

Newmann, Fred M., Thomas A. Bertocci, and Ruthanne M. Landsness. 1977. *Skills in Citizen Action: An English-Social Studies Program for Secondary Schools.* Madison, WI: Citizen Participation Project.

Oliver, Donald W., and James P. Shaver. 1966. *Teaching Public Issues in the High School.* Boston: Houghton Mifflin.

Patrick, John J., and Sharryl Hawke. 1982. "Social Studies Curriculum Materials." In *The Current State of Social Studies: A Report of Project SPAN*, 105–158. Boulder, CO: Social Science Education Consortium.

Pincus, John. 1974. Incentives for innovation in the public schools. *Review of Educational Research.* 44(1): 113–144.

Popkewitz, Thomas S., B. Robert Tabachnick, and Gary Wehlege. 1982. *The Myth of Educational Reform.* Madison: University of Wisconsin Press.

Project SPAN Staff and Consultants. 1982. *The Current State of Social Studies: A Report on Project SPAN.* Boulder, CO: Social Science Education Consortium.

Ravitch, Diane. 1987. Tot sociology: Or what happened to history in the grade schools. *The American Scholar* 56(3): 343–354.

Richburg, James R. 1969. *Curriculum Diffusion: Dissemination and Adoption of Materials in the Anthropology Curriculum Study Project.* Athens: University of Georgia.

Ross, E. Wayne. 1987. "Preservice Teachers' Perspectives Toward Secondary Social Studies Education." Paper presented at the annual meeting of the American Educational Research Association, Washington, DC.

Rusen, Jorn, and Hans Sussmuth, eds. 1980. *Theorien in der Geschichtswissenschaft (Theories of Historical Science).* Dusseldorf: Pädagogischer Verlag Schwann.

Schug, Marc C. 1982. "Why Kids Don't Like Social Studies." Paper presented at the annual meeting of the National Council for the Social Studies, Boston.

Senesh, Lawrence. 1964. *Our Working World.* Chicago: Science Research Associates.

Sewell, G. T. 1988. American history textbooks: Where do we go from here? *Phi Delta Kappan* 69(8): 552–558.

Shafer, Susanne M. 1981. "Social Studies in Other Nations." In *The Social Studies: Eightieth Yearbook of the National Society for the Study of Education*, edited by Howard D. Mehlinger and O. L. Davis, Jr., 82–101. Chicago: University of Chicago Press.

Shaver, James P., O. L. Davis, and Suzanne W. Helburn. 1979. *An Interpretative Report on the Status of Pre-Collegiate Social Studies Education Based on Three NSF-Funded Studies.* Washington, DC: National Science Foundation.

Shaver, James P., and Richard S. Knight. 1986. "Civics and Government in Citizenship Education." In *Social Studies and Social Sciences: A Fifty-Year Perspective, Bulletin no. 78*, edited by Stanley P. Wronski and Donald H. Bragaw, 71–84. Washington, DC: National Council for the Social Studies.

Slavin, Robert E. 1989. PET and the pendulum: Faddism in education and how to stop it. *Phi Delta Kappan.* 70(10): 752–758.

Stake, Robert E., and Jack A. Easley Jr. 1978. *Case Studies in Science Education.* Washington, DC: National Science Foundation.

Stanley, William B. 1985. "Recent Research in the Foundations of Social Education: 1976–1983." In *Review of Research in Social Studies Education, 1976–1983, Bulletin no. 75*, edited by William B. Stanley, 309–397. Washington, DC: National Council for the Social Studies.

Stanley, William B. 1989. Beyond pragmatic inquiry: A critical analysis of Lawrence Metcalf's approach to social education. *The International Journal of Social Education* 3(3): 63–83.

Stodolsky, Susan S. 1988. *The Subject Matters: Classroom Activity in Math and Social Studies.* Chicago: University of Chicago Press.

Superka, Douglas P. 1977. *An Exploration of Social Studies Innovations in Secondary Schools.* Boulder, CO: Social Studies Education Consortium.

Superka, Douglas P., and Sharryl Hawke. 1982. *Social Roles: A Focus for Social Studies in the 1980s.* Boulder, CO: Social Science Education Consortium.

Sussmuth, Hans, ed. 1980. *Soziale Studien in der Grundschule (Social Studies in the Primary School).* Dusseldorf: Pädagogischer Verlag Schwann.

Taylor, Bob L., and Gregory R. Birchell. 1983. "Has the "Back-to-Basics" Movement Influenced Elementary Social Studies Textbooks?" Paper presented at the National Council for the Social Studies Annual Conference, San Francisco, CA.

Thomas, Gordon R., and Jim Parsons. 1984. "Setting the Qualitative Research Agenda in Social Studies Education." Paper presented at the annual meeting of the National Council for the Social Studies, Washington, DC.

Tucker, Jan L., and Howard D. Mehlinger, eds. 1979. *Social Studies in Other Nations.* Washington, DC: National Council for the Social Studies.

Tyson-Bernstein, Harriet. 1988. *A Conspiracy of Good Intentions.* Washington, DC: Council for Basic Education.

U.S. Office of Educational Research and Improvement. 1988. *Youth Indicators 1988: Trends in the Well-Being of American Youth.* Washington, DC: U.S. Department of Education.

Wallen, Norman E., and Jack R. Fraenkel. 1988. An analysis of social studies research over an eight year period. *Theory and Research in Social Education* 16(Winter): 1–22.

White, Jane J. 1985. "What Works for Teachers: A Review of Ethnographic Research Studies as They Inform Issues of Social Studies Curriculum and Instruction." In *Review of Research in Social Studies Education: 1976–1983, Bulletin 75*, edited by William B. Stanley, 215–307. Washington, DC: National Council for the Social Studies.

Wilcox, K. 1982. "Differential Socialization in the Classroom: Implications for Equal Opportunity." In *Doing the Ethnography of Schooling: Educational Anthropology in Action*, edited by George Spindler, 268–309. New York: Holt, Rinehart and Winston.

Wiley, Karen B. 1977. *The Status of Pre-College Science, Mathematics, and Social Science Education: 1955–1975*. Washington, DC: National Science Foundation.

ω 30 ω

RESEARCH IN FOREIGN LANGUAGE CURRICULUM

Myriam Met
MONTGOMERY COUNTY PUBLIC SCHOOLS

Vicki Galloway
GEORGIA INSTITUTE OF TECHNOLOGY

Significant changes in the role of foreign language instruction in our schools, and in the ways the profession views foreign language teaching and learning, have shaped, and continue to shape, curriculum. Since the late 1950s, the debate has continued about why students should learn a foreign language, what they should learn, how they should learn it, how we can assess foreign language learning, and the future directions of this field. Both theory and research, and occasionally a lack of either or both, have influenced the debate. In this chapter we will examine these critical questions from the viewpoint of curriculum.

WHY SHOULD STUDENTS LEARN A FOREIGN LANGUAGE?

Reasons offered for foreign language learning reflect the political, social, and economic realities of the times. These forces influence the perceived needs for learning other languages, the content of the curriculum, and delivery systems.

A Historical Perspective

Foreign language education is both a young and an old profession. Since ancient times the need has existed for people of different languages to communicate. Most often this need was met through direct interaction between speakers of these languages. Direct instruction in languages became an imperative as vernacular forms of Latin evolved in the Middle Ages. The need to read and write classical Latin, the language in which both scholarly and religious works were written, required students to learn a language other than their own. Through much of modern times, formal study of additional languages was limited to learning classical languages as an avenue to reading the literature of ancient Greece and Rome.

In the United States, the foreign language profession has its earliest roots in the early 20th century. Although Latin and Greek predominated, instruction in other languages was certainly available in schools. (For example, the American Association of Teachers of Spanish and Portuguese was founded in 1917.) Classical languages were taught to provide students with access to literature. This purpose was directly related to instructional delivery. Students learned to read languages and occasionally to write in them. Little, if any, attention was paid to developing competence in aural/oral communication.

The launching of Sputnik in the late 1950s stirred the nation to action. Recognizing the Soviet educational advantage in mathematics, science, and foreign languages, the U.S. government actively intervened in promoting foreign language study. In this national drive to improve the learning of foreign languages, purpose was tied to curriculum: Students were to learn to listen, speak, read, and write other languages. Enrollments in Latin declined as modern foreign languages appeared to address the national need more effectively.

As anxieties about the supremacy of the United States

subsided in the late 1960s, so too did views of the role of foreign languages in the total school curriculum. The period that followed saw a massive restructuring of course offerings in both secondary and postsecondary institutions as the cry for "relevance" in course offerings overwhelmed the voices calling for a humanistic, liberal arts education. Foreign language skills, now deemed irrelevant to the needs of the young, were quietly dropped from many postsecondary entrance or exit requirements. Issues of what students should learn, and appropriate related instruction, became increasingly unclear as the purposes of language study became less well defined. Curriculum in foreign language courses drifted in a sea of conflicting views of language learning and effective language teaching (issues that will be examined in greater detail in the next section).

In 1979, the report of the President's Commission on Foreign Languages and International Studies refocused attention on the need for a language-competent America. Highlighting the serious communicative disadvantages our nation faced in global politics, diplomacy, and economics, the Commission called for vigorous action to address the critical needs faced in these arenas.

The Commission's call for foreign language instruction to enable Americans to communicate effectively with other peoples and nations had marked implications for curriculum developers. Curriculum would need to provide for the development of oral and written communicative abilities and ensure that students were competent to communicate in culturally sensitive and appropriate ways. Since communication implies both receptive and productive skills, curriculum would need to enable learners to understand oral and written communications within a cultural context and to produce oral and written communications that were linguistically and culturally appropriate. The rationale for language learning—effective participation in a globally interdependent world—was clearly tied to the linguistic and cultural contents of the curriculum. As we will see in the next section, there has been a significant impact on theory and practice.

In the 1980s economic competitiveness emerged as a major force in molding educational advances and reforms. A renewed emphasis on foreign language competence stemmed directly from concerns about our nation's ability to compete in a global economy. Competitiveness again motivated many educators to examine foreign language curricula in light of the purposes to which learners will put their skills.

Why Learn Foreign Languages in the 1990s?

A more balanced view of the rationale for foreign language in the total curriculum prevails today. This view incorporates geopolitical, domestic, and individual motivations for Americans to learn other languages (for a fuller discussion, see Met 1989b).

For the 1990s economic competitiveness will continue to be a prime factor in the renewed interest in foreign language education. Concerns about America's ability to compete in international markets are highlighted by reports of the inability of business to communicate effectively with potential clients and collaborators abroad. Calls for improved foreign language education have come from a variety of political groups, including the National Governors' Association (1989), the Southern Governors' Association (1986), and commissions on the reform of education. Unlike many other countries that regularly introduce foreign languages early in the school program and usually require a long sequence of foreign language study for graduation, the United States has relatively low foreign language enrollments and minimal graduation requirements. As a result, while other countries can easily participate in trade negotiations and collaborative trade agreements, Americans must rely on the awkward process of interpretation and translation. Further, American students display an insular view of other cultures and countries because they have little exposure to the customs, traditions, history, geography, and contributions of other cultures. Such ignorance only reinforces Americans' difficulties in competing in the world marketplace.

The Governors' reports note that diplomacy and politics are other arenas in which the United States must effectively participate. The number of diplomats and other foreign service personnel stationed abroad who are competent enough in other languages to sustain high-level discussions is low. Relying on interpretation or translation is, as one former diplomat reported, "like hacking one's way through a forest with a feather" (Evans, as cited in Peter 1977, 121). Worse still, the assumption made by some Americans that discussions and negotiations will be carried out in English is often interpreted by both allies and antagonists as blatant cultural arrogance.

Sociocultural diversity in the United States affects both the languages students learn and the curriculum to teach them. Surveys of foreign language enrollments in the last decade have reflected a steady increase in the number of students studying Spanish, for example. Curriculum is changing to reflect the real-life applications to which students plan to put their language into practice.

While all the reasons for studying foreign languages examined above have utilitarian applications, perhaps an even more convincing rationale from the educator's perspective is that foreign language study contributes to the cognitive, academic, and humanistic goals of the overall educational program. Research indicates that students who take a foreign language demonstrate enhanced cognitive functioning in the areas of divergent thinking, cognitive flexibility, and metalinguistic awareness (Ben Zeev 1977; Hakuta 1984; Landry 1974). Similarly, several studies of elementary school students who took a foreign language have shown that such students make greater gains on standardized tests of reading/language arts and, on occasion, mathematics than those who do not. (These studies will be discussed in greater detail later in this chapter). Secondary students who take a foreign language attain higher scores on the verbal section of the Scholastic Aptitude Test (SAT) than those who do not; the longer the sequence of foreign language study, the stronger the relationship with increased SAT scores. Indeed, 5 years of foreign language study has been shown to be associated with higher verbal SAT scores than 5 years of any other academic subject in the secondary curriculum (Cooper 1987).

Foreign languages have long been considered an integral part of a liberal arts education. Recently, this role has been reaffirmed in the position paper issued by the National Endowment for the Humanities, *American Memory* (Cheney 1987). Knowledge of other languages and cultures gives students direct access to the historical and aesthetic contributions of others. Appreciation of world literature is enhanced when reading is unfiltered by translations or interpretations. Access to the arts, such as theater or opera, is increased when students know the language in which the work is performed. Similarly, appreciation of art is increased when students understand the cultural and historical context in which it was produced. And foreign language study can contribute significantly to students' knowledge of world history and geography. Lastly, through such study, students gain insights into the factors that have shaped how we speak, think, behave, and live today.

These personal benefits of foreign language learning that accrue to students may have different implications for curriculum development and instruction than do clearly utilitarian reasons for studying languages. It may be possible for students to attain such benefits solely through the development of receptive skills (i.e., listening and reading) and cultural knowledge. Research has not provided clear answers on which components of language instruction contribute most to the cognitive or academic benefits observed. In contrast, program planners and students themselves may ascertain which aspects of language learning may most closely relate to the humanistic goals of cultural/aesthetic appreciation.

WHERE ARE FOREIGN LANGUAGES STUDIED?

As noted above, the 1979 report of the President's Commission on Foreign Languages and International Studies noted that Americans' lack of competence in foreign languages was scandalous and that the situation was unlikely to improve. The Commission called for a number of initiatives to remedy this alarming state of affairs. In the years that followed, a significant number of reports on the state of American education in general called for expanded and improved foreign language instruction in the schools and included specific recommendations that foreign language instruction be introduced at the elementary school level.

The National Commission on Excellence in Education (1983) highlighted the importance of foreign language study in its report *A Nation at Risk*, noting that it "introduces students to non-English speaking cultures, heightens awareness and comprehension of one's native tongue, and serves the Nation's needs in commerce, diplomacy, defense and education" (21). This attitude was echoed in the report of the Task Force of the Twentieth Century Fund, *Making the Grade* (Peterson 1983), which states that "every American public school student should have the opportunity to acquire proficiency in a second language" (12) and also by the report of the Carnegie Foundation for the Advancement of Teaching, *High School: A Report on Secondary Education in America* (Boyer 1983), which stated that "all students should not only 'learn about' a foreign language, but be proficient in its use" (100).

The reports recognized that the current status of foreign language instruction was inadequate to accomplish those aims. *A Nation at Risk* recommended that foreign language study begin at the elementary school level. The recommendations of the Carnegie Foundation were similar: Foreign language study should begin long before high school, preferably before fourth grade, and it should be sustained. The National Advisory Board on International Education Programs (1983) agreed, recommending that students have the opportunity to begin a foreign language at the earliest possible years. It further recommended a review of curriculum requirements at each educational level.

The period from early 1980 through 1990 saw response to such calls. Foreign language initiatives in a number of states began to radically change the picture of foreign language instruction. Draper (1989) reports that 16 states have some form of secondary school foreign language requirement, and three mandate foreign language instruction in grades K–8. Perhaps the most sweeping of these initiatives has been in New York, where all schools have been required to make foreign language instruction available in grades 7–12 since 1988. In addition, beginning in 1991 students graduating from high school in New York State are required to complete one unit of foreign language prior to grade 9; in 1994 the requirement will be two units (a unit is equivalent to at least 3 hours per week of instruction). New York also implemented high school graduation requirements that differ according to the diploma sought and has initiated a proficiency examination in the skills of listening, speaking, reading, and writing. In another broad stroke, the state of North Carolina has mandated that by 1993 all students in grades K–5 must be studying a foreign language. Both New York and North Carolina have supported these initiatives with additional funding. In November 1989, the Arizona State Board of Education voted to require foreign language instruction in grades 1–8, with programs to be fully in place by 1998.

Other states have demonstrated support for foreign language instruction as well. Some have imposed foreign language requirements for certain types of diplomas: Nebraska requires 2 years for a scholar's diploma, and Virginia requires 2 years of two foreign languages, or 3 years of a single foreign language, for its college-bound students. In 1986 the Tennessee legislature established the Foreign Language Institute to meet the needs of the foreign language community. The Florida legislature has established the Office of International Education and a Commission on International Education, among other agencies, to improve the teaching and learning of foreign languages and international studies. The California International Studies project was initiated by legislative action in 1986 to establish resource centers that focus on international education. Several of the nine resource centers emphasize foreign language learning. Georgia has revised teacher certification standards to expand the range of grades teachers are qualified to teach—from grades 7–12 to K–12—in anticipation of initiation and expansion of elementary school foreign language programs. And the Texas legislature has included in its long-range plans consideration of a K–12 foreign language initiative.

Requirements for entry into or exit from postsecondary institutions are increasing. Although only one in six institutions requires foreign language credits for entrance, two thirds require such credits for graduation. Entrance requirements, however, are increasing (American Council on the Teaching of Foreign Languages 1987b). For example, the California State University system has required 2 years of foreign language study beginning with students entering in the 1988–1989 academic year. By 1991 the University of Minnesota will require 2 years of high school foreign language study; the University of Maryland will require 1 year in 1991 and 2 years by 1992.

Reflecting the increased calls for foreign language study and perhaps increased requirements by postsecondary institutions, enrollments in secondary school foreign language courses have been steadily increasing since the early 1980s. There has also been explosive growth at the elementary school level. These trends will be discussed below.

Foreign Languages in the Secondary Schools

In 1915, 36 percent of high school students took a foreign language; in 1980, only 15 percent did. In 1985, for the first time since 1915, enrollments in modern foreign language courses (which exclude Latin and ancient Greek) once again began to approach the 1915 levels.

A 1987 survey of secondary school foreign language programs conducted by the Center for Applied Linguistics (Rhodes and Oxford 1988) found that 87 percent of secondary schools offer students the opportunity to study a foreign language. While 95 percent of high schools offered foreign language courses, only 72 percent of junior high/middle schools did.

Courses in secondary schools showed relative conformity to a national program model: Almost all secondary modern foreign language courses meet approximately one period daily. In some junior high/middle schools foreign language classes meet on alternate days, while a few secondary schools offer intensive language classes that meet for more than one instructional period daily. Most schools surveyed indicated that they offer instruction in the four common foreign language skill areas (listening, speaking, reading, and writing). Approximately 20 percent of the schools surveyed offer an "exploratory" language course. This course provides students with an introduction to language study and exposure to two or more languages. It is a nonsequential course and often lays the foundation for more in-depth study of a single foreign language in subsequent years. Most exploratory courses are of short duration (e.g., 6 weeks to 1 year). Forty-four percent of them are found at the junior high/middle school level.

At the other end of the foreign language continuum are advanced placement, honors, and accelerated courses. The 1987 survey results showed that 20 percent of private secondary schools and 10 percent of public secondary schools offered advanced placement foreign language courses; 19 percent of the private schools and 10 percent of the public schools offered honors or accelerated foreign language courses. Two percent of all U.S. secondary schools surveyed reported offering a "conversation only" foreign language course.

Enrollments in these secondary course offerings have significantly increased since the late 1970s. Surveys of public secondary school enrollments conducted by the American Council on the Teaching of Foreign Languages (ACTFL) reflect the waxing, waning, and renewed vigor of foreign language enrollments (American Council on the Teaching of Foreign Languages 1984; Dandonoli 1987). While secondary school foreign language enrollments in the post–Sputnik era were relatively strong (32.2 percent), by 1978 this figure had dropped to 17.8 percent. Four years later, in 1982, only a very modest increase, 19 percent, was found in the survey. By 1985 (the latest year for which the ACTFL data are available), secondary school foreign language enrollments had climbed to 24.8 percent.

The figures above mask significant increases in high school enrollments. Since, as noted above, over one fourth of junior high/middle schools do not offer foreign language courses, junior high/middle school data should be separated from those of high schools. This separation reveals that high school foreign language enrollments increased from 23 percent in 1982 to 32.3 percent in 1985.

Additional data regarding foreign language enrollments is furnished by the Educational Testing Service's (ETS) 1989 report, *What Americans Study*. This study found that 1982 high school graduates took an average of 1.05 years of foreign language; 1987 graduates took 1.47 years. Perhaps even more interesting are the demographic data found in the ETS study: Significant differences in foreign language enrollments were found by race/ethnicity and level of parental education. Eleventh graders who took 2 years or more of a foreign language were more likely to come from homes in which parents had a postsecondary education (38.8 percent) than students whose parents were high school graduates (19.2 percent) or had not graduated from high school (14.6 percent). Conversely, students who took one semester or less of foreign language in high school came from homes in which parents had not graduated from high school (65.6 percent) or had had no postsecondary education (58.1 percent). These data are supported by similar patterns of enrollment by eighth graders: 27.6 percent of students whose parents had had postsecondary education were taking a foreign language compared with 13.8 percent of eighth graders whose parents were high school graduates and 14.3 percent of those whose parents were not.

Racial and ethnic patterns were also revealed by the ETS (1989) data. Hispanic students were more likely to take two years or more of a foreign language (32.6 percent) than white (29.8 percent) or black students (22.6 percent). Black students were most likely to take one semester or less of a foreign language (55.2 percent) versus white (45 percent) or Hispanic (40.1 percent) students.

The languages studied by secondary students have not changed substantially over the last decades, although there have been some fluctuations in which languages are most frequently learned. In the ACTFL 1985 survey, Spanish accounted for 57.8 percent of all secondary foreign language enrollments and French for 28 percent. In ACTFL's 1982 survey, these figures were 54 percent and 30 percent, respectively. In both surveys, German (7.5 percent), Latin (4.2 percent), and Italian (1.3 percent) accounted for almost all of the remaining enrollments. Although enrollments in Russian, Chinese, Japanese, Arabic, and other less commonly taught languages rose by 8,000 students from 1982 to 1985, in both surveys these languages accounted for less than 1 percent of all foreign language enrollments.

Foreign Languages in the Elementary Schools

Programs of foreign language instruction in the elementary schools were abundant in the post–Sputnik era. A variety of factors contributed to their near-demise by the early 1970s (see below for further discussion of this issue). Results of a 1987 survey by the Center for Applied Linguistics (Rhodes and Oxford 1988) reveal that approximately one in five elementary schools offered students the opportunity to study a foreign language (34 percent of private schools and 17 percent of public schools). Of those elementary schools offering foreign language, only 42 percent report that at least half of their students are actually enrolled. Again, the data indicate that more private than public schools are enrolling at least half of their students in foreign languages (67 percent of private schools offering such study compared with 24 percent of public schools).

Some of the elementary school programs are magnet programs or schools, specifically intended to attract a racially diverse population; others are local school or school district programs. Few, if any, of these language programs screen students for ability or achievement. Thus, unlike secondary programs, which have tended to attract the college-bound student, elementary school programs include a broad spectrum of students. Although research is not extensive on the foreign language achievement of students in elementary school foreign language programs, extant studies indicate that students of all ability and achievement levels can be successful foreign language learners (Andrade, Kretschmer, and Kretschmer 1989; Curtain and Pesola 1988; Holobow, Genesee, and Lambert 1987a, 1987b; Holobow, Genesee, Lambert, and Chartrand 1988; Holobow, Genesee, Lambert, Gastright, and Met 1987).

Programs of foreign language instruction in the elementary schools may differ substantially from one another in characteristics such as goals and objectives, time allocated to foreign language study, and years of study. In 1987, 86 percent of elementary school foreign language programs provided students with exposure to another language or culture; only 14 percent had some degree of language proficiency as their goal. Thus, only 3 percent of all elementary schools in the United States (i.e., 14 percent of the 22 percent offering languages) provide their students with the opportunity to gain some measure of usable language skill. The various program models and their characteristics are discussed below.

Elementary school foreign language program models range over a continuum of time and intensity. Although there are overlapping features of these program models, they are most frequently described as FLEX, FLES, and immersion (Curtain and Pesola 1988; Met 1985; Met et al. 1983; Schinke-Llano 1986).

FLEX is an acronym that stands for foreign language experience, or exploratory. In elementary schools, it is generally a course of relatively short duration (from several weeks to one year) that meets from 15 to 60 minutes weekly. The goals of FLEX programs are primarily cultural: Students are exposed to one or more other languages and their cultures. Given the brief duration of most FLEX programs, it is not surprising that they have limited language goals. Most educators view the role of FLEX programs as an initiation to foreign language study and its purpose to motivate students to pursue more in-depth study of foreign language. While FLEX programs may be found at any grade level, they are most frequently introduced in the upper elementary grades or in the middle school. Middle school exploratory programs familiarize students with foreign language learning and, through exploration of two or more foreign languages, provide students with a basis for making better informed choices of which language to study later. Although FLEX programs constitute approximately 41 percent of all elementary school foreign language programs (Rhodes and Oxford 1988), little research on their efficacy or long-term results is available.

FLES (foreign language in the elementary school) is a term that covers a broad program model. In FLES, foreign language is taught for a designated period of time during the school day. FLES programs begin at any grade in the elementary school and are usually hierarchical and sequential. Thus, students who begin foreign language study in kindergarten are likely to continue through the elementary grades. FLES classes usually meet from two to five times weekly for 15 to 70 minutes per day. In contrast to FLEX programs, FLES programs have more ambitious language objectives. Although they stress aural/oral skills, most FLES programs also provide some instruction in reading and writing. Like FLEX, FLES objectives include a cultural component.

Although FLES was prevalent in the 1960s and presently accounts for approximately 45 percent of all elementary school foreign language programs, research on the relative benefits of specific program variables is sorely lacking. Little clear evidence exists to indicate the optimum number of minutes per week of instruction or to support programmatic choices between, for example, three 20-minute sessions per week as opposed to two 30-minute sessions. Similarly, research has yet to answer questions related to the interaction among such variables such as program design, learner characteristics, teacher characteristics, and curriculum in relation to the achievement of program objectives (Met and Rhodes 1990).

Foreign language immersion is a program in which students acquire foreign language skills by learning at least half of their school curriculum through the medium of a foreign language. In total immersion, the entire school day (with the occasional exception of art, music, physical education, and library skills) is conducted in the foreign language. Beginning in second grade (although in some schools, third or fifth grade) students are instructed in reading and language arts in English. In most total immersion programs, 20 to 50 percent of the day is in English by grades 5 or 6. In partial immersion, the regular school curriculum is taught in the foreign language for half the school day; the remainder of the day is taught in English. While reading and language arts are always taught in English, the choice of which subjects are taught in the foreign language varies. Although the number of immersion programs grows annually, immersion accounts for only 2 percent of all elementary school foreign language programs in the United States.

Interest in the immersion model was sparked by the landmark study conducted in St. Lambert, Canada (Lambert and Tucker 1972). Since the program's inception in 1965, immersion has become widespread throughout Canada. Although the St. Lambert program was a total immersion program, numerous variations have been designed since. Canada now has middle immersion programs (for students entering at grade 4) and late immersion programs (beginning at grade 6, 7, or even 9). Immersion programs in the United States are almost exclusively early immersion. And while most programs in Canada are total immersion, in the United States there are a large number of partial immersion programs.

Of all the programs of foreign language instruction in North American schools, perhaps none has been as thoroughly researched and its results as well documented as immersion. Numerous studies of the English and foreign language development of immersion students have been conducted; indeed, there are several summaries of this research (Genesee 1987; Swain and Lapkin 1982). These studies have been remarkable in the controlled experimental nature of their design and encouraging in their results. Consistently, studies of immersion have shown that students achieve high levels of foreign language proficiency at no detriment to the development of skills in their native language. When compared with native speakers of French, English-speaking students in immersion programs develop nativelike skills in understanding and reading French. Although their productive skills are quite impressive, immersion students' skills in speaking and writing do not approximate native speaker norms, particularly in the area of grammatical accuracy. Both the cause and remediation of this situation have been the subject of considerable debate in Canada, with some suggesting immersion be abandoned (Hammerly 1987) and most others exploring ways in which the grammatical skills of immersion students can be enhanced (Day and Shapson 1989; Harley and Swain 1984; Snow, Met, and Genesee 1989; Swain 1985).

Studies of the English language skills of immersion students have consistently shown that, in the long run, such students do as well (if not better) than do monolingually educated students. Although students in total immersion programs may initially score below their peers on measures of English language arts, this gap disappears when instruction in English language is formally introduced. In fact, the performance of immersion students on tests in English of reading and language arts skills is impressive when one considers that all their instruction has been in a foreign language. This relatively strong performance is hypothesized to be evidence that students are transferring concepts and processes acquired in one language to performance in the other.

While the results of Canadian immersion programs are extremely well documented, there are relatively few studies of programs in the United States. The results of these studies, however, are consistent with Canadian findings. Studies of the English language achievement of total immersion program students in California, Wisconsin, and Maryland (see Genesee 1987) have found that students achieve at or above expectation in English once English reading and language arts instruction is introduced.

As noted above, partial immersion programs in Canada are less common than in the United States. Further, the racial diversity that characterizes urban schools in this country differs from the ethnic diversity in Canadian schools. A longitudinal study of the partial French immersion program in Cincinnati, Ohio, sought to examine the efficacy of partial immersion in urban schools (Holobow, Genesee, and Lambert 1987a, 1987b; Holobow, Genesee, Lambert, and Chartrand 1988). Baseline data was collected on students during the early months of their kindergarten year. A control group of students in an English-only kindergarten was equated with the experimental group on the basis of entry level achievement (as measured by the Metropolitan Readiness Test), nonverbal reasoning ability (as measured by the Ravens Colored Progressive Matrices), and socioeconomic status and race. Students were followed annually through the end of the third grade. The study found that students in the partial immersion program, who were receiving half of their instruction in French, were performing at par with students instructed entirely in English. When students were compared on their achievement in science, the immersion students, who had received instruction in science exclusively in French, performed as well as those taught in English. The researchers concluded that not only were students transferring concepts and skills from French into English but that immersion was clearly not detrimental to students' development. This finding was of particular interest since both the experimental and control groups were racially mixed and composed of a diverse population in terms of academic achievement and ability. In the domain of French language proficiency the researchers found students had well-developed comprehension skills in French, but their oral proficiency lagged behind that of similar students in Canada. Nonetheless, the researchers concluded that partial immersion is an effective approach to foreign language instruction in urban schools in the United States.

Research has also examined the suitability of immersion for all students. In the Cincinnati study, the performance of the experimental group provides evidence that immersion is a suitable instructional program for all learners. There are conflicting results of studies conducted in Canada (Bruck 1978, 1982; Trites 1976, 1981, 1986; Wiss 1989). Trites suggests that students with learning disabilities are at a disadvantage in immersion programs; in contrast, Bruck indicates that students with learning disabilities fare no better or worse in immersion than in regular instructional programs. Wiss's position falls between the two. Further research is needed to provide more definitive answers to this question.

When Should Foreign Language Instruction Begin?

As we have seen in this section, the overwhelming preponderance of K–12 foreign language enrollment is at the secondary level. Indeed, while foreign language instruction in secondary and postsecondary schools has been common for most of this century, opportunities for early language learning have been much more limited. Today, only one in five elementary schools offers at least some of its students such an opportunity.

In the post–Sputnik era, elementary school foreign language programs flourished. The growth of these programs reflected the belief that the long-range attainment of foreign language objectives could be more feasibly attained through a long sequence of study. Unfortunately, the golden era of elementary school foreign language instruction quickly abated. This was due to a variety of factors, perhaps the most salient of which was that research evidence did not support the earlier belief that an early language learning would result in higher levels of foreign language attainment.

In retrospect, most advocates of elementary school foreign language instruction today recognize that an unfortunate constellation of variables made it virtually impossible for the programs of the late 1950s and 1960s to live up to expectations. While educators' beliefs in the advantages of an early start may have been well founded, school and classroom practices were not. For example, the supply of qualified teachers was extremely limited. Few elementary school foreign language teachers were trained specifically to work with young children. Most elementary school teachers had been reassigned from, or co-assigned to, secondary schools. Methodology between the two levels differed little. In addition, the development of age-appropriate instructional materials did not keep pace with the quick growth of programs in the post–Sputnik era. While a veritable explosion in first and second language acquisition research occurred after the heyday of these programs, it was too late to inform decisions about what should be taught and how. Perhaps the most significant factor that undermined the perceived value of early foreign language instruction was the lack of well-designed articulation between elementary and secondary instruction. A significant proportion of students who began foreign language in the elementary schools found themselves grouped with students who had had no prior foreign language instruction and thus were beginning all over again in the secondary schools. Little wonder, then, that the outcomes of elementary school foreign language programs failed to meet expectations.

In the 1980s there was once again growing interest in early language learning. As noted above, this interest, like that of the post–Sputnik era, stemmed from a chorus of voices concerned with the quality of our nation's education and with the implications of education for America's political and economic survival. Advocates of early foreign language instruction today recognize the lessons to be learned from both past successes and failures and are optimistic about the future of elementary school foreign language programs (Met and Rhodes 1990). These advocates note, for example, that there is a strong research base which supports notions of first and second language development in young children. In addition, the educational field was swept in the late 1980s by an interest in early childhood education. In particular, active professional debate on developmentally appropriate educational practices influences foreign language practices, so that one is no longer likely to find secondary methods and materials imported wholesale into elementary school foreign language classrooms. Major professional foreign language associations, each of which has clearly differentiated the specific needs of those who work in elementary schools, have developed guidelines for the preparation of teachers. Commercial publishers have begun to address the needs of foreign language instructional materials appropriate to younger learners. Networking groups of elementary school foreign language practitioners and advocates provide mutual support and opportunities for the exchange of information and noncommercial materials.

There certainly is abundant documentation to support the cognitive and academic benefits of second foreign language acquisition in childhood. Although in the first half of this century research on the relationship between bilingualism and intelligence did not support a strong positive relationship between these two variables, these early studies suffered from serious flaws and the biases of the researchers who sought to influence political or educational decisions (Hakuta 1986b). A landmark study by Peal and Lambert (1962) launched a series of studies that contradicted earlier ones. Peal and Lambert showed that balanced bilinguals (those who had well-developed skills in both languages) achieved higher scores on measures of verbal intelligence than did monolinguals. Studies by Ben Zeev (1977) and Hakuta (1984) have found advantages for bilingual children in the areas of metalinguistic awareness and mental flexibility. Hakuta (1986a) reports a number of studies that found a strong positive relationship between bilingualism and measures of cognitive ability and asserts that the data suggest a causal relationship between degree of bilingualism and enhanced cognitive functioning. Hakuta's findings have direct implications for foreign language instruction, since his data suggest that even at the earliest stages of bilingualism (i.e., prior to achieving full bilingualism) there is a positive effect on cognition. Thus, school programs in which students begin to acquire proficiency in a foreign language may directly result in improved thinking skills.

The cognitive benefits of foreign language learning in school settings have also been documented. Bamford and Mizokawa (1989) review a number of studies that link foreign language acquisition in school with measurable cognitive benefits. Their own study of young children in a Spanish immersion program found significant differences on a measure of nonverbal problem-solving skills favoring the foreign language students. Other studies comparing students in immersion programs with those in English-only instructional programs have reported similar results. Bruck, Lambert, and Tucker (1974) found that French immersion students outperformed controls on measures of cognitive flexibility. Landry's (1974) study of elementary school students in a FLES program found that sixth grade students who had taken a foreign language since first grade scored higher on a measure of divergent thinking than did a comparable group of non–foreign language students. More recently, Foster (1987) reported that the number of years of elementary school foreign language instruction were directly and positively associated with higher levels of cognitive and metacognitive processing.

The academic benefits of elementary school foreign language learning are also well documented. Although some studies in the 1960s failed to show any relationship between foreign language instruction and academic achievement, a number of studies have, indeed, found a positive relationship. A large-scale study of over 13,000 third, fourth, and fifth grade students in Louisiana (Rafferty 1986) showed that students who had taken a foreign language significantly outperformed those who had not on standardized tests of reading and mathematics. Garfinkel and Tabor (1987) studied the relationship between elementary school foreign language study and academic achievement in students who had taken a foreign language in grades 4 through 6. They found that the foreign language students significantly outperformed comparable students who had not taken a foreign language on a standardized test of reading. Garfinkel and Tabor also found that, within the foreign language cohort, students of average ability made greater gains in reading than students of above-average ability, pointing to the value of foreign language learning for all children.

A recent reanalysis of the longitudinal data on the long-term academic achievement of immersion students yielded similar findings to those of the FLES studies discussed earlier (Swain and Lapkin 1991). Canadian students who participated in immersion programs often outperformed control-group students educated in English-only settings. Within the immersion population itself, higher scores on measures of French language proficiency were associated with higher scores on measures of English achievement.

Additional reasons for introducing foreign language instruction in the elementary grades derive from the important goal of developing positive cross-cultural attitudes. Elementary school foreign language programs are more likely to achieve these goals for a variety of reasons. First, many of the cultural goals of such foreign language programs are consistent with those of the elementary school social studies curriculum; these goals and objectives can be achieved through collaboration and cooperation between foreign language and classroom teachers. For example, a fifth grade social studies unit on the explorers of the New World is the ideal time for exploring the contributions that speakers of the foreign language have made, and continue to make, to our language, our traditions, our history, and our daily lives.

While objectives in the elementary school foreign language and social studies curricula facilitate the development of positive cross-cultural attitudes, research supports the value of developing such attitudes as early as possible. Young children may be receptive to learning about and accepting other peoples and their cultures; emerging adolescents may be less so (Carpenter and Torney 1973; Lambert and Klineberg 1967; Torney 1979). Emerging adolescents value belonging to a group and conformity to group norms. They may be less likely to value differences between themselves and others and, therefore, less likely to identify with those of different cultures. Thus, achievement of the cross-cultural goals of foreign language programs may be more difficult to attain when foreign language study begins later. Further, research by Gardner and Lambert (1972) has shown a clear relationship between cultural attitudes and foreign language achievement. Integrative motivation (the desire to identify/integrate with a target group) is positively related to foreign language learning. Students who develop and maintain positive, integrative attitudes toward the target culture are also more likely to learn the language itself, thus strengthening arguments for introducing foreign language instruction in the elementary school.

Administrative considerations, rather than research findings, may also determine the most appropriate point at which to introduce foreign language in the elementary school. These considerations include curriculum development, teacher availability, program model, language selected, and articulation (Met 1985). These considerations also interact with one another.

An elementary school foreign language program must have a curriculum. When programs begin in kindergarten, school administrators must commit to a 6- (K–5) or 7- (K–6) year sequence of curriculum development; when programs begin in grade 3 or 4 the commitment is clearly of shorter duration. Further, the longer the elementary school sequence, the greater the impact will be on the secondary curriculum, requiring a restructuring of that curriculum as well. Since elementary school foreign language programs should be staffed by teachers qualified to work at this level, and since such teachers are in critically short supply, the duration of the program and the nature of the program model selected should include consideration of the availability of staff. Program models (FLEX, FLES, and immersion) each require different curricula, staffing levels, and provisions for articulation. Programs requiring a significant number of specially trained teachers and extensive instructional models (e.g., immersion) may be more challenging to implement in languages such as Russian, Chinese, or Japanese than in programs that demand fewer human and material resources. And programs with limited language goals (e.g., FLEX) pose fewer articulation problems at the secondary level than do those that aim to develop high levels of foreign language proficiency.

WHAT IS FOREIGN LANGUAGE LEARNING?

Any discussion of curriculum must hinge on a clear definition of what the nature of the discipline is. The content of the foreign language curriculum is defined by our answer to the question, What is foreign language learning? The various answers to this question throughout the last several decades have, in large part, determined the curricular and instructional focus in foreign language classrooms. Notions of the value, nature, and process of other language learning have derived not only from the fields of linguistics, psycholinguistics, and cognitive and social psychology but from broader sociopolitical, environmental, and educational trends. The questions, What is a foreign language? and What is foreign language learning? are centuries old and continue to be debated today with great fervor and intensity within the foreign language teaching profession. Any single summary analysis of this debate will, of necessity, result in a vast oversimplification of the issues, for global approaches to the argument may become reduced to simplistic dichotomies. Yet, in the broadest sense, the history of foreign language education has been characterized by two major responses to the question, What is foreign language learning?: (1) grammatical competence and (2) communicative competence. These labels do not constitute professional camps, however. Rather, within each response, and across responses, are ranges and varieties of notions that have become better defined and refined, especially throughout the past 3 decades. This section will provide a brief historical overview of the extremities of these responses and will conclude with a summary of how and how well these views have coalesced.

Language Learning as Grammatical Competence

According to Grittner (1990), one central fact about grammar is clear: It is the most persistent and durable element in the history of American foreign language teaching. Language, most foreign language educators would agree, involves grammar. But what is grammar? And what role does it play in teaching and learning the language?

During the first half of this century, the predominant view was that language was grammar rules. Perhaps the phrase most often used as a rationale for foreign language learning was "mental discipline." The intricacies of a linguistic system were widely acknowledged as difficult learnings, the realm of scholarly individuals for whom the mere exercise of analysis and memorization served a more universal aim of stretching and sharpening the mind. The title of one Spanish "basal" textbook in use at the turn of the century evidences this orientation by its very title: *Castillian Grammar Founded on Philosophical Principles* (Pons y Argent 1850). Its Preface claims that "grammar is the primary science, by necessity," and among the pages of this little book are sections dealing with "simultaneous or coexistent imperfect preterit" and "the conjunctive relative adjective or pronoun of final denomination." Foreign language learning of this day was indeed heady stuff.

The foreign language teaching profession's more vivid and recordable history begins in the 1950s in a national temper of isolationism, conservatism, and staunch patriotism. In this era, foreign language study was one of the most difficult areas to justify in the school curriculum, where it derived its value from its ability to illuminate English syntax and vocabulary. Classroom and textbook fare consisted primarily of verb conjugation, sentence diagramming, verbatim passage translation, and memorization of alphabetized vocabulary lists. Grammar rules were unabashedly the topic of classroom discussion, and language learning was viewed as the accumulation of expertise in grammatical analysis. Because this was the focus, there was no need to deal with the language in any semblance of real-life context. Models of the language that gave any indication as to how these grammar pieces fit together were, in most cases, limited to the phrase or sentence level. Developing the ability to use the language for anything other than reading had been pronounced an unrealistic and nonproductive pursuit by some and as anti-intellectual activity by others (Galloway 1983b). Grammar rules were what teachers knew and knew well, and reading, when it did not serve as mere grist for grammar analysis, had as its justification the development of the ability to translate literature.

As noted earlier, the fifties, sixties, and early seventies heralded a new orientation in language classrooms that focused curriculum on an ability to use, that is, to speak, other languages. A new methodology, one adapted from the Army Specialized Training Programs and based on the theories of structural linguistics and behaviorist psychology, predominated. Through this approach, which consisted of complex pattern drills, repetition, and dialog memorization, it was expected that students would acquire a stock of representative structural patterns and lexical items, which, if fully practiced, would enable them to create analogs for their own self-expression. Yet, what teachers found was that grammar drill and dialog memorization yielded the ability to do grammar drill and dialog recitation. The method seemed to foster splendidly deceptive examples of splinter learning in these practiced-to-perfection performances. Grittner (1990) summarizes the difference between the grammar translation view and this so-called audiolingual approach: It was more important to "behave" grammatically than to be able to give rules about the language. However, the aim was still grammatical competence, often without an abundance of concern for meaning. The analog of conditioned correctness, conditioned incorrectness, was much to be feared. "Error, like sin, " said Brooks, "is to be avoided" (1960, 41). Language was viewed as a structurally tight and restricted system whose use as a tool depended on appropriateness of stimulus-response behavior. Language learning was viewed as imitation and repetition of correct models and the formation of good grammatical habits through "overlearning."

Although the "method" had left many former advocates disillusioned by the early seventies, the goal of grammatical competence was firmly embedded. Large-scale "methods comparison" studies failed to show any superiority of one method over another (Long 1983), but what teachers intuited and took from use of this method was the notion that practice in *using* (hearing and speaking) the grammar of the language (rather than mere knowledge of its rules) was in some way an important factor in language learning. Grammar had *function*.

Language as Communicative Competence

Disillusionment with packaged methodologies created a desire for renewed focus on goals. In the early 1970s, linguists such as Hymes (1972) and Campbell and Wales (1970) were proposing a broadening of the framework of language. Grammatical competence, they said, is but one component of what a native speaker possesses—language is rules of use as well as notions of sociolinguistic and pragmatic appropriateness. What the native speaker possesses is, in short, "communicative competence." Drawing from this work, Savignon (1972), in one of the most well-known studies of the past two decades, defined "communicative competence" as "the ability to function in a truly communicative setting—that is, in a dynamic exchange in which linguistic competence must adapt itself to the total informational input, both linguistic and paralinguistic, of one or more interlocutors" (8). Thus, the notion of language was significantly expanded to include not only its rules but also its function, context, meaning, humanness, verbal and nonverbal forms, and dynamic, rather than stimulus-response, nature.

While Savignon did not propose a "method" for the goal of communicative competence, her study did describe various classroom techniques designed to help students take risks, create with the language, and use the language for personal expression. And her instrument for comparing the degree of communicative competence achieved by experimental and control groups reflected a somewhat revolutionary notion for the times: Not only was grammatical (or linguistic) accuracy only one criterion in the total assessment but this grammatical accuracy was not broken down into discrete errors; it was summarized as "quality of communication." Interestingly enough, the dividing line in assessment of communicative competence was the question, Is the student communicating?

The notion of communicative competence as being composed of more than just linguistic, or grammatical, competence was, given the tenor of the times, interpreted by many as a rejection of linguistic competence. Added to this was the fact that teachers were being encouraged to place errors in the proper perspective: If students are going to create with the language, errors are going to occur, but these errors, just as in first language acquisition, are not an irrevocable part of the student's linguistic repertoire. The latter notion was in direct opposition to the almost paranoid aversion to error that had characterized the only real training most teachers had ever received: training in audiolingual methodology. As Omaggio (1986) summarizes:

> For a period of years in the early to middle part of the decade, communicative competence became synonymous, in the minds of some researchers and practitioners, with a disregard for grammatical accuracy, and second language learners were considered communicatively competent if they got their meaning across to a listener, even if their grammatical accuracy was relatively low. (2)

"Communicative competence" was a refreshing notion to many; it was a frightening notion to many others; it was misunderstood by most, advocates and adversaries alike, because it was vaguely defined. Later work, most notably that of Canale and Swain (1980), brought to the fore a more refined view of communicative competence, one that included, but was not limited to, grammatical or linguistic competence. This model proposed an integrative view of four components: grammatical competence, sociolinguistic competence, discourse competence, and strategic competence.

But determining the degree to which a person was communicatively competent was, admittedly, a dilemma. Throughout the seventies the notion of communicative competence was explored and debated. Was it possible to tell whether one person was more communicatively competent than another? Several studies examined the extent to which such things as grammatical inaccuracies, pronunciation flaws, or misuse of vocabulary interfered with communicative efforts from a native speaker perspective. The conclusion reached by the end of the 1970s is perhaps best summarized by Higgs and Clifford (1982): "A student cannot merely be declared competent in communication. The functions that he is competent to express must be specified. The degree of proficiency required to survive as a tourist is not the same as that required to negotiate treaties" (60).

At the threshold of the 1980s, several events were occurring that made the time propitious to begin to move toward professional consensus regarding the notion of communicative competence. Efforts by the Council of Europe (Van Ek and Alexander 1975) focused on describing language not merely in discrete grammatical inventory terms but in terms of functions and notions. A series of language-specific publications brought to the fore the concept of a "threshold level" in language use; that is, a view of basic transactional competence as defined by abilities to (1) perform certain functions in the language, such as giving and getting directions, asking favors, expressing desire, expressing like and dislike, and so on; (2) express certain notions in the language, such as time and space; and (3) interact in certain entry-level social situations. While the publications themselves, as inventories, suggested no particular syllabus, the approach to viewing language was enlightening. Not only was the traditional grammar element cast in terms of the myriad functions to which it contributes in language use but communicative functions were displayed as having myriad formal (grammatical) realizations.

Assessing Language Proficiency

Occurring at the same time in the United States was an event of profound significance to the foreign language teaching profession—the formation of the Commission on Foreign Language and International Studies. In the Commission's final report, *Strength Through Wisdom* (1979), appeared a series of recommendations, two of which directly charged foreign language educators with a complex professional agenda:

- Institutions and, where appropriate, state educational systems, should be encouraged to adopt nationally recognized performance or proficiency standards.
- Funding should be secured for the revision and redevelopment of tests for the measurement of proficiencies in the four language skills.

Initial response to this charge began with a borrowing from the government language schools—this time the Foreign Service Institute (FSI) and its well-known oral proficiency scale on which an individual's performance was gauged by means of a face-to-face interview. This scale, composed of 11 nonequidistant levels, had been known to foreign language educators for decades; yet, academic application had been hampered by the facts that (1) government needs demanded a scale that would distinguish between levels of native and near-native speaker competence, and (2) the scale did not discriminate clearly at the lower levels of proficiency where language acquisition progress could be seen by beginning and intermediate classroom learners.

A joint effort by the Educational Testing Service (ETS) and the American Council on the Teaching of Foreign Languages (ACTFL) resulted in an academic version of this scale with nine levels of "proficiency." This scale represented an expansion of the lower end of the FSI scale and a collapsing of the upper levels (the levels of native speaker competence). The level descriptions were expanded to create fuller understanding of the performance parameters of each level. A subsequent project of the ACTFL marshalled the knowledge and expertise of professionals in various facets of language education to produce generic and language-specific scales (for French, German, and Spanish) in the other skill areas as well: listening, reading, writing, and culture. These "Proficiency Guidelines" were published in provisional form in 1982 and subsequently revised in 1986. Accompanying their dissemination was a major effort on the part of ACTFL to (1) train teachers to conduct the oral interview with adult learners and (2) institute a nationwide tester certification system.

The impact of these guidelines was both strong and immediate, and, by the mid-1980s, the words "proficiency movement" rang from every professional conference. There were a number of reasons for the popularity of the guidelines. For one, the speaking guidelines and oral interview procedure had provided, for the first time, a curriculum-free progression to the notion of communicative ability that, for the trained tester, allowed for more discriminating measurement of an individual's global ability to use the spoken language, not in relation to classroom peers but, rather, on the basis of what were deemed to be more real-life criteria. The guidelines responded to the questions raised earlier regarding definitional problems with the notion of communicative competence, for each level of the proficiency progression established language user profiles in terms of ranges of (1) tasks or functions that could be performed—the why of language use; (2) topical or content parameters—the what of language use; (3) context spreadings from tourist-level situations to broader social and professional situations—the where of language; and (4) accuracy expectations—the how and how well of language—which focused not on discrete mistakes but on patterns of error and the notions of concept and partial and full control of the functioning of grammaticality. All of these components were seen as interacting at each range for infinite varieties of individual constellations.

Yet, the question of "to whom" in language use had not been adequately addressed. These speaking guidelines included no direct reference to sociolinguistic appropriateness. Rather, concerns for socially and culturally appropriate speech were indirectly measured only through the accuracy strain of the upper levels of proficiency, thereby severely overloading this component of the profiles. While a separate set of guidelines had been developed for culture and published in provisional form (American Council on the Teaching of Foreign Languages 1982), it was never revised. The orientation, as Allen notes (1985), was much too behavioristic, inconsonant with the global notion of proficiency conveyed by the guidelines in the other skills areas.

The popularity of the Proficiency Guidelines, however, has not meant blind and full acceptance. Attempts at developing an assessment criteria progression in each skill area, given the present knowledge base, must rest on professional consensus, but, as we shall see later, real professional consensus regarding language, language in use, and language learning is limited to only very broad global notions. The guidelines are currently undergoing construct validation (Dandanoli and Henning 1990). Yet, the difficulties in this endeavor are obvious, as they involve the separation of the construct from the instrument used to assess it—both, or either of which, may be invalid but resist separate investigative scrutiny.

The numerous discussions surrounding the existing Proficiency Guidelines defy adequate summary in this chapter. While they have represented some of the greatest debate of the decade, explication of the arguments posed demands a more in-depth presentation of the guidelines themselves, a task beyond the scope of this chapter. What is significant, however, in the discussion of "What Is Foreign Language Learning?" is a clarification of two points regarding the Proficiency Guidelines: (1) what they could not do and (2) what they could do.

What they could not do was meet all of the many and diverse needs of a profession starving for answers—answers about what is involved in language use, how people learn languages, and, especially, how best to teach languages. The guidelines are not a theory, nor are they a developmental hierarchy, nor are they a syllabus or curriculum framework, nor do they suggest an approach or "method" for the classroom. Even their use in assessment (which at this point is limited to the speaking skill) is restrictive in that they are not sensitive to measurement of small increments of learning.

What they could do was give language educators a notion of what people do when they use a language. The oral proficiency interview has elicited rich samplings of discourse from novice to near native language users. This has permitted the observation of apprentice users communicating, affording a glimpse of the myriad elements which come into play at the basal level. What the guidelines could do was begin to explore an identity to each of the skills areas—listening, speaking, reading, and writing—which previous classroom practice had displayed as simply different media for the practice of grammar. And what they could do, as well, was present a measurement system for language proficiency that defined a role for grammatical accuracy in communication.

Grammar in Communication and Communication in Grammar

Whereas early advocates of communicative competence were criticized for underestimating the role of accuracy, the proficiency movement has been cited for overemphasizing this aspect of communicative performance (Savignon 1983). A similar "form/meaning" debate rages (albeit with great civility) in the areas of curriculum and instruction. This debate concerns, once again, the most fundamental of issues—the nature and role of grammar in language and in language learning. The questions are not simple ones: What is accuracy? Is it grammatical correctness? If so, what is grammar? Is it rules? If so, what constitutes a rule? Where do rules come from and what role do they play in foreign language learning?

Perhaps the most profound realization throughout the past 50 years in foreign language teaching has been that of the complexity of language—in its system, in its use, in its acquisition, and in its user. Grammatical competence and communicative competence are hopelessly intertwined. As Canale and Swain note (1980), just as there are rules of grammar that would be useless without rules of language use, so there are rules of language use that would be useless without rules of grammar.

Classrooms of the past saw students memorizing and reciting "grammar rules," rules for "exceptions" and exceptions to the rules for exceptions (called "irregulars"). Today, with what we know about "rules," this would be quite an impossible task, for language and language use are seen as the formation, activation, and interaction of many kinds of rules. There are, it seems, rules in language and rules in learning.

Rules in Language

The notion of rules in language use is greatly expanded if we consider where, with whom, and how communication is carried out. There are, it seems, several governing systems.

1. Textbook Grammar Rules. For lack of a better label, these are what we might all recognize as "traditional" rules for grammatical structures (primarily morphemes): rules for adjective agreement, pluralization, pronoun placement, verb endings, and the like, that have arisen from the structural linguist's laboratory. This type of rule (often divorced from its usage) is what has traditionally been termed "grammar," and the ingestion of these rules (which often limited the view of language to the clausal level) are perhaps what has characterized classroom foreign language study throughout most of its history. These rules are derived basically from an English contrast perspective, so that those aspects targeted as rules for study constitute major points of difference between English and the particular foreign language. They have thus assumed both English language system awareness and English metalinguistic knowledge on the part of learners. In a sense, they have treated the foreign language as a hybrid of English, paradoxically assuming parallelism in their contrast (Galloway and Labarca 1990). A traditional textbook presentation of the present tense, for example, might have contrasted its formation to that of English, yet ignored the differences in its purpose, function, and usage in the language under study. An indirect object pronoun might have been treated in terms of its formation and placement, with the assumption that students would understand its English language function. Not only has this assumption proved false, but more important, it has ignored the target language function of this particular "grammatical structure."

The influence of the "communicative competence/proficiency" movement of the past several years has resulted in some changes in these textbook rules, if not in terms of reconceptualization of the grammar of the language, at least in terms of its "packaging." More so-called functional approaches to the grammar of the language have aimed at conveying not only formation and usage, but real-life use of particular structures. Thus, in many Spanish textbooks and classrooms, for example, lessons such as "the present subjunctive in nominative clauses" have been enhanced by the subtitle, "describing what you want or need people to do." This type of real-life function of the grammar has opened the door, albeit only slightly at present perhaps, to a notion of classroom language learning that displays the grammar not as a series of discrete blocks, but rather as the varied realizations of communicative purposes which expand in depth and complexity.

2. Discourse Rules. The present-day definition of rule is not limited, however, to the more traditional clausal or morpheme level treatment of grammar, but is concerned with how these connect structurally and propositionally. In other words, there are rules of discourse that concern one's ability as a listener, reader, speaker, and writer to use cohesion devices—to link and note linkage, to contrast and note contrast, to illustrate and note illustration, to exemplify and note exemplification—at a structural level. They also concern one's ability, as a speaker, reader, listener, and writer to relate and link ideas at a meaning level and to display coherence, continuity, and consistency in thought.

Recognition of these rule systems, which are only beginning to be addressed in classroom instruction and materials, means that the language presented and practiced in the classroom must, first of all, be authentic in its medium, for the discourse of the spoken word is not the same as the discourse of the written word. Traditional textbook materials have often presented a language that, in real life, would appear in neither oral nor written language use. Classrooms are beginning, as well, to focus on coherence and cohesion devices. In developing students' productive skills, this has meant stretching students beyond the sentence level drill and one-word response in interactive contexts that require use of such things as turn-taking, referencing, and exemplifying devices. In developing receptive skills, a focus on discourse features is fostering improved comprehension through attention to the structural and propositional organizing schemes of oral and written texts.

*3. **Pragmatic Rules***. Real-life communication also adheres roughly to certain situation-appropriate or pragmatic rules. Purposeful, functional use of language, both verbal and nonverbal, is governed by such things as topic; cultural conventions and connotations; social context parameters; transactional protocols; and relationships, roles, ages, and backgrounds of participants. What is said, when it is said, and how it is said will depend on considerations as to where and with whom, and these considerations cannot be adequately addressed without the "cultural context of language use."

Knowledge of pragmatic rules enables speakers to function effectively in a variety of communicative settings. Rules that govern turn-taking, for example, vary from language to language. While in English interrupting the speaker to state one's views is considered ill-mannered, it is a legitimate form of taking one's turn to speak in other languages. Similarly, "scripts" that govern routine communications, such as telephone conversations or greeting salesclerks in a store, are necessary for students to perform in both socioculturally and linguistically appropriate ways. While students may understand intuitively how to adjust their native language in accordance with their relationship to their conversation partner (e.g., classmate versus teacher versus parent versus younger sibling versus unknown adult other), such adjustments need to be explicitly learned in a foreign language. Indeed, it may not be possible to do more than sensitize students to the nature of such pragmatic rules and how they influence the ways in which native speakers interpret what they hear, given the limited amount of exposure most students have to foreign language learning and the extensive amount of time it takes to master such subtleties in a language one has learned.

*4. **Strategic Rules***. There are also governing systems of appropriateness in use of communication strategies, those behaviors applied when individuals' needs or task demands outstrip their linguistic (or sociolinguistic) capabilities. These rules inform the individual how to respond to the situation without shifting the topic or resorting to silence and include, in speaking, appropriate ways of circumlocuting, paraphrasing, approximating, clarifying, and self-correcting. In writing, such strategies involve proper use of dictionaries, simplification of thought, illustration, and exemplification. In reading and listening, strategic application involves informed guessing from available clues.

As can be seen from the above examples, the notion of accuracy in language is no longer confined to drill context observations of the use or misuse of verb endings. Present-day definitions of grammatical competence respond to linguistic behavior within the global system of communication in terms of precision, appropriateness, acceptability, and receptability.

Rules in Learning

While the concept of rule has been greatly expanded by the notion of language in use, the past 20 years have seen increasing attention given to defining another complex governing system—that of learning in process. Observations of language users at various stages of their development has led researchers to posit the notion of *interlanguage*. This theory holds that individuals pass through stages in language learning that are characterized by hybrid forms of language production and hybrid notions of the linguistic system. In other words, learners have personal rules, and these rules are both systematic and variable. How these rules are acquired is the subject of various theories of language acquisition.

Although many microtheories exist to account for specific phenomena in second language learning, there is at present no one universally accepted macrotheory with testable hypotheses that has the power to explain the process of foreign language proficiency development to the satisfaction of linguists, psychologists, and foreign language practitioners. Two theories are selected for discussion here for the insights they provide regarding the role, nature, and process of the concept of rule in adult second language acquisition.

Conscious and Subconscious Rule: The Monitor Model. Undoubtedly, the most ambitious and imaginative, albeit fiercely debated, macrotheory of the development of second language proficiency is that presented by Stephen Krashen's Monitor Model (Krashen 1981, 1982). This deductively formulated theory has as its core a number of assumptions from which five central hypotheses are derived. The first of these hypotheses poses a strong dichotomy in maintaining that there are two very distinct ways of developing second language competence: "learning," which Krashen defines as a conscious process with formal rules and feedback that results in knowing about the language; and "acquisition," which is a subconscious process, brought about through focus on meaning in interaction and much akin to the process used by children in acquiring their first language. Learners, Krashen contends, focus on form and rules for grammaticality; acquirers function on a "feel" for grammaticality. The first corollary of this hypothesis is a notion much debated by researchers and practitioners: Learning, Krashen contends, does not "turn into" acquisition. In other words, conscious rules do not turn into unconscious rules, and rule-governed behavior does not turn into "feel"-governed behavior.

Krashen's second hypothesis relegates the role of formal learning to the development of a mental editing device, or "monitor," which functions solely to make changes in the form of an utterance, after it has been produced by the acquired system. Thus, acquisition initiates the speaker's utterances and is responsible for fluency. The monitor performs a pre- or postproduction altering function. According to this hypothesis, individual differences in performance are explained by different types of monitor use: (1) monitor overusers (victims of grammar-only instruction) who are so concerned with the formal accuracy of their utterances that their fluency suffers; (2) monitor underusers, who are generally inattentive to form and thus produce speech that is fluent but flawed; and (3) optimal monitor users, who may not heavily invoke the monitor in speaking, but in writing and planned speech will attempt to raise their level of accuracy. Krashen's is a production-driven model—rules and formal learning are treated in terms of speaking and writing, not in terms of learnings in reading and listening. This is evident, as well, in his proposed criteria for use of the monitor, for in order for this monitor to function, three conditions must be met:

- Time to call the rule to surface. Since this is not usually available in real-life spoken communication, overemphasis on form, or grammatical correctness, will result in lack of fluency and inability to negotiate meaning due to inattention to communicative partner.
- Attention to correctness. An individual is concerned not only with what she is saying but how it is said.
- Knowledge of the rule. Not only do most students not learn all the rules they are exposed to but existing formal rules can describe only a fragment of what the language is.

Krashen's third hypothesis states that we acquire the rules of a language in predictable order, independently of the order in which rules are taught in language classes. This "natural order" is the acquisition process operating separately from learning or monitor use. At present, conflicting research both supports and contradicts this hypothesis.

A fourth hypothesis states that humans acquire language through natural developmental sequences in only one way—by receiving large amounts of what Krashen terms "comprehensible input," that is, by understanding what they hear (or read). Language growth occurs when input is just beyond the learner's present level of competence. Speech, then, cannot be taught directly but rather emerges as the result of acquisition. There is no need to teach the grammar of the language because it has been internalized via input that was understood.

A final hypothesis in Krashen's theory involves what is termed the "affective filter." Comprehensible input may not be used if there is a mental block that keeps the learner from profiting from it. A more precise definition of this mechanism is needed to allow for its study by researchers in terms of development and function.

One of the major problems with Krashen's theory, from a research standpoint, is that its imprecise terms and tenets make it difficult to test and research. Yet, it is probable that no other theory has had such an immediate, profound, and widespread effect on foreign language teaching in the United States. The reason for its popularity probably stems from the power and attractiveness of its metaphor. Language teachers and proficient language users sense the experiential "realness" of such notions as the monitor and the affective filter, they know the value of accessible input. Most likely it is the direction of Krashen's thought, more than the specific corollaries of his hypotheses, that educators find appealing: It reacts against the isolated study of the grammarian's rules; it focuses on the important role of comprehension in production and the "stretching" potential of listening and reading acts; it stresses the importance of attending to meaning, not just formal structure, in comprehending and creating utterances; and it respects the power of affect.

The theory, however, leaves many unresolved issues—such as learning in listening and reading (learning is defined in grammatical terms that do not relate to receptive tasks); the role of cognition; learner variability; and effectiveness of feedback. In short, while the theory's general orientation has been much embraced by language practitioners, the present specific construction of the theory has had limited guidance for the development of pedagogy. The absolute rejection of a role for learned rules in the acquisition of language is a difficult notion for many to accept without evidence. As Krahnke suggests: "Strategically, much of the effort spent arguing against the teaching of grammar might be better spent on convincing true believers in grammar instruction that grammar has a newly defined but useful role to play in language teaching and in showing them what it is" (1985, 598).

Rules in Active Processing: Cognitive Theory

In contrast to Krashen's macrotheory, which attempts to explain the whole of language acquisition, cognitive theory focuses specifically on the learning process, applying the broader framework of cognitive psychology to second language acquisition. Cognitive theory would stand in stark opposition to Krashen's contention that "learning" cannot lead to "acquisition," for the central premise of the former is that to learn a second language is to learn a complex skill through dynamic problem-solving processes. Two notions that drive cognitive theory are *automaticity* and *restructuring*.

Cognitive theorists establish a continuum for controlled processing and automatic processing as the enablers of performance of the myriad subskills that comprise any communicative task. Controlled processing takes time and energy and involves the individual's active attention (albeit possibly subconscious) in the task. Through practice, however, processing that was once controlled becomes routinized or automatic, thus freeing the individual to devote controlled processing energies to new and higher-level (previously difficult or impossible) tasks. Controlled processes underlie all learning and regulate the transfer of new information into long-term storage.

A second process involved in learning, according to cognitive theory, is that of "restructuring"—the organization and conversion of old cognitive representations into new, more effective and efficient ones. McLaughlin notes that while development of automaticity through practice is a continuous process, restructuring is thought to occur in a discontinuous fashion and may be characterized by sudden "moments of insight and clicks of comprehension" (1988, 138). He speculates that while both automaticity and restructuring occur thoughout learning, gains in automaticity might be more characteristic of early stages of learning and restructuring of later stages.

A further distinction made in cognitive theory is that of declarative (what) knowledge—that is, rules of language and procedural (how) knowledge or strategies used by learners to process these data for use.

At present, it is difficult to say what cognitive theory offers in terms of explanation and prediction in second language learning because it has yet to be correlated with linguistic and social theories of language and acquisition and fully explored through second language acquisition research. However, the notion of learner processing and strategy use is having a strong impact on foreign language instruction, curriculum, and materials development in ways such as the following:

1. Old notions of practice such as drill and repetition as mimicking are yielding to richer and more complex interpretations. Practice is viewed as the scaffolding and fading process toward emerging automaticity, and repetition is now much linked to the notion of recursiveness—forms are transferred for new functions, functions are broadened through new forms, and both are practiced continuously in expanded contexts.
2. Attention to learner products is complemented by focus on learning process—what procedures or strategies learners use and how more efficient and effective tactics can be fostered in the classroom.

While the two theories discussed here have sharp differences, each has intuitive and experiential appeal to researchers, practitioners, and language users. Krashen's theory represents a creative construction model; cognitive process theory represents a skill-learning model. The two theories are compared diagrammatically by Littlewood (1984, 73) (see Figure 30–1).

Since the present research base does not allow us to reject either theory, we must look for ways of reconciling them. Littlewood concludes that to view language learning as either one or the other represents a dangerous simplification: "Between the most subconscious processes of 'acquisition' at one extreme and the most conscious forms of 'learning' at the other, it would probably be more realistic to think in terms of a continuum, in which subconscious and conscious processes are mingled to varying degrees" (77).

WHO ARE THE FOREIGN LANGUAGE LEARNERS?

Is developing foreign language proficiency simply the result of some some special talent or ability or "aptitude"? Why do some people experience great difficulty in learning another language while others do not? Should all individuals have the opportunity and be encouraged to learn another language, or should some be counseled out of this line of study? Is it possible to predict success in foreign language learning? At what age should foreign language instruction begin? These are just some of the very old questions that foreign language educators have asked. Responses to these questions throughout the years will be examined in this section. But we will also probe some newer, and perhaps more interesting, issues that have arisen only through abandoning these old questions and shifting attention away from who should study a foreign language to who are learners and how are they learning?

Who Should Study a Foreign Language?

The history of foreign language study is one of unabashed elitism perpetuated through centuries of emphasis on abstract linguistic notions and belles lettres pursuits (Galloway 1983a). The answer to the question, Who should study a foreign language?, though often unspoken, was a relatively simple one: those who can fit the Procrustean bed of the classroom. Foreign language students were exactly what teachers wanted them to be, expected them to be, and

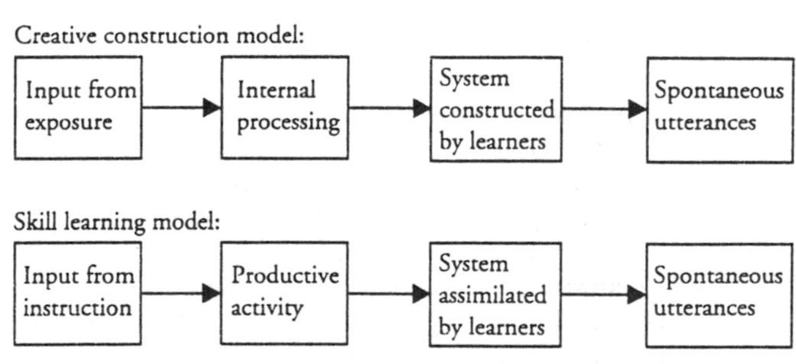

FIGURE 30–1

were trained for them to be: between the ages of 13 and 19, college-bound, holding above a C average in English, highly motivated and achievement oriented, and knowledgeable in English grammar (Galloway 1983a).

The foreign language professional literature is replete with studies attempting to identify "predictors" of success, to define foreign language "aptitude" or to establish some correlations between success in foreign language study and such things as "intelligence" or verbal ability or achievement in other academic areas. For the most part, these studies have come up empty-handed (Izzo 1981). They have also conveyed some rather false and dangerous messages, as Galloway and Labarca (1990) summarize: that we have identified what language learning is and that we are therefore prepared to identify those traits relevant to its pursuit; that we can also predict lack of success and gauge our expectations accordingly; and that the onus belongs on the learner, who, once labeled and classified, may cease to be a relevant consideration in planning and conducting teaching. Galloway continues: "Predictors of success have no place in education when they explain away the learner. Absolute classifications have no value when applied to humans who embody scores of other traits, all of which interact."

The practice of excluding or discouraging students from studying foreign languages is part of a less knowledge-based past. Today's energies are focused on exploring learner variability and on discovering ways to foster learning in all students. Higher expectations are emerging for all learners; in our research and practice students are gauged not in terms of what they have done, but of what, with expert guidance, they can do.

Who Is the Foreign Language Learner?

Throughout the years, many assumptions have been made regarding what the adult learner brings to the foreign language study experience. Yet, much of the learner's background and rich framework of experience has been underexplored through an overemphasis on the linguistic tools that can be brought to bear on the study of another language. It has been typically assumed, for example, that older learners have a first language in which they have received some formal instruction and they will be able to use this knowledge to gain access to another language (Birckbichler 1984). This existing linguistic equipment has thus been seen as the learner's most important characteristic. Yet, while learners will, indeed, have a first language, it can no longer be assumed that this language will be English. Further, learners will display varying degrees of awareness of the structure of their first language and may share neither the ability nor the desire to analyze and describe language as an object. Recent reports indicate, as well, that students may not understand what it means to "write" or "read" or "listen" or "speak" in their first language (Rivers 1990). Perhaps the most difficult notion in this assumption, however, is that of transfer, as languages in use are not parallel but rather unique systems, involving different ways of conceptualizing the world.

Verbal ability is but one thing learners bring to the foreign language learning experience. They also bring with them other knowledge and certain ways of perceiving, thinking, behaving, acting, and reacting in their world. They bring with them their complex personalities, their inherited traits, their social interaction patterns and preferences, and a great deal of academic "conditioning" as products of an educational system. They bring, in short, various learning "styles" to the foreign language classroom.

Research efforts in the examination of learning "styles" in foreign language began initially by testing out certain intuitions regarding the traits of the "good" language learner and, as will be obvious from the summary that follows, were geared heavily to existing notions of language learning as the development of grammatical competence. Thus, the areas of perceptual mode and environmental preferences, as well as social interaction patterns, are quite underresearched. Even in the area of cognitive style, research efforts are hampered by these ties to the past—the motivation to find the style that could predict success—and by the lack of good operational definitions of the traits themselves. Indeed, as is so often the case in education, instruments used to measure traits have become reified; that is, they mathematically embody traits that may or may not have any real physical existence (Galloway and Labarca 1990; Gould 1981).

In the social interaction dimension, Trosborg (1984) found that group interaction resulted not only in increased participation and motivation in language learners but in increased frequency of other-repairs, more flexibility and complexity within exchange patterns, and greater peer cooperation to fill in gaps in one another's vocabulary. In terms of social "style," however, the only trait thus far researched in terms of foreign language learning is that of risk-taking tendency, which is believed to be a positive factor in language acquisition. Beebe (1983) indicates that risk taking is influenced by certain situational factors, among them the degree of "skill" versus "chance" affecting outcomes. Persons with high motivation to achieve are more inclined to take risks if the task depends on skill and they can thus feel in control. In Beebe's studies, skill contexts appeared to stimulate a moderate level of risk taking, whereas a chance context seemed to induce extremely risky or conservative strategies. Other variables included the influence of prior experience, the degree of interest in the task, and the value of the reward. In terms of the latter, the cost of failure appears to be a greater deterrent than the value of success is an incentive. Individuals appeared to take greater risks in group decisions than they did by themselves on the same task and, interestingly, were more likely to take risks in speaking with native speakers than they were in the presence of peers from their own country. Ely (1986) hypothesized that students low in risk-taking tendency would enjoy the "safety" of controlled grammar exercises (drill). His study showed a reverse effect, however, indicating that risk-taking tendency may be linked to error potential, with those exercises in which there is one right answer offering more opportunities for obvious error demonstration, monitoring, teacher correction, and judgment. Research has yet to define this phenomenon clearly. A better sense of what learners perceive to be risk-taking situations is needed, not just in oral performance but in other facets of language use as well.

In terms of cognitive style, those "traits" that have received the most focus in research are degree of field independence, tolerance of ambiguity, and reflectivity, all of which are generally considered to be conducive to language acquisition. Most existing studies of both field independence and tolerance of ambiguity are correlational in nature and are clouded by methodological problems, not the least of which lie in the instruments used to measure these traits. In a study of the relationship between field independence (the ability to separate salient from nonsalient information) and achievement in reading, listening, writing, and gram mar, Bialystock and Frohlich (1978) found that field independence added nothing to the prediction that could not be accounted for by other variables. In addition, they recommended examining the relationship of this and other traits to more functionally oriented and productively based tasks rather than to grammar and comprehension tasks. Another trait held intuitively to be a significant factor in success is that of tolerance of ambiguity, which is seen as the ability to cope effectively and remain unthreatened by novelty, vagueness, uncertainty, or contradiction. Naiman et al. (1975) suggest that those learners who experience extreme difficulty coping with ambiguity may be among the early dropouts in language programs. Yet, at present, there exists no clue as to what learners consider ambiguous, either in the language itself as an arbitrary system or in the classroom presentation of language for learning (Galloway and Labarca 1990). In terms of the latter, for example, Bialystock (1983b) notes that "decontextualizing" the language has been given an important causal role in both the difficulty experienced by adults in learning a second language in an artificial environment and the difficulty experienced by some children in acquiring literacy skills or in coping with schooling in general. Intolerance of ambiguity may, in fact, be construed as a global manifestation of a host of factors, including an individual's persistence, need for structure, concrete/abstract orientation, perceived demands from the teacher or the program, task knowledge, degree and type of motivation, and risk-taking tendencies, as well as one's prior expectations and experiences (Galloway and Labarca 1990).

Another trait that has been examined in terms of cognitive style is that of conceptual tempo; that is, the reflectivity or impulsivity with which an individual responds in situations posing some response uncertainty. Impulsive learners display more spontaneity, but less accuracy; reflective learners will be slower, but more accurate in response. In terms of reading, studies by Hewitt (1989) and Messer (1976) suggest the desirability of reflection in gathering information from texts and evaluating hypotheses. Of attempts to modify impulsive behavior in reading, Hewitt contends that use of scanning strategies appears to hold the most promise for improving comprehension accuracy. Several studies have examined this trait continuum in speaking as well. Holley and King (1971), for example, counseled teachers to wait 5–10 seconds when students hesitated in responding and found that this pause reduced by 50 percent the need for teacher correction. Meredith (1978) imposed a latency period on students and found that when impulsive students were required to delay their responses, gains were found in fluency, amount of relevant information conveyed, and linguistic quality. Performance of reflectives remained relatively stable with gains in levels of fluency.

Other studies, however, suggest that impulsivity may actually be the trait encouraged in the language classroom. Shrum (1985) found that teachers waited, on the average, less than 2 seconds between their elicitation and the student's response and concluded that this amount of time was only enough to allow for sensory storage and short-term processing of very simple elicitations. While, as Shrum explains, this amount of time may be appropriate for drills that do not require extensive thought or attention to meaning, perhaps longer periods of wait time are indicated and would benefit both reflective and impulsive learners if thoughtful communication rather than manipulation of grammar forms is the goal.

For the most part, research on learner styles and characteristics has focused on correlating the perceived existence of a certain trait with various student products or task performances. It has thus not been enormously informative regarding learner processes. While this research begins with the notion that learners are different from each other, it has not fully explored the nature of these differences, not only among learners (interlearner variability) but also within learners (intralearner variability). Questions regarding the mutability and task specificity of "style," the interaction of styles among members of a group, and the relationship of style to strategy comfort zones remain unexplored.

What Do Students Do When Learning?

Many researchers contend that the key distinction between the successful and less successful language learner is the use of learning strategies. Research efforts in the area of learning strategies have been principally directed toward identifying those strategies and combinations of strategies used by "effective" language learners in various contexts in the performance of various language tasks and have explored, as well, the extent to which these strategies may be taught. Most researchers refer to three types of strategies used by learners in order to comprehend, store, retrieve, and use information or in order to plan, regulate, enjoy, or assess learning. These are metacognitive strategies, cognitive strategies, and social and affective strategies.

Educators stress the importance of the use of metacognitive strategies to plan and reflect on the learning process in maintaining and transferring all other strategies. In studies of learner strategy use, Chamot and Kupper (1989) found that intermediate students used metacognitive strategies more frequently than beginners, and, further, that the types of strategies varied. While beginners relied on such strategies as delaying speaking until sufficient confidence is gained, intermediate-level students incorporated self-monitoring and advance preparation strategies, such as use of advance organizers, task survey and analysis, and linguistic inventorying.

In terms of cognitive strategies, or those strategies learners apply directly to the task itself, the most comprehensive inventory is that developed by Oxford-Carpenter (1985), who lists over 40 distinct tactic types. These are summarized below in five categories:

Memory Strategies: These are strategies learners use in order to store and retrieve information and consist of such tactics as grouping and associational schemes, visual or mental imaging, clustering and task decomposition, physical or auditory linkages, and the like.

Emphasis and Summarizing Strategies: Learners use strategies to analyze and synthesize information, to separate salient from nonsalient information through techniques such as highlighting, outlining, note taking, and use of text organizers (e.g., headings).

Inferencing Strategies: These strategies involve the use of available information to conduct informed guessing and may involve use of verbal context clues, knowledge of the world, or topical background.

Elaboration and Transfer: These strategies consist of efforts to make the task more personally meaningful by relating it to everyday life or other academic contexts. Tactics such as transforming information to chart, graph, or diagram; acting out mental scenarios; recognizing cognates from the first language; and anticipating linguistic functions that would be performed in a given context are all examples of strategies whose aim is to relate the new to the known.

Functional Practice: Bialystock (1983a) found that the type of strategy most responsible for achievement on all tasks was that of functional practice: using the language in communicative contexts for the construction of meaning.

Learners also use social and affective strategies to reward and encourage themselves, to lower anxiety or frustration, to seek assistance and validation, or to rehearse and practice (Oxford-Carpenter 1985).

Research is inconclusive at this point as to which strategies or combinations of strategies seem to work best with which learners. Harlow (1988) provides a summary of seven studies that reported significant benefits for use of the following strategies: functional practice, inferencing, self-talk, seeking clarification, seeking verification, self-monitoring, and planning. While use of strategies such as these requires mental engagement on the part of the learner, researchers such as Chamot (1989) report that many foreign language learners, especially beginners, tend to overwork a very narrow repertoire of surface-level strategies such as repetition, translation, rote memorization, and mnemonic devices as artificial memory support. Ehrmann and Oxford (1988) contend that learners have preference or comfort zones according to individual "styles" and that these parameters may determine initial selection of strategies; however, with training, learners can apply new strategies in more deliberate fashion, and these may, with practice, become part of a learner's automatic strategy repertoire. Chamot, an advocate of direct strategy training in the classroom, outlines a seven-stage "scaffolding" plan for integrating strategy use and awareness into the development of listening, speaking, reading, and writing in the foreign language classroom:

1. Identify students' current strategies.
2. Assess students' strategy needs in conjunction with general course objectives and demands of the learning tasks.
3. Model new, more effective strategies through a think-aloud procedure, demonstrating the steps involved in approaching and completing the language task.
4. Label the strategies used so students can identify them and discuss them.
5. Provide guided pratice in use of the strategies.
6. Gradually reduce the reminders to use the strategies on related language tasks.
7. Provide varied practice with other tasks, in other contexts.

Language Learning Strategies of Children

Perhaps the most significant examination of language learning strategies and of individual variation in child language learning was conducted by Wong Fillmore (1976, 1979), who studied five young monolingual Spanish speakers for a year. All of Wong Fillmore's subjects were learning English informally in and out of school; there was no direct instruction in English. Pairing each subject with an English-speaking friend of his or her choosing, Wong Fillmore observed, recorded, and analyzed the data of the paired students' interactions over the course of a year. Wong Fillmore discovered significant variability in the ultimate level of English language attainment of each subject. She attributed this variation to the interaction of three variables: the language task, the strategies used by the subjects, and their personalities.

Personality played a key role in language development. Wong Fillmore's observations of personality differences among the subjects led her to conclude that the following characteristics played a significant role:

- The desire to interact with English speakers. Subjects who learned the most English sought to maximize their interactions with English-speaking peers. This resulted in a greater quantity of interlocutors, increased verbal interactions, and greater variety in the input obtained.
- Uninhibited learners were more successful learners. These children were not concerned about making mistakes, only with engaging in communication with others. In contrast, the more inhibited learners were concerned about saying what they meant and often, therefore, were more limited in their verbal interactions.

- Analytic subjects were more successful learners. Nora, the learner who made the greatest gains, had an analytical approach to tasks that was also reflected in her play with language. While some other subjects would play with the sounds of the language, Nora would play with syntax, exploring structural variations of the language she knew.
- Flexibility led to better language development than rigidity. Since young language learners continually form and test hypotheses of the language they are learning, the willingness to form new hypotheses or modify them on the basis of input data seemed to contribute more to success than the rigid personality of children who, once having decided they knew how to do something, persevered even in the face of conflicting data.

Personality variables interacted strongly with language tasks. To be successful learners, children needed to gather as much English input as possible. Students who actively sought out opportunities to interact with English speakers clearly obtained more input than those whose contacts were more limited. Similarly, the desire to be part of the group and to be an active participant required children to produce language more frequently than those with less social motivation. Output is necessary for children to engage in prolonged linguistic interaction and for hypothesis testing. Thus, subjects who sought to be active participants engaged in greater output activities. Further, the nature of the play activities themselves related to personality. Whereas Nora sought out play activities such as role play or dramatization ("You be the ______, and I'll be the ______"), some of the boys preferred physical activities (e.g., baseball), where the opportunities for verbalization and linguistic interaction were far more limited.

Wong Fillmore identified three social and five cognitive strategies that she believes were formulated by the children and worded as they themselves might express them. The social and cognitive strategies are laid out side by side to demonstrate the interaction between them.

Social Strategies	Cognitive Strategies
S-1 Join a group and act as if you understand what's going on, even if you don't.	*C-1* Assume that what people are saying is directly relevant to the situation at hand or to what they or you are experiencing. Metastrategy: Guess!
S-2 Give the impression—with a few well-chosen words—that you can speak the language.	*C-2* Get some expression you understand and start talking.
S-3 Count on your friends for help.	*C-3* Look for recurring parts in the formulas you know. *C-4* Make the most of what you've got. *C-5* Work on big things first; save the details for later. (1979, 209)

Learning Strategies of Children and Adults

The research on learning strategies of younger and older learners is alike in that it is assumed that more successful learners devise and use such strategies more frequently and effectively than do less successful ones. Some of these strategies, although stated differently, appear to share characteristics. These include inferencing strategies (using background knowledge, assuming that communication is relevant and related to the here and now); elaboration and transfer (relating the new to the old or to other, personal or academic contexts, and children's search for recurring parts in the language they know); and functional practice (using language in communicative tasks, joining a group and talking). Although Wong Fillmore's is an extremely thorough analysis of children's language strategies, it is difficult to state with certainty whether these strategies would apply to classroom foreign language learning and whether her constructs are operationalized in ways similar to the ways in which adult language strategies are used. Similarly, efforts to teach older students language learning strategies have not been replicated with younger students.

As research continues to inform us of the complexity of learners and learning, ways must be explored to adjust classrooms and instructional materials accordingly and to train teachers to shift the focus from what students cannot do to what they can be taught to do in order to learn how to learn, to make learning last, and to enjoy learning.

Age and Foreign Language Learning

Most of the discussion thus far on the foreign language learner has focused on the older learner, examining characteristics that may account for individual variation in language learning. Considerable research has focused on a different question, that of "optimal age": When is the best time to begin to learn another language?

Two reviews of the literature have analyzed in depth the research on the optimum age question. These reviews examine the research evidence that compares the foreign language attainment of learners at different age levels.

Krashen, Scarcella, and Long (1982) examined both long-term (i.e., several years) and short-term (less than 1 year) studies comparing older and younger language learners, examining the relationship among age, rate, and eventual attainment of language. Long-term studies showed that younger learners consistently acquired better pronunciation than older learners. In addition, over the course of time, the ultimate level of language attainment (such as comprehension skills and production of syntax) favored younger learners. Short-term studies that compared adults to children and older children to younger children showed that adults outperformed children and older children outperformed younger children in the rate of language development and in their grammatical skills (syntax and morphology) during the early stages of language development. Krashen, Scarcella, and Long conclude:

> The available literature is consistent with three generalizations concerning the relationship between age, rate, and eventual attainment in second language acquisition: (1) Adults proceed through early stages of syntactic and morphological development faster than children (where time and exposure are held constant). (2) Older children acquire faster than younger children (again, in the early stages of syntactic and morphological development where time and exposure are held constant). (3) Aquirers who begin natural exposure to second languages during childhood generally achieve higher second language proficiency than those beginning as adults. (161)

Harley's (1986) exhaustive review examined both the theoretical perspectives and the empirical evidence to support them. Theoretical perspectives on the relationship between age and second language acquisition differ in the extent to which they posit an innate advantage for either older or younger learners (nature) or incorporate environmental factors (nurture) as well. Some theorists, Harley notes, believe that children are biologically advantaged language learners, while others believe that Piaget's stage of formal operations would make adult learners more successful in the short run in some language tasks, but children more successful in the long run. Harley also cites arguments which favor the view that the cognitive maturity and well-developed first language skills of adults put them at a distinct advantage, particularly in tasks requiring decontextualized, academic language use.

Harley's summary further examines additional measures in language acquisition. Environmental factors include affective and social variables that affect the degree to which the learner wishes to identify with or become part of the target language group. In classroom settings, opportunities for real-life communication and the quantity and quality of input affect differences in second language acquisition. Time as a variable is also assumed to provide younger learners with an advantage in that early foreign language learners have more opportunities for spontaneous language use, can develop greater fluency and comfort levels, and simply have more time available to master language.

Harley's review of the empirical findings on the question of age and second language acquisition indicates that the results often depend on the definition of language proficiency and the language tasks assessed. Using Cummins' (1983) distinctions between interpersonal communication skills and academic language skills, his continuum of context-reduced language tasks (in which the clues to meaning are found only within the language itself), and context-embedded language tasks (in which clues to meaning may be found in the communicative context, the visual input that accompanies language—such as body language or pictures or one's background knowledge), Harley finds that the age/second language acquisition studies demonstrate advantages for older learners in language tasks that are context reduced and require academic language skills. For example, when studies that compare older and younger learners measure language skills through reading tests, a cloze task, translation, comprehension of syntax and morphology, or sentence repetitions, older learners' rate and ultimate level of language attainment is greater. In contrast, on context-embedded tasks focusing on social, interpersonal communication, younger learners are at an advantage. (Measures of language proficiency used in such studies are often face-to-face interviews.)

Lastly, Harley concludes that studies of second language acquisition in natural settings indicate that younger learners are more likely to attain nativelike proficiency than those who begin language learning as adults.

Serious constraints limit the generalizability of the research findings on the younger versus older question. Harley finds that

> a persistent problem in relating theory to empirical findings has been one of interpretation since it is generally impossible within the context of a single study to isolate the variable "age" from the setting in which the L2 [second language] is learned and the way in which L2 progress is assessed. (23)

A most significant problem is the difficulty in designing a controlled experiment that is equitable in its treatment and assessment of both sets of learners. Because learners at different ages have differing needs, abilities, and interests, and because developmentally appropriate instruction is a key to effective teaching and learning, it is difficult to design a valid study in which both younger and older learners receive the same treatment. By definition, equal treatment may bias the results in favor of the population for whom the treatment is more appropriate, and vice versa. For example, an analytical approach to language may favor students with more cognitive maturity and those more able to deal with abstraction; in contrast, a program of interest to young children may be boring to older students, who want to talk about more sophisticated topics.

In a similar vein, methods of assessing learners may be differentially effective with age. Even in their first language, younger and older learners may differ in the range of topics, the sophistication of their lexicon, and their syntactic mastery; they may also demonstrate different levels of sensitivity to appropriate register and other discourse features of the communicative situation. Since such differences are maturational and inherent in the nature of the learner, it may be difficult to distinguish befween these maturational factors and the actual achievement of foreign language skills in an experimental design. Further, most oral assessments require face-to-face testing with an impartial examiner, and younger children may be disadvantaged if they are unfamiliar with such testing or uncomfortable in communicating with unknown adults. Some measures of foreign language proficiency may be assessed through paper-and-pencil tests. While paper-and-pencil tests may be appropriate in some skill areas for older learners, younger learners just acquiring first language literacy skills may be handicapped when tested in their second language.

One additional constraint on the interpretation of the age and language acquisition studies is the variable of time. Studies of relatively short duration, with the maximum period of treatment of approximately 1 year, almost consistently show an advantage for older learners. Research on the long-term relationship between age and language acquisition often shows a different pattern. Indeed, Krashen, Scarcella, and Long suggest that, while older learners may be more efficient in the short run, younger learners may demonstrate stronger and more lasting skill attainment in the long run.

HOW SHOULD FOREIGN LANGUAGES BE TAUGHT?

Having discussed who the foreign language learners are and how they learn, we turn now to what they should learn and how. In this section we will examine the foreign language curriculum: What should be its content, and how should that content be delivered? (The following is a synthesis of the literature on proficiency. For further reading, see Byrnes 1985; Galloway 1987; Heilenman and Kaplan 1984; Medley 1985; Met 1988; and Omaggio 1986).

Teaching for Proficiency

A quick review of curriculum guides from the mid-1950s to the present day reveals few differences in the stated goals of most secondary foreign language programs: Students should be enabled to understand, speak, read, and write the foreign language, particularly when communicating with native speakers of the target language. Students are also expected to develop knowledge of and appreciation for the culture of those who speak the language.

Despite such overt similarities in stated goals, we have seen earlier that definitions of what it means to know another language and another culture have shifted dramatically in the recent decade. Foreign language professionals today use the term "proficiency" to describe the goals and philosophy of modern foreign language programs. Proficency-based programs help students develop language skills that allow them to communicate their own thoughts and feelings in situations they are most likely to encounter. The emphasis is on what students can *do* with language, as opposed to what they *know about* language. Classroom learning experiences should require meaningful use of the language, involve purposeful communication, and connect the learner to authentic language as used in real-life situations. These experiences are intended to develop students' language *proficiency*.

The proficiency-based curriculum answers the question, Proficient to do what? in which situations? and, how well? Proficiency may be defined as the ability to perform oral or written language tasks in given contexts, or in relation to specific contents, with a specified degree of grammatical and cultural accuracy. Proficiency is not an abstract curriculum goal; rather, students are to become proficient to perform certain tasks, in specific situations, with a degree of grammatical accuracy, and in a socioculturally appropriate manner. Proficiency, then, is defined through the performance features of language functions, contexts, contents, and accuracy. Each of these aspects of language use will be discussed more fully below.

Language tasks—or functions—are the purposes for which people use language. As described earlier in this chapter, language functions include, among many others, requesting and giving information, expressing feelings (e.g., likes and dislikes, happiness or anger), persuasion, and socializing. Obviously, language functions cover a broad array of communicative tasks. Language functions, or tasks, may be performed in a variety of situations (contexts) or relate to diverse topics (i.e., contents). For example, likes and dislikes may be expressed with regard to menu selections (a restaurant context) or with regard to clothing (a topic or content). The function of requesting may take place in the context of requesting directions to a given street address, requesting instructions on how to turn on a television set, requesting a description of a missing person, requesting assistance in fixing a flat tire, or requesting a phone number from directory assistance. Language functions may be expressed through a wide array of grammatical structures. For example, in requesting a meal in a restaurant, one might select from among a number of linguistic options (e.g., "I'll have," "Please bring me," "I think I'll order the . . .").

Contexts and contents are the situations or topics about which we communicate. Some survival situations (contexts) in which novice language users may find themselves may include travel, shopping, or dining out. Some topics (contents) about which novice language users may wish to communicate may include food, clothing, the home, or health. Advanced language users may also talk about these same topics, but in addition have a more extensive repertoire of topics, as well as more fully developed linguistic resources for expressing themselves.

Accuracy is both grammatical (linguistic) and sociocultural. Grammatical, or linguistic, accuracy describes the language users' ability to control the syntax and morphology of the language. As learners progress from survival abilities to more advanced skills, they use a wider range of syntactic structures (e.g., various tenses, moods, complex sentences with diverse intersentential and intrasentential connectors) and with ever-increasing accuracy. Accuracy also refers to the learners' growing ability to interpret and convey communication that reflects appropriate sociocultural knowledge and attitudes. For example, students learn early that many modern foreign languages distinguish relationships between speakers through use of formal and informal forms of address. Shared cultural knowledge and assumptions also impact effective communication. For example, the phrase "he's tilting at windmills" can be interpreted accurately only if one is familiar with Cervantes' *Don Quixote*.

Traditionally, foreign language curricula were based on the assumption that mastery of the grammatical rules of a language was tantamount to "knowing" the language. This analytical approach to language presumed that the whole was equal to the sum of the parts, and, thus, mastery of the parts meant mastery of the whole. Analysis of language proceeded from simpler to more complex language structures (as defined by structural linguists). This grammatical approach was linear and hierarchical and focused on "knowing." In contrast, a proficiency-based curriculum focuses on "knowing in action." It is recursive rather than linear—it presumes that at each level students acquire some degree of proficiency and that they are increasingly enabled to perform in the language. Novice-level learners are proficient at performing a limited number of tasks in a restricted number of contexts and with limited syntactic and cultural resources at their disposal. As learners progress through the curriculum, language functions, contexts, and contents are revisited, and students expand their performance repertoire. Students who increase their proficiency expand the ways in which they are able to understand or express language functions, expand the number of functions they understand or express, refine their ability to perform in diverse contexts or to express themselves on diverse topics, and continuously refine the degree to which their interpretation or expression of communication is both grammatically and socioculturally appropriate.

The performance features of function, context and content, and accuracy underlie decisions about curriculum, and curriculum may use any of these as the organizing principle. Curriculum decisions shape the ways in which students become proficient. Curriculum answers the questions: (1) What are students able to do with language? (i.e., which language functions); (2) Under what circumstances? (i.e., the contexts or contents in which they can perform); and (3) With what degree of accuracy can they perform? (grammatical and sociocultural). Curriculum developers must therefore determine with which language functions students will need to become proficient, and in what order; the situations in which students should be enabled to function (e.g., do seventh graders need to know how to request a hotel room in Paris?); and the degree of control expected at each level of instruction.

In the past, when less attention was paid to the real-life uses to which students might put their acquired foreign language skills, curriculum consisted of a hierarchical sequence of grammatical structures and a corpus of vocabulary with which to flesh out language. The sequence of grammar was based on conceptions of simple versus complex, as opposed to the usefulness of the structures to the learner. For example, almost every Spanish or French student learned the forms for giving commands in the first year or two of language study, despite the fact that in real-life most students would never have occasion to command anyone to do anything in the foreign language. Similarly, vocabulary was taught as a convenient vehicle for providing practice for grammatical structures taught. Therefore, many foreign language curricula include daily routines ("I dress myself," "I wash my hands," etc.) with the grammar topic of reflexive verbs.

A proficiency-based curriculum includes vocabulary and grammar, but the specific topics included and the sequence in which these may be presented must also relate to the communicative needs of the learner. These communicative needs are expressed in the curriculum in terms of student performance of functions, in context, and with a specified level of accuracy. Curriculum developers must select from the vast spectrum of possible language uses and real-life purposes those to be taught. Some criteria to be used in selecting grammar to be taught may include the frequency with which the structure occurs in real-life language, the complexity of the concept, the degree to which the students need the structure to communicate effectively, student interest, the versatility of the structure, and the extent to which errors in its use impede effective communication with native speakers (Galloway, as cited in Medley 1985). Because in most secondary schools many students pursue a 2-year course of study, curriculum must focus on those skills that will give foreign language learners the greatest flexibility in communicating in the greatest range of communicative settings.

While several states have developed proficiency-based curriculum frameworks (e.g., Georgia, Maryland, New York, and Wisconsin), local school systems are only just beginning to interpret these frameworks and develop proficiency-based curricula for local use in secondary schools.

Although proficiency-based curricula are only in their infancy at the secondary school level, elements of proficiency-based instruction have characterized elementary school foreign language curricula for some time. Successful elementary school foreign language teachers have long known that students' motivation and on-task behavior is maintained when language instruction is relevant to students' needs to communicate. Since young children are often acquiring concepts such as numbers, colors, and calendar and clock time, identifying appropriate topics and contents for inclusion in the elementary school curriculum has been relatively clear. Language functions—describing, requesting, expressing preferences—are developed, but students' repertoire is limited to a restricted number of mechanisms for expressing these functions. Since most younger learners lack the cognitive maturity to handle the abstractions of grammar rules, most elementary school foreign language curricula have omitted overt instruction in grammar. Rather, syntactic skills have been developed inductively, with students learning from repeated exposure to accurate models and through inductive structured-practice activities.

Culture in the Proficiency-Based Curriculum

Considerable attention has been paid to the role of culture in developing foreign language proficiency. Foreign language curricula have long included instruction in the culture of those who speak the foreign language as a means for enhancing students' world view, as well as a special channel to more effective communication.

In one sense, culture may be defined as the historical, philosophical, and aesthetic heritage of the people(s) who speak the foreign language. The foreign language curriculum includes study of this heritage, as well as knowledge of the geography and related features (e.g., topography, climate, signficant monuments) of the countries in which the language is spoken. In addition, "culture" may also be seen from an anthropological viewpoint, as embodied in the daily lives of a given linguistic, sociocultural group.

Each of these definitions has implications for the foreign language curriculum. Students must be able to identify where the foreign language is spoken and to identify salient features of the cultural heritage associated with the language. In this respect, curriculum trends in today's foreign language programs are not substantially different from those of the past. Where differences emerge, however, is in the increasing emphasis given to developing students' understanding and appreciation of the target culture's lifestyles, customs, values, attitudes, and beliefs, and, specifically, how these interact with effective communication.

Teaching about the daily lives of other cultural groups is fraught with dangers. It is difficult to draw generalizations that are accurate, given the ever-changing nature of modern life. For every accurate generalization there is the equal possibility of identifying a bona fide exception. Further, generalizations draw close to the fine line of stereotyping. In describing the ways in which other cultures organize their daily lives and the belief systems that underlie these lifestyles, teachers also court the danger of overemphasizing cultural differences, often leading to negative attitudes on the part of students toward these differences. Moreover, teachers of languages that are spoken in many different areas (e.g., French and Spanish) are challenged to select some areas for greater emphasis than others and to avoid generalizations that may apply to some parts of the French- or Spanish-speaking world but not to others.

Nonetheless, this aspect of culture is essential to the development of effective communication skills. Students cannot learn to function in real-life situations in the foreign language without also understanding the cultural context within which communication occurs. While the words in one language may be directly translatable into another language, the experiences to which these words refer may differ markedly. The American student who says, "I'll buy some bread on the way home from school" does not refer to the same constellation of events as the French student. The American student probably travels by car or bus, the French student on foot, bicycle, or Metro. The American student buys bread in a convenience store or a huge supermarket, the French student more likely in a small bakery. American bread comes sliced and wrapped in a plastic bag closed with a twist tie. French bread is sold as a long single loaf (baguette), neither sliced nor wrapped in plastic.

Knowing the denotative value of words is only the beginning; students must learn the connotative meanings as well. While the words for "thank you" may be directly translatable, when you may say "thank you" differs. For example, in some cultures, it is inappropriate to use "thank you" in response to a compliment. Because languages differ in how persons of differing social or personal status may be addressed, students may more effectively convey their thoughts and feelings in more socially appropriate ways when students understand the sociocultural rules that underlie communication in the target language.

Because it is important for students to be able to function appropriately in the target culture, proficiency-based instruction incorporates extensive use of authentic materials. Authentic materials are print and nonprint materials and other cultural artifacts drawn directly from the target culture. Authentic texts are print materials written for native speakers; authentic video and film are visual materials developed with a native audience in mind. Artifacts such as train tickets, menus, currency, and bus schedules provide additional opportunities for students to observe and draw inferences about the culture in its most authentic form.

Authentic texts may be used at all levels of instruction and present a range of challenges for students. Novice-level learners may use simple advertisements, menus, or television schedules as the basis for developing reading skills and cultural knowledge. Students' background knowledge and schemata provide contextual clues as to the nature of the text (advertisement versus phone directory) and may be used to facilitate text interpretation. Authentic texts, even such simple ones, provide opportunities for engaging students in observing specific cultural phenomena. A telephone directory from a Spanish-speaking country leads to discussion of practices related to surnames. Television schedules provide insight into the range of viewing opportunities elsewhere and into the role that imported American television shows play in shaping what other peoples believe about life in the United States and in internationalizing lifestyles.

Authentic video brings other cultures to the classroom, especially when students cannot always have direct access to the culture. Even with the sound off, students can vicariously experience the target culture through observation and analysis of typical street scenes. Commercials from other cultures reflect their values and also provide opportunities to learn about goods and services prevalent elsewhere. Video and film allow students to develop and use their listening comprehension skills in authentic and natural situations. Using video and film and guided listening instruction, teachers enable students to interact with native speakers when these speakers are later encountered in real-life contexts.

Just as teachers and curriculum developers are confronted with difficult choices about what language skills to develop if students are to remain in foreign language courses for only a 2-year sequence, so too does the choice of culture become constrained by time. As discussed above, it is impossible to learn a foreign language without understanding the culture through which language is filtered and expressed. Development of an understanding of the cultural context in which language occurs is an essential component of curriculum. Some curricula address this issue by including objectives related to the cultural context with each language objective. While such an approach is critical, there is the danger that other aspects of culture will be shortchanged because of time constraints. Developing a balance between the more traditional (or formal) aspects of culture (i.e., historical and aesthetic heritage) and the sociocultural context of language is a challenge proficiency-based curriculum developers must ultimately address.

Characteristics of Proficiency-Based Instruction

Many of the elements that have characterized foreign language curriculum and instruction in the past continue in a proficiency-based setting. However, the extent to which these characteristics are present and their emphases may differ. These characteristics include, among others, use of the foreign language, use of drill and practice, application activities, error correction, and specific skill development in the areas of listening, speaking, reading, writing, and culture.

In proficiency-based classrooms, curriculum delivery is characterized by extensive use of the foreign language by the teacher and encouragement of students to do so as well.

The proficiency-based foreign language curriculum places renewed emphasis on the role of listening skills. If the goal of instruction is communication, then listening must be an essential skill, since communication evidently involves both receiving and sending messages. Students are guided to develop an understanding of the spoken language, particularly natural language as spoken by native speakers in authentic situations, through a multistep approach. Prelistening activities activate students' schemata and background knowledge. By encouraging students to anticipate what might be heard based on their knowledge of the topic and of the "scripts" that shape communication, teachers enable students to function with growing independence. Repeated listenings allow students to focus on differing aspects of the message, and postlistening experiences extend learnings to new situations and applications.

The proficiency-based curriculum specifies tasks that students can perform in the foreign language. These tasks are communicative in nature, but may be enabled through a variety of classroom activities. Oral activities may be distinguished as rote, mechanical drills that focus on developing specific grammatical or lexical skills; contextualized drills in which the focus is on mechanical drill but set into a meaningful context; and communicative drills, in which the emphasis is on expressing one's own meaning and thoughts. While the answers to mechanical and contextualized drills are almost always predictable (there is only one right answer), responses in communicative drills will often be unpredictable or varied. Communicative activities may involve personalizing questions so that students respond only as appropriate to their own situation ("My eyes are brown"); have truth value for students ("No, I did not walk my dog last night because I do not have a dog"); be reality based ("We celebrate Thanksgiving in November"); and/or be meaningful and purposeful ("What time does the football game start?" "I don't know. I think at 7:30"). Although some communicative activities have predictable responses (e.g., identifying the month in which an event regularly occurs), others do not; further, the linguistic demands made of students may range from nonverbal responses to yes/no to more open-ended possibilities. Communicative activities stand in stark contrast to those that characterized foreign language instruction in earlier periods, activities in which students mechanically conjugated verbs or replaced nouns with object pronouns as specified in the text. The distinction between rote/mechanical or contextual drills and communicative drills parallels the distinction made by Rivers (1975) between skill getting and skill using. Skill-getting activities help students learn about the language; skill-using activities emphasize using that knowledge for meaningful communication. In proficiency-based instruction, skill-using activities predominate. Rote or mechanical drills continue to play a role in the development of basic linguistic tools needed for communication, but these drills form only a small portion of class activities. Rather, students are moved through the continuum of drills, with increased emphasis placed on contextualized drill and the majority of classroom practice devoted to communicative activities.

Because communication is the primary goal of the curriculum, teachers facilitate opportunities for communication within the classroom. In order to provide increased time for students to use these skills, effective foreign language teachers increasingly use small-group and pair work (Nerenz and Knop 1982).

One area of continued debate in the foreign language literature is that of error correction during oral activities. Conflicting evidence in the research about the nature of errors and their amenability to remediation through overt and indirect approaches to correction has left teachers unsure about appropriate responses to student errors. Error correction or feedback in the proficiency-based classroom is provided in a nonthreatening fashion and does not impede the students' efforts to communicate (Omaggio 1986). Errors should not be corrected immediately while students are engaged in communicating; teachers may make mental note of errors and point them out at the appropriate time. When activities focus on mastering a grammatical point, then errors should be corrected immediately.

Reading objectives in a proficiency-based curriculum delineate an ever-increasing ability to interpret print materials in the foreign language through interaction with a variety of text types and using differing reading skills. Students may learn to skim an advertisement or scan newspaper headlines for specific information. In contrast, they must learn to read expository text for details or interpret literary works through inference. To the fullest extent possible, authentic print materials are drawn directly from the target culture in order to increase students' ability to function independently in authentic situations. Because authentic texts may present a myriad of challenges to students at every level of development, teachers guide students to meaningful and appropriate text interpretation through a five-step approach (Phillips 1984). First, teachers activate students' background knowledge and schemata during the preparation stage. Next, students skim for the gist of the text and scan to locate specific information. During the intensive reading stage students actively decode text, using sensible guessing strategies to deduce the meanings of unknown words from context and use other linguistic clues to derive meaning from print. In the comprehension stage, teachers ensure that students have indeed constructed an appropriate interpretation of the text through comprehension checks. In the final stage, information and skills acquired through reading are transferred to other skills and contexts.

Like the speaking objectives of a proficiency-based curriculum, writing objectives describe what students should be able to communicate through the written word. While skill-getting activities allow students to use writing (e.g., note taking) as a form of reinforcing learning, skill-using activities fulfill the curriculum's objectives. These objectives reflect students' ability to communicate in real-life situations and with ever-increasing sophistication. Thus, while writing activities for novice-level learners may include writing lists or brief notes or filling in forms, intermediate learners can write guided descriptions or narrations, brief compositions, journals, or diaries. Advanced writers can develop descriptions with elaboration or detail, engage in dialog journals, and use process approaches to writing, including peer editing (Omaggio 1986). Writing skills in the proficiency-based classroom relate to the real-life purposes for which people write and, therefore, require a sense of audience, communicative task, and selection of appropriate format.

In proficiency-based instruction culture is integrated throughout the curriculum and woven through daily classroom activities and tasks. As noted in our discussion of proficiency, effective communication can take place only when the cultural context is clearly understood.

Teachers assess student progress in ways that are consistent with instruction. Since aural/oral communication is an important component of the curriculum, teachers assess these skills in context. Paper-and-pencil measures of speaking skills are inappropriate. As Omaggio notes, most classroom tests

> tend to be largely discrete-point in nature, reflecting an orientation toward the behavioristic language-learning theories that were popular during the 1960s. . . . This conservative stance in classroom testing has resulted in an ever-widening gap between the description of course goals—often in terms of proficiency statements—and their measurement. (309–310)

Proficiency: Curriculum and Instruction

While proficiency is the stated goal of most foreign language programs, proficiency-based instruction is an approach to teaching, not a methodology. Throughout the 1970s and 1980s various methodologies have been proposed to achieve the goals of the foreign language curriculum. A brief overview of methodologies advocated in the foreign language literature of these 2 decades is provided in Omaggio (1986).

For example, the Total Physical Response method developed by James Asher (1981) emphasizes the importance of developing students' listening skills before requiring oral production. Students physically respond to increasingly complex commands, first acted out with the teacher, and later, independently in response to teacher directives. Asher's research provides convincing evidence that students can, indeed, develop some proficiency through this method, although little of this research has been conducted with students well beyond the initial stages of foreign language development.

The Natural Approach is a method is based on the theoretical work of Krashen (described earlier in this chapter). As developed by Terrell (1977, 1982; Krashen and Terrell 1983), the Natural Approach heavily stresses use of classroom instructional time for communicative activities. Based on Krashen's distinction between learning and acquisition, Terrell advocates classroom activities devoted to fostering language acquisition and out-of-class activities (e.g., homework) focusing on language learning. In this method, then, study and practice of language rules and forms (skill getting) take place outside class; application of rules and forms (skill using) is done in class. Because novice learners can get great mileage from an extensive vocabulary and minimal knowledge of structure in the early stages of language development, the Natural Approach aims toward development of a large corpus of vocabulary early in the curriculum. Grammatical accuracy is built through continued exposure to accurate language models, and students' control of structure emerges slowly over time. This view is in direct opposition to cognitive approaches to foreign language instruction that build knowledge of language structure systematically. The Natural Approach recognizes the important role that Krashen's affective filter plays in facilitating (or inhibiting) language development. Primary emphasis of the Natural Approach is on the development of communication skills.

Content-Based Instruction. Although not strictly a method, content-based instruction is becoming increasingly popular in discussions of elementary school and postsecondary foreign language programs. Content-based instruction uses the foreign language as a medium to learn the content of specific courses (e.g., science, art, or the culture of the target language), shifting the emphasis from language as the content of the course to language as the vehicle. Content-based instruction is highly consistent with proficiency-based approaches, since it logically extends the concepts of language used to convey meaning and the use of language to accomplish specific tasks to the use of language for learning or enriching conceptual learning. At the elementary school level, content-based foreign language instruction substitutes for or enriches instruction in other curriculum areas (Met 1989a). For example, immersion programs substitute the foreign language for English in delivery of instruction of the elementary school curriculum; in some FLES programs one or more content areas may be taught through the foreign language (e.g., art, music, or physical education) instead of in English. Or foreign language instruction may draw practice activities from other content areas, enriching or extending concepts already taught in English. For example, students acquiring foreign language vocabulary for clothing may reinforce graphing skills learned in the mathematics curriculum by developing a graph that depicts what students are wearing.

At the postsecondary level, several institutions offer content-based instruction, including international business, Greek mythology, science and technology, and political science courses taught in a foreign language. A significant study on the language outcomes of content-based instruction was conducted by Edwards et al. (1984; see also Hauptman, Wesche, and Ready 1988). Results of the study showed that students who had taken college psychology in French performed as well as students who had taken the course in their native language: In addition, the experimental group demonstrated significant gains in French listening-comprehension skills. Similarly, Lafayette and Buscaglia (1985) provide insights into a French culture course taught in French at Indiana University. Leaver and Stryker (1989) provide detailed description of the rationale for and implementation of content-based courses at the Foreign Service Institute (FSI). FSI courses allow students to increase their language proficiency by discussing topics regularly included in the curriculum of the FSI's School of Area Studies (e.g., the political system, lifestyles and culture, and policy issues related to the country to which the student is to be assigned). Content-based instruction in topics drawn from area studies have increasingly been included as content in language courses at FSI.

Technology and Foreign Language Instruction

As our society becomes increasingly based on electronic communications, schools lag behind in moving from a print-based approach to the transmission of knowledge to a technology-based approach. For foreign language education, the design of curriculum and its implementation through technologically mediated instruction can be fraught with danger or filled with promise. Unfortunately, little solid evidence exists to inform sound instructional decision making. In the 1950s and 1960s language laboratories, television, and film projectors constituted state-of-the-art technology. While these forms of mediated language learning persist, modern technology has added to the roster computer-assisted language learning (CALL) and has expanded substantially the definition of "television." The role of technology and the specific forms of it available for foreign language instruction are discussed below.

The Language Laboratory. Enthusiasm for foreign languages coupled with readily available funds to improve language instruction provided the impetus for widespread installation of language laboratories in the 1950s and 1960s. Although laboratories are still to be found in a number of secondary schools, a combination of factors—maintenance problems, lack of teacher training, shortage of appropriate courseware, and changing views of language learning—have led to a serious decline in their availability and use in secondary schools today.

However, the future of language laboratories may not be as dismal as the above paragraph might suggest. At the secondary level, language laboratories are being used in conjunction with new courseware. Some textbook programs now include audiotapes that are integral to the learning process and do not simply reiterate what teachers can do equally well without the technology. More important, the laboratory can increase students' opportunities to engage in quality listening experiences. And since a number of contemporary approaches emphasize the critical role that listening comprehension (i.e., comprehensible input) plays in the development of foreign language skills, the language laboratory can serve a significant role in enhancing comprehension skills.

At the postsecondary level, language laboratories are more appropriately termed "multimedia centers" because they provide a variety of opportunities for mediated language learning. Otto (1989) lists a number of benefits that technology, in particular the laboratory, can provide. It can reinforce drill and practice, thus freeing class time for communicative activities. The laboratory can provide opportunities for students to hear (or see) a variety of authentic voices and visuals; it can increase one-on-one instruction since teachers can listen to students reciting individually at their work stations; and it can improve the quality of audio reproduction—particularly important for novice learners.

As we shall see in the following discussions of other uses of technology in foreign language learning, the quality of courseware available for use on increasingly sophisticated hardware plays a critical role in determining the usefulness of the medium.

Computer-Assisted Language Learning (CALL) uses the computer as the medium for supplementing teacher-delivered instruction. In a comprehensive review of research on CALL, Pederson (1987) notes there is no research base to support the general effectiveness of CALL over other methods of curriculum delivery, citing an overreliance on informal observation, use of questionnaires and attitude surveys, and inadequate controls over experimental variables in research studies used as the basis for promoting the use of CALL. Pederson observes that much of the research on CALL compares it to other forms of mediated foreign language instruction or to "traditional" curriculum delivery. Such research generally has found no significant differences between one delivery medium and another. This, Pederson believes, is because researchers have failed to focus on the interaction of learner variables with the design of specific aspects of computer software. "There is little information about how to use the computer's capabilities to enhance CALL lesson delivery" (100), she states.

Research that does look at how CALL software variables differentially interact with learner characteristics seems to indicate that CALL can be effective in promoting achievement on certain language tasks for certain types of learners. Early CALL software was almost exclusively "drill and kill": It was boring, decontextualized, and not designed to enhance students' communicative abilities. Much of the software currently available continues to emphasize mechanical drill and practice, although promising efforts in the United Kingdom are resulting in software that focuses on language tasks instead of forms, group interaction instead of individualized practice, and problem-solving strategies instead of rote memory (Davies 1989).

Perhaps the greatest obstacle to the design of effective software is the unpredictability of real-life communication. If the contributions of each conversationalist were predictable from the outset, social discourse would be exceedingly boring. In real communication, people exchange information. This aspect of communication—an information or opinion gap—characterizes the most challenging of proficiency-based classroom activities. If the computer is to provide enhanced foreign language practice, it must simulate real-life language use. At the Massachusetts Institute of Technology, researchers engaged in project Athena are developing courseware that, through simulations and "structured conversations," allows students to use the computer work station for communication-based language practice (Murray, Morgenstern, and Furstenberg 1989). Although the Athena work station does not include a speech recognition component, students can, through the keyboard, engage in an interactive conversation with the computer as interlocutor. Students can be challenged to negotiate meaning with the computer when it requests clarification, paraphrasing, or further explanations. Although Athena is still in its developmental stage, researchers report encouraging results.

Television. Such a simple term as "television" can hardly do justice to the wide array of technological options available through this medium. Currently, "television" encompasses the use of prerecorded videotape cassettes, international satellite transmissions, interactive video (IAV), and distance learning. Richardson and Scinicariello (1989) note that more teachers currently use television than computers for instruction, but that "there is almost no research on the use of television in foreign language teaching at the present time [in contrast with previous decades]"(62).

(1) Prerecorded videocassettes (whether commercially produced or produced by student penpals) are likely the most prevalent use of television technology in secondary foreign language instruction. Similar to prerecorded video, international broadcasts may be received in schools via satellite and shown immediately or recorded for later use. Both prerecorded video and satellite transmissions address important curriculum objectives in proficiency-based programs. They portray authentic language, used in context by native speakers—language that is up-to-date and natural. They enhance comprehension by providing a visual context for meaning. They improve students' ability to interpret language with cultural accuracy by allowing insight into the nonverbal aspects of communication in the foreign language, such as proxemics and kinesics. Students can be exposed to a range of accents and voices. Lastly, the visual setting of such video materials is laden with both implicit and explicit cultural information.

(2) Interactive video (IAV) is instructional material in which the video presentation is controlled by computer. It is a hybrid technology combining the capability of the computer to both manage and monitor student use linked with the strong visual potential of either videocassette or videodisc. Unlike teacher-controlled total class presentations of prerecorded video, the computer can provide individual or groups of students with a sequenced series of learning activities specifically responsive to their needs and previous performance. The computer can be programmed to present sequences of video, present computer-based tasks to the student and accept students' keyboarded responses, diagnose their responses, and prescribe further video or computer-based learning experiences. The computer can also provide assistance where needed, such as hints, translations, or transcriptions. Lastly, the computer may be programmed to develop and store records on students' usage and performance.

Bush and Crotty (1989) report the experimental use of IAV at a variety of sites, including a joint project among Brigham Young University, the National Security Agency, and the Defense Language Institute in Monterey; at the Naval Academy in Annapolis; and at the Air Force Academy in Colorado Springs. Although enthusiasm for and interest in IAV is high, the use of this technology is so new that little research exists to support its effectiveness in improving language learning. IAV's drawbacks, unfortunately, are numerous: "The hardware is expensive and complicated, support staff often lacks sufficient expertise to work with it, and there is a dearth of software for the computer and recordings for the associated . . . video materials" (Otto 1989, 35). The labor-intensive nature of IAV courseware development is highlighted by Hughes (1989), who reports favorably on the development and implementation of a 10-unit course in survival Spanish at the Central Intelligence Agency Language School in Washington, D.C. Three videodisc units were developed prior to January 1987. The next seven units required 2 full years to complete by a working group composed of nine professionals, plus a camera crew and an outside programming consultant.

(3) Distance learning offers foreign language instruction to students at dispersed sites via television. It is a contemporary extension of instructional television and differs from the visual presentations above in that the content of the video is direct instruction. Not limited to foreign language instruction, distance learning is increasingly used by school systems and postsecondary institutions to offer learning opportunities that cannot be provided in a cost-effective manner by a teacher at a single site or where there is a shortage of qualified instructors.

Distance learning is becoming prevalent in rural areas or small school districts that cannot afford a diversity of courses with low enrollments or that cannot find qualified staff. Two major distance learning networks—Texas-based Ti-In and Oklahoma State University—offer foreign language courses via satellite transmissions. Warriner-Burke (1990) expresses serious reservations about the effectiveness of distance learning in foreign language courses where student-to-student and teacher-student communication are critically important. She notes, for example, that in a Virginia distance-learning Latin class in which students were linked to the teacher by phone, the average student posed an average of only one question per week. In a lengthy discussion of the current state of distance learning in the United States, *Education Week* (West 1989) described and dismissed the concerns of foreign language educators in a single sentence. Citing a report by Bruce Barker in *Research in Rural Education*, the article notes that little research on the effectiveness of distance learning is available because of the relatively recent implementation of the technology in schools (11).

WHERE IS FOREIGN LANGUAGE GOING? RESEARCH NEEDS FOR THE NINETIES AND BEYOND

The study of foreign language teaching and foreign language acquisition is a relatively new field in the United States. Prior to the 1970s much of classroom practice and professional thought was neither fed nor guided by research. There were, perhaps, many reasons for this. First, "language" was considered the domain of the linguist, who, as Heny (1987) points out, was primarily engaged in abstract and formal description of language and who generally had little professional interest in process or in applying theory to practical problems. American linguistics during at least the first half of this century was, according to Fishman (1972), "primarily a formal discipline, almost along the lines of abstract mathematics" (6). A second reason for the paucity of research prior to the 1970s is related to the traditional status of foreign language study in the United States and of language pedagogy in U.S. institutions of higher learning. Research requires time that must be bought, and funders, either government or private, have not often targeted foreign language study, let alone foreign language research, as high priorities. Foreign language departments, composed primarily of literature specialists, have only recently begun to recognize and reward research efforts in the area of language skill development. The process of language acquisition was long taken for granted, for established tradition had defined its ultimate purpose—literary analysis—as the only legitimate level of scholarly activity. Efforts were also severely hampered by the lack of trained researchers. Few institutions in the country offered advanced degrees in foreign language education (as opposed to literature or linguistics) that could provide any kind of in-depth focus on the educator as researcher. Those that did were caught in a web of competing priorities. Further, undergraduate programs in foreign language teacher preparation have suffered from lack of both time and resources to instill in teachers a respect for the contributions of research and to train them to be research consumers. Finally, as in every other field of education, research has been circumscribed by its very definition: Experimental models borrowed from psychology and the biological sciences have reigned as the one true vehicle for legitimate investigation. The "method" thus determined the questions, and research efforts focused on what was considered "scientifically" researchable. The 1970s saw the beginnings of a surge in research into the process and pedagogy of foreign language development, opening both new areas of inquiry and new investigative procedures. In 1980, a national conference on professional priorities, organized by ACTFL, resulted in some consensus on a redefinition of research, opening the field beyond classical empirical investigation to acknowledge the validity of other research models. This section will highlight some of the issues research has yet to fully explore in terms of the major questions presented in this chapter: the why's, what's, where's, when's, who's, and how's of language, language learning, and language teaching. The reader will notice a great degree of overlap, as research in one area will necessarily affect most other areas as well.

Research Needs: Why Study a Foreign Language?

The perceived purposes and goals of foreign language learning drive, directly or indirectly, the entire research agenda. The new goals of the 1990s and beyond demand new thought. A national agenda that addresses the global needs for a multilingual/multicultural populace demands advanced levels of language proficiency. These new purposes for foreign language study beg for a foreign language research agenda that has as one of its foci the advanced language learner and user. Yet much, if not most, of existing research in foreign language study has explored language learning and teaching in terms of the beginner learner, particularly the student in the first or second year of language study. Longitudinal studies are close to nonexistent. Not only must efforts be made to encourage continued language development in learners, but programs must be in place to accommodate the advanced learner, and research efforts must begin to focus on finding out more about these learners and their needs. Such research should not only enhance programs at the advanced level but inform our efforts at the basal levels as well so that instruction may be characterized by a seamless sequence of learning. Research should address questions such as: Who is the advanced language learner (aside from the foreign language teacher)? What are the individual's perceived needs for language use? Which techniques work best at more advanced levels? What is the language of the advanced language learner? What are the advanced learners' internal theories of what language is, how it works, and how it is learned? What are the causes of language attrition, and which aspects of language use are the most fragile, the most subject to attrition?

Perhaps the most important research agenda derived from national needs and increased attention to the advanced language user, however, pertains to the area of cultural knowledge, cross-cultural sensitivity, and culturally appropriate language use in speaking, listening, reading, and writing. Indeed, it hardly seems possible to define what it means to be advanced in one's use of language without making constant reference to the interplay of linguistic and cultural proficiency. As Byrnes (1991) states,

> Whatever the motivation for an emphasis on language usage and use, the inclusive frame of reference is culture, not language. Therefore a focus on the total communicative event inherently recognizes the superordinateness of cultural phenomena in the use of any language as a system for communicating meaning.

Allen (1985) notes that a great deal of past research has been devoted to defining culture as an object of study. Much less attention has been focused on the development of a conceptual framework that would guide its pedagogy and assessment. While some admirable attempts are already underway to define a cultural proficiency progression (Nostrand 1990), there exists at present no professional consensus as to how cultural proficiency would be reflected at various levels, through verbal and nonverbal behavior and through efforts to create meaning in interpreting and participating in communicative events. Likewise, there exist at present no satisfying instruments for observing and assessing these complex phenomena beyond the factual information and surface attitudinal levels. Assuming that cultural understanding can be fostered, at least to a certain level, through direct classroom instruction, the obvious question is how. Proceeding beyond the isolated culture capsule and sporadic teacher anecdote to true integration of language and culture in cognitively engaging activity will require very planned and purposeful pedagogy.

A variety of approaches is currently being suggested by educators. Some combine a focus on knowledge about the culture with the development of investigative skills and a process of discovery (Lange and Crawford-Lange 1984). Some advocate integrating the teaching of culture with the productive skills through attention to the social context of discourse (Kramsch 1987). And some are exploring the power of thematically linked authentic written texts to foster four-skills development while aiding other culture framework building through a guided process of discovery that begins with students' existing cultural schemata (American Council on the Teaching of Foreign Languages 1987). Research comparing these approaches or their combinations at various levels of language learning and that focuses on specific targeted aspects of learner cultural development would not only contribute greatly to our notions of cultural proficiency but would provide a much-needed groundwork for curricular and instructional planning and materials development.

Research Needs: Where Are Foreign Languages Studied?

Foreign languages are, by definition, studied outside the foreign culture, often at great distances from their native users. Contacts with the real language and culture and opportunities for their use are thus limited to the teacher (who is likely not to be a native), the textbook, the tape-recorded voice (with or without its visual coordination or complement), an array of print materials ranging from advertisements to literary works, and, sometimes, native-speaking community members. This becomes an important consideration in interpreting and planning research efforts, for the bulk of past studies of acquisition and classroom-based research focuses not on the learning of foreign languages but rather on the learning and teaching of second languages—usually English as a second language. Foreign languages are learned outside the community in which the language is spoken; in contrast, second languages are those learned within the context of the foreign culture. Second language learners in comparison with foreign language learners may have totally different motivational and attitudinal configurations and totally different acquisition needs and pressures. A vast variety of culturally influenced personal, social, and academic backgrounds converge in second language classrooms. Second language learners, as distinct from foreign language learners, are surrounded by the language and culture under study, both in and out of the classroom.

At times foreign language professionals have been too quick to build a knowledge base on the second language learning research base, often reluctantly dismissing the differences between foreign and second language learning. The primary research agenda suggested by these differences is simple to state, but more overwhelming in its implementation: Replications of existing second language studies with foreign language learners are needed.

Research Needs: What Do We Know About the Efficacy of Foreign Language Programs?

Secondary Programs. Sadly, one of the most under-researched elements of foreign language education concerns the precollegiate setting, particularly the high school. Much foreign language research is of a laboratory nature in that it ignores the programmatic and instructional variables that come to play in any study of learner products. No systematic accounting exists as to what takes place in the foreign language classroom, and one is obviously more inclined to hear about innovation than norm. Ethnographic studies would be of tremendous utility in this regard. Such qualitative research might be followed up by more quantitive studies examining the issue of efficacy by applying proficiency assessment measures to derive a sense of the ranges of communicative abilities of high school students after 2 years and 4 years of study. National goal statements, such as those issued by the College Board for entry-level proficiency, might be used as performance criteria for schools wishing to undergo program self-assessment. And the appropriateness of these and other criteria we establish must be examined. According to Henning (1989), research is needed to ascertain whether students can indeed attain the proficiency levels described in the literature within the constraints of academic programs. Studies conducted at the state-wide, district, or school level as to what students are able to do in the language, as well as their levels of cross-cultural sophistication, would provide for more informed secondary program assessment and curriculum development.

Elementary School Programs. In contrast with the dearth of data on the efficacy of secondary foreign language curriculum and instruction, there has been more research at the elementary school level, although this research has been constrained by limited instrumentation. Two kinds of research questions have been asked about the outcomes of elementary school foreign language programs: (1) How well do programs achieve the goals and objectives they have set for themselves? and (2) How do the foreign language outcomes of the major program models compare with one another?

Until recently, either of these questions was difficult to answer because instrumentation that could appropriately assess the foreign language skills of younger learners was woefully inadequate. Most language assessment instruments were developed for a secondary or postsecondary population. Since even the first language skills of younger students differ substantially from those of older students, it is questionable whether tests developed for one population can be appropriately extended to another. Moreover, standardized tests that can validly and reliably measure language skills date back to the mid-1960s. As such, these tests reflect an emphasis far removed from the realities of today's approaches to skill development and assessment. For example, the Modern Language Association (MLA) Cooperative tests (Educational Testing Service 1963) include a writing section that is primarily a multiple-choice grammar test. Today's approach to writing focuses on writing as a process, as a tool for interpersonal communication, emphasizing the purpose of writing and the audience in the composition of written text.

The development of a common yardstick to measure the foreign language skills of secondary and postsecondary students was a major initiative of ACTFL. While the development of the ACTFL rating scales represents a major step forward in the profession's ability to assess the development of foreign language learners, it is questionable whether the rating scales may be used to assess the efficacy of early language programs. Most significantly, the ACTFL rating scales are predicated upon and derive from the presumed performance of educated adult native speakers. Inherent in the scales, then, is the notion that certain topics (and related language functions) are characteristic of educated adults and, therefore, require a certain degree of cognitive maturity and world knowledge. Clearly, young learners would be at a distinct disadvantage when assessed with such a rating scale. Further, the scales describe mature foreign language learners at progressive developmental stages, stages derived from observations and analysis of adult language learners. Little is known about the generalizability of such descriptive statements of the development of adult learners to the development of child language learners. Lastly, the most widely used of the rating scales, the oral proficiency guidelines, require a face-to-face interview with a trained rater. It is questionable whether such raters are equally competent to work with young children and whether younger learners will respond comfortably and appropriately to unknown adults.

Despite the difficulties in instrumentation described above, a growing body of data provides insights into the language skills of students in elementary school foreign language programs. Since the late 1960s, Canadian researchers have studied the French skills of students in immersion programs. Using a variety of instruments developed specifically for this purpose, researchers have examined the skills of immersion students in comparison with those of students in other kinds of elementary school French programs (Stern, Swain, McLean, Friedman, Harley, and Lapkin 1976) and have also compared the language development of immersion students with those of native Francophone students in Canada (Genesee 1987). In general, the findings of these studies have consistently shown immersion students to outperform students in other program models (such as Core French, the Canadian counterpart to FLES). Longitudinal analysis of the development of students' French skills has shown that participating students develop nativelike abilities in the receptive skills (listening and reading), but rarely approach native-speaker norms in speaking and writing. Characteristically, immersion students are highly proficient in communicating in French, but frequently lack sufficient grammatical accuracy to be considered nativelike in their control. Hypotheses regarding the causes of this situation and approaches to remediation are currently under study in Canada (Day and Shapson 1987, 1989; Harley and Swain 1984; Lapkin and Swain 1984).

In the United States, studies of immersion students have also yielded very positive results. Campbell, Gray, Rhodes, and Snow (1985) used the MLA Cooperative Tests to investigate the foreign language skills of students in FLES and in partial and total immersion programs. Since students in FLES programs spend considerably less time involved with the foreign language than do students in immersion programs, and since partial immersion students receive approximately half as much exposure to the foreign language as do total immersion students, it came as no surprise that total immersion students significantly outperformed partial immersion students, who, in turn, outperformed FLES students. Of greater signficance, however, was the finding that both groups of immersion students scored at the 98th percentile (or above) on the speaking portion of the test, a test normed on secondary students who had completed 2 years of a foreign language. The FLES students, who had studied Spanish from 4 to 7 years, scored better than 60 percent of the second-year high school students on whom the test was normed in 1963. The French FLES students attained speaking scores better than 40 percent of the high school norming group. Perhaps of greatest relevance for future research was the finding that within-group variances were greater than cross-group variances. Further study is needed to identify which program variables may have contributed to the finding that within the total immersion group, for example, there were wide variations in student performance on the MLA test.

Other studies of immersion programs in the United States have consistently shown results that parallel those found in Canadian studies (Genesee 1987).

Attempts to adapt the ACTFL rating scales for use in assessing elementary school foreign language programs in both Canada and the United States have been limited. An informal study of students in a Pittsburgh foreign language program revealed that the ACTFL rating scales were difficult to use with students in the elementary grades and might yield more useful data to evaluate programs than students. In Canada, Rabiteau and Taft (1985) adapted the ACTFL rating scales for use with eighth-grade immersion students and reported satisfactory results.

In an attempt to address the need for valid and reliable measures of elementary school foreign language students' skills, the Center for Applied Linguistics developed two tests: the FLES test and the COPE test. The FLES test for Spanish assesses the listening and reading skills of students who have studied Spanish for a minimum of 30 minutes per week to a maximum of 3 hours per week. The COPE (Clear Oral Proficiency Exam) measures students' ability to comprehend and speak Spanish, particularly in a school context. The COPE requires a role play between two students and measures cognitive/academic and social language skills; its rating scale is adapted from the ACTFL guidelines for oral proficiency interviews.

Thompson, Richardson, Wang, and Rhodes (1988) found that students tested with the FLES test for Spanish demonstrated that they had, indeed, mastered the language objectives typically set in a FLES program: For example, students could correctly comprehend weather expressions and could label foods accurately. Using the COPE test, Rhodes, Thompson, and Snow (1989) reported that immersion students demonstrated a similar skill pattern to that of Canadian French immersion students: Students were most developed in their ability to understand the foreign language, demonstrated strong skills in the area of fluency and vocabulary, and were weakest in grammatical accuracy. Reflecting the findings of the earlier Campbell, Gray, Rhodes, and Snow (1985) study, the COPE test showed significant variability within the immersion program model.

Further research on appropriate instrumentation and on assessing program results is critically needed for several reasons. First, elementary school foreign language programs must be able to substantiate their ability to contribute to the achievement of the foreign language curriculum's goals and objectives. Second, as programs proliferate, articulation with secondary level programs becomes critical. Reliable means of determining how far learners have progressed in their foreign language development are needed to ensure that students will continue to improve and expand the skills they have acquired previously. Lastly, assessment of the development of the foreign language skills of elementary school students may inform decisions about curriculum and instruction at all levels.

Research Needs: What Is Foreign Language Learning?

To date, we have only scanty research in the area of theory testing. As has been noted, predominant theories, only a few of which have been mentioned in this chapter, are, in their present state, quite vague and imprecise. Not only has their lack of clear hypotheses and operational definitions deterred investigative efforts but the nature of the phenomenon of language acquisition itself resists probing, requiring as it does not only getting into the individual mind but staying there for years. Some researchers, such as Anderson (1983), have investigated the role of cognitive processing through artificial intelligence and complex computer task simulations, but unlocking the mystery of second language acquisition remains a futuristic notion. At present, we have only hunches, derived from various other fields, from existing second language research, and from the intuition that comes from experience. These hunches are cast not in terms of the globality of language acquisition but rather in terms of certain of its aspects. The following are just a few of the many notions that suggest themselves for research. An exhaustive account of the research agenda that either these specific categories or the broad topic itself might prompt is well beyond the scope of this (or perhaps any one single) chapter. Further, present questions are limited by present knowledge base. New knowledge will give rise to many new considerations.

Is There a Fixed and Predictable Sequence to Language Acquisition That Functions Apart from Any Instruction Received? It has been suggested that learners are endowed with an internal syllabus for learning the language and that this will psychologically determine their path. Classroom learners are also given an external syllabus, which may be different. In terms of the two, the internal syllabus is stronger and comes to the fore when the learner is placed in spontaneous, uncontrolled communicative situations. Some evidence that purports to support this notion comes from the so-called morpheme studies. These cross-sectional studies (Dulay and Burt 1974; Larsen-Freeman 1975) analyzed the speech of learners at one point in time and found similarities in the accuracy of use of certain morphemes (e.g., "-ing" endings and plural "s," articles such as "the" and "a"). The researchers thus concluded that second language learners display an inherent acquisition sequence. Other researchers (Littlewood 1984; McLaughlin 1988) point out, however, that accuracy order is not a reliable indicator of acquisition order. There are also studies that contradict this observed sequence (Hakuta 1976) and others that point to the contamination of task, method, and performance in the morpheme research. Much more research is needed on this "natural order" hypothesis before it can be accepted by the professional community. Further, such studies must be performed with learners of different languages from different language backgrounds, as well as similar ages, extralinguistic backgrounds, and instructional programs as they communicate spontaneously at different proficiency levels. The notion of natural order, whether universal or personal, is a powerful one and would have implications for all of language pedagogy.

How Can We Best Measure Language Acquisition? In terms of the measurement of proficiency, Henning (1989) suggests the following: Conduct studies related to understanding better the relationship between time spent in language study and the attainment of meaningful proficiency levels, and continue research into the appropriate constructs for language proficiency assessment across languages.

A study recently undertaken by ACTFL (Dandonoli and Henning 1990) sought to determine the construct validity of the proficiency guidelines and oral interview procedures in both French and English as a second language. Though the study warrants replication, results indicate that the guidelines satisfactorily capture an assessment construct in all skills areas but one—listening. Since the guidelines were constructed by professional consensus based on current knowledge bases, the researchers conclude that much more remains to be learned, especially in the area of listening, so that assessment criteria can be devised that more accurately reflect the variables which come to play in this complex process.

The 1989 ACTFL Professional Priorities Conference targeted proficiency assessment issues as a high priority in the coming decade. Further work in this area will open new doors to other types of experimental research. The existence of one reliable and valid framework for assessing language acquired will represent a valuable springboard to probing more deeply into the construct of proficiency.

Research Needs: Who Is the Learner?

It is perhaps the focus on the learners themselves that will have the most impact on all other research topics, informing us on both acquisition issues and promising pedagogy.

Learning Styles. At present, research into the phenomenon of learning styles is severely hampered by several factors: First, only a narrow array of traits has been studied, and some of these traits are of questionable definition. Research that is to inform our pedagogy must begin to address the notion of style by acknowledging the legitimacy of every style. If cognitive traits are to be examined, then research must focus on better identification and definition of what these cognitive traits are. In addition, scores of learning style inventories exist, each with different classifications and labeling systems. The lack of a standard, accepted instrument for use in foreign language research militates against widespread professional sharing and synthesis of results. A better notion of style might be gained by focusing on more understandable and observable learner characteristics, not just in the area of cognition but in social, perceptual, and environmental preferences as well. The latter are just beginning to be explored.

Learning Strategies. Perhaps no other body of research has brought such a breath of fresh air into the classroom as that in the area of learning strategies, for it has helped to dispel the dangerous notion of the inherently less able foreign language learner. According to researchers such as Chamot (1989),

> What distinguished effective from ineffective language learners in the students we studied was that effective students had a range of learning strategies which they used often and which they tailored to the demands of the language task. Ineffective students, on the other hand, used strategies in very limited and often inappropriate ways. Looking at students' abilities in terms of strategies rather than in terms of aptitude has profound implications for instruction. Strategies can be taught and learned, whereas aptitude is generally thought to be innate and unchangeable. (viii)

Intralearner Variability. Research throughout the last two decades has focused on the variability among learners and has allowed a glimpse at the diversity of any given classroom population. Yet, virtually nothing is known about the variability within an individual. Humans are incredibly chaotic creatures, full of unpredictability and irregularity. Their images are not captured on the spot through one glance at one act or one product in one context at one moment of the day; rather, the image of an individual is formed through patterns within ambiguity and contradiction. Research that focuses on observations of microsegments of an individual's classroom life, or that focuses on mass student reaction to pedagogical practices or comparison of student products, will tell us very little about the learner. Hand in hand with ongoing efforts that apply treatments and observation to multitudes of individuals is the need for research that explores the individual, through multitudes of treatments and observations, as he or she engages in complex acts in a variety of contexts. The chaotic nature of humans in a chaotic world may require that we look for ranges and levels and depths in individuals themselves—cognitive ranges, interactional ranges, comfort ranges, development ranges. Learning more about learners may require that we devote more in-depth attention to the learner. Otherwise, all of our seemingly sturdy conclusions and implications for pedagogy may be built on nothing more than shifting sands.

Research Needs: How Should Foreign Languages Be Taught?

Gone are the days when we could provide simplistic answers to the question of how to teach foreign languages. Gone also are the days when our research would look at this question simply as an either/or investigation. Now, the how's are colored by a complex of other considerations, namely, the whats, the whos, the whens, and the whys. The failure of the methods comparison research of the late sixties to identify any one method as superior to any other in secondary classrooms has led to nearly three decades of eclecticism. While the lack of prescriptions for success has caused many teachers frustration, for countless others it has represented the opportunity for responsible exercise of pedagogical freedom.

The pitfalls of confounding variables as revealed by large-scale methods research have left the profession with a research agenda that is less than neatly summarized, for it is as open and far reaching as the researcher's mind will permit. Each new professional learning and leaning could give rise to myriad classroom-based studies. The past two decades have, in fact, seen a plethora of classroom-based research, which has focused not on packaged methodologies but rather on cataloging and analyzing the effects of discrete teacher-student acts in the instructional process. To mention only a few of these topics would be to ignore hundreds of others of equal value in their existing and potential contribution to our knowledge of the effects of classroom instructional variables. What we have learned is that some techniques are effective with some teachers and some learners; others, with others. The questions outlined here, then, provide just a sampling of some of the areas worth investigating in the coming years. Other "how" questions are raised in other portions of this section.

Teaching and Learning. One of the factors that large-scale methods studies failed to consider was learner variability, for in any classroom, one method is going to appeal to some but not all students. Further, many of the packaged methods available today are theoretically derived from notions of base-level learning. Research is needed that builds on what we know about learner variables to assess the compatibility of different methods and instructional approaches with different learners. The question to address is not "What works?" but rather, "What works for whom, and under what circumstances?" For teachers, the development of teaching repertoires to serve diverse populations of learners will not consist as much of collecting classroom activities as it will of being flexibly attuned to learner needs—judging when, why, how, and with whom to use a particular strategy. Among other factors, we might reexamine the age-old deductive-inductive debate in terms of learners, contexts, topic complexity, and proficiency level so that ways may be devised to accommodate the continuous interplay of the two approaches. While we know that learners differ in preferred perceptual modes, we have yet to explore the effects of multisensory presentation, as opposed to practice opportunities, with adult learners. Many other such questions are outlined throughout this section.

Classroom Error. Most of classroom-based research on error has focused on its treatment and correction in controlled versus noncontrolled instructional contexts. Few studies, however, have focused on the classroom as a source of error. We thus have little information as to whether pedagogical practices and textbook delivery systems could actually induce error. Kasper (1982), for example, notes that demands for complete sentence responses in situations in which such behavior would be inappropriate may be teaching students to violate pragmatic and discourse rules of language use. Research is needed to help us identify traditional practice and presentation patterns that may be placing artificial obstacles in the path of the learner's acquisition. For example, all language learners of French and Spanish will recall the frequent use in textbooks of contrastive blocks—such as *ser* versus *estar*; *savoir* versus *connaître*, *por* versus *para*—which have their roots in English translation notions. Yet, with what we know about memory storage and retrieval, the simultaneous, rule-charted storage of these semantically different yet lexically alike concepts may be placing undue burdens on learner memory, actually inducing error in their use. It may be that the very pairing of such contrasts creates undue associations in the learner's mind. Would confusion result if such confusion were not expected and if presentation and practice did not deliberately set students up for confusion? Many more examples such as these could be found in textbooks and teaching practices, and their effects are very researchable.

Functional Presentation and Practice. Research is needed on the question of the relationship between studying grammar and acquiring language. Most teachers still use a structuralist or form-driven model of grammar that does not clarify when a particular form is preferred or what is implied by choosing a particular form over another in various situations. Research may inform us as to whether functional facility is best achieved through practice with linguistic features or through emphasis on linguistic tasks, functions, notions, or situations. While functional language use may be the goal of instruction, the routes to this goal have not yet been fully explored. Research that focuses on different types of learners of different ages and background may show these factors to be highly learner-personal.

Task Design and Expert Guidance. Another interesting and potentially informing area of research concerns the structure and design of language use tasks. Frawley and Lantolf (1984), for example, offer persuasive illustration of the influence of the task itself in deterring or inflating individual performance. Studies of task bias might be complemented by comparative studies of learner-based task design.

Vocabulary and Grammar Learning. Very little research exists in the area of vocabulary presentation and practice. A few studies have begun to explore the complex area of vocabulary storage and retrieval (Thompson 1987); however, identification of instructional techniques and their comparative assessment in isolation and combination remain crucial topics for investigation. Studies that examine materials development need to elucidate the rate of transfer and recursiveness in developing a structural scope and sequence. Advocates of proficiency have long espoused a spiraling grammatical syllabus that would be based on communicative needs and development of learner flexibility, and that would be geared not toward the digestion of discrete chunks of grammar but rather toward learner language use that expands in breadth and fullness. What would such a grammar look like in scope at the different levels? What appear to be the most effective sequencing options?

Further research into topics such as these may allow us a far better sense of the efficacy of classroom instruction. Indeed, we may have only scratched the surface in our notions of what can be taught and learned in our schools.

CONCLUSION

This chapter has reviewed the research on foreign language curriculum from a variety of viewpoints. We have examined the context in which foreign language learning takes place: the reasons for learning languages and the elementary and secondary school settings where instruction occurs. Both the rationale for foreign language learning and the school settings for it interact with how curriculum is designed and delivered. We have seen how differing reasons for language study have resulted in differing emphases on skills development. In the 1980s and continuing into the 1990s, we have seen that global interdependence—both economic and political—have led to curricula that stress communication as an interactive process rooted in the dynamic between listener and speaker or reader/author and text. What students may study, and where and when, depends on where they go to school. Opportunities for language learning increase as students progress from the elementary to the middle to the high school level. And, despite a growing recognition of the importance of a number of world languages, most students still enroll in the languages favored in our schools in the last three or four decades: French, German, Latin, and Spanish.

Most important, this chapter has examined differing definitions of what it means to learn—or know—another language, and has discussed these in light of prevailing, although clearly not definitive, theories of language learning and language acquisition. We have seen that variability among and within learners—how they learn and who they are—interacts significantly with how languages are taught and who teaches them. The delivery system of foreign language instruction includes teachers and technology and reflects instructional design features such as methodology and courseware.

Although the purpose of this chapter has been to review what we know about foreign language curriculum, a significant portion of the chapter has been devoted to a discussion of directions for further research. As we noted early in the chapter, the foreign language profession is a relatively young one. And while we have made considerable progress in a brief period in identifying the elements and agents of curriculum that will result in effective foreign language learning and teaching, there is still much for us to learn.

References

Allen, Wendy W. 1985. "Toward Cultural Proficiency." In *Proficiency, Curriculum, Articulation: The Ties That Bind*, edited by A. C. Omaggio, 137–166. Middlebury, VT: Northeast Conference on the Teaching of Foreign Language.

American Council on the Teaching of Foreign Languages. 1982. *ACTFL Provisional Proficiency Guidelines*. Hastings-on-Hudson, NY: ACTFL.

American Council on the Teaching of Foreign Languages. 1984. ACTFL survey of foreign language enrollments in public secondary schools, Fall 1982. *Foreign Language Annals* 17(6): 611–623.

American Council on the Teaching of Foreign Languages. 1986. *Proficiency Guidelines*. Hastings-on-Hudson, NY: ACTFL.

American Council on the Teaching of Foreign Languages. 1987a. *Faculty Workshops on the Use of Authentic Texts to Develop Cultural Understanding in Foreign Language Programs*. Yonkers, NY: ACTFL.

American Council on the Teaching of Foreign Languages. 1987b. *ACTFL Public Awareness Network Newsletter: A Bimonthly Report on Foreign Language and International Studies*. Hastings-on-Hudson, NY: ACTFL.

American Council on the Teaching of Foreign Languages. 1988a. *ACTFL Teacher Education Guidelines*. Hastings-on-Hudson, NY: ACTFL.

American Council on the Teaching of Foreign Languages. 1988b. Provisional program guidelines for foreign language teacher education. *Foreign Language Annals* 21(1): 71–82.

Anderson, John R. 1983. *The Architecture of Cognition*. Cambridge, MA: Harvard University Press.

Andrade, Carolyn, Richard R. Kretschmer, and Laura W. Kretschmer. 1989. "Two Languages for All Children: Expanding to Low Achievers and the Handicapped." In *Languages in Elementary Schools*, edited by K. E. Muller, 177–203. New York: American Forum.

Asher, James J. 1981. *Learning Another Language Through Actions: The Complete Teacher's Guidebook*. Los Gatos, CA: Sky Oaks.

Bailey, Kathy, Alice Omaggio Hadley, Sally Sieloff Magnan, and Janet Swaffer. 1989. "Priorities for Research in the 1990's: Review, Expand, Initiate." Unpublished paper delivered at the ACTFL Priorities Conference, Boston, MA.

Bamford, Kathleen W., and Donald T. Mizokawa. 1989. "Cognitive and Attitudinal Outcomes of an Additive-Bilingual Program." Paper presented at the annual meeting of the American Educational Research Association, San Francisco, CA.

Beebe, Leslie M. 1983. "Risk-Taking and the Language Learner." In *Classroom Oriented Research in Second Language Acquisition*, edited by H. M. Seliger and Michael H. Long, 39–65. Rowley, MA: Newbury House.

Ben Zeev, S. 1977. "Mechanism by Which Childhood Bilingualism Affects Understanding of Language and Cognitive Structures." In *Bilingualism: Psychological, Social, and Educational Implications*, edited by P. A. Hornby. New York: Academic Press.

Bialystock, Ellen. 1981. The role of conscious strategies in second language proficiency. *Modern Language Journal* 65(1): 24–35.

Bialystock, Ellen. 1983a. "Some Factors in the Selection and Implementation of Communication Strategies." In *Strategies in Interlanguage Communication*, edited by C. Faerch and Gabriele Kaspar, 100–118. London: Longman.

Bialystock, Ellen. 1983b. "Inferencing: Testing the 'Hypothesis-Testing' Hypothesis." In *Classroom Oriented Research in Second Language Acquisition*, edited by H. W. Seliger and Michael H. Long, 104–123. Rowley, MA: Newbury House.

Bialystock, Ellen, and Maria Frohlich. 1978. Variables of classroom achievement in second language learning. *The Modern Language Journal* 62(7): 327–336.

Birckbichler, Diane W. 1984. "The Challenge of Proficiency: Student Characteristics." In *The Challenge for Excellence in Foreign Language Education*, edited by G. A. Jarvis, 47–70. Middlebury, VT: Northeast Conference on the Teaching of Foreign Languages.

Boyer, Ernest L. 1983. *High School: A Report on Secondary Education in America*. New York: Harper & Row.

Brooks, Nelson. 1960. *Language and Language Learning: Theory and Practice*. New York: Harcourt Brace & World.

Bruck, Margaret. 1978. The suitability of early French immersion programs for the language-disabled child. *Canadian Modern Language Review* 34(5): 834–851.

Bruck, Margaret. 1982. Language impaired children's performance in an additive bilingual education program. *Applied Psycholinguistics* 3(1): 45–60.

Bruck, Margaret, Wallace E. Lambert, and Richard Tucker. 1974. Bilingual schooling through the elementary grades: The St. Lambert project at grade seven. *Language Learning* 24(2): 183–204.

Bush, Michael D., and Jill Crotty. 1989. "Interactive Videodisc in Language Teaching." In *Modern Technology in Foreign Language Education: Applications and Projects*, edited by W. F. Smith, 75–95. Lincolnwood, IL: National Textbook.

Byrnes, Heidi. 1985. "Teaching Toward Proficiency: The Receptive Skills." In *Proficiency, Curriculum, Articulation: The Ties That Bind*, edited by Alice Omaggio, 77–107. Middlebury, VT: Northeast Conference on the Teaching of Foreign Languages.

Byrnes, Heidi. October 1989. "Reflections on the Development of Cross-Cultural Communicative Competence in the Foreign Language Classroom." Paper presented at the Conference on Foreign Language Acquisition Research and the Classroom. Philadelphia: University of Pennsylvania and The Consortium for Language Teaching and Learning.

Byrnes, Heidi. November 1989. "Addressing Curriculum Articulation in the Nineties: A Proposal." Paper delivered at the ACTFL Priorities Conference, Boston, MA.

Byrnes, Heidi. 1991. "Reflections on the Development of Cross-Cultural Communicative Competence in the Foreign Language Classroom." In *Foreign Language Acquisition Research and the Classroom*, edited by B. Freed. Boston: Heath.

Campbell, R., and R. Wales. 1970. "The Study of Language Acquisition." In *New Horizons in Linguistics*, edited by J. Lyons. Harmondsworth, England: Penguin.

Campbell, Russell M., T. C. Gray, N. C. Rhodes, and M. A. Snow. 1985. Foreign language learning in the elementary schools: A comparison of three language programs. *Modern Language Journal* 69(1): 44–54.

Canale, Michael, and Merrill Swain. 1980. Theoretical bases of communicative approaches to second language teaching and testing. *Applied Linguistics* 1(1): 1–47.

Carpenter, John A., and Judith Torney. 1973. "Beyond the Melting Pot." In *Children and Intercultural Education*, edited by P. M. Markun and J. L. Land. Washington, DC: Association for Childhood Education International.

Chamot, Anna Uhl. 1987. "The Learning Strategies of ESL Students." In *Learner Strategies in Language Learning*, edited by Anita Wenden and Joan Rubin, 71–83. Englewood Cliffs, NJ: Prentice Hall International.

Chamot, Anna Uhl. 1989. *Learning Strategy Instruction in the Foreign Language Classroom: A Teacher's Resource Guide*. McLean, VA: Interstate Research Associates.

Chamot, Anna Uhl, and Lisa Kupper. 1989. Learning strategies in foreign language instruction. *Foreign Language Annals* 22(1): 13–28.

Cheney, Lynne V. 1987. *American Memory: A Report of the Humanities in the Nation's Public Schools*. Washington, DC: National Endowment for the Humanities.

Cohen, Andrew. 1987. "Studying Learner Strategies: How Do We Get the Information?" In *Learner Strategies in Language Learning,* edited by Anita Wenden and Joan Rubin, 31–42. Englewood Cliffs, NJ: Prentice Hall International.

Collier, Virginia P. 1989. How long: A synthesis of research on academic achievement in second language. *TESOL Quarterly* 23(3): 509–531.

Commission on Foreign Language and International Studies. 1979. *Strength Through Wisdom: A Critique of U.S. Capability*. Washington, DC: Government Printing Office.

Cooper, Thomas. 1987. Foreign language study and SAT verbal scores. *Foreign Language Journal* 71(4): 381–387.

Cortese, Giuseppina. 1985. From receptive to productive in post-intermediate EFL classes: A pedagogical experiment. *TESOL Quarterly* 19(1): 7–23.

Cummins, James. 1981. "The Role of Primary Language Development in Promoting Educational Success for Language Minority Students." In *Schooling and Language Minority Students: A Theoretical Framework,* 3–49. Los Angeles: California State University, Evaluation, Dissemination, and Assessment Center.

Cummins, James. 1983. "Language Proficiency and Academic Achievement." In *Current Issues in Language Testing Research*, edited by J. W. Oller, 108–129. Rowley, MA: Newbury House.

Curtain, Helena, and Carol Ann Pesola. 1988. *Languages and Children: Making the Match*. Reading, MA: Addison-Wesley.

Dandonoli, Patricia. 1987. Report on foreign language enrollment in public secondary schools, fall 1985. *Foreign Language Annals* 20(5): 457–470.

Dandonoli, Patricia, and Grant Henning. 1990. An investigation of the construct validity of the ACTFL proficiency guidelines and oral interview procedure. *Foreign Language Annals* 23(1): 11–22.

Davies, Graham D. 1989. "CALL and NCCALL in the United Kingdom: Past, Present, and Future." In *Modern Technology in Foreign Language Education: Applications and Projects*, edited by W. F. Smith, 161–180. Lincolnwood, IL: National Textbook.

Day, Elaine M., and Stan M. Shapson. 1987. Assessment of oral communicative skills in early French immersion programmes. *Journal of Multilingual and Multicultural Development* 8(3): 237–260.

Day, Elaine M., and Stan M. Shapson. 1989. *Integrating Formal and Functional Approaches in Language Teaching in French Immersion: An Experimental Study*. Vancouver, B.C.: Simon Fraser University.

Draper, Jamie B. 1989. *The State of the States: State Initiatives in Foreign Languages and International Studies, 1979–1989*. Washington, DC: Joint National Committee for Languages.

Dulay, Heidi C., and Marina K. Burt. 1974. Natural sequences in child second language acquisition. *Language Learning* 24(1): 37–53.

Dunn, Rita, J. Beaudry, and Angela Klavas. 1989. Survey of research on learning styles. *Educational Leadership* 46(March): 50–58.

Duquette, Georges. 1988. "Do Cultural Perceptions Facilitate Second-Language Learning?" In *Second Language Acquisition: Selected Readings in Theory and Practice*, edited by G. H. Irons, 343–352. Welland, Ontario, Canada: Canadian Modern Language Review.

Educational Testing Service. 1989. *What Americans Study*. Princeton, NJ: Policy Information Center, Educational Testing Service.

Edwards, Henry, et al. 1984. Second-language acquisition through subject-matter learning: A study of sheltered psychology classes at the University of Ottawa. *The Canadian Modern Language Review* 41(2): 268–282.

Ehrmann, Madeline, and Rebecca Oxford. 1988. "Ants, Grasshoppers, Badgers, and Butterflies: Qualitative Exploration of Adult Language Learning Styles and Strategies." Paper presented at the Ohio State University Symposium on Research and Perspectives on Adult Language Learning and Acquisition, Columbus.

Ely, Christopher. 1986. An Analysis of discomfort, risktaking, sociability and motivation in the second language classroom. *Language Learning* 36(1): 1–25.

Fishman, Joshua A. 1970. *Sociolinguistics: A Brief Introduction*. Rowley, MA: Newbury House.

Fishman, Joshua A. 1972. "Introduction." In *Readings in the Sociology of Language*. The Hague: Mouton.

Foster, Karen M. 1987. "CODOFIL French Instruction and Its Relationships to Higher-Cognitive Processing and Metacognitive Processing." Unpublished doctoral dissertation, University of Southern Mississippi, Hattiesburg.

Frawley, William, and James P. Lantolf. 1984. Second language discourse: A Vygotskyan perspective. *Applied Linguistics* 6(1): 19–44.

Galloway, Vicki B. 1983a. "Foreign Language and the 'Other' Student." In *Foreign Languages: Key Links in the Chain of Learning*, edited by R. G. Mead, Jr., 96–119. Middlebury, VT: Northeast Conference on the Teaching of Foreign Language.

Galloway, Vicki B. 1983b. Foreign language in the schools: Through the looking glass. *Modern Language Journal* 67(4): 342–354.

Galloway, Vicki B. 1987. "From Defining to Developing Proficiency: A Look at the Decision." In *Defining and Developing Proficiency: Guidelines, Implementations and Concepts*, edited by Heidi Byrnes and Michael Canale, 25–73. Lincolnwood, IL: National Textbook.

Galloway, Vicki, and Angela Labarca. 1990. "From Student to Learner: Style, Process and Strategy." In *New Perspectives and New Directions in Foreign Language Education*, edited by Diane Birckbichler, 111–158. Lincolnwood, IL: National Textbook.

Gardner, Robert C., and Wallace E. Lambert. 1972. *Attitudes and Motivation in Second Language Learning*. Rowley, MA: Newbury House.

Garfinkel, Alan, and Kenneth E. Tabor. 1987. "Elementary School Foreign Languages and English Reading Achievement: A New View of the Relationship." Unpublished manuscript, Purdue University, West Lafayette, IN.

Genesee, Fred. 1987. *Learning Through Two Languages*. Rowley, MA: Newbury House.

Gould, Stephen Jay. 1981. *The Mismeasure of Man*. New York: Norton.

Grittner, Frank M. 1990. "Bandwagons Revisited: A Perspective on Movements in Foreign Language Methodology." In *New Perspectives and New Directions in Foreign Language Education*, edited by Diane Birckbichler, 9–43. Lincolnwood, IL: National Textbook.

Hakuta, Kenji. 1976. Becoming bilingual: A case study of a Japanese child learning English. *Language Learning* 26(3): 321–351.

Hakuta, Kenji. 1984. *The Causal Relationship Between the Development of Bilingualism, Cognitive Flexibility, and Social-Cognitive Skills in Hispanic Elementary School Children*. Rosslyn, VA: National Clearinghouse for Bilingual Eduation.

Hakuta, Kenji. 1986a. *Cognitive Development of Bilingual Children*. Los Angeles: UCLA, Center for Language Education and Research.

Hakuta, Kenji. 1986b. *Mirror of Language: The Debate on Bilingualism*. New York: Basic Books.

Hammerly, Hector. 1987. The immersion approach: Litmus test of second language acquisition through classroom communication. *Modern Language Journal* 71(4): 395–401.

Harley, Birgit. 1986. *Age in Second Language Acquisition*. San Diego, CA: College-Hill Press.

Harley, Birgit, and Merrill Swain. 1984. "The Interlanguage of Immersion Students and Its Implications for Second Language Teaching." In *Interlanguage*, edited by A. Davies, C. Criper, and A. P. R. Howatt, 291–311. Edinburgh,Scotland: Edinburgh University Press.

Harlow, Linda L. 1988. The effects of the yellow highlighter—second-language learner strategies and their effectiveness: A research update. *The Canadian Modern Language Review* 45(1): 91–102.

Hauptman, Philip C., Marjorie B. Wesche, and Doreen Ready. 1988. Second-language acquisition through subject-matter learning: A follow-up study at the University of Ottawa. *Language Learning* 38(3): 433–475.

Heilenman, Laura K., and Isabelle Kaplan. 1984. "Proficiency in Practice: The Foreign Language Curriculum." In *Foreign Language Proficiency in the Classroom and Beyond*, edited by Charles James, 55–78. Lincolnwood, IL: National Textbook.

Henning, Grant. 1989. "Priority Issues in the Assessment of Communicative Language Abilities." Paper presented at the ACTFL Priorities Conference, Boston, MA.

Heny, Frank. 1987. "Theoretical Linguistics, Second Language Acquisition, and Language Pedagogy." In *Foreign Language Instruction: A National Agenda*, edited by R. D. Lambert, 194–210. Newbury Park, CA: Sage.

Hewitt, Nancy Maisto. 1989. "Reading, Cognitive Style, and Culture: A Look at Some Relationships in Second Language Acquisition." In *Issues in Second Language: Theory as Practice, Practice as Theory*, edited by Angela Labarca and Leslie Bailey, 62–87. Norwood, NJ: ABLEX.

Higgs, Theodore V., and Ray Clifford. 1982. "The Push Toward Communication." In *Curriculum, Competence, and the Foreign Language Teacher*, edited by Theodore V. Higgs, 57–79. Lincolnwood, IL: National Textbook.

Holley, Freda M., and Janet K. King. 1971. Imitation and correction in foreign language learning. *Modern Language Journal* 55(8): 494–498.

Holobow, Naomi, Fred Genesee, and Wallace E. Lambert. 1987a. *Cincinnati Year 3: The Effectiveness of a Partial French Immersion Program on Students from Different Social Class and Ethnic Backgrounds—Children in Grades 1 and 2*. Montreal: Psychology Department, McGill University.

Holobow, Naomi, Fred Genesee, and Wallace E. Lambert. 1987b. *Learning in a Second Language: The Effects of Partial French Immersion on Children from Middle and Working Class Backgrounds—Cincinnati Year 2*. Montreal: Psychology Department, McGill University.

Holobow, Naomi E., Fred Genesee, Wallace E. Lambert, and Louise Chartrand 1988. *The Cincinnati Study: Report On Year 4: Effectiveness of a Partial French Immersion Program for Students from Different Ethnic and Social Class Backgrounds*. Montreal: Psychology Department, McGill University.

Holobow, Naomi, Fred Genesee, Wallace E. Lambert, J. Gastright, and Myriam Met. 1987. Effectiveness of partial French immersion for children from different social class and ethnic backgrounds. *Applied Psycholinguistics* 8(2): 137–152.

Hughes, Helena. 1989. Conversion of a teacher-delivered course into an interactive videodisc-delivered program. *Foreign Language Annals* 22(3): 283–294.

Hymes, Dell. 1972. "On Communicative Competence." In *Sociolinguistics*, edited by J. B. Pride and J. Holmes, 269–293. Harmondsworth, England: Penguin.

Izzo, Suzanne. 1981. *Second Language Learning: A Review of Related Studies*. Rosslyn, VA: National Clearinghouse for Bilingual Education.

James, Charles J. 1984a. *Foreign Language Proficiency in the Classroom and Beyond*. Lincolnwood, IL: National Textbook.

James, Charles J. 1984b. "Learning from Proficiency: The Unifying Principle." In *Foreign Language Proficiency in the Classroom and Beyond*, 1–8. Lincolnwood, IL: National Textbook.

Kasper, Gabriele. 1982. Teaching-induced aspects of interlanguage discourse. *Studies in Second Language Acquisition* 4(1): 99–113.

Kennedy, Dora, and William De Lorenzo. 1985. *Complete Guide to Exploratory Foreign Language Programs*. Lincolnwood, IL: National Textbook.

Krahnke, Karl. 1985. Review of the natural approach: Language acquisition in the classroom. *TESOL Quarterly* 19(4): 591–603.

Kramsch, Claire. 1987. "Interactive Discourse in Small and Large Groups." In *Interactive Language Teaching*, edited by W. M. Rivers, 17–32. Cambridge, MA: Cambridge University Press.

Krashen, Stephen. 1981. *Second Language Acquisition and Second Language Learning*. Oxford, England: Pergamon.

Krashen, Stephen. 1982. *Principles and Practice in Second Language Acquisition*. New York: Pergamon.

Krashen, Stephen D., Robin C. Scarcella, and Michael H. Long. 1982. *Child-Adult Differences in Second Language Acquisition*. Rowley, MA: Newbury House.

Krashen, Stephen D., and Tracy Terrell. 1983. *The Natural Approach. Language Acquisition in the Classroom*. San Francisco, CA: Alemany Press.

Kubler, Cornelius C. 1987. "Training for High-Level Language Skills." In *Foreign Language Instruction: A National Agenda*, edited by R. D. Lambert, 125–136. Newbury Park, CA: Sage.

Lafayette, Robert C., and Michael Buscaglia. 1985. Students learn language via a civilization course—a comparison of second language classroom environments. *Studies in Second Language Acquisition* 18(3): 323–342.

Lambert, Wallace E., and O. Klineberg. 1967. *Children's Views of Foreign People*. New York: Appleton-Century-Crofts.

Lambert, Wallace E., and Richard Tucker. 1972. *Bilingual Education of Children: The St. Lambert Experiment*. Rowley, MA: Newbury House.

Landry, Richard G. 1974 A comparison of second language learners and monolinguals on divergent thinking tasks at the elementary school level. *Modern Language Journal* 58(1–2): 10–15.

Lange, Dale, and Linda Crawford-Lange. 1984. "Doing the Unthinkable in the Second Language Classroom." In *Teaching for Proficiency, the Organizing Principle*, edited by Theodore V. Higgs, 139–178. Lincolnwood, IL: National Textbook.

Lapkin, Sharon, and Merrill Swain. 1984. *Second Language Maintenance at the Secondary Level. Final Report to the Carleton Board of Education*. Toronto: The Ontario Institute for Studies in Education.

Larsen-Freeman, Diane. 1975. The acquisition of grammatical morphemes by adult ESL students. *TESOL Quarterly* 9(3): 409–414.

Leaver, Betty Lou, and Stephen B. Stryker. 1989. Content-based instruction for foreign language classrooms. *Foreign Language Annals* 22(3): 269–275.

Liskin-Gasparro, Judith. 1984. The ACTFL proficiency guidelines: Gateway to testing and curriculum. *Foreign Language Annals* 17(5): 475–489.

Littlewood, William. 1984. *Foreign and Second Language Learning*. Cambridge, MA: Cambridge University Press.

Long, Michael H. 1983. "Inside the 'Black Box': Methodological Issues in Classroom Research on Language Learning." In *Classroom Oriented Research in Second Language Acquisition*, edited by H. W. Seliger and Michael H. Long, 3–33. Rowley, MA: Newbury House.

McLaughlin, Barry. 1988. *Theories of Second-Language Learning*. London: Edward Arnold.

Magnan, Sally Sieloff. 1985. "Teaching and Testing Proficiency in Writing: Skills to Transcend the Second-Language Classroom." In *Proficiency, Curriculum, Articulation: The Ties That Bind*, edited by Alice Omaggio, 104–136. Middlebury, VT: Northeast Conference on the Teaching of Foreign Languages.

Medley, Frank W., Jr. 1985. "Designing the Proficiency-Based Curriculum." In *Proficiency, Curriculum, Articulation: The Ties That Bind*, edited by Alice Omaggio, 13–40. Middlebury, VT: Northeast Conference on the Teaching of Foreign Languages.

Meredith, Alan R. 1978. Improved oral test scores through delayed response. *Modern Language Journal* 62(7): 321–326.

Messer, S. B. 1976. Reflection-impulsivity: A review. *Psychological Bulletin* 83(6): 1026–1052.

Met, Myriam. 1985. Decisions! Decisions! Decisions! Foreign language in the elementary school. *Foreign Language Annals* 18(6): 469–473.

Met, Myriam. 1988. "Tomorrow's Emphasis in Foreign Language: Proficiency." In *Content of the Curriculum*, edited by R. S. Brandt, 91–108. Alexandria, VA: Association for Supervision and Curriculum Development.

Met, Myriam. 1989a. "Learning Language Through Content: Learning Content Through Language." In *Languages in Elementary Schools*, edited by K. E. Muller, 43–64. New York: American Forum.

Met, Myriam. 1989b. Which foreign languages should students learn? *Educational Leadership* 7(1): 54–58.

Met, Myriam, Helena Anderson, Evelyn Brega, and Nancy Rhodes. 1983. "Elementary School Foreign Language: Key Links in the Chain of Learning." In *Foreign Languages: Key Links in the Chain of Learning*, edited by R. G. Mead, 10–24. Middlebury, VT: Northeast Conference on the Teaching of Foreign Languages.

Met, Myriam, and Nancy Rhodes. 1990. Elementary school foreign language instruction: Priorities for the 1990's. *Foreign Language Annals*.

Modern Language Association (MLA). 1963. *Cooperative tests, French and Spanish versions*. Princeton, NJ: Educational Testing Service.

Murray, Janet H., Douglas Morgenstern, and Gilberte Furstenberg. 1989. "The Athena Language-Learning Project: Design Issues for the Next Generation of Computer-Based Language-Learning Tools." In *Modern Technology in Foreign Language Education: Applications and Projects*, edited by W. F. Smith, 97–118. Lincolnwood, IL: National Textbook.

Naiman, N., Maria Frohlich, and H. H. Stern. 1975. *The Good Language Learner*. Toronto: Ontario Institute for the Study of Education.

National Advisory Board on International Education Programs. 1983. *Critical Needs in International Education: Recommendations for Action*. Washington, DC: Center for International Education.

National Commission on Excellence in Education. 1983. *A Nation at Risk: The Imperative for Educational Reform*. Washington, DC: Government Printing Office. Report No. 065–000-00177.

National Governors' Association. 1989. *America in Transition: The International Frontier. Report of the Task Force on International Education*. Washington, DC: NGA.

Nerenz, Ann G., and Constance K. Knop. 1982. "The Effect of Group Size on Students' Opportunity to Learn in the Second-Language Classroom." In *ESL and the Foreign Language Teacher*, edited by Alan Garfinkel, 47–60. Lincolnwood, IL: National Textbook.

Nostrand, Howard Lee. 1990. "The Intercultural Essential for the Emerging Nationwide Standards of Education." In *Critical Issues in Language Education*, edited by Ellen Silber. New York: Garland.

Omaggio, Alice C. 1986. *Teaching Language in Context:*

Proficiency-Oriented Instruction. Boston, MA: Heinle and Heinle.

Otto, Sue E. K. 1989. "The Language Laboratory in the Computer Age." In *Modern Technology in Foreign Language Education: Applications and Projects*, edited by W. F. Smith, 13–41. Lincolnwood, IL: National Textbook.

Oxford-Carpenter, Rebecca. 1985. *A New Taxonomy of Second Language Learning Strategies*. Washington, DC: Center for Applied Linguistics.

Peal, Elizabeth, and Wallace E. Lambert. 1962. The relation of bilingualism to intelligence. *Psychological Monographs* 76(27), no. 546.

Pederson, Kathleen Marshall. 1987. "Research on CALL." In *Modern Media in Foreign Language Education: Theory and Implementation*, edited by W. F. Smith, 99–131. Lincolnwood, IL: National Textbook.

Peter, Lawrence J. 1977. *Peter's Quotations: Ideas for Our Time*. New York: Morrow.

Peterson, Paul E. 1983. *Making the Grade: Report of the Twentieth Century Fund Task Force on Federal Elementary and Secondary Education Policy*. New York: Twentieth Century Fund.

Phillips, June K. 1984. Practical implications of recent research in reading. *Foreign Language Annals* 17(4): 285–296.

Pons y Argento, Francisco. 1850. *Gramatica Castellana Fundada Sobre Principios Filosoficos*. Barcelona: Gaspar.

Rabiteau, Kathleen, and Hessy Taft. 1985. "Provisional Modified ACTFL/ETS Oral Proficiency Scale for Junior High School Students." Paper presented at the annual meeting of the American Council on the Teaching of Foreign Languages, New York.

Rafferty, Eileen A. 1986. *Second Language Study and Basic Skills in Louisiana*. Baton Rouge: Louisiana Department of Education.

Rhodes, Nancy C., and Rebecca L. Oxford. 1988. Foreign languages in elementary and secondary schools: Results of a national survey. *Foreign Language Annals* 21(1): 51–69.

Rhodes, Nancy C., Lynn Thompson, and Marguerite Ann Snow. 1989. *A Comparison of FLES and Immersion Programs*. Washington, DC: Center for Applied Linguistics.

Richardson, Charles P., and Sharon Guinn Scinicariello. 1989. "Television Technology in the Foreign Language Classroom." In *Modern Technology in Foreign Language Education: Applications and Projects*, edited by W. F. Smith, 43–74. Lincolnwood, IL: National Textbook.

Rivers, Wilga M. 1975. *A Practical Guide to the Teaching of French*. New York: Oxford University Press.

Rivers, Wilga M. 1989. *Ten Principles of Interactive Language Teaching*. Washington, DC: Johns Hopkins University: National Foreign Language Center.

Savignon, Sandra J. 1972. *Communicative Competence: An Experiment in Foreign Language Teaching*. Philadelphia, PA: Center for Curriculum Development.

Savignon, Sandra J. 1983. *Communicative Competence: Theory and Practice*. Reading, MA: Addison-Wesley.

Schinke-Llano, Linda. 1986. *Foreign Language in the Elementary School: State of the Art*. Washington, DC: Center for Applied Linguistics.

Shrum, Judith. 1985. Wait time and the use of target or native language. *Foreign Language Annals* 18(3): 305–313.

Shulman, Lee S. 1987. Knowledge and teaching: Foundation of the new reform. *Harvard Educational Review* 57(1): 1–22.

Slagter, Peter. 1979. *Un Nivel Umbral*. Strasbourg: Council of Europe.

Snow, Ann, Myriam Met, and Fred Genesee. 1989. A conceptual framework for the integration of language and content in second foreign language programs. *TESOL Quarterly* 23(2): 201–217.

Southern Governors' Association's Advisory Council on International Education. 1986. *Cornerstone of Competition*. Washington, DC: Southern Governors' Association.

Stern, H. David, Merrill Swain, L. D. McLean, R. J. Friedman, Birgit Harley, and Sharon Lapkin. 1976. *Three Approaches to Teaching French*. Toronto, Ontario: Minister of Education.

Swain, Merrill. 1985. "Communicative Competence: Some Roles of Comprehensible Input and Comprehensible Output in Its Development." In *Input in Second Language Acquisition*, edited by Susan Gass and Carolyn Madden, 235–253. Rowley, MA: Newbury House.

Swain, Merrill, and Sharon Lapkin. 1982. *Evaluating Bilingual Education: A Canadian Case Study*. Clevedon, England: Multilingual Matters.

Swain, Merrill, and S. Lapkin, 1991. "Additive Bilingualism and French Immersion Education: The Roles of Language Proficiency and Literacy." In *Bilingualism, Multiculturalism, and Second Language Learning: The McGill Conference in Honour of Wallace E. Lambert*, edited by Allan G. Reynolds. Hillsdale, NJ: Erlbaum.

Terrell, Tracy D. 1977. A natural approach to second language acquisition and learning. *Modern Language Journal* 61(7).

Terrell, Tracy D. 1982. The natural approach to language learning: An update. *Modern Language Journal* 66(2): 121–132.

Thompson, Irene. 1987. "Memory in Language Learning." In *Learner Strategies in Language Learning*, edited by Anita Wenden and Joan Rubin, 43–56. Englewood Cliffs, NJ: Prentice Hall.

Thompson, Lynn, et al. 1988. *The Development of the FLES Test—Spanish. Final Report to the U.S. Department of Education, Office of Educational Research and Improvement*. Washington, DC: Center for Applied Linguistics, Center for Language Education and Research.

Torney, Judith V. 1979. "Psychological and Institutional Obstacles in the Global Perspective in Education." In *Schooling for a Global Age*, edited by J. M. Becker, 59–93. New York: McGraw-Hill.

Trites, Ronald L. 1976. Children with learning difficulties in primary French immersion. *The Canadian Modern Language Review* 33(2): 193–216.

Trites, Ronald L. 1981. *Primary French Immersion: Disabilities and Prediction of Success. Review and Evaluation Bulletins*. Toronto, Ontario: Ministry of Education.

Trites, Ronald L. 1986. *Learning Disabilities and Prediction of Success in Primary French Immersion: An Overview*. Toronto, Ontario: Ministry of Education.

Trosborg, Anna. 1984. "Stimulating Interaction in the Foreign Language Classroom through Conversation in Small Groups of Learners." In *Language Learning in Formal and Informal Contexts*, edited by D. M. Singleton and D. G. Little, 177–179. Dublin: Irish Association for Applied Linguistics.

Van Ek, J. A., and L. G. Alexander. 1975. *Threshold Level English* (Council of Europe). New York: Pergamon.

Warriner-Burke, Helen P. 1990. Distance learning: What we don't know can hurt us. *Foreign Language Annals* 23(2): 129–133.

Wells, Gordon. 1986. *The Meaning Makers: Children Learning Language and Using Language to Learn*. Portsmouth, NH: Heinemann.

Wenden, Anita. 1987. "Incorporating Learner Training in the Classroom." In *Learner Strategies in Language Learning*, edited by Anita Wenden and Joan Rubin, 159–168. Englewood Cliffs, NJ: Prentice Hall International.

West, Peter. 1989. Schools' interest in learning by satellite surges. *Education Week* 9(13)(November 29): 1, 10–12.

Wiss, Corrinne. 1989. Early French immersion programs may not be suitable for every child. *The Canadian Modern Language Review* 45 (3): 517–529.

Wong Fillmore, Lily. 1976. "The Second Time Around: Cognitive and Social Structures in Second Language Acquisition." Unpublished Ph.D. dissertation, University of California, Berkeley.

Wong Fillmore, Lily. 1979. "Individual Differences in Second Language Acquisition." In *Individual Differences in Language Ability and Language Behavior*, edited by C. J. Fillmore, W. S. Y. Wang, and D. K. Kempler, 203–228. Academic Press.

31

VOCATIONAL EDUCATION

George H. Copa and Caryl B. Bentley
UNIVERSITY OF MINNESOTA

The evolution of the K–12 curriculum in vocational education from the 18th century to the present mirrors the dramatic shifts experienced by the larger American society as it moved from agricultural beginnings through the Industrial Revolution and into the contemporary electronic and global "Information Age." These shifts in socioeconomic conditions were accompanied by major changes in the demands of work and family roles and responsibilities. Vocational education's focus on preparation for dealing effectively with the practical problems of work and family has challenged its subject matter to be under continual development and renewal in order to be relevant to the needs of this changing society and make best use of knowledge developed from research and practice. While all of education prepares for work and family responsibilities in some measure, directedness toward learning that enhances effectiveness in addressing work and family responsibilities is a unique contribution and challenging mission for vocational education in the K–12 school curriculum.

This chapter presents a historical curricular analysis, reviews current curricular research, and offers suggestions for future curricular research in vocational education. The analysis will treat each of the major subfields separately, as well as vocational education as a whole. While vocational education is practiced extensively in many settings beyond the K–12 public school (i.e., postsecondary institutions, workplaces, community-based organizations), this chapter, in keeping with the rest of this *Handbook*, focuses exclusively on the K–12 public school. The concept of curriculum can be used very broadly to include the subject matter to be taught, who is taught, how it is taught, and how well it is taught (Kliebard 1989); however, in this chapter the focus is primarily on the first of these components—the subject matter to be taught.

DEVELOPMENT OF VOCATIONAL EDUCATION AS A CURRICULAR CATEGORY

As a curricular category, vocational education emerged after the Smith-Hughes Act of 1917, encompassing several separate and definable areas of subject matter (i.e., agriculture, business, home economics, industrial, and marketing education). Many of these subfields of vocational education existed in some form in the secondary school prior to their recognition as part of vocational education. Often the subfields had aims in addition to specific directedness toward preparation for work and family responsibilities. Even today, vocational education as a curricular category is most often taught through these subfields rather than as a fully integrated and cohesive subject.

This section on the historical development of vocational education traces each of the subfields and vocational education as a whole from their beginnings to about the mid-1970s. The challenge of keeping abreast of the shifting nature of the American society, and subsequently work and family responsibilities, over two centuries is readily appar-

The authors wish to acknowledge the careful work of Marylin A. Johnson, who assisted in searching, selecting, and obtaining materials used in this chapter. Acknowledgment is also due to faculty members at the University of Minnesota who reviewed earlier drafts of various sections of this chapter: David Bjorkquist, Judith Lambrecht, Gary Leske, Jane Phihal, James Stone, and Gordon Swanson. The work reported here is part of a research project entitled "The Subject Matter of Vocational Education" and funded by the National Center for Research in Vocational Education, University of California, Berkeley.

ent in the issues and changes in curriculum for vocational education during this time.

Agricultural Education

Promotion of agricultural education in the United States can be traced back to the first society for support of agriculture (the Philadelphia Society for the Promotion of Agriculture), organized in Philadelphia in 1785, with membership including George Washington and Benjamin Franklin. A 1794 committee report of the society provided several alternatives for advancing agricultural education for youth and adults (Stimson and Lathrop 1942). The early history of the development of agricultural education from that date, long before federal legislation for vocational education, is a state-by-state history, with descriptors including "vocational and nonvocational agriculture," "polytechnical education," "education in agriculture," "academic agriculture," "agriculture science," "agriculture of less than college grade," "agriculture clubs," "agriculture academies and schools," "'black' agriculture," and "agricultural extension."

More formal and consistent agricultural education in the secondary schools of the United States dates back to 1862, beginning with high school offerings in land grant colleges and, later, with the development of separate agricultural high schools in several states (True 1929). According to Moore (1985),

> In the 1860s, remedial type agriculture courses were being taught in colleges to prepare students for college-level agriculture courses. This led to a need for an agricultural curriculum for high school students. There was a need to prepare students in high schools for college agriculture courses. (8)

The U.S. Department of Agriculture supported a Committee on Methods of Teaching Agriculture, which developed some basic guidelines for high school study of agriculture during this early period. Topics suggested for study were as follows (Office of Experiment Stations 1902, 5):

Agronomy—climate, soils, fertilizer, botany, varieties, culture, harvesting, preservation, uses, and enemies of farm crops.

Zootechny—theory and practice in animal production, breeding, feeding, hygiene, and management of farm animals.

Dairying—the principles and methods in the handling and sale of milk for consumption and in the making of butter and cheese.

Rural engineering—practices and methods of laying out farms and construction and use of farm buildings, systems for water supply, irrigation, drainage, sewage, roads, and machinery.

Rural economy—history of agriculture, capital, labor systems, costs of production, marketing, records, accounts, and so on, as related to farm management.

The Department of Agriculture, through its Office of Experiment Stations, published a section on secondary agricultural education in their annual reports and a series of special publications during the early 1900s. Titles of special reports included: *The American System of Agricultural Education, A Secondary Course in Agronomy and in Animal Husbandry, Training Courses for Teachers of Agriculture, Applications of Chemistry to Agriculture, Community Work in Rural High Schools*, and *Home Projects in Secondary Agriculture* (True 1929, 330).

The Department urged that collegiate and secondary curriculums be distinguished, that special agricultural high schools be replicated across the country, and that agricultural education be introduced into public high schools, especially in rural communities. Efforts were made to show how agricultural study could be introduced into high schools without disrupting existing school studies—for example, by substituting study of agriculture for some study of Latin or offering agriculture as an elective. The content of the Department of Agriculture's reports reveals concern about agricultural study as general and vocational education, articulation of secondary and collegiate study, and needed preparation of high school agriculture teachers. Experiment station bulletins were a major source of curriculum materials for agriculture teachers during this time (Moore 1987).

The "home project" concept (more recently called the supervised occupational experience) was introduced as an important part of the agricultural education curriculum by Rufus Stimson during this time (Boone, Doerfert, and Elliot 1987). Stimson was hired as the first director of the Smith's Agricultural School at Northampton, Massachusetts, in 1908. He wanted students' study to include a sharp focus on farming problems they were facing on their own home farms. According to Boone, Doerfert, and Elliot (1987), Stimson drew his ideas for the project method from his study under William James at Harvard University and from the thinking of Herbert Spencer.

The U.S. Bureau of Education was also promoting the teaching of agriculture in secondary schools during the period 1900–1915. Among its publications relating to secondary-level agricultural education during the period 1912 to 1917 were reports dealing with topics such as agricultural education in secondary schools, agricultural instruction in high schools, and agricultural teaching. From 1900 to 1915, a large number of high schools across the country introduced instruction in agriculture. A U.S. Bureau of Education survey for the school year 1915–1916 showed 3,675 institutions offering secondary instruction in agriculture, largely in public high schools, and involving about 73,000 students (True 1929, 355–356).

Following passage of the Smith-Hughes Act, also known as the National Vocational Education Act, in 1917 agricultural education began to undergo some major changes. As summarized by Moore (1985), the two major curricular changes that occurred in the 1920s were (1) the use of occupational analysis as a basis for curriculum development and (2) a cross-sectional approach to organizing the curriculum. Prior to the 1920s the curriculum for high school agricultural education was patterned after the college-level curriculum, with little attention to students or the ways in which the learning was to be used. Support for basing curricular content on detailed analysis of agricultural production occupations also came from Rufus W. Stimson (1922), who had progressed to state supervisor of agriculture in Massachusetts to become a recognized national leader in the field of agricultural education; and W. W. Charters (1923), a curriculum expert whose book *Curriculum Construction* advocated use of occupational analysis in developing agricultural curriculum. Moore notes: "From 1922 on, the subject matter bulletins of the Federal Board [for Vocational Education, provided for by the Smith-Hughes legislation] took a task analysis approach to the content instead of the unit approach" (1985, 11).

The cross-sectional strategy for organizing the agriculture curriculum entailed a change from teaching all of the content about a particular topic (i.e., crop production) in a single course (often a year long) to teaching selected parts of the same topic over several years of instruction (i.e., soils and crop selection during the first year, propagation during the second year, and crop marketing and processing during the third year). The format for organizing agricultural education changed from courses on crops, mechanics, and animal husbandry to Agriculture I, II, III, and IV. The advantages of the cross-sectional approach were to relate better to a diversity of student interests each year and to provide the added learning of some repetition of topics. The guidelines for this new approach to organizing the curriculum were developed by Theodore H. Eaton and published by the *Federal Board for Vocational Education* (Eaton 1925) as a federal bulletin entitled *Principles in Making the Vocational Course of Study in Agriculture in the High School*.

In 1928 the national organization of the Future Farmers of America was founded as an intracurricular youth organization for students in vocational agriculture programs. The purpose of the organization was to develop abilities in leadership, cooperation, thrift, and community service, as well as agricultural skills. By 1929, 33 states were represented at the FFA's national convention. During 1935–1936 active membership passed 100,000, and the number of local chapters of the FFA was about 4,000 (Ross 1942). A similar organization, the New Farmers of America, was founded for black students in 1935. By 1940 it had an active membership of 25,000 students (Elam 1942). These youth organizations added a unique component to the curriculum of agricultural education in secondary schools.

During the 1930s, more attention was paid to implementing the cross-sectional approach to organizing the curriculum, using occupational analysis to identify curricular content and moving from a 2-year (ninth and tenth grade) to a complete 4-year curriculum for high school agricultural education (Moore 1985). With the 1940s came further use of the cross-sectional approach to curriculum and a shift of attention to studying the agricultural industry of a local community as a whole rather than specific analyses of occupations as a basis for the content of the agricultural curriculum (Cook 1947). Moore (1985) characterizes the 1950s as a "decade of calm" as it relates to curriculum development in agricultural education. Drawing on Hammonds (1950), Moore describes the situation in agricultural education as follows:

> Today teachers face the difficulty of finding enough time to teach what they would like to teach. Most states now have good school farm shops and devote considerable time to teaching shop work. The Future Farmers of America has come into the picture with its demand for some teaching time. It is now fairly common practice to set aside individual-problem days. Much more teaching time is devoted to supervised farming than formerly. New categories have been developed to be included in the course, such as land use, farm forestry, home food supply, farm-home beautification and improvement, farm improvement, fire protection, farm safety, farm finance, farm organization, and agricultural exploration and guidance. These developments tend to lessen the time that can be given to the enterprises as such and make extremely unwise the use of teaching time in any unnecessary repetition. Conserving time is now a big problem. (88)

In a 50 year history of agricultural education published in 1956, Hamlin notes that the struggle to decide what to teach in secondary vocational agriculture continued. Among the theories and practices being tried he notes: (1) culling from the mass of knowledge about agriculture; (2) using community studies; (3) considering the psychological characteristics and development of high school age youth; (4) relating class work to the actual work of farming through supervised experience programs; (5) using the FFA as a youth organization to stimulate motivation and learn democratic procedures; and (6) recognizing the need to integrate vocational agriculture as a part of the whole of secondary education. He concludes, "We have put all our agricultural education 'eggs' in one vocational 'basket,' apparently unaware that everyone in our society has need for some appropriate form of agricultural education" (105).

Major changes were afoot again for agricultural education during the 1960s and 1970s. With the passage of the Vocational Education Act of 1963, the agricultural curriculum was to give attention to preparing students for both farm *and* off-farm agricultural occupations. The U.S. Office of Education, which had published several earlier reports addressing the purposes and objectives of agriculture education, put out a new version in 1966 (1966a) that specifically addressed this needed change. The new objectives for agricultural education were:

1. To develop agricultural competencies needed by individuals engaged in or preparing to engage in agricultural production.
2. To develop agricultural competencies needed by individuals engaged in or preparing to engage in (off-farm) agricultural occupations other than agricultural production.
3. To develop an understanding of and preparation for career opportunities in agriculture and the preparation needed to enter and progress in agricultural occupations.
4. To develop the ability to secure satisfactory placement and to advance in an agricultural occupation through a program of continuing education.

5. To develop those abilities in human relations which are essential in agricultural occupations.
6. To develop the abilities needed to exercise and follow effective leadership in fulfilling occupational, social, and civic responsibilities. (U.S. Office of Education 1966a, 4–5)

The instructional areas of agricultural education were expanded to include agricultural production, agricultural supplies, agricultural mechanics, agricultural products, ornamental horticulture, forestry, agricultural resources, and other agriculture (Stevens 1967). Occupational analysis was revitalized as an approach for determining the content for the new configuration of work covering the entire agricultural industry. The organization of high school agriculture began to change to accommodate these new thrusts and more divergent group of student interests. The first 2 years of the curriculum often retained the cross-sectional organization and was labeled the "core" curriculum (Roberts 1971). The later 2 years provided for elective specializations that students could choose based on their career interests. Sometimes year-long courses were broken down into semester and quarter offerings to provide more opportunity for choice and greater responsiveness to student interests. In order to provide for the more specialized study, often with a small number of students, neighboring schools sometimes entered into cooperative arrangements to share teachers and facilities and combine students.

In summary, it is clear that agricultural education in secondary schools was initiated well before the Smith-Hughes Act of 1917 (Hillison 1986); however, the Smith-Hughes Act and the Vocational Education Act of 1963 played a very significant role in shaping the agricultural education curriculum (Camp and Crunkilton 1985). The Smith-Hughes legislation substantially increased the amount of agricultural education at the secondary level and increased attention to specific preparation for agricultural work responsibilities in contrast to agricultural education as general education. The Vocational Education Act of 1963 shifted agricultural work to include off-farm as well as farm occupations related to agriculture. Also significant in its impact on curriculum was the use of the "project method" (Boone, Doerfert, and Elliot 1987) and attention to leadership development through use of a youth organization, Future Farmers of America (now called the FFA). Both brought increased attention to individualized instruction and applied learning.

Business Education

Business education started with the purpose of preparing workers for business offices. These workers were engaged in keeping records, writing letters, and accounting for money. While its roots are in the apprenticeship system and stretch back to ancient times, business education (originally called commercial education) as a school curriculum developed first in private business schools in the United States. As noted by Tonne (1971):

> The private business school was a well-established part of the U.S. school system by 1850. A form of business education had been offered well before this time: a few business-type courses had been offered in colonial times, and the academy, the precursor of the U.S. public high school, usually provided courses in business subjects. (507)

In providing business education, private enterprise was responding to an economic development need not being given attention by public high schools. Along with courses designed for specific aspects of office work, private schools introduced more general courses on topics such as the functions of the business enterprise in the U.S. economy and the legal aspects of business (Crank and Crank 1977), as well as the managing, owning, and operating of business enterprises (Daughtrey 1974).

As public schools became more committed to serving a wider range of students and providing a curriculum more relevant to the emerging U.S. economy, business education was introduced into public schools, patterned largely after the curriculum in private business schools. Prior to the 1930s, the public high school curriculum consisted primarily of bookkeeping, typing, and shorthand directed at specific occupational preparation (Crank and Crank 1977). In the early 1920s one of the first and most influential programs of business teacher education was established at New York University by Paul S. Lomax. This program would continue its leadership role through the work of its notable faculty, including Peter L. Agnew, Helen Reynolds, and Herbert A. Tonne (Sapre 1981).

During the 1930s Frederick G. Nichols, professor of commercial education in the School of Education at Harvard University, provided leadership for developing business education as a viable component of the high school curriculum. In his landmark book *Commercial Education in the High School*, Nichols (1933) provided a detailed definition of commercial education, a description of the relationship of commercial education to vocational education, and a curriculum for commercial education to fit a variety of school situations (i.e., junior high, comprehensive high school, specialized high school, and small rural schools). Commercial education was defined as

> A type of training which, while playing its part in the achievement of the general aims of education on any given level, has for its primary objective the preparation of people to enter upon a business career, or having entered upon such a career, to render more efficient service therein and to advance from their present levels of employment to higher levels. (51)

Commercial education was to refer to a comprehensive field of vocational education that addressed "all of the business services that have to do with organizing, financing, staffing, housing, and managing a commercial enterprise as distinguished from those services that have to do with manual productivity in such an enterprise" (51). Commercial education was to include both business knowledge and principles of business (learning the business) as well as business skills (preparation for business). The curriculum for a specific school situation was to be determined locally by specific attention being given to the needs of the people to be trained and the conditions under which instruction was to occur.

Nichols proposed that the junior high (grades 7, 8, and 9) be prevocational in nature and focus on the exploration and tryout of types of work in the field of commerce and the teaching of the fundamentals of business. The senior high was to address vocational commercial education with the following three objectives:

1. Building of an adequate background of general education of a sort which insures a high degree of social understanding; developing right social attitudes and habits of thought and action.
2. Development of a certain amount of occupational intelligence with respect to business organization, management, service, and employment to insure proper functioning in lower levels of employment and ultimate advancement to higher levels.
3. Development of the degree of technical skills required for initial employment (1933, 220–221).

Nichols' curricular recommendations were based on detailed study of commercial work, and he clearly noted that the curriculum needed to change as the nature of commercial work changes. From his viewpoint at the time, the technical subjects making up the core of business education were bookkeeping, commercial arithmetic, business writing, shorthand, and typing. In addition, he supported the need for a series of social-business subjects as being an essential part of a commercial curriculum to give general business knowledge and including commercial geography, commercial law, business organization and management or principles of business, and economics. Nichols also presents a strong argument for sound academic subjects as a part of good commercial education.

The sixth yearbook of the National Commercial Teachers Federation, titled *The Business Curriculum* (Fisk 1940), contained sections on principles of curriculum development (i.e., activity analysis, use of objectives, place of textbooks, core curriculum, relation to business, relation to general education, cooperative practices) and addressed curriculum directly in terms of setting (i.e., with chapters on cosmopolitan high schools, commercial high schools, colleges, junior colleges, private schools, evening schools) and subjects (i.e., with chapters on basic business, bookkeeping and accounting, business arithmetic, business correspondence, business law, consumer education, distributive education, economics, economic geography, everyday business, office practice and machines, personality, Gregg shorthand, and typing).

During the 1930s and 1940s consumer education was added as a significant part of the business education curriculum. Consumer education addressed the "personal use" value of business courses in everyday living (i.e., using checks, calculating interest, planning a budget, taking inventory, preparing tax records). This addition to the business curriculum was assisted by the earlier work of Herbert A. Tonne in "social business," research later completed at Colorado State University at Greeley, and the National Consumer Education Study of the 1940s. As reported by Crank and Crank (1977):

Sponsored by the NASSP [National Association of Secondary School Principals], the Consumer Education Study resulted in the identification of 11 units of study in consumer education, and study booklets were prepared for these 11 units: The Modern American Consumer, Learning to Use Advertising, Time on Your Hands, Investing in Yourself, The Consumer and the Law, Using Standards and Labels, Managing Your Money, Buying Insurance, Using Consumer Credit, Investing in Your Health, and Effective Shopping. (5–6)

The mid-1950s saw the adoption of dual objectives for business education with attention to both preparation for business careers and economic literacy. Economic literacy was seen as the general education component of business education, and the term "basic business" was used to label this area of study, which included economics, general business, consumer economics, and consumer education (Crank and Crank 1977, 7). At about this time, the American Economics Association's concern about economic education in elementary and secondary schools stimulated business education to add economic education to basic business courses. According to Crank and Crank (1977):

The Joint Council on Economic Education, which was organized to promote economic education throughout the nation, gave official recognition to the contribution of business education to economic education; and the entire economic education movement received a vigorous boost from business educators across the land. The problem still remained, however, of identifying specifically the economic concepts and understandings that business education could most effectively develop. (7)

Business education was finally specifically included in federal vocational education legislation and was affected by the resources and direction of the Vocational Education Act of 1963. As a contrast, marketing, or distributive education, which was earlier regarded as a component of business education, began to receive federal vocational education funding in 1948 and grew rapidly after that time as a distinctive vocational education field. With federal funding for business and office education (adding the word "office" to the title was another impact of support from federal vocational education funding) came funds for supervisory personnel at the federal and state levels and partial funding for local programs. These changes were evident in the eighth yearbook of the National Business Education, *The Emerging Content and Structure of Business Education* (Price, Hopkins, and Klaurens 1970), which had chapters addressing the factors affecting the business curriculum (i.e., changing aspects of the social scene, economic scene, world of work, school population, school curriculum, nature of office work) and modifying the business curriculum to better meet student needs (i.e., economic education, secondary and postsecondary programs, programs for disadvantaged students, and career guidance responsibilities and strategies). Interestingly, the yearbook contained chapters addressing both business and office and distributive education curricula.

By the mid-1970s, business educators thought of themselves as making a significant contribution to the curriculum of public schools with attention to occupational exploration and preparation for business careers, as well as consumer and economic education in general. Data processing was entering the curriculum as a new occupational component of business education. The tenth yearbook of the National Business Education (Brendel and Yengel 1972), *Changing Methods of Teaching Business Subjects*, had sections on basic business-economic education (including chapters on basic business, consumer economics, business law, business principles and management, and economics), marketing and distributive education, and office education (including chapters on typing, shorthand, transcription, secretarial procedures, clerical procedures, accounting, data processing, communication, and business mathematics). The career education movement strengthened business education contributions in the areas of career exploration and guidance, as well as economic education. In similar ways, the consumer education movement, through the attention brought by individuals such as Ralph Nader, has maintained the importance of the consumer education content of business education. In the context of vocational education, consumer education is shared with home economics education in the 1968 Amendments to the Vocational Education Act, which provide funds for "consumer and homemaking" education. Crank and Crank (1977) conclude their history of curricular development in business education with the note:

> Business education in the American high schools . . . is strongly vocational in nature and will continue to be so in the future. With proper regard for the importance of education both for earning a living and for using one's financial resources wisely, the dual objectives of high school business education programs will be maintained for many years to come. (10)

A conceptual framework for analyzing the business curriculum (Bahr and Wegforth 1976) presented in the fourteenth yearbook of the National Business Education Association, *Business Education Yesterday, Today, and Tomorrow*, shows the business curriculum as providing education *about* business for *all* students to prepare informed citizens *and* education *for* business for *some* students to prepare effective workers. A critical review of the history of commercial education (Weiss 1978) from 1850 onward, which focused particularly on education for clerical work, concludes that through commercial education high schools affected the development of commercial work by (1) providing a large pool of trained workers at public expense (perhaps keeping the wages down), (2) feminizing clerical work (by encouraging girls to enroll), (3) separating clerical work from manual work (suggesting higher status even though wages might be lower), and (4) encouraging passivity and a sense of inferiority in clerical students in contrast to college preparatory students. She recommended that some discussion of these effects be included in the commercial curriculum as a means of making students aware of the field's liabilities.

Concerning business education in the elementary school, Crank and Crank (1977) note that some business content has been incorporated into career education units in elementary grades and that typing is sometimes included in elementary programs. Junior high school programs are usually in the form of a business exploratory course with attention to typing, general business, and career exploration. The above changes in emphasis and direction for the business education curriculum for the 1960s and 1970s are well documented in policy statements of the Policies Commission for Business and Economic Education (1989).

In summary, business education has two major thrusts in the secondary school: (1) general education about business; and (2) specific education for business occupations. The emphasis on specific preparation for occupations (earlier called commercial education) appeared several decades before the general education emphasis. The general education component now includes consumer economics and economic education as major areas of attention. The areas making up the specific preparation for occupations component have changed over time with changes in the nature of business work (i.e., dropping shorthand, adding data processing).

Home Economics Education

Ideas and beliefs about the nature and purposes of the home economics curriculum were among the most basic notions that early settlers in the United States brought with them from their homelands. The development of ideas about the home economics curriculum from the 17th century until the present closely parallels the development of ideas about appropriate roles for females and males in American society.

The school curriculum in the 17th, 18th, and most of the 19th centuries prepared "young ladies" for household duties, social life, and church participation. Such preparation included the basic skills of reading, writing, and arithmetic, as well as specific training in homemaking tasks, especially sewing. Until the middle of the 19th century, home economics education consisted of a smattering of classes, mostly in sewing, that were taught primarily to young middle-class women.

In the mid-19th century many events and social forces converged, creating, among other things, an expanded role for home economics education. Some of the events and social forces most relevant to the development of home economics include several new waves of immigrants, many of whom lived in abject poverty; the abolition and women's suffrage movements; the establishment of land-grant universities and the manual arts movement; and the rapid expansion of immediately practical applications of scientific discoveries.

Catherine Beecher's *A Treatise on Domestic Economy*, published in 1841, has been called the first textbook in home economics. While Beecher is often remembered today as an apologist for a "separate but equal" position in relation to gender, such recent analysts as Martin (1985) and Thompson (1986) have stressed Beecher's insistence on the crucial importance of education for women in both "reproductive" and "productive" processes as women's part of her proposed educational division of labor between the sexes (1986, 19–20). Furthermore, Beecher's *Domestic Economy* may be the first modern text in any field to assemble and disseminate "state of the art" knowledge for public use (1986, 14), a task that some home economists and other vocational educators continue to take seriously as one of their basic missions today.

In 1857 Edward L. Youmans, a chemist and founder of *Popular Science* magazine, published *Household Science*, the first scientific study of food, air, heat, and light from the standpoint of the home worker. Youmans, who specifically advocated specialized education in home economics, is a typical, although early, example of the kind of male who became interested in home economics in its first years as a profession: a trained scientist who wanted the public to understand, or at least to use, practical applications of science. Benjamin R. Andrews and W. O. Atwater were two men similar to Youmans in their scientific training and commitment to home economics who joined the women, always more numerous in home economics, in developing the field as a full-fledged profession at the end of the 19th and beginning of the 20th centuries (Brown 1985, 269).

By the 1870s, household science departments were being rapidly established in land-grant and other universities, and many private schools of cooking and design were established. There was little consistency or depth in the scattered offerings comprising the home economics "curriculum" until the last quarter of the 19th century when faculty in the new college and university departments of household science began to systematize the subject matter of the field, develop teacher training courses, and write K–12 curricula. By the 1890s, domestic science, as it was then called, had been introduced into many U.S. public schools.

Also in the 1890s the burgeoning field found an energetic and influential leader in Ellen H. Richards, a chemist and author already famous for her applications of science to the household problems of food, clothing, and shelter and for her various social experiments in public lunch rooms, training of household help, and "workingmen's cottages." Richards had entered the Massachusetts Institute of Technology in 1871 as its first woman student. She was a co-founder with Melvil Dewey and the chairman of the Lake Placid Conference of Home Economics, a series of annual discussions about the nature and purpose of home economics that lasted from 1899–1908. Richards was also the first president of the American Home Economics Association (AHEA), from 1909 to 1911, founded as one of the outgrowths of the Lake Placid Conferences (Craig 1945, 22).

The first five Lake Placid conferences "were concerned with purpose, definition, scope, and the relation of the new subject of home economics to education at all levels," while the conferences during the last five years were especially dominated by "formulating the body of knowledge to be implemented in the elementary and secondary schools and in institutions of higher education, gaining acceptance in schools and colleges, and seeking state and federal assistance for program implementation" (American Home Economics Association 1987, 3). At the 1902 conference, a definition of home economics was adopted that is useful to some home economists:

> Home economics in its most comprehensive form is the study of the laws, conditions, principles and ideals which are conceived on the one hand with man's immediate physical environment and on the other hand with his nature as a social being, and in the study especially of the relations between these two factors. (3)

In the 1890s, the K–8 public school home economics curriculum generally included classes focused on the establishment of good health habits and "preparation for home helpfulness" (Bevier 1924, 142). By 1920–1921, following the passage of the Smith-Hughes Act, more than 8,000 secondary schools had home economics departments, as opposed to about 3,000 in 1915–1916 (Craig 1945, 30). Most of the larger school systems required home economics of all seventh and eighth grade girls, and home economics was also commonly taught in the fifth and sixth grades.

In the same period at the end of the 19th and the beginning of the 20th centuries, the curriculum for secondary home economics became both educationally and politically more complex than the K–8 curriculum. In this period lie the roots of an ongoing professional discussion about the nature and relative merits of "general" or "liberal" education and "vocational" education. This discussion continues to the present day in all the subfields of vocational education, especially, perhaps, in home economics and industrial education.

Without detailing the history of the "general" versus "vocational" debate as it has unfolded in the field of home economics, it should nonetheless be pointed out that one important factor in the ongoing discussion is the lack of agreement about the definition of terms. Bevier (1924), an early leader in home economics, was a chemist by training. In 1900 she became director of the Household Science School of the University of Illinois (Brown 1985, 194–195); she was also a participant at many of the Lake Placid conferences as well as a charter member and the second president of the American Home Economics Association (Craig 1945, 13). Bevier differentiated "general" and "vocational" courses within home economics. Concerning secondary home economics in the early 20th century, Bevier wrote:

> The subjects presented in home economics represent almost every phase of home activities, and are combined with science, art, literature, and history so as to give the elements of a liberal education. This type of work is known as general home economics. (1924, 142)

Bevier asserted that such "general" home economics differed from the "vocational" home economics mandated by the Smith-Hughes Act of 1917, which included "'vocational courses' in homemaking'' and ''training in related occupations such as millinery, dressmaking, nursing, lunch room management'' (142).

The first attempt at the development of a national curriculum to address home economics programs at the elementary, secondary, and university levels was prepared in 1913 by a committee of the four-year-old American Home Economics Association in an attempt to bring some order to the rapidly developing field (East 1980, 157). Following the death in 1911 of Ellen Richards, Bevier became chair of the prestigious eight-member committee.

The 1913 curriculum subdivided the field of home economics into the areas of food, clothing, shelter, and household and institution management (158). Under food, clothing, and shelter the committee succinctly recommended the study in each area of ''selection, preparation, use.'' Under household and institution management, the committee said that ''material basis,'' ''social contacts,'' ''activities and functions,'' and ''aims and results'' should be studied.

The 1913 curriculum, which predated the Smith-Hughes Act and its mandate for ''vocational'' home economics, did not raise the issue of ''general'' versus ''vocational'' home economics. The 1913 curriculum is better understood, in fact, as a description of contemporary college and university home economics education as practiced in the more than 250 such institutions that offered 4-year courses leading to a baccalaureate degree in home economics than as a prescription for necessary changes in the curriculum.

The period between 1899 and 1917 is important for three major reasons: (1) home economics came into being as a profession; (2) many of the major themes and issues still critical today surfaced; and (3) home economics became a standard part of the elementary and secondary school curriculum. The dramatic nature of the change in the K–12 curriculum is indicated by a few sketchy facts. For example, in 1898 there were 796 public high schools in the South; of these, only the St. Louis public schools offered home economics (Craig 1945, 7). As another example, in 1896, the year in which the position of director of domestic science was first established in New York City, only 11 public schools offered home economics. By contrast to these low enrollments, in 1914 home economics was taught in the schools of more than 3,500 towns and cities (American Home Economics Association 1987, 4).

The period between 1918 and 1970 was characterized by waves of change in home economics. What often began as a single innovation in home economics curriculum, instructional methodology, administration, or research methodology frequently gathered momentum and became a wave of change.

The single most obvious example is the elaborate bureaucracy of home economics administration developed throughout the middle two quarters of the 20th century. Federal, state, and local government and educational entities, as well as professional organizations and agencies from the private sector, were established to develop, implement, administrate, and, in a few cases, evaluate new home economics programs delivered for new reasons to numerous new audiences.

One example of the way that what began as a ripple became a major wave is the history of the home economics specialization of family relations. While Ellen Richards and others at Lake Placid certainly discussed the needs of contemporary families, the curriculum in both K–12 and higher education included almost no family studies until the 1920s, when child development and parent education emerged from the nursery school and other social movements as new areas of study. In 1920 the U.S. Children's Bureau prepared a set of outlines for study in child development. These outlines were presented at the 1921 AHEA meeting (Craig 1945, 36) and led to the establishment of many new university courses in child care. Since the public school curriculum closely followed the lead of higher education for the first third of the century, secondary schools and then elementary schools began gradually to implement child development units and classes in their own curricula.

In the 1930s the new child and parent education emphasis begun in the previous decade led to a major emphasis on family relations education. The family relations emphasis, in turn, led to the establishment of home economics courses designed for boys and men (American Home Economics Association 1987, 5) as home economists recognized that male members of families also needed family education. Enrollment of boys, estimated at 7,000 in the secondary schools of 42 states in 1930 (Craig 1945, 38), increased to approximately 1 percent of all boys enrolled in secondary schools in 1962 (Paolucci and Shear 1971, 448) and then, according to one study, to 20 percent in 1979 (American Home Economics Association 1987, 9).

Perhaps the most persuasive example of the new emphasis on family relations in the 1930s, however, is represented by the changes in definition of the fields of home economics between the 1913 AHEA unified curriculum project and the AHEA unified curriculum project of the 1930s. Craig (1945) writes, ''*Original* fields were foods, clothing, shelter, household, and institutional management. Revised headings were the family and its relationships; the house, its equipment and management; family economics; food and nutrition; textiles and clothing'' (40).

During the 1940s, the decade of World War II and recovery, the scope of the family relations curriculum began to include for the first time the needs of minority families and handicapped individuals (American Home Economics Association 1987, 7). In the 1950s, a new emphasis on cognitive aspects of child development reflected one of the responses to Sputnik (7). The changing social values of the 1960s, indicated by concern for the environment and for citizens to some degree disenfranchised by poverty, gender, condition of handicap, and/or race, was reflected in home economics education by a new commitment to ''compensatory'' education (8).

The ''ripple-into-wave'' process described briefly in this decade-by-decade development of the family relations component of the home economics education curriculum also applies to such other aspects of home economics education as nutrition education, launched by the school lunch movement in approximately 1914 and resulting in widespread nutrition education in elementary schools by 1943 (Craig 1945, 34, 43); consumer education, launched by classic pioneer studies of consumption economics in the 1920s and resulting in the eventual legislative renaming of the entire field of home economics education as "Consumer and Homemaking Education" by the Vocational Education Act of 1963 (American Home Economics Association 1987, 5, 8); and the expansion of student home economics organizations from scattered clubs at the turn of the century to 287 in 1926 (Craig 1945, 37) and 2,067 in 1945 (45).

The ripple-to-wave phenomenon also applies to home economics curriculum research in the 20th century. Even though reports on curriculum research were by no means an important feature of the AHEA annual meeting in its first years, a report made to the 12th annual meeting in 1919 already "urged" the establishment of a "standardized system of research" to avoid duplication of effort (Craig 1945, 35).

During the 1920s the first curriculum research began to appear. An interesting annotated bibliography of the decade's home economics curriculum research was published in 1930 by Welch and Lingenfelter of the Bureau of Education Research at the Ohio State University. It includes such titles as "Home Economics Teacher Training Under the Smith-Hughes Act 1917 to 1927," [California] "High School Courses in Science of the Household, Nutrition, and Citizen-Homemaking," "Survey of Public School Courses in Child Care for Girls," "Study of Junior High School Home Economics," and "Uses Made of the School Lunch Room by Home Economics Teachers, 1926" (1930, 2, 3, 9, 17, 26).

By the 1930s, curriculum research had moved from lists of courses and a focus on overall subject matter of the field to more specialized studies of the relative merits of the "core" and "unit" approaches to curriculum development (Spafford 1942, 74). This type of curriculum research continued in the 1940s and 1950s, with the addition of curricula developed on the basis of time and motion studies in the home and workplace.

In 1961, home economics historian Marjorie East wrote, "We [in AHEA] tried again to organize and order our subject matter," because "without a structure a subject cannot be learned effectively or economically" (East 1980, 158–159). Although some of the subgroups who first met for a week at French Lick, Indiana, in July 1961 to define basic concepts in their subject matter specialties at K–12, college, and adult levels have continued to meet throughout the years since, there has been, as yet, no attempt by the French Lick project to publish a coordinated list of common and unifying concepts, even though some subgroups of the original group are still meeting (159).

A specific attempt to list common and unifying concepts in secondary home economics was undertaken in 1961 by the Home Economics Education Branch of the U.S. Office of Education (159). Hundreds of home economists met over a period of four years to focus on the content areas of human development and the family, home management and family economics, foods and nutrition, textiles and clothing, and housing. The resulting product, known as "The Bird Book" because of a soaring seagull on the cover, is, according to East, "still the only comprehensive view of our subject matter at any level" (159). The final report identified three major interrelated concepts the committee felt unified the content of all subject matter areas in home economics (American Home Economics Association 1967). These concepts were human development and interpersonal relationships, values, and management.

In 1962 Beulah Coon reported on the home economics content actually being taught in 3,796 public schools in 50 states. She found that two thirds of the class periods in a typical program were devoted to foods and nutrition and clothing and textiles, with the majority of the content of these two areas focused on the concept of coping. The results of Coon's study were discouraging to many in the home economics field who had worked to incorporate family studies, consumer economics, and education about equity issues into the curriculum. Other curriculum research of the 1960s focused on "non-normative family structures," disease prevention, and multicultural approaches to nutrition, clothing, housing, and textiles (American Home Economics Association 1987, 8–9).

In summary, home economics classes were taught as far back in American history as colonial times, but the conscious effort to define the mission and establish the profession of home economics did not begin until the last few years of the 19th century. For the first two decades of the 20th century the home economics curriculum at the elementary and secondary levels developed from a knowledge base taught in higher education. Since the 1930s, however, the elementary and secondary home economics curricula tend to be developed locally and/or to be at least partly based on research into the needs of families and employers and the developmental needs of the students themselves.

Industrial Education

The terminology in industrial education is difficult for someone unfamiliar with the history of the field to understand. At the risk of oversimplification, but in the interests of clarity, this section provides a brief introduction to the history of the terminology of the industrial fields.

Industrial education and vocational education had a common beginning more than a century ago in such historical events as mechanics institutes, Russian manual training, the Slöd system, the arts and crafts movement, the industrial education movement, and the manual training movement. Even though the industrial education movement had strong beginnings well before the turn of the 20th century, this account of the history of the industrial education curriculum begins with the Smith-Hughes Act of 1917. It was at this point that the general education aspects of industrial education—known variously since the 1870s as manual training, manual arts, industrial arts, and now, increasingly since the late 1960s, as industrial technology or simply technology education—were organizationally separated from trade and industrial education (T & I), also known as vocational industrial education.

The Smith-Hughes Act provided funds for trade and industrial education and not for industrial arts education. Trade and industrial education, or vocational industrial education, is analogous to vocational agriculture and vocational home economics; all three have been widely, if not accurately, regarded as providing only specialized education for work or family responsibilities with little relevance or contribution to general education. Industrial arts, on the other hand, has always been strongly identified with general education and its "concern with habits, attitudes, appreciations, leisure time, home mechanics, and consumer knowledge" (Roberts 1965, 428).

Antagonism between representatives of the two fields has continued into the present, manifesting itself, for example, in the creation of entirely separate industrial education professional organizations. In 1972 Congress "authorized the regrouping of these subject fields" (Steeb 1979, 74) through funding industrial arts on a limited basis. While the historical and philosophical differences that separated the two main tributaries of the river of industrial education have not completely merged, there has been a gradual flowing together of the two branches during the last 25 years. Of the two, industrial arts has a much more controversial history and more complex curriculum issues and is the major focus of this section.

Educational practices and curricula within the industrial arts branch of industrial education have been connected to the industrial occupations focus of John Dewey (1899, 1901), whose concepts of the social purposes of education and the psychology of occupations put the study of industrial occupations at the heart of the curriculum of the famous University of Chicago laboratory schools. In fact, the name "industrial arts" began to replace "manual arts" because of the emphasis Dewey and such colleagues as James E. Russell and Frederick G. Bonser of Teachers College, Columbia University, placed on the necessity for children to gain an intelligent understanding of the processes of industrialization and the nature of an industrial society.

During World War I students in industrial arts courses and in trade and industrial programs were encouraged to make articles of direct benefit to the war effort. This involvement had a decidedly positive impact on the attitude of both students and the general public toward industrial arts programs (Barlow 1967b, 241–244).

In the years prior to World War II there was a rapid development of the junior high school movement, which had begun in 1914. Soon the junior high programs became the strongest component of industrial arts education. Junior high school industrial arts educators began to emphasize the concept of the general shop. As Martin and Luetkemeyer (1979) explain it, "The professional literature of this time was concerned with such junior high school-oriented programs as household mechanics, the comprehensive general shop, the general unit shop, and the laboratory of industries" (32).

During this period of rapid expansion, industrial arts educators discussed issues common in times of change in a profession—that is, confusion over terminology, the need for the development of commonly accepted standards for curriculum development in the field, and the development of adequate materials. By the 1930s, in large part due to the influence of Robert W. Selvidge and Verne C. Fryklund, the field of industrial arts emphasized the trade or occupational analysis approach to curriculum development. Selvidge and Fryklund (1930), in a popular teacher training text of the period, presented a "technic of analysis for the purpose of selecting the learning units involved in any subject" (3).

However, the highly detailed curriculum focus of Selvidge conflicted with the Dewey-Bonser tradition, which centered on the interests of the pupils and the needs of society, as well as on the tasks and skills to be learned. A major spokesman for the Dewey-Bonser approach was William E. Warner. Selvidge and Warner held office in different industrial arts organizations that published rival standards, philosophies, and clarifications of terms throughout the 1930s.

Under pressure to develop a document defining the field in a way that would be acceptable to all industrial arts educators, a committee appointed by the U.S. Office of Education published its report, *Industrial Arts: Its Interpretation in American Schools* (U.S. Office of Education 1938). The committee defined industrial arts as a "phase of general education that concerns itself with the materials, processes, and products of manufacture, and with the contribution of those engaged in industry" (1). Martin and Leutkemeyer point out:

> This definition emphasized the position that industrial arts education be considered a curriculum area rather than a specific subject and that it have general values to apply to all levels of education. Although the report was intended to reflect a unified position acceptable to a majority of educators, the efforts of committee members such as William E. Warner and Lois C. Mossman clearly reflected the philosophical position of Dewey and Bonser. (1979, 34)

In 1939 Warner and others founded the Industrial Arts Association to further the cause of industrial arts at all levels of education. The new organization decided to develop a curriculum proposal, which, however, was interrupted by World War II. During the war, industrial arts education again helped substantially with the war effort and in effect functioned as prevocational training, working in closer harmony with educators from trade and industrial education than usual.

In the postwar years the balance of power in industrial education curriculum philosophy again seemed to shift away from the occupational training emphasis of the war years in the direction of a student-focused, general education approach to industrial arts. At the 1947 American Industrial Arts Association conference, Warner (1965) presented a curriculum proposal that eventually became known as *A Curriculum to Reflect Technology*. Lux (1982) writes:

> This proposal probably has had a greater impact than any other upon industrial arts theory. It introduced subject-matter divisions

of communications, construction, management, manufacturing, power, and transportation. Bits and pieces of the ideas and terminology of the proposal gradually filtered into the literature, but the proposal did not affect practice on a widespread basis. Yet, the proposal stimulated curriculum innovation in the 1960s, and today the basic proposal and its terminology are much like what is proposed in a number of states. (859)

Although the 1950s were predominantly a stable period for industrial arts education, there were several innovations during this period: the emphasis on mass production as a unit of study or a method of teaching; the influence of Gestalt psychology on the curriculum, which led to a new focus on problem solving; and the conception of the first large-scale curriculum projects that were to predominate in the 1960s (e.g., Maley 1973, 1979; Olson 1957).

A national study of the industrial arts program in the public secondary schools of the United States was made in 1962–1963 (U.S. Office of Education 1966b). The survey involved a stratified cluster sample of the 25,526 public secondary schools of that time. There were 76 different courses in the area of industrial arts, grouped into general industrial arts, general woods, drafting, general metals, graphic arts, electricity and electronics, crafts, power mechanics, home mechanics, photography, ceramics, industrial arts mathematics and science, plastics, textiles, transportation, and miscellaneous subjects.

During the 1960s a remarkable number of innovative curriculum approaches in both industrial arts and trade and industrial education were fielded, including the American Industry Project, which analyzed various industries to determine both the content for a study of industry and the organization of the content into three project-focused courses for eighth, tenth, and twelfth grades (Face 1965); expansion of the Maryland Plan begun in 1952 (Maley 1973, 1979), a cluster-concept approach that centered on the development of people rather than things; the Industrial Arts Curriculum Project (IACP) (Lux 1979; Towers, Lux, and Ray 1966, 1967), which produced the well-known World of Construction and World of Manufacturing curricula; and the orchestrated systems approach to industrial arts (Yoho 1969).

Of these curricular innovations, the IACP has been most influential in industrial arts education. The IACP curriculum was divided into six parts, each of which was further subdivided: industrial management technology, which includes planning, organizing, and controlling; industrial production technology, which includes preprocessing, processing, and postprocessing; industrial personnel technology, which includes hiring, training, working, advancing, and retiring; industrial material goods, which includes constructed material goods and manufactured material goods; construction technology, which includes initiating the project, developing the project, and implementing it; and manufacturing technology.

In the trade and industrial fields, the Maryland Plan was the most influential curriculum model (Finch 1983). The Maryland Plan's cluster concept approach prepared graduates to enter a wide range of occupations having common work elements. In a 1980 review of the status of the cluster concept, Maley reported that 45 states and territories had cluster concept programs in operation.

In assessing industrial education in the 1960s, Householder (1979) said that a "fundamental re-examination of the functions, purposes, and content of industrial arts education took place" with "simultaneous innovation" occurring in several settings (114, 115). He continued:

As individuals and groups of industrial arts educators undertook to make revisions in existing programs, four major directions were pursued: (a) Industry as a source of content had been the acceptable model for decades; it seemed logical to extrapolate from the past and move to update existing industry-centered programs. (b) As an expanded structure was sought to include the industrial sphere, technology became a logical base; technology could be ordered into a taxonometric matrix and studied as a discipline. (c) The individual assumed a high level of priority during the 1960s; as education focused upon individualized instruction and upon the importance of individual development for social progress, the individual became a logical focal point for efforts in industrial arts program revision. (d) Perhaps the most obvious approach in curriculum improvement is to build directly upon existing programs, modifying them to meet the needs of the times. This approach made it possible to achieve gradual growth within existing situations. (115)

In summary, both industrial arts and trade and industrial education have strong roots in the various educational responses to industrialism in the 19th century and earlier. The two tributaries of the mainstream of industrial education diverged with the passage of the Smith-Hughes Act in 1917, except for the period of the two World Wars. In 1972 the streams became more convergent when Congress began for the first time to award federal funds to industrial arts education. Throughout the years, industrial arts education itself suffered from various philosophic divisions. Nonetheless, industrial arts flourished and was adopted by almost every public school in the United States as part of general education. Industrial arts was characterized by a relatively orderly development until the 1960s when the field began to burst with new activities, ideas, and curriculum approaches as it moved toward a new focus on technological literacy and technology education.

Marketing Education

Ten years before the Smith-Hughes Act of 1917, marketing education was getting its formal start as retail training under the leadership of Lucinda Prince in the Boston area with the support of the Women's Education and Industrial Union. In 1908 she opened the Union School of Salesmanship with financial support from Boston merchants. Interest in the school resulted in a retail training program in the Boston public schools that developed into the Prince School of Store Service (Haas 1939) and, later, a graduate department of Simmons College of Boston. In 1919, Prince authored the first bulletin of the Federal Board for Vocational Education dealing with distributive education, *Retail Selling* (Prince 1919). Retail training programs in public schools spread from Boston to other large cities across the country (Emick 1937). Emick reported that cooperative training between schools and businesses in retail sales was operating in 44 cities and enrolling 4,508 students in 1933 (Emick 1937, 10–12).

Marketing education (then known as distributive education) became a distinctive program separate from business (commercial education) in 1936 with attention and support from the George-Deen Act, which extended the Smith-Hughes legislation. Strengthening distributive education was seen as one way to stimulate a depressed economy in the context of the Great Depression. Under the direction of the George-Deen Act, distributive education began as an adult education program (not in the high school) designed to help those who were unemployed to find work in distribution and marketing occupations, but within a year or two had moved into the high school. Distributive education got its name from Paul H. Nystrom, a marketing professor at Columbia University and member of the Federal Board for Vocational Education (Meyer and Furtado 1976). Nystrom envisioned a program for distributive education similar to the training for agricultural, home economics, and industrial education established by the Smith-Hughes Act (Furtado 1973). Early support also came from Frederick Nichols, noted earlier as a leader in commercial education and also a member of the Federal Board for Vocational Education. He was a strong advocate for increasing attention to retail sales training beyond what it was getting as a part of commercial education. According to Meyer and Furtado (1976), "the retailing backgrounds of the early teacher-coordinators and curriculum bulletins published by the original Federal Board for Vocational Education became the basis for the early program of instruction" (45). The first National Conference for Distributive Education, called the Dunwoody Conference and held in 1939, reaffirmed the adult focus of distributive education and recommended development of instructional materials in five functional areas used to conceptualize retailing: (1) merchandising, (2) promotion, (3) personnel, (4) operations, (5) finance, and (6) control (National Conference for Distributive Education 1939).

Although the early emphasis was primarily on adult programs, secondary school programs in retail selling appeared as early as 1912 and federally supported secondary programs as early as 1937. Later a youth organization, Distributive Education Clubs of America (DECA), was chartered in 1948 with representatives from 17 states (Meyer and Furtado 1976). DECA was seen as an integral part of the high school distributive education curriculum with the purpose of developing leadership, vocational understanding, civic consciousness, and social intelligence (Crawford and Meyer 1972, 184).

Distributive education retained its adult focus until the 1950s, when it began to be viewed as a program for secondary, as well as postsecondary and adult, students. In 1957, John A. Beaumont was appointed director of the Distributive Education Branch of the Division of Vocational Education in the U.S. Office of Education and provided leadership to move marketing beyond the retail field. Specialized curriculum relating to industries such as floristry, home furnishings, and hotel and lodging became a part of the curricular offerings in distributive education (Meyer and Furtado 1976, 57).

The Vocational Education Act of 1963 changed the orientation of distributive education programs by specifically including federal support for preemployment-level training in distributive education and for students under 16 years of age. At a 1963 National Clinic on Distributive Education, Nelson presented a paper entitled "Basis for Curriculum Development in Distribution," which provided the basis for conceptualizing the distributive education curriculum in five competency areas: (1) social competency, (2) basic skill competency, (3) technology competency, (4) marketing competency, and (5) economic competency (1963, 3). In 1966, an article by Nelson, then in the U.S. Office of Education, described a conceptual framework for curricular development in distributive education with attention to distributive competency areas, functions of marketing, and levels of distributive work. During this period several competency studies were done to analyze and describe the tasks done by those employed in marketing occupations. One of the best known of these studies, which started as an examination of competencies required of retail workers as a basis for planning teacher education and later focused on implications for secondary programs in distributive education, was done by Crawford (1967). She stated that teachers must go to the field in order to determine what workers needed to know.

Crawford and Ertel (1970) more specifically described the competency pattern approach to identifying the marketing competencies to be addressed by the curriculum as including three elements: (1) basic concepts relating to marketing and economics, (2) listing of critical tasks for marketing jobs, and (3) listing competencies required to perform these tasks. At the same time, work was going on to develop a standard taxonomy of distributive occupations and distributive education programs (Nelson 1970).

By the end of the 1960s, the U.S. Office of Education (1969) produced a publication entitled *Distributive Education in the High School*, which laid out the curriculum structure, content, and instructional methods for high school, post–high school, and adult levels of distributive education. The preparatory curriculum, designed for a wide range of distributive occupations, was organized to address three levels of occupations: (1) basic jobs curriculum—to develop fundamental techniques in sales and sales-supporting services; (2) career development job curriculum—to develop judgment skills in relation to marketing, merchandising, and management; and (3) specialist job curriculum—to emphasize specific functions, product areas, or service fields.

Integral to the curriculum in distributive education were its two major approaches to instruction, the cooperative plan and the project plan, and its youth organization, Distributive Education Clubs of America. The cooperative plan was used extensively from the beginning of distributive education; the project plan was introduced after 1963.

Crawford and Meyer (1972) describe the cooperative and project plan as follows:

> The cooperative plan is an organized pattern of instruction which involves regularly scheduled part-time employment and which gives students an opportunity to apply classroom learning in practice. It enables them to develop occupational competencies through training on jobs related to their occupational interests.
>
> The project plan is an organizational pattern of instruction which involves a series of selected learning activities or projects related to the field or marketing, merchandising and management and which are related to a student's occupational interests. (11–12)

As is noted, these plans result in actual work issues and problems becoming a central part of the curriculum for distributive education. This focus is reinforced by the typical patterns of offering distributive education by the 1970s, which Crawford and Meyer describe as follows:

> A one-year curriculum based on the cooperative plan and including two class periods based on the cooperative plan and one class period of daily instruction;
> A two-year curriculum with the first year based on the project plan and the second year based on the cooperative plan, each involving one class period of daily instruction;
> A three-year curriculum with the first year based on the project plan and the second and third years based on the cooperative plan;
> A one-year accelerated curriculum based on the project plan and designed for those planning for advanced study beyond the high school;
> A one- or two-year specialized curriculum on either the project or the cooperative plan designed to develop competencies for such specialized areas as fashion merchandising, food distribution, and petroleum distribution. (1972, 7)

The heavy reliance of distributive education on a work experience component integral to the school-based instruction is a unique feature of distributive education among other secondary subject matter areas, including the other vocational education subjects.

By the late 1970s, distributive education was defined as follows:

> Distributive education, one of the seven major vocational education service fields, addresses that part of the world of work concerned with the marketing of goods and services. Distributive education derives its instructional base from the employment field of marketing and has as its mission the preparation of individuals for employment in distributive occupations, including business ownership. (U.S. Office of Education 1978, 7)

The inclusion of attention to business ownership or entrepreneurship was becoming a more explicit aspect of the curriculum by being designated as one of four levels of employment addressed by the curriculum (i.e., threshold entry jobs, career-sustaining jobs, specialization jobs, and entrepreneurial jobs).

The organization of distributive education in terms of scope and occupational responsibility was provided by its listing of instructional program codes, which included advertising and display services; apparel and accessories marketing; automotive, recreational, and agricultural vehicles and accessories marketing; finance and credit services; floristry; farm and garden supplies marketing; food marketing; food service marketing; general merchandise retailing; hardware and building materials marketing; home furnishings marketing; hotel, motel, and lodging services; industrial and institutional marketing; insurance; international marketing; personal service marketing; petroleum marketing; real estate marketing; recreation marketing; transportation and travel marketing; business services marketing; business ownership; and general marketing. Across these occupational areas distributive education's curriculum was described by the U.S. Department of Health, Education and Welfare as consisting of five broad competency areas (similar to those suggested by Nelson cited earlier) made up as follows:

> 1. Marketing skills—knowledge common to all distributive occupations and reflecting the functions of marketing to include selling, sales promotions, buying, operations (sales-supporting activities), marketing research, and marketing management.
> 2. Product or service technology skills—knowledge about particular products or services needed in order to help consumers or users reach buying decisions.
> 3. Social skills—personal effectiveness in relation to customers, to the business, to other employees, and to job activities. Includes ethics, human relations, supervisory skills and leadership.
> 4. Basic skills—skills of mathematics and communication (i.e., reading, listening, speaking, and writing) applied to the practices, terminology, and requirements of each cluster of marketing occupations.
> 5. Economic concepts of private enterprise—knowledge and attitudes about the competitive enterprise system and its impact on marketing; awareness of the importance of marketing in the economic cycle of production, distribution, and consumption; and one's ability to access individual progress with marketing and distribution occupations. (U.S. Office of Education 1978, 21–23)

In summary, marketing education has its heritage in adult education linked closely to the business and industry sector. Its expansion as a separate program from business education came after the George-Deen Act of 1936 and its manifestation as a high school subject after the Vocational Education Act of 1963. The focus on distribution occupations along with the cooperative and project plan of instruction have given it uniqueness as a high school subject and vocational education field.

Health Occupations Education

The development of health occupations education is closely related to the history of the education of working-class women in the United States. During the 19th century, courses in practical nursing, or the nursing arts, were taught in small schools devoted to preparing students for occupations considered suitable for women. Such training in practical nursing was similar to contemporary training for nurse's aides.

After the turn of the century, the National Society for the Promotion of Industrial Education and the Smith-Hughes Act of 1917 provided impetus for programs in the public schools especially designed for women. In addition to home economics courses, classes in practical nursing became part of the curriculum in a few public secondary schools. Developments in the field were slow until World War II, when there was a great increase in the need for health and other kinds of workers (Holloway and Kerr 1969, 3).

The George-Barden Act in 1946 and the Health Amendments Act (Title II of the amended George-Barden Act) in 1956 provided federal funds for educational programs to prepare practical nurses, including the establishment of a supervisor to provide leadership in the field at the state level. The establishment of a high-level state leadership presence resulted in the final separation of health occupations education from industrial education; the two subfields of vocational education had been intermingled for a half century. The Area Redevelopment Act of 1961, the Manpower Development and Training Act of 1962, and the Vocational Education Act of 1963 have furthered the development of practical nursing education (Holloway and Kerr 1969, 3).

Career Education

In the four decades after the Civil War, a new industrial and urban America characterized by a greatly expanded railway system, heavy industries, mining, and mechanized agriculture came into being. In this new society, with its qualities of rapid technological change and increasing occupational and geographical mobility, the old models for teaching people how to perform effectively in their occupations, including education at home, apprenticeship, and on-the-job training, were no longer sufficient (Wirth 1981, 35). The public schools were asked to take an increasingly major role in occupational preparation.

The single individual most responsible for the introduction of career education into the public schools was Frank Parsons. In 1907 he gave an address on choosing an occupation to members of a graduating class from a Boston evening high school. At the end of the address, several of the new graduates asked him for personal appointments to discuss further their occupational choices. Six months later, in January 1907, Dr. Parsons opened the Vocation Bureau to provide vocational counseling. Many people "between 15 and 72 years of age" came to see Parsons in the first few months of the Bureau's operation (Roberts 1965, 338–339), which convinced the Boston public schools to establish the first school-based vocational guidance program in 1909. Also in 1909, a few months after Parsons died, his book, *Choosing a Vocation*, the first textbook in the field of career education, was published (Parsons 1909). Staff in the Boston program included both counselors and teachers who conducted guidance activities on a volunteer basis (Roberts 1965, 340). Thus, from the outset, the activities of career education have been divided between counselors and teachers and have included classroom, group, and individual components. Historically, it has most often been the occupational information component of career education and guidance that has been reserved for classroom teachers or shared between teachers and counselors.

According to Goldhammer and Taylor (1972), statements emphasizing the importance of career education under its various names (including "vocational guidance" and "occupational education") have been included and re-emphasized in practically all of the major statements of goals for American education, including statements by some influential individuals. For example, Senator Carroll S. Page of Vermont gave a 3-hour speech in 1912 introducing an early vocational education bill in which he strongly defended the concept of career education:

> People are beginning to realize that boys and girls must be taught to earn a living and that they cannot spend their entire time in studying so-called classical subjects. All children must be educated for their ethical side and must be taught about the higher things of life, but they must also be taught that they must support themselves and be given lessons in how to earn money. Our schools should be well balanced, with both these ideas kept well to the front. (as quoted in Barlow 1973, 32)

The early influence of vocational education on career guidance was demonstrated with passage of the Smith-Hughes Act, which emphasized the role of supervised work experience and placement. Also, "vocation" was among the seven objectives listed in the 1918 publication by the Commission on Reorganization of Secondary Education entitled *Cardinal Principles of Secondary Education*. According to the Commission, "a good citizen earns his living, contributes to the general welfare by working, and maintains desirable relationships with fellow workers" (quoted in Goldhammer and Taylor 1972, 1–2). Furthermore, the Educational Policies Commission of the National Education Association in 1938 listed four current school objectives—third among them "Economic Efficiency," meaning that "the school should produce an individual who selects his own vocation, understands and lives according to the requirements of his job, improves his working efficiency, and plans his own economic life" (quoted in Goldhammer and Taylor 1972, 2). Finally, the first of 10 imperative needs of youth, according to the Educational Policies Commission of 1944, was:

> All youth need to develop salable skills and those understandings and attitudes that make the worker an intelligent and productive participant in economic life. To this end, most youth need supervised work experience as well as education in the skills and knowledge of their occupation. (2)

Modern theories of career development began appearing in educational research literature during the 1950s. At that time, the occupational choice focus of the first 40 years of career development was beginning to give way to a broader, more comprehensive view of individuals and their occupational development over the life span. Occupational choice was beginning to be seen as a development process. Donald Super (1957, 1984) brought together what was then known about careers as "lifelong sequences of study, work, and related roles" and "helped to put to use in guidance and counseling what others had found in their research" (1984, 28). It was during the late 1950s and the 1960s that the term "vocational development" became popular as a way of describing the broadening view of occupational choice, although, according to Hoyt (1987, 1), the term "career education," so popular in the 1970s, was first coined in the 1956 publication *Manpower and Education*, developed by the Educational Policies Commission of the National Education Association and the American Association of School Administrators (Educational Policies Commission 1956).

Vocational Education

According to Roberts (1965), "The history of vocational education is the history of man's efforts to learn to work" (31). If work is defined broadly to include the work done in and through family life and "man" relates to both men and women, then this statement seems a fair conclusion. The earliest form of vocational education largely involved the "pick-up" method of acquiring competence through observation and imitation, often of an older family member. Later this process was formalized into the apprenticeship method, with a master who was under contract to teach students (apprentices) a vocation. As described by McClure, Christman, and Mock (1985), the apprenticeship system became the major method of vocational education during the late Middle Ages through merchant and craft guilds. The apprenticeship period often lasted 7 years and involved both vocational and moral education. From the status of apprentice, students moved to journeyman and, with successful accomplishments, to the master level. By the 1800s the apprentice system had declined substantially because of (1) mechanization, which reduced the skills required for production and changed skill requirements more rapidly, and (2) expanded commerce, which increased the competition for workers (see Bennett 1926 for more explanation).

During colonial times in America, the apprenticeship system was very strong for a wide variety of occupations, including trades, merchants, housekeeping, law, medicine, and teaching. Apprentices were of two kinds, voluntary and indentured, the latter usually involving children of the poor, orphans, and bastards. Masters were to provide training in the basic skills of reading, writing, and arithmetic as well as specific job skills. With the coming of the Industrial Revolution by the 1860s, the apprenticeship system fell into disuse for the reasons noted above—it was too slow to meet demand, and factory methods needed a different profile of changing skills (McClure, Christman, and Mock 1985).

As noted by Barlow (1967a), vocational education emerged as a composite involving a number of forces, approaches to instruction, instructional settings, and subject matter fields that developed somewhat independently. Bennett (1926, 1937), Hawkins, Prosser, and Wright (1951), McClure, Christman, and Mock (1985), and Roberts (1965) describe early school-based vocational education as including:

1. *Franciscan Mission Schools.* Around 1630 Franciscan missionaries established as many as 25 of these schools in New Mexico. The schools combined work and education with students (primarily Indian) over age 9 trained in areas such as carpentry, metalworking, masonry, and tailoring. The most talented of the students later became teachers in these schools.
2. *Franklin's Academy.* In 1749 Benjamin Franklin proposed that an academy be developed to prepare young people for the problems of making a living. The curriculum included English, mathematics, history, and commerce. However, when established in 1751, the academy was made up of both a Latin school (because of strong advocacy to include classic studies) and an English school (which contained the study of commerce). With the Latin master as head of the academy, the English school was gradually reduced to an elementary school, and the academy became a preparatory school for college.
3. *Mechanics Institutes.* Originally developed in England, mechanics institutes were introduced into the United States in the 1820s, with the first one in New York City. Their purpose was to provide evening classes for adults in a variety of subjects, both academic and vocational.
4. *Lyceums.* Where mechanics institutes addressed the needs of urban workers, lyceums offered similar services for farmers and tradespeople in small towns. Approximately 1,000 local lyceums were in operation by 1833 and were organized by states into a national movement. The local lyceum provided a place and context for working people to gather and discuss topics of mutual interest. Subjects included mechanics, chemistry, botany, mathematics, hydraulics, history, and politics.
5. *Technical Institutes.* Starting with the Rensselaer School in 1824 and later including the Worcester, Massachusetts, Polytechnic Institute (1868), Case School of Applied Science in Cleveland, Ohio (1881), and California School of Mechanics Arts in San Francisco (1895), technical institutes were established to improve the skills of workers by emphasizing the practical application of science. In some of the schools, study included instruction in classrooms combined with work settings on farms and in workshops.
6. *German Drawing Schools.* The Centennial Exposition held in Philadelphia in 1876 included drawings, charts, and diagrams describing machines and mechanical processes used in German industry. American business representatives admired the drawings and, as a result, began to advocate for inclusion of practical drawing (as opposed to artistic drawing) in American schools to assist students in grasping mechanical principles and machines. With this pressure, drawing was added to the curriculum of many public high schools during this time.

7. *Russian Manual Training.* The Centennial Exposition of 1876 also resulted in adoption of the Russian system of using shop training as part of the curriculum in vocational education. The idea, drawn from a display from the Moscow Imperial Technical School, was to use training shops exclusively for teaching and production shops for training and actual production of products for sale. The training shops were very structured with lectures, exercises, and demonstrations. John D. Runkle, president of the Massachusetts Institute of Technology, was so impressed with this concept that he recommended that the Institute establish training shops for engineering and manual and industrial courses. Exhibits from the Centennial Exposition remain at the Smithsonian Museum in Washington, DC.
8. *Slöd System.* American schools, particularly elementary schools, turned to the Slöd system, developed in Scandinavian countries, to improve on the Russian system of training shops. It was difficult to hold the interest of younger students in the highly structured format of the Russian system. The Slöd system combined attention to physical and mental development with learning specific skills. The system relied on instructors who were trained as teachers rather than artisans and was designed for students to complete an entire project with concern for both beauty and usefulness. The Slöd system was adopted widely, with 25 percent of all schools offering manual arts in grades 7 through 12 using the system by 1894.
9. *Arts and Crafts.* The Arts and Crafts Movement, which began in England during the latter 1800s, also was transported to America and influenced the curriculum of manual arts programs. It brought more emphasis to creativity, more variety of materials (i.e., leather and metal), and flexibility (dropping heavy reliance on skill exercises) to vocational education.
10. *Manual Training.* Johann Heinrich Pestalozzi (1746–1827), a Swiss educator, has been considered the "father of manual training" (McClure, Christman, and Mock 1985). He established a school in Europe where manual work was combined with general education. This school served children of the poor. Pestalozzi believed that sound education, particularly for these children, needed to include both vocational and general education. He wrote *Leonard and Gertrude* (Pestalozzi 1910), a romantic novel that described this education with emotional effects. The book was a major success. However, while he exerted considerable influence on the American education system and particularly on industrial education, his school was a financial disaster. One of the American educators influenced by Pestalozzi's ideas and by the Russian and Slöd systems was Calvin Milton Woodward, dean of the Polytechnic faculty at Washington University in St. Louis. In 1890, Woodward initiated the Manual Training School for boys 14 years of age and older. The curriculum included science, mathematics, language, literature, history, drawing, and shop work. Shop work was included as a way to keep instruction more interesting, to provide learning in the use of basic tools common to a variety of jobs, and to increase general education. Woodward was not supportive of specific job training at this age because it narrowed student choices. His school required testing in basic skills before admission and acquired a reputation as a tough and demanding school. In 1915, 35 years later, the school was closed because the St. Louis public schools accepted responsibility for vocational education. But to quote McClure, Christman, and Mock (1985), "Woodward's basic concepts of vocational education in the secondary schools was an accepted part of American education" (25).
11. *Cooperative Training.* The development of cooperative training (as distinguished from cooperative learning) can be traced back to Herman S. Schneider, a civil engineer at Lehigh University who, in 1901, called for a plan to split the study time of engineers between classroom and actual job experience. He believed that existing engineering education lacked practical experience as a key component. He was first able to implement the plan in 1906–1907 at the School of Engineering at the University of Cincinnati—and with its success, by 1927, the cooperative method was being used in 20 to 25 university engineering programs. Introduction of the cooperative plan into the high school curriculum can be documented back to 1908 in Fitchburg, Massachusetts. There, Daniel Simonds, who was excited by Schneider's idea, implemented an industrial cooperative training program at the high school level.

All of the above movements were influencing public high schools prior to 1900. At the same time, the number of young people attending high school was growing rapidly. While in 1870 public high schools were educating a select group, almost all of whom went on to college, by the decade 1910–1920 the percentage going on to earn a college degree dropped to 20 (Roberts 1965, Venn 1964). Increased interest was given to vocational education as a means to meet the needs of those not going on to college and of the labor force for middle-range occupations (between professional and unskilled). The Manual Training School at Washington University was the first school of this type, with the first public manual training school opening in Baltimore in 1884. McClure, Christman, and Mock (1985) note:

> As the nineteenth century drew to a close, the number of publicly supported manual high schools and the number of high schools that included manual training in their general curriculum grew. By 1900, the public school system in over one hundred cities included manual training in the curriculum of their high schools. However, the complete acceptance of vocational training as a part of the general high school curriculum did not come until the twentieth century. (29)

The period 1900 to 1920 was very significant to vocational education in the United States. Some of the initial federal encouragement for vocational education began with the Morrill (Land-Grant Colleges) Act of 1862 and amendments to the Morrill Act of 1890, which provided for colleges with major focus on training for working-class students and emphasizing agriculture and mechanics arts. The Nelson Amendments to the Morrill Act in 1907 increased funding and allowed the use of funds for training agriculture and mechanics arts teachers. By the turn of the century, the federal government was emphasizing funds for practical (i.e., professional and vocational) education over general (i.e., liberal arts and humanities); however, most funds were aimed at institutions that served adults (beyond high school).

In 1906, under the leadership of Charles R. Richards, professor of manual training at Columbia University, and James P. Haney, director of art and manual training in the New York City school system, the National Society for the Promotion of Industrial Education (NSPIE) was initiated. This organization, made up of business and industry representatives and professional educators, would provide the support for later passage of the Smith-Hughes Act and eventually form the American Vocational Association. The NSPIE orchestrated the interests (sometimes conflicting) of agricultural organizations and agencies, the National Education Association, the American Federation of Labor, the National Association of Manufacturers, the Chamber of Commerce, and the spirit of the Progressive era as a means to gain federal support for vocational education in secondary schools. Through the work of a Commission on National Aid to Vocational Education provided for by federal legislation passed in 1914, the Smith-Hughes Bill was drafted after considerable study and discussion (Swanson 1966).

Senator Smith and Representative Hughes, both from Georgia, had been strong advocates of vocational education. They introduced their bill in 1916 with good support in both the Senate and House. In December 1916, President Woodrow Wilson, in his message to Congress, gave special attention to vocational education. After brief congressional debate and action, he signed the bill into law on February 23, 1917. The Smith-Hughes Act provided funds for (1) salaries of teachers, supervisors, and directors of agricultural programs; (2) salaries of teachers of home economics and industrial and trade subjects; and (3) training of teachers, supervisors, and directors of agricultural programs and teachers of home economics and industrial and trade subjects (McClure, Christman, and Mock 1985, 64). Speculation about why commercial (business) education was not included suggests that the congressional leaders felt that private business colleges would be against the bill if it included commercial education. The funds were in the amount of $1,600,000 for 1918, to be increased to $7,167,000 by 1926. States and local districts were required to match these federal funds dollar for dollar. Funds could be used to support vocational education in full-time day schools, part-time schools, and evening schools. The act also provided for a Federal Board of Vocational Education to administer the new federal program. Charles A. Prosser, former secretary to the National Society for the Promotion of Industrial Education, was selected by board members to be the first director of vocational education and chief executive officer of the board. Assistant directors were appointed for each major area assigned to the board; these included agriculture education, trade and industrial education, home economics education, and research services. The board served an important role in curriculum development and direction for each of these areas by holding meetings and publishing a large number of curriculum bulletins.

At the end of the 1910s, the idea that vocational education was an appropriate and integral part of the high school curriculum was confirmed not only by passage of federal legislation but by the Commission on Reorganization of Secondary Education (1918), which issued the famous seven "cardinal principles of secondary education": health, command of fundamental processes, worthy home membership, development of a vocation, civic education, worthy use of leisure time, and ethical character. In 1920 Snedden published his book *Vocational Education*, asking, "Shall we have vocational education in the high school?" and answering:

> Yes, if the floor and grounds of the high school, primarily designed to serve the purposes of liberal education, can be adapted to give practical training to locomotive engineers, coal miners, street car motormen, sailors, printers, shoe machine operators, tractor engine drivers, poultry raisers, carpenters . . . .(24)

In the spirit of social efficiency, he goes on to recommend:

> Any comprehensive program of vocational education must be designed primarily to prepare young persons for the effective exercise of productive vocations as now found; it may be designed secondarily and incidentally to anticipate probable social changes in the character and incidence of vocational activities; and, under some circumstances (taking due account of the relatively fundamental and only slightly controllable character of economic forces), to further desirable, and to restrain undesirable, economic tendencies by its emphasis on one or the other of different possible education objectives. (411)

Earlier, Snedden's positions about the desirability of separate vocational high schools and the conservative stance toward the subject matter of vocational education had been hotly contested by John Dewey in a published debate (Dewey 1915a, 1915b). Dewey profoundly disagreed with Snedden on social and political grounds:

> The kind of vocational education in which I am interested is not one which will "adapt" workers to the existing industrial regime: I am not sufficiently in love with the regime for that. It seems to me that the business of all who would not be educational time-servers is to resist every move in this direction, and to strive for a kind of vocational education which will first alter the existing industrial system, and ultimately transform it. (Dewey 1915b, 42)

The history of the relationship of vocational education to general education from 1845 to 1945 is well laid out by Mays (1946), who concludes, "On the whole, the first two decades of the new century saw the acceptance by the general educator of vocational education as a responsibility of the public secondary school program," (105) and, "By the close of the period studied, most leaders in general education had come to be interested in establishing a relationship between vocational and general education which would be most conducive to the realization of the most desirable outcomes of both'' (107).

During the 1920s and 1930s, vocational education came of age through federal assistance. Federal guidelines called for states to create state boards to administer vocational education funds and for submission of a state plan for federal approval. A major purpose of the federal legislation was to stimulate development of vocational education in states. According to enrollment figures cited by McClure, Christman, and Mock (1985, 73), the federal government was very successful in this purpose. During 1918, there were 165,000 students involved in programs funded under the act. The number participating under the legislative funds grew to 1,249,000 by 1935. The George-Reed Act (1929) and the George-Ellsy Act (1934) provided increased federal funding for vocational education. Charles A. Prosser (Prosser and Allen 1925) introduced his 16 desired characteristics of vocational education in 1925 (later to be known as Prosser's Theorems), which were used widely to guide the planning and development of vocational education. In 1936 the George-Deen Act again increased funding and added distributive education as a program area to be supported for part-time and evening programs, primarily directed at adults.

During the 1940s, vocational education was used as a major strategy to provide training to support the war effort through special federal funding and programs. In 1943, the National Society for the Study of Education entitled its forty-second yearbook *Vocational Education* (Henry 1943). A theme running through the chapters is the rationalizing of a set of objectives for vocational education and the relation of these objectives to the total educational program of schools. Following the war, the country was facing major problems concerning jobs and training for those returning from the war, a more diverse student body, inequity in educational opportunity, and enrollment increases caused by the "baby boom." Debate in Congress over the George-Barden Act (Vocational Education Act of 1946) provided a sense of the issues facing vocational education at that time: (1) the private business schools felt that vocational education was wasteful of funds and not providing adequate training to ensure placement of students; (2) organized labor urged that vocational education was training too narrowly, and poorly at that, and recommended a return to liberal arts, with training to come after school through apprenticeship systems; and (3) provisions for occupational guidance, public service training, office training, supervision of industrial arts, and establishment of area schools below the college level were dropped from early versions of the bill. However, vocational education success in training for the war effort is credited with passage of the George-Barden Act, again increasing funding for vocational education.

The 1950s initiated a period of reexamination of the role of vocational education. In 1953, administration of federal efforts in vocational education moved to the Office of Education in the new cabinet-level Department of Health, Education and Welfare. As a part of the Health Amendments Act of 1956, $5 million was added to vocational education for health occupations education, particularly for practical nursing. In 1958, Title VIII of the National Defense Education Act authorized annual appropriations of $15 million for 4 years to establish area vocational education programs of less than college level to prepare skilled technicians important to national defense and scientific progress.

In 1961, with the changing nature of work caused by technological change, President John F. Kennedy directed the Secretary of Health, Education and Welfare to appoint a Panel of Consultants on Vocational Education to review federal legislation supporting vocational education and suggest future directions. The panel included representatives from agriculture, industry, business, labor, and education and was chaired by Benjamin C. Willis, general superintendent of schools in Chicago. Recommendations of the panel suggested the areas of change needed in vocational education, many with curricular implications. These recommendations called for expanded high school programs, full-time post–high school programs, short-term courses for youth and adults, individualized programs for the handicapped and disadvantaged, and support services (i.e., teacher education, career guidance, basic skills development). Using the panel's recommendations, the new federal legislation was drafted and debated, resulting in the Vocational Education Amendments of 1963, signed into law by President Lyndon B. Johnson. Funding for vocational education was substantially increased (i.e., authorization of $60 million for 1964, rising to $225.5 million in 1967 and each year after that). Attention was shifting from subject matter areas (i.e., agriculture, home economics) to categories of people to be served (i.e, high school, post–high school, handicapped, and disadvantaged). There was increased flexibility in use of funds to meet local needs. New construction of building and facilities (i.e., area vocational schools) and development of new programs were important developments under the act. The sixty-fourth yearbook of the National Society for the Study of Education was again entitled *Vocational Education* (Barlow 1965) and dealt extensively with several of these issues in depth. One of the chapters by Walsh and Seldon (1965), entitled "Vocational Education in the Secondary School," laid out the following principles for planning vocational education:

1. Vocational education should occur as close to the time of application as possible. On the secondary level, vocational courses should be concentrated in eleventh and twelfth grades.
2. There must be sufficient concentration of work in each area to enable the student to develop sufficient competence to hold an entry job in a given occupation upon the completion of the curriculum.
3. A well-planned vocational program integrates vocational education and general education. The vocational development should be built on a sound base of general education.
4. Some diversity of curriculum offerings is needed to provide for individual needs and to give flexibility to the program.
5. All aspects of an occupational area cannot be included in the

curriculum. Those skills which form the core of the occupation and which are necessary for entry into the occupation should be taught.

6. Vocational instruction must be geared to the times, preparing the individual to enter the world of work of today and tomorrow. (Walsh and Seldon 1965, 92)

The authors concluded that there needed to be strong interrelationship among the vocational education fields in order to meet the job requirements of the future. Robert Mager's (1962) book *Preparing Instructional Objectives* was in wide use in curriculum development in vocational education. Writing about curriculum in the secondary school and the role of vocational education at about the same time, Trump and Miller (1968) suggested that vocational educators faced four major problems in planning their curriculum: (1) misguided official attitudes (i.e., school administration and faculty have false and distorted ideas about vocational education); (2) the idea that college preparation represents the only real value in education; (3) the difficulty of keeping pace with ever-changing employment needs; and (4) the need to add vitality and integration to work-study programs.

The report of an Advisory Council on Vocational Education set up under the 1963 act to review its impact provided the basis for reauthorization of federal vocational education in 1968. The Council, chaired by Martin W. Essex, Superintendent of Public Instruction for Ohio, made recommendations to strengthen vocational education, including consolidation of all federal vocational education in one act in order to make it more manageable and substantially increasing its funding. The Vocational Education Amendments of 1968 followed the general direction of the 1963 act with increased funding (i.e., total authorization was to increase from $542 million in 1969 to $910 million in 1972). A new provision of the amendments was the establishment of state and national advisory councils on vocational education to advise on direction, curriculum, and accountability.

In 1972 and 1976 additional amendments were made to the Vocational Education Act of 1963, increasing federal funding for vocational education. The 1972 amendments included provisions for consumer and homemaking education, exemplary programs and projects, and a Bureau of Occupational and Adult Education in the U.S. Office of Education. In 1976, the provisions brought attention to the need for increased external involvement in planning vocational education, designation of one state agency to manage vocational education, reduction of sex stereotyping in programs, and increased efforts at vocational guidance and counseling. By this time Evans' (1971) book, *Foundations of Vocational Education*, was of influence and proposed three major objectives for vocational education: (1) to meet the labor market needs of society, (2) to increase options available to students, and (3) to provide incentives for learning. Criticism of vocational education during this time, exemplified by the report "Work in America" (Special Task Force to the Secretary of Health, Education and Welfare 1972), raised issues of the effectiveness of high school vocational education in terms of occupational placement and cost and the use of federal funds to maintain existing programs, as opposed to stimulating new development.

During the 1970s, career education, advocated by Sidney P. Marland, Jr., the U.S. Commissioner of Education, came into being. Career education (described earlier in this chapter) was to start in the elementary grades and continue after high school, to be integrated into all school subjects, and to prepare people for the world of work. The Office of Education's discretionary resources were used to conduct pilot tests of exemplary career education models. Federal legislation and funding followed during the 1970s to assist states in developing curricula for career education, calling for a state plan for career education, establishing an Office of Career Education in the Office of Education and providing for a National Advisory Council for Career Education, and implementing a national program of career education. However, the career education movement generally lost momentum in the 1980s, and several of its components became a part of vocational education.

In summary, by the late 1970s vocational education had grown substantially in students and funding from its meager start prior to the 1900s (Barlow 1976). By 1978, 19,536,175 students were enrolled, 64 percent in secondary schools. The federal funding level was approximately $413 million (appropriations always fell considerably short of authorizations). State and local funding for vocational education was nearly $6 billion. The federal government was providing $650 million by 1979 (about 9.9 percent of the total). Vocational education was going on throughout the K–12 system, although concentrated in grades 10 through 12, in postsecondary colleges and institutes, and in part-time adult programs. Vocational education in secondary schools was delivered in comprehensive high schools, specialized vocational high schools, and area centers serving several high school districts. The curriculum was still largely subdivided along traditional lines of agriculture, business and office, distributive, health occupations, home economics, and industrial education. Business and office and health occupations education were new areas. Distributive education was moving toward a new name—marketing education. Industrial education was a compromise label, used particularly at the university level, to include a combination of industrial arts, trade, and industrial and technical education. Industrial arts was beginning to examine the desirability of changing its name to industrial technology or technology education. Career education had stimulated the addition of some general vocational education components dealing with vocational development and employability skills. Vocational education had become a commonly identified separate track, along with college preparatory and general, in the high school curriculum. The perception or fact of tracking students into certain kinds of work was a continuing criticism of vocational education (Kantor and Tyack 1982; Oakes 1985; Shor 1987; Tanner and Tanner 1980).

Although the state and local funding contribution to vocational education was considerable, the federal government still had considerable sway and power in setting overall direction, structure, and focus of curriculum in vocational education. Significant impacts of federal legislation were to strengthen vocational education's unique purposes to prepare for work and family responsibilities, rather than to support other areas of instruction in the secondary school, and to focus on occupations requiring less than a college degree for entry, rather than on the full range of occupations. States had assumed a much larger role in developing curriculum guidelines (previously done at the federal level), and local advisory committees, community surveys, and detailed occupational analyses were used as self-correcting, checks and balances mechanisms to tailor the curriculum of local schools to the surrounding community. Vocational education was accepted in the curriculum as a means to "democratize" secondary schools by serving the needs, interests, and abilities of all students in a given geographic area.

REVIEW OF CURRENT CURRICULAR RESEARCH

The review that follows picks up from where the historical development of vocational education and its subfields, described in the previous section, leaves off, and focuses on the period from the mid-1970s to the present. Within subsections on each subfield of vocational education, the review and synthesis reports published by the National Center for Research in Vocational Education will be used as primary source documents for the time periods for which they are available. Generally, these reports include a chapter or section devoted to curricular research, sometimes reviewing several hundred studies. Among the studies cited in these reports, most attention will be given to the more comprehensive studies that have had substantial impact on the field.

Agricultural Education

In the field of agricultural education the major reviews and syntheses of research were authored by L. H. Newcomb at the Ohio State University (1978) and J. H. Lee at Mississippi State University (1985). Newcomb reviewed studies for the period 1969 to 1978 and grouped those related to curriculum into the categories of task analysis, core curriculum, development of curriculum guides, evaluation of curriculum, and determination of employment needs. Significant task analysis studies done during this period were for mechanical competencies for skilled and semiskilled laborers in horticulture, agribusiness (see Berkey, Drake, and Legacy 1972), agricultural mechanics, and retail feed (Hohenhaus 1976) occupations. On a less technical level, task analysis was used to develop a common core of basic skills needed across agribusiness and natural resource occupations (McCracken and Yoder 1975) and for leadership and personal development (Hampson, Newcomb, and McCracken 1977). The areas of leadership and personal development identified were categorized as follows: (1) leading individuals and groups, (2) developing good work habits, (3) participating in social activities, (4) participating in committees and groups, (5) participating in professional business and civic organizations, (6) managing financial resources, (7) developing communications skills, (8) developing citizen skills, and (9) developing personal skills.

The 1970s was also a time when the curricular research in agricultural education began to seek a core curriculum that could be common across agricultural education programs in a state or region. McCracken and Yoder (1975) concluded that use of local advisory committees, task inventories, and community surveys in planning the agricultural education curriculum for a specific school mitigated against development of a core curriculum. Rather, these strategies focused on specific skill requirements for particular occupations and not on more general skills and exploratory experiences. In their study to develop a common core of basic skills across agricultural occupation, they identified 48 occupational tasks that could serve as the basis for a common core in agricultural education. These tasks were grouped under the headings performing office work, following general safety precautions, maintaining equipment, using and maintaining hand and power tools, operating equipment and vehicles, and maintaining buildings and structures. The tasks placed in these categories were selected from over 2,500 tasks needed in the occupations studied. The actual number of tasks that were identified as common (48) and their description led McCracken and Yoder to conclude that (1) the common core tasks represent only a small section of tasks needed for success in agricultural occupations, and (2) few of the common tasks are specifically agricultural in nature. Studies by Horner, Zikmund, and Dillon (1970) and Snowden and McMinn (1971) also sought to identify common areas of subject matter among agricultural occupations. Areas so identified included business management, taxes, credit, marketing, soils, electricity, insurance, accounting, livestock, farm machinery, welding, tractor and other power, agricultural economics, sales, and first aid.

Many curriculum guides were developed during this period, and they varied in the formality of research procedures used in the development process. A major study using more formal development and testing procedures was conducted by Householder, McGhee, and Roediger (1976) for major occupational categories within agribusiness, natural resources, and environmental protection. They developed 10 curriculum guides containing administrative directions and instructional units for use by classroom teachers. Guides were developed based on identification of current and emerging occupations in the above-cited areas and analysis of other existing curriculum guides. Field-test procedures for the guides included monitoring policies and procedures for dissemination of the guides, teachers' opinion of the guides, and student achievement using criterion-referenced tests. While teachers valued the guides for help in selecting teaching objectives, content, and student activities, few significant relationships were found between use of the guides and achievement test performance.

In the category of curriculum evaluation, Newcomb (1978) cites the above study by Householder, McGhee, and Roediger as being well designed and rigorous in approach. He concludes, "There is a need for more systematic and rigorous evaluation of curriculum efforts in agricultural education, aimed at student performance and/or employee performance" (19). Studies looking at more general trends in the agricultural education curriculum during this time concluded that junior high agriculture courses had few exploratory occupational objectives (Dillon 1970) and that agricultural production (farming) was declining as a subject matter area in agricultural programs.

The last curriculum research category used by Newcomb (1978) relates to studies that sought to provide labor market information about agricultural occupations. Few studies were reported, and he concluded that insufficient data exist for sound planning and accountability of agricultural education from the perspective of labor market needs. A major study of labor market needs for agricultural occupations was designed during this period by the U.S. Office of Education, but unfortunately was not funded (McClay 1978).

Lee (1985) reviewed studies in agricultural education for the period 1978 to 1984. In contrast to Newcomb, Lee organizes the studies relating to curriculum into the categories of major thrusts, secondary curriculum, postsecondary curriculum, and adult/young adult curriculum. Only the first two are included here. In the category of major curricular thrusts, the work by Iowa State University in developing Standards for Quality Vocational Programs in Agricultural/Agribusiness Education (1977), sponsored by the U.S. Office of Education, is particularly noted. An initial draft of the standards was developed at a national meeting of agricultural educators from across the country. These standards were then validated separately in each of 46 states by seeking reactions from those with expertise and experience in various areas and levels of agricultural education. Standards were developed that are common to all areas of agricultural education as well as to each instructional cluster of programs (i.e., production agriculture, agricultural supplies and services, agricultural mechanics, agricultural products, ornamental horticulture, agricultural resources, and forestry). A sample of the standards common to all programs and related to curriculum include:

- Validated competencies, needed by students for entry and advancement in employment, are used in developing objectives for the instructional program.
- Students enrolled in vocational education in agriculture/agribusiness are also enrolled in other appropriate courses, including science, mathematics, social science, and oral and written communications.
- The instructional program is articulated with other local secondary, postsecondary, and 4-year programs in agriculture/agribusiness.
- Provisions are made to accommodate students with physical handicaps or other special educational needs.
- Students are engaged in supervised occupational experience programs that are related to their occupational objectives and are appropriate in light of their ability and place of residence.
- Leadership development activities are an integral part of the instructional program.

At about the same time, McClay (1978) was directing a nation-wide study designed to (1) identify the essential agricultural competencies needed for entry employment and advancement in the major agriculture and agribusiness occupations and (2) validate the importance of identified competencies for each occupation. This work was completed for 59 production agriculture and 139 agribusiness occupations. The information for each occupation includes a job description, job competencies and subcompetencies, ratings of competency importance, and descriptions of the group surveyed and the agency conducting the survey. Teacher educators in agricultural education in 40 colleges and universities across the country did most of the survey work. Competency was defined as "behavioral characteristics of knowledge, skills, attitudes and judgment generally required for the successful performance of a task(s) or the sum total of attitudes, knowledge, and skills which enable a person to perform efficiently and effectively in a given function" (7). According to Lee (1985), "The findings of this study have had substantive impact on programming and curriculum in vocational-technical agricultural education in the United States" (3) as evidenced by citations in curriculum guides, in-service activities, and professional literature.

Consistent with the study by McClay (1978) noted above, other curriculum research in agricultural education focused on relating subject matter more closely to the trends and practices in the agricultural industry. For example, Hogue, Carnes, and Briers (1981) identified more than 150 new and emerging occupations related to agriculture that should be taken account of in curriculum development. Comprehensive job descriptions were developed for occupations such as agricultural computer operator, horticultural supply clerk, smoke jumper, and seafood butcher. In keeping with this trend of relating curriculum content more closely to industrial practice, Baggett (1982) proposed an eight-stage model for using information from agriculture program graduates and the agriculture industry to assure a relevant curriculum.

A second approach to curriculum research gaining attention during this time was the use of local community needs assessments relating to agriculture as a basis for curriculum review. Parmley, Wilton, and Bender (1981), in studying school districts in Kansas that did not have high school agriculture programs, found that while rural residents and agribusiness favored adding programs, school administrators were unfavorable for reasons of facilities, finances, student interest, and educational need. An example of a community needs assessment for local districts is provided by Effendi (1984) in West Virginia.

The curriculum research noted by Lee (1985) in the category of secondary curriculum again focuses on competencies needed in agricultural occupations. Some of the clusters of agricultural occupations addressed include agricultural mechanics (Maday 1984), ornamental horticulture and feed, seed, and grain (Bigo 1979). Specific occupations were also examined for their required competencies, for example, dairy farm managers (Stenzel 1979) and agricultural mechanics in retail dealerships (Kesler 1984). During this time, the Vocational-Technical Consortium of States (V-TECS) also began its detailed and extensive work to develop competency lists for occupations addressed by vocational education, including agriculture. The work by Hamilton (1983) for farm machinery set-up mechanics and delivery persons is a good example.

As in previous periods, several states developed curriculum guides during the period 1978 to 1984, often as a basis for a core curriculum in agriculture. Examples of states that had completed or had ongoing research in this area were Illinois (Russel and Courson 1984), Louisiana (Burnett 1983), Michigan (Karelse and Olson 1983), Texas (Brown 1978), and Oklahoma (Hatcher, Frazier, and Miller 1978). Lee concludes his review of secondary curriculum research in agriculture with the admonition, "A weakness in close adherence to competency studies in curriculum development is the lack of 'future orientation.' Competency studies are time bound" (1985, 4).

As one moves to the most recent curricular research in agricultural education, the major study of consideration is the work by the Committee on Agricultural Education of the National Academy of Science (1988). This study, guided by an interdisciplinary team of agricultural scholars, educational scholars, and representatives of schools and agricultural associations, was initiated in 1985 "because of concerns about the declining profitability and international competitiveness of American Agriculture, as well as concerns about declining enrollments, instructional content, and quality in agricultural education programs" (v). With these concerns in mind, the committee drew on expert testimony, reports, field visits, and open hearings to propose goals, subject matter, and policy changes for instruction in agriculture for elementary and secondary schools. The committee concluded: (1) instruction in agriculture must become more than vocational agriculture, and (2) major changes are needed in vocational agriculture. The response to the first conclusion was to introduce the idea of "agricultural literacy," which focuses on education "about" agriculture. Agricultural literacy education for all students is to start in kindergarten and extend through the high school grades. Instruction could occur in separate agriculture courses, but most instruction should be integrated into existing courses in every subject matter area. The goal should be to develop agriculturally literate persons, meaning they have an understanding of the food and fiber system, including its history and current economic, social, and environmental significance. On the other hand, vocational agriculture or education "in" agriculture should retain its focus of preparing for agricultural work, but with a much broader concept of agricultural work and the necessary preparation for that work. In addition to production agriculture, agricultural work is to include agribusiness management and marketing; agricultural research and engineering; food science, processing, and retailing; banking; education; landscape architecture; and urban planning. Agriculture education should be viewed as preparation for effective study of agriculture in postsecondary schools and colleges for many students. While retaining the three basic components of the agricultural education curriculum (i.e., classroom and laboratory instruction, supervised occupational experience, and participation in a youth organization [the Future Farmers of America or FFA]), each of these components should be broadened to reflect the changing nature of agricultural work.

Other curricular research during this most recent time period began to focus on themes and issues that were affecting the secondary school curriculum more generally. For example, Anderson and Boddy (1985) focused on identifying the science (i.e., biology, chemistry, and physics) skills taught in vocational programs, including agriculture, and the importance vocational teachers attached to students possessing science skills on entering and leaving agricultural education programs in secondary schools. The conclusions suggest that the vocational agriculture curriculum consisted of a relatively high number of science skills and that teachers attached importance to the students' possession of science skills.

Relating to another more general curricular theme, Peuse and Swanson (1980) examined factors affecting teacher acceptance of a new instructional unit in international agriculture in Illinois. Earlier work by Field (1976) in Minnesota considered the receptiveness and appropriateness of increasing the awareness and sensitivity of students of agricultural programs to global perspectives and issues relating to agriculture. He found that (1) agriculture students are generally lacking in awareness of and sensitivity to international agricultural issues; (2) agricultural teachers are extremely receptive to instructional materials on the topic and feel it is an appropriate aspect of the curriculum (particularly its technical skill dimensions); and (3) instructors who emphasize the topic significantly affect their students' future involvement in international work.

In summary, the curricular research in agricultural education from the mid-1970s to the present makes it clear that major efforts have been made to base the curriculum on the specific technical knowledge and skills needed for success in agricultural work. Surrounding this focus were studies to provide labor market information about agricultural work (i.e., employment opportunities, needed educational levels, new and emerging occupational titles) and nontechnical skill needs such as leadership and personal abilities. Statewide core-curriculum-guide development coincided with efforts to develop basic or common skills across a wide variety of occupations making up agricultural work. However, rigorous testings of these curriculum guides in terms of student performance were few and, where done, did not produce expected results. Standards for quality agricultural education programs were developed by the profession and were used to guide program planning and review in many states. More recently, curriculum research attention has shifted to examining the science content of agricultural courses and the role of agricultural education in international education. Ending this period was a major review of secondary school agricultural education across the United States, which recommended that the goals of agricultural education be broadened to include (1) agricultural literacy (education about agriculture) for all students in all grade levels and (2) vocational agriculture (education in agriculture), to encompass a wider array of agricultural work and all occupational levels. Curricular research questions that may merit study in the future for agricultural education include (1) What is the meaning of "agricultural literacy" and "vocational agriculture" we have moved from the rural economy of the 1700s to the 1990s when only 3 percent of the American people are farmers? (2) What special curricular challenges are posed in the shift of emphasis from family farming to agribusiness? (3) As the agriculture industry increasingly becomes a global enterprise, what changes are essential in agricultural education?

Business Education

The only review and synthesis of research in business and office education completed after the mid-1970s was done by Judith J. Lambrecht (University of Minnesota–Minneapolis), Marianne J. D'Onofrio (Utah State University), L. Eugene Jones (Northeast Louisiana University), and Patricia A. Merrier (University of Minnesota–Duluth) (1981). They reviewed 1,129 studies for the period 1968 to 1980. The review was organized around the major content areas of business and office education, bookkeeping and accounting, basic business education, communications, business mathematics, business data processing, shorthand and transcription, typing, and word processing.

Studies focused on the content of bookkeeping and accounting used sources such as (1) competency or task analysis, (2) technology applications, (3) teacher opinions, (4) worker opinions, (5) textbooks, and (6) professional literature and reports. The preponderance of studies were competency or task analyses—for example, addressing the data processing duties of bookkeeping and accounting jobs. Examples of other sources of content were highlighted in addressing the changing nature of mechanical equipment for processing financial information, in securing the opinions of college accounting instructors and business representatives concerning electronic accounting concepts, and in identifying difficult bookkeeping topics.

In the content area of basic business education, two studies dealt across the area with textbook analysis to identify the social responsibility content of basic high school business texts and categories of content found in general business, economics, consumer economics, business principles, and business law textbooks. Other studies dealt with the subarea of basic business. For example, among the curriculum-related topics investigated were appropriate content about the code of canon law, legal concepts important to consumers and citizens, and legal issues. In the subarea of personal finance, the topic of personal finance competencies needed by high school graduates as judged by business, home economics, mathematics, and social studies teachers and business representatives was investigated. In the teaching of economics, research focused on the economic concepts important to understanding American business and economic concepts judged important by consumer-related organizations. Teaching of economic concepts in the context of a variety of subject areas was also investigated during this time; the subject matter areas included typing, U.S. history, social studies, and community-based economic education. Competency studies were completed in the area of consumer education, often involving both business and consumer homemaking teachers. Studies of specific areas within consumer education illustrating the nature of the content focused on consumer problems of unmarried high school graduates 4 years after leaving school, personal income aspects of consuming, problems of home buying, management problems of bankrupt households, and consumer awareness rights. One of the conclusions reached by Lambrecht et al. (1981) was that curricular research was needed in the basic business areas to structure, sequence, and interrelate the various subareas.

In the business and office content area of communications, studies focused on communications competencies needed for specific business and office work and issues in particular types of communications content. Competency studies focused on writing communications by secretaries, clerical workers, and paralegal workers and reading in office jobs. Issues investigated in particular areas of communications content included oral communications effectiveness in business, English usage expressions, guidelines for written job applications, writing problems in business offices, writing skills of accountants, types of letters written by business managers, changes in letter-writing procedures with word processing, organizational patterns of letters, report writing, and nonverbal communications.

Again, in the content area of business mathematics, competency studies were the major focus of curricular research. These studies addressed business mathematics competencies needed in the fields of accounting, business administration, and secretarial science; entry-level jobs in retailing; and beginning versus experienced business workers.

Perhaps the emergence of data processing as a content area of business education accounts for the large numbers of curricular studies in this area between 1968 and 1980. Lambrecht et al. (1981) categorized the studies into three groups based on the research approach used: (1) contact with industry users or employed data processing personnel; (2) contrast of competencies used by employed workers versus content of data processing programs; and (3) examination of current data processing programs. Occupations included in the studies were data processing managers, systems analysts, programmers, computer operators, data entry operators, and clerks. Studies with potentially unique implications included changes in job requirements for data processing from 1969 to 1973; data processing jobs attainable with high school training; data processing skills appropriate for all high school students; qualifications, job distinctions, and career ladders in computer production operations; contrast of secondary and postsecondary data processing programs; business computer programming languages; and the data processing program requirements for special groups of students.

Studies in the content area of typewriting involved analysis of business letters to determine structure and design, contrast of office production materials with materials in high school typing textbooks, typing in insurance offices, work performed by beginning office workers, and teaching other content (i.e., economic concepts, reading) in typing classes. In the area of word processing, a very large number of studies were also completed between 1968 and 1980. Lambrecht et al. (1981) classified the curricular research by source of implications for content under the headings job practices in word processing installations; entry-level qualifications, tasks, and/or competencies; and job satisfaction of word processing personnel. As examples, Scriven et al. (1981) reported on the national Delta Pi Epsilon (professional fraternity in business education) survey of current practices in word processing installations across the United States. The studies of entry-level qualifications concluded that English, secretarial, and human relations skills were needed for entry-level word processing jobs. Competency studies revealed that the skills of typing from handwritten, typed, and rough draft copy; applying English and grammar skills; following directions and listening; meeting and greeting people; answering telephones; and using a filing system were important for word processing jobs (Scriven, Holley, Wagoner, and Brown 1981). Based on studies of this kind, Lambrecht, D'Onofrio, Jones, and Merrier (1981) summarize the implications for business education curricula by suggesting that programs should be teaching the following content relating to word processing: grammar and transcription, typing, listening and following directions, using a filing system, scheduling and screening appointments, answering telephone calls, arranging reservations, and composing letters.

At the beginning of the 1980s, the *National Business Education Yearbook* (Newman and Caton 1981) focused on updating the content of secondary business education. The trends noted as affecting the business education curriculum were the career education movement, technology impacts, socioeconomic factors (i.e., demographics, labor force participation, resource limits, problems of youth), relation of accounting and data processing, and attention to entrepreneurship. It was recommended that need assessments conducted to provide a basis for curriculum change draw on the knowledge of local school administrators and teachers, advisory committees with representatives of business, local surveys, and published reports. Separate chapters in the yearbook addressed meeting the needs of the following groups with special needs: physically handicapped; economically, culturally, and educationally disadvantaged; nontraditional-sex students; and the gifted. Following from the review of curricular research during the 1970s, it seems appropriate that the yearbook chapter dealing specifically with general curricular content focused on competency-based business education as the best way to assure that instruction is clear, relevant, accountable, and efficient.

Writing in the *International Encyclopedia of Education*, Hopkins and Lambrecht (1985) describe the curriculum development process in business education as involving two basic approaches: discipline based and competency based. The discipline-based approach is described as involving an analysis of the body of knowledge regarding a particular instructional area and treating it as fairly fixed regardless of where, when, and to whom it is taught. This approach is suggested as being used most often in accounting, economics, and management. Curriculum development efforts exemplifying this approach are (1) the *Master Curriculum Guide in Teaching Economics for the Nation's Schools* (Hansen, Back, Calderwood, and Sanders 1977) and (2) *DPMA Model Curriculum for Undergraduate Computer Information Systems Education* (Adams and Athey 1981). The competency-based approach draws directly on analyses of business work, with many illustrations already having been given for business education.

During the period 1984 to 1987 the National Business Education Association (1987) conducted an extensive project to codify the entire business education curriculum, K–14, in competency format. The final report, entitled *Database of Competencies for Business Curriculum Development, K–14*, lists the proficiency standards for entry-level work in business offices. Validation was done by a task force of some 50 educators from local schools, teacher education institutions, and state education agencies and reviewed by the Education, Employment and Training Committee of the Chamber of Commerce of the United States. Competencies are organized for elementary, middle/junior high, and secondary and postsecondary business education levels. For the elementary and middle/junior high levels, the categories of content are keyboarding, basic economics, computer literacy, career and business exploration, and job attitude and human relations skills. For the secondary and postsecondary levels, the categories of content are more extensive, involving basic skills and core competencies (information skills; personal development skills; economic, consumer, and business concepts skills; technology skills) and specific job skills (i.e., processing text, processing data, accounting and record keeping, entrepreneurship). Each of the hundreds of competencies included is accompanied by a proficiency standard that specifies the conditions under which the student is to perform, what the student is to be able to do, and the minimum acceptable level of proficiency expected. This guide is to be used as a basic reference in developing business education curriculum for specific situations.

Examining the policy statements of the Policies Commission for Business and Economic Education (1989) (which has representatives from the three major business education organizations—Business Education Division of American

Vocational Association, Delta Pi Epsilon, and the National Business Education Association) for the 1980s from a curricular perspective, one sees attention to teaching basic skills, role of student organizations, linkings with business, and general education components of business education. Separate policy statements also address the following content areas of business education: word processing, business data processing, personal finance, computer literacy, keyboarding, business communications, and entrepreneurship. The policy statement about the role of business education in the comprehensive high school (1985) defines the goals of business education as being to:

1. Educate individuals for and about business.
2. Provide opportunities for nonbusiness students to acquire business knowledge, skills, and attitudes needed to function effectively in their careers.
3. Provide a continuous program of planned learning experiences designed to help students effectively fulfill three roles:
   a. Make mature, intelligent socioeconomic decisions as citizens.
   b. Produce and distribute goods and services as workers.
   c. Use the results of production as consumers.
4. Provide career information that will help students relate their interests, needs, and abilities to occupational opportunities in business. (60)

These basic goals are affirmed by Lambrecht (1987) as still representing viable reasons for business education in the secondary school curriculum. However, as this section was being written, one of the leading scholars in business education, Padamaker M. Sapre (1989), called for reconceptualization of the field of business education, including changing the field's name (although he did not suggest a new name). One of the emerging trends related to the area of office education is the changing of its name to "administrative support occupations" education (for example, see Flood 1989). And a review of the current state of business education (O'Neil 1989) suggests the following topics are gaining attention: (1) keyboarding as a new basic skill, (2) management training/entrepreneurship, and (3) closer ties with business. As keyboarding takes on the characteristics of a basic skill, it is increasingly viewed as being appropriately taught at the elementary school level, resulting in considerable rethinking of the curricular responsibilities of business education in the secondary school.

In summary, the current curricular research in business education is predominantly competency based and extensive in detailed examination of all aspects of business work. From a series of more specific studies, the business education profession moved to a comprehensive, nation-wide study of competencies important to business work as a consistent and cohesive basis for curriculum development. Research has affirmed the general education and vocational education purposes of business education. The ramifications of changing social, economic, technological, and educational issues and trends on the business education curriculum were specifically addressed through a series of professional policy statements. Some questions that might guide future research in business education are (1) What are the implications for business education of the dramatic shift from a goods producing to a service economy? (2) What should business education do about the impact of technology and organizational restructuring on the work life of office workers? (3) Should business and office education (the latter now called administrative support occupations) remain components of a single enterprise?

Home Economics Education

Two reviews and syntheses of research in home economics education cover the periods 1970–1979 (Nelson 1979) and 1979–1985 (Redick and Gritzmacher 1986). Like the reviews of the literature in the other subfields of vocational education, the reviews and syntheses in home economics do not use consistent criteria for inclusion and exclusion of curriculum research or employ the same categories of curriculum research from edition to edition. These inconsistencies make it difficult to observe patterns in the development of curriculum research in home economics and the other subfields of vocational education. The 1979 review and synthesis of the research by Helen Y. Nelson contains approximately 120 citations, whereas the number of references cited in the Redick and Gritzmacher (1986) review is nearly 275.

Nelson's review and synthesis covers the following topics: consumer homemaking education, occupational home economics programs in the junior and senior high schools, postsecondary and outreach programs for adults, area vocational schools, and home economics teacher education. Of these categories only the first two are included here. The review

> focused on those studies investigating significant problems that tested theoretically derived hypotheses, those that approached problems in an innovative manner, those that illustrated a continuity of research, those that tended to conceptualize problems, and those that tested experimental or quasi-experimental designs. (1979, 6)

Within the chapter on curriculum, Nelson reported on four types of curriculum research relevant to K–12 home economics education: relation of philosophic position to curriculum beliefs, curriculum for consumer-homemaker programs, curriculum for occupational home economics, and curriculum for learners with special needs.

Nelson chose Swan's study (1975) to address the issue of the relation of philosophic beliefs to curriculum beliefs. Seeing evidence of dissension among home economists about both philosophy and curriculum beliefs in the four different subject matter fields of the College and University Professional Section of the American Home Economics Association, that is, child development/family relations, teacher education, textiles and clothing, and food and nutrition, Swan's purpose was "to identify the nature and range of philosophical beliefs, to examine whether or not these beliefs could be classified as belonging to one of two philosophical positions, and to check for consistency between expressed philosophy and espoused curriculum'' (Nelson 1979, 73).

The two philosophical categories in Swan's study were Position I, which emphasized the primacy of developing self-fulfilled human beings, and Position II, which emphasized attainment of knowledge as an end in and of itself. Position I in curriculum beliefs favors student- or experience-centered curriculum, while Position II favors traditional subject-centered, teacher-directed curriculum. ANOVA results established significant differences among the four teaching areas, although all groups tended to gravitate toward Position I. Child development and family relations faculty were more strongly attracted to Position I, however, while those from home economics teacher education, textiles and clothing, and food and nutrition ranked behind them in the order given. There were high correlations between philosophy of education and curriculum, indicating the importance of philosophy in determining practice.

Nelson discusses several exemplary curriculum research studies in her section on curriculum for consumer homemaking. Of these studies, Murphy's (1974) development of a four-part guide, *Consumer Education Curriculum Modules: A Spiral Process Approach*, is the most significant, both because the ''spiral process'' was innovative and because it brought some order to the rapidly expanding knowledge in consumer education.

Murphy designed four modules for use with learners ranging from ninth graders to adults. A six-step spiral approach was used to provide repeated exposure to the processes of becoming a critical consumer at different levels of complexity in both class and nonclass settings. The four processes of becoming a critical consumer are acquiring information, exploring values, making decisions, and taking action. In addition to providing learners with an opportunity to move through the spiral at least to some extent at their own pace, the spiral curriculum provided teachers with more flexibility than usual in ''responding to the changing interests and increasing ability of learners to deal with abstractions'' (Nelson 1979, 68). The modules were tested on 4,873 learners. Over half of the sample scored higher on post- than on premodule assessment.

The other three studies that Nelson discussed in the consumer homemaking section of her literature review were Vaughn's (1974) development of a list of conceptual statements appropriate for use in designing curricula for grades 5 to 8, Ford's (1976) development of miniunits for coeducational middle school classes that were purportedly free of sex bias, and Fassett's (1977) planning paper for consumer homemaking teachers to use with Future Homemakers of America groups.

Under the category of occupational home economics curriculum Nelson discusses only one study, Beavers' (1979) national study of standards for curriculum development in textiles and clothing. Since Beavers' study had a postsecondary focus, it will not be discussed here except to say that its lattice-ladder approach to curriculum has been an influential and useful approach to curriculum development for the last 15 years. The lattice-ladder approach provides ''stop-out points'' that give people the opportunity to gain work experience before receiving further training. Other occupational home economics curricula from this period continued, for the most part, the competency-based approaches that have been widely used for many years in vocational education curricula.

The final category of Nelson's review, which dealt with curricula developed for K–12, is the section on curriculum for learners with special needs. She discusses two studies of significance to K–12 curriculum developers, one by Nelson, Lowe, and Dalrymple (1975) on preparing disadvantaged students for homemaker and wage-earner roles through a three-state study of the effects of six different curricular approaches on the self-concepts of disadvantaged students in 12 treatment groups and another by Dougherty (1977), who solicited contributions from vocational home economics educators in Wisconsin and then compiled a volume of program procedures, educational strategies, and teaching materials useful in programs for the disadvantaged.

Redick and Gritzmacher's (1986) review and synthesis does not include a list of formal topics covered within the larger field of home economics (e.g., occupational home economics). Instead, their review covers eight aspects of home economics education, including the nature, content, and structure of current curriculum research. The selection criteria included documented validity and reliability of measurement; appropriateness of observation and analysis; quality of sampling design and sample response rate; innovative or interdisciplinary approach; and critical or emerging subject matter. Regarding their decision to include innovative approaches to curriculum development, Redick and Gritzmacher write:

> While most recent curriculum research continues to use the empirical-analytical research to explain or predict the nature, content, and structure of home economics education, significant studies have been done using interpretive and critical science research frameworks. Researchers have uncovered meanings underlying curriculum decisions and have suggested new possibilities for home economics curriculum. (viii)

In their section on the nature of home economics curriculum, Redick and Gritzmacher cite approximately 25 studies, which fall into several types. One type of study they review is the critique of home economics curriculum of which Eyestone's study (1982) of parenthood education is an example. Eyestone examined a selection of parenthood education curriculum guides for secondary students and found them to be something of a conceptual hodgepodge, teaching a variety of different parenthood concepts with different philosophical implications.

A second type of research into the nature of home economics curriculum reviewed by Redick and Gritzmacher addresses the normative question: What should be the nature of home economics education? Based on a conceptual framework model adapted from Brown (1980, 1985) and Brown and Paolucci (1979), Kister (1981) is one of several researchers between 1979 and 1985 who used the critical science mode of inquiry and the dialectical reasoning method as conceptual tools by which to make explicit the assumptions, aims, values, and inconsistencies of a given curriculum. Kister examined the homemaking tasks identified through occupational analysis done by Abt, Lewis, Barnes, and Geiger (1968) and concluded that empirical-rational, hermeneutic, and critical science perspectives should guide home economics curriculum development. Baldwin (1984), in a study related to Kister's analysis, found that the models "were not based on adequately established theoretical frameworks" (Redick and Gritzmacher 1986, 13–14).

A third type of study within the section on home economics curriculum is the common type of curriculum study that identifies standards and content for specific home economics programs such as nutrition education or clothing and textiles. One innovative study within this general type was that done by MacCleave-Frazier and Murray (1983) to reconceptualize clothing curriculum in consumer homemaking programs. Using status and qualitative research approaches, they organized illustrative curriculum materials around "practical problems and questions of families" and "appropriate systems of family action" (Redick and Gritzmacher 1986, 14).

The fourth and last subtype of curriculum research to be carried out under the general heading of the nature of the home economics curriculum is a new arrival in the field. Redick and Gritzmacher (1986) write: "Besides home economics content, mathematics, science, and thinking processes have also become the focus of home economics curriculum research" (14), and they cite several examples of studies about such topics as using formal reasoning in analyzing books and ads for misleading content (Contento 1981; Franz, MacDonald, and Grocott 1985).

Under the category "content of home economics curriculum," Redick and Gritzmacher cite about a dozen examples of recent research into the content of elementary and secondary home economics classes. Of these, the most interesting, although discouraging, results were found by Bakalars (1980) and Bakalars and Petrich (1983), who studied the family life concepts that were taught by elementary teachers. These concepts are structured around (1) learning about self and others, (2) family and society interaction, (3) developing as a family member, and (4) adolescence, "yet none of the factors was taught to a great extent and factors two and four [as well as content on human sexual development] were seldom or never taught" (Redick and Gritzmacher 1986, 15).

Redick and Gritzmacher's third category, "structure of home economics curriculum," and the fourth category, "factors affecting curriculum content and design," present findings from 8 and 15 studies, respectively. Like the first two sections, the last two sections stress the complexity of curriculum development and the importance of testing new or, at least, relatively untested research methodologies and curriculum development principles such as integration of home economics concepts into non–home economics curricula, imaging, focus groups, content analysis, and tape-recorded dialogue.

Since 1985, the theme of accelerating the pace of vocational home economics curriculum development within general home economics curriculum development has taken on strength. Kister (1989), among others, argues that faltering families with increasingly diverse structures and worker shortages in the service sector are two important reasons for increased attention to vocational home economics. Kister discusses a study of working parents (Burden and Googins 1985), which shows that, while 86 percent rate their job performance as good or unusually good, only 62 percent rated their family performance that high. Kister reminds the reader that "strengthening families is inherently the mission of vocational home economics" and points out that "the vulnerability of families is clearly an acute social problem" (Kister 1989, 35).

Although it has not yet showed up in the reviews and syntheses of the research literature, mostly because it is so new, another theme in the home economics curriculum literature of the last 10 years is entrepreneurship education. One modest and enthusiastic study from Montana is typical of studies in this field. The researchers (Goetting and Muggli 1988) searched out 22 "Made in Montana" entrepreneurial home economists, all women, and surveyed them about the nature of their business, the resources needed to start the business, the relationship of their home economics background to their business, and their future plans. The Montana Home Economics Association will continue to seek out home economist entrepreneurs and will ask those identified to serve on discussion panels that focus on starting one's own business and to serve as mentors for other entrepreneurial home economists. Many observers believe that entrepreneurial education is an important dimension of vocational education and that the informal information gathering and networking of the 1980s will lead to the development of formal research and curriculum research at K–12 as well as postsecondary levels in the 1990s.

A third and final theme of the most recent research in home economics curriculum continues the interest first noted in the 1979–1985 period in new conceptual models. A study by Weade and Gritzmacher (1987) developed a conceptual model to test the relationship between personality type preferences, as measured by the Myers-Briggs Type Indicator, and curriculum design preferences, as measured by a curriculum preference survey developed by the authors. Like Swan's somewhat similar attempt (1975) to study the relationship of philosophic beliefs to curriculum beliefs, the results of Weade and Gritzmacher's study are complex and mixed.

In summary, the story of home economics education curriculum development in the 1970s and 1980s is one of both broadening and deepening of the field. One way that the broadening of the home economics education curriculum is evidenced is in the expansion of home economics curricular offerings to increasingly diverse and often quite specialized audiences—for example, teen parents, displaced homemakers, single parents, and bilingual students of all ages. Another indication of the broadening of the field may be seen in the increasing emphasis on expanding the theoretical base and methodological tools of the field. There was by the end of the 1980s an impressive body of curriculum research using interpretive and critical science perspectives, concepts, and tools. A third example of the broadening of the home economics education mission is the expansion of curriculum content to include such topics as entrepreneurial education, development education, expanded consumer economics offerings, domestic and sexual abuse, AIDS education, work/family issues, and various equity topics.

Evidence of the deepening of home economics curricula can be found in the attempts of the field as a whole to develop curriculum development standards in the subfields of home economics education, to critique curricula in some subfields in order to assess the lack of clearly stated assumptions and other conceptual shortcomings, and to use both more innovative and more rigorous curriculum development approaches, such as the lattice-ladder and cluster curricular approaches imported into home economics from other educational subdisciplines.

Several important issues focusing on the philosophy of the K–12 home economics curriculum are raised perennially in the field. While there is no disagreement about the expansion of the curriculum into new areas, there are those who say that this expansion is more driven by the fluctuating and faddish demands of the marketplace than by thoughtful discussion and planning by home economists.

An issue related to the scope of the curriculum is the ongoing discussion about the nature and purpose of home economics. A strong and articulate minority within the field has argued for a broader and more complex understanding of the mission since the Lake Placid Conferences at the end of the 19th and beginning of the 20th centuries. The most influential proponents of this perspective are Brown and Paolucci (1979), who wrote:

> The mission of home economics is to enable families, both as individual units and generally as a social institution, to build and maintain systems of action which lead (1) to maturing in individual self-formation and (2) to enlightened, cooperative participation in the critique and formulation of social goals and means for accomplishing them. (23)

In a similar vein, Brown (1985) expressed concern that home economics has become "limited" through "the self-imposed restriction growing out of the ideology of science and technology" (928–929). The issues raised by Brown and Paolucci (1979) and Brown (1985) are important. Should the field take Brown and Paolucci's definition more seriously in creating K–12 curricula? Is the orientation now dominant in the field the best one by which to help develop family members to become autonomous moral agents?

Industrial Education

The two reviews and syntheses of the research literature in the field of industrial education were written by Dyrenfurth and Householder in 1979 to cover the period 1970–1979 and by McCrory in 1987 to cover the period 1980–1986. Like the other reviews and syntheses in the subfields of vocational education, these two reviews are very different from each other in focus. A separate review in trade and industrial education written by Finch in 1983 focuses on research published between 1977 and 1982 but includes other research published between 1969 and 1977 or even earlier.

Because the Dyrenfurth and Householder (1979) review is so lengthy and detailed, the research literature they discussed will only be highlighted here by extrapolating their general themes. Dyrenfurth and Householder subdivided their discussion of industrial arts curriculum into several major categories, including comprehensive efforts, curriculum processes and analyses, industry-education analyses, instructional units, and Industrial Arts Curriculum Project (IACP) (38). Under comprehensive efforts, one theme the authors identified is a discussion in the industrial arts field of the desirability of a uniform nation-wide industrial arts curriculum. Given the large-scale curriculum projects that began in the late 1950s and gathered momentum in the 1960s, it is not surprising that Carter (1970) decided to survey industrial arts teachers and administrators at all levels about the idea of a national curriculum. The respondents did not favor the idea, but they did advocate establishing a "common core." Other comprehensive curriculum research of the period established a widespread approval for "articulation" of various sorts: between elementary and junior high school curricula, between locally developed secondary curricula and state curricula, and so forth.

Another theme closely connected to the issues of curriculum consolidation and articulation was the role of state curriculum guides. Dyrenfurth and Householder report the development of several different types of these guides and the creation of survey instruments to query industrial educators about their utility and popularity.

Under the category "curriculum processes," Dyrenfurth and Householder begin with a discussion of DeVore's major contribution of 1968, *Structure and Content Foundations for Curriculum Development*, a work that, among other things, "laid the foundation for the case of the technology education thrust" (Dyrenfurth and Householder 1979, 40). DeVore's publication led to numerous studies in the 1970s of such curriculum processes as occupational analysis, criterion-referenced curricula, performance objectives with criterion measures, behavioral objectives, competency-based instruction, systems theory, network and critical path methods, task organization pattern identification, and content identification (40–44).

In their sections on "industry-education analysis" and "instructional units," Dyrenfurth and Householder entered familiar territory in industrial arts curriculum history. They reported that while these sources of curriculum generation did not create new curriculum methodologies, they nonetheless remained useful in establishing such new content areas for the field as energy alternatives, plastics, metal casting, aerospace education, safety education in industrial arts, and industrial pilot mechanics.

The famous Industrial Arts Curriculum Project (IACP), discussed in the history section, has its own category in the Dyrenfurth and Householder review because this curriculum is "one of the few innovative efforts to have reached enough students in a variety of settings to permit substantive research" (50). One such major study was undertaken by the Pontiac City School District (1971) of cognitive content mastery by students. Results from Pontiac, as well as the results from other research, show the Industrial Arts Curriculum Project to be generally effective. Students expressed a positive reaction to the World of Manufacturing curriculum in particular, but were "less than enthusiastic about the more abstract concepts of the program" (Dyrenfurth and Householder 1979, 50). Dyrenfurth and Householder specifically expressed appreciation to Buffer (1971) and Umstattd (1976) for undertaking syntheses of research on the IACP project. They wrote: "While the findings have not always been consistent or favorable for the innovative program, they encouraged subsequent researchers to validate curriculum developments" (Dyrenfurth and Householder 1979, 52).

In summarizing the research of the period covered by their review and synthesis, Dyrenfurth and Householder conclude that much research was going on, particularly in the development of instructional units; that the clearest area of weakness in industrial arts curriculum research is the secondary curriculum; and that another weakness is that much less attention is paid to the *use* of developed curricula than to the development itself (54–55).

McCrory's 1987 review of curriculum research for the period 1980–1986 uses the categories of comprehensive efforts, content, courses and units, learning activities, and curriculum development and implementation to summarize the studies. The most important curriculum project of the 1980s is the Jackson's Mill Industrial Arts Curriculum Theory, derived by 21 industrial arts educators from an analysis of technical human-adaptive systems (Hales and Snyder 1982a, 1982b; Snyder and Hales 1981). The authors promote the view of technology as an integral part of human-adaptive systems. Technology enables us to cope with our natural and humanmade environments. There are six classes of inputs into the system: people, knowledge, materials, energy, capital, and finance. The actions and practices applied to the inputs are defined as the processes used in adaptive behavior, and the outputs take the form of products, services, or desired conditions of the environment. Education then, is one of the feedback mechanisms that allows for assessment, adjustment, and constant redirection of the system.

To provide a single consistent principle for organizing curriculum content, curricular elements were divided into four subsystems of human technological/sociological endeavors: communication, construction, manufacturing, and transportation, each of which has technical and sociocultural components. The subsystems possess these common elements:

1. productive processes—those activities designed by people that utilize selected inputs to reach desired goals;
2. managerial processes—those activities designed by people to ensure that productive processes are performed efficiently and appropriately; and
3. a managed productive system—a system developed by people in which each step in the transformation of inputs to outputs is efficiently planned, organized, directed, and controlled with respect to company goals and in concert with society objectives.

While the degree of innovation in the Jackson's Mill project is debatable, the project's impact has been substantial. McCrory states that "the comprehensive studies and those related to curriculum content," such as those undertaken by Bensen (1979) and the Wisconsin Department of Public Instruction (1984), "give evidence that a consensus has formed" that the Jackson's Mill project is "the curriculum content model for technology education for the next decade." McCrory also states, however, that "as yet specific course outlines and student activities have not been developed [by states] to implement the new technology education curriculum designs" (McCrory 1987, 20).

Under the category "content and instructional units," McCrory discusses the current status of the perennial discussion in industrial education about the content source for industrial arts. McCrory cites recent arguments by Swanson (1983), Wright (1982), and Meyers (1985) that industry should remain the content base. In this section McCrory also refers to Lauda and Wright's article (1983) about the first university technology curriculum in the country, established in the early 1980s at Eastern Illinois University.

Under the category "curriculum development and implementation," McCrory singles out Bensen's 1979 discussion of the cluster, trade analysis, and concept approaches to curriculum development; Ritz's 1980 outline of a systematic process for curriculum consisting of curriculum foundations, content, and evaluation; the International Technology Education Association's 1985 guide for curriculum implementation, which showcased exemplary technology education programs; a curriculum guide for the handicapped; and a curriculum plan to promote sex equity (McCrory 1987, 19).

Finch (1983) analyzed recent curriculum research in the trade and industrial fields under the headings of models and frameworks, content determination, affective and transferable skills, futuristic content considerations, and competency-based education.

The most important curriculum model in trade and industrial education is the Maryland Plan, developed in the late 1960s and discussed in the section on the history of industrial education. Two other models Finch discusses reflect the need to focus on trade and industrial curriculum priorities. Drake, Davis, and Terry (1980) gathered data on a variety of curriculum dimensions and developed a ranking procedure for determining which trade and industrial instructional areas were in most critical need of development. Wichowski (1981) provided a needs-assessment model, the outputs of which include (1) identification of program areas with the greatest curriculum need; (2) weighted decision-making variables used to allocate resources; (3) demographic data; and (4) profiles of existing curricular textbooks.

In the area of content determination, Finch and Crunkilton (1979) identified six strategies for deriving trade and industrial content: philosophical base, introspection, function approach, task analysis, critical incident technique, and the Delphi approach. Ammerman, Pratzner, Essex, and Mead (1977), Berger and Hawkins (1979), and Morsh and Archer (1967) have all developed further approaches to the curriculum task analysis process, including occupational surveys, task inventories, and CODAPs (Comprehensive Occupational Data Analysis Programs).

Affective and transferable skills is an approach to curriculum not exclusively focused on the identification of technical content. Nelson and O'Niel (1977), for example, identified 27 skills important for occupational survival through telephone interviews with workers. Foster (1978) used the critical incident technique to identify essential nontechnical skills for workers in trade and industrial fields. Beach (1978) developed the Affective Work Competencies Inventory, while Swanson (1981) developed a system for analyzing subject matter related to nonobservable work behavior. Pratzner (1978) is one of several researchers who studied adaptability and skill transfer, while Spencer (1979) pioneered job competence assessment (JCA). Reigeluth and Merrill (1980) developed the extended task analysis procedure (ETAP) to encompass component skills and knowledge that must be learned if a whole task is to be mastered.

In the area of futuristic content consideration, several attempts at predicting the future content of trade and industrial curricula are discussed. Finally, research in the area of competency-based education (CBE) is presented. CBE is presented as the most promising and comprehensive approach to trade and industrial curriculum development because it includes key elements of task analysis and other trade and industrial processes. Horne (1981) has begun to sharpen CBE's definition in terms of formal standards that provide a framework for developing CBE in secondary vocational education programs, although Moss (1981) and others have warned against going beyond reasonable limits in applying CBE to education.

In summary, the 1980s appear to have been a time of consolidation rather than innovation in curriculum design in both industrial arts and trade and industrial education. A survey of dissertations and research articles on industrial education curriculum published since 1986 reveals little that had not been introduced earlier. One observation may be made, however, about curriculum development in industrial education during the period 1987–1990, namely, that several states now seem to have developed technology education curriculum guides or curricula as a result of the example of the Jackson's Mill curriculum. Dyrenfurth (1987) for the state of Missouri, the North Carolina State Department of Public Instruction (1987), Cuetara (1988) for the state of New Hampshire, and Savage (1989) for the state of Ohio have developed and reported on their new technological literacy/technical education models, all based on the Jackson's Mill curriculum.

A second type of recent work, of which there are several examples, is the reflective essay or other type of synthesis of the technology education trend within industrial arts. Examples of such work are Zuga's 1987 AERA presentation "Trapped in a Technocratic Ideology," Clark's article in the newly established *Journal of Technology Education* examining the contemporary paradigm shift in industrial education (1989), and Colelli's "primer" on technology education (1989).

Curriculum in industrial education during the 1970s and 1980s still seemed to be catching up to the great burst of creative energy displayed during the 1960s when several large-scale curriculum projects such as the Maryland Plan were undertaken. In the 1970s the Industrial Arts Curriculum Project became the standard against which other curriculum theory and practice were measured, and in the 1980s that role fell to the Jackson's Mill curriculum project. Some industrial arts educators hope for a renewed burst of conceptual vigor, arguing that the 1970s and 1980s reflected a greater emphasis on compromise and consensus than may be healthy for the field.

Marketing Education

Research in the field of marketing education for the period 1969–1978 was reviewed by R. G. Berns (Virginia Polytechnical Institute and State University), J. L. Borrow (University of Northern Iowa), and H. R. Wallace (Colorado State University) (1980). The section on curricular research was subdivided into the areas of competency identification models, analysis of marketing occupations, middle management retail occupations, middle management curriculum, content areas, postsecondary curriculum research, and curricula designed to meet special needs. The authors introduce the section by noting that the basic framework for marketing education curricula was developed from the conceptual work of Nelson (1963), who proposed four areas of subject matter: social skills, basic skills, product or service technology, and marketing skills. In 1969, the U.S. Office of Education published *Distributive Education in the High School*, extending Nelson's work and adding three career levels: basic jobs, career development jobs, and specialist jobs. Following this, in 1978, the U.S. Office of Education issued *Distributive Education Programs*, which added the economic concepts of private enterprise as a fifth area of subject matter and defined four levels of employment: threshold, career sustaining, specialization, and entrepreneur. Twenty-two instructional programs were described to characterize the scope of marketing education.

From the mid-1960s on, competency identification for the occupations making up marketing work was the consistent approach to providing a base for the marketing curriculum. Studies to identify competencies have used methods including mailed surveys, personal interviews of workers and supervisors, and direct observation of workers. The landmark competency studies by Ertel (1966) and Crawford (1967) set the theoretical structure for later studies in focusing on the analysis of occupations within the clusters of marketing work and providing an initial, extensive list of competencies.

To review, Ertel (1966) identified the competencies important to successful employment in three categories of retail businesses. Crawford (1967) developed a list of 983 competencies for marketing work in seven categories of businesses. She classified the competencies into nine competency areas: advertising, display, human relations, communications, mathematics, merchandising, operations and management, product or service technology, and selling. Using Crawford's research, Harrison (1973) directed a 3-year development and testing study for 500 learning activity packages involving nearly 200 teachers and 7,000 students in 11 states. The study involved developing a computer-assisted management system to organize instructional activities in relation to student career objectives.

The competency identification studies that followed can be organized into the following: (1) comprehensive studies of marketing work, (2) studies of one occupational cluster of marketing work, (3) studies of one occupation within an occupational cluster, and (4) studies of one competency area (as defined by Crawford). In the first category of comprehensive studies of marketing work, the work of Lynch and Kohns (1977) is prototypic. They identified competencies for occupations in 19 of the instructional program areas used by the U.S. Office of Education to describe the scope of marketing education. Competency lists were developed from a synthesis of interviews with representatives from business and analysis of previous competency studies. Broad course outlines were developed from the competency lists for the 19 instructional programs. The content for each program was structured for three levels of employment (i.e., entry, midmanagement, and manager/owner) and five instructional areas (i.e., marketing, product or service technology, social skills, basic skills, and economic principles/concepts). Instructional objectives used to describe and communicate the content were reviewed by consultants and business representatives for each employment level and instructional program.

Another comprehensive study aimed at developing competency lists for marketing work was conducted by Harris (1978) as a basis to prepare curriculum guides for marketing education program areas. Harris focused on essential competencies for the most common entry-level jobs and the most common career ladders and promotion criteria in each occupational cluster of marketing work. Information for the study was based on literature review, juries of business executives, and structured interviews of workers.

At about this same time two cooperative efforts among states were also active in assisting to develop and reform the marketing education curriculum using a competency-based approach and avoiding unnecessary duplication of efforts. The Interstate Distributive Education Curriculum Consortium (IDECC) (now known as the Marketing Education Resource Center), formed from the states that developed, field tested, and disseminated the learning activity packages based on Crawford's work (Harris 1978), in 1979 began efforts to update and extend its competency-based curriculum. As a part of the effort, Williams, Berns, and Heath-Sipos (1979) developed a standard procedure for developing competency lists (task inventories) for the curriculum work of the consortium. This procedure was tested by the developers with 16 general merchandising department store occupations.

Another consortium to develop competency-based curriculum in vocational education, including marketing education, was initiated at about this time under the name of Vocational-Technical Education Consortium of States (V-TECS) (1978). Seventeen states made up the initial consortium to strengthen competency-based curricula and avoid duplication of efforts among the states. Again a standard procedure was developed to guide competency identification and description. The studies published by the consortium include performance objectives and criterion-referenced measures to aid in evaluation of teaching and learning.

In their review and synthesis of marketing curricular research, Berns, Borrow, and Wallace (1980) describe several competency studies that focus on only one occupational area of marketing work (as opposed to comprehensively addressing all areas). Among those cited, where persons employed in the occupation were used as a primary source of data, are studies of the hotel, tourism, foods, and fashion industries. A third group of important competency studies cited by Berns, Borrow, and Wallace (1980) addressed particular occupations within occupational areas. Here they cited work on middle managers in retail stores for hotel/motel room clerks and cashiers in the hotel industry.

The last category of competencies studies identified by Berns, Borrow, and Wallace (1980) related to studies of specific competency areas as originally described by Crawford (1976). Although most studies related to a specific occupational area or geographic area, the competency areas addressed in cited studies were mathematics and computation, marketing research, selling, economics, and marketing concepts.

The impact of the Vocational Amendment of 1968, with its attention to better serving the needs of a more diverse group of people in vocational education, is evident in marketing curricular research during the 1970s in studies that focus on special needs groups of learners. Studies on testing a more intensive marketing education program for high school seniors in Detroit, on modifying marketing education programs for the needs of emotionally and mentally handicapped students, and on testing the motivational impact of information about marketing careers with Philadelphia high school students are indicative of efforts to focus on the needs of special learner groups.

At the end of the 1970s, Berns, Borrow, and Wallace concluded their review of curricular research in marketing education as follows:

> Much of the curricular research in the past several years has primarily focused on competency or task analysis. Competency-based instruction has become an accepted element in marketing and distributive education. Future competency research needs to be examined to ensure that representative populations are used to identify competencies, that comprehensive coverage is given to the broad range of marketing occupations, that unneeded duplication is avoided, and that a greater consistency of research design is maintained. Consideration needs to be given to other curriculum models; additional evaluative studies should be conducted to measure the effectiveness of competency-based programs. (164)

The 1980s brought continued work on competency studies, such as work in identifying needed competencies for entry-level jobs and career ladders in the automotive and petroleum industries. However, curriculum research efforts also broadened to include (1) attention to the teaching of basic academic skills (i.e., mathematics and communications) in marketing education; (2) microcomputer applications important to the content of marketing education; (3) teaching entrepreneurship competencies in marketing education; (4) teaching marketing and economic principles; (5) the importance of teaching effective work competencies in marketing education (Stewart and Dill 1987); and (6) the relationship of students' cognitive style to learning in marketing courses.

The 1980s were also a time of reexamining the mission, directions, and standards of quality for marketing education. These scholarly efforts were initiated in 1980 at the National Conference on Marketing Education: Directions for the 1980's in Vail, Colorado. Major papers were presented by Samson ("Distributive Education: Identity and Image"), Egglund ("Program Development in Marketing and Distributive Education"), Rowe ("Leadership in Marketing and Distributive Education"), and Trapnell ("Power and Influence"). The purpose of the conference was "to make critical decisions regarding the future role of marketing and distributive education as a significant delivery system for vocational education" (Burgess and Nelson 1980, 1). Emanating from the conference was verification of a mission statement and premises to guide marketing and distributive education. The mission statement for the 1980s initially drafted by Samson (1980) and modified somewhat at the conference read thus:

> The mission of Marketing and Distributive Education is to develop competent workers in and for the major occupational areas within marketing, assist in the improvement of marketing techniques, and build understandings of the wide range of social and economic responsibilities which accompany the right to engage in marketing businesses in a free enterprise system. (Lynch 1983, 15)

The use of the prepositions "in" and "for" indicates the intention to provide educational programs for those already engaged "in" marketing work as well as preparatory programs "for" those who will be entering such work. The premises adopted for marketing and distributive education programs and in support of the mission statement (also initially developed by Samson [1980]) are as follows:

- The discipline of marketing is the content base for all instruction.
- Instruction will be offered to any personnel and in whatever setting necessary to meet community needs.
- Programs will deliver a range of instruction covering functional skills, career competency development, operational management, and entrepreneurial development.
- Instruction will stress application to, and direct involvement with, marketing businesses and be carried out by a variety of methods.
- Professional personnel in the field of marketing and distributive education will have training in marketing and marketing education, and will possess business experience in marketing.
- Where offered, marketing and distributive education will be considered an integral part of the institution's educational program, with direction and counsel coming largely from a business community advisory group. (Lynch 1983, 2)

The premises particularly important in their curricular implications are the focus on marketing as a content base (i.e., the business activities of market research, product and service planning, promotion, buying and pricing products and services for resale, physical distribution, financing, and management) and attention to a wide range of functional, career, management, and entrepreneurial skills. A high level of nation-wide endorsement for the mission statement and premises was found among state supervisors, teacher educators, teacher coordinators, school administrators, and businesspeople in a 1983 study (Jacobsen 1983).

Lynch (1983) used the results of the conference along with other reports and interviews with educators, business persons, and association executives to develop a national plan for the future of marketing education, which was called for by the conference. Among the 7 recommendations resulting from his work was that the term "marketing education" should be used to name the field because it better described what is taught (distribution being only one component of marketing) and is used more commonly in businesses and colleges and universities. Other recommendations included the development of a Marketing Education Association to bring together all professionals involved in marketing education and the development of a conceptual framework for marketing educators to use, particularly in articulating curricula among the various educational levels.

Another area of continued professional discussion recommended at the 1980 conference was the development of standards for monitoring the quality of marketing education. Development and validation of process standards was addressed by Wubbens (1982). Attention to outcome standards which would better assure "product consistency" for secondary marketing education was provided by Stone (1985). Stone used Delphi procedures with a 20-member advisory panel made up of former students, business people, and marketing educators. Twenty-four outcome standards were judged to be very important; the 5 standards rated most important for graduates of marketing education programs were that they:

1. Exhibit positive attitude toward work and their employers.
2. Demonstrate employability skills.
3. Exhibit pride in their work.
4. Demonstrate work habits appropriate for their marketing occupation.
5. Demonstrate good citizenship.

Among Stone's recommendations are that these standards be used to plan curricula and that states consider developing an extensive evaluation procedure (i.e., a posttest for program completers, an employer follow-up, and a longitudinal follow-up of students) to assess student learning and later success.

During the 1980s, considerable curricular research and development was expended on developing state curriculum guides for marketing education. A content analysis of selected state guides was done by Gleason, Harvey, and Dopo (1985), particularly with regard to the "foundations for marketing education and the function of marketing" developed earlier by the Curriculum Committee of the National Council for Marketing Education. This led to the development of the *National Curriculum Framework and Core Competencies* (National Curriculum Committee for Marketing Education 1987). The *National Framework* recommended conceptualizing curriculum thinking in terms of levels of marketing occupations (i.e., entry level, career sustaining, marketing specialist, marketing supervisor, and manager/entrepreneur), functions of marketing (i.e., distribution, financing, marketing-information management, pricing, product/service planning, promotion, purchasing, risk management, and selling), and foundations of marketing (i.e., economic, marketing and business, and human resources). Core competencies are identified to fill out this framework as specific guides for curriculum development.

Spurred by the National Curriculum Conference in Marketing Education held in 1985, many states initiated curriculum development efforts. An exemplary guide developed after considerable systematic competency development research and professional involvement is the *A Guide to Curriculum Planning in Marketing Education* (Wisconsin Department of Public Instruction 1987). The guide contains sections on philosophy, directions, curriculum, evaluation, sex equity, advisory committees, special needs students, guidance, and Distributive Education Clubs of America. Drawing from the *National Curriculum Framework and Core Competencies*, the curriculum section sets forth a conceptual framework for marketing education made up of "foundations" and "functions" that address marketing education at various career levels. The "foundations" component is composed of human resource foundations (i.e., mathematics, communications, self-understanding, interpersonal skills, career development, and human resource management), economic foundations (i.e., basic economics, economic systems, and entrepreneurship and economic trends), and marketing and business foundations (i.e., business ownership and operations and marketing functions and concepts). The "functions of marketing" component is made up of distribution, financing, marketing information management, pricing, product/service planning, promotion, buying, risk management, and selling.

In summary, the curricular research in marketing education uses study of marketing work as a basis for curriculum development and renewal. Cooperative efforts among states are used to enhance the consistency, efficiency, and frequency of competence assessment as a means to keep the curriculum modern and up-to-date. The field has several widely accepted conceptual frameworks for describing and reflecting on its curricular content, including program categories, competency areas, occupational levels, and foundations. During the early 1980s, professionals in marketing education developed and adopted a new mission statement and premises to set future direction for the field. Scholarly work since that time has sought to develop program standards, curriculum content, and program development consistent with the mission and premises. Curriculum content changes exhibit attention to a wider array of occupational levels, often requiring postsecondary education for entry, with a concurrent shift away from entry-level training as the major focus. Changes have included a new name, marketing education, and a new professional association, the Marketing Education Association. Curricular research in marketing education is an ongoing component of the Marketing Education Resource Center. Questions that might direct curricular research for the future in marketing education are: (1) Since the marketing function cuts across various industrial categories, what should be the relationship between marketing education and other subfields of vocational education such as agriculture, business, and industrial education? (2) Should marketing education more seriously entertain approaches in addition to task analysis/competency-based strategies as a basis for curriculum? (3) What should be the response of marketing education to the large predicted increase in sales workers, particularly in service industries?

Health Occupations Education

In the 1970s and 1980s health occupations education became more and more recognized as a distinct field of vocational education. In fact, health occupations education has now become known by its acronym, HOE, signaling the "arrival" of the field. Other signs of HOE's increasing status may be found in evidence of institutionalization in the last 15 years. For example, the U.S. Department of Education established the position of secondary and postsecondary Health Occupation Education Program Specialist; university departments of education have HOE teacher educators on staff; there is a division of Health Occupation Education within the American Vocational Association, which holds both curriculum and research conferences periodically; the *Journal of Health Occupation Education* has begun publication; and the Health Occupations Students of America (HOSA) has been formed.

As the worth of nonprofessional auxiliary workers in the health occupations very gradually became established since the 1940s, vocational education at the junior high, high school, and postsecondary levels assumed an increasingly important role in training these new workers. Following the pattern established in the earliest years of the 20th century with practical nursing, training in the health occupations continues to stress the importance of on-the-job training. Despite a few studies (Cohelan 1963; Crenshaw 1961; Elmore 1964) suggesting innovative ways to improve the curriculum in health occupations fields, in general, the health occupations curriculum, particularly at the secondary level, was based directly on occupational analysis. This trend lasted until the mid-1960s. Sometimes curriculum developers simply asked people working in the field how they did their job or how it should be done. Sometimes various observation and interview techniques were used.

In the late 1960s, as the field of health occupations education began to expand to include new subfields, researchers began to develop more sophisticated methodologies. Decker (1967), for example, in seeking to develop curriculum in the medical laboratory subfield of health occupations education, also had a broader curricular development goal. He sought to develop a model for determining the goals of instructional programs in general. In a study called *A Functional Analysis of Paramedical Occupations as a Foundation for Curriculum Development*, Decker used a procedure called evental analysis to refine educational goals. Evental analysis describes in simple terms the real "events" that a worker must perform on the job (or in a simulated on-the-job situation) in a specific time frame and with specific accuracy. It will be noted that Decker's work is similar to the work in "behaviorally specified objectives" done by Mager (1962) and others at about the same time, although it is less well known.

Other approaches found useful to some researchers in the development of health occupations curriculum are the "core" and "ladder" concepts. Developers using the "core" concept approach look for commonalities in the curricula of multiple health programs offered by the same or neighboring educational institutions and seek ways to combine these common elements into more economical course offerings (Holloway and Kerr 1969, 31). The "ladder" concept is an extension of the core concept as Holloway and Kerr explain it: "Just as commonalities across several health occupations will be identified for core courses, so will commonalities between levels within a field" (32). Using the ladder concept, training for programs is planned so that trainees will have the opportunity for career development within their health occupation.

Despite the increasing importance of the health occupations fields and an expanding repertoire of useful approaches to curriculum development, there is as yet no unified focus for curriculum in secondary health occupations, according to Catherine Junge, who held the position of Health Occupation Education Program Specialist in 1989 (telephone interview). Junge estimates that 50 percent of both secondary and postsecondary health occupations education is nursing related.

Secondary curriculum can be divided into two categories: exploratory and preparatory. There are regional differences with regard to the number of secondary programs offered and the content of those programs. In the eastern and southern states there are large numbers of programs, and the emphasis is on preparation for job entry. Showcase states include Texas, Florida, and Oklahoma; Texas has several high schools entirely devoted to health occupations education. In the Midwest, the number of secondary programs is not as great, and there tends to be a greater emphasis on exploratory programs. For example, Iowa has only three HOE programs at the secondary level. According to the results of telephone interviews with four leaders in the HOE curriculum field, there are several factors that currently influence or will influence curriculum:

> The Health Occupations Student Organization (HOSA) plays an informal role in standardizing curriculum by providing an opportunity for secondary HOE educators to congregate. The numbers of disadvantaged students in some states drives the curriculum towards preparation for job entry. The movement away from integration with industrial education released what was perceived as a barrier to the emergence of HOE leadership.
>
> Since half of all secondary programs are nursing related, the National Board of Nursing influences program content. The fact that graduates of certain HOE programs are required to have certification or registration in the given occupational area also influences curriculum.
>
> The U.S. Omnibus Reconciliation Act of 1987 has a requirement regarding Medicare/Medicaid reimbursement for employers in long-term nursing care facilities. Nursing assistants employed in those facilities must be prepared using a seventy-five hour nursing assistant curriculum. Given the large numbers of nursing assistant programs, this will have a great impact on curriculum nationally. The national trend toward "back to basics" offers a challenge to the HOE curriculum writers. The HOE leaders interviewed hope that HOE courses can fulfill secondary science credits, thus increasing the viability of some programs in times of cutbacks.
>
> The HOE leadership is moving towards multi-occupational preparation at the secondary level rather than preparation for a single occupation. (Junge 1989)

Other signs of the trends in the emerging fields of health occupations education are found in some recent exploratory and preparatory HOE curricula prepared by state departments of education and university HOE curriculum developers. For example, one exploratory core curriculum was developed in Minnesota (Minnesota Health Occupations Core Curriculum) to be offered to all HOE students (Bralier 1983). It contains units on introduction to health careers, medical terminology, anatomy and physiology, emergency first aid and CPR, conflict resolution and decision making, working with others, career planning, and leadership skills. Another exploratory curriculum from Louisiana (Cassimer 1981) combines concepts from the core and ladder curriculums. It is designed to help health occupations teachers in Louisiana prepare grade 11 and 12 students with beginning-level skills in a variety of health-related occupations. The 10 units are introduction to health careers (60 hours), medical terminology (60 hours), nutrition (60 hours), growth and development (20 hours), infection and disease (30 hours), basic skills (90 hours), emergency care and safety (60 hours), and cooperative health occupations (1 hour daily for 1 year plus 15 hours a week in certifiable health employment).

In summary, health occupations education (HOE) is a growing area of vocational education at both the K–12 and postsecondary levels due to the increasing demand for auxiliary health workers. At present there are several options for HOE programs offered in the public schools, according to the American Vocational Association Health Occupations Division (1985): (1) health careers orientation programs, provided at grades K through 8; (2) health career exploratory programs, provided at grades 9 and 10, in which students are exposed to health options in cluster groupings and given the opportunity to participate in hands-on, related activities; (3) health occupations programs provided at grades 10, 11, and 12, in which students are provided skill development in two or more health occupations; and (4) health occupations programs provided at grades 11 and 12, in which students are offered training in a single health occupation, with nursing-related programs the most prevalent.

Some observers of the HOE curriculum options believe they have so far been defined too narrowly. More than some fields, health occupations offer an opportunity for students to grapple with issues of ethnic diversity. Beliefs and values about health, disease, hygiene, touching, and other related issues differ greatly from culture to culture. Multicultural approaches to health care could be an important component of the HOE curriculum options.

Career Education

In the 1960s, knowledge about occupational choice as a developmental process increased dramatically. By the end of the decade, the terms "career" and "career development" began to become popular, so that today many people prefer them to "vocation" and "vocational development" (Gysbers 1984, 620). In 1964, the Sixty-fourth Yearbook of the National Society for the Study of Education focused on vocational education. For example, Franklin J. Keller (1964), a well-known vocational educator since the 1940s, wrote an article titled "Vocational and Educational Guidance" for the yearbook (135–167). The article seems to stand at a historical crossroads, on the one hand emphasizing vocational guidance and the provision of occupational information as the responsibility of both classroom teachers and counselors within the context of both general and vocational education and, on the other hand, recognizing the new emphasis on the developmental nature of career education and the need for specialized testing, research, and counseling.

Although there is no necessary conflict between the two "positions" taken by Franklin, the career educators who became so powerful during the decade of the 1970s emphasized career development as an important education goal for *all* of education and reached beyond traditional vocational education. Goldhammer and Taylor (1972) state:

> While occupational and career development have been included in earlier statements of educational purpose, it should be emphasized that career education is not more of the same. It is not a synonym for vocational education. It is not a reiteration of traditional . . . educational goals. It retains the essentials of education but introduces a new sense of purposefulness—career development. It places career development as the central unifying element for education. (2)

They continue:

> Specifically, career education is designed to capacitate individuals for their several life roles: economic, community, home, avocational, religious, and aesthetic. . . . Designed for all students, career education should be viewed as lifelong and pervasive, permeating the entire school program and even extending beyond it.
>
> Career education is a systematic attempt to increase the career options available to individuals and to facilitate more rational and valid career planning and preparation. (6)

In a similar vein, Herr (1972) writes:

> Vocational education has been called the Bridge Between Man and His Work (*The General Report of the Advisory Council on Vocational Education*, 1968). If a career development theme is to be viable, such an appellation must come to describe the total educational enterprise—not just a segment of it. . . . More than narrowly defined job training is involved. It is this very specificity of trade or job training which has led to cries of obsolescence in vocational education and unresponsiveness to the dynamics of the occupational structure. (98)

The "new and exciting adventure" (Keller 1972, 185) of career education that began in 1971 was spearheaded by Sidney P. Marland, U.S. Commissioner of Education, who made career education the highest priority of his administration. Marland passionately advocated the developmental approach to career education. He established a new Office of Career Education (McCrory 1976, 63), wrote and spoke extensively about the value of career education (Marland 1972a, 1972b), and lobbied successfully among vocational educators to use vocational education funds to support 112 K–12 career education demonstration projects (Hoyt 1980, 179) and to establish and test the viability of four different types of career education models (Hoyt 1987).

The career education reform movement was indirectly funded through the Education Amendments of 1972 and directly funded through Section 406 of the Education Amendments of 1974 and the Career Education Incentive Act of 1978 (Halasz 1988, 2). In 1981 Congress repealed the Career Education Incentive Act. While career education advocates were worried in advance that the repeal of federal funding would cause the demise of career education, career and other educators seem to disagree after the fact about the impact of the repeal. Some educators (e.g., Hoyt 1980; Malpiedi and Hillison 1986) say that the career education movement was a success as evidenced by the integration or "infusion" of career education material into all levels of the curriculum. "Invisibility" in this case, they argue, indicates success. Other educators see career education as an essentially conservative reaction to education reform ideas of the 1960s (Shor 1987) and assert that, like many other reform movements in education, it has run its course.

A third opinion among educators is that while the career education movement represented a period of unusually intense interest in a theme that has been and will continue to be crucially important in 20th-century American education, career education as a reform movement has peaked and is in decline (Halasz 1988; Herr 1987b). Evidence for the latter position includes decreasing numbers of citations of "career education" or "career development" as descriptors in the ERIC database and the total absence of articles or conference presentations about career education in American Vocational Association publications and activities since 1976, despite much AVA interest in the subject during the 5-year period preceding 1976 (Hoyt 1980, 179).

Just as there are different evaluations of the impact of the career education movement of the 1970s, so there are different assessments of the viability of career education in the 1980s. In his 1987 review of the career education literature, Hoyt says there are 7 basic ways in which persons "commonly" define the goals of contemporary career education. These are:

- to promote and implement private sector/education system partnerships;
- to equip persons with general employability/adaptability/promotability skills;
- to help persons in career awareness/exploring/decision making;
- to reform education by infusing a "careers" emphasis in classrooms;
- to make work a meaningful part of the total lifestyle;
- to relate education and work so that better choices of both can be made; and
- to reduce bias and stereotyping and thus protect freedom of career choice. (5–6)

While Hoyt's goals were the major goals of the leading members of the career education reform movement, it is doubtful that they are "commonly" seen as current goals of something called "career education." Rather, the seven goals have been reassigned to different parts of the contemporary educational agenda. Thus, there is great current interest in partnerships or collaboration between industry and education, for example, but this interest is probably not connected in the minds of either professional educators or the public to the career education movement.

As is often the case when federal dollars are involved, the career education focus in the 1980s is the most visible in curricula explicitly developed for one or more special populations designated for special funding by the Carl D. Perkins Vocational Education Act of 1984. While most of these groups are adults, funds are also available for career exploration and guidance for at-risk youth.

In summary, the career education "movement" of the 1970s is too close to the present moment to assess with precision. It is possible that Herr (1987a) is correct when he argues that the legacy of the career education movement of the 1970s is to be found in the amorphous but strong commitment of some educators in the 1980s to "basic skills." Herr links the career education movement to the back-to-the-basics reform movement of the 1980s, which began with the publication of *A Nation at Risk* in 1983. Even though *A Nation at Risk* does not include career education in its recommendations for reform, Herr believes that his broad—and possibly overly optimistic—interpretation of the current emphasis on basic skills to include commitment to career education is supported by the 1985 report of the Committee for Economic Development, "which indicates that specific occupational skills are less crucial for entry-level employment than a generally high level of literacy, responsible attitudes toward work, the ability to communicate well, and the ability to learn" (Halasz 1988, 5).

However, Halasz probably comes closer to expressing the views of most contemporary vocational educators when she comments in the conclusion of her 1988 review of career education:

> Much of the [career education] literature seems to take a defensive posture in attempting to prove that career education exists, that it is successful, that it is a critical aspect of educational reform, that it was the precursor and definer of the reform movements of the 1980s, and that its value should be recognized. Perhaps it is time to accept its existence as a relevant construct or strategy and to move on to more useful pursuits, such as conducting research that can answer the many unanswered questions about career development in this complex and changing society. (21)

Vocational Education

The curricular research from the mid-1970s to the present that deals with vocational education as a whole or with particular dimensions not generally addressed within specific fields is described in this section. The review is organized into components dealing with studies of the whole vocational education enterprise, studies of selected curricular topics, and exemplary state-level curricular studies.

Studies of the Whole Vocational Education Enterprise. The Educational Amendment of 1976, Public Law 94–482, also known as the Vocational Education Act of 1976, directed the National Institute of Education to do a national evaluation and study of vocational education conducted under the Vocational Education Act of 1963 and other related legislation. The study was particularly to focus on the distribution of funds, compliance with laws, program quality and effectiveness, and consumer and homemaking programs and make recommendations for future federal legislation. The final report of the Vocational Education Study, directed by Henry David and involving several million dollars over 3 years, was issued in September 1981 as the drafting of legislation later to become the Carl D. Perkins Vocational Education Act of 1984 was underway. Several of the findings and recommendations of the study had implications for the curriculum of secondary vocational education.

The study concluded that the vocational education enterprise "is pluralistic and diversified in structure and governance and constitutes a multiplicity of different systems" (David 1981, xxi). Results of examining the effectiveness of secondary vocational education were inconclusive because of limitations in data available at the time and the difficulty of the research problem. From a federal perspective the report poses three options for improving vocational education: (1) extend and improve the quality of programs, (2) improve services to students with special needs, and (3) equalize the capacity of local schools to provide vocational education. These options were provided to assist in framing the policy issues about vocational education for the federal government, essentially noting that the federal government had attempted to do too much about vocational education with too little resources and therefore needed to make some choices about how vocational education could best be improved—increasing quality or increasing access and doing this for all or for a special group of potential students. At about this time, Swanson (1982) was pointing out:

> Vocational education has not developed as a system but rather as a collection of enterprises identified to a greater or lesser degree with every type of education and most types of institutions. Yet the most distinguishable characteristic of various forms of occupational preparation is not the type of education chosen, but rather its duration or length. (22)

The idea of vocational education being designed and planned as "short" education was for Swanson a tragedy, as short education leads to lower expenditures per student, having a disproportionate number of disadvantaged students enrolled, and lower-status occupational positions than "long" education. He concluded that the major policy issues important to vocational education at the time were (1) federal versus state versus local control, (2) limiting programs to the postsecondary level versus extending into the secondary level, and (3) closing versus maintaining the gap between liberal arts and vocational education.

Another overview of the vocational education enterprise was prepared by Bottoms and Copa (1983) describing the many changes which were underway in vocational education, including its curriculum. They pointed out that vocational education at the secondary level was occurring in a wide variety of institutional types: general high schools (10,851), comprehensive high schools (4,878), vocational high schools ([illegible]), secondary area vocational centers (1,395), and, through articulation agreements, several types of postsecondary institutions. The curriculum in vocational education was categorized into consumer/homemaking, prevocational, prevocational basic skills, related instructions, and employability skills programs. The employability skills programs were, in turn, classified into occupational-cluster, occupationally specific, job-specific, and employer-specific programs. Issues facing vocational education, each with curricular implications, were (1) need for intensive vocational education for advanced work responsibilities involving longer-term training, continuous on-the-job experience, and active involvement of employers in curricular planning; (2) an integrated approach to instruction, bringing together the basic (i.e., mathematics, science, communications) and applied (i.e., vocational subjects) disciplines; and (3) vigorous pursuit of excellence in vocational education, which would include the quality of basic skills instruction, teaching an understanding of "why" as well as how to "do," and maintaining breadth (i.e., effects of technology, changing nature of work) as well as depth in vocational education.

An extensive review of vocational education, particularly in high schools, was completed by the National Commission on Secondary Vocational Education (1984), chaired by Harry F. Silberman and entitled *The Unfinished Agenda*. Its charge was to examine the role and function of secondary vocational education in American high schools, especially in the context of educational reform reports such as *A Nation at Risk* (National Commission on Excellence 1983). The Commission based its response on site visits to schools, public hearings, solicited opinions, and its own deliberations. The Commission called for educational diversity as the more responsive action to promoting excellence and equity in high schools. Vocational education's role was seen as making youth more employable, with *all* students needing a mix of academic and vocational education (National Commission on Secondary Vocational Education 1984, 3).

Vocational education was described as both a body of knowledge and an educational process. Speaking directly to curriculum, the Commission concluded that the content should include "career guidance and exploration, general employability skills, broad concepts of work and family, and general and specific occupational skill training" (14). Content should be addressed in classrooms, community internships, part-time work, projects, independent studies, and youth organizations. The Commission concludes that quality should be the major issue in secondary vocational education. Within the context of improving quality, the Commission makes recommendations regarding access; equity; curriculum; teacher recruitment and preparation; standards and accountability; articulation; leadership; business, labor, and community; and field-based learning. With respect to curriculum, the recommendations for finishing the agenda for vocational education include (1) reducing curricular mandates that limit opportunity for students to participate in vocational education; (2) including instruction and practice in reading, writing, arithmetic, speaking, listening, and problem solving in vocational education; (3) developing self-esteem, positive attitudes toward work, safe work habits, job-seeking skills and other general employability skills, in addition to occupationally specific skills;

(4) enriching and diversifying courses to make them attractive to all students; (5) allowing students to satisfy some graduation requirements through study of vocational education; and (6) providing opportunities for students to participate in vocational youth organizations.

The second major assessment of vocational education mandated by the Congress, entitled the *National Assessment of Vocational Education*, and under the direction of John G. Wirt, was called for by the Carl D. Perkins Vocational Education Act of 1984. The purpose of the study was to describe and evaluate the effects of the Act in terms of vocational education's relation to special populations, modernization, academic skills, employment opportunities, and other topics. The final report of the several-million-dollar study (Wirt, Muraskin, Goodwin, and Meyer 1989), using methods ranging from field study to sophisticated empirical investigations, includes a section specifically addressing secondary vocational education. Many of the findings and recommendations have curricular implications.

Among the findings on secondary vocational education is that participation in vocational education is nearly universal in serving all students, including the college bound. Vocational education was described conceptually as being made up of three major types of programs: (1) consumer and homemaking education, (2) general vocational education (i.e., typing I, introductory industrial arts, work experience, and general skills courses), and (3) occupationally specific vocational education (i.e., training in the 11 subject areas of agriculture, business support, business management, marketing and distribution, health, occupational home economics, technical and communications, construction, mechanics and repair, precision production, and transportation). On average, students took more credits of vocational education in high school than any other subject (i.e., English, mathematics, social studies). The breadth of participation provides a challenge for vocational education curriculum in balancing attention to job-specific and transferable occupational skills. Because students going directly to work after high school and those going on to postsecondary school both take a large amount of vocational education, its role in teaching basic academic skills is also a curricular challenge.

The 1989 *National Assessment* concluded that academically disadvantaged and handicapped students take more vocational education than academically advantaged and nonhandicapped students. However, academically disadvantaged and handicapped females and students from schools with high concentrations of academically and disadvantaged students participate in different-quality (lower) vocational education, as measured by breadth and depth of courses offered. Based on this finding, the report recommends targeting of program improvement (including curriculum) efforts in schools with a relatively high number of poor and low-achieving students.

With respect to the job-specific dimension of the curriculum for secondary vocational education, the *National Assessment* concludes that vocational education at the secondary level needs to include *both* job-specific and broad occupational training and integrated academic and vocational instruction. There are students with both types of needs in secondary schools, and all of these students should be provided with high-quality programs. Specifically concerning the curriculum for job-specific programs, the report recommends attention to learning that is closely aligned with the needs of employers, focuses on higher-skilled jobs, and includes aggressive job placement assistance.

In its examination of the effects of vocational education on achievement in basic academic skills, the *National Assessment* specifically investigated the area of mathematics. The findings support the conclusion that significant gains in mathematics achievement can be made in curricular areas of an applied nature when the courses are heavily enriched with mathematics content. This conclusion is particularly significant for students not bound for college after high school since they do not take a lot of traditional mathematics, experience significant mathematics gains in applied learning settings, and take a relatively large amount of vocational education. However, the report concludes that traditional vocational education courses would need to be substantially revised to include more mathematics content if they are to play a larger role in boosting mathematics proficiency (Wirt, Muraskin, Goodwin, and Meyer 1989).

Studies of Selected Curricular Topics. A series of topics that received focused attention during the 1980s can be identified in the curricular research addressing vocational education as a whole. The topics selected for inclusion here are vocational education and basic skills, emerging skill needs, at-risk students, tracking, competency studies, higher-order thinking skills, generalizable skills, and international education. Exemplary studies relating to each topic will be briefly reviewed to illustrate the nature of the curricular research conducted.

Lotto (1983) addressed the topic of teaching basic skills through vocational education. She found strong support for the generalizations: "Academic students are substantially more proficient across all basic skill areas than vocational students" (3) and "Secondary school curriculum enrollment distinguishes among students by academic achievement and ability" (5). Using case descriptions of actual programs or projects designed to reinforce and remediate basic skills through vocational education, Lotto identified four basic strategies being used at the secondary level: (1) compensatory or remedial programs (special programs for low-achieving, disadvantaged, low socioeconomic-status students who are not succeeding in regular classrooms), (2) support-oriented programs (reinforcing basic skills instruction to support learning in vocational education), (3) alternative school programs (separate schools for students who are disaffected, alienated, or "turned off" by regular school), (4) in-service training programs (strengthening basic skills teaching competence for vocational teachers). Work by Stern, Dayton, Paik, Weisberg, and Evans (1988) illustrates the evaluation of one of these curricular strategies, the alternative school, as a means to reduce high school dropout rates. The study focuses on high schools that replicate the California peninsula academies, which combine core academic curricula with vocational instruction in selected occupational fields for dropout prone students. Results of analysis suggest that student effects in these alternative schools can be replicated and that generally the students in these schools had better grades and completed more course credits than comparison group students.

Harrington (1988), in a review of research and cases of integrating academic and vocational education, states that "vocational education does not exist apart from academics" (2). She goes on to pose three categories of basic skills needed by students in vocational education: (1) common-core basic skills (i.e., mathematics, science, and communications), (2) job-specific basic skills (i.e., specific to an occupation), and (3) academics for the whole person (i.e., liberal studies). However, the reinforcement and enhancement of basic academic skills in vocational education classrooms requires clear and sustained attention if it is to actually occur (Weber, Puleo, and Kurth 1989). Based on observation in vocational and nonvocational classes in 120 secondary schools in 24 states, these authors concluded that there are many opportunities to attend to basic skills, but they are often ignored by vocational teachers.

The curricular topic of vocational education and emerging skills and the changing workplace is illustrated by the work of Halfin and Nelson (1982) and Pratzner and Russell (1984). Citing the rapid rate of technological change and change in work environments, Halfin and Nelson conclude that vocational education must examine multiple approaches to identifying curriculum content if its programs are to be kept modern and up-to-date. The approaches they describe and analyze include advisory committee; creative insight; DACUM process (developing a curriculum); Delphi process; evaluation study; industrial work experience; labor market survey; study, survey, conference; and task analysis. They conclude that the curriculum development procedures for vocational education must be flexible, efficient, and responsive to emerging skills and make use of historical, current, and future-based data.

An example of curricular research that appears future oriented is the work by Pratzner and Russell (1984), which examines the implications of the quality of work life movement for vocational education. Using a review of current literature and research, and interviews and observations at nine firms recognized as leaders in developing and implementing quality of work life activities, they recommend needed changes in the content of vocational education. Quality of work life activities address ways of structuring jobs and organizing work to make the work economically viable and more satisfying. The key point made by Pratzner and Russell is

> to function effectively in high-involvement, participative work settings, workers and managers not only need good basic skills and technical job skills, but they will also increasingly need improved skills and knowledge in group problem solving (e.g., in such areas as interpersonal and group process skills, problem solving and decision making, planning, and communication), and in the organization and management of production (e.g., in such areas as business economics, business operations, statistical quality control, and quality of work life developments. (xi–xii)

The term "sociotechnical literacy" is coined to characterize the purpose of educational programs with the above focus. A vocational education with the goal of developing sociotechnical literacy would be much broader in its content base, appropriate for all students, and involve cooperative learning procedures and experiential learning.

Curricular research in vocational education that addresses the needs of at-risk or special needs groups is reviewed by Copa (1984) and Tindall (1988). Copa's review focuses on vocational education and youth unemployment in the United States. Results of review of an extensive series of studies in youth unemployment suggest that youth unemployment has multiple causes (categorized as demand side, supply side, and transition from school to work). While the most important cause is cited as not enough jobs, the unequal distribution of youth unemployment among different groups of young people (i.e., gender, race, socioeconomic status, geographic area of residence) is related to supply side and transition causes. Copa concludes, "Ready access to sufficient, high-quality vocational education, with needed support services, has potential for impact in this context" (xiv). In order for vocational educators to be most effective in dealing with the issue of youth unemployment, it must be seen as part of a comprehensive portfolio of services categorized as follows: (1) access related (i.e., outreach, recruitment, assessment, guidance), (2) education related (i.e., general education, employability or job-readiness training, skill training), (3) information related (i.e., labor market information, education information), (4) transition related (i.e., age integration, role model development, testing, credentialing and licensing, job placement, support services, community involvement, laws and regulations, geographic relocation, alternatives to work, coordination of services), and (5) work experience related (i.e., work experience, job development). Vocational education was seen as a major provider of the education-related services, and to some extent, other categories of services, with opportunity to alter its capacity, scope, and mix of services.

The work by Tindall (1988) reviews the literature relevant to the issues of career and vocational education's role in retaining at-risk students in school. There are multiple definitions of at-risk students, with typical characteristics including one or more years behind grade level in reading and mathematics achievement; three or more credits behind their age/grade level; chronic truancy; school-age parents; personal and/or family drug and alcohol abuse; physical, sexual, or emotional abuse; and low self-concept and social maturity. Focusing on the area of school retention (dropout prevention), Tindall concludes that a comprehensive program is needed to address the needs of at-risk students and involving the components of (1) administrative support, (2) community support, (3) family support, (4) funding support, and (5) at-risk program development. The component of at-risk program development has the most direct implications for the content of vocational education.

Another topic in the research related to vocational education during the 1980s focuses on the potential of "tracking" students in vocational education with negative consequences for students. The research by Oakes (1983) has been particularly significant as it relates to tracking in general and its implications for vocational education. Using data collected from 25 secondary schools across the country from the study on schooling by Goodlad (1984), she investigated the relationship between student race and ethnicity and differences in the scope and substance of courses taken in vocational education. Her findings were that, in contrasting schools with large nonwhite populations versus those with all-white populations, there was no difference in emphasis on the subject matter of vocational education and that, in schools with large nonwhite populations, there was not a disproportionate number of nonwhite students in vocational education courses. However, she did find that there were marked differences in the kind of vocational education (i.e., curricular content and organizational arrangements) whites and nonwhites experienced within vocational education. The differences led her to conclude that more nonwhites were being directed toward more job-specific training for work with lower-class social and economic futures. One of her recommendations with curricular implications was to question the appropriateness of job-specific training at the high school level.

In contrast to Oakes's interpretation, Plihal, Ernst, and Rehm (1986) studied the practice of equity in terms of access to and treatment in secondary vocational education programs in Minnesota. The authors conclude:

> Vocational education does provide increased opportunity for students. Vocational education apparently serves a variety of student needs, some of which might not be met through other classroom experiences. Vocational education also helps in making winners out of students by laying the foundations for other learning and by increasing their self-esteem. The students themselves generally see vocational education as providing them with opportunities for employment and education. (79)

From yet another perspective concerning tracking, Kantor and Tyack (1982), in an edited book dealing with historical perspectives on vocationalism in American education, conclude that the idea that school should assist in preparing young people for work has been commonly accepted and provides support for vocational programs. They note, "Historians of education . . . generally applauded the rise of vocational schooling, viewing it a democratic movement to liberate the educational system from outmoded practices" (2). On the other hand, "Revisionist historians have argued that vocational education was part of a middle- and upper-class movement for social control and order in a corporate state" (3). Several of the authors in the book edited by Kantor and Tyack argue that attention to increasing vocationalism in schools has not provided the expected results in increased economic opportunity and has diverted attention from basic economic structural problems in this country that cause reproduction of class structure.

The topic of conducting competency or task analyses as a basis for curriculum in vocational education continued during the 1980s, although it was not so pervasive relative to other areas of research. Exemplifying curricular research of this kind is the work of the Vocational Technical Education Consortium of States (V-TECS) (McCage 1986), initiated in 1973. As of 1989, V-TECS had 24 state members and produced 185 catalogs of performance objectives and performance guides addressing more than 500 occupations using very careful and explicit procedures. The catalogs contain lists of duties for each occupation and specific tasks making up each duty (the catalogs of V-TECS now contain over 25,000 tasks). For each task there is a performance guide describing how the task is typically done, the standard for acceptable performance, and the conditions under which standard performance is to occur. Based on these catalogs of objectives and performance, V-TECS has developed curricular guides (45 available at the time of this writing and another 45 under development). The guides formulate the contents of the catalogs into teaching activities, resources, and procedures for evaluation. To assist in curriculum development, this information has recently been computerized into an automated cross-reference occupational system (ACROS). The last component of the V-TEC system, responding to the pressure for accountability for learning, is the development of validated criterion-referenced test item banks to complement the curriculum guides (20 item banks have been developed and others are underway). Test banks are developed under very specific procedures and are field tested. Again, a computerized data base is being used to assist teachers in constructing criterion-referenced tests for specific occupations.

Teaching higher-order thinking skills is another topic of focused curricular research in vocational education. Thomas and Litowitz (1986) proposed an "agenda for inquiry" concerning vocational education and higher-order thinking skills in response to 5 persistent educational problems: (1) inert knowledge, (2) transfer of learning, (3) integration of knowledge, (4) going beyond the givens, and (5) identifying and understanding different types of problems. The agenda for research on higher-order thinking, described as referring to the "more complex levels of intellectual functioning" (Thomas and Litowitz 1986, 6), in relation to vocational education, was described in three parts:

> 1. Identifying and organizing problems and contexts central in vocational education and their requirements.
> 2. Describing, documenting, and understanding knowledge, cognitive abilities, and dispositions required by problems and contexts central in vocational education.
> 3. Identifying, developing, and assessing curricular designs and instructional processes that facilitate development of the knowledge, cognitive abilities, and dispositions required by problems and contexts central in vocational education. (28–29)

The role and development of higher-order thinking skills is addressed from diverse perspectives in an edited report by Thomas (1987), using home economics as a context.

Later work by Thomas, Cooke, and Johnson (1988), undertaking aspects of the proposed agenda, focused on thinking underlying expertise in specific knowledge domains (i.e., electrical troubleshooting, or parenting) and its implications for vocational education. In another study, Thomas and Englund (1989) observe that during practice, an important aspect of vocational education, attention is given to the integration of knowledge and thinking. This concern by vocational education with not simply understanding but application in particular contexts requires strong attention to teaching higher-order thinking skills.

Also relating to higher-order thinking in vocational education, Claus (1988) used a critical science research approach to investigating the curriculum and administration of secondary vocational education in New York using survey and ethnographic techniques. He called for a "renegotiated" vocational education in which (1) problem solving, decision making, and analytical thinking were an explicit part of the subject matter; (2) basic skills are integrated into all vocational courses; and (3) opportunity is provided for group management of entrepreneurial projects. All of these changes are thought to be important in empowering students to understand and manage important aspects of their lives. The need for increased attention to more complex thinking skills and the context of application for vocational education and the rest of education is substantiated by Berryman (1988). The "New Basics" for the workplace identified in joint work supported by the American Society for Training and Development and the U.S. Department of Labor (Carnevale, Gainer and Meltzer 1988) are described as (1) knowing how to learn; (2) reading, writing, computation; (3) listening and oral communication; (4) creative thinking/problem solving; (5) self-esteem/goal setting and motivation/personal and career development; (6) interpersonal skills/negotiation/teamwork; and (7) organizational effectiveness/leadership. The importance of higher-order thinking to these basics is evident.

Another curricular topic selected to be illustrated relates to teaching generalizable skills in vocational education. Generalizable skills are described in various ways by different authors. A fairly comprehensive taxonomy proposed by Nemko (1986) uses these categories: (1) basic skills (i.e., English language, critical thinking, and mathematics), (2) preemployment skills (i.e., lifelong career planning and job acquisition), and (3) work maturity traits (i.e., interpersonal skills and personal management skills). Greenan (1983, 1986, 1987) and Greenan and Winters (1989) conducted a program of research to specifically identify and measure extent of knowledge in several of the basic skill areas (i.e., mathematics, communications, interpersonal). However, Moss (1987) questions an overbalance of attention to generalizable occupational skills (i.e., technical content that is common to a cluster of occupations). He argues that as content is made more generalizable its occupational commonality may decrease along with its economic advantage to students. An alternative strategy would be to retain strong emphasis on more job-specific skills, but with attention to improving a student's adaptability by focusing on a learning process that facilitates transfer and attitudes that acknowledge the need to continuously change and update occupational skills.

Curricular research involving international perspectives on vocational education also became increasingly frequent during the 1980s. For example, a good description of the place of vocational education in the educational system of member states of the European community was done in 1984 (Angress and Hammelmann). A collection of national perspectives on youth, unemployment, and training (Fiddy 1985) included attention to vocational education for Great Britain, France, Germany, Norway, North America, China, and Fiji. In the 1987 World Yearbook of Education, entitled *Vocational Education*, editors Twining, Nisbet, and Megarry (1987) note, "Vocational education, worldwide, is rich and diverse . . . . The content of vocational education is the 'hidden hand' behind most aspects of everyday life . . . ." (10). After discussing topics addressing the need for definitions (i.e., general versus vocational education, vocational education versus vocational training), contrasts in cultures, immense changes occurring in vocational education, and the knowledge gap between developed and developing countries, the book presents chapters dealing with various aspects of vocational education in Australia, England and Wales, Scotland, Germany, the U.S.S.R., Brazil, East Asia, New Zealand, the Netherlands, South Africa, the United States, Kenya, India, and Japan. In a book series on comparative and international education, the volume relating to vocational education was entitled *Vocationalizing Education: An International Perspective* (Lauglo and Lillis 1988). Vocationalizing is described as changing curriculum in a practical or vocational direction. The editors note that this change is transcending the differing educational systems of rich and poor countries and different political systems. Chapters in the book deal with this change under the headings of goals and justification, context for policy formation, policy implementation, and empirical evaluation studies while dealing with the educational systems of countries such as Britain, France, Germany, the United States, Sierra Leone, Sweden, the U.S.S.R., Brazil, Zimbabwe, Kenya, Tanzania, Colombia, and Trinidad and Tobago.

State-Level Curricular Studies. Several states have made major efforts to revise and reform vocational education to be more effective in secondary schools. These efforts have involved a wide diversity of research approaches, varying from formal, with detailed data collection and analysis, to informal and depending on study groups, conferences, and hearings. Two states will be used to illustrate curriculum renewal projects that are well underway: New York and Minnesota.

The work in New York is described by Kadamus and Daggett (1986), who provided leadership for the effort. Using a group of "futuring committees" for each occupational area in vocational education and an overall administrative committee, the project resulted in recommendations to:

1. Develop a curriculum that would meet the needs of all students and the needs of business and industry.

2. Incorporate a group of core competencies with components relating to personal development, social systems, information skills, resource management, and technology.
3. Integrate the vocational fields into a coordinated program of instruction.

Key features of the curriculum were:

1. A continuous, lifelong vocational development perspective with programming starting in the elementary grades and specific vocational education courses initiated in grades 7 and 8 and required for all students; the coursework that follows in grades 9 through 12 is tuned to the expanding and intensifying vocational development needs of students.
2. Increased integration of vocational and academic coursework and integration among the traditional vocational program areas where appropriate; traditional areas are retained and emphasized in grades 11 through 12; vocational education is seen and designed as a *part* of general education.
3. Major attention to modernization of programs in terms of subject matter, but retaining vocational education's use of experiential methods.
4. Flexibility in curriculum structure (i.e., shorter-length courses, modules within courses) to fit a wide variety of school situations (and student needs).
5. Provision for vocational education in graduation requirements in terms of required courses, sequences of courses, and use of vocational education to meet part of graduation requirements in mathematics, communication, and science. Student "program of study" core to resemble college programs with balanced attention to foundational, core, and specialized study.
6. Development of a very focused assessment process to demonstrate quality and accountability.

After reviewing major technical, economic, demographic, and societal changes affecting work and family life in the United States and their experience with the curriculum reform process in New York, Kadamus and Daggett outlined new directions for secondary vocational education, including:

1. A decrease in emphasis on specialized training;
2. Less expenditure on specialized equipment and more on staff development;
3. Change in emphasis from trade and industry to information and service occupations;
4. New linkages with business and industry; and
5. A closer relationship with general education for a coordinated, integrated curriculum (1986, vii).

In Minnesota, the curriculum reform for secondary vocational education occurred through the work of two major state-level committees. The first effort by the Commissioner's (of Education) Task Force on Education for Employment resulted in a report entitled *Work-Readiness: A New Promise in Minnesota's Education* (1988). A major finding noted in the preface to the report was:

> The unshakable conclusion reached by the Task Force is that work readiness is a critical teaching element that must take root in the pre-K–12 education curriculum as integrated, experienced-based learning. This is a new promise we feel that the Minnesota education system must now make to its young people. (iii)

The recommendations of the Task Force were as follows:

1. The legislative and state board of education mission for pre-K–12 education in Minnesota should be reviewed and updated to include the following: "Graduates from Minnesota's pre-K–12 educational system will be work-ready, in that they will have the appropriate skills, information, experience, and attitudes to pursue productive work lives in a rapidly changing society/economy" (15).
2. Although the pre-K–12 educational system is primarily responsible for achieving the goal of work-ready high school graduates, the task requires sharing, strong support, and involvement from key stakeholders.
3. The State Board of Education will define and evaluate specific state-wide pre-K–12 work-readiness learner outcomes in every curricular area.
4. Every local school district should assure work-readiness learner outcomes through an integrated, experiential pre-K–12 curriculum, which encompasses the relationship between education activities and the real world of students and which promotes valued workplace behaviors. School/business/community partnerships should be encouraged as resources to integrate and increase work-readiness learning.
5. State and local systems should be redesigned to ensure a process that is relevant, readily accessible, and able to improve the ability of administrators, teachers, and support staff to ensure work readiness of students.
6. State and local systems will need to restructure education delivery systems to ensure that an environment is created that guarantees students will be work ready. This would include accountability, decentralization, flexibility, and improved access to work readiness.

As described, work readiness is a responsibility of the entire school curriculum and forms a larger "umbrella" for the functions of vocational education. Vocational education was described as needing to play a leadership role in helping to implement the work-readiness goal in other curricular areas. More directly, work readiness is a primary focus of vocational education.

The second major component of planning for reform in secondary vocational education in Minnesota was the result of a legislatively commissioned study involving general and vocational educators, school administrators, representatives of business, industry and labor, the general public, and teacher educators. The study report, *A Restructured Model for Secondary Vocational Education* (Minnesota Department of Education 1988), contained the following recommendations:

1. The legislature and state board of education must move to an outcome-based design for all of Minnesota's students.
2. The legislature and state board of education must remove barriers that impede achieving these goals. They must support local program designs that address individual student needs and interests and local conditions.
3. State and local leadership must ensure the support necessary to redirect curriculum, develop supportive structures, and design effective evaluation approaches.
4. The legislature, state board, and local districts must implement some critical changes immediately, as well as provide for the active participation of all stakeholders in a long-range restructuring of the total school experience.
5. The legislature must provide the necessary resources to assure implementation of the proposed restructured model.

The principles guiding the reform include (1) integration (including basic and higher-order thinking skills), (2) articulation (nonduplicative transition between secondary and postsecondary programs), (3) modernization (updating and upgrading curriculum and instructional support), (4) equity (equal access and treatment), and (5) redirected curriculum priorities (focus on technical skills, career development, work readiness, preparation for family roles, and technological competence). These recommendations and principles have since been accepted by the Minnesota legislature and state board of education, and implementation is underway.

Summary

As should be apparent from this review of curricular research in vocational education as a whole, there was a considerable increase in attention to vocational education as an integrated instructional system, along with the previously reviewed attention to specific subfields during the 1980s. Curricular research efforts have worked across the fields in areas such as reinforcing basic skills, teaching higher-order thinking, and better serving at-risk youth. Research has shifted to focus on the relationship of vocational education to the rest of the educational system in purposes and curriculum. Major changes, reform, and restructuring of vocational education is being considered, along with the refinement of existing programs in the context of economic, social, and educational change affecting schools, workplaces, and families. Some questions that curricular research in vocational education might consider more seriously in the future are (1) What should be the future structure of vocational education in the context of changing social and economic conditions? (2) How should vocational education be supportive of other general education goals, as well as provide a unique contribution to general education with aims of its own? (3) How can vocational education be made more responsive to the wants and needs of *all* students in K–12 education? (4) What conceptual approaches to curriculum development are most appropriate to vocational education?

IMPLICATIONS FOR FURTHER RESEARCH

Analysis of the historical development and recent research with respect to curriculum in vocational education suggests several research questions that are continuing and/or emerging as significant for future educational research. Some questions persist over time, though responses must change with changing social, economic, and educational context. Other questions are newly emerging as seemingly more important within this changing context.

General versus Specific Education

What content of vocational education should be considered as general, and what is specific education? Some areas of content in vocational education should be part of the common or general education of *all* students for successful participation in our society. Examples of this content include technology education, consumer education, family life education, career education, and economic education. Other areas of the content of vocational education are specific to particular occupational clusters or occupations, and while these areas should be made available to students in an equitable way, they would be selected by students based on their interests and ability to benefit. Examples of this content include secretarial education, sales education, agribusiness education, health occupations education, and transportation occupations education. With this view, vocational education, is both general and specific education, and the traditional categories such as agriculture, business, and marketing have aspects of both types of education. The recent research by Beck (1990a, 1990b, 1990c) provides in-depth insights into the relation between vocational and general education and, particularly, ways that the subject matter of vocational education could be used to strengthen general education. Also, distinctively viewing education for, about, and through work and family responsibilities may have promise in facilitating thinking about curriculum in vocational education. The work of Gardner (1983), initially described in his book *Frames of Mind*, suggest that individuals have multiple intelligences, some of which are directly (and perhaps uniquely) addressed by vocational education in the K–12 curriculum.

Vocational Education and Higher-Order Thinking

What should be done about teaching higher-order thinking skills through vocational education? It is obvious on examining the content of vocational education that it does and needs to include teaching higher-order thinking skills such as problem solving, decision making, and critical judgment. These skills extend well beyond technical (how to) skills to the areas of ethical (moral) and aesthetic issue resolution. More research is needed to describe the problems confronted in work and family responsibilities and the higher-order thinking content that needs to be learned in successfully dealing with these problems. Special attention should be given to facilitating the transfer of learning to resolving the same problems over time or in different contexts, as well as to resolving different problems. Sternberg and Wagner's (1986) work on practical intelligence provides a promising way to think about vocational education and higher-order thinking skills in the context of developing competence for the everyday world.

Vocational Education and Basic Skills

What should be done about initially teaching, reinforcing, and enriching basic skills in vocational education? Effective accomplishment of work and family responsibilities requires sound basic skills in communication and computation along with higher-order and more specific skills. The opportunities for strengthening basic skills and ways of doing it effectively by providing a functional context for learning need to be identified for use by vocational educators.

As basic skills are extended to include a working knowledge of science and social studies, the applied aspects of these curricular areas can become an important aspect of vocational education (i.e., technology as the applied aspects of science). The problems and issues of vocational education can, in a similar way, be used to strengthen the effectiveness of subjects not typically labeled as vocational education. In this way, perhaps, the line between vocational and academic education can be productively blurred. The restructuring initiatives now being developed and tested in education represent a major new approach to viewing all of the curriculum of the public schools. The work of Berryman (1988), drawing on the results of investigating the changing nature of work and research in cognitive psychology, suggests significant changes are needed in all of K–12 education regarding the teaching of basic skills with important implications for the role of vocational education.

Integration Within Vocational Subfields

What should be done about the relationships among the content and purposes of the subfields of vocational education (i.e., agriculture, business, home economics)? Can these commonalities and uniquenesses be used to reinforce and strengthen one another? Feasible programs of study for students drawing on the content of several subfields should be developed. Can vocational education be thought of as one fully integrated system? Consideration should be given to more effective ways of structuring and categorizing the content of vocational education. Schemes such as work oriented and family oriented; general, occupational cluster specific, occupation specific, and employer specific; and goods versus services production-related education structures should be investigated as ways to think and talk about vocational education. The interrelation of work and family responsibilities is an increasingly important concern for successful living as both men and women are involved in and try to balance both responsibilities.

Keeping Vocational Education Up to Date

What should be done about keeping the content of vocational education modern and up to date? Technological change, global interdependence, and changing economic and social conditions and values result in the need for the continuous changes in the content of vocational education. How can these changes best be monitored and translated into an effective curriculum for vocational education? Attention needs to be given to strategies for content identification as well as curricular change. Competency studies and local advisory committees have been used in the past as means to ensure up-to-date curriculum modification, and additional mechanisms need to be considered for the future.

Articulation Among Levels of Vocational Education

What should be done about specifying and interrelating the content of vocational education offered at various school levels (i.e., elementary, junior high, high school, postsecondary)? What content is most appropriate for each level, that is, what should be the scope and sequence of vocational education? There may well be areas of needed duplication, and responses may vary depending on the context of particular geographic areas and institutional arrangements. Students need to be able to progress in an orderly fashion, experiencing neither gaps nor unnecessary duplication.

Coordination Among Providers of Vocational Education

What should be done about coordinating the vocational education provided in school with that in other settings, including family, workplace, and community? Consideration needs to be given to other settings for learning the content of vocational education beyond the school. What content is best learned where? What are effective and important partnerships and collaborative relations for providing vocational education? What needs to be done to access what learning has occurred and assure attention to what is missing and essential? It may well be that important dimensions of the content of vocational education are best learned in settings other than school.

Transition from School to Work and Family Life

What should be done about facilitating the transition from school to work and family responsibilities for students? Recognition needs to be given to the fact that the transition to work and family life often occurs before schooling is complete and that the transition may also involve movement from work and family responsibilities *to* school. Attention to successful placement of students as an aspect of the content of vocational education is being increasingly recognized as important to assure program accountability.

Attention to Full Range of Work and Family Responsibilities

What should be done about assuring that vocational education addresses the full range of work and family responsibilities? The range of work responsibilities includes all occupational levels from unskilled to professional, employee to employer, paid to unpaid. The attention to entrepreneurial education and community service education for young people are manifestations of this concern. Similarly, for family responsibilities, the range includes child, parent, grandparent, sibling, and extended family, as well as various manifestations of family (i.e., single, married, divorced, joint residents). How would the content of vocational education need to change if it extended the range of work and family responsibilities given attention? What are the consequences of restricting or extending this range?

Vocational Education's Role as Change Agent

What should be done about vocational education's role in improving the conditions of workplaces and families? Consideration needs to be given to the content of vocational education that would empower students to be active and responsible change agents for making workplaces and families safer and healthier, fairer, more just, and more nurturing and caring settings. Vocational education's stance with respect to existing conditions, that is, whether it acts as a mirror or a change agent, becomes especially clear in this area. Here also is a place for working out vocational education's role beyond the school in community development, both social and economic. The ideas proposed by Wirth (1983) in his book *Productive Work in Industry and School* is a stimulating place to start.

Vocational Education and At-Risk Students

What should be done about at-risk students with vocational education? It may well be that the future economic and social program of the United States is dependent at least as much on the effectiveness of education with these students as with those who are very successful in the present educational system. What content of vocational education would be most important and effective in dealing with the needs of at-risk students? What are the consequences of emphasizing this content and these students for other students to be served by vocational education? Who should vocational education be serving in the secondary school? The necessary support services, in addition to vocational education for providing the comprehensive services often needed for at-risk students, must be identified and coordinated. The findings of the William T. Grant Foundation (1988), as described in the report *The Forgotten Half*, and Schorr and Schorr (1988) in their book *Within Our Research: Breaking the Cycle of Disadvantage* provide hope and specific actions that have implications for reaching at-risk students through vocational education.

Vocational Education and Stratification

What should be done about vocational education as a potential means to stratify or track students into less-valued social and economic opportunities? Is vocational education being used in this way? How would its content and organizational arrangement need to change to remedy this situation if it exists? The historical analysis of vocational education made by Tanner and Tanner (1980) and the critical analysis by Oakes (1985) raise useful ideas for investigation.

Mission and Purpose of Vocational Education

What should be the mission and purpose of vocational education in the K–12 school setting? Should it emphasize broad development? general education? specific skills? Should it focus on preparation for short-term goals (i.e., immediate work and family responsibilities) or longer-term goals (i.e., postsecondary education, advancement, and maturity)? Consideration needs to be given to balanced attention to both work and family responsibilities as important aspects of vocational education's mission. The program of research conducted by the Minnesota Research and Development Center for Vocational Education (Copa et al. 1985a, 1985b; Copa, Plihal, and Johnson 1986) provides multiple perspectives on important questions in this regard.

State versus Local Curriculum Content and Guides

What should be done to balance state-wide curriculum specifications and assurances with localized curriculum needs in vocational education? The role of the state education agency in assuring equitable access to high-quality vocational education, in contrast to tailoring curriculum to diverse local school situations, needs further investigation. Where should state responsibility for the curriculum content in vocational education leave off and local responsibility begin? What are the most salient features at each level of responsibility? How is articulation between levels best accomplished in the interests of teachers and students as well as those responsible for funding and accountability? The current movement toward outcome-based education (Spady 1988) provides an opportunity and need to reexamine these issues within new structural arrangements for education.

Interaction of Content and Methods of Vocational Education

What should be done to extend the content of vocational education to recognize its interrelation with and contribution to the methods of vocational education? A dichotomy between instructional content and instructional methods is artificial and often counterproductive in addressing curricular issues. Vocational education's reliance on cooperative and experiential methods may well be a very significant aspect of its content. This interrelationship needs to be clarified and explicitly recognized in research on curriculum in vocational education. The research findings on learning styles (Dunn and Dunn 1978; Keefe 1987) should be examined carefully to identify vocational education's unique contributions to education as a *way* of learning.

Summary

In summary, while the curricular research in the subfields of vocational education and vocational education as a whole is extensive and disciplined, it is in large part (with some notable exceptions) still narrowly focused on technical competence, lacking in an overall conceptual framework, and heavily reliant on a single approach to curriculum development (e.g., instrumental/technical). If this critique is sound, curricular research in vocational education could benefit in important ways from (1) considering a broader and more expansive view of educational excellence (see, for example, Greene [1988], *The Dialectic of Freedom*; Scheffler [1985], *Of Human Potential*; and Shor and Freire [1987], *A Pedagogy for Liberation*); (2) approaching curriculum change and development from several different conceptual and philosophical perspectives (see, for example, McNeil [1977], *Curriculum: A Comprehensive Introduction*; Eisner [1979], *The Educational Imagination*; Schubert [1986], *Curriculum: Perspective, Paradigm, and Possibility*; and Ornstein and Hunkins [1988], *Curriculum: Foundations, Principles, and Issues*); and (3) reconsidering the role of researcher and practitioner in the curriculum research and development process (see, for example, Schön [1983], *The Reflective Practitioner*; and Carr and Kemmis [1986], *Becoming Critical: Education, Knowledge and Action Research*). With vocational education's unique focus toward preparing individuals for effectively dealing with work and family responsibilities in a rapidly changing, multicultural, and global society, the challenge to its curricular research is immense, as are the benefits to its good scholarship and practice.

References

Abt, Phyllis, W. Lewis, W. Barnes, and B. Geiger. 1968. *Occupational Analysis of Colorado Homemakers Utilizing the DACUM Approach*. Fort Collins: Colorado State University.

Adams, David R., and Thomas H. Athey, eds. 1981. *Model Curriculum for Undergraduate Computer Information Systems Education*. Park Ridge, IL: Data Processing Management Association Education Foundation.

American Home Economics Association. 1967. *Concepts and Generalizations: Their Place in High School Home Economics Curriculum Development*. Washington, DC: AHEA.

American Home Economics Association. 1987. *Definitive Themes in Home Economics and Their Impact on Families, 1909–1984*, rev. ed. Washington, DC: AHEA.

American Vocational Association, Health Occupations Division. 1985. *Vocational Health Occupations in High Schools: A Fact Sheet*. Arlington, VA: AVA.

Ammerman, Harry, F. Pratzner, Duane W. Essex, and Michael A. Mead. 1977. *Performance Content for Job Training*. Research and development series nos. 121–125. Columbus: Center for Vocational Education, Ohio State University (ERIC no. ED 146369–373).

Anderson, B. H., and R. Boddy. 1985. *The Identification of Science Competencies Included in the Curriculum of Secondary Vocational Education Programs*. Denver: Department of Vocational Education, Colorado State University.

Angress, Gina, and I. Hammelmann, eds. 1984. *Vocational Training Systems in the Member States of the European Community*. Berlin: European Center for the Development of Vocational Training.

Baggett, C. D. 1982. "The Influence of Selected Career Information Material on Career Interest of Secondary Students." Unpublished Ph.D. dissertation, Pennsylvania State University, College Station.

Bahr, G., and R. P. Wegforth. 1976. "A Historical Development of an Economic Emphasis in Business Education." In *Business Education Yesterday, Today, and Tomorrow*, edited by R. B. Woolschlager and E. E. Harris, 20–40. National Business Education Association Yearbook no. 14. Reston, VA: National Business Education Association.

Bakalars, Rita L. 1980. "Home Economics, Child Development and Family Concepts in Elementary Schools: A Conceptual Structure." Unpublished Ph.D. dissertation, University of Wisconsin, Madison.

Bakalars, Rita L., and Beatrice Petrich. 1983. Family life and child development concepts in elementary schools: A factor analysis. *Home Economics Research Journal* 12(1): 49–56.

Baldwin, Edith E. 1984. "The Nature of Home Economics Curriculum in Secondary Schools." Unpublished Ph.D. dissertation, Oregon State University, Corvallis.

Barlow, Melvin L., ed. 1965. *Vocational Education*. Sixty-fourth Yearbook of the National Society for the Study of Education, Part I. Chicago: University of Chicago Press.

Barlow, Melvin L. 1967a. Foundations of vocational education. *American Vocational Journal* 42(3): 16–19.

Barlow, Melvin L. 1967b. *History of Industrial Education in the United States*. Peoria, IL: Charles A. Bennett.

Barlow, Melvin L. 1973. "Historical Antecedents to Career Education." In *Career Education*, edited by J. H. Magisos, 30–39. Third Yearbook of the American Vocational Association. Washington, DC: American Vocational Association.

Barlow, Melvin L. 1976. Two hundred years of vocational education, 1776–1976. *American Vocational Journal* 51(5): 21–88.

Beach, David. 1978. "The Effects of Competency/Evaluation Profile Feedback on Achievement in Electronics." Unpublished Ph.D. dissertation, University of Missouri, Columbia.

Beavers, Irene. 1979. *Standards for Postsecondary Programs in Textiles and Clothing*. Ames: Department of Home Economics Education, Iowa State University.

Beck, Robert. 1990a. *Polytechnic Education: A Step*. Berkeley, CA: National Center for Research in Vocational Education.

Beck, Robert. 1990b. *Vocational Preparation and General Education*. Berkeley, CA: National Center for Research in Vocational Education.

Beck, Robert. 1990c. *General Education: Vocational and Academic Collaboration*. Berkeley, CA: National Center for Research in Vocational Education.

Beecher, Catharine E. 1841. *A Treatise on Domestic Economy*. New York: Harper & Brothers.

Bennett, Charles A. 1926. *History of Manual and Industrial Education up to 1870*. Peoria, IL: Manual Arts Press.

Bennett, Charles A. 1937. *History of Manual and Industrial Education, 1870 to 1917*. Peoria, IL: Charles A. Bennett.

Bensen, M. J. 1979. Clusters or concepts in selecting industrial arts content. *Journal of Epsilon Pi Tau*, 5(1): 33–39.

Berger, Michael, and Helmut Hawkins. 1979. "Occupational Analysis: An Automated Approach." In *Handbook of Vocational Education Evaluation*, edited by Theodore Abramson, Carol Tittle, and Lee Cohen, 275–301. Beverly Hills, CA: Sage.

Berkey, Arthur, William Drake, and James Legacy. 1972. *A Model for Task Analysis in Agribusiness*. Project Study, Cornell University, Ithaca, NY (ERIC no. ED 065 686).

Berns, R. G., J. L. Borrow, and H. R. Wallace. 1980. *Marketing and Distributive Education: Review and Synthesis of the Research*. Information Series no. 213. Columbus, OH: National Center for Research in Vocational Education.

Berryman, Susan E. 1988. *Education and the Economy: What Should We Teach? When? How? To Whom?* Occasional Paper, No. 4. New York: National Center on Education and Employment, Columbia University, New York.

Bevier, Isabel. 1924. *Home Economics in Education*. Family Life Series, edited by Benjamin R. Andrews. Philadelphia, PA: Lippincott.

Bigo, C. H. 1979. "Entry Level Competency Needs of the Utah Feed, Seed and Grain Workers as Perceived by Vocational Agriculture Educators and Industry." Unpublished master's thesis, Utah State University, Logan. (microfiche).

Boone, H. N., D. L. Doerfert, and J. Elliot. 1987. Supervised occupational experience programs: History, philosophy, current status, and future implications. *Journal of the American Association of Teacher Educators in Agriculture* 28(4): 57–64.

Bottoms, Eugene, and Patricia Copa. 1983. A perspective on vocational education today. *Phi Delta Kappan* 64(5): 348–351.

Bruhn, M. [illegible] *Minnesota Health Occupations Core Curriculum*. St. Paul: Minnesota Department of Education.

Brendel, L., and H. Yengel, eds. 1972. *Changing Methods of Teaching Business Subjects*. National Business Education Yearbook, no. 10. Washington, DC: National Business Education Association.

Brown, Herman D. 1978. *An Assessment of the Basic Curriculum Guide for Teaching Vocational Agriculture in Texas*. College Station: Department of Agricultural Education, Texas A & M University. (ERIC no. ED 182 541).

Brown, Marjorie M. 1980. *What Is Home Economics Education?* St. Paul: Minnesota Research and Development Center for Vocational Education.

Brown, Marjorie M. 1985. *Philosophical Studies of Home Economics in the United States: Our Practical-Intellectual Heritage*. 2 vols. East Lansing: Michigan State University.

Brown, Marjorie M., and Ben Paolucci. 1979. *Home Economics: A Definition*. Washington, DC: American Home Economics Association.

Buffer, James J. 1971. *A Junior High School Industrial Technology Curriculum Project: A Final Evaluation of the Industrial Arts Curriculum Project (IACP) 1965–1971*. Columbus: Ohio State University Research Foundation.

Burden, D., and B. Googins. 1985. *Boston University: Balancing Job and Homelife Study*. Boston, MA: School of Social Work, Boston University.

Burgess, E. F., and E. L. Nelson. May 1980. "Directions for the 1980s." Preconference mimeographed material prepared for the National Conference on Marketing and Distributive Education.

Burnett, M. F. 1983. "Instructional Materials for the Basic Program of Vocational Agriculture in Louisiana." Staff study, Louisiana State University, Baton Rouge.

Camp, William G., and John R. Crunkilton. 1985. History of agricultural education in America: The great individuals and events. *Journal of the American Association of Teacher Educators in Agriculture* 26(1): 57–63.

Carnevale, Anthony P., Leila J. Gainer, and Ann S. Meltzer. 1988. *Workplace Basics: The Skills Employers Want*. Alexandria, VA: American Society for Training and Development and U.S. Department of Labor Employment and Training Administration.

Carr, Wilfred, and Stephen Kemmis. 1986. *Becoming Critical: Education, Knowledge and Action Research*. Philadelphia, PA: Falmer.

Carter, P. John. 1970. "An Investigation of Attitudes Held by Industrial Arts Educators Toward the Question of a Uniform Nationwide Curriculum for Industrial Arts." Unpublished Ed.D. dissertation, Greeley: University of Northern Colorado.

Cassimer, M. H. 1981. *Health Occupations Curriculum Guide, 1981*. Bulletin no. 1635. Baton Rouge: Louisiana Department of Education.

Charters, W. W. 1923. *Curriculum Construction*. New York: Macmillan.

Clark, Stephen C. 1989. The industrial arts paradigm: Adjustment, replacement, or extinction? *Journal of Technology Education* 1(1): 7–21.

Claus, Jeff. 1988. "Renegotiating Vocational Instruction." Paper presented at the annual meeting of the American Educational Research Association, New Orleans, LA.

Cohelan, Evelyn E. 1963. "Nursing Activities Described by Students as Useful for Providing Emotionally Supportive Care to Patients." Unpublished Ph.D. dissertation. University of California, Berkeley.

Colelli, L. A. [illegible] *Technology Education: A Primer*. Reston, VA: International Technology Education Association.

Commission on the Reorganization of Secondary Education (appointed by the National Education Association). 1918. *Cardinal Principles of Secondary Education*. Bulletin no. 35. Washington, DC: U.S. Bureau of Education.

Commissioner's Task Force on Education for Employment. 1988.

Work-Readiness: A New Promise in Minnesota's Education. St. Paul: Minnesota Department of Education.

Committee on Agricultural Education in Secondary Schools, National Research Council, National Academy of Sciences. 1988. *Understanding Agriculture: New Directions for Education*. Washington, DC: National Academy Press.

Contento, Isabel. 1981. Thinking about nutrition: Assessing and enhancing the reasoning skills of college non-major nutrition students. *Home Economics Research Journal* 10(2): 160–174.

Cook, Glen C. 1947. *A Handbook on Teaching Vocational Agriculture*. Danville, IL: Interstate.

Coon, Beulah I. 1962. *Home Economics in the Public Secondary Schools: A Report of a National Study*. U.S. Office of Education Circular No. 661. Washington, DC: Government Printing Office.

Copa, George H. 1984. *Vocational Education and Youth Employment*. Columbus, OH: National Center for Research in Vocational Education.

Copa, George H., Jeanette Daines, Linda Ernst, James Knight, Gary Leske, John Persico, Jane Plihal, and Steve Scholl. 1985a. *Purpose of Vocational Education in the Secondary School*. St. Paul: Minnesota Research and Development Center for Vocational Education.

Copa, George H., Jane Plihal, Steve Scholl, Linda Ernst, Marsha Rehm, and Patricia M. Copa. 1985b. *An Untold Story: Purposes of Vocational Education in Secondary Schools*. St. Paul: Minnesota Research and Development Center for Vocational Education.

Copa, George H., Jane Plihal, and Marilyn A. Johnson. 1986. *Re-Visioning Vocational Education in the Secondary School*. St. Paul: Minnesota Research and Development Center for Vocational Education.

Craig, Hazel T. 1945. *The History of Home Economics*. New York: Practical Home Economics.

Crank, F., and D. Crank. 1977. "Historical Perspectives of Education for Business." In *Curriculum Development in Education for Business*, edited by J. W. Crews and Z. S. Dickerson, Jr., 1–18. National Business Education Association Yearbook, no. 15. Reston, VA: National Business Education Association.

Crawford, Lucy C. 1967. *A Competency Pattern Approach to Curriculum Construction in Distributive Teacher Education*, Vols. 1–4. Blacksburg: Virginia Polytechnic Institute (ERIC nos. ED 032 383, 4, 5, 6).

Crawford, Lucy C. 1976. *Developing and Testing Simulated Occupational Experiences for Distributive Education Students in Rural Communities*. Blacksburg: Virginia Polytechnic Institute and State University (ERIC no. ED 118 997).

Crawford, Lucy C., and Kenneth A. Ertel. 1970. "Methods of Identifying Marketing Competencies." In *The Emerging Content and Structure of Business Education*, edited by R. G. Price, C. R. Hopkins, and M. Klaurens. National Business Education Association Yearbook, no. 8. Washington, DC: National Business Education Association.

Crawford, Lucy C., and Warren G. Meyer. 1972. *Organization and Administration of Distributive Education*. Columbus, OH: Merrill.

Crenshaw, Virginia P. 1961. "An Inquiry into Students' Competencies in Nursing and Suggested Guidelines for Curriculum Improvement." Unpublished Ph.D. dissertation, George Peabody College for Teachers, Nashville, TN.

Cuetara, Paul. 1988. *A Guide for Change—Making the Transition from Industrial Arts to Technology Education*. Concord: Christa McAuliffe Trust of the State of New Hampshire. (ERIC no. ED 305517)

Daughtrey, Ann S. 1974. *Methods of Basic Business and Economic Education*. Cincinnati, OH: South-Western.

David, Henry, ed. 1981. *The Vocational Education Study: The Final Report*. Vocational education study publication no. 8. Washington, DC: National Institute of Education, U.S. Department of Education.

Decker John P. 1967. *A Functional Analysis of Paramedical Occupations as a Foundation for Curriculum Development*. Phoenix: Arizona Health Services Education Association (ERIC no. ED 012 790).

DeVore, Paul W. 1968. *Structure and Content Foundations for Curriculum Development*. Washington, DC: American Industrial Arts Association.

Dewey, John. 1899. *The School and Society*. Chicago: University of Chicago Press.

Dewey, John. 1901. The place of manual training in the elementary course of study. *Manual Training Magazine* 2(4): 193–199.

Dewey, John. 1915a. Splitting up the school system. *The New Republic* 2(24): 283–284.

Dewey, John. 1915b. Education vs. trade-training—Dr. Dewey's reply. *The New Republic* 3(28): 42–43.

Dillon, Ray. 1970. Are Local Teachers of Agriculture Teaching Relevant Junior High Vocational Courses? Staff study, University of Nebraska, Lincoln.

Dougherty, Barbara. 1977. *Wisconsin: Consumer and Homemaking Programs—Compilation of Program Procedures, Educational Strategies and Teaching Materials Related to Consumer and Homemaking Disadvantaged Programs in Wisconsin*. Final report. Madison: Wisconsin Board of Vocational, Technical, and Adult Education.

Drake, Bob, Paul Davis, and Thomas Terry. 1980. A demonstrated model for establishing curriculum development priorities in trade and industrial education. *Journal of Industrial Teacher Education* 17 (Summer): 28–35.

Dunn, Kenneth, and Rita Dunn. 1978. *Teaching Students Through Their Individual Learning Styles: A Practical Approach*. Reston, VA: Reston.

Dyrenfurth, Michael J. 1987. *Missouri Industrial Technology Guide*. Columbia: Division of Vocational Education, Missouri State Department of Elementary and Secondary Education and University of Missouri.

Dyrenfurth, Michael J., and Daniel L. Householder. 1979. *Industrial Arts Education: A Review and Synthesis of the Research*. Information Series no. 183. Columbus, OH: National Center for Research in Vocational Education.

East, Marjorie. 1980. *Home Economics: Past, Present, and Future*. Boston, MA: Allyn & Bacon.

Eaton, Theodore H. 1925. *Principles of Making the Vocational Course of Study in Agriculture in the High School*. Bulletin no. 28, Agricultural Series no. 22. Washington, DC: Federal Board for Vocational Education.

Educational Policies Commission of the National Education Association and American Association of School Administrators. 1956. *Manpower and Education*. Washington, DC: Government Printing Office.

Effendi, Maklar N. 1984. "Crops Information Needs of Farmers as Perceived by Selected West Virginia Farmers, County Extension Agents, and Vocational Agriculture Teachers." Unpublished master's thesis, West Virginia University, Morgantown.

Egglund, Steven A. 1980. "Program Development in Marketing and Distributive Education." Paper presented to the National Conference on Directions in Marketing and Distributive Education, Vail, CO.

Eisner, Elliot W. 1979. *The Educational Imagination*. New York: Macmillan.

Elam, William N. 1942. "New Farmers of America." In *History of Agricultural Education of Less Than College Grade in the*

United States, compiled by Rufus W. Stimson and Frank W. Lothrop, 551–558. Vocational Divsion Bulletin no. 217, Agricultural Series No. 55. Washington, DC: Office of Education.

Elmore, Marjorie J. 1964. "Proposals Relating to the Selection and Organization of Learning Experiences for Nursing Students in the Care of Older Patients." Unpublished Ph.D. dissertation, Columbia University, New York.

Emick, Glenn O. 1937. *Cooperative Training in Retail Selling in the Public Secondary Schools*. Vocational Education Bulletin no. 186. Washington, DC: Government Printing Office.

Ertel, Kenneth. 1966. *Identification of Major Tasks Performed by Merchandising Employers Working in Three Standard Industrial Classifications*. Moscow: University of Idaho (ERIC no. ED 010 657).

Evans, Rupert N. 1971. *Foundations of Vocational Education*. Columbus, OH: Merrill.

Eyestone, Virginia G. 1982. "An Evaluation of Selected Parenthood Education Curriculum Guides for Consumer and Homemaking Programs." Unpblished Ed.D. dissertation, Pennsylvania State University, College Station.

Face, William L. 1965. "Conceptual Approach to American Industry." In *Approaches and Procedures in Industrial Arts*, 2nd ed., edited by G. S. Wall. Fourteenth Yearbook of the American Council on Industrial Arts Teacher Education. Bloomington, IL: McKnight.

Fassett, Diane. 1977. *Future Homemakers of America Planning Paper for Consumer and Homemaking Education*. Washington, DC: Future Homemakers of America (ERIC no. 211 724).

Fiddy, Rob. 1985. *Youth, Unemployment and Training: A Collection of National Perspectives*. Philadelphia, PA: Falmer.

Field, William E. 1976. "Estimating the Need to Increase the Emphasis on Topics Relating to the World Food Crisis and International Agriculture in the Vocational Agricultural Curriculum." Unpublished master's thesis, University of Minnesota, St. Paul.

Finch, Curt R. 1983. *Review and Synthesis of Research in Trade and Industrial Education*. Information series no. 260. Columbus, OH: National Center for Research in Vocational Education.

Finch, Curt R., and John Crunkilton. 1979. "Curriculum Development Content for the 1980's and Beyond." In *Vocational-Technical Education for the Eighties*, edited by C. Bradley and J. Friedenberg. Miami, FL: International Dynamics.

Fisk, Margaret, ed. 1940. *The Business Curriculum*, Sixth Yearbook of National Commercial Teachers Federation. Bowling Green, KY: National Commercial Teachers Federation.

Flood, Joan. 1989. *Minnesota Post-Secondary Business and Office Curriculum Guide: Administrative Support Career Program*. St. Paul: Minnesota State Board of Vocational and Technical Education.

Ford, Roxanne. 1976. *Middle School/Junior High Co-Educational Mini-units in Home Economics*. St. Paul: Division of Vocational and Technical Education, Minnesota Department of Education.

Foster, G. 1978. "Identification of Workers' Affective Skills Using the Critical Incident Technique." Ed.D. dissertation, Virginia Polytechnic Institute and State University, Blacksburg.

Franz, Wanda, Nora J. MacDonald, and Pat Grocott. 1985. The importance of mathematical and logical skills to clothing construction. *Illinois Teacher of Home Economics* [illegible](1): 35–38.

Furtado, Lorraine T. 1973. "An interpretative history of distributive education, 1936–1972, as seen by selected leaders." Unpublished Ph.D. dissertation, Michigan State University, East Lansing.

Gardner, Hannah. 1983. *Frames of Mind*. New York: Basic Books.

Gleason, James B., Beth Harvey, and Debbi Dopo, eds. 1985. *Content Analysis of Selected State Curriculum Guides*. Columbus: Ohio State University, Interstate Distributive Education Curriculum Consortium.

Goetting, M. A., and G. Y. Muggli. 1988. *Journal of Home Economics* 80(1): 7–10.

Goldhammer, Keith, and Robert E. Taylor. 1972. "Introduction: Career Education Perspectives." In *Career Education: Perspective and Promise*, edited by Keith Goldhammer and Robert E. Taylor, 1–12. Columbus, OH: Merrill.

Goodlad, John I. 1984. *A Place Called School*. New York: McGraw-Hill.

Greenan, James P. 1983. Identification and validation of generalizable skills in vocational programs. *Journal of Vocational Education Research* 8(3): 46–71.

Greenan, James P. 1986. The relationship between student self-ratings and teacher ratings of students' generalizable mathematics skills in vocational programs. *Journal of Industrial Teacher Education* 24(1): 47–55.

Greenan, James P. 1987. The correlation between student self-ratings and teacher ratings of generalizable communications skills. *Occupational Education Forum* 16(2): 9–13.

Greenan, James P., and Michael R. Winters. 1989. The relationship between students' self-ratings and teacher ratings of vocational students' interpersonal relations skills. *Journal of Studies in Technical Careers* 11(2): 111–118.

Greene, Maxine. 1988. *The Dialectic of Freedom*. New York: Teachers College Press.

Gysbers, Norman C. 1984. "Major Trends in Career Development Theory and Practice." In *Designing Careers: Counseling to Enhance Education, Work, and Leisure*, edited by Norman C. Gysbers, 618–632. San Francisco, CA: National Vocational Guidance Association and Jossey-Bass.

Haas, Kenneth B. 1939. *Cooperative Part-Time Retail Training Programs, Supervision, Coordination, and Teaching*. Vocational Division Bulletin no. 205. Washington, DC: Government Printing Office.

Halasz, Ida M. 1988. *Trends and Issues in Career Education*. Columbus: Center on Education and Training for Employment, Ohio State University.

Hales, James A., and James F. Snyder. 1982a. Jackson's Mill industrial arts curriculum theory: A base for curriculum conceptualization. Part 1 of a two-part series. *Man/Society/Technology* 41(5): 6–10.

Hales, James A., and James F. Snyder. 1982b. Jackson's Mill industrial arts curriculum theory: A base for curriculum conceptualization. Part 2 of a two-part series. *Man/Society/Technology* 41(6): 6–8.

Halfin, Harold, and Orville Nelson. 1982. *Emerging Skills: Implications for Voc Ed*. Columbus, OH: National Center for Research in Vocational Education.

Hamilton, William H. 1983. "Farm Machinery Set-Up Mechanics, a V-TECS Catalog." Staff study, Purdue University, Lafayette.

Hamlin, Herbert M. 1956. 50 years of progress in agricultural education. *American Vocational Journal*, 31(9): 39–46, 105.

Hammonds, Carsie. 1950. *Teaching Agriculture*. New York: McGraw-Hill.

Hampson, Michael, L. Newcomb, and J. David McCracken. 1977, *Essential Leadership and Personal Development Competencies Needed in Agricultural Occupations as Identified by Agriculture Leaders in Ohio*. Staff study. Columbus: Ohio State University (ERIC ED no. 141 645).

Hansen, W. Lee, G. L. Back, J. D. Calderwood, and P. Sanders. 1977. *Master Curriculum Guide in Economics for the Nation's Schools. Part 1: A Framework For Teaching Economics: Basic Concepts*. New York: Joint Council on Economic Education.

Harrington, Lois G. 1988. Making common cause: Integrating academic and vocational studies. *Curriculum Report* 18(1): 1–8.

Harris, Edward. 1978. *Curriculum Research for the Development of Marketing and Distributive Education Curriculum Guides in the State of Illinois*. Dekalb: Northern Illinois University.

Harrison, W., Jr. 1973. Learning activity packages: A progress report. *DE Today* 7(February): 2.

Hatcher, Elizabeth, Don Frazier, and Carolyn Miller. 1978. *Validation of Agricultural Mechanics Curriculum Manual*. Stillwater: Oklahoma Vocational Research Coordinating Unit (ERIC no. ED 160 819).

Hawkins, Layton S., Charles A. Prosser, and John C. Wright. 1951. *Development of Vocational Education*. Chicago: American Technical Society.

Henry, Nelson B., ed. 1943. *Vocational Education*. Forty-second Yearbook of the National Society for the Study of Education, Part I. Chicago: University of Chicago.

Herr, Edmund L. 1972. "Unifying an Entire System of Education Around a Career Development Theme." In *Career education: Perspective and Promise*, edited by Keith Goldhammer and Robert E. Taylor, 63–106. Columbus, OH: Merrill.

Herr, Edmund L. 1987a. Comprehensive career guidance and vocational education: Natural allies. *Vocational Education Journal* 62(6): 30–33.

Herr, Edmund L. 1987b. Education as preparation for work: Contributions of career education and vocational education. *Journal of Career Development* 13(3): 16–30.

Hillison, John. 1986. Agricultural teacher education preceding the Smith-Hughes Act. *Journal of the American Association of Teacher Educators in Agriculture* 28(2): 8–17.

Hogue, Ken, John Carnes, and Gary Briers. 1981. *Identification and analysis of emerging occupations in vocational agriculture. Final report*. College Station: Department of Agricultural Education, Texas A & M University (ERIC no. ED 234 188).

Hohenhaus, William. 1976. "Developing and Evaluating a Procedure for Identifying, Sequencing, and Determining an Instructional Environment for Competencies Needed at Various Occupational Levels in the Retail Feed Industry of Minnesota." Unpublished Ph.D. dissertation, University of Minnesota, St. Paul.

Holloway, Lewis D., and E. E. Kerr. 1969. *Review and Synthesis of Research in Health Occupations Education*. Columbus: Center for Research and Leadership Development, Ohio State University.

Hopkins, Charles, and Judith Lambrecht. 1985. "Business Education." In *International Encyclopedia of Education*, edited by T. Husen and T. N. Postlethwaite, 607–618. New York: Pergamon.

Horne, Ralph. 1981. *A Guide for Implementing Competency-Based Education in Vocational Programs*. Richmond: Virginia Department of Education.

Horner, James, D. Zikmund, and Roy Dillon. 1970. "A Determinant of Occupational Commonalities to Serve as a Base for Course Construction. Staff study. Lincoln: University of Nebraska.

Householder, Daniel L. 1979. "Curriculum Movements of the 1960s." In *Industrial Arts Education: Retrospect, Prospect*, edited by G. Eugene Martin, 113–132. Twenty-eighth Yearbook of the American Council on Industrial Arts Teacher Education. Bloomington, IL: McKnight.

Householder, Larry, Max McGhee, and Roger Roediger. 1976. *Curriculum Development Basic to the Training of Individuals for Employment in Agribusiness, Natural Resources, and Environmental Protection*. Final Report. Staff study. Columbus: Ohio State University (ERIC no. ED 131 297).

Hoyt, Kenneth B. 1980. Career education and vocational education: A re-examination. *Journal of Career Education* 6(3): 178–186.

Hoyt, Kenneth B. 1987. "Trends in Career Education: Implications for the Future." In *Education in Transition: Trends and Implications for the Future*, edited by Kenneth B. Hoyt and K. R. Shylo, 5–32 Columbus, OH: National Center for Research in Vocational Education.

International Technology Education Association. 1985. *Standards for Technology Education Programs*. South Holland, IL: Goodhart-Wilcox.

Iowa State University, Agriculture Education Department. 1977. *Standards for Quality Vocational Programs in Agricultural/ Agribusiness Education*. Ames: Iowa State University.

Jacobsen, W. 1983. "A National Study to Ascertain the Level of Unanimity among Five Selected Groups for the Mission Statement and Six Premise Statements for Marketing and Distributive Education." Unpublished doctoral dissertation, University of Wisconsin, Madison.

Junge, Cathrine B. 1989, spring. Telephone interview by Marsha Walsh. University of Minnesota, St. Paul.

Kadamus, James A., and William R. Daggett. 1986. *New Directions for Vocational Education at the Secondary Level*. Columbus, OH: National Center for Research in Vocational Education.

Kantor, Harvey, and David B. Tyack, eds. 1982. *Work, Youth and Schooling: Historical Perspectives on Vocationalism in American Education*. Stanford, CA: Stanford University Press.

Karelse, R., and C. Olson. 1983. *Task Based Curriculum for Production Agriculture. Final Report*. East Lansing: Michigan State University.

Keefe, James W. 1987. *Learning Style: Theory and Practice*. Reston, VA: National Association of Secondary School Principals.

Keller, Franklin J. 1964. "Vocational and Educational Guidance." In *Vocational Education*. Sixty-fourth Yearbook of the National Society for the Study of Education, Part I, edited by Melvin L. Barlow, 135–167. Chicago: National Society for the Study of Education.

Keller, Louise J. 1972. "Career Development—An Integrated Curriculum Approach, K–12." In *Career Education: Perspective and Promise*, edited by Keith Goldhammer and Robert E. Taylor, 185–208. Columbus, OH: Merrill.

Kesler, Kevin. 1984. "An Analysis of the Tasks Performed by Agricultural Mechanics at a Retail Agricultural Equipment Dealership in Utah." Master's thesis, Utah State University, Logan (microfilm).

Kister, Joanna. 1981. "An Empirical/Interpretive Perspective of Home and Family Life: An Application of the Metascientific Theory of Jurgen Habermas." Ph.D. dissertation, Ohio State University, Columbus.

Kister, Joanna. 1989. Home economics education: We need it! *Vocational Education Journal* 64(4): 35–36.

Kliebard, Herbert M. 1989. Problems of definition in curriculum. *Journal of Curriculum and Supervision* 5(1): 1–5.

Lambrecht, Judith L. 1987. Where does business education fit in the information society? *NABTE Review* 14: 11–17.

Lambrecht, Judith L., et al. 1981. *Business and Office Education: Review and Synthesis*. Information Series no. 232. Columbus, OH: National Center for Research in Vocational Education.

Lauda, Donald P., and J. Wright. 1983. *Eastern's Technology Education Plan*. Charleston: Eastern Illinois University.

Lauglo, Jon, and Kevin Lillis, eds. 1988. *Vocationalizing Education: An International Perspective*. Pergamon Comparative and International Education Series, Vol. 6. New York: Pergamon.

Lee, Jasper H. 1985. *Agricultural Education: Review and Synthesis of the Research*. Information Series no. 298. Columbus, OH: National Center for Research in Vocational Education.

Lotto, Linda. 1983. *Building Basic Skills: Results from Vocational Education*. Columbus, OH: National Center for Research in Vocational Education.

Lux, Donald G. 1979. "The Industrial Arts Curriculum Project." In *Industrial Arts Education: Retrospect, Prospect*, edited by G. Eugene Martin, 149–168. Twenty-eighth Yearbook of the American Council on Industrial Arts Teacher Education. Bloomington, IL: McKnight.

Lux, Donald G. 1982. "Industrial Arts Education." In *Encyclopedia of Educational Research*, edited by Harold E. Mitzel, 859–863. New York: Free Press.

Lynch, Richard L. 1983. *Marketing Education: A Future Perspective*. Special Publication Series no. 37. Columbus, OH: National Center for Research in Vocational Education.

Lynch, Richard L., and Donald Kohns. 1977. *Proposed Design and Broad Content Outlines for Teacher and Professional Educator Materials in the Field of Marketing and Distribution*. Blacksburg: Virginia Polytechnic Institute and State University.

McCage, Ronald D. 1986. Using the V-TECS databases. *Vocational Education Journal* 61(8): 39–41.

McClay, David R. 1978. *Identifying and Validating Essential Competencies Needed for Entry and Advancement in Major Agriculture and Agribusiness Occupations. Final Report*. State College, PA: Instructional Consulting and Research Associates (ERIC no. ED 151 521).

MacCleave-Frazier, Anne, and Eloise C. Murray. 1983. *Reconceptualizing the Teaching of Clothing in Consumer and Homemaking Programs: Implications for Teacher Preparation*. University Park: Division of Occupational and Vocational Studies, Pennsylvania State University, College Station. (ERIC no. ED 236 345).

McClure, Arthur F., James R. Christman, and Perry Mock. 1985. *Education for Work: The Historical Evolution of Vocational and Distributive Education in America*. London: Associated University Presses.

McCracken, David J., and Edgar Yoder. 1975. *Determination of a Common Core of Basic Skills for Agribusiness and Natural Resources*. Staff study. Columbus: Ohio State University (ERIC no. ED 115 791).

McCrory, David L. 1976. "Career Education: A Working Definition." In *The Career Educator*, edited by D. P. Garner, 63–68. Charleston: Eastern Illinois University.

McCrory, David L. 1987. *Technology Education: Industrial Arts in Transition, a Review and Synthesis of the Research*, 4th ed. Information Series no. 325. Columbus, OH: National Center for Research in Vocational Education.

McNeil, John D. 1977. *Curriculum: A Comprehensive Introduction*. Boston, MA: Little, Brown.

Maday, J. A. 1984. *Develop and Field Test Written and Performance Student Achievement Measures for Agricultural Machinery and Equipment Operator and Maintenance Person*. Gainesville: University of Florida.

Mager, Robert F. 1962. *Preparing Instructional Objectives*. Palo Alto, CA: Fearon.

Maley, Donald. 1973. *The Maryland Plan*. New York: Bruce.

Maley, Donald. 1979. "The Maryland Plan." In *Industrial Arts Education: Retrospect, Prospect*, edited by G. Eugene Martin, 132–148. Twenty-eighth Yearbook of the American Council on Industrial Arts Teacher Education. Bloomington, IL: McKnight.

Malpiedi, B. J., and John Hillison. 1986. Career education: A time of change. *Journal of Career Development* 12(4): 327–337.

Marland, Sidney P., Jr. 1972a. "Career Education Now." In *Career Education: Perspective and Promise*, edited by Keith Goldhammer and Robert E. Taylor, 33–42. Columbus, OH: Merrill.

Marland, Sidney P., Jr. 1972b. "Career Education: More Than a Name." In *Career Education: Perspective and Promise*, edited by Keith Goldhammer and Robert E. Taylor, 43–54. Columbus, OH: Merrill.

Martin, G. Eugene, and J. F. Luetkemeyer. 1979. "The Movements That Led to Contemporary Industrial Arts Education." In *Industrial Arts Education: Retrospect, Prospect*, edited by G. Eugene Martin, 17–42. Twenty-eighth Yearbook of the American Council on Industrial Arts Teacher Education. Bloomington, IL: McKnight.

Martin, Jane R. 1985. *Reclaiming a Conversation: The Ideal of the Educated Woman*. New Haven, CT: Yale University Press.

Mays, Arthur B. 1946. *The Concept of Vocational Education in the Thinking of the General Educator, 1845 to 1945*. University of Illinois Bulletin no. 65. Urbana: University of Illinois.

Meyer, G. Warren, and Lorraine T. Furtado. 1976. "A Historical Development of Distributive Education." In *Business Education Yesterday, Today, and Tomorrow*, edited by R. B. Woolschager and E. E. Harris, 41–75. National Business Education Association Yearbook no. 14. Reston, VA: National Business Education Association.

Meyers, Arthur. 1985. Productivity as the content base for industrial arts. *Technology Teacher* 44(5). 1[illegible]0.

Minnesota Department of Education. 1988. *A Restructured Model for Secondary Vocational Education*. St. Paul: Minnesota Department of Education.

Moore, Gary E. 1985. The secondary vocational agriculture curriculum from 1890 to 1980. *Journal of the American Association of Teacher Educators in Agriculture* 27(3): 8–19.

Moore, Gary E. 1987, May. "To Tell the Truth: The Impact of the Hatch Act on Secondary Agricultural Education." Paper presented at meeting of American Association of Teacher Educators in Agriculture, Las Vegas, NV (ERIC no. ED 290 030).

Morsh, J., and W. Archer. 1967. *Procedural Guide for Conducting Occupational Surveys in the United States Air Force*. Lakeland Air Force Base, TX: Personnel Research Laboratory.

Moss, Jerome, Jr. 1981. LCBE: Limiting competency-based education (or) Let's curb behavioral excesses. *Journal of Industrial Teacher Education*. 19(1): 14–18.

Moss, Jerome, Jr. 1987. Teaching "generalizable" occupational skills: It's a puzzlement. *Journal of Industrial Teacher Education* 24(3): 59–66.

Murphy, Patricia D. 1974. *Consumer Education Modules: A Spiral-Process Approach*. Curriculum Development in Vocational and Technical Education, North Dakota State University, Fargo. Washington, DC: Office of Education.

National Business Education Association. 1987. *Database of Competencies for Business Curriculum Development, K–14*. Reston, VA: National Business Education Association.

National Commission on Excellence in Education. 1983. *A Nation at Risk: The Imperative for Educational Reform*. Washington, DC: National Commission on Excellence in Education.

National Commission on Secondary Vocational Education. 1984. *The Unfinished Agenda: The Role of Vocational Education in the High School*. Columbus, OH: National Center for Research in Vocational Education (ERIC no. ED 251622).

National Conference for Distributive Education (Dunwoody Conference). 1939. *Preliminary Report of Committee on Methods*. Minneapolis, MN: William Hood Dunwoody Industrial Institute.

National Curriculum Committee for Marketing Education. 1987. *National Curriculum Framework and Core Competencies*. Columbus, OH: Marketing Education Resource Center.

Nelson, Edwin L. 1963. "Basis for Curriculum Development in Distribution." Paper presented at the meeting of the National Clinic on Distributive Education, Washington, DC.

Nelson, Edwin L. 1966. A conceptual framework for curriculum development in distributive education. *Business Education Forum* 20(7): 10–13.

Nelson, Edwin L. 1970. "The Taxonomy of Distributive Education and Distributive Occupations." In *The Emerging Content and Structure of Business Education*, edited by R. G. Price, C. R. Hopkins, and M. Klaurens. National Business Education Association Yearbook, no. 8. Washington, DC: National Business Education Association.

Nelson, Helen Y. 1979. *Home Economics Education: A Review and Synthesis of the Research*. Information Series No. 134. Columbus, OH: National Center for Research in Vocational Education.

Nelson, Helen Y., P. L. Lowe, and J. I. Dalrymple. 1975. Preparing disadvantaged pupils for homemaker and wage-earner roles. *Home Economics Research Journal* 4(2): 103–114.

Nelson, Robert, and Sharon O'Niel. 1977. Worker perceptions of occupational survival skills. *Journal of Industrial Teacher Education*. 14(2): 34–42.

Nemko, Barbara. 1986. "Model General Occupational/Employability Skills." Draft. Davis: University of California.

Newcomb, L. H. 1978. *Agricultural Education: Review and Synthesis of Research*. Information Series no. 139. Columbus, OH: National Center for Research in Vocational Education.

Newman, Charles A., and J. Joyce Caton, eds. 1981. *Updating Content in Secondary Business Education*. National Business Education Yearbook, no. 19. Reston, VA: National Business Education Association.

Nichols, Frederick G. 1933. *Commercial Education in the High School*. New York: Appleton-Century.

North Carolina State Department of Public Instruction, Division of Vocational Education. 1987. *Industrial Arts/Technology Education: A Guide for Developing Contemporary Industrial Arts/Technology Education Curricula*. Raleigh: Department of Public Instruction.

Oakes, Jeannie. 1983. Limiting opportunity: Student race and curricular differences in secondary vocational education. *American Journal of Education* 91(3): 328–355.

Oakes, Jeannie. 1985. *Keeping Track: How Schools Structure Inequality*. New Haven, CT: Yale University Press.

Office of Experiment Stations, USDA. 1902. *Extract of 7th Report of the Committee on Methods of Teaching Agriculture*. Circular no. 29. Washington, DC: Government Printing Office.

Olson, Delmar W. 1957. *Technology and Industrial Arts: A Derivation of Subject Matter from Technology*. Ann Arbor, MI: University Microfilms.

O'Neil, J. 1989. Business education: Implementing technology dominates new agenda. *Curriculum Update* (September): 1–2, 6–8.

Ornstein, Allan C., and Francis P. Hunkins. 1988. *Curriculum: Foundations, Principles, and Issues*. Englewood Cliffs, NJ: Prentice Hall.

Paolucci, Bea, and Twyla Shear. 1971. "Home Economics Education: Overview." In *Encyclopedia of Educational Research*, edited by L. C. Deighton, 447–451. New York: Macmillan and the Free Press.

Parmley, J. D., R. F. Wilton, and M. Bender. 1981. *Opinion of Agriculture Teachers, School Administrators, Students and Parents Concerning Females as Agriculture Students, Teachers and Workers in Agriculture*. Manhattan: Department of Adult and Occupational Education, Kansas State University (ERIC no. ED 209 488).

Parsons, Frank. 1909. *Chosing a Vocation*. Boston: Houghton Mifflin.

Pestalozzi, Johann H. 1910. *Pestalozzi's Leonard and Gertrude*, translated and abridged by E. Channing. Boston, MA: Heath.

Peuse, H. Gene, and Burton E. Swanson. 1980. Illinois vocational agriculture teachers' acceptance of an instructional unit on international agriculture. *Journal of the American Association of Teacher Educators in Agriculture* 21(3): 29–34, 65.

Plihal, Jane, Linda Ernst, and Marsha Rehm. 1986. *The Practice of Equity: Access to, Treatment in, and Outcomes of Vocational Education in the Secondary School*. St. Paul: Minnesota Research and Development Center for Vocational Education.

Policies Commission for Business and Economic Education. 1989. *Policy Statements, 1959–1989*. Cincinnati, OH: South-Western.

Pontiac City School District. 1971. *The World of Manufacturing, 1970–71: A Junior High School Industrial Technology Exemplary Program, Final Report*. Pontiac, MI: Pontiac City School District.

Pratzner, Frank C. 1978. *Occupational Ability and Transferable Skills: Project Final Report*. Information series no. 129. Columbus, OH: National Center for Research in Vocational Education (ERIC no. ED 186717).

Pratzner, Frank C., and Jill F. Russell. 1984. *The Changing Workplace: Implications of Quality of Work Life for Vocational Education*. Columbus, OH: National Center for Research in Vocational Education.

Price, Raymond A., Charles R. Hopkins, and Mary Klaurens, eds. 1970. *The Emerging Content and Structure of Business Education*. National Business Education Association Yearbook, no. 8. Washington, DC: National Business Education Association.

Prince, Lucinda W. 1919. *Retail Selling*. Bulletin no. 22, Commercial Education Service no. 1. Washington, DC: Federal Board for Vocational Education.

Prosser, Charles A., and C. R. Allen. 1925. *Vocational Education in a Democracy*. New York: Century.

Redick, Sharon S., and Joan E. Gritzmacher. 1986. *Home Economics Education: A Review and Synthesis of the Research*, 5th ed. Information Series no. 313. Columbus, OH: National Center for Research in Vocational Education.

Reigeluth, Charles, and M. Merrill. 1980. *Extended Task Analysis Procedures User's Manual*. Fort Monroe, VA: U.S. Army Training Development Institute.

Ritz, John M. 1980. Technology as the content base for industrial arts. *Man/Society/Technology* 41(1): 2–4.

Roberts, Roy W. 1965. *Vocational and Practical Arts Education: History, Development, and Principles*, 2nd ed. New York: Harper & Row.

Roberts, Roy W. 1971. *Vocational and Practical Arts Instruction*. New York: Harper & Row.

Ross, W. A. 1942. "Future Farmers of America Organization." In *History of Agriculture Education of Less Than College Grade in the United States*, compiled by Rufus W. Stimson and Frank W. Lothrop, 532–551. Vocational Division Bulletin no. 217, Agricultural Series no. 55. Washington, DC: Office of Education.

Rowe, Kenneth L. 1980. "Leadership in Marketing and Distributive Education." Paper presented to National Conference on Directions in Marketing and Distributive Education, Vail, CO.

Russell, Earl B., and R. L. Courson. 1984. *Illinois Core Curriculum in Agriculture—Phase V*. Staff study. University of Illinois, Urbana.

Samson, Harlan E. 1980. "Distributive Education: Identity and Image." Paper presented to National Conference on Directions in Marketing and Distributive Education, Vail, CO.

Sapre, Padamaker M., ed. 1981. *Early Leaders in Business Education at New York University*. Reston, VA: National Business Education Association.

Sapre, Padamaker M. 1989. *Toward a Redefinition of Business Education*. 13th Annual Peter L. Agnew Memorial Lecture, Alpha Chapter Delta Pi Epsilon, March 15, 1988, New York University. Pamphlet edited by Daniel S. Marone and Ronald Colefield, New York University, New York.

Savage, E. A. 1989. *A Model for Technology Education in Ohio: A Product of the Model Industrial Technology Systems Project*. Bowling Green: Bowling Green State University and Ohio Department of Education, Division of Elementary and Secondary Education and Vocational and Career Education.

Scheffler, Israel. 1985. *Of Human Potential*. Boston, MA: Routledge & Kegan Paul.

Schön, Donald A. 1983. *The Reflective Practitioner*. New York: Basic Books.

Schorr, Lisbeth B., and Daniel Schorr. 1988. *Within Our Reach: Breaking the Cycle of Disadvantage*. New York: Anchor Press.

Schubert, William H. 1986. *Curriculum: Perspective, Paradigm, and Possibility*. New York: Macmillan.

Scriven, Jolene D., J. L. Holley, K. P. Wagoner, and R. D. Brown. 1981. *National Study of Word Processing Installations in Selected Business Organizations*. A Report of the National Word Processing Research Study of Delta Pi Epsilon. St. Paul, MN: Delta Pi Epsilon (ERIC no. CE 028 787).

Selvidge, Robert W., and Verne C. Fryklund. 1930. *Principles of Trade and Industrial Teaching*. Peoria, IL: Manual Arts Press.

Shor, Ira. 1987. *Culture Wars: School and Society in the Conservative Restoration, 1969–1984*. New York: Routledge & Kegan Paul.

Shor, Ira, and Paolo Freire. 1987. *A Pedagogy for Liberation*. South Hadley, MA: Bergin and Garvey.

Snedden, David. 1915. Vocational education. *The New Republic* 3(28): 40–42.

Snedden, David. 1920. *Vocational Education*. New York: Macmillan.

Snowden, Obed L., and J. H. McMinn. 1971. *In-Service Development of Vocational Teachers for Competencies in Non-Farm Occupations*. Vocational Agriculture Special Project Report. Mississippi State University. (ERIC no. ED 065 673).

Snyder, J. A., and J. F. Hales, eds. 1981. *Jackson's Mill Industrial Arts Curriculum Theory*. Charleston: West Virginia Department of Education.

Spady, William G. 1988. Organizing for results: The basis of authentic restructuring and reform. *Educational Leadership* (October): 4–8.

Spafford, Ivol. 1942. *Fundamentals in Teaching Home Economics*, 2nd ed. New York: Wiley.

Special Task Force to Secretary of Health, Education and Welfare. 1972. *Work in America*. Cambridge, MA: MIT Press.

Spencer, Lyle. 1979, August. "Identifying, Measuring, and Training 'Soft Skill' Competencies Which Predict Performance in Professional, Managerial, and Human Service Jobs." Paper presented at the Soft Skill Analysis Symposium, Army Training Development Institute, Fort Monroe, VA.

Steeb, R. V. 1979. "Industrial Arts and Its Relationship to Vocational Education." In *Industrial Arts Education: Retrospect, Prospect*, edited by G. Eugene Martin, 73–85. Twenty-eighth Yearbook of the American Council on Industrial Arts Teacher Education. Bloomington, IL: McKnight.

Stenzel, K. R. 1979. "A Study Attempting to Establish the Validity of Dairy Farm Manager Competencies," Master's thesis, University of Minnesota, St. Paul.

Stern, David, C. Dayton, I. Paik, A. Weisberg, and J. Evans. 1988. Combining academic and vocational courses in an integrated program to reduce high school dropout rates: Second-year results from replications of the California Peninsula Academics. *Educational Evaluation and Policy Analysis* 10(2): 161–170.

Sternberg, Robert J., and Richard K. Wagner. 1986. *Practical Intelligence*. New York: Cambridge University Press.

Stevens, Glenn Z. 1967. *Agricultural Education*. New York: Center for Applied Research in Education.

Stewart, Bob R., and Gary V. Dill. 1987. Affective work competencies of marketing education students. *Marketing Educator's Journal* 13(1): 36–45.

Stimson, Rufus W. 1922. The relationship of occupational analysis to the project method. *Vocational Education Magazine* 1(1): 12–14.

Stimson, Rufus W., and Frank W. Lathrop. 1942. *History of Agricultural Education of Less Than College Grade in the United States*. Vocational Division Bulletin no. 217, Agricultural Series no. 55. Washington, DC: Office of Education.

Stone, James R. 1985. Outcome standards for secondary marketing education. *Marketing Educators' Journal* 2(1): 32–41.

Super, Donnie E. 1957. *The Psychology of Careers*. New York: Harper & Row.

Super, Donnie E. 1984. "Perspectives on the Meaning and Value of Work." In *Designing Careers: Counseling to Enhance Education, Work, and Leisure*, edited by N. C. Gysbers, 27–53. San Francisco, CA: National Vocational Guidance Association and Jossey-Bass.

Swan, F. F. 1975. "Relation of Home Economics Professors' Philosophic Positions to their Curriculum Beliefs." Unpublished Ph.D. dissertation, Pennsylvania State University, University Park.

Swanson, Gordon I. 1982. "Vocational Education Patterns in the United States." In *Education and Work*, edited by H. F. Silberman, 15–48. Eighty-first Yearbook of the National Society for the Study of Education. Chicago: University of Chicago Press.

Swanson, I. Chester. 1966. *Development of Federal Legislation for Vocational Education*. Chicago: American Technical Society.

Swanson, Richard A. 1981, Summer. Analyzing non-observable work behavior. *Journal of Industrial Teacher Education*. 18: 11–23.

Swanson, Richard A., ed. 1983. *A View of Industry*. St. Paul: University of Minnesota.

Tanner, Daniel, and Laurel N. Tanner. 1980. "The Curriculum and the Emergent Technological Society." Chap. 13 in *Curriculum Development: Theory into Practice*, 2nd ed. New York: Macmillan.

Thomas, Ruth G., ed. 1987. *Higher Order Thinking: Definition, Meaning and Instructional Approaches*. Washington, DC: Home Economics Education Association.

Thomas, Ruth G., Betty D. Cooke, and Scott D. Johnson. 1988. *Thinking Underlying Expertise in Specific Knowledge Domains: Implications for Vocational Education*, edited by R. G. Thomas. St. Paul, MN: MRDCVE.

Thomas, Ruth G., and Len Litowitz. 1986. *Vocational Education and Higher Order Thinking Skills: An Agenda for Inquiry*. St. Paul: Minnesota Research and Development Center for Vocational Education.

Thomas, Ruth G., and Michelle Englund. 1989. *Instructional Design for Developing Higher Order Thinking. Vol. I: Knowledge Domain Development*. St. Paul: Minnesota Research and Development Center for Vocational Education.

Th[illegible] "H[illegible] Hermeneutics: A Lens of Analysis for Home Economics." Paper presented at the Annual Meeting of the American Educational Research Association, San Francisco, CA, 16–20 April (ERIC no. ED 278 614).

Tindall, Lloyd W. 1988. *Retaining At-Risk Students: The Role of Career and Vocational Education*. Columbus, OH: Center on Education and Training for Employment.

Tonne, Herbert A. 1971. "Business Education: Overview." In *The Encyclopedia of Education*, edited by L. Deighton, 507–511. New York: Macmillan and the Free Press.

Towers, Edward R., D. J. Lux, and W. E. Ray. 1966. *A Rationale and Structure for Industrial Arts Subject Matter*. Columbus: Ohio State University Research Foundation.

Towers, Edward R., D. J. Lux, and W. E. Ray. 1967. *Industrial Arts Curriculum Project for the Junior High School: A Final Report*. Columbus: Ohio State University.

Trapnell, Gail. 1980. "Power and Influence." Paper presented to National Conference on Directions in Marketing and Distributive Education, Vail, CO.

True, Alfred C. 1929. *A History of Agricultural Education in the United States, 1785–1925*. Washington, DC: Government Printing Office.

Trump, J. Lloyd, and Delmas F. Miller. 1968. *Secondary School Curriculum Improvement: Proposals and Procedures*. Boston, MA: Allyn & Bacon.

Twining, John, Stanley Nisbet, and Jacquetta Megarry, eds. 1977. *World Yearbook of Education 1987: Vocational Education*. New York: Nichols.

Umstattd, William D. 1976. "Manufacturing Education Curriculum Project." Paper presented at the American Industrial Arts Association Conference, Des Moines, IA.

U.S. Office of Education. 1938. *Industrial Arts: Its Interpretation in American Schools*. Bulletin 1937, no. 34. Washington, DC: Government Printing Office.

U.S. Office of Education. 1966a. *Objectives for Vocational and Technical Eduction in Agriculture*, no. 4. Washington, DC: Government Printing Office.

U.S. Office of Education. 1966b. *Industrial Arts Education: A Survey of Programs, Teachers, Students, and Curriculum*. Circular no. 791. Washington, DC: Government Printing Office.

U.S. Office of Education. 1969. *Distributive Education in the High School: A Suggested Guide*. Washington, DC: Government Printing Office.

U.S. Office of Education. 1978. *Distributive Education Programs: A Program Information Publication*. Washington, DC: Government Printing Office.

Vaughn, Gladys G. 1974. Development of a Conceptual Base for Home Economics Curriculum in Grades Five Through Eight. Unpublished Ph.D. dissertation, University of Maryland, College Park.

Venn, Grant. 1964. *Man, Education, and Work: Postsecondary Vocational and Technical Education*. Washington, DC: American Council on Education.

V-TECS. Vocational-Technical Education Consortium of States. 1978. *Fourth Progress and Information Report*. Atlanta, GA: Southern Association of Colleges and Schools (ERIC no. ED 154 109).

Walsh, John P., and William Selden. 1965. "Vocational Education in the Secondary School." In *Vocational education*, edited by Melvin I. Barlow, 88–134. Sixty-fourth Yearbook of the National Society for the Study of Education, Part I. Chicago: University of Chicago Press.

Warner, William E. 1965. *A Curriculum to Reflect Technology*. Columbus, OH: Epsilon Pi Tau.

Weade, Regina, and Joan Gritzmacher. 1987. Personality characteristics and curriculum design preferences of vocational home economics educators. *Journal of Vocational Education Research* 12(2): 1–18.

Weber, James W., Nancy Puleo, and Paula Kurth. 1989. A look at basic academic skills reinforcement/enhancement efforts in secondary vocational classrooms. *Journal of Vocational Education Research* 14(1): 27–47.

Weiss, Janice H. 1978. "Educating for Clerical Work: A History of Commercial Education in the United States Since 1850." Unpublished Ph.D. dissertation, Harvard University, Cambridge, MA.

Welch, Lila M., and Mary R. Lingenfelter, comps. 1930. *Studies of the Home Economics Curriculum: An Annotated Bibliography*. Columbus: Bureau of Educational Research, Ohio State University.

Wichowski, Chester. 1981, December. "Curriculum Needs Assessment: A Model for Trade and Industrial Education Decision-Making." Paper presented at the American Vocational Association convention, Atlanta, GA. (ERIC no. ED 226 169).

William T. Grant Foundation Commission on Work, Family and Citizenship. 1988. *The Forgotten Half: Pathways to Success for America's Youth and Young Families*. Washington, DC: William T. Grant Commission on Work, Family and Citizenship.

Williams, Terry, Robert Berns, and Betty Heath-Sipos. 1979. *Task Validation of 16 General Merchandising Department Store Occupations*. Washington, DC: Office of Education.

Wirt, John G., L. D. Muraskin, D. A. Goodwin, and R. H. Meyer. 1989. *Summary of Findings and Recommendations*. Vol. 1, Final Report. Washington, DC: National Assessment of Vocational Education.

Wirth, Arthur G. 1972. *Education in the Technological Society*. Scranton, NJ: Intext.

Wirth, Arthur G. 1974. Philosophical issues in the vocational-liberal studies controversy (1900–1927): John Dewey vs. the social efficiency philosophers. *Studies in Philosophy and Education* 8(3): 105–118.

Wirth, Arthur G. 1981. "The Historical and Social Context of Career Education." In *Readings in Career Education*, edited by H. C. Kazanas, 34–44. Peoria, IL: Bennett.

Wirth, Arthur G. 1983. *Productive Work in Industry and School*. Lanham, MD: University Press of America.

Wisconsin Department of Public Instruction. 1984. *Industry and Technology Education: A Guide for Developing Contemporary Industrial Arts/Technology Education Curricula*. Madison: Wisconsin Department of Public Instruction.

Wisconsin Department of Public Instruction. 1987. *A Guide to Curriculum Planning in Marketing Education*. Madison: Wisconsin Department of Public Instruction.

Wright, R. Thomas. 1982. Industry as the content base for industrial arts. *Man/Society/Technology* 41(4): 2–4.

Wubbens, Dennis. 1982. Fifty-seven program standards identified as very important—a peer review. *Marketing and Distributive Educator's Digest* 7(2): 8–14.

Yoho, Lewis W. 1969. Systems, concepts with implications for industrial and technical education. *Journal of Industrial Teacher Education* 6(2): 5–19.

Zuga, Karen F. 1987. "Trapped in a Technocratic Ideology." Paper presented at the American Educational Research Association Conference, Washington, DC.

32

BECOMING KNOWLEDGE: THE EVOLUTION OF ART EDUCATION CURRICULUM

Dennie Palmer Wolf
HARVARD GRADUATE SCHOOL OF EDUCATION

THE EMERGENCE OF THE ARTS AS WAYS OF KNOWING

There has been a major shift in the curriculum and the conduct of arts education over the last century. This shift might be registered in the statistics that suggest the arts are gaining wider acceptance: Music is taught in 93 percent of schools, art in 90 percent; by 1989, 22 states will have graduation requirements that include the arts (Lehman and Sinatra 1988). But those numbers tell too simple a story of "spread" when deeper changes have occurred.

Since the formation of the common curriculum for public schools at the turn of the last century, arts educators have struggled to have the arts taken seriously. Recurrently, arts education has had the place of an exponent of values and citizenship (think of the posters and essays students contribute to current substance-abuse campaigns); a special program (such as bilingual education or black history) to be funded in flush, politically generous, and fully enrolled times; or an accessory (such as French club or a swimming pool). As such, it has been both marginal and vulnerable, often shifting in chameleonlike ways simply to survive: arguing at one moment that drawing teaches industrially relevant skills, that dance or theater training yields self-confidence, or that the presence of an arts program is a sign of a "good" school. To counter the view of arts education as little else than catechism, therapy, or merit badge—a handmaiden to *other* causes—arts educators have had to make Yeats's point:

> Better go down upon your marrow bones
> And scrub a kitchen pavement, or break stones
> Like an old pauper, in all kinds of weather;
> For to articulate sweet sounds together
> Is to work harder than all these.

In short, they have had to become increasingly articulate about *the arts as a distinct form of knowledge*, requiring sustained and demanding work and yielding kinds of empathy, understanding, and skill both equal to and distinctive from those available in chemistry, civics, or shop.

It is the emergence of this point of view about the place of the arts in schools that marks a radical change in arts education. What now arises is the question of whether, given the history of the arts in the schools, this point of view can be realized in classrooms, not just in literature reviews. Can it inform curriculum, teaching, and learning?

Overview

The first portion of this chapter outlines the gradual creation of the outlook and practices that treat the arts as a

The preparation of this chapter was made possible by a grant from the Rockefeller Foundation and conversations with colleagues willing to share expertise that was not originally mine: Lyle Davidson, Howard Gardner, Steve Seidel, Nancy Smith, and Thomas Wolf among them.

way of knowing and the school as a place where that kind of knowledge can be acquired. I will argue that this took place in four major steps or shifts, each of which yielded both contributions and lasting tensions for curriculum in arts education. The evolution began with the inclusion of drawing and music in the common curriculum of the comprehensive public school at the end of the 19th century. Later, with the appearance of progressive education and the child study movement, arts educators began to argue for the *distinctive* role of arts education. That role was essentially a psychological one: The arts, it was argued, were *the* occasion within schooling to engage in self-discovery and to become creative. Subsequently, it was the work in child development and the arts, carried out largely since the 1960s, that provided a vivid picture of how art, music, theater, and dance involve more than the expression of interest or talent. Through research and naturalistic observation, arts educators came to argue that painting, acting, dancing, or music making schooled children in how to articulate their experience via symbol systems, using the rules, conventions, and value systems their culture offered. Neither symbolization nor rule making was a matter of spontaneous unfolding. As such, the arts inevitably involved *active thought* and demanded *thoughtful instruction*. Building on this picture of the arts as thought provoking, arts educators have questioned aspects of the older, child- and studio-centered notions of arts education and raised questions about the integrity of a "school art" that is cut off from the expert practices of artists, historians, critics, and philosophers of art. Put differently, the central image, or the imagined endpoint for arts education, has shifted from craftsman to artist to symbol user and thinker and, now, to a much more composite and fully dimensional figure: the painter informed by art history or the concert goer whose hearing is informed by the risks and demands of playing an instrument (Eisner 1972; Smith 1987).

The shifts in imagery outlined above amount to more than changing fashions in arts education. Far from being just fluctuations, each of these phases has contributed distinctively to the development of arts education. Thus, at this moment, arts education can be said to have a place in the common curriculum, a distinctive body of knowledge and practices, a growing sense for plausible sequences of development and learning, and, finally, an incipient relation to expert practice in a range of arts and art-related disciplines. But along with this kind of self-definition have come all the complex outcomes of maturity—recurrent debates, different camps, and the responsibility not to carp from the margin but to design and sustain long-term, consistent efforts at serious instruction. Like science education (American Association for the Advancement of Science 1989) or foreign language teaching (Hirsch 1989), arts education is now coherent enough to be marked by the tensions of its own history and evolution. From its earliest conceptualization as craftsmanship, arts education remains marked by an emphasis on exercise and skills that is deeply at odds with the long-term, restless, and thoughtful nature of mature production or perception in the arts. Dating from the period in which arts educators argued that the arts taught creativity, there has been a tension about the preciousness of arts education: Are standards destructive? Shouldn't we protect children's imaginations from the rigors of formal notation or the rules of perspective? Isn't encouragement more important than critique? The intensely developmental work of the 1960s and 1970s, with its assumptions about universal sequences of learning, yielded lasting questions about whose growth was to be taken as normative and whose art was to serve as exemplar and endpoint. This is the problem of how, having been forged so much out of modern and Western concerns, art education in America can make space for either the art of much earlier or much different cultures. As arts educators turn their attention to the expert practices of a range of arts-related disciplines, they face the danger of turning arts education experiences into exercises in higher-order thinking skills that "happen" to use the content of the arts as chief illustrations.

By way of conclusion, the final section focuses on arts education in the larger context of schools as institutions and curricula as tools. Together the institutional fabric of schools and the implicit values of curricula teach much more than specific content (the nines table or the Civil War) or distinct processes (how to write a book report; how to take apart a word problem). They convey fundamental attitudes to learning (Henry 1963; Katz 1973). So, in these last pages, the question is, "What could the presence of a full-fledged arts curriculum provoke as questions or worthwhile experiments within schooling or curriculum design understood more broadly?"

A Point of View

Like all stories, the one told here neatens and shapes the facts in order to give a compelling, or at least a coherent, account. In the living of it, there was no such neat layer-cake emergence to arts education—each of the moments described has more ancient roots, and each of them continues on, very much alive.

A Focused Account. None of the periods described here was, in fact, a wholesale swing to an utterly new point of view—at most, there was a shift only in the center of gravity, with many dissenting opinions still vocal. Consequently, they are not really neat periods but more like four slices into time. And the four moments described here are certainly not stages in the sense of being progressive developments. Rather, the debates and efforts of the later period have the advantages of retrospection and of building on the work of earlier teachers and researchers—that is all.

The account is also lopsided. Visual arts and music take the lion's share in the school day—quite simply because the traditions of history, professional writing, and curriculum research are older and better established in those fields than in dance or theater, not to mention film or photography. Consequently, theater, dance, and other forms are mentioned less often, but when they are mentioned, they are powerfully relevant. To avoid clumsiness in the writing, the term "arts education" is used when talking about broad trends in education, while more specific terms, such as "music education," appear when that particular discipline is focal. In order to demonstrate the influence of the shifting images of artistry on curriculum, each section contains a central example of curriculum that comes from each period of change. This is not meant to exclude, only to provide a way of offering closely argued and detailed material rather than a cursory examination of the critical issues.

It is also true that this story, like any other, is told from a certain vantage point. Here the perspective includes the belief that the arts *are* a kind of knowledge, just as distinctive, coherent, and powerfully organized as the knowledge of science or history (Habermas 1971). From a psychological perspective, work in the arts has, time and again, been shown to demand higher-order thinking: analysis, inference, problem finding, and problem solving (Getzels and Csikszentmihalyi 1976; Resnick 1987). Even among students, who are still learning the ropes, we have strong evidence that choreographing a dance, making a series of woodblock prints, or listening closely to a piece of music engages not just the hand or the ears but also the mind (Barylick 1983; Reimer 1989; Wolf 1988a, 1989a, 1989b; Zessoules 1990). Similarly, we know that practices like rehearsal or revision demand strategic and metacognitive operations—self-monitoring, perspective taking, standard setting—all too often associated only with logic, chess, or higher mathematics (Brown and Smiley 1978; Scribner 1984). Similar points can also be made from a more academic vantage. Even though the arts have often been argued to be ends in themselves, quite unlike carpentry or gardening, they also have long and consistent histories of scholarship, which raise and pursue issues about the universality and variation in human experience that are just as large, and applicable, as the mathematician's questions about order and pattern in the universe. At the same time, the arts are a distinct way of knowing, characterized by specific tools, practices, and beliefs about what makes a performance or an object handsome, moving, or worth returning to time and time again (College Entrance Examination Board 1980; Eisner 1972). As will be described later, the particular nature of the art work concerns expression, fashioning, and the capacity to invent realities.

THE EMERGENCE OF ARTS EDUCATION AS A FIELD OF KNOWLEDGE

What follows is one account of the evolution of the arts education curriculum. But it is not the story of the making of a field in the sense of a history of certification, the appearance of arts education in the curricula of normal schools or graduate programs, or the emergence of professional organizations like Music Educators National Conference (MENC), National Art Educators Association (NAEA), or the National Dance Association. Nor is it an account of the shifts in the daily "stuff" of arts education: shifts in the songs taught to children, the practices for teaching painting, or the entry of dance or photography into the curriculum. Both of those histories are vital, but different from the one told here. The focus here falls on the gradual appearance of a conceptual framework for a curriculum in arts education. This framework includes the argument that the arts represent a distinctive form of knowledge, but it is more extensive. It also includes the belief that the arts should be a part of the common curriculum for *all*, not just talented individuals. The framework has entailed developmental research to show that there are sequences of development typical for anyone learning an art form and, consequently, that artistic and aesthetic knowledge can be learned and taught. They are not simply matters of genes or inspiration. Finally, this argument has also involved an effort to connect what occurs in classrooms with the sophisticated practices coming from studios, museums, performance halls, and universities.

The Arts Enter the Common Curriculum: Art and Music for All

(Good music tends) to improve the heart, and thus to be instrumental in promoting the cause of human happiness, virtue, and religion. (Lowell Mason, *Manual of the Boston Academy of Music*, 1843; quoted in Choksy et al. 1986, 6)

In the late 19th century, American politicians and taxpayers at last took on large-scale social responsibilities: caring for the sick, attending to the mentally ill, offering services to the poor, and providing public education to all children, not just the well-to-do and willing (Katz 1973; Tyack 1974). In that framework, public schools were conceived and designed as an organized effort to cope with a pressing social problem: an ethnically and economically diverse population of unemployed and potentially unemployable youth, all too likely to become a drain on other social institutions, such as hospitals and poorhouses. Together with the order of a scheduled class day, the curriculum was envisioned as the chief tool for social change or control within schools. It would convey not just job skills but also forms of social organization, work habits, and an intimate knowledge of rewards and risks. The debate over the curriculum was shaped by several competing rhetorics. On the one hand, there was the ennobling amalgam of Jeffersonian ideals of a wise and literate electorate and the tough Jacksonian myth of access for all (meaning hard-working white boys with the mettle of a Lincoln, an Edison, or an Horatio Alger). This was counterbalanced by a determination to found and run an efficient social institution that would turn out civil, reliable, and skilled workers for offices and factories. It is in this crucible that American public education, and with it arts education, took its original shape.

The results were in many respects jarring and incompatible. What issued forth was a line of argument about the place of the arts—not just as culture or knowledge (Korzenik 1985) but as carriers of moral values (Freedman and Popkewitz 1988; Wygant 1983). Schools, and arts education as a curricular tool, were to be institutions of Americanization; they were to help immigrant children shed feudal and class-riddled values they brought with them, along with their strange last names. Becoming American meant turning away from European culture and values.

Nowhere is this Americanizing impulse more evident than in one of the earliest forms of aesthetic education: von Rydingsvard's system of picture study. In this system art was deracinated from its European status and tamed by being transformed into something closer to bible or tract. Mass-produced sets of artists' reproductions were sold to the schools, accompanied by manuals instructing teachers how to use the images and their implied narratives to teach the worth of hard work, struggle, and perseverance and to portray the greatness of the emerging American nature. Thus, von Rydingsvard suggests that, using a portrait of a peasant girl, teachers should instruct children:

> The peasants in Europe are very poor. That is why so many of them like to come to our country. . . . Think how many things you have to be thankful for, to which those peasant children are not born! Do you believe you are grateful enough for having been born in so glorious a country as the United States, where the best in education and art, as well as freedom of life and thought, is the birthright of all her sons and daughters? If you have not begun to express your gratitude and show your love for your country, begin today, and you will grow up to be a better citizen, a credit to your native land, and a help to your fellow-men. (quoted in Logan 1955)

In this way, traditions and images that had their roots in European art became a tool for turning away from Europe and its culture. But when one looks at von Rydingsvard's picture study, what is perhaps most striking is the particular role carved out for arts education: It was not a field of study, so much as it was a tool or an occasion for producing citizens, a way to smooth, to civilize, and to inculcate. It was, in this respect, more a catechism or a civics than a history or a mathematics. It was a handmaiden and an amplifier, not a field of study in its own right.

Similar conceptions of arts education pervaded moments when students engaged in studio practice. There the arts were used in the service of job training, with classroom time spent in practices designed to train journeymen rather than artists or concert goers. In 1870, Walter Smith, an English art teacher and headmaster, came to Boston to fill the position of state art director. His program was centered on the notion that the public schools should develop drawing skills useful to industry and that they did so best by practicing isolated elements of design (the curves, symmetrical bursts, and bandings present in fabric, brick ornament, and wallpaper) repetitively until they achieved a machinelike dependability. Invention, according to Smith, was to be restricted to combinations of previously practiced elements. Like Mason, his musical counterpart, Smith argued for elevation and practiced guildwork, writing:

> Experience has proved that the surest way of elevating public taste and improving all manufacturing industries is to educate all people in the elements of art and science . . . [and] that the mental habit of scientific accuracy . . . will be of social advantage. (quoted in Wygant 1983, 226–227)

Systems like Smith's were to give school children the tools with which to be industrious and to rise beyond what their social origins might predict for them—without encouraging either authorship or invention.

Nor was the situation any different in the field of music education. Horace Mann, in his fury of school reform, insisted that the public schools he was designing should introduce to all what had been the privilege of children of leisured and comfortable parents: drawing, music, and the study of natural objects. Lowell Mason, as one of the earliest and most avid proponents of music in the schools, wrote a deluge of popular articles and song books, each arguing for the power of music to instill virtue in all children who would open their mouths and sing. And yet the dominant practice was to teach music by means of rote repetition—that is, without giving students access to reading music or to playing instruments (Choksy et al. 1986). Musical literacy for all turned out to be little more than reading lyrics and following the teacher's beat.

In this context, arts educators struggled to find basic elements of instruction, routine practices, and modules of activity that resembled the "scientific" and "efficient" kinds of practices being developed concurrently in factories, municipal bureaucracies, and other areas of the curriculum, especially reading and mathematics (Callahan 1962). With the rise of public schools there developed a new market—the production of pupil texts and teachers' materials. Methods and their accompanying materials, like those developed by Smith and von Rydingsvard, appeared, competed hard with one another, and filled classrooms. In effect, they served to spread a view of learning as the partitioned and highly rationalized acquisition of a series of separable skills. In arts curricula, the hallmarks were the lists of *the* elements of design or *the* components of music, along with the accompanying exercises constructed just to highlight quarter-note rests or visual balance—as if rests were not a tool in creating an entire rhythmic pattern that underscores a melodic line.

But it is important to point out that it is with Smith and von Rydingsvard, Mann, and Mason that art and music become part of a *common* curriculum—a conveyer of values rather than a form of knowledge, to be sure—but necessary, not just nice. It was a strange kind of Faustian bargain. The arts were admitted to the common curriculum—so long as they served virtue, religion, citizenship, and industry and so long as they assumed the look, the practices, and the diction of industrial or clerical work. The arts were in the schools, but in classrooms rather than rehearsal spaces or studios, as exercises rather than as sustained artistic projects, judged by neatness and precision rather than by insight or imagination. In essence, the arts were present, but in disguise.

It is all too easy to deride the industrial model of arts education and to vilify its originators. But without the bargain they struck and lived by, it is unlikely that the arts would have become a part of our definition of the school curriculum. In all probability the arts would have stayed where they were centuries before: in the private preserve of those who had leisure enough for trips to paint watercolors of the Italian ruins and money enough for instruments in the sitting room.

The Psychological Contributions of Arts Education

In art education art is used only as a means to an end and not as an end in itself. It is the aim of art education to use the creative process to make people more creative regardless of where this creativeness will be applied. (Viktor Lowenfeld, *Creative and Mental Growth*, 1957, 4–5)

From the Romantics, like Wordsworth and Byron, arts educators inherited an image of art quite different from Mason's virtuous psalms or von Rydingsvard's moral catechism. In the Romantic view, the arts were the result of highly individual acts of imagination. The artist was the ultimate imaginer, and imagination was virtually the antithesis of industrial craft—it was, in Wordsworth's phrase, "the spontaneous overflow of strong feeling."

At the opening of the 20th century, those notions took on new and fiercer meanings. Stravinsky and Schoenberg shattered conventional musical structures, playing with bitonality and atonality. Cézanne's geometry dissolved even further, yielding the tilted tables and multiple faces of late cubism, and modernist poetry (as well as psychoanalysis) insisted on another, different semantics—one of dreams, ancient images, and free association. World War I pierced American isolationism, and many of these ideas reached "home," as Europeans fled the devastation and Americans returned.

At the same time, the arts and crafts movements in Europe and in America, drawing on the influence of figures like William Morris, pulled away in horror and disgust from the manufacturing and manufactured environment, calling for art to act as the antidote, the protection, and the refuge from the ugly maw of the industrial wasteland. Handmade dishes, printed fabrics, and, eventually, the customized and carefully detailed architecture of Frank Lloyd Wright appeared.

By the late 19th century, there was considerable interest in the origins of many things—species, civilizations, and human thought. Early on, this interest focused on things like archaeology and evolution. Later, it turned to childhood. Social reformers like Jane Addams and Lewis Hine drew attention to the plight of the industrial poor of cities, with a poignant emphasis on the waste of children's lives. Their work came back repeatedly to the refrain of how early young lives could be warped by poverty, disease, and alcohol. From an entirely different vantage point, Freud proposed that very sophisticated mechanisms of mind—dreaming, defenses, symbolization, and sexuality—had their origins in the early years. He even argued for the analogy between the poet daydreaming and the child at play (Freud 1958). The upshot was a picture of childhood as utterly formative. Between Victorian times and the 1930s, children went from being "seen and not heard" to being viewed as the great originals. So profoundly was this the case that years later, Picasso (with who knows what degree of irony) could quip that he had "spent many years learning to draw like a child."

Traditional educational paradigms dissolved and shifted, just as pictorial space or the language of poetry fractured. In Vienna, in a cabin, in a garden, Erik Erikson taught Anna Freud's patients, throwing away the classical chalkboard and texts in favor of "projects" in which all forms of knowledge were brought together through field trips from which drawings, essays, and questions flowed. In America, John Dewey and his colleagues developed the tenets of progressive education, drawing on an older tradition of child-centered education initiated by European educators like Froebel (1887) and Pestalozzi (Green 1978).

In the wake of these broader cultural changes, arts education took on a new shape. No longer a route into social values, it became a safeguard against the routine, the regular, and the predictable, something like an occasion, or a medium, for the development of creativity. Given their openness to invention, the plasticity of their raw materials, and their ability to carry multiple messages, arts experiences were envisioned as *the* ground for self-discovery, invention, and expression (Wolf, Smith, and Gardner 1982). In this light, the dominant image for arts education became the studio. Children were artists. And they were to play, discover, and invent rather than to be taught, to practice, or to copy. Teachers were not masters but keepers of the ateliers. Far from silent, they were active but not authoritarian. They arranged materials, engaged students in thought-provoking talk, probed, asked questions, and helped children formulate evaluations. The arts were an ideal site for this kind of collaboration, largely because there were "no right answers." As realms in which it was possible to invent forms and meanings, educators argued that the arts were healing, confirming, and even therapeutic. In addition, they argued that from the spontaneous playfulness of young children we could deduce that growth in the arts would occur naturally (Barkan 1966; Feldman 1986, 1987; Smith 1987). But chiefly and centrally, arts educators lobbied for a view of painting, singing, dancing, and pretending as extending the child's creativity. Moreover, they promised that the creative spark seeded by the arts would, with time and permission, become a part of the child's personality.

The argument is interesting for how far from and how close to the earlier rationales for arts education it is. At the far reaches of this promise of creativity was the implication that painting would produce inventive policymakers, patent procurers, and homemakers who could furnish a nifty living room on a shoestring. But there is also a new element: Another impulse behind Lowenfeld (1957) is the idea that the arts are not just apt occasions for the practice of general skills. They should have a distinct place in the curriculum since they make a unique contribution.

Perhaps nowhere is this impulse to release the natural creativity of children more evident than in the burst of music education methods that came to influence curriculum in American schools by midcentury, particularly those pioneered by Jaques-Dalcroze, Orff, and Kodaly. The earliest of these music educators, Jaques-Dalcroze was, after his own conservatory training in Vienna, at odds with the abstract manner in which musical understanding was taught by means of exercises in the principles of theory and notation, to the exclusion of work in expression and interpretation. He was convinced that the source of musical understanding was in emotions, not technique. In his search to understand the sound–feeling connection, he was captivated by the intuitive and unconscious behaviors he observed in his students: their facial expressions, swaying, and foot tapping as they played or listened to music. He was convinced that these were the primitive forms of the emotive musical understanding he sought. Throughout the rest of his career he explored the possibility of several aspects of body–emotion–music connections. In his techniques of eurhythmics and kinesthesia, he used the body's motions as the fundamental text for learning the essence of rhythm. In solfege, or sight singing, he used the voice as the entry to teaching pitch and melodic contour. In his work with improvisation he insisted that children begin their encounters with composition, not with formal patterns but with playful explorations. His notions of keyboard training provide clear samples of this approach: Rather than scales or arpeggios, Jaques-Dalcroze insisted that beginning students play with the piano strings—plucking, striking, stroking—and silencing the sounds in experimental ways. Later they were to play note clusters on black keys with the entire palm so as to avoid the strain and boredom of early single-finger playing. These clusters rapidly turned into compositions in melodramas (improvisations accompanying stories) and improvised dialog (improvisations built from conversational patterns).

In Hellerau, Germany, Jaques-Dalcroze established a theater and a school devoted to new methods of performance. To that theater came many artists and educators. Among them was Carl Orff, a young German composer who was intrigued by the improvisational techniques and innovative styles of "the New Dance Wave." In collaboration with a dancer, Dorothy Gunther, Orff began to explore how young dancers and players might be trained to take an active role in the innovative theater he envisioned. But if performers were to break free of scores to improvise, they had to be skilled, independent thinkers in charge of the materials. Orff invented what he came to call the "elemental style," in which both dance and music were distilled into their most basic components (beat, meter, tempo, etc.) and mastered *through performance*. To make this possible, Orff and his colleagues developed an entire line of simplified instruments, based on African xylophones and Indonesian percussion pieces. Later, when he added voices to his *Musik fur Kinder* it was not the typical adult lyrics written for children. Instead, he turned to what he saw as the "natural" sounds of childhood: shouts, chants, and children's rhymes.

Orff developed what Jaques-Dalcroze began. Both pictured music as fundamentally creative rather than re-creative, as expressive rather than technical, and as a personally fulfilling rather than a conventional activity. The methods they invented assume children's innate musical capacities and their ability to create novel musical patterns given only their bodies and voices. It is musical training that is child centered and experiential and that has as its cornerstone an image of the child as a composer and a performing artist (Choksy et al. 1986).

There were similar developments in theater, where the interest in children as small adult actors, learning lines and stage mannerisms, gave way to a focus on imaginative play and creative dramatics. Theater educators were concerned about the damage that could be done to children, and their understanding of drama, if they were put through the rigors of doing a rehearsed piece for adults, according to rules and for reasons they might not understand (Bolton 1989; Slade 1954; Way 1967). The new focus settled instead on the uses of drama for personal development, particularly the unfolding of a dramatic imagination. Just as Jaques-Dalcroze and Orff shifted attention away from scores onto improvisation, theater educators also turned to improvisation as a more spontaneous and child-centered entry to an art form (Courtney 1968). Rather than lines and literary delivery, they wanted children to understand how to create imagined worlds and how to stand in another's shoes. But much as in the adult theater of the period, following the lead of Stanislavsky, and later Method acting, filling another's shoes involved much more than learning a part and the accompanying stage business. It meant becoming the character, entering not just his "here and now" but his psychological skin. This sort of activity, like being an Orff musician, demanded improvisation. Hence, even as actors, students were meant to be playwrights of a kind, "finding" the right gestures, postures, and motions to sustain their characters (Heathcote 1980).

From the vantage point of 1990, it has become fashionable to question and doubt our most immediate ancestors—notably the generation of arts educators who saw in dance, theater, music, or painting the opportunity for all children to become creative (Barkan 1966; Getty Center for Arts Education 1985; Feldman 1987). From the position of educators interested in school reform, excellence, expert systems, and cultural literacy, the earlier emphasis on feeling, discovery, and a child-centered curriculum appears loose and undisciplined. The belief in the unfolding of the child's innate understanding of rhythm or images strikes educators as naively unaware of the social conventions and issues of craft, which are an inevitable part of the making of images, poems, or dances (Wilson and Wilson 1977) or the ways in which arts learning require rigorous, continuous instruction (Feldman 1986, 1987). The image of the child as artist seems romantic, overblown, and misplaced, given how few adults ever become musicians, dancers, actors, or painters compared to listeners, audience members, or viewers (Feldman 1967, 1970, 1985; Reimer 1989; Smith 1987). Even on their own chosen grounds, educators who argued that the arts were *the* occasion for the development of creativity were frankly wrong. The capacity for improvisation or invention is certainly a part of science (American Association for the Advancement of Science 1989) and essential to good history (Holt 1990; Woodward 1989).

But a critique that goes no further misunderstands or caricatures the seminal contribution of the child study movement and progressive education. This is the widespread conviction that the arts are not merely an occasion for inculcating values or conveying industrially useful skills. Instead, they require that individuals make use of a quite different sort of process than the understanding that underlies either daily problem solving, or work in science, mathematics, or languages. These include the emotional availability, playful exploration, and improvisation stressed by Jaques-Dalcroze and Orff and the empathy and perspective taking underscored by early theater educators.

Arts Education as an Instance of Development: Symbols and Rules

> Perhaps most notable about sequence in drawings is the degree of order and consistency children reveal, even as young as three, four, or five. At a time when in much of their other behavior they appear whimsical, irrational, or easily distracted by the least thing to come along, their drawings reveal a great deal of order. In a sense they proceed according to plan. To me, the discovery of this orderly sequence is as important as the finding that young children's language follows discernible rules. . . . In all these cases children's behavior follows an identifiable principle that can be seen to change with age. So the apparent disorder in children's behavior—its apparent lack of principles or rules—is due to our own ignorance of the principles they work by. (Goodnow 1977, 51)

During the 1960s and 1970s, researchers documented the early, and stunning, regularities in children's language acquisition (Brown 1973). Simultaneously, the Swiss psychologist Jean Piaget provided careful observations of children counting stones, pouring water, or playing marbles and, in so doing, described them not as free spirits at play but as incipient scientists and philosophers chipping away at the major cognitive and moral issues of life (Piaget 1963, 1965). In this context, the image of 5-year-olds or adolescents as trainable blank slates faded, replaced by a conception of them as active, constructive problem solvers and world makers (Bruner 1968). The consequences for the continuing construction of a rationale and theory of curriculum for arts education were enormous. In that context, arts education was, at least partially, reconceptualized as an occasion for thoughtfulness.

As in previous periods, this shift in arts education did not occur *sui generis*. It was part of a broader network of changes in a society at large. In this period, a rather different kind of artist and artistry emerged. The romantic view of the emotionally motivated artist that still dominated movements like abstract expressionism was complemented, if not replaced, by an image of artists as thinkers and systematizers. This is evident in work by composers like Milton Babbitt and Philip Glass, choreographers like Cunningham and Tharp, or painters like Josef Albers and Agnes Martin, who explored the mystery of apparently rational geometries in which a clean perceptual order gave both beauty and feeling. At the same time, many psychologists broke with associationist and behaviorist frameworks and took a new interest in issues like thought, mind, and representation. Educators, meanwhile, in reaction to the mixed results of progressive education and in the wake of the Russians sending the first satellite into orbit, became concerned with getting back to "the basics" and to the pursuit of excellence rather than individuality or expression.

What was in the 1920s and 1930s a view of arts education as the unfolding of children's creativity shifted to a view of the arts as an instance of *earned* conceptual development. Observers looked beyond the "whimsical" and "irrational" for the "great deal of order" that Goodnow refers to. Researchers and educators contended that children gradually *constructed* (not discovered) the possibilities of reference and the rule systems of music, art, theater, and dance in their culture. This was as true for perceptual activities as it was for painting, singing, or dancing. A young viewer had to do the complex work of understanding that aesthetic perception was a different enterprise from simple observation, or even careful investigation. Clearly, then, the arts were a matter of learning, not discovery, and they deserved careful instruction, not just mere opportunity.

Some of the strongest examples of this reconceptualization come from the visual arts. A number of researchers and educators became involved in an effort to describe the stages of development *in order to provide a reasoned basis for arts instruction*. This was hardly the first effort of its kind, since similar investigations had been going on for nearly a hundred years. But what was new was the emphasis on how children *worked* their way from stage to stage, rather than "just" discovering new possibilities for reference and expression in their paintings and drawings (Arnheim 1969, 1974; Goodnow 1977; Werner and Kaplan 1963). Unlike earlier accounts by descriptive researchers like Luquet (1917) and Kellogg (1969), these portraits stressed the mechanisms and sources of children's changing notions of pictorial possibilities: the properties of media (Arnheim 1969, 1974; Golomb 1974; Smith 1982); copying and interacting with peers (Wilson and Wilson 1977); and the ability to plan and execute sequences of behavior (Freeman 1980; Goodnow 1977). The resulting portrait of children's drawings did not change radically: The drawing stages described still went from scribbling to marking to shape making and picturing. But there was a major revolution in the description of development as *achieved* rather than as *assured*. Since that was the case, moment-to-moment instruction (not just an overall philosophy or a generous environment) played a significant role. Arts curriculum was reconceived, not as simply enabling development but as drawing it forward by providing the kinds of materials and interactions that would help children growing up in a relatively artless culture to understand the place of expression or the exploration of the qualitative aspects of experience. This work was to *combine* enabling and explicit tuition about art and materials.

An excellent example comes from the materials that grew out of Follow-Through, the Bank Street model for the continuation of the Head Start Program through the primary school years. (The version used here is that published a number of years later in *Experience and Art*, a book for teachers by N. R. Smith 1982.)

While acknowledging that the arts are distinctive "because in them, it is important to consider the expressive qualities of form," the introduction continues, "In the past much attention has been paid to understanding the emotions that underlie children's art work. However, this book emphasizes the *thinking or cognitive processes* behind children's painting" (Smith 1982, xiii). In addition, the author distinguishes her approach from earlier romantic images of the child as an analog to the adult artist: "A clear distinction is drawn between the creativity of adult artists and that of children. The effort of children to find means of organizing and making images is the creativity of the child" (xiv). Later, she makes clear why developmental studies can inform instruction:

> Children exercise . . . aesthetic understandings within developmental limits, and adults must learn to recognize the types of meaning and organization appropriate to each phase in the sequence of development. In order to be able to do this, it is important to study the course of children's art closely. (Smith 1982, 12)

What follows is a series of chapters, each devoted to a particular period of painting development, illustrated with careful field notes on the process of actual paintings. Each chapter closes with a discussion of how teachers can get children started thinking about the paintings they want to make and how they can sustain children's work through thought-provoking comments and responses to that work.

In the chapter on 9- through 12-year-olds, Smith observes:

> Another pictorial device that appears with the advent of more complex thought is the metaphorical use of images. . . . The ability to use visual images for nonconcrete entities like concepts . . . depends on being able to entertain two levels of symbolization at one time. The artist must decide which object best represents the concept and then which lines, shapes, and colors best represent the object. (88–89)

Later, in discussing a young girl's stylized painting of a cat on a cushion, she suggests the kind of response that would both recognize and teach: "You simplified the shapes of the cat and the cushion, made a strong pattern for the wallpaper, and a strong texture for the rug. These make your composition strong and bold, but the shapes and textures you made are soft. The result is a strong painting about a soft and tender subject." Here teaching is an act that balances an understanding of the issues of art (e.g., visual metaphor, not neatness) and the developmental state of the child. It is not simply nurturance; instead, it is a kind of dialogue *structured* to focus the child's attention on the visual and aesthetic properties of her painting and, so, of painting more generally.

In the case of music, there was a similar effort to create a map of the cognitive changes in musical *understanding*, as opposed to the acquisition of technical performance. Researchers turned away (to some extent) from studies of children's pitch matching and note recognition and sought out the kinds of products and performances that would expose the principles on which children organized their musical ideas and systems. Consequently, there was considerable interest in the way children learned new songs, the way they notated musical patterns, and the structures they gave to songs they invented. The search was to infer the underlying *rules* or conceptual frameworks that characterized beginning versus more sophisticated performances (Bamberger 1982; Davidson and Colley 1987; Dowling and Harwood 1986; Kratus 1985, 1989; McKernon 1979; Miller 1987; Moorhead and Pond 1941–1944; Upitis 1987; Webster in press a, in press b). The emergent picture of music, musical development, and young musicians owed much to the work of Jaques-Dalcroze and Orff, who had insisted that students be understood as young musicians. But their emphasis on basic urges and playfulness gave way to a description of music as a language, with an underlying grammar and musical learning as investigation rather than discovery (Lehman 1987; Leonhard 1984).

Musical development in this model took place quite gradually rather than in glorious bursts and very much in collaboration with other minds and models. Some musical aptitudes, such as tonal and musical imagery, sensitivity to musical structures as wholes, and the originality of musical ideas, are evident as early as birth and, as far as we can tell, are sensitive to considerable influence from the environment (Webster in press a and in press b) until they appear to stabilize between the ages of 9 and 11. We also know that basic musical conceptions, such as those governing surface and underlying rhythms, or the scale structure of Western music, mature prior to adolescence (Bamberger 1982; Davidson and Scripp 1989; Upitis 1987). However, it appears that other aspects of a generative musical thought, such as the ability to *use* these aptitudes in new contexts (such as in composition, or in listening to utterly unfamiliar works), are difficult and require considerable support from families, teachers, and musical models.

Further, in contrast to earlier models for arts education, developmentally based research insisted that the active, restless quality of cognition described acts of perception, as well as moments of production in visual and musical realms. In this way, looking and listening were radically reconceptualized. Perception, like production, was described not as passive consumption but as a matter of activity and rule-governed thought. Eisner puts it nicely:

> There is no equivalent of Bach's Mass in B Minor. Words cannot convey what the music has to say. But the messages in these works are not there simply for the taking. They must, so to speak, be recovered. They must be read. The works themselves must be unwrapped to be experienced. . . . I used the term "read" in the previous sentence. I did this intentionally. Visual and musical forms are forms that are patterned. They are forms that reflect a history. They are forms influenced by purpose, shaped by technology, and possess the signature of their authors. To recover the meaning these forms possess requires the ability to read the language they employ. (65).

In this light, music perception was understood as demanding close observation, comparisons, and hypothesis formation (Gordon 1971, 1979; Reimer 1989; Schafer 1979). Viewing paintings, dances, or sculpture, or even reading, came to be understood as involving the understanding and generative application of such complex notions as style or even more fundamental conceptions of art, value, and beauty (Barthes 1974; Eisner and Ecker 1966; Gardner, Winner, and Kircher 1975; Johnson 1982; Parsons 1987).

What emerges is a more complex argument about the nature of arts curriculum. First, rather than being handmaidens to other skills or additional sites for the exercise of reasoning and close observation, the arts were described as calling on both these general skills and more domain-specific abilities (such as the qualitative aspects of experience or, more specifically, visual metaphor or melodic line). Second, the studio metaphor of the progressive era was complemented, if not displaced, by the understanding that looking and listening were also acts of cognition that could inform and challenge a student's understanding of the arts. Finally, the place of teaching and the role of instruction were acknowledged. More than designing generous environments or productive methods, educators were clearly responsible for sustaining and informing their students' work.

The sociolinguist William Labov once commented on how hard it appears to be for researchers working in social science to stand on the shoulders, rather than the faces, of those who have come before. This surely might be said of curriculum work in arts education. At this moment, as a still different paradigm is emerging for arts education, the temptation is to belittle and caricature the developmentalists' hope that basic research would yield a sufficient map on which curriculum could be based. But from the developmental point of view comes the crucial understanding that artistry or aesthetic understanding is the result of learning, not the spontaneous combustion of inspiration or the guaranteed operation of gift. Without this foundation it seems unlikely that the current reconceptualizations of school arts as continuous with, and intimately connected to, the practices of mature producers and consumers would have emerged.

Becoming an Apprentice: Arts Education as Expertise

By the middle of the 20th century, arts education had enough history and purchase to become the ground of major debates. As always, these debates were a part of larger conversations about the nature of art and the artistic process. They were also shaped and colored by changing concepts of cognition and knowledge that took place [illegible] in fields like anthropology and psychology. In the period between 1960 and 1990, at least three serious controversies developed about classical aspects of educational practice: These were discussions about the necessity of explicit tuition, the difficulties of established canons, and the place of thoughtfulness in artistry. Their conduct has yielded still another image for arts education: that of the apprentice.

Teaching and Development. Critics of developmentally motivated arts research and curriculum were quick to point out the important difference between development and education. What occurs "naturally" provides only one kind of blueprint for instruction—there remains the entire, difficult, and value-laden question of what we *want* students to know. In the usual course of events, few children acquire enough musical proficiency to play an instrument as an adult. Unlike speaking, few children would reach a fluency in choreography without explicit tuition in the technique, vocabulary, and interpretative skills of dance. Given the choice, most Americans would not "naturally" become involved with the arts (Lasch 1984; Steiner 1980). But if none of these are conditions we want, then as both Barkan (1966) and Ecker (1963) have pointed out, there is no reason to confuse "is" with "ought." What occurs "naturally" is not necessarily the foundation for a curriculum. Development establishes only a footing—it cannot dictate matters of value. This was a serious critique of both the psychological and the developmental motives behind arts education of the previous decades. Essentially, it argues for a radically revised view of teaching—if development does not unfold in an assured way, or if it provides only the foundations for artistic achievement, then teaching is much more than enabling or filling out a preordained design. Such a view suggests that students need not just opportunities and materials but mentors capable of exhibiting and sharing the working and thinking processes of mature participants in the arts.

The Canons of Art and Intellect. Volumes like the classic Janson and Janson *History of Art* or Groves's *Dictionary of Music* document the arts as fashioned by—as the slang phrase would have it—"dead white men." The absences of female, Asian, African, and Latin American artists and musicians are startling. The late 20th century was marked by a reaction to these absences: a museum of African-American art in Washington, D.C., an African wing at the Metropolitan Museum, Judy Chicago's feminist art projects, and the growing number of exhibits and books about indigenous and folk art traditions (Alland 1983). But more than sheer access was at stake. As the insistence that varied, indigenous, and popular arts be acknowledged has grown, so has the corresponding argument that inclusion means acknowledgment, not easy appropriation. Borrowing and incorporation are part of art making: Moorish idioms became a part of Spanish architecture; Indian paisley was literally woven into the fabric of British life. Russian folk dance influenced Diaghilev, and Brecht stole from folk theater. But how appropriate is it for Western arts educators to just insert African masks or Inca sculpture as illustrations in their frameworks and analyses (Lovano-Kerr 1985; McFee and Degge 1977)? Similar versions of this debate about insider and outsider art occur about the exclusion of popular arts in favor of elite forms—for instance, why illustrations from film but not from television? Why medieval manuscripts and not graffiti? Where is jazz and rock and country western (Chapman 1982; Congdon 1985; McFee 1961)?

Just as the notion of a monolithic artistic canon has come under fire, so have received notions about the homogenized nature of thought and intellect come to be questioned in the fields of psychology and education. Familiar and virtually unquestioned notions of "intellect" or "IQ" have come under fire. In their place, researchers are suggesting a much more modular or diversified conception of mind (Fischer 1980; Gardner 1982; Sternberg and Wagner 1986) characterized by multiple forms of knowing or intelligences. Just as the art world has rejected a view of the arts confined to theaters and museums, anthropologists and ethnographers have argued that "schoolish" or academic forms of knowledge are only a slice of the kinds of wisdom people possess (Gee 1985; Heath 1983; Rogoff 1989; Scribner 1984). A dairy worker can perform remarkable calculations in loading cases for delivery, but score poorly on a paper-and-pencil test of mathematical abilities (Scribner 1984). This has raised questions about whether we ought, as we have long supposed, to teach "general education" and "thinking skills." There is increasing evidence that human knowledge, particularly outside school, is not a matter of generalized skills. Increasingly, it looks as if most skills are highly specific: adapted for use with certain materials, in a particular context, for a given purpose—even in subjects as apparently omnibus as the literate skills of reading and writing (Bruner, Olver, and Goldfield 1966; Scribner and Cole 1981; Wolf 1988b). Moreover, it has proven difficult to demonstrate that individuals can transfer learning from one domain to another (Resnick 1987), suggesting that knowledge is more local than we originally supposed. There are consequences here for arts education as much as for mathematics and foreign languages. If the arts are a form of local knowledge, what are the distinguishing characteristics of that knowledge?

Artistic knowledge has at least three major (and overlapping) characteristics that distinguish it in an inevitably blurred but essential way from the humanities, mathematics, and social and natural sciences. These characteristics go beyond pointing out that the arts are concerned with a distinctive class of objects: dances, plays, frescoes, porticos, or films. What is critical is *how* informed or experienced participants in the arts observe, question, and understand these items (Aspin 1986; Assessment of Performance Unit [APU] 1983; Cassirer 1979; Greene 1981; Langer 1942, 1953; Ross 1984; Witkin 1974).

To begin, the arts evoke as much as they refer. They express as often as they describe. That is the difference between a story and an account. An account has only the obligation to say what happened when. A story includes much that was never witnessed: Many of those invisibles have to do with the internal world of experience: emotion, sensation, hunch, belief, and dream. Consider the difference between what a drivers' education manual and a novel have to say about a traffic accident:

If you are involved in an accident as the driver of a vehicle, you must give your name, address and registration number to any person injured and to the owner or person in charge of the property damaged and you must show your Driver's License if asked to do so. . . . You must report an accident in which someone is killed, hurt, or there are damages in excess of $1,000.00 to a car or other property. A written accident report must be sent to the Registrar of Motor Vehicles and to the Police Department in the city or town where the accident happened within five days of the accident. Accident report forms are available at all police stations. (Commonwealth of Massachusetts 1989, 60)

A moment later she rushed out into the dusk, waving her hands and shouting—before he could move from his door the business was over.

The "death car" as the newspapers called it, didn't stop; it came out of the gathering darkness, wavered tragically for a moment, and then disappeared around the next bend. Michaelis wasn't even sure of its color—he told the first policemen that it was light green. The other car, the one going to New York, came to rest a hundred yards beyond, and its driver hurried back to where Myrtle Wilson, her life violently extinguished, knelt in the road and mingled her thick dark blood with the dust. (Fitzgerald 1925, 138)

The topic is the "same," but the content is entirely different. The accident Fitzgerald gives us is full of human intentions; the drivers' manual is picked clean of them. The Fitzgerald is a crisscross of human perceptions: what Michaelis, the newspaper reporter, the evident narrator, and the implied narrator make of the sudden, brutal event (Bruner 1986; Iser 1978). The manual speaks of all and any accidents, the novel of *the* accident, with all its gruesome and ironic particulars. It is not just the detail but a sense of an author choosing those specific items so as to force our eyes and ears to take in not just the random or the usual but this particular death, in this way, of this woman. Moreover, as we read, we say to ourselves, "He was up to something. He means for his words to reach into my memories or images or fears of hurtling cars and to do their work." The arts are, both in what they refer to and in how they operate, about arousal. The arts mean to take effect.

But the arts achieve their effect by making meaning in ways that are different from the force of logic underlying a mathematical proof or the historical precedents of civil rights laws. In the arts, meaning, either as it is made or understood, involves the *qualitative* aspects of experience (Eisner 1972, 1985; Greene 1981). This has many ingredients, but all of them are related to a willingness to see how *thick* an object or a performance can be: how handsomely and expressively a thing is made (Arnheim 1969, 1974; Goodman 1968); how semantically dense or rich in meanings it is (Goodman 1968; Parsons 1987; Winner 1982); and how recursively and thoughtfully it draws on the materials of culture, the images and resources of history, and the hubbub of the immediate world (Gardner 1989; Gombrich 1969; Panofsky 1982; Wollheim 1980). Thus, Fitzgerald makes his meaning by *how* he writes—his "gathering dark" and "thick blood" rather than simply by gathering and arranging the facts concerning Myrtle Wilson's death.

Despite their resemblance to the flashy summer colonies and industrial wastelands outside New York, Fitzgerald's East and West Egg are inventions—just like Italo Calvino's cities or Ray Bradbury's galaxies. The arts are concerned with a particular kind of truth. The arts deal in invented and multiple realities or possible worlds—whether those worlds are constructed with words or gesture or line (Bruner 1986). Stanislavsky's "naturalism," the mime's "faithfulness," or Vermeer's "reach out and touch it" goblet entail selection and stylization just as surely as do Meyerhold's fabulist theatricals or Aboriginal dream paintings. Equally important are the many, overlapping worlds of *versions* of reality the arts afford. Fitzgerald gives us many *versions* of the accident at once: the implied, but always absent, actual collision; the faulty, riddled account Michaelis gave a policeman; the journalist's tabloid write-up; Nick Carraway's strangely earnest collection of all the bits of reportage; and what may be his own irony hidden in the strange, eclectic whole. It is not unlike the final sense we have of Frida Kahlo's self looking across the wild array of all her self-portraits. Versions are also at the heart of performance and perception in the arts. One performance of Langston Hughes's *Black Nativity* may occur in modern dress and another in classical robes and swaddling. Each will hear a different message about saviors, religion, and belief. Toscanini's mercurial tempos for Beethoven expose quite a different aspect of the works than do Klemperer's slowed renditions of the "same" pieces. The "same" painting by Degas looks quite different after Marxist criticism has raised questions about the mercantile world it reflects or after a feminist critique insists that we see the women in the bath, or behind the bar, as held there by the gaze of the 19th-century man about town (Clark 1985; Lipton 1986). There are also versions of response to the realities an artist invents: The film *It Happened One Night* can strike one viewer as an entertaining comedy and another as a critique of gender relations. And there is the play of versions that comes as a part of one culture's taking up the tales, songs, or fabrics of another. (Think about how ballet changes once it stands in contrast to African and Latin forms of dance: how much more sharply we understand the gender relations, the conception of the body, and the particular definition of grace it involves.) The point here is that central to arts is a laminated, crisscrossed version of truth rather than a search for a *single*, parsimonious account of the world and how it works (Eisner 1972; Greene 1981; Wittgenstein 1953). Certainly part of the "work" of the arts occurs because of these possible and multiple worlds: Both conjuring these worlds and comprehending them demand remarkably active, restless, problem finding and solving (Getzels and Csikszentmihalyi 1976).

Thus, artistic or aesthetic knowledge is different from other kinds of knowing in fundamental ways: in intention, in modes of making meaning, in its method and view of truth or excellence.

Thoughtfulness in Arts Education. In the late 20th century, increasing numbers of artists have claimed the theoretical and historical aspects of artistry. Postmodern architecture is rife with references to other buildings. Both dance and painting have been invaded by text. Ideas about art have become a medium almost akin to clay or motion. The intellectual side of the arts, always present, has been claimed. At the same time, there is considerable discussion, both in psychology and education, about critical thinking, reflection, and problem solving (Newell and Simon 1972). Earlier notions of mind as simply memory or encyclopedia have expanded to include notions of planning, reflection, and metacognition, or the ability to think about thinking. This reconceptualization has led to a radical critique of the gap between "school skills" and "real thinking."

Typically, in schools we insist upon teaching basic skills first, leaving for later the "higher-order" skills of a domain (Resnick 1987; Resnick and Klopfer 1989). The result is that children's formative introduction to a field comes in terms of practices that have no authenticity in the domain (as in the case of tracing forms, filling in the blanks in rhythm exercises, or drawing pictures that "go" with the music). Moreover, they spend the maximum amount of time with activities that water down the issues and problems that are central to a field. Young musicians shouldn't be singing simplified arrangements; they ought to be rehearsing genuine (if simple) pieces of music and learning to think about pulse, meter, and accent in that authentic context (Brown, Collins, and Duguid 1989; Rogoff 1989). When school children go to a museum they shouldn't "find all the bird pictures." Perhaps they should talk about what they notice, what surprises them, and the reasons why. Child centered should not translate into "childish." The presence of the arts in schools should not mean that the arts taught are "schoolish."

There are many implications for the familiar forms of arts education. In 1976, Arthur Efland, writing in *Studies in Art Education*, gave voice to these concerns within the context of visual arts education. In describing what he called the "school art style," Efland offered a critique of what "is"—the mixed blandness and indifference of most school art practices and the poor art that issues from them. First, he illustrated the flat uniformity of what hangs on bulletin boards in Fort Worth, Litchfield, and Albuquerque. Second, he argued that those images of houses, sunsets, and shoes were different, and discontinuous, from the landscapes and observational sketches that artists, or even children working outside school, produce. Anticipating much of current critique of curriculum in any number of areas (Holt 1990; McNeill 1988; Silver 1990), he underscored the homogenization and pasteurization of arts teaching that takes place when school instruction is cut off or protected from the demands of more authentic kinds of learning (Efland 1976; Jackson 1968). In essence, he pointed out that school art is a domesticated and narrowed version of art as it is practiced by experts, whether those experts are painters, collectors, museum goers, or art historians. And what he had to say was not unique to visual art. One has only to think of the differences between band practice and a quartet "really" rehearsing (raising questions, trying different interpretations, playing through mistakes in order to get a sense for the line) to have a sense for how generally Efland's criticisms apply (Blum 1986). The presence of the arts in public schooling is marginal—not only in hours and resources but in depth (Arts, Education, and the Americans [AEA] 1977; Fowler 1988).

Also in the wake of this interest in thoughtfulness has come the discussion of whether or not arts education should be limited to studio work or performance. Increasingly, arts educators have asked whether the emphasis on creation was narrow and inappropriate. The result has been a far-reaching discussion of whether arts education will continue to be rooted chiefly in *knowing how* to make art, or whether it should expand to include *knowing about*—for example, gathering information from the arts-related disciplines of art history, criticism, and aesthetics (College Entrance Examination Board 1980; National Endowment for the Arts 1988; Smith 1987). This latter view of arts education, while having a long tradition in European and American academic training in the United States, (Broudy 1972; Chapman 1982; Feldman 1967, 1970, 1985), was crystallized by the publication in 1985 of the Getty Center's monograph *Beyond Creating* in which the following statement appears:

> We increase our understanding of the meaning of an artwork if we have worked with materials and processes that artists use to create art. We also broaden our understanding if we know when and where a work was made, something about its creator, the function it served in society, and what art experts have said about it. Artists, art historians, art critics, and aestheticians contribute different perspectives about an artwork. These perspectives are instructive and useful because each one deepens our understanding and heightens our appreciation of the various levels of meaning the work of art conveys. (Getty Center for Arts Education 1985)

Taken together, these three discussions—about the necessity of teaching, the distinctiveness of artistic knowledge, and the place of thoughtfulness—has led to a new definition of arts education. In this definition, the root image for arts education is one of an apprenticeship in which students learn the full range of works and practices that would make for expertise in the arts.

Across any number of academic, political, and institutional statements, this new image is apparent (Getty Center for Arts Education 1985; National Education Association 1988; National Endowment for the Arts 1988). The language is revealing: The National Education Association, for example, calls for the arts to be taught as *disciplines*, to be made available through *creating*, *studying*, and *experiencing*. The call is for the *development of skills in and knowledge of* the arts. The statement also calls for school instruction to be combined with "the highest quality arts experiences both in schools and in theaters, concert halls and museums." In this context, there has been a struggle to rethink the contents and structure of arts knowledge.

The results of this shift are perhaps most visible and remarkable in a field like dance, which has been heavily performance oriented. In this light, it is striking to read the most recent materials from the National Dance Association, which argue (along with dance scholars) that dance consists of three types of knowledge: dance as a way of knowing dance as something to know, and dance as the experience of dancing (Barylick 1983; Hannah 1979; National Dance Association 1988.) As a way of knowing, dance is, like other arts, a way of understanding oneself and of making sense of one's experiences in the world by capturing interior or observed experience in a particular kind of medium: the body in time through space with energy (Laban Art of Movement Guild 1953; Russell 1975). As such, dance entails aesthetic perception that enables a participant to become attuned to shapes, rhythms, and timings that might otherwise go unnoticed (Mettler 1970, 1974, 1980).

At the same time, dance is something to know: Dancers should understand the forms and styles of movement that are the kinetic expressions of cultures as different as West Africa and the plains states of North America, and of periods as different as 18th-century minuets and the 20th-century jitterbug. To know dance is also to be a keen observer of dance: to have a rich enough vocabulary and to have standards by which to judge dance that is as modern as this evening's concert.

Finally, there is the experience of dancing that involves performing, creating, and responding to dance (American Alliance for Health, Physical Education, Recreation, and Dance [AAHPERD] 1981; Hannah 1979):

> It is apparent that dancing, creating dance, and responding to dance are not discrete areas. Many experiences overlap from one area to another. For example, a student may both create a dance composition and perform: responding to one's dance and performing it are part of the process of refining the choreography. (AAHPERD, 8)

To understand all that is implied by the rhythms and body positions of a "dip tango," chances are that students who clasp a partner, stand with shoulders drawn back, and move to the music will, by virtue of that performance, understand more of the cultural meaning of the steps.

In an effort to connect school arts with sophisticated practice, at least two quite different approaches to curriculum have emerged. The first is what is known as "discipline-based arts education," which has been sponsored and nurtured in the visual arts by the Getty Center for Arts Education. Although the Getty Center has sponsored a range of projects, at the core of each is a commitment to expose even the youngest children to four major modes of artistic knowledge: studio work, art history, art criticism, and aesthetics (Getty Center for Arts Education 1985). A core idea is visual literacy: what Eisner (1985) referred to as the ability to "recover meaning" from works of art. As a result, skills such as the ability to notice the relevant visual characteristics of a work (known as "scanning") play an prominent role in many classrooms. The following excerpt from a classroom interaction provides a sample of what such an interchange sounds like. (The students are eighth graders in an Illinois classroom, observed by Robert Stake.)

> The teacher projected a painting by Edward Hopper entitled *Gas* and said, "You probably haven't seen this before."
>
> A student quickly asked, "Is it Rockwell?"
>
> The teacher replied, "No, but from the same period, probably the early forties. It's an American scene. You recognize the Mobil sign. It's by Hopper."
>
> A student said, "It isn't realistic. It's too clean and perfect."
>
> "Would you say it's *too* perfect?"

"Maybe. Maybe it's something from the Twilight Zone."

"What makes you say that?"

"Well, there's no grease on the station. And the road disappears into the blackness of the trees."

"What is the artist expressing?"

"Distance." (Getty Center for Arts Education 1985, 35)

What is immediately evident is the engagement of worthwhile works of art, the acquisition of art historical information (it is by Hopper, painted in the 1940s), and the development of a vocabulary that permits discussion and debate about works ("realistic," "expressing"). Also clear is the interest in urging students to think about what they behold. The exchange goes well beyond the obvious to a discussion of the strange, overly ordered reality that Hopper invents. At its richest and best, this approach uses the tools of studio work, art history, criticism, and aesthetics as a means to offer students a range of knowledge and forms of inquiry not unlike those of a connoisseur (Clark, Day, and Greer 1987).

This class, like many other discipline-based classes, meets the critique of "school arts" by making an eighth grade class resemble a good, upper-level art history course. There is an abundance of high-quality works (rather than just the tattered Gilbert Stuart portrait of Washington and van Gogh's *Sunflowers*). The questions are authentic ones for the domain and the particular work (many Hopper scholars have discussed the atmosphere vacuumed of all disturbance and texture). The conversation is about an aspect of what makes the arts distinctive: the expressive properties of the work.

A different approach is represented by ARTS PROPEL, a collaboration between the teachers of Pittsburgh and researchers at Harvard Project Zero and Educational Testing Service. Like discipline-based arts education, PROPEL is concerned with widening and deepening the ways that students come to know the arts. However, the vehicles and the emphases are considerably different.

PROPEL, now being applied to visual arts, music, and creative writing, has much in common with contemporary movements toward what has been called "everyday" or "situated cognition" (Brown, Collins, and Duguid 1989). The central concern is to involve students in *doing* the work of a field. This is accomplished by involving students in a semester- or year-long series of projects and the formation of a portfolio. Projects are sustained involvements with a piece of aesthetic work. They involve making or performing works, but they are in no way limited to what has traditionally been called "creation." They also entail building up a deep enough understanding of a work to perform it, or a diverse enough set of questions and approaches to a work to understand it.

The underlying model of artistic cognition is one of conversation between different authentic perspectives or stances (Vygotsky 1978, 1986). During each project, students are encouraged to take up the stances of producer, perceiver, and reflective critic, by turns, much as do skilled practitioners in the arts (Wolf 1989a). A composer hardly confines himself to work of translating the sounds inside his head into the notational conventions of his culture. While at work on a composition, he also draws on what he knows from the performer's perspective (Can the cellist make these sounds articulately at this tempo?), borrows from his own musical heritage, applies rigorous standards, and possibly wonders, as he leans back from his desk, about the changing relationship between music and sound. These stances are different from formal disciplines, insofar as they entail an approach to a work, rather than the acquisition of a particular body of information.

The following is an excerpt from an interview with a high school senior who is part of a PROPEL classroom. The student is describing a sustained project in which she did a series of portraits of family members. Toward the end of the project, the student grew restless with her original intention of portraits. She wanted to reach beyond specifics to renditions that would capture something more universal about the nature of family bonds. As a part of pursuing that issue, she visited the museum where she was struck by a work of Giacometti, *Walking Man*. Here she comments on what she learned from the intersection of her own questions and the encounter with the statue:

Well, as much as I like my family series, I was beginning to get bored. . . . There is only so far you can take it, and I was trying for something that I could still keep that family quality and make it universal, so that everybody could see a part of themselves in it. . . . [I remembered] the sculpture of the Walking Man. He didn't have a face really, sort of an indication of a nose, or something. Not very . . . where it could be any man, anybody struggling. It looked like a very struggling piece. [I wrote in my journal:] "In Walking Man, the figure of the man appeared to be held back as his back foot tried to advance forward." Basically, what I was saying is . . . if you notice . . . the back foot is . . . appears to be stuck in something. And he's leaning forward, he's trying to get away but something is holding him back. I think, the fact that [same artist] didn't put in any figures—features that is, in the face could mean anybody who is trying to get away from something, trying to advance forward in life. But something's holding them back.

Following this encounter with a sophisticated work that shows her other possibilities for representation, the student turns from portraits to a series of much more abstract works in collage and plaster sculpture that highlight basic forms expressive of the intimacy and differentiation that occur between parents and children. Here the model is the sustained work of an artist-perceiver who moves deliberately between studio, museum, and journal (Wolf 1988a).

Common to both discipline-based arts education and ARTS PROPEL is the effort to confront much of what was implied in Efland's 1976 criticism of the "school art style." Central to this is the effort to connect arts in schools to the contours and demands of authentic work in the arts. However, if either approach (or some different one) were pursued, it would mean that the arts in schools lose their isolation—and their protection. It ceases to be comfortable or appropriate to accept the institutional or instructional structures that are a matter of habit or routine practice in schools when they constrain and distort the serious work to be done. The ramifications are many: Arts classes cannot be crammed into 40-minute periods once a week; arts classes cannot be cut off from access to authentic examples, be they works in museums or performances of Ailey's "Revelations"; students must encounter adults who can be models for such engaged work. These are steep demands for a subject still considered only marginal in many settings. But they will prove necessary, rather than nice, if the arts are to be more than "schoolish."

CONTINUING TENSIONS

Origins are tenacious: Much of the history of arts education still hangs on, creating the basic tensions, difficulties, and opportunities for change in the field.

At the turn of the century the arts became part of the common curriculum of the public schools. The power of this event was that the arts were treated as a kind of intellectual or cultural capital that ought to belong to all. But the bargain had its Faustian side. The arts became part of common schooling—with a consequent loss of their distinctiveness as a form of knowledge and as a set of practices. Access and inclusion in the school world has meant the arts, just like arithmetic or history, have succumbed to an exercise-driven approach to instruction that gives us, to this day, art and music textbooks with numbered objectives, lists of materials needed, time required printed at the top, and exercises at the close of each lesson instead of the more authentic, full-scale problems and projects characteristic of artists, composers, dancers, or set designers. By far the bulk of music education continues to focus on what Webster (in press a, in press b) refers to as the enabling skills of technical proficiency with voice or instrument or listening skills (e.g., the ability to recognize pitches, to discriminate elements, to predict patterns, to identify periods or composers).

The Faustian bargain isn't unique to "way back then." In the recent wave of educational reform, there has been considerable support for the arts in the common curriculum. In *Academic Preparation for College* (1980), and again emphatically in *Academic Preparation in the Arts* (1983), the College Entrance Examination Board has declared that the arts are subjects worthy of study on a level with foreign languages, mathematics, or English. In 1986, the U.S. Department of Education published its study of elementary school, *First Lessons*, which was, for all its emphasis on the traditional values of schooling, surprisingly supportive of the presence of the arts in early education. The report states, "The arts are an essential element of education, just like reading, writing, arithmetic. . . . Music, dance, painting, and theater are keys that unlock profound human understanding and accomplishment." The parallel report on high schools, *James Madison High: A Model High School Curriculum*, also supports the arts. Similar positions emerged from Goodlad's extensive studies of schools and from *A Nation at Risk*. In all of these documents it is worth observing how often the arts are portrayed as conveying a kind of basic *literacy*. Yet just as reading and writing can be, and often have been, taught as little more than decoding and inscribing, the same could become true of the arts; hence, being labeled a literacy is a mixed blessing (Wolf 1988b). It can mean that the arts are a fundamental and undeniable part of the curriculum or that they are susceptible to the same dilution into basic skills taught by rote that plagues other areas of the curriculum. High on a wall in a high school art studio, more than a hundred years after Walter Smith's heyday, there hangs this list of the criteria on which student work will be evaluated:

1. Work is turned in complete and on time.
2. Work is neat.
3. Workspace and materials have been taken care of.
4. The student has cooperated with others.
5. The student shows evidence of having tried the techniques and problems that were introduced.
6. Work is original.

With the possible exception of the last item, these are characteristics that a foreman or supervisor could use in an electronic components assembly line or for job training candidates in an insurance firm. There is nothing here that argues artwork demands attention to specific or unique dimensions of process or outcome or that excellence is an issue.

Progressive education and the child study movement saw in the arts a distinctive kind of educational opportunity: the option for students learning to be creative. The contribution was enormous. It raised the possibility that the arts had a distinctive role within education. Drawing was not just manual skill, and music was not just preparation for church choir. But here too, the legacy is complicated. Part of the vision of the arts in the progressive era included a vision of the child as a "natural artist" whose talents and intuitions should be left to unfold. What emerged at best was a keen attention to a series of studiolike processes that permitted engagement, sustained attention, and problem finding. What emerged at worst was a kind of preciousness about children and a laissez-faire attitude about teaching. If we look closely at visual arts education, we see the lasting fingerprints of this attitude. Throughout their elementary school careers, children are encouraged to draw almost exclusively from memory or imagination. They are kept away from observation drawing—even though much of mature artistic practice, in the form of figure drawing or *plein air* landscape, thrives on matching mark to model. The rationale remains that the demands of an observed object will crush and defeat the child's creative instincts. But the real question is whether it crushes or narrows and falsifies visual arts education in the name of a romantic and too simple vision of childhood (Smith 1983; Smith and Fucigna 1987).

Developmentally oriented researchers and educators sought to correct the too simple romanticism of the progressive era by arguing that the arts were learned, and artistic understandings were constructed; they were not simply discovered or uncovered. Insofar as the developmental perspective portrayed the series of acquisitions involved in learning to sing, dance, engage in dramatic play, or paint, it made a clear argument for the arts as matters of learning rather than "just play" or talent. However, like preceding arguments, the developmental perspective leaves behind a checkered set of assumptions and practices.

If developmental studies and resulting curricula are understood as universal, they are frankly problematic. They are, by nature, concerned with average, and therefore general, patterns of development. "The child" doesn't exist, nor does "the sequence for learning about music." Moreover, the bulk of developmental information was and continues to be collected on a narrow sample: middle-class, Caucasian children. If taken literally, developmentally based curricula can be hard on issues of diversity. This is particularly problematic in a school system where diversity of backgrounds is the rule rather than the exception. Music curricula presume the elements and emphases of Western music. But many of the children in music classes come from Asian backgrounds where very different scale organizations prevail, or African-influenced cultures where rhythm rather than melody may dominate musical composition. The issue is whether their "take" on music comes to be seen in the light of "difference" or "deficit."

Moreover, developmentally founded curricula are frankly problematic when and if they are misunderstood to imply a rigid ladder (scope and sequence) leading from "basic" to "higher-order thinking skills" (Resnick 1987). The result can be that children's initial encounters with the arts can be elemental exercises, which are barely disguised rote drills in quarter notes, cutting shapes, or skipping, with fundamental issues about quality, expression, and meaning left for "later, when the fundamentals are in place." The issue is not that there aren't basics but that from the very outset students have to encounter the fundamental problems of "understanding art," in the same sense that we would talk about "doing history" or "acting like a scientist."

The child-centered quality of much progressive and developmental curricula has stirred concern about the insulation of arts education from the authentic practices of adults who are engaged in or expert at the arts. Efforts in the direction of aesthetic knowledge, a discipline base, sustained projects, and portfolios all address a basic concern for arts education to "grow up" toward or reach for the knowledge structures characteristic of the arts when they are seriously pursued. But here, too, the bargain can be driven too hard (Ewens 1988; Zessoules, Wolf, and Gardner 1988). The point is not academics or the cultivation of a curatorial stance in school children. In asking a young musician to keep a journal about her rehearsals, the point is not to make a junior-grade critic, capable of spouting the "right" analytic terms. When we ask a young dancer to consider what he might learn from watching video tapes of Ted Shawn or reading dance reviews, the point cannot be to make him a scholar—to elevate reading and writing above dance. The point has to be to inform him about cultural traditions and questions that can inform his *performance*.

CONCLUSION: THE ARTS AS MORE THAN MINOR DISTURBANCES

In the opening to *The Child and the Curriculum*, John Dewey writes:

> Profound differences in theory are never gratuitous or invented. They grow out of conflicting elements in a genuine problem—a problem which is genuine just because the elements, taken as they stand, are conflicting. Any significant problem involves conditions that for the moment contradict each other. (Dewey 1969, 3–4)

Dewey was speaking about an educational problem very much on his own mind at the time, the conflicts between the needs of children and the "social aims, meanings, and values" that adults want to impart. But he could easily have been writing about arts education. Its very name signals conflict: Arts education is about giving a genuine understanding of painting, song, theater, or dance in the institutional setting of schools. The effort to resolve that conflict, either by redefining the arts or by challenging the values and structures of schools, has been the history of arts education. It is difficult, this tension between schooling as we know it and the arts as we would have them taught. But it is, in Dewey's terms, a genuine conflict, and, so, worth our pursuit. The arts do not fit easily into schools, but once there, their presence raises important questions. As the arts move in from the margin, their presence exposes certain issues almost relentlessly. Two instances are symptomatic.

As mentioned earlier, much of school instruction is characterized by practices and forms of knowledge that occur only in classrooms, not in real-life settings or in forms of expert practice in professions or disciplines. School history is chronology rather than inference and investigation (Holt 1990); school science is verification rather than experimentation (Mestre 1990); school art is stained glass ornaments assembled from precut pieces. Part of changing this situation has to do with modeling instruction on complex and sustained problem finding and problem solving, rather than exercises, excerpts, and abridgements. Until schooling comes to be characterized by these more authentic and difficult practices, it offers lessons in civility and basic skills—not an introduction to learning or the possession of knowledge. The arts, at least in pockets, have preserved many authentic practices: studio classrooms, museum visits, rehearsals, critiques, performances, and artist residencies. In these practices are embedded complex tasks, sustained work, and instances of assessment that function as episodes of learning. Rather than regarding these practices as marginalia or oddities, educators in any number of subject areas might learn from them.

Moreover, the vulnerable situation of the arts alerts us to the fact that schooling, as we know it, honors one very particular kind of knowledge. As cross-cultural studies have shown, individuals who go to school more than passingly, learn to take on problems and to offer answers even when information comes in a remarkably decontextualized format (Bruner, Olver, and Goldfield 1966; Luria 1976; Scribner and Cole 1981). In effect, what schooling may teach is a kind of distance from the particularities of information. In addition, much of schooling is an apprenticeship in logical-deductive thinking of the kind that underlies either everyday problem solving (Where was the last place I saw my keys?) or much more rigorous tasks (the empirical investigations characteristic of laboratory science). In either case, what is at issue is arriving at the one right and verifiably correct answer (Bruner 1986). The arts do not subscribe: They are concerned with invention rather than verification, with versions rather than a single truth, and with qualitative aspects of experience as much as with the content of experience. The arts raise the question, Can a way of knowing gain access to the curriculum as we know it and retain its distinctiveness? More than a local issue, its answer has deep implications for whether history can go from time lines to the reading and interpretation of original sources, or whether science instruction could focus on a series of linked experiments rather than the series of chapters in the text.

The playwright George Bernard Shaw is said to have remarked, "There are only two great teachers, art and torture, and since one is illegal, we have to depend on the other." If the arts are taken seriously within education, they may have much to teach, not just students, but schools.

References

Alland, Alexander. 1983. *Playing with Form*. New York: Columbia University Press.

American Alliance for Health, Physical Education, Recreation, and Dance (AAHPERD). 1981. *Children's Dance*. Reston, VA: AAHPERD.

American Association for the Advancement of Science. 1989. *Science for All Americans: A Project 2061 Report on Literacy Goals in Science, Mathematics, and Technology*. Washington, DC: AAAS.

Arnheim, Rudolf. 1969. *Visual Thinking*. Berkeley: University of California Press

Arnheim, Rudolf. 1974. *Art and Visual Perception: The New Version*. Berkeley: University of California Press.

Arts, Education, and the Americans (AEA). 1977. *Coming to Our Senses: The Significance of the Arts for American Education*. New York: McGraw-Hill.

Aspin, David. 1986, summer. Objectivity and assessment in the arts: The problem of aesthetic development. *Inspection and Advice* 22(1).

Assessment of Performance Unit (APU). 1983. *Aesthetic Development*. London: DES.

Bamberger, Jeanne. 1982. "Revisiting Children's Drawings of Simple Rhythms: A Function for Reflection in Action." In *U-Shaped Behavioral Growth*, edited by S. Strauss. New York: Academic Press.

Barkan, Manuel. 1966. Prospects for change in the teaching of art. *Art Education* 19(4–8).

Barthes, Roland. 1974. *S/Z*. New York: Hill & Wang.

Barylick, Martha. 1983. Both artist and instrument: An approach to dance education. *Daedalus* 112(3): 113–128.

Blum, David. 1986. *The Art of Quartet Playing*. New York: Knopf.

Bolton, Gavin. 1989. "Drama." In *Children and the Arts*, edited by D. Hargreaves, 119–137. Milton Keyes, England: Open University Press.

Broudy, Harry S. 1972. *Enlightened Cherishing: An Essay on Aesthetic Education*. Urbana: University of Illinois Press.

Brown, Ann L., and Sandra S. Smiley. 1978. The development of strategies for studying texts. *Child Development* 49: 1076–1088.

Brown, John S., Allan Collins, and Paul Duguid. 1989. Situated cognition and the culture of learning. *Educational Researcher* 18(1): 32–42.

Brown, Roger. 1973. *A First Language*. Cambridge, MA: Harvard University Press.

Bruner, Jerome. 1968. *Towards a Theory of Instruction*. New York: Norton.

Bruner, Jerome. 1986. *Actual Minds, Possible Worlds*. Cambridge, MA: Harvard University Press.

Bruner, Jerome, Rose Olver, and Patricia Goldfield. 1966. *Studies in Cognitive Growth: A Collaboration at the Center for Cognitive Studies*. New York: Wiley.

Callahan, Raymond. 1962. *Education and the Cult of Efficiency*. Chicago: University of Chicago Press.

Cassirer, Ernst. 1979. *Symbol, Myth, and Culture: Essays and Lectures of Ernst Cassirer*. New Haven, CT: Yale University Press.

Chapman, Laura. 1982. *Instant Art, Instant Culture*. Wolfeboro, NH: Teachers College Press.

Choksy, Lois, et al. 1986. *The Teaching of Music in the Twentieth Century*. Englewood Cliffs, NJ: Prentice Hall.

Clark, Gilbert, Michael Day, and W. Dwaine Greer. 1987. Discipline-based art education: Becoming students of art. *Journal of Aesthetic Education* 21(2): 129–186.

Clark, Timothy J. 1985. *Painting and Modern Life*. New York: Knopf.

College Entrance Examination Board. 1980. *Academic Preparation for College*. New York: College Entrance Examination Board.

College Entrance Examination Board. 1983. *Academic Preparation in the Arts*. New York: College Entrance Examination Board.

Commonwealth of Massachusetts. 1989. *Motor Vehicle Operator's Manual*. Boston: Commonwealth of Massachusetts.

Congdon, Kristin. 1985. The study of folk art in our school's art classrooms: Some problems and considerations. *Multi-Cultural and Cross-Cultural Research in Art Education* 3(1): 65–75.

Courtney, Richard. 1968. *Play, Drama and Thought: The Intellectual Background to Dramatic Education*. London: Cassell.

Davidson, Lyle, and Bernadette Colley. 1987. "Children's Rhythmic Development from Age 5 to 7." In *Music and Child Development*, edited by J. Peery, I. Peery, and T. Draper, 107–136. New York: Springer-Verlag.

Davidson, Lyle, and Larry Scripp. 1989. "Education and Development in Music from a Cognitive Perspective." In *Children and the Arts*, edited by D. Hargreaves, 59–86. Milton Keyes, England: Open University Press.

Dewey, John. 1969. *The Child and the Curriculum*. Chicago: University of Chicago Press.

Dowling, W. Jay, and Dane Harwood. 1986. *Music Cognition*. Orlando, FL: Academic Press.

Ecker, David. 1963. Some inadequate doctrines in art education and a proposed resolution. *Studies in Art Education* 5(1): 71–81.

Efland, Arthur. 1976. The school art style: A functional analysis. *Studies in Art Education* 17(2): 37–44.

Eisner, Elliot. 1972. *Educating Artistic Vision*. New York: Macmillan.

Eisner, Elliot. 1985. *The Educational Imagination: On the Design and Evaluation of School Programs*. New York: Macmillan.

Eisner, Elliot, and David Ecker. 1966. *Readings in Art Education*. Waltham, MA: Blaisdell.

Ewens, Thomas. 1988. "Flawed Understandings: On Getty, Eisner and DBAE." In *Beyond DBAE: The Case for Multiple Visions of Art Education*, edited by J. Burton, A. Lederman, and P. London, 5–25. University Council on Art Education.

Feldman, David. 1986. *Nature's Gambit: Child Prodigies and the Development of Human Potential*. New York: Basic Books.

Feldman, David. 1987. Developmental psychology and art education: Two fields at the crossroads. *Journal of Aesthetic Education* 21(2). 243–259.

Feldman, Edmund. 1967. *Art as Image and Idea*. Englewood Cliffs, NJ: Prentice Hall.

Feldman, Edmund. 1970. *Becoming Human through Art: Aesthetic Experience in the School*. Englewood Cliffs, NJ: Prentice Hall.

Feldman, Edmund. 1985. *Thinking about Art*. Englewood Cliffs, NJ. Prentice Hall.

Fischer, Kurt W. 1980. A theory of cognitive development: The control and construction of hierarchies of skills. *Psychological Review* 87: 477–531.

Fitzgerald, F. Scott 1925. *The Great Gatsby*. New York: Scribner.

Fowler, Charles. 1988. *Can We Rescue the Arts for America's Children: Coming to Our Senses—10 Years Later*. New York: American Council for the Arts.

Freedman, Kerry, and Thomas S. Popkewitz. 1988. Art education and social interests in the development of American schooling: Ideological origins of curriculum theory. *Journal of Curriculum Studies* 20(5). 387–405.

Freeman, Norman. 1980. *Strategies of Representation in Young Children*. London: Academic Press.

Freud, Sigmund. 1958. "The Relation of the Poet to Daydreaming." In *On Creativity and the Unconscious*. New York: Harper & Row.

Froebel, Friedrick. 1887. *The Education of Man*. New York: Appleton.

Gardner, Howard. 1982. *Frames of Mind*. New York: Basic Books.

Gardner, Howard. 1989. *To Open Minds*. New York: Basic Books.

Gardner, Howard, Ellen Winner, and Mary Kircher. 1975. Children's conceptions of the arts. *Journal of Aesthetic Education* 9(3): 60–77.

Gee, James P. 1985. The narrativization of experience in the oral style. *Journal of Education* 167(1): 9–35.

Getty Center for Arts Education. 1985. *Beyond Creating*. Los Angeles: Getty Trust.

Getzels, Jacob, and Mihaly Csikszentmihalyi. 1976. *The Creative Vision: A Longitudinal Study of Problem-Finding in Art*. New York: Wiley.

Golomb, Claire. 1974. *Young Children's Drawings and Sculptures*. Cambridge, MA: Harvard University Press.

Gombrich, Ernst. 1969. *Art and Illusion*. Princeton, NJ: Princeton University Press.

Goodman, Nelson. 1968. *Languages of Art*. Indianapolis, IN: Bobbs-Merrill.

Goodnow, Jacqueline. 1977. *Children Drawing*. Cambridge, MA: Harvard University Press.

Gordon, Edwin. 1971. *The Psychology of Music Teaching*. Englewood Cliffs, NJ: Prentice Hall.

Gordon, Edwin. 1979. Developmental Music Aptitude as Measured by Primary Measures of Music Audiation. *Psychology of Music* 7(1): 42–49.

Green, John, ed. 1978. *Pestalozzi's Educational Writings*. University Publications of America.

Greene, Maxine. 1981. "Aesthetic Literacy in General Education." In *Philosophy and Education, 80th Yearbook of the National Society for the Study of Education*, edited by J. F. Soltis, 115–141. Chicago: University of Chicago Press.

Habermas, Jürgen. 1971. *Knowledge and Human Interests*. Boston, MA: Beacon Press.

Hannah, Judith L. 1979. *To Dance is Human*. Austin: University of Texas Press.

Heath, Shirley B. 1983. *Ways with Words: Language, Life and Work in Communities and Classrooms*. Cambridge: Cambridge University Press.

Heathcote, Dorothy. 1980. *Drama as Context*. Sheffield, England: National Association for Teaching English.

Henry, Jules. 1963. *Culture Against Man*. New York: Random House.

Hirsch, Bette. 1989. *Languages of Thought*. New York: College Entrance Examination Board.

Holt, Thomas. 1990. *Teaching History: Narrative, Imagination and Questioning*. New York: College Entrance Examination Board.

Iser, Wolfgang. 1978. *The Act of Reading: A Theory of Aesthetic Response*. Baltimore, MD: Johns Hopkins University Press.

Jackson, Philip W. 1968. *Life in Classrooms*. New York: Holt, Rinehart and Winston.

Johnson, Nancy. 1982. Children's meanings about art. *Studies in Art Education* 23(2): 61–67.

Katz, Michael. 1973. *Education in History. Readings on Social Issues*. New York: Praeger.

Kellogg, Rhoda. 1969. *Analyzing Children's Drawings*. Palo Alto, CA: National Books Press.

Korzenik, Diana. 1985. *Drawn to Art*. Hanover, NH: University Press of New England.

Kratus, Jay. 1985. "Rhythm, Melody, Motive and Phrase Characteristics of Original Songs by Children Aged Five to Thirteen." Unpublished doctoral dissertation, Northwestern University, Evanston, IL.

Kratus, Jay. 1989. A time analysis of the compositional processes used by children 7 to 11. *Journal of Research in Music Education* 37(1): 5–20.

Laban Art of Movement Guild. 1953. *The Art of Movement in Education and Recreation*. London: MacDonald and Evans.

Langer, Susanne. 1942. *Philosophy in a New Key*. Cambridge, MA: Harvard University Press.

Langer, Susanne. 1953. *Feeling and Form*. New York: Scribner.

Lasch, Christopher. 1984. "The Degradation of Work and the Apotheosis of Art." In *The Future of Musical Education in America: In Memoria for Howard Hansen*, edited by D. J. Shetler, 11–13. Rochester, NY: Eastman School of Music.

Lehman, Paul. 1987. *Music in Today's Schools: Rationale and Commentary*. Reston, VA: Music Educators' National Conference.

Lehman, Paul, and Richard Sinatra. 1988. "Assessing Arts Curricula in the Schools: Their Roles, Content, and Purpose." In *Toward a New Era in Arts Education: The Interlochen Sym-*

posium, edited by J. McLaughlin. New York: American Council on the Arts.

Leonhard, Charles. 1984. "The Future of Musical Education in America: A Pragmatist's View." In *The Future of Musical Education in America: In Memoria for Howard Hansen*, edited by Donald J. Shetler, 60–72. Rochester, NY: Eastman School of Music.

Lipton, Eunice. 1986. *Looking into Degas*. Berkeley, CA: University of California Press.

Logan, Frederick M. 1955. *Growth of Art in American Schools*. New York: Harper Brothers.

Lovano-Kerr, Jessie. 1985. Cultural diversity and art education: A global perspective. *Multi-Cultural and Cross-Cultural Research in Art Education* 3(1): 25–33.

Lowenfeld, Viktor. 1939. *The Nature of Creative Activity*. New York: Harcourt, Brace.

Lowenfeld, Viktor. 1957. *Creative and Mental Growth*. New York: Macmillan.

Luquet, Georges H. 1917. *Les Dessins d'un Enfant*. Paris: Alcan.

Luria, A. R. 1976. *Cognitive Development*. Cambridge, MA: Harvard University Press.

McFee, June. 1961. *Preparation for Art*. San Francisco, CA: Wadsworth.

McFee, June, and Rogena Degge. 1977. *Art, Culture and Environment: A Catalyst for Teaching*. New York: Wadsworth.

McKernon, Patricia. 1979. "First Songs." In *Early Symbolization: New Directions in Child Development*, edited by Dennie Wolf and Howard Gardner, 43–58. San Francisco: Jossey-Bass.

McNeill, Linda. 1988. *The Contradictions of Control*. London: Routledge Chapman and Hall.

Mestre, Joseph. 1990. *Academic Preparation in Science*, rev. ed. New York: College Entrance Examination Board.

Mettler, Barbara. 1970. *Children's Creative Dance Book*. Tucson, AZ: Mettler Studios.

Mettler, Barbara. 1974. *Materials of Dance as a Creative Art Activity*. Tucson, AZ: Mettler Studios.

Mettler, Barbara. 1980. *The Nature of Dance as a Creative Art Activity*. Tucson, AZ: Mettler Studios.

Miller, Linda B. 1987. "Children's Musical Behaviors." In *Music and Child Development*, edited by J. Peery, I. Peery, and T. Draper, 206–224. New York: Springer-Verlag.

Moorhead, George, and Donald Pond. 1941–1944. *Music of Young Children*. Santa Barbara, CA: Pillsbury Foundation for the Advancement of Music Education.

National Dance Association. 1988. *Dance: Curricula Guidelines, K–12*. Reston, VA: National Dance Association.

National Education Association. 1988. "Concepts for Strengthening Arts Education in Schools." In *Dance: Curricula Guidelines, K–12*. Reston, VA: National Education Association.

National Endowment for the Arts 1988. *Towards Civilization: A Report on Arts Education*. Washington, DC: National Endowment for the Arts.

Newell, Allen, and Herbert A. Simon. 1972. *Human Problem-Solving*. Englewood Cliffs, NJ: Prentice Hall.

Panofsky, Erwin. 1982. *Meaning in the Visual Arts*. Chicago: University of Chicago Press.

Parsons, Michael. 1987. *How We Understand Art*. Cambridge: Cambridge University Press.

Piaget, Jean. 1963. *The Origins of Intelligence in Children*. New York: Norton.

Piaget, Jean. 1965. *The Moral Judgment of the Child*. New York: Free Press.

Reimer, Bennett. 1989. *Philosophy of Music Education*. Englewood Cliffs, NJ: Prentice Hall.

Resnick, Lauren. 1987. *Education and Learning to Think*. Washington, DC: National Academy Press.

Resnick, Lauren, and Leopold Klopfer. 1989. *Toward the Thinking Curriculum: 1989 Yearbook of the Association for Supervision and Curriculum Development*. Reston, VA: ASCD.

Rogoff, Barbara. 1989. *Apprenticeships in Thinking*. New York: Oxford University Press.

Ross, Malcolm. 1984. *The Aesthetic Impulse*. Oxford: Pergamon.

Russell, Joan. 1975. *Creative Movement and Dance for Children*. Boston, MA: Plays.

Schafer, Murray. 1979. *Creative Music Education*. New York: Schirmer.

Scribner, Sylvia. 1984. "Studying Practical Intelligence." In *Everyday Cognition*, edited by B. Rogoff and J. Lave. Cambridge, MA: Harvard University Press.

Scribner, Sylvia, and Michael Cole. 1981. *The Psychology of Literacy*. Cambridge, MA: Harvard University Press.

Silver, Edward. 1990. *Thinking through Mathematics*. New York: College Board.

Slade, Peter. 1954. *Child Drama*. Oxford: Oxford University Press.

Smith, Nancy R. 1982. *Experience and Art*. New York: Teachers' College Press.

Smith, Nancy R. 1983. Drawing conclusions: Do children draw what they see? *Art Education* 36(5): 22–25.

Smith, Nancy R., and C. Fucigna. 1987, August. "Drawing Systems in Children's Pictures: Contour and Form." Paper presented at the Meeting of the American Psychological Association, New York.

Smith, Ralph. 1987. The changing image of art education: Theoretical antecedents of discipline-based art education. *Journal of Aesthetic Education* 21(2): 3–34.

Steiner, George. 1980. The archives of Eden. *Salmagundi*. 50–51(Fall 1980–Winter 1981): 57–89.

Sternberg, Robert, and Richard Wagner, eds. 1986. *Practical Intelligence*. New York: Cambridge University Press.

Tyack, David. 1974. *The One Best System*. Cambridge, MA: Harvard University Press.

Upitis, Rena. 1987. "Toward a Model for Rhythm Development." In *Music and Child Development*, edited by J. Peery, I. Peery, and T. Draper. New York: Springer-Verlag.

Vygotsky, Lev. 1978. *Mind in Society*. Cambridge, MA: Harvard University Press.

Vygotsky, Lev. 1986. *Thought and Language*. Cambridge, MA: MIT Press.

Way, Brian. 1967. *Development through Drama*. Humanities Press.

Webster, Peter. In press a. "Refinement of a Measure of Creative Thinking in Music." In *Research in Music Behavior: Applications and Extensions*, edited by C. Madsen. Tuscaloosa: University of Alabama Press.

Webster, Peter. In press b. "Creative Thinking in Music: Approaches to Research." In *Music, Society and Education in the United States*, edited by T. Gates. Tuscaloosa: University of Alabama Press.

Werner, Heinz, and Bernard Kaplan. 1963. *Symbol Formation*. New York: International Universities Press.

Wilson, Brent, and Marjorie Wilson. 1977. An iconoclastic view of the imagery sources in the drawings of young people. *Art Education* 8(1): 33–42.

Winner, Ellen. 1982. *Invented Worlds*. Cambridge, MA: Harvard University Press.

Witkin, Robert. 1974. *Intelligence of Feeling*. London: Heinemann.

Wittgenstein, Ludwig. 1953. *Philosophical Investigations*. New York: Macmillan.

Wolf, Dennie. 1988a. Opening up assessment: Ideas from the arts. *Educational Leadership* 45(4): 24–29.

Wolf, Dennie. 1988b. *Reading Reconsidered*. New York: College Entrance Examination Board.

Wolf, Dennie. 1989a. "Artistic Learning as Conversation." In *Children and the Arts*, edited by D. Hargreaves. Milton Keynes, England: Open University Press.

Wolf, Dennie. 1989b. Portfolio assessment: Sampling student work. *Educational Leadership* 46(7): 35–49.

Wolf, Dennie, Ann Smith, and Howard Gardner. 1982. "Max and Molly: Individual Differences in Artistic Symbols." Reprinted in *Art, Mind and Brain*, edited by Howard Gardner. New York: Basic Books.

Wollheim, Richard. 1980. *Art and Its Objects*. New York: Cambridge University Press.

Woodward, C. Vann. 1989. *The Future of the Past*. New York: Oxford University Press.

Wygant, Foster. 1983. *Art in American Schools in the Nineteenth Century*. Cincinnati, OH: Interwood.

Zessoules, Rieneke. 1990. *Portfolio: The Newsletter of ARTS PROPEL* (Winter): 5.

Zessoules, Rieneke, Dennie Wolf, and Howard Gardner. 1988. "A Better Balance: ARTS PROPEL as an Alternative to Discipline-Based Arts Education." In *Beyond DBAE: The Case for Multiple Visions of Art Education*, edited by J. Burton, A. Lederman, and P. London, 117–130. University Council on Art Education.

∽ 33 ∽

PHYSICAL EDUCATION

Mary A. Steinhardt
THE UNIVERSITY OF TEXAS AT AUSTIN

As in other subject areas, physical education programs throughout the past century have been influenced by an array of trends, issues, organizations, research studies, and public policies. In general, program development in physical education is responsive to the needs and concerns of society. The review of physical education curriculum is particularly important at this time, given the widespread public concern regarding the content of existing physical education programs and the fitness levels of American youth.

The study of physical education curriculum is complex in that it involves issues of value (e.g., what should we teach?) as well as issues of control (e.g., who makes decisions about what is taught?). The fact that physical educators hold different opinions with respect to the definition of a quality physical education program (Bain 1988b) has often led to confusion rather than enlightenment (Kirk 1988) and has been one of the major reasons for the lack of "public education" with regard to the value of physical education. At present, most physical education programs continue to struggle to become respected and basic components of public education. This struggle is heightened by the lack of expectations for significant outcomes in physical education by principals and parents, especially at the high school level (Siedentop 1987). Despite the struggle, one can readily find examples across the United States of exemplary physical education programs "that are gaining the respect of their school, administrators, teaching colleagues, communities, and most importantly, their students" (24).

This chapter examines the curriculum in physical education and is limited in scope to a focus on school and college physical education programs. For a more complete understanding of physical education curriculum, the reader should also be familiar with general curriculum perspectives and paradigms (Kimpston and Rogers 1986; Schubert 1986), the relation of curriculum to instruction (Giroux, Penna, and Pinar 1981), research on teaching (Wittrock 1986) and teacher education (Bain 1990a; Lanier and Little 1986), and determinants of exercise behavior (Dishman 1990; Sallis and Hovell 1990).

The chapter is divided into four sections. The first section provides a historical perspective of the physical education curriculum and how it has changed over the years. The second section examines different theoretical perspectives regarding the proposed subject matter of quality physical education programs. The third section provides a review of research related to the study of curriculum in physical education. Finally, the fourth section discusses future directions and points to curriculum research that is still needed in the field of physical education.

HISTORICAL PERSPECTIVE

An understanding of the historical impact of past events and concerns of society is necessary in order to examine the present curriculum and develop sound curricular programs for the future. A brief review will provide a perspective for the discussion of curriculum theory, curriculum research, and future directions for quality physical education programs. More comprehensive reviews of the history of physical education can be found elsewhere (Leonard and Affleck 1947; Lumpkin 1990; Siedentop 1980).

The first physical education programs in the United States evolved during the 1820s. Charles Beck, who taught

The author wishes to express her appreciation to James F. Sallis, who provided a thoughtful review to an earlier draft of this chapter. A special thanks goes to Linda L. Bain for her comments and to Philip W. Jackson for this opportunity.

at Round Hill School in Northhampton, Massachusetts, was the first officially recognized physical education teacher. Beck's program was based on the German gymnastics system, which used equipment to develop strength, although popular sports and games were also included. Catharine Beecher was the first American to advocate daily physical education in the public schools. In the mid-1800s, borrowing from the concepts of Swedish gymnastics, she introduced girls to calisthenics designed to contribute to their health, beauty, and strength.

During the 1860s, Dio Lewis, dissatisfied with the strength and skill necessary for executing German gymnastics and inspired by the work of Catharine Beecher, promoted a "new gymnastics" that utilized light equipment to promote flexibility, agility, carriage, and grace. The development of a teaching school to train teachers in the Lewis system also aided in the promotion and spread of this new gymnastics approach. During the same time period, the first college department of physical education was developed at Amherst under the leadership of Edward Hitchcock. In the 1870s, Dudley Sargent developed a similar program at Harvard, although he expanded the program to include exercise machines that allowed each student to develop an exercise program based on his individual needs. This approach to physical development is similar to the physical fitness programs of today, which emphasize personal fitness (Blair, Pate, and McClenaghan 1982; Corbin and Lindsey 1985; Stokes and Moore 1986) and criterion-referenced standards (Cureton and Warren 1990).

At the 1889 Boston Conference on Physical Training, all known physical education programs were described, demonstrated, and discussed. Since none of these fully met the diverse needs of American schools and colleges, a "battle of the systems" raged for years. Although German and Swedish gymnastics predominated, the concept of "new physical education" was gaining wide acceptance. New physical education emphasized sports, games, dance, and recreational pastimes and promoted "education through the physical," rather than training and development of the body. Although physical fitness was important, fitness was assumed to be a by-product of participation in sports, games, and other activities. The education-through-the-physical approach, which included instruction in social and emotional values, dominated the profession for the first half of the 20th century. It was, however, challenged by various leaders who advocated more of an emphasis on skill development and physical fitness.

Periodic attention has been given to increased physical fitness at both the elementary and secondary levels. Just as the U.S.S.R.'s launching of Sputnik created a concern about the quality of mathematics and science instruction in the United States, results from the Kraus–Weber test (Kraus and Hirschland 1954) created a renewed emphasis on the physical fitness of American youth. The results from this test revealed that American children ($N = 4,264$) failed a battery of six muscular fitness tests at a much higher rate (57.9 percent) than did the European children ($N = 2,870$; 8.7 percent). As a result, there was increased public concern with regard to the fitness of American youth, especially in the late 1950s and 1960s. An increased focus on physical fitness also occurred in the 1980s in response to the public health aim of reducing risk factors for cardiovascular heart disease (Paffenbarger, Hyde, and Wing 1990; Powell et al. 1987; Simons-Morton et al. 1987; Wilmore 1982). Concern for the activity and physical fitness levels of children and adolescents expressed in the 1990 *Objectives for the Nation* and issued by the U.S. Department of Health and Human Services (DHHS) was an attempt to set goals for the establishment of activity patterns early in life that could be carried into adulthood (U.S. Department of Health and Human Services 1980). The 11 objectives listed below relate to physical activity and exercise in school-aged children and are outlined in the midcourse review (U.S. Department of Health and Human Services 1986) of the 1990 physical fitness and exercise, *Objectives for the Nation*. The schools are the appropriate institution to supervise the implementation of these objectives (Dishman and Dunn 1988).

1. By 2000, 75 percent or more of children and adolescents ages 10 to 17 years will participate 3 or more times per week for at least 30 minutes per session in activities requiring 50 percent or more VO_2 max and which are most commonly or easily performed by adults.
2. By 2000, 90 percent or more of children and adolescents ages 10 to 17 years will participate 3 or more times per week for at least 30 minutes per session in an activity at least as vigorous as a sustained slow walk.
3. By 2000, 75 percent or more of children and adolescents ages 10 to 17 years will participate 3 or more times per week for at least 15 minutes per session in activities that promote the development and maintenance of flexibility and muscular strength and endurance.
4. By 2000, population-based descriptive information about the levels of physical fitness and physical activity patterns of children ages 6 to 9 years will be available.
5. By 2000, 50 percent or more of children and adolescents 6 to 17 years of age will participate in daily school PE programs.
6. By 2000, 90 percent or more of high schools will have PE classes devoting at least 50 percent of class time to activities that are commonly done by adults.
7. By 2000, 80 percent or more of persons 10 years of age and older will be able to correctly identify the variety, frequency, and duration of exercise thought to promote most effectively cardiorespiratory fitness for their age group.
8. By 2000, 80 percent or more of persons 10 years of age and older will know that regular physical activity reduces the risk of heart disease, helps maintain appropriate body weight, and reduces the symptoms of depression and anxiety.
9. By 2000, practical methods to measure the health-related components of fitness and desirable and reasonable norms for those measures will be established for

age- and sex-specific groups for both children and adults.

10. By 2000, the levels of achievement of the health-related components of fitness for various age- and sex-specific segments of children and adults will be known.
11. By 2000, 70 percent of children and adolescents 10–17 years of age will receive recognition for their participation in a test of physical fitness without regard to their level of achievement. (U.S. Department of Health and Human Services 1986)

Several components of this historical perspective influence the physical education curriculum as it exists today. Physical education still struggles to define its professional cognate. The lack of consensus with respect to a few specific, meaningful goals that can be reasonably accomplished in physical education programs has limited progress in physical education curriculum research. At present, more effort has been devoted to developing theoretical models and debating the value of physical education than to actual research.

The inability to agree on a common curriculum is not unique to physical education. For example, in the recent *Handbook of Research on Teacher Education* (Houston 1990), similar concerns were expressed for science education, mathematics education, and reading education. With respect to science education, Yager and Penick (1990) comment: "Worst of all, there is no common agreement as to the basic meaning of science as a part of the education of all youth" (671). Brown, Cooney, and Jones (1990) discuss mathematics teacher education in terms of two research paradigms, analytic and humanistic, and encourage mathematics educators "to consider pedagogical problems in different lights and from different perspectives" (652). Finally, Alvermann (1990) describes three contrasting conceptions of reading teacher education (e.g., traditional-craft, competency based, and inquiry oriented), each of which has very different implications for curriculum development.

Because physical educators differ with respect to their beliefs regarding the subject matter of a quality physical education program, an understanding of the different curriculum models is important. Kirk (1988) suggests that "most curriculum work in physical education shares some of the basic, underlying notions that Jewett and Bain's approach to curriculum theory and practice demonstrates" (22). In their text *The Curriculum Process in Physical Education*, Jewett and Bain (1985) identify and critique seven different physical education curriculum models, each of which will be briefly described in the next section.

THEORETICAL PERSPECTIVE

Kirk (1988) suggests that unless we specifically define the term "curriculum," confusion will result as we attempt to understand "curriculum study," "curriculum theory," and "curriculum research." He further suggests that definitions of curriculum (see Barrow 1984) are too broad and thus extremely difficult to use in developing a conceptual framework for curriculum study. For purposes of this chapter, the term "curriculum" includes the "characteristics of subject matter, the pedagogic interactions of teachers and learners, and the sociocultural milieu in which these interactions take place" (Kirk 1988, 9). Thus, the three characteristics of curriculum in abbreviated form are knowledge, interaction, and context. Curriculum study focuses on the problems and issues of day-to-day curriculum created by the fusion of these three characteristics. In addition to what actually occurs, this includes the study of what educational practitioners intend to do and factors that influence and shape these intentions.

The selection of a curriculum model should be consistent with a individual's value orientation (Sanders and McCutcheon 1986) and thus characterized by the priorities given to various outcomes of the teaching-learning process (Ennis and Zhu 1991). Jewett and Bain (1985) have proposed that the value orientations underlying the models be made explicit. Five different value orientations have been identified and include *disciplinary mastery*, *social reconstruction*, *learning process*, *self-actualization*, and *ecological integration* (Jewett and Bain 1985; Jewett and Ennis 1990). Although the Jewett and Bain text was the only one found that specifically addressed value orientations in physical education, other texts acknowledged that value judgments are a necessary part of the curricular process (Dauer and Pangrazi 1989). Because curricular goals are derived from personal beliefs, a first important step toward developing program goals should be to clarify beliefs relative to the subject matter (Siedentop, Mand, and Taggart 1986). The five value orientations identified and described below reflect the work of Jewett and Bain (1985) and, as noted by Jewett (1980), have been adapted from the work of Eisner and Vallance (1974). Ennis and Hooper (1988) have developed and validated an instrument for assessing these value orientations.

Disciplinary mastery is the most traditional value orientation and places greatest priority on mastery of subject matter. The continuing focus on back-to-the-basics and proficiency reflects a disciplinary mastery approach. Although a disciplinary mastery approach is the most widely endorsed value orientation, of concern is the extent to which students actually master the taught curriculum. Furthermore, a question still strongly debated is "what knowledge is of most worth?" (Broudy 1982; Jewett and Bain 1985). Programs in which students are expected to become proficient in a variety of sport skills (Rink 1985) or develop and maintain minimum health-related physical fitness standards (U.S. Department of Health and Human Services 1988) represent a disciplinary mastery value orientation. *Social reconstruction* emerged as a popular value orientation in the 1940s. From this perspective, the school curriculum is viewed as a vehicle for creating a better society. Societal needs take priority over individual needs, and these needs are reflected in the curriculum. A high value is placed on democratic principles, and students are encouraged to analyze contemporary issues and ask critical questions related to the social, political, and economic development of society (Apple 1982; Freire 1983). An example of social reconstruction was reflected during the 1940s when World War II demanded teamwork and leadership skills. More recently, issues of discrimination by race, class, gender, physical ability, and physical appearance reflect a social reconstruction value orientation and are being increasingly addressed by critical theorists (Bain 1990a; Dewar 1987, 1990; Dodds 1986; Griffin 1983, 1985b, Sherlock 1987). Examples of social reconstruction include the passage of Title IX in 1972, which addressed issues of sex equity, and Public Law 94-142 in 1975, which addressed issues of equal access for all children to a free and appropriate public education.

The *learning process* value orientation emphasizes the process of learning. This value orientation is based on the premise that, because of the large volume of knowledge and rapid changes due to technology, developing process skills for continued learning are as important as what we learn (Bloom 1981). *Self-actualization* is a child-centered value orientation emphasizing individual autonomy, personal growth, and self-direction. Curricular decisions are centered around helping students achieve their potential (Maslow 1979). The final value orientation, *ecological integration*, incorporates self-actualization as described in the fourth value orientation, but goes beyond this view to include the individual as a integral part of a constantly changing environment. Learning is achieved by working with other individuals in the environment to help create the future of the world in which we live (Dewey 1916; Jewett and Ennis 1990).

Each curriculum model differs in terms of the overall program goal, the structure of the program, program content, and value orientation. The physical education curriculum models presented below include (1) developmental education, (2) humanistic physical education, (3) movement education, (4) kinesiological studies, (5) sports education, (6) personal meaning, and (7) health-related physical fitness (Jewett and Bain 1985).

Developmental Education

The developmental model is currently the most widely endorsed physical education curriculum model, although some professionals feel that developmental education is infused throughout all models rather than being a separate curriculum model. The philosophy of the model is often described by the popular expression "education through the physical," and the program is characterized by physical activities used to contribute to the total development of the individual socially, emotionally, intellectually, and physically (Melograno 1979; Pangrazi and Darst 1985; Thompson and Mann 1977). The primary value orientation is self-actualization. The physical education teacher, as developmental expert, is responsible for selecting and determining the sequence of learning tasks based on research describing developmental patterns of children and children's interests and skill capabilities (Thomas, Lee, and Thomas 1988). A more in-depth discussion of developmental education at the elementary level can be obtained from *Meaningful Movement for Children* (Hoffman, Young, and Klesius 1981) and, at the secondary level, *Designing Curriculum and Learning: A Physical Coeducational Approach* (Melograno 1979).

Jewett and Bain (1985) describe critics of this approach as questioning whether physical education programs can produce the broad developmental goals that are claimed while at the same time individualizing instruction (Lawson and Placek 1981; Siedentop 1980). There appears to be an assumption that participation in sports and games results in broad developmental outcomes, although these outcomes have not been empirically tested. Siedentop, Mand, and Taggart (1986) have omitted a discussion of developmental education in their most recent physical education text, *Physical Education Teaching and Curriculum Strategies for Grades 5–12*, and instead described a multiactivity program they refer to as the "historical backbone of physical education curriculum" (161). The philosophy of a multiactivity program is to expose students to as many activities as possible in hopes of creating an interest in pursuing lifetime activity. Although teachers can teach in their area of expertise in a multiactivity program, a common pitfall is that teachers sometimes roll out the ball and have supervised recreation.

Humanistic Education

The humanistic curriculum model also emphasizes the total well-being of the individual, but the approach is student oriented. The value orientation may include both self-actualization and social reconstruction, depending upon the priority of the teacher. The work of Hellison over the last 15 years represents the most complete description of a humanistic physical education curriculum (Jewett and Bain 1985; Siedentop, Mand, and Taggart 1986). Hellison's social development model has been field tested in inner-city schools, detention programs, and after-school programs with at-risk youth and, as a result, has undergone several revisions (DeBusk and Hellison 1989; Hellison 1978, 1983a, 1983b, 1985, 1989). Although the model has been implemented predominantly with at-risk youth, it is applicable for all students. The primary focus of the model is to promote the social development of students from irresponsibility to caring. *Self-* and *social* responsibility goals are presented as developmental levels and taught through a process of awareness, decision making, and self-reflection. Self-responsibility goals focus on empowering students to take more control of their lives despite such external forces as peer pressure, self-doubt, lack of skill, and vision. Social responsibility goals focus on developing a sensitivity to the rights and feelings of others, as well as service to and concern for others (DeBusk and Hellison 1989; Hellison 1989b). The developmental levels and teaching strategies for achieving each level are outlined below, as adapted from DeBusk and Hellison (1989). Together, these developmental levels and strategies provide a framework for teacher planning and evaluation.

Developmental Levels

Level O: *Irresponsibility*—describes students who are unmotivated and undisciplined.

Level I: *Self-Control*—describes students who may not participate in the day's activity or show much mastery or improvement, but who are able to control their behavior.

Level II: *Involvement*—describes students who demonstrate self-control and are involved in the subject matter.

Level III: *Self-Direction*—describes students who learn to take more responsibility for their choices and for linking these choices to their own identities; these students are able to work without direct supervision.

Level IV: *Caring*—describes students who are motivated to extend their sense of responsibility by cooperating, giving support, showing concern, and helping others.

Self-Responsibility Strategies

Teacher Talk—explaining levels, posting them, referring to them during a teachable moment;

Modeling—modeling developmental attitudes and behaviors;

Reinforcement—any act by the teacher that strengthens a level-related attitude or behavior of an individual student;

Reflection Time—time students spend thinking about their attitudes and behavior in relation to the levels;

Student Sharing—asking students to give their opinions about some aspect of the program;

Specific Level-Related Strategies—activities that increase interaction with a specific level; for example, student contracts may help students operate at Level III; and reciprocal teaching, whereby students pair up and teach each other, may help students to operate at Level IV (DeBusk and Hellison 1989, 112).

As described by Jewett and Bain (1985), critics originally expressed concern regarding the lack of evidence for clearly defined program concepts and goals (Siedentop 1980), as well as personal and social outcomes (Lawson and Placek 1981). More recent concerns relate to the notion that, although the concepts of the model are important, they are important for all subject areas and thus should not be the focus of subject matter content in physical education.

Movement Education

Movement education programs have had the greatest impact on elementary schools, and, depending on the priorities of the teacher, emphasize some combination of the value orientations disciplinary mastery (i.e., emphasis on learning about movement), learning process (i.e., emphasis on learning how to move), and self-actualization (i.e., emphasis on the child). Movement education programs in the United States began in the early 1960s and are based on the work of Rudolph Laban (1963). Laban's framework includes the concepts of body awareness (what the body does), effort (how the body moves), space (where the body moves), and relationships (what relationships occur). From each of these aspects of movement, objectives and learning activities are designed and typically use a problem-solving, guided discovery, or exploratory style of teaching (Logsdon et al. 1984). For example, Pangrazi and Darst (1985) suggest that in using this approach, which they call movement analysis theory, students would analyze levels of movement while dribbling a basketball or discover court positions and awareness while playing racquetball. In the text *Moving and Learning—The Elementary School Physical Education Experience*, Nichols (1990) has proposed an integrated curriculum in which children are taught the relationship between what they learn about movement and a variety of physical education activities.

Jewett and Bain (1985) point out that efforts to teach movement education have been criticized for unfounded claims of transfer of learning as well as decreased physical activity time due to an emphasis on teaching concepts. Critics also have identified the lack of a research base to support the practice of using discovery teaching styles to teach athletic skills (Dauer and Pangrazi 1989; Siedentop 1980). Although some secondary school programs include Laban's (1963) movement concepts of time, space, force, and flow, most interest in the movement education approach has been at the elementary level. At least two secondary texts have omitted a discussion of movement education as a viable curricular alternative (Lawson and Placek 1981; Siedentop, Mand, and Taggart 1986).

Kinesiological Studies

A kinesiological studies model is similar to movement education in value orientation, but uses movement activities to study the disciplinary foundations of human movement (e.g., exercise physiology, biomechanics, kinesiology). Emphasis is placed on developing problem-solving skills, typically using a combination of classroom lectures and activities in the gymnasium. The primary goal of this conceptually based model is that each student develop a cognitive understanding of the *how* and *why* of physical education (Siedentop, Mand, and Taggart 1986). Hal Lawson and Judith Placek have been the primary spokespersons for this model, and much of their work is described in the book *Physical Education in the Secondary Schools: Curricular Alternatives* (Lawson and Placek 1981). Two organizational approaches are typically used in a kinesiological studies curriculum. In the first approach, the content is organized by activity units, and disciplinary concepts are integrated with skill instruction. In the second approach, activity units are organized around specific concepts that take priority over skill instruction.

Most interest in the kinesiological studies approach has been at the secondary level. Although many schools have included one or two concept units in their curriculum, typically associated with health-related physical fitness (Pangrazi and Darst 1985), few school physical education programs consist solely of a kinesiological studies approach.

The National Association for Sports and Physical Education (NASPE) *Basic Stuff* series (Carr 1987; Kneer 1981), published by the American Alliance for Health, Physical Education, Recreation and Dance (AAHPERD), represents the most complete example of a kinesiological studies curriculum. Although NASPE has not endorsed the kinesiological studies curriculum model, the *Basic Stuff* series clearly represents this approach. The series identifies basic concepts and learning activities in six disciplinary areas (exercise physiology, kinesiology, motor learning, psychosocial aspects, humanities, and motor development).

Critics of the kinesiological studies model have expressed concern that the model focuses on concept units that emphasize intellectual development at the expense of participation in physical activities. These concerns are similar to those raised regarding a movement education curriculum (Jewett and Bain 1985; Siedentop 1980). As described by Siedentop, Mand, and Taggart (1986), advocates of the kinesiological studies approach feel that physical education course offerings must require intellectual rigor as well as physical exertion "if we are to be viewed as worthy in the hierarchy of education" (Marsh 1983, 9).

Sports Education

The sports education model, formerly *play education* as described by Jewett and Bain (1985), portrays sport as intrinsically valuable and voluntarily entered into for its own sake. Daryl Siedentop, the primary spokesperson for this model, defines the main objective of physical education as helping "students become skilled sports participants and good sportspersons" (Siedentop, Mand, and Taggart 1986, 185). Physical education is conceptualized and implemented in such a manner that student experiences are similar to the experiences of students in interscholastic sport programs. Sport is defined as playful competition in which the emphasis is upon becoming proficient at some activity for its own sake rather than using the activity for personal improvement or physical fitness. The value orientation for sports education is disciplinary mastery and increasing subject matter approach tendencies is seen as the ultimate objective (Bain 1980; Siedentop 1980). Siedentop, Mand, and Taggart (1986) identify the following 6 characteristics that distinguish the sports education model from the more traditional physical education programs: (1) programs involve seasons rather than units, (2) students quickly become members of teams, (3) a formal schedule of competition is provided, (4) culminating events are present, (5) records are kept and publicized, and (6) teachers assume the roles of coaches.

Although few physical education teachers publicly endorse the sports education model, in practice many agree with the concepts. Pangrazi and Darst (1985) in their text *Dynamic Physical Education Curriculum and Instruction for Secondary School Students* refer to sports education as a subset of the more traditional or activity-centered approach, advocating "movement forms for the intrinsic meaning and satisfaction they provide people" (32). A concern even for those physical educators who believe in the model is justifying the curriculum to administrators. Critics of the model claim that sports education and physical education are different in focus because physical education programs are product oriented rather than nonproductive and necessary rather than voluntary (Lawson and Placek 1981). Melograno (1979) feels that philosophically the approach is sound, although impractical from both an educational and lifestyle focus. "Persons have and always will respond to both intrinsic and extrinsic motivation . . . it would be unnatural and incongruent with today's society to de-emphasize extrinsic values in favor of intrinsic values" (52). Other concerns are related to the assumption that improved skill will increase the tendency to participate in physical activities, the notion that sport behaviors learned in youth will carry over into the adult years, and the lack of a research base to support the model (Jewett and Bain 1985).

Personal Meaning

A personal meaning curriculum model asserts that, for an experience to be educational, it must have meaning and significance for the individual. Ann Jewett has been the primary spokesperson for this model and purports that "the role of the educator is to analyze potential sources of meaning, to provide a wide range of opportunities, and to respond supportively to the individual's search for meaning" (Jewett and Bain 1985, 72). The model is based on the ecological integration (Jewett and Ennis 1990) and learning process value orientations, and the Purpose Process Curriculum Framework (PPCF) provides the most thorough description of the model (Jewett and Mullan 1977). The PPCF is a theoretical framework composed of two major dimensions, a *purpose* dimension and a *process* dimension, and is intended for use in physical education curricular decision making. The purpose dimension serves as a guide for assisting planners with decisions concerning the nature and scope of curriculum content. This dimension includes 22 purpose statements, which represent students' motives or purposes for participating in movement activities. These 22 purposes can also be viewed as physical education objectives (Jewett 1980). The second dimension of the PPCF, the process dimension, serves as a classification scheme for identifying the processes through which individuals learn movement. Seven movement process categories are described and provide a taxonomy of instructional goals in the psychomotor domain. These process categories include perceiving, patterning, adapting, refining, varying, improvising, and composing (Jewett and Mullan 1977).

Most of the criticism of the PPCF has centered around the dilemma of understanding and translating the model into practice. There are very few examples of the model in practice, and practitioners have difficulty in translating purposes for engaging in physical activity into statements of program goals (Jewett and Bain 1985). At least two recent texts (Pangrazi and Darst 1985; Thomas, Lee, and Thomas

1988), however, have included personal meaning as a viable curriculum model for consideration.

Health-Related Physical Fitness

A physical fitness curriculum is similar to the developmental and humanistic education models in that all three models view physical education as a means to contribute to the well-being of students. The distinguishing characteristic of the physical fitness model is that benefits to the individual are limited to the area of health, and the value orientation is disciplinary mastery. Getchell (1982) defines physical fitness as the capability of the heart, blood vessels, lungs, and muscles to function at optimal efficiency. Optimal efficiency is defined as the most favorable health needed for enthusiastic and pleasurable participation in daily tasks and recreation. The President's Council on Physical Fitness and Sports defines physical fitness as "the ability to carry out daily tasks with vigor and alertness, without undue fatigue, and with ample energy to enjoy leisure time pursuits and to meet unusual situations and unforeseen emergencies" (Clark 1971, 4). Thus, a physically fit person is better able to withstand stress and persevere under difficult physical circumstances than an unfit person.

Throughout most of the 20th century, youth fitness in America has been synonymous with skill-related fitness and is often referred to as athletic fitness. Skill-related fitness abilities include agility, balance, coordination, power, reaction time, and speed. At present, however, many youth fitness programs include only those fitness components that promote health and/or prevent disease (Blair, Kohl, and Powell 1987; Blair, Pate, and McClenaghan 1982; Pate 1983). These components include cardiovascular fitness, muscular strength, muscular endurance, flexibility, and body composition.

The focus on health-related fitness has largely resulted from the fact that coronary heart disease (CHD) is the major cause of morbidity and mortality in the United States at the present time (Despres, Bouchard, and Malina 1990; Pollock and Wilmore 1990; Rowland 1990; Sallis 1987), as well as recent studies that have effectively linked sedentary living habits (Powell et al. 1987) and low levels of physical fitness (Blair et al. 1989; Paffenbarger and Hyde 1988; Paffenbarger, Hyde, and Wing 1990) with an increased risk for CHD. Furthermore, programs that reward children for speed and power provide the implicit message that "if you want to be physically fit, you must be fast, agile, and powerful as well as strong and enduring" (Pate 1983, 80). This creates a system that has a strong genetic component. Although many physical educators feel that an emphasis on motor performance is no longer the state of the art (Blair, Pate, and McClenaghan 1982), there is concern that programs which do not emphasize skill development will "end up with a person who runs and only runs" (Legwold 1983, 155). Some physical educators support the inclusion of performance skills in a health-related fitness curriculum for this reason, and one such curriculum model has been proposed (Steinhardt and Stueck 1986). However, because the focus of the model is on developing and maintaining physical fitness, the sport skill lesson should be designed such that participation contributes to the development and maintenance of physical fitness.

Critics of health-related physical fitness programs feel that the focus of the program is too narrow (Lawson and Placek 1981) and for many students and teachers dull, restrictive, and boring (Siedentop, Mand, and Taggart 1986). Although the focus is less narrow in fitness programs that include performance skills, classes which meet every other day or every third day are limited in the time that can be devoted to developing and perfecting performance skills and still achieve health-related fitness goals (Koslow 1988).

Kirk and Colquhuon (1989) point to the concern that many health-based physical education programs are based on a number of assumptions focused within an "exercise = fitness = health" triplex. As they point out, "the triplex [exercise = fitness = health] reveals the health orientation in physical education to rest on a much more strongly bonded relationship among these components. The implicit belief among many physical educators is that exercise, through the mediating notion of fitness, *leads* to health, that exercise is *essential* to health, and that being fit and having a slender body are *proof* of health" (426). "Individuals must develop a health ethic which involves making sacrifices of time and effort to 'work' on their health, perseverance to maintain their practices and habits, and a motivation to curb their interests, excesses and inclinations" (Colquhoun 1990, 227). Crawford (1977, 1986) has labeled this rationale "healthism," which is the belief that health can be achieved through individual effort and discipline and is primarily directed at regulating the physical appearance of the body.

Summary

Seven different physical education curriculum models have been described, each providing a framework for the selection, scope, and sequence of learning experiences based upon a different view. In practice, elementary physical education programs sometimes emphasize a movement education curriculum, occasionally provide opportunities to learn various sports and games in the form of a multiactivity program, and often provide instruction in fundamental motor skills. Secondary physical education programs typically portray a multiactivity curriculum consisting of games and instruction in sport skills, especially team sports. Within the last 10 years, health-related physical fitness testing also has become a fundamental component of this multiactivity program. It is often difficult to determine which curriculum model is present in a given school physical education program, and quite often it appears that more than one model is present. Although the concept of a balanced program incorporating a variety of objectives has received support (Dauer and Pangrazi 1989; Legwold 1983), concerns regarding accountability and objective standards from which to evaluate these programs remain unresolved. Also of concern, given a multiactivity program, is that minimal student learning takes place because students are exposed to such a wide array of objectives for short periods of time.

In response to these concerns, Lawson (1986b) has suggested the need to develop a national curriculum that would consist of intended learning outcomes which define a physically educated person. These outcomes would provide a structure for competing curriculum models to find harmony. Although Bain (1986) agrees that structural changes in physical education are needed, she questions the feasibility and desirability of a national curriculum. Feasibility issues relate to the concern that statements of intended outcomes would have to be general enough to achieve consensus, yet specific enough to guide practice. Also of concern would be the dissemination of curriculum materials and accreditation of school programs. The issue of desirability raises both technical and moral–ethical questions. From a technical standpoint, it must be determined that a national curriculum would produce the desired results and that such a curriculum would improve the quality of teaching at the local level. Moral–ethical questions relate to the concern of having a common curriculum in a pluralistic society.

As in other subject areas, it is not unusual that physical educators disagree on the answer to the basic question, What knowledge is of most worth and why? However, it also is necessary for physical educators to take responsibility for educating the public with regard to the purpose of physical education. A recent report sponsored by NASPE, *Definition of the Physically Educated Person—Outcomes of Quality Physical Education Programs*, identifies 20 characteristics of a physically educated student upon completion of appropriately designed and conducted school physical education programs (National Association for Sport and Physical Education 1990, 1–2).

A PHYSICALLY EDUCATED PERSON:

HAS learned skills necessary to perform a variety of physical activities

1. . . . moves using concepts of body awareness, space awareness, effort and relationships.
2. . . . demonstrates competence in a variety of manipulative, locomotor and non-locomotor skills.
3. . . . demonstrates competence in combinations of manipulative, locomotor and non-locomotor skills performed individually and with others.
4. . . . demonstrates competence in many different forms of physical activity.
5. . . . demonstrates proficiency in a few forms of physical activity.
6. . . . has learned how to learn new skills.

DOES participate regularly in physical activity

7. . . . participates in health enhancing physical activity at least three times a week.
8. . . . selects and regularly participates in lifetime physical activities.

IS physically fit

9. . . . assesses, achieves and maintains physical fitness.
10. . . . designs safe, personal fitness programs in accordance with principles of training and conditioning.

KNOWS the implications of and the benefits from involvement in physical activities

11. . . . identifies the benefits, costs and obligations associated with regular participation in physical activity.
12. . . . recognizes the risk and safety factors associated with regular participation in physical activity.
13. . . . applies concepts and principles to the development of motor skills.
14. . . . understands that wellness involves more than being physically fit.
15. . . . knows the rules, strategies and appropriate behaviors for selected physical activities.
16. . . . recognizes that participation in physical activity can lead to multi-cultural and international understanding.
17. . . . understands that physical activity provides the opportunity for enjoyment, self-expression and communication.

VALUES physical activity and its contributions to a healthful lifestyle

18. . . . appreciates the relationships with others that result from participation in physical activity.
19. . . . respects the role that regular physical activity plays in the pursuit of life-long health and well-being.
20. . . . cherishes the feelings that result from regular participation in physical activity.

It can be noted that the NASPE outcomes reflect each of the seven curriculum models briefly described in this chapter, and together these outcomes comprise three broader curricular perspectives: *activity oriented*, *concept oriented*, and *individual oriented*. These perspectives are not mutually exclusive, as components of each approach can be found in the other approaches. Activity-oriented programs emphasize games, sports, and dance and most often exemplify the sports education and health-related physical fitness curriculum models. Activity-oriented programs represent what a physically educated person HAS, DOES, and IS. Concept-oriented programs emphasize an understanding of the principles and concepts of our discipline and most often exemplify the movement education and kinesiological studies curriculum models. Concept-oriented programs represent what a physically educated person KNOWS. Individual-oriented programs emphasize the benefits of physical activity and exemplify the developmental education, humanistic education, and personal meaning curriculum models. Individual-oriented programs represent what a physically educated person VALUES.

The notion of defining a few, specific and meaningful goals that can be reasonably accomplished in physical education programs has merit. Historically, physical educators have tried to achieve such a wide range of outcomes that the resulting physical education programs have lacked a central focus, and thus student learning has been compromised. Although the NASPE outcomes represent an example of a document that can be used to heighten the public's awareness regarding the value of physical education, the outcomes also reinforce past concerns with respect to program focus and intended learning outcomes.

REVIEW OF RESEARCH

The link between curriculum-as-theory and practice is enhanced if evidence is presented that a particular program can be successfully implemented. As Hellison (1989) points out, "although research cannot tell us what's worth doing, research can tell us if a particular model can achieve its goals in real settings with real kids—in other words, whether it works" (113). Historically, physical education curriculum research has been criticized for being involved in a great deal of theorizing, and producing very few empirical studies to support this theorizing. To a certain extent, this criticism is accurate, as there has not been a lot of empirical research related to physical education curriculum. However, as can be noted from examining the presentations from the last six *Proceedings* of the Curriculum Theory Conferences in Physical Education sponsored by Ann Jewett and held at the University of Georgia from 1979 to 1989, the percentage of data-based presentations has increased while the percentage of theoretical presentations has decreased. At the first three conferences, 9 data-based papers (18 percent of the presentations) were presented, whereas the last three conferences included 29 data-based papers (45 percent of the presentations).

Research studies in physical education curriculum can be described as using one of four generally accepted research methods (Borg and Gall 1983). These include experimental or controlled studies, quasi-experimental or uncontrolled studies, descriptive studies, and qualitative or naturalistic studies. Experimental designs provide the most rigorous test of causal hypotheses and with the exception of controlled epidemiological studies (Caspersen 1989; Paffenbarger 1988) are necessary to determine cause and effect. Empirical scientists start with specific hypotheses, manipulate certain aspects of the environment, and measure the impact of these manipulations. Quasi-experimental designs are useful in uncovering relationships between variables, and, although these types of studies are uncontrolled, the external validity is strengthened if findings are reported across time and in various settings. Quasi-experimental designs are often used in curriculum research when the investigator cannot directly manipulate the independent variables. Descriptive studies, which describe and interpret certain conditions or relationships that exist, are the most common in physical education curriculum research and typically include case studies, surveys, and correlational studies. Finally, qualitative or naturalistic studies attempt to describe what happens within the context of the physical education environment from the perspective of both teachers and students (Earls 1985; Goetz and LeCompte 1984; Sage 1989; Schutz 1989). Qualitative researchers do not start with specific hypotheses; rather, they describe the context or environment and determine how certain aspects of the environment interact with both the teacher and learner to influence behavior (Bain 1989b; Earls 1986). Locke (1989) has provided a summary for those unfamiliar with qualitative research. Qualitative designs are most useful in generating ideas and new perspectives about what to study, as well as in assisting the researcher in understanding the behavioral dynamics of the gym (Siedentop 1989).

As described by Bain (1989a), qualitative studies in physical education often have been based on one of four theoretical perspectives. These include *functionalist theory*, *correspondence theory*, *symbolic interaction theory*, and *critical theory*. Functionalist and correspondence theory are similar in that both view schools as teaching certain values whether or not they concur with teacher and student values, and both view schools as functioning to preserve society. However, they differ in their opinion regarding whether such a society is fundamentally just or unjust. *Functionalist theory* suggests that the schools are an effective place for students to learn societal norms and prepare to be effective participants in adult society. *Correspondence theory* proposes that "the hierarchically structured patterns of values, norms and skills that characterize the work force and the dynamics of class interaction under capitalism are mirrored in the social dynamics of the daily classroom" (Giroux 1981a, 6). *Symbolic interaction theory* focuses on the interactions of individuals and the process by which these individuals negotiate and subsequently agree upon a set of rules. Finally, *critical theory* is based on the assumption that all research is value based rather than value free. The goal of critical research is to empower the participants being studied to free themselves from sources of domination and repression (Anderson 1989). The researcher attempts to help subjects critically examine the social circumstances surrounding their lives and empower them to choose actions that improve their lives. Although the primary research focus is setting specific, the final step is to identify actions that might assist in the transformation of both schools and society, often referred to as emancipatory or radical pedagogy (Bain 1989b; Giroux 1981a, 1981b). As Bain (1990b) states, "the hope is not that the results can be directly applied in other settings, but that reading the study will inspire others to critically examine their own circumstances" (10).

The review of research will be organized into the following four sections: (1) curriculum perspectives, (2) curriculum models, (3) curriculum development, and (4) curriculum practice. The first section, curriculum perspectives, will examine how physical education curriculum is thought about and talked about. The second section, curriculum models, will focus on studies that examined the conceptual framework of one of the seven curriculum models described earlier. The third section, curriculum development, will include studies that examined curriculum documents and the dissemination of curriculum materials.

Collaborative models of curriculum research and development and the process of curriculum change also will be included. Finally, the fourth section, curriculum practice, will include descriptive studies of physical education programs and the effects of physical education programs on activity level, health-related physical fitness, motor skills, and "other" outcomes. Also included in this section will be studies related to the implicit curriculum.

Curriculum Perspectives

This section is divided into three parts. The first part examines the beliefs, values, and thought processes of teachers, as well as their day-to-day struggles in developing and implementing quality programs. The second part reviews the beliefs, values, and thought processes of students with respect to school physical education programs and physical activity in general. Finally, the third part considers outsiders' perceptions of the physical education curriculum.

Teacher Perspectives. Peterson (1988) has suggested that in order to truly understand what makes teachers effective, research needs to examine teachers' and students' thought processes, in addition to measuring teacher behavior and student achievement. One aspect of teacher cognition considered to influence the philosophical thought process of teachers is that of educational value orientations (Eisner and Vallance 1974; Jewett and Bain 1985). Ennis and Zhu (1991) have examined the extent to which decisions made by physical education teachers ($N = 90$) are consistent with their value orientations. Also examined was whether significant differences in value orientation were related to gender, teaching level, and teaching experience. For example, it is often assumed that a self-actualization value orientation, which emphasizes nurturing and caring, will more clearly characterize elementary as opposed to high school educators and female as opposed to male educators. A similar expectation is that more experienced educators will exemplify a disciplinary mastery orientation, as opposed to younger educators, who will choose to critically question current views and embrace a social reconstruction value orientation that challenges perceived oppression in the schools. A final hypothesis examined whether or not the majority of teachers could be classified within the most traditional value orientation of disciplinary mastery. Ninety out of 175 physical educators from three different school districts completed a Value Orientation Inventory (VOI) (Ennis and Hooper 1988) administered through the mail. The VOI contained 75 items arranged in 15 sets of 5 items. One item per set represented each of the 5 value orientations. Teachers rank ordered their preferences within each set of 5 items to reflect the curriculum knowledge they valued to be of most worth. Thus, a five-score value-orientation profile was constructed. All scores were converted to T-scores and classified into high- and low-priority orientations using T-tests. Chi-square tests were used to determine if differences in value orientation existed by gender, teaching level, and years of experience. Results revealed that approximately 97 percent of the teachers demonstrated a consistent position on at least one of the 5 value orientations, indicating that teachers do select learning outcomes reflective of a consistent value orientation. A summary of T-score data revealed that the following percentage of teachers consistently ranked (e.g., either high or low priority) each of the value orientations as follows: ecological validity, 63 percent; learning process, 58.9 percent; social reconstruction, 56.6 percent; self-actualization, 47.8 percent; and disciplinary mastery, 45.5 percent. Often, teachers placed a high priority on two or more value orientations, indicating that physical education teachers' belief systems included a variety of value perspectives and goals for teaching. The chi-square analyses revealed no significant difference by gender, teaching level, or years of experience, and thus the stereotypes sometimes proposed were not confirmed. Also, the hypothesis that disciplinary mastery would be the predominate value orientation was not supported, although most teachers did place a high priority on knowledge of subject matter. One explanation for this finding is that in some schools unique personal and social problems of students are of such magnitude that placing a priority on individual or context goals versus mastery of sport skill or knowledge goals is necessary.

In a related study, Ennis, Mueller, and Hooper (1990) examined the extent to which teachers' value orientations influenced their receptiveness to an in-service education program. Seven in-service sessions, based on a movement education curriculum (Logsdon et al. 1984), were designed for purposes of increasing teachers' use of movement terminology, shared decision making, and students' cognitive involvement with the lesson. All elementary physical education teachers ($N = 25$) in the Madison, Wisconsin, Metropolitan School District served as subjects. Success of the in-service program was measured by changes in the pre/post lesson plans of subjects. The authors hypothesized that efforts to implement a theoretically based movement education curriculum would be met with limited success by those teachers for whom the program conflicted with their value orientations. Although analysis of variance (ANOVA) results revealed no significant differences in the use of terminology from the first lesson plan to the second, a mean terminology use of 18.19 times prior to the in-service as opposed to 21.67 times following the in-service indicated that these teachers were already using movement terminology in their lesson planning. ANOVA results further indicated that teachers with weak disciplinary mastery orientations and strong social reconstruction orientations provided significantly more opportunities for shared decision making than did other teachers. Finally, with the exception of teachers possessing a strong disciplinary mastery orientation, most teachers changed their lesson plans to reflect more opportunities for student cognitive involvement. Results from this study indicate that value orientations mediate the extent to which teachers are willing to incorporate certain teaching strategies into their lesson planning.

A number of studies have also examined teachers' beliefs with respect to stated goals and objectives for physical education programs. Avery and Lumpkin (1987) have provided a historical review of the study of objectives in physical education. In general, most physical education teachers hold a wide range of goals (Rosentswieg 1969; Tillman 1976) and feel they have the knowledge and ability to teach these goals (Lambdin and Steinhardt in press). Loucks (1979) provided a summary of physical education professionals' objectives, which indicated that neuromuscular skills, self-realization, mental and emotional development, and the development of organic vigor were considered to be important objectives. Reed (1983) surveyed elementary and secondary school physical education teachers and found that secondary teachers ranked fitness first, the development of affective qualities second, and motor skill development third in order of importance, while elementary teachers ranked the development of affective qualities first, motor skills second, and fitness third.

Haag (1983) had teachers ($N = 560$) in the Federal Republic of Germany list the aims and objectives of physical education and also found that teachers hold a wide range of goals. The following 8 categories of objectives and their corresponding frequencies were listed: health and fitness (17.7 percent); personality and character development (17.2 percent); development of movement behavior (16.4 percent); social behavior and social learning (13.8 percent); affective domain (11.5 percent); development of recreational behavior (8.5 percent); general sport-specific objectives (10.1 percent); and cognitive-oriented objectives (3.9 percent). When asked to rank these physical education objectives in order of importance, the top 6 responses were as follows: preparation for recreation; fun and enjoyment; health; physical fitness; self-competency; and movement. It is interesting to note that although outcomes related to health and fitness were listed more frequently as goals for physical education, these outcomes were listed third and fourth in order of importance.

Several studies support the notion that physical education teachers generally teach using more than one curriculum model and incorporating aspects from all three curricular perspectives (e.g., activity, concept, individual). Caldwell and Bain (1985) used a Q sort consisting of 54 items to determine if university physical educators' ($N = 158$) perceptions of physical education curriculum were consistent with three selected curriculum models: fitness, sports education, and human movement. An equal number of statements describing the values, conceptual framework, and program design were written for each model. Results indicated that rather than supporting one model, physical education teachers considered the three models equally important. Mean scores for fitness (73.3), sports education (74.0), and human movement (69.6) were very close.

Ennis and Hooper (1990) conducted four studies that also support the multidimensionality of curriculum models. Although these studies are discussed in the curriculum models research section, one conclusion has relevance here. The authors state that the lack of a strong theoretical research base to guide practice is a likely reason for the efforts by physical educators to teach an eclectic curriculum. They further note that teaching an eclectic curriculum also may contribute to the difficulties teachers presently experience in implementing quality physical education programs.

A related body of research has addressed teachers' concerns with respect to the day-to-day struggles and limitations under which they train and work. Several studies have examined the curriculum from various perspectives and found that the functional or real curriculum does not always match the curriculum as recommended in the literature or the curriculum as intended to be taught by teachers. Williams (1980) compared the curriculum as recommended in the literature and by a teacher-training program to the curriculum actually practiced by junior high school teachers ($N = 36$). The recommended curriculum included objectives related to developmental education, social development, movement education, and kinesiological studies. Based upon interview data, Williams noted several discrepancies between the recommended curriculum and day-to-day practice. For example, recommendations for teaching were not based on empirical data, and the expectations of transfer from theory to practice were different from what was realistically attainable. Williams suggests that the model upon which contemporary junior high physical education programs are based may not be feasible due to constraints of the environment in which teachers train and work. This viewpoint supports Reid's (1978) assertion that theoretical discussions of physical education curriculum can be described as idealized practice in that curriculum theorists paint "a picture of what practice should be which tends to differ from what practitioners see as realistically attainable" (Williams 1980, 97). Placek (1983, 1984) conducted a naturalistic study of teacher planning in physical education using a multicase approach and found that teachers ($N = 4$), each with varying levels of experience, spent only a brief amount of time planning. Yet, as noted by Placek, all four teachers held well-organized classes in which students were on task and discipline problems were minimal. Placek concluded that teachers planned immediately prior to teaching and focused on the immediate act of teaching rather than on goals related to student learning, due to practical considerations and unpredictable teaching environments.

Kneer (1986) cited reasons specialists in Illinois secondary schools ($N = 128$) gave for not using the following eight teaching practices on a regular basis: goal-directed tasks, cueing, incentives, feedback, varied practice time, maximum active learning time, variety of learning experiences, and mastery learning. Reasons most often cited for not using these practices included "takes too much time" (36.19 percent) and "not necessary" (29.14 percent). Thirty-four percent cited "other" reasons, including such comments as "depends upon the activity" and "not practical." Although several responses may represent real barriers, others may represent lack of interest or perceived importance. For example, only 3.57 percent of the teachers stated "inability" as a reason for not using the teaching practices. Another example of lack of perceived importance is illustrated by Griffin (1985b) using ethnographic and phenomenological methodologies in an effort to identify and describe teachers' perceptions of and responses to sex equity problems. Griffin spent 84 hours observing in a New England elementary school and described one teacher's resentment of being required to teach coed classes:

> It just takes too much energy, too much fighting, and too much wasting time to do that. You have to decide what's important. Is it more important to get these boys and girls to interact together or more important for me to get the skills done? There's not time and energy to get everything in. Sure, you know what should happen. There are 800 things all at once and you can act on some of them and some of them you can't. You set priorities, and whether a boy takes a girl as a partner is not my priority, to be honest. (Griffin 1985b, 106)

In a related study (Lambdin and Steinhardt in press), 60 physical education teachers completed a questionnaire that assessed their level of agreement with 14 commonly identified goals for physical education. For each goal, participants also indicated their knowledge and ability to teach the goal, whether they taught the goal in their present curriculum, and whether their students achieved the goal. Results indicated that most teachers hold a wide range of goals and feel they have the knowledge and ability to teach these goals. A trend was evident, however, of a decrease in agreement from goal and knowledge statements to what was actually taught and then another decrease to what was learned by students. The fact that teachers actually perceive these three areas so differently is crucial to future study of what goes on in the gym. Obvious questions arise, such as, Why do teachers perceive these areas so differently, and how closely do teachers' perceptions match the perceptions of outside observers and students with respect to what is happening in the gym? One suggestion was for future research to focus on identifying barriers that stop teachers from teaching what they would like to and feel prepared to teach. This study suggests that teacher intentions are not the greatest problem. Questions remain as to how teachers actually move from intent to action in their own curriculum and what barriers prevent them from teaching what they intend to teach.

A recent series of papers, *Profiles of Struggles* (Locke and Griffin 1986), describes some of the obstacles and prevailing themes in teachers' struggles to change the barriers to quality teaching and quality programs. The series profiles five elementary and two secondary physical education teachers based upon interviews and observations. Seven common themes of coping strategies used to overcome systemic obstacles to excellence are identified and represent a teacher's attempt to gain control over a generally unresponsive environment. These include compromising, substituting, ignoring, giving up, tinkering, challenging, overcoming, and getting out. Griffin (1986) suggests that over a teacher's career many, if not all, of these strategies will be used. Although a few teachers profiled were able to overcome systemic obstacles to quality and develop exceptional programs, in general the norm emphasized mediocrity, compliance, and smooth operations rather than student achievement. These barriers are not limited to teachers in the United States, as physical education specialists ($N = 560$) in the Federal Republic of Germany listed 2,174 barriers to quality teaching, the most common being lack of time (27.6 percent), oversized classes (21.1 percent), inadequate facilities (10.0 percent), and no interest on the part of pupils (4.3 percent) (Haag 1983).

Preservice and classroom teachers also have expressed day-to-day struggles that affect quality teaching. In a study of preservice teachers ($N = 6$), in which 30 classes were randomly observed, the curriculum as observed by the investigators differed from the student teachers' intentional curriculum (Steinhardt et al. in press). The main reasons teachers gave for not teaching according to their intentions included student apathy toward participation, problems with student behavior, lack of adequate facilities and equipment, large class sizes, and students with English as a second language. In many cases ideals were compromised, and "getting through the day" appeared to be more important than student achievement.

Faucette, McKenzie, and Patterson (1990) conducted observations of kindergarten through sixth grade physical education classes ($N = 226$) in California taught by classroom teachers. Classes primarily consisted of low-organization games or free play, although frequently physical education was dropped from the daily schedule. The authors presented interview data revealing that environmental conditions such as facilities and equipment did not enable classroom teachers to provide an adequate physical education class. In addition, the reward structure of the schools emphasized academic instruction and provided little or no accountability for physical education. Finally, most classroom teachers did not feel adequately prepared to teach physical education and were not convinced that physical education was an integral part of children's education. Although Faucette and Patterson (1990) suggest that intensive in-service training should be provided for nonspecialists teaching physical education until school districts are able to hire specialists, Williams (1980) has stated that unless adequate courses are taken initially in teacher training, deficiencies are not likely to be rectified at a later date. A more accountable approach, as suggested by Faucette and Patterson (1990), would be for preservice teacher education programs to "require sufficient levels of knowledge and practical experience in elementary physical education before nonspecialists can be credentialed to teach this subject" (113).

Student Perspectives. A better understanding of students' attitudes and beliefs about physical education can greatly influence teacher effectiveness and the design of programs to address the needs of students. It is presumed that children's physical activity habits and preferences are developed in childhood (Baranowski et al. 1987; Gilliam and MacConnie 1984). Generally, children have a positive attitude toward physical education, although Shephard and Godin (1986) found that as students moved from grades 7 to 9, they were less likely to perceive exercise as being fun. The current research literature that focuses on participation during youth as an antecedent to adult activity participation is equivocal (Dishman 1990), and a better standardization of measures, as well as control for confounding variables, selection bias, and quality of programs, is needed (Powell and Dysinger 1987). Most of this research has focused on participation in sports rather than physical education, although one abstract (Ho et al. 1981) did find a positive relationship between men (*N* = 48) participating in a voluntary jogging program and a perceived positive experience in elementary school physical education. Greenockle, Lee, and Lomax (1990) suggest that education in health and fitness concepts and positive experiences in physical activity settings during primary school may have a profound effect on future activity behavior.

Smoll and Schutz (1980) used a multiple longitudinal design to assess the attitudes of children (boys = 58; girls = 56) in grades 4 through 6. A semantic differential inventory (Simon and Smoll 1974) adapted from the work of Kenyon (1968a, 1968b) measured children's attitudes toward physical activity (CATPA) on three repeated occasions (grades 4, 5, and 6) for two birth cohorts. The following 6 subdomains were used to describe reasons why children engage in physical activity: (1) as a social experience, (2) as health and fitness, (3) as pursuit of vertigo, (4) as an aesthetic experience, (5) as catharsis, and (6) as an ascetic experience. Although results revealed a nonsignificant grade by sex interaction, girls had more favorable attitudes toward the aesthetic subdomain, and boys had more favorable attitudes toward the pursuit of vertigo and catharsis subdomains. Group CATPA scores were generally positive and appeared stable across grades, although scores within individuals were not stable. Patterson and Faucette (1990) also used the CATPA inventory to compare the attitudes of fourth- and fifth-grade children (*N* = 414) in classes taught by specialists versus nonspecialists. Although their results found minimal differences in children's attitudes toward physical activity, the authors did acknowledge that factors such as curricular experiences, teacher characteristics, and the school environment were not controlled.

Macintosh and Albinson (1982) conducted a study of attitudes toward physical education using eighth grade students (*N* = 670) in selected eastern Ontario schools. The attitudes of students opting out of secondary school physical education were compared with those of students who elected to take physical education. Students who chose not to take physical education were found to (1) have lower academic grades; (2) perceive themselves as being less healthy, more often overweight, less fit, and less skillful than students participating in physical education; (3) have lower self-concepts; (4) denote less positive attitudes toward physical activity and physical education; (5) perceive physical education as a threat to their perceived fitness and skill adequacies; (6) receive less encouragement to take physical education from significant others; and (7) be less pleased with aspects of the program such as program development, grading, and levels of competition. These findings also were confirmed at a 3-year follow-up during the eleventh grade. Of the students available to participate (*N* = 509), 83 percent (*N* = 424) participated in the 3-year follow-up. The more positive attitudes that initially distinguished those students who signed up for physical education in grade 8 remained remarkably consistent at grade 11. Macintosh and Albinson (1982) conclude that grade 8 is a critical period with respect to student election of secondary school physical education.

The identification of expected outcomes and perceived barriers to participation in physical activity during adolescence is an important step toward increasing the likelihood that an active lifestyle will be adopted and maintained. This approach also provides a primary data source from which to design a physical education curriculum with a personal orientation. Godin and Shephard (1986) surveyed students (*N* = 698) attending two junior high schools in Toronto and found that girls associated "looking better" as an expected outcome of physical activity more than boys did, whereas boys associated "being healthy," "being tired," and "having fun" as positive outcomes of physical activity more than girls did. Students in grade 7 had more positive feelings regarding "being tired" as a result of activity and were more likely to perceive exercise as "fun" and as helping them "to be physically fit" than students in grade 9. This finding was also supported by Greenockle, Lee, and Lomax (1990), who found ninth grade students to have a wide range of complaints regarding participation in a fitness unit, including such comments as (1) "it's too hot," (2) "it's too cold," (3) "I don't want to dress out," (4) "I don't want to get sweaty," and (5) "I don't want to mess up my hair or make-up." Welsh and Labbe (1989) surveyed school-aged children (boys = 49; girls = 27) from 5 to 17 years of age (average = 9.6 years) to determine if "fun runs" were really fun. The authors concluded that children participate in fun runs for fun as contrasted with adults who participate for fitness or weight control; therefore, future programs for children that strive to influence long-term activity patterns should emphasize the enjoyable and social aspects of activity. Tappe, Duda, and Ehrnwald (1989) examined the barriers to exercise among high school students (*N* = 236) by gender (41 percent male, 59 percent female) and self-reported levels of physical activity. The major barriers to exercise included time constraints, unsuitable weather, school and schoolwork, and lack of interest or desire. Univariate ANOVAs revealed that high school males were less likely to exercise due to "use of alcohol or drugs" or "having a girlfriend," whereas high school females were less likely to exercise due to "time constraints." Finally, low-active students were significantly less likely to exercise due to perceived "time constraints" and "lack of desire or interest."

Similar expected outcomes and perceived barriers to exercise have been reported by university students. Lander (1983) developed an Incentive Values Inventory in an effort to explain motives for participation and to predict preferences for physical activity among college students (*N* = 684). The hypothesized model of incentive values for participation in physical activity consisted of 162 items that included 18 incentive value dimensions or reasons for participating in physical activity. A principal components analysis with varimax rotation yielded the following 12 factors, explaining 66 percent of the total variance: socialization, dominance, aesthetic expression, body cathexis, excellence, independence, stress-reduction, esteem, thrill seeking, joy, aggression, and leadership. A high correlation among several of the value dimensions indicated that certain incentive values are closely related; thus preference for and participation in physical activity may involve a group of similar incentive values. Interestingly, when the value dimensions were arranged vertically according to their intercorrelations, a similarity to Maslow's (1954) hierarchy of needs was noted. The first level of Maslow's hierarchy, physiological needs, corresponds to the incentive values, body cathexis, and stress reduction. The second level, need for belonging, reflects the incentive values socialization and independence. The third level, need for esteem, reflects the incentive values esteem and leadership. Finally, the highest level in Maslow's hierarchy, self-actualization, corresponds to the incentive values joy, aesthetic expression, and thrill seeking.

A two-way ANOVA (gender by incentive value) indicated that excellence, body cathexis, and stress reduction were the most likely valued reasons for engaging in physical activity. Males valued dominance, aggression, leadership, esteem, and thrill seeking significantly more than females, whereas females valued body cathexis, aesthetic expression, and stress reduction significantly more than males. The least valued dimensions for the total group were dominance and aggression. Discriminant function analysis also was performed to determine if the incentive value scores could effectively discriminate between high- and low-preference groups for the following activities: individual, rhythmic, nature, running, target, water/snow, martial arts, team/ball, racquet sports, team/implement. Classification was equal to or above 69 percent for five of these activities. Lander (1983) suggests that the Incentive Values Inventory can be used to assist in the design of personalized physical education curricula that encourage clarification of personal intentions and provide experiences in human movement which have personal significance.

In a similar study, Steinhardt and Dishman (1989) conducted a prospective investigation to examine the reliability and validity of self-report scales for assessing outcome-expectancy values and barriers for participating in physical activity. College students from two sections of a jogging course ($N = 80$) and a health-related concepts and physical activity course ($N = 163$) served as subjects for the study. A principal components analysis identified three outcome-expectancy factors (psychological, body image, health) and three perceived barrier factors (time, effort, obstacles). The four most common expected outcomes were stay in shape, make me feel better in general, good health, and maintain proper body weight. The four most common perceived barriers were lack of motivation, too lazy, too busy, and not enough time. At week 9, students with higher estimates of energy expenditure in supervised running ([illegible]) were less likely to perceive barriers of time and effort ($R^2 = .27$).

Although student perceptions of physical education classes are influenced by a variety of factors, two main influences that appear to have a significant impact on behavior are teacher characteristics and student perceptions of the actual activity experience. Melville and Maddalozzo (1988) examined whether a male physical education teacher's appearance of body fatness influenced students' (1) attitudes toward the instructor, (2) perceptions of the instructor's knowledge, (3) performance on a knowledge-based exam, and (4) intentions to try to improve their level of physical fitness. Also measured was the belief that a physical education instructor should be an appropriate role model. Students ($N = 850$) from six schools in the northwestern part of the United States aged 14 to 19 were randomly assigned by class to watch one of two videotapes. Each tape was 20 minutes long, and the only difference between the tapes was that in one the physical education instructor wore a "fat suit" to present the image of an overweight teacher. The first half of the tape consisted of a lecture and demonstration regarding the concepts and importance of flexibility, and the second half discussed the role of diet and exercise with respect to body composition. Results revealed that students liked the fit instructor ($t = 26.37$, $p < .01$) more than the overweight instructor and perceived the former as more knowledgeable ($t = 14.44$, $p < .01$). Based on a 5-point Likert scale, students also felt that it was important for a physical education teacher to be a good role model (average = 4.10), and further analysis did not support the hypothesis that overweight students would rate the fat instructor more positively than their thin counterparts. Finally, a two-by-two (instructor fitness level by concept area) ANOVA revealed that students who watched the fit tape made significantly fewer errors on the exam than viewers of the overweight tape ($F = 206.66$, $p < .01$) and were more likely to report that they planned to improve their future fitness level as a result of watching the tape ($t = 5.74$, $p < .01$).

Students' perceptions of their activity experiences also influence attitudes and participation patterns. Worsley et al. (1984) conducted two studies investigating 10-year-old children's perceptions of physical education and other school activities. Study one involved students ($N = 600$) who attended 50 classes in 22 different schools in Australia. Classes were randomly assigned to receive either daily physical education or the conventional, less active physical education. Pre- and post-testing consisted of an attitudinal measure and a body fat index measure. The questionnaire, consisting of forms one and two, measured attitudes toward a variety of physical activities and academic subjects. Form one contained the following questions: "Do you like it? Does your best friend(s) like it? Are you good at it? In the future will you try harder at it?" (202). Form two contained the following questions: "Is it fun? Is it good for you? Is it difficult? If you try hard, will you be good at it?" (202). Body fat was determined from the sum of four skinfold measurements (triceps, biceps, subscapular, and suprailiac), and test-retest reliability over a 7-day period was $r = .95$. Differences in perceptions for slim and obese children accounted for 71.2 percent and 76.3 percent of the variance, respectively. In general, obese girls and boys found distance running more difficult, and they evaluated it less favorably, whereas they found flexibility and rhythmic dance activities more favorable than their slim counterparts. Slim children tended to feel that if they tried hard at physical activities they could excel. They also perceived their best friends as having more positive attitudes toward physical activity. Obese children were more pessimistic regarding the daily physical education treatment, particularly with regard to endurance activities, whereas the opinions of slim children regarding physical education were unaltered. A second study, which served as a replication, involved 528 children in grades 4 and 5 living in a metropolitan city in Australia. Results were basically the same as in study one, although the findings were more pronounced for boys and less pronounced for girls. In general, these children liked activities they perceived as easy, and they were willing to try hard at these activities. Worsley et al. (1984) suggest that daily physical education programs that incorporate endurance activities may in fact cause obese children to develop less favorable attitudes toward physical education.

There is some evidence to indicate that physical education classes are less effective in changing activity patterns of less fit students (Macintosh and Albinson 1982). Sherrill and Holguin (1989) examined the attitudes toward physical education in two elementary schools in Texas. All children ($N = 393$) enrolled in grades 4 and 5 of these two schools were administered the Texas Physical Fitness Test (Governor's Commission on Physical Fitness 1973) and a Children's Attitude Inventory Toward Physical Education, developed by the authors. Fitness scores were converted to T scores and summed to identify high- and low-fit girls and boys. Overall, level of fitness was not significantly correlated with attitudes toward physical education. However, when subjects ($N = 204$) were divided into the upper 26 percent and lower 27 percent of fitness level in their classes, a one-way ANOVA revealed significant differences among these four groups on attitude toward physical education ($F = 4.86$, $p < .003$). A Scheffe post hoc test indicated that highly fit girls had significantly more positive attitudes toward physical education classes than did the least fit boys.

As a participant observer in a university exercise class on fitness and weight control, Bain (1985a) examined students' ($N = 34$) expectations and reactions to the class. As expected, most students enrolled in the course to improve their level of fitness and lose weight; however, the less fit, overweight students were not as successful in changing their exercise behavior. Bain suggests that the lack of success for less fit students may be due in part to the structure of the course. The course reflected a technical-rational view, which assumed that information and knowledge would change behavior. In contrast, student reactions reflected a subjective-affective view, which posits that behavior is influenced by feelings and emotions. Although body-cathexis scores were significantly related to body fat ($r = .43$, $p < .02$) for moderately overweight students ($N = 15$), the course expectations differed. The expected outcomes for students with more positive body images related to fun and relaxation, whereas moderately overweight students with less positive body images emphasized goals related to weight loss.

Outsiders' Perspectives. Physical education is often perceived by outsiders as a nonacademic subject (Bain 1990a). As a result, physical education teachers have low subject status, a fact that students in physical education teacher education quickly perceive (Hendry 1975). Teacher/coach role conflict, as well as the low status of pedagogy within physical education departments, further intensifies the marginal status of physical education (Bain 1990a).

In 1972, a National Adult Fitness Survey (Clark 1973) found that of the 76 million Americans who had had school physical education, most adults felt they had a positive experience. Only 1.1 million adults felt physical education was a bad experience, while 9.8 million adults were neutral in their opinion. The impact of physical education programs on adult activity patterns was less clear. Although approximately 91 percent of adults felt children should have school physical education from elementary school through college, 45 percent of the population surveyed was sedentary. Of present concern, however, is that more recent polls suggest a decline in the number of Americans who feel that physical education should be a required course in school. A 1984 Gallup Poll measuring attitudes of Americans toward the public schools found that only 43 to 44 percent felt physical education should be required for high school students, irrespective of their plans for college (Gallup 1984). Moreover, this rate has remained unchanged from earlier Gallup surveys of 1981 and 1983 (Dishman and Dunn 1988). With respect to subject matter importance, physical education follows health education and ranks eighth in terms of importance. This is of primary concern given that the biggest drop in physical activity across the age span occurs in late adolescence as youth leave school (Dishman and Dunn 1988; Stephens, Jacobs, and White 1985).

Dishman and Dunn (1988) state that the lack of perceived importance for physical education may be due in part to a lack of knowledge with respect to the amounts of physical activity necessary for health and fitness. For example, although the Perrier Fitness in America Survey (Harris 1979) indicated that health was the top perceived benefit of exercise, 33 percent of adults believed that golf or bowling three times each week was sufficient for fitness, and 57 percent felt that baseball three times each week was sufficient for fitness. Nonetheless, only 3 percent of Americans stated that further knowledge of the benefits of exercise would motivate them to increase their activity patterns.

Curriculum Models

This section focuses on studies whose purpose was to examine the conceptual framework of one of the physical education curriculum models described earlier. Although seven models were described, studies examining the structural framework were found for only two of the models, social development and personal meaning.

Social Development. The social development model has evolved from a 15-year process of goal clarification, search for appropriate strategies necessary to successfully implement the model, and evaluation of results. Much of Hellison's initial work with the model is summarized in *Beyond Balls and Bats* (Hellison 1978). Since this time, additional projects have been completed in a variety of field settings, including inner-city high schools, alternative schools, housing projects, a residential boys' home, and an after-school dropout prevention program (Hellison 1989b, 1990a; Hellison and Templin 1991). Research projects to date have been "based on a model that teaches self and social responsibility through a process of awareness, experience, decision-making, and self-reflection" (Hellison 1990a, 38). Bain (1989b) notes that much of Hellison's work can be described from a critical theory perspective, since his aim is not merely to describe students but to empower them to increase their self-responsibility and caring for others.

DeBusk and Hellison (1989) investigated the efficacy of the social development model for teaching self-responsibility to delinquency-prone youth. Ten fourth grade boys referred by school officials as behavior problems participated in a special physical education program conducted for three 1-hour periods each week for 6 weeks. Approximately 200 pages of transcribed qualitative data were collected from six data sources, and results were summarized in terms of behavior, affective, and knowledge changes. In general, the data supported the efficacy of the model as a channel for improving social development for delinquency-prone youth. Although no changes occurred in referrals for any of the boys as a result of the special program, both the teacher-researcher and the two teaching assistants noted several behavior changes by the end of the special program, especially in self-control (Level I) and caring (Level IV). Additionally, classroom teachers reported positive behavior changes in the classroom in 5 of the 10 boys, and playground supervisors reported positive changes in self-control for 8 of the 10 boys. With respect to affective changes, pre- and postinterviews revealed that the boys preferred the special program to their regular physical education class, even though the instructor was the same for both classes. Student journal entries and postinterviews supported a more open and sharing attitude, despite some internal struggle at each of the levels. For example, one student reported, "When he hit me I was going to hit him back but Level Zero [irresponsibility] suddenly flashed in my head!" (DeBusk and Hellison 1989, 109). Both the interview data and journal entries also demonstrated that the students had developed an understanding of the levels, particularly Level I (self-control) and Level IV (caring). Fewer changes occurred in both the model and the teacher-researcher. With the exception of strategies for transfer, the model retained its validity. The teacher-researcher came to view the model as applicable with students in regular physical education class in addition to the delinquency-prone youth.

Hellison (1990a, 1990b), Lifka (1990), and Georgiadis (1990) have recently published a series of articles describing and evaluating the effectiveness of the Physical Education At-Risk Youth Program at the University of Illinois at Chicago. In general, they report many success stories, although Hellison notes that when working with disadvantaged youth, "no amount of interaction with this model will rectify the poverty, lack of job opportunities, and related urban problems" (Hellison 1990b, 44)

Lifka (1990) implemented the social development model in an after-school physical education program for sixth, seventh, and eighth grade students in a low-socioeconomic neighborhood marked with high gang activity. Several strategies were used, including problem solving at Level I, positive reinforcement at Level II, proximal goal setting at Level III, group discussion at Level IV, and self-reflection for all levels. Although Lifka admittedly stated that he "struggled mightily along the way" (41), he felt the program did successfully affect his students. "It's harder to teach this way but so much more rewarding," commented Lifka—"I'll never go back" (41). The following student interview response is an example of the success of the program:

> This program is trying to help us look at life another way, trying to help us express our feelings, trying to help us understand what the world is all about. We came here [to the United States] to get a better life, to get a better job. The program teach[es] us to go to high school and not drop out. To try even though you get bad grades, to try and get good grades. (41)

Teachers of the students also described a change in student behavior. During one of the interviews a teacher commented, "their cursing, the name-calling, that has changed a lot. And I thought it had a lot to do with the gym program" (41).

Georgiadis (1990) developed and implemented a basketball program at an inner-city residential boys' home. The program consisted of two practices a week and game play on Saturday mornings. The racial mixture of the team was an equal ratio of blacks, hispanics, and whites. Initially, the teacher struggled as he learned how important his actions were in influencing behavior. He realized that he had adopted the goals of the model but not the strategies when his emphasis on winning reinforced highly skilled players' complaining about the less skilled players' lack of ability, and less skilled players' complaining about not getting any playing time. The social development model implemented involved levels of self-control, inclusion of everyone, goal setting, and cooperating as a team. In addition, all practice sessions emphasized the strategies of reflection and problem-solving barriers to team progress. Success at Level I was reported by both the recreational therapist and the counselor at the residential home in that the players were discussing self-control and respect in the home and their self-control around the home had improved. During one game a player who became frustrated after being harassed by the opposing team remarked during a time out, "Coach, take me out. I don't want to lose my self-control!" (43). Levels III and IV were also incorporated, as evidenced by players working for 15–20 minutes individually and modifying drills as a team when needed.

Personal Meaning. Over the past 20 years, the Purpose Process Curriculum Framework (PPCF) has produced the largest body of research in physical education curriculum relative to the testing of a given curriculum model. The personal meaning model has evolved through a series of approximately 30 research studies, many of which are summarized in a special monograph in the *Journal of Teaching in Physical Education* (Jewett and Bain 1987). Jewett and Mullan (1977) suggest that the PPCF be used to provide the scope for appropriate instruction so that individuals can pursue related but varying individual goals. Several studies have confirmed the presence of the purpose concepts defined in the PPCF. Chapman (1974) devised the Movement Purposes Attitude Inventory (MPAI) to evaluate the affective responses of secondary students to each purpose concept of the PPCF. The MPAI, which is a semantic differential instrument, revealed two dimensions of attitude, likeability (e.g., fun, interesting) and utility (e.g., beneficial, worthwhile). Mangham (1979) replicated Chapman's (1974) study and was also able to identify these two dimensions (Lander and Chapman 1987). Ennis (1985, 1987) designed the Middle School Movement Purposes Inventory (MSMPI) to assess the presence of purpose concepts in an operational middle school curriculum. Ennis confirmed the presence of purpose concepts in the operational curriculum as well as the dimension of utility as identified by Chapman (1974).

Similar studies have been conducted with college students and a variety of purposes acknowledged as reasons for engaging in physical activity. Norton (1982, 1987) examined personal reasons college students enrolled in Fitness for Life physical education classes and found students consider the following as the most meaningful purposes for engaging in activity: musculoskeletal efficiency, attractiveness, mechanical efficiency, circulo-respiratory efficiency, weight control, vitality, and enjoyment. Kisabeth (1985) identified the most and least meaningful PPCF purposes for physical education majors and college students enrolled in physical education activity classes. This study required subjects to rank order their top seven and bottom seven movement purposes. The most meaningful purposes were musculoskeletal efficiency, catharsis, and weight control, whereas the least meaningful purposes were cultural understanding, leadership, and teamwork. Neikirk (1985) determined the characteristics of reentry women students and their reasons for participating in physical activity. Results revealed a significant relationship between health status and the purposes spatial orientation and joy of movement. Significant chi-square values also were reported for 15 of the purposes as related to skill level.

Although much of the work related to the PPCF has focused on theory, the psychometric properties of the conceptual framework also have been examined. The content validity of the 22 purposes as defined in the PPCF has been established using a Delphi technique (LaPlante 1973; LaPlante and Jewett 1987). Recently, the results of LaPlante's study were supported by a cross-cultural (i.e., United States, England, Japan) study investigating comparisons of the 22 purpose items as desired student outcomes for the present as well as the future (Speakman-Yearta 1987). Several studies using various populations and instruments have been designed using the list of 22 purpose items, most of which have focused on further validation of the PPCF (Ennis and Hooper 1990; Jewett and Bain 1987; Steinhardt, Jewett, and Mullan 1988).

Ennis and Hooper (1990) conducted three studies in an effort to develop an instrument that would examine physical education teachers' priorities for making curricular decisions. The PPCF served as the theoretical framework from which to base decisions regarding content. Study one was conducted with secondary physical education teachers ($N = 10$) to determine whether the aims and goals listed on a questionnaire were relevant and applicable for their physical education classes. Five items were written for each of the 22 purpose concepts, and each teacher was asked to write qualitative statements for a subsample of 60 items indicating the relevance of the item for their classes. Once the items had been revised, study two consisted of an evaluation by curriculum experts of the theoretical consistency of the items with the PPCF purposes using a 5-point Likert scale ranging from poorly represents to strongly represents. Thirty-nine members of NASPE who had attended one or more of the biannual Physical Education Curriculum Theory Conferences between 1979 and 1985 served as subjects for this study. Items with a mean score greater than 3.70 and alpha coefficients for categories greater than or equal to .70 were retained. Only 8 of the 22 purpose categories had alpha coefficients that met this criterion, suggesting that the other 14 concepts were multidimensional. Study three was originally designed to examine the reliability of the purpose concepts in school settings; however, because of the low internal consistency in study two, public school teachers ($N = 94$) were asked to rank order 84 items representing 22 purpose concepts arranged in 12 sets. Each set represented 7 different concepts in the PPCF. Results of this study indicated that using a ranking format did not increase the likelihood that purpose concepts were internally consistent but rather further supported the multidimensionality of the PPCF. Only one category, joy of movement, met the internal consistency criterion of .70.

In a related study, the PPCF served as the hypothesized theoretical structure for attempting to validate the Purposes for Engaging in Physical Activity Scale (PEPAS) (Steinhardt, Jewett, and Mullan 1988). This instrument was based on the personal meaning model and contained 22 items representing the three key concepts (Individual Development, Environmental Coping, Social Interaction) of the PPCF. The PEPAS was administered to fourth ($N = 259$) and sixth grade ($N = 392$) students participating in coeducational physical education classes in Georgia. Although the instrument had sufficient internal consistency and test-retest reliability, principal components analysis failed to confirm the hypothesized structure of the scale. A recent study (Shifflett et al. 1990) conducted in California also examined the structure of the PEPAS and found similar results. These studies suggest that either the PEPAS needs revision to more accurately represent the conceptual framework or the conceptual framework needs restructuring to represent more accurately the factor structure derived in these studies.

Although the overall structure of the PPCF has not been established, it should be noted that lack of support for the hypothesized structure does not mean the 22 purposes are not valid. It is possible that each purpose might be valid individually even though clusters of purpose items might not be valid (Steinhardt, Jewett, and Mullan 1988). For example, the content validity of the PPCF has been established, as previously discussed, and several studies have addressed the construct validity of individual purpose items (Rady et al. 1987). Jones (1972) conducted a construct validity study of the purpose awareness, Tiburzi (1979) validated the major purpose of physiological efficiency, Rady (1981) validated a theoretical construct for relationships, and Segall (1984) developed and validated a model of the construct teamwork.

Curriculum Development

This section focuses on curriculum development and is divided into two parts. The first part examines research related to curriculum documents and the dissemination of curriculum materials. The second part considers collaborative models for research and development and the process of curriculum change.

Curriculum Documents. One approach to studying physical education curriculum development is to examine how the curriculum is described in textbooks and curriculum guides. Only one study was found that focused on curriculum materials, this being a content analysis of textbooks in elementary physical education. Barrett (1987, 1988b) examined elementary physical education texts between 1917 and 1986 in order to determine the conceptualization of elementary school physical education subject matter. After examining over 60 textbooks, she concluded that physical educators currently perceive the subject matter from two different perspectives—a physical activity perspective and a human movement perspective. A physical activity perspective emphasizes a balanced range of activities, such as simple games and relays, fitness activities, and sport skills organized in a progression from simple to complex across grade levels. A human movement perspective emphasizes movement forms and an analysis of relationships in space, such as pathways, extensions, meeting/parting, and in front/behind. Barrett suggests that rather than continue to try to merge these two perspectives or debate the question of which perspective should be the subject matter of children's physical education, we should acknowledge that the two perspectives are different and, as such, allow physical education teachers to build their programs around one basic perspective. She further states that textbooks can be chosen that support either of these two perspectives. It should be noted that this viewpoint supports the unidimensionality of curriculum models rather than the multidimensionality of models.

A second way to examine the impact of curriculum documents is through the effectiveness of the dissemination process and its subsequent use at the local level. Although several states have mandated physical education content to be covered in the curriculum, the development of a national curriculum seems unlikely. Bain (1990a) suggests that the absence of two mechanisms for controlling school curriculum (e.g., textbooks and standardized achievement tests) accounts for the autonomy regarding curriculum development at the local level. The current emphasis on health-related physical fitness at the local level is perhaps due in part to the availability of health-related physical fitness texts for school-aged children, such as *Personal Fitness and You* (Stokes and Moore 1986), and five nationally distributed health-related youth fitness tests, including the Physical Best Program (American Alliance for Health, Physical Education, Recreation, and Dance 1988), FITNESSGRAM (Institute for Aerobics Research 1987), Fit Youth Today (American Health and Fitness Foundation 1986), the Presidential Physical Fitness Awards Program (U.S. Department of Health and Human Services 1988), and the YMCA Youth Fitness Test (Franks 1989).

Two studies were found that examined the effectiveness of the dissemination process. One of these related to the dissemination and use of health-related physical fitness materials and the other to the dissemination and use of the Basic Stuff Series. In both cases, the dissemination of national materials to the local level has not been very effective. Safrit and Wood (1986) administered a Health-Related Physical Fitness Test Opinionnaire (Safrit and Wood 1983) to a stratified random sample of physical education teachers in Illinois ($N = 1625$), Oregon ($N = 338$), and Arizona ($N = 950$) to examine the use of the AAHPERD Health-Related Physical Fitness Test (HRPFT) (American Alliance for Health, Physical Education, Recreation, and Dance 1980). The overall return response was 31 percent. Of the total sample ($N = 895$), 19 percent of the teachers had used the HRPFT and 81 percent had not. Those teachers who used the test reported motivation, evaluation, and diagnosis of fitness as major benefits, although 11 percent of this group did not feel that health-related physical fitness was an important part of the physical education curriculum. Safrit and Wood (1986) concluded that the HRPFT received limited use in these three states and therefore that increased publicity of the test and efforts to educate teachers with respect to the availability and rationale for using the HRPFT are needed.

Placek (1989) conducted an evaluation of the implementation of the Basic Stuff Series, published by AAHPERD in 1981. Distribution of survey questionnaires were limited to individuals ($N = 966$) who had purchased the Basic Stuff Series between 1982 and 1986. Results indicated that approximately two thirds of the respondents had read the Basic Stuff Series, and over half reported using both Series I (66 percent) and Series II (55 percent) in their present work. However, the return response rate was a moderately low 20.5 percent, and of those responding, the majority of teachers only "somewhat" used the Series (Series I, 54 percent; Series II, 47 percent), "very little" used the Series

(Series I, 20 percent; Series II, 26 percent), or "not at all" used the Series (Series I, 14 percent; Series II, 19 percent). Although there was no description of the use of Basic Stuff materials at the local level, 31 percent of respondents were elementary teachers, 22 percent secondary teachers, 28 percent college or university teachers, and 16 percent taught at more than one level.

Collaborative Models. Examples of successful collaborative programming in which teachers and researchers have merged university and public school resources are becoming more evident. The *Journal of Teaching in Physical Education* recently published a special monograph describing two types of collaborative programs, program assistance models and research-bonded models (Martinek and Schempp 1988). Program assistance models typically provide support to preservice and in-service programs through teaching centers, workshops, and resource centers. In research-bonded models, practitioners and researchers work together in proposing research questions and in carrying out the research process. Graham (1988) points to several benefits of university–school collaboration, including improved preservice and in-service education, improved research consumption, increased communication between university and public schools, and effective assistance in times of urgency. Although the two models will be discussed separately, they are not independent as research questions, and studies are a natural extension as the collaborative relationship grows. Further, program assistance models, which tend to focus on the practical side of teachers' work, keep university personnel in touch with the realities of schools.

Examples of program assistance models include the Physical Education Development Center at Teachers College, Columbia University (Anderson 1982, 1987, 1988), the Second Wind Program at the University of Massachusetts (Griffin and Hutchinson 1988), and the Teacher Education Center for Children at the University of North Carolina at Greensboro (Barrett 1988a). These programs are similar in that they (1) are designed to enhance physical education programs in surrounding schools, (2) have a faculty member assigned to work in the program, and (3) are based on a mutually respectful relationship. Nonetheless, the structure of the programs is slightly different at each site. At Columbia University, access to the school districts is pursued only if the director of physical education for K–12 programs is interested in joining. Once a district joins, that district is asked to complete a self-assessment of current programs and establish priorities for program development. The teachers in the district are viewed as the key decision makers, and research is considered a byproduct of the program and clearly subordinate to curriculum development efforts. Although the other two programs are similar in scope and focus, a few points are worthy of mention. In addition to providing resources for the expressed needs of teachers, the Second Wind program specifically encourages isolated or disenchanted teachers to get involved in an effort to renew their commitment to teaching. These efforts support Templin's (1988) recommendation for formal structures that function to reduce isolation and promote colleagueship. The North Carolina program also is unique in that university faculty taught the physical education classes for children in the schools while classroom teachers at first observed, later assisted, and eventually taught one, two, and finally, three lessons each week. Once this phase of the center was completed, a similar training process continued for university students, with classroom teachers serving as the model teachers.

Five examples of research-bonded models are included in the *Journal of Teaching in Physical Education* special monograph on collaboration (Martinek and Schempp 1988). In the first example, Martinek and Butt (1988) present an action research model that is used as part of a collaborative arrangement between the University of North Carolina at Greensboro and Greensboro public school teachers. The "philosophy that embraces action research methodology advocates a team concept whereby teachers, researchers, and administrators engage concurrently in the formulation and conduct of research. The primary focus is on resolving the concerns of the practitioners" (215). In the present study, 12 middle school teachers participated in a fall workshop before school began and subsequently a second workshop midway through the fall semester. These workshops were followed by a series of planned sessions in which research strategies to help teachers address instructional concerns involved the following five stages: (1) identification of instructional problems, (2) development of a research strategy, (3) implementation of the action research project, (4) discussion of results, and (5) future recommendations. Martinek and Butt (1988) present case study results of one middle school teacher who studied the effects that reciprocal teaching (Mosston and Ashworth 1986) and assigning students as squad captains had on on-task and off-task behavior. Three of the teacher's most disruptive students served as subjects, and event recording was used to monitor the effects of the intervention. Baseline measures were collected followed by 8 instructional periods and post-intervention measures. All coding was done by the university researcher, and results indicated that on-task behavior for the 3 target students increased from 73 percent to 80 percent, while off-task behavior decreased from 27 percent to 19 percent.

Several studies were related to the success of various program development projects. In a study by Almond and Thorpe (1988), teachers agreed to monitor and critically reflect on their teaching of games as related to student understanding. As a result, teachers reported learning more about themselves, their students, and the teaching process. The authors suggest that successful reflective practice requires teachers to keep journals of their experiences and reflections, meet regularly to share ideas, and have an outsider available to act as a facilitator. In a related study that examined teachers' reactions to program development activities over a 6-year period at Columbia University (Schwager and Doolittle 1988), checklist and interview data revealed that teachers most valued the opportunity to meet with other teachers from various districts to discuss practical concerns. Contrary to the Almond and Thorpe (1988) study, however, the additional writing of activities that was not a part of teachers' normal duties was seen as an added burden that required too much time. Other important features of successful programs included teacher "ownership" of program development projects, voluntary participation on the part of teachers, and an emphasis on practical ideas that could be readily adapted to the school setting.

The two final studies representing research-bonded models addressed effects of program development programs on teacher behavior and the process of change. Ratliffe (1988) used a multiple baseline design to examine the effects of two evaluation procedures on class management time and student activity time: the principals' subjective observation of gym class and observation following a videotaped training session using systematic observation. Results indicated that the subjective observation procedures used by the principals did not produce a positive and reliable change of class management and activity time, whereas positive changes were seen in classes followed by evaluations using systematic evaluation. Ratliffe suggests that principals can benefit from information regarding essential components of quality physical education programs and that the supervision skills gained can be effectively used to help physical education teachers. An additional important benefit is that the physical educators in this study expressed enthusiasm and appreciation for principals showing some attention to their classes.

Faucette (1988) used a Concerns-Based Adoption Model to study teachers' concerns when participating in an in-service program. The in-service program consisted of four training sessions over a 3-month period conducted for elementary physical education teachers ($N = 7$) within one school district. Special attention was devoted to using a movement approach to curriculum development and to increasing students' activity levels. During the in-service program, data were collected using a Stages of Concern Questionnaire (SoCQ), followed by an open-ended statement of concerns, and interview data. These data were not shared with the university consultant leading the in-service program or the elementary teachers. Results of the concern data were discouraging in that five of the seven teachers never implemented the changes (Faucette 1987). Of these teachers, two were identified as "resisters" by the SoCQ profiles, and the other three teachers reflected scores expressing informational or personal concerns. The two teachers that successfully implemented the innovations had SoCQ profiles consistent with those of users of innovations. These teachers had higher levels of concern, such as concerns that the success of the program depended not only on their performance but on a collaborative effort by both teachers and administrators. These teachers also felt that their principals supported and appreciated their efforts, believed in their abilities, and desired the program to be a success (Faucette and Graham 1986). Thus, Faucette (1988) concludes that, in addition to focusing on the outcomes of training programs, teachers' concerns with respect to proposed programs must be identified, respected, and responded to if successful implementation of innovative change programs is to occur.

Curriculum Practice

This section is divided into five parts and examines descriptive studies of physical education classes, as well as the effects of physical education programs on students. The first part presents descriptive studies of physical education classes in schools and children's level of activity within these classes. The second part presents studies that examined the impact of physical education programs on the health-related physical fitness of children. The third part describes studies that examined the effects of physical education programs on motor skills, and the fourth part examines a general category of "other" outcomes of physical education programs. Finally, the fifth part focuses on studies related to the implicit curriculum in physical education.

School Physical Education Programs. Physical education is the only subject matter with the potential to have a direct impact on the physical health and well-being of children and adolescents. Presently, most states mandate at least some physical education in school settings (Iverson et al. 1985). The best available data describing children's participation in school physical education programs is from the National Children and Youth Fitness Studies (NCYFS) (U.S. Department of Health and Human Services 1985, 1987). NCYFS I was cross-sectional and involved a national random sample of 8,800 school children from grades 5 through 12. Although the percentage of children attending physical education classes in this study (80.3 percent) was virtually the same as the percentage involved in physical activity through community organizations (Kleiber and Roberts 1983), no community group has the capacity for impacting all children with structured physical activity as physical education programs have (Simons-Morton et al. 1987). As noted by Bar-or (1987), however, there was a rapid and continuous decline in the number of boys and girls enrolled in physical education from grade 5 (boys, 98.0 percent; girls, 97.4 percent) to grade 12 (boys, 55.7 percent; girls, 48.5 percent). Furthermore, the average percentage of children receiving daily physical education from grades 5 through 12 (36.3 percent) was well below the recommended *Objective for the Nation* of 60 percent for the year 1990 (U.S. Department of Health and Human Services 1980), and the now lowered, more realistic objective of 50 percent for the year 2000 (U.S. Department of Health and Human Services 1986). As expected, the physical education curriculum primarily consisted of sports and games (U.S. Department of Health and Human Services 1985). An average of 47.6 percent of the curriculum was devoted to lifetime activities, and 5.6 different lifetime activities were included in the curriculum each year.

Dishman and Dunn (1988) have discussed three additional activity trends resulting from NCYFS I that are disturbing from a public health perspective. First, when activity is defined according to the minimum standard of 20 minutes of aerobic activity 3 or more times weekly, and at an intensity level equal to or greater than 60 percent of aerobic capacity (American College of Sports Medicine 1991), only half of the children in the study met this criterion. Furthermore, only 41 percent of children describe a level of activity such that they breathe hard and sweat. This level falls short of the year 2000 *Objective for the Nation*, which calls for 75 percent of children and adolescents to participate 3 or more times per week for at least 30 minutes per session in activities requiring 50 percent or more of VO_2 max (U.S. Department of Health and Human Services 1986). Second, the percentage of the active student population rises during the spring and summer and then declines substantially during the fall and winter months. Dishman and Dunn (1988) caution that this inconsistent pattern of activity behavior may set an unhealthy precedent for adult behavior. Third, and finally, American children in the NCYFS I study appeared significantly fatter (2 to 3 millimeters), as indicated by the triceps brachii skinfold assessment, when contrasted with a comparable sample of American children from the 1960s. This finding suggests that current activity levels are not adequate to offset dietary habits, a finding one study suggests results from excessive television watching and insufficient activity (Dietz and Gortmaker 1985). However, Safrit (1986) notes that increases in percentage of fat could possibly be due to measurement and methodological issues and thus be insignificant from a practical or epidemiological standpoint (Dishman and Dunn 1988).

The NCYFS II was conducted using a nationally representative sample of children ($N = 4,678$) in 19 states from grades 1 through 4. The average class lasted 33.4 minutes and was composed of movement education primarily in grades 1 and 2, with a shift in focus to team sports by grade 3 or 4. The percentage of children enrolled in physical education was relatively high (boys, 97.5 percent; girls, 96.4 percent), although a bimodal distribution similar to that found in NCYFS I for fifth and sixth grade students was found with respect to frequency of participation. The percentage of students receiving physical education 1 or 2 days a week (37.2 percent) was similar to those receiving daily physical education (36.4 percent). Physical education met on the average 3.1 times weekly, as compared to 3.6 weekly meetings in grades 5 through 12 in NCYFS I (U.S. Department of Health and Human Services 1986). The average days per week in which physical education was taught by a classroom teacher (0.8 days per week) was quite high when one considers that the time spent with a physical education specialist was only 2.3 days a week. Also, only 39.3 percent of physical education classes were held in a gymnasium, and many students had physical education class in less than ideal environments, such as a cafeteria, auditorium, or regular classroom. Most classes were held outside on school grounds (52.4 percent). Interestingly, students who had physical education in a gymnasium saw a classroom teacher less for physical education instruction (.21 days per week) than students who had physical education outside a gymnasium (1.37 days per week). Finally, as noted by Simons-Morton et al. (1988), children's fitness as measured by the mile run/walk was related to their amount of physical activity, especially out-of-school activity and their mother's level of physical activity, and inversely related to total time spent watching television. Several studies have described children's participation in free-living physical activity. Simons-Morton et al. (1987) summarized six such studies in their review *Children and Fitness: A Public Health Perspective*. However, because participation in structured physical education programs was not the focus, these studies will not be described. It should be noted, however, that because of inconsistencies in the definition of physical activity, the authors note that any conclusions that can be drawn are at best speculative.

Several studies were found that provided descriptions of what occurred in physical education classes. The monograph *What's Going On in Gym: Descriptive Studies of Physical Education Classes*, edited by Anderson and Barrette (1978), represents the largest set of videotapes of physical education classes to date. This project, the Videotape Data Bank Project (VDBP), was conducted in three states spread throughout a 100-mile radius of New York City and represented 83 randomly selected classes from 60 schools in 20 school districts. The collection of videotapes includes 40 elementary school classes, 20 high school girls' classes, 20 high school boys' classes, and 3 high school coeducational classes. Each class was taught indoors by a different physical education specialist (men = 47; women = 36), who did not know in advance which day or which class would be videotaped. Subsequently, an observational system was developed to describe objectively the BEhavior of STudents in Physical EDucation classes (BESTPED). This system was designed to describe the following four dimensions: (1) what the students were doing, (2) whether the students were moving or not moving, (3) the activities in which the students were participating, and (4) the duration of each behavior. To determine reliability and validity of the system, three coders were trained and independently coded a random sample of a wide variety of classes. The overall interobserver reliability of the system was 94.5 percent, and intraobserver reliability was 94.1 percent. The coding system is described in detail in the monograph (Anderson and Barrette 1978).

Interestingly, the distribution of physical activities in the VDBP was very similar to the distribution of activities in the more recent NCYFS. In fact, of the four activities receiving the highest percentage of total class time, three (e.g., calisthenics, basketball, and volleyball) were the same for both studies. With respect to total class time, students spent 63.2 percent in nonmovement activity and 36.8 percent in movement activity. Of the nonmovement activity, students spent the largest portion waiting (35.4 percent) and receiving information (25.4 percent). Of the time spent in movement activity, approximately 28 percent of this time was spent in movement directly related to accomplishing an objective related to physical education. For example, 15 percent of the time was spent practicing motor skills, 10 percent was spent playing games, 4 percent was spent exercising, and 0.2 percent was spent in movement education activities, such as exploring. Substantive activity time ranged from a low of 19.3 percent for gymnastics to a high of 78.7 percent for hula hoop activities. Students in game-related activities (basketball, soccer, field hockey, etc.) usually engaged in substantive activity 50 percent or more of the time. Surprisingly, very little time was spent in movement education activities, despite the fact that during the 1960s and 1970s movement education was included in many teacher education programs. Finally, although small classes are frequently advocated by educators, the results of the VDBP do not support this viewpoint, as students in smaller classes spent more time waiting, and students in larger classes spent more time in skill practice, game play, and exercise. Anderson and Barrette (1978) speculate that perhaps teachers of larger classes learned to organize their classes more efficiently and thus involved students in activity more quickly.

With respect to the general organization of class, the data revealed that teachers spent a larger percentage of time in certain activities during some segments of class as opposed to others. For example, calisthenics/exercises occurred almost exclusively at the beginning of class (95.6 percent). Students were also more likely to receive information at the beginning of class (44.1 percent) than in the middle (29.9 percent) and at the end (26.0 percent). Students also spent more time waiting in the middle of class (38.8 percent) than near the beginning (26.1 percent). Finally, practice time usually occurred during the middle of class (39.6 percent), and game play usually occurred during the latter part of class (51.3 percent).

More recently, Parcel et al. (1987) assessed the amount of moderate to vigorous physical activity (MVPA) among randomly selected third through fifth grade children ($N = 409$) enrolled in daily physical education in four elementary schools. Trained observers recorded one of four levels of successively higher energy expenditure. Level 3, slow trunk movement such as walking, and level 4, body movement across space such as running or skipping and weight transfer such as push-ups or jump rope, represented MVPA. An interobserver reliability of 96.8 percent was obtained for a subset of children ($N = 16$). Results revealed that 50.2 percent of total class time was spent in MVPA, which was lower than the time spent in MVPA during recess (72.8 percent) for a subsample of students ($N = 48$). Twenty percent of the available class time, or 6.4 minutes, was spent in level 4 activity, and boys received only slightly more MVPA than did girls. Analysis of class content for a subsample of classes ($N = 14$) revealed that of the total class time, 32.8 percent was spent in management/organization, 8.6 percent was spent in instruction, 13.5 percent was spent in skills practice, 27.5 percent was spent in games, sports, and free play, 11.4 percent was spent in nonaerobic fitness activity, and 6.1 percent was spent in aerobic fitness activity. Based on these data, Parcel et al. (1987) suggest that, in addition to increasing the number of children who receive physical education and the number of total class sessions, an equally important objective is to increase the quality of concentration of MVPA during physical education class.

The amount of MVPA found in the Parcel et al. (1987) study is similar to that found in other studies. Greenockle, Lee, and Lomax (1990) described activity patterns of 10 intact ninth and tenth grade high school fitness classes in an effort to explore relationships between student characteristics and exercise behavior. All 10 teachers of these classes were in-serviced and given detailed instructions for teaching an 8-week fitness unit. However, of concern was that students spent the majority of time walking as opposed to jogging. In a similar study, UNIQ heartwatches were used to monitor the total class time children spent in physical education above 60 percent of their predicted heart rate reserve (HRR). Subjects were children ($N = 184$) at three different elementary schools in grades 3 through 5. The total class time at or above 60 percent of HRR was 15 percent, 16 percent, and 26 percent, corresponding to 6 (out of 40), 6.9 (out of 43), and 6.4 (out of 24.7) minutes of available class time for grades 3, 4, and 5, respectively (Best and Steinhardt 1990).

Klausen, Rasmussen, and Schibye (1986) investigated the effect of increasing the number of physical education lessons from two to five over a 3-year period in an effort to motivate children in Danish public schools to engage in regular exercise once they left school. Four classes, two experimental and two control, in grades 4 and 6 were followed through grades 6 and 8, respectively. Although no deliberate attempts were made to increase the physical activity in these physical education classes, the paper reported the activity level at the end of the 3-year period, and several interesting observations were found. First, the average heart rate (HR) for the two experimental sixth grade classes was approximately 10 beats higher than for the two eighth grade classes. Eighth graders tended to have higher HRs during warm-up than during the rest of the lesson, whereas sixth graders had higher HRs following the warm-up period of class. Second, a MEMOLOG heartwatch system recording heart rates every 30 seconds found the sixth graders to have a higher percentage of HRs greater than 150 and 170. Third, the amount of active time in this study, ranging between 50 and 60 percent, was similar to the amount of MVPA reported in other studies. Finally, children is this study were relatively high-fit children, and no difference in fitness was found between the experimental and control groups. Although increasing motivation to exercise after school was the focus of the study, rather than increasing intensity of exercise during physical education class, it was pointed out that a significant ($p < .05$) negative correlation was found between HR during physical education and aerobic power ($ml \cdot min^{-1} \cdot kg^{-1}$). Thus, the authors concluded that the physical education lessons did not provide sufficient physical activity to improve fitness levels, even with the increase in number of classes from two to five. The percentage of time in which HRs were above 150 beats per minute was approximately 20 percent for both the experimental and control classes, although grade 6 had slightly higher values than grade 8. These values correspond well with the results of other studies relative to vigorous activity and also correspond with data by Baranowski et al. (1987) in which a decrease in free-living physical activity from grades 3 and 4 to grades 5 and 6 was found. However, these results are not supported by the extensive VDBP, which found that students in lower grades spent more time waiting than students in upper grades, and students in upper grades spent more time involved in skill practice and game play than did students in lower grades. One limitation of these data, however, are that level of intensity was not measured. Saris et al. (1986) found different results when intensity was measured among boys ($N = 217$) and girls ($N = 189$) followed longitudinally from age 6 to age 12. These children participated in a health education program in the Netherlands. Although total energy expenditure increased with age, energy expenditure above 50 percent of aerobic power was found to decrease as these children got older. Further, contrary to previous reports, relative to aerobic capacity unfit children were more active than fit children.

The available data suggest that although children generally have a relatively high level of cardiovascular fitness, they do not obtain a high level of MVPA during physical education classes. However, because of the difficulty of measuring children's level of activity (Freedson 1989; Saris 1985), Saris (1986) suggests the need for much more research before we conclude that today's seemingly healthy children are not active at sufficient levels.

Because of the number of school districts that are increasing the proportion of physical education classes taught by classroom teachers (nonspecialists), the available research in this area also needs to be considered. Current findings indicate that physical education classes are more effective when taught by specialists than nonspecialists. Faucette and Patterson (1990) observed four specialists and seven nonspecialists using a Teacher Observation Schedule (TOS) with momentary time sampling to examine seven categories of teacher behavior. Forty-two fourth and fifth grade classes were observed over a 3-month period. Results indicated that specialists had significantly more effective teaching behaviors in the following 6 categories: (1) feedback/reward, (2) correcting, prohibiting, (3) questioning, (4) directing/explaining/informing, (5) monitoring/attending, and (6) managing. Students of specialists also had significantly higher levels of activity (34.6 percent) when compared with students taught by nonspecialists (16.5 percent). In a similar study, kindergarten through sixth grade classes taught by nonspecialists ($N = 226$) from 84 elementary schools were observed to determine the organization of class and types of activities available to children. Results revealed that nonspecialists usually organized activity to be played by the entire class (71.9 percent) and involved game-type activities (58.7 percent) such as relays, kickball, and dodgeball. Frequently, physical education was dropped from the day's schedule, or children were allowed in engage in free play (18.6 percent) (Faucette, McKenzie, and Patterson 1990).

Health-Related Physical Fitness. Many experimental and quasi-experimental studies have focused on involving children in more MVPA to improve health-related physical fitness. This emphasis is related to the increased awareness and concern with respect to child and adolescent health promotion and CHD risk reduction (Riopel et al. 1986). The *Objectives for the Nation* (U.S. Department of Health and Human Services 1980, 1986) call for 90 percent of children ages 10–17 to participate regularly in appropriate physical activity, especially cardiovascular activities that may be carried into adulthood. Vogel (1986) has described three studies that reported positive effects of physical education programs on activity level. Physical activity was assessed using heart rate (HR) monitoring in two of the studies (Drake and Kuntzleman 1988; Gilliam et al. 1982) and a diary in the third study (Shephard et al. 1980). Increases in physical activity were found within the physical education program as well as out of class, particularly with respect to participation in vigorous exercise. Although out-of-class activity did not significantly increase in the Drake and Kuntzleman (1988) study, shifts in activity from light and moderate to heavy and very heavy were reported. Vogel (1986) notes than failure to find significance in the experimental group may have been due to independently testing levels of activity rather than the overall effect. It should be noted that although the effects of the three studies were similar, the treatments were different. Two of the studies (Drake and Kuntzleman 1988; Gilliam et al. 1982) had a significant amount of class time devoted to instruction associated with the relationship of activity to overall health, whereas the Shephard et al. (1980) study did not include a cognitive component.

Simons-Morton et al. (1988) have summarized eight studies that reported evaluations of physical education programs whose objective was to increase cardiovascular fitness. The programmatic intervention in these types of studies typically focused on walk/jog programs, aerobic dance, calisthenics, and high-intensity aerobic games and sports. All but one study (Cooper et al. 1975) involved elementary school children. These studies collectively demonstrate that improvements in health-related physical fitness can result from involving students in physical education programs which focus on increasing MVPA. Such favorable outcomes include (1) improvements in physical working capacity (Dwyer et al. 1983), as well as distance and timed runs (Cooper et al. 1975; Duncan et al. 1983; Dwyer et al. 1983; Siegel and Manfredi 1984); (2) elevated heart rates during physical education (MacConnie et al. 1982) and throughout the day (Geenan et al. 1982); and (3) decreased skinfolds (Dwyer et al. 1983). One study (Simons-Morton et al. 1987) also provided evidence of successful implementation of a teacher-training program.

Whereas the above studies demonstrate the efficacy of immediate fitness outcomes, of major concern, albeit difficult to assess, is that none of these studies have addressed the long-term effectiveness of the intervention. This is of primary concern given that the Fit Youth Today (FYT) study, which included 20,707 students from grades 4 through 12, found a downward trend in fitness levels as children got older (Haydon and Squires 1988). As pointed out by Simons-Morton et al. (1988), at present, studies have not addressed the effects of physical fitness programs on students' attitudes toward physical activity and maintenance of activity following the intervention. Given the current conditions of some physical education programs, such as only meeting one to two times a week or classes being taught by classroom teachers, developing behavioral skills that encourage engagement in MVPA outside of physical education class is necessary (American College of Sports Medicine 1988). Behavioral skills are especially important for physical education as compared to other subject matter areas given that physical fitness cannot be "stored up" for a lifetime. Presently, a rapid decrease in activity patterns occurs as students leave the school setting (Dishman and Dunn 1988; Stephens, Jacobs, and White 1985).

Motor Skills. Motor skill performance is generally defined as the ability to perform fundamental motor and sport skills (Vogel 1986) and includes such skill-related abilities as agility, balance, coordination, power, reaction time, and speed. In the chapter "Effects of Physical Education on Children," Vogel (1986) has summarized 12 studies that have reported evaluations of physical education programs on motor performance. Each study included one or more of three types of outcome measures (e.g., skill-related abilities, fundamental skills, and specific sport-related skills), which reflects the lack of standardization with respect to how motor performance is measured. Studies that assessed *skill-related abilities* as outcome measures included specific skill-related tests, such as the stork stand to measure balance, or tests used as indicators of skill-related abilities, such as the shuttle run, obstacle race, or 50-yard dash. Because these test scores are limited by other factors, such as the genetic potential of students, the effects of physical education programs on the development of motor performance abilities may be inaccurate. Although only one study (Shephard et al. 1980) found a significant program effect, Vogel (1986) states that the available evidence does not suggest that physical education programs cannot improve skill-related attributes, but rather supports the effectiveness of long-term programs that contain activities similar to the capabilities tested. The physical education program in the Shephard et al. (1980) study emphasized sport skills and was taught 5 days a week for several years.

Mixed findings were reported with respect to the second type of outcome measure, *fundamental skills*, such as the long jump, softball throw, and vertical jump. However, because of methodological concerns with respect to program design, such as program intervention of short duration (Franks and Moore 1969), lack of similarity between program content and measured outcomes (Johnson 1969), and lack of control with respect to program delivery (Duncan et al. 1983; Kemper et al. 1978), it is inappropriate to conclude that physical education programs are ineffective in improving fundamental skills. Furthermore, in some instances, changes in fundamental movement skills were examined out of convenience because pre- and postmeasures happened to be available.

The third outcome, *specific sport-related skills*, is more closely linked to the acquisition of sport skills and represents more complex motor skill performance. Such outcomes as basketball, soccer, volleyball, and gymnastics skills were measured, and again the results are equivocal. However, as previously stated, methodological concerns in the studies with nonsignificant findings yield no reasons sufficient to negate the studies that found physical education classes to significantly enhance motor skill performance.

Other Outcomes. Several other outcomes of participation in physical education programs have been examined, and many of these are summarized by Vogel (1986). Among these outcomes are academic achievement, knowledge of subject matter, attitude, personal-social characteristics, and diet. Vogel reported four studies that examined the effects of physical education programs on student performance as measured by teacher grades and standardized tests (Lipton 1970; Moore, Guy, and Reeve 1984; Shephard et al. 1984; Thomas et al. 1975). Although the results from the studies yielded mixed findings, the data support the fact that extra time devoted to physical education, and thus taken away from other academic subjects, did not decrease academic performance. When the cognitive information examined was taught in physical education classes, such as information related to cardiovascular exercise, motor skills, and the development of healthy lifestyles, physical education programs had a significant positive effect on academic achievement (Drake and Kuntzleman 1988; Vogel 1986). Furthermore, Vogel (1986) discussed two unpublished reports which provide evidence that physical education programs which had a positive effect on motor performance and knowledge of subject matter also positively influenced how children felt about physical activity. However, the available evidence does not indicate that physical education programs can influence self-concept or personality (Drake and Kuntzleman 1988; Moore, Guy, and Reeve 1984; Thomas et al. 1975).

Because physical activity combined with a healthful diet is most prudent in decreasing overweight conditions, obesity, and ill health, the effect of physical education on diet is of interest. Drake and Kuntzleman (1988) have reported the effects of the *Feelin' Good* physical education program (Drake and Kuntzleman 1988) on total calories, single carbohydrates, sodium, potassium, and fat. In general, little evidence supports the hypothesis that participation in physical education classes alters the nutritional practices of students.

Implicit Curriculum. Unlike the explicit curriculum, in which teachers overtly state intended outcomes, the implicit curriculum is characterized by teaching through the context of the learning environment. The implicit values communicated may or may not be congruent with the explicit philosophy espoused by teachers. According to Dodds (1983), the implicit curriculum involves covert, hidden, and null levels. The covert curriculum is characterized by intended outcomes held by teachers that are not shared verbally with students. These actions are often planned very carefully and consistently implemented. For example, when teachers ask students to work with new partners, although the teacher is consciously intending for students to learn to work cooperatively with peers, the objective may not be directly stated. When teachers emphasize structured practice, completing tasks thoroughly and well, and always striving to improve personal performance, students receive messages that learning and personal performance are important (Dodds 1983). The hidden curriculum is "comprised of unplanned and unrecognized values taught and learned through the process of schooling" (Bain 1975, 92), and the research in this area has been summarized in recent chapters by Bain (1989a, 1990c). Finally, the null curriculum consists of everything the teacher either consciously or unconsciously leaves out of the curriculum (Eisner 1977). The most potent message given by the null curriculum is that "teacher decisions to exclude particular activities, social behaviors, role models, appreciations and so on from the explicit or covert curricula mean in the end deliberate denial to students of these opportunities to experience and to learn parts of their world" (Dodds 1983, 221–222).

The research in physical education related to the implicit curriculum has focused on the hidden curriculum. Two types of research studies have been completed. The first describes patterns of behavior in physical education, whereas the second not only describes patterns of behavior but also examines the meanings participants attach to their experiences in physical education (Bain 1985b). This section examines the hidden curriculum from the perspective of teacher behavior, student behavior and experiences, and program structure. For a more complete analysis of the hidden curriculum in physical education the reader is referred to a summary chapter by Bain (1989a) and a later chapter that analyzes three themes (meritocracy, technocentric ideology, and social relations) that emerge from a critical analysis of this literature (Bain 1990c).

Bain (1976b) first described the hidden curriculum in physical education by using systematic observation (Bain 1976a) to identify implicit values present in secondary classes. Twenty-four teachers in the Chicago area were observed three times for data regarding verbal behavior and class organization. Teachers also completed a questionnaire concerning class regulations and grading procedures. Six predetermined value dimensions were selected for study: achievement, autonomy, orderliness, privacy, specificity, and universalism. Results indicated that order and control were more important than achievement. For example, 58 percent of teacher verbal behavior dealt with procedural matters, as opposed to 35 percent that was related to the subject matter and 7 percent that was unrelated to class. Women teachers were more concerned with students' privacy, particularly at urban schools, and were more likely to interact with students about skill rather than personal issues (e.g., specificity). Students in urban schools received less autonomy and were more likely to be treated as group members than as individuals (e.g., universalism), despite the smaller class sizes in the urban schools. With respect to grading procedures, both men and women placed more emphasis on attitudes and compliance than on skill and knowledge, and men based a smaller percentage of students' grades on skill (men = 17.9 percent, women = 30.8 percent) and knowledge (men = 8.1 percent, women = 18.3 percent) than did women.

Following minor revisions in instrumentation to clarify the achievement dimension as either competitive achievement or instructional achievement, Bain (1978) replicated her initial investigation and expanded the research design to include teachers and coaches in secondary schools. Twenty physical education teachers and 20 coaches were observed on three separate occasions. In general, the results supported the previous investigation. Women teachers and coaches safeguarded the privacy of their students more so than male teachers and coaches. Women subjects also scored higher on instructional achievement. Coaches scored higher than teachers on three dimensions: privacy, instructional achievement, and specificity; teachers scored higher than coaches on universalism. Although differences among teachers were reported, both studies indicated an emphasis on order and control over achievement.

Bain (1989a) noted that other related research on teachers' perceptions of "life in the gym" also revealed an emphasis on order and control. Placek (1983, 1984) found that student behavior and practical concerns were the two greatest influences in teacher planning. Teachers "seemed to define the teaching situation in terms of keeping students busy, happy, and good" (Placek 1983, 49). Earls (1981) conducted extensive interviews with 12 middle school teachers and likewise found teachers to emphasize student participation and enjoyment. Veal (1988) studied teachers' assessment practices and found that teachers tend to evaluate participation and effort rather than skill development. Among the reasons Bain (1989a) gives for this emphasis on order and control include (1) the conservative nature of physical education teachers (Sage 1980), (2) conflicts and time demands experienced by the dual roles of teacher and coach (Bain 1983; Locke and Massengale 1978), and (3) inadequate professional socialization programs (Lawson 1986a; Siedentop 1986). If changes in the hidden curriculum are intended, Bain suggests the need for increased attention to recruits, to the content of teacher education programs, and to situational factors that affect teachers' performances.

Another research area related to teacher behavior that has considerable relevance to research on the hidden curriculum in physical education is that of teachers' perceptions and attitudes toward students and the resulting impact on student behavior and performance (Bain 1985b). Research related to teacher expectations in physical education has primarily focused on the characteristics of students and the learning context. The work of Martinek (1989) and his colleagues (Martinek, Crowe, and Rejeski 1982) has demonstrated that teachers' perceptions of students are influenced by a set of teacher expectations described as impression cues. These cues are typically identified as either static (e.g., sex or race) or dynamic (e.g., performance or behavioral disposition) and form the basis from which teachers' expectations emerge.

Several specific teaching behaviors identified in physical education classes have been related to teacher expectations. Martinek and Karper (1981) found that physical educators have significantly lower expectations for handicapped students with regard to both social relations and physical performance as compared to nonhandicapped students. Teachers also typically give less verbal and nonverbal praise to low-expectancy students (Crowe 1977; Martinek and Johnson 1979; Rejeski, Darracott, and Hutslar 1979), ask these students fewer analytic questions, and provide fewer response opportunities (Crowe 1977; Martinek and Johnson 1979). Further, low-expectancy students receive fewer evaluative comments, less probing and time to respond to unanswered questions (Crowe 1977), fewer dyadic contacts (Martinek 1983; Martinek and Johnson 1979), more criticism (Templin 1981), and less acceptance and use of their ideas (Martinek and Johnson 1979; Martinek and Karper 1982). The physical attractiveness of students has also influenced teacher expectations. In one study, Martinek (1981) found that teacher expectations for physical and social skills were higher for more attractive students. Teachers also paid greater attention to the ideas of attractive students. In a follow-up study, Martinek and Karper (1984) found that the relationship between physical attractiveness and performance expectations strengthened as children got older.

A final impression cue that influences teacher expectancy relates to participation during physical education class. According to Rejeski and Lowe (1980), teachers are influenced by the amount of perceived effort that students exhibit during instruction, a finding also supported by the work of Martinek and Karper (1982, 1984). This finding has particular relevance when we consider the many ways teachers reinforce and discipline students "in order to elicit higher levels of motivation and participation rather than better performance" (Martinek 1989, 63). Bain (1989a) notes that the research on teacher expectations supports an emphasis on order and control. For example, Templin's (1981) study of student socialization found that teachers were more favorable toward students who were conforming, cooperative, and high achieving.

Several studies have focused their investigation of the hidden curriculum on student behavior and perceptions. Most of these studies have been qualitative in research design and have attempted to describe student experiences and participation patterns. Each study has illustrated that students are active agents in their environment, often having different views of the instructional process and perceptions of social and moral values. In a participant-observation study of a fifth grade physical education class, Wang (1977) discovered that the explicit curriculum espoused by the teacher differed from the student-imposed curriculum. Although the teacher promoted cooperation, equality, and social responsibility, the student-imposed curriculum discriminated among individuals based on gender, race, social class, personality, and skill performance. Wang suggests that a more intense instructional skills program may help to counter the student-imposed discrimination.

Tousignant and Siedentop (1983) used ethnographic research techniques to analyze task structures and participation patterns in four secondary physical education classes. Four categories of student behavior were identified: (1) task as stated by the teacher, (2) modified task, (3) deviant off-task behavior, and (4) competent bystanders. Student behavior appeared to be determined more by teacher-active supervision and accountability than by teacher instruction. Students learned to distinguish when minimal participation and effort were required versus a particular level of skill or knowledge. This was often accomplished through a process of investigation with respect to the formal task requirements.

Two other investigations have also reported emerging patterns or categories of participation. In a study previously discussed (Bain 1985a), student expectations and reactions to a university exercise class on fitness and weight control were examined. Four patterns of student participation emerged: (1) serious runners, (2) serious walkers, (3) social interactors, and (4) absentees. In general, less fit overweight students were not as successful in changing their exercise behavior. Bain suggested that this may be due in part to the structure of the course, which reflected a technical-rational view of behavior rather than a subjective-affective view.

Griffin (1983, 1984, 1985a, 1985b) observed a seventh and eighth grade coeducational physical education program in a white, middle-class community for a 3-month period. The primary emphasis of her work related to issues of sex equity and gender, and several implicit values were reflected in student participation patterns. Participation was influenced by the perceived appropriateness of the activity and the personal characteristics of the students, such as size, skill, and sex. Boys' participation in "girl-appropriate" gymnastic events was characterized as either frivolous or reluctant. Girls' participation in "boy-appropriate" gymnastic events was characterized as either exploratory or reluctant (Griffin 1983). With respect to team sports, girls' styles of participation ranged from "athletic" to "system beaters," and boys' styles of participation ranged from "machos" to "wimps" (Griffin 1984, 1985a). Teachers accepted the different participation patterns as unavoidable and attempted to respond to the various groups in the most appropriate manner.

Two other investigations have described patterns of student behavior and participation and have also examined participant perceptions and reactions to their experiences. Tindall (1975) conducted an ethnographic study of the hidden curriculum by organizing and supervising a school-wide high school basketball tournament. He concluded that the hidden curriculum represents a lesson in how to behave according to the principles of one's culture. For example, although the basketball tournament was explicitly organized in an educationally sound manner, implicitly each organizational step was controlled by someone else. In short, the tournament was "a lesson in how people should organize their behavior—that behavior reflecting established sets of relationships between categories of people, events, and things" (26). Tindall points out that the consequences of such hidden curricula are that we are sustaining a society that distributes knowledge and skill, and thus power and wealth, based on social identity and characteristics. This premise was accepted by all students in this study with the exception of those for whom the premise conflicted with their native culture. For example, although the premise underlying the tournament recognized the legitimacy of individuals to control other individuals, basketball games played by Mormons were characterized by group effort, whereas Native Americans tended to emphasize individual performances.

Kollen (1981, 1983) used a phenomenological methodology to interview 20 high school seniors concerning their K–12 experiences in physical education. Based on student responses in her interviews, she concluded that the physical education environment is "characterized by embarrassing situations, public humiliation, not being believed, unrealistic expectations . . . " (Kollen 1983, 87) and that being "out of place is the norm of the nonathlete" (88). Students responded in a variety of ways, including "minimal compliance, lack of involvement, manipulation of the teacher, false enthusiasm, rebellion, leaving, failing class, isolation, or giving up" (88). Kollen points out that movement experiences in physical education tend to be fragmented rather than integrated and suggests that this stems from our deeply embedded ideals, which foster a masculine-athletic-competitive image as our standard. Integrated movement exists when competition is based solely on physical capabilities. Fragmentation exists when competition is used "to make psychological distinctions and status is placed on these distinctions" (92). Kollen suggests the need for physical educators to examine whether we wish to promote the enjoyment of physical activity or the rewards gained from participation.

Each of the studies just described has enhanced the knowledge of the hidden curriculum by examining the social construction of knowledge and the meaning that various experiences in physical education classes have for individuals. Bain (1989a) suggests, however, that such examination is only the first step; the final step should be to compare the hidden curriculum with the explicit educational philosophy of the physical education program, the school, and society at large. Inconsistencies that are identified should then be addressed. This approach is based on the assumption that a goal of research is to empower those individuals being researched, to assist them in critiquing their own social circumstances, and then to encourage them to act in such a manner as to improve their lives (Bain 1985b). Apple (1978) suggests that the omission in research that examines the social construction of knowledge may in fact lend support to the existing social order.

The amount of emphasis on competition in physical education programs, especially as compared to informal sport and organized sport, has also received much attention. Bain (1989a) discussed several studies (Chalip et al. 1984; Coakley 1980; Dubois 1986; Fine 1987) that examined student experiences in these three settings and summarized several findings. First, informal sport was seen as playful, action centered, and incorporating individual differences. Organized sport, on the other hand, was viewed as exciting, intense, and achievement oriented. The concern was raised that although most physical education programs explicitly espoused a philosophy which accentuates both achievement and allowance for individual difference, observation of these programs and interviews of students indicate that programs may not be consistent with the explicit philosophy. Rather, physical education programs appear to be characterized by an emphasis on structure and control without a clear focus on student achievement.

FUTURE DIRECTIONS

One approach to addressing recommendations for further study is to reflect on the three most basic curriculum questions proposed by Schubert (1986): "What knowledge is most worthwhile? Why is it worthwhile? How is it acquired or created?" (1). Much of the work to date in physical education curriculum has focused on curriculum theorizing in an attempt to answer Schubert's first two questions, What knowledge is of most worth and why? The proceedings of the six Physical Education Curriculum Theory Conferences held at the University of Georgia contain much of this work, and at present these two questions remain unresolved. The NASPE outcomes project is the most recent attempt to address these two questions. One strength of the NASPE project is that concepts and values are listed as important objectives in addition to outcomes related to motor skill and physical fitness. This implies that these objectives must be planned for and taught, as opposed to naturally occuring as a byproduct of activity. Although this project is a step in the right direction, much work remains to be done. For example, it can be argued that the NASPE outcomes have simply reinforced a troubled multiactivity approach in that physical educators are expected to achieve a broad-based array of outcomes rather than prioritizing objectives that can be realistically achieved. If Siedentop's (1987) observations are correct, and quality programs have a specific focus as well as teachers who are excited about that focus, then perhaps the NASPE outcomes are too broad based.

Research that addresses Schubert's (1986) third question, How is knowledge acquired or created? has been largely descriptive in nature. The work that Hellison has done over the last 15 years and continues to do in revising and validating the social development model is perhaps the most well-documented effort to answer this question for a specific curriculum model. Experimental studies to date have primarily focused on health-related fitness and have largely been completed by faculty from schools of medicine and departments of public health rather than by physical education curriculum specialists. The implicit assumption of these research studies has been that health-related physical fitness is the knowledge of most worth.

Although "the bottom line will always be that people choose what to do based on value positions" (Rink 1987, 208), it is critical to the future of the profession that a common set of objectives be identified from which all physical educators are expected to teach, and research, using multiple paradigms, is expected to determine how best to achieve these objectives. This will be a value-laden process and will require much deliberation; however, it is a crucial step if our profession is to move forward. Hellison (1987a) has referred to a 51 percent rule, in which teachers concentrate on their strengths and values (the 51 percent) while also teaching toward goals they feel obligated, as physical educators, to share with students, such as priorities of the local community and outcomes identified by research and professional judgment to be of greatest value to children (the other 49 percent). If physical education is to remain a viable subject in the future, students will need to be exposed to a somewhat similar body of knowledge and set of behavioral objectives. This common curriculum, as well as the other 51 percent, should be guided by the following recommendations for future research: (1) a focus on impact and research-supported curriculum, (2) a more thorough investigation of the implicit curriculum, and (3) a broadening of the empirical-analytical research paradigm to include the interpretive and critical paradigms.

Focus on Impact

In an opening address to the Fifth Curriculum Theory Conference in Physical Education, entitled "Future Directions in Curriculum Theorizing—Being Accountable for 'Impact,'" Razor (1987) highlighted current trends in which subdisciplines are increasingly being held accountable for their impact and contribution to society, in addition to the quality of their work. Razor asserts that it is not enough "to theorize or build theory in the absence of research on the development of programs which demonstrate some 'impact,' if not value" (4). Future research needs to be directed toward the impact of existing physical education programs. If new curriculum models are proposed, they too must demonstrate an impact. In addition, Rink (1987) suggests that just as important and perhaps more critical than questions of "what should we do" are questions of "what can we do"? For example,

> volleyball is not meaningful when a served ball does nothing but drop to the other side of the net or someone fists it back over the net. Physical education is just not meaningful when teachers find themselves teaching the same thing year after year because students have never spent enough time on anything to learn it. (204)

We also must more actively voice our position and justification of that position with respect to health-related physical fitness. The research in this area has had the strongest impact to date, and little of that research has been done by physical education curriculum experts. Health-related physical fitness also appears to have strong federal support. The midcourse review of the Public Health Service 1990 Objectives for the Nation (U.S. Department of Health and Human Sciences 1980) extended and expanded the recommended objectives for the year 2000, many of which relate to the activity patterns and fitness of children (U.S. Department of Health and Human Sciences 1986).

Specific recommendations for further study that focus on impact include the following:

1. Define a common set of objectives (psychomotor, cognitive, affective, social) that our profession can agree on to be taught in physical education classes. These objectives should be theoretically based and periodically revised based on professional judgment and research that focuses on impact. The recent outcomes project by NASPE is an example of efforts related to this recommendation (National Association for Sport and Physical Education 1990).
2. For curriculum research to make an impact, it must include all three aspects of curriculum study as described by Kirk (1988): (1) the characteristics of subject matter, (2) the pedagogic interactions of teachers and learners, and (3) the sociocultural milieu in which these interactions occur.
3. Greater attention should be focused on helping children develop positive attitudes toward physical activity (Corbin 1987; Fox 1988). Programs that have sufficient MVPA but do not instill positive attitudes toward physical activity may have little influence on adult activity patterns.
4. Research should continue to examine the impact of physical education classes taught by physical education specialists as compared to classroom teachers (Faucette and Patterson 1989, 1990).
5. Typically, studies that have addressed increases in health-related physical fitness in school settings have been limited to the effects of increased physical activity and physical training programs on cardiovascular fitness. More effort needs to be directed toward the effects of physical education programs on other health-promoting behaviors and risk factors for cardiovascular disease (Cureton 1987; Montoye 1985).

Focus on Implicit Curriculum

A second recommended area of further study in physical education curriculum is that of the implicit curriculum. Just as important as what teachers overtly state as intended outcomes are "the things students learn which are not at the level of specifically stated and shared teacher intentions" (Dodds 1983, 217). All three dimensions of the implicit curriculum as defined by Dodds (1983)—covert, hidden, and null—teach children through the context of the learning environment and need to be further studied as they relate to the functional or "real" curriculum. Research related to the hidden curriculum in physical education has examined descriptions of physical education classes, teachers' perceptions and attitudes toward students, and student behavior and perceptions of their experiences. This work needs to be continued and expanded, especially with respect to health-related physical fitness.

Carlyon (1984) argues that instead of promoting healthier lifestyles, educators have advocated constant lifestyle scrutiny in a search for risk factors and a denial of pleasure, which misses the point of being human. Kreuter, Parsons, and McMurray (1982) contend that more attention needs to be paid to the ethical dimensions of health promotion and that moral sensitivity needs to be heightened. They add that people have a right to make their own choices, and that, although "unhealthy lifestyles may be unwise, . . . they are not necessarily immoral" (13). Because educators paradoxically see the individual as "both the cause and cure of whatever ails him" (Carlyon 1984, 30), they often resort to teaching methods known as "blaming the victim" (Allegrante and Sloan 1986; Wikler 1987). In this case, social problems are believed to be located within the individual rather than in social influences or the environment (Burdine, McLeroy, and Gottlieb 1987), a situation that can be remedied by being more sensitive and ceasing to make moral judgments regarding who is at fault. Hellison (1987a) notes that reforms in physical education should require wellness to be redefined such that "the needs of the inside self and the development of humanitarian concerns were not only included but ranked higher in importance than disease prevention" (149).

Much of the theoretical basis from which health-related programs result emphasize a perspective of health and wellness behavior characterized by "self-control," and although this perspective may not be the most effective means of attaining wellness, it does help explain the current state of affairs. Examples of this self-control orientation are readily found within the literature. The fear drive model (Higbee 1969; Janis 1967) asserts that an emotional fear response that creates discomfort or tension is necessary to motivate actual changes in behavior. In this model, individuals attempt to allay feelings of tension by rehearsing various recommended actions. Similarly, the Health Belief Model (Rosenstock 1974) posits that coping responses are based on objective health threats and that health actions by individuals are influenced by (1) the perceived vulnerability of the health threat, (2) perceptions of the severity of the threat, (3) perceptions of the benefits versus the costs of taking the recommended action, and (4) cues to action. Social learning theory (Bandura 1977), which asserts that behavior is a function of the individual, the environment, and the behavior itself, also promotes greater individual self-control. This theory posits that individuals will change their behavior if they believe the outcome will be positive, and if they value the outcome. Within social learning theory, the self-regulatory process of self-monitoring, self-evaluation, and self-reinforcement (Kanfer and Gaelick 1986) plays an important role. Schunk and Carbonari (1984) point out that social learning theory is a product of "the idea that people self-regulate their environment and actions" (230) and that behavior change requires severe environmental restrictions and the avoidance of high-risk situations (Wolinsky 1982). This results in improved health for those able to "exert a measure of control over their lives" (Schunk and Carbonari 1984, 244). Finally, theoretical perspectives of relapse prevention (Marlatt 1986) view environmental restriction as a means of bolstering self-efficacy. However, the tendency of these techniques to imply deprivation and punishment would seem to make their effectiveness at enhancing wellness, increasing self-efficacy and self-esteem, and establishing long-term behavior change questionable.

In addition to the promotion of self-control from a theoretical perspective, we are also beginning to see societal evidence of this perspective in some individuals who exercise excessively. These individuals have been labeled compulsive exercisers in the popular literature. Others have called them negatively addicted (Morgan 1979), exercise dependent (de Coverley Veale 1987), obligatory runners (Yates, Leehey, and Shisslak 1983), and fitness fanatics (Little 1969), who experience withdrawal symptoms (e.g., depression, irritability, fatigue) when they are unable to exercise (Morgan 1979). This condition is an extreme example of the self-control perspective and becomes harmful when an individual's obsessive physical demands lead to debilitating injury or the neglect of other personal or social needs (Blumenthal, Rose, and Chang 1985). An alternative, "self-trust" orientation would advocate positive health behaviors and exercise as a means to nurture oneself and experience pleasure rather than being necessary for improving health or preventing disease.

Although there is no research with school-aged children that examines these two perspectives, the notion of self-trust is in general agreement with a study by Wankel (1985), which demonstrated the importance of exercise enjoyment. Further, a recent study (Davis, Cowles, and Hastings 1990) found that in a sample of regularly exercising women ($N = 112$), 40 percent reported they "are constantly dieting" as opposed to 38 percent who reported they "rarely feel the need to diet." Dieters were significantly more likely to (1) engage in more physical activity, (2) place greater emphasis on exercise as a means of controlling their weight, (3) be more emotionally reactive as indicated by the Eysenck Personality Inventory, and (4) score higher on all subscales of an eating disorder inventory.

Specific recommendations for future study that focus on the implicit curriculum include the following:

1. To examine whether health-related physical fitness, characterized by the current dominant perspective of "self-control," in a technological society (Bain 1990c) is more effective than a broad perspective of wellness and health-related behaviors characterized by "self-trust." This recommendation relates to Kollen's (1983) suggestion to examine whether we wish to promote the enjoyment of physical activity (e.g., process) or the rewards gained from participation (e.g., product) (Meredith 1988).

2. To examine inequities related to class, race, gender, and physical ability and physical appearance and ways in which cultural beliefs are transmitted or changed (Bain 1989a).

Focus on Broadening of Research Paradigms

The research paradigms available to curriculum experts to address the proposed questions have expanded beyond an emphasis on empirical-analytical research to include research based on interpretive and critical paradigms (Bain 1988a, 1989b; Bain and Jewett 1987; Lincoln and Guba 1985; Locke 1989). The interpretive paradigm examines the construction of meaning in various physical education settings. For example, much of the research base related to the PPCF was designed using an interpretive paradigm. Critical theory paradigms examine how physical education programs reproduce or transform society. Critical theorists are interested in the production of a more democratic, egalitarian society and acknowledge the existence of values in all research efforts.

Specific recommendations that focus on the broadening of research paradigms include:

1. Both scholars and practitioners should work together as a productive discipline to design programs and environments in which individuals can achieve their own movement potential (Bressan 1979).
2. One way of ensuring a broadening of research paradigms is to have journals revise their policies and procedures to include qualitative manuscripts.

In closing, we should look to the future with optimism. No other subject matter has the potential to influence the physical health and well-being of our children as does physical education. However, to gain the respect this profession rightly deserves, physical education curriculum researchers must make an impact. Research accompanied by methodological rigor and from multiple paradigms must become the driving force for our field. This research should help guide, and modify when needed, a common set of objectives that can be taught in all physical education classes.

References

Allegrante, John P., and Richard P. Sloan. 1986. Ethical dilemmas in workplace health promotion. *Preventive Medicine* 15(3): 313–320.

Almond, Len, and Rod Thorpe. 1988. Asking teachers to research. *Journal of Teaching in Physical Education* 7(3): 221–227.

Alvermann, Donna E. 1990. "Reading Teacher Education." In *Handbook for Research on Teacher Education*, edited by W. Robert Houston, 687–704. New York: Macmillan.

American Alliance for Health, Physical Education, Recreation and Dance. 1980. *Health Related Physical Fitness Test Manual*. Reston, VA: AAHPERD.

American Alliance for Health, Physical Education, Recreation and Dance. 1988. *Physical Best*. Reston, VA: AAHPERD.

American College of Sports Medicine. 1988. Opinion statement on physical fitness in children and youth. *Medicine and Science in Sports and Exercise* 20(4): 422–423.

American College of Sports Medicine. 1991. *Guidelines for Exercise Testing and Prescription*. Philadelphia, PA: Lea & Febiger.

American Health and Fitness Foundation. 1986. *Fit Youth Today*. Austin, TX: The Foundation.

Anderson, Gary L. 1989. Critical ethnography in education: Origins, current status, and new directions. *Review of Educational Research* 59(3): 249–270.

Anderson, William G. 1982. Working with inservice teachers: Suggestions for teacher educators. *Journal of Teaching in Physical Education* 1(3): 15–22.

Anderson, William G. 1987. "Five Years of Program Development: A Retrospective." In *Myths, Models and Methods in Sport Pedagogy*, edited by Gary T. Barrett, Ronald S. Feingold, C. Roger Rees, and Maurice Pieron, 123–133. Champaign, IL: Human Kinetics.

Anderson, William G. 1988. A school-centered collaborative model for program development. *Journal of Teaching in Physical Education* 7(3): 176–183.

Anderson, William G., and Gary T. Barrette, eds. 1978. What's going on in gym: Descriptive studies of physical education classes. *Motor Skills: Theory Into Practice Monograph 1*.

Apple, Michael W. 1978. The new sociology of education: Analyzing cultural and economic reproduction. *Harvard Educational Review* 48(4): 495–503.

Apple, Michael W. 1982. *Education and Power*. Boston: Routledge & Kegan Paul.

Avery, Marybell, and Angela Lumpkin. 1987. Students' perceptions of physical education objectives. *Journal of Teaching in Physical Education* 7(1): 5–11.

Bain, Linda L. 1975. The hidden curriculum in physical education. *Quest* 24 (Summer): 92–101.

Bain, Linda L. 1976a. An instrument for identifying implicit values in physical education programs. *Research Quarterly* 47(3): 307–315.

Bain, Linda L. 1976b. Description of the hidden curriculum in secondary physical education. *Research Quarterly* 47(2): 154–160.

Bain, Linda L. 1978. Differences in values implicit in teaching and coaching behaviors. *Research Quarterly* 49(1): 5–11.

Bain, Linda L. 1980. Socialization into the role of participant: Physical education's ultimate goal. *Journal of Physical Education and Recreation* 51(7): 48–50.

Bain, Linda L. 1983. "Teacher/Coach Role Conflict: Factors Influencing Role Performance." In *Teaching in Physical Education*, edited by Thomas J. Templin and Janice K. Olson, 94–101. Champaign, IL: Human Kinetics.

Bain, Linda L. 1985a. A naturalistic study of students' responses to an exercise class. *Journal of Teaching in Physical Education* 5(1): 2–12.

Bain, Linda L. 1985b. The hidden curriculum re-examined. *Quest* 37(2): 145–153.

Bain, Linda L. 1986, April. "Risks of a National Curriculum." Paper presented at the Annual Convention of the American Alliance for Health, Physical Education, Recreation and Dance, Cincinnati, OH. ERIC Document no. ED 273 601.

Bain, Linda L. 1988a. Beginning the journey: Agenda for 2001. *Quest* 40(2): 96–106.

Bain, Linda L. 1988b. "Curriculum for Critical Reflection in Physical Education." In *Content of the Curriculum*, edited by Ronald S. Brandt, 133–147. Alexandria, VA: Association for Supervision and Curriculum Development.

Bain, Linda L. 1989a. "Implicit Values in Physical Education." In *Socialization into Physical Education: Learning to Teach*, edited by Thomas J. Templin and Paul G. Schempp, 289–314. Indianapolis, IN: Benchmark Press.

Bain, Linda L. 1989b. Interpretive and critical research in sport and physical education. *Research Quarterly for Exercise and Sport* 60(1): 21–24.

Bain, Linda L. 1990a. "Physical Education Teacher Education." In *Handbook for Research on Teacher Education*, edited by W. Robert Houston, 758–781. New York: Macmillan.

Bain, Linda L. 1990b, April. "The Impact and Implications of Research on Teaching and Teacher Education in Physical Education." Paper presented at the annual meeting of the American Educational Research Association, Boston, MA.

Bain, Linda L. 1990c. "A Critical Analysis of the Hidden Curriculum in Physical Education." In *Physical Education, Curriculum and Culture: Critical Issues in the Contemporary Crisis*, edited by David Kirk and Richard Tinning, 23–42. London: Falmer.

Bain, Linda L., and Ann E. Jewett. 1987. Future research and theory-building. *Journal of Teaching in Physical Education* 6(3): 346–364.

Bandura, Albert. 1977. *Social Learning Theory*. Englewood Cliffs, NJ: Prentice Hall.

Baranowski, Tom, et al. 1987. Aerobic physical activity among third- to sixth-grade children. *Developmental and Behavioral Pediatrics* 8(4): 203–206.

Bar-or, Obed. 1987. A commentary to children and fitness: A public health perspective. *Research Quarterly for Exercise and Sport* 58(4): 304–307.

Barrett, Kate R. 1987. "The Subject Matter of Children's Physical Education or 'No Gap to Bridge—No Race to Run.'" In *Proceedings of the Fifth Conference on Curriculum Theory in Physical Education*, edited by M. Martha Carnes and Patricia Stueck, 211–223. Athens: University of Georgia.

Barrett, Kate R. 1988a. A teaching center for children's physical education: "The dream and the reality." *Journal of Teaching in Physical Education* 7(3): 190–196.

Barrett, Kate R. 1988b. Two views. The subject matter of children's physical education. *Journal of Physical Education, Recreation and Dance* 59(2): 42–46.

Barrow, Robin. 1984. *Giving Teaching Back to Teachers: A Critical Introduction to Curriculum Theory*. Brighton, England: Wheatsheaf.

Best, Richard W., and Mary A. Steinhardt. 1990. The accuracy of heart rate monitoring in elementary school children [abstract]. *Medicine and Science in Sports and Exercise* 22(2): S10.

Blair, Steven N., et al. 1989. Physical fitness and all-cause mortality. *American Medical Association Journal* 262(17): 2395–2401.

Blair, Steven N., Harold W. Kohl, and Kenneth E. Powell. 1987. "Physical Activity, Physical Fitness, Exercise, and the Public's Health." In *The Academy Papers*, edited by Margaret J. Safrit and Helen M. Eckert, 53–69. Champaign, IL: Human Kinetics.

Blair, Steven N., Russell R. Pate, and Bruce McClenaghan. 1982. "Current Approaches to Physical Fitness Education." In *Advances in School Psychology*, Vol. II, edited by Thomas R. Kratochwill, 315–361. Hillsdale, NJ: Erlbaum.

Bloom, Benjamin S. 1981. *All Our Children Learning*. New York: McGraw-Hill.

Blumenthal, James A., Sandra Rose, and Jonathan L. Chang. 1985. Anorexia nervosa and exercise implications from recent findings. *Sports Medicine* 2(4): 237–247.

Borg, Walter R., and Meredith D. Gall. 1983. *Educational Research: An Introduction*. New York: Longman.

Bressan, Elizabeth S. 1979. 2001: The profession is dead—was it murder or suicide? *Quest* 31(1): 77–82.

Broudy, Harry S. 1982. What knowledge is of most worth? *Educational Leadership* 39(8): 574–578.

Brown, Stephen O., Thomas J. Cooney, and Doug Jones. 1990. "Mathematics Teacher Education." In *Handbook for Research on Teacher Education*, edited by W. Robert Houston, 639–656. New York: Macmillan.

Burdine, James N., Kenneth B. McLeroy, and Nell H. Gottlieb. 1987. Ethical dilemmas in health promotion: An introduction. *Health Education Quarterly* 14(1): 7–9.

Caldwell, Patsy, and Linda L. Bain. 1985. "The Multidimensionality of Curriculum Models." In *Proceedings of the Fourth Conference on Curriculum Theory in Physical Education*, edited by M. Martha Carnes, 223–239. Athens: University of Georgia.

Carlyon, William H. 1984. Disease prevention/health promotion—bridging the gap to wellness. *Health Values: Achieving High Level Wellness* 8(3): 27–30.

Carr, Norma J., ed. 1987. *Basic Stuff in Action Grades 4–8*. Reston, VA: AAHPERD.

Caspersen, Carl J. 1989. "Physical Activity Epidemiology: Concepts, Methods, and Applications to Exercise Science." In *Exercise and Sport Science Reviews*, edited by Kent B. Pandolf, 423–473. Baltimore, MD: Williams & Wilkins.

Chalip, Laurence, et al. 1984. Variations of experience in formal and informal sport. *Research Quarterly for Exercise and Sport* 55(2): 109–116.

Chapman, Peggy A. 1974. "Evaluation of Affective Responses of Students to a Selected List of Purposes for Human Movement." Unpublished doctoral dissertation, University of Wisconsin, Madison.

Clark, H. H., ed. 1971. *Physical Fitness Research Digest*. Washington, DC: President's Council on Physical Fitness and Sports, Series 1, no. 1.

Clark, H. H., ed. 1973, May. *National Adult Physical Fitness Survey* (special edition). Washington, DC: President's Council on Physical Fitness and Sports.

Coakley, Jay J. 1980. Play, games and sports: Developmental implications for young people. *Journal of Sport Behavior* 3(3): 99–118.

Colquhoun, Derek. 1990. "Images of Healthism in Health-based Physical Education." In *Physical Education, Curriculum and Culture: Critical Issues in the Contemporary Crisis*, edited by David Kirk and Richard Tinning, 225–251. London: Falmer.

Cooper, Kenneth H., et al. 1975. An aerobic conditioning program for the Fort Worth Texas School District. *Research Quarterly* 46(3): 345–350.

Corbin, Charles B. 1987. Youth fitness, exercise and health: There is much to be done. *Research Quarterly for Exercise and Sport* 58(4): 308–314.

Corbin, Charles B., and Ruth Lindsey. 1985. *Concepts of Physical Fitness with Laboratories*. Dubuque, IA: Brown.

Crawford, R. 1977. You are dangerous to your health: There is much to be done. *International Journal of Health Services* 7(4): 663–680.

Crawford, R. 1986. "A Cultural Account of 'Health': Control, Release, and the Social Body.'' In *Issues in the Political Economy of Health Care*, edited by J. B. McKinley, 60–103. London: Tavistock.

Crowe, Patricia B. 1977. ''An Observational Study of Expectancy Effects and their Mediation Mechanisms on Students of Physical Education Activity Classes.'' Unpublished doctoral dissertation, University of North Carolina at Greensboro.

Cureton, Kirk J. 1987. Commentary on ''Children and fitness: A public health perspective.'' *Research Quarterly for Exercise and Sport* 58(4): 315–320.

Cureton, Kirk J., and Gordon L. Warren. 1990. Criterion-referenced standards for youth health-related fitness tests: A tutorial. *Research Quarterly for Exercise and Sport* 61(1): 7–19.

Dauer, Victor P., and Robert P. Pangrazi. 1989. *Dynamic Physical Education for Elementary School Children*. New York: Macmillan.

Davis, C., M. P. Cowles, and P. Hasting. 1990. A study of relationships among exercise participation, psychological factors, and weight preoccupation in women. *Medicine and Science in Sports and Exercise* 22(2): S92.

De Coverley Veale, D. M. W. 1987. Exercise dependence. *British Journal of Addiction* 82(7): 735–740.

DeBusk, Michael, and Don Hellison. 1989. Implementing a physical education self-responsibility model for delinquency-prone youth. *Journal of Teaching in Physical Education* 8(2): 104–111.

Despres, Jean-Pierre, Claude Bouchard, and Robert M. Malina. 1990. ''Physical Activity and Coronary Heart Disease Risk Factors During Childhood and Adolescence.'' In *Exercise and Sport Sciences Reviews*, edited by Kent B. Pandolf and John O. Holloszy, 243–261. Baltimore, MD: Williams & Wilkins.

Dewar, Alison M. 1987. The social construction of gender in a physical education programme. *Women's Studies International Forum* 10(4): 453–466.

Dewar, Alison M. 1990. ''Oppression and Privilege in Physical Education: Struggles in the Negotiation of Gender in a University Programme.'' In *Physical Education, Curriculum and Culture: Critical Issues in the Contemporary Crisis*, edited by David Kirk and Richard Tinning, 67–99. London: Falmer.

Dewey, John. 1916. *Democracy and Education*. New York: MacMillan.

Dietz, William H., and Steven L. Gortmaker. 1985. Do we fatten our children at the television set? Obesity and television viewing in children and adolescent. *Pediatrics* 75(5): 807–812.

Dishman, Rod K. 1990. ''Determinants of Participation in Physical Activity.'' In *Exercise, Fitness, and Health*, edited by Claude Bouchard et al., 75–101. Champaign, IL: Human Kinetics.

Dishman, Rod K., and Andrea Dunn. 1988. ''Exercise Adherence in Children and Youth: Implications for Adulthood.'' In *Exercise Adherence: Its Impact on Public Health*, edited by Rod K. Dishman, 155–200. Champaign, IL: Human Kinetics.

Dodds, Patt. 1983. ''Consciousness Raising in Curriculum: A Teacher's Model for Analysis.'' In *Proceedings of the Third Conference on Curriculum Theory in Physical Education*, edited by Ann E. Jewett, M. Martha Carnes, and Maureen Speakman, 213–234. Athens: University of Georgia.

Dodds, Patt. 1986. ''Stamp Out the Ugly 'Isms' in Your Gym.'' In *Sport Pedagogy*, edited by Maurice Pieron and George Graham, 141–150. Champaign, IL: Human Kinetics.

Drake, Debra D., and Charles T. Kuntzleman. 1988. ''Early Intervention/Prevention in Childhood.'' In *Epidemiology, Behavior Change, and Intervention in Chronic Disease*, edited by Linda K. Hall and G. Curt Meyer, 25–38. Champaign, IL: Life Enhancement.

Dubois, Paul E. 1986. The effect of participation in sport on the value orientations of young athletes. *Sociology of Sport Journal* 3(1): 29–42.

Duncan, Burris, et al. 1983. A controlled trial of a physical fitness program for fifth grade students. *Journal of School Health* 53(8): 467–471.

Dwyer, T., et al. 1983. An investigation of the effects of daily physical activity on the health of primary school students in South Australia. *International Journal of Epidemiology* 12(3): 308–313.

Earls, Neal F. 1981. Distinctive teachers' personal qualities, perceptions of teacher education and the realities of teaching. *Journal of Teaching in Physical Education* 1(1): 59–70.

Earls, Neal F. 1985. ''Criteria for Disciplined Naturalistic Inquiry in Physical Education.'' In *Proceedings of the Fourth Curriculum Theory Conference in Physical Education*, edited by M. Martha Carnes, 84–98. Athens: University of Georgia.

Earls, Neal F. 1986. Research design, data collection, and analysis. *Journal of Teaching in Physical Education* 6(1): 40–49.

Eisner, Elliot W. 1977. *The Educational Imagination: On the Design and Evaluation of School Programs*. New York: Macmillan.

Eisner, Elliot W., and Elizabeth Vallance, eds. 1974. *Conficting Conceptions of Curriculum*. Berkeley, CA: McCutchan.

Ennis, Catherine D. 1985. Purpose concepts in an existing physical education curriculum. *Research Quarterly for Exercise and Sport* 56(4): 323–333.

Ennis, Catherine D. 1987. Properties of purpose concepts in an operational middle-school curriculum. *Journal of Teaching in Physical Education* 6(3): 287–300.

Ennis, Catherine D., and Linda M. Hooper. 1988. Development of an instrument for assessing educational value orientations. *Journal of Curriculum Studies* 20(3): 277–280.

Ennis, Catherine D., and Linda M. Hooper. 1990. An analysis of the PPCF as a theoretical framework for an instrument to examine teacher prioritites for selecting curriculum content. *Research Quarterly for Exercise and Sport* 61(1): 50–58.

Ennis, Catherine D., Leslie K. Mueller, and Linda M. Hooper. 1990. The influence of teacher value orientations on curriculum planning within the parameters of a theoretical framework. *Research Quarterly for Exercise and Sport* 61(4): 360–368.

Ennis, Catherine D., and Weimo Zhu. 1991. Value orientations: A description of teachers' goals for student learning. *Research Quarterly for Exercise and Sport* 62(1): 33–40.

Faucette, Nell. 1987. Teachers' concerns and participation styles during in-service education. *Journal of Teaching in Physical Education* 6(4): 425–440.

Faucette, Nell. 1988. Stages of concern: A model for enhancing the change process. *Journal of Teaching in Physical Education* 7(3): 235–239.

Faucette, Nell, and George Graham. 1986. The impact of principals on teachers during inservice education: A qualitative analysis. *Journal of Teaching in Physical Education* 5(2): 79–90.

Faucette, Nell, Thomas L. McKenzie, and Patricia Patterson. 1990. Descriptive analysis of nonspecialist elementary physical education teachers' curricular choices and class organization. *Journal of Teaching in Physical Education* 9(4): 284–293.

Faucette, Nell, and Patricia Patterson. 1989. Classroom teachers and physical education: What they are doing and how they feel about it. *Education* 110(1): 108–114.

Faucette, Nell, and Patricia Patterson. 1990. Comparing teaching behaviors and student activity levels in classes taught by p.e. specialists versus nonspecialists. *Journal of Teaching in Physical Education* 9(2): 106–114.

Fine, Gary A. 1987. *With the Boys: Little League Baseball and Preadolescent Culture*. Chicago: University of Chicago Press.

Fox, Kenneth R. 1988. The self-esteem complex and youth fitness. *Quest* 40(3): 230–246.

Franks, B. Don. 1989. *YMCA Youth Fitness Test Manual*. Champaign, IL: Human Kinetics.

Franks, B. Don, and George C. Moore. 1969. Effects of calisthenics and volleyball on the AAHPER fitness tests and volleyball skill. *Research Quarterly* 40(2): 288–292.

Freedson, Patty S. 1989. Field monitoring of physical activity in children. *Pediatric Exercise Science* 1(1): 8–18.

Freire, Paulo. 1983. *Pedagogy of the Oppressed*. New York: Continuum.

Gallup, George. 1984. The 16th annual Gallup poll of the public's attitudes toward the public schools. *Phi Delta Kappan*, September, 23–28.

Geenan, David L., et al. 1982. Echocardiographic measures in 6 to 7 year old children after an 8 month exercise program. *The American Journal of Cardiology* 49: 1990–1995.

Georgiadis, Nikos. 1990. Does basketball have to be all W's and L's? An alternative program at a residential boys' home. *Journal of Health, Physical Education, Recreation and Dance* 61(6): 42–43.

Getchell, Bud. 1982. *Physical Fitness a Way of Life*. New York: Wiley.

Gilliam, Thomas B., et al. 1982. Exercise program for children: A way to prevent heart disease? *The Physician and Sportsmedicine* 10(9): 96–101, 105–106, 108.

Gilliam, Thomas B., and S. E. MacConnie. 1984. Coronary heart disease risk in children and their physical activity patterns. In *Advances in Pediatric Sport Sciences*, edited by Richard A. Boileau. Champaign, IL: Human Kinetics.

Giroux, Henry A. 1981a. Hegemony, resistance, and the paradox of educational reform. *Interchange* 12(2–3): 3–26.

Giroux, Henry A. 1981b. *Ideology, Culture and the Process of Schooling*. London: Falmer.

Giroux, Henry A., Anthony N. Penna, and William F. Pinar. 1981. *Curriculum and Instruction Alternatives in Education*. Berkeley, CA: McCutchan.

Godin, Gaston, and Roy J. Shephard. 1986. Psychosocial factors influencing intentions to exercise of young students from grades 7 to 9. *Research Quarterly for Exercise and Sport* 57(1): 41–52.

Goetz, Judith P., and Margaret D. LeCompte. 1984. *Ethnography and Qualitative Design in Educational Research*. Orlando, FL: Academic Press.

Governor's Commission on Physical Fitness. 1973. *Texas Physical Fitness—Motor Ability Test*. Austin: Governor's Commission on Physical Fitness.

Graham, George. 1988. Collaboration in physical education: A lot like marriage? *Journal of Physical Education* 7(3): 165–174.

Greenockle, Karen M., Amelia L. Lee, and Richard Lomax. 1990. The relationship between selected student characteristics and activity patterns in a required high school physical education class. *Research Quarterly for Exercise and Sport* 61(1): 599–669.

Griffin, Patricia S. 1983. " 'Gymnastics Is a Girls' Thing': Student Participation and Interaction Patterns in a Middle School Gymnastics Unit." In *Teaching in Physical Education*, edited by Thomas J. Templin and Janice K. Olson, 71–85. Champaign, IL: Human Kinetics.

Griffin, Patricia S. 1984. Girls' participation patterns in a middle school team sports unit. *Journal of Teaching in Physical Education* 4(1): 30–38.

Griffin, Patricia S. 1985a. Boys' participation styles in a middle school physical education sports unit. *Journal of Teaching in Physical Education* 4(2): 100–110.

Griffin, Patricia S. 1985b. Teacher's perceptions of and responses to sex equity problems in a middle school physical education program. *Research Quarterly for Exercise and Sport* 56(2): 103–110.

Griffin, Patricia S. 1986. What have we learned? *Journal of Physical Education, Recreation and Dance* 57(4): 57–59.

Griffin, Patricia, and Gayle Hutchinson. 1988. Second wind: A physical education program development network. *Journal of Teaching in Physical Education* 7(3): 184–189.

Haag, Herbert. 1983. "Data Based Curriculum Development: Perception of Aims and Objectives by Physical Education Teachers." In *Proceedings of the Third Conference on Curriculum Theory in Physical Education*, edited by Ann E. Jewett, M. Martha Carnes, and Maureen Speakman, 279–299. Athens: University of Georgia.

Harris, Louis. 1979. *The Perrier Study: Fitness in America*. New York: Perrier.

Haydon, Donald F., and William G. Squires. 1988. Fit youth today. *Texas Alliance for Health, Physical Education, Recreation, and Dance Journal* 56(2): 41–50.

Hellison, Don R. 1978. *Beyond Balls and Bats: Alienated Youth in the Gym*. Washington, DC: AAHPERD.

Hellison, Don R. 1983a. *Humanistic Physical Education*. Englewood Cliffs, NJ: Prentice Hall.

Hellison, Don R. 1983b. "It Only Takes One Case to Prove a Possibility . . . and Beyond." In *Teaching in Physical Education*, edited by Thomas J. Templin and Janet K. Olson, 102–106. Champaign, IL: Human Kinetics.

Hellison, Don R. 1985. *Goals and Strategies for Teaching Physical Education*. Champaign, IL: Human Kinetics.

Hellison, Don R. 1987. "Dreaming the Possible Dream: The Rise and Triumph of Physical Education." In *Trends Toward the Future in Physical Education*, edited by John D. Massengale, 137–151. Champaign, IL: Human Kinetics.

Hellison, Don R. 1989a. "A Qualitative Case Study of the Qualitative Case Study in Physical Education Curriculum Research." In *Proceedings of the Sixth Conference on Curriculum Theory in Physical Education*, edited by Marie R. Mullan, 113–122. Athens: University of Georgia.

Hellison, Don R. 1989b. *An Alternative Model for Teaching Sport and Exercise to At-Risk Youth*. Unpublished manuscript.

Hellison, Don R. 1990a. Teaching p. e. to at-risk youth in Chicago: A model. *Journal of Physical Education, Recreation and Dance* 61(6): 38–39.

Hellison, Don R. 1990b. Making a difference: Reflections on teaching urban at-risk youth. *Journal of Physical Education, Recreation and Dance* 61(6): 44–45.

Hellison, Don R., and Thomas J. Templin. 1991. *A Reflective Approach to Teaching Physical Education*. Champaign, IL: Human Kinetics.

Hendry, L. B. 1975. The role of the physical education teacher. *Educational Research* 17(2): 115–121.

Higbee, Kenneth L. 1969. Fifteen years of fear arousal: Research on threat appeals: 1953–1968. *Psychological Bulletin* 72(6): 426–444.

Ho, P., et al. 1981. Adherence prediction and psychological/behavioral changes following one-year randomized exercise programs (abstract). *Proceedings of Pan American Congress and International Course on Sports Medicine and Exercise Science*, Miami, FL, May: 9.

Hoffman, Herbert A., Jane Young, and Stephen E. Klesius. 1981. *Meaningful Movement for Children*. Boston, MA: Allyn & Bacon.

Houston, W. Robert, ed. 1990. *Handbook for Research on Teacher Education*. New York: Macmillan.

Institute for Aerobics Research. 1987. *FITNESSGRAM User's Manual*. Dallas, TX: Institute for Aerobics Research.

Iverson, Donald C., et al. 1985. The promotion of physical activity in the United States population: The status of programs in medical, worksite, community, and school settings. *Public Health Reports* 100(2): 212–224.

Janis, Irving L. 1967. "Effects of Fear Arousal on Attitude Change: Recent Developments in Theory and Experimental Research." In *Advances in Experimental Social Psychology*, Vol. 3, edited by Leonard Berkowitz, 167–224. New York: Academic Press.

Jewett, Ann E. 1980. The status of physical education curriculum theory. *Quest* 32(2): 163–173.

Jewett, Ann E., and Linda L. Bain. 1985. *The Curriculum Process in Physical Education*. Dubuque, IA: Brown.

Jewett, Ann E., and Linda L. Bain, eds. 1987. The purpose process curriculum framework: A personal meaning model for physical education, special monograph. *Journal of Teaching in Physical Education* 6(3): 195–366.

Jewett, Ann E., and Catherine D. Ennis. 1990. Ecological integration as a value orientation for curricular decision making. *Journal of Curriculum and Supervision* 5(2): 120–131.

Jewett, Ann E., and Marie R. Mullan. 1977. *Curriculum Design: Purposes and Processes in Physical Education Teaching-Learning*. Washington, DC: AAHPER.

Johnson, La Von C. 1969. Effects of 5-day-a-week vs. 2- and 3-day-a-week physical education class on fitness, skill, adipose tissue and growth. *Research Quarterly* 40(1): 93–98.

Jones, LaVetta S. 1972. "The Construct of Body Awareness in Space as Reflected Through Children's Ability to Discriminate Direction, Levels, and Pathways in Movement." Unpublished doctoral dissertation, University of Wisconsin, Madison.

Kanfer, F. H., and L. Gaelick. 1986. "Self-Management Methods." In *Helping People Change*, edited by Frederick H. Kanfer and Arnold P. Goldstein, 283–345, New York: Pergamon.

Kemper, H. C. G., et al. 1978. Investigation into the effects of two extra physical education lessons per week during one school year upon the physical development of 12–13-year-old boys. *Medicine Sport* 11: 159–166.

Kenyon, Gerald S. 1968a. A conceptual model for characterizing physical activity. *Research Quarterly* 39(1): 96–104.

Kenyon, Gerald S. 1968b. Six scales for assessing attitude toward physical activity. *Research Quarterly* 39(3): 566–574.

Kimpston, Richard D., and Karen B. Rogers. 1986. A framework for curriculum research. *Curriculum Inquiry* 16(4): 463–474.

Kirk, David. 1988. *Physical Education and Curriculum Study*. New York: Croom Helm.

Kirk, David, and Derek Colquhoun. 1989. Healthism and Physical Education. *British Journal of Sociology of Education* 10(4): 417–434.

Kisabeth, K. L. 1985. "Personal Purposes for Meanings in Movement. A Q sort." In *Proceedings of the Fourth Conference of Curriculum Theory in Physical Education*, edited by M. Martha Carnes, 204–212. Athens: University of Georgia.

Klausen, Klaus, Birger Rasmussen, and Bente Schibye. 1986. "Evaluation of the Physical Activity of School Children During a Physical-Education Lesson." In *Children and Exercise XII*, edited by Joseph Rutenfranz, Rolf Mocellin, and Ferdinand Klimt, 93–101. Champaign, IL: Human Kinetics.

Kleiber, Douglas A., and Glynn C. Roberts. 1983. The relationship between game and sport involvement in later childhood: A preliminary investigation. *Research Quarterly for Exercise and Sport* 54(2): 200–203.

Kneer, Marion E., ed. 1981. *Adolesence Basic Stuff Series*. Reston, VA: AAHPERD.

Kneer, Marion E. 1986. Description of physical education instructional theory/practice gap in selected secondary schools. *Journal of Teaching in Physical Education* 5(2): 91–106.

Kollen, Patsy P. 1981. "The Experience of Movement in Physical Education: A Phenomenology." Unpublished doctoral dissertation, University of Michigan, Ann Arbor.

Kollen, Patsy P. 1983. "Fragmentation and Integration in Movement." In *Teaching in Physical Education*, edited by Thomas J. Templin and Janice K. Olson, 86–93. Champaign, IL: Human Kinetics.

Koslow, Robert E. 1988. Can physical fitness be a primary objective in a balanced pe program? *Journal of Physical Education, Recreation and Dance* 59(4): 75–77.

Kraus, Hans, and Ruth P. Hirschland. 1954. Minimum muscular fitness tests in school children. *The Research Quarterly* 25(2): 178–188.

Kreuter, Marshall W., Michael J. Parsons, and Martha P. McMurry. 1982. Moral sensitivity in health promotion. *Health Education* 13(6): 11–13.

Kuntzleman, Charles T., Debra A. Drake, and B. A. Kuntzleman. 1984. *Feelin' Good: Youth Fitness Report—Summary*. Spring Arbor, MI: Fitness Finders.

Laban, Rudolph. 1963. *Modern Educational Dance*, 2nd ed. New York: Praeger.

Lambdin, Dolly, and Mary Steinhardt. In press. "Elementary and secondary physical education teachers' perceptions of their goals, expertise, curriculum, and students' achievement." *Journal of Teaching in Physical Education*.

Lander, Linda M. 1983. "A Conceptual Model of Incentive Values for Designing Physical Education Curricula." In *Proceedings of the Third Conference on Curriculum Theory in Physical Education*, edited by Ann E. Jewett, Martha M. Carnes, and Maureen Speakman, 339–355. Athens: University of Georgia.

Lander, Linda M., and Peggy A. Chapman. 1987. The likeability and utility dimensions of the purpose elements. *Journal of Teaching in Physical Education* 6(3): 234–242.

Lanier, Judith E., and Judith W. Little. 1986. "Research on Teacher Education." In *Handbook of Research on Teaching*, 3rd ed., edited by Merlin C. Wittrock, 527–569. New York: Macmillan.

LaPlante, Marilyn J. 1973. "Evaluation of a Selected List of Purposes for Physical Education using a Modified Delphi Technique." Unpublished doctoral dissertation, University of Wisconsin, Madison.

LaPlante, Marilyn J., and Ann E. Jewett. 1987. Content validation of the purpose dimension. *Journal of Teaching in Physical Education* 6(3): 214–223.

Lawson, Hal A. 1986a. Occupational socialization and the design of teacher education programs. *Journal of Teaching in Physical Education* 5(2): 107–116.

Lawson, Hal A. 1986b, April. "Toward a National Curriculum in Physical Education." Paper presented at the Annual Convention of the American Alliance for Health, Physical Education, Recreation and Dance, Cincinnati, OH. ERIC Document no. ED 273 601.

Lawson, Hal A., and Judith Placek. 1981. *Physical Education in the Secondary Schools: Curricular Alternatives*. Boston: Allyn & Bacon.

Legwold, Gary. 1983. New verse, same chorus: Children aren't fit. *The Physician and Sportsmedicine* 11(5): 153–155.

Leonard, F. E., and G. Affleck. 1947. *A Guide to the History of Physical Education*. Philadelphia: Lea and Febiger.

Lifka, Bobby. 1990. Hiding beneath the stairwell: A dropout prevention program for hispanic youth. *Journal of Health, Physical Education, Recreation and Dance* 61(6): 40–41.

Lincoln, Yvonna S., and Egon G. Guba. 1985. *Naturalistic Inquiry*. Beverly Hills, CA: Sage.

Lipton, Edward D. 1970. A perceptual-motor development program's effect on visual perception and reading readiness of first grade children. *Research Quarterly* 41(3): 402–405.

Little, J. Crawford. 1969. The athlete's neurosis—a deprivation crisis. *Acta Psychiatrica Scandinavica* 45(2): 187–197.

Locke, Lawrence F. 1989. Qualitative research as a form of scientific inquiry in sport and physical education. *Research Quarterly for Exercise and Sport* 60(1): 1–20.

Locke, Lawrence F., and Patricia Griffin, eds. 1986. Profiles of struggle. *Journal of Physical Education, Recreation and Dance* 57(4): 32–63.

Locke, Lawrence F., and John D. Massengale. 1978. Role-conflict in teacher-coaches. *Research Quarterly* 49(2): 162–174.

Logsdon, Bette J., et al. 1984. *Physical Education for Children: A Focus on the Teaching Process*. Philadelphia, PA: Lea and Febiger.

Loucks, H. Donald. 1979. New professionals reorder objectives. *Journal of Physical Education and Recreation* 50(7): 64–65.

Lumpkin, Angela. 1990. *Physical Education and Sport: A Contemporary Introduction*. St. Louis, MO: Times Mirror/Mosby.

MacConnie, S. E., et al. 1982. Daily physical activity patterns of prepubertal children involved in a vigorous exercise program. *International Journal of Sports Medicine* 4(3): 202–207.

Macintosh, Donald, and John Albinson. 1982. Physical education in Ontario secondary schools. *Canadian Association for Health, Physical Education and Recreation Journal* 48(3): 14–17.

Mangham, Patsy N. 1979. "Attitudes of Selected Secondary School Students Toward Purposes of Human Movement." Unpublished master's thesis, University of Georgia, Athens.

Marlatt, G. Alan. 1986. "Relapse Prevention: Theoretical Rationale and Overview of the Model." In *Relapse Prevention: Maintenance Strategies in the Treatment of Addicted Behaviors*, edited by G. Alan Marlatt and Judith R. Gordon, 3–70. New York: Guilford.

Marsh, David. 1983. Issues and insights. *Journal of Physical Education, Recreation and Dance* 54(7): 9.

Martinek, Thomas J. 1981. Physical attractiveness: Effects of teacher expectations and dyadic interactions in elementary age children. *Journal of Sport Psychology* 3(3): 196–205.

Martinek, Thomas J. 1983. "Creating Golem and Galatea Effects during Physical Education Instruction: A Social Psychological Perspective." In *Teaching in Physical Education,* edited by Thomas J. Templin and Janice K. Olson, 46–56. Champaign, IL: Human Kinetics.

Martinek, Thomas J. 1989. "The Psycho-Social Dynamics of the Pygmalion Phenomenon in Physical Education and Sport." In *Socialization into Physical Education: Learning to Teach*, edited by Thomas J. Templin and Paul G. Schempp, 199–217. Indianapolis, IN: Benchmark.

Martinek, Thomas, J., and Karen Butt. 1988. An application of an action research model for changing instructional practice. *Journal of Teaching in Physical Education* 7(3): 214–220.

Martinek, Thomas J., Patricia B. Crowe, and Walter J. Rejeski. 1982. *Pygmalion in the Gym: Causes and Effects of Expectations in Teaching and Coaching*. West Point, NY: Leisure Press.

Martinek, Thomas, and Susan B. Johnson. 1979. Teacher expectations: Effects on dyadic interactions and self-concept in elementary age children. *Research Quarterly* 50(1): 60–70.

Martinek, Thomas, and William Karper. 1981. Teacher expectations for handicapped and non-handicapped children in mainstreamed physical education classes. *Perceptual and Motor Skills* 53(1): 327–330.

Martinek, Thomas, and William Karper. 1982. Canonical relationships among motor ability, expression of effort, teacher expectations and dyadic interactions in elementary age children. *Journal of Teaching in Physical Education* 1(2): 26–39.

Martinek, Thomas, and William Karper. 1984. Multivariate relationships of specific impression cues with teacher expectations and dyadic interactions in elementary education classes. *Research Quarterly for Exercise and Sport* 55(1): 32–40.

Martinek, Thomas J., and Paul G. Schempp, eds. 1988. Collaboration for instructional improvement: Models for school-university partnerships. *Journal of Teaching in Physical Education* 7(3): 157–263.

Maslow, Abraham H. 1954. *Motivation and Personality*. New York: Harper & Row.

Maslow, Abraham H. 1979. Humanistic education. *Journal of Humanistic Psychology* 19(3): 13–25.

Melograno, Vincent. 1979. *Designing Curriculum and Learning: A Physical Coeducation Approach*. Dubuque, IA: Kendall/Hunt.

Melville, D. Scott, and John G. F. Maddalozzo. 1988. The effects of a physical educator's appearance of body fatness on communicating exercise concepts to high school students. *Journal of Teaching in Physical Education* 7(4): 343–352.

Meredith, Marilu D. 1988. Activity or fitness: Is the process or the product more important for public health? *Quest* 40(3): 180–186.

Montoye, Henry J. 1985. "Risk Indicators for Cardiovascular Disease in Relation to Physical Activity in Youth." In *Children and Exercise XI*, edited by Rob A. Binkhorst, Han C. G. Kemper, and Wim H. M. Saris, 3–25. Champaign, IL: Human Kinetics.

Moore, Jane B., Linda M. Guy, and T. Gilmour Reeve. 1984. Effects of the capon perceptual-motor program on motor ability, self-concept, and academic readiness. *Perceptual and Motor Skills* 58(3): 711–714.

Morgan, William P. 1979. Negative addiction in runners. *The Physician and Sportsmedicine* 7(2): 57–70.

Mosston, Muska, and Sara Ashworth. 1986. *Teaching Physical Education*. Columbus, OH: Merrill.

National Association for Sport and Physical Education. 1990. *Definition of the Physically Educated Person: Outcomes of Quality Physical Education Programs. Report of the Physical Education Outcomes Committee to the Association Delegate Assembly*. Reston, VA: AAHPERD.

Neikirk, Mary M. 1985. "Characteristics of Reentry Women Students and their Purposes for Participating in Movement Activities." Unpublished doctoral dissertation, University of Georgia, Athens.

Nichols, Beverly. 1990. *Moving and Learning: The Elementary School Physical Education Experience*. St. Louis, MO: Times Mirror/Mosby.

Norton, Candice J. 1982. "Student Purposes for Engaging in Fitness Activities." Unpublished doctoral dissertation, University of Georgia, Athens.

Norton, Candice J. 1987. Meaningfulness for adult participants. *Journal of Teaching in Physical Education* 6(3): 243–251.

Paffenbarger, Ralph S. 1988. Contributions of epidemiology to exercise science and cardiovascular health. *Medicine and Science in Sports and Exercise* 20(5): 426–438.

Paffenbarger, Ralph S., and Roberet T. Hyde. 1988. "Exercise Adherence, Coronary Heart Disease, and Longevity." In *Exercise Adherence: Its Impact on Public Health*, edited by Rod K. Dishman, 1–73. Champaign, IL: Human Kinetics.

Paffenbarger, Ralph S., Robert T. Hyde, and Alvin L. Wing. 1990. "Physical Activity and Physical Fitness as Determinants of Health and Longevity." In *Exercise, Fitness, and Health*, edited by Claude Bouchard et al., 33–48. Champaign, IL: Human Kinetics.

Pangrazi, Robert P., and Paul W. Darst. 1985. *Dynamic Physical Education Curriculum and Instruction for Secondary Students*. Minneapolis, MN: Burgess.

Parcel, Guy S., et al. 1987. School promotion of healthful diet and exercise behavior: An integration of organizational change and social learning theory interventions. *Journal of School Health* 57(4): 150–156.

Pate, Russell R. 1983. A new definition of youth fitness. *The Physician and Sportsmedicine* 11(4): 77–83.

Patterson, Patricia, and Nell Faucette. 1990. Children's attitudes toward physical activity in classes taught by specialist versus nonspecialist p.e. teachers. *Journal of Teaching in Physical Education* 9(4): 324–331.

Peterson, Penelope L. 1988. Teachers' and students' cognitional knowledge for classroom teaching and learning. *Educational Researcher* 17(5): 5–14.

Placek, Judith H. 1983. "Conceptions of Success in Teaching: Busy, Happy, and Good?" In *Teaching in Physical Education*, edited by Thomas J. Templin and Janice K. Olson, 46–56. Champaign, IL: Human Kinetics.

Placek, Judith H. 1984. A multi-case study of teacher planning in physical education. *Journal of Teaching in Physical Education* 4(1): 39–49.

Placek, Judith H. 1989. An evaluation of the implementation of basic stuff. *Journal of Teaching in Physical Education* 8(2): 152–161.

Pollock, Michael L., and Jack H. Wilmore. 1990. *Exercise in Health and Disease: Evaluation and Prescription for Prevention and Rehabilitation*, 2nd ed. Philadelphia, PA: Saunders.

Powell, Kenneth E., et al. 1987. Physical activity and the incidence of coronary heart disease. *Annual Review of Public Health* 8: 253–287.

Powell, Kenneth E., and Wayne Dysinger. 1987. Childhood participation in organized school sports and physical education as precursors of adult physical activity. *American Journal of Preventive Medicine* 3(5): 276–281.

Rady, Amy M. 1981. "A Construct Validation of Spatial Relationships." Unpublished doctoral dissertation, University of Georgia, Athens.

Rady, Amy M., et al. 1987. Individual purpose components. *Journal of Teaching in Physical Education* 6(3): 259–286.

Ratliffe, Tom. 1988. Principal training for effective staff development. *Journal of Teaching in Physical Education* 7(3): 228–234.

Razor, Jack E. 1987. "Future Directions in Curriculum Theorizing—Being Accountable for 'Impact'." In *Proceedings of the Fifth Conference on Curriculum Theory in Physical Education*, edited by M. Martha Carnes and Patricia M. Stueck, 1–4. Athens: University of Georgia.

Reed, B. 1983. "The Importance and Attainment of Selected Physical Education Objectives as Perceived by Educators and Non-Educators." Unpublished dissertation, University of Maryland, College Park.

Reid, W. A. 1978. *Thinking about the Curriculum*. London: Routledge & Kegan Paul.

Rejeski, Walter J., Charles Darracott, and Sally Hutslar. 1979. Pygmalion in youth sport: A field study. *Journal of Sport Psychology* 1(4): 311–319.

Rejeski, Walter J., and Charles A. Lowe. 1980. The role of ability and effort in sport achievement. *Journal of Personality* 48(2): 233–244.

Rink, Judith E. 1985. *Teaching Physical Education for Learning*. St. Louis, MO: Times Mirror/Mosby.

Rink, Judith E. 1987. "When Should Be Becomes Can We in Curriculum." In *Proceedings of the Fifth Conference on Curriculum Theory in Physical Education*, edited by Martha Carnes and Patricia M. Stueck, 203–210. Athens: University of Georgia.

Riopel, Donald A., et al. 1986. Coronary risk factor modification in children: Exercise. *Circulation* 74(5): 1189A-1191A.

Rosenstock, I. M. 1974. Historical origins of the health belief model. *Health Education Monographs* 2: 328–335.

Rosentswieg, Joel. 1969. A ranking of the objectives of physical education. *Research Quarterly* 40(4): 783–787.

Rowland, Thomas W. 1990. *Exercise and Children's Health*. Champaign, IL: Human Kinetics.

Safrit, Margaret J. 1986. "Health-Related Fitness Levels of American Youth." In *American Academy of Physical Education Papers*, edited by G. A. Stull and H. M. Eckert, 153–166. Champaign, IL: Human Kinetics.

Safrit, Margaret J., and Terry M. Wood. 1983. The health-related fitness test opinionnaire: A pilot survey. *Research Quarterly for Exercise and Sport* 54(2): 204–207.

Safrit, Margaret J., and Terry M. Wood. 1986. The health-related physical fitness test: A tri-state survey of users and non-users. *Research Quarterly for Exercise and Sport* 57(1): 27–32.

Sage, George H. 1980. Sociology of physical educator/coaches: Personal attributes controversy. *Research Quarterly for Exercise and Sport* 51(1): 110–121.

Sage, George H. 1989. A commentary on qualitative research as a form of scientific inquiry in sport and physical education. *Research Quarterly for Exercise and Sport* 60(1): 25–29.

Sallis, James F. 1987. A commentary on children and fitness: A public health perspective. *Research Quarterly for Exercise and Sport* 58(4): 326–330.

Sallis, James F., and Melbourne F. Hovell. 1990. "Determinants of Exercise Behavior." In *Exercise and Sport Sciences Reviews*, edited by Kent B. Pandolf and John O. Holloszy, 307–330. Baltimore, MD: Williams & Wilkins.

Sanders, Donald P., and Gail McCutcheon. 1986. The development of practical theories of teaching. *Journal of Curriculum and Supervision* 2(1): 50–67.

Saris, Wim H. M. 1985. The assessment and evaluation of daily physical activity in children: A review. *Acta Paediatrica Scandinavica Supplement* 318(1): 37–48.

Saris, Wim H. M. 1986. Habitual physical activity in children: Methodology and findings in health and disease. *Medicine and Science in Sports and Exercise* 18(3): 253–263.

Saris, Wim H. M., et al. 1986. "Changes in Physical Activity of Children Aged 6 to 12 Years." In *Children and Exercise XII*, edited by Joseph Rutenfranz, Rolf Mocellin, and Ferdinand Klimt, 121–130. Champaign, IL: Human Kinetics.

Schubert, William H. 1986. *Curriculum: Perspective, Paradigm, and Possibility*. New York: Macmillan.

Schunk, Dale H., and Joseph P. Carbonari. 1984. "Self-Efficacy Models." In *Behavioral Health*, edited by Joseph D. Matarazzo, et al., 230–247. New York: Wiley.

Schutz, Robert W. 1989. Qualitative research: Comments and controversies. *Research Quarterly for Exercise and Sport* 60(1): 30–35.

Schwager, Susan M., and Sarah A. Doolittle. 1988. Teachers' reactions to activities in ongoing program development. *Journal of Teaching in Physical Education* 7(3): 240–249.

Segall, Brenda K. [illegible]. "Development and Validation of a Teamwork Construct." Unpublished doctoral dissertation, University of Georgia, Athens.

Shephard, Roy J., and Gaston Godin. 1986. "Behavioral Intentions and Activity of Children." In *Children and Exercise XII*, edited by Joseph Rutenfranz, Rolf Mocellin, and Ferdinand Klimt, 103–109. Champaign, IL: Human Kinetics.

Shephard, Roy J., Jean-Claude Jequier, Hugues Lavallée, Robert LaBarre, and Mirjana Rajic. 1980. Habitual physical activity: Effects of sex, milieu, season and required activity. *Journal of Sports Medicine and Physical Fitness* 20(1): 55–66.

Shephard, Roy J., M Volle, Hugues Lavallée, Robert LaBarre, Jean-Claude Jequier, and Mirjana Rajic. 1984. "Required Physical Activity and Academic Grades: A Controlled Study." In *Children and Sport: Paediatric Work Physiology*, edited by J. Ilmarinen and I. Vaelimaeki, 58–63. Berlin: Springer-Verlag.

Sherlock, Joyce. 1987. Issues of masculinity and femininity in British physical education. *Women's Studies International Forum* 10(4): 443–451.

Sherrill, Claudine, and Omar Holguin. 1989. Fitness, attitude toward physical education, and self-concept of elementary school children. *Perceptual and Motor Skill* 69(2): 411–414.

Shifflett, Bethany, et al. 1990. "Reliability and Validity for the Purposes for Engaging in Physical Activity Survey." In *Abstracts Research Papers AAHPERD*, edited by Jane E. Clark, 252. Reston, VA: AAHPERD.

Siedentop, Daryl. 1980. *Physical Education Introductory Analysis*. Dubuque, IA: Brown.

Siedentop, Daryl. 1986. "The Modification of Teacher Behavior." In *Sport Pedagogy*, edited by Maurice Pieron and George Graham, 3–18. Champaign, IL: Human Kinetics.

Siedentop, Daryl. 1987. High school physical education still an endangered species. *Journal of Physical Education, Recreation and Dance* 58(2): 24–25.

Siedentop, Daryl. 1989. Do the lockers really smell? *Research Quarterly for Exercise and Sport* 60(1): 36–41.

Siedentop, Daryl, Charler Mand, and Andrew Taggart. 1986. *Physical Education: Teaching and Curriculum Strategies for Grades 5 to 12*. Columbus, OH: Mayfield.

Siegel, Judith A., and Thomas G. Manfredi. 1984. Effects of a ten-month fitness program on children. *The Physician and Sportsmedicine* 12(5): 91–97.

Simon, Julie A., and Frank L. Smoll. 1974. An instrument for assessing children's attitudes toward physical activity. *Research Quarterly* 45(4): 407–415.

Simons-Morton, Bruce G., et al. 1987. Children and fitness: A public health perspective. *Research Quarterly for Exercise and Sport* 58(4): 295–302.

Simons-Morton, Bruce G., et al. 1988. Health-related physical fitness in childhood: Status and recommendations. *Annual Review of Public Health* 9: 403–425.

Smoll, Frank L., and Robert W. Schutz. 1980. Children's attitudes toward physical activity: A longitudinal analysis. *Journal of Sport Psychology* 2(2): 137–147.

Speakman-Yearta, Maureen A. 1987. Cross-cultural comparisons of physical education purposes. *Journal of Teaching in Physical Education* 6(3): 252–258.

Steinhardt, Mary, et al. In press. An analysis of student teachers' intentional, perceived and operational motor skills and physical fitness curriculum. *Journal of Teaching in Physical Education*.

Steinhardt, Mary A., and Rod K. Dishman. 1989. Reliability and validity of expected outcomes and barriers for habitual physical activity. *Journal of Occupational Medicine* 31(6): 536–546.

Steinhardt, Mary A., Ann E. Jewett, and Marie R. Mullan. 1988. An analysis of the purposes for engaging in physical activity scale (pepas) as an instrument for curriculum research. *Research Quarterly for Exercise and Sport* 59(4): 339–350.

Steinhardt, Mary A., and Patricia M. Stueck. 1986. Personal fitness a curriculum model. *Journal of Physical Education, Recreation and Dance* 57(7): 23–32.

Stephens, Thomas, David R. Jacobs, and Craig C. White. 1985. A descriptive epidemiology of leisure-time physical activity. *Public Health Reports* 100(2): 147–158.

Stokes, Roberta, and Clancy Moore. 1986. *Personal Fitness and You*. Winston-Salem, NC: Hunter Textbooks.

Tappe, Marlene K., Joan L. Duda, and Patricia M. Ehrnwald. 1989. Perceived barriers to exercise among adolescents. *Journal of School Health* 59(4): 153–155.

Templin, Thomas J. 1981. Student as socializing agent. *Journal of Teaching in Physical Education*, introductory issue, 71–79.

Templin, Thomas J. 1988. Teacher isolation: A concern for the collegial development of physical educators. *Journal of Teaching in Physical Education* 7(3): 197–205.

Thomas, Jerry R., et al. 1975. Effects of perceptual motor training on preschool children: A multivariate approach. *Research Quarterly* 46(4): 505–513.

Thomas, Jerry R., Amelia M. Lee, and Katherine T. Thomas. 1988. *Physical Education for Children: Concepts into Practice*. Champaign, IL: Human Kinetics.

Thompson, M. M., and B. A. Mann. 1977. *An Holistic Approach to Physical Education Curricula: Objectives Classification System for Elementary Schools*. Champaign, IL: Stipes.

Tiburzi, Antonionette. 1979. "Validation of the Construct Physiological Fitness." Unpublished doctoral dissertation, University of Georgia, Athens.

Tillman, K. 1976. Value shifts by physical educators. *The Reporter: Journal of the New Jersey AHPER* 22(2): 12–15.

Tindall, B. Allan. 1975. Ethnography and the hidden curriculum in sport. *Behavioral and Social Science Teacher* 2(2): 5–28.

Tousignant, Marielle, and Daryl Siedentop. 1983. A qualitative analysis of task structures in required secondary physical education classes. *Journal of Teaching in Physical Education* 3(1): 47–57.

U.S. Department of Health and Human Services. 1980. *Promoting Health/Preventing Disease: Objectives for the Nation*. Washington, DC: Government Printing Office.

U.S. Department of Health and Human Services. 1985. Summary of findings from national children and youth fitness study. *Journal of Physical Education, Recreation and Dance* 56(1): 44–90.

U.S. Department of Health and Human Services. 1986. *Midcourse Review, 1990 Physical Fitness and Exercise Objectives*. President's Council on Physical Fitness and Sports and Behavioral Epidemiology Branch, Center for Health Promotion, Centers for Disease Control. Washington, DC: Government Printing Office.

U.S. Department of Health and Human Services. 1987. Summary of findings from national children and youth fitness study II. *Journal of Physical Education, Recreation and Dance* 58(9): 49–96.

U.S. Department of Health and Human Services. 1988. *The New Expanded President's Challenge Youth Physical Fitness Awards Program*. President's Council on Physical Fitness and Sports. Washington, DC: Government Printing Office.

Veal, Mary L. 1988. Pupil assessment: Perceptions and practices of secondary teachers. *Journal of Teaching in Physical Education* 7(4): 327–342.

Vogel, Paul G. 1986. "Effects of Physical Education Programs on Children." In *Physical Activity and Well-Being*, edited by Vern Seefeldt, 456–501. Reston, VA: AAHPERD.

Wang, Bulah M. 1977. "An Ethnography of a Physical Education Class: An Experiment in Integrated Living." Unpublished doctoral dissertation, University of North Carolina, Greensboro.

Wankel, Leonard M. 1985. Personal and situational factors affecting exercise involvement: The importance of enjoyment. *Research Quarterly for Exercise and Sport* 56(3): 275–282.

Welsh, M. Cay, and Elise E. Labbe. 1989. Are fun runs fun for kids? A survey of school-aged participants. *Perceptual and Motor Skills* 69(1): 74.

Wikler, Daniel. 1987. Who should be blamed for being sick? *Health Education Quarterly* 14(1): 11–25.

Williams, Anne. 1980. Intention versus transaction—the junior school physical education curriculum. *Physical Education Review* 3(2): 96–104.

Wilmore, Jack H. 1982. Objectives for the Nation—Physical Fitness and Exercise. *Journal of Physical Education, Recreation and Dance* 53(3): 41–43.

Wittrock, Merlin C., ed. 1986. *Handbook of Research on Teaching*, 3rd ed. New York: Macmillan.

Wolinsky, J. 1982. Responsibility can delay aging. *American Psychological Association Monitor* 13(3): 14–41.

Worsley, A., et al. 1984. Slim and obese children's perceptions of physical activities. *International Journal of Obesity* 8(3): 201–211.

Yager, Robert E., and John E. Penick. 1990. "Science Teacher Education." In *Handbook for Research on Teacher Education*, edited by W. Robert Houston, 657–673. New York: Macmillan.

Yates, Alayne, Kevin Leehey, and Catherine M. Shisslak. 1983. Running—an analogue of anorexia? *New England Journal of Medicine* 308(5): 251–255.

34

THE EXTRACURRICULUM

Laura E. Berk
ILLINOIS STATE UNIVERSITY

This chapter provides a broad overview of historical and current research on the wide array of school-sponsored activities that typically take place outside the formal academic program. Common examples of extracurricular pursuits include athletic competitions; music associations, such as orchestra, band, and chorus; student publications; drama; debate; student government; assemblies; and social, hobby, and service clubs. This list is by no means exhaustive, nor is it possible to create an all-inclusive ennumeration. Indeed, the task of defining and delimiting the domain encompassed by the extracurriculum is difficult, for extracurricular offerings vary considerably from school to school.

In addition, although the curriculum and extracurriculum are commonly viewed as separate domains of education, the line between them is a fuzzy one. For example, educational objectives commonly ascribed to the extracurriculum—learning to work cooperatively with others, to be a responsible and productive contributor to society, to use leisure time effectively, and to develop one's own abilities to their fullest—can also be applied to a great many formally sponsored school learning experiences. In fact, the tendency for certain extracurricular activities, such as academically oriented clubs, to extend formal curricular concerns and for others, such as band, orchestra, choir, and drama, to be incorporated into the regular schedule of credit-generating classes attests to the widespread acceptance of student activities as an important part of American education.

In view of the interconnection between formal classroom and activity concerns, the word "extracurricular" is somewhat of a misnomer, although it has been, and continues to be, the most widely used designation in the professional and research literature. The prefix "extra" implies a set of pursuits apart from and unrelated to the curriculum, as well as something of peripheral importance. The negative connotations of this label, and other existing substitutes, such as extraschool, noncurricular, semicurricular, paracurricular, and collateral, have led educators to generate a set of more neutral terms, including school activities, student activities, the informal curriculum, the third curriculum, and the other curriculum. At least one referent with a distinctively positive valence has come into frequent usage—cocurricular activities. This designation is preferred by enthusiasts who stress the importance of integrating student activities with classroom studies and who believe that extracurricular pursuits are as vital a part of educational experience as regular academic work.

Despite the proliferation of terms, general agreement exists that extracurricular pursuits differ in essential ways from most formal classroom work. First, they are more social than cognitive in orientation, constituting the major portion of the organized social life of the school. Second, at least in theory if not always in practice, they are student planned and maintained rather than teacher directed, with teachers serving as advisers and guides rather than instructors and students assuming important leadership roles. Third, they generally, although not always, take place outside normally scheduled school hours, such as at lunch time, before and after school, or on weekends. Finally, participation is voluntary rather than required, leading the extracurricular program to be a domain of schooling that is especially responsive to individual differences in student interests and abilities.

The extracurriculum is primarily the province of secondary education. Although a few student activities, such as intramural athletics, music-related pursuits, and student government, have infiltrated elementary schools, they never flourished to the same extent as they did in middle schools, junior high, and high schools. The interests and skills of young elementary school pupils are probably not mature enough to support a differentiated extracurricular program, and their social needs seem better served by the smaller, simpler peer organization of the self-contained classroom. Consequently, the focus of this chapter is on the junior and senior high school and largely on the latter, where activity programs are more extensively developed.

RISE OF THE EXTRACURRICULUM

Extracurricular activities are, in one form or another, as old as the educational system itself, but prior to the 20th century, they emerged haphazardly in secondary schools, without a regularly formulated plan or educational rationale. Before 1900, athletic competitions, school socials, and special interest clubs and musical, literary, and debating societies were carried on largely at the initiative and under the control of students (Gutowski 1988; Jordan 1928; Roemer and Allen 1926). Many principals and teachers of the 19th century took a dim view of these out-of-class, school-affiliated pursuits, fearing that they would encroach on the time students devoted to academic learning (Faunce 1960; Graham 1969; Jones 1935; Krug 1964).

From 1900 to 1915, American educators became more tolerant of student-planned social and athletic activities. Opinion articles written by principals and teachers proliferated, and their content reflected greater awareness of the value of extracurricular pursuits in fostering worthwhile leisure interests and positive social inclinations, such as cooperation and civic responsibility (for examples, see Botkin 1910; Halleck 1902; Johnson 1909; McLinn 1911). Moreover, legitimate school organizations, under the watchful eye of school officials, began to be seen as an important means for combating the negative consequences of adolescent self-generated affiliations. Fraternities and sororities, prevalent in American high schools during the late 19th and early 20th centuries, were widely condemned by educators because of their exclusionary practices, anti-intellectual values, and promotion of undesirable habits, such as smoking, alcohol consumption, and monetary extravagance. School-sponsored organizations were regarded as one way to drive out these secret societies. It was suggested that if enough faculty-supervised organizations were available and if they were responsive to student interests and "democratic and aggressive in spirit," then spontaneously formed cliques and clubs would no longer flourish (Keller 1905, 11; see also Gutowski 1988; Morrison 1905).

Budding recognition that extracurricular organizations could serve as a powerful mechanism of adolescent socialization and social control surfaced in turn-of-the-century educational literature, but it was not until the end of World War I that organized extracurricular programs permeated virtually every American urban junior and senior high school. By the 1920s the extracurricular movement had taken on the status of an "educational cult" (Spring 1986, 204). During the succeeding decade, a wide variety of books and articles were published on the topic, and two specialized journals were established, *School Activities* (1929) and *Student Life* (1934). Leaders of the movement emerged, among them Elbert K. Fretwell of Columbia University, who authored one of the first textbooks on the subject (Fretwell 1931) and devoted much of his career to promoting the educational importance of extracurricular programming in American schools (Graham 1969). Teacher-training institutions added preservice and in-service courses on how to develop and operate extracurricular programs, and a beginning research literature appeared, consisting largely of questionnaires sent to school administrators requesting information on characteristics of activity programs, student participation rates, and beliefs about the benefits of student involvement (see, for example, Jones 1935; Reavis and Van Dyke 1933; Shannon 1929). In 1926, the National Society for the Study of Education devoted Part II of its twenty-fifth yearbook to a description of extracurricular practices and current opinion (Whipple 1926).

Modern educational historians rank the extracurriculum as one of the foremost educational innovations of the early 20th century, alongside compulsory school attendance, vocational education, and the comprehensive high school (Spring 1986; Violas 1978). Indeed, the extracurriculum arose in response to the very same changes in the American social fabric that brought these other well-known educational reforms into being. Urbanization of the population, industrialization of the work force, and a rising tide of immigration at the turn of the century introduced new social problems. Crime, corruption, and poverty became threats to a peaceful and orderly city life. The passage of child labor laws released many youngsters onto the streets, where they were in danger of being influenced by and contributing to urban social degeneration. Moreover, the development of assembly line manufacturing techniques meant that many new jobs required a much narrower range of skills and offered less personal control over the production process than the work of 19th-century artisans. Boredom and alienation were threats to worker productivity and created the potential for widespread industrial unrest. Lower-class and immigrant children, regarded as the industrial work force of the coming generation, were believed to be in need of educational experiences that would prevent the unleashing of these disruptive forces into society.

Compulsory school attendance through midadolescence kept youngsters off the streets and gradually raised the literacy level of the American populace, and expansion of high school courses of study to include vocational education offered direct preparation for new urban-industrial work roles. At the same time, government officials, business and industrial leaders, and educators agreed that education for good citizenship—inculcation of a cooperative spirit, an ability to work as a member of a productive team, and a willingness to subordinate the self to group goals—was needed to produce a socially efficient and content work force.

In 1918, the Commission on the Reorganization of Secondary Education of the National Education Association released its widely influential report *Cardinal Principles of Secondary Education*, which attempted to shape the American high school to meet the needs of the modern corporate state. Besides recommending the establishment of comprehensive high schools with a wide variety of curricula designed to suit the abilities and interests of different types of students, it placed greater emphasis on the social aims of education than any previous educational document in English-speaking nations (Connell 1980). Bringing students of all walks of life together in the same school building, where each would be trained to perform tasks of benefit to society, seemed to offer ideal conditions under which cooperation, cohesion, and social solidarity could be promoted. To assure the attainment of these social goals and to counteract the separation of students from diverse backgrounds and enrolled in different courses of study, the Commission called for "participation of pupils in common activities in which they should have a large measure of responsibility, such as athletic games, social activities, and the government of the school" (National Education Association 1918, 23). Thus, the report endorsed the extracurriculum as the central means for building unification among social strata and cultivating industrious and prosocial personalities (Krug 1964; Spring 1986; Violas 1978). Besides their promise to improve the quality of the American work force, extracurricular activities were believed by the authors of the *Cardinal Principles* to offer all children, and immigrant youth in particular, essential opportunities to experience and identify with American ideals and standards of citizenship. The report stated: "Through loyalty to a school which includes many groups [children] are prepared for loyalty to State and Nation" (National Education Association 1918, 24–26).

Related to the concept of education for citizenship in a new industrial age were new, turn-of-the-century ideas about the social development of adolescents. The most influential American developmental psychologist of this period was G. Stanley Hall. According to his theory of evolutionary recapitulation, each stage of individual development reenacted a stage of human evolution. During puberty, a flood of instinctual passions envelops the person; the child recapitulates the life of savagery. In his classic work *Adolescence*, Hall (1904, xv) wrote, "The whole future of life depends on how new powers given suddenly and in profusion [during puberty] are husbanded." The sexual-social passions of adolescence could lead the young person into a life of decadence and conflict with society, or they could be harnessed and directed toward some socially useful function. Hall's theory underscored the belief of many educators that the high school years were an especially important period for the development of a sense of cooperation and social service required for success in modern society (Spring 1986) and provided an additional impetus for the development of wholesome extracurricular activities that could capture and channel the drives of teenagers.

Although some historians regard the goals of the early extracurricular movement as entirely limited to social control and indoctrination of students in patriotic values (see, for example, Violas 1978), an examination of the early 20th-century literature on the topic reveals that extracurricular leaders did not lose sight of individual student needs. Throughout the *Cardinal Principles*, the premise that "each individual has a right to the opportunity to develop the best that is in him" was emphasized (National Education Association, 1918, 32). In 1926, Koos published a content analysis of 40 journal articles authored by school administrators and teachers, who reported on their opinions of and experiences with extracurricular activities. Examining the values each author claimed were fostered by the extracurriculum, Koos found that the most frequently mentioned goals (in 37 of the 40 articles) did deal with civic, social, and moral matters. At the same time, the importance of extracurricular programming for meeting individual needs was noted. Recognition of student interests and ambitions appeared in 10 articles, intellectual development in 7, and exploration in 5. Moreover, educators recognized that direct coercion was not an effective means through which the goals of the extracurriculum could be achieved. A number of authors stated that teachers who supervised extracurricular activities by dominating them (as many were accustomed to doing in the regular classroom) instead of granting students an appropriate measure of self-determination undermined the democratic values on which extracurricular programming ought to be based. Finally, the wide range of activities offered in American junior high and high schools by the early 1920s (a total of 135 different ones were mentioned in the articles reviewed by Koos) reflected a concerted effort by administrators and teachers to provide sufficient choice so that each student could find at least one activity that fit with his or her capacities and interests.

The functional relationship among the developing individual, the school, and society, so apparent in early 20th-century rationales for extracurricular programming, is strongly reminiscent of John Dewey's progressive educational philosophy, which created the intellectual climate that fostered the educational innovations of which the extracurriculum was a part. Dewey's (1916) vision of education for a democratic society and belief in the educative value of direct experience, along with the NEA's *Cardinal Principles*, were widely read and quoted abroad during succeeding decades, and both helped set the pace for a utilitarian approach to education in other industrialized nations (Connell 1980). For example, the Spens Report (1939), in reformulating the goals of British secondary education, paid considerably more attention to the social functions of schooling than previous national statements. In line with Dewey's philosophy and the *Cardinal Principles*, it recommended that the school be conceived "not merely as a 'place of learning' but as a social unit" (Spens et al. 1939, 197), offering opportunities to practice the virtues of willing cooperation and service to the larger society. To achieve this goal, the Spens Report suggested that extracurricular activities mirror on a smaller scale features of the complex political and corporate organization of industrialized nations. Students were to be assigned to houses, multiage groupings representing a cross section of the larger school community and providing the organizational basis for competitive games and other activities. Groups smaller than the house were to serve as a meeting ground for students with common interests, in the form of clubs and societies of many kinds. The small group, the house, and finally the school offered a differentiated social organization in which adolescents could learn to recognize themselves as members of a community with common interests, purposes, and loyalties.

Similarly, Japanese educators devoted more attention to social development during the mid-20th century. During the pre–World War II period, a wide variety of after-school clubs emerged in Japanese secondary schools. Initially, strict authoritarian control by older students over younger ones characterized these organizations, and adult supervision was frequently lacking. During the postwar occupation, extracurricular activities took on a more central educational role and, following the American example, were viewed as valuable training ground for participation in a democratic society. Contemporary Japanese extracurricular activities, which continue to consist largely of after-school clubs of various kinds, have not maintained the authoritarian flavor of their prewar antecedents. However, they continue to be characterized by less faculty involvement as well as lower rates of student participation than exist in the United States, perhaps because of the pressures many Japanese high school students experience in preparing for university entrance examinations (Rohlen 1983).

Soviet secondary schools, modeled after those of Western Europe, also sponsor extracurricular activities, largely under the control of the Komsomol (Communist Youth League). Peer tutoring programs to encourage academic accomplishment, student government organizations, essay-writing contests on social and political topics, politically oriented clubs, work experiences on collective farms, and academic and technical–agricultural contests and exhibits are extracurricular pursuits commonly available to Soviet adolescents. Some of the stated goals of Komsomol activities resemble those enumerated in the American extracurricular literature—development of cooperative, industrious workers, patriotic citizens, and capable adult leaders, as well as prevention of premature school leaving among non-academically inclined pupils. However, Soviet extracurricular activities, far more than those of the Western nations described above, are admittedly aimed at "political and ideological indoctrination" (Muratov 1975, 10). Their highly centralized sponsorship and unambiguous commitment to the inculcation of Communist ideals is a stark illustration of how extracurricular programs mirror salient features of life in the larger, out-of-school political and social system.

Extracurricular programming appears to have been a common response by educational systems in industrialized nations to rapid increases in secondary school enrollments, divergent needs of a heterogeneous student population, and the prospect that young people might lose a sense of social solidarity when exposed to the forces of modern industrialization (Kandel 1933). Although the extracurricular movement infiltrated the educational systems of many developed nations, in no country did it develop as quickly and flourish with as much intensity and variety as it did in American high schools. For this reason, it has been characterized as "a peculiarly . . . American (educational) innovation" (Graham 1969, 1368).

ORGANIZATION AND OPERATION OF THE EXTRACURRICULUM

Early on, American educators were concerned with problems of how to organize and operate the extracurriculum effectively. They recognized that crucial to a successful extracurricular program were a carefully delineated school policy, clear procedures for implementing it, well-trained and committed faculty sponsors, appropriate scheduling of activities, mechanisms to encourage broad-based student participation, and sufficient financial support. Leaders of the extracurricular movement were also aware of the need for procedures to evaluate the extent to which extracurricular programs were achieving their intended goals (Koos 1926). The literature on these pragmatic concerns—how to organize, operate, and evaluate the secondary school extracurriculum—is addressed in the sections that follow.

Structure and Content of the Extracurriculum

Survey research in which high school administrators have been asked to report their extracurricular offerings has documented the existence of literally hundreds of different activities in American junior and senior high schools since the first such studies were conducted during the 1920s. To summarize the breadth of extracurricular offerings within and across schools, investigators have devised taxonomies in which activities are grouped according to their general function. Classification systems differ, and not all are exhaustive. The left-hand side of Table 34–1 displays a synthesis of three taxonomies (along with authors' definitions and examples) published in the 1930s that, when combined, offer a complete account of activity types reported in the earliest studies. The right-hand side of the table shows a current taxonomy, devised by Gholson and Buser in 1983. A comparison of the two category systems reveals that extracurricular activities have remained remarkably stable in range and content over the course of this century. Home rooms and class organizations, originally developed to help students adjust to life in a new school (Spring 1986) and to serve as havens for those who might be lost and confused by departmental teaching, are the only type of extracurricular offering to have faded from modern American junior and senior high schools. Where they still exist, they have, for the most part, been reduced to attendance, announcement, and record rooms (Faunce 1960). However, home room programs serving important adolescent developmental and educational needs—assisting students in understanding their own individuality, in selecting appropriate courses of study, and in developing good study habits and desirable social

TABLE 34–1. Classification and Examples of Commonly Available Exracurricular Activities in the 1930s and 1980s

Millard (1930), Terry (1930), Reavis and Van Dyke (1932)	Gholson and Buser (1983)
School government organizations—governing bodies and organizations that perform services for the school as an entire unit rather than for smaller groups of individuals. Student council, interclub council, library squad, boosters club, cafeteria squad, and pep club are examples.	*Governance related*—activities through which students participate in the direction and management of the local school. Examples include student council, student senate, interclub council, class officers, and student-faculty-administrator-parent advisory groups. *Cheerleading/pep club related*—cheerleading, pep clubs, and pom pom groups that are closely associated with support of interscholastic (primarily athletic) teams.
Academic or departmental clubs—organizations whose primary purpose is supplementing or extending the work of specific courses in the regular curriculum or courses organized in such a way that their activities are related in a definite manner to a specific course in the regular curriculum. Examples include book lovers, history, science, foreign language, social studies, typing, stenography, industrial arts, and home economics clubs.	*Class related*—activities that are primarily subject-, school-, and career-oriented. Examples are science, social studies, mathematics, Future Business Leaders of America, Future Homemakers of America, Future Farmers of America, human relations, environment-ecology, language, and future nurses clubs.
Special interest clubs—activities that are avocational or hobby clubs, conducted for the purpose of providing members with desirable ways of spending leisure time under school sponsorship and guidance. Examples include chess, handicraft, dancing, book, collections, cooking, woodcraft, and photography.	*Hobby/leisure related*—activities designed for personal interest that are primarily avocational in nature, such as photography, chess, skiing, auto, riding, judo-karate, and roller skating.
Major voluntary organizations—athletic, dramatic, music, and forensic associations. Specific examples are football, soccer, basketball, track, hockey, tennis, and swimming teams; athletic councils and honor societies; dramatic clubs and plays; chorus, glee club, orchestra, and band; and debating and public speaking societies.	*Athletic/sport related*—individual and team sports, intrascholastic and intramural sports, and activities directly related to their support. Included are activities such as basketball, bowling, golf, handball, aquatics, volleyball, baseball, soccer, cross country, and letter clubs. *Music related*—performance- or leisure-oriented activities such as band, orchestra, chorus, ensembles, drum-bugle corps, pep band, madrigal singers, color/honor guards, twirlers, musical productions, and folksinging and barbershop groups. *Speech/drama related*—performance-oriented activities, such as class plays, school plays, debate clubs, National Forensics League, National Thespian Society, and those that support production activities, such as stage, sound, and lighting crews.

Millard (1930), Terry (1930), Reavis and Van Dyke (1932)	Gholson and Buser (1983)
Assembly programs and activities	*Special events days*—special school assemblies, awards programs, baccalaureate, commencement, prom, pageants/festivals, and trips/tours.
Social, moral, leadership, and guidance clubs—clubs and activities organized primarily for the purpose of developing desirable characteristics of personality, manners, moral attitudes, and leadership qualities. Examples are Girl Scouts, Boy Scouts, Hi-Y, social dancing club, and leaders club.	*Service related*—activities that have as a primary purpose serving the needs of the school and society, such as audiovisual, library, student patrol, and usher clubs, as well as the National Junior Red Cross, color guards, student assistants to teachers/administrators and support staff, peace club, model United Nations, and service to the aging.
Social activities—parties and dances	*Social related*—activities designed to develop the socialization skills and the personal interests of students, including dances, YMCA, YWCA, Hi-Y, and Y-Teens.
Honorary organizations—honorary societies and letter clubs in which membership is restricted to students meeting certain requirements.	*Honors related*—activities that acknowledge individual student achievement in academics or school service. Included are National Honor Society, Beta Club, Key Club, Quill and Scroll, and foreign language honor societies.
Organizations in which all pupils of the school are included—home room, class organizations, and any other organization in which membership is offered to or required of all pupils.	

skills—continue to be prevalent in the educational systems of some other countries, such as Japan (Kataoka 1985; Okihara 1986).

The broad activity categories displayed in Table 34–1 differ from one another in the variety of specific activities available within them. Buser and Humm (1980) asked administrators (who were typically principals) of all public secondary schools in Illinois to respond to a survey on extracurricular offerings and student participation. A total of 91 percent of the junior high and 84 percent of the high schools responded. As indicated in Table 34–2, class-related activities were associated with the largest array of activity titles, followed by athletic, music, service, and social activities. The breadth of activity offerings linked to the remaining activity classifications—governance, cheerleading/pep, speech/drama, publications, honors, and hobby/leisure—was much more restricted.

Proliferation of varied activities within a category is not a perfect indicator of the attractiveness of a particular type of activity to students. For example, in a recent nation-wide survey of a representative sample of American youth, 31 percent of high school students mentioned sports as a major reason they like school, second only to the opportunity to associate with friends (Giroux 1984). Table 34–2 reveals that approximately half of students' extracurricular selections are concentrated in the athletics/sports category, with an additional 3 to 4 percent participating indirectly through cheerleading and pep club activities. Far fewer selections are class related, despite the fact that class-related organizations are the most varied subtype of extracurricular offerings in public high schools. Neither leadership nor membership in academic and vocational clubs brings with it the same kind of visibility and social prestige, both within the school and in the surrounding community, that accrues from athletic participation, a factor that undoubtedly contributes to the allure of athletic pursuits found repeatedly in studies of high school social life (see the pioneering studies of Barker and Gump 1964; Coleman 1961; and Hollingshead 1949). Table 34–2 also indicates that although the number of specific extracurricular titles increases from junior high to high school, the overall breadth of offerings, as well as the proportion of participants who select different kinds of activities, is remarkably similar at both levels of secondary education.

Despite uniformity in general functions of extracurricular offerings over time and across levels of secondary education, specific activities available vary considerably from school to school and are undoubtedly affected by such

TABLE 34–2. Number of Activity Titles and Percentage of Students Participating by Activity Category in Illinois Junior and Senior High Schools, 1977

	Junior High		High School	
Activity Category	Number of Activity Titles	Percentage of Students Participating	Number of Activity Titles	Percentage of Students Participating
Athletic/sport related	41	56	67	49
Music related	23	20	39	22
Class related	65	6	95	20
Service related	25	4	36	4
Governance related	2	5	4	4
Cheerleading/pep club related	4	3	4	4
Speech/drama related	4	3	7	5
Publications related	2	2	4	3
Honors related	4	1	6	4
Social related	19	1	25	1
Hobby/leisure related	9	1	8	1

Source: Buser & Humm (1980).

contextual factors as faculty–student interests, school size, local policies, and community expectations. In addition, several investigations reveal that the number of specific activity offerings increases with high school size (Barker and Gump 1964; Schoggen and Schoggen 1988; Turner and Thrasher 1970), especially in the class-, athletic-, service-, and social-related categories (Buser and Humm 1980). However, even very small secondary schools—those with enrollments below 300—offer the full range of activity types given in Table 34–2 (Vornberg et al. 1981). Moreover, the number of unique activity titles does not increase at a rate commensurate with size of the student body, a finding that bears on the relationship of high school size to student participation rates, to be discussed later in this chapter (Barker and Gump 1964; Buser and Humm 1980; Heath 1970; Campbell et al. 1981). For example, Buser and Humm (1980) reported a total of 25 different class-related and 20 athletic-related activities in high schools with enrollments under 200; the respective counts were 62 and 49 for schools enrolling 1,700 to 2,599 students. Student body size increased 8- to 13-fold; specific activity offerings rose only 2- to 3-fold in these two areas, and the increase was far less in most other activity categories. In fact, the number of specific titles began to decline as school size exceeded 2,600 students, especially in the areas of class, music, service, and hobby/leisure, with musical pursuits showing the greatest drop-off, from 31 to 16 offerings. There may be a threshold of student body size above which further enrollments are actually detrimental to the diversity of extracurricular offerings, a possibility that warrants further research.

Overlap and interchange exist between the curricular and extracurricular domains of schooling. For example, academic clubs are a clear extension of curricular concerns into the extracurricular life of the school. Moreover, as soon as extracurricular activities became commonplace in American secondary education, they induced modifications and expansions in traditional curricular offerings. Certain activities were quickly incorporated into the regular, credit-generating courses of the school. In an extensive investigation addressing the extent to which activities changed status (from extracurricular to curricular, and vice versa) since their introduction into American secondary education, Jones (1935) surveyed 505 high school principals believed to be administering strong extracurricular programs, 53.5 percent of whom replied. Respondents indicated whether 28 commonly available activities were first introduced in their school as curricular or extracurricular, which ones had since changed status, and, if they had changed, in what school year. Results showed that a substantial proportion of schools (from 40 to 53 percent) initially introduced the school newspaper, glee club, chorus, orchestra, and band as regular curricular offerings. A lesser number (12 to 16 percent) did so with dramatic and forensic pursuits. With few exceptions, there was little tendency for schools to grant credit for participation in athletic activities or clubs at the time of their inception. Those activities initially welcomed into the regular curriculum by a large proportion of schools were also the ones most likely to shift from extracurricular to curricular status. By 1933, the overwhelming majority of schools gave credit for musical activities, and about half did so for newspaper, debating, and dramatics. Interestingly, although certain extracurricular activities did become curricular, the reverse direction of movement never occurred. That is, at no time were credit-generating courses subsequently relegated to the extracurricular life of the school.

Band, chorus, student publications, drama, and, to some extent, athletic pursuits retain their credit-generating status in many contemporary middle, junior high, and high schools (Gholson and Buser 1983; Sinks, Mclure, Malinka, and Pozdol 1978). Strictly speaking, under these conditions they are not extracurricular but are part of the regular program of studies. However, they continue to be identified with the extracurriculum, probably because they retain a number of distinguishing features of extracurricular programming. Students participate by choice rather than requirement, and both participants and faculty sponsors must be prepared to devote substantial quantities of regularly scheduled, out-of-class time.

It is difficult to identify any long-term, secular trends in scope of extracurricular offerings or extent of student participation, due to an absence of survey data collected from representative samples of schools at regular time intervals using comparable procedures. For example, in 1973, Buser, Long, and Tweedy (1975) asked 2,000 Illinois students enrolled in 25 different high schools about their activity participation. A comparison of their findings to Buser and Humm's (1980) 1977 survey of Illinois high school administrators suggests a decline in intramural athletic participation and an increase in interscholastic sports over the decade of the seventies, a change that the latter authors attribute to increased opportunities for girls to engage in interscholastic competition. Participation also appeared to diminish in class-, service-, drama-, hobby/leisure-, publications-, and honor-related endeavors. However, the validity of these trends is called into question by the use of different informants in the investigations. Compared to students, administrators may underreport participation in less prestigious and publicly visible pursuits, such as academic clubs of various kinds. In line with this supposition, a comparison of self-reported activity participation by two nationally representative samples of high school seniors, one collected in 1972 and the other in 1980, revealed fairly comparable involvement across all nonathletic pursuits, along with a 7 percent increase in athletic participation (Peng, Fetters, and Kolstad 1981). With regard to the latter figure, since wording of the athletic survey items was slightly different in each year of study, it may not accurately reflect extent of sports-related change. A special need exists for continuous, systematic assessments of characteristics of extracurricular programs that note the addition and deletion of particular activities in relation to participation patterns, as reported by administrators, activity sponsors, and students.

Aside from systematic documentation of changes in the extracurriculum, there is a need for research on factors that contribute to program variability (beyond the school size findings noted earlier). In this regard, Kapferrer (1978) offers an analysis of Australian extracurricular programs that merits additional scrutiny. In comparison to state schools, extracurricular offerings in Australian private schools are much more elaborate in scope, organization, and participation, and many more activities have been incorporated as electives into the formal program of studies. Kapferrer conjectures that the character of the extracurriculum is a function of extent to which a close ideological liaison exists between the school and community, as well as the extent to which this liaison is promoted and sustained by the extracurriculum itself.

> The private school parental community is, to a much greater degree than that of any state school, a homogeneous group subscribing to many of the same cultural values. In large state schools, on the other hand, school-community interaction is reduced to a minimum, because of conflicting demands and beliefs of teachers within the school, of parents and other citizens outside the school, and of the two groups in interaction. (266)

Kapferrer's analysis suggests that the more discordant student backgrounds are from the central values of the school, the less well developed the extracurriculum is likely to be. At the same time, strong, effective extracurricular administration has the potential for building bridges between school and community, since the locus of the extracurriculum is at the interface between the two. From this perspective, variations in extracurricular planning and implementation may serve as vital intervening determinants of the extent to which pupils from diverse backgrounds enrolled in large educational settings seek social success and confirmation of their identity within, rather than outside, the confines of the school. The available research on this potentially crucial administrative side of the extracurriculum is addressed in the section that follows.

Administration of Extracurricular Activities

The literature on administration of the extracurriculum consists, for the most part, of opinion-based, how-to articles relying on descriptions of a single successful program or practice (for examples, see Gorton 1976; Grady 1981). There is a dearth of systematic evidence on how extracurricular programs are actually administered in secondary schools.

An exception is Vornberg, Zukowski, Gipson, and Southern's (1981) descriptive study of public high school extracurricular programming in Arkansas, Kansas, Missouri, Oklahoma, and Texas. Administrators (who were usually principals) in 300 secondary schools representing the states in terms of student body size and location were surveyed about the presence or absence of administrative components. Responses were received from 102 schools (34 percent). Findings revealed substantial variation in how the extracurriculum is administered. For example, although the majority of schools (76 percent) had philosophy or objectives statements for their activities programs, nearly a fourth had none. In slightly more than half the schools, the principal was responsible for the operation of the activity program. About a third of the schools had a special activities director; in a few instances, administration was delegated to the athletic director, assistant principal, student council adviser, or the student council as a whole. In 45 percent of the schools, a policy committee made up of teachers and/or students existed to help give direction to the activities program. In almost a third, selection of sponsors occurred by principal appointment; in 4 percent, students recruited sponsors, while in 16 percent, faculty members volunteered. The remaining half relied on some combination of these alternatives. Nearly a fourth of the schools did not provide faculty with compensation for extracurricular sponsorship. Slightly over half offered extra salary, while 6 percent had lighter class loads; 11 percent provided both kinds of benefits. Just over a third of the schools had some kind of in-service training for extracurricular sponsors, but in most schools (63 percent) faculty members were not specially prepared. More often than faculty, student leaders received training (in two thirds of the schools surveyed), either through state-wide workshops for student council members, local training sessions, or enrollment in a semester-long leadership class. Financial support for activities consisted of some combination of money-raising projects, admissions charges, and appropriated funds. Appropriated monies were usually channeled into the most externally visible and costly activities; 95 percent of the schools used them to support athletics, 79 percent to support drama and music, and over 50 percent to support school publications.

Based on the figures given above, the extent to which schools have carefully articulated administrative plans for realizing a set of clearly stated extracurricular objectives is disappointing at best. In fact, the findings of Vornberg, Zukowski, Gipson, and Southern (1981) probably overestimated the quality of extracurricular administration, since the large number of nonresponding schools may have had the least effective programs. The Vornberg et al. results are also limited by the fact that each administrative dimension was examined independently. Little is known about their interrelationships—that is, the extent to which good things, such as articulated goals, compensation for activity sponsors, in-service training for faculty and student leaders, adequate financial support, and systematic evaluation, go hand in hand and depend on larger contextual factors, such as community characteristics and school size.

Earlier it was noted that administrative factors may serve as crucial mediating links in the power of the extracurriculum to affect the involvement and, ultimately, the development of its participants. To date, no research exists on how administrative variables, considered either in isolation or collectively, affect the day-to-day functioning of extracurricular activities. A special topic meriting consideration is the delicate balance between adult authority and pupil control, regarded by educational reformers of the early 20th century to be essential for certain social goals to be realized among student participants. One can plausibly argue that young people who are centrally involved in managing and financing their own activities learn more about making decisions, cooperating with others, handling responsibility, and leading effectively, partly as the result of being given the opportunity to make mistakes, than do students who affiliate with more efficiently run, faculty-controlled clubs. Administrative arrangements that promote adult guidance rather than directiveness in sponsor-student relations need to be identified and their association with important developmental consequences established empirically.

The scarcity of empirical evidence on extracurricular administration is partly due to the fact that school practice far exceeds theory in this area. Few conceptual frameworks exist to offer structure and guidance to the process of extracurricular development in schools and, in turn, to research endeavors. Conyne (1983a, 1; 1983b) has developed one, called the CORE model, aimed at "advanc[ing] student development through positive alteration of student organizations." Although designed to apply to the college environment, essential features of the model may generalize to the secondary school extracurriculum. As indicated in Figure 34–1, the CORE model consists of three concentric rings, with the center one containing four social–psychological conditions that motivate an organization to meet its needs. These are:

(a) *cohesion*, the glue that binds members to the organization, as evidenced by their involvement and participation, group affiliation and commitment, shared sense of mission, feelings of belongingness, and friendship and helpfulness.
(b) *organization*, or mechanisms for maintaining and improving activity functioning. These include well-defined and agreed-upon goals, a division of labor and set of reporting lines; clear policies and procedures to guide organizational behavior and practice; and rewards for members who perform well.
(c) *resourcefulness*, which refers to working knowledge and skills needed to maintain the student group. Examples are a membership well informed about relevant school rules and available resources and interpersonally skilled leaders who encourage positive working relationships.
(d) *energy*, or a high level of membership support for the general organizational direction and operating conditions, as reflected in work motivation, initiation of innovative projects, acceptance of responsibility, cooperation, and openness to change within the framework of agreed-upon organizational goals.

Indicators of group success, which are products of CORE conditions, comprise the second ring of the model. These include fund raising, attendance, recruitment, motivating members, assuming leadership, improving communication, and group unity. They were derived from a needs-assessment survey of student organizations conducted by Conyne; the relative endorsement of each area's importance by respondents is reflected by its proportionate size in the model and may vary from one educational setting to another. Finally, the outer ring of the model contains 10 student development domains that represent both immediate and long-range outcomes of extracurricular involvement, assumed to depend on conditions in the inner concentric circles.

Conyne (1983a) has developed the *CORE Conditions Checklist*, a 100-item instrument that permits organization members, as well as sponsors and administrators, to rate student activities for presence of the four CORE conditions. These assessments provide an indication of the effectiveness of organizational functioning from the perspective of different affiliates. Responses can be used to pinpoint problem areas, initiate appropriate interventions, and evaluate their effectiveness. The model locates assessment of extracurricular functioning squarely within the internal environment of the student organization itself. However, Conyne notes that internal conditions can be related to variations in the contextual environment of which the organization is a part, such as school policies, administrative structures, and availability of financial resources, as well as to both proximal and distal outcomes represented in the outer concentric rings of the model. The CORE framework is a promising conceptual

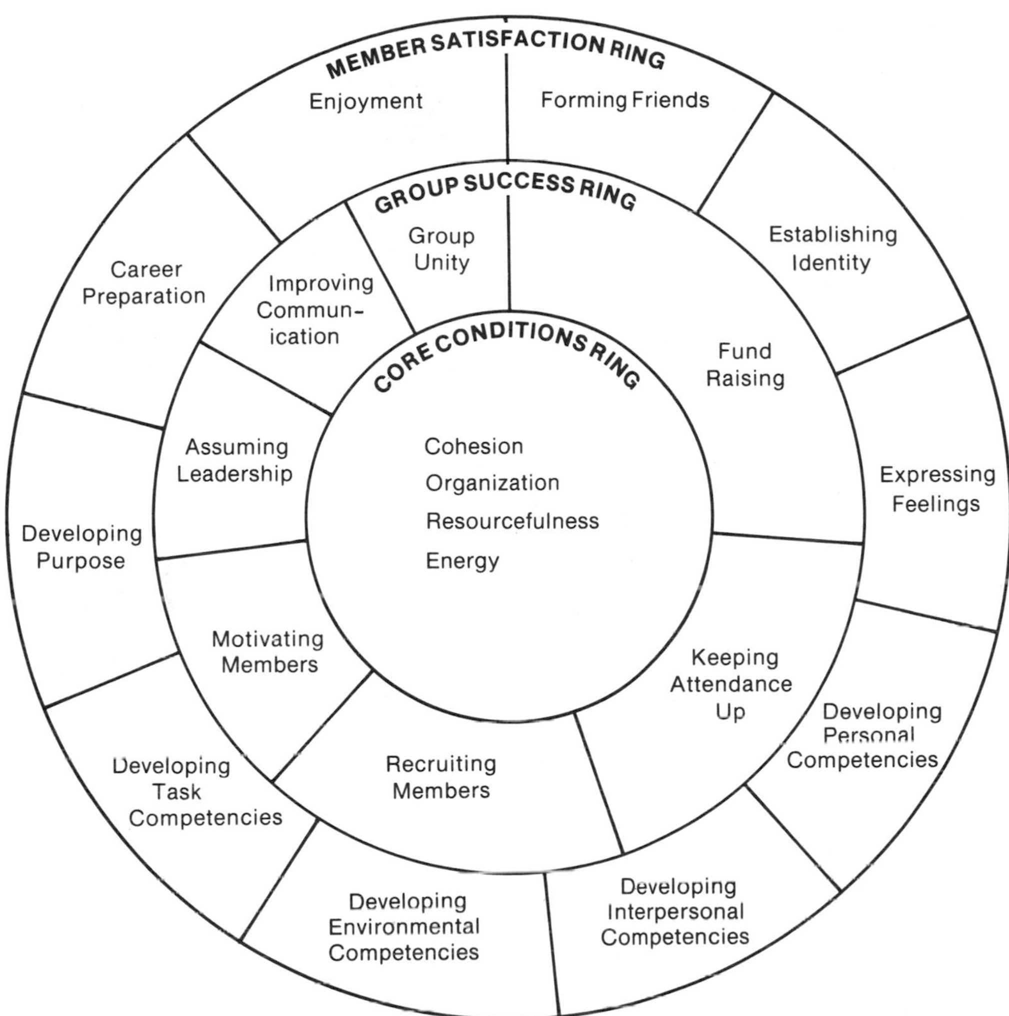

FIGURE 34–1. Conyne's CORE model

tool for integrating aspects of the extracurriculum that have, as yet, either been studied in isolation or hardly investigated at all—namely, program administration, functioning of the activity organization, and developmental consequences of extracurricular participation.

Evaluation of Extracurricular Programming

As early as the 1920s, educators saw the need for efficient procedures that would permit school administrators to determine if student activities were meeting their stated objectives and that could serve as the basis for redesigning and improving extracurricular programs. However, few convenient instruments were available for measuring program quality or immediate psychological and interpersonal benefits. Therefore, initial evaluative efforts seldom went beyond documenting participation rates, comparing the academic accomplishments of involved and uninvolved students, and soliciting sponsor opinion on the extent to which student growth occurred (Koos 1926).

Unfortunately, school-based evaluative efforts are not much more refined today. In the Vornberg et al. (1981) survey described earlier, only 29 percent of responding administrators indicated that they engaged in any type of formal evaluation of their student activities program; the vast majority (71 percent) made no attempt to evaluate the extracurriculum at all. Among those who did evaluate, in 64 percent of the cases a committee consisting of faculty sponsors, the activity director, the principal, and students performed the evaluation; but in 29 percent of the schools the principal was the only person involved. As the authors indicate, "a void is apparent in [this aspect of] the administrative process" (16), a conclusion documented by other survey studies as well (Jung and Fox 1952; Mullins 1962).

Evaluation of activity programs is hampered by the absence of clear objectives for extracurricular activities in many schools. In addition, few ready-made instruments exist to assist school personnel in conducting systematic evaluations. Conyne's (1983a) CORE checklist, described earlier, is an efficient tool for looking at activity processes that could easily be adapted for the secondary school level. Another, *The Student Activities Evaluative Instrument*, has been developed by the National Study of School Evaluation (1983) as part of its publication, *Evaluative Criteria*, a comprehensive self-study and evaluation package that can be used by individual schools. Respondents are asked to rate a set of common extracurricular objectives in terms of degree of acceptance and implementation. The instrument also asks for basic descriptive information on characteristics of extracurricular programming, including a list of organizations and activities, names of their sponsors, and numbers of participants. Finally, a form requesting information on specific activity objectives and efforts to meet them, finances, requirements for and extent of student participation, sponsor selection procedures, and meeting schedules is filled out by each activity adviser.

Negri (1973) has demonstrated the importance of obtaining evaluative information from multiple sources. In a survey of school personnel and students using the 1969 edition of *The Student Activities Evaluative Instrument*, striking group differences in perceptions emerged. Compared to teachers and administrators, students regarded activity programs as less actively supported by the school staff, viewed themselves as having far fewer opportunities to assist with resolution of school problems and issues, and less often felt that the program provided membership opportunities to students on a democratic basis. The reasons for such large disparities in staff-student views of how the extracurriculum is managed and implemented merit investigation, especially since administrators regard student opinion as the most important source of information on the success of extracurricular programming (Vornberg et al. 1981).

Widespread availability of efficient evaluative instruments is likely to increase the willingness of school administrators to initiate periodic evaluations of their extracurricular programs and to institute changes based on evaluative feedback. At the same time, use of comparable instrumentation across many schools would offer researchers a valuable beginning data base for answering many of the pressing questions raised above. Evaluative efforts could also be encouraged through the ready availability of comprehensive sources that school personnel could consult on the topics of planning, implementing, and evaluating the extracurriculum. Many professional texts were written on extracurricular programming from the 1920s into the 1950s (see, for example, Frederick 1959; Fretwell 1931; Kilzer, Stephenson, and Nordberg 1956; McKown 1952; Millard 1930; and Trump 1944). However, a search of literature published during the past two decades revealed no comparable sourcebooks, although a variety of short articles and pamphlets with practical recommendations continue to appear on a regular basis.

Summary

The overall range and content of the secondary school extracurriculum has remained remarkably stable over the course of this century. Although breadth of activity programming is similar from school to school, specific activities vary substantially. Yet little research has examined community, school, and student characteristics that contribute to this variability. Identification of long-term secular trends in extracurricular offerings is hampered by the absence of periodic data collection on representative samples of schools using comparable procedures. School variations in administration of the extracurriculum have been documented, but their impact on the daily functioning of activity settings and on student outcomes remains uninvestigated. Finally, few instruments are available for school personnel to apply in evaluating extracurricular programming, and the large majority of schools do not conduct such evaluations. Consequently, little in the way of school-based data is available to address the myriad of unanswered questions about the organization and operation of the extracurriculum.

WHO BENEFITS FROM THE EXTRACURRICULUM? CHARACTERISTICS OF PARTICIPANTS AND FACTORS MODERATING PARTICIPATION

Although extracurricular activities were envisioned as settings in which youngsters from different walks of life would intermingle and learn that common interests could override group differences and antagonisms, early proponents were aware that participation might be highly selective and that many youngsters might not be reached at all (Dee 1928; Koos 1926). The largest body of research on the extracurriculum has been directed at identifying factors that influence adolescents' voluntary entry into activities. Recent estimates indicate that, on the average, about a third to a fifth of students in secondary schools take no part in the extracurriculum (Craig and Pasewark 1981; Nover 1981; U.S. Office of Education 1986; Yarworth and Gauthier 1978). The rate of nonparticipation is as high as half of the student body in some schools (Schoggen and Schoggen 1988) and as low as 15 percent in others (Craig and Pasewark 1981). Variables associated with participation include demographic characteristics (socioeconomic status, racial–ethnic classification, student employment status, sex, and grade in school), psychological factors (academic performance, educational aspirations, self-esteem, interests, attitudes, and personality characteristics), and ecological determinants (school size, school grade-level organization, and community characteristics). In a few studies, investigators have approached the problem of activity involvement quite directly, by asking students why they do or do not participate in extracurricular offerings.

The evidence is limited in a variety of ways. First, the large majority of studies are correlational in design. Consequently, causes, consequences, and concomitants of participation are frequently not distinguishable, and inappropriate causal interpretation pervades a substantial portion of the research literature. In an effort to separate antecedents from concomitants and consequences of participation, some investigators have employed comparison groups presumed to be equivalent on all relevant characteristics except the causal variable in question. For example, Steinberg et al. (1982), in examining the impact of adolescent employment on extracurricular participation, compared employed students with both job-seeking and non-job-seeking unemployed students. A worker–nonworker difference due to factor(s) other than working should be reflected in comparable differences between job seekers (presumed to be like working students in background characteristics) and nonseekers. Other investigators, such as Schafer and Armer (1968), have used regression procedures to demonstrate the relationship of a particular variable—in this case, academic achievement—to participation, after adjusting for a collection of relevant prior variables, such as years of school completed, intelligence, father's occupation, previous grade point average (GPA), and curricular track. This approach reduces the probability that the variable in question is merely a concomitant rather than cause or effect of participation, but it does not permit clear discrimination between the latter two possibilities. However, as Schafer and Armer point out, once background variables are controlled, when groups not disposed toward a particular behavior (e.g., achievement) show a stronger relationship between participation and the behavior than those who are so disposed (as these investigators found for students from blue-collar versus white-collar homes), then the probability increases that the behavior in question is consequent rather than antecedent to participation. Path analytic techniques have also been used to tease out causal associations from correlational evidence, as Eyler (1982) has done in testing a model relating student political attitudes to extracurricular participation. The literature contains comparatively few instances of designs that permit more effective separation of pre- and postparticipation variables. These include experimental or quasi-experimental interventions aimed at augmenting extracurricular participation and longitudinal studies that assess students prior, during, and subsequent to opportunities for activity involvement.

A second limitation of existing research, noted by Holland and Andre (1987) in a recent review, is that samples vary widely in quality, from studies of single schools to broad sampling from a variety of schools to a handful of studies based on nationally representative data bases, such as information collected in conjunction with administration of the ACT (see Baird 1969; Downey 1978) or obtained from the data bank of *The High School and Beyond*, a longitudinal study of a national probability sample of American high school students (see Lindsay 1984; Trent and McPartland 1982; U.S. Office of Education 1986). Across all types of studies, many samples are incompletely described in terms of variables known to be associated with extracurricular participation, such as socioeconomic status and size of school attended. In these instances, the potential, moderating impact of such factors on the central variable(s) in question remains undetermined. Moreover, to date no meta-analyses have been conducted to synthesize empirical evidence on demographic, psychological, and ecological factors and to overcome the limitations of generalization from small and potentially biased samples.

A third limitation is that the research conducted to date, with few exceptions, focuses on molar input variables and gross measures of participation, such as counts of number of activities entered and leadership positions held. The impact of antecedent conditions on length and quality of involvement has seldom been addressed. Undoubtedly, this is because theory of student activity choice and participation maintenance is not yet well developed. Aside from ecological theory on the impact of school size (Barker and Gump 1964), little in the way of explicit theorizing exists, and for the most part research has been empirically rather than conceptually driven.

Finally, the larger context of activity participation has been given scant attention—either within the school, in terms of organization and administration of the school's activity program (as mentioned earlier in this chapter), or without, in terms of the social class makeup of neighborhoods from which the school draws, substitute activities available to adolescents in the community, proximity of competing schools, busing of students, and other relevant contextual variables (Holland and Andre 1987). With these reservations in mind, the current state of knowledge on factors influencing adolescent extracurricular involvement is reviewed below.

Demographic Characteristics

Socioeconomic Status. The social class gap in extracurricular participation was first highlighted by Hollingshead (1949) in his classic investigation of Elmtown, a typical midwestern small town selected as the site for a case study of the extent to which adult social organization carries over into the behavior of adolescents. Descriptive findings painted a picture of vicious exclusionary practices by wealthier students against those from the wrong side of town. For example, a clique of popular football players mistreated lower-class team members, who, although initially attracted to athletics in about the same proportion as their more advantaged counterparts, tended to drop out. The student council was dominated by the higher classes, with the lowest class of students having not a single representative. As one low-income student described the situation, "Frankly, for a lot of us there is nothing here but just going to classes, listening to the teacher, reciting, studying, and going home again. We are pushed out of things" (150).

Hollingshead's study was carried out in an era in which low-income adolescents constituted a much smaller proportion of the high school student body than they do today. Subsequent research by Coleman (1961) showed that extracurricular activities are not dominated by middle-class students unless the student body is primarily middle class as well. Examining 10 schools in varying types of communities, one of which was Elmtown (revisited almost 15 years after Hollingshead's research), Coleman found that middle-class domination varied substantially from school to school.

In Elmtown, it was quite small, due to enrollment of more working-class teenagers, who in greater numbers successfully penetrated the school's social system.

Recent correlational evidence based on large samples of students from diverse schools and communities (including one Canadian and one Israeli study) indicates that the overall relationship between socioeconomic status and participation is positive but not large (Cuccia 1981; Ichilov and Chen 1978; Macintosh 1982; Otto 1975, 1976a; Rehberg and Schafer 1973; U.S. Office of Education 1986). This is the case even for leadership positions, where the social class/participation association might be expected to be greatest. Hynes, Richardson, and Asher (1986) studied 13 predictors of self-reported high school leadership utilizing Project TALENT's nationally representative sample of nearly 3,000 high school students. The impact of social class was weak, and it did not predict leadership as effectively as did student personality characteristics.

Nevertheless, a cautious approach to these findings is appropriate, since at least one study deviates from the pattern of results described above. In a large, representative survey of high school students in 19 school districts in a large northeastern state, Serow (1979) reported a strong association between social class and extracurricular involvement. Higher-status students showed twice the participation rate of their lower-status counterparts. Furthermore, few investigations have examined the relationship of social class to participation in specific activities. If low- and middle-income youngsters sort themselves into different extracurricular environments, their overall participation rates may look fairly equivalent, despite the fact that their extracurricular experiences are substantially different. In line with this idea, Hollingshead (1949) found a class-graded system of academic clubs in Elmtown—for example, a homemaker's club consisting of predominantly lower-class youth and a French club comprised of middle-income youngsters. This segregated arrangement was a function of the fact that middle-class adolescents enrolled in the college preparatory curriculum, whereas lower-class students were sorted into general and commercial tracks. Consequently, each socioeconomic stratum was drawn into different academically related activities. A recent analysis of the extracurricular choices of a nationally representative sample of high school seniors from *The High School and Beyond* study revealed participation rates to favor higher-income youngsters in all types of activities except hobby and vocational clubs, where the social classes were equivalent (U.S. Office of Education 1986).

Finally, when low socioeconomic status is combined with certain other factors—namely, below average intelligence, very low school grades, and enrollment in a large high school—that, taken together, lead a young person to be poorly adapted to school life, extracurricular participation is either extremely low or nonexistent (Bell 1967; Willems 1967; Yudin et al. 1973). Under these conditions, adolescents have a high probability of dropping out of school. Once such students leave school, they become unavailable as subjects, a circumstance that clearly attenuates the social class/extracurricular participation relationship.

Racial–Ethnic Classification. The most extensive information available on participation rates by racial-ethnic group, gathered as part of *The High School and Beyond* study, is limited to a comparison of black and white students. Findings revealed that the percentage of 1980 sophomores participating in four different types of extracurricular pursuits (drama/debate, band/orchestra, hobby clubs, and subject matter clubs) was reasonably comparable for the two racial groups. Participation rates tended to favor blacks over whites in some areas—chorus and dance for both sexes, cheerleading for females, and athletics for males (Trent and McPartland 1982). These trends suggest that, on a national basis, black students are represented in the activity life of schools to an equivalent degree, and, in the case of athletics and music, to an even greater extent than are white students. However, it is important to note that the basis of comparison here was a gross one; students simply indicated, for a variety of activities, if they participated or not. Whether there are broad racial-ethnic differences in quality of participation—for example, in variety of activities entered or in positions of responsibility and leadership—is not made clear by the findings. School related variables affecting participation rates of black students are considered in a later section of this chapter on the extracurriculum and school desegregation.

Sex. Coleman's (1961) study is well known for an analysis of high school students' responses to the question of how they would prefer to be remembered in school. Boys were asked to choose among "brilliant student," "athletic star," and "most popular," girls among "brilliant student," "most popular," and "leader in activities." Findings indicated that the image of athletic star was especially attractive to boys, and the images of activities leader and most popular were particularly attractive to girls. These choices were also associated with student views of what it took to be well liked by age mates. Among student elites—that is, those identified by student respondents as admired by large numbers of peers—football players were overrepresented among boys, and club and activity participants were especially prevalent among girls.

An impressive number of studies have documented sex differences in participation rates resembling the pattern of student preferences identified by Coleman (1961). Surveying more than 600,000 high school students in the state of Illinois, Gholson and Buser (1981) found female participation to exceed male participation in all activity categories listed in Table 34–2 except athletic/sport and hobby/leisure, where males were more prevalent. The female advantage was especially marked in drama, honors, service, cheerleading/pep, publications, and social-related areas. Although still present, it was not as great in class- and governance-related pursuits. These trends generalize across school size (Gholson and Buser 1981), surface repeatedly in many studies of high school youth (Bender 1978; Eyler 1982; Grabe 1975, 1981; Grabe and Latta 1977; Gump and Friesen 1964; Lindsay 1982; Nover 1981; Peng, Fetters, and Kolstad 1981; U.S. Office of Education 1986; Yarworth and Gauthier 1978), and also emerge when college students are asked to recollect their high school group memberships (Berk and Goebel 1987a, 1987b; Cross and Moreland 1985). However, the differences may not generalize across cultures. A study of extracurricular involvement in 31 comprehensive secondary schools in England showed boys to have greater overall participation rates than girls (Reid 1970, 1972), although sex differences in entry into different types of activities were not examined.

Coleman (1961) attributed sex differences in participation to variations in the behaviors required of males and females to achieve status within the peer group. In line with this idea, research indicates that sex stereotyping of school activities emerges in early elementary school and intensifies over childhood and adolescence, with athletics and mechanical skills considered more appropriate for boys and artistic, social, and domestic pursuits more appropriate for girls (Sagaria and Sagaria 1984; Stein 1971; Stein and Smithells 1969). Sex-stereotyped interests are particularly pronounced during early adolescence, a period during which young people are preoccupied with what others think of them and have an especially strong need to conform to sex-typed peer social conventions (Ullian 1976). Another explanation, suggested by Cross and Moreland (1985), is that commonly reported sex differences in sociability carry over to high school group memberships. In comparison to men, entering college women in their study reported belonging to more groups and larger groups in high school, as well as enjoying them more and regarding them as more important.

A longitudinal investigation by Rehberg and Schafer (1973) designed to separate antecedents from consequents of extracurricular involvement sheds additional light on sex differences in participation. The investigators surveyed approximately 3,000 members of the class of 1970 in seven high school systems from the freshman year to several months post–high school. Path analysis was used to explore the causal association among parental socialization practices, student educational aspirations, extracurricular participation, and post–high school education pursued. Findings revealed striking differences between boys and girls in determinants of participation. Parental achievement pressures and student educational aspirations were direct and fairly strong predictors of extracurricular involvement for boys, but not for girls. The authors concluded that extracurricular participation has different meanings for the two sexes. For males, it is an instrumental, achievement-oriented activity; for females, it has more expressive, interpersonal connotations, an interpretation that is consistent with a large body of research on sex differences in parental socialization practices and children's motivational dispositions (Block 1983). Boys' more instrumental, strategic approach to activity choices may underlie their heavy extracurricular focus on athletics, which in more recent research has been shown to carry even more status than it did among Coleman's sample of the late 1950s (Eitzen 1975).

In fact, a study by Olen (1971) of three Catholic high schools—one with an all-male, the second with an all-female, and the third with a coeducational student body—suggests that boys' heavy emphasis on athletics may be at the heart of their reduced participation in other activities. From this perspective, one sex difference can lead to others for ecological rather than sex-stereotypic reasons. Olen found that athletics dominated the all-male environment. In this school, the number of athletic offerings was almost 5 times as great as in the all-girls' school and nearly 1.5 times as great as in the coeducational environment. Moreover, sports events were scheduled more frequently and lasted considerably longer than other activities. Consquently, many boys found themselves immersed in activities that demanded so much of their time and energy that little remained to devote to other extracurricular pursuits.

In two studies examining carry-over of extracurricular participation from high school to college (one conducted in a large multipurpose university and the other in a small liberal arts college), Berk and Goebel (1987a, 1987b) showed that girls eventually lose their general participatory advantage. Males in the large university, where there was little press for continued participation, maintained the same level of involvement in academic honors and student government they had in high school, whereas females declined in all activity areas. In the small college, males gained in two highly visible, talent-related pursuits (performing arts and sports); females showed no gains and lost the edge they held in five extracurricular categories. In line with Rehberg and Schafer's (1973) interpretation noted above, Berk and Goebel regarded the instrumental orientation of males—their greater self-confidence, competitiveness, and drive toward mastery—as responsible for their involvement gains during college and females' expressiveness and dependence on external supports for participation as responsible for their eventual disadvantage.

Student Employment Status. Current estimates place the proportion of employed 16-year-old high school youth at nearly 60 percent, with 40 to 50 percent of these students working more than 14 hours a week (Steinberg et al. 1982). Substantial investments of time and energy in the workplace may weaken the young person's commitment to school, resulting in reduced extracurricular participation as one among a number of indicators of school involvement.

Two types of student employment have been investigated. The first are credit-generating work-study programs designed to serve youth whose low socioeconomic status and poor school record in terms of attendance and academic performance is associated with little or no extracurricular participation and high drop-out rates (Bardley 1977). Research indicates that work-study arrangements may facilitate the general school commitment of these youngsters. In one study, potential dropouts participating in work-study programs not only entered more school activities but also gained in attitudes toward school, participation in class projects, and school attendance (Schneider 1971).

A second type of student employment consists of student-initiated entry into jobs in the private sector, a form that, in contrast to work-study, applies to youth of all socioeconomic and ethnic backgrounds. Evidence on the impact of these work arrangements is ambiguous. In a well-designed investigation, Steinberg, Greenberger, Garduque, and McAuliffe (1982) used regression analysis to study the impact of work status on the school commitment of more than 500 tenth and eleventh graders, controlling for the effects of grade in school and social class. Workers were more often absent from school, reported enjoying school less, and spent less time on homework than both job-seeking and nonseeking nonworking students; also, increased time on the job was associated with a lower grade point average (GPA). Yet surprisingly, the reduced commitment of working students to the academic life of the school did not generalize to the extracurriculum. Gade and Peterson (1980) also found that employment status was unrelated to extracurricular participation. However, in both of these investigations, a very crude measure of extracurricular involvement was used—gross student estimates of time devoted to activities—that may limit the validity of the findings.

In a study reporting contrary results, Mueller (1984) asked over 300 tenth, eleventh, and twelfth graders to indicate the number of noncredit activities in which they participated and found the mean to be significantly lower for working (.92) than nonworking students (1.31). However, when students were divided into top, middle, and bottom thirds by academic ability, the trade-off between employment and extracurricular participation held only for the bottom third, a finding that contrasts sharply with the evidence on work–study programs described above. Taken together, research suggests that poorly achieving youth are most affected by work status, with consequences varying from detrimental to beneficial, depending on the type of employment arrangement.

Nevertheless, even these findings may underestimate the impact of employment on participation, since in studies in which students have been asked to explain their lack of involvement, out-of-school employment has consistently ranked as an important reason (Bullock 1965; Draeger 1972; Vornberg et al. 1983). In one investigation, it was the most frequently given explanation, mentioned by 68 percent of a sample of 1,500 students. In this study, principals also reported that scheduling conflicts and time demands of student jobs interfere with extracurricular involvement (Long, Buser, and Jackson 1977).

Grade Level. Studies examining grade-related changes are consistent: Frequency and variety of extracurricular participation increases over the junior high and high school years (Bardley 1977; Coleman, Hoffer, and Kilgore 1981; Eyler 1982; Grabe 1975, 1976, 1981; LeGault 1985). More extracurricular opportunities are probably available to older students, who also possess the maturity and ability to take advantage of them. Little evidence is available on how participation in different types of activities changes with grade. Grabe (1975, 1976, 1981) found that younger high school students reported a higher incidence of participation in athletics, while older students listed more academic pursuits, social activities, and clubs. In a Canadian study that focused on the physical activity of over 600 girls in grades 6 to 10, participation in interscholastic teams and intramural athletics was high throughout junior high, but dropped sharply in grade 10, at the beginning of senior high (Butcher 1983). The school district studied was Catholic and largely low income, and therefore the results may not be generalizable to other settings. Moreover, no comparative information was available for boys. Nevertheless, these findings are intriguing, and more needs to be known about grade-related patterns of activity participation, both normatively and in terms of individual differences, along with developmental changes and the external pressures that contribute to them.

Psychological Variables

Academic Performance and Educational Aspirations. Coleman (1961) concluded that academics were pushed from importance by students' preoccupation with the extracurricular life of school. According to his findings, students ranked getting good grades as a much less important dimension of peer popularity than athletics for boys and school clubs for girls. However, a close look at Coleman's results, as well as recent evidence on the relationship between academic performance and participation, does not support the general thesis that the academic and extracurricular domains of schooling are at odds with one another. Instead, they appear to be mutually facilitating.

Responses of Coleman's subjects clearly indicated that doing well in school counted for something. Although athletic star was selected by a plurality of boys (40 percent) and activities leader by a plurality of girls (36 percent) as the way they wanted to be remembered, 32 percent of the boys and 28 percent of the girls did choose brilliant student in response to this question. Moreover, athletics and scholarship were not mutually exclusive. Athlete–scholars in Coleman's sample far outdistanced pure athletes and pure scholars in recognition and respect accorded by peers (although pure athletes fared much better than pure scholars). In addition, an inverse association between the emphasis students placed on extracurricular activities and such academically relevant pursuits as hours spent on homework or college aspirations did not emerge in Coleman's findings. For example, in 6 of his 10 schools, the mean GPA of top athletes was higher than the average of the male student body. In only three schools did athletes perform more poorly, and in one school the performance of athletes and nonathletes was equivalent. These results suggest that schools differ in the extent to which good grades are emphasized and serve as antecedents and/or possible consequents of extracurricular participation.

Many other investigations report a positive association between academic orientation and extracurricular involvement. Frederick (1959) reviewed the literature from the 1920s into the 1950s and concluded that students with the highest grades were the most active. Subsequent studies show this same trend (Bender 1978; Bourgon 1967; Galiardo 1982; Haensly, Lupkowski, and Edlind 1986; Hedgpeth 1981; Rogers 1970; U.S. Office of Education 1986) and also reveal that participation is related to the high school tracking system. Students enrolled in college preparatory curricula, as opposed to vocational and general programs, and those expressing high aspirations for post–high school education are the most involved participants (Burton 1973; McCray 1967; Rehberg and Schafer 1973; Spady 1961; Yarworth and Gauthier 1978).

Additional investigations have restricted their comparisons to athletes versus nonathletes (a global category that includes nonathletic participants plus nonparticipants), because of a widespread belief that sports activities attract less serious students and divert them further from their studies. Most research indicates that male athletes actually score higher in achievement and educational aspirations than their nonsports-oriented counterparts (Aivoldi, Peterson, and Webb 1967; Connor 1954; Eidsmore 1963; Phillips and Schafer 1971; Rehberg and Schafer 1968; Schafer 1969; Schafer and Armer 1968; Schafer and Rehberg, 1970; Spreitzer and Pugh 1973). However, conflicting findings do exist. A variety of studies report no association between academic performance as measured by GPA and boys' or girls' athletic involvement (Bullock 1965; Feltz and Weiss 1984; Hanks and Eckland 1976; Rehberg and Schafer 1968; Snyder and Spreitzer 1977; Spreitzer and Pugh 1973), and one Canadian investigation found a positive relationship only for curricular track, not for grades (Macintosh 1982). In addition, some evidence suggests that boys who are narrowly focused on sports obtain scores below the national average on the Scholastic Aptitude Test, while those who are more diverse in their extracurricular pursuits score above average (Landers and Landers 1978). Rehberg and Cohen (1975) reported similar results for several additional academically related measures, including intelligence, self-rated importance of being a good student, time spent on homework, and educational aspirations. Moreover, when the two extracurricular domains are directly compared, academic orientation bears a stronger relationship to nonathletic than to athletic activity pursuits (Hanks and Eckland 1976; Rogers 1970; Yarworth and Gauthier 1978). For example, Yarworth and Gauthier reported that among a variety of variables entered into a stepwise regression equation, curricular track membership was the strongest predictor of both athletic and nonathletic participation, but it predicted nonathletic involvement more effectively.

Nevertheless, for extracurricular activities in general as well as athletics in particular, it is possible that the relationship between academic orientation and participation is a spurious one—that is, due to one or more temporally antecedent conditions common to both variables (Rehberg 1969). Few investigators have entered the myriad of relevant preexisting conditions (socioeconomic status, intelligence, previous GPA, and others) as control variables into their analyses. However, when they do, the effect has been to reduce but not totally eliminate academic differences between participants and nonparticipants, suggesting that the relationship is, in fact, real. For example, Schafer and Armer (1968) controlled for intelligence, father's occupation, previous GPA, and curriculum track in their study of 585 sophomore boys. The GPA disparity between athletes and nonathletes was small but persisted, at 2.35 versus 2.24 on a 4-point scale. In Rehberg and Schafer's (1968) investigation of 785 senior males, controlling for class rank, socioeconomic status, and parental educational encouragement reduced the correlation between educational aspirations and athletic participation only minimally, from .28 to .24.

Whether participation is cause or consequence of academic orientation is not made clear by these findings, but other evidence suggests that a bidirectional relationship is probably closest to the truth. Using path analysis, Hanks and Eckland (1976) examined the impact of academic variables among a national sample of over 4,000 high school sophomores, asked to recount their high school and college extracurricular experiences 15 years later. Sophomore grades served as the strongest direct predictor of subsequent high school nonathletic participation, although they were inconsequential for involvement in varsity sports. These results suggest that overall participation is promoted by an academic orientation, a conclusion that is supported by other longitudinal findings. Rehberg and Schafer's (1973) path-analytic study, described in the previous section on sex differences, indicated that parental achievement pressures and student educational aspirations exert a direct effect on male students' subsequent high school activity involvement. At the same time, the findings of both of these investigations, along with others, suggest that participation is not just affected by, but also contributes to, academic performance and educational aspirations, a set of evidence that will be taken up later in this chapter.

School priorities originating with staff, student body, and/or community have, for the most part, not been taken into account in past and current research on the achievement/participation connection. Variations among Coleman's (1961) 10 schools, as well as the mixed findings of other studies examining the relationship between achievement and athletics, suggest that school valuation of academic excellence may play a role in the relationship. In England, where the value placed on academic success may be higher than in the United States, Reid (1970, 1972) reported academic aptitude to be a very strong predictor of involvement in a wide variety of activities. The trend was especially marked in the schools' major extracurricular offerings of sports, music, art, and subject-based pursuits. Reid suggested that the strength of this association may have resulted from a variety of subtle, school-based selection practices, such as a tendency on the part of staff to choose academically successful students for highly visible teams, choirs, and dramatic productions and a general lack of encouragement for less able youngsters to take part. An extracurricular bias favoring academically able students may have also been promoted by some heads who believed the primary purpose of activities was to raise the prestige of the school or supplement the curricular work of the classroom.

Under conditions like these, institutional forces combine with the needs and interests of academically inclined youngsters to elevate the achievement/participation relationship, and the social integration function of the extracurriculum is sacrificed for a higher level of student performance. In the

United States, this same trade-off is at the heart of the current debate over no pass–no play rules, which set minimum GPA requirements for participation in interscholastic sports, an issue considered in greater detail later in this chapter. At this point, it is important to note that the prevalence of academic eligibility requirements for athletic participation, and more recently for nonathletic extracurricular involvement as well, may be responsible for a substantial portion of the relationship between academic variables and extracurricular involvement in American research. Yet so far no investigation examining this association has reported information on eligibility standards or attempted to control for them.

Self-Esteem. Positive relationships between self-esteem and extracurricular participation have been reported in many studies (Grabe 1975, 1976, 1981; Hedgpeth 1981; Leonardson 1986; Rosenberg 1965; Yarworth and Gauthier 1978). Like academic performance, self-esteem has been conceptualized as both antecedent and consequent to extracurricular involvement. For example, Grabe's (1975) model of mutual influence between activity participation and self-esteem suggests that participation should lead to a rise in self-esteem if students are successful, which, in turn, should facilitate continued involvement. His short-term longitudinal analyses tested only the first, but not the second, part of the model. Based on 1- and 2-year longitudinal data sets, Grabe used regression procedures to demonstrate a unique relationship between five different types of participation (athletics, academics, fine arts, clubs, and social activities) and self-esteem uncontaminated by prior self-esteem. Aside from this study, existing research on the self-esteem/participation connection has not been very effective in sorting out cause from effect. In addition, rarely have relevant control variables, such as achievement and socioeconomic status, been entered into data analyses.

Yarworth and Gauthier's (1978) research is unique in taking into account a number of control conditions and in investigating the relationship of a differentiated measure of self-esteem to extracurricular involvement. Nine separate self-esteem scores gathered on over 450 high school students, along with academic achievement, curricular track, sex, and grade, were regressed against athletic, nonathletic, and total participation. Results revealed that, except for social self, which showed positive associations with all three measures of participation, self-esteem indexes were differentially related to kind of activity involvement. For example, for athletic participation, the physical self, behavioral self, and personal self reached significance, whereas for nonathletic participation, total self-esteem and moral-ethical self were important. Yarworth and Gauthier's study extends previous research by showing that dimensions of self-esteem are related to functionally similar types of student activity and, when combined with Grabe's results, it establishes that self-esteem predicts a wide variety of extracurricular pursuits. However, Yarworth and Gauthier's design, like most other studies on the topic, does not permit the separation of antecedents from consequents in the self-esteem/participation relationship.

Interests, Attitudes, and Personality Characteristics. School activities do not appeal equally to all students. Administering aptitude and interest batteries to over 900 high school seniors who reported on their extracurricular activities, Dawis and Sung (1984) found that abilities and interests were differentially related to patterns of activity participation, with relationships being stronger for interests than for abilities. Similarly, Eylon et al. (1985) reported that Israeli high school students who enrolled in extracurricular science clubs, when compared to randomly selected nonparticipants from the same schools, were not only higher in scientific ability but also displayed greater scientific interest, especially in terms of a desire for independent research experiences not available in their regular classrooms. Research suggests that interest in academic clubs can be inspired by positive regular classroom experiences. Tamir, Welch, and Rakow (1985) measured perceptions of science class experiences among a nationally representative sample of 2,000 13- and 17-year-olds. Class attitudes were a strong predictor of participation in extracurricular science activities, accounting for 33 percent of the variance after ability was removed.

That interests are important in students' extracurricular choices is also evident in the reasons they give for joining or not joining school organizations. In a survey of 2,500 high school students, Gholson (1979) found that over 90 percent checked intrinsic motives for becoming involved, such as personal achievement, fun and enjoyment, outlets for individual needs and interests, and experiences not available in the regular school program. However, an equally large number of students also cited extrinsic factors (opportunities to earn letters, awards, or prizes and to establish status among peers). In another similar study, irrelevance of activities to the interests and needs of students was checked by 51 percent of respondents and ranked second only to out-of-school employment as the most frequently mentioned reason for nonparticipation (Long, Buser, and Jackson 1977).

Among student attitudes, political dispositions have been the most commonly studied variables. Although considerable evidence exists to support a relationship between extracurricular participation and political attitudes (Cuccia 1981; see review by Ehman 1980), the research is largely correlational, and causal inferences are, for the most part, not possible. Eyler's (1982) path analytic study is an exception. According to her model, students who come to school with favorable attitudes toward the larger political system transfer these feelings of confidence to the school as a substitute political arena. As a result, they seek out governance and extracurricular activities. Analyses of attitudinal and extracurricular responses of over 3,000 students attending 13 urban, suburban, and rural high schools revealed direct paths from general political attitudes to school political attitudes and from school attitudes to participation, in support of the model. Moreover, political attitudes differentiated governance participants, nongovernance participants, and uninvolved students more effectively than did social attitudes (general feelings of trust in and integration with others). These findings support Eyler's assumption that choosing to become involved in student government is of political significance to students. Eyler acknowledged that positive political attitudes probably emanate from, as well as support, extracurricular involvement. There is, in fact, some support for a bidirectional association, as will be evident in a subsequent section on attitudinal outcomes of participation.

Finally, limited evidence suggests that students who participate in certain extracurricular pursuits have more favorable personality characteristics than nonparticipants. Hynes, Richardson, and Asher (1986) investigated 13 cognitive and personality predictors of self-reported high school leadership, using the Project TALENT nationally representative sample. Cognitive variables (reading comprehension, creativity, abstract reasoning, and arithmetic reasoning) were, for the most part, unrelated to leadership criteria. In contrast, several personality indexes—personal maturity, self-confidence, and spontaneity (e.g., liking to do things on the spur of the moment)—were consistently predictive. Mowbray (1980) gave 181 tenth graders Rotter's locus of control scale and reported that those who were internal on world control but external in personal control (i.e., who believed in the power of individual effort, but viewed themselves as lacking in this power) were least involved in school activities, had low feelings of belongingness, and experienced difficulties getting along with others. Similarly, among a sample of over 500 sophomores, juniors, and seniors, Burbach (1972) found that non-office holders, when compared with their office-holding peers, had significantly greater feelings of societal and school powerlessness. Moreover, an overall index of extracurricular participation was negatively associated with both forms of powerlessness, although the correlations were low. Socioeconomic status is known to be linked to measures of perceived control (e.g., Bartel 1971; Battle and Rotter 1963) as well as to extracurricular participation (see the discussion earlier in this chapter). However, in neither the Mowbray nor the Burbach studies was it, or other possible antecedent conditions, entered into the analyses as a control variable.

In the realm of athletics, research is evenly divided on whether athletes and nonathletes differ in personality characteristics (Andrews 1971; Holland and Andre 1987; Stevenson 1975). Schendel's (1965, 1968) studies comprise the only longitudinal evidence available. Students were given the California Psychological Inventory in ninth grade, again in twelfth grade, and (in one study) a third time during college. Findings revealed that on nine scales, ninth grade athletes possessed more positive psychological characteristics. However, differences between the two groups were more limited in twelfth grade, and, interestingly, in college the trend reversed itself: Nonathletes possessed a variety of more positive characteristics. When athletes rated by their coaches as outstanding, regular players, or substitutes were compared, there were few differences, except in twelfth grade, where those with lower athletic ratings generally possessed more positive qualities. Unfortunately, despite collection of longitudinal data, Schendel's analyses of personality/participation relationships are all concurrent. No attempt was made to predict later participation or stability of participation from earlier personality tendencies, or vice versa. Consequently, the extent to which athletic as well as other activity pursuits attract students with particular personality traits is not clarified by the correlational evidence available.

Ecological Factors

School Size. The most consistent finding in the literature on antecedents of extracurricular participation is the strong negative impact of school size. Barker and Gump (1964) were the first to thoroughly investigate this phenomenon and to develop a theoretical rationale to account for it. Student involvement in school activities, they reasoned, could be explained in terms of ecological pressure to participate, which increases as the ratio of students per activity environment declines. According to this idea, since the activity settings of small high schools are underpeopled in comparison to those of large schools, the inhabitants of small schools (1) are pressed by stronger social forces to participate and (2) are pressed in more varied directions. Consequently, more students in small schools should become involved, and, in comparison to their large-school counterparts, should enter a greater number and variety of activities and take on more responsible roles in them. These hypotheses were confirmed by Barker, Gump, and their collaborators using a diverse array of dependent measures. As expected, students from small schools more often entered interschool, regional, and state extracurricular contests and participated in a slightly greater average number and variety of activities. But the greatest difference between small- and large-school students was in quality rather than quantity of participation. When small-school students entered activities, they were twice as likely as their large-school counterparts to contribute actively by holding positions of responsibility. When central leadership roles were considered, small-school students performed such functions, on the average, in nearly four different activities; large-school students did so in less than one. In contrast, large-school students far surpassed small-school students in the number of settings they entered as audience persons or members—that is, in passive, spectator roles.

A great many subsequent investigations have reported findings in agreement with those of Barker and Gump (Baird 1969; Berk and Goebel 1987a, 1987b; Campbell, Cotterell, Robinson, and Sadler 1981; Downey 1978; Gholson and Buser 1981; Grabe 1981; Grabe and Latta 1977; Kleinert 1969; Lindsay 1982, 1984; Morgan and Alwin 1980; Rogers 1987; Schoggen and Schoggen 1988; Serow 1979; Wicker 1968, 1969a). In fact, the influence of school size on participation is far more powerful than the impact of any of the demographic and academic variables discussed earlier in this chapter (Lindsay 1984), and sometimes it can completely overcome their effects. Gump and Friesen (1964) examined the extent to which students of different levels of intellectual ability participated in small and large schools. "Slow" girls in small schools held positions of responsibility and leadership far more often than their large-school counterparts at any level of intellectual ability. At the same time, the danger of overinvolvement in student activities is not greater in small schools. In a study of 63 randomly selected southern Michigan high schools, Kleinert (1969) found that small schools had more students participating actively in several activities (two to five) in a given year than did large ones, but no relationship with school size existed for students joining in six or more extracurricular pursuits.

Variations in subjective experiences of participants in small and large schools provide additional support for ecological pressure theory. Willems (1964, 1967) analyzed the reasons given by students for entering activities and found that those in small schools described both more external forces (e.g., "I knew that I'd have to help if the thing was going to work"; or "My friends urged me to go") and personal forces (e.g., "I just wanted to go"; "I like basketball"). However, external forces, along with statements reflecting a sense of obligation to participate ("We all ought to take part"; or "I felt I should"), varied more with school size than did personal forces, and they were also more strongly correlated with actual participation. In addition, Willems found that in small schools, marginal students—those whose low IQ, poor academic performance, and low-income family background left them at high risk for dropping out—did not differ from regular students in number of external and personal forces. However, large-school marginal students described fewer forces of either kind, and in the case of external forces the difference was marked. In line with differences in reasons for participating, marginal students in small schools have been found to hold more positions of leadership and responsibility than do comparable students in large schools (Gump and Friesen 1964; Willems 1965).

School size is confounded with other variables that could account for the findings described above. Since small schools tend to be located in rural towns and large schools in cities and metropolitan areas, a major rival hypothesis is community size. Wicker (1968) discounted this possibility by demonstrating that participation is a function of the ratio of available participants to number of people required to operate an activity, regardless of whether comparisons are made between activities within a school or between schools of different sizes. He then argued that number of students, rather than other factors associated with size, produced the participation differences observed by Barker and Gump (1964). Additional research supports Wicker's conclusion by demonstrating that school-size effects persist when community size is held relatively constant (Berk and Goebel 1987a, 1987b; Campbell 1964; Lindsay 1982). Size is also related to member participation and satisfaction in nonschool organizations, such as churches and corporations, that do not covary as strongly with community characteristics (Talacchi 1960; Wicker 1969c; Wilken 1971).

Another proposal is that warmer, more student-oriented educational climates account for the vigor of small-school extracurricular participation. Rideout (1974) found that students in small high schools regarded the educational climate of their school to be more open—lively, energetic, active, and satisfying—than those in large schools, and student perceptions of openness were significantly correlated with their perceptions of opportunities to participate and actual participation in extracurricular activities. Rideout suggested that students in small schools perceive their school as fulfilling its service obligation to meet their personal needs. Consequently, they respond in kind, participating in nonrequired activities because they feel wanted and needed, not because (as ecological pressure theory assumes) they are pressed into participation. However, feeling wanted and needed may, to a large extent, be a function of environmental press. Campbell, Cotterell, Robinson, and Sadler (1981) found that small school size, positive school climate, and underpeopled activity settings are strongly intercorrelated. As they point out, the relationship between student participation and school climate is likely to be a two-way street. The provision of a warm and challenging climate may foster high involvement, but high involvement may also contribute to a school's climate as well as to students' perceptions of it. According to this view, both climate and ecological pressure serve as related intervening variables in the school size/participation relationship.

A refinement of ecological pressure theory has recently been proposed, based on findings that functionally different activity settings are not equally affected by variations in school size. Morgan and Alwin (1980) hypothesized that the impact of school size varies with the centrality (importance to the institution) and elasticity (ability to expand to accommodate more students) of the activity. Those activities highly central to the organization, but that are inelastic (e.g., journalism) should be characterized by the strongest negative association between school size and participation. In contrast, activities both central and elastic (e.g., athletics) or noncentral and inelastic (e.g., debate) should show a much weaker relationship. In the case of the former, the activity's importance leads schools of all sizes to invest resources in it, and it can easily expand to keep pace with available participants. In the case of the latter, the activity is neither important nor expandable, and there should be relatively little change in participation across schools. Finally, Morgan and Alwin expected that activities low in centrality but high in elasticity (e.g., hobby clubs) should show a reverse pattern—increased rates of participation with increases in school size—because of their ability to expand as the need arises. Surveying students in 30 schools, the investigators reported findings consistent with their expectations. Supportive evidence also appeared for music and sports (central and elastic activities) in Berk and Goebel's (1987b) study. However, other investigators have found strong school-size effects for some activity areas (e.g., sports and music) that, according to Morgan and Alwin, should show little interschool variation and minimal school-size effects for others (e.g. hobby clubs) that should show a great deal (Gholson and Buser 1981; Kleinert 1969; Lindsay 1982). Consequently, Morgan and Alwin's theory has not received clear confirmation, and the underlying basis for variations among activities in the school-size effect requires further study.

In view of the evidence that small schools are effective in drawing marginal students into the mainstream of extracurricular life, several investigators have asked the related question of whether utilization of extracurricular resources is more evenly balanced among all social strata in schools enrolling fewer pupils. The available findings are largely negative on this issue. Surveying students in 19 school districts in a large northeastern state, Serow (1979) reported that a reduction in ratio of students to activities did not lessen the participation advantage of higher social class youth. Instead, underpeopled activity settings led students of each social class to gain in participation rates to the same degree. Several additional studies indicate that females are more sensitive to small-school social pressures to join in activities and that small school size accentuates rather than minimizes sex differences in participation. Wicker (1969a) found greater involvement among females than males in small schools, but no sex difference in a large-school environment. Similarly, Lindsay (1982) reported a larger participation gender gap in favor of females in small than in large schools. The tendency of small-school students to enter a wider variety of activity settings is also more characteristic of females than males (Grabe and Latta 1977). Finally, based on Willems's (1967) marginality hypothesis—that small schools must utilize a greater proportion of students of lesser talents to keep their activities in operation—Grabe (1976) anticipated that students in the lower grades would be more involved in the extracurriculum in small- than in large-school settings. However, he found support for this expectation only in the case of underclass females.

An important implication of the school-size literature is that attending a small school should have a greater impact on development, as a result of a more intense and richer extracurricular experience. The ability of small schools to integrate marginal students into the extracurriculum, as well as the generally positive psychological consequences thought to emanate from small-school participation, is underscored by those who argue against the current trend toward school consolidation (Campbell, Cotterell, Robinson, and Sadler 1981; Garbarino 1980; Kleinert 1969; Lindsay 1982). Research indicates that when schools enroll more than 500 to 700 students, it is difficult to ensure that many can participate at a high level and that there will be few who are uninvolved. In other words, the decline in proportion of the student body that participates accelerates rapidly above this threshold (Campbell, Cotterell, Robinson, and Sadler 1981; Downey 1978; Garbarino 1980; Turner and Thrasher 1970). Garbarino suggests that this optimal school-size figure be adjusted in accordance with student characteristics. As the number of socially and academically marginal students increases, ideal school size should decrease. However, as Campbell, Cotterell, Robinson, and Sadler (1981) and Kleinert (1969) point out, it is unlikely that any movement to return to smaller-size high schools will gain much momentum in the near future. Along with Wicker (1969b), these authors recommend active experimentation with different internal school structures, such as the school-within-a-school or house plan, to increase extracurricular involvement. Unfortunately, efforts to experiment with such arrangements have not been very successful, largely because a common practice in such schools is to retain the activity program at a school-wide level rather than reorganizing it on a unit basis. As a result, the critical feature that induces greater participation, fewer people per activity, does not occur. In addition to more effective house-plan arrangements, Wicker suggests that deliberate efforts be made to create more activities in large schools so more students can hold responsible positions. As yet, no research exists on the efficacy of such interventions.

School Grade-Level Organization. A limited literature exists on the relationship of school grade-level organization to extracurricular participation. Over the course of this century, education in the United States and in other industrialized nations has undergone a shift from a kindergarten to eighth grade (K–8) school structure and associated 4-year secondary school to a kindergarten to sixth grade (K–6) elementary school followed by junior and senior high schools. Blyth, Simmons, and Bush (1978) followed a sample of 239 pupils from sixth to seventh grade, some who remained in the same K–8 schools they had attended the previous year and others who transferred from K–6 into junior high school. Although both groups participated equally often in the extracurriculum during sixth grade, at seventh grade there were dramatic differences. Eighty one percent of those remaining in K–8 schools were involved in some kind of student activity, compared to only 39 percent in junior high, despite the greater number of activities available in junior high schools. Much the same findings were reported by Ichilov and Chen (1978) in a similarly designed Israeli study. However, in both of these investigations, school grade-level organization was confounded with school size. In Blyth et al.'s research, the junior highs were, on the average, more than three times as large as the K–6 schools, making it difficult to determine whether school size alone or size in combination with school transition was responsible for the results. That school transition, as a stressful event in the life of young adolescents, probably contributes to reduced extracurricular participation is suggested by another study in which the effect of simultaneous life changes (school transition, pubertal maturation, early dating behavior, residential mobility, and family disruption) was examined. Participation in extracurricular activities declined linearly with an increase in number of stressful life conditions, as did students' GPA and self-esteem (Simmons et al. 1987).

At present, no studies have examined variations in junior to senior high grade-level organization. Comparisons of a grades 7–9, 10–12 combination with a 7–8, 9–12 grade structure offer the possibility of examining the impact of school transition independently of school size, since enrollments of junior and senior high schools in the same community are more comparable than those of elementary and junior highs.

Community Characteristics. Although, as indicated earlier, community size is not a viable alternative explanation for school-size variations in overall participatory behavior, there is evidence that community characteristics do affect several aspects of extracurricular involvement. Baird (1969) reported that degree of urbanization influences the achievements of students in certain extracurricular areas. Analyses of data obtained from the American College Testing Program (ACT) revealed that, in music, the influence of community setting was larger than the effect of high school size, with students from small cities and towns receiving the greatest number of honors and awards and those from large cities, the least. Also, dramatic arts achievement was highest in rural communities.

Eitzen (1975) attempted to separate the impact of school and community characteristics on sports participation by collecting data from male students in nine different school and community settings. Asking, as Coleman (1961) did, how students would like to be remembered (as an athletic star, brilliant student, or most popular), Eitzen reported that greater status was accorded to sports participation in smaller communities, in communities with fewer professionals and more poverty, and in those with relatively little industrialization. Unfortunately, this study is weakened by the strong possibility that the community characteristics under investigation were confounded with one another and with school size.

Nevertheless, the available evidence is consistent with the widespread belief that small rural communities are especially enthusiastic about and supportive of their local high school athletic teams and musical and dramatic productions. In an ethnographic investigation of a small community of 2,200 persons with just over 500 students in its K–12 school system, Peshkin (1978) provided additional support for this assumption. The school is described as the one place in the community that simultaneously keeps youth busy and serves as a primary source of entertainment for adults. As Peshkin put it, "The high school is Mansfield's hub of activity, the place where when the lights are out in other public settings, save for the Laundromat and the taverns, there is very likely something happening" (147).

Stability of a community's population also affects extracurricular involvement. Craig and Pasewark (1981) compared participation of juniors attending two large and two small Wyoming high schools. The large schools were located in relatively large rural communities, one of which had experienced a population boom—a growth rate of 77 percent between 1970 and 1975—along with considerable transience in population. The two small schools were located in somewhat smaller towns that remained stable in population. Rural boom towns have been characterized as engendering a strong sense of interpersonal anonymity and alienation. Consequently, the investigators expected that high school students in the boom town would be less involved in the extracurriculum than their peers in an equally large but stable high school. This prediction held true only for transient boom town students, who tended not to participate in any activities. The remaining results were surprising. For both athletic and nonathletic activities, average participation rates for the student body as a whole were as great in the large boom town school as they were in the two small stable high schools, and they were considerably greater than in the large stable high school.

Why this unusual pattern of results occurred is a matter of speculation. The authors surmised that recreational resources in the boom community may have been limited, causing students to turn instead toward organized school activities. It is also possible that the large number of uninvolved transient students in the boom town school led students with stable residency to experience increased pressures to participate. If the latter explanation is correct, then Craig and Pasewark's investigation shows how special community circumstances—in this case, a large, uncommitted transient population—can cause a relatively large school environment to become underpeopled.

Student Perspectives on Participation

A handful of investigations have collected self-reports on why students do and do not participate, along with perceptions of the value of extracurricular offerings. As indicated in earlier sections of this chapter, intrinsic reasons for extracurricular involvement are prevalent in student replies, suggesting that the desire for social status, emphasized by Hollingshead (1949) and Coleman (1961), is only one among a number of motives for entering the extracurriculum. Among Gholson's (1979) 2,500 survey respondents, besides personal needs and interests and quests for peer recognition, social motives were at the heart of extracurricular participation: 90 percent of the sample ranked broadening personal and social contacts among the most important reasons for involvement. In addition to out-of-school employment, competing community activities were a primary reason given by Gholson's subjects for nonparticipation.

Long, Buser, and Jackson's (1977) survey of 1,500 students from a nationally stratified sample of 65 high schools adds to the list of student-perceived factors that discourage participation. Inconvenient after-school scheduling of activities was mentioned by 51 percent of the respondents. Significant numbers of students also cited the following reasons for not joining school organizations: control by social groups or cliques (47 percent); failure to be selected to participate (41 percent); grades not high enough to allow participation (41 percent); apathy on the part of faculty sponsors (40 percent); and lack of awareness of available activities (40 percent). Activity costs, parental disapproval of participation, and domination of activities by teachers were less salient reasons for noninvolvement. Findings in basic agreement with these were reported by Allen and Gansneder (1976) in a small-scale survey of student perceptions. Finally, in a study of a stratified random sample of high schools in five southwestern states in which uninvolved students were asked for information about why they did not participate, lack of activities relevant to their needs and interests was by far the most frequently checked response (76.7 percent). All other reasons were much lower in frequency; they were checked by less than half the sample (Vornberg et al. 1983).

Since student perceptions can be expected to affect participation and their content sheds light on the reasons behind individual differences in involvement, they are important. To date, except for the attention given by Wicker (1968) and Willems (1964, 1967) to student subjective experiences as intervening links between school size and extent of participation, no research has looked at student perceptions of extracurricular activities as a function of environmental factors and student characteristics, or at the relationship of perceptions to actual extracurricular involvement.

Summary

The largest body of evidence on the extracurriculum is devoted to the study of factors influencing student participation. The most serious limitations of current research include difficulties in separating antecedents from consequents and concomitants in correlational studies, poorly described samples, use of undifferentiated measures of extracurricular involvement, and a paucity of well-developed theory in the area of student activity choice and participation maintenance to guide empirical endeavors. Studies based on longitudinal designs and those using regression and path analysis to test causal models offer the most promising findings to date. The evidence as a whole reveals that student characteristics and ecological variables combine with one another to influence extracurricular participation. The academic and extracurricular dimensions of schooling are not, as has sometimes been assumed, antithetical. Instead, the most involved extracurricular participants score higher in academic performance and educational aspirations. Participating students are also advantaged in a variety of additional ways, including socioeconomic status, self-esteem, political attitudes, and personality characteristics. Participation has been found to increase over the junior high and high school years as students gain in maturity and ability and are offered a wider array of extracurricular opportunities. Of the two sexes, female students are the more involved participants, except in the areas of athletics and hobby clubs, where males predominate. Moreover, research suggests that participation has a more instrumental, achievement-oriented meaning for males and a more expressive, affiliative meaning for females, a difference that may contribute to the fact that by college females lose their general extracurricular advantage. School value priorities, such as the emphasis placed on academic excellence, may moderate the relationships between student characteristics and participation noted above, but as yet they have not been systematically investigated.

School size is the most consistent and powerful determinant of extracurricular participation. The greater depth and variety of involvement in smaller schools, along with their power to draw socially and academically marginal students into the extracurriculum, can be explained in terms of intense social pressures to participate in underpeopled environments. Community size is not a viable alternative explanation for school-size variations in activity involvement, but the importance of other community as well as school contextual variables requires further study. Finally, student self-reports offer a potentially rich source of information about motivations for extracurricular involvement, but few studies have examined them as intervening links between individual and ecological variables and actual student participation.

DEVELOPMENTAL CONSEQUENCES OF EXTRACURRICULAR INVOLVEMENT

The 1985 Gallup Poll of the public's attitude toward the public schools reported that 80 percent of Americans regard extracurricular activities as important to a young person's education, a pattern of response that duplicated the results of polls conducted during the prior decade. When adults surveyed in 1978 were asked, "What subjects that you studied or experiences that you gained in high school have you found to be most useful in later life?" extracurricular activities ranked fourth, right behind English, mathematics, and commercial subjects, such as typing and bookkeeping (Gallup 1978). A unique feature of the extracurriculum, in contrast to most formal classroom experiences where absorption of teacher- and text-conveyed knowledge is the major mode of learning, is the opportunity for active engagement—emotionally, physically, and intellectually—in a wide variety of shared pursuits that duplicate on a smaller scale meaningful activities in the wider society. Because of its responsiveness to individual interests and abilities and its encouragement of involved, expressive activity, the extracurriculum may have especially important implications for many aspects of psychosocial and intellectual development. As Gump (1981) argues, the "opportunity to function," to play a key role in an important human enterprise, provided by extracurricular activities should enhance young people's sense of personal satisfaction, their perceptions of themselves, and their knowledge of how the world works.

Research on consequences of extracurricular participation suffers from many of the same problems as the body of evidence on antecedents—namely, limited correlational designs; variations in sampling quality; lack of attention to process variables, such as degree of involvement and quality of experience within the activity; a paucity of longitudinal research; and a total absence of experimental and quasi-experimental intervention studies. In the sections that follow, studies using longitudinal designs and instituting controls that increase the possibility, if not the certainty, that dependent measures are consequents, rather than antecedents or concomitants of participation are selected out for special review.

Investigations of extracurricular consequences cover a wide range of outcome variables. Most researchers focus on intellectual and psychosocial factors assessed during or shortly after the extracurricular experience, including subsequent extracurricular involvement, academic performance, educational aspirations, student retention, prevention of adolescent antisocial acts, personality characteristics, and current psychological well-being and life satisfaction. A few take a long-term view of extracurricular experiences and examine benefits that persist into early and middle adulthood. In this category of research, occupational attainment and community participation and leadership in adulthood have been the major targets of study. In general, findings suggest that the predictive value of participation varies with both type of activity and student characteristics. Although the bulk of research reveals a wide variety of beneficial effects, results are not invariably positive. Some forms of extracurricular involvement for some kinds of students appear to be associated with either an absence of gains or negative rather than favorable outcomes. Finally, given the powerful impact of school size on participatory behavior and associated subjective experiences, one question that arises from time to time in the outcome literature is whether extracurricular experiences in small schools are more facilitating of student development than those in larger-school environments.

Future Extracurricular Participation

One possible short-term outcome of participation is that students involved in the extracurriculum may be more likely to contribute to the extracurricular life of their school in the future. Several investigators have examined the stability of participation from high school to college, recognizing that the extracurriculum is unlikely to exert a long-term impact on student development if involvement is fleeting and inconsistent from one time period to another.

There are two ways of looking at the stability of any measure of behavior: (1) in terms of correlations, or the degree to which subjects maintain their relative standing in a sample assessed repeatedly over time; and (2) in terms of absolute performance, which involves within-subject analyses of the consistency of participation scores over a series of repeated assessments. Both approaches have been used in studies of the stability of extracurricular participation.

In Rehberg and Schafer's (1973) longitudinal study described earlier in this chapter, the strongest correlate of participation during the last year of high school was participation in the second year, a finding which suggests that variations among students in degree of involvement are established early and tend to persist. Two additional investigations provide evidence that high school participation is correlated with college extracurricular involvement. Examining the interrelationship of retrospective accounts of high school and college participation provided by over 2,000 subjects, Hanks and Eckland (1976) reported correlations of .44 and .53 for athletic activities and .48 and .36 for nonathletic pursuits for males and females, respectively. Moreover, path-analytic findings revealed a strong direct relationship between high school and college participation after several other relevant variables (socioeconomic status, high school academic aptitude, and high school and college grades) were controlled. Focusing on a more restricted sample, Hiss, Woodcock, and McGrath (1984) asked 355 students at Bates College to evaluate the extent of their involvement in a variety of extracurricular areas at both the high school and college levels. Strong correlations were obtained for varsity sports (.65), individual athletics (.66), and intramural sports (.60). In addition, all artistic pursuits (music, theater, art, and dance) showed significant positive relationships, the strongest of which was visual arts (.66). However, involvement in community service organizations (for which there was substantial encouragement at Bates) showed weak high school to college correlational stability, probably because many nonservice-oriented high school students responded to the press of the college environment and took advantage of new opportunities for volunteer work.

In contrast to correlational evidence, findings on the stability of absolute level of participation are less encouraging. Baird (1969) examined the extracurricular achievements of 5,000 students in 29 colleges and found little difference in rate of college achievement between students from large and small high schools, a result suggesting that the higher level of participation of students in smaller environments does not carry over to the college years. Similar findings were reported by Berk and Goebel (1987a) in a study of students enrolled in a small liberal arts college and in a second investigation conducted at a large, multipurpose university (Berk and Goebel 1987b). Both Baird and Berk and Goebel concluded that students' absolute level of extracurricular participation is largely under the control of the immediate situation, since in all three studies college extracurricular performance was a function of college size, independent of size of high school attended. Moreover, Berk and Goebel found that level of extracurricular participation declined from high school to college in both college environments, but the decline was greater for students in the large university. However, high school students at the lower level who entered the small college deviated from the general pattern and actually gained in participation over time.

The evidence summarized above suggests that, although there is reasonable consistency in who participates most and who participates least from high school to college, immediate contextual factors powerfully affect the overall level of student participation. Nevertheless, it is important to note that the persisting influence of small high school environments on subsequent level of involvement may be masked temporarily by the pressing developmental tasks of late adolescence and young adulthood (establishing an occupational identity and developing intimate relationships) that cause participation to decline during the college years. From this perspective, the lasting participatory advantage of attending a small school may not surface until later in life. Although correlational evidence on adolescent to adult organizational involvement is available (see the section on adult community participation later in this chapter), studies that chart extent and type of participation over several decades are needed to explore this issue. As yet, they have not been conducted.

Finally, only one investigation has addressed the question of what underlies the correlational continuity of extracurricular participation from high school to college. Pavelchak, Moreland, and Levine (1986) point out that many variables may be influential, including students' personality characteristics, interest in and talent for group activities and goals, and favorableness of prior extracurricular experiences. Concentrating on the last of these factors, the investigators explored the impact of high school extracurricular experiences on the group-joining behavior of freshmen college students at a large university. Tests of causal modeling were applied to students' questionnaire responses, revealing that those with positive high school group experiences judged such groups to be useful for achieving future personal goals, which, in turn, made them more willing to consider joining similar organizations in college. In a practical vein, these results suggest that finding ways to strengthen students' beliefs in the personal utility of extracurricular memberships may enhance their interest in new groups, even if prior extracurricular experiences were negative.

Academic Performance, Educational Aspirations, and Educational Attainment

Longitudinal analyses suggest that nonathletic and overall extracurricular participation has direct, beneficial consequences for later high school grades, educational aspirations, and post–high school educational attainment (Hanks and Eckland 1976, 1978; Otto 1975, 1976b; Rehberg and Schafer 1973; Snyder 1969, 1975; Spady 1970, 1971). In a longitudinal study of nearly 300 boys surveyed in their senior year of high school and again 4 years later, Spady (1970) compared the impact of extracurricular participation, achievement motivation, and grades while controlling for socioeconomic status and intelligence and found that extracurricular involvement had, by far, the strongest association with college success and realization of educational expectations. High school students without a major extracurricular interest, when compared to their involved counterparts, were much less likely to have college aspirations and, if they did, to fulfill them. Similarly, in a longitudinal investigation of over 300 high school senior males studied again 15 years later, extracurricular participation accounted for more variability in educational attainment than did socioeconomic status, academic ability, or high school academic performance (Otto 1976a). The power of the extracurriculum to influence academic outcomes appears to carry over to activity participation during the college years. In Hanks and Eckland's (1976) path-analytic 15-year follow-up study, among males, college nonathletic participation exerted as strong a direct effect as aptitude and grades on ultimate educational attainment; among females, it was the strongest direct predictor of educational attainment.

With respect to athletic involvement in particular, investigators disagree on whether it facilitates the academic mission of education (Otto and Alwin 1977; Phillips and Schafer 1971), is counterproductive to it (Spady 1970), or neither depresses nor especially enhances academic performance (Hanks and Eckland 1976). Phillips and Schafer (1971) reviewed research prior to 1970 and concluded that the positive association of athletics with high school grades and educational aspirations is greater for male athletes from lower-class homes, a finding which suggests that athletic participation may have an especially salutary effect for students who tend to do poorly in school and are often not college bound. Other more recent investigations report similar findings (Otto 1975, 1976a; Spady 1970, 1971). In contrast, Hanks and Eckland (1976) reported that high school athletic participation had no direct consequences for later grades, curriculum track, or ultimate educational attainment. Moreover, Spady (1970) found that, although participation in athletics predicted high levels of educational aspiration by the end of high school, it was not associated with eventual translation of those goals into effective action when socioeconomic status and grades were low. However, low-income and poorly achieving students who immersed themselves in service activities and leadership roles not only had high levels of aspiration but also tended to fulfill them. Analyzing 15-year longitudinal follow-up data, Otto and Alwin (1977) reported results in opposition to those of Hanks and Eckland and Spady—namely, that athletic participation contributed positively to both educational aspirations and attainment. However, Otto and Alwin did not separate involvement in athletics from participation in other activities, as Hanks and Eckland and Spady did. Therefore, the possibility remains that athletes in their study may have been immersed in additional facets of the extracurriculum that account for their favorable findings.

The precise process by which participation facilitates academic outcomes has been of interest to investigators, although very little research has addressed the topic. Phillips and Schafer (1971) and Rehberg (1969) conjectured that the salutary effect of participation is largely a function of increased contacts with school personnel as well as peer group pressure. In the case of athletics, academically less-inclined boys are thought to first gain peer respect through athletic performance. Subsequently, they become better students because they learn that such behavior is expected by other athletic elites as well as by adult mentors with whom they interact at school. Hanks and Eckland (1976) tested this hypothesis by looking at amount of contact with teachers and with college-bound peers as possible intervening variables between participation and academic outcomes. Strong support was found for the model in the case of nonathletic activities for males, but not for females. In contrast, little evidence emerged to support the notion that athletics exposes students of either sex to social pressures that elevate academic performance. However, Snyder (1975), in a study of male basketball players, found that contact with teachers was a function of degree of team involvement. Stars were more likely than starters, and starters more likely than substitutes, to receive advice from their coaches about attending college, to feel that their coaches were a great influence on them, and to plan to continue their education, although the extent to which they realized their aspirations was not investigated. Spady's (1970, 1971) contention is that service and leadership activities, as opposed to athletics, promote the development of important personal resources and capacities that facilitate the realization of educational goals. In his research, boys who participated only in athletics tended to have inflated rather than accurate perceptions of their own peer status, and a considerable proportion of their failure to realize educational goals could be traced to their exaggerated self-perceptions. Spady concluded that, because of its high visibility and short-term status rewards, sports stimulates the desire for further recognition, expressed through college aspirations, but it does not provide the kinds of experiences that contribute to college academic success. Exactly what attitudes and skills are promoted by extracurricular experiences that facilitate the realization of educational aspirations, and why they are fostered by some activities and not by others, requires additional research.

Finally, limited evidence is available on the question of whether participatory experiences in small high schools are more facilitating of future academic performance than those in large high schools. In a retrospective study, Downey (1978) collected academic data during the first four semesters of college on a sample of 400 Kansas State University students, randomly stratified by size of high school attended. ACT survey data obtained before college entry showed small-school students to have had a higher level of high school extracurricular accomplishment, but there were no significant differences in mean college cumulative GPAs by high school size. In fact, students from the very smallest high schools (graduating classes of 24 or less) actually showed a greater tendency to drop out of college. These findings are consistent with general trends in the literature on the relationship between high school size and college performance (Pantages and Creedon 1978). However, in Downey's and in other studies, relevant control variables (e.g., socioeconomic status, intelligence, high school GPA) were not entered into the analyses, nor was there an effort to directly assess the extent to which extracurricular experiences serve as intervening variables between high school size and college academic record.

Student Retention

Estimates indicate that over 60 percent of high school dropouts were not involved in any extracurricular activities during their high school years (Beacham 1980; Hewitt and Johnson 1979). The effectiveness of small high schools in involving marginal students in the extracurriculum has led to the hypothesis that participation helps prevent early school attrition by sparking interest in and commitment to the school environment. The sense of obligation and responsibility engendered is believed to be at least partly responsible for the lower dropout rates in small as opposed to large high schools (Garbarino 1980; Rogers 1987).

Research addressing the assumption that participation promotes student retention is sparse but supportive. Using longitudinal data collected over a 5-year period, Doss (1986) examined courses selected by high-risk students in ninth grade, including credit-generating extracurricular offerings such as band and sports, for their relationship to subsequent school attrition. Discriminant analyses on two data sets revealed that varsity sports was the only course associated with above average holding power in both analyses. Similarly, Schafer and Armer (1968) compared 164 athletes and nonathletes, matched on intelligence, fathers' occupation, curriculum track, and GPA in the final semester of junior high. Only 2 percent of the athletes failed to finish high school in comparison to 9 percent of the nonathletes.

Timberlake (1982) approached the problem by examining self-reports of 66 black female students identified as at risk for dropping out on the basis of three criteria—suspension from school, accumulation of a high rate of unexcused absences, and referral for discipline problems at least three times during the school year. Responses to open-ended questions revealed no significant differences between persisters (who eventually graduated from high school) and nonpersisters in after-school extracurricular participation. However, more persisters reported engaging in recreational activities held in the school building during evening hours, a finding which suggests that they were more involved in the out-of-class life of their school. After-school employment, which favored the persisters, may be responsible for the pattern of activity findings appearing in this study.

Research on the significance of activity involvement for student retention is more abundant at the college level, but the literature is contradictory, with some studies supporting its importance, others reporting no relationship, and at least one study suggesting that activity involvement can be detrimental (Demitroff 1974; see the review by Pantages and Creedon 1978). In contrast, increased opportunity for personalized interaction with faculty, especially around course work, consistently predicts college retention (Pantages and Creedon 1978; Terenzini and Pascarella 1980). Whether a similar experiential factor, instead of, in addition to, or as part of extracurricular involvement, is responsible for the lower attrition rates in small high schools is not yet known.

Prevention of Antisocial Behavior

The social control function emphasized by early advocates of extracurricular activities has stimulated a small body of research on the extent to which participation prevents adolescent antisocial behavior. In one of the first studies to address this issue, Schafer (1969) reported that among students with poor academic records and low socioeconomic status (where delinquency rates tend to be highest), high school athletes had a lower incidence of court-recorded crime than did nonathletes. Schafer's study does not shed light on the relative effectiveness of sports versus other extracurricular pursuits in reducing the rate of adolescent delinquency, but a study by Landers and Landers (1978) provides additional information. A comparison of participants in sports only, service-leadership only, both types of activities, and neither revealed the three participant groups to be equivalent; only nonparticipants committed significantly more delinquent acts. These findings suggest that whatever prosocial lessons are learned from athletics can also be acquired in other extracurricular activities. However, Landers and Landers did not control for background variables, such as academic performance and socioeconomic status, known to be related to both nonparticipation and adolescent crime. Therefore, selection factors rather than extracurricular experiences may be responsible for their findings. Similar problems plague investigations reporting that extracurricular participation is inversely related to adolescent drug and alcohol use (Fischler 1975–1976; Gibbons, Wylie, Echterling, and French 1986; Igra and Moos 1979). Gender, religiosity, and socioeconomic status are among the known correlates of substance abuse not controlled in these studies.

If involvement in the extracurriculum plays some role in deterring adolescent antisocial behavior, the opportunities it affords students to contribute to school governance may be an important ingredient of its effectiveness. McPartland and McDill (1977) analyzed responses of over 3,000 students in 14 high schools to determine the relationship of student offenses to their satisfaction with participation in school rule making and with the rules themselves, controlling for age, sex, race, socioeconomic status, and perceived quality of school instruction. Small but significant associations were found, with the most satisfied students reporting that they engaged in fewer antisocial acts. Other dimensions of participation may also contribute to a reduction in student offenses, including relief from boredom, legitimate opportunities to attain peer status and other rewards, exposure to nondeviant role models, and acquisition of interpersonal skills, but they await more conclusive evidence on the causal role of the extracurriculum in preventing antisocial behavior. Finally, after controlling for a wide variety of student demographic characteristics, McPartland and McDill found school size to be positively associated with a wide range of principal-reported student offenses. However, the extent to which the lower incidence of antisocial acts in smaller schools is mediated by extracurricular opportunities, as opposed to other school-related variables, has not been studied.

Personality Characteristics

Building upon Barker and Gump's (1964) ecological pressure theory, Campbell, Cotterell, Robinson, and Sadler (1981) hypothesized that the greater press to participate and the [illegible], more challenging educational climate associated with small schools would foster certain positive aspects of personal–social development. These include (1) a sense of group cohesion and concern for other persons; (2) a positive attitude toward school; (3) a sense of functional identity (seeing oneself as an achiever irrespective of how one's abilities and aptitudes stack up against those of others); (4) an internal locus of control (from experiencing the effects of personal effort on activity success); and (5) cognitive complexity (as the result of participating in a wide range of activities at a high level of involvement). However, Barker and Gump (1964), Campbell, Cotterell, Robinson, and Sadler (1981), and Grabe (1976, 1981) have also highlighted several interrelated negative outcomes that may accrue from participatory experiences in small as opposed to large schools. Because small-school students engage in more varied and difficult extracurricular tasks, they are exposed to more success as well as failure opportunities. Their increased vulnerability to failure should promote greater feelings of insecurity (Barker and Gump 1964) and a higher fear of failure (Campbell, Cotterell, Robinson, and Sadler 1981). In addition, when students do fail at activity performances in small schools, they should experience greater alienation from the school environment than their large-school counterparts. This is because greater pressure toward successful participation forces a more negative evaluation under failure conditions, and students repeatedly forced to face such feedback should soon begin to create psychological distance between themselves and the source of those evaluations (Grabe 1976, 1981).

To date, very little research has been conducted to test these propositions. The most comprehensive study available is that of Campbell, Cotterell, Robinson, and Sadler (1981), who assessed all of the positive characteristics noted above, and also fear of failure, among 122 seventh graders enrolled in both large and small schools. Controlling for age, sex, intelligence, years of attendance at their current school, and socioeconomic status of family and community, regression analyses revealed that participation was related to a number of personality outcomes, including functional identity, internal locus of control for success experiences, concern for persons, and fear of failure. However, small-school participants were advantaged over their large-school counterparts only on personality dimensions that reflected affiliative orientation—sense of cohesion and concern for persons. As Campbell, Cotterell, Robinson, and Sadler pointed out, small-school youngsters appeared "gentler, more conscious of responsibilities to others" (226) than large-school students. Otherwise, participation was associated with similar personality outcomes in both types of school environments.

Campbell, Cotterell, Robinson, and Sadler's decision to focus on seventh graders may have limited the power of their analyses, since more time may be needed for the differential effects of participation in large and small schools to accrue. Along these lines, Wicker (1969a) examined the impact of school size as mediated by participation on the cognitive complexity of a more mature sample—high school juniors. The measure of cognitive complexity was a modified version of the one used by Campbell, Cotterell, Robinson, and Sadler in that the score was the number of constructs generated by students when asked to evaluate school activities instead of persons. Findings revealed that frequency of activities entered and number of responsible positions held predicted cognitive complexity. Moreover, students from small schools had higher cognitive complexity scores than those from large schools, after a variety of background variables (father's occupation, parental education, intelligence, and school grades) had been controlled. Wicker's findings can be explained by the fact that students holding central positions can be described as "'in' on the business of their settings" (Gump 1981, 109). They become part of occasions and places that are usually closed to their classmates, such as behind-the-scenes conferences, meetings, and rehearsals devoted to activity planning and maintenance. Because these events offer exposure to how activity settings work, they may be largely responsible for the higher cognitive complexity scores of extracurricular leaders and performers, in comparison to club members, spectators, and nonparticipants.

Although Campbell, Cotterell, Robinson, and Sadler (1981) did not find that participants in small schools feared failure to a greater extent than those in large schools, in two studies Grabe (1975, 1981) reported that they felt more alienated from the school setting. However, Grabe did not assess alienation as a function of success and failure experiences in extracurricular activities, a design feature essential for validating his intriguing hypothesis. Consequently, it is impossible to tell if small-school students scored higher in alienation because (as Grabe interprets) intense pressure toward extracurricular success leads poorly performing youngsters to protect their self-images by withdrawing psychologically from the school environment.

Self-Esteem, Identity Development

Grabe's (1975) findings on self-esteem, introduced in an earlier section of this chapter, lend support to the supposition that participation in the extracurriculum contributes to a generally positive self-image. Grabe (1981) was also interested in whether greater ecological pressure in small schools, with its associated opportunities for extracurricular success, would have the effect of strengthening the participation/self-esteem connection. Positive results were obtained for a sample of over 1,500 students attending 20 different high schools. Relationships between participation frequency and self-esteem were consistently stronger in small institutions. They were also stronger for students in the upper grades, who, because of increased maturity, undoubtedly have more extracurricular success experiences than their younger counterparts.

Rehberg (1969) hypothesized that self-esteem may serve as an intervening variable between athletic participation and high school academic orientation. According to this idea, sports enhances feelings of accomplishment and self-worth of participants, who respond by raising their scholastic performance and educational aspirations. Rehberg suggested that the validity of this hypothesis be tested by comparing longitudinal gains in self-esteem of athletes and nonathletes, but, to date, no such study has been conducted. In an ex post facto investigation, Dowell, Badgett, and Hunkler (1972) assessed degree of high school athletic achievement among 475 male college freshmen, who were also given a differentiated measure of self-esteem. Athletic achievement correlated positively (but at a low level) with college physical and motivational self-esteem, but negatively with intellectual self-esteem. Since types of self-esteem are known to be related to functionally similar forms of behavior (Harter 1983), these findings suggest that athletics may not promote the kinds of self-image qualities that contribute to subsequent academic success. Differentiated measures of self-esteem are needed in future longitudinal studies to test this idea, as well as to explore the long-term significance of self-esteem advantages accruing from extracurricular involvement.

According to Erikson (1950, 1968), self-development takes on a new direction during the adolescent years. It moves toward a sense of identity, a coherent conception of values, beliefs, and future goals to which the young person is solidly committed. Erikson noted that the search for identity can serve as an important motivator of participation in youth organizations, and such involvement may, in turn, contribute importantly to identity consolidation. However, only one investigation has addressed the relationship between student participation and identity development. Weston and Stein (1977) studied women students attending a small private college and found that being active in one or more campus organizations was positively associated with identity achievement. However, the number of organizations to which students belonged and whether they held leadership positions was not. The authors suggested that their limited findings may be due to the fact that most college students are in the later stages of identity development and may have passed the point at which participation exerts its greatest impact. Correlational research on high school students of both sexes, as well as longitudinal studies that simultaneously track participation and identity progress, still need to be conducted.

Political Attitudes and Behavior

Extracurricular activities are regarded as a major educational vehicle for teaching political attitudes that motivate participation in a democratic society. It has been argued that student government is the activity of greatest relevance to such political learning, since it is the most obvious direct analog of the adult political world (Dawson and Prewitt 1969). In addition, interscholastic competition is believed to be important in the political socialization process, because it mirrors the struggle between groups for political power and trains students to work for group rather than individual ends, thereby fostering socially responsible, publicly oriented values (Jennings 1974). As indicated earlier in this chapter, there is considerable evidence to support a linkage between school participation and political attitudes. However, at present, only one longitudinal study has addressed the proposition that participation contributes to the socialization of political attitudes and interests. Dailey (1983) examined the impact of school-based variables, one of which was a count of extracurricular activities, on the development of political attitudes among a sample of over 700 Caucasian males surveyed repeatedly from their sophomore year in high school until 5 years after high school graduation. Controlling for socioeconomic status, intelligence, prior political attitudes, and other school-related variables (curriculum track, GPA, and educational aspirations), she reported that extracurricular participation had a weak but unexpected negative impact on adult political interest.

Dailey's (1983) findings are limited by the fact that her index of extracurricular involvement was a global, undifferentiated one. Less powerfully designed, nonlongitudinal studies suggest that type of extracurricular experience may make an important difference. Jennings (1974) studied the relationship of two extracurricular indexes—engagement in interscholastic competition (which included athletics, music, and speech–debate teams) and seeking of elective office—to political attitudes in 77 schools, using a sample of nearly 21,000 students and controlling for a wide variety of family background, community, and school-related variables. A unique feature of this study was the use of school rather than student as the unit of the analysis, an approach that controls for idiosyncratic school influences on the behavior of individual members of the sample (Hopkins 1982). Results revealed strong positive relationships between running for office and political efficacy and trust, while involvement in interschool competition was negatively associated with these variables. However, a reverse and inexplicable trend emerged for tendency to engage in political conversations: Engagement in interschool competition was positively associated with this index, while political office seeking was negatively predictive. In general, Jennings found that family socioeconomic status was a more powerful predictor of political attitudes than any school-based variable, but among school-related factors, extracurricular participation was more strongly related to political orientations than a variety of academic dimensions. Consequently, Jennings' study provides some support for the contention that nonacademic experiences are at least as important as academic ones in shaping positive political orientations. In fact, a number of investigations have established fairly strong connections between opportunities for peer interaction and adolescent political attitudes (see Ehman's 1980 review). Since the school's extracurricular milieu is a context in which extensive peer contact occurs, peer associations may be an important mechanism through which activity involvement exerts its impact on political beliefs.

Only a few studies have addressed the relationship between extracurricular involvement and actual political participation. Lewellen (1974) examined the impact of four school factors on the extent to which 1,800 high school students attending a special educational program in Washington, D.C., were politically active outside the school context (e.g., talked with others about politics, expressed political opinions by writing letters to newspapers and political officials, made campaign contributions, and worked for a political party or candidate). Two of the school influences were extracurricular—number of school organizational memberships and involvement in school partisan political activities (running for elective office, helping someone run for office, being a club officer or committee chairperson). The remaining two were academic—total number of social studies courses taken and student answers to the question of whether any such courses involved real political experiences, such as working in a local campaign or political action project. Controlling for seven potentially influential background variables (sex, race, socioeconomic status, rural-urban residence, school size, parental interest in politics, and exposure to political affairs through the mass media), Lewellen found extracurricular indexes to have small positive effects on political participation, whereas number of social studies courses exerted no impact. The strongest school-related predictor of student partisan political behavior was exposure to real political activities.

Two studies employing longitudinal data sets yield stronger associations between extracurricular involvement and political participation than those reported by Lewellen (1974). Hanks and Eckland (1978) and Hanks (1981) found that adolescent participation had both direct and indirect effects (mediated through adult membership in voluntary associations) on several political participation indexes, including tendency to vote, to participate actively in election campaigns, and to discuss political issues. Moreover, Hanks's analysis revealed that participation in adolescent "instrumental" organizations—those whose primary activities serve as a means to an end (e.g., student government, academic and vocational clubs) rather than ends in themselves (e.g., athletics, hobby clubs)—had the strongest impact on adult political behavior. This was especially true for campaign participation, the most effortful form of adult political involvement. Taken together, Hanks and Lewellen's results underscore the relevance of quality of students' learning experiences, rather than mere counts of organizational memberships, to student political development.

Finally, school climate and student political orientation are related. A variety of investigations show that schools encouraging student involvement in decision making also promote political trust, civic tolerance, and student negotiation rather than confrontational tactics to effect change (see Ehman 1980). As indicated earlier in this chapter, warm, open school climates are associated with intense extracurricular involvement, and the quality of extracurricular experiences in such schools may be especially effective in fostering positive attitudes and skills that transfer to the wider political arena. In this way, extracurricular experiences may be responsible for some or all of the association between school climate and political socialization, a possibility that merits future research.

Psychological Well-Being and Life Satisfaction

It is possible that adolescents who participate actively in the community life of their school are more satisfied with their general life circumstances than their less involved counterparts. Using *The High School and Beyond* 1980 sophomore data base and controlling for several demographic variables (sex, race, geographic region, and socioeconomic status), Trent and McPartland (1982) concluded that the impact of extracurricular participation on psychological well-being was much stronger than its effect on either self-esteem or sense of control over the environment. Interestingly, among black students the importance of activity involvement for all three of these outcome measures, but especially for sense of well-being, was substantially greater in desegregated than in segregated high schools. This finding suggests that participation takes on a very different psychological meaning for black students in racially mixed environments.

Different satisfactions also emanate from participation in large and small schools that may be responsible for the small-school self-esteem advantage reported earlier. Gump and Friesen (1964) asked high school juniors to indicate what they enjoyed about or got out of activity settings. In small schools, a greater number of responses dealt with developing competence (e.g., "Being in the junior play gave me more confidence"), surmounting challenge ("The magazine sale gave me a chance to see if I could be a good salesman"), engaging in important actions ("You are supporting your school"), contributing to group functioning ("For the school play, we worked together as a group, which I enjoyed very much"), and achieving worthwhile moral and cultural values ("I feel the basketball games bring people closer together"). In contrast, large-school students' gratifications were more passive, vicarious, and external. They more often mentioned the pleasures of watching others perform ("I like waiting to see who's beat"), affiliating with large crowds ("I could yell and have a good time with my friends"), opportunities for relaxation and distraction ("Watching something that interests me helps me to relax and takes my mind off small troubles"), and gaining points for participating. These school differences were traced to the greater proportion of small-school students occupying positions of responsibility and leadership. Most large- and small-school variations in satisfactions disappeared when investigators held setting position constant (Gump and Friesen 1964; Wicker 1968).

Little is known about the long-term impact of adolescent activity participation on individuals' satisfaction with the quality of their adult lives. Daniels and Wallace (1978) attempted to address this question with reference to college extracurricular involvement. A stratified random sample of alumni from a large southern university, half of whom had been heavy participants as undergraduates and half of whom had been uninvolved, were asked to respond to questionnaires about college experiences important to their life satisfaction 10 years after graduation. Findings revealed that participants rated college extracurricular participation as more important, while nonparticipants rated academic experiences as more important. The results of this study suggest that extracurricular involvement may have long-term psychological significance for at least some individuals—namely, those who were campus leaders and awards recipients. However, the investigators did not ascertain whether participants were actually more satisfied with their adult life circumstances than their nonparticipating counterparts.

Community Participation in Adulthood

Longitudinal investigations examining the extent to which adolescent extracurricular involvement is a determinant of adult community participation have come to remarkably similar conclusions. Otto (1976b) estimated the long-term stability of social participation from activities reported by males in the senior year of high school to community organizational memberships 15 years later, controlling for socioeconomic status, academic ability, and academic performance. The coefficient was .33, a substantial association in view of the extended time period between assessments. Moreover, tests of a complex path-analytic model designed to account for adult social involvement indicated that high school participation not only had a significant direct effect but also mediated a substantial proportion of the effect of the mother's education and academic performance on adult social integration. Among a host of adolescent and adult indicators of status attainment measured in this study, high school extracurricular participation had the strongest total effect on adult social involvement. In studies based on larger samples, Hanks and Eckland (1978) and Hanks (1981) replicated Otto's results and showed that they were valid for females as well. Also, Hanks's investigation, along with two additional studies, revealed that types of extracurricular involvement and accomplishment in high school were modestly but significantly correlated with similar areas of social participation and achievement during adulthood (Munday and Davis 1974; Roberts 1977).

The results described above are consistent with the idea that the high school extracurriculum is an important socialization context in which interpersonal skills are learned that facilitate community involvement and productive use of leisure time. However, it is still possible that the adolescent/adulthood participation connection is a function of some other underlying variable or process, such as a sociable personality, not entered into the path-analytic models tested above. Analyzing information obtained from *The High School and Beyond* 1972 data bank on nearly 9,000 seniors followed up 5 years after high school graduation, Lindsay (1984) expanded the range of antecedent variables entered into a model of how adolescent involvement affects adult participation by including a rough measure of adolescent sociability. In addition, Lindsay included size of the community in which the young adult resided, since community size has been found to affect adult participation in the same way that high school size affects student participation—namely, the smaller the community, the greater the social pressure on residents to become involved in its activities (Barker 1978). With these additional controls, both direct effects of high school involvement on adult participation and indirect effects, mediated in this case through educational attainment, persisted, supporting the conclusion that the extracurriculum has long-term consequences for voluntary participation in adult life.

Lindsay (1984) also addressed the question of whether smaller high schools, through their impact on high school involvement, promote adult community participation more effectively than larger ones. The school-size effect was very small, suggesting that participatory experiences in small high schools are not more effective precursors of adult community involvement. However, as is the case with most extracurricular outcome research, the participatory measures entered into Lindsay's analyses, as well as the other studies described above, were gross ones. No effort was made to search for linkages between specific qualities of high school participation, such as leadership experiences or breadth of activity involvement (known to be more prevalent in small than in large schools) and adult participatory behavior.

Occupational Attainment and Income

Evidence that high school extracurricular participation has long-term benefits for educational attainment has led to the hypothesis that it may also facilitate occupational achievement and income. Otto (1976a) found that high school activity involvement contributed modestly to occupational prestige in middle adulthood, mediating a small portion of the effect of background socioeconomic status. Nevertheless, the role of participation in influencing occupational attainment paled when compared to such academically related variables as intelligence and GPA, which played substantially greater roles. Interestingly, whereas academic ability and performance in high school had no impact on income in adulthood, the direct effect of high school participation on income was small but significant. Otto reasoned that interpersonal relations learned in the context of extracurricular involvement have some value in the occupational arena, as jobs with high prestige and high income generally require considerable skill in working with others. However, Hanks and Eckland's (1978) effort to replicate these findings was unsuccessful. Their path-analytic results revealed no direct effects of high school participation on either occupational prestige or income. Instead, the impact of participation was small and indirect, entirely mediated through educational attainment.

Although these findings are mixed and ambiguous, many employers report that they find information about extracurricular participation helpful when making hiring decisions, although they do not regard it as important as GPA, previous work experience, or specific courses taken (Bryan, Mann, Nelson, and North 1981). Much like academic course work, particular kinds of activities may be especially relevant for particular kinds of work, but as yet no studies have examined these fine-grained associations.

Summary

Research on consequences of extracurricular participation suffers from the same limitations as the correlational research literature addressing antecedents reviewed earlier in this chapter. Nevertheless, longitudinal evidence combined with well-controlled studies of single age sectors suggests that extracurricular participation has positive implications for many aspects of individual development, including academic performance, educational aspirations, school retention, prosocial personality characteristics, political attitudes and behavior, self-esteem, current psychological well-being and satisfaction, and future extracurricular and community participation. Findings are least conclusive with respect to whether participation prevents adolescent antisocial behavior or facilitates occupational attainment and income in adulthood. Research addressing the special benefits of athletics suggests that it has a salutary impact on the high school academic orientations of low-achieving students, although it is not as effective as nonathletic pursuits, such as service activities and student organization leadership roles. Moreover, the short-term status rewards of athletic involvement may promote unrealistically high educational aspirations without equipping students with the necessary skills for translating them into effective action. Finally, the limited evidence available on the special developmental value of participatory experiences in small high schools reveals advantages in the areas of self-esteem, affiliative tendencies, cognitive complexity in social situations, and current life satisfaction. Small- and large-school participants do not differ in college academic performance or in a number of additional personal-social characteristics that appear to be enhanced by extracurricular involvement.

Future studies need to pay far greater attention to the impact of variations in type and quality of extracurricular participation. In addition to assessments of the internal life of activity environments as they currently exist, intervention studies that examine the consequences of augmenting student participation and that systematically vary aspects of student extracurricular experience would add immeasurably to existing knowledge.

THE EXTRACURRICULUM AND SOCIETY

As indicated in earlier sections of this chapter, the literature on objectives and outcomes of extracurricular participation has repeatedly emphasized its special role in preparing young people for citizenship in a democracy. Yet the extracurriculum, like the school environment as a whole, not only affects but also reflects contemporary societal problems. Over the past 25 years, increased public attention has been devoted to the school's authority to regulate student participation in extracurricular activities. A variety of cases addressing student constitutional rights have reached the courts. Disputes have centered around First Amendment rights to free speech, press, and assembly and Fourteenth Amendment liberty, property, and due process guarantees.

Although the Supreme Court has identified school attendance as a property right under the First Amendment, debate continues over whether students have a comparable right to participate in the extracurriculum or whether participation is a privilege extended at the discretion of the school, which may establish entry and conduct requirements (Mondschein and Greene 1981). Court rulings have at times been contradictory, but most decisions have supported the position that judgments about participation should be left to the discretion of school officials, a perspective that sanctions extracurricular entry requirements like no pass–no play rules, discussed below. Student challenges to administrative decisions have, for the most part, been unsuccessful. In the majority of cases, courts have ruled that either no due process, or only minimal due process (e.g., prior notice of the rule, an explanation of the reason behind the school's action, and an opportunity for the student to tell his or her side of the story) need be accorded before removing a student from extracurricular activities or preventing a student from joining in the first place. However, school officials do not have complete free rein. Courts have been willing to step in where the most basic constitutional freedoms are at stake (Cromartie 1986; Strope 1984). Nevertheless, given the general reluctance of the courts to become involved, substantial variation exists in extracurricular regulations instituted by schools, and the consequences of these differences for student participatory behavior and development remain almost entirely uninvestigated. It is possible that negotiations between administrators and students over individual rights in the domain of the extracurriculum may be especially important for inculcating democratic attitudes and values and related styles of interpersonal behavior.

The sections below afford a brief look at the extracurriculum in its broader societal context. The focus is on efforts to redress social grievances by intervening in extracurricular programming. Where available, research evaluating the impact of such interventions is considered; where not, new lines of investigation are suggested.

No Pass–No Play: Academic Eligibility Requirements for Extracurricular Participation

High school extracurricular activities have come under close public scrutiny because of the increasing prevalence of rules requiring a minimum level of academic performance for participation in interscholastic sports, a trend encouraged by a number of recent developments in American education. In 1983, the National Collegiate Athletic Association (NCAA) adopted academic eligibility standards requiring incoming freshman athletes to have graduated from high school with a cumulative C average. The policy led many high schools to institute similar rules, in an effort to assure that their graduating athletes would qualify for college teams. In addition, the need for improved academic standards emphasized in recent reports on the quality of American education (Dossey et al. 1988; National Assessment of Educational Progress 1985; National Commission on Excellence in Education 1983) has stimulated many state legislatures, as well as state and local boards of education, to move toward no pass–no play rules and, in many instances, toward academic requirements for participating in any extracurricular pursuit (Joekel 1985).

Proponents of these measures believe that making extracurricular participation contingent on academic performance will motivate students to bring up their grades. Critics counter that such policies will prevent many low-income and ethnic minority students from developing their athletic and artistic talents and will also lower their morale. Opponents also point out that students who stand to benefit most from activities offering enhanced educational opportunities, such as school publications, drama, and debate, already tend not to join them. For such students, academic requirements would only institutionalize and exaggerate existing forms of extracurricular discrimination (Clark 1986; U.S. Office of Education 1986). Moreover, critics believe that excluding poorly achieving students because of low grades will remove the most important incentive they have for staying in school, thereby increasing dropout rates. In addition, it has been speculated that some students will be discouraged from enrolling in challenging courses for fear of losing their eligibility, that cheating will increase among those at risk for being excluded, and that classroom teachers who also sponsor extracurricular activities will offer less challenging courses and inflate students' grades (Frith and Clark 1984; Ostro 1980).

Most states have adopted minimum eligibility requirements for extracurricular participation. The National Federation of High School Activities recommends a base standard of at least four passing grades for the student's previous semester of attendance. At this writing, 31 states follow this guideline, 9 have imposed a more stringent rule, and 11 have less restrictive requirements (Brown 1988). Since some form of grade requirement for participating in the most prestigious extracurricular activities of sports, cheerleading, and student government existed in many school districts prior to the NCAA ruling (Horn 1972; Weber and McBee 1982), the current controversy focuses less on whether to have such requirements than it does on how stringent they should be (Brown 1988).

The groups hardest hit by C-average eligibility standards are black and Hispanic students. Recently, as part of a package of educational reforms, the Texas legislature adopted into law a rule prohibiting students with a grade below 70 in any academic class from participating in the extracurriculum. Demographic statistics were collected in 1985 at the end of the first 6-week grading period to which the law applied. Fifteen percent of all varsity athletes failed at least one course. Among subvarsity players, the rate was as high as 30 to 50 percent. Additional information obtained in 1986 showed that 35 percent of black and 38 percent of Hispanic students failed, compared to only 26 percent of whites (Cromartie 1986).

Aside from limited statistical information, there is virtually no research on the impact of academic eligibility requirements. The majority of authors expressing an opinion on the subject believe that imposing standards above the minimum will be counterproductive. But whether they actually result in dilution rather than strengthening of academic standards and promote cheating, school attrition, and restriction of extracurricular participation along social class and racial–ethnic lines is desperately in need of systematic study. Current variations in stringency of participation requirements across school districts and states offer contexts for comparative study of different academic criteria—for example, an average GPA for all courses or a passing grade in each course; a standard based on all courses or one based only on core academic courses; a requirement that applies to all extracurricular pursuits or one that applies only to the most prestigious and publicly visible of extraclass endeavors; and sanctions that range from complete suspension to suspension only from formal events to a probationary period that gives students a chance to rectify an inadequate academic record. In view of pressures exerted by special interest groups toward revision of NCAA eligibility requirements and current state and local regulations, answers to such questions would provide an alternative to totally opinion-based development of social policy in this area.

The Extracurriculum and Freedom of Religion and Speech

Court-ordered protection of First Amendment rights in the context of the extracurriculum has largely revolved around regulation of religious activities, student-initiated forums and public meetings, and school publications. With regard to religious pursuits, most cases have involved suits against school boards permitting the exercise of religion in public schools. In these instances, the courts have, for the most part, sided with plaintiffs and regarded prayer at school events to violate the constitutional mandate of separation of church and state. However, narrow exceptions have been recognized, as in graduation exercises, where ceremonial rather than educative functions predominate, and attendance of students is not required. In the 1980s came a series of different challenges—suits against schools that did not allow religious activities, rather than suits to stop them. For example, a number of cases involved attempts to organize voluntary prayer and Bible study groups and to have them recognized as official student activities. The courts upheld the decisions of school boards in all of these cases except one, where a federal district court arrived at the opposite conclusion, and the Supreme Court refused to review the decision (Strope 1984).

A similar contradictory message has been delivered with respect to freedom of speech and press at school. Until recently, students have enjoyed a high degree of court protection in these areas. Beginning with the 1969 landmark student expression case of *Tinker v. Des Moines Independent School District* (396 U.S. 864), virtually all court decisions protected students' rights to assemble, invite guest speakers, and discuss controversial topics. Although school officials could regulate the time, place, and manner of student expression, they were not permitted to control its content beyond the minimum necessary to ensure protection of the rights of others and maintain school discipline (Ornstein 1980). However, a 1988 ruling challenged these earlier decisions. In *Hazelwood School District v. Kuhlmeier* (108 U.S. 562) by a vote of 5 to 3 the Supreme Court granted school officials the right to exercise control over both the style and content of school-sponsored student publications. The majority opinion justified the ruling as a necessary means for ensuring that educators maintain control over the curriculum (of which the school newspaper was judged to be a part), shield young people from sensitive material (in this case, on adolescent pregnancy and parental divorce), and dissociate the institution from student expression that school officials find objectionable. Dissenting justices pointed out that the decision makes student publications, as well as other extracurricular forms of expression, vulnerable to flagrant censorship that can easily be justified as a benign effort on the part of school personnel to protect students from sensitive issues. Recent analyses of the opinion advise administrators to continue the prior tradition of exercising restraint in controlling the content of the student press (American School Board Journal 1988; Sendor 1988), for how schools choose to supervise such activities may teach powerful lessons in freedom versus oppression, responsible journalism, and legal and moral understanding (Fager 1978).

The turn against student rights in the context of the extracurriculum is part of a national trend toward restricting constitutional protections accorded children and youth. This rollback of basic freedoms may be due to the fact that public institutions, including schools and the juvenile justice system, have experienced a rash of youth violence and disciplinary problems in recent years. However, attempting to solve these problems by clamping down on student rights in an authoritarian fashion may have the unfortunate side effect of undermining adolescents' basic faith in the democratic process. A current danger is that an atmosphere will emerge in which American youth become cynical about the worth of democratic principles, rather than deeply appreciative of their value and the importance of protecting them (Melton 1987; Salamone 1989).

The Extracurriculum and Sex Equity in Education

Concerns about gender equality in the extracurriculum largely revolve around the substantially lower rates of female participation in athletics. The most recent nationally representative evidence available, based on the *High School and Beyond* sample of seniors surveyed in 1980, revealed that 64 percent of males but only 41 percent of females participated actively in school sports (Peng, Fetters, and Kolstad 1981). The male–female gap of 23 percent was substantial, although there was evidence of progress. This figure was reduced by more than a third when compared to a similar statistic compiled a decade earlier (36 percent).

Title IX of the Education Amendments of 1972 requires that educational institutions receiving federal funds provide equal opportunities for males and females to participate in educational programs and activities, including sports. Since its passage, services available to female athletes have expanded, and participation of girls on interscholastic athletic teams has become commonplace (Abrams 1982; East 1978). However, simply providing more opportunities does not change basic inequalities in school and community support for male and female athletics. Eder and Parker (1987) conducted an in-depth ethnographic study of student out-of-class experiences in a middle school, placing particular emphasis on athletic practices and games. They observed an almost total lack of interest in female sports both within and beyond the confines of the school. For example, audiences for such events rarely exceeded a handful spectators. The authors suggested that because of the low visibility accorded girls' athletics, females are not provided avenues for extracurricular achievement and peer and community status equivalent to those of males. Moreover, Eder and Parker's observations, as well as those of others (Kessler et al. 1985), indicate that interscholastic sport activities are important contexts in which endurance, competitiveness, assertiveness, and effective teamwork are taught, learning experiences less available to females because of the low stature of girls' athletics in schools. Consistent with this conclusion, some research indicates that interscholastic sports is defined more in affiliative than in competitive terms by adolescent girls than boys (Borman and Kurdek 1987). In view of these findings, besides providing more athletic opportunities, special attempts should be made to increase the external visibility and social importance of girls' interscholastic sports, and to document the consequences of such interventions for girls' psychosocial development.

The Extracurriculum and School Desegregation

Research suggests that students participating in interracial activities experience unique psychological and social benefits. As indicated in the section above on outcomes of extracurricular involvement, black participants in integrated schools show special enhancement of their sense of well-being. Also, both black and white students who have been active in the same extracurricular activities are more likely to report other-race friendships (Crain, Mahard, and Narot 1982; Patchen et al. 1977) and to continue to engage in cross-race interaction after entering college (Damico and Scott 1984).

Earlier in this chapter it was noted that, based on the most recent nationally representative survey data, there is no widespread evidence of white domination of extracurricular activities in interracial schools. At the same time, substantial differences among schools exist in the extent to which interracial mixing occurs in the extracurriculum (Crain et al. 1982; see Collins 1978 for an ethnographic description of racial segregation in student activities of an urban high school in the Deep South that persisted for 5 years after court-ordered desegregation). Some investigators have hypothesized that certain features of the school environment—namely, the enrollment balance of black and white students and the rapidity with which desegregation occurs—may affect the extent to which racially different students intermingle.

Findings on the relationship of student body racial composition to cross-race contact in the extracurriculum are contradictory. Comparing three schools in different stages of racial change, one of which was predominantly white, one racially balanced, and a third predominantly black, Gottlieb and TenHouten (1965) found that blacks were less involved in extracurricular activities in the mostly white school than in the racially balanced and black majority environments. For whites, both the racially balanced and black majority schools were associated with reduced extracurricular participation. Moreover, the low rate of cross-race friendship choices found in the balanced school suggested that despite school integration, two social systems divided along racial lines had emerged. Conflicting evidence was reported by St. John (1964), who observed that blacks enrolled in two high schools where they comprised only about 17 percent of the student body did not participate in fewer extracurricular activities than their white peers.

Dardan and Jacob (1981) hypothesized that the disparity in these early findings may have been due to the desegregation history of the schools studied. They pointed out that Gottlieb and TenHouten (1965) chose schools undergoing rapid change in racial balance, whereas St. John selected schools where the transition was gradual. Analyzing participation rates reflected in yearbook pictures of six high schools, three of which had undergone relatively rapid change in racial composition and three of which had experienced slow change, Dardan and Jacob found no support for the supposition that rapid desegregation leads to greater racial segregation in school activities, although rapidly changing schools did show an overall lower level of extracurricular involvement by both blacks and whites than did gradually changing environments.

It is possible that black student participation in integrated settings increases over time, irrespective of the racial balance and rapidity of desegregation in the school. In support of this idea, Hall and Gentry (1969) questioned 377 black students attending 16 different integrated high schools in a southeastern state and found that black student participation rose with each year of attendance, from 58 percent in the first year to 61 percent in the second year to 71 percent in the third. Also, with the passage of time an increasingly larger percentage of black students responded affirmatively to the question of whether they had been invited by white classmates to participate in school activities. These findings suggest that racial isolation has a tendency to subside as students (and the community at large) become accustomed to a biracial school environment.

Additional research indicates that the internal social organization of the school plays a crucial role in the success of extracurricular integration. According to Allport (1954), several factors must be present to promote positive intergroup contact: (1) the members of both groups must have equal social status; (2) the environment must engender cooperative interaction in the service of shared goals; and (3) authority figures must be supportive of interracial interaction. Research in elementary school classrooms reveals that these conditions are highly successful in producing cross-race peer acceptance (Johnson, Johnson, and Maruyama 1984). However, there may be fewer opportunities for these qualities of social organization to develop in the secondary school formal curriculum, where classroom resegregation due to curriculum tracking and ability grouping is a more serious problem than it is in the lower grades (Trent 1980). Consequently, the extracurriculum may be the single most effective arena the high school has for improving race relations, since many extracurricular endeavors may spontaneously engender cooperative interaction and equal social status among students of different racial-ethnic backgrounds. Unfortunately, there are no systematic observational studies of teacher-student and student-student interaction in the domain of the extracurriculum of any sort, let alone ones aimed at determining how patterns of communication among racially and ethnically different youngsters vary from the formal classroom to the extracurriculum, or from one extracurricular activity to another.

The Extracurriculum and Mainstreaming of the Handicapped

Section 504 of the Rehabilitation Act of 1973 mandates that in institutions receiving federal financial assistance, handicapped students capable of participating in school activities should be provided with opportunities to do so in the same settings as their nonhandicapped peers. Separate or different experiences are to be offered only if they are consistent with the educational needs and abilities of the handicapped youngster. The few court cases calling for interpretation of this act with respect to the extracurriculum all involve athletic participation, and the decisions rendered are divided in terms of whether they have sided with handicapped plaintiffs or school officials. In one case, a school's policy of prohibiting students with vision in only one eye from engaging in contact sports was judged not to violate the Rehabilitation Act or the Fourteenth Amendment, since it was justified by the high risk of eye injury in such activities. In another case, a student who had established residency with his grandparents was granted the right to participate in interscholastic athletics in a school system other than the one in which his parents resided. The court argued that because of the youth's emotional problems, there were compelling reasons for living with the grandparents as well as for athletic participation (Abbott 1980). Concern has also been expressed about the extent to which no pass–no play policies may bar many otherwise eligible handicapped students, especially those in mainstreamed classrooms, from extracurricular activities (e.g., Frith and Clark 1984). However, at least some established rules, such as the Texas legislation discussed earlier, recognize the potential problem and exempt these youngsters from compliance (Cromartie 1986).

Despite supportive legislation, there is no broad-based information available on the extent to which handicapped youngsters actually participate in school activities and on how they are received by nonhandicapped peers. Limited evidence on learning disabled adolescents suggests that despite widespread mainstreaming of these students into regular classrooms, they engage in very few extracurricular pursuits. In one study, learning disabled students reported participating in such activities less than once per month, whereas their normally achieving counterparts participated on a weekly basis and spent three times as many hours per week immersed in the extracurriculum (Deshler, Schumaker, Alley, Warner, and Clark 1981). Sarkees (1983) has observed that despite a 90 percent increase in handicapped students enrolling in vocational curricular tracks in the decade following passage of the Rehabilitation Act of 1972, there has been a lack of parallel participation in vocational student organizations.

A common assumption in much of the literature on youngsters with mild handicapping conditions is that they are deficient in social skills, a characteristic that could contribute to their diminished involvement in the out-of-class life of the school. Whereas there is good evidence that mainstreamed mildly retarded and learning disabled elementary school pupils suffer from social inadequacies when compared to their normal classmates (Bryan and Bryan 1981; Taylor, Asher, and Williams 1987), the evidence is not as clear on older-aged handicapped youth. By adolescence, many may have caught up with their peers in the social realm (Deshler et al. 1981). Whether lower rates of participation of these students have their origins in social incompetencies, in lack of encouragement by administrators and teachers, or in inadequate support services to accommodate their special needs merits investigation. In addition, the immediate and long-term consequences of participation for the social and academic development of handicapped youth is yet another entirely uncharted area of study.

CONCLUSIONS AND FUTURE DIRECTIONS

Extracurricular activities proliferated in secondary schools in the early part of this century because of the widespread belief that public education in a new industrial age should direct its attention to the development of facets of the individual other than just academic knowledge. Today, the extracurriculum continues to thrive as a prime context at the secondary educational level for nurturing prosocial values and behavior, individual interests and talents, and worthwhile use of leisure time.

An analysis of the published literature cited in this chapter indicates that a rise in systematic research on antecedents and consequences of extracurricular participation occurred during the decade of the 1970s, largely conducted by sociologists interested in exploring its causal role in the status attainment process. This flourish of research activity did not persist through the 1980s. In fact, a lull in systematic inquiry has occurred during the past 10 years, perhaps because of the recent preoccupation of educational researchers with the quality of the American formal academic program. Consequently, recent advances in knowledge have been minimal, and only a few recently published investigations have directly extended the work of the earlier time period.

In addition, research on the extracurriculum does not display the same breadth of theoretical perspectives and methodologies that have permeated investigations of student experiences in formal classrooms. Instead, it has been largely limited to gross estimates of degree of involvement and similarly global antecedent and consequent student conditions. The comprehensive review of the empirical literature presented in this chapter yielded few ethnographic accounts and not one systematic observational study aimed at discerning the quality of students' experiences with peers, teachers, and instructional tasks in extracurricular activities. The current state of knowledge is analogous to that which prevailed in the 1960s and early 1970s for the formal aspects of schooling. During that time period, researchers' preoccupation with a narrow range of school characteristics and student outcome variables, such as expenditures per child, teacher-student ratios, and achievement test scores (e.g., Coleman et al. 1966; Jencks et al. 1972), led them to underestimate the impact of school experiences on student development. Once investigators turned to the study of the school as a complex social system in which the joint impact of physical resources, educational philosophies, teacher-student interaction patterns, and community contexts was explored, it became apparent that schooling exerted powerful influences on many aspects of individual development (Minuchin and Shapiro 1983). This chapter calls for a similar expansion of inquiry in the domain of the extracurriculum.

Despite the limitations of existing knowledge, the weight of current evidence indicates that extracurricular activities contribute in vital ways to adolescent development and that they do not, as has often been assumed, undermine students' commitment to the academic side of secondary school life. In fact, research suggests the existence of bidirectional relationships between participation and a variety of academic and psychosocial outcomes, including school achievement, educational aspirations, self-esteem, political attitudes, and personality characteristics. In other words, students advantaged in these qualities tend to be attracted to and/or encouraged into the extracurriculum to a greater extent than their less advantaged schoolmates, and they benefit further from extracurricular opportunities. Moreover, extracurricular participation is related to higher school retention rates, promotes students' current sense of well-being and life satisfaction, and carries over to community participation in adulthood.

The existing body of research provides sufficient justification for encouraging nonparticipating students, particularly those at risk for social and academic problems, to become involved in extracurricular activities. However, research documenting the efficacy of such interventions is badly needed. Other areas identified in this chapter as requiring further study include (1) the impact of larger social-contextual factors, such as community priorities and school administrative practices, on extracurricular offerings, student participation, and developmental outcomes; (2) research designs permitting more effective separation of extracurricular antecedents and consequents, including continuous longitudinal assessments of students prior to, during, and subsequent to participation, as well as experimental and quasi-experimental manipulations of participation; (3) meta-analyses that synthesize existing findings on extracurricular antecedents and consequents; (4) more definitive work on the comparative advantages and liabilities of small-school versus large-school extracurricular experiences; and (5) increased attention to process measures of participation, including student perceptions of extracurricular experiences, length and type of activity involvement, and quality of sponsor-student and student-student relationships. In addition, practically no research exists to guide ongoing policy development in the realm of the extracurriculum, such as the establishment of academic eligibility requirements for participation, efforts to mainstream handicapped youngsters into student activities, or attempts to provide equal extracurricular opportunities to male and female students and to students of different racial-ethnic backgrounds.

Although the value of the extracurriculum is appreciated by educators and the general public alike, it nevertheless continues to be regarded as a peripheral feature of American education. For example, analyses of student activities have been entirely overlooked in recent national reports on the quality and condition of American education. Moreover, the extracurriculum is often placed in the unfortunate position of having to compete with the academic curriculum for scarce institutional resources. Many teachers feel overburdened by the roles and responsibilities of extracurricular sponsorship, which drain time and energy away from central instructional concerns (Mendez 1984). Faced with funding cutbacks, school boards across the nation immediately address the possibility of eliminating costly extracurricular offerings. Activities most often curtailed may be precisely those identified in research as most supportive of the academic mission of the school—namely, nonathletic class-related organizations and school and community service pursuits. Given the positive contributions of extracurricular activities to the quality of students' everyday life in school and to their academic and social development, it seems wise to exercise caution before substantially reducing or eliminating them. At the same time, applied research on the impact of policies aimed at alleviating curricular and extracurricular conflict, such as mandatory student activity fees instituted in times of economic retrenchment, scheduling of activities in ways that reduce interference with academic instruction, and compensations accorded faculty for extracurricular sponsorship, would assist school personnel in making sound decisions that support the breadth and quality of both curricular and extracurricular offerings.

In view of the widespread image of the extracurriculum as worthwhile but expendable, research documenting its value is especially crucial for its continued survival and development, particularly in an era in which the quality of

American formal education has been judged to require time-consuming and costly reforms. In addition to summarizing the existing state of knowledge, a major purpose of this chapter has been to inspire a new wave of educational research on characteristics, functioning, and developmental consequences of student activities in the final decade of the 20th century.

References

Abbott, Jeff H. 1980. "The Developing Case Law of Public School Extracurricular Activities. In *School Law in Contemporary Society*, edited by M. A. McGhehey, 233–243. Topeka, KS: National Organization on Legal Problems of Education.

Abrams, Mary. 1982. Title IX—A modest success. *Graduate Woman* 76 (January/February): 23–25.

Aivoldi, Norman, Barbara Peterson, and Dwight Webb. 1967. Junior high school athletes excel in scholarship. *Personnel and Guidance Journal* 45 (June): 1021–1024.

Allen, Howard W., and Bruce Gansneder. 1976. Student perceptions about student activities. *High School Journal* 55 (October): 10–16.

Allport, Gordon. 1954. *The Nature of Prejudice*. New York: Addison-Wesley.

American School Board Journal. 1988. Civics or censorship: It's your choice. *American School Board Journal* 175 (April): 12.

Andrews, J. C. 1971. Personality, sporting interest and achievement. *Educational Review* 23 (February): 126–134.

Baird, Leonard L. 1969. Big school, small school: A critical examination of the hypothesis. *Journal of Educational Psychology* 60 (August): 253–260.

Bardley, Rosella M. Hughes. 1977. "A Study of the Relationship Between School Attendance Patterns, Attitude Toward School, Self-Concept, and Activities Participation Among Junior High Students." Ph.D. dissertation, Catholic University of America, Washington, DC.

Barker, Roger G. 1978. *Habitats, Environments, and Human Behavior*. San Francisco, CA: Jossey-Bass.

Barker, Roger G. and Paul V. Gump. 1964. *Big School, Small School: High School Size and Student Behavior*. Stanford, CA: Stanford University Press.

Bartel, Nettie R. 1971. Locus of control and achievement in middle-class and lower-class children. *Child Development* 42 (October): 1099–1107.

Battle, Esther S., and Julian B. Rotter. 1963. Children's feeling of personal control as related to social class and ethnic group. *Journal of Personality* 31 (December): 482–490.

Beacham, Herbert C. 1980. *Reading and Helping High School Dropouts and Potential School Leavers*. Tallahassee: Florida A and M University.

Bell, James W. 1967. A comparison of dropouts and non-dropouts on participation in school activities. *Journal of Educational Research* 60 (February): 248–251.

Bender, David S. 1978, March. "Extracurricular Activities and Achievement Orientation of Adolescent Males and Females." Paper presented at the annual meeting of the American Educational Research Association, Toronto, Ontario.

Berk, Laura E., and Barbara L. Goebel. 1987a. High school size and [illegible] a study of a small college environment. *Environment and Behavior* 19 (January): 53–76.

Berk, Laura E., and Barbara L. Goebel. 1987b. Patterns of extracurricular participation from high school to college. *American Journal of Education* 95 (May): 468–485.

Block, Jeanne H. 1983. Differential premises arising from differential socialization of the sexes: Some conjectures. *Child Development* 54 (December): 1335–1354.

Blyth, Dale A., Roberta G. Simmons, and Diane Bush. 1978. The transition into early adolescence: A longitudinal comparison of youth in two educational contexts. *Sociology of Education* 51 (July): 149–162.

Borman, Kathryn M., and Lawrence A. Kurdek. 1987. Gender differences associated with playing high school varsity soccer. *Journal of Youth and Adolescence* 16 (August): 379–400.

Botkin, Alice Sinclair. 1910. The relation of outside interests to major subjects in the high school. *Education* 31 (October): 103–107.

Bourgon, J. Kenneth. 1967. Which students are active? *School Activities* 38 (May): 15.

Brown, John W. 1988. Should eligibility standards go beyond minimum requirements? *NASSP Bulletin* 72 (April): 46–49.

Bryan, Tanis H., and James H. Bryan. 1981. "Some Personal and Social Experiences of Learning Disabled Children." In *Advances in Special Education*, edited by Barbara Keough, 147–186. Greenwich, CT: JAI Press.

Bryan, William A., Greg T. Mann, Robert B. Nelson, and Richard A. North. 1981. The co-curricular transcript—what do employers think? A national survey. *NASPA Journal* 19 (Summer): 29–36.

Bullock, Kenneth Vernon. 1965. Certain Characteristics of Participants and Nonparticipants in Extracurricular School Activities. Ph.D. dissertation, University of Southern California, Los Angeles.

Burbach, Harold J. 1972. An empirical study of powerlessness among high school students. *High School Journal* 55 (April): 343–354.

Burton, Joel I. 1973. Participation and college aspirations: Complex effects of community size. *Rural Sociology* 38 (Spring): 7–16.

Buser, Robert L., and William L. Humm. 1980. *Special Report on Co-curricular Offerings and Participation*. Springfield: Illinois State Board of Education.

Buser, Robert L., Ruth Long, and Hewey Tweedy. 1975. The who, what, why, and why not of student activity participation. *Phi Delta Kappan* 57 (October): 124–126.

Butcher, Janice. 1983. Socialization of adolescent girls into physical activity. *Adolescence* 28 (Winter): 753–766.

Campbell, W. J. 1964. "Some Effects of High School Consolidation." In *Big School, Small School: High School Size and Student Behavior*, edited by Roger G. Barker and Paul V. Gump, 139–153. Stanford, CA: Stanford University Press.

Campbell, W. J., J. L. Cotterell, N. M. Robinson, and D. R. Sadler. 1981. Effects of school size upon some aspects of personality. *Journal of Educational Administration* 19 (Summer): 201–231.

Clark, Vernon L. [illegible] *Journal of Negro Education* 55 (Spring): 162–170.

Coleman, James S. 1961. *The Adolescent Society*. Glencoe, IL: Free Press.

Coleman, James S., Ernest Q. Campbell, Carol J. Hobson, James McPartland, Alexander M. Mood, Frederic D. Weinfeld, and

Robert L. York. 1966. *Equality of Educational Opportunity*. Washington, DC: Government Printing Office.

Coleman, James S., Thomas Hoffer, and Sally Kilgore. 1981. *Public and Private Schools*. A report to the National Center for Education Statistics. Chicago: National Opinion Research Center.

Collins, Thomas W. 1978. Reconstructing a high school society after court-ordered desegregation. *Anthropology and Education Quarterly* 9 (Winter): 248–257.

Connell, William Fraser. 1980. *A History of Education in the Twentieth Century World*. New York: Teachers College, Columbia University.

Connor, Tom. 1954. Varsity athletes make superior scholars. *Scholastic Coach* 24 (November): 56–57.

Conyne, Robert K. 1983a, March. "CORE Conditions for Student Organization Development." Paper presented at the annual meeting of the American College Personnel Association, Houston, TX.

Conyne, Robert K. 1983b, March. "The CORE Model to Student Organization Development." Paper presented at the annual meeting of the American College Personnel Association, Houston, TX.

Craig, Paul L., and Richard A. Pasewark. 1981. Extracurricular participation in a rural boom town. *Journal of Rural Community Psychology* 2 (Fall): 12–22.

Crain, Robert L., Rita E. Mahard, and Ruth E. Narot. 1982. *Making Desegregation Work: How Schools Create Social Climates*. Cambridge, MA: Ballinger.

Cromartie, Martha. 1986. No pass–no play: Academic requirements for extracurricular activities. *School Law Bulletin* 17 (Fall): 13–18.

Cross, Michael, and Richard Moreland. 1985, May. "Sex Differences in Group Memberships." Paper presented at the annual meeting of the Midwestern Psychological Association, Chicago.

Cuccia, Nick J. 1981. Sociopolitical attitude differences between school activity participants and nonparticipants. *Adolescence* 16 (Winter): 871–880.

Dailey, Ann Ricks. 1983. Educational attainment and political attitudes: An effect of schools and schooling? *Theory and Research in Social Education* 9 (Summer): 35–52.

Damico, Sandra Bowman, and Elois Skeen Scott. 1984. Role of extracurricular activities in the promotion of cross-race contact by white students from high school to college. *Urban Review* 16 (November): 165–176.

Daniels, Jack L., and Dan Wallace. 1978. A comparative follow-up study of life satisfaction and college impact on college leaders and non-leaders ten years after graduation. *Southern Journal of Educational Research* 12 (Summer): 161–172.

Dardan, Joe T., and Susan Jacob. 1981. Court-ordered desegregation and extracurricular activities: Impact on racial participation and segregation in high school clubs and organizations. *Urban Education* 16 (April): 37–64.

Dawis, René V., and Yong H. Sung. 1984. The relationship of participation in school activities to abilities and interests in a high school student sample. *Journal of Vocational Behavior* 24 (April): 159–168.

Dawson, Richard E., and Kenneth Prewitt. 1969. *Political Socialization*. Boston, MA: Little, Brown.

Dee, M. Barbara. 1928. Extra-curriculum sctivities in Massachusetts high schools. *School Review* 36 (January): 44–47.

Demitroff, John F. 1974. Student persistence. *College and University* 49 (Summer): 553–567.

Deshler, Donald D., Jean B. Schumaker, Gordon R. Alley, Michael M. Warner, and Frances L. Clark. 1981. "Social Interaction Deficits in Learning Disabled Adolescents—Another Myth?" In *Bridges to Tommorow, vol. 2. The Best of ACLD*, edited by William M. Cruickshank and Archie A. Silver, 57–65. Syracuse, NY: Syracuse University Press.

Dewey, John. 1916. *Democracy and Education*. New York: Macmillan.

Doss, David A. 1986, April. "Ninth Grade Course Enrollment and Dropping Out." Paper presented at the annual meeting of the American Educational Research Association, San Francisco, CA.

Dossey, John A., Ina V. S. Mullis, Mary M. Lindquist, and Donald L. Chambers. 1988. *The Mathematics Report Card: Are We Measuring Up?* Princeton, NJ: Educational Testing Service.

Dowell, Linus, John Badgett, and Richard Hunkler. 1972. The relationship between high school athletic achievement and the variables of self-concept and academic achievement. *Psychology* 9 (November): 48–52.

Downey, Ronald G. 1978. Differences between entering freshmen from different size high schools. *Journal of College Student Personnel* 19 (July): 353–358.

Draeger, Russell, Jr. 1972. "Increasing Student Participation in Student Activities." Ph.D. dissertation, University of Wisconsin, Madison.

East, Elizabeth R. 1978. "Federal Civil Rights Legislation and Sport." In *Women and Sport: From Myth to Reality*, edited by C. A. Oglesby, 205–219. Philadelphia, PA: Lea and Febiger.

Eder, Donna, and Stephen Parker. 1987. The cultural production and reproduction of gender: The effect of extracurricular activities on peer-group culture. *Sociology of Education* 60 (July): 200–213.

Ehman, Lee H. 1980. The American school in the political socialization process. *Review of Educational Research* 50 (Spring): 99–119.

Eidsmore, Russell M. 1963. High school athletes are brighter. *School Activities* 35 (November): 75–77.

Eitzen, D. Stanley. 1975. Athletics in the status system of male adolescents. A replication of Coleman's *The Adolescent Society*. *Adolescence* 10 (Summer): 267–276.

Erikson, Erik H. 1950. *Childhood and Society*. New York: Norton.

Erikson, Erik H. 1968. *Identity: Youth and Crisis*. New York: Norton.

Eyler, Janet. 1982. A model relating political attitudes to participation in high school activities. *Theory and Research in Social Education* 10 (Spring): 43–62.

Eylon, Bat-Sheva, Avi Hofstein, Netta Maoz, and Moshe Rishpon. 1985. Extracurricular science courses: Filling a gap in school science education. *Research in Science and Technological Education* 3 (May): 81–89.

Fager, Christopher. 1978. The emerging student press. *Update on Law-related Education* 2 (Winter): 23–26.

Faunce, Roland C. 1960. "Extracurricular Activities." In *Encyclopedia of Educational Research*, edited by Chester W. Harris, 506–511. New York: Macmillan.

Feltz, Deborah L., and Maureen R. Weiss. 1984. The impact of girls' interscholastic sport participation on academic orientation. *Research Quarterly for Exercise and Sport* 55 (December): 332–339.

Finn, J. D. 1989. Withdrawing from school. *Review of Educational Research* 59, 117–142.

Fischler, M. L. 1975–1976. Drug usage in rural, small town New England. *Journal of Altered States of Consciousness* 2(2): 171–183.

Frederick, Robert W. 1959. *The Third Curriculum*. New York: Appleton-Century-Crofts.

Fretwell, Elbert K. 1931. *Extracurricular Activities in Secondary Schools*. Boston, MA: Houghton Mifflin.

Frith, Greg H., and Reba Clark. 1984. Extracurricular activities: Academic incentives or nonessential functions? *The Clearing House* 57 (March): 325–327.

Gade, Eldon, and Lois Peterson. 1980. A comparison of working and nonworking high school students on school performance, socioeconomic status, and self-esteem. *Vocational Guidance Quarterly* 29 (September): 65–69.

Galiardo, Ronald John. 1982. "A Study of Seventh and Eighth Grade Student Feelings about Instructional Activities in District 202, Lisle, Illinois." Ed.D. dissertation, University of Illinois, Urbana-Champaign.

Gallup, George H. 1978. The 10th annual Gallup Poll of the public's attitude toward the public schools. *Phi Delta Kappan* 60 (September): 33–45.

Gallup, George H. 1985. The 17th annual Gallup Poll of the public's attitude toward the public schools. *Phi Delta Kappan* 67 (September): 35–47.

Garbarino, James. 1980. Some thoughts on school size and its effects on adolescent development. *Journal of Youth and Adolescence* 9 (February): 19–31.

Gholson, Ronald E. 1979. Extracurricular activities: Different perceptions but strong support. *Phi Delta Kappan* 61 (September): 67–60.

Gholson, Ronald E., and Robert L. Buser. 1981. Student activities: A guide for determining who is participating in what. *NASSP Bulletin* 65 (May): 43–47.

Gholson, Ronald E., and Robert L. Buser. 1983. *Co-curricular Activity Programs in Secondary Schools.* Reston, VA: National Association of Secondary School Principals.

Gibbons, Stephen, Mary Lou Wylie, Linnis Echterling, and Joan French. 1986. Patterns of alcohol use among rural and small-town adolescents. *Adolescence* 21 (Winter): 887–900.

Giroux, Terry. 1984. *The Mood of American Youth.* Reston VA: National Association of Secondary School Principals.

Gorton, Richard A. 1976. How to run an efficient and effective student activities program. *NASSP Bulletin* 60 (December): 69–76.

Gottlieb, David, and Warren D. TenHouten. 1965. Racial composition and the social systems of three high schools. *Journal of Marriage and the Family* 27 (May): 204–212.

Grabe, Mark D. 1975. "Big School, Small School: Impact of the High School Environment." Ph.D. dissertation, Iowa State University, Ames.

Grabe, Mark D. 1976. Big school, small school: Impact of the high school environment. *Contemporary Educational Psychology* 1 (Spring): 20–25.

Grabe, Mark D. 1981. School size and the importance of school activities. *Adolescence* 16 (Spring): 21–31.

Grabe, Mark D., and R. Michael Latta 1977. *School Size and School Press: Attempts to Quantify Differences in the High School Environment.* ERIC Document Reproduction Service, no. 138 380.

Grady, Joan B. 1981. *Student Activities . . . An Extension of the Curriculum.* Reston, VA: National Association of Secondary School Principals.

Graham, Grace. 1969. "Student Organizations and Activities: Elementary and Secondary." In *Encyclopedia of Educational Research*, edited by Robert Ebel, 1367–1376. New York: [illegible]

Gump, Paul V. 1981. Adolescence and the significance of function. *Character* 3 (November): 1–4.

Gump, Paul V., and Wallace V. Friesen. 1964. "Satisfactions Derived from Nonclass Settings." In *Big School, Small School: High School Size and Student Behavior*, edited by Roger G. Barker and Paul V. Gump, 75–93. Stanford, CA: Stanford University Press.

Gutowski, Thomas W. 1988. Student initiative and the origins of the high school extracurriculum: Chicago, 1880–1915. *History of Education Quarterly* 28 (Spring): 49–72.

Haensly, Patricia A., Ann E. Lupkowski, and Elaine P. Edlind 1986. The role of extracurricular activities in education. *High School Journal* 69 (January): 110–119.

Hall, G. Stanley. 1904. *Adolescence.* Vol. 1–2. New York: Appleton-Century-Crofts.

Hall, Morrill M., and Harold W. Gentry. 1969. Isolation of Negro students in integrated public schools. *Journal of Negro Education* 38 (Spring): 156–161.

Halleck, Reuben Post. 1902. "The Social Side of High-School Life." In *National Education Association Addresses and Proceedings* 41 (July): 459–461.

Hanks, Michael. 1981. Youth, voluntary associations and political socialization. *Social Forces* 60 (1981): 211–223.

Hanks, Michael, and Bruce K. Eckland. 1976. Athletics and social participation in the educational attainment process. *Sociology of Education* 49 (October): 271–294.

Hanks, Michael, and Bruce K. Eckland. 1978. Adult voluntary associations and adolescent socialization. *Sociological Quarterly* 19 (Summer): 481–490.

Harter, Susan. 1983. "Developmental Perspectives on the Self-System." In *Handbook of Child Psychology. Vol. 4. Socialization, Personality, and Social Development*, edited by E. Mavis Hetherington, 275–385. New York: Wiley.

Heath, Douglas H. 1970. Student alienation and school. *School Review* 78 (August): 515–528.

Hedgpeth, Walker David. 1981. "A Comparison among Students' Extracurricular Involvement, School Attendance, Grade Point Average, and Other Selected Variables as Measured in Four Large Urban High Schools in Texas." Ed.D. dissertation, East Texas State University, Commerce.

Hewitt, John D., and William S. Johnson. 1979. Dropping out in Middletown. *The High School Journal* 62 (March): 252–256.

Hiss, William C., Elizabeth C. Woodcock, and Alice C. McGrath. 1984. (At least) 20 questions: Academic criteria, personal qualities, and college admissions. *Journal of College Admissions* 104 (Spring): 3–6.

Holland, Alyce, and Thomas Andre. 1987. Participation in extracurricular activities in secondary school: What is known, What needs to be known. *Review of Educational Research* 57 (Winter): 437–466.

Hollingshead, August B. 1949. *Elmstown's Youth.* New York: Wiley.

Hopkins, Kenneth D. 1982. The unit of analysis: Group means versus individual observations. *American Educational Research Journal* 19 (Spring): 5–18.

Horn, Gunnar. 1972. Extracurricular activities—Right or privilege? *Today's Education* 61 (May): 45.

Hynes, Kevin, William B. Richardson, and William Asher. 1986. Project TALENT revisited: Cross-validating self-report measures of leadership. *Journal of Experimental Education* 47 (Winter): 106–111.

Ichilov, Orit, and Michael Chen. 1978. A comparison of school-club activity in two educational frameworks. *Educational Research* [illegible]

Igra, A., and R. Moos. 1979. Alcohol use among college students: Some competing hypotheses. *Journal of Youth and Adolescence* 8 (December): 393–405.

Jencks, Christopher S., Marshall Smith, Henry Acland, Mary Jo Bane, David Cohen, Herbert Gintis, Barbara Heyns, and Stephan

Michelson. 1972. *Inequality: A Reassessment of the Effects of Family and Schooling in America*. New York: Basic Books.

Jennings, M. Kent. 1974. An aggregate analysis of home and school effects on political socialization. *Social Science Quarterly* 55 (September): 394–410.

Joekel, Ronald G. 1985. Student activities and academic eligibility requirements. *NASSP Bulletin* 69 (October): 3–9.

Johnson, David W., Roger T. Johnson, and Geoffrey Maruyama. 1984. "Goal Interdependence and Interpersonal Attraction in Heterogeneous Classrooms: A Meta-Analysis." In *The Psychology of Desegregation*, edited by Norman Miller and Marilyn B. Brewer, 187–212. New York: Academic Press.

Johnson, Franklin Winslow. 1909. The social organization of the high school. *The School Review* 17 (December): 665–680.

Jones, Galen. 1935. *Extra-Curricular Activities in Relation to the Curriculum*. New York: Teachers College, Columbia University.

Jordan, Riverda Harding. 1928. *Extra-classroom Activities in Elementary and Secondary Schools*. New York: Crowell.

Jung, Christian W., and William H. Fox. 1952. *Extracurricular Activities in Indiana High Schools: The Club Program*. Bloomington: Indiana University School of Education.

Kandel, Isaac Leon. 1933. *Comparative education*. Boston, MA: Houghton Mifflin.

Kapferrer, Judith. 1978. Social control and the extracurriculum. *Australian Journal of Education* 22 (October): 262–276.

Kataoka, Tokuo. 1985. *The Influence of Class Management and Student Guidance upon Academic Work at the Elementary and Lower Secondary Education Levels in Japan*. Report to the Office of Educational Research and Improvement. Washington, DC: Government Printing Office.

Keller, Paul G. W. 1905. Open school organizations. *The School Review* 13 (January): 10–13.

Kessler, S., D. Ashenden, R. Connell, and G. Dowsett. 1985. Gender relations in secondary schooling. *Sociology of Education* 58 (January): 34–47.

Kilzer, Louis, Harold H. Stephenson, and H. Orville Nordberg. 1956. *Allied Activities in the Secondary School*. New York: Harper.

Kleinert, E. John. 1969. Effects of high school size on student activity participation. *NASSP Bulletin* 53 (March): 34–46.

Koos, Leonard V. 1926. "Analysis of the General Literature on Extra-Curricular Activities." In *Twenty-fifth Yearbook of the National Society for the Study of Education*, edited by Guy Montrose Whipple, 9–22. Bloomington, IL: Public School.

Krug, Edward A. 1964. *The Shaping of the American High School*. New York: Harper & Row.

Landers, Daniel M., Deborah L. Feltz, George E. Obermeier, and Thomas R. Brouse. 1978. Socialization via interscholastic athletics: Its effects on educational attainment. *Research Quarterly* 49 (December): 475–483.

Landers, Daniel M., and Donna M. Landers. 1978. Socialization via interscholastic athletics: Its effects on delinquency. *Sociology of Education* 51 (October): 299–303.

LeGault, Dorothy Ann Lea. 1985. "An Analysis of the Relationship of One- and Two-Parent Family Students with Junior High School Academic Achievement, Attendance, Discipline, and Extracurricular Participation." Ph.D. dissertation, University of Minnesota, Minneapolis.

Leonardson, Gary R. 1986. The relationship between self-concept and selected academic and personal factors. *Adolescence* 21 (Summer): 467–474.

Lewellen, James R. 1974, November. "Adolescent Political Education and Political Participation." Paper presented at the National Council for the Social Studies meeting, Chicago.

Lindsay, Paul. 1982. The effect of high school size on student participation, satisfaction, and attendance. *Educational Evaluation and Policy Analysis* 4 (Spring): 57–65.

Lindsay, Paul. 1984. High school size, participation in activities, and young adult social participation: Some enduring effects of schooling. *Educational Evaluation and Policy Analysis* 6 (Spring): 73–83.

Long, Ruth, Robert Buser, and Michael Jackson. 1977. *Student Activities in the Seventies: A Survey Report*. Reston, VA: National Association of Secondary School Principals.

McCray, James Calvin. 1967. "Factors Related to Student Participation in Co-Curricular Activities in Gary High Schools." Ph.D. dissertation, Indiana University, Bloomington.

Macintosh, Donald. 1982. Socio-economic, educational, and status characteristics of Ontario interschool athletes. *Canadian Journal of Applied Sports Sciences* 7 (December): 272–283.

McKown, Harry C. 1952. *Extracurricular Activities*, 3rd ed. New York: Macmillan.

McLinn, Charles B. 1911. The social side of high school life. *Journal of Education* 74 (October): 345–346.

McPartland, James M., and Edward L. McDill. 1977. "Research on Crime in Schools." In *Violence in Schools*, edited by James M. McPartland and Edward L. McDill, 3–33. Lexington, MA: Lexington Books.

Melton, Gary B. 1987. The clashing of symbols: Prelude to child and family policy. *American Psychologist* 42 (April): 345–354.

Mendez, Roy. 1984. Extracurricular activities in today's school—Have we gone too far? *NASSP Bulletin* 68 (March): 60–64.

Millard, Cecil Vernon. 1930. *The Organization and Administration of Extracurricular Activities*. New York: A. S. Barnes.

Minuchin, Patricia P., and Edna K. Shapiro. 1983. "The School as a Context for Social Development." In *Handbook of Child Psychology. Vol. 4. Socialization, Personality, and Social Development*, edited by E. Mavis Hetherington, 197–274. New York: Wiley.

Mondschein, Eric, and Loel Greene. 1981. "Title IX and Extracurricular Activities." In *School Law for a New Decade*, edited by M. A. McGhehey, 142–153. Topeka, KS: National Organization on Legal Problems of Education.

Morgan, David L., and Duane F. Alwin. 1980. When less is more: School size and student social participation. *Social Psychology Quarterly* 43 (June): 241–252.

Morrison, Gilbert B. 1905. Social ethics in high school life. *School Review* 13 (May): 363–367.

Mowbray, Carol T. 1980. Adaptation in the high school: Investigation of locus of control in differing suburban high school environments. *Adolescence* 58 (Summer): 321–339.

Mueller, Lester Dean. 1984. "A Study of Working High School Students and an Analysis of the Relationships Between Part-Time Work and their Educational Programs." Ph.D. dissertation, University of Colorado, Boulder.

Mullins, J. Dale. 1962. Activity programs in Oklahoma—A report to the profession. *School Activities* 33 (March): 197–199.

Munday, Leo A., and Jeanne C. Davis. 1974. *Varieties of Accomplishment after College: Perspectives on the Meaning of Academic Talent*. ACT Research Report no. 62, Iowa City, IA.

Muratov, Iu. I. 1975. The alliance of the school and the Komsomol in the education of young builders of communism. *Soviet Education* 17 (March): 4–21.

National Assessment of Educational Progress. 1985. *The Reading Report Card: Progress Toward Excellence in Our Schools*. Princeton, NJ: Educational Testing Service.

National Commission on Excellence in Education. 1983. *A Nation at Risk: The Imperative for Educational Reform*. Washington, DC: Government Printing Office.

National Education Association. 1918. *Cardinal Principles of Sec-*

ondary Education. Report of the Commission on the Reorganization of Secondary Education. Washington, DC: Bureau of Education Bulletin.

National Study of School Evaluation. 1983. *Evaluative criteria*. Falls Church, VA: National Study of School Evaluation.

Negri, Richard. 1973. "The Perceptions of Students, Teachers, and Administrators Toward Selected Aspects of the Student Activity Program in High Schools in St. Louis County, Missouri." Ph.D. dissertation, Southern Illinois University, Carbondale.

Nover, Michael L. 1981, August. "Student Involvement and the Psychological Experience of the High School." Paper presented at the annual meeting of the American Psychological Association, Los Angeles.

Okihara, Yutaka. 1986. The wide-ranging nature of the Japanese curriculum and its implications for teacher-training. *Comparative Education* 22 (January): 13–18.

Olen, Dale R. 1971. "Environmental Offerings and Students' Behavior in All Boy, All Girl and Coeducational Catholic High Schools." Master's thesis, University of Kansas, Lawrence.

Ornstein, Allan C. 1980. An update of student rights. *High School Journal* 64 (November): 60–64.

Ostro, H. 1980. Eligibility standards. *Scholastic Coach* 50 (September): 6–14.

Otto, Luther B. 1975. Extracurricular activities in the educational attainment process. *Rural Sociology* 40 (Summer): 162–176.

Otto, Luther B. 1976a. Extracurricular activities and aspirations in the status attainment process. *Rural Sociology* 41 (Summer): 217–233.

Otto, Luther B. 1976b. Social integration and the status-attainment process. *American Journal of Sociology* 81 (May): 1360–1361.

Otto, Luther B., and Duane F. Alwin. 1977. Athletics, aspirations, and attainments. *Sociology of Education* 42 (April): 102–113.

Pantages, Timothy J., and Carol F. Creedon. 1978. Studies of college attrition: 1950–1975. *Review of Educational Research* 48 (Winter): 49–101.

Patchen, Martin, James D. Davidson, Gerhard Hofman, and William R. Brown. 1977. Determinants of students' interracial behavior and opinion change. *Sociology of Education* 50 (January): 55–75.

Pavelchak, Mark A., Richard L. Moreland, and John M. Levine. 1986. Effects of prior group memberships on subsequent reconnaissance activities. *Journal of Personality and Social Psychology* 50 (January): 56–66.

Peng, Samuel S., William B. Fetters, and Andrew J. Kolstad. 1981. *A Capsule Description of High School Students*. Washington, DC: Department of Education, National Center for Education Statistics.

Peshkin, Alan. 1978. *Growing Up American: Schooling and the Survival of the Community*. Chicago: University of Chicago Press.

Phillips, John C., and Walter E. Schafer. 1971. Consequences of participation in interscholastic sports. *Pacific Sociological Review* 14 (July): 328–338.

Reavis, William C., and George E. Van Dyke. 1933. *Nonathletic Extra-curriculum Activities*. Bulletin 1932, no. 17. National Survey of Secondary Education, Monograph no. 26. Washington, DC: Government Printing Office.

Rehberg, Richard A. 1969. Behavioral and attitudinal consequences of high school interscholastic sports: A speculative consideration. *Adolescence* 4 (Spring): 69–88.

Rehberg, Richard A., and Michael Cohen. 1975. Athletes and scholars: An analysis of the compositional characteristics and images of these two culture categories. *International Review of Sports Sociology* 10 (Winter): 91–107.

Rehberg, Richard A., and Walter E. Schafer. 1968. Participation in interscholastic athletics and college expectations. *American Journal of Sociology* 73 (May): 732–740.

Rehberg, Richard A., and Walter E. Schafer. 1973, February. "Participation in Student Activities as a Variable in the Educational Attainment and Expectation Process." Paper presented at the annual meeting of the American Educational Research Association.

Reid, Margaret I. 1970. "Voluntary Extra-curricular Activities." In *Comprehensive Education in Action*, edited by T. G. Monks, 128–168. Slough, England: National Foundation for Educational Research in England and Wales.

Reid, Margaret I. 1972. Comprehensive integration outside the classroom. *Educational Research* 14 (February): 128–134.

Rideout, Bill Wayne. 1974. "A Study of the Relationship of Size of High Schools and Student Perceptions of School Climate, Student Alienation, Teacher-Student Relationships, Student Deviant Behavior, and Voluntary Participation in Extra-class Activities." Ed.D. dissertation, University of Kentucky, Louisville.

Roberts, Fred L. 1977. "The Relationship of Nonacademic Accomplishments of Students from Selected High Schools to Their Comparable Adult Accomplishments Ten Years Later." Ed.D. dissertation, Memphis State University, Memphis, TN.

Roemer, Joseph, and Charles Forrest Allen. 1926. *Extracurricular Activities in Junior and Senior High Schools*. Boston, MA: Heath.

Rogers, Carroll Wayne. 1970. "A Study of the Relationship Between Participation in Student Activities and Scholastic Achievement in Selected Oklahoma High Schools." Ph.D. dissertation, University of Oklahoma, Norman.

Rogers, Robert G. 1987, February. "Is Big Better? Fact or Fad Concerning School District Organization." Paper presented at the annual meeting of the American Educational Research Association, New Orleans, LA.

Rohlen, Thomas P. 1983. *Japan's High Schools*. Berkeley: University of California Press.

Rosenberg, Morris. 1965. *Society and the Adolescent Self-Image*. Princeton, NJ: Princeton University Press.

Sagaria, Mary Ann D., and Sabato D. Sagaria. 1984. Sex-role stereotyping and freshman students' intended extracurricular activities. *Journal of College Student Personnel* 25 (March): 133–138.

Salamone, Rosemary C. 1989. "Children Versus the State: The Status of Students' Constitutional Rights." In *Caring for America's Children*, edited by Frank J. Macchariola and Alan Gartner, 182–200. New York: Academy of Political Science.

Sarkees, Michelle D. 1983. Vocational student organizations: Benefits for handicapped students. *Teaching Exceptional Children* 16 (Fall): 60–64.

Schafer, Walter E. 1969. Participation in interscholastic athletics and delinquency: A preliminary study. *Social Problems* 17 (Summer): 40–47.

Schafer, Walter E., and J. Michael Armer. 1968. Athletes are not inferior students. *Transaction* 6 (November): 21–26.

Schafer, Walter E., and Richard A. Rehberg. 1970. Athletic participation, college aspirations, and college encouragement. *Pacific Sociological Review* 13 (Summer): 182–186.

Schendel, Jack S. 1965. Psychological differences between athletes and nonparticipants in athletics at [illegible] school levels. *Re- search Quarterly* 36 (March): 52–57.

Schendel, Jack S. 1968. "The Psychological Characteristics of High School Athletes and Nonparticipants in Athletics: A Three-Year Longitudinal Study." In *Contemporary Psychology of Sport*, edited by Gerald S. Kenyon, 79–96. Washington, DC: International Society of Sport Psychology.

Schneider, Stanley 1971. "The Effect of Work-Study Programs on

Certain Student Behaviors." Ed.D. dissertation, University of New Mexico, Albuquerque.

Schoggen, Phil, and Maxine Schoggen. 1988. Student voluntary participation and high school size. *Journal of Educational Research* 81 (May–June): 288–293.

Sendor, Benjamin. 1988. Managing the student press: Consider carefully before you unsheath the censor's scissors. *American School Board Journal* 175 (April): 24–25.

Serow, Robert C. 1979. The high school extracurriculum: *Cui bono? NASSP Bulletin* 632 (April): 90–94.

Shannon, J. R. 1929. The post-school careers of high school leaders and high school scholars. *School Review* 37 (November): 656–665.

Simmons, Roberta G., Richard Burgeson, Steven Carlton-Ford, and Dale A. Blyth. 1987. The impact of cumulative change in early adolescence. *Child Development* 58 (October): 1220–1234.

Sinks, Thomas A., John W. Mclure, Robert Malinka, and Marvin Pozdol. 1978. What's happening in middle schools in the upper midwest? *Clearing House* 51 (May): 444–448.

Snyder, Eldon E. 1969. A longitudinal analysis of the relationship between high school student values, social participation, and educational-occupational achievement. *Sociology of Education* 42 (Summer): 261–270.

Snyder, Eldon E.. 1975. Athletic team involvement, educational plans, and the coach-player relationship. *Adolescence* 10 (Summer): 191–200.

Snyder, Eldon E., and Elmer Spreitzer. 1977. Participation in sports as related to educational expectations among high school girls. *Sociology of Education* 50 (January): 47–55.

Spady, William G. 1970. Lament for the letterman: Effects of peer status and extracurricular activities on goals and achievement. *American Journal of Sociology* 75 (January): 680–702.

Spady, Willam G. 1971. Status, achievement, and motivation in the American high school. *School Review* 79 (May): 379–403.

Spens, Will, et al. 1939. *Report of the Consultative Committee on Secondary Education with Special Reference to Grammar Schools and Technical High Schools*. London: His Majesty's Stationery Office.

Spreitzer, Elmer, and Meredith Pugh. 1973. Interscholastic athletics and educational expectations. *Sociology of Education* 46 (Spring): 171–182.

Spring, Joel. 1986. *The American School 1642–1985*. New York: Longman.

St. John, Nancy Hoyt. 1964. De facto segregation and interracial association in high school. *Sociology of Education* 37 (Summer): 326–344.

Stein, Aletha Huston. 1971. The effects of sex-role standards for achievement and sex-role preference on three determinants of achievement motivation. *Developmental Psychology* 4 (March): 219–231.

Stein, Aletha Huston, and Janis Smithells. 1969. Age and sex differences in children's sex-role standards about achievement. *Developmental Psychology* 1 (May): 252–259.

Steinberg, Laurence D., Ellen Greenberger, Laurie Garduque, and Sharon McAuliffe. 1982. High school students in the labor force: Some costs and benefits to schooling and learning. *Educational Evaluation and Policy Analysis* 4 (Fall): 363–372.

Stevenson, Christopher L. 1975. Socialization effects of participation in sport: A critical review of the research. *Research Quarterly* 46 (March): 287–301.

Strope, John L., Jr. 1984. *School Activities and the Law.* Reston, VA: National Association of Secondary School Principals.

Talacchi, Sergio. 1960. Organizational size, individual attitudes, and behavior: An empirical study. *Administrative Science Quarterly* 5 (December): 398–420.

Tamir, Pinchas, Wayne W. Welch, and Steven J. Rakow. 1985. The influence of science class attitudes and teacher image on student outcomes. *Journal of Research and Development in Education* 18 (Winter): 26–32.

Taylor, Angela R., Steven R. Asher, and Gladys A. Williams. 1987. The social adaptation of mainstreamed mildly retarded children. *Child Development* 58 (October): 1321–1334.

Terenzini, Patrick T., and Ernest T. Pascarella. 1980. Toward the validation of Tinto's model of college student attrition: A review of recent studies. *Research in Higher Education* 12 (Issue 3): 271–282.

Terry, Paul W. 1930. *Supervising Extra-curricular Activities in the American Secondary School*. New York: McGraw-Hill.

Timberlake, Constance H. 1982. Demographic factors and personal resources that black female students identified as being supportive in attaining their high school diplomas. *Adolescence* 65 (Spring): 107–115.

Trent, William T. 1980. *Contrasts, Trends and Implications of Student Course Enrollments and Extra-curricular Memberships in Desegregated High Schools*. Report to the National Institute of Education. Center for Social Organization of Schools, Johns Hopkins University, Baltimore, MD.

Trent, William T., and James M. McPartland. 1982. The Sense of Well-Being and Opportunity of America's Youth: Some Sources of Race and Sex Differences in Early Adolescence. ERIC Document Reproduction Service, no. 242 798.

Trump, J. Lloyd. 1944. *High-School Extracurricular Activities*. Chicago: University of Chicago Press.

Turner, C. Claude, and James M. Thrasher. 1970. *School Size Does Make a Difference*. San Diego, CA: Institute for Educational Management.

Ullian, Dorothy Z. 1976. "The Development of Conceptions of Masculinity and Femininity." In *Exploring Sex Differences*, edited by B. Lloyd and J. Archer, 25–47. London: Academic Press.

U.S. Office of Education, Office of Educational Research and Improvement. 1986. *Extracurricular Activity Participants Outperform Other Students*. OERI Bulletin. Washington, DC: Government Printing Office.

Violas, Paul C. 1978. *The Training of the Urban Working Class: A History of Twentieth Century American Education*. Chicago: Rand McNally.

Vornberg, James A., James J. Zukowski, Vance W. Gipson, and J. Stephen Southern. 1981. *A Model for Student Activity Programs*. Phi Delta Kappa, East Texas State Chapter, Commerce.

Vornberg, James A., James J. Zukowski, J. Stephen Southern, and Vance W. Gipson. 1983. Student activities: What are the problems now? *Clearing House* 56 (February): 269–270.

Weber, Larry J., and Janice K. McBee. 1982. Policy and practice on the exclusion of students from school activities. *Clearing House* 56 (December): 171–177.

Weston, Louise C., and Sandra L. Stein. 1977. The relationship of identity achievement of college women and campus participation. *Journal of College Student Personnel* 18 (January): 21–24.

Whipple, Guy Montrose, ed. 1926. *Twenty-fifth Yearbook of the National Society for the Study of Education*. Bloomington, IL: Public School Co.

Wicker, Allan W. 1968. Undermanning, performances, and students' subjective experiences in behavior settings of large and small high schools. *Journal of Personality and Social Psychology* 10 (November): 255–261.

Wicker, Allan W. 1969a. Cognitive complexity, school size, and participation in school behavior settings: A test of the frequency of interaction hypothesis. *Journal of Educational Psychology* 60 (June): 200–203.

Wicker, Allan W. 1969b. School size and students' experience in extracurricular activities: Some possible implications for school planning. *Educational Technology* 9 (May): 44–47.

Wicker, Allan W. 1969c. Size of church membership and members' support of church behavior settings. *Journal of Personality and Social Psychology* 13 (November): 278–288.

Wilken, Paul H. 1971. Size of organization and member participation in church congregations. *Administrative Science Quarterly* 16 (June): 173–179.

Willems, Edwin P. 1964. "Forces Toward Participation in Behavior Settings." In *Big School, Small School: High School Size and Student Behavior*, edited by Roger G. Barker and Paul V. Gump, 115–135. Stanford, CA: Stanford University Press.

Willems, Edwin P. 1965. "Participation in Behavior Settings in Relation to Three Variables: Size of Behavior Settings, Marginality of Persons, and Sensitivity to Audiences." Ph.D. dissertation, University of Kansas, Lawrence.

Willems, Edwin P. 1967. Sense of obligation to high school activities as related to school size and marginality of student. *Child Development* 38 (December): 1247–1260.

Yarworth, Joseph S., and William J. Gauthier, Jr. 1978. Relationship of student self-concept and selected personal variables to participation in school activities. *Journal of Educational Psychology* 70 (June): 335–344.

Yudin, Lee W., Stephen I. Ring, Myra Nowakiwska, and Shirley H. Heinemann. 1973. School dropout or college bound: A study in contrast. *Journal of Educational Research* 67 (October): 87–93.

NAME INDEX

A

Abagi, J., 143, 144, 147
Abbott, J. H., 1035
Abbs, P., 558
Abelson, R., 708
Abelson, R. P., 519
Abimbola, I. O., 474
Abraham, J., 592
Abrams, M., 1034
Abt, P., 917
Aceland, R., 330
Achievement Council, 596
Acioly, N., 753
Ackerman, J., 708
Acland, H., 1036
Ad Hoc Committee on the Social Studies, 258
Ada, A. F., 633
Adams, D., 558
Adams, D. R., 914
Adams, D. W., 628
Adams, M. J., 529, 531, 711, 713
Addams, J., 557, 665, 671
Adelman, C., 493
Adelson, J., 547, 560
Ader, M., 738
Adey, P., 801
Adkisson, J., 836
Adler, A., 274
Adler, M., 18, 19, 197, 281, 290, 296, 297, 309, 310, 311, 316, 573, 674, 735, 740
Adler, M. J., 339
Adler, S., 842
Affleck, G., 964
Afflerbach, P., 527, 617
Agostine, V. R., 839
Agulla, A., 465
Ahier, J., 438, 440
Ahlbrand, W., 236
Ahlquist, R., 259
Aikenhead, G., 794, 804–805
Aikin, W., 62, 340, 419–421, 422, 427
Airasian, P. W., 135, 136, 141, 142, 143
Aivoldi, N., 1017
Alberty, H., 339
Albinson, J., 976, 978
Alder, D. D., 836–837
Aldrich, M. L., 671
Aldridge, B. G., 282
Aleksandrov, A. D., 750
Alessi, S. J., Jr., 3*n*
Alexander, G., 557
Alexander, K. L., 577, 591–593
Alexander, L. G., 861
Alexander, R., 549
Alexander, W. M., 3*n*, 4, 82
Alford, L., 227, 228
Alland, A., 953
Allard, F., 522
Allegrante, J. P., 992
Allen, C. F., 1003
Allen, C. R., 908
Allen, D. C., 729
Allen, H. W., 1022
Allen, J., 531
Allen, K. R., 555
Allen, W. W., 862, 880
Alley, G. R., 1028, 1035
Allington, R. L., 583, 617, 695, 699, 705, 711, 714
Allport, G., 1034
Almond, S. M., 983
Alpert, J. L., 583
Alston, W. G., 553
Altbach, P. G., 442
Alton-Lee, A., 505
Alvermann, D. E., 500, 966
Alwin, D. F., 1019–1020, 1025
Amaral, M., 361, 365, 416, 419, 422, 427, 431
American Alliance for Health, Physical Education, Recreation, and Dance, 956, 969, 981
American Association for the Advancement of Science, 439, 800, 812, 818
American Association of Teachers of Spanish and Portuguese, 852
American College of Sports Medicine, 987
American Council on Educa tion, 446
American Council on the Teaching of Foreign Languages, 854–855, 862, 880
American Health and Fitness Foundation, 981
American Home Economics Association, 897, 898–899
Ammann, R., 258
Ammerman, H., 920
Ammon, M. S., 645, 649
Ammon, P., 531, 640, 645, 649
Anderson, B. H., 912
Anderson, C., 205, 593
Anderson, C. S., 64
Anderson, C. W., 498
Anderson, D., 703, 706–707
Anderson, D. H., 376
Anderson, D. S., 103
Anderson, H., 856
Anderson, I. H., 703
Anderson, J., 231, 238, 375, 708
Anderson, J. H., 517
Anderson, J. R., 54, 518, 519, 521, 522, 524, 525, 529, 533, 774, 882
Anderson, L., 64
Anderson, L. M., 505, 711
Anderson, R., 56, 306, 714
Anderson, R. [illegible]
Anderson, R. C., 136, 422, 520, 711–712, 744–745
Anderson, T. H., 493, 494
Anderson, W. G., 972, 982, 984–985
Andersson, B., 810
Andersson, T., 627
Andre, T., 1013, 1019
Andrew, L. D., 254
Andrews, J. C., 1019
Angus, D. L., 177, 180, 592
Annas, P. J., 670
Anrig, G. R., 482
Antler, J., 665
Anyon, J., 87–89, 206, 236, 242, 254, 259, 260, 294, 322, 478, 486, 499, 556, 585, 589, 835–836, 839, 843
Anzai, Y., 527
Aoki, T. T., 80, 92
Apple, M., 772, 793
Apple, M. W., 18, 35, 80, 84, 87–89, 93, 102, 108, 158, 174, 195, 205, 206, 226, 233, 238, 254, 277, 280, 282, 290, 294, 295, 305, 311, 315, 338, 378, 478, 483, 493, 499, 561, 580, 585, 672, 767, 967
Applebee, A., 227
Applebee, A. N., 236, 500, 691, 708–710, 712, 716, 726, 728–729, 731, 733–736, 740–742, 745
Applebee, R. K., 702–703, 709
Applebee, R. N., 737–739
Aquinas, T., 271, 284
Archer, W., 920
Argyle, M., 546
Argyris, C., 105
Aries, P., 121
Aristotle, 31, 273, 284, 286, 309, 318, 550
[illegible]
Armento, B. J., 836, 843
Armer, J. M., 1013, 1017, 1026
Armstrong, D. G., 330, 336
Armstrong, J. M., 667
Armstrong, M., 386
Armstrong, S., 385

Arnheim, R., 283, 951, 954
Arnold, M., 122, 272
Arnold, T., 556
Aron, J., 573, 586
Aronowitz, S., 315
Artley, A. S., 704
Arts, Education, and the Americans, 955
Arzi, H., 799
Ascher, C., 612–613, 616–617, 618–620
Ashenden, D., 1034
Ashenden, D. J., 295, 586
Asher, J., 876
Asher, S. R., 1035
Asher, W., 1014, 1019
Ashton, P. T., 376
Ashton-Warner, S., 386
Ashworth, S., 982
Aspin, D., 954
Association for Science Education, 798, 804
Association for Supervision and Curriculum Development, 330, 335
Association for the Evaluation of Educational Achievement, 744
Athey, T. H., 914
Atkin, J. M., 220, 227
Atkin, M., 188, 199, 200, 239
Atkinson, R. C., 707
Attanucci, J., 554
Atwell, N., 392
Atwood, V. A., 836, 841
Au, K., 599
Au, K. H., 257, 262, 474, 475, 501, 645, 711
Auerbach, N., 665, 670
Aulls, M. W., 506
Austerfield, V., 385
Austin, G. A., 519, 699, 703
Austin, M. C., 707, 714
Ausubel, D. P., 52, 53, 523, 531
Avery, M., 974
Axtell, J., 347, 348, 350
Ayers, W., 386
Ayres, L. P., 121, 122, 129

B

Bachrach, P., 189
Back, G. L., 914
Bacon, F., 99, 273, 284
Badgett, J., 1028
Baggett, C. D., 911
Bagley, W. C., 125, 441, 446, 696, 698
Bahr, G., 896
Bail, L. L., 981
Bailey, C., 287, 551
Bailey, M., 441
Bailey, S., 487, 670
Bailyn, B., 159, 181, 348
Bain, A., 693
Bain, L. L., 557, 964, 966–969, 971–974, 978–980, 988, 989–990, 992–993
Bain, R. K., 668
Baird, J., 799
Baird, L. L., 1013, 1019, 1022, 1024
Baker, D. P., 572, 593
Baker, E. L., 333, 384
Baker, F. L., 727, 729
Baker, F. T., 689, 692
Baker, G., 620
Baldwin, E. E., 917
Baldwin, J. M., 49
Ball, D. L., 210, 496, 498
Ball, S. J., 252, 260, 487, 572, 576, 577, 583–585, 589, 592
Ballou, F., 122, 129
Balow, J. H., 594
Baltimore Feminist Project, 259
Bamberger, J., 952
Bamford, K. W., 859
Bandura, A., 49, 546, 992
Bane, M. J., 1036
Banks, C. A. M., 54
Banks, J. A., 54, 259, 445
Bantock, G. H., 103, 271, 297
Baranes, R., 498
Baranowski, T., 975, 986
Baratz, M., 189
Barbeau, E., 750
Barber, B., 814
Bardeen, C. W., 452
Barden, R., 821
Bardley, R. M., 1015, 1016
Barham, I. H., 743
Barkan, M., 949, 950, 953
Barker, R. G., 1008, 1013, 1019–1020, 1027, 1030
Barker Lunn, J. C., 592
Barlow, M. L., 900, 904–905, 908–909
Barnard, D. P., 713
Barnard, H., 454, 489
Barnes, D., 500, 738
Barnes, W., 917
Barnet, B., 371
Barnhart, C., 257
Barone, T. E., 107, 108
Barone, W. P., 839
Barr, A. S., 491
Barr, M. A., 739
Barr, R., 229, 494, 495, 573, 574, 583, 587, 591–594, 714, 832
Barrett, K. R., 981
Barrett, T. C., 704, 713
Barrette, G. T., 984–985
Barrow, H. M., 557
Barrow, R., 3, 33, 36
Barth, J. L., 551
Barth, R., 218
Barth, V., 832
Barthes, R., 953
Bartholomae, D., 708
Bartlett, F. C., 54, 55, 711
Barton, A., 707
Barton, L., 35
Barylick, M., 947
Barzun, J., 99, 385, 441
Basch, C., 403
Basic Aims Committee, 735
Bassok, M., 55, 517, 526, 528, 532, 533
Bassuk, E., 611
Bateman, D., 700
Bateman, D. R., 743
Bates, T., 375
Battiste, M., 250, 256
Battistich, V., 554
Battistoni, R. M., 556
Bauer, B., 744
Bauer, G. L., 556
Bay, M., 436
Bayles, E. E., 489, 493
Bazerman, C., 708
Beach, B., 733
Beach, D., 920
Beachman, H. C., 1026
Beady, C., 69
Beane, J. A., 3*n*
Beard, M., 662
Beaton, A., 136
Beauchamp, G. S., 486, 487, 492
Beauvoir, S. de, 662
Beavers, I., 916
Bebeau, M. J., 668
Beck, C., 551, 554
Beck, I. L., 493, 531, 705, 707, 711, 713
Beck, M. D., 143
Beck, R., 933
Becker, A., 699
Becker, E., 673
Becker, H. S., 105, 133, 583
Becker, J., 847
Becker, J. M., 338
Becker, J. P., 770
Becker, J. R., 671
Beckner, W., 376
Beebe, L. M., 867
Beebe, V. N., 629
Beecher, C., 664
Beezer, B., 258
Begle, E. G., 750
Belenky, M. F., 93, 678
Bell, A. W., 779
Bell, B., 802
Bell, D., 279, 735, 771
Bell, E., 753
Bell, J. W., 1014
Bell, R., 123, 144
Bell, S. G., 666–667
Bellack, A., 103, 161, 365, 573, 776, 781
Bellah, R., 274, 574, 595
Bellah, R. N., 551, 553, 559
Bellarmine, 124
Belli, G., 221, 229, 231
Belok, M. V., 450, 454
Belth, M., 334
Belugi, U., 711
Ben-Peretz, M., 367, 372, 374, 376, 794
Ben-Peretz, M. R., 56
Ben-Zvi, R., 517
Benavot, A., 227, 228
Benbow, C. P., 667
Bender, D. S., 1014, 1016
Bender, I. C., 692
Bender, M., 911
Benhabib, S., 676
Benjamin, H., 22
Benjamin, L. T., Jr., 455
Benne, K. D., 492
Bennett, A. T., 633
Bennett, C., 253, 613
Bennett, C. A., 905
Bennett, C. T., 842
Bennett, N., 505, 506
Bennett, W., 197, 208, 712
Bennett, W. J., 257, 271, 281, 296, 297, 443, 444, 543, 552, 559, 738
Bennis, W. G., 492
Bensen, M. J., 919
Benson, C., 593, 600, 601
Bentham, J., 139
Bentley, D., 808
Bentzen, M. M., 411
Bereiter, C., 283, 284, 497, 523, 525–527, 530, 533–535, 537, 543, 559, 670, 704, 708
Berends, M., 206, 576, 583, 585, 591, 592, 594, 599
Berg, I., 593
Berger, M., 920
Berger, P. L., 487
Berk, L., 108
Berk, L. E., 1015, 1019–1020, 1024
Berk, R. A., 136
Berkenkotter, C., 708
Berkey, A., 910
Berkheimer, G., 810
Berkowitz, M. W., 547, 549
Berkson, W., 281
Berlak, A., 197
Berlak, H., 197
Berlin, G., 611–612
Berlin, J., 688–689, 691–693, 699, 708
Berliner, D. C., 56, 64, 65, 518, 711, 714, 765
Berlyne, D. E., 531
Berman, E. H., 90
Berman, P., 201, 364, 365, 369, 372–374, 404, 411–413, 415–417
Bernal, H. H., 668
Bernard-Powers, J., 670
Bernd, J. M., 733
Bernhardt, N. W., 692, 702

Berns, R. G., 920–921
Bernstein, B., 195, 205, 206, 231, 233, 294, 295, 296, 318, 478, 711
Bernstein, M., 367, 405, 406, 411, 416, 417, 430
Berryman, S. E., 593, 931, 934
Berthoff, A., 699
Bertocci, T. A., 838
Best, R. W., 985
Bestor, A., 334
Bestor, A. E., 446
Bestor, A. E., Jr., 174
Bettelheim, B., 525, 547, 589
Beust, N. E., 704
Bevier, I., 897
Beyer, B., 556
Beyer, L., 255
Beyer, L. E., 90, 91, 174, 175
Bhattacharyya, N., 144
Bialystock, E., 868–869
Bibb, E. R., 734
Biber, D., 642
Bickel, F., 613
Biddle, B. J., 63–65, 103, 492
Bidwell, C., 217, 233, 240, 587
Bidwell, C. E., 347
Bierstedt, R., 437, 439, 445, 446
Bigelow, R. C., 258
Biggs, E., 768
Biggs, J. B., 526, 527
Bigo, C. H., 912
Biklen, S. K., 105, 668
Binet, A., 61
Birchell, G. R., 840
Bird, T., 412, 417, 418
Birkhoff, G., 766
Birman, B. F., 714
Birmingham, J., 231
Biroux, H. A., 338
Bishop, A. I., 752, 762
Bishop, A. J., 258
Bishop, J., 208
Biss, J., 367, 369
Bissex, G., 392, 716
Bjorkquist, D., 891
Black, H., 147, 227, 229, 436
Black, J. B., 518, 523
Black, P., 819, 821–822
Black, P. J., 280
Blackmore, D. E., 375
Blades, C., 385
Blair, H., 688
Blair, S. N., 965, 970
Blanco, G., 638
Blank, R., 571
Blankenship, G., 445
Blanshard, J., 557
Blasi, A., 549
Blatchford, P., 628
Blatt, M., 549
Blau, P. M., 357
Bleich, D., 708
Bleier, R., 92, 94, 291, 671
Bleir, R., 80, 81
Bloch, M. N., 179
Block, J. H., 669, 1015
Block, K. K., 713
Bloom, A., 197, 208, 315, 545, 559, 660
Bloom, B. S., 57, 100, 102, 110, 123, 129, 340, 517, 704, 796, 967
Bloome, D., 501, 506
Bloomfield, L. J., 703, 705
Bloor, B. S., 333
Blosser, P., 199, 790
Blum, A., 370
Blum, D., 955
Blum, L. A., 676
Blumberg, F., 796
Blumenfeld, P. C., 504–506
Blumenthal, J. A., 992
Blyth, D. A., 1021
Bobbitt, F., 6–9, 11, 13, 14, 19–28, 30–34, 36, 37, 59, 81, 101, 110, 125, 129, 160–162, 167–170, 173, 197, 198, 231, 239, 278, 332, 333, 366, 378, 490, 491, 580, 768
Boben, D., 816
Bobrow, D. G., 524
Boddy, R., 912
Bode, B., 173
Boeha, B., 795
Bogdan, D., 550, 551, 556
Bogdan, R. C., 105
Boggs, C., 93
Boggs, S. T., 644–645
Bok, S., 94, 551, 553
Bolger, N., 135
Bolin, F., 486, 492
Bolinger, D. L. M., 54
Bolton, G., 950
Bolvin, J. O., 705, 707
Bond, G. L., 705
Bondi, J., 3*n*
Boney, C., 712
Bonjour, L., 269
Bonser, F. G., 337
Book, C., 842–843
Boomer, G., 377
Boone, H. N., 892, 894
Booth, W., 385
Bordelon, K. W., 445
Borg, W. R., 972
Boring, E., 312
Borko, H., 714
Borman, K. M., 1034
Bormuth, J. R., 711
Borrow, J. L., 920–921
Borwick, D., 451, 713
Bossert, S., 503
Bossing, N. L., 339
Boston School Committee, 578
Boston Women's Teachers' Group, 668
Botkin, A. S., 1003
Bottani, N., 120
Bottoms, E., 927
Bouchard, C., 970
Bourdieu, P., 195, 205, 292, 293, 294, 296, 315, 321, 478, 580, 793
Bourgon, J. K., 1016
Bourne, E. L., 752
Bovet, M., 50
Bowe, R., 252
Bower, G. H., 54, 520
Bower, G., 708
Bowlby, J., 547
Bowler, R., 121, 142, 144, 147
Bowles, S., 206, 226, 238, 254, 255, 256, 276, 322, 544, 580, 585, 594, 672
Bowsher, C. A., 6
Boyd, D., 547, 550, 551
Boyd, J., 143
Boyd, W., 187, 189, 195, 201, 203, 204
Boyd, W. L., 221, 224, 227, 229
Boyer, E., 251, 573, 589, 598, 789, 834
Boyer, E. L., 340, 732, 779, 854
Boyer, M., 627
Boyle, C. F., 533
Brabeck, M. M., 554, 668
Bracht, G. H., 103, 104
Braddock, R., 700
Braden, A. C., 63
Bradley, R. H., 53
Brady, E. H., 330
Brady, L., 376
Bralier, M., 924
Brandl, J., 192
Branscombe, A., 599
Bransford, J. D., 525
Braun, H. I., 589
Braun, M., 50
Braybrooke, D., 189
Bredo, A. E., 411
Bredo, E. R., 411
Brega, E., 856
Brendel, L., 896
Breneman, B., 709, 716
Brenner, C., 274
Brenzel, B. M., 664–665
Bressan, E. S., 993
Brewer, W. F., 524
Brians, P., 558
Brickell, H. M., 220
Bricker, D. C., 551
Bridenbaugh, C., 349, 350
Bridge, C., 710
Bridgeford, N. J., 126, 127
Briers, G., 911
Briggs, L., 57, 110
Brigham, C., 61
Britton, J., 708, 711
Britton, J. N., 738
Broadbelt, S., 835
Broadfoot, P., 144
Broder, D. E., 174
Broder, L. J., 517
Brody, P., 741, 745
Bromage, B., 53
Bromley, H., 89
Bromme, R., 56
Bronfenbrenner, U., 318, 547
Brookover, W. B., 69
Brooks, C., 620, 736, 745
Brooks-Gunn, J., 611–612, 669
Brophy, J., 467, 486, 496, 573, 585, 620, 711
Brophy, J. E., 48, 50, 55, 64, 65, 369, 559
Brosseau, B. A., 842–843
Broudy, E., 443
Broudy, H. S., 90, 103, 255, 283, 284, 365, 370, 956, 966
Brown, A., 56, 613, 711
Brown, A. L., 497, 525, 536, 537
Brown, B., 617
Brown, D., 947
Brown, E. E., 166
Brown, J. P., 557
Brown, J. S., 56, 469, 486, 497, 498, 525, 532, 534, 536, 955, 957
Brown, J. W., 1032
Brown, L., 555
Brown, M., 591, 593
Brown, M. M., 897, 912, 917–918
Brown, R., 699, 951
Brown, R. D., 914
Brown, R. W., 711
Brown, S., 369, 376, 377
Brown, S. O., 966
Brown, W. B., 339
Brown, W. R., 1034
Brubacher, J. S., 129
Bruber, H., 303
Bruck, M., 858
Bruggen, J. C. van, 328
Brumby, M., 813
Brunelli, P., 145
Bruner, H. B., 226, 234
Bruner, J., 43, 50, 51, 54, 63, 123, 283, 286, 304, 329, 335, 366, 368, 556, 678, 735–736, 791–792, 951, 954, 960
Bruner, J. S., 443, 519, 531, 699, 701, 703
Brush, L. R., 667
Bryan, J. H., 1035
Bryan, W. A., 1031
Bryan, W. J., 447
Bryant, M., 293
Bryk, A. S., 69, 70, 559, 575, 583, 591, 668
Brynes, H., 880
Bucat, R., 800
Buchmann, M., 297, 713
Buck, C., 621
Buck, G., 690, 716
Bud, R., 273
Buescher, T. M., 90

Buffer, J., 816
Buffer, J. J., 919
Bugliarello, G., 281
Buka, S. L., 562
Bulkin, B. J., 671
Bullivant, B. M., 259
Bullock, K. V., 1016–1017
Bullock, R., 392
Bullough, R. V., 385
Bunder, W., 806
Bunderson, C. V., 375
Bunnell, R., 251
Burbach, H. J., 1019
Burden, D., 917
Burdine, J. N., 992
Bureau of the Census, 609–610
Burge, L., 375
Burgeson, R., 1021
Burgess, E. F., 9222
Burgess, R. G., 105, 508, 583
Burgess, T., 708
Burke, C., 370, 716
Burke, P. E., 757
Burlbaw, L. M., 446
Burnett, L. W., 339
Burnett, M. F., 912
Burnett, N., 522
Burnham, J. C., 491
Burns, G., 223
Burns, G. T., 164–166, 275
Buros, O. K., 125, 135, 136, 490
Burstein, L., 69, 72
Burt, M. K., 882
Burton, E., 121
Burton, J., 1017
Burton, R. R., 533
Burton, R. V., 545
Buscaglia, M., 877
Buser, R., 1016, 1018, 1022
Buser, R. L., 1006–1009, 1014, 1019–1020
Bush, R. N., 64
Business and Economic Education, 896
Bussis, A., 416, 419, 422, 427, 431
Bussis, A. M., 364, 365
Buswell, G. T., 101, 441, 444
Butcher, J., 1016
Butler, B., 671
Butler, J. A., 228
Butler, M., 753
Butt, K., 982
Butt, R. L., 385
Butterfield, R. A., 713
Bybee, R., 804
Bybee, R. W., 179, 447
Byers, J. L., 713, 842–843
Bynum, C. W., 662
Byrnes, H., 872

C

Caduto, M., 557
Cahn, E. S., 258
Cairns, L. G., 376
Calderwood, J. D., 914
Caldwell, P., 974
Calfee, R., 54, 56, 129, 497, 796
Calfee, R. C., 438, 444, 714
Calhoun, D., 348, 349
California State Department of Education, 709
Calkins, L., 708
Calkins, L. M., 385
Callahan, R. E., 58, 60, 66, 81, 82, 125, 198, 225, 239, 312, 313, 359, 732, 948
Camarena, M., 576, 585
Camp, L. S. de, 436, 447
Camp, W. G., 894
Campbell, D. S., 3*n*, 4, 8
Campbell, D. T., 101, 103–108, 113, 114, 145, 288
Campbell, E., 67
Campbell, E. Q., 1036
Campbell, G., 688
Campbell, R., 86
Campbell, R. F., 251
Campbell, R. M., 882
Campbell, W. J., 1019, 1020, 1021, 1027–1028
Campione, J., 613
Campione, J. C., 525
Canale, M., 861, 863
Canisius, 124
Cannell, J. J., 70, 145, 146
Cantarella, E., 660–661
Caramazza, A., 517
Carbonari, J. P., 992
Carbone, F., Jr., 160, 164
Card, C., 292
Carey, M., 437
Carey, N., 68, 120, 128, 131, 132
Carey, S., 524
Carlisle, R. S., 640
Carlow, C., 371
Carlson, D., 254, 796
Carlson, R. O., 63
Carlton-Ford, S., 1021
Carlyon, W. H., 992
Carman, P., 556
Carmichael, L. N., 279, 281
Carnegie Council on Adolescent Development, 596
Carnegie Forum on Education and the Economy, 192
Carnegie Foundation for the Advancement of Teaching, 217, 612, 630–632, 649, 789
Carnegie Task Force on Teaching as a Profession, 630, 677
Carnes, J., 911
Carnevale, A. P., 931
Carnoy, M., 226, 236, 238, 594, 672, 776
Carpenter, C., 441, 452
Carpenter, G. R., 689, 692, 727, 729
Carpenter, J. A., 859, 869
Carpenter, P. A., 519
Carpenter, T. B., 223
Carpenter, T. P., 499, 759, 780
Carpenter, T. R., 765
Carper, J. C., 446
Carr, N. J., 969
Carr, R., 376
Carr, W., 105, 385, 493, 936
Carr-Saunders, A. M., 125
Carriedo, R. A., 69
Carroll, J. B., 136, 521, 711–712
Carss, M., 770
Carter, J. P., 918
Carter, K., 210, 486, 504, 506, 507, 509
Carter, L. F., 617–618, 711
Case, R., 53, 110, 304, 529–531, 801, 53110
Case Studies in Science Education, 790
Casement, W., 551, 556
Caspersen, C. J., 972
Casserly, P., 667
Cassidy, T., 105
Cassimer, M. H., 924
Cassirer, E., 304, 318, 520, 954
Caswell, H., 160
Caswell, H. I., 403, 419
Caswell, H. L., 3*n*, 4, 7, 8, 21
Caton, J. J., 914
Cattell, J., M., 669
Caul, J., 713
Cavallo, D., 557
Cavell, S., 10, 286
Cawelti, G., 836
Caywood, C. L., 670
Cazden, C., 589
Cazden, C. B., 49, 249, 250, 253, 255, 474, 475, 493, 500, 711
Cazwell, 378
Center on Budget and Policy Priorities, 612
Centra, J. A., 64
Centre for Educational Research and Innovation, 370
Cerjak, J., 558
Chafe, W., 708
Chaffe-Stenger, P., 791
Chalip, L., 990
Chall, J., 229
Chall, J. S., 444, 698, 703, 706, 712–713, 716
Chamberlin, D., 62, 421, 422
Chamberlin, E., 62
Chamberlin, E. S., 421, 422
Chambers, B., 127
Chambliss, M. J., 438, 444
Chamont, A. U., 649
Chamot, A. U., 868–869, 883
Champagne, A., 801, 810
Champagne, A. B., 223, 517
Chandrasekhar, S., 286, 288, 291
Chang, J. L., 992
Chapman, L., 954, 956
Chapman, P., 235
Chapman, P. A., 980
Charms, R. de, 448
Charness, N., 522
Charters, W. W., 101, 125, 129, 160, 162, 167–170, 198, 216, 231, 239, 333, 367, 378, 411, 490, 545, 768, 893
Chartrand, L., 857
Chase, F., 224
Chase, W. G., 522
Chazan, B. I., 558
Chen, M., 1014, 1021
Cheney, L., 311
Cheney, L. V., 854
Cherry, R., 708
Cherryholmes, C., 288, 295
Cherryholmes, C. H., 80, 86, 91, 174, 493, 494, 496
Chevallard, Y., 761, 781
Chi, M., 55
Chi, M. T. H., 518, 522, 526, 528, 534
Child, D. A., 56
Children's Defense Fund, 613
Childs, J., 224
Chin, R., 492
Chipman, S. F., 667
Chisholm, R., 269
Chittenden, E., 416, 419, 422, 427, 431
Chittenden, E. A., 364, 365
Chodorow, N., 673–675
Choksy, L., 947–948, 950
Chomsky, C., 711
Chomsky, N., 292, 519, 536, 708, 736, 743
Choy, S., 593
Christ, C. P., 674
Christenbury, J., 738
Christian-Smith, L. K., 295, 555, 556
Christiansen, B. A., 750, 756
Christie, D., 558
Christman, J. R., 905–908
Cicchetti, P., 126
Cicero, 271, 272, 273
Cicourel, A. V., 575, 577, 589, 596, 711
Clancey, W. J., 519, 533, 534
Clandinin, D. J., 33, 282, 322, 365, 370, 373, 385, 486, 488, 493
Clandinin, J., 108
Claparede, E., 49, 51
Clapp, J. M., 732
Clark, B. R., 359

Clark, C., 56, 63, 66, 708, 716
Clark, C. M., 363, 498, 500
Clark, D., 103, 130, 199, 200, 305
Clark, D. L., 81
Clark, F. L., 1035, 1038
Clark, G., 957
Clark, H. H., 970, 978
Clark, T. J., 954
Clark, V. L., 1032
Clarke, D., 765
Clarke, D. L., 130
Clarke, E., 665
Claus, J., 931
Clay, M. M., 531, 617
Clegg, A. A., 370
Clement, J., 534
Clements, B. S., 506
Clennell, S., 375
Clifford, G. J., 231, 367, 440, 451
Clifford, J., 481
Clifford, R., 861
Clinchy, B. M., 678
Clore, G. L., 520
Clune, W., 192, 210, 598
Coakley, J. J., 990
Cobb, L., 694
Cobb, P. E., 780
Cobb, R., 187
Cobb, S., 167
Cochran-Smith, M., 425, 478
Cochrane, D., 562
Cockburn, A., 505, 506
Cody, C., 442–444
Cohelan, E. E., 924
Cohen, A., 636–637, 639
Cohen, D., 188, 190, 198, 207, 208, 210, 221, 223, 581, 627, 1036
Cohen, D. K., 166, 171, 174, 237, 260, 339, 360, 373, 374, 385, 417, 573, 574, 578, 580–585, 595, 598, 776
Cohen, E., 645
Cohen, E. G., 591, 599, 645–646
Cohen, G. A., 296
Cohen, K., 53
Cohen, L., 105
Cohen, M., 190, 417, 1017
Cohen, P. C., 351
Cohen, R. B., 53
Cohen, R. D., 162
Cohen, S. G., 650
Coker, H., 65
Colby, A., 547–549
Colby, K. M., 521
Coldevin, G., 376
Cole, A., 800
Cole, C., 304
Cole, M., 482, 531, 536, 716, 739, 954, 960
Cole, N., 482
Cole, R. R., 556
Cole, R. W., 248, 249, 250, 260
Coleman, E. B., 711
Coleman, J., 320
Coleman, J. S., 53, 67, 69, 131, 553, 1007, 1013–1016, 1017, 1022, 1036
Coles, R., 364, 385, 386, 387, 388, 389, 391, 392
College Entrance Examination Board, 756
Colley, B., 952
Collier, V. P., 647–648, 651
Collings, E., 102
Collins, A., 56, 469, 486, 497, 498, 525, 532, 536, 955, 957
Collins, A. M., 711
Collins, G. C., 671
Collins, R., 196, 207, 574
Collins, T. W., 1034
Colquhuon, D., 970
Colvin, N. R., 693
Comber, L., 796
Comenius, 497
Comer, J. P., 620
Commager, H. S., 450
Commissioners of National Education in Ireland, 122
Commission for the Reorganization of Secondary Education, 578
Commission on English, 701, 737
Commission on Mathematics, 142
Commission on National Aid to Vocational Education, 598
Commission on Secondary School Curriculum, 735
Commission on the English Curriculum, 735, 739
Commission on the English Curriculum of the National Council of Teachers of English, 700
Commission on the Reorganization of Secondary Education, 907, 1003
Committee of Inquiry into the Teaching of Mathematics in Schools, 749, 756
Committee on the Status of Women in Sociology, 291
Common, D. L., 367
Commonwealth of Massachusetts, 954
Commonwealth Secretariat, 789, 814
Comte, A., 309
Conant, F. R., 646
Conant, J., 573, 574, 594
Conant, J. B., 229
Conference Board of Mathematical Sciences, 761, 765
Confrey, J., 497, 508
Congdon, K., 954
Conklin, J., 456
Conklin, N. F., 126
Conle, C., 385
Conlon, J. B., 448
Connell, R., 1034
Connell, R. W., 295, 297, 370, 586
Connell, W. F., 1004
Connelley, F. M., 108
Connelly, F. M., 33, 282, 322, 328, 365, 367, 370–374, 385, 486, 493
Connelly, M., 85, 794, 797
Connor, J., 669
Connor, T., 1017
Connors, R. J., 690
Conrad, S., 229
Contento, I., 917
Conyne, R. K., 1010–1011
Cooey, P. M., 676
Cook, F., 224
Cook, G. C., 893
Cook, M., 577, 591, 592
Cook, M. A., 577, 591, 593
Cook, T. D., 104, 106
Cook, V., 613
Cook, W. W., 328
Cook-Gumperz, G., 708
Cooke, B. D., 930
Coolahan, J. M., 121
Cooley, C. H., 169
Cooley, W. W., 711, 714
Coomer, D. L., 128, 133
Cooney, T. J., 67, 69, 577, 583, 966
Coop, R. H., 53
Cooper, B., 493
Cooper, C., 53
Cooper, C. R., 708–709, 716
Cooper, K. H., 986
Cooper, M., 518
Cooper, T., 854
Coote, E., 350
Copa, G. H., 929, 935
Copa, P., 927
Copley, B., 708
Corbeil, G., 526
Corbett, E., 52, 699, 701
Corbett, H. D., 234, 235, 236, 249, 257, 258, 259
Corbin, C. B., 965, 991
Corbitt, M. K., 759
Corey, K. E., 492
Cornbleth, C., 486, 492, 499, 506, 834
Cornell, D., 674
Cornell, E. R., 590, 591
Corno, L., 56, 505
Corwe, P. B., 989
Corwin, R., 417
Cosmides, L., 537
Cotterell, J. L., 1019–1021, 1027–1028
Coulter, D., 65
Coulthard, R. M., 708
Council for Basic Education, 596
Council on Interracial Books for Children, 259
Counts, G. S., 18, 102, 103, 125, 224, 231–233, 235, 236, 239, 278, 311, 333, 338, 378, 403, 693
Courson, R. L., 912
Court, F. E., 556
Courtis, S. A., 101, 403
Courtney, R., 950
Coverley Veale, D. M. W. de, 992
Cowan, D., 281, 282
Cowden, P., 417
Cowles, M. P., 992
Coxford, A. F., 766
Craig, D., 556
Craig, H. T., 897–899
Craig, P. L., 1012, 1022
Craig, R. L., 1022
Crain, R. L., 583, 1034
Cram, D., 375
Crandall, D., 417
Crandall, D. P., 369, 374, 376, 377, 405, 409, 416, 417
Crandall, J., 641
Crank, D., 894–896
Crank, F., 894–896
Crawford, J., 628–629
Crawford, L. C., 902–903
Crawford, R., 970
Crawley, S. J., 845
Creedon, C. F., 1026
Cremin, L., 222–226, 226, 230, 231, 237, 238, 302, 311, 312, 314, 419
Cremin, L. A., 8, 11, 12, 14, 16, 58, 61, 62, 100, 159, 160, 162, 163, 328, 333, 347–356, 360, 365, 367, 368, 372, 377, 379, 449, 558, 578, 579
Crenshaw, V. P., 924
Crittenden, B. S., 551
Crocker, R., 797
Cromartie, M., 1032, 1035
Crombie, A. C., 286
Cronbach, L. J., 45, 61, 64, 66, 69, 100, 104, 106, 111, 112, 123, 127, 131, 132, 135, 136, 141, 339, 436, 442, 443
Cronin, J., 225
Crooks, T. J., 127, 135, 143
Cross, M., 1015
Crosswhite, F. J., 67, 69, 577, 583
Crowe, P. B., 989
Crowell, D. C., 645
Crummey, L., 493, 494

Crunkilton, J., 920
Cruse, K. L., 135, 140
Csikszentmihalyi, M., 947, 955
Cuban, L., 131, 142, 144, 167, 174, 204, 224, 226, 231, 232, 236, 237, 239, 263, 275, 310, 314, 366–370, 374, 378, 467, 715
Cubberley, E. P., 61, 81, 83, 100, 159, 162, 224, 452, 490, 579
Cuccia, N. J., 1014, 1018
Cuetara, P., 920
Cuevas, G. J., 641
Cuff, T., 105
Culler, J., 304, 508
Cullinan, B., 614, 621
Cummings, W., 571
Cummings, W. K., 144
Cummins, J., 629, 631–633, 637–639, 651, 871
Cunningham, A. E., 144, 146
Cureton, E. E., 140
Cureton, K. J., 965, 991
Curriculum and Evaluation Standards for School Mathematics, 750, 754–755
Curriculum Task Force, 833
Curtain, H., 856
Curti, M., 164, 444, 445, 450, 453
Curtis, M. E., 56
Cusick, P., 223, 231, 237, 260, 369, 467, 559, 585, 586, 588
Cusick, P. A., 208, 506
Cutright, P., 403

D

Daggett, W. R., 931
Dailey, A. R., 1029
Dairymple, J. I., 916
Dale, T. C., 641
Daly, M., 663, 675–676
D'Amato, J., 474
D'Ambrosio, U., 753, 762, 778
Damerow, P., 757, 775, 778
Damico, S. B., 1034
Dandonoli, P., 855, 862, 883
Daniel, J. S., 376
Daniels, J. L., 1030
Daniels, M. T., 592
Danley, R., 371
Dapra, R. A., 143
Dardan, J. T., 1034
Darling-Hammond, L., 42, 45, 58, 65, 71, 234, 589
Darlington, R., 617
Darracott, C., 989
Darrow, C., 447
Darst, P. W., 967–968
Darwin, C., 312, 447, 665
Datta, L., 134
Dauer, V. P., 966, 968, 970
Davenport, S., 137, 571, 575, 576, 589, 590, 600
David, H., 927
Davidson, C., 441
Davidson, J. D., 1034
Davidson, L., 952
Davies, A., 393, 808
Davies, G. D., 878
Davies, I. K., 531
Davies, L., 555, 589
Davies, W. J., 452
Davis, A., 671
Davis, C., 992
Davis, F. B., 704
Davis, J. C., 1030
Davis, J. E., 374, 376
Davis, O. L., 831, 832, 834–835
Davis, O. L., Jr., 161, 436, 446, 670
Davis, P., 920
Davis, P. J., 751
Davis, R., 56, 523
Davis, R. B., 770
Davis, R. J., 750
Davis, S. A., 576, 577, 595
Davison, A., 531
Davy, D., 273
Davydov, V. V., 536
Dawes, R., 178
Dawes, R. M., 503
Dawis, R. V., 1018
Dawson, R. E., 1028
Day, D., 671
Day, E. M., 857, 881
Day, M., 957
Dayton, C., 928
Deadman, J. A., 532
Deans, E., 51
Dearborn, W. F., 703
Dearden, R. F., 551
DeAvila, E., 599
DeAvila, E. A., 645–646, 650
DeBoer, J. J., 705
DeBusk, M., 967–968, 979
Decker, J. P., 924
DeClark, G., 53
Dee, M. B., 1012
DeForest, M., 531, 536
Deforges, C., 506
DeFrain, J., 51
DeFries, J. C., 536
Degge, R., 953
DeGracie, J., 713
deGroot, A. D., 522
Deitroff, J. F., 1026
deKleer, J., 534
Delamont, S., 790, 803
DeLany, B., 575, 576, 589
Delaney, H. D., 523
DelFattore, J., 444, 446
Delgado-Gaitan, C., 474
Delisle, R. G., 619
Della-Piana, G. M., 704, 711
Delpit, L., 730
DeMartino, R., 275
DeMilo, C., 741, 745
Demmin, P., 280
Demos, E. S., 713
Demos, J., 348
Dempsey-Atwood, N., 64, 65
Dennett, D. C., 518, 521
Dennis, L., 556
Dennison, G., 385
Denny, J. V., 689
Denscombe, M., 237
Denton, N. A., 612
Denzin, N., 104
Department of Education, 815
Department of Education and Science, 129, 147
Department of Education and Science and the Welsh Office, 820
Department of Superintendence, 403
Descartes, R., 99, 271, 272
Desforges, C. A., 505, 506
Deshler, D. D., 1035
Designs for Change, 252
Despres, J. P., 970
Devaney, K., 201
DeVault, M. V., 756
DeVitis, J. L., 551
Dewar, A. M., 967
Dewey, E., 378
Dewey, J., 6–8, 10, 11, 13, 14, 19, 20, 22, 31, 42–45, 48, 58, 61, 72, 82, 84, 100, 102, 103, 128, 160, 162, 163, 170–174, 220, 224, 230, 236, 269, 275, 278, 279, 284, 293, 297, 311, 312, 313, 316, 321, 333, 334, 335, 339, 356, 364, 365, 368, 369, 378, 379, 380, 432, 436, 444, 465–468, 476, 489, 493, 536, 545, 547, 550, 556, 570, 574, 598, 716, 751–752, 760, 907, 967
Dewey, V., 1004
Dexter, E. G., 693, 714
Deyhle, D., 474
Diaz, R., 716
Diaz, S., 475, 577, 589, 598, 599, 640
Dickens, C., 387
Dietz, W. H., 984
Dillard, J. L., 614
Diller, A., 555
Dillon, D., 500
Dillon, D. R., 257, 259, 262
Dillon, J. T., 236
Dillon, R., 910–911
DiMaggio, P., 293, 295
DiMaggio, P. J., 240
Diorio, J. A., 555, 556
Dippo, D., 104
Dishman, R. K., 964–965, 976–978, 984, 987
Dittman, F., 370, 371
Dixon, J., 737
Dodds, P., 967, 988, 991
Doebler, L. K., 641
Doerfert, D. L., 892, 894
Doherty, V. W., 127
Dolch, E., 695
Doll, R. C., 3n
Donaldson, J., 808
Donaldson, M., 52
Donmoyer, R., 108
Donovan, B., 761
Donow, C., 557
Donsky, B. V. B., 692
Doolittle, S. A., 982
Dooren, I. van, 752
Dopo, D., 923
Doris, J., 416
Dorman, G., 145
Dornbusch, S. M., 240
Dorow, E. B., 506
Dorr-Bremme, D. W., 127, 613, 616
Dorsten, L., 591, 593
Doss, D. A., 1026
Dossett, W. A., 407
Dossey, J. A., 67, 69, 577, 583, 1032
Dougan, A. M., 831
Dougherty, B., 916
Doughty, P., 743
Douglas, J. D., 662
Dow, G., 377
Dow, P. B., 448
Dowell, L., 1028
Dowling, J., 240
Dowling, J. W., 952
Downey, M. E., 551
Downey, M. T., 836, 837
Downey, R. G., 1013, 1019, 1021, 1026
Downie, D., 671
Downing, C., 674
Downing, J. A., 531
Downs, A., 220
Dowsett, G., 1034
Dowsett, G. W., 295, 586
Doyle, D., 618
Doyle, W., 51, 63–66, 103, 108, 210, 231, 263, 280, 416, 486, 488, 492, 493, 500, 503–507, 509
Draeger, R., Jr., 1016
Drake, B., 910, 920
Drake, D. D., 986–987
Draper, J. B., 854
Dreeben, R., 8, 9, 222, 229, 233, 237, 240, 250, 276, 305, 306, 467, 478, 488, 495, 573, 574, 583, 587, 591, 592, 594, 668, 756
Dressel, P. L., 330

Dressel, R. J., 668
Dreyfus, H. L., 523
Dreyfus, S. E., 523
Driver, R., 789, 801–803, 814
Drost, W. H., 164, 169
Drought, N., 62, 421, 422
Drum, P., 497
Duari, P., 144
Dubey, S. D., 144
DuBois, E. C., 662, 670
Dubois, P. E., 990
Ducharme, D., 371
Duchastel, P. C., 130
Duck, L., 560
Duckworth, E., 135, 385, 392
Duda, J. L., 976
Duffin, R. G., 371
Duffy, G. G., 711
Dufresne, R., 534
Duguid, P., 56, 469, 486, 497, 498, 536, 955, 957
Duit, R., 802
Duke, D. L., 241
Dulay, H. C., 882
Dumont, R. V., 257
Dumont, R. V., Jr., 474
Duncan, B., 986, 987
Duncan, S. E., 646, 650
Dunkel, H. B., 368
Dunkin, M. J., 63–65, 492
Dunlop, O. J., 269
Dunn, A., 965, 978, 984, 987
Dunn, K., 936
Dunn, R., 936
Dunn, S., 481, 500
Durkheim, E., 180, 205, 270, 271, 346, 544
Durkin, D., 229, 493, 495, 504, 529, 713–714
Durkin, M. J., 494
Duruy, V., 293
Dwyer, C. A., 670
Dwyer, D., 217, 219, 224
Dwyer, D. C., 367, 368
Dwyer, T., 986
Dykstra, R., 705
Dynneson, T. L., 833
Dyrenfurth, M. J., 918–920
Dysinger, W., 976
Dyson, A., 53, 708
Dyson, A. H., 475

E

Eagleton, T., 304
Earls, N. F., 972, 988
Easley, J., 199, 220, 227, 236, 477, 758, 765
Easley, J. A., 841–842
Easley, J. A., Jr., 491
East, E. R., 1034
East, M., 898–899
Eastabrook, G., 367
Eaton, T. H., 893
Ebbinghaus, H., 54
Ebel, R., 104
Ebel, R. L., 140
Eccles, J., 52, 671
Echterling, L., 1027
Ecker, D., 953
Eckland, B. K., 1017, 1024–1025, 1029–1031
Economic Cooperation and Development, 789
Eddington, A., 288, 291
Edelman, M., 180, 187, 595
Edelman, M. W., 611–612
Edelsky, C., 640
Eder, D., 500, 583, 585, 592, 1034
Edington, E. D., 376
Edlind, E. P., 1016
Edmonds, R., 69, 417, 612, 712
Edmonds, R. R., 123
Edmonson, J. B., 441
Edmund, N. R., 702
Education and Technology Task Force, 818
Education of the National Education Association, 833
Education Products Information Exchange, 713
Education Week, 251
Educational Testing Service, 856, 881
Edwards, A. C., 171, 278, 279, 378, 379
Edwards, A. D., 500
Edwards, J., 803
Edwards, K., 53
Effendi, M. N., 911
Efland, A., 955, 957
Egan, D. E., 522
Egan, K., 3, 36, 37, 43, 297, 368, 531, 547
Egan, S., 836
Eggleston, E., 349
Eggleston, J., 276, 295, 377
Ehman, L. H., 833, 847, 1018, 1029
Ehrenpreis, E., 733
Ehrenreich, B., 290, 663
Ehrmann, M., 869
Ehrnwald, P. M., 976
Eidsmore, R. M., 1017
Eijkelhof, H., 805, 813
Einstein, A., 273, 291, 292, 443
Eireann, D., 139
Eisemon, T., 814
Eisemon, T. O., 143, 144, 146
Eisner, E., 196, 224, 227, 231, 442, 946, 947, 953–955, 956
Eisner, E. W., 3, 9, 13, 15, 16, 20, 46, 80, 90, 92, 102–104, 107, 108, 130, 131, 133, 250, 261, 287, 305, 306, 314, 317, 318, 319, 323, 327, 333, 334, 370, 375, 377, 378, 379, 380, 381, 392, 466, 467, 487, 936, 966, 973, 988
Eitzen, D. S., 1015
Eitzen, J. S., 1021
Ekeland, I., 750
Ekstrom, R. B., 589–591
Elam, W. N., 893
Elbaz, F., 33, 108, 385, 486, 488, 492, 499
Elboim-Dror, R., 189, 195
Elbow, P., 197, 374, 699
Elder, C., 187
Elementary and Secondary Education Act, 705
Elgin, C. Z., 286
Elias, P., 64, 65
Eliot, C., 60
Eliot, C. W., 163–167, 176, 197, 436, 451, 729
Elkind, D., 544
Elley, W. B., 743
Elliot, J., 892
Elliott, 100
Elliott, D. L., 442–444
Elliott, E. C., 125
Elliott, J., 377, 381, 382, 383
Elliott, R., 550
Ellman, F., 615
Ellrod, F. A., 553
Ellrod, F. E., 553
Elmore, M. J., 924
Elmore, R., 187, 189–191, 195, 199–201, 203, 417
Elmore, R. F., 228, 240, 241, 601
Elson, R. M., 235, 449, 451, 452, 454, 457
Elstein, A., 55, 56, 72
Ely, C., 867
Emerson, 122
Emerson, H. P., 692
Emick, G. O., 902
Emig, J., 708
Emmer, E. T., 506
Emrick, J., 201
Emrick, J. A., 416, 417
Endo, G. T., 704, 711
Endres, W. B., 556
Enelow, A., 274
Engelhart, M., 57
Engestrom, Y., 520
England, D. A., 726
Engle, P., 638
Engle, S., 832
Engle, S. H., 556
Englert, R. M., 204
English, D., 290, 663
Englund, M., 931
Englund, T., 223, 232, 237
Ennis, C., 969
Ennis, C. D., 966, 967, 973, 980
Ennis, R., 56
Ennis, R. H., 551
Enns, R., 372
Enns-Connolly, E., 385
EPIE (Educational Products Information Exchange) Institute, 444
Epstein, C. F., 668
Epstein, J., 257
Epstein, M., 796
Epstein, N., 629
Epstein, T., 323
Erasmus, 271, 272
Erickson, E., 50
Erickson, F., 249, 250, 253, 257, 258, 469, 474, 475, 493, 500, 501, 503, 506, 518, 577, 589
Erickson, G., 801
Erickson, G. L., 392
Ericksson, K. A., 105
Erikson, E. H., 547, 554, 674, 1028
Erlwanger, S., 48, 759
Ernest, P., 750–751, 762
Ernst, L., 930
Ertel, K., 902, 921
Erting, C., 258
Esley, R. E., 832
Eslinger, M. v., 842
Esposito, D., 590, 591
Essex, D. W., 920
Estabrook, G., 369
Estes, J. J., 523
Estes, T. H., 523
Ethington, C. A., 237
Etzioni, A., 488
Eubanks, E. E., 618, 623
Evaluation of Educational Achievement, 796
Evans, B., 736
Evans, H. M., 226, 234
Evans, J., 928
Evans, L. J., 853
Evans, R. N., 909
Evans, R. W., 257
Evans, W. H., 700, 702
Everhart, R., 206
Everhart, R. B., 253, 254, 255, 256, 474, 499
Evertson, C., 64, 65, 711
Evertson, C. M., 501
Ewens, T., 959
Ewert, O. M., 51
Exman, E., 444
Eyestone, V. G., 916
Eyler, B., 1018
Eyler, J., 613, 1013, 1014, 1016
Eylon, B., 1018
Eylon, B. S., 517, 802

F

Face, W. L., 901
Fader, D. N., 737
Fager, C., 1033
Faigley, L., 708

FairTest, 615
Fallows, J., 146
Faraday, 443
Faraday, M., 273, 275
Farish, W., 124
Farmer, H. S., 672
Farmer, R., 842
Farmer, S. A., 676
Farnham, J. F., 556
Farr, M., 55
Farr, M. J., 522
Farr, R., 444
Farrar, E., 166, 171, 174, 208, 221, 223, 260, 339, 573, 574, 578, 581, 583–585, 595, 598
Farrell, A. P., 124
Fasold, R. W., 614
Fassett, D., 916
Fassett, J. H., 451
Faucette, N., 976, 983, 986, 991
Faunce, R. C., 1003, 1005
Fawcett, H., 102
Fawns, R., 793
Fay, B., 85, 89, 133
Fay, R. S., 731
Featherman, D. L., 572, 591
Febvre, L., 452
Fechner, G., 312
Feeley, J., 619, 621
Fehr, H., 806
Feiman-Nemser, S., 242, 263, 496, 559
Fein, L. J., 252
Feinberg, W., 756–757
Feistritzer, C. E., 763
Felderhof, M. C., 558
Feldhusen, J. F., 456
Feldman, D., 319, 949
Feldman, E., 950, 956
Felker, D. B., 143
Feltovich, P. J., 55, 518, 528
Feltz, D. L., 1017
Fennema, E., 499, 780
Fennessey, G., 53
Fensham, P., 81, 280, 791, 793–794, 799–800, 802, 804, 805, 807, 811, 814
Fenstermacher, G., 597
Fenstermacher, G. D., 66, 487, 507
Fenton, 562
Fenton, E., 838
Ferrara, R. A., 525
Ferrara, S., 127, 142
Ferreiro, E., 531
Ferris, F. L., Jr., 63
Fetterley, J., 670
Fetterman, D. M., 105, 106
Fetters, W. B., 1009, 1014, 1033
Fey, J., 765
Feyerabend, P. K., 99
Field, W. E., 912
Fielding, L., 714
Fiesch, R., 703
Fifty-Fourth Yearbook of the National Society for the Study of Education, The, 268
Filler, L., 544
Fillmore, W., 869
Filmore, C. J., 638, 708
Finch, C. R., 901, 919, 920
Finch, M. E., 376
Fine, G. A., 990
Fine, M., 623, 632
Finegan, E., 728
Finkelstein, B., 226, 233
Finkelstein, J. M., 841
Finlay, G. C., 63
Finley, M. K., 575, 583, 589
Finn, C. E., Jr., 739, 757
Finney, R., 580
Firestone, W. A., 249, 257, 258
Firth, G. R., 3*n*
Fisch, R., 218
Fischer, H., 50
Fischer, K. W., 954
Fischler, M. L., 1027
Fish, S., 10, 19
Fisher, C., 64
Fisher, G., 122
Fishman, J., 700
Fishman, J. A., 879
Fitzgerald, F., 206, 229, 293, 436, 445, 446, 493
Fitzgerald, F. S., 954
Flagg, B., 110, 111
Flanagan, O., 676
Flanders, J., 764
Flanders, J. K., 228
Flanders, J. R., 436
Flanders, N., 65
Flavell, J. H., 525
Flax, E., 255
Flax, J., 675
Fleischer, S., 708
Fleming, D. B., 835
Fleming, J. T., 704
Fleming, M., 127
Fleming, R., 804, 806
Flesch, R., 447, 705, 713
Flew, A., 551
Flinders, D. J., 9
Floden, R., 55, 188, 194, 195, 204, 221, 227–229, 231
Floden, R. E., 131, 141, 242, 263, 297, 493, 494, 559
Flood, J., 713, 915
Flood, P., 69
Florander, J., 328
Flores, B., 639
Florio, S., 500, 501, 708, 716
Florio-Ruane, S., 481, 500
Flower, L., 781
Flower, L. S., 518, 526, 708
Flygare, T. J., 258
Fodor, J. A., 519, 535
Fogarty, D., 708
Ford, G. W., 102
Ford, P. L., 452, 453, 727
Ford, P. M., 557
Ford, R., 916
Ford, W. W., 766
Fordham, S., 474
Forkner, H. L., 337
Forrest, J. D., 555
Fortune, R., 708
Foshay, A., 103
Foshay, A. S., 487
Foshay, A. W., 3, 328, 334, 433
Foshay, W. R., 487
Foster, E. M., 704
Foster, G., 920
Foster, G. E., 69
Foster, K. M., 859
Foster, P. J., 260
Foucault, M., 84, 88, 137–139, 148, 284, 296, 469
Foulds, K., 808
Fouts, J. T., 845
Fowler, C., 955
Fox, K. R., 991
Fox, W. H., 1011
Fraenkel, J. R., 548, 847
Framer, R., 836
Frangedis, H., 556
Frank, B., 61, 419
Frankel, C., 171
Franklin, B., 164, 226, 234, 237, 273, 275, 445
Franklin, B. M., 80–82, 87, 161, 169, 174, 175, 368, 372, 488, 490, 580
Franks, B. D., 981, 987
Franz, W., 917
Fraser, B., 803
Fraser, D. M., 335
Fraser, N., 673
Frawley, W., 884
Frazier, D., 912
Frechtling, J. A., 147
Frederick, R. W., 1012, 1016
Frederiksen, J. R., 530, 532
Frederiksen, N., 135, 136, 142, 143, 280
Freedman, K., 293, 948
Freedman, S. E., 509
Freedman, S. W., 475, 708
Freedson, P. S., 986
Freeman, D., 195, 198, 202, 204, 221, 227- 229, 231
Freeman, D. J., 131, 141, 493, 494, 495
Freeman, E. A., 727
Freeman, J. H., 358
Freeman, Y., 712
Frei, A., 110
Freidson, E., 488
Freire, P., 255, 292, 316, 633, 652, 936, 967
French, B. S., 506
French, J., 803, 1027
French, M., 670
French, P., 500
Fretwell, E. K., 1003, 1012
Freud, S., 31, 81, 274, 519, 545, 674, 949
Freudenthal, H., 751, 755–756, 758, 760, 766, 769, 770
Frey, K., 110, 814
Frey, O., 670
Freyberg, P., 799, 801
Friedan, B., 673
Friedman, K., 179
Friedman, R. J., 881
Friedrich, P., 256
Friere, P., 88, 89
Fries, C., 700, 703
Friesen, W. V., 1014, 1019–1020
Frisbie, D. A., 126
Frith, G. H., 1032, 1035
Froebel, F., 49, 101, 102, 122, 236, 489, 493, 949
Frohlich, M., 868
Fromm, E., 275
Frost, J., 51, 53, 63
Frost, J. W., 446
Frost, R., 557
Frye, N., 735
Fryklund, V. C., 900
Frymier, J., 330, 331
Fucigna, C., 958
Fuhrman, S., 190
Fulkerson, R., 708
Fullan, M., 131, 228, 367, 368, 369, 376, 403–406, 411, 413, 416, 417, 418, 429, 431, 492, 601
Fuller, F. F., 406
Fuller, T., 297
Fuller, W. E., 355, 359
Furlong, V., 474, 585, 586, 589
Furlong, V. J., 500
Furst, E., 57
Furst, E. J., 140
Furst, N., 64
Furstenberg, F. F., 611–612
Furstenberg, G., 878
Furtado, L. T., 902
Fuson, K. C., 770
Futrell, M. H., 622, 779

G

Gabler, M., 446
Gabler, N., 446
Gadamer, H. G., 88, 91, 286, 289
Gade, E., 1016
Gaelick, L., 992
Gage, N. L., 42, 44, 45, 49, 53, 63, 64, 66, 72, 103, 491, 492
Gagné, R. M., 57, 110, 330, 331, 335, 339, 766
Gagnon, P., 840–841, 848

Gainer, L. J., 931
Galambos, J. A., 518
Galambos, R., 52
Galanter, W. L., 417
Galiardo, R. J., 1016
Galileo, 99, 273
Gall, J., 376
Gall, M. D., 972
Gallagher, J. J., 63, 506
Gallimore, R., 475, 644–645, 645
Gallistel, C. R., 536
Galloway, J., 872–873
Galloway, V., 860, 863, 866–867
Gallup, A., 305
Gallup, A. M., 130
Gallup, G., 978
Gallup, G. H., 1023
Galton, F., 273, 312
Gambell, T., 556
Gambrell, L., 714
Gammon, E. M., 494
Gamoran, A., 43, 206, 290, 345, 573, 575–577, 583–587, 589–592, 594, 599, 600, 714
Gansneder, B., 1022
Gant, M., 204
Garbarino, J., 1021, 1026
Garden, R. A., 769
Gardner, H., 53, 56, 252, 303, 318, 319, 323, 519, 521, 644, 933, 949, 953–954, 959
Gardner, L., 130
Gardner, P., 558
Gardner, R. C., 859
Garduque, L., 1013, 1015
Garet, M., 575, 576, 589
Garet, M. S., 776
Garfinkel, A., 859
Garfinkle, N., 449, 450
Garner, R., 518, 525, 526
Garrison, J. W., 493
Garry, R., 370, 371
Garza-Lubeck, M., 446
Gaskell, J., 226
Gaskell, P. J., 793, 799
Gass, S., 643
Gass, W. H., 286
Gates, 374
Gaumnitz, W. H., 60
Gauthier, J. S., 1012
Gauthier, M. G., 91
Gauthier, W., 1017–1018
Gauthier, W. J., 142, 1014, 1017
Gayen, A. K., 144
Geadelmann, P. L., 671
Gee, J. P., 954
Gee, T., 376
Geel, T. van, 201, 203
Geel, T. von, 227, 228, 234
Geenan, D. L., 986
Geertz, C., 10, 597
Geiger, B., 917
Gelman, R. S., 536
Gendler, T., 69
Genesse, F., 857, 881
Genishi, C., 53
Gentner, D., 523, 524
Gentry, H. W., 1034
Genung, J. F., 692
Geoffrey, W., 104, 237, 242, 306
George, A. A., 408
George, R., 613
Georgiadis, N., 979
Gerace, W., 534
Gerbrich, J. R., 140
Gere, A. R., 692, 701, 708
Gergen, K., 292
Gertzog, W. A., 110, 497, 508
Gesell, A., 50
Getchell, B., 970
Getty Center for Arts Education, 950, 956- 957
Getzels, J., 303, 947, 955
Getzels, J. W., 217, 369, 491, 526
Geuss, R., 286
Gewirtz, J. L., 545
Ghent, P., 534
Gholson, R. E., 1006–1007, 1008, 1014, 1018- 1020, 1022
Giacquinta, J., 367, 405, 406, 411, 416, 430
Giacquinta, J. B., 417
Gibbons, S., 1027
Gibbs, J. C., 548
Gibson, J. J., 536
Gibson, M., 474
Gilbert, J., 801
Giles, H., 421
Gille, K., 473
Gillespie, R., 800
Gilliam, T. B., 975
Gilliam, T. M., 986
Gilligan, C., 93, 545, 547, 548, 554, 555, 558, 668, 673, 676, 807
Gillman, L., 114
Gilmartin, K. J., 671
Gilmore, A., 835, 836
Gilmore, P., 474, 585, 589
Gilroy, M. K., 668
Ginsburg, A., 553, 615
Ginsburg, H., 51
Ginsburg, H. P., 529
Gintis, H., 206, 226, 238, 254, 255, 276, 322, 544, 580, 585, 591, 672, 793, 1036
Giordan, A., 802
Gipps, C., 120, 143
Gipson, V. W., 1009–1011, 1016, 1022
Girls and Science and Technology, 806
Giroux, H., 9, 561, 562
Giroux, H. A., 35, 80, 84, 88, 89, 238, 254, 255, 257, 259, 263, 294, 311, 315, 321, 334, 378, 474, 482, 632–633, 964, 972
Girouz, H. H., 672
Girouz, T., 1007
Glaser, R., 18, 55, 56, 130, 135, 340, 517, 518, 520–522, 526–528, 532–534
Glass, G. V., 65, 103, 104–106, 112
Glatthorn, A. A., 492
Glazer, N., 629
Gleason, J. R., 923
Glinchy, B. M., 93
Glueck, G., 671
Goddard, H., 61
Goddijn, H., 770
Goebel, B. L., 1015, 1019, 1020, 1024
Goertz, M. E., 589
Goetsch, D., 821
Goetting, M. A., 917
Goetz, E. T., 522
Goetz, J. P., 972
Goffman, I., 104
Gold, B. A., 417
Goldberg, M., 586, 593
Goldberger, N. R., 93, 678
Golden, J. M., 486, 501, 502, 503, 508
Goldfield, P., 954, 960
Goldhammer, K., 925
Goldman, A. H., 269
Goldman, S. V., 533
Goldstein, B., 588, 589
Goldstein, H., 120
Goldstein, I., 54
Golomb, C., 951
Gombrich, E., 954
Gonzalez, E., 643, 649
Gonzalez, G., 636
Gonzalez, L., 509
Good, T., 573, 585, 590, 760
Good, T. L., 369, 467, 496, 559
Good, T. S., 48, 51, 55, 61, 64
Goodin, G., 975, 976
Goodlad, J., 834
Goodlad, J. I., 3, 10, 12, 21, 103, 127, 128, 161, 171, 205, 222, 227, 231, 233, 234, 236, 242, 252, 306, 316, 328, 329, 331, 335, 338, 340, 365, 367, 368, 378, 403, 411, 444, 467, 482, 506, 560, 573, 585, 586, 590, 594, 596–598, 598, 776, 930
Goodman, D., 531
Goodman, J., 49, 392, 842
Goodman, K., 639
Goodman, K. S., 537, 621, 704, 712
Goodman, N., 286, 287, 288, 289, 304, 318, 954
Goodman, P., 102, 269, 467
Goodman, Y., 53, 639, 713
Goodman, Y. M., 537
Goodnow, J., 951
Goodnow, J. J., 519
Goodnow, J. L., 699, 703
Goodson, I., 33, 493
Goodson, I. F., 178, 179, 224, 235, 257, 293, 346, 487
Goodwin, D. A., 928
Googins, B., 917
Gordon, C., 711
Gordon, D., 9, 276, 500
Gordon, E., 953
Gordon, P., 144
Gordon, R. M., 558
Gordon, S. C., 121
Gormley, W., 192
Gortmaker, S. L., 984
Gorton, R. A., 1009
Goswami, D., 708
Gott, R., 808
Gottlieb, D., 1034
Gottlieb, N. H., 992
Goud, S. J., 867
Gould, S. J., 596
Goulston, W., 670
Gove, W., 80, 81
Governor's Commission on Physical Fitness, 978
Gowin, D. B., 368
Grabe, M. D., 1014, 1016, 1018–1019, 1021, 1027–1028
Grady, J. B., 1009
Graff, G., 385
Grafton, A., 272, 273, 293
Grafton, T., 260
Graham, G., 982, 983, 1003, 1005
Graham, J., 385
Graham, K., 501
Graham, P. A., 167
Grambs, J. D., 668
Grammatical Institute of the English Language, 727
Grandjean, B. D., 668
Grant, C., 236
Grant, C. A., 259, 260
Grant, G., 559, 592
Grant, G. E., 504
Grant, G. W., 713
Grant, L., 633
Grant, M., 88, 806
Grant, N., 123, 144
Grasso, J., 593
Graue, M. E., 116
Graves, D., 633
Graves, D. H., 500, 708, 710–711
Gray, P. S., 115
Gray, T. C., 882
Gray, W. S., 695, 696–698, 699, 704, 705

Greaney, V., 139, 143, 145, 146
Greeley, A. M., 69
Green, A., 206, 585
Green, B. F., 517
Green, D., 639
Green, J., 500, 949
Green, J. L., 500, 501, 502, 503
Green, T., 196, 202, 207, 208
Green, T. F., 369, 370, 551, 558
Greenan, M., 931
Greenbaum, W., 629
Greenberg, D. H., 134
Greenberg, H., 778
Greenberg, S., 669
Greenberger, E., 1013, 1015
Greene, H., 140
Greene, L., 1032
Greene, M., 18, 90, 108, 335, 338, 365, 368, 370, 378, 678, 760, 936, 954–955
Greenfield, T. B., 371
Greeno, J., 56, 774, 777, 779, 802
Greeno, J. G., 129
Greenockle, K. M., 976, 985
Greenwood, P., 201
Greenwood, P. W., 372, 373
Greer, D. W., 957
Greer, E. A., 493, 494
Gress, J. R., 3*n*, 4, 561
Griffin, P., 482, 716
Griffin, P. S., 967, 974–975, 982, 989
Griffin, S., 531
Griffiths, M., 287
Grimshaw, J., 292, 663, 676
Grimshaw, P., 665
Griswold, P.A., 126
Grittner, F. M., 860
Gritzmacher, J., 917
Gritzmacher, J. E., 915–917
Grizzell, E. D., 353, 354
Grobman, H., 63, 370, 374
Grocott, P., 917
Groen, G., 504
Groff, P., 592
Grommon, A. H., 729
Gromoll, E. W., 493, 494, 531
Groos, K., 49
Gross, B., 560
Gross, N., 367, 405, 406, 411, 416, 417, 430
Gross, R., 560
Gross, R. E., 833, 836
Grossman, P., 202
Grossman, P. L., 498, 499
Grouws, D. A., 64
Grubb, N., 225
Grubb, W. N., 578
Grube, G. M. A., 758
Grumet, M., 311, 673, 673–674, 678
Grumet, M. R., 79, 80, 91–93, 102, 108, 392
Grundmann, H., 661–662
Guardado, S., 555
Guarini, G., 272, 273
Guba, E., 199, 200
Guba, E. G., 81, 86, 88, 91, 92, 94, 131, 133, 993
Gudmundsdottir, S., 498, 499
Guesne, E., 801
Guinn, R., 176
Guiton, G., 72, 576, 577
Gump, P. V., 1007–1008, 1013–1014, 1019- 1020, 1023, 1027–1028, 1030
Gumperz, J., 708, 711
Gunstone, R., 801, 810
Gunstone, R. F., 223
Gusfield, J. R., 180
Guskey, T. R., 377
Gutek, G. L., 164
Guthrie, J., 71
Guthrie, L. F., 583, 714
Gutman, C. J., 523
Gutowski, T. W., 231, 1003
Guy, L. M., 987
Gwynn, J. M., 489
Gysbers, N. C., 925

H

Haag, H., 974, 975
Haas, J. D., 832
Haas, J. P., 838–839
Haas, K. B., 901
Habermas, J., 85, 88, 133, 205, 286, 287, 333, 338, 543, 947
Hacker, M., 821
Hadley, C., 121
Haensley, P. A., 1016
Haertel, E., 127, 129, 137, 138, 142, 145
Haertel, G. D., 53
Haggerty, M. E., 123
Hagstrom, W. O., 753
Hahn, C. L., 445, 670, 671, 832–834, 836, 839, 841–843, 847
Haines, D. F., 279, 281
Hakuta, K., 858, 882
Hakuta, S. K., 853
Haladyna, T., 473
Haladyna, T. M., 145, 147, 845
Halasz, I. M., 925–926
Hale, J., 615
Hales, J., 816
Hales, J. A., 919
Haley, M., 230
Halfin, H., 929
Halkes, R., 56
Hall, E. T., 131
Hall, G., 405–407, 407, 408, 417
Hall, G. E., 368, 377, 492
Hall, G. R., 69
Hall, G. S., 165, 176, 197, 224, 451, 666
Hall, J., 147
Hall, J. L., 419
Hall, M. M., 1004, 1034
Hall, O., 668
Hall, P. W., 671
Hall, S. G., 731, 733
Hall, W., 805
Halleck, R. P., 1003
Haller, E., 56
Haller, E. J., 576, 577, 595
Halliday, M., 743
Halliday, M. A. K., 53, 708
Hallinan, M. T., 576, 587, 592
Hallinger, P., 585, 591
Ham, M., 770
Hamerow, T. S., 556
Hamilton, D., 5, 103, 108, 131, 180, 226, 236, 275, 479
Hamilton, S., 208
Hamilton, S. F., 572
Hamilton, W., 121
Hamilton, W. H., 912
Hamlyn, D., 258
Hamm, C. M., 548
Hamm, M., 558
Hammer, T., 555
Hammer, T. H., 558
Hammerly, H., 857
Hammersley, M., 179
Hammond, K., 56
Hammonds, C., 893
Hampel, R., 226
Hampson, D. H., 335
Hampson, M., 910
Handscombe, J., 639
Haney, C., 613
Haney, W., 70, 71, 126, 135, 137, 139, 141, 146, 147, 223, 235
Hanks, M., 1017, 1024–1025, 1029–1031
Hanna, P., 447
Hannabus, S., 556
Hannah, J. L., 956
Hannan, D. F., 592
Hannan, M., 358
Hansell, S., 592, 593
Hansen, C., 228
Hansen, J., 713
Hansen, J. H., 711
Hansen, L. W., 914
Hanson, R. A., 573, 583
Hanson, S., 553, 585, 588, 589
Hanson, T., 202
Hansot, E., 122, 219, 223, 225, 226, 232, 239, 367, 368, 488, 544, 665, 669–670
Harap, H., 3, 339
Harasim, L. M., 375, 376
Hardiman, P. T., 534
Harding, J., 92, 806, 808
Harding, S., 290, 291, 671
Harding, S. S., 674–675
Hare, R. M., 543, 550–552
Hare, S., 576, 577, 589
Hargreaves, A., 236, 295
Hargreaves, D., 236, 561
Hargreaves, D. H., 583, 585, 589, 592, 597
Harker, J. O., 500, 501
Harlen, W., 814
Harley, B., 857, 871, 881
Harlow, L. L., 869
Harmin, M., 549, 550, 560
Harper, G. F., 145
Harper, W. R., 222
Harre, R., 520, 536
Harrington, G. M., 491
Harrington, L. G., 929
Harris, A. S., 671
Harris, C., 386
Harris, E., 921
Harris, J. J., III, 613
Harris, L., 978
Harris, W. T., 101, 164, 356, 357, 370, 403, 441
Harris-Sharples, S., 229
Harrison, B., 258
Harrison, G., 819, 821–822
Harrison, W., 921
Harrod, P. M. F., 500
Harste, J., 370, 716
Hart, C. W. M., 255
Harter, S., 1028
Hartley, J., 531
Hartley, S., 65
Hartshorne, H., 545, 556
Hartsock, N., 675
Harvard University, 729
Harvey, B., 923
Harvey, F. R., 752
Harvey, J. G., 761
Harwood, D., 952
Harylick, M., 956
Hashweh, M. Z., 498
Haskins, C., 271
Hass, G., 3*n*
Hass, N. S., 145, 147
Hastings, P., 992
Hastings, T., 123, 129
Hatch, T., 53, 56
Hatcher, E., 912
Hatfield, W. W., 691, 733
Hauptman, P. C., 877
Haussler, M., 53
Havelock, R., 200
Havelock, R. G., 410
Havighurst, R., 242
Havighurst, R. J., 550, 552, 557
Hawke, S., 832, 835, 841
Hawkes, H. E., 136
Hawkins, D., 385
Hawkins, H. P., 920
Hawkins, L. S., 905
Hawkins, M., 592
Hawkins, M. L., 835–836
Hawthorne, R., 367
Hayakawa, S. I., 628

Haycock, K., 627
Haydon, D. F., 987
Hayes, D. H., 500
Hayes, E., 729
Hayes, J. R., 518, 526, 528, 708
Hays, A. G., 447
Hays, S. P., 489
Hayvren, M., 451, 713
Hazlett, J. S., 161, 163
Head, J., 807
Heaney, W., 141
Heap, J. L., 502, 503
Hearn, W. E., 121, 135
Hearold, S., 65
Heartman, C. F., 453
Heath, R. W., 287
Heath, S., 206, 598, 599
Heath, S. B., 257, 475, 621, 644, 708, 711, 716, 954
Heath, T. L., 751
Heath-Sipos, B., 921
Heathcote, D., 742, 950
Heathers, G., 590
Hebb, D. O., 52
Heckert, B. L., 671
Heckert, M., 671
Heclo, H., 190
Hedgpath, W. D., 1016, 1018
Hegel, G. W., 312
Hegelson, S., 790
Heidegger, 91
Heikkinen, H., 807, 812
Heilenman, L. K., 872
Heinemann, S. H., 1043
Helburn, S., 670
Helburn, S. W., 436, 832, 834–835
Held, V., 676
Helgeson, S., 199
Hellison, D. R., 967–968, 972, 979, 992
Helmholtz, H. von, 312
Hemmings, A., 574, 595
Hendry, L. B., 978
Hening, G., 882
Henkin, L., 114
Henley, N., 670
Henning, G., 862, 880, 882
Henry, J., 467, 478, 588, 946
Henry, N., 224, 268
Henry, N. B., 444, 706, 908
Henslow, J., 274
Heny, F., 879
Herald, K., 416, 417
Herbart, J. F., 101, 122
Herber, H., 704
Herman, J. L., 127, 613, 616
Herman, W. L., 836
Herman, W. L., Jr., 839
Herr, E. L., 926
Herrick, V. E., 331, 340, 703, 706–707
Herrington, A. J., 708
Herriott, R. E., 417
Hersh, R., 751
Hersh, R. J., 750
Hertweck, A., 467
Hertzberg, H. W., 835, 841–842
Hess, M., 553
Hess, R. D., 615
Hesse, M., 80
Hester, S., 597
Heubner, D., 3, 21, 28, 316
Hewer, A., 548
Hewitt, J. D., 1026
Hewitt, N. M., 868
Hewson, M. G., 258
Hewson, P. W., 110, 497, 508
Heyneman, S. P., 143
Heyns, B., 577, 593, 617, 1036
Hidi, S. E., 531
Hiebert, E. H., 451, 583, 590, 591, 710, 712
Higbee, K. L., 992
Higgins, A., 549, 561
Higgs, T. V., 861
Hildreth, G., 706
Hilgard, E. R., 520
Hill, P. T., 69
Hill, T., 813
Hill, W., 57
Hillard, A., 620
Hiller, R. J., 629
Hillison, J., 894, 926
Hillocks, G., 256, 258, 708, 716
Hilmo, I., 807
Hines, J., 805
Hintikka, M., 671
Hirsch, B., 946
Hirsch, E. D., Jr., 171, 174, 286, 296, 297, 310, 311, 315, 332, 523, 632, 647, 715, 728, 738
Hirsch, J. D., 208
Hirschland, R. P., 965
Hirsh, S. A., 258
Hirst, A., 770
Hirst, K., 770
Hirst, P. H., 52, 103, 278, 279, 287, 318, 319, 323, 551, 558
Hiss, W. C., 1024
Hitchcock, A. M., 692
Ho, P., 976
Hoachlander, E. G., 593
Hobbes, T., 284, 285, 286
Hobson, C. J., 1036
Hochchild, A., 667
Hodges, W., 417
Hodgins, J. G., 276
Hodgkinson, H. L., 367
Hodson, D., 158, 180, 793, 802
Hoetker, J., 236, 742
Hoff Sommers, C., 545, 561
Hoffer, T., 69, 320, 1016
Hoffman, M., 545, 547
Hofman, G., 1034
Hofstadter, R., 163
Hofstein, A., 370, 808, 1018
Hogan, D., 225, 230, 238, 472
Hogan, D. J., 356
Hogan, P., 393
Hogue, K., 911
Hohenhaus, W., 910
Holguin, O., 978
Hollaender, A., 51
Holland, A., 1013, 1019
Holland, J. G., 47
Holland, J. H., 521
Holland, P. B., 69
Holley, F. M., 618, 868
Holley, J. L., 914
Hollingshead, A., 242, 581
Hollingshead, A. B., 1007, 1013–1014, 1022
Hollingsworth, A. M., 728–729
Hollis, M., 289
Holloway, L. D., 904, 924
Holly, P., 377
Holman, J., 805, 813
Holmberg, B., 376
Holmes Group, 313, 843
Holmes, C., 249
Holmes, E. E., 144
Holobow, N., 857
Holt, J., 102, 467
Holt, T., 950, 955, 959
Holyoak, K. J., 521
Holzman, M., 518
Homer, 271
Honey, J. R., 277
Honig, B., 557, 618
Hood, B. L., 489, 493
Hook, J. N., 691, 726, 731
Hook, S., 269
Hooper, F. H., 51
Hooper, L. M., 973, 980
Hoover, E., 671
Hopkins, C., 895, 914
Hopkins, D., 105, 377
Hopkins, K. D., 140, 1029
Hopper, R., 615
Horace, 368
Horak, V. M., 48
Hord, S. M., 377, 408, 410, 417
Horio, T., 262, 308
Horn, E., 101, 696
Horn, G., 1032
Horner, J. D., 910
Horner, M., 668
Horney, K., 274
Horwitz, R. A., 53, 64, 65
Horwood, R. H., 802
Hosic, J., 692–693
Hosic, J. F., 690, 731–732, 741
Hoskins, K., 124, 125
Hostetler, J. A., 255, 256, 454
Hotchkiss, L., 591, 593
Hotyat, F., 142
Hounshell, P., 274
House, E., 188, 199, 200, 220, 224, 227, 239, 241
House, E. R., 112, 128, 377, 410
Householder, D. L., 901, 918–919
Houston, J., 94
Houston, R. W., 966
Hovell, M. E., 964
Howard, A., 256
Howe, F., 677
Howe, R., 199, 790
Howe, S. G., 59, 122
Howlett, N., 714
Howson, A. G., 750, 756, 759, 769, 772
Hoyt, K. B., 905, 925–926
Hsieh, H-C., 592
Huberman, A. M., 405, 409, 430
Huberman, M., 105, 369, 374
Huckin, T., 708
Huddle, E., 410
Hudelson, E., 693
Hudelson, S., 640–641
Hueber, C., 452
Huebner, D., 83, 91, 334, 338
Huey, E. B., 695, 716
Huff, R., 53
Hufstedler, S., 804
Hughes, H., 878
Hughes, R. N., 121
Huling-Austin, S., 410, 417
Hull, D. L., 280, 284, 287, 288
Hull, T., 546, 573
Humble, S., 383
Humm, W. L., 1007–1009
Hungerford, H., 805
Hunkins, F. P., 335, 336, 936
Hunkler, R., 1028
Hunt, A., 813
Hunt, M. P., 832
Hunter, G. W., 455
Hunter, M., 210, 373, 377
Hurd, P., 199, 227
Hurtado, A., 613
Husen, T., 769
Husserl, 91
Hustler, D., 105
Hutchcroft, C. R., 226, 234
Hutchins, R., 309, 310, 311
Hutchins, R. M., 18, 19, 197, 309, 333, 334, 735, 758
Hutchinson, G., 982
Hutchinson, P., 807
Hutslar, S., 989
Huxley, T., 455
Hyde, J., 807
Hyde, J. S., 667
Hyde, R. T., 965, 970
Hyman, R., 573
Hymes, D., 474, 509, 711, 861
Hynes, K., 1014, 1019

I

Iadicola, P., 613
Ichilov, O., 1014, 1021
Igra, A., 1027

Illich, 561
Imber, M., 180, 241
Inglis, A. J., 353–357
Ingraham, P., 191
Ingram, D., 546
Inhelder, B., 50, 72, 699, 703
Inlow, G. M., 3*n*
International Council of Scientific Unions, 789
International Technology Education Association, 817
Intili, J. K., 645
Iran-Nejad, A., 520, 521
Irwin, S., 227, 228
Isaacs, S., 49
Ives, W., 52
Izzo, S., 867

J

Jackson, K., 676
Jackson, M., 1016, 1018, 1022
Jackson, M. M. B., 365
Jackson, P., 104, 107, 108, 174, 222, 233, 236, 237, 305, 306
Jackson, P. W., 4, 8, 45, 63, 83, 84, 89, 126, 130, 193, 199, 250, 270, 273, 276, 369, 370, 378, 379, 380, 381, 385, 467, 469, 491, 498, 500, 558, 559, 561, 562, 573, 574, 585, 750, 760, 765, 955, 964
Jackson, S., 444
Jacob, E., 108, 133, 134, 589
Jacob, S., 1034
Jacobs, D. R., 978, 987
Jacobs, H., 758
Jacobs, V. A., 716
Jacobsen, W., 922
Jacobson, R., 637
Jaeger, R., 140
Jaeger, R. M., 66
Jaffee, A., 781
Jaggar, A., 621
Jaggar, A. M., 292
Jahnke, H., 752
Jahnke, H. N., 757, 764
James, J., 228
James, M., 121
James, T., 227, 558
James, W., 46, 80, 100, 106
Jamison, D., 340
Janis, I. R., 992
Janke, H. N., 767
Jantz, R. K., 841–843
Jardine, L., 272, 273, 293
Jarolimek, J., 834
Jencks, C., 576, 591, 593, 1036
Jenkins, D., 3*n*, 33
Jenkins, E., 792, 793, 803, 813
Jenkins, F., 794
Jenkinson, E. B., 258
Jennings, J. F., 771
Jennings, K. H., 711
Jennings, L., 252
Jennings, M. K., 204, 1028, 1029
Jennings, S. H. M., 711
Jensen, A., 260
Jensen, A. R., 614
Jensen, F. A., 444
Jersild, A. T., 377
Jewett, A. E., 557, 966–969, 973, 980, 993
Jiminez, E., 668
Joekel, R. G., 1032
John, V. P., 474
Johnson, C., 350, 452, 727
Johnson, C. D., 561
Johnson, D. D., 711–713
Johnson, D. W., 558, 591
Johnson, E. W., 1003
Johnson, H. C., Jr., 544
Johnson, J., 818
Johnson, L. C., 987, 989
Johnson, M., Jr., 486
Johnson, M. A., 891, 935
Johnson, Marietta, 167
Johnson, Mark, 369, 393
Johnson, N., 953
Johnson, N. B., 242
Johnson, R., 293, 558, 591
Johnson, S. D., 930
Johnson, S. M., 230, 231
Johnson, W. S., 1026
Johnson-Laird, P. N., 523
Johnston, C. H., 419
Johnston, K., 810
Johnston, P. A., 527, 617, 711, 714
Johnston, V. M., 473, 474
Johnston, W. B., 772
Johnstone, J. N., 120
Joint Committee on Standards for Educational Evaluation, 120
Joncich, G. M., 489, 490, 491
Jones, A., 231
Jones, D., 966
Jones, G., 1003, 1008
Jones, G. A., 764
Jones, J. D., 576, 577, 583, 585, 591, 593
Jones, L. S., 980
Jones, L. V., 68, 439, 444
Jones, P. S., 756
Jordan, C., 257, 258, 262, 475, 589, 599, 645, 711
Jordan, R. H., 1003
Jorg, T., 806
Jorgensen, A., 140
Journal of Legal Education, 676
Joyce, B. R., 3, 53, 373, 377, 491
Judd, C. H., 100, 123, 125, 224, 239, 278, 444, 489
Judy, S. N., 726
Jung, C., 274, 674
Jung, C. W., 1011
Jurkowitz, C. M., 234, 235
Just, M. A., 519
Justman, J., 140, 586, 593

K

Kadamus, J. A., 931
Kaestle, C. F., 134, 137, 159, 175, 205, 218, 223, 228, 293, 348, 351, 352, 450, 694, 698
Kagan, J., 53, 553
Kagan, S., 633, 645
Kahane, J. R., 772
Kahn, J. L., 425
Kalh, S., 65
Kalk, J., 65
Kamii, C., 53, 144
Kamin, L. J., 61
Kaminski, J., 147
Kammen, M., 574
Kandel, I. L., 1005
Kane, C. H., 248, 256
Kanger, F. H., 992
Kant, I., 543, 547, 663
Kantor, H., 225, 581, 909
Kantor, H. A., 173, 175
Kantowski, M. G., 770
Kapferrer, J., 1009
Kaplan, A., 113
Kaplan, B., 951
Kaplan, I., 872
Karelse, K., 912
Kariya, T., 208, 571, 593
Karoly, L., 576, 577, 594
Karper, W., 989
Karplus, 368
Kasarda, J., 587
Kaser, J. S., 147
Kasper, G., 884
Kass, H., 375, 797
Kataoka, T., 1007
Katz, M. B., 159, 223–226, 238, 472, 473, 727, 946–947
Katznelson, I., 238, 472, 473
Kauchak, D., 65
Kaulfers, W. V., 734
Kazemek, F. E., 555
Kazipedes, T., 551
Kean, C. J., 173
Kearney, M. C., 328
Keating, P., 482
Keddie, N., 206, 499, 583–588, 597, 600
Keefe, J. W., 936
Keegan, D., 376
Keels, O. M., Jr., 830
Keerr, E. F., 904
Keeves, J., 796
Keeves, J. P., 103
Kegler, S. B., 705
Keislar, E., 52
Keisler, H. J., 753
Keitel, C., 752, 757, 759, 778
Keith, P., 405, 411, 412–415, 417
Keith, P. M., 367
Kellaghan, T., 135, 136, 143, 146
Keller, C., 676
Keller, E. F., 81, 92, 291, 292, 671, 675
Keller, F. J., 925
Keller, P. G., 1003
Keller, S., 586
Kellerman, H., 520, 521
Kellogg, B., 691
Kellogg, R., 951
Kelly, 125
Kelly, A., 806–808
Kelly, A. V., 132, 144, 551
Kelly, G. P., 662, 670
Kelly, L. G., 691, 728
Kelly, M., 588
Kelly, P., 790
Kelly, P. J., 532
Kelly, T. E., 558
Kemerer, F. R., 258
Keming, J. S., 837
Kemmis, S., 385, 493, 936
Kempa, R., 808
Kemper, H. C. G., 987
Kennard, B., 392
Kennedy, E. L., 662, 670
Kennedy, M., 417
Kenney, A. M., 555
Kenway, J., 93
Kenyon, G. S., 976
Kepler-Zumwalt, K., 659
Kepner, H. S., 759
Kerckhoff, A. C., 572, 576, 591, 594
Keroes, J., 709
Kerr, E. E., 924
Kesler, K., 912
Kessler, H. L., 339
Kessler, S., 295, 1034
Kickbusch, K. W., 253, 254, 255, 256, 499
Kidder, S., 53
Kieren, T., 375
Kifer, E., 577, 583
Kifer, S. O., 67, 69
Kiger, J., 229, 230
Kilbourn, B., 385, 392
Kilgore, S., 69, 1016
Killens, J., 227
Kilpatrick, J., 759, 776
Kilpatrick, W. H., 102, 103, 125, 167, 168, 173, 178, 224, 278, 337, 348, 551, 733
Kilzer, L., 1012
Kim, M. S., 770
Kimball, B., 197, 271
Kimball, S. T., 253, 254
Kimpston, R. D., 376, 964
Kinakin, D., 376
Kincheloe, J. L., 256
Kineberg, O., 859

King, A. R., Jr., 763
King, J. K., 868
King, K., 814
King, M. L., Jr., 553
King, N. R., 88
Kingdon, J., 189, 190
Kingsley, C., 163
Kingston, P. W., 842
Kinnear, M., 662
Kinneavy, J., 708
Kirby, D., 544
Kircher, M., 953
Kirk, D., 966, 970, 991
Kirp, D. L., 228, 234, 239
Kirsch, A., 497, 507
Kirst, M., 188, 189, 195, 204, 221, 224, 227–229, 234, 417
Kirst, M. W., 102, 251, 367, 368, 377
Kisabeth, K. L., 980
Kister, J., 917
Kitcher, P., 751, 753
Kitsuse, J. I., 575, 577, 589
Kitzhaber, A., 708
Klahr, D., 519
Klainin, S., 807, 808
Klaits, J., 662
Klare, G. R., 696, 711
Klatis, J., 663
Klaurens, M., 895
Klausen, K., 985
Klausmeier, H. J., 330, 410
Klawiller, K., 841–843
Klein, F., 103
Klein, M. F., 128, 328, 329, 335, 336, 338, 368, 411, 761
Klein, S. S., 555, 671
Klein, T. W., 645
Kleine, P. F., 367, 368
Kleine, P., 217, 219, 224
Kleinert, E. J., 1019
Kleinert, J. E., 1020–1021
Kleinig, J., 551
Kliebard, H. M., 3, 7, 13, 15, 16, 18, 22, 28, 31, 46, 60, 81, 82, 84, 87, 102, 103, 159–161, 165, 171, 174, 175, 180, 196, 197, 223, 224, 225, 229, 231, 239, 270, 293, 331, 334, 356, 360, 365, 366, 378, 447, 487, 488, 489, 490, 492, 493, 570, 573, 574, 578, 580–582, 585, 588, 595, 598, 749, 761, 765, 767, 776, 891
Klimpston, R. D., 3*n*
Kline, C., 55
Kline, M., 750, 751, 756
Klitgaard, R. E., 69
Klopfer, L. E., 16, 223, 517, 801, 810, 955
Kloss, H., 627
Kluckholn, C., 481
Knapp, C. E., 557
Knappen, T., 221, 229, 231
Kneer, M. E., 969, 974
Kneeshaw, S., 556
Knigga, M., 671
Knight, G., 753
Knight, R. S., 837
Knop, C. K., 875
Knowles, M. S., 375
Knowles, R. T., 553
Kochman, T., 615
Koerner, J. D., 144
Kogan, N., 53
Kohl, H., 231, 467, 481
Kohl, H. W., 970
Kohlberg, L., 50, 543, 545–551, 553, 554, 557, 560–562, 676, 832, 837
Kohler, W., 52
Kohns, D., 921
Kollen, P. P., 990, 992
Kolmogorov, A. N., 750
Kolstad, A. J., 1009, 1014, 1033
Koltnow, J., 671
Komoski, K. P., 229
Koos, L. V., 1005, 1011–1012
Koretz, D., 70, 71, 146
Korpi, M., 127, 142
Korsemeyer, C. W., 662, 670
Korth, W., 506
Kortland, K., 805, 813
Korzenik, D., 948
Koslin, B. L., 136
Koslin, S., 136
Koslow, R. E., 970
Kozol, J., 258
Kramarae, C., 670
Kramer, E. E., 780
Kramer, J., 256
Kramsch, S., 880
Krashen, S. D., 642–643, 864, 870, 876
Krathwohl, D., 57
Krathwohl, D. R., 123, 129
Kratus, J., 952
Kratzmann, A., 251
Kraus, H., 965
Krausz, M., 289
Kreeft-Peyton, J., 640
Kreinberg, N., 671
Kreitzer, A. E., 146, 147
Kremer, L., 376
Kreutter, M. W., 992
Kridel, C., 161
Kristeva, J., 674
Krogh, S. L., 556, 559
Kroll, B., 700
Kroma, S., 385
Krug, E. A., 100, 162, 163, 165, 166, 168, 224, 225, 574, 580, 598, 1003, 1004
Kuhn, D., 50
Kuhn, T. S., 99, 101, 107, 288, 442, 443, 753
Kuhs, L., 221, 229, 231
Kuhs, T., 198
Kuhs, T. M., 493, 494
Kulik, C.-L., 591, 594
Kulik, J., 591, 594
Kulik, J. A., 64, 65
Kulkarni, V., 795, 803
Kundsin, R. B., 671
Kung, G., 548
Kung, H., 94
Kuntz, J. F., 307, 320
Kuntzleman, C. T., 986–987
Kupper, L., 868
Kurdek, L. A., 1034
Kurtines, W. M., 545
Kutnick, P., 560
Kyle, D. W., 713
Kyle, W. C., Jr., 474
Kyte, G. C., 696, 698

L

Laban, R., 968
Labarca, A., 863, 867
Labaree, D. F., 175, 176, 196, 207, 225, 254, 356, 580–582, 595
LaBelle, T. J., 254, 261
Laboratory of Comparative Human Cognition, 503
Labov, W., 614, 700, 711, 743, 953
Lacan, J., 674
Lacey, C., 583, 585, 589, 592
Ladner, J., 258
LaFarge, P., 558
Lafayette, R. C., 877
Laffer, A. B., 121
Lafleur, C., 375
LaFollette, J., 574–576, 583, 589
Lagemann, E. C., 231, 489, 490, 492
Laird, J. E., 521
Lajoie, S., 521
Lakatos, I., 99, 288, 519, 535, 751
Lakoff, G., 369, 708
Lakomski, G., 9, 276, 500
Lamb, H., 743
Lambdin, D., 974
Lambert, R., 480
Lambert, W. E., 629, 637, 643, 857–859
Lambrecht, J. L., 891, 913–915
Lamon, S. J., 779
Lampert, M., 197, 392, 477, 481, 497, 498, 507, 526, 533, [illegible], [illegible], 700
Lamport, H. B., 452
Lancaster, J., 472
Landau, M., 187
Lander, L. M., 976, 980
Landers, D. L., 1017
Landers, D. M., 1017
Landry, R. C., 853
Landsheere, G. De, 100
Landsness, R. M., 838
Lane, H., 560
Lange, J. de, 750, 769, 778
Langeheine, R., 110
Langenburg, D. N., 804
Langer, J.,766
Langer, J. A., 227, 236, 699, 708, 711–712, 716, 738-741, 745
Langer, S., 304, 318, 954
Langland, E., 80, 81
Langley, P., 519
Lanier, J. E., 385, 562, 964
Lantolf, J. P., 884
Lantz, O., 328
Lapkin, S., 643, 651, 857, 859, 881
LaPlante, M. J., 980
Lapointe, A. E., 439, 482, 772
Lapp, D., 713
Larkin, J., 55, 524, 528, 802
Larkins, G. A., 835–836
Larsen-Freeman, D., 882
Lasch, C., 953
Lashley, K. S., 52
Lather, P., 86, 89, 92, 254
Lathronp, F. W., 892
Latta, R. M., 1014, 1019, 1021
Lauda, D. P., 919
Laudan, L., 288
Laughlin, M. A., 831
Lauglo, J., 931
Lauritzen, P., 93
Lauter, P., 666
Lauterbach, R., 814
Lave, J., 56, 258, 498, 536, 753
LaVigne, L., 251
Lavrent'ev, M. A., 750
Lawn, M., 35
Lawn, N., 383
Lawson, A., 801
Lawson, H. A., 967–968, 970–971, 988
Lawton, D., 144, 295, 367, 847
Layton, D., 158, 178, 273, 274, 293, 789, 791, 793, 818
Layton, E., Jr., 822–823
Lazar, I., 617
Lazerson, M., 205, 225, 487, 578
Lazonby, J., 806
Le Bold, W. K., 671
Leacock, E., 585, 588
Leary, B., 698
Leaver, B. L., 877
Leavis, F. R., 556
LeCompte, M. D., 972
Lectures on Rhetoric and Belles Lettres, 728
Lee, A. L., 976, 985
Lee, A. M., 967, 969
Lee, C. C., 615
Lee, G. C., 365
Lee, J. H., 911

Lee, J. M., 140
Lee, P., 52
Lee, S. Y., 772
Lee, V. E., 69, 70, 575, 576, 583, 591, 600, 668
Leehey, K., 992
Legacy, J., 910
Legaretta, D. M., 636–637
LeGault, D. A. L., 1016
Legwold, G., 970
Lehman, P., 945, 952
Lehr, F., 713
Leibowitz, A. H., 627
Leinhardt, G., 56, 132, 141, 404, 498, 711, 714, 765
Leither, K. C., 711
Leithwood, K., 417
Leithwood, K. A., 367, 376
LeMahieu, P. G., 143
Leming, J. S., 550, 556, 557, 562, 832, 835, 838, 840, 844, 846
Lemke, J. L., 501, 503, 507, 803
Lengel, J. G., 832, 836
Lennenberg, E. H., 52
Lenrow, E., 734
Leon, C. D. De, 287
Leonard, F. E., 964
Leonard, J. P., 330
Leonard, S. A., 728, 732
Leonardson, G. R., 1018
Leonhard, C., 952
LePage, R. B., 261
Leplin, J., 288
LeRiche, L. W., 836
Lerner, B., 121
Lerner, G., 671
Lesgold, A. M., 521
Leske, G., 891
Lesko, N., 600
Leslie, L. L., 258
Leventhal, C., 583
Levin, D. M., 557
Levin, H., 206, 226, 236, 238, 594, 672
Levin, H. M., 57, 252, 776
Levin, J., 321
Levin, J. R., 520, 523, 525
Levin, M., 292
Levine, D., 669
Levine, D. M., 121
Levine, D. O., 99
Levine, D. U., 618, 623
Levine, J. M., 1025
Levine, L., 295
Levine, L. W., 727
Levines, C., 548
Lewellen, J. R., 1029
Lewis, A. J., 419
Lewis, J., 790, 805
Lewis, M. W., 526, 528
Lewis, S., 808
Lewis, W., 917
Lewis, W. D., 692
Lezama, J., 643, 649
Liberman, K., 258
Lickona, T., 548, 553, 554
Lieb-Brilhart, B., 670
Lieberman, A., 373, 377, 378, 393
Lieberman, M., 488
Lifka, B., 979
Lightfoot, M., 370, 385
Lightfoot, S., 585, 592
Lightfoot, S. L., 222, 369, 559
Lillis, K., 931
Lincoln, Y. S., 41, 80, 81, 84, 86, 88, 91, 92, 94, 993
Lindberg, S. W., 450, 452
Lindblom, C., 189
Linder, S., 191
Lindquist, E. F., 136
Lindquist, M. M., 759
Lindsay, P., 1013, 1014, 1019–1021, 1030- 1031
Lindsey, R., 965
Linn, M., 802, 807
Linn, M. C., 667
Linn, R. L., 126, 134, 146
Linton, R., 250
Lipman, I., 669
Lippincott, W., 812
Lipsky, M., 193–195
Lipton, E., 955
Lipton, M., 596
Litowitz, L., 930
Little, A., 135, 144
Little, C. J., 964
Little, J., 417
Little, J. W., 376, 385, 562
Littlefield, G. E., 452
Littlewood, W., 882
Livengood, W. W., 444
Livermore, A. H., 63
Livingston, S., 53
Lloyd-Jones, R., 700, 709, 716, 739, 741
Locke, H. D., 972
Locke, J., 46, 101
Locke, L. F., 975, 988, 993
Lockheed, M. E., 668
Lockwood, A. L., 550, 551, 553, 837
Loef, M., 499
Loehlin, J. C., 536
Logan, F. M., 948
Logan, T., 377
Logsdon, B. J., 968, 973
Lohman, D. F., 129
Lomax, R., 976, 985
Long, M., 445
Long, M. H., 643, 861, 869
Long, R., 1009, 1016, 1018, 1022
Longstreet, W. S., 831–832
Loren, K., 260
Lorge, I., 101
Lorimer, R., 445
Lortie, D. C., 193, 233, 236, 367, 583, 668
Lotto, L., 928
Loucks, D. H., 974
Loucks, S., 405–409, 417
Loucks, S. F., 368, 369, 377, 492
Louis, K. S., 416, 417
Lovano-Kerr, J., 953
Lowe, C. A., 989
Lowe, P. L., 916
Lowe, R., 226, 293
Lowenfeld, V., 949
Lowyck, J., 51
Luckmann, T., 487
Ludwig, E., 258
Luetkemeyer, J. F., 900
Luke, A., 438, 440, 444, 452, 706–707
Lukes, S., 289, 290
Lull, H. G., 727
Lumpkin, A., 964, 974
Lumsden, C. J., 520, 536
Lundgren, U. P., 494, 500, 509, 761
Lunetta, V., 808
Lunsford, A., 709, 716, 739, 741
Lupkowski, A. E., 1016
Luquet, G. H., 951
Luria, A. R., 960
Luther, M., 124
Lutz, F. W., 104
Lux, D. G., 900–901
Lybeck, L., 802
Lyman, R. L., 691, 692
Lynch, J., 251, 259
Lynch, J. J., 702, 736
Lynch, P. P., 438
Lynch, R. L., 921–922
Lynd, H. M., 167, 233, 581
Lynd, R. S., 167, 233, 581
Lyons, C. A., 617
Lyons, N. P., 555, 558
Lyons, R., 126, 137, 139, 147
Lytle, S. L., 478

M

Mabry, J., 47, 48
Macbeth, D., 647, 650, 652
MacCleave-Frazier, A., 917
MacConnell, C. M., 339
MacConnie, S. E., 975, 986
MacDonald, B., 32, 381, 382, 383, 384
MacDonald, C. T., 671
MacDonald, J. B., 3, 34, 85, 88, 89, 93, 103, 130, 316, 338, 363, 486
MacDonald, N. J., 917
MacDonald, R., 368, 376
MacDonald, W., 796
Macdonald, S. C., 93
MacDonald-Ross, M., 130
MacGinitie, W. H., 494
Machlup, F., 284
Macintosh, D., 976, 978, 1014, 1017
MacIntyre, A., 553, 559, 676
Mack, R., 228
Mackenzie, G., 224, 229
MacKenzie, G. N., 367
Mackey, G., 556
Mackey, J., 258
Mackey, W. F., 629
Mackinson-Smyth, J., 640
MacLure, M., 500
Macnamara, J., 125, 142, 144
Macrorie, K., 231
Madaus, G. F., 70, 71, 120–126, 129, 131, 132, 134–147, 223, 236, 508
Maday, J. A., 912
Maddalozzo, J. G. F., 977
Madden, C., 643
Madden, N. A., 671
Madison, J., 308
Madsden, R., 551, 553, 559
Madsen, R., 274, 574, 595
Maehr, M. L., 249, 250
Mager, R., 909
Mager, R. F., 130, 375, 924
Maguire, D. C., 676
Mahard, R. E., 1034
Mahowald, M. B., 663–664
Maisels, S. J., 144
Malcolm, C., 811
Maley, D., 901
Malina, R. M., 970
Malinka, R., 1008
Malkus, U., 319
Malone, D., 729
Malone, K., 728
Malpiedi, B. J., 926
Mand, A., 966
Mand, C., 967–968, 970
Mandell, B. J., 738
Mandler, J. M., 531, 536
Manen, M. van, 91, 105, 108
Manfredi, T. G., 986
Mangham, P. N., 980
Manheim, K., 158
Manion, L., 105
Mann, A., 629
Mann, B. P., 967
Mann, C. H., 355–357
Mann, C. R., 136
Mann, D., 201
Mann, G. T., 1031
Mann, H., 103, 122, 125, 141, 454, 489, 544
Mann, J. A., 553
Mann, J. S., 85
Manzer, R. A., 382
Maoz, N., 1018
March, J., 190, 217, 220
March, J. G., 219, 239, 240
Marchman, V. A., 506
Mardis, L. J., 641
Mare, R. D., 576, 577, 589–592, 600
Margolis, G., 258

Margolis, R. J., 441
Marker, G. W., 443, 841, 843, 847
Markova, A. K., 744
Markowitz, H., Jr., 376
Marks, H. M., 668
Marland, P., 803
Marland, S. P., 925
Marlatt, G. A., 992
Marler, C. D., 128
Marrett, C. B., 668
Marrou, H. I., 270, 271
Marsh, C. J., 377
Marsh, D., 260
Marsh, D. D., 367
Marshall, C., 204
Marshall, S., 590
Martin, G. E., 897, 900
Martin, H., 455
Martin, H. J., 452
Martin, J. R., 278, 292, 561, 598, 660–661, 663–664, 672, 677
Martin, L. S., 9, 48
Martin, M., 557
Martin, N., 370, 385, 708
Martin, S., 147
Martinand, J. L., 802
Martinek, T. J., 982, 989
Marton, F., 486, 497
Marx, K., 286, 296, 315
Marx, R. W., 504, 526
Masia, B. B., 123, 129
Maslow, A. H., 335, 967, 977
Mason, J., 257, 262
Mason, J. H., 731
Mason, J. M., 475, 531, 645
Mason, L., 947
Mason, W. S., 668
Massachusetts Advocacy Center, 596
Massaro, D. W., 711
Massengale, J. D., 988
Massey, C. R., 592, 593
Massey, D. S., 612
Mathematical Sciences Education Board, 756, 768, 771
Mathematics Curriculum, 754
Mathematics Education, 754
Mathematics Sciences Education Board, 772
Mathematics Tomorrow, 754
Mather, C., 349
Matthews, M. M., 694, 698
Matute-Bianchi, M. E., 644
Maughan, B., 417, 559, 586, 589
May, H. F., 163
May, J., 804
May, M. A., [illegible]
Mayer, J. W., 600
Mayer, R., 53, 55, 56
Mayer, R. E., 52, 53, 520
Mayer, W. V., 63
Mayhew, D., 187
Mayhew, K. C., 171, 278, 279, 378, 379
Mays, A. B., 907
McAuliffee, S., 1013, 1015
McBee, J. K., 1032
McCage, R. D., 930
McCarthy, L., 708
McCartney, K., 536
McCaslin, E. S., 493, 494
McClay, D. R., 911
McClelland, D. C., 448
McClelland, J. L., 535
McClelland, W. A., 775
McClenaghan, B., 965, 970
McClintock, B., 292
McClintock Collective, The, 808
McCloskey, D., 286
McCloskey, M., 517
McClung, M. S., 140
McClure, A. F., 905, 905–908
McClure, M. L., 905
McClure, S., 32
McConnell, M., 813
McCormick, R., 121
McCracken, D. J., 910
McCray, J. C., 1017
McCrory, D. L., 918–919, 925
McCutchen, S., 421
McCutcheon, G., 492, 966
McDade, J. E., 699
McDermott, J., 55, 524, 528, 708
McDermott, R. P., 467, 469, 471, 500, 573, 583, 586, 589, 596, 711
McDiarmid, G. W., 498
McDill, E. L., 577, 593, 1027
McDonagh, J. T., 138
McDonald, F. J., 64, 65
McDonald, J. P., 493
McDonnell, L., 191, 201
McDonnell, L. M., 66, 68, 71, 72
McDowell, E., 456
McFadden, C., 810
McFee, J., 953, 954
McGill-Franzen, A. M., 705, 714
McGilly, K., 613
McGrath, A. C., 1024
McGuffey, W. H., 450, 451
McHoul, A., 500
McIntyre, D., 369, 376, 377
McIntyre, L. D., 711
McKay, R., 711
McKeachie, 56, 64, 65
McKee, P., 705, 706
McKee, S. J., 841–842
McKenna, B. H., 64, 143
McKenzie, T. L., 986
McKeown, M. G., 493, 494, 531, 711
McKernan, J., 105
McKernon, P., 952
McKim, M. G., 337
McKinney, W. L., 176, 178, 232, 236, 237, 368
McKnight, C. C., 67, 69, 577, 583, 772
McKown, H. C., 1012
McLaren, P., 255, 648
McLaughlin, B., 645, 882
McLaughlin, D. A., 671
McLaughlin, E. C., 661–662
McLaughlin, J. B., 487
McLaughlin, M. W., 189, 195, 199–201, 203, 228, 240, 241, 364, 365, 367, 369, 372–374, 404, 411–413, 415–417, 601
McLean, L. D., 112, 375, 881
McLean, R. S., 533
McLeod, A., 648, 652
McLeroy, K., 992
McLinn, C. B., 1003
Mclure, J. W., 1008
McMinn, J. H., 910
McMurray, F., 443
McMurray, M. P., 992
McMurry, C. A., 160, 378
McMurry, F., 160
McNeil, J. D., 3*n*, 4, 13, 15, 16, 224, 936
McNeil, L. M., 131, 145, 171, 193, 195, 206, 234, 237, 329, 506, 561, 955
McNemar, Q., 55
McNett, I., 815
McPartland, J. M., 583, 1013–1014, 1027, 1030, 1036
McPhall, P., 546
McPherson, B., 487
McTaggart, R., 144
McVeagh, H. E., 376
Mead, 546, 556
Mead, G. H., 169
Mead, M., 472
Mead, M. A., 920
Mead, N., 439
Mead, N. A., 772
Measor, L., 254, 257, 260, 474
Medin, D. L., 517
Medley, D. M., 63, 64, 65
Medley, F. W., Jr., 872, 873
Meece, J. L., 505, 506
Meek, M., 385
Megarry, J., 931
Megill, A., 286
Mehan, H., 231, 249, 250, 253, 255, 467, 474, 500, 577, 596, 640, 711
Mehlinger, H. D., 833, 839, 847
Mehrens, W. A., 147
Meichenbaum, D. H., 49
Meier, D., 135
Meighan, P., 115
Meihls, J. L., 467
Meikle, H. W., 729
Meiland, J. W., 289
Meister, G., 368, 377
Melancthon, P., 121
Melle, M., 417
Mellin-Olsen, S., 762
Mellon, J., 700, 743
Mellor, F., 597
Melograno, V., 967
Melton, G. B., 1033
Meltzer, A. S., 931
Melville, D. S., 977
Mendelson, L. J., 251
Mendez, R., 1036
Menkel-Meadow, C. J., 672, 673
Menyuk, P., 699
Meredith, A. R., 868
Meredith, M. D., 992
Merelman, R., 189, 195
Merelman, R. M., 556
Mergendoller, J. R., 504–506
Merrill, M., 920
Merrill, P. F., 130
Mersand, J., 729
Messer, S. B., 868
Mestre, J., 959
Mestre, J. P., 534
Met, M., 853, 856–859, 872, 876
Metcalf, L. E., 831–832
Mettler, B., 956
Metz, M. H., 228, 242, 249, 250, 253, 263, 306, 467, 571, 574, 576, 583–586, 588, 589, 592, 594, 595
Meyer Precup, L., 643, 651
Meyer, J., 194, 195, 217, 220, 224, 234, 237, 240, 241
Meyer, J. W., 178, 358, 360, 597
Meyer, L., 651
Meyer, L. A., 493, 494
Meyer, L. M., 647, 650, 652
Meyer, M., 240
Meyer, M. W., 357
Meyer, N. R., 693
Meyer, R. H., 928
Meyer, W. B., 902, 903
Meyers, W. G., 919
Michael, W. B., 335
Michaels, S., 500, 502–504, 507
Michell, M., 814
Michelson, S., 1036
Michigan Interagency Committee on the Black Child, 610
Michigan State Board of Education, 835
Middleton, D., 546
Miel, A., 377
Miles, M., 105, 201
Miles, M. B., 409, 417, 449
Mill, J. S., 135, 139
Millar, R., 802, 814
Millard, C. V., 1006–1007, 1012
Miller, C., 912
Miller, D. F., 909
Miller, G. A., 519, 529
Miller, J., 322
Miller, J. B., 675
Miller, J. D., 844
Miller, J. L., 93, 555

Miller, L., 377
Miller, L. B., 952
Miller, M. D., 69
Miller, N., 670
Miller, R., 286
Miller, W. S., 590
Millett, K., 670
Mills, C. W., 762
Mills, J. S., 80
Milne, A. M., 615
Milton, D., 549
Minnich, H. C., 452
Minsky, M. L., 523
Minuchin, P. P., 1036
Miracle, A. W., Jr., 583
Mirel, J. E., 177, 180, 592
Mischel, T., 551
Mischel, W., 546
Mitchell, 600, 601
Mitchell, D., 204
Mitchell, I., 799
Mitman, A. L., 506
Mizokawa, D. T., 859
Mock, P., 905, 905–908
Mock, R., 905
Modgil, C., 547
Modgil, S., 259, 547
Modiano, N., 638
Modra, H., 93
Moeller, G. H., 448
Moffett, J., 53, 446, 708, 738, 742
Mohan, B. A., 650
Mohatt, G., 474
Mohr, J., 295
Moi, T., 670
Moll, L., 577, 589, 598, 599, 640–641, 716
Moll, L. C., 475
Molnar, A., 35, 85, 555
Monaghan, E. J., 445, 450, 452, 493
Mondschein, E., 1032
Monette, M. L., 634
Monford, R., 612–613
Monroe, W. S., 125
Montague, W. E., 520
Montana State Department of Public Education, 691
Montessori, M., 49
Montgomery, M., 761
Montgomery, R. J., 121
Montoye, H. J., 991
Mood, A. M., 1036
Moody, C. D., 613
Moon, B., 180
Mooney, R. L., 85
Moore, C., 965, 981
Moore, C. G., 987
Moore, D. R., 137
Moore, D., 571, 575, 576, 589, 590, 600
Moore, D. W., 704
Moore, G. E., 892, 893
Moore, H., 613
Moore, M., 189
Moore, W. E., 217
Moorhead, G., 952
Moos, R., 1027
Moran, R. F., 633–634
Moreland, R., 1015
Moreland, R. L., 1025
Morgan, D. L., 1019, 1020
Morgan, E. S., 347, 348
Morgan, G., 81
Morgan, R. T., 444
Morgan, S. P., 611–612
Morgan, W. P., 992
Morgenstern, D., 878
Morison, S. E., 349
Morris, G. C., 142
Morris, N., 144
Morrison, A., 126
Morrison, C., 707, 714
Morrison, G. B., 1003
Morrissett, I., 832, 842
Morsch, J., 920
Morse, J., 445
Mortimer, P., 417
Mortimore, P., 559, 586, 589
Mosely, H., 274
Mosenthal, P., 502, 504, 520
Moser, J., 761
Mosher, R. L., 545, 547
Mosier, R. D., 449, 450, 697
Moss, A., 446
Moss, J., 920, 931
Mosston, M., 982
Mowbray, C. T., 1019
Moy, P. S., 713
Mueller, L. D., 1016
Mueller, L. K., 973
Muggli, G. Y., 917
Mukerji, S. N., 144
Mullahy, P., 274
Mullan, M. R., 969
Mullen, N. A., 652
Muller, D. K., 293
Muller, H. J., 737
Mullins, J. D., 1011
Mullis, H. J., 739
Mullis, I., 227, 236, 796
Munby, H., 377
Munday, L. A., 1030
Munski, M., 144
Muraskin, L. D., 928
Muratov, I. I., 1005
Murnane, R. J., 66–68, 70, 71, 146, 796
Murphy, G. L., 517
Murphy, J., 573, 585, 591
Murphy, J. E., 548
Murphy, P. D., 916
Murphy, R., 120
Murphy, S., 712
Murphy, S. B., 505
Murray, E. C., 917
Murray, J. A., 878
Murray, L., 450
Musgrave, A., 288
Musgrave, P. W., 158
Musgrove, F., 255, 262
Mussen, P. H., 50
Myers, D. E., 615
Myers, G. W., 379
Myers, M., II, 525

N

Nachtrieb, N., 279, 281
Nagel, T., 292
Nails, D., 554
Naiman, N., 868
Naisbitt, J., 376, 771
Nakayama, K., 639
Nalin, K., 711
Nanda, P. D., 144
Narot, R. E., 1034
Nasaw, D., 580
Natalicio, D. S., 615
National Advisory Board on International Education Programs, The, 854
National Alliance of Black School Educators, 622
National Assessment of Education Performance, 796
National Assessment of Educational Progress, 333, 710, 715, 716
National Association for Sport and Physical Education, 969, 971
National Association of Secondary School Principals, 895
National Black Child Development Institute, 610
National Board for Professional Teaching Standards, 544
National Business Education Association, 914, 915
National Center for Educational Statistics, 589, 590
National Center of Effective Secondary Schools, 142
National Children and Youth Fitness Studies, 983
National Clearinghouse for Bilingual Education, 635
National Coalition of Advocates for Students, 614, 616, 627
National Commission on Excellence in Education, 252, 314, 339, 439, 574, 598, 630, 854, 927
National Commission on Secondary Vocational Education, The, 815, 927
National Commission on Testing and Public Policy, 123
National Council for the Social Studies, 258
National Council of Teachers of English, 670, 693, 704, 731–732, 735, 739
National Council of Teachers of Mathematics, 749, 756–758, 776–777
National Curriculum Council, 809, 811
National Dance Association, 956
National Defense Act, 705
National Education Association, 544, 689- 690, 695, 699, 715, 729–730
National Governors' Association Center for Policy Research and Analysis, 782
National Governors' Association, 715, 853
National League for Nursing, 331
National Research Council, 482, 807
National Science Board, 252
National Science Foundation, 589, 789, 797
National Society for the Promotion of Industrial Education, 907
Natkins, L. G., 385
Nauman, C., 600
Navarro, M. S., 627
Nay, M., 375
Nazario, S. L., 630, 634
Neches, R., 519, 526
Neckerman, K. M., 610
Needels, M. C., 63, 66
Needham, J. G., 455
Negri, R., 1012
Neikirk, M. M., 980
Neill, A. S., 311, 339, 560
Neisser, U., 536
Nelkin, D., 203, 447
Nelson, C., 757
Nelson, E. L., 902, 920, 922
Nelson, H. Y., 915–916
Nelson, J., 286, 821
Nelson, J. L., 831, 832, 841, 845–846
Nelson, K., 509
Nelson, L., 558
Nelson, L. N., 340
Nelson, M. R., 160
Nelson, O., 929
Nelson, R., 920
Nelson, R. B., 1031
Nemko, B., 931
Nemser, C., 671
Nerenz, A. G., 875
Nespor, J., 475, 505
Neufeld, B., 207, 581
Neufville, J. I. De, 66
New England Journal of Education, 727

New England Primer, The, 727
New York State Department of Education, 690- 691, 701, 704, 705, 709, 712
Newcomb, L., 910–911
Newell, A., 55, 517, 519, 521, 526–529, 955
Newlon, J. H., 412, 418, 419
Newman, C. A., 914
Newman, D., 533
Newman, J. R., 750
Newman, S. E., 525, 532
Newmann, F. M., 601, 838, 843
Newmann, J. R., 755
Newton, E., 376
Newton, I., 273, 443
Ng, K., 527
Nichols, F. G., 894
Nicholson, L., 672
Nickerson, J., 505
Nickerson, R., 752
Nietz, J. A., 450, 452
Nightingale, A. F., 166, 176
Nisbet, R. A., 217, 368
Nisbet, S., 931
Nisbett, R. E., 521
Nitko, A., 131, 141
Noblit, G., 573
Nochlin, L., 671
Noddings, N., 9, 374, 393, 545, 555, 562, 661, 663, 668, 672, 676, 678
Nolen, S. B., 145, 147
Noll, V. H., 140
Nordberg, H. O., 1012
Norsworthy, F., 371
North, R. A., 1031
Northfield, J., 803
Norton, C. J., 980
Nostrand, H. L., 880
Novak, J., 801
Nover, M. L., 1012, 1014
Novick, S., 778
Novitz, D., 289
Novotney, J. M., 338
Nowakiwska, M., 1043
Nucci, L. P., 546, 547
Nussbaum, J., 524, 531, 778
Nuthall, G., 491, 505
Nuttall, D. L., 120, 132, 147
Nystrand, M., 584, 599

O

Oakes, J., 43, 61, 64, 66, 69, 120, 128, 131, 132, 164, 165, 206, 231, 242, 260, 293, 345, 469, 499, 574–577, 583- 586, 589, 590, 594–598, 601, 613–614, 631–633, 647, 909, 930, 935
Oakeshott, M., 289, 297, 328
Oaxaca, J., 772
Oberg, A., 33, 385
Oberteuffer, D., 557
O'Brien, M. M., 672
O'Brien, S., 441
Ocha, A. S., 556
Ochoa, A., 832
Ochs, E., 644
O'Connor, C. A., 226, 368
Odden, A., 260
Odell, L., 53, 708
Offen, K. M., 666–667
Ogbu, J. U., 261, 475, 586, 614, 615, 644
Ogle, D., 614
Ohanian, S., 257
O'Hare, F., 700, 743
Oja, S. N., 105
Okakok, L., 471, 472
Okihara, Y., 1007
Okin, S. M., 659, 660, 663–664, 668, 676
Olave, M. de, 633
Oldham, V., 802
Olen, D. R., 1015
Olexa, C., 577, 592
Oliva, P. F., 5
Oliver, A. I., 276
Oliver, A. J., 3*n*
Oliver, D. W., 832, 837–838
Oliver, R., 954
Olneck, M. O., 180
Olsen, D., 304, 313
Olsen, J. P., 190, 219, 239, 240
Olsen, L., 647, 652
Olsen, T., 481, 482, 670
Olshavsky, J. E., 526
Olson, D. W., 901, 912
Olson, J. K., 369, 374, 376
Olson, J. W., 734
Olson, W. C., 703
Olver, R., 960
Omaggio, A. C., 861, 872, 875–876
O'Malley, J. M., 649
Omanson, R. C., 711
O'Neal, L., 376
O'Neil, J., 915
Ong, W. J., 158, 271, 293
O'Niel, J., 920
Ontario Ministry of Education, 376
Opper, S., 51
O'Rand, A. M., 291
Orfield, G., 228, 612–613
Organization for Economic Cooperation and Development, 269
Orland, M. E., 610, 612
Orlich, D., 199
Orlonsky, D. E., 3*n*
Orme, N., 271
Ornstein, A. C., 936
Orpwood, G., 794
Orr, E. W., 614
Ortony, A., 369, 521
Osborn, J., 493, 713
Osborne, A., 765
Osborne, R., 801, 802
Oser, F. K., 543, 551
O'Shea, W., 225
Osin, L., 456
Ostro, H., 1032
Oswald, H., 572, 593
Otte, J. P., 750
Otte, M., 756
Otto, H. J., 590
Otto, L. B., 1014, 1025, 1030–1031
Otto, S. E. K., 878
Otto, W., 705
Ouston, J., 417, 559, 586, 589
Ovando, C. J., 647–648, 6511
Overing, G. R., 670
Overly, N. V., 8
Owen, D. B., 556
Oxford, C., 855, 869
Oxford-Carpenter, J. A., 869
Oxtoby, D., 279, 281

P

Packer, A. E., 772
Packer, K. H., 453
Packer, M. J., 506
Padgham, R. E., 90
Paffenbarger, R. S., 965, 970, 972
Pagano, J. A., 678
Page, R., 43, 345, 574, 577, 583–589, 592, 594, 598, 600
Paik, I., 928
Paine, T., 443
Paley, V. G., 364, 385, 386, 389–392, 481, 669
Palinscar, A. S., 56, 497, 536, 711
Palmer, D. J., 727, 728
Palmer, E. L., 110
Palmer, G. H., 170
Palmer, J. R., 365, 370
Pangrazi, R., 966–970
Panofsky, E., 954
Pantages, T. J., 1026
Paolucci, B., 898, 917–918
Papert, S., 54
Pappademos, J., 647
Parallel Distributed Processing Research Group, 535
Parcel, G. S., 985
Paris, C. L., 418, 419, 425–427
Paris, S. G., 525
Parish, R., 409
Parke, M., 702
Parke, R., 66, 67
Parker, A., 201
Parker, D., 1034
Parker, F., 122, 224
Parker, J., 370
Parker, L., 807
Parker, W. R., 728
Parlett, M., 103, 131
Parmley, J. D., 911
Parrish, T. M., 452, 454
Parsons, F., 904
Parsons, J., 835
Parsons, M., 953–954
Parsons, M. J., 992
Parsons, P. W., 256
Parsons, W., 556
Parvey, C. F., 661
Pascarella, E. T., 1026
Pascual-Leone, J., 529, 531
Pasewark, R. A., 1012, 1022
Passeron, C., 580
Passeron, J. C., 195, 205, 292, 294, 295, 478, 793
Passmore, J., 544
Passow, A. H., 337, 586, 593, 594, 597
Patchen, M., 1034
Pate, R. R., 965, 970
Patel, V. L., 143, 144, 147
Pateman, C., 555
Patrick, J. J., 835, 841
Pattenson, J., 598
Patterson, P., 975–976, 986, 991
Paucette, N., 975
Pauley, E., 404
Paulos, J. A., 750
Paulston, R. G., 219
Pavan, B. N., 48
Pavelchak, M. A., 1025
Pavlov, I., 47, 546
Payne, W. H., 489
Pea, R. D., 533, 772
Peak, G. W., 204
Peal, E., 858
Pearce, J., 743
Pearson, P. D., 370, 711, 712, 716, 745
Pease, S. R., 45, 65
Peck, R. F., 550, 552, 557
Peddiwell, J. A., 766
Pederson, K. M., 877
Pekarsky, D., 172
Pellegrin, R. J., 367, 411
Pendleton, C. S., 732
Peng, S. S., 1009, 1014, 1033
Penick, J. E., 966
Penkov, B., 769
Penna, A. N., 35, 334, 338, 964
Perez, A. L., 713
Perkins, D., 56
Perl, T., 663
Perreiah, A. R., 124
Perry, I., 480, 481
Perry, L. R., 560
Perry, M., 772
Persell, C., 577, 585, 593
Peshkin, A., 108, 255, 256, 257, 260, 262, 304, 307, 308, 558, 1022
Pesola, C. A., 856
Pestalozzi, J. H., 49, 101, 102, 122, 236, 489, 493, 497

Peters, G., 191
Peters, J., 375
Peters, R., 318, 319, 323
Peters, R. S., 278, 283, 545, 546, 548, 550- 553
Petersen, A. C., 667
Petersen, K., 671
Peterson, B., 1017
Peterson, K., 65, 251
Peterson, L., 1016
Peterson, P. E., 224, 231, 854
Peterson, P. L., 48, 51–53, 55, 56, 63–66, 363, 477, 497, 498, 499, 507, 755, 780, 973
Peterson, S. M., 416, 417
Petrie, H. G., 369
Petty, M. C., 592
Peuse, G. H., 912
Pfeffer, J., 239, 240
Pfundt, H., 802
Phenix, P. H., 287, 318, 319, 323
Phihal, J., 891
Philips, S. U., 474, 500, 501, 644
Phillips, D. C., 47, 52, 56, 104, 105, 107, 287, 288, 369, 766
Phillips, G. W., 439, 772
Phillips, J. A., 367, 661
Phillips, J. C., 1017, 1025
Phillips, J. K., 875
Piaget, J., 42, 49–52, 63, 72, 197, 269, 275, 303, 312, 330, 335, 519, 520, 530, 536, 543, 545, 547, 548, 554, 557, 699, 703, 951
Piattelli-Palmarini, M., 536
Piche, G. L., 726
Pickwell, F. G., 419
Pierce, C., 660
Pierstorff, L., 703, 706–707
Pike, K., 699
Pilkington, J. P., 454
Piltz, A., 271
Pimm, D., 750
Pinar, W. F., 35, 36, 79, 80, 82–86, 92, 93, 102, 108, 311, 316, 322, 334, 338, 392, 678, 964
Pincoffs, E., 559
Pincus, J., 240, 372, 373, 847
Pines, A. L., 517
Pines, L., 801, 802
Pinnell, G. S., 617
Pintner, R., 699
Pinxten, R., 752
Piontkowski, D. C., 714
Pipho, C., 121, 760
Placek, J. H., 967–968, 970, 981, 988
Placetter, E., 385
Plank, D., 229, 234
Plato, 10, 269, 270, 271
Plattor, E., 385
Player, J., 254
Plihal, J., 930, 935
Pliny, 272
Plomin, R., 536
Plowden Report, 314
Plummer, A., 270
Plutchick, R., 520, 521
Poincaré, 286
Polanyi, M., 270, 273, 284, 523
Policies Commission of Business and Economic Education, 914
Pollack, J., 589
Pollak, H., 775
Pollard, R., 708
Pollock, J., 269
Pollock, M. L., 970
Polson, M. C., 533
Polya, G., 760
Pomfret, A., 367, 403–406, 413, 429, 431
Pond, D., 952
Ponder, G. A., 263, 416, 446
Pons y Argent, 860
Popham, W. J., 102, 110, 130, 135, 138, 140- 142, 333, 364, 375, 796
Popkewitz, T. S., 174, 179, 220, 224, 293, 411, 412, 414–417, 428, 487, 489, 493, 506, 750, 753, 842, 948
Popp, H. M., 713
Popper, K. R., 99, 104, 105, 288, 523
Portelli, J. P., 10
Porter, A. C., 131, 141, 194, 195, 198, 204, 205, 221, 227–229, 231, 436, 493, 494, 495
Posner, G. J., 110, 468, 486, 492, 497, 504, 505, 508, 799, 801
Posner, M. I., 54
Postman, N., 550
Potter, D. A., 64
Poussaint, A., 619
Powell, A. G., 166, 171, 174, 208, 221, 223, 231, 339, 467, 471, 573, 574, 578, 581, 583–585, 595, 598
Powell, K. E., 965, 970, 976
Powell, V., 279, 281
Powell, W. W., 240
Power, C., 547, 549, 561
Power, C. N., 61
Pozdol, M., 1008
Prakash, M. S., 553, 804
Pratt, H., 417, 492
Pratte, R., 315
Pratzner, F. C., 920, 929
Prawat, R. S., 505
Prescott, B., 127, 142
Prescott, D., 337
Preskill, S., 165
Pressey, S. L., 47, 333, 374, 455
Pressley, M., 520, 523, 525
Pressman, J., 187, 188
Prewitt, K., 1028
Price, D. S., 804
Price, G. G., 775
Price, K., 103
Price, R. A., 895
Prince, L.W., 901
Pring, R. A., 546, 551, 552
Pritchard, I., 552, 553
Proefriedt, W. A., 559
Prophet, R. B., 158, 180
Prosser, C., 163, 171, 177
Prosser, C. A., 905, 908
Provenzo, E., 776
Provenzo, E. F., 771
Prunty, J., 217, 219, 224
Prunty, J. J., 367, 368
Prusak, B. P., 661
Puck, T., 281, 282
Pugh, M., 1017
Pugno, L., 102
Pullin, D. C., 208
Pulsifer, W. E., 444
Purdy, D., 779
Purkey, S., 239
Puro, P., 506
Purpel, D., 543, 562
Purpel, D. E., 3*n*, 4, 9, 561
Purves, A., 574
Purves, A. C., 68, 727, 733, 739–740, 741- 745
Purvis, J., 259, 260
Putnam, H., 288, 289
Putnam, H. C., 88
Putnam, R., 105
Putnam, R. T., 477, 497, 507, 509, 755
Pylyshyn, Z. W., 518–520, 535

Q

Quick, S., 227, 229
Quilling, M. R., 711
Quintilian, 271, 272
Quirk, D. L., 744
Quirk, T. J., 711

R

Rabinow, P., 296
Rabiteau, K., 882
Rachlin, S., 770
Rady, A. M., 981
Radzikhovskii, L. A., 536
Rafferty, E. A., 859
Rafferty, M., 144
Raizen, S., 601, 796
Raizen, S. A., 68, 147, 439, 444
Rajchman, J., 296
Rakow, S. J., 1018
Ramsey, K., 576, 577, 589
Ramsey, M. A., 104
Ramsey, P. D. K., 367
Randall, J. H., Jr., 273
Randolph, 374
Rankin, S. C., 135, 140
Rasher, S. P., 48, 71
Rasmussen, B., 985
Raths, L., 549, 550, 560
Ratliffe, T., 983
Raudenbush, S. W., 69
Ravetz, J., 273
Ravitch, D., 226, 444, 531, 579, 739, 836, 840
Rawls, J., 551
Ray, W. E., 901
Raymond, D., 385
Raywid, M-A., 551
Razor, J. E., 991
Readence, J. E., 556, 704
Ready, D., 877
Reavis, W. C., 1003, 1006–1007
Reddy, M. J., 369, 370
Redfield, R., 113
Redick, S. S., 915, 916–917
Redsun, A., 845
Reed, A., 691
Reed, B., 974
Reeder, R. R., 452, 727
Rees, E., 55
Rees, M., 759
Reese, W., 224
Reese, W. L., 80
Reeve, T. G., 987
Regan, E., 367
Rehberg, R. A., 577, 593, 595, 1014–1015, 1017, 1024–1025, 1028
Rehberg, R. D., 1017
Rehm, M., 930
Reich, W., 560
Reid, J. M., 441, 444, 455
Reid, M. I., 1015, 1017
Reid, W., 224, 232
Reid, W. A., 32, 33, 178, 179, 370, 487, 508, 974
Reigeluth, C., 920
Reimann, P., 526, 528
Reimer, B., 947, 953
Reis, R., 518, 525
Reise, B. J., 518
Reisman, D., 552
Rejeki, W. J., 989
Remsen, I., 282
Rennie, L., 807
Reorganization of Education in French Equatorial Africa, 260
Rescher, N., 774
Resnick, D. P., 122, 131, 147, 222, 223, 234, 235, 241, 613, 767, 796
Resnick, L. B., 16, 51, 52, 71, 147, 222, 223, 234, 235, 241, 482, 497, 504, 525–528, 536, 537, 613, 619, 649, 758, 766, 767, 772, 796, 947, 954, 955

Resnick, T., 959
Reubens, B. G., 593
Reverby, S., 665, 671
Reynolds, A. W., 772
Reynolds, J., 130, 250, 251, 253, 508
Reynolds, R. E., 422
Reys, E., 759
Rheinboldt, W. C., 772
Rhodes, N. C., 641, 855–858, 882
Rice, E. W., 454
Rice, J. M., 60, 101, 197, 222, 491, 768
Rich, A., 670, 677
Rich, J. M., 551
Richards, C. M., 3*n*
Richards, I. A., 735
Richards, O. W., 455
Richardson, C. P., 878
Richardson, J. J., 533
Richardson, V., 492
Richardson, W. B., 1014, 1019
Richburg, J. R., 847
Richert, A. E., 498
Rickelman, R. J., 704
Rickoff, A., 441
Rickover, H., 216
Rickover, H. G., 446
Ricouer, P., 84, 88
Rideout, B. W., 1020
Rieff, P., 274, 385
Riesman, D., 449, 595
Rihn, B. A., 526
Riley, J., 110
Ring, S. I., 1043
Ringel, P. J., 368
Ringer, F., 293
Rink, J. E., 966, 991
Rinne, R., 223
Riopel, D. A., 986
Ripley, R., 186
Rishpon, M., 1018
Rist, R., 206, 231, 242, 573, 576, 583, 586, 589, 592, 597
Rist, R. C., 64, 104, 106–108, 467
Rivers, W. M., 867, 875
Rivlin, A. M., 404
Robbins, I., 140
Roberts, D., 794
Roberts, F. L., 1030
Roberts, G. K., 273
Roberts, H. D., 734
Roberts, R. W., 894, 900, 904, 904–905, 905
Robins, P., 134
Robinson, A., 753
Robinson, F. G., 53, 416
Robinson, F. P., 704
Robinson, H. A., 704
Robinson, J. T., 330
Robinson, L. S., 662, 670
Robinson, N. M., 1019–1021, 1027–1028
Robitaille, D. F., 769
Rock, D., 667
Rock, D. A., 589
Rodriguez, R., 256, 629
Roemer, J., 1003
Rogers, C., 18, 48, 550
Rogers, C. W., 1016
Rogers, K. B., 964
Rogers, R. G., 1017, 1019, 1026
Rogers, T., 739, 743
Rogoff, B., 536, 954, 955
Rohlen, T. P., 571, 593
Rohlen, T. R., 1005
Rohrkemper, M., 56, 505
Rolls, I. F., 557
Roman, L. G., 80
Romberg, T. A., 72, 223, 752, 761, 763, 764- 767, 769–770, 774–775, 779, 782
Rorabaugh, W. A., 452
Rorabaugh, W. J., 269
Rorty, R., 10, 287, 288, 289
Rosaldo, R., 481
Rose, H., 291, 675
Rose, M., 467, 480, 481
Rose, S., 992
Rosebery, A. S., 530, 646
Rosen, H., 708
Rosenbach, A. S. W., 452
Rosenbaum, J., 208
Rosenbaum, J. E., 571, 574–577, 583, 585, 588, 589, 592–594, 596
Rosenbaum, P. R., 589
Rosenbaur, J., 260
Rosenberg, M., 1018
Rosenblatt, L. M., 733, 744
Rosenbloom, P. S., 521, 529
Rosenblum, S., 416, 417
Rosenholtz, S., 596
Rosenshine, B., 64, 65, 373, 467, 488, 491, 493, 494, 714
Rosenshine, B. V., 142
Rosenstock, I. M., 992
Rosenthal, D. B., 179, 447
Rosenthal, E. R., 577, 593, 595
Rosentswieg, J., 974
Rosier, P., 639
Ross, C. C., 140
Ross, D. D., 107
Ross, E. A., 168, 169
Ross, J., 371
Ross, M., 954
Ross, M. E., 676
Ross, W. E., 842
Rossi, A., 675
Rossi, R. J., 671
Rossiter, M. W., 665
Rossman, G., 202
Rossman, G. B., 249, 257, 258, 259
Rossmiller, R. A., 440
Roszak, T., 106
Roth, D. R., 711
Roth, K., 205
Roth, K. J., 526
Rothblatt, S., 124, 138, 272
Rothe, J. P., 375
Rothman, A. I., 63
Rothman, R., 259, 713
Rotter, 546
Rousseau, J. J., 16, 49, 101, 269, 282, 436, 443, 556
Rowan, B., 194, 195, 217, 224, 234, 237, 240, 241, 583, 597, 714
Rowell, A. G., 260
Rowell, P., 793
Rowland, S., 385, 386
Rowland, T. G., 51, 53, 63
Rowland, T. W., 970
Royal Commission on Education, 122
Royal Society and the Institute of Physics, 807
Royal Society for the Encouragement of Arts, Manufacturing and Commerce, 815
Rubin, L., 611
Rubinson, R., 226, 239
Ruch, G. M., 136, 140
Rudduck, J., 383
Rudolph, F., 726, 729
Rugg, H., 4, 222, 224, 233, 234, 239, 277, 278, 279, 280, 282, 311, 403, 579
Rugg, H. O., 100–103, 125, 160, 165, 167, 333, 338, 365, 378, 446, 447
Ruggles, R. H., 375
Rumelhart, D. E., 521, 535, 708
Rundle, L., 549
Rusen, J., 847
Rusk, R. R., 49
Ruskin, J., 556
Russel, E. B., 912
Russell, B., 72, 560
Russell, D., 690
Russell, J., 5, 774, 956
Russell, J. F., 929
Russell, R. L., 529
Russell, T. L., 377, 392
Russell, W., 438
Rutherford, E., 288
Rutter, M., 559, 586, 589
Rutter, M. B., 417
Ryan, D. W., 369, 376
Ryan, K., 385, 543, 544, 553, 560, 562
Ryerson, E., 367, 370
Ryle, G., 283, 523

S

Sabar, N., 370, 376
Sadler, D. R., 1019, 1020, 1020–1021, 1021, 1027–1028
Sadow, M. W., 494, 714
Safrit, M. J., 981, 984
Sagaria, M. A. D., 1015
Sagaria, S. D., 1015
Sage, G. H., 972, 988
Sahling, M., 672
Saily, M., 440
Salamon, L., 191
Salamone, R. C., 1033
Salle, J. B. de la, 138
Sallis, J. F., 964, 970
Salmon-Cox, L., 127, 143
Salomon, G., 56
Sampson, E. E., 520
Samson, H. E., 922
San Francisco Unified School District, 648
Sand, O., 331, 370
Sandell, R., 671
Sanders, D. P., 966
Sanders, J. R., 120, 124
Sanders, N., 574–576, 583, 589, 593, 597
Sanders, N. M., 146
Sanders, P., 914
Sandieson, R., 531
Sandifer, P. D., 135, 140
Sanford, J. P., 504–507
Sangren, P. V., 140
Santibanez, J., 258
Sapir, E., 304
Sapre, P. M., 894, 915
Sarason, S. B., 227, 232, 237, 242, 378, 411, 416, 573, 589, 597
Saris, W. H. M., 986
Sartre, J.-P., 31, 543
Sassen, G., 668
Saul, E. W., 493
Saunders, M., 508
Savage, E. A., 920
Saveth, E. N., 442, 445
Savignon, S. J., 863
Saxe, G., 753
Sayigh, R., 256
Saylor, J. G., 3*n*, 4, 82
Scarcella, R. C., 870
Scardamalia, M., 283, 284, 497, 525–527, 533, 534, 537, 670, 704, 708
Scarr, S., 536
Schaaf, W. L., 752
Schaeger, R. J., 328
Schafer, M., 953
Schafer, W. E., 577, 592, 1013–1015, 1017, 1024–1026
Schaffarzick, J., 130, 197, 203, 310, 335, 367, 491
Schallert, D. L., 422
Schalock, D., 491
Schank, R., 708
Schank, R. C., 519
Schaps, E., 554
Schau, C. G., 670
Schauber, E., 508

Scheffler, I., 283
Schein, E. N., 251
Scheman, N., 675
Schempp, P. G., 982
Schendel, J. S., 1019
Schibye, B., 985
Schiefflin, B., 644
Schiller, D., 53
Schindler, D., 553
Schinke-Llano, L., 856
Schlechty, P., 589
Schlesinger, A. M., 439
Schliemann, A., 753
Schlossman, S., 226
Schmacher, A., 102
Schmalohr, E., 51
Schmerkotte, H., 51
Schmidt, P., 255
Schmidt, W., 195, 198, 221, 227–229, 231
Schmidt, W. H., 131, 141, 493, 494, 713
Schmits, D. W., 574
Schmuck, P., 554
Schnapp-Matthews, W., 669
Schneider, E. E., 1015
Schneider, W., 529, 530
Schoeff, D., 576, 577, 589
Schoenfeld, A., 223
Schoenfeld, A. H., 48, 440, 497, 506, 525, 750
Schoenherr, R., 357
Schoer, J., 700
Schoggen, M., 1008, 1019
Schoggen, P., 1008, 1012, 1019
Schoggen, T., 1012
Schommer, M., 145
Schön, D. A., 199, 200, 369, 378, 799
School Activities, 1003
School Review, 740
Schoolboys of Barbiana, 481
Schools Council, 817
Schorr, D., 935
Schorr, L. B., 935
Schostak, J. F., 377
Schrag, F., 271, 274, 281, 555, 560, 766
Schramm, W., 443
Schrodinger, E., 443
Schubert, W., 103
Schubert, W. H., 3*n*, 6, 8, 13, 36, 80, 82, 162, 164, 174, 221, 231, 268, 269, 332, 333, 334, 487, 936, 964, 990
Schug, M. C., 845
Schulman, L. S., 104
Schultz, J., 469, 506
Schultz, R. E., 573, 583
Schumaker, J. B., 1035
Schunk, D. H., 992
Schunke, G. M., 556
Schutz, R. E., 711
Schutz, R. W., 972, 976
Schwab, J., 280, 287, 792, 802
Schwab, J. J., 3, 4, 21, 22, 27–37, 41, 52, 53, 82, 83, 103, 109, 128, 329, 332, 333, 334, 366, 367, 368, 369, 370, 378, 379, 380, 381
Schwager, S. M., 982
Schwartz, B. J., 522
Schwartz, F., 585, 586, 589, 592
Schwartz, J. L., 766, 780
Schweitzer, J., 69
Schwille, J., 188, 194, 195, 204, 205, 221, 227, 229, 231, 297
Schwille, J. A., 231
Schwille, J. R., 131, 141, 493, 494
Science Council of Canada, 797
Science Research Associates, 707
Scinicariello, S. G., 878
Scopes, J., 455
Scopes, J. T., 447
Scott, E. S., 1034
Scott, F. N., 689, 692, 727, 729
Scott, J., 712
Scott, J. A., 451
Scott, K. P., 670
Scott, L., 135
Scott, M., 816
Scott, W., 62, 421, 422
Scott, W. R., 239, 240
Scribner, J., 204
Scribner, S., 531, 536, 739, 947, 954, 960
Scripp, L., 952
Scriven, J. D., 914
Scriven, M., 120, 544, 818
Scriven, M. S., 130, 139
Searle, D., 500
Searle, D. E., 708
Searle, D. J., 500
Sears, J. B., 490
Secada, W. G., 641
Secondary Science Curriculum Review, The, 809
Seddon, T., 376
Seddon, T. L., 158, 181
Sedlak, M., 208, 226, 231
Seewald, A. M., 132
Seguel, M. L., 160, 365, 378, 489, 490
Selden, S., 81, 88, 180, 580
Seldon, W., 908
Selvidge, R. W., 900
Selvin, M. J., 576, 577, 589, 594
Selznick, P., 219
Sendov, B., 769
Senesh, L., 838
Senior Secondary Assessment Board of South Australia, 818
Serbin, L., 669
Serow, R. C., 1014, 1021
Sewall, G. T., 254
Sewart, D., 375, 376
Sewell, G. T., 254, 841
Sexton, P. C., 669
Seybolt, R. F., 348–351
Shaevitz, M. H., 737
Shafer, S. M., 831
Shafriri, N., 376
Shakeshaft, C., 249, 668
Shakespeare, W., 8, 47, 284
Shanahan, T., 716
Shane, H., 230, 231
Shane, H. I., 771
Shanker, A., 121, 145
Shannon, J. R., 1003
Shannon, P., 695–696, 698, 703, 707, 712, 715
Shapiro, B., 790, 799, 803
Shapiro, E. K., 1036
Shapson, S. M., 857, 881
Sharp, R., 206, 585
Shaughnessy, J., 845
Shaughnessy, J. M., 473
Shavelson, R. J., 54, 55, 64–66, 68, 71, 72, 126, 714
Shaver, J. P., 436, 545, 556, 557, 670, 832, 834, 837–838, 845–846
Shaver, L. P., 835
Shavit, Y., 572, 591, 593
Shaw, C. M., 671
Shaw, J. C., 519
Shaw, T. B., 728
Shayer, M., 801
Shea, J., 593
Shear, T., 898
Sheingold, K., 533
Sheldon, E. B., 66, 67
Shepard, L., 712
Shepard, L. A., 144–147, 623
Shepard, R. J., 975, 976, 986, 987
Sher, J. P., 376
Sherlock, J., 967
Sherman, A., 671
Sherman, A. S., 692
Shermis, S., 832
Shermis, S. S., 551
Sherretz, L., 65
Sherrill, C., 978
Sherwin, J. S., 728, 743
Shields, L., 668
Shifflett, B., 980
Shiffrin, R. M., 529
Shils, E., 217
Shimozawa, J., 794
Shinkfield, A. J., 120
Shipman, M. D., 3*n*, 33, 370
Shipman, V. C., 615
Shirreffs, J. H., 445
Shisslak, C. M., 992
Shor, I., 278, 279, 715, 909, 926, 936
Shores, J. H., 3*n*, 82, 250, 330, 338
Short, D. J., 649–650
Short, E. C., 84–86, 90, 227
Short, K., 617
Showers, B., 373, 377
Shrum, J., 868
Shugrue, M. F., 735–736
Shulman, L., 52, 55, 56, 72, 196, 486, 560, 799
Shulman, L. S., 493, 496, 498
Shultz, J., 500, 501
Shumaker, A., 277, 278, 279, 311
Shure, M. B., 546
Shuy, R., 700, 708
Shymansky, J. A., 474
Sichel, B., 547–549, 555, 559, 560
Sichel, B. A., 676
Sicinski, A., 255
Sidney, J. S., 672
Sieber, S. D., 416, 446
Siedentop, D., 964, 966–970, 989–990
Siegel, J. A., 986
Siegler, R. S., 529, 531
Sigel, I. E., 53
Sikes, P. K., 381
Silberman, C., 218, 227, 235
Silberstein, J., 517
Silberstein, M., 376
Silver, E., 955
Silver, H., 180
Silverman, J., 555
Siman, J., 804
Simmons, D., 557
Simmons, R. G., 1021
Simon, B., 293
Simon, D., 55
Simon, D. P., 524, 528
Simon, H. A., 55, 105, 517–519, 522, 524, 526–529, 955
Simon, H. D., 708
Simon, J. A., 976
Simon, R. I., 89, 634, 652
Simon, S. B., 549, 550, 560
Simons, H., 383
Simons, M., 248, 256
Simons-Morton, B. G., 965, 983–984, 986–987
Simpson, C., 596
Simpson, D. J., 365
Simpson, E., 550
Simpson, H., 668
Simpson, R. L., 668
Sims, R., 620
Sinatra, R., 945
Sinclair, H., 50
Sinclair, J., 708
Sinclair, K. E., 376
Sinclair, R. L., 584
Singer, H., 440
Singer, J. D., 228

Singer, R., 53
Sinks, T. A., 1008
Sirotnik, K., 271
Sirotnik, K. A., 340, 367, 368, 601
Siverton, S. C., 180
Sizer, T., 164, 171, 229, 252, 369, 589, 712, 729
Sizer, T. R., 316, 339, 467, 471
Sjoberg, S., 806, 823
Skemp, R. R., 765
Skilbeck, M., 132, 250, 251, 253, 328, 378
Skinner, B. F., 46–48, 333, 374, 443, 455, 545, 546, 704, 710
Skoog, G., 447
Skov, P., 328
Slade, P., 950
Slavin, R., 617, 621
Slavin, R. E., 340, 575, 585, 590, 591, 594, 597, 600, 843
Sleeter, C., 236
Sleeter, C. E., 259, 260
Slesnick, T., 671
Sliepcevish, E., 403
Sloan, R. P., 992
Sloat, K. C., 645
Smail, B., 807–808
Small, B., 807
Small, W. H., 349, 350
Smallwood, M. L., 271
Smart, P., 551
Smiley, S. S., 947
Smith, A., 135, 139, 417, 556, 559
Smith, A. D., 239
Smith, B. H., 10
Smith, B. O., 3*n*, 250, 338
Smith, C. D., 671
Smith, D. A., 498
Smith, D. E., 670, 675
Smith, D. G., 91
Smith, D. M., 105
Smith, D. T., 307, 308
Smith, D. V., 694, 734, 737, 740
Smith, E., 62, 82, 83, 205, 420, 421
Smith, E. R., 102, 123, 141
Smith, F. F., Jr., 573
Smith, H., 176
Smith, J., 518, 529
Smith, K. L., 254
Smith, L., 217, 219, 224, 237, 242, 306, 405, 411, 412–415, 417
Smith, L. M., [illegible], 370, 385
Smith, M., 228, 239, 1036
Smith, M. B., 446
Smith, M. L., 105, 133, 134, 144, 146, 712
Smith, M. S., 137
Smith, N., 812
Smith, N. B., 451, 452, 694, 697–698, 727
Smith, N. L., 339
Smith, N. R., 949, 951–952, 958
Smith, R., 670, 946, 949–950
Smith, S., 753
Smith, W., 808
Smithells, J., 1015
Smolensky, P., 535
Smoll, F. R., 976
Smoot, R. C., 279, 281
Smulyan, L., 105
Smyth, J., 493
Snedden, D., 163, 167–173, 239, 293, 580
Snook, I., 491
Snook, I. A., 551
Snow, A., 857, 881
Snow, C. P., 556
Snow, M. A., 882
Snow, R. E., 61, 64, 122, 129
Snowden, O. L., 910
Snyder, B. R., 9
Snyder, E. E., 1017, 1025
Snyder, J., 486, 492, 816
Snyder, J. F., 919
Soar, R. M., 65
Soar, R. S., 65
Sockett, H. T., 553, 562
Socrates, 270, 272, 274
Sola, M., 633
Solomon, D., 554
Solomon, J., 554, 803–805, 806
Soltis, J., 47, 52, 56, 235, 283
Soltis, J. F., 756–757, 766
Sorensen, A. B., 571, 573, 575, 576, 587, 592, 594
Sortiskey, M., 708
Sosniak, L. A., 237
Soter, A., 739, 743
Souque, J. P., 794
Southern, J., 1016
Southern, J. S., 1009–1010
Southern, S., 1011, 1022
Southern Governors' Association, 853
Southworth, G., 377
Soutter, D., 384
Spade, J. Z., 576, 577, 583, 585, 591, 593
Spady, W., 204
Spady, W. G., 367, 936, 1017, 1025–1026
Spafford, I., 899
Spanos, G., 641
Spaulding, F., 60, 198, 224, 225
Spaulding, F. T., [illegible]
Speakman-Yearta, M. A., 980
Speidel, G., 645
Spelke, E. S., 536
Spencer, H., 157
Spencer, L, 920
Spender, D., 670, 807
Spens Report, 1004
Spens, W., 1004
Sperber, R., 549
Sperling, M., 475
Spiegel-Rosing, I., 804
Spieseke, A. W., 438, 454
Spindler, G., 105, 106, 220, 242, 574
Spindler, L., 220, 242, 574
Spiro, R. J., 55, 520
Spivak, G., 546
Spolsky, E., 508
Spreitzer, E., 1017
Spretnak, C., 674
Spring, J., 169, 176, 226, 238, 580, 594, 703, 705, 715, 1003–1005
Squire, J. R., 444, 493, 583, 702–703, 709, 736-738, 742
Squires, W. G., 987
Srinivasan, J. T., 144
St. John, J., 452, 1034
Stachnik, T., 47, 48
Stafford, J. M., 555
Stage, E. K., 671
Stahl, S. A., 713
Stake, J. A., 832
Stake, R., 103, 108, 199, 220, 227, 236, 758, 765
Stake, R. E., 128, 131, 133, 142, 143, 144, 841, 842
Stallings, J., 417, 617
Stallings, J. A., 560
Standing, E. M., 277
Stanek, G. M. A., 179
Stanic, G., 759
Stankiewicz, M-A., 556
Stanley, J., 101, 103–108, 113, 114
Stanley, J. C., 140, 531, 667
Stanley, W. B., 832, 841
Stanley, W. O., 3*n*, 82, 250, 338
Stanovich, K. E., 529
Starch, D., 125, 448
Starkey, P., 536
Starratt, R. J., 554
Staszewski, J., 55
Staver, J. R., 436
Steady, F. C., 671
Stedman, L. C., 134, 137
Steeb, R. V., 900
Steedman, C., 385
Steen, L. A., 750–751
Stefano, A. di, 549
Stefik, M., 533
Stein, A. H., 1015
Stein, N. L., 711
Stein, E. L., 1020
Steinbach, R., 525
Steinberg, L. D., 1013, 1015
Steiner, G., 953
Steiner, R., 309
Steinhardt, M., 974
Steinhardt, M. A., 970, 977, 980, 985
Stella, F., 508
Stenhouse, L., 102, 132, 316, 377, 378, 381, 382, 383, 384, 551
Stenhouse, L. A., 32, 33
Stenmark, J. K., 671
Stenzel, K. R., 912
Stephens, T., 978, 987
Stephens, W. M., 761
Stephenson, H. H., 1012
Stern, D., 593, 928
Stern, H. D., 881
Stern, P., 56, 66, 126, 714
Stern, W., 49
Sternberg, R., 954
Sternberg, R. J., 53, 71, 934
Stetz, F. P., 143
Stevens, A. L., 523, 524
Stevens, D. D., 505
Stevens, E., 561
Stevens, G. Z., 894
Stevens, L. B., 219
Stevens, R., 714
Stevens, R. J., 493, 494
Stevenson, C. L., 1019
Stevenson, D. L., 572, 593
Stevenson, H. W., 772
Steward, W., 621
Stewart, J. S., 550
Stich, S. P., 521, 522
Stickel, G., 556
Stiggins, R. J., 126, 127
Stigler, J. W., 498, 770, 772
Stimpson, C., 668
Stimson, R. W., 892, 893
Stinchcombe, A. L., 219, 358, 592
Stipek, D., 560
Stoddard, 136
Stodolsky, S. S., 65, 135, 142, 144, 145, 205, 229, 436, 481, 494, 495, 714, 842
Stoephasius von, R., 335
Stokes, R., 965, 981
Stone, C., 53, 585, 600
Stone, F., 588
Stone, J. R., 922
Stone, N., 574–576, 583, 589
Stones, J., 891
Stotsky, S., 713
Stout, J. E., 160, 579, 726, 729
Stout, J. W., 562
Stratemeyer, F. B., 3*n*, 17, 337
Straughan, R., 549
Straw, B., 219
Stray, C., 275
Strayer, 160
Streit, R., 770
Strickland, D., 53, 619, 621
Strickland, R. G., 702
Strieb, L., 481
Strike, K., 287, 594
Strike, K. A., 110, 497, 508
Strom, M. S., 549, 556

Strope, J. L., 1032–1033
Stroud, M. A., 376
Strube, P. D., 438
Stryker, S. B., 877
Student Life, 1003
Stueck, P. M., 970
Stufflebeam, D. L., 120, 122–124, 128, 133
Stuhr, D., 549
Styer, S., 555
Suan, M. Z., 803
Subelman, I., 531
Suchman, J. R., 53
Sugarman, B., 552
Sullivan, 546
Sullivan, E. V., 330, 553
Sullivan, H. J., 333
Sullivan, M., 440
Sullivan, W., 574, 595
Sullivan, W. M., 274, 551, 553, 559
Sulzby, E., 708
Sum, A., 611–612
Sumner, W. G., 113
Sung, Y. H., 1018
Super, D., 905
Superka, D. P., 832, 836, 842–843, 847
Suppe, F., 288
Suppes, P., 100, 340
Sussmuth, H., 847
Sutherland, G., 121, 122
Suttle, B., 551
Suttle, B. B., 549
Sutton, C., 803
Sutton, F. X., 260
Sutton, W., 454
Suydam, M., 115, 220, 236, 765
Suzuki, D. T., 275
Svobodny, D., 452
Swafford, J. O., 577, 583
Swafford, S. O., 67, 69
Swain, M., 629, 637, 639, 643, 857, 859, 861, 863, 881
Swallow, J., 533
Swan, F. F., 915
Swanson, B. E., 912
Swanson, G., 891
Swanson, G. I., 907, 927
Swanson, R. A., 919, 920
Swarthout, D. W., 504, 505
Sweller, J., 527, 528, 534
Swetz, F., 752
Swetz, F. J., 751, 764, 767
Swidler, A., 274, 551, 553, 559, 574, 595
Swing, S. R., 52, 55, 66
Switzer, T. J., 843, 847

T

Taba, H., 3*n*, 3, 82, 85, 129, 330, 331, 734
Tabachnick, B. R., 411, 412, 414–417, 428, 506, 750, 842
Tabler, M. B., 771
Tabor, K. E., 859
Taerum, T., 375
Taft, H., 882
Taggart, A., 966, 967–968, 970
Talacchi, S., 1020
Talbott, J. E., 159
Talmage, H., 48, 71
Tamir, P., 110, 367, 370, 376, 790, 794, 808, 1018
Tanner, D., 3*n*, 9, 13, 17, 63, 67, 80, 83, 85, 103, 161, 165, 334, 336, 447, 455, 579, 909, 935
Tanner, L. N., 3*n*, 9, 13, 17, 63, 67, 80, 83, 85, 103, 161, 165, 171, 334, 336, 909, 935
Tappe, M. K., 976
Tarule, J. M., 93
Task Force on Education for Economic Growth, 252
Tasker, R., 799
Taxel, J., 295
Taylor, 374
Taylor, A. R., 1035
Taylor, B. L., 840
Taylor, F., 81, 197, 224
Taylor, F. W., 169
Taylor, G., 417
Taylor, M. E., 713
Taylor, P. H., 3*n*
Taylor, R. E., 925
Teale, W. T., 716
Tebbel, J., 445, 453, 454
Teberosky, A., 531
Teitelbaum, K., 158
Teitlebaum, H., 629
Tempes, F., 641
Templin, T. J., 979, 982, 989
TenHouten, W. D., 1034
Terenzini, P. T., 1026
Terman, L., 61, 596
Terman, L. W., 123
Terman, S., 703
Terrell, T., 643
Terrell, T. D., 876
Terry, P. W., 1006–1007
Terry, T., 920
TeSelle, S., 258
Tetreault, M. K., 670, 678
Tetreault, M. K. T., 554–556, 670
Thagard, P. R., 521
Tharp, R., 644–645
Tharp, R. G., 645
Thelen, L. J., 557
Theobald, P., 142
Theodorou, E., 501, 506
Thier, H., 813
Thiessen, D., 377
Thomas, B. R., 340
Thomas, G. R., 835
Thomas, I., 812
Thomas, J. A., 969
Thomas, J. R., 967, 969, 987
Thomas, K. T., 967
Thomas, L. G., 368
Thomas, M. C., 392, 667
Thomas, R. G., 930–931
Thomas, V. G., 667
Thomas, W. B., 259
Thompson, H., 50
Thompson, J. A., 601
Thompson, J. B., 296
Thompson, J. R., 376
Thompson, L., 882, 884
Thompson, M. G., 560, 562
Thompson, M. M., 967
Thompson, P., 677
Thompson, P. J., 897
Thompson, S. K., 669
Thompson, W., 445
Thonis, E. W., 639
Thorndike, E. L., 18, 47, 48, 61, 100, 101, 122, 123, 129, 197, 224, 230, 231, 293, 335, 443, 489, 490, 492, 496, 519, 522, 535, 695–696, 696, 710, 758
Thorne, B., 670
Thornton, G., 743
Thornton, S. J., 9
Thorpe, R., 982–983
Thrasher, J. M., 1021
Thurschwell, A., 674
Thurstone, L. L., 535
Tiberghien, A., 801
Tiburzi, A. M., 981
Tiedt, S., 228
Tierney, R. J., 711, 716
Tietze, W., 51
Tikunoff, W., 637
Tikunoff, W. J., 64
Tilman, K., 974
Timar, T. B., 228, 234, 239
Time, 258
Timerlake, C. H., 1026
Timpane, P. M., 404
Tindall, B. A., 989
Tindall, L. W., 929
Tingelstad, O. A., 448
Tipton, S., 574, 595
Tipton, S. M., 274
Tipton, S. N., 551, 553, 559
Tisher, R., 809
Tisher, R. P., 223
Tobias, S., 671
Tobin, B. M., 545
Tobin, K., 506
Tocqueville, A. de, 113
Toepfer, C. F., Jr., 3*n*
Toffler, A., 771
Tolman, E. C., 546
Tom, A., 544
Tomberlin, J. E., 269
Tomkins, G., 364, 365, 367, 368, 370, 378
Tompkins, E., 60
Tonne, H. A., 894
Torney, J., 859
Torrance, H., 120
Tough, J., 651
Toulmin, S., 288, 708
Toure, S., 262
Tousignant, M., 989
Towers, E. R., 901
Trabasso, T., 711
Trafton, P. R., 758
Tran, C., 639
Traub, R., 64
Travers, K. J., 67, 69, 577, 583, 769
Travers, R. M. W., 103, 123–125, 138, 143, 374, 491
Travers, R. W., 66
Trecker, J. L., 445
Treisman, P. U., 114
Trent, W. T., 1013–1014, 1030
Trimble, K., 584
Trisman, D. A., 711
Trites, R. L., 858
Troen, S., 231
Troen, S. K., 353, 354, 356
Troike, R., 629
Trono, J., 676
True, A. C., 892
Trump, J. L., 909, 1012
Tryon, C., 337, 338
Tuana, N., 92
Tucker, G. R., 629, 637, 643
Tucker, J. L., 847
Tucker, M., 619
Tucker, R., 859
Tuer, A. W., 452
Tufte, E. R., 438
Tully, M. A., 444
Tulving, J., 708
Turner, C. C., 1008, 1021
Turner, G., 144, 250
Turner, M. J., 843, 847
Turner, R., 593
Turney, C., 376
Tweedy, H., 1009
Twining, J., 931
Tyack, D., 58–60, 122, 159, 181, 196, 218, 219, 223–228, 230–232, 239, 359, 596, 659, 665, 669–670, 947
Tyack, D. B., 365, 367, 368, 451, 487, 488, 544, 558, 909
Tye, K. A., 128, 329, 338
Tyler, L. L., 329, 333, 335
Tyler, R., 67, 230, 231, 239, 316, 317
Tyler, R. W., 21, 24–28, 30–33, 36, 62, 82- 87, 102, 110, 120, 123, 127–129, 140-142, 144, 329, 331–333, 338, 365, 366, 369, 420, 421, 490, 523, 630, 633–634

Tynan, M., 124
Typer, R. W., 330
Tyson-Bernstein, H., 713, 841

U

Uhl, W., 579
Uhrmacher, B., 309
Ullian, D. Z., 1015
Ulrich, R., 47, 48
Umstattd, W. D., 919
UNESCO, 376, 638, 790, 797, 803
Ungoed-Thomas, J. R., 546
Updegraff, H., 349, 350, 353, 359
Upitis, R., 952
Urban, W., 368
Urban, W. J., 176, 177
Urch, G. E., 261
Urwin, 385
U.S. Department of Education, 627, 923
U.S. Department of Health, 983
U.S. Department of Health and Human Services, 981, 983
U.S. National Assessment of Educational Progress, 769
U.S. Office of Education, 838, 902–903, 920, 1016
U.S. Office of Educational Research and Improvement, 844
Usiskin, Z., 765
Usiskin, Z. P., 766

V

Valance, E., 3
Valdes, G., 640
Valdes-Fallis, G., 636
Valentine, J. A., 741
Vallance, E., 3, 9, 13, 15, 16, 20, 46, 196, 276, 334, 487, 561, 966, 973
Valli, L., 576, 583, 585, 586, 588, 589, 594, 600
Van de Ven, P., 730
Van Dyke, G. E., 1003, 1006–1007
Van Ek, J. A., 861
Van Kirk, J., 801
Vandenberg, D., 287
Vanfossen, B. E., 576, 577, 583, 585, 591, 593
VanLehn, K., 530
Varelas, M., 237
Varenne, H., 570, 573, 574, 586, 588, 589, 595
Vasudex, J., 554
Veal, M. L., 988
Veatch, J., 703, 712
Veblen, T., 113
Velez, W., 571, 593
Venezky, R. L., 439, 448, 452, 453, 456, 694, 697–698
Verdonk, A., 811
Vergnaud, G., 774
Verhave, T., 47
Verney, 600, 601
Vico, G., 272, 297
Viennot, L., 517
Villedieu, A. de, 121
Vining, A., 189
Vinovskis, M., 694
Vinovskis, M. A., 359
Violas, P. C., 1003, 1004
Virgil, 272
Vitz, P. C., 670
Vocational Education Act of 1963, 895
Voege, H. W., 229
Vogel, M., 416, 417
Vogel, P. G., 986, 987
Vondruska, R. J., 520
Vornberg, J. A., 1008, 1009–1012, 1016, 1022
Vos, W. de, 811
Vose, R. M., 690, 694
Vosniadou, S., 524
Voss, J. F., 522, 527, 528
Vries, M. de, 817
Vygotsky, L., 957
Vygotsky, L. S., 52, 312, 313, 470, 536, 699

W

Waggener, W. J., 282
Wagner, B. J., 53
Wagner, J. J., 258
Wagner, R., 954
Wagner, R. K., 934
Wagoner, K. P., 914
Wahlquist, J. T., 251
Waitrowski, M. D., 592, 593
Waks, L., 804
Walberg, H. J., 53, 56, 63, 553
Walcutt, C. C., 703
Wales, R., 861
Walford, G., 807
Walker, A., 573
Walker, D., 3, 103, 110, 130, 188, 189, 195, 198, 202, 204, 221, 224, 227, 229, 303, 310
Walker, D. F., 3, 32, 33, 112, 160, 340, 370, 491
Walker, J. L., 700
Walker, L. J., 554
Walker, M., 781
Walker, R., 32, 105, 382, 383, 384
Wallerstein, V., 141
Walkling, P. H., 254
Wall, R. E., 835
Wallace, D., 1030
Wallace, H. R., 920–921
Wallace, J., 803
Wallace, R. C., Jr., 407
Wallen, N. E., 491
Waller, W., 236, 242, 467, 585, 589
Wallin, M., 367
Walmsley, S. A., 711, 713
Walp, T. P., 711, 713
Walsh, C., 633
Walsh, J., 504
Walsh, J. P., 908
Walsh, M., 249
Walworth, A., 446
Wang, B. M., 989
Wankel, L. M., 992
Waples, D., 123
Ward, C. H., 692
Ward, L., 613
Wardle, D., 293
Ware, S., 812
Waring, M., 793
Warner, M., 385, 661
Warner, M. M., 1035, 1038
Warner, W. E., 900
Warnock, M., 551
Warren, B., 646
Warren, B. M., 530
Warren, C., 965
Warren, D. R., 66
Warren, P. A., 745
Warren, R. P., 736
Warriner-Burke, H. P., 878
Washburne, C., 102
Watson, J., 676
Watson, J. B., 47
Watson, M., 546, 554
Watters, D. H., 452, 453
Watts, M., 801, 808
Watzlawick, P., 218
Waugh, E., 480
Way, B., 950
Wayland, S. R., 233, 235
Weade, R., 493, 500, 501, 917
Weakland, J., 218
Weatherly, R., 194
Weaver, J. F., 756
Weaver, R., 701
Webb, L. J., 1017
Webb, N., 51
Webb, N. M., 591
Webb, R. B., 376
Webber, L. S., 613
Weber, L. J., 1032
Weber, M., 81
Webster, P., 952
Webster, W. J., 124, 129
Weeks, R. M., 690
Wegforth, R. P., 896
Wegner, G., 229, 447
Wehlage, G., 411, 412, 414, 417, 428, 506, 585, 588, 600, 842
Wehlage, G. G., 750
Weick, K., 194, 217, 240, 241
Weick, K. E., 79
Weidman, C., 56
Weil, M., 53, 491
Weimer, D., 189
Weinberg, S., 711
Weiner, C., 291
Weinfeld, F. D., 1036
Weingartner, C., 550
Weinstein, C. E., 56, 520
Weinstein, R. S., 591
Weintraub, S., 714
Weir, M., 238, 472, 473
Weir, R., 699
Weis, L., 35, 478, 483
Weisberg, A., 928
Weiskopf, V., 286
Weisner, T. S., 475
Weiss, I., 199, 220, 227, 765
Weiss, I. R., 436
Weiss, J., 64
Weiss, J. H., 896
Weiss, M. R., 1017
Welch, A., 452
Welch, S. D., 676
Welch, W., 63, 103, 112, 188, 199, 794
Welch, W. W., 336, 1018
Welford, G., 808
Well, C. G., 53
Wells, J., 672
Wells, S., 340
Welsh, W., 765
Welter, B., 473
Welton, M., 543
Wendell, B., 692
Wenham, P., 384
Wepner, S., 619
Werner, H., 951
Wertheimer, M., 52
Werthman, C., 588
Wertsch, J. V., 469
Wesbury, I., 570, 574
Wesche, M. B., 877
West, L., 802, 807
West, L. H. T., 517
West, P., 594, 879
Westat, Inc., 202
Westbury, I., 103, 176, 178, 223, 232, 236, 237, 240, 367, 368, 380, 442, 443, 445, 573, 574, 598, 757, 769, 775, 778
Westerhoff, J. H., III, 441, 445, 450–452
Westlake, P., 728
Weston, L. C., 1028
Weston, W. J., 446
Wettersten, J., 281
Wexler, P., 294
Weyl, H., 286, 288
Whately, R., 600
Wheeler, C. W., 208, 559
Wheeler, D., 751
Wheeler, D. K., 129
Wheelock, A., 145
Whipple, G., 704–707
Whipple, G. M., 101, 378, 380, 441, 1003

Whitbeck, C., 676
White, B., 110
White, B. Y., 532
White, C. C., 978, 987
White, E. E., 125, 144
White, J. J., 236, 840–841
White, J. P., 551
White, M., 171, 571
White, N., 270
White, P., 598
White, R., 799, 801, 809–810
White, R. T., 223
White, S. H., 562
White, W. T., Jr., 489, 490
Whitehead, A. N., 330, 525
Whitty, G., 252, 276, 295
Whorf, B. L., 304
Whyte, J., 807, 807–808
Wichowski, C., 920
Wicker, A. W., 1020–1021, 1023, 1027, 1030
Wiebe, R. H., 488
Wieting, M. C., 226, 234
Wigginton, E., 231, 339
Wikler, D., 992
Wilcox, K., 583, 586, 588, 835, 840
Wildavsky, A., 187–189
Wilder, D. E., 707
Wiles, J., 3*n*
Wiley, K. B., 841
Wilken, P. H., 1020
Wilkerson, I. A., 712
Wilkinson, B., 505, 506
Wilkinson, I. A. G., 451
Wilkinson, L. C., 617
Wilkof, N. J., 380
Willems, E. P., 1014, 1020–1021, 1023
Williams, 374
Williams, A., 974–975
Williams, B., 676
Williams, F., 615
Williams, G. A., 1035
Williams, N., 552
Williams, P. L., 135, 140
Williams, R., 158, 159, 205, 293, 294, 295, 296, 437, 438, 445, 572, 580, 593, 727
Williams, R. A., 592
Williams, T., 921
Williamson, O., 357
Willingham, R. M., 452
Willingham, R. M., Jr., 454
Willis, P., 133, 174, 206, 226, 231, 242, 254, 295, 321, 474, 478, 586, 589, 592
Willis, P. E., 499
Willows, D. M., 451, 713
Wilmore, J. H., 965, 970
Wilson, B., 795, 950–951
Wilson, B. J., 574
Wilson, B. L., 234, 235, 236
Wilson, C., 795
Wilson, D. L., 592
Wilson, D. M., 667
Wilson, E. O., 520, 536
Wilson, H. B., 696
Wilson, J., 549, 551, 552
Wilson, J. S., 671
Wilson, M., 950–951
Wilson, P., 714
Wilson, P. A., 125
Wilson, S., 799
Wilson, S. M., 498, 499
Wilson, W. J., 610–611
Wilton, R. F., 911
Winant, T., 292
Winchester, I., 10
Wind, A. L., 965
Wineburg, S. S., 498, 499, 536
Wing, A. L., 970
Winkelmann, W., 51
Winne, P. H., 526
Winner, E., 953, 954
Winner, L., 131, 138
Winograd, T., 708
Winters, M. R., 931
Wirszup, I., 770
Wirt, F., 102, 204, 229
Wirt, F. M., 224, 228, 234
Wirt, J., 199
Wirt, J. G., 928
Wirt, W., 198
Wirth, A. G., 165, 904, 935
Wisconsin Department of Public Instruction, 923
Wise, A., 193, 195, 234
Wise, A. E., 42, 44, 45, 58, 65, 71, 131
Wise, L. L., 671
Wiseman, S., 124
Wisenbaker, J., 69
Wiske, M. S., 780
Wiss, C., 858
Witherell, C., 678
Witkin, R., 954
Witt, P. D., 726–728
Witt, P. W. F., 375
Witte, G. B., 261
Wittgenstein, L., 955
Wittrock, M., 802
Wittrock, M. C., 66, 103, 520, 521, 964
Wodtke, K. H., 145
Wolcott, H., 236, 237, 242
Wolcott, H. F., 104, 257, 376
Wolf, D., 947, 949, 954, 957–958
Wolf, J., 959
Wolf, L. C., 556
Wolf, R. M., 68
Wolfram, W., 614
Wolfson, B., 46
Wolinksy, J., 992
Wollheim, R., 954
Wollnough, B. E., 180
Wollstonecraft, M., 664
Women's Studies Quarterly, 677
Womer, F., 796
Wong Fillmore, L., 637, 643, 645, 649
Wongthonglour, S., 810
Wood, G. H., 561
Wood, H. B., 226, 234
Wood, S., 437
Wood, T., 780
Wood, T. M., 981
Woodcock, E. C., 1024
Woodring, P., 489
Woodruff, E., 533
Woods, P., 105, 226, 231, 242, 392
Woods, W., 708
Woodward, A., 441, 442, 444, 704, 707
Woodward, V., 370, 716
Woodward, V. C., 950
Woody, C., 140
Wooton, W., 370
Worfram, W., 700
World Affairs Council of Northern California, 651
Worsely, A., 977–978
Worthen, B. R., 120, 124
Wright, J., 919
Wright, S., 228
Wright, T. R., 905, 919
Wrightstone, W. J., 140
Wrigley, J., 205, 238
Wubbels, T., 806
Wubbens, D., 922
Wundt, W., 312
Wylie, M. L., 1027
Wyllie, M., 743
Wynne, E., 553, 562
Wynne, E. A., 553

Y

Yachinsky, J., 143
Yackel, E., 780
Yager, R. E., 966
Yalow, E., 122
Yambert, P. A., 557
Yarworth, J. S., 1014, 1017–1018
Yarworth, W. J., 1012
Yates, A., 992
Yates, J., 147
Yeazell, M. I., 556
Yengel, H., 896
Yerkes, R., 61
Yerushalmy, M., 766, 780
Yin, R. K., 105, 416, 417
Yinger, R., 56
Yoder, E., 910
Yogev, A., 572, 592
Yoho, L. W., 901
Yonemura, M. V., 385
York, R. L., 1036
Yost, G., 533
Young, I. M., 676
Young, J. A., 281
Young, J. H., 376, 377
Young, M. F. D., 102, 294, 295, 296, 478
Young, M., 205, 750, 760, 776, 793
Young, M. J., 444
Young, P., 617
Young, R., 699, 708
Yudin, L. W., 1014

Z

Zacharias, J., 227, 237, 368
Zahorik, J. A., 35, 85
Zais, R. S., 3*n*, 10, 487
Zarinnia, E. A., 779
Zec, P., 257
Zechiel, A., 421
Zeev, B., 853, 858
Zeidler, D. L., 557
Zelan, K., 525
Zelizer, V. A., 472
Zeno, S., 136
Zessoules, R., 947, 959
Zhu, W., 966, 973
Zidonis, F., 700, 743
Ziefuss, H., 817, 819
Ziegler, H., 204
Zikmund, D., 910
Zilversmit, A., 226
Ziman, J., 273
Zimet, S., 442, 445, 448
Zinchenko, V. P., 536
Zirbes, L., 703
Zoller, U., 805
Zuga, K. F., 249, 920
Zukowski, J. J., 1009–1011, 1016, 1022
Zumwalt, K. K., 9, 392, 427, 486, 492, 493
Zweng, M., 770

SUBJECT INDEX

A

Ability grouping, 469, 472, 577, 613
Absolute Curriculum, The (Bowsher), 6
Abstractness, of mathematics, 755
Academic orientation, 15
Academic performance
  and extracurriculum, 1016–1017, 1025–1026
  See also Achievement
Academic Preparation for College, 958
Academic Preparation in the Arts, 958
Academic track, 578
Academy, 354
  Franklin's, 905
  Plato's, 270
Accelerated school, 321
Accreditation, impact on curriculum stability/change, 234
Achievement
  and curriculum differentiation, 590–592
  and gender differences, 668
  research on, 67–68
  school effects, 68–70
  and tracking, 594
Action research, teachers in, 377–378
Active instruction, and poor African-Americans, 620
"Activities Basic to Learning Mathematics" (Romberg), 755
Activity curriculum, 337
Add-on programs, 617–618
  studies of effectiveness, 617
Adolescence (Hall), 731, 1004
Advances in Instructional Psychology (Glaser), 532
Aesthetic criticism of curriculum, 90–91
  and ethics, 91
Aesthetics, contributions to curricular theory, 90–91
Affective revolution, and social studies curriculum, 839
African-Americans
  anti-achievement ethic, 615
  barriers to excellence, 613–614, 616
  black male joblessness, 611
  black underclass, 610–611
  and cultural dissonance, 615
  educational isolation, 612–613
  effects of poverty, 615–616
  female-headed family, 611–612
  genetic differences issue, 614
  linguistic differences issue, 614–615
  and racism, 615
  in urban areas, 610
African-Americans and curriculum
  higher-order thinking skills, 619
  instructional organization, 616–618
  instructional strategies, 621
  language development, 621
  mathematics, 618–619
  multicultural education, 620
  parental involvement, 621
  reading, 618–619
  recommendations for, 622–623
  use of computers, 619–620
Age
  age-grading, 59, 61
  and foreign language learning, 870–872
Agenda for Action, An, 754
Agricultural education
  curricular research, 910–913
  historical view, 892–894
  home project concept, 892
  standards for, 911
Aims of education, 128–129
Aldine Readers, 697
American Association for the Advancement of Science, 229
American Book Company, 455
American Council of Learned Societies, 230
American Federation of Teachers, 145, 230
American Institute for Biological Sciences, 229–230
American Mathematical Society, 230
American Memory (Cheney), 311, 854
American Preceptor (Bingham), 453
American Psychological Association, 61
American System of Agricultural Education, 892
American Vocational Association, 907
Anatomy of an Educational Innovation, 411
And Madly Teach: A Layman Looks at Public School Education (Smith), 446
Animal Intelligence (Thorndike), 100
Annehurst Curriculum Classification System, 330–331
Anthroposophy, 309
Antisocial behavior, and extracurriculum, 1026–1027
Apperceptive mass, 333
Appleton Readers, 441
Applications, in mathematics, 755–756
Applications of Chemistry to Agriculture, 892
Apprenticeship, 269–271
  characteristics of, 269–270
  colonial era, 348
  historical perspective, 124
  model for art education, 953
  and vocational education, 270, 905
Area Redevelopment Act, 904
Army Specialized Training Program, 860
Art
  development as school subject, 179
  and higher order thinking, 947
  meaning in, 954
  as way of knowing, 947
Art education
  apprenticeship model, 953
  ARTS PROPEL, 957
  conflict related to, 959–960
  Delacroze method, 950
  and development, 951–953
  developmentally based curricula, 958–959
  discipline-based method, 956–957
  divergent views of, 956
  exclusions from, 953–954
  historical view, 947–949

Art education *(Continued)*
  Orff method, 950
  and progressive education movement, 958–959
  psychological contributions of, 949–951
  and school art style, 955
Articulation, cognitive method, 532
Artificial intelligence, 519
  and computer-assisted instruction, 533
  expert systems, 522–523
Arithmetic (Ray), 454
Artistic approaches, qualitative evaluation, 133
Arts and Crafts Movement, and manual arts programs, 906
Asians
  bilingual education, 642
  performance compared to Mexican-Americans, 644
  work styles of, 645
  See also Japanese schools
Assessment
  definition of, 120
  empirical approach to, 57–72
  foreign language study, 862–863, 881, 882
  and language arts curriculum, 741
  and science curriculum, 795–796, 811–812
Assessment of Performance Unit
  tasks of, 796
  technology education, 819–820
Athena project, 878
Athletes
  personality traits, 1019
  See also Extracurriculum
At-risk students
  characteristics of, 929
  and physical education, 979
  and vocational education, 929–930
Audio-lingual approach, foreign language study, 860–861
Australian Science Education Project, 803
Authority, and curriculum policy, 187–188
Automaticity
  in cognitive theory, 866
  and decoding, 529, 530
  and information processing, 529, 530
  training for, 530
Average daily attendance formula, state aid, 612

B

Background knowledge, purpose of, 522
Back-to-basics-movement, 135, 547, 705–706, 760
  social studies curriculum, 839–840
Bank Street model, 951
Basal readers, 703, 706
  decoding skills, 713
  report on, 712, 713
Basic Issues in the Teaching of English, 736
Basic Principles of Curriculum and Instruction (Tyler), 24–25, 28, 83, 86, 129, 330, 365
Basic skills approach
  language arts, 738
  mathematics, 760
  and vocational education, 934
Basic Stuff, 969, 981
Bay Area Global Education Program, 651
Becoming a Nation of Readers, 712
Becoming Critical: Education, Knowledge and Action Research (Carr and Kemmis), 936
Beginning Teacher Evaluation Study, 64
Behavioral approaches
  and education, 489–490
  and science curriculum, 791
  Thorndike's laws, 695
Behavioral objectives, 761
  behavioral objectives movement, 129–130
  problems related to use, 130
Behavioral theory
  contributions to curriculum study, 48–49
  curriculum studies, 47–49
  history of, 46–47, 102
Beloe Report, 144
Better Science—Making It Happen, 809
Beyond Balls and Bats (Hellison), 979
Beyond Creating, 956
Bilingual Education: History, Politics, Theory and Practice (Crawford), 629
Bilingual education, 628–629
  Canadian immersion programs, 637–638, 643
  concurrent methods, 637
  development of, 629–630
  early efforts, 627
  literacy in dominant language, 638–639
  mathematics, 641
  national/regional centers for, 635
  opposition to, 627–628
  philosophical issues, 630–634
  and reading, 639–640
  and Title VII of ESEA, 629
  writing, 640–641
  See also Language minorities
Bilingual Education Act, 629
Bilingual Education Multifunction Support Centers, 635
Bilingual Education Service Centers, 635
Bilingualism in Education: Aspects of Theory, Research and Practice (Cummins and Swain), 629–630
Biological Science Curriculum Study, 53, 63, 227, 792
Black English, 621, 743
Blue-Backed Speller, 727
Boston Conference on Physical Training, 965
Boston English High School, 729
Boston Latin School, 729
British infant schools, 53
British model, curriculum development, 32–33
Broad-field pattern, curriculum organization, 336
Brookline Moral Education Project, 549
Brown v. Topeka Board of Education, 228, 615
Building America, 447
Bureaucracy, street-level bureaucracy concept, 193–194
Business Curriculum, The, 895
Business education
  curricular research, 913–915
  goals of, 915
  historical view, 894–896
Business Education Yesterday, Today, and Tomorrow, 896

C

Calgary Listening Inquiry Project, 385
California School of Mechanics Arts, 905
Call of Stories: Teaching and Moral Imagination (Coles), 386
Capacity building, 191
Capital, curriculum as capital view, 195, 196–198
Cardinal Principles of Secondary Education, The, 61, 161, 162, 163, 164, 578, 579, 904, 1003, 1004
Career choice, and individual expression, 19
Career education, 909
  curricular research, 925–926
  goals of, 926
  historical view, 904–905
Career Education Incentive Act, 925
Career Oriented Modules to Explore Technology and Science, 808
Carnegie Foundation, 60, 61, 229, 252
Carnegie units, 60, 62
Case School of Applied Science, 905
Case studies, 847
  approaches to, 479
Castillian Grammar Founded on Philosophical Principles, 860
Censorship, and curriculum, 258
Centennial Exposition, 905, 906
Center for Restructuring, 252
Central tendency theory, textbook content analysis, 449
Changes in School Mathematics (Romberg), 755
Changing Methods of Teaching Business Subjects, 896
Character education, 552–554
  goal of, 553
  moral person in, 553
  movement for, 553
  in school and classroom, 553–554
Cheche Konnen model, 646
Chemical Education Materials Study, 63
Chemical Manipulation (Faraday), 273
Chemicals in Public Places project, 813
Chemistry, organization of material, 279–280, 281, 282

Chemistry in a Thousand Questions, 811
Chemistry in the Community, 806, 812
Chicanos: Mexican American Voices, The (Ludwig and Santibanez), 258
Child and the Curriculum, The (Dewey), 6–7, 172, 378, 959
Child-centered school, compared to conventional school, 278
Child-Centered School, The (Rugg and Shumacher), 102, 277–278, 311
Child Development Project, 554
Children and Fitness: A Public Health Perspective, 984
Children's Learning in Science project, 810
Children's School Project, 619
Christianity
  Christian schools, 256, 261–262
  on education of women, 661–662
Chunking, 55, 529
Citizenship education, 699, 845
Civic Biology (Hunter), 455
Class conflict, in educational history, 159–160
Classical conditioning, 47
Classical Rhetoric for the Modern Student (Corbett), 701
Classics, 100
  aspects of classical curriculum, 727–729
  Great Books approach, 741
Classroom
  aim of classroom life, 469
  communication processes, 500–501
  dynamics and curriculum differentiation, 585–589
  impact of structures on curriculum stability/change, 237
  issues related to social system, 470–471
  social changes, impact of, 473
  sociolinguistic studies of, 474–475
  and student experience of curriculum, 469–471
  student rankings in, 469–470
  students' interpretations of classroom culture, 508
  teacher attention, 470
"Classroom Knowledge" (Keddie), 587
Classrooms and Corridors: The Crisis of Authority in Desegregated Secondary Schools (Metz), 588
Classroom tasks, 503–507
  components of, 504
  elements of, 468–469
  meaning of task, 503–504
  procedural tasks, 506
  students' versions of, 505–506
  and task system, 504
  location of effects in classroom, 504
  types of, 506–507
  types of task research, 504–507
Closing of the American Mind, The (Bloom), 315
Cloze method, 711
Coaching, cognitive method, 532
Coalition of Essential Schools, 252
Cognition and curriculum
  cognitive apprenticeship, 532
  cognitive skills and curriculum, 335
  cognitive teaching, 532–533
  computer environments, 533
  curriculum sequencing, 531
  design of transitional forms, 531–532
  development of procedural knowledge, 524–525
  discourse comprehension, 521–522
  education for expertise, 534–535
  expertise as knowledge, 522
  formal knowledge, 525
  implications for curriculum, 523
  information processing, 529–530
  learning from intelligent systems, 523
  mental models, 523–524
  metacognition, 525–529
Cognition and Instruction, 497, 532
Cognitive Academic Language Learning Approach, 649–650
Cognitive apprenticeship, 497
  teaching methods of, 532
Cognitive pluralism, 317–319
  characteristics of, 317–318
  influences of, 318–319
  research in, 323
Cognitive process orientation, curriculum content, 15, 16
Cognitive science
  connectionism, 535
  and culture, 520
  ecological cognitive science, 536
  and emotion, 520–521
  historical view of study, 519–520
  meaning of, 518
  mental level of description, meaning of, 518–519
  and nativism, 537–538
  role of computers in, 520
  scope of, 521
  situated learning, 536
Cognitive Science and Mathematics Education (Schoenfeld), 750
Cognitive strategies
  elaboration and transfer, 869
  emphasis and summarizing strategies, 869
  functional practice, 869
  inferencing strategies, 869
  memory strategies, 869
Cognitive structuralist theory
  concepts in, 52–53
  curriculum issues related to, 54
  history of, 52
  implications for curriculum, 53–54
  language in, 52, 53
Cognitive style, and foreign language learning, 868
Cognitive theory
  areas of exploration, 517–518
  automaticity in, 866
  basic concepts, 54–55
  and foreign language study, 865–866
  implications for curriculum, 55–56
  language learning, 865–866
  and mathematics, 777–778
  and reading curriculum, 711
  research question in, 55
  restructuring in, 866
  and writing curriculum, 708
Cold war, impact on curriculum stability/change, 226–227
Coleman Report, 67
Collaborative models, physical education, 982–983
College admission, and the intended curriculum, 234–235
College Entrance Examination Board, 235
College level, foreign language study, 877
Colonial schools, 347–350
  apprenticeship, 348
  institutionalization of schooling, 349
  private education, 350–351
  Puritan values, 347–348
  textbooks of, 453
  and urbanization, 350
Commercial Education in the High School (Nichols), 894
Commission on National Aid to Vocational Education, 907
Commission on the English Curriculum, 700–701
Commission on the Reorganization of Secondary Education, 166, 229, 368, 833
Committee of Eight, 840
Committee of Fifteen, 696, 699
Committee of Ten, 60, 162–163, 164, 165, 166, 175, 229, 235, 368, 578, 689, 690, 693, 699, 729–730
Committee on Agricultural Education of the National Academy of Science, 912
Committee on College-Entrance Requirements, 164, 166, 167, 175
Committee on Methods of Teaching Agriculture, 892
Committee on Minimal Essentials in Elementary School Subjects, 696, 732
Committee on Reading, 712
Committee on the Economy of Time in Learning, 696, 732
Committee on Types of Organization of High School English, 693
Committee reports
  areas of interpretation for, 162–164
  and curriculum history, 162–167
"Common Curriculum for Mathematics" (Romberg), 755
Common Learnings Program, 174, 234
Communication
  communication processes, classroom, 500–501
  communicative competence and foreign language learning, 861, 863

Communication *(Continued)*
and computers, 533
language skills for, 735
Community, and extracurriculum, 1021–1022
Community Work in Rural High Schools, 892
Composition (Weaver), 701
Comprehensive School Improvement Program, 229
Computer-assisted instruction, 533, 617
development of, 456
as teacher-proof curricula, 375
Computer-assisted language learning, foreign language study, 877–878
Computer-mediated communication systems, as teacher-proof curricula, 375
Computers
and cognitive science, 520, 533
communication networks, 533
and language arts, 742–743
programs for poor African-Americans, 619–620
tutoring programs, 533
Concept of Mind, The (Ryle), 283
Conceptual empiricists, 82
Concerns-Based Adoption Model, 377
stages in, 406–408
Condition of Education, The, 67
Conduit metaphor in education, 369–374
characteristics of, 369
Rand Corporation study, 372–374
teacher in, 370, 371–372
teacher proof curriculum in, 374
Confederates, in formative research, 111
Conference on Home Economics, 897
Conformists, students, 256
Connectionism, 535
connectionist technology, 535
Consortium on Restructuring, 252
Constitutional rights, and extracurriculum, 1033
Constructivism
and language arts, 738–739
nature of constructivist schools, 415
"Consumer and Homemaking Education," 899
Consumer Education Curriculum Modules: A Spiral Process Approach (Murphy), 916
Content
adaptations, bilingual education, 647–652
content pedagogy, 497
of differentiated curriculum, 573–574
pedagogical content knowledge, 498–499
social studies curriculum, 836–837
Content-based instruction, foreign language study, 876–877
Content Determinants Project, 204
Continuity, curriculum organization, 330
Control
curriculum as control view, 195, 203–207
curriculum differentiation as, 580
ideologies of, 367–368
Cooperative learning strategies, and poor African-Americans, 620–621
Cooperative movement, 690
Cooperative Research Program, 705
Cooperative Test Service, 136
Cooperative training, nature of, 906
COPE exam, 882
Core curriculum
curriculum organization, 338–339
nature of, 631
CORE model, for extracurriculum, 1010–1011
Correlated Curriculum, 690
Correlated-subject design, curriculum organization, 336
Correspondence education
as teacher-proof curricula, 375–376
UNESCO definition of, 376
Correspondence theory, basis of, 972
Council of Europe, 861
Course of Practical Instruction in Elementary Biology (Huxley and Martin), 455
Covert curriculum, nature of, 988
Craft, Design and Technology, 817
Creative Power (Hook), 691
Creative Youth (Mearns), 691
Criterion-referenced tests, 135, 136
Critical/emancipatory approaches, qualitative evaluation, 133–134
Critical inquiry, and curriculum organization, 333–334
Critical Legal Studies, 671
Critical literacy, 648
Critical studies, 86
Critical Teaching and Everyday Life (Shor), 278
Critical theory, 314–316
basis of, 972
characteristics of, 314–315
feminist theory, 671–672
influences of, 315–316
research in, 321–322
Cross Commission, 144
Cross-cultural view
curriculum development, 370–371
curriculum differentiation, 571–572, 600
extracurriculum, 1005
language arts, 730
mathematics, 768–770
physical education, 974, 975
science curriculum, 790, 794, 796–797, 798–799, 800, 801–803, 806, 808, 809–811, 815
technology curriculum, 815–820
vocational education, 931
Cross-national studies, 847
Cross-sectional research, 480
Cultural artifacts, textbooks as, 437
Cultural assimilation, and bilingual education, 630, 631
Cultural capital, 206
and social class, 292–293
Cultural dissonance, and African-Americans, 615
Cultural literacy, 745
Cultural Literacy (Hirsch), 310, 311, 523, 632
Cultural pluralism, and bilingual education, 630, 631
Culture
and cognitive science, 520
definition of, 873–874
and foreign language study, 873–874
and language, 256–257
and mathematics, 752–754, 762
and subculture, 249–250
use of term, 249–250
See also Curriculum and culture
Culture fair tests, 615
Current English Usage, 732
Curriculum: A Comprehensive Introduction (McNeil), 936
Curriculum: Foundations, Principles, and Issues (Ornstein and Hunkins), 936
Curriculum: Perspective, Paradigm, and Possibility (Schubert), 936
Curriculum
aesthetic critics on, 90–91
Bobbit's view, 7–8, 11, 13–14, 22–24, 26, 34, 36, 81
cycles of reform, 365
definitional issues, 4–12
definitional shifts, 9–12
definition of, 4–6, 7, 9, 221, 276–277, 346, 364–365, 427
delivered curriculum, 439
desired curriculum, 439
Dewey's view, 6–7, 8, 13–14, 22
as educative experience, 7–8
enacted curriculum, 9
feminist theory, 92–94
first text on, 21
hidden curriculum, 8–9, 12
historical curriculum, 223
historical view, 21–32
institutional curriculum, 487–488
intended curriculum, 222
learned curriculum, 222–223
most influential text, 24
needed curriculum, 439
null curricula, 9
official curriculum, 9
out-of-school curriculum, 7–8, 11–12
phenomenologists on, 91–92
political analysts' contribution to, 88–90
prescribed curriculum, 439
principles derived from court cases, 203
problems of reformists, 87
and psychological nature of learner, 14
received curriculum, 439–440
reconceptualist's view, 83–86
Schwab's view, 28–32, 34, 35
and social conditions, 14
sources of influence, 22

taught curriculum, 222
teacher's acceptance of, 17–18
Tyler's view, 24–28, 82–83, 231
views of curricular historians, 87–88
Curriculum, The (Bobbit), 21, 22, 24–28, 82–83
Curriculum adaptation project, 370
Curriculum alignment, 199, 201–203, 280
examples of practices, 205
Curriculum and Evaluation Standards for School Mathematics, 750, 754, 773
Curriculum components
broad educational aims, 128–129
context, 128
curricular materials, 130
objectives of specific learning units, 129–130
outcomes, 131–132
transactions and processes, 130–131
Curriculum Construction (Charters), 893
Curriculum content
academic orientation, 15
cognitive process orientation, 15, 16
humanistic orientation, 15, 41
interpretation of differing views, 16–21
multiple perspectives in writings, 11–21
self-actualization orientation, 15
social reconstruction orientation, 15
technological orientation, 15
traditional versus modernized views about, 12–14
Curriculum and culture
areas for research, 261–263
and concept of fit, 250–252
macrolevel referents for curriculum, 253–255
microlevel referents for curriculum, 255–261
relationship between, 252–261
Curriculum design, methods of, 279–281
Curriculum development
British model, 32–33
cross-cultural study, 370–371
enterprises in, 198
naturalistic methods, 110
school-based and staff-development, 377
systematic methods, 110
Curriculum differentiation
and access to knowledge, 583–585
and achievement, 590–592
and attitudes toward school, 592–593
and classroom dynamics, 585–589
consequences of, 582–593
contexts of, 570–571
cross cultural view, 571–572, 600
differentiation of content, 573–574
in elementary schools, 575, 590–591
fairness-justice question, 595–597
future research, 599–601
historical view, 577–578
issues related to, 572, 593–599
and language arts, 740–741
multiple functions of, 594–595
organizational patterns, 574–575
and peer groups, 592
and postsecondary education, 592–593
and quality of schooling, 597–599
revisionist view, 580
in secondary schools, 575–577, 591–592, 594
as social control, 580
societal context, 577–582
and sociodemographic stratification, 589–590, 595–597, 600
student assignment practices, 575–577
Curriculum documents
and acquisition of knowledge, 281
and knowledge, 277
nature of, 277
physical education research, 981–982
Curriculum enactment
Denver Curriculum Project as example, 418–419
issues in, 418
meaning of, 402
Curriculum evaluation
by teachers, 126–127, 132
effects on curricula, 142–147
essay examinations, 125
evaluation of products, 124
formal evaluation, 127–132, 133
high-stakes testing, 141, 144–147
historical perspective, 121–126
instruction-driven measurement, 140–141
low-stakes testing, 143–144
measurement-driven instruction, 141–142
as mechanism of power, 137–140
multiple-choice questions, 125
multiple-choice tests, 134–137
objective measures, 133
oral examinations, 124
and policy, 137–140
qualitative evaluation, 133–134
qualitative ranking, 124
quantitative marks, 124–125
short-answer examinations, 125
standardized testing, 126, 134
terminology related to, 121–122
written examinations, 124
Curriculum Field: Its Formative Years, The (Seguel), 160
Curriculum history
as area of scholarship, 159–162
Dewey's impact, 171–173
methodological variance in, 173–178
questions/issues related to, 157–159
role of committee reports in, 162–167
school subjects, 178–180
scientific curriculum, 167–170
scope and direction of, 181
See also Curriculum and school organization
Curriculum ideologies
cognitive pluralism, 317–319
critical theory, 314–316
operational ideology, 305–306
progressive ideology, 311–314
rational humanist ideology, 309–311
reconceptualism, 316–317
religious orthodox ideologies, 307–309
research in, 319–323
Curriculum implementation
affecting factors, 415–418
conceptual issues, 427–430
contexts of curriculum change study, 425–427
critical view of, 414–415
curriculum enactment, 418–427
degree of implementation, 429–430
Dessemination Efforts Supporting School Improvement (DESSI), 408–410
fidelity perspective, 404–410
future research, 431–433
historical overview, 403–404
inhibiting factors, 430
methodological issues, 430–431
mutual adaptation, 410–418
open education study, 422–425
rationale for studies in, 404
role of change in, 429
study of educational innovation, 413–414
and teacher, 405–408, 429
use of term, 428
versus adaptation by local users, 428
Curriculum indicators, 43, 59–61
definition of, 66
early indicators, 59–60
functions of, 66
historical view, 66–67
research projects on, 67–69
Curriculum in Elementary Education, The (Weet), 6
Curriculum Inquiry, 107, 370
Curriculum knowledge, nature of, 418
Curriculum Laboratory, survey by, 234
Curriculum materials, assessment of, 130
Curriculum organization
activity curriculum, 337
approach to sequence in, 330
broad-field pattern, 336
continuity, 330
core curriculum, 338–339
correlated-subject design, 336
and critical inquiry, 333–334
definition of, 328
developmental tasks pattern, 337
discipline position, 334
essentialist position, 334
and experimentalism, 333
fused curriculum, 336
hybrid organizational patterns, 338–339
integration, 330–331
and intellectual traditionalism, 332
levels of, 328–329
around modes of thought, 334
organizing centers, 331
organizing elements, 331
orientation to students' interests/development, 336–338

Curriculum organization *(Continued)*
perennialist position, 334
reconceptualism, 338
research on, 339–340
scope, 329–330
sequence, 330
single-subject pattern, 335
and social behaviorism, 332–333
around social issues, 338
and social reconstructionism, 333
around subject disciplines, 335–336
themes of, 334–339
topics of, 329–331
Curriculum and pedagogy
and educational science, 489–490
institutional level, 487
integrated conception of, 507–509
pedagogical research, 490–491
and professionalization of teaching, 488–489
and scientific method, 490
Curriculum Perspectives, 370
Curriculum policy
and access to knowledge, 211
agenda formation, sources of policy, 188–190
authority for control of curriculum, 203–204
conditions of policy making, 189–191
configurational perspective, 200
curriculum alignment, 201–203
curriculum as capital aspects, 207–208
curriculum as control aspects, 203–207
curriculum as rational system aspects, 198–202
curriculum as worthwhile knowledge aspects, 196–198
curriculum enactment as policy concern, 210–212
curriculum perspectives on public policy, 195–203
forms of authority in, 187
future research needs, 208–210
government action, 191–192
as ideologies for organization of authority, 187–188
institutional design based on, 211–212
intent versus action in, 186–187
levels of, 221
linear R & D model, 199–200
nature of, 186–188
networking strategy, 200–201
process streams of, 190–191
relationship to practice, 192–194
sources of tension, 186
as symbolic actions, 187
Curriculum potential, meaning of, 794
Curriculum Process in Physical Education, The (Jewett and Bain), 966
Curriculum-referenced tests, 135, 136
Curriculum research
character of, 109
empirical approach to curriculum, 57–72
evolution of curriculum theory, 492
formative research, example of, 110–113
history of, 101–103
improvement, role of methodology, 113–115
method, emergence of concern for, 100
nature of, 109–110
qualitative methods, 106–108
scientific approach to curriculum, 41–72
teacher in, 366–367
Curriculum research in reading
curriculum materials in, 697–698, 706–707, 713
curriculum recommendations in, 695–697, 704–705, 712–713
curriculum research in, 694–695, 703–704, 710–711
instructional approaches, 698–699, 707, 713–714
research directions, 716–717
Curriculum research in writing
curriculum materials in, 691–692, 701–702, 709
curriculum recommendations in, 690–691, 700–701, 708–709
curriculum research in, 688–690, 699–700, 707–708
instructional approaches, 692–694, 702–703, 709–710
research directions, 716–717
Curriculum and school organization, historical context
centralization of schools, 355–356
colonial era, 347–350
18th century colonies, 351–352
and Laboratory School, 356
market-driven diversification of schools, 353–354
19th century, 353–357
and St. Louis schools, 356–357
unitary system, 354–355
Curriculum specialists
authority as advice givers, 26–28
as consultants, 32–34
curriculum chairperson, role of, 29, 30
curriculum professor, role of, 29–30, 35
as generalists, 34–37
knowledge requirements of, 30
precursors to, 22
reconceptualists, 34–35
relationship with practitioners, 33
team approach, 29
terms related to, 21
university-based specialist, 33
work of, 21
Curriculum stability and change
and accreditation, 234
and activities within school system, 231–232
basic questions related to, 216
beliefs related to, 217–218
and classroom structures, 237
and cold war, 226–227
determinants of, 232–238
first-order changes, 218
and foundations, 229
and functions of schooling, 233–235
and historical curriculum, 237
and influential individuals, 230–231
and legal decisions, 227–229
maintenance of continuity by schools, 219–221
organizational perspective on, 239–242
and parents, 231
pluralist political perspective on, 238–239
and professional associations, 229–230
and progressive movement, 224–226
and publishers, 229
second-order changes, 218
and students/teachers/principles, 236–237
and teachers, 236–237, 368–369
and testing agencies, 235
and textbooks, 235–236
Curriculum and teacher
action research, 377–378
and change/stability in schools, 368–369
conduit metaphor, 369–372
Dewey's view, 378–379
Eisner's view, 380–381
Humanities Curriculum Project, 381–384
Jackson's view, 379–380
mutual adaptation concept, 372–374
origin of concept, 366
and school reform through curriculum development, 366–367
Schwab's view, 380
studies of teachers in reform settings, 376–377
and teacher practices, 369
teacher-proof curriculum, 374–376
teachers' stories of curriculum making, 385–392
Curriculum Theorizing: The Reconceptualists (Pinar), 83
Curriculum Theory Conferences in Physical Education, 972
Curriculum Theory Network, 102, 370
Curriculum to Reflect Technology, A, 900
Curriculum traditions of inquiry
curriculum as capital, 195, 207–208
curriculum as control, 195, 203–207
curriculum as rational system, 195, 198–203
curriculum as worthwhile knowledge, 195, 196–198
Curriculum treatments, 61, 62
Customized publishing, development of, 456

D

Dare the School Build a New Social Order (Counts), 102
Database of Competencies for Business Curriculum Development, K–14, 914
Death at an Early Age: the Destruction of

Hearts and Minds of Negro Children in the Boston Public Schools (Kozol), 258
Death of White Sociology, The (Ladner), 258
Debra P. v. Turlington, 132, 140, 141
Declarative knowledge, 524, 866
Decoding, 706
automaticity, 529, 530
and basal readers, 713
Definition of the Physically Educated Person-Outcomes of Quality Physical Education Programs, 971
Degrees of Reading Power Test, The, 136
Delacroze method, 950
Delinquency Prevention Research and Development Program, 417–418
Delivered curriculum, 439
Democracy and Education (Dewey), 172, 231
Democracy in America (de Tocqueville), 113
De Musica (Boethius), 452
Denver Curriculum Project, and curriculum enactment, 418–419
Department of Education, 61
beginning of, 66
Descartes' Dream (Davis and Hirsch), 750
Desegregation, and extracurriculum, 1034–1035
Design and technology, technology education, 820
Designing Curriculum and Learning: A Physical Coeducational Approach (Melograno), 967
Desired curriculum, 439
De Studiis Adolescentum (Melancthon), 121
Developing Mathematical Processes (Romberg, Harvey, Moser, and Montgomery), 761
Developmental model, physical education, 967
Developmental tasks pattern, curriculum organization, 337
Developmental theory
curricular issues, 49–50
debates related to, 50–51
developmentalists, focus of, 16, 49
developmental stages, 50–51
history of, 49–50
implications for curriculum research, 51–52
Piagetian theory, 49–52
research issues, 49, 50–51
Development of High-School Curricula in the North Central States from 1860 to 1918, The (Stout), 160
Dewey School, The (Mayhew and Edwards), 378
Diagnostic prescriptive method, 705, 711
curriculum materials related to, 707
Dialectic of Freedom, The (Greene), 936
Dictionary of Cultural Literacy (Hirsch), 315
Didactical Phenomenology of Mathematical Structures (Freudenthal), 754
Digest of Educational Statistics, 67
Direct instruction
effectiveness of, 65
nature of, 65
Disciplinary mastery orientation, physical education, 966
Discipline-oriented approach, language arts, 736–737
Discipline position, curriculum organization, 334
Disciplines
differentiation between, 284, 286–287
and truth, 287–289
Discourse rules, language learning rules, 863–864
Discovery learning, 51, 52
and cognitive structuralist theory, 53
Dissemination Efforts Supporting School Improvement (DESSI), curriculum implementation, 408–410, 416–417
Distance education
foreign language study, 878–879
major networks for, 878
as teacher-proof curricula, 376
DISTAR, 374, 707
Distraction technique, in formative research, 111
Distributive education. *See* Marketing education
Distributive Education Clubs of America, 902
Distributive Education in the High School, 902, 920
Distributive Education Programs, 920
Doctrinal (de Velledieu), 121
Donat, 121
Douglas Commission report of 1906, 177
DPMA Model Curriculum for Undergraduate Computer Information Systems Education, 914
Drama/theater, and language arts, 742
Dunwoody Conference, 902
Dynamic Physical Education Curriculum and Instruction for Secondary School Students (Pangrazi and Darst), 969

E

Early intervention programs, 617
Ecological approach, to education, 11–12
Ecological cognitive science, 536
Ecological integration orientation, physical education, 967
Ecological research, 63, 65
focus in, 66
Economic Education Councils, 843
Economic Opportunity Act, 228
Education
ecological approach to, 11–12
and politics, 290–291
research methods, historical view, 100
science of, 42, 100, 489–490
Educational Conference Board, 200
Educational Imagination, The (Eisner), 107, 936
Educational indicators, 43
use of, 120
Educational Indicators, 67
Educational Innovations: Then and Now (Smith et al.)385
Educational objectives, sources of, 25
Educational outcomes, and Eight Year Study, 123
Educational process, principles of, 59–60
Educational psychology
cognitive research, 520
curriculum field, 490
development of, 489–490
pedagogical research, 490–491
Thordike's laws, 695, 698
Educational Research Analysts, 446
Educational Researcher, 103
Educational Science Institute, 261
Educational Wastelands (Bestor), 446
Education Amendments, Title IX, 228, 1033–1034
Education and Freedom (Rickover), 446–447
Education for All Handicapped Children Act, 131, 228
Education for Capability, 815
Education in the Forming of American Society (Bailyn), 159
Education of Man, The (Froebel), 101
Education Reform Act, 819
Educative experience, curriculum as, 7–8
Eight Year Study, 62–63, 67, 83, 84, 102, 123, 129, 144, 231, 235, 340, 419–422
categories measured, 420
descriptive categories of, 421
inputs needed for curriculum building, 421
purposes of evaluation, 420
statements related to curriculum development, 422
Elementary and Secondary Education Act, 131, 228, 616, 626
Elementary (Mulcaster), 452
Elementary schools
and curriculum differentiation, 575, 590–591
foreign language study, 856–858, 881–882
science curriculum, 813–815
Elements of Rhetoric (Whately), 688
Eligibility requirements, and extracurriculum, 1032–1033
Elitism, rational humanist ideology, 310
Ellis Island experiments, 61
Elson Readers, 698
Emancipatory action, 133–134
Emerging Content and Structure of Business Education, The, 895
Emile (Rousseau), 101, 663–664
Emotion, and cognitive science, 520–521
Empirical approach to curriculum, 57–72
curriculum indicators, 59–61
Dewey on, 61
Eight Year Study, 62–63

Empirical approach to curriculum *(Continued)*
goals of inquiries, 57–58
history of, 59–61
need for improved measures, 71–72
and Progressive Education Association, 61–62
quantification of curriculum, 59
research approaches, 63–66
statistical research, 66–70
Employment status of students, and extracurricular, 1015–1016
Empowering Minority Students (Cummins), 629
Enacted curriculum, 9, 466
Enactment perspective
curriculum implementation, 418–427
curriculum knowledge in, 429
future research on, 432–433
Encyclopedia of Educational Research, 161
English Coalition Conference: Democracy Through Language, 709, 739
English Composition and Rhetoric (Bain), 693
English Composition as a Mode of Behavior (Scott), 689
English Reader, 450
English Round Table, 693
English school, 354
English Schoole-Maister, The (Coote), 350, 452
Enlightenment, education of women in, 663–664
Environmentalism, 19th century, 664–665
Environmental studies, 806
Epistemological view, feminist theory, 674–676
Equality of Educational Opportunity Survey, 67
EQUALS, 671
Erikson's theory, 547
stages in, 547
"Eros and Education" (Schwab), 380
Essay examinations, historical perspective, 125
Essentialist position, curriculum organization, 334
Ethical perspective, feminist theory, 676
Ethics, and aesthetic curriculum, 91
Ethnic Heritage Act, 228
Ethnicity
and curriculum development, 258–259
studies of, 258
Eugenics movement, 87–88
Eugenics Research Association, 61
European schools, tracking, 572
Evaluation, definition of, 121
Evening schools, 351
Everybody Counts, 750, 754
Evolution issue, textbooks, 447
Evolution of Educational Thought: Lectures on the Formation and Development of Secondary Education in France (Durkheim), 180
Exemplars of Teaching Method (Broudy and Palmer), 365
Expanding Your Horizons Conferences, 671
Experience
curriculum centered around, 334, 691, 693–694, 707
and language arts curriculum, 733–734
and manifest curriculum, 473–474
and social studies, 837–838
See also Student experience
Experience and Art (Smith), 952
Experience and Education (Dewey), 173, 312
Experience-Based Career Education, 200
Experience Curriculum in English, An, 691, 733
Experienced curriculum, 492–493
studies of, 493
Experimentalism, and curriculum organization, 333
Expertise
education for expertise, 534–535
expert-novice studies, 55–56
expert versus novice problem solving, 528
as knowledge, 522
research on, 518
Expert systems, 522–523
Explaining "Teaching Machines" and Programming (Cram), 375
Exploration, cognitive method, 532
Expressive objectives, 130
Extracurriculum
academic eligibility requirements, 1032–1033
and academic performance, 1016–1017, 1025–1026
administration of, 1009–1010
and adult community participation, 1030–1031
and community, 1021–1022
and constitutional rights, 1033
CORE model, 1010–1011
cross-cultural view, 1005
and desegregation, 1034–1035
developmental outcomes of, 1023–1013
evaluation of programming, 1011–1012
examples of activities, 1006–1007, 1008
future directions, 1035–1036
and future participation, 1024–1025
gender differences, 1014–1015
and gender equality, 1033–1034
and grade-level organization, 1021
historical view, 1003–1005
and identity development, 1028
and life satisfaction, 1029–1030
and mainstreaming of handicapped, 1035
and occupational achievement/income, 1031
and personality traits, 1019, 1027–1028
and political attitudes, 1018–1019, 1028–1029
psychological variables, 1016–1018
racial/ethnic factors, 1014
research limitations, 1013
and school size, 1019–1021
and self-esteem, 1018, 1028
social control function, 1026–1027
and socioeconomic factors, 1013–1014
structure and content of, 1005, 1007–1009
and student attitudes, 1018
and student employment status, 1015–1016
and student interests, 1018
and student retention, 1026
students perspectives on, 1022–1023

F

Family life programs, 555
Federal Board of Vocational Education, 902, 907
Federal funding
curriculum reform projects, 443
vocational education, 908
Federal influences
social studies curriculum, 843–844
textbooks, 443–444
Federal Programs Supporting Educational Change, 372–374
Feelin' Good program, 987
Female-headed household, black families, 611–612
Feminist science, 291–292, 807–808
Feminist theory
contributions to curricular theory, 92–94
critical theories, 671–672
epistemological view, 674–676
ethical perspective, 676
feminist empiricism, 675
feminist standpoints, 675
Marxist theory, 672–673
object relations theory, 673, 675
power sources in, 92
psychoanalytic view, 673–674
transformational view, 677–678
Fidelity perspective
curriculum implementation, 404–410
curriculum knowledge in, 428
future research on, 432
Films, and language arts, 742
Finding Out/Descubrimiento programs, 641, 650
First Lessons, 958
FITNESSGRAM, 981
Fit Youth Today, 981, 986–987
FLES program, 856, 859, 881–882
Flexible purposing, 313
FLEX programs, 856, 859, 860
Folk psychology, 521, 522
Folkways (Sumner), 113
Follow Through, 199, 200, 617, 951
"Forces for Change in the Mathematics Curriculum" (Steen), 754
Ford Foundation, 229
Foreign language study
age and learning, 870–872

assessment, 862–863, 881, 882
audio-lingual approach, 860–861
authentic materials, use of, 874
child language learning variables, 869–870
and cognition, 865–866
and cognitive style, 868
college level, 877
and communicative competence, 861, 863
computer-assisted language learning, 877–878
content-based instruction, 876–877
and culture, 873–874
distance learning, 878–879
elementary schools, 856–858, 881–882
and grammatical competence, 860–861, 863, 884–885
historical view, 852–853
immersion programs, 857–858, 881–882
and individual variables, 883
interactive video, 878
internal syllabus concept, 882
language laboratory, 877
learning strategies of, 868–870, 883
and metacognition, 868–869
Natural Approach, 876
proficiency-based approach, 872–876
Proficiency Guidelines, 862
profile of foreign language learner, 867–868
rationale for, 852–854
research needs, 879–884
rules in language, 863–864
rules in learning, 864–865
scaffolding plan, 869
and Scholastic Aptitude Test, 853–854
secondary schools, 855–856, 880
time to begin study, 858–860
Total Physical Response method, 876
video, use of, 878
weaknesses related to, 854

Foreign Service Institute, 862, 877
Forgotten Half, The, 935
Formal knowledge
development of, 524
role of, 524–525
Formative research
basis for credibility, 111
example of, 110–113
generalizability problem, 111
methodological issues in, 111–112
methods used in, 111
Foundations, impact on curriculum stability/change, 229
Foundations for Learning: Language, 619
Foundations of Curriculum Making, 125
Foundations of Method (Kilpatrick), 102
Foundations of Vocational Education (Evans), 909
Frame factors, 761
Frames of Mind (Gardner), 933
Frameworks, 811
Freedom and Discipline in English, 701, 737
Functional Analysis of Paramedical Occupations as a Foundation for Curriculum Development, A, 923
Functionalism
basis of theory, 972
and language arts, 732–733
and mathematics, 756–758
Fund for the Advancement of Education, 229
Fused curriculum, curriculum organization, 336
Future Farmers of America, 893

G

Gateway English, 737
Gender and curriculum
early research, 666–667
gender and school subjects, 669–672
gender bias, textbooks, 445, 670
intervention programs, 671
single-sex schooling, effects of, 668–669
women's studies programs, 676
Gender bias
science curriculum, 806–808
social studies textbooks, 835
Gender differences
and achievement, 668
attitudes toward science, 474
in educational research, 667–668
extracurriculum, 1014–1015
and language, 670
and mathematics, 667–668
moral development, 554–555, 676
and science curriculum, 806
use of term, 667
Gender equality, and extracurriculum, 1033–1034
General Biology (Needham), 455
General Curriculum, 177
Generalizability problem, formative research, 111
Generalizable skills, in vocational education, 931
General track, 578
Generation of Animals (Aristotle), 661
Genetic factors, issue related to African-Americans, 614
Geography (Morse), 453
"Geometry for All: No Geometry at All?" (de Lange), 757
George-Barden Act, 904, 908
George-Deen Act, 902, 908
German drawing schools, 905
Gestalt psychology, 52, 53, 63
Getty Center for Arts Education, 956
Girls and Technology Education project, 816
Goal-free evaluation, 130
Government action
capacity building, 191
inducements, 191
institutional choice, 192
mandates, 191
policy instruments, 191–192
systemic changes, 191
See also Federal influences
Grammar, 691–692, 693, 729
foreign language learning, 860–861, 863, 884–885
textbook grammar rules, 863
transformational, 743
Grammatical Institute of the English Language (Webster), 727
Great Books movement, 19, 741
Great Depression, 61, 81, 101, 177, 902
Greek, 852
Greeks, on education of women, 659–660
Group learning, and language minorities, 645–646
Group problem solving, mathematics, 775
Growth Through English, 738
Guardians of Tradition (Elson), 235, 449
Guide to Curriculum Planning in Marketing Education, A, 923
Gymnastics, and physical education movement, 965

H

Half Way Covenant, 349
Handbook for Achieving Sex Equity Through Education, 671
Handbook of Research on Teacher Education, 966
Handbook of Research on Teaching (Gage), 103
Hazelwood School District v. Kuhlmeier, 1033
Head Start, 200, 228, 951
Health Amendments Act, 904, 908
Healthism, 970
Health occupations education
curricular research, 923–925
historical view, 903–904
types of programs, 925
Health-related physical fitness, and physical education, 970, 986
Health-Related Physical Fitness Test, 981
Hidden curriculum, 8–9, 12, 87, 89, 206
characteristics of, 314
dimensions of, 561
and ethos of schools, 561
physical education, 988–990
social studies, 840
studies on, 474–475
Hierarchy of needs, 977
Highbrow/Lowbrow (Levine), 295
Higher Learning in America, The (Hutchins), 735
Higher Lessons in English (Reed and Kellogg), 691
Higher-order thinking
and art, 947
and multiple choice tests, 135
programs for poor African-Americans, 619

Higher-order thinking *(Continued)*
and vocational education, 930–931, 933–934
High School: A Report on Secondary Education in America, 789, 854
High School and Beyond, 67, 575, 577, 1013, 1014, 1029, 1030, 1033
High School Instruction Today, 737
High-stakes testing, 141, 144–147
effects of, 144
effects on teaching, 144–145
historical view, 144
problems related to, 145–147
Hispanic students
dropout rate, 627
work styles of, 645
Historical curriculum, 223
impact on curriculum stability/change, 237–238
Historical Inquiry in Education: A Research Agenda, 161
Hobson v. Hansen, 228
Holmes Group, 779
Home economics education
curricular research, 915–918
historical view, 896–899
Home project concept, agricultural education, 892
Home Projects in Secondary Agriculture, 892
Hooked on Books, 737
Household Science (Youmans), 897
How to Make a Curriculum (Bobbit), 27, 366
How to Read a Book (Adler), 735
How to Solve It (Polya), 754
How to Teach Reading and What to Read in School (Hall), 731
Humanistic approach
curriculum content, 15, 41
definitions of humanism, 80
humanists, focus of, 15–16
nature of, 80–82
physical education, 967–968
secular humanism, 80
Humanities, and moral education, 556
Humanities Curriculum Project, 381–384
early teacher stories of, 382–383
emergence of, 382
importance of, 381
induction of teachers into, 382–383
setting for, 381–382
teachers stories of participation in, 383–384
training of future trainers, 383
types of teachers at time of, 381
view of teachers as curriculum makers, 384–385
Hutterites, schooling of, 256
Hybridization concept, 174

I

Ideological curriculum, 329
Identity development, and extracurriculum, 1028
Ideology
and curriculum policy, 187–188
role in education, 302–305
See also Curriculum ideologies
Illusory schools, nature of, 415
Immersion programs
foreign language study, 857–858, 881–882
research on language and instruction, 637–638, 643
Imperiled Education, An, 631, 632
Implicit curriculum
nature of, 987–988
physical education research, 987–990, 991–992
and student experience, 474–475
studies, 474–475
Incidental learning, 8
In-class programs, 618
Indicators. *See* Curriculum indicators
Indirect instruction, 65
effectiveness of, 65
Individualized Education Plan, 228
Individualized reading, 703
Individually Guided Education, 200
adaptation and response to, 414–415
Individually Guided Mathematics (Romberg), 755
Individually Prescribed Instruction, 707
Indoctrination, and moral education, 551
Inducements, 191
Industrial Arts: Its Interpretation in American Schools, 900
Industrial Arts Curriculum Project, 901, 918, 919
Industrial education
curricular research, 918–920
historical view, 899–901
nature of, 900
scope of, 900
Information-based society, impact for school mathematics, 771–772
Information processing, 529–530
and automaticity, 529, 530
basis of model, 54
cognitive structuralist approach, 52–54
cognitive theory, 54–57
overcoming limitations to, 529–530
Innovations: The Social Consequences of Science and Technology, 813
Innovations
Eight Year Study, 419–422
innovation-adoption process, 406
life cycle of, 220
open education, study of, 422–425
students benefiting from, 221
See also Curriculum implementation
Innovations in Science and Technology Education, 789
Innumeracy (Paulos), 750
In Place of Confusion: Technology and Science in the High School Curriculum (Black and Harrison), 819
Input-output studies, 67, 69
Insights and Illusions of Philosophy (Piaget), 519
Institute for the Promotion of Science and Technology, 809
Institutional choice, government action, 192
Institutional curriculum, 328
nature of, 487
Institutionalization of schooling, historical view, 349, 353
Instruction
direct instruction, 65
in empirical studies on curriculum, 63–66
indirect instruction, 65
Instructional curriculum, 328–329
Instruction-driven measurement, 140–141
Integration, curriculum organization, 330–331
Intellectualism, in curriculum writings, 31–32, 34
Intellectual traditionalism, and curriculum organization, 332
Intelligence tests, 60–61
Intended curriculum, 222
Interactive video, foreign language study, 878
International Assessments of Educational Progress, 68, 69
International Association for the Evaluation of Educational Achievement, 67–68, 744, 796–797
International Education Act, 228
International movements, science curriculum, 803–806
International Union for the Conservation of Nature, 803
Interpretive approaches, qualitative evaluation, 133
Interpretive community concept, 19–20
Interstate Distributive Education Curriculum Consortium, 921
Introduction to Arithmetic (Root), 453
Invention, in mathematics, 755
Investigations in Mathematics Education (Suydam), 115
Iowa Every-Pupil Testing Program, 136
Irish Intermediate Education Act of 1878, 139
Irish Primary Certificate examination, 145–146
Issues in Biology, 813
"Is There a Best Way of Teaching Harold Bateman?" (Jackson), 107

J

Jackson's Mill Industrial Arts Curriculum symposium, 816, 919
James Madison High: A Model High School Curriculum, 958
Japanese schools, 600
educational policies, 308
extracurricular activities, 1005
juku schools, 146
tracking, 571–572

Jews, religious systems of, 307
Job analysis, 129
Joint Council for Economic Education, 843
Joint Dissemination Review Panel, 201
Joplin plan, 575, 590
Journal of Curriculum Theorizing, The, 34, 102, 317
Journal of Higher Education, 101
Juku schools, 146
Jungian theory, and feminist theory, 674
Junior high school movement, 900
Just community, 558, 560–561
Juvenile Delinquency and Youth Offenses Act, 228

K

Kamehameha Early Education Project (KEEP), 645
Key School, 319
Kinesiological studies, physical education, 968–969
Knowledge
  curriculum as worthwhile knowledge view, 195, 196–198
  and curriculum differentiation, 583–585
  and disciplines, 284–289
  expertise as, 522
  from formal to procedural knowledge, 524
  and instructional practice, 197–198
  intermediate states of, 530–532
  knowledge production in lessons, 502–503
  mapping of knowledge, 283–284
  and mathematics, 763–764, 774
  organization of, 278–279
  and politics, 290–292
  and social stratification, 292–294
  and textbooks, 442–443
  and truth, 287–289
Knowledge acquisition
  apprenticeship tradition, 269–271
  comparison of traditions, 275
  and curriculum, 275–282
  mystical tradition, 274–275
  philosophical tradition, 270–271
  psychotherapeutic tradition, 274
  rhetorical tradition, 271–273
  scientific tradition, 273–274
Knowledge and Human Interest (Habermas), 88
Knowledge engineering, 523
Kohlberg's theory, 547–549
  criticisms, of, 548–549
  development of, 548
  school based projects, 549
  stages in, 548

L

Laboratory School, 100, 171, 279, 356, 378, 900
Lake Wobegon effect, 146
Language
  and cognitive structuralist theory, 52, 53
  and culture, 256–257
  and gender differences, 670
  issue related to African-Americans, 614–615
  of theories, changes over time, 16
  and thought, 52–53
Language adaptations, of bilingual students, 635–644
Language arts
  academic resurgence movement, 735–737
  and assessment, 741
  basic skills approach, 738
  communication approach, 735
  and computers, 742–743
  constructivist theory, 738–739
  cross-cultural view, 730
  current issues, 739–745
  and curriculum differentiation, 740–741
  discipline-based approach, 736–737
  drama/theater, 742
  English coalition reports, 739
  ethical tradition, 726–727
  experiential movement, 733–734
  films/video, 742
  and formal study of language, 743–744
  functional movement, 732–733
  general principles for curriculum, 740
  institutionalization of curriculum, 729–730
  and literary criticism, 744–745
  and New Criticism, 735–736
  nonacademic tradition, 729
  nonprint media, role of, 741–743
  and progressive movement, 732–734
  and Reorganization Reports, 731
  as school subject, 731
  social living approach, 734–735
  and social relevance, 737–738
  status studies, 740
  and study of classics, 727–729
Language development
  and personality, 869–870
  and poor African-Americans, 621
Language in General Education, 735
Language laboratory, foreign language study, 877
Language learning
  cognitive theory, 865–866
  discourse rules, 863–864
  and interlanguage concept, 864
  monitor model, 864–865
  pragmatic rules, 864
  strategic rules, 864
  textbook grammar rules, 863
Language minorities
  adaptations in scope of curriculum, 648–651
  alienation from family and assimilation, 628
  bilingual education, 628–629
  Cheche Konnen model, 646
  Cognitive Academic Language Learning Approach, 649–650
  and compensatory programs, 629
  content adaptations, 647–652
  and group learning, 645–646
  Kamehameha Early Education Project (KEEP), 645
  language adaptations, 635–644
  and minority dialects, 700
  modifications in language use, 643
  pedagogical/structural adaptations, 644–646
  problems of, 627
  research agenda, 652–653
  time span for assimilation, 628
  See also Bilingual education
Latent content of textbooks
  achievement based surveys, 448
  central tendency theory, 449
  nature of, 438
  social approach to analysis, 449–450
  specialized element of, 438
Latin, 852
  study of, 272–273
Latin grammar school, 354
Lau v. Nichols, 629, 648
Law of Effect, 695
Law of Exercise, 695
Law of Identical Elements, 695
Laws of Learning, 695, 698
Laws (Plato), 660
Learned curriculum, 222–223
Learning
  and problem solving, 527–528
  psychological processes in, 496
Learning environment, 51
Learning Laboratory Districts, 252
Learning process value orientation, physical education, 967
Learning Research and Development Center, 340
Learning sets, 339–340
Learning theory, and science curriculum, 791
Lectures on Rhetoric and Belles Lettres (Blair), 688, 728
Legal decisions, impact on curriculum stability/change, 227–229
Legislated Learning (Wise), 193
Leonard and Gertrude (Pestalozzi), 101, 906
Lessons
  construction of, 501–502
  knowledge production in, 502–503
Letter to A Teacher, 481
Leviathan (Hobbes), 284
Life adjustment education, 174
Life in Classrooms (Jackson), 380
Light house schools, 843
Linear R & D model, 199–200
Linguistic approach, 705
Linguistics, and curriculum, 743–744
Literacy, high-literacy and low-literacy schools, 767
Literary criticism, and language arts, 744–745

Literature
  anthologies, 734
  classics, 257
  experience curriculum, 733–734
  gender images in, 670
  literary appreciation movement, 729
  in textbooks, 451–452
Literature as Exploration (Rosenblatt), 733, 744
Logic Theorist, 519
Longitudinal studies, 847
  methods in, 480
Low-stakes testing, 143–144
Lyceums, 905

M

McGuffey Readers, 59, 235, 440, 441, 450–451, 453, 697, 727
Mainstreaming of handicapped, and extracurriculum, 1035
Making the Grade, 854
Man: A Course of Study (MACOS), 53, 54, 545, 838–839
Man and His Changing Society, 447
Man and the Biosphere, 803
Mandates, 191
Manifest curriculum
  and student experience, 473–474
  studies, of, 473–474
  of textbooks, 437–438
Manpower Development and Training Act, 904
Manual Training School, 906
Mapping, of knowledge, 282–284
Marketing education
  curricular research, 920–923
  historical view, 901–903
  mission statement for, 922
  standards for, 923
Marketing Education Resource Center, 921
Marxist theory, feminist theory, 672–673
Maryland Plan, 901, 919–920
Master Curriculum Guide in Teaching Economics for the Nation's Schools, 914
Mastery in Learning Project, 252
Mastery learning, 340
Materials Development Centers, 635
Mathematical Discovery (Polya), 754
Mathematical Experience, The (Davis and Hersh), 750
Mathematical Thought from Ancient to Modern Times (Kline), 750
Mathematics: A Human Endeavor (Jacobs), 758
Mathematics: Its Content, Methods, and Meaning (Aleksandrov, Kolmogorov, and Lavrent'ev), 750
Mathematics
  abstractness of, 755
  aim and practice gap, 760–761
  applications in, 755–756
  authentic curriculum, scope of, 771–780
  challenges to current system, 775–776
  and cognition, 777–778
  cross-cultural view, 768–770
  and culture, 752–754, 762
  current teaching practices, 763
  definition of, 751
  development as school subject, 179–180
  different mathematical emphases issue, 759–760
  doing mathematics, meaning of, 754–756
  functionalist view, 756–758
  and gender bias, 671
  and gender differences, 667–668
  goals-statements for mathematics education, 772–773
  group problem solving, 775
  impact of information-based society on, 771–772
  influential scholars, 754–755
  invention in, 755
  and knowledge, 763–764, 774
  materials for study, 766
  mathematical knowledge, nature of, 751–752
  modern mathematics movement, 766
  nature of study, 750–751
  new math, 178
  philosophy of mathematics, 751
  problematic features of, 750
  problem-solving, 775, 777–778
  problems with rationales for teaching, 759–762
  programs for poor African-Americans, 618–619
  proof in, 755
  rationale for teaching of, 756–759
  second language learners, 641
  students role in learning, 765–766, 774
  and teachers role in teaching, 764–765, 774–775, 778–780
  textbooks, 760, 770
  traditions related to, 766–768
Mathematics and Plausible Reasoning (Polya), 754
Mathematics and the Unexpected (Ekeland), 750
Mathematics as an Educational Task (Freudenthal), 754
Mathematics Counts, 750, 773
"Mathematics for All Is No Mathematics at All" (de Lange), 757
Mathematics, Insight, and Meaning (de Lange), 750
Mathematics Tomorrow (Steen), 750, 754
Math/Science Network, 671
Matter and Molecules, 810
Meaningful Movement for Children (Hoffman, Young and Klesius), 967
Measurement-driven instruction, 141–142
  favorable view of, 142
  and policy, 142
Measurement issues, scientific approach to curriculum, 44
Mechanics institutes, 905
Mediating variable paradigm, of learning, 51
Medieval university, 271
Memory
  chunking, 529
  long-term, use in learning, 529
  study of, 54
Meno, 660
Mental level of description, meaning of, 518–519
Mental models, 523–524
Mental Models (Getner and Stevens), 523–524
Mental Models (Johnson-Laird), 523–524
Metacognition, 525–529
  and foreign language learning, 868–869
  implicit theories of learning, 525–526
  nature of, 525
  nature/purpose of what is learned, 525
  problem solving, 526–528
  during teacher directed learning, 526
  teacher preemption of, 526
  types of research, 525
Method of hypothesis, 270
Methodolatry, 675
Methodology
  and curriculum research, 101–103, 113–115
  and educational research, 100
  historical perspective, 101–103
  qualitative methods, 103–108
  scientific, 100–101
  and study of human affairs, 99
Mexican-Americans, performance compared to Asians, 644
Middletown (Lynd and Lynd), 167
Mind's New Science, The (Gardner), 521
Minimum-competency, 147
Minorities
  and academic eligibility for extracurricular, 1032–1033
  bias in textbooks, 445–446
  and curriculum differentiation, 589–590, 595–597
  and racism in education, 615
  and segregation, 615, 617
  and textbooks, 648
  See also Language minorities; specific minority groups
Mirror of Language: The Debate on Bilingualism (Hakuta), 630
Missing Half: Girls and Science Education, 806
Mission schools, 905
Modeling, cognitive method, 532
Monitoring of School Mathematics: Background Papers (Romberg), 755
Monitor model, language learning, 864–865
Montessori method, 53, 277
Moral education
  character education, 552–554
  components of morally educated person, 551–552
  and contemporary issues, 544
  and controversial issues, 558
  and education of teachers, 544
  and ethos of schools, 559–560

Gilligan's work, 554–555
hidden curriculum, 561
historical view, 544–547
and humanities, 556
and indoctrination, 551
just community, 560–561
Kohlberg's work, 547–549
personal/social education, 552
and physical education, 557
politics of, 543
and religious education, 558
research directions, 561–562
research methodology for, 562
and science, 557–558
situational atmosphere approach, 549
and social studies, 556–557
and teachers, 544, 560, 562
values clarification, 549–551
and women, 554–555, 676
Morill Act, 906–907
Moscow Imperial Technical School, 906
Motor skills, physical education, 987
Movement education, 968
Movement Purposes Attitude Inventory, 980
Moving and Learning-The Elementary School Physical Education Experience (Nichols), 968
Mozert v. Hawkins County Public Schools, 446
Multicultural education, 254, 259
aspects of, 620
Bay Area Global Education Program, 651
and black learners, 620
Stanford Program on International and Cross-Cultural Education, 651
Multimedia centers, foreign language study, 877
Multiple-choice tests, 134–137
electronic scoring, 136–137
historical perspective, 125
issues related to format, 135
lower order and higher order skills, 135
and norm referencing, 135–136
Mutual adaptation, 373
criticism of methodology, 431
curriculum implementation, 410–418
curriculum knowledge in, 428–429
development of, 431–432
documentation of mutual phenomenon, 412–413
emergence as concept, 411–412
future research on, 432
process of, 412–413
research questions in, 412
"My Pedagogical Creed" (Dewey), 367, 378
Mystical tradition, knowledge acquisition, 274–275

N

National Academy of Sciences, 68
National Adult Fitness Survey, 978
National Assessment of Educational Progress, 67, 120, 252
National Assessment of Vocational Education, 928
National Board for Professional Teaching Standards, 192
National Center for Bilingual Research, 635
National Center for Education Statistics data bases, 70
National Children and Youth Fitness Studies, 983, 984
National Clearinghouse for Bilingual Education, 635
National Clinic on Distributive Education, 902
National Commission on Excellence in Education, 142
National Committee on Reading, 696
National Computer Systems, 126
National Conference on Marketing Education, 922
National Council of Teachers of English, 700, 731
National Curriculum, Great Britain, 130, 811, 812, 822
National Curriculum Framework and Core Compentencies, 923
National defense, impact on curriculum stability/change, 226–227
National Defense Education Act, 131, 227, 228, 251, 700, 736, 908
National Diffusion Network, 201, 203, 419
Research, Development, and dissemination approach, 405, 408–410
role of administrators, 409
role of principles, 410
steps in, 409
study of implementation of, 408–410
National Dissemination Center, 635
National Education Association, 61, 230
National Education Longitudinal Studies, 67
National Herbart Society, 100
National Institute of Education, 228
creation of, 199
National Institute of Educational Science, 261
Nationalistic content, textbooks, 446, 449
National Merit Scholarship, 235, 251
National Network for Educational Renewal, 252
National Research Center for Educational Development, 261
National Research Council, 61
National Science Foundation, 63, 68, 794
curriculum development, 199, 203, 227
surveys of, 227
National Society for the Promotion of Industrial Education, 907
National Society for the Scientific Study of Education, 100
National Survey of Science and Mathematics, 589
National Vocational Act (Smith-Hughes Act), 891, 892, 894, 899, 900
Nation at Risk, A, 189, 252, 314, 339, 854, 926, 958
Native Americans, 256–257
education of, historical view, 628
Nativism, and cognitive science, 537–538
Natural Approach, foreign language study, 876
Naturalistic methods, curriculum development, 110
Nature of Proof, The (Fawcett), 102
Needed curriculum, 439
Networking strategy, curriculum policy, 200–201
Neural modeling, 535
"New Agenda for Mathematics Education" (Steen), 754
New Basics, 931
New Criticism, and language arts, 735–737, 744–745
New England Primer, 451, 452, 453, 694, 727
New Farmers of America, 893, 894
New York Trade School, 225
Normative issues, scientific approach to curriculum, 44
Norm referencing, and multiple-choice tests, 135–136
North American Readers (Cobb), 694
Nuffield Foundation, 794
Null curricula, 9

O

Objective-referenced tests, 135, 136
Objectives, of specific learning units, 129–130
Objectives for the Nation, 965, 983–984, 986
Object relations theory, and feminist theory, 673, 675
Occupational achievement/income, and extracurriculum, 1031
Office of Educational Research and Improvement, 228
Official curriculum, 9
Of Human Potential (Scheffler), 936
Old World in the New, The (Ross), 168
"On the Classification and Framing of Educational Knowledge" (Bernstein), 294
On their Own in Reading (Gray), 705
On the Liberal Arts and Sciences (Cassiodorus), 452
On the Shoulders of Giants, 750, 754
Open Education, 51
study of, 422–425
Operant conditioning, 47
Operational ideology, of schooling, 305–306
Opportunity-to learn, 69
Optical scanning
optical mark reading companies, 126
standardized tests, 136–137
Oral examinations, historical perspective, 124
Orbis Sensualium Pictus (Comenius), 452
Orff method, 950
Organizational perspective, perspective on curricular change/stability, 239–241

Organization for Economic Cooperation and Development, 68
Organizing centers, curriculum organization, 331
Organizing elements, curriculum organization, 331
Our Brother's Keeper (Cahn), 258
Outcomes, measurement of, 131–132
"Out from Underachievement" (Steen), 754
Outlines of English Literature (Shaw), 728
Out-of-school curriculum, 7–8, 11–12
Oz paradigm, in formative research, 111

P

Paideia Programs, 281, 321
Paideia Proposal (Adler), 290, 309, 740–741
Paradigm wars, 42, 45, 48, 63
Parallel distributed processing, 535
Parental involvement, and poor African-Americans, 621
Parents, impact on curriculum stability/change, 231
Paternalism, defined, 203
Pattern curriculum, 733
Payment by Results, 121–122, 135, 144
Pedagogy
  content pedagogy, 497
  pedagogical content knowledge, 498–499
  teachers' theories and knowledge, 509
  See also Curriculum and pedagogy
Pedagogy for Liberation, A (Shor and Freire), 936
Pedagogy of the Oppressed (Friere), 88
Peer groups, and curriculum differentiation, 592
Peer tutoring, and poor African-Americans, 621
People in Classrooms: Teacher Evaluations of the Humanities Curriculum Project (Elliott and MacDonald), 381
Perception, and learning, 53
Perennialist position, curriculum organization, 334
"Permanence of Learning" (Tyler), 102
Perrier Fitness in America Survey, 978
Personal and Social Education in the Curriculum (Pring), 546
Personal education, 552
Personal Fitness and You (Stokes and Moore), 981
Personality traits
  athletes, 1019
  and extracurriculum, 1019, 1027–1028
  and language development, 869–870
Personal meaning orientation, physical education, 969–970, 980–981
Perspectives on Mathematics Education (Christiansen, Howson and Otte), 750
Pestalozzian principles, 697, 698, 906
Phenomenology
  contributions to curricular theory, 91–92
  nature of, 91
Philosophical approach, basic questions in, 41
Philosophical influences, science curriculum, 791–792, 802–803
Philosophical tradition, knowledge acquisition, 270–271
Philosophy and Framework of Curriculum, 754
"Philosophy and Teaching" (Greene), 365
Philosophy of Mathematics Education, 750
Philosophy of Rhetoric (Campbell), 688
Physica (Aristotle), 452
Physical Best Program, 981
Physical education
  aspects of physically educated person, 971
  and at-risk students, 979
  collaborative models, 982–983
  cross-cultural view, 974, 975
  developmental model, 967
  disciplinary mastery orientation, 966
  ecological integration orientation, 967
  health-related physical fitness, 970, 986
  hidden curriculum, 988–990
  historical view, 964–966
  humanistic model, 967–968
  kinesiological studies, 968–969
  learning process value orientation, 967
  and moral education, 557
  motor skills, 987
  movement education, 968
  personal meaning orientation, 969–970, 980–981
  program assistance models, 982
  program development projects, 982–983
  self-actualization orientation, 967
  social development model, 979
  sports education, 969
  state mandates, 983
  teacher expectations, 988–989
Physical Education At-Risk Youth Program, 979
Physical Education Curriculum Theory Conferences, 990
Physical Education in the Secondary Schools: Curricular Alternatives (Lawson and Placek), 968
Physical education research
  curriculum documents, 981–982
  curriculum models, 978–981
  curriculum perspectives, 973–978
  curriculum practice, 983–990
  future directions, 990–993
  implicit curriculum, 987–990, 991–992
  methods used, 972
  outsiders' perspectives, 978
  student perspectives, 975–978
  teacher perspectives, 973–975
  theoretical perspectives in, 972
Physical Education Teaching and Curriculum Strategies for Grades 5–12 (Siedentop, Mand and Taggart), 967
Physical fitness, meaning of, 970
Physical Sciences Study Committee, 63, 792
Physics Curriculum Development Project, 812–813
Piagetian theory, 49–52, 335, 519, 791
  criticisms of, 52
  educational implications, 50, 63
  genetic epistemology, 551
  research methods of, 50
  and science curriculum, 801
Pictorial Eclectic Primer, 451
Planned Variations Study, 617
Platonic method, 270–271
PLATO system, 375
Pluralism
  and control, 204–205
  perspective on curricular change/stability, 238
Policy
  and curriculum evaluation, 137–140
  curriculum perspectives on, 195–203
  and indicators, 66–67
  indicators of policy strength, 204
  and measurement-driven instruction, 142
  policy instruments, government action, 191–192
  state curriculum policy, 202–203
  and statistical research, 70–71
  See also Curriculum policy; Public policy
Political analysts, contributions to curricular theory, 88–90
Political attitudes, and extracurriculum, 1018–1019, 1028–1029
Politics
  and education, 290–291
  and science, 291–292
Pollard Synthetic Method, 697
Polytechnic Institute, 905
Portland Public School Multiethnic Curriculum Project, 620
Poverty
  and African-Americans, 610–612
  effects of, 615–616
  and schooling, 617–618
  and social isolation, 610–611
  and urban schools, 612
Power, curriculum evaluation as mechanism of, 137–140
"Practical: A Language for Curriculum, The," (Schwab), 28
"Practical: Arts of Eclectic, The," (Schwab), 28
"Practical 3: Translation into Curriculum," (Schwab), 28
"Practical 4: Something for Curriculum Professors To Do," (Schwab), 28, 29, 380
Practical Criticism (Richards), 735–736
Practice, relationship to curriculum policy, 192–195
Pragmatic rules, language learning, 864
Preparing Instructional Objectives (Mager), 909
Preparing Objectives for Programmed Instruction (Mager), 375
Prescribed curriculum, 439
Presidential Physical Fitness Awards Program, 981

President's Commission on Foreign Languages and International Studies, 853, 854
Preview-review method, 649
Primary Reader, 438
Principals, impact on curriculum stability/change, 237
Principle of affected interests, 203
Principles in Making the Vocational Course of Study in Agriculture in the High School, 893
Principles of Curriculum and Instruction (Tyler), 239
Principles of Psychology (James), 100
Principles of Rhetoric and Their Applications, The (Hill), 692
Private education, colonial era, 350–351
Problem solving, 526–528
  learning as, 527
  learning through, 527–528
  learning to solve problems, 528
  mathematics, 775, 777–778
Procedural knowledge, 866
  development of, 524–525
Procedural tasks, 506
Process Approach to Science, 814
Processing load, 529–530
Process of Education, The (Bruner), 366, 791, 792
Process-oriented approach, 716
  writing curriculum, 709
Process-product research, 63, 64–67
  Beginning Teacher Evaluation Study, 64
  criticism of, 65, 66
Process-tracing research, 517–518
Process versus content, 62
Productive Work in Industry and School (Wirth), 935
Professional associations, impact on curriculum stability/change, 229–230
Professionalization, in education, 488–489
Proficiency-based approach
  characteristics of, 875–876
  foreign language study, 872–876
Proficiency Guidelines, foreign language study, 862
Profiles of Struggles (Locke and Griffin), 975
Program assistance models, physical education, 982
Program development projects, physical education, 982–983
Programmed learning, 281
Programmed textbooks
  development of, 455–456
  as teacher-proof curricula, 375
Progressive Education Association, 16, 167
  314
  and empirical approach to curriculum, 61–62
Progressive education movement, 14, 62–63
  and art education, 958–959
  and concept of curriculum, 278
  Dewey's influence, 171–173, 311–313
  impact on curriculum stability/change, 224–226
  influential school reformers, 224
  and language arts, 732–734
  position on curriculum, 171–173
  scope of, 224
  and social studies curriculum, 834
  themes related to schools, 225
  and vocational education, 225
Progressive ideology, 311–314
  characteristics of, 311–313
  research in, 321
  roots of, 312
Project 2061, 800–801
  Technology Panel, 818
Project Child, 619
Project English Demonstration and Curriculum Centers, 700
Project method, agriculture education, 894
Project Physics, 63
Project Technology, 817
Project to Enhance Effective Learning, 799
Project Zero, 957
Proof, in mathematics, 755
Properties of Matter, 810
Protestant ethic, and textbooks, 445, 450
Prussian system, 59
Psychoanalytic theories
  and education, 547
  Erikson's theory, 547
  and feminist theory, 673–674
Psychology of Intelligence (Piaget), 519
Psychology of learning, and curriculum, 14, 25
Psychology of Teaching Reading, The (Anderson and Dearborn), 703
Psychotherapeutic tradition, knowledge acquisition, 274
Pull-out programs
  effective methods for, 617
  negative effects of, 617
Pupils' Attitudes Towards Technology, 817
Puritan values, colonial schools, 347–348
Purpose Process Curriculum Framework, 969, 980
Purposes for Engaging in Physical Activity Scale, 980–981

Q

Quaker schools, 447
Qualitative evaluation
  artistic approaches, 133
  critical/emancipatory approaches, 133–134
  interpretive approaches, 133
  systematic approaches, 133
  theory driven approaches, 133
Qualitative methods, 103–108
  in curriculum research, 106–108
  debates related to, 103–108
  in educational research, 103–108
  standards of quality, 105
Qualitative ranking, historical perspective, 124
Quantitative marks, historical perspective, 124–125
Quantification of curriculum, 59
Questionnaires surveys, 479–480

R

Racial/ethnic factors. *See* Minorities
Rand Change Agent Study, 411
  implementation measures, 413, 416, 417
  and mutation phenomenon, 412–413
Rand Corporation, *Federal Programs Supporting Educational Change*, 372–374
Rational humanist ideology, 309–311
  elitism, 310
  influences of, 310–311
  research in, 320–321
  roots of, 309–310
Rational Method of Reading, 697
Rational system, curriculum as rational system view, 195, 198–203
Readability formulas, and textbook production, 713
Readability research, 696
Reader's Guide to Prose Fiction, 734
Reader, the Text, the Poem, The (Rosenblatt), 744–745
Reading, 497
  historical view of teaching. *See* Curriculum research in reading
  programs for poor African-Americans, 618–619
  second language learners, 639–640
  united with writing in curriculum, 716
  See also Language arts
Reading Ladders for Human Relations, 734
Reading Recovery, 617
Received curriculum, 439–440
  immobility of, 714–715
Reciprocal teaching, 51
Reconceptualism, 34–35, 316–317
  assumptions of, 83–84
  categories of, 84–85
  characteristics of, 316–317
  criticism of, 85–86
  curriculum organization, 338
  influence of, 317
  research in, 322–323
  views of, 83
Rediscovery of Ethnicity, The (TeSelle), 258
Red shirting, kindergartners, 146
Reflection, cognitive method, 532
Reflective Practitioner, The (Sch_n), 936
Reformation, education of women in, 662–663
Reforming of General Education, The (Bell), 279
Rehabilitation Act, 1035
Religious content, textbooks, 446, 449
Religious education, and moral education, 558
Religious orthodox ideologies, 307–309
  characteristics of, 307

Religious orthodox ideologies *(Continued)*
influences of, 307
research in, 320
Remediation
add-on programs, 617–618
in-class programs, 618
pull-out programs, 617
replacement programs, 618
Title I programs, 705
Renaissance, education of women in, 662–663
Renewing US Mathematics: Critical Resource for the Future, 750
Reorganization of English in the Secondary Schools, 690–691, 731–732
Replacement programs, 618
Replication, research studies, 847
Report Card on Basal Readers, 712
Report of the Committee of Ten, 689, 690
See also Committee of Ten
Republic (Plato), 203, 659, 660, 758
Research, Development, and Dissemination approach, study of curriculum implementation, 405, 408–410
Reshaping School Mathematics, 750
Resources in Technology, 816–817
Restructured Model for Secondary Vocational Education, 932–933
Restructuring, in cognitive theory, 866
Restructuring Schools Project, 252
Retail Selling (Prince), 901
Revisionists, on curriculum differentiation, 580
Rhetorical tradition
knowledge acquisition, 271–273
teaching classical rhetoric, 688–689, 728–729
Roman Catholic schools, 307
Romans, on education of women, 660
Rotenberry Act, 447
Royal Society, 273
Rugby School, 273
Russian manual training schools, 906

S

Saber-Tooth Curriculum, The (Peddiwell), 766
St. Louis, rise of school district, 356–357
Salters Chemistry, 806, 812
Scaffolding
cognitive method, 532
foreign language learning, 869
Scan-Tron Corporation, 126
Schemata, 56
schema-based comprehension, 521–522
Scholastic Aptitude Test, 235, 252
decline in scores, 844
and foreign language learning, 853–854
School and Society (Dewey), 378
School Curriculum Improvement Study, 51
School effects, statistical research on, 68–70
Schooling
goals and functions of, 233
professionalization of, 488–489
Schooling and The Acquisition of Knowledge (Anderson, Spiro and Montague), 520
School Mathematics: Options for the 1990s (Romberg and Stewart), 755
School Mathematics Study Group, 51, 63
School organization
definition of, 346
See also Curriculum and school organization
School production, and tracking, 587
Schools, ethos of, 559–560
Schools Council Humanities Project, 371
Schools Council Integrated Science Project, 805
School size, and extracurriculum, 1019–1021
Schools of To-Morrow (Dewey and Dewey), 100, 378
Science
development as school subject, 178–179
feminist science, 291–292, 807–808
and gender bias, 671, 806–808
gender differences in attitude towards, 474
and moral education, 557–558
and politics, 291–292
relationship to technology, 821–823
Science and Technology in Society, 813
Science as Inquiry, 802
Science curriculum
and academic scientists, 791, 799–801
and assessment, 795–796, 811–812
as construction of meaning, 810–811
cross-cultural view, 790, 794, 796–797, 798–799, 800, 801–803, 806, 808, 809–811, 815
curriculum competition, 793–794
curriculum emphases, 794
elementary education, 813–815
environmental studies, 806
equipment/technology in, 808–809
and gender differences, 806
guidelines approach to, 811
historical analysis of, 792–794
and input of science educators, 798–799
and input of science teachers, 797–798
international movements, 803–806
isolated modular approach, 813
new approach, Science, Technology, and Society, 804–806
and new learners, 794–795
and philosophical ideas of science, 791–792, 802–803
and psychological theories of learning, 791, 801–802
reforms, 791, 797
secondary education, 794–795
and teacher expertise, 809–810
textbooks, 810–811
whole course approach, 812–813
See also Technology education
Science for All, 797, 798, 800, 812
Science for All Americans, 800–801, 812
Science for Every Citizen, 797
Science Is for Everybody, 800
Science of Education, The (Hebart), 101
"Science of Patterns," "The" (Steen), 754
Science Plus, 810
Science, Technology, and Society
materials, 812–813
scope of, 804–806
and technological understanding, 822
whole courses in, 812
Scientific approach to curriculum, 41–72
behaviorist perspective, 46–49, 490
cognitive science perspective, 54–56
cognitive structuralist perspective, 52–54
and conceptions of teaching, 45–46
contributions of, 56–57
debates related to, 42, 103–108
developmental perspective, 49–52
empirical approach to curriculum, 57–72
history of, 100–101, 167–170
instruction and assessment in, 42–43
measurement issues, 44
methodology in, 41
normative issues, 44
possibilities and limitations of, 43–44
scientism in, 44–45
sources of conflict in, 42
theoretical issues, 44
Tyler Rationale, 490
Scientific management movement, 225
applied to education, 59–60, 61, 81, 82
taxonomies of mathematical knowledge, 763–764
Scientific tradition, knowledge acquisition, 273–274
Scope, curriculum organization, 329–330
Scopes trial, 447
Secondary Course in Agronomy and in Animal Husbandry, 892
Secondary Schools 1960 (Snedden), 170
Secondary schools
and curriculum differentiation, 575–577, 591–592, 595
foreign language study, 855–856, 880
science curriculum, 794–795
Secondary Science Curriculum Review, 795, 809
Second Handbook of Research on Teaching (Travers), 103
Second International Mathematics Study, 68
Second International Math Study, 577
Segregation
and minorities, 615, 617
single-sex schooling, 668–669
Self-actualization orientation
curriculum content, 15
physical education, 967
self-actualizing curriculum, 335
Self-esteem, and extracurriculum, 1028
Self-fulfilling prophesy, 598
Sequence, 531
cognitive view, 531
curriculum organization, 330
and knowledge building, 847
Sex education, 555

Sex-role stereotyping, textbooks, 445
Shadow and Substance: Afro-American Experience in Contemporary Children's Fiction (Sims), 620
Shadowing, in formative research, 111
Shopping Mall High School, The (Powell, Farrar and Cohen), 166
Short-answer examinations, historical perspective, 125
Short Introduction to the Latin Tongue, A (Cheever), 453
Significant Bilingual Instructional Features Study, 637
Silent reading era, 698–699
Silent Reading Workbook, 698
Single-sex schooling, effects of, 668–669
Single-subject pattern, curriculum organization, 335
Situated learning, cognitive science, 536
Situational atmosphere approach, moral education, 549
Skill learning, fallacies related to, 530
Slöd system, 906
Smith-Hughes Act, 228, 891, 892, 894, 899, 900, 907
Smith v. Board of School Commissioners of Mobile County, 307
Social aspects, of curriculum, 499–500
Social behaviorism, and curriculum organization, 332–333
Social class
  and content of schooling, 238, 242
  and cultural capital, 292–293
  and curriculum, 293
  and curriculum design, 294–296
  and curriculum differentiation, 589–590, 600
  and extracurriculum, 1013–1014
Social conditions, and curriculum, 14
Social control
  and extracurriculum, 1026–1027
  and schools, 81–82, 87
  of textbooks, 445–448
Social Control (Ross), 168
Social development model, physical education, 979
Social education, 552
Social Education, 556
Social efficiency movement, 168–170
  focus of, 16
Social indicators, 66–67
Social interaction theory, and moral education, 546
Social isolation, and poverty, 610–611
Socialization, and learning mode, 644
Social learning theory, nature of, 546
Social living, language arts for, 734–735
Social meliorists, focus of, 16
Social Objectives of School English (Pendleton), 732
Social reconstructionism
  and curriculum content, 15
  and curriculum organization, 333
Social relevance, and language arts, 737–738
Social Responsibility of Science, 803
Social science, and development of school subjects, 179
Social stratification, and knowledge, 292–294
Social studies
  goals of, 835–838
  and moral education, 556–557
  purpose of, 831–832
  reduction of gender bias, 670–671
Social studies curriculum
  and affective revolution, 839
  back-to-basics-movement, 839–840
  citizenship education, 845
  content, 836–837
  control of, 840–844
  effects of learning social studies, 844–845
  factors affecting curriculum research, 845–847
  government influences, 843–844
  hidden curriculum, 840
  lack of research about, 834–835
  Man: A Course of Study (MACOS), 838–839
  New Social Studies, 838–839
  and progressive education movement, 834
  research needs, 847
  skill development, 837
  and special interest groups, 843
  state curriculum, framework for, 833–834, 842
  and student participation, 837–838
  teacher preparation, 842–843
  teachers' role, 841–842
  textbooks, 835, 840–841
Societal curriculum, 328
Society for Curriculum Study, 447
Society for the Study of Curriculum History, 161
Socioeconomic factors, and extracurriculum, 1013–1014
Sociolingustic studies, of classrooms, 474–475
Sociological analysis, of curriculum, 793, 803
Sociology of education, new sociology, 294–295
Sociotechnical literacy, 929
Some Thoughts Concerning Education (Locke), 101
SPAN study, 846
Speaking Mathematically (Pimm), 750
Special Interest Group, 801–802
Speller (Webster), 453, 697
Spiral curriculum, 735
  nature of, 916
Spiritual Milk for American Babes (Cotton), 453
Sports education, 969
Sputnik, 791, 852, 965
SQ3R study skills method, 704
SRA Skill Builders, 707
Staff-development, and school-based curriculum development, 377
Stage theory. *See* Developmental theory
Staggered case studies, in formative research, 111
Standardized tests and testing
  basic testing concepts related to, 134
  bureaucratic functions, 613
  growing popularity of, 126
  multiple-choice tests, 134–137
  as outcome measure, 131
  and poor students, 613–614
  preparation for, 145, 147
Standards of quality, qualitative methods, 105
Standpoint epistemologies, feminist theory, 675
Stanford Program on International and Cross-Cultural Education, 651
States
  calculation of state aid, 612
  control of textbooks, 444
  curriculum guidelines, 709, 712–713
  impact on curriculum stability/change, 227–228, 234
  and physical education, 983
  policy and curriculum policy, 202–203
  social studies curriculum, 833–834, 842
  and vocational education, 931–933, 935–936
Statistical research
  history of, 66–67
  indicator movements, 66–67
  major research projects, 66–69
  on curriculum, 66–70
  on school effects, 68–70
  and policy formation, 70–71
  search for better measures, 71–72
Status studies, language arts, 740
Stimulated recall, in formative research, 111
Stimulus substitution, 47
Story Hour Readers, 697
Strategic rules, language learning, 864
Street-Level Bureaucracy (Lipsky), 193
Structure and Content Foundations for Curriculum Development (DeVore), 918
Student Activities Evaluative Instrument, 1012
Student experience
  classroom as site of, 469–471
  Dewey's view, 466
  historical perspective, 471–473
  immediate curricular engagement, 468–469
  and implicit curriculum, 474–475
  and manifest curriculum, 473–474
  research limitations, 467–468
  research needs, 475–481
Student retention, and extracurriculum, 1026

Students
  conformists, 256
  impact on curriculum stability/change, 231, 236
  implicit theories of learning, 525–526
  student authors, 480–481
Student Teams-Achievement Divisions, 620–621
Studies in Arts Education (Efland), 955
Study of Thinking, A (Gruner, Goodnow and Austin), 519
Study skills, SQ3R study skills method, 704
Subcultures, 249–250, 262–263
Subjects
  content pedagogy, 497
  curriculum of school subjects, 178–180
  gender in, 669–672
  process of evolution of, 179
Sullivan Programmed Readers, 707
Summa Theologica (Aquinas), 271
Summative evaluation, 139
Summerhill, 560
Summer school, effectiveness of, 617
Supreme Council for Scientific Research, 261
Surveys, uses of, 479–480
Symbolic action, and curriculum policy, 187
Symbolic interaction theory, basis of, 972
Symposium (Xenophon), 660
Synod of 1662, 349
Systematic approaches
  curriculum development, 110
  qualitative evaluation, 133
Systemic changes, government action, 191

T

Talks to Teachers on Psychology (James), 100
Task analysis, 468
Taught curriculum, 222
Taunton Commission, 144
Teacher as Philosopher, The (Simpson and Jackson), 365
Teacher as Stranger (Greene), 365
Teacher Center Program, 201
Teacher Councils, 230
Teacher effectiveness, 467
  nature of research related to, 491
Teacher expectations, and physical education, 988–989
"Teacher in John Dewey's Works, The" (Greene), 365
Teacher preparation, and social studies, 842–843
Teacher-proof curriculum
  computer-assisted instruction, 375
  computer-mediated communication systems, 375
  correspondence education, 375–376
  distance education, 376
  programmed textbooks, 375
  programs related to, 374
  teaching machines, 374–375
Teachers
  acceptance of curriculum, 17–18
  assessment activities, 126–127
  and curriculum implementation, 405–408, 429
  impact on curriculum stability/change, 231, 236–237
  influence on social studies curriculum, 841–842
  information about teacher practices, 369
  and mathematics teaching, 764–765, 774–775, 778–780
  as moral educators, 544, 560, 562
  as researcher, 385–386
  study of thought processes, 66
  See also Curriculum and teacher
Teacher's Word Book (Thorndike), 696
Teaching, conceptions of and scientific inquiry, 45–46
Teaching and Mastery of Language, The (Markova), 744
Teaching machines
  early machines, 47
    as teacher-proof curricula, 374–375
Teaching of English in the Elementary and Secondary Schools (Carpenter, Baker and Scott), 689
Team approach, curriculum, 29
Technical institutes, 905
  nature of, 415
Technology
  curriculum as technology, 335
  and curriculum content, 15
  relationship to science, 821–823
Technology and You (Goetsch and Nelson), 821
Technology education
  Assessment of Performance Unit, 819–820
  capability approach, 815–816
  cross-cultural view, 815–820
  design and technology, 820
  industry related, 818–819
  learning about technology typology, 821
  models from industrial arts, 816–818
  social theories on, 818
  textbooks, 821
  uncertainty related to, 815
  and women, 816, 817
Technology in Your World (Hacker and Barden), 821
Technology Learning Activities, 821
Testing
  impact on curriculum stability/change, 235
  teaching for test results, 796, 842
  test design, 280
  See also Curriculum evaluation and assessment; Standardized tests and testing
Testing movement, 123
Test preparation activities, 147
  classification based on ethicalness, 145
Textbooks
  alternative formats, 455–456
  authorship of, 440–441
  central tendency theory, 449
  of colonial period, 453
  as cultural artifacts, 437
  and curricular chain, 438–440
  and curriculum, 403
  difficulty level of, 444
  earliest texts, 452
  economics of, 444
  and educational research, 440
  evolution issue, 447
  federal influences, 443–444
  gender bias, 445, 670
  historical evolution of, 441, 453–455
  impact on curriculum stability/change, 235–236
  intertextuality of, 438
  and knowledge, 442–443
  latent content of, 448–452
  latent curriculum of, 438
  levels of validation in, 438
  literary selections, 451–452
  lobby for civil rights in, 448
  manifest curriculum of, 437–438
  marketing aspects, 440, 445
  mathematics, 760, 770
  and minorities, 648
  mode of production, 437
  modern era, 454–455
  nationalistic content, 446, 449
  pedagogical apparatus of, 438
  and pedagogy, 494
  pre-Civil War period, 454
  and Protestant ethic, 445, 450
  publishers' control of, 444–445
  publishers' impact on curriculum stability/change, 229
  racial/ethnic bias, 445–446
  religious content, 446, 449
  science, 810–811
  sex-role stereotyping, 445
  social control of, 445–448
  social studies, 835, 840–841
  states' influences, 444
  studies of, 441–442
  as surrogate curriculum, 437
  and teacher needs, 442–443
  technology education, 821
  variations in content of, 494
  variations in uses of, 495–497
  writing textbooks, 692, 702
Textbooks and Schooling in the United States (Elliot and Woodward), 442
Text Materials in Modern Society, 442
Text Material Study, 442
That Men May Understand (Rugg), 100
Theoretical issues, scientific approach to curriculum, 44
Theory-driven approaches, qualitative evaluation, 133
Theory of the Leisure Class, The (Veblen), 113

Think-aloud technique, in formative research, 111
Think and Do Book, 698
Thinking
  and language, 52–53
  and mathematics, 758
Ti-In, 878
Time-Shared, Interactive Computer Controlled Information Television, 375
Tinker v. De Moines Independent School District, 1033
Title I programs, 705
Title IX, 228, 1033–1034
Topics (Aristotle), 124
Total Physical Response method, foreign language study, 876
Tracking, 61
  and achievement, 594
  and classroom dynamics, 587–589
  and equality of opportunity, 594
  and homogeneous groups, 594
  and poor black students, 614
  and school production, 587
  and teachers' perceptions, 597–598
  and vocational education, 935
  See also Curriculum differentiation
Tradition and Reform in the Teaching of English (Applebee), 745
Training Courses for Teachers of Agriculture, 892
Transformational grammar, 743
Transformationists, 254, 255
  view of feminist theory, 677–678
Transitional knowledge, 531–532
"Trapped in a Technocratic Ideology" (Zuga), 920
Treatise on Domestic Economy, A (Beecher), 896–897
Tutoring programs, computers, 533
Tyler Rationale, 331, 490

U

Underclass, blacks, 610
Understanding Poetry (Brooks and Warren), 736, 744
Unemployment, black men, 611
Unitary system, 354–355
University Centers for Economic Education, 843
Urban areas
  problems of blacks in, 610
  schools in poor areas, 612
  and segregated schools, 613
U. S. Office of Education, 63, 66

V

Validity, instructional/curricular, 140–141
Values and Teaching (Raths, Harmin and Simon), 549, 550
Values clarification, 549–551
  approach in, 549–550
  criticism of, 550–551
  and indoctrination, 551
  popularity of, 550
Verstehen, 133
Video
  foreign language study, 874, 878
  language arts, 742
Vidoetape Data Bank Project, 984, 985, 986
Vindication of the Rights of Woman, A (Wollstonecraft), 664
Vocabulary control, readers, 698
Vocational Amendments, 921
"Vocational and Educational Guidance," (Keller), 925
Vocational education, 173
  and apprenticeship, 270
  and at-risk students, 935
  and basic skills, 934
  as change agent, 935
  content/methods interaction, 936
  coordination and educators, 935
  cross-cultural view, 931
  curricular research, 927–933
  development of, 579
  Dewey on, 171–172
  early models of, 905–906
  federal funding, 908
  general versus specific content, 933
  and higher-order thinking skills, 930–931, 933–934
  historical view, 905–910
  institutional settings for, 927
  integration of subfields in, 934
  issues related to, 927
  mission of, 935
  planning principles, 908–909
  and progressive movement, 225
  and social class, 260
  state curriculum, 931–933, 935–936
  and tracking, 935
  types of programs in, 928
  See also Technology education
Vocational Education Act, 893, 894, 896, 902, 904, 909, 926, 927, 928
Vocational Education Amendments, 909
Vocational education, historical view
  agricultural education, 892–894
  business education, 894–896
  career education, 904–905
  health occupations education, 903–904
  home economics education, 896–899
  industrial education, 899–901
  marketing education, 901–903
  origins, 891
  vocational education, 905–910
Vocational education research
  agricultural education, 910–913
  business education, 913–915
  career education, 925–926
  health occupations education, 923–925
  home economics education, 915–918
  industrial education, 918–920
  marketing education, 920–923
  vocational education, 927–933
Vocational Education (Snedden), 907
Vocational Education Study, 927
Vocationalizing Education: An International Perspective, 931
Vocational-Technical Education Consortium, 921, 930
Vocational track, 578
Vocation Bureau, 904

W

Waldorf schools, 309
Way Out of Educational Confusion, The (Dewey), 173
Weeding and Sowing (Freudenthal), 754
Western Farmer's Almanac (Hall), 453
Western Primer (Hall), 453
Western Reader (Hall), 453
What Americans Study, 855
What's Going On in Gym: Descriptive Studies of Physical Education Classes (Anderson and Barrett), 984
Whole child approach, 313
Whole group instruction, factors related to use of, 472
Whole language approach, and cognitive structuralist theory, 53–54
Whole piece writing approach, 709
Why Johnny Can't Read (Flesch), 447, 705
Within Our Research: Breaking the Cycle of Disadvantage, 935
Women
  changing roles, impact on schools, 473
  and curriculum, 259
  development of curriculum for, 169
  moral development, 554–555
  women's studies programs, 676
  See also Gender and curriculum; Gender differences
Women and Minorities in Science and Engineering, 807
Women in Science, 806
Women's educational history
  in 19th and 20th century, 664–666
  age of Christianity, 661–662
  Greek and Roman era, 659–661
  during Renaissance and Reformation, 662–663
Woods Hole Conference, 443, 791
"Work in America," 909
Working Group, 820
Work-Readiness: A New Promise in Minnesota's Education, 932
World of Construction curricula, 901
World of Manufacturing curricula, 901, 919
World of Mathematics (Newman), 750
Writing, 497, 502–503
  Committee of Ten, work of, 690
  historical view of teaching. *See* Curriculum research in writing
  second language learners, 640–641
  united with reading in curriculum, 716
  women writers as models in teaching of, 670

Writing *(Continued)*
  writing process approach, 708
  writing textbooks, 70, 692
Writing Trends Across the Decade, 710
Writing Without Teachers (Elbow), 374
Written examinations, historical perspective, 124

Y

Yale Child Study Center School Development Program, Social Skills Curriculum for Inner-City Children, 620
YMCA Youth Fitness Test, 981
Youth Dictionary of Technology-Humane and Ecological Technologies, 806

YORK COLLEGE OF PENNSYLVANIA 17403
0 2003 0033706 6

DISCARDED
YORK COLLEGE
PENNSYLVANIA
Servire est vivere
LIBRARY